NEW! 3D Animations of Origins, Insertions, Actions, and Innervations with Gradab

Link from more than 65 muscle images in the PAL 2.0 Human Cadaver module to these 3D Animations of Origins, Insertions, Actions, and Innervations. Quizzes for the Animations are included in the Quizzes section of PAL 2.0. The customizable and gradable Quizzes are also available on myA&P™ with CourseCompass.™

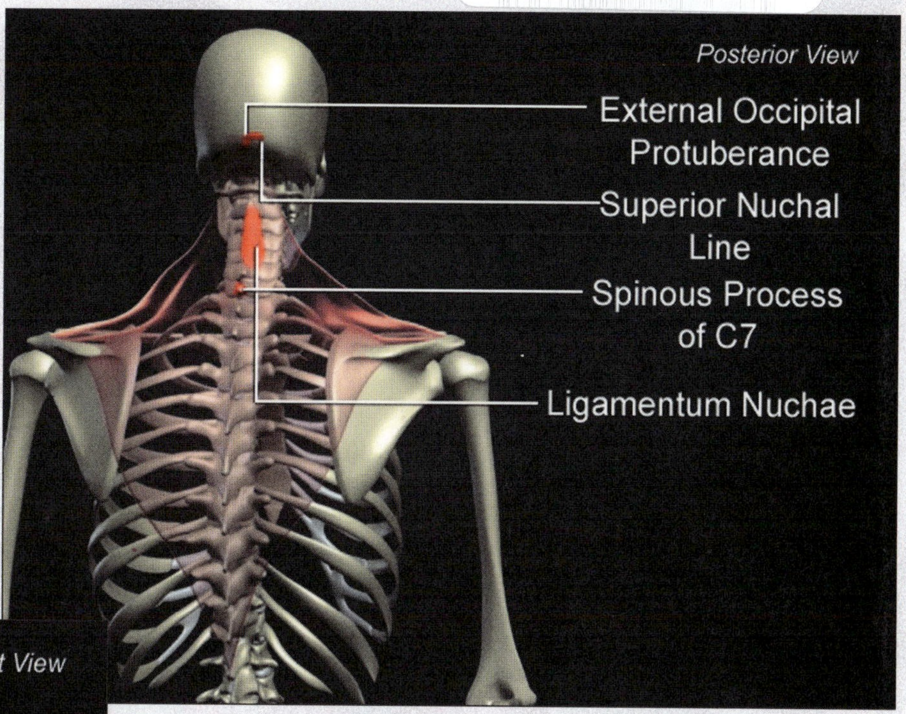

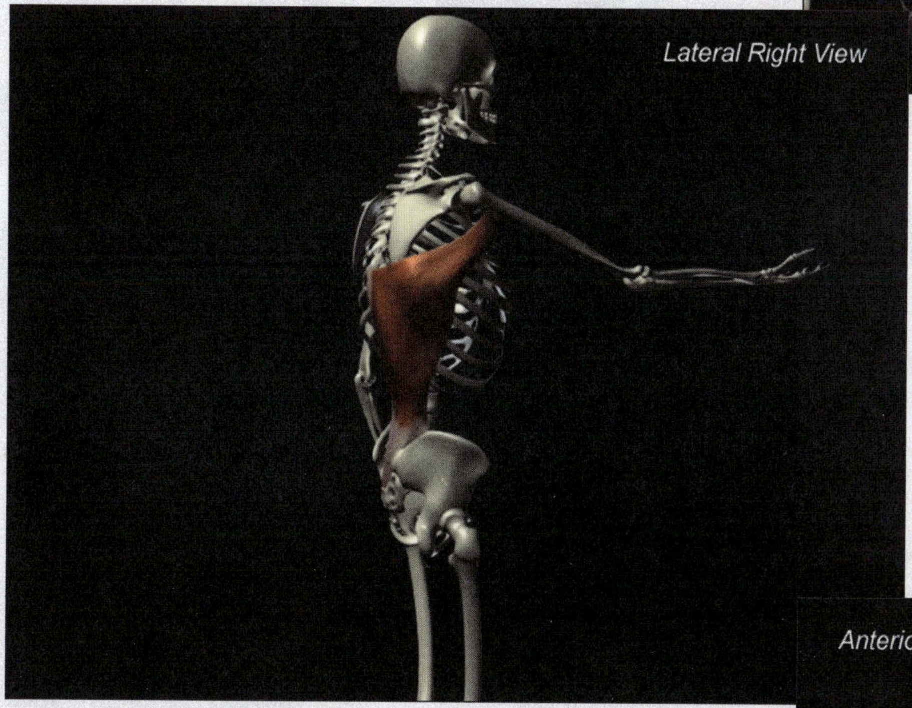

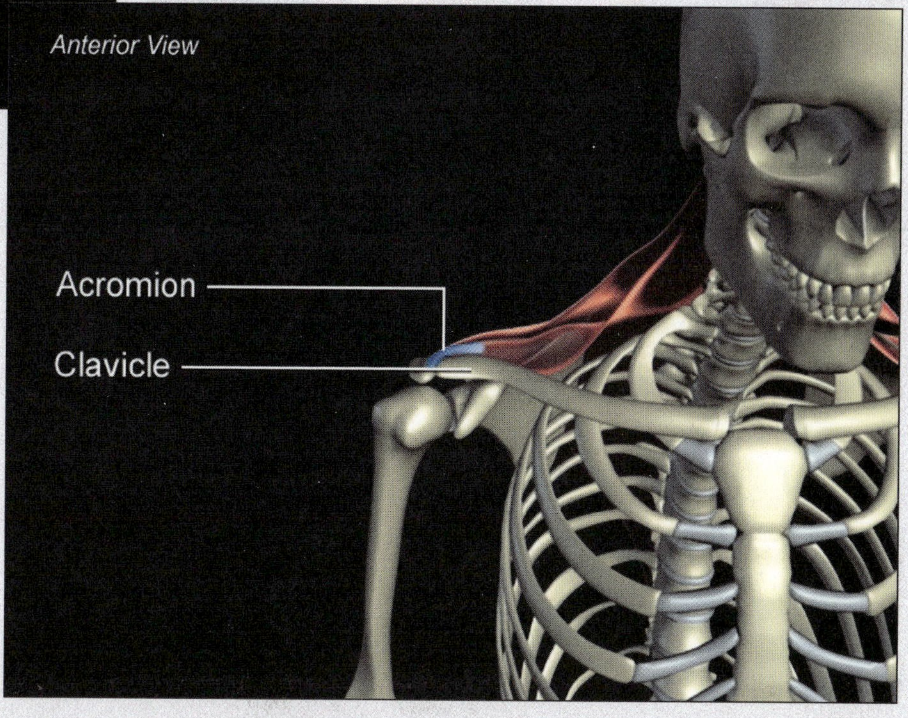

myA&P www.myaandp.com

A WEALTH OF RESOURCES AND TOOLS, ALL IN ONE CONVENIENT LOCATION

myA&P™

This companion website for ***Human Anatomy*, Sixth Edition** includes chapter guides, learning activities, self-study quizzes, brand-new anatomy animations with quizzes, interactive flashcards, bone review, muscle review, histology review, web links, and a glossary with pronunciations. This greatly expanded website provides the online versions of the new Practice Anatomy Lab™ (PAL) 2.0 and ***Get Ready for A&P* Media Update**. It also includes a password-protected Instructor's Resource Section.

myA&P with CourseCompass™

myA&P with CourseCompass combines the strength of the content of the myA&P website with state-of-the-art eLearning tools. CourseCompass is a nationally hosted, dynamic, interactive online course management system powered by Blackboard, the leading platform for Internet-based learning tools. This easy-to-use and customizable program enables professors to tailor content and functionality to meet individual course needs. The course includes all of the content found on the myA&P website together with course management functionality.

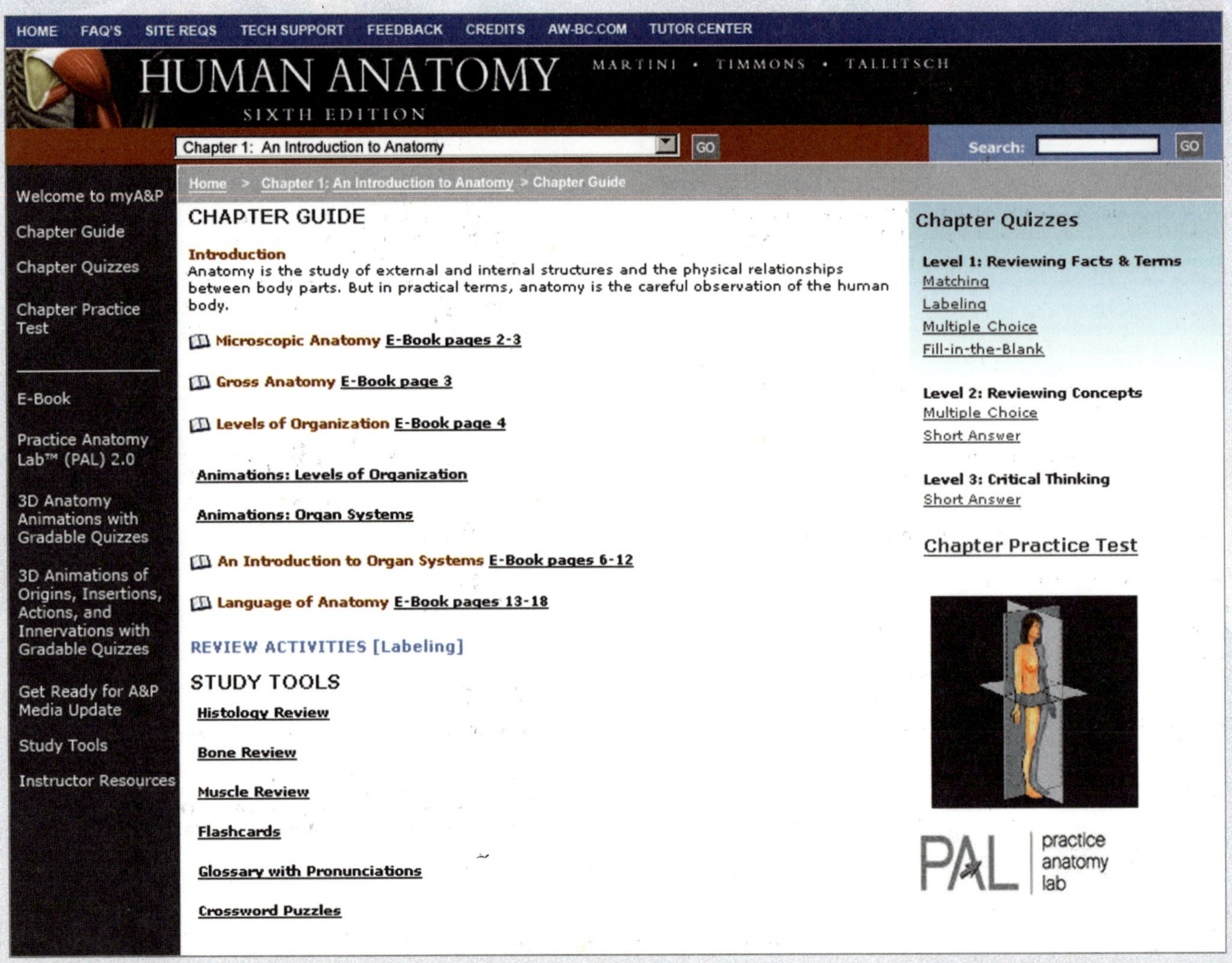

www.myaandp.com

Your steps to success.

STEP 1: Register

All you need to get started is a valid email address and the access code below. To register, simply:

1. Go to www.myaandp.com.
2. Click the appropriate book cover. Cover must match the textbook edition being used for your class.
3. Click **"Register"** under **"First Time User?"**
4. Leave **"No, I Am a New User"** selected.
5. Using a coin, scratch off the silver coating below to reveal your access code. *Do not use a knife or other sharp object, which can damage the code.*
6. Enter your access code in lowercase or uppercase, without the dashes.
7. Follow the on-screen instructions to complete registration.

   During registration, you will establish a personal login name and password to use for logging into the website. You will also be sent a registration confirmation email that contains your login name and password.

Your Access Code is:

USWHM-MUSIL-ROBLE-OMAGH-TERZA-WWRSE

Note: If there is no silver foil covering the access code, it may already have been redeemed, and therefore may no longer be valid. In that case, you can purchase access online using a major credit card. To do so, go to www.myaandp.com, click "students" under "First Time Users," click "I need to buy access" under "myA&P," click the cover of your textbook, then click "**Buy Now,**" and follow the on-screen instructions.

STEP 2: Log in

1. Go to www.myaandp.com. and click **"myA&P"** under **"Returning Users."**
2. Click the appropriate book cover.
3. Under **"Established User?"** Enter the login name and password that you created during registration. *If unsure of this information, refer to your registration confirmation email.*
4. Click **"Log In."**

STEP 3: (Optional) Join a class

Instructors have the option of creating an online class for you to use with this website. If your instructor decides to do this, you'll need to complete the following steps using the Class ID your instructor provides you. By "joining a class," you enable your instructor to view the scored results of your work on the website in his or her online gradebook.

To join a class:

1. Log into the website. For instructions, see **"STEP 2: Log in."**
2. Click **"Join a Class."**
3. Enter your instructor's **"Class ID"** and then click **"Next."**
4. At the Confirm Class page you will see your instructor's name and class information. If this information is correct, click **"Next."**
5. Click **"Enter Class Now"** from the Class Confirmation page.

- *To confirm your enrollment in the class, check for your instructor and class name at the top right of the page. You will be sent a class enrollment confirmation email.*
- *As you complete activities on the website from now through the class end date, your results will post to your instructor's gradebook, in addition to appearing in your personal view of the Results Reporter.*

To log into the class later, follow the instructions under **"STEP 2: Log in."**

Got technical questions?

Customer Technical Support: To obtain support, please visit us online anytime at http://247.aw.com where you can search our knowledgebase for common solutions, view product alerts, and review all options for additional assistance.

SITE REQUIREMENTS

For the latest updates on Site Requirements, go to www.myaandp.com, click "myA&P" under "Returning Users."Pick your book and click the lower right link to "Site Requirements." Or you can click the "Books Available" tab at the top of the page, click your book cover, then click the lower right link "Site Requirements."

WINDOWS
OS: Windows 2000, XP
Resolution: 1024 x 768
Plugins: Latest Version of Flash/QuickTime/Shockwave (as needed)
Browsers: Internet Explorer 6.x; Firefox 1.x
Internet connection: 56K minimum

MACINTOSH
OS: 10.2.4, 10.3.2
Resolution: 1024 x 768
Plugins: Latest Version of Flash/QuickTime/Shockwave (as needed)
Browsers: Firefox 1.x; Safari 1.3
Internet connection: 56K minimum

Register and log in

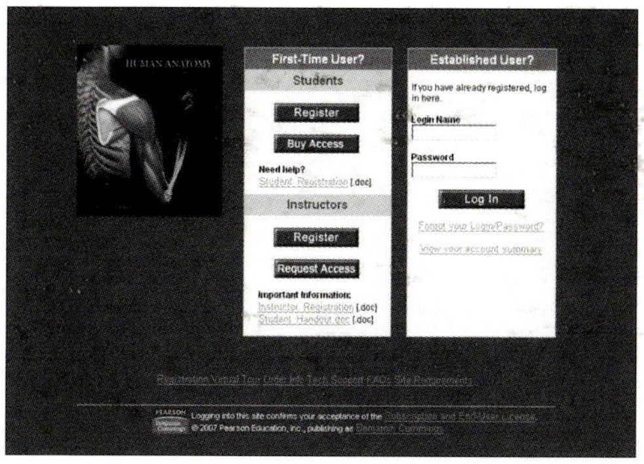

Join a class

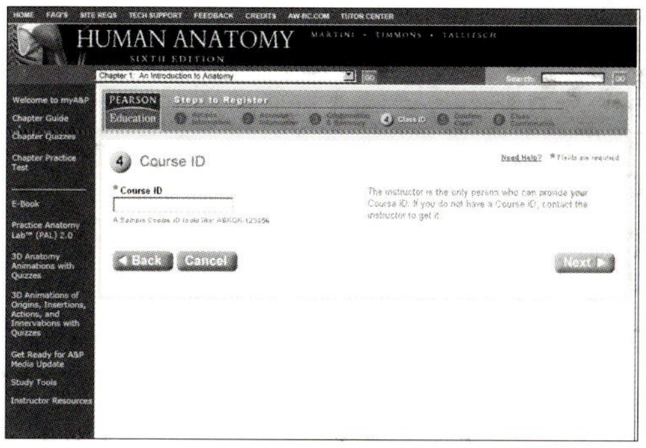

Important: Please read the Subscription and End-User License agreement, accessible from the book website's login page, before using the *myA&P* website. By using the website, you indicate that you have read, understood, and accepted the terms of this agreement.

Human Anatomy

SIXTH EDITION

Frederic H. Martini, Ph.D.
University of Hawaii

Michael J. Timmons, M.S.
Moraine Valley Community College

Robert B. Tallitsch, Ph.D.
Augustana College

with

William C. Ober, M.D.
Art Coordinator and Illustrator

Claire W. Garrison, R.N.
Illustrator

Kathleen Welch, M.D.
Clinical Consultant

Ralph T. Hutchings
Biomedical Photographer

PEARSON
Benjamin Cummings

San Francisco Boston New York
Cape Town Hong Kong London Madrid Mexico City
Montreal Munich Paris Singapore Sydney Tokyo Toronto

Executive Editor: Leslie Berriman
Project Editor: Katy German
Development Manager: Claire Alexander
Associate Editor: Robin Pille
Editorial Assistant: Kelly Reed
Director, Media Development: Lauren Fogel
Media Producers: Sarah Young-Dualan, Aimee Pavy
Associate Media Producer: Suzanne Rasmussen
Managing Editor: Deborah Cogan
Production Supervisor: Caroline Ayres
Copyeditor: Michael Rossa
Production Management and Composition: S4Carlisle Publishing Services
Art Coordinator: Jean Lake
Interior and Cover Designer: Side by Side Design
Photo Researcher: Clare Maxwell
Director, Image Resource Center: Melinda Patelli
Image Rights and Permissions Manager: Zina Arabia
Senior Manufacturing Buyer: Stacey Weinberger
Marketing Manager: Gordon Lee
Text printer: RR Donnelly Willard
Cover printer: Phoenix Cover
Cover Photo Credit: John Bagley, Rich Tauber, Pearson Benjamin Cummings
Cover Illustrator: Blakely Kim, Pearson Benjamin Cummings

Library of Congress Cataloging-in-Publication Data
Martini, Frederic.
Human anatomy/Frederic H. Martini, Michael J. Timmons, Robert B. Tallitsch; with William C. Ober, art coordinator and illustrator; Claire W. Garrison, illustrator; Kathleen Welch, clinical consultant; Ralph T. Hutchings, biomedical photographer.—6th ed.
p. ; cm.
Includes bibliographical references and index.
ISBN: 978-0-321-50042-7
1. Human anatomy. 2. Human anatomy—Atlases.
[DNLM: 1. Anatomy—Atlases. QS 17 M386h 2008] I. Timmons, Michael J. II. Tallitsch, Robert B. III. Title.
QM23.2.M356 2008
611—dc22 2007024341

1 2 3 4 5 6 7 8 9 10—DOW—12 11 10 09 08

PEARSON
Benjamin Cummings

www.aw-bc.com

ISBN-10: 0-321-63201-X (Student Edition)
ISBN-13: 978-0321-63201-2 (Student Edition)

ISBN-10: 0-321-51197-2 (P-copy)
ISBN-13: 978-0321-51197-3 (P-copy)

Text and Illustration Team

Frederic (Ric) Martini

Author

Dr. Martini received his Ph.D. from Cornell University in comparative and functional anatomy for work on the pathophysiology of stress. His publications include journal articles and contributed chapters, technical reports, and magazine articles. He is the coauthor of six other undergraduate texts on anatomy and physiology or anatomy. He is currently affiliated faculty of the University of Hawaii and remains connected with the Shoals Marine Laboratory, a joint venture between Cornell University and the University of New Hampshire. Dr. Martini is now a President Emeritus of the Human Anatomy and Physiology Society after serving as President-Elect, President, and Past-President over 2004–2007. He is also a member of the American Physiological Society, the American Association of Anatomists, the Society for Integrative and Comparative Biology, the Australia/New Zealand Association of Clinical Anatomists, and the International Society of Vertebrate Morphologists.

Michael J. Timmons

Author

Michael J. Timmons received his degrees from Loyola University, Chicago. For more than three decades he has had a strong commitment to teaching nursing and pre-professional students at Moraine Valley Community College. In 2005–2006 Professor Timmons was honored with the Professor of the Year Award by Moraine Valley College and the Excellence Award from the National Institute for Staff and Organizational Development for his outstanding contributions to teaching, leadership, and student learning. He was the recipient of the Excellence in Teaching Award by the Illinois Community College Board of Trustees. Professor Timmons has authored several anatomy and physiology lab manuals and dissection guides. His areas of interest include biomedical photography, crafting illustration programs, and developing instructional technology learning systems. He chaired the Midwest Regional Human Anatomy and Physiology Conference and is also a national and regional presenter at the League for Innovation Conferences on Information Technology for Colleges and Universities and at Human Anatomy and Physiology Society meetings.

Robert B. Tallitsch

Author

Dr. Tallitsch received his Ph.D. in physiology with an anatomy minor from the University of Wisconsin—Madison at the ripe old age of 24. Since then, Dr. Tallitsch has been on the biology faculty at Augustana College in Rock Island, Illinois. His teaching responsibilities include Human Anatomy, Neuroanatomy, Histology, and Kinesiology. He is also a member of the Asian Studies faculty at Augustana College and teaches a course in Traditional Chinese Medicine. In seven out of the last nine years, Dr. Tallitsch has been designated as one of the "unofficial teachers of the year" by the graduating seniors at Augustana College. Dr. Tallitsch is a member of the American Physiological Society, American Association of Anatomists, AsiaNetwork, and the Human Anatomy and Physiology Society. In addition to his teaching responsibilities at Augustana College, Dr. Tallitsch has served as a visiting faculty member at the Foreign Languages Faculty at the Beijing University of Chinese Medicine and Pharmacology (Beijing, PRC), and the Foreign Languages Faculty at Central China Normal University (Wuhan, PRC).

William C. Ober

Art Coordinator and Illustrator

Dr. William C. Ober received his undergraduate degree from Washington and Lee University and his M.D. from the University of Virginia. While in medical school, he also studied in the Department of Art as Applied to Medicine at Johns Hopkins University. After graduation, Dr. Ober completed a residency in Family Practice and later was on the faculty at the University of Virginia in the Department of Family Medicine. He is currently an Affiliate Professor of Biology at Washington and Lee University and is part of the Core Faculty at Shoals Marine Laboratory, where he teaches Biological Illustration every summer. The textbooks illustrated by Medical & Scientific Illustration have won numerous design and illustration awards.

Claire W. Garrison

Illustrator

Claire W. Garrison, R.N., B.A., practiced pediatric and obstetric nursing before turning to medical illustration as a full-time career. She returned to school at Mary Baldwin College where she received her degree with distinction in studio art. Following a five-year apprenticeship, she has worked as Dr. Ober's partner in Medical & Scientific Illustration since 1986. She is on the Core Faculty at Shoals Marine Laboratory and co-teaches the Biological Illustration course.

Kathleen Welch

Clinical Consultant

Dr. Welch received her M.D. from the University of Washington in Seattle and did her residency in Family Practice at the University of North Carolina in Chapel Hill. For two years, she served as Director of Maternal and Child Health at the LBJ Tropical Medical Center in American Samoa and subsequently was a member of the Department of Family Practice at the Kaiser Permanente Clinic in Lahaina, Hawaii. She has been in private practice since 1987. Dr. Welch is a Fellow of the American Academy of Family Practice and a member of the Hawaii Medical Association and the Human Anatomy and Physiology Society. With Dr. Martini, she has coauthored both a textbook on anatomy and physiology and the *A & P Applications Manual* available as a supplement to the eighth edition of *Fundamentals of Anatomy & Physiology*.

Ralph T. Hutchings

Biomedical Photographer

Mr. Hutchings was associated with The Royal College of Surgeons of England for 20 years. An engineer by training, he has focused for years on photographing the structure of the human body. The result has been a series of color atlases, including the *Color Atlas of Human Anatomy*, the *Color Atlas of Surface Anatomy*, and *The Human Skeleton* (all published by Mosby-Yearbook Publishing). For his anatomical portrayal of the human body, the International Photographers Association has chosen Mr. Hutchings as the best photographer of humans in the twentieth century. He lives in North London, where he tries to balance the demands of his photographic assignments with his hobbies of early motor cars and airplanes.

Preface

Welcome to the Sixth Edition of *Human Anatomy!* In preparing this edition, the authors and illustrators focused on two questions:

1) How can the presentation be improved to increase student comprehension and interest?

To increase *student comprehension*, we paid particular attention to the most difficult topics in human anatomy and to areas identified by students and reviewers. Some of the changes are major, some are minor, but all reflect careful deliberation based on the authors' collective classroom experience. To increase *student interest*, we expanded the clinical content throughout the chapters and added new clinical case studies at the conclusion of each body system.

2) How can the best textbook illustration program for the undergraduate human anatomy course be made even better for teaching and learning?

This textbook has always been known for its distinctive atlas-style format and unsurpassed visual presentation of anatomical concepts. In the Sixth Edition, the illustration colors are more saturated to better attract students' attention, and the contrast between colors has been enhanced to more clearly delineate and distinguish structures for easier teaching and learning.

As in previous editions, the text and art are closely integrated to provide a seamless learning system. The illustrations do more than provide occasional support for the narrative; they are partners with the text in conveying information and helping students understand structures and relationships in a way that distinguishes this human anatomy textbook from all others.

These first pages in the Preface describe global and chapter-specific text and art revisions. The visual walkthrough that follows presents key features in the textbook and in the unparalleled media support materials.

Global Revisions

Text Revisions

The Sixth Edition of *Human Anatomy* introduces **Clinical Cases** at the conclusion of each body system. They appear at the end of Chapters 4 (The Integumentary System), 8 (The Skeletal System), 11 (The Muscular System), 18 (The Nervous System), 19 (The Endocrine System), 22 (The Cardiovascular System), 23 (The Lymphoid System), 24 (The Respiratory System), 25 (The Digestive System), 26 (The Urinary System), and 27 (The Reproductive System). The goal of anatomy isn't rote memorization—it's understanding. These Clinical Cases are designed to show how the various topics covered in this text are closely linked and integrated. Not every student enrolled in a Human Anatomy course intends to become a health professional. However, we hope that these Clinical Cases will show students how every system of the body interacts and plays an important role in presenting the signs and symptoms of an illness. This interaction among systems enables a physician to piece together the various clues that will lead to a correct diagnosis of the patient. One of the core elements contributing to the physician's success is a thorough understanding of basic anatomical concepts. It is our intent that the style and content of the Clinical Cases will help students *learn* the anatomical concepts presented in this text rather than simply memorize isolated facts without understanding their interrelationships.

We increased the number of **Clinical Notes** within the chapters. These Clinical Notes present clinical material that is pertinent to the anatomical material in each chapter.

We wanted to improve the presentation of the **Embryology Summaries** in previous editions. To create a more integrated presentation, Embryology Summaries have been moved to two key chapters within the text. Embryology Summaries now appear at the end of Chapter 3 (Tissues and Early Embryology) and within Chapter 28 (Embryology and Human Development).

The Sixth Edition of *Human Anatomy* continues to incorporate the terminology endorsed by the International Federation of Associations of Anatomists as published in the 1998 *Terminologia Anatomica* (TA). Wherever practical, we have used terms in the TA and terms internationally recognized and supported by the American Association of Anatomists and other professional organizations in preference to the older, often idiosyncratic terms in common use. Histology and cytology, as subspecialties of anatomy, have lacked a commonly agreed-upon terminology. In 2008, the Federative International Committee on Anatomical Terminology published the *Terminologia Histologica: International Terms for Human Cytology and Histology* (TH). We have incorporated this new histological terminology throughout the Sixth Edition of *Human Anatomy*.

Art Revisions

The art program in the Sixth Edition of *Human Anatomy* has undergone a significant revision. Each figure was evaluated on how well it visually presented the anatomical material in the chapter. Approximately 85% of the figures in this edition are either new or have been revised.

The art palette utilizes new, stronger colors and more dimensionality (e.g., Figures 2.3, 2.15, 5.7, 9.9, 13.5, 13.8, 13.12, 14.1, 14.8, 14.13, 14.14, and 14.17).

Many innovations have been continued and expanded in the Sixth Edition. You'll recognize the **Side-by-Side Figures** and **Macro-to-Micro Figures** that are hallmarks of this book. The **Step-by-Step Figures** facilitate the understanding of sequential anatomical processes and thereby enhance student learning (e.g., Figures 5.5 and 5.11). The areas of detail in many figures have been revised to improve clarity. In addition, boxes and banners have been used to better organize many figures (e.g., Figures 9.5, 25.1, and 26.6). The overlay of line art on surface anatomy photos has been expanded in the Sixth Edition (e.g., Figures 10.10, 11.2, 11.3, 11.5, 11.6, 14.10, 14.11b,c, 15.26, 15.28, 15.29, 15.30, 21.4, 22.16, 23.4, and 23.10) to provide students with a better understanding of where structures are located within the human body. The information derived from superficial and deep dissections is more easily understood as a result of a new heading style that has been incorporated into many of the figures (e.g., Figure 23.14b).

Chapter-by-Chapter Revisions

Specific chapter-by-chapter revisions, with select examples, include:

Chapter 1 (An Introduction to Anatomy)

- Twelve illustrations in this chapter are either new or have been significantly revised.
- Changes were made in terminology according to the TA.

Chapter 2 (The Cell)

- Fifteen illustrations in this chapter are either new or have been significantly revised.
- Changes were made in terminology according to the TA and TH.
- The presentation order of some material was rearranged in order to facilitate student learning.

Chapter 3 (Tissues and Early Embryology)

- Twelve illustrations in this chapter are either new or have been significantly revised.
- Changes were made in terminology according to the TA and TH.
- The presentation order of some material was rearranged in order to facilitate student learning.
- New material was added to update the chapter according to current histological research.
- Embryology Summaries that appeared intermittently throughout the chapters of previous editions of *Human Anatomy* have been brought together in this chapter and in Chapter 28, thereby providing students with a more integrated discussion of embryology and human development.

Chapter 4 (The Integumentary System)

- Twelve illustrations in this chapter are either new or have been significantly revised.
- Changes were made in terminology according to the TA and TH.
- New material was added to the discussion of the epidermis, and the existing material was revised for easier comprehension.

Chapter 5 (The Skeletal System: Osseous Tissue and Skeletal Structure)

- Twelve illustrations in this chapter are either new or have been significantly revised.
- New material was added to the discussion of bone remodeling and repair, and the existing material was revised for easier reading and comprehension.
- New material was added to the discussion of the cells of bone to match current histological terminology and research.

Chapter 6 (The Skeletal System: Axial Division)

- Twelve illustrations in this chapter are either new or have been significantly revised.
- New material was added to the discussion of the bones of the cranium to match current anatomical terminology and research.
- New material was added, and existing material has been clarified, in the discussions of the vertebral regions.

Chapter 7 (The Skeletal System: Appendicular Division)

- Five illustrations in this chapter are either new or have been significantly revised.
- New material was added, and existing material has been clarified, in the discussions of the clavicle, scapula, humerus, pelvic girdle, patella, tibia, and the arches of the foot.

Chapter 8 (The Skeletal System: Articulations)

- Eleven illustrations in this chapter are either new or have been significantly revised.
- An extensive revision of this chapter was undertaken, with new material added and existing material clarified in almost every section of the chapter.

Chapter 9 (The Muscular System: Skeletal Muscle Tissue and Muscle Organization)

- Eleven illustrations in this chapter are either new or have been significantly revised.
- A new section entitled "Levers and Pulleys: A Systems Design for Movement" was added to this chapter. This section provides examples of anatomical pulleys and outlines the function of these structures and how they enhance the functioning of skeletal muscles.

Chapter 10 (The Muscular System: Axial Musculature)

- Eleven illustrations in this chapter are either new or have been significantly revised.
- The sections entitled "Muscles of the Vertebral Column" and "Muscles of the Perineum and the Pelvic Diaphragm" have been updated and clarified.

Chapter 11 (The Muscular System: Appendicular Musculature)

- Seventeen illustrations in this chapter are either new or have been significantly revised.
- A new section entitled "Factors Affecting Appendicular Muscle Function" has been added to this chapter. This section helps students work through the process of *understanding* the actions of skeletal muscles at a joint. This section also explains the concept of the *action line of a muscle*, and how students, once they have determined the action line, may apply three simple rules in order to determine the action of a muscle at that joint.

Chapter 12 (Surface Anatomy and Cross-Sectional Anatomy)

- Seven new cross-sectional images from the Visible Human Project (subsequently enhanced) have been added to the chapter. These new images will assist students in the development of their three-dimensional understanding of anatomical concepts.

Chapter 13 (The Nervous System: Neural Tissue)

- Eight illustrations in this chapter are either new or have been significantly revised.
- The sections entitled "Neuroglia of the CNS" and "Synaptic Communication" were updated in order to match current research findings in the field.

Chapter 14 (The Nervous System: The Spinal Cord and Spinal Nerves)

- Twelve illustrations in this chapter are either new or have been significantly revised.
- The discussion of the meninges of the spinal cord was expanded.
- The discussion of the sectional anatomy of the spinal cord was expanded, with particular emphasis on the revision of the section on "Organization of the Gray Matter."
- The section on "Spinal Nerves" has been rewritten in order to facilitate student learning and comprehension.
- The sections on "The Brachial Plexus" and "The Lumbar and Sacral Plexuses" were rewritten to make them easier to understand.

Chapter 15 (The Nervous System: The Brain and Cranial Nerves)

- Twenty illustrations in this chapter are either new or have been significantly revised.
- All sections of this chapter were revised, either partially or totally, to make them easier to understand.

Chapter 16 (The Nervous System: Pathways and Higher-Order Functions)
- Seven illustrations in this chapter are either new or have been significantly revised.
- All sections of this chapter were revised, either partially or totally, to make them easier to understand.

Chapter 17 (The Nervous System: Autonomic Division)
- Eleven illustrations in this chapter are either new or have been significantly revised.
- All sections of this chapter were revised, either partially or totally, to make them easier to understand.

Chapter 18 (The Nervous System: General and Special Senses)
- Twenty-three illustrations in this chapter are either new or have been significantly revised.
- All sections of this chapter were revised, either partially or totally, to make them easier to understand.

Chapter 19 (The Endocrine System)
- Eleven illustrations in this chapter are either new or have been significantly revised.
- All sections of this chapter were revised, either partially or totally, to make them easier to understand.

Chapter 20 (The Cardiovascular System: Blood)
- Six illustrations in this chapter are either new or have been significantly revised.
- All sections of this chapter were updated in order to match current research findings in the field.

Chapter 21 (The Cardiovascular System: The Heart)
- Seven illustrations in this chapter are either new or have been significantly revised.
- The sections on "The Intercalated Discs," "Orientation and Superficial Anatomy of the Heart," and "Coronary Blood Vessels" were rewritten in order to reflect new research findings in the field and to make them easier to understand.

Chapter 22 (The Cardiovascular System: Vessels and Circulation)
- Twenty illustrations in this chapter are either new or have been significantly revised.
- All sections of this chapter were updated in order to match current research findings in the field.
- All sections of this chapter were revised, either partially or totally, to make them easier to understand.

Chapter 23 (The Lymphoid System)
- Fifteen illustrations in this chapter are either new or have been significantly revised.
- All sections of this chapter were updated in order to match current research findings in the field.
- All sections of this chapter were revised, either partially or totally, to make them easier to understand.

Chapter 24 (The Respiratory System)
- Thirteen illustrations in this chapter are either new or have been significantly revised.
- Revisions have been made to reflect the current histological information on the respiratory system.
- All sections of this chapter were revised, either partially or totally, to make them easier to understand.

Chapter 25 (The Digestive System)
- Twenty-one illustrations in this chapter are either new or have been significantly revised.
- Revisions were made to reflect the current histological information on the various organs of the digestive system.
- All sections of this chapter were revised, either partially or totally, to make them easier to understand.

Chapter 26 (The Urinary System)
- Six illustrations in this chapter are either new or have been significantly revised.
- Revisions were made to reflect the current histological information on the various organs of the digestive system.
- All sections of this chapter were revised, either partially or totally, to make them easier to understand.

Chapter 27 (The Reproductive System)
- Seventeen illustrations in this chapter are either new or have been significantly revised.
- Revisions were made to reflect the current histological information on the various organs of the male and female reproductive systems.
- All sections of this chapter were revised, either partially or totally, to make them easier to understand.

Chapter 28 (The Reproductive System: Embryology and Human Development)
- All of the Embryology Summaries in this chapter have been significantly revised.
- Embryology Summaries that appeared intermittently throughout the chapters of previous editions of *Human Anatomy* have been brought together in this chapter and in Chapter 3, thereby providing students with a more integrated discussion of embryology and human development.

The Ultimate Anatomy Practice Tool

Practice Anatomy Lab (PAL) 2.0 is an indispensable virtual anatomy practice tool that gives students 24/7 access to the most widely used lab specimens, including the **human cadaver, anatomical models, histology slides, cat, and fetal pig.** Each of the five specimen modules includes hundreds of images as well as interactive tools for reviewing the specimens, hearing the names of anatomical structures, and taking multiple choice quizzes and fill-in-the-blank lab practical exams. Specimen images are also linked to animations.

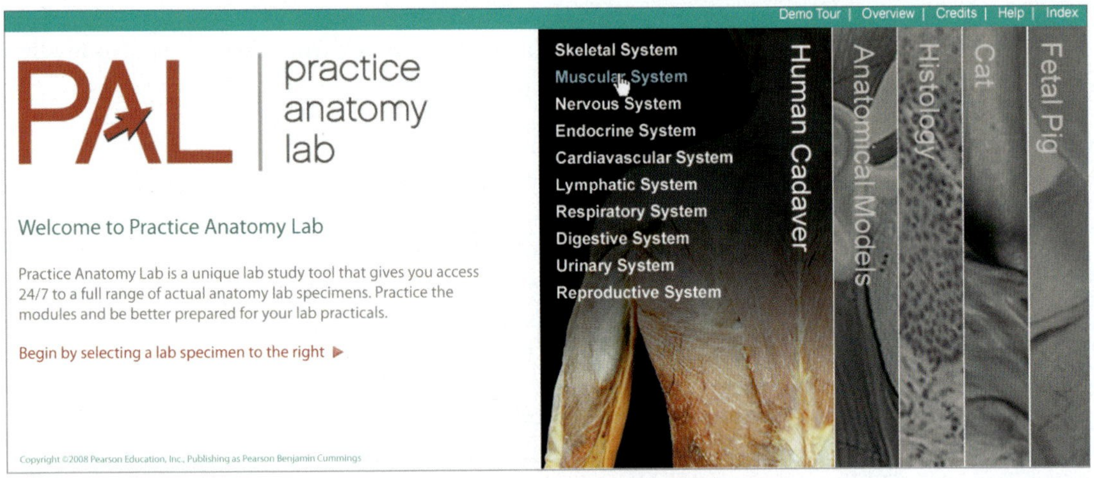

NEW! PAL 2.0 features:

- **The all-new Human Cadaver module** includes hundreds of specially-commissioned cadaver photos in all three activity sections in the module. This module also provides a **fully rotatable human skull** and 17 other rotatable skeletal structures.
- **3D Animations of Origins, Insertions, Actions, and Innervations** depict more than 65 muscles in the Human Cadaver module. These 3D Animations are viewable as students learn and hear the name of a muscle, thereby giving students a **one-stop learning experience**. Gradable Quizzes for the Animations are included.
- **Customizable and gradable Quizzes and Lab Practicals** allow instructors to customize the online gradable Quizzes and Lab Practicals to reflect only those structures on which they want their students to be tested. The Quizzes and Lab Practicals are available in the Computerized Test Bank (and in Microsoft® Word®) and in CourseCompass,™ Blackboard, and WebCT.
- **A greatly expanded Histology module** includes more images of different types of tissues.
- **Two new body systems, Endocrine and Lymphoid,** have been added to the Human Cadaver and Anatomical Models modules.

Specially-commissioned Cadaver Photos

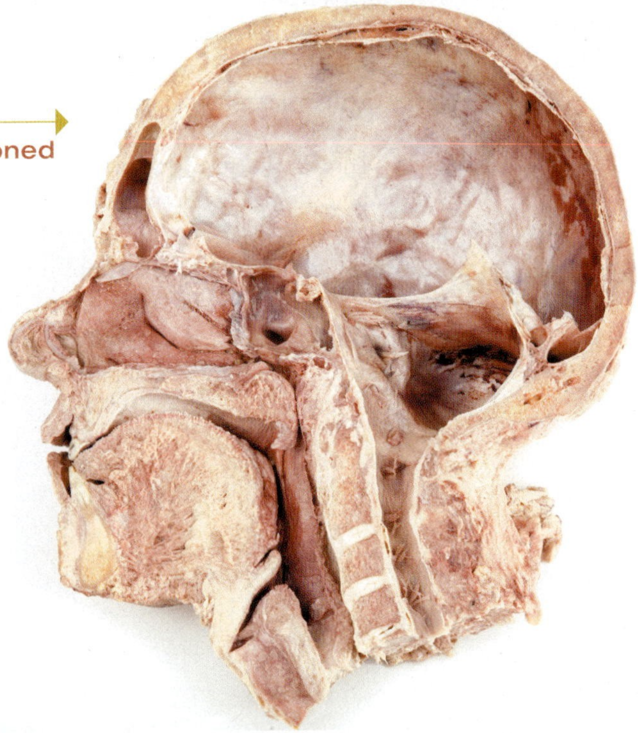

Fully Rotatable Human Skull

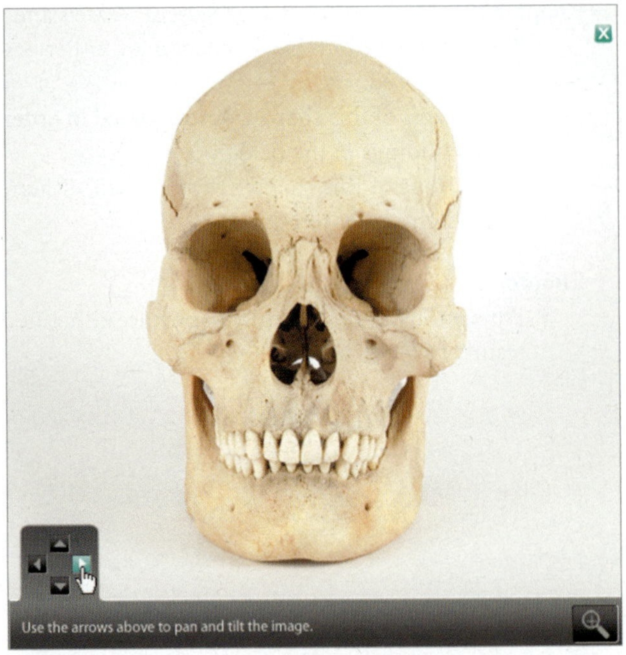

PAL 2.0 is on the myA&P™ Companion Website **(www.myaandp.com)**.
The **PAL 2.0 CD-ROM** can also be packaged with the book for no additional charge.

Everything Students Need to Prepare for their Lab Practical

Three Activity Sections

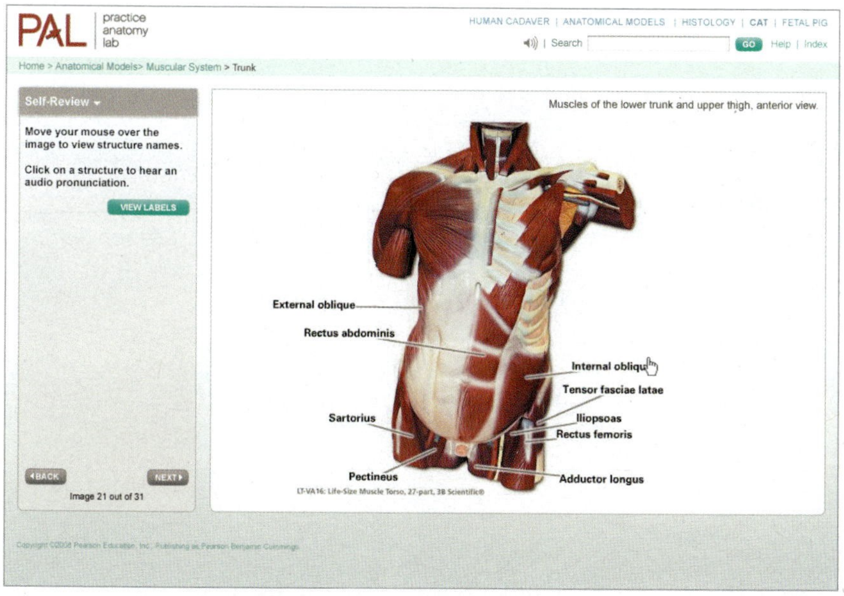

Self-Review allows students to review the names of structures, see structures highlighted, hear pronunciations of anatomical terms, and turn labels on and off.

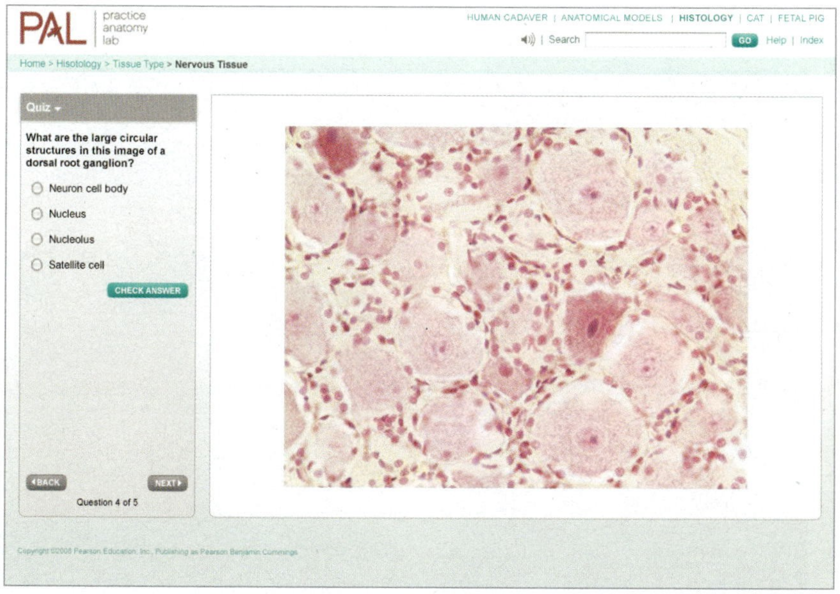

Quizzes let students quiz themselves on their knowledge of anatomical structures and functional anatomy. Students can receive immediate feedback to their answers, or they can wait to see a summary of results with the correct answers next to the images.

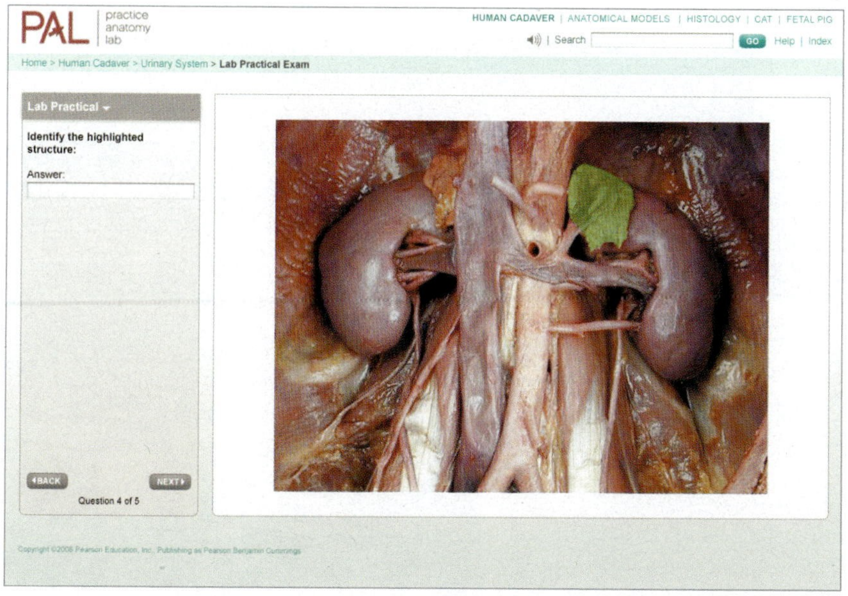

Lab Practicals simulate a real lab practical exam. Fill-in-the-blank exam questions ask students to identify and spell the names of a series of structures.

The **Instructor's Resource DVD for PAL 2.0** includes labeled and unlabeled images from PAL 2.0 in both JPEG and PowerPoint® formats. The PowerPoint Label Edit feature, with editable labels and leader lines, is built into every image. PowerPoint image slides include embedded links to the relevant 3D Animations of Origins, Insertions, Actions, and Innervations (see next page).

NEW! 3D Animations of Origins, Insertions, Actions, and Innervations with Gradable Quizzes

Link from more than 65 muscle images in the PAL™ 2.0 Human Cadaver module to these 3D Animations of Origins, Insertions, Actions, and Innervations. Quizzes for the Animations are included in the Quizzes section of PAL 2.0 (see previous page). The customizable and gradable Quizzes are also available on myA&P™ with CourseCompass.™

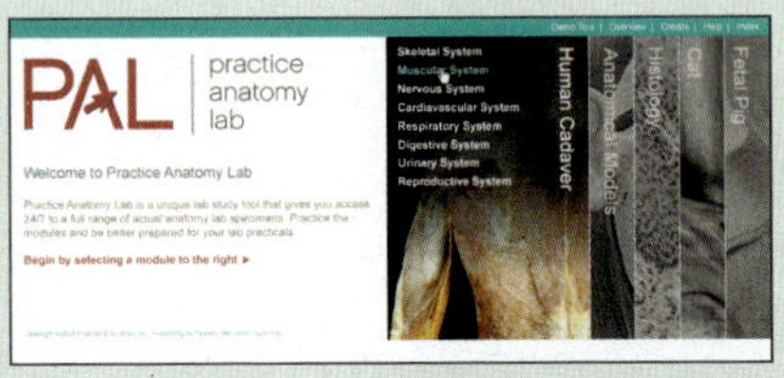

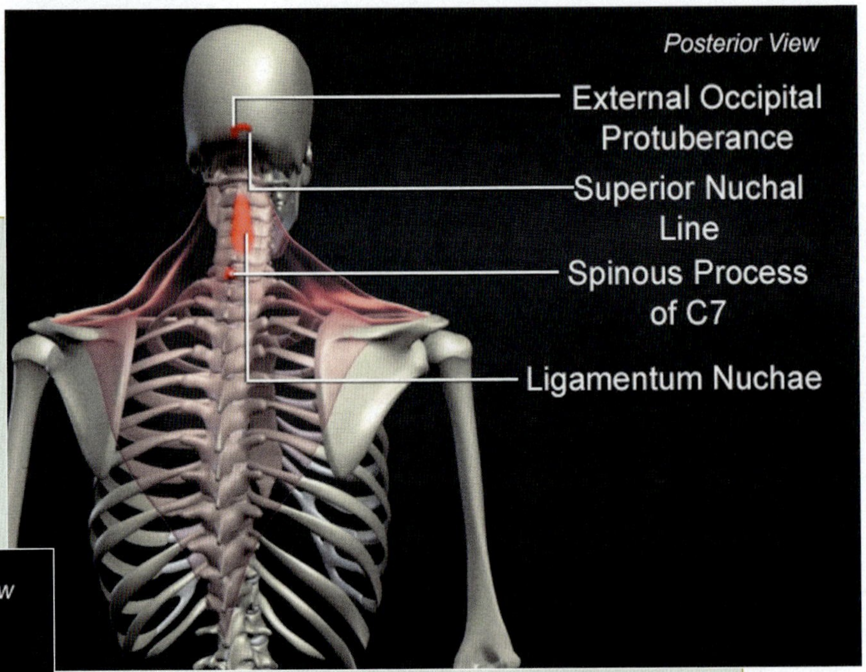

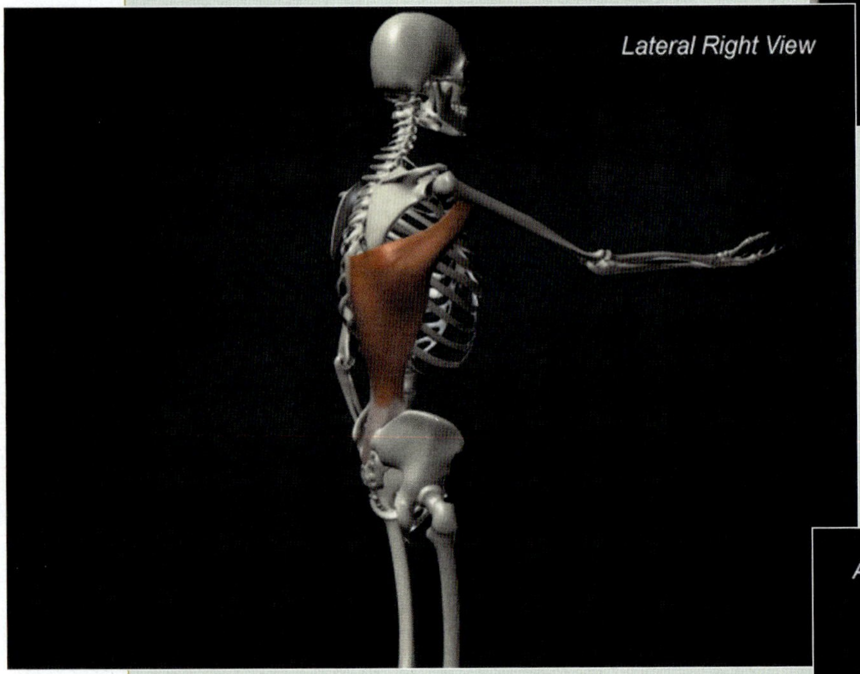

Available on PAL 2.0, myA&P, and the instructor's Media Manager (see next spread).

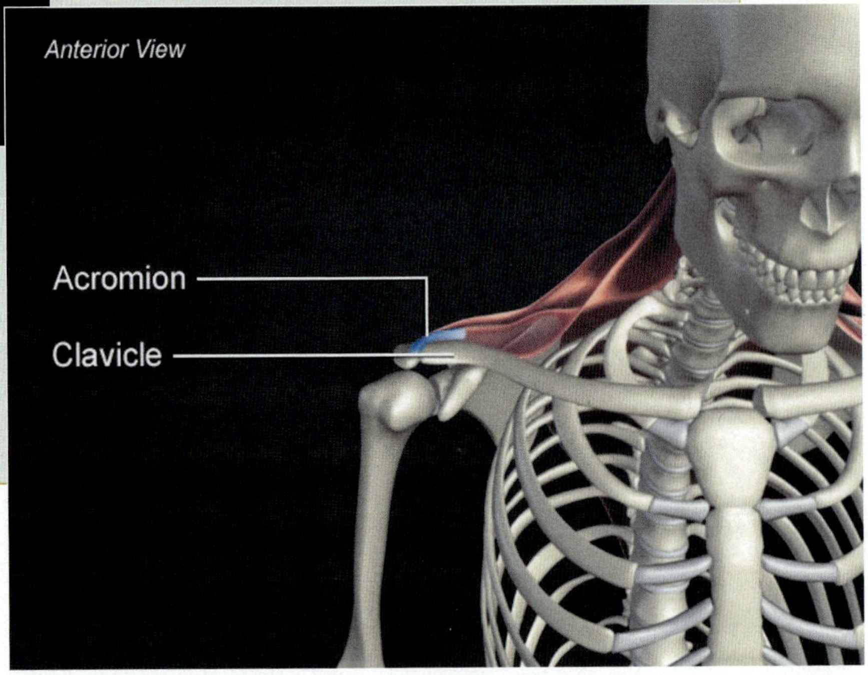

NEW! 3D Anatomy Animations with Gradable Quizzes

These 50 animations **help students understand muscle and joint actions** and appear on **both** the myA&P™ Companion Website and on the instructor's Media Manager (see next spread). The customizable and gradable Quizzes are also available on myA&P™ with CourseCompass.™

myA&P™ Companion Website

Every animation is accompanied by a gradable quiz.

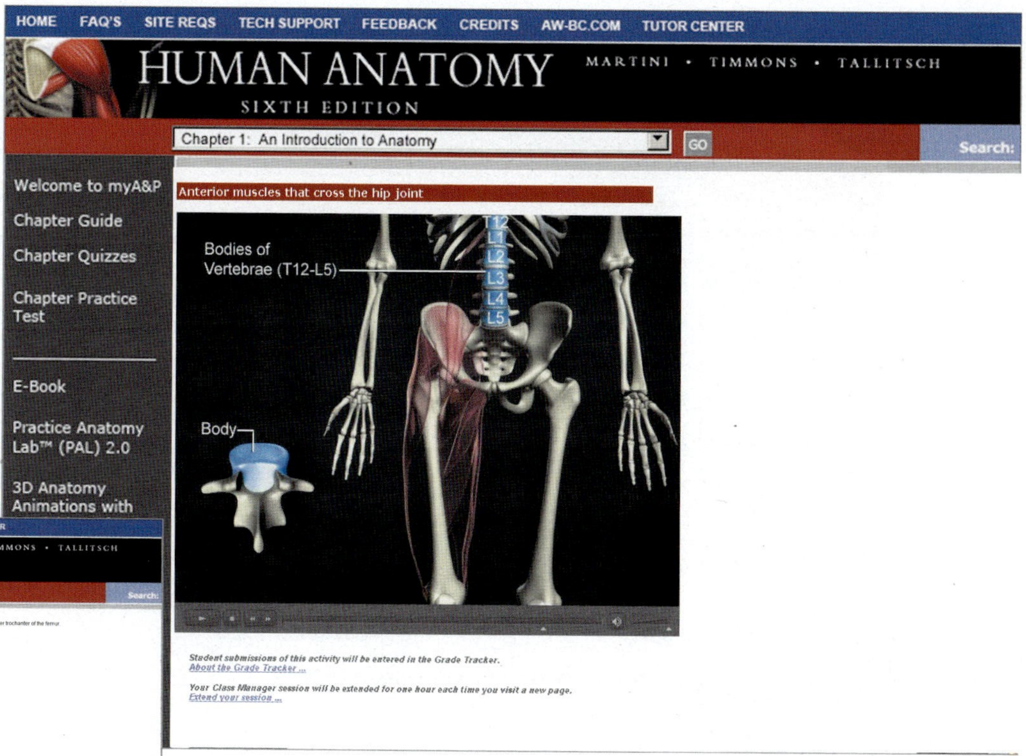

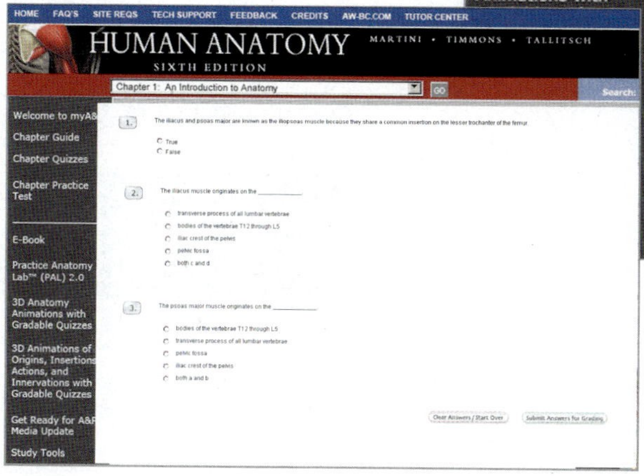

Available on myA&P and the instructor's Media Manager (see next spread).

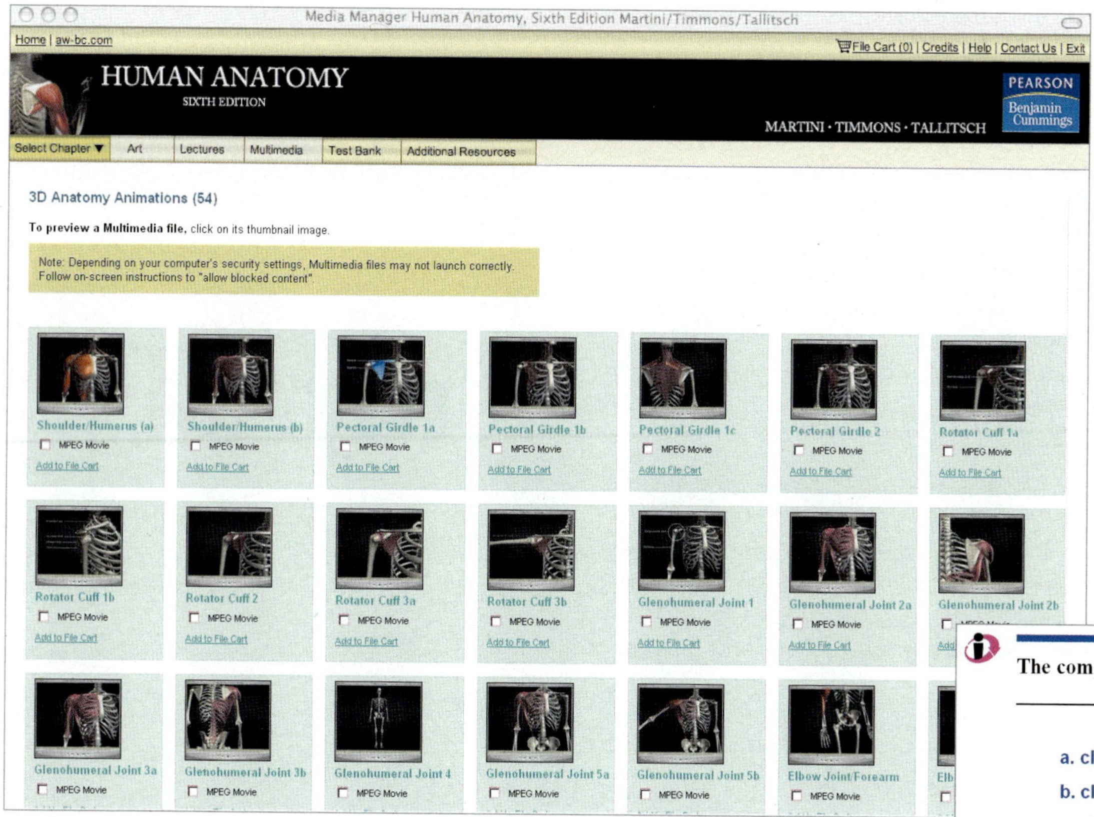

Instructor's Media Manager

Thumbnail images let instructors quickly select animations for a classroom presentation. All animation quiz items from the myA&P Companion Website are available as PRS-enabled Clicker Questions.

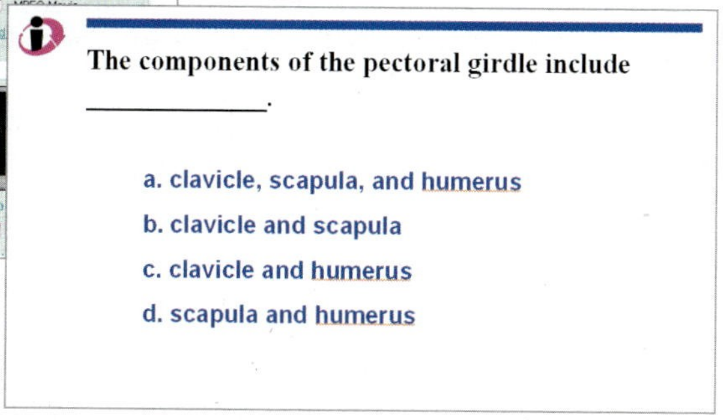

3D Anatomy Animations

myA&P™ Companion Website

Learning through Practice

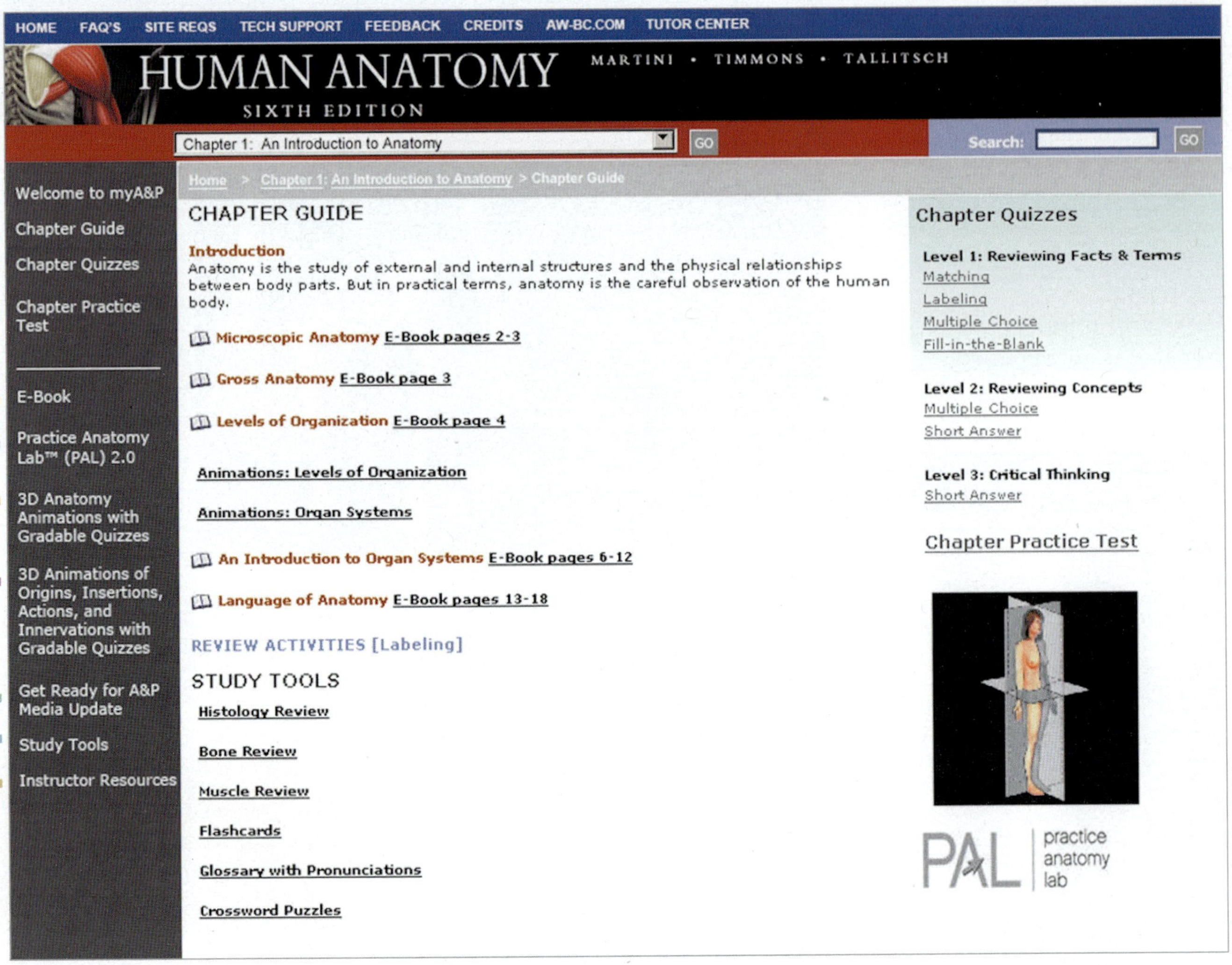

Features of myA&P™ Companion Website:

- **Chapter Guides** organize all chapter-specific activities and assessments by learning unit on one page.
- **Chapter Quizzes** now include more visuals for labeling practice.
- **Chapter Practice Tests** assess students' overall understanding of the chapter and include a timer feature.
- **The E-book** of ***Human Anatomy*, Sixth Edition** is a full electronic version.
- **Practice Anatomy Lab™ (PAL) 2.0** gives 24/7 access to the most widely used lab specimens (see previous spread).
- **3D Anatomy Animations with Gradable Quizzes** illustrate and test students on muscle and joint movements (see previous spread).
- **3D Animations of Origins, Insertions, Actions, and Innervations with Gradable Quizzes** illustrate and test students on these topics (see previous spread).
- ***Get Ready for A&P* Media Update** includes diagnostic quizzes and access to the ***Get Ready for A&P*** website so students can get up to speed with the basics.
- **Study Tools** include Histology Review, Bone Review, Muscle Review, Flashcards, Glossary with Pronunciations, Crossword Puzzles, and more.
- **A Gradebook** tracks students' progress and grades.

myA&P

www.myaandp.com

NEW! Media Manager 2.1

All Instructor Media Resources in One Convenient Place

The **Media Manager** organizes all instructor media resources by chapter into **one convenient and easy-to-use package**.

New to Media Manager 2.1:

- **A "shopping cart" functionality** that allows instructors to quickly search, select, and download any item
- **"Quiz Game" chapter reviews** (in PRS-enabled Clicker Question format) that encourage student interaction and facilitate discussion
- **More than 50 new 3D Anatomy Animations with Quizzes** (in PRS-enabled Clicker Question format) that focus on hard-to-visualize anatomical concepts, especially muscle actions and joint movements (see previous spread)
- **3D Animations of Origins, Insertions, Actions, and Innervations with Quizzes** (in PRS-enabled Clicker Question format) that help students understand these topics (see previous spread)

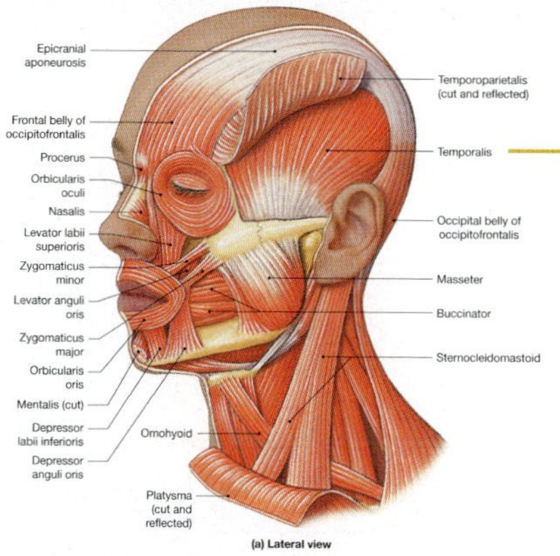

Customizable Art

Label Edit feature

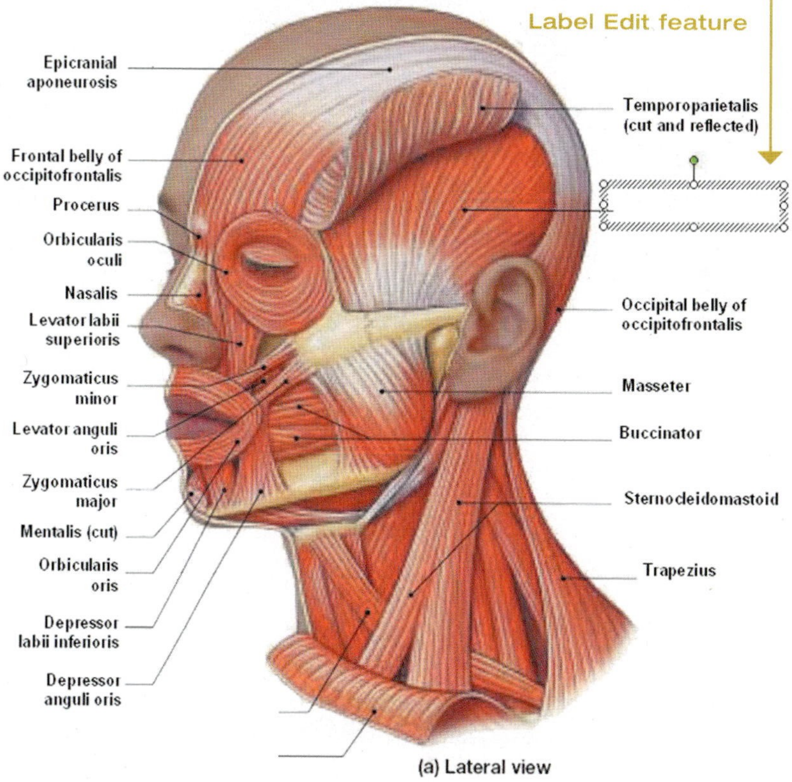

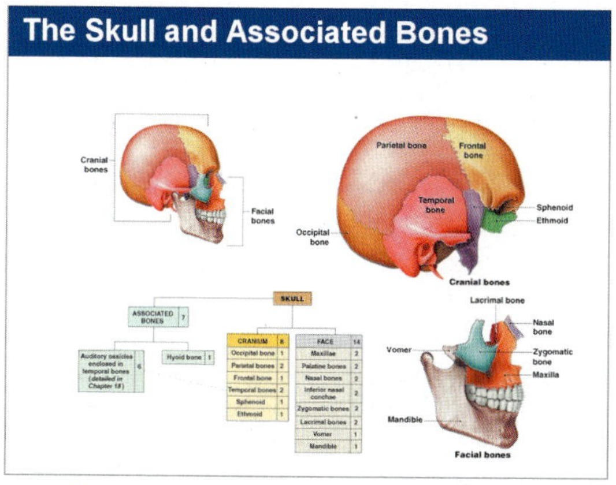

Customizable PowerPoint® Lecture Slides

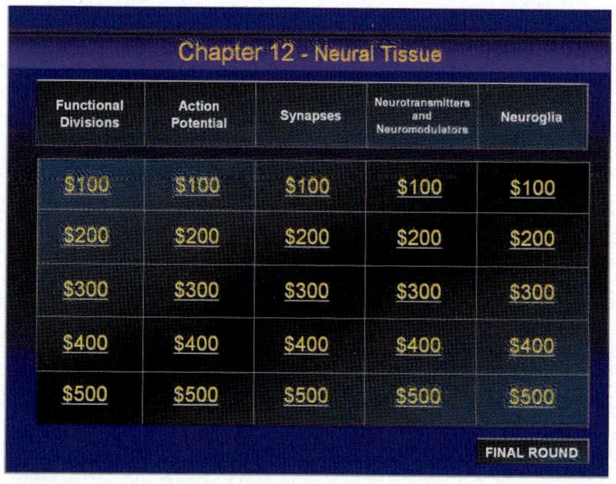

Quiz Game Chapter Reviews

The **Instructor's Resource DVD for PAL 2.0** includes labeled and unlabeled images from PAL 2.0 in both JPEG and PowerPoint® formats. The PowerPoint Label Edit feature, with editable labels and leader lines, is built into every image. PowerPoint image slides include embedded links to the relevant 3D Animations of Origins, Insertions, Actions, and Innervations.

The Media Manager also includes:

- **Customizable art** including all illustrations and photos from the textbook. The optional **Label Edit** feature allows instructors to choose which structures to present.
- **All tables from the textbook**.
- **A bank of additional images** (not in the textbook) including MRI/CT scans, histology slides, and muscle origins and insertions.
- **All images from *Martini's Atlas of the Human Body***.
- **Select *Interactive Physiology*® (IP) slides** on anatomy topics.
- **Active Lecture Questions** that stimulate effective classroom discussions and check comprehension, in PRS-enabled Clicker Question format.
- **Customizable PowerPoint® Lecture Slides**, available for every chapter, combining lecture notes, illustrations, photos, tables, and animations.
- **The Computerized Test Bank**.

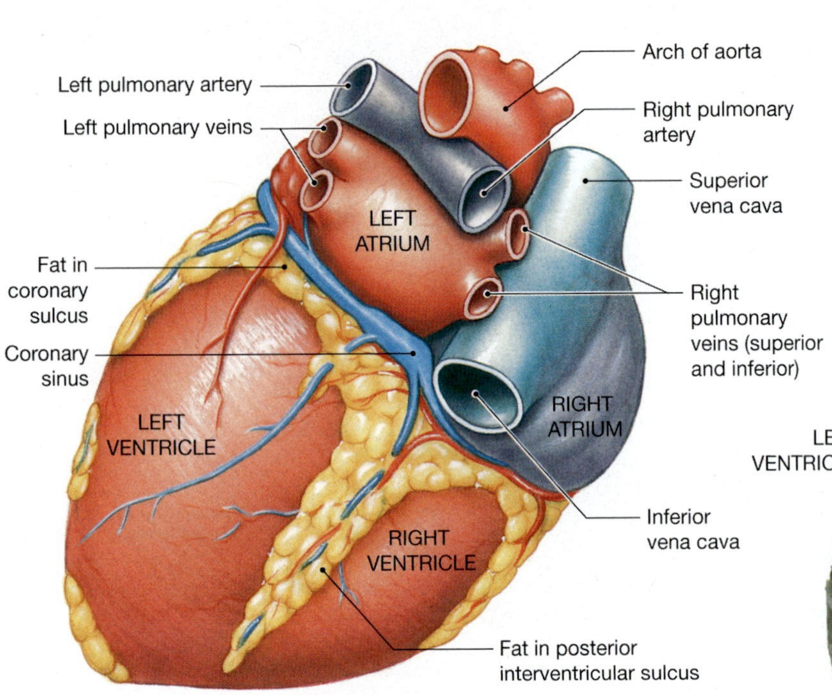

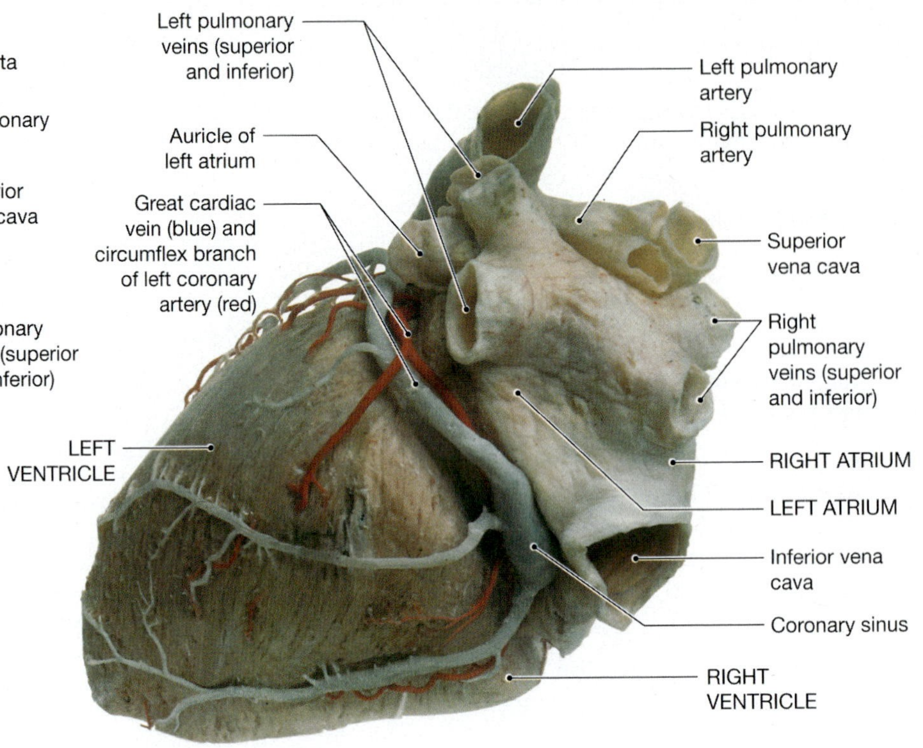

"Side-by-Side" Figures

Multiple views of the same structure or tissue allow students to compare an illustrator's rendering with a photo of the actual structure or tissue as it may be seen in a laboratory or operating room.

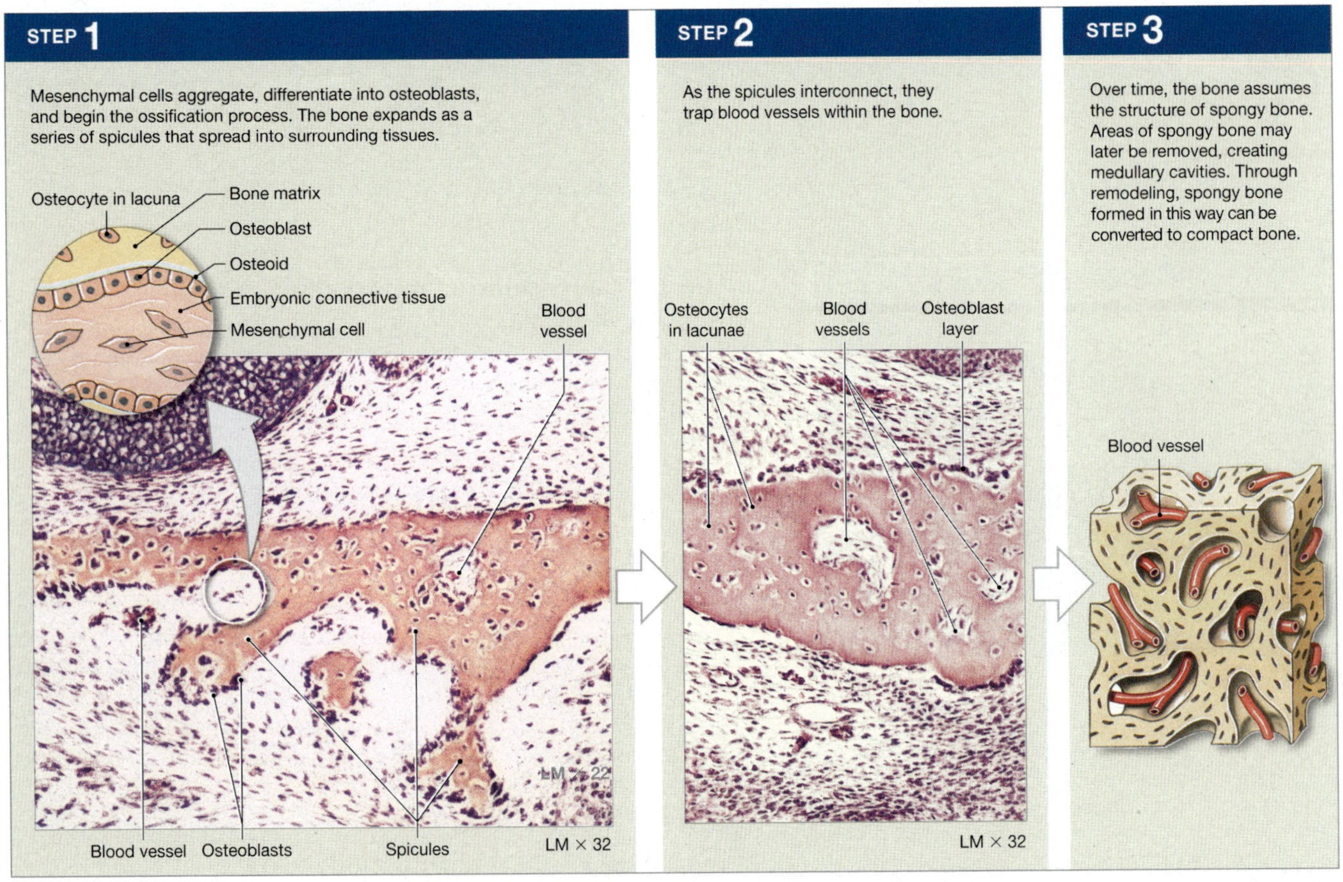

"Step-by-Step" Figures

These figures break down multifaceted processes into numbered step-by-step illustrations that coordinate with the authors' narrative descriptions.

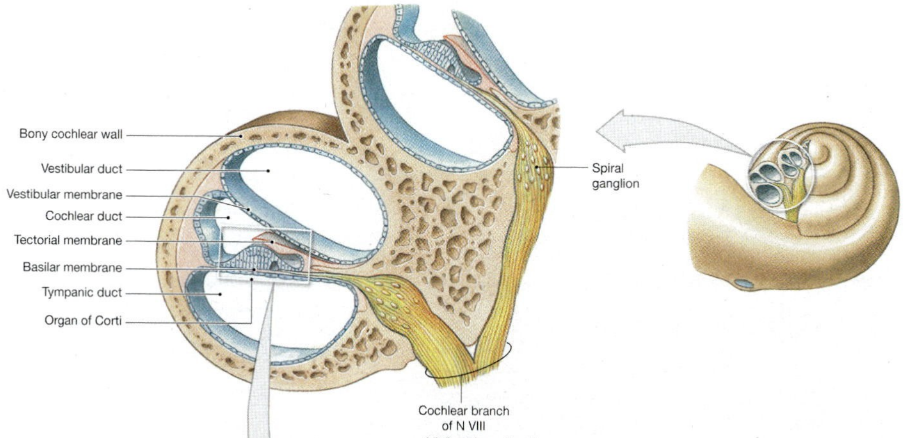

(d) Cochlear chambers

"Macro-to-Micro" Figures

These figures help students to bridge the gap between familiar and unfamiliar structures by sequencing anatomical views from whole organs or other structures to their smaller parts.

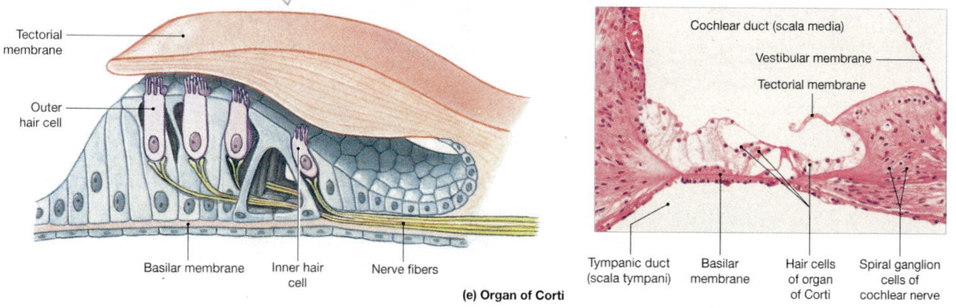

(e) Organ of Corti

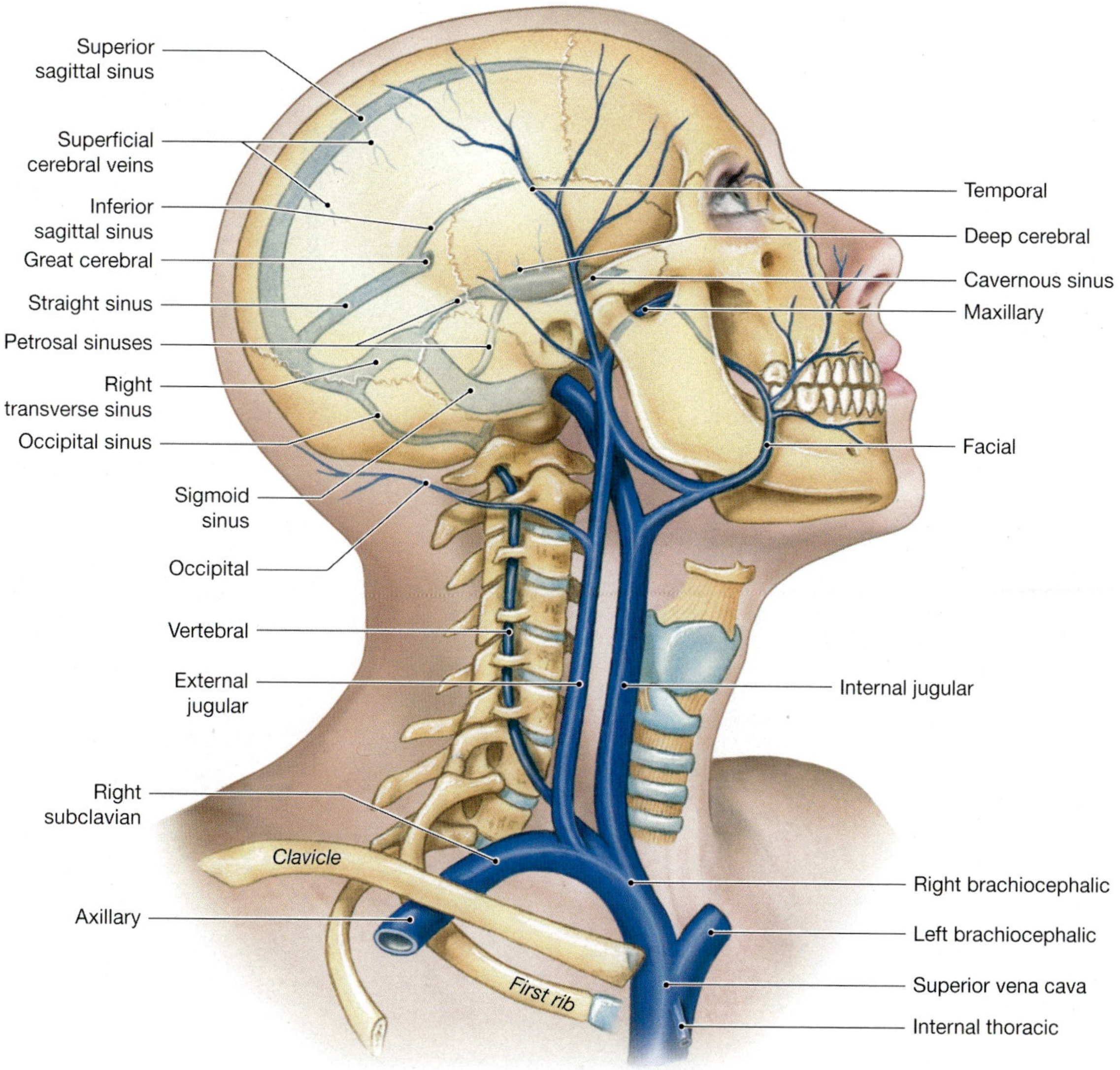

"Illustration-over-Photo" Figures

This method of presenting images brings depth, dimensionality, and visual interest to the page and ensures that the illustrated structures are proportional in size to the human body.

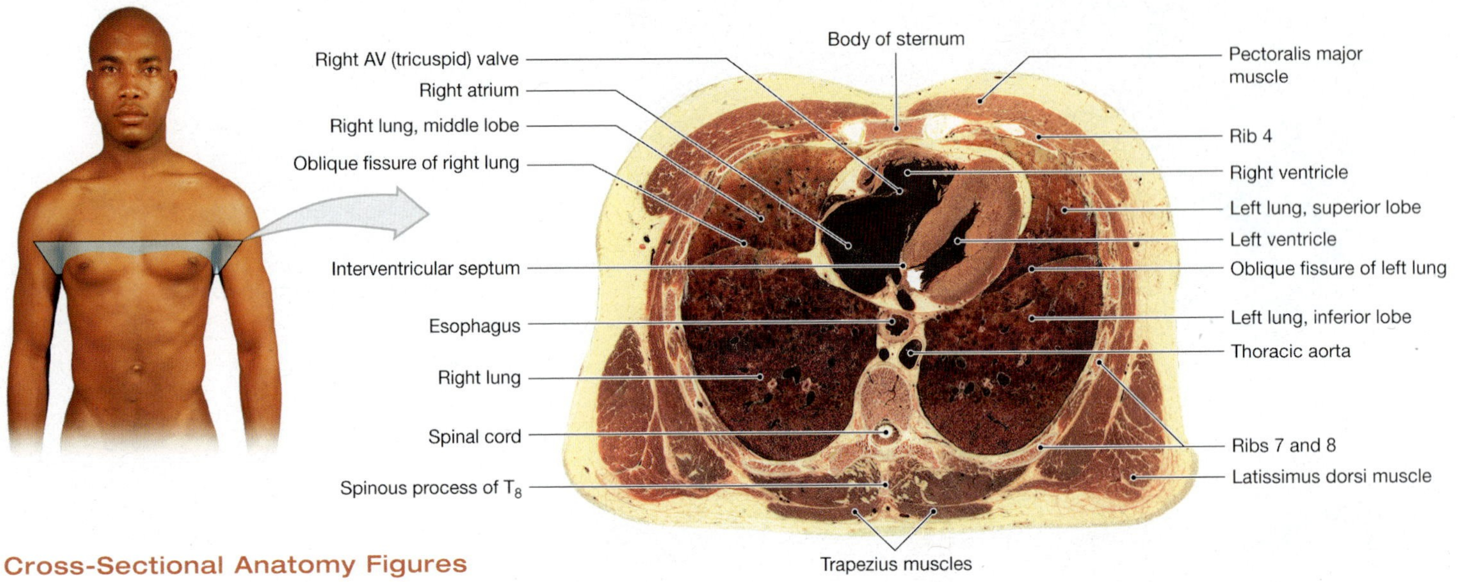

NEW! Cross-Sectional Anatomy Figures

Expanded Chapter 12, now titled "Surface Anatomy and Cross-Sectional Anatomy," includes seven new and subsequently enhanced cross-sectional images from the Visible Human Project to give students another perspective on the human body.

Embryology Summary Figures

Highlighting the developmental stages of significant organs, structures, and systems, the Embryology Summaries that previously appeared with each body system throughout the book have been consolidated into two substantial sections in Chapter 3 and Chapter 28.

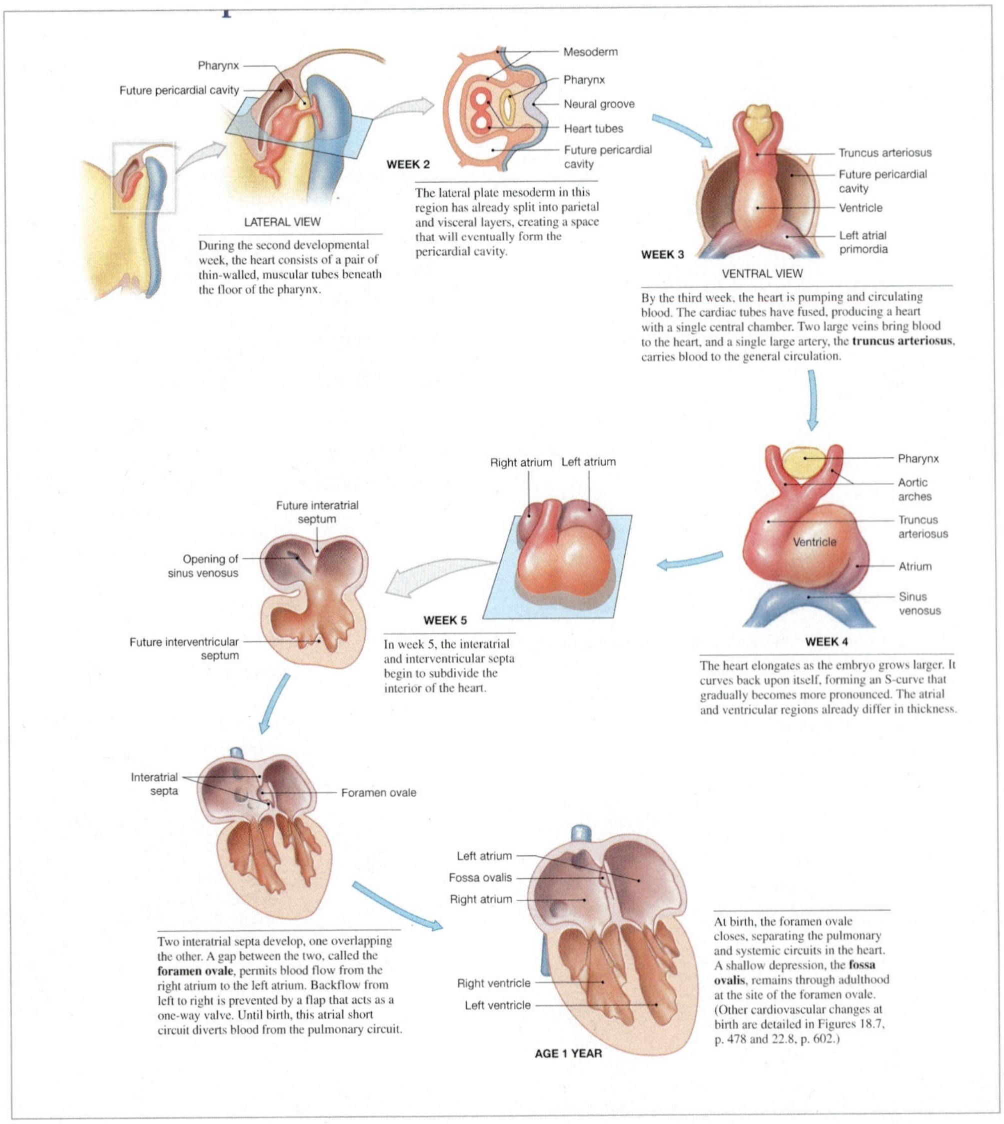

Increased Clinical Coverage

Clinical Case — THE ENDOCRINE SYSTEM

WHY CAN'T I KEEP UP ANYMORE?

Joan is a 35-year-old college professor. She is a regular runner, averaging 35–40 miles per week. Joan has always been interested in running, and she continued to improve throughout high school and college. Her running career peaked when Joan earned cross-country all-American honors during her third and fourth years of intercollegiate running at the University of Wisconsin–Madison. Since joining the faculty at her college five years ago, Joan has enjoyed running during the week and on weekends with several of the male faculty members. She has always taken pride in the fact that she can, and does, run much faster than her male counterparts. For the past six months, however, Joan has noticed that it has become increasingly difficult to sustain her normal running tempo and pace, even on runs as short as 2–3 miles. This, combined with frequent muscle cramps, joint pains, cold-like symptoms, and chronic fatigue has forced her to think of herself as an "old runner" and someone who can't keep up with her normal running partners any more. Joan finally decides to make an appointment with her family physician when she is turned down as a blood donor due to anemia and elevated total cholesterol and triglyceride levels.

Initial Examination

Joan is examined by her family physician. The physical examination yields the following information:

- cold symptoms and a hoarse voice that have persisted for 2–3 weeks
- frequent problems with constipation
- yellow coloration to the skin, but no scleral involvement
- cool, dry, rough, and scaly skin
- presence of a puffy face and periorbital edema
- thickened and brittle nails
- slight, diffuse hair loss involving the scalp and the lateral third of the eyebrows
- blood pressure 110/80 mm Hg
- diminished deep tendon reflexes with prolonged muscle relaxation as observed by the Achilles tendon reflex
- slightly enlarged thyroid gland that is rubbery to palpation without any tenderness

Joan's physician orders the following laboratory tests:

- complete blood count (CBC)
- lipid profile
- urine test
- TSH levels
- free T_4 levels

Follow-up Examination

Joan and her physician meet the next week to discuss the results of her lab tests. The test results demonstrate the following:

- CBC is consistent with iron deficiency anemia.
- Lipid profile confirms high total cholesterol, high low-density lipoprotein, and high triglyceride levels.
- Plasma TSH levels are 20 mU/L.
- Free T_4 levels are 0.6 ng/dl.

CLINICAL CASE TERMS

anemia: Any condition in which the number of red blood cells or the concentration of hemoglobin is clinically reduced.
autoimmune disease: A condition in which an individual's lymphoid system produces cells and/or antibodies against the individual's own tissues.
cholesterol: The most abundant steroid in animal tissues, especially in bile, and present in food, especially food rich in animal fat.
complete blood count: Count of all the red and white blood cells and platelets found within a specific amount of blood.
deep tendon reflexes *(myotatic reflex)*: A contraction of muscles in response to a stretching force resulting from stimulation of proprioceptors.
lipid profile: A lab test that examines the concentrations and chemical characteristics of the lipids suspended within the blood of an individual.
periorbital edema: An accumulation of an excessive amount of watery fluid in the interstitial spaces of the skin surrounding the eyes.
sclera: A portion of the fibrous layer forming the outer layer of the eyeball; the white of the eye.
triglyceride: Fatty acid linked to glycerol; the most important form of lipid in the body. Also known as triacylglycerol.

NEW! Clinical Cases

Clinical Cases, found at the end of each chapter that closes a body system, lead students from a description of a patient's symptoms, through the results of physical exams and lab work, through engaging questions that encourage them to review related content in the preceding chapters, through a brief analysis and interpretation of the case, and ultimately to a diagnosis.

continued

...der

...e body, at one time or another, plays an important ...signs or symptoms, thereby enabling a physician to ...various clues that will, ideally, lead to a correct diag... ...t. Both the patient's presenting symptoms and the ...s and interpretation of the symptoms contribute to ...

...meaning of the information presented in the case ...review the anatomical material covered in Chapter ...ine System. The questions below will guide you in ...k about and answer each one, referring back to ...eed help.

...e, all of Joan's symptoms seem to be random and un... ...t do all of these symptoms have in common?

...n's symptoms develop slowly over such a long pe...

...oan's lipid profile confirm high total cholesterol, high ...ipoprotein, and high triglyceride levels?

...terpretation

...elow answers the questions raised in the "Points to ... To review the material, refer to the pages referenced ...

... hormones secreted by the endocrine system have ...metabolic effects. All of Joan's symptoms are related ...ll cellular metabolic level and rate of oxygen con... ...p. 513–515).

...r cavities within the follicles of the thyroid gland ...ne (T_4) and triiodothyronine (T_3) (p. 513). The re... ...hormones will slowly decrease as Joan's condition ...nce the slow development of her symptoms.

...ofile, high total cholesterol, high low-density lipopro... ...triglyceride levels are the result of a decreased meta... ...d the decreased absorption of lipids by peripheral ...tissues. Many of the hormones secreted by the endocrine system affect various aspects of the body's metabolism (pp. 518–521).

Diagnosis

After further testing for anti-thyroid antibodies and an MRI (Figure 19.12), Joan is diagnosed with an autoimmune disease: **Hashimoto thyroiditis**. This disease is characterized by the slow destruction of the thyroid cells by various cell- and antibody-mediated immune processes. The result of this autoimmune disease is inadequate thyroid hormone synthesis and release. However, the symptoms of this disease develop slowly over time due to the "leakage" of previously formed thyroxine and triiodothyronine from the thyroid follicles slowly being damaged by the autoimmune disease.

Hashimoto thyroiditis is the most common cause of hypothyroidism in residents of the United States over 6 years of age. Worldwide, the most common cause of hypothyroidism is iodine deficiency. However, Hashimoto thyroiditis is the most common cause of spontaneous hypothyroidism worldwide in areas with adequate dietary iodine intake.

Joan's physician used her knowledge of the individual endocrine organs and their functions to predict the symptoms of specific endocrine disorders. For example, Joan's symptoms, as unrelated as they might have appeared initially, indicated to the physician that Joan's metabolism was not normal. Thyroid hormones increase basal metabolic rate, body heat production, perspiration, and heart rate. An elevated metabolic rate, increased body temperature, weight loss, nervousness, excessive perspiration, and an increased or irregular heartbeat are symptoms of hyperthyroidism. Conversely, a low metabolic rate, decreased body temperature, weight gain, lethargy, dry skin, and a reduced heart rate typically accompany hypothyroidism. However, many signs and symptoms related to endocrine disorders are less definitive. For example, polyuria, or increased urine production, can result from hyposecretion of ADH (diabetes insipidus) or the hyperglysuria caused by diabetes mellitus; a symptom such as hypertension (high blood pressure) can be caused by a variety of cardiovascular or endocrine problems. In these instances, many diagnostic decisions are based on blood and other tests, which can confirm the presence of an endocrine disorder by detecting abnormal levels of circulating hormones or metabolic products resulting from hormone action. Follow-up tests can determine whether the primary cause of the problem lies with the endocrine gland, the regulatory mechanism(s), or the target tissues. Often, a pattern of several different test results leads to the diagnosis. Table 19.6 provides a clinical overview of endocrine malfunctions, and Table 19.7 outlines some anatomical tests used in the diagnosis of endocrine disorders such as Joan's. ■

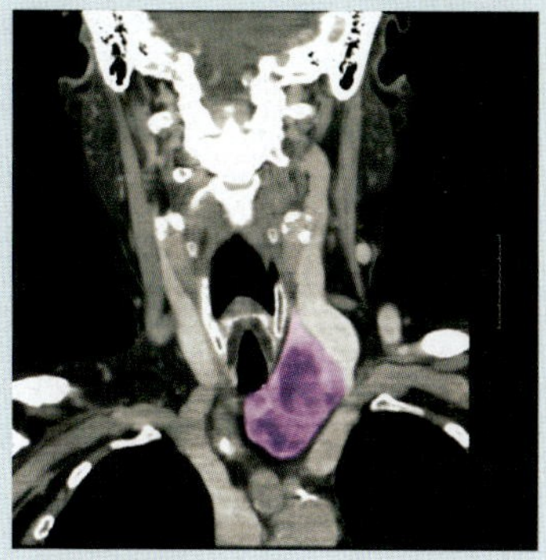

Figure 19.12 Joan's MRI

Clinical Note

Traumatic Brain Injuries *Traumatic brain injury (TBI)* may result from harsh contact between the head and another object or from a severe jolt. Head injuries account for more than half the deaths attributed to trauma. Every year roughly 1.5 million cases of TBI occur in the United States. Approximately 50,000 people die, and another 80,000 have long-term disability.

Concussions may accompany even minor head injuries. A concussion may involve transient confusion with abnormal mental status, temporary loss of consciousness, and some degree of amnesia. Physicians examine concussed individuals quite closely and may x-ray or CT-scan the skull to check for fractures or cranial bleeding. Mild concussions produce a brief interruption of consciousness and little memory loss. Severe concussions produce extended periods of unconsciousness and abnormal neurological functions. Severe concussions are typically associated with contusions (bruises), hemorrhages, or lacerations (tears) of the brain tissue; the possibilities for recovery vary with the areas affected. Extensive damage to the reticular formation can produce a permanent state of unconsciousness, and damage to the lower brain stem generally proves fatal.

Wearing helmets during activities such as bike, horse, skateboard, or motorcycle riding; contact sports such as football and hockey; and when batting and base running in baseball provides protection for the brain. Seat belts give similar protection in the event of a motor vehicle accident. If a concussion does occur, restricted activities, including delay in return to the activity that led to the injury, is recommended.

Clinical Notes

The Clinical Notes embedded in the running narrative of each chapter present pathologies and their relation to normal physiological function, while the larger boxed versions address important medical or social topics. The number of Clinical Notes has been increased in this edition.

NEW! Full-Color Laboratory Manual

This new full-color laboratory manual combines illustrations (modified, as needed) and photos from ***Human Anatomy*, Sixth Edition** with Michael G. Wood's easy-to-follow writing style and student-focused features to make it the most learner-centered Human Anatomy laboratory manual available.

Ideal in combination with ***Human Anatomy,* Sixth Edition**, it is also a perfect companion to any other Human Anatomy textbook.

Key features include:

- *QuickCheck* questions
- *Making Connections* boxes
- *Clinical Correlations* sections
- *A Regional Look* pages

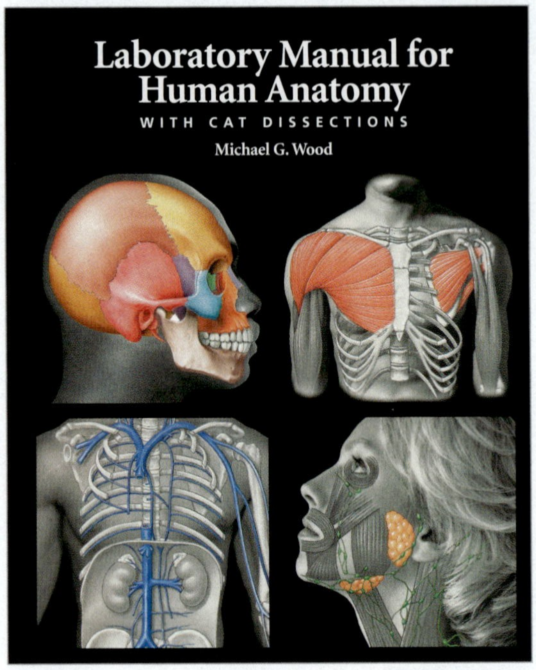

Laboratory Manual for Human Anatomy with Cat Dissections
by Michael G. Wood
© 2009 • 512 pages
978-0-8053-7375-2 • 0-8053-7375-6

Instructor Supplements

Media Manager 2.1 (Includes Computerized Test Bank)
978-0-321-51232-1 • 0-321-51232-4

Instructor Visual Guide
978-0-321-51196-6 • 0-321-51196-4

Instructor Manual
978-0-321-51191-1 • 0-321-51191-3

Printed Test Bank
978-0-321-51193-5 • 0-321-51193-X

Transparency Acetates
978-0-321-51192-8 • 0-321-51192-1

Website and Course Management Programs

myA&P™
www.myaandp.com
Gateway to the myA&P Companion Website and the myA&P with CourseCompass course management program

WebCT
www.aw-bc.com/webct

Blackboard
www.aw-bc.com/blackboard

Student Supplements

Practice Anatomy Lab 2.0 CD-ROM
Available for packaging with the textbook for no additional charge

***Get Ready for A&P* Media Update**
by Lori K. Garrett
Available for packaging with the textbook for no additional charge

Martini's Atlas of the Human Body
by Frederic H. Martini
Available for packaging with the textbook for no additional charge

A&P Applications Manual
by Frederic H. Martini and Kathleen Welch
Available for packaging with the textbook for no additional charge

Martini Study Card
978-0-321-53601-3 • 0-321-53601-0
Available for packaging with the textbook for no additional charge

Acknowledgments

We would like to acknowledge the many users, reviewers, survey respondents, and focus group members whose advice, comments, and collective wisdom helped shape this text into its final form. Their passion for the subject, their concern for accuracy and method of presentation, and their experience with students of widely varying abilities and backgrounds have made the revision process interesting and educating.

Reviewers

Frank Baker, *Golden West College*
Gillian Bice, *Michigan State University*
William Brothers, *San Diego Mesa College*
Jett Chinn, *College of Marin*
Cynthia Herbrandson, *Kellogg Community College*
Kelly Johnson, *University of Kansas*
Philip Osborne, *San Diego City College*
Heather Roberts, *Sierra College*
Dean J. Scherer, *Oklahoma State University*
Judith L. Schotland, *Boston University*
Elena Stark, *Santa Monica College*
Edward Williams, *Minnesota State University*
Sally Wilson, *Marshalltown Community College*
David Woodman, *University of Nebraska*
Scott D. Zimmerman, *Missouri State University*
John M. Zook, *Ohio University*
Joan Ellen Zuckerman, *Long Beach City College*

Technical Reviewers

Wendy Lackey, *Michigan State University*
Alan D. Magid, *Duke University School of Medicine*
Larry A. Reichard, *Metropolitan Community College*
Mark Seifert, *Indiana University-Purdue University Indianapolis*
Lance Wilson, *Triton College*
Michele Zimmerman, *Indiana University Southeast*

The creative talents brought to this project by our artist team, William Ober, M.D., and Claire Garrison, R.N., are inspiring and valuable beyond expression. Bill and Claire worked intimately and tirelessly with us, imparting a unity of vision to the book while making each illustration both clear and beautiful. Their superb art program is greatly enhanced by the incomparable bone and cadaver photographs of Ralph T. Hutchings, formerly of The Royal College of Surgeons of England and coauthor of the best-selling McMinn's *Color Atlas of Human Anatomy.* In addition, Dr. Pietro Motta, Professor of Anatomy, University of Roma, La Sapienza, provided several superb SEM images for use in the text.

A special note of thanks to Delia Hamidzada, P.A., and Elizabeth Wilson, R.N., for assisting Mike Timmons with organizing portions of the manuscript and review.

We are deeply indebted to the Benjamin Cummings staff, whose efforts were vital to the creation of this edition. A special note of thanks and gratitude goes to the editorial staff at Benjamin Cummings, especially Leslie Berriman, Executive Editor, for her dedication to the success of this project; Katy German, Project Editor, for her management of the text and its components; and Robin Pille, Associate Editor, and Kelly Reed, Editorial Assistant, for their work on the supplements. We express thanks to Sarah Young-Dualan, Media Producer, Aimee Pavy, Media Producer, and Suzanne Rassmussen, Associate Media Producer, for their work across all of the media programs that support *Human Anatomy.* Thanks also to Caroline Ayres, Production Supervisor, for her steady hand managing this complex text; and Norine Strang, Angie Hamilton, Mark Wyngarden, and Laura Davis for their roles in the production of the text. We appreciate the phenomenal art and design contributions of Mark Ong, Design Manager; and Blake Kim, Art Developer. We are very grateful to Linda Davis, President, Frank Ruggirello, Editorial Director, and Lauren Fogel, Director of Media Development for their continued enthusiasm and support of this project. We appreciate the contributions of Gordon Lee, Marketing Manager, who keeps his finger on the pulse of the market and helps us meet the needs of our users, and the remarkable and tireless Pearson Science sales reps.

We are also grateful that the contributions of all of the aforementioned people have led to this text receiving the following awards: The Association of Medical Illustrators Award, The Text and Academic Authors Award, the New York International Book Fair Award, and the 35th Annual Bookbuilders West Book Show.

Finally, we would like to thank our families for their love and support during the revision process. We could not have accomplished this without the help of our wives—Kitty, Judy, and Mary—and the patience of our children—P.K., Molly, Kelly, Patrick, Katie, Ryan, Molly, and Steven.

No three people could expect to produce a flawless textbook of this scope and complexity. Any errors or oversights are strictly our own rather than those of the reviewers, artists, or editors. In an effort to improve future editions, we ask that readers with pertinent information, suggestions, or comments concerning the organization or content of this textbook send their remarks to us directly, by the e-mail below, or care of Publisher, Applied Sciences, Benjamin Cummings, 1301 Sansome Street, San Francisco, CA 94111.

Frederic H. Martini, Haiku, HI
Michael J. Timmons, Orland Park, IL
Robert B. Tallitsch, Rock Island, IL
(RobertTallitsch@augustana.edu)

Contents in Brief

Contents

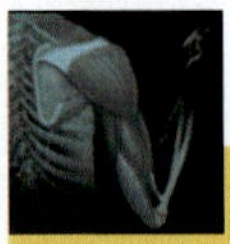

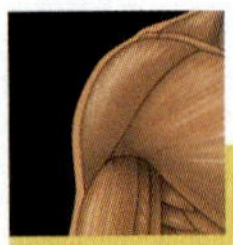

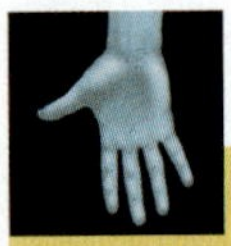

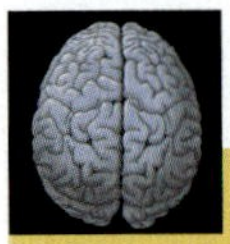

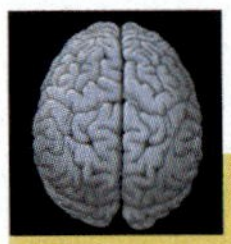

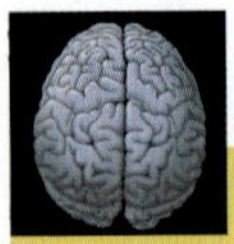

17

The Nervous System: Autonomic Division 451

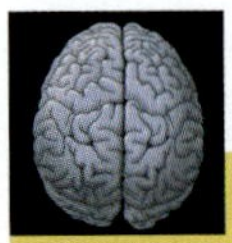

18

The Nervous System: General and Special Senses 470

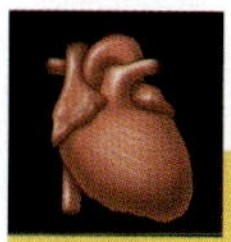

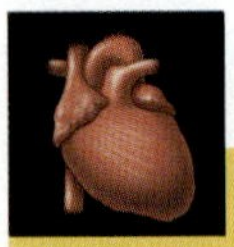

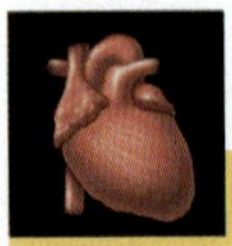

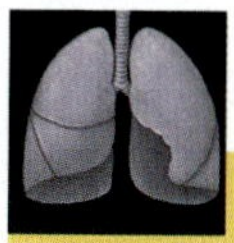

24 The Respiratory System 629

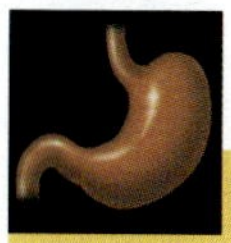

25 The Digestive System 655

1

An Introduction to Anatomy

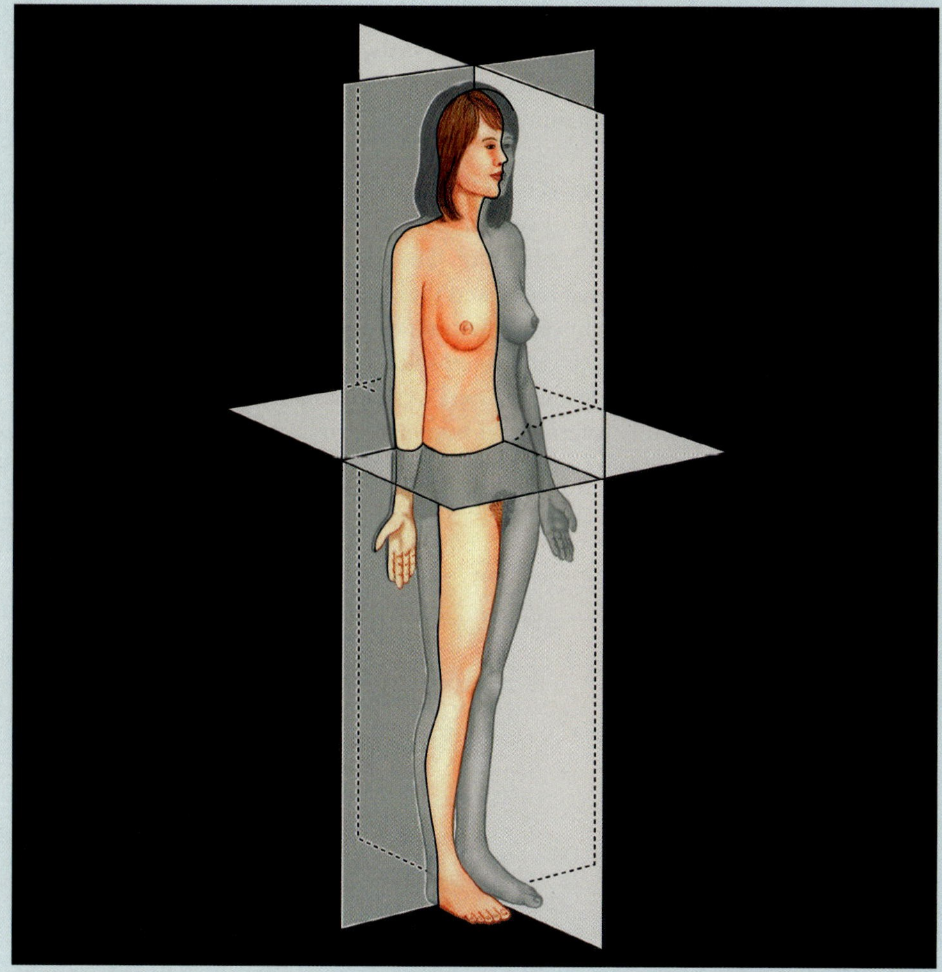

CHAPTER OBJECTIVES

1. Understand the reasons for studying anatomy and describe the relationship between structure and function.
2. Define the limits of microscopic anatomy and briefly describe cytology and histology.
3. Describe various ways to approach gross anatomy.
4. Define the various specialties of anatomy.
5. Identify the major levels of organization in living organisms.
6. Describe the basic life functions of an organism.
7. Identify the organ systems of the human body and understand their major functions.
8. Use anatomical terms to describe body sections, body regions, relative positions, and the anatomical position.
9. Identify the major body cavities and understand their functions.

We are all anatomists in our daily lives, if not in the classroom. For example, we rely on our memories of specific anatomical features to identify our friends and family, and we watch for subtle changes in body movement or position that give clues to what others are thinking or feeling. To be precise, anatomy is the study of external and internal structures and the physical relationships between body parts. But in practical terms, anatomy is the careful observation of the human body. Anatomical information provides clues about probable functions; physiology is the study of function, and physiological mechanisms can be explained only in terms of the underlying anatomy. *All specific functions are performed by specific structures.* For instance, filtering, warming, and humidifying inspired air are functions of the nasal cavity. The shapes of the bones projecting into the nasal cavity cause turbulence in the inhaled air, making it swirl against the moist lining. This contact warms and humidifies the air, and any suspended particles stick to the moist surfaces. In this way, the air is conditioned and filtered before it reaches the lungs.

The link between structure and function is always present, but not always understood. For example, the superficial anatomy of the heart was clearly described in the 15th century, but almost 200 years passed before the pumping action of the heart was demonstrated. On the other hand, many important cell functions were recognized decades before the electron microscope revealed the anatomical basis for those functions.

This text will discuss the anatomical structures and functions that make human life possible. The goals are to help you develop a three-dimensional understanding of anatomical relationships as well as prepare you for more advanced courses in anatomy, physiology, and related subjects, and to help you make informed decisions about your personal health.

Microscopic Anatomy [Figure 1.1]

Microscopic anatomy considers structures that cannot be seen without magnification. The boundaries of microscopic anatomy, or *fine anatomy*, are established by the limits of the equipment used (**Figure 1.1**). A simple hand lens shows details that barely escape the naked eye, while an electron microscope demonstrates structural details that are less than one-millionth as large. As we proceed through the text, we will be considering details at all levels, from macroscopic to microscopic. (Readers unfamiliar with the terms used to describe measurements and weights over this size range should consult the reference tables in the Appendix, pp. 820–821.)

Microscopic anatomy can be subdivided into specialties that consider features within a characteristic range of sizes. **Cytology** (sī-TOL-ō-jē) analyzes the internal structure of **cells**, the smallest units of life. Living cells are composed of complex chemicals in various combinations, and our lives depend on the chemical processes occurring in the trillions of cells that form our body.

Histology (his-TOL-ō-jē) takes a broader perspective and examines **tissues**, groups of specialized cells and cell products that work together to perform specific functions. The cells in the human body can be assigned to four basic tissue types, and these tissues are the focus of Chapter 3.

Tissues in combination form **organs** such as the heart, kidney, liver, and brain. Organs are anatomical units that have multiple functions. Many tissues and most organs are examined easily without a microscope, and at this point we cross the boundary from microscopic anatomy into gross anatomy.

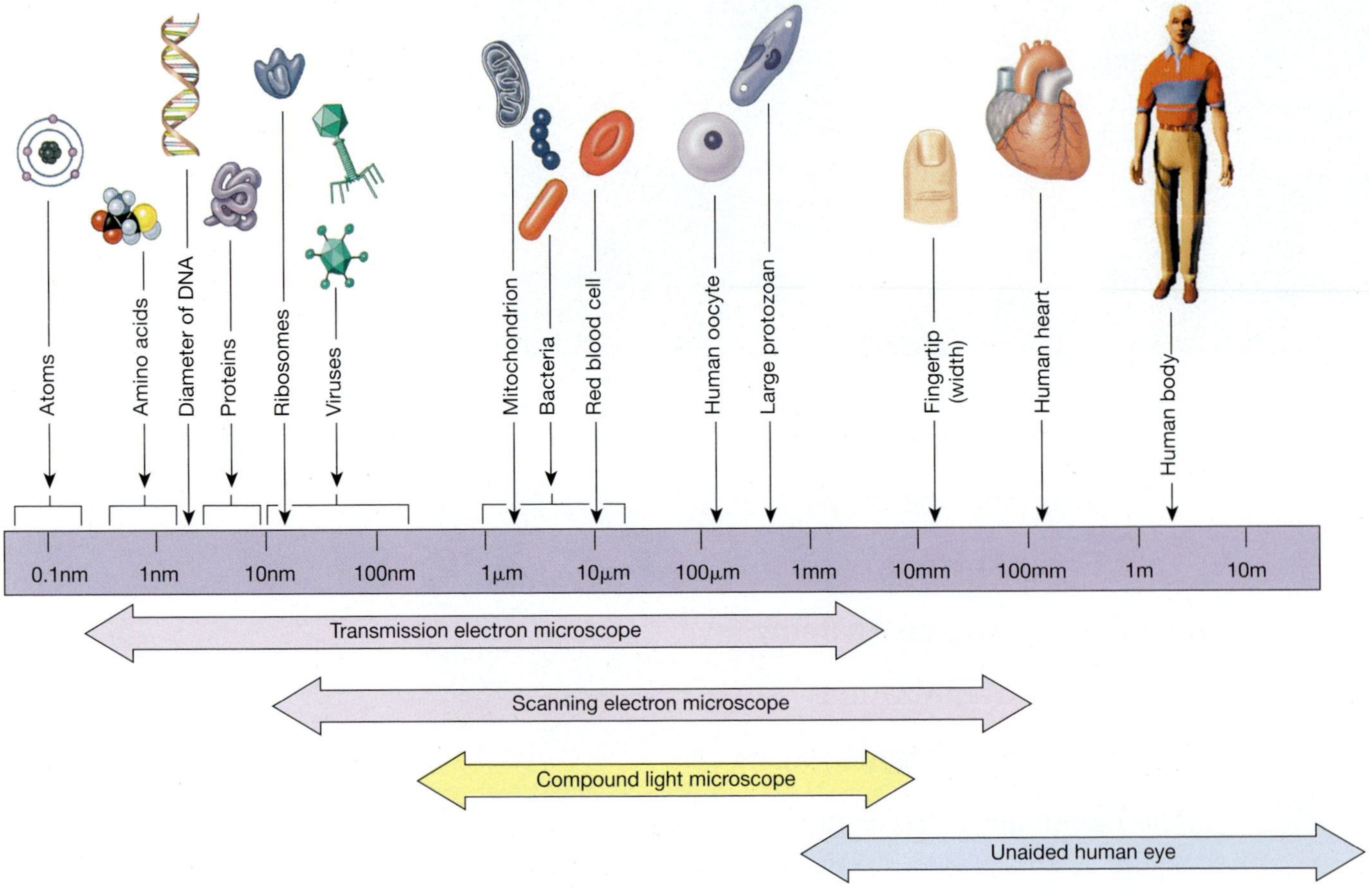

Figure 1.1 The Study of Anatomy at Different Scales
The amount of detail recognized depends on the method of study and the degree of magnification.

Gross Anatomy

Gross anatomy, or **macroscopic anatomy**, considers relatively large structures and features visible to the unaided eye. There are many ways to approach gross anatomy:

- *Surface anatomy* refers to the study of general form, or *morphology*, and superficial anatomical markings.
- *Regional anatomy* considers all of the superficial and internal features in a specific area of the body, such as the head, neck, or trunk. Advanced courses in anatomy often stress a regional approach because it emphasizes the spatial relationships among structures already familiar to the students.
- *Systemic anatomy* considers the structure of major *organ systems*, such as the skeletal or muscular systems. Organ systems are groups of organs that function together to produce coordinated effects. For example, the heart, blood, and blood vessels form the *cardiovascular system*, which distributes oxygen and nutrients throughout the body. There are 11 organ systems in the human body, and they will be introduced later in the chapter. Introductory texts in anatomy, including this one, use a systemic approach because it provides a framework for organizing information about important structural and functional patterns.

Other Perspectives on Anatomy [Figure 1.2]

Other anatomical specialties will be encountered in this text.

- *Developmental anatomy* examines the changes in form that occur during the period between conception and physical maturity. Because it considers anatomical structures over such a broad range of sizes (from a single cell to an adult human), developmental anatomy involves the study of both microscopic and gross anatomy. Developmental anatomy is important in medicine because many structural abnormalities can result from errors that occur during development. The most extensive structural changes occur during the first two months of development. **Embryology** (em-brē-OL-ō-jē) is the study of these early developmental processes.
- *Comparative anatomy* considers the anatomical organization of different types of animals. Observed similarities may reflect evolutionary relationships. Humans, lizards, and sharks are all called *vertebrates* because they share a combination of anatomical features that is not found in any other group of animals. All vertebrates have a spinal column composed of individual elements called *vertebrae*. Comparative anatomy uses techniques of gross, microscopic, and developmental anatomy. Information on developmental anatomy has demonstrated that related animals typically go through very similar developmental stages (Figure 1.2).

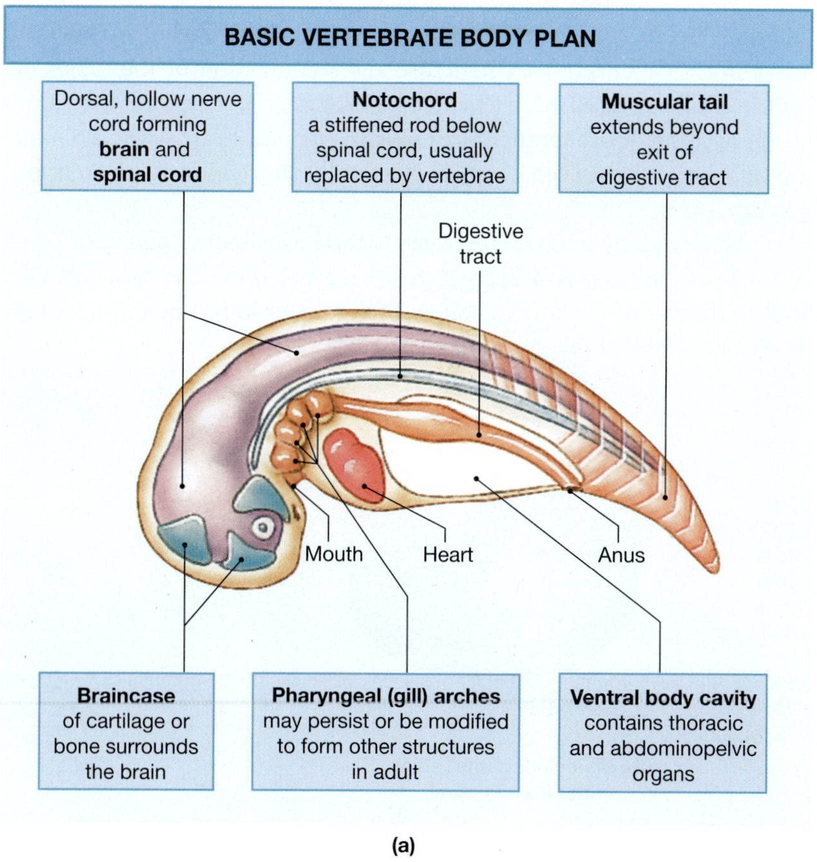

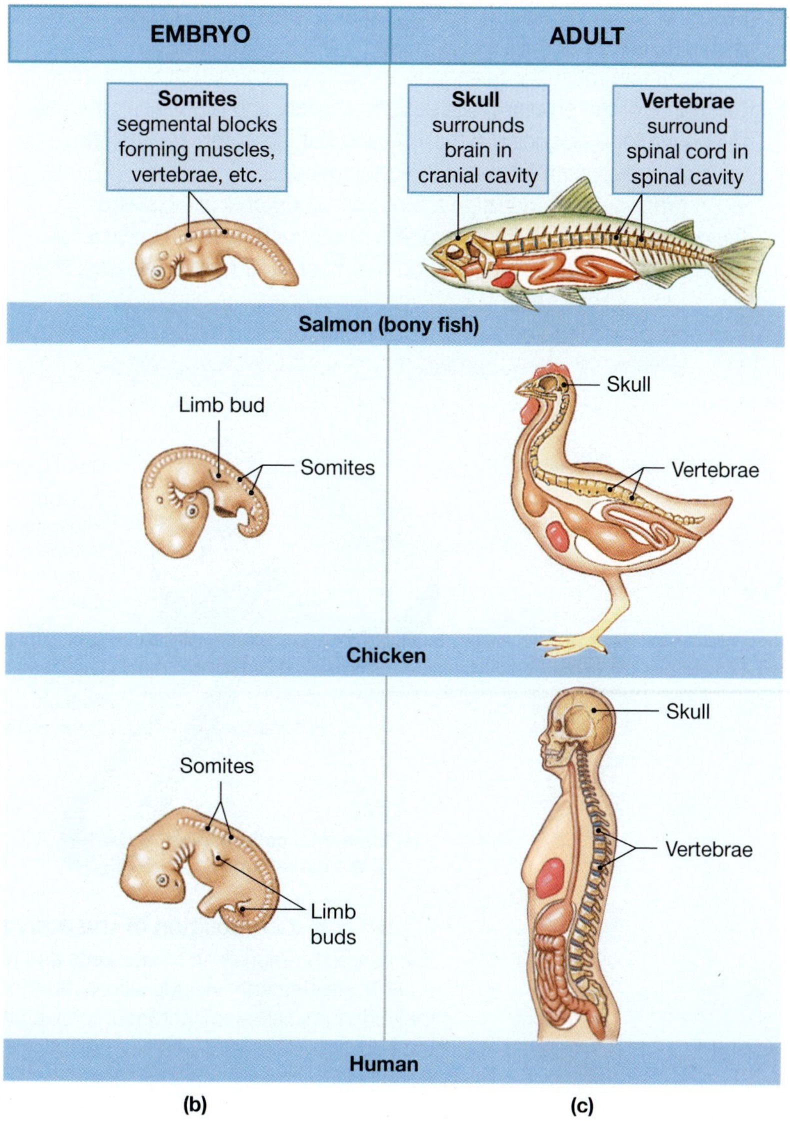

Figure 1.2 Comparative Anatomy
(a) Humans are classified as *vertebrates*, a group that also includes animals as different in appearance as fish, chickens, and cats. All vertebrates share a basic pattern of anatomical organization that differs from that of other animals. The similarities are often most apparent when comparing embryos at comparable stages of development **(b)** rather than when comparing adult vertebrates **(c)**.

Several other gross anatomical specialties are important in medical diagnosis.

- *Clinical anatomy* focuses on anatomical features that may undergo recognizable pathological changes during illness.
- *Surgical anatomy* studies anatomical landmarks important for surgical procedures.
- *Radiographic anatomy* involves the study of anatomical structures as they are visualized by x-rays, ultrasound scans, or other specialized procedures performed on an intact body.
- *Cross-sectional anatomy* has emerged as a new subspecialty of gross anatomy as new advances in radiographic anatomy, such as CT (computerized tomography) and MRI (magnetic resonance imaging) scans, have emerged.

Clinical Note

Disease, Pathology, and Diagnosis The formal name for the study of disease is **pathology.** Different diseases typically produce similar signs and symptoms. For example, a person whose lips are paler than normal and who complains of a lack of energy and breathlessness might have (1) respiratory problems that prevent normal oxygen transfer to the blood (as in *emphysema*); (2) cardiovascular problems that interfere with normal blood circulation to all parts of the body (heart failure); or (3) an inability to transport adequate amounts of oxygen in the blood, due to blood loss or problems with blood formation. In such cases, doctors must ask questions and collect information to determine the source of the problem. The patient's history and physical exam may be enough for a diagnosis in many cases, but laboratory testing and imaging studies such as x-rays are often needed.

A **diagnosis** is a decision about the nature of an illness. The diagnostic process is often a process of elimination, in which several potential causes are evaluated and the most likely one is selected. This brings us to a key concept: *All diagnostic procedures presuppose an understanding of the normal structure and function of the human body.*

CONCEPT CHECK

1. A histologist investigates structures at what level of organization?
2. Which level(s) of organization does a gross anatomist investigate?
3. How does the study of regional anatomy differ from the study of systemic anatomy?

See blue "Answers" tab at back of book.

Levels of Organization [Figures 1.3/1.4]

Our study of the human body will begin with an overview of cellular anatomy and then proceed to the anatomy, both gross and microscopic, of each organ system. When considering events from the microscopic to macroscopic scales, we are examining several interdependent *levels of organization.*

We begin at the *chemical* or *molecular level of organization.* The human body consists of more than a dozen different elements, but four of them (hydrogen, oxygen, carbon, and nitrogen) account for more than 99 percent of the total number of atoms (**Figure 1.3a**). At the chemical level, atoms interact to form three-dimensional compounds with distinctive properties. The major classes of compounds in the human body are indicated in **Figure 1.3b**.

Figure 1.4 presents an example of the relationships between the chemical level and higher levels of organization. The *cellular level of organization* includes *cells,* the smallest living units in the body. Cells contain internal structures called *organelles.* Cells and their organelles are made up of complex chemicals. Cell structure and the function of the major organelles will be presented in Chapter 2. In **Figure 1.4**, chemical interactions produce complex proteins within a *muscle cell* in the heart. Muscle cells are unusual because they can contract powerfully, shortening along their longitudinal axis.

Heart muscle cells are connected to form a distinctive *muscle tissue,* an example of the *tissue level of organization.* Layers of muscle tissue form the bulk of the wall of the heart, a hollow, three-dimensional organ. We are now at the *organ level* of organization.

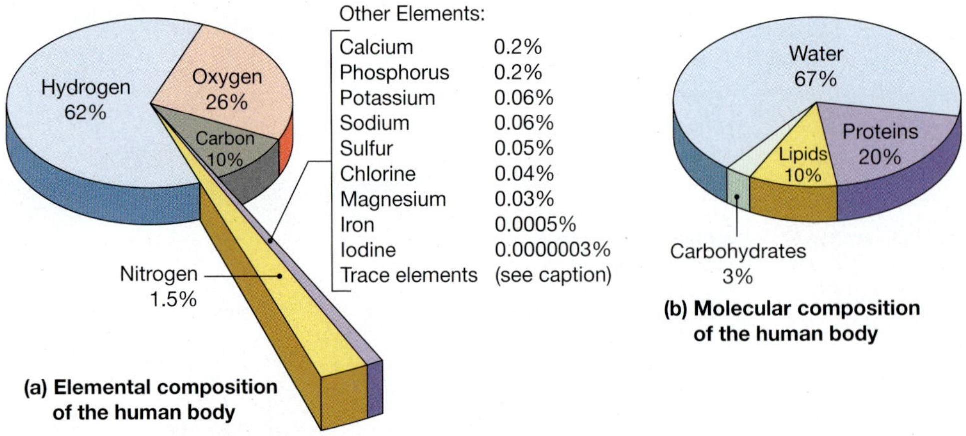

Figure 1.3 Composition of the Body at the Chemical Level of Organization
The percent composition of elements and major molecules. **(a)** Elemental composition of the body. Trace elements include silicon, fluorine, copper, manganese, zinc, selenium, cobalt, molybdenum, cadmium, chromium, tin, aluminum, and boron. **(b)** Molecular composition of the body.

Figure 1.4 Levels of Organization
Interacting atoms form molecules that organize themselves into complex contractile protein fibers within heart muscle cells. These cells interlock, forming cardiac muscle tissue that constitutes the bulk of the walls of the heart, a three-dimensional organ. The heart is one component of the cardiovascular system, which also includes the blood and blood vessels. All of the organ systems must work together for the person to remain alive and healthy.

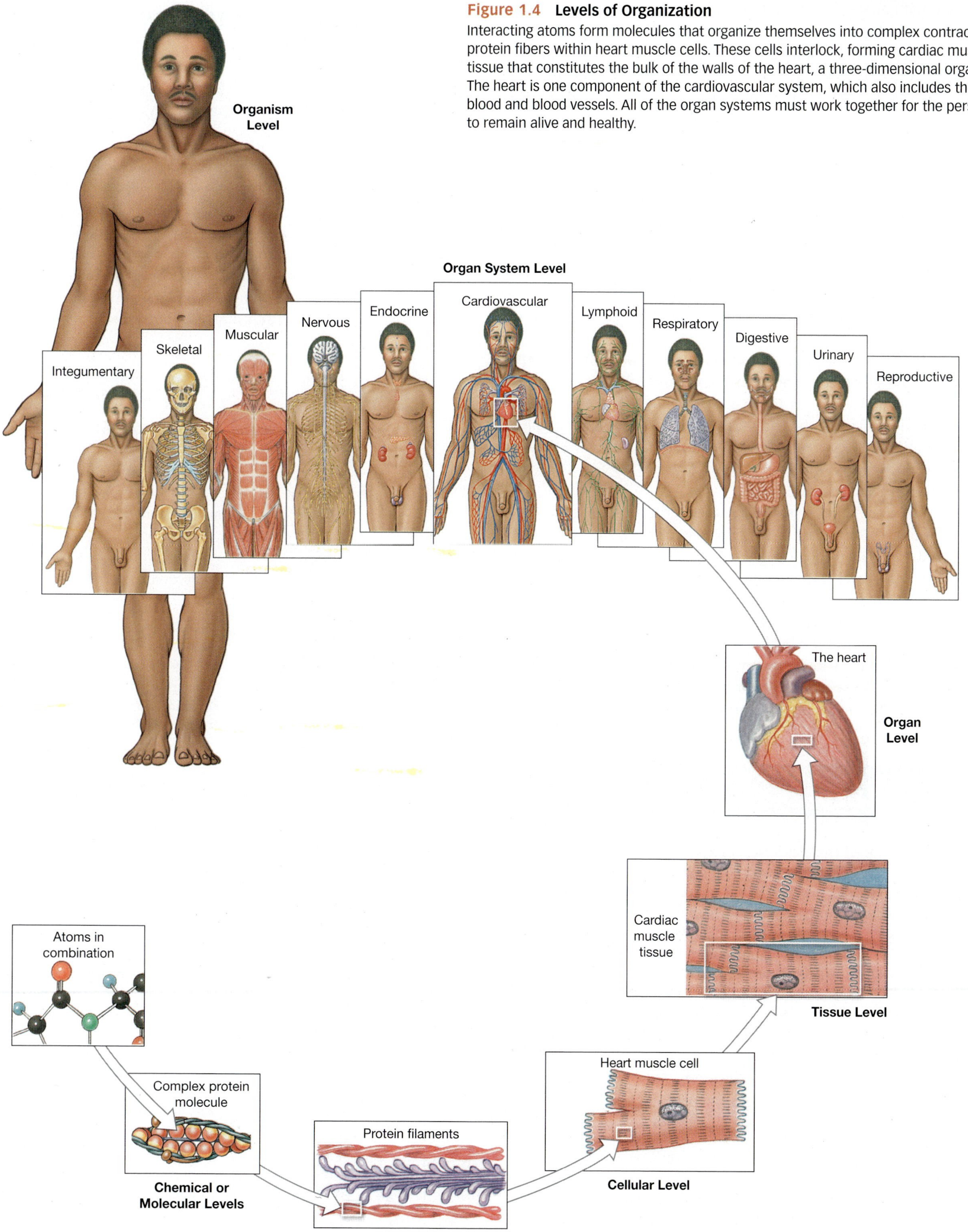

Normal functioning of the heart depends on interrelated events at the chemical, cellular, tissue, and organ levels of organization. Coordinated contractions in the adjacent muscle cells of cardiac muscle tissue produce a heartbeat. When that beat occurs, the internal anatomy of the organ enables it to function as a pump. Each time it contracts, the heart pushes blood into the *circulatory system*, a network of blood vessels. Together the heart, blood, and circulatory system form an *organ system*, the *cardiovascular system (CVS)*.

Each level of organization is totally dependent on the others. For example, damage at the cellular, tissue, or organ level may affect the entire system. Thus, a chemical change in heart muscle cells may cause abnormal contractions or even stop the heartbeat. Physical damage to the muscle tissue, as in a chest wound, can make the heart ineffective even when most of the heart muscle cells are intact and uninjured. An inherited abnormality in heart structure can make it an ineffective pump, although the muscle cells and muscle tissue are perfectly normal.

Finally, it should be noted that something that affects the system will ultimately affect all of its components. For example, the heart may not be able to pump blood effectively after a massive blood loss due to damage of a major blood vessel somewhere in the body. If the heart cannot pump and blood cannot flow, oxygen and nutrients cannot be distributed. In a very short time, the tissue begins to break down as heart muscle cells die from oxygen and nutrient starvation.

Of course, the changes that occur when the heart is not pumping effectively will not be restricted to the cardiovascular system; all of the cells, tissues, and organs in the body will be damaged. This observation brings us to another, higher level of organization, that of the *organism*; in this case a human being. This level reflects the interactions among organ systems. All are vital; every system must be working properly and in harmony with every other system, or survival will be impossible. When those systems are functioning normally, the characteristics of the internal environment will be relatively stable at all levels. This vital state of affairs is called **homeostasis** (hō-mē-ō-STĀ-sis; *homeo*, unchanging + *stasis*, standing).

Clinical Note

The Diagnosis of Disease *Homeostasis* is the maintenance of a relatively constant internal environment suitable for the survival of body cells and tissues. A failure to maintain homeostatic conditions constitutes **disease**. The disease process may initially affect a specific tissue, an organ, or an organ system, but it will ultimately lead to changes in the function or structure of cells throughout the body. Some diseases can be overcome by the body's defenses. Others require intervention and assistance. For example, when trauma has occurred and there is severe bleeding or damage to internal organs, surgical intervention may be necessary to restore homeostasis and prevent fatal complications.

An Introduction to Organ Systems [Figures 1.5/1.6]

Figure 1.5 provides an overview of the 11 organ systems in the human body. **Figure 1.6** introduces the major organs in each system. All living organisms share vital properties and processes:

- **Responsiveness:** Organisms respond to changes in their immediate environment; this property is also called *irritability*. You move your hand away from a hot stove; your dog barks at approaching strangers; fish are scared by loud noises; and amoebas glide toward potential prey. Organisms also make longer-lasting changes as they adjust to their environments. For example, as winter approaches, an animal may grow a heavier coat or migrate to a warmer climate. The capacity to make such adjustments is termed *adaptability*.

ORGAN SYSTEM		MAJOR FUNCTIONS
	**Integumentary system**	Protection from environmental hazards; temperature control
	**Skeletal system**	Support, protection of soft tissues; mineral storage; blood formation
	**Muscular system**	Locomotion, support, heat production
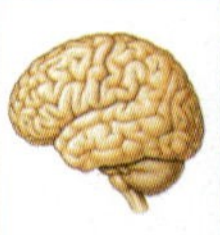	**Nervous system**	Directing immediate responses to stimuli, usually by coordinating the activities of other organ systems
	**Endocrine system**	Directing long-term changes in the activities of other organ systems
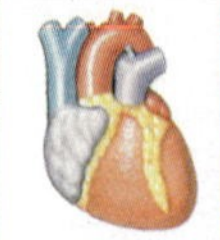	**Cardiovascular system**	Internal transport of cells and dissolved materials, including nutrients, wastes, and gases
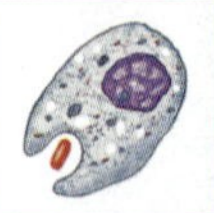	**Lymphoid system**	Defense against infection and disease
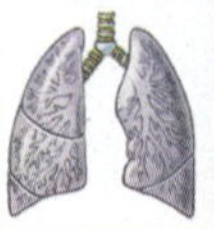	**Respiratory system**	Delivery of air to sites where gas exchange can occur between the air and circulating blood
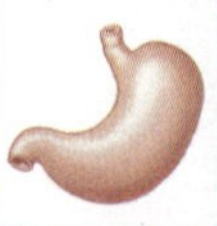	**Digestive system**	Processing of food and absorption of organic nutrients, minerals, vitamins, and water
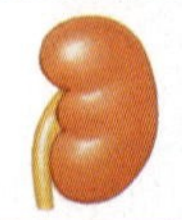	**Urinary system**	Elimination of excess water, salts, and waste products; control of pH
	**Reproductive system**	Production of sex cells and hormones

Figure 1.5 An Introduction to Organ Systems
An overview of the 11 organ systems and their major functions.

Figure 1.6 The Organ Systems of the Body

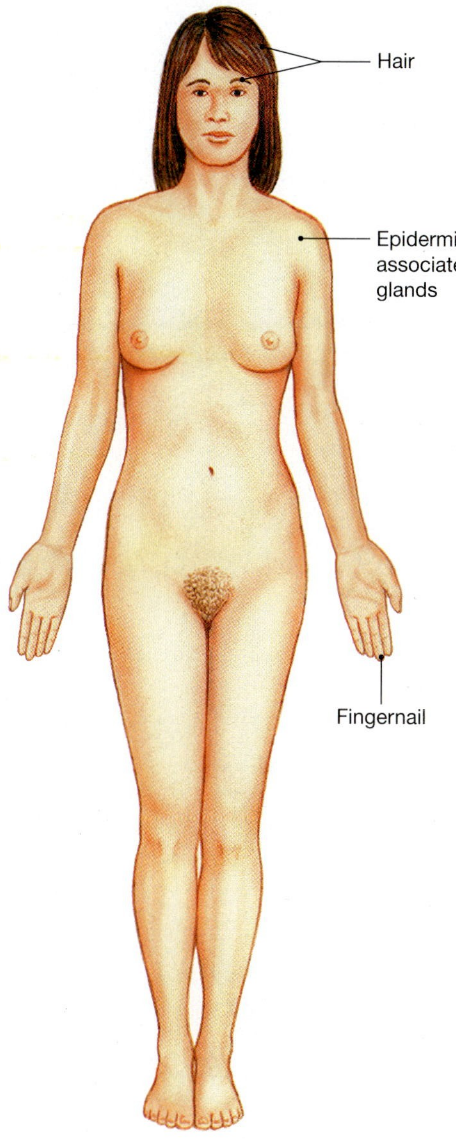

(a) The Integumentary System

Protects against environmental hazards; helps control body temperature

Organ/Component	Primary Functions
CUTANEOUS MEMBRANE	
Epidermis	Covers surface; protects deeper tissues
Dermis	Nourishes epidermis; provides strength; contains glands
HAIR FOLLICLES	Produce hair; innervation provides sensation
Hairs	Provide some protection for head
Sebaceous Glands	Secrete lipid coating that lubricates hair shaft and epidermis
SWEAT GLANDS	Produce perspiration for evaporative cooling
NAILS	Protect and stiffen distal tips of digits
SENSORY RECEPTORS	Provide sensations of touch, pressure, temperature, pain
SUBCUTANEOUS LAYER	Stores lipids; attaches skin to deeper structures

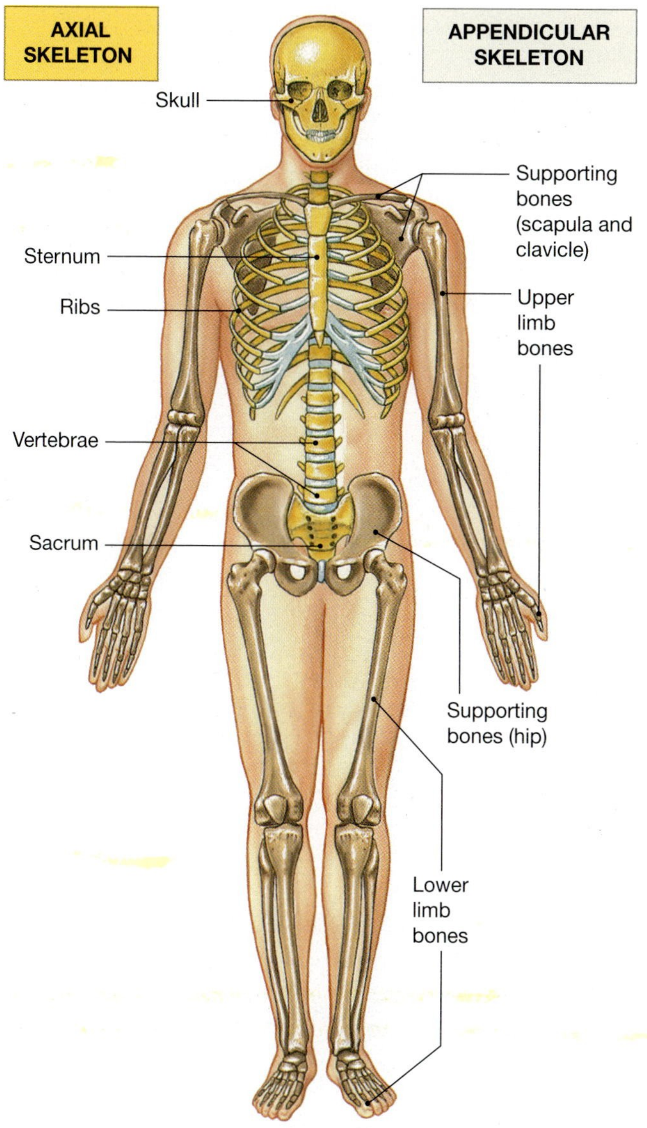

(b) The Skeletal System

Provides support; protects tissues; stores minerals; forms blood cells

Organ/Component	Primary Functions
BONES, CARTILAGES, AND JOINTS	Support, protect soft tissues; bones store minerals
Axial skeleton (skull, vertebrae, sacrum, coccyx, sternum, supporting cartilages and ligaments)	Protects brain, spinal cord, sense organs, and soft tissues of thoracic cavity; supports the body weight over the lower limbs
Appendicular skeleton (limbs and supporting bones and ligaments)	Provides internal support and positioning of the limbs; supports and moves axial skeleton
BONE MARROW	Primary site of blood cell production (red marrow); storage of energy reserves in fat cells (yellow marrow)

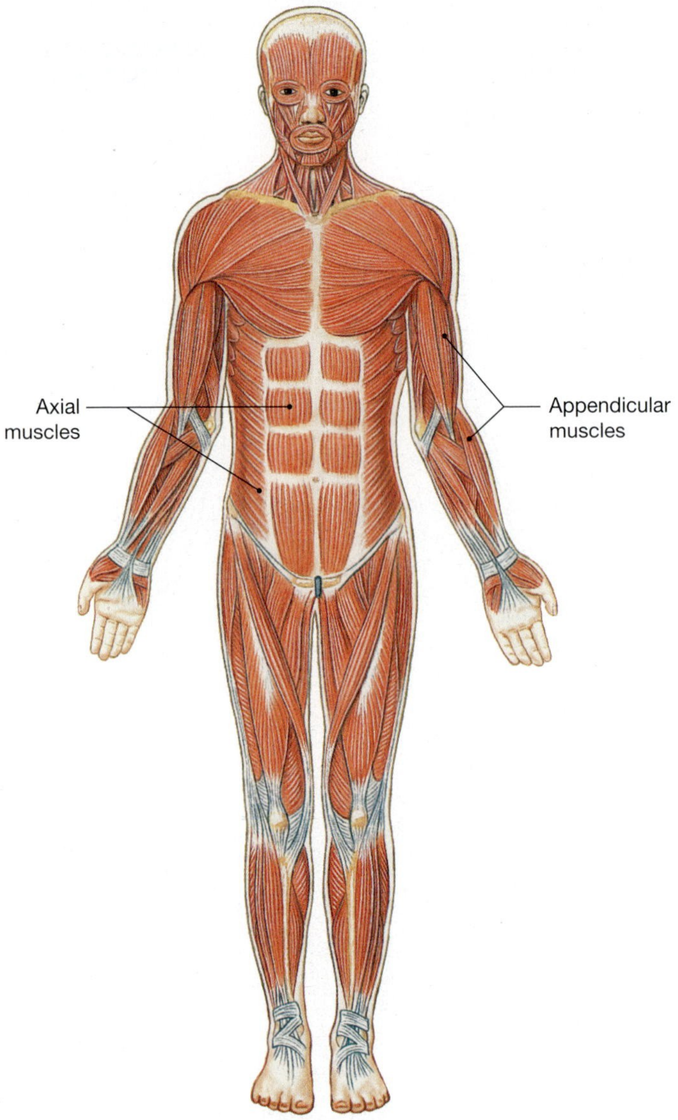

(c) The Muscular System

Allows for locomotion; provides support; produces heat

Organ/Component	Primary Functions
SKELETAL MUSCLES (700)	Provide skeletal movement; control entrances to digestive and respiratory tracts and exits of digestive and urinary tracts; produce heat; support skeleton; protect soft tissues
Axial muscles	Support and position axial skeleton
Appendicular muscles	Support, move, and brace limbs
TENDONS, APONEUROSES	Harness forces of contraction to perform specific tasks

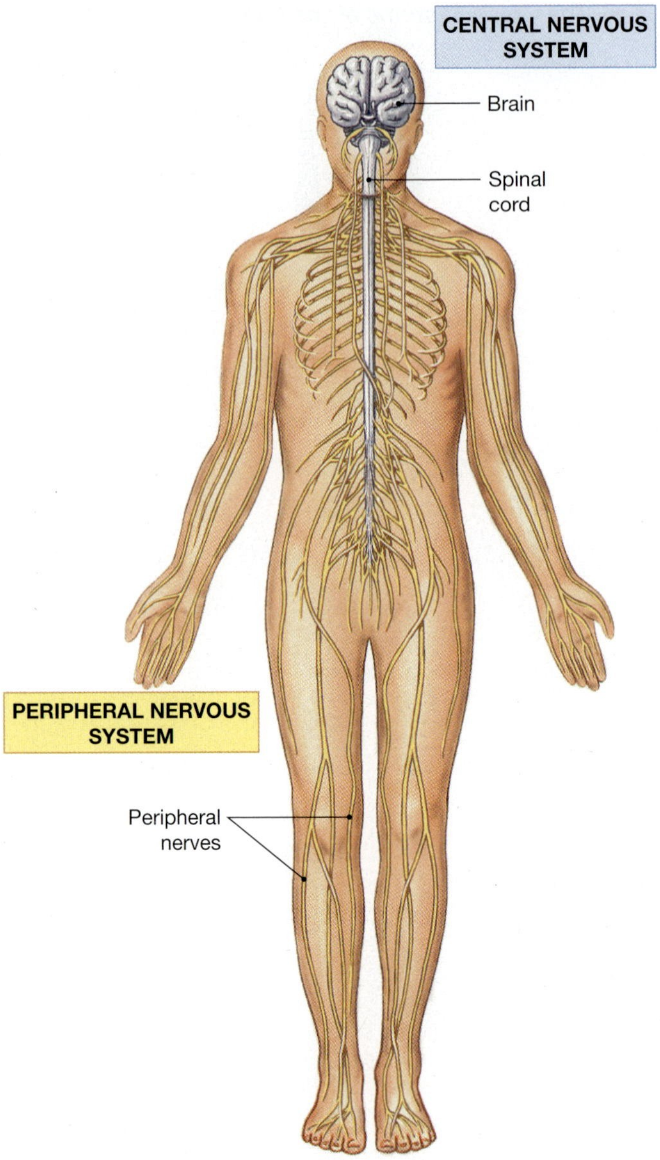

(d) The Nervous System

Directs immediate responses to stimuli; usually by coordinating the activities of other organ systems

Organ/Component	Primary Functions
CENTRAL NERVOUS SYSTEM (CNS)	Acts as control center for nervous system: processes information; provides short-term control over activities of other systems
Brain	Performs complex integrative functions; controls both voluntary and autonomic activities
Spinal cord	Relays information to and from brain; performs less-complex integrative functions; directs many simple involuntary activities
Special senses	Provide sensory input to the brain relating to sight, hearing, smell, taste, and equilibrium
PERIPHERAL NERVOUS SYSTEM (PNS)	Links CNS with other systems and with sense organs

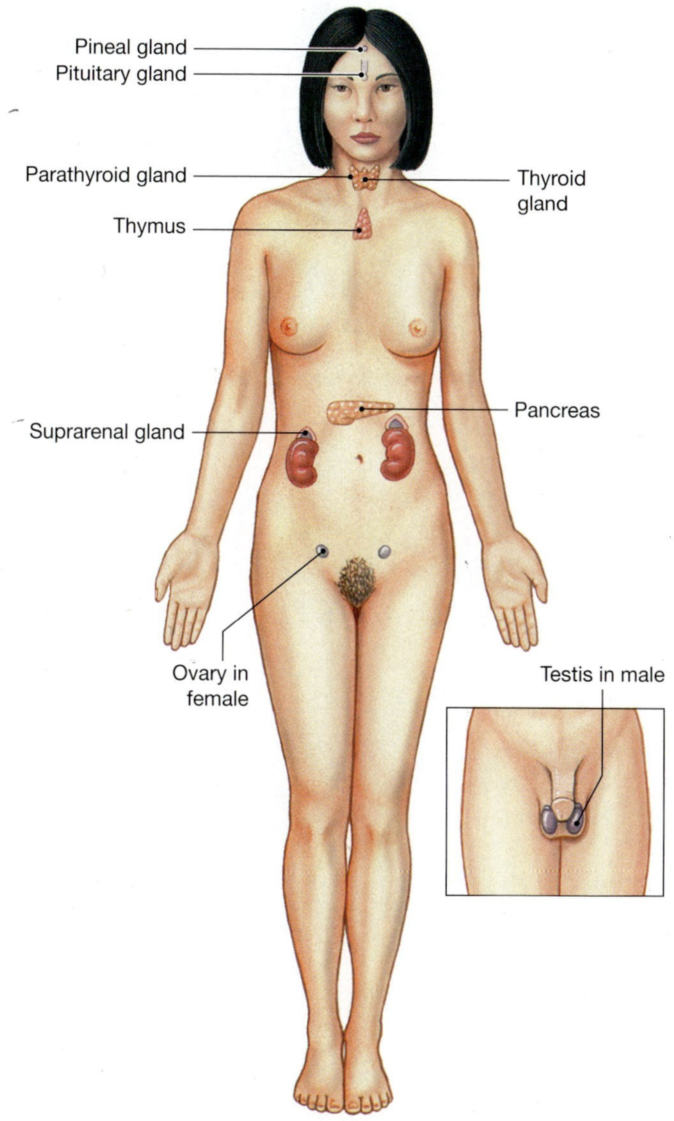

(e) The Endocrine System
Directs long-term changes in activities of other organ systems

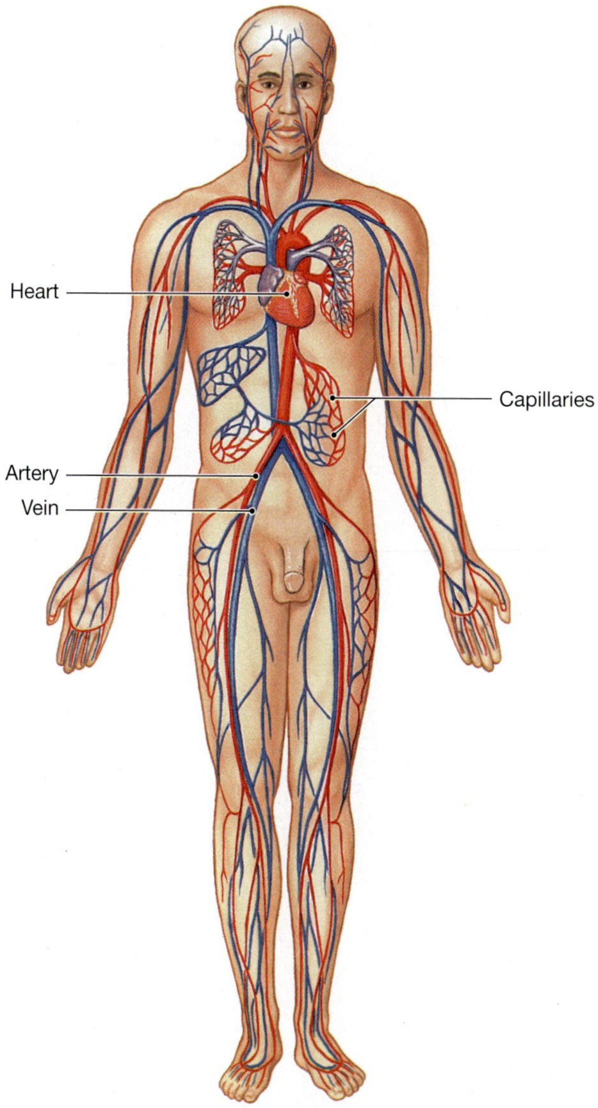

(f) The Cardiovascular System
Transports cells and dissolved materials, including nutrients, wastes, and gases

Organ/Component	Primary Functions
PINEAL GLAND	May control timing of reproduction and set day–night rhythms
PITUITARY GLAND	Controls other endocrine glands; regulates growth and fluid balance
THYROID GLAND	Controls tissue metabolic rate; regulates calcium levels
PARATHYROID GLANDS	Regulate calcium levels (with thyroid)
THYMUS	Controls maturation of lymphocytes
SUPRARENAL GLANDS (adrenal)	Adjust water balance, tissue metabolism, cardiovascular and respiratory activity
KIDNEYS	Control red blood cell production and elevate blood pressure
PANCREAS	Regulates blood glucose levels
GONADS	
Testes	Support male sexual characteristics and reproductive functions *(see Figure 1.6k)*
Ovaries	Support female sexual characteristics and reproductive functions *(see Figure 1.6l)*

adrenal gland adjust water balance...

Organ/Component	Primary Functions
HEART	Propels blood; maintains blood pressure
BLOOD VESSELS	Distribute blood around the body
Arteries	Carry blood from heart to capillaries
Capillaries	Permit diffusion between blood and interstitial fluids
Veins	Return blood from capillaries to the heart
BLOOD	Transports oxygen, carbon dioxide, and blood cells; delivers nutrients and hormones; removes waste products; assists in temperature regulation and defense against disease

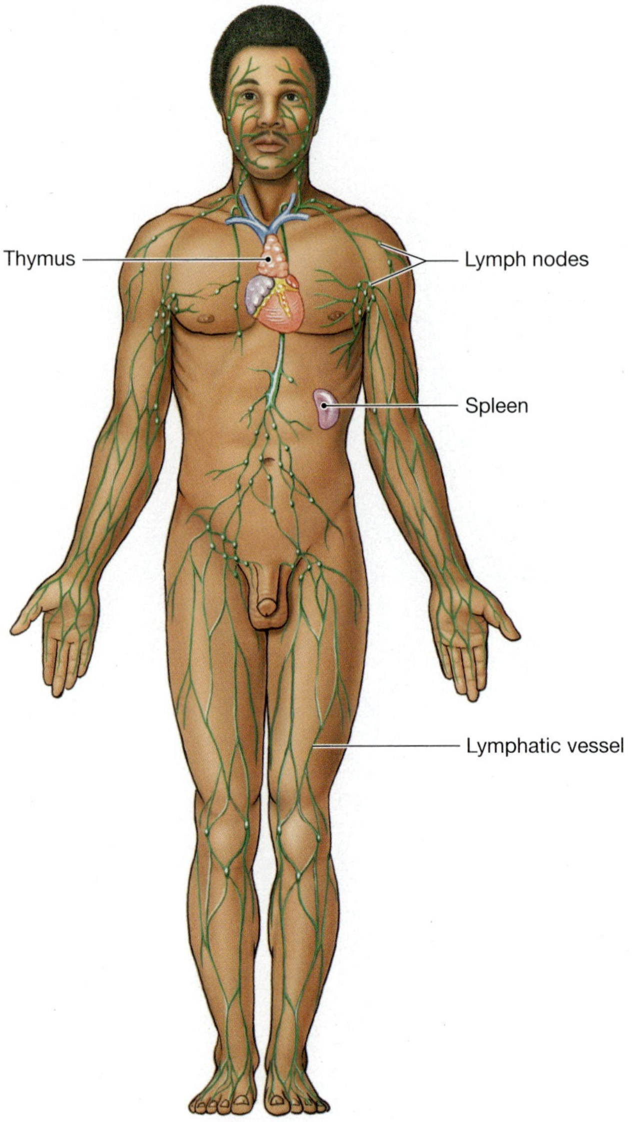

(g) The Lymphoid System

Defends against infection and disease; returns tissue fluid to the bloodstream

Organ/Component	Primary Functions
LYMPHATIC VESSELS	Carry lymph (water and proteins) and lymphocytes from peripheral tissues to veins of the cardiovascular system
LYMPH NODES	Monitor the composition of lymph; engulf pathogens; stimulate immune response
SPLEEN	Monitors circulating blood; engulfs pathogens and recycles red blood cells; stimulates immune response
THYMUS	Controls development and maintenance of one class of lymphocytes (T cells)

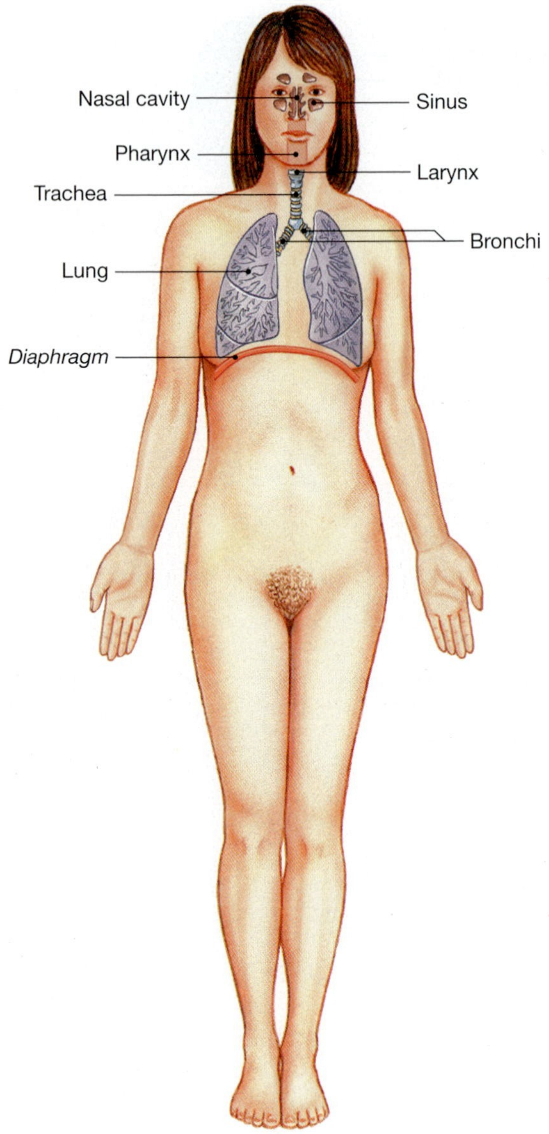

(h) The Respiratory System

Delivers air to sites where gas exchange can occur between the air and circulating blood

Organ/Component	Primary Functions
NASAL CAVITIES, PARANASAL SINUSES	Filter, warm, humidify air; detect smells
PHARYNX	Conducts air to larynx; a chamber shared with the digestive tract *(see Figure 1.6i)*
LARYNX	Protects opening to trachea and contains vocal cords
TRACHEA	Filters air, traps particles in mucus; cartilages keep airway open
BRONCHI	(Same functions as trachea) through volume changes
LUNGS	Responsible for air movement during movements of ribs and diaphragm; include airways and alveoli
Alveoli	Act as sites of gas exchange between air and blood

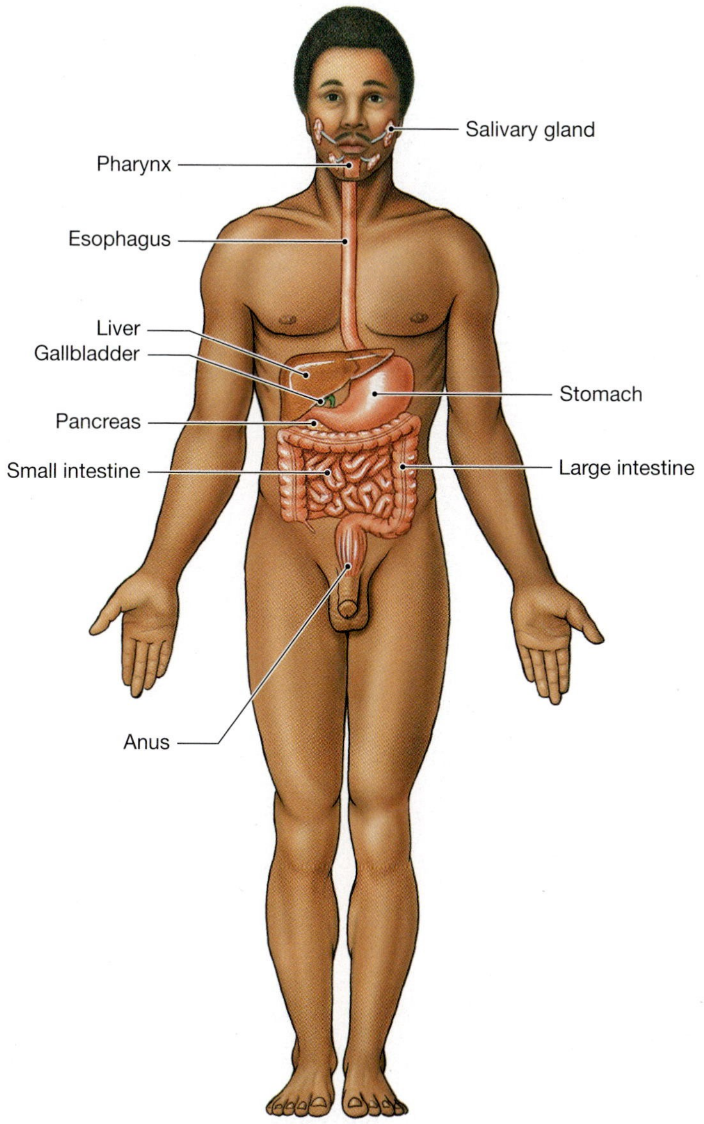

(i) The Digestive System

Processes food and absorbs nutrients

Organ/Component	Primary Functions
MOUTH	Receptacle for food; works with associated structures (teeth, tongue) to break up food and pass food and liquids to pharynx
SALIVARY GLANDS	Provide buffers and lubrication; produce enzymes that begin digestion
PHARYNX	Conducts solid food and liquids to esophagus; chamber shared with respiratory tract *(see Figure 1.6h)*
ESOPHAGUS	Delivers food to stomach
STOMACH	Secretes acids and enzymes
SMALL INTESTINE	Secretes digestive enzymes, buffers, and hormones; absorbs nutrients
LIVER	Secretes bile; regulates nutrient composition of blood
GALLBLADDER	Stores and concentrates bile for release into small intestine
PANCREAS	Secretes digestive enzymes and buffers; contains endocrine cells *(see Figure 1.6e)*
LARGE INTESTINE	Removes water from fecal material; stores wastes

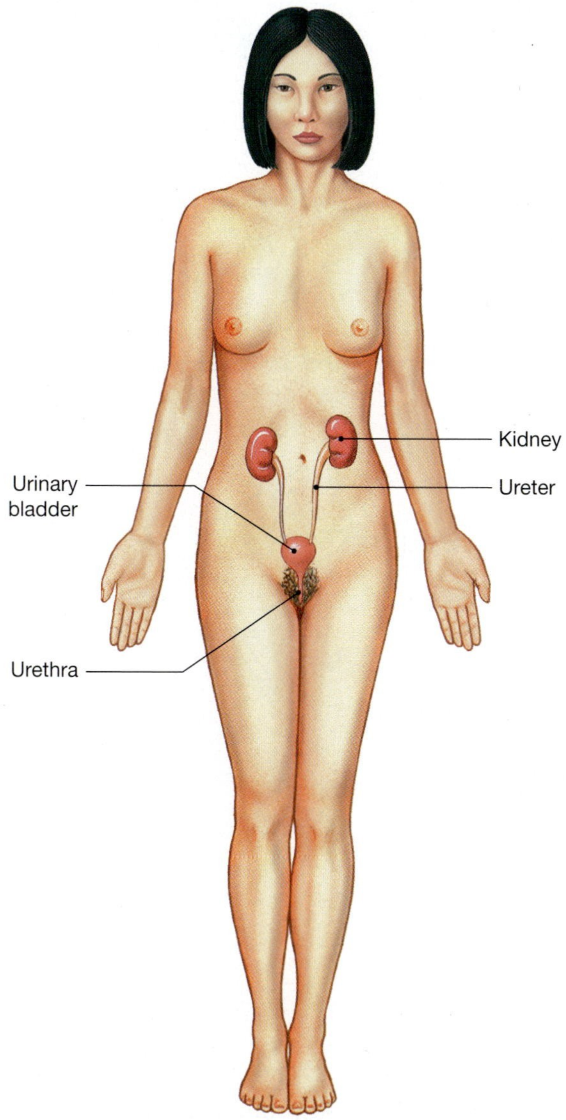

(j) The Urinary System

Eliminates excess water, salts, and waste products

Organ/Component	Primary Functions
KIDNEYS	Form and concentrate urine; regulate blood pH and ion concentrations; perform endocrine functions *(see Figure 1.6e)*
URETERS	Conduct urine from kidneys to urinary bladder
URINARY BLADDER	Stores urine for eventual elimination
URETHRA	Conducts urine to exterior

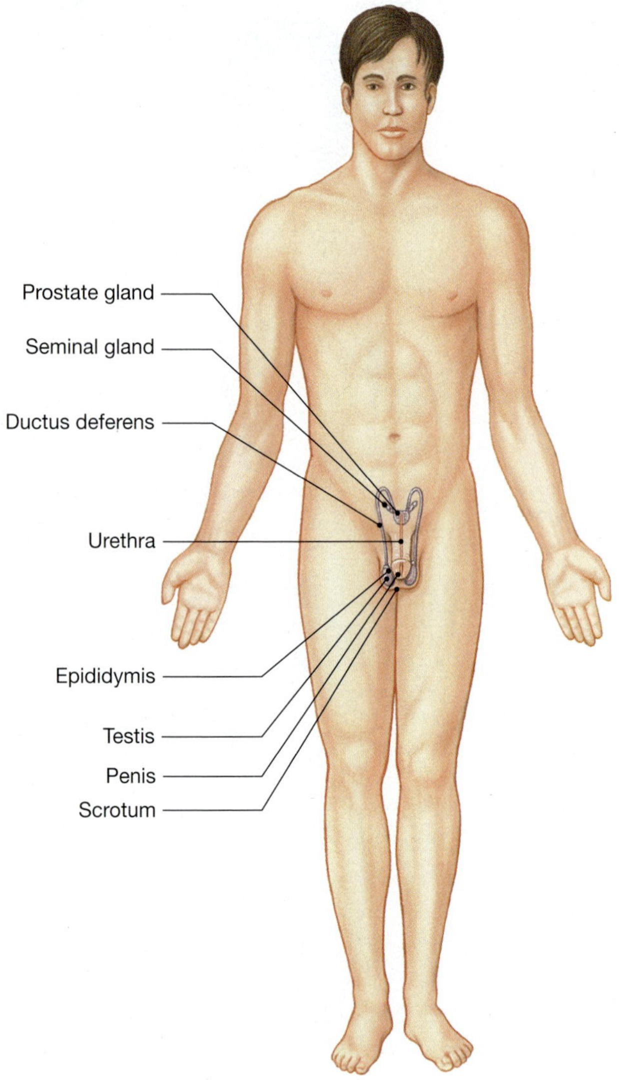

(k) The Male Reproductive System

Produces sex cells and hormones

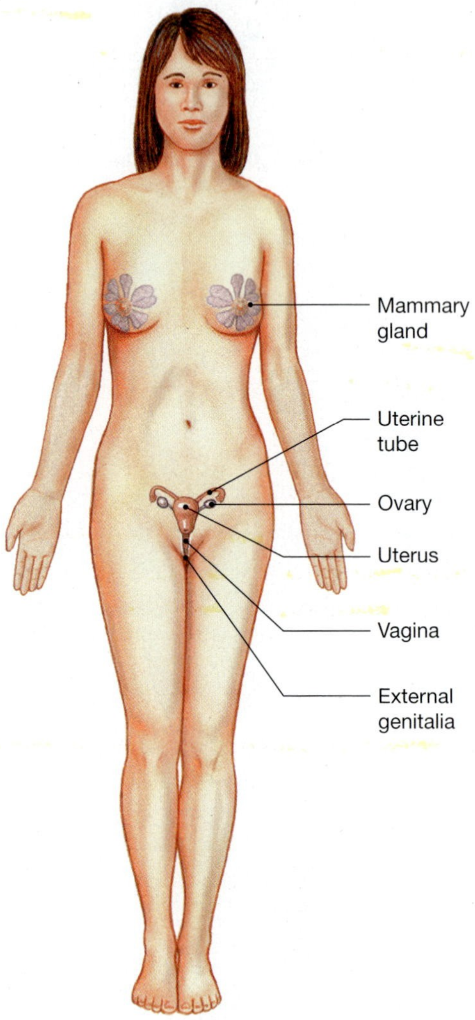

(l) The Female Reproductive System

Produces sex cells and hormones; supports embryonic development from fertilization to birth

Organ/Component	Primary Functions
TESTES	Produce sperm and hormones *(see Figure 1.6e)*
ACCESSORY ORGANS	
Epididymis	Acts as site of sperm maturation
Ductus deferens (sperm duct)	Conducts sperm from the epididymis and merges with the duct of the seminal gland
Seminal glands	Secrete fluid that makes up much of the volume of semen
Prostate gland	Secretes fluid and enzymes
Urethra	Conducts semen to exterior
EXTERNAL GENITALIA	
Penis	Contains erectile tissue; deposits sperm in vagina of female; produces pleasurable sensations during sexual activities
Scrotum	Surrounds the testes and controls their temperature

Organ/Component	Primary Functions
OVARIES	Produce oocytes and hormones *(see Figure 1.6e)*
UTERINE TUBES	Deliver oocyte or embryo to uterus; normal site of fertilization
UTERUS	Site of embryonic development and exchange between maternal and embryonic bloodstreams
VAGINA	Site of sperm deposition; acts as birth canal at delivery; provides passageway for fluids during menstruation
EXTERNAL GENITALIA	
Clitoris	Contains erectile tissue; produces pleasurable sensations during sexual activities
Labia	Contain glands that lubricate entrance to vagina
MAMMARY GLANDS	Produce milk that nourishes newborn infant

- **Growth and Differentiation:** Over a lifetime, organisms grow larger, increasing in size through an increase in the size or number of their cells. In multicellular organisms, the individual cells become specialized to perform particular functions. This specialization is called **differentiation**. Growth and differentiation in cells and organisms often produce changes in form and function. For example, the anatomical proportions and physiological capabilities of an adult human are quite different from those of an infant.
- **Reproduction:** Organisms reproduce, creating subsequent generations of their own kind, whether unicellular or multicellular.
- **Movement:** Organisms are capable of producing movement, which may be internal (transporting food, blood, or other materials inside the body) or external (moving through the environment).
- **Metabolism and Excretion:** Organisms rely on complex chemical reactions to provide energy for responsiveness, growth, reproduction, and movement. They must also synthesize complex chemicals, such as proteins. The term **metabolism** refers to all the chemical operations under way in the body: *Catabolism* is the breakdown of complex molecules into simple ones, and *anabolism* is the synthesis of complex molecules from simple ones. Normal metabolic operations require the **absorption** of materials from the environment. To generate energy efficiently, most cells require various nutrients, as well as oxygen, an atmospheric gas. The term **respiration** refers to the absorption, transport, and use of oxygen by cells. Metabolic operations often generate unneeded or potentially harmful waste products that must be removed through the process of **excretion**.

For very small organisms, absorption, respiration, and excretion involve the movement of materials across exposed surfaces. But creatures larger than a few millimeters seldom absorb nutrients directly from their environment. For example, human beings cannot absorb steaks, apples, or ice cream directly—they must first alter the foods' chemical structure. That processing, called **digestion**, occurs in specialized areas where complex foods are broken down into simpler components that can be absorbed easily. Respiration and excretion are also more complicated for large organisms, and we have specialized organs responsible for gas exchange (the lungs) and waste excretion (the kidneys). Finally, because absorption, respiration, and excretion are performed in different portions of the body, there must be an internal transportation system, or **cardiovascular system**.

CONCEPT CHECK

1. What system includes the following structures: sweat glands, nails, and hair follicles?
2. What system has structures with the following functions: production of hormones and ova, site of embryonic development?
3. What is differentiation?

See blue "Answers" tab at back of book.

The Language of Anatomy [Figure 1.7]

If you discovered a new continent, how would you begin collecting information so that you could report your findings? You would have to construct a detailed map of the territory. The completed map would contain (1) prominent landmarks, such as mountains, valleys, or volcanoes; (2) the distance between them; and (3) the direction you traveled to get from one place to another. The distances might be recorded in miles, and the directions recorded as compass bearings (north, south, northeast, southwest, and so on). With such a map, anyone could go directly to a specific location on that continent.

Early anatomists faced similar communication problems. Stating that a bump is "on the back" does not give very precise information about its location. So anatomists created maps of the human body. The landmarks are prominent anatomical structures, and distances are measured in centimeters or inches. In effect, anatomy uses a special language that must be learned at the start. It will take some time and effort but is absolutely essential if you want to avoid a situation like that shown in **Figure 1.7**.

New anatomical terms continue to appear as technology advances, but many of the older words and phrases remain in use. As a result, the vocabulary of this science represents a form of historical record. Latin and Greek words and phrases form the basis for an impressive number of anatomical terms. For example, many of the Latin names assigned to specific structures 2000 years ago are still in use today.

A familiarity with Latin roots and patterns makes anatomical terms more understandable, and the notes included on word derivation are intended to assist you in that regard. In English, when you want to indicate more than one of something, you usually add an *s* to the name—*girl/girls* or *doll/dolls*. Latin words change their endings. Those ending in *-us* convert to *-i*, and other conversions involve changing from *-um* to *-a*, and from *-a* to *-ae*. Additional information on foreign word roots, prefixes, suffixes, and combining forms can be found in the Appendix on p. 822.

Latin and Greek terms are not the only foreign terms imported into the anatomical vocabulary over the centuries. Many anatomical structures and clinical conditions were initially named after either the discoverer or, in the case of diseases, the most famous victim. The major problem with this practice is that it is difficult for someone to remember a connection between the structure or disorder and the name. Over the last 100 years most of these commemorative names, or *eponyms*, have been replaced by more precise terms. For those interested in historical details, the Appendix titled "Eponyms in Common Use" provides information about the commemorative names in occasional use today.

Figure 1.7 The Importance of Precise Vocabulary
Would you want to be this patient? *[©The New Yorker Collection 1990 Ed Fisher from cartoonbank.com. All Rights Reserved.]*

Superficial Anatomy

A familiarity with major anatomical landmarks and directional references will make subsequent chapters more understandable, since none of the organ systems except the integument can be seen from the body surface. You must create your own mental maps and extract information from the anatomical illustrations that accompany this discussion.

Anatomical Landmarks [Figure 1.8]

Important anatomical landmarks are presented in Figure 1.8. You should become familiar with the adjectival form as well as the anatomical term. Understanding the terms and their origins will help you to remember the location of a particular structure, as well as its name. For example, the term **brachium** refers to the arm, and later chapters discuss the *brachialis muscle* and branches of the *brachial artery.*

Standard anatomical illustrations show the human form in the **anatomical position**. In the anatomical position, the person stands with the legs together and the feet flat on the floor. The hands are at the sides, and the palms face forward. The individual shown in Figure 1.8 is in the anatomical position as seen from the front (Figure 1.8a) and back (Figure 1.8b). The anatomical position is the standard by which the language of anatomy, regardless of level, from basic to clinical, is communi-

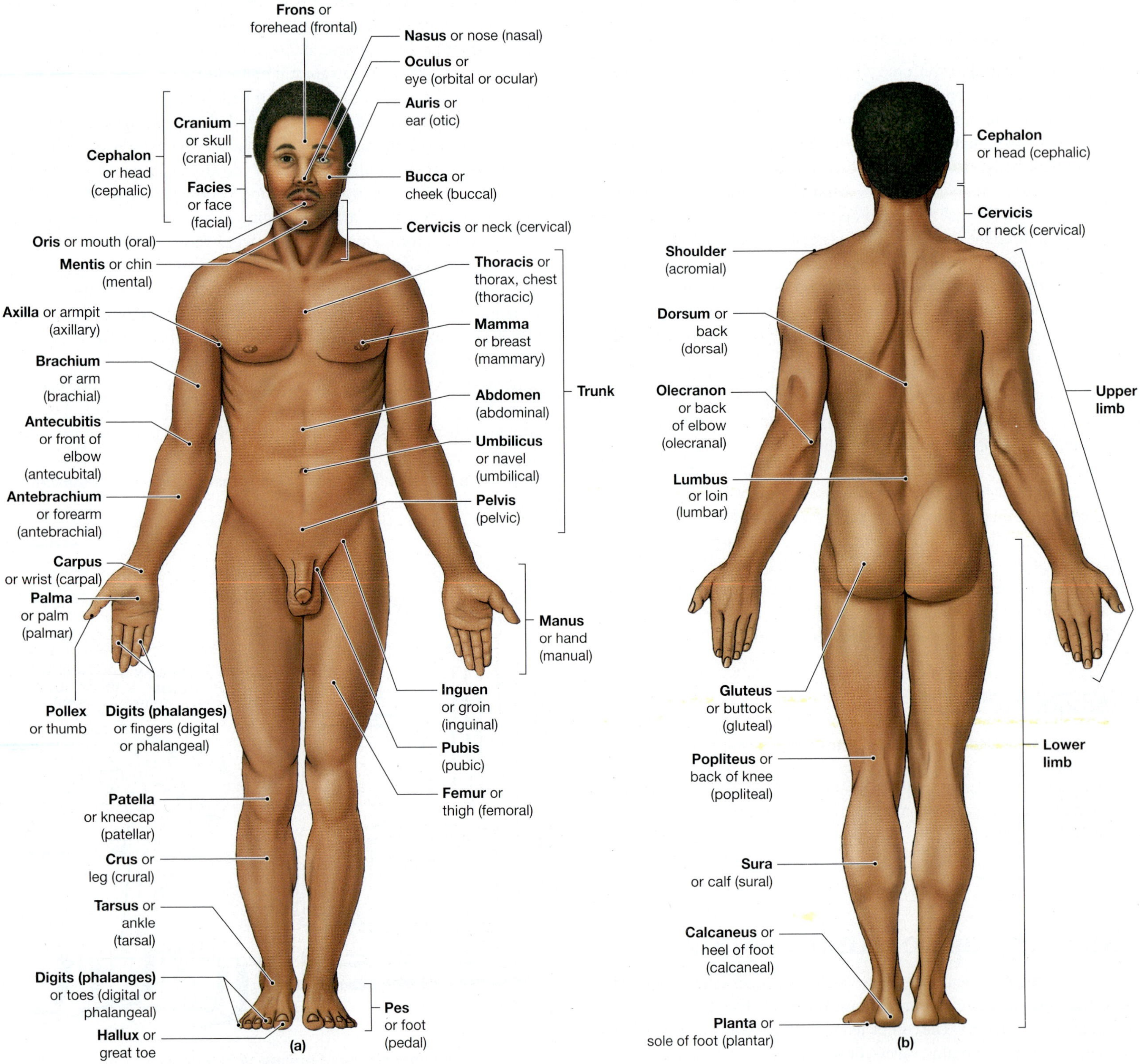

Figure 1.8 Anatomical Landmarks
The anatomical terms are shown in boldface type, the common names are in plain type, and the anatomical adjectives are in parentheses. **(a)** Anterior view in the anatomical position. **(b)** Posterior view in the anatomical position.

TABLE 1.1 Regions of the Human Body*

Anatomical Name	Anatomical Region	Area Indicated
Cephalon	Cephalic	Area of head
Cervicis	Cervical	Area of neck
Thoracis	Thoracic	The chest
Brachium	Brachial	The segment of the upper limb closest to the trunk; the arm
Antebrachium	Antebrachial	The forearm
Carpus	Carpal	The wrist
Manus	Manual	The hand
Abdomen	Abdominal	The abdomen
Pelvis	Pelvic	The pelvis (in general)
Pubis	Pubic	The anterior pelvis
Inguen	Inguinal	The groin (crease between thigh and trunk)
Lumbus	Lumbar	The lower back
Gluteus	Gluteal	The buttock
Femur	Femoral	The thigh
Patella	Patellar	The kneecap
Crus	Crural	The leg, from knee to ankle
Sura	Sural	The calf
Tarsus	Tarsal	The ankle
Pes	Pedal	The foot
Planta	Sole	Plantar region of foot

* See Figures 1.8 and 1.9.

cated. Therefore, unless otherwise noted, all of the descriptions given in this text refer to the body in the anatomical position. A person lying down in the anatomical position is said to be **supine** (soo-PĪN) when lying face up and **prone** when lying face down.

Anatomical Regions [Figures 1.8/1.9 and Table 1.1]

Major regions of the body are indicated in Table 1.1. These and additional regions and anatomical landmarks are noted in **Figure 1.8**. Anatomists and clinicians often use specialized regional terms to indicate a specific area of the abdominal or pelvic regions. There are two different methods in use. One refers to the **abdominopelvic quadrants**. The abdominopelvic surface is divided into four segments using a pair of imaginary lines (one horizontal and one vertical) that intersect at the *umbilicus* (navel). This simple method, shown in **Figure 1.9a**, provides useful references for the description of aches, pains, and injuries. The location can assist the doctor in deciding the possible cause; for example, tenderness in the right lower quadrant (RLQ) is a symptom of appendicitis, whereas tenderness in the right upper quadrant (RUQ) may indicate gallbladder or liver problems.

Regional distinctions are used to describe the location and orientation of internal organs more precisely. There are nine **abdominopelvic regions**,

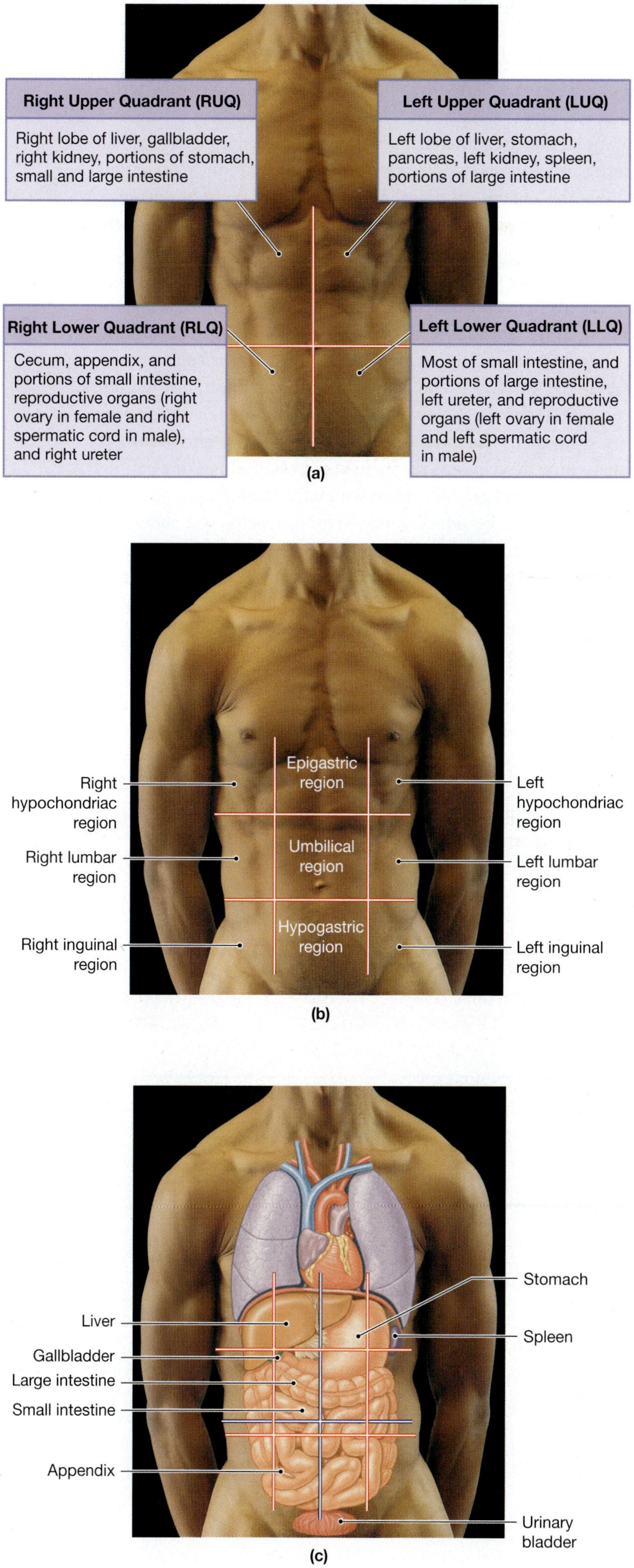

Figure 1.9 Abdominopelvic Quadrants and Regions
The abdominopelvic surface is separated into sections to identify anatomical landmarks more clearly and to define the location of contained organs more precisely. **(a)** Abdominopelvic quadrants divide the area into four sections. These terms, or their abbreviations, are most often used in clinical discussions. **(b)** More precise anatomical descriptions are provided by reference to the appropriate abdominopelvic region. **(c)** Quadrants or regions are useful because there is a known relationship between superficial anatomical landmarks and underlying organs.

shown in Figure 1.9b. Figure 1.9c shows the relationship between quadrants, regions, and internal organs.

Anatomical Directions [Figure 1.10 and Table 1.2]

Figure 1.10 and Table 1.2 show the principal directional terms and examples of their use. There are many different terms, and some can be used interchangeably. As you learn these directional terms, it is important to remember that all anatomical directions utilize the anatomical position as the standard point of reference. For example, *anterior* refers to the front of the body; in humans, this term is equivalent to *ventral*, which actually refers to the belly side. Although your instructor may have additional terminology, the terms that appear frequently in later chapters have been emphasized in Table 1.2. When following anatomical descriptions, you will find it useful to remember that the terms *left* and *right* always refer to the left and right sides of the subject, not the observer. You should also note that although some reference terms are equivalent—*posterior* and *dorsal*, or *anterior* and *ventral*—anatomical descriptions use them in opposing pairs. For example, a discussion will give directions with reference either to posterior versus anterior, or dorsal versus ventral. Finally, you should be aware that some of the reference terms listed in Table 1.2 are either not used or have different meanings in veterinary anatomy.

Sectional Anatomy

A presentation in sectional view is sometimes the only way to illustrate the relationships between the parts of a three-dimensional object. An understanding of sectional views has become increasingly important since the development of electronic imaging techniques that enable us to see inside the living body without resorting to surgery.

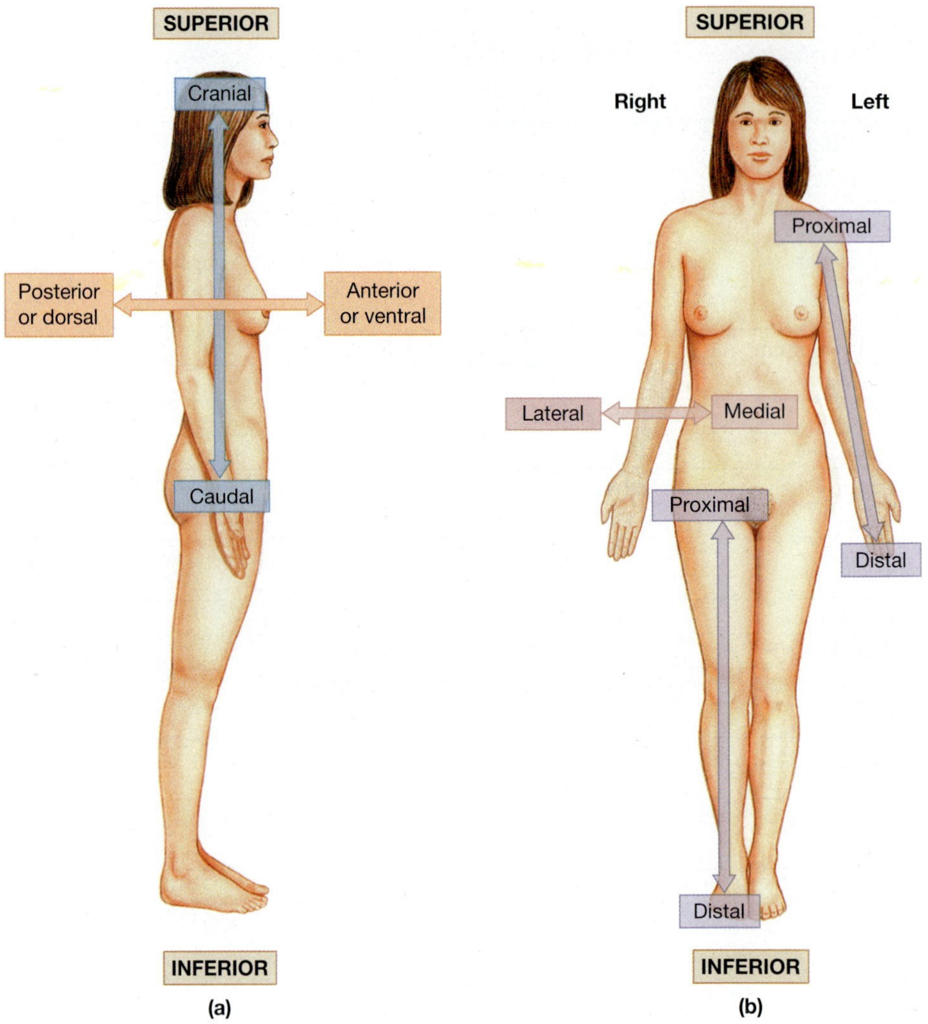

Figure 1.10 Directional References
Important directional references used in this text are indicated by arrows; definitions and descriptions are included in Table 1.2. **(a)** Lateral view. **(b)** Anterior view.

TABLE 1.2 Regional and Directional Terms (see Figure 1.10)

Term	Region or Reference	Example
Anterior	The front; before	The navel is on the *anterior* surface of the trunk.
Ventral	The belly side (equivalent to anterior when referring to human body)	The navel is on the *ventral* surface.
Posterior	The back; behind	The scapula (shoulder blade) is located *posterior* to the rib cage.
Dorsal	The back (equivalent to posterior when referring to human body)	The scapula (shoulder blade) is located on the *dorsal* side of the body.
Cranial	Toward the head	The *cranial*, or *cephalic*, border of the pelvis is *superior* to the thigh.
Cephalic	Same as cranial	
Superior	Above; at a higher level (in human body, toward the head)	
Caudal	Toward the tail (coccyx in humans)	The hips are *caudal* to the waist.
Inferior	Below; at a lower level; toward the feet	The knees are *inferior* to the hips.
Medial	Toward the midline (the longitudinal axis of the body)	The *medial* surfaces of the thighs may be in contact.
Lateral	Away from the midline (the longitudinal axis of the body)	The femur articulates with the *lateral* surface of the pelvis.
Proximal	Toward an attached base	The thigh is *proximal* to the foot.
Distal	Away from an attached base	The fingers are *distal* to the wrist.
Superficial	At, near, or relatively close to the body surface	The skin is *superficial* to underlying structures.
Deep	Toward the interior of the body; farther from the surface	The bone of the thigh is *deep* to the surrounding skeletal muscles.

Planes and Sections [Figures 1.11/1.12 and Table 1.3]

Any slice through a three-dimensional object can be described with reference to three **sectional planes,** indicated in Table 1.3 and Figure 1.11. The **transverse plane** lies at right angles to the longitudinal axis of the part of the body being studied. A division along this plane is called a **transverse section,** or *cross section.* The **frontal plane**, or **coronal plane**, and the **sagittal plane** parallel the longitudinal axis of the body. The frontal plane extends from side to side, dividing the body into **anterior** and **posterior** sections. The sagittal plane extends from anterior to posterior, dividing the body into *left* and *right* sections. A section that passes along the midline and divides the body into left and right halves is a **midsagittal section**, or a **median sagittal section**; a section parallel to the midsagittal line is a **parasagittal section**.

Sometimes it is helpful to compare the information provided by sections made along different planes. Each sectional plane provides a different perspective on the structure of the body; when combined with

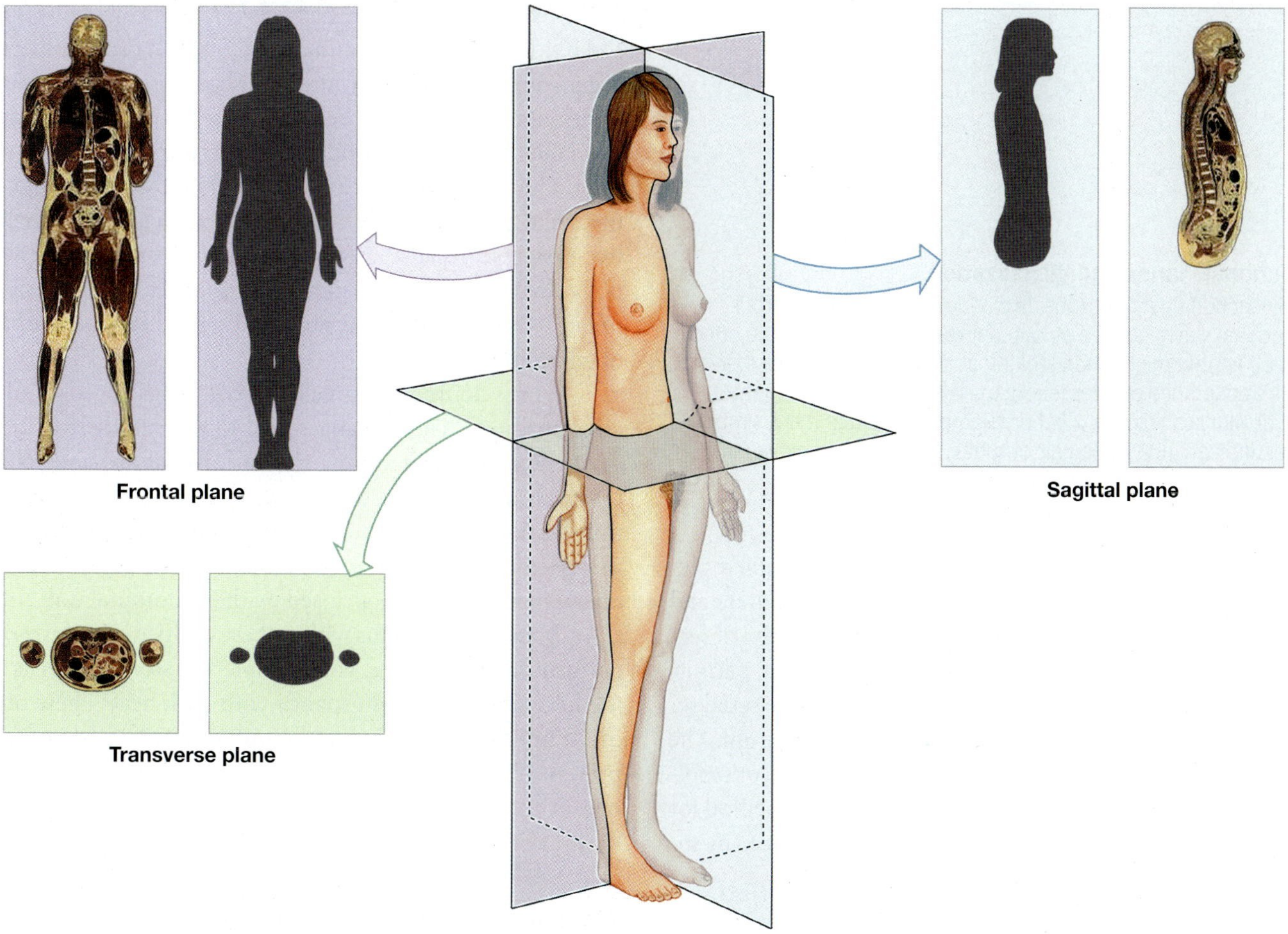

Figure 1.11 Planes of Section
The three primary planes of section are indicated here. The photographic images are derived from the Visible Human data set, described on p. 18. Table 1.3 defines and describes these terms.

TABLE 1.3 Terms That Indicate Planes of Section (see Figure 1.11)

Orientation of Plane	Adjective	Directional Term	Description
Perpendicular to long axis	Transverse or horizontal or cross-sectional	Transversely or horizontally	A *transverse*, or *horizontal section* separates superior and inferior portions of the body; sections typically pass through head and trunk regions.
Parallel to long axis	Sagittal	Sagittally	A *sagittal section* separates right and left portions. You examine a sagittal section, but you section sagittally.
	Midsagittal		In a *midsagittal section*, the plane passes through the midline, dividing the body in half and separating right and left sides.
	Parasagittal		A *parasagittal section* misses the midline, separating right and left portions of unequal size.
	Frontal or coronal	Frontally or coronally	A *frontal*, or *coronal*, *section* separates anterior and posterior portions of the body; coronal usually refers to sections passing through the skull.

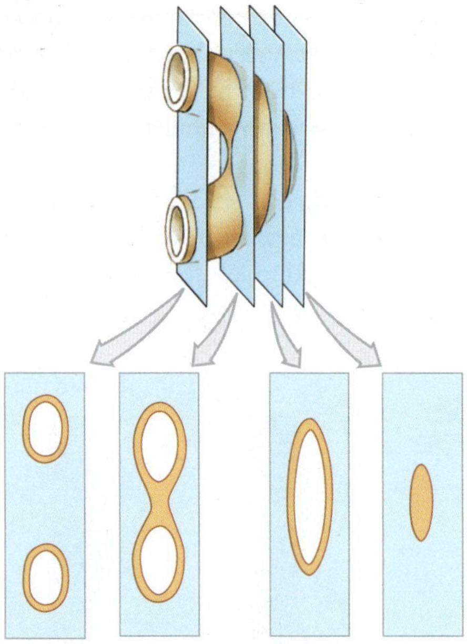

Figure 1.12 Sectional Planes and Visualization
Here we are serially sectioning a bent tube, like a piece of elbow macaroni. Notice how the sectional views change as one approaches the curve; the effects of sectioning must be kept in mind when looking at slides under the microscope. They also affect the appearance of internal organs when seen in a sectional view, through a CT or MRI scan (see p. 22). For example, although it is a simple tube, the small intestine can look like a pair of tubes, a dumbbell, an oval, or a solid, depending on where the section was taken.

observations on the external anatomy, they create a reasonably complete picture (see the Clinical Note below). You could develop a more accurate and complete picture by choosing one sectional plane and making a series of sections at small intervals. This process, called **serial reconstruction**, permits the analysis of relatively complex structures. Figure 1.12 shows the serial reconstruction of a simple bent tube, such as a piece of elbow macaroni. The procedure could be used to visualize the path of a small blood vessel or to follow a loop of the intestine. Serial reconstruction is an important method for studying histological structure and for analyzing the images produced by sophisticated clinical procedures (see the Clinical Note on p. 21).

Clinical Note

The Visible Human Project The goal of the Visible Human Project, funded by the U.S. National Library of Medicine, has been to create an accurate computerized human body that can be studied and manipulated in ways that would be impossible using a real body. The data set in its current form consists of the digital images of cross sections painstakingly prepared (by Dr. Victor Spitzer and colleagues at the University of Colorado Health Sciences Center) at 1-mm intervals for the visible male and 0.33-mm intervals for the visible female. Even the relatively "low-resolution" data sets are enormous—the male sections total 14 GB and the female sections total 40 GB. These images can be viewed on the Web at **http://www.nlm.nih.gov/research/visible/visible_human.html**. These data have subsequently been used to generate a variety of enhanced images, such as those appearing in Figure 1.11, and for interactive educational projects, such as the Digital Cadaver.

CONCEPT CHECK

1. What type of section would separate the two eyes?
2. You fall and break your antebrachium. What part of the body is affected?
3. What is the anatomical name for each of the following areas: groin, buttock, hand?

See blue "Answers" tab at back of book.

Body Cavities [Figures 1.13/1.14]

Viewed in sections, the human body is not a solid object, and many vital organs are suspended in internal chambers called **body cavities**. These cavities protect delicate organs from accidental shocks and cushion them from the thumps and bumps that occur during walking, jumping, and running. The **ventral body cavity**, or *coelom* (SĒ-lom; *koila*, cavity), contains organs of the respiratory, cardiovascular, digestive, urinary, and reproductive systems. Because they project partly or completely into the ventral body cavity, there can be significant changes in the size and shape of these organs without distorting surrounding tissues or disrupting the activities of adjacent organs.

As development proceeds, internal organs grow and change their relative positions. These changes lead to the subdivision of the ventral body cavity. Relationships among the various subdivisions of the ventral body cavity are diagrammed in Figures 1.13a and 1.14. The **diaphragm** (DĪ-a-fram), a dome-shaped muscular sheet, separates the ventral body cavity into a superior *thoracic cavity*, enclosed by the chest wall, and an inferior *abdominopelvic cavity*, enclosed by the abdominal wall and pelvis.

Many of the organs within these cavities change size and shape as they perform their functions. For example, the stomach swells at each meal, and the heart contracts and expands with each beat. These organs project into moist internal chambers that permit expansion and limited movement, but prevent friction. There are three such chambers in the thoracic cavity and one in the abdominopelvic cavity. The internal organs that project into these cavities are called **viscera** (VIS-er-a).

The Thoracic Cavity The lungs and heart, associated organs of the respiratory, cardiovascular, and lymphoid systems, as well as the thymus and inferior portions of the esophagus, are contained within the **thoracic cavity**. The boundaries of the thoracic cavity are established by the muscles and bones of the chest wall and the diaphragm, a muscular sheet that separates the thoracic cavity from the abdominopelvic cavity (see Figure 1.13a,c). The thoracic cavity is subdivided into the left and right *pleural cavities* separated by the **mediastinum** (mē-dē-as-TĪ-num or mē-dē-AS-ti-num) (Figure 1.13a,c,d).

Each **pleural cavity** contains a lung. The cavity is lined by a shiny, slippery *serous membrane*, which reduces friction as the lung expands and recoils during respiration. The serous membrane lining a pleural cavity is called a *pleura* (PLOOR-ah). The *visceral pleura* covers the outer surfaces of a lung, and the *parietal pleura* covers the opposing mediastinal surface and the inner body wall.

The mediastinum consists of a mass of connective tissue that surrounds, stabilizes, and supports the esophagus, trachea, and thymus, and the major blood vessels that originate or end at the heart. It also contains the **pericardial cavity**, a small chamber that surrounds the heart (Figure 1.13d). The relationship between the heart and the pericardial cavity resem-

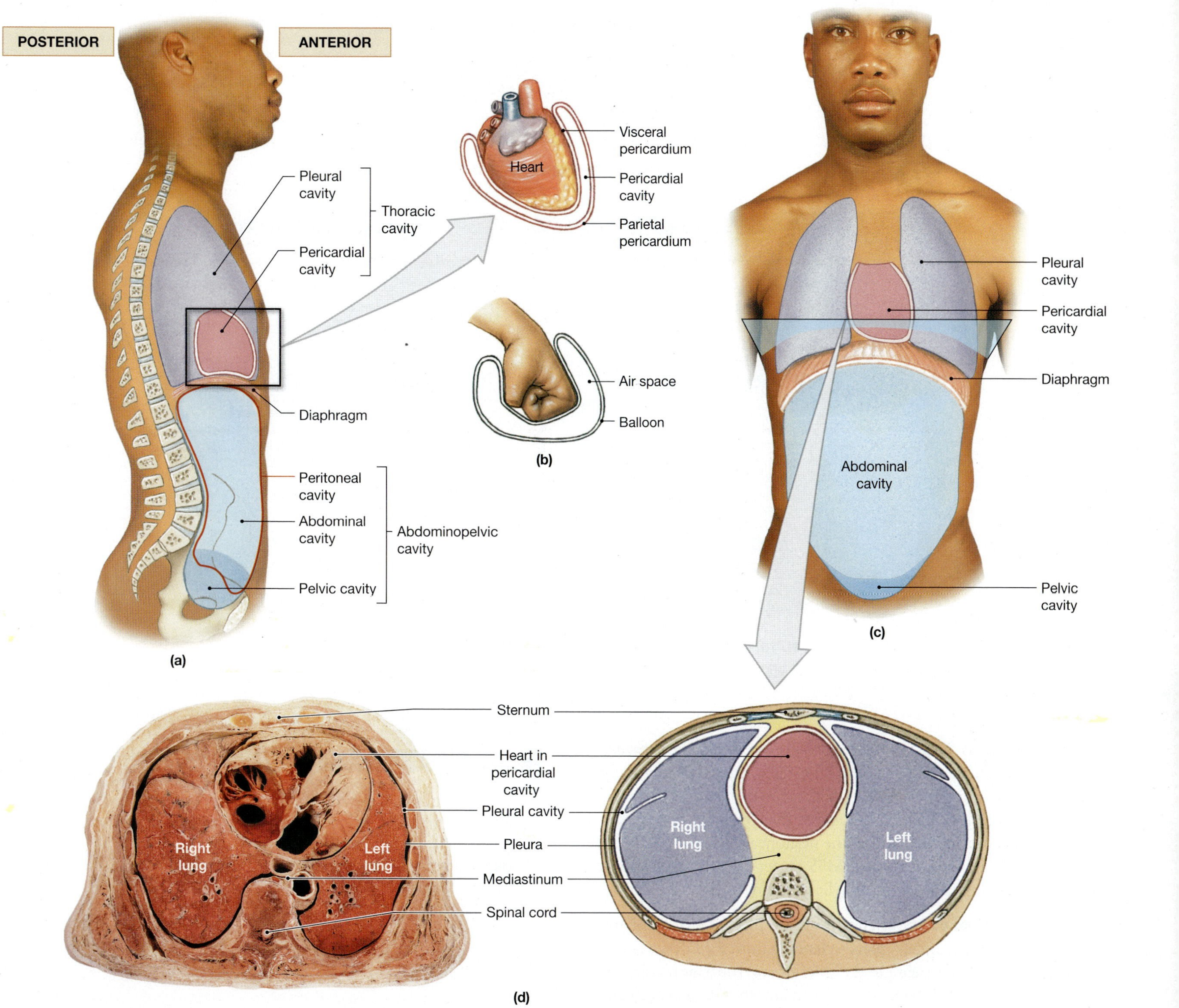

Figure 1.13 Body Cavities
(a) Lateral view of the subdivisions of the ventral body cavities. The muscular diaphragm divides the ventral body cavity into a superior thoracic (chest) cavity and an inferior abdominopelvic cavity. **(b)** The heart projects into the pericardial cavity like a fist pushed into a balloon. **(c)** Anterior view of the ventral body cavity and its subdivisions. **(d)** Sectional view of the thoracic cavity. Unless otherwise noted, all sectional views are presented in inferior view. (See Clinical Note on pp. 21–23 for more details.)

bles that of a fist pushing into a balloon (Figure 1.13b). The wrist corresponds to the base (attached portion) of the heart, and the balloon corresponds to the serous membrane that lines the pericardial cavity. The serous membrane covering the heart is called the **pericardium** (*peri-*, around + *kardia*, heart). The layer covering the heart is the *visceral pericardium*, and the opposing surface is the *parietal pericardium*. During each beat, the heart changes in size and shape. The pericardial cavity permits these changes, and the slippery pericardial lining prevents friction between the heart and adjacent structures in the mediastinum.

The Abdominopelvic Cavity Figures 1.13a and 1.14 demonstrate that the **abdominopelvic cavity** can be divided into a superior *abdominal cavity* and an inferior *pelvic cavity*. The abdominopelvic cavity contains the **peritoneal** (per-i-tō-NĒ-al) **cavity**, an internal chamber lined by a serous

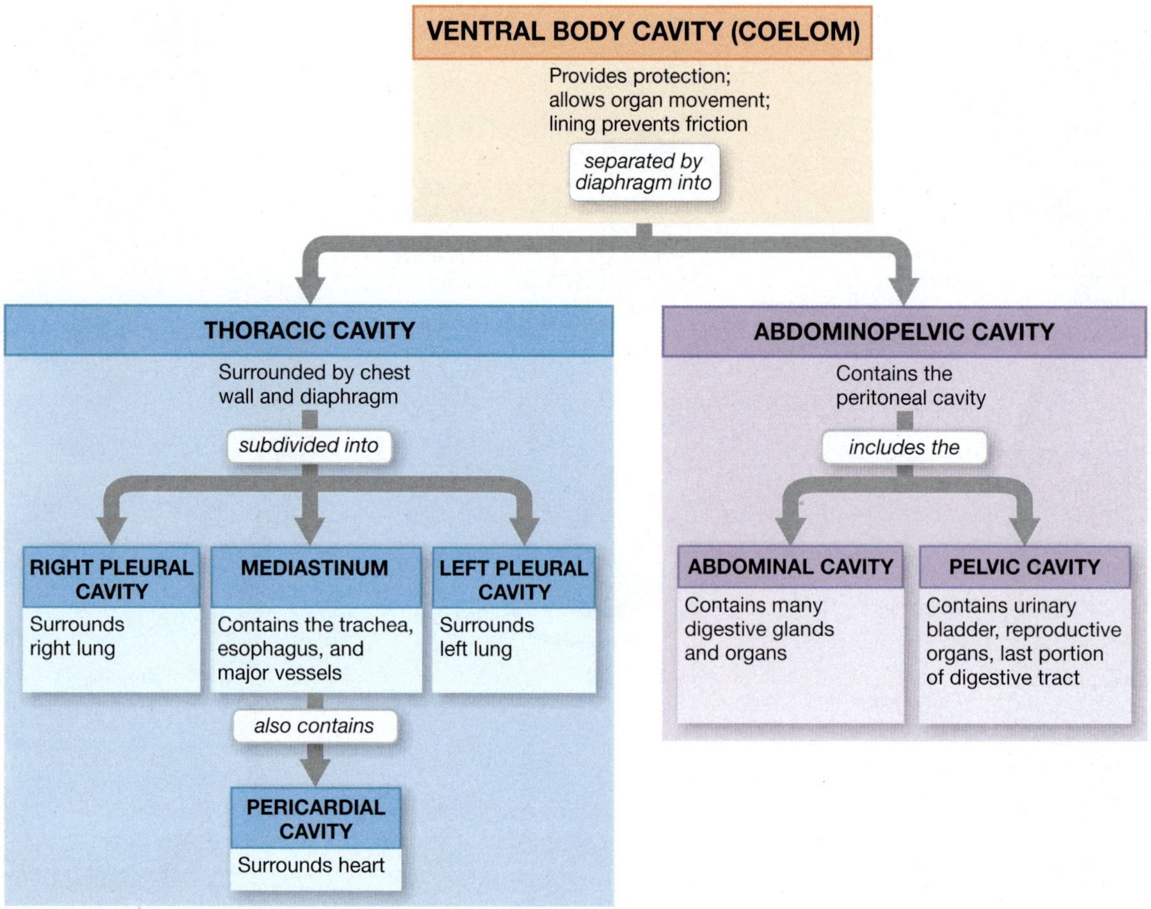

Figure 1.14 The Ventral Body Cavity
Relationships, contents, and some selected functions of the subdivisions of the ventral body cavity.

membrane known as the **peritoneum** (per-i-tō-NĒ-um). The *parietal peritoneum* lines the body wall. A narrow, fluid-filled space separates the parietal peritoneum from the *visceral peritoneum* that covers the enclosed organs. Organs such as the stomach, small intestine, and portions of the large intestine are suspended within the peritoneal cavity by double sheets of peritoneum, called **mesenteries** (MES-en-ter-ēs). Mesenteries provide support and stability while permitting limited movement.

- The **abdominal cavity** extends from the inferior surface of the diaphragm to an imaginary plane extending from the inferior surface of the lowest spinal vertebra to the anterior and superior margins of the pelvic girdle. The abdominal cavity contains the liver, stomach, spleen, kidneys, pancreas, and small intestine, and most of the large intestine. (The positions of many of these organs can be seen in **Figure 1.9c**, p. 15). These organs project partially or completely into the peritoneal cavity, much as the heart and lungs project into the pericardial and pleural cavities, respectively.
- The portion of the ventral body cavity inferior to the abdominal cavity is the **pelvic cavity**. The pelvic cavity, enclosed by the bones of the pelvis, contains the last segments of the large intestine, the urinary bladder, and various reproductive organs. For example, the pelvic cavity of a female contains the ovaries, uterine tubes, and uterus; in a male, it contains the prostate gland and seminal glands. The inferior portion of the peritoneal cavity extends into the pelvic cavity. The superior portion of the urinary bladder in both sexes, and the uterine tubes, the ovaries, and the superior portion of the uterus in females are covered by the peritoneum.

CONCEPT CHECK

1. What is the general function of the mesenteries?
2. If a surgeon makes an incision just inferior to the diaphragm, which body cavity will be opened?
3. Use a directional term to describe the following:
   (a) The toes are ______________ to the tarsus.
   (b) The hips are ______________ to the head.

See blue "Answers" tab at back of book.

This chapter provided an overview of the locations and functions of the major components of each organ system, and it introduced the anatomical vocabulary needed for you to follow the more detailed anatomical descriptions in later chapters. Modern methods of visualizing anatomical structures in living individuals are summarized in the Clinical Note and **Figure 1.17**. A true understanding of anatomy involves integrating the information provided by sectional images, interpretive artwork based on sections and dissections, and direct observation. This text will give you the basic information and show you interpretive illustrations, sectional views, and "real-life" photos. But it will be up to you to integrate these views and develop your ability to observe and visualize anatomical structures. As you proceed, don't forget that every structure you encounter has a specific function. The goal of anatomy isn't simply to identify and catalog structural details, but to understand how those structures interact to perform the many and varied functions of the human body.

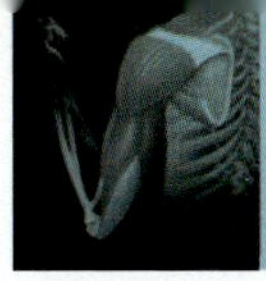

Clinical Note [Figures 1.15/1.16/1.17]

Sectional Anatomy and Clinical Technology **Radiological procedures** include various noninvasive techniques that use radioisotopes, radiation, and magnetic fields to produce images of internal structures. Physicians who specialize in the performance and analysis of these diagnostic images are called **radiologists**. Radiological procedures can provide detailed information about internal systems and structures. Figures 1.15 through 1.17 compare the views provided by several different techniques. Most of the procedures produce black-and-white images on film sheets. Colors can be added by computer to illustrate subtle variations in contrast and shading. Note that when anatomical diagrams or scans present cross-sectional views, the sections are presented as though the observer were standing at the feet and looking toward the head of the subject.

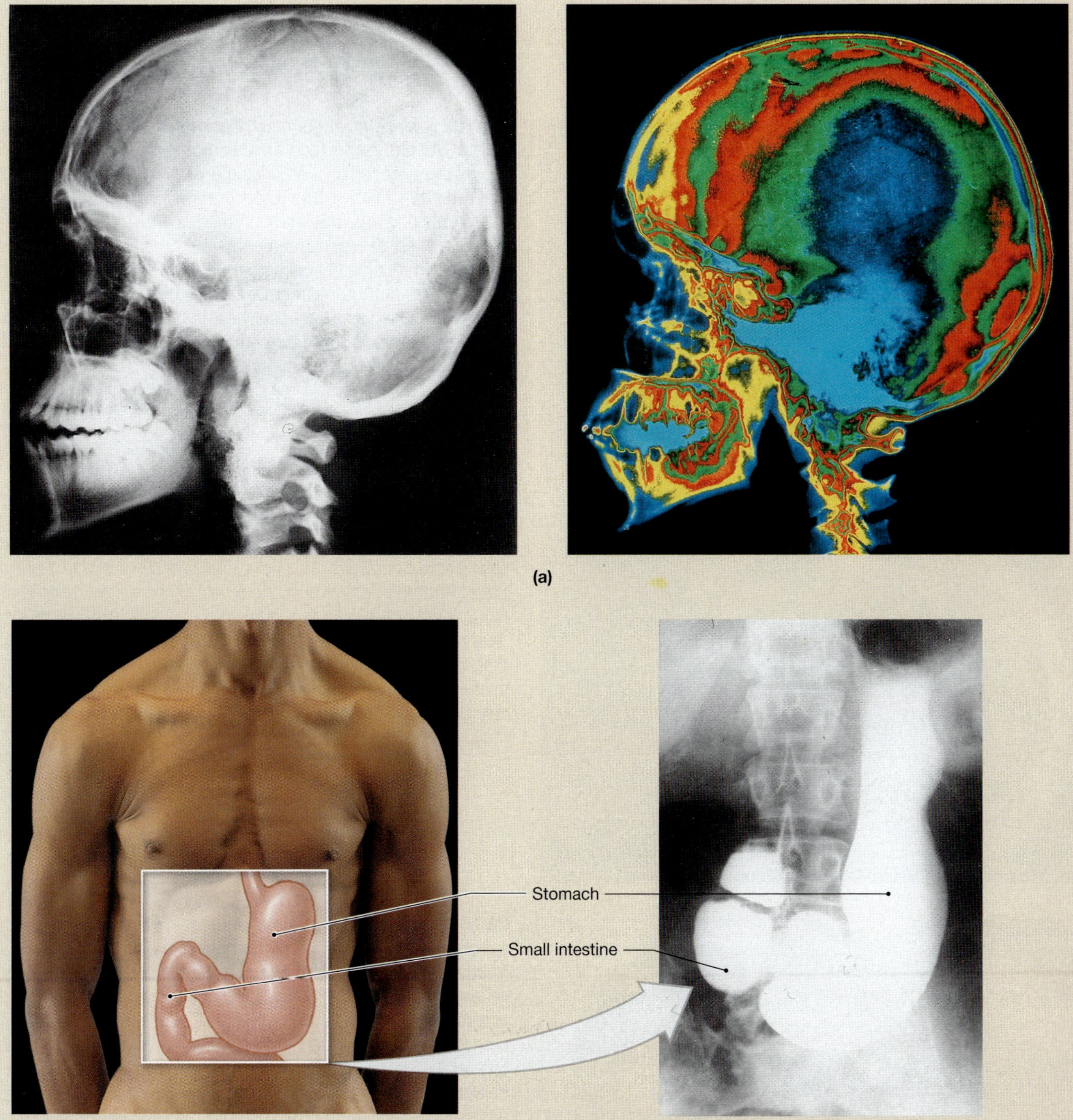

Figure 1.15 X-Rays
(a) An x-ray of the skull and color-enhanced x-ray of the skull, taken from the left side. X-rays are a form of high-energy radiation that can penetrate living tissues. In the most familiar procedure, a beam of x-rays travels through the body and strikes a photographic plate. Not all of the projected x-rays arrive at the film; some are absorbed or deflected as they pass through the body. The resistance to x-ray penetration is called **radiodensity**. In the human body, the order of increasing radiodensity is as follows: air, fat, liver, blood, muscle, bone. The result is an image with radiodense tissues, such as bone, appearing white, while less dense tissues are seen in shades of gray to black. (The image to the right has been scanned and digitally color enhanced.) A typical x-ray is a two-dimensional image of a three-dimensional object; it is usually difficult to decide whether a particular feature is on the left side (toward the viewer) or on the right side (away from the viewer). **(b)** A **barium-contrast x-ray** of the upper digestive tract. Barium is very radiodense, and the contours of the gastric and intestinal lining can be seen outlined against the white of the barium solution.

Clinical Note *(continued)*

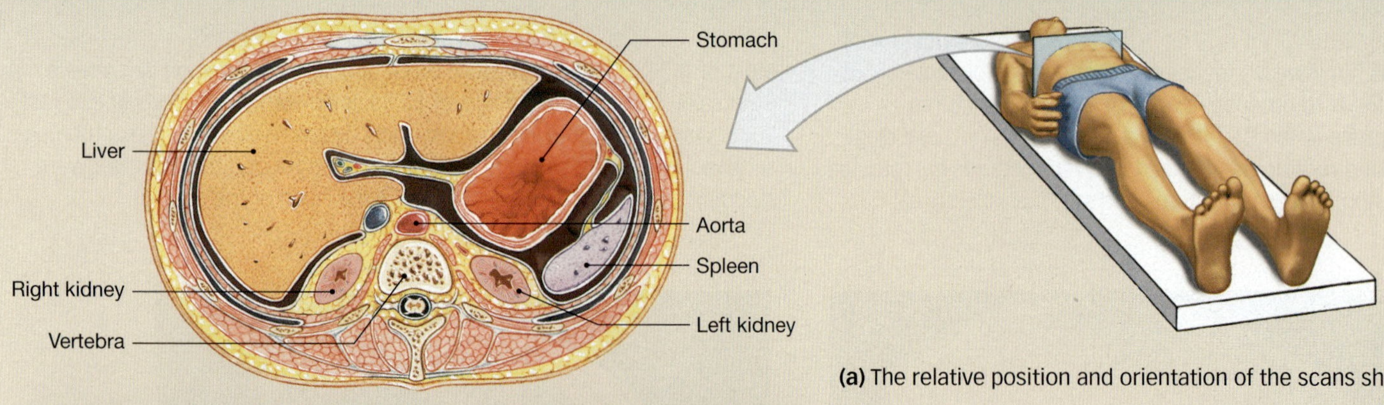

(a) The relative position and orientation of the scans shown in parts (b)–(d).

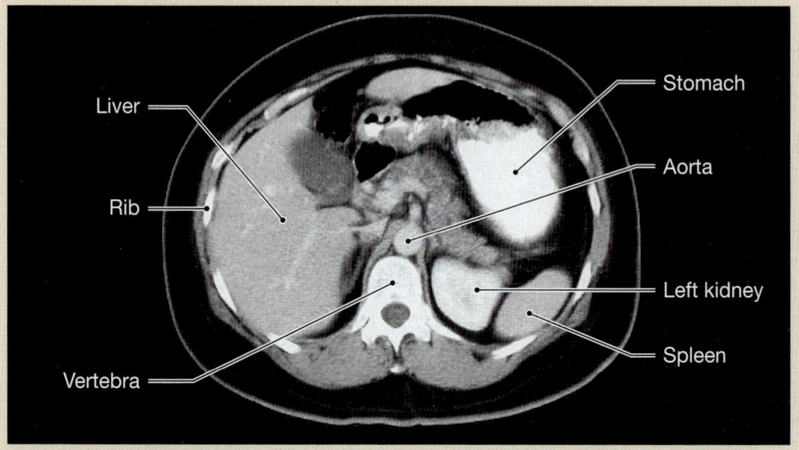

(b) A CT scan of the abdomen. **CT (computerized tomography)** formerly called **CAT (computerized axial tomography)** uses computers to reconstruct sectional views. A single x-ray source rotates around the body, and the x-ray beam strikes a sensor monitored by the computer. The source completes one revolution around the body every few seconds; it then moves a short distance and repeats the process. By comparing the information obtained at each point in the rotation, the computer reconstructs the three-dimensional structure of the body. The result is usually displayed as a sectional view in black and white, but it can be colorized. CT scans show three-dimensional relationships and soft tissue structure more clearly than standard x-rays.

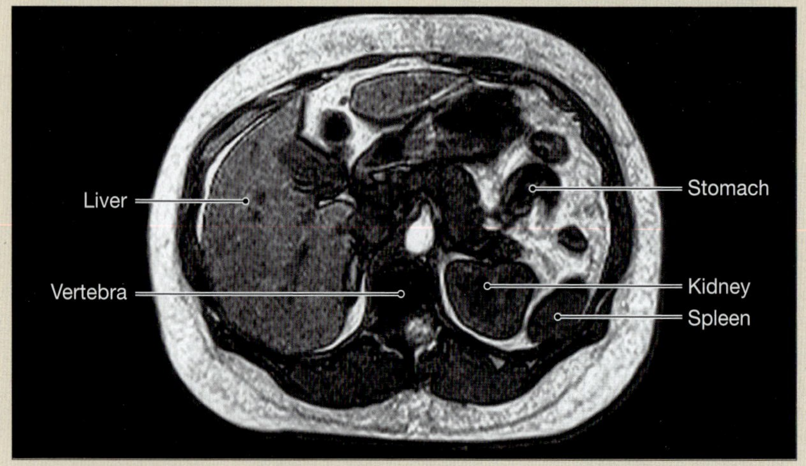

(c) An **MRI (magnetic resonance imaging)** scan of the same region. MRI surrounds part or all of the body with a magnetic field about 3000 times as strong as that of Earth. This field affects protons within atomic nuclei throughout the body, which line up along the magnetic lines of force like compass needles in Earth's magnetic field. When struck by a radio wave of the proper frequency, a proton will absorb energy. When the pulse ends, that energy is released, and the energy source of the radiation is detected by the MRI computers. Each element differs in terms of the radio frequency required to affect its protons. Note the differences in detail between this image, the CT scan, and the x-rays in **Figure 1.15**.

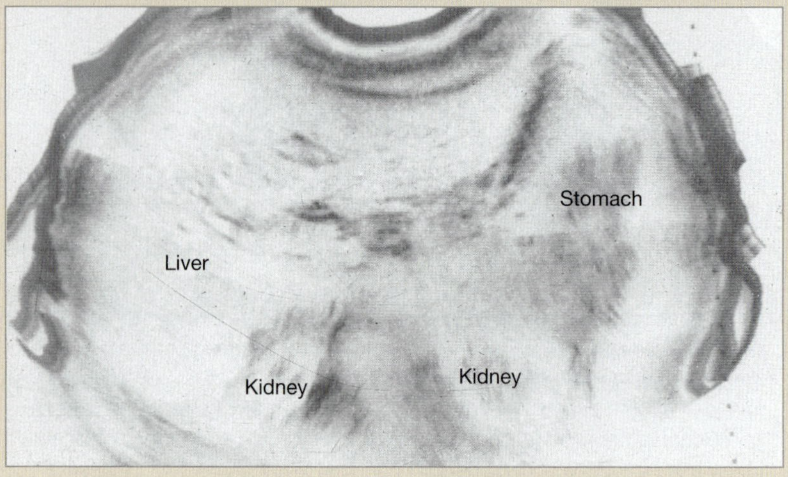

(d) An ultrasound scan of the abdomen. In **ultrasound** procedures, a small transmitter contacting the skin broadcasts a brief, narrow burst of high-frequency sound and then picks up the echoes. The sound waves are reflected by internal structures, and a picture, or **echogram**, can be assembled from the pattern of echoes. These images lack the clarity of other procedures, but no adverse effects have been attributed to the sound waves, and fetal development can be monitored without a significant risk of birth defects. Special methods of transmission and processing permit structural analysis of the beating heart, without the complications that can accompany dye injections.

Figure 1.16 Scanning Techniques

Clinical Note *(continued)*

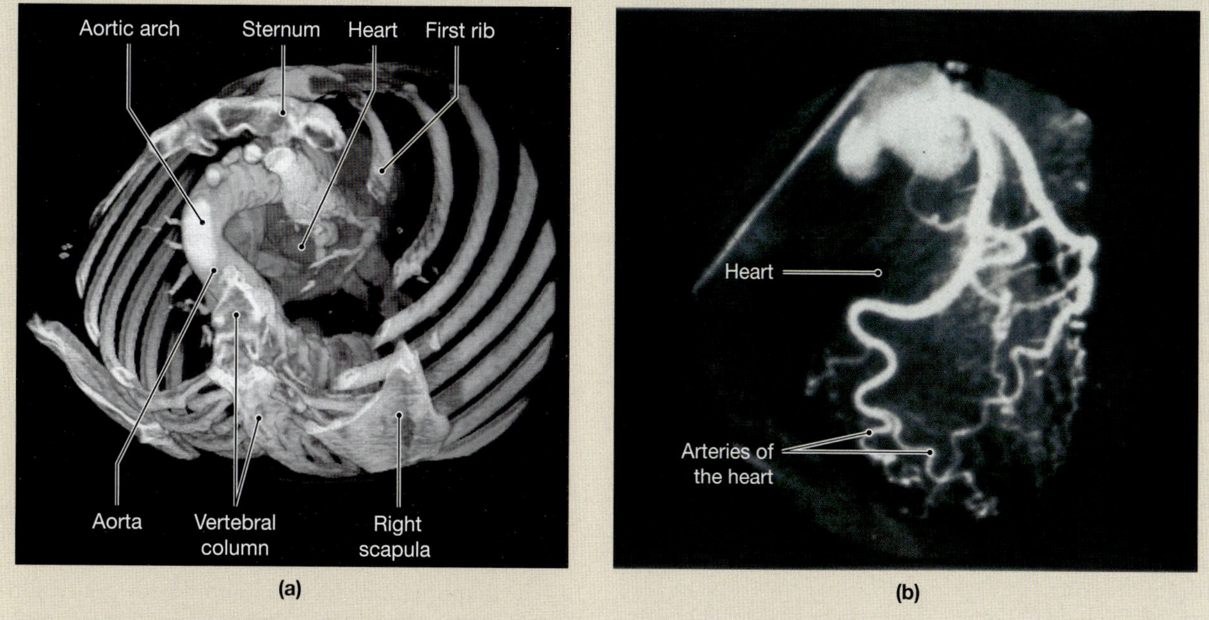

Figure 1.17 Special Scanning Methods
(a) A **spiral-CT** scan of the chest. Such an image is created by special processing of CT data. It permits rapid three-dimensional visualization of internal organs. Spiral-CT scans are becoming increasingly important in clinical settings.
(b) Digital subtraction angiography (DSA) is used to monitor blood flow through specific organs, such as the brain, heart, lungs, and kidneys. X-rays are taken before and after radiopaque dye is administered, and a computer "subtracts" details common to both images. The result is a high-contrast image showing the distribution of the dye.

CLINICAL TERMS

abdominopelvic quadrant: One of four divisions of the abdominal surface.

abdominopelvic region: One of nine divisions of the abdominal surface.

CT, CAT (computerized [axial] tomography): An imaging technique that reconstructs the three-dimensional structure of the body.

diagnosis: A decision about the nature of an illness.

disease: A failure of the body to maintain homeostatic conditions.

MRI (magnetic resonance imaging): An imaging technique that employs a magnetic field and radio waves to portray subtle structural differences.

pathology: The formal name for the study of disease.

radiologist: A physician who specializes in performing and analyzing diagnostic imaging procedures.

ultrasound: An imaging technique that uses brief bursts of high-frequency sound reflected by internal structures.

x-rays: High-energy radiation that can penetrate living tissues.

STUDY OUTLINE

Introduction 2

1. **Anatomy** is the study of internal and external structures and the physical relationships between body parts. Specific anatomical structures perform specific functions.

Microscopic Anatomy 2

1. The boundaries of **microscopic anatomy** are established by the limits of the equipment used. **Cytology** is the study of the internal structure of individual cells, the smallest units of life. **Histology** examines **tissues**, groups of cells that work together to perform specific functions. Specific arrangements of tissues form **organs**, anatomical units with multiple functions. A group of organs that function together forms an **organ system**. *(see Figure 1.1)*

Gross Anatomy 3

1. **Gross (macroscopic) anatomy** considers features visible without a microscope. It includes **surface anatomy** (general form and superficial markings); **regional anatomy** (superficial and internal features in a specific area of the body); and **systemic anatomy** (structure of major organ systems).

Other Perspectives on Anatomy 3

1. **Developmental anatomy** examines the changes in form that occur between conception and physical maturity. **Embryology** studies the processes that occur during the first two months of development.
2. **Comparative anatomy** considers the similarities and relationships in anatomical organization of different animals. *(see Figure 1.2)*

3. Anatomical specialties important to clinical practice include **clinical anatomy** (anatomical features that undergo characteristic changes during illness), **surgical anatomy** (landmarks important for surgical procedures), **radiographic anatomy** (anatomical structures that are visualized by specialized procedures performed on an intact body), and **cross-sectional anatomy**. *(see Figures 1.15 to 1.17)*

Levels of Organization 4

1. Anatomical structures are arranged in a series of interacting levels of organization ranging from the chemical/molecular level, through cell/tissue levels, to the organ/system/organism level. *(see Figures 1.3/1.4)*

An Introduction to Organ Systems 6

1. All living organisms are recognized by a set of vital properties and processes: They **respond** to changes in their environment; they show *adaptability* to their environment; they **grow**, **differentiate**, and **reproduce** to create future generations; they are capable of producing **movement**; and they absorb materials from the environment, and use them in **metabolism.** Organisms absorb and consume oxygen during **respiration**, and discharge waste products during **excretion. Digestion** breaks down complex foods for use by the body. The **cardiovascular system** forms an internal transportation system between areas of the body. *(see Figures 1.5/1.6)*
2. The 11 organ systems of the human body perform these vital functions to maintain **homeostasis**. *(see Figure 1.5)*

The Language of Anatomy 13

1. Anatomy utilizes a special language that includes many terms and phrases derived from foreign languages, especially Latin and Greek. *(see Figures 1.7 to 1.14)*

Superficial Anatomy 14

2. Standard anatomical illustrations show the body in the **anatomical position**. Here, a person stands with the legs together and the feet flat on the floor. The hands are at the sides and the palms face forward. *(see Figures 1.8/1.10)*
3. A person lying down in the anatomical position may be **supine** (face up) or **prone** (face down).
4. Specific terms identify specific anatomical regions; for example, *cephalic* (area of head), *cervical* (area of neck), and *thoracic* (area of chest). Other terms, including *abdominal, pelvic, lumbar, gluteal, pubic, brachial, antebrachial, manual, femoral, patellar, crural, sural,* and *pedal,* are applied to specific regions of the body. *(see Figure 1.8 and Table 1.1)*
5. **Abdominopelvic quadrants** and **abdominopelvic regions** represent two different approaches to describing locations in the abdominal and pubic areas of the body. *(see Figure 1.9)*
6. Specific directional terms are used to indicate relative location on the body; for example, *anterior* (front, before), *posterior* (back, behind), and *dorsal* (back). Other directional terms encountered throughout the text include *ventral, superior, inferior, medial, lateral, cranial, cephalic, caudal, proximal,* and *distal. (see Figure 1.10 and Table 1.2)*

Sectional Anatomy 16

7. There are three **sectional planes: frontal plane** or **coronal plane** (anterior versus posterior), **sagittal plane** (right versus left sides), and **transverse plane** (superior versus inferior). These sectional planes and related reference terms describe relationships between the parts of the three-dimensional human body. *(see Figure 1.11)*
8. **Serial reconstruction** is an important technique for studying histological structure and analyzing images produced by radiological procedures. *(see Figure 1.12)*
9. **Body cavities** protect delicate organs and permit changes in the size and shape of visceral organs. The **ventral body cavity**, or **coelom**, surrounds organs of the respiratory, cardiovascular, digestive, urinary, and reproductive systems.
10. The **diaphragm** divides the ventral body cavity into the superior **thoracic** and inferior **abdominopelvic cavities.** *(see Figures 1.13/1.14)*
11. The **abdominal cavity** extends from the inferior surface of the diaphragm to an imaginary line drawn from the inferior surface of the most inferior spinal vertebra to the anterior and superior margin of the pelvic girdle. The portion of the ventral body cavity inferior to this imaginary line is the **pelvic cavity**. *(see Figures 1.13/1.14)*
12. The ventral body cavity contains narrow, fluid-filled spaces lined by a *serous membrane.* The thoracic cavity contains two **pleural cavities** (each surrounding a lung) separated by the **mediastinum.** *(see Figures 1.13/1.14)*
13. The mediastinum contains the thymus, trachea, esophagus, blood vessels, and the **pericardial cavity**, which surrounds the heart. The membrane lining the pleural cavities is called the **pleura**; the membrane lining the pericardial cavity is called the **pericardium**. *(see Figures 1.13/1.14)*
14. The **abdominopelvic cavity** contains the **peritoneal cavity**, which is lined by the **peritoneum**. Many digestive organs are supported and stabilized by **mesenteries.**
15. Important **radiological procedures**, which can provide detailed information about internal systems, include **x-rays, CT scans, MRI**, and **ultrasound**. Physicians who perform and analyze these procedures are called **radiologists**. *(see Figures 1.15 to 1.17)*

CHAPTER REVIEW

For answers to the Concept Check and Chapter Review questions, go to the blue "Answers" tab at the back of the book.

Level 1 Reviewing Facts and Terms

Match each numbered item with the most closely related lettered item. Use letters for answers in the spaces provided.

Column A	Column B
___1. supine	a. study of tissues
___2. cytology	b. face down
___3. homeostasis	c. thoracic and abdominopelvic
___4. lumbar	d. all chemical activity in body
___5. prone	e. study of cells
___6. metabolism	f. face up
___7. ventral body cavity	g. constant internal environment
___8. histology	h. lower back

9. A plane that passes perpendicular to the longitudinal axis of the part of the body being studied is
   (a) sagittal (b) coronal
   (c) transverse (d) frontal

10. Body cavities
    (a) are internal chambers containing many vital organs
    (b) include a ventral space and its subdivisions
    (c) allow visceral organs to change size and shape
    (d) all of the above

11. The major function of the ______________________ system is the internal transport of nutrients, wastes, and gases.
    (a) digestive
    (b) cardiovascular
    (c) respiratory
    (d) urinary

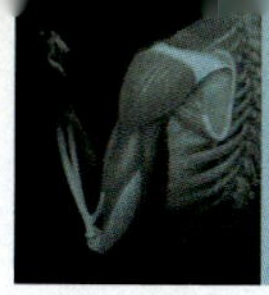

12. Which of the following includes only structures enclosed within the mediastinum?
    (a) lungs, esophagus, heart
    (b) heart, trachea, lungs
    (c) esophagus, trachea, thymus
    (d) pharynx, thymus, major vessels

13. Making a sagittal section results in the separation of
    (a) anterior and posterior portions of the body
    (b) superior and inferior portions of the body
    (c) dorsal and ventral portions of the body
    (d) right and left portions of the body

14. The primary site of blood cell production is within the
    (a) cardiovascular system
    (b) skeletal system
    (c) integumentary system
    (d) lymphatic system

15. Which of the following regions corresponds to the arm?
    (a) cervical
    (b) brachial
    (c) femoral
    (d) pedal

Level 2 Reviewing Concepts

1. From the following selections, identify the directional terms equivalent to *ventral, posterior, superior,* and *inferior* in the correct sequence.
   (a) anterior, dorsal, cephalic, caudal
   (b) dorsal, anterior, caudal, cephalic
   (c) caudal, cephalic, anterior, posterior
   (d) cephalic, caudal, posterior, anterior
2. What properties and processes are associated with all living things?
3. Utilizing proper anatomical terminology, describe the relationship of the hand to the arm.
4. The body system that performs crisis management by directing rapid, short-term, very specific responses is the
   (a) lymphatic system
   (b) nervous system
   (c) cardiovascular system
   (d) endocrine system
5. Which sectional plane could divide the body so that the face remains intact?
   (a) sagittal section
   (b) coronal section
   (c) midsagittal section
   (d) none of the above
6. Why must large organisms have circulatory systems?

Level 3 Critical Thinking

1. How might a disruption in the normal cellular division processes of cells within the bone marrow support the view that all levels of organization within an organism are interdependent?
2. A child born with a severe cleft palate may require surgery to repair the nasal cavity and reconstruct the roof of the mouth. What body systems are affected by the cleft palate? Also, studies of other mammals that develop cleft palates have helped us understand the origins and treatment of such problems. What anatomical specialties are involved in identifying and correcting a cleft palate?

2

The Cell

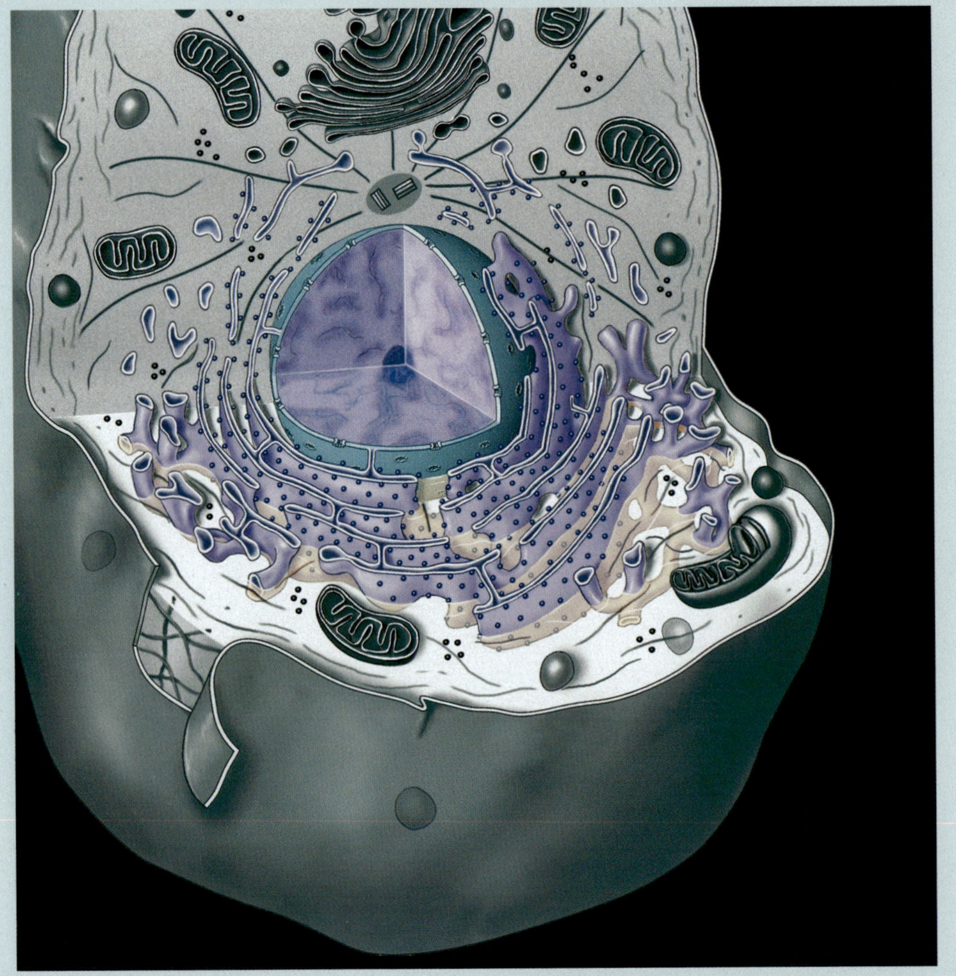

CHAPTER OBJECTIVES

1. Discuss the basic concepts of the cell theory.
2. Compare the perspectives provided by LMs, TEMs, and SEMs in the study of cell and tissue structure.
3. Explain the structure and significance of the plasmalemma.
4. Relate the structure of a membrane to its functions.
5. Describe how materials move across the plasmalemma.
6. Compare the fluid contents of a cell with the extracellular fluid.
7. Describe the structure and function of the various nonmembranous organelles.
8. Compare the structure and functions of the various membranous organelles.
9. Discuss the role of the nucleus as the cell's control center.
10. Discuss how cells can be interconnected to maintain structural stability in body tissues.
11. Describe the cell life cycle and how cells divide through the process of mitosis.

If you walk through a building supply store, you see many individual items—bricks, floor tiles, wall paneling, and a large assortment of lumber. Each item by itself is unremarkable and of very limited use. Yet if you have all of them in sufficient quantity, you can build a functional unit, in this case a house. The human body is also composed of a multitude of individual components called *cells*. Much as individual bricks and lumber collectively form a wall of a house, individual cells work together to form *tissues*, such as the muscular wall of the heart.

Cells were first described by the English scientist Robert Hooke, around 1665. Hooke used an early light microscope to examine dried cork. He observed thousands of tiny empty chambers, which he named *cells*. Later, other scientists observed cells in living plants and realized that these spaces were filled with a gelatinous material. Research over the next 175 years led to the *cell theory*, the concept that cells are the fundamental units of all living things. Since the 1830s, when it was first proposed, the cell theory has been expanded to incorporate several basic concepts relevant to our discussion of the human body:

1. Cells are the structural "building blocks" of all plants and animals.
2. Cells are produced by the division of preexisting cells.
3. Cells are the smallest structural units that perform all vital functions.

The human body contains trillions of cells. All our activities, from running to thinking, result from the combined and coordinated responses of millions or even billions of cells. Yet each individual cell remains unaware of its role in the "big picture"—it is simply responding to changes in its local environment. Because cells form all of the structures in the body, and perform all vital functions, our exploration of the human body must begin with basic cell biology.

Two types of cells are contained in the body: sex cells and somatic cells. **Sex cells** (*germ cells* or *reproductive cells*) are either the sperm of males or the oocytes of females. **Somatic cells** (*soma*, body) include all the other cells in the body. In this chapter we will discuss somatic cells; and in the chapter on the reproductive system (Chapter 27) we will discuss sex cells.

The Study of Cells [Figures 2.1/2.2]

Cytology is the study of the structure and function of cells. Over the past 40 years we have learned a lot about cellular physiology and the mechanism of homeostatic control. The two most common methods used to study cell and tissue structure are *light microscopy* and *electron microscopy*.

Light Microscopy

Historically, most information has been provided by light microscopy, a method in which a beam of light is passed through the object to be viewed. A photograph taken through a light microscope is called a light micrograph (LM) (see **Figure 2.1a**). Light microscopy can magnify cellular structures about 1000 times and show details as fine as 0.25 μm. (The symbol μm stands for micrometer; 1 μm = 0.001 mm, or 0.0004 in.) With a light microscope, one can identify cell types and see large intracellular structures. Cells have a variety of sizes and shapes, as indicated in **Figure 2.2**. The relative proportions of the cells in **Figure 2.2** are correct, but all have been magnified roughly 500 times. Unfortunately, you cannot simply pick up a cell, slap it onto a microscope slide, and take a photograph. Because individual cells are so small, you must work with large numbers of them. Most tissues have a three-dimensional structure, and small pieces of tissue can be removed for examination. The component cells are prevented from decomposing by first exposing the tissue sample to a poison that will stop metabolic operations, but will not alter cellular structures.

Even then, you still cannot look at the tissue sample through a light microscope, because a cube only 2 mm (0.078 in.) on a side will contain several million cells. You must slice the sample into thin sections. Living cells are relatively thick, and cellular contents are not transparent. Light can pass through the section only if the slices are thinner than the individual cells. Making a section that slender poses interesting technical problems. Most tissues are not very sturdy, so an attempt to slice a fresh piece will destroy the sample. (To appreciate the problem, try to slice a marshmallow into thin sections.) Thus, before you can make sections, you must embed the tissue sample in something that will make it more stable, such as wax, plastic, or epoxy. These materials will not interact with water molecules, so your sample must first be dehydrated (typically by immersion in 30 percent, 70 percent, 95 percent, and, finally, 100 percent alcohol). If you are embedding the sample in wax, the wax must be hot enough to melt; if you are using plastic or epoxy, the hardening process generates heat on its own.

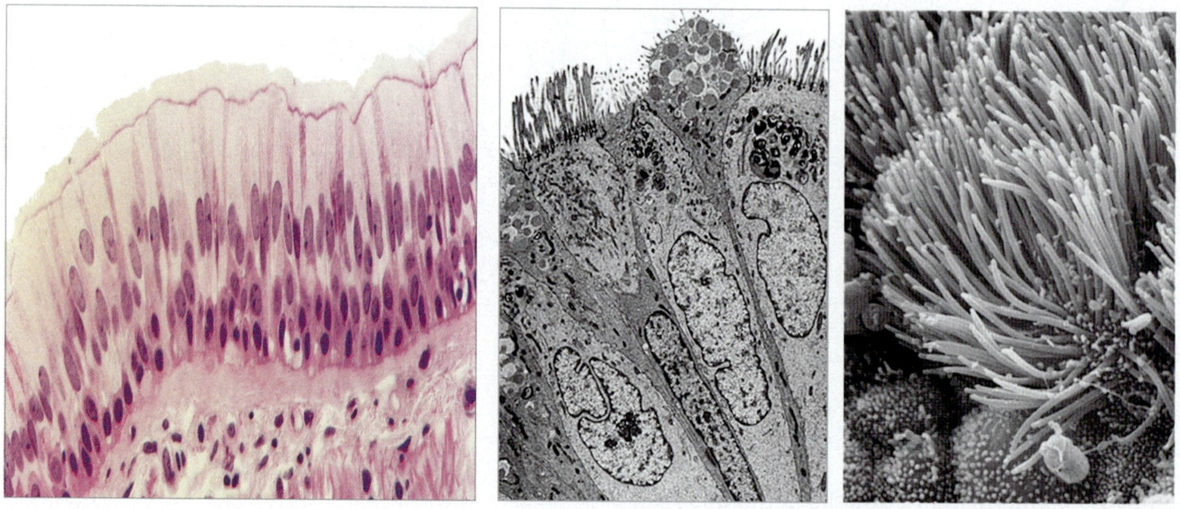

(a) (b) (c)

Figure 2.1 Different Techniques, Different Perspectives
Cells as seen in **(a)** light microscopy (respiratory tract), **(b)** transmission electron microscopy (intestinal tract), and **(c)** scanning electron microscopy (respiratory tract).

After embedding the sample, you can section the block with a machine called a microtome, which uses a metal, glass, or diamond knife. For viewing by light microscopy, a typical section is about 5 μm (0.002 in.) thick. The thin sections are then placed on microscope slides. If the sample was embedded in wax, you can now remove the wax with a solvent, such as xylene. But you are not done yet: In thin sections, the cell contents are almost transparent; you cannot yet distinguish intracellular details by using an ordinary light microscope. You must first add color to the internal structures by treating the slides with special dyes called stains. Some stains are dissolved in water and others in alcohol. Not all types of cells pick up a given stain to the same degree—if they pick it up at all; nor do all types of cellular organelles. For example, in a sample scraped from the inside of the cheek, one stain might dye only certain types of bacteria; in a semen sample, another stain might dye only the flagella of the sperm. If you try too many stains at one time, they all run together, and you must start over. Following staining, you can put coverslips over the sections (generally after you have dehydrated them again) and can see what your labors have accomplished.

Any single section can show you only a part of a cell or tissue. To reconstruct the tissue structure, you must look at a series of sections made one after the other. After examining dozens or hundreds of sections, you can understand the structure of the cells and the organization of your tissue sample—or can you? Your reconstruction has left you with an understanding of what these cells look like after they have (1) died an unnatural death; (2) been dehydrated; (3) been impregnated with wax or plastic; (4) been sliced into thin sections; (5) been rehydrated, dehydrated, and stained with various chemicals; and (6) been viewed with the limitations of your equipment. A good cytologist or histologist is extremely careful, cautious, and self-critical and realizes that much of the laboratory preparation is an art as well as a science.

Electron Microscopy

Individual cells are relatively transparent and difficult to distinguish from their neighbors. They become easier to see if they are treated with dyes that stain specific intracellular structures. Although special staining techniques can show the general distribution of protein, lipid, carbohydrate, or nucleic acids in the cell, many fine details of intracellular structure remained a mystery until investigators began using electron microscopy. This technique uses a focused beam of electrons, rather than a beam of light, to examine cell structure. In **transmission electron microscopy**, electrons penetrate an ultrathin section of tissue to strike a photographic plate. The result is a transmission electron micrograph (TEM). Transmission electron microscopy shows the fine structure of a plasmalemma (cell membrane) and the details of intracellular structures (Figure 2.1b). In **scanning electron microscopy**, electrons bouncing off exposed surfaces that have been coated with a gold-carbon film create a scanning electron micrograph (SEM). Although scanning electron microscopy provides less magnification than transmission electron microscopy, it provides a three-dimensional perspective on cell structure (Figure 2.1c).

This level of detail poses problems of its own. At the level of the light microscope, if you were to slice a large cell as you would slice a loaf of bread, you might produce 10 sections from the one cell. You could review the entire series under a light microscope in a few minutes. If you sliced the same cell for examination under an electron microscope, you would have 1000 sections, each of which could take several hours to inspect!

Many other methods can be used to examine cell and tissue structure, and examples will be found in the pages that follow and throughout the book. This chapter describes the structure of a typical cell, some of the ways in which cells interact with their environment, and how cells reproduce.

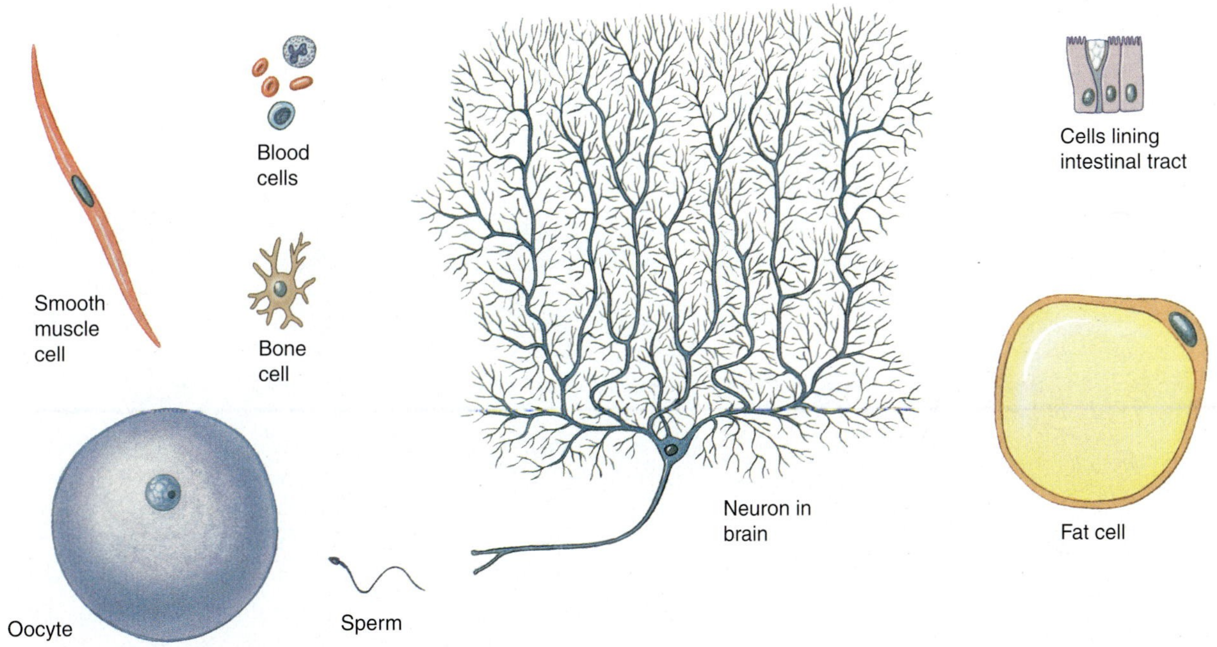

Figure 2.2 The Diversity of Cells in the Body

The cells of the body have many different shapes and a variety of special functions. These examples give an indication of the range of forms and sizes; all of the cells are shown with the dimensions they would have if magnified approximately 500 times.

Figure 2.3 Anatomy of a Typical Cell
See Table 2.1 for a summary of the functions associated with the various cell structures.

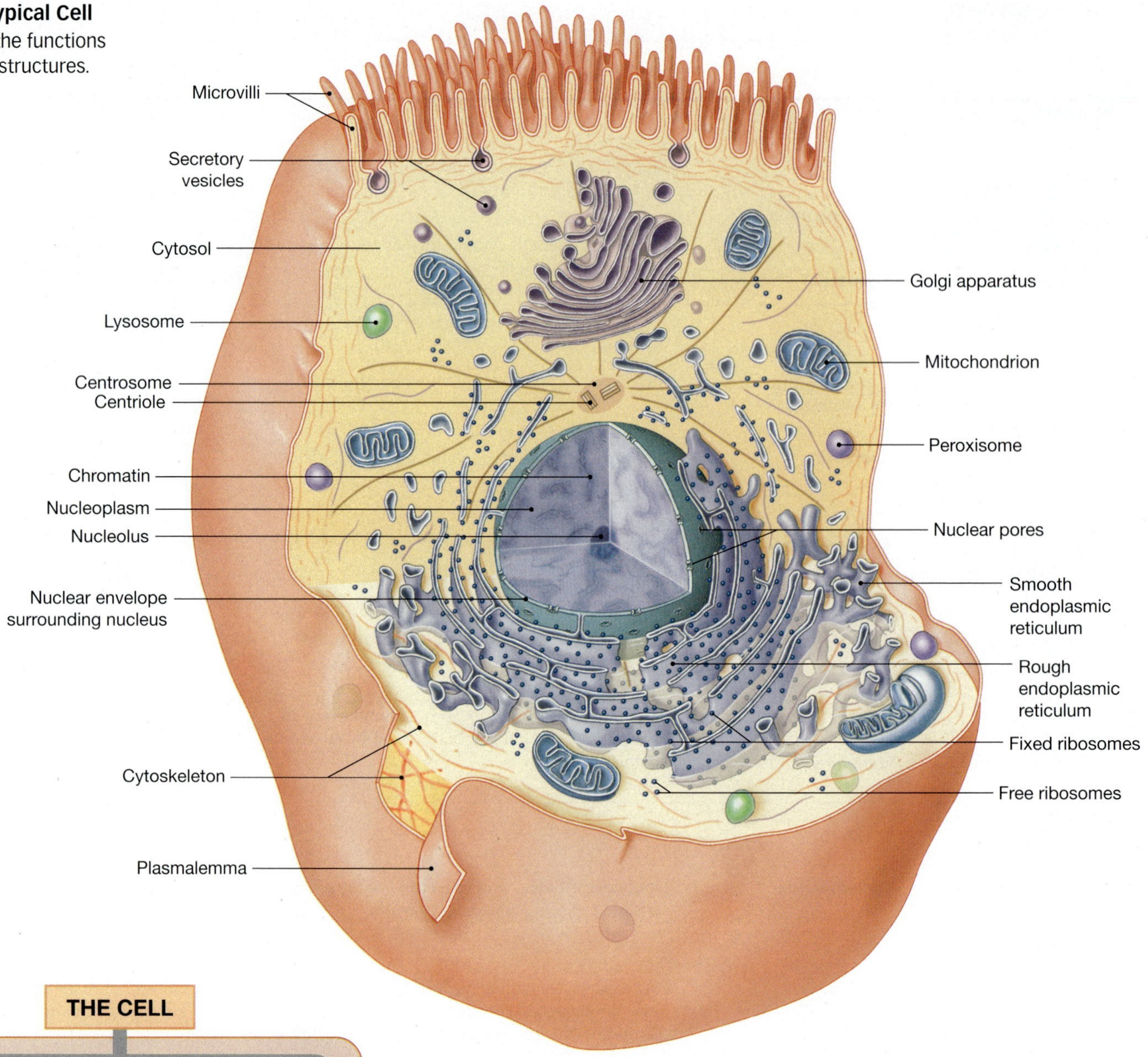

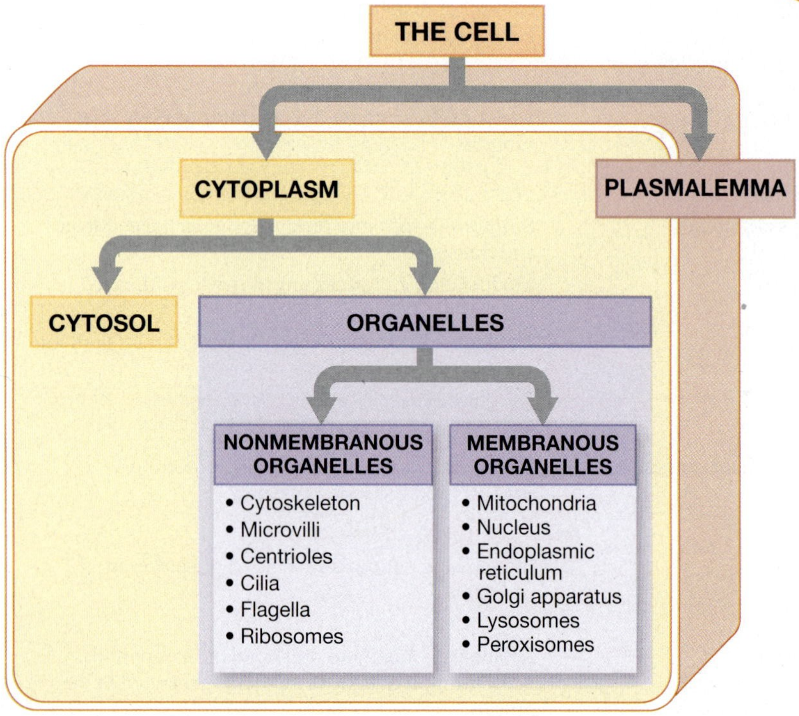

Figure 2.4 A Flow Chart for the Study of Cell Structure
Cytoplasm is subdivided into cytosol and organelles. Organelles are subdivided into nonmembranous organelles and membranous organelles.

Cellular Anatomy [Figures 2.3/2.4 and Table 2.1]

The "typical" cell is like the "average" person. Any description can be thought of only in general terms because enormous individual variations occur. Our typical model cell will share features with most cells of the body without being identical to any. Figure 2.3 shows such a cell, and Table 2.1 summarizes the major structures and functions of its parts.

Figure 2.4 previews the organization of this chapter. Our representative cells float in a watery medium known as the **extracellular fluid**. A *plasmalemma* separates the cell contents, or *cytoplasm*, from the extracellular fluid. The cytoplasm can be further subdivided into a fluid, the *cytosol*, and intracellular structures collectively known as *organelles* (or-ga-NELS, "little organs").

TABLE 2.1 Anatomy of a Representative Cell

Appearance	Structure	Composition	Function(s)
PLASMALEMMA AND CYTOSOL			
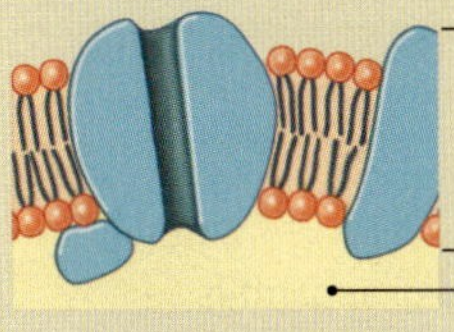	**Plasmalemma**	Lipid bilayer, containing phospholipids, steroids, proteins, and carbohydrates	Isolation; protection; sensitivity; support; control of entrance/exit of materials
	Cytosol	Fluid component of cytoplasm; may contain inclusions of insoluble materials	Distributes materials by diffusion; stores glycogen, pigments, and other materials
NONMEMBRANOUS ORGANELLES			
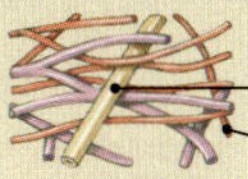	**Cytoskeleton** Microtubule Microfilament	Membrane extensions containing microfilaments	Increase surface area to facilitate absorption of extracellular materials
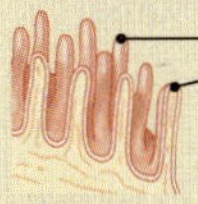	**Microvilli**	Membrane extensions containing microtubule doublets in a 9 + 2 array	Movement of materials over cell surface
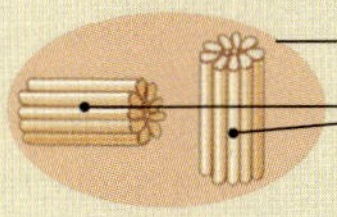	**Centrosome** Centrioles	Proteins organized in fine filaments or slender tubes	Strength and support; movement of cellular structures and materials
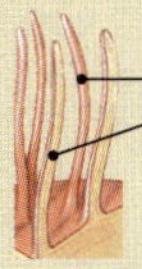	**Cilia**	Cytoplasm containing two centrioles, at right angles; each centriole is composed of nine microtubule triplets	Essential for movement of chromosomes during cell division; organization of microtubules in cytoskeleton
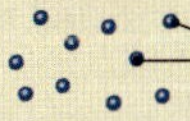	**Ribosomes**	RNA + proteins; fixed ribosomes bound to rough endoplasmic reticulum, free ribosomes scattered in cytoplasm	Protein synthesis
MEMBRANOUS ORGANELLES			
	**Mitochondria**	Double membrane, with inner membrane folds (cristae) enclosing metabolic enzymes	Produce 95 percent of the ATP required by the cell
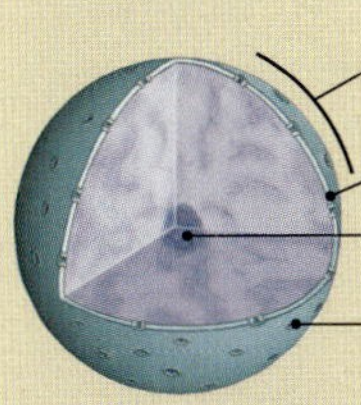	**Nucleus**	Nucleoplasm containing nucleotides, enzymes, nucleoproteins, and chromatin; surrounded by double membrane (nuclear envelope) containing nuclear pores	Control of metabolism; storage and processing of genetic information; control of protein synthesis
	Nuclear envelope		
	Nucleolus	Dense region in nucleoplasm containing DNA and RNA	Site of rRNA synthesis and assembly of ribosomal subunits
	Nuclear pore		
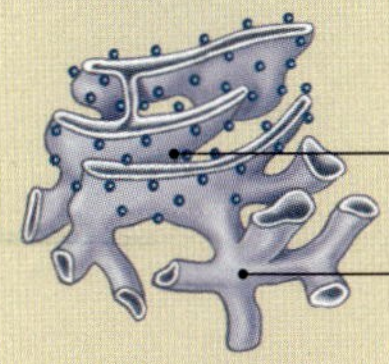	**Endoplasmic reticulum (ER)**	Network of membranous channels extending throughout the cytoplasm	Synthesis of secretory products; intracellular storage and transport
	Rough ER	Has ribosomes bound to membranes	Modification and packaging of newly synthesized proteins
	Smooth ER	Lacks attached ribosomes	Lipid, steroid, and carbohydrate synthesis; calcium ion storage
	**Golgi apparatus**	Stacks of flattened membranes (cisternae) containing chambers	Storage, alteration, and packaging of secretory products and lysosomal enzymes
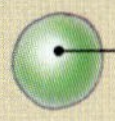	**Lysosome**	Vesicles containing digestive enzymes	Intracellular removal of damaged organelles or of pathogens
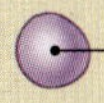	**Peroxisome**	Vesicles containing degradative enzymes	Catabolism of fats and other organic compounds; neutralization of toxic compounds generated in the process

The Plasmalemma [Figure 2.5]

The outer boundary of a cell is termed the **plasmalemma**, which may also be termed the **cell membrane** or *plasma membrane.* It is extremely thin and delicate, ranging from 6 to 10 nm (1 nm = 0.001 μm) in thickness. Nevertheless, it has a complex structure composed of phospholipids, proteins, glycolipids, and cholesterol. The structure of the plasmalemma is shown in Figure 2.5.

The plasmalemma is called a **phospholipid bilayer** because its phospholipids form two distinct layers. In each layer the phospholipid molecules lie so that the heads are at the surface and the tails are on the inside. Dissolved ions and water-soluble compounds cannot cross the lipid portion of a plasmalemma because the lipid tails will not associate with water molecules. This feature makes the membrane very effective in isolating the cytoplasm from the surrounding fluid environment. Such isolation is important because the composition of the cytoplasm is very different from that of the extracellular fluid, and that difference must be maintained.

There are two general types of membrane proteins. **Peripheral proteins** are attached to either the inner or the outer membrane surface. **Integral proteins** are embedded in the membrane. Most integral proteins span the entire width of the membrane one or more times, and are therefore called *transmembrane proteins.* Some of the integral proteins form **channels** that let water molecules, ions, and small water-soluble compounds into or out of the cell. Most of the communication between the interior and exterior of the cell occurs through these channels. Some of the channels are called **gated** because they can open or close to regulate the passage of materials. Other integral proteins may function as catalysts or receptor sites or in cell–cell recognition.

The inner and outer surfaces of the plasmalemma differ in protein and lipid composition. The carbohydrate (*glyco-*) component of the glycolipids and glycoproteins that extend away from the outer surface of the plasmalemma form a viscous, superficial coating known as the **glycocalyx** (*calyx*, cup). Some of these molecules function as receptors: When bound to a specific molecule in the extracellular fluid, a membrane receptor can trigger a change in cellular activity. For example, cytoplasmic enzymes on the inner surface of the plasmalemma may be bound to integral proteins, and the activities of these enzymes may be affected by events on the membrane surface.

The general functions of the plasmalemma include the following:

1. *Physical isolation:* The lipid bilayer of the plasmalemma forms a physical barrier that separates the inside of the cell from the surrounding extracellular fluid.
2. *Regulation of exchange with the environment:* The plasmalemma controls the entry of ions and nutrients, the elimination of wastes, and the release of secretory products.
3. *Sensitivity:* The plasmalemma is the first part of the cell affected by changes in the extracellular fluid. It also contains a variety of receptors that allow the cell to recognize and respond to specific molecules in its environment, and to communicate with other cells. Any alteration in the plasmalemma may affect all cellular activities.
4. *Structural support:* Specialized connections between plasmalemmae or between membranes and extracellular materials give tissues a stable structure.

Membrane structure is fluid. Cholesterol helps stabilize the membrane structure and maintain its fluidity. Integral proteins can move within the membrane like ice cubes drifting in a bowl of punch. In addition, the composition of the plasmalemma can change over time, through the removal and replacement of membrane components.

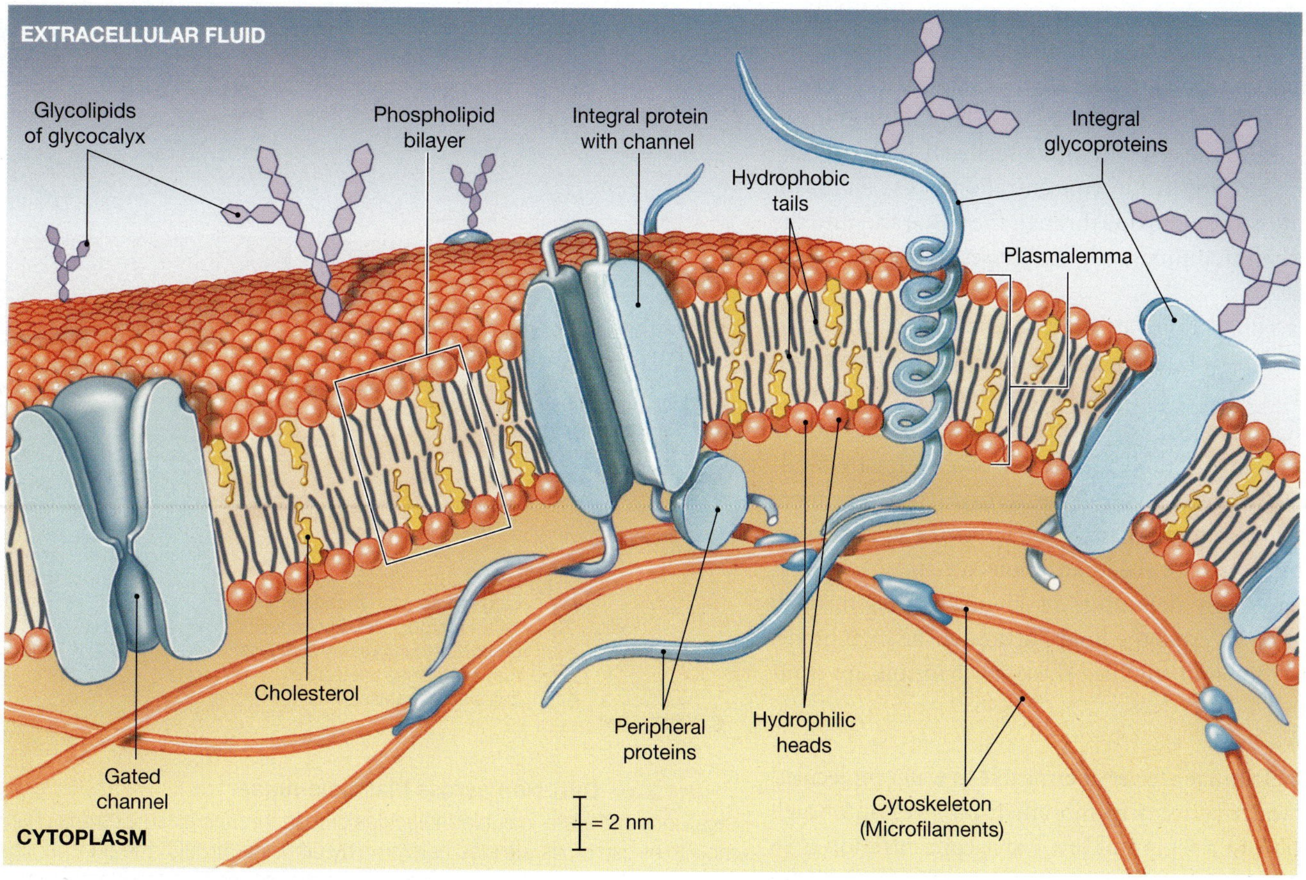

Figure 2.5 **The Plasmalemma**

Membrane Permeability: Passive Processes

The **permeability** of a membrane is a property that determines its effectiveness as a barrier. The greater the permeability, the easier it is for substances to cross the membrane. If nothing can cross a membrane, it is described as **impermeable**. If any substance can cross without difficulty, the membrane is **freely permeable**. Plasmalemmae fall somewhere in between and are said to be **selectively permeable**. A selectively permeable membrane permits the free passage of some materials and restricts the passage of others. The distinction may be on the basis of size, electrical charge, molecular shape, solubility of the substance, or any combination of these factors.

The permeability of a plasmalemma varies depending on the organization and characteristics of membrane lipids and proteins. The processes involved in the passage of a substance across the membrane may be active or passive. Active processes, discussed later in this chapter, require that the cell draw on an energy source, usually *adenosine triphosphate*, or *ATP*. Passive processes move ions or molecules across the plasmalemma without any energy expenditure by the cell. Passive processes include *diffusion*, *osmosis*, and *facilitated diffusion*.

Diffusion [Figure 2.6] Ions and molecules in solution are in constant motion, bouncing off one another and colliding with water molecules. The result of the continual collisions and rebounds that occur is the process called diffusion. **Diffusion** can be defined as the net movement of material from an area where its concentration is relatively high to an area where its concentration is relatively low. The difference between the high and low concentrations represents a **concentration gradient**, and diffusion continues until that gradient has been eliminated. Because diffusion occurs from a region of higher concentration to one of lower concentration, it is often described as proceeding "down a concentration gradient." When a concentration gradient has been eliminated, an equilibrium exists. Although molecular motion continues, there is no longer a net movement in any particular direction.

Diffusion is important in body fluids because it tends to eliminate local concentration gradients. For example, an active cell generates carbon dioxide and absorbs oxygen. As a result, the extracellular fluid around the cell develops a relatively high concentration of CO_2 and a relatively low concentration of O_2. Diffusion then distributes the carbon dioxide through the tissue and into the bloodstream. At the same time, oxygen diffuses out of the blood and into the tissue.

In the extracellular fluids of the body, water and dissolved solutes (substances dissolved in water) diffuse freely. A plasmalemma, however, acts as a barrier that selectively restricts diffusion. Some substances can pass through easily, whereas others cannot penetrate the membrane at all. Only two routes are available for an ion or molecule to diffuse across a plasmalemma: through one of the membrane channels or across the lipid portion of the membrane. The size of the ion or molecule and any electrical charge it might carry determine its ability to pass through membrane channels. To cross the lipid portion of the membrane, the molecule must be lipid soluble. These mechanisms are summarized in Figure 2.6.

Osmosis Plasmalemmae are very permeable to water molecules. The diffusion of water across a membrane from a region of high water concentration to a region of low water concentration is so important that it is given a special name, **osmosis** (oz-MŌ-sis; *osmos*, thrust). Whenever an osmotic gradient exists, water molecules will diffuse rapidly across the plasmalemma until the osmotic gradient is eliminated. For convenience, we will always use the term *osmosis* when considering water movement and restrict use of the term *diffusion* to the movement of solutes.

Facilitated Diffusion Many essential nutrients, such as glucose and amino acids, are insoluble in lipids and too large to fit through membrane channels. These compounds can be passively transported across the membrane by special **carrier proteins** in a process called **facilitated diffusion**. The molecule to be transported first binds to a **receptor site** on an integral membrane protein. It is then moved to the inside of the plasmalemma and released into the cytoplasm. No ATP is expended in facilitated diffusion or simple diffusion; in each case, molecules move from an area of higher concentration to one of lower concentration.

Membrane Permeability: Active Processes

All **active membrane processes** require energy. By spending energy, usually in the form of ATP, the cell can transport substances *against their concentration gradients*. We will consider two active processes: *active transport* and *endocytosis*.

Active Transport When the high-energy bond in ATP provides the energy needed to move ions or molecules across the membrane, the process is termed **active transport**. The process is complex, and specific enzymes must be present in addition to carrier proteins. Although it requires energy, active transport offers one great advantage: It is not dependent on a concentration gradient. As a result the cell can import or export specific materials *regardless of their intracellular or extracellular concentrations*.

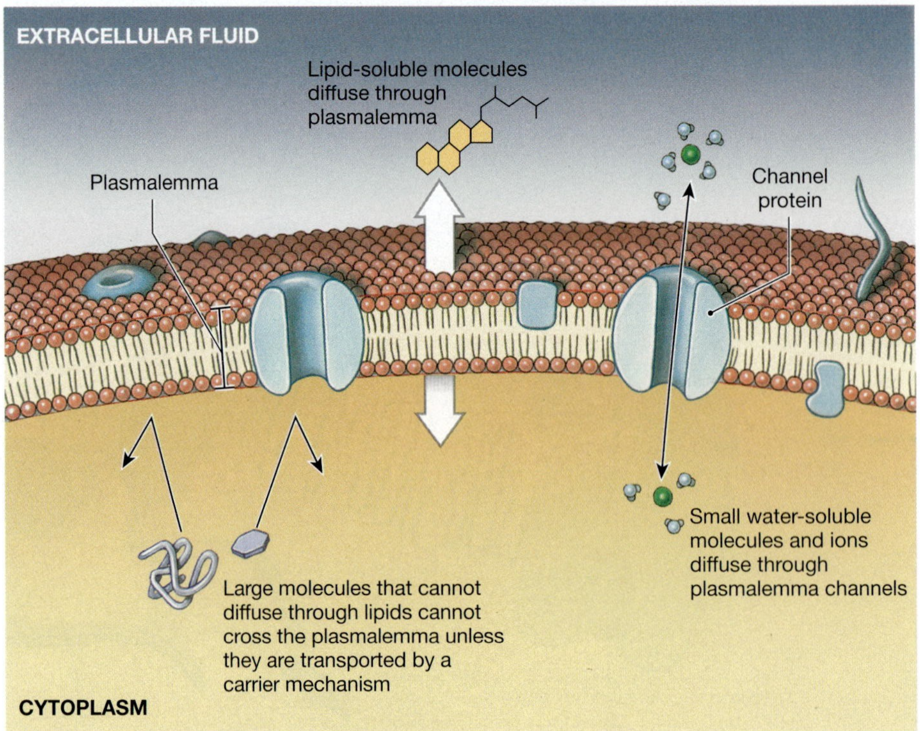

Figure 2.6 Diffusion across Plasmalemmae
Small ions and water-soluble molecules diffuse through plasmalemma channels. Lipid-soluble molecules can cross the plasmalemma by diffusing through the phospholipid bilayer. Large molecules that are not lipid soluble cannot diffuse through the plasmalemma at all.

All living cells show active transport of sodium (Na^+), potassium (K^+), calcium (Ca^{2+}), and magnesium (Mg^{2+}). Specialized cells can transport additional ions such as iodide (I^-) or iron (Fe^{2+}). Many of these carrier mechanisms, known as **ion pumps**, move a specific cation or anion in one direction, either into or out of the cell. If one ion moves in one direction while another moves in the opposite direction, the carrier is called an **exchange pump**. The energy demands of these pumps are impressive; a resting cell may use up to 40 percent of the ATP it produces to power its exchange pumps.

Endocytosis The packaging of extracellular materials into a vesicle at the cell surface for importation into the cell is termed **endocytosis** (EN-dō-sī-TŌ-sis). This process, which involves relatively large volumes of extracellular material, is sometimes called *bulk transport*. There are three major types of endocytosis: *pinocytosis*, *phagocytosis*, and *receptor-mediated endocytosis*. All three require energy in the form of ATP and so are classified as active processes. The mechanism is presumed to be the same in all three cases, but the mechanism itself remains unknown.

All forms of endocytosis produce small, membrane-bound compartments called *endosomes*. Once a vesicle has formed through endocytosis, its contents will enter the cytosol only if they can pass through the vesicle wall. This passage may involve active transport, simple or facilitated diffusion, or the destruction of the vesicle membrane.

Pinocytosis [Figure 2.7a] The formation of *pinosomes*, or vesicles filled with extracellular fluid, is the result of a process termed **pinocytosis** (PIN-ō-sī-TŌ-sis), or "cell drinking." In this process, a deep groove or pocket forms in the plasmalemma and then pinches off (Figure 2.7a). Nutrients, such as lipids, sugars, and amino acids, then enter the cytoplasm by diffusion or active transport from the enclosed fluid. The membrane of the pinosome then returns to the cell surface.

Virtually all cells perform pinocytosis in this manner. In a few specialized cells, the pinosomes form on one side of the cell and travel through the cytoplasm to the opposite side. There they fuse with the plasmalemma and discharge their contents through the process of *exocytosis*, described further on page 42. This method of bulk transport is found in cells lining capillaries, the most delicate blood vessels. These cells use pinocytosis to transfer fluid and solutes from the bloodstream to the surrounding tissues.

Phagocytosis [Figure 2.7b] Solid objects are taken into cells and enclosed within vesicles by **phagocytosis** (FAG-ō-sī-TŌ-sis), or "cell eating." This process produces vesicles that may be as large as the cell itself, and is shown in Figure 2.7b. Cytoplasmic extensions called **pseudopodia** (soo-dō-PŌ-dē-a; *pseudo-*, false + *podon*, foot) surround the object, and their membranes fuse to form a vesicle known as a *phagosome*. The phagosome may then fuse with a lysosome, whereupon its contents are digested by lysosomal enzymes.

Most cells display pinocytosis, but phagocytosis, especially the entrapment of living or dead cells, is performed only by specialized cells of the immune system. The phagocytic activity of these cells will be considered in chapters dealing with blood cells (Chapter 20) and the lymphoid system (Chapter 23).

Receptor-Mediated Endocytosis [Figure 2.8 and Table 2.2] A process that resembles pinocytosis, but is far more selective, is termed

Figure 2.7 Pinocytosis and Phagocytosis
(a) An electron micrograph showing pinocytosis. **(b)** Material brought into the cell through phagocytosis is enclosed in a pinosome and subsequently exposed to lysosomal enzymes. After absorption of nutrients from the vesicle, the residue is discharged through exocytosis.

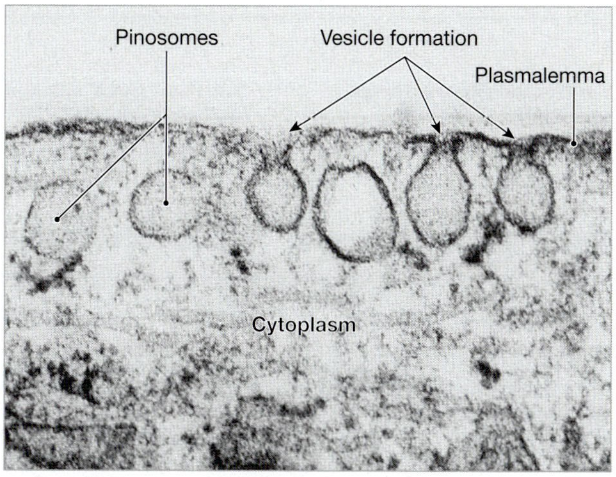

(a)

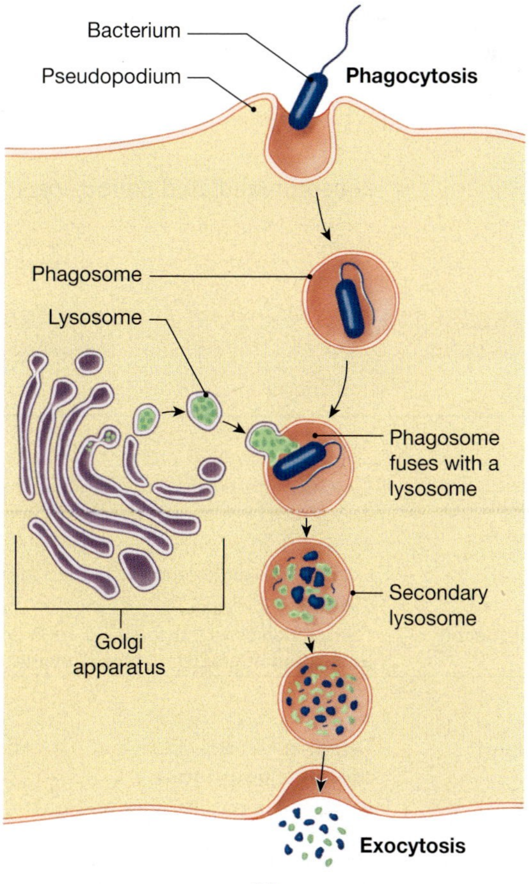

(b)

receptor-mediated endocytosis (Figure 2.8). Pinocytosis produces pinosomes filled with extracellular fluid; receptor-mediated endocytosis produces *coated vesicles* that contain a specific target molecule in high concentrations. The target substances, called *ligands*, are bound to receptors on the membrane surface. Many important substances, including cholesterol and iron ions (Fe^{2+}), are distributed through the body attached to special transport proteins. The proteins are too large to pass through membrane pores, but they can enter the cell through receptor-mediated endocytosis. The vesicle eventually returns to the cell surface and fuses with the plasmalemma. As the coated vesicle fuses with the plasmalemma, its contents are released into the extracellular fluid. This release is another example of the process of exocytosis. A summary and comparison of the mechanisms involved in movement across plasmalemmae is presented in Table 2.2.

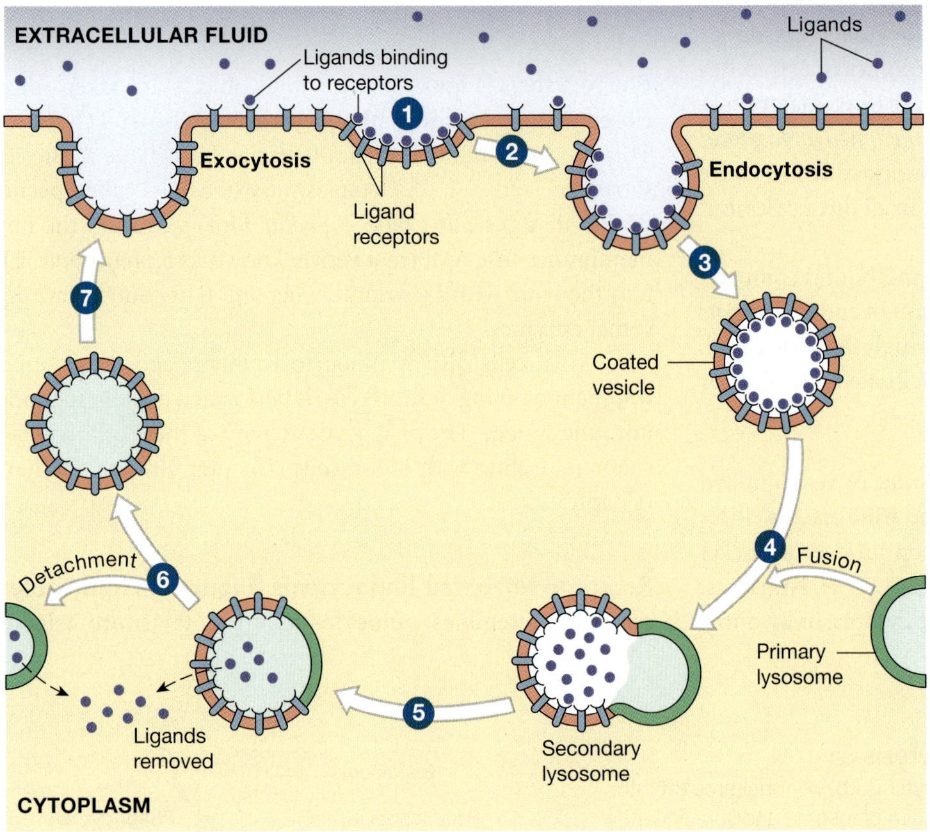

Receptor-Mediated Endocytosis

1. Target molecules (ligands) bind to receptors in plasmalemma.
2. Areas coated with ligands form deep pockets in plasmalemma surface.
3. Pockets pinch off, forming endosomes known as coated vesicles.
4. Coated vesicles fuse with primary lysosomes to form secondary lysosomes.
5. Ligands are removed and absorbed into the cytoplasm.
6. The lysosomal and endosomal membranes separate.
7. The endosome fuses with the plasmalemma, and the receptors are again available for ligand binding.

Figure 2.8 **Receptor-Mediated Endocytosis**

TABLE 2.2 Summary of Mechanisms Involved in Movement across Plasmalemmae

Mechanism	Process	Factors Affecting Rate	Substances Involved
PASSIVE			
Diffusion	Molecular movement of solutes; direction determined by relative concentrations	Size of gradient, molecular size, charge, lipid protein solubility, temperature	Small inorganic ions, lipid-soluble materials (all cells)
Osmosis	Movement of water (solvent) molecules toward high solute concentrations; requires membrane	Concentration gradient; opposing pressure	Water only (all cells)
Facilitated diffusion	Carrier molecules transport materials down a concentration gradient; requires membrane	As above, plus availability of carrier protein	Glucose and amino acids (all cells)
ACTIVE			
Active transport	Carrier molecules work despite opposing concentration gradients	Availability of carrier, substrate, and ATP	Na^+, K^+, Ca^{2+}, Mg^{2+} (all cells); probably other solutes in special cases
Endocytosis	Formation of membranous vesicles (endosomes) containing fluid or solid material at the plasmalemma	Stimulus and mechanism not understood; requires ATP	Fluids, nutrients (all cells); debris, pathogens (special cells)
Exocytosis	Fusion of vesicles containing fluids and/or solids with the plasmalemma	Stimulus and mechanism incompletely understood; requires ATP and calcium ions	Fluid and wastes (all cells)

Extensions of the Plasmalemma: Microvilli

Microvilli [Figure 2.9a,b] Small, finger-shaped projections of the plasmalemma are termed **microvilli**. They are found in cells that are actively engaged in absorbing materials from the extracellular fluid, such as the cells of the small intestine and kidneys (**Figure 2.9a,b**). Microvilli are important because they increase the surface area exposed to the extracellular environment for increased absorption. A network of microfilaments stiffens each microvillus and anchors it to the *terminal web*, a dense supporting network within the underlying cytoskeleton. Interactions between these microfilaments and the cytoskeleton can produce a waving or bending action. Their movements help circulate fluid around the microvilli, bringing dissolved nutrients into contact with receptors on the membrane surface.

CONCEPT CHECK

1. What term is used to describe the permeability of plasmalemmae?
2. Describe the processes of osmosis and diffusion. How do they differ?
3. What are the three major types of endocytosis? How do they differ?
4. Cells lining the small intestine have numerous fingerlike projections on their free surfaces. What are these structures, and what is their function?

See blue "Answers" tab at back of book.

The Cytoplasm

The general term for all of the material inside the cell is **cytoplasm**. Cytoplasm contains many more proteins than the extracellular fluid; proteins account for 15–30 percent of the weight of the cell. The cytoplasm includes two major subdivisions:

1. *Cytosol*, or intracellular fluid. The cytosol contains dissolved nutrients, ions, soluble and insoluble proteins, and waste products. The plasmalemma separates the cytosol from the surrounding extracellular fluid.
2. *Organelles* (or-gan-ELS) are intracellular structures that perform specific functions.

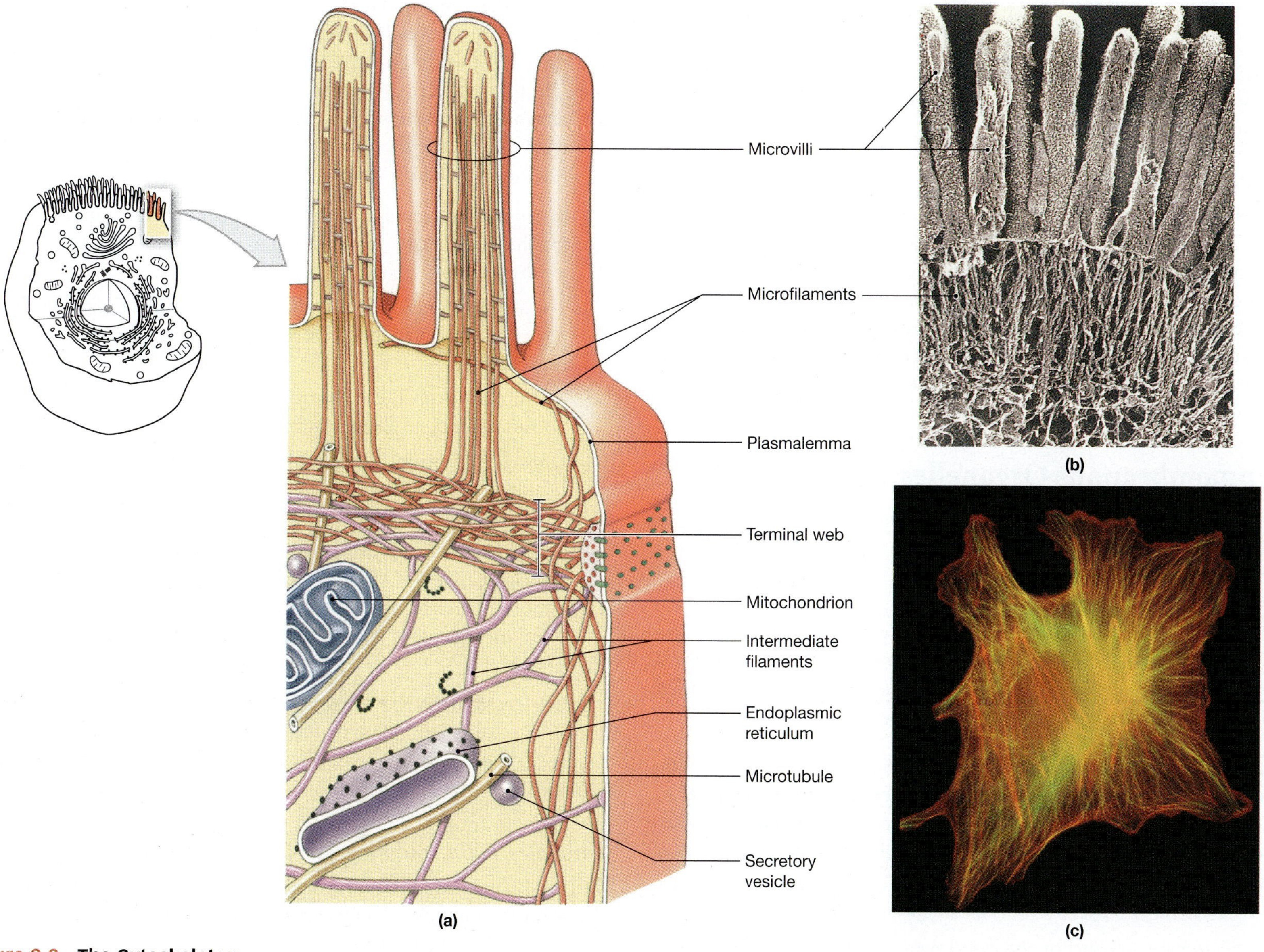

Figure 2.9 The Cytoskeleton
(a) The cytoskeleton provides strength and structural support for the cell and its organelles. Interactions between cytoskeletal elements are also important in moving organelles and in changing the shape of the cell. **(b)** A SEM image of the microfilaments and microvilli of an intestinal cell. **(c)** Microtubules in a living cell, as seen after special fluorescent labeling. (LM × 3200)

The Cytosol

Cytosol is significantly different from extracellular fluid. Three important differences are:

1. The cytosol contains a high concentration of potassium ions, whereas extracellular fluid contains a high concentration of sodium ions. The numbers of positive and negative ions are not in balance across the membrane; the outside has a net excess of positive charges, and the inside a net excess of negative charges. The separation of unlike charges creates a *transmembrane potential*, like a miniature battery. The significance of the transmembrane potential will become clear in Chapter 13.
2. The cytosol contains a relatively high concentration of dissolved and suspended proteins. Many of these proteins are enzymes that regulate metabolic operations, while others are associated with the various organelles. These proteins give the cytosol a consistency that varies between that of thin maple syrup and almost-set gelatin.
3. The cytosol contains relatively small quantities of carbohydrates and large reserves of amino acids and lipids. The carbohydrates are broken down to provide energy, and the amino acids are used to manufacture proteins. The lipids stored in the cell are used primarily as an energy source when carbohydrates are unavailable.

The cytosol of cells contains masses of insoluble materials known as **inclusions**, or *inclusion bodies*. The most common inclusions are stored nutrients: for example, glycogen granules in liver or skeletal muscle cells, and lipid droplets in fat cells.

Organelles [Figure 2.3]

Organelles are found in all body cells (**Figure 2.3**, p. 29) although the types and numbers of organelles differ among the various cell types. Each organelle performs specific functions that are essential to normal cell structure, maintenance, and/or metabolism. Cellular organelles can be divided into two broad categories (Table 2.1, p. 30): (1) **nonmembranous organelles**, which are always in contact with the cytosol; and (2) **membranous organelles** surrounded by membranes that isolate their contents from the cytosol, just as the plasmalemma isolates the cytosol from the extracellular fluid.

Nonmembranous Organelles

Nonmembranous organelles include the *cytoskeleton*, *centrioles*, *cilia*, *flagella*, and *ribosomes*.

The Cytoskeleton [Figure 2.9]

The internal protein framework that gives the cytoplasm strength and flexibility is the **cytoskeleton**. It has four major components: *microfilaments*, *intermediate filaments*, *thick filaments*, and *microtubules*. None of these structures can be seen with the light microscope.

Microfilaments [Figure 2.9] Slender strands composed primarily of the protein **actin** are termed **microfilaments**. In most cells, microfilaments are scattered throughout the cytosol and form a dense network under the plasmalemma. **Figure 2.9a,b** shows the superficial layers of microfilaments in an intestinal cell.

Microfilaments have two major functions:

1. Microfilaments anchor the cytoskeleton to integral proteins of the plasmalemma. This function stabilizes the position of the membrane proteins, provides additional mechanical strength to the cell, and firmly attaches the plasmalemma to the underlying cytoplasm.
2. Actin microfilaments can interact with microfilaments or larger structures composed of the protein **myosin**. This interaction can produce active movement of a portion of a cell, or a change in the shape of the entire cell.

Intermediate Filaments Intermediate filaments are defined chiefly by their size; their composition varies from one cell type to another. Intermediate filaments (1) provide strength, (2) stabilize the positions of organelles, and (3) transport materials within the cytoplasm. For example, specialized intermediate filaments, called **neurofilaments**, are found in neurons, where they provide structural support within *axons*, long cellular processes that may be up to a meter in length.

Thick Filaments [Figure 2.9a] Relatively massive filaments composed of myosin protein subunits, which are not shown in **Figure 2.9**, are termed **thick filaments**. Thick filaments are abundant in muscle cells, where they interact with actin filaments to produce powerful contractions.

Microtubules [Figures 2.9a,c/2.10] All cells possess hollow tubes termed **microtubules**. These are built from the protein **tubulin**. **Figure 2.9a,c** and **Figure 2.10** show microtubules in the cytoplasm of representative cells. A microtubule forms through the aggregation of tubulin molecules; it persists for a time and then disassembles into individual tubulin molecules once again. The microtubular array is centered near the nucleus of the cell, in a region known as the *centrosome*. Microtubules radiate outward from the centrosome into the periphery of the cell.

Microtubules have a variety of functions:

1. Microtubules form the primary components of the cytoskeleton, giving the cell strength and rigidity and anchoring the positions of major organelles.
2. The assembly and/or disassembly of microtubules provides a mechanism for changing the shape of the cell, perhaps assisting in cell movement.
3. Microtubules can attach to organelles and other intracellular materials and move them around within the cell.
4. During cell division, microtubules form the *spindle apparatus* that distributes the duplicated chromosomes to opposite ends of the dividing cell. This process will be considered in more detail in a later section.
5. Microtubules form structural components of organelles such as *centrioles*, *cilia*, and *flagella*. Although these organelles are associated with the plasmalemma, they are considered among the nonmembranous organelles because they do not have their own enclosing membrane.

The cytoskeleton as a whole incorporates microfilaments, intermediate filaments, and microtubules into a network that extends throughout the cytoplasm. The organizational details are as yet poorly understood, because the network is extremely delicate and difficult to study in an intact state.

Centrioles, Cilia, and Flagella [Figure 2.10 and Table 2.3]

The cytoskeleton contains numerous microtubules that function individually. Groups of microtubules form *centrioles*, *cilia*, and *flagella*. These structures are summarized in Table 2.3

Centrioles [Figure 2.10a] A **centriole** is a cylindrical structure composed of short microtubules (**Figure 2.10a**). There are nine groups of mi-

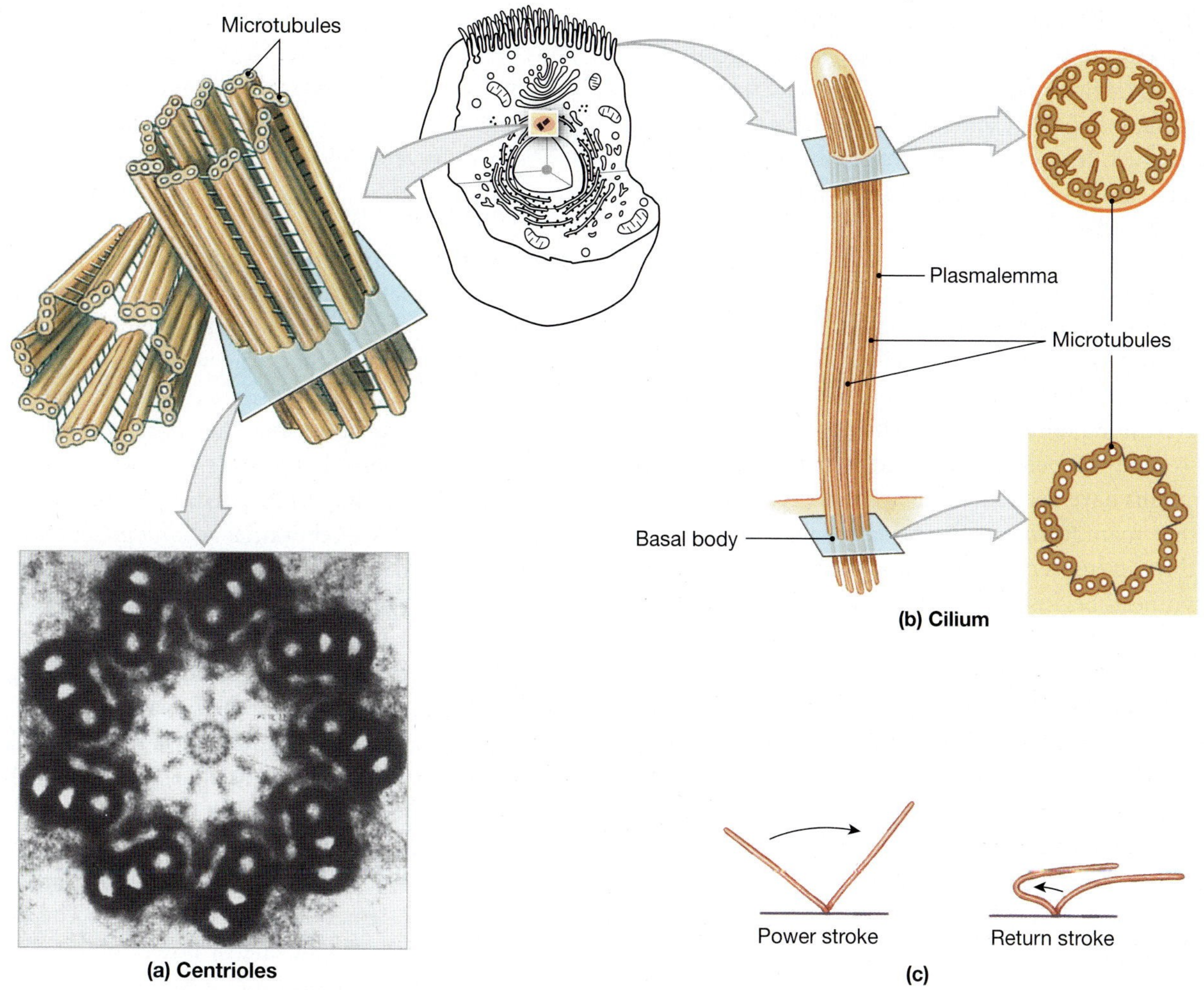

Figure 2.10 Centrioles and Cilia
(a) A centriole consists of nine microtubule triplets (9 + 0 array). The centrosome contains a pair of centrioles oriented at right angles to one another. **(b)** A cilium contains nine pairs of microtubules surrounding a central pair (9 + 2 array). **(c)** A single cilium swings forward and then returns to its original position. During the power stroke, the cilium is relatively stiff, but during the return stroke, it bends and moves parallel to the cell surface.

TABLE 2.3 A Comparison of Centrioles, Cilia, and Flagella

Structure	Microtubule Organization	Location	Function
Centriole	Nine groups of microtubule triplets form a short cylinder	In centrosome near nucleus	Organizes microtubules in the spindle to move chromosomes during cell division
Cilium	Nine groups of long microtubule doublets form a cylinder around a central pair	At cell surface	Propels fluids or solids across cell surface
Flagellum	Same as cilium	At cell surface	Propels sperm cells through fluid

crotubules and each group is a triplet of microtubules. Because there are no central microtubules, this is called a *9 + 0 array*. This identification reflects the number of peripheral groups of microtubules oriented in a ring, with the number of microtubules at the center of the ring. However, some preparations show an axial structure that runs parallel to the long axis of the centriole, with radial spokes extending outward toward the microtubule groups. The function of this complex is not known. Cells capable of cell division contain a pair of centrioles arranged at right angles to each other. Centrioles direct the movement of chromosomes during cell division (discussed later in this chapter). Cells that do not divide, such as mature red blood cells and skeletal muscle cells, lack centrioles. The **centrosome** is the region of cytoplasm surrounding this pair of centrioles. It directs the organization of the microtubules of the cytoskeleton.

Cilia [Figure 2.10b,c]

Cilia (singular, *cilium*) contain nine groups of microtubule doublets surrounding a central pair (**Figure 2.10b**). This is known as a *9 + 2 array*. Cilia are anchored to a compact **basal body** situated just beneath the cell surface. The structure of the basal body resembles that of a centriole. The exposed portion of the cilium is completely covered by the plasmalemma. Cilia "beat" rhythmically, as depicted in **Figure 2.10c**, and their combined efforts move fluids or secretions across the cell surface. Cilia lining the respiratory tract beat in a synchronized manner to move sticky mucus and trapped dust particles toward the throat and away from delicate respiratory surfaces. If the cilia are damaged or immobilized by heavy smoking or some metabolic problem, the cleansing action is lost, and the irritants will no longer be removed. As a result, chronic respiratory infections develop.

Flagella **Flagella** (fla-JEL-ah; singular, *flagellum*, "whip") resemble cilia but are much longer. A flagellum moves a cell through the surrounding fluid, rather than moving the fluid past a stationary cell. The sperm cell is the only human cell that has a flagellum, and it is used to move the cell along the female reproductive tract. If sperm flagella are paralyzed or otherwise abnormal, the individual will be sterile because immobile sperm cannot reach and fertilize an oocyte (female gamete).

Ribosomes [Figure 2.11]

Ribosomes are small, dense structures that cannot be seen with the light microscope. In an electron micrograph, ribosomes are dense granules roughly 25 nm in diameter (Figure 2.11a). They are found in all cells, but their number varies depending on the type of cell and its activities. Each ribosome consists of roughly 60 percent RNA and 40 percent protein. At least 80 ribosomal proteins have been identified. These organelles are intracellular factories that manufacture proteins, using information provided by the DNA of the nucleus. A ribosome consists of two subunits that interlock as protein synthesis begins. When protein synthesis is complete, the subunits separate.

There are two major types of ribosomes: free ribosomes and fixed ribosomes (Figure 2.11a). **Free ribosomes** are scattered throughout the cytoplasm; the proteins they manufacture enter the cytosol. **Fixed ribosomes** are attached to the *endoplasmic reticulum*, a membranous organelle. Proteins manufactured by fixed ribosomes enter the *lumen*, or internal cavity, of the endoplasmic reticulum, where they are modified and packaged for export. These processes are detailed later in this chapter.

CONCEPT CHECK

1. How would the absence of a flagellum affect a sperm cell?
2. Identify the two major subdivisions of the cytoplasm and the function of each.

See blue "Answers" tab at back of book.

Membranous Organelles

Each membranous organelle is completely surrounded by a phospholipid bilayer membrane similar in structure to the plasmalemma. The membrane isolates the contents of a membranous organelle from the surrounding cytosol. This isolation allows the organelle to manufacture or store secretions, enzymes, or toxins that could adversely affect the cytoplasm in general. Table 2.1 on p. 30 includes six types of membranous organelles: *mitochondria, the nucleus, the endoplasmic reticulum, the Golgi apparatus, lysosomes,* and *peroxisomes.*

Mitochondria [Figure 2.12]

Mitochondria (mī-tō-KON-drē-ah; singular, *mitochondrion*; *mitos*, thread + *chondrion*, small granules) are organelles that have an unusual double membrane (Figure 2.12). An outer membrane surrounds the entire organelle, and a second, inner membrane contains numerous folds, called **cristae**. Cristae increase the surface area exposed to the fluid contents, or **matrix**, of the mitochondrion. The matrix contains metabolic enzymes that perform the reactions that provide energy for cellular functions.

Enzymes attached to the cristae produce most of the ATP generated by mitochondria. Mitochondrial activity produces about 95 percent of the energy needed to keep a cell alive. Mitochondria produce ATP through the breakdown of organic molecules in a series of reactions that also consume oxygen (O_2) and generate carbon dioxide (CO_2).

Mitochondria have various shapes, from long and slender to short and fat. Mitochondria control their own maintenance, growth, and reproduction. The number of mitochondria in a particular cell varies depending on the cell's energy demands. Red blood cells lack mitochondria—they obtain energy in other ways—but liver and skeletal muscle cells typically contain as many as 300 mitochondria. Muscle cells have high rates of energy consumption, and over time the mitochondria respond to the increased energy demands by reproducing. The increased numbers of mitochondria can provide energy faster and in greater amounts, improving muscular performance.

The Nucleus [Figures 2.13/2.14]

The **nucleus** is the control center for cellular operations. A single nucleus stores all the information needed to control the synthesis of the approximately 100,000 different proteins in the human body. The nucleus determines the structural and functional characteristics of the cell by controlling what proteins are synthesized, and in what amounts. Most cells contain a single nucleus, but there are exceptions. For example, skeletal muscle cells are called *multinucleate* (*multi-*, many) because they have many nuclei,

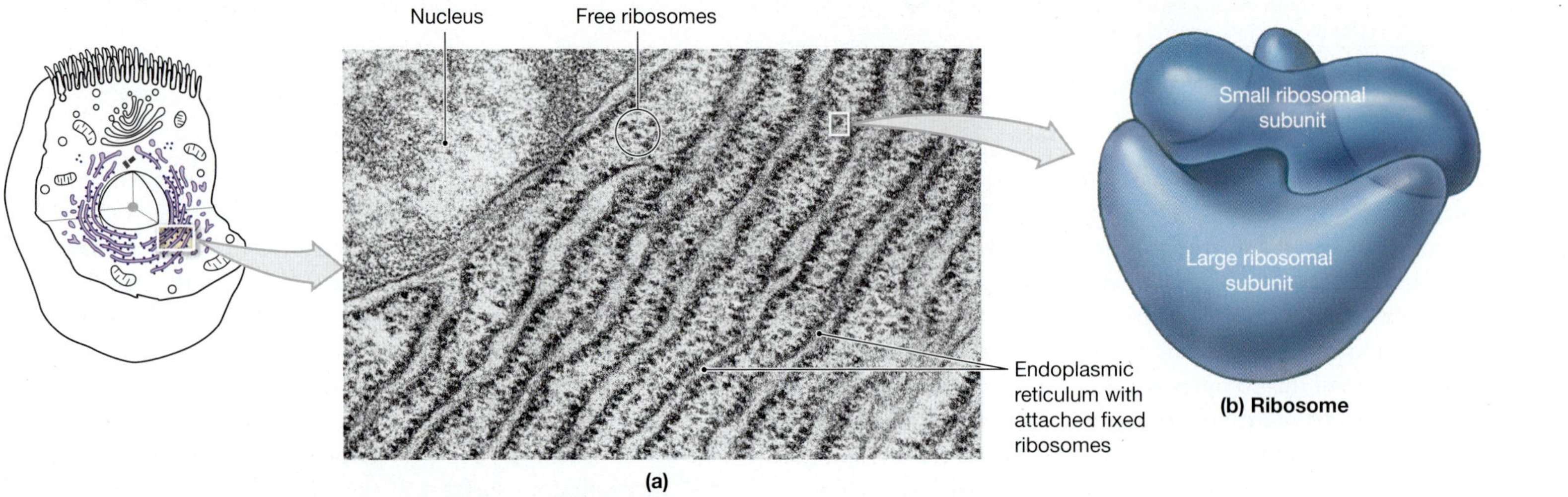

Figure 2.11 Ribosomes
These small, dense structures are involved in protein synthesis. **(a)** Both free and fixed ribosomes can be seen in the cytoplasm of this cell. (TEM × 73,600) **(b)** An individual ribosome, consisting of small and large subunits.

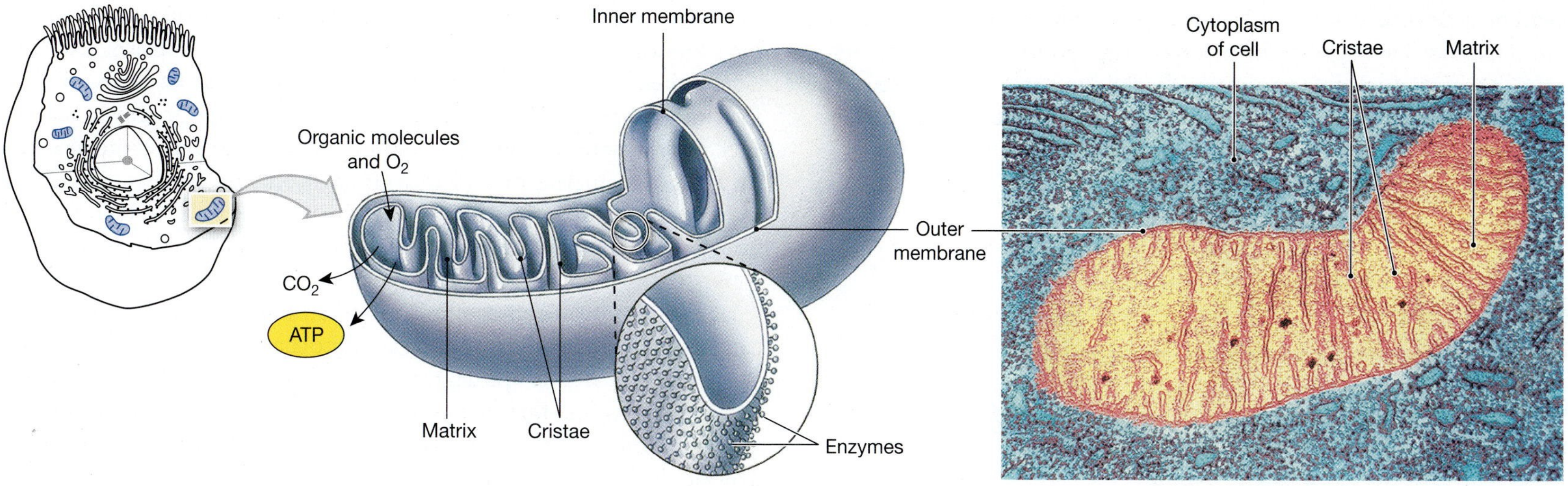

Figure 2.12 Mitochondria
The three-dimensional organization of a mitochondrion, and a color-enhanced TEM showing a typical mitochondrion in section. (TEM × 61,776)

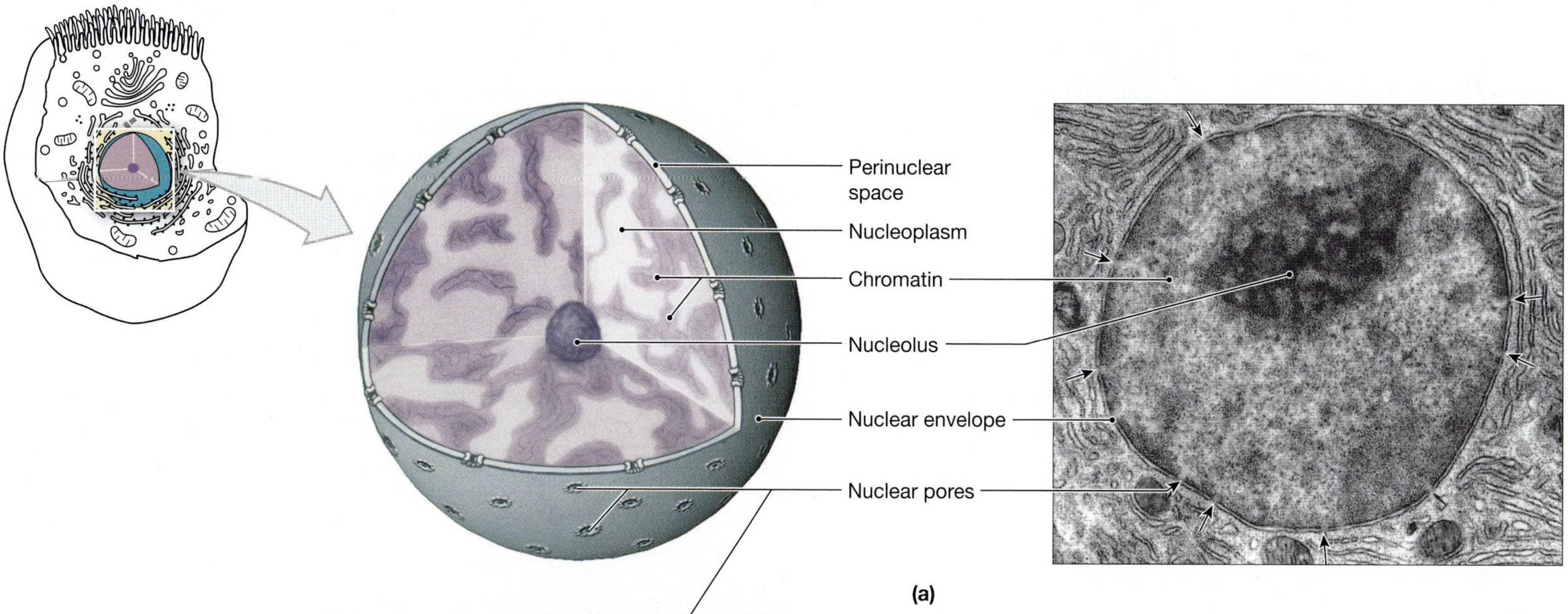

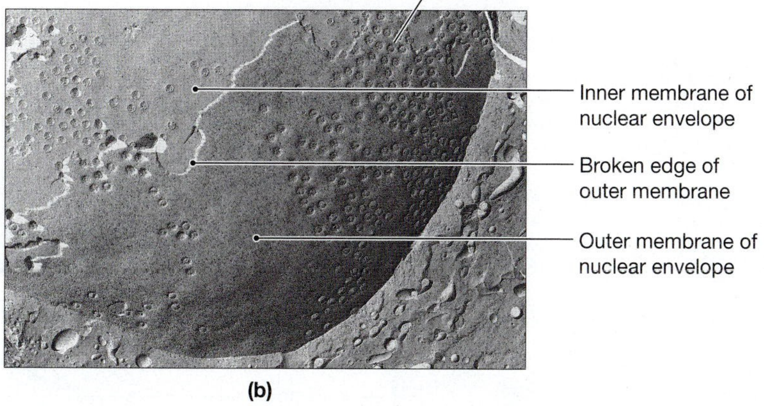

Figure 2.13 The Nucleus
The nucleus is the control center for cellular activities. **(a)** TEM showing important nuclear structures. (TEM × 4828) **(b)** The cell seen in this SEM was frozen and then broken apart so that internal structures could be seen. This technique, called freeze-fracture, provides a unique perspective on the internal organization of cells. The nuclear envelope and nuclear pores are visible; the fracturing process broke away part of the outer membrane of the nuclear envelope, and the cut edge of the nucleus can be seen. (SEM × 9240)

whereas mature red blood cells are called *anucleate* (*a*-, without) because they lack nuclei. A cell without a nucleus could be compared to a car without a driver. However, a car can sit idle for years, but a cell without a nucleus will survive only three to four months.

Figure 2.13 details the structure of a typical nucleus. A **nuclear envelope** surrounds the nucleus and separates it from the cytosol. The nuclear envelope is a double membrane enclosing a narrow **perinuclear space** (*peri*-, around). At several locations, the nuclear envelope is connected to the rough endoplasmic reticulum, as shown in Figure 2.3, p. 29.

The nucleus directs processes that take place in the cytosol and must in turn receive information about conditions and activities in the cytosol. Chemical communication between the nucleus and cytosol occurs through **nuclear pores**, a complex of proteins that regulates movement of macromolecules into and out of the nucleus. These pores, which account for about 10 percent of the surface of the nucleus, permit the movement of water, ions, and small molecules but regulate the passage of large proteins, RNA, and DNA.

The term **nucleoplasm** refers to the fluid contents of the nucleus. The nucleoplasm contains ions, enzymes, RNA and DNA nucleotides, proteins, small amounts of RNA, and DNA. The DNA strands form complex structures known as *chromosomes* (*chroma*, color). The nucleoplasm also contains a network of fine filaments, the **nuclear matrix**, that provides structural support and may be involved in the regulation of genetic activity. Each **chromosome** contains DNA strands bound to special proteins called **histones**. The nucleus of each of your cells contains 23 pairs of chromosomes; one member of each pair was derived from your mother and one from your father. The structure of a typical chromosome is diagrammed in Figure 2.14.

At intervals the DNA strands wind around the histones, forming a complex known as a **nucleosome**. The entire chain of nucleosomes may coil around other histones. The degree of coiling determines whether the chromosome is long and thin or short and fat. Chromosomes in a dividing cell are very tightly coiled, and so can be seen clearly as separate structures in light or electron micrographs. In cells that are not dividing, the chromosomes are loosely coiled, forming a tangle of fine filaments known as **chromatin** (KRŌ-ma-tin). Each chromosome may have some coiled regions, and only the coiled areas stain clearly. As a result, the nucleus has a clumped, grainy appearance.

The chromosomes also have direct control over the synthesis of RNA. Most nuclei contain one to four dark-staining areas called **nucleoli** (noo-KLĒ-ō-lī; singular, *nucleolus*). Nucleoli are nuclear organelles that synthesize the components of ribosomes. A nucleolus contains histones and enzymes as well as RNA, and it forms around a chromosomal region containing the genetic instructions for producing ribosomal proteins and RNA. Nucleoli are most prominent in cells that manufacture large amounts of proteins, such as liver cells and muscle cells, because these cells need large numbers of ribosomes.

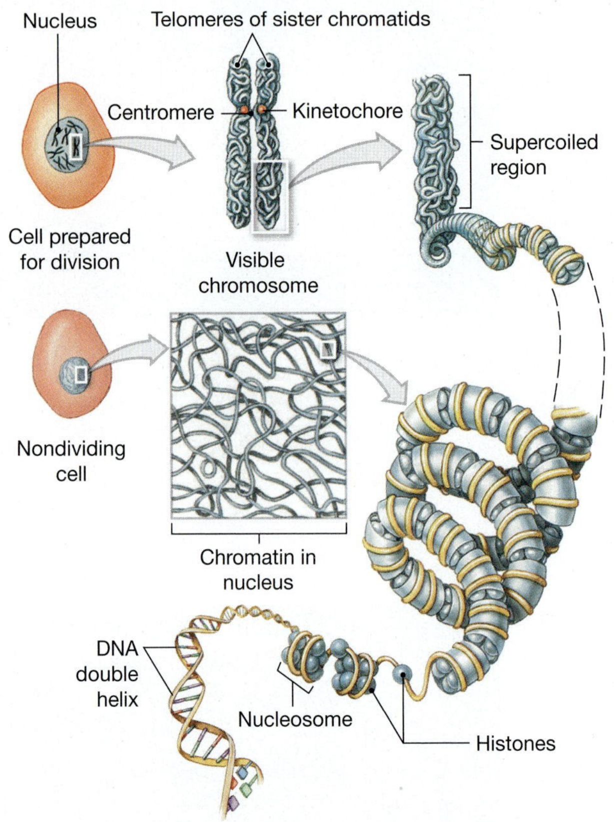

Figure 2.14 Chromosome Structure
DNA strands are coiled around histones to form nucleosomes. Nucleosomes form coils that may be very tight or rather loose. In cells that are not dividing, the DNA is loosely coiled, forming a tangled network known as chromatin. When the coiling becomes tighter, as it does in preparation for cell division, the DNA becomes visible as distinct structures called chromosomes.

The Endoplasmic Reticulum [Figure 2.15]

The **endoplasmic reticulum** (en-dō-PLAZ-mik re-TIK-ū-lum), or **ER**, is a network of intracellular membranes that forms hollow tubes, flattened sheets, and rounded chambers (Figure 2.15). The chambers are called **cisternae** (sis-TUR-nē; singular, *cisterna*, a reservoir for water).

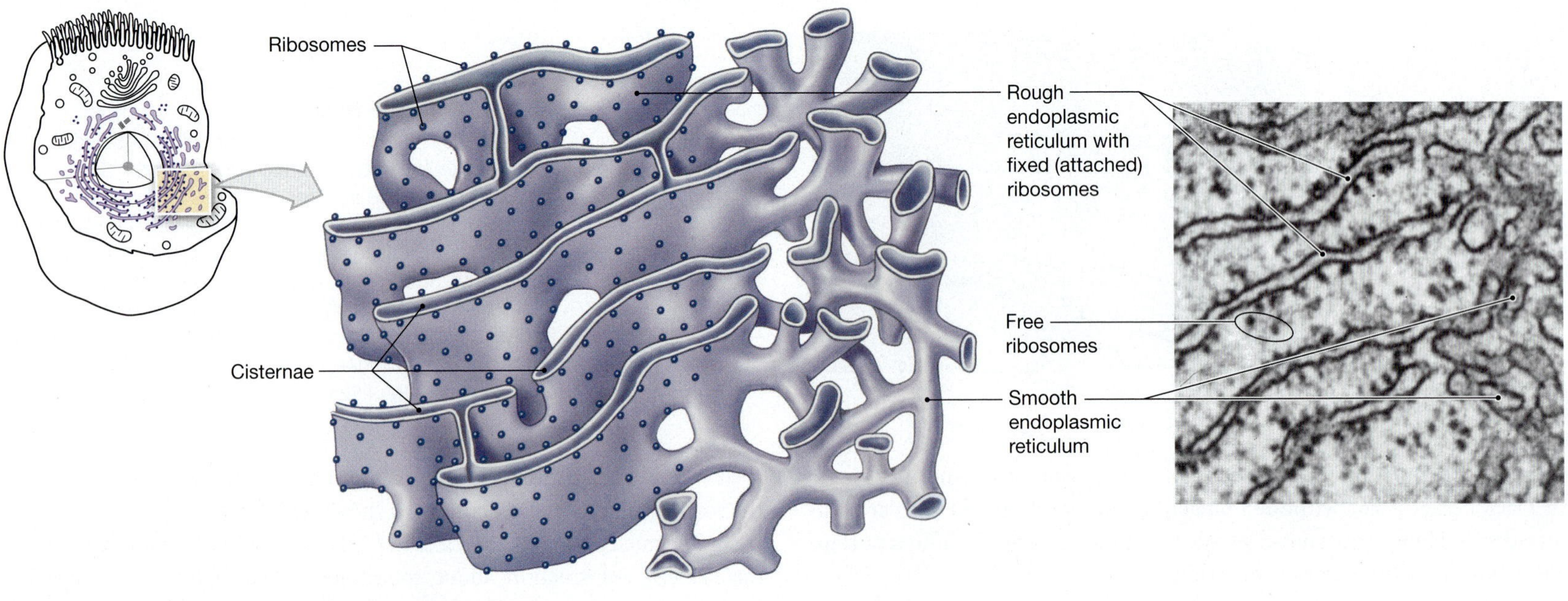

Figure 2.15 The Endoplasmic Reticulum
This organelle is a network of intracellular membranes. Here, a diagrammatic sketch shows the three-dimensional relationships between the rough and smooth endoplasmic reticulum.

The ER has four major functions:

1. *Synthesis:* The membrane of the endoplasmic reticulum contains enzymes that manufacture carbohydrates, steroids, and lipids; areas with fixed ribosomes synthesize proteins. These manufactured products are stored in the cisternae of the ER.
2. *Storage:* The ER can hold synthesized molecules or substances absorbed from the cytosol without affecting other cellular operations.
3. *Transport:* Substances can travel from place to place within the cell inside the endoplasmic reticulum.
4. *Detoxification:* Cellular toxins can be absorbed by the ER and neutralized by enzymes found on its membrane.

The ER thus functions as a combination workshop, storage area, and shipping depot. It is where many newly synthesized proteins undergo chemical modification and where they are packaged for export to their next destination, the *Golgi apparatus.* There are two distinct types of endoplasmic reticulum, **rough endoplasmic reticulum (RER)** and **smooth endoplasmic reticulum (SER)**.

The outer surface of the rough endoplasmic reticulum contains fixed ribosomes. Ribosomes synthesize proteins using instructions provided by a strand of RNA. As the polypeptide chains grow, they enter the cisternae of the endoplasmic reticulum, where they may be further modified. Most of the proteins and glycoproteins produced by the RER are packaged into small membrane sacs that pinch off the edges or surfaces of the ER. These **transport vesicles** deliver the proteins to the Golgi apparatus.

No ribosomes are associated with smooth endoplasmic reticulum. The SER has a variety of functions that center on the synthesis of lipids, steroids, and carbohydrates; the storage of calcium ions; and the removal and inactivation of toxins.

The amount of endoplasmic reticulum and the proportion of RER to SER vary depending on the type of cell and its ongoing activities. For example, pancreatic cells that manufacture digestive enzymes contain an extensive RER, and the SER is relatively small. The situation is reversed in cells that synthesize steroid hormones in reproductive organs.

The Golgi Apparatus [Figure 2.16]

The **Golgi** (GŌL-jē) **apparatus**, or *Golgi complex*, consists of flattened membrane discs called *cisternae.* A typical Golgi apparatus, shown in Figure 2.16, consists of five to six cisternae. Cells that are actively secreting have larger and more numerous cisternae than resting cells. The most actively secreting cells contain several sets of cisternae, each resembling a stack of dinner plates. Most often these stacks lie near the nucleus of the cell.

The major functions of the Golgi apparatus are:

1. Synthesis and packaging of secretions, such as mucins or enzymes.
2. Packaging of special enzymes for use in the cytosol.
3. Renewal or modification of the plasmalemma.

The Golgi cisternae communicate with the ER and with the cell surface. This communication involves the formation, movement, and fusion of vesicles.

Figure 2.16 The Golgi Apparatus
(a) A sectional view of the Golgi apparatus of an active secretory cell. (TEM × 83,520) **(b)** A three-dimensional view of the Golgi apparatus with a cut edge corresponding to part (a).

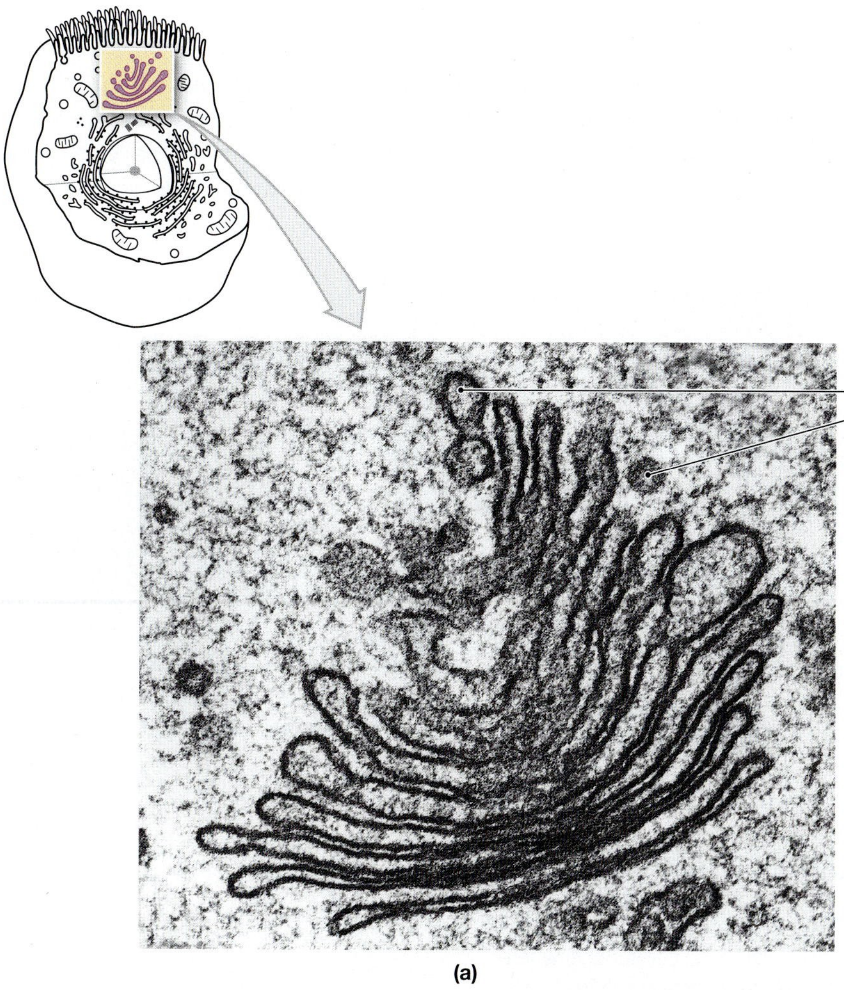

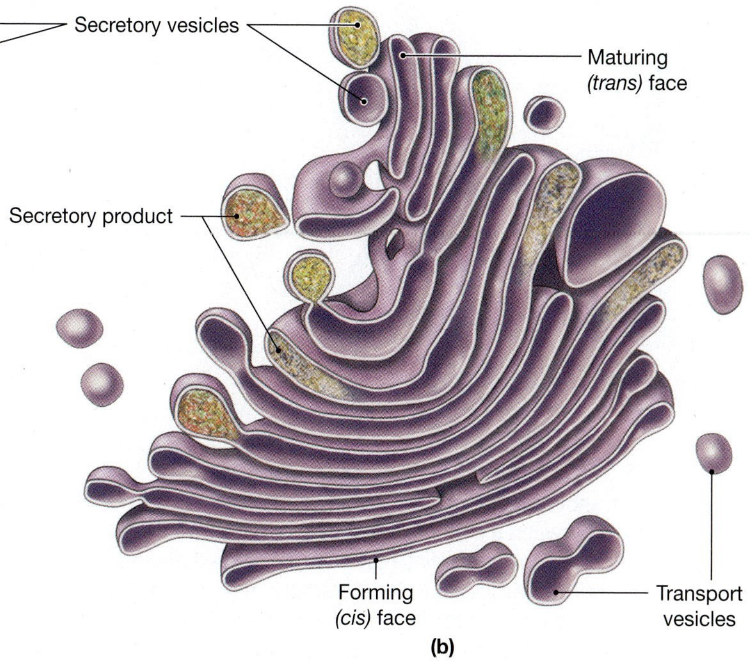

Vesicle Transport, Transfer, and Secretion [Figure 2.17] The role played by the Golgi apparatus in packaging secretions is illustrated in Figure 2.17a. Protein and glycoprotein synthesis occurs in the RER, and transport vesicles (packages) then move these products to the Golgi apparatus. The vesicles usually arrive at a convex cisterna known as the *forming face* (or *cis face*). The transport vesicles then fuse with the Golgi membrane, emptying their contents into the cisternae, where enzymes modify the arriving proteins and glycoproteins.

Material moves between cisternae by means of small **transfer vesicles**. Ultimately the product arrives at the *maturing face* (or *trans face*). At the maturing face, vesicles form that carry materials away from the Golgi. Vesicles containing secretions that will be discharged from the cell are called **secretory vesicles**. Secretion occurs as the membrane of a secretory vesicle fuses with the plasmalemma. This discharge process is called **exocytosis** (ek-sō-sī-TŌ-sis) (Figure 2.17b).

Membrane Turnover Because the Golgi apparatus continually adds new membrane to the cell surface, it has the ability to change the properties of the plasmalemma over time. Such changes can profoundly alter the sensitivity and functions of the cell. In an actively secreting cell, the Golgi membranes may undergo a complete turnover every 40 minutes. The membrane lost from the Golgi is added to the cell surface, and that addition is balanced by the formation of vesicles at the membrane surface. As a result, an area equal to the entire membrane surface may be replaced each hour.

Lysosomes [Figure 2.18]

Many of the vesicles produced at the Golgi apparatus never leave the cytoplasm. The most important of these are lysosomes. **Lysosomes** (LĪ-sō-sōms; *lyso-*, dissolution + *soma*, body) are vesicles filled with digestive enzymes formed by the rough endoplasmic reticulum and then packaged within the lysosomes by the Golgi apparatus. Refer to Figure 2.18 as we describe the types of lysosomes and lysosomal functions. *Primary lysosomes* contain inactive enzymes. Activation occurs when the lysosome fuses with the membranes of damaged organelles, such as mitochondria or fragments of the endoplasmic reticulum. This fusion creates a *secondary lysosome*, which contains active enzymes. These enzymes then break down the lysosomal contents. Nutrients reenter the cytosol, and the remaining waste material is eliminated by exocytosis.

Lysosomes also function in the defense against disease. By the process of endocytosis, cells may remove bacteria, as well as fluids and organic debris, from their surroundings and isolate them within vesicles. Lysosomes may fuse with vesicles created in this way, and the digestive enzymes within the secondary lysosome then break down the contents and release usable substances such as sugars or amino acids. In this way the cell not only protects itself against pathogenic organisms but obtains valuable nutrients.

Lysosomes also perform essential cleanup and recycling functions inside the cell. For example, when muscle cells are inactive, lysosomes gradually break down their contractile proteins; if the cells become active once again, this destruction ceases. This regulatory mechanism fails in a damaged or dead cell. Lysosomes then disintegrate, releasing active enzymes into the cytosol. These enzymes rapidly destroy the proteins and organelles of the cell, a process called **autolysis** (aw-TOL-i-sis; *auto-*, self). Because the breakdown of lysosomal membranes can destroy a cell, lysosomes have been called cellular "suicide packets." We do not know how to control lysosomal activities, or why the enclosed enzymes do not digest the lysosomal membranes unless the cell is damaged. Problems with lysosomal enzyme production cause more than 30 serious diseases affecting children. In these conditions, called *lysosomal storage diseases*, the lack of a specific lysosomal enzyme results in the buildup of waste products and debris normally removed and recycled by lysosomes. Affected individuals may die when vital cells, such as those of the heart, can no longer continue to function.

Peroxisomes

Peroxisomes are smaller than lysosomes and carry a different group of enzymes. Peroxisome enzymes are formed by free ribosomes within the cytoplasm. These enzymes are then inserted into the membranes of preexisting peroxisomes. Therefore, new peroxisomes are the result of the cell recycling older, preexisting peroxisomes that no longer contain active enzymes.

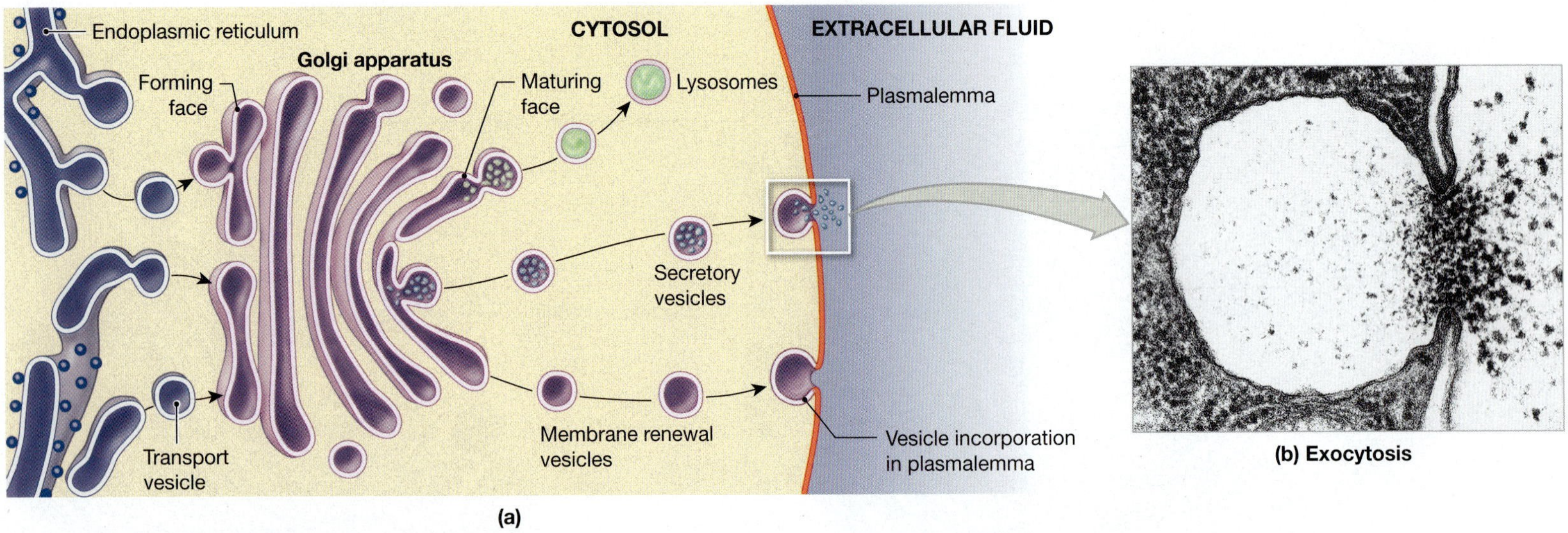

Figure 2.17 The Function of the Golgi Apparatus
(a) This diagram shows the functional link between the ER and the Golgi apparatus. Golgi structure has been simplified to clarify the relationships between the membranes. Transport vesicles carry the secretory product from the endoplasmic reticulum to the Golgi apparatus, and transfer vesicles move membrane and materials between the Golgi cisternae. At the maturing face, three functional categories of vesicles develop. Secretory vesicles carry the secretion from the Golgi to the cell surface, where exocytosis releases the contents into the extracellular fluid. Other vesicles add surface area and integral proteins to the plasmalemma. Lysosomes, which remain in the cytoplasm, are vesicles filled with enzymes. **(b)** Exocytosis at the surface of a cell.

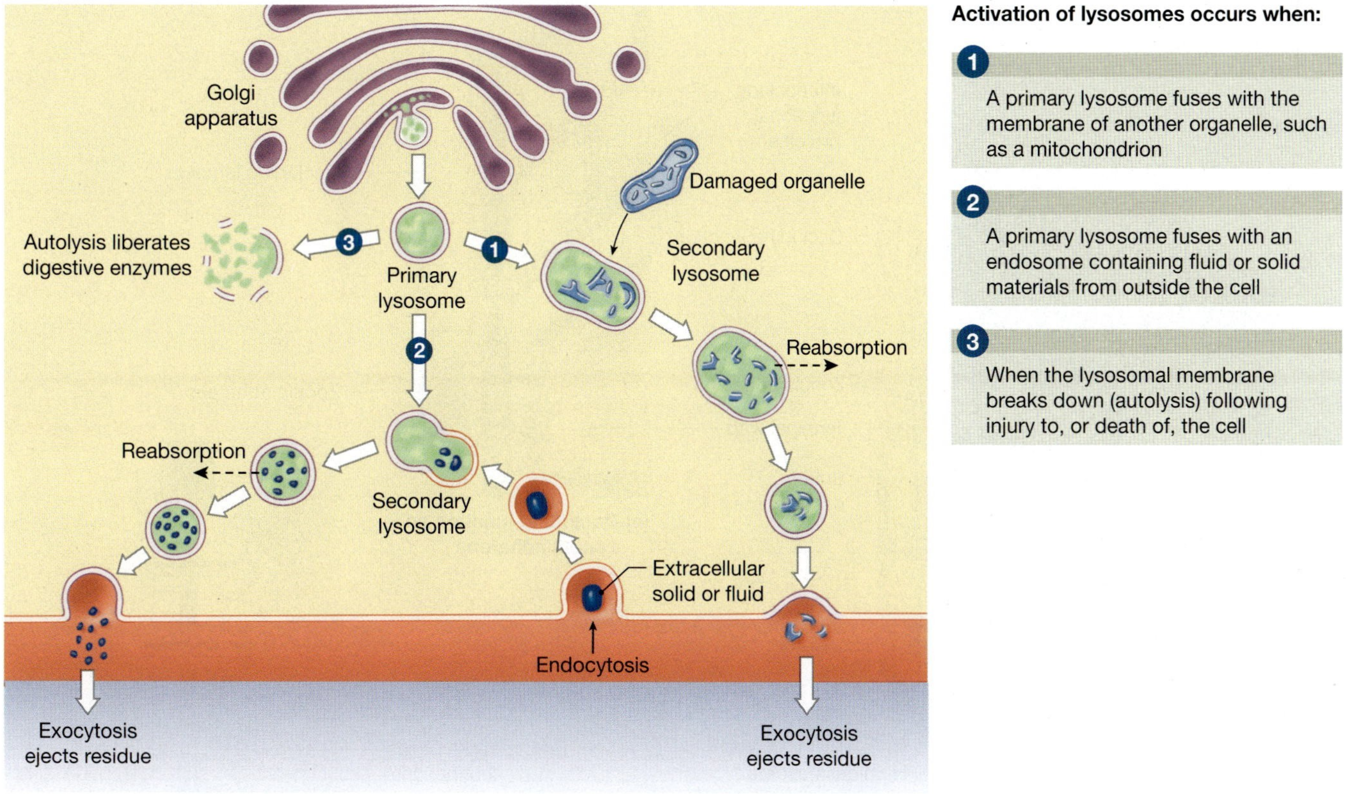

Figure 2.18 Lysosomal Functions
Primary lysosomes, formed at the Golgi apparatus, contain inactive enzymes. Activation may occur under three basic conditions: **(1)** when the primary lysosome fuses with the membrane of another organelle, such as a mitochondrion; **(2)** when the primary lysosome fuses with an endocytotic vesicle containing fluid or solid materials from outside the cell; or **(3)** in autolysis, when the lysosomal membrane breaks down following injury to or death of the cell.

Peroxisomes absorb and break down fatty acids and other organic compounds. Enzymatic activity within a peroxisome may form toxins such as hydrogen peroxide as a by-product; other enzymes then convert the hydrogen peroxide to water. Peroxisomes are most abundant in liver cells, which remove and neutralize toxins absorbed in the digestive tract.

Membrane Flow

With the exception of mitochondria, all the membranous organelles in the cell are either interconnected or in communication through the movement of vesicles. The RER and SER are continuous and connected to the nuclear envelope. Transport vesicles connect the ER with the Golgi apparatus, and secretory vesicles link the Golgi apparatus with the plasmalemma. Finally, vesicles forming at the exposed surface of the cell remove and recycle segments of the plasmalemma. This continual movement and exchange is called **membrane flow**.

Membrane flow is another example of the dynamic nature of cells. It provides a mechanism for cells to change the characteristics of their plasmalemmae—lipids, receptors, channels, anchors, and enzymes—as they grow, mature, or respond to a specific environmental stimulus.

CONCEPT CHECK

1. Microscopic examination of a cell reveals that it contains many mitochondria. What does this observation imply about the cell's energy requirements?
2. Cells in the ovaries and testes contain large amounts of smooth endoplasmic reticulum (SER). Why?
3. What occurs if lysosomes disintegrate in a damaged cell?

See blue "Answers" tab at back of book.

Intercellular Attachment [Figure 2.19]

Many cells form permanent or temporary attachments to other cells or extracellular materials (Figure 2.19). Intercellular connections may involve extensive areas of opposing plasmalemmae, or they may be concentrated at specialized attachment sites. Large areas of opposing plasmalemmae may be interconnected by transmembrane proteins called **cell adhesion molecules (CAMs)**, which bind to each other and to other extracellular materials. For example, CAMs on the attached base of an epithelium help bind the basal surface (where the epithelium is attached to underlying tissues) to the underlying basal lamina. The membranes of adjacent cells may also be held together by **intercellular cement**, a thin layer of proteoglycans. These proteoglycans contain polysaccharide derivatives known as *glycosaminoglycans*, most notably **hyaluronan** *(hyaluronic acid)*.

There are three major types of **cell junctions**: (1) *tight junctions*, (2) *communicating junctions*, and (3) *anchoring junctions*.

- At a **tight junction** (also termed an *occluding junction*), the lipid portions of the two plasmalemmae are tightly bound together by interlocking membrane proteins (Figure 2.19b). At an occluding junction the apical plasmalemmae of adjacent cells come into close contact with each other, thereby sealing off any intercellular space between the cells and preventing the passage of material into the intercellular space between the two cells. This diffusion barrier prevents the passage of

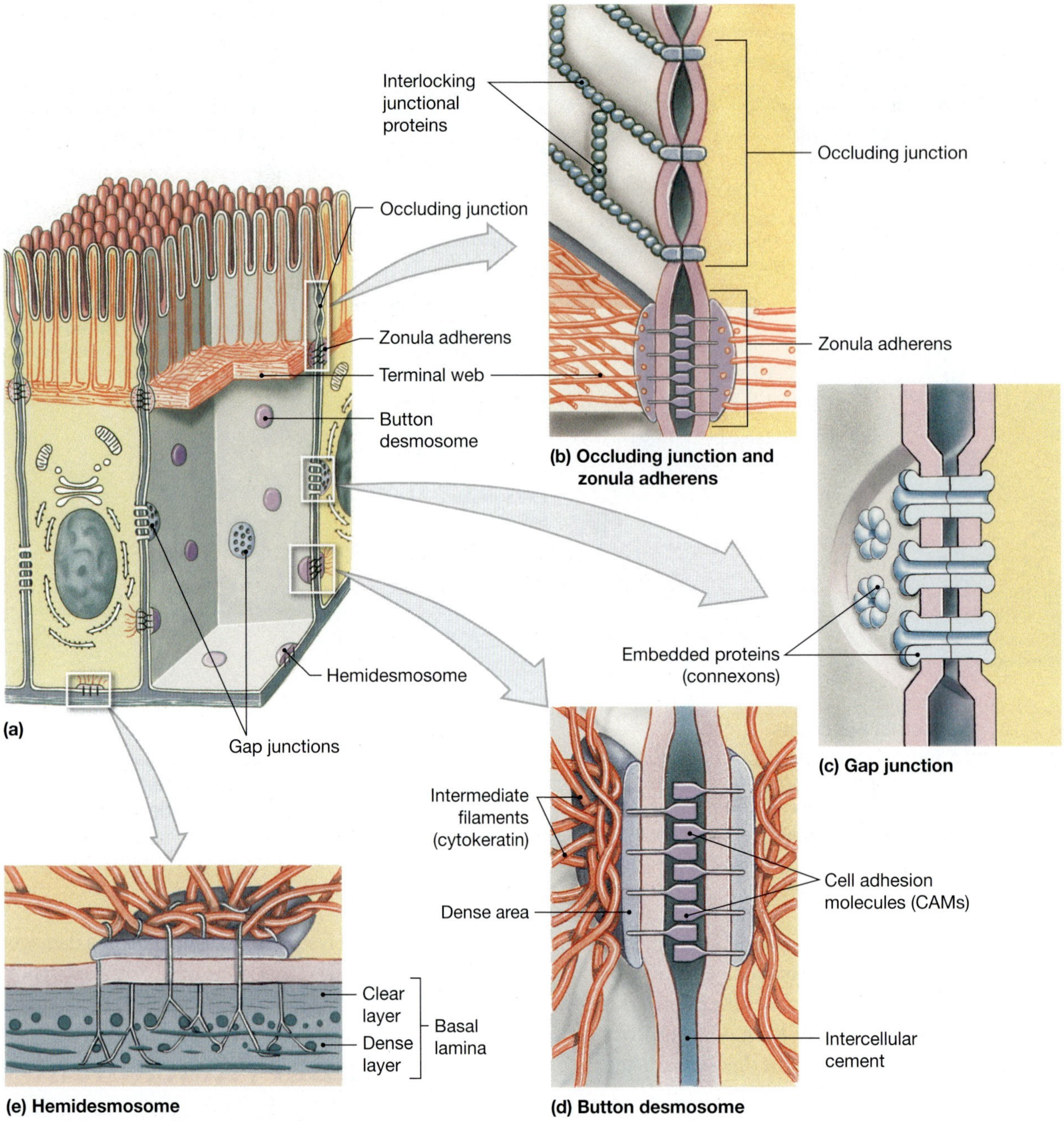

Figure 2.19 Cell Attachments
(a) A diagrammatic view of an epithelial cell, showing the major types of intercellular connections. **(b)** A tight junction is formed by the fusion of the outer layers of two plasmalemmae. Tight junctions prevent the diffusion of fluids and solutes between the cells. **(c)** Communicating junctions permit the free diffusion of ions and small molecules between two cells. **(d)** Anchoring junctions attach one cell to another. A macula adherens has a more organized network of intermediate filaments. An adhesion belt is a form of anchoring junction that encircles the cell. This complex is tied to the microfilaments of the terminal web. **(e)** Hemidesmosomes attach an epithelial cell to extracellular structures, such as the protein fibers in the basal lamina.

material from one side of an epithelial cell to another via this intercellular space, thereby requiring cells to utilize some active (energy requiring) process to pass material from cell to cell.

- At **communicating junctions** (also termed *gap junctions* or *nexuses*), two cells are held together by membrane proteins called *connexons* (Figure 2.19c). Because these are channel proteins, the result is a narrow passageway that lets ions, small metabolites, and regulatory molecules pass from cell to cell. Communicating junctions are common among epithelial cells, where they help coordinate functions such as the beating of cilia. These junctions are also abundant in cardiac muscle and smooth muscle tissue, where they are essential to the coordination of muscle cell contractions.
- **Anchoring junctions** provide mechanical linkages between two adjacent cells at their lateral or basal surfaces (Figure 2.19d). These mechanical linkages are accomplished by CAMs and proteoglycans that link the opposing membranes and form a junction with the cy-

toskeleton within the adjoining cells. Anchoring junctions are very strong, and they can resist stretching and twisting. At an anchoring junction each cell contains a layered protein complex known as a *dense area* on the inside of the plasmalemma. Cytoskeleton filaments composed of the protein *cytokeratin* are bound to this dense area. Two types of anchoring junctions have been identified at the lateral surfaces of cells: *zonula adherens* (also termed an *adhesion belt*) and *macula adherens* (also termed a *desmosome*, DEZ-mō-sōm; *desmos*, ligament + *soma*, body). A zonula adherens is a sheet-like anchoring junction that serves to stabilize nonepithelial cells, while a macula adherens provides small, localized spot-like anchoring junctions that stabilize adjacent epithelial cells (**Figure 2.19d**). These connections are most abundant between cells in the superficial layers of the skin, where zonula adherens create links so strong that dead skin cells are shed in thick sheets rather than individually. Two additional forms of anchoring junctions have been found where epithelial tissue rests on the connective tissue of the basal lamina. *Focal adhesions* (also termed *focal contacts*) are responsible for connecting intracellular microfilaments to protein fibers of the basal lamina. These types of anchoring junctions are found in epithelial tissue that is undergoing a dynamic change, such as the migration of epithelial cells during the process of wound repair. *Hemidesmosomes* (**Figure 2.19e**) are found in epithelial tissue that is subjected to a significant amount of abrasion and shearing forces, and require a strong attachment to the underlying basal lamina. Hemidesmosomes are found in tissues such as the cornea of the eye, skin, and the mucosal surfaces of the vagina, oral cavity, and esophagus.

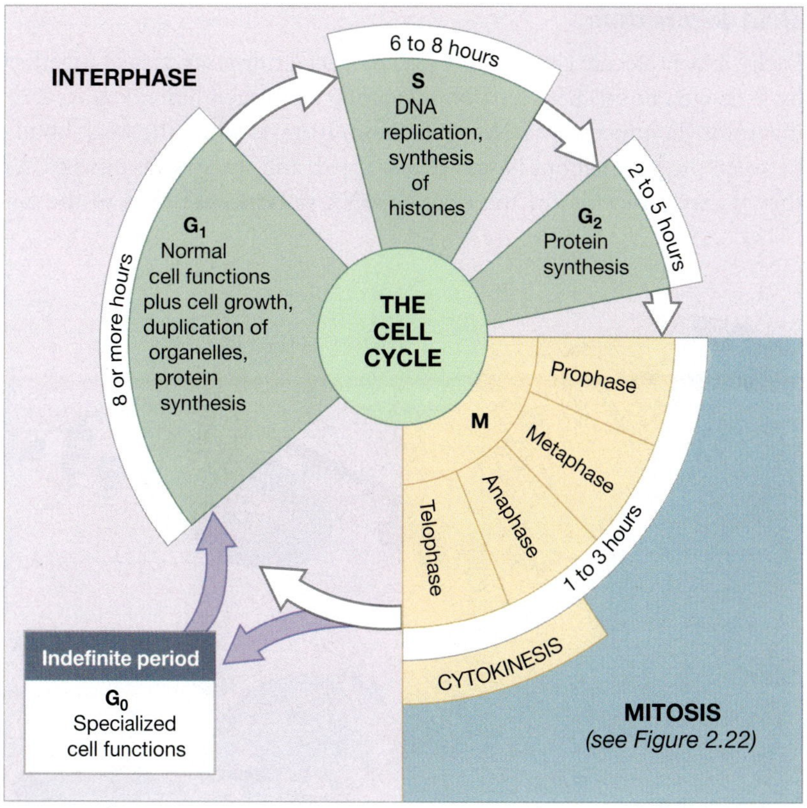

Figure 2.20 The Cell Life Cycle
The cell cycle is divided into interphase, comprising G_1, S, and G_2 stages, and the G_M phase, which includes mitosis and cytokinesis. The result is the production of two identical daughter cells.

The Cell Life Cycle [Figure 2.20]

Between fertilization and physical maturity a human being increases in complexity from a single cell to roughly 75 trillion cells. This amazing increase in number occurs through a form of cellular reproduction called **cell division**. The division of a single cell produces a pair of *daughter cells*, each half the size of the original. Thus, two new cells have replaced the original one.

Even when development has been completed, cell division continues to be essential to survival. Although cells are highly adaptable, they can be damaged by physical wear and tear, toxic chemicals, temperature changes, and other environmental hazards. Cells are also subject to aging. The life span of a cell varies from hours to decades, depending on the type of cell and the environmental stresses involved. A typical cell does not live nearly as long as a typical person, so over time cell populations must be maintained by cell division.

The most important step in cell division is the accurate duplication of the cell's genetic material, a process called *DNA replication*, and the distribution of one copy of the genetic information to each of the two new daughter cells. The distribution process is called **mitosis** (mī-TŌ-sis). Mitosis occurs during the division of somatic (*soma*, body) cells. Somatic cells include all of the cells in the body other than the reproductive cells, which give rise to sperm or oocytes. Sperm and oocytes are called *gametes*; they are specialized cells containing half the number of chromosomes present in somatic cells. Production of gametes involves a distinct process, *meiosis* (mī-Ō-sis), which will be described in Chapter 28. An overview of the life cycle of a typical somatic cell is presented in **Figure 2.20**.

Interphase [Figures 2.20/2.21/2.22]

Most cells spend only a small part of their time actively engaged in cell division. Somatic cells spend the majority of their functional lives in *interphase*. During **interphase** the cell is performing all of its normal functions and, if necessary, preparing for division. In a cell preparing for division, interphase can be divided into the G_1, *S*, and G_2 phases (**Figure 2.20**). An interphase cell in the **G_0 phase** is not preparing for mitosis, but is performing all other normal cell functions. Some mature cells, such as skeletal muscle cells and most neurons, remain in G_0 indefinitely and may never undergo mitosis. In contrast, *stem cells*, which divide repeatedly with very brief interphase periods, never enter G_0.

In the **G_1 phase** the cell manufactures enough mitochondria, centrioles, cytoskeletal elements, endoplasmic reticulum, ribosomes, Golgi membranes, and cytosol to make two functional cells. In cells dividing at top speed, G_1 may last as little as 8–12 hours. Such cells pour all of their energy into mitosis, and all other activities cease. If G_1 lasts for days, weeks, or months, preparation for mitosis occurs as the cells perform their normal functions. When G_1 preparations have been completed, the cell enters the **S phase**. Over the next six to eight hours, the cell replicates its chromosomes, a process that involves the synthesis of both DNA and the associated histones.

Throughout the life of a cell, the DNA strands in the nucleus remain intact. DNA synthesis, or **DNA replication**, occurs in cells preparing to undergo mitosis or meiosis. The goal of replication is to copy the genetic information in the nucleus so that one set of chromosomes can be distributed to each of the two cells produced. Several different enzymes are needed for the process.

DNA Replication

Each DNA molecule consists of a pair of nucleotide strands held together by hydrogen bonds between complementary nitrogen bases. **Figure 2.21** diagrams the process of DNA replication. It starts when the weak bonds between the nitrogenous bases are disrupted, and the strands unwind. As they do so, molecules of the enzyme **DNA polymerase** bind to the exposed nitrogenous bases. This enzyme promotes bonding between the nitrogenous bases of the DNA strand and complementary DNA nucleotides suspended in the nucleoplasm.

Many molecules of DNA polymerase are working simultaneously along different portions of each DNA strand. This process produces short complementary nucleotide chains that are then linked together by enzymes called **ligases** (LĪ-gās-ez; *liga,* to tie). The final result is a pair of identical DNA molecules.

Once DNA replication has been completed, there is a brief (2–5 hours) **G_2 phase** devoted to last-minute protein synthesis. The cell then enters the **M phase**, and mitosis begins (**Figures 2.20** and **2.22**).

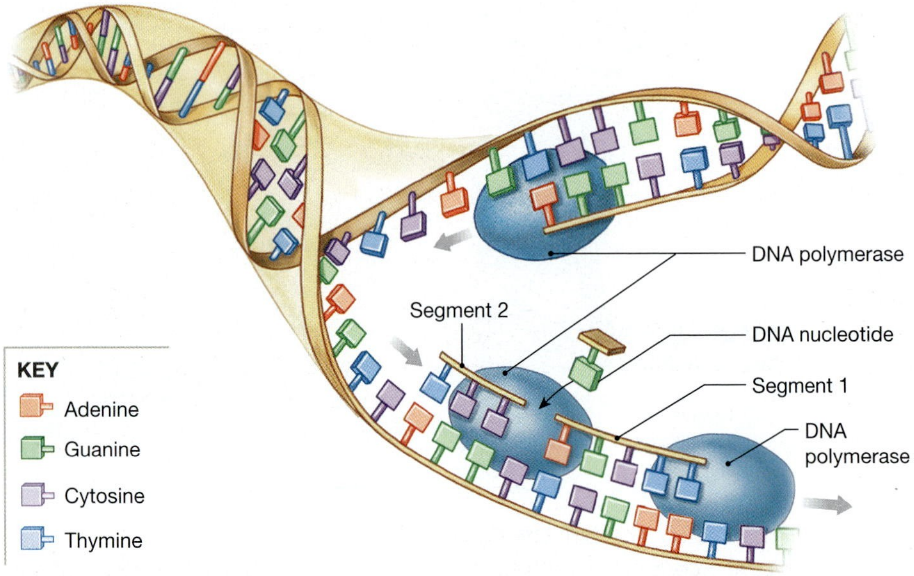

Figure 2.21 DNA Replication
In DNA replication the original paired strands unwind, and DNA polymerase begins attaching complementary DNA nucleotides along each strand. This process produces two identical copies of the original DNA molecule.

Mitosis [Figure 2.22]

Mitosis consists of four stages, but the transitions from stage-to-stage are seamless. The stages are detailed in **Figure 2.22**.

STEP 1. ***Prophase.*** (PRŌ-fāz; *pro,* before; **Figure 2.22**) Prophase begins when the chromosomes coil so tightly that they become visible as individual structures. As a result of DNA replication during the S phase, there are two copies of each chromosome, called **chromatids** (KRŌ-ma-tids), connected at a single point, the **centromere** (SEN-trō-mēr). The centrioles replicated in the G_1 phase; the two pairs of centrioles move apart during prophase. **Spindle fibers** extend between the centriole pairs; smaller microtubules called *astral rays* radiate into the surrounding cytoplasm. Prophase ends with the disappearance of the nuclear envelope. The spindle fibers now form among the chromosomes and the kinetochore of each chromatid becomes attached to a spindle fiber called a *chromosomal microtubule.*

Figure 2.22 Interphase and Mitosis
The appearance of a cell in interphase and at the various stages of mitosis. (LM × 775)

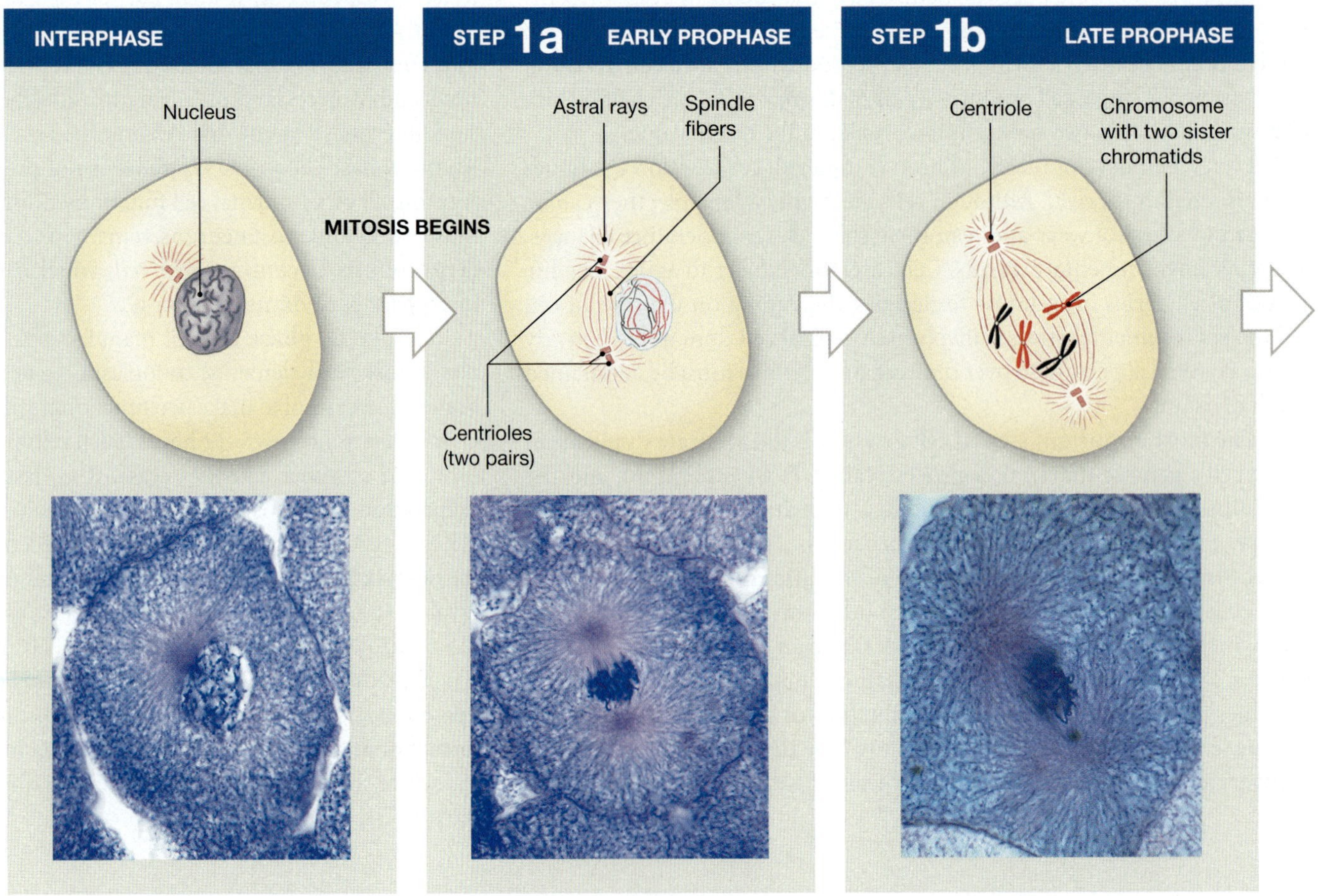

Clinical Note

Cell Division and Cancer In normal tissue the rate of cell division balances cell loss or destruction. When that balance breaks down, the tissue begins to enlarge. A **tumor**, or **neoplasm**, is a mass or swelling produced by abnormal cell growth and division. In a **benign tumor** the cells remain within a connective tissue capsule. Such a tumor seldom threatens an individual's life. Surgery can usually remove the tumor if its size or position disturbs adjacent tissue function.

Cells in a **malignant tumor** are no longer responding to normal control mechanisms. These cells divide rapidly, spreading into the surrounding tissues, and they may also spread to other tissues and organs. This spread is called **metastasis** (me-TAS-ta-sis). Metastasis is dangerous and difficult to control. Once in a new location, the metastatic cells produce secondary tumors.

The term **cancer** refers to an illness characterized by malignant cells. Cancer cells gradually lose their resemblance to normal cells. They change size and shape, often becoming unusually large or abnormally small. Organ function begins to deteriorate as the number of cancer cells increases. The cancer cells may not perform their original functions at all, or they may perform normal functions in an unusual way. They also compete for space and nutrients with normal cells. They do not use energy very efficiently, and they grow and multiply at the expense of normal tissues. This activity accounts for the starved appearance of many patients in the late stages of cancer.

STEP 2. ***Metaphase.*** (MET-a-fāz; *meta*, after; Figure 2.22) Spindle fibers now pass among the chromosomes, and the kinetochore of each chromatid becomes attached to a spindle fiber called a *chromosomal microtubule*. The chromosomes composed of chromatid pairs now move to a narrow central zone called the **metaphase plate**. A microtubule of the spindle apparatus attaches to each centromere.

STEP 3. ***Anaphase.*** (AN-uh-fāz; *ana*, back; Figure 2.22) As if responding to a single command, the chromatid pairs separate, and the **daughter chromosomes** move toward opposite ends of the cell. Anaphase ends as the daughter chromosomes arrive near the centrioles at opposite ends of the dividing cell.

STEP 4. ***Telophase.*** (TEL-ō-fāz; *telo*, end; Figure 2.22) This stage is in many ways the reverse of prophase, for in it the cell prepares to return to the interphase state. The nuclear membranes form and the nuclei enlarge as the chromosomes gradually uncoil. Once the chromosomes disappear, nucleoli reappear and the nuclei resemble those of interphase cells.

Telophase marks the end of mitosis proper, but the daughter cells have yet to complete their physical separation. This separation process, called **cytokinesis** (sī-tō-ki-NĒ-sis; *cyto-*, cell + *kinesis*, motion), usually begins in late anaphase. As the daughter chromosomes near the ends of the spindle apparatus, the cytoplasm constricts along the plane of the metaphase plate, forming a *cleavage furrow*. This process continues through telophase, and the completion of cytokinesis (Figure 2.22) marks the end of cell division and the beginning of the next interphase period.

The frequency of cell division can be estimated by the number of cells in mitosis at any given time. As a result, the term **mitotic rate** is often used when discussing rates of cell division. In general, the longer the life

Figure 2.22 ***(continued)***

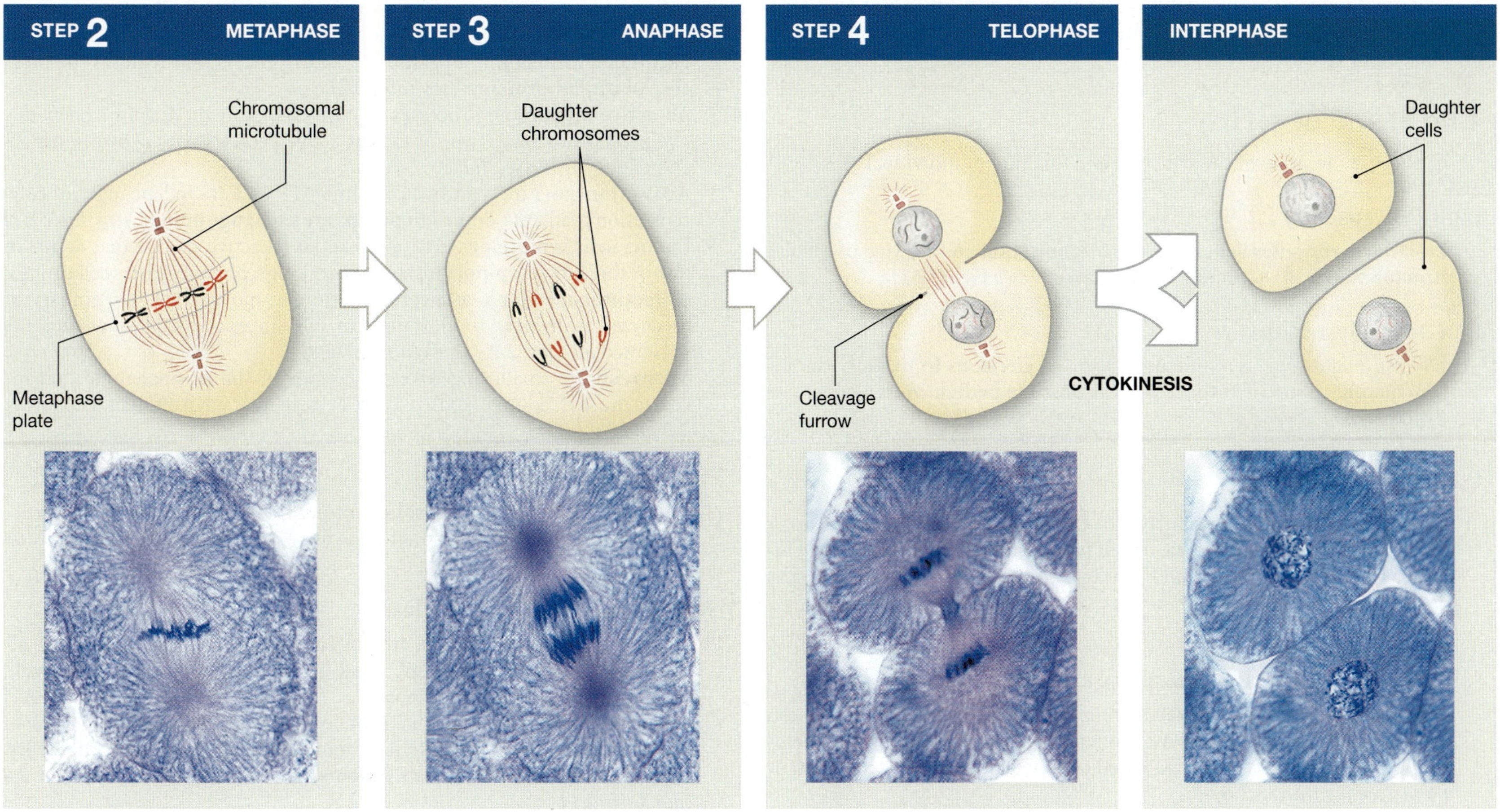

expectancy of a cell type, the slower the mitotic rate. Relatively long-lived cells, such as muscle cells and neurons, either never divide or do so only under special circumstances. Other cells, such as those lining the digestive tract, survive only for days or even hours because they are constantly subjected to attack by chemicals, pathogens, and abrasion. Special cells called **stem cells** maintain these cell populations through repeated cycles of cell division.

CONCEPT CHECK

1. What is cell division?
2. Prior to cell division, mitosis must occur. What is mitosis?
3. List, in order of appearance, the stages of interphase and mitosis and the events that occur in each.

See blue "Answers" tab at back of book.

CLINICAL TERMS

benign tumor: A mass or swelling in which the cells remain within a connective tissue capsule; rarely life-threatening.

cancer: An illness characterized by malignant cells.

carcinogen (kar-SIN-ō-jen): An environmental factor that stimulates the conversion of a normal cell to a cancer cell.

hereditary predisposition: The condition of an individual born with genes that increase the likelihood of a specific disease.

malignant tumor: A mass or swelling in which the cells no longer respond to normal control mechanisms, but divide rapidly.

metastasis(me-TAS-ta-sis): The spread of malignant cells into surrounding and distant tissues and organs.

mutagen (MŪ-ta-jen): A factor that can damage DNA strands and sometimes cause chromosomal breakage, stimulating the development of cancer cells.

oncogene (ON-kō-jēn): A cancer-causing gene created by a somatic mutation in a normal gene (proto-oncogene) involved with growth, differentiation, or cell division.

tumor (neoplasm): A mass or swelling produced by abnormal cell growth and division.

tumor-suppressing genes (TSG) or **antioncogenes:** Genes that suppress mitosis and growth in normal cells.

STUDY OUTLINE

Introduction 27

1. All living things are composed of **cells**, and contemporary *cell theory* incorporates several basic concepts: (1) Cells are the building blocks of all plants and animals; (2) cells are produced by the division of preexisting cells; (3) cells are the smallest units that perform all vital functions.
2. The body contains two cell types: **sex cells** (germ cells or reproductive cells) and **somatic cells** (body cells).

The Study of Cells 27

1. *Cytology* is the study of the structure and function of individual cells.

Light Microscopy 27

2. *Light microscopy* uses light to permit magnification and viewing of cellular structures up to 1000 times their natural size. *(see Figure 2.1)*

Electron Microscopy 28

3. *Electron microscopy* uses a focused beam of electrons to magnify cell ultrastructure up to 1000 times what is possible by light microscopy. *(see Figure 2.1b,c)*

Cellular Anatomy 29

1. A cell is surrounded by a thin layer of **extracellular fluid**. The cell's outer boundary is the **plasmalemma**, or **cell membrane**. It is a **phospholipid bilayer** containing proteins and cholesterol. *Table 2.1* summarizes the anatomy of a typical cell. *(see Figures 2.3/2.4)*

The Plasmalemma 31

2. **Integral proteins** are embedded in the phospholipid bilayer of the membrane, while **peripheral proteins** are attached to the membrane but can separate from it. **Channels** allow water and ions to move across the membrane; some channels are called **gated channels** because they can open or close. *(see Figures 2.5/2.6)*
3. Plasmalemmae are **selectively permeable**; that is, they permit the free passage of some materials.
4. **Diffusion** is the net movement of material from an area where its concentration is high to an area where its concentration is lower. Diffusion occurs until the **concentration gradient** is eliminated. *(see Figure 2.6 and Table 2.2)*
5. Diffusion of water across a membrane in response to differences in water concentration is called **osmosis**. *(see Table 2.2)*
6. **Facilitated diffusion** is a passive transport process that requires the presence of **carrier proteins**. *(see Table 2.2)*
7. All **active membrane processes** require energy in the form of *adenosine triphosphate*, or ATP. Two important active processes are active transport and endocytosis. *(see Table 2.2)*
8. **Active transport** mechanisms consume ATP and are independent of concentration gradients. Some **ion pumps** are **exchange pumps**. *(see Table 2.2)*
9. **Endocytosis** is movement into a cell and is an active process that occurs in one of three forms: **pinocytosis** (cell drinking), **phagocytosis** (cell eating), or **receptor-mediated endocytosis** (selective movement). A summary of mechanisms involved in movement of substances across plasmalemmae is presented in *Table 2.2. (see Figures 2.7/2.8)*
10. **Microvilli** are small, fingerlike projections of the plasmalemma that increase the surface area exposed to the extracellular environment. *(see Figure 2.9 and Table 2.1)*

The Cytoplasm 35

11. The **cytoplasm** contains **cytosol**, an intracellular fluid that surrounds structures that perform specific functions, called **organelles**. *(see Figure 2.3 and Table 2.1)*

Nonmembranous Organelles 36

12. **Nonmembranous organelles** are not enclosed in membranes, and are always in contact with the cytosol. These include the cytoskeleton, microvilli, centrioles, cilia, flagella, and ribosomes. *(see Figures 2.9 to 2.11 and Table 2.1)*
13. The **cytoskeleton** is an internal protein network that gives the cytoplasm strength and flexibility. It has four components: **microfilaments**, **intermediate filaments**, **thick filaments**, and **microtubules**. *(see Figure 2.9 and Table 2.1)*

14. **Centrioles** are small, microtubule-containing cylinders that direct the movement of chromosomes during cell division. *(see Figure 2.10 and Table 2.1)*
15. **Cilia**, anchored by a **basal body**, are microtubules containing hairlike projections from the cell surface that beat rhythmically to move fluids or secretions across the cell surface. *(see Figure 2.10 and Table 2.1)*
16. A whiplike **flagellum** moves a cell through surrounding fluid, rather than moving the fluid past a stationary cell. *Table 2.3* presents a comparison of centrioles, cilia, and flagella.
17. **Ribosomes** are intracellular factories consisting of small and large subunits; together they manufacture proteins. Two types of ribosomes, **free** (within the cytosol) and **fixed** (bound to the *endoplasmic reticulum*), are found in cells. *(see Figure 2.11 and Table 2.1)*

Membranous Organelles 38

18. **Membranous organelles** are surrounded by lipid membranes that isolate them from the cytosol. They include: mitochondria, the nucleus, the endoplasmic reticulum (rough and smooth), the Golgi apparatus, lysosomes, and peroxisomes.
19. **Mitochondria** are responsible for producing 95 percent of the ATP within a typical cell. *(see Figure 2.12 and Table 2.1)*
20. The **nucleus** is the control center for cellular operations. It is surrounded by a **nuclear envelope**, through which it communicates with the cytosol through **nuclear pores**. The nucleus contains 23 pairs of **chromosomes**. *(see Figures 2.13/2.14 and Table 2.1)*
21. The **endoplasmic reticulum (ER)** is a network of intracellular membranes involved in synthesis, storage, transport, and detoxification. The ER forms hollow tubes, flattened sheets, and rounded chambers termed **cisternae**. There are two types of ER: rough and smooth. **Rough endoplasmic reticulum (RER)** has attached ribosomes; **smooth endoplasmic reticulum (SER)** does not. *(see Figure 2.15 and Table 2.1)*
22. The **Golgi apparatus** packages materials for **lysosomes**, **peroxisomes**, **secretory vesicles**, and membrane segments that are incorporated into the plasmalemma. Secretory products are discharged from the cell through the process of **exocytosis**. *(see Figures 2.16/2.17 and Table 2.1)*
23. **Lysosomes** are vesicles filled with digestive enzymes. The process of endocytosis is important in ridding the cell of bacteria and debris. The endocytic vesicle fuses with a lysosome, resulting in the digestion of its contents. *(see Figure 2.18 and Table 2.1)*
24. **Peroxisomes** carry enzymes used to break down organic molecules and neutralize toxins.

Membrane Flow 43

25. There is a continuous movement of membrane among the nuclear envelope, Golgi apparatus, endoplasmic reticulum, vesicles, and the plasmalemma. This is called **membrane flow.**

Intercellular Attachment 43

1. Cells attach to other cells or to extracellular protein fibers by three different types of cell junctions: occluding junctions, communicating junctions, and anchoring junctions.
2. Cells in some areas of the body are linked by combinations of cell junctions. *(see Figure 2.19)*
3. At an **occluding junction**, the lipid portions of the two plasmalemmae are bound together to seal off the intercellular space between cells. *(see Figure 2.19b)*
4. In a **communicating junction**, two cells are held together by interlocked membrane proteins. These are channel proteins, which form a narrow passageway. *(see Figure 2.19c)*
5. An **anchoring junction** provides a mechanical linkage between two adjacent cells at their lateral or basal surfaces. *(see Figure 2.19d)*
6. A *hemidesmosome* attaches a cell to extracellular filaments and fibers. *(see Figure 2.19e)*

The Cell Life Cycle 45

1. **Cell division** is the reproduction of cells. Reproductive cells produce *gametes* (sperm or oocytes) through the process of *meiosis. (see Figures 2.20/2.22)* In a dividing cell, an interphase or growth period alternates with a nuclear division phase, termed **mitosis**. *(see Figure 2.20)*

Interphase 45

2. Most somatic cells spend most of their time in **interphase**, a time of growth. *(see Figure 2.20)*

Mitosis 46

3. **Mitosis** refers to the nuclear division of somatic cells.
4. Mitosis proceeds in four distinct, contiguous stages: **prophase**, **metaphase**, **anaphase**, and **telophase**. *(see Figure 2.22)*

CHAPTER REVIEW

For answers to the Concept Check and Chapter Review questions, go to the blue "Answers" tab at the back of the book.

Level 1 Reviewing Facts and Terms

Match each numbered item with the most closely related lettered item. Use letters for answers in the spaces provided.

Column A	Column B
___1. ribosomes	a. DNA replication
___2. lysosomes	b. flattened membrane discs, packaging
___3. integral proteins	c. adjacent plasmalemmae bound by bands of interlocking proteins
___4. Golgi apparatus	d. packaging of materials for import into cell
___5. endocytosis	e. RNA and protein; protein synthesis
___6. cytoskeleton	f. control center; stores genetic information
___7. tight junction	g. cell vesicles with digestive enzymes
___8. nucleus	h. embedded in the plasmalemma
___9. S phase	i. internal protein framework in cytoplasm

10. All of the following membrane transport mechanisms are passive processes except
    (a) facilitated diffusion (b) vesicular transport
    (c) filtration (d) diffusion

11. The viscous, superficial coating on the outer surface of the plasmalemma is the
    (a) phospholipid bilayer (b) gated channel network
    (c) glycocalyx (d) plasmalemma

12. The interphase of a cell's life cycle is divided into the following phases:
    (a) prophase, metaphase, anaphase, and telophase
    (b) G_0, G_1, S, and G_2
    (c) mitosis and cytokinesis
    (d) replication, rest, division

13. Which organelle is prevalent in cells involved in many phagocytic events?
    (a) free ribosomes (b) lysosomes
    (c) peroxisomes (d) microtubules

14. In comparison with the intracellular fluid, the extracellular fluid contains
    (a) equivalent amounts of sodium ions
    (b) consistently highter concentration of potassium ions
    (c) many more enzymes
    (d) a lower concentration of dissolved proteins
15. Membrane flow provides a mechanism for
    (a) continual change in the characteristics of membranes
    (b) increase in the size of the cell
    (c) response of the cell to a specific environmental stimulus
    (d) all of the above
16. If a cell lacks mitochondria, the direct result will be that it cannot
    (a) manufacture proteins
    (b) produce substantial amounts of ATP
    (c) package proteins manufactured by the fixed ribosomes
    (d) reproduce itself
17. Some integral membrane proteins form gated channels that open or close to
    (a) regulate the passage of materials into or out of the cell
    (b) permit water movement into or out of the cell
    (c) transport large proteins into the cell
    (d) communicate with neighboring cells
18. The three major functions of the endoplasmic reticulum are
    (a) hydrolysis, diffusion, osmosis
    (b) detoxification, packaging, modification
    (c) synthesis, storage, transport
    (d) pinocytosis, phagocytosis, storage
19. The function of a selectively permeable plasmalemma is to
    (a) permit only water-soluble materials to enter or leave the cell freely
    (b) prohibit entry of all materials into the cell at certain times
    (c) permit the free passage of some materials but restrict passage of others
    (d) allow materials to enter or leave the cell only using active processes
20. The presence of invading pathogens in the extracellular fluid would stimulate immune cells to engage the mechanism of
    (a) pinocytosis
    (b) phagocytosis
    (c) receptor-mediated pinocytosis
    (d) bulk transport

Level 2 Reviewing Concepts

1. What advantage does a cell have if its nucleus is enclosed within a membrane?
2. List the three basic concepts that make up modern cell theory.
3. By what four passive processes do substances get into and out of cells?
4. Explain the similarities and differences between facilitated diffusion and active transport.
5. What three major factors determine whether a substance can diffuse across a plasmalemma?
6. What are organelles? Identify the two broad categories into which organelles may be divided and describe the main difference between these groups.
7. What is the relationship between mitotic rate and the frequency of cell division?
8. List the stages of mitosis in order and briefly describe the events that occur in each.
9. What are four general functions of the plasmalemma?
10. Discuss the two major functions of microfilaments.

Level 3 Critical Thinking

1. Why does the skin of your hands get swollen and wrinkled if you soak them in fresh water for a long time?
2. When skin that is damaged by sunburn "peels," large areas of epidermal cells are often shed simultaneously. Why does the shedding occur this way?
3. What is the benefit of having some organelles enclosed by a membrane similar to a cellular membrane?
4. Experimental evidence demonstrates that the transport of a certain molecule exhibits the following characteristics: (1) The molecule moves against its concentration gradient, and (2) cellular energy is required for transport to occur. What type of transport process is at work?

3

Tissues and Early Embryology

CHAPTER OBJECTIVES

1. Describe the structural and functional relationships between cells and tissues and classify the tissues of the body into four major categories.
2. Describe the relationship between structure and function for each epithelial type.
3. Define gland and glandular epithelium.
4. Describe modes and types of gland secretion; compare and contrast gland structures.
5. Compare and contrast the structural and functional characteristics of connective tissue elements.
6. Describe the general characteristics and locations of different connective tissue types.
7. Compare embryonic and adult connective tissues.
8. Explain how epithelia and connective tissues combine to form membranes and specify the functions of each membrane type.
9. Describe how connective tissues establish the framework of the body.
10. Compare and contrast the three types of muscle tissue in terms of structure, function, and location.
11. Discuss the basic structure and function of neural tissue.
12. Distinguish between neurons and neuroglia; discuss the functions of each.
13. Describe how nutrition and aging affect tissues.

A big corporation is a lot like a living organism, although it depends on its employees, rather than cells, to ensure its survival. It may take thousands of employees to keep the corporation going, and their duties vary—no one employee can do everything. So, corporations usually have divisions with broad functions such as marketing, production, and maintenance. The functions performed by the body are much more diverse than those of corporations, and no single cell contains the metabolic machinery and organelles needed to perform all of those functions. Instead, through the process of differentiation, each cell develops a characteristic set of structural features and a limited number of functions. These structures and functions can be quite distinct from those of nearby cells. Nevertheless, cells in a given location all work together. A detailed examination of the body reveals a number of patterns at the cellular level. Although the body contains trillions of cells, there are only about 200 types of cells. These cell types combine to form **tissues**, collections of specialized cells and cell products that perform a relatively limited number of functions. *Histology* is the study of the minute structure of cells, tissues, and organs in relation to their function. There are four **primary tissue types**: *epithelial tissue, connective tissue, muscle tissue,* and *neural tissue.* The basic functions of these tissue types are introduced in Figure 3.1.

This chapter will discuss the characteristics of each major tissue type, focusing on the relationship between cellular organization and tissue function. As noted in Chapter 2, histology is the study of groups of specialized cells and cell products that work together to perform specific functions.

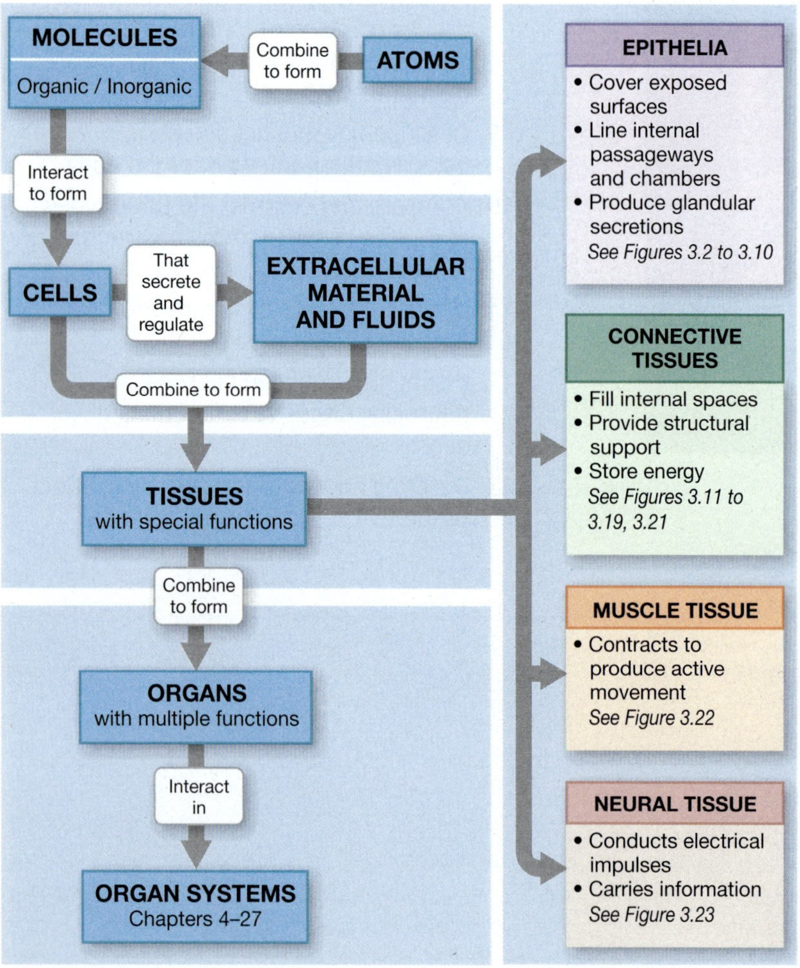

Figure 3.1 An Orientation to the Tissues of the Body
An overview of the levels of organization in the body, and an introduction to some of the functions of the four tissue types.

This chapter introduces the basic histological concepts needed to understand the patterns of tissue interaction in the organs and systems considered in later chapters.

It is important to realize at the outset that tissue samples usually undergo considerable manipulation before microscopic examination. For example, the photomicrographs appearing in this chapter are of tissue samples that were removed, preserved in a fixative solution, and embedded in a medium that made thin sectioning possible. The plane of section is determined by the orientation of the embedded tissue with respect to the knife blade. By varying the sectional plane, one can obtain useful information about the three-dimensional anatomy of a structure (Figure 1.11, ∞ p. 17). However, the appearance of a tissue in histological preparations will vary markedly depending upon the plane of section, as indicated in Figure 1.12, ∞ p. 18 . Even within a single plane of section, the internal organization of a cell or tissue will vary as the level of section changes. You should keep these limitations in mind as you review the micrographs found throughout this text.

Epithelial Tissue

Epithelial tissue includes epithelia and glands; glands are secretory structures derived from epithelia. An **epithelium** (ep-i-THĒ-lē-um; plural, *epithelia*) is a sheet of cells that covers an exposed surface or lines an internal cavity or passageway. Each epithelium is a barrier with specific properties. Epithelia cover every exposed body surface. The surface of the skin is a good example, but epithelia also line the digestive, respiratory, reproductive, and urinary tracts—passageways that communicate with the outside world. Epithelia also line internal cavities and passageways, such as the chest cavity, fluid-filled chambers in the brain, eye, inner ear, and the inner surfaces of blood vessels and the heart.

Important characteristics of epithelia include the following:

1. *Cellularity:* Epithelia are composed almost entirely of cells bound closely together by cell junctions. There is little or no intercellular space between the cells in epithelial tissues. (In most other tissues, extracellular fluid or fibers separate the individual cells.)
2. *Polarity:* An epithelium always has an exposed *apical surface* that faces the exterior of the body or some internal space. It also has an attached *basal surface,* where the epithelium is attached to adjacent tissues. The surfaces differ in plasmalemma structure and function. Whether the epithelium contains a single layer of cells or multiple layers, the organelles and other cytoplasmic components are not evenly distributed between the exposed and attached surfaces. **Polarity** is the term for this uneven distribution.
3. *Attachment:* The basal surface of a typical epithelium is bound to a thin **basal lamina**. The basal lamina is a complex structure produced by the epithelium and cells of the underlying connective tissue.
4. *Avascularity:* Epithelia do not contain blood vessels. Because of this **avascular** (ā-VAS-kū-lar; *a-*, without + *vas*, vessel) condition, epithelial cells must obtain nutrients by diffusion or absorption across the apical or basal surfaces.
5. *Arranged into sheets or layers:* All epithelial tissue is composed of a sheet of cells one or more layers thick.
6. *Regeneration:* Epithelial cells damaged or lost at the surface are continually replaced through the divisions of stem cells within the epithelium.

Functions of Epithelial Tissue

Epithelia perform several essential functions:

1. *Provide physical protection:* Epithelia protect exposed and internal surfaces from abrasion, dehydration, and destruction by chemical or biological agents.
2. *Control permeability:* Any substance that enters or leaves the body has to cross an epithelium. Some epithelia are relatively impermeable, whereas others are permeable to compounds as large as proteins. Many epithelia contain the molecular "machinery" needed for selective absorption or secretion. The epithelial barrier can be regulated and modified in response to various stimuli. For example, hormones can affect the transport of ions and nutrients through epithelial cells. Even physical stress can alter the structure and properties of epithelia—think of the calluses that form on your hands when you do rough work for a period of time.
3. *Provide sensation:* Most epithelia are extensively innervated by sensory nerves. Specialized epithelial cells can detect changes in the environment and convey information about such changes to the nervous system. For example, touch receptors in the deepest epithelial layers of the skin respond to pressure by stimulating adjacent sensory nerves. A **neuroepithelium** is a specialized sensory epithelium. Neuroepithelia are found in special sense organs that provide the sensations of smell, taste, sight, equilibrium, and hearing.
4. *Produce specialized secretions:* Epithelial cells that produce secretions are called **gland cells.** Individual gland cells are often scattered among other cell types in an epithelium. In a **glandular epithelium**, most or all of the epithelial cells produce secretions.

Specializations of Epithelial Cells [Figure 3.2]

Epithelial cells have several specializations that distinguish them from other body cells. Many epithelial cells are specialized for (1) the production of secretions, (2) the movement of fluids over the epithelial surface, or (3) the movement of fluids through the epithelium itself. These specialized epithelial cells usually show a definite polarity along the axis that extends from the *apical surface*, where the cell is exposed to an internal or external environment, to the *basolateral surface*, where the epithelium contacts the basal lamina and neighboring epithelial cells. This polarity means that (1) the intracellular organelles are unevenly distributed, and (2) the apical and basolateral plasmalemmae differ in terms of their associated proteins and functions. The actual arrangement of organelles varies depending on the functions of the individual cells.

Most epithelial cells have microvilli on their exposed apical surfaces; there may be just a few, or they may carpet the entire surface. Microvilli are especially abundant on epithelial surfaces where absorption and secretion occur, such as along portions of the digestive and urinary tracts. p. 35 The epithelial cells in these locations are transport specialists, and a cell with microvilli has at least 20 times the surface area of a cell without them. Increased surface area provides the cell with a much greater ability to absorb or secrete across the plasmalemma. Microvilli are shown in Figure 3.2. **Stereocilia** are very long microvilli (up to 250 μm) that are incapable of movement. Stereocilia are found along portions of the male reproductive tract and on receptor cells of the inner ear.

Figure 3.2b shows the apical surface of a **ciliated epithelium**. A typical ciliated cell contains about 250 cilia that beat in a coordinated fashion. Substances are moved over the epithelial surface by the synchronized

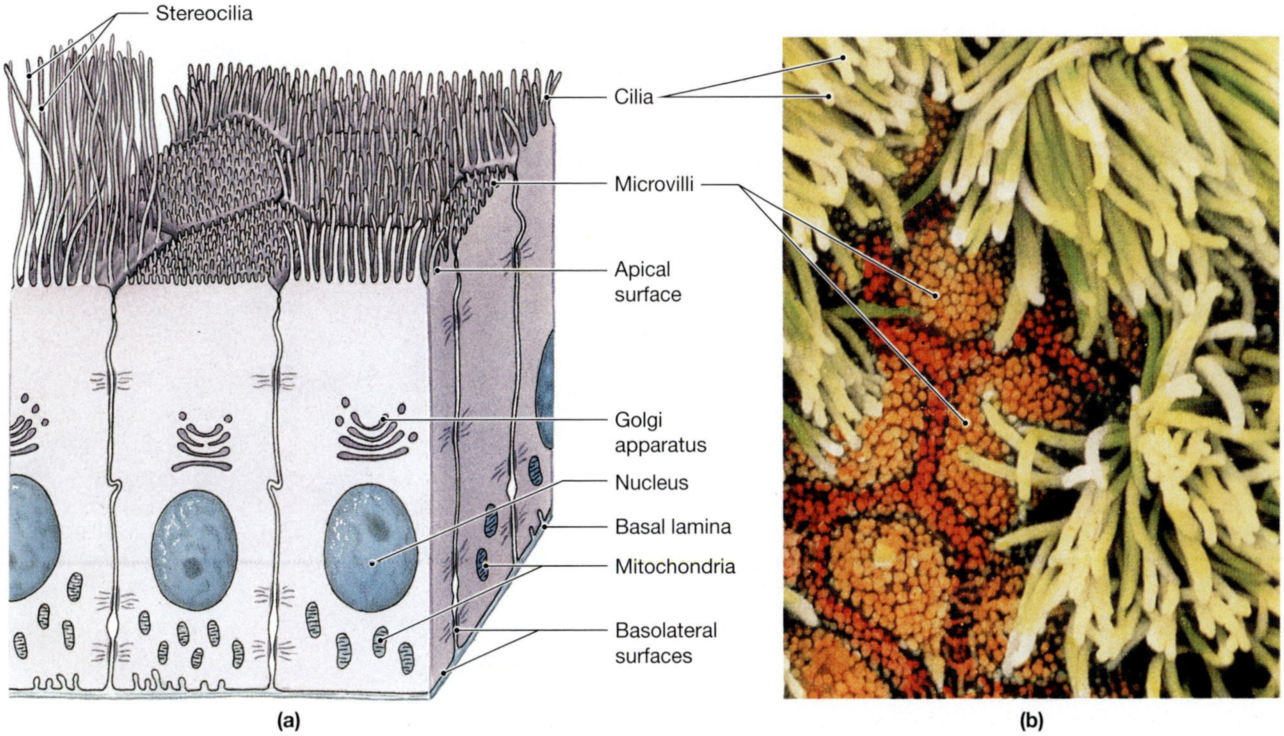

Figure 3.2 Polarity of Epithelial Cells
(a) Many epithelial cells differ in internal organization along an axis between the apical surface and the basal lamina. The apical surface frequently bears microvilli; less often, it may have cilia or (very rarely) stereocilia. A single cell typically has only one type of process; stereocilia and microvilli are shown together to highlight their relative proportions. *(All three would not normally be on the same group of cells but are depicted here for purposes of illustration.)* Tight junctions prevent movement of pathogens or diffusion of dissolved materials between the cells. Folds of plasmalemma near the base of the cell increase the surface area exposed to the basal lamina. Mitochondria are typically concentrated at the basolateral region, probably to provide energy for the cell's transport activities. **(b)** An SEM showing the surface of the epithelium that lines most of the respiratory tract. The small, bristly areas are microvilli found on the exposed surfaces of mucus-producing cells that are scattered among the ciliated epithelial cells. (SEM × 15,846)

beating of cilia, like a continuously moving escalator. For example, the ciliated epithelium that lines the respiratory tract moves mucus from the lungs toward the throat. The mucus traps particles and pathogens and carries them away from more delicate surfaces deeper in the lungs.

Maintaining the Integrity of the Epithelium

Three factors are involved in maintaining the physical integrity of an epithelium: (1) intercellular connections, (2) attachment to the basal lamina, and (3) epithelial maintenance and renewal.

Intercellular Connections [Figure 3.3]

Cells in epithelia are usually bound together by a variety of cell junctions, as detailed in **Figure 2.19**, p. 44. There is often an extensive infolding of opposing plasmalemmae that both interlocks the cells and increases the surface area of the cell junctions. Note the degree of interlocking between plasmalemmae in **Figure 3.3a,c**. The extensive connections between cells hold them together and may deny access to chemicals or pathogens that may contact their free surfaces. The combination of cell junctions, CAMs (cell adhesion molecules), intercellular cement, and physical interlocking gives the epithelium great strength and stability (**Figure 3.3b**).

Attachment to the Basal Lamina [Figure 3.3b]

Epithelial cells not only hold onto one another, they also remain firmly connected to the rest of the body. The basal surface of a typical epithelium is attached to the **basal lamina** (LAM-i-na; *lamina*, thin layer). The superficial portion of the basal lamina consists of the *clear layer* (also termed the lamina lucida; *lamina*, layer + *lucida*, clear), a region dominated by glycoproteins and a network of fine microfilaments. The clear layer of the basal lamina provides a barrier that restricts the movement of proteins and other large molecules from the underlying connective tissue into the epithelium. In most epithelial tissues, the basal lamina has a second, deeper layer, called the *dense layer* (lamina densa), that is secreted by the underlying connective tissue cells. The dense layer contains bundles of coarse protein fibers that give the basal lamina its strength. Attachments between the protein fibers of the clear layer and the dense layer bind them together.

Epithelial Maintenance and Renewal

An epithelium must continually repair and renew itself. The rate of cell division varies depending on the rate of loss of epithelial cells at the surface. Epithelial cells lead hard lives, for they may be exposed to disruptive enzymes, toxic chemicals, pathogenic bacteria, and mechanical abrasion. Under severe conditions, such as those encountered inside the small intestine, an epithelial cell may survive for just a day or two before it is destroyed. The only way the epithelium can maintain its integrity over time is through continual division of stem cells. These stem cells, also known as **germinative cells**, are usually found close to the basal lamina.

CONCEPT CHECK

1. Identify the four primary tissue types.
2. List four characteristics of epithelia.
3. What are two specializations of epithelial cells?

See blue "Answers" tab at back of book.

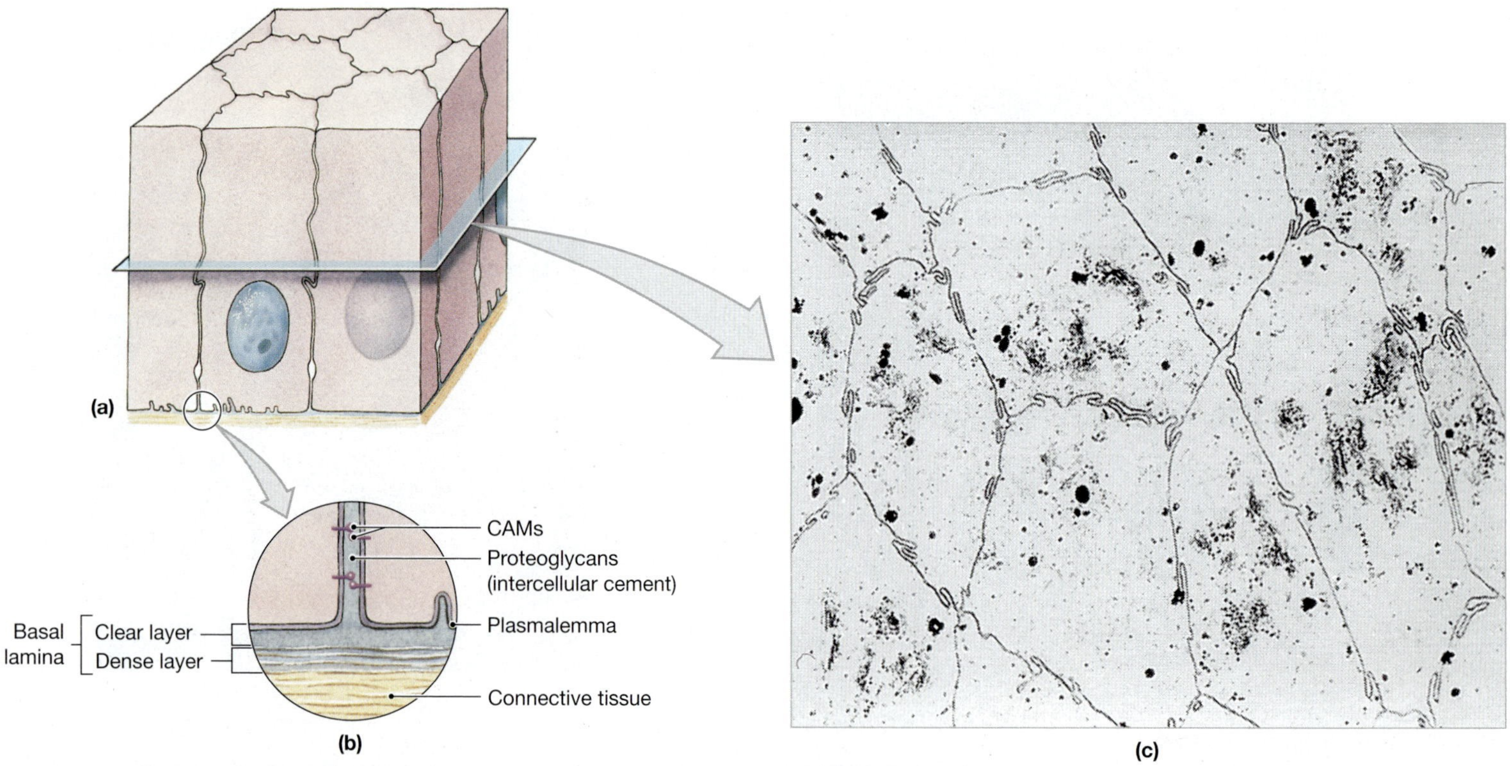

Figure 3.3 Epithelia and Basal Laminae
The integrity of the epithelium depends on connections between adjacent epithelial cells and their attachment to the underlying basal laminae. **(a)** Epithelial cells are usually packed together and interconnected by intercellular attachments. (*See Figure 2.19*) **(b)** At their basal surfaces, epithelia are attached to a basal lamina that forms the boundary between the epithelial cells and the underlying connective tissue. **(c)** Adjacent epithelial plasmalemmae are often interlocked. The TEM, magnified 2600 times, shows the degree of interlocking between columnar epithelial cells.

Classification of Epithelia

Epithelia are classified according to the number of cell layers and the shape of the cells at the exposed surface. The classification scheme recognizes two types of layering—*simple* and *stratified*—and three cell shapes—*squamous*, *cuboidal*, and *columnar*.

If there is only a single layer of cells covering the basal lamina, the epithelium is a **simple epithelium**. Simple epithelia are relatively thin, and because all the cells have the same polarity, the nuclei form a row at roughly the same distance from the basal lamina. Because they are so thin, simple epithelia are also relatively fragile. A single layer of cells cannot provide much mechanical protection, and simple epithelia are found only in protected areas inside the body. They line internal compartments and passageways, including the ventral body cavities, such as the chambers of the heart, and all blood vessels.

Simple epithelia are also characteristic of regions where secretion, absorption, or filtration occurs, such as the lining of the intestines and the gas-exchange surfaces of the lungs. In these places, the thin single layer of simple epithelia provides an advantage, for it lessens the distance involved and thus the time required for materials to pass through or across the epithelial barrier.

A **stratified epithelium** has two or more layers of cells above the basal lamina. Stratified epithelia are usually found in areas subject to mechanical or chemical stresses, such as the surface of the skin and the lining of the mouth. The multiple layers of cells in a stratified epithelium make it thicker and sturdier than a simple epithelium. Regardless of whether an epithelium is simple or stratified, the epithelium must regenerate, replacing its cells over time. The germinative cells are always at or near the basal lamina. This means that in a simple epithelium, the germinative cells form part of the exposed epithelial surface, whereas in a stratified epithelium, the germinative cells are covered by more superficial cells.

Combining the two basic epithelial layouts (simple and stratified) and the three possible cell shapes (squamous, cuboidal, and columnar) enables one to describe almost every epithelium in the body.

Squamous Epithelia [Figure 3.4]

In a **squamous epithelium** (SKWĀ-mus; *squama*, plate or scale), the cells are thin, flat, and somewhat irregular in shape—like puzzle pieces (**Figure 3.4a**). In a sectional view the nucleus occupies the thickest portion of each cell, and has a flattened shape similar to that of the cell as a whole; from the surface, the cells look like fried eggs laid side by side. A **simple squamous epithelium** is the most delicate type of epithelium in the body. This type of epithelium is found in protected regions where absorption takes place or where a slick, slippery surface reduces friction. Examples include the respiratory exchange surfaces (*alveoli*) of the lungs, the serous membranes lining the ventral body cavities, and the inner surfaces of the circulatory system.

Special names have been given to simple squamous epithelia that line chambers and passageways that do not communicate with the outside world. The simple squamous epithelium that lines the ventral body cavities is known as a **mesothelium** (mez-ō-THĒ-lē-um; *mesos*, middle). The pleura, peritoneum, and pericardium each contain a superficial layer of mesothelium. The simple squamous epithelium lining the heart and all blood vessels is called an **endothelium** (en-dō-THĒ-lē-um).

SIMPLE SQUAMOUS EPITHELIUM

LOCATIONS: Mesothelia lining ventral body cavities; endothelia lining heart and blood vessels; portions of kidney tubules (thin sections of nephron loops); inner lining of cornea; alveoli of lungs

FUNCTIONS: Reduces friction; controls vessel permeability; performs absorption and secretion

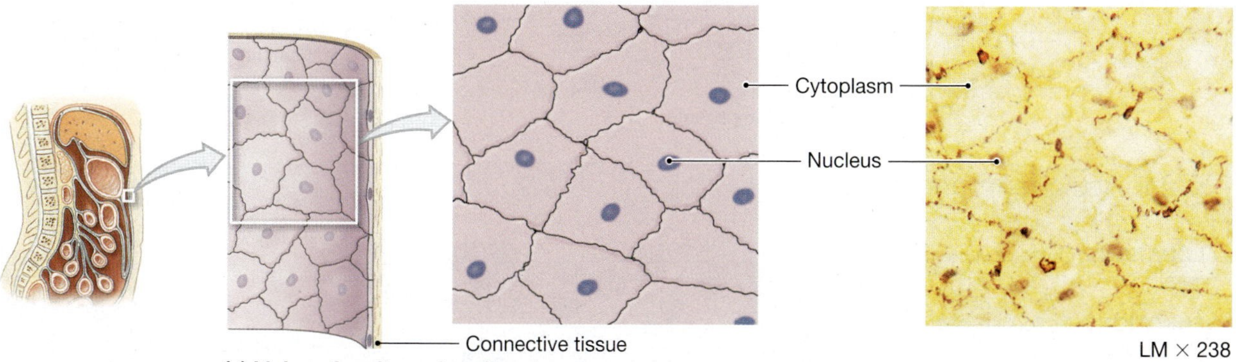

(a) Lining of peritoneal cavity

STRATIFIED SQUAMOUS EPITHELIUM

LOCATIONS: Surface of skin; lining of mouth, throat, esophagus, rectum, anus, and vagina

FUNCTIONS: Provides physical protection against abrasion, pathogens, and chemical attack

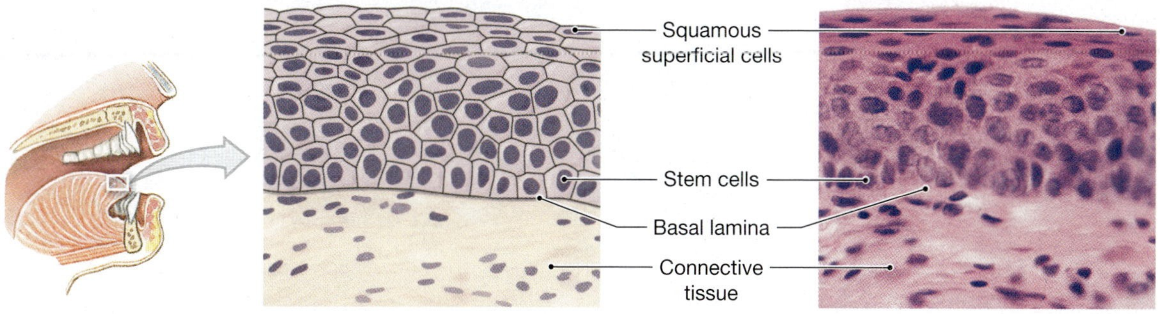

(b) Surface of tongue

Figure 3.4 Histology of Squamous Epithelia
(a) Simple Squamous Epithelium. A superficial view of the simple squamous epithelium (*mesothelium*) that lines the peritoneal cavity. The three-dimensional drawing shows the epithelium in superficial and sectional view. **(b)** Stratified Squamous Epithelium. Sectional views of the stratified squamous epithelium that covers the tongue.

A **stratified squamous epithelium** (Figure 3.4b) is usually found where mechanical stresses are severe. Note how the cells form a series of layers, like a stack of plywood sheets. The surface of the skin and the lining of the mouth, throat, esophagus, rectum, vagina, and anus are areas where this epithelial type provides protection from physical and chemical attack. On exposed body surfaces, where mechanical stress and dehydration are potential problems, the apical layers of epithelial cells are packed with filaments of the protein *keratin*. As a result, the superficial layers are both tough and water resistant, and the epithelium is said to be **keratinized**. A **nonkeratinized** stratified squamous epithelium provides resistance to abrasion, but will dry out and deteriorate unless kept moist. Nonkeratinized stratified squamous epithelia are found in the oral cavity, pharynx, esophagus, rectum, anus, and vagina.

Cuboidal Epithelia [Figure 3.5]

The cells of a **cuboidal epithelium** resemble little hexagonal boxes; they appear square in typical sectional views. Each nucleus is near the center of the cell, with the distance between adjacent nuclei roughly equal to the height of the epithelium. **Simple cuboidal epithelia** provide limited protection and occur in regions where secretion or absorption takes place. Such an epithelium lines portions of the kidney tubules, as seen in Figure 3.5a. In the pancreas and salivary glands, simple cuboidal epithelia secrete enzymes and buffers and line the ducts that discharge those secretions. The thyroid gland contains chambers called *thyroid follicles* that are lined by a cuboidal secretory epithelium. Thyroid hormones, especially *thyroxine*, accumulate within the follicles before they are released into the bloodstream.

SIMPLE CUBOIDAL EPITHELIUM

LOCATIONS: Glands; ducts; portions of kidney tubules; thyroid gland

FUNCTIONS: Limited protection, secretion, absorption

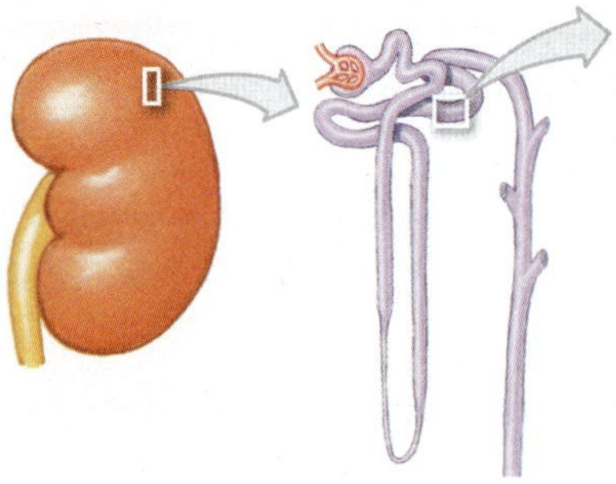

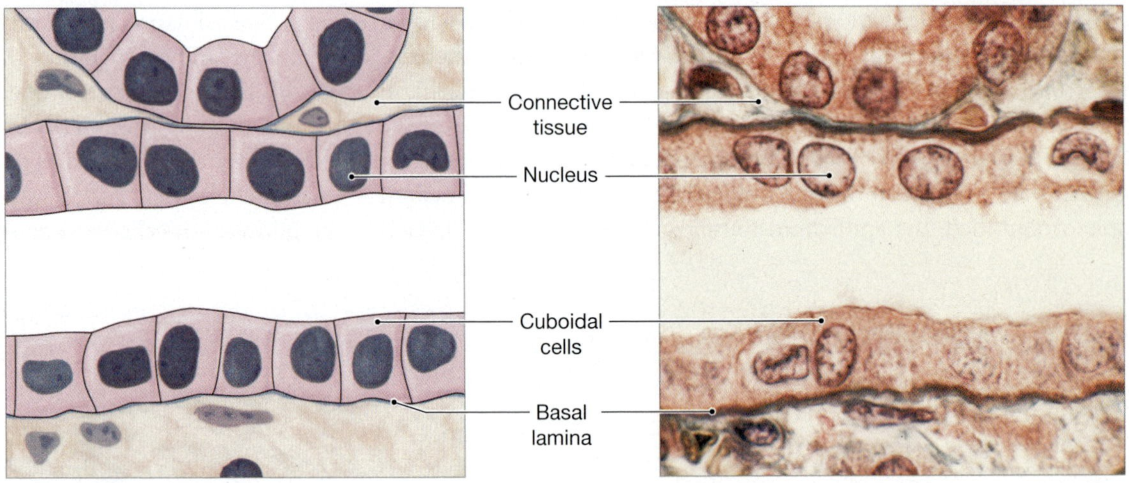

(a) Kidney tubule

STRATIFIED CUBOIDAL EPITHELIUM

LOCATIONS: Lining of some ducts (rare)

FUNCTIONS: Protection, secretion, absorption

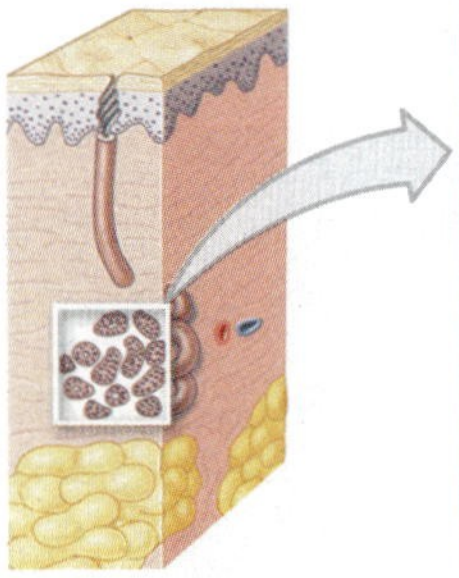

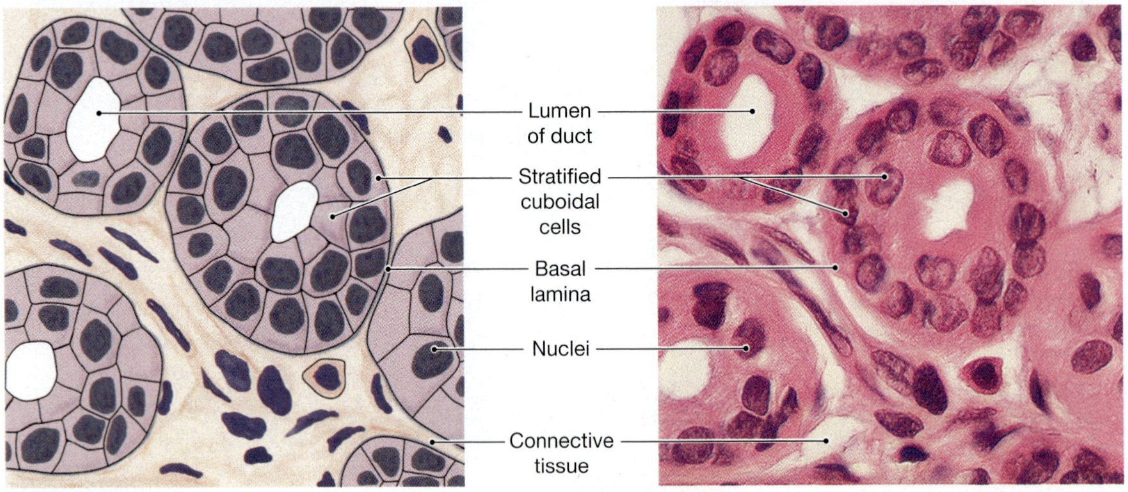

(b) Sweat gland duct

Figure 3.5 Histology of Cuboidal Epithelia
(a) Simple Cuboidal Epithelium. A section through the simple cuboidal epithelium lining a kidney tubule. The diagrammatic view emphasizes structural details that permit the classification of an epithelium as cuboidal. **(b)** Stratified Cuboidal Epithelium. A sectional view of the stratified cuboidal epithelium lining a sweat gland duct in the skin.

Stratified cuboidal epithelia are relatively rare; they are often found along the ducts of sweat glands (Figure 3.5b) and in the larger ducts of some other exocrine glands, such as the mammary glands.

Columnar Epithelia [Figure 3.6]

Columnar epithelial cells, like cuboidal epithelial cells, are also hexagonal in cross section, but in contrast to cuboidal cells their height is much greater than their width. The nuclei are crowded into a narrow band close to the basal lamina, and the height of the epithelium is several times the distance between two nuclei (Figure 3.6a). A **simple columnar epithelium** provides some protection and may also be encountered in areas where absorption or secretion occurs. This type of epithelium lines the stomach, intestinal tract, uterine tubes, and many excretory ducts.

Stratified columnar epithelia are relatively rare, providing protection along portions of the pharynx, urethra, and anus, as well as along a few large excretory ducts. The epithelium may have two layers (Figure 3.6b) or multiple layers; when multiple layers exist, only the superficial cells have the classic columnar shape.

Pseudostratified and Transitional Epithelia [Figure 3.7]

Two specialized forms of epithelia are found lining the passageways of the respiratory system and the hollow conducting organs of the urinary system.

Portions of the respiratory tract contain a specialized columnar epithelium, called a **pseudostratified columnar epithelium**, which includes a mixture of cell types. Because their nuclei are situated at varying distances from the surface, the epithelium appears to be layered or stratified. Because

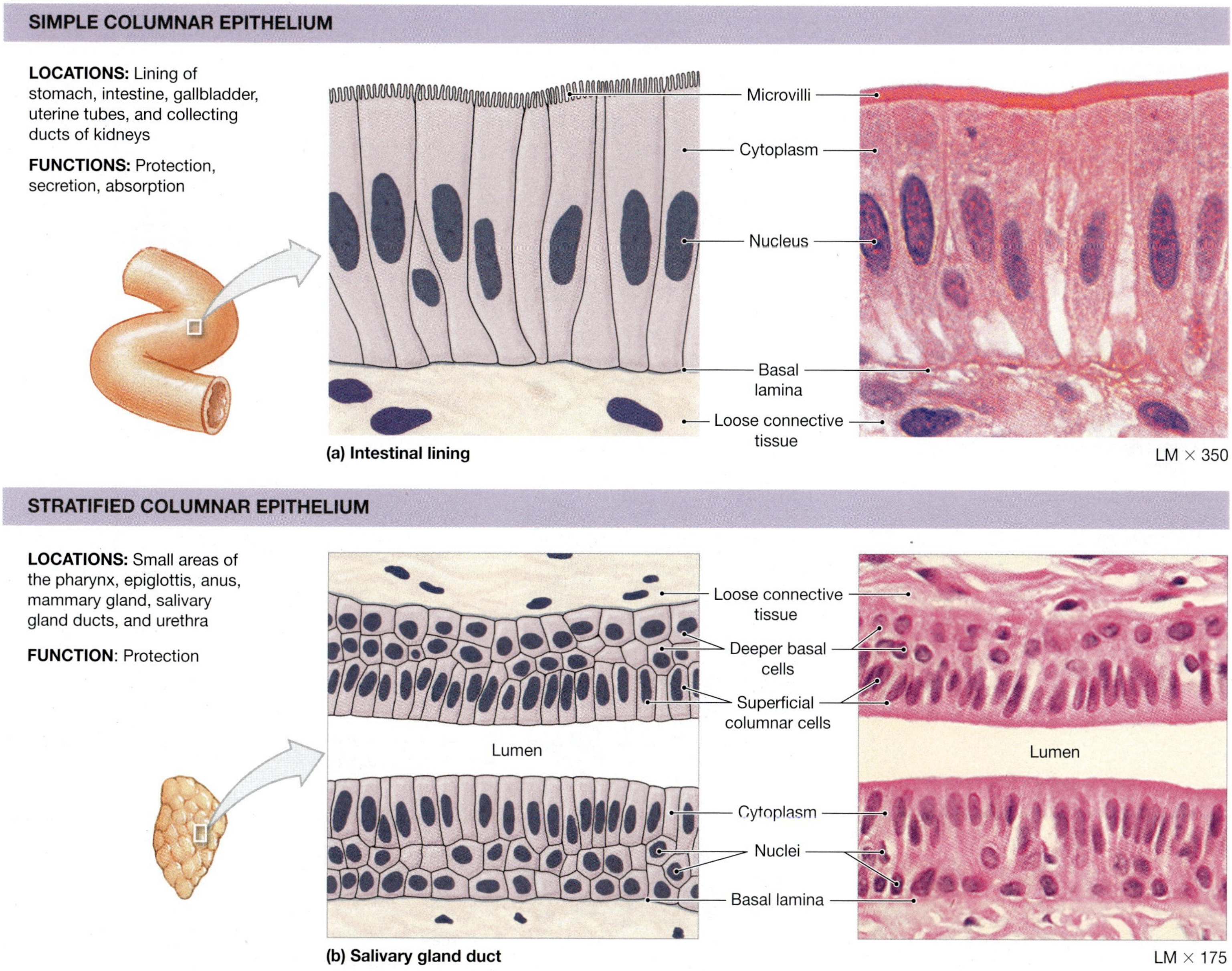

Figure 3.6 Histology of Columnar Epithelia
(a) Simple Columnar Epithelium. A light micrograph showing the characteristics of simple columnar epithelium. In the diagrammatic sketch, note the relationships between the height and width of each cell; the relative size, shape, and location of nuclei; and the distance between adjacent nuclei. Contrast these observations with the corresponding characteristics of simple cuboidal epithelia. **(b)** Stratified Columnar Epithelium. A stratified columnar epithelium is sometimes found along large ducts, such as this salivary gland duct. Note the overall height of the epithelium and the location and orientation of the nuclei.

all of the cells rest on the basal lamina, this epithelium is actually a simple epithelium; therefore, it is known as a pseudostratified columnar epithelium. The exposed epithelial cells typically possess cilia, so this is often called a **pseudostratified ciliated columnar epithelium** (Figure 3.7a). This type of epithelium lines most of the nasal cavity, the trachea (windpipe), bronchi, and also portions of the male reproductive tract.

Transitional epithelia, shown in Figure 3.7b, line the renal pelvis, the ureters, and the urinary bladder. Transitional epithelium is a stratified epithelium with special characteristics that allow it to distend, or stretch. When stretched, transitional epithelia resemble a stratified, nonkeratinized epithelium with two or three layers. In an empty bladder (Figure 3.7b), the epithelium seems to have many layers, and the outermost cells are typically rounded cuboidal cells. The design of transitional epithelium allows for considerable distention of the epithelium without damage to the component cells.

Glandular Epithelia

Many epithelia contain gland cells that produce secretions. *Exocrine glands* discharge their secretions onto an epithelial surface. Exocrine glands are classified by the type of secretions released, the structure of the gland, and the mode of secretion. Exocrine glands, which may be either unicellular or multicellular, secrete mucins, enzymes, water, and waste products. These secretions are released at the apical surfaces of the individual gland cells.

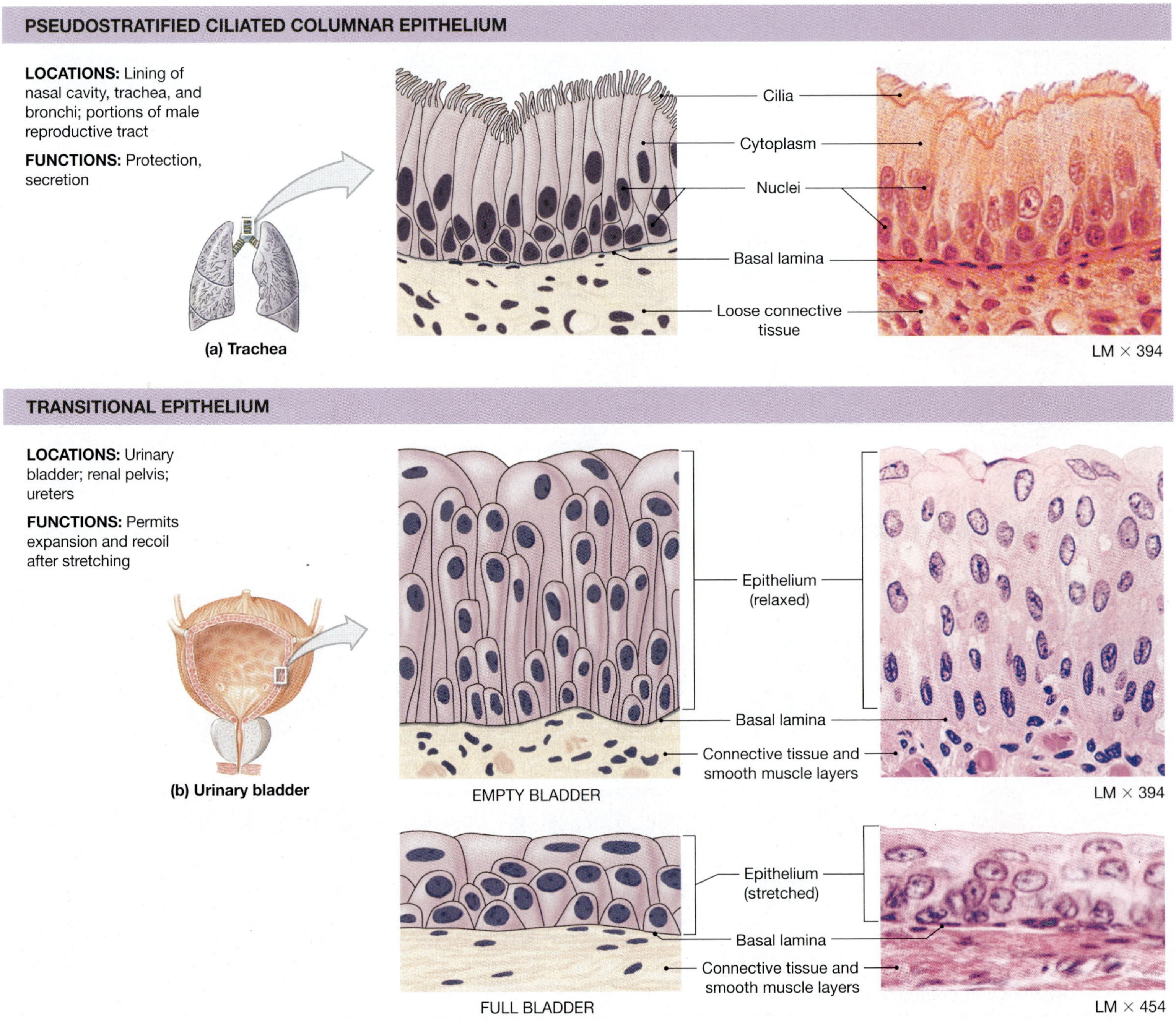

Figure 3.7 Histology of Pseudostratified Ciliated Columnar and Transitional Epithelia
(a) Pseudostratified Ciliated Columnar Epithelium. The pseudostratified, ciliated, columnar epithelium of the respiratory tract. Note the uneven layering of the nuclei. **(b)** Transitional Epithelium. A sectional view of the transitional epithelium lining the urinary bladder. The cells from an empty bladder are in the relaxed state, while those lining a full urinary bladder show the effects of stretching on the arrangement of cells in the epithelium.

Endocrine glands are ductless glands that release their secretions directly into the interstitial fluids, lymph, or blood.

Types of Secretion

Exocrine (*exo-*, outside) secretions are discharged onto the surface of the skin or onto an epithelial surface lining one of the internal passageways that communicates with the exterior through an epithelial **duct** that is connected to the surface of the skin or epithelial surface. These ducts may release the secretion unaltered, or may alter it by a variety of mechanisms, including reabsorption, secretion, or countertransport. Enzymes entering the digestive tract, perspiration on the skin, and the milk produced by mammary glands are examples of exocrine secretions.

Exocrine glands may be categorized according to the nature of the secretion produced:

- *Serous glands* secrete a watery solution that usually contains enzymes, such as the salivary amylase in saliva.
- *Mucous glands* secrete glycoproteins called **mucins** (MŪ-sins) that absorb water to form a slippery *mucus*, such as the mucus in saliva.
- *Mixed exocrine glands* contain more than one type of gland cell and may produce two different exocrine secretions, one serous and the other mucous.

Endocrine (*endo-*, inside) secretions are released by exocytosis from the gland cells into the fluid surrounding the cell. These secretions, called **hormones**, diffuse into the blood for distribution to other regions of the body, where they regulate or coordinate the activities of various tissues, organs, and organ systems. Endocrine cells, tissues, organs, and hormones are considered further in Chapter 19.

Gland Structure [Figures 3.8/3.9]

In epithelia that contain scattered gland cells, the individual secretory cells are called **unicellular glands**. **Multicellular glands** include glandular epithelia and aggregations of gland cells that produce exocrine or endocrine secretions.

Unicellular exocrine glands secrete mucins. There are two types of unicellular glands, *goblet cells* and *mucous cells*. Goblet cells and mucous

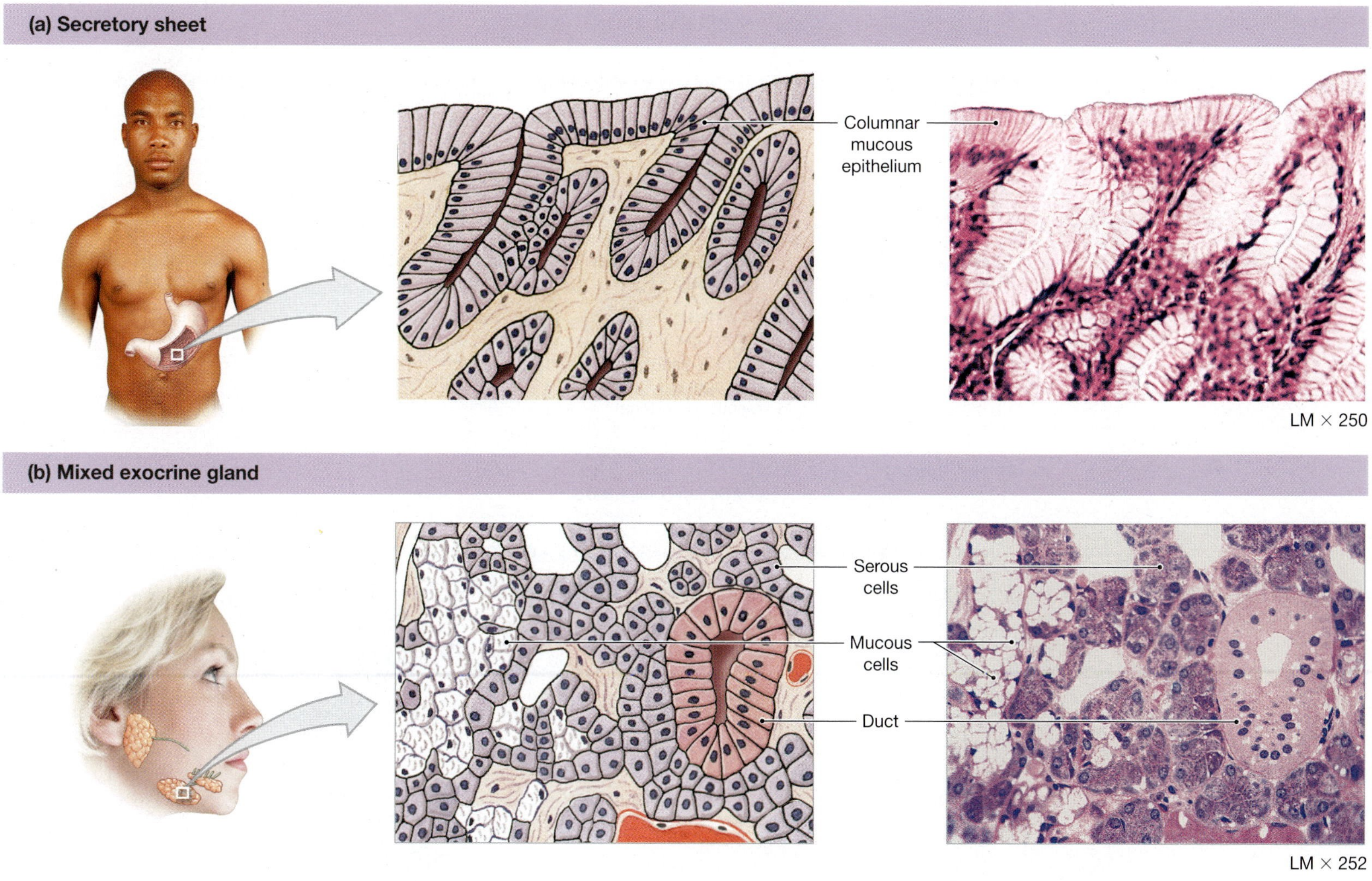

Figure 3.8 Histology of Mucous and Mixed Glandular Epithelia
(a) The interior of the stomach is lined by a secretory sheet whose secretions protect the walls from acids and enzymes. (The acids and enzymes are produced by glands that discharge their secretions onto the mucous epithelial surface.)
(b) The submandibular salivary gland is a mixed gland containing cells that produce both serous and mucous secretions. The mucous cells contain large vesicles containing mucins, and they look pale and foamy. The serous cells secrete enzymes, and the proteins stain darkly.

cells are found scattered among other epithelial cells. For example, mucous cells are found in the pseudostratified ciliated columnar epithelium that lines the trachea, while the columnar epithelium of the small and large intestines contains an abundance of goblet cells.

The simplest **multicellular exocrine gland** is called a **secretory sheet**. In a secretory sheet, glandular cells dominate the epithelium and release their secretions into an inner compartment (Figure 3.8a). The mucus-secreting cells that line the stomach are an example of a secretory sheet. Their continual secretion protects the stomach from the acids and enzymes it contains.

Most other multicellular glands are found in pockets set back from the epithelial surface. Figure 3.8b shows one example, a salivary gland that produces mucus and digestive enzymes. These multicellular exocrine glands have two epithelial components: a glandular portion that produces the secretion and a duct that carries the secretion to the epithelial surface.

Two characteristics are used to describe the organization of a multicellular gland: (1) the shape of the secretory portion of the gland and (2) the branching pattern of the duct.

1. Glands made up of cells arranged in a tube are **tubular**; those made up of cells in a blind pocket are **alveolar** (al-VĒ-ō-lar; *alveolus*, sac) or **acinar** (AS-i-nar; *acinus*, chamber). Glands that have a combination of the two arrangements are called **tubuloalveolar** or **tubuloacinar**.
2. A duct is referred to as **simple** if it does not branch and **compound** if it branches repeatedly. Each glandular area may have its own duct; in the case of branched glands, several glands share a common duct.

Figure 3.9 diagrams this method of classification based on gland structure. Specific examples of each gland type will be discussed in later chapters.

Modes of Secretion [Figure 3.10]

A glandular epithelial cell may use one of three methods to release its secretions: *merocrine secretion*, *apocrine secretion*, or *holocrine secretion*. In **merocrine secretion** (MER-ō-krin; *meros*, part + *krinein*, to separate), the secretory product is released through exocytosis (Figure 3.10a). This is the most common mode of secretion. For example, goblet cells release **mucus** through merocrine secretion. **Apocrine secretion** (AP-ō-krin; *apo-*, off) involves the loss of cytoplasm as well as the secretory product (Figure 3.10b). The apical portion of the cytoplasm becomes packed with secretory vesicles before it is shed. Milk production by the lactiferous glands in the breasts involves a combination of merocrine and apocrine secretion.

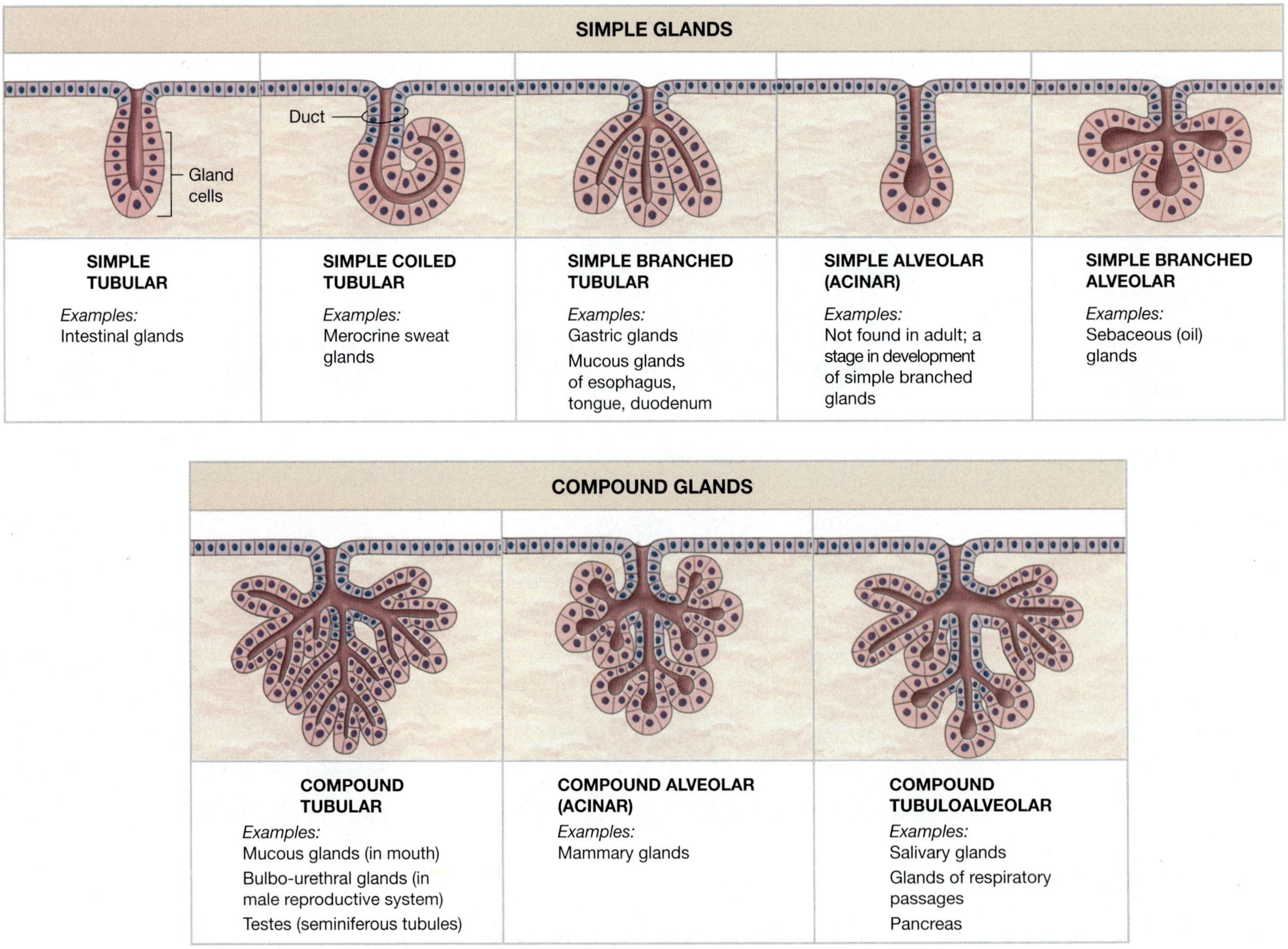

Figure 3.9 A Structural Classification of Simple and Compound Exocrine Glands

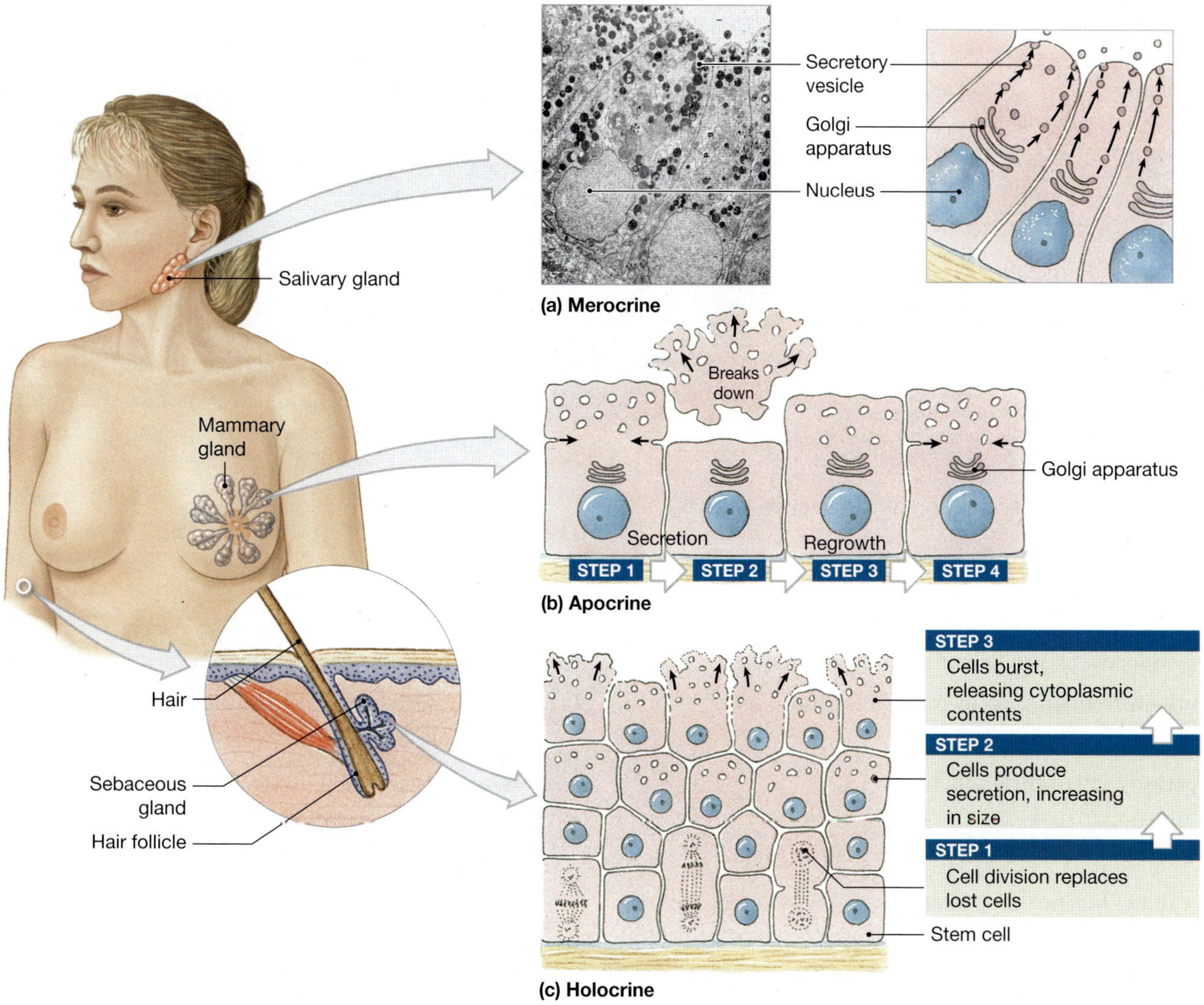

Figure 3.10 Mechanisms of Glandular Secretion
Diagrammatic representation of the mechanisms of exocrine gland secretion. **(a)** In merocrine secretion, secretory vesicles are discharged at the surface of the gland cell through exocytosis. **(b)** Apocrine secretion involves the loss of cytoplasm. Inclusions, secretory vesicles, and other cytoplasmic components are shed at the apical surface of the cell. The gland cell then undergoes a period of growth and repair before releasing additional secretions. **(c)** Holocrine secretion occurs as superficial gland cells break apart. Continued secretion involves the replacement of these cells through the mitotic division of underlying stem cells.

Merocrine and apocrine secretions leave the nucleus and Golgi apparatus of the cell intact, so it can perform repairs and continue secreting. **Holocrine secretion** (HOL-ō-krin; *holos*, entire) destroys the gland cell. During holocrine secretion, the entire cell becomes packed with secretory products and then bursts apart (Figure 3.10c). The secretion is released and the cell dies. Further secretion depends on gland cells being replaced by the division of stem cells. Sebaceous glands, associated with hair follicles, produce a waxy hair coating by means of holocrine secretion.

CONCEPT CHECK

1. You look at a tissue under a microscope and see a simple squamous epithelium. Can it be a sample of the skin surface?
2. Why is epithelium regeneration a necessity in a gland that releases its product by holocrine secretion?
3. Ceruminous glands of the external acoustic meatus of the ear release their products by apocrine secretion. What occurs in this mode of secretion?
4. What functions are associated with a simple columnar epithelium?

See blue "Answers" tab at back of book.

Connective Tissues

Connective tissues are found throughout the body but are never exposed to the environment outside the body. Connective tissues include bone, fat, and blood, tissues that are quite different in appearance and function. Nevertheless, all connective tissues have three basic components: (1) specialized cells, (2) extracellular protein fibers, and (3) a fluid known as the **ground substance**. The extracellular fibers and ground substance constitute the **matrix** that surrounds the cells. Although epithelial tissue consists almost entirely of cells, connective tissue consists mostly of extracellular matrix.

Connective tissues perform a variety of functions that involve far more than just connecting body parts together. Those functions include the following:

1. establishing a structural framework for the body;
2. transporting fluids and dissolved materials from one region of the body to another;
3. providing protection for delicate organs;
4. supporting, surrounding, and interconnecting other tissue types;

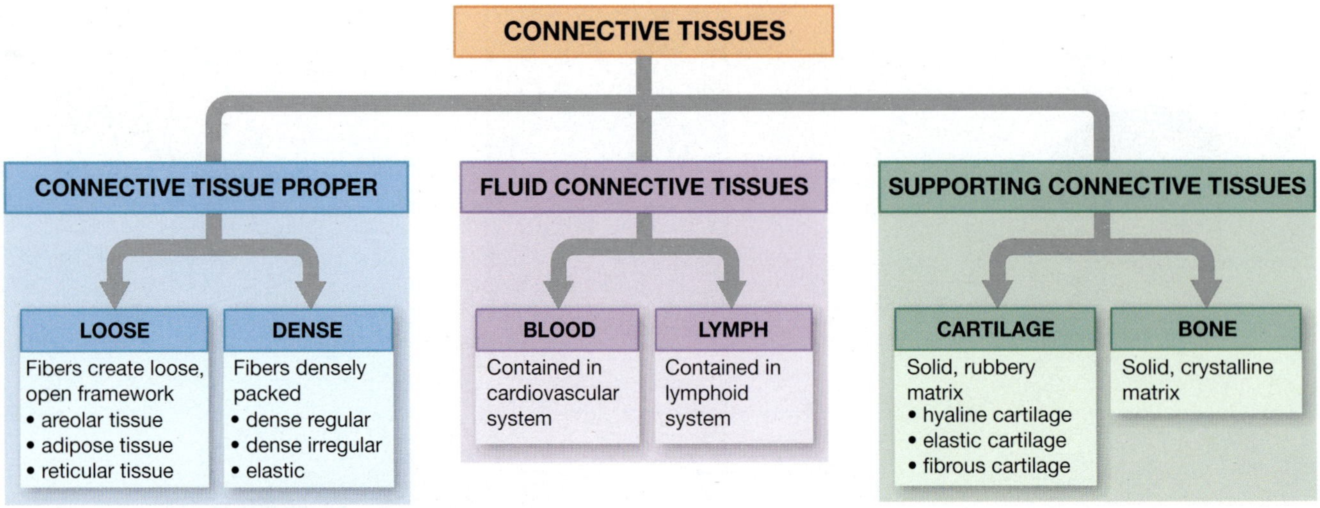

Figure 3.11 **A Classification of Connective Tissues**

5. storing energy reserves, especially in the form of lipids; and
6. defending the body from invasion by microorganisms.

Although most connective tissues have multiple functions, no single connective tissue performs all of these functions.

Classification of Connective Tissues [Figure 3.11]

Connective tissue can be classified into three categories: (1) *connective tissue proper*, (2) *fluid connective tissues*, and (3) *supporting connective tissues*. These categories are introduced in **Figure 3.11**.

1. *Connective tissue proper* refers to connective tissues with many types of cells and extracellular fibers in a syrupy ground substance. These connective tissues may differ in terms of the number of cell types they contain and the relative properties and proportions of fibers and ground substance. *Adipose* (fat) *tissue*, *ligaments*, and *tendons* differ greatly, but all three are examples of connective tissue proper.
2. *Fluid connective tissues* have a distinctive population of cells suspended in a watery matrix that contains dissolved proteins. There are two types of fluid connective tissues: *blood* and *lymph*.
3. *Supporting connective tissues* have a less diverse cell population than connective tissue proper and a matrix that contains closely packed fibers. There are two types of supporting connective tissues: *cartilage* and *bone*. The matrix of cartilage is a gel whose characteristics vary depending on the predominant fiber type. The matrix of bone is said to be **calcified** because it contains mineral deposits, primarily calcium salts. These minerals give the bone strength and rigidity.

Connective Tissue Proper [Figure 3.12 and Table 3.1]

Connective tissue proper contains extracellular fibers, a viscous (syrupy) ground substance, and two classes of cells. **Fixed cells** are stationary and are involved primarily with local maintenance, repair, and energy storage. **Wandering cells** are concerned primarily with the defense and repair of damaged tissues. The number of cells at any given moment varies depending on local conditions. Refer to **Figure 3.12** and Table 3.1 as we describe the cells and fibers of connective tissue proper.

Cells of Connective Tissue Proper

Fixed Cells Fixed cells include *mesenchymal cells*, *fibroblasts*, *fibrocytes*, *fixed macrophages*, *adipocytes*, and, in a few locations, *melanocytes*.

- *Mesenchymal* (MES-en-kī-mul) *cells* are stem cells that are present in many connective tissues. These cells respond to local injury or infection by dividing to produce daughter cells that differentiate into fibroblasts, macrophages, or other connective tissue cells.
- *Fibroblasts* (FĪ-bro-blasts) are one of the two most abundant fixed cells in connective tissue proper and are the only cells always present. These slender or *stellate* (star-shaped) cells are responsible for the production of all connective tissue fibers. Each fibroblast manufactures and secretes protein subunits that interact to form large extracellular fibers. In addition, fibroblasts secrete *hyaluronan*, which gives the ground substance its viscous consistency.
- *Fibrocytes* (FĪ-bro-sīts) differentiate from fibroblasts, and are the second most abundant fixed cell in connective tissue proper. These stellate cells maintain the connective tissue fibers of connective tissue proper. Because their synthetic activity is quite low, the cytoplasm stains quite poorly, and only the nucleus is visible in a standard histological preparation.
- *Fixed macrophages* (MAK-rō-fā-jez; *phagein*, to eat) are large, amoeboid cells that are scattered among the fibers. These cells engulf damaged cells or pathogens that enter the tissue. Although they are not abundant, they play an important role in mobilizing the body's defenses. When stimulated, they release chemicals that activate the immune system and attract large numbers of wandering cells involved in the body's defense mechanisms.
- *Adipocytes* (AD-i-pō-sīts) are also known as fat cells, or *adipose cells*. A typical adipocyte is a fixed cell containing a single, enormous lipid droplet. The nucleus and other organelles are squeezed to one side, so that in section the cell resembles a class ring. The number of fat cells varies from one type of connective tissue to another, from one region of the body to another, and from individual to individual.
- *Melanocytes* (MEL-an-ō-sīts or me-LAN-ō-sīts) synthesize and store a brown pigment, **melanin** (MEL-a-nin), that gives the tissue

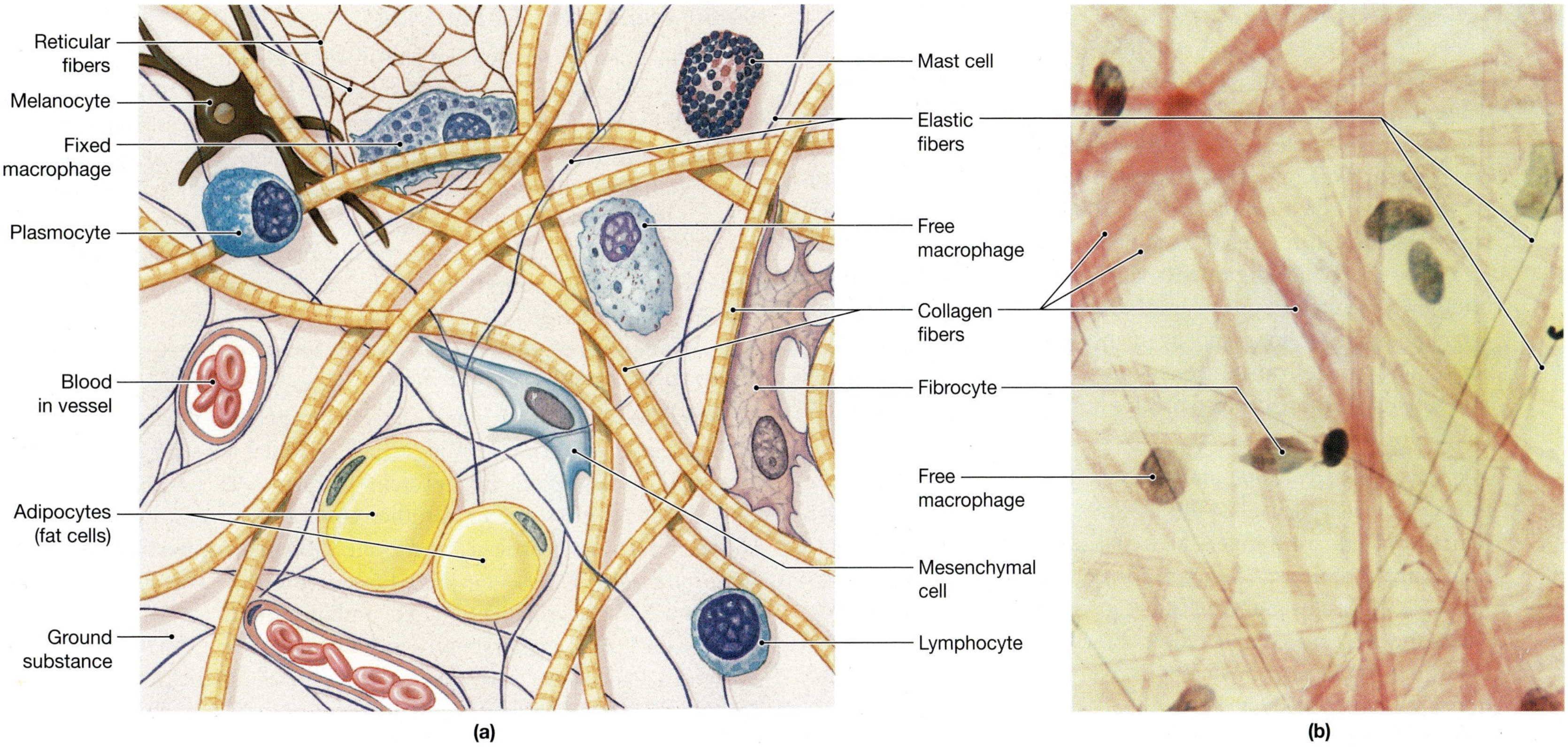

Figure 3.12 Histology of the Cells and Fibers of Connective Tissue Proper
(a) Diagrammatic view of the cells and fibers in areolar tissue, the most common type of connective tissue proper. **(b)** A light micrograph showing the areolar tissue that supports the mesothelium lining the peritoneum. (LM × 502)

TABLE 3.1 A Comparison of Some Functions of Fixed Cells and Wandering Cells

Cell Types	Functions
FIXED CELLS	
Fibroblasts	Produce connective tissue fibers
Fibrocytes	Maintain connective tissue fibers and matrix
Fixed macrophages	Phagocytize pathogens and damaged cells
Adipocytes	Store lipid reserves
Mesenchymal cells	Connective tissue stem cells that can differentiate into other cell types
Melanocytes	Synthesize melanin
WANDERING CELLS	
Free macrophages	Mobile/traveling phagocytic cells (derived from monocytes of the blood)
Mast cells	Stimulate local inflammation
Lymphocytes	Participate in immune response
Neutrophils and eosinophils	Small, phagocytic blood cells that mobilize during infection or tissue injury

a dark color. Melanocytes are common in the epithelium of the skin, where they play a major role in determining skin color. They are also found in the underlying connective tissue (the *dermis*), although their distribution varies widely due to regional, individual, and racial factors. Melanocytes are also abundant in connective tissues of the eyes.

Wandering Cells *Free macrophages*, *mast cells*, *lymphocytes*, *plasmocytes*, *neutrophils*, and *eosinophils* are wandering cells.

- *Free macrophages* are relatively large phagocytic cells that wander rapidly through the connective tissues of the body. When circulating within the blood, these cells are called *monocytes*. In effect, the few fixed macrophages in a tissue provide a "front-line" defense that is reinforced by the arrival of free macrophages and other specialized cells.
- *Mast cells* are small, mobile connective tissue cells often found near blood vessels. The cytoplasm of a mast cell is filled with secretory granules of **histamine** (HIS-ta-mēn) and **heparin** (HEP-a-rin). These chemicals, which are released after injury or infection, stimulate local inflammation.
- *Lymphocytes* (LIM-fō-sīts), like free macrophages, migrate throughout the body. Their numbers increase markedly wherever tissue damage occurs, and some may then develop into **plasmocytes** (plasma cells). Plasmocytes are responsible for the production of *antibodies*, proteins involved in defending the body against disease.
- *Neutrophils* and *eosinophils* are phagocytic blood cells that are smaller than monocytes. These cells migrate through connective tissues in small numbers. When an infection or injury occurs, chemicals released by macrophages and mast cells attract neutrophils and eosinophils in large numbers.

Connective Tissue Fibers [Figures 3.12/3.14/3.15]

Three types of fibers are found in connective tissue: *collagen*, *reticular*, and *elastic fibers*. Fibroblasts produce all three types of fibers through the synthesis and secretion of protein subunits that combine or aggregate within the matrix. Fibrocytes are responsible for maintaining these connective tissue fibers.

1. *Collagen fibers* are long, straight, and unbranched (Figure 3.12). These are the most common, and the strongest, fibers in connective tissue proper. Each collagen fiber consists of three fibrous protein subunits wound together like the strands of a rope; like a rope, a collagen fiber is flexible, yet it is very strong when pulled from either end. This kind of applied force is called *tension*, and the ability to resist tension is called *tensile strength*. **Tendons** (Figure 3.15a, p. 67) consist almost entirely of collagen fibers; they connect skeletal muscles to bones. Typical **ligaments** (LIG-a-ments) resemble tendons, but they connect one bone to another. The parallel alignment of collagen fibers in tendons and ligaments allows them to withstand tremendous forces; uncontrolled muscle contractions or skeletal movements are more likely to break a bone than to snap a tendon or ligament.
2. *Reticular fibers* (*reticulum*, network) contain the same protein subunits as collagen fibers, but the subunits interact in a different way. Reticular fibers are thinner than collagen fibers, and they form a branching, interwoven framework that is tough but flexible. These fibers are especially abundant in organs such as the spleen and liver, where they create a complex three-dimensional network, or *stroma*, that supports the *parenchyma* (pa-RENG-ki-ma), or distinctive functional cells, of these organs (Figures 3.12a and 3.14c). Because they form a network, rather than sharing a common alignment, reticular fibers can resist forces applied from many different directions. They are thus able to stabilize the relative positions of the organ's cells, blood vessels, and nerves despite changing positions and the pull of gravity.
3. *Elastic fibers* contain the protein *elastin*. Elastic fibers are branching and wavy, and after stretching up to 150 percent of their resting length, they recoil to their original dimensions. **Elastic ligaments** contain more elastin rather than collagen fibers. They are relatively rare, but are found in areas requiring more elasticity, such as those interconnecting adjacent vertebrae (Figure 3.15b, p. 67).

Ground Substance [Figure 3.12a]

The cellular and fibrous components of connective tissues are surrounded by a solution known as the ground substance (Figure 3.12a). Ground substance in normal connective tissue proper is clear, colorless, and similar in consistency to maple syrup. In addition to hyaluronan, the ground substance contains a mixture of various proteoglycans and glycoproteins that interact to determine its consistency.

Connective tissue proper can be divided into *loose connective tissues* and *dense connective tissues* based on the relative proportions of cells, fibers, and ground substance.

Embryonic Tissues [Figure 3.13]

Mesenchyme is the first connective tissue to appear in the developing embryo. Mesenchyme contains star-shaped cells that are separated by a matrix that contains very fine protein filaments. This connective tissue (Figure 3.13a) gives rise to all other connective tissues, including fluid connective tissues, cartilage, and bone. **Mucous connective tissue**, or *Wharton's Jelly* (Figure 3.13b), is a loose connective tissue found in many regions of the embryo, including the umbilical cord.

Neither of these embryonic connective tissues is found in the adult. However, many adult connective tissues contain scattered mesenchymal (stem) cells that assist in repairs after the connective tissue has been injured or damaged.

Loose Connective Tissues

Loose connective tissues are the "packing material" of the body. These tissues fill spaces between organs, provide cushioning, and support epithelia. Loose connective tissues also surround and support blood vessels and nerves, store lipids, and provide a route for the diffusion of materials. There are three types of loose connective tissues: *areolar tissue*, *adipose tissue*, and *reticular tissue*.

Areolar Tissue [Figure 3.14a] The least specialized connective tissue in the adult body is **areolar tissue** (*areola*, a little space). This tissue, shown in Figure 3.14a, contains all of the cells and fibers found in any

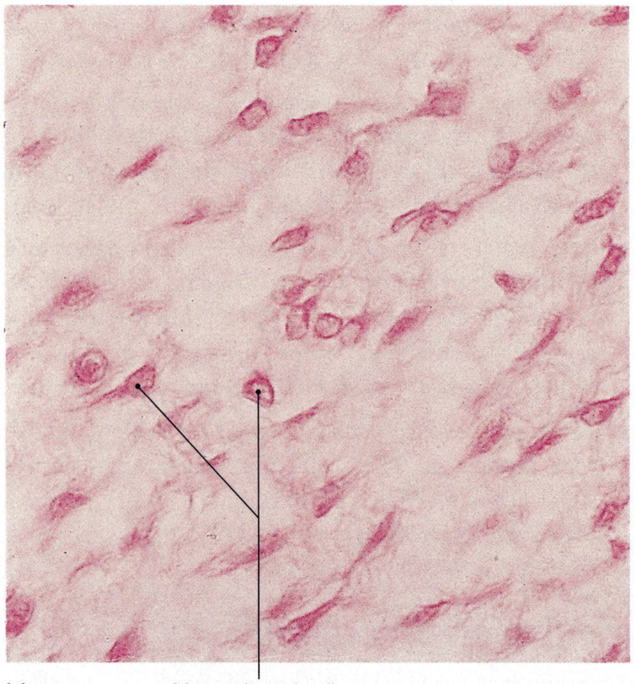

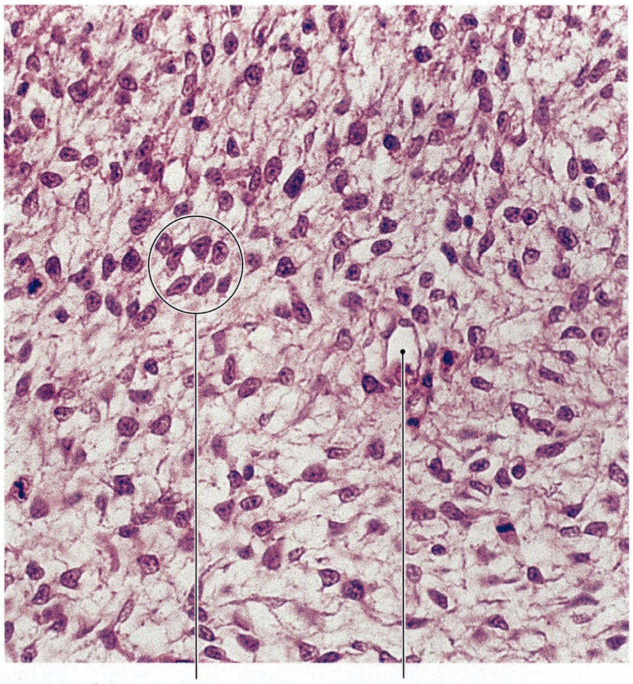

Figure 3.13 Histology of Embryonic Connective Tissues
These connective tissue types give rise to all other connective tissue types. **(a)** Mesenchyme. This is the first connective tissue to appear in the embryo. (LM × 1036) **(b)** Mucous Connective Tissue (*Wharton's Jelly*). This sample was taken from the umbilical cord of a fetus. (LM × 650)

AREOLAR TISSUE

LOCATIONS: Within and deep to the dermis of skin, and covered by the epithelial lining of the digestive, respiratory, and urinary tracts; between muscles; around blood vessels, nerves, and around joints

FUNCTIONS: Cushions organs; provides support but permits independent movement; phagocytic cells provide defense against pathogens

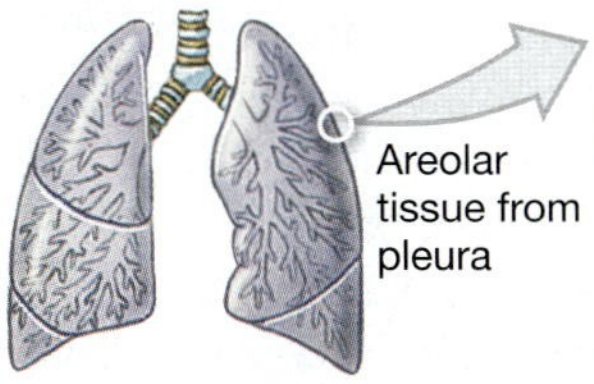

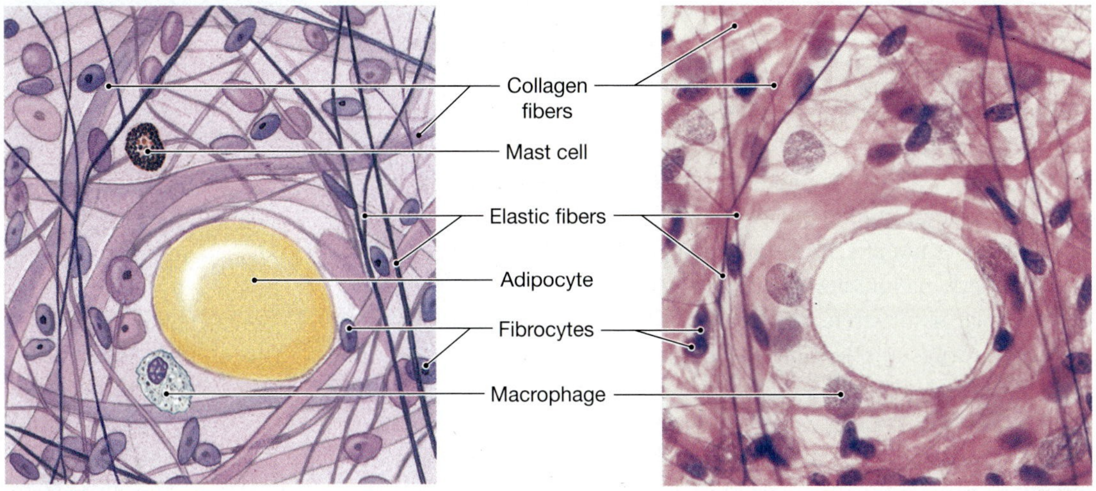

(a) Areolar tissue

LM × 380

ADIPOSE TISSUE

LOCATIONS: Deep to the skin, especially at sides, buttocks, breasts; padding around eyes and kidneys

FUNCTIONS: Provides padding and cushions shocks; insulates (reduces heat loss); stores energy

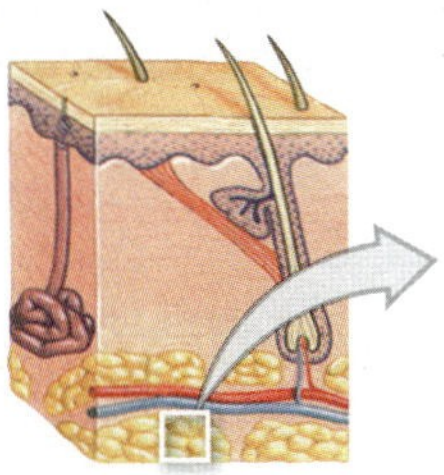

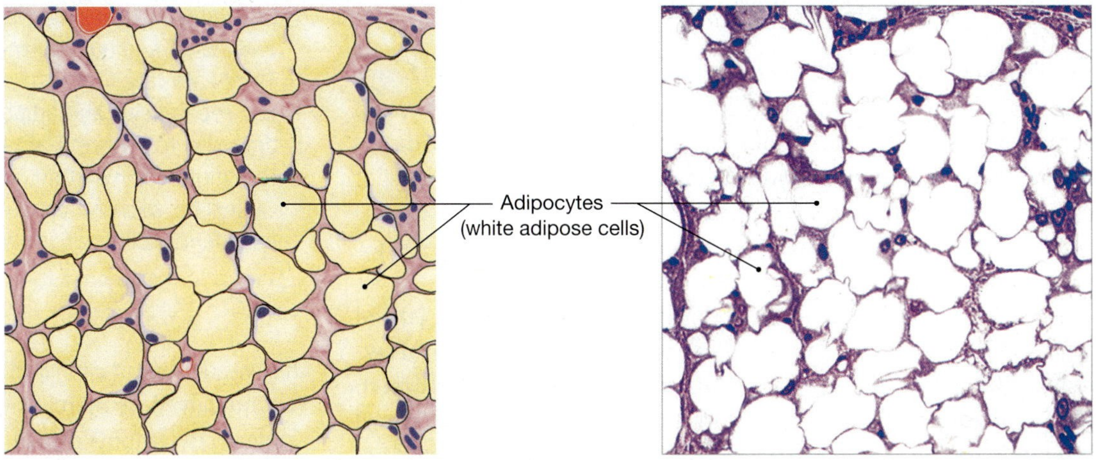

(b) Adipose tissue

LM × 133

RETICULAR TISSUE

LOCATIONS: Liver, kidney, spleen, lymph nodes, and bone marrow

FUNCTIONS: Provides supporting framework

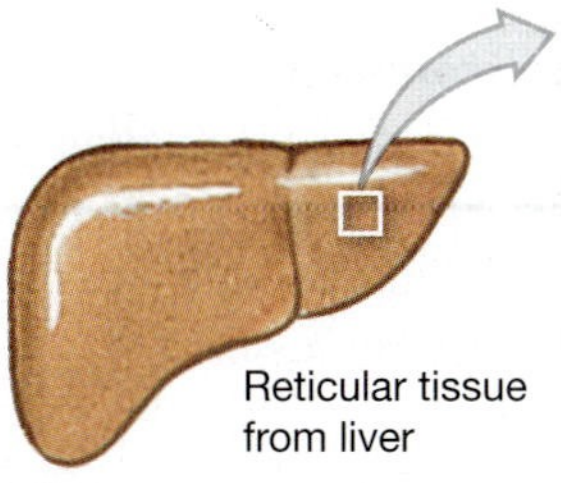

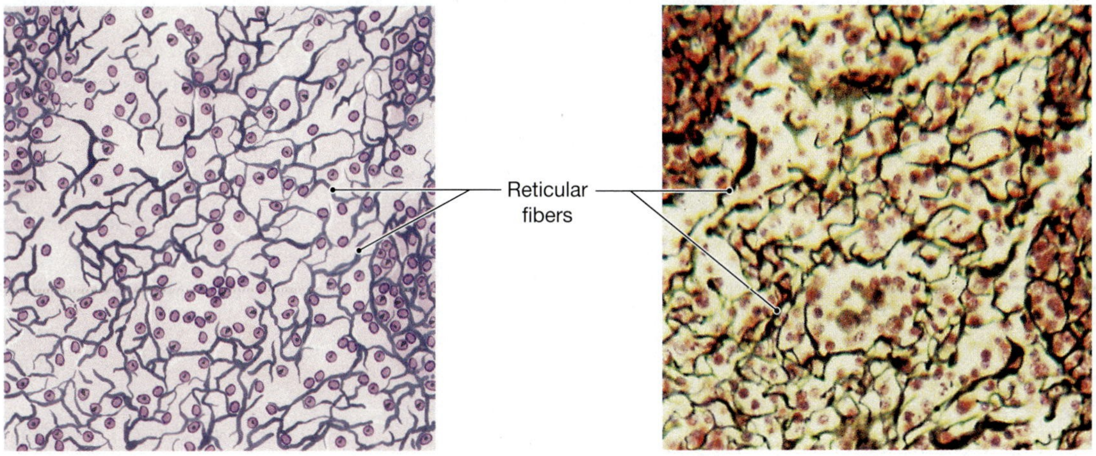

(c) Reticular tissue

LM × 375

Figure 3.14 Histology of Loose Connective Tissues
This is the "packing material" of the body, filling spaces between other structures. **(a)** Areolar Tissue. Note the open framework; all the cells of connective tissue proper are found in areolar tissue. **(b)** Adipose Tissue. Adipose tissue is a loose connective tissue dominated by adipocytes. In standard histological views, the cells look empty because their lipid inclusions dissolve during slide preparation. **(c)** Reticular Tissue. Reticular tissue consists of an open framework of reticular fibers. These fibers are usually very difficult to see because of the large numbers of cells organized around them.

connective tissue proper. Areolar tissue has an open framework, and ground substance accounts for most of its volume. This viscous fluid cushions shocks, and because the fibers are loosely organized, areolar tissue can be distorted without damage. The presence of elastic fibers makes it fairly resilient, so this tissue returns to its original shape after external pressure is relieved.

Areolar tissue forms a layer that separates the skin from deeper structures. In addition to providing padding, the elastic properties of this layer allow a considerable amount of independent movement. Thus, pinching the skin of the arm does not affect the underlying muscle. Conversely, contractions of the underlying muscles do not pull against the skin—as the muscle bulges, the areolar tissue stretches. Because this tissue has an extensive circulatory supply, drugs injected into the areolar tissue layer under the skin are quickly absorbed into the bloodstream.

In addition to delivering oxygen and nutrients and removing carbon dioxide and waste products, the capillaries (the smallest blood vessels) in areolar tissue carry wandering cells to and from the tissue. Epithelia usually cover a layer of areolar tissue, and fibrocytes are responsible for maintaining the dense layer of the basal lamina. The epithelial cells rely on diffusion across the basal lamina, and the capillaries in the underlying connective tissue provide the necessary oxygen and nutrients.

Adipose Tissue [Figure 3.14b] Adipocytes are found in almost all forms of areolar connective tissues. In several locations, adipocytes can become so abundant that any resemblance of normal areolar connective tissue disappears. It is then called **adipose tissue**. In areolar connective tissue, most of the tissue volume consists of intercellular fluids and fibers. In adipose tissue most of the tissue volume consists of adipocytes, which are clustered together like tightly packed grapes (Figure 3.14b).

There are two types of adipose tissue, generally known as white fat and brown fat. **White fat**, which is more common in adults, has a pale, yellow-white color. The adipocytes (termed *white adipose cells*) are relatively inert. These cells contain a single large lipid droplet, and therefore are also termed *unilocular adipose cells* (*uni*, one + *locular*, chamber). The lipid droplet occupies most of the cytoplasm, squeezing the nucleus and other organelles to one side, so that the cell resembles a class ring in a histological preparation. White adipose tissue provides padding, cushions shocks, acts as an insulator to slow heat loss through the skin, and serves as packing or filler around structures. White adipose tissue is common under the skin of the groin, sides, buttocks, and breasts. It also fills the bony sockets behind the eyes, surrounds the kidneys, and dominates extensive areas of loose connective tissue in the pericardial and abdominal cavities.

Brown fat is more abundant in infants and children than adults. Fat is stored in numerous cytoplasmic vacuoles in *brown adipose cells*, and therefore these cells are also termed *multilocular adipose cells*. This tissue is highly vascularized, and the individual cells contain numerous mitochondria, which gives the tissue a deep, rich color from which the name brown fat is derived. Brown fat is very active biochemically, and is important in temperature regulation of newborns and young children. At birth, an infant's temperature-regulating mechanisms are not fully functional. Brown fat provides a mechanism for raising body temperature rapidly, and is found between the shoulder blades, around the neck, and possibly elsewhere in the upper body of newborn children. Brown fat cells are innervated by sympathetic autonomic fibers. When these nerves are stimulated, lipolysis accelerates in brown fat. The energy released through fatty acid catabolism radiates into the surrounding tissues as heat. This heat quickly warms the blood that passes through brown fat, and it is then distributed throughout the body. In this way, an infant can accelerate metabolic heat generation by 100 percent very quickly. With increasing age and size, body temperature becomes more stable, so the importance of brown fat declines. Therefore, adults have little if any brown fat.

Clinical Note

Liposuction One much-publicized method of battling obesity is the process of liposuction. **Liposuction** is a surgical procedure for the removal of unwanted adipose tissue. Adipose tissue is flexible but not as elastic as areolar tissue, and it tears relatively easily. In liposuction, a small incision is made through the skin and a tube is inserted into the underlying adipose tissue. Suction is then applied. Because adipose tissue tears easily, chunks of tissue containing adipocytes, other cells, fibers, and ground substance can be vacuumed away. Liposuction is the most commonly performed cosmetic surgical procedure in the United States, with an estimated 400,000 procedures performed annually since 2003.

This practice has received a lot of news coverage, and many advertisements praise the technique as easy, safe, and effective. In fact, it is not always easy, and it can be dangerous and have limited effectiveness. The density of adipose tissue varies from place to place in the body and from individual to individual, and it is not always easy to suck through a tube. Blood vessels are stretched and torn, and extensive bleeding can occur. An anesthetic must be used to control pain, and anesthesia always poses risks; heart attacks, pulmonary embolism, and fluid balance problems can develop, with fatal results. The death rate for this procedure is 1 in 5000. Finally, adipose tissue can repair itself, and adipocyte populations recover over time. The only way to ensure that fat lost through liposuction will not return is to adopt a lifestyle that includes a proper diet and adequate exercise. Over time, such a lifestyle can produce the same weight loss, *without liposuction*, eliminating the surgical expense and risk.

Reticular Tissue [Figure 3.14c] Connective tissue consisting of reticular fibers, macrophages, fibroblasts, and fibrocytes is termed **reticular tissue** (Figure 3.14c). The fibers of reticular tissue form the stroma of the liver, the spleen, lymph nodes, and bone marrow. The fixed macrophages, fibroblasts, and fibrocytes of reticular tissue are seldom visible because they are vastly outnumbered by the parenchymal cells of these organs.

Dense Connective Tissues

Most of the volume of **dense connective tissues** is occupied by fibers. Dense connective tissues are often called **collagenous** (ko-LAJ-in-us) **tissues** because collagen fibers are the dominant fiber type. Two types of dense connective tissue are found in the body: (1) *dense regular connective tissue* and (2) *dense irregular connective tissue*.

Dense Regular Connective Tissue [Figures 3.7b/3.15a,b] In dense regular connective tissue the collagen fibers are packed tightly and aligned parallel to applied forces. Four major examples of this tissue type are *tendons*, *aponeuroses*, *elastic tissue*, and *ligaments*.

1. *Tendons* (Figure 3.15a) are cords of dense regular connective tissue that attach skeletal muscles to bones and cartilage. The collagen fibers run along the longitudinal axis of the tendon and transfer the pull of

DENSE REGULAR CONNECTIVE TISSUE

LOCATIONS: Between skeletal muscles and skeleton (tendons and aponeuroses); between bones or stabilizing positions of internal organs (ligaments); covering skeletal muscles; deep fasciae

FUNCTIONS: Provides firm attachment; conducts pull of muscles; reduces friction between muscles; stabilizes relative positions of bones

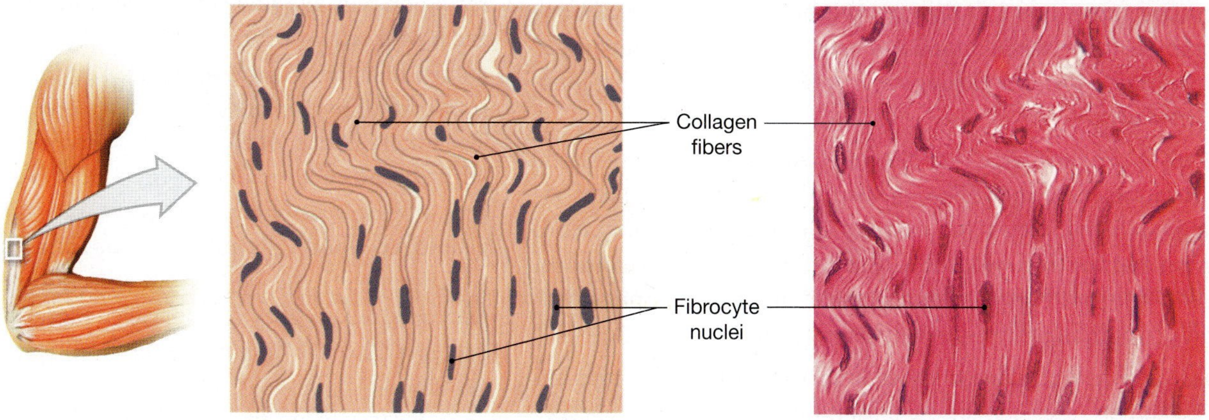

(a) Tendon LM × 440

ELASTIC TISSUE

LOCATIONS: Between vertebrae of the spinal column (ligamentum flavum and ligamentum nuchae); ligaments supporting penis; ligaments supporting transitional epithelia; in blood vessel walls

FUNCTIONS: Stabilizes positions of vertebrae and penis; cushions shocks; permits expansion and contraction of organs

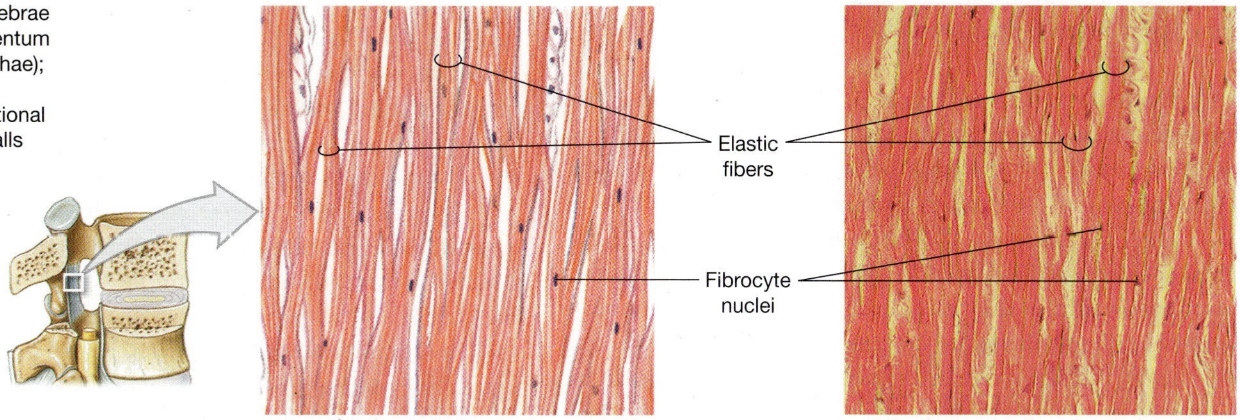

(b) Elastic ligament LM × 887

DENSE IRREGULAR CONNECTIVE TISSUE

LOCATIONS: Capsules of visceral organs; periostea and perichondria; nerve and muscle sheaths; dermis

FUNCTIONS: Provides strength to resist forces applied from many directions; helps prevent overexpansion of organs such as the urinary bladder

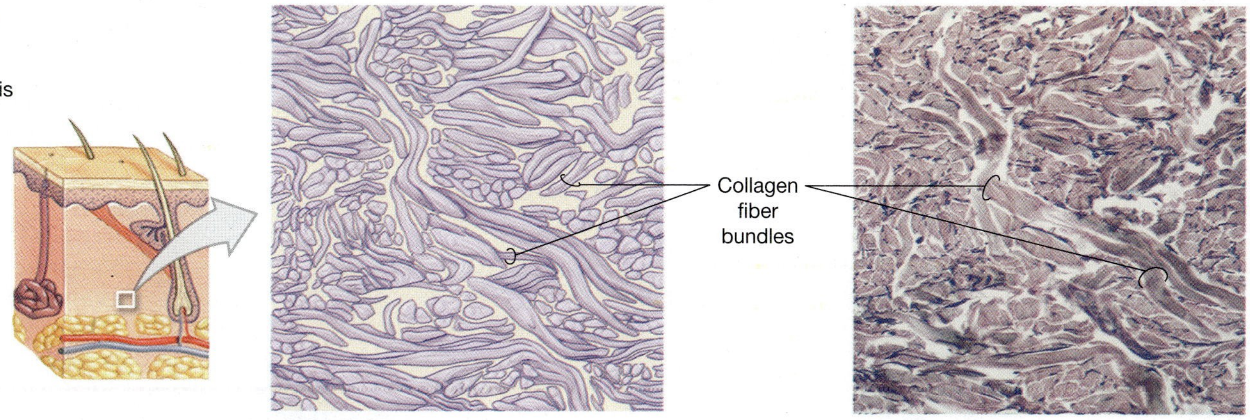

(c) Deep dermis LM × 111

Figure 3.15 Histology of Dense Connective Tissues
(a) Dense Regular Connective Tissue: Tendon. The dense regular connective tissue in a tendon consists of densely packed, parallel bundles of collagen fibers. The fibrocyte nuclei can be seen flattened between the bundles. Most ligaments resemble tendons in their histological organization. **(b)** Dense Regular Connective Tissue: Elastic Ligament. Elastic ligaments extend between the vertebrae of the spinal column. The bundles of elastic fibers are fatter than the collagen fiber bundles of a tendon or typical ligament. **(c)** Dense Irregular Connective Tissue. The deep portion of the dermis of the skin consists of a thick layer of interwoven collagen fibers oriented in various directions.

the contracting muscle to the bone or cartilage. Large numbers of fibrocytes are found between the collagen fibers.

2. *Aponeuroses* (ap-ō-noo-RŌ-sēz) are collagenous sheets or ribbons that resemble flat, broad tendons. Aponeuroses may cover the surface of a muscle and assist in attaching superficial muscles to another muscle or structure.
3. *Elastic tissue* contains large numbers of elastic fibers. Because elastic fibers outnumber collagen fibers, the tissue has a springy, resilient nature. This ability to stretch and rebound allows it to tolerate cycles of expansion and contraction. Elastic tissue often underlies transitional epithelia (Figure 3.7b, p. 58); it is also found in the walls of blood vessels and surrounding the respiratory passageways.
4. *Ligaments* resemble tendons, but they usually connect one bone to another. Ligaments often contain significant numbers of elastic fibers as well as collagen fibers, and they can tolerate a modest amount of stretching. An even higher proportion of elastic fibers is found in elastic ligaments, which resemble tough rubber bands. Although uncommon elsewhere, elastic ligaments along the vertebral column are very important in stabilizing the positions of the vertebrae (Figure 3.15b).

Dense Irregular Connective Tissue [Figure 3.15c] The fibers in **dense irregular connective tissue** form an interwoven meshwork and do not show any consistent pattern (Figure 3.15c). This tissue provides strength and support to areas subjected to stresses from many directions. A layer of dense irregular connective tissue, the *dermis*, gives skin its strength; a piece of cured leather (the dermis of animal skin) provides an excellent illustration of the interwoven nature of this tissue. Except at joints, dense irregular connective tissue forms a sheath around cartilage (the perichondrium) and bone (the periosteum). Dense irregular connective tissue also forms the thick fibrous **capsule** that surrounds internal organs, such as the liver, kidneys, and spleen, and encloses the cavities of joints.

Fluid Connective Tissues [Figure 3.16]

Blood and *lymph* are connective tissues that contain distinctive collections of cells in a fluid matrix. The watery matrix of blood and lymph contains cells and many types of suspended proteins that do not form insoluble fibers under normal conditions.

Blood contains blood cells and fragments of cells collectively known as *formed elements* (Figure 3.16). Three types of formed elements exist: (1) red blood cells, (2) white blood cells, and (3) platelets. A single cell type, the **red blood cell**, or **erythrocyte** (e-RITH-rō-sīt; *erythros*, red), accounts for almost half the volume of blood. Red blood cells are responsible for the transport of oxygen and, to a lesser degree, of carbon dioxide in the blood. The watery matrix of blood, called **plasma**, also contains small numbers of **white blood cells**, or **leukocytes** (LOO-kō-sīts; *leukos*, white). White blood cells include *neutrophils, eosinophils, basophils, lymphocytes,* and *monocytes.* The white blood cells are important components of the immune system, which protects the body from infection and disease. Tiny membrane-enclosed packets of cytoplasm called **platelets** contain enzymes and special proteins. Platelets function in the clotting response that seals breaks in the vessel wall.

Extracellular fluid includes three major subdivisions: *plasma, interstitial fluid,* and *lymph. Plasma* is normally confined to the vessels of the circulatory system, and contractions of the heart keep it in motion. **Arteries** are vessels that carry blood away from the heart toward fine, thin-walled vessels called **capillaries. Veins** are vessels that drain the capillaries and return the blood to the heart, completing the circuit of blood. In tissues, filtration moves water and small solutes out of the capillaries and into the interstitial fluid, which bathes the body's cells. The major difference between the plasma and interstitial fluid is that plasma contains a large number of suspended proteins.

Lymph forms as interstitial fluid and then enters **lymphatic vessels**, small passageways that return it to the cardiovascular system. Along the way, cells of the immune system monitor the composition of the lymph and respond to signs of injury or infection. The number of cells in lymph may vary, but ordinarily 99 percent of them are lymphocytes. The rest are primarily phagocytic macrophages, eosinophils, and neutrophils.

Supporting Connective Tissues

Cartilage and bone are called **supporting connective tissues** because they provide a strong framework that supports the rest of the body. In these connective tissues, the matrix contains numerous fibers and, in some cases, deposits of insoluble calcium salts.

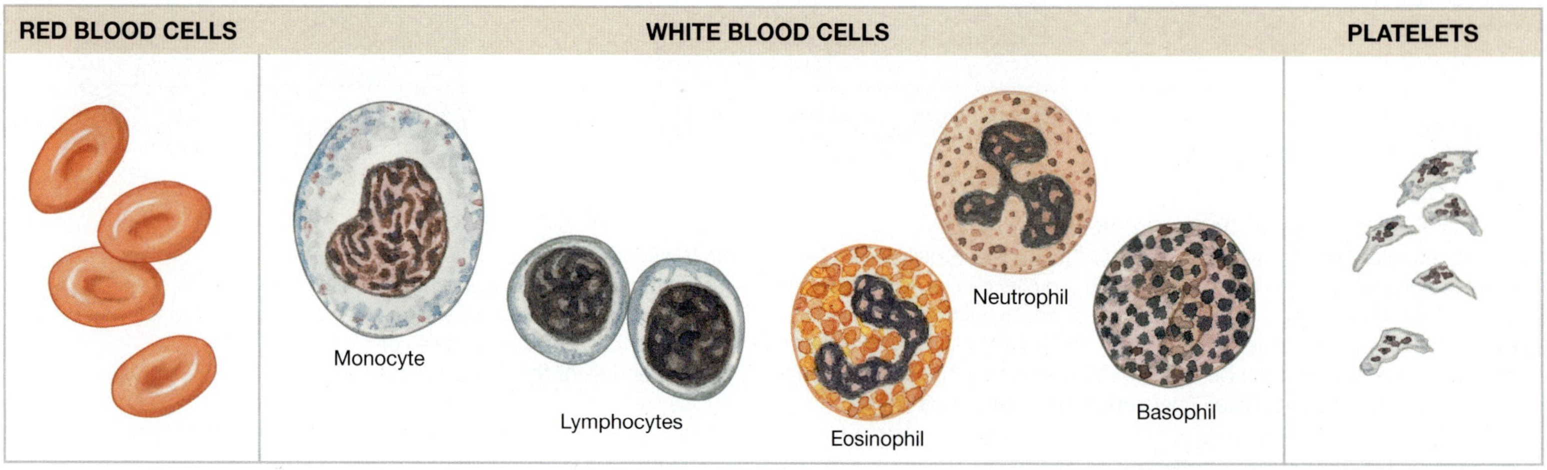

Figure 3.16 Formed Elements of the Blood

Cartilage [Figure 3.17]

The matrix of **cartilage** is a firm gel that contains complex polysaccharides called **chondroitin sulfates** (kon-DRO-y-tin; *chondros*, cartilage). The chondroitin sulfates form complexes with proteins, forming proteoglycans. Cartilage cells, or **chondrocytes** (KON-drō-sīts), are the only cells found within the cartilage matrix. These cells live in small chambers known as **lacunae** (la-KOO-nē; *lacus*, pool). The physical properties of cartilage depend on the nature of the matrix. Collagen fibers provide tensile strength, and the combined characteristics of the extracellular fibers and the ground substance give it flexibility and resilience.

Cartilage is avascular because chondrocytes produce a chemical that discourages the formation of blood vessels. All nutrient and waste-product exchange must occur by diffusion through the matrix. Cartilage is usually set apart from surrounding tissues by a fibrous **perichondrium** (per-ē-KON-drē-um; *peri*, around) (Figure 3.17a). The perichondrium contains two distinct layers: an outer, *fibrous layer* of dense irregular connective tissue and an inner, *cellular layer*. The fibrous layer provides mechanical support and protection and attaches the cartilage to other structures. The cellular layer is important to the growth and maintenance of the cartilage.

Cartilage grows by two mechanisms (Figure 3.17b,c). In **appositional growth**, stem cells of the inner layer of the perichondrium undergo repeated cycles of division. The innermost cells differentiate into chondroblasts, which begin producing cartilage matrix. After they are completely surrounded by matrix, the chondroblasts differentiate into chondrocytes. This growth mechanism gradually increases the dimensions of the cartilage by adding to its surface. Additionally, chondrocytes within the cartilage matrix can undergo division, and their daughter cells produce additional matrix. This cycle enlarges the cartilage from within, much like the inflation of a balloon; the process is called **interstitial growth**. Neither appositional nor interstitial growth occurs in adult cartilages, and most cartilages cannot repair themselves after a severe injury.

Clinical Note

Cartilages and Knee Injuries The knee is an extremely complex joint that contains both hyaline cartilage and fibrous cartilage. The hyaline cartilage caps bony surfaces, while pads of fibrous cartilage within the joint prevent bone-to-bone contact when movements are under way. Many sports injuries involve tearing of the fibrous cartilage pads or supporting ligaments; the loss of support and cushioning places more strain on the hyaline cartilages within joints and leads to further joint damage. Articular cartilages not only are avascular, but also lack a perichondrium. As a result, they heal even more slowly than other cartilages. Surgery usually produces only a temporary or incomplete repair. For this reason, most competitive sports have rules designed to reduce the number of knee injuries. For example, in football "clipping" is outlawed because it produces stresses that can tear the fibrous cartilages and the supporting ligaments at the knee.

Recent advances in tissue culture have enabled researchers to grow fibrous cartilage in the laboratory. Chondrocytes removed from the knees of injured patients are cultured in an artificial framework of collagen fibers. Eventually, they produce masses of fibrous cartilage that can be inserted into the damaged joints. Over time, the pads change shape and grow, restoring normal joint function. This labor-intensive technique has been used to treat severe joint injuries, particularly in athletes.

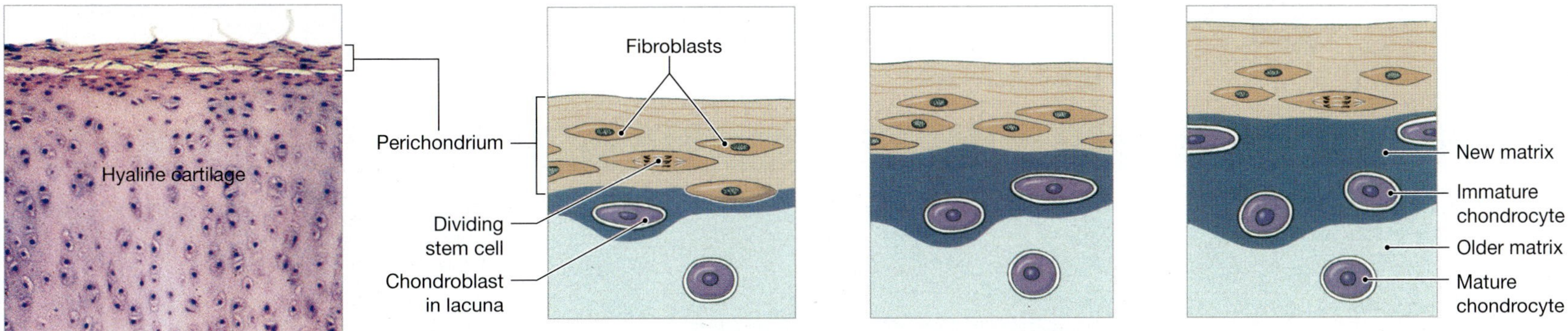

(a) The perichondrium

Cells in the cellular layer of the perichondrium differentiate into chondroblasts.

These immature chondroblasts secrete new matrix.

As the matrix enlarges, more chondroblasts are incorporated; they are replaced by divisions of stem cells in the perichondrium.

(b) Appositional growth

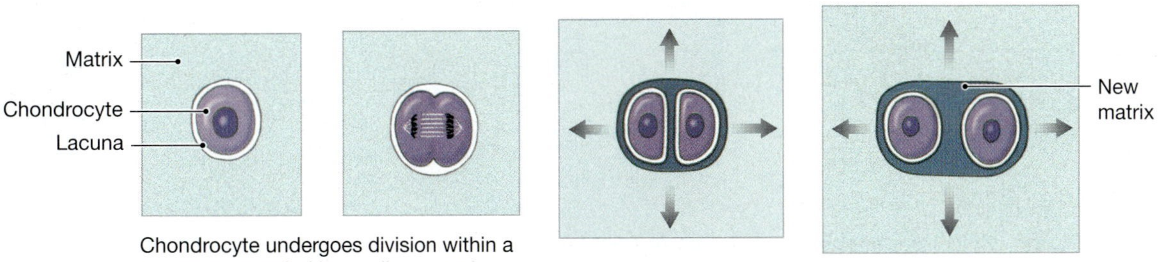

Chondrocyte undergoes division within a lacuna surrounded by cartilage matrix.

As daughter cells secrete additional matrix, they move apart, expanding the cartilage from within.

(c) Interstitial growth

Figure 3.17 The Formation and Growth of Cartilage
(a) This light micrograph shows the organization of a small piece of hyaline cartilage and the surrounding perichondrium. **(b)** Appositional Growth. The cartilage grows at its external surface through the differentiation of fibroblasts into chondrocytes within the cellular layer of the perichondrium. **(c)** Interstitial Growth. The cartilage expands from within as chondrocytes in the matrix divide, grow, and produce new matrix.

HYALINE CARTILAGE

LOCATIONS: Between tips of ribs and bones of sternum; covering bone surfaces at synovial joints; supporting larynx (voice box), trachea, and bronchi; forming part of nasal septum

FUNCTIONS: Provides stiff but somewhat flexible support; reduces friction between bony surfaces

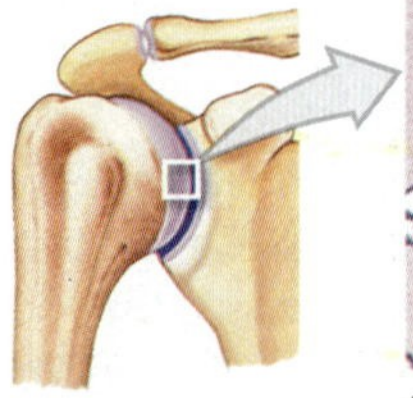

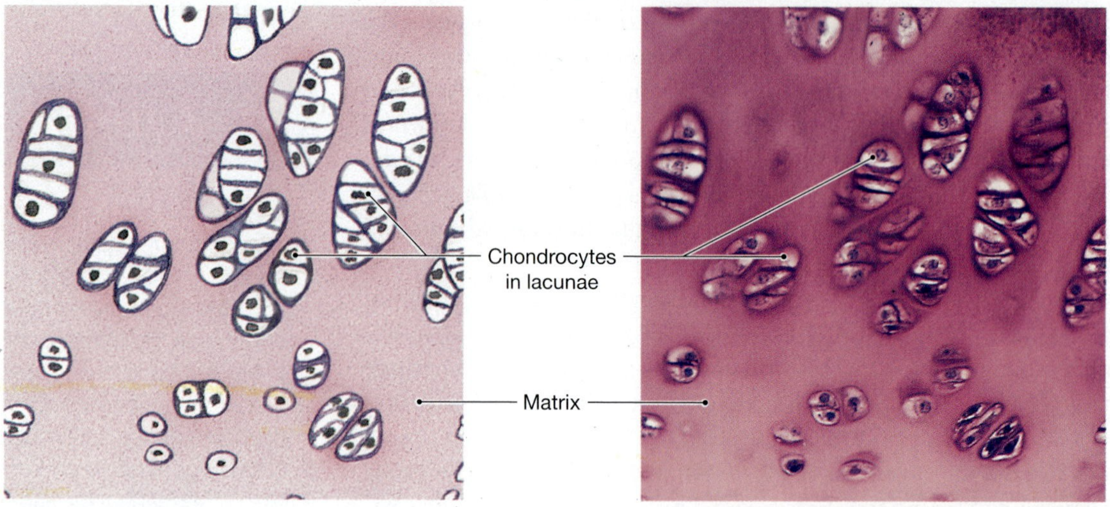

(a) Hyaline cartilage

LM × 500

ELASTIC CARTILAGE

LOCATIONS: Auricle of external ear; epiglottis; auditory canal; cuneiform cartilages of larynx

FUNCTIONS: Provides support, but tolerates distortion without damage and returns to original shape

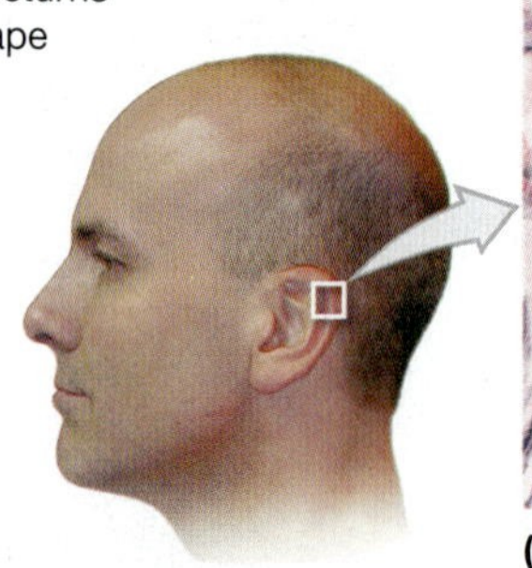

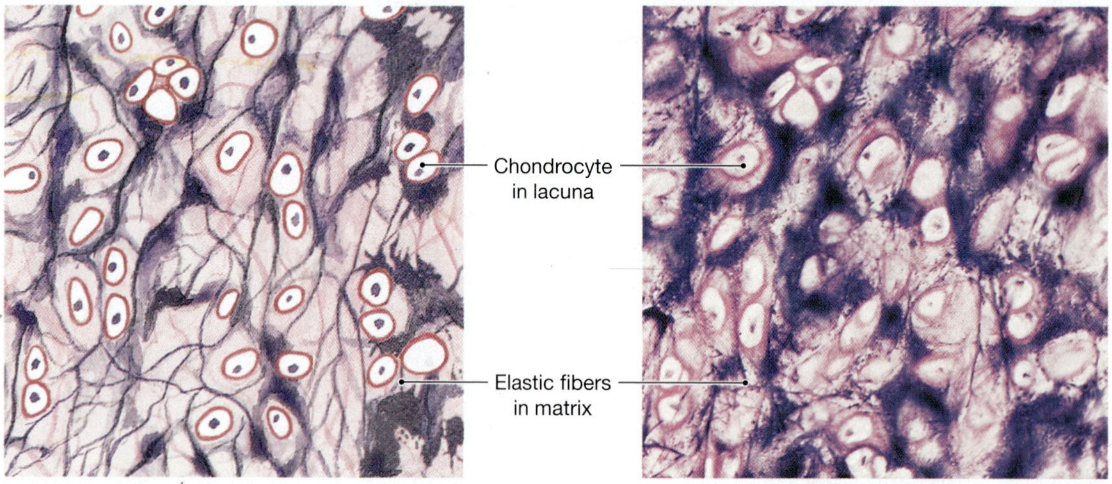

(b) Elastic cartilage

LM × 358

FIBROUS CARTILAGE

LOCATIONS: Pads within knee joint; between pubic bones of pelvis; intervertebral discs

FUNCTIONS: Resists compression; prevents bone-to-bone contact; limits relative movement

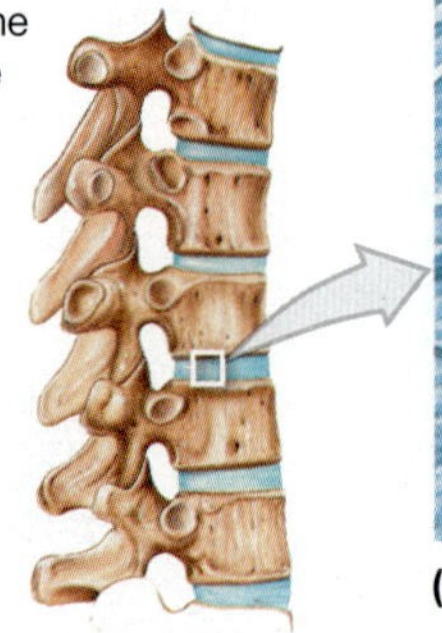

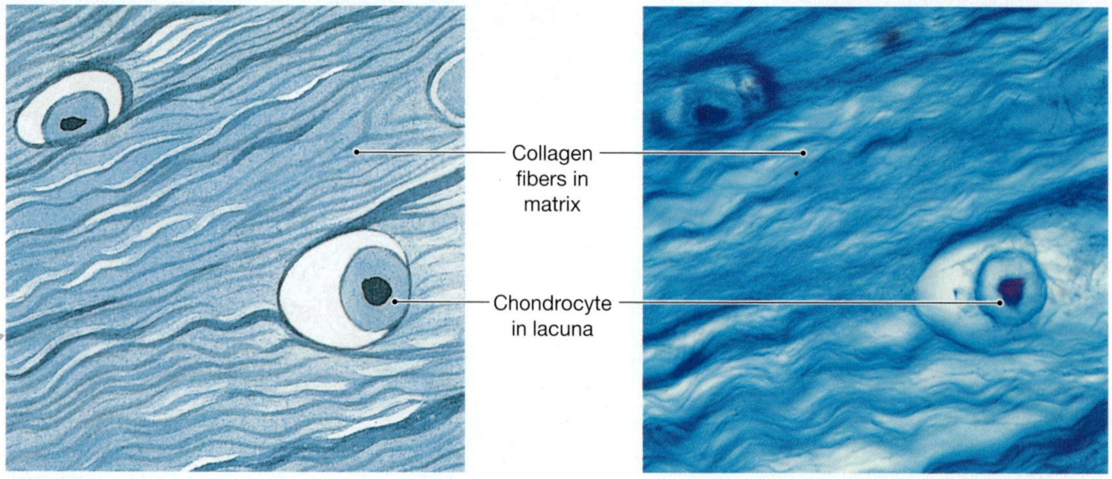

(c) Fibrous cartilage

LM × 1000

Figure 3.18 Histology of the Three Types of Cartilage
Cartilage is a supporting connective tissue with a firm, gelatinous matrix. **(a)** Hyaline Cartilage. Note the translucent matrix and the absence of prominent fibers. **(b)** Elastic Cartilage. The closely packed elastic fibers are visible between the chondrocytes. **(c)** Fibrous cartilage. The collagen fibers are extremely dense, and the chondrocytes are relatively far apart.

Types of Cartilage [Figure 3.18] There are three major types of cartilage: (1) *hyaline cartilage*, (2) *elastic cartilage*, and (3) *fibrous cartilage*.

1. **Hyaline cartilage** (HĪ-a-lin; *hyalos*, glass) is the most common type of cartilage. The matrix of hyaline cartilage contains closely packed collagen fibers. Although it is tough but somewhat flexible, this is the weakest type of cartilage. Because the collagen fibers of the matrix do not stain well, they are not always apparent in light microscopy (**Figure 3.18a**). Examples of this type of cartilage in the adult body include (1) the connections between the ribs and the sternum, (2) the supporting cartilages along the conducting passageways of the respiratory tract, and (3) the *articular cartilages* covering opposing bone surfaces within synovial joints, such as the elbow or knee.
2. **Elastic cartilage** contains numerous elastic fibers that make it extremely resilient and flexible. Among other structures, elastic cartilage forms the external flap (*auricle* or *pinna*) of the external ear (**Figure 3.18b**), the epiglottis, the airway to the middle ear (*auditory tube*), and small (*cuneiform*) cartilages of the larynx. Although the cartilages at the tip of the nose are very flexible, there is disagreement as to whether they should be classified as "true" elastic cartilages because their elastic fibers are not as abundant as at the auricle or epiglottis.
3. **Fibrous cartilage**, or *fibrocartilage*, has little ground substance, may lack a perichondrium, and the matrix is dominated by collagen fibers (**Figure 3.18c**). Fibrocartilaginous pads lie in areas of high stress, such as between the spinal vertebrae, between the pubic bones of the pelvis, and around or within a few joints and tendons. In these positions fibrous cartilage resists compression, absorbs shocks, and prevents damaging bone-to-bone contact. The collagen fibers within fibrous cartilage follow the stress lines encountered at that particular location, and therefore are more regularly arranged than those of hyaline or elastic cartilage. Cartilages heal slowly and poorly, and damaged fibrous cartilage in joints can interfere with normal movements.

Bone [Figure 3.19 and Table 3.2]

Because the detailed histology of **bone**, or *osseous tissue* (OS-ē-us; *os*, bone), will be considered in Chapter 5, this discussion will focus on significant differences between cartilage and bone. Table 3.2 summarizes the similarities and differences between cartilage and bone. Roughly one-third of the matrix of bone consists of collagen fibers. The balance is a mixture of calcium salts, primarily calcium phosphate with lesser amounts of calcium carbonate. This combination gives bone truly remarkable properties. By themselves, calcium salts are strong but rather brittle. Collagen fibers are weaker, but relatively flexible. In bone, the minerals are organized around the collagen fibers. The result is a strong, somewhat flexible combination that is very resistant to shattering. In its overall properties, bone can compete with the best steel-reinforced concrete.

The general organization of osseous tissue can be seen in **Figure 3.19**. *Lacunae* within the matrix contain bone cells, or **osteocytes** (OS-tē-ō-sīts). The lacunae are often organized around blood vessels that branch through the bony matrix. Although diffusion cannot occur through the calcium

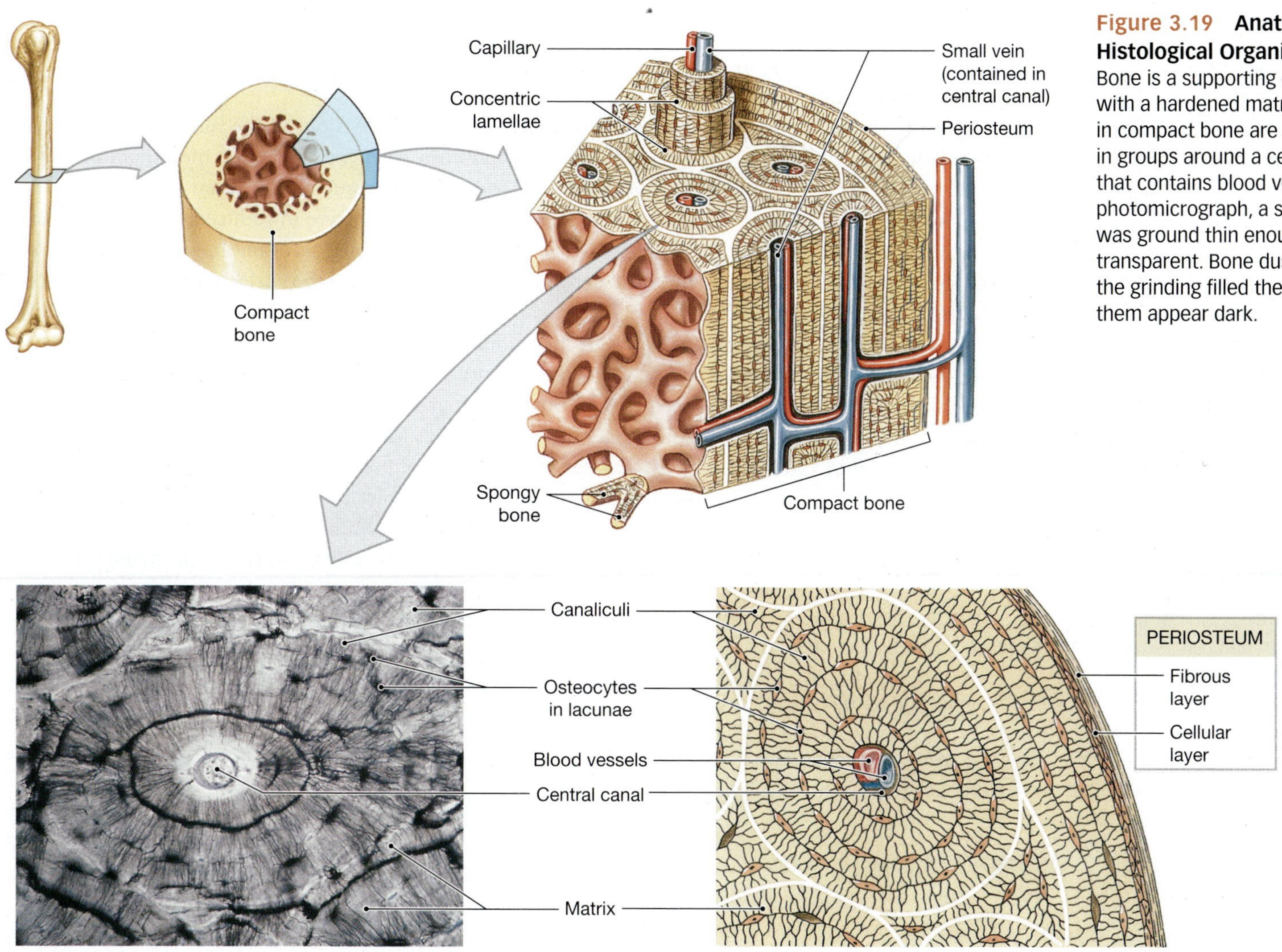

Figure 3.19 Anatomy and Histological Organization of Bone
Bone is a supporting connective tissue with a hardened matrix. The osteocytes in compact bone are usually organized in groups around a central space that contains blood vessels. For the photomicrograph, a sample of bone was ground thin enough to become transparent. Bone dust produced during the grinding filled the lacunae, making them appear dark.

TABLE 3.2 A Comparison of Cartilage and Bone

Characteristic	Cartilage	Bone
STRUCTURAL FEATURES		
Cells	Chondrocytes in lacunae	Osteocytes in lacunae
Matrix	Chondroitin sulfates with proteins, forming hydrated proteoglycans	Insoluble crystals of calcium phosphate and calcium carbonate
Fibers	Collagen, elastic, reticular fibers (proportions vary)	Collagen fibers predominate
Vascularity	None	Extensive
Covering	Perichondrium, two layers	Periosteum, two layers
Strength	Limited: bends easily but hard to break	Strong: resists distortion until breaking point is reached
Growth	Interstitial and appositional	Appositional only
Repair capabilities	Limited ability	Extensive ability
Oxygen demands	Low	High
Nutrient delivery	By diffusion through matrix	By diffusion through cytoplasm and fluid in canaliculi

salts, osteocytes communicate with blood vessels and with one another through slender cytoplasmic extensions. These extensions run through long, slender passages in the matrix. These passageways, called **canaliculi** (kan-a-LIK-ū-lē; "little canals"), form a branching network for the exchange of materials between the blood vessels and the osteocytes. There are two types of bone: *compact bone*, which contains blood vessels trapped within the matrix, and *spongy bone*, which does not.

Almost all bone surfaces are sheathed by a **periosteum** (per-ē-OS-tē-um) composed of a fibrous outer layer and a cellular inner layer. The periosteum is incomplete only at joints, where bones articulate. The periosteum assists in the attachment of a bone to surrounding tissues and to associated tendons and ligaments. The cellular layer functions in bone growth and participates in repairs after an injury. Unlike cartilage, bone undergoes extensive remodeling on a regular basis, and complete repairs can be made even after severe damage has occurred. Bones also respond to the stresses placed upon them, growing thicker and stronger with exercise, and thin and brittle with inactivity.

CONCEPT CHECK

1. Identify the three basic components of all connective tissues.
2. What is a major difference between connective tissue proper and supporting connective tissue?
3. What are the two general classes of cells in connective tissue proper? What cells are found in each class?
4. Lack of vitamin C in the diet interferes with the ability of fibroblasts to produce collagen. What effect might this limited ability to produce collagen have on connective tissue?

See blue "Answers" tab at back of book.

Membranes

Epithelia and connective tissues combine to form **membranes**. Each membrane consists of an epithelial sheet and an underlying connective tissue layer. Membranes cover and protect other structures and tissues in the body. There are four types of membranes: (1) *mucous membranes*, (2) *serous membranes*, (3) *the cutaneous membrane (skin)*, and (4) *synovial membranes*.

Mucous Membranes [Figure 3.20a]

Mucous membranes line passageways that communicate with the exterior, including the digestive, respiratory, reproductive, and urinary tracts (Figure 3.20a). Mucous membranes, or mucosae (mū-KŌ-sē; singular, *mucosa*), form a barrier that resists the entry of pathogens. The epithelial surfaces are kept moist at all times; they may be lubricated by mucus or other glandular secretions or by exposure to fluids such as urine or semen. The areolar tissue component of a mucous membrane is called the **lamina propria** (PRŌ-prē-a). The lamina propria forms a bridge that connects the epithelium to underlying structures. It also provides support for the blood vessels and nerves that supply the epithelium. We will consider the organization of specific mucous membranes in greater detail in later chapters.

Many mucous membranes are lined by simple epithelia that perform absorptive or secretory functions. One example is the simple columnar epithelium of the digestive tract. However, other types of epithelia may be involved. For example, the mucous membrane of the mouth contains a stratified squamous epithelium, and the mucous membrane along most of the urinary tract has a transitional epithelium.

Serous Membranes [Figure 3.20b]

Serous membranes line the subdivisions of the ventral body cavity. There are three serous membranes, each consisting of a mesothelium (p. 55) supported by areolar connective tissue rich in blood and lymphatic vessels (Figure 3.20b). These membranes were introduced in Chapter 1: (1) The *pleura* lines the pleural cavities and covers the lungs; (2) the *peritoneum* lines the peritoneal cavity and covers the surfaces of the enclosed organs; and (3) the *pericardium* lines the pericardial cavity and covers the heart. p. 18 Serous membranes are very thin, and they are firmly attached to the body wall and to the organs they cover. When you are looking at an organ, such as the heart or stomach, you are really seeing the tissues of the organ through a transparent serous membrane.

The parietal and visceral portions of a serous membrane are in close contact at all times. Minimizing friction between these opposing surfaces is the primary function of serous membranes. Because the mesothelia are very thin, serous membranes are relatively permeable, and tissue fluids diffuse onto the exposed surface, keeping it moist and slippery.

The fluid formed on the surfaces of a serous membrane is called a **transudate** (TRANS-ū-dāt; *trans-*, across). Specific transudates are called *pleural fluid*, *peritoneal fluid*, or *pericardial fluid*, depending on their source. In normal healthy individuals, the total volume of transudate at any given time is extremely small, just enough to prevent friction between the walls of the cavities and the surfaces of internal organs. But after an injury or in certain disease states, the volume of transudate may increase dramatically, complicating existing medical problems or producing new ones.

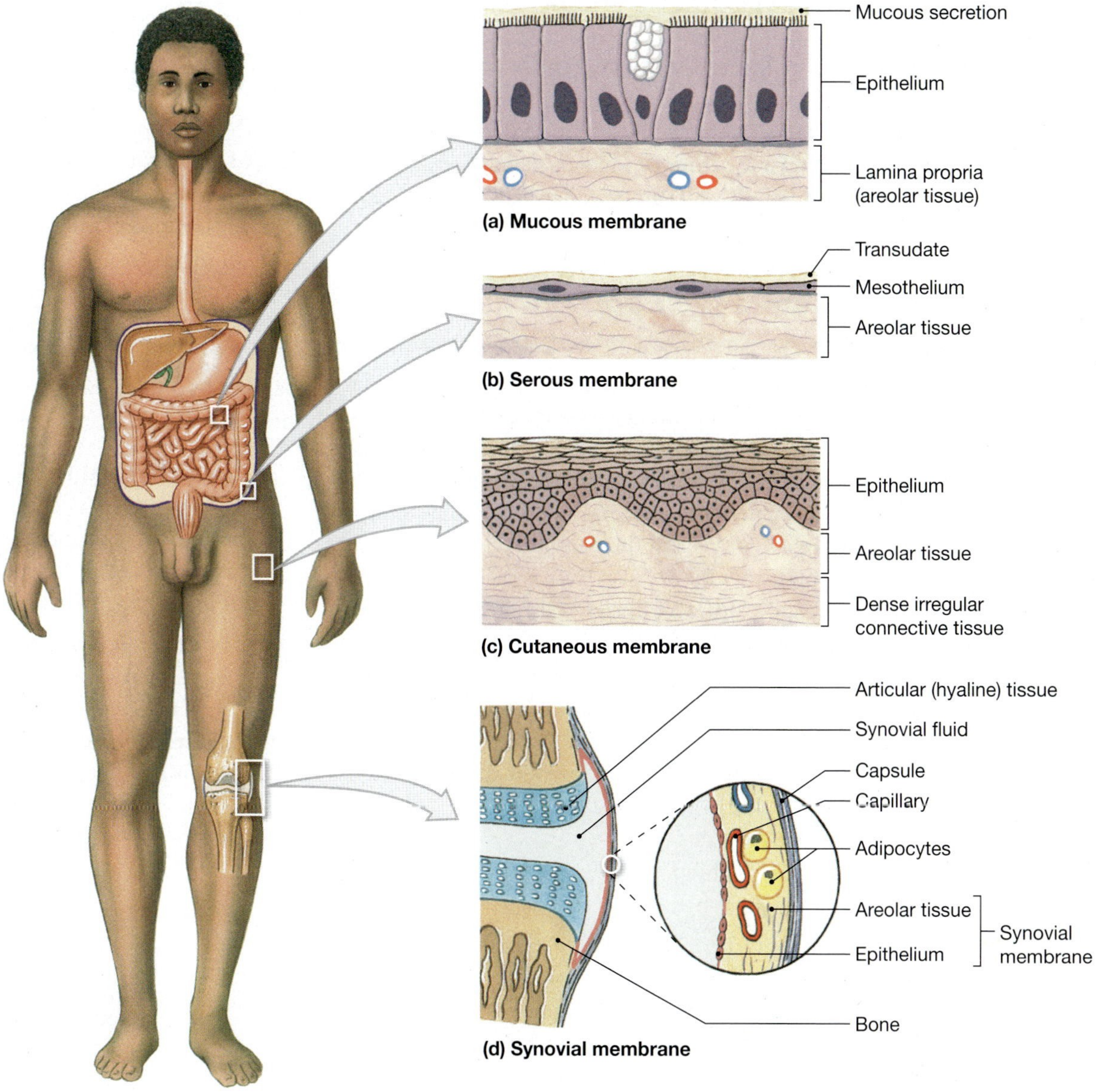

Figure 3.20 Membranes
Membranes are composed of epithelia and connective tissues, which act to cover and protect other tissues and structures. **(a)** Mucous membranes are coated with the secretions of mucous glands. Mucous membranes line most of the digestive and respiratory tracts and portions of the urinary and reproductive tracts. **(b)** Serous membranes line the ventral body cavities (the peritoneal, pleural, and pericardial cavities). **(c)** The cutaneous membrane, the skin, covers the outer surface of the body. **(d)** Synovial membranes line joint cavities and produce the fluid within the joint.

Clinical Note

Problems with Serous Membranes Several clinical conditions, including infection and chronic inflammation, can cause the abnormal buildup of fluid in a body cavity. Other conditions can reduce the amount of lubrication, causing friction between opposing layers of serous membranes. This can promote the formation of adhesions—fibrous connections that eliminate the friction by locking the membranes together. Adhesions may also severely restrict the movement of the affected organ or organs and may compress blood vessels or nerves.

Pleuritis, or *pleurisy*, is an inflammation of the pleural cavities. At first the opposing membranes become drier and scratch against one another, producing a sound known as a *pleural rub*. Adhesions seldom form between the serous membranes of the pleural cavities. More commonly, continued rubbing and inflammation leads to a gradual increase in fluid production to levels well above normal. Fluid then accumulates in the pleural cavities, producing a condition known as *pleural effusions*. Pleural effusions are also caused by heart conditions that elevate the pressure within the pulmonary blood vessels. Fluid then leaks into the alveoli and into the pleural spaces as well, compressing the lungs and making breathing difficult. This combination can be lethal.

Pericarditis is an inflammation of the pericardium. This condition typically leads to *pericardial effusion*, an abnormal accumulation of the fluid in the pericardial cavity. When sudden or severe, the fluid buildup can seriously reduce the efficiency of the heart and restrict blood flow through major vessels.

Peritonitis, an inflammation of the peritoneum, can follow infection of, or injury to, the peritoneal lining. Peritonitis is a potential complication of any surgical procedure in which the peritoneal cavity is opened or of a disease that perforates the walls of the intestines or stomach. Adhesions are common following peritoneal infections and may lead to constriction and blockage of the intestinal tract.

Liver disease, kidney disease, or heart failure can cause an accumulation of fluid in the peritoneal cavity. Called *ascites* (ā-SĪ-tēz), this accumulation creates a characteristic abdominal swelling. The pressure and distortion of internal organs by the excess fluid can lead to symptoms such as heartburn, indigestion, shortness of breath, and low back pain.

The Cutaneous Membrane [Figure 3.20c]

The **cutaneous membrane**, or the skin, covers the surface of the body. It consists of a keratinized stratified squamous epithelium and an underlying layer of areolar connective tissue reinforced by a layer of dense connective tissue (Figure 3.20c). In contrast to serous or mucous membranes, the cutaneous membrane is thick, relatively waterproof, and usually dry. (The skin is discussed in detail in Chapter 4.)

Synovial Membranes [Figure 3.20d]

A **synovial membrane** (si-NŌ-vē-al) consists of extensive areas of areolar tissue bounded by an incomplete superficial layer of squamous or cuboidal cells (Figure 3.20d). Bones contact one another at joints, or *articulations*. Joints that permit significant movement are surrounded by a fibrous capsule and contain a joint cavity lined by a synovial membrane. Although usually called an epithelium, the synovial membrane lining develops within connective tissue and differs from other epithelia in three respects: (1) There is no basal lamina or reticular lamina, (2) the cellular layer is incomplete, with gaps between adjacent cells, and (3) the "epithelial cells" are derived from macrophages and fibroblasts of the adjacent connective tissue. Some of the lining cells are phagocytic and others are secretory. The phagocytic cells remove cellular debris or pathogens that could disrupt joint function. The secretory cells regulate the composition of the **synovial fluid** within the joint cavity. The synovial fluid lubricates the cartilages in the joint, distributes oxygen and nutrients, and cushions shocks at the joint.

The Connective Tissue Framework of the Body [Figure 3.21]

Connective tissues create the internal framework of the body. Layers of connective tissue connect the organs within the body cavities with the rest of the body. These layers (1) provide strength and stability, (2) maintain the relative positions of internal organs, and (3) provide a route for the distribution of blood vessels, lymphatics, and nerves.

Fascia (FASH-ē-a; plural *fasciae*) is a general term for a layer or sheet of connective tissue that can be seen on gross dissection. These layers and wrappings can be divided into three major components: the superficial fascia, the deep fascia, and the subserous fascia. The functional anatomy of these layers is illustrated in Figure 3.21:

- The **superficial fascia**, or **subcutaneous layer** (*sub*, below + *cutis*, skin) is also termed the *hypodermis* (*hypo*, below + *derma*, skin). This layer of loose connective tissue separates the skin from underlying tissues and organs. It provides insulation and padding and lets the skin or underlying structures move independently.
- The **deep fascia** consists of dense regular connective tissue. The fiber organization resembles that of plywood: All the fibers in an individual layer run in the same direction, but the orientation of the fibers changes from one layer to another. This variation helps the tissue resist forces applied from many different directions. The tough *capsules* that surround most organs, including the organs in the thoracic and peritoneal cavities, are

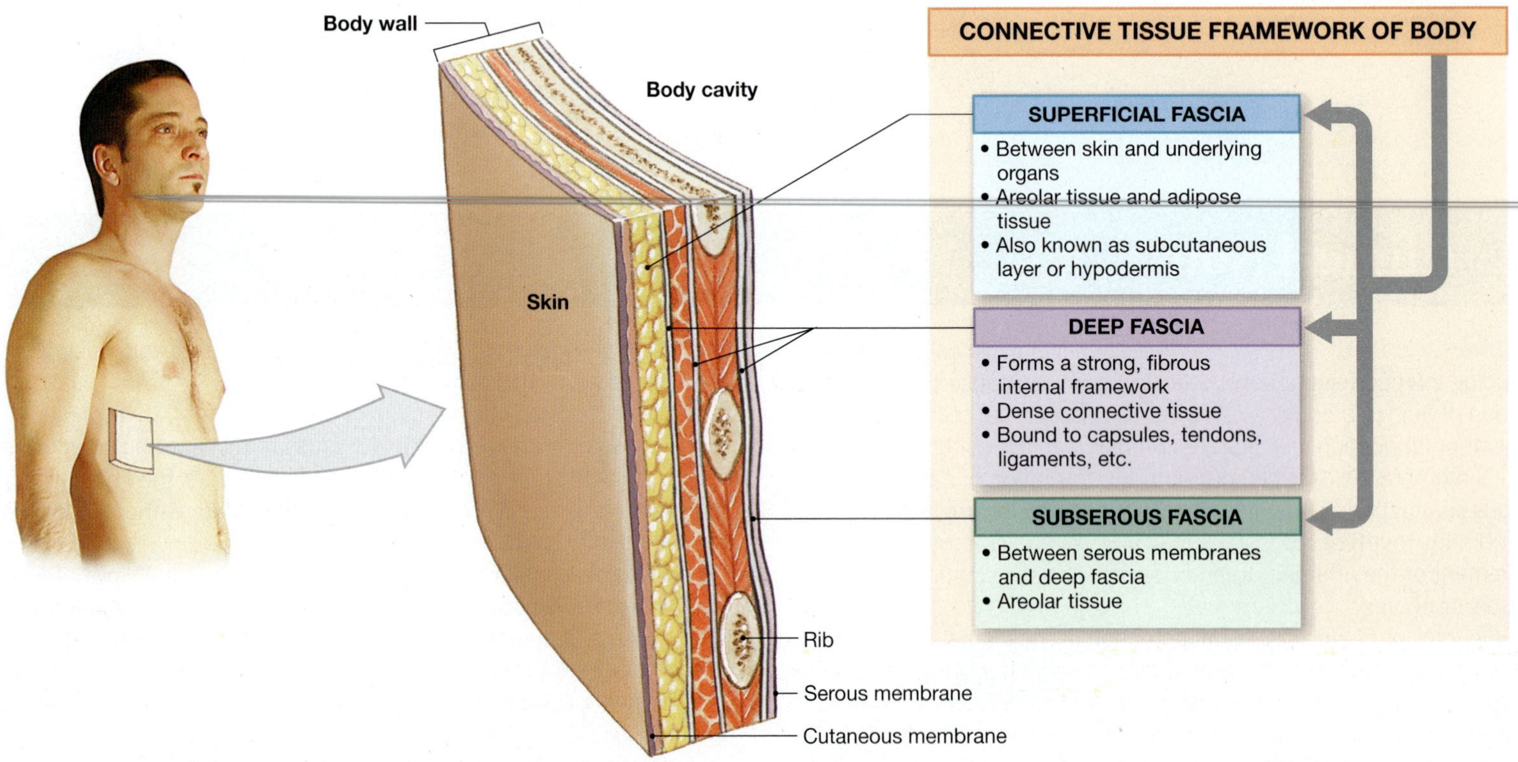

Figure 3.21 The Fasciae
The anatomical relationship of connective tissue elements in the body.

bound to the deep fascia. The perichondrium around cartilages, the periosteum around bones, and the connective tissue sheaths of muscle are also connected to the deep fascia. The deep fascia of the neck and limbs pass between groups of muscles as *intermuscular fascia*, and this divides the muscles into compartments or groups that are different functionally and developmentally. These dense connective tissue components are interwoven; for example, the deep fascia around a muscle blends into the tendon, whose fibers intermingle with those of the periosteum. This arrangement creates a strong, fibrous network for the body and ties structural elements together.

- The **subserous fascia** is a layer of loose connective tissue that lies between the deep fascia and the serous membranes that line body cavities. Because this layer separates the serous membranes from the deep fascia, movements of muscles or muscular organs do not severely distort the delicate lining.

CONCEPT CHECK

1. What type of membrane lines passageways of the respiratory and digestive systems? Why is this type of membrane suited to these areas?
2. Provide another name for the superficial fascia. What does it do?
3. You are asked to locate the pericardium. What type of membrane is this, and where would you find it?
4. What are the functions of the cutaneous membrane?

See blue "Answers" tab at back of book.

Muscle Tissue [Figure 3.22]

Muscle tissue is specialized for contraction (**Figure 3.22**). Muscle cells possess organelles and properties distinct from those of other cells. They are capable of powerful contractions that shorten the cell along its longitudinal axis. Because they are different from "typical" cells, the term **sarcoplasm** is used to refer to the cytoplasm of a muscle cell, and **sarcolemma** is used to refer to the plasmalemma.

Three types of muscle tissue are found in the body: (1) *skeletal*[1], (2) *cardiac*, and (3) *smooth*. The contraction mechanism is similar in all three, but they differ in their internal organization. We will describe each muscle type in greater detail in later chapters (skeletal muscle in Chapter 9, cardiac muscle in Chapter 21, and smooth muscle in Chapter 25). This discussion will focus on general characteristics rather than specific details.

Skeletal Muscle Tissue [Figure 3.22a]

Skeletal muscle tissue contains very large muscle cells. Because individual skeletal muscle cells are relatively long and slender, they are usually called **muscle fibers**. Skeletal muscle fibers are very unusual because they may be a foot (0.3 m) or more in length, and each cell is **multinucleate**, containing hundreds of nuclei lying just under the surface of the sarcolemma (**Figure 3.22a**). Skeletal muscle fibers are incapable of dividing, but new muscle fibers can be produced through the division of **myosatellite cells** (also termed satellite cells), mesenchymal cells that persist in adult skeletal muscle tissue. As a result, skeletal muscle tissue can at least partially repair itself after an injury.

Skeletal muscle fibers contain *actin* and *myosin* filaments arranged in parallel within organized functional groups. As a result, skeletal muscle fibers appear to have a banded, or *striated*, appearance (**Figure 3.22a**). Normally, skeletal muscle fibers will not contract unless stimulated by nerves, and the nervous system provides voluntary control over their activities. Thus, skeletal muscle is called **striated voluntary muscle**.

Skeletal muscle tissue is bound together by areolar connective tissue. The collagen and elastic fibers surrounding each cell and group of cells blend into those of a tendon or aponeurosis that conducts the force of contraction, usually to a bone of the skeleton. When the muscle tissue contracts, it pulls on the bone, and the bone moves.

Cardiac Muscle Tissue [Figure 3.22b]

Cardiac muscle tissue is found only in the heart. A typical **cardiac muscle cell** is smaller than a skeletal muscle fiber, and has one centrally placed nucleus. The prominent striations, seen in **Figure 3.22b**, resemble those of skeletal muscle. Cardiac muscle cells form extensive connections with one another; these connections occur at specialized regions known as **intercalated discs**. As a result, cardiac muscle tissue consists of a branching network of interconnected muscle cells. The anchoring junctions help channel the forces of contraction, and gap junctions at the intercalated discs help coordinate the activities of individual cardiac muscle cells. Like skeletal muscle fibers, cardiac muscle cells are incapable of dividing, and because this tissue lacks myosatellite cells, cardiac muscle tissue damaged by injury or disease cannot regenerate.

Cardiac muscle cells do not rely on nerve activity to start a contraction. Instead, specialized cardiac muscle cells called **pacemaker cells** establish a regular rate of contraction. Although the nervous system can alter the rate of pacemaker activity, it does not provide voluntary control over individual cardiac muscle cells. Therefore, cardiac muscle is called **striated involuntary muscle**.

Smooth Muscle Tissue [Figure 3.22c]

Smooth muscle tissue can be found at the base of hair follicles; in the walls of blood vessels; around hollow organs such as the urinary bladder; and in layers around the respiratory, circulatory, digestive, and reproductive tracts. A smooth muscle cell is a small cell with tapering ends, containing a single, centrally located, oval nucleus (**Figure 3.22c**). Smooth muscle cells can divide, and smooth muscle tissue can regenerate after an injury. The actin and myosin filaments in smooth muscle cells are organized differently from those of skeletal and cardiac muscle, and as a result there are no striations; it is the only *nonstriated* muscle tissue. Smooth muscle cells usually contract on their own, through the action of *pacesetter cells*. Although smooth muscle contractions may be triggered by neural activity, the nervous system does not usually provide voluntary control over those contractions. Consequently, smooth muscle is called **nonstriated involuntary muscle**.

[1] The *Terminologia Histologica: International Terms for Human Cytology and Histology* (TH, © 2008) splits this category into skeletal striated muscle and noncardiac visceral striated muscle, based on location and function.

SKELETAL MUSCLE TISSUE

Cells are long, cylindrical, striated, and multinucleate.

LOCATIONS: Combined with connective tissues and neural tissue in skeletal muscles

FUNCTIONS: Moves or stabilizes the position of the skeleton; guards entrances and exits to the digestive, respiratory, and urinary tracts; generates heat; protects internal organs

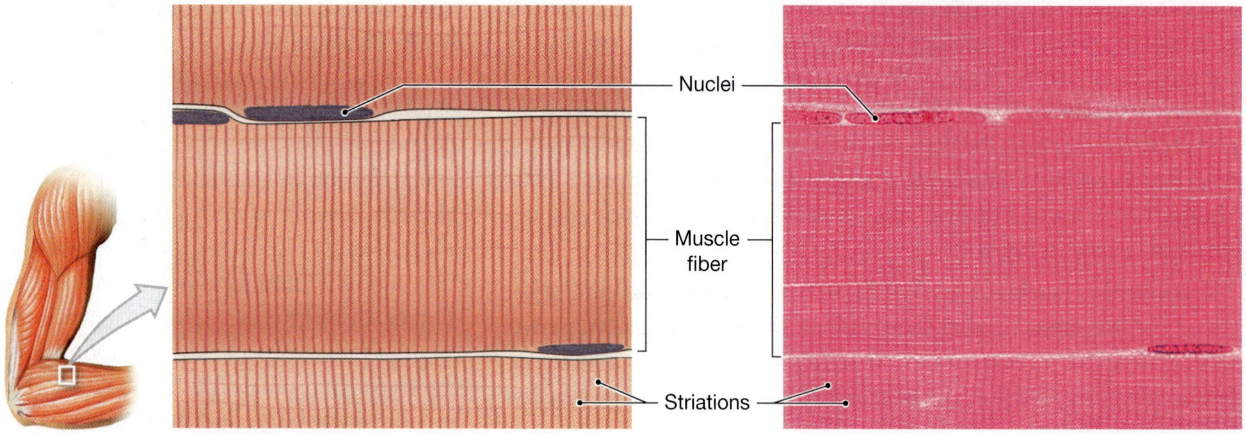

(a) Skeletal muscle LM × 180

CARDIAC MUSCLE TISSUE

Cells are short, branched, and striated, usually with a single nucleus; cells are interconnected by intercalated discs.

LOCATION: Heart

FUNCTIONS: Circulates blood; maintains blood (hydrostatic) pressure

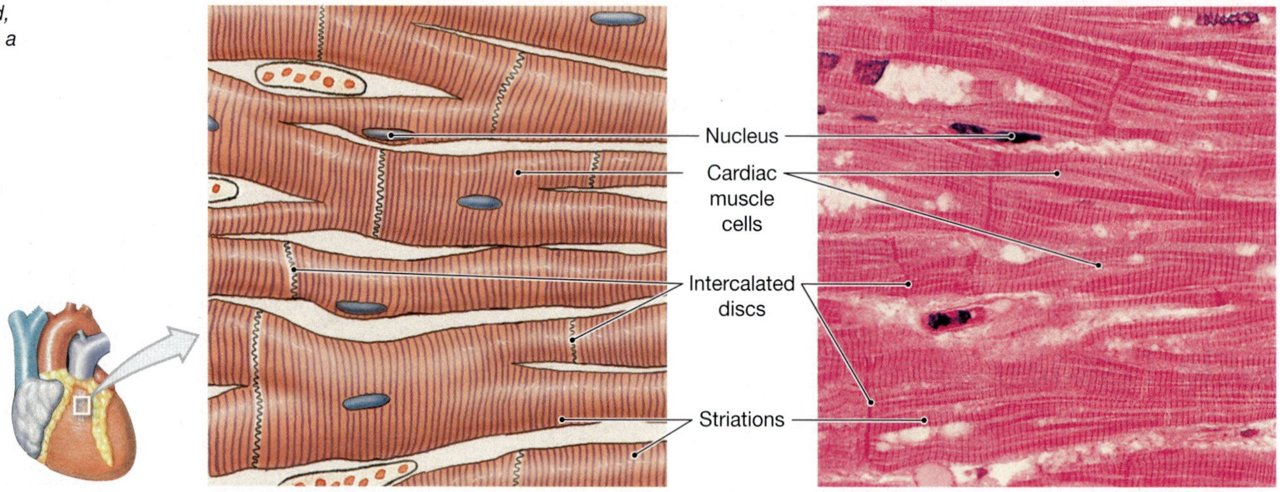

(b) Cardiac muscle LM × 450

SMOOTH MUSCLE TISSUE

Cells are short, spindle-shaped, and nonstriated, with a single, central nucleus

LOCATIONS: Found in the walls of blood vessels and in digestive, respiratory, urinary, and reproductive organs

FUNCTIONS: Moves food, urine, and reproductive tract secretions; controls diameter of respiratory passageways; regulates diameter of blood vessels

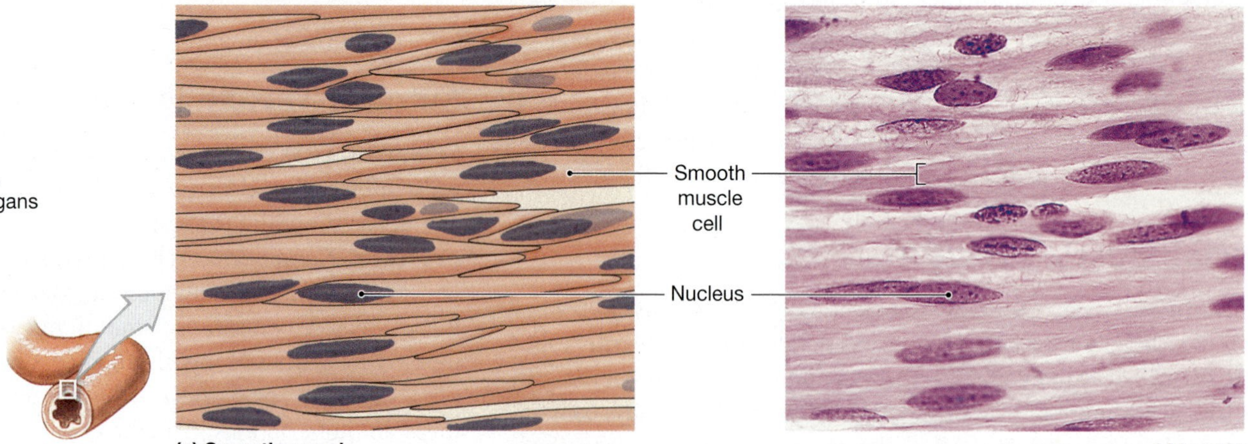

(c) Smooth muscle LM × 235

Figure 3.22 Histology of Muscle Tissue
(a) Skeletal Muscle Fibers. Note the large fiber size, prominent banding pattern, multiple nuclei, and unbranched arrangement. **(b) Cardiac Muscle Cells**. Cardiac muscle cells differ from skeletal muscle fibers in three major ways: size (cardiac muscle cells are smaller), organization (cardiac muscle cells branch), and number of nuclei (a typical cardiac muscle cell has one centrally placed nucleus). Both contain actin and myosin filaments in an organized array that produces the striations seen in both types of muscle cell. **(c) Smooth Muscle Cells**. Smooth muscle cells are small and spindle shaped, with a central nucleus. They do not branch, and there are no striations.

Neural Tissue [Figure 3.23]

Neural tissue, also known as **nervous tissue** or *nerve tissue*, is specialized for the conduction of electrical impulses from one region of the body to another. Most of the neural tissue in the body (roughly 96 percent) is concentrated in the brain and spinal cord, the control centers for the nervous system. Neural tissue contains two basic types of cells: **neurons** (NOOR-ons; *neuro*, nerve), or *nerve cells*, and several different kinds of supporting cells, collectively called **neuroglia** (noo-ROG-lē-a; *glia*, glue). Neurons transmit electrical impulses along their plasmalemmae. All of the functions of the nervous system involve changes in the pattern and frequency of the impulses carried by individual neurons. Neuroglia have varied functions, such as providing a supporting framework for neural tissue, regulating the composition of the interstitial fluid, and providing nutrients to neurons.

Neurons are the longest cells in the body, many reaching a meter in length. Most neurons are incapable of dividing under normal circumstances, and they have a very limited ability to repair themselves after injury. A typical neuron has a **cell body**, or *soma*, that contains a large prominent nucleus (Figure 3.23). Typically, the cell body is attached to several branching processes, called **dendrites** (DEN-drīts; *dendron*, tree), and a single **axon**. Dendrites receive incoming messages; axons conduct outgoing messages. It is the length of the axon that can make a neuron so long; because axons are very slender, they are also called **nerve fibers**. In Chapter 13 we will discuss the properties of neural tissue and provide additional histological and cytological details.

Tissues, Nutrition, and Aging

Tissues change with age. In general, repair and maintenance activities grow less efficient, and a combination of hormonal changes and alterations in lifestyle affect the structure and chemical composition of many tissues. Epithelia get thinner and connective tissues more fragile. Individuals bruise easily and bones become brittle; joint pains and broken bones are common complaints. Because cardiac muscle cells and neurons cannot be replaced, over time, cumulative losses from relatively minor damage can contribute to major health problems such as cardiovascular disease or deterioration in mental function.

In future chapters we will consider the effects of aging on specific organs and systems. Some of these changes are genetically programmed. For example, the chondrocytes of older individuals produce a slightly different form of proteoglycan than those of younger people. The difference probably accounts for the observed changes in the thickness and resilience of cartilage. In other cases the tissue degeneration may be temporarily slowed or even reversed. The age-related reduction in bone strength in women, a condition called **osteoporosis**, is often caused by a combination of inactivity, low dietary calcium levels, and a reduction in circulating estrogens (female sex hormones). A program of exercise and calcium supplements, sometimes combined with hormonal replacement therapies, can usually maintain normal bone structure for many years. (The risks versus potential benefits of hormone replacement therapies must be carefully evaluated on an individual basis.)

In this chapter we have introduced the four basic types of tissue found in the human body. In combination these tissues form all of the organs and systems that will be discussed in subsequent chapters.

CONCEPT CHECK

1. What type of muscle tissue has small, tapering cells with single nuclei and no obvious striations?
2. Why is skeletal muscle also called striated voluntary muscle?
3. Which tissue is specialized for the conduction of electrical impulses from one body region to another?

See blue "Answers" tab at back of book.

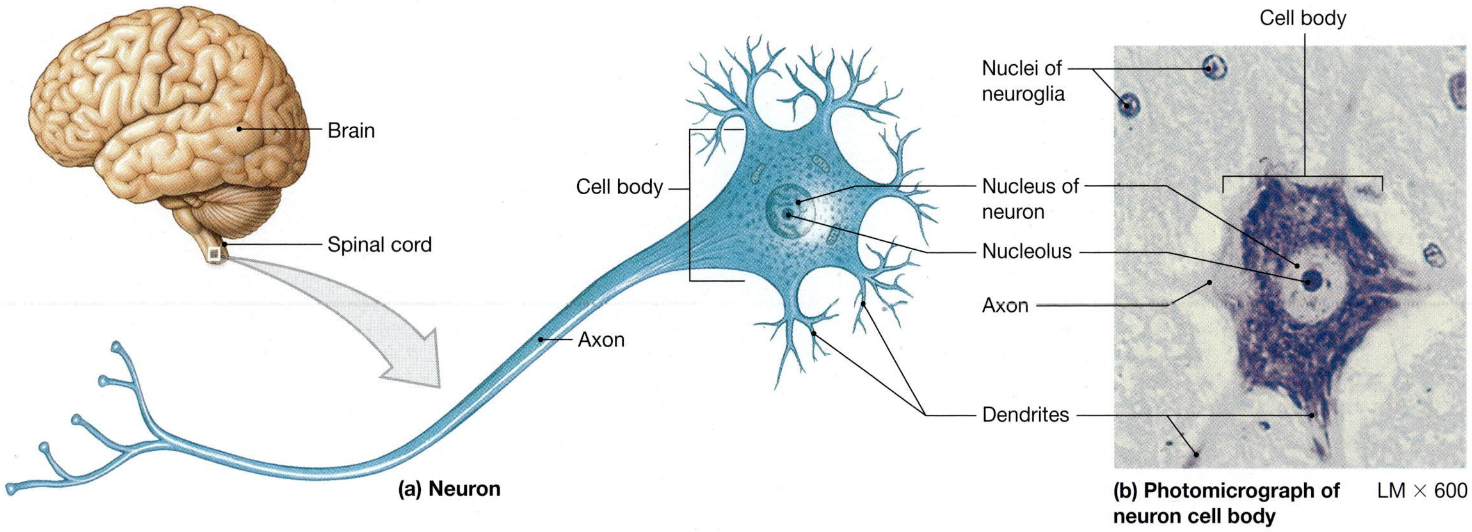

Figure 3.23 Histology of Neural Tissue
Diagrammatic **(a)** and histological **(b)** views of a representative neuron. Neurons are specialized for conduction of electrical impulses over relatively long distances within the body.

Clinical Note

Tumor Formation and Growth Physicians who specialize in the identification and treatment of cancers are called **oncologists** (ōn-KŌL-ō-jists; *onkos*, mass). Pathologists and oncologists classify cancers according to their cellular appearance and their sites of origin. Over a hundred kinds have been described, but broad categories are used to indicate the usual location of the primary tumor. Table 3.3 summarizes information concerning benign and malignant tumors (cancers) associated with the tissues discussed in this chapter.

Cancer develops in a series of steps, diagrammed in Figure 3.24. Initially the cancer cells are restricted to a single location, called the **primary tumor** or **primary neoplasm**. All of the cells in the tumor are usually the daughter cells of a single malignant cell. At first the growth of the primary tumor simply distorts the tissue, and the basic tissue organization remains intact. Metastasis begins as tumor cells "break out" of the primary tumor and invade the surrounding tissue. When this invasion is followed by penetration of nearby blood vessels, the cancer cells begin circulating throughout the body.

Responding to cues that are as yet unknown, these cells later escape from the circulatory system and establish **secondary tumors** at other sites. These tumors are extremely active metabolically, and their presence stimulates the growth of blood vessels into the area. The increased circulatory supply provides additional nutrients and further accelerates tumor growth and metastasis. Death may occur because vital organs have been compressed, because nonfunctional cancer cells have killed or replaced the normal cells in vital organs, or because the voracious cancer cells have starved normal tissues of essential nutrients.

TABLE 3.3 Benign and Malignant Tumors in the Major Tissue Types

Tissue	Description
EPITHELIA	
Carcinomas	Any cancer of epithelial origin
Adenocarcinomas	Cancers of glandular epithelia
Angiosarcomas	Cancers of endothelial cells
Mesotheliomas	Cancers of mesothelial cells
CONNECTIVE TISSUES	
Fibromas	Benign tumors of fibroblast origin
Lipomas	Benign tumors of adipose tissue
Liposarcomas	Cancers of adipose tissue
Leukemias, lymphomas	Cancers of blood-forming tissues
Chondromas	Benign tumors in cartilage
Chondrosarcomas	Cancers of cartilage
Osteomas	Benign tumors in bone
Osteosarcomas	Cancers of bone
MUSCLE TISSUES	
Myomas	Benign muscle tumors
Myosarcomas	Cancers of skeletal muscle tissue
Cardiac sarcomas	Cancers of cardiac muscle tissue
Leiomyomas	Benign tumors of smooth muscle tissue
Leiomyosarcomas	Cancers of smooth muscle tissue
NEURAL TISSUES	
Gliomas, neuromas	Cancers of neuroglial origin

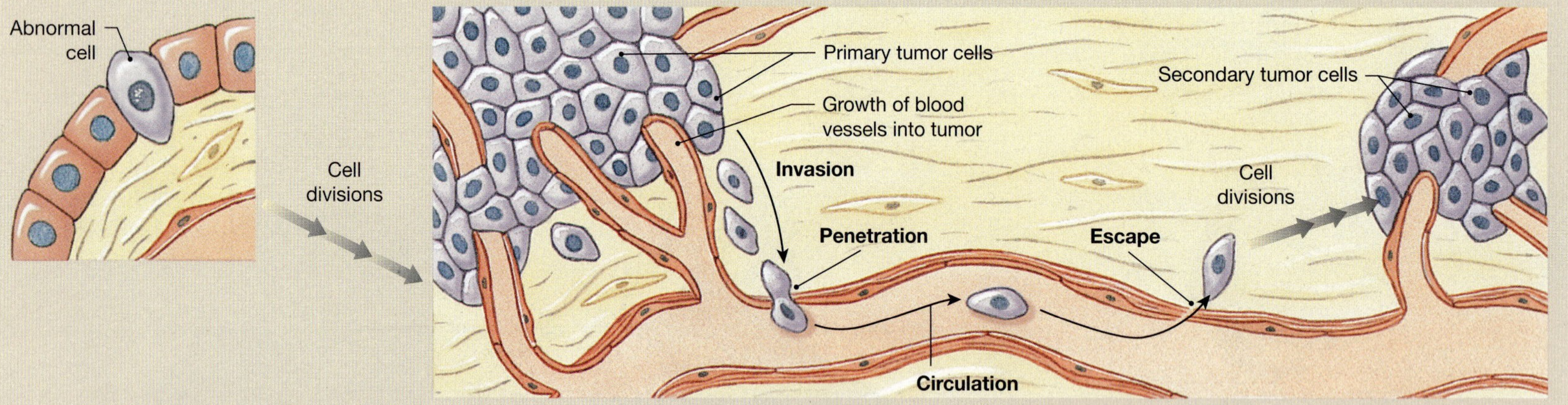

Figure 3.24 The Development of Cancer
Diagram of abnormal cell divisions leading to the formation of a tumor. Blood vessels grow into the tumor, and tumor cells invade the blood vessels to travel throughout the body.

The Formation of Tissues

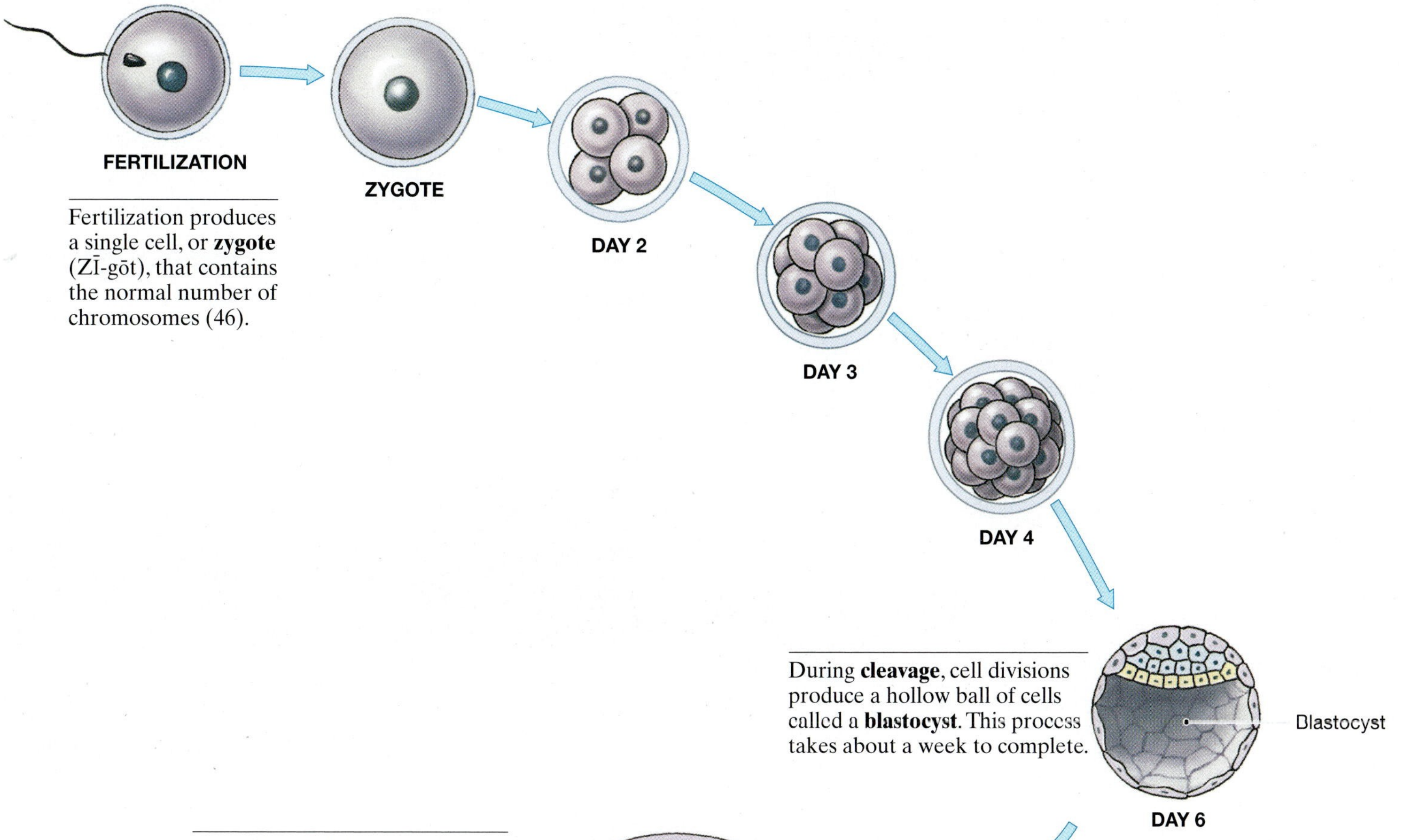

Fertilization produces a single cell, or **zygote** (ZĪ-gōt), that contains the normal number of chromosomes (46).

During **cleavage**, cell divisions produce a hollow ball of cells called a **blastocyst**. This process takes about a week to complete.

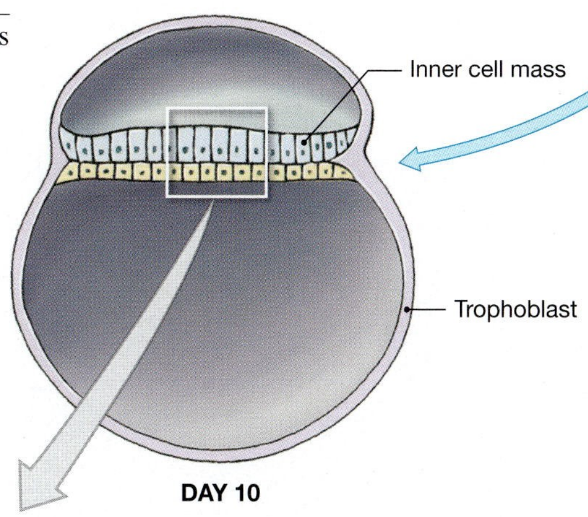

In section, the blastocyst contains two groups of cells with very different fates. The outer layer, or **trophoblast** (TRŌ-fō-blast; *trophos*, food + *blast*, precursor), will form the placenta, which nourishes the developing embryo. The **inner cell mass** will form the actual embryo.

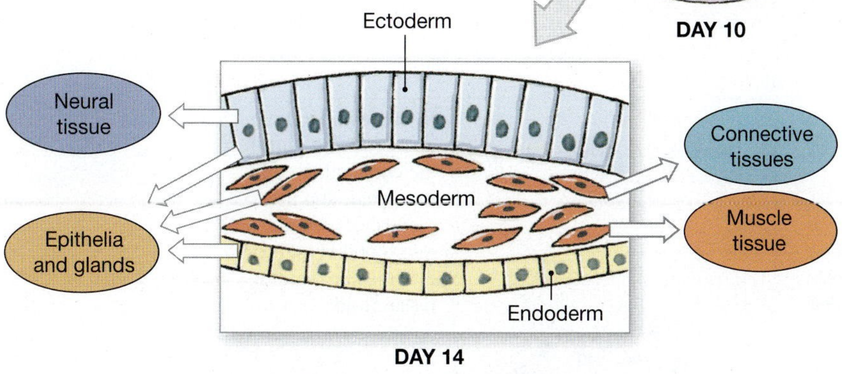

During the second week of development, different populations of cells can be seen in the inner cell mass. These cells are organized into three **primary germ layers**: the **ectoderm**, **mesoderm**, and **endoderm**. Further differentiation of the primary germ layers will produce the major tissue types.

All three germ layers participate in the formation of functional organs and organ systems. Their interactions will be detailed in later Embryology Summaries dealing with specific systems.

The Development of Epithelia

All epithelia begin as simple epithelia that may later become stratified.

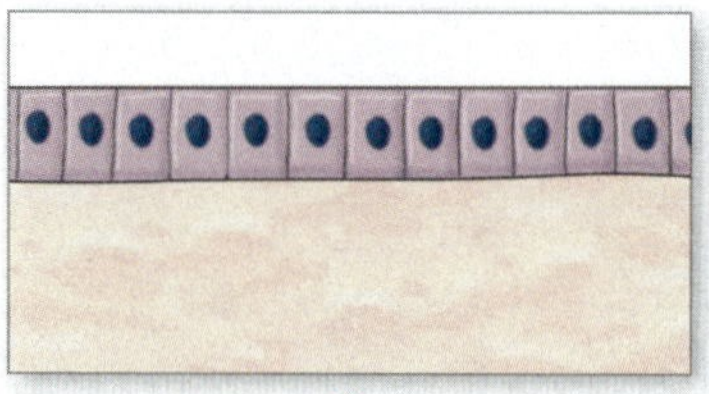

These cells differentiate into functional epithelial cells and gland cells that may have endocrine or exocrine functions.

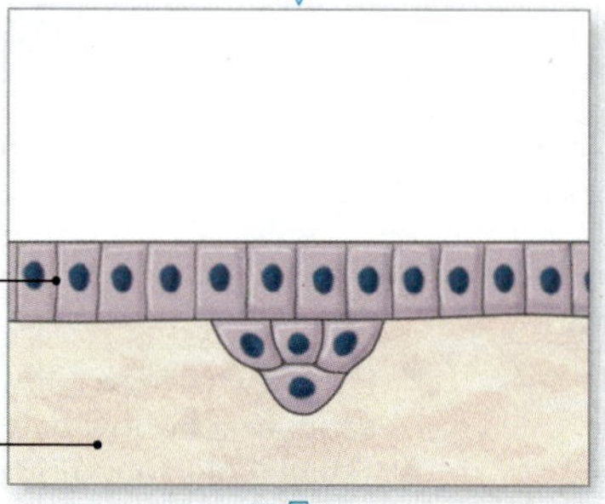

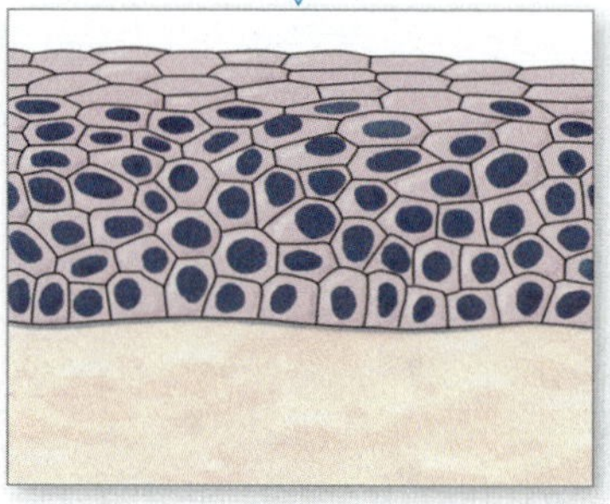
Skin

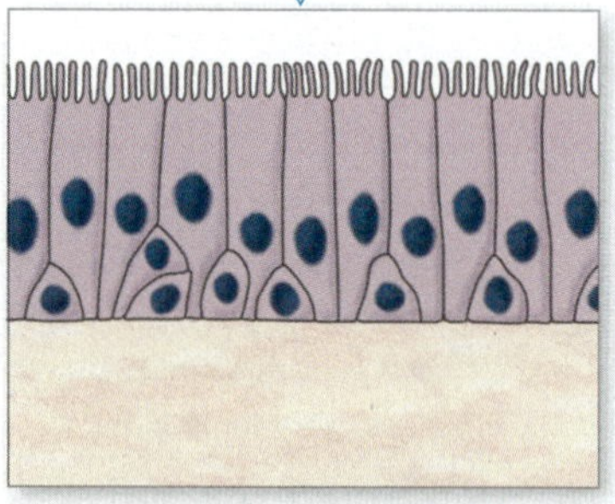
Respiratory epithelium

Complex glands begin to form as epithelial cells grow into the underlying connective tissue.

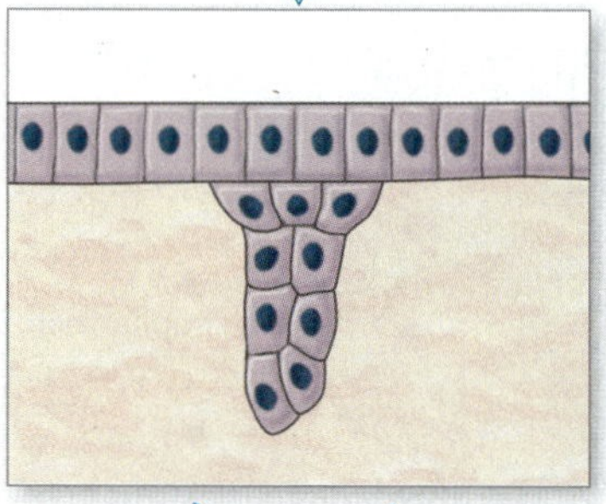

In the formation of an **exocrine gland**, the cells connecting the secretory cells to the surface form the duct that carries the secretions of the gland cells to the epithelial surface.

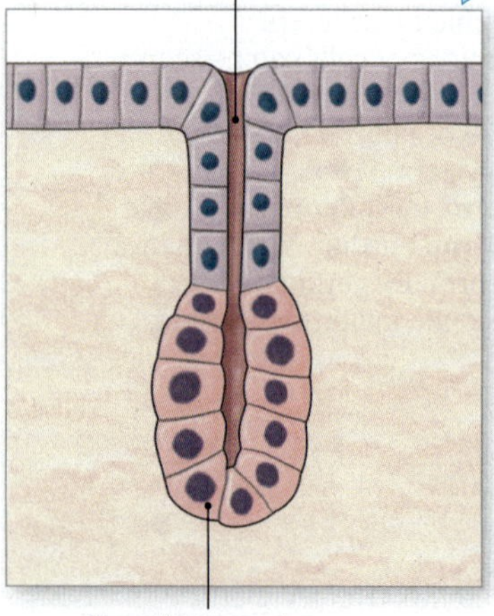

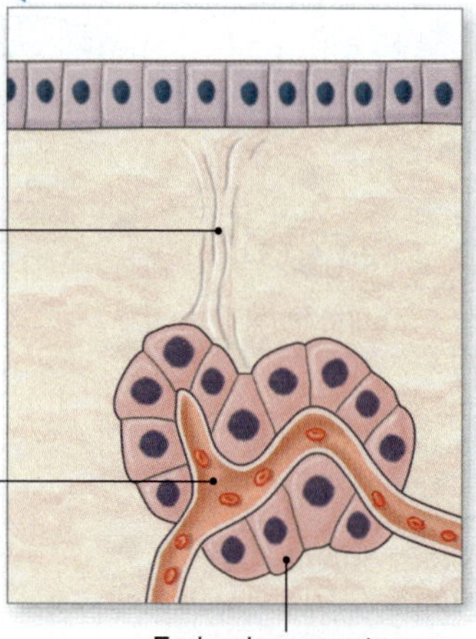

In the formation of an **endocrine gland**, the connecting cells disappear, and the gland cells secrete into blood vessels or into the surrounding tissue fluids.

Origins of Connective Tissues

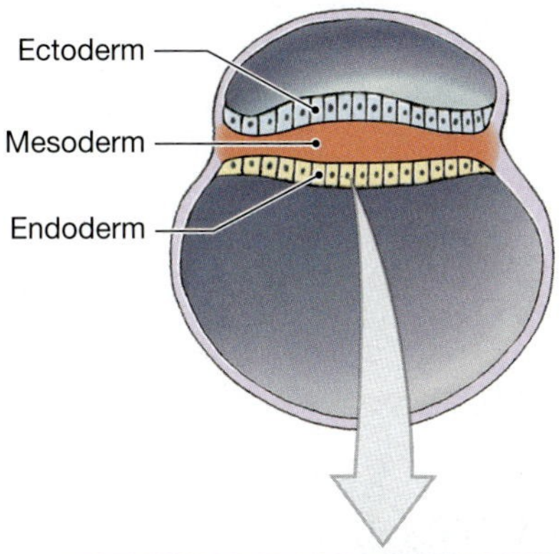

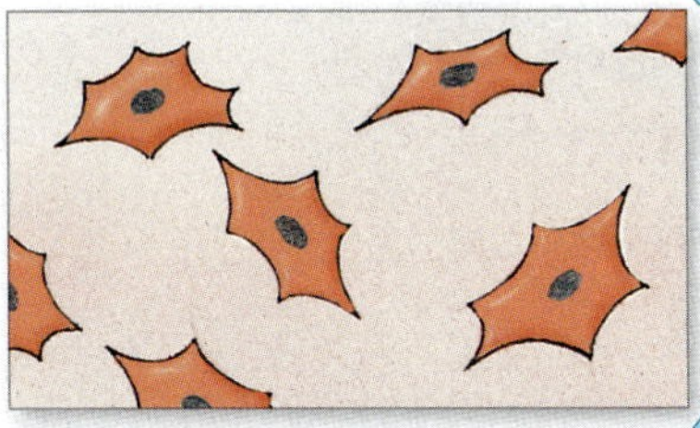

Mesenchyme is the first connective tissue to appear in the developing embryo. Mesenchyme contains star-shaped cells that are separated by a ground substance that contains fine protein filaments. Mesenchyme gives rise to all other forms of connective tissue, and scattered mesenchymal cells in adult connective tissues participate in their repair after injury.

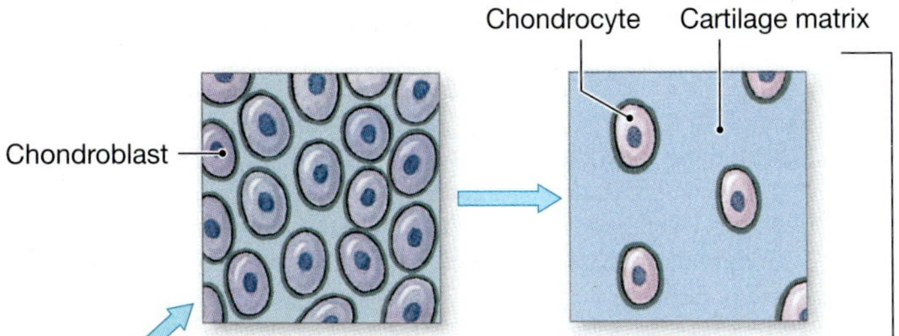

Cartilage develops as mesenchymal cells differentiate into **chondroblasts** that produce cartilage matrix. These cells later become chondrocytes.

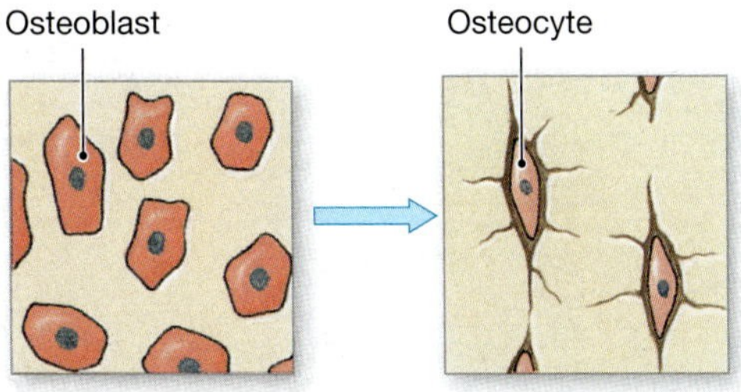

Bone formation begins as mesenchymal cells differentiate into **osteoblasts** that lay down the matrix of bone. These cells later become trapped as osteocytes.

Supporting connective tissue

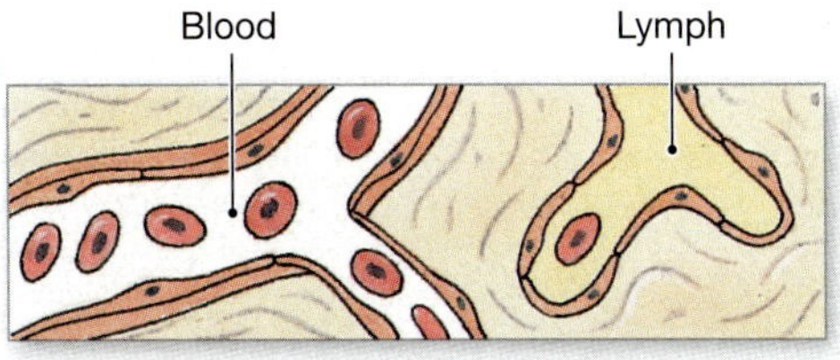

Fluid connective tissues form, as mesenchymal cells create a network of interconnected tubes. Cells trapped in those tubes differentiate into red and white blood cells.

Fluid connective tissue

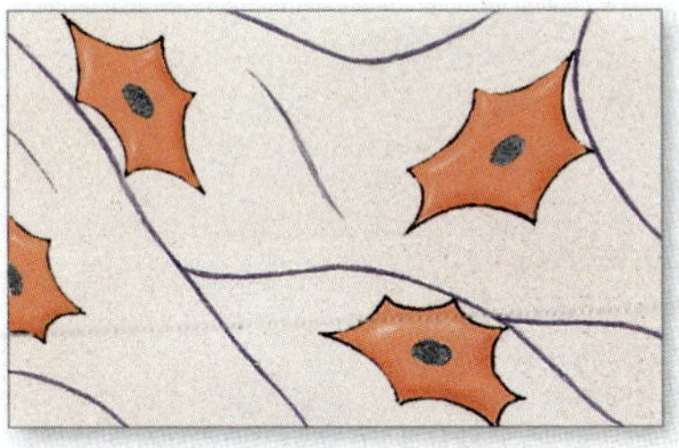

Embryonic connective tissue develops as the density of fibers increases. Embryonic connective tissue may differentiate into any of the connective tissues proper.

Loose connective tissue

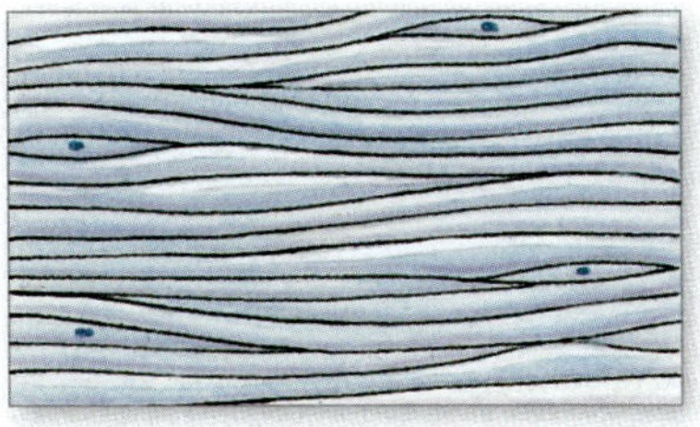

Dense connective tissue

The Development of Organ Systems

For a summary of the development of the muscular and nervous systems, see Chapter 28 (Embryology and Human Development).

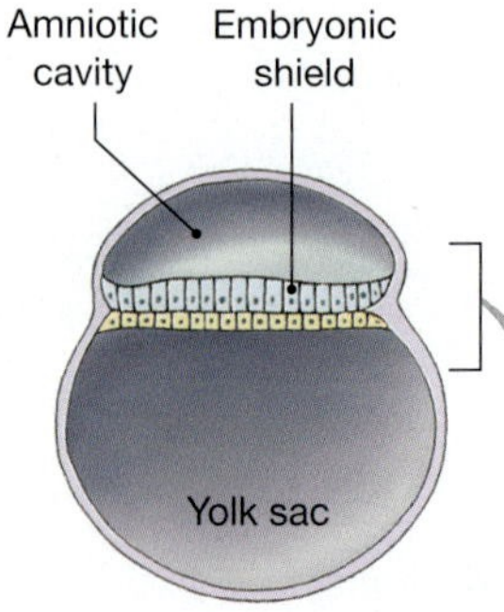

Many different organ systems show similar patterns of organization. For example, the digestive, respiratory, urinary, and reproductive systems each include passageways lined by epithelia and surrounded by layers of smooth muscle. These patterns are the result of developmental processes under way in the first two months of embryonic life.

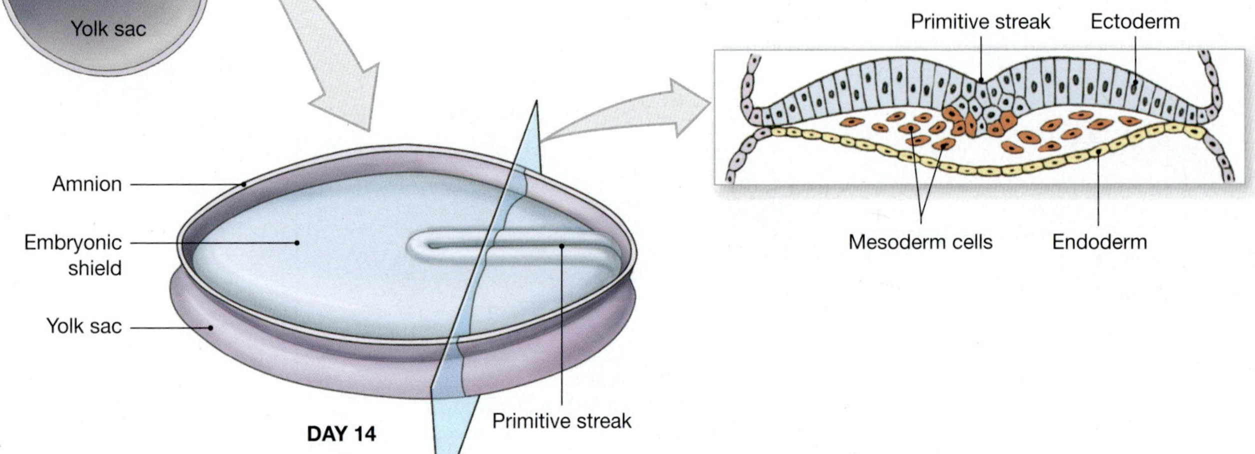

After roughly two weeks of development, the inner cell mass is only a millimeter in length. The region of embryonic development is called the **embryonic shield**. It contains a pair of epithelial layers: an upper ectoderm and an underlying endoderm. At a region called the **primitive streak**, superficial cells migrate between the two, adding to an intermediate layer of mesoderm.

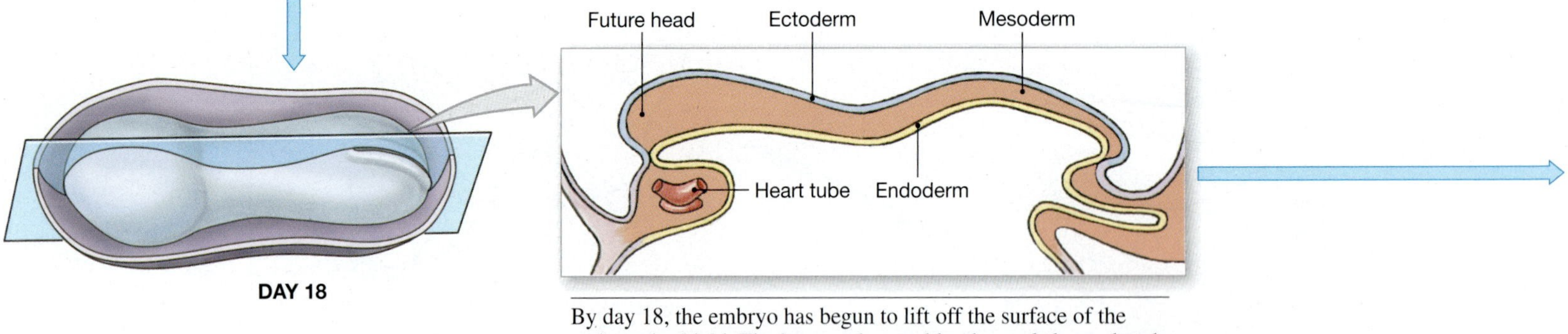

By day 18, the embryo has begun to lift off the surface of the embryonic shield. The heart and many blood vessels have already formed, well ahead of the other organ systems. Unless otherwise noted, discussions of organ system development in later chapters will begin at this stage.

DERIVATIVES OF PRIMARY GERM LAYERS	
Ectoderm Forms:	Epidermis and epidermal derivatives of the integumentary system, including hair follicles, nails, and glands communicating with the skin surface (sweat, milk, and sebum) Lining of the mouth, salivary glands, nasal passageways, and anus Nervous system, including brain and spinal cord Portions of endocrine system (pituitary gland and parts of suprarenal glands) Portions of skull, pharyngeal arches, and teeth
Mesoderm Forms:	Dermis of integumentary system Lining of the body cavities (pleural, pericardial, peritoneal) Muscular, skeletal, cardiovascular, and lymphoid systems Kidneys and part of the urinary tract Gonads and most of the reproductive tract Connective tissues supporting all organ systems Portions of endocrine system (parts of suprarenal glands and endocrine tissues of the reproductive tract)
Endoderm Forms:	Most of the digestive system: epithelium (except mouth and anus), exocrine glands (except salivary glands), the liver and pancreas Most of the respiratory system: epithelium (except nasal passageways) and mucous glands Portions of urinary and reproductive systems (ducts and the stem cells that produce gametes) Portions of endocrine system (thymus, thyroid gland, parathyroid glands, and pancreas)

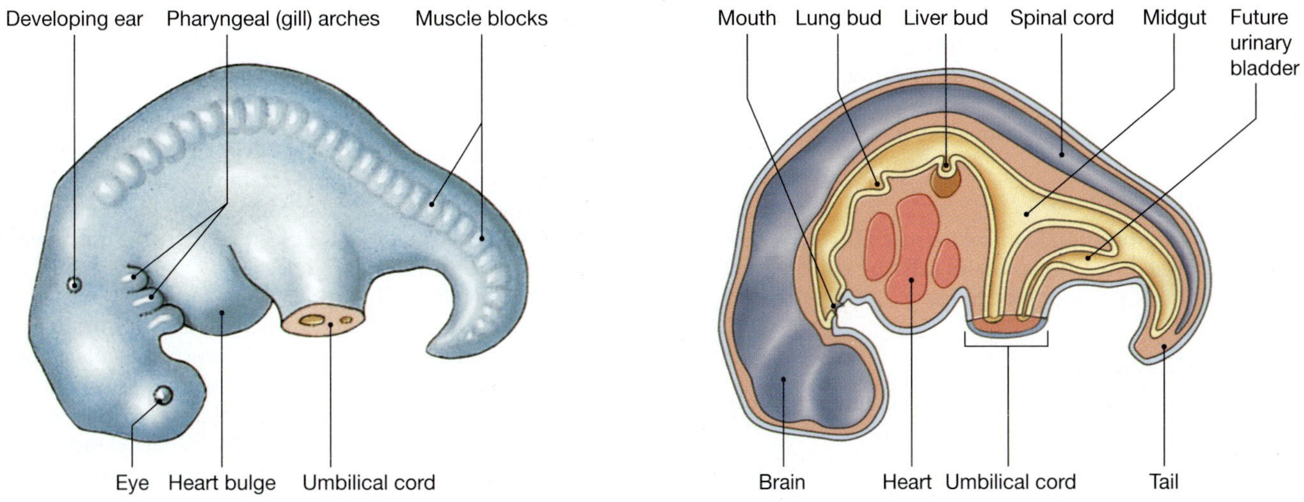

DAY 28

After one month, you can find the beginnings of all major organ systems. The role of each of the primary germ layers in the formation of organs is summarized in the accompanying table; details are given in later Embryology Summaries.

CLINICAL TERMS

adhesions: Restrictive fibrous connections that can result from surgery, infection, or other injuries to serous membranes.

anaplasia (an-a-PLĀ-zē-a): An irreversible change in the size and shape of tissue cells.

ascites (a-SĪ-tēz): An accumulation of peritoneal fluid that creates a characteristic abdominal swelling.

chemotherapy: The administration of drugs that either kill cancerous tissues or prevent mitotic divisions.

dysplasia (dis-PLĀ-zē-a): A change in the normal shape, size, and organization of tissue cells.

effusion: The accumulation of fluid in body cavities.

immunotherapy: The administration of drugs that help the immune system recognize and attack cancer cells.

liposuction: A surgical procedure to remove unwanted adipose tissue by sucking it through a tube.

metaplasia (met-a-PLĀ-zē-a): A structural change that alters the character of a tissue.

oncologists (on-KOL-ō-jists): Physicians who specialize in identifying and treating cancers.

pathologists (pa-THOL-ō-jists): Physicians who specialize in the diagnosis of diseases, primarily from an examination of body fluids, tissue samples, and other anatomical clues.

pericarditis: An inflammation of the pericardium.

peritonitis: An inflammation of the peritoneum.

pleuritis (pleurisy): An inflammation of the lining of the pleural cavities.

primary tumor (primary neoplasm): The site at which a cancer initially develops.

remission: A stage in which a tumor stops growing or grows smaller; the goal of cancer treatment.

secondary tumor: A colony of cancerous cells formed by metastasis, the spread of cells from a primary tumor.

STUDY OUTLINE

Introduction 52

1. **Tissues** are collections of specialized cells and cell products that are organized to perform a relatively limited number of functions. There are four **primary tissue types**: *epithelial tissue*, *connective tissue*, *muscle tissue*, and *neural tissue*. *(see Figure 3.1)*
2. **Histology** is the study of tissues.

Epithelial Tissue 52

1. **Epithelial tissues** include *epithelia*, which cover surfaces, and *glands*, which are secretory structures derived from epithelia. An **epithelium** is an **avascular** sheet of cells that forms a surface, lining, or covering. Epithelia consist mainly of tightly bound cells, rather than extracellular materials. *(see Figures 3.2 to 3.10)*
2. Epithelial cells are replaced continually through stem cell activity.

Functions of Epithelial Tissue 53

3. Epithelia provide physical protection, control permeability, provide sensation, and produce specialized secretions. **Gland cells** are epithelial cells (or cells derived from them) that produce secretions.

Specializations of Epithelial Cells 53

4. Epithelial cells are specialized to maintain the physical integrity of the epithelium and perform secretory or transport functions.
5. Epithelia may show **polarity** from the *basal* to the *apical* surface; cells connect neighbor cells on their *lateral surfaces*; some epithelial cells have microvilli on their apical surfaces. There are often structural and functional differences between the apical surface and the *basolateral* surfaces of individual epithelial cells. *(see Figure 3.2)*
6. The coordinated beating of the cilia on a **ciliated epithelium** moves materials across the epithelial surface. *(see Figure 3.2)*

Maintaining the Integrity of the Epithelium 54

7. All epithelial tissue rests on an underlying **basal lamina** consisting of a *clear layer* (lamina lucida), produced by the epithelial cells and usually a deeper *dense layer* (lamina densa) secreted by the underlying connective tissue. In areas exposed to extreme chemical or mechanical stresses, divisions by **germinative cells** replace the short-lived epithelial cells. *(see Figure 3.3a)*

Classification of Epithelia 55

8. Epithelia are classified both on the basis of the number of cell layers in the epithelium and the shape of the exposed cells at the surface of the epithelium. *(see Figures 3.4 to 3.7)*
9. A **simple epithelium** has a single layer of cells covering the basal lamina. A **stratified epithelium** has several layers. In a **squamous epithelium** the surface cells are thin and flat; in a **cuboidal epithelium** the cells resemble short hexagonal boxes; in a **columnar epithelium** the cells are also hexagonal, but they are relatively tall and slender. **Pseudostratified columnar epithelium** contains columnar cells, some of which possess cilia and mucous (secreting) cells that appear stratified, but are not. A **transitional epithelium** is characterized by a mixture of what appears to be both cuboidal and squamous cells arranged to permit stretching. *(see Figures 3.4 to 3.7)*

Glandular Epithelia 58

10. Glands may be classified by the type of secretion produced, the structure of the gland, or their mode of secretion. *(see Figures 3.8 to 3.10)*
11. **Exocrine** secretions are discharged through **ducts** onto the skin or an epithelial surface that communicates with the exterior; **endocrine** secretions, known as **hormones**, are released by gland cells into the interstitial fluid surrounding the cell.
12. Exocrine glands may be classified as **serous** (producing a watery solution usually containing enzymes), **mucous** (producing a viscous, sticky mucus), or **mixed** (producing both types of secretions).
13. In epithelia that contain scattered gland cells, the individual secretory cells are called **unicellular glands**. **Multicellular glands** are glandular epithelia or aggregations of gland cells that produce exocrine or endocrine secretions. *(see Figures 3.8/3.9)*
14. A glandular, epithelial cell may release its secretions through a merocrine, apocrine, or holocrine mechanism. *(see Figure 3.10)*
15. In **merocrine secretion**, the most common method of secretion, the product is released by exocytosis. **Apocrine secretion** involves the loss of both secretory product and some cytoplasm. Unlike the other two methods, **holocrine secretion** destroys the cell, which had become packed with secretory product before bursting. *(see Figure 3.10)*

Connective Tissues 61

1. All connective tissues have three components: specialized cells, extracellular **protein fibers**, and **ground substance**. The combination of protein fibers and ground substance forms the **matrix** of the tissue.

2. Whereas epithelia consist almost entirely of cells, the extracellular matrix accounts for most of the volume of a connective tissue. Therefore connective tissues, with the exception of adipose tissue, are identified by the characteristics of the extracellular matrix.
3. **Connective tissue** is an internal tissue with many important functions, including establishing a structural framework; transporting fluids and dissolved materials; protecting delicate organs; supporting, surrounding, and interconnecting tissues; storing energy reserves; and defending the body from microorganisms.

Classification of Connective Tissues 62

4. **Connective tissue proper** refers to all connective tissues that contain varied cell populations and fiber types suspended in a viscous ground substance. *(see Figure 3.11)*
5. **Fluid connective tissues** have a distinctive population of cells suspended in a watery ground substance containing dissolved proteins. *Blood* and *lymph* are examples of fluid connective tissues. *(see Figure 3.11)*
6. **Supporting connective tissues** have a less diverse cell population than connective tissue proper. Additionally, they have a dense matrix that contains closely packed fibers. The two types of supporting connective tissues are *cartilage* and *bone. (see Figure 3.11)*

Connective Tissue Proper 62

7. Connective tissue proper is composed of extracellular fibers, a viscous ground substance, and two categories of cells: **fixed cells** and **wandering cells**. *(see Figure 3.12 and Table 3.1)*
8. There are three types of fibers in connective tissue: **collagen fibers**, **reticular fibers**, and **elastic fibers**. *(see Figures 3.12/3.14/3.15)*
9. All connective tissues are derived from embryonic **mesenchyme**. *(see Figure 3.13)*
10. Connective tissue proper includes **loose** and **dense connective tissues**. There are three types of loose connective tissues: **areolar tissue**, **adipose tissue**, and **reticular tissue**. Most of the volume of loose connective tissue is ground substance, a viscous fluid that cushions shocks. Most of the volume in dense connective tissue consists of extracellular protein fibers. There are two types of dense connective tissue: **dense regular connective tissue**, in which fibers are parallel and aligned along lines of stress, and **dense irregular connective tissue**, in which fibers form an interwoven meshwork. *(see Figures 3.14/3.15)*

Fluid Connective Tissues 68

11. **Blood** and **lymph** are examples of fluid connective tissues, each with a distinctive collection of cells in a watery matrix. Both blood and lymph contain cells and many different types of dissolved proteins that do not form insoluble fibers under normal conditions. *(see Figure 3.16)*
12. Extracellular fluid includes the **plasma** of blood; the **interstitial fluid** within other connective tissues and other tissue types; and lymph, which is confined to vessels of the lymphoid system.

Supporting Connective Tissues 68

13. Cartilage and bone are called **supporting connective tissues** because they support the rest of the body. *(see Figures 3.17/3.18)*
14. The matrix of **cartilage** is a firm gel that contains **chondroitin sulfates**. It is produced by immature cells called **chondroblasts**, and maintained by mature cells called **chondrocytes**. A fibrous covering called the **perichondrium** separates cartilage from surrounding tissues. Cartilage grows by two different mechanisms, **appositional growth** (growth at the surface) and **interstitial growth** (growth from within). *(see Figure 3.18)*
15. There are three types of cartilage: **hyaline cartilage**, **elastic cartilage**, and **fibrous cartilage**. *(see Figure 3.18 and Table 3.2)*
16. **Bone (osseous tissue)** has a matrix consisting of collagen fibers and calcium salts, giving it unique properties. *(see Figure 3.19)*
17. **Osteocytes** in **lacunae** depend on diffusion through intercellular connections or **canaliculi** for nutrient intake. *(see Figure 3.19 and Table 3.2)*
18. All bone surfaces except those inside joint cavities are covered by a **periosteum** that has fibrous and cellular layers. The periosteum assists in attaching the bone to surrounding tissues, tendons, and ligaments, and it participates in the repair of bone after an injury.

Membranes 72

1. Membranes form a barrier or interface. Epithelia and connective tissues combine to form membranes that cover and protect other structures and tissues. There are four types of membranes: *mucous*, *serous*, *cutaneous*, and *synovial. (see Figure 3.20)*

Mucous Membranes 72

2. **Mucous membranes** line passageways that communicate with the exterior, such as the digestive and respiratory tracts. These surfaces are usually moistened by mucous secretions. They contain areolar tissue called the **lamina propria**. *(see Figure 3.20a)*

Serous Membranes 72

3. **Serous membranes** line internal cavities and are delicate, moist, and very permeable. Examples include the pleural, peritoneal, and pericardial membranes. Each serous membrane forms a fluid called a **transudate**. *(see Figure 3.20b)*

The Cutaneous Membrane 74

4. The **cutaneous membrane**, or **skin**, covers the body surface. Unlike other membranes, it is relatively thick, waterproof, and usually dry. *(see Figure 3.20c)*

Synovial Membranes 74

5. The **synovial membrane**, located within the cavity of synovial joints, produces **synovial fluid** that fills joint cavities. Synovial fluid helps lubricate the joint and promotes smooth movement in joints such as the knee. *(see Figure 3.20d)*

The Connective Tissue Framework of the Body 74

1. All organ systems are interconnected by a network of connective tissue proper that includes the **superficial fascia** (the **subcutaneous layer** or **hypodermis**, separating the skin from underlying tissues and organs), the **deep fascia** (dense connective tissue), and the **subserous fascia** (the layer between the deep fascia and the serous membranes that line body cavities). *(see Figure 3.21)*

Muscle Tissue 75

1. **Muscle tissue** consists primarily of cells that are specialized for contraction. There are three different types of muscle tissue: *skeletal muscle*, *cardiac muscle*, and *smooth muscle. (see Figure 3.22)*

Skeletal Muscle Tissue 75

2. **Skeletal muscle tissue** contains very large cylindrical **muscle fibers** interconnected by collagen and elastic fibers. Skeletal muscle fibers have striations due to the organization of their contractile proteins. Because we can control the contraction of skeletal muscle fibers through the nervous system, skeletal muscle is classified as **striated voluntary muscle**. New muscle fibers are produced by the division of **myosatellite cells**. *(see Figure 3.22a)*

Cardiac Muscle Tissue 75

3. **Cardiac muscle tissue** is found only in the heart. It is composed of unicellular, branched short cells. The nervous system does not provide voluntary control over cardiac muscle cells. Thus, cardiac muscle is classified as **striated involuntary muscle**. *(see Figure 3.22b)*

Smooth Muscle Tissue 75

4. **Smooth muscle tissue** is composed of short, tapered cells containing a single nucleus. It is found in the walls of blood vessels, around hollow organs, and in layers around various tracts. It is classified as **nonstriated involuntary muscle**. Smooth muscle cells can divide and therefore regenerate after injury. *(see Figure 3.22c)*

Neural Tissue 77

1. **Neural tissue** or **nervous tissue** (*nerve tissue*) is specialized to conduct electrical impulses from one area of the body to another.
2. Neural tissue consists of two cell types: neurons and neuroglia. **Neurons** transmit information as electrical impulses. There are different kinds of **neuroglia**, and among their other functions these cells provide a supporting framework for neural tissue and play a role in providing nutrients to neurons. *(see Figure 3.23)*
3. Neurons have a **cell body**, or **soma**, that contains a large prominent nucleus. Various branching processes termed **dendrites** and a single **axon** or **nerve fiber** extend from the cell body. Dendrites receive incoming messages; axons conduct messages toward other cells. *(see Figure 3.23)*

Tissues, Nutrition, and Aging 77

1. Tissues change with age. Repair and maintenance grow less efficient, and the structure and chemical composition of many tissues are altered.

CHAPTER REVIEW

For answers to the Concept Check and Chapter Review questions, go to the blue "Answers" tab at the back of the book.

Level 1 Reviewing Facts and Terms

Match each numbered item with the most closely related lettered item. Use letters for answers in the spaces provided.

Column A	Column B
___ 1. skeletal muscle	a. all epithelia
___ 2. mast cell	b. single cell layer
___ 3. avascular	c. urinary bladder
___ 4. transitional	d. cell destroyed
___ 5. goblet cell	e. connective tissue component
___ 6. collagen	f. unicellular, exocrine gland
___ 7. cartilage	g. tendon
___ 8. simple epithelium	h. wandering cell
___ 9. ground substance	i. lacunae
___ 10. holocrine secretion	j. striated

11. Epithelial cells do not
    (a) cover every exposed surface of the body
    (b) line the digestive, respiratory, reproductive, and urinary tracts
    (c) line the outer surfaces of blood vessels and the heart
    (d) line internal cavities and passageways

12. Which of the following refers to the dense connective tissue that forms the capsules that surround many organs?
    (a) superficial fascia (b) hypodermis
    (c) deep fascia (d) subserous fascia

13. The reduction of friction between the parietal and visceral surfaces of an internal cavity is the function of
    (a) cutaneous membranes (b) mucous membranes
    (c) serous membranes (d) synovial membranes

14. Which of the following is not a characteristic of epithelial cells?
    (a) They may consist of a single or multiple cell layer.
    (b) They always have a free surface exposed to the external environment or some inner chamber or passageway.
    (c) They are avascular.
    (d) They consist of a few cells but have a large amount of extracellular material.

15. Functions of connective tissue include each of the following, except
    (a) establishing a structural framework for the body
    (b) transporting fluids and dissolved materials
    (c) storing energy reserves
    (d) providing sensation

16. Which of the following is not a property of smooth muscle tissue?
    (a) is composed of small cells with tapering ends
    (b) has cells with many, irregularly shaped nuclei
    (c) can replace cells and regenerate after an injury
    (d) contracts with or without nervous stimulation

17. Tissue changes with age include
    (a) decreased ability to repair
    (b) less efficient tissue maintenance
    (c) thinner epithelia
    (d) all of the above

18. What type of supporting tissue is found in the pinna of the ear and the tip of the nose?
    (a) bone (b) fibrous cartilage
    (c) elastic cartilage (d) hyaline cartilage

19. An epithelium is connected to underlying connective tissue by
    (a) a basal lamina (b) canaliculi
    (c) stereocilia (d) proteoglycans

20. Which of the following are wandering cells found in connective tissue proper?
    (a) fixed macrophages
    (b) mesenchymal cells and adipocytes
    (c) fibroblasts and melanocytes
    (d) eosinophils, neutrophils, and mast cells

Level 2 Reviewing Concepts

1. How does the role of a tissue in the body differ from that of a single cell?
2. A layer of glycoproteins and a network of fine protein filaments that perform limited functions together act as a barrier that restricts the movement of proteins and other large molecules from the connective tissue to epithelium. This describes the structure and function of
    (a) interfacial canals (b) the reticular lamina
    (c) the basal lamina (d) areolar tissue

3. Connective tissue cells that respond to injury or infection by dividing to produce daughter cells that differentiate into other cell types are
   (a) mast cells (b) fibroblasts
   (c) plasmocytes (d) mesenchymal cells
4. How does a tendon function?
5. What is the difference between exocrine and endocrine secretions?
6. What is the significance of the cilia on the respiratory epithelium?
7. Why does pinching the skin usually not distort or damage the underlying muscles?
8. How does a tendon differ from an aponeurosis?
9. What are germinative cells, and what is their function?

Level 3 Critical Thinking

1. Analysis of a glandular secretion indicates that it contains some DNA, RNA, and membrane components such as phospholipids. What kind of secretion is this and why?
2. During a laboratory examination, a student examines a tissue section that is composed of many parallel, densely packed protein fibers. There are no nuclei or striations, and there is no evidence of other cellular structures. The student identifies the tissue as skeletal muscle. Why is the student's choice wrong, and what tissue is being observed?
3. Smoking destroys the cilia found on many cells of the respiratory epithelium. How does this contribute to a "smoker's cough"?
4. Why is ischemia (lack of oxygen) of cardiac muscle more life-threatening than ischemia of skeletal muscle?

4

The Integumentary System

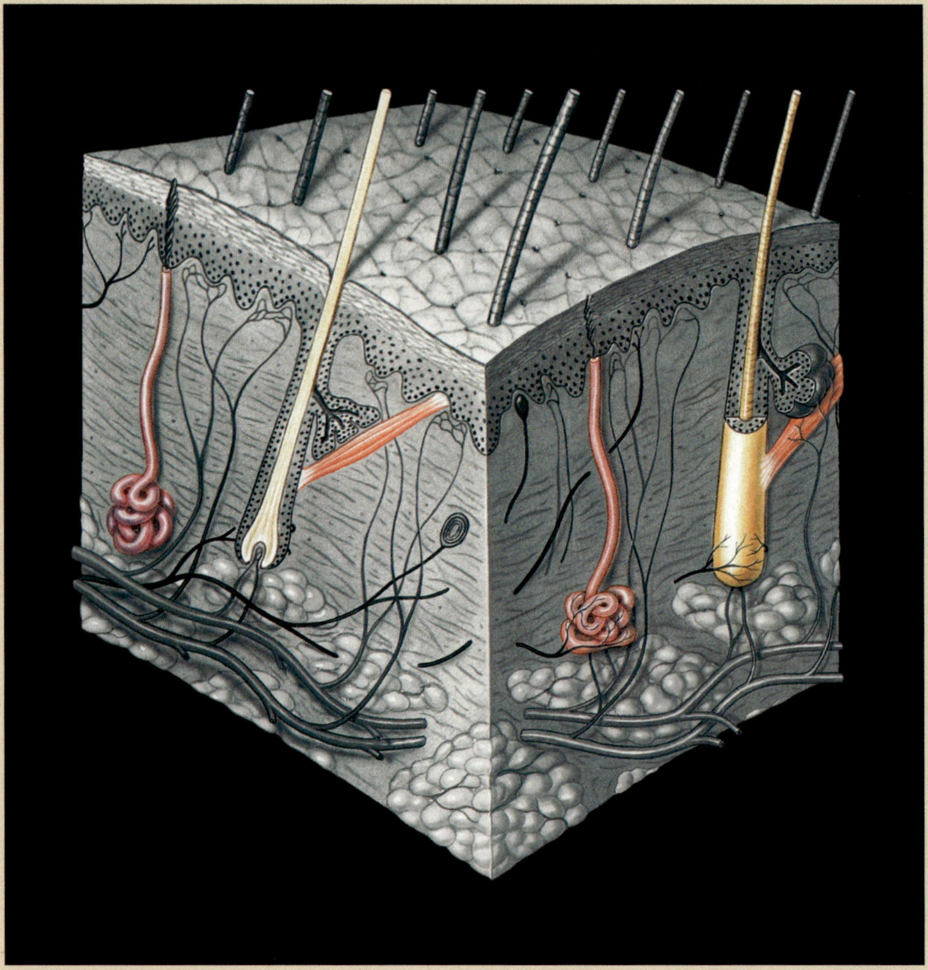

CHAPTER OBJECTIVES

1. Describe and compare the structure and functions of the skin with the underlying connective tissue.
2. Describe the four primary cell types found in the epidermis.
3. Explain the factors that contribute to individual and racial differences in skin, such as skin color.
4. Discuss the effects of ultraviolet radiation on the skin and the role played by melanocytes in this regard.
5. Describe the organization of the dermis.
6. Discuss dermal components, including blood supply and nerve supply.
7. Describe the structure of the subcutaneous layer (hypodermis) and its importance.
8. Discuss the anatomy and functions of the skin's accessory structures: hair, glands, and nails.
9. Describe the mechanisms that produce hair and determine hair texture and color.
10. Compare and contrast sebaceous and sweat glands.
11. Describe how the sweat glands of the integumentary system function in the regulation of body temperature.
12. Explain how the skin responds to injuries and repairs itself.
13. Summarize the effects of aging on the skin.

The **integumentary system,** or *integument,* is composed of the skin and its derivatives: hair, nails, sweat, oil, and mammary glands. This system is probably the most closely watched yet underappreciated organ system. It is the only system we see every day, almost in its entirety. Because others see this system as well, we devote a lot of time to improving the appearance of the integument and associated structures. Washing the face, brushing and trimming hair, taking showers, and applying makeup are activities that modify the appearance or properties of the integument.

Most people use the general appearance of the skin to estimate the overall health and age of a new acquaintance—healthy skin has a smooth sheen, and young skin has few wrinkles. The skin also gives clues to your emotional state, as when you blush with embarrassment or flush with rage. When something goes wrong with the skin, the effects are immediately apparent. Even a relatively minor condition or blemish will be noticed at once, whereas more serious problems in other systems are often ignored. (That's probably why TV advertising devotes so much time to the control of minor acne, a temporary skin condition that is publicly displayed, rather than to the control of blood pressure, a potentially fatal cardiovascular problem that is easier to ignore.) The skin also mirrors the general health of other systems, and clinicians can use the appearance of the skin to detect signs of underlying disease. For example, the skin color changes from the presence of liver disease.

The skin has more than a cosmetic role, however. It protects you from the surrounding environment; its receptors tell you a lot about the outside world; and it helps regulate your body temperature. You will encounter several more important functions as we examine the functional anatomy of the integumentary system in this chapter.

Clinical Note

Examination of the Skin When examining a patient a dermatologist uses a combination of investigative questions ("What has been in contact with your skin lately?" or "How does it feel?") and a physical examination to arrive at a diagnosis. The condition of the skin is carefully observed. Notes are made about the presence of **lesions**, which are changes in skin structure caused by trauma or disease processes. Lesions are also called **skin signs** because they are measurable, visible abnormalities of the skin surface.

The distribution of lesions can be an important clue to the source of the problem. For instance, in *shingles (herpes zoster),* blisters on the skin occur in the area(s) innervated by peripheral sensory nerves. A ring of slightly raised, scaly (papular) lesions is typical of fungal infections that may affect the trunk, scalp, or nails. Signs on the surface of the skin, as well as those involving the accessory organs of the skin can also be important. For instance:

- Nails have a characteristic shape that can change due to an underlying disorder. An example is *clubbing* of the fingernails, commonly a sign of *emphysema* or *congestive heart failure*. In these conditions, the fingertips broaden and the nails become distinctively curved.
- The condition of the hair can be an indicator of a person's overall health. For example, depigmentation and coarseness of hair occur in the protein deficiency disease *kwashiorkor*.

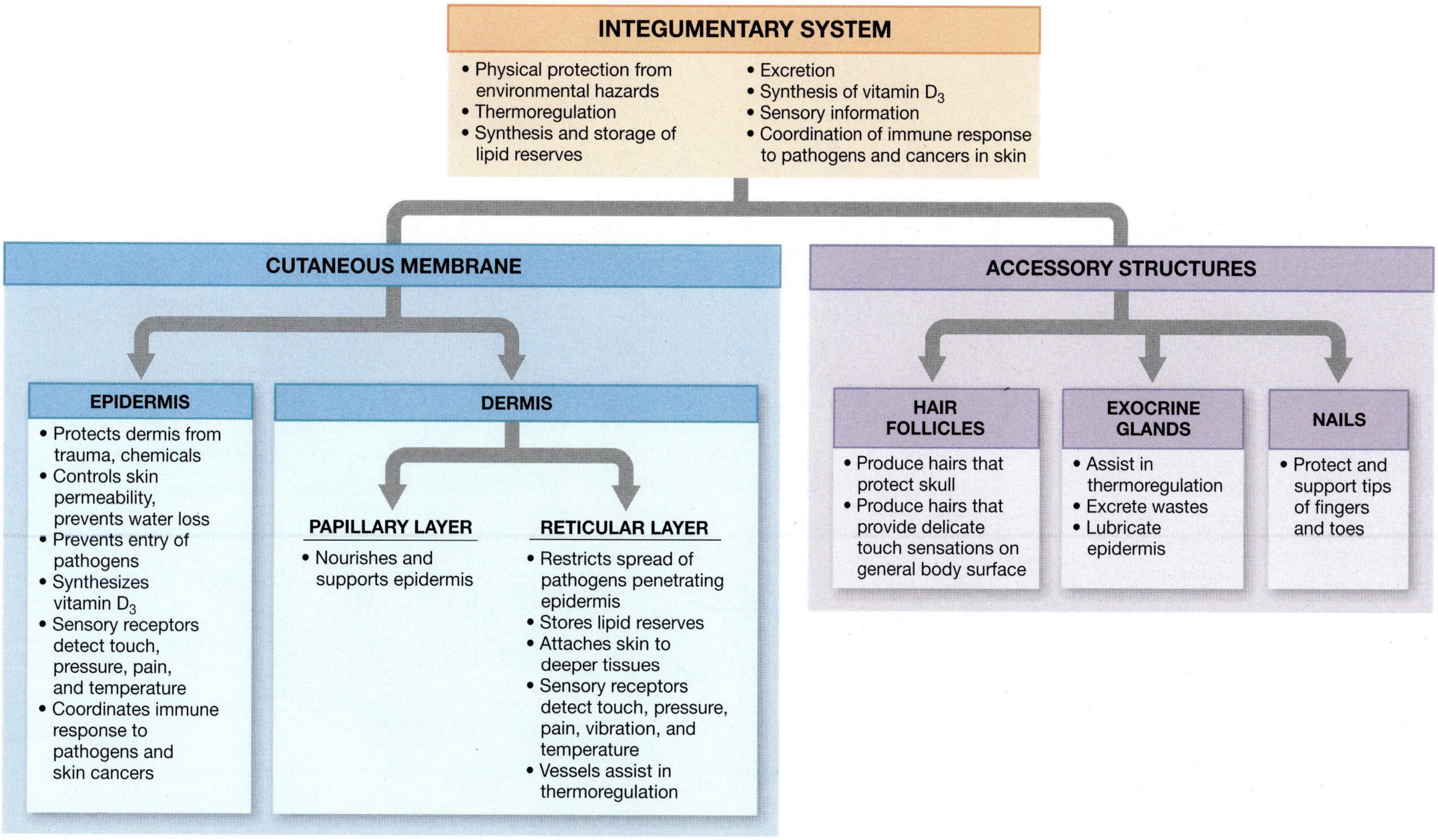

Figure 4.1 Functional Organization of the Integumentary System
Flowchart showing the relationships among the components of the integumentary system.

Integumentary Structure and Function [Figure 4.1]

The integument covers the entire body surface, including the anterior surfaces of the eyes and the tympanic membranes (eardrums) at the ends of the external auditory canals. At the nostrils, lips, anus, urethral opening, and vaginal opening the integument turns inward, meeting the mucous membranes lining the respiratory, digestive, urinary, and reproductive tracts, respectively. At these sites the transition is seamless, and the epithelial defenses remain intact and functional.

All four tissue types are found within the integument. An epithelium covers its surface, and underlying connective tissues provide strength and resiliency. Blood vessels within the connective tissue nourish the epidermal cells. Smooth muscle tissue within the integument controls the diameters of the blood vessels and adjusts the positions of the hairs that project above the body surface. Neural tissue controls these smooth muscles and monitors sensory receptors providing sensations of touch, pressure, temperature, and pain.

The integument has numerous functions, including physical protection, regulation of body temperature, excretion (secretion), nutrition (synthesis), sensation, and immune defense. Figure 4.1 shows the functional organization of the integumentary system. The integument has two major components, the *skin* (cutaneous membrane) and the *accessory structures.*

1. The **skin** has two components, the superficial epithelium, termed the **epidermis** *epi-*, above + *derma*, skin) and the underlying connective tissues of the **dermis.** Deep to the dermis, the loose connective tissue of the subcutaneous layer, also known as the superficial fascia, or *hypodermis*, separates the integument from the deep fascia around other organs, such as muscles and bones. ∞ p. 74 Although it is not usually considered part of the integument, we will consider the subcutaneous layer in this chapter because of its extensive interconnections with the dermis.

2. The **accessory structures** include hair, nails, and a variety of multicellular exocrine glands. These structures are located in the dermis and protrude through the epidermis to the surface.

The Epidermis [Figure 4.2]

The epidermis of the skin consists of a stratified squamous epithelium, as seen in Figure 4.2. There are four cell types in the epidermis: *keratinocytes, melanocytes, Merkel cells,* and *Langerhans cells.* The most abundant epithelial cells, the **keratinocytes** (ke-RAT-i-nō-sīts), form several different layers. The precise boundaries between them are often difficult to see in a light micrograph. In *thick skin*, found on the palms of the hands and soles of the feet, five layers can be distinguished. Only four layers can be distinguished in the *thin skin* that covers the rest of the body. Melanocytes are pigment-producing cells in the epidermis. Merkel cells have a role in detecting sensation, whereas Langerhans cells are phagocytic cells. All of these cell types are scattered among keratinocytes.

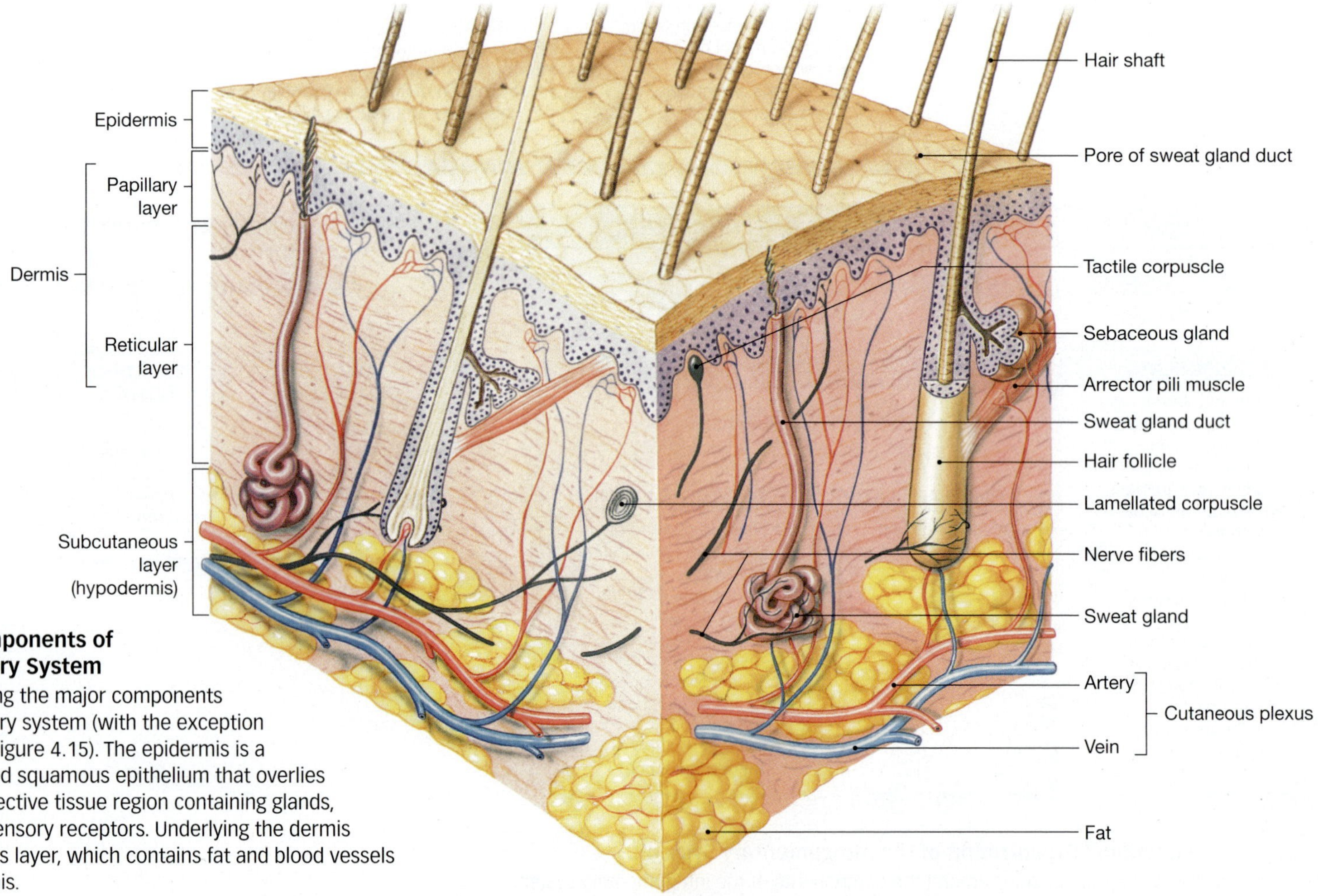

Figure 4.2 Components of the Integumentary System
Relationships among the major components of the integumentary system (with the exception of nails, shown in Figure 4.15). The epidermis is a keratinized stratified squamous epithelium that overlies the dermis, a connective tissue region containing glands, hair follicles, and sensory receptors. Underlying the dermis is the subcutaneous layer, which contains fat and blood vessels supplying the dermis.

Layers of the Epidermis [Figure 4.3 and Table 4.1]

Refer to Figure 4.3 and Table 4.1 as we describe the layers in a section of thick skin. Beginning at the basal lamina and traveling toward the outer epithelial surface, we find the *stratum germinativum*, the *stratum spinosum*, the *stratum granulosum*, the *stratum lucidum*, and the *stratum corneum*.

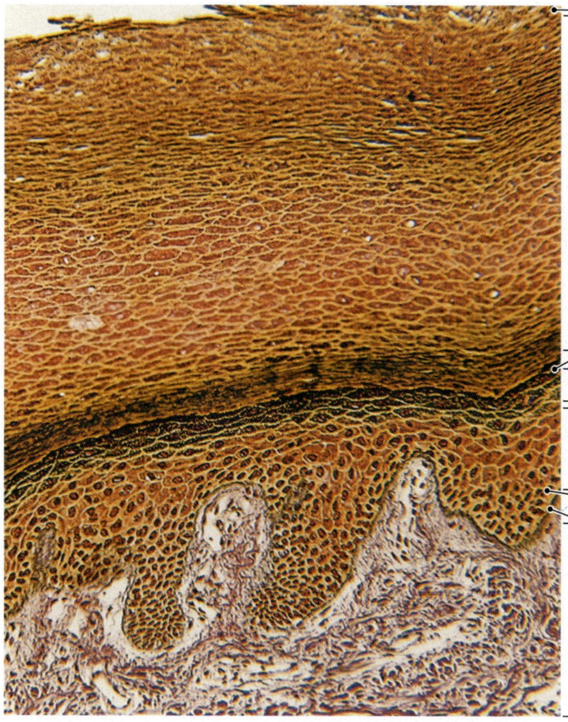

Figure 4.3 The Structure of the Epidermis
A light micrograph showing the major stratified layers of epidermal cells in thick skin.

TABLE 4.1 Epidermal Layers

Layer	Characteristics
Stratum germinativum	Innermost, basal layer Attached to basal lamina Contains epidermal stem cells, melanocytes, and Merkel cells
Stratum spinosum	Keratinocytes are bound together by macula adherens attached to tonofibrils of the cytoskeleton Some keratinocytes divide in this layer Langerhans cells and melanocytes are often present
Stratum granulosum	Keratinocytes produce keratohyalin and keratin Keratin fibers develop as cells become thinner and flatter Gradually the cell membranes thicken, the organelles disintegrate, and the cells die
Stratum lucidum	Appears as a "glassy" layer in thick skin only
Stratum corneum	Multiple layers of flattened, dead, interlocking keratinocytes Typically relatively dry Water resistant, but not waterproof Permits slow water loss by insensible perspiration

Stratum Germinativum

The innermost epidermal layer is the **stratum germinativum** (STRĀ-tum jer-mi-na-TĒ-vum), or *stratum basale*. This layer is firmly attached to the basal lamina that separates the epidermis from the loose connective tissue of the adjacent dermis. Large stem cells, or *basal cells*, dominate the stratum germinativum. The divisions of stem cells replace the more superficial keratinocytes that are lost or shed at the epithelial surface. The brown tones of the skin result from the synthetic activities of *melanocytes*, pigment cells introduced in Chapter 3. ∞ p. 62 Melanocytes are scattered among the basal cells of the stratum germinativum. They have numerous cytoplasmic processes that inject *melanin*, a black, yellow-brown, or brown pigment, into the keratinocytes in this layer and in more superficial layers. The ratio of melanocytes to germinative cells ranges between 1:4 and 1:20, depending on the region examined. They are most abundant in the cheeks and forehead, in the nipples, and in the genital region. Individual and racial differences in skin color result from different levels of melanocyte activity, not different numbers of melanocytes. Even *albino* individuals have normal numbers of melanocytes. (Albinism is an inherited condition in which melanocytes are incapable of producing melanin; it affects approximately one person in 10,000.)

Skin surfaces that lack hair contain specialized epithelial cells known as **Merkel cells.** These cells are found among the deepest cells of the stratum germinativum. They are sensitive to touch, and when compressed, Merkel cells release chemicals that stimulate sensory nerve endings, providing information about objects touching the skin. (There are many other kinds of touch receptors, but they are located in the dermis and will be introduced in later sections. All of the integumentary receptors are described in Chapter 18.)

Stratum Spinosum

Each time a stem cell divides, one of the daughter cells is pushed into the next, more superficial layer, the **stratum spinosum** ("spiny layer"), where it begins to differentiate into a keratinocyte. The stratum spinosum is several cells thick. Each keratinocyte in the stratum spinosum contains bundles of protein filaments that extend from one side of the cell to the other. These bundles, called *tonofibrils*, begin and end at macula adherens (desmosomes) that connect the keratinocyte to its neighbors. The tonofibrils thus act as cross braces, strengthening and supporting the cell junctions. All of the keratinocytes in the stratum spinosum are tied together by this network of interlocked macula adherens and tonofibrils. Standard histological procedures, used to prepare tissue for microscopic examination, shrink the cytoplasm but leave the tonofibrils and macula adherens intact. This makes the cells look like miniature pincushions, which is why early histologists used the term "spiny layer" in their descriptions.

Some of the cells entering this layer from the stratum germinativum continue to divide, further increasing the thickness of the epithelium. Melanocytes are common in this layer, as are **Langerhans cells,** although the latter cells cannot be distinguished in standard histological preparations. Langerhans cells, which account for 3–8 percent of the cells in the epidermis, are most common in the superficial portion of the stratum spinosum. These cells play an important role in initiating an immune response against (1) pathogens that have penetrated the superficial layers of the epidermis and (2) epidermal cancer cells.

Stratum Granulosum

The layer of cells superficial to the stratum spinosum is the **stratum granulosum** ("granular layer"). The stratum granulosum consists of keratinocytes displaced from the stratum spinosum. By the time cells reach this layer, they have begun to manufacture large quantities of the proteins

Clinical Note

Disorders of Keratin Production Not all skin signs are the result of infection, trauma, or allergy; some are the normal response to environmental stresses. One common response is the excessive production of keratin, a process called **hyperkeratosis** (hī-per-ker-a-TŌ-sis). The most obvious effects—calluses and corns—are easily observed. Calluses are thickened patches that appear on already thick-skinned areas, such as the palms of the hands or the soles or heels of the feet, in response to chronic abrasion and distortion. Corns are more localized areas of excessive keratin production that form in areas of thin skin on or between the toes.

In **psoriasis** (so-RI-a-sis), stem cells in the stratum germinativum are unusually active, causing hyperkeratosis in specific areas, often the scalp, elbows, palms, soles, groin, or nails. Normally, an individual stem cell divides once every 20 days, but in psoriasis it may divide every day and a half. Keratinization is abnormal and typically incomplete by the time the outer layers are shed. The affected areas have red bases covered with vast numbers of small, silvery scales that continuously flake off. Psoriasis develops in 20–30 percent of individuals with an inherited tendency for the condition. Roughly 5 percent of the U.S. population has psoriasis to some degree, frequently aggravated by stress and anxiety. Most cases are painless and controllable, but not curable.

Xerosis (zē-RŌ-sis), or dry skin, is a common complaint of the elderly and people who live in arid climates. In xerosis, plasmalemmae in the outer layers of skin gradually deteriorate and the stratum corneum becomes more a collection of scales than a single sheet. The scaly surface is much more permeable than an intact layer of keratin, and the rate of insensible perspiration increases. In persons with severe xerosis, the rate of insensible perspiration may increase by up to 75 times.

Pressure on the skin, another form of stress, can produce *decubitis ulcers*, or *bedsores*. *Decubitis* means "to lie down"; an *ulcer* is a localized loss of epithelium. Decubitis ulcers form where dermal blood vessels are compressed against deeper structures such as bones or joints, so that local circulation is reduced enough to damage dependent tissues.

keratohyalin (ker-a-tō-HĪ-a-lin) and **keratin** (KER-a-tin; *keros*, horn). Keratohyalin accumulates in electron-dense granules called *keratohyalin granules*. These granules form an intracellular matrix that surrounds the keratin filaments. As large keratin filaments are developing within them, the keratinocytes gradually become thinner and flatter. The cell membranes thicken and become less permeable. The nuclei and other organelles then disintegrate, the cells die, and their subsequent dehydration creates a tightly interlocked layer of keratin fibers surrounded by keratohyalin and sandwiched between phospholipid membranes.

The rate of synthesis of keratohyalin and keratin by keratinocytes is often influenced by environmental factors. Increased friction against the skin stimulates increased keratohyalin and keratin synthesis by keratinocytes within the stratum granulosum. This results in a localized thickening of the skin and the formation of a *callus* (also termed a *clavus*), such as that seen on the palm of the hands of weightlifters or the knuckles of boxers and karate students.

In humans, keratin forms the basic structural component of hair and nails. It is a very versatile material, however, and in other vertebrates it forms the claws of dogs and cats, the horns of cattle and rhinos, the feathers of birds, the scales of snakes, the baleen of whales, and a variety of other interesting epidermal structures.

Stratum Lucidum

In the thick skin of the palms and soles, a glassy **stratum lucidum** ("clear layer") covers the stratum granulosum. The cells in this layer are flattened, densely packed, and filled with keratin, but they do not stain well in standard histological preparations.

Stratum Corneum

The **stratum corneum** (KŌR-nē-um; *cornu*, horn) is found at the surface of both thick and thin skin. It consists of 15–30 layers of flattened, dead, and interlocking cells. Because the interconnections established in the stratum spinosum remain intact, the cells are usually shed in large groups or sheets, rather than individually.

An epithelium containing large amounts of keratin is said to be **keratinized** (KER-a-ti-nīzd), or *cornified* (KŌR-ni-fīd; *cornu*, horn + *facere*, to make). Normally the stratum corneum is relatively dry, which makes the surface unsuitable for the growth of many microorganisms. Maintenance of this barrier involves coating the surface with the secretions of integumentary glands (sebaceous and sweat glands, discussed in a later section). The process of **keratinization** occurs everywhere on exposed skin surfaces except over the anterior surfaces of the eyes.

Although the stratum corneum is water resistant, it is not waterproof, and water from the interstitial fluids slowly penetrates the surface, to be evaporated into the surrounding air. This process, called insensible perspiration, accounts for a loss of roughly 500 ml (about 1 pt) of water per day.

It takes 15–30 days for a cell to move from the stratum germinativum to the stratum corneum. The dead cells usually remain in the exposed stratum corneum layer for an additional two weeks before they are shed or washed away. Thus the deeper portions of the epithelium—and all underlying tissues—are always protected by a barrier composed of dead, durable, and expendable cells.

The protective nature of the skin is most easily seen and understood when large areas of the skin have been lost following injury, such as a serious burn. Following second degree (partial thickness) burns or third degree (full thickness) burns, physicians must be concerned about the absorption of toxic substances, the loss of excess fluids, and infection at the site of the burn, all of which are medical problems resulting from the loss of the protective role of the skin.

CONCEPT CHECK

1. Excessive shedding of cells from the outer layer of skin in the scalp causes dandruff. What is the name of this layer of skin?
2. As you pick up a piece of lumber, a splinter pierces the palm of your hand and lodges in the third layer of the epidermis. Identify this layer.
3. What are the two major subdivisions of the integumentary system, and what are the components of each subdivision?
4. What is keratinization? What are the stages of this process?

See blue "Answers" tab at back of book.

Clinical Note

Transdermal Drug Administration Drugs in oils or other lipid-soluble carriers can penetrate the epidermis. The movement is slow, particularly through the layers of cell membranes in the stratum corneum, but once a drug reaches the underlying tissues, it will be absorbed into the circulation. A useful technique involves placing a sticky patch containing a drug over an area of thin skin. To overcome the relatively slow rate of diffusion, the patch must contain an extremely high concentration of the drug. This procedure, called *transdermal drug administration*, has the advantage that a single patch may work for several days, making daily pills unnecessary. *Scopolamine*, a drug that affects the nervous system, is administered transdermally to control the nausea associated with motion sickness. Transdermal *nitroglycerin* can be used to improve blood flow within the heart muscle and prevent a heart attack. Transdermal *estrogen* can be used to reduce bone loss in postmenopausal women. Transdermal *nicotine* can be used to control the craving for tobacco and make it easier to quit smoking.

Thick and Thin Skin [Figure 4.4]

In descriptions of the skin, the terms *thick* and *thin* refer to the relative thickness of the epidermis, not to the integument as a whole. Most of the body is covered by **thin skin.** In a sample of thin skin, only four layers are present because the stratum lucidum is typically absent. Here the epidermis is a mere 0.08 mm thick, and the stratum corneum is only a few cell layers deep (Figure 4.4a,b). **Thick skin** on the palms of the hands may be covered by 30 or more layers of keratinized cells. As a result, the epidermis in these locations exhibits all five layers and may be as much as six times as thick as the epidermis covering the general body surface (Figure 4.4c).

Epidermal Ridges [Figures 4.4/4.5]

The stratum germinativum layer of the epidermis forms **epidermal ridges** that extend into the dermis, increasing the area of contact between the two regions. Projections from the dermis toward the epidermis, called **dermal papillae** (singular, *papilla*; "nipple-shaped mound") extend between adjacent ridges, as indicated in Figure 4.4a,c.

The contours of the skin surface follow the ridge patterns, which vary from small conical pegs (in thin skin) to the complex whorls seen on the thick skin of the palms and soles. Ridges on the palms and soles increase the surface area of the skin and increase friction, ensuring a secure grip. Ridge shapes are genetically determined: Those of each person are unique and do not change in the course of a lifetime. Fingerprint-ridge patterns on the tips of the fingers (Figure 4.5) can therefore be used to identify individuals, and they have been so used in criminal investigation for over a century.

Skin Color [Figure 4.6]

The color of the epidermis is due to a combination of (1) the dermal blood supply, (2) the thickness of the stratum corneum, and (3) variable quantities of two pigments: *carotene* and *melanin*. Blood contains red blood cells that carry the protein hemoglobin. When bound to oxygen, hemoglobin has a bright red color, giving blood vessels in the dermis a reddish tint that is seen most easily in lightly pigmented individuals. When those vessels are dilated, as during inflammation, the red tones become much more pronounced.

The amount of melanin and carotene produced is under genetic control. A variation in the expression of these inherited genes determines an individual's skin color.

Dermal Blood Supply When the circulatory supply is temporarily reduced, the skin becomes relatively pale; a frightened Caucasian may "turn white" because of a sudden drop in blood supply to the skin. During a sustained reduction in circulatory supply, the blood in the superficial vessels loses oxygen and the hemoglobin changes color to a much darker red tone. Seen from the surface, the skin takes on a bluish coloration called **cyanosis** (sī-a-NŌ-sis; *kyanos*, blue). In individuals of any skin color, cyanosis is most apparent in areas of thin skin, such as the lips or beneath the nails. It can be a response to extreme cold or a result of circulatory or respiratory disorders, such as heart failure or severe asthma.

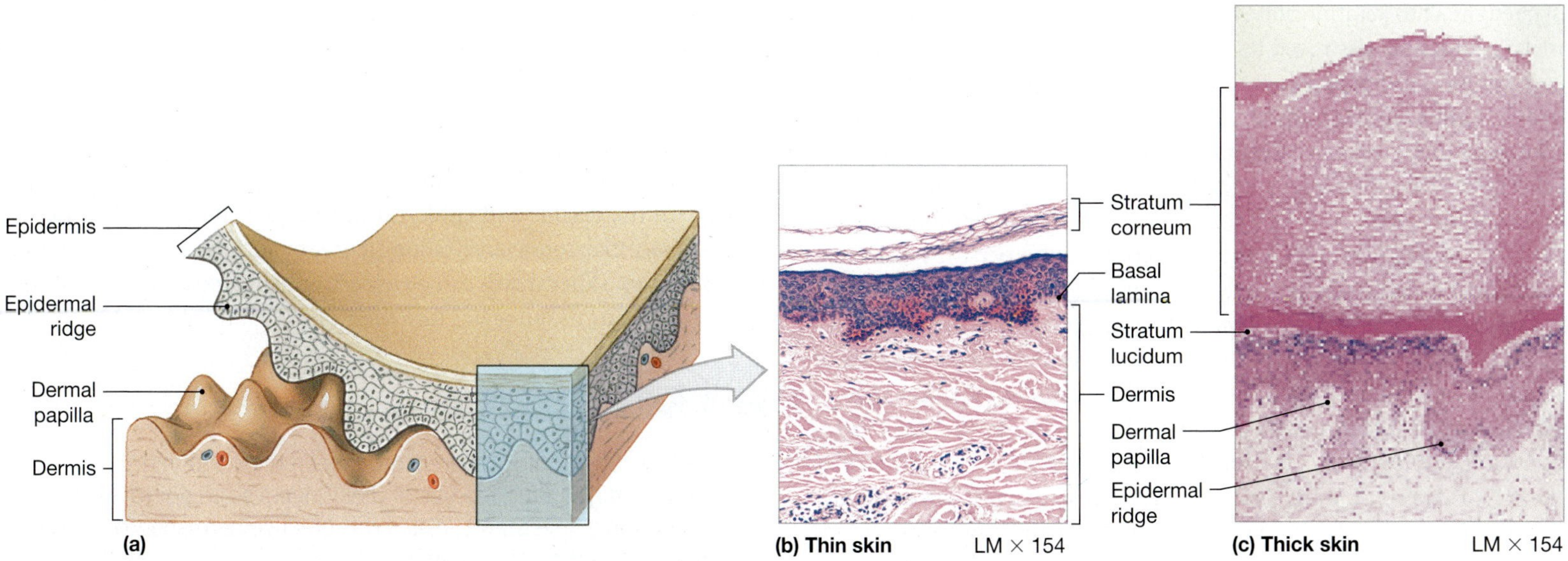

Figure 4.4 Thin and Thick Skin
The epidermis is a stratified squamous epithelium, which varies in thickness. **(a)** The basic organization of the epidermis. The thickness of the epidermis, especially the thickness of the stratum corneum, changes radically depending on the location sampled. **(b)** Thin skin covers most of the exposed body surface. (During sectioning the stratum corneum has pulled away from the rest of the epidermis.) **(c)** Thick skin covers the surfaces of the palms and soles.

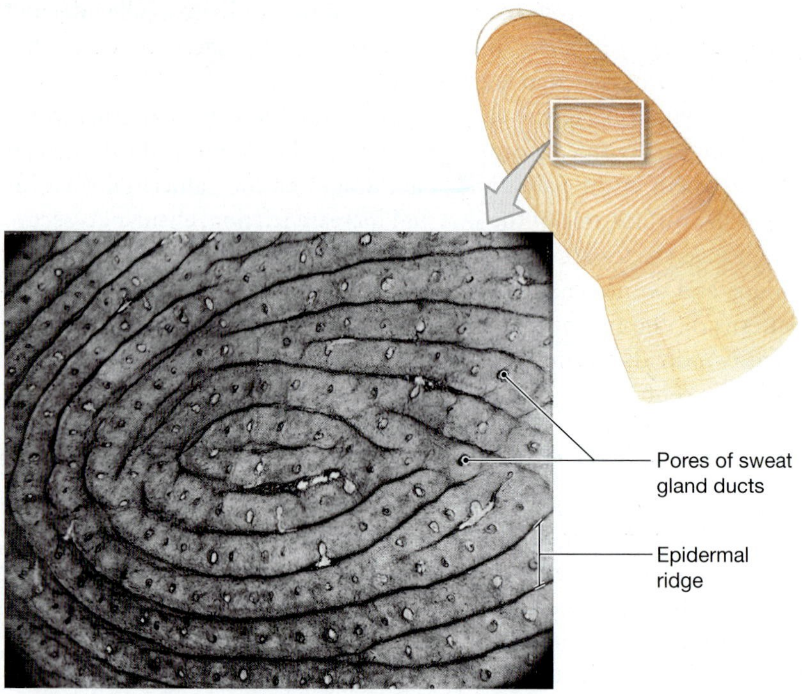

Figure 4.5 The Epidermal Ridges of Thick Skin
Fingerprints reveal the pattern of epidermal ridges in thick skin. This scanning electron micrograph shows the ridges on a fingertip. The pits are the pores of sweat gland ducts. (SEM × 25) *[© R. G. Kessel and R. H. Kardon, "Tissues and Organs: A Text-Atlas of Scanning Electron Microscopy", W. H. Freeman & Co., 1979. All Rights Reserved.]*

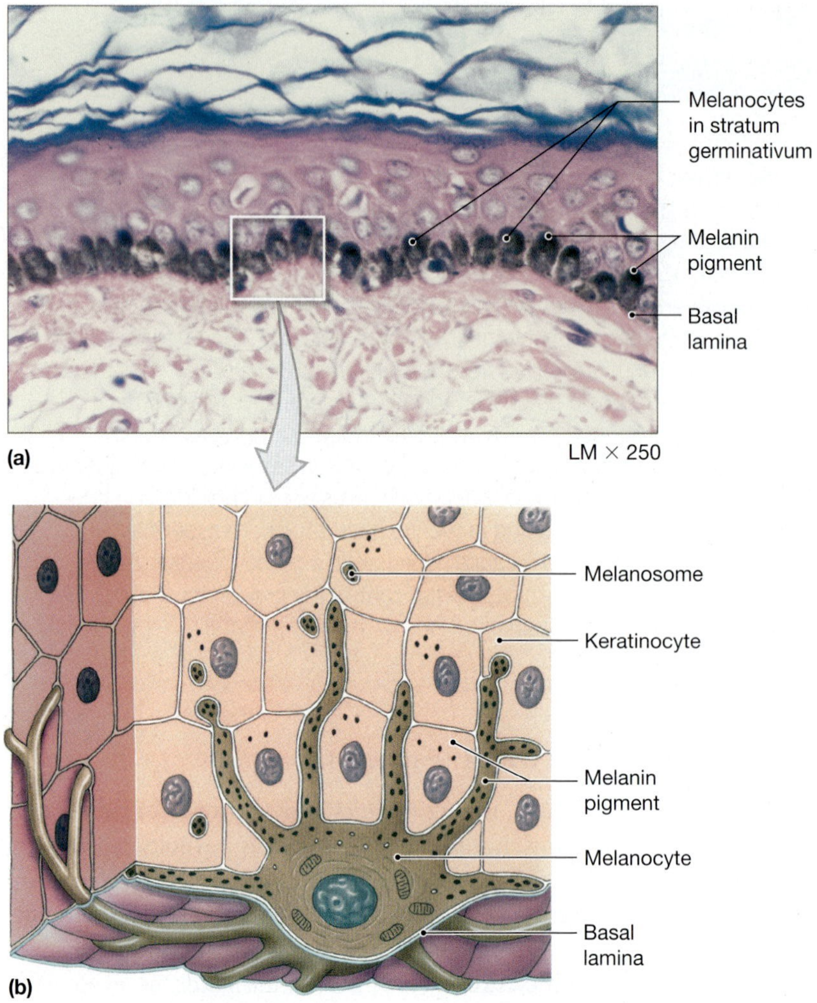

Figure 4.6 Melanocytes
The micrograph and accompanying drawing indicate the location and orientation of melanocytes in the stratum germinativum of a dark-skinned person.

Epidermal Pigment Content **Carotene** (KAR-ō-ten) is an orange-yellow pigment that is found in various orange-colored vegetables, such as carrots, corn, and squashes. It can be converted to vitamin A, which is required for epithelial maintenance and the synthesis of visual pigments by the photoreceptors of the eye. Carotene normally accumulates inside keratinocytes, and it becomes especially evident in the dehydrated cells of the stratum corneum and in the subcutaneous fat. **Melanin** (MEL-a-nin) is produced and stored in melanocytes (**Figure 4.6**). The black, yellow-brown, or brown melanin forms in intracellular vesicles called *melanosomes.* These vesicles, which are transferred intact to keratinocytes, color the keratinocytes temporarily, until the melanosomes are destroyed by lysosomes. The cells in more superficial layers gradually lighten in color as the number of intact melanosomes decreases. In light-skinned individuals, melanosome transfer occurs in the stratum germinativum and stratum spinosum, and the cells of more superficial layers lose their pigmentation. In dark-skinned individuals, the melanosomes are larger and the transfer may occur in the stratum granulosum as well; the pigmentation is thus darker and more persistent. Melanin pigments help prevent skin damage by absorbing **ultraviolet (UV) radiation** in sunlight. A little ultraviolet radiation is necessary because the skin requires it to convert a cholesterol-related steroid precursor into a member of the family of hormones collectively known as vitamin D.[1] Vitamin D is required for normal calcium and phosphorus absorption by the small intestine; inadequate supplies of vitamin D lead to impaired bone maintenance and growth. However, too much UV radiation may damage chromosomes and cause widespread tissue damage similar to that caused by mild to moderate burns. Melanin in the epidermis as a whole protects the underlying dermis. Within each keratinocyte, the melanosomes are most abundant around the cell's nucleus. This increases the likelihood that the UV radiation will be absorbed before it can damage the nuclear DNA.

Melanocytes respond to UV exposure by increasing their rates of melanin synthesis and transfer. Tanning then occurs, but the response is not quick enough to prevent a sunburn on the first day at the beach; it takes about 10 days. Anyone can get a sunburn, but dark-skinned individuals have greater initial protection against the effects of UV radiation. Repeated UV exposure sufficient to stimulate tanning can result in long-term skin damage in the dermis and epidermis. In the dermis, damage to fibrocytes causes abnormal connective tissue structure and premature wrinkling. In the epidermis, skin cancers can develop from chromosomal damage in germinative cells or melanocytes (see the Clinical Note on p. 96).

CONCEPT CHECK

1. Describe the primary difference between thick and thin skin.
2. Some criminals sand the tips of their fingers so as not to leave recognizable fingerprints. Would this practice permanently remove fingerprints? Why or why not?
3. Identify the sources of color of the epidermis.
4. Describe the relationship between epidermal ridges and dermal papillae.

See blue "Answers"tab at back of book.

[1]Specifically, vitamin D_3 or *cholecalciferol,* which undergoes further modification in the liver and kidneys before circulating as the active hormone *calcitriol.*

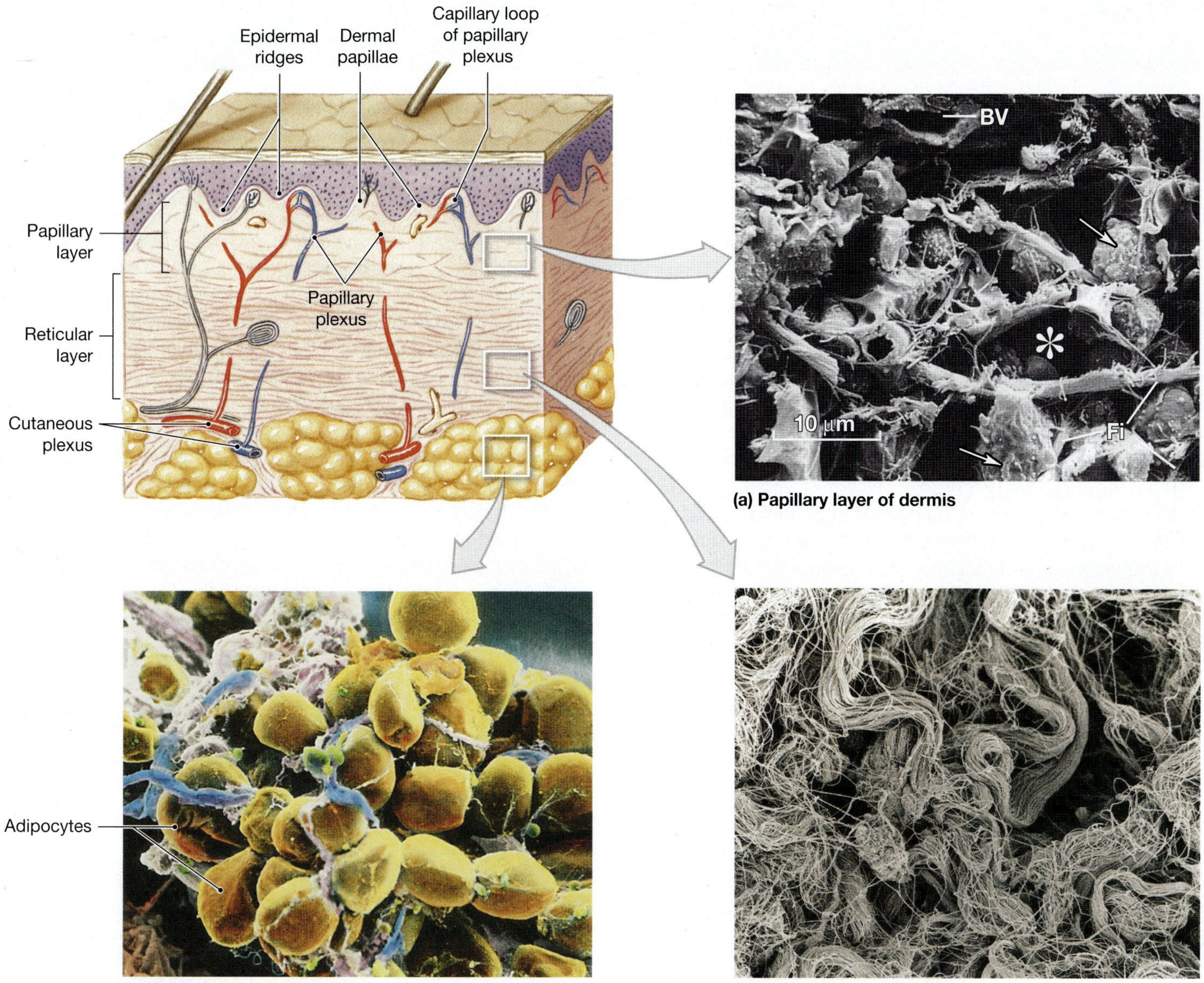

(a) Papillary layer of dermis

(c) Subcutaneous layer

(b) Reticular layer of dermis

Figure 4.7 The Structure of the Dermis and the Subcutaneous Layer
The dermis is a connective tissue layer deep to the epidermis; the subcutaneous layer (hypodermis) is a connective tissue layer deep to the dermis. **(a)** The papillary layer of the dermis consists of loose connective tissue that contains numerous blood vessels (BV), fibers (Fi), and macrophages (arrows). Open spaces, such as the one marked by an asterisk, would be filled with fluid ground substance. (SEM × 649) **(b)** The reticular layer of the dermis contains dense, irregular connective tissue. (SEM × 1340) **(c)** The subcutaneous layer contains large numbers of adipocytes in a framework of loose connective tissue fibers. (SEM × 268) *[(a) © R. G. Kessel and R. H. Kardon, "Tissues and Organs: A Text-Atlas of Scanning Electron Microscopy", W. H. Freeman & Co., 1979. All Rights Reserved.]*

The Dermis [Figure 4.2]

The dermis lies deep to the epidermis (Figure 4.2, p. 90). It has two major components: a superficial *papillary layer* and a deeper *reticular layer*.

Dermal Organization [Figures 4.4/4.7]

The superficial **papillary layer** consists of loose connective tissue (Figure 4.7a). This region contains the capillaries supplying the epidermis and the axons of sensory neurons that monitor receptors in the papillary layer and the epidermis. The papillary layer derives its name from the dermal papillae that project between the epidermal ridges (Figure 4.4).

The deeper **reticular layer** consists of fibers in an interwoven meshwork of dense irregular connective tissue that surrounds blood vessels, hair follicles, nerves, sweat glands, and sebaceous glands (Figure 4.7b). The name of the layer derives from the interwoven arrangement of collagen fiber bundles in this region (*reticulum*, a little net). Some of the collagen fibers in the reticular layer extend into the papillary layer, tying the two layers together. The boundary line between these layers is therefore indistinct. Collagen fibers of the reticular layer also extend into the deeper subcutaneous layer (Figure 4.7c).

Wrinkles, Stretch Marks, and Lines of Cleavage [Figure 4.8]

The interwoven collagen fibers of the reticular layer provide considerable tensile strength, and the extensive array of elastic fibers enables the dermis

Clinical Note

Skin Cancers Almost everyone has several benign lesions of the skin; freckles and moles are examples. Skin cancers are the most common form of cancer, and the most common skin cancers are caused by prolonged exposure to sunlight.

A **basal cell carcinoma** is a malignant cancer that originates in the germinativum (basal) layer. This is the most common skin cancer, and roughly two-thirds of these cancers appear in areas subjected to chronic UV exposure. These carcinomas have recently been linked to an inherited gene.

Squamous cell carcinomas are less common, but almost totally restricted to areas of sun-exposed skin. Metastasis seldom occurs in squamous cell carcinomas and almost never in basal cell carcinomas, and most people survive these cancers. The usual treatment involves surgical removal of the tumor, and at least 95% of patients survive 5 years or more after treatment. (This statistic, the 5-year survival rate, is a common method of reporting long-term prognoses.) Compared with these common and seldom life-threatening cancers, **malignant melanomas** (mel-a-NŌ-maz) are extremely dangerous. In this condition, cancerous melanocytes grow rapidly and metastasize throughout the lymphoid system. The outlook for long-term survival is dramatically different, depending on when the condition is diagnosed. If the condition is localized, the 5-year survival rate is 90%; if widespread, the survival rate drops to 14%.

Fair-skinned individuals who live in the tropics are most susceptible to all forms of skin cancer, because their melanocytes are unable to shield them from the ultraviolet radiation. Sun damage can be prevented by avoiding exposure to the sun during the middle hours of the day and by using clothing, a hat, and a sunblock (not a tanning oil or sunscreen)— a practice that also delays the cosmetic problems of sagging and wrinkling. Everyone who expects to be out in the sun for any length of time should choose a broad-spectrum sunblock with a sun protection factor (SPF) of at least 15; blonds, redheads, and people with very fair skin are better off with a sun protection factor of 20 to 30. (One should also remember the risks before spending time in a tanning salon or tanning bed.) The use of sunscreens has now become even more important as the ozone gas in the upper atmosphere is destroyed by our industrial emissions. Ozone absorbs UV before it reaches the earth's surface, and in doing so, it assists the melanocytes in preventing skin cancer. Australia, which is most affected by the depletion of the ozone layer near the South Pole (the "ozone hole"), is already reporting an increased incidence of skin cancers.

to stretch and recoil repeatedly during normal movements. Age, hormones, and the destructive effects of ultraviolet radiation reduce the thickness and flexibility of the dermis, producing wrinkles and sagging skin. The extensive distortion of the dermis that occurs over the abdomen during pregnancy or after a substantial weight gain often exceeds the elastic capabilities of the skin. Elastic and collagen fibers then break, and although the skin stretches, it does not recoil to its original size after delivery or a rigorous diet. The skin then wrinkles and creases, creating a network of **stretch marks**.

Tretinoin (Retin-A) is a derivative of vitamin A that can be applied to the skin as a cream or gel. This drug was originally developed to treat acne, but it also increases blood flow to the dermis and stimulates dermal repairs. As a result, the rate of wrinkle formation decreases, and existing wrinkles become smaller. The degree of improvement varies from individual to individual.

At any one location, the majority of the collagen and elastic fibers are arranged in parallel bundles. The orientation of these bundles depends on the stress placed on the skin during normal movement; the bundles are aligned to resist the applied forces. The resulting pattern of fiber bundles establishes the **lines of cleavage** of the skin. Lines of cleavage, shown in Figure 4.8, are clinically significant because a cut parallel to a cleavage line will usually remain closed, whereas a cut at right angles to a cleavage line will be pulled open as cut elastic fibers recoil. Surgeons choose their incision patterns accordingly, since an incision parallel to the cleavage lines will heal fastest and with minimal scarring.

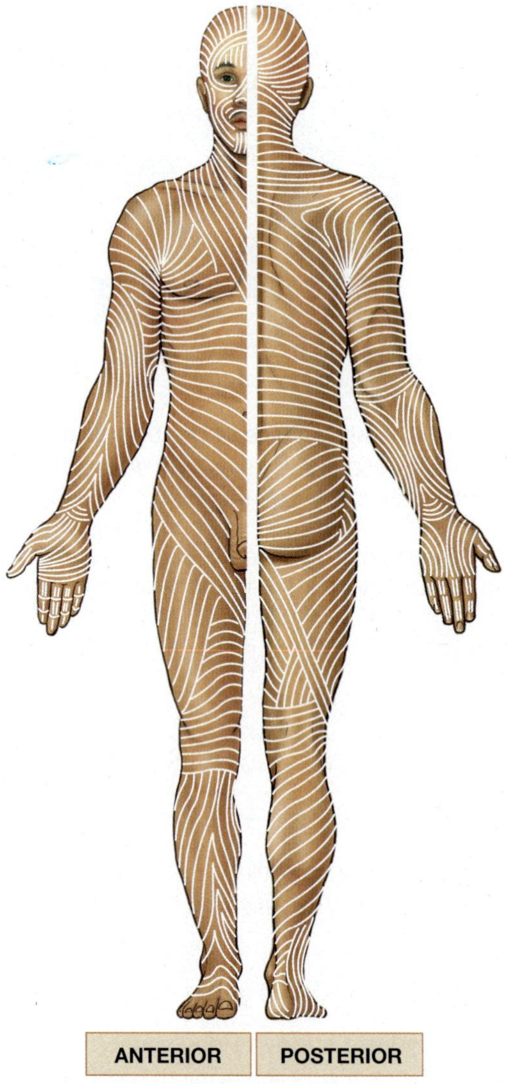

Figure 4.8 Lines of Cleavage of the Skin
Lines of cleavage follow lines of tension in the skin. They reflect the orientation of collagen fiber bundles in the dermis.

Other Dermal Components [Figures 4.2/4.9]

In addition to extracellular protein fibers, the dermis contains all of the cells of connective tissue proper. p. 62 Accessory organs of epidermal origin, such as hair follicles and sweat glands, extend into the dermis

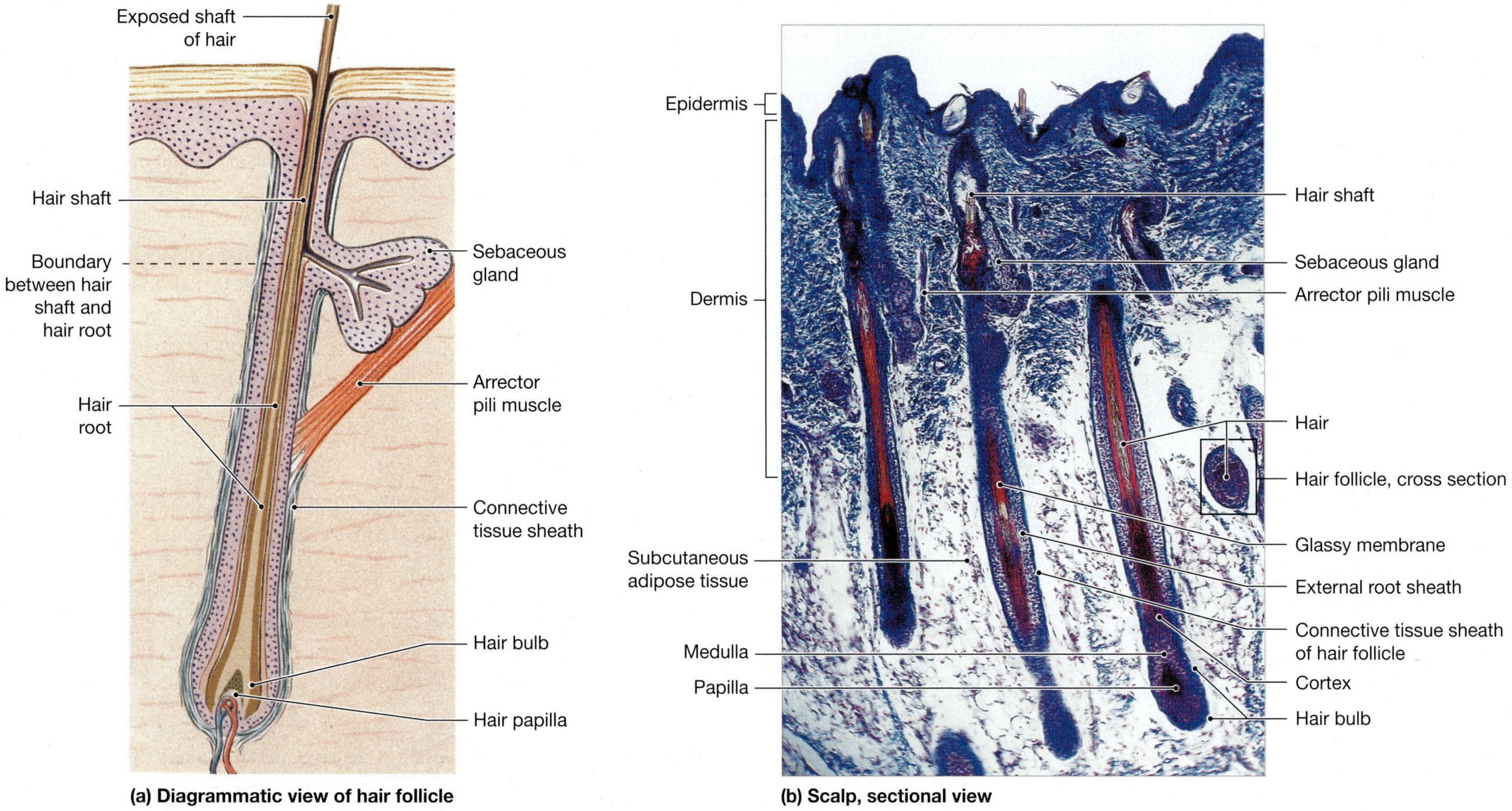

Figure 4.9 Accessory Structures of the Skin
(a) A diagrammatic view of a single hair follicle. **(b)** A light micrograph showing the sectional appearance of the skin of the scalp. Note the abundance of hair follicles and the way they extend into the dermis. (LM $\times$ 66)

(**Figure 4.9**). In addition, the reticular and papillary layers of the dermis contain networks of blood vessels, lymph vessels, and nerve fibers (**Figure 4.2**, p. 90).

The Blood Supply to the Skin [Figures 4.2/4.7]

Arteries and veins supplying the skin form an interconnected network in the subcutaneous layer along the border with the reticular layer. This network is called the **cutaneous plexus** (**Figure 4.2**, p. 90). Branches of the arteries supply the adipose tissue of the subcutaneous layer as well as the tissues of the skin. As small arteries travel toward the epidermis, branches supply the hair follicles, sweat glands, and other structures in the dermis. Upon reaching the papillary layer, these small arteries enter another branching network, the **papillary plexus**, or *subpapillary plexus.* From there, capillary loops follow the contours of the epidermal–dermal boundary (**Figure 4.7a**, p. 95). These capillaries empty into a network of delicate veins (*venules*) that rejoin the papillary plexus. From there, larger veins drain into a network of veins in the deeper cutaneous plexus.

There are two reasons why the circulation to the skin must be tightly regulated. First, it plays a key role in *thermoregulation,* the control of body temperature. When body temperature increases, increased circulation to the skin permits the loss of excess heat, whereas when body temperature decreases, reduced circulation to the skin promotes retention of body heat. Second, because the total blood volume is relatively constant, increased blood flow to the skin means a decreased blood flow to some other organ(s). The nervous, cardiovascular, and endocrine systems interact to regulate blood flow to the skin while maintaining adequate blood flow to other organs and systems.

The Nerve Supply to the Skin

Nerve fibers in the skin control blood flow, adjust gland secretion rates, and monitor sensory receptors in the dermis and the deeper layers of the epidermis. We have already noted the presence of Merkel cells in the deeper layers of the epidermis. These cells are touch receptors monitored by sensory nerve endings known as *tactile discs.* The epidermis also contains the dendrites of sensory nerves that probably respond to pain and temperature. The dermis contains similar receptors as well as other, more specialized receptors. Examples discussed in Chapter 18 include receptors sensitive to light touch (*tactile corpuscles,* located in dermal papillae and the *root hair plexus* surrounding each hair follicle), stretch (*Ruffini corpuscles,* in the reticular layer), and deep pressure and vibration (*lamellated corpuscles,* in the reticular layer).

The Subcutaneous Layer [Figures 4.2/4.7c]

The connective tissue fibers of the reticular layer are extensively interwoven with those of the **subcutaneous layer**, also referred to as the *hypodermis* or the *superficial fascia,* and the boundary between the two layers is usually indistinct (**Figure 4.2**, p. 90). Although the subcutaneous layer is sometimes not considered to be a part of the integument, it is important in stabilizing the position of the skin in relation to underlying tissues, such as skeletal muscles or other organs, while still permitting independent movement.

The subcutaneous layer consists of loose connective tissue with abundant adipocytes (**Figure 4.7c**, p. 95). Infants and small children usually have extensive "baby fat," which helps reduce heat loss. Subcutaneous fat also serves as a substantial energy reserve and a shock absorber for the rough-and-tumble activities of our early years.

As we grow, the distribution of subcutaneous fat changes. Men accumulate subcutaneous fat at the neck, on the upper arms, along the lower back, and over the buttocks. In women the breasts, buttocks, hips, and thighs are the primary sites of subcutaneous fat storage. In adults of either sex, the subcutaneous layer of the backs of the hands and the upper surfaces of the feet contain few adipocytes, whereas distressing amounts of adipose tissue can accumulate in the abdominal region, producing a prominent "pot belly."

The subcutaneous layer is quite elastic. Only the superficial region of the subcutaneous layer contains large arteries and veins; the remaining areas contain a limited number of capillaries and no vital organs. This last characteristic makes *subcutaneous injection* a useful method for administering drugs. The familiar term *hypodermic needle* refers to the region targeted for injection.

Accessory Structures [Figure 4.2]

The accessory structures of the integument include *hair follicles*, *sebaceous glands*, *sweat glands*, and *nails* (**Figure 4.2**, p. 90). During embryological development, these structures form through invagination or infolding of the epidermis.

Hair Follicles and Hair

Hairs project beyond the surface of the skin almost everywhere except over the sides and soles of the feet, the palms of the hands, the sides of the fingers and toes, the lips, and portions of the external genitalia.[2] There are about 5 million hairs on the human body, and 98 percent of them are on the general body surface, not the head. Hairs are nonliving structures that are formed in organs called **hair follicles**.

Hair Production [Figures 4.9b/4.10]

Hair follicles extend deep into the dermis, often projecting into the underlying subcutaneous layer. The epithelium at the follicle base surrounds a small **hair papilla**, a peg of connective tissue containing capillaries and nerves. The **hair bulb** consists of epithelial cells that surround the papilla.

Hair production involves a specialization of the keratinization process. The **hair matrix** is the epithelial layer involved in hair production. When the superficial basal cells divide, they produce daughter cells that are pushed toward the surface as part of the developing hair. Most hairs have an inner *medulla* and an outer *cortex*. The medulla contains relatively soft and flexible **soft keratin**. Matrix cells closer to the edge of the developing hair form the relatively hard **cortex** (**Figures 4.9b** and **4.10**). The cortex contains **hard keratin** that gives hair its stiffness. A single layer of dead, keratinized cells at the outer surface of the hair overlap and form the **cuticle** that coats the hair.

The **hair root** extends from the hair bulb to the point where the internal organization of the hair is complete. The hair root attaches the hair to the hair follicle. The **shaft**, the part we see on the surface, extends from this point, usually halfway to the skin surface, to the exposed tip of the hair. The size, shape, and color of the hair shaft are highly variable.

Follicle Structure [Figure 4.10a]

The cells of the follicle walls are organized into concentric layers (**Figure 4.10a**). Beginning at the hair cuticle, these layers include the following:

- **The internal root sheath:** This layer surrounds the hair root and the deeper portion of the shaft. It is produced by the cells at the periphery of the hair matrix. Because the cells of the internal root sheath disintegrate relatively quickly, this layer does not extend the entire length of the follicle.
- **The external root sheath:** This layer extends from the skin surface to the hair matrix. Over most of that distance it has all of the cell layers found in the superficial epidermis. However, where the external root sheath joins the hair matrix, all of the cells resemble those of the stratum germinativum.
- **The glassy membrane:** This is a thickened basal lamina, wrapped in a dense connective tissue sheath.

Functions of Hair [Figures 4.9/4.10a]

The 5 million hairs on the human body have important functions. The roughly 100,000 hairs on the head protect the scalp from ultraviolet light, cushion a blow to the head, and provide insulation for the skull. The hairs guarding the entrances to the nostrils and external auditory canals help prevent the entry of foreign particles and insects, and eyelashes perform a similar function for the surface of the eye. A **root hair plexus** of sensory nerves surrounds the base of each hair follicle (**Figure 4.10a**). As a result, the movement of the shaft of even a single hair can be felt at a conscious level. This sensitivity provides an early-warning system that may help prevent injury. For example, you may be able to swat a mosquito before it reaches the skin surface.

A ribbon of smooth muscle, called the **arrector pili** (a-REK-tor PĪ-lī; plural, *arrectores pilorum*) extends from the papillary dermis to the connective tissue sheath surrounding the hair follicle (**Figures 4.9** and **4.10a**). When stimulated, the arrector pili pulls on the follicle and elevates the hair. Contraction may be caused by emotional states, such as fear or rage, or as a response to cold, producing characteristic "goose bumps." In a furry mammal, this action increases the thickness of the insulating coat, rather like putting on an extra sweater. Although we do not receive any comparable insulating benefits, the reflex persists.

[2] The glans penis and prepuce of the male; the clitoris, labia minora, and inner surfaces of the labia majora in the female.

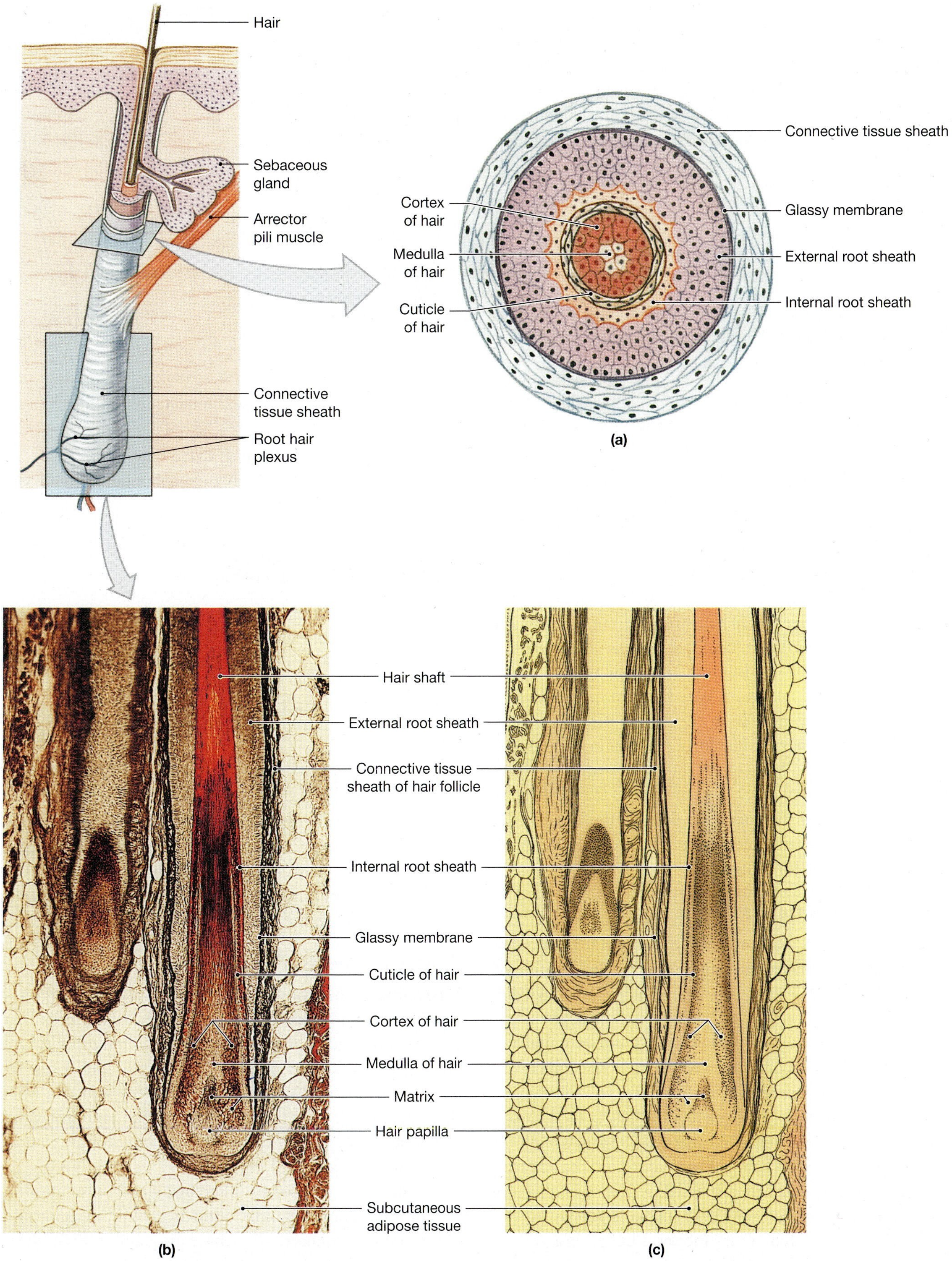

Figure 4.10 Hair Follicles

Hairs originate in hair follicles, which are complex organs. **(a)** A longitudinal section and a cross section through a hair follicle. Histological **(b)** and diagrammatic **(c)** sections along the longitudinal axis of a hair follicle. (LM × 60)

Types of Hairs

Hairs first appear after roughly three months of embryonic development. These hairs, collectively known as *lanugo* (la-NOO-gō), are extremely fine and unpigmented. Most lanugo hairs are shed before birth. They are replaced by one of the three types of hairs in the adult. The three major types of hairs in the integument of an adult are *vellus hairs*, *intermediate hairs*, and *terminal hairs*.

- *Vellus hairs* are the fine "peach fuzz" hairs found over much of the body surface.
- *Intermediate hairs* are hairs that change in their distribution, such as the hairs of the upper and lower limbs.
- *Terminal hairs* are heavy, more deeply pigmented, and sometimes curly. The hairs on your head, including your eyebrows and eyelashes, are examples of terminal hairs.

The description of hair structure earlier in the chapter was based on an examination of terminal hairs. Vellus and intermediate hairs are similar, though neither has a distinct medulla. Hair follicles may alter the structure of the hairs they produce in response to circulating hormones. Thus a follicle that produces a vellus hair today may produce an intermediate hair tomorrow; this accounts for many of the changes in hair distribution that begin at puberty.

Hair Color

Variations in hair color reflect differences in hair structure and variations in the pigment produced by melanocytes at the papilla. These characteristics are genetically determined, but the condition of your hair may be influenced by hormonal or environmental factors. Whether your hair is black or brown depends on the density of melanin in the cortex. Red hair results from the presence of a biochemically distinct form of melanin. As pigment production decreases with age, the hair color lightens toward gray. White hair results from the combination of a lack of pigment and the presence of air bubbles within the medulla of the hair shaft. Because the hair itself is dead and inert, changes in coloration are gradual; your hair can't "turn white overnight," as some horror stories suggest.

Growth and Replacement of Hair [Figure 4.11]

A hair in the scalp grows for 2–5 years, at a rate of around 0.33 mm/day (about 1/64 inch). Variations in the hair growth rate and in the duration of the **hair growth cycle,** illustrated in Figure 4.11, account for individual differences in uncut hair length.

While hair growth is under way, the root of the hair is firmly attached to the matrix of the follicle. At the end of the growth cycle, the follicle becomes inactive, and the hair is now termed a **club hair**. The follicle gets smaller, and over time the connections between the hair matrix and the root of the club hair break down. When another growth cycle begins, the follicle produces a new hair, and the old club hair gets pushed toward the surface.

In healthy adults, about 50 hairs are lost each day, but several factors may affect this rate. Sustained losses of more than 100 hairs per day usually indicate that something is wrong. Temporary increases in hair loss can result from drugs, dietary factors, radiation, high fever, stress, and hormonal factors related to pregnancy. Collecting hair samples can be helpful in diagnosing several disorders. For example, hairs of individuals with lead poisoning or other heavy-metal poisoning contain high quantities of those metal ions. In males, changes in the level of the sex hormones circulating in the blood can affect the scalp, causing a shift from terminal hair to vellus hair production. This alteration is called **male pattern baldness**.

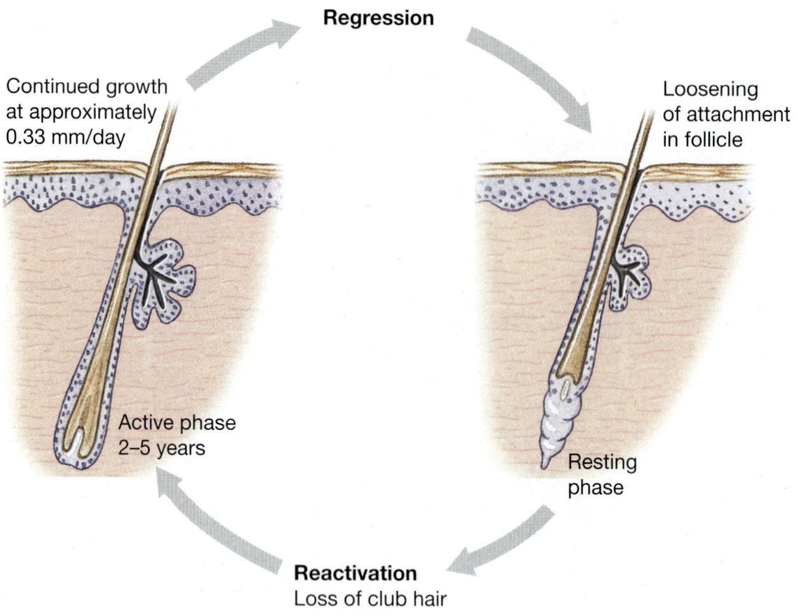

Figure 4.11 The Hair Growth Cycle
Each hair follicle goes through growth cycles involving active and resting stages.

CONCEPT CHECK

1. What happens to the dermis when it is excessively stretched, as in pregnancy or obesity?
2. What condition is produced by the contraction of the arrector pili?
3. Describe the major features of a hair.

See blue "Answers" tab at back of book.

Glands in the Skin [Figure 4.12]

The skin contains two types of exocrine glands: *sebaceous glands* and *sweat (sudoriferous) glands*. Sebaceous glands produce an oily lipid that coats hair shafts and the epidermis. Sweat glands produce a watery solution and perform other special functions. Figure 4.12 summarizes the functional classification of the exocrine glands of the skin.

Sebaceous Glands [Figure 4.13]

Sebaceous (se-BĀ-shus) **glands**, or *oil glands*, discharge a waxy, oily secretion into hair follicles (Figure 4.13). The gland cells manufacture large quantities of lipids as they mature, and the lipid product is released through holocrine secretion. pp. 60–61 The ducts are short, and several sebaceous glands may open into a single follicle. Depending on whether the glands share a common duct, they may be classified as *simple alveolar glands* (each gland has its own duct) or *simple branched alveolar glands* (several glands empty into a single duct). p. 60

The lipids released by sebaceous gland cells enter the open passageway, or *lumen*, of the gland. Contraction of the arrector pili muscle that elevates the hair squeezes the sebaceous gland, forcing the waxy secretions into the follicle and onto the surface of the skin. This secretion, called **sebum** (SĒ-bum), provides lubrication and inhibits the growth of bacteria. Keratin is a tough protein, but dead, keratinized cells become dry and brittle once exposed to the environment. Sebum lubricates and protects the keratin of the hair shaft and conditions the surrounding skin. Shampooing removes the natural oily coating, and excessive washing can make hairs stiff and brittle.

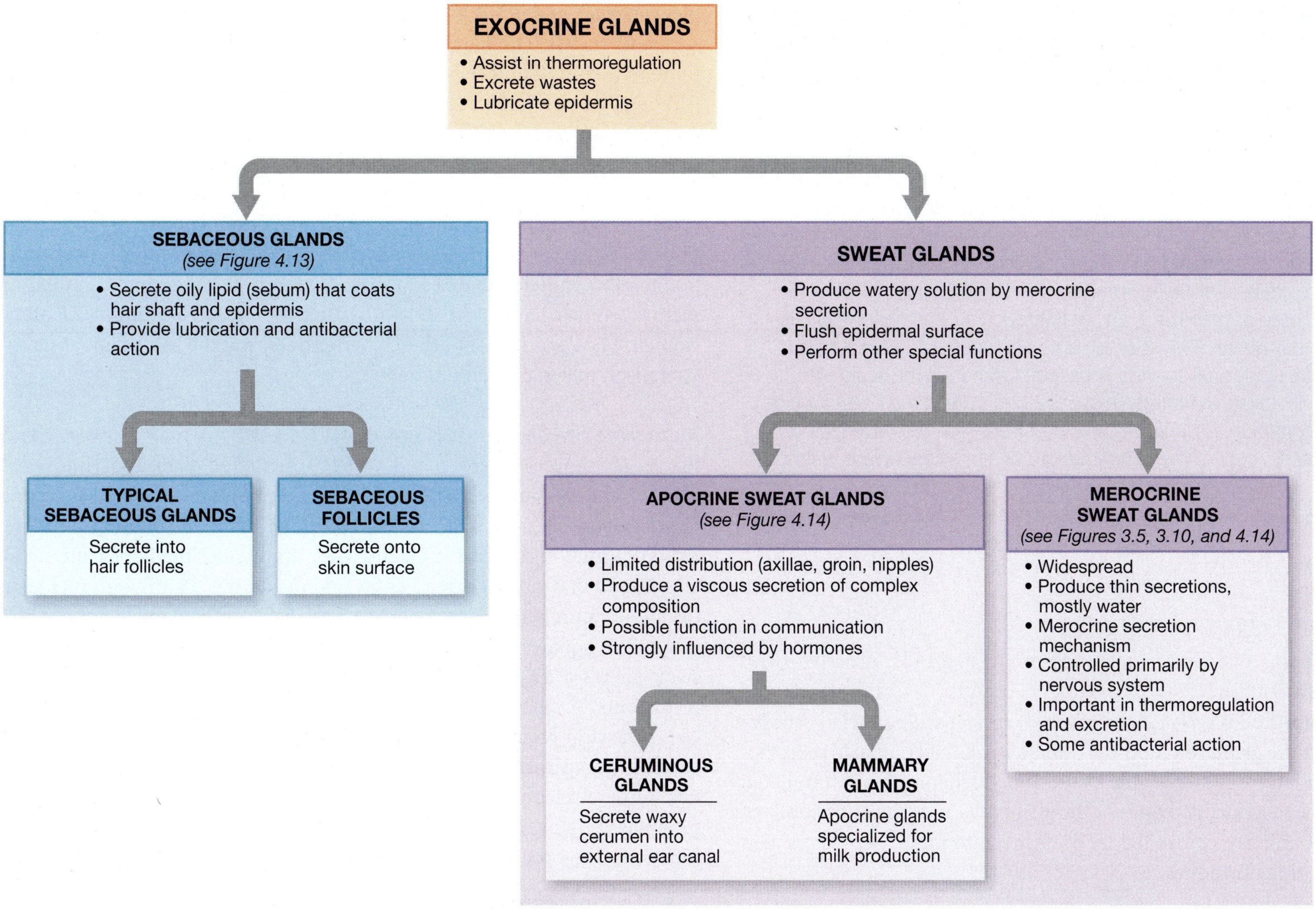

Figure 4.12 A Classification of Exocrine Glands in the Skin
Relationship of sebaceous glands and sweat glands, and some characteristics and functions of their secretory products.

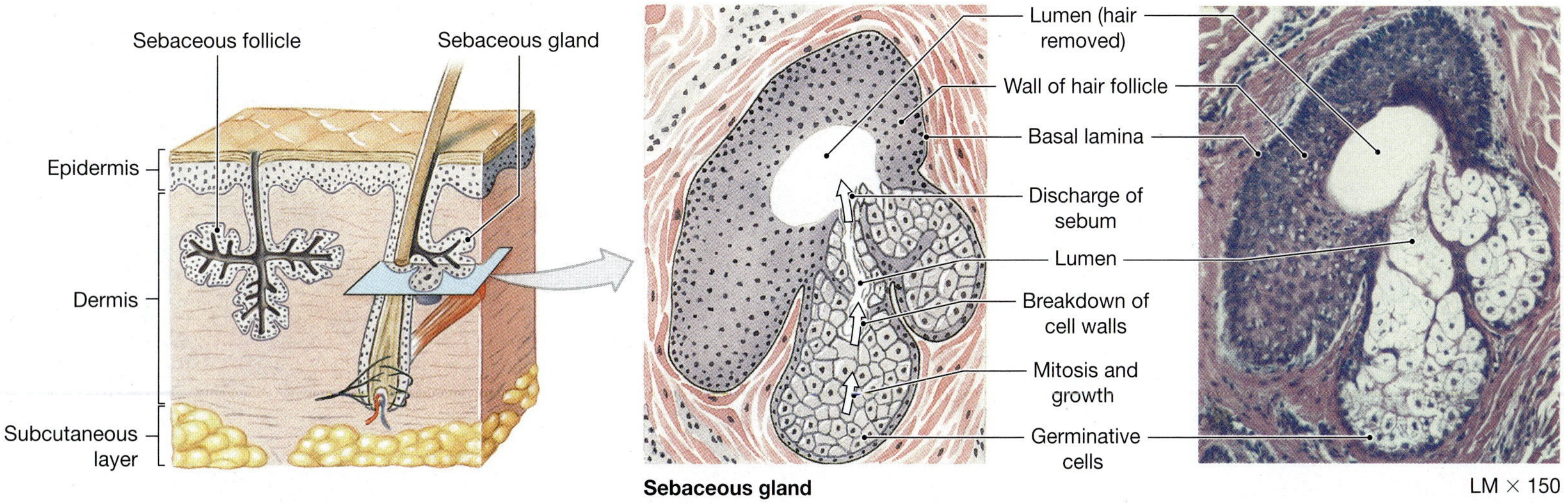

Figure 4.13 Sebaceous Glands and Follicles
The structure of sebaceous glands and sebaceous follicles in the skin.

Sebaceous follicles are large sebaceous glands that communicate directly with the epidermis. These follicles, which never produce hairs, are found on the integument covering the face, back, chest, nipples, and male sex organs. Although sebum has bactericidal (bacteria-killing) properties, under some conditions bacteria can invade sebaceous glands or follicles. The presence of bacteria in glands or follicles can produce a local inflammation known as **folliculitis** (fo-lik-ū-LĪ-tis). If the duct of the gland becomes blocked, a distinctive abscess called a **furuncle** (FU-rung-kl), or "boil," develops. The usual treatment for a furuncle is to cut it open, or "lance" it, so that normal drainage and healing can occur.

Clinical Note

Acne and Seborrheic Dermatitis Sebaceous glands and sebaceous follicles are very sensitive to changes in the concentrations of sex hormones, and their secretory activities accelerate at puberty. For this reason an individual with large sebaceous glands may be especially prone to develop acne during adolescence. In **acne**, sebaceous ducts become blocked and secretions accumulate, causing inflammation and providing a fertile environment for bacterial infection.

Seborrheic dermatitis is an inflammation around abnormally active sebaceous glands. The affected area becomes red, and there is usually some epidermal scaling. Sebaceous glands of the scalp are most often involved. In infants, mild cases are called *cradle cap*. Adults know this condition as *dandruff*. Anxiety, stress, and food allergies can increase the severity of the inflammation, as can a concurrent fungal infection.

Sweat Glands [Figures 4.12/4.14]

The skin contains two different groups of sweat glands: *apocrine sweat glands* and *merocrine sweat glands* (Figures 4.12 and 4.14). Both gland types contain **myoepithelial cells** (*myo*-, muscle), specialized epithelial cells located between the gland cells and the underlying basal lamina. Myoepithelial cell contractions squeeze the gland and discharge the accumulated secretions. The secretory activities of the gland cells and the contractions of myoepithelial cells are controlled by both the autonomic nervous system and by circulating hormones.

Apocrine Sweat Glands [Figures 4.9a/4.14a] Sweat glands that release their secretions into hair follicles in the axillae (armpits), around the nipples (*areolae*), and in the groin are termed **apocrine sweat glands** (Figures 4.9a and 4.14a). The name *apocrine* was originally chosen because it was thought that the gland cells used an apocrine method of secretion. p. 60 Although we now know that their secretory products are produced through merocrine secretion, the name has not changed. Apocrine sweat glands are coiled tubular glands that produce a viscous, cloudy, and potentially odorous secretion. They begin secreting at puberty; the sweat produced may be acted upon by bacteria, causing a noticeable odor. Apocrine gland secretions may also contain *pheromones*, chemicals that communicate information to other individuals at a subconscious level. The apocrine secretions of mature women have been shown to alter the menstrual timing of other women. The significance of these pheromones, and the role of apocrine secretions in males, remain unknown.

Merocrine Sweat Glands [Figures 4.12/4.14b] A type of sweat gland that is far more numerous and widely distributed than apocrine sweat glands is the **merocrine** (MER-ō-krin) **sweat glands,** also known as *eccrine sweat glands* (Figures 4.12 and 4.14b). The adult integument contains around 3 million merocrine glands. They are smaller than apocrine sweat glands, and they do not extend as far into the dermis. Palms and soles have the highest numbers; estimates are that the palm of the hand has about 500 glands per square centimeter (3000 glands per square inch). Merocrine sweat glands are coiled tubular glands that discharge their secretions directly onto the surface of the skin.

The clear secretion produced by merocrine glands is termed **sweat,** or **sensible perspiration.** Sweat is mostly water (99 percent), but it does contain some electrolytes (chiefly sodium chloride), metabolites, and waste products. The presence of sodium chloride gives sweat a salty taste. The functions of merocrine sweat gland activity include the following:

- **Thermoregulation.** Sweat cools the surface of the skin and reduces body temperature. This cooling is the primary function of sensible perspiration, and the degree of secretory activity is regulated by neural

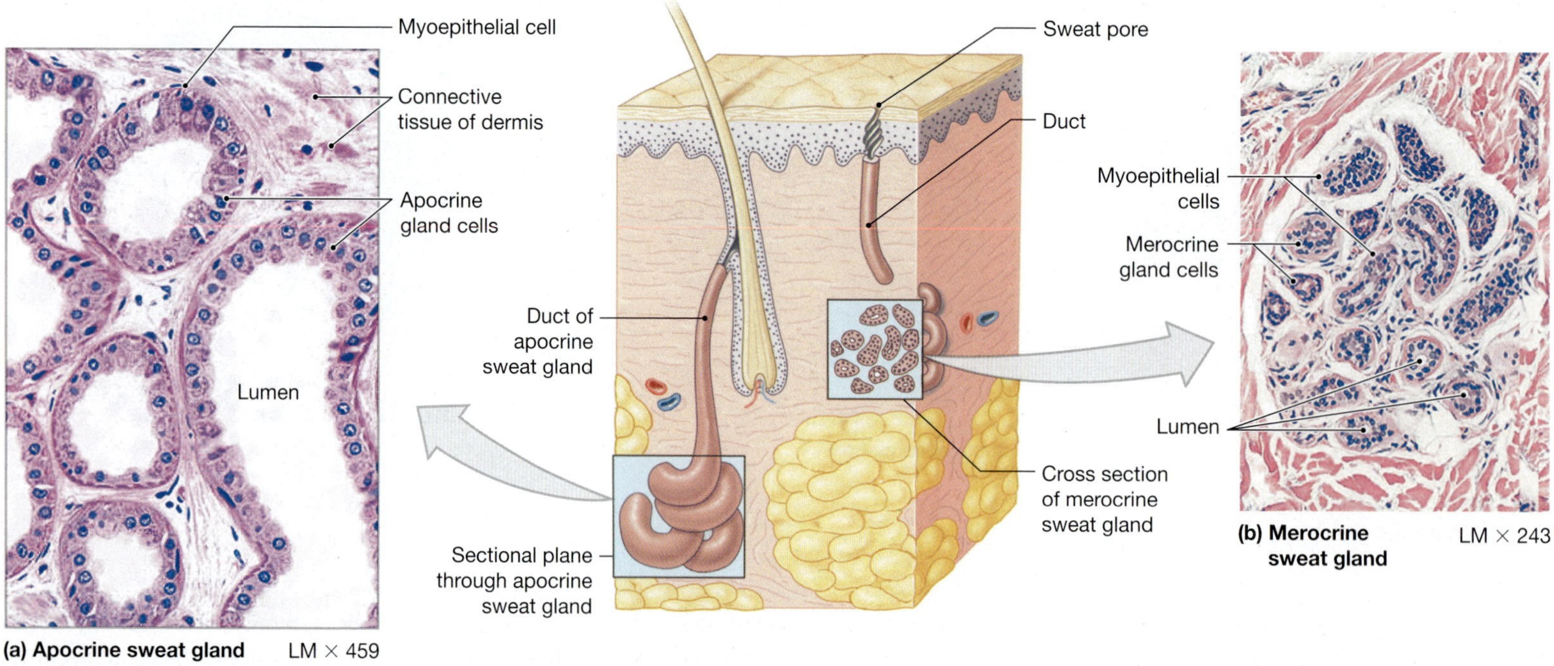

Figure 4.14 Sweat Glands
(a) Apocrine sweat glands are found in the axillae (armpits), groin, and nipples. They produce a thick, potentially odorous fluid. **(b)** Merocrine sweat glands produce a watery fluid commonly called sensible perspiration or sweat.

and hormonal mechanisms. When all of the merocrine sweat glands are working at maximum, the rate of perspiration may exceed a gallon per hour, and dangerous fluid and electrolyte losses can occur. For this reason athletes in endurance sports must pause frequently to drink fluids.

- **Excretion.** Merocrine sweat gland secretion can also provide a significant excretory route for water and electrolytes, as well as for a number of prescription and nonprescription drugs.
- **Protection.** Merocrine sweat gland secretion provides protection from environmental hazards by diluting harmful chemicals and discouraging the growth of microorganisms.

Control of Glandular Secretions

Sebaceous glands and apocrine sweat glands can be turned on or off by the autonomic nervous system, but no regional control is possible—this means that when one sebaceous gland is activated, so are all the other sebaceous glands in the body. Merocrine sweat glands are much more precisely controlled, and the amount of secretion and the area of the body involved can be varied independently. For example, when you are nervously awaiting an anatomy exam, your palms may begin to sweat.

Other Integumentary Glands

Sebaceous glands and merocrine sweat glands are found over most of the body surface. Apocrine sweat glands are found in relatively restricted areas. The skin also contains a variety of specialized glands that are restricted to specific locations. Many will be encountered in later chapters; two important examples will be noted here.

1. The **mammary glands** of the breasts are anatomically related to apocrine sweat glands. A complex interaction between sexual and pituitary hormones controls their development and secretion. Mammary gland structure and function will be discussed in Chapter 27.
2. **Ceruminous** (se-ROO-mi-nus) **glands** are modified sweat glands located in the external auditory canal. They differ from merocrine sweat glands in that they have a larger lumen and their gland cells contain pigment granules and lipid droplets not found in other sweat glands. Their secretions combine with those of nearby sebaceous glands, forming a mixture called **cerumen,** or simply "earwax." Earwax, together with tiny hairs along the ear canal, probably helps trap foreign particles or small insects and keeps them from reaching the eardrum.

CONCEPT CHECK

1. Compare the secretions of apocrine and merocrine sweat glands. Which produces secretions targeted by the deodorant industry?
2. What is sensible perspiration?
3. How does the control of merocrine gland secretion differ from the control of sebaceous and apocrine gland secretion?

See blue "Answers" tab at back of book.

Nails [Figure 4.15]

Nails form on the dorsal surfaces of the tips of the fingers and toes. The nails protect the exposed tips of the fingers and toes and help limit distortion when the digits are subjected to mechanical stress—for example,

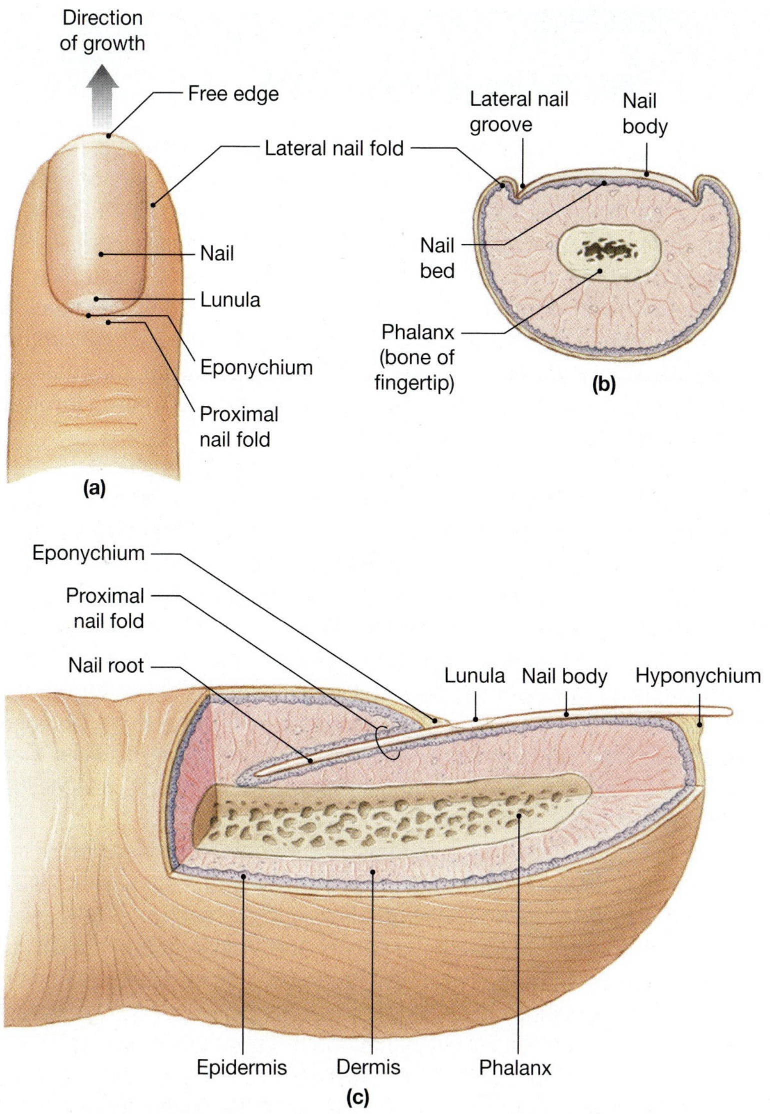

Figure 4.15 Structure of a Nail
These drawings illustrate the prominent features of a typical fingernail as viewed **(a)** from the surface, **(b)** in cross section, and **(c)** in longitudinal section.

in grasping objects or running. The structure of a nail can be seen in Figure 4.15. The **nail body** covers the **nail bed**, but nail production occurs at the **nail root**, an epithelial fold not visible from the surface. The deepest portion of the nail root lies very close to the periosteum of the bone of the fingertip.

The nail body is recessed beneath the level of the surrounding epithelium, and it is bounded by **nail grooves** and **nail folds.** A portion of the stratum corneum of the nail fold extends over the exposed nail nearest the root, forming the **eponychium,** (ep-ō-NIK-ē-um; *epi-*, over + *onyx*, nail) or *cuticle.* Underlying blood vessels give the nail its characteristic pink color, but near the root these vessels may be obscured, leaving a pale crescent known as the **lunula** (LOO-nūla; *luna*, moon). The free edge of the nail body extends over a thickened stratum corneum, the **hyponychium** (hī-pō-NIK-ē-um).

Changes in the shape, structure, or appearance of the nails are clinically significant. A change may indicate the existence of a disease process affecting metabolism throughout the body. For example, the nails may turn yellow in patients who have chronic respiratory disorders, thyroid gland disorders, or AIDS. They may become pitted and distorted in psoriasis and concave in some blood disorders.

Clinical Note

Repairing Injuries to the Skin The skin can regenerate effectively, even after considerable damage has occurred, because stem cells persist in both the epithelial and connective tissue components. Germinative cell divisions replace lost epidermal cells, and mesenchymal cell divisions replace lost dermal cells. The process can be slow. When large surface areas are involved, problems of infection and fluid loss complicate the situation. The relative speed and effectiveness of skin repair vary with the type of wound involved. A slender, straight cut, or *incision,* may heal relatively quickly compared with a deep scrape, or *abrasion,* which involves a much greater surface area to be repaired.

The regeneration of the skin after an injury involves four stages. When damage extends through the epidermis and into the dermis, bleeding generally occurs (STEP 1). The blood clot, or **scab**, that forms at the surface temporarily restores the integrity of the epidermis and restricts the entry of additional microorganisms into the area (STEP 2). The bulk of the clot consists of an insoluble network of *fibrin,* a fibrous protein that forms from blood proteins during the clotting response. The clot's color reflects the presence of trapped red blood cells. Cells of the stratum germinativum undergo rapid divisions and begin to migrate along the edges of the wound in an attempt to replace the missing epidermal cells. Meanwhile, macrophages patrol the damaged area of the dermis, phagocytizing any debris and pathogens.

If the wound occupies an extensive area or involves a region covered by thin skin, dermal repairs must be underway before epithelial cells can cover the surface. Divisions by fibroblasts and mesenchymal cells produce mobile cells that invade the deeper areas of injury. Endothelial cells of damaged blood vessels also begin to divide, and capillaries follow the fibroblasts, enhancing circulation. The combination of blood clot, fibroblasts, and an extensive capillary network is called **granulation tissue**.

Over time, deeper portions of the clot dissolve, and the number of capillaries declines. Fibroblast activity leads to the appearance of collagen fibers and typical ground substance (STEP 3). The repairs do not restore the integument to its original condition, however, because the dermis will contain an abnormally large number of collagen fibers and relatively few blood vessels. Severely damaged hair follicles, sebaceous or sweat glands, muscle cells, and nerves are seldom repaired, and they too are replaced by fibrous tissue. The formation of this rather inflexible, fibrous, noncellular **scar tissue** can be considered a practical limit to the healing process (STEP 4).

We do not know what regulates the extent of scar tissue formation, and the process is highly variable. For example, surgical procedures performed on a fetus do not leave scars, perhaps because damaged fetal tissues do not produce the same types of growth factors that adult tissues do. In some adults, most often those with dark skin, scar tissue formation may continue beyond the requirements of tissue repair. The result is a thickened mass of scar tissue that begins at the site of injury and grows into the surrounding dermis. This thick, raised area of scar tissue, called a **keloid** (KĒ-loyd), is covered by a shiny, smooth epidermal surface. Keloids most commonly develop on the upper back, shoulders, anterior chest, or earlobes. They are harmless; in fact, some aboriginal cultures intentionally produce keloids as a form of body decoration.

In fact, people in societies around the world adorn the skin with culturally significant markings of one kind or another. Tattoos, piercings, keloids and other scar patterns, and even high-fashion makeup are all used to "enhance" the appearance of the integument. Scarification is performed in several African cultures, resulting in a series of complex, raised scars on the skin. Polynesian cultures have long preferred tattoos

STEP 1

Bleeding occurs at the site of injury immediately after the injury, and mast cells in the region trigger an inflammatory response.

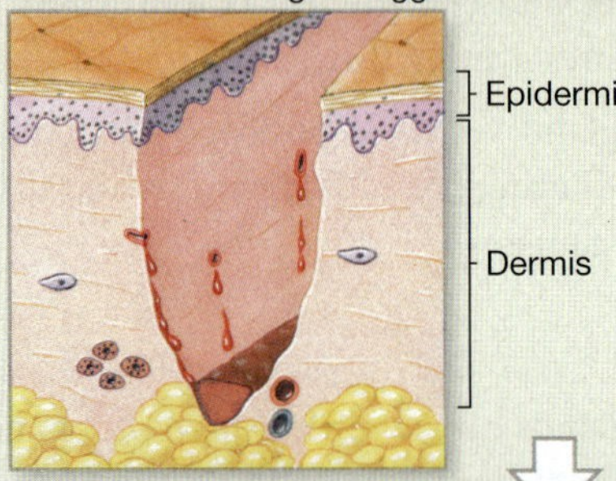

STEP 2

After several hours, a scab has formed and cells of the stratum germinativum are migrating along the edges of the wound. Phagocytic cells are removing debris, and more of these cells are arriving via the enhanced circulation in the area. Clotting around the edges of the affected area partially isolates the region.

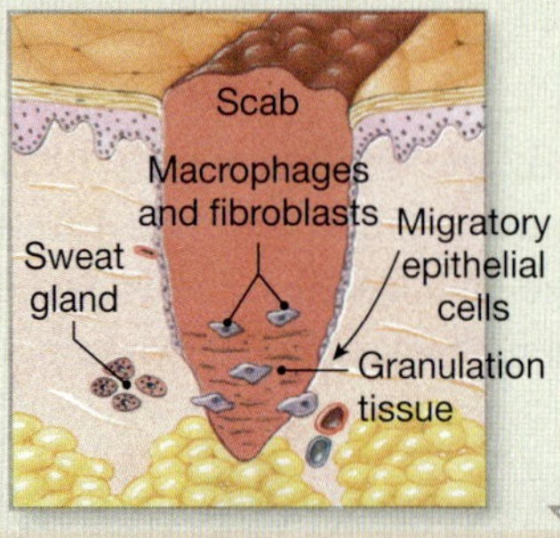

STEP 3

One week after the injury, the scab has been undermined by epidermal cells migrating over the meshwork produced by fibroblast activity. Phagocytic activity around the site has almost ended, and the fibrin clot is disintegrating.

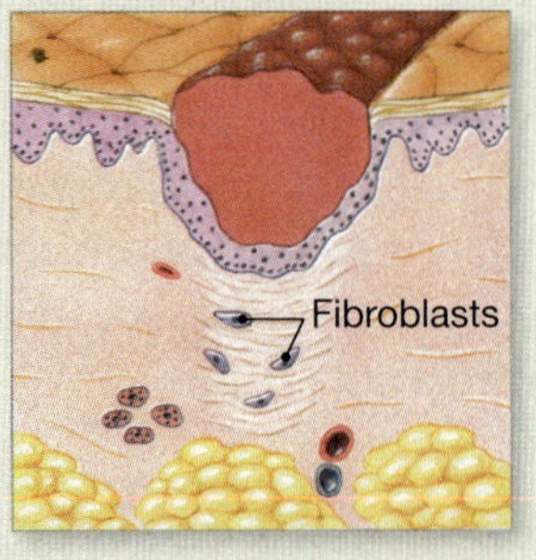

STEP 4

After several weeks, the scab has been shed, and the epidermis is complete. A shallow depression marks the injury site, but fibroblasts in the dermis continue to create scar tissue that will gradually elevate the overlying epidermis.

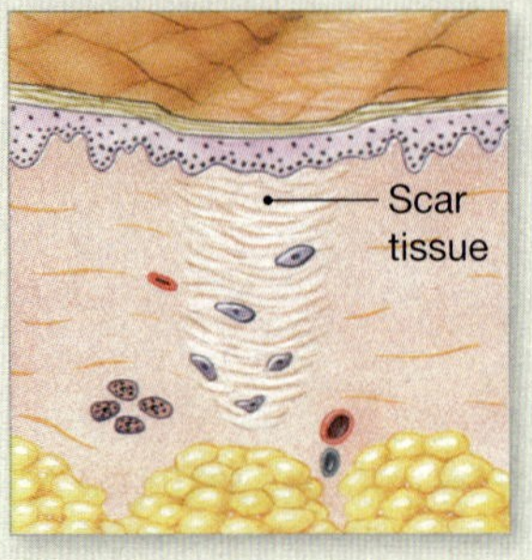

Clinical Note *(continued)*

as a sign of status and beauty. A dark pigment is inserted deep within the dermis of the skin by tapping on a needle, shark tooth, or bit of bone. Because the pigment is inert, if infection does not occur (a potentially serious complication), the markings remain for the life of the individual, clearly visible through the overlying epidermis. American popular culture has recently rediscovered tattoos as a fashionable form of body adornment. The colored inks that are commonly used are less durable, and older tattoos can fade or lose their definition.

Tattoos can now be partially or completely removed. The removal process takes time (10 or more sessions may be required to remove a large tattoo), and scars often remain. To remove the tattoo, an intense, narrow beam of light from a laser breaks down the ink molecules in the dermis. Each blast of the laser that destroys the ink also burns the surrounding dermal tissue. Although the burns are minor, they accumulate and result in the formation of localized scar tissue.

Local Control of Integumentary Function

The integumentary system displays a significant degree of functional independence. It responds directly and automatically to local influences without the involvement of the nervous or endocrine systems. For example, when the skin is subjected to mechanical stresses, stem cells in the stratum germinativum divide more rapidly, and the depth of the epithelium increases. That is why *calluses* form on your palms when you perform manual labor. A more dramatic display of local regulation can be seen after an injury to the skin.

After severe damage, the repair process does not return the integument to its original condition. The injury site contains an abnormal density of collagen fibers and relatively few blood vessels. Damaged hair follicles, sebaceous or sweat glands, muscle cells, and nerves are seldom repaired, and they too are replaced by fibrous tissue. The formation of this rather inflexible, fibrous, noncellular **scar tissue** is a practical limit to the healing process. Skin repairs proceed most rapidly in young, healthy individuals. For example, it takes 3–4 weeks to complete the repairs to a blister site in a young adult. The same repairs at age 65–75 take 6–8 weeks. However, this is just one example of the changes that occur in the integumentary system as a result of the aging process.

Aging and the Integumentary System [Figure 4.16]

Aging affects all of the components of the integumentary system. These changes are summarized in Figure 4.16.

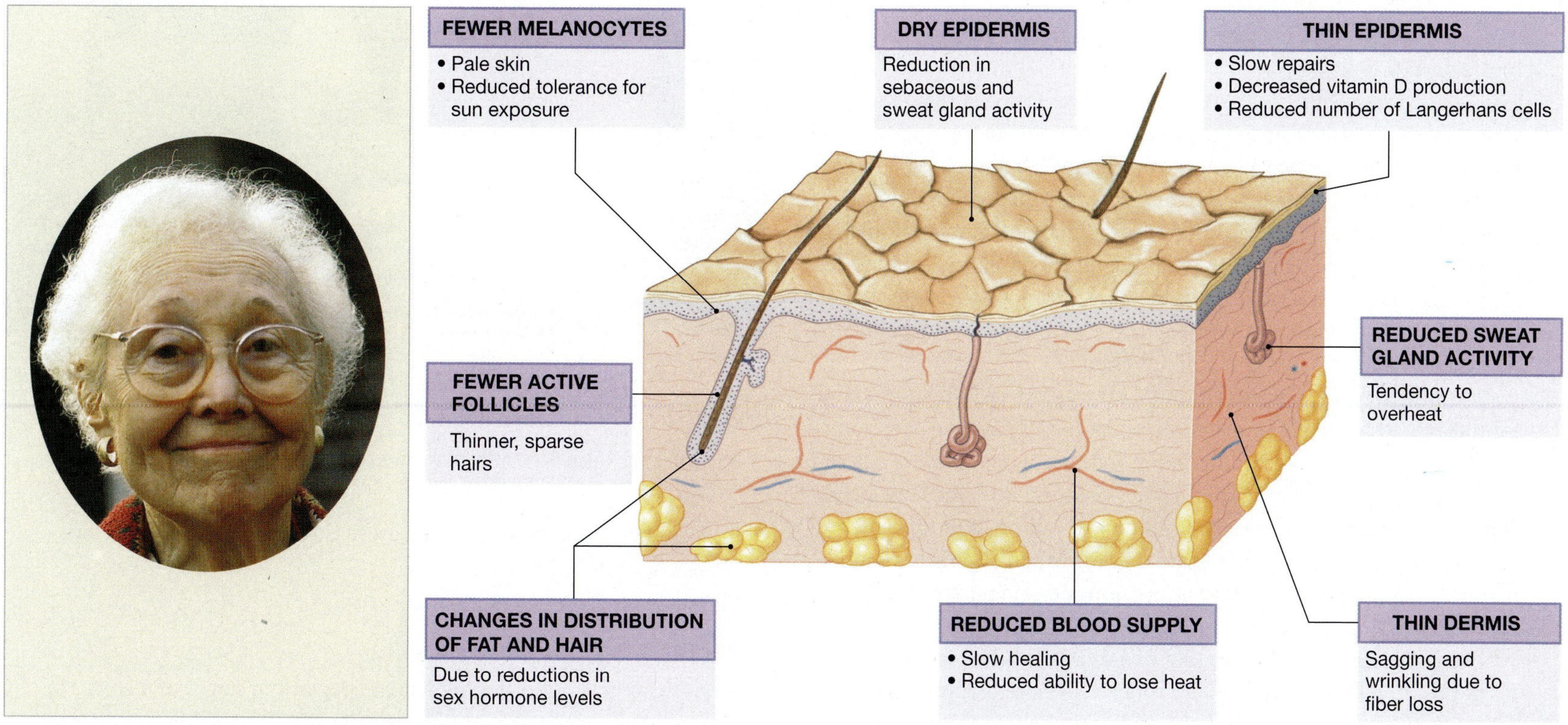

Figure 4.16 The Skin during the Aging Process
Characteristic changes in the skin during aging; some causes and some effects.

1. *The epidermis thins* as germinative cell activity declines, making older people more prone to injury and skin infections.
2. *The number of Langerhans cells decreases* to around 50 percent of levels seen at maturity (approximately age 21). This decrease may reduce the sensitivity of the immune system and further encourage skin damage and infection.
3. *Vitamin D production declines* by around 75 percent. The result can be muscle weakness and a reduction in bone strength.
4. *Melanocyte activity declines*, and in Caucasians the skin becomes very pale. With less melanin in the skin, older people are more sensitive to sun exposure and more likely to experience sunburn.
5. *Glandular activity declines.* The skin becomes dry and often scaly because sebum production is reduced; merocrine sweat glands are also less active. With impaired perspiration, older people cannot lose heat as fast as younger people can. Thus, the elderly are at greater risk of overheating in warm environments.
6. *The blood supply to the dermis is reduced* at the same time that sweat glands become less active. This combination makes the elderly less able to lose body heat, and overexertion or overexposure to warm temperatures (such as a sauna or hot tub) can cause dangerously high body temperatures.
7. *Hair follicles stop functioning* or produce thinner, finer hairs. With decreased melanocyte activity, these hairs are gray or white.
8. *The dermis becomes thinner*, and the elastic fiber network decreases in size. The integument therefore becomes weaker and less resilient; sagging and wrinkling occur. These effects are most pronounced in areas exposed to the sun.
9. *Secondary sexual characteristics in hair and body fat distribution begin to fade* as the result of changes in levels of sex hormones. In consequence, people age 90–100 of both sexes and all races look very much alike.
10. *Skin repairs proceed relatively slowly*, and recurring infections may result.

Clinical Case — THE INTEGUMENTARY SYSTEM

ANXIETY IN THE ANATOMY LABORATORY

John is a third-year English and Psychology major who hopes to go to medical school following graduation. He is enrolled in a variety of classes this term, including Abnormal Psychology, Milton, Professional Writing, Sociology of Deviant Behavior, and Human Anatomy. Of all of these courses, Human Anatomy and its associated cadaver laboratory are occupying the largest percentage of his time. To prepare for his laboratory midterm examination, John is spending many hours in the laboratory. The extra time that John needs to spend on the course and the pressure he feels about the upcoming examination are combining to make John increasingly nervous during his time in the laboratory. While working in the laboratory late into the evening before the examination, John hears rumors about the difficulty of the examination. John is now in high anxiety. Despite doing his best to relax, he finds himself soaked in sweat. He changes out of his laboratory clothes, washes up, and heads to the college union for a snack break. While sitting at a table, John notices that the skin on his hands has become a bit itchy and red.

The next day, before the laboratory midterm examination starts, John sees that the redness and itching on his hands have subsided somewhat. As he enters the laboratory, John puts on his laboratory coat and opens a new box of examination gloves. Because his hands are sweaty from nervousness, the gloves are difficult to put on, and they rip and tear. John discards them and goes back to the brand of powdered gloves that he has been wearing for the entire semester. He settles in and takes the laboratory examination.

Two days later John notices that he has a red, itchy rash on both of his hands. In addition, his eyes are watery, his nose is running, and his voice has become hoarse. As the day progresses the symptoms intensify, and John goes to the RediMed office.

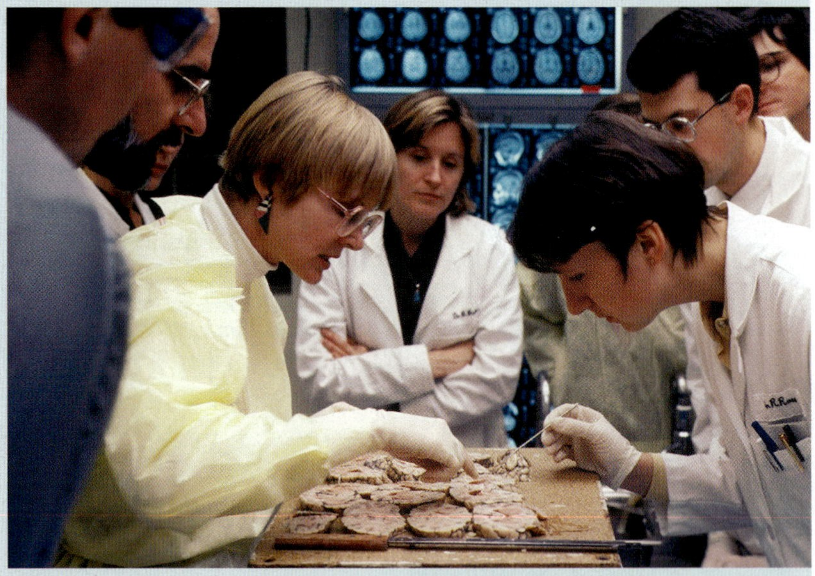

Initial Examination

The physician in the clinic notes the following:

- Both of John's hands demonstrate erythema and are slightly swollen.
- John's eyes are watery, and his nose is running, both characteristics of a cold.
- His voice is hoarse and raspy.
- His temperature is 37°C (98.6°F).

The physician tells John that he has the beginning stages of a cold. He recommends an over-the-counter antihistamine for the cold symptoms and hydrocortisone for the rash on his hands.

Clinical Case *continued*

As the next week progresses, John continues his studies in the cadaver laboratory. Neither medication seems to be working, and the rash and itching on his hands intensify. Within another week, John is unable to wear gloves at all because the symptoms intensify within minutes of putting them on. John returns to RediMed for a second examination.

Follow-up Examination

The physician notes the following:

- John's hands are swollen and red (**Figure 4.17**).
- All values for joint range of motion (ROM) are normal, and joint movement is not accompanied by any pain or discomfort.
- Papules and vesicles are noted on both the palmar and dorsal surfaces of his hands.
- The skin on John's hands appears to have thickened and is demonstrating pigment changes.
- John's previous symptoms of a runny nose, watery eyes, and hoarseness of the voice are still present.

The physician is concerned that John has developed either a talc irritation or an allergy to one or more of the working conditions in the cadaver laboratory. An allergy to latex gloves or to the formalin used to preserve cadavers are both possibilities. The physician:

- Precribes an antihistamine and a stronger steroid cream for the skin rash to help alleviate John's symptoms.
- Recommends that he avoid hand contact with either latex or formalin.
- Prescribes an epinephrine pen for John and recommends that he carry it at all times in the event that John undergoes an anaphylactic reaction in the laboratory.
- Requests that John return to the office within the next 48 hours and provide the physician with a sample of the gloves used in the cadaver laboratory as well as a list of the chemicals utilized to preserve the cadavers.
- Tells John to call the physician's office within 72 hours if the symptoms have not diminished.

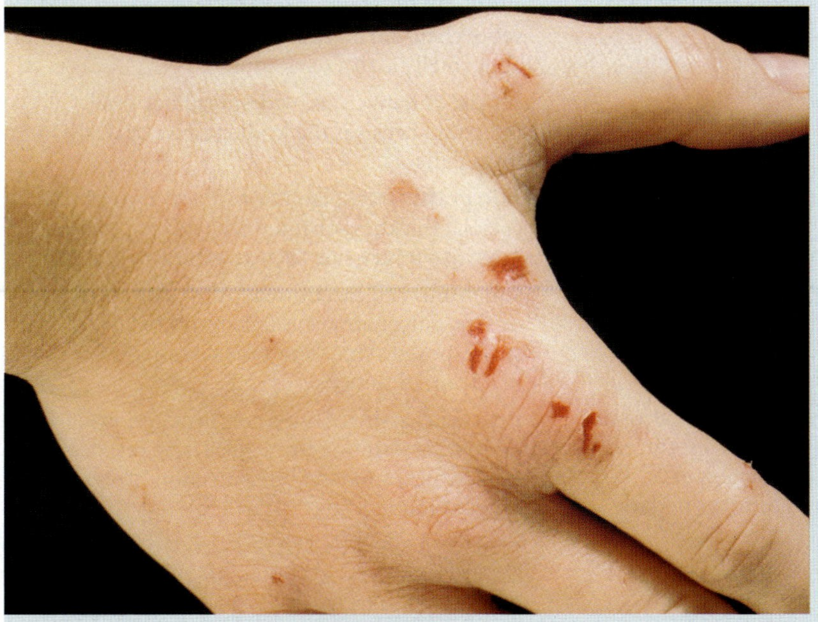

Figure 4.17 Dorsum of John's Hand

Points to Consider

Every system of the body does, at one time or another, play an important role in presenting signs or symptoms, thereby enabling a physician to piece together the various clues that will, ideally, lead to a correct diagnosis of the patient. Both the patient's presenting symptoms and the physician's analysis and interpretation of the symptoms contribute to the detective work.

To consider the meaning of the information presented in the case above, you need to review the anatomical material covered in this chapter. The questions below will guide you in your review. Think about and answer each one, referring back to this chapter if you need help.

1. What are the anatomical characteristics of the skin on the palmar and dorsal surfaces of the hands?
2. What anatomical structures of the skin are responsible for the protective characteristics of the skin? What are the anatomical characteristics of these cells and tissues that would account for these protective characteristics?
3. What anatomical structures are responsible for the formation of sweat?
4. The skin on John's hands appears to have thickened and is demonstrating pigment changes. What anatomical process would account for these changes?

Analysis and Interpretation

The information below answers the questions raised in the "Points to Consider" section. To review the material, refer to the pages in the chapter indicated by the link icons.

1. The skin on the palms of the hands and soles of the feet is thick skin, which may be covered by 30 or more layers of keratinized cells. pp. 90–92
2. The epidermis of the skin, especially the stratum corneum, is responsible for the protective characteristics of the skin. pp. 92–93
3. Sweat glands in the skin produce sweat. These glands are controlled by the autonomic nervous system, which would be more active than normal due to John's nervousness about the upcoming examination. pp. 102–103
4. Although slight, the repetitive irritation of John's hands by the rubber gloves will increase the synthesis of keratohyalin and keratin within the stratum granulosum of the skin. pp. 91–92 As a result of the thickening of the epidermis of the skin, the color of the skin in the affected region will become lighter. p. 93

Diagnosis

John is experiencing an increasingly common allergic reaction among health care-workers, students, and anyone who may be exposed to latex-containing products: John has developed a latex allergy. Advanced

Clinical Case *continued*

stages of latex allergies, which John is experiencing due to his continued use of latex gloves in the cadaver lab throughout the term, are accompanied by a runny nose, watery eyes, and a hoarse voice due to the widespread involvement of the mucous membranes of the nose, eyes, and throat. These mucous membranes form a barrier to the entrance of pathogens (p. 72), and John's latex allergy is affecting the anatomical structure and function of these membranes.

Allergies to natural rubber latex are becoming more common in children and adults. In addition, latex allergies are becoming a serious medical problem for health-care workers.

Latex is the milky fluid derived from rubber trees. It is composed primarily of benign organic compounds. These compounds are responsible for most of the strength and elasticity of latex. Latex also contains a large variety of sugars, lipids, nucleic acids, and proteins.

After being produced at the factory, latex gloves are dried and rinsed in an effort to reduce the number of proteins and impurities on the surfaces of the gloves. Latex gloves are often lubricated with constarch or talc powder. The cornstarch or talc powder that is used to lubricate the gloves has the ability to absorb any residual latex proteins remaining from the manufacturing process. These residual latex proteins contribute to the possibility of an allergic reaction for the user of the gloves.

Latex is used in a wide variety of products today. In addition, latex has been used in an increasing number of medical devices in the past 20 years. In the late 1980s the use of latex in the medical industry skyrocketed as latex gloves were widely recommended to prevent the transmission of blood-borne pathogens, including the human immunodeficiency virus (HIV), in health-care workers. Billions of pairs of medical gloves are imported to the United States annually. This widespread use of latex has caused latex allergies to become an increasing problem in the health-care industry, not only in the United States but worldwide. ■

CLINICAL CASE TERMS

anaphylactic reaction: An induced systemic or generalized sensitivity.

epinephrine pen (also known as an epi-pen): An instrument that enables the rapid injection of a predetermined amount of epinephrine into an individual without the presence of a health professional.

erythema (er-i-THĒ-ma): Redness due to capillary dilation.

papule (PAP-yul): A circumscribed, solid elevation up to 100 cm in diameter on the skin.

vesicle: A small (less than l cm) circumscribed elevation of the skin containing fluid.

CLINICAL TERMS

acne: A sebaceous gland inflammation caused by an accumulation of secretions.

basal cell carcinoma: A malignant tumor that originates in the stratum germinativum. This is the most common skin cancer, and roughly two-thirds of these cancers appear in areas subjected to chronic UV exposure. Metastasis rarely occurs.

capillary hemangioma: A birthmark caused by a tumor in the capillaries of the papillary layer of the dermis. It usually enlarges after birth, but subsequently fades and disappears.

cavernous hemangioma ("port-wine stain"): A birthmark caused by a tumor affecting larger vessels in the dermis. Such birthmarks usually last a lifetime.

contact dermatitis: A dermatitis usually caused by strong chemical irritants. It produces an itchy rash that may spread to other areas if scratching distributes the chemical agent; poison ivy is an example.

contraction: A pulling together of the edges of a wound during the healing process.

decubitis ulcers ("bedsores"): Ulcers that occur in areas subjected to restricted circulation, especially common in bedridden people.

dermatitis: An inflammation of the skin that involves primarily the papillary region of the dermis.

diaper rash: A localized dermatitis caused by a combination of moisture, irritating chemicals from fecal or urinary wastes, and flourishing microorganisms.

eczema (EK-se-ma): A dermatitis that can be triggered by temperature changes, fungus, chemical irritants, greases, detergents, or stress, and that can be related to hereditary or environmental factors.

erysipelas (er-i-SIP-e-las): A widespread inflammation of the dermis caused by bacterial infection.

erythema (er-i-THĒ-ma): Redness due to capillary dilation.

granulation tissue: A combination of fibrin, fibroblasts, and capillaries that forms during tissue repair following inflammation.

hypodermic needle: A needle used to administer drugs via subcutaneous injection.

keloid (KĒ-loyd): A thickened area of scar tissue covered by a shiny, smooth epidermal surface. Keloids most often develop on the upper back, shoulders, anterior chest, and earlobes in dark-skinned individuals.

malignant melanoma (mel-a-NŌ-ma): A skin cancer originating in malignant melanocytes. A potentially fatal metastasis often occurs.

papule (pap-ūl): A circumscribed, solid elevation up to 100 cm in diameter on the skin.

psoriasis (sū-RĪ-a-sis): A painless condition characterized by rapid stem cell divisions in the stratum germinativum of the scalp, elbows, palms, soles, groin, and nails. Affected areas appear dry and scaly.

scab: A fibrin clot that forms at the surface of a wound to the skin.

seborrheic dermatitis: An inflammation around abnormally active sebaceous glands.

sepsis: A dangerous, widespread bacterial infection. Sepsis is the leading cause of death in burn patients.

skin graft: Transplantation of a section of skin (partial thickness or full thickness) to cover an extensive injury site, such as a third-degree burn.

squamous cell carcinoma: A less common form of skin cancer almost totally restricted to areas of sun-exposed skin. Metastasis seldom occurs except in advanced tumors.

urticaria (ur-ti-KAR-e-a) or *hives:* An extensive dermatitis resulting from an allergic reaction to food, drugs, an insect bite, infection, stress, or other stimulus.

vesicle: A small (less than 1 cm) circumscribed elevation of the skin containing fluid.

xerosis (zē-RŌ-sis): "Dry skin," a common complaint of older people and almost anyone living in an arid climate.

STUDY OUTLINE

Introduction 89

1. The **integumentary system**, or *integument*, serves to protect an individual from the surrounding environment. Its receptors also tell us about the outside world; and it helps to regulate body temperature.

Integumentary Structure and Function 90

1. The **integumentary system**, or **integument**, consists of the **cutaneous membrane** or *skin*, which includes the superficial **epidermis** and deeper **dermis**, and the **accessory structures**, including **hair follicles**, **nails**, and **exocrine glands**. The subcutaneous layer is deep to the cutaneous membrane. *(see Figures 4.1/4.2)*

The Epidermis 90

1. There are four cell types in the epidermis: **keratinocytes**, the most abundant epithelial cells; **melanocytes**, pigment-producing cells; **Merkel cells**, involved in detecting sensation; and **Langerhans cells**, which are phagocytic cells of the immune system. Melanocytes, Merkel cells, and Langerhans cells are scattered among the keratinocytes.
2. The epidermis is a *stratified squamous epithelium*. There are five layers of keratinocytes in the epidermis in **thick skin** and four layers in **thin skin**. *(see Figure 4.4)*

Layers of the Epidermis 91

3. Division of basal cells in the **stratum germinativum** produces new keratinocytes, which replace more superficial cells. *(see Figures 4.2 to 4.6)*
4. As new committed epidermal cells differentiate, they pass through the **stratum spinosum**, the **stratum granulosum**, the **stratum lucidum** (of thick skin), and the **stratum corneum**. The keratinocytes move toward the surface, and through the process of keratinization the cells accumulate large amounts of **keratin**. Ultimately the cells are shed or lost at the epidermal surface. *(see Figure 4.3)*

Thick and Thin Skin 93

5. **Thin skin** covers most of the body; **thick skin** covers only the heavily abraded surfaces, such as the palms of the hands and the soles of the feet. *(see Figure 4.4)*
6. **Epidermal ridges**, such as those on the palms and soles, improve our gripping ability and increase the skin's sensitivity. Their pattern is determined genetically. The ridges interlock with **dermal papillae** of the underlying dermis. *(see Figures 4.4/4.5)*
7. The color of the epidermis depends on a combination of three factors: the dermal blood supply, the thickness of the stratum corneum, and variable quantities of two pigments: *carotene* and *melanin*. Melanin helps protect the skin from the damaging effects of excessive **ultraviolet radiation**. *(see Figure 4.6)*

The Dermis 95

Dermal Organization 95

1. Two layers compose the dermis: the superficial **papillary layer** and the deeper **reticular layer**. *(see Figures 4.2/4.4/4.7 to 4.9)*
2. The papillary layer derives its name from its association with the dermal papillae. It contains blood vessels, lymphatics, and sensory nerves. This layer supports and nourishes the overlying epidermis. *(see Figures 4.4/4.7)*
3. The reticular layer consists of a meshwork of collagen and elastic fibers oriented in all directions to resist tension in the skin. *(see Figure 4.8)*

Other Dermal Components 96

4. An extensive blood supply to the skin includes the **cutaneous** and **papillary plexuses**. The papillary layer contains abundant capillaries that drain into the veins of these plexuses. *(see Figure 4.2)*
5. Sensory nerves innervate the skin. They monitor touch, temperature, pain, pressure, and vibration. *(see Figure 4.2)*

The Subcutaneous Layer 97

1. The **subcutaneous layer** is also referred to as the **hypodermis** or the **superficial fascia**. Although not part of the integument, it stabilizes the skin's position against underlying organs and tissues yet permits limited independent movement. *(see Figures 4.2/4.7)*

Accessory Structures 98

Hair Follicles and Hair 98

1. Hairs originate in complex organs called **hair follicles**, which extend into the dermis. Each hair has a **bulb**, **root**, and **shaft**. Hair production involves a special keratinization of the epithelial cells of the **hair matrix**. At the center of the matrix, the cells form a soft core, or **medulla**; cells at the edge of the hair form a hard **cortex**. The **cuticle** is a hard layer of dead, keratinized cells that coats the hair. *(see Figures 4.2/4.9 to 4.11)*
2. The lumen of the follicle is lined by an **internal root sheath** produced by the hair matrix. An **external root sheath** surrounds the internal root sheath, between the skin surface and hair matrix. The **glassy membrane** is the thickened basal lamina external to the external root sheath; it is wrapped by a dense connective tissue layer. *(see Figure 4.10)*
3. A **root hair plexus** of sensory nerves surrounds the base of each hair follicle and detects the movement of the shaft. Contraction of the **arrector pili muscle** elevates the hair by pulling on the follicle. *(see Figures 4.9/4.10a)*
4. **Vellus hairs** ("peach fuzz"), **intermediate hairs**, and heavy **terminal hairs** make up the hair population on our bodies. *(see Figure 4.11)*
5. Hairs grow and are shed according to the **hair growth cycle**. A single hair grows for 2–5 years and is subsequently shed. *(see Figure 4.11)*

Glands in the Skin 100

6. **Sebaceous (oil) glands** discharge a waxy, oily secretion (**sebum**) into hair follicles. **Sebaceous follicles** are large sebaceous glands that produce no hair; they communicate directly with the epidermis. *(see Figure 4.13)*
7. **Apocrine sweat glands** produce an odorous secretion; the more numerous **merocrine sweat glands**, or *eccrine sweat glands*, produce a thin, watery secretion known as **sensible perspiration**, or **sweat**. *(see Figures 4.12/4.14)*
8. The **mammary glands** of the breast resemble larger and more complex apocrine sweat glands. Active mammary glands secrete milk. **Ceruminous glands** in the ear canal are modified sweat glands, which produce waxy **cerumen**.

Nails 103

9. The **nails** protect the exposed tips of the fingers and toes and help limit their distortion when they are subjected to mechanical stress.
10. The **nail body** covers the **nail bed**, with nail production occurring at the **nail root**. The **cuticle**, or **eponychium**, is formed by a fold of the stratum corneum, the **nail fold**, extending from the **nail root** to the exposed nail. *(see Figure 4.15)*

Local Control of Integumentary Function 105

1. The skin can regenerate effectively even after considerable damage, such as severe cuts or moderate burns.
2. Severe damage to the dermis and accessory glands cannot be completely repaired, and fibrous **scar tissue** remains at the injury site.

Aging and the Integumentary System 105

1. Aging affects all layers and accessory structures of the integumentary system. *(see Figure 4.16)*

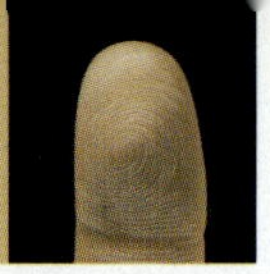

CHAPTER REVIEW

For answers to the Concept Check and Chapter Review questions, go to the blue "Answers" tab at the back of the book.

Level 1 Reviewing Facts and Terms

Match each numbered item with the most closely related lettered item. Use letters for answers in the spaces provided.

Column A	Column B
___ 1. hypodermis	a. fibrous, noncellular
___ 2. dermis	b. holocrine; oily secretion
___ 3. stem cell	c. pigment cells
___ 4. keratinized/cornified	d. stratum germinativum
___ 5. melanocytes	e. superficial fascia
___ 6. epidermis	f. papillary layer
___ 7. sebaceous gland	g. stratum corneum
___ 8. sweat gland	h. stratified squamous epithelium
___ 9. scar tissue	i. merocrine; clear secretion

10. Anatomically, "thick skin" and "thin skin" refer to differences in the thickness of the
    (a) papillary layer (b) dermis
    (c) hypodermis (d) epidermis
11. The effects of aging on the skin include
    (a) a decline in the activity of sebaceous glands
    (b) increased production of vitamin D
    (c) thickening of the epidermis
    (d) an increased blood supply to the dermis
12. Skin color is the product of
    (a) the dermal blood supply
    (b) pigment composition
    (c) pigment concentration
    (d) all of the above
13. Sensible perspiration
    (a) cools the skin surface to reduce body temperature
    (b) provides an excretory route for water and electrolytes
    (c) dilutes harmful chemicals and discourages bacterial growth on the skin
    (d) all of the above
14. The layer of the skin that contains both interwoven bundles of collagen fibers and the protein elastin, and is responsible for the strength of the skin, is the
    (a) papillary layer (b) reticular layer
    (c) epidermal layer (d) hypodermal layer
15. The layer of the epidermis that contains cells undergoing division is the
    (a) stratum corneum (b) stratum germinativum
    (c) stratum granulosum (d) stratum lucidum
16. Water loss due to penetration of interstitial fluid through the surface of the skin is termed
    (a) sensible perspiration (b) insensible perspiration
    (c) latent perspiration (d) active perspiration
17. All of the following are effects of aging except
    (a) the thinning of the epidermis of the skin
    (b) an increase in the number of Langerhans cells
    (c) a decrease in melanocyte activity
    (d) a decrease in glandular activity
18. Each of the following is a function of the integumentary system except
    (a) protection of underlying tissue (b) excretion
    (c) synthesis of vitamin C (d) thermoregulation
19. Carotene is
    (a) an orange-yellow pigment that accumulates inside epidermal cells
    (b) another name for melanin
    (c) deposited in stratum granulosum cells to protect the epidermis
    (d) a pigment that gives the characteristic color to hemoglobin
20. Which statement best describes a hair root?
    (a) It extends from the hair bulb to the point where the internal organization of the hair is complete
    (b) It is the nonliving portion of the hair
    (c) It encompasses all of the hair deep to the surface of the skin
    (d) It includes all of the structures of the hair follicle

Level 2 Reviewing Concepts

1. Epidermal ridges
   (a) are at the surface of the epidermis only
   (b) cause ridge patterns on the surface of the skin
   (c) produce patterns that are determined by the environment
   (d) interconnect with macula adherens of the stratum spinosum
2. Why do fair-skinned individuals have to shield themselves from the sun more than do dark-skinned individuals?
3. How and why do calluses form?
4. Stretch marks may result from pregnancy. What makes stretch marks occur?
5. How does the protein keratin affect the appearance and function of the integument?
6. What characteristic(s) make(s) the subcutaneous layer a region frequently targeted for hypodermic injection?
7. Why do washing the skin and applying deodorant reduce the odor of apocrine sweat glands?
8. What is happening to an individual who is cyanotic, and what body structures would show this condition most easily?
9. Why are elderly people less able to adapt to temperature extremes?
10. Skin can regenerate effectively even after considerable damage has occurred because
    (a) the epidermis of the skin has a rich supply of small blood vessels
    (b) fibroblasts in the dermis give rise to new epidermal germinal cells
    (c) contraction in the injured area brings cells of adjacent strata together
    (d) stem cells persist in both the epithelial and connective tissue components of the skin even after injury

Level 3 Critical Thinking

1. In a condition called sunstroke, the victim appears flushed, the skin is warm and dry, and the body temperature rises dramatically. Explain these observations based on what you know concerning the role of the skin in thermoregulation.
2. You are about to undergo surgery. Why is it important that your physician have an excellent understanding of the lines of cleavage of the skin?
3. Many medications can be administered transdermally by applying patches that contain the medication to the surface of the skin. These patches can be attached anywhere on the skin except the palms of the hands and the soles of the feet. Why?

5

The Skeletal System

Osseous Tissue and Skeletal Structure

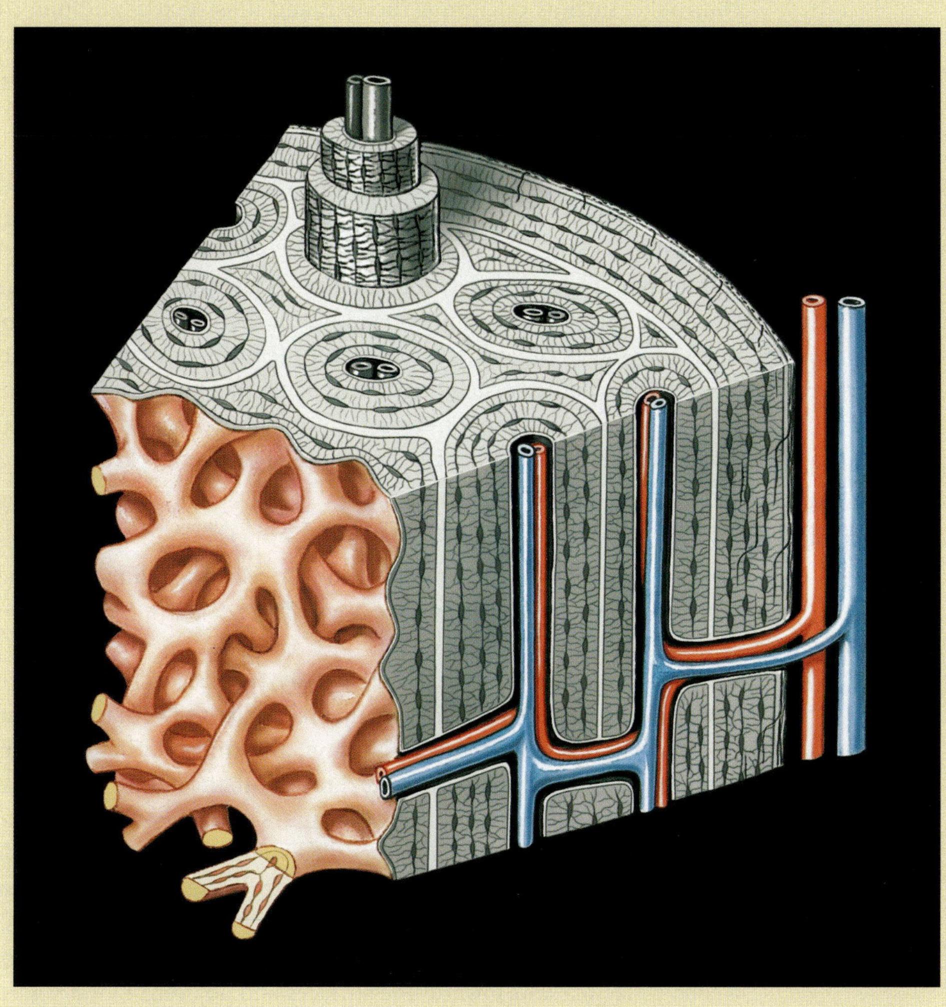

CHAPTER OBJECTIVES

1. Describe the functions of the skeletal system.
2. Describe the types of cells found in mature bone and compare their functions.
3. Compare the structures and functions of compact and spongy bone.
4. Locate and compare the structure and function of the periosteum and endosteum.
5. Discuss the steps in the processes of bone development and growth that account for variations in bone structure.
6. Discuss the nutritional and hormonal factors that affect growth.
7. Describe the remodeling of the skeleton, including the effects of nutrition, hormones, exercise, and aging on bone development and the skeletal system.
8. Describe the different types of fractures and explain how fractures heal.
9. Classify bones according to their shapes and give examples for each type.

The skeletal system includes the varied bones of the skeleton and the cartilages, ligaments, and other connective tissues that stabilize or interconnect them. Bones are more than racks that muscles hang from; they support our weight and work together with muscles to produce controlled, precise movements. Without a framework of bones to hold onto, contracting muscles would just get shorter and fatter. Our muscles must pull against the skeleton to make us sit, stand, walk, or run. The skeleton has many other vital functions; some may be unfamiliar to you, so we will begin this chapter by summarizing the major functions of the skeletal system.

1. *Support:* The skeletal system provides structural support for the entire body. Individual bones or groups of bones provide a framework for the attachment of soft tissues and organs.
2. *Storage of Minerals:* The calcium salts of bone represent a valuable mineral reserve that maintains normal concentrations of calcium and phosphate ions in body fluids. Calcium is the most abundant mineral in the human body. A typical human body contains 1–2 kg (2.2–4.4 lb) of calcium, with more than 98 percent of it deposited in the bones of the skeleton.
3. *Blood Cell Production:* Red blood cells, white blood cells, and platelets are produced in the *red marrow,* which fills the internal cavities of many bones. The role of the bone marrow in blood cell formation will be described in later chapters that discuss the cardiovascular and lymphoid systems (Chapters 20 and 23).
4. *Protection:* Delicate tissues and organs are often surrounded by skeletal elements. The ribs protect the heart and lungs, the skull encloses the brain, the vertebrae shield the spinal cord, and the pelvis cradles delicate digestive and reproductive organs.
5. *Leverage:* Many bones of the skeleton function as levers. They can change the magnitude and direction of the forces generated by skeletal muscles. The movements produced range from the delicate motion of a fingertip to powerful changes in the position of the entire body.

This chapter describes the structure, development, and growth of bone. The two chapters that follow organize bones into two divisions: the *axial skeleton* (consisting of the bones of the skull, vertebral column, sternum, and ribs) and the *appendicular skeleton* (consisting of the bones of the limbs and the associated bones that connect the limbs to the trunk at the shoulders and pelvis). The final chapter in this group examines articulations or joints, structures where the bones meet and may move with respect to each other.

The bones of the skeleton are actually complex, dynamic organs that contain osseous tissue, other connective tissues, smooth muscle tissue, and neural tissue. We will now consider the internal organization of a typical bone.

Structure of Bone

Bone, or **osseous tissue**, is one of the supporting connective tissues. (You should review the sections on dense connective tissues, cartilage, and bone at this time.) pp. 66–72 Like other connective tissues, osseous tissue contains specialized cells and an extracellular matrix consisting of protein fibers and a ground substance. The matrix of bone tissue is solid and sturdy due to the deposition of calcium salts around the protein fibers.

Osseous tissue is usually separated from surrounding tissues by a fibrous *periosteum.* When osseous tissue surrounds another tissue, the inner bony surfaces are lined by a cellular *endosteum.*

The Histological Organization of Mature Bone

The basic organization of bone tissue was introduced in Chapter 3. pp. 71–72 We will now take a closer look at the organization of the matrix and cells of bone.

The Matrix of Bone

Calcium phosphate, $Ca_3(PO_4)_2$, accounts for almost two-thirds of the weight of bone. The calcium phosphate interacts with calcium hydroxide [$Ca(OH)_2$] to form crystals of hydroxyapatite (hī-DROK-sē-ap-a-tīt), $Ca_{10}(PO_4)_6(OH)_2$. As they form, these crystals also incorporate other calcium salts, such as calcium carbonate, and ions such as sodium, magnesium, and fluoride. These inorganic components enable bone to resist compression. Roughly one-third of the weight of bone is from collagen fibers, which contribute tensile strength to bone. Osteocytes and other cell types account for only 2 percent of the mass of a typical bone.

Calcium phosphate crystals are very strong, but relatively inflexible. They can withstand compression, but the crystals are likely to shatter when exposed to bending, twisting, or sudden impacts. Collagen fibers are tough and flexible. They can easily tolerate stretching, twisting, and bending, but when compressed, they simply bend out of the way. In bone, the collagen fibers provide an organic framework for the formation of mineral crystals. The hydroxyapatite crystals form small plates that lie alongside the collagen fibers. The result is a protein–crystal combination with properties intermediate between those of collagen and those of pure mineral crystals.

The Cells of Mature Bone [Figure 5.1]

Bone contains a distinctive population of cells, including *osteoprogenitor cells, osteoblasts, osteocytes,* and *osteoclasts* (Figure 5.1a).

Osteocytes Mature bone cells are **osteocytes** (*osteon,* bone). They maintain and monitor the protein and mineral content of the surrounding matrix. As you will see in a later section, the minerals in the matrix are continually recycled. Each osteocyte directs both the release of calcium from bone to blood and the deposition of calcium salts in the surrounding matrix. Osteocytes occupy small chambers, called **lacunae**, that are sandwiched between layers of calcified matrix. These matrix layers are known as **lamellae** (la-MEL-lē; singular, lamella; a thin plate) (Figure 5.1b–d). Channels called **canaliculi** (kan-a-LIK-ū-lī; "little canals") radiate through the matrix from lacuna to lacuna and toward free surfaces and adjacent blood vessels. The canaliculi, which contain fine cytoplasmic processes and ground substance, interconnect the osteocytes situated in adjacent lacunae. Tight junctions interconnect these processes and provide a route for the diffusion of nutrients and waste products from one osteocyte to another across gap junctions.

Osteoblasts Cells that are cuboidal in shape and found on the inner or outer surfaces of a bone are **osteoblasts** (OS-tē-ō-blasts; *blast,* precursor). These cells secrete the organic components of the bone matrix. This material, called **osteoid** (OS-tē-oyd), later becomes mineralized through an unknown mechanism. Osteoblasts are responsible for the production of new bone, a process called **osteogenesis** (os-tē-ō-JEN-e-sis; *gennan,* to produce). Although the exact stimulus is unknown, it is thought that osteoblasts may respond to mechanical or hormonal stimuli to initiate osteogenesis. If an osteoblast becomes surrounded by matrix, it differentiates into an osteocyte.

Osteoprogenitor Cells Bone tissue also contains small numbers of **osteoprogenitor cells** (os-tē-ō-prō-JEN-i-tor; *progenitor,* ancestor).

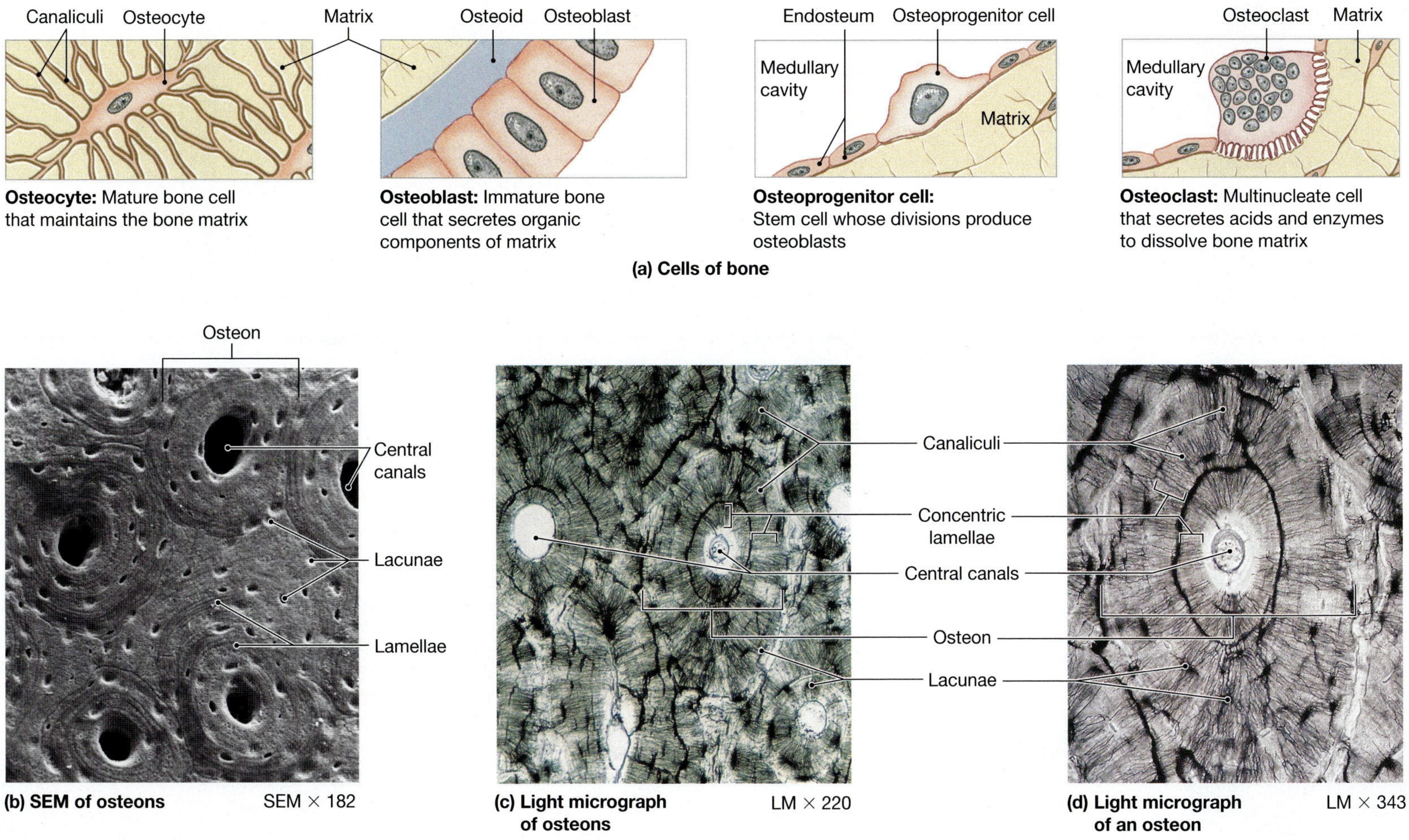

Figure 5.1 Histological Structure of a Typical Bone
Osseous tissue contains specialized cells and a dense extracellular matrix containing calcium salts. **(a)** The cells of bone. **(b)** A scanning electron micrograph of several osteons in compact bone. **(c)** A thin section through compact bone; in this procedure the intact matrix and central canals appear white, and the lacunae and canaliculi are shown in black. **(d)** A single osteon at higher magnification. *[(b) © R. G. Kessel and R. H. Kardon, "Tissues and Organs: A Text-Atlas of Scanning Electron Microscopy", W. H. Freeman & Co., 1979. All Right Reserved.]*

Osteoprogenitor cells differentiate from mesenchyme and are found on the innermost layer of the periosteum and in the *endosteum* lining the medullary cavities. Osteoprogenitor cells can divide to produce daughter cells that differentiate into osteoblasts. The ability to produce additional osteoblasts becomes extremely important after a bone is cracked or broken. We will consider the repair process further in a later section.

Osteoclasts **Osteoclasts** (OS-tē-ō-klasts) are large, multinucleate cells. They are derived from the same stem cells that produce monocytes and neutrophils. pp. 62–63 They secrete acids through the exocytosis of lysosomes. The acids dissolve the bony matrix and release amino acids and the stored calcium and phosphate. This erosion process, called **osteolysis** (os-tē-OL-i-sis), increases the calcium and phosphate concentrations in body fluids. Osteoclasts are always removing matrix and releasing minerals, and osteoblasts are always producing matrix that quickly binds minerals. The balance between the activities of osteoblasts and osteoclasts is very important; when osteoclasts remove calcium salts faster than osteoblasts deposit them, bones become weaker. When osteoblast activity predominates, bones become stronger and more massive.

Compact and Spongy Bone [Figure 5.2]

There are two types of osseous tissue: *compact bone*, or dense bone; and *spongy bone*, or *trabecular* (tra-BEK-ū-lar) *bone*. **Compact bone** is relatively dense and solid, whereas **spongy bone** forms an open network of struts and plates. Both compact and spongy bone are present in typical bones of the skeleton, such as the *humerus*, the proximal bone of the upper limb, and the *femur*, the proximal bone of the lower limb. Compact bone tissue forms the walls, and an internal layer of spongy bone surrounds the **medullary** (marrow) **cavity** (Figure 5.2a). The medullary cavity contains **bone marrow**, a loose connective tissue that may be dominated by adipocytes (**yellow marrow**) or by a mixture of mature and immature red and white blood cells, and the stem cells that produce them (**red marrow**).

Structural Differences between Compact and Spongy Bone

The matrix composition in compact bone is the same as that of spongy bone, but they differ in the three-dimensional arrangement of osteocytes, canaliculi, and lamellae.

Compact Bone [Figures 5.1b–d/5.2] The basic functional unit of mature compact bone is the cylindrical **osteon** (OS-tē-on), or *Haversian system* (Figure 5.1b–d). Within an osteon the osteocytes are arranged in concentric layers around a **central canal**, or *Haversian canal*, which contains the blood vessels that supply the osteon. Central canals usually run parallel to the surface of the bone (Figure 5.2a). Other passageways, known as **perforating canals**, or the *Volkmann's canals*, extend roughly perpendicular to the surface (Figure 5.2b). Blood vessels in the perforating canals deliver blood to osteons deeper in the bone and service the interior medullary cavity. The lamellae of each osteon are cylindrical and aligned parallel to the long axis of the bone.

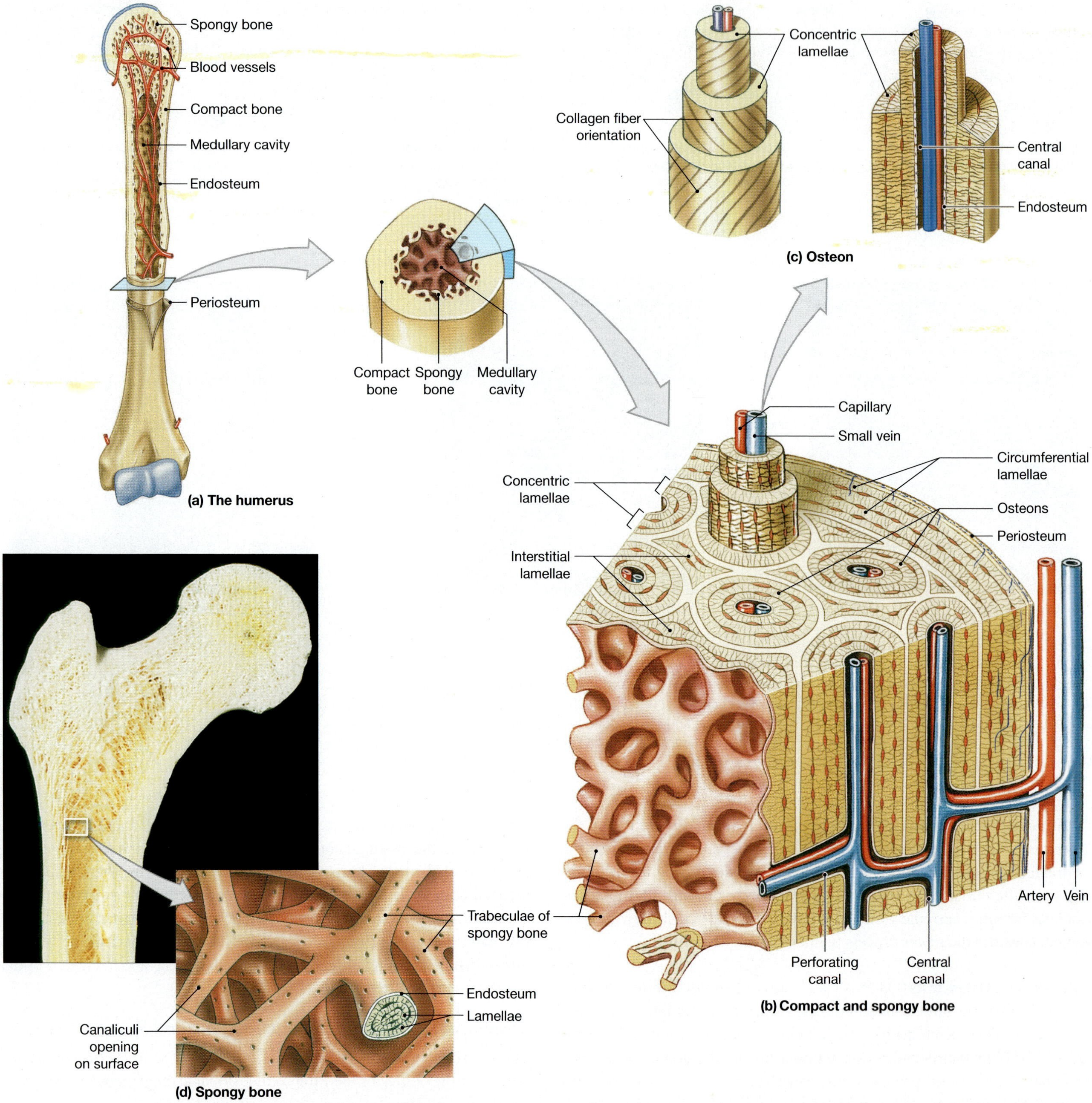

Figure 5.2 The Internal Organization in Representative Bones
The structural relationship of compact and spongy bone in representative bones. **(a)** Gross anatomy of the humerus. **(b)** Diagrammatic view of the histological organization of compact and spongy bone. **(c)** The organization of collagen fibers within concentric lamellae. **(d)** Location and structure of spongy bone. The photo shows a sectional view of the proximal end of the femur.

These are known as *concentric lamellae.* Collectively, concentric lamellae form a series of concentric rings, resembling a "bull's-eye" target, around the central canal (**Figure 5.2b,c**). The collagen fibers spiral along the length of each lamella, and variations between the direction of spiraling in adjacent lamellae strengthen the osteon as a whole. Canaliculi interconnect the lacunae of an osteon and form a branching network that reaches the central canal. *Interstitial lamellae* fill in the spaces between the osteons in compact bone. Depending on their location, these lamellae either may have been produced during the growth of the bone, or may represent remnants of osteons whose matrix components have been recycled by osteoclasts during repair or remodeling of the bone. A third type of lamellae, the *circumferential lamellae,* occur at the external and internal surfaces of the bone. In a limb bone such as the humerus or femur, the circumferential lamellae form the outer and inner surfaces of the shaft (Figure 5.2b).

Spongy Bone [Figure 5.2d] The major difference between compact bone and spongy bone (also termed *trabecular bone* or *cancellous bone*) is the arrangement of spongy bone into parallel struts or thick, branching plates called trabeculae (tra-BEK-ū-lē; "a little beam") or *spicules*. Numerous interconnecting spaces are found between the trabeculae in spongy bone. Spongy bone possesses lamellae and, if the trabeculae are sufficiently thick, osteons will be present.

In terms of the associated cells and the structure and composition of the lamellae, spongy bone is no different from compact bone. Spongy bone forms an open framework (Figure 5.2d), and as a result it is much lighter than compact bone. However, the branching trabeculae give spongy bone considerable strength despite its relatively light weight. Thus, the presence of spongy bone reduces the weight of the skeleton and makes it easier for muscles to move the bones. Spongy bone is thus found wherever bones are not stressed heavily or where stresses arrive from many directions.

Functional Differences between Compact and Spongy Bone [Figure 5.3]

A layer of compact bone covers bone surfaces; the thickness of this layer varies from region to region and from one bone to another. This superficial layer of compact bone is in turn covered by the *periosteum,* a connective tissue wrapping that is connected to the deep fascia. The periosteum is complete everywhere except within a joint, where the edges or ends of two bones contact one another. In some joints, the two bones are interconnected by collagen fibers or a block of cartilage. In more mobile fluid-filled (*synovial*) joints, hyaline *articular cartilages* cover the opposing bony surfaces.

Compact bone is thickest where stresses arrive from a limited range of directions. Figure 5.3a shows the general anatomy of the *femur,* the proximal bone of the lower limb. The compact bone of the **cortex** surrounds the

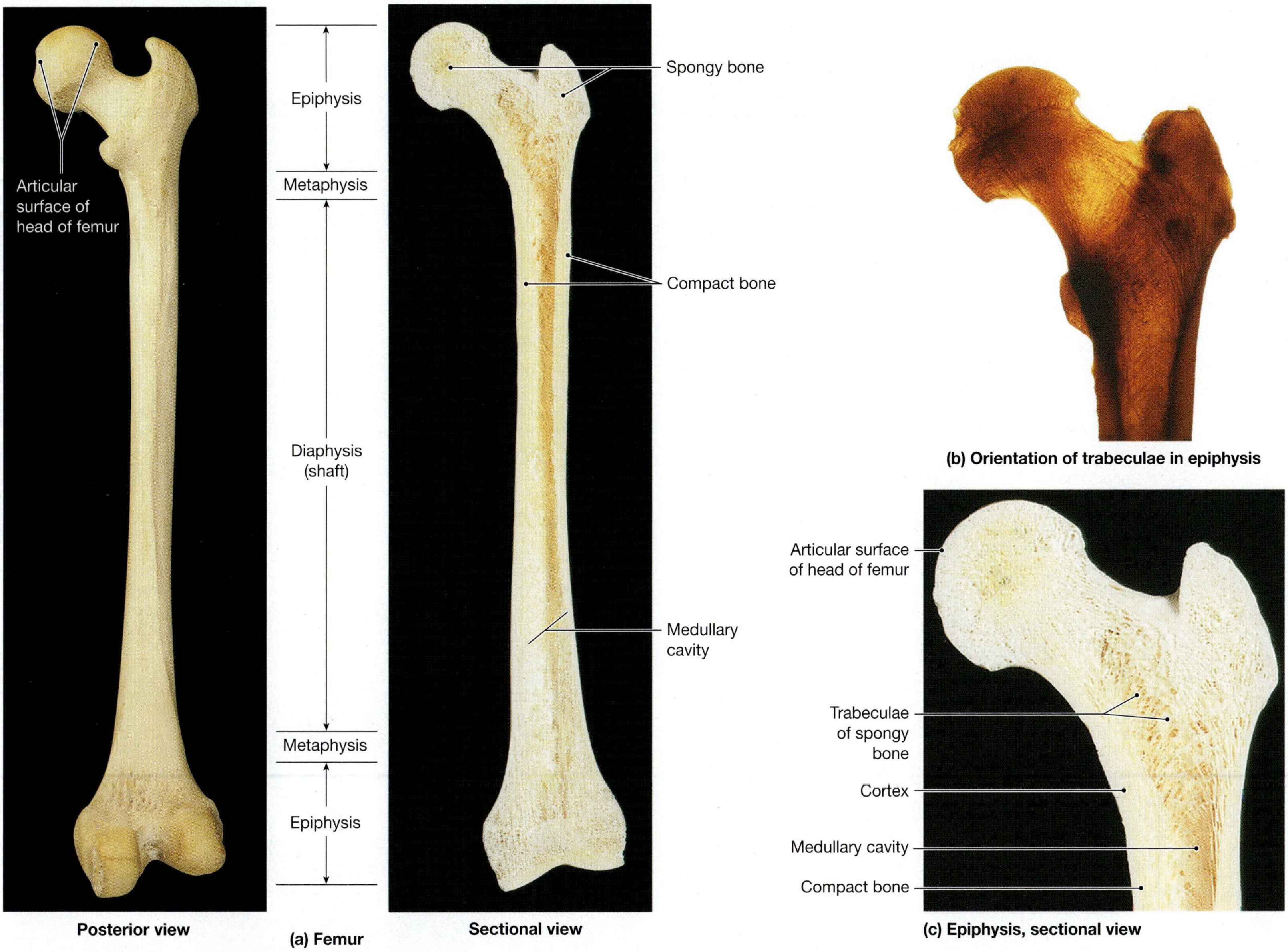

Figure 5.3 Anatomy of a Representative Bone
(a) The femur, or thigh bone, in superficial and sectional views. The femur has a diaphysis (shaft) with walls of compact bone and epiphyses (ends) filled with spongy bone. A metaphysis separates the diaphysis and epiphysis at each end of the shaft. The body weight is transferred to the femur at the hip joint. Because the hip joint is off center relative to the axis of the shaft, the body weight is distributed along the bone so that the medial portion of the shaft is compressed and the lateral portion is stretched. **(b)** An intact femur chemically cleared to show the orientation of the trabeculae in the epiphysis.
(c) A photograph showing the epiphysis after sectioning.

medullary cavity, also known as the *marrow cavity* (*medulla*, innermost part). The bone has two ends, or **epiphyses** (e-PIF-i-sēs; singular, *epiphysis*; *epi*, above + *physis*, growth), separated by a tubular **diaphysis** (dī-AF-i-sis; "a growing between"), or **shaft**. The diaphysis is connected to the epiphysis at a narrow zone known as the **metaphysis** (me-TAF-i-sis). Figure 5.3 shows the organization of compact and spongy bone within the femur. The shaft of compact bone normally conducts applied stresses from one epiphysis to another. For example, when you are standing, the shaft of the femur conducts your body weight from your hip to your knee. The osteons within the shaft are parallel to its long axis, and as a result the femur is very strong when stressed along that axis. You might envision a single osteon as a drinking straw with very thick walls. When you try to push the ends of a straw together it seems quite strong. However, if you hold the ends and push the side of the straw, it will break easily. Similarly, a long bone does not bend when forces are applied to either end, but an impact to the side of the shaft can easily cause a break, or *fracture*.

Spongy bone is not as massive as compact bone, but it is much more capable of resisting stresses applied from many different directions. The epiphyses of the femur are filled with spongy bone, and the trabecular alignment of the proximal epiphysis is shown in Figure 5.3b,c. The trabeculae are oriented along the stress lines, but with extensive cross-bracing. At the proximal epiphysis, the trabeculae transfer forces from the hip across the metaphysis to the femoral shaft; at the distal epiphysis, the trabeculae direct the forces across the knee joint to the leg. In addition to reducing weight and handling stress from many directions, the open trabecular framework provides support and protection for the cells of the bone marrow. Yellow marrow, often found in the medullary cavity of the shaft, is an important energy reserve. Extensive areas of red marrow, such as that found in the spongy bone of the femoral epiphyses, are important sites of blood cell formation.

The Periosteum and Endosteum [Figure 5.4]

The outer surface of a bone is usually covered by a **periosteum** (Figure 5.4a). The periosteum (1) isolates and protects the bone from surrounding tissues, (2) provides a route and a place of attachment for circulatory and nervous

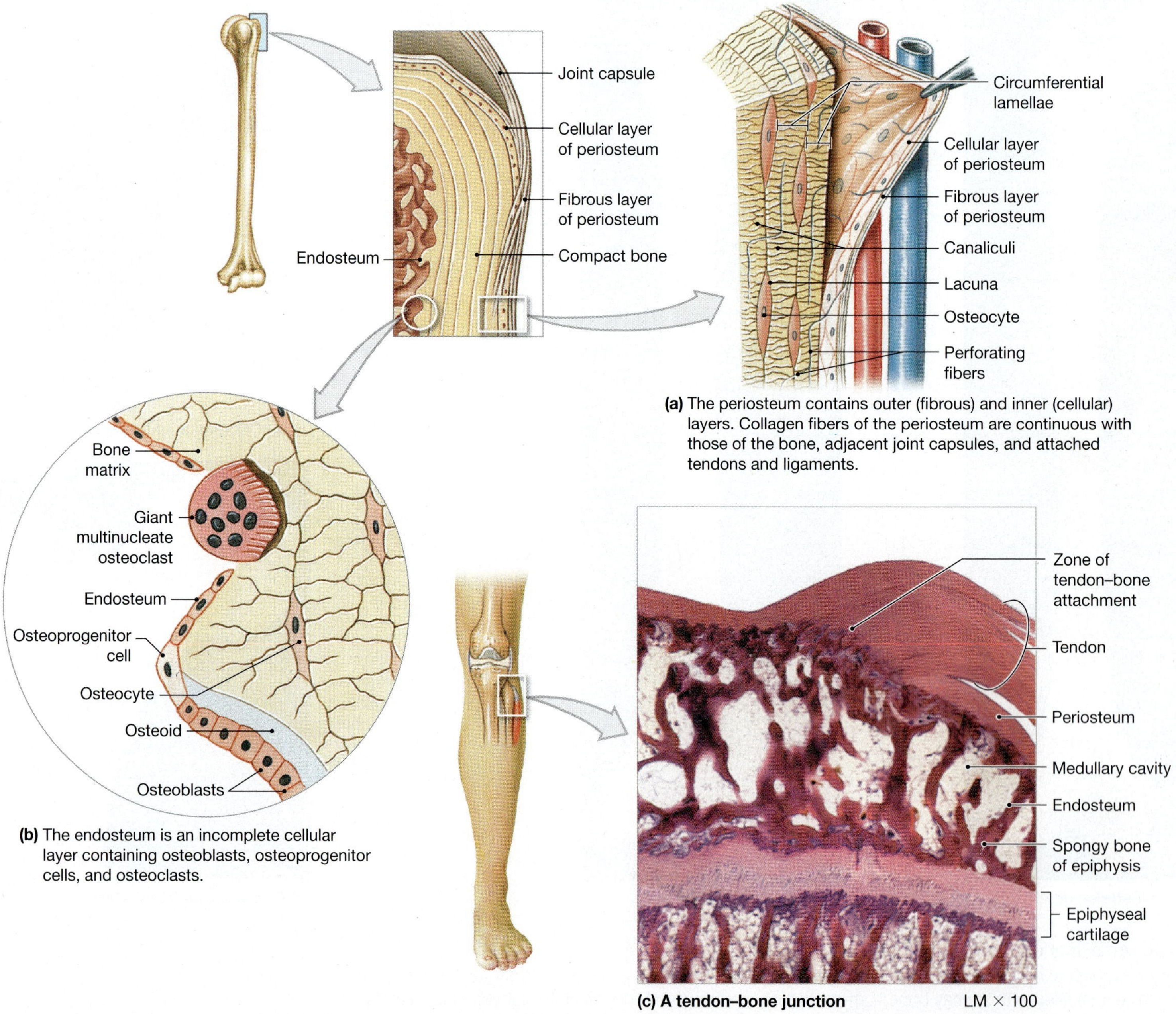

(a) The periosteum contains outer (fibrous) and inner (cellular) layers. Collagen fibers of the periosteum are continuous with those of the bone, adjacent joint capsules, and attached tendons and ligaments.

(b) The endosteum is an incomplete cellular layer containing osteoblasts, osteoprogenitor cells, and osteoclasts.

(c) A tendon–bone junction

Figure 5.4 Anatomy and Histology of the Periosteum and Endosteum
Diagrammatic representation of periosteum and endosteum locations and their association with other bone structures; histology section shows both periosteum and endosteum. **(a)** The periosteum. **(b)** The endosteum. **(c)** A tendon–bone junction.

Clinical Note

Rickets The hip joint consists of the head of the femur and a corresponding socket on the lateral surface of the hip bone. The femoral head projects medially, and body weight compresses the medial side of the diaphysis. Because the force is applied off center, the bone has a tendency to bend into a lateral bow. The other side of the shaft, which resists this bending, is placed under a stretching load, or *tension*. Bending occurs in disorders that reduce the amount of calcium salts in the skeleton. **Rickets** usually develops in children as a result of a vitamin D deficiency; this vitamin is essential to normal calcium absorption and deposition in the skeleton. In rickets, the bones are poorly mineralized, and they become very flexible. Affected individuals develop a bowlegged appearance as the thigh and leg bones bend under the weight of the body.

supply, (3) actively participates in bone growth and repair, and (4) attaches the bone to the connective tissue network of the deep fascia. A periosteum does not surround sesamoid bones, nor is it present where tendons, ligaments, or joint capsules attach, nor where bone surfaces are covered by articular cartilages.

The periosteum consists of an outer fibrous layer of dense fibrous connective tissue and an inner cellular layer containing osteoprogenitor cells. When a bone is not undergoing growth or repair, few osteoprogenitor cells are visible within the cellular layer.

Near joints, the periosteum becomes continuous with the connective tissue network that surrounds and helps stabilize the joint. At a fluid-filled (*synovial*) joint, the periosteum is continuous with the *joint capsule* that encloses the joint complex. The fibers of the periosteum are also interwoven with those of the tendons attached to the bone (Figure 5.4c). As the bone grows, these tendon fibers are cemented into the superficial lamellae by osteoblasts from the cellular layer of the periosteum. The collagen fibers incorporated into bone tissue from tendons and from the superficial periosteum are called *perforating fibers* or *Sharpey's fibers* (Figure 5.4a). The cementing process makes the tendon fibers part of the general structure of the bone, providing a much stronger bond than would otherwise be possible. An extremely powerful pull on a tendon or ligament will usually break the bone rather than snap the collagen fibers at the bone surface.

Inside the bone, a cellular **endosteum** lines the medullary cavity (Figure 5.4b). This layer, which contains osteoprogenitor cells, covers the trabeculae of spongy bone and lines the inner surfaces of the central canals and perforating canals. The endosteum is active during the growth of bone and whenever repair or remodeling is under way. The endosteum is usually only one cell thick and is an incomplete layer, and the bone matrix is occasionally exposed.

CONCEPT CHECK

1. How would the strength of a bone be affected if the ratio of collagen to calcium salts (hydroxyapatite) increased?
2. A sample of bone shows concentric lamellae surrounding a central canal. Is the sample from the cortex or the medullary cavity of a long bone?
3. If the activity of osteoclasts exceeds the activity of osteoblasts in a bone, how is the mass of the bone affected?
4. If the osteoprogenitor cells in bone tissue were selectively destroyed by a poison, what future, normal process may be impeded?

See blue "Answers" tab at back of book.

Bone Development and Growth

The growth of the skeleton determines the size and proportions of our body. The bony skeleton begins to form about six weeks after fertilization, when the embryo is approximately 12 mm (0.5 in.) long. (Before this time all of the skeletal elements are either mesenchymal or cartilaginous.) During subsequent development, the bones undergo a tremendous increase in size. Bone growth continues through adolescence, and portions of the skeleton usually do not stop growing until age 25. The entire process is carefully regulated, and a breakdown in regulation will ultimately affect all of the body systems. In this section we will consider the physical process of *osteogenesis* (bone formation) and bone growth. The next section will examine the maintenance and replacement of mineral reserves in the adult skeleton.

During embryonic development, either mesenchyme or cartilage is replaced by bone. This process of replacing other tissues with bone is called **ossification**. The process of **calcification** refers to the deposition of calcium salts within a tissue. Any tissue can be calcified, but only ossification results in the formation of bone. There are two major forms of ossification. In *intramembranous ossification*, bone develops from mesenchyme or fibrous connective tissue. In *endochondral ossification*, bone replaces an existing cartilage model. The bones of the limbs and other bones that bear weight, such as the vertebral column, develop by endochondral ossification. Intramembranous ossification occurs in the formation of bones such as the clavicle, mandible, and the flat bones of the face and skull.

Intramembranous Ossification [Figures 5.5/5.6]

Intramembranous (in-tra-MEM-bra-nus) **ossification**, also called *dermal ossification*, begins when mesenchymal cells differentiate into osteoblasts within embryonic or fibrous connective tissue. This type of ossification normally occurs in the deeper layers of the dermis, and the bones that result are often called **dermal bones**, or *membrane bones*. Examples of dermal bones include the roofing bones of the skull (the *frontal* and *parietal bones*), the *mandible* (lower jaw), and the *clavicle* (collarbone). *Sesamoid bones* form within tendons; the *patella* (kneecap) is an example of a sesamoid bone. Membrane bone may also develop in other connective tissues subjected to chronic mechanical stresses. For example, cowboys in the 19th century sometimes developed small bony plates in the dermis on the insides of their thighs from friction and impact against their saddles. In some disorders affecting calcium ion metabolism or excretion, intramembranous bone formation occurs in many areas of the dermis and deep fascia. Bones in abnormal locations are called *heterotopic bones* (*heteros*, different + *topos*, place).

Intramembranous ossification starts approximately during the eighth week of embryonic development. The steps in the process of intramembranous ossification are illustrated in Figure 5.5 and may be summarized as follows:

STEP 1. Mesenchymal tissue becomes highly vascularized, and the mesenchymal cells enlarge and differentiate into osteoblasts. The osteoblasts then cluster together and start to secrete the organic components of the matrix. The resulting mixture of collagen fibers and osteoid then becomes mineralized through the crystallization of calcium salts. The location in a bone where ossification begins is called an **ossification center**. As ossification proceeds, it traps some osteoblasts inside bony pockets; these cells differentiate into osteocytes. Although the osteocytes have become separated by the secreted matrix, they remain connected by thin cytoplasmic processes.

Clinical Note

Heterotopic Bone Formation *Heterotopic* (*heteros*, different + *topos*, place), or *ectopic* (*ektos*, outside), *bones* are bones that develop in unusual places. Such bones dramatically demonstrate the adaptability of connective tissues. Mesenchymal stem cells can develop into bone, cartilage, or even fat and muscle. Physical or chemical events can stimulate the development of osteoblasts in normal connective tissues. For example, sesamoid bones develop within tendons near points of friction and pressure. Bone can also form within a large blood clot at the site of an injury or within portions of the dermis subjected to chronic abuse. Other triggers include foreign chemicals and problems that affect calcium excretion and storage.

Almost any connective tissue can be affected. Ossification within a tendon or around joints can painfully interfere with movement. Bones can also form within the kidneys, between skeletal muscles, in the pericardium, in the walls of arteries, and around the eyes.

Myositis ossificans (mī-ō-SĪ-tis os-SIF-i-kanz) involves the deposition of bone around skeletal muscles. A muscle injury can trigger a minor case. Severe cases, which have a genetic basis, provide the most dramatic demonstrations of heterotopic bone formation. If the process does not reverse itself, the muscles of the back, neck, and upper limbs will gradually be replaced by bone.

STEP 2. The developing bone grows outward from the ossification center in small struts called **spicules**. Although osteoblasts are still being trapped in the expanding bone, mesenchymal cell divisions continue to produce additional osteoblasts. Bone growth is an active process, and osteoblasts require oxygen and a reliable supply of nutrients. As blood vessels branch within the region and grow between the spicules, the rate of bone growth accelerates.

STEP 3. Over time, multiple ossification centers form, and the newly deposited bone assumes the structure of spongy bone. Continued deposition of bone by osteoblasts located close to blood vessels, as well as the remodeling of this newly formed bone by osteoclasts, results in the formation of compact bone seen in the mature bones of the skull.

Figure 5.6a shows skull bones forming through intramembranous ossification in the head of a 10-week fetus.

Endochondral Ossification [Figures 5.6/5.7]

Endochondral ossification (en-dō-KON-dral; *endo*, inside + *chondros*, cartilage) begins with the formation of a hyaline cartilage model. Limb bone development is a good example of this process. By the time an embryo is six weeks old, the proximal bone of the limb, either the *humerus* (upper limb) or *femur* (lower limb), has formed, but it is composed entirely of cartilage.

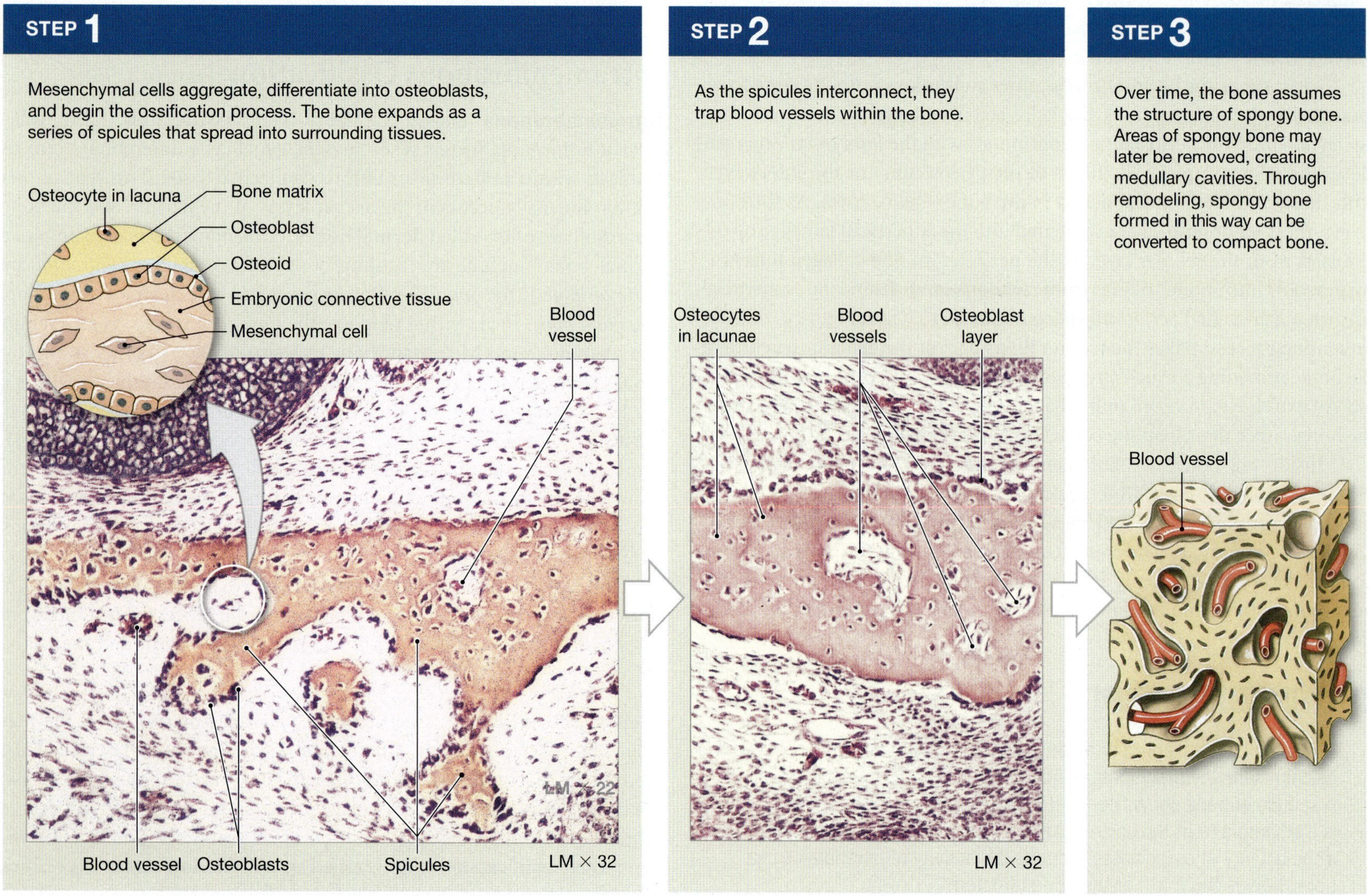

Figure 5.5 Histology of Intramembranous Ossification
Stepwise formation of intramembranous bone from mesenchymal cell aggregation to spongy bone. The spongy bone may later be remodeled to form compact bone.

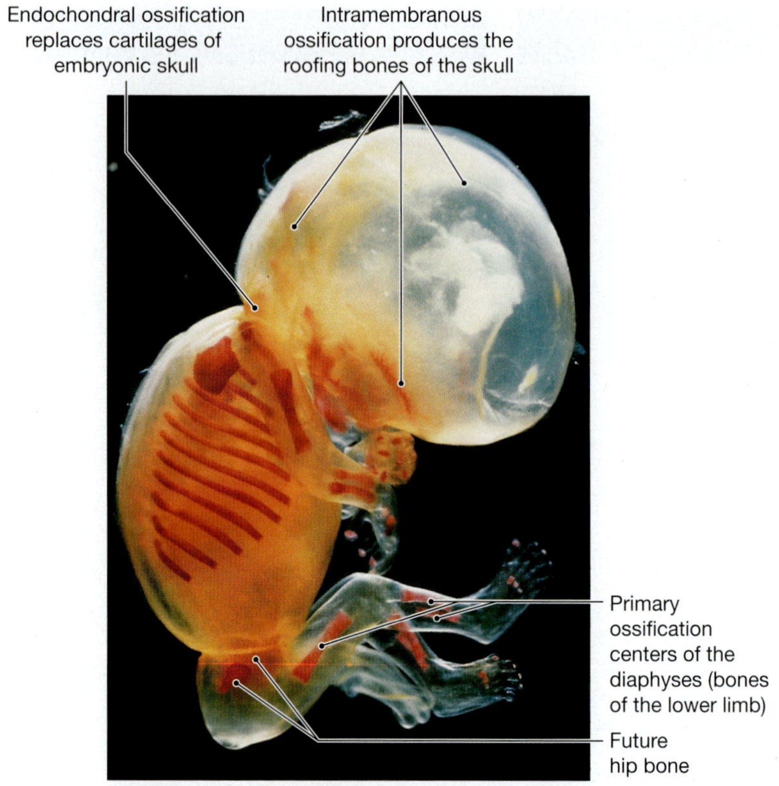

(a)

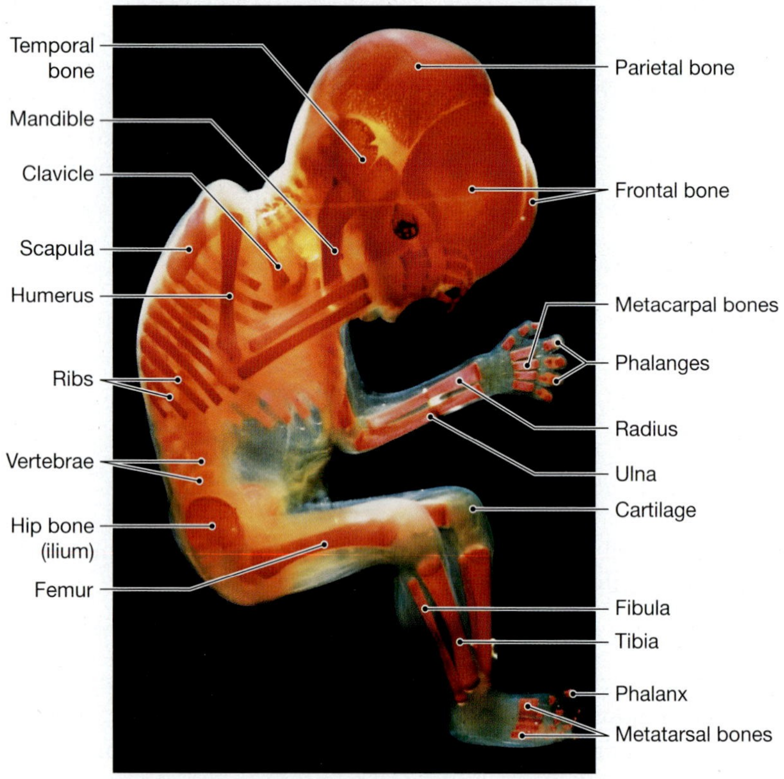

(b)

Figure 5.6 Fetal Intramembranous and Endochondral Ossification
These 10- and 16-week human fetuses have been specially stained (with alizarin red) and cleared to show developing skeletal elements. **(a)** At 10 weeks the fetal skull clearly shows both membrane and cartilaginous bone, but the boundaries that indicate the limits of future skull bones have yet to be established. **(b)** At 16 weeks the fetal skull shows the irregular margins of the future skull bones. Most elements of the appendicular skeleton form through endochondral ossification. Note the appearance of the wrist and ankle bones at 16 weeks versus at 10 weeks.

This model continues to grow by expansion of the cartilage matrix (*interstitial growth*) and the production of more cartilage at the outer surface (*appositional growth*). These growth mechanisms were introduced in Chapter 3. p. 69 **Figure 5.6b** shows the extent of endochondral ossification occurring in the limb bones of a 16-week fetus. Steps in the growth and ossification of one of the limb bones are diagrammed in **Figure 5.7a**.

STEP 1. As the cartilage enlarges, chondrocytes near the center of the shaft increase greatly in size, and the surrounding matrix begins to calcify. Deprived of nutrients, these chondrocytes die and disintegrate.

STEP 2. Cells of the perichondrium surrounding this region of the cartilage differentiate into osteoblasts. The perichondrium has now been converted into a periosteum, and the inner **osteogenic layer** (os-tē-ō-JEN-ik) soon produces a *bone collar*, a thin layer of compact bone around the shaft of the cartilage.

STEP 3. While these changes are under way, the blood supply to the periosteum increases, and capillaries and osteoblasts migrate into the heart of the cartilage, invading the spaces left by the disintegrating chondrocytes. The calcified cartilaginous matrix then breaks down, and osteoblasts replace it with spongy bone. Bone development proceeds from this **primary ossification center** in the shaft, toward both ends of the cartilaginous model.

STEP 4. While the diameter is small, the entire diaphysis is filled with spongy bone, but as it enlarges, osteoclasts erode the central portion and create a medullary cavity. Further growth involves two distinct processes: an increase in *length* and an enlargement in *diameter*.

Increasing the Length of a Developing Bone [Figures 5.7/5.8]

During the initial stages of osteogenesis, osteoblasts move away from the primary ossification center toward the epiphyses. But they do not manage to complete the ossification of the model immediately, because the cartilages of the epiphyses continue to grow. The region where the cartilage is being replaced by bone lies at the metaphysis, the junction between the diaphysis (shaft) and epiphyses of the bone. On the shaft side of the metaphysis, osteoblasts are continually invading the cartilage and replacing it with bone. But on the epiphyseal side, new cartilage is being produced at the same rate. The situation is like a pair of joggers, one in front of the other. As long as they are running at the same speed, they can run for miles without colliding. In this case, the osteoblasts and the epiphysis are both "running away" from the primary ossification center. As a result, the osteoblasts never catch up with the epiphysis, although the skeletal element continues to grow longer and longer.

STEP 5. The next major change occurs when the centers of the epiphyses begin to calcify. Capillaries and osteoblasts then migrate into these areas, creating **secondary ossification centers**. The time of appearance of secondary ossification centers varies from one bone to another and from individual to individual. Secondary ossification centers may occur at birth in both ends of the humerus (arm), femur (thigh), and tibia (leg), but the ends of some other bones remain cartilaginous through childhood.

STEP 6. The epiphyses eventually become filled with spongy bone. A thin cap of the original cartilage model remains exposed to the joint cavity as the **articular cartilage**. This cartilage prevents damaging bone-to-bone contact within the joint. At the metaphysis, a relatively narrow cartilaginous region called the **epiphyseal cartilage**, or *epiphyseal plate*, now separates the epiphysis from the diaphysis. **Figure 5.7b** shows the interface between the degenerating cartilage and the advancing osteoblasts. As long as the rate of cartilage

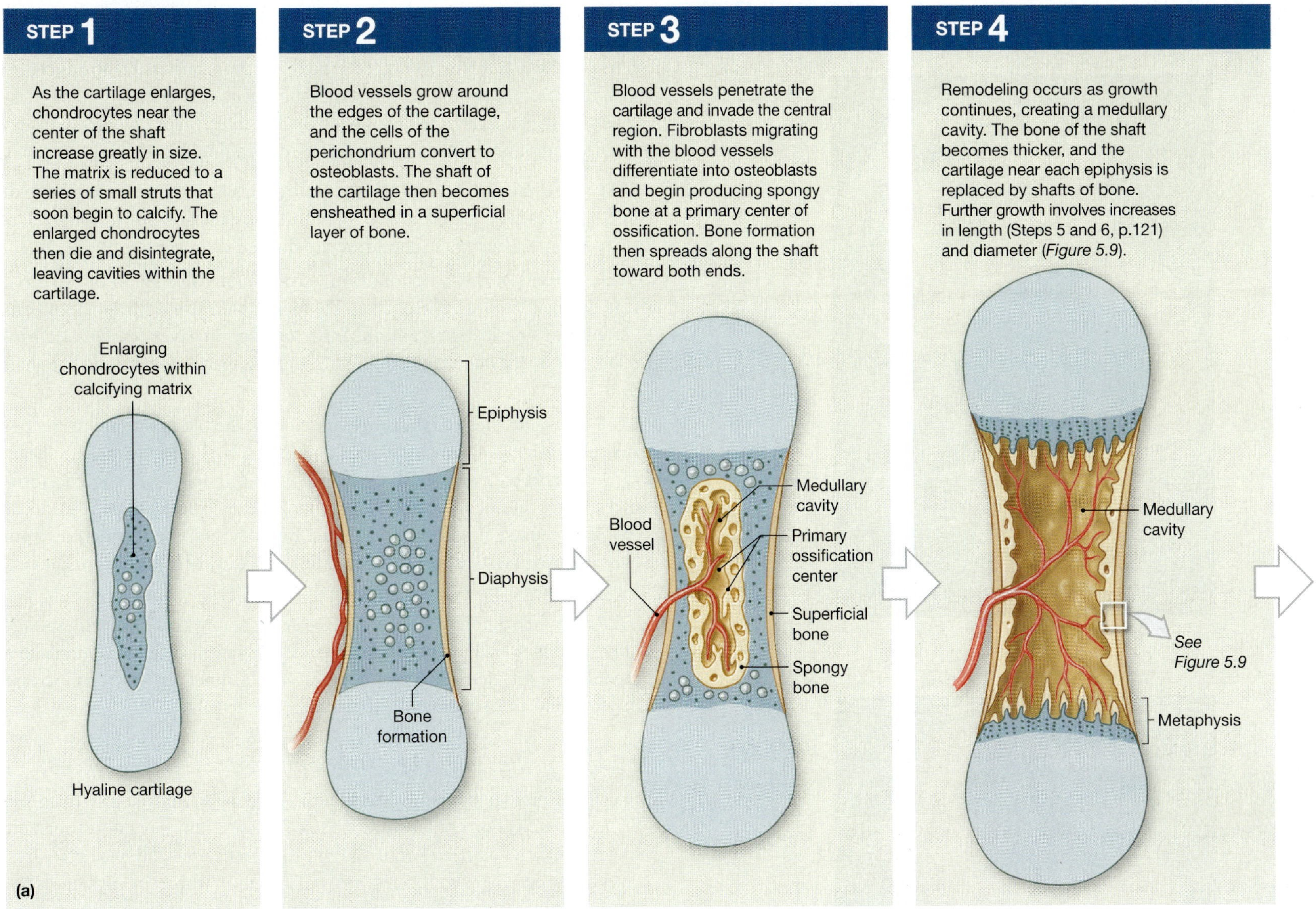

Figure 5.7 Anatomical and Histological Organization of Endochondral Ossification
(a) Steps in the formation of a long bone from a hyaline cartilage model.

growth keeps pace with the rate of osteoblast invasion, the shaft grows longer but the epiphyseal cartilage survives.

Within the epiphyseal cartilage, the chondrocytes are organized into zones (**Figure 5.7b**). Chondrocytes at the epiphyseal side of the cartilage continue to divide and enlarge, while cartilage at the diaphyseal side of the cartilage is gradually replaced by bone. Overall, the thickness of the epiphyseal cartilage does not change. The continual expansion of the epiphyseal cartilage forces the epiphysis farther from the shaft. As the daughter cells mature, they become enlarged, and the surrounding matrix becomes calcified. On the shaft side of the epiphyseal cartilage, osteoblasts and capillaries continue to invade these lacunae and replace the cartilage with newly formed bone organized as a series of trabeculae. **Figure 5.8a** shows an x-ray of epiphyseal cartilages in the hand of a young child.

STEP 7. At maturity, the rate of epiphyseal cartilage production slows and the rate of osteoblast activity accelerates. As a result, the epiphyseal cartilage gets narrower and narrower, until it ultimately disappears. This event is called *epiphyseal closure.* The former location of the epiphyseal cartilage can often be detected in x-rays as a distinct *epiphyseal line* that remains after epiphyseal growth has ended (**Figure 5.8b**).

Increasing the Diameter of a Developing Bone [Figure 5.9]

The diameter of a bone enlarges through appositional growth at the outer surface. In appositional growth, osteoprogenitor cells of the inner layer of the periosteum differentiate into osteoblasts and add bone matrix to the surface. This adds successive layers of circumferential lamellae to the outer surface of the bone. Over time, the deeper lamellae are recycled and replaced with the osteons typical of compact bone.

However, blood vessels and collagen fibers of the periosteum can and do become enclosed within the matrix. Where this occurs, the process of appositional bone growth is somewhat more complex, as indicated in **Figure 5.9a**.

Step 1. Where blood vessels run along the bone surface, the new bone is deposited in ridges oriented parallel to the blood vessels.

Step 2. As these longitudinal ridges enlarge, they grow toward each other, and the vessel now lies in a deep pocket.

STEP 5

Capillaries and osteoblasts migrate into the epiphyses, creating secondary ossification centers.

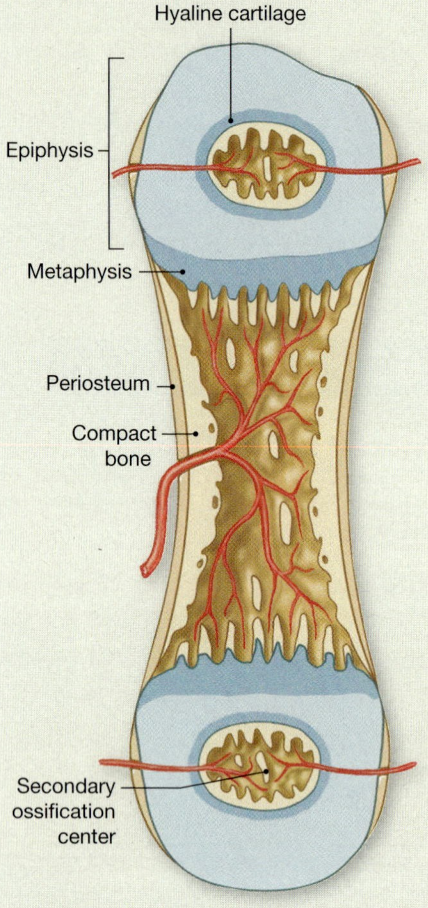

STEP 6

Soon the epiphyses are filled with spongy bone. An articular cartilage remains exposed to the joint cavity; over time it will be reduced to a thin superficial layer. At each metaphysis, an epiphyseal cartilage separates the epiphysis from the diaphysis.

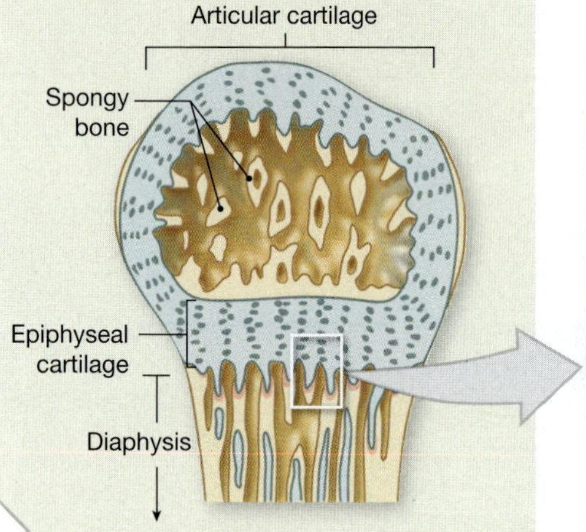

Figure 5.7 Anatomical and Histological Organization of Endochondral Ossification *(continued)*
(b) Light micrograph showing the zones of cartilage and the advancing osteoblast at an epiphyseal cartilage.

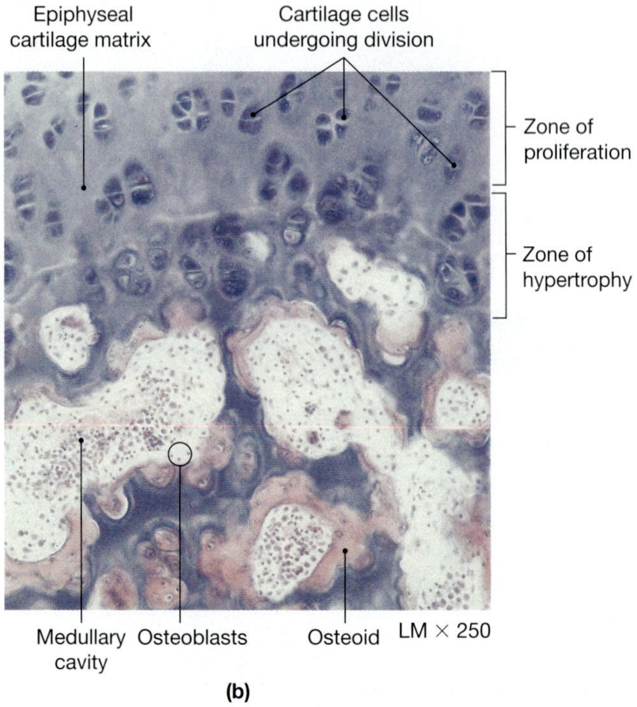

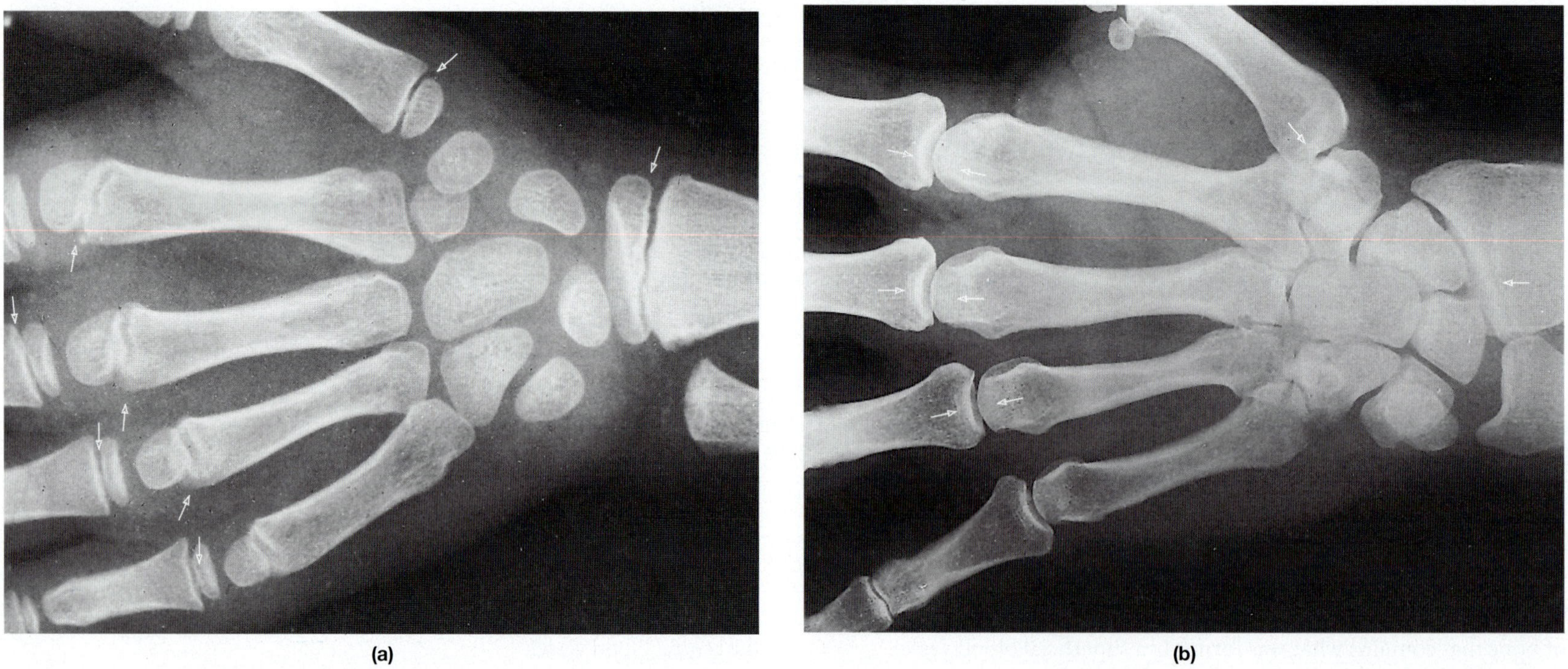

Figure 5.8 Epiphyseal Cartilages and Lines
The epiphyseal cartilage is the location of long bone growth in length prior to maturity; the epiphyseal line marks the former location of the epiphyseal cartilage after growth has ended. **(a)** X-ray of the hand of a young child. The arrows indicate the locations of the epiphyseal cartilages. **(b)** X-ray of the hand of an adult. The arrows indicate the locations of epiphyseal lines.

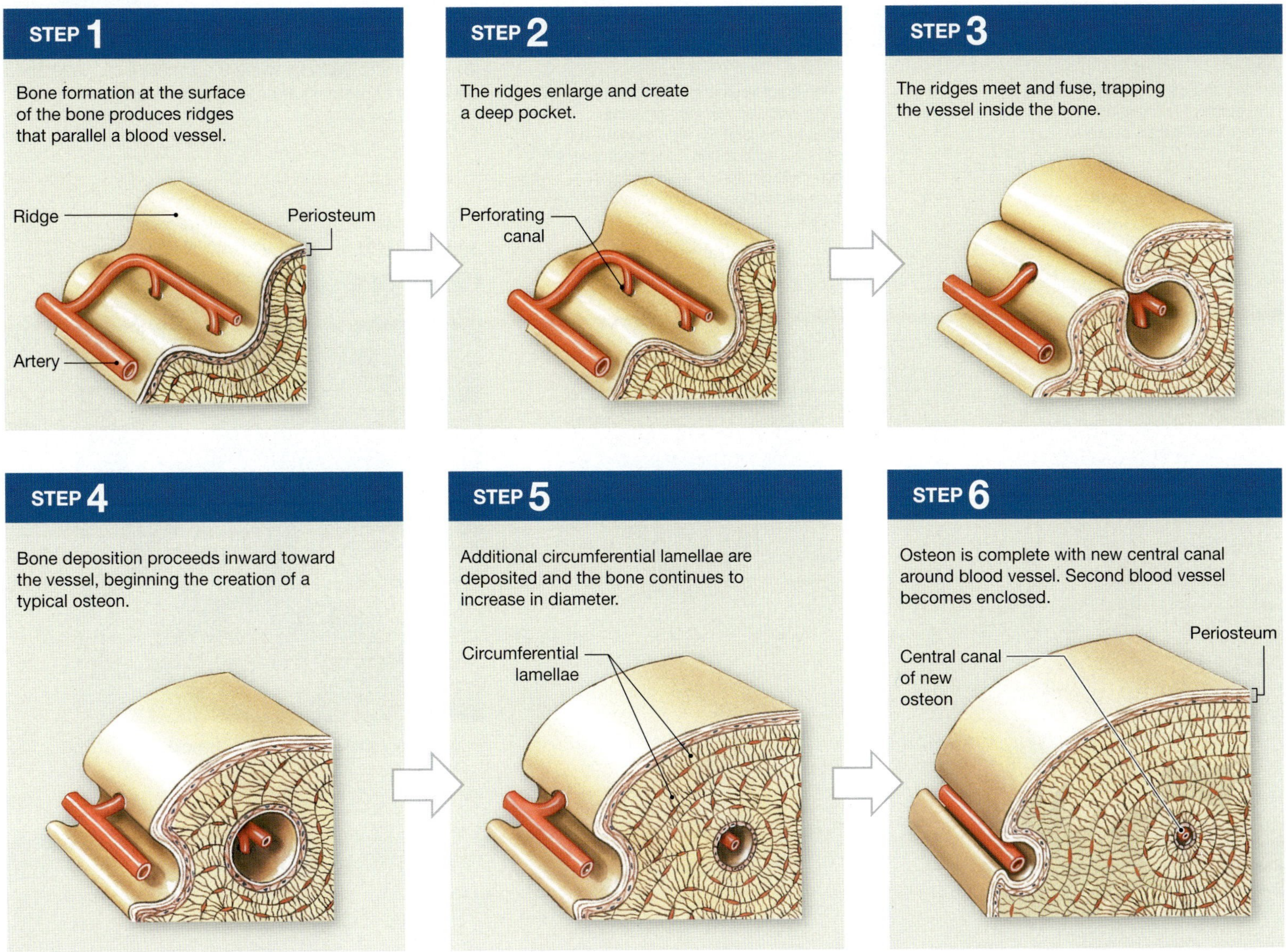

(a) Steps in appositional bone growth

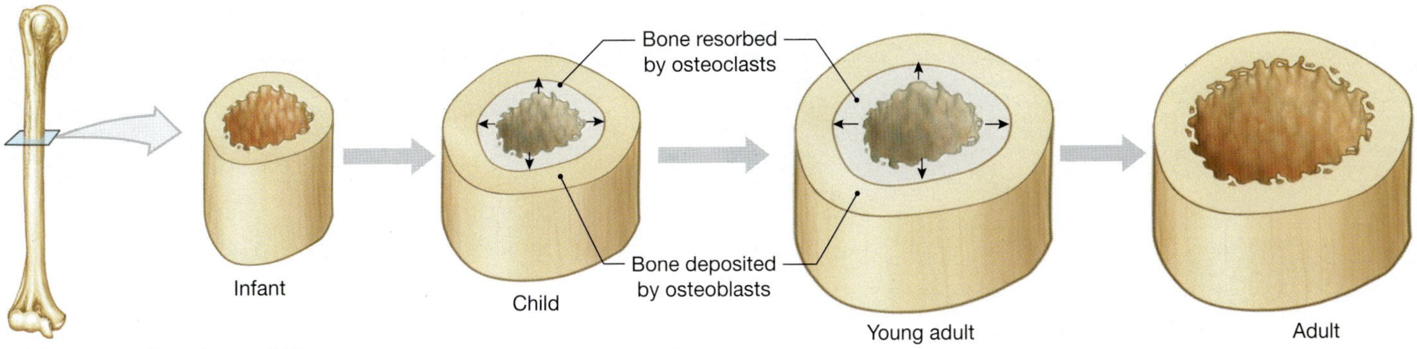

(b) Appositional growth and remodeling

Figure 5.9 Appositional Bone Growth
(a) Three-dimensional diagrams illustrating the mechanism responsible for increasing the diameter of a growing bone. **(b)** A bone grows in diameter as new bone is added to the outer surface. At the same time, osteoclasts resorb bone on the inside, enlarging the medullary cavity.

Step 3. The two ridges eventually meet and fuse together, forming a tunnel of bone that contains what was formerly a superficial blood vessel.

Steps 4–6. The tunnel is lined by cells that were, until STEP 3, part of the periosteum. Osteoprogenitor cells in this layer now differentiate into osteoblasts. These cells secrete new bone on the walls of the tunnel, forming concentric lamellae that eventually produce a new osteon organized around the central blood vessel.

While bone is being added to the outer surface, osteoclasts are removing bone matrix at the inner surface. As a result, the medullary cavity gradually enlarges as the bone increases in diameter (Figure 5.9b).

Clinical Note

Congenital Disorders of the Skeleton In **acromegaly** (*akron*, extremity + *megale*, great) an excessive amount of growth hormone is released after puberty, when most of the epiphyseal cartilages have already closed. Cartilages and small bones respond to the hormone, however, resulting in abnormal growth at the hands, feet, lower jaw, skull, and clavicle. Excessive growth resulting in **gigantism** occurs if there is hypersecretion of growth hormone before puberty. Inadequate production of growth hormone before puberty, by contrast, produces **pituitary dwarfism**. People with this condition are very short, but unlike *achondroplastic dwarfs* (discussed below), their proportions are normal.

In **osteomalacia** (os-tē-ō-ma-LĀ-shē-uh; *malakia*, softness) the size of the skeletal elements does not change, but their mineral content decreases, softening the bones. The osteoblasts work hard, but the matrix doesn't accumulate enough calcium salts. This condition, **rickets**, occurs in adults or children whose diet contains inadequate levels of calcium or vitamin D_3.

The excessive formation of bone is termed **hyperostosis** (hī-per-os-TŌ-sis). In **osteopetrosis** (os-tē-ō-pe-TRŌ-sis; *petros*, stone), the total mass of the skeleton gradually increases as a result of a decrease in osteoclast activity. Remodeling stops, and the shapes of the bones gradually change. Osteopetrosis in children produces a variety of skeletal deformities. The primary cause of this relatively rare condition is unknown.

There are more than 200 recognized inheritable disorders of connective tissues. Individual cases frequently result from a spontaneous mutation in either the oocyte or sperm of unaffected parents. Individuals with such conditions may transmit the disorder to their children. *Osteogenesis imperfecta*, *Marfan's syndrome*, and *achondroplasia* are examples of inherited conditions characterized by abnormal bone formation.

Osteogenesis imperfecta, appearing in roughly 1 individual in 20,000, affects the organization of collagen fibers. Osteoblast function is impaired, growth is abnormal, and in severe forms the bones are very fragile, leading to repeated fractures and progressive skeletal deformation. Fibroblast activity is also affected, and the ligaments and tendons can be very "loose," permitting excessive movement at the joints. There are four recognized types and large variations occur in symptom severity. The lifetime fracture count can range from just a few to hundreds, with the worst form often fatal soon after birth.

Marfan's syndrome is also linked to defective connective tissue structure. Extremely long and slender limbs, the most obvious physical indication of this disorder, result from excessive cartilage formation at the epiphyseal cartilages. An abnormality of a gene on chromosome 15 that affects the protein fibrillin is responsible. The skeletal effects are striking, but associated arterial wall weaknesses are more dangerous.

Achondroplasia (a-kon-drō-PLĀ-sē-uh) also results from abnormal epiphyseal activity. The child's epiphyseal cartilages grow unusually slowly, and the adult has short, stocky limbs. Although other skeletal abnormalities occur, the trunk is normal in size, and sexual and mental development remain unaffected. An adult with achondroplasia is known as an *achondroplastic dwarf*. The condition results from an abnormal gene on chromosome 4 that affects a fibroblast growth factor. Most cases are the result of spontaneous mutations. If both parents have achondroplasia, the chances are that 25 percent of their children will be unaffected, 50 percent will be affected to some degree, and 25 percent will inherit two abnormal genes, leading to severe abnormalities and early death.

Formation of the Blood and Lymphatic Supply [Figures 5.2b/5.9/5.10]

Osseous tissue is very vascular, and the bones of the skeleton have an extensive blood supply. In a typical bone such as the humerus, four major sets of blood vessels develop (Figure 5.10).

1. *The nutrient artery and vein:* These vessels form as blood vessels invade the cartilage model at the start of endochondral ossification. There is usually only one **nutrient artery** and one **nutrient vein** entering the diaphysis through a *nutrient foramen*, although a few bones, including the femur, have two or more. These vessels penetrate the shaft to reach the medullary cavity. The nutrient artery will divide into ascending and descending branches, which approach the epiphyses. These vessels then re-enter the compact bone by perforating canals and extend along the central canals to supply the osteons of the compact bone. (Figure 5.2b, p. 114).
2. *Metaphyseal vessels:* These vessels supply blood to the inner (diaphyseal) surface of each epiphyseal cartilage, where bone is replacing cartilage.
3. *Epiphyseal vessels:* The epiphyseal ends of long bones often contain numerous smaller foramina. The vessels that use these foramina supply the osseous tissue and medullary cavities of the epiphyses.
4. *Periosteal vessels:* Blood vessels from the periosteum are incorporated into the developing bone surface as described and illustrated in Figure 5.9. These vessels provide blood to the superficial osteons of the shaft. During endochondral bone formation, branches of periosteal vessels enter the epiphyses, providing blood to the secondary ossification centers. The periosteum also contains an extensive network of lymphatic vessels, and many of these have branches that enter the bone and reach individual osteons through numerous perforating canals.

Following the closure of the epiphyses, all three sets of blood vessels become extensively interconnected, as indicated in Figure 5.10.

Bone Innervation

Bones are innervated by sensory nerves, and injuries to the skeleton can be very painful. Sensory nerve endings branch throughout the periosteum, and sensory nerves penetrate the cortex with the nutrient artery to innervate the endosteum, medullary cavity, and epiphyses.

Factors Regulating Bone Growth

Normal bone growth depends on a combination of nutritional and hormonal factors:

- Normal bone growth cannot occur without a constant dietary source of calcium and phosphate salts, as well as other ions such as magnesium, citrate, carbonate, and sodium.

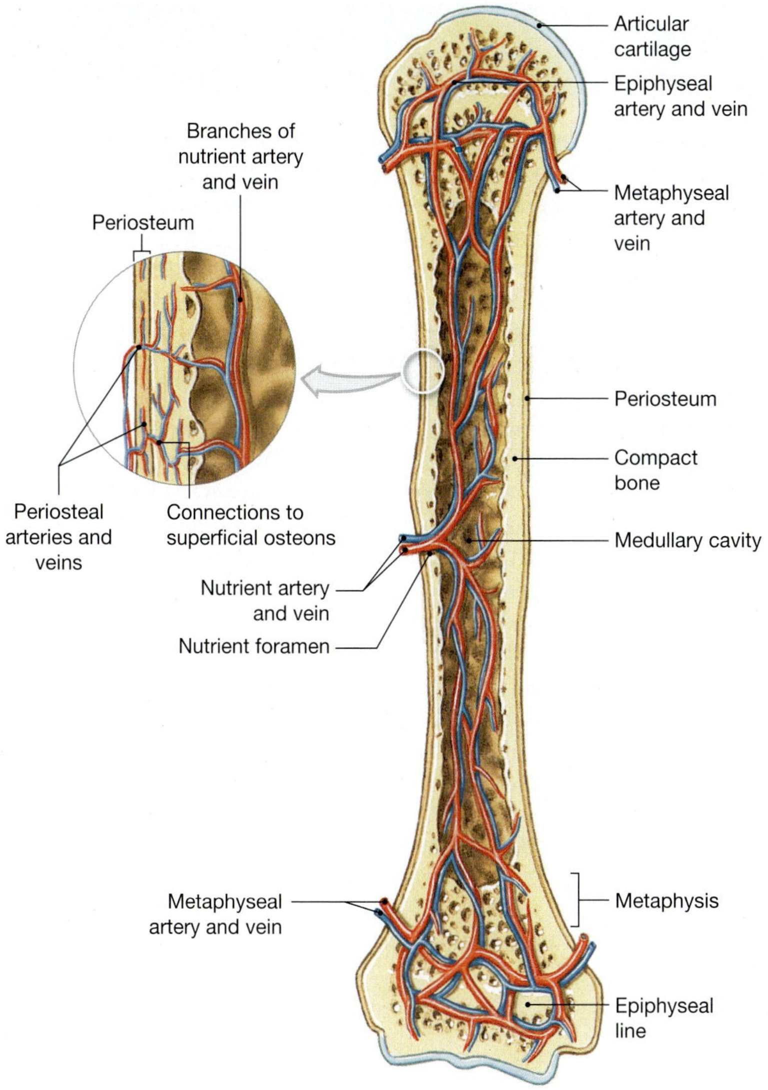

Figure 5.10 Circulatory Supply to a Mature Bone
Arrangement and association of blood vessels supplying the humerus.

- *Vitamins A* and *C* are essential for normal bone growth and remodeling. These vitamins must be obtained from the diet.
- The group of related steroids collectively known as **vitamin D** plays an important role in normal calcium metabolism by stimulating the absorption and transport of calcium and phosphate ions into the blood. The active form of vitamin D, *calcitriol*, is synthesized in the kidneys; this process ultimately depends on the availability of a related steroid, *cholecalciferol*, that may be absorbed from the diet or synthesized in the skin in the presence of UV radiation. p. 94

Hormones regulate the pattern of growth by changing the rates of osteoblast and osteoclast activity:

- The parathyroid glands release **parathyroid hormone**, which stimulates osteoclast and osteoblast activity, increases the rate of calcium absorption along the small intestine, and reduces the rate of calcium loss in the urine. The action of parathyroid hormone on the intestine requires the presence of *calcitriol*, a hormone produced at the kidneys. p. 94
- *C thyrocytes* (also termed *C cells*) within the thyroid glands of children and pregnant women secrete the hormone **calcitonin** (kal-si-TŌ-nin), which inhibits osteoclasts and increases the rate of calcium loss in the urine. Calcitonin is of uncertain significance in the healthy nonpregnant adult.
- *Growth hormone*, produced by the pituitary gland, and **thyroxine**, from the thyroid gland, stimulate bone growth. In proper balance, these hormones maintain normal activity at the epiphyseal cartilages until roughly the time of puberty.
- At puberty, bone growth accelerates dramatically. The **sex hormones** (*estrogen* and *testosterone*) stimulate osteoblasts to produce bone faster than the rate of epiphyseal cartilage expansion. Over time, the epiphyseal cartilages narrow and eventually ossify, or "close." The continued production of sex hormones is essential to the maintenance of bone mass in adults.

There are differences from bone to bone and individual to individual as to the timing of epiphyseal cartilage closure. The toes may complete their ossification by age 11, whereas portions of the pelvis or the wrist may continue to enlarge until age 25. Differences in the male and female sex hormones account for the variation between the sexes and for related variations in body size and proportions.

CONCEPT CHECK

1. How can x-rays of the femur be used to determine whether a person has reached full height?
2. Briefly describe the major steps in the process of intramembranous ossification.
3. Describe how bones increase in diameter.
4. What is the epiphyseal cartilage? Where is it located? Why is it significant?

See blue "Answers" tab at back of book.

Bone Maintenance, Remodeling, and Repair

Bone growth occurs when osteoblasts are creating more bone matrix than osteoclasts are removing. Bone remodeling and repair may involve a change in the shape or internal architecture of a bone or a change in the total amount of minerals deposited in the skeleton. In the adult, osteocytes are continually removing and replacing the surrounding calcium salts. But osteoblasts and osteoclasts also remain active throughout life, not just during the growth years. In young adults osteoblast activity and osteoclast activity are in balance, and the rate of bone formation is equal to the rate of bone reabsorption. As one osteon forms through the activity of osteoblasts, another is destroyed by osteoclasts. The rate of mineral turnover is quite high; each year almost one-fifth of the adult skeleton is demolished and then rebuilt or replaced. Every part of every bone may not be affected, as there are regional and even local differences in the rate of turnover. For example, the spongy bone in the head of the femur may be replaced two or three times each year, whereas the compact bone along the shaft remains largely untouched. This high turnover rate continues into old age, but in older individuals osteoblast activity decreases faster than osteoclast activity. As a result, bone resorption exceeds bone deposition, and the skeleton gradually gets weaker and weaker.

Remodeling of Bone

Although bone is hard and dense, it is able to change its shape in response to environmental conditions. Bone remodeling involves the simultaneous process of adding new bone and removing previously formed bone. For

example, bone remodeling occurs following the realignment of teeth by an orthodontist. As the teeth are moved the shape of the tooth socket changes by the resorption of old bone and the deposition of new bone according to the tooth's new position. In addition, increased muscular development (as in weight training) will involve the remodeling of bones to meet the new stress imposed at the site of muscular and tendon attachment.

Bones adapt to stress by altering the turnover and recycling of minerals. Osteoblast sensitivity to electrical events has been hypothesized as the mechanism that controls the internal organization and structure of bone. Whenever a bone is stressed, the mineral crystals generate minute electrical fields. Osteoblasts are apparently attracted to these electrical fields, and once in the area they begin to produce bone. (Electrical fields may also be used to stimulate the repair of severe fractures.)

Because bones are adaptable, their shapes and surface features reflect the forces applied to them. For example, bumps and ridges on the surface of a bone mark the sites where tendons attach to the bone. If muscles become more powerful, the corresponding bumps and ridges enlarge to withstand the increased forces. Heavily stressed bones become thicker and stronger, whereas bones not subjected to ordinary stresses will become thin and brittle. Regular exercise is therefore important as a stimulus that maintains normal bone structure, especially in growing children, postmenopausal women, and elderly men.

Degenerative changes in the skeleton occur after relatively brief periods of inactivity. For example, using a crutch while wearing a cast takes weight off the injured limb. After a few weeks, the unstressed bones lose up to about a third of their mass. However, the bones rebuild just as quickly when normal loading resumes.

Injury and Repair [Figure 5.11]

Despite its mineral strength, bone may crack or even break if subjected to extreme loads, sudden impacts, or stresses from unusual directions. The damage produced constitutes a **fracture**. Healing of a fracture usually occurs even after severe damage, provided the blood supply and the cellular components of the endosteum and periosteum survive. Steps in the repair of a fracture are illustrated in Figure 5.11. The final repair will be slightly thicker and probably stronger than the original bone; under comparable stresses, a second fracture will usually occur at a different site.

Aging and the Skeletal System [Figure 5.12]

The bones of the skeleton become thinner and relatively weaker as a normal part of the aging process. Inadequate ossification is called **osteopenia** (os-tē-ō-PĒ-nē-a; *penia*, lacking), and everyone becomes slightly osteopenic as they age. This reduction in bone mass occurs between ages 30 and 40. Over this period, osteoblast activity begins to decline while osteoclast activity continues at previous levels. Once the reduction begins, women lose roughly 8 percent of their skeletal mass every decade; the skeletons of men

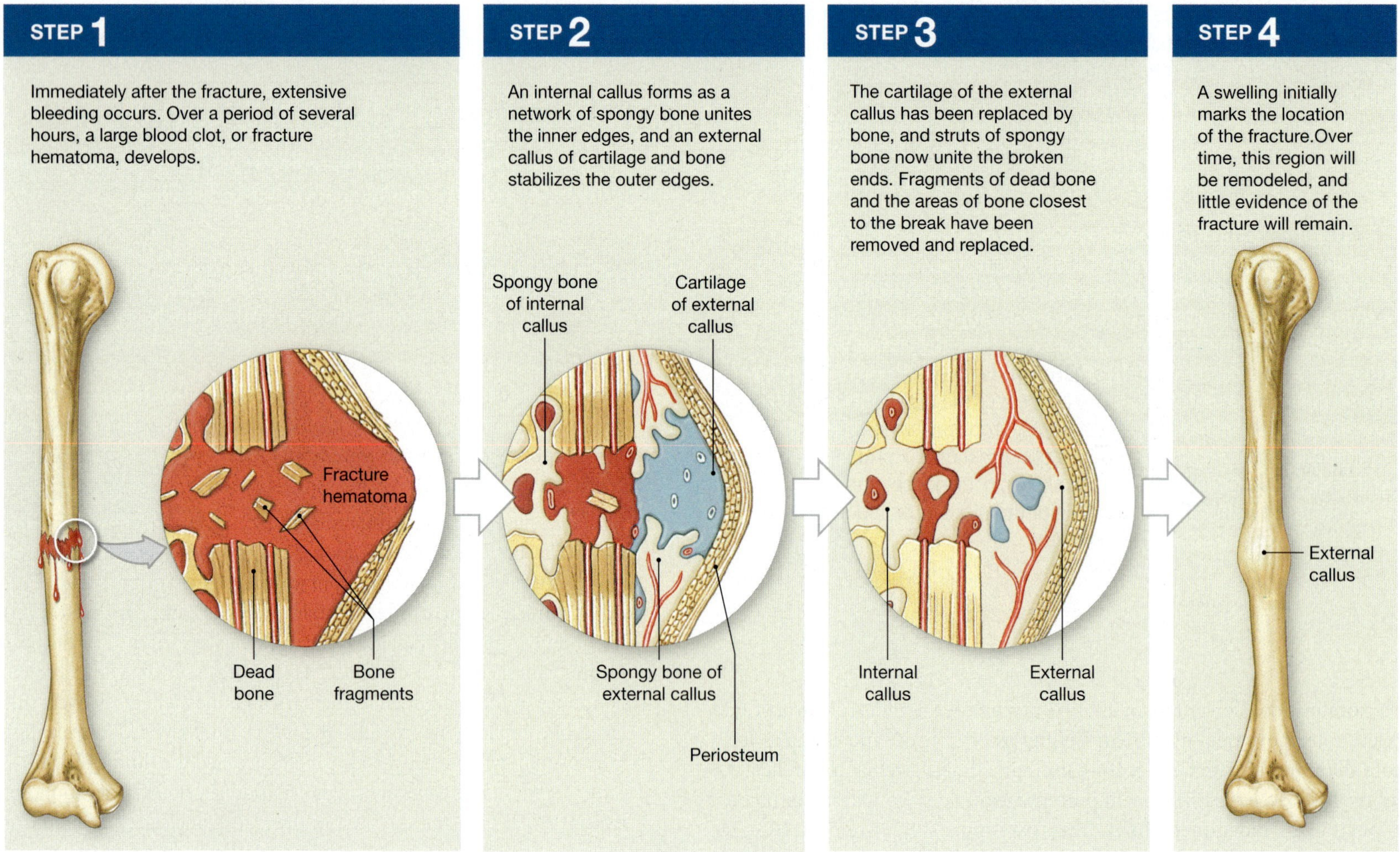

Figure 5.11 Fracture Repair
Steps involved in the repair of a fracture.

Clinical Note

Osteoporosis and Age-Related Skeletal Abnormalities

In **osteoporosis** (os-tē-ō-pō-RŌ-sis; *porosus*, porous), there is a reduction in bone mass sufficient to compromise normal function. Our maximal bone density is reached in our early twenties and decreases as we age. Inadequate calcium intake in teenagers reduces peak bone density and increases the risk of osteoporosis. The distinction between the "normal" osteopenia of aging and the clinical condition of osteoporosis is a matter of degree.

Current estimates indicate that 29 percent of women between ages 45 and 79 can be considered osteoporotic. The increase in incidence after menopause has been linked to a decrease in the production of estrogens (female sex hormones). The incidence of osteoporosis in men of the same age is estimated at 18 percent.

The excessive fragility of osteoporotic bones commonly leads to breakage, and subsequent healing is impaired. Vertebrae may collapse, distorting the vertebral articulations and putting pressure on spinal nerves. Supplemental estrogens, dietary changes to elevate calcium levels in blood, exercise that stresses bones and stimulates osteoblast activity, and the administration of calcitonin by nasal spray appear to slow, but not prevent, the development of osteoporosis. The inhibition of osteoclast activity by drugs called *bisphosphonates*, such as Fosamax, can reduce the risk of spine and hip fractures in elderly women and improve bone density. For long-term use, exercise, dietary calcium, and bisphosphonates are currently preferred.

Osteoporosis can also develop as a secondary effect of some cancers. Cancers of the bone medullary, breast, or other tissues may release a chemical known as **osteoclast-activating factor**. This compound increases both the number and activity of osteoclasts and may produce severe osteoporosis.

Infectious diseases that affect the skeletal system become more common as individuals age. In part, this fact reflects the higher incidence of fractures, combined with slower healing and the reduction of immune defenses.

Osteomyelitis (os-tē-ō-mī-e-LĪ-tis; *myelos*, marrow) is a painful and destructive bone infection generally caused by bacteria. This condition, most common in people over age 50, can lead to dangerous systemic infections. Heredity and environmental factors, including the possibility of a viral infection, appear to be responsible for **Paget's disease**, also known as **osteitis deformans** (os-tē-Ī-tis de-FOR-manz). This condition may affect up to 10 percent of the population over 70. Localized osteoclast activity accelerates, producing areas of acute osteoporosis, and osteoblasts produce abnormal matrix proteins. The result is a gradual deformation of the skeleton. Bisphosphonate treatment may slow the progression of the disease, as it does osteoporosis, by reducing osteoclast activity.

deteriorate at the slower rate of about 3 percent per decade. All parts of the skeleton are not equally affected. Epiphyses, vertebrae, and the jaws lose more than their fair share, resulting in fragile limbs, a reduction in height, and the loss of teeth. A significant percentage of older women and a smaller proportion of older men suffer from **osteoporosis** (os-tē-ō-pō-RŌ-sis; *porosus*, porous). This condition is characterized by a reduction in bone mass and microstructural changes that compromise normal function and increase susceptibility to fractures (Figure 5.12).

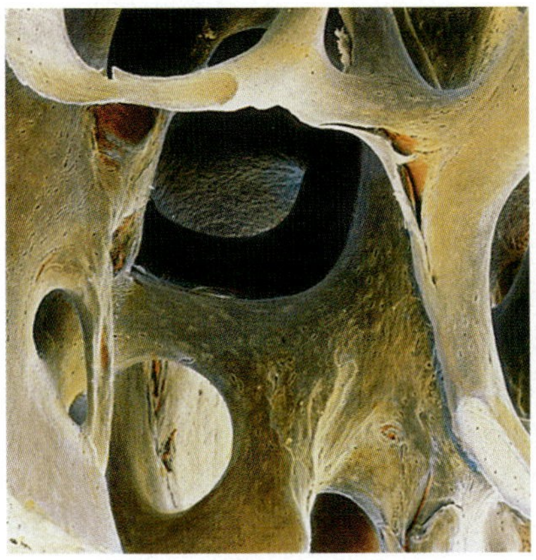

(a) Normal spongy bone

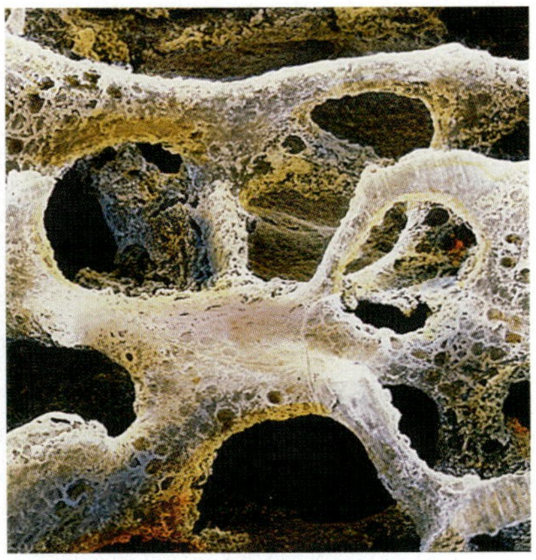

(b) Spongy bone in osteoporosis

Figure 5.12 The Effects of Osteoporosis
(a) Normal spongy bone from the epiphysis of a young adult. (SEM × 25)
(b) Spongy bone from a person with osteoporosis. (SEM × 21)

CONCEPT CHECK

1. Would you expect to see any difference in the bones of an athlete before and after extensive training to increase muscle mass? Why or why not?
2. Which vitamins and hormones regulate bone growth?
3. What major difference might we expect to find when comparing bone growth in a 15-year-old and that of a 30-year-old?

See blue "Answers" tab at back of book.

Anatomy of Skeletal Elements

The human skeleton contains 206 major bones. We can divide these bones into six broad categories according to their individual shapes.

Classification of Bones [Figures 5.3/5.13]

Refer to Figure 5.13 as we describe the anatomical classification of bones.

1. *Long bones* are relatively long and slender (Figure 5.13a). They have a diaphysis, two metaphyses, two epiphyses, and a medullary (marrow) cavity, as detailed in Figure 5.3, p. 115. Long bones are found in the upper and lower limbs. Examples include the *humerus, radius, ulna, femur, tibia,* and *fibula.*
2. *Flat bones* have thin, roughly parallel surfaces of compact bone. In structure a flat bone resembles a spongy bone sandwich; such bones are strong but relatively light. Flat bones form the roof of the skull (Figure 5.13b), the sternum, the ribs, and the scapulae. They provide protection for underlying soft tissues and offer an extensive surface area for the attachment of skeletal muscles. Special terms are used when describing the flat bones of the skull, such as the parietal bones. Their relatively thick layers of compact bone are called the *internal* and *external tables,* and the layer of spongy bone between the tables is called the **diploë** (DIP-lō-ē). *Sutural (Wormian) bones* are small, flat, oddly shaped bones found between the flat bones of the skull in the suture line. They develop from separate centers of ossification, and are regarded to be a type of flat bone.
3. *Pneumatized bones* are bones that are hollow or contain numerous air pockets, such as the ethmoid (Figure 5.13c).

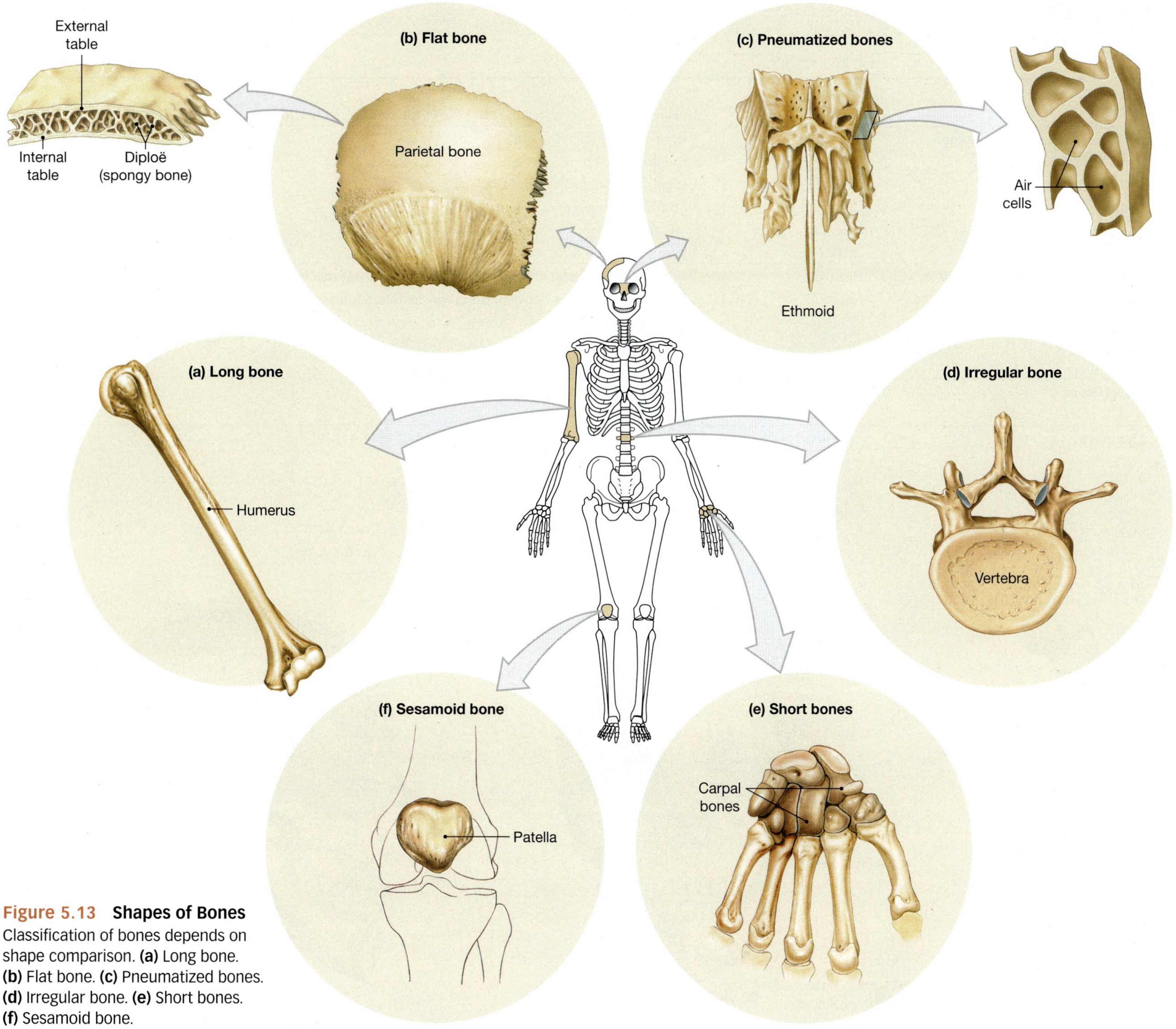

Figure 5.13 Shapes of Bones Classification of bones depends on shape comparison. **(a)** Long bone. **(b)** Flat bone. **(c)** Pneumatized bones. **(d)** Irregular bone. **(e)** Short bones. **(f)** Sesamoid bone.

4. *Irregular bones* have complex shapes with short, flat, notched, or ridged surfaces (Figure 5.13d). Their internal structure is equally varied. The vertebrae that form the spinal column and several bones in the skull are examples of irregular bones.
5. *Short bones* are boxlike in appearance (Figure 5.13e). Their external surfaces are covered by compact bone, but the interior contains spongy bone. Examples of short bones include the *carpal bones* (wrists) and *tarsal bones* (ankles).
6. *Sesamoid bones* are usually small, round, and flat (Figure 5.13f). They develop inside tendons and are most often encountered near joints at the knee, the hands, and the feet. Few individuals have sesamoid bones at every possible location, but everyone has sesamoid *patellae* (pa-TEL-ē), or kneecaps.

Bone Markings (Surface Features)

[Figure 5.14 and Table 5.1]

Each bone in the body has a distinctive shape and characteristic external and internal features. Elevations or projections form where tendons and ligaments attach and where adjacent bones articulate. Depressions, grooves, and tunnels in bone indicate sites where blood vessels and nerves lie alongside or penetrate the bone. Detailed examination of these **bone markings**, or *surface features*, can yield an abundance of anatomical information. For example, forensic anthropologists can often determine the age, size, sex, and general appearance of an individual on the basis of incomplete skeletal remains. (This topic will be discussed further in Chapter 6.) Bone marking terminology is presented in Table 5.1 and illustrated in Figure 5.14.

TABLE 5.1 Common Bone Marking Terminology

General Description	Anatomical Term	Definition and Example *(See Figure 5.14)*
Elevations and projections (general)	Process	Any projection or bump (b)
	Ramus	An extension of a bone making an angle to the rest of the structure (b, e)
Processes formed where tendons or ligaments attach	Trochanter	A large, rough projection (a)
	Tuberosity	A rough projection (d)
	Tubercle	A small, rounded projection (a, d)
	Crest	A prominent ridge (e)
	Line	A low ridge (e)
	Spine	A pointed process (e)
Processes formed for articulation with adjacent bones	Head	The expanded articular end of an epiphysis, often separated from the shaft by a narrower neck (a, d)
	Neck	A narrower connection between the epiphysis and diaphysis (a, d)
	Condyle	A smooth, rounded articular process (a, d)
	Trochlea	A smooth, grooved articular process shaped like a pulley (d)
	Facet	A small, flat articular surface (a)
Depressions	Fossa	A shallow depression (d, e)
	Sulcus	A narrow groove (d)
Openings	Foramen	A rounded passageway for blood vessels and/or nerves (b, e)
	Fissure	An elongated cleft (b)
	Meatus or canal	A passageway through the substance of a bone (c)
	Sinus or antrum	A chamber within a bone, normally filled with air (c)

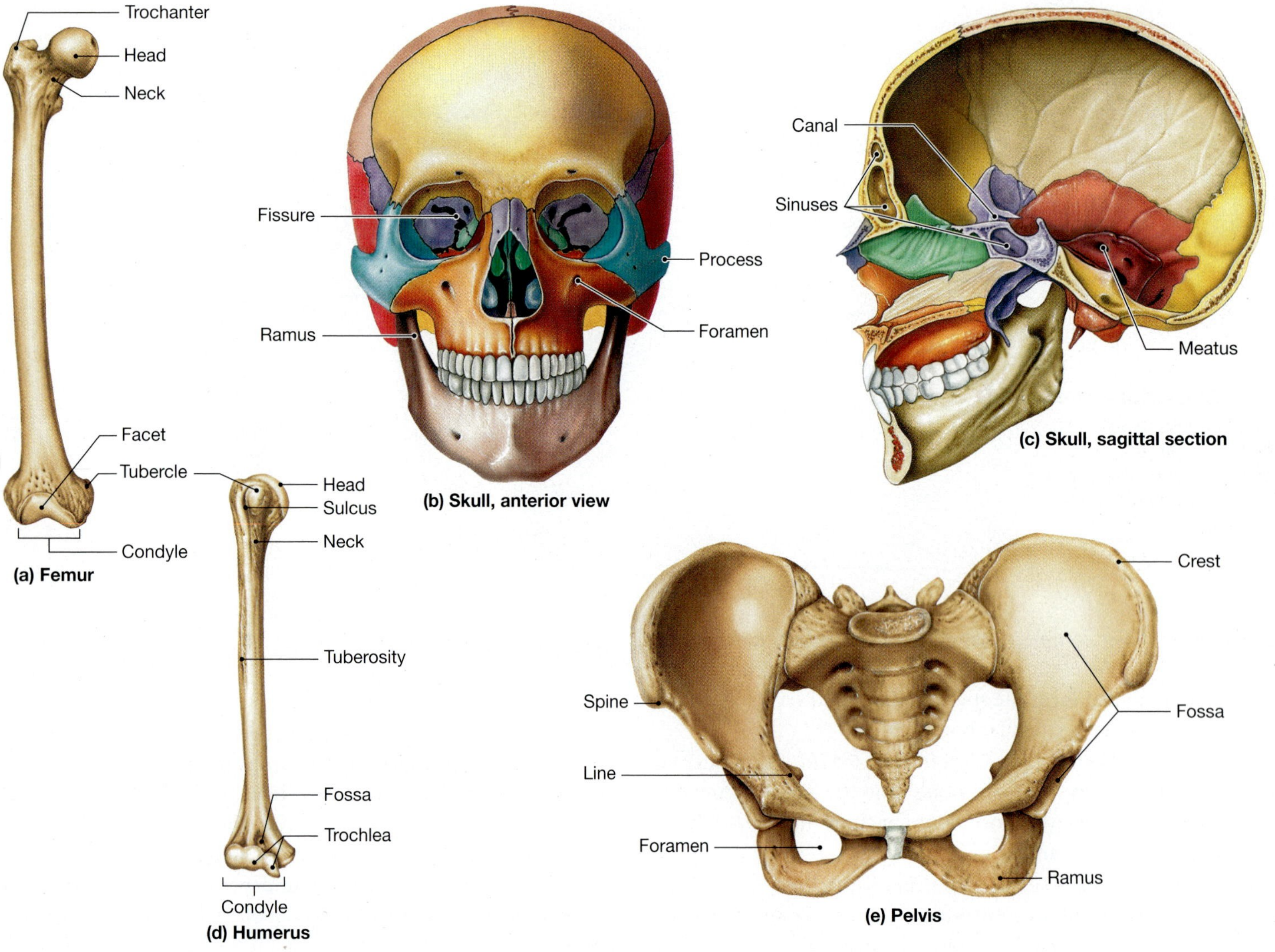

Figure 5.14 Examples of Bone Markings (Surface Features)
Bone markings provide distinct and characteristic landmarks for orientation and identification of bones and associated structures.

Clinical Note

A Classification of Fractures Fractures are classified according to their external appearance, the site of the fracture, and the nature of the crack or break in the bone. Important fracture types are described here, with representative x-rays. Many fractures fall into more than one category. For example, a Colles' fracture is a transverse fracture, but depending on the injury, it may also be a comminuted fracture that can be either open or closed. **Closed**, or *simple*, **fractures** are completely internal; they do not involve a break in the skin. **Open**, or *compound*, **fractures** project through the skin; they are more dangerous because of the possibility of infection or uncontrolled bleeding.

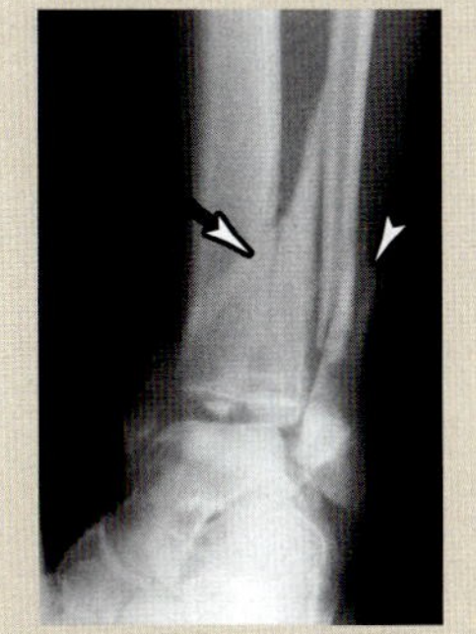

A **Pott's fracture** occurs at the ankle and affects both the tibia and the fibula.

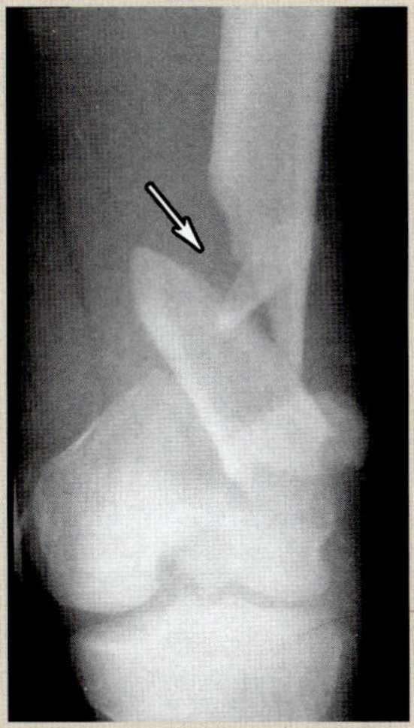

Comminuted fractures, such as this fracture of the femur, shatter the affected area into a multitude of bony fragments.

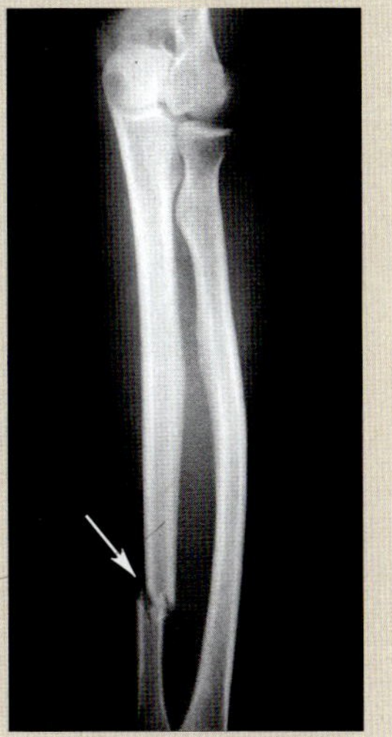

Transverse fractures, such as this fracture of the ulna, break a bone across its long axis.

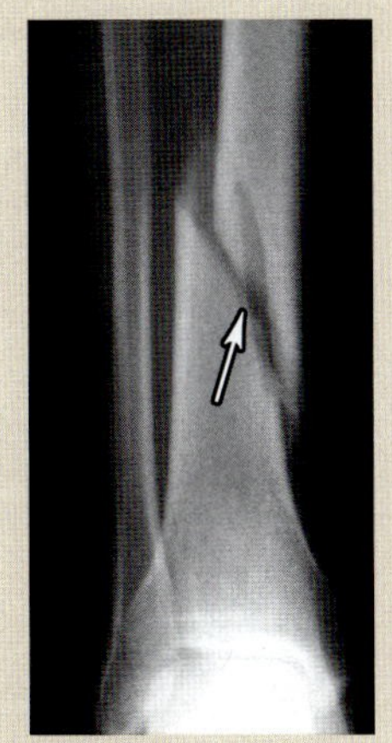

Spiral fractures, such as this fracture of the tibia, are produced by twisting stresses that spread along the length of the bone.

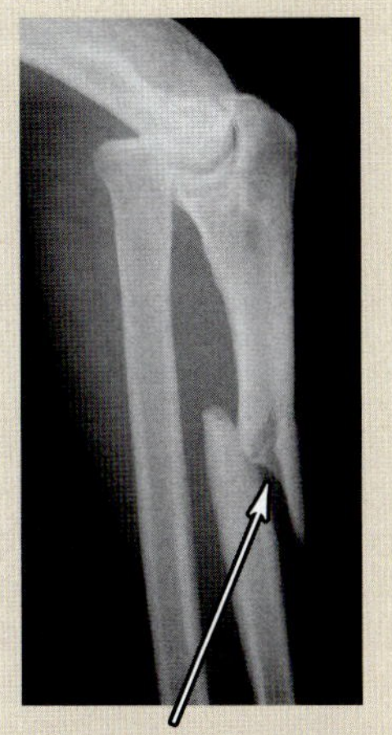

Displaced fractures, such as this ulnar fracture, produce new and abnormal bone arrangements; **nondisplaced fractures** retain the normal alignment of the bones or fragments.

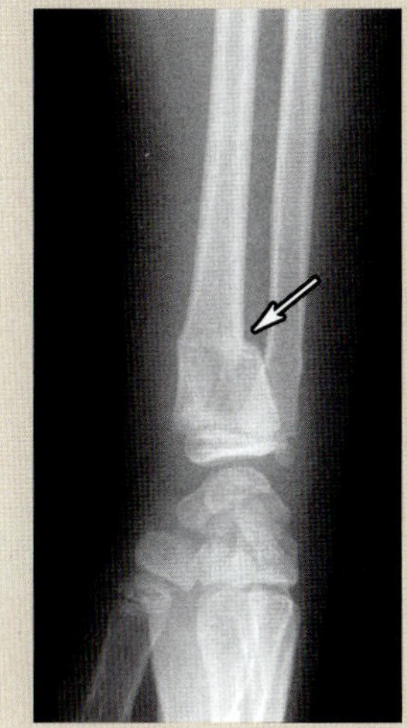

A **Colles' fracture**, a break in the distal portion of the radius, is typically the result of reaching out to cushion a fall.

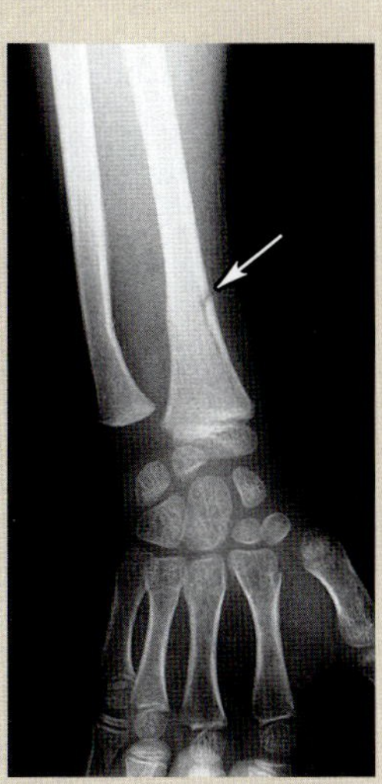

In a **greenstick fracture**, such as this fracture of the radius, only one side of the shaft is broken, and the other is bent. This type generally occurs in children, whose long bones have yet to ossify fully.

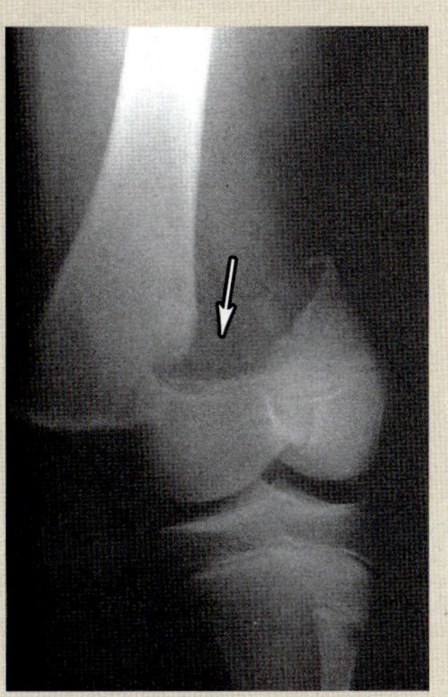

Epiphyseal fractures, such as this fracture of the femur, tend to occur where the bone matrix is undergoing calcification and chondrocytes are dying. A clean transverse fracture along this line generally heals well. Unless carefully treated, fractures between the epiphysis and the epiphyseal cartilage can permanently stop growth at this site.

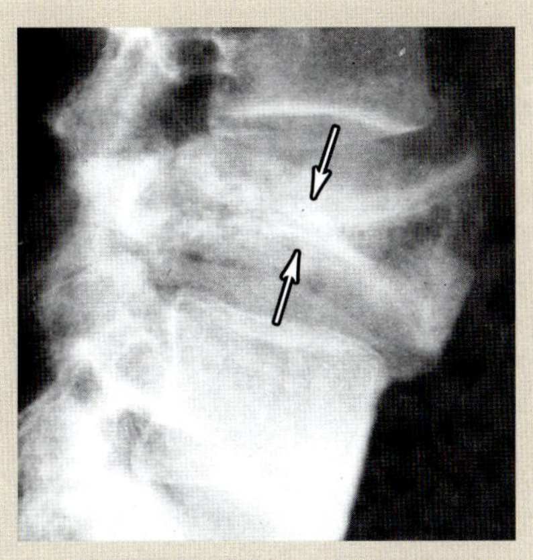

Compression fractures occur in vertebrae subjected to extreme stresses, as when you land on your seat in a fall. They are more common when bones are weakened by osteoporosis.

Our discussion will focus on prominent features that are useful in identifying a bone. These markings are also useful because they provide fixed landmarks that can help in determining the position of the soft tissue components of other systems. Specific anatomical terms are used to describe the various elevations and depressions.

✓ CONCEPT CHECK

1. Why is a working knowledge of bone markings important in a clinical setting?
2. What is the primary difference between sesamoid and irregular bones?
3. Where would you look for sutural bones in a skeleton?

See blue "Answers" tab at back of book.

Integration with Other Systems

Although bones may seem inert, you should now realize that they are quite dynamic structures. The entire skeletal system is intimately associated with other systems. Bones are attached to the muscular system, extensively connected to the cardiovascular and lymphoid systems, and largely under the physiological control of the endocrine system. Also, the digestive and excretory systems play important roles in providing the calcium and phosphate minerals needed for bone growth. In return, the skeleton represents a reserve of calcium, phosphate, and other minerals that can compensate for changes in the dietary supply of these ions.

CLINICAL TERMS

achondroplasia (a-kon-drō-PLĀ-sē-uh): A condition resulting from abnormal epiphyseal cartilage activity; the epiphyseal cartilages grow unusually slowly, and the individual develops short, stocky limbs. The trunk is normal in size, and sexual and mental development remain unaffected.

acromegaly (ak-rō-MEG-a-lē): A condition caused by excessive secretion of growth hormone after puberty and closure of epiphyseal cartilage. Skeletal abnormalities develop, affecting the cartilages and various small bones, notably in the face, hands, and feet.

external callus: A toughened layer of connective tissue that encircles and stabilizes a bone at a fracture site.

fracture: A crack or break in a bone.

fracture hematoma: A large blood clot that closes off the injured vessels and leaves a fibrous meshwork in the damaged area.

gigantism: A condition resulting from an overproduction of growth hormone before puberty.

hyperostosis (hī-per-os-TŌ-sis): The excessive formation of bone tissue.

internal callus: A bridgework of trabecular bone that unites the broken ends of a bone on the marrow side of the fracture.

Marfan's syndrome: An inherited condition linked to defective production of a connective tissue glycoprotein. Extreme height and long, slender limbs are the most obvious physical indications of this disorder.

osteoclast-activating factor: A compound released by cancers of the bone marrow, breast, and other tissues. It produces severe osteoporosis.

osteogenesis imperfecta (im-per-FEK-ta): An inherited condition affecting the organization of collagen fibers. Osteoblast function is impaired, growth is abnormal, and the bones are very fragile, leading to progressive skeletal deformation and repeated fractures.

osteomalacia (os-tē-ō-ma-LĀ-shē-uh): A softening of bone due to a decrease in the mineral content.

osteomyelitis (os-tē-ō-mī-e-LĪ-tis): A painful infection in a bone, usually caused by bacteria.

osteopenia (os-tē-ō-PĒ-nē-a): A reduction in bone mass and density.

osteopetrosis (os-tē-ō-pe-TRŌ-sis): A condition caused by a decrease in osteoclast activity, causing increased bone mass and various skeletal deformities.

osteoporosis (os-tē-ō-pō-RŌ-sis): A disease characterized by deterioration in the histological organization of bone tissue, leading to a reduction in bone mass to a degree that compromises normal function.

Paget's disease (osteitis deformans) (os-tē-Ī-tis de-FOR-manz): A condition characterized by gradual deformation of the skeleton.

pituitary growth failure: A type of dwarfism caused by inadequate growth hormone production.

rickets: A disorder that reduces the amount of calcium salts in the skeleton; often characterized by a "bowlegged" appearance.

STUDY OUTLINE

Introduction 112

1. The skeletal system includes the bones of the skeleton and the cartilages, ligaments, and other connective tissues that stabilize or interconnect bones. Its functions include structural support, storage of minerals and lipids, blood cell production, protection of delicate tissues and organs, and leverage.

Structure of Bone 112

1. **Osseous (bone) tissue** is a supporting connective tissue with specialized cells and a solid, extracellular **matrix** of protein fibers and a ground substance.

The Histological Organization of Mature Bone 112

2. Bone matrix consists largely of crystals of **hydroxyapatite**, accounting for almost two-thirds of the weight of bone. The remaining third is dominated by collagen fibers and small amounts of other calcium salts; bone cells and other cell types contribute only about 2 percent to the volume of bone tissue.
3. **Osteocytes** are mature bone cells that are completely surrounded by hard bone matrix. Osteocytes reside in spaces termed **lacunae**. Osteocytes in lacunae are interconnected by small, hollow channels called **canaliculi**. **Lamellae** are layers of calcified matrix. *(see Figure 5.1)*

4. **Osteoblasts** are immature, bone-forming cells. By the process of **osteogenesis**, osteoblasts synthesize **osteoid**, the matrix of bone prior to its calcification. *(see Figure 5.1)*
5. **Osteoprogenitor cells** are mesenchymal cells that play a role in the repair of bone fractures. *(see Figure 5.1)*
6. **Osteoclasts** are large, multinucleated cells that help dissolve the bony matrix through the process of **osteolysis**. They are important in the regulation of calcium and phosphate concentrations in body fluids. *(see Figure 5.1)*

Compact and Spongy Bone 113

7. There are two types of bone: **compact**, or *dense*, bone, and **spongy**, or *trabecular*, bone. The matrix composition in compact bone is the same as that of spongy bone, but they differ in the three-dimensional arrangement of osteocytes, canaliculi, and lamellae. *(see Figures 5.1/5.2)*
8. The basic functional unit of compact bone is the **osteon**, or *Haversian system*. Osteocytes in an osteon are arranged in concentric layers around a **central canal**. *(see Figures 5.1b–d/5.2)*
9. Spongy bone contains struts or plates called **trabeculae**, often in an open network. *(see Figure 5.2)*
10. Compact bone covers bone surfaces. It is thickest where stresses come from a limited range of directions. Spongy bone is located internally in bones. It is found where stresses are few or come from many different directions. *(see Figure 5.3)*

The Periosteum and Endosteum 116

11. A bone is covered externally by a two-layered **periosteum** (outer fibrous, inner cellular) and lined internally by a cellular **endosteum**. *(see Figure 5.4)*

Bone Development and Growth 117

1. **Ossification** is the process of replacing other tissue by bone; **calcification** is the process of deposition of calcium salts within a tissue.

Intramembranous Ossification 117

2. **Intramembranous ossification**, also called **dermal ossification**, begins when osteoblasts differentiate within a mesenchymal or fibrous connective tissue. This process can ultimately produce spongy or compact bone. Such ossification begins at an **ossification center**. *(see Figures 5.5/5.6)*

Endochondral Ossification 118

3. **Endochondral ossification** begins with the formation of a cartilaginous model. This hyaline cartilage model is gradually replaced by osseous tissue. *(see Figures 5.6/5.7)*
4. The length of a developing bone increases at the **epiphyseal cartilage**, which separates the epiphysis from the diaphysis. Here, new cartilage is added at the epiphyseal side, while osseous tissue replaces older cartilage at the diaphyseal side. The time of closure of the epiphyseal cartilage differs among bones and among individuals. *(see Figure 5.8)*
5. The diameter of a bone enlarges through appositional growth at the outer surface. *(see Figure 5.9)*

Formation of the Blood and Lymphatic Supply 123

6. A typical bone formed through endochondral ossification has four major sets of vessels: the *nutrient vessels, metaphyseal vessels, epiphyseal vessels,* and *periosteal vessels.* Lymphatic vessels are distributed in the periosteum and enter the osteons through the nutrient and perforating canals. *(see Figures 5.7/5.10)*

Bone Innervation 123

7. Sensory nerve endings branch throughout the periosteum, and sensory nerves penetrate the cortex with the nutrient artery to innervate the endosteum, medullary cavity, and epiphyses.

Factors Regulating Bone Growth 123

8. Normal osteogenesis requires a continual and reliable source of minerals, vitamins, and hormones.
9. **Parathyroid hormone**, secreted by the parathyroid glands, stimulates osteoclast and osteoblast activity. In contrast, **calcitonin**, secreted by *C cells* in the thyroid gland, inhibits osteoclast activity and increases calcium loss in the urine. These hormones control the rate of mineral deposition in the skeleton and regulate the calcium ion concentrations in body fluids.
10. **Growth hormone**, **thyroxine**, and **sex hormones** stimulate bone growth by increasing osteoblast activity.
11. There are differences between individual bones and between individuals with respect to the timing of epiphyseal cartilage closure.

Bone Maintenance, Remodeling, and Repair 124

1. The turnover rate for bone is quite high. Each year almost one-fifth of the adult skeleton is broken down and then rebuilt or replaced.

Remodeling of Bone 124

2. Bone remodeling involves the simultaneous process of adding new bone and removing previously formed bone.
3. Mineral turnover and recycling allow bone to adapt to new stresses.
4. Calcium is the most common mineral in the human body, with more than 98 percent of it located in the skeleton.

Injury and Repair 125

5. A **fracture** is a crack or break in a bone. Healing of a fracture can usually occur if portions of the blood supply, endosteum, and periosteum remain intact. *(see Figure 5.11)* For a classification of fracture types, see the Clinical Note on 131.

Aging and the Skeletal System 125

6. The bones of the skeleton become thinner and relatively weaker as a normal part of the aging process. **Osteopenia** usually develops to some degree, but in some cases this process progresses to **osteoporosis** and the bones become dangerously weak and brittle. *(see Figure 5.12)*

Anatomy of Skeletal Elements 126

Classification of Bones 126

1. Categories of bones are based on anatomical classification; they are *long bones, flat bones, pneumatized bones, irregular bones, short bones,* and *sesamoid bones. (see Figure 5.13)*

Bone Markings (Surface Features) 127

2. **Bone markings** (or *surface features*) can be used to identify specific elevations, depressions, and openings of bones. Common bone marking terminology is presented in *Table 5.1. (see Figure 5.14)*

Integration with Other Systems 130

1. The skeletal system is anatomically and physiologically linked to other body systems and represents a reservoir for calcium, phosphate, and other minerals.

CHAPTER REVIEW

For answers to the Concept Check and Chapter Review questions, go to the blue "Answers" tab at the back of the book.

Level 1 Reviewing Facts and Terms

1. Which type of cell is capable of dividing to produce new osteoblasts?
   (a) osteocyte
   (b) osteoprogenitor
   (c) osteoblast
   (d) osteoclast
2. Spongy bone is formed of
   (a) osteons
   (b) struts and plates
   (c) concentric lamellae
   (d) spicules only
3. The basic functional unit of mature compact bone is the
   (a) osteon
   (b) canaliculus
   (c) lamella
   (d) central canal
4. Endochondral ossification begins with the formation of
   (a) a fibrous connective tissue model
   (b) a hyaline cartilage model
   (c) a membrane model
   (d) a calcified model
5. When sexual hormone production increases, bone production
   (a) slows down
   (b) accelerates rapidly
   (c) increases slowly
   (d) is not affected
6. The presence of an epiphyseal line indicates that
   (a) epiphyseal growth has ended
   (b) epiphyseal growth is just beginning
   (c) growth in bone diameter is just beginning
   (d) the bone is fractured at that location
7. The inadequate ossification that occurs with aging is called
   (a) osteopenia
   (b) osteomyelitis
   (c) osteitis
   (d) osteoporosis
8. The process by which the diameter of a developing bone enlarges is
   (a) appositional growth at the outer surface
   (b) interstitial growth within the matrix
   (c) lamellar growth
   (d) Haversian growth
9. The sternum is an example of a(n)
   (a) flat bone
   (b) long bone
   (c) irregular bone
   (d) sesamoid bone
10. A small, rough projection of a bone is termed a
    (a) ramus
    (b) tuberosity
    (c) trochanter
    (d) spine

Level 2 Reviewing Concepts

1. How would decreasing the proportion of organic molecules to inorganic components in the bony matrix affect the physical characteristics of bone?
   (a) the bone would be less flexible
   (b) the bones would be stronger
   (c) the bones would be more brittle
   (d) the bones would be more flexible
2. Premature closure of the epiphyseal cartilages could be caused by
   (a) elevated levels of sex hormones
   (b) high levels of vitamin D
   (c) too little parathyroid hormone
   (d) an excess of growth hormone
3. What factors determine the type of ossification that occurs in a specific bone?
4. What events signal the end of long bone elongation?
5. What are the advantages of spongy bone over compact bone in an area such as the expanded ends of long bones?
6. How does a bone grow in diameter?
7. Why is a healed area of bone less likely to fracture in the same place again from similar stresses?
8. Why will a diet that consists mostly of junk foods hinder the healing of a fractured bone?
9. What properties are used to distinguish a sesamoid bone from a sutural bone?
10. Contrast the processes of ossification and calcification.

Level 3 Critical Thinking

1. A small child falls off a bicycle and breaks an arm. The bone is set correctly and heals well. After the cast is removed, an enlarged bony bump remains at the region of the fracture. After several months this enlargement disappears, and the arm is essentially normal in appearance. What happened during this healing process?
2. Most young children who break a bone in their upper or lower limbs experience a greenstick fracture. This type of fracture is quite rare in an adult. What is the reason for this difference?
3. As individuals age bones break more easily, often as the result of quite normal movements, such as twisting or getting up suddenly from a chair. Why are these types of fractures so common in elderly people? Activity of what type(s) of bone cells is implicated in this result? How might these conditions be improved?

6

The Skeletal System
Axial Division

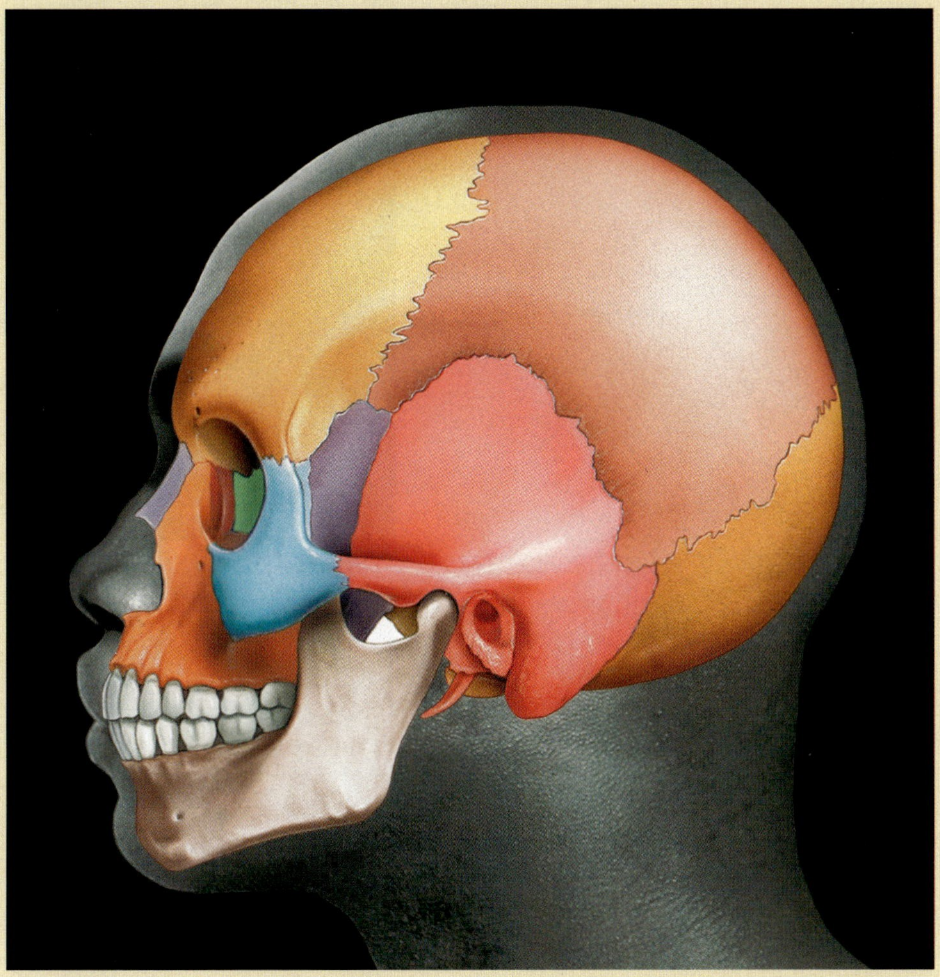

CHAPTER OBJECTIVES

1. Identify the bones of the axial skeleton and their functions.
2. Identify the bones of the skull and explain the significance of the markings on the individual bones.
3. Locate and describe the major cranial sutures.
4. Describe the structure of the nasal complex and the functions of the individual elements.
5. Describe the bones associated with the skull and discuss their functions.
6. Distinguish structural differences among the skulls of infants, children, and adults.
7. Describe the general structure of the vertebral column.
8. Identify and describe the various spinal curves and their functions.
9. Identify and describe the parts of a representative vertebra.
10. Identify the vertebral groups and describe the differences among them in structural and functional terms.
11. Describe the features and landmarks of a representative rib, and be able to differentiate between true ribs and false ribs.
12. Explain the significance of the articulations of the thoracic vertebrae, the ribs, and the sternum.

The basic features of the human skeleton have been shaped by evolution, but because no two people have exactly the same combination of age, diet, activity pattern, and hormone levels, the bones of each individual are unique. As discussed in Chapter 5, bones are continually remodeled and reshaped, and your skeleton changes throughout your lifetime. Examples include the proportional changes at puberty and the gradual osteoporosis of aging. This chapter provides other examples of the dynamic nature of the human skeleton, such as the changes in the shape of the vertebral column during the transition from crawling to walking.

The skeletal system is divided into *axial* and *appendicular divisions*; the axial division components are shown in yellow and blue in **Figure 6.1**. The skeletal system includes 206 separate bones and a number of associated

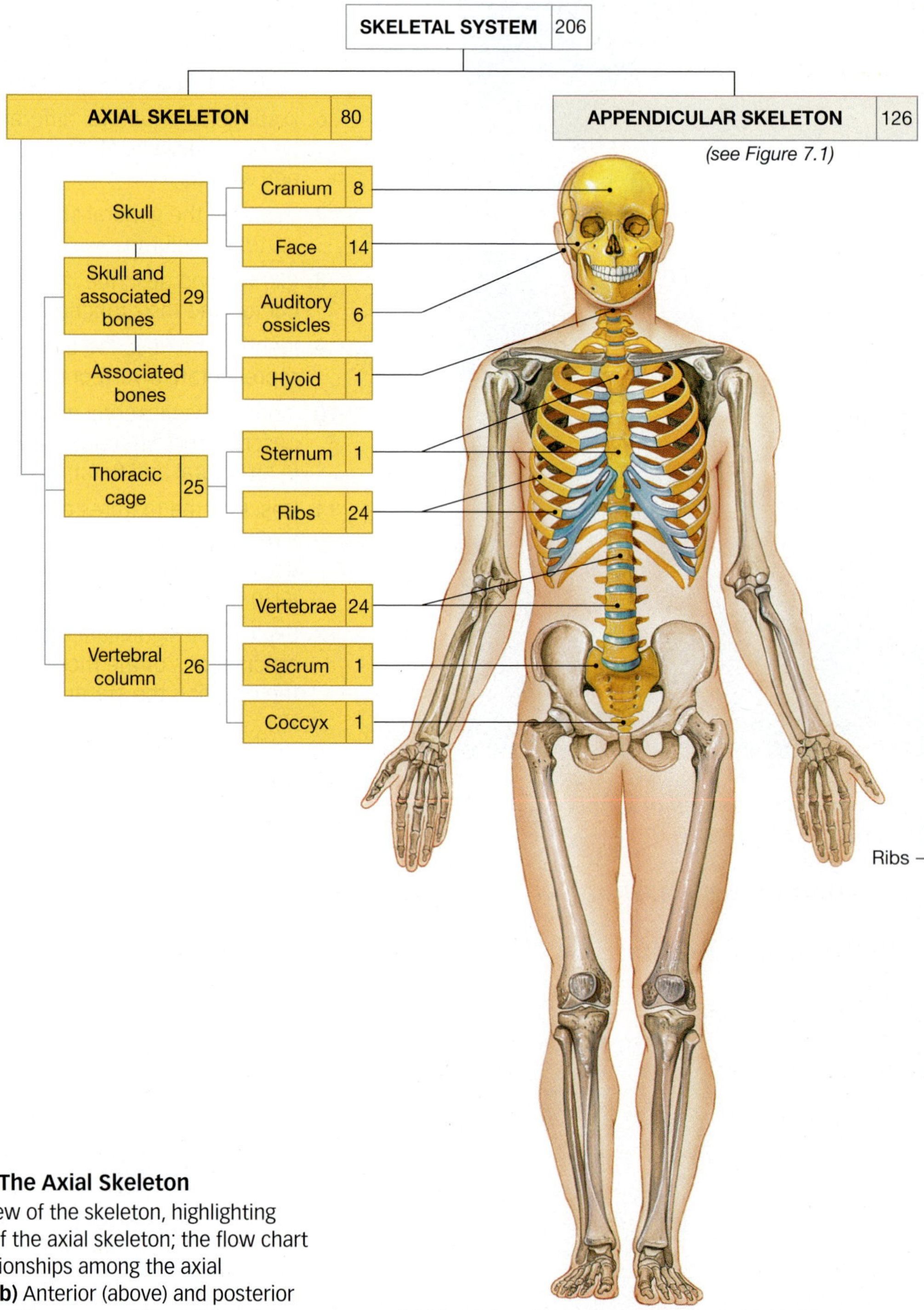

(a) Skeletal system, axial components highlighted

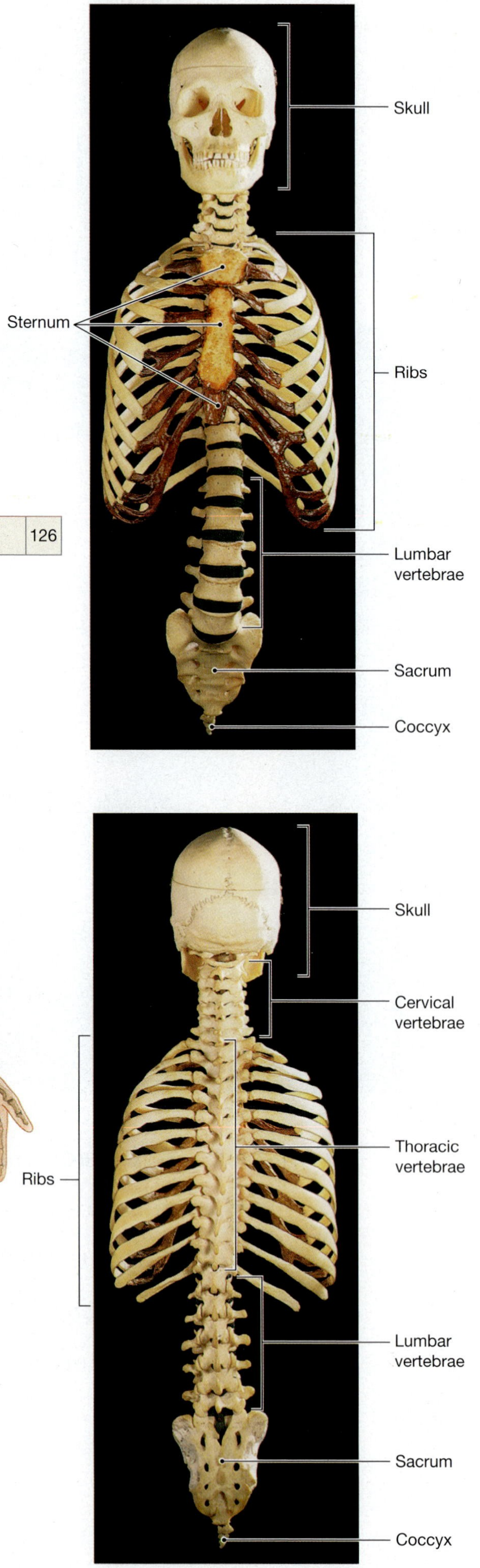

(b) Axial skeleton

Figure 6.1 The Axial Skeleton
(a) Anterior view of the skeleton, highlighting components of the axial skeleton; the flow chart indicates relationships among the axial components. **(b)** Anterior (above) and posterior (below) views of the bones of the axial skeleton.

cartilages. The **axial skeleton** consists of the bones of the skull, thorax, and vertebral column. These elements form the longitudinal axis of the body. There are 80 bones in the axial skeleton, roughly 40 percent of the bones in the human body. The axial components include

- the **skull** (22 bones),
- bones associated with the skull (6 auditory ossicles and 1 hyoid bone),
- the **vertebral column** (24 vertebrae, 1 sacrum, and 1 coccyx), and
- the **thoracic cage** (24 ribs and 1 sternum).

The axial skeleton functions as a framework that supports and protects organs in the ventral body cavities. It houses special sense organs for taste, smell, hearing, balance, and sight. Additionally, it provides an extensive surface area for the attachment of muscles that (1) adjust the positions of the head, neck, and trunk, (2) perform respiratory movements, and (3) stabilize or position structures of the appendicular skeleton. The joints of the axial skeleton permit limited movement, but they are very strong and often heavily reinforced with ligaments. Finally, some parts of the axial skeleton, including portions of the vertebrae, sternum, and ribs, contain red marrow for blood cell production, as do many of the long bones of the appendicular skeleton.

This chapter describes the structural anatomy of the axial skeleton, and we will begin with the skull. Before proceeding, you may find it helpful to review the directional references included in Tables 1.1 and 1.2 ∞ pp. 15, 16 and the terms introduced in Table 5.1. ∞ p. 128 The remaining 126 bones of the human skeleton constitute the **appendicular skeleton**. This division includes the bones of the limbs and the **pectoral** and **pelvic girdles** that attach the limbs to the trunk. The appendicular skeleton will be examined in Chapter 7.

The Skull and Associated Bones [Figures 6.2 to 6.7a]

The skull contains 22 bones: 8 form the **cranium**, or "*braincase*," and 14 are associated with the face (Figures 6.2 to 6.5).

The cranium surrounds and protects the brain. It consists of the *occipital*, *parietal*, *frontal*, *temporal*, *sphenoid*, and *ethmoid* bones. These cranial bones enclose the **cranial cavity**, a fluid-filled chamber that cushions and supports the brain. Blood vessels, nerves, and membranes that stabilize the position of the brain are attached to the inner surface of the cranium. Its outer surface provides an extensive area for the attachment of muscles that move the eyes, jaws, and head. A specialized joint between the occipital bone and the first spinal vertebra stabilizes the positions of the cranium and vertebral column while permitting a considerable range of head movements.

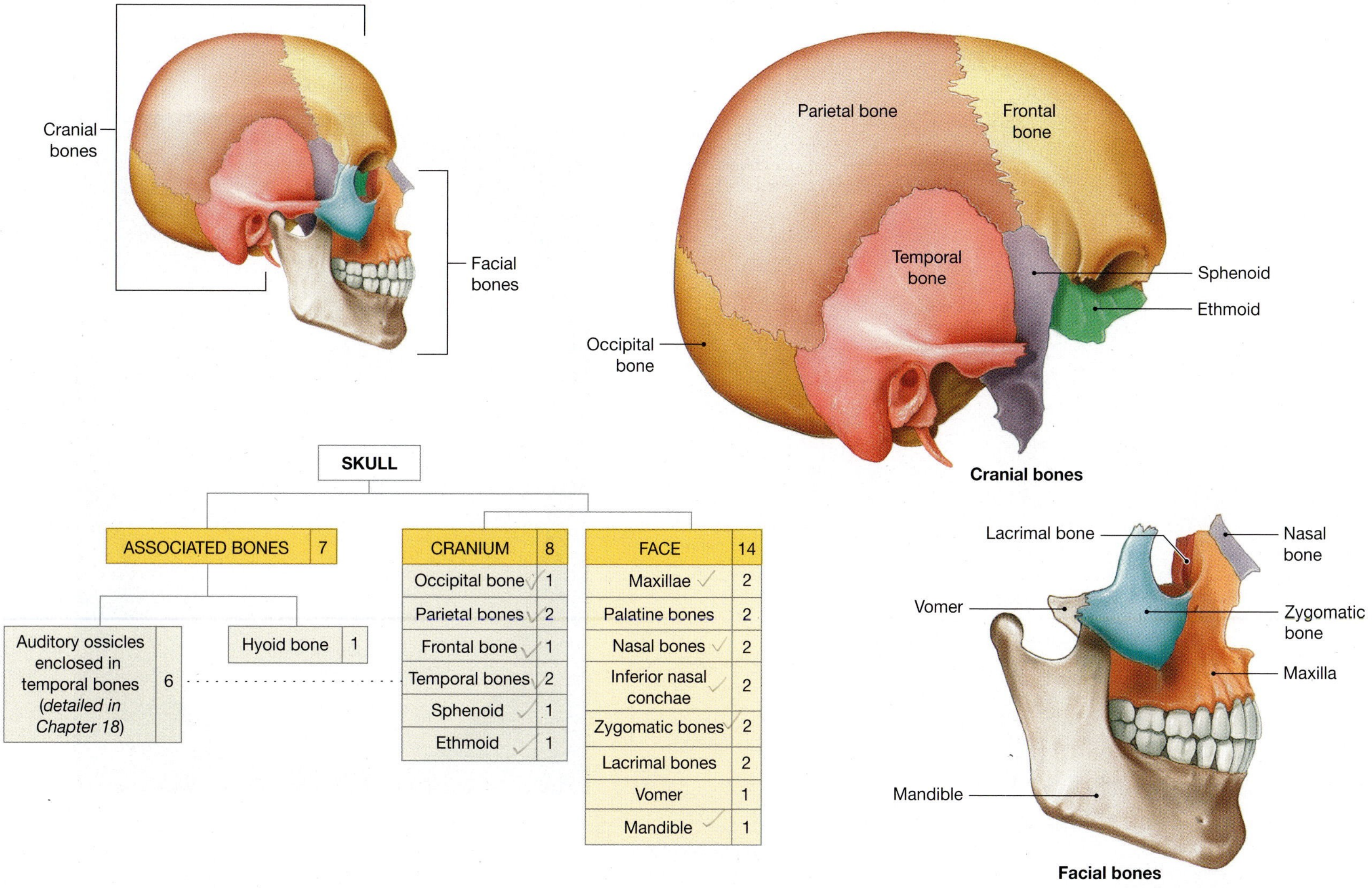

Figure 6.2 Cranial and Facial Subdivisions of the Skull
The skull can be divided into the cranial and the facial divisions. The palatine bones and the inferior nasal conchae of the facial division are not visible from this perspective. The seven associated bones are not shown.

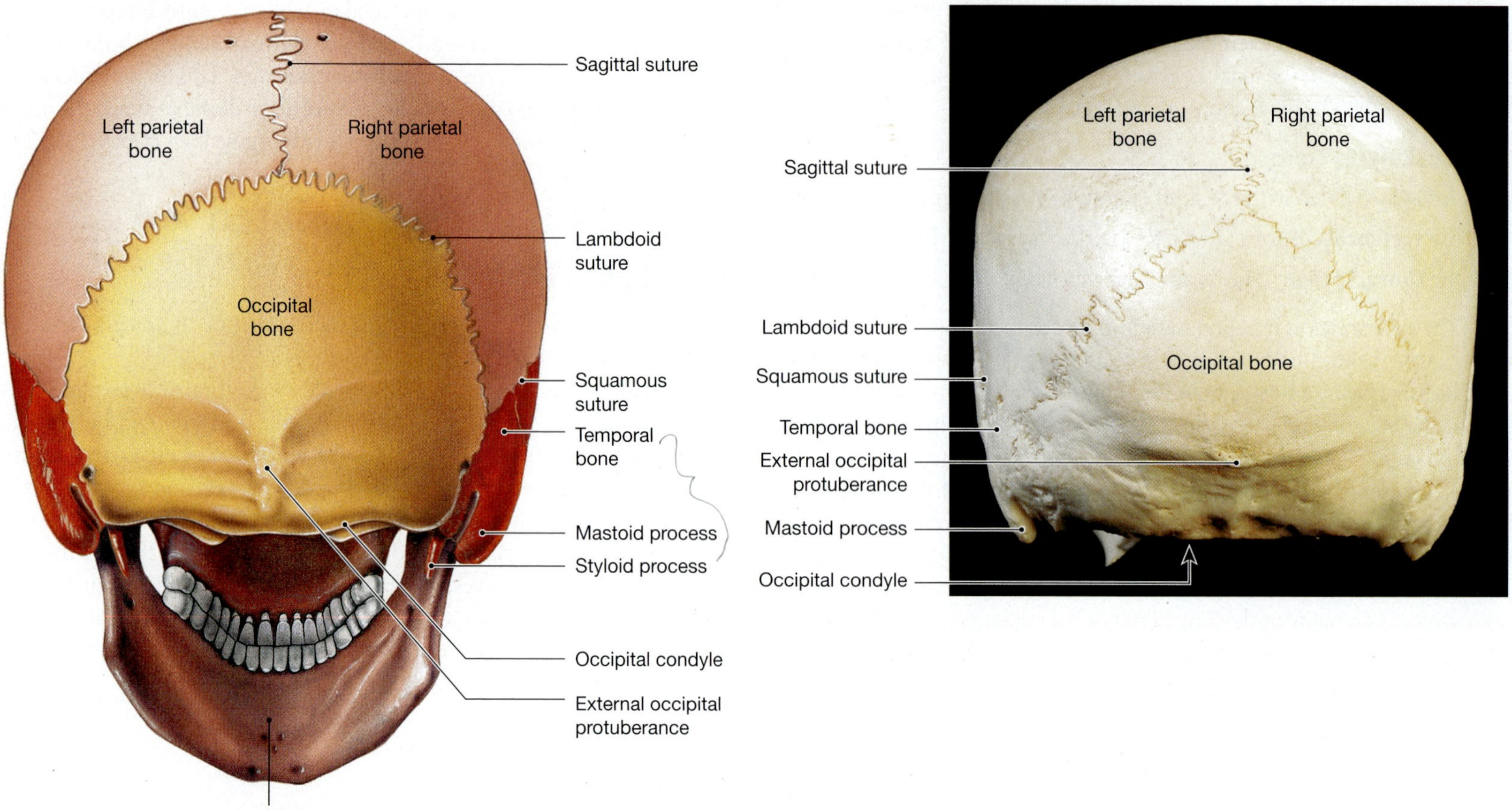

(a) Posterior view

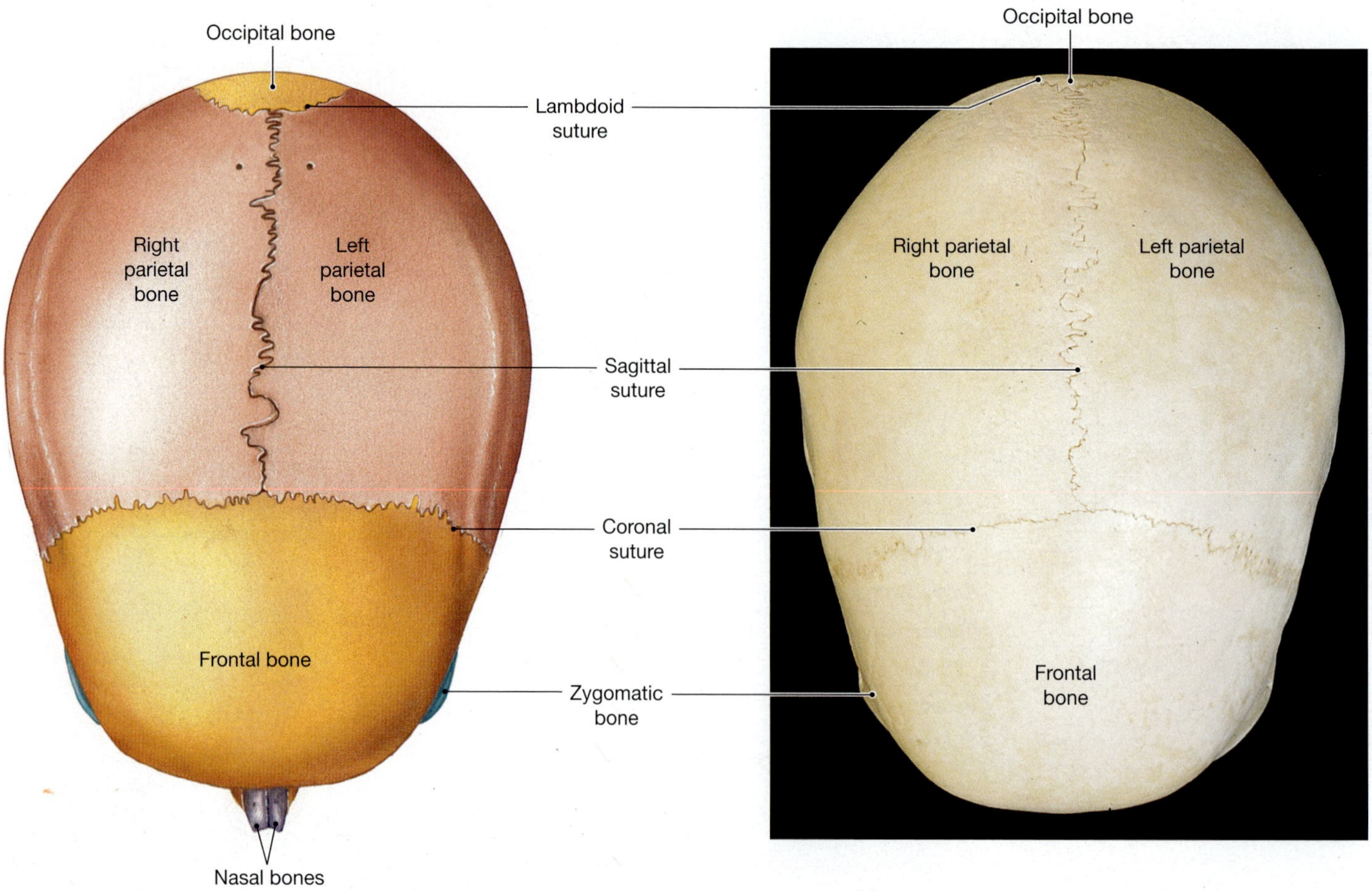

(b) Superior view

Figure 6.3 The Adult Skull
The bones in an adult skull are shown in **(a)** posterior view, **(b)** superior view, **(c)** lateral view, **(d)** anterior view, and **(e)** inferior view.

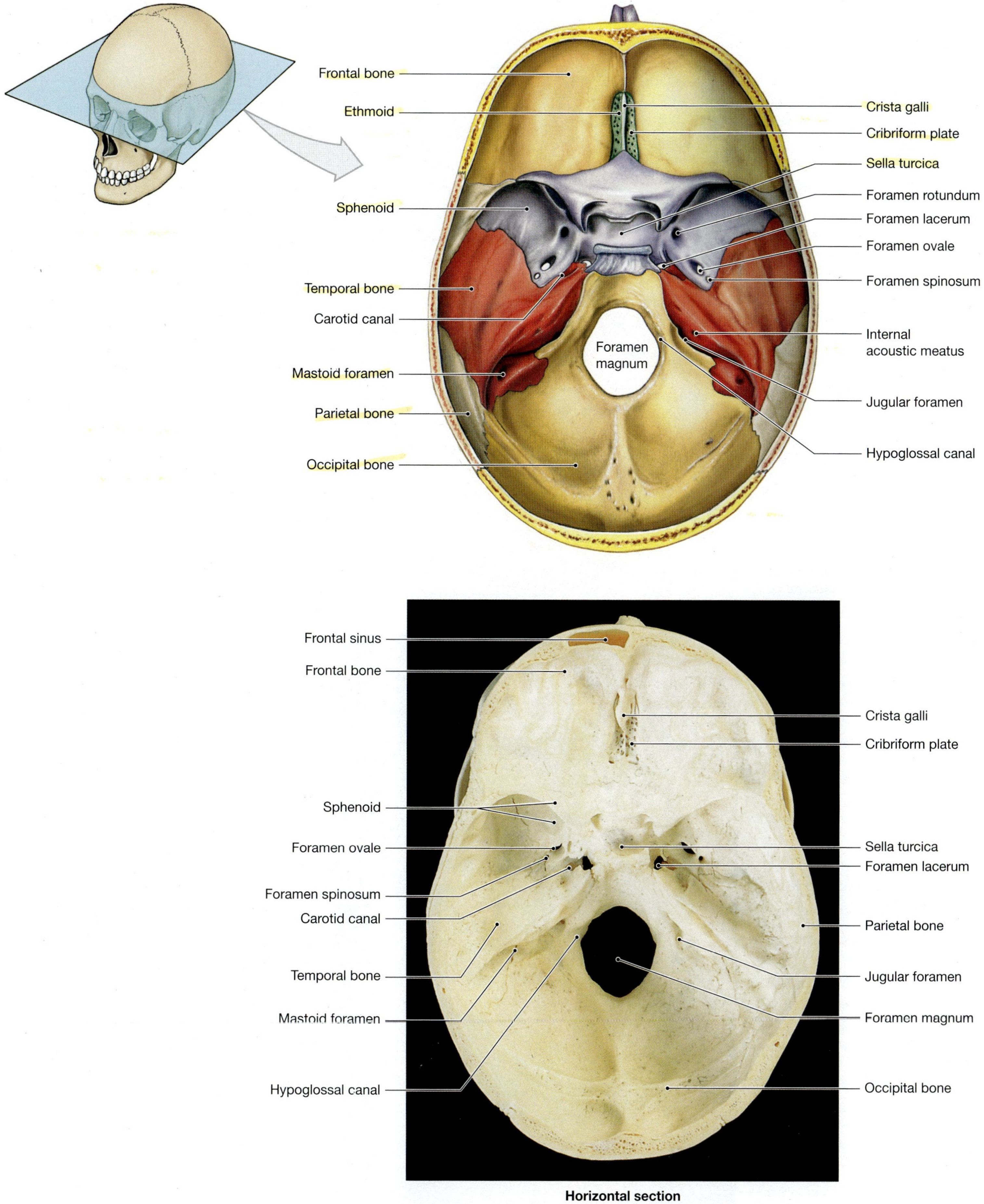

Figure 6.4 Sectional Anatomy of the Skull, Part I
Horizontal section: A superior view showing major landmarks in the floor of the cranial cavity.

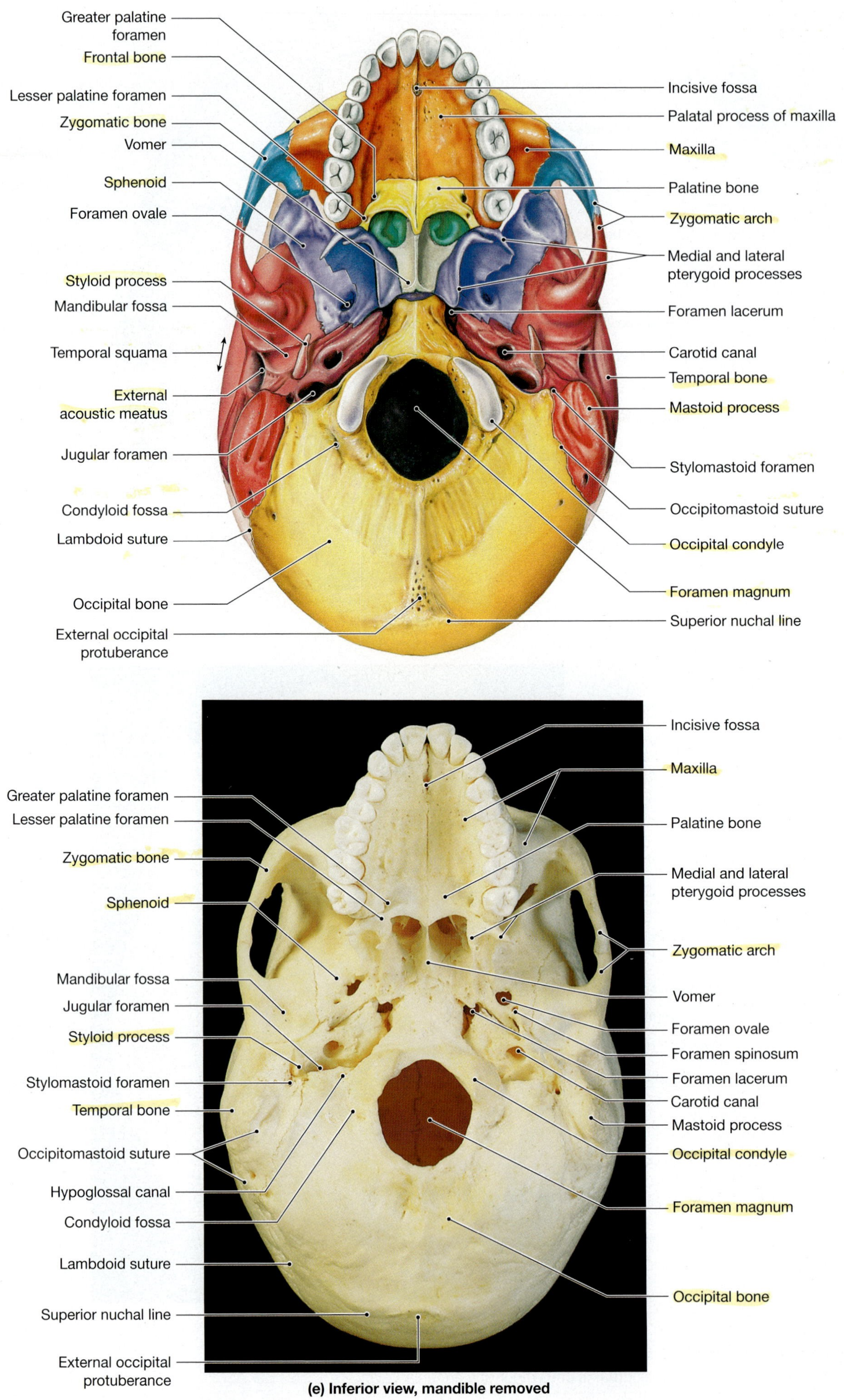

(e) Inferior view, mandible removed

Figure 6.3 ***(continued)***

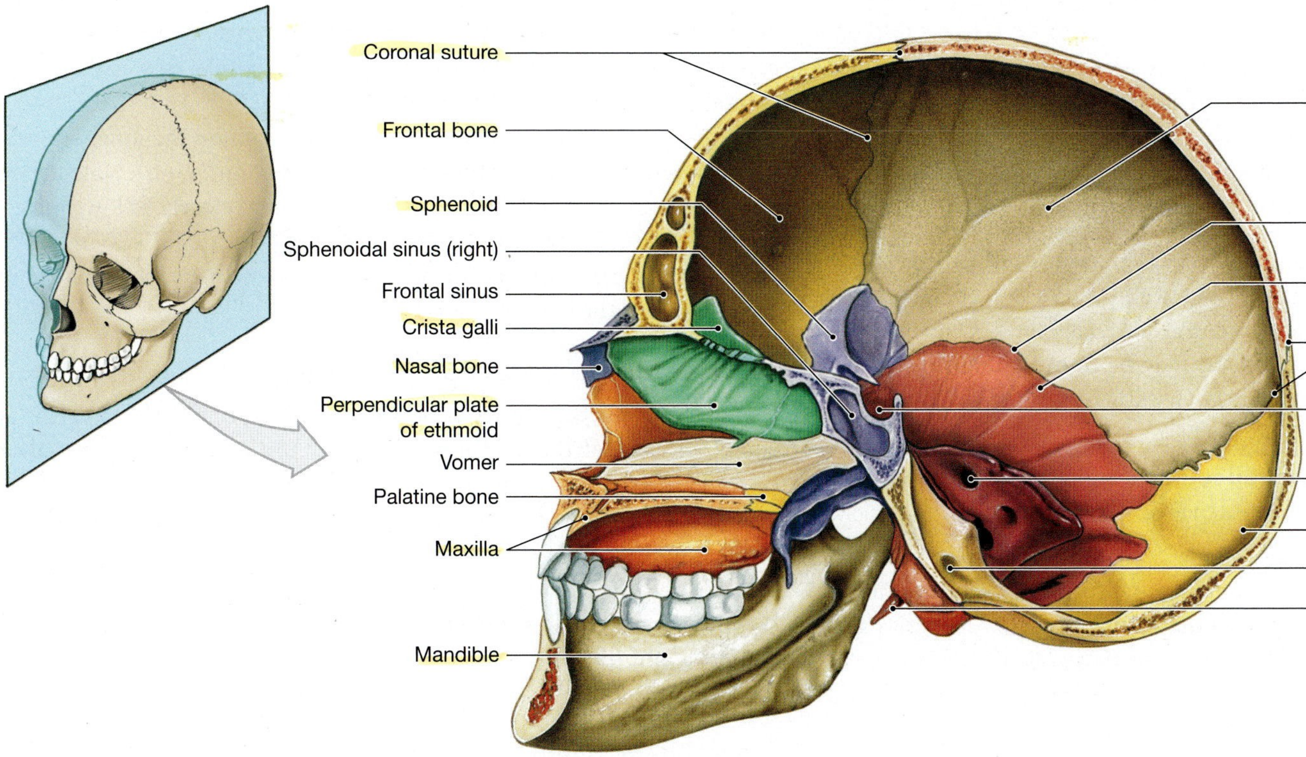

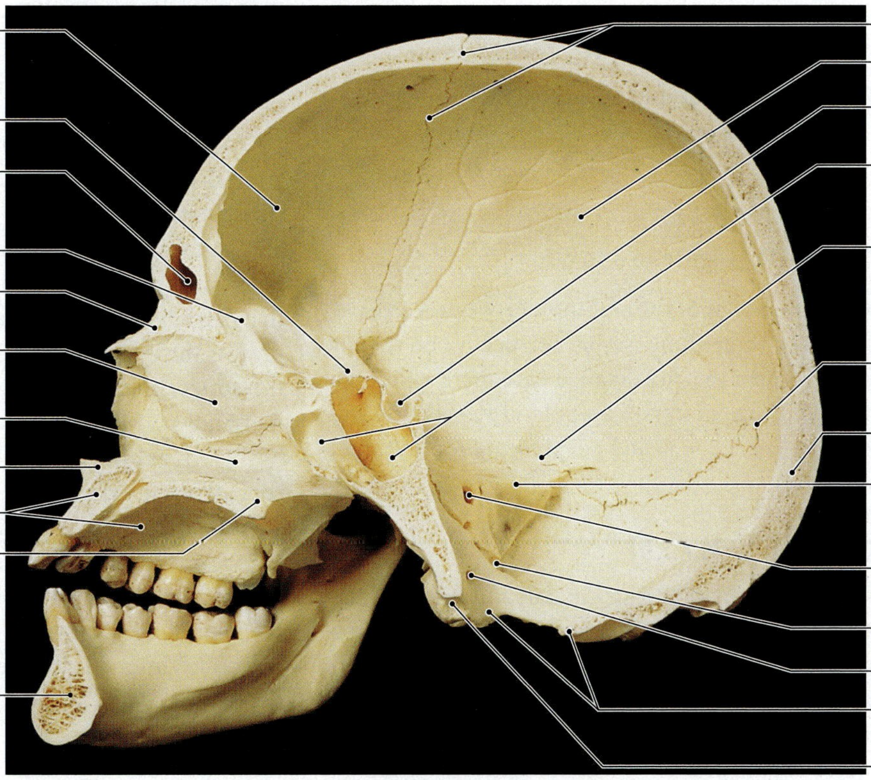

Sagittal section

Figure 6.5 Sectional Anatomy of the Skull, Part II
Sagittal section: A medial view of the right half of the skull. Because the bony nasal septum is intact, the right nasal cavity cannot be seen.

If the cranium is the house where the brain resides, the *facial complex* is the front porch. The **facial bones** protect and support the entrances to the digestive and respiratory tracts. The superficial facial bones—the *maxillae, palatine, nasal, zygomatic, lacrimal, vomer,* and *mandible* (Figure 6.2, p. 135)—provide areas for the attachment of muscles that control facial expressions and assist in the manipulation of food.

The boundaries between skull bones are immovable joints called **sutures**. At a suture, the bones are joined firmly together with dense fibrous connective tissue. Each of the sutures of the skull has a name, but you need to know only five major sutures at this time: the *lambdoid, sagittal, coronal, squamous,* and *frontonasal* sutures.

- **Lambdoid (lam-DOYD) suture.** The **lambdoid suture** arches across the posterior surface of the skull (Figure 6.3a, p. 136), separating the *occipital bone* from the *parietal bones.* One or more **sutural bones** (*Wormian bones*) may be found along this suture; they range from a bone the size of a grain of sand to one as large as a quarter. ∞ p. 128
- **Sagittal suture.** The **sagittal suture** begins at the superior midline of the lambdoid suture and extends anteriorly between the parietal bones to the coronal suture (Figure 6.3b).
- **Coronal suture.** Anteriorly, the sagittal suture ends when it intersects the coronal suture. The **coronal suture** crosses the superior surface of the skull, separating the anterior *frontal bone* from the more posterior parietal bones (Figure 6.3b). The occipital, parietal, and frontal bones form the **calvaria** (kal-VAR-ē-a), also called the *cranial vault* or "skullcap."
- **Squamous suture.** A **squamous suture** on each side of the skull marks the boundary between the *temporal bone* and the parietal bone of that side. The squamous sutures can be seen in Figure 6.3a, where they intersect the lambdoid suture. The path of the squamous suture on the right side of the skull can be seen in Figure 6.3c.
- **Frontonasal suture.** The **frontonasal suture** is the boundary between the superior aspects of the two nasal bones and the frontal bone (Figure 6.3c,d).

Bones of the Cranium [Figures 6.3 to 6.5]

We will now consider each of the bones of the cranium. As we proceed, use the figures provided to develop a three-dimensional perspective on the individual bones. Ridges and foramina that are detailed here mark either the attachment of muscles or the passage of nerves and blood vessels that will be studied in later chapters. Figures 6.3, 6.4, and 6.5 present the adult skull in superficial and sectional views.

Occipital Bone [Figures 6.3a–c,e/6.6a,b]

The **occipital bone** contributes to the posterior, lateral, and inferior surfaces of the cranium (Figure 6.3a–c,e). The inferior surface of the occipital bone contains a large circular opening, the **foramen magnum** (Figure 6.3e), which connects the cranial cavity with the spinal cavity enclosed by the vertebral column. At the adjacent **occipital condyles**, the skull articulates with the first cervical vertebra. The posterior, external surface of the occipital bone (Figure 6.6a) bears a number of prominent ridges. The **external occipital crest** extends posteriorly from the foramen magnum, ending in a small midline bump called the **external occipital protuberance**. Two horizontal ridges intersect the crest, the **inferior** and **superior nuchal** (NOO-kal) **lines**. These lines mark the attachment of muscles and ligaments that stabilize the articulation between the first vertebra and the skull at the occipital condyles and balance the weight of the head over the vertebrae of the neck. The occipital bone forms part of the wall of the large **jugular foramen** (Figure 6.3e). The *internal jugular vein* passes through this foramen to drain venous blood from the brain. The **hypoglossal canals** begin at the lateral base of each occipital condyle, just superior to the condyles (Figure 6.6a). The *hypoglossal nerves,* cranial nerves that control the tongue muscles, pass through these canals.

Inside the skull, the hypoglossal canals begin on the inner surface of the occipital bone near the foramen magnum (Figure 6.6b). Note the concave internal surface of the occipital bone, which closely follows the contours of the brain. The grooves follow the path of major vessels, and the ridges mark the attachment site of membranes (the *meninges*) that stabilize the position of the brain.

Parietal Bones [Figures 6.3b–c/6.5/6.6c]

The paired **parietal** (pa-RĪ-e-tal) **bones** contribute to the superior and lateral surfaces of the cranium and form the major part of the calvaria (Figure 6.3b,c). The external surface of each parietal bone (Figure 6.6c) bears a pair of low ridges, the **superior** and **inferior temporal lines**. These lines mark the attachment of the *temporalis muscle,* a large muscle that closes the mouth. The smooth parietal surface superior to these lines is called the **parietal eminence**. The internal surfaces of the parietal bones retain the impressions of cranial veins and arteries that branch inside the cranium (Figure 6.5).

Frontal Bone [Figures 6.3b–d/6.5/6.7]

The **frontal bone** forms the forehead and roof of the orbits (Figure 6.3b–d). During development, the bones of the cranium form through the fusion of separate centers of ossification, and at birth the fusions have not been completed. At this time there are two frontal bones that articulate along the **frontal** (*metopic*) **suture**. Although the suture usually disappears by age 8 with the fusion of the bones, the frontal bone of an adult often retains traces of the suture line.

The frontal suture, or what remains of it, runs down the center of the **frontal eminence** of the frontal bone (Figure 6.7a). The convex anterior surface of the frontal part is called the *squamous part,* or forehead. The lateral surfaces contain the anterior continuations of the superior temporal lines. The frontal part of the frontal bone ends at the **supra-orbital margins** that mark the superior limits of the orbits, the bony recesses that support and protect the eyeballs. Above the supra-orbital margins are thickened ridges, the **superciliary arches**, which support the eyebrows. The center of each margin is perforated by a single **supra-orbital foramen** or **notch**.

The **orbital part** of the frontal bone forms the roughly horizontal roof of each orbit. The inferior surface of the orbital part is relatively smooth, but it contains small openings for blood vessels and nerves heading to or from structures in the orbit. This is often called the *orbital surface* of the frontal bone. The shallow **lacrimal fossa** marks the location of the *lacrimal* (tear) *gland* that lubricates the surface of the eye (Figure 6.7b).

The internal surface of the frontal bone roughly conforms to the shape of the anterior portion of the brain (Figure 6.7c). The inner surface of the frontal part bears a prominent **frontal crest** that marks the attachment of membranes that, among their other functions, prevent contact between the delicate brain tissues and the bones of the cranium.

The **frontal sinuses** (Figures 6.5 and 6.7b) are variable in size and in time of appearance. They usually develop after age 6, but some people never develop them at all. The frontal sinuses and other sinuses will be described in a later section.

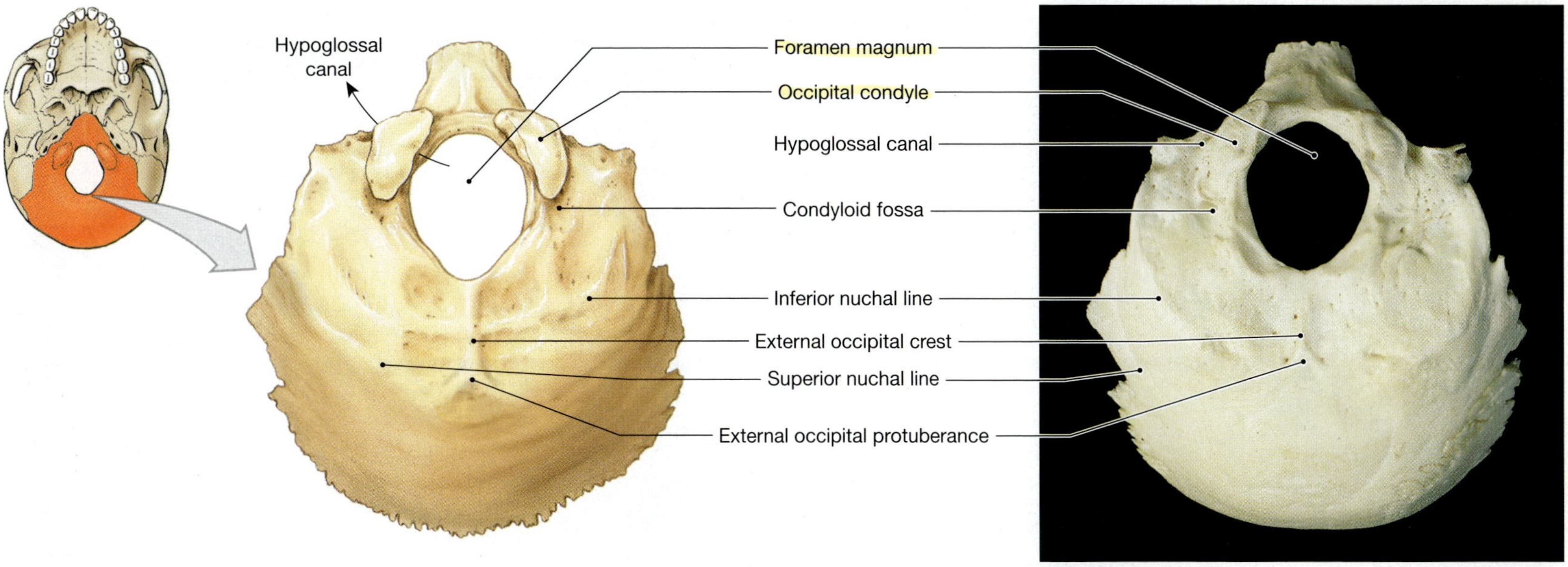

(a) Occipital bone, inferior (external) view

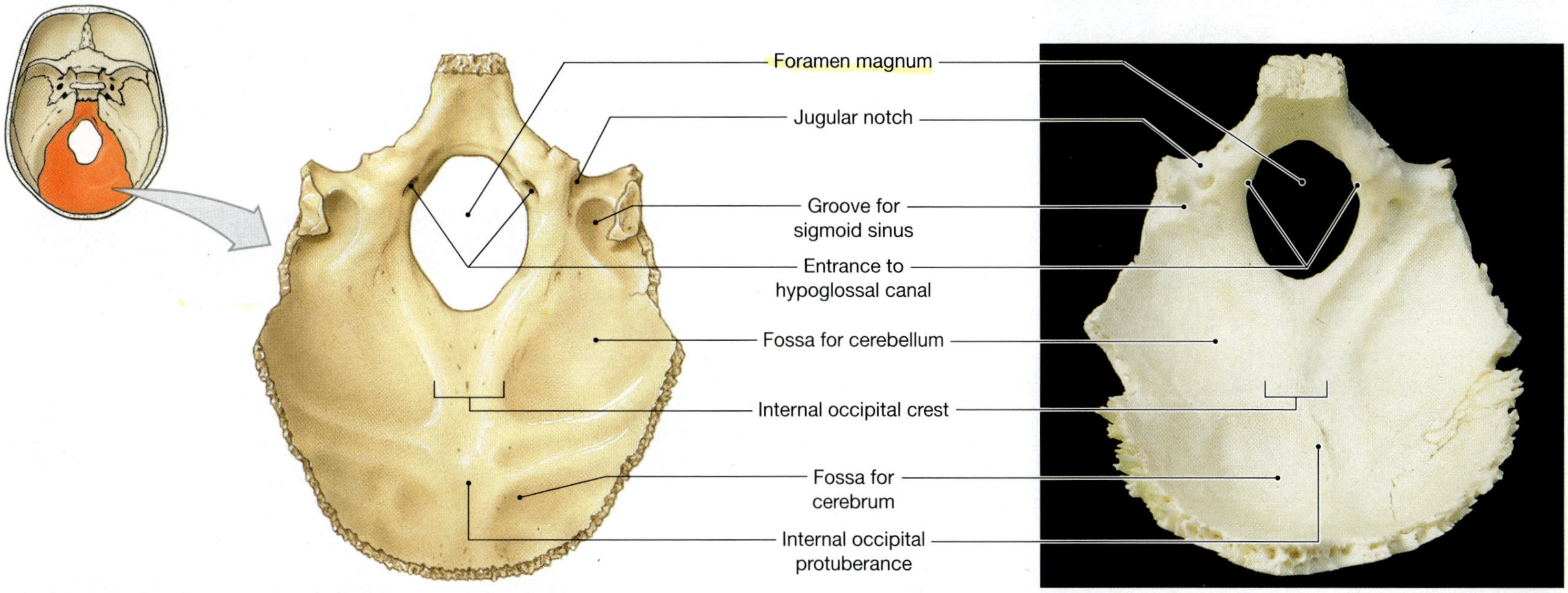

(b) Occipital bone, superior (internal) view

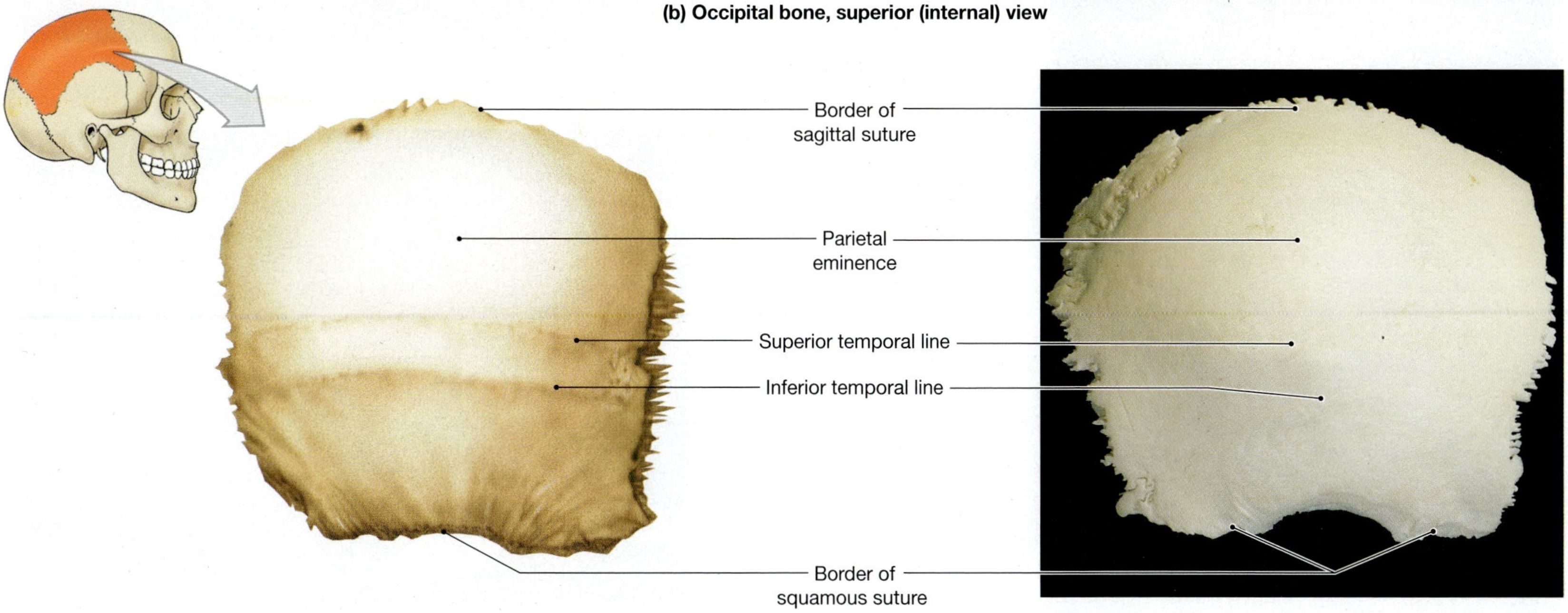

(c) Parietal bone, external surface

Figure 6.6 The Occipital and Parietal Bones
The occipital bone is shown in **(a)** inferior (external) view and **(b)** superior (internal) view. **(c)** A lateral view of the right parietal bone; for a medial view, *see Figure 6.5*.

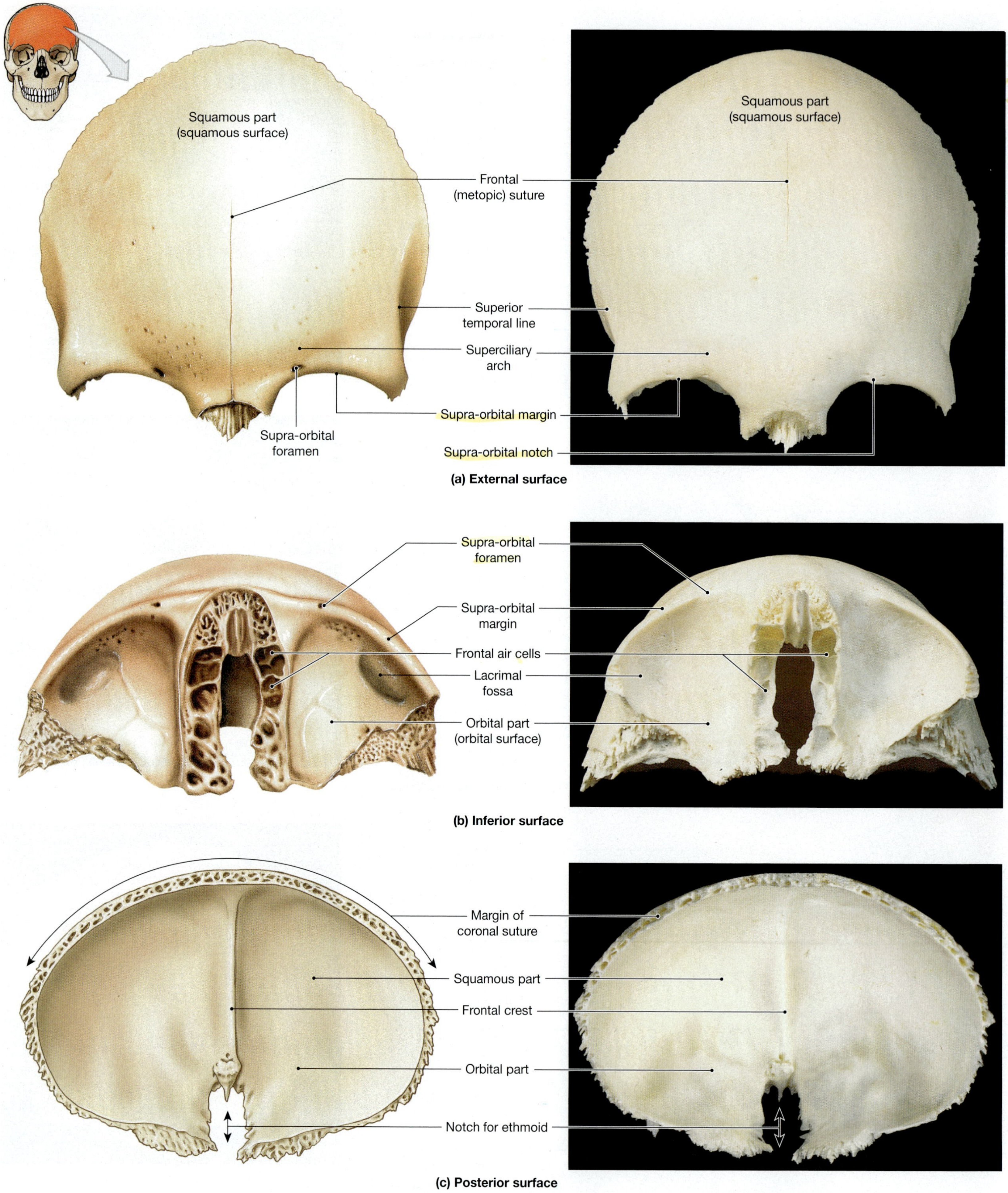

Figure 6.7 The Frontal Bone
The frontal bone is shown in **(a)** anterior view, **(b)** inferior view, and **(c)** posterior (internal) view.

Temporal Bones [Figures 6.3c–e/6.8]

The paired **temporal bones** contribute to the lateral and inferior walls of the cranium; contribute to the *zygomatic arches* of the cheek; form the only articulations with the mandible; and protect the sense organs of the inner ear. In addition, the convex surfaces inferior to each parietal bone form an extensive area for the attachment of muscles that close the jaws and move the head (Figure 6.3c, p. 137). The temporal bones articulate with the zygomatic, parietal, and occipital bones and with the sphenoid and mandible. Each temporal bone has squamous, tympanic, and petrous parts.

The **squamous part** of the temporal bone is the lateral surface bordering the squamous suture (Figure 6.8a,d). The convex external surface of the squamous part is the *squama;* the concave internal surface, whose curvature parallels the surface of the brain, is the *cerebral surface.* The inferior margin of the squamous part is formed by the prominent **zygomatic process**. The zygomatic process curves laterally and anteriorly to meet the **temporal process** of the *zygomatic bone.* Together these processes form the **zygomatic arch**, or cheekbone. Inferior to the base of the zygomatic process, the temporal bone articulates with the mandible. A depression called the **mandibular fossa** and an elevated **articular tubercle** mark this site (Figure 6.8a,c).

Immediately posterior and lateral to the mandibular fossa is the **tympanic part** of the temporal bone (Figure 6.8b). This region surrounds the entrance to the **external acoustic meatus**, or *external auditory canal.* In life, this passageway ends at the delicate **tympanic membrane**, or eardrum, but the tympanic membrane disintegrates during the preparation of a dried skull.

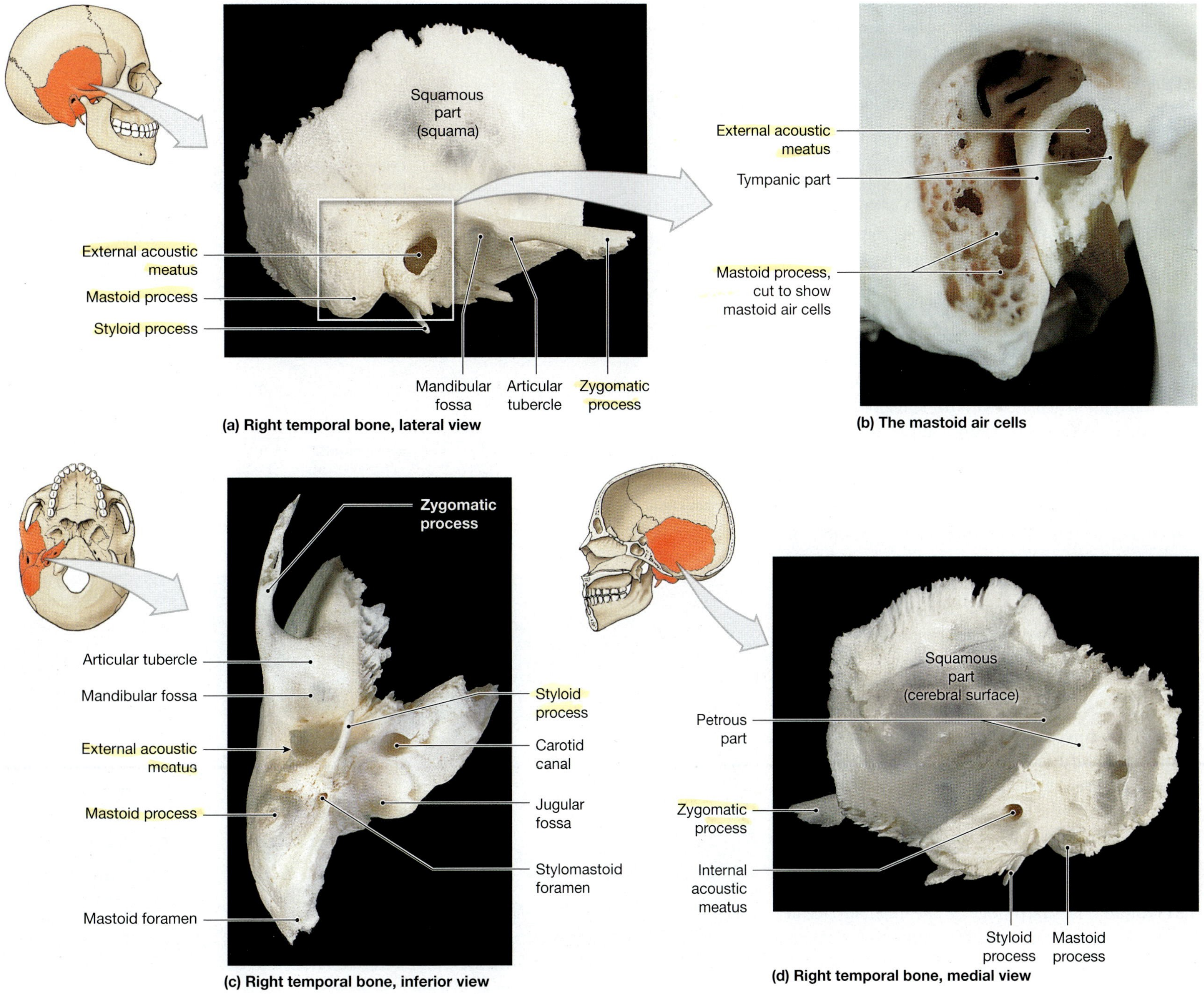

Figure 6.8 The Temporal Bone
Major anatomical landmarks are shown on a right temporal bone: **(a)** lateral view, **(b)** cutaway view of the mastoid air cells, **(c)** inferior view, **(d)** medial view.

The most massive portion of the temporal bone is the **petrous part** (*petrous*, stone). The petrous part of the temporal bone surrounds and protects the sense organs of hearing and balance. On the lateral surface, the bulge just posterior and inferior to the external acoustic meatus is the **mastoid process** (Figure 6.8a–c). This process provides an attachment site for muscles that rotate or extend the head. Numerous interconnected mastoid sinuses, termed *mastoid air cells*, are contained within the mastoid process (Figure 6.8b). Infections in the respiratory tract may spread to these air cells, and such an infection is called *mastoiditis*.

Several other landmarks on the petrous part of the temporal bone can be seen on its inferior surface (Figure 6.8c). Near the base of the mastoid process, the **mastoid foramen** penetrates the temporal bone. Blood vessels travel through this passageway to reach the membranes surrounding the brain. Ligaments that support the hyoid bone attach to the sharp **styloid process** (STĪ-loyd; *stylos*, pillar), as do muscles of the tongue, pharynx, and larynx. The **stylomastoid foramen** lies posterior to the base of the styloid process. The *facial nerve* passes through this foramen to control the facial muscles. Medially, the **jugular fossa** is bounded by the temporal and occipital bones (Figure 6.3e, p. 139). Anterior and slightly medial to the jugular foramen is the entrance to the **carotid canal**. The *internal carotid artery*, a major artery that supplies blood to the brain, penetrates the skull through this passageway. Anterior and medial to the carotid canal, a jagged slit, the **foramen lacerum** (LA-se-rum; *lacerare*, to tear), extends between the occipital and temporal bones. In life, this space contains hyaline cartilage and small arteries supplying the inner surface of the cranium.

Lateral and anterior to the carotid foramen, the temporal bone articulates with the sphenoid. A small canal begins at that articulation and ends inside the mass of the temporal bone (Figure 6.8c). This is the *musculotubal canal*, which surrounds the **auditory tube**, an air-filled passageway. The auditory tube, also known as the *Eustachian* (ū-STĀ-kē-an) *tube*, or *pharyngotympanic tube*, begins at the pharynx and ends at the **tympanic cavity**, a chamber inside the temporal bone. The tympanic cavity, or *middle ear*, contains the **auditory ossicles**, or ear bones. These tiny bones transfer sound vibrations from the eardrum toward the receptor complex in the inner ear, which provides the sense of hearing.

The petrous part dominates the medial surface of the temporal bone (Figure 6.8d). The **internal acoustic meatus** carries blood vessels and nerves to the inner ear and the facial nerve to the stylomastoid foramen. The entire medial surface of the temporal bone is marked by grooves that indicate the location of blood vessels passing along the inner surface of the cranium. The sharp ridge on the inner surface of the petrous part marks the attachment of a membrane that helps stabilize the position of the brain.

Sphenoid [Figures 6.3c–e/6.4/6.9]

The **sphenoid**, or *sphenoidal bone*, articulates with every other cranial bone and extends from one side to the other across the floor of the cranium. Although it is relatively large, much of the sphenoid is hidden by more superficial bones. It acts as a bridge uniting the cranial and facial bones; it articulates with the frontal, occipital, parietal, ethmoid, and temporal bones of the cranium, and the palatine bones, zygomatic bones, maxillae, and vomer of the facial complex (Figure 6.3c–e, pp. 137–139). The sphenoid also acts as a brace, strengthening the sides of the skull. The **body** forms the central portion of the bone.

The general shape of the sphenoid has been compared to a giant bat with its wings extended. The wings can be seen most clearly on the superior surface (Figures 6.4 and 6.9a). A prominent central depression between the wings cradles the pituitary gland below the brain. This recess is called the **hypophysial** (hī-pō-FIZ-ē-al) **fossa**, and the bony enclosure is

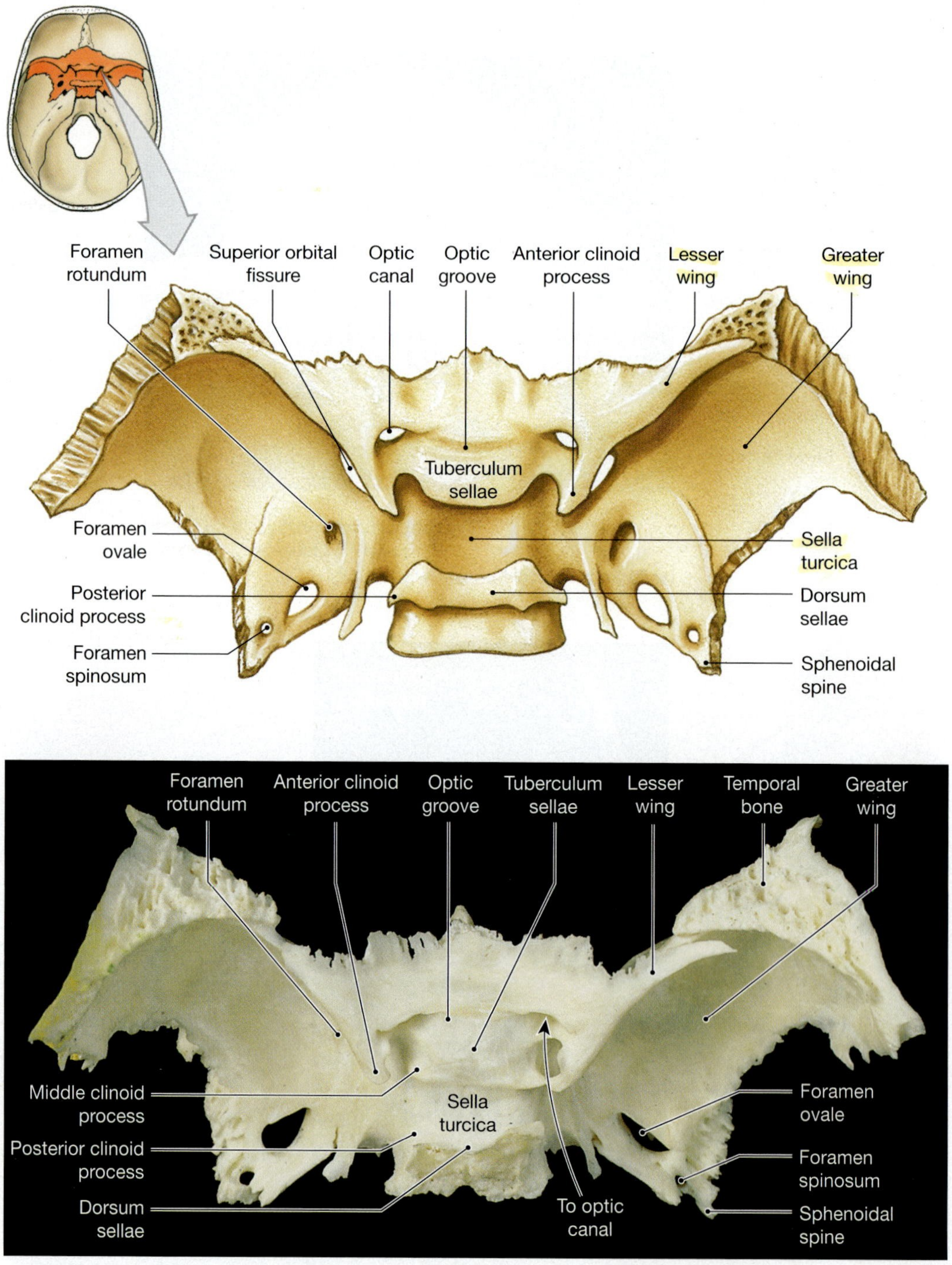

(a) Superior surface

Figure 6.9 The Sphenoid
Views of the sphenoid showing major anatomical landmarks on the **(a)** superior surface and **(b)** anterior surface.

called the **sella turcica** (TUR-si-ka) because it supposedly resembles a "Turkish saddle." A rider facing forward could grasp the **anterior clinoid** (KLĪ-noyd) **processes** on either side. The anterior clinoid processes are posterior projections of the **lesser wings** of the sphenoid. The **tuberculum sellae** forms the anterior border of the sella turcica; the **dorsum sellae** forms the posterior border. A **posterior clinoid process** extends laterally on either side of the dorsum sellae. The lesser wings are triangular in shape, with the superior surfaces supporting the frontal lobe of the brain. The inferior surfaces form part of the orbit and the superior part of the **superior orbital fissure**, which serves as a passageway for blood vessels and cranial nerves of the eye.

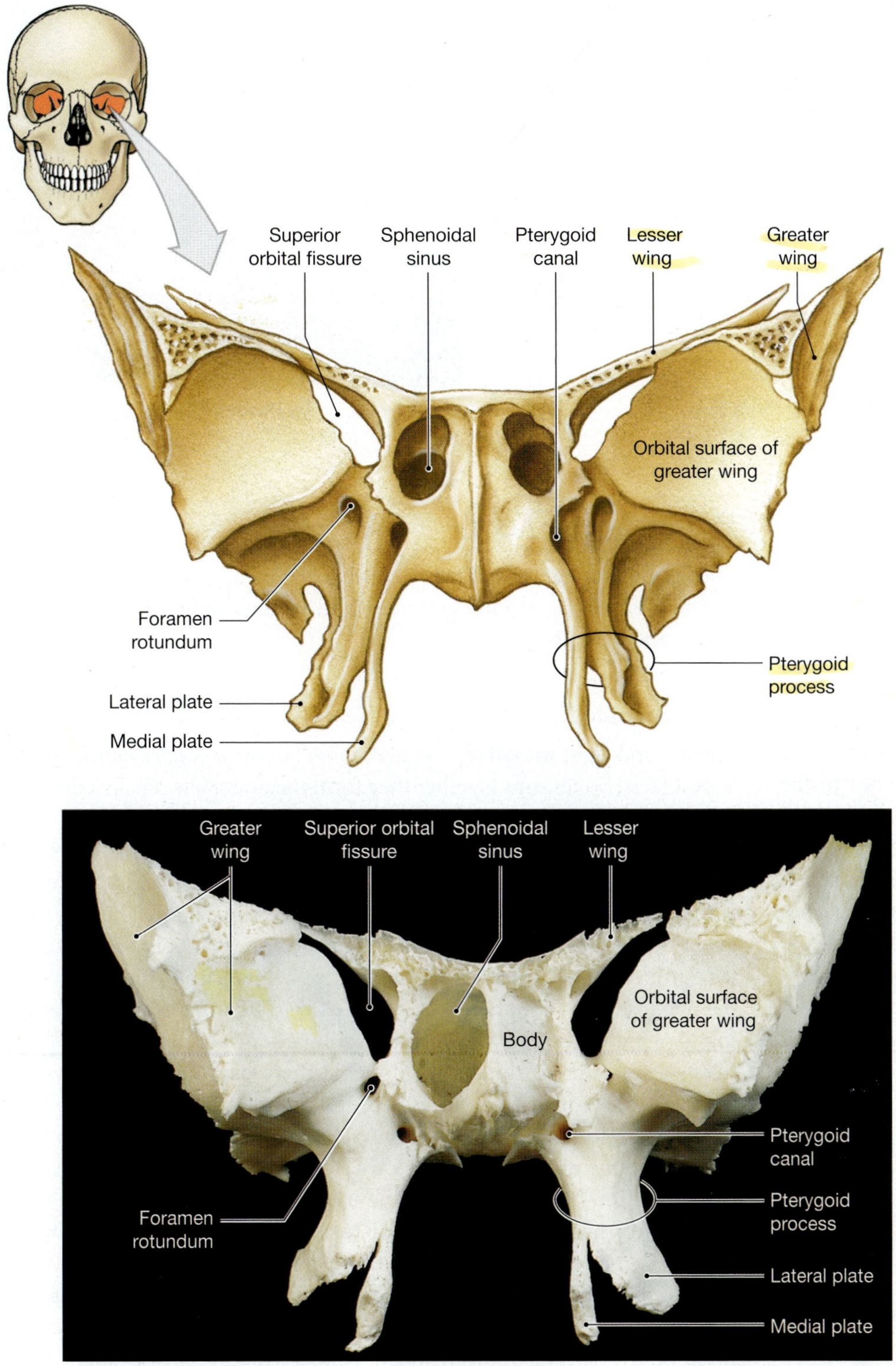

(b) Anterior surface

Figure 6.9 ***(continued)***

The transverse groove that crosses to the front of the saddle, above the level of the seat, is the **optic groove**. At either end of this groove is an **optic canal**. The *optic nerves* that carry visual information from the eyes to the brain travel through these canals. On either side of the sella turcica, the **foramen rotundum**, the **foramen ovale** (ō-VAH-lē), and the **foramen spinosum** penetrate the **greater wings** of the sphenoid. These passages carry blood vessels and cranial nerves to structures of the orbit, face, and jaws. Posterior and lateral to these foramina the greater wings end at a sharp **sphenoidal spine**. The superior orbital fissures and the left and right foramen rotundum can also be seen in an anterior view (Figure 6.9b).

The **pterygoid processes** (TER-i-goyd; *pterygion*, wing) of the sphenoid are vertical projections that begin at the boundary between the greater and lesser wings. Each process forms a pair of *plates* that are important sites for the attachment of muscles that move the lower jaw and soft palate. At the base of each pterygoid process, the **pterygoid canal** provides a route for a small nerve and an artery that supply the soft palate and adjacent structures.

Ethmoid [Figures 6.3d/6.4/6.5/6.10]

The **ethmoid**, or *ethmoidal bone*, is an irregularly shaped bone that forms part of the orbital wall (Figure 6.3d, p. 139), the anteromedial floor of the cranium (Figure 6.4, p. 140), the roof of the nasal cavity, and part of the nasal septum (Figure 6.5, p. 141). The ethmoid has three parts: the *cribriform plate*, the *ethmoidal labyrinth*, and the *perpendicular plate* (Figure 6.10).

The superior surface of the ethmoid (Figure 6.10a) contains the **cribriform plate**, an area perforated by the *cribriform foramina*. These openings allow passage of the branches of the *olfactory nerves*, which provide the sense of smell. A prominent ridge, the **crista galli** (*crista*, crest + *gallus*, chicken; "cock's comb") separates the right and left sides of the cribriform plate. The *falx cerebri*, a membrane that stabilizes the position of the brain, attaches to this bony ridge.

The ethmoidal labyrinth, dominated by the **superior nasal conchae** (KON-kē; singular, *concha*; "a snail shell") and the **middle nasal conchae**, is best viewed from the anterior and posterior surfaces of the ethmoid (Figure 6.10b,c). The **ethmoidal labyrinth** is an interconnected network of ethmoidal air cells. These air cells are continuous with the air cells found in the inferior portion of the frontal bone. The ethmoidal air cells also open into the nasal cavity on each side. Mucous secretions from these air cells flush the surfaces of the nasal cavities.

The nasal conchae are thin scrolls of bone that project into the nasal cavity on either side of the perpendicular plate. The projecting conchae break up the airflow, creating swirls and eddies. This mechanism slows air movement, but provides additional time for warming, humidification, and dust removal before the air reaches more delicate portions of the respiratory tract.

The **perpendicular plate** forms part of the *nasal septum*, a partition that also includes the vomer and a piece of hyaline cartilage. Olfactory receptors are located in the epithelium covering the inferior surfaces of the cribriform plate, the medial surfaces of the superior nasal conchae, and the superior portion of the perpendicular plate.

Figure 6.10 The Ethmoid
Views of the ethmoid showing major anatomical landmarks on the **(a)** superior surface, **(b)** anterior surface, and **(c)** posterior surface.

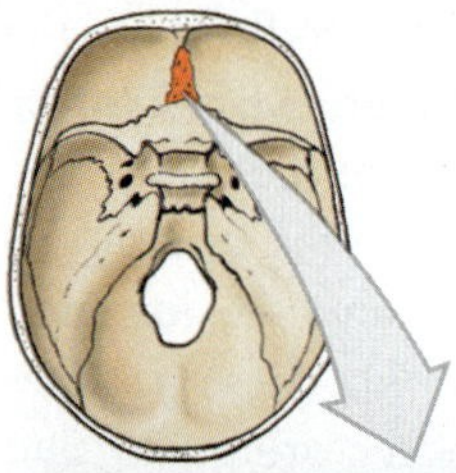

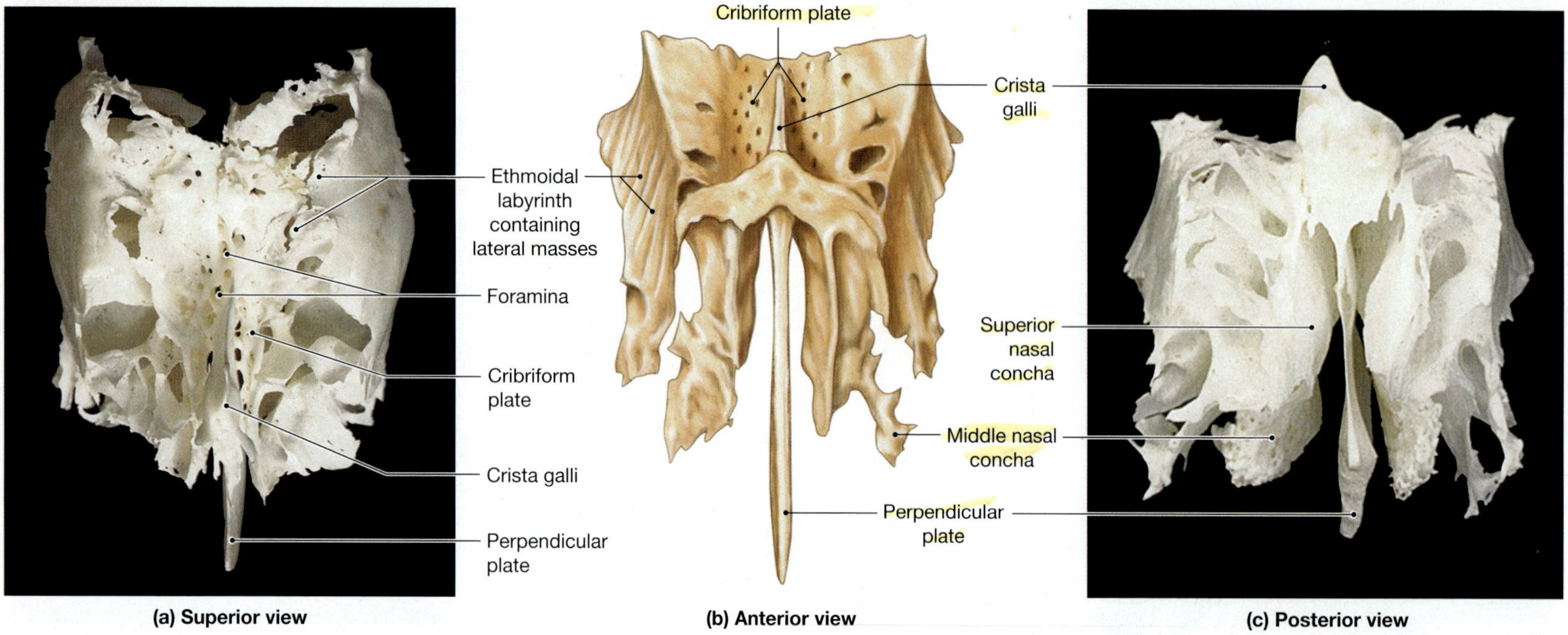

The Cranial Fossae [Figure 6.11]

The contours of the cranium closely follow the shape of the brain. Proceeding from anterior to posterior, the floor of the cranium is not horizontal; it descends in two steps (Figure 6.11a). Viewed from the superior surface (Figure 6.11b), the cranial floor at each level forms a curving depression known as a **cranial fossa**. The **anterior cranial fossa** is formed by the frontal bone, the ethmoid, and the lesser wings of the sphenoid. The anterior cranial fossa cradles the frontal lobes of the cerebral hemispheres. The **middle cranial fossa** extends from the "step" at the lesser wings to the petrous portion of the temporal bone. The sphenoid, temporal, and parietal bones form this fossa, which cradles the temporal lobes of the cerebral hemispheres, the *diencephalon*, and the anterior portion of the brain stem (*mesencephalon*). The more inferior **posterior cranial fossa** extends from the petrous parts of the temporal bones to the posterior surface of the skull. The posterior fossa is formed primarily by the occipital bone, with contributions from the temporal and parietal bones. The posterior cranial fossa supports the occipital lobes of the cerebral hemispheres, the cerebellum, and the posterior brain stem (*pons* and *medulla oblongata*).

CONCEPT CHECK

1. The internal jugular veins are important blood vessels of the head. Through what opening do these blood vessels pass?
2. What bone contains the depression called the sella turcica? What is located in the depression?
3. Which of the five senses would be affected if the cribriform plate of the ethmoid failed to form?
4. Identify the bones of the cranium.

See blue "Answers" tab at back of book.

Bones of the Face

The facial bones are the paired maxillae, palatine bones, nasal bones, inferior nasal conchae, zygomatic bones, and lacrimal bones, and the single vomer and mandible.

The Maxillae [Figures 6.3d,e/6.12a,b,c/6.15]

The left and right **maxillae** (singular, *maxilla*), or *maxillary bones*, are the largest facial bones, and together they form the upper jaw. The maxillae articulate with all other facial bones except the mandible (Figure 6.3d, p. 138). The **orbital surface** (Figure 6.12a) provides protection for the eye and other structures in the orbit. The **frontal process** of each maxilla articulates with the frontal bone of the cranium and with a nasal bone. The oral margins of the maxillae form the **alveolar processes** that contain the upper teeth. An elongated **inferior orbital fissure** within each orbit lies between the maxillae and the sphenoid (Figure 6.3d). The **infra-orbital foramen** that penetrates the orbital rim marks the path of a major sensory nerve from the face. In the orbit, it runs along the **infra-orbital groove** (shown in Figure 6.15) before passing through the inferior orbital fissure and the foramen rotundum to reach the brain stem.

The large **maxillary sinuses** are evident in medial view and in horizontal section (Figure 6.12b,c). These are the largest sinuses in the skull; they lighten the portion of the maxillae superior to the teeth and produce mucous secretions that flush the inferior surfaces of the nasal cavities. The sectional view also shows the extent of the **palatine processes** that form most of the bony roof, or *hard palate*, of the mouth. The **incisive fossa** on the inferior midline of the palatal process marks the openings of the *incisive canals* (Figure 6.3e), which contain small arteries and nerves.

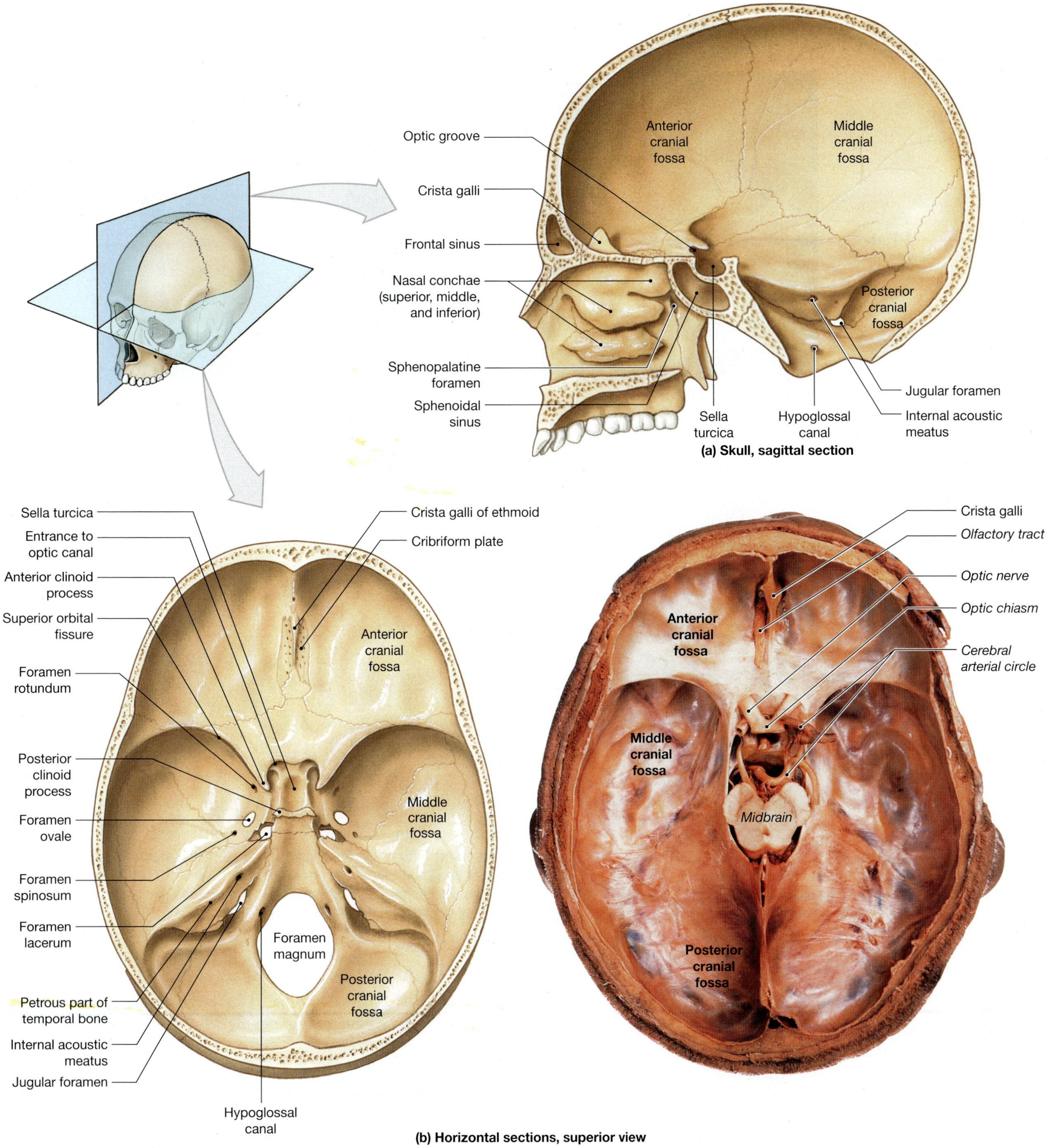

Figure 6.11 The Cranial Fossae
Cranial fossae are curved depressions in the floor of the cranium. **(a)** A sagittal section through the skull, showing the relative positions of the cranial fossae. **(b)** Horizontal sections, superior view. The superior portion of the brain has been removed, but portions of the brain stem and associated nerves and blood vessels remain.

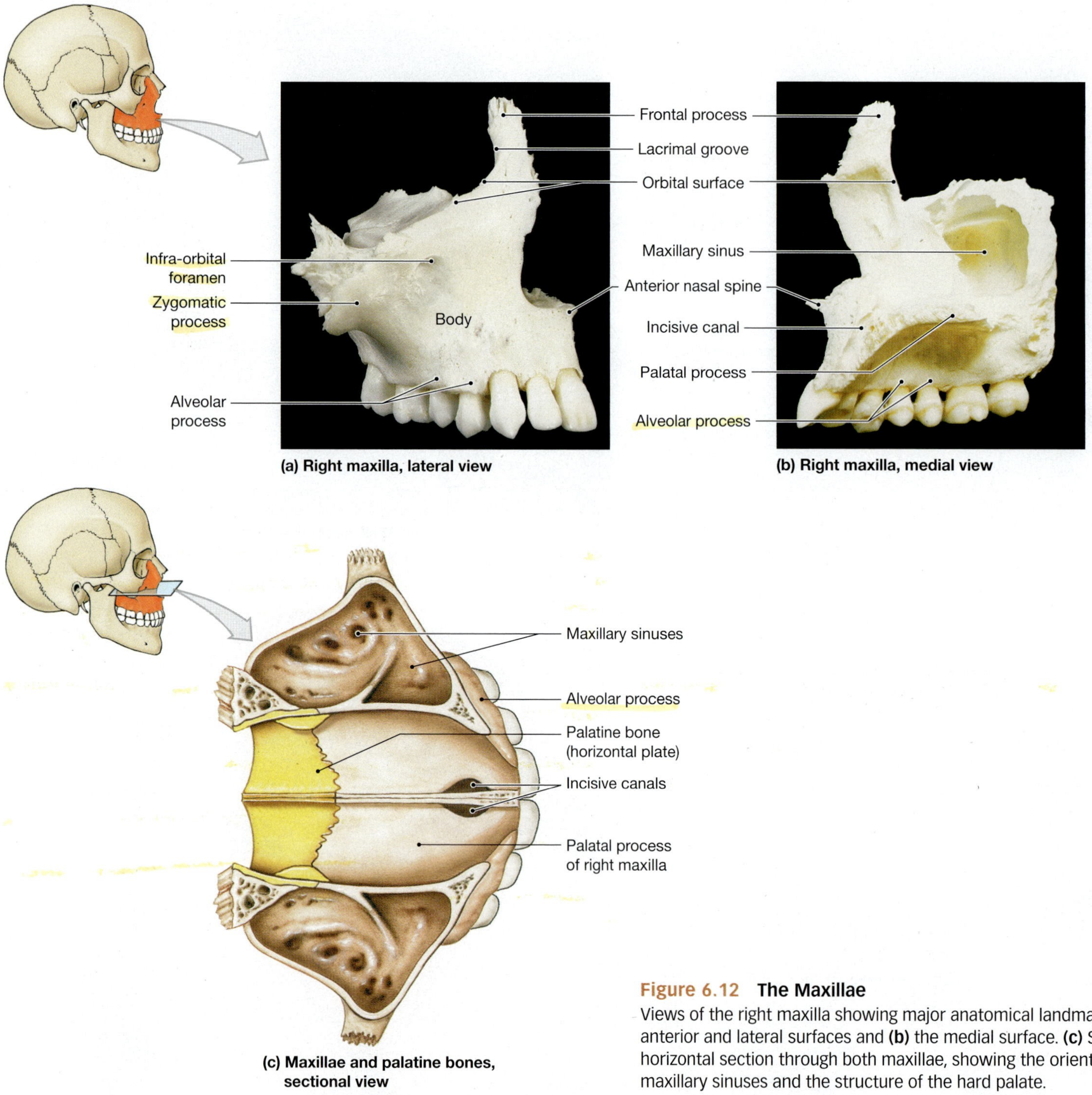

Figure 6.12 The Maxillae
Views of the right maxilla showing major anatomical landmarks on **(a)** the anterior and lateral surfaces and **(b)** the medial surface. **(c)** Superior view of a horizontal section through both maxillae, showing the orientation of the maxillary sinuses and the structure of the hard palate.

The Palatine Bones [Figures 6.3e/6.12c/6.13/6.15]

The **palatine bones** are small, L-shaped bones (Figure 6.13). The *horizontal plates* articulate with the maxillae to form the posterior portions of the hard palate (Figure 6.12c). On its inferior surface, a *greater palatine groove* lies between the palatine bone and the maxilla on each side (Figure 6.3e, p. 139). One or more *lesser palatine foramina* are usually present in the inferior surface as well. The *nasal crest*, a ridge that forms where the left and right palatine bones interconnect, marks the articulation with the vomer. The vertical portion of the "L" is formed by the *perpendicular plate* of the palatine bone. This portion of the palatine bone articulates with the maxillae, sphenoid, and ethmoid, and with the inferior nasal concha. The medial surface of the perpendicular plate has two ridges: (1) the *conchal crest*, marking the articulation with the inferior nasal concha, and (2) the *ethmoidal crest*, marking the articulation with the middle nasal concha of the ethmoid. The *orbital process*, based on the perpendicular plate, forms a small portion of the posterior floor of the orbit (Figure 6.15).

The Nasal Bones [Figures 6.3c,d/6.15]

The paired **nasal bones** articulate with the frontal bone at the midline of the face at the *frontonasal suture* (Figure 6.3c,d). Cartilages attached to the inferior margins of the nasal bones support the flexible portion of the nose, which extends to the **external nares** (NA-rēz), or nasal openings. The lateral edge of each nasal bone articulates with the frontal process of a maxilla (Figures 6.3c and 6.15).

The Inferior Nasal Conchae [Figures 6.3d/6.16]

The **inferior nasal conchae** are paired scroll-like bones that resemble the superior and middle conchae of the ethmoid. One inferior concha is located

Figure 6.13 The Palatine Bones
Views of the palatine bones, showing major anatomical landmarks on **(a)** the anterior surfaces of the palatine bones, **(b)** the medial surface of the right palatine bone, and **(c)** the lateral surface of the right palatine bone.

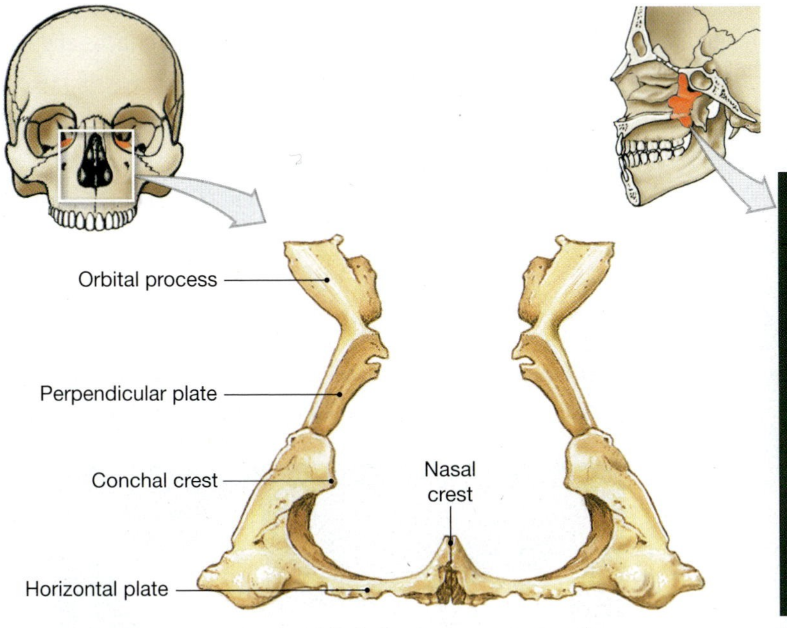

(a) Palatine bones, anterior view

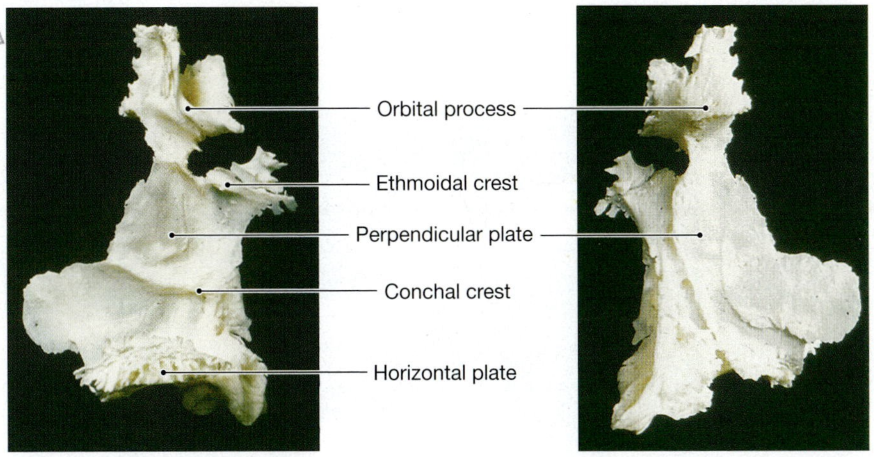

(b) Palatine bone, medial view

(c) Palatine bone, lateral view

on each side of the nasal septum, attached to the lateral wall of the nasal cavity (**Figures 6.3d**, p. 138, and **6.16**). They perform the same functions as the conchae of the ethmoid.

The Zygomatic Bones [Figures 6.3c,d/6.15]

As noted earlier, the temporal process of the **zygomatic bone** articulates with the zygomatic process of the temporal bone to form the zygomatic arch (**Figure 6.3c,d**). A **zygomaticofacial foramen** on the anterior surface of each zygomatic bone carries a sensory nerve innervating the cheek. The zygomatic bone also forms the lateral rim of the orbit (**Figure 6.15**) and contributes to the inferior orbital wall.

The Lacrimal Bones [Figures 6.3c,d/6.15]

The paired **lacrimal bones** (*lacrima*, tear) are the smallest bones of the skull. The lacrimal bone is situated in the medial portion of each orbit, where it articulates with the frontal bone, maxilla, and ethmoid (**Figures 6.3c,d** and **6.15**). A shallow depression, the **lacrimal groove**, or *lacrimal sulcus*, leads to a narrow passageway, the **nasolacrimal canal**, formed by the lacrimal bone and the maxilla. This canal encloses the tear duct as it passes toward the nasal cavity.

The Vomer [Figures 6.3d,e/6.5]

The **vomer** forms the inferior portion of the nasal septum (**Figure 6.5**, p. 141). It is based on the floor of the nasal cavity and articulates with both the maxillae and palatine bones along the midline. The vertical portion of the vomer is thin. Its curving superior surface articulates with the sphenoid and the perpendicular plate of the ethmoid, forming a bony **nasal septum** (*septum*, wall) that separates the right and left nasal cavities (**Figure 6.3d,e**). Anteriorly, the vomer supports a cartilaginous extension of the nasal septum that continues into the fleshy portion of the nose and separates the external nares.

The Mandible [Figures 6.3c,d/6.14]

The **mandible** forms the entire lower jaw (**Figures 6.3c,d**, pp. 137–138, and **6.14**). This bone can be subdivided into the horizontal **body** and the ascending **rami of the mandible** (singular, *ramus*; "branch"). The teeth are supported by the mandibular body. Each ramus meets the body at the **angle of the mandible.** The **condylar processes** extend to the smooth articular surface of the *head* of the mandible. The head articulates with the mandibular fossae of the temporal bone at the *temporomandibular joint (TMJ)*. This joint is quite mobile, as evidenced by jaw movements during chewing or talking. The disadvantage of such mobility is that the jaw can easily be dislocated by forceful movement of the mandible anteriorly or laterally.

At the **coronoid** (kor-Ō-noyd) **processes,** the *temporalis muscle* inserts onto the mandible. This is one of the most forceful muscles involved in closing the mouth. Anteriorly, the **mental foramina** (*mentalis*, chin) penetrate the body on each side of the chin. Nerves pass through these foramina, carrying sensory information from the lips and chin back to the brain. The **mandibular notch** is the depression that lies between the condylar and coronoid processes.

The **alveolar part** of the mandible is a thickened area that contains the alveoli and the roots of the teeth (**Figure 6.14b**). A **mylohyoid line** lies on the medial aspect of the body of the mandible. It marks the origin of the *mylohyoid muscle* that supports the floor of the mouth and tongue. The *submandibular salivary gland* nestles in the **submandibular fossa,** a depression inferior to the mylohyoid line. Near the posterior, superior end of the mylohyoid line, a prominent **mandibular foramen** leads into the **mandibular canal**. This is a passageway for blood vessels and nerves that service the lower teeth. The nerve that uses this passage carries sensory information from the teeth and gums; dentists typically anesthetize this nerve before working on the lower teeth.

The Orbital and Nasal Complexes

Several of the facial bones articulate with cranial bones to form the *orbital complex* surrounding each eye and the *nasal complex* that surrounds the nasal cavities.

The Orbital Complex [Figure 6.15]

The **orbits** are the bony recesses that enclose and protect the eyes. In addition to the eye, each orbit also contains a lacrimal gland, adipose tissue, muscles that move the eye, blood vessels, and nerves. Seven bones fit together to create the **orbital complex** that forms each orbit (**Figure 6.15**). The frontal bone forms the roof, and the maxilla forms most of the orbital floor. Proceeding from medial to lateral, the orbital surface and the first portion of the wall are contributed by the maxilla, the lacrimal bone, and the

Figure 6.14 The Mandible
Views of the mandible showing major anatomical landmarks on **(a)** the superior and lateral surfaces and **(b)** the medial surface of the right half of the mandible.

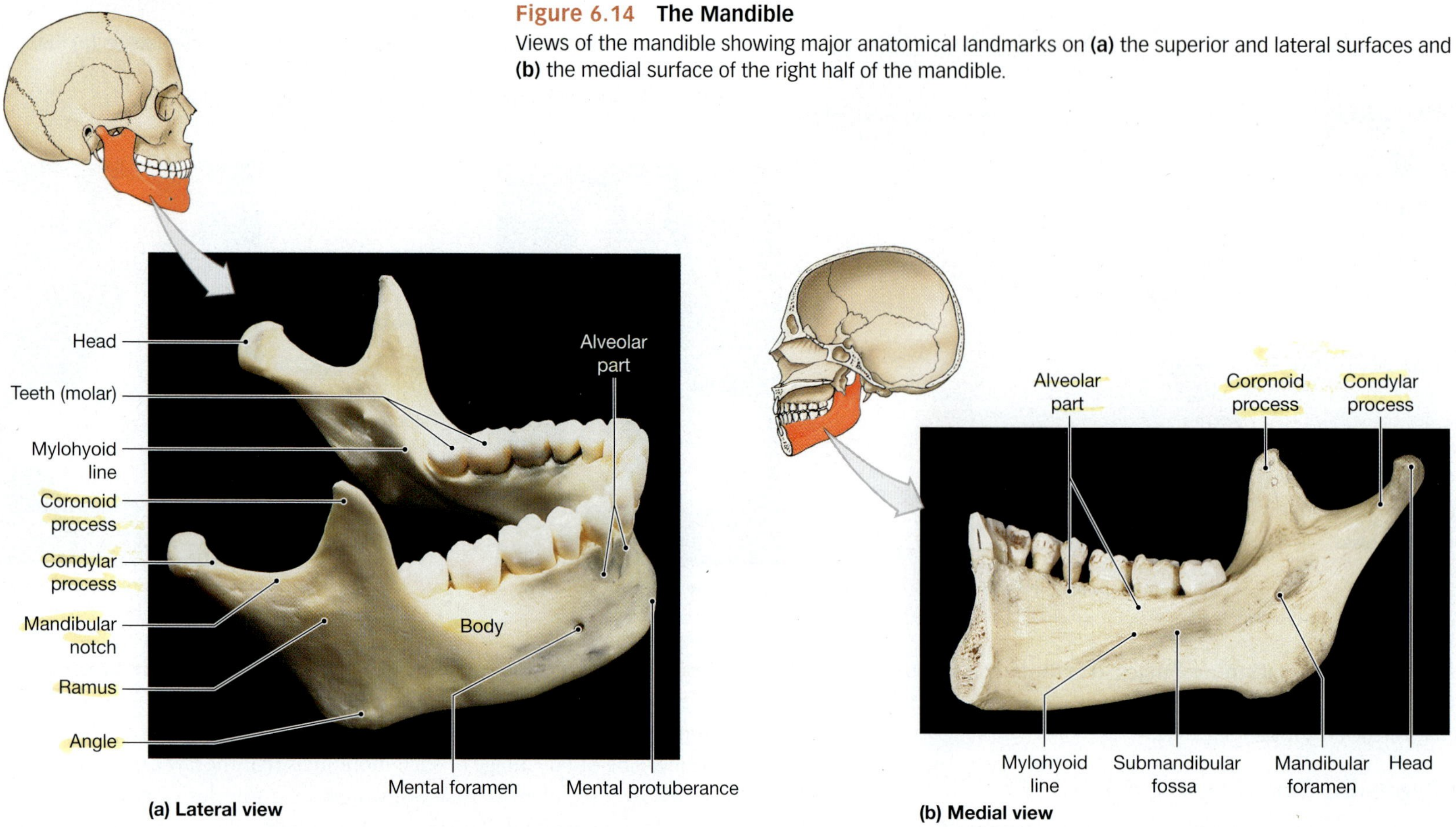

Figure 6.15 The Orbital Complex
The structure of the orbital complex on the right side. Seven bones form the bony orbit that encloses and protects the right eye.

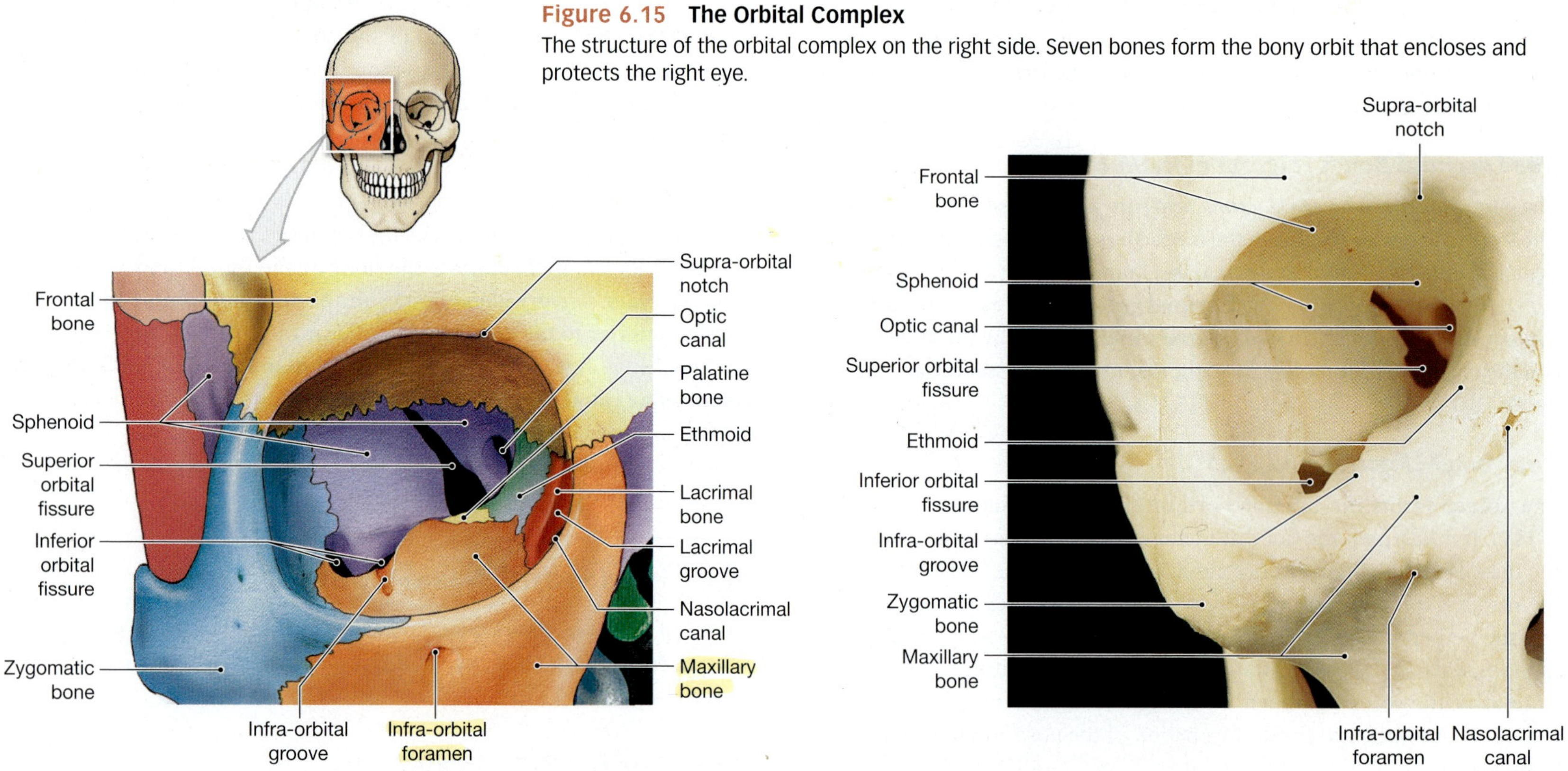

lateral mass of the ethmoid, which articulates with the sphenoid and a small process of the palatine bone. The sphenoid forms most of the posterior orbital wall. Several prominent foramina and fissures penetrate the sphenoid or lie between the sphenoid and maxilla. Laterally, the sphenoid and maxilla articulate with the zygomatic bone, which forms the lateral wall and rim of the orbit.

The Nasal Complex [Figures 6.5/6.16]

The **nasal complex** (Figure 6.16) includes the bones and cartilage that enclose the nasal cavities and the *paranasal sinuses*, air spaces connected to the nasal cavities. The frontal bone, sphenoid, and ethmoid form the superior wall of the nasal cavities. The perpendicular plate of the ethmoid and the vomer form the bony portion of the nasal septum (see Figures 6.5, p. 141, and 6.16a). The lat-

Figure 6.16 The Nasal Complex
Sections through the skull showing relationships among the bones of the nasal complex. **(a)** Sagittal section with the nasal septum in place. **(b)** Diagrammatic sagittal section with the nasal septum removed to show major features of the wall of the right nasal cavity. **(c)** A coronal section of the head showing the position of the paranasal sinuses. **(d)** A diagrammatic frontal section showing the positions of the paranasal sinuses.

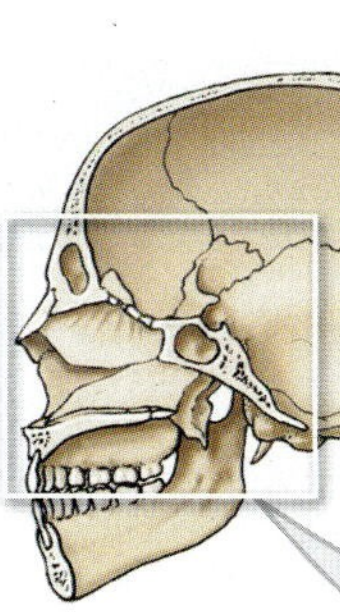

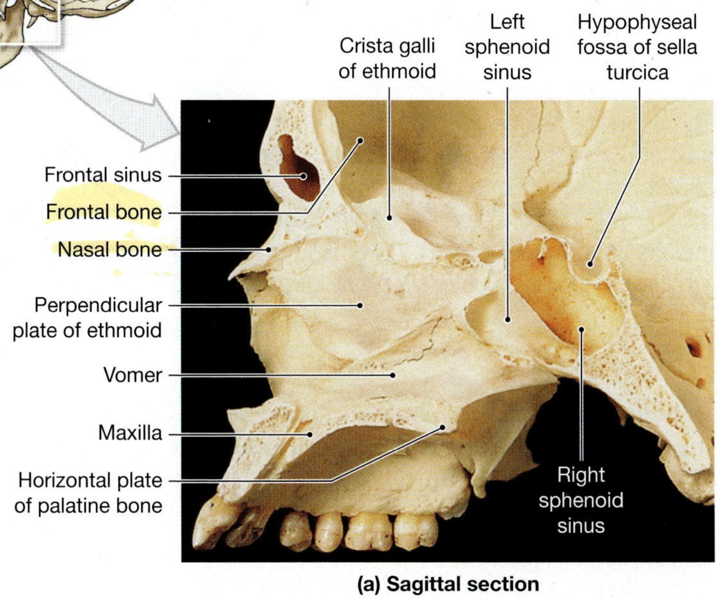

(a) Sagittal section

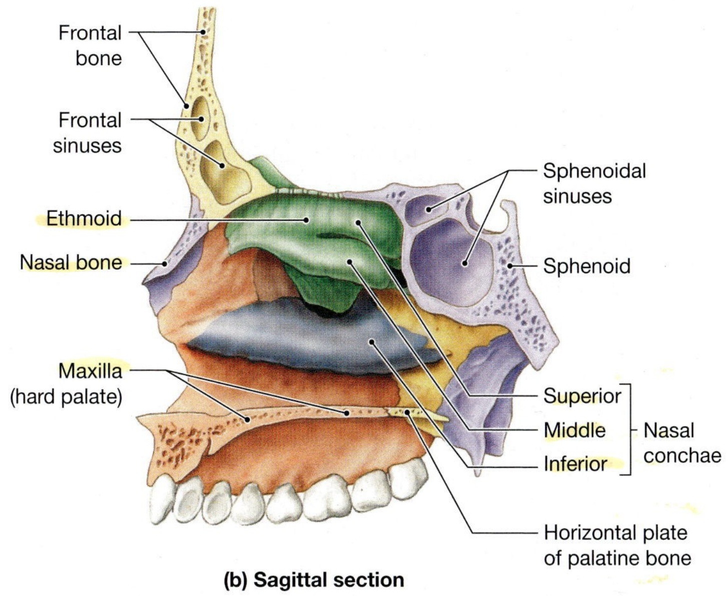

(b) Sagittal section

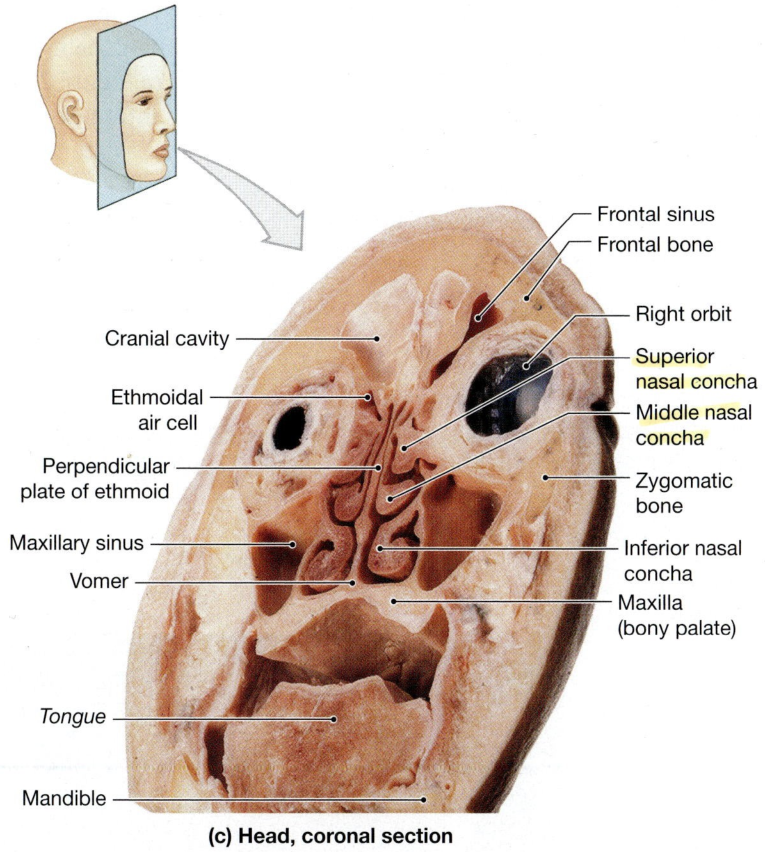

(c) Head, coronal section

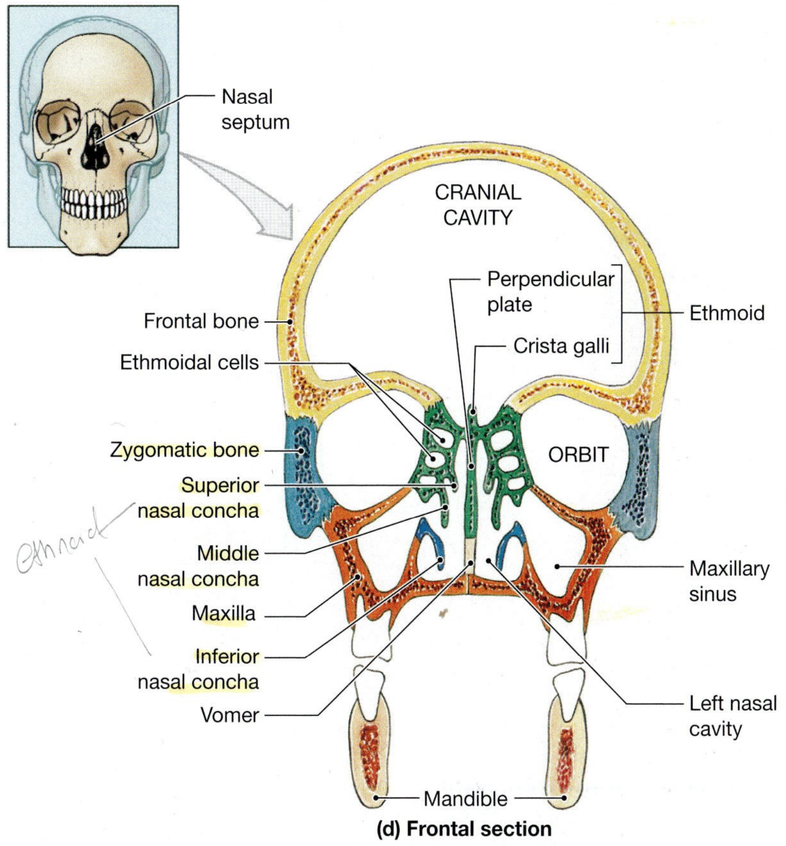

(d) Frontal section

eral walls are primarily formed by the maxillae, the lacrimal bones, the ethmoid, and the inferior nasal conchae (Figure 6.16b–d). The bridge of the nose is supported by the maxillae and nasal bones. The soft tissues of the nose enclose anterior extensions of the nasal cavities. These are supported by cartilaginous extensions of the bridge of the nose and the nasal septum.

The Paranasal Sinuses [Figure 6.16] The frontal bone, sphenoid, ethmoid, and maxilla contain the **paranasal sinuses**, air-filled chambers that act as extensions of and open into the nasal cavities. Figure 6.16 shows the location of the **frontal** and **sphenoidal sinuses**. The **ethmoidal air cells** (or *ethmoidal sinuses*) and **maxillary sinuses** are shown in Figure 6.16c,d. These sinuses lighten skull bones, produce mucus, and resonate during sound production. The mucous secretions are released into the nasal cavities, and the ciliated epithelium passes the mucus back toward the throat, where it is eventually swallowed. Incoming air is humidified and warmed as it flows across this carpet of mucus. Foreign particulate matter, such as dust

Clinical Note

Sinus Problems The mucous membrane of the paranasal sinuses responds to environmental stress by accelerating the production of mucus. The mucus flushes irritants off the walls of the nasal cavities. A variety of stimuli produce this result, including sudden changes in temperature or humidity, irritating vapors, and bacterial or viral infections. The flushing action often succeeds in removing a mild irritant. But a viral or bacterial infection produces an inflammation of the mucous membrane of the nasal cavity. As swelling occurs, the communicating passageways narrow. Mucus drainage slows, congestion increases, and the victim experiences headaches and a feeling of pressure within the facial bones. This condition of sinus inflammation and congestion is called *sinusitis*. The maxillary sinuses are often involved because gravity does little to assist mucus drainage from these sinuses.

Temporary sinus problems may accompany allergies or exposure of the mucous epithelium to chemical irritants or invading microorganisms. Chronic sinusitis may occur as the result of a *deviated* (nasal) *septum*. In this condition the nasal septum has a bend in it, most often at the junction between the bony and cartilaginous regions. Septal deviation often blocks drainage of one or more sinuses, producing chronic cycles of infection and inflammation. A deviated septum can result from developmental abnormalities or injuries to the nose, and the condition can usually be corrected or improved by surgery.

and microorganisms, becomes trapped in this sticky mucus and then swallowed. This mechanism helps protect the delicate exchange surfaces of the fragile lung tissue portions of the respiratory tract.

The Hyoid Bone [Figure 6.17]

The **hyoid bone** lies inferior to the skull, suspended by the **stylohyoid ligaments**, but not in direct contact with any other bone of the skeleton (Figure 6.17). The body of the hyoid serves as a base for several muscles concerned with movements of the tongue and larynx. Because muscles and ligaments form the only connections between the hyoid and other skeletal structures, the entire complex is quite mobile. The larger processes on the hyoid are the **greater horns**, which help support the larynx and serve as the base for muscles that move the tongue. The **lesser horns** are connected to the stylohyoid ligaments, and from these ligaments the hyoid and larynx hang beneath the skull like a swing from the limb of a tree.

Many superficial bumps and ridges in the axial skeleton are associated with the skeletal muscles described in Chapter 10; learning the names now will help you organize the material in that chapter. Tables 6.1 and 6.2 summarize information concerning the foramina and fissures introduced thus far. Use Table 6.1 as a reference for foramina and fissures of the skull and Table 6.2 as a reference for surface features and foramina of the skull. These references will be especially important in later chapters dealing with the nervous and cardiovascular systems.

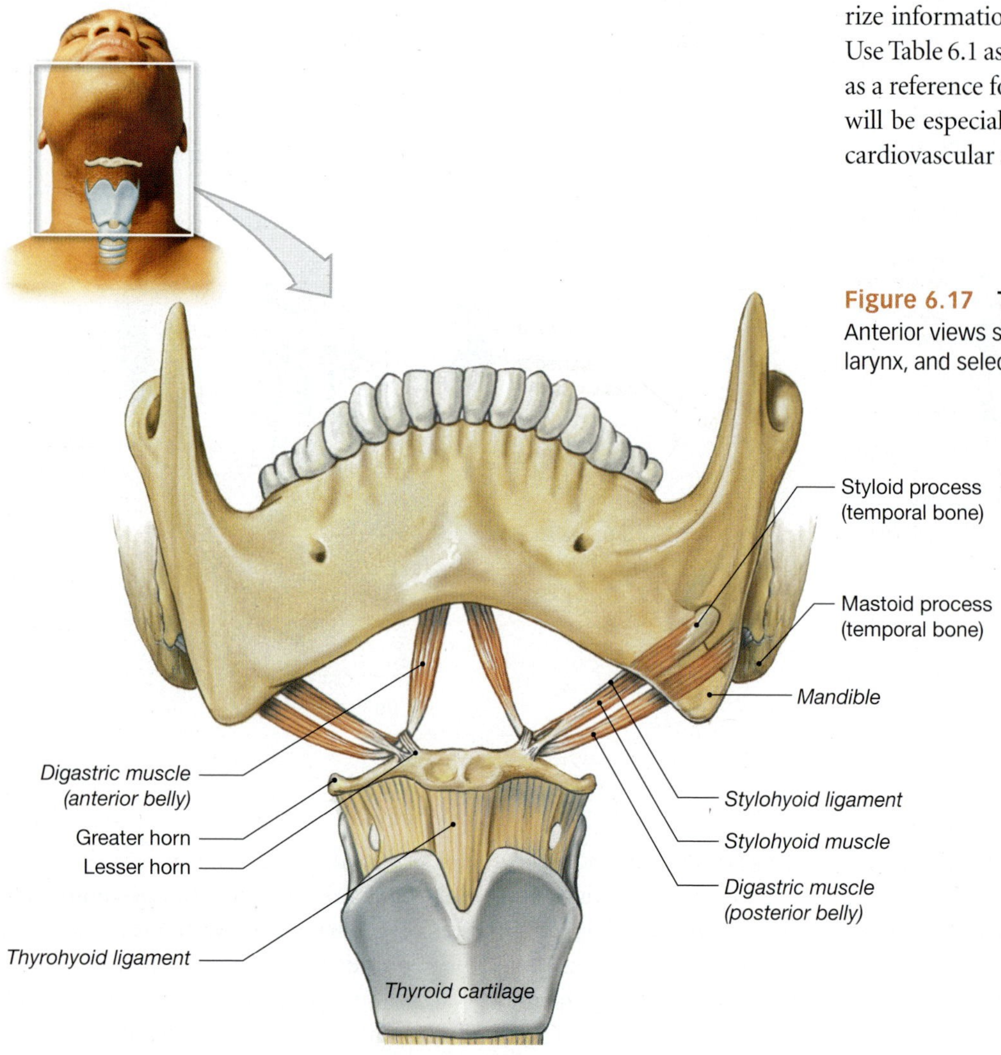

(a) Anterior view

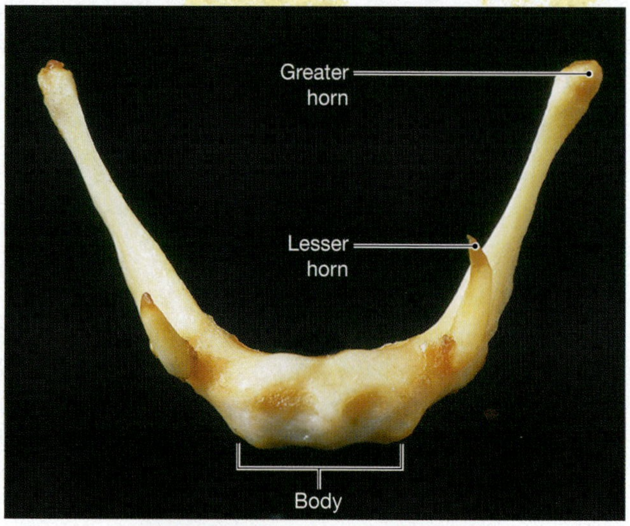

(b) Hyoid bone, anterosuperior view

Figure 6.17 The Hyoid Bone
Anterior views showing **(a)** the relationship of the hyoid bone to the skull, the larynx, and selected skeletal muscles; **(b)** the isolated hyoid bone.

TABLE 6.1 A Key to the Foramina and Fissures of the Skull

Bone	Foramen/Fissure	Major Structures Using Passageway: Neural Tissue	Major Structures Using Passageway: Vessels and Other Structures
OCCIPITAL BONE	Foramen magnum	Medulla oblongata (last portion of brain) and accessory nerve (XI) controlling several muscles of the back, pharynx, and larynx*	Vertebral arteries to brain and supporting membranes around CNS
	Hypoglossal canal	Hypoglossal nerve (XII) provides motor control to muscles of the tongue	
With temporal bone	Jugular foramen	Glossopharyngeal nerve (IX), vagus nerve (X), accessory nerve (XI). Nerve IX provides taste sensation; X is important for visceral functions; XI innervates important muscles of the back and neck	Internal jugular vein; important vein returning blood from brain to heart
FRONTAL BONE	Supra-orbital foramen (or notch)	Supra-orbital nerve, sensory branch of the ophthalmic nerve, innervating the eyebrow, eyelid, and frontal sinus	Supra-orbital artery delivers blood to same region
TEMPORAL BONE	Mastoid foramen		Vessels to membranes around CNS
	Stylomastoid foramen	Facial nerve (VII) provides motor control of facial muscles	
	Carotid canal		Internal carotid artery; major arterial supply to the brain
	External acoustic meatus		Air conducts sound to eardrum
	Internal acoustic meatus	Vestibulocochlear nerve (VIII) from sense organs for hearing and balance. Facial nerve (VII) enters here, exits at stylomastoid foramen	Internal acoustic artery to inner ear
SPHENOID	Optic canal	Optic nerve (II) brings information from the eye to the brain	Ophthalmic artery brings blood into orbit
	Superior orbital fissure	Oculomotor nerve (III), trochlear nerve (IV), ophthalmic branch of trigeminal nerve (V), abducens nerve (VI). Ophthalmic nerve provides sensory information about eye and orbit; other nerves control muscles that move the eye	Ophthalmic vein returns blood from orbit
	Foramen rotundum	Maxillary branch of trigeminal nerve (V) provides sensation from the face	
	Foramen ovale	Mandibular branch of trigeminal nerve (V) controls the muscles that move the lower jaw and provides sensory information from that area	
With temporal and occipital bones	Foramen spinosum		Vessels to membranes around CNS
	Foramen lacerum		Internal carotid artery leaves carotid canal, passes along superior margin of foramen lacerum
With maxillae	Inferior orbital fissure	Maxillary branch of trigeminal nerve (V). *See Foramen rotundum* of the sphenoid	
ETHMOID	Cribriform foramina	Olfactory nerve (I) provides sense of smell	
MAXILLA	Infra-orbital foramen	Infra-orbital nerve, maxillary branch of trigeminal nerve (V) from the inferior orbital fissure to face	Infra-orbital artery with the same distribution
	Incisive canals	Nasopalatine nerve	Small arteries to the palatal surface
ZYGOMATIC BONE	Zygomaticofacial foramen	Zygomaticofacial nerve, sensory branch of maxillary nerve to cheek	
LACRIMAL BONE	Lacrimal groove, nasolacrimal canal (with maxilla)		Tear duct drains into the nasal cavity
MANDIBLE	Mental foramen	Mental nerve, sensory nerve branch of the mandibular nerve, provides sensation for the chin and lower lip	Mental vessels to chin and lower lip
	Mandibular foramen	Inferior alveolar nerve, sensory branch of the mandibular nerve, provides sensation for the gums, teeth	Inferior alveolar vessels supply same region

*We are using the classical definition of cranial nerves based on the nerve's anatomical structure as it leaves the brain stem.

Clinical Note

Problems with Growth of the Skull The growth of the cranium is usually coordinated with the expansion of the brain. Unusual distortions of the skull result from the premature fusion of the frontal or other sutures; this condition is called **craniostenosis** (krā-nē-ō-sten-Ō-sis; *stenosis*, narrowing). As the brain continues to enlarge, the rest of the skull accommodates it. A long and narrow head will be produced by early closure of the sagittal suture, whereas a very broad skull results if the coronal suture fuses prematurely. Closure of all of the cranial sutures restricts the development of the brain, and surgery must be performed to prevent brain damage. However, if the brain enlargement stops because of genetic or developmental abnormalities, skull growth ceases as well. This condition, which results in a very undersized head, is called **microcephaly** (mī-krō-SEF-a-lē).

TABLE 6.2 Surface Features of the Skull

			Surface Features			
Region	**Bone**	**Articulates with**	**Structures**	**Functions**	**Foramina**	**Functions**
CRANIUM (8)						
	Occipital bone (1) *(Figure 6.6)*	Parietal bone, temporal bone, sphenoid	**External:** Occipital condyles	Articulate with first cervical vertebra	Jugular foramen (with temporal)	Carries blood from smaller veins in the cranial cavity
			Occipital crest, external occipital protuberance, and inferior and superior nuchal lines	Attachment of muscles and ligaments that move the head and stabilize the atlantooccipital joint	Hypoglossal canal	Passageway for hypoglossal nerve that controls tongue muscles
			Internal: Internal occipital crest	Attachment of membranes that stabilize position of the brain		
	Parietal bones (2) *(Figure 6.6)*	Occipital, frontal, temporal bones, sphenoid	**External:** Superior and inferior temporal lines	Attachment of major jaw-closing muscle		
			Parietal eminence	Attachment of scalp to skull		
	Frontal bone (1) *(Figure 6.7)*	Parietal, nasal, zygomatic bones, sphenoid, ethmoid, maxillae	Frontal suture	Marks fusion of frontal bones in development	Supra-orbital foramina	Passageways for sensory branch of ophthalmic nerve and supra-orbital artery to the eyebrow and eyelid
			Squamous part	Attachment of muscles of scalp		
			Supra-orbital margin	Protects eye		
			Lacrimal fossae	Recesses containing the lacrimal glands		
			Frontal sinuses	Lighten bone and produce mucous secretions		
			Frontal crest	Attachment of stabilizing membranes (meninges) within the cranium		
	Temporal bones (2) *(Figure 6.8)*	Occipital, parietal, frontal, zygomatic bones, sphenoid and mandible; enclose auditory ossicles and suspend hyoid bone by stylohyoid ligaments	**External:** *Squamous part:* Squama	Attachment of jaw muscles	**External:** Carotid canal	Entryway for carotid artery bringing blood to the brain
			Mandibular fossa and articular tubercle	Form articulation with mandible	Stylomastoid foramen	Exit for nerve that controls facial muscles
			Zygomatic process	Articulates with zygomatic bone	Jugular foramen (with occipital bone)	Carries blood from smaller veins in the cranial cavity
			Petrous part: Mastoid process	Attachment of muscles that extend or rotate head	External acoustic meatus	Entrance and passage to tympanum
			Styloid process	Attachment of stylohyoid ligament and muscles attached to hyoid bone	Mastoid foramen	Passage for blood vessels to membranes of brain
			Internal: Mastoid air cells	Lighten mastoid process	**External:** Foramen lacerum between temporal and occipital bones	Cartilage and small arteries to the inner surface of the cranium
			Petrous part	Protects middle and inner ear	**Internal:** Auditory tube	Connects air space of middle ear with pharynx
					Internal acoustic meatus	Passage for blood vessels and nerves to the inner ear and stylomastoid foramen

TABLE 6.2 Surface Features of the Skull *(Continued)*

Region	Bone	Articulates with	Surface Features: Structures	Functions	Foramina	Functions
	Sphenoid (1) (*Figure 6.9*)	Occipital, frontal, temporal, zygomatic, palatine bones, maxillae, ethmoid, and vomer	**Internal:**			
			Sella turcica	Protects pituitary gland	Optic canal	Passage of optic nerve
			Anterior and posterior clinoid processes, optic groove	Protect pituitary gland and optic nerve	Superior orbital fissure	Entrance for nerves that control eye movements
			External:			
			Pterygoid processes and spines	Attachment of jaw muscles	Foramen rotundum	Passage for sensory nerves from face
					Foramen ovale	Passage for nerves that control jaw movement
					Foramen spinosum	Passage of vessels to membranes around brain
	Ethmoid (1) (*Figure 6.10*)	Frontal, nasal, palatine, lacrimal bones, sphenoid, maxillae, and vomer	Crista galli	Attachment of membranes that stabilize position of brain	Cribriform foramina	Passage of olfactory nerves
			Ethmoidal labyrinth	Lightens bone and site of mucus production		
			Superior and middle conchae	Create turbulent airflow		
			Perpendicular plate	Separates nasal cavities (with vomer and nasal cartilage)		
FACE (14)	**Maxillae (2)** (*Figure 6.12*)	Frontal, zygomatic, palatine, lacrimal bones, sphenoid, ethmoid, and inferior nasal concha	Orbital margin	Protects eye	Inferior orbital fissure and infra-orbital foramen	Exit for nerves entering skull at foramen rotundum
			Palatal process	Forms most of the bony palate	Greater and lesser palatine foramina	Passage of sensory nerves from face
			Maxillary sinus	Lightens bone, secretes mucus	Nasolacrimal canal (with lacrimal bone)	Drains tears from lacrimal sac to nasal cavity
			Alveolar process	Surrounds articulations with teeth		
	Palatine bones (2) (*Figure 6.13*)	Sphenoid, maxillae, and vomer		Contribute to bony palate and orbit		
	Nasal bones (2) (*Figures 6.3c,d; 6.15*)	Frontal bone, ethmoid, maxillae		Support bridge of nose		
	Vomer (1) (*Figures 6.3d,e; 6.5; 6.16*)	Ethmoid, maxillae, palatine bones		Form inferior and posterior part of nasal septum		
	Inferior nasal conchae (2) (*Figures 6.3d; 6.16*)	Maxillae and palatine bones		Create turbulent airflow		
	Zygomatic bones (2) (*Figures 6.3c,d; 6.15*)	Frontal and temporal bones, sphenoid, maxillae	Temporal process	With zygomatic process of temporal, completes zygomatic arch for attachment of jaw muscles		
	Lacrimal bones (2) (*Figures 6.3c,d; 6.15*)	Ethmoid, frontal bones, maxillae, inferior nasal conchae			Nasolacrimal groove	Contains lacrimal sac
	Mandible (1) (*Figure 6.14*)	Temporal bones	Ramus		Mandibular foramen	Passage for sensory nerve from teeth and gums
			Condylar process	Articulates with temporal bone	Mental foramen	Passage for sensory nerve from chin and lips
			Coronoid process	Attachment of temporalis muscle from parietal surface	Mandibular foramen	Passage of sensory nerve from teeth and gums

(continued)

TABLE 6.2 Surface Features of the Skull *(Continued)*

Region	Bone	Articulates with	Surface Features			
			Structures	Functions	Foramina	Functions
	Mandible (1) (*Figure 6.14*)		Alveolar part	Protects articulations with teeth		
			Mylohyoid line	Attachment of muscle supporting floor of mouth		
			Submandibular fossa	Protects submandibular salivary gland		
ASSOCIATED BONES (7)	**Hyoid bone** (1) (*Figure 6.17*)	Suspended by ligaments from styloid process of temporal bone; connected by ligaments to larynx	Greater horns	Attachment of tongue muscles and ligaments to larynx		
			Lesser horns	Attachment of stylohyoid ligaments		
	Auditory ossicles (6)	3 are enclosed by the petrous part of each temporal bone		Conduct sound vibrations from tympanic membrane to fluid-filled chambers of inner ear		

CONCEPT CHECK

1. What are the names and functions of the facial bones?
2. Identify the functions of the paranasal sinuses.
3. What bones form the orbital complex?

See blue "Answers" tab at back of book.

The Skulls of Infants, Children, and Adults [Figure 6.18]

Many different centers of ossification are involved in the formation of the skull, but as development proceeds, fusion of the centers produces a smaller number of composite bones. For example, the sphenoid begins as 14 separate ossification centers. At birth, fusion has not been completed, and there are two frontal bones, four occipital bones, and a number of sphenoid and temporal elements.

The skull organizes around the developing brain, and as the time of birth approaches, the brain enlarges rapidly. Although the bones of the skull are also growing, they fail to keep pace, and at birth the cranial bones are connected by areas of fibrous connective tissue. These connections are quite flexible, and the skull can be distorted without damage. Such distortion normally occurs during delivery and eases the passage of the infant along the birth canal. The largest fibrous regions between the cranial bones are known as **fontanels** (fon-tah-NELS; sometimes spelled *fontanelles*) (Figure 6.18):

- The *anterior fontanel* is the largest fontanel. It lies at the intersection of the frontal, sagittal, and coronal sutures.
- The *posterior fontanel* is at the junction between the lambdoid and sagittal sutures.
- The *sphenoidal fontanels* are at the junctions between the squamous sutures and the coronal suture.
- The *mastoid fontanels* are at the junctions between the squamous sutures and the lambdoid suture.

The skulls of infants and adults differ in terms of the shape and structure of cranial elements, and this difference accounts for variations in proportions as well as in size. The most significant growth in the skull occurs before age 5; at that time the brain stops growing and the cranial sutures develop. As a result, when compared with the skull as a whole, the cranium of a young child is relatively larger than that of an adult.

The Vertebral Column [Figure 6.19]

The rest of the axial skeleton is subdivided into the vertebral column and rib cage. The adult **vertebral column** consists of 26 bones, including the vertebrae (24), the sacrum, and the coccyx. The vertebrae provide a column of support, bearing the weight of the head, neck, and trunk, and ultimately transferring that weight to the appendicular skeleton of the lower limbs. They also protect the spinal cord, provide a passageway for spinal nerves that begin or end at the spinal cord, and help maintain an upright body position, as in sitting or standing.

The vertebral column is divided into regions. Beginning at the skull, the regions are *cervical*, *thoracic*, *lumbar*, *sacral*, and *coccygeal* (Figure 6.19). Each region of the vertebral column has different functions and, as a result, vertebrae within each region have anatomical specializations that allow for these functional differences. In addition, the vertebrae located at the junction between two regions of the vertebral column will share some anatomical characteristics of the region above and the region below.

Seven *cervical vertebrae* constitute the neck and extend inferiorly to the trunk. The first cervical vertebra forms a pair of joints, or articulations, with the occipital condyles of the skull. The seventh cervical vertebra articulates with the first thoracic vertebra. Twelve *thoracic vertebrae* form the midback region, and each articulates with one or more pairs of ribs. The twelfth thoracic vertebra articulates with the first lumbar vertebra. Five *lumbar vertebrae* form the lower back; the fifth articulates with the sacrum, which in turn articulates with the coccyx. The cervical, thoracic, and lumbar regions consist of individual vertebrae. During development, the *sacrum* originates as a group of five vertebrae, and the *coccyx* (KOK-siks), or "tailbone," begins as three to five very small vertebrae. The vertebrae of the

Figure 6.18 The Skull of an Infant
The flat bones in the infant skull are separated by fontanels, which allow for cranial expansion and the distortion of the skull during birth. By about age 4 these areas will disappear, and skull growth will be completed. **(a)** Lateral view. **(b)** Superior view. **(c)** Anterior view. **(d)** Posterior view.

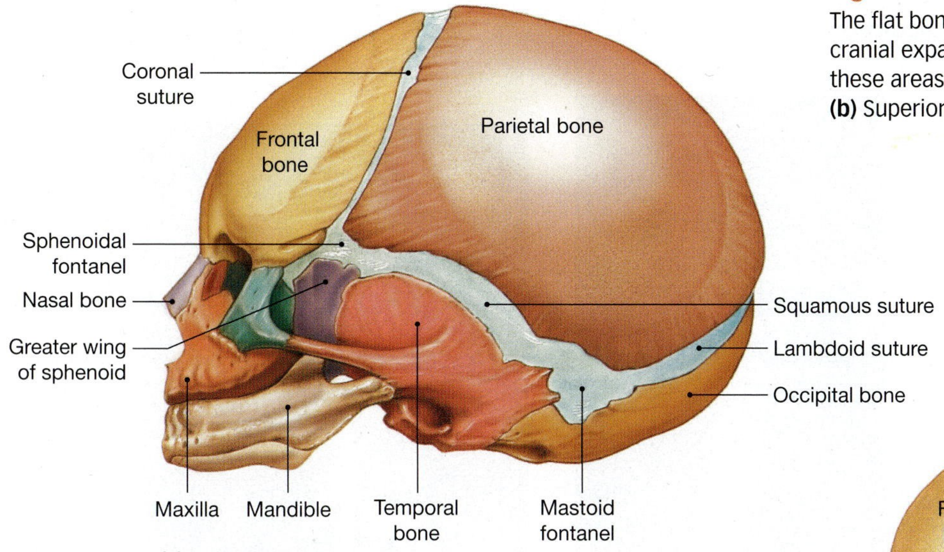

(a) Lateral view

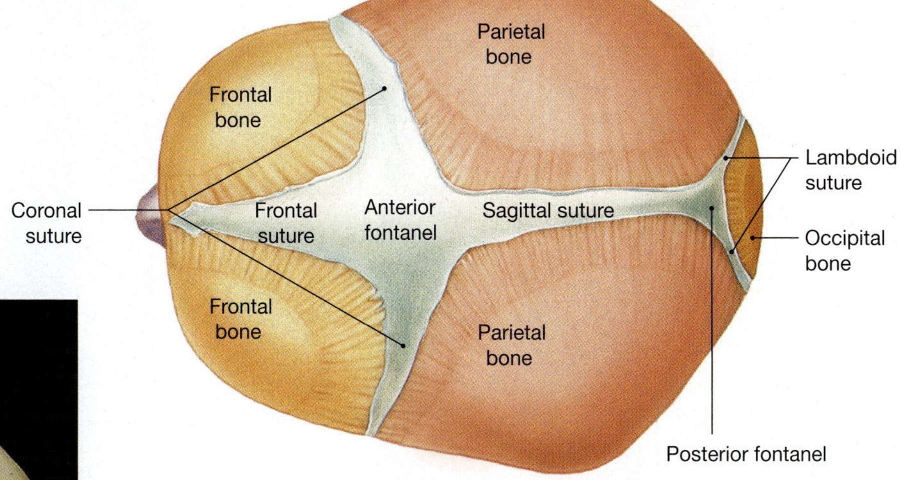

(b) Superior view

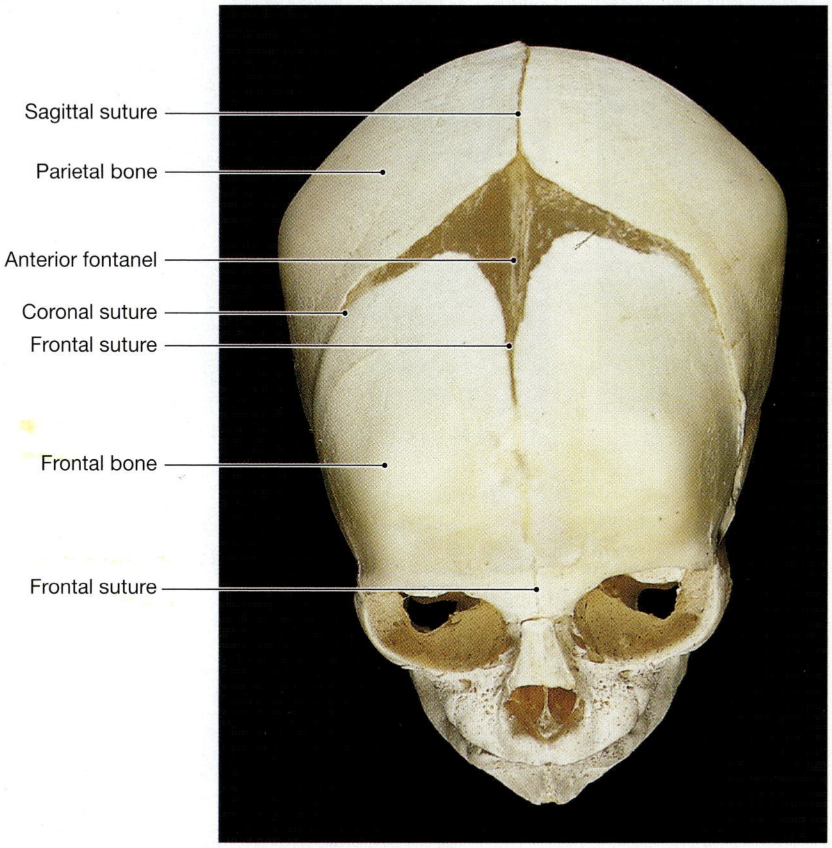

(c) Anterior/superior view

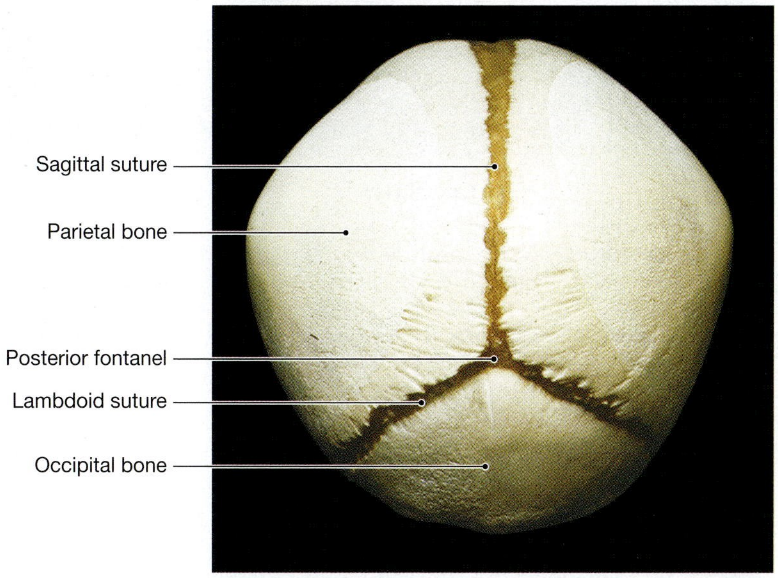

(d) Posterior view

sacrum usually complete their fusion by age 25. The distal coccygeal vertebrae do not complete their ossification before puberty, and thereafter fusion occurs at a variable pace. The total length of the vertebral column of an adult averages 71 cm (28 in.).

Spinal Curves [Figure 6.19]

The vertebral column does not form a straight and rigid structure. A side view of the adult vertebral column shows four **spinal curves** (Figure 6.19a–c): (1) **cervical curve**, (2) **thoracic curve**, (3) **lumbar curve**, and (4) **sacral curve**. The sequence of appearance of the spinal curves from fetus, to newborn, to child, and to adult is illustrated in Figure 6.19d. The thoracic and sacral curves are called **primary curvatures** because they appear late in fetal development. These are also called **accommodation curvatures** because they accommodate the thoracic and abdominopelvic viscera. The vertebral column in the newborn is C-shaped in contrast to the reversed S-shape of the adult, because only the primary curvatures are present. The lumbar and cervical curves, known as **secondary curvatures**, do not appear until several months after birth. These are also called **compensation curvatures** because they help shift the trunk weight over the legs as the child begins to stand. They become accentuated as the toddler learns to walk and run. All four curves are fully developed by the time a child is 10 years old.

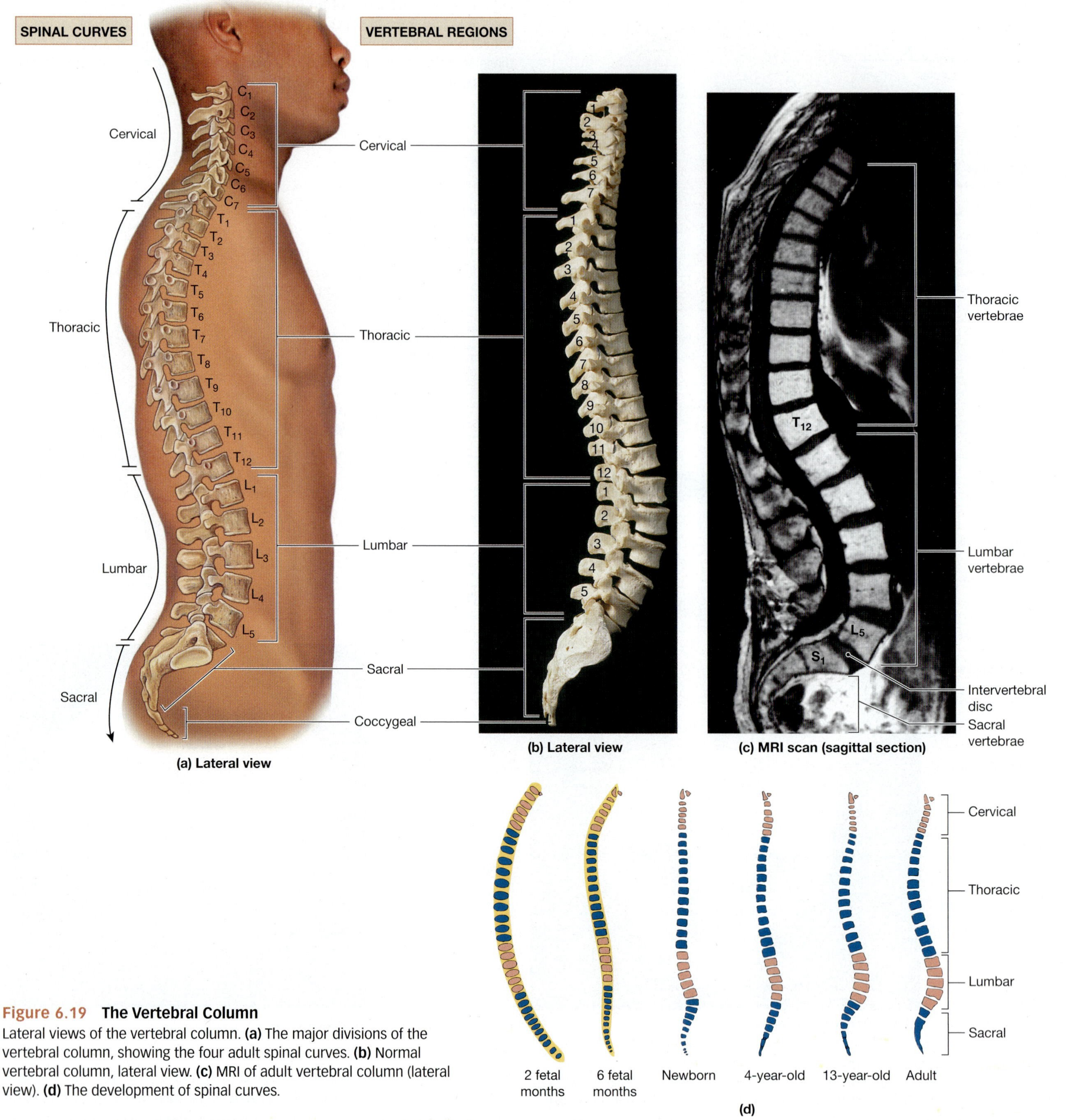

Figure 6.19 The Vertebral Column
Lateral views of the vertebral column. **(a)** The major divisions of the vertebral column, showing the four adult spinal curves. **(b)** Normal vertebral column, lateral view. **(c)** MRI of adult vertebral column (lateral view). **(d)** The development of spinal curves.

When standing, the weight of the body must be transmitted through the vertebral column to the hips and ultimately to the lower limbs. Yet most of the body weight lies in front of the vertebral column. The various curves bring that weight in line with the body axis and its center of gravity. Consider what people do automatically when they stand holding a heavy object. To avoid toppling forward, they exaggerate the lumbar curve, bringing the weight and center of gravity closer to the body axis. This posture can lead to discomfort at the base of the spinal column. Similarly, women in the last three months of pregnancy often develop chronic back pain from the changes in the lumbar curve that adjust for the increasing weight of the fetus. No doubt you have seen pictures of African or South American people carrying heavy objects balanced on their heads. Such a practice increases the

Clinical Note

Kyphosis, Lordosis, and Scoliosis (Figure 6.20) The vertebral column has to move, balance, and support the trunk and head, with multiple bones and joints involved. Conditions or events that damage the bones, muscles, or nerves can result in distorted shapes and impaired function. In **kyphosis** (kī-FŌ-sis), the normal thoracic curve becomes exaggerated posteriorly, producing a "round-back" appearance (Figure 6.20). This condition can be caused by (1) osteoporosis with compression fractures affecting the anterior portions of vertebral bodies, (2) chronic contractions in muscles that insert on the vertebrae, or (3) abnormal vertebral growth.

In **lordosis** (lōr-DŌ-sis), or "swayback," both the abdomen and buttocks protrude abnormally (Figure 6.20b). The cause is an anterior exaggeration of the lumbar curve. This may result from abdominal wall obesity or weakness in the muscles of the abdominal wall.

Scoliosis (skō-lē-Ō-sis) is an abnormal lateral curvature of the spine (Figure 6.20c). This lateral deviation can occur in one or more of the movable vertebrae. Scoliosis is the most common distortion of the spinal curvature. This condition may result from developmental problems, such as incomplete vertebral formation, or from muscular paralysis affecting one side of the back (as in some cases of polio). The "Hunchback of Notre Dame" suffered from severe scoliosis, which prior to the development of antibiotic therapies was often caused by a tuberculosis infection of the spine. In four out of five cases, the structural or functional cause of the abnormal spinal curvature is impossible to determine. This idiopathic scoliosis generally appears in girls during adolescence, when periods of growth are most rapid. Treatment may consist of a combination of exercises and braces that offer limited, if any, benefit. Severe cases can be treated through surgical straightening with implanted metal rods or cables.

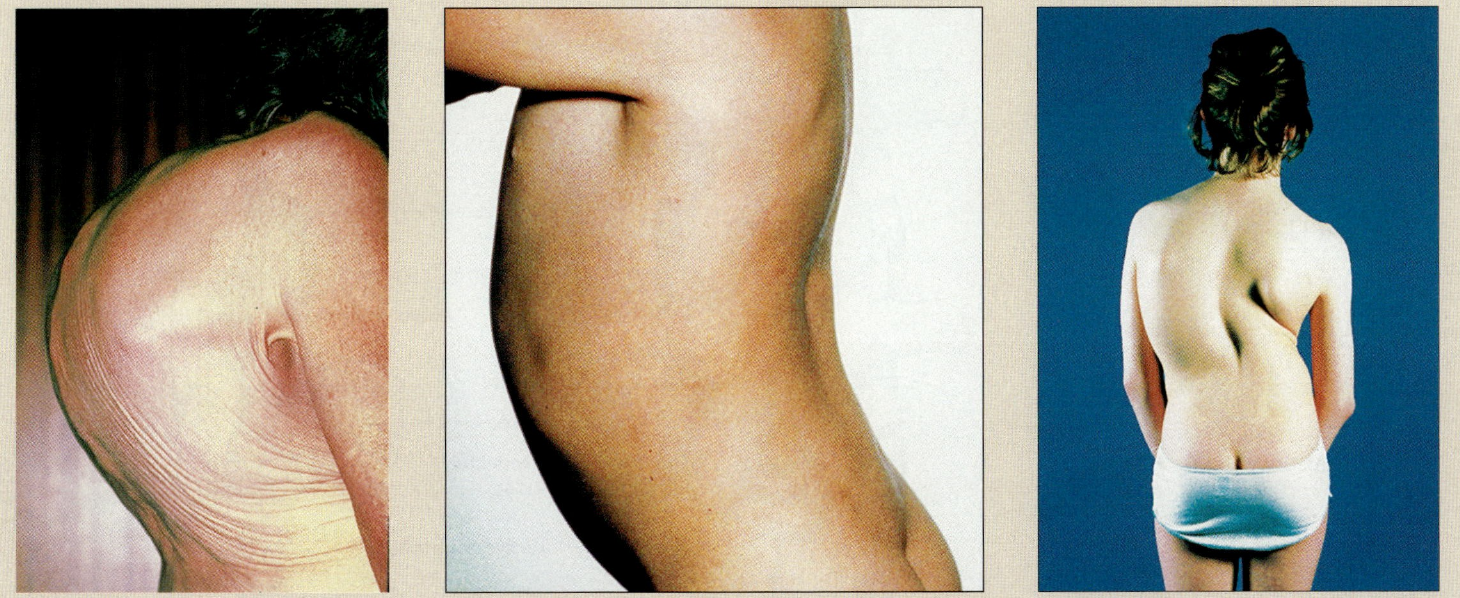

(a) Kyphosis (b) Lordosis (c) Scoliosis

Figure 6.20 Abnormal Curves of the Vertebral Column

load on the vertebral column, but because the weight is aligned with the axis of the spine, the spinal curves are not affected and strain is minimized.

Vertebral Anatomy [Figure 6.21]

Generally, vertebrae have a common structural plan (Figure 6.21). Anteriorly, each vertebra has a relatively thick, spherical to oval *body*, from which a *vertebral arch* extends posteriorly. Various processes either for muscle attachment or for rib articulation extend from the vertebral arch. Paired *articular processes* on both the superior and inferior surfaces project from the vertebral arch. These points represent the articulation between adjacent vertebrae (Figure 6.21d,e).

The Vertebral Body [Figure 6.21e]

The **vertebral body**, or *centrum* (plural, *centra*), is the part of a vertebra that transfers weight along the axis of the vertebral column (Figure 6.21e). Each vertebra articulates with neighboring vertebrae; the bodies are interconnected by ligaments and separated by pads of fibrous cartilage, the **intervertebral discs**.

The Vertebral Arch [Figure 6.21]

The **vertebral arch** (Figure 6.21), also called the **neural arch**, forms the lateral and posterior margins of the **vertebral foramen** that in life surrounds a portion of the spinal cord. The vertebral arch has a floor (the posterior surface of the body), walls (the *pedicles*), and a roof (the *laminae*) (LAM-i-nē; singular, *lamina*; "a thin layer"). The **pedicles** (PED-i-kls) arise along the posterolateral (posterior and lateral) margins of the body. The **laminae** on either side extend dorsomedially (dorsally and medially) to complete the roof. From the fusion of the laminae, a **spinous process**, also known as a *spinal process*, projects dorsally and posteriorly from the midline. These processes can be seen and felt through the skin of the back. **Transverse processes** project laterally or dorsolaterally on both sides from the point where the laminae join the pedicles. These processes are sites of muscle attachment, and they may also articulate with the ribs.

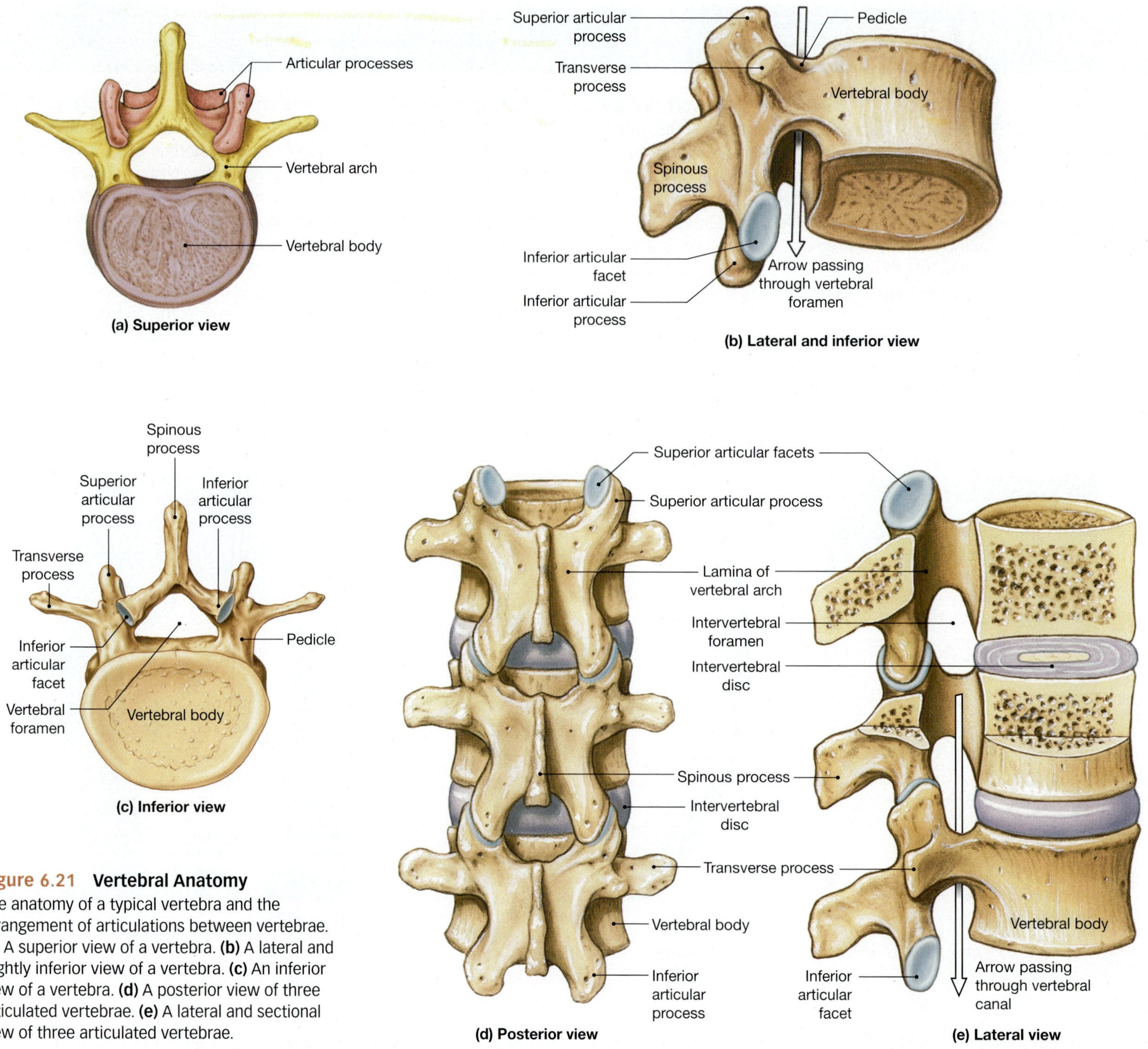

Figure 6.21 Vertebral Anatomy
The anatomy of a typical vertebra and the arrangement of articulations between vertebrae. **(a)** A superior view of a vertebra. **(b)** A lateral and slightly inferior view of a vertebra. **(c)** An inferior view of a vertebra. **(d)** A posterior view of three articulated vertebrae. **(e)** A lateral and sectional view of three articulated vertebrae.

The Articular Processes [Figure 6.21]

The **articular processes** also arise at the junction between the pedicles and laminae. There is a superior and inferior articular process on each side of the vertebra. The **superior articular processes** project cranially; the **inferior articular processes** project caudally (Figure 6.21).

Vertebral Articulation [Figure 6.21]

The inferior articular processes of one vertebra articulate with the superior articular processes of the more caudal vertebra. Each articular process has a polished surface called an **articular facet**. The superior processes have articular facets on their dorsal surfaces, whereas the inferior processes articulate along their ventral surfaces.

The vertebral arches of the vertebral column together form the **vertebral canal**, a space that encloses the spinal cord. However, the spinal cord is not completely encased in bone. The vertebral bodies are separated by the intervertebral discs, and there are gaps between the pedicles of successive vertebrae. These **intervertebral foramina** (Figure 6.21) permit the passage of nerves running to or from the enclosed spinal cord.

Vertebral Regions [Figure 6.19a and Table 6.3]

In references to the vertebrae, a capital letter indicates the vertebral region, and a subscript number indicates the vertebra in question, starting with the cervical vertebra closest to the skull. For example, C_3 refers to the third cervical vertebra, with C_1 in contact with the skull; L_4 is the fourth lumbar vertebra, with L_1 in contact with the last thoracic vertebra (Figure 6.19a). This shorthand will be used throughout the text.

Although each vertebra bears characteristic markings and articulations, focus on the general characteristics of each region and how the regional variations determine the vertebral group's basic function. Table 6.3 compares typical vertebrae from each region of the vertebral column.

Cervical Vertebrae [Figure 6.22 and Table 6.3]

The seven **cervical vertebrae** are the smallest of the vertebrae (Figure 6.22). They extend from the occipital bone of the skull to the thorax. As you will see, the first, second, and seventh cervical vertebrae possess unique characteristics and are considered to be atypical cervical vertebrae, while the third through the sixth display similar characteristics and are considered to be typical cervical vertebrae. Notice that the body of a cervical vertebra is relatively small as compared with the size of the triangular vertebral foramen. At this level the spinal cord still contains most of the nerves that connect the brain

TABLE 6.3 Regional Differences in Vertebral Structure and Function

Type (Number)	Vertebral Body	Vertebral Foramen	Spinous Process	Transverse Process	Functions
Cervical vertebrae (7) *(see Figure 6.22)*	Small; oval; curved faces	Large	Long; split; tip points inferiorly	Has transverse foramen	Support skull, stabilize relative positions of brain and spinal cord, allow controlled head movement
Thoracic vertebrae (12) *(see Figure 6.24)*	Medium; heart-shaped; flat faces; facets for rib articulations	Smaller	Long; slender; not split; tip points inferiorly	All but two (T_{11}, T_{12}) have facets for rib articulations	Support weight of head, neck, upper limbs, organs of thoracic cavity; articulate with ribs to allow changes in volume of thoracic cage
Lumbar vertebrae (5) *(see Figure 6.25)*	Massive; oval; flat faces	Smallest	Blunt; broad tip points posteriorly	Short; no articular facets or transverse foramen	Support weight of head, neck, upper limbs, organs of thoracic and abdominal cavities

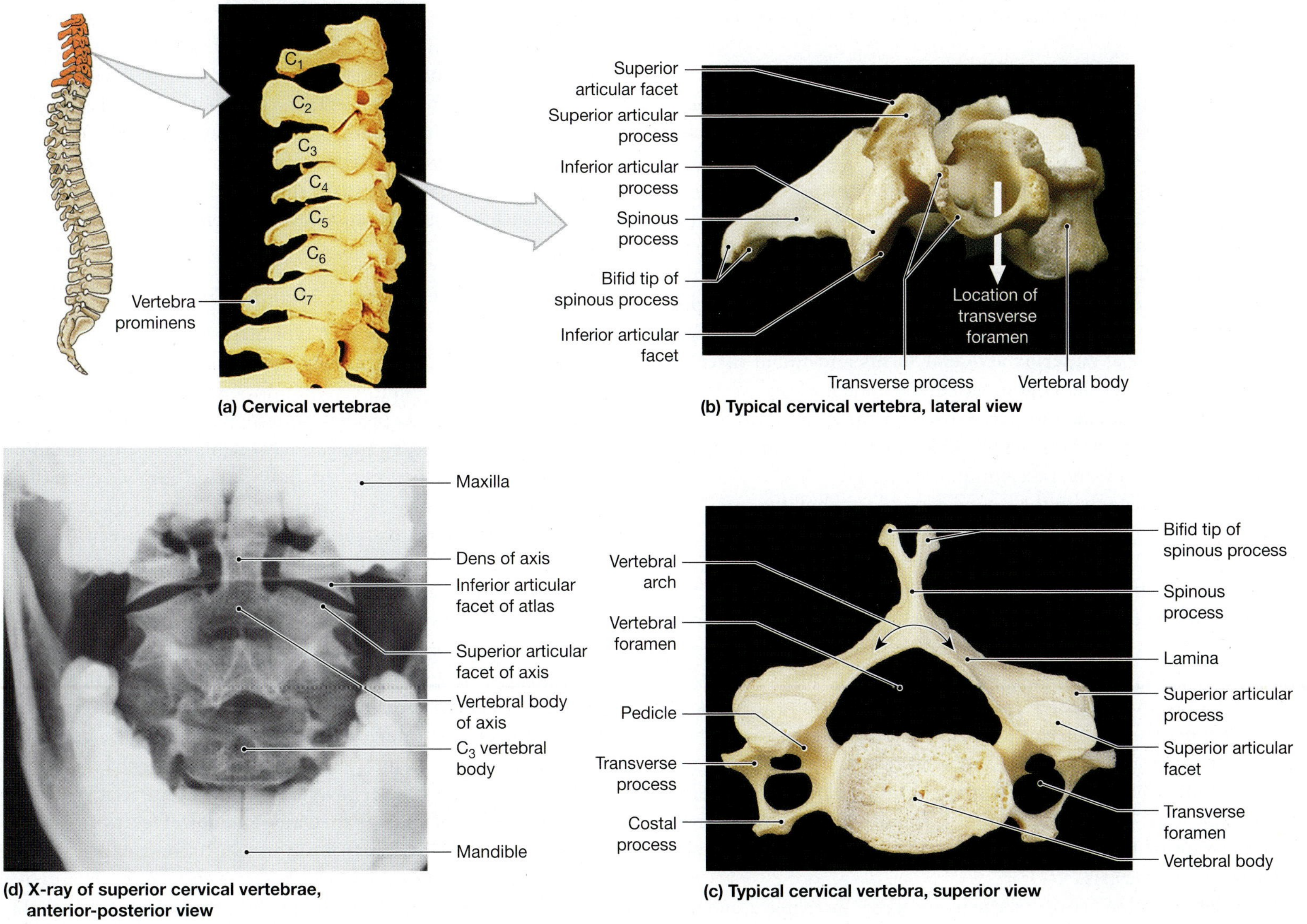

Figure 6.22 Cervical Vertebrae

These are the smallest and most superior vertebrae. **(a)** Lateral view of the cervical vertebrae. **(b)** Lateral view of a typical (C_3–C_6) cervical vertebra. **(c)** Superior view of the same vertebra. Note the characteristic features listed in Table 6.3. **(d)** An x-ray of the superior cervical vertebrae, anterior-posterior view. The mouth is open and the lower teeth are visible.

to the rest of the body. As you continue along the vertebral canal, the diameter of the spinal cord decreases, and so does the diameter of the vertebral arch. On the other hand, cervical vertebrae support only the weight of the head, so the vertebral bodies can be relatively small and light. As you continue caudally along the vertebral column, the loading increases and the vertebral bodies gradually enlarge.

In a typical cervical vertebra(C_3–C_6), the superior surface of the body is concave from side to side, and it slopes, with the anterior edge inferior to the posterior edge. The spinous process is relatively stumpy, usually shorter than the diameter of the vertebral foramen. The tip of each process other than C_7 bears a prominent notch. A notched spinous process is described as *bifid* (BĪ-fid; *bifidus*, cut into two parts). Laterally, the transverse processes are fused to the **costal processes** that originate near the ventrolateral portion of the body. *Costal* refers to a rib, and these processes represent the fused remnants of cervical ribs. The costal and transverse processes encircle prominent, round, **transverse foramina**. These passageways protect the *vertebral arteries* and *vertebral veins*, important blood vessels supplying the brain.

This description would be adequate to identify all but the first two cervical vertebrae. When cervical vertebrae C_3–C_7 articulate, their interlocking vertebral bodies permit a relatively greater degree of flexibility than do those of other regions. The first two cervical vertebrae are unique and the seventh is modified. Table 6.3 summarizes the features of cervical vertebrae.

The Atlas (C_1)[Figure 6.23a,b] Articulating with the occipital condyles of the skull at the superior articular facet of the superior articular process, the **atlas** (C_1) holds up the head (**Figure 6.23a,b**). It is named after Atlas, a figure in Greek mythology who held up the world. The articulation between the occipital condyles and the atlas is a joint that permits nodding (as when indicating "yes") but prevents twisting. The atlas can be distinguished from the other vertebrae by the following features: (1) the lack of a body, (2) the possession of semicircular **anterior** and **posterior vertebral arches**, each containing **anterior** and **posterior tubercles**, (3) the presence of oval **superior articular facets** and round **inferior articular facets** and (4) the largest vertebral foramen of any vertebra. These modifications provide more free space for the spinal cord, which prevents damage to the cord during the wide range of movements possible in this region of the vertebral column.

The atlas articulates with the second cervical vertebra, the *axis*. This articulation permits rotation (as when shaking the head to indicate "no").

The Axis (C_2) [Figure 6.23c–f] During development, the body of the atlas fuses to the body of the second cervical vertebra, called the **axis** (C_2) (**Figure 6.23c,d**). This fusion creates the prominent **dens** (*denz*, tooth), or *odontoid process* (ō-DON-toyd; *odontos*, tooth) of the axis. Thus, there is no intervertebral disc between the atlas and the axis. A *transverse ligament* binds the dens to the inner surface of the atlas, forming a pivot for rotation of the atlas and skull relative to the rest of the vertebral column. This permits the turning of the head from side to side (as when indicating "no"; **Figure 6.23e,f**). Important muscles controlling the position of the head and neck attach to the especially robust spinous process of the axis.

In a child the fusion between the dens and axis is incomplete, and impacts or even severe shaking can cause dislocation of the dens and severe damage to the spinal cord. In the adult, a blow to the base of the skull can be equally dangerous because a dislocation of the axis–atlas joint can force the dens into the base of the brain, with fatal results.

Vertebra Prominens (C_7) [Figures 6.22a/6.24a] The transition from one vertebral region to another is not abrupt, and the last vertebra of one region usually resembles the first vertebra of the next. The **vertebra prominens** (C_7) has a long, slender spinous process that ends in a broad tubercle that can be felt beneath the skin at the base of the neck. This vertebra, shown in **Figures 6.22a** and **6.24a**, is the interface between the cervical curve, which arches anteriorly, and the thoracic curve, which arches posteriorly. The transverse processes are large, providing additional surface area for muscle attachment, and the transverse foramina may be reduced or absent. A large elastic ligament, the **ligamentum nuchae** (lig-a-MEN-tum NOO-kā; *nucha*, nape) begins at the vertebra prominens and extends cranially to an insertion along the external occipital crest. Along the way, it attaches to the spinous processes of the other cervical vertebrae. When the head is upright, this ligament acts like the string on a bow, maintaining the cervical curvature without muscular effort. If the neck has been bent forward, the elasticity in this ligament helps return the head to an upright position.

The head is relatively massive, and it sits atop the cervical vertebrae like a soup bowl on the tip of a finger. With this arrangement, small muscles can produce significant effects by tipping the balance one way or another. But if the body suddenly changes position, as in a fall or during rapid acceleration (a jet taking off) or deceleration (a car crash), the balancing muscles are not strong enough to stabilize the head. A dangerous partial or complete dislocation of the cervical vertebrae can result, with injury to muscles and ligaments and potential injury to the spinal cord. The term **whiplash** is used to describe such an injury, because the movement of the head resembles the cracking of a whip.

Thoracic Vertebrae [Figure 6.24 and Table 6.3]

There are 12 **thoracic vertebrae**. A typical thoracic vertebra (**Figure 6.24**) has a distinctive heart-shaped body that is more massive than that of a cervical vertebra. The round vertebral foramen is relatively smaller, and the long, slender spinous process projects posterocaudally. The spinous processes of T_{10}, T_{11}, and T_{12} increasingly resemble those of the lumbar series, as the transition between the thoracic and lumbar curvatures approaches. Because of the weight carried by the lower thoracic and lumbar vertebrae, it is difficult to stabilize the transition between the thoracic and lumbar curves. As a result, compression fractures or compression–dislocation fractures after a hard fall most often involve the last thoracic and first two lumbar vertebrae.

Each thoracic vertebra articulates with ribs along the dorsolateral surfaces of its body. The location and structure of the articulations vary somewhat from vertebra to vertebra (**Figure 6.24b,c**). Thoracic vertebrae T_1 to T_8 have **superior** and **inferior costal facets**, as they articulate with two pairs of ribs. Vertebrae T_9 to T_{12} have only a single costal facet on each side.

The transverse processes of vertebrae T_1 to T_{10} are relatively thick, and their anterolateral surfaces contain **transverse costal facets** for articulation with the tubercles of ribs. Thus, ribs 1 through 10 contact their vertebrae at two points, at a costal facet and at a transverse costal facet. This dual articulation with the ribs limits the mobility of the thoracic vertebrae. Table 6.3, p. 163, summarizes the features of the thoracic vertebrae.

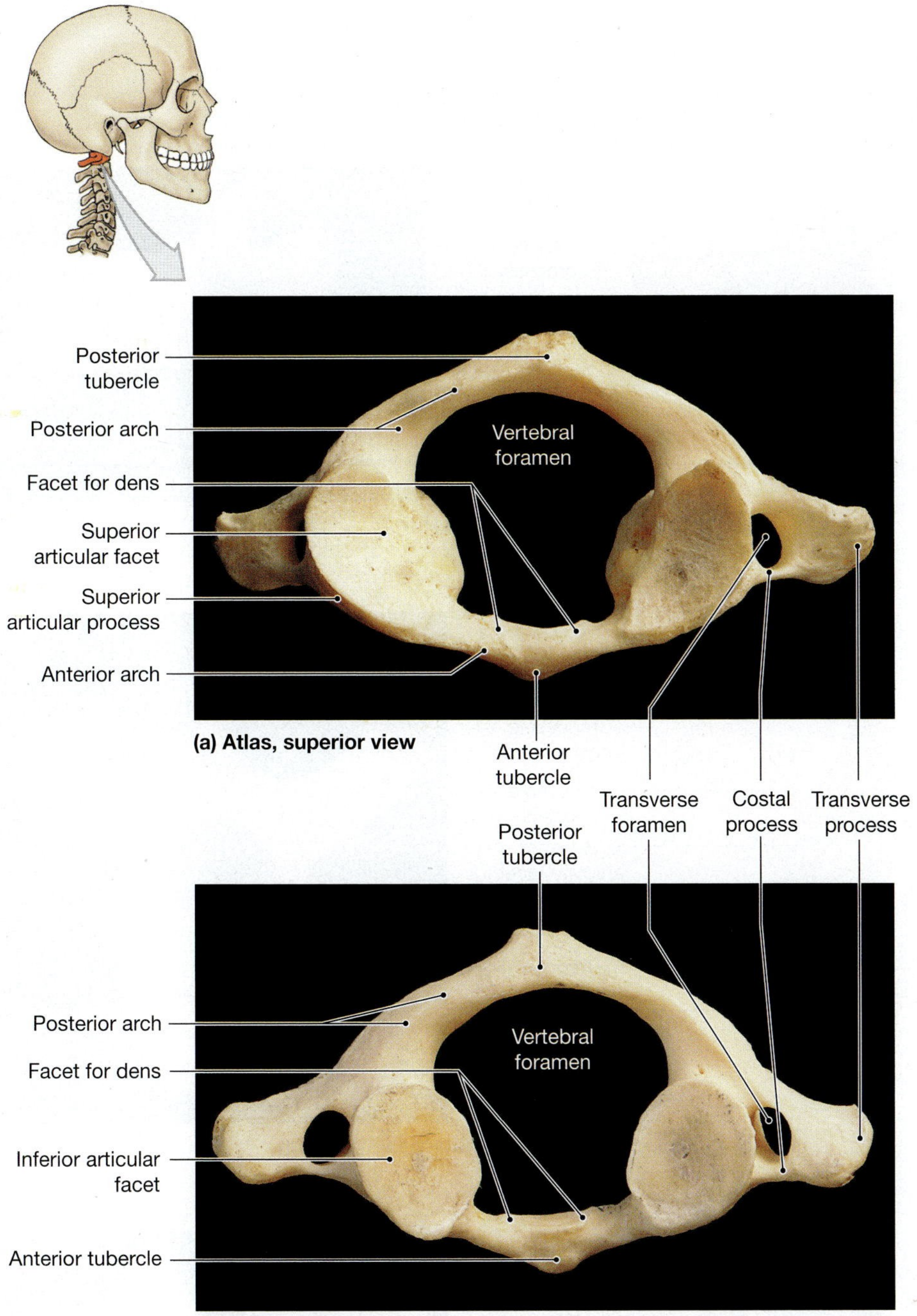

(a) Atlas, superior view

(b) Atlas, inferior view

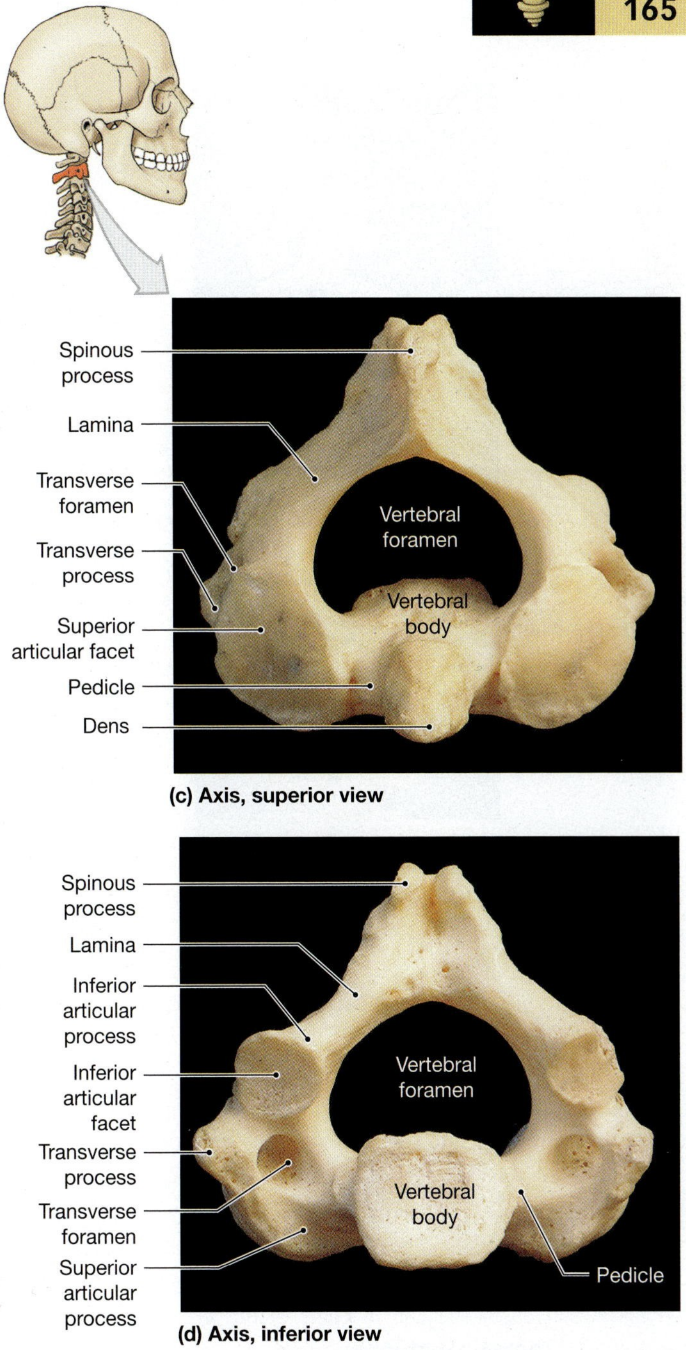

(c) Axis, superior view

(d) Axis, inferior view

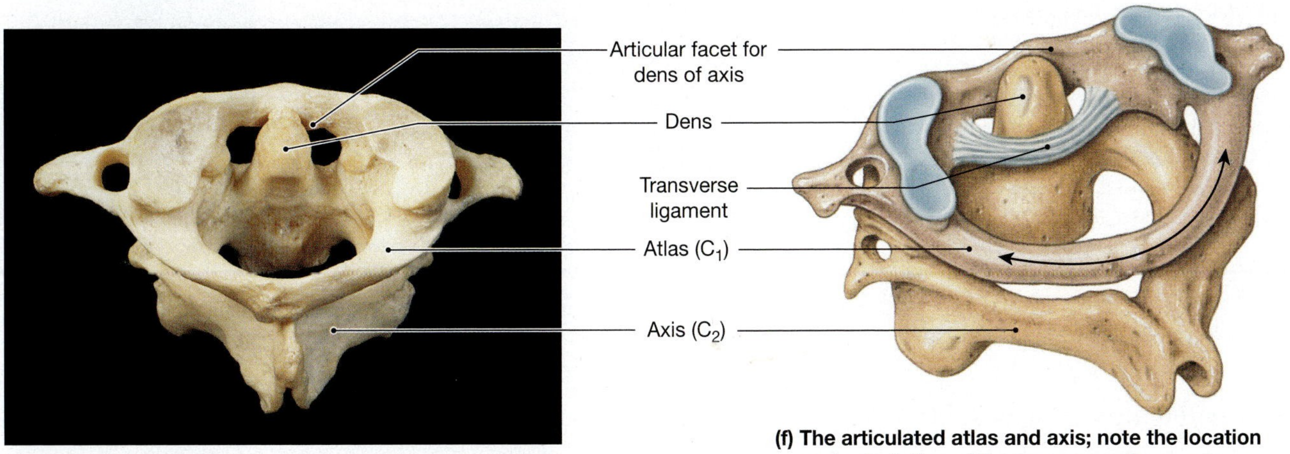

(e) Articulated atlas and axis, superior and posterior view

(f) The articulated atlas and axis; note the location and orientation of the transverse ligament

Figure 6.23 Atlas and Axis

Unique anatomical characteristics of vertebrae C_1 (atlas) and C_2 (axis). The atlas is seen in **(a)** superior view and **(b)** inferior view. The axis is seen in **(c)** superior view and **(d)** inferior view. **(e)** The articulated atlas and axis, in superior and posterior view. **(f)** The articulated atlas (C_1) and axis (C_2), showing the transverse ligament that holds the dens of the axis in position at the articular facet of the atlas.

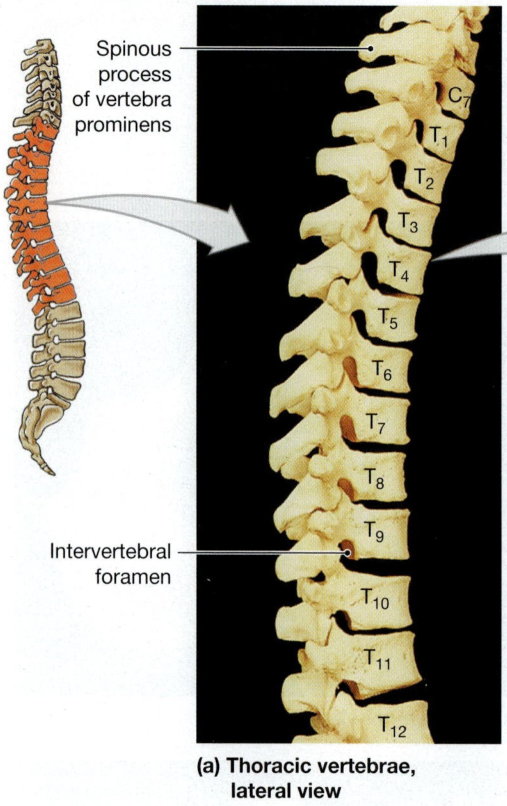

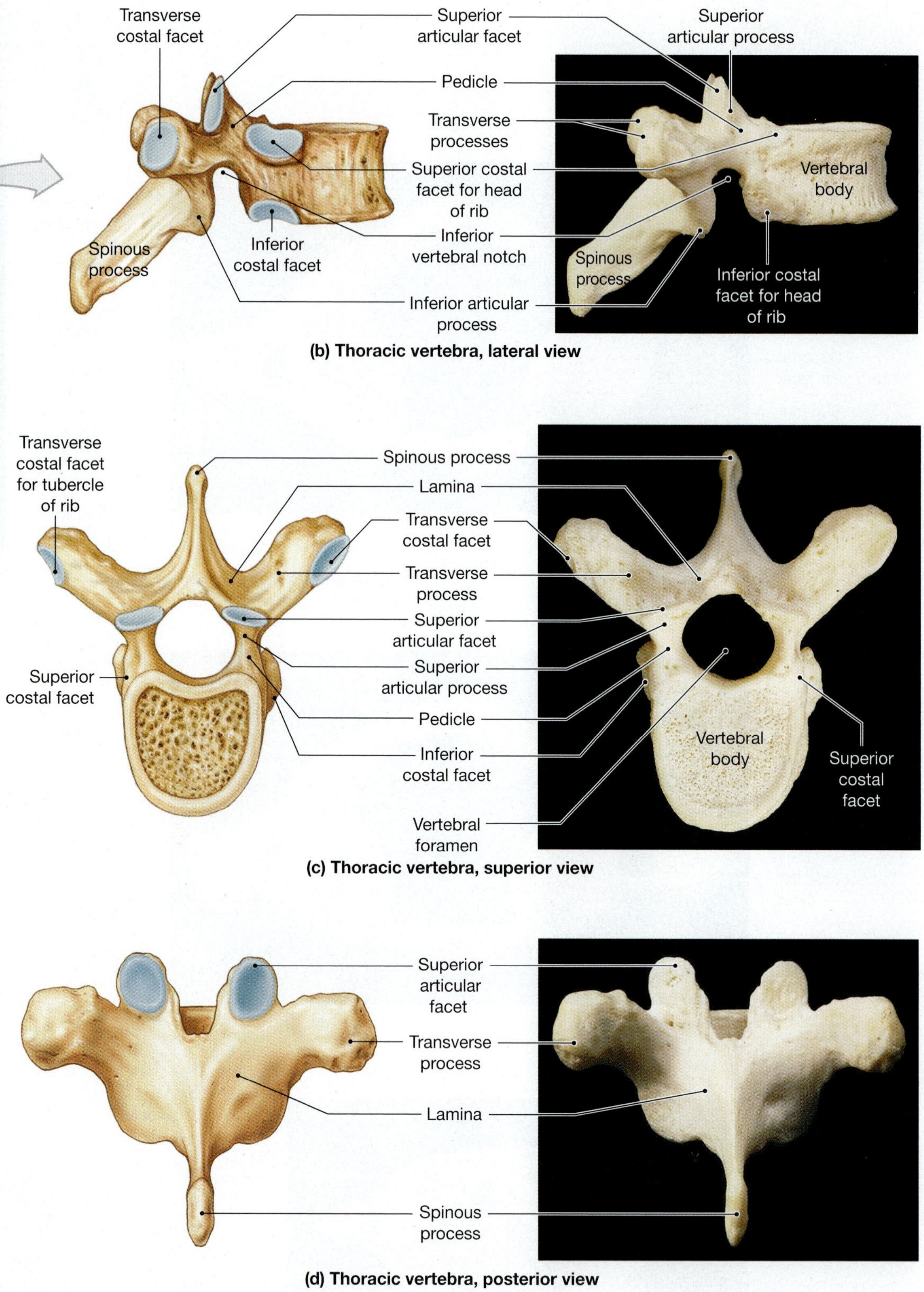

Figure 6.24 Thoracic Vertebrae
The body of each thoracic vertebra articulates with ribs. Note the characteristic features listed in Table 6.3. **(a)** Lateral view of the thoracic region of the vertebral column. The vertebra prominens (C_7) resembles T_1, but it lacks facets for rib articulation. Vertebra T_{12} resembles the first lumbar vertebra (L_1), but it has a facet for rib articulation. A representative thoracic vertebra is shown in **(b)** lateral view, **(c)** superior view, and **(d)** posterior view.

Lumbar Vertebrae [Figure 6.25 and Table 6.3]

The **lumbar vertebrae** are the largest of the vertebrae. The body of a typical lumbar vertebra (**Figure 6.25**) is thicker than that of a thoracic vertebra, and the superior and inferior surfaces are oval rather than heart shaped. There are no articular facets on either the body or the transverse processes, and the vertebral foramen is triangular. The transverse processes are slender and project dorsolaterally, and the stumpy spinous processes project dorsally.

The lumbar vertebrae bear the most weight. Thus a compression injury to the vertebrae or intervertebral discs most often occurs in this region. The most common injury is a tear or rupture in the connective tissues of the intervertebral disc; this condition is known as a herniated disc. The massive spinous processes of the lumbar vertebrae provide surface area for the attachment of lower back muscles that reinforce or adjust the lumbar curvature. Table 6.3, p. 163, summarizes the characteristics of lumbar vertebrae.

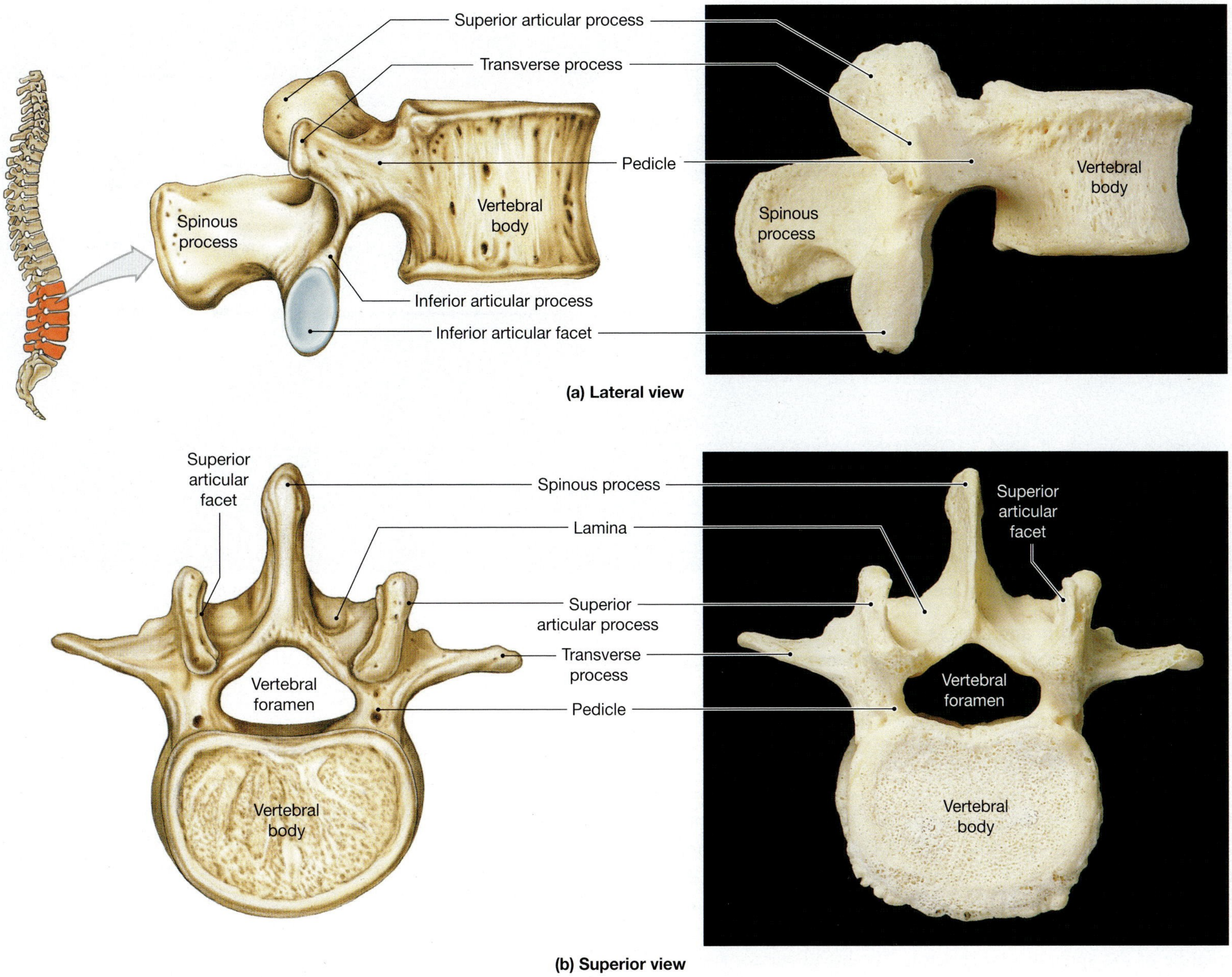

Figure 6.25 Lumbar Vertebrae
The lumbar vertebrae are the largest vertebrae and bear the most weight. A representative lumbar vertebra is shown in **(a)** lateral view and **(b)** superior view.

Clinical Note

Spina Bifida During the third week of embryonic development, the vertebral arches form around the developing spinal cord. In the condition called **spina bifida** (SPĪ-nuh BI-fi-duh; *bifidus*, cut into two parts), the most common neural tube defect (NTD), a portion of the spinal cord develops abnormally such that the adjacent vertebral arches do not form. Because the vertebral arch is incomplete, the membranes (or meninges) that line the dorsal body cavity bulge outward. This is the most common developmental abnormality of the nervous system, occurring at a rate of up to 4 cases per 1000 births. (See the Embryology Summary in Chapter 28 for illustrations of this condition.) Both heredity and maternal diet, particularly the amount of folic acid present before and during early pregnancy, have been linked to NTDs. Women who may become pregnant are advised to take 400 micrograms of folic acid daily, and to assist in this, food in the United States containing wheat, rice, and corn has been fortified with folic acid since 1998. Probably as a result, the incidence of NTDs in the United States dropped 19 percent between 1998 and 2001.

The region affected and the severity of the condition vary widely. It is most common in the inferior thoracic, lumbar, or sacral region, typically involving 3–6 vertebrae. Variable degrees of paralysis occur distal to the affected vertebrae. Mild cases involving the sacral and lumbar regions may pass unnoticed, because neural function is not compromised significantly and "baby fat" may mask the fact that some of the spinous processes are missing. When spina bifida is detected, surgical repairs can close the gap in the vertebral wall. Severe cases, involving the entire spinal column and skull, reflect major problems with the formation of the spinal cord and brain. These neural problems usually kill the fetus before delivery; infants born with such developmental defects seldom survive more than a few hours or days.

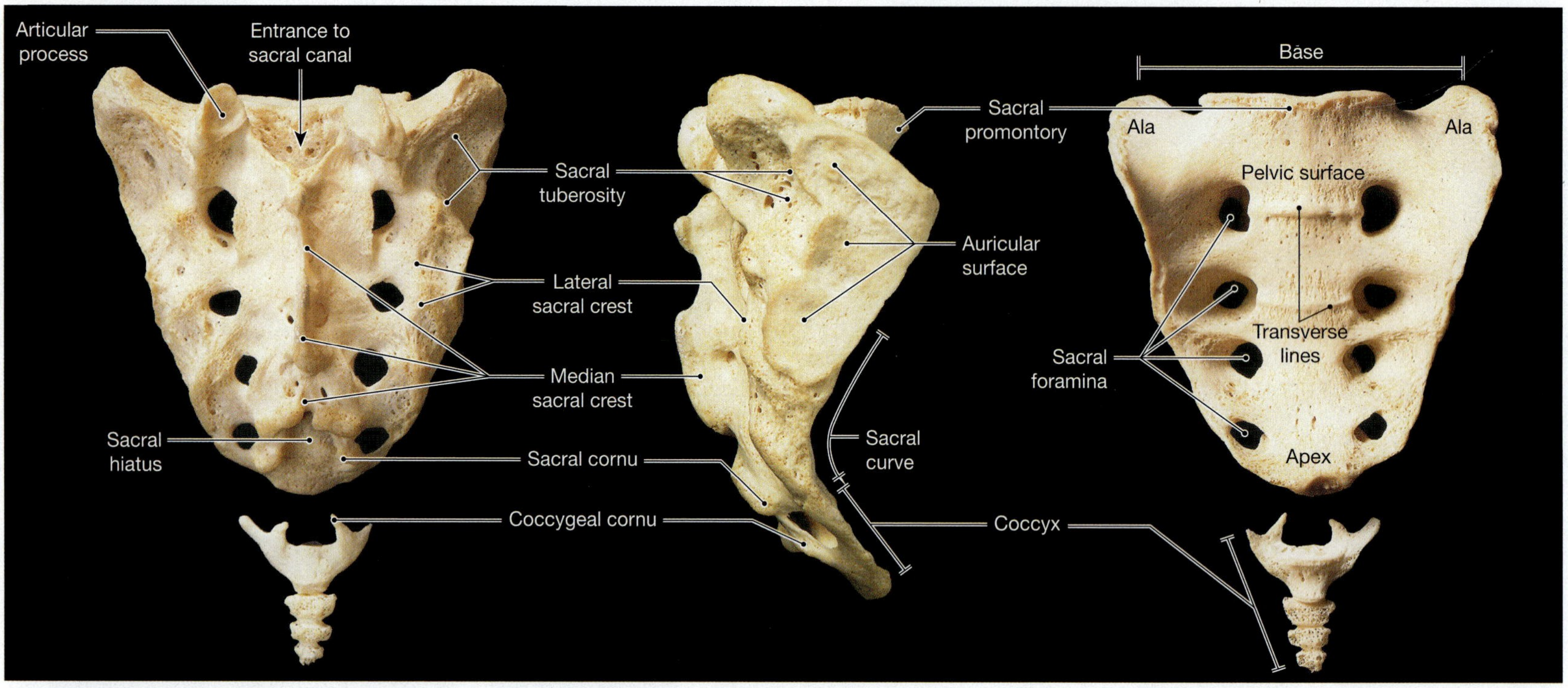

Figure 6.26 The Sacrum and Coccyx
Fused vertebrae form the adult sacrum and coccyx. These bones are shown in **(a)** posterior view, **(b)** lateral view from the right side, and **(c)** anterior view.

The Sacrum [Figure 6.26]

The **sacrum** (Figure 6.26) consists of the fused components of five sacral vertebrae. These vertebrae begin fusing shortly after puberty and are usually completely fused between ages 25 and 30. Once this fusion is complete, prominent *transverse lines* mark the former boundaries of individual vertebrae. This composite structure protects reproductive, digestive, and excretory organs and, via paired articulations, attaches the axial skeleton to the pelvic girdle of the appendicular skeleton. The broad surface area of the sacrum provides an extensive area for the attachment of muscles, especially those responsible for movement of the thigh.

The sacrum is curved, with a convex dorsal surface (Figure 6.26a). The narrow, caudal portion is the sacral **apex**, whereas the broad superior surface forms the **base**. The **sacral promontory**, a prominent bulge at the anterior tip of the base, is an important landmark in females during pelvic examinations and during labor and delivery. The **superior articular processes** form synovial articulations with the last lumbar vertebra. The **sacral canal** begins between those processes and extends the length of the sacrum. Nerves and membranes that line the vertebral canal in the spinal cord continue into the sacral canal.

The spinous processes of the five fused sacral vertebrae form a series of elevations along the **median sacral crest**. The laminae of the fifth sacral vertebra fail to contact one another at the midline, and they form the **sacral cornua**. These ridges establish the margins of the **sacral hiatus** (hī-Ā-tus), the end of the sacral canal. In life, this opening is covered by connective tissues. On either side of the median sacral crest are the **sacral foramina**. The intervertebral foramina, now enclosed by the fused sacral bones, open into these passageways. A broad sacral *wing*, or **ala**, extends laterally from each **lateral sacral crest**. The median and lateral sacral crests provide surface area for the attachment of muscles of the lower back and hip.

Viewed laterally (Figure 6.26b), the *sacral curve* is more apparent. The degree of curvature is greater in males than in females (see Table 7.1, p. 201). Laterally, the **auricular surface** of the sacrum articulates with the pelvic girdle at the **sacro-iliac joint**. Dorsal to the auricular surface is a roughened area, the **sacral tuberosity**, which marks the attachment of a ligament that stabilizes this articulation. The anterior surface, or *pelvic surface*, of the sacrum is concave (Figure 6.26c). At the apex, a flattened area marks the site of articulation with the *coccyx*. The wedgelike shape of the mature sacrum provides a strong foundation for transferring the weight of the body from the axial skeleton to the pelvic girdle.

The Coccyx [Figure 6.26]

The small **coccyx** consists of three to five (most often four) coccygeal vertebrae that have usually begun fusing by age 26 (Figure 6.26). The coccyx provides an attachment site for a number of ligaments and for a muscle that constricts the anal opening. The first two coccygeal vertebrae have transverse processes and unfused vertebral arches. The prominent laminae of the first coccygeal vertebra are known as the **coccygeal cornua**; they curve to meet the cornua of the sacrum. The coccygeal vertebrae do not complete their fusion until late in adulthood. In males, the adult coccyx points anteriorly, whereas in females, it points inferiorly. In very elderly people, the coccyx may fuse with the sacrum.

The Thoracic Cage [Figure 6.27]

The skeleton of the chest, or **thoracic cage**, consists of the thoracic vertebrae, the *ribs*, and the *sternum* (Figure 6.27a,c). The *ribs*, or **costae**, and the sternum form the **rib cage** and support the walls of the thoracic cavity. This cavity is narrow superiorly, broad inferiorly, and somewhat flattened in an anterior-posterior direction. The thoracic cage serves two functions:

- It protects the heart, lungs, thymus, and other structures in the thoracic cavity; and
- It serves as an attachment point for muscles involved with (1) respiration, (2) the position of the vertebral column, and (3) movements of the pectoral girdle and upper limbs.

Figure 6.27 The Thoracic Cage
(a) Anterior view of the rib cage and sternum. **(b)** A superior view of the articulation between a thoracic vertebra and the vertebral end of a right rib. **(c)** Posterior view of the rib cage. **(d)** A posterior and medial view showing major anatomical landmarks on an isolated left rib (rib 10).

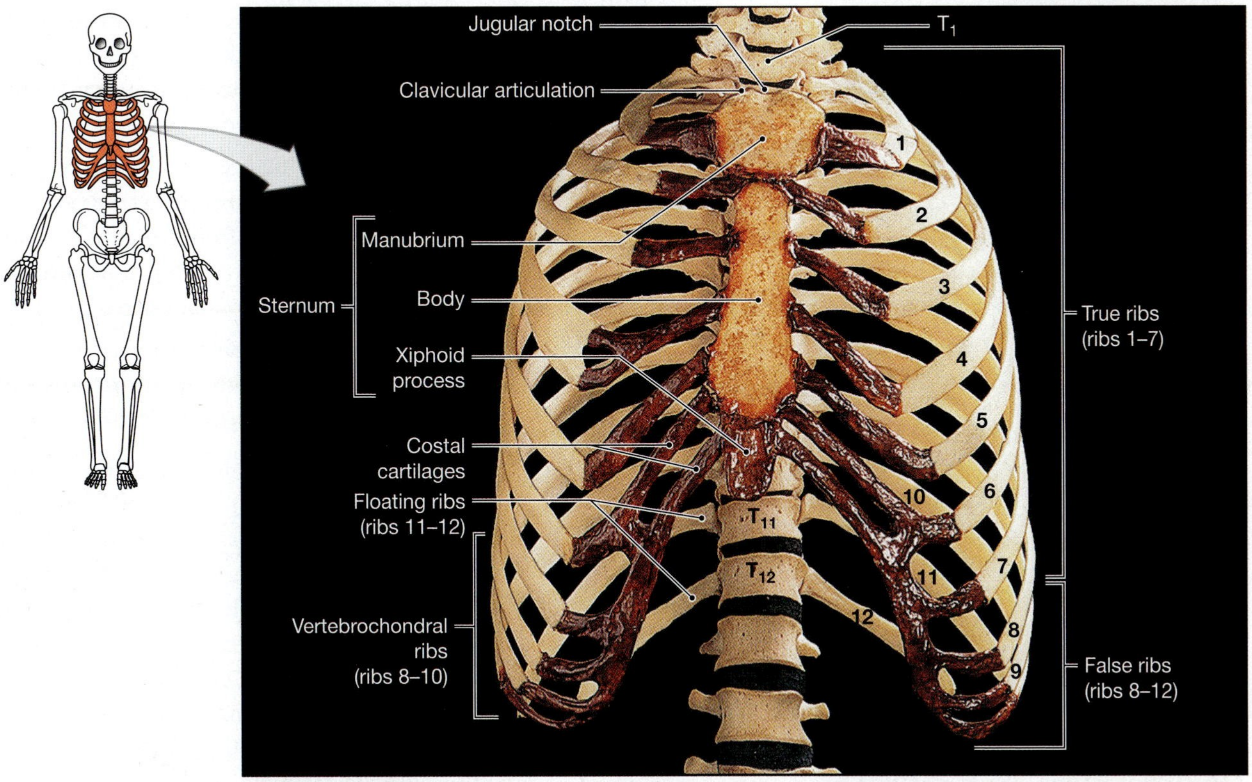

(a) Anterior view

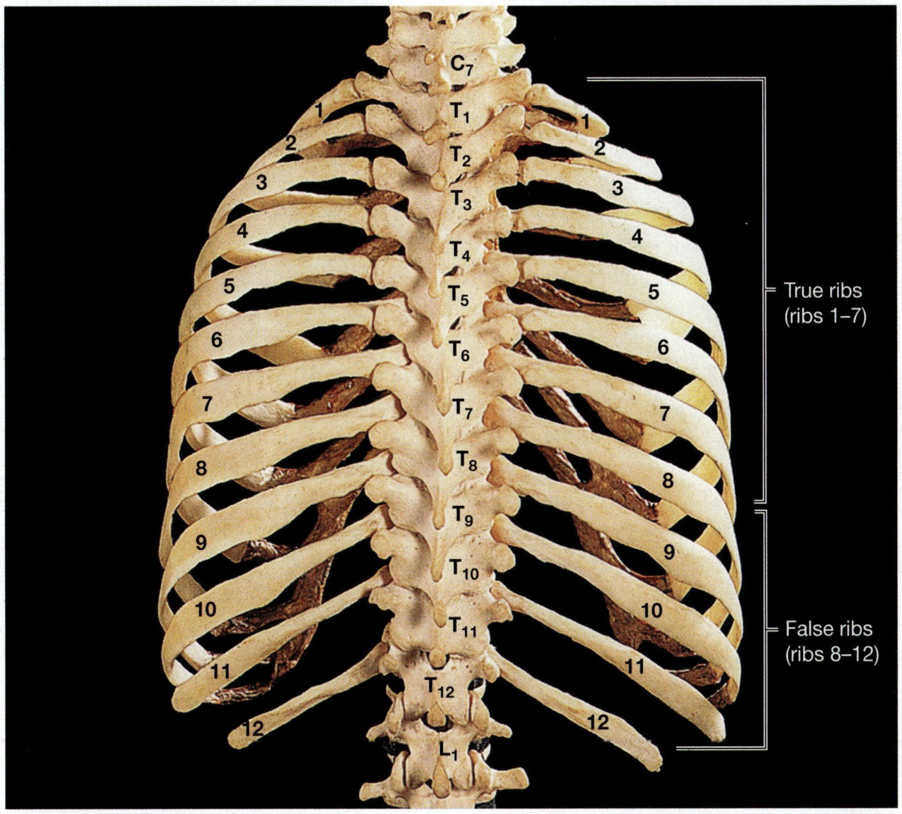

(c) Posterior view

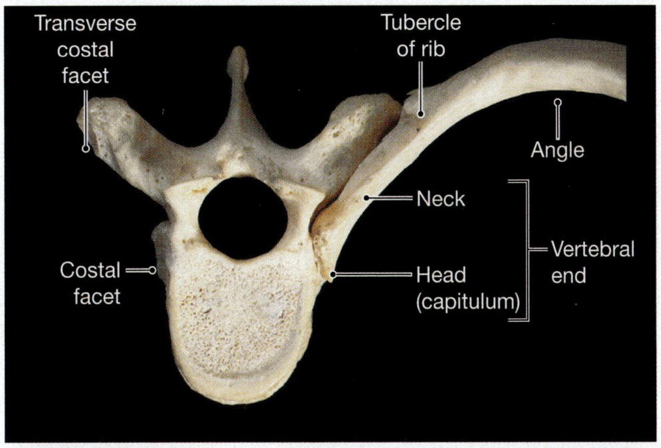

(b) Superior view

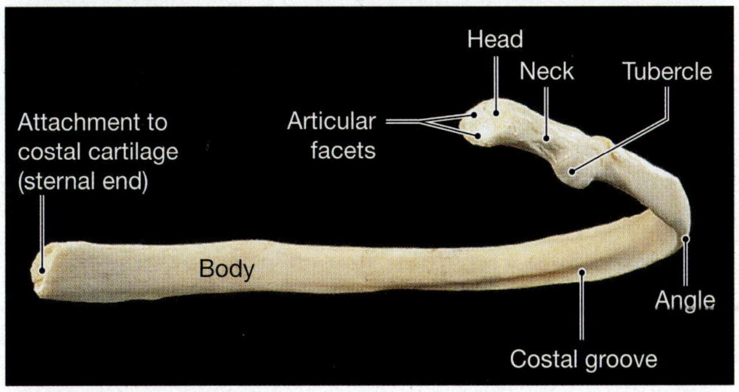

(d) Posterior view

The Ribs [Figures 6.24/6.27]

Ribs, or *costae*, are elongated, curved, flattened bones that (1) originate on or between thoracic vertebrae and (2) end in the wall of the thoracic cavity. There are 12 pairs of ribs (Figure 6.27). The first seven pairs are called **true ribs**, or *vertebrosternal ribs*. At the anterior body wall the true ribs are connected to the sternum by separate cartilages, the **costal cartilages**. Beginning with the first rib, the vertebrosternal ribs gradually increase in length and in the radius of curvature.

Ribs 8–12 are called **false ribs** or *vertebrochondral ribs*, because they do not attach directly to the sternum. The costal cartilages of ribs 8–10 fuse together before reaching the sternum (Figure 6.27a). The last two pairs of ribs are sometimes called **floating ribs** because they have no connection with the sternum.

Figure 6.27b shows the superior surface of the *vertebral end* of a representative rib. The **head**, or *capitulum* (ka-PIT-ū-lum) of each rib articulates with the body of a thoracic vertebra or between adjacent vertebral bodies. After a short **neck**, the **tubercle**, or *tuberculum* (too-BER-kū-lum),

Clinical Note

Cracked Ribs A hockey player is checked into the boards; a basketball player flies out of bounds after a loose ball, slamming into the first row of seats; a wide receiver is hit hard after catching a pass over the middle. Sudden impacts in the chest such as these are relatively common, and the ribs usually take the full force of the contact.

The ribs are composed of spongy bone with a thin outer covering of compact bone. They are firmly bound in connective tissues and are interconnected by layers of muscle. As a result, displaced fractures are uncommon, and rib injuries usually heal swiftly and effectively. In extreme injuries, a broken rib can be forced into the thoracic cavity and can damage internal organs. The entry of air into one of the pleural cavities, a condition known as a **pneumothorax** (noo-mō-THŌR-aks), may lead to a collapsed lung. Damage to a blood vessel or even the heart can cause bleeding into the thoracic cavity, a condition called a hemothorax. A **hemothorax** can also impair lung function because fluid may accumulate and compress a lung.

projects dorsally. The inferior portion of the tubercle contains an articular facet that contacts the transverse process of the thoracic vertebra. When the rib articulates between adjacent vertebrae, the articular surface is divided into **superior** and **inferior articular facets** by the **interarticular crest** (Figure 6.27c,d). Ribs 1 through 10 originate at costal facets on the bodies of vertebrae T_1 to T_{10}, and their tubercular facets articulate with the transverse costal facets of their respective vertebrae. Ribs 11 and 12 originate at costal facets on T_{11} and T_{12}. These ribs do not have tubercular facets and they do not articulate with transverse processes. The difference in rib orientation and articulation with the vertebral column can be seen by comparing Figure 6.24, p. 166, and 6.27c,d.

The bend, or **angle**, of the rib indicates the site where the tubular **body**, or *shaft*, begins curving toward the sternum. The internal rib surface is concave, and a prominent **costal groove** along its inferior border marks the path of nerves and blood vessels. The superficial surface is convex and provides an attachment site for muscles of the pectoral girdle and trunk. The *intercostal muscles* that move the ribs are attached to the superior and inferior surfaces.

With their complex musculature, dual articulations at the vertebrae, and flexible connection to the sternum, the ribs are quite mobile. Note how the ribs curve away from the vertebral column to angle downward. Functionally, a typical rib acts as if it were the handle on a bucket, lying just below the horizontal plane. Pushing it down forces it inward; pulling it up swings it outward. In addition, because of the curvature of the ribs, the same movements change the position of the sternum. Depressing the ribs moves the sternum posteriorly (inward), whereas elevation moves it anteriorly (outward). As a result, movements of the ribs affect both the width and the depth of the thoracic cage, increasing or decreasing its volume accordingly.

The Sternum [Figure 6.27a]

The adult **sternum** is a flat bone that forms in the anterior midline of the thoracic wall (Figure 6.27a). The sternum has three components:

- The broad, triangular **manubrium** (ma-NOO-brē-um) articulates with the *clavicles* (or collarbones) of the appendicular skeleton and the costal cartilages of the first pair of ribs. The manubrium is the widest and most superior portion of the sternum. The **jugular notch** is the shallow indentation on the superior surface of the manubrium. It is located between the clavicular articulations.
- The tongue-shaped **body** attaches to the inferior surface of the manubrium and extends caudally along the midline. Individual costal cartilages from rib pairs 2–7 are attached to this portion of the sternum. The rib pairs 8–10 are also attached to the body, but by a single pair of cartilages shared with rib pair 7.
- The **xiphoid** (ZĪ-foyd) **process**, the smallest part of the sternum, is attached to the inferior surface of the body. The muscular *diaphragm* and the *rectus abdominis muscle* attach to the xiphoid process.

Ossification of the sternum begins at 6 to 10 different centers, and fusion is not completed until at least age 25. Before age 25, the sternal body consists of four separate bones. Their boundaries can be detected as a series of transverse lines crossing the adult sternum. The xiphoid process is usually the last of the sternal components to undergo ossification and fusion. Its connection to the body of the sternum can be broken by an impact or strong pressure, creating a spear of bone that can severely damage the liver. To reduce the chances of that happening, strong emphasis is placed on the proper positioning of the hand during cardiopulmonary resuscitation (CPR) training.

Clinical Note

The Thoracic Cage and Surgical Procedures Surgery on the heart, lungs, or other organs in the thorax often involves entering the thoracic cavity. The mobility of the ribs and the cartilaginous connections with the sternum allow the ribs to be temporarily moved out of the way. Special rib spreaders are used, which push them apart in much the same way that a jack lifts a car off the ground for a tire change. If more extensive access is required, the sternal cartilages can be cut and the entire sternum can be folded out of the way. Once replaced, the cartilages are reunited by scar tissue, and the ribs heal fairly rapidly.

After thoracic surgery, **chest tubes** may penetrate the thoracic wall to permit drainage of fluids. To install a chest tube or obtain a sample of pleural fluid, the wall of the thorax must be penetrated. This process, called **thoracentesis** (thō-ra-sen-TĒ-sis), involves the penetration of the thoracic wall along the superior border of one of the ribs. Penetration at this location avoids damaging vessels and nerves within the costal groove.

CONCEPT CHECK

1. Joe suffered a hairline fracture at the base of the odontoid process. What bone is fractured, and where would you find it?
2. Improper administration of CPR (cardiopulmonary resuscitation) could result in a fracture of what bone?
3. What are the five vertebral regions? What are the identifying features of each region?
4. List the spinal curves in order from superior to inferior.

See blue "Answers" tab at back of book.

CLINICAL TERMS

chest tube: A drain installed after thoracic surgery to permit removal of blood and pleural fluid.

craniostenosis (krā-nē-ō-sten-Ō-sis): Premature closure of one or more sutures, which can lead to unusual distortions of the skull.

deviated nasal septum: A bent nasal septum that may slow or prevent sinus drainage

hemothorax: Bleeding into the thoracic cavity.

kyphosis (kī-FŌ-sis): Abnormal exaggeration of the thoracic curvature that produces a "roundback" appearance.

lordosis (lōr-DŌ-sis): Abnormal lumbar curvature giving a "swayback" appearance.

microcephaly (mī-krō-SEF-a-lē): An undersized head resulting from genetic or developmental abnormalities.

pneumothorax (noo-mō-THŌR-aks): The entry of air into a pleural cavity.

scoliosis (skō-lē-Ō-sis): Abnormal lateral curvature of the spine.

sinusitis: Inflammation and congestion of the paranasal sinuses.

spina bifida (SPĪ-nuh BI-fi-duh): A condition resulting from failure of the vertebral laminae to unite during development; it is often associated with developmental abnormalities of the brain and spinal cord.

thoracentesis (thō-ra-sen-TĒ-sis) or **thoracocentesis:** The penetration of the thoracic wall along the superior border of one of the ribs.

whiplash: An injury resulting from a sudden change in body position that can injure the cervical vertebrae.

STUDY OUTLINE

Introduction 134

1. The skeletal system consists of the axial skeleton and the appendicular skeleton. The **axial skeleton** can be subdivided into the **skull** and associated bones (the **auditory ossicles** and **hyoid bone**), the **vertebral column**, and the **thoracic cage** composed of the **ribs** and **sternum**. *(see Figure 6.1)*
2. The **appendicular skeleton** includes the **pectoral** and **pelvic girdles** that support and attach the upper and lower limbs to the trunk. *(see Figure 6.1)*

The Skull and Associated Bones 135

1. The **skull** consists of the *cranium* and the *bones of the face.* Skull bones protect the brain and guard entrances to the digestive and respiratory systems. Eight skull bones form the **cranium**, which encloses the **cranial cavity**, a division of the dorsal body cavity. The **facial bones** protect and support the entrances to the respiratory and digestive systems. *(see Figures 6.2 to 6.15 and Tables 6.1/6.2)*
2. Prominent superficial landmarks on the skull include the **lambdoid**, **sagittal**, **coronal**, **squamous**, and **frontonasal** sutures. **Sutures** are immovable joints that form boundaries between skull bones. (see *Figure 6.3a–d and Tables 6.1/6.2)*

Bones of the Cranium 142

3. For articulations of cranial bones with other cranial bones and/or facial bones, *see Table 6.2.*
4. The **occipital bone** forms part of the base of the skull. It surrounds the **foramen magnum** and forms part of the wall of the **jugular foramen**. (*see Figures 6.3a–c,e/6.6a,b)*
5. The **parietal bones** form part of the superior and lateral surfaces of the cranium. *(see* Figures 6.3b,c/6.5/6.6c*)*
6. The **frontal bone** forms the forehead and roof of the orbits. *(see Figures 6.3b–d/6.5/6.7)*
7. The **temporal bone** forms part of the wall of the jugular foramen and houses the **carotid canal**. The thick **petrous part** of the temporal bone houses the tympanic cavity containing the **auditory ossicles**. The auditory ossicles transfer sound vibrations from the tympanic membrane to a fluid-filled chamber in the inner ear. *(see Figures 6.3c–e/Figures 6.8/Figures 18.10)*
8. The **sphenoid** contributes to the floor of the cranium. It is a bridge between the cranial and facial bones. **Optic nerves** pass through the **optic canal** in the sphenoid to reach the brain. **Pterygoid processes** form **plates** that serve as sites for attachment of muscles that move the mandible and soft palate. *(see Figures 6.3c–e/6.4/6.9)*
9. The **ethmoid** is an irregularly shaped bone that forms part of the orbital wall and the roof of the nasal cavity. The **cribriform plate** of the ethmoid contains perforations for olfactory nerves. The **perpendicular plate** forms part of the *nasal septum. (see Figures 6.3d/6.4/6.5/6.10)*
10. **Cranial fossae** are curving depressions in the cranial floor that closely follow the shape of the brain. The **anterior cranial fossa** is formed by the frontal bone, the ethmoid, and the **lesser wings** of the sphenoid. The **middle cranial fossa** is created by the sphenoid, temporal, and parietal bones. The **posterior cranial fossa** is primarily formed by the occipital bone, with contributions from the temporal and parietal bones. *(see Figure 6.11)*

Bones of the Face 148

11. For articulations of facial bones with other facial bones and/or cranial bones, *see Table 6.2.*
12. The left and right **maxillae**, or *maxillary bones*, are the largest facial bones and form the upper jaw. *(see Figures 6.3d/6.12)*
13. The **palatine bones** are small, L-shaped bones that form the posterior portions of the hard palate and contribute to the floor of the orbit. *(see Figures 6.3e/6.13)*
14. The paired **nasal bones** articulate with the frontal bone at the midline and articulate with cartilages that form the superior borders of the **external nares**. *(see Figures 6.3c,d/6.15/6.16)*
15. One **inferior nasal concha** is located on each side of the **nasal septum**, attached to the lateral wall of the nasal cavity. They increase the epithelial surface area and create turbulence in the inspired air. The superior and middle conchae of the ethmoid perform the same functions. *(see Figures 6.3d/6.16)*
16. The **temporal process** of the **zygomatic bone** articulates with the **zygomatic process** of the temporal bone to form the **zygomatic arch** (*cheekbone*). *(see Figures 6.3c,d/6.15)*
17. The paired **lacrimal bones** are the smallest bones in the skull. They are situated in the medial portion of each orbit. Each lacrimal bone forms a **lacrimal groove** with the adjacent maxilla, and this groove leads to a **nasolacrimal canal** that delivers tears to the nasal cavity. *(see Figures 6.3c,d/6.16)*
18. The **vomer** forms the inferior portion of the nasal septum. It is based on the floor of the nasal cavity and articulates with both the maxillae and the palatines along the midline. *(see Figures 6.3c,d/6.5/6.16)*
19. The **mandible** is the entire lower jaw. It articulates with the temporal bone at the *temporomandibular joint* (TMJ). *(see Figures 6.3c,d/6.14)*

The Orbital and Nasal Complexes 151

20. Seven bones form the **orbital complex**, a bony recess that contains an eye: frontal, lacrimal, palatine, and zygomatic bones and the ethmoid, sphenoid, and maxillae. *(see Figure 6.16)*
21. The **nasal complex** includes the bones and cartilage that enclose the nasal cavities and the **paranasal sinuses**. Paranasal sinuses are hollow airways that interconnect with the nasal passages. Large paranasal sinuses are present in the frontal bone and the sphenoid, ethmoid, and maxillae. *(see Figures 6.5/6.16)*

The Hyoid Bone 154

22. The **hyoid bone**, suspended by **stylohyoid ligaments**, consists of a **body**, the **greater horns**, and the **lesser horns**. The hyoid bone serves as a base for several muscles concerned with movements of the tongue and larynx. *(see Figure 6.17)*

The Skulls of Infants, Children, and Adults 158

1. Fibrous connections at **fontanels** permit the skulls of infants and children to continue growing. *(see Figure 6.18)*

The Vertebral Column 158

1. The adult **vertebral column** consists of 26 bones (24 individual *vertebrae*, the *sacrum*, and the *coccyx*). There are 7 *cervical vertebrae* (the first articulates with the occipital bone), 12 *thoracic vertebrae* (which articulate with the ribs), and 5 *lumbar vertebrae* (the fifth articulates with the *sacrum*). The sacrum and coccyx consist of fused vertebrae. *(see Figures 6.19 to 6.26)*

Spinal Curves 159

2. The spinal column has four **spinal curves:** the **thoracic** and **sacral curves** are called **primary**, or **accommodation curvatures**; the **lumbar** and **cervical curves** are known as **secondary**, or **compensation**, **curvatures**. *(see Figure 6.19)*

Vertebral Anatomy 161

3. A typical vertebra has a thick, supporting **body**, or *centrum*; it has a **vertebral arch** (**neural arch**) formed by walls (**pedicles**) and a roof (**lamina**) that provide a space for the spinal cord; and it articulates with other vertebrae at the **superior** and **inferior articular processes**. *(see Figure 6.21)*
4. Adjacent vertebrae are separated by **intervertebral discs**. Spaces between successive pedicles form the **intervertebral foramina** through which nerves pass to and from the spinal cord. *(see Figure 6.21)*

Vertebral Regions 162

5. **Cervical vertebrae** are distinguished by the shape of the vertebral body, the relative size of the vertebral foramen, the presence of **costal processes** with **transverse foramina**, and bifid **spinous processes**. *(see Figures 6.19/6.22/6.23 and Table 6.3)*
6. **Thoracic vertebrae** have distinctive heart-shaped bodies; long, slender spinous processes; and articulations for the ribs. *(see Figures 6.19/6.24)*
7. The **lumbar vertebrae** are the most massive and least mobile; they are subjected to the greatest strains. *(see Figures 6.19/6.25)*
8. The **sacrum** protects reproductive, digestive, and excretory organs. It has an **auricular surface** for articulation with the pelvic girdle. The sacrum articulates with the fused elements of the **coccyx**. *(see Figure 6.26)*

The Thoracic Cage 168

1. The skeleton of the **thoracic cage** consists of the *thoracic vertebrae*, the *ribs*, and the *sternum*. The ribs and sternum form the **rib cage**. *(see Figure 6.27a,c)*

The Ribs 169

2. **Ribs** 1–7 are **true**, or *vertebrosternal*, **ribs**. Ribs 8–12 are called **false**, or *vertebrochondral*, **ribs**. The last two pairs of ribs are **floating ribs**. The *vertebral end* of a typical rib articulates with the vertebral column at the **head**, or **capitulum**. After a short **neck**, the **tubercle**, or *tuberculum*, projects dorsally. A bend, or **angle**, of the rib indicates the site where the tubular **body**, or **shaft**, begins curving toward the sternum. A prominent, inferior **costal groove** marks the path of nerves and blood vessels. *(see Figures 6.24/6.27)*

The Sternum 170

3. The **sternum** consists of a **manubrium**, a **body**, and a **xiphoid process**. *(see Figure 6.27a)*

CHAPTER REVIEW

For answers to the Concept Check and Chapter Review questions, go to the blue "Answers" tab at the back of the book.

Level 1 Reviewing Facts and Terms

Match each numbered item with the most closely related lettered item. Use letters for answers in the spaces provided.

Column A	Column B
b 1. suture	a. mandible
e 2. foramen magnum	b. boundary between skull bones
h 3. mastoid process	c. maxillae
___ 4. optic canal	d. cervical vertebrae
i 5. crista galli	e. occipital bone
a 6. condylar process	f. sternum
___ 7. transverse foramen	g. thoracic vertebrae
___ 8. costal facets	h. temporal bone
___ 9. manubrium	i. ethmoid
c 10. upper jaw	j. sphenoid

11. Which of the following is/are true of the ethmoid?
    (a) it contains the crista galli
    (b) it contains the cribriform plate
    (c) it serves as the anterior attachment of the falx cerebri
    (d) all of the above
12. Which of the following applies to the sella turcica?
    (a) it supports and protects the pituitary gland
    (b) it is bounded directly laterally by the foramen spinosum
    (c) as is true for the mastoid process and air cells, it does not develop until after birth
    (d) it permits passage of the optic nerves
13. The lower jaw articulates with the temporal bone at the
    (a) mandibular fossa
    (b) mastoid process
    (c) superior clinoid process
    (d) cribriform plate

14. The hyoid bone
    (a) serves as a base of attachment for muscles that move the tongue
    (b) is part of the mandible
    (c) is located inferior to the larynx
    (d) articulates with the maxillae
15. The vertebral structure that has a pedicle and a lamina, and from which the spinous process projects, is the
    (a) centrum (b) transverse process
    (c) inferior articular process (d) vertebral arch
16. The role of fontanels is to
    (a) allow for compression of the skull during childbirth
    (b) serve as ossification centers for the facial bones
    (c) serve as the final bony plates of the skull
    (d) lighten the weight of the skull bones
17. The sacrum
    (a) provides protection for reproductive, digestive, and excretory organs
    (b) bears the most weight in the vertebral column
    (c) articulates with the pectoral girdle
    (d) is composed of vertebrae that are completely fused by puberty
18. The side walls of the vertebral foramen are formed by the
    (a) body of the vertebra (b) spinous process
    (c) pedicles (d) laminae
19. The portion of the sternum that articulates with the clavicles is the
    (a) manubrium (b) body
    (c) xiphoid process (d) angle
20. The prominent groove along the inferior border of the internal rib surface
    (a) provides an attachment for intercostal muscles
    (b) is called the costal groove
    (c) marks the path of nerves and blood vessels
    (d) both b and c are correct

Level 2 Reviewing Concepts

1. The primary spinal curves
    (a) are also called compensation curves
    (b) include the lumbar curvature
    (c) develop several months after birth
    (d) accommodate the thoracic and pelvic viscera
2. As you move inferiorly from the atlas, you will note that free space for the spinal cord is greatest at C_1. What function would this increased space serve?
3. What is the relationship between the pituitary gland and the sphenoid bone?
4. The secondary curves of the vertebral column develop several months after birth. With their development they shift the trunk weight over the legs. What does this shifting of weight help accomplish?
5. Describe the relationship between the ligamentum nuchae and the axial skeleton with respect to holding the head in the upright position.
6. Discuss factors that can cause increased mucus production by the mucous membranes of the paranasal sinuses.
7. Why are the largest vertebral bodies found in the lumbar region?
8. What is the relationship between the temporal bone and the ear?
9. What is the purpose of the many small openings in the cribriform plate of the ethmoid bone?

Level 3 Critical Thinking

1. Elise is in her last month of pregnancy and is suffering from lower back pain. Since she is carrying her excess weight in front of her, she wonders why her back hurts. What would you tell her?
2. Jeff gets into a brawl at a sports event and receives a broken nose. After the nose heals, he starts to have sinus headaches and discomfort in the area of his maxillae. What is the probable cause of Jeff's discomfort?
3. Some of the symptoms of the common cold or flu include an ache in all of the teeth in the maxillae, even though there is nothing wrong with them, as well as a heavy feeling in the front of the head. What anatomical response to the infection causes these unpleasant sensations?
4. A model is said to be very photogenic, and is often complimented on her high cheekbones and large eyes. Would these features have an anatomical basis, or could they be explained in another manner?

7

The Skeletal System

Appendicular Division

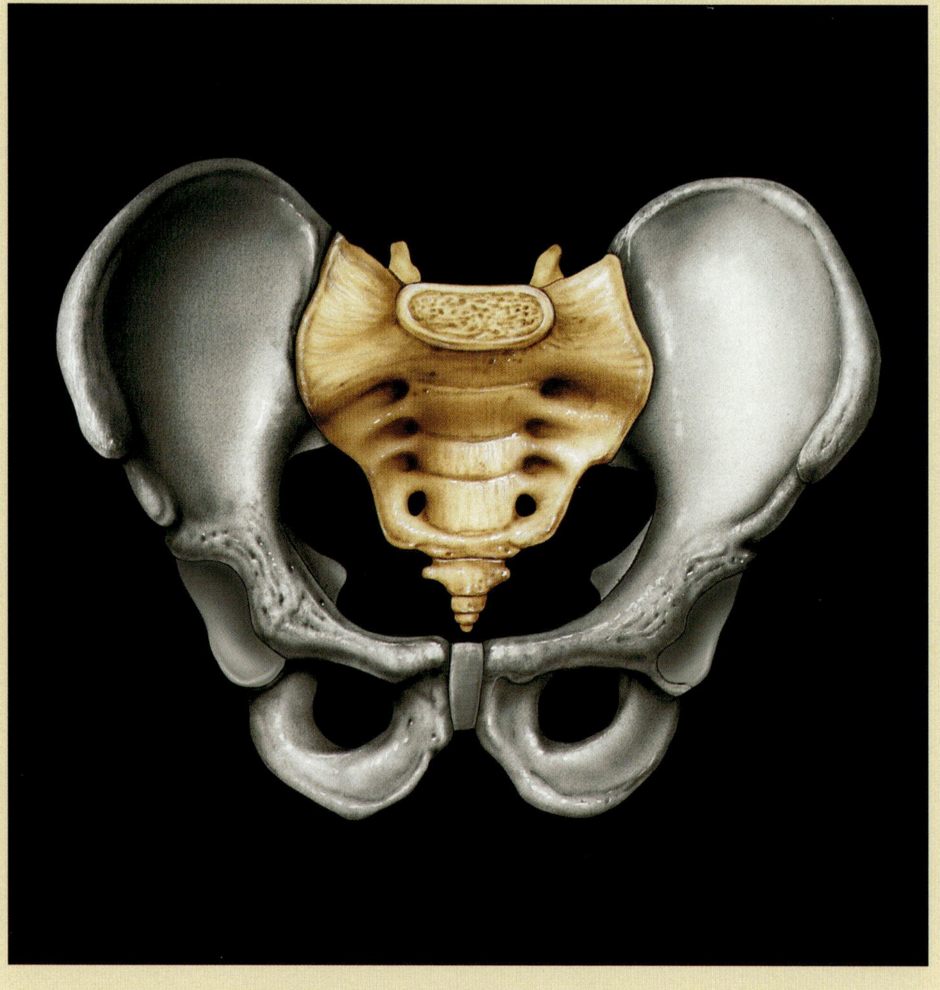

CHAPTER OBJECTIVES

1. Identify the bones of the pectoral girdle and upper limb and their prominent surface features.
2. Identify the bones that form the pelvic girdle and lower limb and their prominent surface features.
3. Discuss the structural and functional differences between the pelvis of a female and that of a male.
4. Explain how studying the skeleton can reveal important information about an individual.
5. Summarize the skeletal differences between males and females.
6. Briefly describe how the aging process affects the skeletal system.

If you make a list of the things you've done today, you will see that your appendicular skeleton plays a major role in your life. Standing, walking, writing, eating, dressing, shaking hands, and turning the pages of a book—the list goes on and on. Your axial skeleton protects and supports internal organs, and it participates in vital functions, such as respiration. But your appendicular skeleton gives you control over your environment, changes your position in space, and provides mobility.

The **appendicular skeleton** includes the bones of the upper and lower limbs and the supporting elements, called *girdles*, that connect them to the trunk (**Figure 7.1**). This chapter describes the bones of the appendicular skeleton. As in Chapter 6, the descriptions emphasize surface features that have functional importance and highlight the interactions among the skeletal system and other systems. For example, many of the anatomical features noted in this chapter are attachment sites for skeletal muscles or openings for nerves and blood vessels that supply the bones or other organs of the body.

There are direct anatomical connections between the skeletal and muscular systems. As noted in Chapter 5, the connective tissue of the deep fascia that surrounds a skeletal muscle is continuous with that of its tendon, which continues into the periosteum and becomes part of the bone matrix

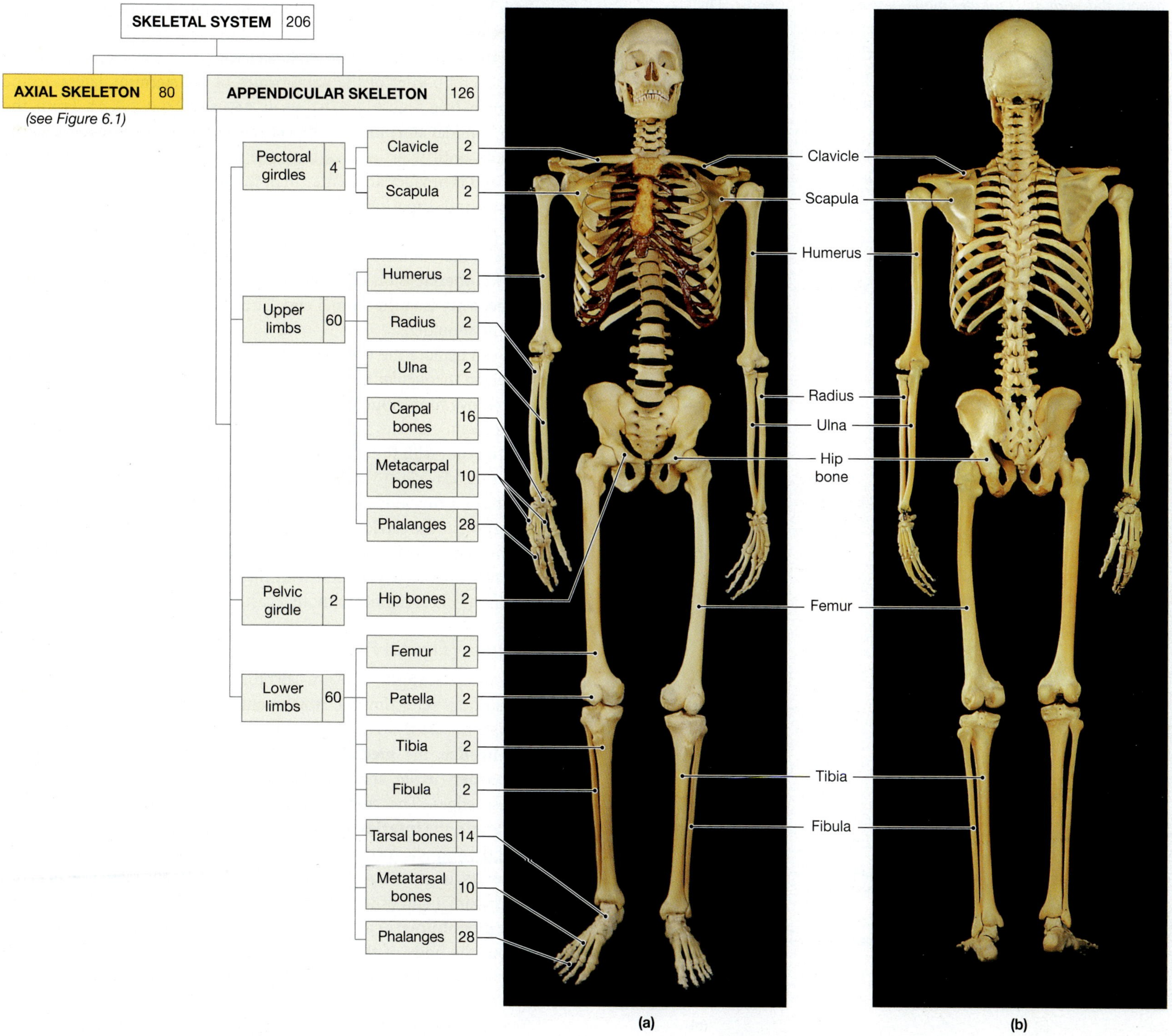

Figure 7.1 The Appendicular Skeleton
A flowchart showing the relationship of the components of the appendicular skeleton: pectoral and pelvic girdles, and upper and lower limbs. **(a)** Anterior view of the skeleton, highlighting the appendicular components. The numbers in the boxes indicate the total number of bones of that type or category in the adult skeleton. **(b)** Posterior view of the skeleton.

at its attachment site. pp. 116–117 Muscles and bones are also physiologically linked, because muscle contractions can occur only when the extracellular concentration of calcium remains within relatively narrow limits. The skeleton contains most of the body's calcium, and these reserves are vital to calcium homeostasis.

The Pectoral Girdle and Upper Limb [Figure 7.2]

Each arm articulates with the trunk at the **pectoral girdle**, or *shoulder girdle*. The pectoral girdle consists of the S-shaped *clavicle (collarbone)* and a broad, flat *scapula (shoulder blade)*, as seen in Figure 7.2. The clavicle articulates with the manubrium of the sternum, and this is the *only* direct connection between the pectoral girdle and the axial skeleton. Skeletal muscles support and position the scapula, which has no direct bony or ligamentous connections to the thoracic cage. Each upper limb consists of the *brachium* (arm), the *antebrachium* (forearm), the wrist, and the hand. The skeleton of the upper limb consists of the *humerus* of the arm, the *ulna* and *radius* of the forearm, the *carpal bones* of the *carpus* (wrist), and the *metacarpal bones* and *phalanges* of the hand.

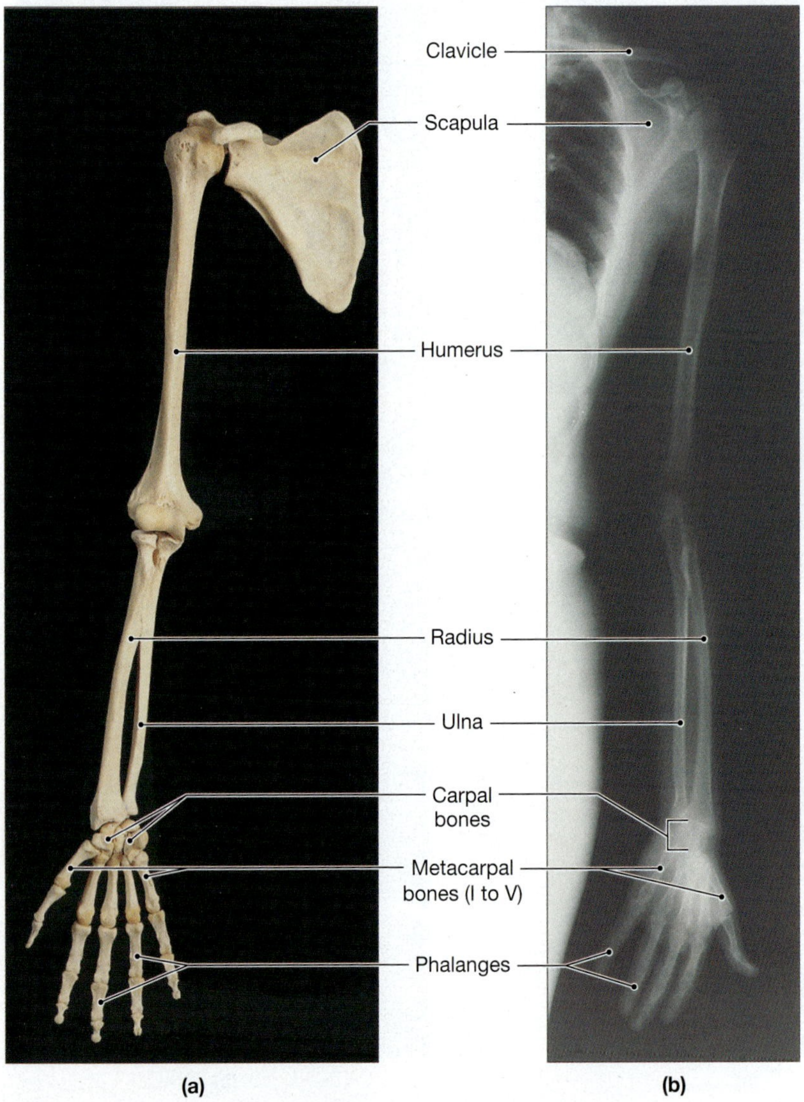

Figure 7.2 The Pectoral Girdle and Upper Limb
Each upper limb articulates with the axial skeleton at the trunk through the pectoral girdle. **(a)** Right upper limb, anterior view. **(b)** X-ray of right pectoral girdle and upper limb, posterior view.

The Pectoral Girdle

Movements of the clavicle and scapula position the shoulder joint and provide a base for arm movement. Once the shoulder joint is in position, muscles that originate on the pectoral girdle help move the upper limb. The surfaces of the scapula and clavicle are therefore extremely important as sites for muscle attachment. Where major muscles attach, they leave their marks, creating bony ridges and flanges. Other bone markings, such as grooves or foramina, indicate the position of nerves or blood vessels that control the muscles and nourish the muscles and bones.

The Clavicle [Figures 7.3/7.4]

The **clavicle** (KLAV-i-kl) (Figure 7.3) connects the pectoral girdle and the axial skeleton. The clavicle braces the shoulder and transfers some of the weight of the upper limb to the axial skeleton. Each clavicle originates at the craniolateral border of the manubrium of the sternum, lateral to the jugular notch (see Figure 6.27a, p. 169 and Figure 7.4). From the roughly pyramidal **sternal end**, the clavicle curves in an S-shape laterally and dorsally until it articulates with the acromion of the scapula. The **acromial end** is broader and flatter than the sternal end.

The smooth superior surface of the clavicle lies just deep to the skin; the rough inferior surface of the acromial end is marked by prominent lines and tubercles that indicate the attachment sites for muscles and ligaments. The **conoid tubercle** is on the inferior surface at the acromial end, and the **costal tuberosity** is at the sternal end. These are attachment sites for ligaments of the shoulder.

You can explore the interaction between scapulae and clavicles. With your fingers in the *jugular notch*, locate the clavicle to either side. p. 169 When you move your shoulders, you can feel the clavicles change their positions. Because the clavicles are so close to the skin, you can trace one laterally until it articulates with the scapula. Shoulder movements are limited by the position of the clavicle at the *sternoclavicular joint*, as shown in Figure 7.4. The structure of this joint will be described in Chapter 8. Fractures of the medial portion of the clavicle are common because a fall on the palm of the hand of an outstretched arm produces compressive forces that are conducted to the clavicle and its articulation with the manubrium. Fortunately, these fractures usually heal rapidly without a cast.

The Scapula [Figures 7.4/7.5]

The **body** of the **scapula** (SCAP-ū-lah) forms a broad triangle with many surface markings reflecting the attachment of muscles, tendons, and ligaments (Figure 7.5a,d). The three sides of the scapular triangle are the **superior border**; the **medial**, or *vertebral*, **border**; and the **lateral**, or *axillary*, **border** (*axilla*, armpit). Muscles that position the scapula attach along these edges. The corners of the scapular triangle are called the **superior angle**, the **inferior angle**, and the **lateral angle**. The lateral angle, or *head* of the scapula, forms a broad process that supports the cup-shaped **glenoid cavity**, or *glenoid fossa*. At the glenoid cavity, the scapula articulates with the proximal end of the *humerus*, the bone of the arm. This articulation is the **glenohumeral joint**, or **shoulder joint**. The lateral angle is separated from the body of the scapula by the rounded **neck**. The relatively smooth, concave **subscapular fossa** forms most of the anterior surface of the scapula.

Two large scapular processes extend over the superior margin of the glenoid cavity, superior to the head of the humerus. The smaller, anterior projection is the **coracoid** (KOR-a-koyd; *korakodes*, like a crow's beak) **process**. This process projects anteriorly and slightly laterally, and serves as an attachment site for the short head of the *biceps brachii muscle*, a

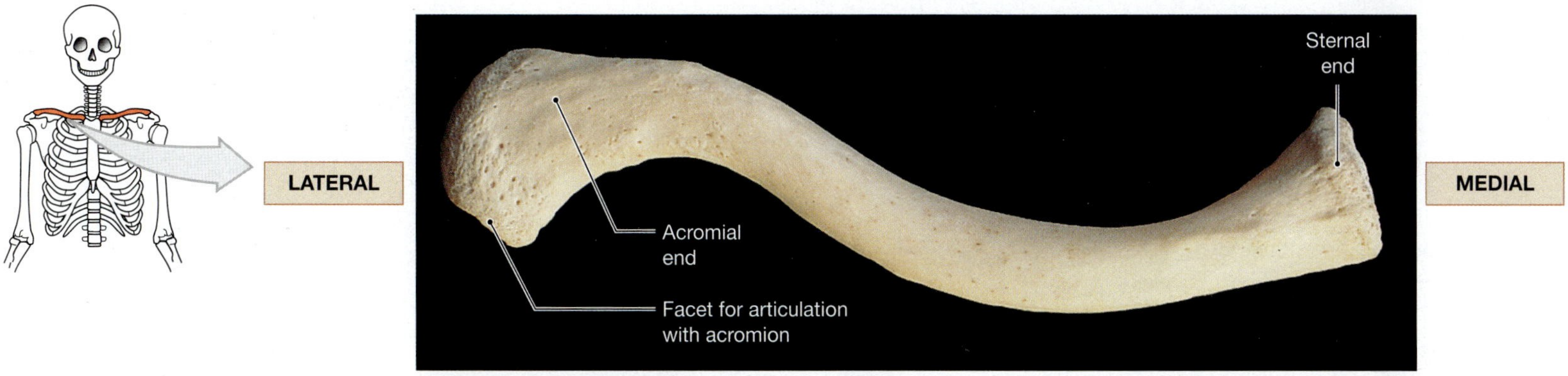

(a) Superior view

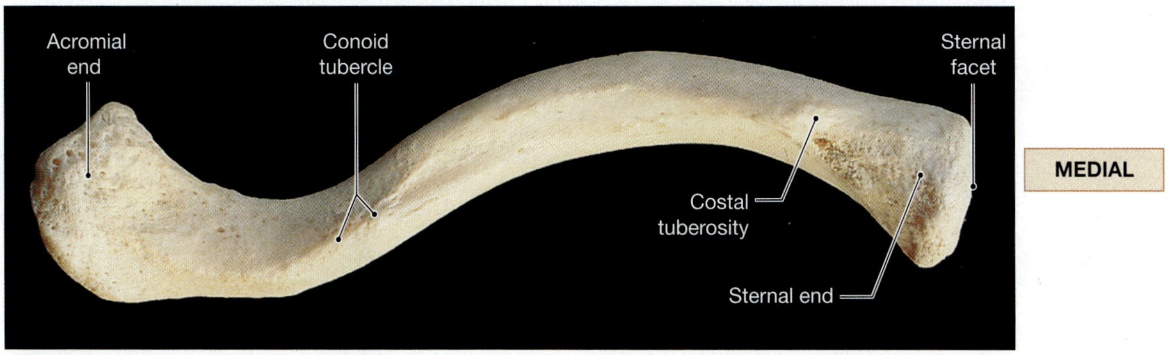

(b) Inferior view

Figure 7.3 The Clavicle
The clavicle is the only direct connection between the pectoral girdle and the axial skeleton. **(a)** Superior and **(b)** inferior views of the right clavicle.

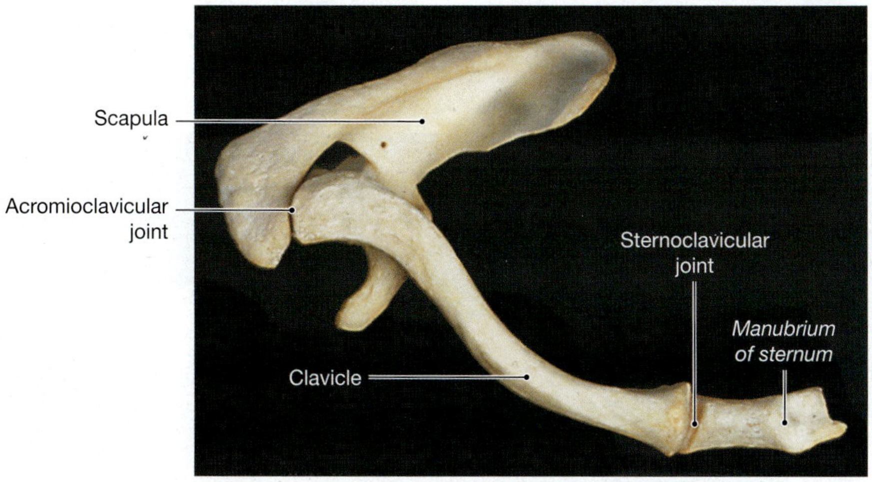

(a) Bones of the right pectoral girdle, superior view

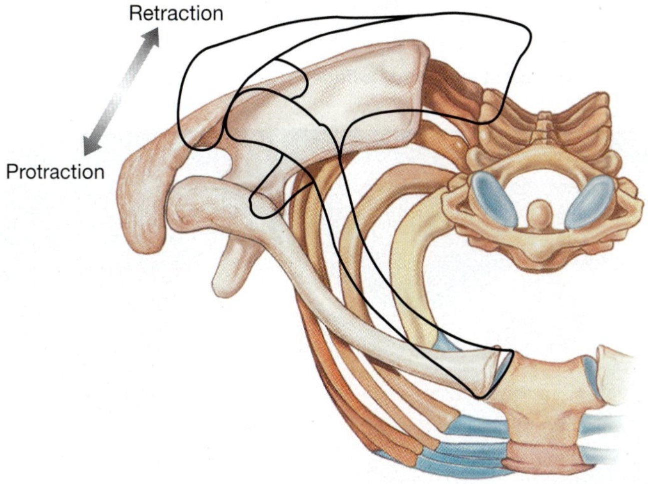

(b) Superior view

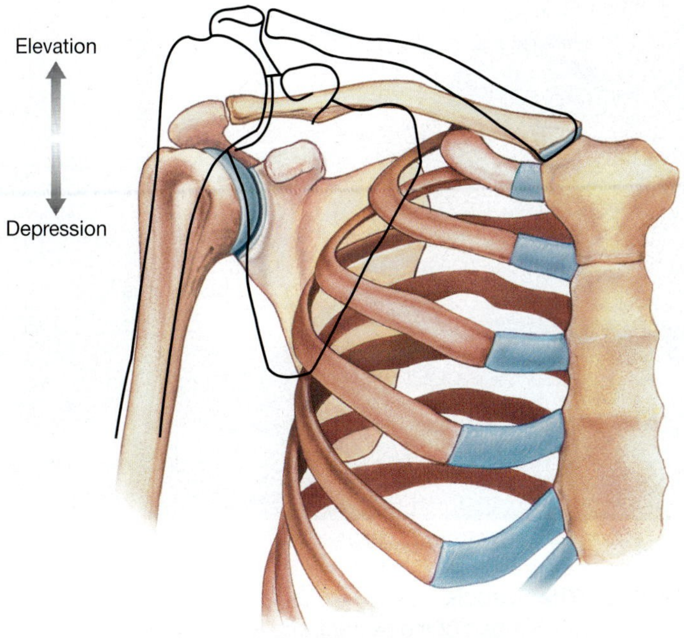

(c) Anterior view

Figure 7.4 Mobility of the Pectoral Girdle
Diagrammatic representation of normal movements of the pectoral girdle. **(a)** Bones of the right pectoral girdle. **(b)** Alterations in the position of the right shoulder that occur during *protraction* (movement anteriorly) and *retraction* (movement posteriorly). **(c)** Alterations in the position of the right shoulder that occur during *elevation* (superior movement) and *depression* (inferior movement). In each instance, note that the clavicle is responsible for limiting the range of motion. *(see Figure 8.5d,f)*

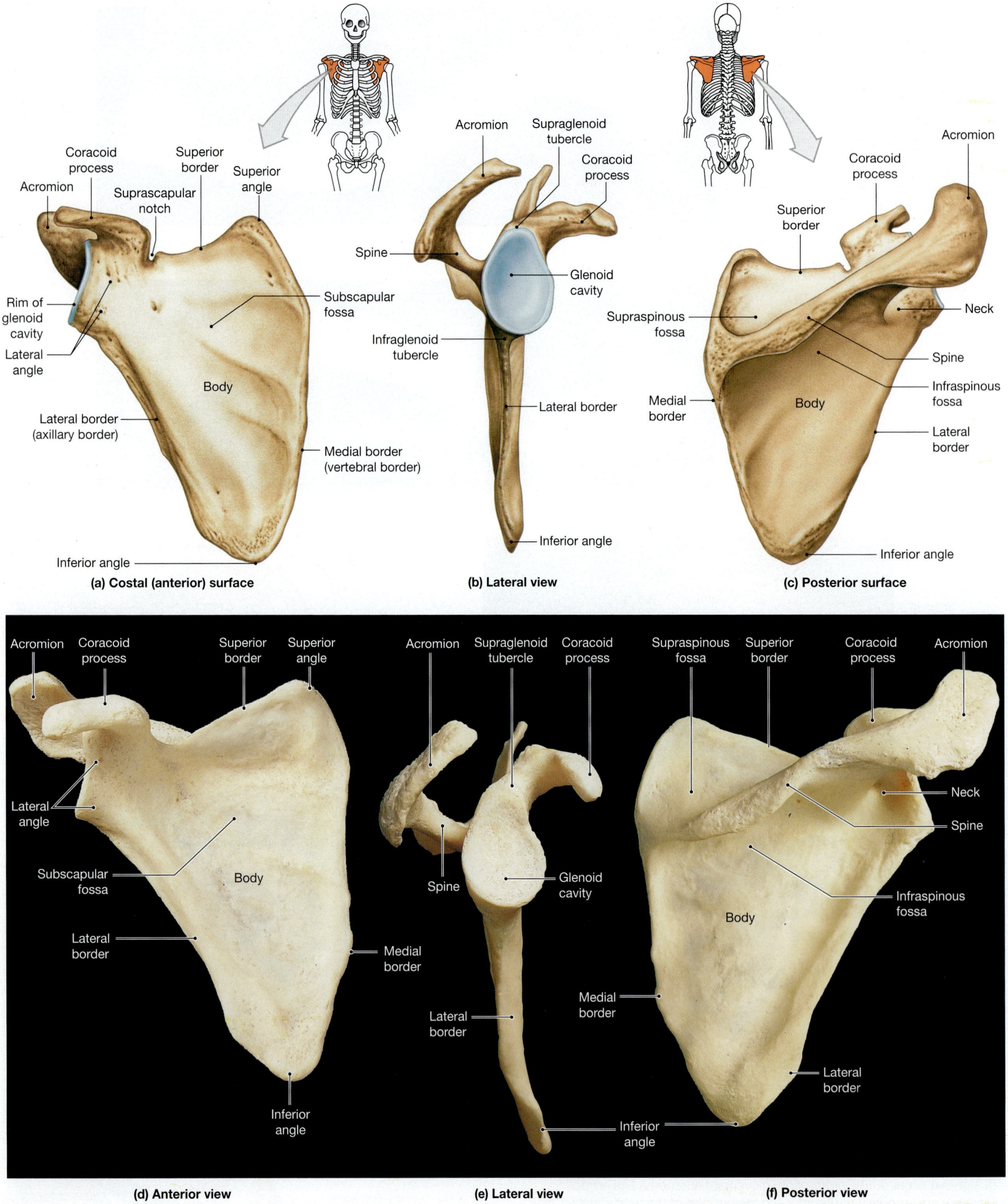

Figure 7.5 The Scapula
The scapula, which is part of the pectoral girdle, articulates with the upper limb. **(a,d)** Anterior, **(b,e)** lateral, and **(c,f)** posterior views of the right scapula.

prominent muscle on the anterior surface of the arm. The **suprascapular notch** is an indentation medial to the base of the coracoid process. The **acromion** (a-KRŌ-mē-on; *akron*, tip + *omos*, shoulder), the larger, posterior process, projects anteriorly at a 90° angle from the lateral end of the *scapular spine*, and serves as an attachment point for part of the *trapezius muscle* of the back. If you run your fingers along the superior surface of the shoulder joint, you will feel this process. The acromion articulates with the clavicle at the **acromioclavicular joint** (Figure 7.4a). Both the acromion and the coracoid process are attached to ligaments and tendons associated with the shoulder joint, which will be described further in Chapter 8.

Most of the surface markings of the scapula represent the attachment sites for muscles that position the shoulder and arm. For example, the **supraglenoid tubercle** marks the origin of the long head of the *biceps brachii muscle.* The **infraglenoid tubercle** marks the origin of the long head of the *triceps brachii muscle*, an equally prominent muscle on the posterior surface of the arm. The **scapular spine** crosses the scapular body before ending at the medial border. The scapular spine divides the convex dorsal surface of the body into two regions. The area superior to the spine constitutes the **supraspinous fossa** (*supra*, above); the region inferior to the spine is the **infraspinous fossa** (*infra*, beneath). The faces of the scapular spine separate the *supraspinatus muscle* from the *infraspinatus muscle*, and the prominent posterior ridge of the scapular spine serves as an attachment site for the *deltoid* and *trapezius muscles.*

The Upper Limb [Figure 7.2]

The bones of each upper limb consist of a humerus, an ulna and radius, the carpal bones of the wrist, and the metacarpal bones and phalanges of the hand (Figure 7.2, p. 176).

The Humerus [Figure 7.6]

The **humerus** is the proximal bone of the upper limb. The superior, medial portion of the proximal epiphysis is smooth and round. This is the **head** of the humerus, which articulates with the scapula at the glenoid cavity. The lateral edge of the epiphysis bears a large projection, the **greater tubercle** of the humerus (Figure 7.6a,b). The greater tubercle forms the lateral margin of the shoulder; you can find it by feeling for a bump situated a few centimeters anterior and inferior to the tip of the acromion. The greater tubercle bears three smooth, flat impressions that serve as the attachment sites for three muscles that originate on the scapula. The *supraspinatus muscle* inserts onto the uppermost impression, the *infraspinatus muscle* onto the middle, and the *teres minor muscle* inserts onto the lowermost. The **lesser tubercle** lies on the anterior and medial surface of the epiphysis. The lesser tubercle marks the insertion point of another scapular muscle, the *subscapularis.* The lesser tubercle and greater tubercle are separated by the **intertubercular sulcus**, or *intertubercular groove.* A tendon of the *biceps brachii muscle* runs along this sulcus from its origin at the supraglenoid tubercle of the scapula. The **anatomical neck**, a constriction inferior to the head of the humerus, marks the distal limit of the articular capsule of the shoulder joint. It lies between the tubercles and the smooth articular surface of the head. Distal to the tubercles, the narrow **surgical neck** corresponds to the metaphysis of the growing bone. This name reflects the fact that fractures often occur at this site.

The proximal **shaft**, or *body*, of the humerus is round in cross section. The elevated **deltoid tuberosity** runs along the lateral border of the shaft, extending more than halfway down its length. The deltoid tuberosity is named after the *deltoid muscle* that attaches to it. On the anterior surface of the shaft, the intertubercular sulcus continues alongside the deltoid tuberosity.

The articular **condyle** dominates the distal, inferior surface of the humerus (Figure 7.6a,c). A low ridge crosses the condyle, dividing it into two distinct articular regions. The **trochlea** (*trochlea*, pulley) is the spool-shaped medial portion that articulates with the *ulna*, the medial bone of the forearm. The trochlea extends from the base of the **coronoid fossa** (KOR-ō-noyd; *corona*, crown) on the anterior surface to the **olecranon fossa** on the posterior surface (Figure 7.6a,d). These depressions accept projections from the surface of the ulna as the elbow approaches full *flexion* (elbow bent) or full *extension* (elbow straight). The rounded **capitulum** forms the lateral surface of the condyle. The capitulum articulates with the head of the *radius*, the lateral bone of the forearm. A shallow **radial fossa** superior to the capitulum accommodates a small part of the radial head as the forearm approaches the humerus.

On the posterior surface (Figure 7.6d), the **radial groove** runs along the posterior margin of the deltoid tuberosity. This depression marks the path of the *radial nerve*, a large nerve that provides sensory information from the back of the hand and motor control over large muscles that straighten the elbow. The radial groove ends at the inferior margin of the deltoid tuberosity, where the nerve turns toward the anterior surface of the arm. Near the distal end of the humerus, the shaft expands to either side, forming a broad triangle. *Epicondyles* are processes that develop proximal to an articulation and provide additional surface area for muscle attachment. The **medial** and **lateral epicondyles** project to either side of the distal humerus at the elbow joint (Figure 7.6c,d). The *ulnar nerve* crosses the posterior surface of the medial epicondyle. Bumping the humeral side of the elbow joint can strike this nerve and produce a temporary numbness and paralysis of muscles on the anterior surface of the forearm. It causes an odd sensation, so this area is sometimes called the *funny bone.*

The Ulna [Figures 7.2/7.7]

The **ulna** and **radius** are parallel bones that support the forearm (Figure 7.2). In the anatomical position, the ulna lies medial to the radius (Figure 7.7a). The **olecranon** (ō-LEK-ra-non), or *olecranon process*, of the ulna forms the point of the elbow (Figure 7.7b). This process is the superior and posterior portion of the proximal epiphysis. On its anterior surface, the **trochlear notch** (or *semilunar notch*) interlocks with the trochlea of the humerus (Figure 7.7c–e). The olecranon forms the superior lip of the trochlear notch, and the **coronoid process** forms its inferior lip. When the elbow is straightened (*extension*), the olecranon projects into the olecranon fossa on the posterior surface of the humerus. When the elbow is bent (*flexion*), the coronoid process projects into the coronoid fossa on the anterior humeral surface. Lateral to the coronoid process, a smooth **radial notch** (Figure 7.7d,e) accommodates the head of the radius at the *proximal radioulnar joint.*

The shaft of the ulna is roughly triangular in cross section, with the smooth medial surface at the base of the triangle and the lateral margin at the apex. A fibrous sheet, the **antebrachial interosseous membrane**, connects the lateral margin of the ulna to the medial margin of the radius and provides additional surface area for muscle attachment (Figure 7.7a,d). Distally, the ulnar shaft narrows before ending at a disc-shaped **ulnar head** whose posterior margin supports a short **styloid process** (*styloid*, long and pointed). A triangular articular cartilage attaches to the styloid process, isolating the ulnar head from the bones of the wrist. The *distal radioulnar joint* lies near the lateral border of the ulnar head (Figure 7.7f).

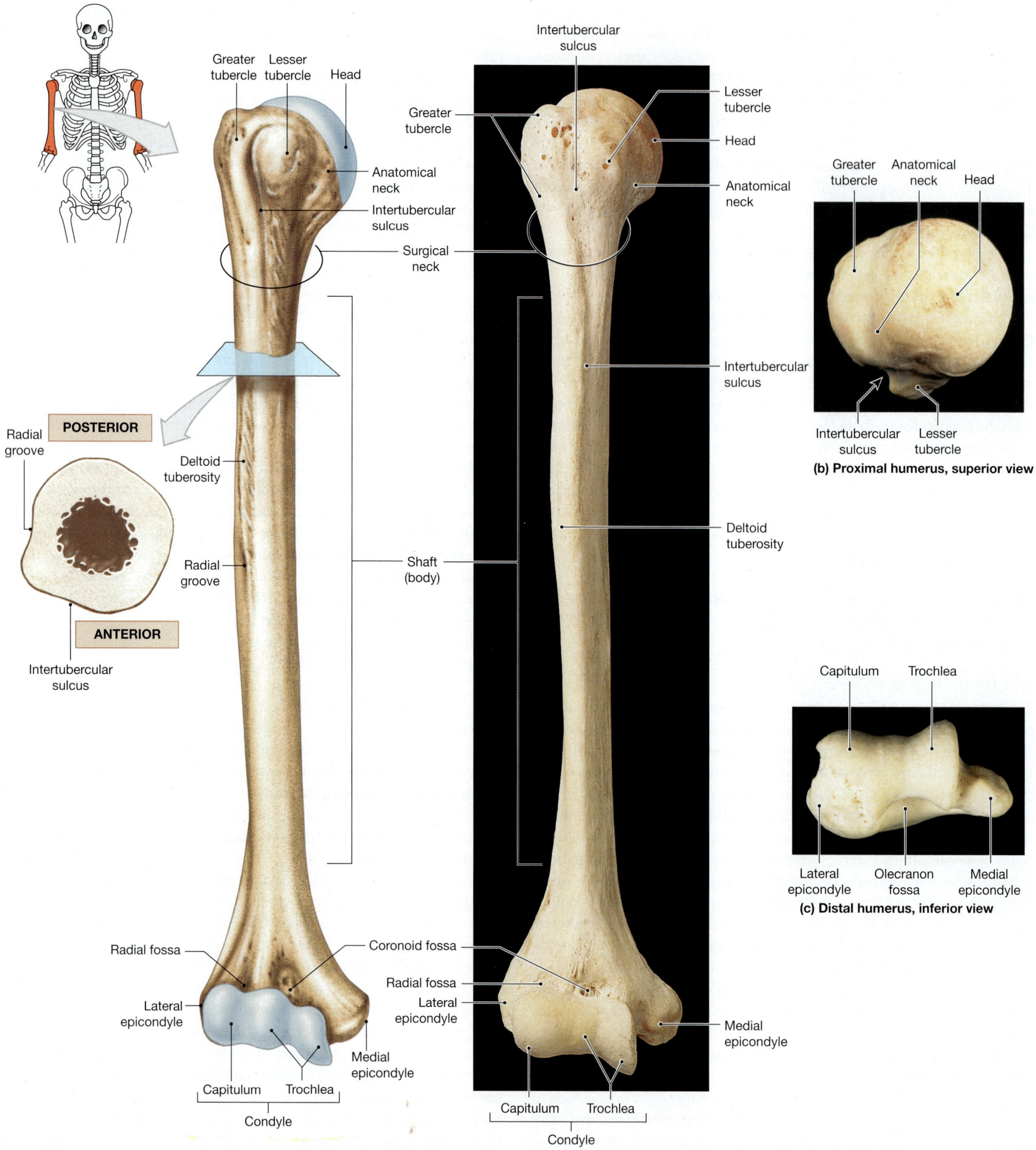

(a) Anterior surface

Figure 7.6 The Humerus
(a) Anterior views. **(b)** Superior view of the head of the humerus. **(c)** Inferior view of the distal humerus. **(d)** Posterior views.

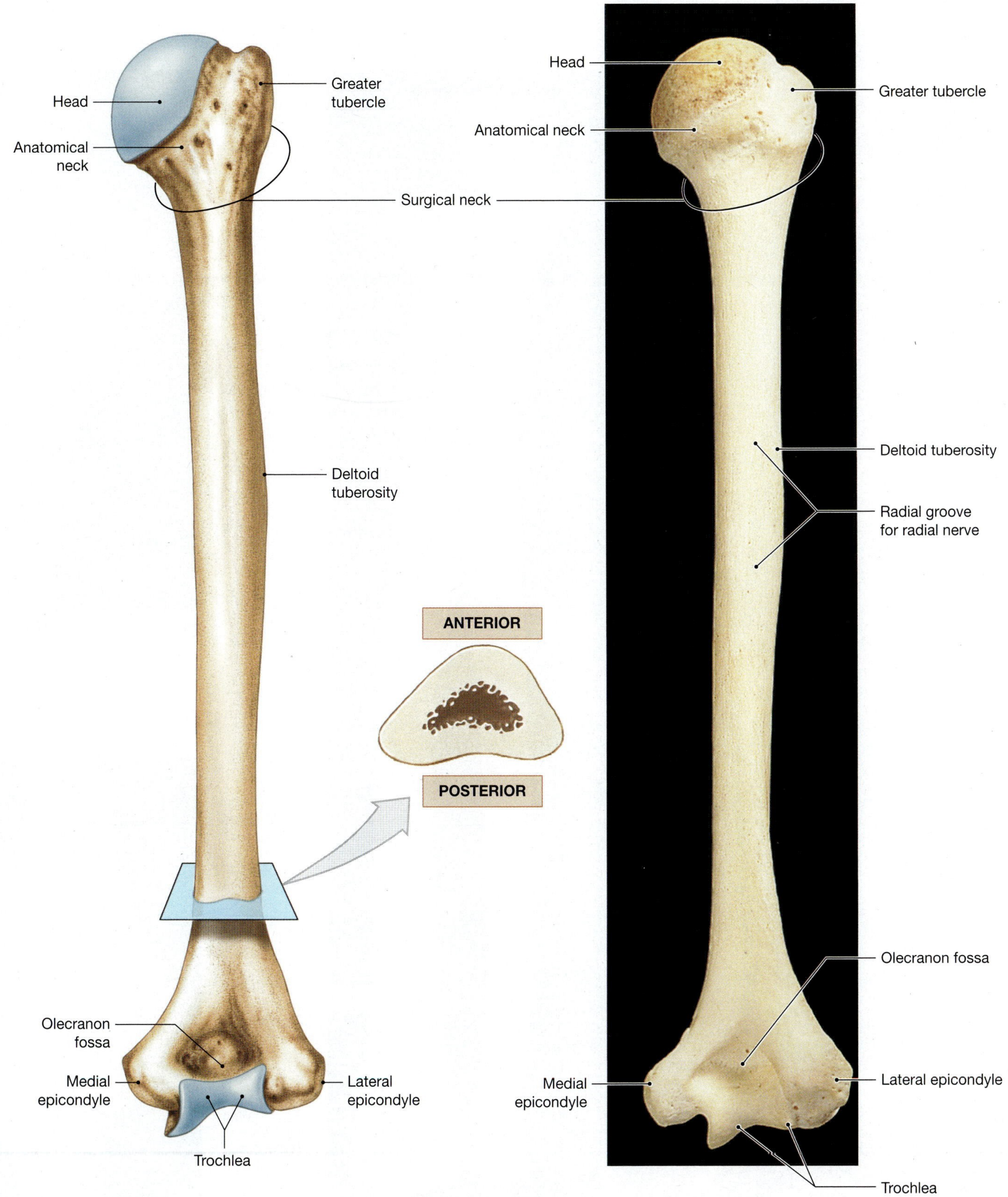

(d) Posterior surface

Figure 7.6 ***(continued)***

The *elbow joint* is a stable, two-part joint that functions like a hinge (**Figure 7.7b,c**). Much of the stability comes from the interlocking of the trochlea of the humerus with the trochlear notch of the ulna; this is the *humeroulnar joint.* The other portion of the elbow joint consists of the *humeroradial joint* formed by the capitulum of the humerus and the flat superior surface of the head of the radius. We will examine the structure of the elbow joint in Chapter 8.

The Radius [Figure 7.7]

The radius is the lateral bone of the forearm (**Figure 7.7**). The disc-shaped **head** of the radius, or *radial head,* articulates with the capitulum of the humerus. A narrow *neck* extends from the radial head to a prominent **radial tuberosity** that marks the attachment site of the *biceps brachii muscle.* This muscle bends (flexes) the elbow, swinging the forearm toward the arm. The shaft of the radius curves along its length, and

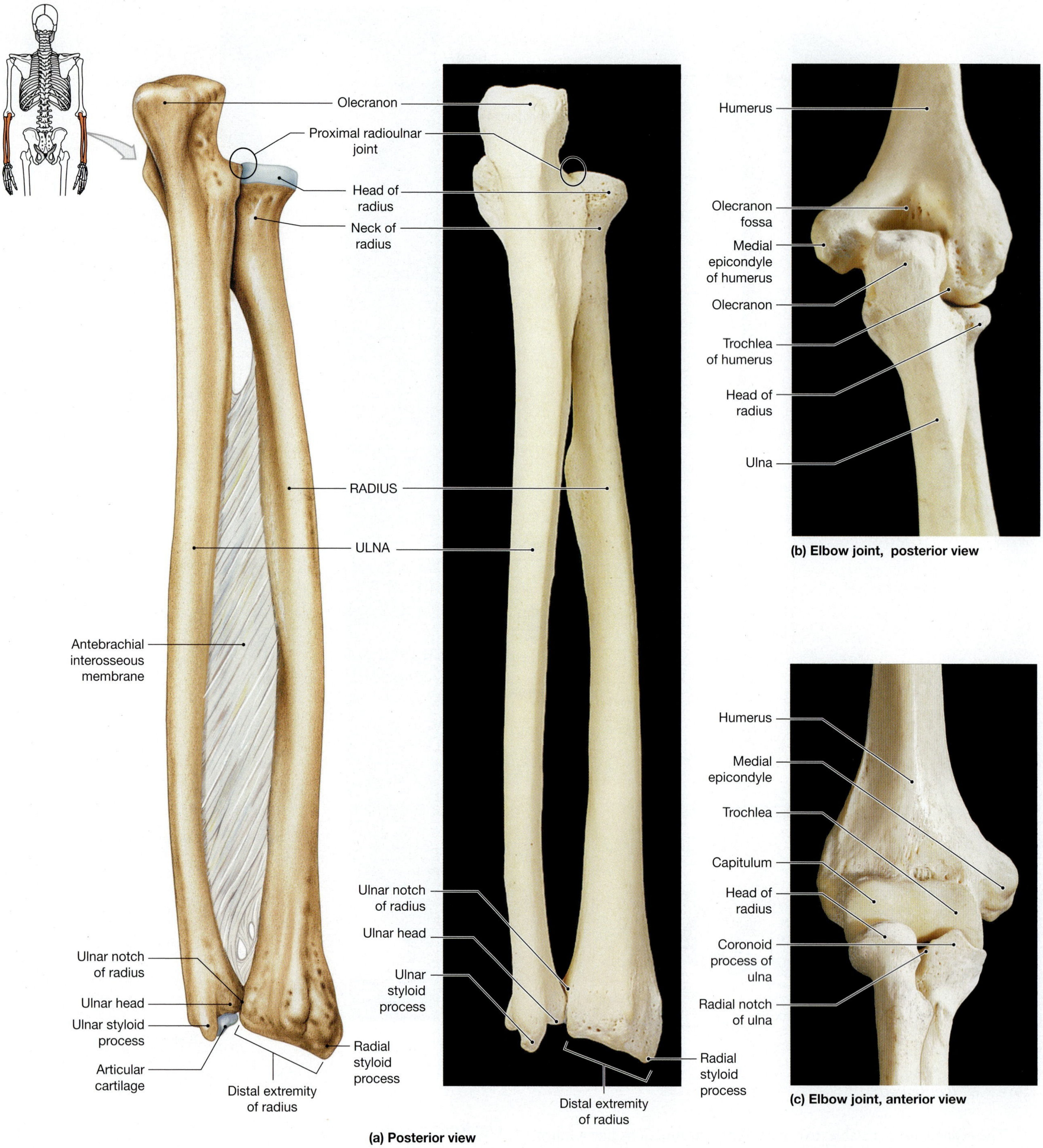

Figure 7.7 The Radius and Ulna

The radius and ulna are the bones of the forearm. **(a)** Posterior view of the right radius and ulna. **(b)** Posterior view of the elbow joint, showing the interlocking of the participating bones. **(c)** Anterior view of the elbow joint. **(d)** Anterior view of the radius and ulna. **(e)** Lateral view of the proximal end of the ulna. **(f)** Anterior view of the distal portions of the radius and ulna, and the distal radioulnar joint.

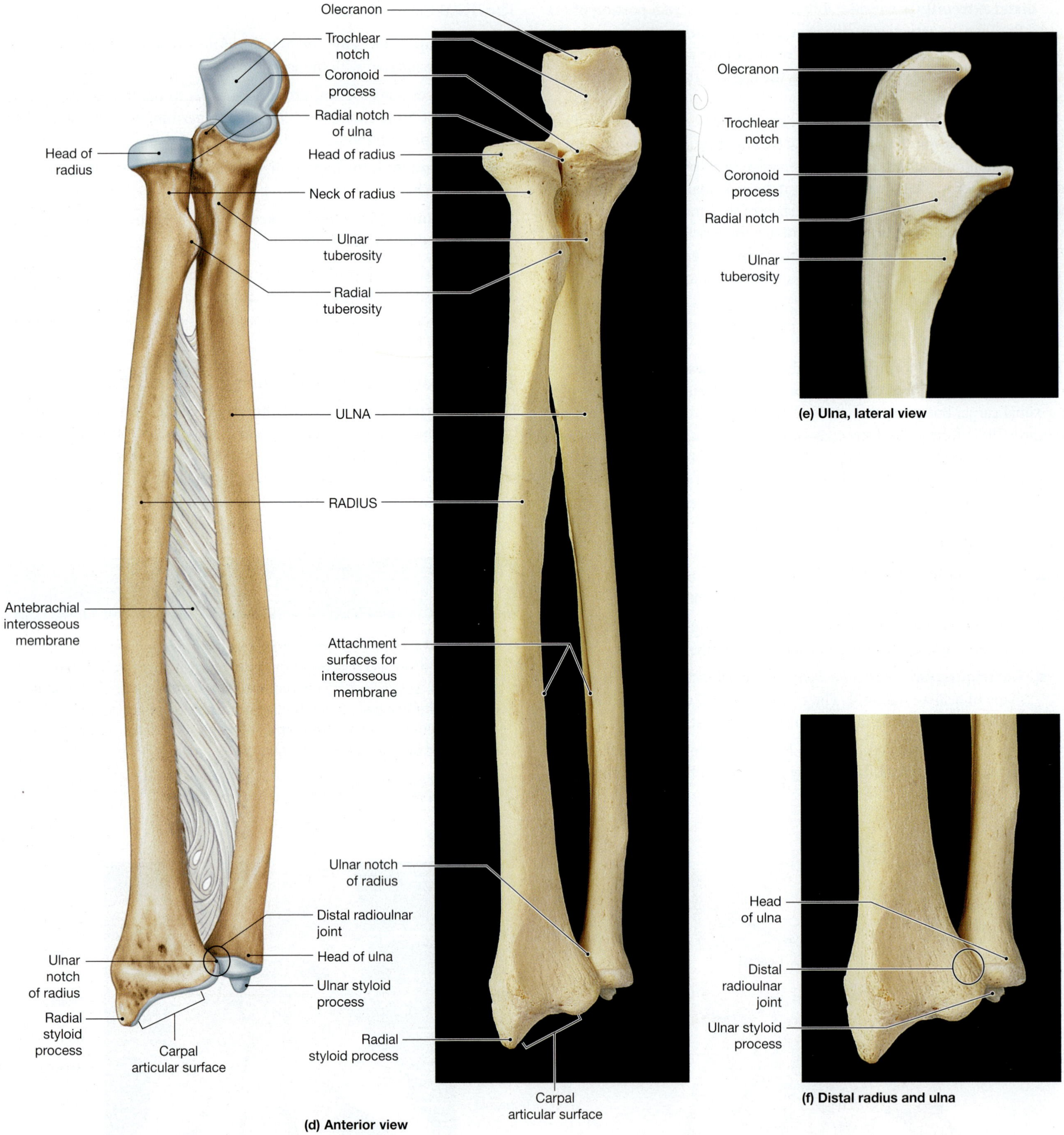

Figure 7.7 ***(continued)***

the **distal extremity** is considerably larger than the distal portion of the ulna. Because the articular cartilage and an articulating disc separate the ulna from the wrist, only the distal extremity of the radius participates in the wrist joint. The **styloid process** on the lateral surface of the distal extremity helps stabilize the wrist.

The medial surface of the distal extremity articulates with the ulnar head at the **ulnar notch of the radius**, forming the distal radioulnar joint. The proximal radioulnar joint permits *medial* or *lateral rotation* of the radial head. When medial rotation occurs at the proximal radioulnar joint, the ulnar notch rolls across the rounded surface of the ulnar head. Medial rotation at the radioulnar joints in turn rotates the wrist and hand medially, from the anatomical position. This rotational movement is called *pronation*. The reverse movement, which involves lateral rotation at the radioulnar joints, is called *supination*.

The Carpal Bones [Figure 7.8]

The wrist, or *carpus*, is formed by the eight **carpal bones**. The bones form two rows, with four **proximal carpal bones** and four **distal carpal bones**. The proximal carpal bones are the *scaphoid*, the *lunate*, the *triquetrum*, and the *pisiform* (PĪS-i-form). The distal carpal bones are the *trapezium*, the *trapezoid*, the *capitate*, and the *hamate* (Figure 7.8). The carpal bones are linked with one another at joints that permit limited sliding and twisting movements. Ligaments interconnect the carpal bones and help stabilize the wrist.

The Proximal Carpal Bones

- The **scaphoid** is the proximal carpal bone located on the lateral border of the wrist adjacent to the styloid process of the radius.
- The comma-shaped **lunate** (*luna*, moon) lies medial to the scaphoid. Like the scaphoid, the lunate articulates with the radius.
- The **triquetrum** (*triangular bone*) is medial to the lunate. It has the shape of a small pyramid. The triquetrum articulates with the cartilage that separates the ulnar head from the wrist.
- The small, pea-shaped **pisiform** lies anterior to the triquetrum and extends farther medially than any other carpal bone in the proximal or distal rows.

The Distal Carpal Bones

- The **trapezium** is the lateral bone of the distal row. It forms a proximal articulation with the scaphoid.
- The wedge-shaped **trapezoid** lies medial to the trapezium; it is the smallest distal carpal bone. Like the trapezium, it has a proximal articulation with the scaphoid.
- The **capitate** is the largest carpal bone. It sits between the trapezoid and the hamate.
- The **hamate** (*hamatum*, hooked) is a hook-shaped bone that is the medial distal carpal bone.

A phrase to help you remember the names of the carpal bones in the order given is: "**S**am **l**ikes **t**o **p**ush **t**he **t**oy **c**ar **h**ard." The first letter of each word is the first letter of the bone, proceeding lateral to medial; the first four are proximal, the last four distal.

The Metacarpal Bones and Phalanges [Figure 7.8b,c]

Five **metacarpal** (met-a-KAR-pal) **bones** articulate with the distal carpal bones and support the palm of the hand (Figure 7.8b,c). Roman numerals I–V are used to identify the metacarpal bones, beginning with the lateral metacarpal bone. Each metacarpal bone looks like a miniature long bone, possessing a wide, concave, proximal *base*, a small *body*, and a distal *head*.

Clinical Note

Scaphoid Fractures The scaphoid is the most frequently fractured carpal bone, usually resulting from a fall onto an outstretched hand. The fracture usually occurs perpendicular to the long axis of the bone. Because the blood supply to the proximal portion of the scaphoid decreases with age, a fracture to this segment of the bone usually heals poorly, and often results in necrosis of the proximal segment of the scaphoid.

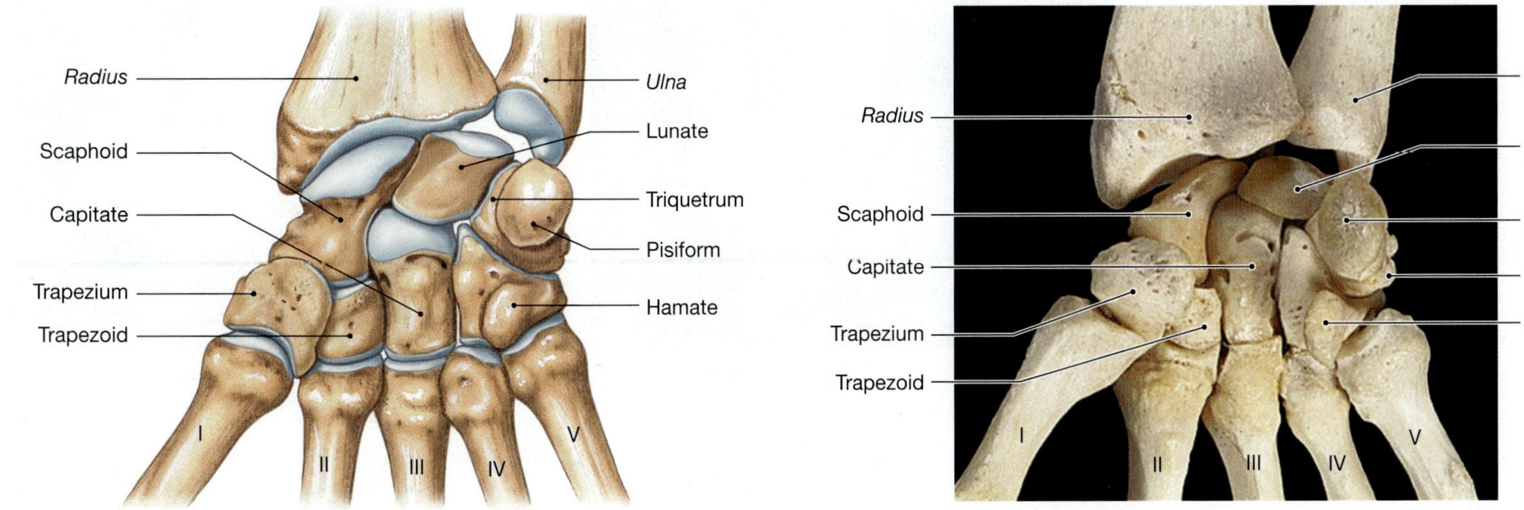

(a) Right wrist, anterior (palmar) view

Figure 7.8 The Bones of the Wrist and Hand
Carpal bones form the wrist; metacarpal bones and phalanges form the hand. **(a)** Anterior (palmar) view of the bones of the right wrist. **(b)** Anterior (palmar) view of the bones of the right wrist and hand. **(c)** Posterior (dorsal) view of the bones of the right wrist and hand.

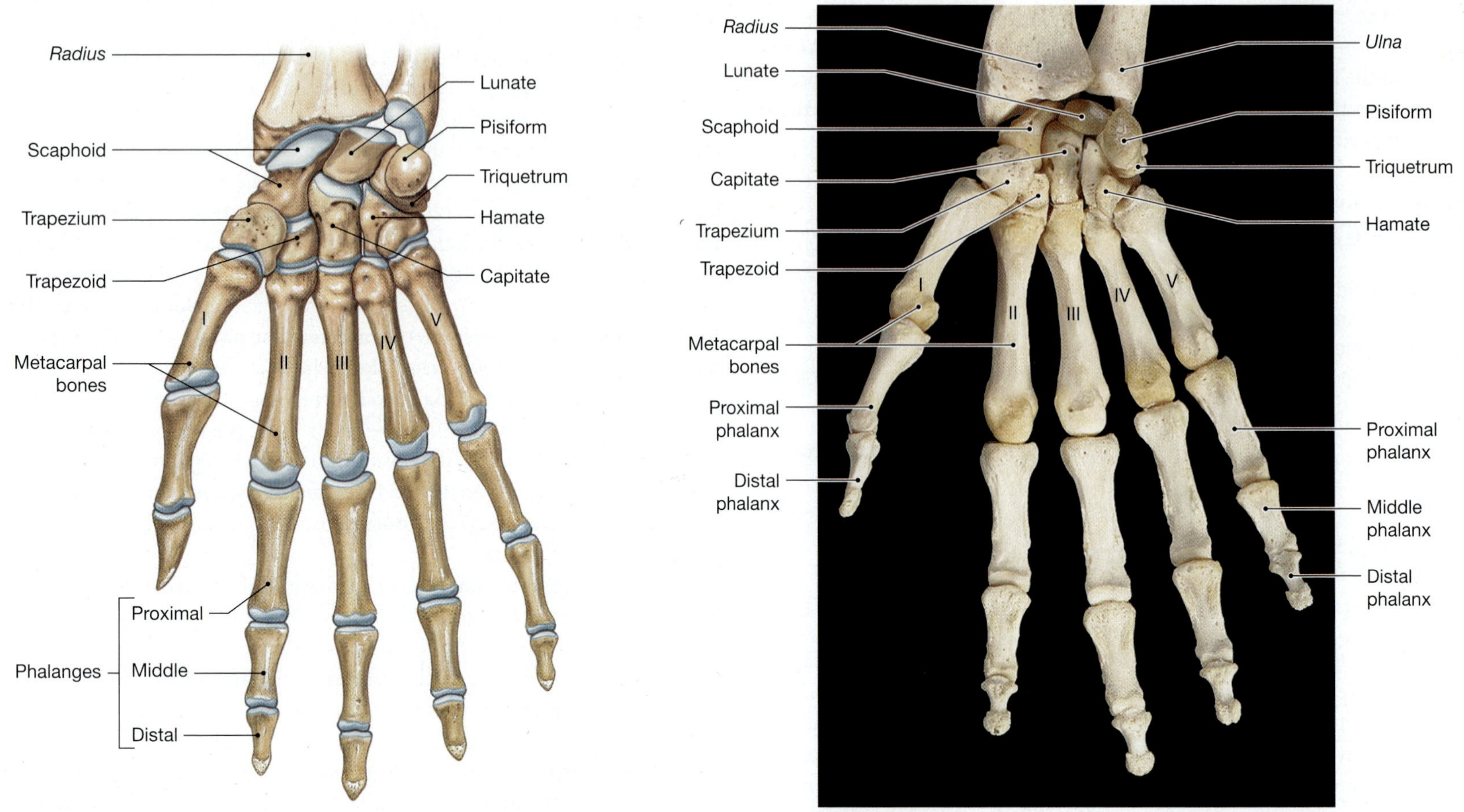

(b) Right wrist and hand, anterior (palmar) view

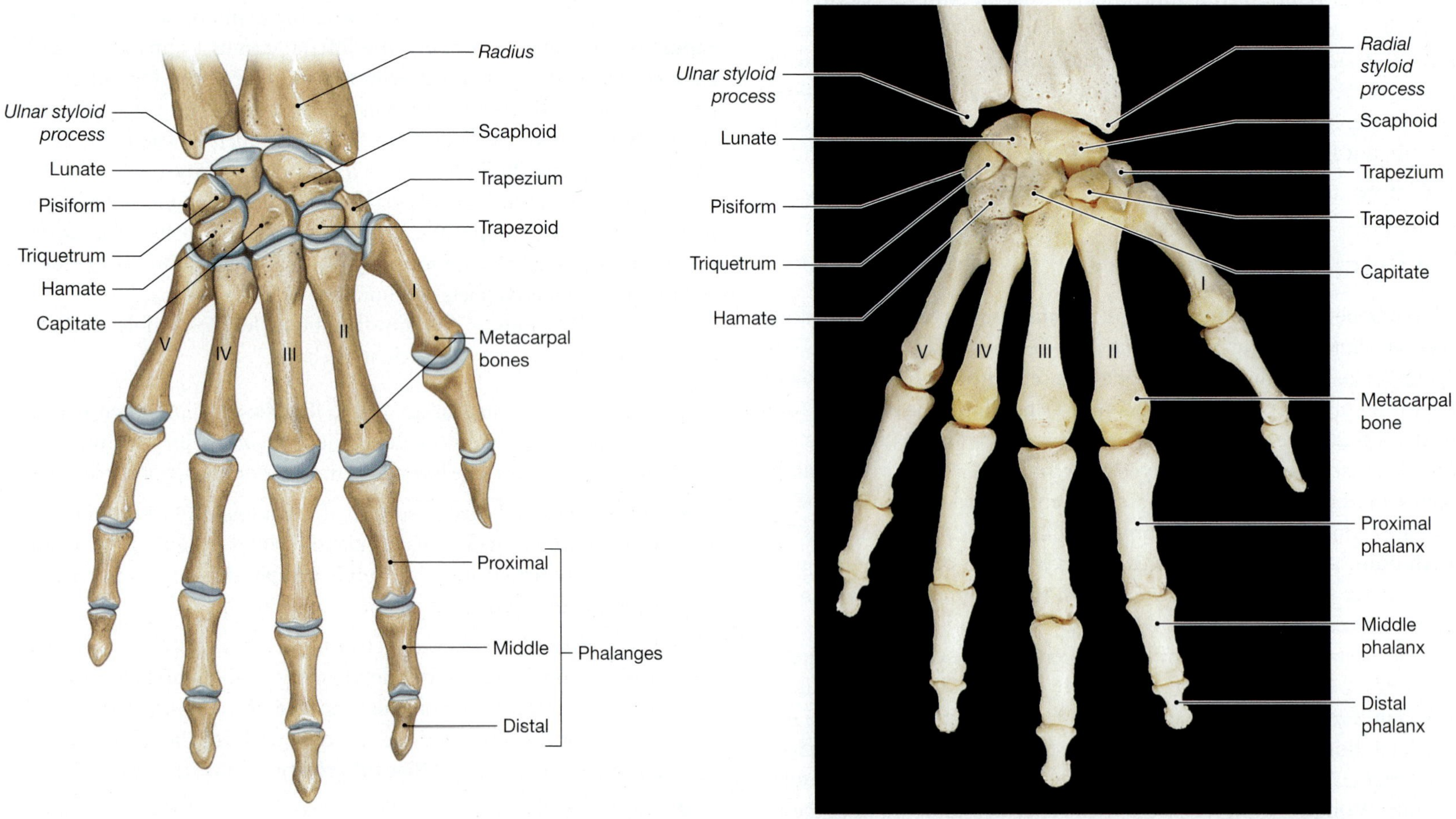

(c) Right wrist and hand, posterior (dorsal) view

Figure 7.8 ***(continued)***

Distally, the metacarpal bones articulate with the finger bones, or **phalanges** (fa-LAN-jēz; singular, *phalanx*). There are 14 phalangeal bones in each hand. The thumb, or **pollex** (POL-eks), has two phalanges (proximal phalanx and distal phalanx), and each of the other fingers has three phalanges (proximal, middle, and distal).

CONCEPT CHECK

1. Why would a broken clavicle affect the mobility of the scapula?
2. Which antebrachial bone is lateral in the anatomical position?
3. What is the function of the olecranon?
4. Which bone is the only direct connection between the pectoral girdle and the axial skeleton?

See blue "Answers" tab at back of book.

The Pelvic Girdle and Lower Limb [Figure 7.9]

The bones of the **pelvic girdle** support and protect the lower viscera, including the reproductive organs and developing fetus in females. The pelvic bones are more massive than those of the pectoral girdle because of the stresses involved in weight bearing and locomotion. The bones of the lower limbs are more massive than those of the upper limbs for similar reasons. The pelvic girdle consists of two **hip bones**, also called *coxal bones* or *innominate bones*. The *pelvis* is a composite structure that includes the hip bones of the appendicular skeleton and the sacrum and coccyx of the axial skeleton. The skeleton of each lower limb includes the *femur* (thigh), the *patella* (kneecap), the *tibia* and *fibula* (leg), and the bones of the ankle (*tarsal bones*) and foot (*metatarsal bones* and *phalanges*) (Figure 7.9). In anatomical terms, *leg* refers only to the distal portion of the limb, not to the entire lower limb. We use *thigh* for *upper leg* and *leg* for *lower leg*.

The Pelvic Girdle [Figure 7.10]

Each hip bone of the adult pelvic girdle forms through the fusion of three bones: an *ilium* (IL-ē-um), an *ischium* (IS-kē-um), and a *pubis* (PŪ-bis) (Figure 7.10). At birth the three bones are separated by hyaline cartilage. Growth and fusion of the three bones into a single hip bone is usually completed by age 25. The articulation between a hip bone and the auricular surfaces of the sacrum occurs at the posterior and medial aspect of the ilium, forming the *sacro-iliac joint*. The anterior and medial portions of the hip bones are connected by a pad of fibrous cartilage at the *pubic symphysis*. The **acetabulum** (as-e-TAB-ū-lum; *acetabulum*, a vinegar cup) is found on the lateral surface of the hip bone. The head of the femur articulates with this curved surface, at the *hip joint*.

The acetabulum lies inferior and anterior to the center of the pelvic bones (Figure 7.10a). The space enclosed by the walls of the acetabulum is the **acetabular fossa**, which has a diameter of approximately 5 cm (2 in.). The acetabulum contains a smooth curved surface that forms the shape of the letter C. This is the **lunate surface**, which articulates with the head of the femur. A ridge of bone forms the lateral and superior margins of the acetabulum. There is no ridge marking the anterior and inferior margins. This gap is called the *acetabular notch*.

The Hip Bones [Figures 7.10/7.11a]

The ilium, ischium, and pubis meet inside the acetabular fossa, as if it were a pie sliced into three pieces. The **ilium** (plural, *ilia*), the largest of the bones, provides the superior slice that includes around two-fifths of the acetabular surface. Superior to the acetabulum, the broad, curved, lateral surface of the ilium provides an extensive area for the attachment of muscles, tendons, and ligaments (Figure 7.10a). The **anterior**, **posterior**, and **inferior gluteal lines** mark the attachment sites for the *gluteal muscles* that move the femur. The iliac expansion begins superior to the **arcuate** (AR-kū-āt) **line** (Figure 7.10b). The anterior border includes the **anterior inferior iliac spine**, superior to the **inferior iliac notch**, and continues anteriorly to the **anterior superior iliac spine**. Curving posteriorly, the superior border supports the **iliac crest**, a ridge marking the attachments of ligaments and muscles. The iliac crest ends at the **posterior superior iliac spine**. Inferior to the spine, the posterior border of the ilium continues inferiorly to the rounded **posterior inferior iliac spine** that is superior to the **greater sciatic** (sī-AT-ik) **notch**, through which the sciatic nerve passes into the lower limb.

Near the superior and posterior margin of the acetabulum, the ilium fuses with the **ischium**, which accounts for the posterior two-fifths of the acetabular surface. The ischium is the strongest of the coxal bones. Posterior to the acetabulum, the prominent **ischial spine** projects superior to the **lesser sciatic notch**. The rest of the ischium forms a sturdy process that turns medially and inferiorly. A roughened projection, the **ischial tuberosity**, forms its posterolateral border. When seated, the body weight is borne by the ischial tuberosities. The narrow **ischial ramus** (branch) of the ischium continues toward its anterior fusion with the **pubis**.

At the point of fusion, the ramus of the ischium meets the **inferior ramus** of the pubis. Anteriorly, the inferior ramus begins at the **pubic tubercle**, where it meets the **superior ramus** of the pubis. The anterior, superior surface of the superior ramus bears a roughened ridge, the **pubic crest**, which extends medially from the pubic tubercle. The pubic and ischial rami encircle the **obturator** (OB-too-rā-tor) **foramen**. In life, this space is closed by a sheet of collagen fibers whose inner and outer surfaces provide a firm base for the attachment of muscles of the hip. The superior ramus originates at the anterior margin of the acetabulum. Inside the acetabulum, the pubis contacts the ilium and ischium.

Figures 7.10b and 7.11a show additional features visible on the medial and anterior surfaces of the right hip bone:

- The concave medial surface of the **iliac fossa** helps support the abdominal organs and provides additional surface area for muscle attachment. The arcuate line marks the inferior border of the iliac fossa.
- The anterior and medial surface of the pubis contains a roughened area that marks the site of articulation with the pubis of the opposite side. At this articulation, the **pubic symphysis**, the two pubic bones are attached to a median pad of fibrous cartilage.
- The **pectineal** (pek-TIN-ē-al) **line** begins near the symphysis and extends diagonally across the pubis to merge with the arcuate line, which continues toward the **auricular surface** of the ilium. The auricular surfaces of the ilium and sacrum unite to form the *sacro-iliac joint*. Ligaments arising at the **iliac tuberosity** stabilize this joint.
- On the medial surface of the superior ramus of the pubis lies the **obturator groove**. Upon dissection, the obturator blood vessels and nerves would be found within this groove.

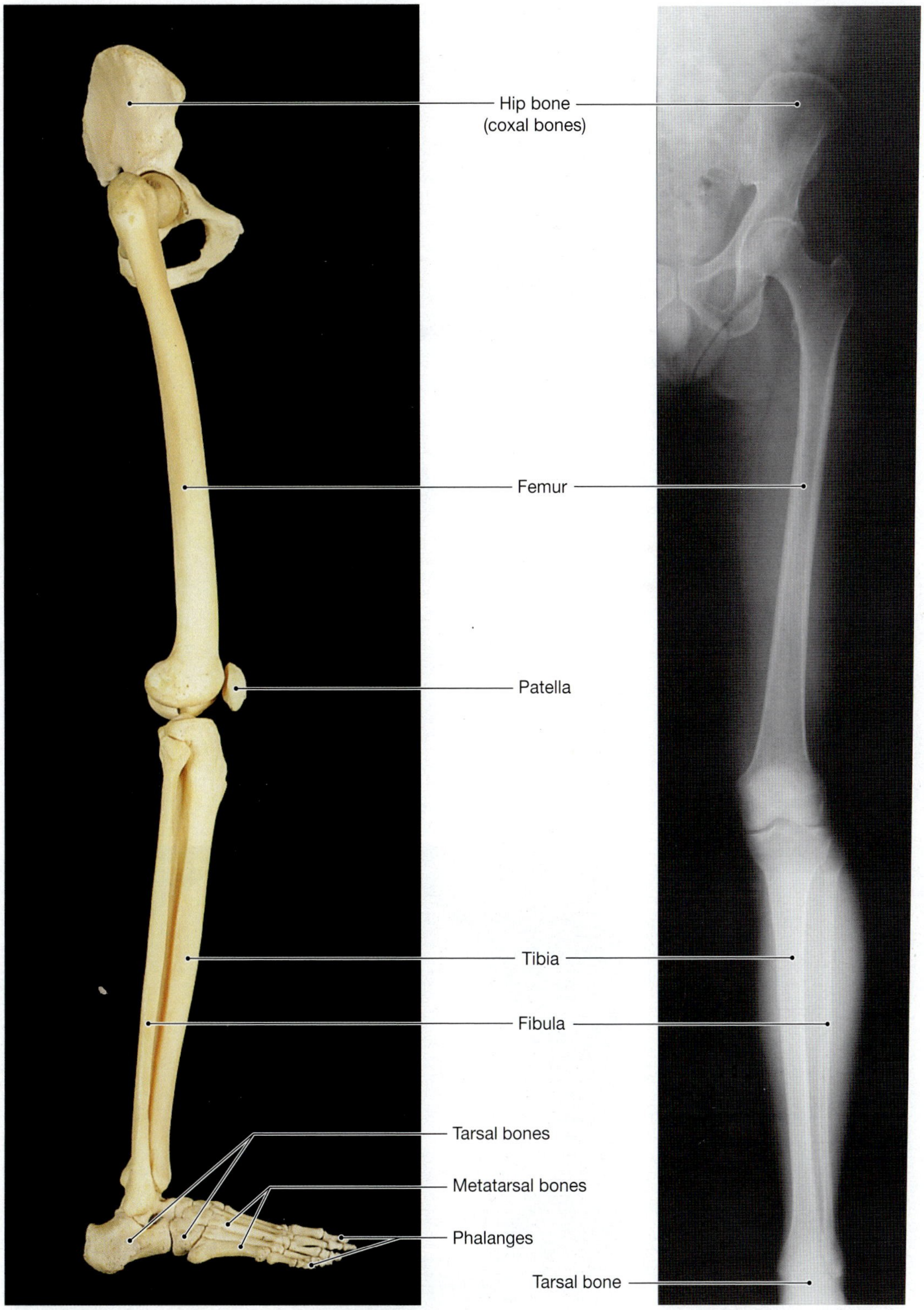

(a) Lateral view

(b) X-ray, anterior/posterior projection

Figure 7.9 The Pelvic Girdle and Lower Limb
Each lower limb articulates with the axial skeleton at the trunk through the pelvic girdle. **(a)** Right lower limb, lateral view. **(b)** X-ray, pelvic girdle and lower limb, anterior/posterior projection.

The Pelvis [Figures 7.11 to 7.13]

Figure 7.11 shows anterior and posterior views of the **pelvis**, which consists of four bones: the two hip bones, the sacrum, and the coccyx. The pelvis is a ring of bone, with the hip bones forming the anterior and lateral parts, the sacrum and coccyx the posterior part. An extensive network of ligaments connects the lateral borders of the sacrum with the iliac crest, the ischial tuberosity, the ischial spine, and the iliopectineal line. Other ligaments bind the ilia to the posterior lumbar vertebrae. These interconnections increase the stability of the pelvis.

Figure 7.10 The Pelvic Girdle
The pelvic girdle consists of the two hip bones. Each hip bone forms as a result of the fusion of an ilium, an ischium, and a pubis. **(a)** Lateral view. **(b)** Medial view.

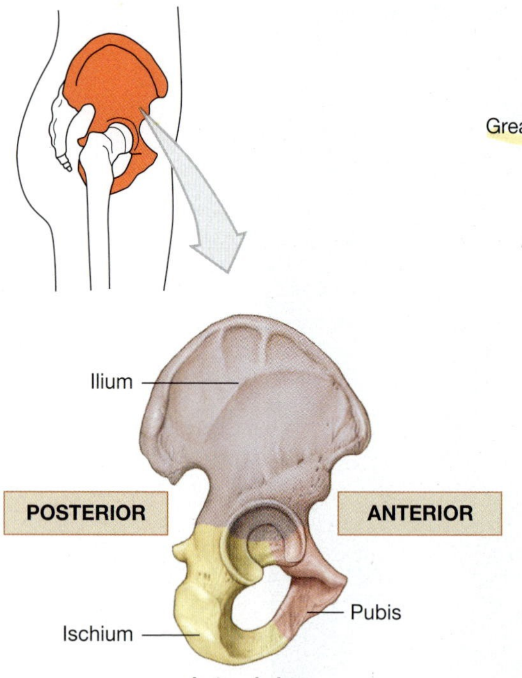

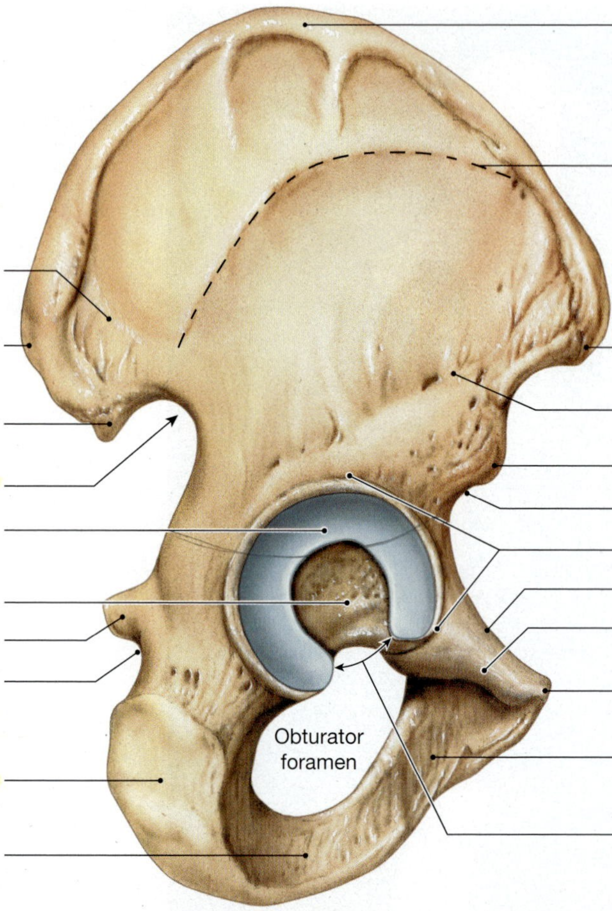

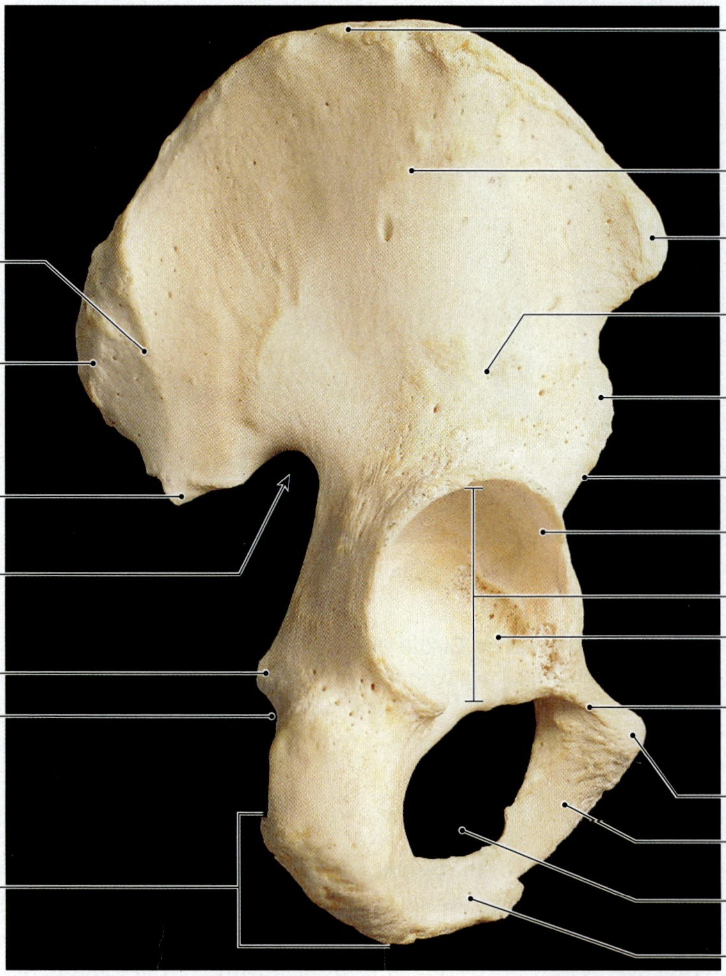

(a) Lateral view

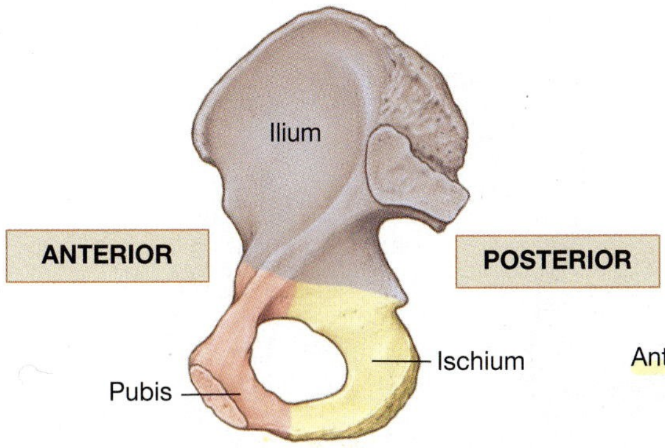

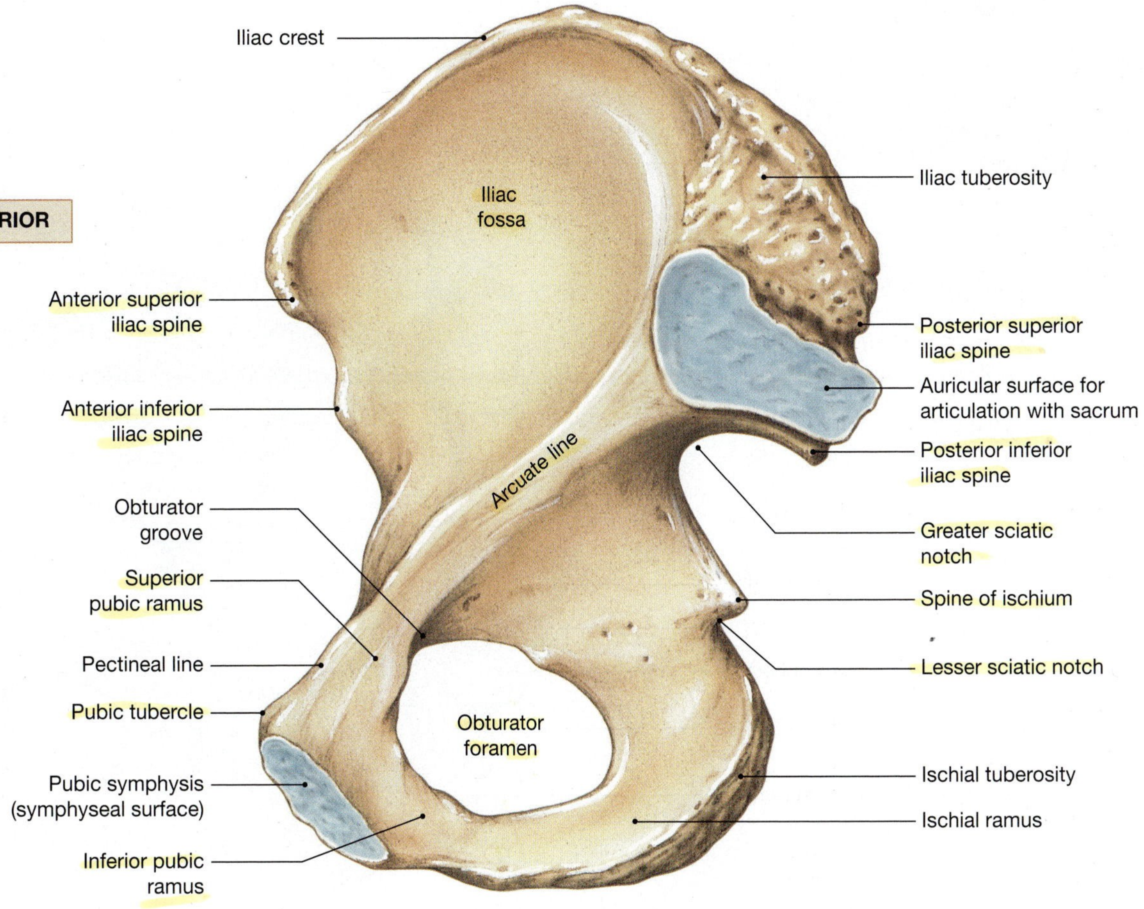

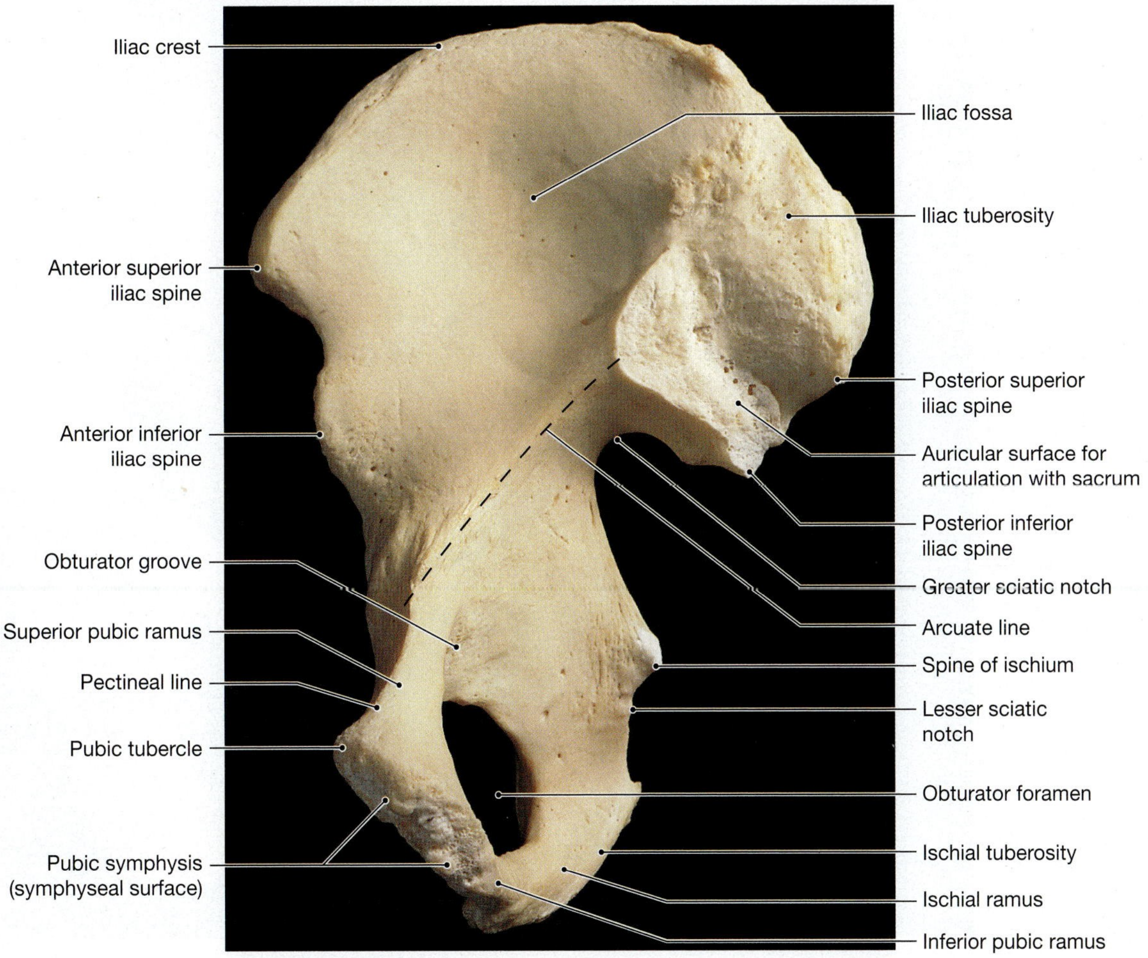

(b) Medial view

Figure 7.10 ***(continued)***

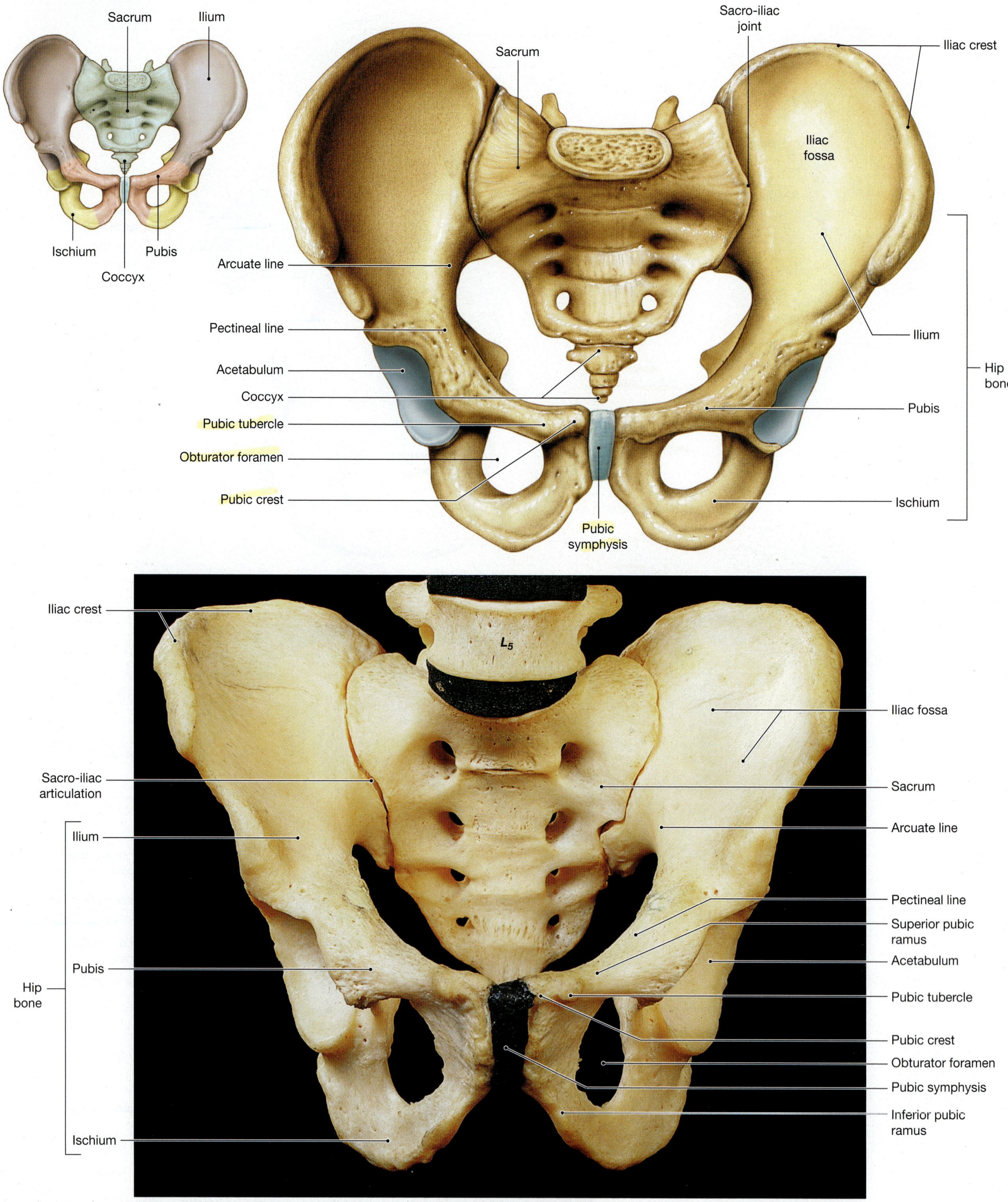

(a) Anterior view

Figure 7.11 The Pelvis
A pelvis consists of two hip bones, the sacrum, and the coccyx. **(a)** Anterior view of the pelvis of an adult male. **(b)** Posterior view.

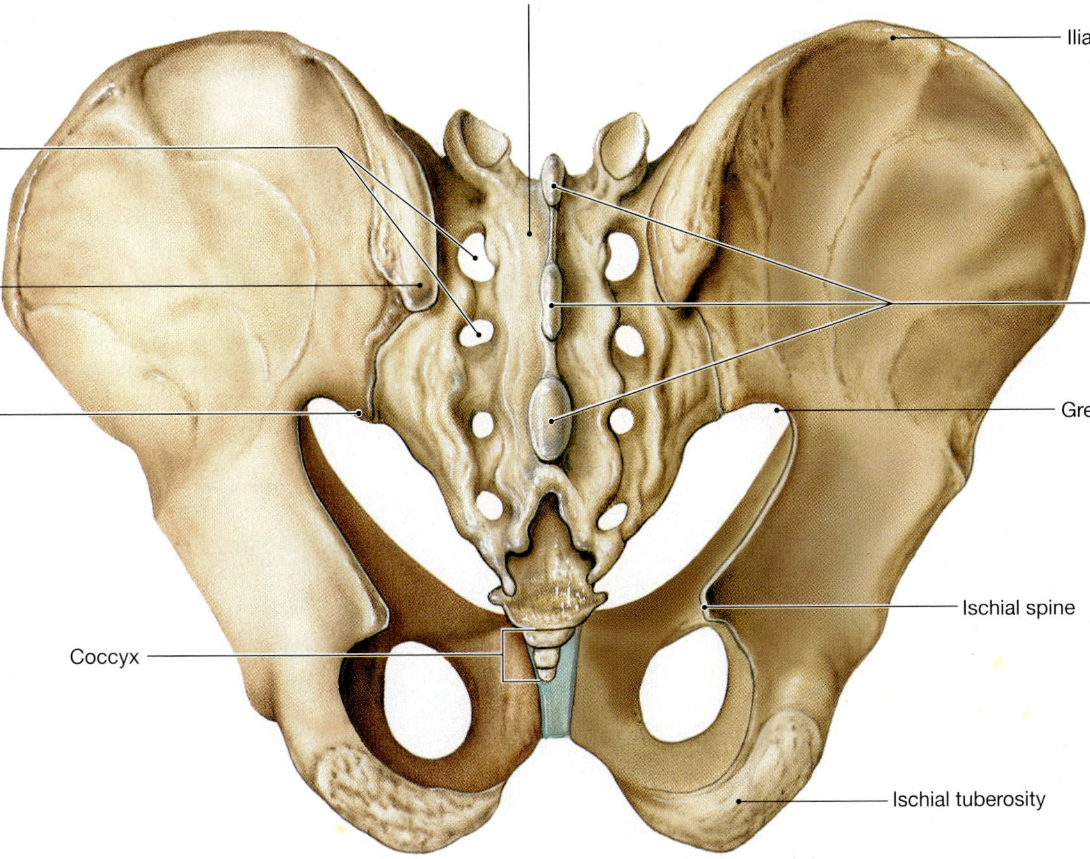

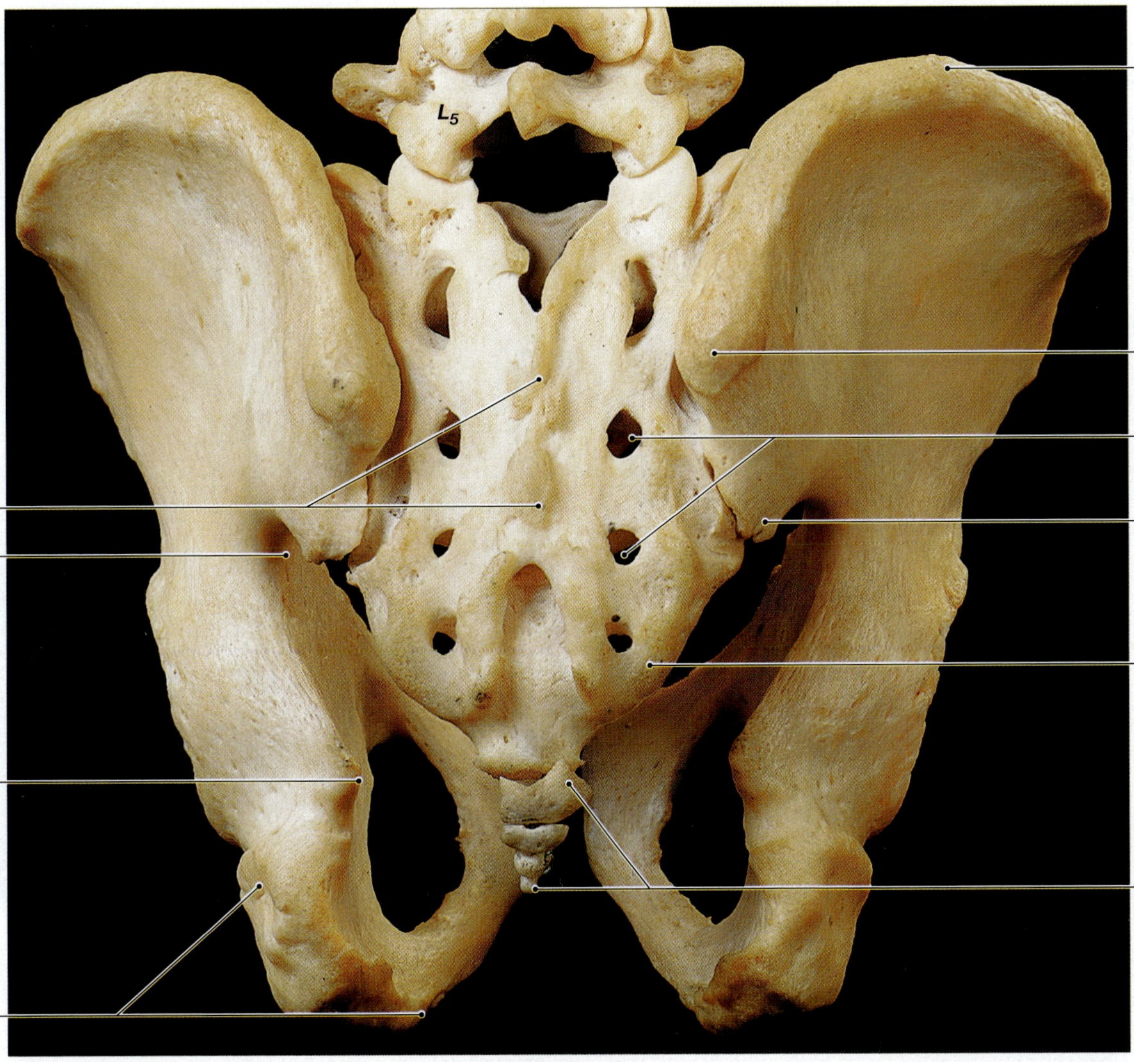

(b) Posterior view

Figure 7.11 ***(continued)***

The pelvis may be subdivided into the **greater** (*false*) **pelvis** and the **lesser** (*true*) **pelvis**. The boundaries of each are indicated in **Figure 7.12**. The greater pelvis consists of the expanded, bladelike portions of each ilium superior to the iliopectineal line. The greater pelvis encloses organs within the inferior portion of the abdominal cavity. Structures inferior to the iliopectineal line form the lesser pelvis, which forms the boundaries of the

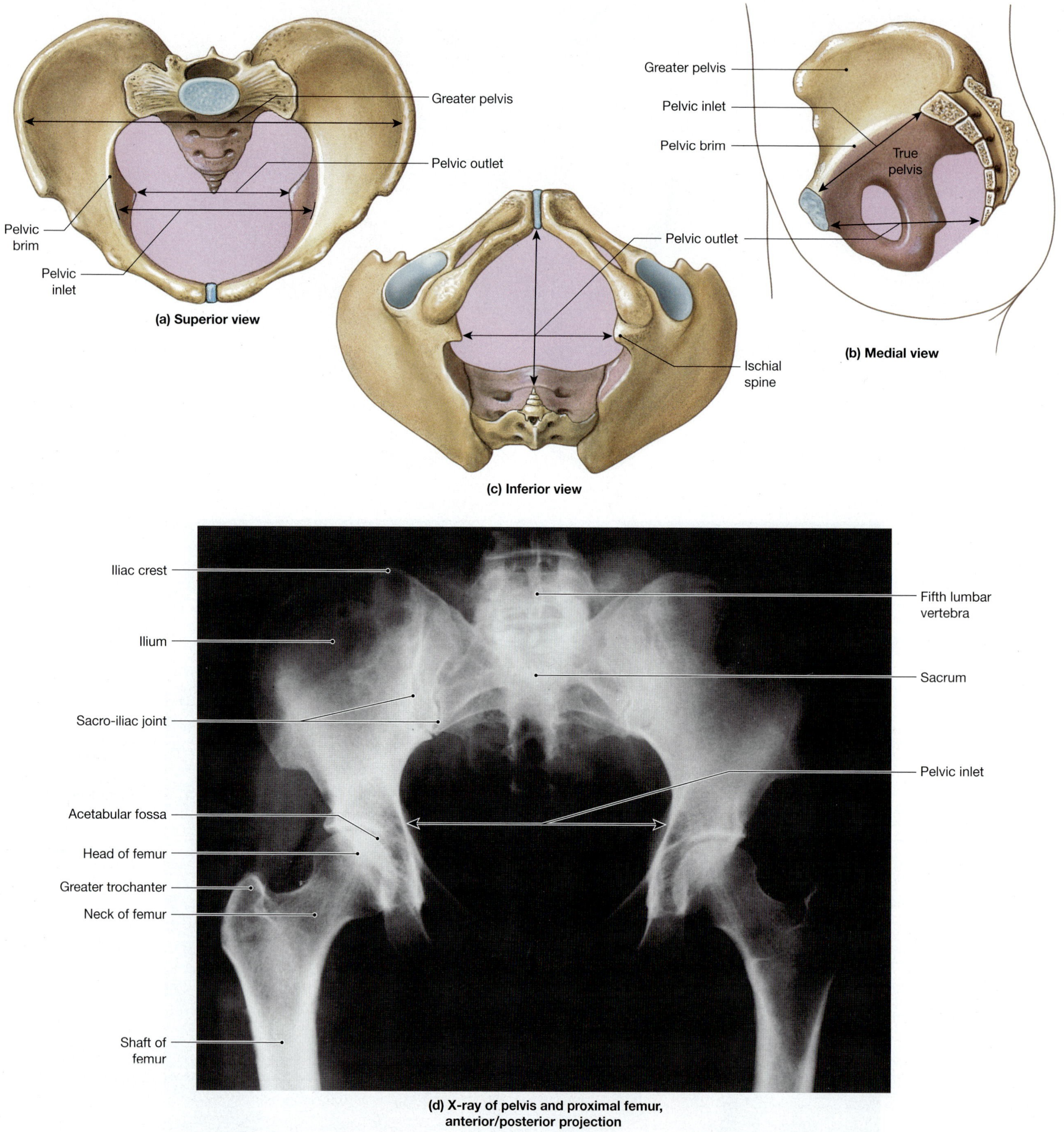

Figure 7.12 Divisions of the Pelvis

A pelvis is subdivided into the true (lesser) and false (greater) pelvis. **(a)** Superior view, showing the pelvic brim and pelvic inlet of a male. **(b)** Lateral view, showing the boundaries of the true (lesser) and false (greater) pelvis. **(c)** Inferior view, showing the limits of the pelvic outlet. **(d)** X-ray (anterior/posterior projection) of the pelvis and femora.

pelvic cavity. pp. 19–20 These pelvic structures include the inferior portions of each ilium, both pubic bones, the ischia, the sacrum, and the coccyx. In medial view (Figure 7.12b), the superior limit of the lesser pelvis is a line that extends from either side of the base of the sacrum, along the iliopectineal lines to the superior margin of the pubic symphysis. The bony edge of the lesser pelvis is called the **pelvic brim**. The space enclosed by the pelvic brim is the **pelvic inlet**.

The **pelvic outlet** is the opening bounded by the inferior margins of the pelvis (Figure 7.12a–c), specifically the coccyx, the ischial tuberosities, and the inferior border of the pubic symphysis. In life, the region of the pelvic outlet is called the *perineum* (per-i-NĒ-um). Pelvic muscles form the floor of the pelvic cavity and support the enclosed organs. These muscles are described in Chapter 10.

Figure 7.12d shows the appearance of the pelvis in anterior view. The shape of the female pelvis is somewhat different from that of the male pelvis (Figure 7.13). Some of these differences are the result of variations in body size and muscle mass. Because women are typically less muscular than men, the pelvis of the adult female is usually smoother and lighter and has less prominent markings where muscles or ligaments attach. Other differences are adaptations for childbearing, including the following:

- an enlarged pelvic outlet, due in part to greater separation of the ischial spines;
- less curvature on the sacrum and coccyx, which in the male arc into the pelvic outlet;
- a wider, more circular pelvic inlet;
- a relatively broad, low pelvis;
- ilia that project farther laterally, but do not extend as far superior to the sacrum; and
- a broader *pubic angle*, with the inferior angle between the pubic bones greater than 100°.

These adaptations are related to (1) supporting of the weight of the developing fetus and uterus and (2) easing the passage of the newborn through the pelvic outlet at the time of delivery. In addition, a hormone produced during pregnancy loosens the pubic symphysis, allowing relative movement between the hip bones that can further increase the size of the pelvic inlet and outlet and thus facilitate delivery.

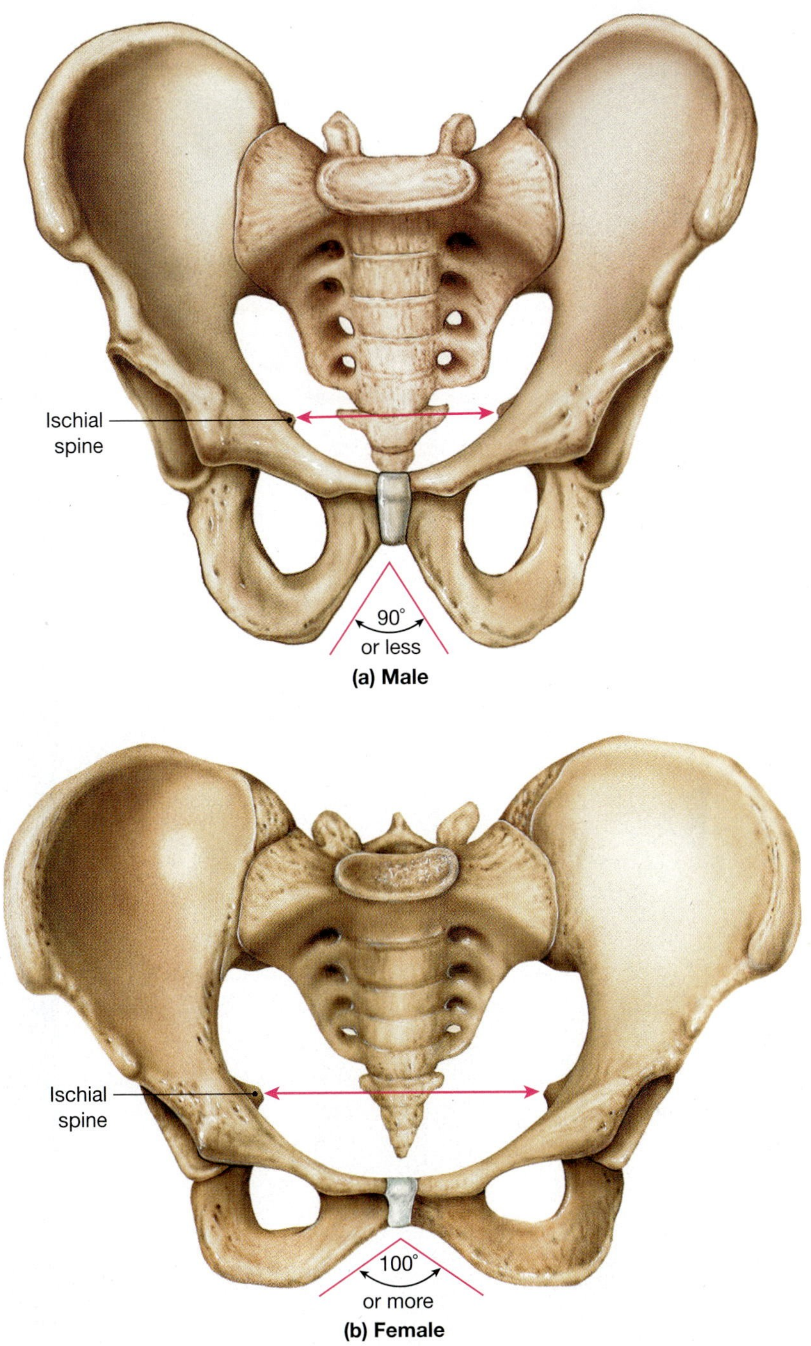

Figure 7.13 Anatomical Differences in the Male and Female Pelvis The black arrows indicate the pubic angle. Note the much sharper pubic angle in the pelvis of a **(a)** male compared to a **(b)** female. The red arrows indicate the width of the pelvic outlet *(see Figure 7.12)*. The female pelvis has a much wider pelvic outlet.

The Lower Limb [Figure 7.9]

The skeleton of the lower limb consists of the femur, patella (kneecap), tibia and fibula, tarsal bones of the ankle, and metatarsal bones and phalanges of the foot (Figure 7.9). The functional anatomy of the lower limb is very different from that of the upper limb, primarily because the lower limb must transfer the body weight to the ground.

The Femur [Figures 7.9/7.12a/7.14]

The **femur** (Figure 7.14) is the longest and heaviest bone in the body. Distally, the femur articulates with the tibia of the leg at the knee joint. Proximally, the rounded **head** of the femur articulates with the pelvis at the acetabulum (Figures 7.9 and 7.12a). A stabilizing ligament (the *ligament of the head*) attaches to the femoral head at a depression, the **fovea** (Figure 7.14b). Distal to the head, the **neck** joins the shaft at an angle of about 125°. The shaft is strong and massive, but curves along its length (Figure 7.14a,d,e). This lateral bow facilitates weight bearing and balance, and becomes greatly exaggerated if the skeleton weakens; a bowlegged stance is characteristic of rickets, a metabolic disorder discussed in Chapter 5. p. 117

The **greater trochanter** (trō-KAN-ter) projects laterally from the junction of the neck and shaft. The **lesser trochanter** originates on the posteromedial surface of the femur. Both trochanters develop where large tendons attach to the femur. On the anterior surface of the femur, the raised **intertrochanteric** (in-ter-trō-kan-TER-ik) **line** marks the distal edge of the articular capsule (Figure 7.14a,c). This line continues around to the posterior surface, passing inferior to the trochanters as the **intertrochanteric crest** (Figure 7.14b,d). Inferior to the intertrochanteric crest, the **pectineal line** (medial) and the **gluteal tuberosity** (lateral) mark the attachment of the *pectineus muscle* and the *gluteus maximus muscle*, respectively. A prominent elevation, the **linea aspera** (*aspera*, rough), runs along the center of the posterior surface of the femoral shaft. This ridge marks the attachment site of other powerful hip muscles (the *adductor muscles*). Distally, the linea aspera

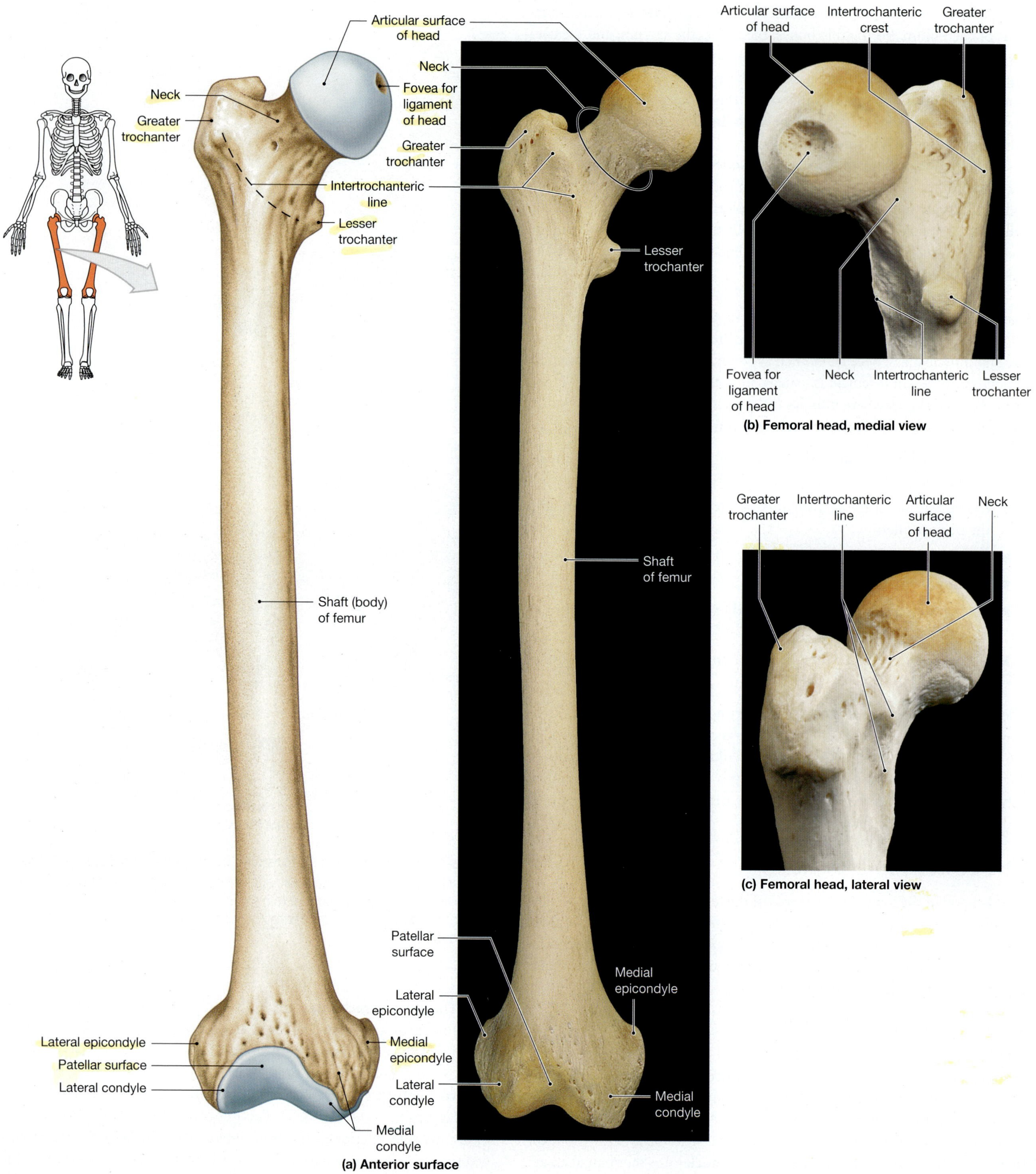

Figure 7.14 The Femur
(a) Landmarks on the anterior surface of the right femur. **(b)** A medial view of the femoral head. **(c)** A lateral view of the femoral head. **(d)** Landmarks on the posterior surface of the right femur. **(e)** A superior view of the femur. **(f)** An inferior view of the right femur, showing the articular surfaces that participate in the knee joint.

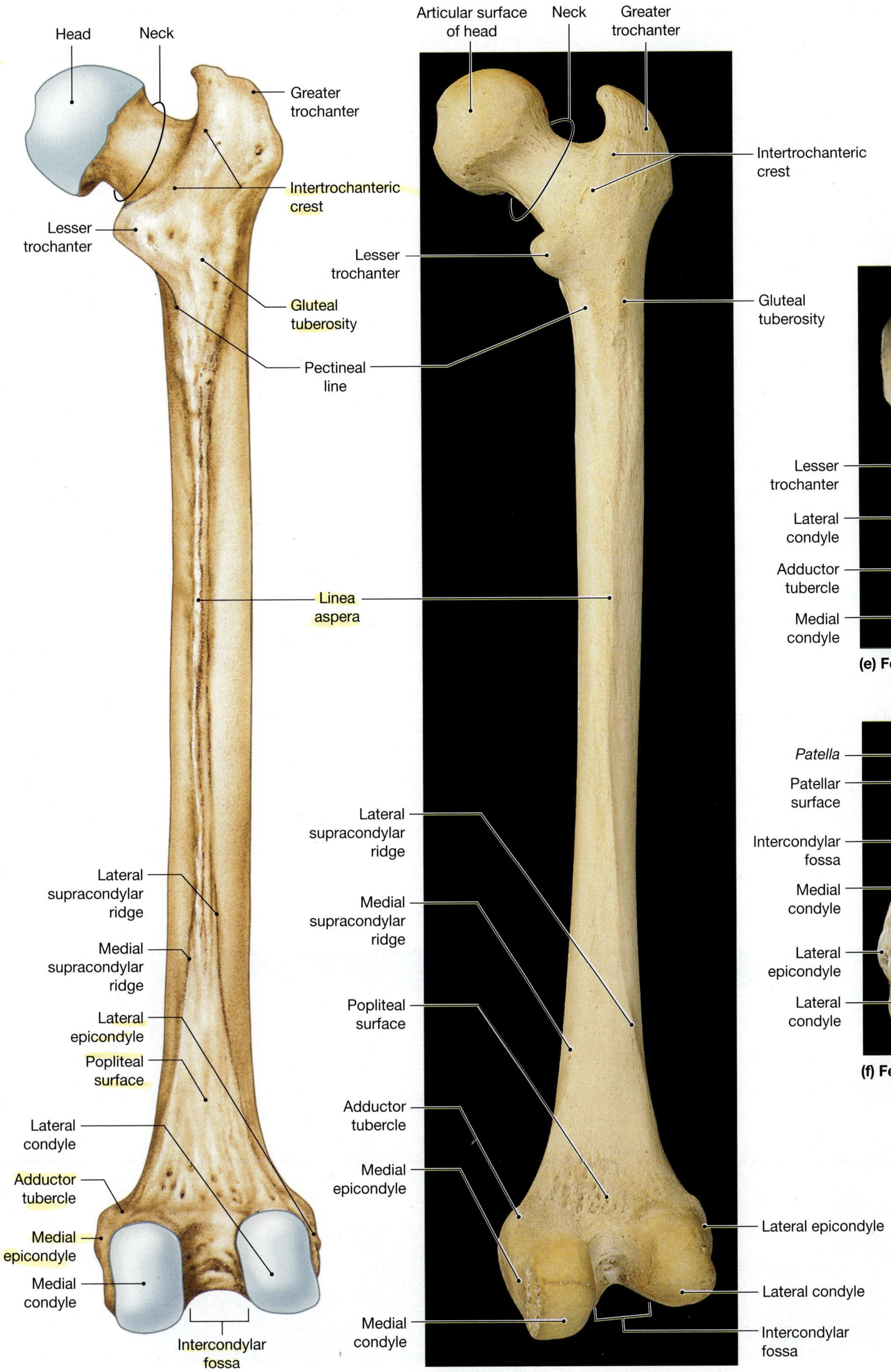

(d) Posterior surface

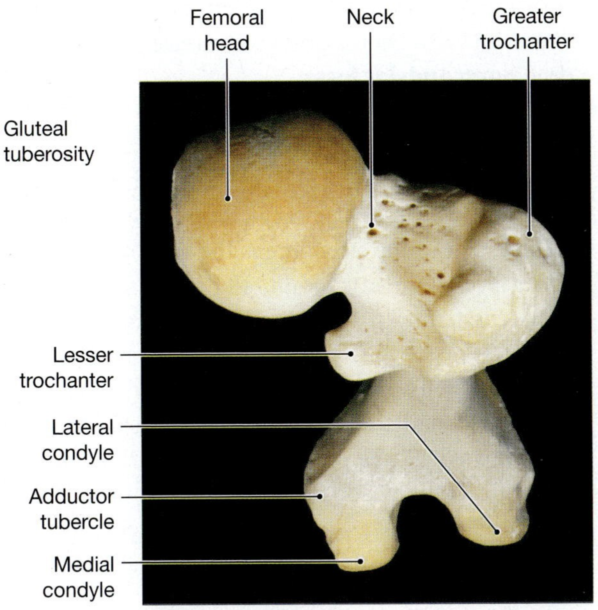

(e) Femur, superior view

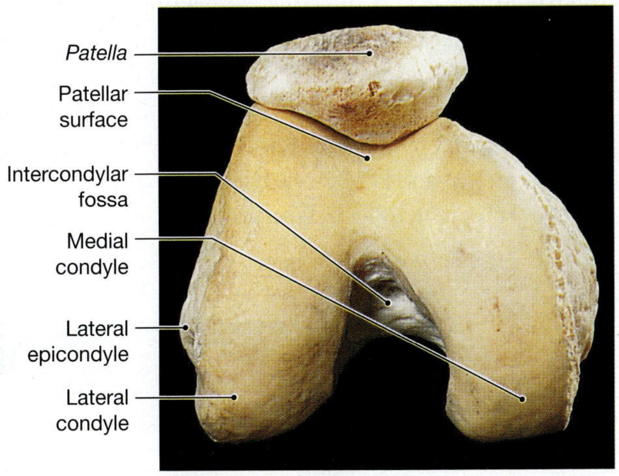

(f) Femur, inferior view

Figure 7.14 ***(continued)***

divides into a **medial** and **lateral supracondylar ridge** to form a flattened triangular area, the **popliteal surface**. The medial supracondylar ridge terminates in a raised, rough projection, the **adductor tubercle**, on the **medial epicondyle**. The lateral supracondylar ridge ends at the **lateral epicondyle**. The smoothly rounded **medial** and **lateral condyles** are primarily distal to the epicondyles. The condyles continue across the inferior surface of the femur to the anterior surface, but the intercondylar fossa does not. As a result, the smooth articular faces merge, producing an articular surface with elevated lateral borders. This is the **patellar surface** over which the patella glides (Figure 7.14a,f). On the posterior surface, the two condyles are separated by a deep **intercondylar fossa**.

The Patella [Figures 7.14a,f/7.15]

The **patella** (pa-TEL-a) is a large sesamoid bone that forms within the tendon of the *quadriceps femoris*, a group of muscles that straightens (extends) the knee. This bone strengthens the *quadriceps tendon*, protects the anterior surface of the knee joint, and increases the contraction force of the quadriceps femoris. The triangular patella has a rough, convex anterior surface (Figure 7.15a). It has a broad, superior **base** and a roughly pointed inferior **apex**. The roughened surface and broad base reflect the attachment of the quadriceps tendon (along the anterior and superior surfaces) and the *patellar ligament* (along the anterior and inferior surfaces). The patellar ligament extends from the apex of the patella to the tibia. The posterior patellar surface (Figure 7.15b) presents two concave **facets** (*medial* and *lateral*) for articulation with the medial and lateral condyles of the femur (Figure 7.14a,f).

The Tibia [Figure 7.16]

The **tibia** (TIB-ē-a) is the large medial bone of the leg (Figure 7.16). The medial and lateral condyles of the femur articulate with the **medial** and **lateral condyles** of the proximal end of the tibia. The lateral condyle is more prominent, and possesses a facet for the articulation with the fibula at the *superior tibiofibular joint*. A ridge, the **intercondylar eminence**, separates the medial and lateral condyles of the tibia (Figure 7.16b,d). There are two **tubercles** (**medial** and **lateral**) on the intercondylar eminence. The anterior surface of the tibia near the condyles bears a prominent, rough **tibial tuberosity** that can easily be felt beneath the skin of the leg. This tuberosity marks the attachment of the stout patellar ligament.

The **anterior margin**, or *border*, is a ridge that begins at the distal end of the tibial tuberosity and extends distally along the anterior tibial surface. The anterior margin of the tibia can be felt through the skin. The lateral margin of the shaft is the **interosseous border**; from here, a collagenous sheet extends to the medial margin of the fibula. Distally, the tibia narrows, and the medial border ends in a large process, the **medial malleolus** (ma-LĒ-ō-lus; *malleolus*, hammer). The inferior surface of the tibia (Figure 7.16c) forms a hinge joint with the *talus*, the proximal bone of the ankle. Here the tibia passes the weight of the body, received from the femur at the knee, to the foot across the ankle joint, or *talocrural joint*. The medial malleolus provides medial support for this joint, preventing lateral sliding of the tibia across the talus. The posterior surface of the tibia bears a prominent **soleal line**, or *popliteal line* (Figure 7.16d). This marks the attachment of several leg muscles, including the *popliteus* and the *soleus*.

The Fibula [Figure 7.16]

The slender **fibula** (FIB-ū-la) parallels the lateral border of the tibia (Figure 7.16). The **head** of the fibula, or *fibular head*, articulates along the lateral margin of the tibia on the inferior and posterior surface of the lateral tibial condyle. The medial border of the thin shaft is bound to the tibia by the *crural interosseous membrane*, which extends from the **interosseous border** of the fibula to that of the tibia. A sectional view through the shafts of the tibia and fibula (Figure 7.16e) shows the locations of the tibial and fibular interosseous borders and the fibrous *crural interosseous membrane* that extends between them. This membrane helps stabilize the positions of the two bones and provides additional surface area for muscle attachment.

The fibula is excluded from the knee joint and does not transfer weight to the ankle and foot. However, it is an important site for muscle attachment. In addition, the distal tip of the fibula provides lateral support to the ankle joint. This fibular process, the **lateral malleolus**, provides stability to the ankle joint by preventing medial sliding of the tibia across the surface of the talus.

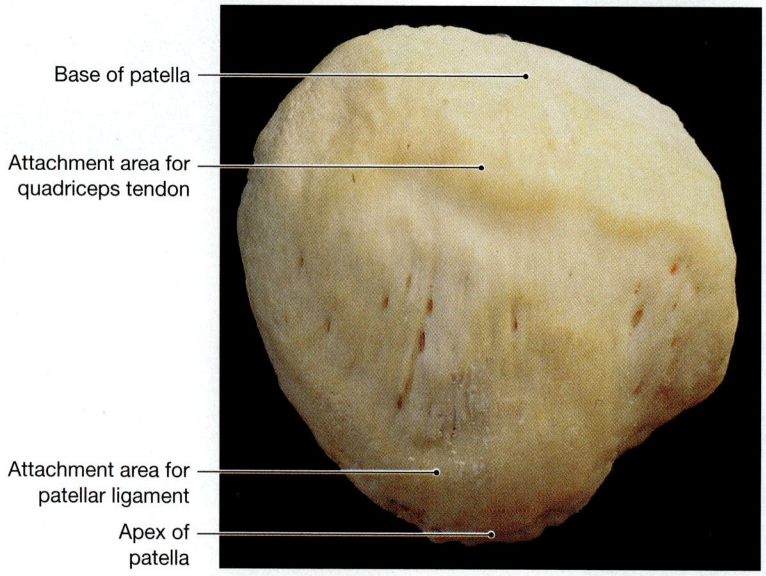

(a) Anterior view

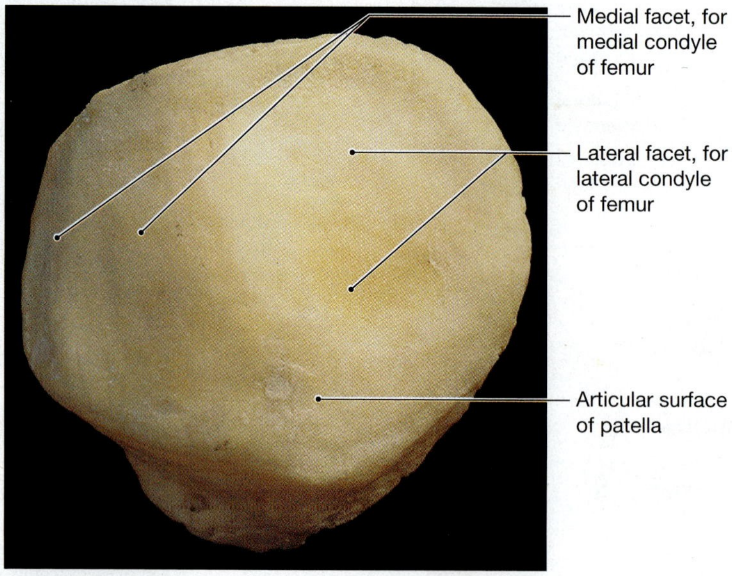

(b) Posterior view

Figure 7.15 The Patella
This sesamoid bone forms within the tendon of the *quadriceps femoris*. **(a)** Anterior surface of the right patella. **(b)** Posterior surface.

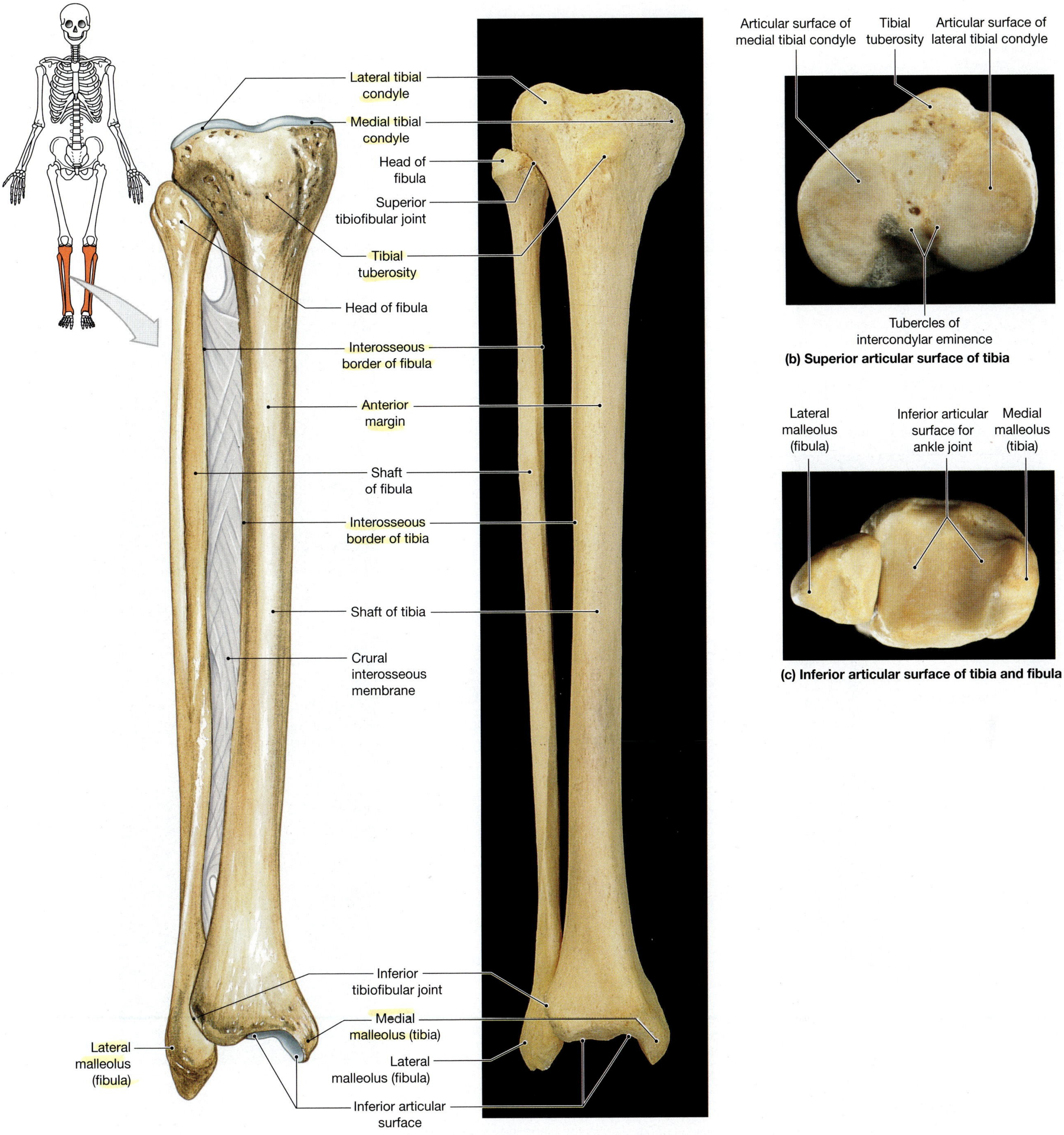

(a) Anterior views

(b) Superior articular surface of tibia

(c) Inferior articular surface of tibia and fibula

Figure 7.16 The Tibia and Fibula

(a) Anterior views of the right tibia and fibula. **(b)** Superior view of the proximal end of the tibia. **(c)** Inferior view of the distal surfaces of the tibia and fibula, showing the surfaces that participate in the ankle joint. *(Continues on next page)*

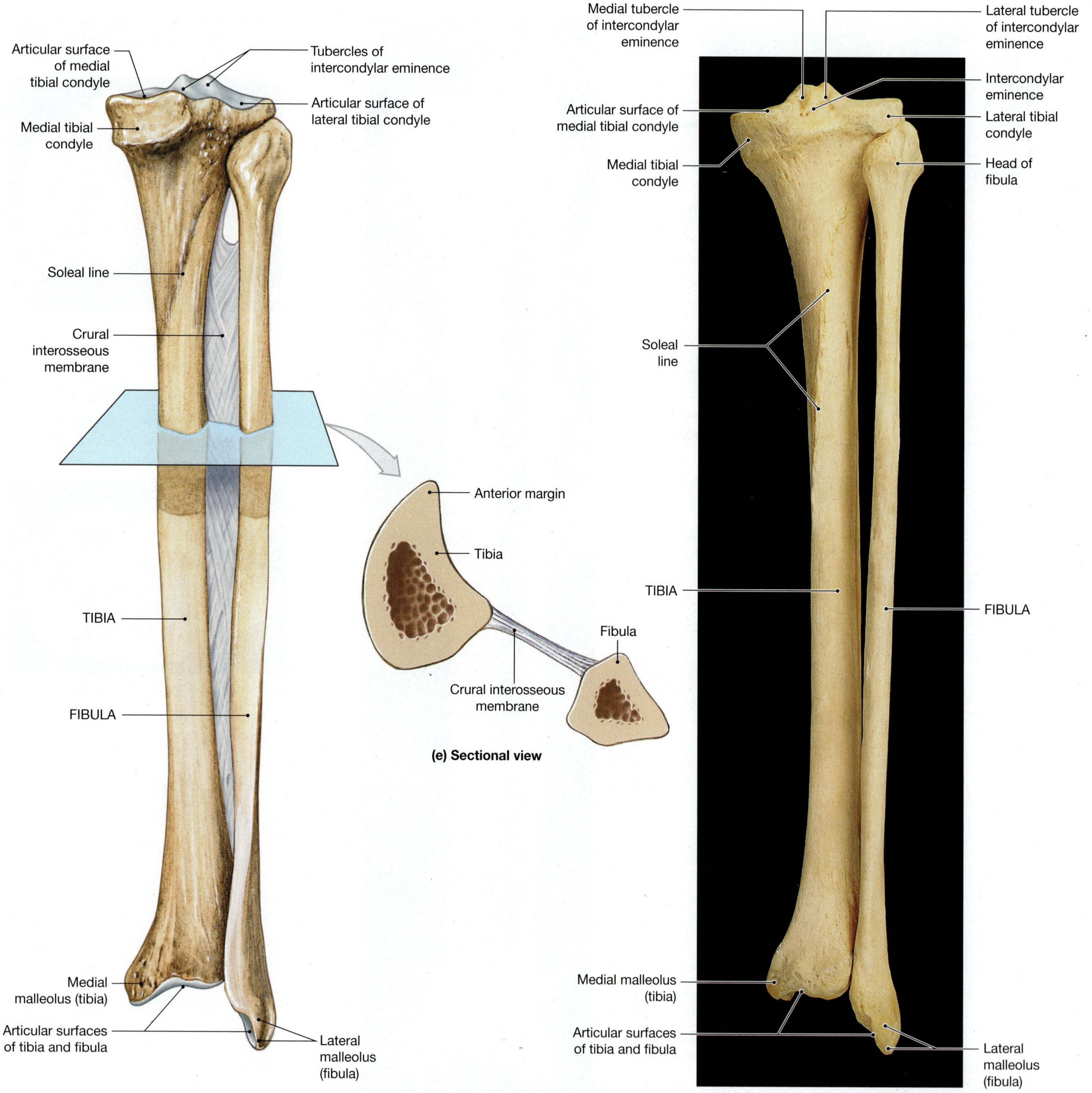

(e) Sectional view

(d) Posterior views

Figure 7.16 ***(continued)***
(d) Posterior views of the right tibia and fibula. **(e)** A cross-sectional view at the plane indicated in part (d).

The Tarsal Bones [Figures 7.17/7.18]

The ankle, or **tarsus**, contains seven **tarsal bones**: the *talus*, the *calcaneus*, the *cuboid*, the *navicular*, and three *cuneiform bones* (**Figures 7.17** and **7.18**).

- The **talus** is the second largest bone in the foot. It transmits the weight of the body from the tibia anteriorly, toward the toes. The primary tibial articulation is between the talus and the tibia; this involves the smooth superior surface of the **trochlea** of the talus. The trochlea has

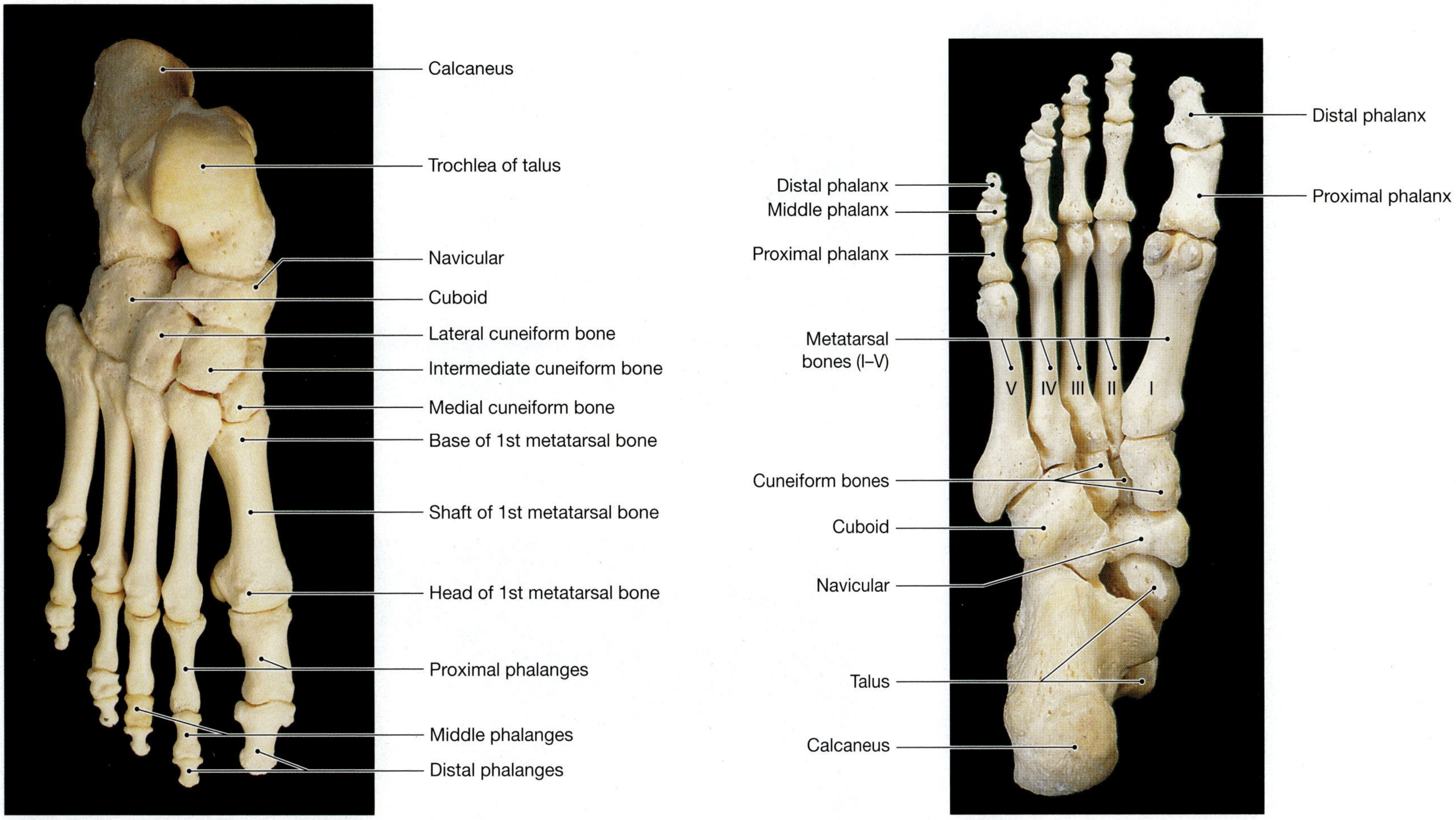

Figure 7.17 Bones of the Ankle and Foot, Part I
(a) Superior view of the bones of the right foot. Note the orientation of the tarsal bones that convey the weight of the body to both the heel and the plantar surfaces of the foot. **(b)** Inferior (plantar) view.

lateral and medial extensions that articulate with the lateral malleolus (fibula) and medial malleolus (tibia). The lateral surfaces of the talus are roughened where ligaments connect it to the tibia and fibula, further stabilizing the ankle joint.

- The **calcaneus** (kal-KĀ-nē-us), or heel bone, is the largest of the tarsal bones and may be easily palpated. When you are standing normally, most of your weight is transmitted from the tibia to the talus to the calcaneus, and then to the ground. The posterior surface of the calcaneus is a rough, knob-shaped projection. This is the attachment site for the *calcaneal tendon* (*calcanean tendon* or *Achilles tendon*) that arises at the strong calf muscles. These muscles raise the heel and lift the sole of the foot from the ground, as when standing on tiptoe. The superior and anterior surfaces of the calcaneus bear smooth facets for articulation with other tarsal bones.
- The **cuboid** articulates with the anterior, lateral surface of the calcaneus.
- The **navicular**, located on the medial side of the ankle, articulates with the anterior surface of the talus. The distal surface of the navicular articulates with the three cuneiform bones.
- The three **cuneiform bones** are wedge-shaped bones arranged in a row, with articulations between them, located anterior to the navicular. They are named according to their position: **medial cuneiform**, **intermediate cuneiform**, and **lateral cuneiform bones**. Proximally, the cuneiform bones articulate with the anterior surface of the navicular. The lateral cuneiform bone also articulates with the medial surface of the cuboid. The distal surfaces of the cuboid and the cuneiform bones articulate with the metatarsal bones of the foot.

The Metatarsal Bones and Phalanges [Figures 7.17/7.18]

The **metatarsal bones** are five long bones that form the *metatarsus* (or distal portion) of the foot (Figures 7.17 and 7.18). The metatarsal bones are identified with Roman numerals I–V, proceeding from medial to lateral across the sole. Proximally, the first three metatarsal bones articulate with the three cuneiform bones, and the last two articulate with the cuboid. Distally, each metatarsal bone articulates with a different proximal phalanx. The metatarsals help support the weight of the body during standing, walking, and running.

The 14 **phalanges**, or toe bones, have the same anatomical organization as the phalanges of the fingers. The great toe, or **hallux**, has two phalanges (proximal phalanx and distal phalanx), and the other four toes have three phalanges each (proximal, middle, and distal).

Arches of the Foot [Figure 7.18b] The arches of the foot are designed to accomplish two contrasting tasks. First, the foot must accept the weight of the body while simultaneously adapting to varying surfaces during walking or running. To do this, the arches must be flexible enough to dampen forces while still adapting to the contours of the surface of the ground. Second, the foot must function as a stable platform that is able to support the weight of the body while standing. In order to do this the arches of the foot must function as a rigid lever while distributing the weight of the body throughout the foot.

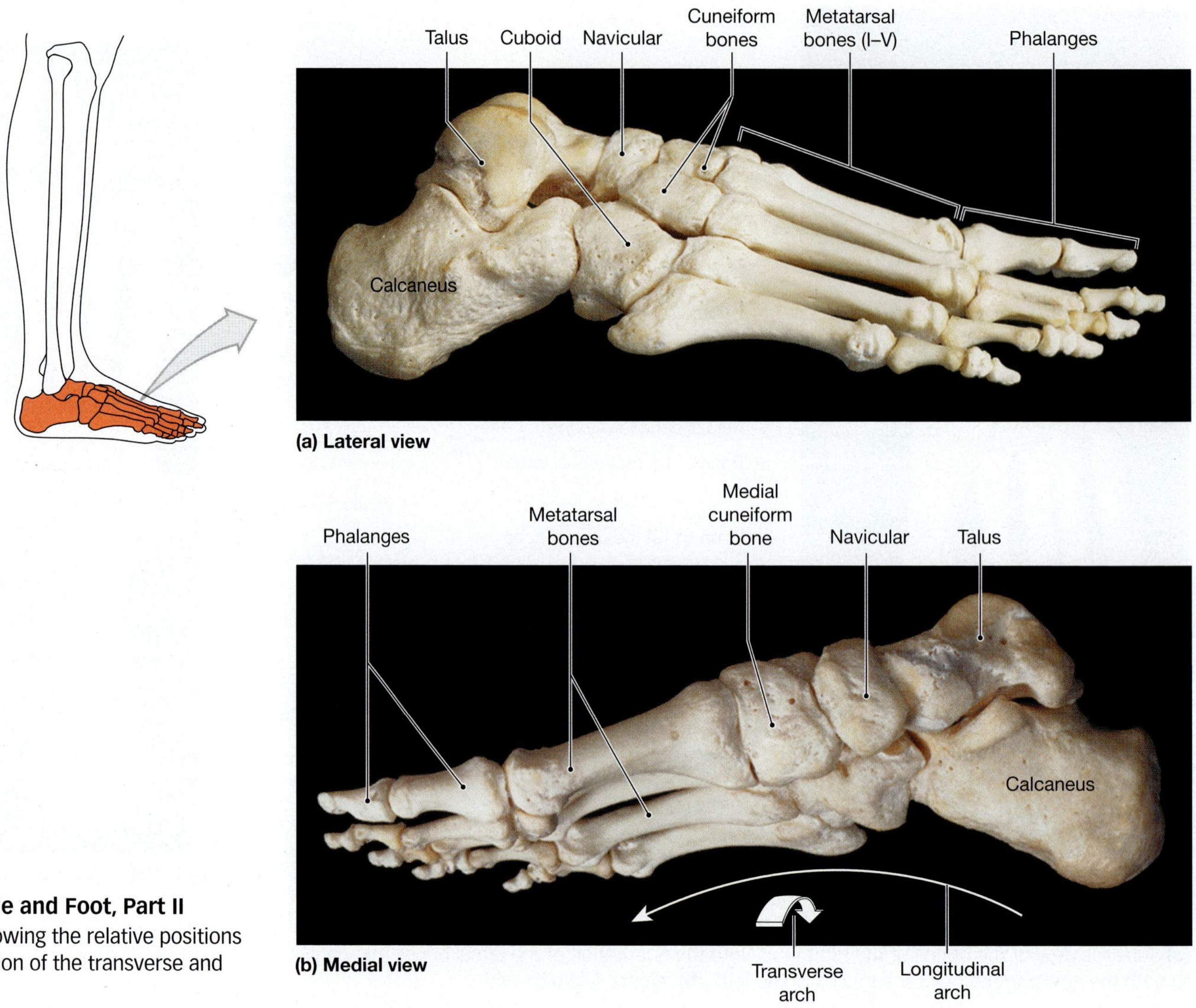

Figure 7.18 Bones of the Ankle and Foot, Part II
(a) Lateral view. **(b)** Medial view, showing the relative positions of the tarsal bones and the orientation of the transverse and longitudinal arches.

Weight transfer occurs along the **longitudinal arch** of the foot (**Figure 7.18b**). Ligaments and tendons maintain this arch by tying the calcaneus to the distal portions of the metatarsal bones. The lateral side of the foot carries most of the weight of the body while standing normally. This calcaneal portion of the arch has less curvature than the medial, talar portion. The talar portion also has more elasticity than the calcaneal portion of the longitudinal arch. As a result, the medial, plantar (sole) surface remains elevated, and the muscles, nerves, and blood vessels that supply the inferior surface of the foot are not squeezed between the metatarsal bones and the ground. This elasticity also helps absorb the shocks that accompany sudden changes in weight loading. For example, the stresses involved with running or ballet dancing are cushioned by the elasticity of this portion of the longitudinal arch. Because the degree of curvature changes from the medial to the lateral borders of the foot, a **transverse arch** also exists. In the condition known as *flatfeet*, normal arches are lost ("fall") or never form. Individuals with this condition cannot walk long distances.

When you stand normally, your body weight is distributed evenly between the calcaneus and the distal ends of the metatarsal bones. The amount of weight transferred forward depends on the position of the foot and the placement of body weight. During dorsiflexion of the foot, as when "digging in the heels," all of the body weight rests on the calcaneus. During plantar flexion and "standing on tiptoe," the talus and calcaneus transfer the weight to the metatarsal bones and phalanges through more anterior tarsal bones.

CONCEPT CHECK

1. What three bones make up the hip bone?
2. The fibula does not participate in the knee joint, nor does it bend; but when it is fractured, walking is difficult. Why?
3. While jumping off the back steps of his house, 10-year-old Mark lands on his right heel and breaks his foot. What foot bone is most likely broken?
4. Describe at least three differences between the female and male pelvis.
5. Where does the weight of the body rest during dorsiflexion? During plantar flexion?

See blue "Answers" tab at back of book.

Individual Variation in the Skeletal System [Tables 7.1/7.2]

A comprehensive study of a human skeleton can reveal important information about the individual. For example, there are characteristic racial differences in portions of the skeleton, especially the skull, and the development of various ridges and general bone mass can permit an estimation of muscular development. Details such as the condition of the teeth or the presence of healed fractures can provide information about the individual's medical history. Two important details, sex and age, can be determined or closely estimated on the basis of measurements indicated in Tables 7.1 and 7.2. Table 7.1

Clinical Note

Problems with the Ankle and Foot The arches of the foot are usually present at birth. Sometimes, however, they fail to develop properly. In **congenital talipes equinovarus (clubfoot)**, abnormal muscle development distorts growing bones and joints. One or both feet may be involved, and the condition can be mild, moderate, or severe. In most cases, the tibia, ankle, and foot are affected; the longitudinal arch is exaggerated, and the feet are turned medially and inverted. If both feet are involved, the soles face one another. This condition, which affects 2 in 1000 births, is roughly twice as common in boys as in girls. Prompt treatment with casts or other supports in infancy helps alleviate the problem, and fewer than half the cases require surgery.

Someone with **flatfeet** loses or never develops the longitudinal arch. "Fallen arches" develop as tendons and ligaments stretch and become less elastic. Up to 40 percent of adults may have flatfeet, but no action is necessary unless pain develops. Individuals with abnormal arch development are most likely to suffer metatarsal injuries. Obese individuals and those who must constantly stand or walk on the job are likely candidates. Children have very mobile articulations and elastic ligaments, so they commonly have flexible, flat feet. Their feet look flat only while they are standing, and the arch appears when they stand on their toes or sit down. In most cases, the condition disappears as growth continues.

Claw feet are produced by muscular abnormalities. In individuals with a claw foot, the median longitudinal arch becomes exaggerated because the plantar flexors overpower the dorsiflexors. Causes include muscle degeneration and nerve paralysis. The condition tends to get progressively worse with age.

Even the normal ankle and foot are subjected to a variety of stresses during daily activities. In a **sprain**, a ligament is stretched to the point at which some of the collagen fibers are torn. The ligament remains functional, and the structure of the joint is not affected. The most common cause of a sprained ankle is a forceful inversion of the foot that stretches the lateral ligament. An ice pack is generally required to reduce swelling. With rest and support, the ankle should heal in about three weeks.

In more serious incidents, the entire ligament can be torn apart, or the connection between the ligament and the lateral malleolus can be so strong that the bone breaks instead of the ligament. In general, a broken bone heals more quickly and effectively than does a completely torn ligament. A dislocation may accompany such injuries.

In a **dancer's fracture**, the proximal portion of the fifth metatarsal is broken. Most such cases occur while the body weight is being supported by the longitudinal arch of the foot. A sudden shift in weight from the medial portion of the arch to the lateral, less elastic border breaks the fifth metatarsal close to its distal articulation.

TABLE 7.1 Sexual Differences in the Adult Human Skeleton

Region/Feature	Male	Female
SKULL		
General appearance	Heavier; rougher surface	Lighter; smoother surface
Forehead	More sloping	More vertical
Sinuses	Larger	Smaller
Cranium	About 10% larger (average)	About 10% smaller
Mandible	Larger, more robust	Lighter, smaller
Teeth	Larger	Smaller
PELVIS		
General appearance	Narrow; robust; heavier; rougher surface	Broad; light; smoother surface
Pelvic inlet	Heart shaped	Oval to round
Iliac fossa	Deeper	Shallower
Ilium	More vertical; extends farther superior	Less vertical; less extension superior to the sacro-iliac joint
Angle inferior to pubic symphysis	Less than 90°	100° or more
Acetabulum	Directed laterally	Faces slightly anteriorly as well as laterally
Obturator foramen	Oval	Triangular
Ischial spine	Points medially	Points posteriorly
Sacrum	Long, narrow triangle with pronounced sacral curvature	Broad, short triangle with less curvature
Coccyx	Points anteriorly	Points inferiorly
OTHER SKELETAL ELEMENTS		
Bone weight	Heavier	Lighter
Bone markings	More prominent	Less prominent

identifies characteristic differences between the skeletons of males and females, but not every skeleton shows every feature in classic detail. Many differences, including markings on the skull, cranial capacity, and general skeletal features, reflect differences in average body size, muscle mass, and muscular strength. The general changes in the skeletal system that take place with age are summarized in Table 7.2. Note how these changes begin at age 3 months and continue throughout life. For example, fusion of the epiphyseal cartilages begins at about age 3, while degenerative changes in the normal skeletal system, such as a reduction in mineral content in the bony matrix, do not begin until age 30–45.

Embryology Summary

For a summary of the development of the appendicular skeleton, see Chapter 28 (Embryology and Human Development).

TABLE 7.2 Age-Related Changes in the Skeleton

Region/Structure	Event(s)	Age (Years)
GENERAL SKELETON		
Bony matrix	Reduction in mineral content	Begins at age 30–45; values differ for males versus females between ages 45 and 65; similar reductions occur in both sexes after age 65
Markings	Reduction in size, roughness	Gradual reduction with increasing age and decreasing muscular strength and mass
SKULL		
Fontanels	Closure	Completed by age 2
Frontal suture	Fusion	2–8
Occipital bone	Fusion of ossification centers	1–6
Styloid process	Fusion with temporal bone	12–16
Hyoid bone	Complete ossification and fusion	25–30 or later
Teeth	Loss of "baby teeth"; appearance of permanent teeth; eruption of permanent molars	Detailed in Chapter 25 (Digestive System)
Mandible	Loss of teeth; reduction in bone mass; change in angle at mandibular notch	Accelerates in later years (age 60)
VERTEBRAE		
Curvature	Appearance of major curves	3 months–10 years *(see Figure 6.19, p. 160)*
Intervertebral discs	Reduction in size, percentage contribution to height	Accelerates in later years (age 60)
LONG BONES		
Epiphyseal cartilages	Fusion	Ranges vary according to specific bone under discussion, but general analysis permits determination of approximate age (3–7, 15–22, etc.)
PECTORAL AND PELVIC GIRDLES		
Epiphyseal cartilages	Fusion	Overlapping ranges are somewhat narrower than the above, including 14–16, 16–18, 22–25 years

CLINICAL TERMS

congenital talipes equinovarus (clubfoot): A congenital deformity affecting one or both feet. It develops secondary to abnormalities in neuromuscular development.

dancer's fracture: A fracture of the fifth metatarsal, usually near its proximal articulation.

flatfeet: The loss or absence of a longitudinal arch.

sprain: Condition caused when a ligament is stretched to the point where some of the collagen fibers are torn. Unless torn completely, the ligament remains functional, and the structure of the joint is not affected.

STUDY OUTLINE

Introduction 175

1. The **appendicular skeleton** includes the bones of the upper and lower limbs and the pectoral and pelvic girdles that support the limbs and connect them to the trunk. *(see Figure 7.1)*

The Pectoral Girdle and Upper Limb 176

1. Each upper limb articulates with the trunk through the **pectoral girdle**, or *shoulder girdle*, which consists of the **clavicle** (collarbone) and the **scapula** (shoulder blade). *(see Figures 7.2 to 7.5)*

The Pectoral Girdle 176

2. The clavicle and scapula position the shoulder joint, help move the upper limb, and provide a base for muscle attachment. *(see Figures 7.3/7.4)*
3. The **clavicle** is an S-shaped bone that extends between the manubrium of the sternum and the **acromion** of the scapula. This bone provides the only direct connection between the pectoral girdle and the axial skeleton.
4. The **scapula** articulates with the round head of the humerus at the **glenoid cavity** of the scapula, the **glenohumeral joint** (*shoulder joint*). Two scapular processes, the **coracoid** and the **acromion**, are attached to ligaments and tendons associated with the shoulder joint. The acromion articulates with the clavicle at the **acromioclavicular joint**. The acromion is continuous with the **scapular spine**, which crosses the posterior surface of the scapular body. *(see Figure 7.5)*

The Upper Limb 179

5. The **humerus** articulates with the glenoid cavity of the scapula. The articular capsule of the shoulder attaches distally to the humerus at its **anatomical neck**. Two prominent projections, the **greater tubercle** and **lesser tubercle**, are important sites for muscle attachment. Other prominent surface features include the **deltoid tuberosity**, site of *deltoid muscle* attachment; the articular **condyle**, divided into two articular regions, the **trochlea** (medial) and **capitulum** (lateral); the **radial groove**, marking the path of the *radial nerve*; and the **medial** and **lateral epicondyles** for other muscle attachment. *(see Figures 7.2/7.6 to 7.8)*
6. Distally the humerus articulates with the ulna (at the trochlea) and the radius (at the capitulum). The trochlea extends from the **coronoid fossa** to the **olecranon fossa**. *(see Figure 7.6)*
7. The **ulna** and **radius** are the parallel bones of the forearm. The olecranon fossa of the humerus accommodates the **olecranon** of the ulna during straightening (extension) of the elbow joint. The coronoid fossa accommodates the **coronoid process** of the ulna during bending (flexion) of the elbow joint. *(see Figures 7.2/7.7)*
8. The **carpal bones** of the wrist form two rows, **proximal** and **distal**. From lateral to medial, the proximal row consists of the **scaphoid**, **lunate**,

triquetrum, and **pisiform**. From lateral to medial, the distal row consists of the **trapezium**, **trapezoid**, **capitate**, and **hamate**. *(see Figure 7.8)*

9. Five **metacarpal bones** articulate with the distal carpal bones. Distally, the metacarpal bones articulate with the phalanges. Four of the fingers contain three **phalanges**; the **pollex** (thumb) has only two. *(see Figure 7.8)*

The Pelvic Girdle and Lower Limb 186

The Pelvic Girdle 186

1. The pelvic girdle consists of two **hip bones**, also called *coxal bones* or *innominate bones*; each hip bone forms through the fusion of three bones—an ilium, an ischium, and a pubis. *(see Figures 7.9/7.10)*
2. The **ilium** is the largest of the hip bones. Inside the **acetabulum** (the fossa on the lateral surface of the hip bone that accommodates the **head** of the femur) the ilium is fused to the **ischium** (posteriorly) and to the **pubis** (anteriorly). The **pubic symphysis** limits movement between the pubic bones of the left and right hip bones. *(see Figures 7.11/7.13)*
3. The **pelvis** consists of the two hip bones, the sacrum, and coccyx. It may be subdivided into the **greater** (*false*) **pelvis** and the **lesser** (*true*) **pelvis**. The lesser pelvis encloses the **pelvic cavity**. *(see Figures 7.11 to 7.13)*

The Lower Limb 193

4. The **femur** is the longest bone in the body. At its rounded **head**, it articulates with the pelvis at the acetabulum, and at its distal end its **medial** and **lateral condyles** articulate with the tibia at the knee joint. The **greater** and **lesser trochanters** are projections near the head where large tendons attach to the femur. *(see Figures 7.9/7.12d/7.14)*
5. The **patella** is a large sesamoid bone that forms within the tendon of the *quadriceps femoris* muscle group. The patellar ligament extends from the patella to the **tibial tuberosity**. *(see Figures 7.14f/7.15)*
6. The **tibia** is the large medial bone of the leg. The prominent rough surface markings of the tibia include the **tibial tuberosity**, the **anterior margin**, the **interosseous border**, and the **medial malleolus**. The medial malleolus is a large process that provides medial support for the **talocrural joint** (ankle). *(see Figure 7.16)*
7. The **fibula** is the slender leg bone lateral to the tibia. The **head** articulates with the tibia inferior to the knee, inferior and slightly posterior to the lateral tibial condyle. A fibular process, the **lateral malleolus**, stabilizes the ankle joint by preventing medial movement of the tibia across the talus. *(see Figures 7.16/7.17)*
8. The **tarsus**, or ankle, includes seven **tarsal bones**; only the smooth superior surface of the trochlea of the talus articulates with the tibia and fibula. It has lateral and medial extensions that articulate with the lateral and medial malleoli of the fibula and tibia, respectively. When standing normally, most of the body weight is transferred to the calcaneus, and the rest is passed on to the **metatarsal bones**.
9. The basic organizational pattern of the **metatarsal bones** and **phalanges** of the foot is the same as that of the metacarpal bones and phalanges of the hand. *(see Figures 7.17/7.18)*
10. Weight transfer occurs along the **longitudinal arch** and **transverse arch** of the foot. *(see Figures 7.17/7.18)*

Individual Variation in the Skeletal System 200

1. Studying a human skeleton can reveal important information such as race, medical history, gender, body size, muscle mass, and age. *(see Tables 7.1/7.2)*
2. A number of age-related changes and events take place in the skeletal system. These changes begin at about age 3 and continue throughout life. *(see Tables 7.1/7.2)*

CHAPTER REVIEW

For answers to the Concept Check and Chapter Review questions, go to the blue "Answers" tab at the back of the book.

Level 1 Reviewing Facts and Terms

Match each numbered item with the most closely related lettered item. Use letters for answers in the spaces provided.

Column A	Column B
___ 1. shoulder	a. tibia
___ 2. hip	b. pectoral girdle
___ 3. scapula	c. radius
___ 4. trochlea	d. phalanges
___ 5. ulnar notch	e. pelvic girdle
___ 6. one coxal bone	f. femur
___ 7. greater trochanter	g. infraspinous fossa
___ 8. medial malleolus	h. calcaneus
___ 9. heel bone	i. ilium
___10. toes	j. humerus

11. Structural characteristics of the pectoral girdle that adapt it to a wide range of movement include
    (a) heavy bones
    (b) relatively weak joints
    (c) limited range of motion at the shoulder joint
    (d) joints stabilized by ligaments and tendons to the thoracic cage
12. The broad, relatively flat portion of the clavicle that articulates with the scapula is the
    (a) sternal end (b) conoid tubercle
    (c) acromial end (d) costal tuberosity
13. What bone articulates with the hip bone at the acetabulum?
    (a) sacrum (b) humerus
    (c) femur (d) tibia
14. The protuberance that can be palpated on the lateral side of the ankle is the
    (a) lateral malleolus (b) lateral condyle
    (c) tibial tuberosity (d) lateral epicondyle
15. Structural characteristics of the pelvic girdle that adapt it to the role of bearing the weight of the body include
    (a) heavy bones
    (b) stable joints
    (c) limited range of movement
    (d) all of the above at some joints
16. Which of the following is a characteristic of the male pelvis?
    (a) triangular obturator foramen
    (b) coccyx points into the pelvic outlet
    (c) sacrum broad and short
    (d) ischial spine points posteriorly
17. Which of the following is not a carpal bone?
    (a) scaphoid (b) hamate
    (c) cuboid (d) triquetrum
18. The ___ of the radius assists in the stabilization of the wrist joint.
    (a) olecranon (b) coronoid process
    (c) styloid process (d) radial tuberosity
19. The olecranon is found on the
    (a) humerus (b) radius
    (c) ulna (d) femur

20. The small, anterior projection of the scapula that extends over the superior margin of the glenoid cavity is the
    (a) scapular spine
    (b) acromion
    (c) coracoid process
    (d) supraspinous process

Level 2 Reviewing Concepts

1. The observable differences between the male and female pelvis are a result of which of the following?
   (a) smoother surface and lighter bones of the female pelvis
   (b) less curvature of the sacrum and coccyx in the female
   (c) a more circular pelvic outlet
   (d) all of the above
2. Identification of an individual by examination of the skeleton can be made by use of which of the following?
   (a) matching of dental records from prior to death
   (b) relative density of the bones
   (c) strength of the ligamentous attachments of the bones
   (d) relative length of the elements of the hands and feet
3. Characteristics that specifically identify a skeletal element as belonging to a male include
   (a) heavy orbital ridges on the frontal bones
   (b) a more vertical forehead
   (c) a relatively shallow iliac fossa
   (d) a smaller cranial cavity
4. In determining the age of a skeleton, what pieces of information would be helpful?
5. What is the importance of maintaining the correct amount of curvature of the longitudinal arch of the foot?
6. Why are fractures of the clavicle so common?
7. Why is the tibia, but not the fibula, involved in the transfer of weight to the ankle and foot?
8. What is the function of the olecranon of the ulna?
9. How is body weight passed to the metatarsal bones?

Level 3 Critical Thinking

1. Why would a person who has osteoporosis be more likely to suffer a broken hip than a broken shoulder?
2. Archaeologists find the pelvis of a primitive human and are able to tell the sex, the relative age, and some physical characteristics of the individual. How is this possible from the pelvis only?
3. How would a forensic scientist decide whether a partial skeleton found in the forest is that of a male or female?
4. The condition of lower-than-normal longitudinal arches is known as "flatfeet." What structural problem causes flatfeet?

8

The Skeletal System

Articulations

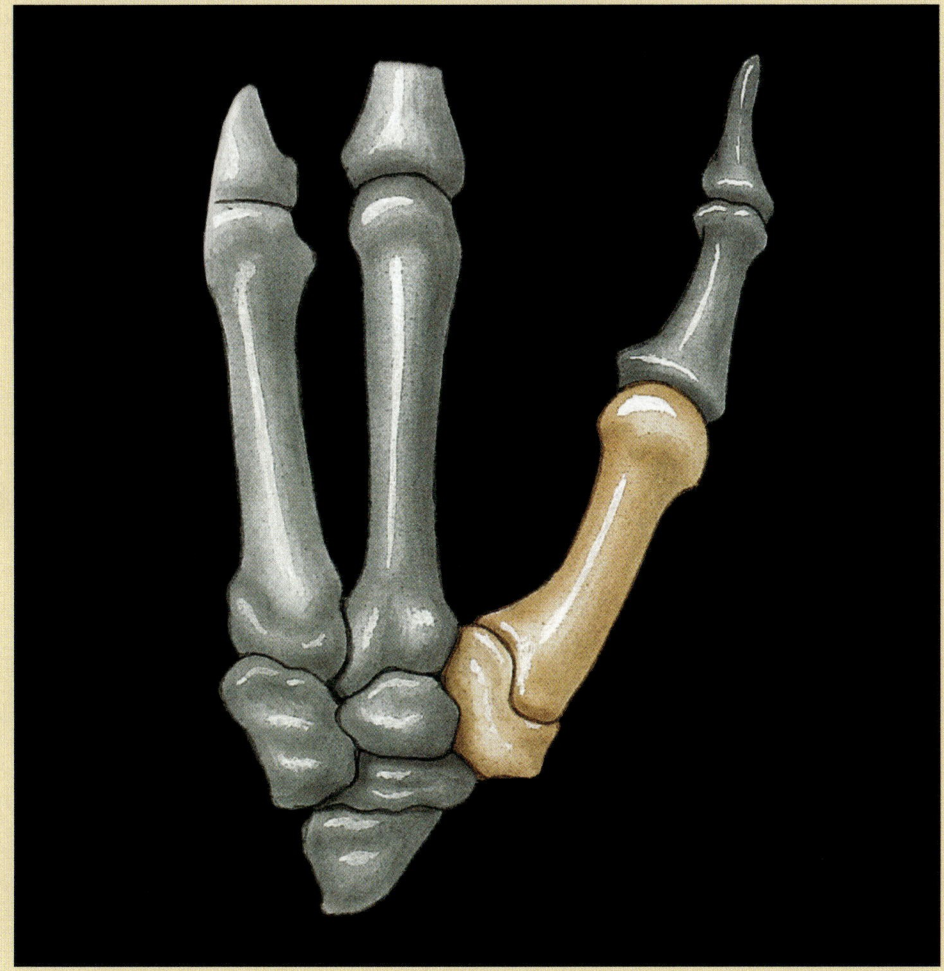

CHAPTER OBJECTIVES

1. Distinguish among different types of joints, link anatomical design to joint functions, and describe accessory joint structures.
2. Describe the dynamic movements of the skeleton.
3. Describe the six types of synovial joints based on their movement.
4. Describe the structure and function of the joints between (1) the mandible and the temporal bone, (2) adjacent vertebrae along the vertebral column, and (3) the clavicle and sternum.
5. Describe the structure and function of the joints of the upper limb: shoulder, elbow, wrist, and hand.
6. Describe the structure and function of the joints of the lower limb: hip, knee, ankle, and foot.

We depend on our bones for support, but support without mobility would leave us little better than statues. Body movements must conform to the limits of the skeleton. For example, you cannot bend the shaft of the humerus or femur; movements are restricted to joints. Joints (*arthroses*), or **articulations** (ar-tik-ū-LĀ-shuns), exist wherever two or more bones meet; they may be in direct contact or separated by fibrous tissue, cartilage, or fluid. Each joint tolerates a specific range of motion, and a variety of bony surfaces, cartilages, ligaments, tendons, and muscles work together to keep movement within the normal range. In this chapter we will focus on how bones are linked together to give us freedom of movement. The function and range of motion of each joint depend on its anatomical design. Some joints are interlocking and completely prohibit movement, whereas other joints permit either slight movement or extensive movement. Immovable and slightly movable joints are more common in the axial skeleton, whereas the freely movable joints are more common in the appendicular skeleton.

Classification of Joints [Tables 8.1/8.2]

Three functional categories of joints are based on the range of motion permitted (Table 8.1). An immovable joint is a **synarthrosis** (sin-ar-THRŌ-sis; *syn*, together + *arthros*, joint); a slightly movable joint is an **amphiarthrosis** (am-fē-ar-THRŌ-sis; *amphi*, on both sides); and a freely movable joint is a **diarthrosis** (dī-ar-THRŌ-sis; *dia*, through). Subdivisions within each functional category indicate significant structural differences. Synarthrotic or amphiarthrotic joints are classified as fibrous or cartilaginous, and diarthrotic joints are subdivided according to the degree of movement permitted. An alternative classification scheme is based on joint structure only (bony fusion, fibrous, cartilaginous, or synovial). This classification scheme is presented in Table 8.2. We will use the functional classification here, as our focus will be on the degree of motion permitted, rather than the histological structure of the articulation.

Synarthroses (Immovable Joints)

At a synarthrosis the bony edges are quite close together and may even interlock. A **suture** (*sutura*, a sewing together) is a synarthrotic joint found only between the bones of the skull. The edges of the bones are interlocked and bound together at the suture by connective tissue. This connective tissue is termed the *sutural ligament* or *sutural membrane*. The sutural membrane is the unossified remnants of the embryonic mesenchymal membrane in which the bones developed. A synarthrosis is designed to allow forces to be spread easily from one bone to another with minimal joint movement, thereby decreasing the chance of injury. A **gomphosis** (gom-FŌ-sis; *gomphosis*, a bolting together) is a specialized form of fibrous synarthrosis that binds each tooth to the surrounding bony socket. This fibrous connection is the **periodontal ligament** (per-ē-ō-DON-tal; *peri*, around + *odontos*, tooth).

In a growing bone, the diaphysis and each epiphysis are bound together by an epiphyseal cartilage, an example of a cartilaginous synarthrosis. This rigid connection is called a **synchondrosis** (sin-kon-DRŌ-sis; *syn*, together + *chondros*, cartilage). Sometimes two separate bones actually fuse together, and the boundary between them disappears. This creates a **synostosis** (sin-os-TŌ-sis), a totally rigid, immovable joint.

Amphiarthroses (Slightly Movable Joints)

An amphiarthrosis permits very limited movement, and the bones are usually farther apart than they are at a synarthrosis. The bones may be connected by collagen fibers or cartilage. At a **syndesmosis** (sin-dez-MŌ-sis; *desmo*, band or ligament), the articulating bones are connected by a ligament that limits movement of the articulating bones. Examples include the distal articulation between the tibia and fibula and the interosseous membrane between the radius and ulna. At a **symphysis** the bones are separated by a wedge or pad of fibrous cartilage. The articulations between adjacent vertebral bodies (via the *intervertebral disc*) and the anterior connection between the two pubic bones (the *pubic symphysis*) are examples of this type of joint.

Diarthroses (Freely Movable Joints) [Figure 8.1]

Diarthroses, or **synovial** (si-NŌ-vē-al) **joints**, are specialized for movement, and permit a wide range of motion. Under normal conditions, the bony sur-

TABLE 8.1 A Functional Classification of Articulations

Functional Category	Structural Category	Description	Example
SYNARTHROSIS (no movement)	**Fibrous**		
	Suture	Fibrous connections plus extensive interlocking	Between the bones of the skull
	Gomphosis	Fibrous connections plus insertion in alveolar process	Periodontal ligaments between the teeth and jaws
	Cartilaginous		
	Synchondrosis	Interposition of cartilage plate	Epiphyseal cartilages
	Bony fusion		
	Synostosis	Conversion of other articular form to a solid mass of bone	Portions of the skull, such as along the frontal suture; epiphyseal lines
AMPHIARTHROSIS (little movement)	**Fibrous**		
	Syndesmosis	Ligamentous connection	Between the tibia and fibula
	Cartilaginous		
	Symphysis	Connection by a pad of fibrous cartilage	Between right and left hip bones of pelvis; between adjacent vertebral bodies
DIARTHROSIS (free movement)	**Synovial**	Complex joint bounded by joint capsule and containing synovial fluid	Numerous; subdivided by range of movement *(see Figures 8.3 to 8.6)*
	Monaxial	Permits movement in one plane	Elbow, ankle
	Biaxial	Permits movement in two planes	Ribs, wrist
	Triaxial	Permits movement in all three planes	Shoulder, hip

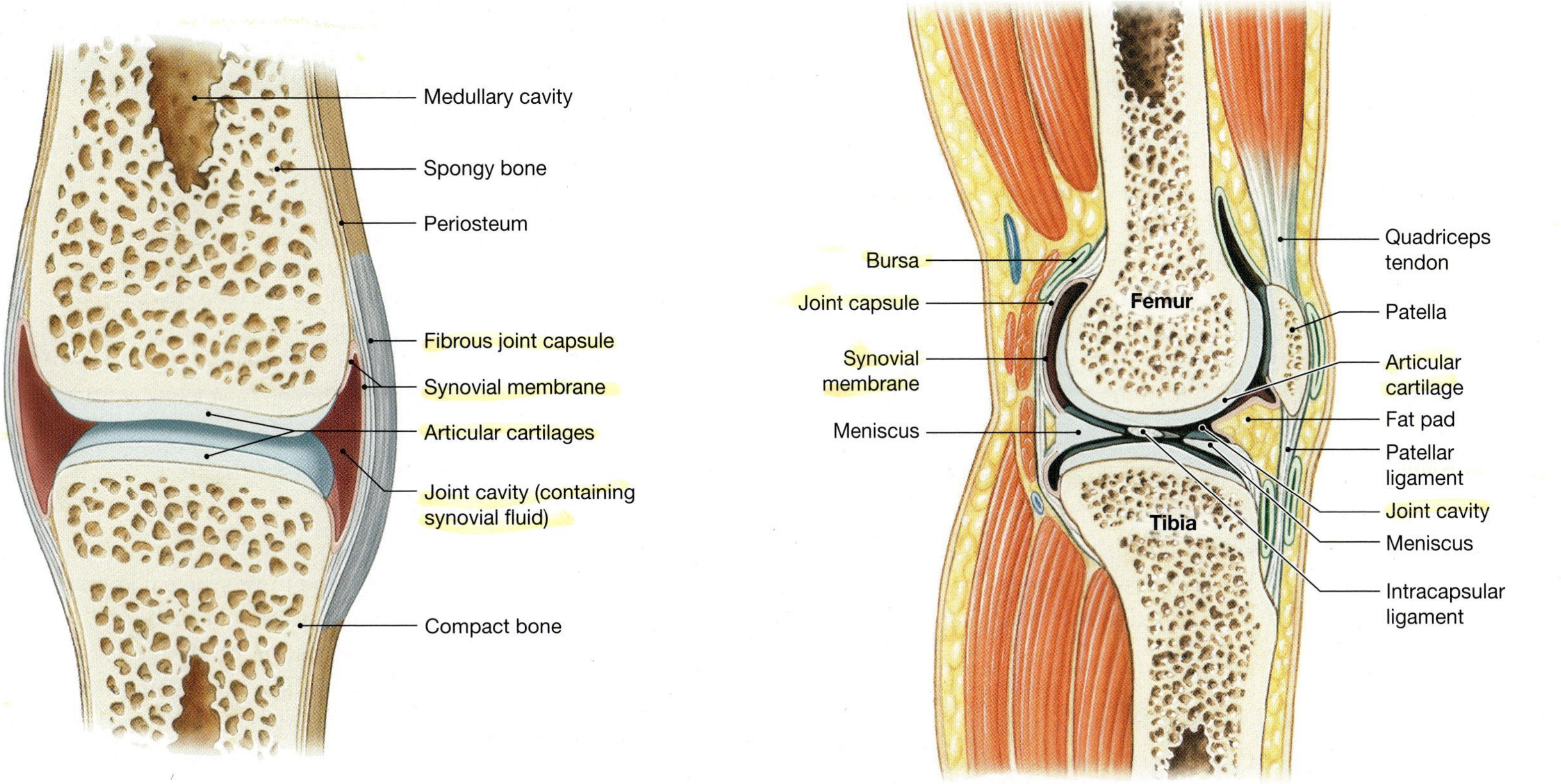

(a) Synovial joint, sagittal section

(b) Knee joint, sagittal section

Figure 8.1 Structure of a Synovial Joint
Synovial joints are diarthrotic joints that permit a wide range of motion. **(a)** Diagrammatic view of a simple articulation. **(b)** A simplified sectional view of the knee joint.

faces within a synovial joint do not contact one another because those surfaces are covered by the **articular cartilages**. These cartilages act as shock absorbers and also help reduce friction. These articular cartilages resemble hyaline cartilages in many respects. However, articular cartilages lack a perichondrium and the matrix contains more fluid than typical hyaline cartilage. Synovial joints are typically found at the ends of long bones, such as those of the upper and lower limbs.

Figure 8.1 introduces the structure of a typical synovial joint. All synovial joints have the same basic characteristics: (1) a *joint capsule*; (2) *articular cartilages*; (3) a *joint cavity* filled with *synovial fluid*; (4) a *synovial membrane* lining the joint capsule; (5) *accessory structures*; and (6) *sensory nerves* and *blood vessels* that supply the exterior and interior of the joint.

Synovial Fluid

A synovial joint is surrounded by a **joint capsule**, or **articular capsule**, composed of a thick layer of dense connective tissue. A *synovial membrane* lines the joint cavity but stops at the edges of the articular cartilages. ∞ p. 74 Synovial membranes produce the **synovial fluid** that fills the joint cavity. Synovial fluid serves three functions:

1. *Provides lubrication:* The thin layer of synovial fluid covering the inner surface of the joint capsule and the exposed surfaces of the articular cartilages provides lubrication and

TABLE 8.2 A Structural Classification of Articulations

Structure	Type	Functional Category	Example*
BONY FUSION	Synostosis	Synarthrosis	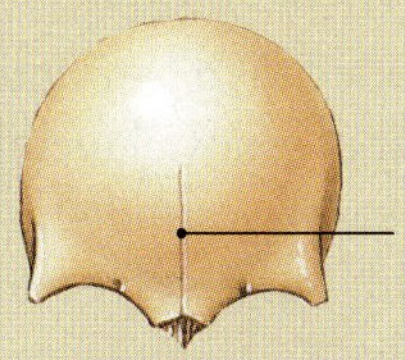
FIBROUS JOINT	Suture Gomphosis Syndesmosis	Synarthrosis Synarthrosis Amphiarthrosis	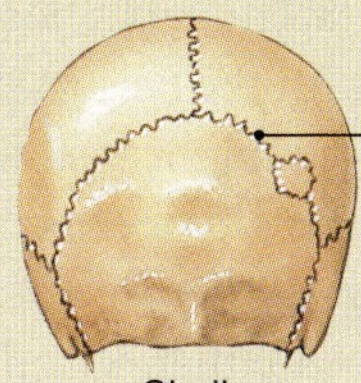
CARTILAGINOUS JOINT	Synchondrosis Symphysis	Synarthrosis Amphiarthrosis	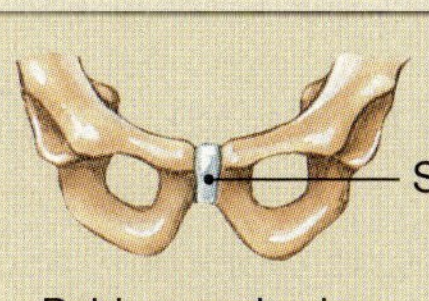
SYNOVIAL JOINT	Monaxial Biaxial Triaxial }	All diarthroses	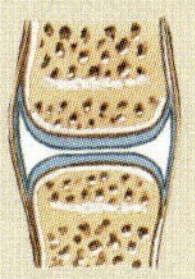

*For other examples, see Table 8.1.

reduces friction. This is accomplished by the *hyaluronan* and *lubricin* within synovial fluid, which reduce friction between the cartilage surfaces in a joint to around one-fifth of that between two pieces of ice.

2. *Nourishes the chondrocytes:* The total quantity of synovial fluid in a joint is normally less than 3 ml, even in a large joint such as the knee. This relatively small volume of fluid must circulate to provide nutrients and a route for waste disposal for the chondrocytes of the articular cartilages. Synovial fluid circulation is driven by joint movement, which also causes cycles of compression and expansion in the opposing articular cartilages. On compression, synovial fluid is forced out of the articular cartilages; on reexpansion, synovial fluid is pulled back into the cartilages. This flow of synovial fluid out of and into the articular cartilages provides nourishment for their chondrocytes.
3. *Acts as a shock absorber:* Synovial fluid cushions shocks in joints that are subjected to compression. For example, the hip, knee, and ankle joints are compressed during walking, and they are severely compressed during jogging or running. When the pressure suddenly increases, the synovial fluid absorbs the shock and distributes it evenly across the articular surfaces.

Accessory Structures [Figure 8.1]

Synovial joints may have a variety of accessory structures, including pads of cartilage or fat, ligaments, tendons, and bursae (**Figure 8.1**).

Cartilages and Fat Pads [Figure 8.1b] In complex joints such as the knee (**Figure 8.1b**), accessory structures may lie between the opposing articular surfaces and modify the shapes of the joint surfaces. These include the following:

- *Menisci* (me-NIS-kē; singular *meniscus*, crescent), or **articular discs**, are pads of fibrous cartilage that may subdivide a synovial cavity, channel the flow of synovial fluid, allow for variations in the shapes of the articular surfaces, or restrict movements at the joint.
- *Fat pads* are often found around the periphery of the joint, lightly covered by a layer of synovial membrane. Fat pads provide protection for the articular cartilages and serve as packing material for the joint as a whole. Fat pads fill spaces created when bones move and the joint cavity changes shape.

Ligaments [Figure 8.1b] The joint capsule that surrounds the entire joint is continuous with the periostea of the articulating bones. **Accessory ligaments** support, strengthen, and reinforce synovial joints. **Intrinsic ligaments**, or **capsular ligaments**, are localized thickenings of the joint capsule. **Extrinsic ligaments** are separate from the joint capsule. These ligaments may be located either outside or inside the joint capsule, and are called *extracapsular* and *intracapsular ligaments*, respectively (**Figure 8.1b**).

Tendons [Figure 8.1b] While typically not part of the articulation itself, tendons (**Figure 8.1b**) usually pass across or around a joint. Normal muscle tone keeps these tendons taut, and their presence may limit the range of motion. In some joints, tendons are an integral part of the joint capsule, and provide significant strength to the capsule.

Bursae [Figure 8.1b] Small, fluid-filled pockets in connective tissue are called **bursae** (**Figure 8.1b**). They are filled with synovial fluid and lined by a synovial membrane. Bursae may be connected to the joint cavity, or they may be completely separate from it. Bursae form where a tendon or ligament rubs against other tissues. Their function is to reduce friction and act as a shock absorber. Bursae are found around most synovial joints, such as the shoulder joint. **Synovial tendon sheaths** are tubular bursae that surround tendons where they pass across bony surfaces. Bursae may also appear beneath the skin covering a bone or within other connective tissues exposed to friction or pressure. Bursae that develop in abnormal locations, or due to abnormal stresses, are called *adventitious bursae*.

Clinical Note

Dislocation of a Synovial Joint When a **dislocation**, or **luxation** (luk-SĀ-shun), occurs, the articulating surfaces are forced out of position. This displacement can damage the articular cartilages, tear ligaments, or distort the joint capsule. Although the *inside* of a joint has no pain receptors, nerves that monitor the capsule, ligaments, and tendons are quite sensitive, and dislocations are very painful. The damage accompanying a partial dislocation, or **subluxation** (sub-luk-SĀ-shun), is less severe. People who are said to be "double-jointed" have joints that are weakly stabilized. Although their joints permit a greater range of motion than those of other individuals, they are more likely to suffer partial or complete dislocations.

Strength versus Mobility

A joint cannot be both highly mobile and very strong. The greater the range of motion at a joint, the weaker it becomes. A synarthrosis, the strongest type of joint, does not permit any movement, whereas any mobile diarthrosis may be damaged by movement beyond its normal range of motion. Several factors combine to limit mobility and reduce the chance of injury:

- the presence of accessory ligaments and the collagen fibers of the joint capsule;
- the shapes of the articulating surfaces that prevent movement in specific directions;
- the presence of other bones, bony processes, skeletal muscles, or fat pads around the joint; and
- tension in tendons attached to the articulating bones. When a skeletal muscle contracts and pulls on a tendon, it may either encourage or oppose movement in a specific direction.

CONCEPT CHECK

1. Distinguish between a synarthrosis and an amphiarthrosis.
2. What is the main advantage of a synovial joint?
3. Identify two functions of synovial fluid.
4. What are bursae? What is their function?

See blue "Answers" tab at back of book.

Articular Form and Function

To *understand* human movement you must become aware of the relationship between structure and function at each articulation. To *describe* human movement you need a frame of reference that permits accurate and precise communication. The synovial joints can be classified according to their anatomical and functional properties. To demonstrate the basis for that classification, we will describe the movements that can occur at a typical synovial joint, using a simplified model.

Describing Dynamic Motion [Figure 8.2]

Take a pencil (or pen) as your model, and stand it upright on the surface of a desk or table, as shown in Figure 8.2a. The pencil represents a bone, and the desk is an articular surface. A little imagination and a lot of twisting, pushing, and pulling will demonstrate that there are only three ways to move the model. Considering them one at a time will provide a frame of reference for analyzing any complex movement.

Possible Movement 1: Moving the point. If you hold the pencil upright but do not secure the point, you can push the pencil across the surface. This kind of motion is called *gliding* (Figure 8.2b), and it is an example of **linear motion**. You could slide the point forward or backward, from one side to the other, or diagonally. However you choose to move the pencil, the motion can be described using two lines of reference. One line represents forward/backward motion, and the other represents left/right movement. For example, a simple movement along one axis could be described as "forward 1 cm" or "left 2 cm." A diagonal movement could be described using both axes, as in "backward 1 cm and to the right 2.5 cm."

Possible Movement 2: Changing the angle of the shaft. While holding the tip in position, you can still move the free (eraser) end forward and backward or from side to side. These movements, which change the angle between the shaft and the articular surface, are examples of **angular motion** (Figure 8.2c). Any angular movement can be described with reference to the same two axes (forward/backward, left/right) and the angular change (in degrees). However, in one instance a special term is used to describe a complex angular movement. Grasp the free end of the pencil, and move it until the shaft is no longer vertical. Now with the point held firmly in place, move the free end through a complete circle (Figure 8.2d). This movement is very difficult to describe. Anatomists avoid the problem entirely by using a special term, **circumduction** (ser-kum-DUK-shun; *circum*, around), for this type of angular motion.

Possible Movement 3: Rotating the shaft. If you prevent movement of the base and keep the shaft vertical, you can still spin the shaft around its longitudinal axis. This movement is called **rotation** (Figure 8.2e). Several articulations will permit partial rotation, but none can rotate freely; such a movement would hopelessly tangle the blood vessels, nerves, and muscles that cross the joint.

An articulation that permits movement along only one axis is called **monaxial** (mon-AKS-ē-al), or *uniaxial* (ū-nē-AKS-ē-al). In the preceding model, if an articulation permits angular movement only in the forward/backward plane, or prevents any movement other than rotation around its longitudinal axis, it is monaxial. If movement can occur along two axes, the articulation is **biaxial** (bī-AKS-ē-al). If the pencil could undergo angular motion in the forward/backward or left/right plane, but not in some combination of the two, it would be biaxial. **Triaxial** (trī-AKS-ē-al) joints permit a combination of rotational and angular motion.

Types of Movements

All movements, unless otherwise indicated, are described with reference to a figure in the anatomical position. In descriptions of motion at synovial joints, anatomists use descriptive terms that have specific meanings. We will consider these movements with regard to the basic categories of movement considered in the previous section.

Linear Motion (Gliding) [Figure 8.2b]

In **gliding**, two opposing surfaces slide past one another (Figure 8.2b). Gliding occurs between the surfaces of articulating carpal bones and tarsal bones and between the clavicles and the sternum. The movement can occur in almost any direction, but the amount of movement is slight, and rotation is usually prevented by the capsule and associated ligaments.

Angular Motion [Figure 8.3]

Examples of angular motion include *abduction*, *adduction*, *flexion*, and *extension*. The description of each movement is based on reference to an individual in the anatomical position (Figure 8.3).

- **Abduction** (*ab*, from) is movement *away from the longitudinal axis of the body* in the frontal plane. For example, swinging the upper limb away from the side is abduction of the limb; moving it back constitutes

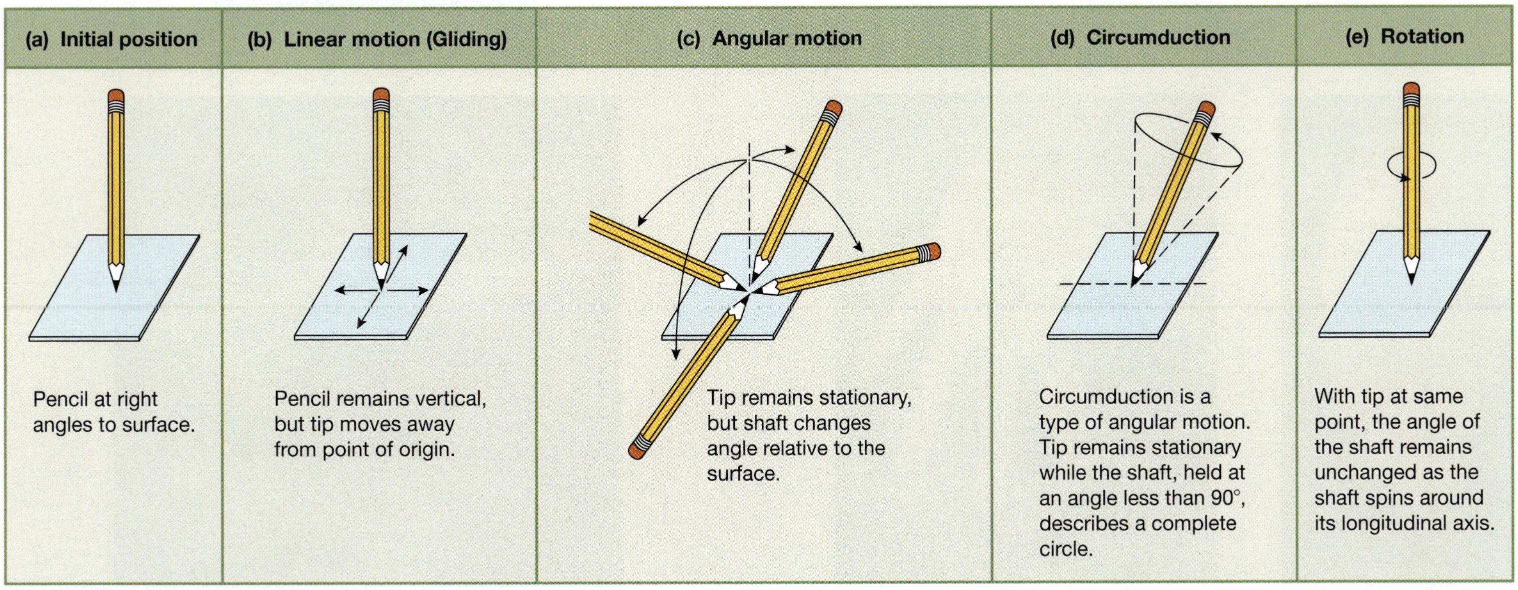

Figure 8.2 A Simple Model of Articular Motion
Three types of dynamic motion are described: **(a)** initial position of the model; **(b)** possible movement 1, showing gliding, an example of linear motion; **(c)** possible movement 2, showing angular motion; **(d)** possible movement 2, showing a special type of angular motion called circumduction; and **(e)** possible movement 3, showing rotation.

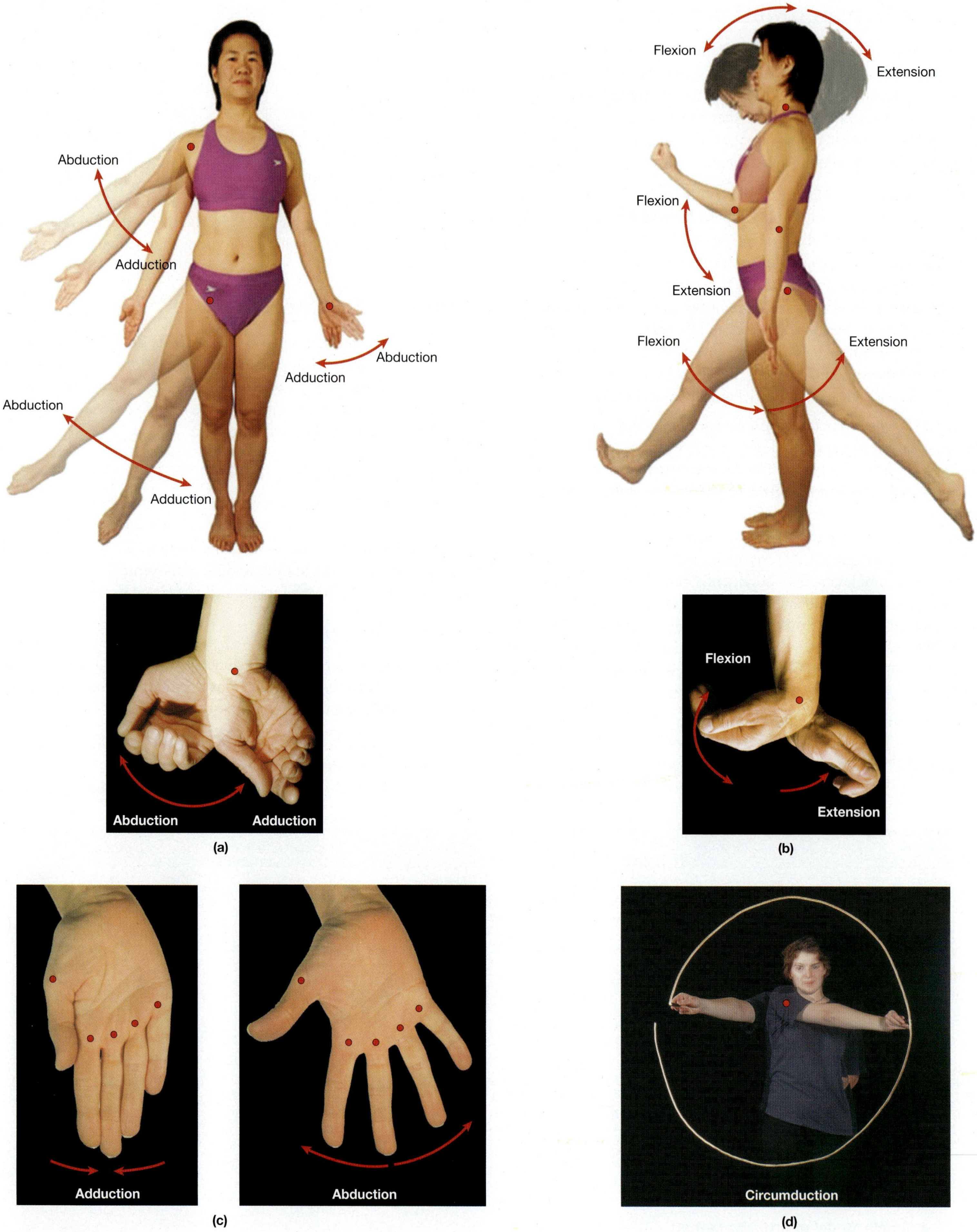

Figure 8.3 Angular Movements

Examples of movements that change the angle between the shaft and the articular surface. The red dots indicate the locations of the joints involved in the illustrated movement. **(a)** abduction/adduction, **(b)** flexion/extension, **(c)** adduction/abduction, and **(d)** circumduction.

adduction (*ad*, to). Abduction of the wrist moves the heel of the hand away from the body, whereas adduction moves it toward the body. Spreading the fingers or toes apart abducts them, because they move *away* from a central digit (finger or toe). Bringing them together constitutes adduction. Abduction and adduction always refer to movements of the appendicular skeleton (**Figure 8.3a,c**).

- **Flexion** (FLEK-shun) can be defined as movement in the anterior-posterior plane that *reduces the angle between the articulating elements.* **Extension** occurs in the same plane, but it *increases the angle between articulating elements* (**Figure 8.3b**). When you bring your head toward your chest, you flex the intervertebral articulations of the neck. When you bend down to touch your toes, you flex the intervertebral articulations of the entire vertebral column. Extension is a movement in the same plane as flexion, but in the opposite direction. Extension may return the limb to or beyond the anatomical position. **Hyperextension** is a term applied to any movement where a limb is extended beyond its normal limits, resulting in joint damage. Hyperextension is usually prevented by ligaments, bony processes, or surrounding soft tissues.

  Flexion at the shoulder or hip swings the limbs anteriorly, whereas extension moves them posteriorly. Flexion at the wrist moves the palm forward, and extension moves it back.

- A special type of angular motion, *circumduction* (**Figure 8.3d**), was also introduced in our model. A familiar example of circumduction is moving your arm in a loop, as when drawing a large circle on a chalkboard.

Rotation [Figure 8.4]

Rotation of the head may involve **left rotation** or **right rotation**, as in shaking the head "no." In analysis of movements of the limbs, if the anterior aspect of the limb rotates *inward*, toward the ventral surface of the body, you have **internal rotation**, or **medial rotation**. If it turns *outward*, you have **external rotation**, or **lateral rotation**. These rotational movements are illustrated in **Figure 8.4**.

The articulations between the radius and ulna permit the rotation of the distal end of the radius from the anatomical position across the anterior surface of the ulna. This moves the wrist and hand from palm-facing-front to palm-facing-back. This motion is called **pronation** (prō-NĀ-shun); the opposing movement, which turns the palm forward, is **supination** (soo-pi-NĀ-shun).

Special Movements [Figure 8.5]

A number of special terms apply to specific articulations or unusual types of movement (**Figure 8.5**).

- **Eversion** (ē-VER-zhun; *e*, out + *vertere*, to turn) is a twisting motion of the foot that turns the sole outward (**Figure 8.5a**). The opposite movement, turning the sole inward, is called **inversion** (*in*, into).
- **Dorsiflexion** and **plantar flexion** (*planta*, sole) also refer to movements of the foot (**Figure 8.5b**). Dorsiflexion, or *ankle flexion*, elevates the distal portion of the foot and the toes, as when "digging in the heels." Plantar flexion, or *ankle extension*, elevates the heel and proximal portion of the foot, as when standing on tiptoe.
- **Lateral flexion** occurs when the vertebral column bends to the side. This movement is most pronounced in the cervical and thoracic regions (**Figure 8.5c**). Lateral flexion to the left is counteracted by lateral flexion to the right.
- **Protraction** entails moving a part of the body anteriorly in the horizontal plane. **Retraction** is the reverse movement (**Figure 8.5d**). You protract your jaw when you grasp your upper lip with your lower teeth, and you protract your clavicles when you cross your arms.

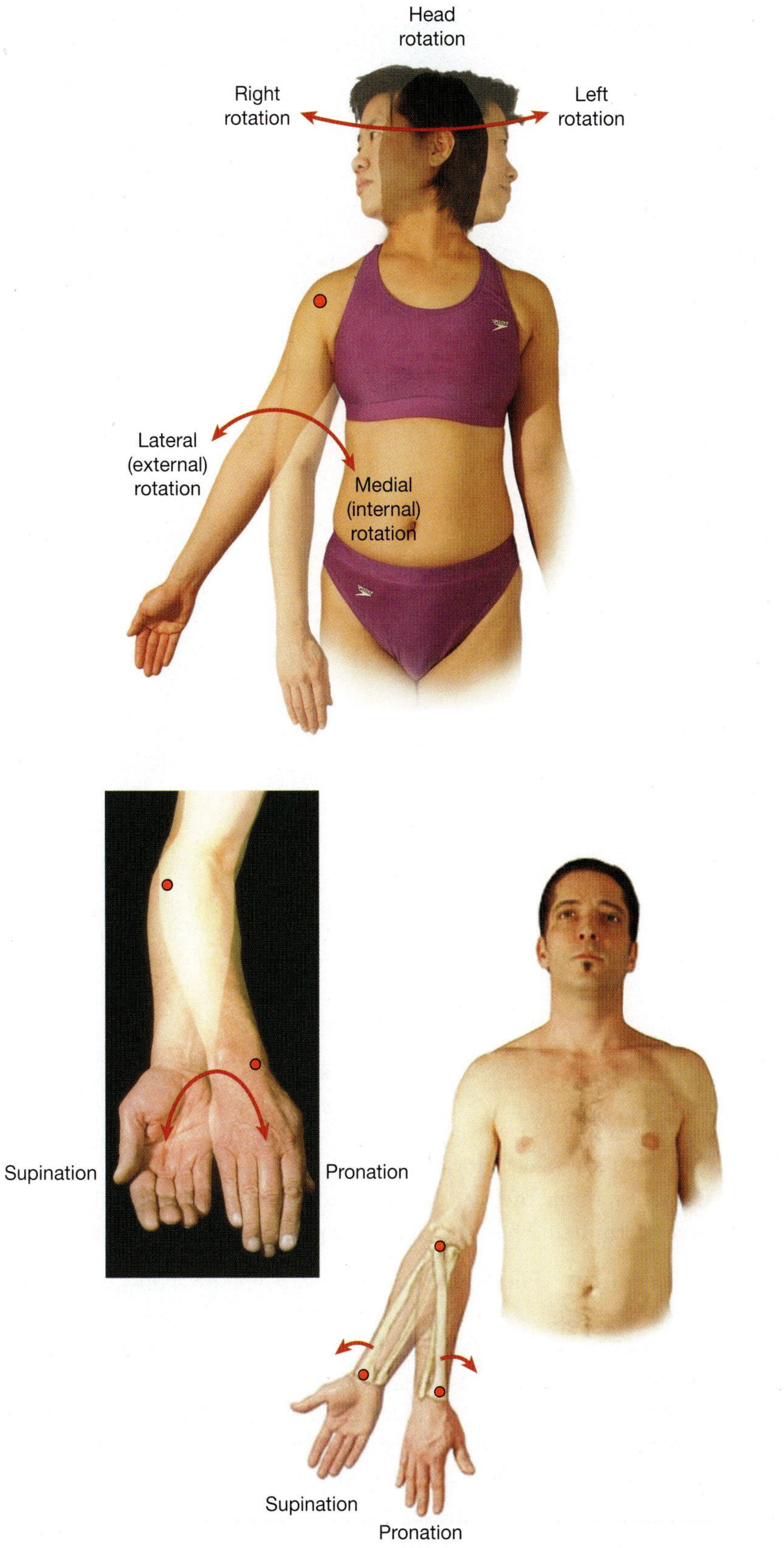

Figure 8.4 Rotational Movements
Examples of motion in which the shaft of the bone rotates.

- **Opposition** is the special movement of the thumb that produces pad-to-pad contact of the thumb with the palm or any other finger. Flexion of the fifth metacarpal bone can assist this movement. The reverse of opposition is called *reposition* (**Figure 8.5e**).
- **Elevation** and **depression** occur when a structure moves in a superior or inferior direction. You depress your mandible when you open your mouth and elevate it as you close it (**Figure 8.5f**). Another familiar elevation occurs when you shrug your shoulders.

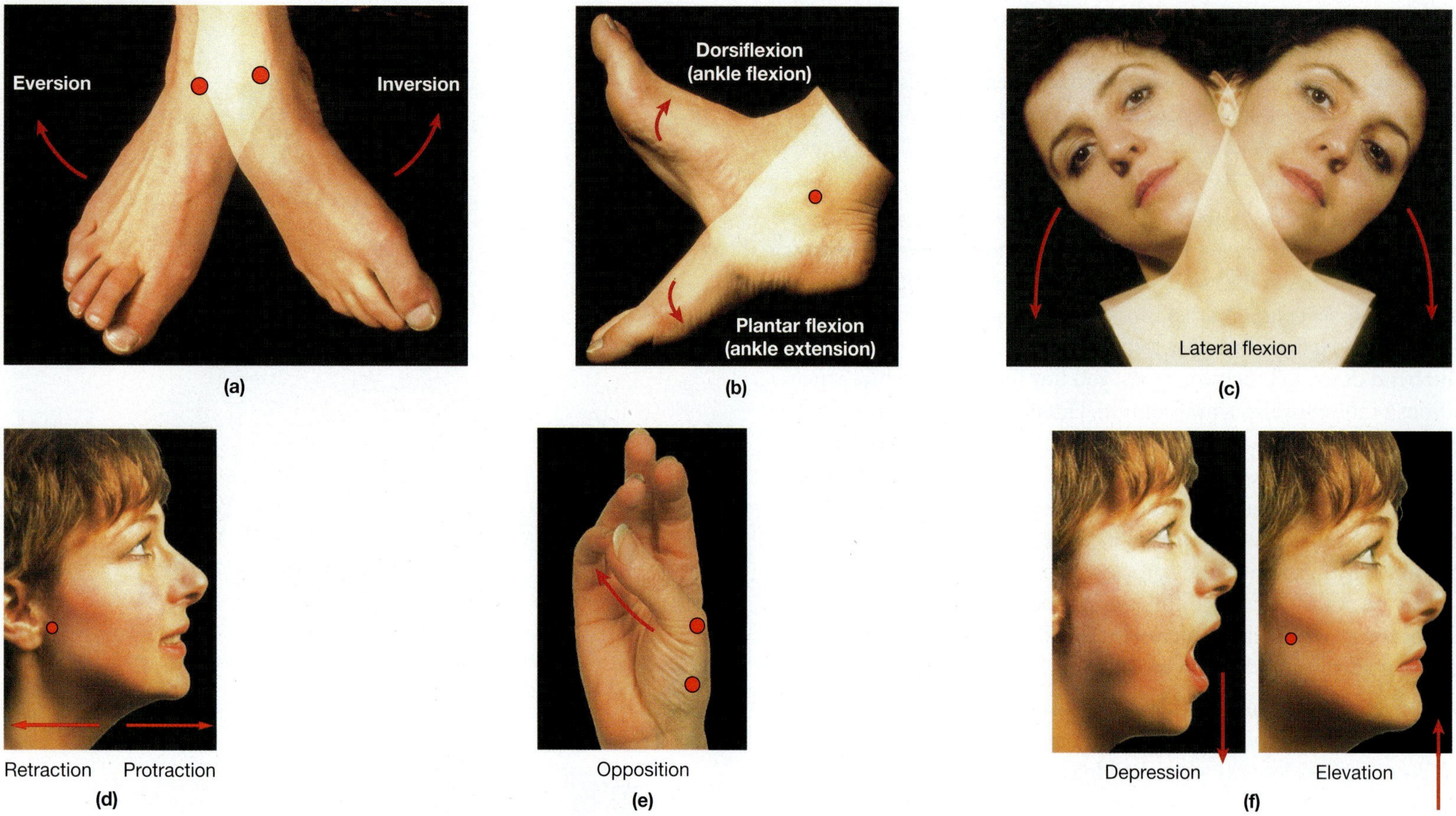

Figure 8.5 Special Movements
Examples of special terms used to describe movement at specific joints or unique directions of movement: **(a)** eversion/inversion, **(b)** dorsiflexion/plantar flexion, **(c)** lateral flexion, **(d)** retraction/protraction, **(e)** opposition, **(f)** depression/elevation.

A Structural Classification of Synovial Joints [Figure 8.6]

Synovial joints are freely movable diarthrotic joints. Since they permit a wide range of motion, they are classified according to the type and range of movement permitted. The structure of the joint defines its movement.

- **Plane joints:** **Plane joints**, also called *planar* or *gliding joints*, have flattened or slightly curved faces (Figure 8.6a). The relatively flat articular surfaces slide across one another, but the amount of movement is very slight. Ligaments usually prevent or restrict rotation. Plane joints are found at the ends of the clavicles, between the carpal bones, between the tarsal bones, and between the articular facets of adjacent vertebrae. Plane joints may be *nonaxial*, which means that they permit only small sliding movements, or *multiaxial*, which means that they permit sliding in any direction.
- **Hinge joints:** **Hinge joints** permit angular movement in a single plane, like the opening and closing of a door (Figure 8.6b). A hinge joint is an example of a monaxial joint. Examples of hinged joints would be the elbow and knee.
- **Pivot joints:** **Pivot joints** are also monaxial, but they permit only rotation (Figure 8.6c). A pivot joint between the atlas and axis allows you to rotate your head to either side.
- **Condylar joints:** In a **condylar joint**, or *ellipsoidal joint*, an oval articular face nestles within a depression on the opposing surface (Figure 8.6d). With such an arrangement, angular motion occurs in two planes, along or across the length of the oval. It is thus an example of a biaxial joint. Condylar joints connect the fingers and toes with the metacarpal bones and metatarsal bones, respectively.
- **Saddle joints:** **Saddle joints** (Figure 8.6e) have complex articular faces. Each one resembles a saddle because it is concave on one axis and convex on the other. Saddle joints are extremely mobile, allowing extensive angular motion without rotation. They are usually classified as biaxial joints. Moving the saddle joint at the base of your thumb is an excellent demonstration that also provides an excuse for twiddling your thumbs during a lecture.
- **Ball-and-socket joints:** In a **ball-and-socket joint** (Figure 8.6f), the round head of one bone rests within a cup-shaped depression in another. All combinations of movements, including rotation, can be performed at ball-and-socket joints. These are triaxial joints, and examples include the shoulder and hip joints.

CONCEPT CHECK

1. In a newborn infant, the large bones of the skull are joined by fibrous connective tissue. What type of joint is this? These bones later grow, interlock, and form immovable joints. What type of joints are these?
2. Give the proper term for each of the following types of motion: (a) moving the humerus away from the midline of the body; (b) turning the palms so that they face forward; (c) bending the elbow.

See blue "Answers" tab at back of book.

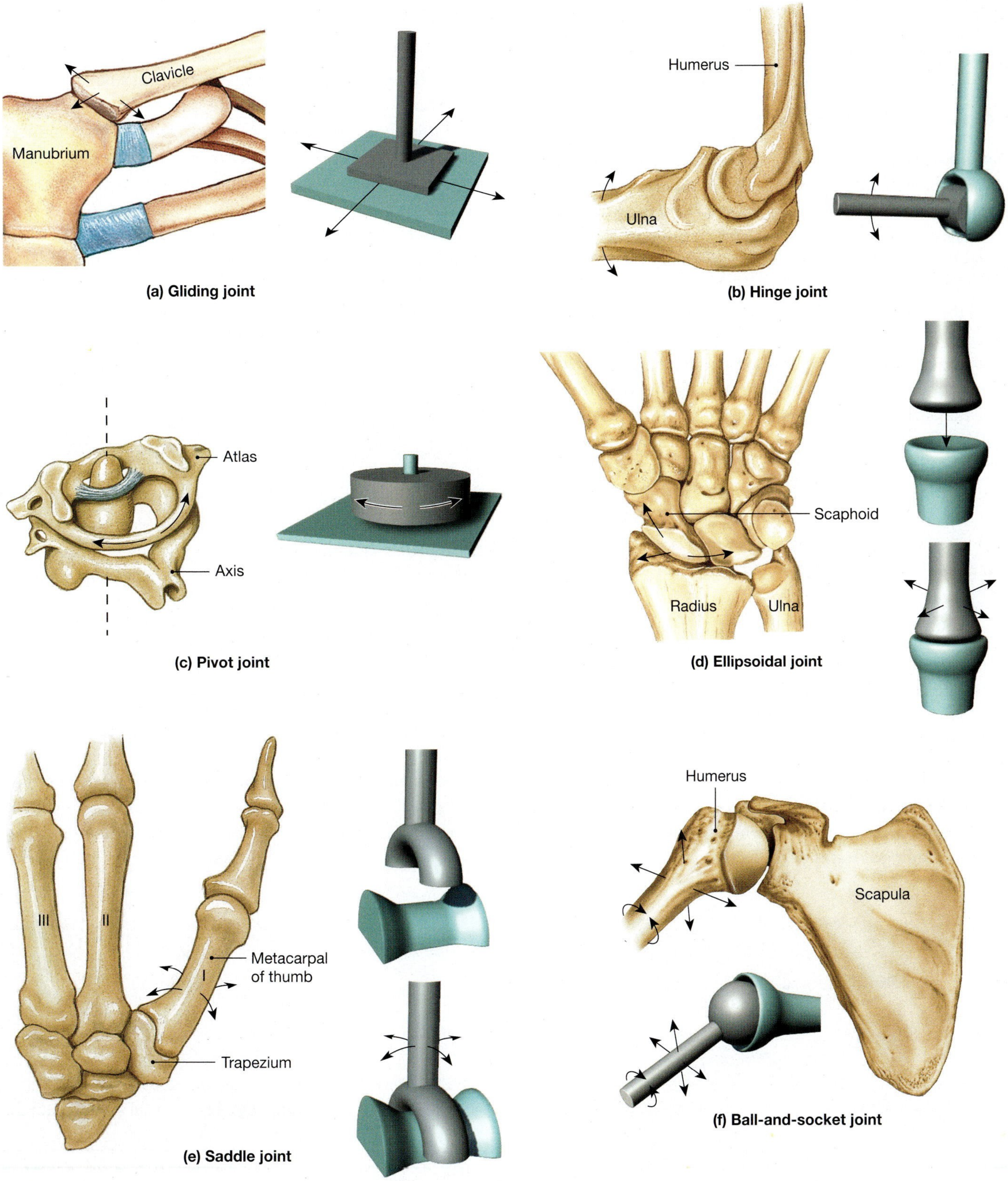

Figure 8.6 A Structural Classification of Synovial Joints
This classification scheme is based on the amount of movement permitted.

Representative Articulations

This section considers examples of articulations that demonstrate important functional principles. We will first consider several articulations of the axial skeleton: (1) the *temporomandibular joint* (TMJ), between the mandible and the temporal bone, (2) the *intervertebral articulations* between adjacent vertebrae, and (3) the *sternoclavicular joint* between the clavicle and the sternum. Next, we will examine synovial joints of the appendicular skeleton. The shoulder has great mobility, the elbow has great strength, and the wrist makes fine adjustments in the orientation of the palm and fingers. The functional requirements of the joints in the lower limb are very different from those of the upper limb. Articulations at the hip, knee, and ankle must transfer the body weight to the ground, and during movements such as running, jumping, or twisting, the applied forces are considerably greater than the weight of the body. Although this section considers representative articulations, Tables 8.3, 8.4, and 8.5 summarize information concerning the majority of articulations in the body.

The Temporomandibular Joint [Figure 8.7]

The **temporomandibular joint** (Figure 8.7) is a small but complex multiaxial articulation between the mandibular fossa of the temporal bone and the condylar process of the mandible. pp. 145, 151–152 The articulating bones are separated by a thick disc of fibrous cartilage. This cartilage, which extends horizontally, divides the joint cavity into two separate chambers. As a result, the temporomandibular joint is really two synovial joints, one between the temporal bone and the articular disc, and the second between the articular disc and the mandible.

The articular capsule surrounding this joint complex is not well defined. The portion of the capsule superior to the neck of the condyle is relatively loose, while the portion of the capsule inferior to the cartilage disc is quite tight. The structure of the capsule permits an extensive range of motion. However, because the joint is poorly stabilized, a forceful lateral or anterior movement of the mandible can result in a partial or complete dislocation.

The lateral portion of the articular capsule, which is relatively thick, is called the **lateral** (*temporomandibular*) **ligament**. There are also two extracapsular ligaments:

- the **stylomandibular ligament**, which extends from the styloid process to the posterior margin of the angle of the mandibular ramus;
- the **sphenomandibular ligament**, which extends from the sphenoidal spine to the medial surface of the mandibular ramus. Its insertion covers the posterior portion of the mylohyoid line.

The temporomandibular joint is primarily a hinge joint, but the loose capsule and relatively flat articular surfaces also permit small gliding and rotational movements. These secondary movements are important when positioning food on the grinding surfaces of the teeth.

Intervertebral Articulations [Figure 8.8]

The articulations between the superior and inferior articular processes of adjacent vertebrae are plane joints that permit small movements associated with flexion and extension, lateral flexion, and rotation of the vertebral column. Little gliding occurs between adjacent vertebral bodies. Figure 8.8 illustrates the structure of the intervertebral joints. From axis to sacrum, the vertebrae are separated and cushioned by pads of fibrous cartilage called **intervertebral discs**. Intervertebral discs are not found in the sacrum and coccyx, where vertebrae have fused, nor are they found between the first and second cervical vertebrae. The articulation between C_1 and C_2 was described in Chapter 6. p. 164

The Intervertebral Discs [Figures 8.8/8.9a]

The intervertebral discs have two functions: (1) to separate individual vertebrae, and (2) to transmit the load from one vertebra to another. Each intervertebral disc (Figures 8.8 and 8.9a) is composed of two parts. The first is a tough outer layer of fibrous cartilage, the **anulus fibrosus** (AN-ū-lus fī-BRŌ-sus). The anulus surrounds the second part of the intervertebral disc, the **nucleus pulposus** (pul-PŌ-sus). The nucleus pulposus is a soft, elastic, gelatinous core, composed primarily of water (about 75 percent) with scattered reticular and elastic fibers. The nucleus pulposus gives the disc resiliency and enables it to act as a shock absorber. The superior and inferior surfaces of the disc are almost completely covered by thin *vertebral end plates.* These end plates are composed of hyaline and fibrous cartilage. They are bound to the annulus fibrosus of the intervertebral disc, and weakly attached to the adjacent vertebrae. The vertebral attachments are sufficient to help stabilize the position of the intervertebral disc, and additional reinforcement is provided by the intervertebral ligaments considered in the next section.

Movements of the vertebral column compress the nucleus pulposus and displace it in the opposite direction. This displacement permits smooth gliding movements by each vertebra while still maintaining the alignment of all the vertebrae. The discs make a significant contribution to an individual's

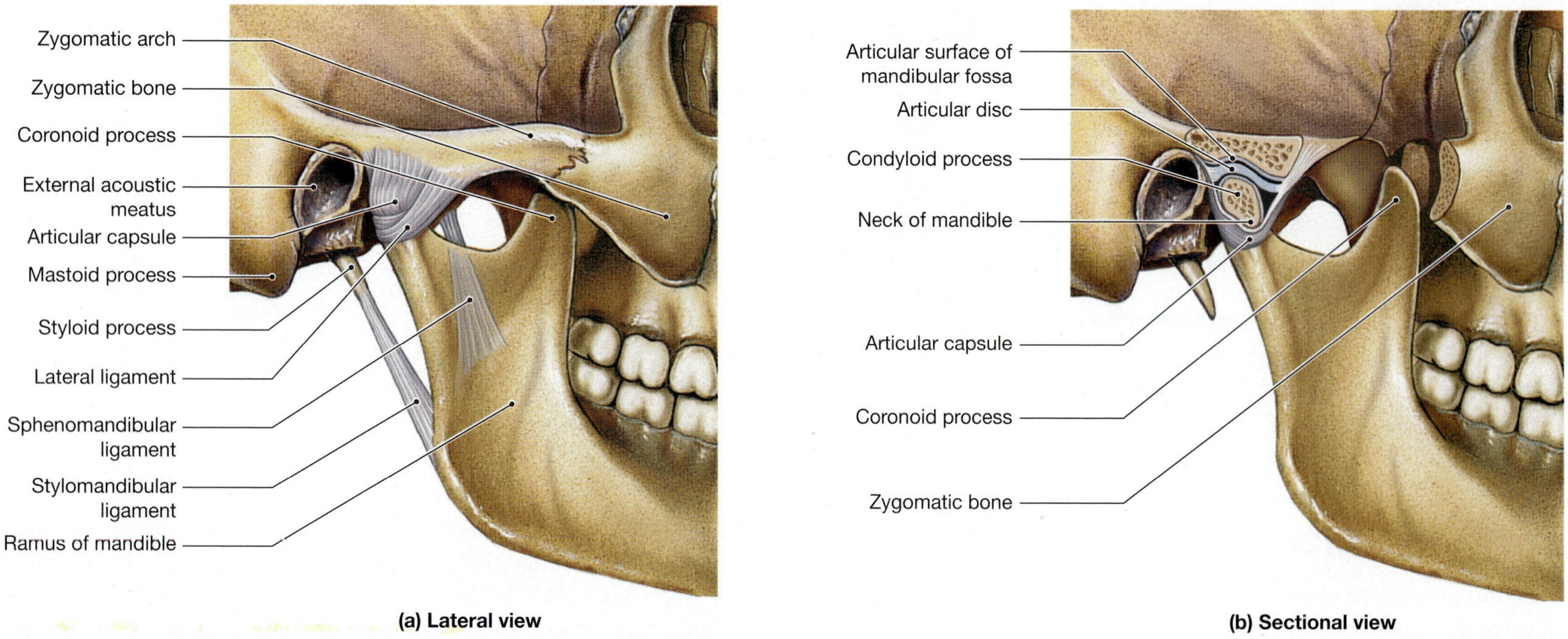

Figure 8.7 The Temporomandibular Joint
This hinge joint forms between the condylar process of the mandible and the mandibular fossa of the temporal bone. **(a)** Lateral view of the right temporomandibular joint. **(b)** Sectional view of the same joint.

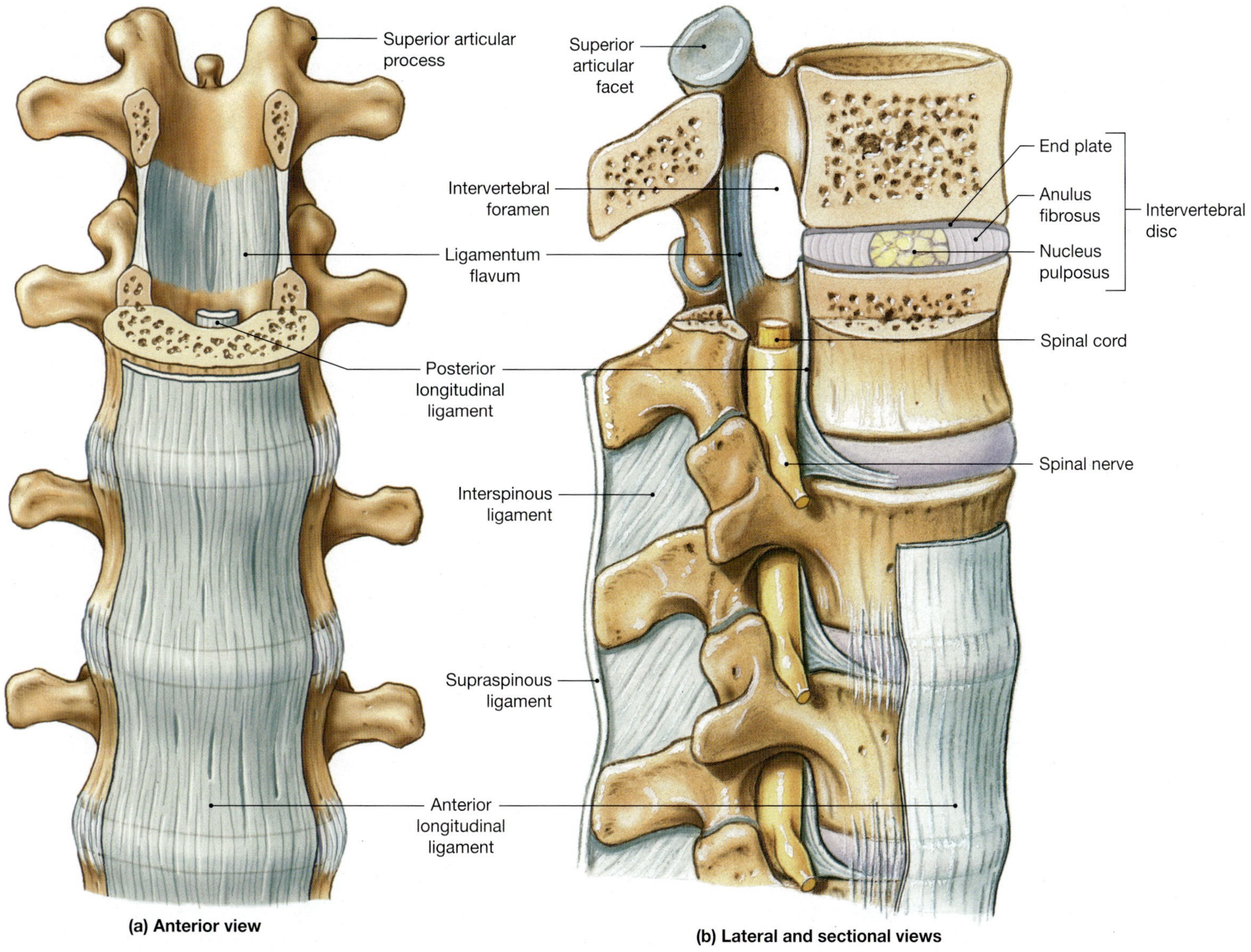

Figure 8.8 Intervertebral Articulations
Adjacent vertebrae articulate at their superior and inferior articular processes; their bodies are separated by intervertebral discs. **(a)** Anterior view. **(b)** Lateral and sectional views.

height; they account for roughly one-quarter of the length of the vertebral column above the sacrum. As we grow older, the water content of the nucleus pulposus within each disc decreases. The discs gradually become less effective as a cushion, and the chances for vertebral injury increase. Loss of water by the discs also causes shortening of the vertebral column; this shortening accounts for the characteristic decrease in height with advanced age.

Intervertebral Ligaments [Figure 8.8]

Numerous ligaments are attached to the bodies and processes of all vertebrae to bind them together and stabilize the vertebral column (Figure 8.8). Ligaments interconnecting adjacent vertebrae include the *anterior longitudinal ligament*, the *posterior longitudinal ligament*, the *ligamentum flavum*, the *interspinous ligament*, and the *supraspinous ligament*.

- The *anterior longitudinal ligament* connects the anterior surfaces of each vertebral body.
- The *posterior longitudinal ligament* parallels the anterior longitudinal ligament but passes across the posterior surfaces of each body.
- The *ligamentum flavum* (plural, *ligamenta flava*) connects the laminae of adjacent vertebrae.
- The *interspinous ligament* connects the spinous processes of adjacent vertebrae.
- The *supraspinous ligament* interconnects the tips of the spinous processes from C_7 to the sacrum. The *ligamentum nuchae*, discussed in Chapter 6, is a supraspinous ligament that extends from C_7 to the base of the skull. p. 164

Vertebral Movements [Table 8.3]

The following movements of the vertebral column are possible: (1) **anterior flexion**, bending forward; (2) **extension**, bending backward; (3) **lateral flexion**, bending to the side; and (4) **rotation**, or twisting.

Table 8.3 summarizes information concerning the articulations and movements of the axial skeleton.

The Sternoclavicular Joint [Figure 8.10]

The **sternoclavicular joint** is a synovial joint between the medial end of the clavicle and the manubrium of the sternum. This joint serves to anchor the scapula to the axial skeleton, and is considered to be a functional component of the shoulder joint.

Clinical Note

Problems with the Intervertebral Discs An intervertebral disc compressed beyond its normal limits may become temporarily or permanently damaged. If the posterior longitudinal ligaments are weakened, as often occurs with advancing age, the compressed nucleus pulposus may distort the anulus fibrosus, partially forcing it into the vertebral canal. This condition is often called a **slipped disc** (Figure 8.9a), although disc slippage does not actually occur. The most common sites for disc problems are at C_5–C_6, L_4–L_5, and L_5–S_1.

Under severe compression the nucleus pulposus may break through the anulus fibrosus and enter the vertebral canal. This condition is called a **herniated disc** (Figure 8.9b). When a disc herniates, sensory nerves are distorted, producing pain; the protruding mass can also compress the nerves passing through the intervertebral foramen. **Sciatica** (sī-AT-i-ka) is the painful result of compression of the roots of the sciatic nerve. The acute initial pain in the lower back is sometimes called **lumbago** (lum-BĀ-gō).

Most lumbar disc problems can be treated successfully with some combination of rest, back braces, analgesic (painkilling) drugs, and physical therapy. Surgery to relieve the symptoms is required in only about 10 percent of cases involving lumbar disc herniation. In this procedure, the disc is removed and the vertebral bodies are fused together to prevent movement. To access the offending disc, the surgeon may remove the nearest vertebral arch by shaving away the laminae. For this reason, the procedure is known as a **laminectomy** (lam-i-NEK-tō-mē).

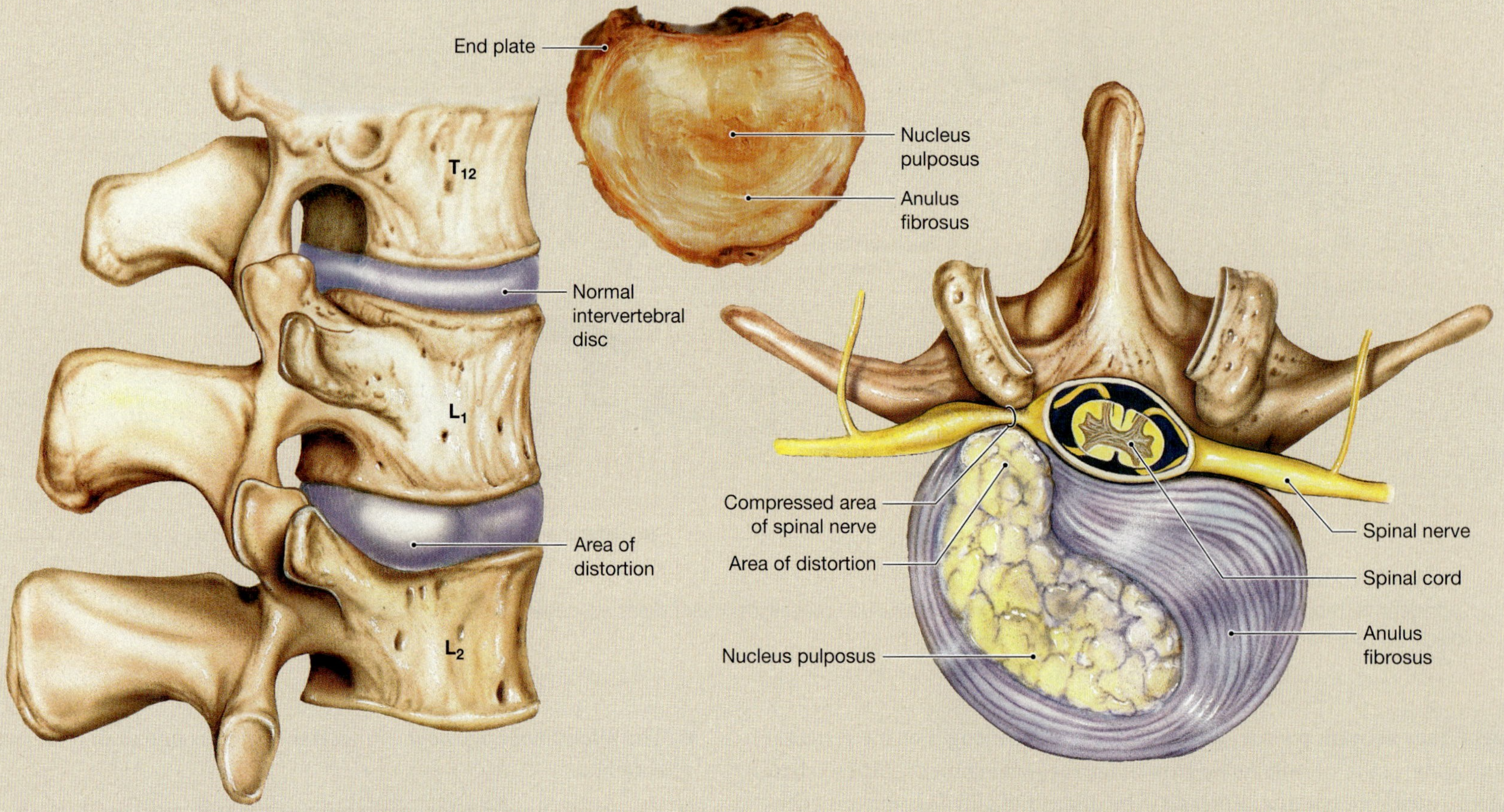

(a) Lateral view of distorted intervertebral disc **(b) Herniated disc, superior view**

Figure 8.9 Damage to the Intervertebral Discs
(a) Lateral view of the lumbar region of the spinal column, showing normal and distorted ("slipped") intervertebral discs. The superior surface of an isolated normal intervertebral disc is shown for comparison with **(b)**, a sectional view through a herniated disc, showing displacement of the nucleus pulposus and its effect on the spinal cord and adjacent nerves.

As at the temporomandibular joint (p. 214), an articular disc divides the sternoclavicular joint and separates two synovial cavities (Figure 8.10). The articular capsule is both tense and dense, providing stability but limiting movement. The capsule is reinforced by two accessory ligaments, the **anterior sternoclavicular ligament** and the **posterior sternoclavicular ligament**. There are also two extracapsular ligaments:

- The **interclavicular ligament** interconnects the clavicles and reinforces the superior portions of the adjacent articular capsules. This ligament, which is also firmly attached to the superior border of the manubrium, prevents dislocation when the shoulder is depressed.
- The broad **costoclavicular ligament** extends from the costal tuberosity of the clavicle, near the inferior margin of the articular capsule, to the superior and medial borders of the first rib and the first costal cartilage. This ligament prevents dislocation when the shoulder is elevated.

The sternoclavicular joint is primarily a plane joint, but the capsular fibers permit a slight rotation and circumduction of the clavicle.

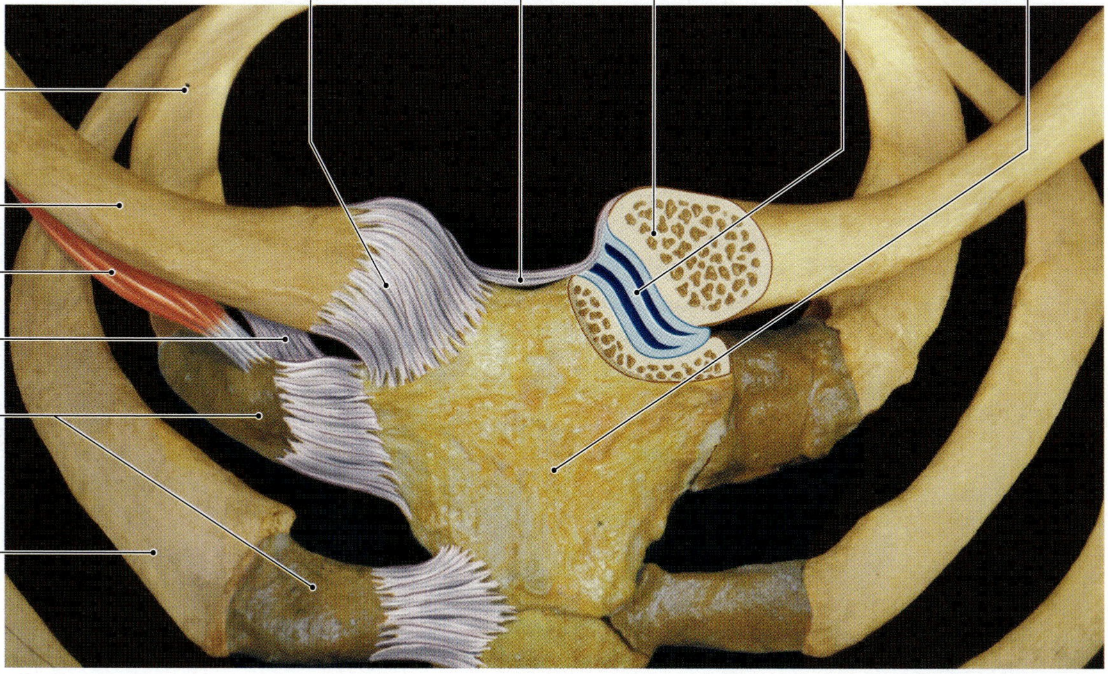

Figure 8.10 The Sternoclavicular Joint An anterior view of the thorax showing the bones and ligaments of the sternoclavicular joint. This joint is classified as a stable, heavily reinforced plane diarthrosis.

The Shoulder Joint [Figure 8.11]

The **shoulder joint**, or **glenohumeral joint**, is a loose and shallow joint that permits the greatest range of motion of any joint in the body. The shape of these articulating structures, and the accompanying wide range of motion, enables us to position the hand for a wide variety of functions. Because the shoulder joint is also the most frequently dislocated joint, it provides an excellent demonstration of the principle that strength and stability must be sacrificed to obtain mobility.

This joint is a ball-and-socket type, formed by the articulation of the head of the humerus with the glenoid cavity of the scapula (Figure 8.11). In life, the margin of the glenoid cavity is covered by the **glenoid labrum** (*labrum*, lip or edge) (Figure 8.11c,d), which deepens the joint. The glenoid labrum is a ring of dense, irregular connective tissue that is attached to the margin of the glenoid cavity by fibrous cartilage. In addition to enlarging the joint cavity, the glenoid labrum serves as an attachment site for the glenohumeral ligaments and the long head of the biceps brachii muscle, a flexor of the shoulder and elbow.

The articular capsule extends from the scapular neck to the humerus. It is a relatively oversized capsule that is weakest at its inferior surface. When the upper limb is in the anatomical position, the capsule is tight superiorly and loose inferiorly and anteriorly. The construction of the capsule contributes to the extensive range of motion of the shoulder joint. The bones of the pectoral girdle provide some stability to the superior surface, because the acromion and coracoid process project laterally superior to the humeral head. However, most of the stability at this joint is provided by (1) ligaments and (2) surrounding skeletal muscles and their associated tendons.

Ligaments [Figure 8.11]

Major ligaments involved with stabilizing the glenohumeral joint are shown in Figure 8.11a–c and described next.

- The capsule surrounding the shoulder joint is relatively thin, but it thickens anteriorly in regions known as the **glenohumeral ligaments**. Because the capsular fibers are usually loose, these ligaments participate in joint stabilization only as the humerus approaches or exceeds the limits of normal motion.
- The large **coracohumeral ligament** originates at the base of the coracoid process and inserts on the head of the humerus. This ligament strengthens the superior part of the articular capsule and helps support the weight of the upper limb.
- The **coracoacromial ligament** spans the gap between the coracoid process and the acromion, just superior to the capsule. This ligament provides additional support to the superior surface of the capsule.
- The strong **acromioclavicular ligament** binds the acromion to the clavicle, thereby restricting clavicular movement at the acromial end. A *shoulder separation* is a relatively common injury involving partial or complete dislocation of the acromioclavicular joint. This injury can result from a blow to the superior surface of the shoulder. The acromion is forcibly depressed, but the clavicle is held back by strong muscles.
- The **coracoclavicular ligaments** tie the clavicle to the coracoid process and help limit the relative motion between the clavicle and scapula.
- The **transverse humeral ligament** extends between the greater and lesser tubercles and holds down the tendon of the long head of the biceps brachii muscle in the intertubercular groove of the humerus.

Skeletal Muscles and Tendons

Muscles that move the humerus do more to stabilize the glenohumeral joint than all the ligaments and capsular fibers combined. Muscles originating on the trunk, pectoral girdle, and humerus cover the anterior, superior, and posterior surfaces of the capsule. Tendons passing across the joint reinforce the anterior and superior portions of the capsule. The tendons of specific appendicular muscles support the shoulder and limit its movement range. These muscles, collectively called the *rotator cuff*, are a frequent site of sports injury.

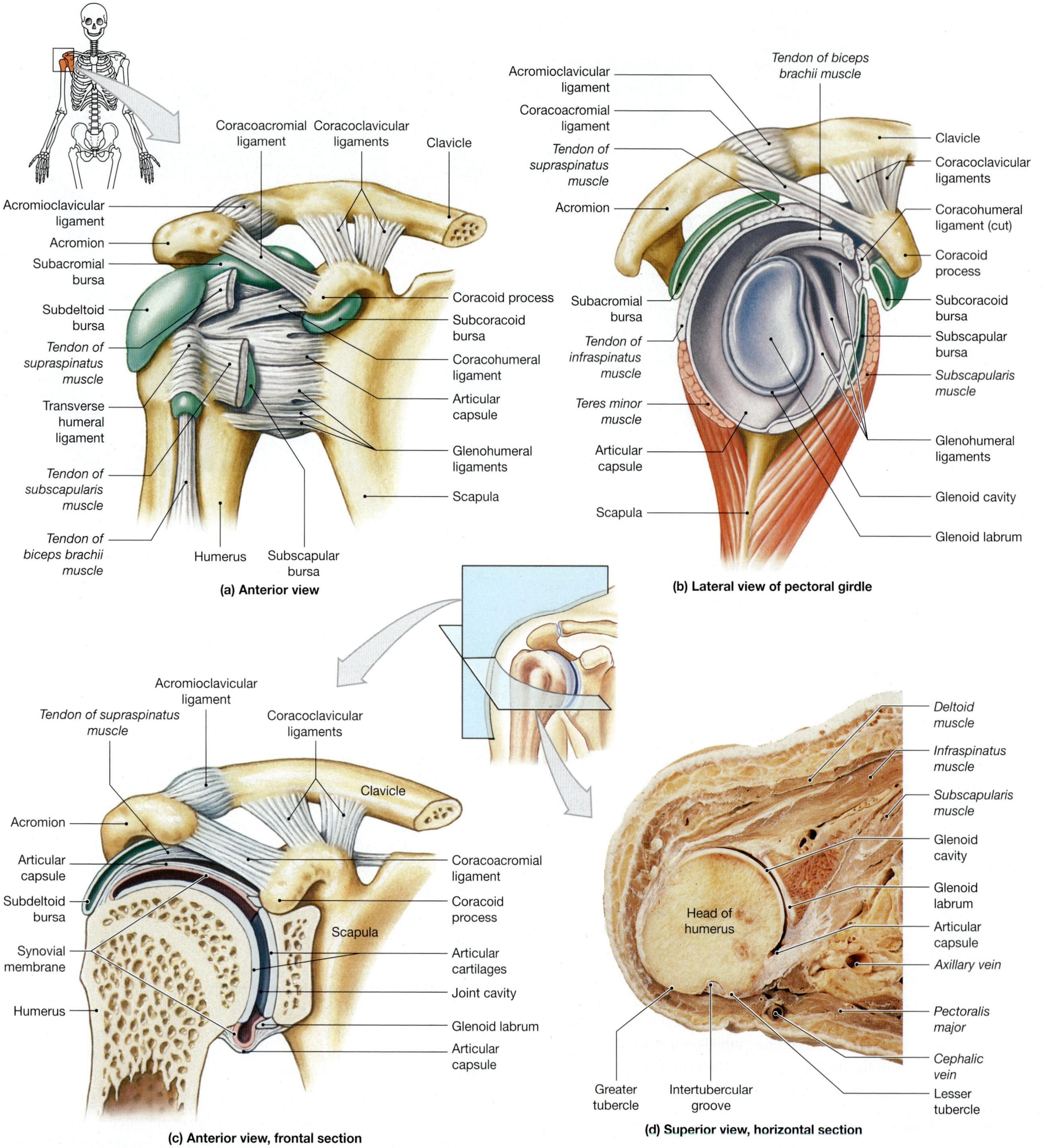

Figure 8.11 The Glenohumeral Joint
A ball-and-socket joint formed between the humerus and the scapula. **(a)** Anterior view of the right shoulder joint. **(b)** Lateral view, right shoulder joint (humerus removed). **(c)** A frontal section through the right shoulder joint, anterior view. **(d)** Horizontal section of the right shoulder joint, superior view.

Clinical Note

Shoulder Injuries When a head-on charge leads to a collision, such as a block (in football) or check (in hockey), the shoulder usually lies in the impact zone. The clavicle provides the only fixed support for the pectoral girdle, and it cannot resist large forces. Because the inferior surface of the shoulder capsule is poorly reinforced, a dislocation caused by an impact or violent muscle contraction most often occurs at this site. Such a dislocation can tear the inferior capsular wall and the glenoid labrum. The healing process often leaves a weakness and inherent instability of the joint that increases the chances for future dislocations.

Bursae [Figure 8.11a–c]

As at other joints, *bursae* at the shoulder reduce friction where large muscles and tendons pass across the joint capsule. p. 208 The shoulder has a relatively large number of important bursae. The **subacromial bursa** and the **subcoracoid bursa** (Figure 8.11a,b) prevent contact between the acromion and coracoid process and the capsule. The **subdeltoid bursa** and the **subscapular bursa** (Figure 8.11a–c) lie between large muscles and the capsular wall. Inflammation of one or more of these bursae can restrict motion and produce the painful symptoms of **bursitis**.

The Elbow Joint [Figure 8.12]

The **elbow joint** is complex and composed of the joints between (1) the humerus and the ulna, and (2) the humerus and the radius. These joints enable flexion and extension of the elbow. These movements, when combined with the radioulnar joints discussed below, allow for positioning of the hand, thereby allowing for a wide variety of activities, such as feeding, grooming, or defense simply by changing the position of the hand with respect to the trunk.

The largest and strongest articulation at the elbow is the *humeroulnar joint*, where the trochlea of the humerus projects into the trochlear notch of the ulna. pp. 179, 183 At the smaller *humeroradial joint*, which lies lateral to the humeroulnar joint, the capitulum of the humerus articulates with the head of the radius (Figure 8.12).

The elbow joint is extremely stable because (1) the bony surfaces of the humerus and ulna interlock to prevent lateral movement and rotation, (2) the articular capsule is very thick, and (3) the capsule is reinforced by strong ligaments. The medial surface of the joint is stabilized by the **ulnar collateral ligament**. This ligament extends from the medial epicondyle of the humerus anteriorly to the coronoid processes of the ulna, and posteriorly to the olecranon (Figure 8.12a,b). The **radial collateral ligament** stabilizes the lateral surface of the joint. It extends between the lateral epicondyle of the humerus and the **annular ligament** that binds the proximal radial head to the ulna (Figure 8.12e).

Despite the strength of the capsule and ligaments, the elbow joint can be damaged by severe impacts or unusual stresses. For example, when you fall on a hand with a partially flexed elbow, contractions of muscles that extend the elbow may break the ulna at the center of the trochlear notch. Less violent stresses can produce dislocations or other injuries to the elbow, especially if epiphyseal growth has not been completed. For example, parents in a hurry may drag a toddler along behind them, exerting an upward, twisting pull on the elbow joint that can result in a partial dislocation known as "nursemaid's elbow."

The Radioulnar Joints [Figure 8.13]

The *proximal radioulnar* and *distal radioulnar* joints allow for supination and pronation of the forearm. At the proximal radioulnar joint, the head of the radius articulates with the *radial notch of the ulna.* pp. 179, 183 The head of the radius is held in place by the **annular ligament** (Figure 8.13a). The distal radioulnar joint is a pivot diarthrosis. The articulating surfaces include the *ulnar notch of the radius*, the *radial notch of the ulna*, and a piece of hyaline cartilage termed the *articular disc.* These articulating surfaces are held together by a series of radioulnar ligaments and the *antebrachial interosseous membrane* (Figure 8.13b).

Pronation and supination at the radioulnar joints is controlled by muscles that insert on the radius. The largest of these is the *biceps brachii muscle,* which covers the anterior surface of the arm. Its tendon is attached to the radius at the *radial tuberosity*, and contraction of this muscle produces both flexion at the elbow and supination of the forearm. The muscles responsible for movement at the elbow and radioulnar joints will be detailed in Chapter 11.

The Joints of the Wrist [Figure 8.14]

The carpus, or wrist, contains the **wrist joint** (Figure 8.14). The wrist joint consists of the **radiocarpal joint** and the **intercarpal joints**. The radiocarpal joint involves the distal articular surface of the radius and three proximal carpal bones: the scaphoid, lunate, and triquetrum. The radiocarpal joint is a condylar articulation that permits flexion/extension, adduction/abduction, and circumduction. The intercarpal joints are plane joints that permit sliding and slight twisting movements.

Stability of the Wrist [Figure 8.14b,c]

Carpal surfaces that do not participate in articulations are roughened by the attachment of ligaments and for the passage of tendons. A tough connective tissue capsule, reinforced by broad ligaments, surrounds the wrist and stabilizes the positions of the individual carpal bones (Figure 8.14b,c). The major ligaments include the following:

- the *palmar radiocarpal ligament*, which connects the distal radius to the anterior surfaces of the scaphoid, lunate, and triquetrum;
- the *dorsal radiocarpal ligament*, which connects the distal radius to the posterior surfaces of the same carpal bones (not seen from the palmar surface);
- the *ulnar collateral ligament*, which extends from the styloid process of the ulna to the medial surface of the triquetrum; and
- the *radial collateral ligament*, which extends from the styloid process of the radius to the lateral surface of the scaphoid.

In addition to these prominent ligaments, a variety of *intercarpal ligaments* interconnect the carpal bones, and *digitocarpal ligaments* bind the distal carpal bones to the metacarpal bones (Figure 8.14c). Tendons that pass across the wrist joint provide additional reinforcement. (There are many tendons involved, and they are not illustrated in the accompanying figure; we will examine these tendons and associated muscles in

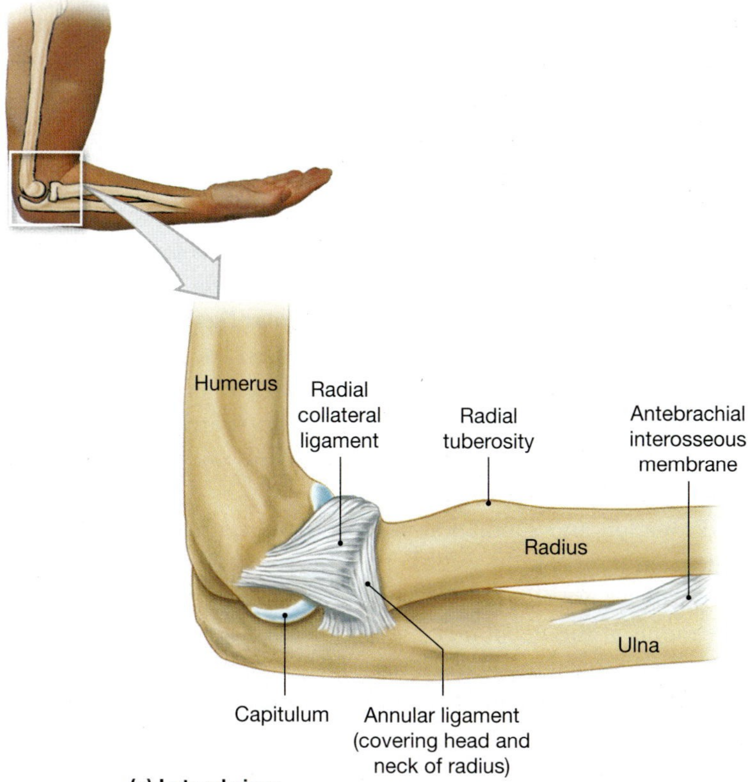

(a) Lateral view

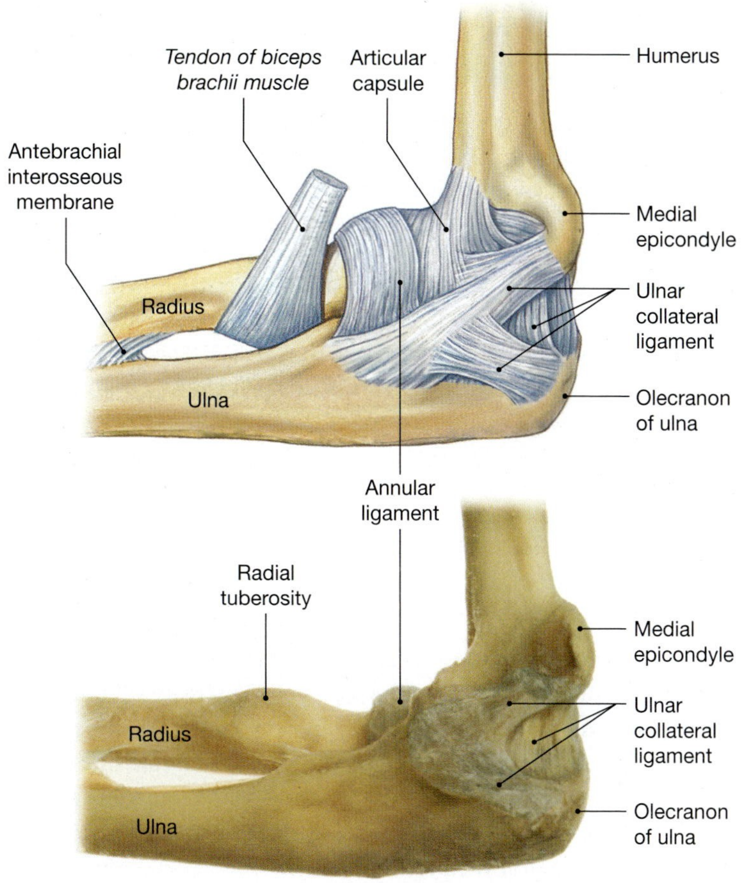

(b) Medial view

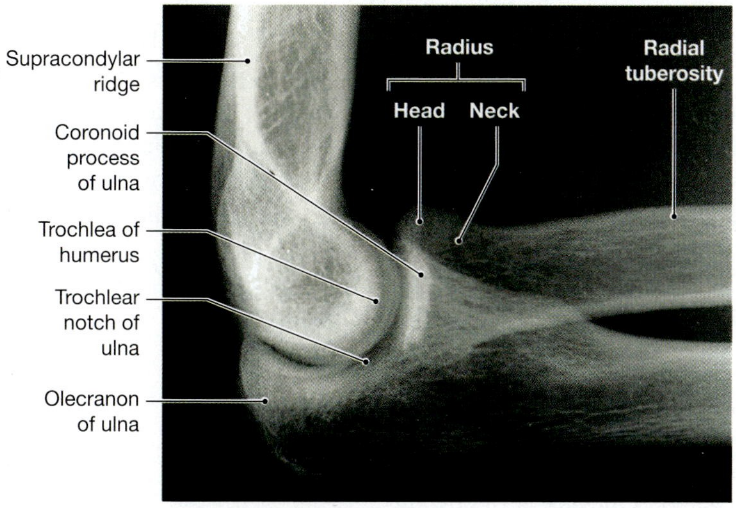

(c) X-ray, right elbow

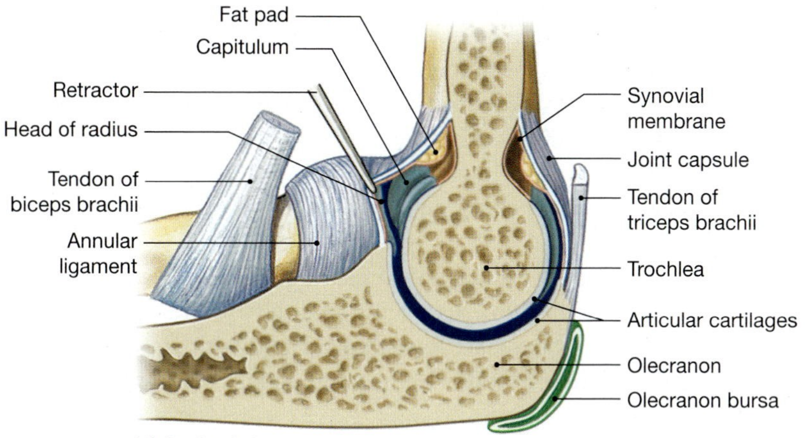

(d) Sagittal view

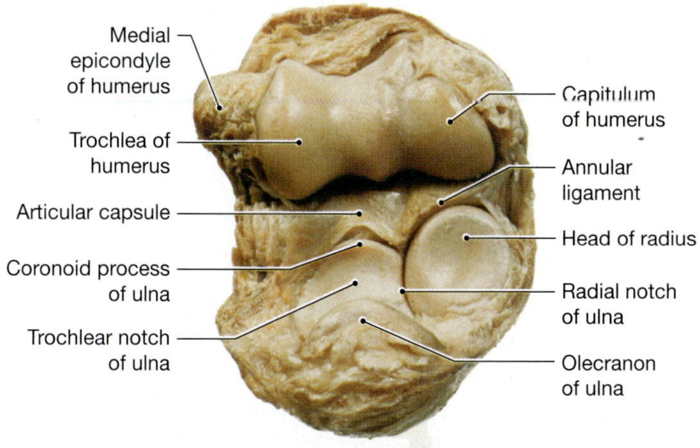

(e) Articular surfaces within the right elbow joint

Figure 8.12 The Elbow Joint
The elbow joint is a complex hinge joint formed between the humerus and the ulna and radius. All views are of the right elbow joint. **(a)** Lateral view. **(b)** Diagrammatic medial view. The radius is shown pronated; note the position of the biceps brachii tendon, which inserts on the radial tuberosity. **(c)** X-ray. **(d)** Sagittal view of the elbow. **(e)** A posterior view; the posterior portion of the capsule has been cut and the joint cavity opened to show the opposing surfaces.

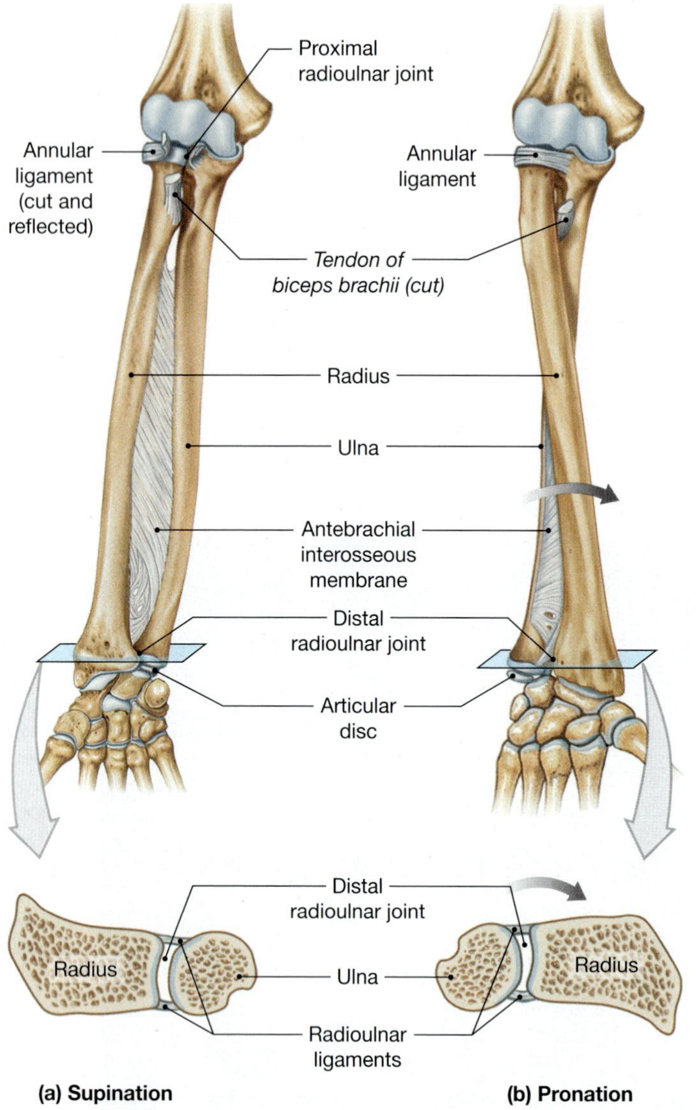

Figure 8.13 The Radioulnar Joints

Chapter 11.) Tendons of muscles producing flexion of the wrist and finger joints pass over the anterior surface of the wrist joint superficial to the ligaments of the wrist joint. Tendons of muscles producing extension pass across the posterior surface in a similar fashion. A pair of broad transverse ligaments arch across the anterior and posterior surfaces of the wrist superficial to these tendons, holding the tendons in position.

The Joints of the Hand [Figure 8.14 and Table 8.4]

The carpal bones articulate with the metacarpal bones of the palm (Figure 8.14a). The first metacarpal bone has a saddle-type articulation at the wrist, the **carpometacarpal joint** of the thumb (Figure 8.14b,d). All other carpal/metacarpal articulations are plane joints. An **intercarpal joint** is formed by carpal/carpal articulation. The articulations between the metacarpal bones and the proximal phalanges (**metacarpophalangeal joints**) are condylar, permitting flexion/extension and adduction/abduction. The **interphalangeal joints** are hinge joints that allow flexion and extension (Figure 8.14d).

Tables 8.3 and 8.4 summarize the characteristics of the articulations of the axial skeleton and the upper limb, respectively.

CONCEPT CHECK

1. Who would be more likely to develop inflammation of the subscapular bursa—a tennis player or a jogger? Why?
2. Mary falls on the palms of her hands with her elbows slightly flexed. After the fall, she can't move her left arm at the elbow. If a fracture exists, what bone is most likely broken?

See blue "Answers" tab at back of book.

TABLE 8.3 Articulations of the Axial Skeleton

Element	Joint	Type of Articulation	Movements
SKULL			
Cranial and facial bones of skull	Various	Synarthroses (suture or synostosis)	None
Maxillae/teeth	Alveolar	Synarthrosis (gomphosis)	None
Mandible/teeth	Alveolar	As above	None
Temporal bone/mandible	Temporomandibular	Combined plane joint and hinge diarthrosis	Elevation/depression, lateral gliding, limited protraction/retraction
VERTEBRAL COLUMN			
Occipital bone/atlas	Atlanto-occipital	Condylar diarthrosis	Flexion/extension
Atlas/axis	Atlanto-axial	Pivot diarthrosis	Rotation
Other vertebral elements	Intervertebral (between vertebral bodies)	Amphiarthrosis (symphysis)	Slight movement
	Intervertebral (between articular processes)	Planar diarthrosis	Slight rotation and flexion/extension
Thoracic vertebrae/ribs	Vertebrocostal	Planar diarthrosis	Elevation/depression
Rib/costal cartilage		Synchondrosis	None
Costal cartilage/sternum	Sternocostal	Synchondrosis (rib 1)	None
		Planar diarthrosis (ribs 2–7)	Slight gliding movement
L_5/sacrum	Between body of L_5 and sacral body	Amphiarthrosis (symphysis)	Slight movement
	Between inferior articular processes of L_5 and articular processes of sacrum	Planar diarthrosis	Slight flexion/extension
Sacrum/os coxae	Sacro-iliac	Planar diarthrosis	Slight gliding movement
Sacrum/coccyx	Sacrococcygeal	Planar diarthrosis (may become fused)	Slight movement
Coccygeal bones		Synarthrosis (synostosis)	None

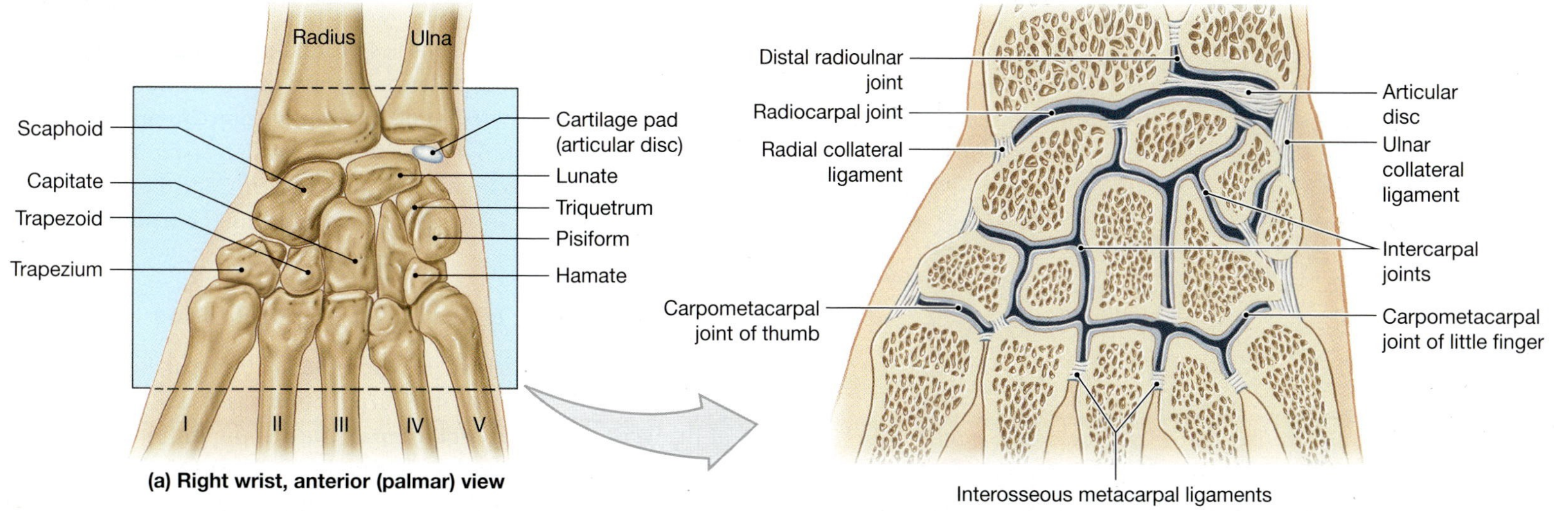

(a) Right wrist, anterior (palmar) view

(b) Wrist joints, coronal section

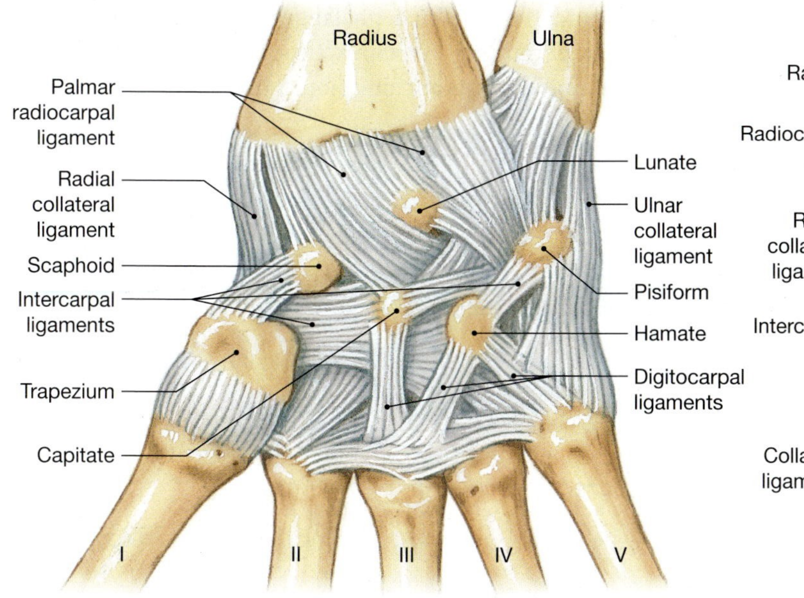

(c) Ligaments of the wrist, anterior (palmar) view

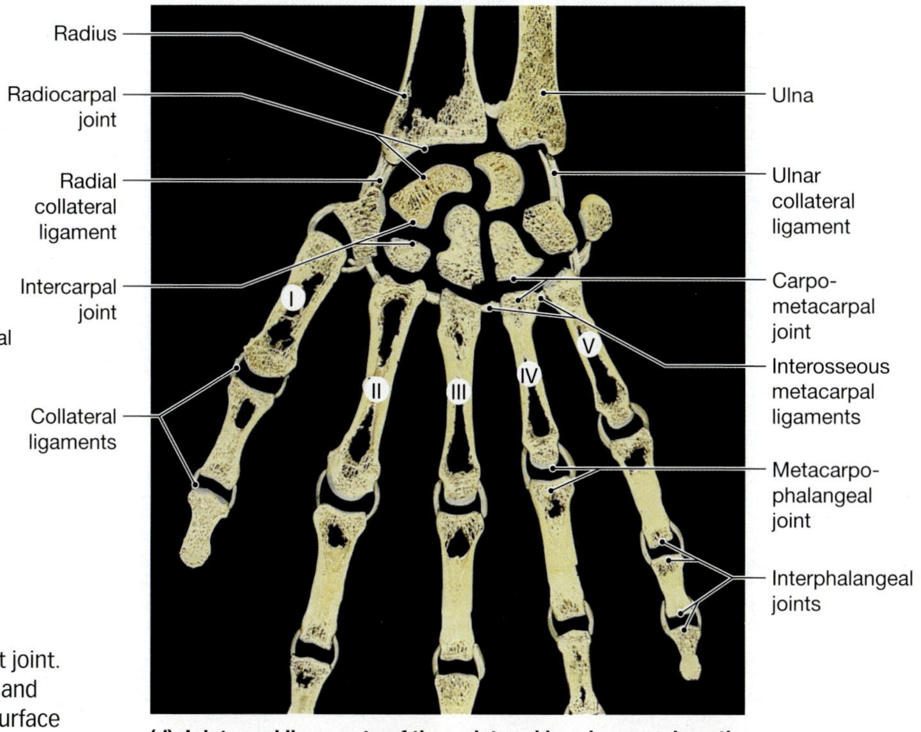

(d) Joints and ligaments of the wrist and hand, coronal section

Figure 8.14 The Joints of the Wrist and Hand
(a) Anterior view of the right wrist, identifying the components of the wrist joint. **(b)** Sectional view through the wrist, showing the radiocarpal, intercarpal, and carpometacarpal joints. **(c)** Stabilizing ligaments on the anterior (palmar) surface of the wrist. **(d)** Sectional view of the bones that form the wrist and hand.

TABLE 8.4 Articulations of the Pectoral Girdle and Upper Limb

Element	Joint	Type of Articulation	Movements
Sternum/clavicle	Sternoclavicular	Planar diarthrosis (a double "plane joint," with two joint cavities separated by an articular cartilage)	Protraction/retraction, depression/elevation, slight rotation
Scapula/clavicle	Acromioclavicular	Planar diarthrosis	Slight gliding movement
Scapula/humerus	Glenohumeral (shoulder)	Ball-and-socket diarthrosis	Flexion/extension, adduction/abduction, circumduction, rotation
Humerus/ulna and humerus/radius	Elbow (humeroulnar and humeroradial)	Hinge diarthrosis	Flexion/extension
Radius/ulna	Proximal radioulnar Distal radioulnar	Pivot diarthrosis Pivot diarthrosis	Rotation Pronation/supination
Radius/carpal bones	Radiocarpal	Condylar diarthrosis	Flexion/extension, adduction/abduction, circumduction
Carpal bone/carpal bone	Intercarpal	Planar diarthrosis	Slight gliding movement
Carpal bone/first metacarpal bone	Carpometacarpal of thumb	Saddle diarthrosis	Flexion/extension, adduction/abduction, circumduction, opposition
Carpal bones/metacarpal bones II–V	Carpometacarpal	Planar diarthrosis	Slight flexion/extension, adduction/abduction
Metacarpal bones/phalanges	Metacarpophalangeal	Condylar diarthrosis	Flexion/extension, adduction/abduction, circumduction
Phalanx/phalanx	Interphalangeal	Hinge diarthrosis	Flexion/extension

The Hip Joint [Figure 8.15]

Figure 8.15 introduces the structure of the **hip joint**. In this ball-and-socket joint, a pad of fibrous cartilage covers the articular surface of the acetabulum and extends like a horseshoe along the sides of the **acetabular notch** (**Figure 8.15a**). A fat pad covered by a synovial membrane covers the central portion of the acetabulum. This pad acts as a shock absorber, and the adipose tissue stretches and distorts without damage.

The Articular Capsule [Figure 8.15a–c]

The articular capsule of the hip joint is extremely dense, strong, and deep (**Figure 8.15b,c**). Unlike the capsule of the shoulder joint, the capsule of the hip joint contributes extensively to joint stability. The capsule extends from the lateral and inferior surfaces of the pelvic girdle to the intertrochanteric line and intertrochanteric crest of the femur, enclosing both the femoral head and neck. This arrangement helps keep the head from moving away from the acetabulum. Additionally, a circular rim of fibrous cartilage, called the **acetabular labrum** (**Figure 8.15a**), increases the depth of the acetabulum.

Stabilization of the Hip [Figures 8.15/8.16]

Four broad ligaments reinforce the articular capsule (**Figure 8.15b,c**). Three of them are regional thickenings of the capsule: the **iliofemoral**, **pubofemoral**, and **ischiofemoral ligaments**. The **transverse acetabular ligament** crosses the acetabular notch and completes the inferior border of the acetabular fossa. A fifth ligament, the **ligament of the femoral head**, or *ligamentum capitis femoris*, originates along the transverse acetabular ligament and attaches to the center of the femoral head (**Figures 8.15a** and **8.16**). This ligament tenses only when the thigh is flexed and undergoing external rotation. Additional stabilization of the hip joint is

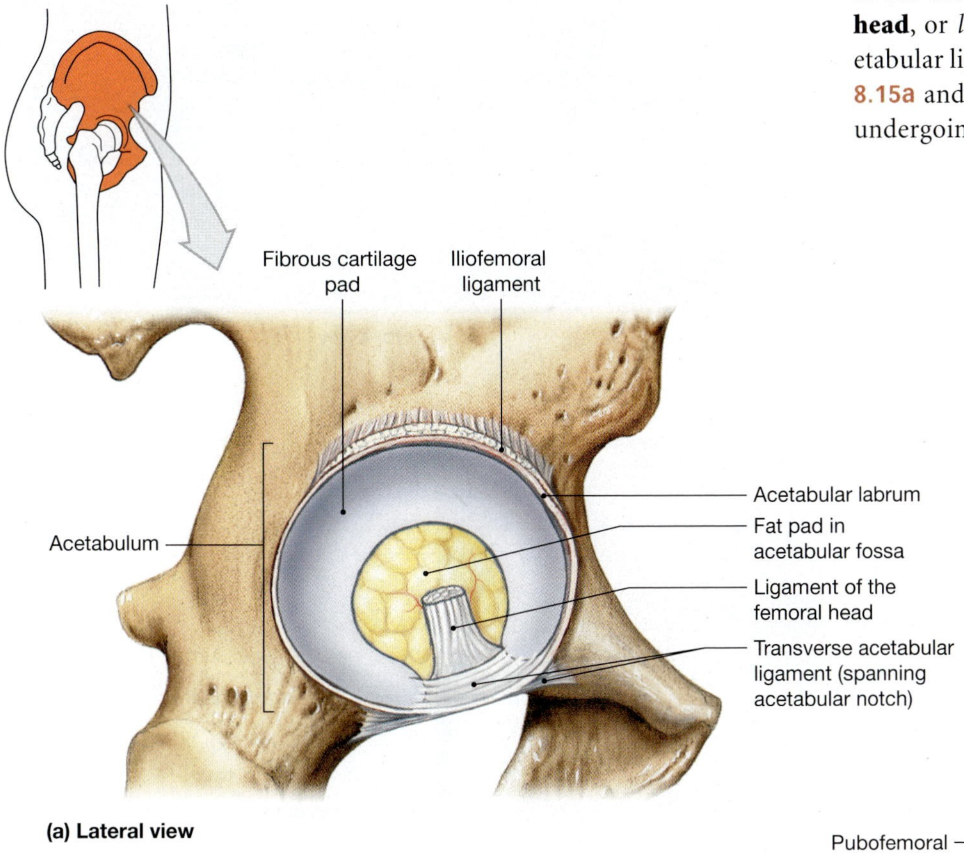

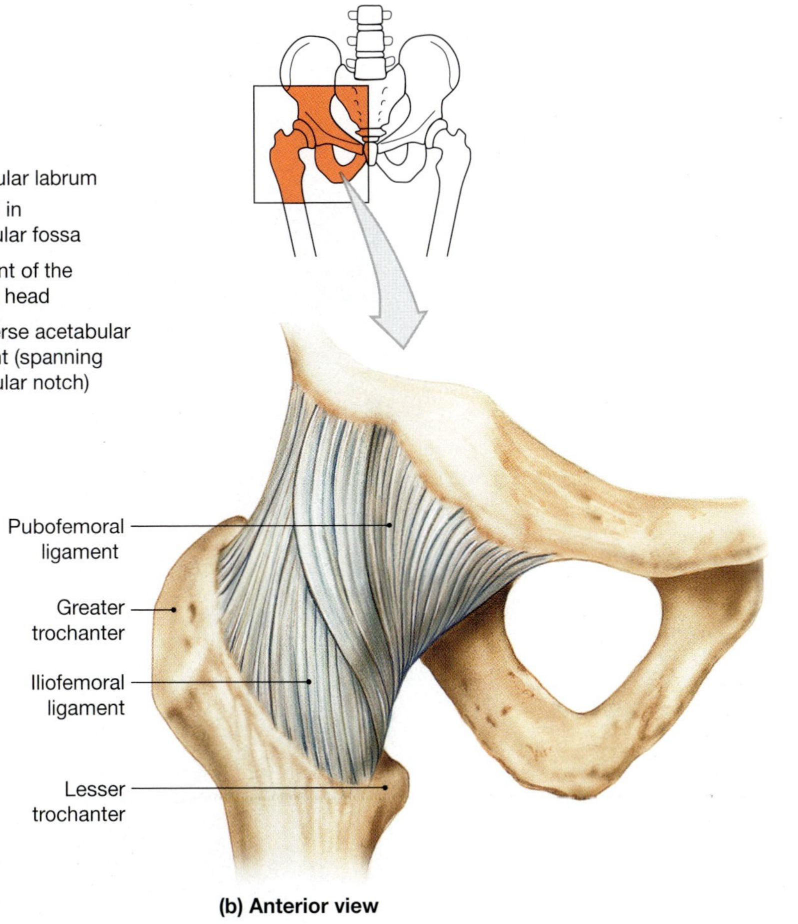

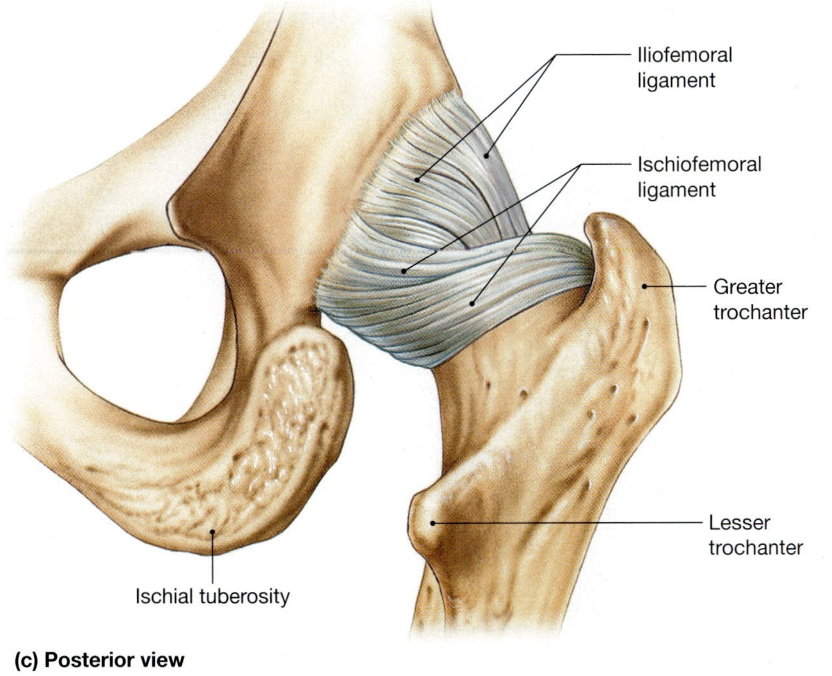

Figure 8.15 The Hip Joint
Views of the hip joint and supporting ligaments. **(a)** Lateral view of the right hip joint with the femur removed. **(b)** Anterior view of the right hip joint. This joint is extremely strong and stable, in part because of the massive capsule. **(c)** Posterior view of the right hip joint, showing additional ligaments that add strength to the capsule.

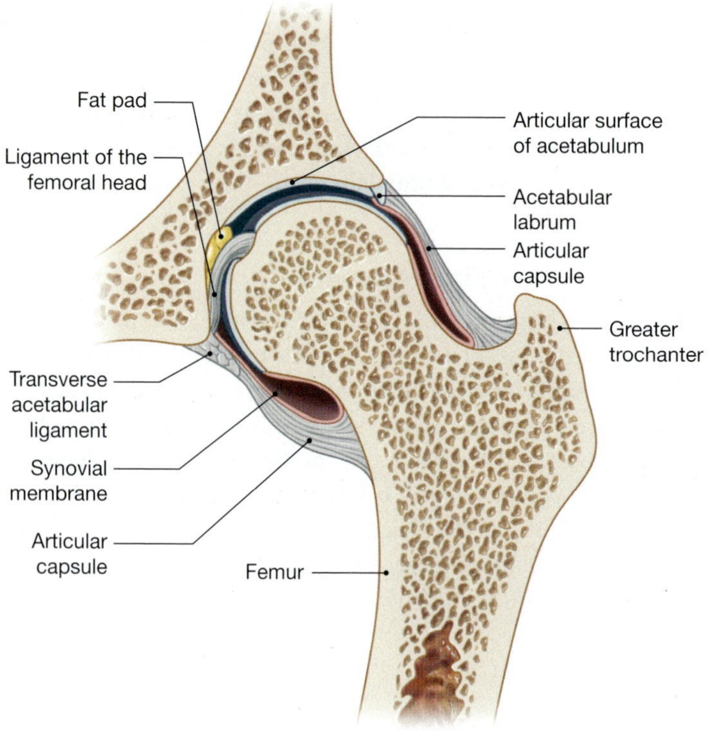

(a) Sectional view

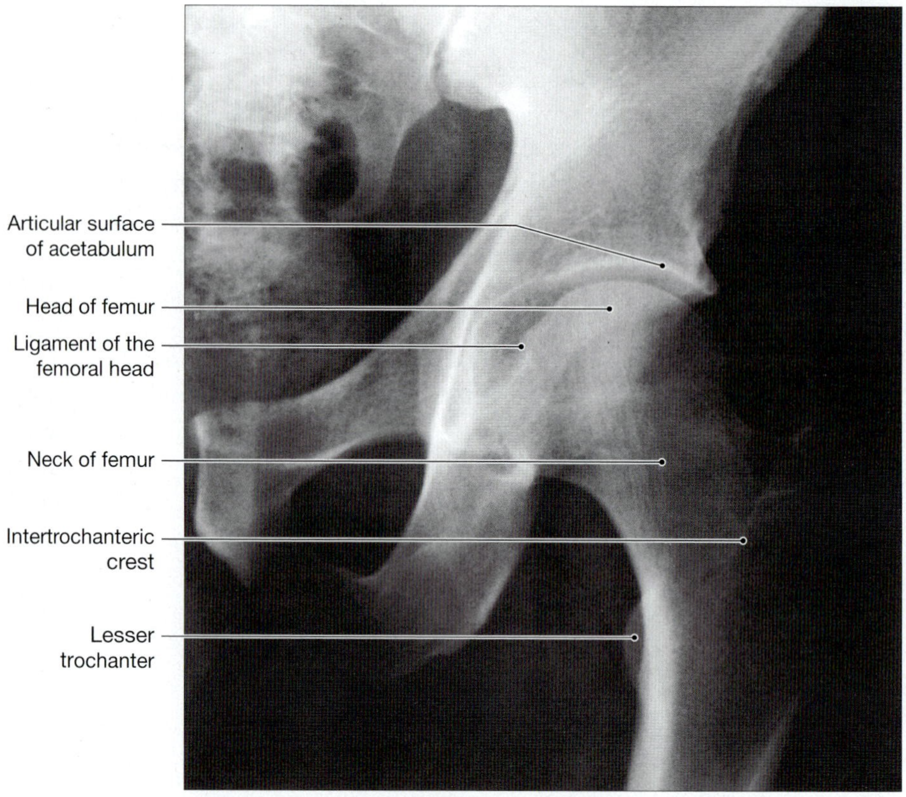

(b) X-ray

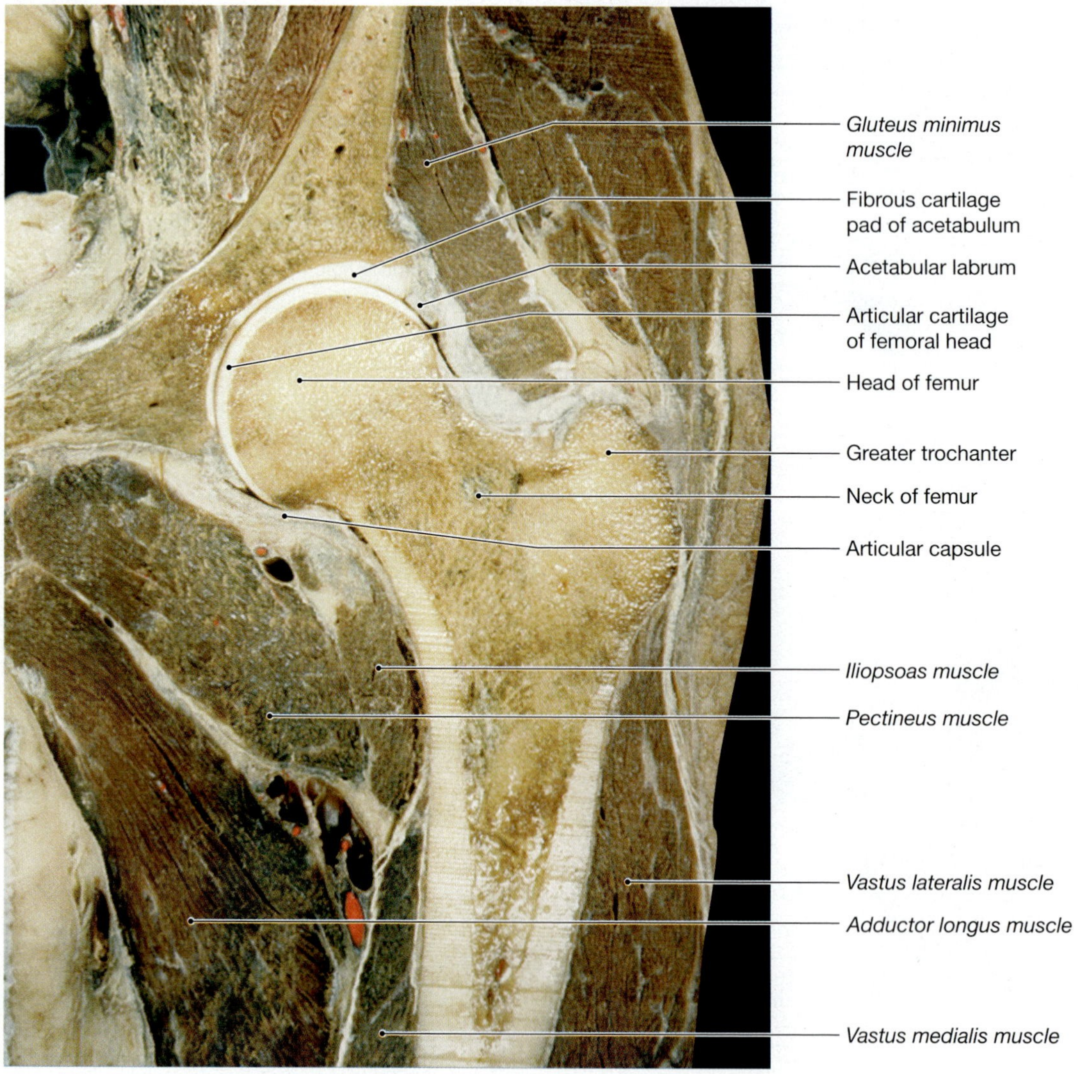

(c) Coronal section through the hip

Figure 8.16 Articular Structure of the Hip Joint

Coronal sectional views of the hip joint. **(a)** View showing the position and orientation of the ligament of the femoral head. **(b)** X-ray of right hip joint, anterior/posterior view. **(c)** Coronal section through the hip.

provided by the bulk of the surrounding muscles. Although flexion, extension, adduction, abduction, and rotation are permitted, hip flexion is the most important normal movement. All of these movements are restricted by the combination of ligaments, capsular fibers, the depth of the bony socket, and the bulk of the surrounding muscles.

The almost complete bony socket enclosing the head of the femur, the strong articular capsule, the stout supporting ligaments, and the dense muscular padding make this an extremely stable joint. Fractures of the femoral neck or between the trochanters are actually more common than hip dislocations.

The Knee Joint

The knee joint is responsible, in conjunction with the hip and ankle joints, for supporting the body's weight during a variety of activities, such as standing, walking, and running. However, the anatomy of the knee must provide this support while (1) having the largest range of motion (up to 160 degrees) of any joint of the lower limb, (2) lacking the large muscle mass that supports and strengthens the hip, and (3) lacking the strong ligaments that support the ankle joint.

Although the knee functions as a hinge joint, the articulation is far more complex than that of the elbow. The rounded femoral condyles roll across the superior surface of the tibia, so the points of contact are constantly changing. The knee is much less stable than other hinge joints, and some degree of rotation is permitted in addition to flexion and extension. Structurally the knee is composed of two joints within a complex synovial capsule: a joint between the tibia and femur (the *tibiofemoral joint*) and one between the patella and the patellar surface of the femur, (the *patellofemoral joint*). ∞ pp. 193–196

The Articular Capsule [Figures 8.17/8.18b,c]

There is no single unified capsule in the knee, nor is there a common synovial cavity (Figure 8.17). A pair of fibrous cartilage pads, the **medial** and **lateral menisci**, lie between the femoral and tibial surfaces (Figure 8.18b,c). The menisci (1) act as cushions, (2) conform to the shape of the articulating surfaces as the femur changes position, (3) increase the surface area of the tibiofemoral joint, and (4) provide some lateral stability to the joint. Prominent **fat pads** provide padding around the margins of the joint and assist the bursae in reducing friction between the patella and other tissues (Figure 8.17a,b,d).

Supporting Ligaments [Figures 8.17/8.18]

Seven major ligaments stabilize the knee joint, and a complete dislocation of the knee is an extremely rare event.

- The tendon from the muscles responsible for extending the knee passes over the anterior surface of the joint (Figure 8.17a,d). The patella is embedded within this tendon, and the **patellar ligament** continues to its attachment on the anterior surface of the tibia. The patellar ligament provides support to the anterior surface of the knee joint (Figure 8.17b), where there is no continuous capsule.

The remaining supporting ligaments are grouped either as extracapsular ligaments or intracapsular ligaments, depending on the location of the ligament with respect to the articular capsule. The extracapsular ligaments include the following:

- The **tibial collateral ligament** reinforces the medial surface of the knee joint, and the **fibular collateral ligament** reinforces the lateral surface (Figures 8.17a and 8.18). These ligaments tighten only at full extension, and in this position they act to stabilize the joint.
- Two superficial **popliteal ligaments** extend between the femur and the heads of the tibia and fibula (Figure 8.18). These ligaments reinforce the back of the knee joint.
- The intracapsular ligaments include the **anterior cruciate ligament (ACL)** and **posterior cruciate ligament (PCL)**, which attach the intercondylar area of the tibia to the condyles of the femur. *Anterior* and *posterior* refer to their sites of origin on the tibia, and they cross one another as they proceed to their destinations on the femur (Figure 8.18b,c). (The term *cruciate* is derived from the Latin word *crucialis*, meaning "a cross.") These ligaments limit the anterior and posterior movement of the femur and maintain the alignment of the femoral and tibial condyles.

Locking of the Knee [Figure 8.18/Table 8.5]

The knee joint can "lock" in the extended position. At full extension a slight external rotation of the tibia tightens the anterior cruciate ligament and jams the meniscus between the tibia and femur. This mechanism allows you to stand for prolonged periods without using (and tiring) the extensor muscles. Unlocking the joint requires muscular contractions that produce internal rotation of the tibia or external rotation of the femur.

Table 8.5 summarizes information about the articulations of the lower limb.

TABLE 8.5 Articulations of the Pelvic Girdle and Lower Limb

Element	Joint	Type of Articulation	Movements
Sacrum/hip bones	Sacro-iliac	Planar diarthrosis	Gliding movements
Hip bones/hip bones	Pubic symphysis	Amphiarthrosis	None*
Hip bones/femur	Hip	Ball-and-socket diarthrosis	Flexion/extension, adduction/abduction, circumduction, rotation
Femur/tibia	Knee	Complex, functions as hinge	Flexion/extension, limited rotation
Tibia/fibula	Tibiofibular (proximal) Tibiofibular (distal)	Planar diarthrosis Planar diarthrosis and amphiarthrotic syndesmosis	Slight gliding movements Slight gliding movements
Tibia and fibula with talus	Ankle, or talocrural	Hinge diarthrosis	Dorsiflexion/plantar flexion
Tarsal bone to tarsal bone	Intertarsal	Planar diarthrosis	Slight gliding movements
Tarsal bones to metatarsal bones	Tarsometatarsal	Planar diarthrosis	Slight gliding movements
Metatarsal bones to phalanges	Metatarsophalangeal	Condylar diarthrosis	Flexion/extension, adduction/abduction
Phalanx/phalanx	Interphalangeal	Hinge diarthrosis	Flexion/extension

*During pregnancy, hormones weaken the symphysis and permit movement important to childbirth (see Chapter 28).

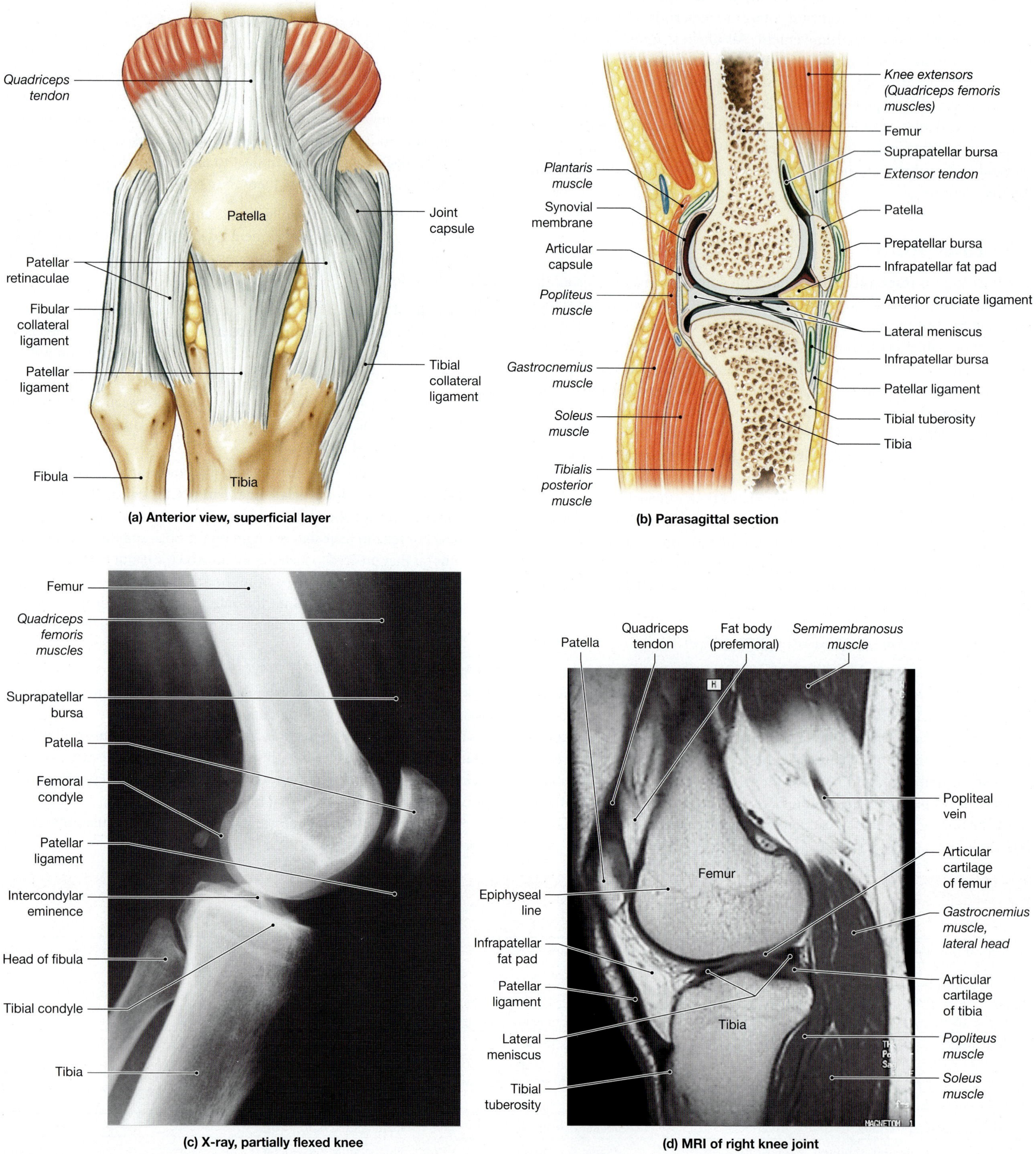

Figure 8.17 The Knee Joint, Part I

(a) Anterior view of a superficial dissection of the extended right knee. **(b)** A diagrammatic parasagittal section through the extended right knee. **(c)** X-ray of the partially flexed right knee joint, lateral projection. **(d)** MRI scan of the right knee joint, parasagittal section, lateral to medial sequence.

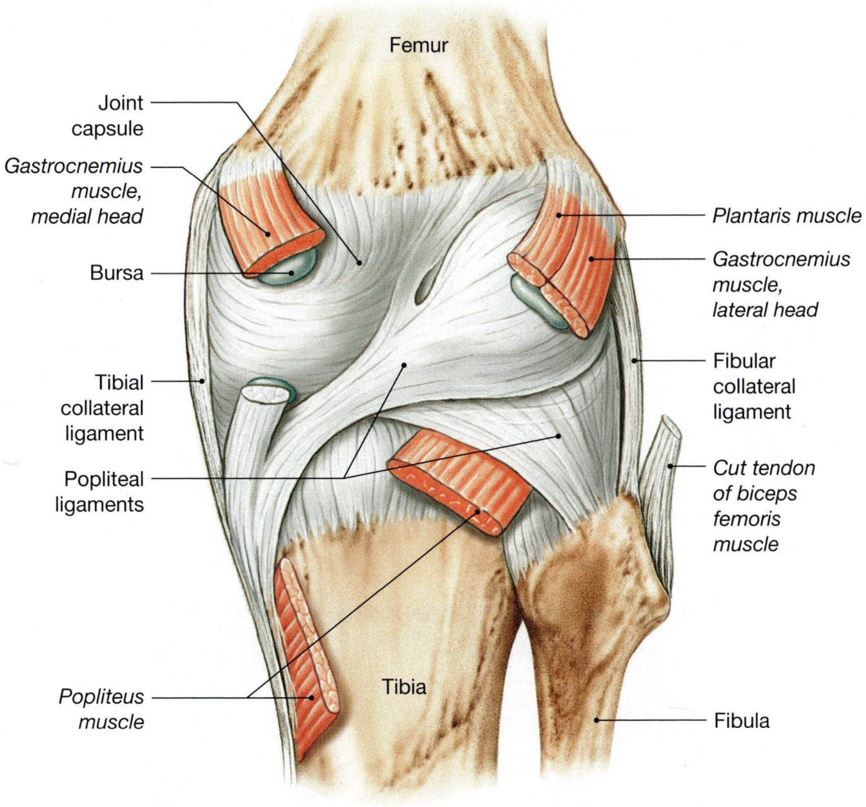

(a) Posterior view, superficial layer

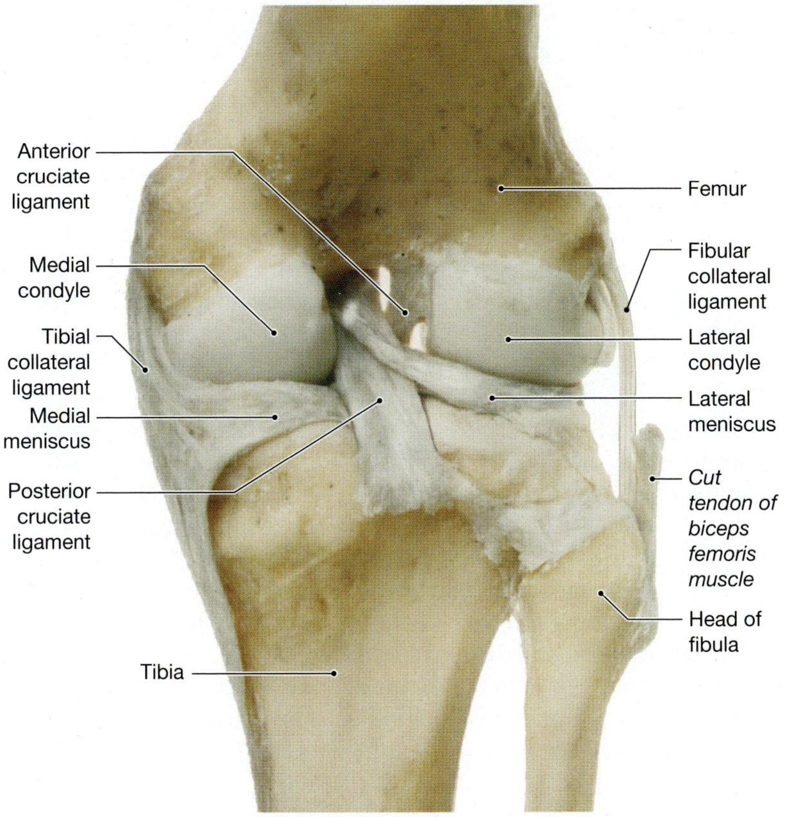

(b) Posterior view, deep layer

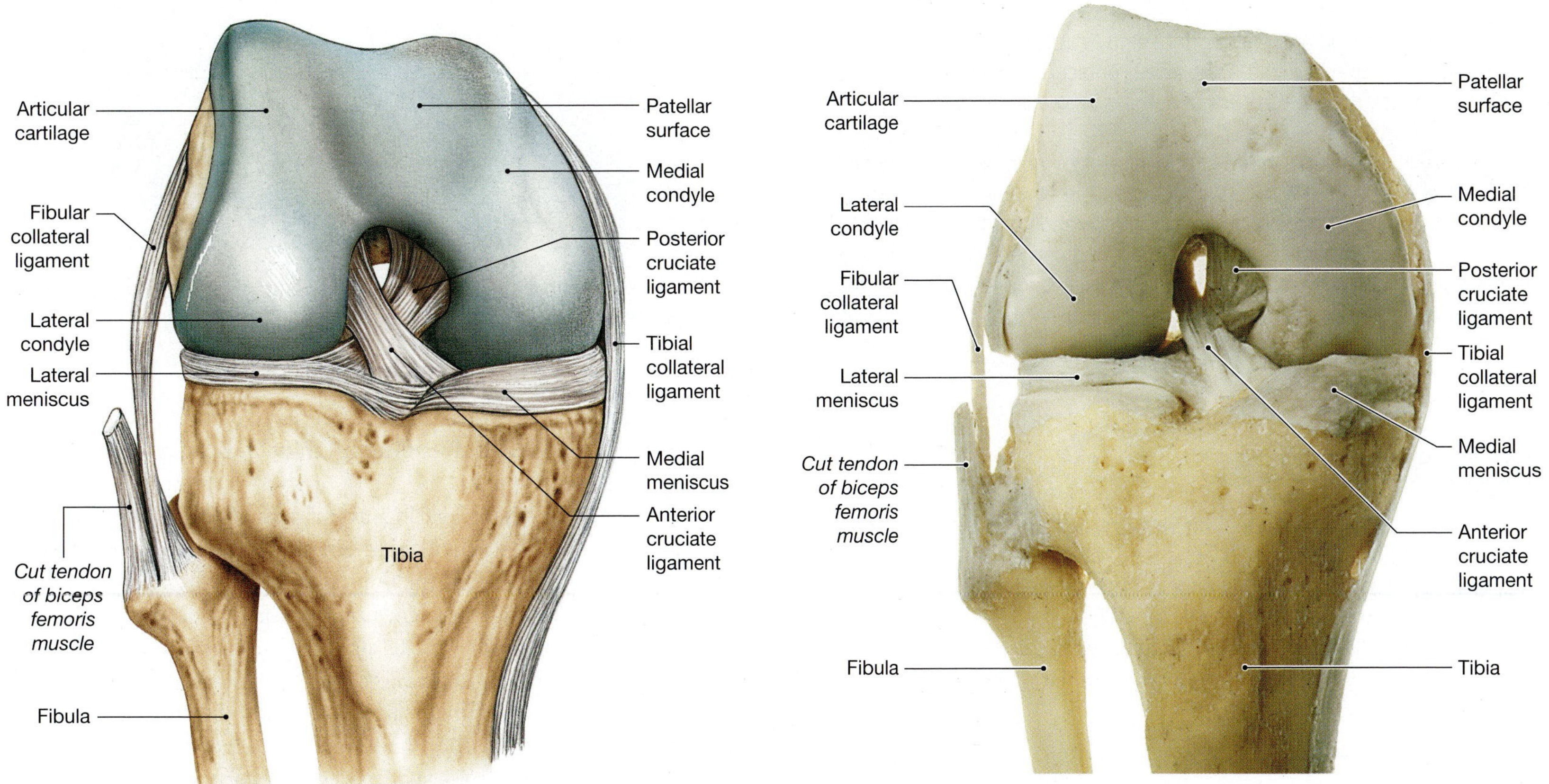

(c) Anterior views, flexed knee

Figure 8.18 The Knee Joint, Part II
(a) Posterior view of a dissection of the extended right knee, showing the ligaments supporting the capsule. **(b)** Posterior view of the right knee at full extension after removal of the joint capsule. **(c)** Anterior views of the right knee at full flexion after removal of the joint capsule, patella, and associated ligaments.

Clinical Note

Knee Injuries Athletes place tremendous stresses on their knees. Ordinarily, the medial and lateral menisci move as the position of the femur changes. Placing a lot of weight on the knee while it is partially flexed can trap a meniscus between the tibia and femur, resulting in a break or tear in the cartilage. In the most common injury, the lateral surface of the leg is driven medially, tearing the medial meniscus. In addition to being quite painful, the torn cartilage may restrict movement at the joint. It can also lead to chronic problems and the development of a "trick knee"—a knee that feels unstable. Sometimes the meniscus can be heard and felt popping in and out of position when the knee is extended. To prevent such injuries, most competitive sports outlaw activities that generate side impacts to the knee, and athletes wishing to continue exercising with injured knees may use a brace that limits lateral movement.

Other knee injuries involve tearing one or more stabilizing ligaments or damaging the patella. Torn ligaments can be difficult to correct surgically, and healing is slow. Rupture of the anterior cruciate ligament (ACL) is a common sports injury that affects women two to eight times as often as men. Twisting on an extended weight-bearing knee is frequently the cause. Nonsurgical treatment with exercise and braces is possible, but requires a change in activity patterns. Reconstructive surgery using part of the patellar tendon or an allograft from a cadaver tendon may allow a return to active sports.

The patella can be injured in a number of ways. If the leg is immobilized (as it might be in a football pileup) while you try to extend the knee, the muscles are powerful enough to pull the patella apart. Impacts to the anterior surface of the knee can also shatter the patella. Treatment of a fractured patella is difficult and time consuming. The fragments must be surgically removed and the tendons and ligaments repaired. The joint must then be immobilized. Total knee replacements are rarely performed on young people, but they are becoming increasingly common among elderly patients with severe arthritis.

Physicians often evaluate knee injuries by *arthroscopic examination*. An arthroscope uses fiber optics to permit the exploration of a joint without major surgery. Optical fibers are thin threads of glass or plastic that conduct light. The fibers can be bent around corners, so they can be introduced into a knee or other joint and moved around, enabling the physician to see and diagnose problems inside the joint. Arthroscopic surgical treatment of the joint is possible at the same time. This procedure, called **arthroscopic surgery**, has greatly simplified the treatment of knee and other joint injuries. Figure 8.19 is an arthroscopic view of the interior of an injured knee, showing a damaged meniscus. Small pieces of cartilage can be removed and the meniscus surgically trimmed. A total **meniscectomy**, the removal of the affected cartilage, is generally avoided, because it leaves the joint prone to develop degenerative joint disease. New tissue-culturing techniques may someday permit the replacement of the meniscus or even the articular cartilage.

Arthroscopy is an invasive procedure with some risks. Magnetic resonance imaging (MRI) is a safe, noninvasive, and cost-effective method of viewing and examining soft tissues around the joint. It improves the diagnostic accuracy of knee injuries, and reduces the need for diagnostic arthroscopies. It can also help guide the arthroscopic surgeon.

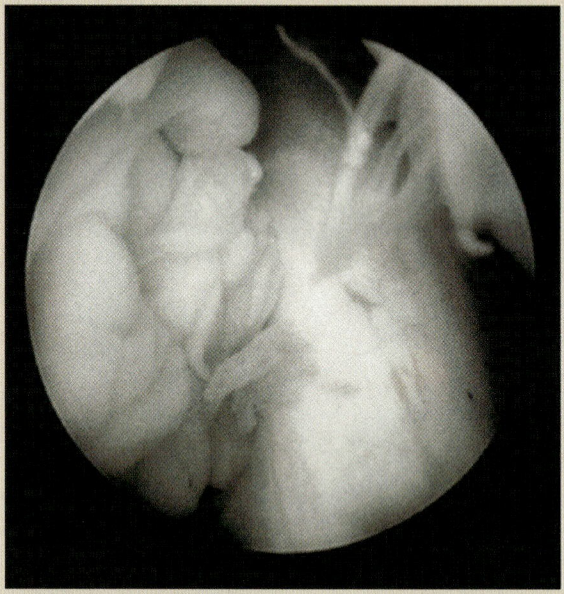

Figure 8.19 An arthroscopic view of the interior of an injured knee, showing a damaged meniscus

CONCEPT CHECK

1. Where would you find the following ligaments: iliofemoral ligament, pubofemoral ligament, and ischiofemoral ligament?
2. What symptoms would you expect to see in an individual who has damaged the menisci of the knee joint?
3. How is the knee joint affected by damage to the patellar ligament?
4. How do both the tibial and fibular collateral ligaments function to stabilize the knee joint?

See blue "Answers" tab at back of book.

The Joints of the Ankle and Foot

The Ankle Joint [Figures 8.20/8.21]

The ankle joint, or **talocrural joint**, is a hinge joint formed by articulations among the tibia, the fibula, and the talus (Figures 8.20 and 8.21). The ankle joint permits limited dorsiflexion (ankle flexion) and plantar flexion (ankle extension). p. 211

The primary weight-bearing articulation of the ankle is the *tibiotalar joint*, between the distal articular surface of the tibia and the trochlea of the talus. Normal functioning of the tibiotalar joint, including range of motion and weight-bearing, is dependent upon medial and lateral stability at this joint. Three joints provide this stability: (1) the proximal tibiofibular joint, (2) the distal tibiofibular joint, and (3) the fibulotalar joint.

The *proximal tibiofibular joint* is a plane joint formed between the posterolateral surface of the tibia and the head of the fibula. The *distal tibiofibular joint* is a fibrous syndesmosis between the distal facets of the tibia and fibula. The joint formed between the lateral malleolus of the fibula and the lateral articular surface of the talus is termed the *fibulotalar joint*. A series of ligaments along the length of the tibia and fibula hold these two bones in place, and this limits movement at the two tibiofibular joints and the fibulotalar joint. Maintaining the proper amount of movement at these joints provides the medial and lateral stability of the ankle.

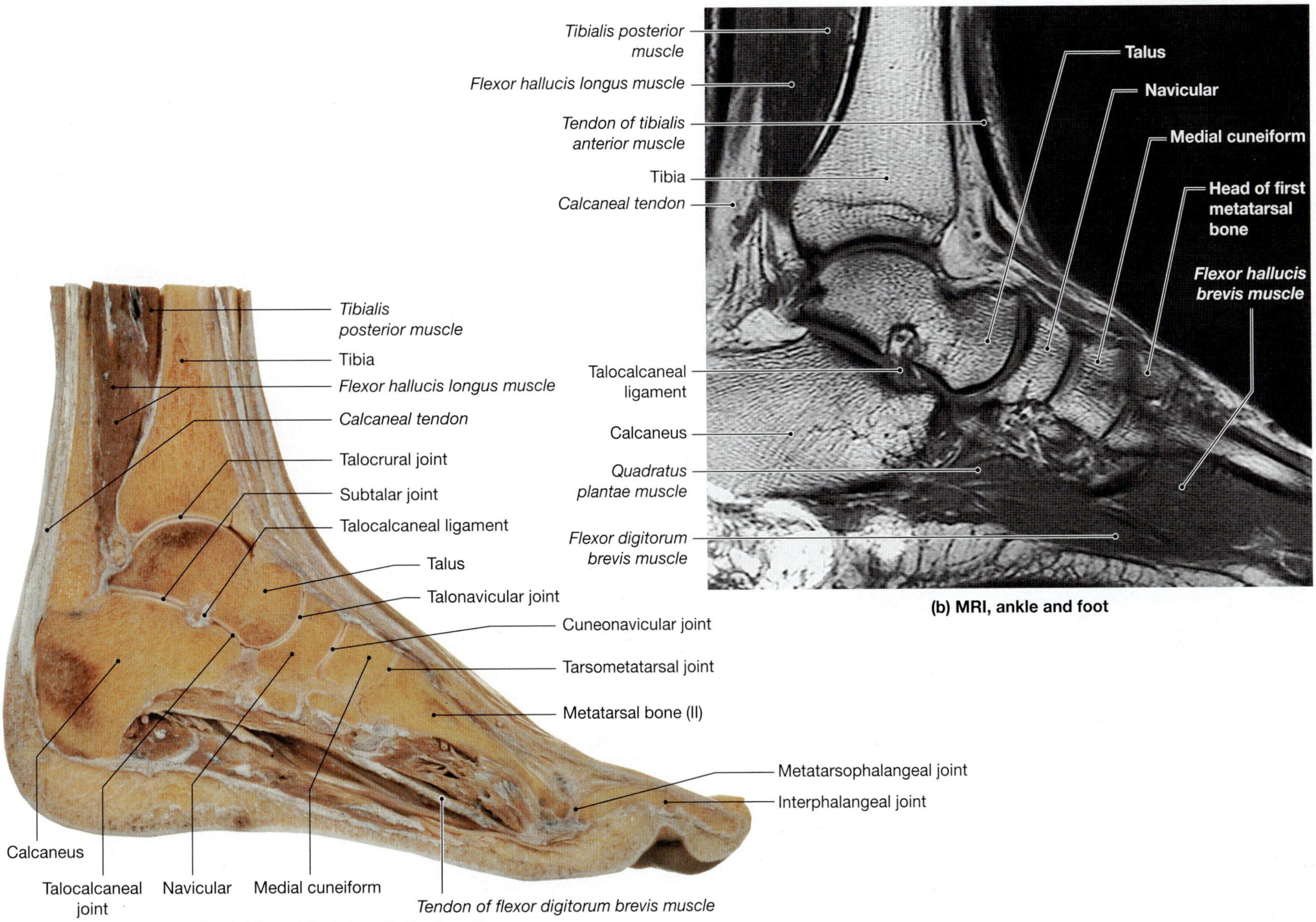

(b) MRI, ankle and foot

(a) Ankle and foot, longitudinal section

Figure 8.20 The Joints of the Ankle and Foot, Part I
(a) Longitudinal section of the left foot identifying major joints and associated structures. **(b)** A corresponding MRI scan of the left ankle and proximal portion of the foot.

The articular capsule of the ankle joint extends between the distal surfaces of the tibia and the medial malleolus of the tibia, the lateral malleolus of the fibula, and the talus. The anterior and posterior portions of the articular capsule are thin, but the lateral and medial surfaces are strong and reinforced by stout ligaments shown in Figure 8.21b–d. The major ligaments are the medial **deltoid ligament** and the three **lateral ligaments**. The malleoli, supported by these ligaments and bound together by the *tibiofibular ligaments*, prevent the ankle bones from sliding from side to side.

The Joints of the Foot [Figures 8.20/8.21]

Four groups of synovial joints are found in the foot (Figures 8.20 and 8.21):

1. Tarsal bone to tarsal bone (**intertarsal joints**). These are plane joints that permit limited sliding and twisting movements. The articulations between the tarsal bones are comparable to those between the carpal bones of the wrist.
2. Tarsal bone to metatarsal bone (**tarsometatarsal joints**). These are plane joints that allow limited sliding and twisting movements. The first three metatarsal bones articulate with the medial, intermediate, and lateral cuneiform bones. The fourth and fifth metatarsal bones articulate with the cuboid.
3. Metatarsal bone to phalanx (**metatarsophalangeal joints**). These are condylar joints that permit flexion/extension and adduction/abduction. Joints between the metatarsal bones and phalanges resemble those between the metacarpal bones and phalanges of the hand. Because the first metatarsophalangeal joint is condylar, rather than saddle-shaped like the first metacarpophalangeal joint of the hand, the great toe lacks the mobility of the thumb. A pair of sesamoid bones often forms in the tendons that cross the inferior surface of this joint, and their presence further restricts movement.
4. Phalanx to phalanx (**interphalangeal joints**). These are hinge joints that permit flexion and extension.

Aging and Articulations

Joints are subjected to heavy wear and tear throughout our lifetime, and problems with joint function are relatively common, especially in older individuals. **Rheumatism** (ROO-muh-tizm) is a general term that indicates

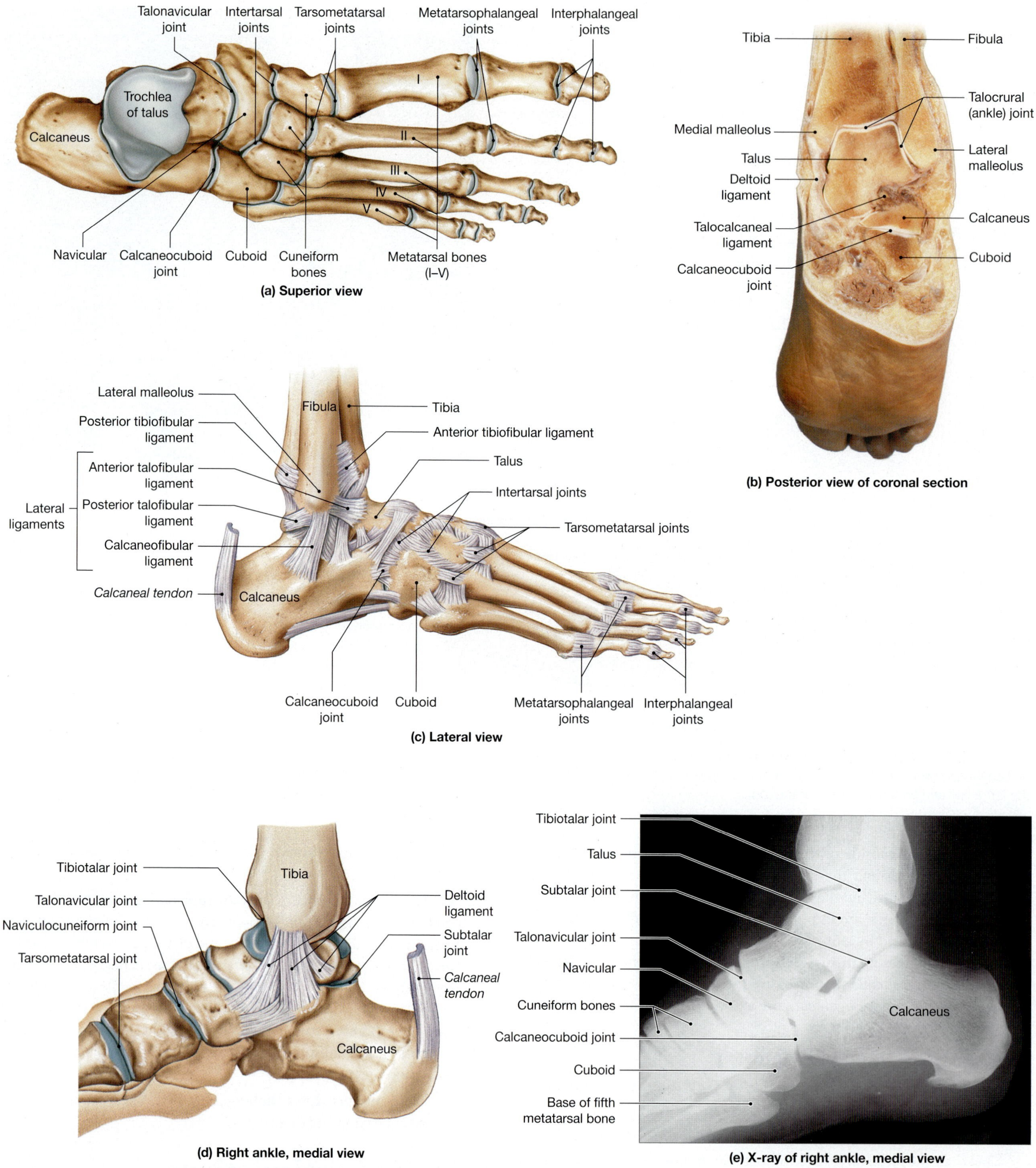

Figure 8.21 The Joints of the Ankle and Foot, Part II

(a) Superior view of bones and joints of the right foot. **(b)** Posterior view of a coronal section through the right ankle after plantar flexion. Note the placement of the medial and lateral malleoli. **(c)** Lateral view of the right foot, showing ligaments that stabilize the ankle joint. **(d)** Medial view of the right ankle, showing the medial ligaments. **(e)** X-ray of right ankle, medial/lateral projection.

pain and stiffness affecting the skeletal system, the muscular system, or both. Several major forms of rheumatism exist. **Arthritis** (ar-THRĪ-tis) encompasses all the rheumatic diseases that affect synovial joints. Arthritis always involves damage to the articular cartilages, but the specific cause can vary. For example, arthritis can result from bacterial or viral infection, injury to the joint, metabolic problems, or severe physical stresses.

With age, bone mass decreases and bones become weaker, so the risk of fractures increases. If osteoporosis develops, the bones may weaken to the point at which fractures occur in response to stresses that could easily be tolerated by normal bones. Hip fractures are among the most dangerous fractures seen in elderly people. These fractures, most often involving individuals over age 60, may be accompanied by hip dislocation or by pelvic fractures.

Healing proceeds very slowly, and the powerful muscles that surround the hip joint often prevent proper alignment of the bone fragments. Fractures at the greater or lesser trochanter generally heal well if the joint can be stabilized; steel frames, pins, screws, or some combination of these devices may be needed to preserve alignment and to permit healing to proceed normally.

Although hip fractures are most common among those over age 60, in recent years the frequency of hip fractures has increased dramatically among young, healthy professional athletes.

Bones and Muscles

The skeletal and muscular systems are structurally and functionally interdependent; their interactions are so extensive that they are often considered to be parts of a single *musculoskeletal system.*

There are direct physical connections, because the connective tissues that surround the individual muscle fibers are continuous with those that establish the tissue framework of an attached bone. Muscles and bones are also physiologically linked, because muscle contractions can occur only when the extracellular concentration of calcium remains within relatively narrow limits, and most of the body's calcium reserves are held within the skeleton. The next three chapters will examine the structure and function of the muscular system and discuss how muscular contractions perform specific movements.

Clinical Case — THE SKELETAL SYSTEM AND SKELETAL ARTICULATIONS

THE ROAD TO DAYTONA

NASCAR racing is one of the most rapidly growing spectator sports in the United States. Each week the track, and corresponding race strategy, is different. That, combined with the "down home" nature of the drivers and America's fascination with the automobile, has resulted in the rapidly growing interest in the sport. The ultimate goal for many drivers is obtaining "a ride." They start racing at the local county dirt track and are hopeful to move up the ladder to the Busch Series and, ultimately, NASCAR. Because drivers on the dirt track circuit don't have the highly financed sponsors seen with the Busch Series or NASCAR, some high-priced safety systems are omitted from the automobile or from the driver's equipment.

Elliott is a young racer who is making it big in the local stock car circuit. He has a string of 20 consecutive top-five finishes in the Illinois-Indiana-Wisconsin-Michigan dirt track circuit. Tonight he will be driving his car at the Wisconsin State Fair, and several scouts for the Busch Series will be in the crowd looking for promising young drivers to fill the anticipated vacancies in next year's racing circuit.

The race is going well for Elliott—he is currently in first place on lap 45 of the 50-lap feature race. As Elliott comes out of turn 3 and accelerates, he is rapidly gaining on the last car in the field. The #99 car immediately in front of him blows a right-front tire, sending it up and into the wall, and then down toward the infield. Elliott locks up his brakes and is unable to avoid the #99 car. He broadsides the car at a little more than 110 mph, causing a rapid deceleration. The #12 car, which was in second place, also locks up its brakes and slams into the back of Elliott's car at a little more than 90 mph, sandwiching it between the #99 and #12 cars. When the emergency crews get to Elliott's car, he is unconscious and must be extricated from the vehicle.

After he is removed from his car, the EMS crew fits Elliott with a cervical collar. They place him on the stretcher and head to the infield hospital.

Initial Examination

A preliminary examination at the track field hospital notes the following:

- Elliott is slowly regaining consciousness and is becoming more responsive.
- Elliott is complaining of blurred vision and keeps asking "When does the race start?"

The EMS crew decides to transfer Elliott to St. Mary's Hospital in Milwaukee.

Follow-up Examination

The emergency room physicians begin an examination and note the following:

- In addition to the mild **concussion** suffered in the accident, the attending physicians are immediately concerned with the possibility of a neck injury. Therefore, a full X-ray series of Elliott's head and neck is ordered.

Clinical Case *continued*

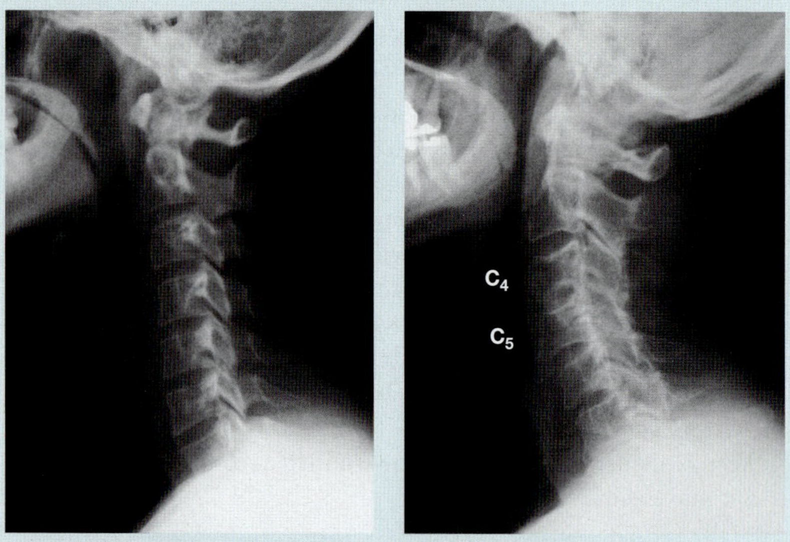

(a) X-ray of a normal cervical spine **(b) X-ray of Elliott's cervical spine**

Figure 8.22 X-ray of Cervical Vertebrae
(a) X-ray of normal cervical vertebrae. **(b)** X-ray of cervical vertebrae demonstrating a disappearance of the normal cervical region curvature and the presence of bony spurs around the intervertebral foramina between C_4 and C_5.

- The results of a screening neurological examination, including evaluation of **deep tendon reflexes** and **plantar responses**, are normal.
- Cervical X-rays demonstrate a disappearance of normal cervical region curvature (Figure 8.22).
- Evidence of slight degenerative changes at the middle cervical vertebrae, with some **bony spurs** around the intervertebral foramina between C_4 and C_5, is noted.
- No cervical fractures are noted.
- Upon removal of the cervical collar, the physicians conduct a cervical palpation and manipulation involving extension and rotation. This part of the exam demonstrates significant stiffness and pain. Tenderness is noted over the area of the transverse processes of C_4 and C_5.

Points to Consider

As you examine the information presented above, review the material covered in Chapters 5–8, and determine what anatomical information will enable you to sort through the information given to you about Elliott and his condition.

1. What are the normal curves of the vertebral column?
2. What are the anatomical characteristics of the cervical vertebrae, with particular reference to C_4 and C_5?
3. What soft-tissue structures would be found in association with the cervical region of the vertebral column, and what are the functions of these structures?
4. What are the anatomical characteristics of the intervertebral articulations?

Analysis and Interpretation

The information below answers the questions raised in the "Points to Consider" section. To review the material, refer to the indicated pages in the chapter.

1. The vertebral column exhibits four normal curves. The thoracic and sacral curves are termed primary curves, and the cervical and lumbar curves are termed secondary curves. pp. 159–160
2. The shape of the vertebral body, vertebral foramen, spinous processes and transverse processes enable you to distinguish cervical vertebrae from those of other regions of the vertebral column. pp. 162–166 In addition, the anatomical characteristics of a "typical" vertebra (C_3 through C_6) differ from those of C_1, C_2, and C_7. p. 164
3. A considerable amount of soft tissue found in association with the cervical region of the vertebral column may have been damaged in the accident.
4. The articulations between the superior and inferior articular processes of adjacent cervical vertebrae, as well as the intervertebral discs, may have been damaged in the accident. pp. 214–215

Diagnosis

Elliott is diagnosed with cervical syndrome resulting from a hyperextension-hyperflexion (also termed whiplash) injury caused by the combined front-end and rear-end collision during the race. As a result of this whiplash injury, Elliott probably strained several muscles in the neck region, causing the observed neck stiffness. In addition to strained muscles, Elliott might have injured one or more of the ligaments associated with the cervical region of the vertebral column, including the anterior longitudinal ligament, the posterior longitudinal ligament, the ligamentum flavum, or the interspinous ligament. p. 215 The sudden and extreme flexion and extension of the cervical region of the vertebral column might have ruptured one or more of the intervertebral discs in the cervical region of the vertebral column. p. 216 The slight degenerative changes at C_4 and C_5 (pp. 163–164) could be due to at least two circumstances:

1. These alterations might be the result of one or more previous neck injuries related to prior crashes.
2. Such alterations in vertebrae are often the result of the wear and tear that comes with advanced age. However, because Elliott is only 25, such a reason for this finding is highly unlikely. ■

CLINICAL CASE TERMS

concussion: An injury to soft tissue, such as the brain, resulting from a blow or violent shaking.

deep tendon reflexes (*myotatic reflex*): A contraction of muscles in response to a stretching force resulting from stimulation of proprioceptors.

plantar responses: A response to a stimulation, usually a stroking of the plantar surface of the foot from the heel to the ball of the foot. A normal plantar response would be a flexion of the toes. An abnormal response is termed a Babinski sign and consists of extension of the big toe and abduction of the remaining toes.

bony spurs: An abnormal thickening on a bone, usually in response to a traumatic event; often associated with pain due to movement of the bone or pressure on the bony growth.

CLINICAL TERMS

ankylosis (an-ki-lō-sis): An abnormal fusion between articulating bones in response to trauma and friction within a joint.

arthritis (ar-THRĪ-tis): Rheumatic diseases that affect synovial joints. Arthritis always involves damage to the articular cartilages, but the specific cause may vary. The diseases of arthritis are usually classified as either **degenerative** or **inflammatory** in nature.

arthroscope: An instrument that uses fiber optics to explore a joint without major surgery.

arthroscopic surgery: The surgical modification of a joint using an arthroscope.

bony spur: An abnormal thickening on a bone, usually in response to a traumatic event; often associated with pain due to movement of the bone or pressure on the bony growth.

concussion: An injury to a soft tissue, as in the brain, resulting from a blow or violent shaking.

continuous passive motion (CPM): A therapeutic procedure involving passive movement of an injured joint to stimulate circulation of synovial fluid. The goal is to prevent degeneration of the articular cartilages.

deep tendon reflex (*myotatic reflex*): Tonic contraction of the muscles in response to a stretching force.

herniated disc: A common name for a condition caused by distortion of an intervertebral disc. The distortion applies pressure to spinal nerves, causing pain and limiting range of motion.

laminectomy (lam-i-NEK-tō-mē): Removal of vertebral laminae; may be performed to access the vertebral canal and relieve symptoms of a herniated disc.

luxation (luk-SĀ-shun): A dislocation; a condition in which the articulating surfaces are forced out of position.

meniscectomy: The surgical removal of an injured meniscus.

osteoarthritis (os-tē-ō-ar-THRĪ-tis) (*degenerative arthritis, or degenerative joint disease [DJD]*): An arthritic condition resulting from (1) cumulative wear and tear on joint surfaces or (2) genetic predisposition.

plantar response (*plantar reflex*): The response to tactile stimulation to the ball of the foot; normally plantar flexion of the toes.

rheumatism (ROO-ma-tizm): A general term that indicates pain and stiffness affecting the skeletal system, the muscular system, or both.

rheumatoid arthritis: An inflammatory arthritis that affects roughly 2.5 percent of the adult population. The cause is uncertain, although allergies, bacteria, viruses, and genetic factors have all been proposed.

sciatica (sī-AT-i-ka): The painful result of compression of the roots of the sciatic nerve.

shoulder separation: The partial or complete dislocation of the acromioclavicular joint.

subluxation (sub-luk-SĀ-shun): A partial dislocation; displacement of articulating surfaces sufficient to cause discomfort, but resulting in less physical damage to the joint than during a complete dislocation.

STUDY OUTLINE

Introduction 206

1. **Articulations** (joints) exist wherever two bones interact. The function of a joint is dependent on its anatomical design. Joints may permit (1) no movement, (2) slight movement, or (3) extensive movement.

Classification of Joints 206

1. Three categories of joints are based on range of movement. *Immovable joints* are **synarthroses**, *slightly movable joints* are **amphiarthroses**, and *freely movable joints* are **diarthroses**. Joints may be classified by function *(see Table 8.1)* or by structure *(see Table 8.2)*.

Synarthroses (Immovable Joints) 206

2. In a **synarthrosis**, bony edges are close together and may interlock. Examples of synarthroses include a **suture** between skull bones, a **gomphosis** between teeth and jaws, a **synchondrosis** between bone and cartilage in an epiphyseal plate, and a **synostosis** where two bones fuse and the boundary between them disappears.

Amphiarthroses (Slightly Movable Joints) 206

3. Very limited movements are permitted in an **amphiarthrosis.** Examples of amphiarthroses are a **syndesmosis**, where collagen fibers connect bones of the leg, and a **symphysis**, where bones are separated by a pad of cartilage.

Diarthroses (Freely Movable Joints) 206

4. A wide range of movement is permitted at a **diarthrosis**, or **synovial joint**. These joints possess seven common characteristics: a **joint capsule**; **articular cartilages**; a fluid-filled **synovial cavity**; a **synovial membrane**; **accessory capsular ligaments**; **sensory nerves**; and **blood vessels** that supply the synovial membrane. The articular cartilages are lubricated by **synovial fluid.** Other synovial and accessory structures can include **menisci** or **articular discs**; **fat pads**; **tendons**; **ligaments**; **bursae**; and **tendon sheaths**. *(see Figure 8.1)*
5. A joint cannot have both great strength and great mobility at the same time. The greater the strength of a joint, the lesser its mobility, and vice versa.

Articular Form and Function 208

Describing Dynamic Motion 209

1. Possible movements of a bone at an articulation can be classified as **linear motion** (back-and-forth motion), **angular motion** (movement in which the angle between the shaft and the articular surface changes), and **rotation** (spinning of the shaft on its longitudinal axis). *(see Figure 8.2)*
2. Joints are described as **monaxial**, **biaxial**, or **triaxial** depending on the number of axes along which they permit movement. *(see Figure 8.6)*

Types of Movements 209

3. In **gliding**, the opposing surfaces at an articulation slide past each other. *(see Figure 8.2b)*
4. Several important terms describe angular motion: **abduction** (movement away from the longitudinal axis of the body), **adduction** (movement toward the longitudinal axis of the body), **flexion** (reduction in angle between articulating elements), **extension** (increase in angle between articulating elements), **hyperextension** (extension beyond normal anatomical limits, thereby producing joint damage), and **circumduction** (a special type of angular motion that includes flexion, abduction, extension, and adduction). *(see Figure 8.3)*
5. Description of rotational movements requires reference to a figure in the anatomical position. **Rotation** of the head to the left or right is observed when shaking the head "no." An **internal (medial)** or **external (lateral) rotation** is observed in limb movements if the anterior aspect of the limb either turns toward or away from the ventral surface of the body. The bones in the forearm permit **pronation** (motion to bring palm facing back) and **supination** (motion to bring palm facing front). *(see Figure 8.4)*
6. Several special terms apply to specific articulations or unusual movement types. Movements of the foot include **eversion** (bringing the sole of the foot outward) and **inversion** (bringing the sole of the foot inward). The ankle undergoes **dorsiflexion** (ankle flexion, "digging in the heels") and **plantar**

flexion (ankle extension, "standing on tiptoe"). **Lateral flexion** occurs when the vertebral column bends to the side. **Protraction** involves moving a body part anteriorly (jutting out the lower jaw); **retraction** involves moving it posteriorly (pulling the jaw back). **Opposition** is the thumb movement that enables us to grasp objects. **Elevation** and **depression** occur when we move a structure inferiorly or superiorly (occurs with opening and closing of the mouth). *(see Figure 8.5)*

A Structural Classification of Synovial Joints 212

7. **Plane joints** permit limited movement, usually in a single plane. *(see Figure 8.6 and Table 8.2)*
8. **Hinge joints** and **pivot joints** are monaxial joints that permit angular movement in a single plane. *(see Figure 8.6 and Table 8.2)*
9. Biaxial joints include **condylar (ellipsoidal) joints** and **saddle joints**. They allow angular movement in two planes. *(see Figure 8.6 and Table 8.2)*
10. Triaxial, or **ball-and-socket joints**, permit all combinations of movement, including rotation. *(see Figure 8.6 and Table 8.2)*

Representative Articulations 213

The Temporomandibular Joint 214

1. The **temporomandibular joint (TMJ)** involves the mandibular fossa of the temporal bone and the condylar process of the mandible. This joint has a thick pad of fibrous cartilage, the articular disc. Supporting structures include the dense capsule, the **temporomandibular ligament**, the **stylomandibular ligament**, and the **sphenomandibular ligament**. This relatively loose hinge joint permits small amounts of gliding and rotation. *(see Figure 8.7)*

Intervertebral Articulations 214

2. The superior and inferior articular processes of vertebrae form plane joints with those of adjacent vertebrae. The bodies form symphyseal joints. They are separated by **intervertebral discs** containing an inner soft, elastic gelatinous core, the **nucleus pulposus**, and an outer layer of fibrous cartilage, the **anulus fibrosus**. *(see Figures 8.8/8.9)*
3. Numerous ligaments bind together the bodies and processes of all vertebrae. *(see Figure 8.8)*
4. The articulations of the vertebral column permit **flexion** and **extension** (anterior-posterior), **lateral flexion**, and **rotation**.
5. Articulations of the axial skeleton are summarized in *Table 8.3*.

The Sternoclavicular Joint 215

6. The **sternoclavicular joint** is a plane joint that lies between the sternal end of each clavicle and the manubrium of the sternum. An articular disc separates the opposing surfaces. The capsule is reinforced by the **anterior** and **posterior sternoclavicular ligaments**, plus the **interclavicular** and **costoclavicular ligaments**. *(see Figure 8.10)*

The Shoulder Joint 217

7. The shoulder, or **glenohumeral joint**, formed by the glenoid fossa and the head of the humerus, is a loose, shallow joint that permits the greatest range of motion of any joint in the body. It is a ball-and-socket diarthrosis. Strength and stability are sacrificed to obtain mobility. The ligaments and surrounding muscles and tendons provide strength and stability. The shoulder has a large number of **bursae** that reduce friction as large muscles and tendons pass across the joint capsule. *(see Figure 8.11)*

The Elbow Joint 219

8. The **elbow joint** is composed of the joints between (1) the humerus and the ulna, and (2) the humerus and the radius.
9. The **elbow** is a hinge joint that permits flexion and extension. It is really two joints, one between the humerus and the ulna (*humeroulnar joint*) and one between the humerus and the radius (*humeroradial joint*). **Radial** and **ulnar collateral ligaments** and **annular ligaments** aid in stabilizing this joint. *(see Figure 8.12)*

The Radioulnar Joints 219

10. The *proximal radioulnar* and *distal radioulnar joints* allow for supination and pronation of the forearm. The head of the radius is held in place by the **annular ligament**, while the distal radioulnar articulating surfaces are held in place by a series of radioulnar ligaments and the antebrachial interosseous membrane. *(see Figure 8.13)*

The Joints of the Wrist 219

11. The **wrist joint** is formed by the **radiocarpal joint** and the **intercarpal joints**. The radiocarpal articulation is a condylar articulation that involves the distal articular surface of the radius and three proximal carpal bones (scaphoid, lunate, and triquetrum). The radiocarpal joint permits flexion/extension, adduction/abduction, and circumduction. A connective tissue capsule and broad ligaments stabilize the positions of the individual carpal bones. The intercarpal joints are plane joints. *(see Figure 8.14)*

The Joints of the Hand 221

12. Five types of diarthrotic joints are found in the hand: (1) carpal bone/carpal bone (**intercarpal joints**); plane diarthrosis; (2) carpal bone/first metacarpal bone (**carpometacarpal joint of the thumb**); saddle diarthrosis, permitting flexion/extension, adduction/abduction, circumduction, opposition; (3) carpal bones/metacarpal bones II–V (**carpometacarpal joints**); plane diarthrosis, permitting slight flexion/extension and adduction/abduction; (4) metacarpal bone/phalanx (**metacarpophalangeal joints**); condylar diarthrosis, permitting flexion/extension, adduction/abduction, and circumduction; and (5) phalanx/phalanx (**interphalangeal joints**); hinge diarthrosis, permitting flexion/extension. *(see Figure 8.14)*

The Hip Joint 223

13. The **hip joint** is a ball-and-socket diarthrosis that is formed by the union of the acetabulum of the os coxae with the head of the femur. The joint permits flexion/extension, adduction/abduction, circumduction, and rotation. *(see Figures 8.15/8.16)*
14. The articular capsule of the hip joint is reinforced and stabilized by four broad ligaments: the **iliofemoral**, **pubofemoral**, **ischiofemoral**, and **transverse acetabular ligaments**. Another ligament, the **ligament of the femoral head** *(ligamentum capitis femoris)*, also helps stabilize the hip joint. *(see Figures 8.15/8.16)*

The Knee Joint 225

15. The knee joint functions as a hinge joint, but is more complex than standard hinge joints such as the elbow. Structurally, the knee resembles three separate joints: (1) the medial condyles of the femur and tibia, (2) the lateral condyles of the femur and tibia, and (3) the patella and patellar surface of the femur. The joint permits flexion/extension and limited rotation. *(see Figures 8.17/8.18/8.19)*
16. The articular capsule of the knee is not a single unified capsule with a common synovial cavity. It contains (1) **fibrous cartilage pads**, the **medial** and **lateral menisci**, and (2) **fat pads**. *(see Figures 8.17/8.18)*
17. Seven major ligaments bind and stabilize the knee joint: the **patellar**, **tibial collateral**, **fibular collateral**, **popliteal** (two), and **anterior** and **posterior cruciate ligaments** (ACL and PCL). *(see Figures 8.17/8.18)*

The Joints of the Ankle and Foot 228

18. The ankle joint, or **talocrural joint**, is a hinge joint formed by the inferior surface of the tibia, the lateral malleolus of the fibula, and the trochlea of the talus. The primary joint is the tibiotalar joint. The tibia and fibula are bound together by **anterior** and **posterior tibiofibular ligaments**. With these stabilizing ligaments holding the bones together, the medial and lateral malleoli can prevent lateral or medial sliding of the tibia across the trochlear surface. The ankle joint permits dorsiflexion/plantar flexion. The medial **deltoid ligament** and three **lateral ligaments** further stabilize the ankle joint. *(see Figures 8.20/8.21)*
19. Four types of diarthrotic joints are found in the foot: (1) tarsal bone/tarsal bone (**intertarsal joints**, named after the participating bone), plane diarthro-

sis; (2) tarsal bone/metatarsal bone (**tarsometatarsal joints**), plane diarthrosis; (3) metatarsal bone/phalanx (**metatarsophalangeal joints**), condylar diarthrosis, permitting flexion/extension and adduction/abduction; and (4) phalanx/phalanx (**interphalangeal joints**), hinge diarthrosis, permitting flexion/extension. *(see Figures 8.20/8.21 and Table 8.5)*

Aging and Articulations 229

1. Problems with joint function are relatively common, especially in older individuals. **Rheumatism** is a general term for pain and stiffness affecting the skeletal system, the muscular system, or both; several major forms exist. **Arthritis** encompasses all the rheumatic diseases that affect synovial joints. Both conditions become increasingly common with age.

Bones and Muscles 231

1. The skeletal and muscular systems are structurally and functionally interdependent and constitute the *musculoskeletal system.*

CHAPTER REVIEW

For answers to the Concept Check and Chapter Review questions, go to the blue "Answers" tab at the back of the book.

Level 1 Reviewing Facts and Terms

Match each numbered item with the most closely related lettered item. Use letters for answers in the spaces provided.

Column A	Column B
___ 1. no movement	a. wrist joint
___ 2. synovial	b. dorsiflexion
___ 3. increased angle	c. fluid-filled pockets
___ 4. bursae	d. diarthrosis
___ 5. palm facing anteriorly	e. knee
___ 6. digging in heels	f. intervertebral discs
___ 7. fibrous cartilage	g. supination
___ 8. carpus	h. extension
___ 9. menisci	i. synarthrosis

10. The function of a bursa is to
    (a) reduce friction between a bone and a tendon
    (b) absorb shock
    (c) smooth the surface outline of a joint
    (d) both a and b are correct

11. All of the following are true of the movement capabilities of joints except
    (a) great stability decreases mobility
    (b) they may be directed or restricted to certain directions by the shape of articulating surfaces
    (c) they may be modified by the presence of accessory ligaments and collagen fibers of the joint capsule
    (d) the strength of the joint is determined by the strength of the muscles that attach to it and its joint capsule

12. Which of the following is not a function of synovial fluid?
    (a) absorb shocks
    (b) increase osmotic pressure within joint
    (c) lubricate the joint
    (d) provide nutrients

13. A joint in which the articular surfaces can slide in any direction is called
    (a) uniaxial (b) biaxial
    (c) multiaxial (d) monaxial

14. Which of the following ligaments is not associated with the hip joint?
    (a) iliofemoral ligament
    (b) pubofemoral ligament
    (c) ligament of the femoral head
    (d) ligamentum flavum

15. The back of the knee joint is reinforced by
    (a) tibial collateral ligaments
    (b) popliteal ligaments
    (c) posterior cruciate ligament
    (d) patellar ligaments

16. The shoulder joint is primarily stabilized by
    (a) ligaments and muscles that move the humerus
    (b) the scapula
    (c) glenohumeral ligaments only
    (d) the clavicle

17. A twisting motion of the foot that turns the sole inward is
    (a) dorsiflexion (b) eversion
    (c) inversion (d) protraction

18. Which of the following correctly pairs structures of the elbow joint?
    (a) lateral epicondyle, radial tuberosity
    (b) capitulum of humerus, head of radius
    (c) radial collateral ligament, medial epicondyle
    (d) olecranon, radial notch

19. Luxations are painful due to stimulation of pain receptors in all locations except the following
    (a) inside the joint cavity
    (b) in the capsule
    (c) in the ligaments around the joint
    (d) in the tendons around the joint

20. The ligaments that limit the anterior and posterior movement of the femur and maintain the alignment of the femoral and tibial condyles are the
    (a) cruciate ligaments
    (b) fibular collateral ligaments
    (c) patellar ligaments
    (d) tibial collateral ligaments

Level 2 Reviewing Concepts

1. When a baseball pitcher "winds up" prior to throwing a pitch, he or she is taking advantage of the ability of the shoulder joint to perform
   (a) rotation (b) protraction
   (c) extension (d) supination

2. Compare and contrast the strength and stability of a joint with respect to the amount of mobility in the joint.

3. How does the classification of a joint change when an epiphysis fuses at the ends of a long bone?

4. How do the malleoli of the tibia and fibula function to retain the correct positioning of the tibiotalar joint?

5. How do articular cartilages differ from other cartilages in the body?
6. What factors are responsible for limiting the range of motion of a mobile diarthrosis?
7. What role is played by capsular ligaments in a complex synovial joint? Use the humeroulnar joint to illustrate your answer.
8. What is the common mechanism that holds together immovable joints such as skull sutures and the gomphoses, holding teeth in their alveoli?
9. How can pronation be distinguished from circumduction of a skeletal element?
10. What would you tell your grandfather about his decrease in height as he grows older?

Level 3 Critical Thinking

1. When a person involved in an automobile accident suffers from "whiplash," what structures have been affected and what movements could be responsible for this injury?
2. A marathon runner steps on an exposed tree root, causing a twisted ankle. After being examined, she is told the ankle is severely sprained, not broken. The ankle will probably take longer to heal than a broken bone would. Which structures were damaged, and why would they take so long to heal?
3. Almost all football knee injuries occur when the player has the knee "planted" rather than flexed. What anatomical facts would account for this?

9

The Muscular System

Skeletal Muscle Tissue and Muscle Organization

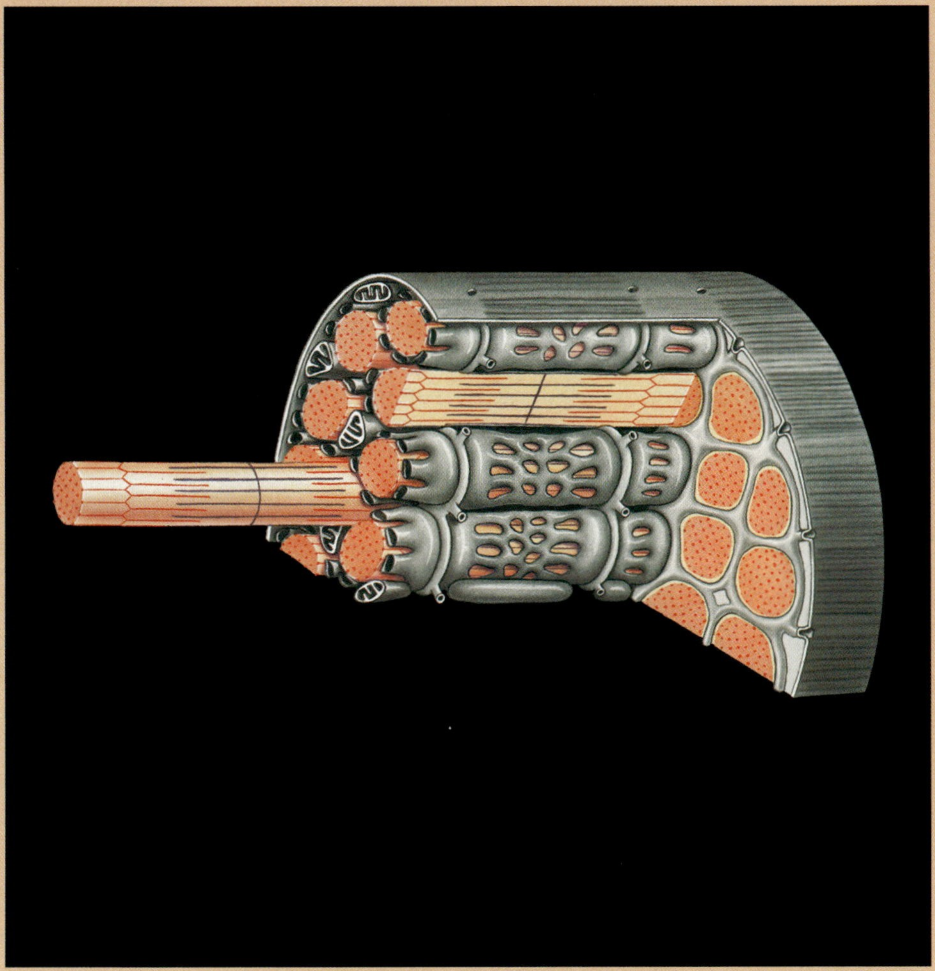

CHAPTER OBJECTIVES

1. Describe the distinguishing characteristics of muscle tissue.
2. Describe the functions of skeletal muscle tissue.
3. Discuss the organization of connective tissues, blood supply, and innervation of skeletal muscle.
4. Describe the arrangement of the sarcoplasmic reticulum, transverse tubules, myofibrils and myofilaments, and sarcomere organization within skeletal muscle fibers.
5. Describe the role of the sarcoplasmic reticulum and transverse tubules in contraction.
6. Discuss the structure of the neuromuscular synapse and summarize events that occur at the junction.
7. Summarize the process of muscular contraction.
8. Describe a motor unit and the control of muscle fibers.
9. Relate the distribution of various types of skeletal muscle fibers to muscular performance.
10. Describe the arrangement of fascicles in the various types of muscles and explain the resulting functional differences.
11. Predict the actions of a muscle on the basis of its origin and insertion.
12. Explain how muscles interact to produce or oppose movements.
13. Use the name of a muscle to help identify and remember its orientation, unusual features, location, appearance, and function.
14. Describe the relationship between muscles and bones, the different classes of levers, and anatomical pulleys, and how they make muscles more efficient.
15. Describe the effects of exercise and aging on skeletal muscle.

It is hard to imagine what life would be like without muscle tissue. We would be unable to sit, stand, walk, speak, or grasp objects. Blood would not circulate, because there would be no heartbeat to propel it through the vessels. The lungs could not rhythmically empty and fill nor could food move along the digestive tract. In fact, there would be practically no movement through any of our internal passageways.

This is not to say that all life depends on muscle tissue. There are large organisms that get by very nicely without it—we call them plants. But life as *we* live it would be impossible, for many of our physiological processes, and virtually all our dynamic interactions with the environment, involve muscle tissue. Muscle tissue, one of the four primary tissue types, consists chiefly of *muscle fibers*—elongate cells, each capable of contracting along its longitudinal axis. Muscle tissue also includes the connective tissue fibers that harness those contractions to perform useful work. There are three types of muscle tissue: *skeletal muscle*,* *cardiac muscle*, and *smooth muscle*. p. 75

The primary role of **skeletal muscle** tissue is to move the body by pulling on bones of the skeleton, making it possible for us to walk, dance, or play a musical instrument. **Cardiac muscle** tissue pushes blood through the arteries and veins of the circulatory system; **smooth muscle** tissues push fluids and solids along the digestive tract and perform varied functions in other systems. These muscle tissues share four basic properties:

1. *Excitability:* the ability to respond to stimulation. For example, skeletal muscles normally respond to stimulation by the nervous system, and some smooth muscles respond to circulating hormones.
2. *Contractility:* the ability to shorten actively and exert a pull or tension that can be harnessed by connective tissues.
3. *Extensibility:* the ability to continue to contract over a range of resting lengths. For example, a smooth muscle cell can be stretched to several times its original length and still contract when stimulated.
4. *Elasticity:* the ability of a muscle to rebound toward its original length after a contraction.

This chapter focuses attention on skeletal muscle tissue. Cardiac muscle tissue will be considered in Chapter 21, which deals with the anatomy of the heart, and smooth muscle tissue will be considered in Chapter 25, in our discussion of the digestive system.

Skeletal muscles are organs that include all four basic tissue types but consist primarily of skeletal muscle tissue. The **muscular system** of the human body consists of more than 700 skeletal muscles and includes all of the skeletal muscles that can be controlled voluntarily. This system will be the focus of the next three chapters. This chapter considers the function, gross anatomy, microanatomy, and organization of skeletal muscles, as well as muscle terminology. Chapter 10 discusses the gross anatomy of the axial musculature, skeletal muscles associated with the axial skeleton; Chapter 11 discusses the gross anatomy of the appendicular musculature, skeletal muscles associated with the appendicular skeleton.

Functions of Skeletal Muscle

Skeletal muscles are contractile organs directly or indirectly attached to bones of the skeleton. Skeletal muscles perform the following functions:

1. *Produce skeletal movement:* Muscle contractions pull on tendons and move the bones of the skeleton. The effects range from simple motions, such as extending the arm, to the highly coordinated movements of swimming, skiing, or typing.
2. *Maintain posture and body position:* Contraction of specific muscles also maintains body posture—for example, holding the head in position when reading a book or balancing the weight of the body above the feet when walking involves the contraction of muscles that stabilize joints. Without constant muscular contraction, we could not sit upright without collapsing or stand without toppling over.
3. *Support soft tissues:* The abdominal wall and the floor of the pelvic cavity consist of layers of skeletal muscle. These muscles support the weight of visceral organs and protect internal tissues from injury.
4. *Regulate entering and exiting of material:* Openings, or **orifices**, of the digestive and urinary tracts are encircled by skeletal muscles. These muscles provide voluntary control over swallowing, defecation, and urination.
5. *Maintain body temperature:* Muscle contractions require energy, and whenever energy is used in the body, some of it is converted to heat. The heat lost by contracting muscles keeps our body temperature in the range required for normal functioning.

Anatomy of Skeletal Muscles

When naming structural features of muscles and their components, anatomists often used the Greek words *sarkos* ("flesh") and *mys* ("muscle"). These root words should be kept in mind as our discussion proceeds. We will first discuss the gross anatomy of skeletal muscle and then describe the microstructure that makes contraction possible.

Gross Anatomy [Figure 9.1]

Figure 9.1 illustrates the appearance and organization of a typical skeletal muscle. We begin our study of the gross anatomy of muscle with a description of the connective tissues that bind and attach skeletal muscles to other structures.

Connective Tissue of Muscle [Figure 9.1]

Each skeletal muscle has three concentric layers, or wrappings, of connective tissue: an outer *epimysium*, a central *perimysium*, and an inner *endomysium* (Figure 9.1).

- The **epimysium** (ep-i-MIS-ē-um; *epi*, on + *mys*, muscle) is a dense irregular connective tissue layer that surrounds the entire skeletal muscle. The epimysium, which separates the muscle from surrounding tissues and organs, is connected to the *deep fascia*. p. 74
- The connective tissue fibers of the **perimysium** (per-i-MIS-ē-um; *peri-*, around) divide the muscle into a series of internal compartments, each containing a bundle of muscle fibers called a **fascicle** (FAS-i-kul; *fasciculus*, bundle). In addition to collagen and elastic fibers, the perimysium contains numerous blood vessels and nerves that branch to supply each individual fascicle.
- The **endomysium** (en-dō-MIS-ē-um; *endo*, inside + *mys*, muscle) surrounds each skeletal muscle fiber, binds each muscle fiber to its neighbor, and supports capillaries that supply individual fibers. The endomysium consists of a delicate network of reticular fibers. Scattered **myosatellite cells** lie between the endomysium and the muscle fibers. These cells function in the repair of damaged muscle tissue.

Tendons and Aponeuroses The connective tissue fibers of the endomysium and perimysium are interwoven, and those of the perimysium blend into the epimysium. At each end of the muscle, the collagen fibers of the epimysium, perimysium, and endomysium often converge to form a fibrous

*The *Terminologia Histologica: International Terms for Human Cytology and Histology* (TH, © 2008) splits this category into skeletal striated muscle and noncardiac visceral striated muscle.

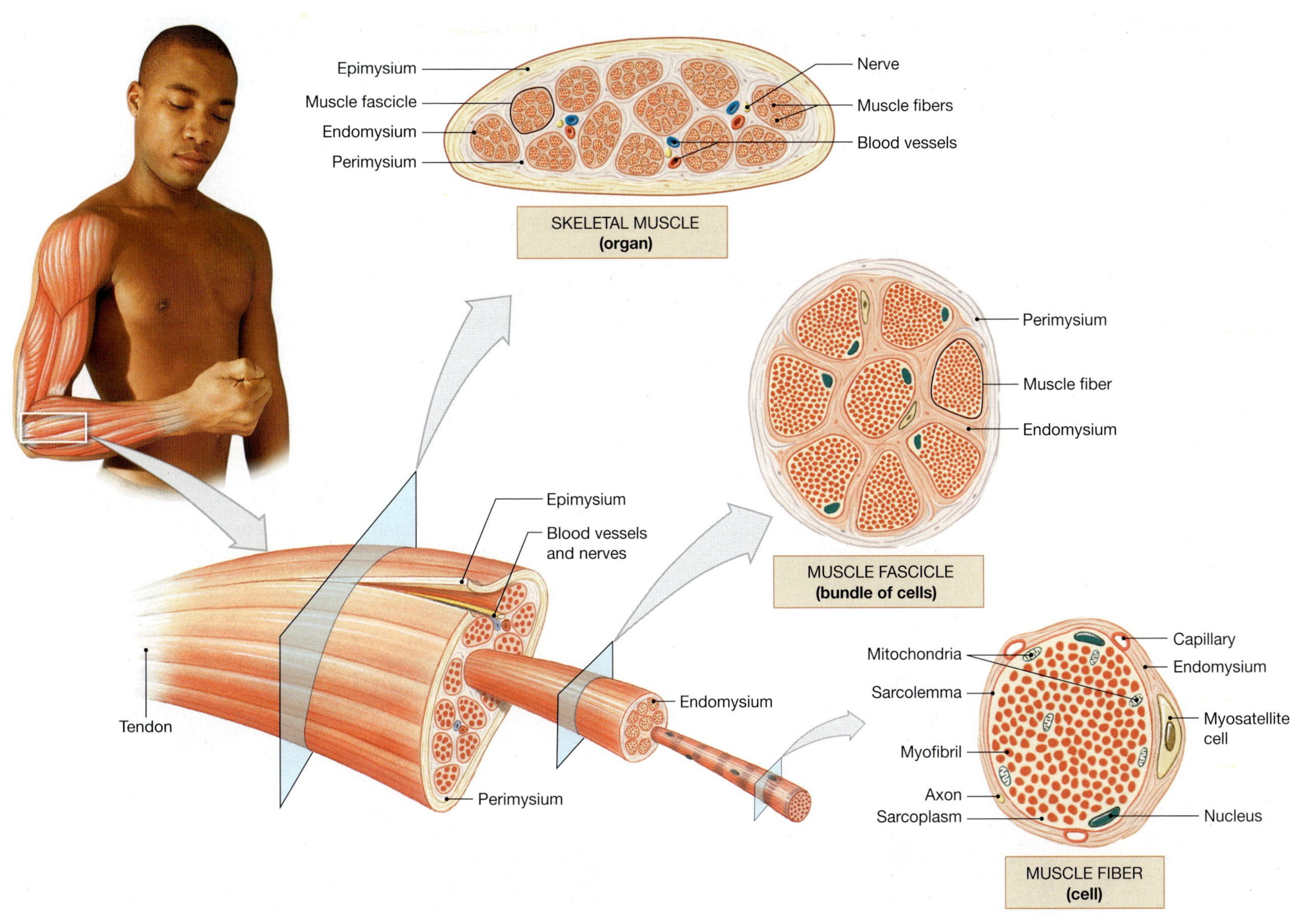

Figure 9.1 Structural Organization of Skeletal Muscle
A skeletal muscle consists of bundles of muscle fibers (fascicles) enclosed within a connective tissue sheath, the epimysium. Each fascicle is then ensheathed by the perimysium, and within each fascicle the individual muscle fibers are surrounded by the endomysium. Each muscle fiber has many nuclei as well as mitochondria and other organelles seen here and in *Figure 9.3*.

tendon that attaches the muscle to bone, skin, or another muscle. Tendons often resemble thick cords or cables. Tendons that form thick, flattened sheets are called **aponeuroses**. The structural characteristics of tendons and aponeuroses were considered in Chapter 3. pp. 65–68

The tendon fibers are interwoven into the periosteum and matrix of the associated bone. This meshwork provides an extremely strong bond, and any contraction of the muscle exerts a pull on the attached bone.

Nerves and Blood Vessels [Figure 9.2]

The connective tissues of the epimysium, perimysium, and endomysium contain the nerves and blood vessels that supply the muscle fibers. Skeletal muscles are often called *voluntary muscles* because their contractions can be consciously controlled. This control is provided by the nervous system. Nerves, which are bundles of axons, penetrate the epimysium, branch through the perimysium, and enter the endomysium to innervate individual muscle fibers. Chemical communication between a synaptic terminal of the neuron and a skeletal muscle fiber occurs at a site called the **neuromuscular synapse**, or *myoneural junction*. Several neuromuscular synapses are shown in Figure 9.2. Each muscle fiber has one neuromuscular synapse, usually located midway along its length. At a neuromuscular synapse, the synaptic terminal of the neuron is bound to the *motor end plate* of the skeletal muscle fiber. The motor end plate is a specialized area of the muscle cell membrane within a neuromuscular synapse. (A later section will consider the structure of the motor end plate and its role in nerve–muscle communication.)

Muscle contraction requires tremendous quantities of energy, and an extensive vascular supply delivers the oxygen and nutrients needed for the production of ATP in active skeletal muscles. These blood vessels often enter the muscle alongside the associated nerves, and the vessels and nerves follow the same branching pattern through the perimysium. Once within the endomysium, the arteries supply an extensive capillary network around each muscle fiber. Because these capillaries are coiled rather than straight, they are able to tolerate changes in the length of the muscle fiber.

CONCEPT CHECK

1. What are the three types of muscle tissue, and what is the function of each?
2. What is the perimysium? What structures would be located here?
3. Describe the difference between a tendon and an aponeurosis.
4. What is the difference between a myoneural junction and a motor end plate?

See blue "Answers" tab at back of book.

Clinical Note

Fibromyalgia and Chronic Fatigue Syndrome **Fibromyalgia** (-algia, pain) is a disorder that has formally been recognized only since the mid-1980s. Although first described in the early 1800s, the condition is still somewhat controversial, because the symptoms cannot be definitively linked to any anatomical or physiological abnormalities. However, physicians now recognize a distinctive pattern of symptoms with the diagnostic criteria of widespread musculoskeletal pain for three months or more, and tenderness in 11 or more of 18 specific tender points. Sleep disorders, depression, and irritable bowel syndrome also occur alongside fibromyalgia.

Fibromyalgia may be the most common musculoskeletal disorder affecting women under age 40; from 3 to 6 million individuals in the United States may have this condition. The four most common tender points are (1) the medial surface of the knee, (2) the area distal to the lateral epicondyle of the humerus, (3) the area near the external occipital crest of the skull, and (4) the junction between the second rib and its costal cartilage. An additional clinical criterion is that the pains and stiffness cannot be explained by other mechanisms.

Most of the symptoms mentioned could be attributed to other problems. For example, chronic depression can, by itself, lead to fatigue and poor-quality sleep. As a result, the pattern of tender points is the diagnostic key to fibromyalgia. This symptom distinguishes fibromyalgia from **chronic fatigue syndrome (CFS)**. The current symptoms accepted as a definition of CFS include (1) a sudden onset, generally following a viral infection, (2) disabling fatigue, (3) muscle weakness and pain, (4) sleep disturbance, (5) fever, and (6) enlargement of cervical lymph nodes. Roughly twice as many women as men are diagnosed with CFS.

Attempts to link either fibromyalgia or CFS to a viral infection, suprarenal gland dysfunction, or some physical or psychological trauma have not been successful, and the causes remain unknown. For both conditions, treatment is at present limited to relieving symptoms when possible. For example, anti-inflammatory medications may help relieve pain, antidepressant medications may improve sleep patterns and reduce depression, and exercise programs may help maintain a normal range of motion. Reassurance that fibromyalgia is not progressive, crippling, or life-threatening may help those who have it.

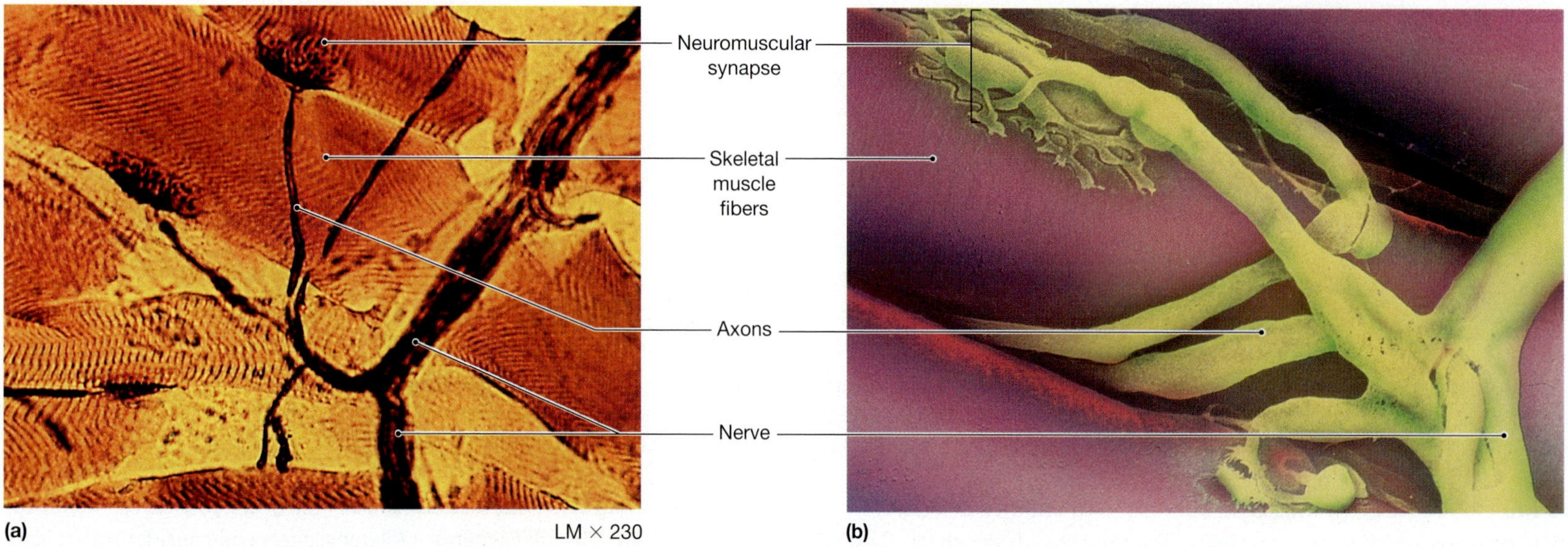

Figure 9.2 Skeletal Muscle Innervation
Each skeletal muscle fiber is stimulated by a nerve fiber at a neuromuscular synapse. **(a)** Several neuromuscular synapses are seen on the muscle fibers of this fascicle. **(b)** Colorized SEM of neuromuscular synapse.

Microanatomy of Skeletal Muscle Fibers [Figures 9.1/9.3]

The cell membrane, or **sarcolemma** (sar-kō-LEM-a; *sarkos*, flesh + *lemma*, husk) of a skeletal muscle fiber surrounds the cytoplasm, or **sarcoplasm** (SAR-kō-plazm). Skeletal muscle fibers differ in several other respects from the "typical" cell described in Chapter 2.

- Skeletal muscle fibers are very large. A fiber from a leg muscle could have a diameter of 100 μm and a length equal to that of the entire muscle (30–40 cm, or 10–16 in.).
- Skeletal muscle fibers are *multinucleate*. During development, groups of embryonic cells called **myoblasts** fuse together to create individual skeletal muscle fibers (Figure 9.3a). Each nucleus in a skeletal muscle fiber reflects the contribution of a single myoblast. Each skeletal muscle fiber contains hundreds of nuclei just inside the sarcolemma (Figure 9.3b,c). This characteristic distinguishes skeletal muscle fibers from cardiac and smooth muscle fibers. Some myoblasts do not fuse with developing muscle fibers, but remain in adult skeletal muscle tissue as *myosatellite cells* (Figures 9.1 and 9.3a). When a skeletal muscle is injured, myosatellite cells may differentiate and assist in the repair and regeneration of the muscle.
- Deep indentations in the sarcolemmal surface form a network of narrow tubules that extend into the sarcoplasm. Electrical impulses conducted by the sarcolemma and these **transverse tubules**, or **T tubules**, help stimulate and coordinate muscle contractions.

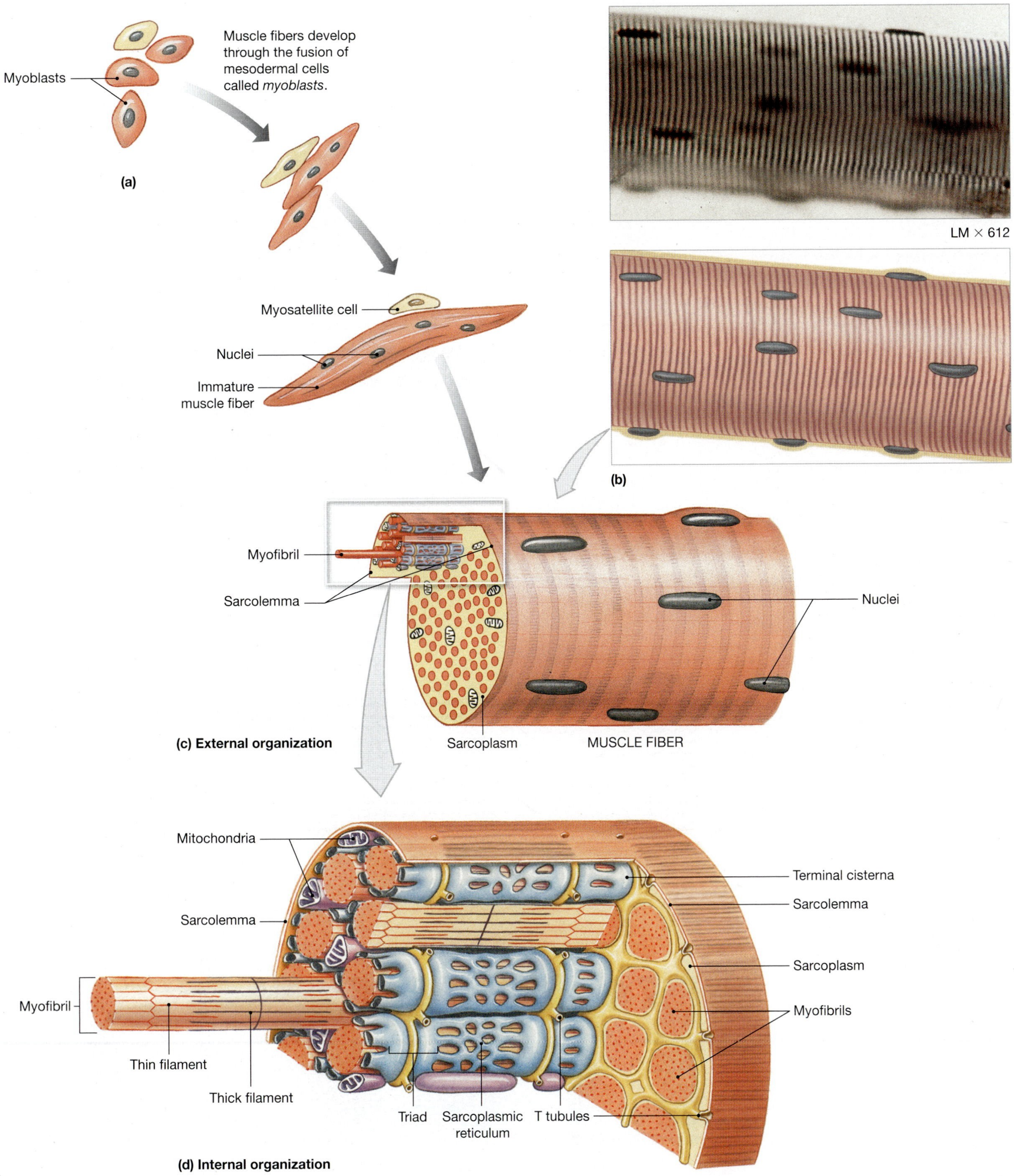

Figure 9.3 The Formation and Structure of a Skeletal Muscle Fiber
(a) Development of a skeletal muscle fiber. **(b)** External appearance and histological view. **(c)** The external organization of a muscle fiber. **(d)** Internal organization. Note the relationships among myofibrils, sarcoplasmic reticulum, mitochondria, triads, and thick and thin filaments.

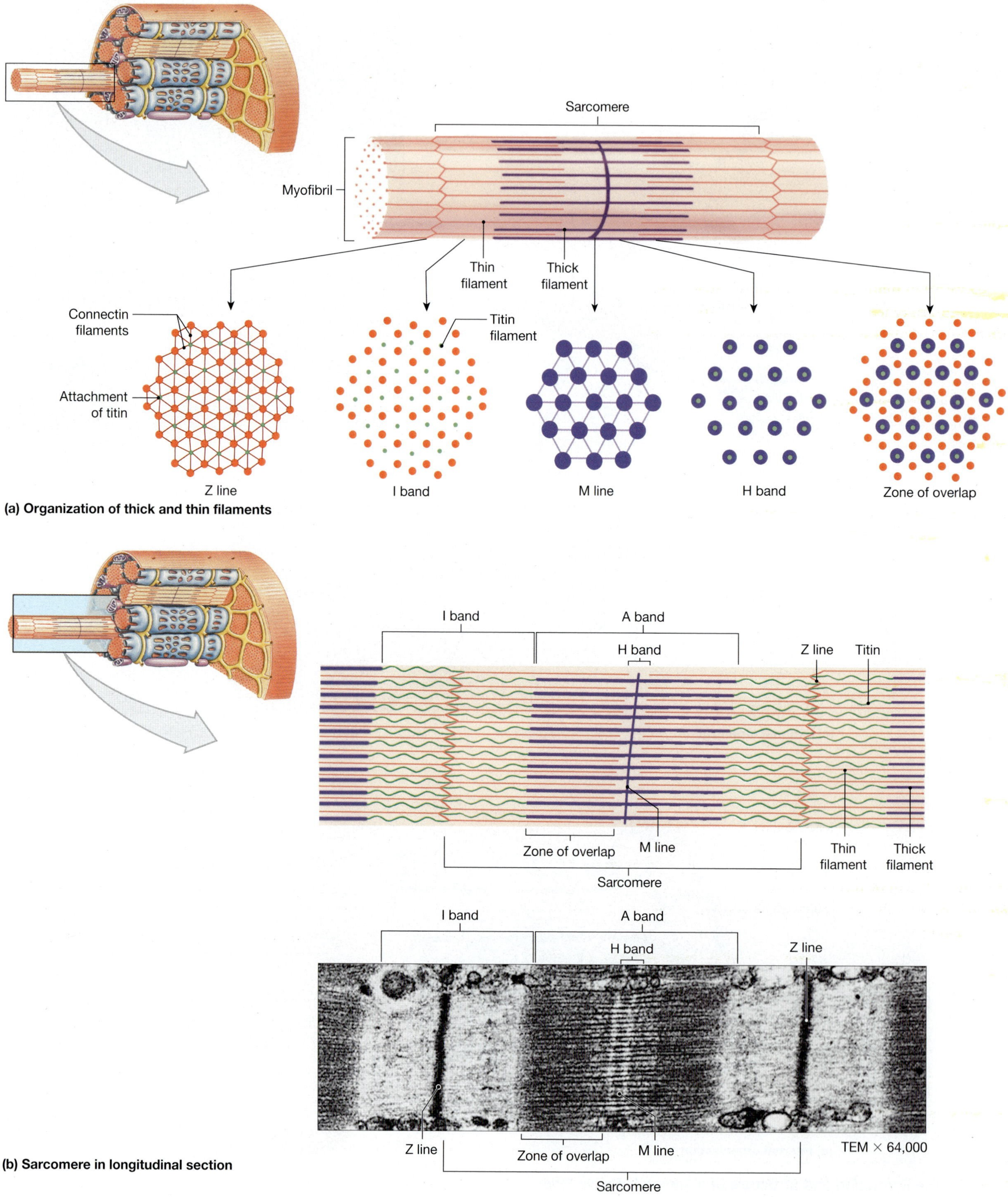

Figure 9.4 Sarcomere Structure
(a) The basic arrangement of thick and thin filaments within a sarcomere and cross-sectional views of each region of the sarcomere. **(b)** A corresponding view of a sarcomere in a myofibril in the gastrocnemius muscle of the calf and a diagram showing the various components of this sarcomere.

Myofibrils and Myofilaments [Figure 9.3c,d]

The sarcoplasm of a skeletal muscle fiber contains hundreds to thousands of **myofibrils**. Each myofibril is a cylindrical structure 1–2 μm in diameter and as long as the entire cell (Figure 9.3c,d). Myofibrils can shorten, and these are the structures responsible for skeletal muscle fiber contraction. Because the myofibrils are attached to the sarcolemma at each end of the cell, their contraction shortens the entire cell.

Surrounding each myofibril is a sleeve made up of membranes of the **sarcoplasmic reticulum (SR)**, a membrane complex similar to the smooth endoplasmic reticulum of other cells (Figure 9.3d). This membrane network, which is closely associated with the transverse tubules, plays an essential role in controlling the contraction of individual myofibrils. On either side of a transverse tubule, the tubules of the SR enlarge, fuse, and form expanded chambers called **terminal cisternae**. The combination of a pair of terminal cisternae plus a transverse tubule is known as a **triad**. Although the membranes of the triad are in close contact and tightly bound together, there is no direct connection between them.

Mitochondria and glycogen granules are scattered among the myofibrils. The breakdown of glycogen and the activity of mitochondria provide the ATP needed to power muscular contractions. A typical skeletal muscle fiber has hundreds of mitochondria, more than most other cells in the body.

Myofibrils consist of bundles of **myofilaments**, protein filaments consisting primarily of the proteins *actin* and *myosin*. The actin filaments are found in *thin filaments*, and the myosin filaments are found in *thick filaments*. ∞ p. 36 The actin and myosin filaments are organized in repeating units called **sarcomeres** (SAR-kō-mērz; *sarkos*, flesh + *meros*, part).

Sarcomere Organization [Figures 9.2/9.3/9.4/9.5]

Thick and thin filaments within a myofibril are organized in the sarcomeres. The arrangement of thick and thin filaments within the sarcomere gives it a banded appearance. All of the myofibrils are arranged parallel to the long axis of the cell, with their sarcomeres lying side by side. As a result, the entire muscle fiber has a banded appearance corresponding to the bands of the individual sarcomeres (see Figures 9.2 and 9.3).

Each myofibril consists of a linear series of approximately 10,000 sarcomeres. Sarcomeres are the smallest functional units of the muscle fiber—interactions between the thick and thin filaments of sarcomeres are responsible for skeletal muscle fiber contractions. Figure 9.4 diagrams the structure of an individual sarcomere. The thick filaments lie in the center of the sarcomere, linked by proteins of the **M line**. Thin filaments at either end of the sarcomere, attached to interconnecting proteins that make up the **Z lines**, extend toward the M line. The Z lines delineate the ends of the sarcomere. In the **zone of overlap**, the thin filaments pass between the thick filaments. Figure 9.4a shows cross sections through different portions of the sarcomere. Note the relative sizes and arrangement of thick and thin filaments at the zone of overlap. Each thin filament sits in a triangle formed by three thick filaments, and each thick filament is surrounded by six thin filaments.

The differences in the size and density of thick filaments and thin filaments account for the banded appearance of the sarcomere. The **A band** is the area containing thick filaments (Figure 9.4b). The A band includes the M line, the **H band** (thick filaments only), and the zone of overlap (thick and thin filaments). The region between the A band and the Z line is part of the **I band**, which contains only thin filaments. From the Z lines at either end of the sarcomere, thin filaments extend into the zone of overlap toward the M line. The terms *A band* and *I band* are derived from *anisotropic* and *isotropic*, which refer to the appearance of these bands when viewed under polarized light. You may find it helpful to remember that A bands are dark and I bands are light. Figure 9.5 reviews the levels of organization we have considered thus far.

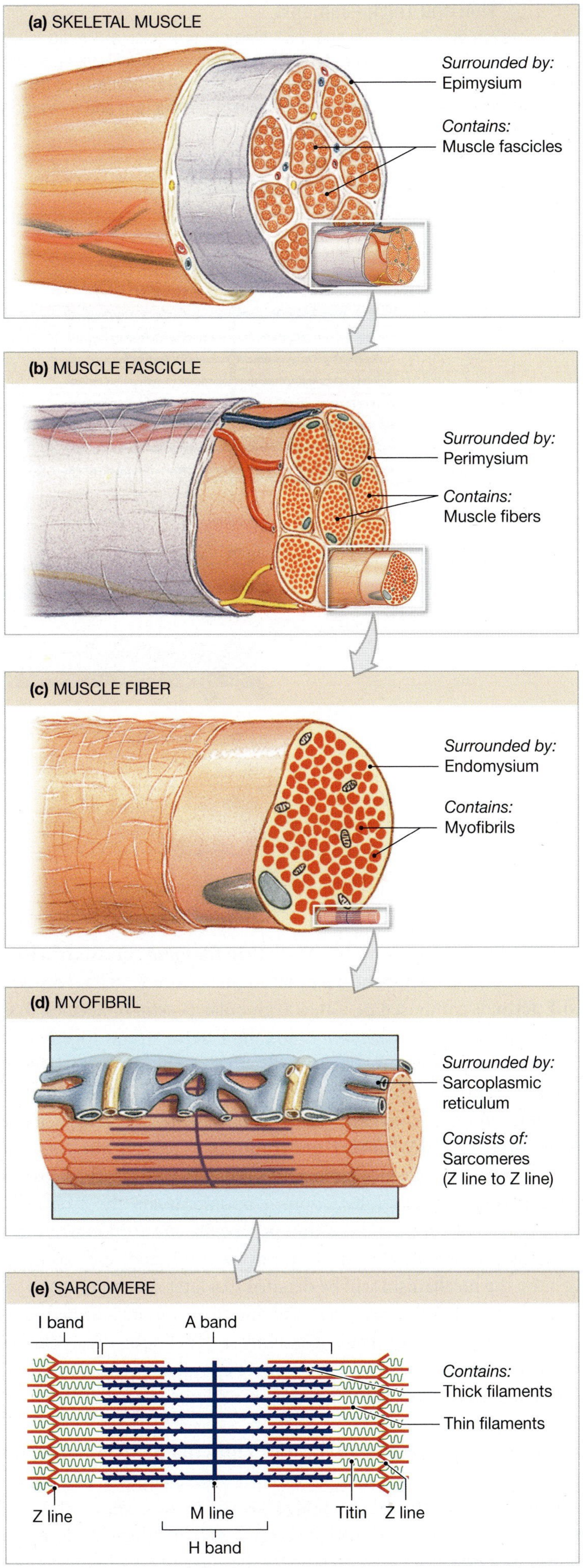

Figure 9.5 Levels of Functional Organization in a Skeletal Muscle Fiber

Figure 9.6 Thin and Thick Filaments
Myofilaments are bundles of thin and thick filament proteins. **(a)** The attachment of thin filaments to the Z line. **(b)** The detailed structure of a thin filament, showing the organization of G actin, troponin, and tropomyosin. **(c)** The structure of thick filaments. **(d)** A single myosin molecule, detailing the structure and movement of the myosin head after cross-bridge binding occurs.

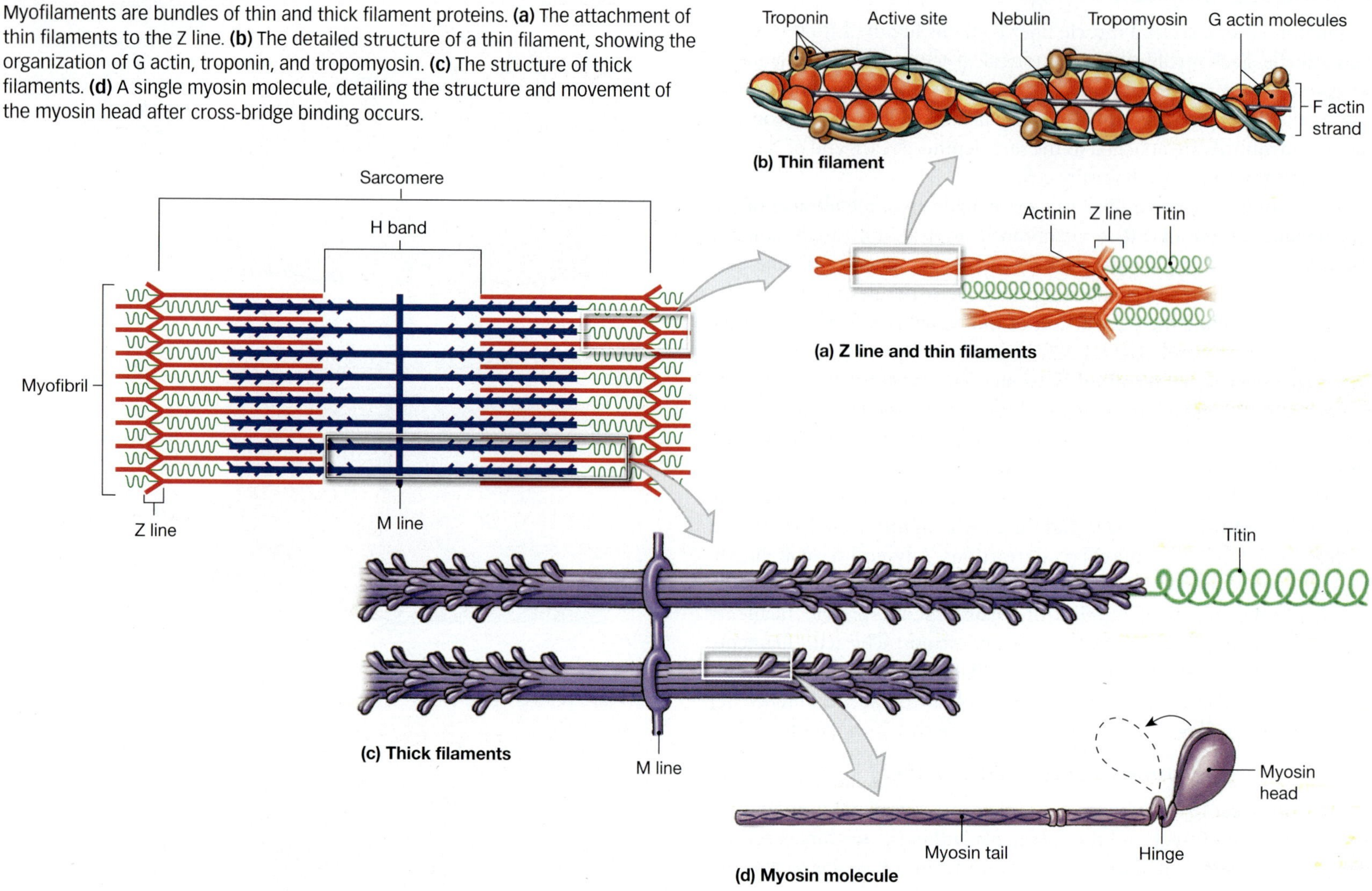

Thin Filaments [Figure 9.6a,b] Each **thin filament** consists of a twisted strand 5–6 nm in diameter and 1 μm in length (Figure 9.6a,b). This strand, called **F actin**, is composed of 300–400 globular *G actin* molecules. A slender strand of the protein *nebulin* holds the F actin strand together. Each molecule of G actin contains an **active site** that can bind to a thick filament in much the same way that a substrate molecule binds to the active site of an enzyme. A thin filament also contains the associated proteins **tropomyosin** (trō-pō-MĪ-ō-sin) and **troponin** (TRŌ-pō-nin; *trope*, turning). Tropomyosin molecules form a long chain that covers the active sites, preventing actin–myosin interaction. Troponin holds the tropomyosin strand in place. Before a contraction can begin, the troponin molecules must change position, moving the tropomyosin molecules and exposing the active sites; the mechanism will be detailed in a later section.

At either end of the sarcomere, the thin filaments are attached to the Z line. Although called a *line* because it looks like a dark line on the surface of the myofibril, in sectional view the Z line is more like an open meshwork created by proteins called *actinins*. For this reason, the Z line is often called the *Z disc*.

Thick Filaments [Figure 9.4a/9.6c,d] **Thick filaments** are 10–12 nm in diameter and 1.6 μm long (Figure 9.6c). They are composed of a bundle of myosin molecules. Each of the roughly 500 myosin molecules within a thick filament consists of a double myosin strand with an attached, elongate *tail* and a free globular *head* (Figure 9.6d). Adjacent thick filaments are interconnected midway along their length by proteins of the M line. The myosin molecules are oriented away from the M line, with the heads projecting outward toward the surrounding thin filaments. Myosin heads are also known as **cross-bridges**, because they connect thick filaments and thin filaments during a contraction.

Each thick filament has a core of *titin* (Figures 9.4a and 9.6c). On either side of the M line, a strand of titin extends the length of the filament and continues past the myosin portion of the thick filament to an attachment at the Z line. The portion of the titin strand exposed within the I band is highly elastic and will recoil after stretching. In the normal resting sarcomere, the titin strands are completely relaxed; they become tense only when some external force stretches the sarcomere. When this occurs, the titin strands help maintain the normal alignment of the thick and thin filaments, and when the tension is removed, the recoil of the titin fibers helps return the sarcomere to its normal resting length.

✓ CONCEPT CHECK

1. Why does skeletal muscle appear striated when viewed with a microscope?
2. What are myofibrils? Where are they found?
3. Myofilaments consist primarily of what proteins?
4. What is the functional unit of skeletal muscle?
5. What two proteins help regulate actin and myosin interaction?

See blue "Answers" tab at back of book.

Muscle Contraction

A contracting muscle fiber exerts a pull, or **tension**, and shortens in length. Muscle fiber contraction results from interactions between the thick and thin filaments in each sarcomere. The mechanism for muscle contraction is explained by the *sliding filament theory*. The trigger for a contraction is the presence of calcium ions (Ca^{2+}), and the contraction itself requires the presence of ATP.

The Sliding Filament Theory [Figures 9.7/9.8]

Direct observation of contracting muscle fibers indicates that in a contraction, (1) the H band and I band get smaller, (2) the zone of overlap gets larger, and (3) the Z lines move closer together, but (4) the width of the A band remains constant throughout the contraction (Figure 9.7). The explanation for these observations is known as the **sliding filament theory**. The sliding filament theory explains the physical changes that occur between thick and thin filaments during contraction.

Sliding occurs when the myosin heads of thick filaments bind to active sites on thin filaments. When cross-bridge binding occurs, the myosin head pivots toward the M line, pulling the thin filament toward the center of the sarcomere. The cross-bridge then detaches and returns to its original position, ready to repeat the cycle of "attach, pivot, detach, and return." When the thick filaments pull on the thin filaments, the Z lines move toward the M line, and the sarcomere shortens.

When many people are pulling on a rope, the amount of tension produced is proportional to the number of people involved. In a muscle fiber, the amount of tension generated during a contraction depends on the number of cross-bridge interactions that occur in the sarcomeres of the myofibrils. The number of cross-bridges is in turn determined by the degree of overlap between thick and thin filaments. Only myosin heads within the zone of overlap can bind to active sites and produce tension. The tension produced by the muscle fiber can therefore be related directly to the structure of an individual sarcomere (Figure 9.8). At optimal lengths the muscle fiber develops maximum tension (Figure 9.8c). The normal range of sarcomere lengths is from 75 to 130 percent of this optimal length. During normal movements, our muscle fibers perform over a broad range of

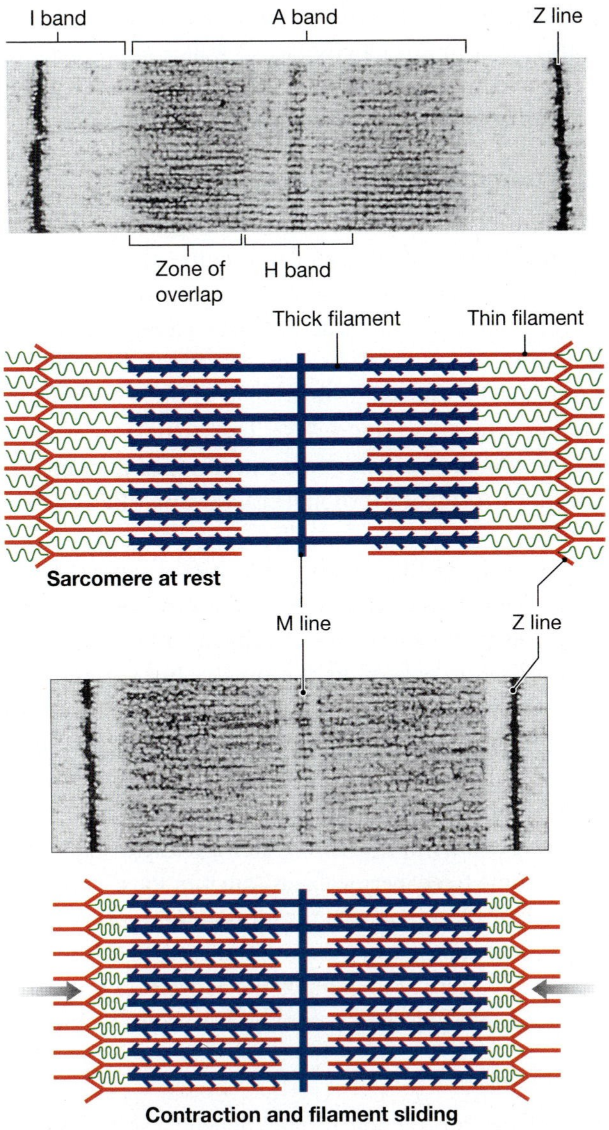

Figure 9.7 Changes in the Appearance of a Sarcomere during Contraction of a Skeletal Muscle Fiber
During a contraction, the A band stays the same width, but the Z lines move closer together and the I band and H band are reduced in width.

Figure 9.8 The Effect of Sarcomere Length on Tension
If sarcomeres are too short or too long, the efficiency of contraction is affected. When the sarcomeres are too short, contraction cannot occur, because either **(a)** the thick filaments come in contact with the Z lines or **(b)** the thin filaments overlap across the center of the sarcomere. **(c)** The tension produced by a contracting skeletal muscle fiber reaches a maximum when the zone of overlap is large, but the thin filaments do not extend across the center of the sarcomere. If the sarcomeres are stretched too far, the zone of overlap is reduced **(d)** or disappears **(e)**, and the cross-bridge interactions are reduced or cannot occur.

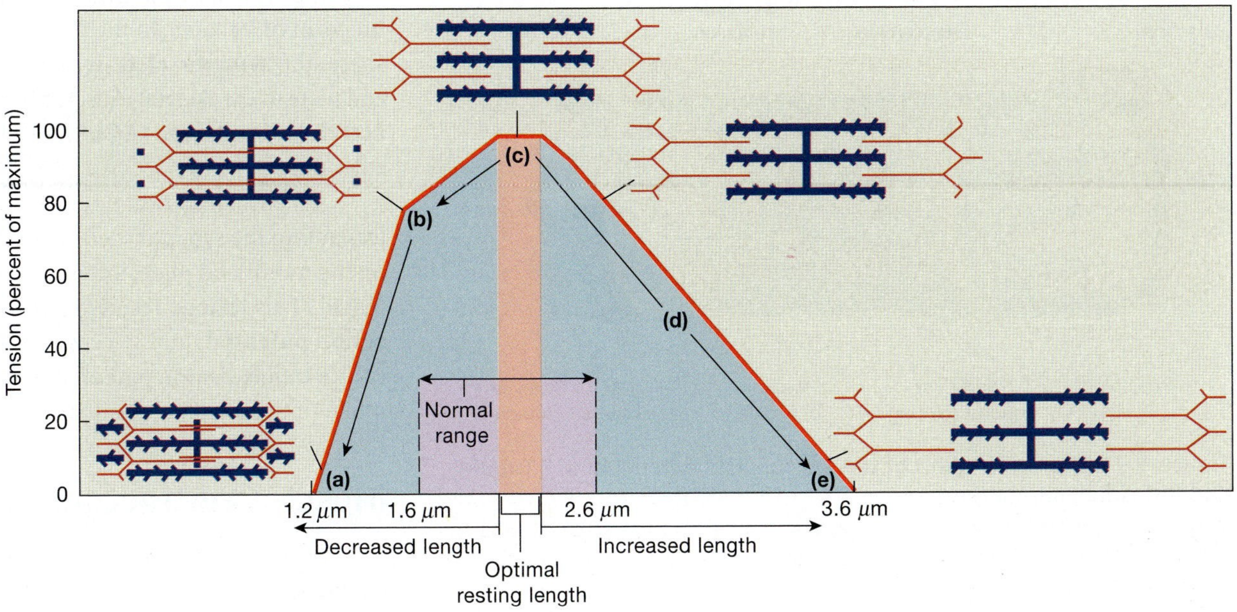

intermediate lengths, and the tension produced therefore varies from moment to moment. During an activity such as walking, in which muscles contract and relax in a cyclical fashion, muscle fibers are stretched to a length very close to optimal before they are stimulated to contract.

The Start of a Contraction [Figures 9.3d/9.9]

The immediate trigger for contraction is the appearance of free calcium ions in the sarcoplasm. The intracellular calcium ion concentration is usually very low. In most cells, this is because any calcium ions entering the cytoplasm are immediately pumped across their cell membranes and into the extracellular fluid. Although skeletal muscle fibers do pump Ca^{2+} out of the cell in this way, they also transport them into the terminal cisternae of the sarcoplasmic reticulum (**Figure 9.9**). The sarcoplasm of a resting skeletal muscle fiber contains very low concentrations of calcium ions, but the Ca^{2+} concentration inside the terminal cisternae may be as much as 40,000 times higher.

Electrical events at the sarcolemmal surface cause a contraction by triggering the release of calcium ions from the terminal cisternae. The electrical "message," or impulse, is distributed by the transverse tubules that extend deep into the sarcoplasm of the muscle fiber. A transverse tubule begins at the sarcolemma and travels inward at right angles to the membrane surface (**Figure 9.3d**, p. 241). Along the way, branches from the transverse tubule encircle each of the individual sarcomeres at the boundary between the A band and the I band.

When an electrical impulse travels along a nearby T tubule, the terminal cisternae become freely permeable to calcium ions. These calcium ions diffuse into the zone of overlap, where they bind to troponin. This results in a change in the shape of the troponin molecule, and this alters the position of the tropomyosin strand and exposes the active sites on the actin molecules. Cross-bridge binding then occurs, and the contraction begins.

The End of a Contraction

The duration of the contraction usually depends on the duration of the electrical stimulation. The change in calcium permeability at the terminal cisternae is only temporary, so if the contraction is to continue, additional electrical impulses must be conducted along the T tubules. If the electrical stimulation ceases, the sarcoplasmic reticulum will recapture the calcium ions, the troponin–tropomyosin complex will cover the active sites, and the contraction will end.

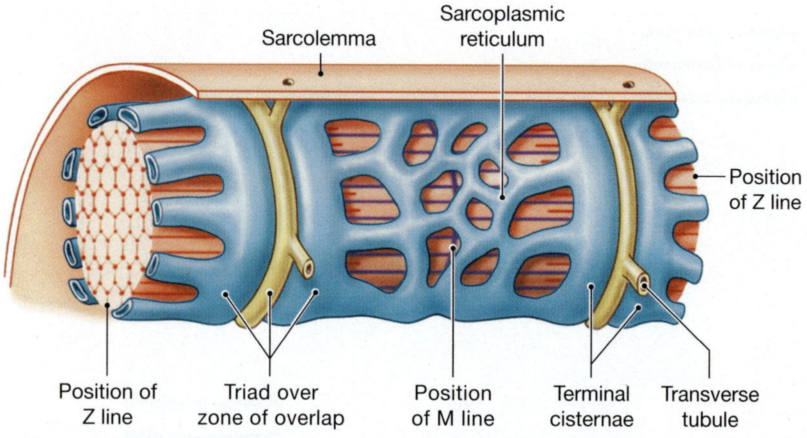

Figure 9.9 The Orientation of the Sarcoplasmic Reticulum, T Tubules, and Individual Sarcomeres
A triad occurs where a T tubule encircles a sarcomere between two terminal cisternae. Compare with *Figure 9.3d*; note that triads occur at the zones of overlap.

The binding and breakdown of ATP is what "cocks" the myosin head and prepares it for binding to an active site on actin. Once a cross-bridge has formed, the myosin head pivots and pulls the thin filament toward the center of the sarcomere. Another ATP must now bind to the myosin head before it will detach and re-cock for another cycle. Thus, even with continued stimulation, muscle fibers will eventually stop contracting as they run out of ATP. Each myosin head may cycle five times each second, and there are hundreds of myosin heads on each thick filament, hundreds of thick filaments in a sarcomere, thousands of sarcomeres in a myofibril, and hundreds to thousands of myofibrils in each muscle fiber. In other words, a muscle fiber contraction consumes enormous amounts of ATP!

Although muscle contraction is an active process, the return to resting length is entirely passive. Muscles cannot push; they can only pull. Factors that help return a shortened muscle to its normal resting length include elastic forces (such as the recoil of elastic fibers in the epimysium, perimysium, and endomysium), the pull of other muscles, and gravity.

The Neural Control of Muscle Fiber Contraction [Figures 9.2/9.10]

The basic sequence of events in the process can be summarized as follows:

1. Chemicals released by the motor neuron at the neuromuscular synapse alter the transmembrane potential of the sarcolemma. This change sweeps across the surface of the sarcolemma and into the transverse tubules.
2. The change in the transmembrane potential of the T tubules triggers the release of calcium ions by the sarcoplasmic reticulum. This release initiates the contraction, as detailed previously.

Each skeletal muscle fiber is controlled by a *motor neuron* whose cell body is located inside the central nervous system. p. 77 The axon of this motor neuron extends into the periphery to reach the neuromuscular synapse of that muscle fiber. The general appearance of a neuromuscular synapse was shown in **Figure 9.2**, p. 240. **Figure 9.10** provides additional details. The expanded tip of the axon at the neuromuscular synapse is called the **synaptic terminal**. The cytoplasm of the synaptic terminal contains numerous mitochondria and small secretory vesicles, called **synaptic vesicles**, filled with molecules of **acetylcholine (ACh)** (as-e-til-KŌ-lēn).

Acetylcholine is an example of a *neurotransmitter*, a chemical released by a neuron to communicate with another cell. That communication takes the form of a change in the transmembrane potential of that cell. A narrow space, the **synaptic cleft**, separates the synaptic terminal from the motor end plate of the skeletal muscle fiber. The synaptic cleft contains the enzyme **acetylcholinesterase (AChE)**, or *cholinesterase*, which breaks down molecules of ACh.

When an electrical impulse arrives at the synaptic terminal, ACh is released into the synaptic cleft. The ACh released then binds to receptor sites on the motor end plate, initiating a change in the local transmembrane potential. This change results in the generation of an electrical impulse, or **action potential**, that sweeps over the surface of the sarcolemma and into each T tubule. Action potentials will continue to be generated, one after another, until acetylcholinesterase removes the bound ACh.

Muscle Contraction: A Summary [Figure 9.11]

The entire sequence of events from neural activation to the completion of a contraction is visually summarized in **Figure 9.11**.

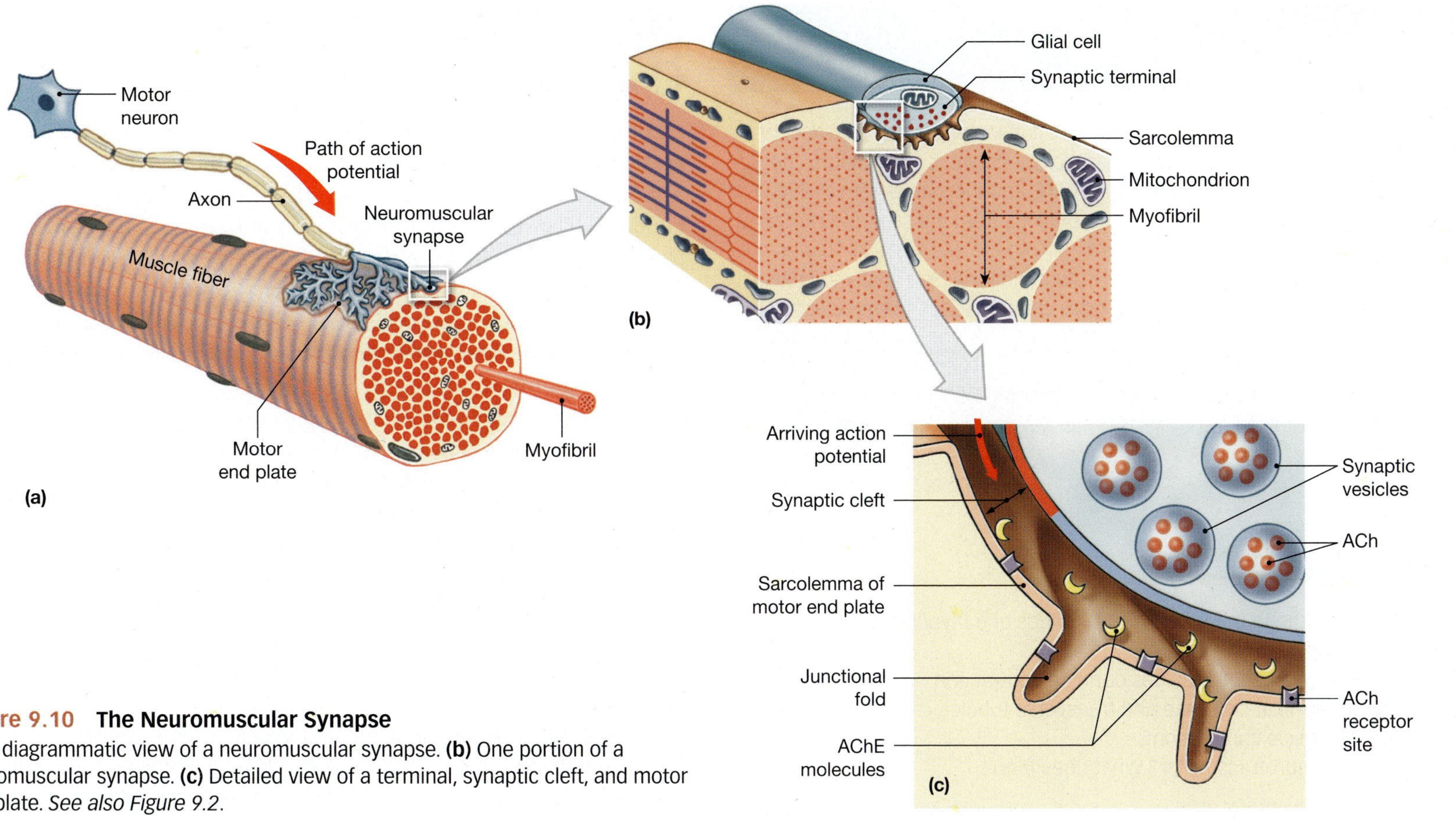

Figure 9.10 The Neuromuscular Synapse
(a) A diagrammatic view of a neuromuscular synapse. **(b)** One portion of a neuromuscular synapse. **(c)** Detailed view of a terminal, synaptic cleft, and motor end plate. *See also Figure 9.2.*

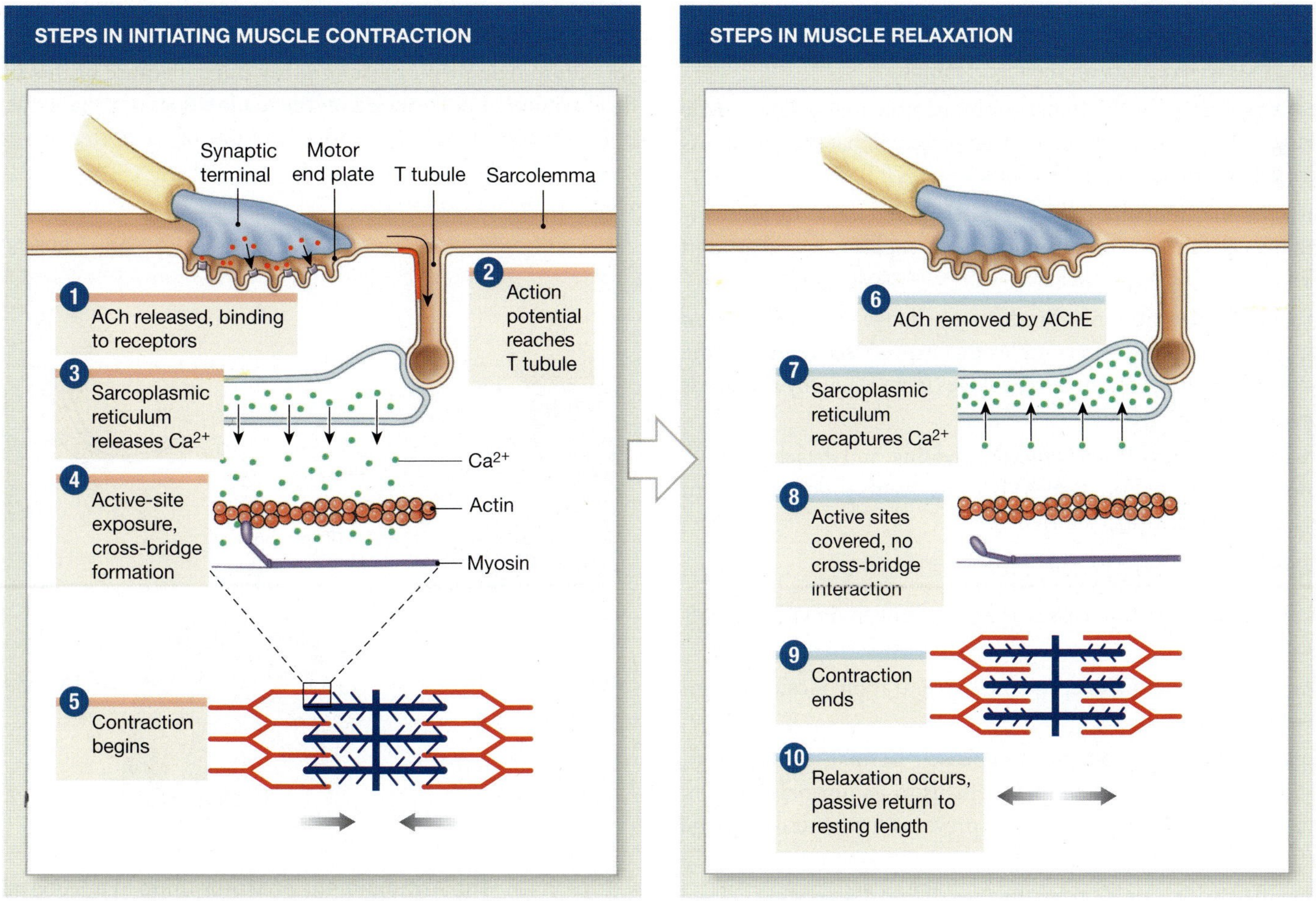

Figure 9.11 The Events in Muscle Contraction
A summary of the sequence of events in a muscle contraction.

Clinical Note

Rigor Mortis When death occurs, circulation ceases and the skeletal muscles are deprived of nutrients and oxygen. Within a few hours, the skeletal muscle fibers have run out of ATP, and the sarcoplasmic reticulum becomes unable to remove calcium ions from the sarcoplasm. Calcium ions diffusing into the sarcoplasm from the extracellular fluid or leaking out of the sarcoplasmic reticulum then trigger a sustained contraction. Without ATP, the cross-bridges cannot detach from the active sites, and the muscle locks in the contracted position. All of the body's skeletal muscles are involved, and the individual becomes "stiff as a board." This physical state, called **rigor mortis**, lasts until the lysosomal enzymes released by autolysis break down the myofilaments 15–25 hours later.

CONCEPT CHECK

1. What happens to the A bands and I bands of a myofibril during a contraction?
2. List the sequence of activities during a contraction.
3. How do terminal cisternae and transverse tubules interact to cause a skeletal muscle contraction?
4. What is a neurotransmitter? What does it do?

See blue "Answers" tab at back of book.

Key steps in the initiation of a contraction include the following:

1. At the neuromuscular synapse (NMS), ACh released by the synaptic terminal binds to receptors on the sarcolemma.
2. The resulting change in the transmembrane potential of the muscle fiber leads to the production of an action potential that spreads across its entire surface and along the T tubules.
3. The sarcoplasmic reticulum (SR) releases stored calcium ions, increasing the calcium concentration of the sarcoplasm in and around the sarcomeres.
4. Calcium ions bind to troponin, producing a change in the orientation of the troponin–tropomyosin complex that exposes active sites on the thin (actin) filaments. Myosin cross-bridges form when myosin heads bind to active sites.
5. Repeated cycles of cross-bridge binding, pivoting, and detachment occur, powered by the hydrolysis of ATP. These events produce filament sliding, and the muscle fiber shortens.

This process continues for a brief period, until:

6. Action potential generation ceases as ACh is broken down by acetylcholinesterase (AChE).
7. The SR reabsorbs calcium ions, and the concentration of calcium ions in the sarcoplasm declines.
8. When calcium ion concentrations approach normal resting levels, the troponin–tropomyosin complex returns to its normal position. This change covers the active sites and prevents further cross-bridge interaction.
9. Without cross-bridge interactions, further sliding does not take place, and the contraction ends.
10. Muscle relaxation occurs, and the muscle fiber returns passively to resting length.

Motor Units and Muscle Control [Figure 9.12]

All of the muscle fibers controlled by a single motor neuron constitute a **motor unit**. A typical skeletal muscle contains thousands of muscle fibers. Although some motor neurons control a single muscle fiber, most control hundreds. The size of a motor unit is an indication of how fine the control of movement can be. In the muscles of the eye, where precise control is extremely important, a motor neuron may control two or three muscle fibers. We have much less precise control over power-generating muscles, such as our leg muscles, where up to 2000 muscle fibers may be controlled by a single motor neuron.

A skeletal muscle contracts when its motor units are stimulated. The amount of tension produced depends on two factors: (1) the frequency of stimulation and (2) the number of motor units involved. A single, momentary contraction is called a **muscle twitch**. A twitch is the response to a single stimulus. As the rate of stimulation increases, tension production will rise to a peak and plateau at maximal levels. Most muscle contractions involve this type of stimulation.

Each muscle fiber either contracts completely or does not contract at all. This characteristic is called the *all or none principle.* All of the fibers in a motor unit contract at the same time, and the amount of force exerted by the muscle as a whole thus depends on how many motor units are activated. By varying the number of motor units activated at any one time, the nervous system provides precise control over the pull exerted by a muscle.

When a decision is made to perform a movement, specific groups of motor neurons are stimulated. The stimulated neurons do not respond simultaneously, and over time, the number of activated motor units gradually increases. Figure 9.12 shows how the muscle fibers of each motor unit are intermingled with those of other units. Because of this intermingling, the direction of pull exerted on the tendon does not change as more motor units are activated, but the total amount of force steadily increases. The

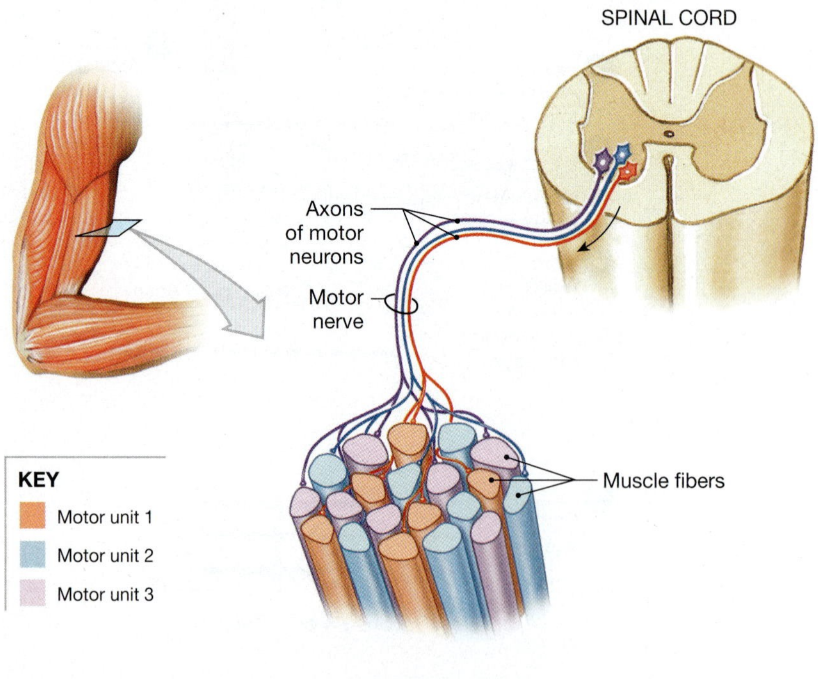

Figure 9.12 The Arrangement of Motor Units in a Skeletal Muscle
Muscle fibers of different motor units are intermingled, so that the net distribution of force applied to the tendon remains constant even when individual muscle groups cycle between contraction and relaxation. The number of muscle fibers in a motor unit ranges from as few as one to more than 2000.

smooth but steady increase in muscular tension produced by increasing the number of active motor units is called **recruitment**, or **multiple motor unit summation**.

Peak tension occurs when all of the motor units in the muscle are contracting at the maximal rate of stimulation. However, such powerful contractions cannot last long, because the individual muscle fibers soon use up their available energy reserves. To lessen the onset of fatigue during periods of sustained contraction, motor units are activated on a rotating basis, so that some of them are resting and recovering while others are actively contracting.

Muscle Tone

Even when a muscle is at rest, some motor units are always active. Their contractions do not produce enough tension to cause movement, but they do tense the muscle. This resting tension in a skeletal muscle is called **muscle tone**. Motor units are randomly stimulated, so that there is a constant tension in the attached tendon but individual muscle fibers can have some time to relax. Resting muscle tone stabilizes the position of bones and joints. For example, in muscles involved with balance and posture, enough motor units are stimulated to produce the tension needed to maintain body position. Specialized muscle cells called **muscle spindles** are monitored by sensory nerves that control the muscle tone in the surrounding muscle tissue. Reflexes triggered by activity in these sensory nerves play an important role in the reflex control of position and posture, a topic that we will discuss in Chapter 14.

Muscle Hypertrophy

Exercise increases the activity of muscle spindles and may enhance muscle tone. As a result of repeated, exhaustive stimulation, muscle fibers develop a larger number of mitochondria, a higher concentration of glycolytic enzymes, and larger glycogen reserves. These muscle fibers have more myofibrils, and each myofibril contains a larger number of thick and thin filaments. The net effect is an enlargement, or **hypertrophy** (hī-PER-trō-fē), of the stimulated muscle. Hypertrophy occurs in muscles that have been repeatedly stimulated to produce near-maximal tension; the intracellular changes that occur increase the amount of tension produced when these muscles contract. A champion weight lifter or bodybuilder is an excellent example of hypertrophied muscular development.

Muscle Atrophy

When a skeletal muscle is not stimulated by a motor neuron on a regular basis, it loses muscle tone and mass. The muscle becomes flaccid and the muscle fibers become smaller and weaker. This reduction in muscle size, tone, and power is called **atrophy**. Individuals paralyzed by spinal injuries or other damage to the nervous system will gradually lose muscle tone and size in the areas affected. Even a temporary reduction in muscle use can lead to muscular atrophy; this loss of tone and size may easily be seen by comparing limb muscles before and after a cast has been worn. Muscle atrophy is initially reversible, but dying muscle fibers are not replaced, and in extreme atrophy the functional losses are permanent. That is why physical therapy is crucial in cases where people are temporarily unable to move normally.

Types of Skeletal Muscle Fibers [Figure 9.13]

Skeletal muscles are designed for various actions. The types of fibers that compose a muscle will, in part, determine its action. There are three major types of skeletal muscle fibers in the body: *fast*, *slow*, and *intermediate*. Fast and slow muscle fibers are shown in **Figure 9.13**. The differences among these groups reflect differences in the way they obtain the ATP to support their contractions.

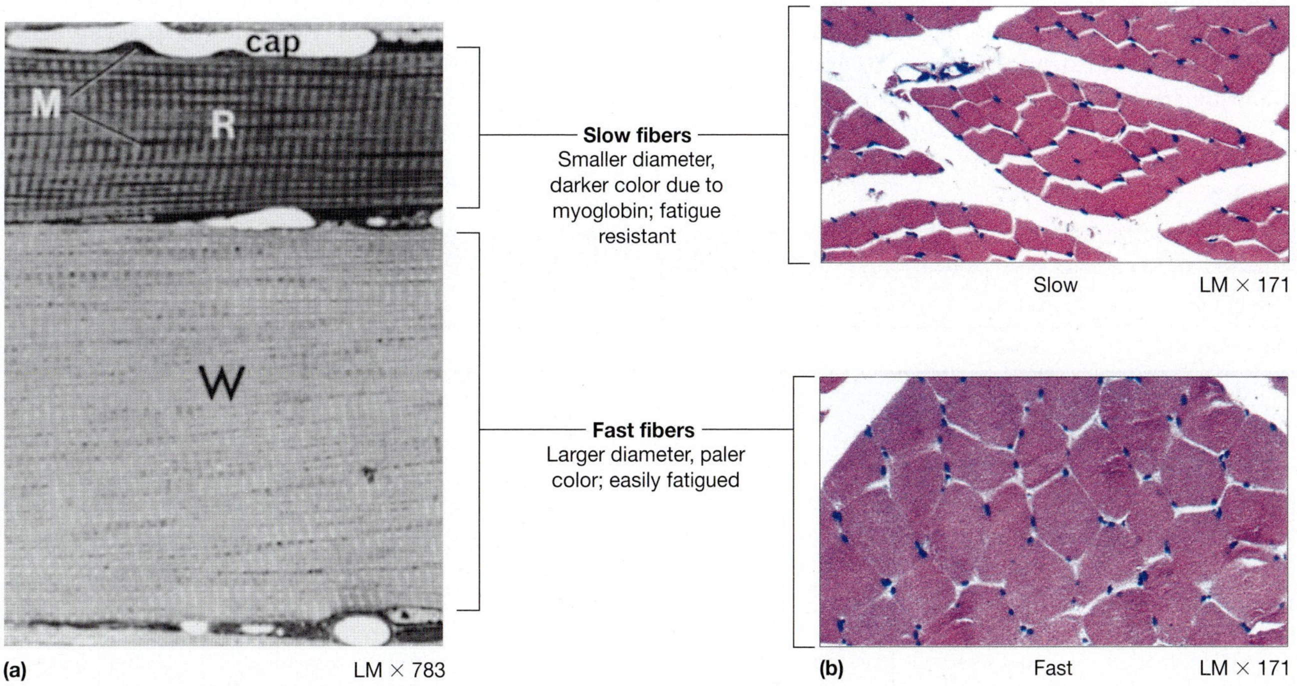

Figure 9.13 Types of Skeletal Muscle Fibers
Fast fibers are for rapid contractions and slow fibers are for slower, but extended contractions. **(a)** The relatively slender slow muscle fiber (R) has more mitochondria (M) and a more extensive capillary supply (cap) than the fast muscle fiber (W). **(b)** Note the difference in the size of slow muscle fibers (above) and fast muscle fibers (below).

Fast fibers, or *white fibers*, are large in diameter; they contain densely packed myofibrils, large glycogen reserves, and relatively few mitochondria. Most of the skeletal muscle fibers in the body are called fast fibers because they can contract in 0.01 seconds or less following stimulation. The tension produced by a muscle fiber is directly proportional to the number of sarcomeres, so fast-fiber muscles produce powerful contractions. However, these contractions use enormous amounts of ATP, and their mitochondria are unable to meet the demand. As a result, their contractions are supported primarily by *anaerobic* (*an*, without + *aer*, air + *bios*, life) *glycolysis*. This reaction pathway, which does not require oxygen, converts stored glycogen to lactic acid. Fast fibers fatigue rapidly, both because their glycogen reserves are limited and because lactic acid builds up, and the acid pH interferes with the contraction mechanism.

Slow fibers, or *red fibers*, are only about half the diameter of fast fibers, and they take three times as long to contract after stimulation. Slow fibers are specialized to continue contracting for extended periods, long after a fast muscle would have become fatigued. They can do so because their mitochondria are able to continue producing ATP throughout the contraction. As you will recall from Chapter 2, mitochondria absorb oxygen and generate ATP. The reaction pathway involved is called *aerobic metabolism*. The oxygen required comes from two sources:

1. Skeletal muscles containing slow muscle fibers have a more extensive network of capillaries than do muscles dominated by fast muscle fibers. This means that there is greater blood flow, and the red blood cells can deliver more oxygen to the active muscle fibers.
2. Slow fibers are red because they contain the red pigment **myoglobin** (MĪ-ō-glō-bin). This globular protein is structurally related to hemoglobin, the oxygen-binding pigment found in red blood cells. Myoglobin binds oxygen molecules as well. Thus, resting slow muscle fibers contain substantial oxygen reserves that can be mobilized during a contraction.

Slow muscles also contain a relatively larger number of mitochondria than do fast muscle fibers. Whereas fast muscle fibers must rely on their glycogen reserves during peak levels of activity, the mitochondria in slow muscles can break down carbohydrates, lipids, or even proteins. They can therefore continue to contract for extended periods; for example, the leg muscles of marathon runners are dominated by slow muscle fibers.

Intermediate fibers have properties intermediate between those of fast fibers and slow fibers. For example, intermediate fibers contract faster than slow fibers but slower than fast fibers. Histologically, intermediate fibers are very similar to fast fibers, although they have more mitochondria, a slightly increased capillary supply, and a greater resistance to fatigue.

The properties of the various types of skeletal muscles are detailed in Table 9.1.

Distribution of Fast, Slow, and Intermediate Fibers

The percentage of fast, slow, and intermediate muscle fibers varies from one skeletal muscle to another. Most muscles contain a mixture of fiber types, although all of the fibers within one motor unit are of the same type. However, there are no slow fibers in muscles of the eye and hand, where swift but brief contractions are required. Many back and calf muscles are dominated by slow fibers; these muscles contract almost continually to maintain an upright posture.

The percentage of fast versus slow fibers in each muscle is genetically determined, and there are significant individual differences. These variations have an effect on endurance. A person with more slow muscle fibers in a particular muscle will be better able to perform repeated contractions under aerobic conditions. For example, marathon runners with high proportions of slow muscle fibers in their leg muscles outperform those with more fast muscle fibers. For brief periods of intense activity, such as a sprint or a weight-lifting event, the individual with a higher percentage of fast muscle fibers will have the advantage.

The characteristics of the muscle fibers change with physical conditioning. Repeated, intense workouts promote the enlargement of fast muscle fibers and muscular hypertrophy. Training for endurance events, such as cross-country or marathon running, increases the proportion of intermediate fibers in the active muscles. This occurs through the gradual conversion of fast fibers to intermediate fibers.

Endurance training does not promote hypertrophy, and many athletes train using a combination of aerobic activity, such as swimming, with anaerobic activities, such as weight lifting or sprinting. This combination, known as *interval training*, enlarges muscles and improves strength and endurance.

TABLE 9.1 Properties of Skeletal Muscle Fiber Types

Property	Slow	Intermediate	Fast
Cross-sectional diameter	Small	Intermediate	Large
Tension	Low	Intermediate	High
Contraction speed	Slow	Fast	Fast
Fatigue resistance	High	Intermediate	Low
Color	Red	Pink	White
Myoglobin content	High	Low	Low
Capillary supply	Dense	Intermediate	Scarce
Mitochondria	Many	Intermediate	Few
Glycolytic enzyme concentration in sarcoplasm	Low	High	High
Substrates used for ATP generation during contraction	Lipids, carbohydrates, amino acids (aerobic)	Primarily carbohydrates (anaerobic)	Carbohydrates (anaerobic)
Alternative names	Type I, S (slow), red, SO (slow oxidizing), slow-twitch oxidative	Type II-A, FR (fast resistant), fast-twitch oxidative	Type II-B, FF (fast fatigue), white, fast-twitch glycolytic

Clinical Note

Delayed-Onset Muscle Soreness You have probably experienced muscle soreness the day after a period of physical exertion. Considerable controversy exists over the source and significance of this pain, which is known as *delayed-onset muscle soreness (DOMS)* and has several interesting characteristics:

- DOMS is distinct from the soreness you experience immediately after you stop exercising. The initial short-term soreness is probably related to the biochemical events associated with muscle fatigue.
- DOMS generally begins several hours after the exercise period ends and may last three or four days.
- The amount of DOMS is highest when the activity involves eccentric contractions. Activities dominated by concentric or isometric contractions produce less soreness.
- Levels of CPK and myoglobin are elevated in the blood, indicating damage to muscle sarcolemmae. The nature of the activity (eccentric, concentric, or isometric) has no effect on these levels, nor can the levels be used to predict the degree of soreness experienced.

Three mechanisms have been proposed to explain DOMS:

1. Small tears may exist in the muscle tissue, leaving muscle fibers with damaged membranes. The sarcolemma of each damaged muscle fiber permits the loss of enzymes, myoglobin, and other chemicals that may stimulate nearby pain receptors.
2. The pain may result from muscle spasms in the affected skeletal muscles. In some studies, stretching the muscle involved after exercise reduced the degree of soreness.
3. The pain may result from tears in the connective tissue framework and tendons of the skeletal muscle.

Some evidence supports each of these mechanisms, but it is unlikely that any one tells the entire story. For example, muscle fiber damage is certainly supported by biochemical findings, but if that were the only factor, the type of activity and the level of intracellular enzymes in the circulation would be correlated with the level of pain experienced, and this is not the case.

CONCEPT CHECK

1. Why does a sprinter experience muscle fatigue after a few minutes, while a marathon runner can run for hours?
2. What type of muscle fibers would you expect to predominate in the large leg muscles of someone who excels at endurance activities such as cycling or long-distance running?
3. Why do some motor units control only a few muscle fibers, whereas others control many fibers?
4. What is recruitment?

See blue "Answers" tab at back of book.

The Organization of Skeletal Muscle Fibers [Figures 9.1/9.14]

Although most skeletal muscle fibers contract at comparable rates and shorten to the same degree, variations in microscopic and macroscopic organization can dramatically affect the power, range, and speed of movement produced when a muscle contracts.

Muscle fibers within a skeletal muscle form bundles called *fascicles* (**Figure 9.1**, p. 239). The muscle fibers of each fascicle lie parallel to one another, but the organization of the fascicles in the skeletal muscle can vary, as can the relationship between the fascicles and the associated tendon. Four different patterns of fascicle arrangement or organization produce *parallel muscles*, *convergent muscles*, *pennate muscles*, and *circular muscles*. **Figure 9.14** illustrates the fascicle organization of skeletal muscle fibers.

Parallel Muscles [Figure 9.14a]

In a **parallel muscle**, the fascicles are parallel to the long axis of the muscle. The functional characteristics of a parallel muscle resemble those of an individual muscle fiber. Consider the skeletal muscle shown in **Figure 9.14a**. It has a firm attachment by a tendon that extends from the free tip to a movable bone of the skeleton. Most of the skeletal muscles in the body are parallel muscles. Some form flat bands, with broad aponeuroses at each end; others are spindle shaped, with cordlike tendons at one or both ends. Such a muscle has a central **body**, also known as the *belly*, or *gaster* (GAS-ter; *gaster*, stomach). When this muscle contracts, it gets shorter and the body increases in diameter. The *biceps brachii muscle* of the arm is an example of a parallel muscle with a central body. The bulge of the contracting biceps can be seen on the anterior surface of the arm when the elbow is flexed.

A skeletal muscle cell can contract effectively until it has been shortened by roughly 30 percent. Because the muscle fibers are parallel to the long axis of the muscle, when they contract together, the entire muscle shortens by the same amount. For example, if the skeletal muscle is 10 cm long, the end of the tendon will move 3 cm when the muscle contracts. The tension developed by the muscle during this contraction depends on the total number of myofibrils it contains. Because the myofibrils are distributed evenly through the sarcoplasm of each cell, the tension can be estimated on the basis of the cross-sectional area of the resting muscle. A parallel skeletal muscle 6.45 cm^2 (1 in^2) in cross-sectional area can develop approximately 23 kg (50 lb) of tension.

Convergent Muscles [Figure 9.14b]

In a **convergent muscle**, the muscle fibers are based over a broad area, but all the fibers come together at a common attachment site. They may pull on a tendon, a tendinous sheet, or a slender band of collagen fibers known as a **raphe** (RĀ-fē; seam). The muscle fibers often spread out, like a fan or a broad triangle, with a tendon at the tip, as shown in **Figure 9.14b**. The prominent *pectoralis muscles* of the chest have this shape. This type of muscle has versatility; the direction of pull can be changed by stimulating only one group of muscle cells at any one time. However, when they all contract at once, they do not pull as hard on the tendon as a parallel muscle of the same size because the muscle fibers on opposite sides of the tendon pull in different directions rather than all pulling in the same direction.

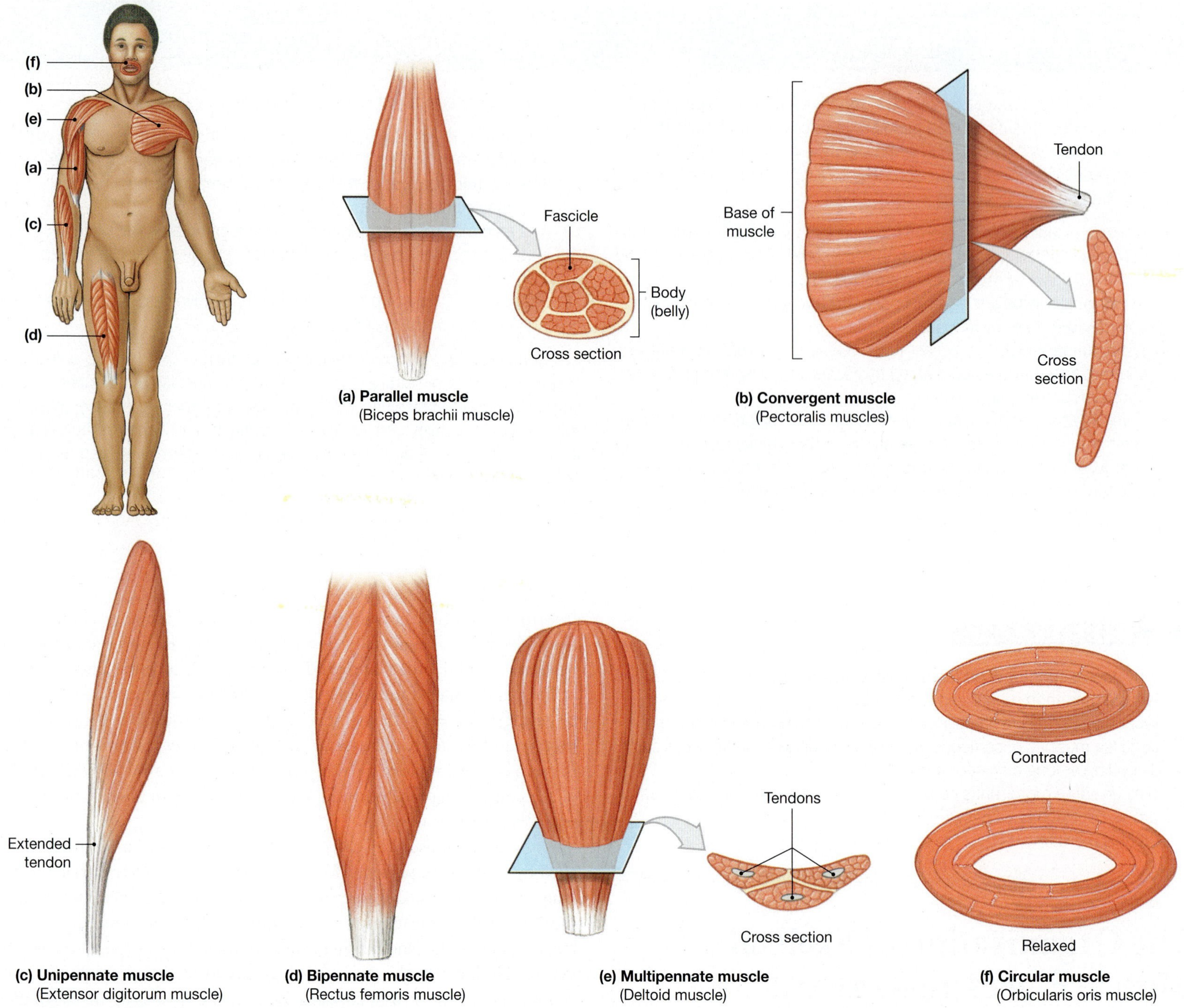

Figure 9.14 Skeletal Muscle Fiber Organization
Four different arrangements of muscle fiber patterns are observed: **(a)** parallel, **(b)** convergent, **(c, d, e)** pennate, and **(f)** circular.

Pennate Muscles [Figure 9.14c–e]

In a **pennate muscle** (*penna*, feather), one or more tendons run through the body of the muscle, and the fascicles form an oblique angle to the tendon. Because they pull at an angle, contracting pennate muscles do not move their tendons as far as parallel muscles do. However, a pennate muscle will contain more muscle fibers than a parallel muscle of the same size, and as a result, the contraction of the pennate muscle generates more tension than that of a parallel muscle of the same size.

If all of the muscle cells are found on the same side of the tendon, the muscle is **unipennate** (Figure 9.14c). A long muscle that extends the fingers, the *extensor digitorum muscle*, is an example of a unipennate muscle. More commonly, there are muscle fibers on both sides of the tendon. A prominent muscle of the thigh, the *rectus femoris muscle*, is a **bipennate muscle** (Figure 9.14d) that helps extend the knee. If the tendon branches within the muscle, the muscle is multipennate (Figure 9.14e). The triangular *deltoid muscle* that covers the superior surface of the shoulder joint is an example of a **multipennate muscle**.

Circular Muscles [Figure 9.14f]

In a **circular muscle**, or **sphincter** (SFINK-ter), the fibers are concentrically arranged around an opening or recess (Figure 9.14f). When the muscle contracts, the diameter of the opening decreases. Circular muscles guard entrances and exits of internal passageways such as the digestive and urinary tracts. An example is the *orbicularis oris muscle* of the mouth.

Muscle Terminology [Table 9.2]

Each muscle begins at an **origin**, ends at an **insertion**, and contracts to produce a specific **action**. Terms indicating the actions of muscles, specific regions of the body, and structural characteristics of muscle are presented in Table 9.2.

Origins and Insertions

Typically, the origin remains stationary and the insertion moves, or the origin is proximal to the insertion. For example, the triceps inserts on the olecranon and originates closer to the shoulder. Such determinations are made during normal movement with the individual in the anatomical position. Part of the fun of studying the muscular system is that you can actually do the movements and think about the muscles involved. (Laboratory discussions of the muscular system often resemble a poorly organized aerobics class.)

When the origins and insertions cannot be determined easily on the basis of movement or position, other criteria are used. If a muscle extends between a broad aponeurosis and a narrow tendon, the aponeurosis is considered to be the origin, and the tendon is attached to the insertion. If there are several tendons at one end and just one at the other, there are multiple origins and a single insertion. These simple rules cannot cover every situation, and knowing which end is the origin and which is the insertion is ultimately less important than knowing where the two ends attach and what the muscle does when it contracts.

Actions

Almost all skeletal muscles either originate or insert on the skeleton. When a muscle moves a portion of the skeleton, that movement may involve *abduction, adduction, flexion, extension, circumduction, rotation, pronation, supination, eversion, inversion, dorsiflexion, plantar flexion, lateral flexion, opposition, protraction, retraction, elevation,* and *depression.* Before proceeding, consider reviewing the discussion of planes of motion and Figures 8.3 to 8.5. pp. 210–212

There are two methods of describing actions. The first references the bone region affected. Thus the biceps brachii muscle is said to perform "flexion of the forearm." The second method specifies the joint involved. Thus, the action of the biceps brachii muscle is described as "flexion of (or at) the elbow." Both methods are valid, and each has its advantages, but we will primarily use the latter method when describing muscle actions in later chapters.

Muscles can be grouped according to their **primary actions** into three types:

1. *Prime movers (agonists):* A **prime mover**, or **agonist**, is a muscle whose contraction is chiefly responsible for producing a particular movement, such as flexion at the elbow. The biceps brachii muscle is an example of a prime mover or agonist producing flexion at the elbow.
2. *Synergists:* When a **synergist** (*syn*-, together + *ergon*, work) contracts, it assists the prime mover in performing that action. Synergists may provide additional pull near the insertion or stabilize the point

TABLE 9.2 Muscle Terminology

Terms Indicating Direction Relative to Axes of the Body	Terms Indicating Specific Regions of the Body*	Terms Indicating Structural Characteristics of the Muscle	Terms Indicating Actions
Anterior (front)	Abdominis (abdomen)	**ORIGIN**	**GENERAL**
Externus (superficial)	Anconeus (elbow)	Biceps (two heads)	Abductor
Extrinsic (outside)	Auricularis (auricle of ear)	Triceps (three heads)	Adductor
Inferioris (inferior)	Brachialis (brachium)	Quadriceps (four heads)	Depressor
Internus (deep, internal)	Capitis (head)	**SHAPE**	Extensor
Intrinsic (inside)	Carpi (wrist)	Deltoid (triangle)	Flexor
Lateralis (lateral)	Cervicis (neck)	Orbicularis (circle)	Levator
Medialis/medius (medial, middle)	Cleido-/-clavius (clavicle)	Pectinate (comblike)	Pronator
Oblique (angular)	Coccygeus (coccyx)	Piriformis (pear-shaped)	Rotator
Posterior (back)	Costalis (ribs)	Platys- (flat)	Supinator
Profundus (deep)	Cutaneous (skin)	Pyramidal (pyramid)	Tensor
Rectus (straight, parallel)	Femoris (femur)	Rhomboideus (rhomboid)	**SPECIFIC**
Superficialis (superficial)	Genio- (chin)	Serratus (serrated)	Buccinator (trumpeter)
Superioris (superior)	Glosso/glossal (tongue)	Splenius (bandage)	Risorius (laugher)
Transversus (transverse)	Hallucis (great toe)	Teres (long and round)	Sartorius (like a tailor)
	Ilio- (ilium)	Trapezius (trapezoid)	
	Inguinal (groin)	**OTHER STRIKING FEATURES**	
	Lumborum (lumbar region)	Alba (white)	
	Nasalis (nose)	Brevis (short)	
	Nuchal (back of neck)	Gracilis (slender)	
	Oculo- (eye)	Lata (wide)	
	Oris (mouth)	Latissimus (widest)	
	Palpebrae (eyelid)	Longissimus (longest)	
	Pollicis (thumb)	Longus (long)	
	Popliteus (behind knee)	Magnus (large)	
	Psoas (loin)	Major (larger)	
	Radialis (radius)	Maximus (largest)	
	Scapularis (scapula)	Minimus (smallest)	
	Temporalis (temples)	Minor (smaller)	
	Thoracis (thoracic region)	-tendinosus (tendinous)	
	Tibialis (tibia)	Vastus (great)	
	Ulnaris (ulna)		
	Uro- (urinary)		

*For other regional terms, refer to Figure 1.8, p. 14, which identifies anatomical landmarks.

of origin. Their importance in assisting a particular movement may change as the movement progresses; in many cases they are most useful at the start, when the prime mover is stretched and its power is relatively low. For example, the *latissimus dorsi muscle* and the *teres major muscle* pull the arm inferiorly. With the arm pointed at the ceiling, the muscle fibers of the massive latissimus dorsi muscle are at maximum stretch, and they are aligned parallel to the humerus. The latissimus dorsi muscle cannot develop much tension in this position. However, the orientation of the teres major muscle, which originates on the scapula, can contract more efficiently, and it assists the latissimus dorsi muscle in starting an inferior movement. The importance of this smaller "assistant" decreases as the inferior movement proceeds. In this example, the latissimus dorsi muscle is the agonist and the teres major muscle is the synergist. Synergists may also assist an agonist by preventing movement at a joint and thereby stabilizing the origin of the agonist. These muscles are called *fixators*.

3. *Antagonists:* **Antagonists** are muscles whose actions oppose that of the agonist; if the agonist produces flexion, the antagonist will produce extension. When an agonist contracts to produce a particular movement, the corresponding antagonist will be stretched, but it will usually not relax completely. Instead, its tension will be adjusted to control the speed of the movement and ensure its smoothness. For example, the biceps brachii muscle acts as an agonist when it contracts, thereby producing flexion of the elbow. The triceps brachii muscle, located on the opposite side of the humerus, acts as an antagonist to stabilize the flexion movement and to produce the opposing action, extension of the elbow.

Names of Skeletal Muscles [Table 9.2]

You will not need to learn every one of the nearly 700 muscles in the human body, but you will have to become familiar with the most important ones. Fortunately, the names of most skeletal muscles provide clues to their identification (Table 9.2). Skeletal muscles are named according to several criteria, including specific body regions, orientation of muscle fibers, specific or unusual features, identification of origin and insertion, and primary functions. The name may indicate a specific region (the *brachialis muscle* of the arm), the shape of the muscle (*trapezius* or *piriformis muscles*), or some combination of the two (*biceps femoris muscle*).

Some names include reference to the orientation of the muscle fibers within a particular skeletal muscle. For example, **rectus** means "straight," and rectus muscles are parallel muscles whose fibers generally run along the long axis of the body. Because there are several rectus muscles, the name usually includes a second term that refers to a precise region of the body. The *rectus abdominis muscle* is found on the abdomen, and the *rectus femoris muscle* on the thigh. Other directional indicators include **transversus** and **oblique** for muscles whose fibers run across or at an oblique angle to the longitudinal axis of the body.

Other muscles were named after specific and unusual structural features. A *biceps* muscle has two tendons of origin (*bi-*, two + *caput*, head), the *triceps* has three, and the *quadriceps* four. Shape is sometimes an important clue to the name of a muscle. For example, the names *trapezius* (tra-PĒ-zē-us), *deltoid*, *rhomboideus* (rom-BOYD-ē-us), and *orbicularis* (or-bik-ū-LA-ris) refer to prominent muscles that look like a trapezoid, a triangle, a rhomboid, and a circle, respectively. Long muscles are called **longus** (long) or **longissimus** (longest), and **teres** muscles are both long and round. Short muscles are called **brevis**; large ones are called **magnus** (big), **major** (bigger), or **maximus** (biggest); and small ones are called **minor** (smaller) or **minimus** (smallest).

Muscles visible at the body surface are external and often called **externus** or **superficialis** (superficial), whereas those lying beneath are internal, termed **internus** or **profundus**. Superficial muscles that position or stabilize an organ are called **extrinsic** muscles; those that operate within the organ are called **intrinsic** muscles.

The names of many muscles identify their origins and insertions. In such cases, the first part of the name indicates the origin and the second part the insertion. For example, the *genioglossus muscle* originates at the chin (*geneion*) and inserts in the tongue (*glossus*).

Names that include *flexor, extensor, retractor*, and so on indicate the primary function of the muscle. These are such common actions that the names almost always include other clues concerning the appearance or location of the muscle. For example, the *extensor carpi radialis longus muscle* is a long muscle found along the radial (lateral) border of the forearm. When it contracts, its primary function is extension at the wrist.

A few muscles are named after the specific movements associated with special occupations or habits. For example, the *sartorius* (sar-TŌR-ē-us) *muscle* is active when crossing the legs. Before sewing machines were invented, a tailor would sit on the floor cross-legged, and the name of the muscle was derived from *sartor*, the Latin word for "tailor." On the face, the *buccinator* (BUK-si-nā-tor) *muscle* compresses the cheeks, as when pursing the lips and blowing forcefully. *Buccinator* translates as "trumpet player." Finally, another facial muscle, the *risorius* (ri-SOR-ē-us) *muscle*, was supposedly named after the mood expressed. However, the Latin term *risor* means "laughter," while a more appropriate description for the effect would be "grimace."

Except for the *platysma* and the *diaphragm*, the complete names of all skeletal muscles include the term *muscle*. Although we will generally use the full name of the muscle in the text, to save space and reduce clutter we will use only the descriptive portion of the name in the accompanying figures (*triceps brachii*, instead of *triceps brachii muscle*).

Levers and Pulleys: A Systems Design for Movement [Figures 9.15/9.16]

Skeletal muscles do not work in isolation. When a muscle is attached to the skeleton, the nature and site of the connection will determine the force, speed, and range of the movement produced. These characteristics are interdependent, and the relationships can explain a great deal about the general organization of the muscular and skeletal systems.

Classes of Levers [Figure 9.15]

The force, speed, or direction of movement produced by contraction of a muscle can be modified by attaching the muscle to a lever. The applied force is the effort produced by the muscle contraction. This effort is opposed by a resistance, which is a load or weight. A **lever** is a rigid structure—such as a board, a crowbar, or a bone—that moves on a fixed point called the **fulcrum**. In the body, each bone is a lever and each joint a fulcrum. The teeter-totter, or seesaw, at the park provides a more familiar example of lever action. Levers can change (1) the direction of an applied force, (2) the distance and speed of movement produced by a force, and (3) the strength of a force.

Three classes of levers are found in the human body:

1. *First-class levers:* The seesaw is an example of a **first-class lever**—one in which the fulcrum lies between the applied force and the resistance, as seen in **Figure 9.15a**. There are not many examples of first-class

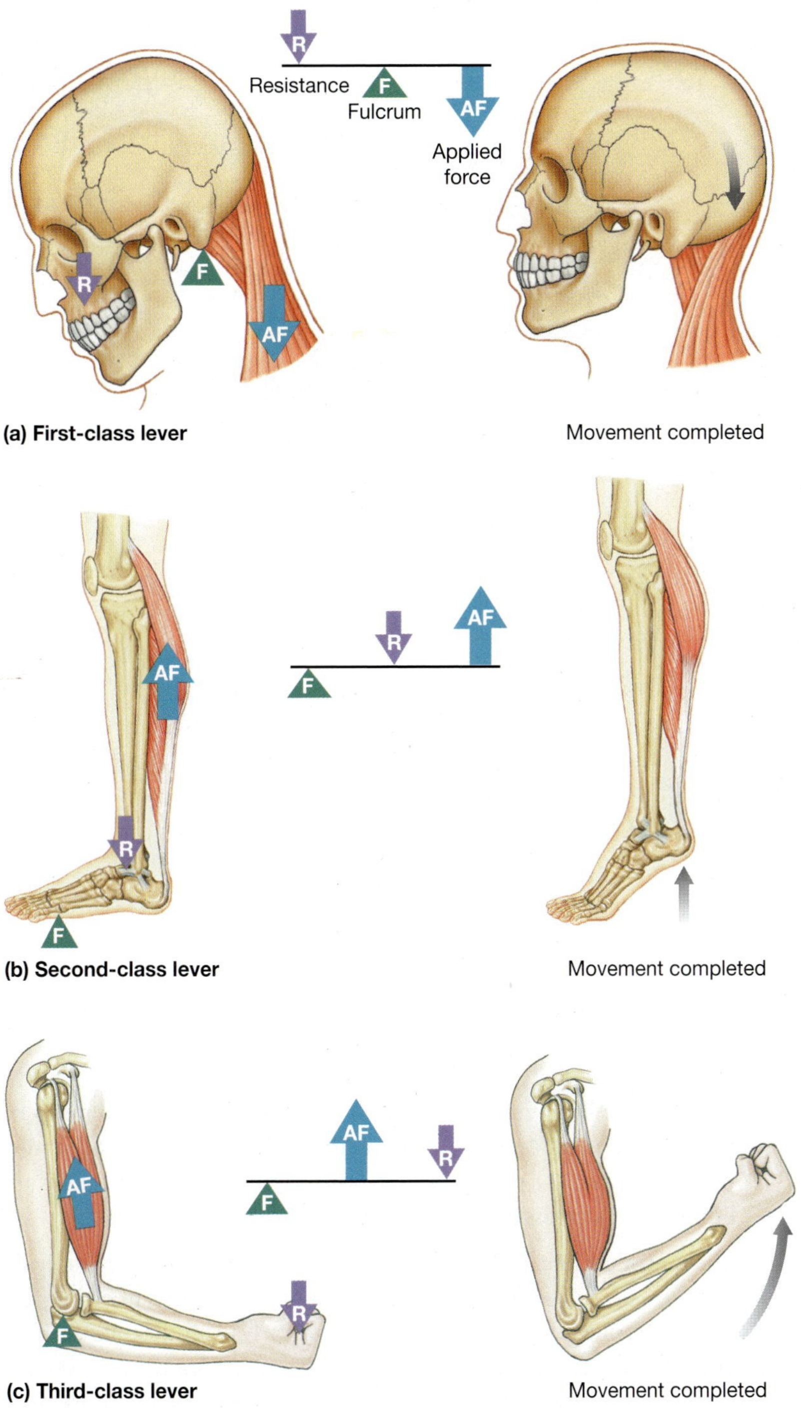

Figure 9.15 The Three Classes of Levers
Levers are rigid structures that move on a fixed point called a fulcrum. **(a)** In a first-class lever, the applied force and the resistance are on opposite sides of the fulcrum. This lever can change the amount of force transmitted to the resistance and alter the direction and speed of movement. **(b)** In a second-class lever, the resistance lies between the applied force and the fulcrum. This arrangement magnifies force at the expense of distance and speed; the direction of movement remains unchanged. **(c)** In a third-class lever, the force is applied between the resistance and the fulcrum. This arrangement increases speed and distance moved but requires a larger applied force.

levers in the body. One, involving the muscles that extend the neck, is shown in this figure.

2. *Second-class levers:* In a **second-class lever**, the resistance is located between the applied force and the fulcrum. A familiar example of such a lever is a loaded wheelbarrow. The weight of the load is the resistance, and the upward lift on the handle is the applied force. Because in this arrangement the force is always farther from the fulcrum than the resistance, a small force can balance a larger weight. In other words, the force is magnified. Notice, however, that when a force moves the handle, the resistance moves more slowly and covers a shorter distance. There are few examples of second-class levers in the body. In performing plantar flexion, the calf muscles act across a second-class lever (Figure 9.15b).
3. *Third-class levers:* In a **third-class lever** system, a force is applied between the resistance and the fulcrum (Figure 9.15c). Third-class levers are the most common levers in the body. The effect of this arrangement is the reverse of that produced by a second-class lever: Speed and distance traveled are increased at the expense of force. In the example illustrated (the biceps brachii muscle, which flexes the elbow), the resistance is six times farther away from the fulcrum than the applied force. The biceps brachii muscle can develop an effective force of 180 kg, which now will be reduced from 180 kg to 30 kg. However, the distance traveled and the speed of movement are *increased* by the same ratio (6:1): The resistance travels 45 cm while the insertion point moves only 7.5 cm.

Although every muscle does not operate as part of a lever system, the presence of levers provides speed and versatility far in excess of what we would predict on the basis of muscle physiology alone. Skeletal muscle cells resemble one another closely, and their abilities to contract and generate tension are quite similar. Consider a skeletal muscle that can contract in 500 ms and shorten 1 cm while exerting a 10-kg pull. Without using a lever, this muscle would be performing efficiently only when moving a 10-kg weight a distance of 1 cm. But by using a lever, the same muscle operating at the same efficiency could move 20 kg a distance of 0.5 cm, 5 kg a distance of 2 cm, or 1 kg a distance of 10 cm. Thus, the lever system design produces the maximum movements with the greatest efficiency.

Anatomical Pulleys [Figure 9.16]

Mechanical pulleys are often used to change the direction of a force in order to accomplish a task more easily and efficiently. On a sailboat, a sailor pulls down on a rope to raise the sail. The sail goes up because a pulley at the top of the mast changes the direction of the force applied to the rope. Similarly, a flag goes *up* a flagpole when you pull the line *down* because the line passes through a pulley at the top of the pole (Figure 9.16a). In the body, tendons act like lines that convey the forces produced by muscle contraction. The path taken by a tendon may be changed by the presence of bones or bony processes. These bony structures, which change the direction of applied forces, are called **anatomical pulleys**.

The lateral malleolus of the fibula is an example of an anatomical pulley. The tendon of insertion for the fibularis longus muscle does not follow a direct path. Instead, it curves around the posterior margin of the lateral malleolus. This redirection of the contractile force is essential to the normal function of the fibularis longus—producing plantar flexion at the ankle (Figure 9.16b).

The patella is another example of an anatomical pulley. The *quadriceps femoris* is a group of four muscles that form the anterior musculature of the thigh. These four muscles attach to the patella by the quadriceps tendon. The patella is, in turn, attached to the tibial tuberosity by the patellar ligament. The quadriceps femoris muscles produce extension at the knee by this two-link system. As illustrated in Figure 9.16c, the patella acts as an anatomical pulley when extending a flexed knee. The quadriceps tendon pulls on the patella in one direction throughout the movement, but the direction of force applied to the tibia by the patellar ligament changes constantly as the movement proceeds.

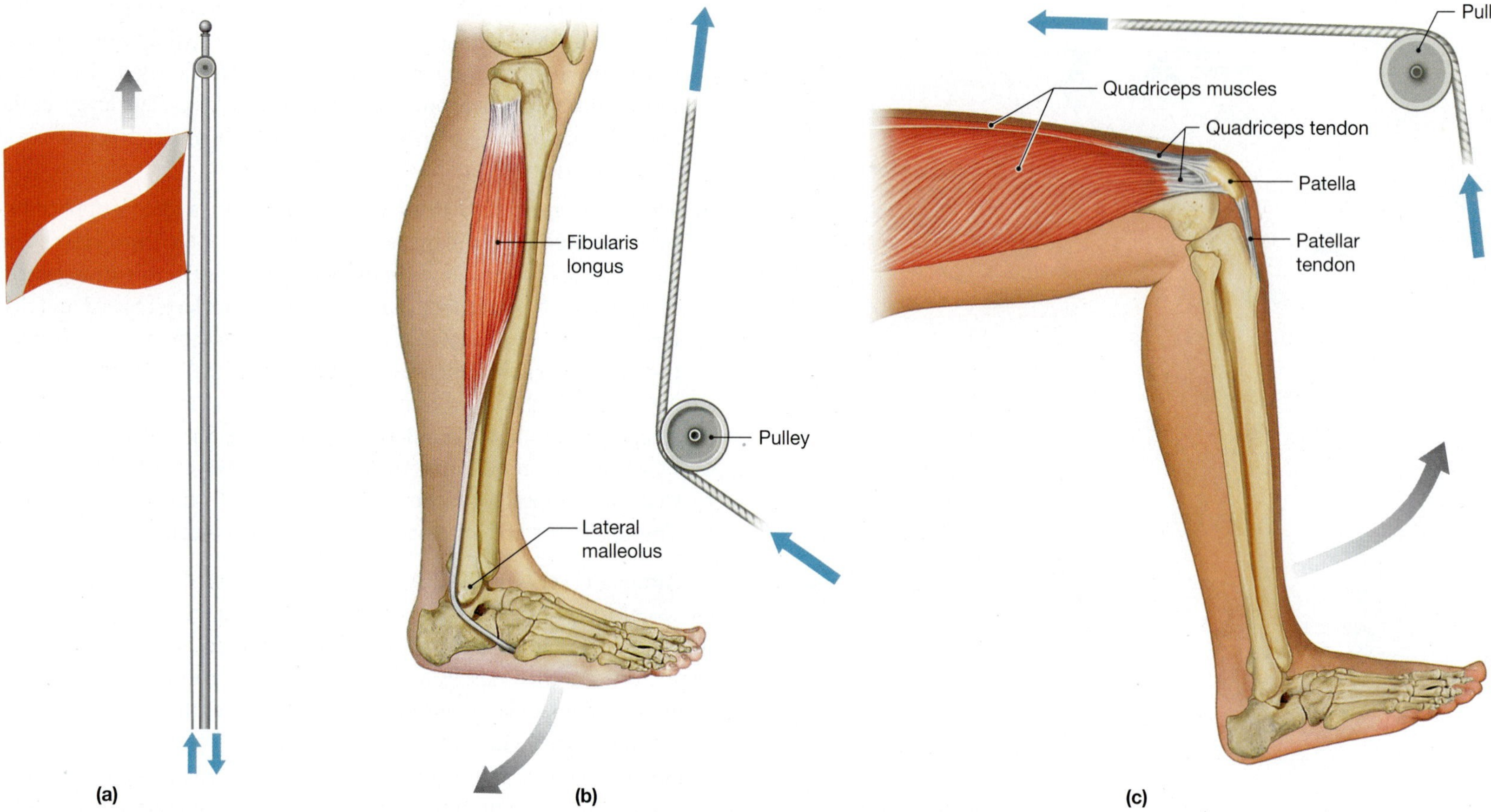

Figure 9.16 Anatomical Pulleys
(a) Bony structures that change the direction of applied forces, just as the pulley at the top of a flag pole, are called anatomical pulleys. **(b)** The lateral malleolus of the fibula acts as an anatomical pulley in the normal functioning of the fibularis longus in the production of plantar flexion at the ankle. **(c)** The patella acts as an anatomical pulley in the production of extension at the knee by the quadriceps femoris muscles.

Aging and the Muscular System

As the body ages, there is a general reduction in the size and power of all muscle tissues. The effects of aging on the muscular system can be summarized as follows:

1. *Skeletal muscle fibers become smaller in diameter:* This reduction in size reflects primarily a decrease in the number of myofibrils. In addition, the muscle fibers contain less ATP, glycogen reserves, and myoglobin. The overall effect is a reduction in muscle strength and endurance and a tendency to fatigue rapidly. Because cardiovascular performance also decreases with age, blood flow to active muscles does not increase with exercise as rapidly as it does in younger people.
2. *Skeletal muscles become smaller in diameter and less elastic:* Aging skeletal muscles develop increasing amounts of fibrous connective tissue, a process called **fibrosis**. Fibrosis makes the muscle less flexible, and the collagen fibers can restrict movement and circulation.
3. *Tolerance for exercise decreases:* A lower tolerance for exercise results in part from the tendency for rapid fatigue and in part from the reduction in the ability to eliminate the heat generated during muscular contraction. ∞ pp. 105, 238
4. *Ability to recover from muscular injuries decreases:* The number of myosatellite cells steadily decreases with age, and the amount of fibrous tissue increases. As a result, when an injury occurs, repair capabilities are limited, and scar tissue formation is the usual result.

The rate of decline in muscular performance is the same in all individuals, regardless of their exercise patterns or lifestyle. Therefore, to be in good shape late in life, one must be in very good shape early in life. Regular exercise helps control body weight, strengthens bones, and generally improves the quality of life at all ages. Extremely demanding exercise is not as important as regular exercise. In fact, extreme exercise in the elderly may lead to problems with tendons, bones, and joints. Although it has obvious effects on the quality of life, there is no clear evidence that exercise prolongs life expectancy.

CONCEPT CHECK

1. What does the name *flexor digitorum longus* tell you about this muscle?
2. Describe the difference between the origin and insertion of a muscle.
3. What type of a muscle is a synergist?
4. What is the difference between *major* and *minor* designations for a muscle?

See blue "Answers" tab at back of book.

Clinical Note

Trichinosis **Trichinosis** (trik-i-NŌ-sis; trichos, hair + nosos, disease) results from infection by the parasitic nematode *Trichinella spiralis*. Symptoms include diarrhea, weakness, and muscle pain. These are caused by the invasion of skeletal muscle tissue by larval worms, which create small pockets within the perimysium and endomysium (Figure 9.17).

Trichinella larvae are common in the flesh of pigs, horses, dogs, and other mammals. The larvae are killed when the meat is cooked; people are most often exposed by eating undercooked infected pork. Once eaten, the larvae mature within the human intestinal tract, where they mate and produce eggs. The new generations of larvae then enter the lymphoid and cardiovascular systems and migrate through the body tissues to reach highly vascularized skeletal muscles, where they complete their early development. The larvae settle in the most metabolically active skeletal muscles, and so muscles of the tongue, eyes, diaphragm, chest, and legs are most often affected.

The migration and subsequent settling produce a generalized achiness, muscle and joint pain, and swelling in infected tissues. An estimated 1.5 million Americans carry *Trichinella* in their muscles, and up to 300,000 new infections occur each year. The mortality rate for people who have symptoms severe enough to require treatment is approximately 1 percent.

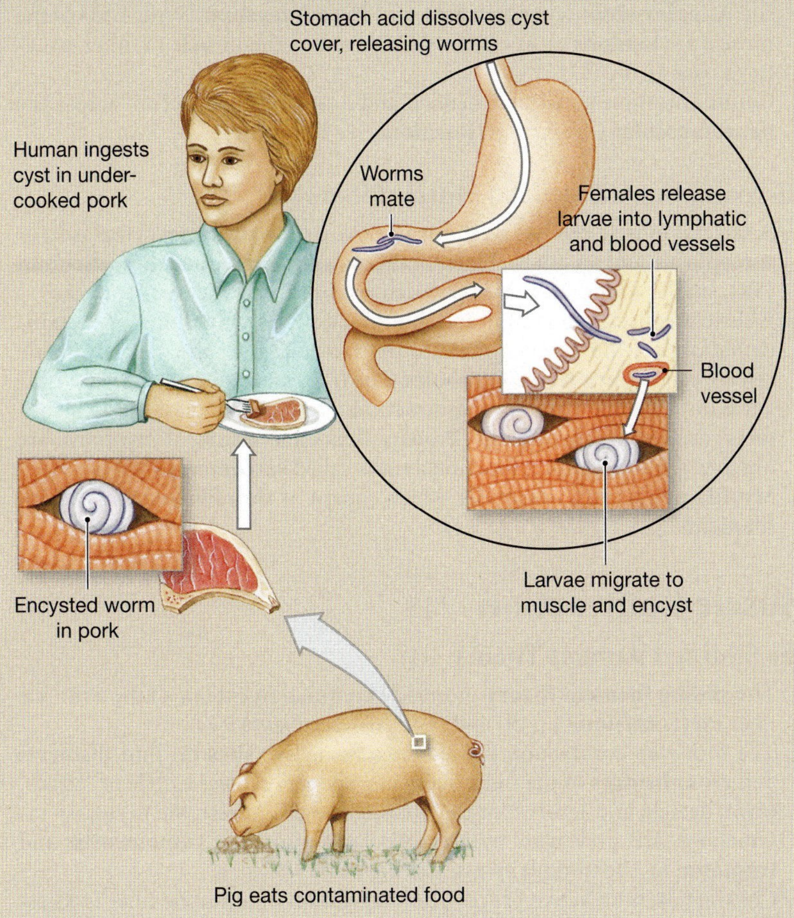

Figure 9.17 The Life Cycle of *Trichinella spiralis*

CLINICAL TERMS

fibrosis: A process in which increasing amounts of fibrous connective tissue develop, making muscles less flexible.

muscular dystrophy: Several congenital conditions characterized by a generalized muscular weakness most evident in the upper limbs, head, and chest; caused by a reduction in the number of ACh receptors on motor end plates.

myasthenia gravis: A disease that produces progressive muscular weakness due to the loss of ACh receptors at the motor end plate.

polio: Progressive paralysis due to destruction of CNS motor neurons by the polio virus.

rigor mortis: A state following death during which muscles are locked in the contracted position, making the body extremely stiff.

STUDY OUTLINE

Introduction 238

1. There are three types of muscle tissue: **skeletal muscle**, **cardiac muscle**, and **smooth muscle**. The muscular system includes all the skeletal muscle tissue that can be controlled voluntarily.

Functions of Skeletal Muscle 238

1. **Skeletal muscles** attach to bones directly or indirectly and perform these functions: (1) produce skeletal movement, (2) maintain posture and body position, (3) support soft tissues, (4) regulate the entering and exiting of materials, and (5) maintain body temperature.

Anatomy of Skeletal Muscles 238

Gross Anatomy 238

1. Each muscle fiber is wrapped by three concentric layers of connective tissue: an **epimysium**, a **perimysium**, and an **endomysium**. At the ends of the muscle are **tendons** or **aponeuroses** that attach the muscle to other structures. *(see Figure 9.1)*
2. Communication between a neuron and a muscle fiber occurs across the **neuromuscular** (*myoneural*) **junction.** *(see Figure 9.2)*

Microanatomy of Skeletal Muscle Fibers 240

3. A skeletal muscle cell has a cell membrane, or **sarcolemma**; cytoplasm, or **sarcoplasm**; and an internal membrane system, or **sarcoplasmic reticulum (SR)**, similar to the endoplasmic reticulum of other cells. *(see Figure 9.3)*
4. A skeletal muscle cell is large and multinucleate. Invaginations, or deep indentations, of the sarcolemma into the sarcoplasm of the skeletal muscle cell are called **transverse (T) tubules.** The transverse tubules carry the electrical impulse that stimulates contraction into the sarcoplasm, which contains numerous **myofibrils.** Protein filaments inside a myofibril are organized into repeating functional units called **sarcomeres.**
5. **Myofilaments** form myofibrils, which consist of **thin filaments** and **thick filaments.** *(see Figures 9.3 to 9.6)*

Muscle Contraction 245

The Sliding Filament Theory 245

1. The **sliding filament theory** of muscle contraction explains how a muscle fiber exerts **tension** (a pull) and shortens. *(see Figure 9.7)*
2. The four-step contraction process involves **active sites** on thin filaments and **cross-bridges** of the thick filaments. Sliding involves a cycle of "attach, pivot, detach, and return" for the myosin bridges. At rest, the necessary interactions are prevented by the associated proteins, **tropomyosin** and **troponin**, on the thin filaments. *(see Figures 9.5/9.7)*
3. Contraction is an active process, but elongation of a muscle fiber is a passive process that can occur either through elastic forces or through the movement of other, opposing muscles.
4. The amount of tension produced during a contraction is proportional to the degree of overlap between thick and thin filaments. *(see Figure 9.8)*

The Neural Control of Muscle Fiber Contraction 246

5. Neural control of muscle function involves a link between release of chemicals by the neurons and electrical activity in the sarcolemma leading to the initiation of a contraction.
6. Each muscle fiber is controlled by a neuron at a *neuromuscular (myoneural) synapse*; the synapse includes the **synaptic terminal**, **synaptic vesicles**, and the **synaptic cleft. Acetylcholine (ACh)** release leads to the stimulation of the motor end plate and the generation of electrical impulses that spread across the sarcolemma. **Acetylcholinesterase (AChE)** breaks down ACh and limits the duration of stimulation. *(see Figures 9.2/9.10)*

Muscle Contraction: A Summary 246

7. The steps involved in contraction are as follows: ACh release from synaptic vesicles → binding of ACh to the motor end plate → generation of an electrical impulse in the sarcolemma → conduction of the impulse along T tubules release of calcium ions by the SR → exposure of active sites on thin filaments → cross-bridge formation and contraction. *(see Figure 9.11)*

Motor Units and Muscle Control 248

1. The number and size of a muscle's **motor units** indicate how precisely controlled its movements are. *(see Figure 9.12)*
2. A single momentary muscle contraction is called a **muscle twitch** and is the response to a single stimulus.
3. Each muscle fiber either contracts completely or does not contract at all. This characteristic is the *all or none principle.*

Muscle Tone 249

4. Even when a muscle is at rest, motor units are randomly stimulated so that a constant tension is maintained in the attached tendon. This resting tension in a skeletal muscle is called **muscle tone.** Resting muscle tone stabilizes bones and joints.

Muscle Hypertrophy 249

5. Excessive repeated stimulation to produce near-maximal tension in skeletal muscle can lead to **hypertrophy** (enlargement) of the stimulated muscles.

Muscle Atrophy 249

6. Inadequate stimulation to maintain resting muscle tone causes muscles to become flaccid and undergo **atrophy.**

Types of Skeletal Muscle Fibers 249

1. The three types of skeletal muscle fibers are *fast fibers, slow fibers,* and *intermediate fibers. (see Figure 9.13)*
2. **Fast fibers** are large in diameter; they contain densely packed myofibrils, large glycogen reserves, and relatively few mitochondria. They produce rapid and powerful contractions of relatively brief duration.
3. **Slow fibers** are only about half the diameter of fast fibers, and they take three times as long to contract after stimulation. Slow fibers are specialized to enable them to continue contracting for extended periods.
4. **Intermediate fibers** are very similar to fast fibers, although they have a greater resistance to fatigue.

Distribution of Fast, Slow, and Intermediate Fibers 250

5. The percentage of fast, slow, and intermediate fibers varies from one skeletal muscle to another. Muscles contain a mixture of fiber types, but the fibers within one motor unit are of the same type. The percentage of fast versus slow fibers in each muscle is genetically determined.

The Organization of Skeletal Muscle Fibers 251

1. A muscle can be classified according to the arrangement of fibers and fascicles as a *parallel muscle, convergent muscle, pennate muscle,* or *circular muscle (sphincter).*

Parallel Muscles 251

2. In a **parallel muscle**, the fascicles are parallel to the long axis of the muscle. Most of the skeletal muscles in the body are parallel muscles, for example, the *biceps brachii muscle. (see Figure 9.14a)*

Convergent Muscles 251

3. In a **convergent muscle**, the muscle fibers are based over a broad area, but all the fibers come together at a common attachment site. The *pectoralis group* of the chest is a good example of this type of muscle. *(see Figure 9.14b)*

Pennate Muscles 252

4. In a **pennate muscle**, one or more tendons run through the body of the muscle, and the fascicles form an oblique angle to the tendon. Contraction of pennate muscles generates more tension than that of parallel muscles of the same size. A pennate muscle may be **unipennate**, **bipennate**, or **multipennate.** *(see Figure 9.14c–e)*

Circular Muscles 252

5. In a **circular muscle (sphincter)**, the fibers are concentrically arranged around an opening or recess. *(see Figure 9.14f)*

Muscle Terminology 253

Origins and Insertions 253

1. Each muscle may be identified by its **origin**, **insertion**, and primary **action**. Typically, the *origin* remains stationary and the *insertion* moves, or the origin is proximal to the insertion. Muscle contraction produces a specific action.

Actions 253

2. A muscle may be classified as a **prime mover** or **agonist**, a **synergist**, or an **antagonist**.

Names of Skeletal Muscles 254

3. The names of muscles often provide clues to their location, orientation, or function. *(see Table 9.2)*

Levers and Pulleys: A Systems Design for Movement 254

1. A **lever** is a rigid structure that moves on a fixed point called a **fulcrum**. Levers can change the direction, speed, or distance of muscle movements, and they can modify the force applied to the movement.

Classes of Levers 254

2. Levers may be classified as **first-class**, **second-class**, or **third-class levers**; third-class levers are the most common type of lever in the body. *(see Figure 9.15)*

Anatomical Pulleys 255

3. Bony structures that change the direction of a muscle's contractile force are termed **anatomical pulleys**. The lateral malleolus of the fibula and the patella are excellent examples of anatomical pulleys. *(see Figure 9.16)*

Aging and the Muscular System 256

1. The aging process reduces the size, elasticity, and power of all muscle tissues. Exercise tolerance and the ability to recover from muscular injuries both decrease as the body ages.

CHAPTER REVIEW

For answers to the Concept Check and Chapter Review questions, go to the blue "Answers" tab at the back of the book.

Level 1 Reviewing Facts and Terms

1. Each of the following changes in skeletal muscles is a consequence of aging except
   (a) muscle fibers become smaller in diameter
   (b) muscles become less elastic
   (c) muscle fibers increase their reserves of glycogen
   (d) the number of myosatellite cells decreases
2. Active sites on the actin become available for binding when
   (a) calcium binds to troponin
   (b) troponin binds to tropomyosin
   (c) calcium binds to tropomyosin
   (d) actin binds to troponin
3. The function of a neuromuscular synapse is
   (a) to generate new muscle fibers if the muscle is damaged
   (b) to facilitate chemical communication between a neuron and a muscle fiber
   (c) to unite motor branches of nerves from different muscle fibers to one another
   (d) to provide feedback about muscle activity to sensory nerves
4. The direct energy supply produced by the skeletal muscles in order to enable them to contract is
   (a) derived from fat, carbohydrate, and cholesterol
   (b) independent of the supply of oxygen
   (c) ATP
   (d) infinite, as long as muscle activity is required
5. In a pennate muscle, the fibers are
   (a) based over a broad area
   (b) concentrically arranged
   (c) oblique to the tendon
   (d) parallel to the tendon
6. Another name for the muscle that is the prime mover is
   (a) agonist (b) antagonist
   (c) synergist (d) none of the above
7. Interactions between actin and myosin filaments of the sarcomere are responsible for
   (a) muscle fatigue
   (b) conduction of neural information to the muscle fiber
   (c) muscle contraction
   (d) the striated appearance of skeletal muscle
8. The theory that explains muscle contraction is formally known as the
   (a) muscle contraction theory
   (b) striated voluntary muscle theory
   (c) rotating myosin head theory
   (d) sliding filament theory
9. The bundle of collagen fibers at the end of a skeletal muscle that attaches the muscle to bone is called a(n)
   (a) fascicle (b) tendon
   (c) ligament (d) epimysium
10. All of the muscle fibers controlled by a single motor neuron constitute a
   (a) fascicle (b) myofibril
   (c) motor unit (d) none of the above

Level 2 Reviewing Concepts

1. To lessen the rate at which muscles fatigue during a contraction, motor units are activated
   (a) to less than their peak tension each time they contract
   (b) in a stepwise fashion
   (c) on a rotating basis
   (d) quickly, to complete the contraction before they fatigue
2. The ability to recover from injuries in older individuals decreases because
   (a) the number of myosatellite cells decreases with age
   (b) myosatellite cells become smaller in size
   (c) the amount of fibrous tissue in the muscle increases
   (d) both a and c are correct
3. In which of the following would the ratio of motor neurons to muscle fibers be the greatest?
   (a) large muscles of the arms
   (b) postural muscles of the back
   (c) muscles that control the eye
   (d) leg muscles
4. If a person is cold, a good way to warm up is to exercise. What is the mechanism of this warming?
   (a) moving faster prevents the person from feeling the cold air because it moves past him or her more quickly
   (b) exercise moves blood faster, and the friction keeps tissues warm
   (c) muscle contraction uses ATP, and the utilization of this energy generates heat, which helps warm the body
   (d) the movement of the actin and myosin filaments during the contraction generates heat, which helps warm the body
5. What do the following names of muscles tell us about the muscles: *rectus*, *externus*, *flexor*, *trapezius*?
6. Summarize the basic sequence of events that occurs at a neuromuscular synapse.
7. What is the role of connective tissue in the organization of skeletal muscle?
8. A motor unit from a skeletal muscle contains 1500 muscle fibers. Would this muscle be involved in fine, delicate movements or powerful, gross movements? Explain.
9. What is the role of the zone of overlap in the production of tension in a skeletal muscle?

Level 3 Critical Thinking

1. Tom broke his leg in a soccer game, and after six weeks in a cast, the cast is finally removed. Afterward, as he steps down from the table, he loses his balance and falls. Why?
2. Several anatomy students take up weight lifting and bodybuilding. After several months, they notice many physical changes, including an increase in muscle mass, lean body weight, and greater muscular strength. What anatomical mechanism is responsible for these changes?
3. Within the past 10–20 years, several countries have initiated the practice of taking leg muscle biopsies of track athletes in an effort to determine their chances of success at sprints or long-distance events. What anatomical fact is the basis of this assumption?

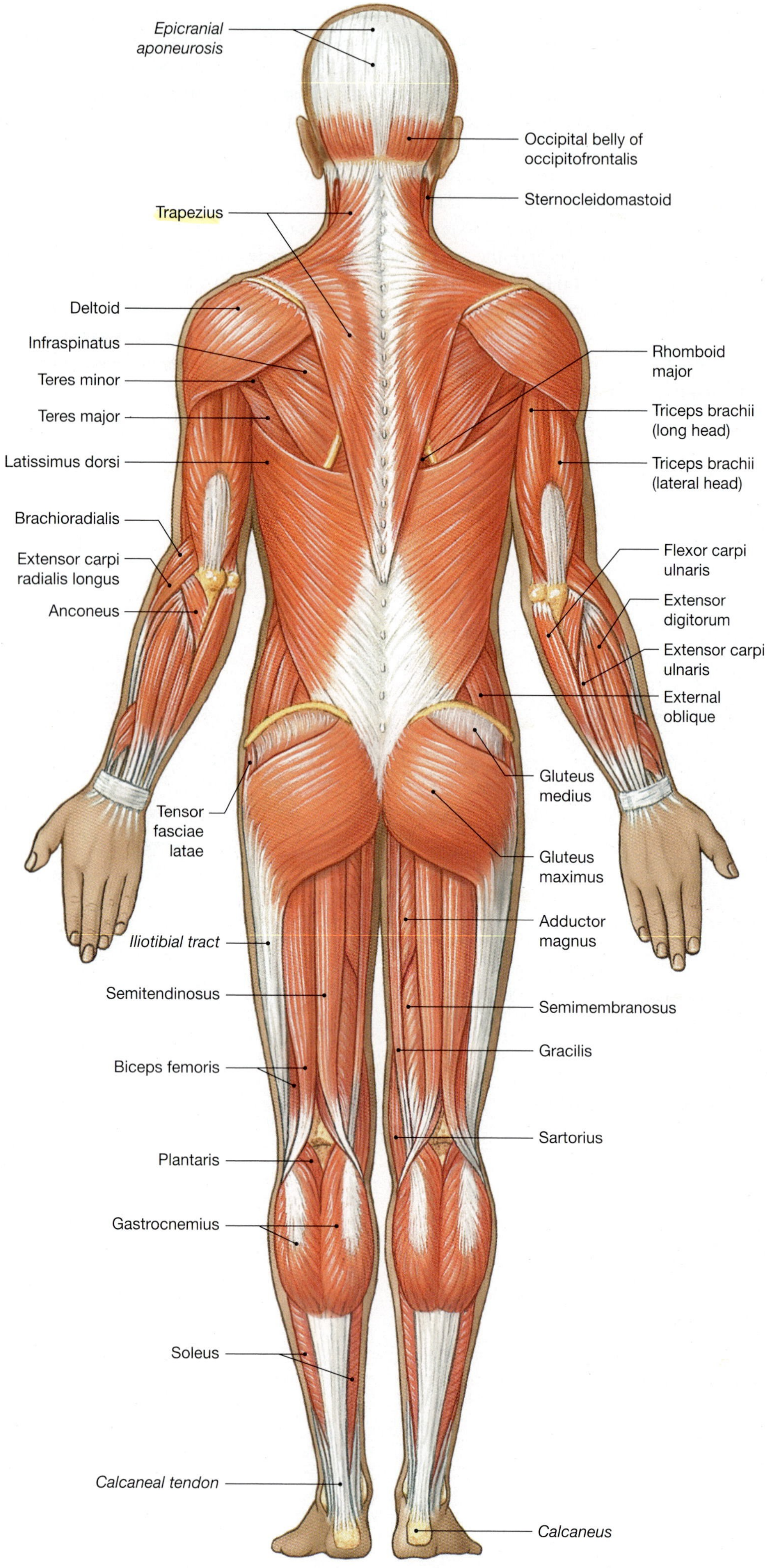

2. The second group, the *muscles of the vertebral column*, includes numerous flexors and extensors of the axial skeleton.
3. The third group, the *oblique* and *rectus muscles*, forms the muscular walls of the thoracic and abdominopelvic cavities between the first thoracic vertebra and the pelvis. In the thoracic area, these muscles are partitioned by the ribs, but over the abdominal surface, they form broad muscular sheets. There are also oblique and rectus muscles in the neck. Although they do not form a complete muscular wall, they are included in this group because they share a common developmental origin. The diaphragm is placed within this group because it is developmentally linked to other muscles of the chest wall.
4. The fourth group, the *muscles of the perineum and the pelvic diaphragm*, extend between the sacrum and pelvic girdle and close the pelvic outlet. pp. 192–193

Figures 10.1 and 10.2 provide an overview of the major axial and appendicular muscles of the human body. These are the superficial muscles, which tend to be relatively large. The superficial muscles cover deeper, smaller muscles that cannot be seen unless the overlying muscles are removed or *reflected*—that is, cut and pulled out of the way. Later figures that show deep muscles in specific regions will indicate whether superficial muscles have been removed or reflected for the sake of clarity.

To facilitate the review process, information concerning the origin, insertion, and action of each muscle has been summarized in tables. These tables also contain information about the *innervation* of individual muscles. The term **innervation** refers to the nerve supply to a particular structure or organ, and the one or more motor nerves that control each skeletal muscle. The names of the nerves provide clues to the distribution of the nerve or the site at which the nerve leaves the cranial cavity or vertebral canal. For example, the *facial nerve* innervates the facial musculature, and the various *spinal nerves* leave the vertebral canal by way of the intervertebral foramina. pp. 162, 166 To help you understand the relationships between the skeletal muscles and the bones of the skeleton, we have included skeletal icons showing the origins and insertions of representative muscles in each group. On each icon, the areas where muscles originate are shown in red, and the areas where muscles insert are shown in blue.

Muscles of the Head and Neck

The muscles of the head and neck can be subdivided into several groups. The *muscles of facial expression*, the *extraocular muscles*, the *muscles of mastication*, the *muscles of the tongue*, and the *muscles of the pharynx* originate on the skull or hyoid bone. Other muscles involved with sight and

Figure 10.2 Superficial Skeletal Muscles, Posterior View
A diagrammatic view of the major axial and appendicular muscles.

hearing originate on the skull. These muscles are discussed in Chapter 18 (general and special senses), along with muscles associated with the ear and hearing. The *anterior muscles of the neck* are concerned primarily with altering the position of the larynx, hyoid bone, and floor of the mouth.

Muscles of Facial Expression [Figures 10.2/10.3/10.4 and Table 10.1]

The muscles of facial expression originate on the surface of the skull. View Figures 10.3 and 10.4 as we describe their structure. Table 10.1 provides a detailed summary of their characteristics. At their insertions, the collagen fibers of the epimysium are woven into those of the superficial fascia and the dermis of the skin; when they contract, the skin moves. These muscles are innervated by the seventh cranial nerve, the *facial nerve.*

The largest group of facial muscles is associated with the mouth (Figure 10.3). The **orbicularis oris** (OR-is) **muscle** constricts the opening, while other muscles move the lips or the corners of the mouth. The **buccinator muscle** has two functions related to feeding (in addition to its importance to musicians). During chewing, it cooperates with the masticatory muscles by moving food back across the teeth from the space inside the cheeks. In infants, the buccinator is responsible for producing the suction required for suckling at the breast.

Smaller groups of muscles control movements of the eyebrows and eyelids, the scalp, the nose, and the external ear. The *epicranium* (ep-i-KRĀ-nē-um; *epi-*, on + *kranion*, skull), or scalp, contains the **temporoparietalis muscle** and the **occipitofrontalis muscle**, which has two bellies, the **frontal belly** and the **occipital belly**, separated by a collagenous sheet, the *epicranial aponeurosis* (Figures 10.2 and 10.3). The superficial **platysma** (pla-TIZ-ma; *platys*, flat) covers the anterior surface of the neck, extending from the base of the neck to the periosteum of the mandible and the fascia at the corners of the mouth (Figures 10.3 and 10.4).

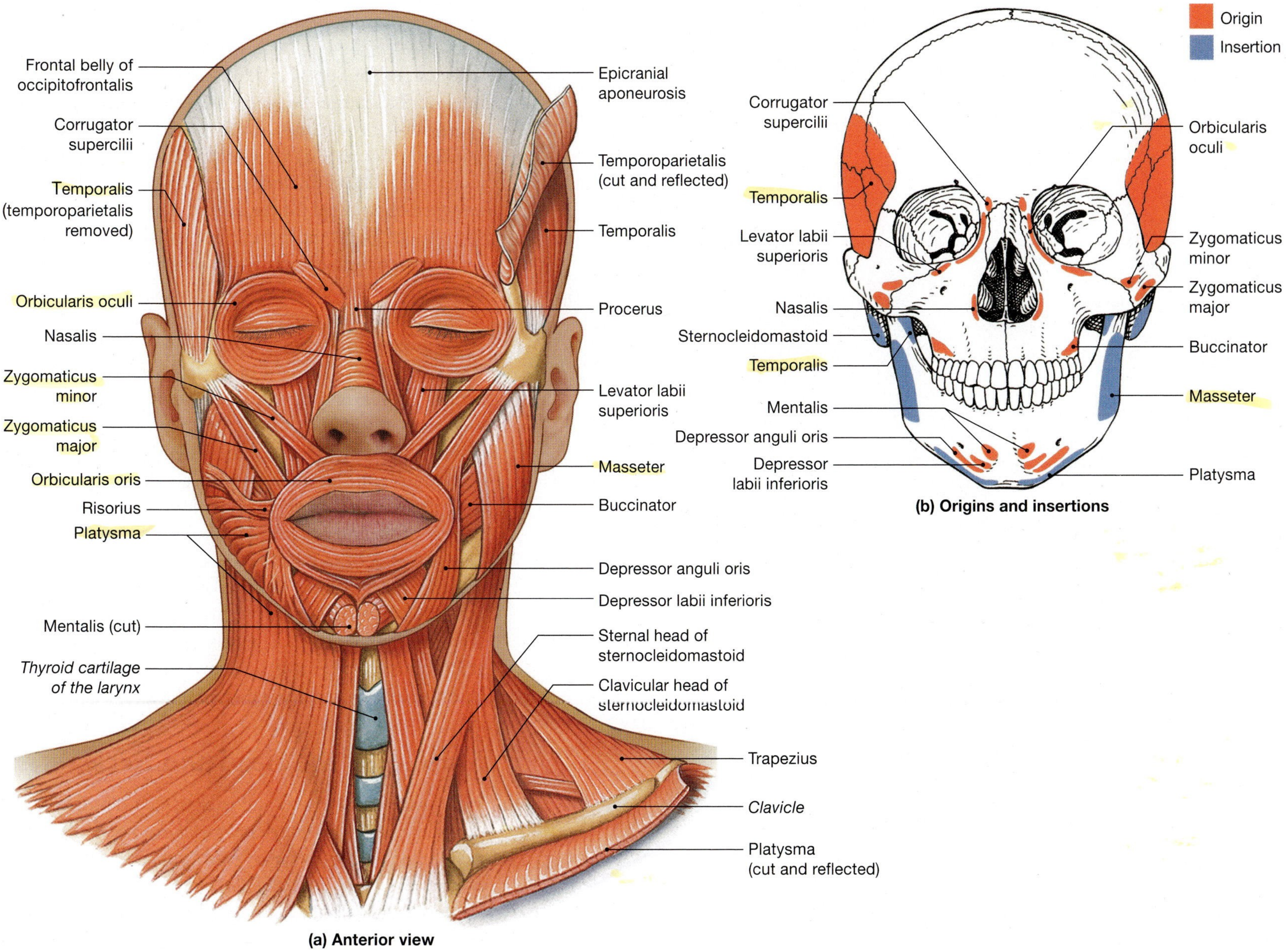

Figure 10.3 Muscles of the Head and Neck, Part I
(a) Anterior view. **(b)** Origins and insertions of selected muscles.

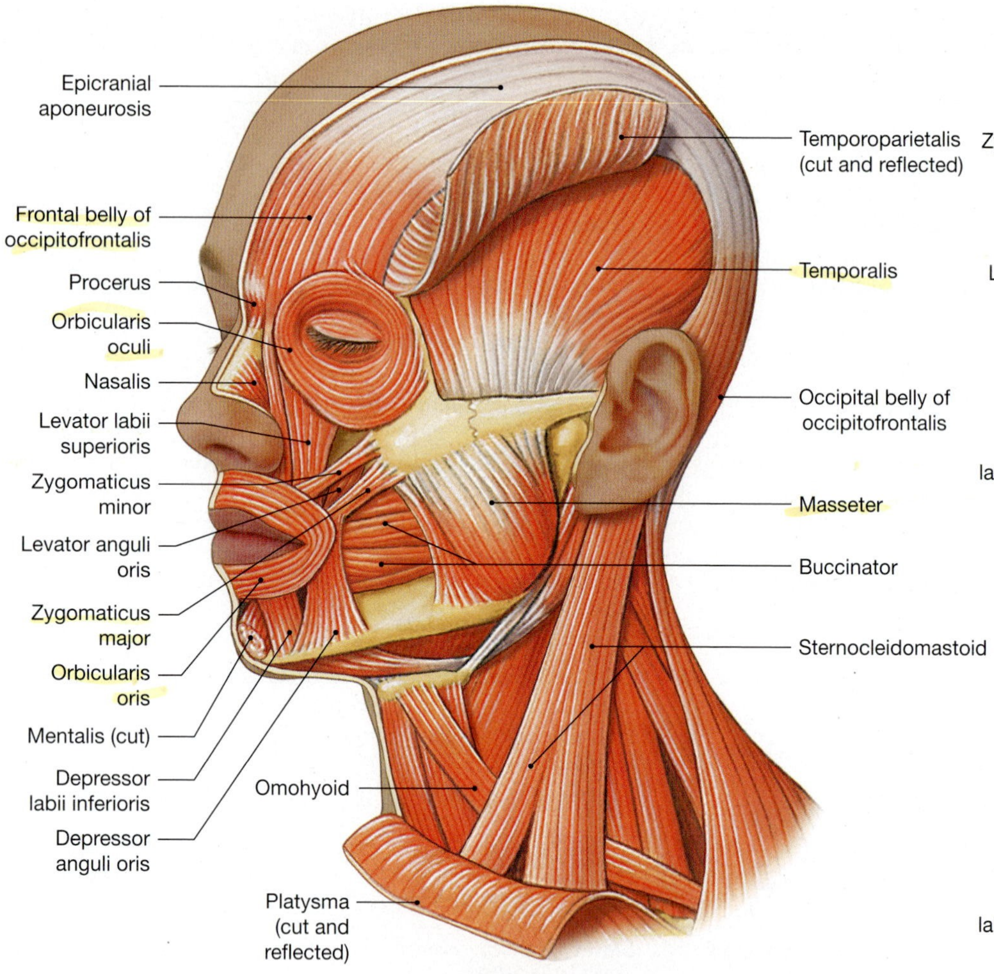

(a) Lateral view

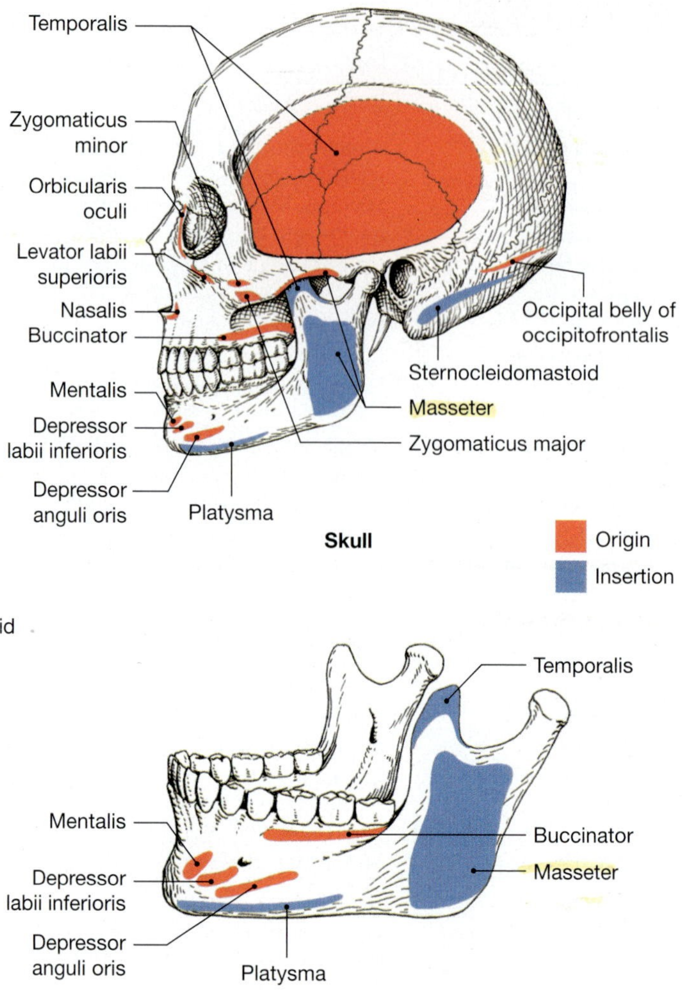

(c) Origins and insertions

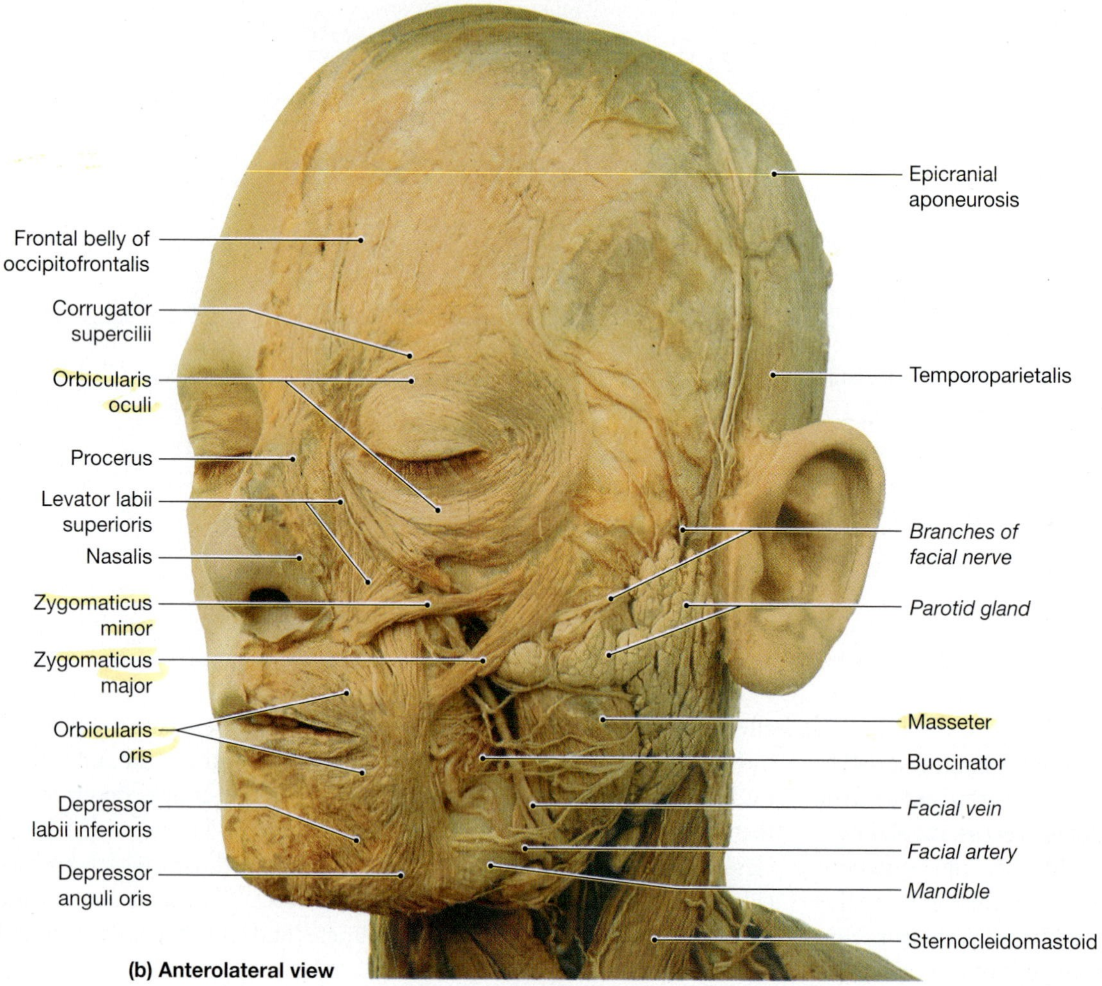

(b) Anterolateral view

Figure 10.4 Muscles of the Head and Neck, Part II
(a) A diagrammatic lateral view. **(b)** A corresponding view of a dissection showing many of the muscles of the head and neck. **(c)** Origins and insertions of representative muscles on the lateral surface of the entire skull (above) and the isolated mandible (below). *See also Figure 6.3.*

TABLE 10.1 Muscles of Facial Expression

Region/Muscle	Origin	Insertion	Action	Innervation
MOUTH				
Buccinator	Alveolar processes of maxilla and mandible opposite the molar teeth	Blends into fibers of orbicularis oris	Compresses cheeks	Facial nerve (N VII)
Depressor labii inferioris	Mandible between the anterior midline and the mental foramen	Skin of lower lip	Depresses lower lip	As above
Levator labii superioris	Inferior margin of orbit, superior to the infra-orbital foramen	Orbicularis oris	Elevates upper lip	As above
Mentalis	Incisive fossa of mandible	Skin of chin	Elevates and protrudes lower lip	As above
Orbicularis oris	Maxilla and mandible	Lips	Compresses, purses lips	As above
Risorius	Fascia surrounding parotid salivary gland	Angle of mouth	Draws corner of mouth to the side	As above
Levator anguli oris	Maxilla inferior to infra-orbital foramen	Skin at angle of mouth	Raises corner of mouth	As above
Depressor anguli oris	Anterolateral surface of mandibular body	Skin at angle of mouth	Depresses corner of mouth	As above
Zygomaticus major	Zygomatic bone near the zygomaticotemporal suture	Angle of mouth	Retracts and elevates corner of mouth	As above
Zygomaticus minor	Zygomatic bone posterior to zygomaticomaxillary suture	Upper lip	Retracts and elevates upper lip	As above
EYE				
Corrugator supercilii	Orbital rim of frontal bone near frontonasal suture	Eyebrow	Pulls skin inferiorly and anteriorly; wrinkles brow	As above
Levator palpebrae superioris	Inferior aspect of lesser wing of the sphenoid superior to and anterior to optic canal	Upper eyelid	Elevates upper eyelid	Oculomotor nerve (N III)[a]
Orbicularis oculi	Medial margin of orbit	Skin around eyelids	Closes eye	Facial nerve (N VII)
NOSE				
Procerus	Lateral nasal cartilages and the aponeuroses covering the inferior portion of the nasal bones	Aponeurosis at bridge of nose and skin of forehead	Moves nose, changes position, shape of nostrils	As above
Nasalis	Maxilla and alar cartilage of nose	Bridge of nose	Compresses bridge, depresses tip of nose; elevates corners of nostrils	As above
SCALP (EPICRANIUM)[b]				
Occipitofrontalis				
Frontal belly	Epicranial aponeurosis	Skin of eyebrow and bridge of nose	Raises eyebrows, wrinkles forehead	As above
Occipital belly	Superior nuchal line and adjacent region of mastoid portion of the temporal bone	Epicranial aponeurosis	Tenses and retracts scalp	As above
Temporoparietalis	Fascia around external ear	Epicranial aponeurosis	Tenses scalp, moves auricle of ear	As above
NECK				
Platysma	Fascia of the superior thorax between cartilage of second rib and acromion of scapula	Mandible and skin of cheek	Tenses skin of neck, depresses mandible	As above

[a]This muscle originates in association with the extra-ocular muscles, so its innervation is unusual, as detailed in Chapter 15.
[b]Includes the epicranial aponeurosis, temporoparietalis, and occipitofrontalis muscles.

Extra-ocular Muscles [Figure 10.5 and Table 10.2]

Six **extra-ocular muscles**, sometimes called the *oculomotor* (ok-ū-lō-MŌ-ter) or *extrinsic eye muscles*, originate on the surface of the orbit and control the position of each eye. These muscles are the **inferior rectus**, **medial rectus**, **superior rectus**, **lateral rectus**, **inferior oblique**, and **superior oblique muscles** (Figure 10.5 and Table 10.2). The rectus muscles move the eyes in the direction indicated by their names. Additionally, the superior and inferior rectus muscles also cause a slight movement of the eye medially, whereas the superior and inferior oblique muscles cause a slight lateral movement. Thus, to roll the eye straight up, one contracts the superior rectus and the inferior oblique muscles; to roll the eye straight down requires the inferior rectus and the superior oblique muscles. The extra-ocular muscles are innervated by the third (*oculomotor*), fourth (*trochlear*), and sixth (*abducens*) cranial nerves. The *intrinsic eye muscles*, which are smooth muscles inside the eyeball, control pupil diameter and lens shape. These muscles are discussed in Chapter 18.

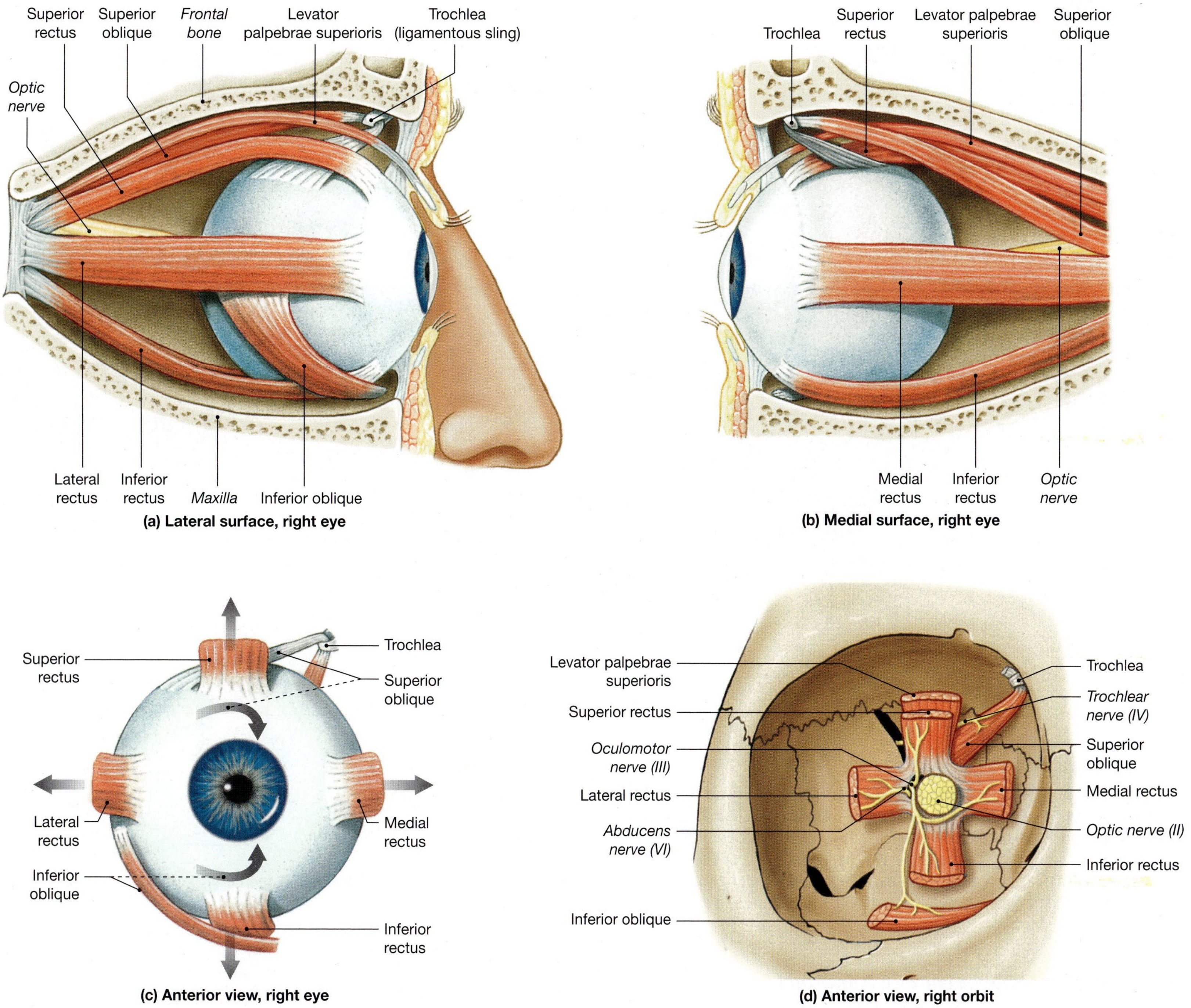

Figure 10.5 Extra-ocular Muscles
(a) Muscles on the lateral surface of the right eye. **(b)** Muscles on the medial surface of the right eye. **(c)** Anterior view of the right eye, showing the orientation of the extra-ocular muscles and the directions of eye movement produced by contractions of the individual muscles. **(d)** Anterior view of the right orbit showing the origins of the extra-ocular muscles. *See also Figure 6.3*.

TABLE 10.2 Extra-ocular Muscles

Muscle	Origin	Insertion	Action	Innervation
Inferior rectus	Sphenoid around optic canal	Inferior, medial surface of eyeball	Eye looks down	Oculomotor nerve (N III)
Medial rectus	As above	Medial surface of eyeball	Eye looks medially	As above
Superior rectus	As above	Superior surface of eyeball	Eye looks up	As above
Lateral rectus	As above	Lateral surface of eyeball	Eye looks laterally	Abducens nerve (N VI)
Inferior oblique	Maxilla at anterior portion of orbit	Inferior, lateral surface of eyeball	Eye rolls, looks up and laterally	Oculomotor nerve (N III)
Superior oblique	Sphenoid around optic canal	Superior, lateral surface of eyeball	Eye rolls, looks down and laterally	Trochlear nerve (N IV)

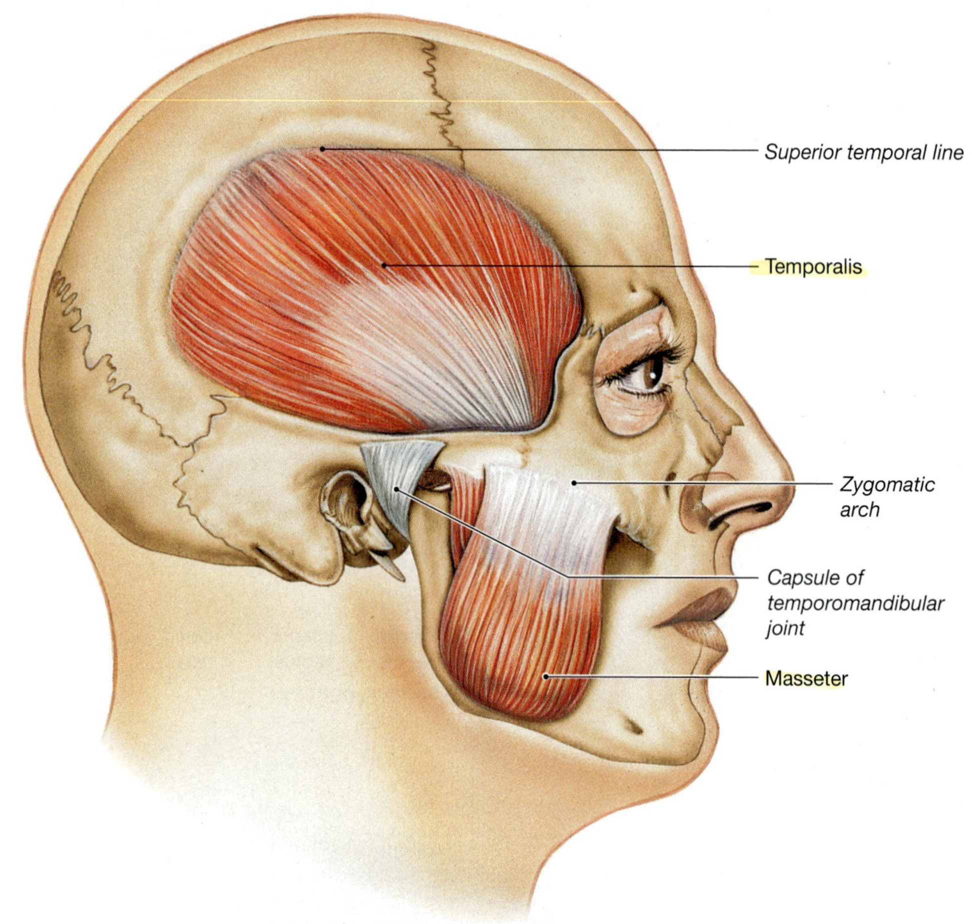

(a) Lateral view

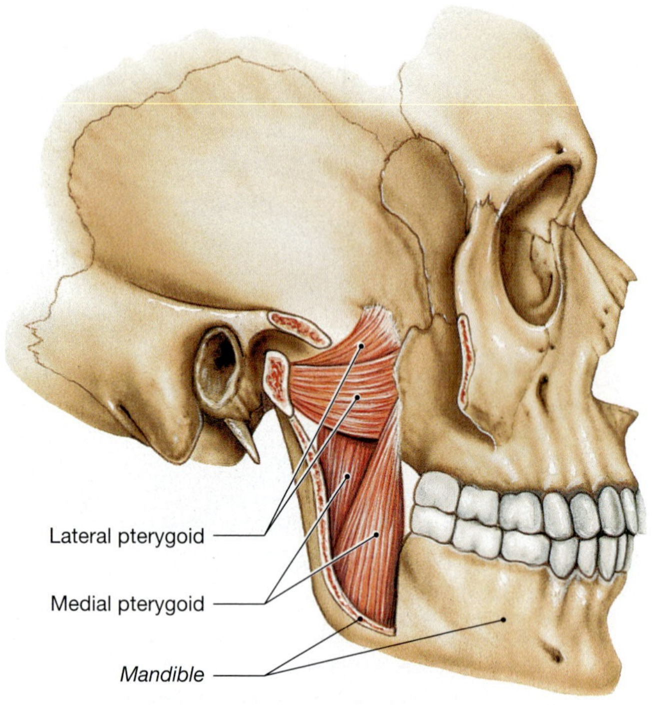

(b) Lateral view, pterygoid muscles exposed

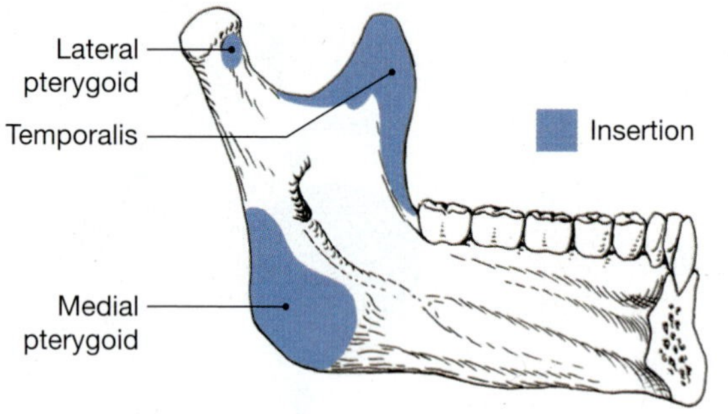

(c) Insertions, medial view of left mandibular ramus

Figure 10.6 Muscles of Mastication
The muscles of mastication move the mandible during chewing. **(a)** The temporalis and masseter are prominent muscles on the lateral surface of the skull. The temporalis passes medial to the zygomatic arch to insert on the coronoid process of the mandible. The masseter inserts on the angle and lateral surface of the mandible. **(b)** The location and orientation of the pterygoid muscles can be seen after removing the overlying muscles, along with a portion of the mandible. **(c)** Selected insertions on the medial surface of the mandible. *See also Figures 6.3 and 6.14.*

Muscles of Mastication [Figure 10.6 and Table 10.3]

The muscles of mastication (Figure 10.6 and Table 10.3) move the mandible at the temporomandibular joint. ∞ p. 214 The large **masseter** (ma-SĒ-ter) **muscle** elevates the mandible and is the most powerful and important of the masticatory muscles. The **temporalis** (tem-po-RA-lis) **muscle** assists in elevation of the mandible, whereas the medial and lateral **pterygoid** (TER-i-goyd) **muscles**, when used in various combinations, can elevate the mandible, protract it, or slide it from side to side; such a movement is called *lateral excursion.* These movements are important in maximizing the efficient use of the teeth while chewing or grinding foods of various consistencies. The muscles of mastication are innervated by the fifth cranial nerve, the *trigeminal nerve.*

TABLE 10.3 Muscles of Mastication

Muscle	Origin	Insertion	Action	Innervation
Masseter	Zygomatic arch	Lateral surface and angle of mandibular ramus	Elevates mandible and closes jaws	Trigeminal nerve (N V), mandibular branch
Temporalis	Along temporal lines of skull	Coronoid process of mandible	As above	As above
Pterygoids	Lateral pterygoid plate	Medial surface of mandibular ramus		
Medial pterygoid	Lateral pterygoid plate and adjacent portions of palatine bone and maxilla	Medial surface of mandibular ramus	Elevates the mandible and closes the jaws, or moves mandible side to side	As above
Lateral pterygoid	Lateral pterygoid plate and greater wing of sphenoid	Anterior part of the neck of the mandibular condyle	Opens jaws, protrudes mandible, or moves mandible side to side	As above

Clinical Note

What's New? You may have heard someone comment that "there's nothing new in anatomy." That statement reflects a popular opinion that every anatomical structure in the human body was described centuries ago. Many people were therefore surprised when, in 1996, anatomical researchers at the University of Maryland documented the existence of a "new" skeletal muscle. This muscle, the *sphenomandibularis muscle* (Figure 10.7), assists the muscles of mastication; it extends from the lateral surface of the sphenoid to the mandible. The work was begun through computer analysis of the Visible Human database, a digitized photographic atlas of cross-sectional anatomy. The initial work was then supported by careful cadaver dissections. Although some controversy remains about this muscle (for example, it may have been described previously as a portion of the temporalis muscle), this is a good example of how modern technologies are providing new perspectives on the human body.

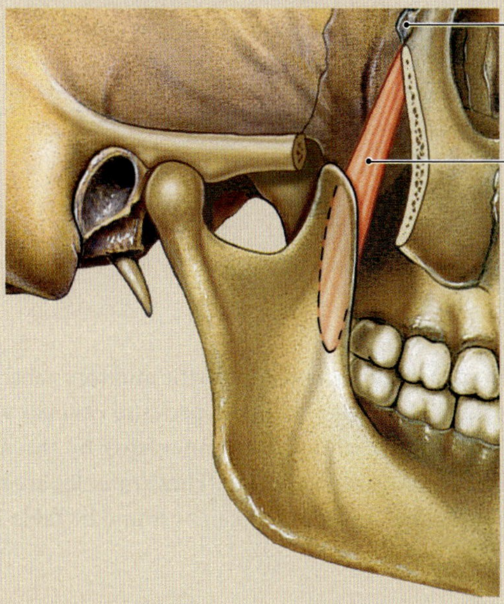

Figure 10.7 The Sphenomandibularis Muscle

Muscles of the Tongue [Figure 10.8 and Table 10.4]

The muscles of the tongue have names ending in *-glossus,* meaning "tongue." Once you can recall the structures referred to by *genio-*, *hyo-*, *palato-*, and *stylo-*, you shouldn't have much trouble with this group. The **genioglossus muscle** originates at the chin, the **hyoglossus muscle** at the hyoid bone, the **palatoglossus muscle** at the palate, and the **styloglossus muscle** at the styloid process (Figure 10.8). These muscles, the extrinsic tongue muscles, are used in various combinations to move the tongue in the delicate and complex patterns necessary for speech. They also manipulate food within the mouth in preparation for swallowing. The intrinsic tongue muscles, located entirely within the tongue, assist in these activities. Most of these muscles are innervated by the twelfth cranial nerve, the *hypoglossal nerve*; its name indicates its function as well as its location (Table 10.4).

Muscles of the Pharynx [Figure 10.9 and Table 10.5]

The paired pharyngeal muscles are important in the initiation of swallowing. The **pharyngeal constrictors** begin the process of moving a *bolus*, or chewed

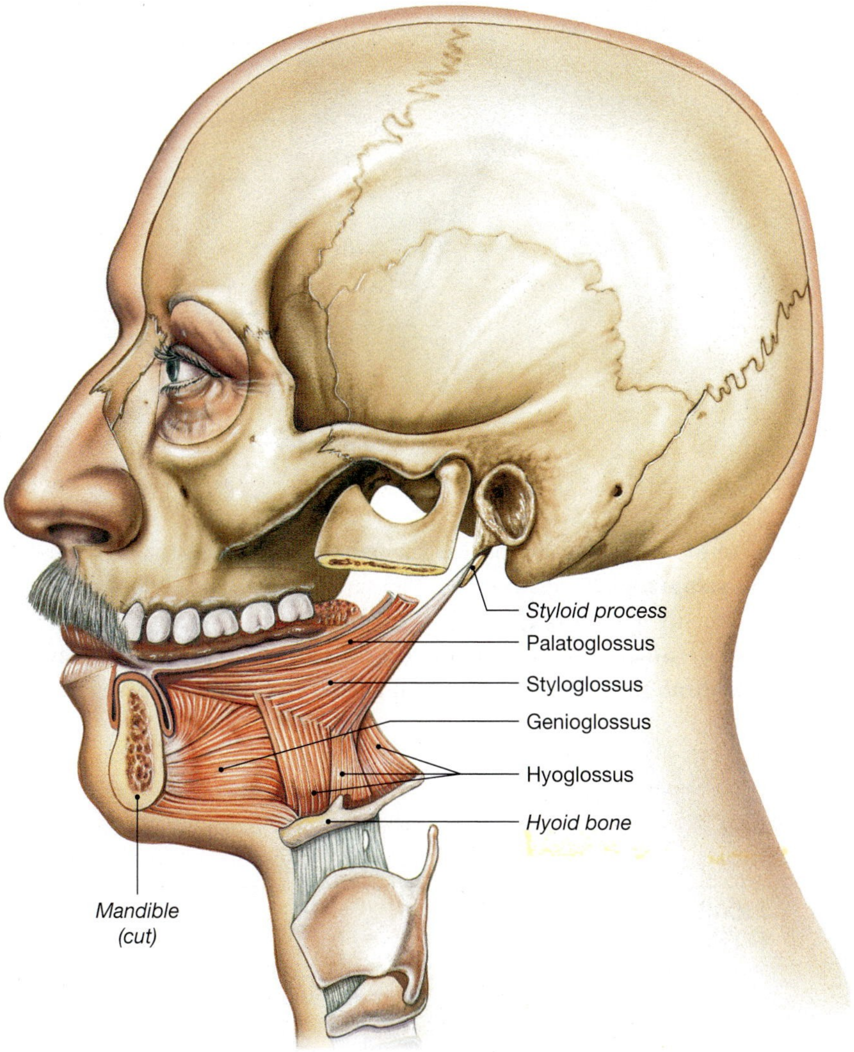

Figure 10.8 Muscles of the Tongue
The left mandibular ramus has been removed to show the muscles on the left side of the tongue.

TABLE 10.4 Muscles of the Tongue

Muscle	Origin	Insertion	Action	Innervation
Genioglossus	Medial surface of mandible around chin	Body of tongue, hyoid bone	Depresses and protracts tongue	Hypoglossal nerve (N XII)
Hyoglossus	Body and greater horn of hyoid bone	Side of tongue	Depresses and retracts tongue	As above
Palatoglossus	Anterior surface of soft palate	As above	Elevates tongue, depresses soft palate	Branch of pharyngeal plexus (N X)
Styloglossus	Styloid process of temporal bone	Along the side to tip and base of tongue	Retracts tongue, elevates sides	Hypoglossal nerve (N XII)

Figure 10.9 Muscles of the Pharynx
Pharyngeal muscles initiate swallowing. **(a)** Lateral view. **(b)** Midsagittal view.

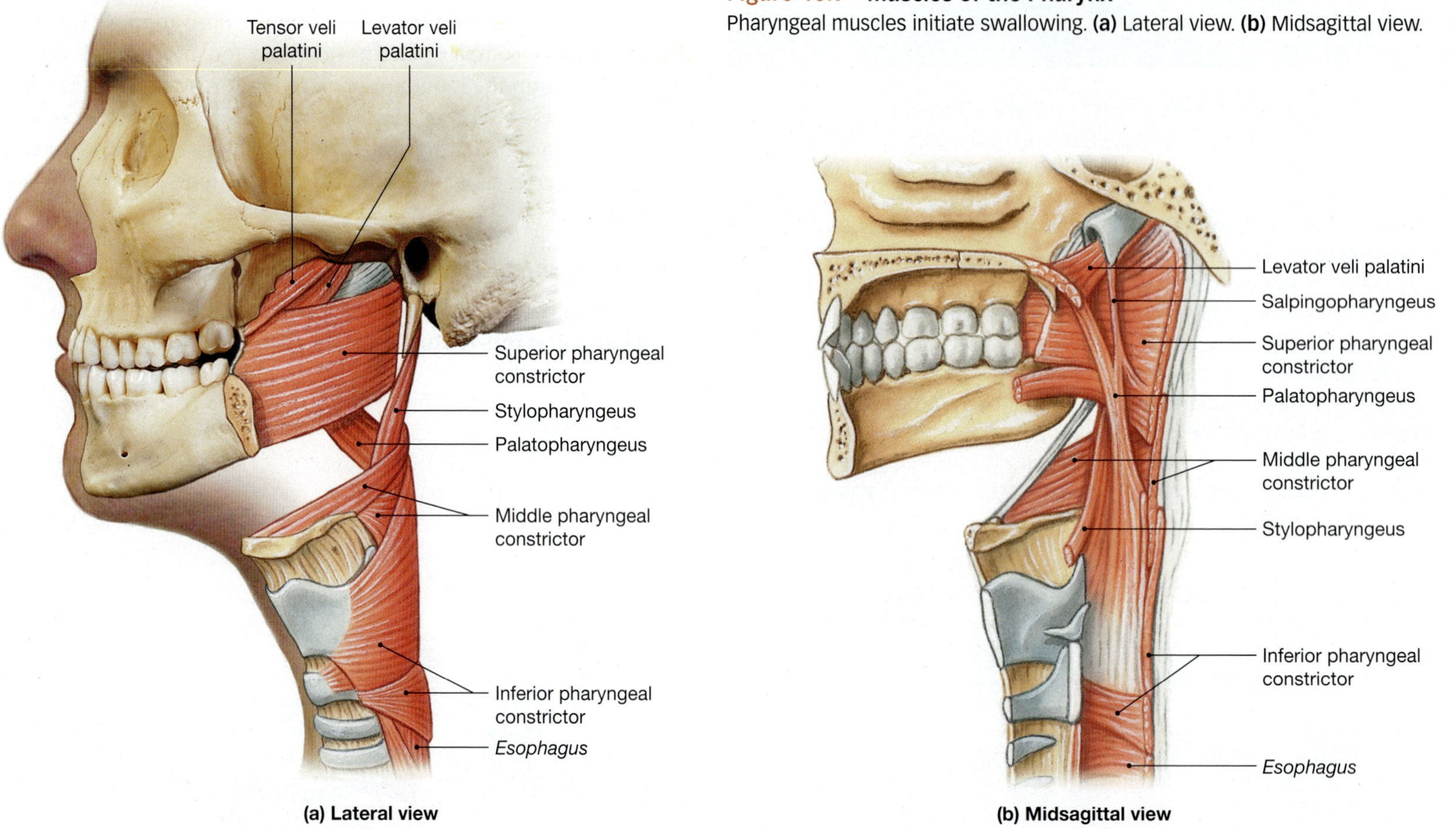

mass of food, into the esophagus. The **palatopharyngeus** (pal-āt-ō-far-IN-jē-us), **salpingopharyngeus** (sal-pin-gō-far-IN-jē-us), and **stylopharyngeus** (stī-lō-far-IN-jē-us) **muscles** elevate the larynx and are grouped together as *laryngeal elevators.* The **palatal muscles**, the **tensor veli palatini** and **levator veli palatini**, raise the soft palate and adjacent portions of the pharyngeal wall. The latter muscles also pull open the entrance to the auditory tube. As a result, swallowing repeatedly can help one adjust to pressure changes when flying or SCUBA diving. Pharyngeal muscles are innervated by the ninth (*glossopharyngeal*) and tenth (*vagus*) cranial nerves. These muscles are illustrated in **Figure 10.9**, and additional information can be found in Table 10.5.

TABLE 10.5 Muscles of the Pharynx

Muscle	Origin	Insertion	Action	Innervation
PHARYNGEAL CONSTRICTORS			Constrict pharynx to propel bolus into esophagus	Branches of pharyngeal plexus (N X)
Superior constrictor	Pterygoid process of sphenoid, medial surfaces of mandible, and the side of the tongue	Median raphe attached to occipital bone		N X
Middle constrictor	Horns of hyoid bone	Median raphe		N X
Inferior constrictor	Cricoid and thyroid cartilages of larynx	Median raphe		N X
LARYNGEAL ELEVATORS*			Elevate larynx	Branches of pharyngeal plexus (N IX & X)
Palatopharyngeus	Soft and hard palates	Thyroid cartilage		N X
Salpingopharyngeus	Cartilage around the inferior portion of the auditory tube	Thyroid cartilage		N X
Stylopharyngeus	Styloid process of temporal bone	Thyroid cartilage		N IX
PALATAL MUSCLES				
Levator veli palatini	Petrous part of temporal bone, tissues around the auditory tube	Soft palate	Elevate soft palate	Branches of pharyngeal plexus (N X)
Tensor veli palatini	Sphenoidal spine, pterygoid process, and tissues around the auditory tube	Soft palate	As above	N V

*Assisted by the thyrohyoid, geniohyoid, stylohyoid, and hyoglossus muscles, discussed in Tables 10.4 and 10.6.

Anterior Muscles of the Neck [Figures 10.10/10.11 and Table 10.6]

The anterior muscles of the neck control the position of the larynx, depress the mandible, tense the floor of the mouth, and provide a stable foundation for muscles of the tongue and pharynx (Figures 10.10 and 10.11, and Table 10.6). The anterior neck muscles that position the larynx are called *extrinsic* muscles, while those that affect the vocal cords are termed *intrinsic* muscles. (The vocal cords will be discussed in Chapter 24.) Additionally, the muscles of the neck are either *suprahyoid* or *infrahyoid* based on their location relative to the hyoid bone. The **digastric** (dī-GAS-trik) **muscle** has two bellies, as the name implies (*di-*, two + *gaster*, stomach). One belly extends from the chin to the hyoid bone, and the other continues from the hyoid bone to the mastoid portion of the temporal bone. This muscle opens the mouth by depressing the mandible. The anterior belly overlies the broad, flat **mylohyoid** (mī-lō-HĪ-oyd) **muscle**, which provides muscular support to the floor of the mouth. The **geniohyoid muscles**, which lie superior to the mylohyoid muscle, provide additional support. The **stylohyoid** (stī-lō-HĪ-oyd) **muscle** forms a muscular connection between the hyoid bone and the styloid process of the skull. The **sternocleidomastoid** (ster-nō-klī-dō-MAS-toid) **muscle** extends from the clavicle and the sternum to the mastoid process of the skull. It originates at two heads, a *sternal head* and a *clavicular head* (Table 10.6). The **omohyoid** (ō-mō-HĪ-oyd) **muscle** attaches to the scapula, the clavicle and first rib, and hyoid bone. These extensive muscles are innervated by more than one nerve, and specific regions can be made to contract independently. As a result, their actions are quite varied. The other members of this group are straplike muscles that run between the sternum and the larynx (*sternothyroid*) or hyoid bone (*sternohyoid*) and between the larynx and hyoid bone (*thyrohyoid*).

CONCEPT CHECK

1. Where do muscles of facial expression originate?
2. What is the general function of the muscles of mastication?
3. Describe the general function(s) of the extra-ocular muscles.
4. What is the importance of the pharyngeal muscles?

See blue "Answers" tab at back of book.

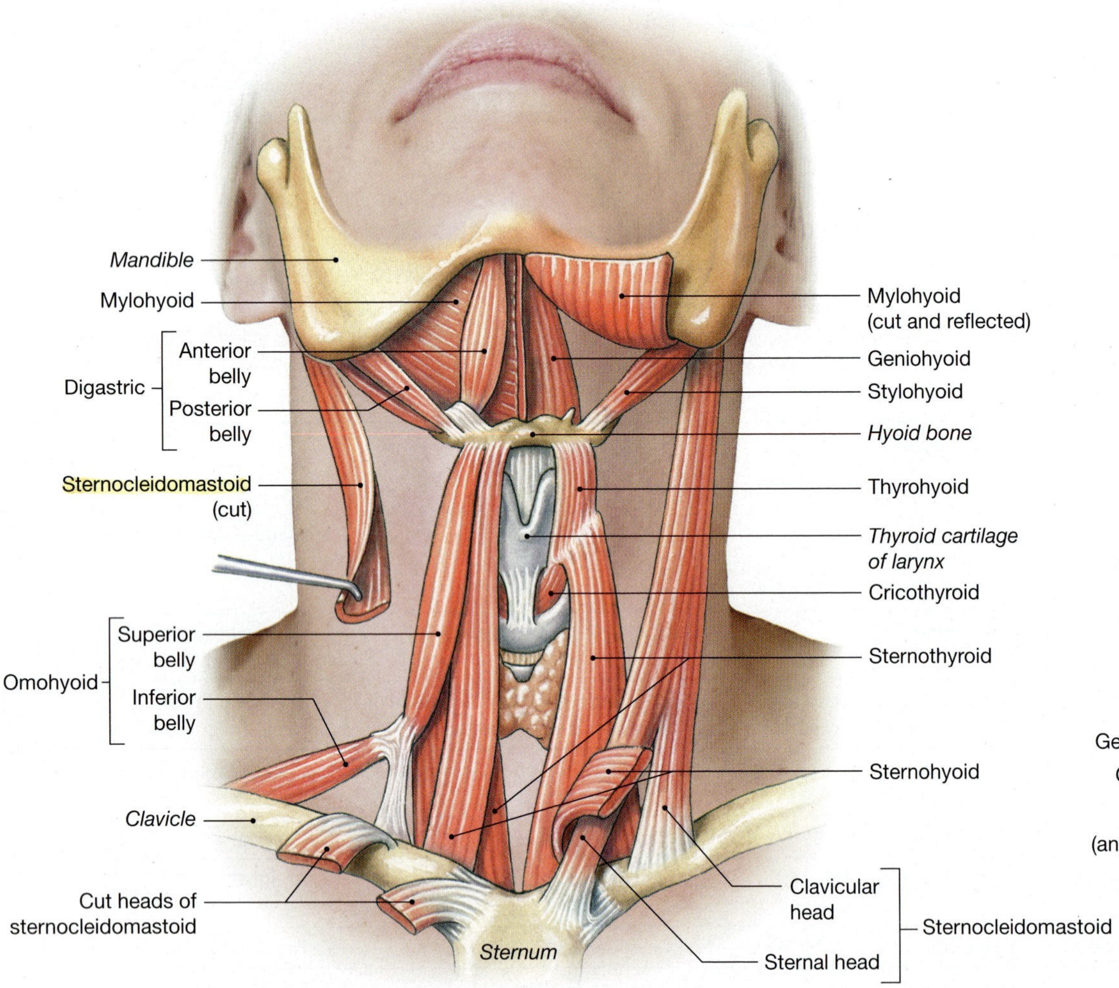

(a) Anterior view

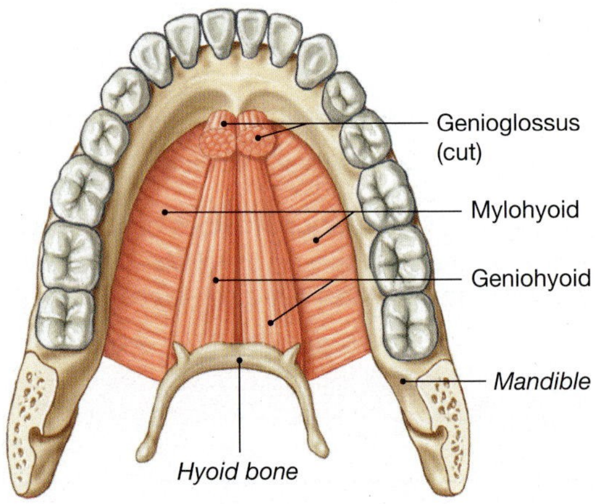

(b) Superior view

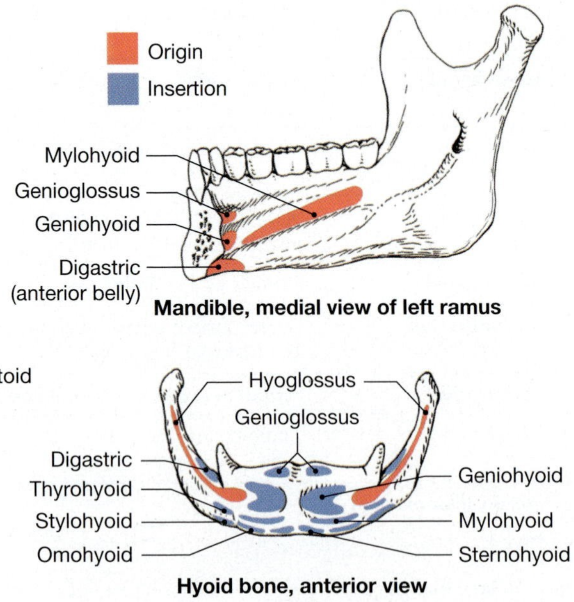

(c) Origins and insertions

Figure 10.10 Anterior Muscles of the Neck, Part I
The anterior muscles of the neck adjust the position of the larynx, mandible, and floor of the mouth and establish a foundation for attachment of both tongue and pharyngeal muscles. **(a)** Anterior view of neck muscles. **(b)** Muscles that form the floor of the oral cavity, superior view. **(c)** Origins and insertions on the mandible and hyoid. *See also Figures 6.3, 6.4, and 6.17.*

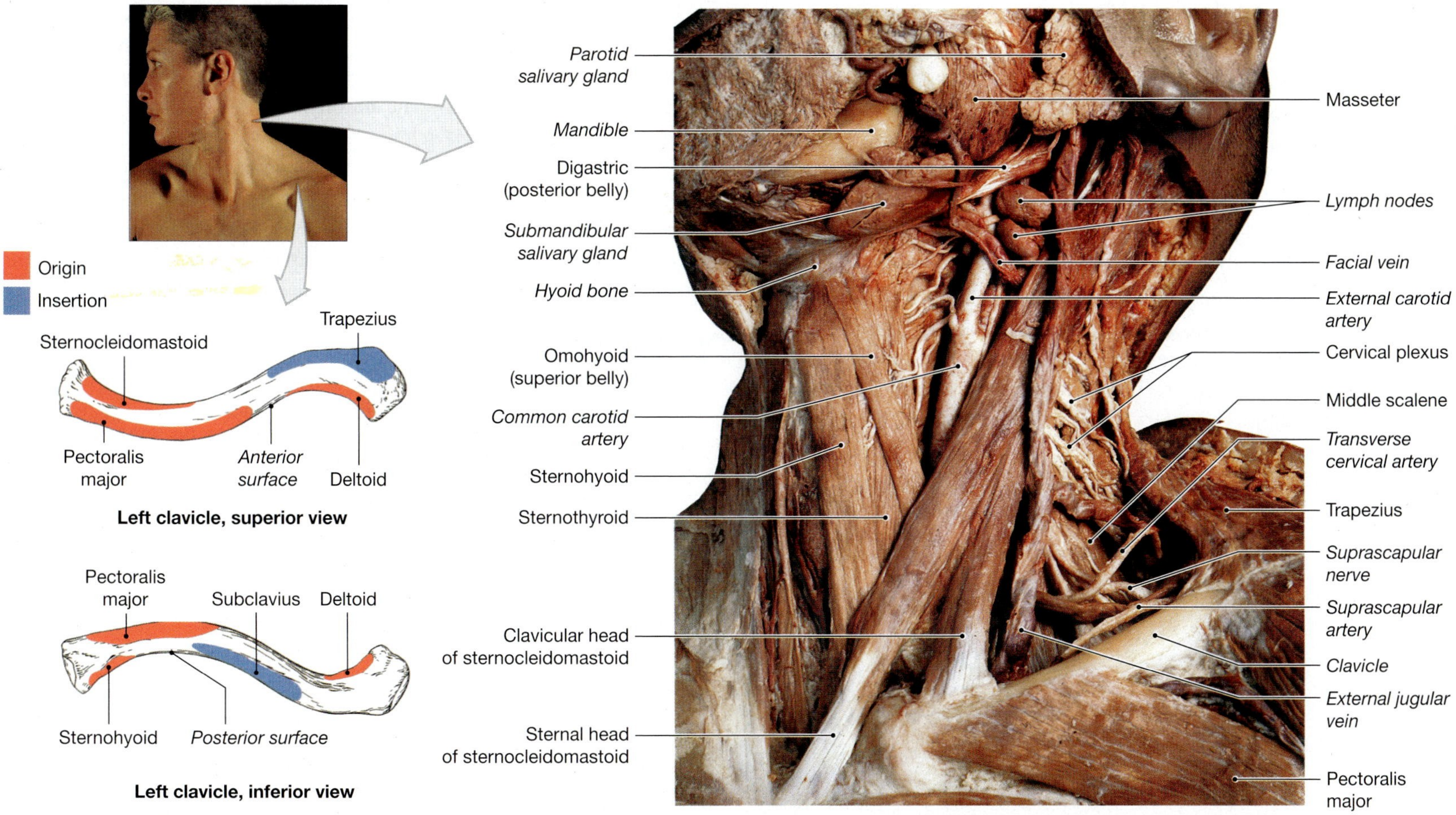

(a) Origins and insertions **(b) Anterolateral view**

Figure 10.11 Anterior Muscles of the Neck, Part II
(a) Origins and insertions on the clavicle. **(b)** An anterolateral view of a dissection of the neck, showing neck muscles and adjacent structures. *See also Figures 6.17 and 7.3.*

TABLE 10.6 Anterior Muscles of the Neck

Muscle	Origin	Insertion	Action	Innervation
Digastric		Hyoid bone	Depresses mandible, opening mouth, and/or elevates larynx	
Anterior belly	From inferior surface of mandible at chin			Trigeminal nerve (N V), mandibular branch
Posterior belly	From mastoid region of temporal bone			Facial nerve (N VII)
Geniohyoid	Medial surface of mandible at chin	Hyoid bone	As above and retracts hyoid bone	Cervical nerve C_1 via hypoglossal nerve (N XII)
Mylohyoid	Mylohyoid line of mandible	Median connective tissue band (raphe) that runs to hyoid bone	Elevates floor of mouth, elevates hyoid bone, and/or depresses mandible	Trigeminal nerve (N V), mandibular branch
Omohyoid*	Superior border of the scapula near the scapular notch	Hyoid bone	Depresses hyoid bone and larynx	Cervical spinal nerves C_2–C_3
Sternohyoid	Clavicle and manubrium	Hyoid bone	As above	Cervical spinal nerves C_1–C_3
Sternothyroid	Dorsal surface of manubrium and first costal cartilage	Thyroid cartilage of larynx	As above	As above
Stylohyoid	Styloid process of temporal bone	Hyoid bone	Elevates larynx	Facial nerve (N VII)
Thyrohyoid	Thyroid cartilage of larynx	Hyoid bone	Elevates larynx, depresses hyoid bone	Cervical spinal nerves C_1–C_2 via hypoglossal nerve (N XII)
Sternocleidomastoid		Mastoid region of skull and lateral portion of superior nuchal line	Together, they flex the neck; alone, one side bends neck toward shoulder and turns face to opposite side	Accessory nerve (N XI) and cervical spinal nerves (C_2–C_3) of cervical plexus
Clavicular head	Attaches to sternal end of clavicle			
Sternal head	Attaches to manubrium			

*Superior and inferior bellies, united at central tendon anchored to clavicle and first rib.

Muscles of the Vertebral Column

[Figures 10.2/10.12 and Table 10.7]

The muscles of the back are arranged into three distinct layers (superficial, intermediate, and deep). The muscles within the first two layers are termed the *extrinsic back muscles.* These muscles, which are innervated by the ventral rami of the associated spinal nerves, extend from the axial skeleton to the upper limb or the rib cage. The muscles of the superficial layer, the trapezius, latissimus dorsi, levator scapulae, and rhomboid muscles, will be discussed in Chapter 11 because they position the pectoral girdle and upper limb. The intermediate layer of the extrinsic back muscles consists of the serratus posterior muscles, whose primary function is assisting in rib movement during respiration. These muscles are discussed later in this chapter.

The deepest muscles of the back are the *intrinsic* (or *true*) *back muscles* (Figure 10.12 and Table 10.7). Intrinsic back muscles are innervated by the dorsal rami of the spinal nerves. These muscles interconnect and stabilize the vertebrae.

The intrinsic back muscles are also arranged in superficial, intermediate, and deep layers. These three muscle layers are found lateral to the vertebral column within the space between the spinous processes and the transverse processes of the vertebrae. Although this mass of muscles extends from the sacrum to the skull overall, it is important to remember that each muscle group is composed of numerous separate muscles of varying length.

The Superficial Layer of the Intrinsic Back Muscles

The superficial layer of intrinsic back muscles consists of the splenius muscles (the **splenius capitis** and **splenius cervicis muscles**). The splenius capitis muscles have their origin on the ligamentum nuchae and the spines of the upper four thoracic vertebrae, and insert onto the skull. The splenius cervicis muscles originate on the ligamentum nuchae and the spines of the upper cervical vertebrae, and also insert onto the skull. These two muscle groups perform extension or lateral flexion of the neck.

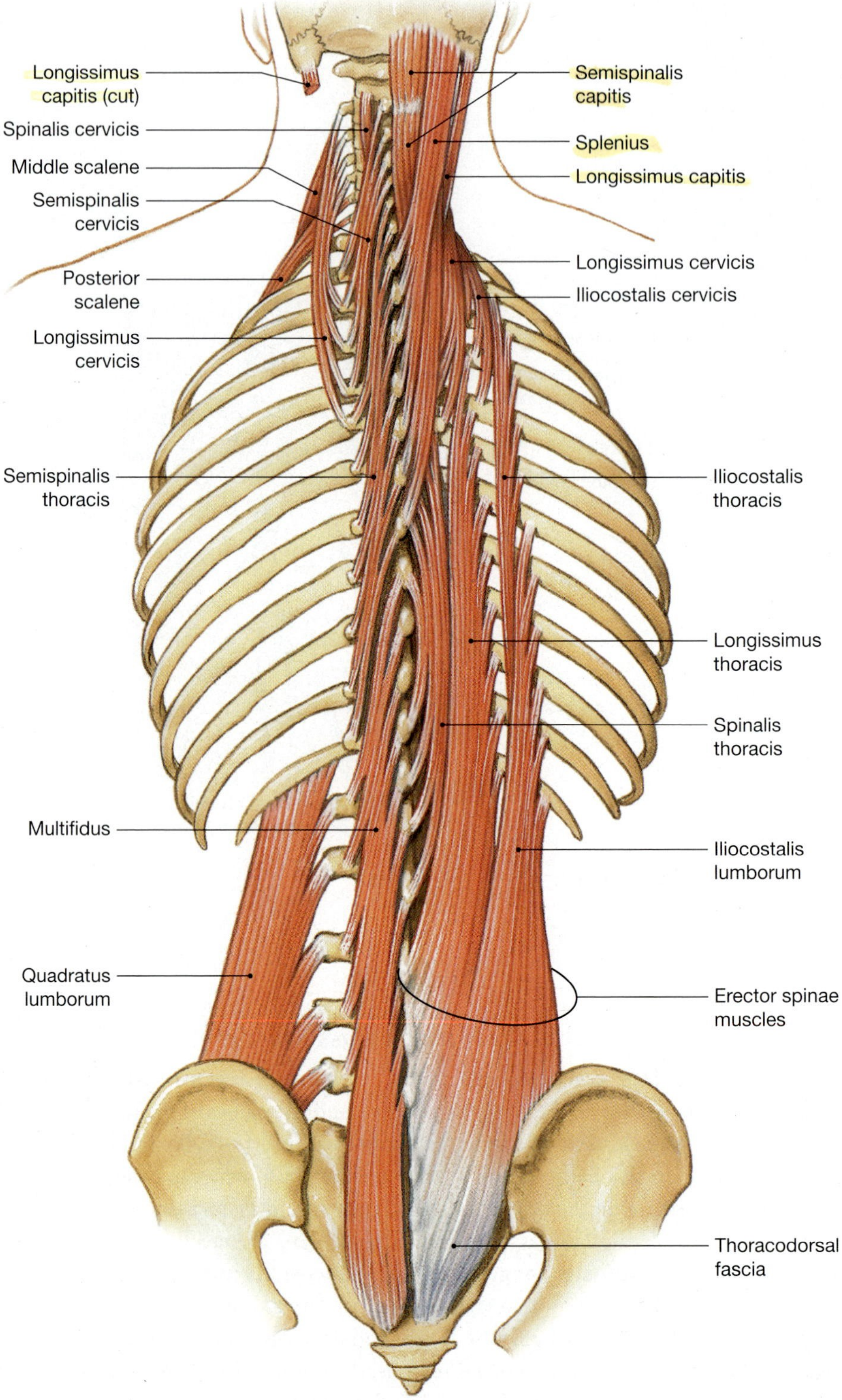

(a) The erector spinae, posterior view

Figure 10.12 Muscles of the Vertebral Column
Collectively, these muscles adjust the position of the vertebral column, head, neck, and ribs. Selected origins and insertions are shown. **(a)** Posterior view of superficial (right) and deeper (left) muscles of the vertebral column. **(b)** Posterior view of the intervertebral muscles. **(c)** Muscles on the anterior surfaces of the cervical and superior thoracic vertebrae.

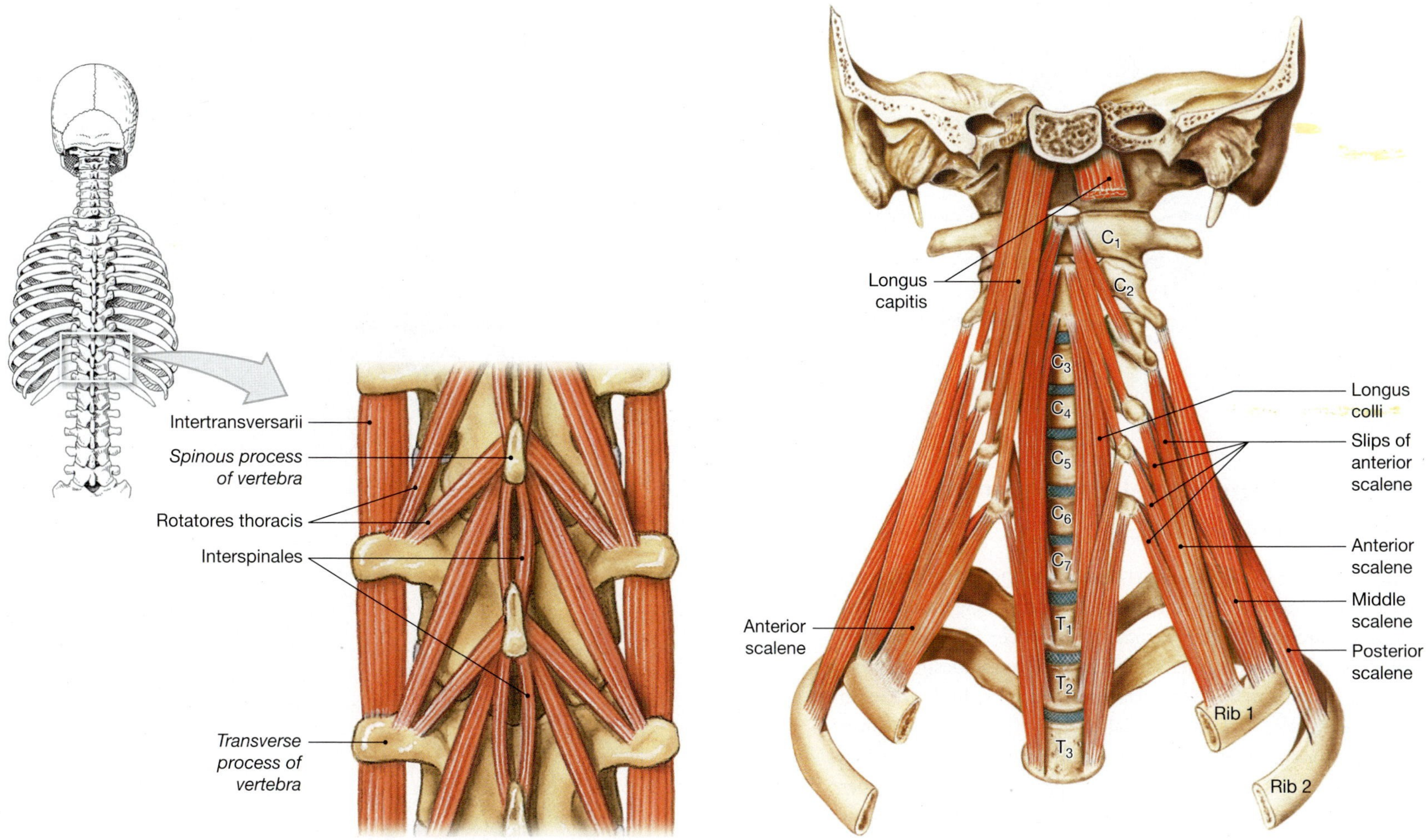

(b) Intervertebral muscles, posterior view

(c) Muscles on the anterior surfaces of the cervical and upper thoracic vertebrae

Figure 10.12 ***(continued)***

The Intermediate Layer of the Intrinsic Back Muscles

The intermediate layer consists of the spinal extensors, or **erector spinae**. These muscles originate on the vertebral column, and the names of the individual muscles provide useful information about their insertions. For example, a muscle with the name *capitis* inserts on the skull, whereas *cervicis* indicates an insertion on the upper cervical vertebrae and *thoracis* an insertion on the lower cervical and upper thoracic vertebrae. The erector spinae are subdivided into **spinalis**, **longissimus**, and **iliocostalis muscle** groups (**Figure 10.12a**). These divisions are based on proximity to the vertebral column, with the spinalis group being the closest and the iliocostalis the farthest away. In the inferior lumbar and sacral regions, the boundaries between the longissimus and iliocostalis muscles become difficult to distinguish. When contracting together, the erector spinae extend the vertebral column. When the muscles on only one side contract, there is lateral flexion of the vertebral column.

The Deep Layer of the Intrinsic Back Muscles

Deep to the spinalis muscles, the muscles of the deepest layer interconnect and stabilize the vertebrae. These muscles, sometimes called the *transversospinalis muscles*, include the **semispinalis** group and the **multifidus**, **rotatores**, **interspinales**, and **intertransversarii muscles** (**Figure 10.12a,b**). These are all relatively short muscles that work in various combinations to produce slight extension or rotation of the vertebral column. They are also important in making delicate adjustments in the positions of individual vertebrae and stabilizing adjacent vertebrae. If injured, these muscles can start a cycle of pain → muscle stimulation → contraction → pain. This can lead to pressure on adjacent spinal nerves, leading to sensory losses as well as limiting mobility. Many of the warmup and stretching exercises recommended before athletic events are intended to prepare these small but very important muscles for their supporting roles.

Spinal Flexors

The muscles of the vertebral column include many extensors but few flexors. The vertebral column does not need a massive series of flexor muscles because (1) many of the large trunk muscles flex the vertebral column when they contract, and (2) most of the body weight lies anterior to the vertebral column, and gravity tends to flex the spine. However, a few spinal flexors are associated with the anterior surface of the vertebral column. In the neck (**Figure 10.12c**) the **longus capitis** and the **longus colli** rotate or flex the neck, depending on whether the muscles of one or both sides are contracting. In the lumbar region, the large **quadratus lumborum** muscles flex the vertebral column and depress the ribs.

TABLE 10.7 Muscles of the Vertebral Column

Group/Muscle	Origin	Insertion	Action	Innervation
SUPERFICIAL LAYER				
Splenius (Splenius capitis, splenius cervicis)	Spinous processes and ligaments connecting inferior cervical and superior thoracic vertebrae	Mastoid process, occipital bone of skull, superior cervical vertebrae	The two sides act together to extend neck; either alone rotates and laterally flexes neck to that side	Cervical spinal nerves
Erector Spinae				
SPINALIS GROUP				
Spinalis cervicis	Inferior portion of ligamentum nuchae and spinous process of C_7	Spinous process of axis	Extends neck	As above
Spinalis thoracis	Spinous processes of inferior thoracic and superior lumbar vertebrae	Spinous processes of superior thoracic vertebrae	Extends vertebral column	Thoracic and lumbar spinal nerves
LONGISSIMUS GROUP				
Longissimus capitis	Transverse processes of inferior cervical and superior thoracic vertebrae	Mastoid process of temporal bone	The two sides act together to extend neck; either alone rotates and laterally flexes neck to that side	Cervical and thoracic spinal nerves
Longissimus cervicis	Transverse processes of superior thoracic vertebrae	Transverse processes of middle and superior cervical vertebrae	As above	As above
Longissimus thoracis	Broad aponeurosis and at transverse processes of inferior thoracic and superior lumbar vertebrae; joins iliocostalis	Transverse processes of superior thoracic and lumbar vertebrae and inferior surfaces of lower 10 ribs	Extension of vertebral column; alone, each produces lateral flexion to that side	Thoracic and lumbar spinal nerves
ILIOCOSTALIS GROUP				
Iliocostalis cervicis	Superior borders of vertebrosternal ribs near the angles	Transverse processes of middle and inferior cervical vertebrae	Extends or laterally flexes neck, elevates ribs	Cervical and superior thoracic spinal nerves
Iliocostalis thoracis	Superior borders of ribs 6–12 medial to the angles	Superior ribs and transverse processes of last cervical vertebra	Stabilizes thoracic vertebrae in extension	Thoracic spinal nerves
Iliocostalis lumborum	Iliac crest, sacral crests, and lumbar spinous processes	Inferior surfaces of ribs 6–12 near their angles	Extends vertebral column, depresses ribs	Inferior thoracic nerves and lumbar spinal nerves
DEEP MUSCLES OF THE SPINE (TRANSVERSOSPINALIS)				
Semispinalis				
Semispinalis capitis	Processes of inferior cervical and superior thoracic vertebrae	Occipital bone, between nuchal lines	Together the two sides extend neck; alone, each extends and laterally flexes neck and turns head to opposite side	Cervical spinal nerves
Semispinalis cervicis	Transverse processes of T_1–T_5 or T_6	Spinous processes of C_2–C_5	Extends vertebral column and rotates toward opposite side	As above
Semispinalis thoracis	Transverse processes of T_6–T_{10}	Spinous processes of C_5–T_4	As above	Thoracic spinal nerves
Multifidus	Sacrum and transverse process of each vertebra	Spinous processes of the third or fourth more superior vertebra	As above	Cervical, thoracic, and lumbar spinal nerves
Rotatores (cervicis, thoracis, and lumborum)	Transverse processes of the vertebrae in each region (cervical, thoracic, and lumbar)	Spinous process of adjacent, more superior vertebra	As above	As above
Interspinales	Spinous process of each vertebra	Spinous processes of more superior vertebra	Extends vertebral column	As above
Intertransversarii	Transverse processes of each vertebra	Transverse process of more superior vertebra	Lateral flexion of vertebral column	As above
SPINAL FLEXORS				
Longus capitis	Transverse processes of cervical vertebrae	Base of the occipital bone	Together the two sides flex the neck; alone each rotates head to that side	Cervical spinal nerves
Longus colli	Anterior surfaces of cervical and superior thoracic vertebrae	Transverse processes of superior cervical vertebrae	Flexes and/or rotates neck; limits hyperextension	As above
Quadratus lumborum	Iliac crest and iliolumbar ligament	Last rib and transverse processes of lumbar vertebrae	Together they depress ribs; alone, each produces lateral flexion of vertebral column; fixes floating ribs (11 and 12) during forced exhalation	Thoracic and lumbar spinal nerves

Oblique and Rectus Muscles

[Figures 10.12 to 10.14 and Table 10.8]

The muscles of the oblique and rectus groups (Figures 10.12 to 10.14, and Table 10.8) lie between the vertebral column and the ventral midline. The oblique muscles can compress underlying structures or rotate the vertebral column, depending on whether one or both sides are contracting. The rectus muscles are important flexors of the vertebral column, acting in opposition to the erector spinae. The oblique and rectus muscles of the trunk and the diaphragm that separates the abdominopelvic and thoracic cavities are united by their common embryological origins. The oblique and rectus muscles can be divided into cervical, thoracic, and abdominal groups.

The oblique group includes the **scalene** (SKĀ-lēn) **muscles** of the cervical region and the **intercostal** (in-ter-KOS-tul) and **transversus muscles** of the thoracic region. In the neck, the *anterior, middle,* and *posterior scalene muscles* elevate the first two ribs and assist in flexion of the neck (Figure 10.12a,c). In the thorax, the oblique muscles, which lie between the ribs, are called *intercostal muscles.* The **external intercostal muscles** are superficial to the **internal intercostal muscles** (Figure 10.13a). Both sets of intercostal muscles are important in respiratory movements of the ribs. A small **transversus thoracis muscle** crosses the inner surface of the rib cage and is covered by the serous membrane (*pleura*) that lines the pleural cavities.

In the abdomen, the same basic pattern of musculature extends unbroken across the abdominopelvic surface. The cross-directional arrangement

TABLE 10.8 Oblique and Rectus Muscles

Group/Muscle	Origin	Insertion	Action	Innervation
OBLIQUE GROUP				
Cervical region				
Scalenes (anterior, middle, and posterior)	Transverse and costal processes of cervical vertebrae C_2–C_7	Superior surface of first two ribs	Elevate ribs and/or flex neck; one side bends neck and rotates head and neck to opposite side	Cervical spinal nerves
Thoracic region				
External intercostals	Inferior border of each rib	Superior border of more inferior rib	Elevate ribs	Intercostal nerves (branches of thoracic spinal nerves)
Internal intercostals	Superior border of each rib	Inferior border of the more superior rib	Depress ribs	As above
Transversus thoracis	Posterior surface of sternum	Cartilages of ribs	As above	As above
Serratus posterior				
superior	Spinous processes of C_7–T_3 and ligamentum nuchae	Superior borders of ribs 2–5 near angles	Elevates ribs, enlarges thoracic cavity	Thoracic nerves (T_1–T_4)
inferior	Aponeurosis from spinous processes of T_{10}–L_3	Inferior borders of ribs 8–12	Pulls ribs inferiorly; also pulls outward, opposing diaphragm	Thoracic nerves (T_9–T_{12})
Abdominal region				
External oblique	External and inferior borders of ribs 5–12	External oblique aponeuroses extending to linea alba and iliac crest	Compresses abdomen; depresses ribs; flexes, laterally flexes, or rotates vertebral column to the opposite side	Intercostal nerves 5–12, iliohypogastric, and ilioinguinal nerves
Internal oblique	Thoracolumbar fascia and iliac crest	Inferior surfaces of ribs 9–12, costal cartilages 8–10, linea alba, and pubis	As above, but rotates vertebral column to same side	As above
Transversus abdominis	Cartilages of ribs 6–12, iliac crest, and thoracolumbar fascia	Linea alba and pubis	Compresses abdomen	As above
RECTUS GROUP				
Cervical region	*Includes the geniohyoid, omohyoid, sternohyoid, sternothyroid, and thyrohyoid muscles in Table 10.6*			
Thoracic region				
Diaphragm	Xiphoid process, ribs 7–12 and associated costal cartilages, and anterior surfaces of lumbar vertebrae	Central tendinous sheet	Contraction expands thoracic cavity, compresses abdominopelvic cavity	Phrenic nerves (C_3–C_5)
Abdominal region				
Rectus abdominis	Superior surface of pubis around symphysis	Inferior surfaces of cartilages (ribs 5–7) and xiphoid process of sternum	Depresses ribs, flexes vertebral column and compresses abdomen	Intercostal nerves (T_7–T_{12})

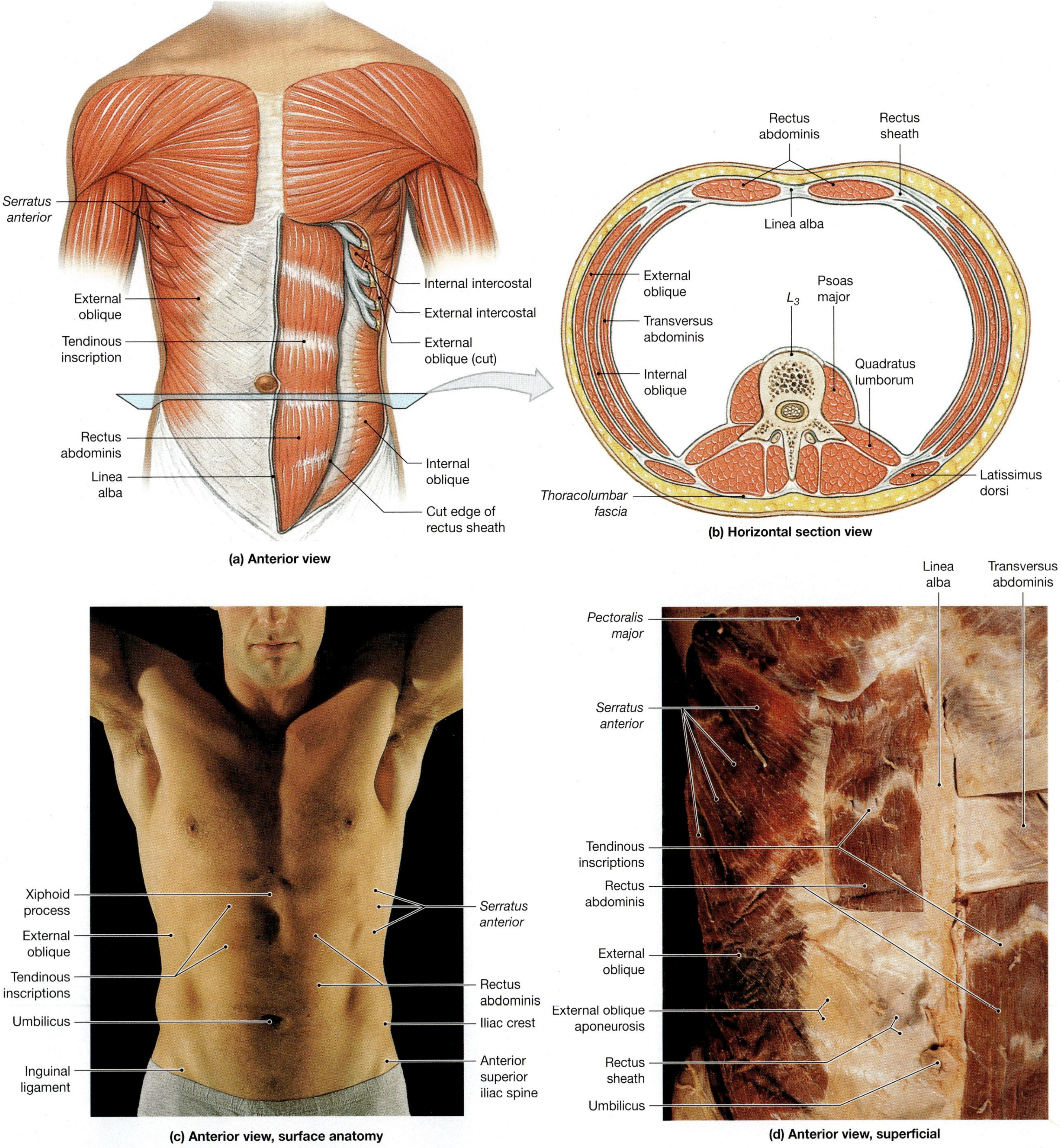

Figure 10.13 The Oblique and Rectus Muscles

Oblique muscles compress underlying structures between the vertebral column and the ventral midline; rectus muscles are flexors of the vertebral column. **(a)** Anterior view of the trunk, showing superficial and deep members of the oblique and rectus groups, and the sectional plane shown in part (b). **(b)** Diagrammatic horizontal section through the abdominal region. **(c)** Surface anatomy of the abdominal wall, anterior view. The *serratus anterior muscle*, seen in parts (a) and (c), is an appendicular muscle detailed in Chapter 11. **(d)** Cadaver, anterior superficial view of the abdominal wall. *See also Figures 6.19, 6.26, and 7.11.*

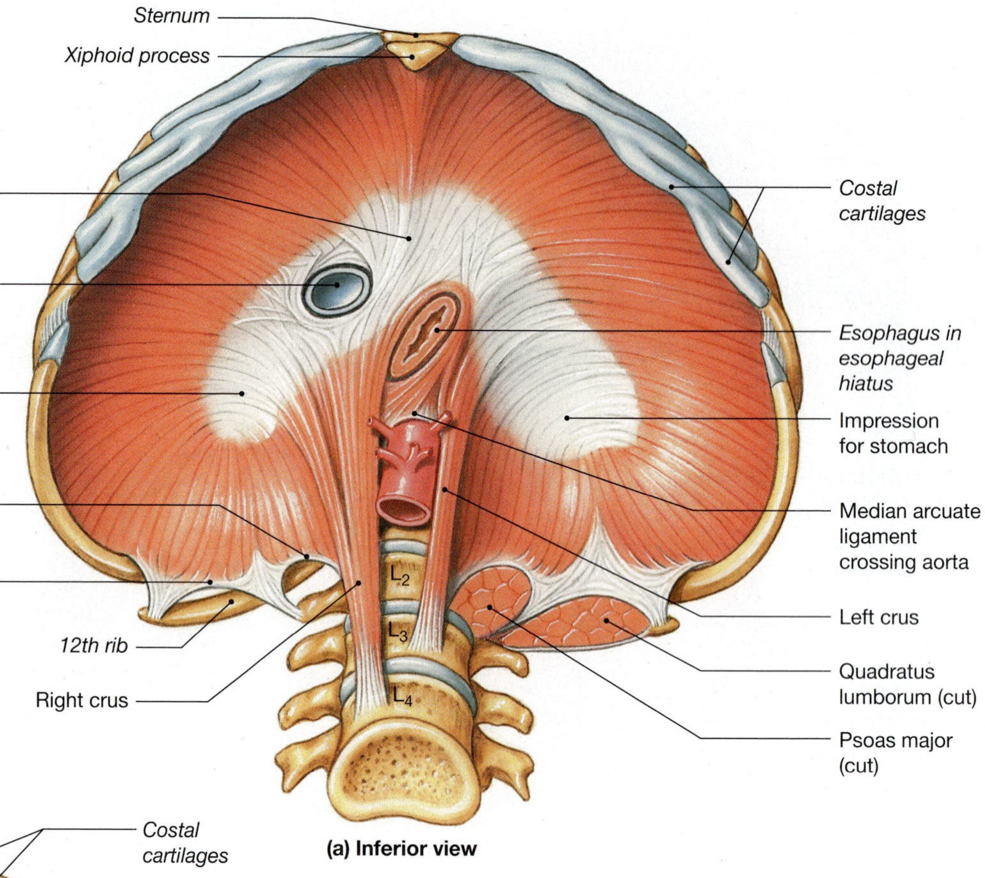

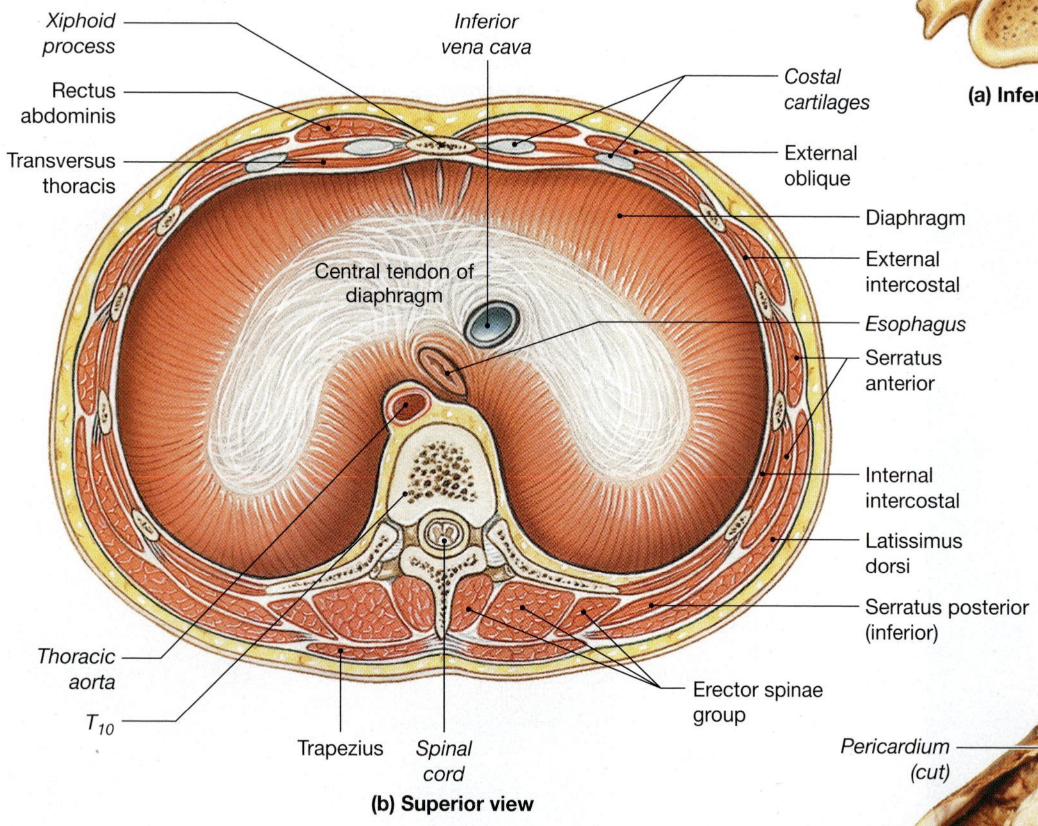

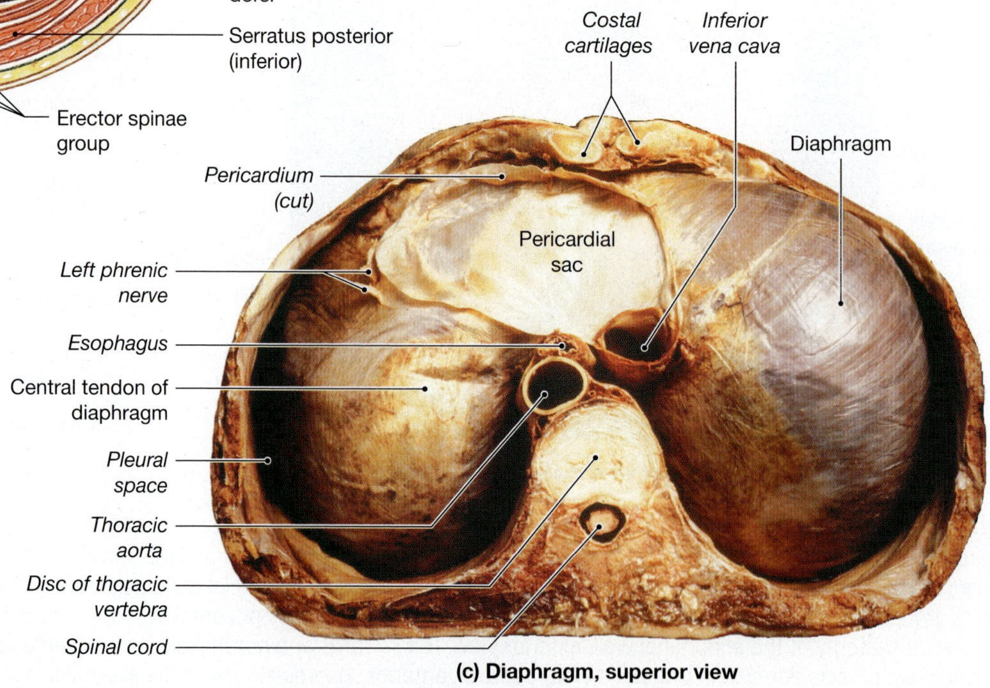

Figure 10.14 The Diaphragm
This muscular sheet separates the thoracic cavity from the abdominopelvic cavity. **(a)** Inferior view. **(b)** Diagrammatic superior view. **(c)** Superior view of a transverse section through the thorax, with other organs removed to show the location and orientation of the diaphragm.

of muscle fibers in these muscles strengthens the wall of the abdomen. These muscles are the **external** and **internal oblique muscles** (also called the *abdominal obliques*), the **transversus abdominis** (ab-DOM-i-nus) **muscles**, and the **rectus abdominis muscle** (Figure 10.13a–d). An excellent way to observe the relationship of these muscles is to view them in horizontal section (Figure 10.13b). The rectus abdominis muscle begins at the xiphoid process and ends near the pubic symphysis. This muscle is divided longitudinally by a median collagenous partition, the **linea alba** (white line). The transverse **tendinous inscriptions** are bands of fibrous tissue that divide this muscle into four repeated segments (Figure 10.13a,d). The surface anatomy of the oblique and rectus muscles of the thorax and abdomen is shown in Figure 10.13c.

The Diaphragm [Figure 10.14]

The term *diaphragm* refers to any muscular sheet that forms a wall. When used without a modifier, however, the **diaphragm**, or *diaphragmatic muscle*, specifies the muscular partition that separates the abdominopelvic and thoracic cavities (Figure 10.14). The diaphragm is a major muscle of respiration: Its contraction increases the volume of the thoracic cavity to promote inspiration; its relaxation decreases the volume to facilitate expiration (the muscles of respiration will be examined in Chapter 24).

Muscles of the Perineum and the Pelvic Diaphragm [Figure 10.16 and Tables 10.9/10.10]

The muscles of the pelvic perineum and the pelvic diaphragm extend from the sacrum and coccyx to the ischium and pubis. These muscles (1) support the organs of the pelvic cavity, (2) flex the joints of the sacrum and coccyx, and (3) control the movement of materials through the urethra and anus (Figure 10.16 and Tables 10.9/10.10).

The boundaries of the **perineum** (the pelvic floor and associated structures) are established by the inferior margins of the pelvis. If you draw a line between the ischial tuberosities, you will divide the perineum into two triangles: an anterior or **urogenital triangle**, and a posterior or **anal triangle** (Figure 10.16b). The superficial muscles of the anterior triangle

Clinical Note

Hernias When the abdominal muscles contract forcefully, pressure in the abdominopelvic cavity can increase dramatically. That pressure is applied to internal organs. If the individual exhales at the same time, the pressure is relieved because the diaphragm can move upward as the lungs collapse. But during vigorous isometric exercises or when lifting a weight while holding one's breath, pressure in the abdominopelvic cavity can rise to 106 kg/cm^2, roughly 100 times the normal pressure. A pressure that high can cause a variety of problems, including hernias. A **hernia** develops when a visceral organ or part of an organ protrudes abnormally through an opening in a surrounding muscular wall or partition. There are many types of hernias; here we will consider only *inguinal* (groin) *hernias* and *diaphragmatic hernias*.

Late in the development of male fetuses, the testes descend into the scrotum by passing through the abdominal wall at the **inguinal canals**. In adult males, the sperm ducts and associated blood vessels penetrate the abdominal musculature at the inguinal canals as the *spermatic cords,* on their way to the abdominal reproductive organs. In an **inguinal hernia**, the inguinal canal enlarges and the abdominal contents, such as a portion of the greater omentum, small intestine, or (more rarely) urinary bladder, enter the inguinal canal (Figure 10.15). If the herniated structures become trapped or twisted, surgery may be required to prevent serious complications. Inguinal hernias are not always caused by unusually high abdominal pressures; injuries to the abdomen or inherited weakness or distensibility of the canal can have the same effect.

The esophagus and major blood vessels pass through openings in the diaphragm, the muscle that separates the thoracic and abdominopelvic cavities. In a **diaphragmatic hernia**, abdominal organs slide into the thoracic cavity. If entry is through the *esophageal hiatus,* the passageway used by the esophagus, a *hiatal hernia* (hī-Ā-tal; *hiatus,* a gap or opening) exists. The severity of the condition depends on the location and size of the herniated organ or organs. Hiatal hernias are very common, and most go unnoticed, although they may increase the severity of gastric acid entry into the esophagus (gastroesophageal reflux disease, or GERD, commonly known as heartburn). Radiologists see them in about 30 percent of individuals whose upper gastrointestinal tracts are examined with barium-contrast techniques.

When clinical complications other than GERD develop, they generally do so because abdominal organs that have pushed into the thoracic cavity are exerting pressure on structures or organs there. Like inguinal hernias, a diaphragmatic hernia can result from congenital factors or from an injury that weakens or tears the diaphragm. If abdominal organs occupy the thoracic cavity during fetal development, the lungs may be poorly developed at birth.

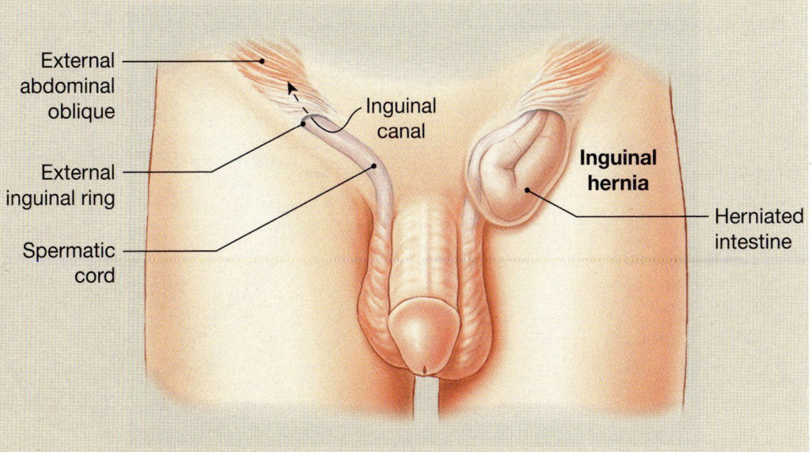

Figure 10.15 An Inguinal Hernia

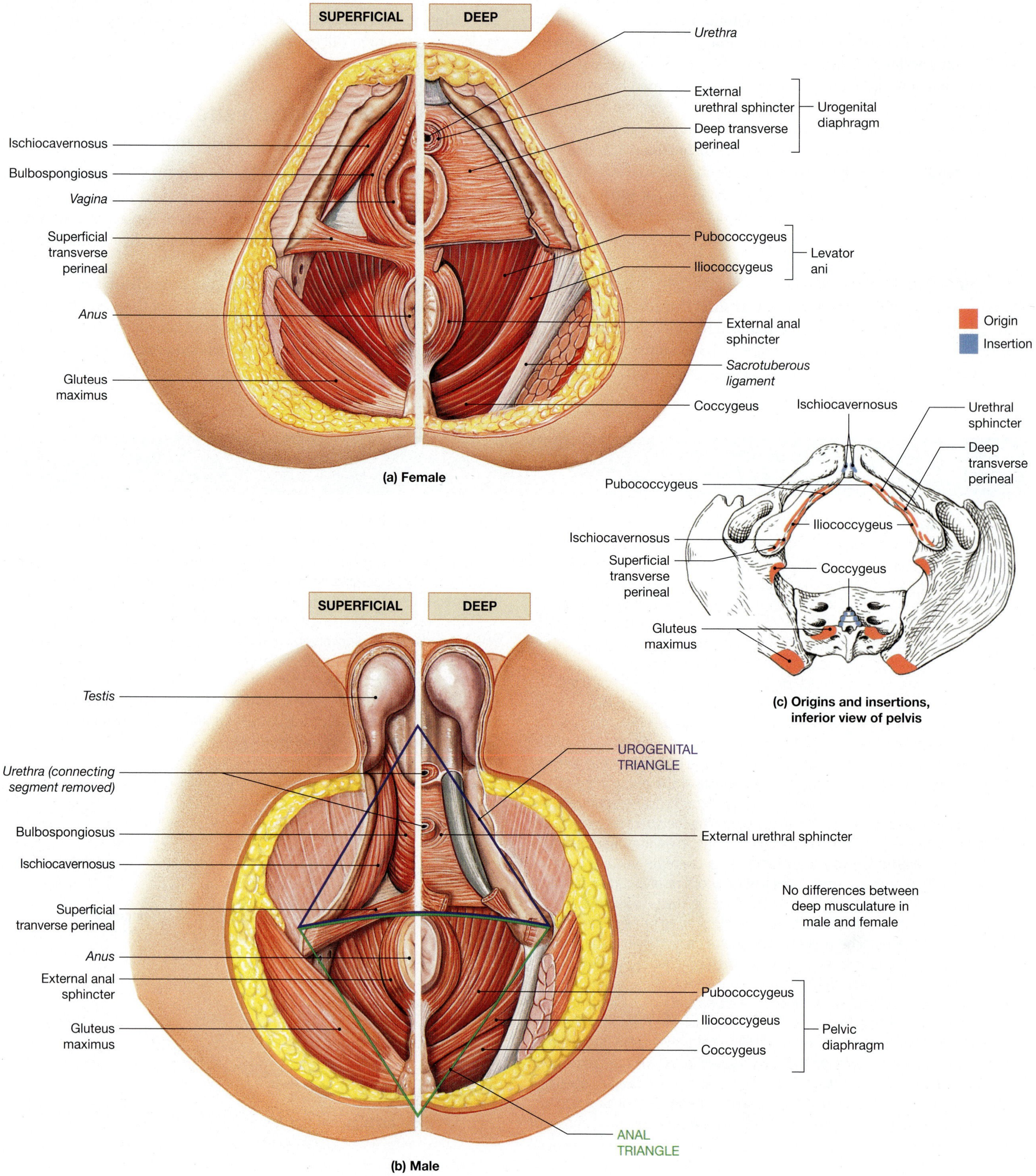

Figure 10.16 Muscles of the Pelvic Floor
The muscles of the pelvic floor form the urogenital triangle and anal triangle to support organs of the pelvic cavity, flex the sacrum and coccyx, and control material movement through the urethra and anus. **(a)** Inferior view, female. **(b)** Inferior view, male. **(c)** Selected origins and insertions. *See also Figures 7.10 to 7.12.*

TABLE 10.9 Muscles of the Perineum

Group/Muscle	Origin	Insertion	Action	Innervation
UROGENITAL TRIANGLE				
Superficial muscles				
Bulbospongiosus				
Male	Perineal body (central tendon of perineum) and medium raphe	Corpus spongiosum, perineal membrane and corpus cavernosum	Compresses base, stiffens penis, ejects urine or semen	Pudendal nerve, perineal branch $(S_2–S_4)$
Female	Perineal body (central tendon of perineum)	Bulb of vestibule, perineal membrane, body of clitoris, and corpus cavernosum	Compresses and stiffens clitoris, narrows vaginal opening	As above
Ischiocavernosus	Ramus and tuberosity of ischium	Corpus cavernosum of penis or clitoris; also to ischiopubic ramus (in female only)	Compresses and stiffens penis or clitoris, helping to maintain erection	As above
Superficial transverse perineal	Ischial ramus	Central tendon of perineum	Stabilizes central tendon of perineum	As above
Deep muscles				
Deep transverse perineal	Ischial ramus	Median raphe of urogenital diaphragm	As above	As above
External urethral sphincter:				
Male	Ischial and pubic rami	To median raphe at base of penis; inner fibers encircle urethra	Closes urethra; compresses prostate and bulbo-urethral glands	As above
Female	Ischial and pubic rami	To median raphe; inner fibers encircle urethra	Closes urethra; compresses vagina and greater vestibular glands	As above

TABLE 10.10 Muscles of the Pelvic Diaphragm

Group/Muscle	Origin	Insertion	Action	Innervation
ANAL TRIANGLE				
Coccygeus	Ischial spine	Lateral, inferior borders of the sacrum and coccyx	Flexes coccygeal joints; elevates and supports pelvic floor	Inferior sacral nerves $(S_4–S_5)$
Levator ani:				
Iliococcygeus	Ischial spine, pubis	Coccyx and median raphe	Tenses floor of pelvis, supports pelvic organs, flexes coccygeal joints, elevates and retracts anus	Pudendal nerve $(S_2–S_4)$
Pubococcygeus	Inner margins of pubis	As above	As above	As above
External anal sphincter	Via tendon from coccyx	Encircles anal opening	Closes anal opening	Pudendal nerve; hemorrhoidal branch $(S_2–S_4)$

are the muscles of the external genitalia. They overlie deeper muscles that strengthen the pelvic floor and encircle the urethra. These deep muscles constitute the **urogenital diaphragm**, a muscular layer that extends between the pubic bones.

An even more extensive muscular sheet, the **pelvic diaphragm**, forms the muscular foundation of the anal triangle. This layer extends anteriorly superior to the urogenital diaphragm as far as the pubic symphysis.

The urogenital and pelvic diaphragms do not completely close the pelvic outlet, because the urethra, vagina, and anus pass through them to open on the external surface. Muscular sphincters surround their openings and permit voluntary control of urination and defecation. Muscles, nerves, and blood vessels also pass through the pelvic outlet as they travel to or from the lower limbs.

CONCEPT CHECK

1. Damage to the external intercostal muscles would interfere with what important process?
2. If someone hit you in your rectus abdominis muscle, how would your body position change?
3. What is the function of the muscles of the pelvic diaphragm?
4. What is the function of the diaphragm?

See blue "Answers" tab at back of book.

Embryology Summary

For a summary of the development of the axial musculature, see Chapter 28 (Embryology and Human Development).

CLINICAL TERMS

diaphragmatic hernia (hiatal hernia): A hernia that occurs when abdominal organs slide into the thoracic cavity through an opening in the diaphragm.

hernia: A condition involving an organ or body part that protrudes through an abnormal opening.

inguinal hernia: A condition in which the inguinal canal enlarges and abdominal contents are forced into the inguinal canal.

STUDY OUTLINE

Introduction 262

1. The separation of the skeletal system into axial and appendicular divisions provides a useful guideline for subdividing the muscular system as well. The **axial musculature** arises from and inserts on the axial skeleton. It positions the head and spinal column and assists in moving the rib cage, which makes breathing possible.

The Axial Musculature 262

1. The axial musculature originates and inserts on the axial skeleton; it positions the head and spinal column and moves the rib cage. The appendicular musculature stabilizes or moves components of the appendicular skeleton. *(see Figures 10.1/10.2)*
2. The axial muscles are organized into four groups based on their location and/or function. These groups are (1) *muscles of the head and neck*, (2) *muscles of the vertebral column*, (3) *oblique* and *rectus muscles*, including the *diaphragm*, and (4) *muscles of the pelvic diaphragm*.
3. Organization of muscles into the four groups includes descriptions of innervation. **Innervation** refers to the identity of the nerve that controls a given muscle, and is also included in all muscle tables.

Muscles of the Head and Neck 263

4. Muscles of the head and neck are divided into several groups: (1) the *muscles of facial expression*, (2) the *extrinsic eye muscles*, (3) the *muscles of mastication*, (4) the *muscles of the tongue*, (5) the *muscles of the pharynx*, and (6) the *anterior muscles of the neck*.
5. Muscles involved with sight and hearing are based on the skull.
6. The muscles of facial expression originate on the surface of the skull. The largest group is associated with the mouth; it includes the **orbicularis oris** and **buccinator**. The **frontal** and **occipital bellies** of the **occipitofrontalis muscle** control movements of the eyebrows, forehead, and scalp. The **platysma** tenses skin of the neck and depresses the mandible. *(see Figures 10.3 to 10.6 and Table 10.1)*
7. The six **extra-ocular eye muscles** (*oculomotor muscles*) control eye position and movements. These muscles are the **inferior**, **lateral**, **medial**, and **superior recti** and the **superior** and **inferior obliques**. *(see Figure 10.5 and Table 10.2)*
8. The muscles of mastication (chewing) act on the mandible. They are the **masseter**, **temporalis**, and **pterygoid** (*medial* and *lateral*) muscles. *(see Figure 10.6 and Table 10.3)*
9. The muscles of the tongue are necessary for speech and swallowing, and they assist in mastication. They have names that end in *-glossus*, meaning "tongue." These muscles are the **genioglossus**, **hyoglossus**, **palatoglossus**, and **styloglossus**. *(see Figure 10.8 and Table 10.4)*
10. Muscles of the pharynx are important in the initiation of the swallowing process. These muscles include the **pharyngeal constrictors**, the laryngeal elevators (**palatopharyngeus**, **salpingopharyngeus**, and **stylopharyngeus**), and the **palatal muscles**, which raise the soft palate. *(see Figure 10.9 and Table 10.5)*
11. The anterior muscles of the neck control the position of the larynx, depress the mandible, and provide a foundation for the muscles of the tongue and pharynx. These include the **digastric**, **mylohyoid**, **stylohyoid**, and **sternocleidomastoid**. *(see Figures 10.3/10.4/10.10/10.11 and Table 10.6)*

Muscles of the Vertebral Column 273

12. The muscles of the back are arranged into three distinct layers (superficial, intermediate, and deep). The more superficial *extrinsic back muscles* are divided into two muscle layers, both of which are innervated by the ventral rami of the spinal nerves. The more superficial extrinsic back muscles extend from the axial skeleton to the upper limb, and are concerned with movement of the upper limb.
13. Only the deepest of these layers is composed of the *intrinsic* (or *true*) *back muscles*. These intrinsic back muscles are innervated by the dorsal rami of the spinal nerves, and interconnect the vertebrae.
14. The intrinsic back muscles are also arranged into layers (superficial, intermediate, and deep). The superficial layer contains the **splenius muscles** of the neck and upper thorax, while the intermediate group is composed of the *erector spinae* muscles of the trunk. The deep layer is composed of the *transversospinalis muscles*, which include the **semispinalis group** and the **multifidus, rotatores, interspinales,** and **intertransversarii muscles**. These muscles interconnect and stabilize the vertebrae. *(see Figure 10.12 and Table 10.7)*
15. Other muscles of the vertebral column include the **longus capitis** and **longus colli**, which rotate and flex the neck, and the **quadratus lumborum muscles** in the lumbar region, which flex the spine and depress the ribs. *(see Figure 10.12 and Table 10.7)*

Oblique and Rectus Muscles 276

16. The oblique and rectus muscles lie between the vertebral column and the ventral midline. The abdominal oblique muscles (**external oblique** and **internal oblique muscles**) compress underlying structures or rotate the vertebral column; the **rectus abdominis muscle** is a flexor of the vertebral column.
17. The oblique muscles of the neck and thorax include the **scalenes**, the **intercostals**, and the **transversus** muscles. The **external intercostals** and **internal intercostals** are important in respiratory movements of the ribs. *(see Figure 10.13 and Table 10.8)*
18. The **diaphragm** (*diaphragmatic muscle*) is also important in respiration. It separates the abdominopelvic and thoracic cavities. *(see Figure 10.14)*

Muscles of the Perineum and the Pelvic Diaphragm 279

19. Muscles of the perineum and pelvic diaphragm extend from the sacrum and coccyx to the ischium and pubis. These muscles (1) support the organs of the pelvic cavity, (2) flex the joints of the sacrum and coccyx, and (3) control the movement of materials through the urethra and anus.
20. The **perineum** (the pelvic floor and associated structures) can be divided into an anterior or **urogenital triangle** and a posterior or **anal triangle**. The pelvic floor consists of the **urogenital diaphragm** and the **pelvic diaphragm**. *(see Figure 10.16 and Tables 10.9/10.10)*

CHAPTER REVIEW

For answers to the Concept Check and Chapter Review questions, go to the blue "Answers" tab at the back of the book.

Level 1 Reviewing Facts and Terms

Match each numbered item with the most closely related lettered item. Use letters for answers in the spaces provided.

Column A	Column B
___ 1. spinalis	a. compresses cheeks
___ 2. perineum	b. elevates larynx
___ 3. buccinator	c. tenses skin of neck
___ 4. extra-ocular	d. pelvic floor/associated structures
___ 5. intercostals	e. elevates mandible
___ 6. stylohyoid	f. move ribs
___ 7. inferior rectus	g. retracts tongue
___ 8. temporalis	h. extends neck
___ 9. platysma	i. eye muscles
___10. styloglossus	j. makes eye look down

11. Which of the following muscles does not compress the abdomen?
    (a) diaphragm (b) internal intercostal
    (c) external oblique (d) rectus abdominis

12. The muscle that arises from the pubis is the
    (a) internal oblique (b) rectus abdominis
    (c) transversus abdominis (d) scalene

13. The iliac crest is the origin of the
    (a) quadratus lumborum (b) iliocostalis cervicis
    (c) longissimus cervicis (d) splenius

14. Which of the following describes the action of the digastric muscle?
    (a) elevates the larynx
    (b) elevates the larynx and depresses the mandible
    (c) depresses the larynx
    (d) elevates the mandible

15. Which of the following muscles has its insertion on the cartilages of the ribs?
    (a) diaphragm (b) external intercostal
    (c) transversus thoracis (d) scalene

16. Some of the muscles of the tongue are innervated by the
    (a) hypoglossal nerve (N XII)
    (b) trochlear nerve (N IV)
    (c) abducens nerve (N VII)
    (d) both b and c are correct

17. All of the following are true of the muscles of the pelvic floor except
    (a) they extend between the sacrum and the pelvic girdle
    (b) they form the perineum
    (c) they "fine-tune" the movements of the thigh with regard to the pelvis
    (d) they encircle the openings in the pelvic outlet

18. The axial muscles of the spine control the position of the
    (a) head, neck, and pectoral girdle
    (b) head, neck, and vertebral column
    (c) vertebral column only
    (d) vertebral column and pectoral and pelvic girdles

19. The scalenes have their origin on the
    (a) transverse and costal processes of cervical vertebrae
    (b) inferior border of the previous rib
    (c) cartilages of the ribs
    (d) thoracolumbar fascia and iliac crest

20. Which cranial nerve is most likely to have been damaged if a person cannot move the right eye to look laterally?
    (a) oculomotor nerve (b) trigeminal nerve
    (c) facial nerve (d) abducens nerve

Level 2 Reviewing Concepts

1. During abdominal surgery, the surgeon makes a cut through the muscle directly to the right of the linea alba. The muscle that is being cut would be the
   (a) digastric (b) external oblique
   (c) rectus abdominis (d) scalenus

2. Ryan hears a loud noise and quickly raises his eyes to look upward in the direction of the sound. To accomplish this action, he must use his ___ muscles.
   (a) superior rectus (b) inferior rectus
   (c) superior oblique (d) lateral rectus

3. Which of the following muscles plays no role in swallowing?
   (a) superior constrictor (b) pterygoids
   (c) palatopharyngeus (d) stylopharyngeus

4. Which of the following features are common to the muscles of mastication?
   (a) they share innervation through the oculomotor nerve
   (b) they are also muscles of facial expression
   (c) they move the mandible at the temporomandibular joint
   (d) they enable a person to smile

5. The muscles of the vertebral column include many dorsal extensors but few ventral flexors. Why?

6. What role do the muscles of the tongue play in swallowing?

7. What is the effect of contraction of the internal oblique muscle?

8. What are the functions of the anterior muscles of the neck?

9. What is the function of the diaphragm? Why is it included in the axial musculature?

10. What muscles are involved in controlling the position of the head on the vertebral column?

Level 3 Critical Thinking

1. How do the muscles of the anal triangle control the functions of this area?

2. Mary sees Jill coming toward her and immediately contracts her frontalis and procerus muscles. Is Mary glad to see Jill? How can you tell?

11

The Muscular System

Appendicular Musculature

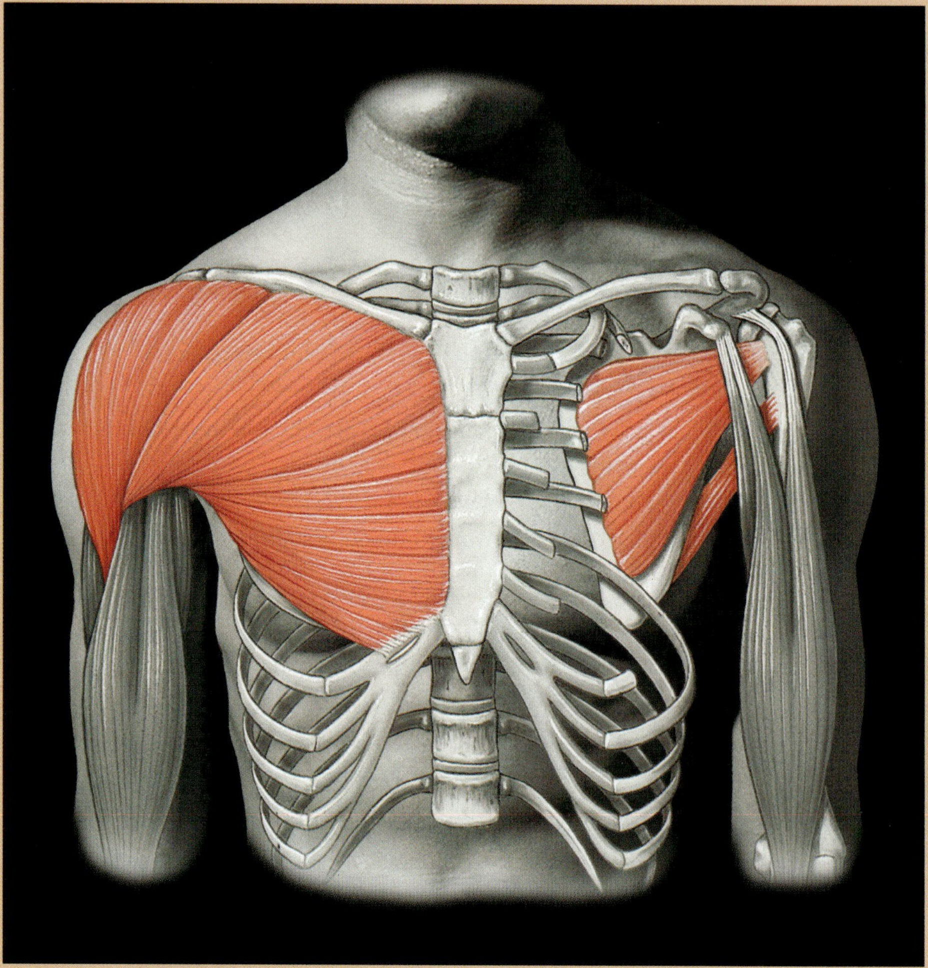

CHAPTER OBJECTIVES

1. Describe the functions of the appendicular musculature.
2. Identify and locate the principal appendicular muscles of the body, together with their origins and insertions, and describe their innervation and actions.
3. Compare the major muscle groups of the upper and lower limbs and relate the differences to variations in their functional roles.
4. Describe and compare the fascia compartments of the arm, forearm, thigh, and leg.

In this chapter, we will describe the **appendicular musculature**. These muscles are responsible for stabilizing the pectoral and pelvic girdles and for moving the upper and lower limbs. Appendicular muscles account for roughly 40 percent of the skeletal muscles in the body.

This discussion assumes an understanding of skeletal anatomy, and you may find it helpful to review figures in Chapters 6 and 7 as you proceed. The appropriate figures are referenced in the figure captions throughout this chapter.

There are two major groups of appendicular muscles: (1) the muscles of the pectoral girdle and upper limbs, and (2) the muscles of the pelvic girdle and lower limbs. The functions and required ranges of motion differ greatly between these groups. The muscular connections between the pectoral girdle and the axial skeleton increase upper limb mobility because the skeletal elements are not locked in position relative to the axial skeleton. The muscular connections also act as shock absorbers. For example, people can jog and still perform delicate hand movements because the appendicular muscles absorb the shocks and jolts, smoothing the bounces in their stride. In contrast, the pelvic girdle has evolved a strong skeletal connection to transfer weight from the axial to the appendicular skeleton. The emphasis is on strength rather than versatility, and the very features that strengthen the joints limit the range of movement. pp. 208–210

Factors Affecting Appendicular Muscle Function

In this chapter, you will learn the origins, insertions, actions, and innervations of the appendicular muscles. To prevent getting lost in the details, you will need to remember to relate the anatomical information to the muscle functions. The goal of anatomy isn't rote memorization—it's understanding. Use what you know to make predictions and test yourself. If you know the origin and insertion, you should be able to predict the action; if you know the origin and action, you can approximate the likely insertion. The many figures in this chapter will assist you in learning the important information and appreciating the three-dimensional relationships involved.

The action produced by a muscle at any one joint is largely dependent upon the structure of the joint and the location of the insertion of the muscle relative to the axis of movement at the joint. The range of motion of a joint, and whether a joint is monaxial, biaxial, or triaxial depends on the anatomical design of the joint. pp. 206, 209 Knowing what movements the anatomy of a particular joint allows will help you understand or predict the actions of a particular muscle at that joint. For example, since the elbow is a hinge joint, none of the associated muscles can cause rotation at the elbow.

Once you know the range of possible movements, the orientation of a muscle relative to a joint will help you determine the action of the muscle at that joint. Muscles develop tension by shortening. If you were to place one end of a string at the muscle's origin, and the other end at the insertion, the string would follow the direction of the applied tension. This is known as the *action line* of the muscle. Once you have determined the action line of a muscle, the following general rules can be applied:

1. At joints that permit flexion and extension, muscles whose action lines cross the anterior aspect of a joint are flexors of that joint, and muscles whose action lines cross the posterior aspect of a joint are extensors of that joint.
2. At joints that permit adduction and abduction, muscles whose action lines cross the medial aspect of a joint are adductors of that joint, and muscles whose action lines cross the lateral aspect of a joint are abductors of that joint.
3. At joints that permit rotation, muscles whose action lines cross on the medial aspect of a joint may produce medial rotation at that joint, whereas muscles whose action lines pass on the lateral aspect of a joint may produce lateral rotation at that joint.

Determining the location of the insertion of a muscle relative to the axis of the joint will provide additional details about the functions of the muscle at that joint. The primary action of a muscle whose insertion is close to the joint will be the production of movement at that joint. However, a muscle whose insertion is considerably farther from the joint will generally help to stabilize that joint *in addition to* producing motion at that joint (**Figure 11.1**).

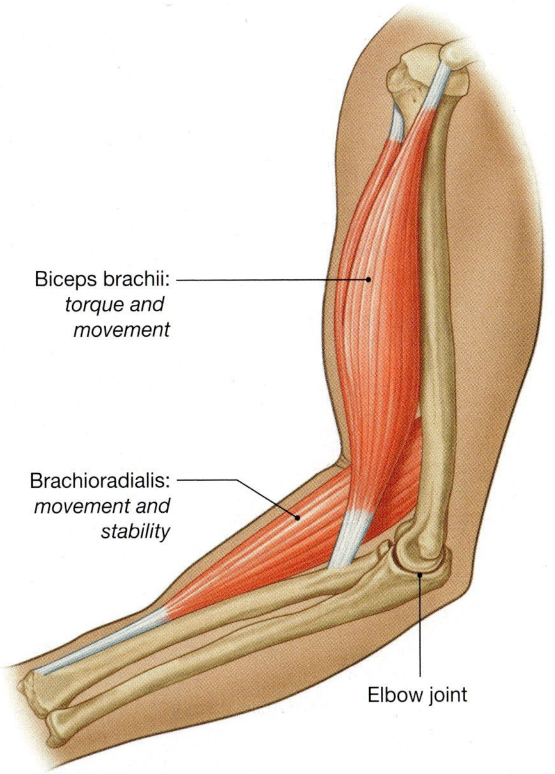

Figure 11.1 Diagram Illustrating the Insertion of the Biceps Brachii Muscle and the Brachioradialis Muscle
The primary action of a muscle whose insertion is close to the joint will be the production of movement at that joint, as illustrated by the biceps brachii muscle. However, a muscle whose insertion is considerably farther from the joint, such as the brachioradialis muscle in this figure, will generally help to stabilize that joint in addition to producing motion at that joint.

Muscles of the Pectoral Girdle and Upper Limbs [Figures 11.2/11.5]

Muscles associated with the pectoral girdle and upper limbs can be divided into four groups: (1) *muscles that position the pectoral girdle*, (2) *muscles that move the arm*, (3) *muscles that move the forearm and hand*, and (4) *muscles that move the hand and fingers*. As we describe the various muscles of the pectoral girdle and upper limbs, refer first to **Figure 11.2**, then to **Figure 11.5** for the general location of the muscle under study.

Muscles That Position the Pectoral Girdle [Figures 11.2 to 11.6 and Table 11.1]

Muscles that position the pectoral girdle work in coordination with the muscles that move the arm. Full range of motion of the arm requires simultaneous movement of the pectoral girdle. Movements of the pectoral girdle are the result of the muscles found in **Figures 11.2** to **11.6** and Table 11.1.

The large **trapezius** (tra-PĒ-zē-us) **muscles** cover the back and portions of the neck, extending to the base of the skull. These muscles originate along the middle of the neck and back and insert upon the clavicles and the scapular spines. Together, these triangular muscles form a broad diamond (**Figures 11.2** and **11.3**). The trapezius muscles are innervated by more than one nerve (Table 11.1). Because specific regions of the trapezius can be made to contract independently, its actions are quite varied.

Removing the trapezius reveals the **rhomboid** (ROM-boyd) and the **levator scapulae** (SKAP-ū-lē) **muscles** (**Figures 11.2** and **11.3**). These muscles are attached to the dorsal surfaces of the cervical and thoracic vertebrae. They insert along the vertebral border of each scapula, between the superior and inferior angles. Contraction of the rhomboid muscles adducts (retracts) the scapula, pulling it toward the center of the back. Contraction of the rhomboid muscles also rotates the scapula downward, an action that

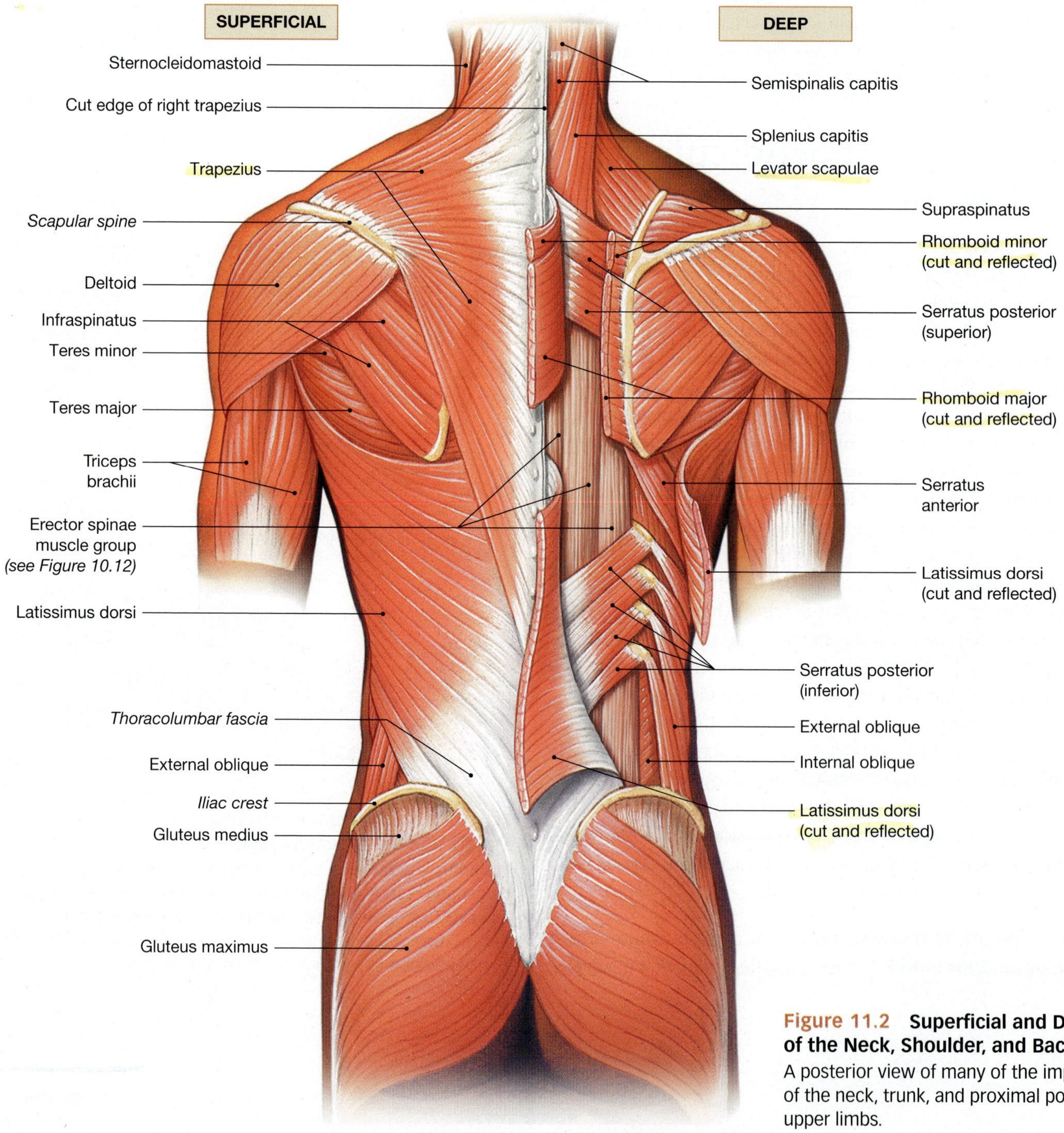

Figure 11.2 Superficial and Deep Muscles of the Neck, Shoulder, and Back
A posterior view of many of the important muscles of the neck, trunk, and proximal portions of the upper limbs.

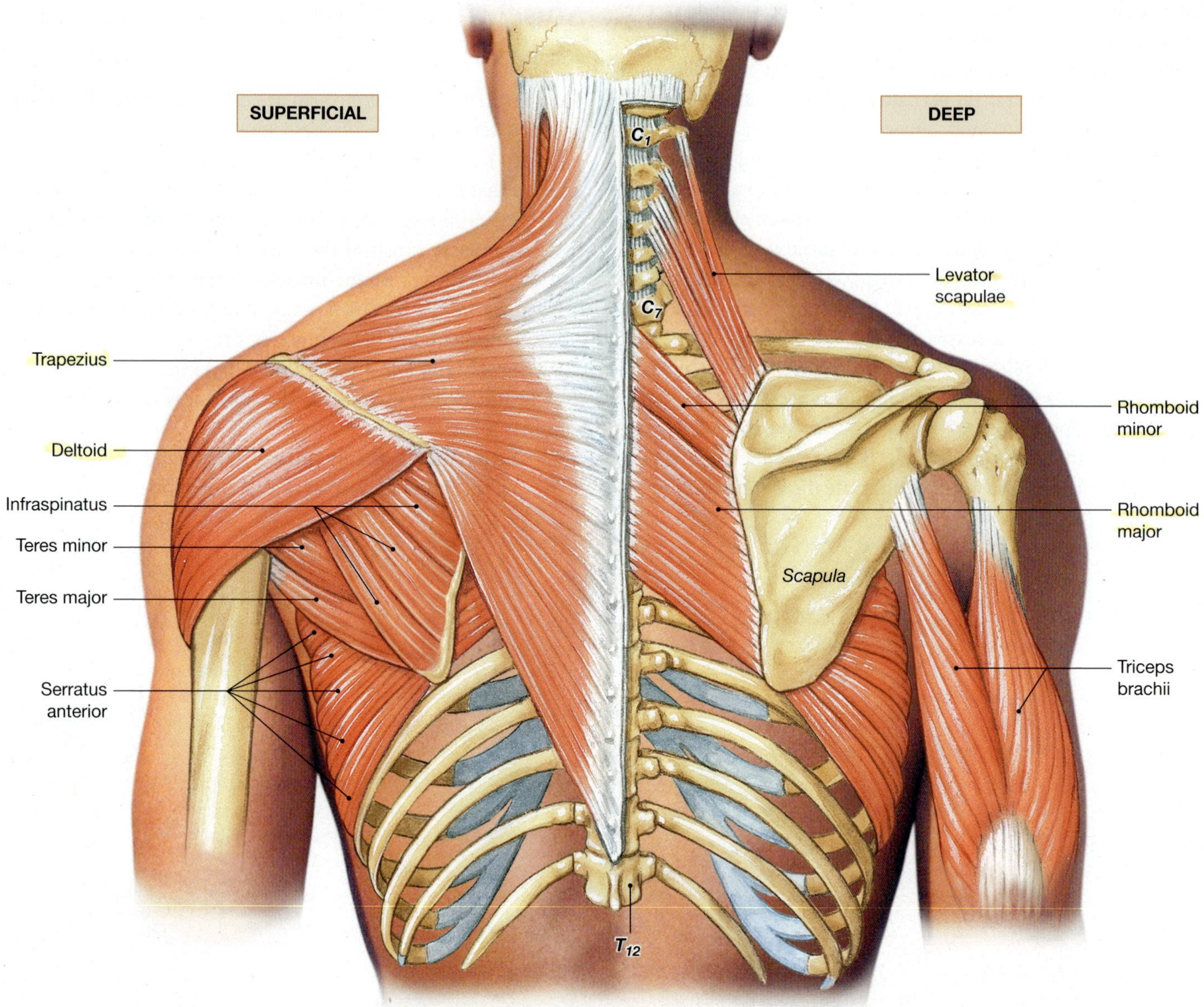

Figure 11.3 Muscles That Position the Pectoral Girdle, Part I
Posterior view, showing superficial muscles and deep muscles of the pectoral girdle. *See also Figures 6.26, 7.4, and 8.11. See Figure 11.6c for insertions of some of the muscles shown in this figure*.

TABLE 11.1 Muscles That Position the Pectoral Girdle

Muscle	Origin	Insertion	Action	Innervation
Levator scapulae	Transverse processes of first four cervical vertebrae	Vertebral border of scapula near superior angle	Elevates scapula	Cervical nerves C_3–C_4 and dorsal scapular nerve (C_5)
Pectoralis minor	Anterior surfaces and superior margins of ribs 3–5 and fascia covering the associated external intercostal muscles	Coracoid process of scapula	Depresses and protracts shoulder; rotates scapula so glenoid cavity moves inferiorly (downward rotation); elevates ribs if scapula is stationary	Medial pectoral nerve (C_8, T_1)
Rhomboid major	Spinous processes of superior thoracic vertebrae	Vertebral border of scapula from spine to inferior angle	Adducts and performs downward rotation of the scapula	Dorsal scapular nerve (C_5)
Rhomboid minor	Spinous processes of vertebrae C_7–T_1	Vertebral border of scapula	As above	As above
Serratus anterior	Anterior and superior margins of ribs 1–8 or 1–9	Anterior surface of vertebral border of scapula	Protracts shoulder; rotates scapula so glenoid cavity moves superiorly (upward rotation)	Long thoracic nerve (C_5–C_7)
Subclavius	First rib	Clavicle (inferior border)	Depresses and protracts shoulder	Nerve to subclavius (C_5–C_6)
Trapezius	Occipital bone, ligamentum nuchae, and spinous processes of thoracic vertebrae	Clavicle and scapula (acromion and scapular spine)	Depends on active region and state of other muscles; may elevate, retract, depress, or rotate scapula upward and/or clavicle; can also extend neck	Accessory nerve (N XI)

causes the glenoid cavity to move inferiorly and the inferior angle of the scapula to move medially and superiorly (Figure 7.5). ∞ p. 178 The levator scapulae muscles elevate the scapula, as in shrugging the shoulders.

On the lateral wall of the chest, the **serratus** (se-RĀ-tus) **anterior muscle** originates along the anterior and superior surfaces of several ribs (Figures 11.3 and 11.4). This fan-shaped muscle inserts along the anterior margin of the vertebral border of the scapula. When the serratus anterior contracts, it abducts (protracts) the scapula and swings the shoulder anteriorly.

Two deep chest muscles arise along the ventral surfaces of the ribs. The **subclavius** (sub-KLĀ-vē-us; *sub*, below + *clavius*, clavicle) **muscle** inserts upon the inferior border of the clavicle (Figures 11.4 and 11.5). When it contracts, it depresses and protracts the scapular end of the clavicle. Because ligaments connect this end to the shoulder joint and scapula, those structures move as well. The **pectoralis** (pek-tō-RĀ-lis) **minor muscle** attaches to the coracoid process of the scapula (Figures 11.4 and 11.5). Its contraction usually complements that of the subclavius. Table 11.1 identifies the muscles that move the pectoral girdle and the nerves that innervate those muscles.

Muscles That Move the Arm [Figures 11.2/11.5 to 11.7 and Table 11.2]

The muscles that move the arm are easiest to remember when grouped by primary actions. Some of these muscles are best seen in posterior view (Figure 11.2) and others in anterior view (Figure 11.5). Information on the muscles that move the arm is summarized in Table 11.2. The **deltoid muscle** is the major abductor of the arm, but the **supraspinatus** (soo-pra-spī-NĀ-tus) **muscle** assists at the start of this movement. The **subscapularis** and **teres** (TER-ēz) **major muscles** rotate the arm medially, whereas the **infraspinatus** (in-fra-spī-NĀ-tus) and **teres minor muscles** perform lateral rotation. All of these muscles originate on the scapula. The small **coracobrachialis**(kor-a-kō-brā-ke-A-lis) **muscle** (Figure 11.6a) is the only muscle attached to the scapula that produces flexion and adduction at the shoulder joint.

The **pectoralis major muscle** extends between the anterior portion of the chest and the crest of the greater tubercle of the humerus. The

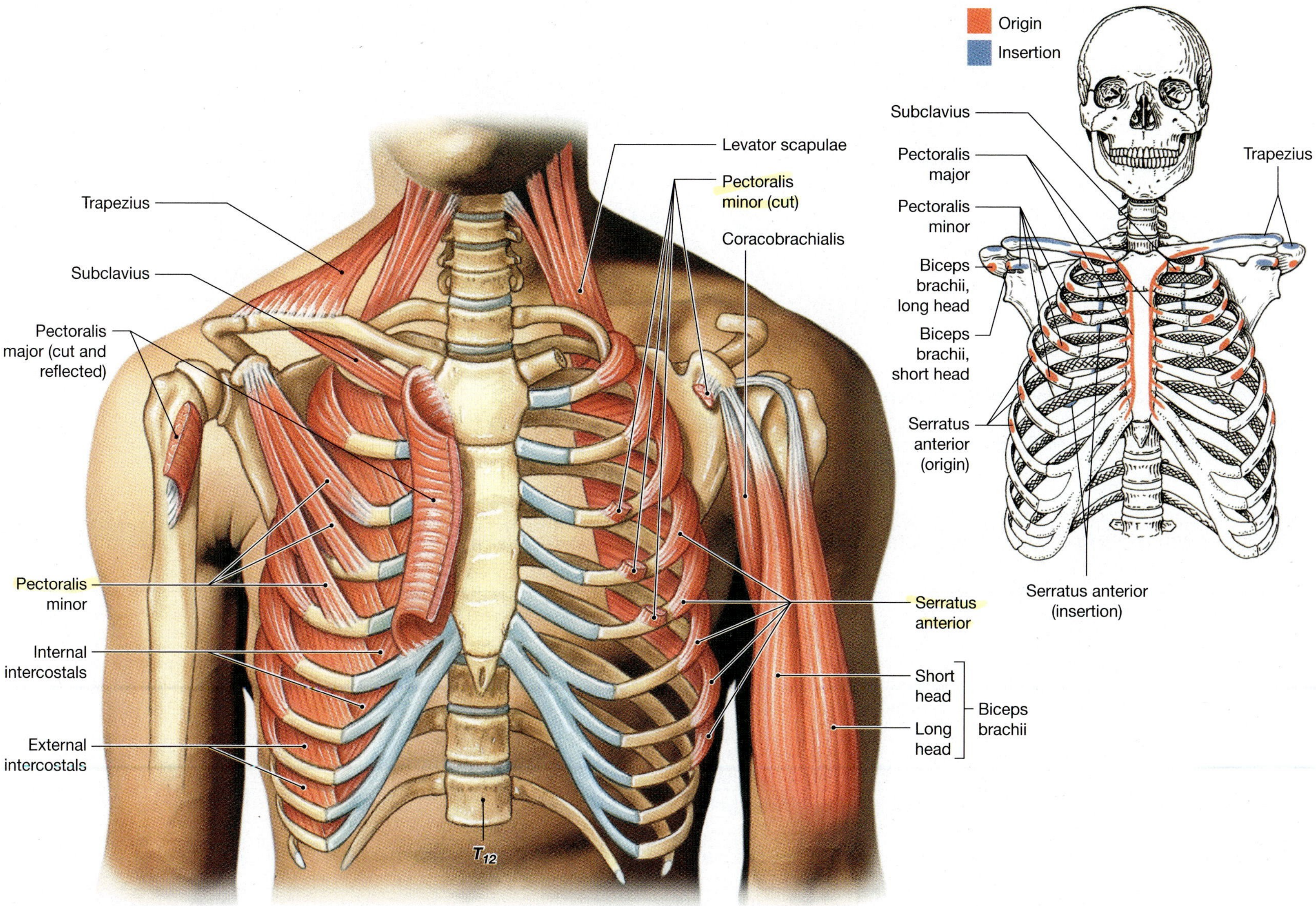

Figure 11.4 Muscles That Position the Pectoral Girdle, Part II
Anterior view, showing superficial muscles and deep muscles of the pectoral girdle. Selected origins and insertions are detailed.

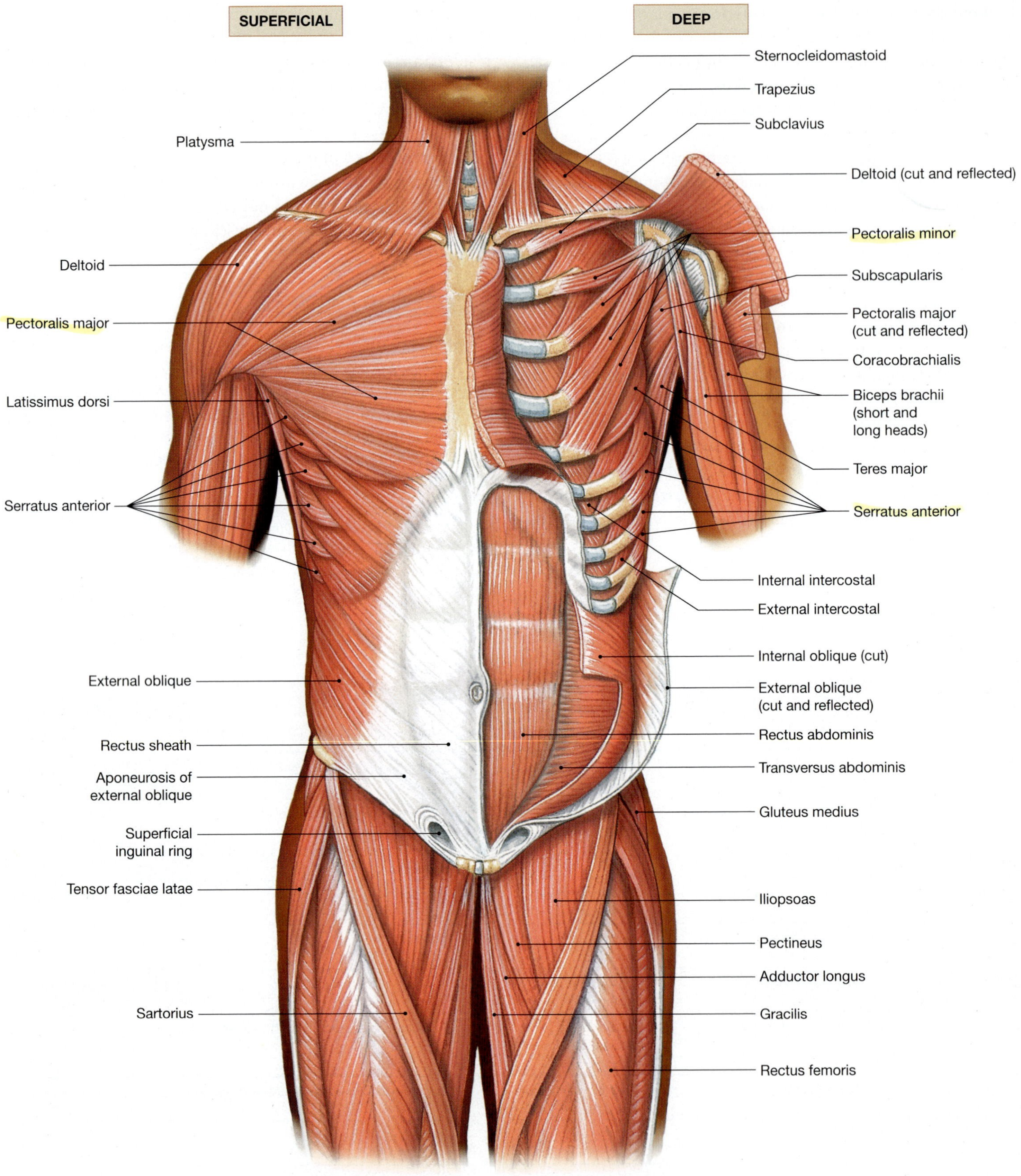

Figure 11.5 Superficial and Deep Muscles of the Trunk and Proximal Limbs
Anterior view of the axial muscles of the trunk and the appendicular musculature associated with the pectoral and pelvic girdles and the proximal portions of the limbs.

latissimus dorsi (la-TIS-i-mus DOR-sē) **muscle** extends between the thoracic vertebrae at the posterior midline and the floor of the intertubercular sulcus of the humerus (**Figures 11.3** to **11.6**). The pectoralis major muscle flexes the shoulder joint, and the latissimus dorsi muscle extends it. These two muscles can also work together to produce adduction and medial rotation of the humerus at the shoulder joint.

The shoulder is a highly mobile but relatively weak joint (**Figures 7.5, 7.6,** and **8.11**). pp. 178, 180–181, 218 The tendons of the supraspinatus, infraspinatus, subscapularis, and teres minor muscles merge with the connective tissue of the shoulder joint capsule and form the *rotator cuff*. The rotator cuff supports and strengthens the joint capsule throughout a wide range of motion. Powerful, repetitive arm movements common in many sports (such as pitching a fastball at 96 mph for many innings) can place intolerable strains on the muscles of the rotator cuff, leading to tendon damage, muscle strains, bursitis, and other painful injuries.

Earlier in the chapter, we discussed how the action line of a muscle could be used to predict the muscle action, and three general rules were introduced. **Figure 11.7** shows the positions of the biceps brachii, triceps brachii, and deltoid muscles in relation to the shoulder joint; it also restates those rules. The action line of the biceps brachii muscle passes anterior to the axis of the shoulder joint, and the action line of the triceps brachii muscle passes posterior to the axis. Although neither inserts on the humerus, the biceps brachii muscle is a flexor of the shoulder, while the triceps brachii muscle is an extensor of the shoulder. The action line of the clavicular, or anterior, portion of the deltoid also crosses anterior to the axis of the shoulder joint to its insertion on the humerus. This portion of the deltoid muscle produces flexion and medial rotation at the shoulder. The action line of the scapular, or posterior, portion of the deltoid muscle passes posterior to the axis of the shoulder joint. The scapular portion of the deltoid muscle produces extension and lateral rotation of the shoulder. Contraction of the entire deltoid muscle produces abduction of the shoulder because the action line for the muscle as a whole passes lateral to the axis of the joint.

CONCEPT CHECK

1. Sometimes baseball pitchers suffer from rotator cuff injuries. What muscles are involved in this type of injury?
2. Identify the fan-shaped muscle that inserts along the anterior margin of the scapula at its vertebral border and acts to protract the scapula.
3. What is the primary muscle producing abduction at the shoulder joint?
4. What two muscles produce extension, adduction, and medial rotation at the shoulder joint?

See blue "Answers" tab at back of book.

TABLE 11.2 Muscles That Move the Arm

Muscle	Origin	Insertion	Action	Innervation
Coracobrachialis	Coracoid process	Medial margin of shaft of humerus	Adduction and flexion at shoulder	Musculocutaneous nerve (C_5–C_7)
Deltoid	Clavicle and scapula (acromion and adjacent scapular spine)	Deltoid tuberosity of humerus	*Whole muscle*: abduction of shoulder; *anterior part*: flexion and medial rotation of humerus; *posterior part*: extension and lateral rotation of humerus	Axillary nerve (C_5–C_6)
Supraspinatus	Supraspinous fossa of scapula	Greater tubercle of humerus	Abduction at shoulder	Suprascapular nerve (C_5)
Infraspinatus	Infraspinous fossa of scapula	Greater tubercle of humerus	Lateral rotation at shoulder	Suprascapular nerve (C_5–C_6)
Subscapularis	Subscapular fossa of scapula	Lesser tubercle of humerus	Medial rotation at shoulder	Subscapular nerve (C_5–C_6)
Teres major	Inferior angle of scapula	Medial lip of intertubercular sulcus of humerus	Extension and medial rotation at shoulder	Lower subscapular nerve (C_5–C_6)
Teres minor	Lateral border of scapula	Greater tubercle of humerus	Lateral rotation and adduction at shoulder	Axillary nerve (C_5)
Triceps brachii (long head)	*See Table 11.3*		Extension at elbow	
Biceps brachii	*See Table 11.3*		Flexion at elbow	
Latissimus dorsi	Spinous processes of inferior thoracic and all lumbar vertebrae, ribs 8–12, and thoracolumbar fascia	Floor of intertubercular sulcus of the humerus	Extension, adduction, and medial rotation at shoulder	Thoracodorsal nerve C_6–C_8
Pectoralis major	Cartilages of ribs 2–6, body of sternum, and inferior, medial portion of clavicle	Crest of greater tubercle and lateral lip of intertubercular sulcus of humerus	Flexion, adduction, and medial rotation at shoulder	Pectoral nerves (C_5–T_1)

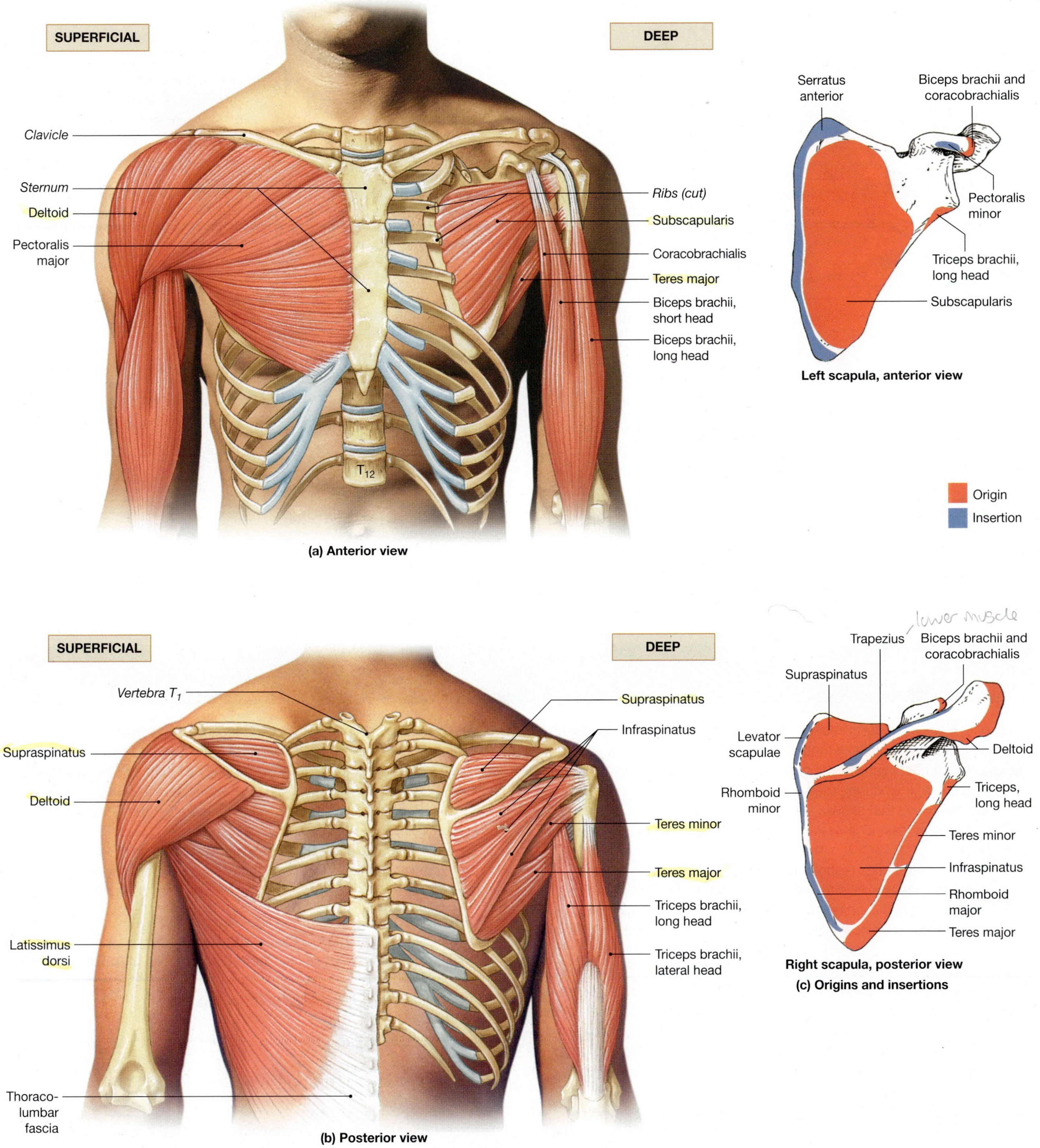

Figure 11.6 Muscles That Move the Arm
(a) Anterior view. **(b)** Posterior view. **(c)** Anterior and posterior views of the scapula, showing selected origins and insertions. *See also Figures 7.4 to 7.6 and 8.11.*

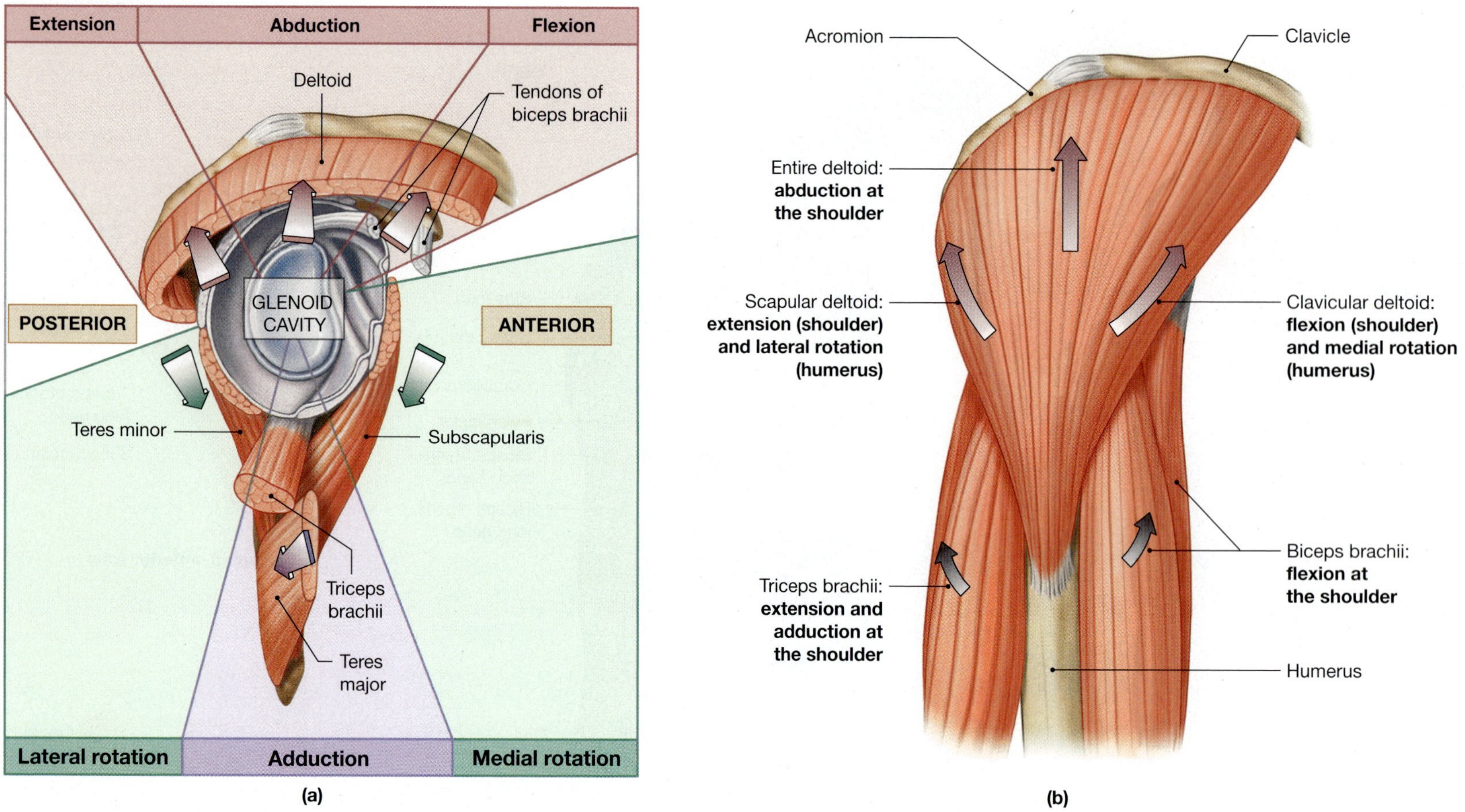

Figure 11.7 Action Lines for Muscles That Move the Arm
(a) Lateral view of the shoulder joint demonstrating the action lines of muscles that move the arm. **(b)** Action lines of the biceps brachii muscle, triceps brachii muscle, and the three parts of the deltoid muscle.

Clinical Note

Sports Injuries Sports injuries affect amateurs and professionals alike. A five-year study of college football players indicated that 73.5 percent experienced mild injuries, 21.5 percent moderate injuries, and 11.6 percent severe injuries during their playing careers. Contact sports are not the only activities that show a significant injury rate: A study of 1650 joggers running at least 27 miles (43 km) a week reported 1819 injuries in a single year.

Muscles and bones respond to increased use by enlarging and strengthening. Poorly conditioned individuals are therefore more likely than people in good condition to subject their bones and muscles to intolerable stresses. Training is also important in minimizing the use of antagonistic muscle groups and in keeping joint movements within the intended ranges of motion. Planned warm-up exercises before athletic events stimulate circulation, improve muscular performance and control, and help prevent injuries to muscles, joints, and ligaments. Stretching exercises after an initial warm-up will stimulate blood flow to muscles and help keep ligaments and joint capsules supple. Such conditioning extends the range of motion and may prevent sprains and strains when sudden loads are applied.

Dietary planning can also be important in preventing injuries to muscles during endurance events, such as marathon running. Emphasis has commonly been placed on the importance of carbohydrates, leading to the practice of "carbohydrate loading" before a marathon. But while operating within aerobic limits, muscles also utilize amino acids extensively, so an adequate diet must include both carbohydrates and proteins.

Improved playing conditions, equipment, and regulations also play a role in reducing the incidence of sports injuries. Jogging shoes, ankle and knee braces, helmets, mouth guards, and body padding are examples of equipment that can be effective. The substantial penalties now earned for personal fouls in contact sports have reduced the numbers of neck and knee injuries.

Several traumatic injuries common to those engaged in active sports can also affect nonathletes, although the primary causes may be very different. A partial listing of activity-related conditions includes the following:

- **Bone bruise**: bleeding within the periosteum of a bone
- **Bursitis**: an inflammation of the bursae at joints
- **Muscle cramps**: prolonged, involuntary, and painful muscular contractions
- **Sprains**: tears or breaks in ligaments or tendons
- **Strains**: tears in muscles
- **Stress fractures**: cracks or breaks in bones subjected to repeated stresses or trauma
- **Tendinitis**: an inflammation of the connective tissue surrounding a tendon

Finally, many sports injuries would be prevented if people who engage in regular exercise would use common sense and recognize their personal limitations. It can be argued that some athletic events, such as the ultramarathon, place such excessive stresses on the cardiovascular, muscular, respiratory, and urinary systems that these events cannot be recommended, even for athletes in peak condition.

Muscles That Move the Forearm and Hand [Figures 11.5/11.6/11.8/11.9 and Table 11.3]

Most of the muscles that move the forearm and hand originate on the humerus and insert upon the forearm and wrist. There are two noteworthy exceptions: The *long head* of the **triceps brachii** (TRĪ-seps BRĀ-kē-ī) **muscle** originates on the scapula and inserts on the olecranon; the *long head* of the **biceps brachii muscle** originates on the scapula and inserts on the radial tuberosity of the radius (Figures 11.5, 11.6, 11.8, and 11.9). Although contraction of the triceps brachii or biceps brachii exerts an effect on the shoulder, their primary actions are at the elbow joint. The triceps brachii muscle extends the elbow when, for example, we do push-ups. The biceps brachii muscle both flexes the elbow and supinates the forearm. With the forearm pronated, the biceps brachii muscle cannot function effectively due to the position of its muscular insertion. As a result, we are strongest when flexing the elbow with the forearm supinated; the biceps brachii muscle then makes a prominent bulge. Muscles that move the forearm and hand along with their nerve innervations are detailed in Table 11.3.

TABLE 11.3 Muscles That Move the Forearm and Hand

Muscle	Origin	Insertion	Action	Innervation
ACTION AT THE ELBOW				
FLEXORS				
Biceps brachii	*Short head* from the coracoid process; *long head* from the supraglenoid tubercle (both on the scapula)	Radial tuberosity	Flexion at elbow and shoulder; supination	Musculocutaneous nerve (C_5–C_6)
Brachialis	Anterior, distal surface of humerus	Ulnar tuberosity	Flexion at elbow	As above and radial nerve (C_7–C_8)
Brachioradialis	Ridge superior to the lateral epicondyle of humerus	Lateral aspect of styloid process of radius	As above	Radial nerve (C_6–C_8)
EXTENSORS				
Anconeus	Posterior surface of lateral humerus	Lateral margin of olecranon and ulnar shaft	Extension at elbow	Radial nerve (C_6–C_8)
Triceps brachii				
lateral head	Superior, lateral margin of humerus	Olecranon of ulna	Extension at elbow	Radial nerve (C_6–C_8)
long head	Infraglenoid tubercle of scapula	As above	As above plus extension and adduction at shoulder	As above
medial head	Posterior surface of humerus, inferior to radial groove	As above	Extension at elbow	As above
PRONATORS/SUPINATORS				
Pronator quadratus	Anterior and medial surfaces of distal ulna	Anterolateral surface of distal portion of radius	Pronates forearm and hand by medial rotation of radius at radioulnar joints	Median nerve (C_8–T_1)
Pronator teres	Medial epicondyle of humerus and coronoid process of ulna	Middle of lateral surface of radius	As above, plus flexion at elbow	Median nerve (C_6–C_7)
Supinator	Lateral epicondyle of humerus and ridge near radial notch of ulna	Anterolateral surface of radius distal to the radial tuberosity	Supinates forearm and hand by lateral rotation of radius at radioulnar joints	Deep radial nerve (C_6–C_8)
ACTION AT THE WRIST				
FLEXORS				
Flexor carpi radialis	Medial epicondyle of humerus	Bases of second and third metacarpal bones	Flexion and abduction at wrist	Median nerve (C_6–C_7)
Flexor carpi ulnaris	Medial epicondyle of humerus; adjacent medial surface of olecranon and anteromedial portion of ulna	Pisiform, hamate, and base of fifth metacarpal bone	Flexion and adduction at wrist	Ulnar nerve (C_8–T_1)
Palmaris longus	Medial epicondyle of humerus	Palmar aponeurosis and flexor retinaculum	Flexion at wrist	Median nerve (C_6–C_7)
EXTENSORS				
Extensor carpi radialis longus	Lateral supracondylar ridge of humerus	Base of second metacarpal bone	Extension and abduction at wrist	Radial nerve (C_6–C_7)
Extensor carpi radialis brevis	Lateral epicondyle of humerus	Base of third metacarpal bone	As above	As above
Extensor carpi ulnaris	Lateral epicondyle of humerus; adjacent dorsal surface of ulna	Base of fifth metacarpal bone	Extension and adduction at wrist	Deep radial nerve (C_6–C_8)

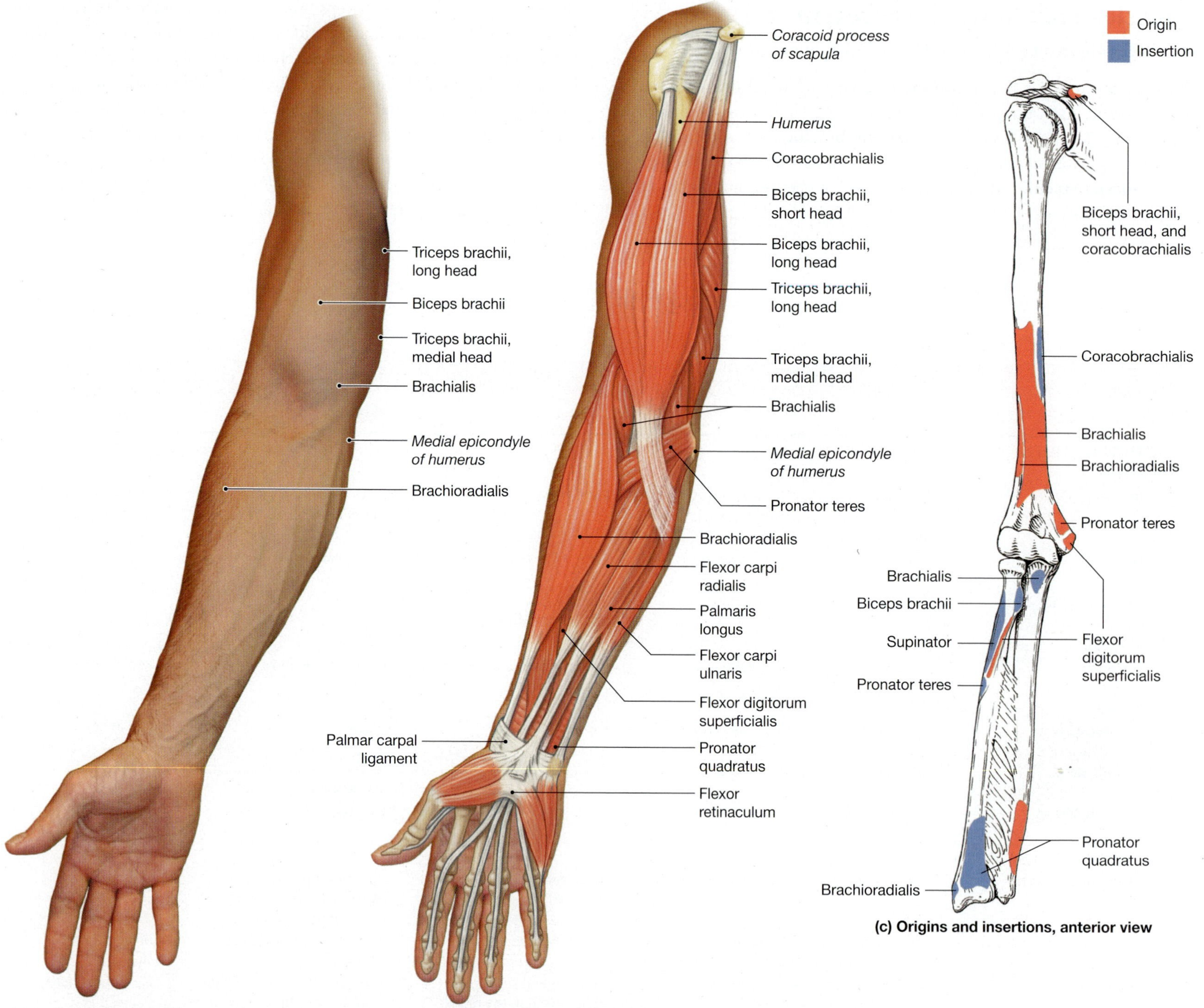

(a) Surface anatomy, anterior view **(b) Superficial muscles, anterior view** **(c) Origins and insertions, anterior view**

Figure 11.8 Muscles That Move the Forearm and Hand, Part I
Relationships among the muscles of the right upper limb are shown. **(a)** Surface anatomy of the right upper limb, anterior view. **(b)** Superficial muscles of the right upper limb, anterior view. **(c)** Anterior view of bones of the right upper limb, showing selected muscle origins and insertions.

The **brachialis** (BRĀ-kē-Ā-lis) and **brachioradialis** (BRĀ-kē-ō-rā-dē-a-lis) **muscles** also flex the elbow; they are opposed by the **anconeus** (an-KŌ-nē-us) and the triceps brachii muscles. The **flexor carpi ulnaris**, the **flexor carpi radialis**, and the **palmaris longus** are superficial muscles that work together to produce flexion of the wrist (Figures 11.8b–e and 11.9b–e). Because of differences in their sites of origin and insertion, the flexor carpi radialis muscle flexes and abducts while the flexor carpi ulnaris muscle flexes and adducts the wrist. The **extensor carpi radialis muscle** and the **extensor carpi ulnaris muscle** have a similar relationship; the former produces extension and abduction, the latter extension and adduction of the wrist.

The **pronator teres muscle** and the **supinator muscle** are antagonistic muscles that originate on both the humerus and the ulna. They insert on the radius and cause rotation without flexing or extending the elbow. The **pronator quadratus muscle** originates on the ulna and assists the pronator teres muscle in opposing the actions of the supinator muscle or biceps brachii muscle. The muscles involved in pronation and supination can be seen in Figures 11.8f and 11.9f. Note the changes in orientation that occur as the pronator teres and pronator quadratus muscles contract. During pronation the tendon of the biceps brachii muscle rolls under the radius, and a bursa prevents abrasion against the tendon. p. 208

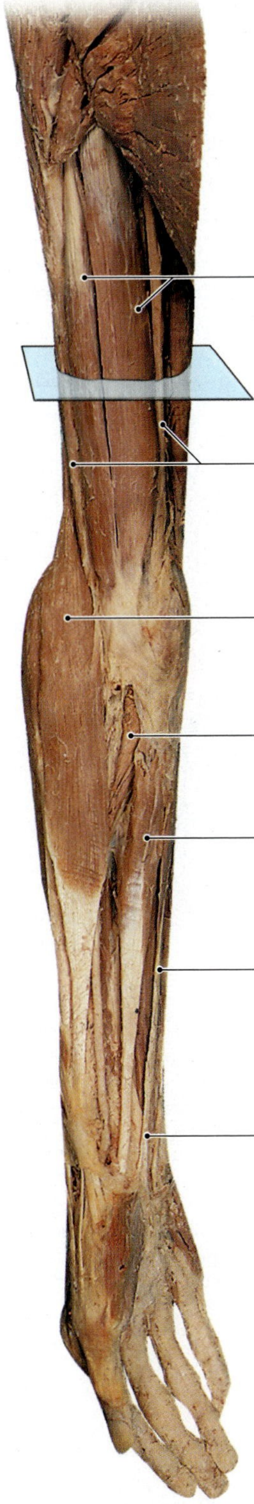

(d) Anterior view

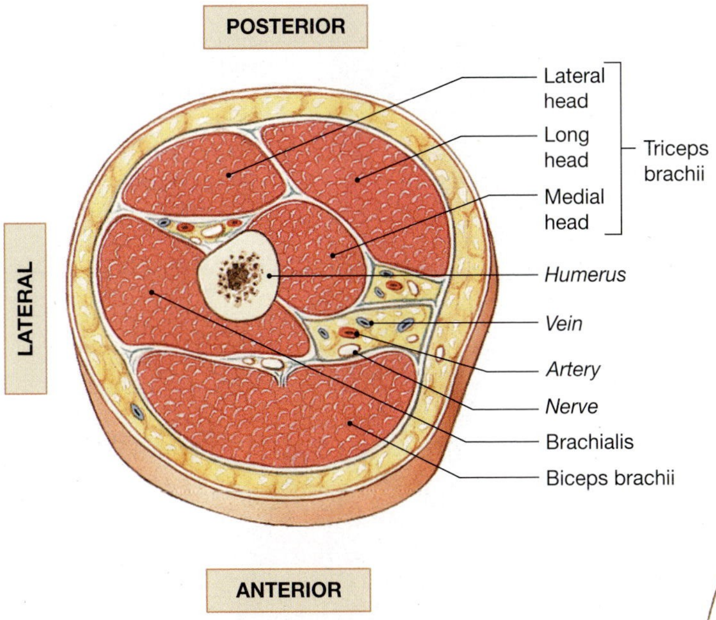

(e) Arm, cross-sectional view

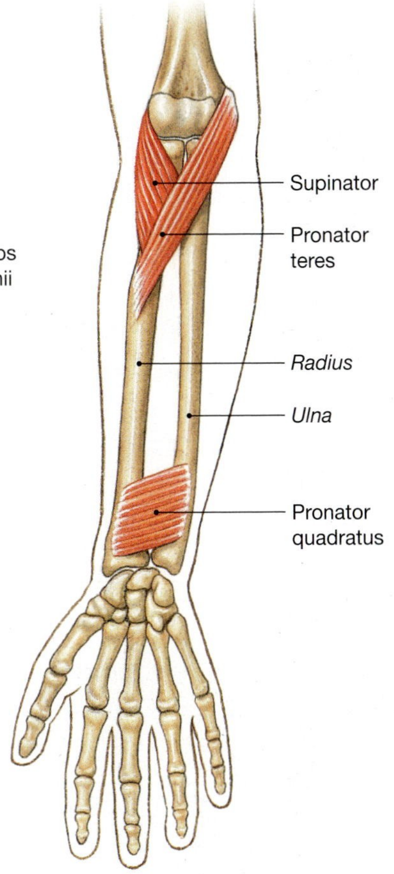

(f) Anterior view of forearm, deep muscles

Figure 11.8 ***(continued)***
(d) Anterior view of a dissection of the muscles of the right upper limb. The palmaris longus and flexor carpi muscles (radialis and ulnaris) have been partly removed, and the flexor retinaculum has been cut. **(e)** The relationships among the deeper muscles of the arm are best seen in the sectional view. For additional perspectives on sectional views, see *Figures 11.22 and 11.23.* **(f)** Anterior view of the deep muscles of the supinated forearm. *See also Figures 7.6, 7.7, and 7.8.*

As you study the muscles in Table 11.3, note that in general, extensor muscles lie along the posterior and lateral surfaces of the forearm, and flexors are found on the anterior and medial surfaces. Many of the muscles that move the forearm and hand can be seen from the body surface (**Figures 11.8a** and **11.9a**).

Muscles That Move the Hand and Fingers

Extrinsic Muscles of the Hand [Figures 11.8 to 11.11 and Table 11.4]

Several superficial and deep muscles of the forearm (Table 11.4) perform flexion and extension at the joints of the fingers. These muscles, which provide strength and crude control of the hand and fingers, are called the *extrinsic muscles of the hand.* Only the tendons of these muscles extend across the wrist joint. These are relatively large muscles (**Figures 11.8** to **11.10**), and keeping them clear of the joints ensures maximum mobility at both the wrist and hand. The tendons that cross the dorsal and ventral surfaces of the wrist pass through **synovial tendon sheaths**, elongated bursae that reduce friction. These muscles and their tendons are shown in anterior view in **Figures 11.8b,d** and **11.11d,g**, and in posterior view in **Figures 11.9b,d, 11.10d–f**, and **11.11a,e**. The fascia of the forearm thickens on the posterior surface of the wrist to form a wide band of connective tissue, the **extensor retinaculum** (ret-i-NAK-ū-lum) (**Figure 11.11a**). The extensor retinaculum holds the tendons of the extensor

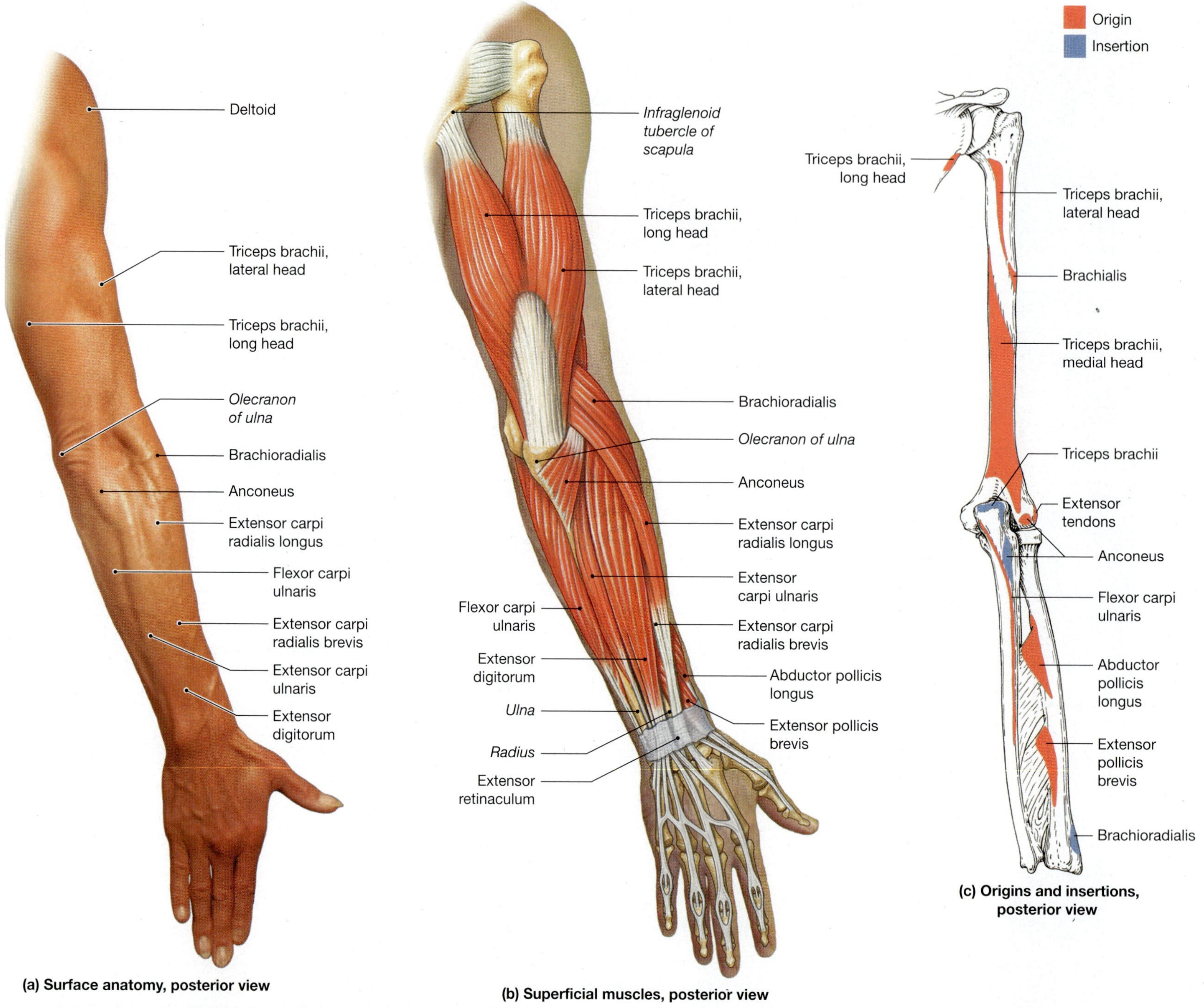

Figure 11.9 Muscles That Move the Forearm and Hand, Part II
Relationships among the muscles of the right upper limb are shown. **(a)** Surface anatomy of the right upper limb, posterior view. **(b)** A diagrammatic view of a dissection of the superficial muscles. **(c)** Posterior view of the bones of the upper limb, showing the origins and insertions of selected muscles. **(d)** A posterior view of superficial dissection of the forearm. **(e)** Relationships among deeper muscles are best seen in this sectional view. The deep digital extensors and flexors are shown in *Figure 11.10*; additional sectional views can be found in *Figures 11.22 and 11.23*. **(f)** Deep muscles involved with pronation and supination. *See also Figure 7.7.*

muscles in place. On the anterior surface, the fascia also thickens to form another wide band of connective tissue, the **flexor retinaculum**, which retains the tendons of the flexor muscles (**Figure 11.11d,f**). Inflammation of the retinacula and tendon sheaths can restrict movement and irritate the *median nerve*, a sensory and motor nerve that innervates the hand. This condition, known as *carpal tunnel syndrome*, causes chronic pain.

Intrinsic Muscles of the Hand [Figure 11.11 and Table 11.5]

Fine control of the hand involves small *intrinsic muscles of the hand* that originate on the carpal and metacarpal bones (**Figure 11.11**). These intrinsic muscles are responsible for (1) flexion and extension of the fingers at the metacarpophalangeal joints, (2) abduction and adduction of the fingers at the metacarpophalangeal joints, and (3) opposition and reposition of the thumb. No muscles originate on the phalanges, and only tendons extend across the distal joints of the fingers. The intrinsic muscles of the hand are detailed in Table 11.5.

The four **lumbrical muscles** originate in the palm of the hand on the tendons of the flexor digitorum profundus muscle. They insert onto the tendons of the extensor digitorum muscle. These muscles produce flexion at the metacarpophalangeal joints, as well as extension at the interphalangeal joints of the fingers.

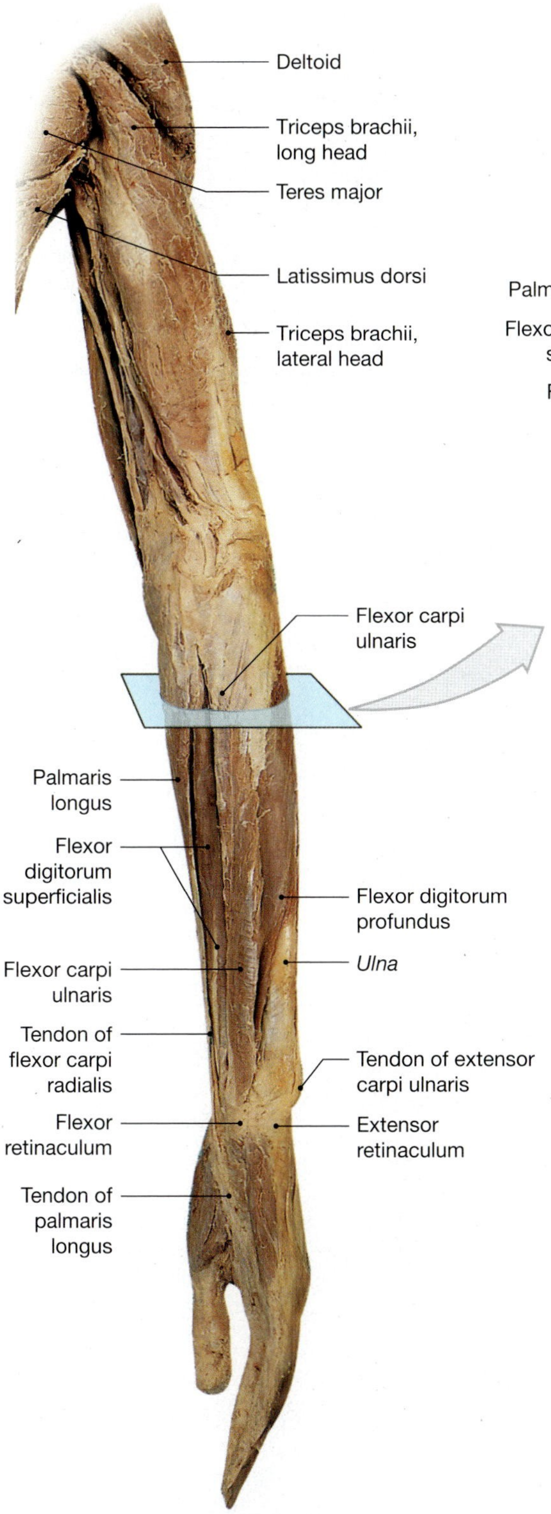

(d) Superficial muscles, posterior view

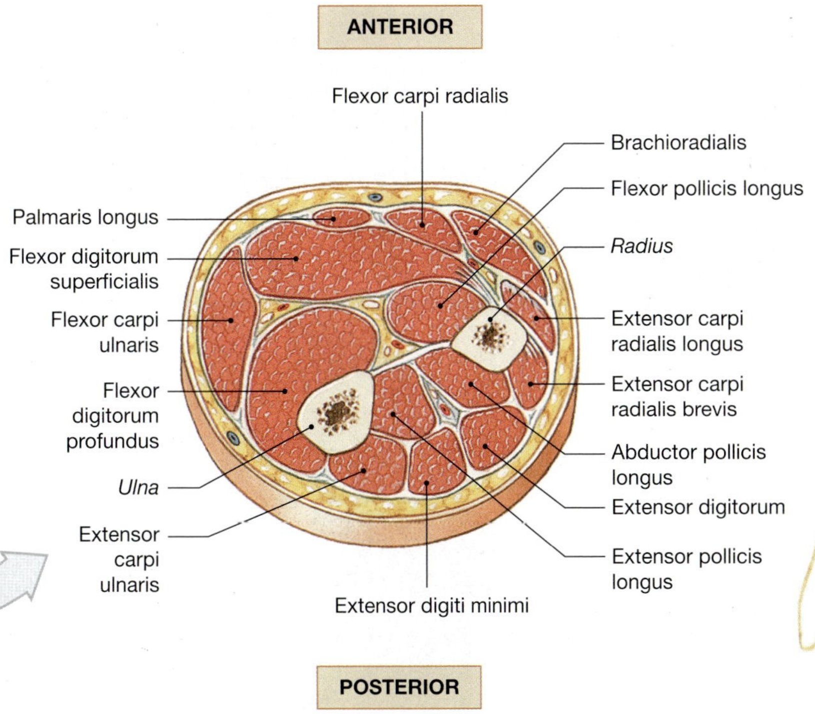

(e) Forearm, cross-sectional view

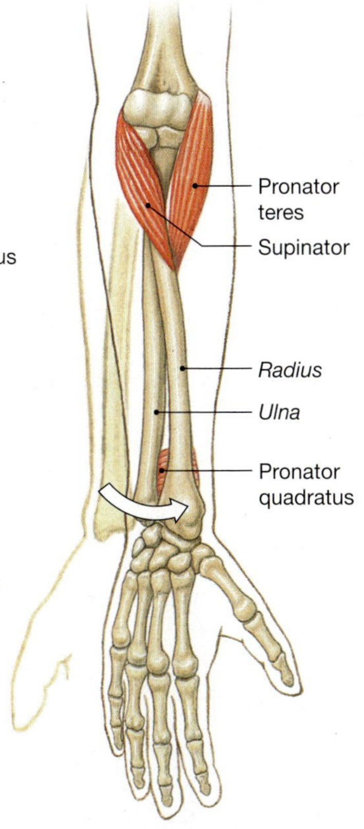

(f) Pronation

Figure 11.9 ***(continued)***

Abduction of the fingers is accomplished by the four **dorsal interossei muscles**. The **abductor digiti minimi muscle** abducts the little finger, and the **abductor pollicis brevis muscle** abducts the thumb. The **adductor pollicis muscle** adducts the thumb, and the four **palmar interossei muscles** adduct the fingers at the metacarpophalangeal joints.

Opposition of the thumb is the movement where the thumb, starting from the anatomical position, is flexed and medially rotated at the carpometacarpal joint. This movement brings the tip of the thumb in contact with the tip of any other finger. This action is accomplished by the **opponens pollicis muscle**. Reposition of the thumb is accomplished by two extrinsic muscles of the hand, the extensor pollicis longus muscle and the abductor pollicis longus muscle (see Table 11.4).

Clinical Note

Carpal Tunnel Syndrome In **carpal tunnel syndrome**, inflammation within the sheath surrounding the flexor tendons of the palm leads to compression of the *median nerve*, a mixed (sensory and motor) nerve that innervates the palm and palmar surfaces of the thumb, index, and middle fingers. Symptoms include pain, especially on wrist flexion, a tingling sensation or numbness on the palm, and weakness in the abductor pollicis brevis. This condition is fairly common and often affects those involved in hand movements that place repetitive stress on the tendons crossing the wrist. Activities commonly associated with this syndrome include typing at a computer keyboard, playing the piano, or, as in the case of carpenters, repeated use of a hammer. Treatment involves administration of anti-inflammatory drugs, such as aspirin, and use of a splint to prevent wrist movement and stabilize the region. A number of specially designed computer keyboards are available to reduce the stresses associated with typing.

CONCEPT CHECK

1. Injury to the flexor carpi ulnaris muscle would impair what two movements?
2. Identify the muscles that rotate the radius without flexing or extending the elbow.
3. What structure do the tendons that cross the dorsal and ventral surfaces of the wrist pass through before reaching the point of insertion?
4. Identify the thickened fascia on the posterior surface of the wrist that forms a wide band of connective tissue.

See blue "Answers" tab at back of book.

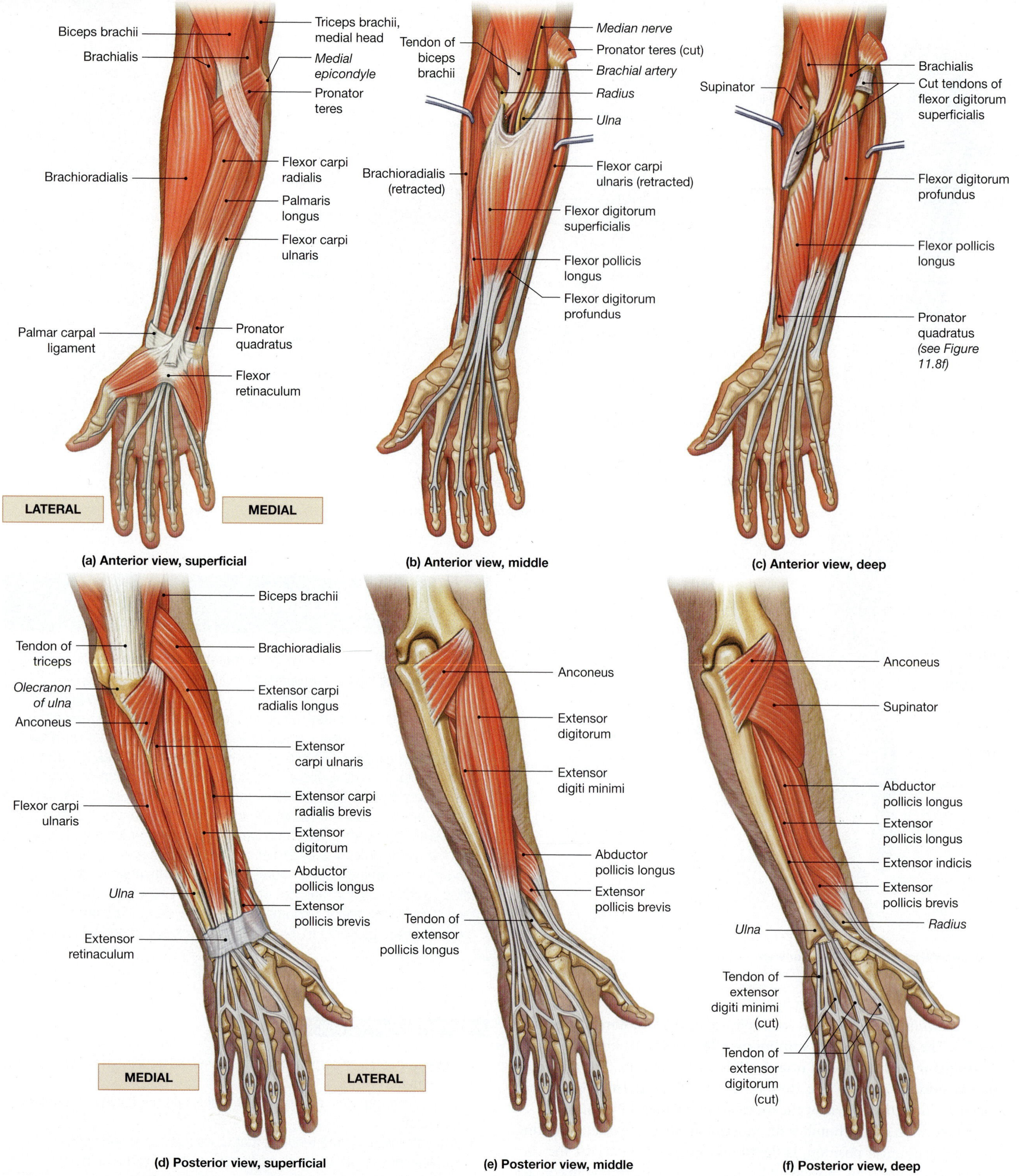

Figure 11.10 Extrinsic Muscles That Move the Hand and Fingers

(a) Anterior view, showing superficial muscles of the right forearm. **(b)** Anterior view of the middle layer of muscles. The flexor carpi radialis muscle and palmaris longus muscle have been removed. **(c)** Anterior view of the deep layer of muscles. **(d)** Posterior view, showing superficial muscles of the right forearm. **(e)** Posterior view of the middle layer of muscles. **(f)** Posterior view of the deep layer of muscles. *See also Figures 7.7, 7.8, and 11.9.*

TABLE 11.4 Muscles That Move the Hand and Fingers

Muscle	Origin	Insertion	Action	Innervation
Abductor pollicis longus	Proximal dorsal surfaces of ulna and radius	Lateral margin of first metacarpal bone	Abduction at joints of thumb and wrist	Deep radial nerve (C_6–C_7)
Extensor digitorum	Lateral epicondyle of humerus	Posterior surfaces of the phalanges, digits 2–5	Extension at finger joints and wrist	Deep radial nerve (C_6–C_8)
Extensor pollicis brevis	Shaft of radius distal to origin of abductor pollicis longus and the interosseous membrane	Base of proximal phalanx of thumb	Extension at joints of thumb; abduction at wrist	Deep radial nerve (C_6–C_7)
Extensor pollicis longus	Posterior and lateral surfaces of ulna and interosseous membrane	Base of distal phalanx of thumb	As above	Deep radial nerve (C_6–C_8)
Extensor indicis	Posterior surface of ulna and interosseous membrane	Posterior surface of proximal phalanx of index finger (2), with tendon of extensor digitorum	Extension and adduction at joints of index finger	As above
Extensor digiti minimi	Via extensor tendon to lateral epicondyle of humerus and from intermuscular septa	Posterior surface of proximal phalanx of little finger	Extension at joints of little finger; extension at wrist	As above
Flexor digitorum superficialis	Medial epicondyle of humerus; adjacent anterior surfaces of ulna and radius	To bases of middle phalanges of digits 2–5	Flexion at proximal interphalangeal, metacarpophalangeal, and wrist joints	Median nerve (C_7–T_1)
Flexor digitorum profundus	Medial and posterior surfaces of ulna, medial surfaces of coronoid process, and interosseous membrane	Bases of distal phalanges of digits 2–5	Flexion at distal interphalangeal joints, and, to a lesser degree, proximal interphalangeal joints and wrist	Anterior interosseous branch of median nerve and ulnar nerve (C_8–T_1)
Flexor pollicis longus	Anterior shaft of radius, interosseous membrane	Base of distal phalanx of thumb	Flexion at joints of thumb	Median nerve (C_8–T_1)

TABLE 11.5 Intrinsic Muscles of the Hand

Muscle	Origin	Insertion	Action	Innervation
Adductor pollicis	Metacarpal and carpal bones	Proximal phalanx of thumb	Adduction of thumb	Ulnar nerve, deep branch (C_8–T_1)
Opponens pollicis	Trapezium and flexor retinaculum	First metacarpal bone	Opposition of thumb	Median nerve (C_6–C_7)
Palmaris brevis	Palmar aponeurosis	Skin of medial border of hand	Moves skin on medial border toward midline of palm	Ulnar nerve, superficial branch (C_8)
Abductor digiti minimi	Pisiform	Proximal phalanx of little finger	Abduction of little finger and flexion at its metacarpophalangeal joint	Ulnar nerve, deep branch (C_8–T_1)
Abductor pollicis brevis	Transverse carpal ligament, scaphoid and trapezium	Radial side of base of proximal phalanx of thumb	Abduction of thumb	Median nerve (C_6–C_7)
Flexor pollicis brevis*	Flexor retinaculum, trapezium, capitate, and ulnar side of first metacarpal bone	Radial and ulnar sides of proximal phalanx of thumb	Flexion and adduction of thumb	Branches of median and ulnar nerves
Flexor digiti minimi brevis	Hamate	Proximal phalanx of little finger	Flexion at fifth metacarpophalangeal joint	Ulnar nerve, deep branch (C_8–T_1)
Opponens digiti minimi	As above	Fifth metacarpal bone	Flexion at metacarpophalangeal joint; brings digit into opposition with thumb	As above
Lumbrical (4)	The four tendons of flexor digitorum profundus	Tendons of extensor digitorum to digits 2–5	Flexion at metacarpophalangeal joints; extension at proximal and distal interphalangeal joints	No. 1 and no. 2 by median nerve; no. 3 and no. 4 by ulnar nerve, deep branch
Dorsal interosseus (4)	Each originates from opposing faces of two metacarpal bones (I and II, II and III, III and IV, IV and V)	Bases of proximal phalanges of digits 2–4	Abduction at metacarpophalangeal joints of digits 2–4, flexion at metacarpophalangeal joints; extension at interphalangeal joints	Ulnar nerve, deep branch (C_8–T_1)
Palmar interosseus (4)	Sides of metacarpal bones II, IV, and V	Bases of proximal phalanges of digits 2, 4, and 5	Adduction at metacarpophalangeal joints of digits 2, 4, and 5; flexion at metacarpophalangeal joints; extension at interphalangeal joints	As above

*The portion of the flexor pollicis brevis originating on the first metacarpal bone is sometimes called the *first palmar interosseus muscle*, which inserts on the ulnar side of the proximal phalanx and is innervated by the ulnar nerve.

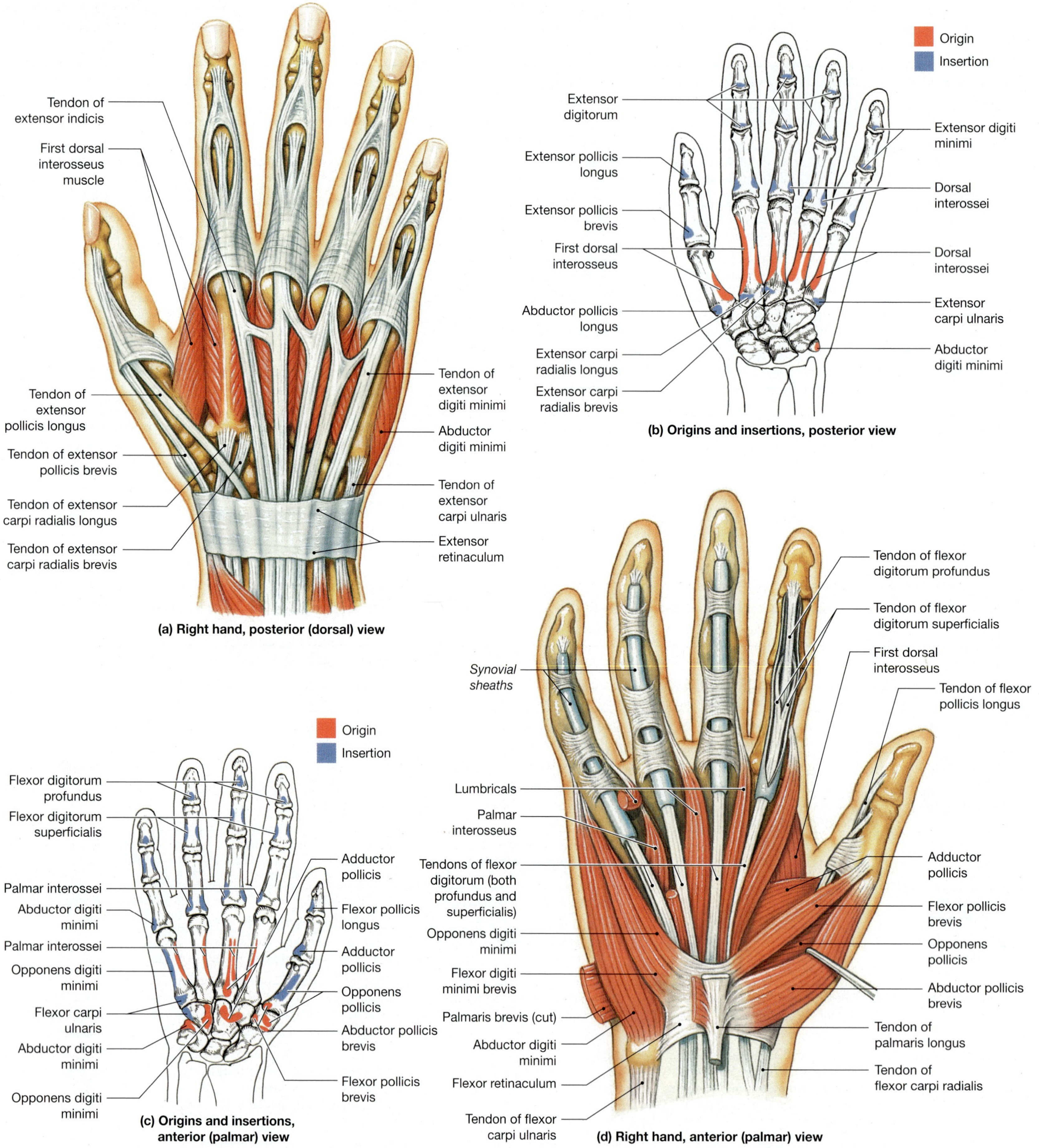

Figure 11.11 Intrinsic Muscles, Tendons, and Ligaments of the Hand
Anatomy of the right wrist and hand. **(a)** Posterior (dorsal) view. **(b)** Posterior view of the bones of the right hand, showing the origins and insertions of selected muscles. **(c)** Anterior view of the bones of the right hand, showing the origins and insertions of selected muscles. **(d)** Anterior (palmar) view. **(e)** Right hand, transverse sectional view through metacarpal bones. **(f)** Anterior view of a superficial palmar dissection of the right hand. **(g)** Anterior view of a deep palmar dissection of the right hand.

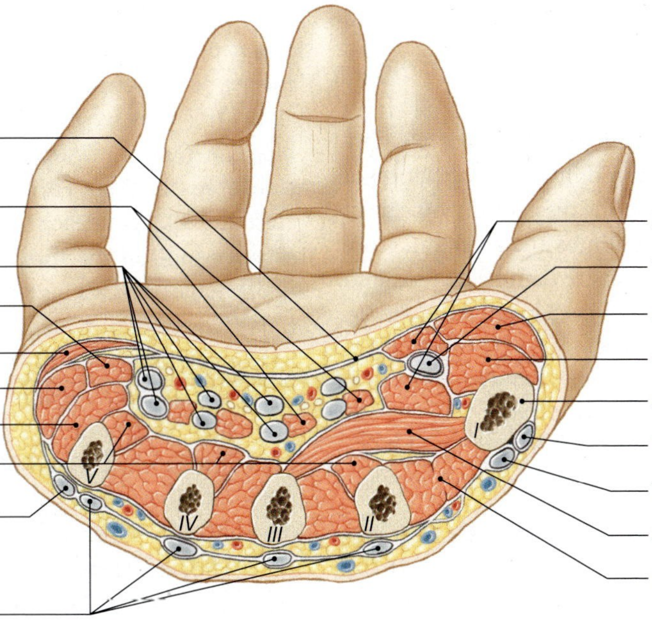

(e) Right hand, sectional view through metacarpal bones

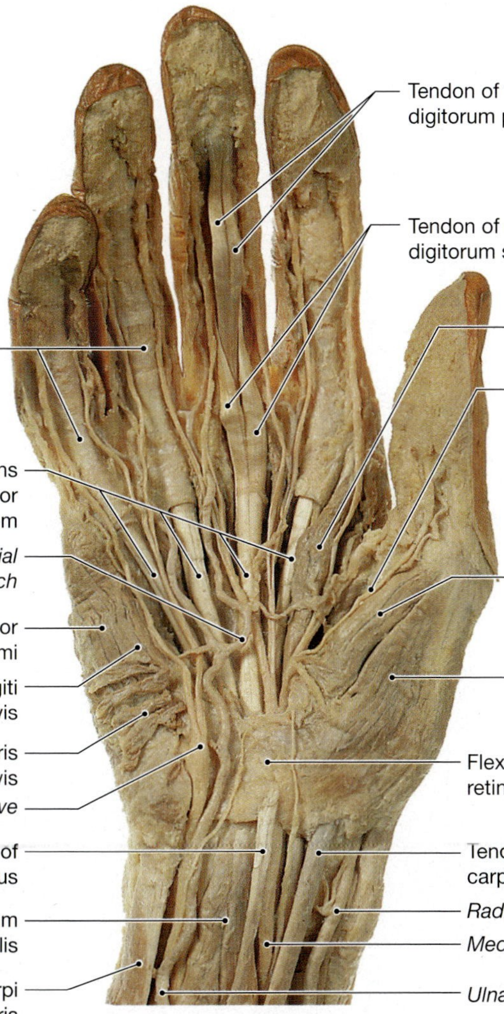

(f) Right hand, anterior (palmar) view

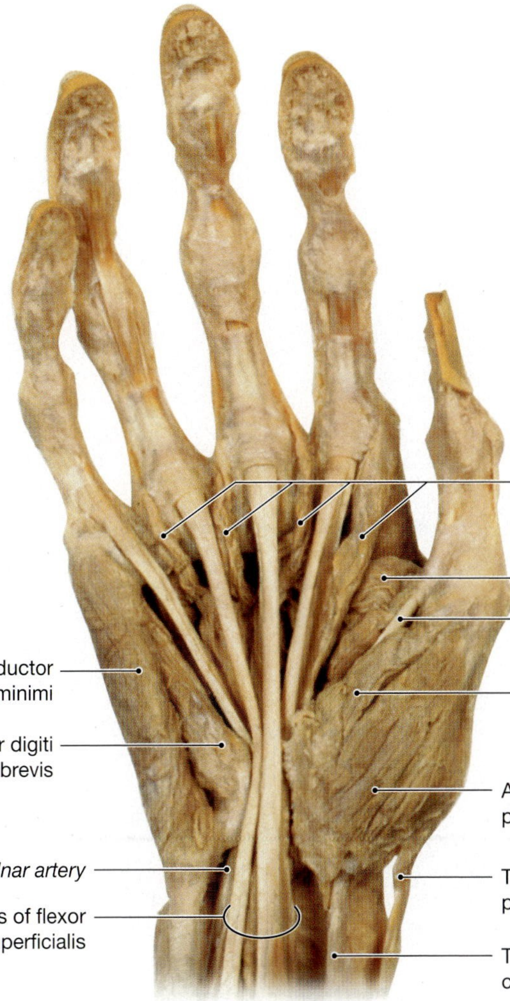

(g) Right hand, anterior view (deep)

Figure 11.11 ***(continued)***

Muscles of the Pelvic Girdle and Lower Limbs

The pelvic girdle is tightly bound to the axial skeleton, and relatively little movement is permitted. The few muscles that can influence the position of the pelvis were considered in Chapter 10, during the discussion of the axial musculature. p. 279 The muscles of the lower limbs are larger and more powerful than those of the upper limbs. These muscles can be divided into three groups: (1) *muscles that move the thigh*, (2) *muscles that move the leg*, and (3) *muscles that move the foot and toes.*

Muscles That Move the Thigh [Figures 11.2/11.5/11.12 to 11.14 and Table 11.6]

The muscles that move the thigh originate on the pelvis; many are large and powerful. The muscles that move the thigh are grouped into (a) the gluteal group, (b) the lateral rotator group, (c) the adductor group, and (d) the iliopsoas group. **Gluteal muscles** cover the lateral surface of the ilium (Figures 11.2, 11.5, and 11.12). The **gluteus maximus muscle** is the largest and most superficial of the gluteal muscles. It originates along the posterior gluteal line and adjacent portions of the iliac crest; the sacrum, coccyx, and associated ligaments; and the thoracolumbar fascia. Acting alone, this massive muscle produces extension and lateral rotation at the hip. The gluteus maximus muscle shares an insertion with the **tensor fasciae latae** (TEN-sor FASH-ē-ē LĀ-tē) **muscle**, which originates on the iliac crest and lateral surface of the anterior superior iliac spine. Together these muscles pull on the **iliotibial** (il-ē-ō-TIB-ē-al) **tract**, a band of collagen fibers that extends along the lateral surface of the thigh and inserts upon the tibia. This tract provides a lateral brace for the knee that becomes particularly important when a person balances on one foot.

The **gluteus medius** and **gluteus minimus muscles** (Figure 11.12) originate anterior to the gluteus maximus and insert upon the greater trochanter of the femur. Both produce abduction and medial rotation at the hip joint. The anterior gluteal line on the lateral surface of the ilium marks the boundary between these muscles. p. 188

The six **lateral rotators** (Figures 11.12a,c and 11.13) originate at, or are inferior to, the horizontal axis of the acetabulum and insert on the femur. All cause lateral rotation of the thigh; additionally, the **piriformis** (pir-i-FOR-mis) **muscle** produces abduction at the hip. The piriformis

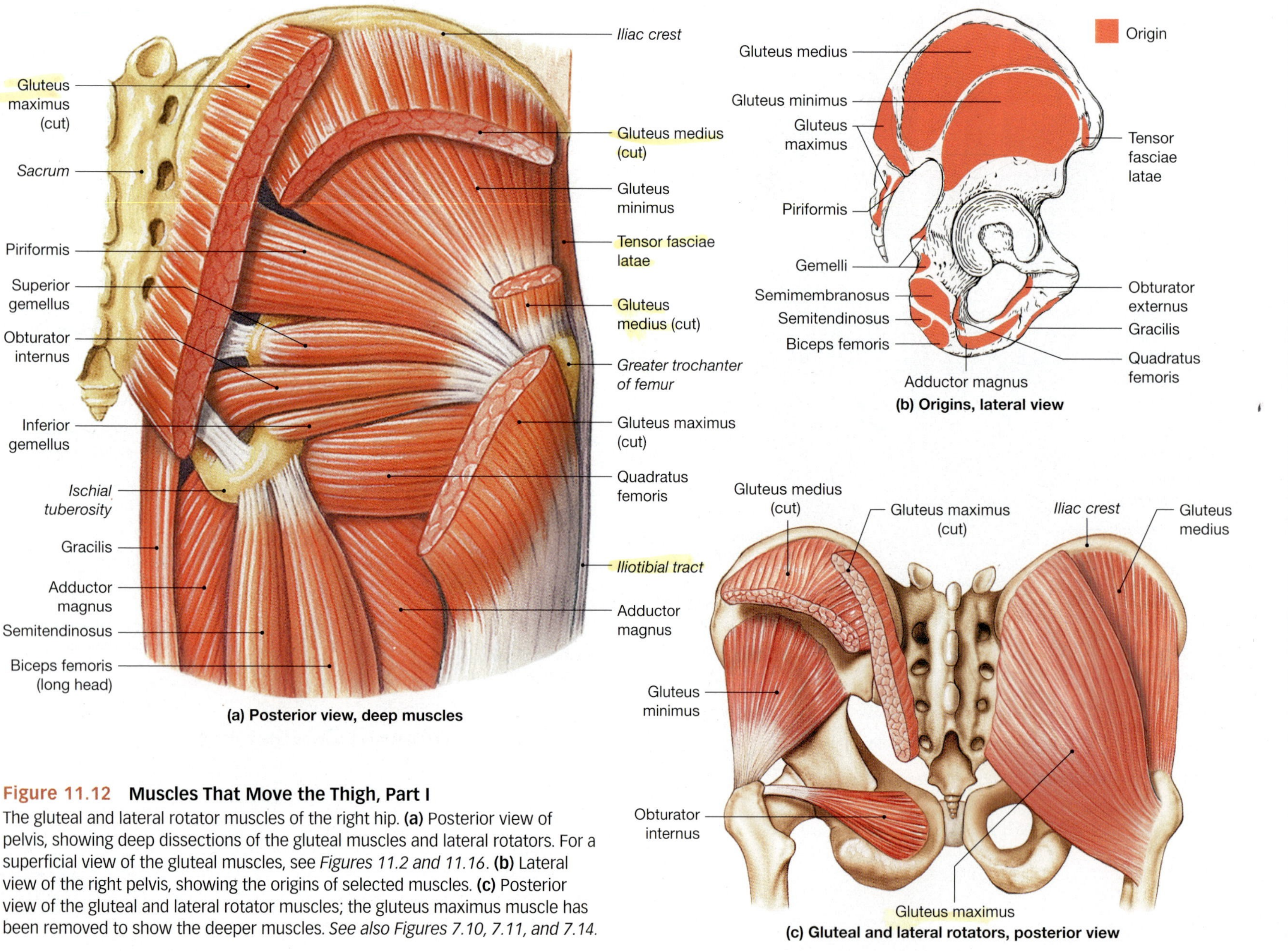

Figure 11.12 Muscles That Move the Thigh, Part I
The gluteal and lateral rotator muscles of the right hip. **(a)** Posterior view of pelvis, showing deep dissections of the gluteal muscles and lateral rotators. For a superficial view of the gluteal muscles, see *Figures 11.2 and 11.16*. **(b)** Lateral view of the right pelvis, showing the origins of selected muscles. **(c)** Posterior view of the gluteal and lateral rotator muscles; the gluteus maximus muscle has been removed to show the deeper muscles. *See also Figures 7.10, 7.11, and 7.14.*

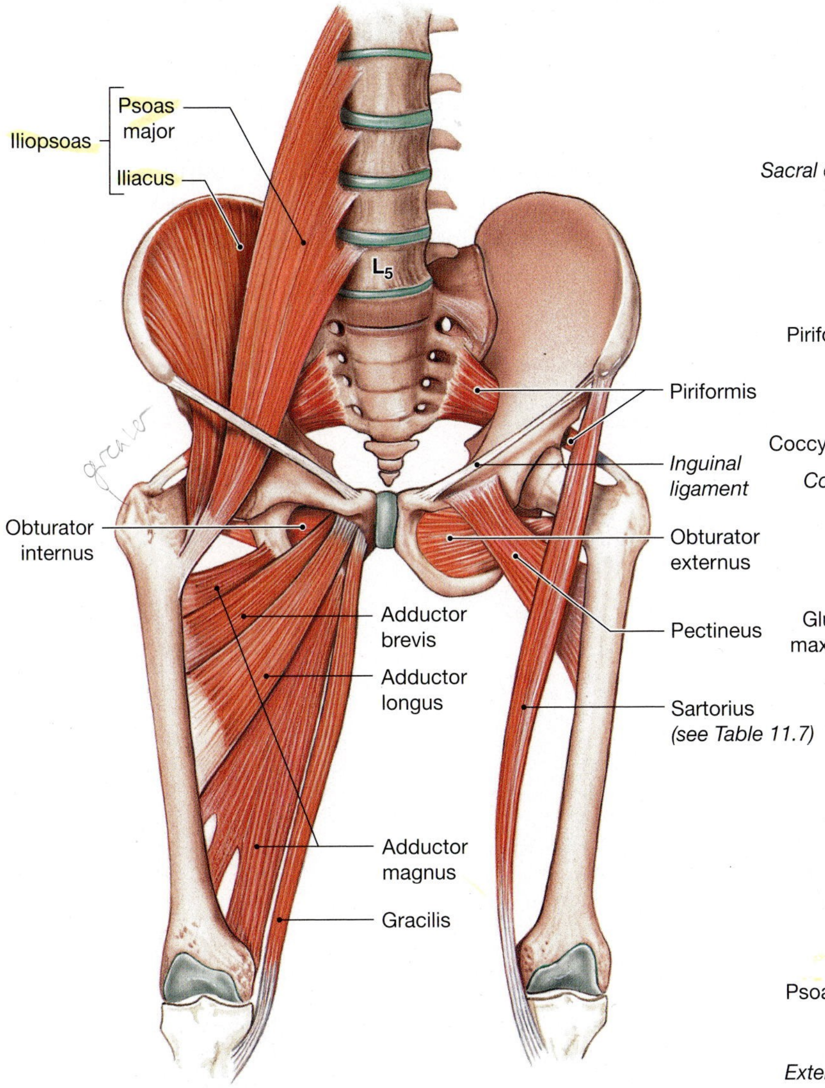

(a) Anterior view

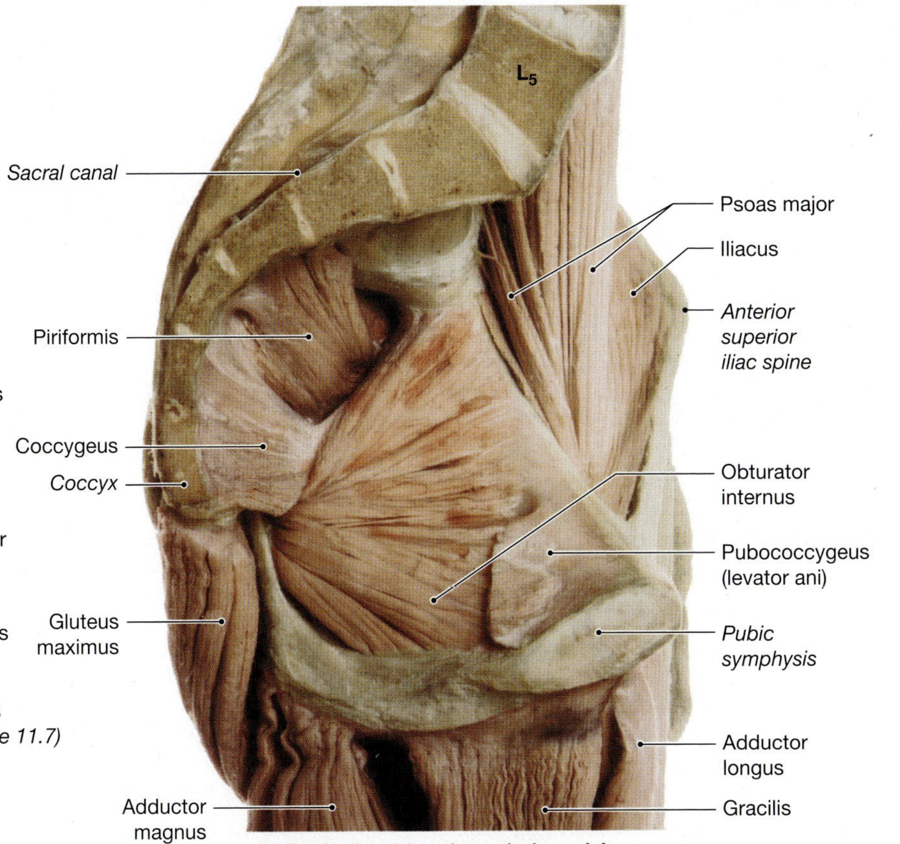

(b) Sagittal section through the pelvis

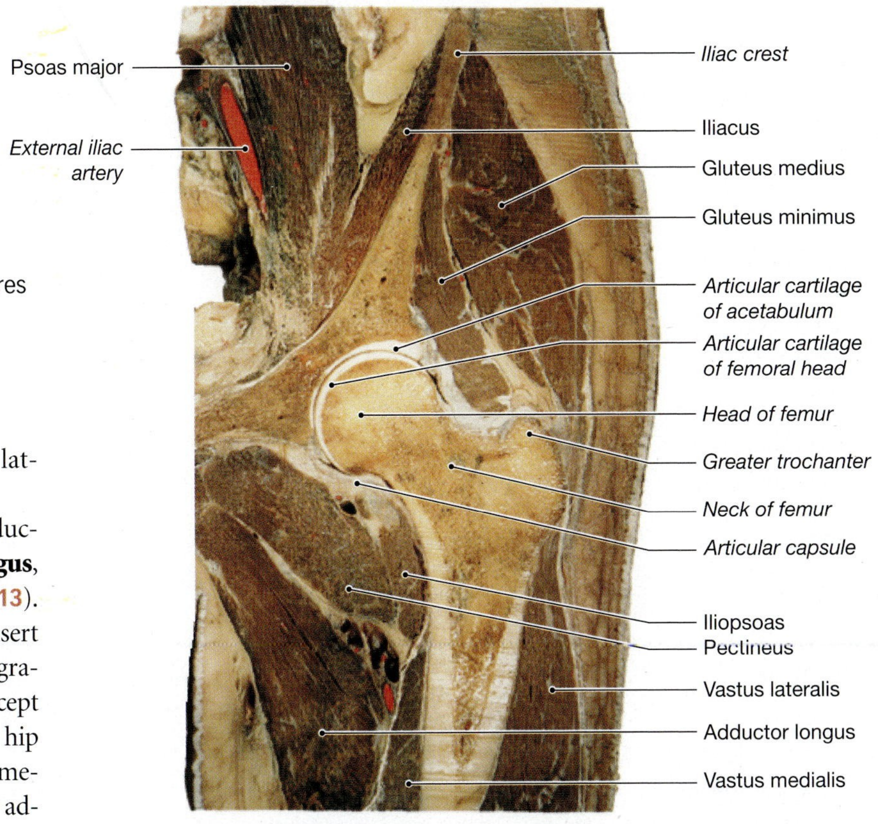

(c) Coronal section through the pelvis

Figure 11.13 Muscles That Move the Thigh, Part II
The iliopsoas muscle and adductors of the right hip. **(a)** Anterior view of the iliopsoas muscle and the adductor group. **(b)** Muscles and associated structures seen in a sagittal section through the pelvis. *See also Figures 7.10, 7.11, and 7.14.* **(c)** Coronal section through the hip, showing the hip joint in relation to surrounding muscles.

and the **obturator muscles** (*externus* and *internus*) are the dominant lateral rotators.

The **adductors** are located inferior to the acetabular surface. The adductors include the **adductor magnus**, **adductor brevis**, **adductor longus**, **pectineus** (pek-TI-nē-us), and **gracilis** (GRAS-i-lis) **muscles** (Figure 11.13). All originate on the pubis; all of the adductors except the gracilis muscle insert on the linea aspera, a ridge along the posterior surface of the femur. (The gracilis inserts on the tibia.) Their actions are varied. All of the adductors except the adductor magnus muscle originate both anterior and inferior to the hip joint, so they produce hip flexion as well as adduction. They also produce medial rotation at the hip. The adductor magnus muscle can produce either adduction and flexion or adduction and extension, depending on the region stimulated. It may also produce either medial or lateral rotation. When an athlete suffers a *pulled groin*, the problem is a *strain*—a muscle tear or break—in one of these adductor muscles.

The medial surface of the pelvis is dominated by a single pair of muscles. The **psoas** (SŌ-us) **major muscle** originates alongside the inferior thoracic and lumbar vertebrae, and its insertion lies on the lesser trochanter of the femur. Before reaching this insertion, its tendon merges with that of the **iliacus** (il-Ē-a-kus) **muscle**, which lies nestled within the iliac fossa. These two muscles, which are powerful flexors of the hip, pass deep to the *inguinal ligament*, and are often referred to as the **iliopsoas** (i-lē-ō-SŌ-us) **muscle** (Figure 11.13).

One method for organizing the information about these diverse muscles is to consider their orientation around the hip joint. Muscles originating on the surface of the pelvis and inserting on the femur will produce characteristic movements determined by their position relative to the acetabulum (Table 11.6).

As with our analysis of the shoulder muscles (pp. 290–292), the relationships between the action lines and the axis of the hip joint can be used to predict the actions of the various muscles and muscle groups. When considering the action lines of the muscles that act at the hip you must remember that (1) the neck of the femur angles inferiorly and laterally away from the acetabulum of the hip, (2) the femur is bent and twisted as you move inferiorly from the hip to the knee, (**Figures 8.14** and **8.15**), pp. 222, 223 and (3) many of the muscles that act on the hip are very large, and they have insertions that extend over a broad area. As a result, these muscles often have more than one action line, and therefore produce more than one action at the hip (**Figure 11.14a**). For example, consider the adductor magnus, a large hip muscle that has three action lines (**Figure 11.14b**). One or another may apply, depending on what portion of the muscle is activated; when the entire muscle contracts, it produces a combination of flexion, extension, and adduction at the hip.

TABLE 11.6 Muscles That Move the Thigh

Muscle	Origin	Insertion	Action	Innervation
GLUTEAL GROUP				
Gluteus maximus	Iliac crest, posterior gluteal line, and lateral surface of ilium; sacrum, coccyx, and thoracolumbar fascia	Iliotibial tract and gluteal tuberosity of femur	Extension and lateral rotation at hip; helps stabilize the extended knee; abduction at the hip (superior fibers only)	Inferior gluteal nerve (L_5–S_2)
Gluteus medius	Anterior iliac crest, lateral surface of ilium between posterior and anterior gluteal lines	Greater trochanter of femur	Abduction and medial rotation at hip	Superior gluteal nerve (L_4–S_1)
Gluteus minimus	Lateral surface of ilium between inferior and anterior gluteal lines	As above	As above	As above
Tensor fasciae latae	Iliac crest and lateral surface of anterior superior iliac spine	Iliotibial tract	Abduction and medial rotation at hip; extension and lateral rotation at knee; tenses fasciae latae, which laterally supports the knee	As above
LATERAL ROTATOR GROUP				
Obturators (externus and internus)	Lateral and medial margins of obturator foramen	Trochanteric fossa of femur (externus); medial surface of greater trochanter (internus)	Lateral rotation and abduction of hip; help to maintain stability and integrity of the hip	Obturator nerve (externus: L_3–L_4) and special nerve from sacral plexus (internus: L_5–S_2)
Piriformis	Anterolateral surface of sacrum	Greater trochanter of femur	As above	Branches of sacral nerves (S_1–S_2)
Gemelli (superior and inferior)	Ischial spine (superior gemellus) and ischial tuberosity (inferior gemellus)	Medial surface of greater trochanter via tendon of obturator internus	As above	Nerves to obturator internus and quadratus femoris
Quadratus femoris	Lateral border of ischial tuberosity	Intertrochanteric crest of femur	Lateral rotation of hip	Special nerves from sacral plexus (L_4–S_1)
ADDUCTOR GROUP				
Adductor brevis	Inferior ramus of pubis	Linea aspera of femur	Adduction and flexion at hip	Obturator nerve (L_3–L_4)
Adductor longus	Inferior ramus of pubis, anterior to adductor brevis	As above	Adduction, flexion, and medial rotation at hip	As above
Adductor magnus	Inferior ramus of pubis posterior to adductor brevis and ischial tuberosity	Linea aspera and adductor tubercle of femur	Whole muscle produces adduction at the hip; anterior part produces flexion and medial rotation; posterior part produces extension	Obturator and sciatic nerves
Pectineus	Superior ramus of pubis	Pectineal line inferior to lesser trochanter of femur	Flexion and adduction at hip	Femoral nerve (L_2–L_4)
Gracilis	Inferior ramus of pubis	Medial surface of tibia inferior to medial condyle	Flexion and medial rotation at knee; adduction and medial rotation at hip	Obturator nerve (L_3–L_4)
ILIOPSOAS GROUP				
Iliacus	Iliac fossa	Femur distal to lesser trochanter; tendon fused with that of psoas major	Flexion at hip and/or lumbar intervertebral joints	Femoral nerve (L_2–L_3)
Psoas major	Anterior surfaces and transverse processes of vertebrae (T_{12}–L_5)	Lesser trochanter in company with iliacus	As above	Branches of the lumbar plexus (L_2–L_3)

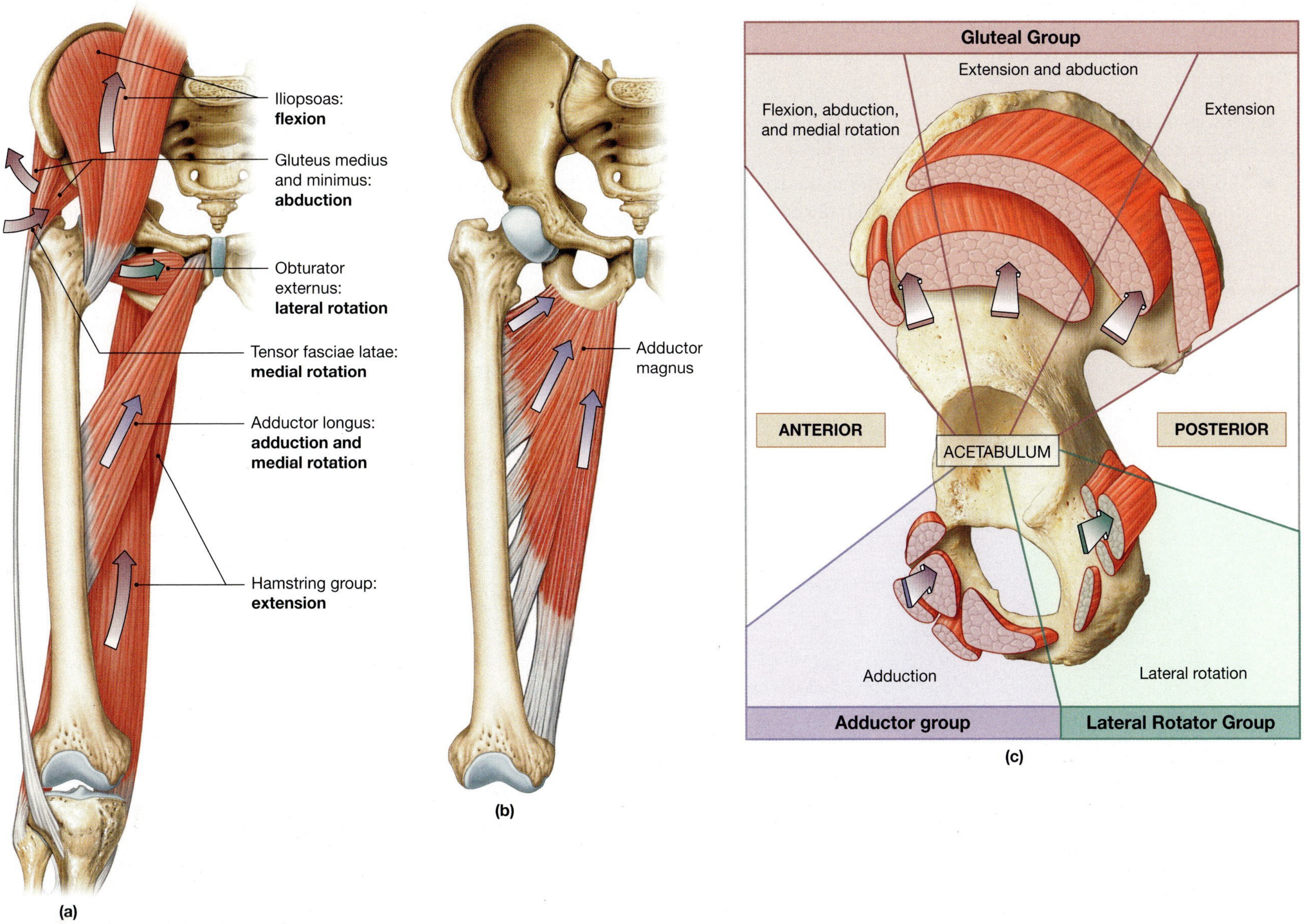

Figure 11.14 The Relationships between the Action Lines and the Axis of the Hip Joint
(a) Examples of several muscles that have more than one action line crossing the axis of the hip. **(b)** Action lines of the adductor magnus. **(c)** Lateral view of the hip joint demonstrating the action lines of muscles that move the thigh.

Clinical Note

Intramuscular Injections Drugs are commonly injected through hollow needles into tissues rather than directly into the bloodstream (accessing blood vessels may be technically more complicated). An *intramuscular (IM) injection* introduces a fairly large amount of a drug, which will then enter the circulation gradually. The drug is introduced into the mass of a large skeletal muscle. Uptake is generally faster and accompanied by less tissue irritation than when drugs are administered intradermally or subcutaneously (injected into the dermis or subcutaneous layer, respectively). Depending on the size of the muscle, up to 5 ml of fluid may be injected at one time, and multiple injections are possible. A decision on the injection technique and the injection site is based on the type of drug and its concentration.

For IM injections, the most common complications involve accidental injection into a blood vessel or piercing of a nerve. The sudden entry of massive quantities of a drug into the bloodstream can have fatal consequences, and damage to a nerve can cause motor paralysis or sensory loss. Thus, the site of injection must be selected with care. Bulky muscles that contain few large vessels or nerves are ideal sites. The gluteus medius muscle or the posterior, lateral, superior part of the gluteus maximus muscle is commonly selected. The deltoid muscle of the arm, about 2.5 cm (1 in.) distal to the acromion, is another effective site. Probably most satisfactory from a technical point of view is the vastus lateralis muscle of the thigh; an injection into this thick muscle will not encounter vessels or nerves, but may cause pain later when the muscle is used in walking. This is the preferred injection site in infants before they start walking, as their gluteal and deltoid muscles are relatively small. The site is also used in elderly patients or others with atrophied gluteal and deltoid muscles.

The hip joint, like the shoulder joint, is a multiaxial synovial joint that permits flexion/extension, adduction/abduction, and medial/lateral rotation. In general terms, the muscle actions can be summarized as (Figure 11.14c):

- Muscles that have action lines that pass posterior to the axis of the hip joint, such as the hamstrings, are extensors of the hip.
- Muscles that have action lines that pass anterior to the axis of the hip joint, such as the iliopsoas group and the anterior fibers of the gluteus medius, are flexors of the hip.
- Muscles that have action lines that pass medial to the axis of the hip joint, such as the adductor longus muscle, are adductors of the hip.
- Muscles that have action lines that pass lateral to the axis of the hip joint, such as the gluteus medius and gluteus minimus, are abductors of the hip.

Muscles whose action lines pass medial to the axis of the hip joint, such as the tensor fasciae latae or adductor longus (Figures 11.14 and 11.15), may produce medial rotation at that joint, whereas muscles whose action lines pass lateral to the axis of the hip, such as the obturator externus, may produce lateral rotation at that joint.

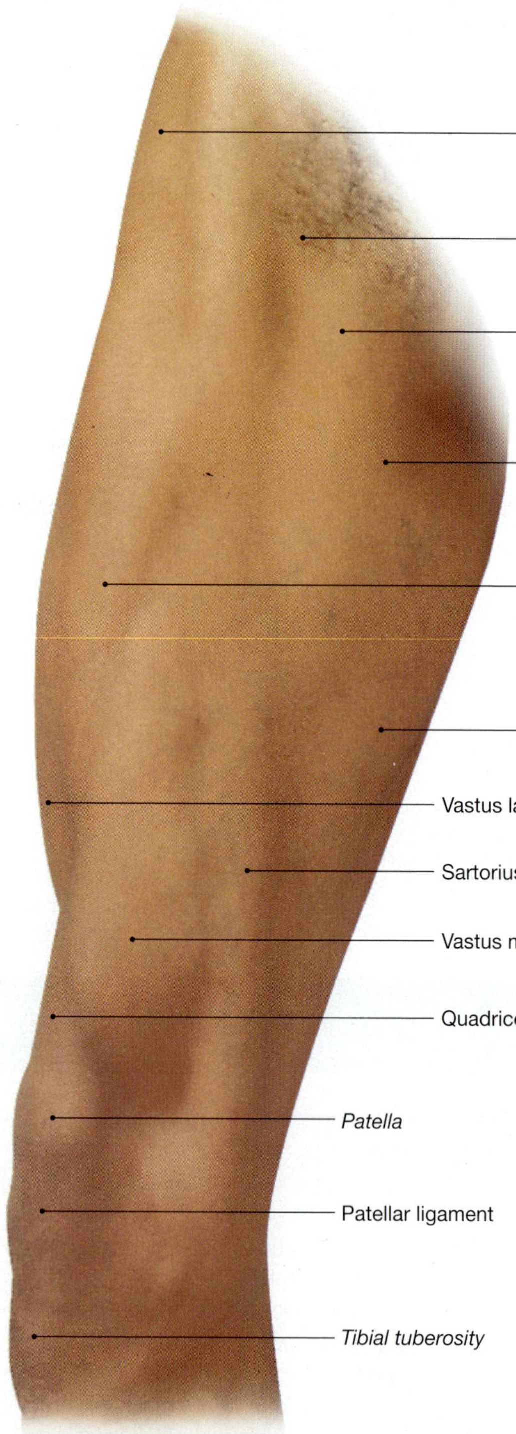

(a) Surface anatomy, anteromedial view

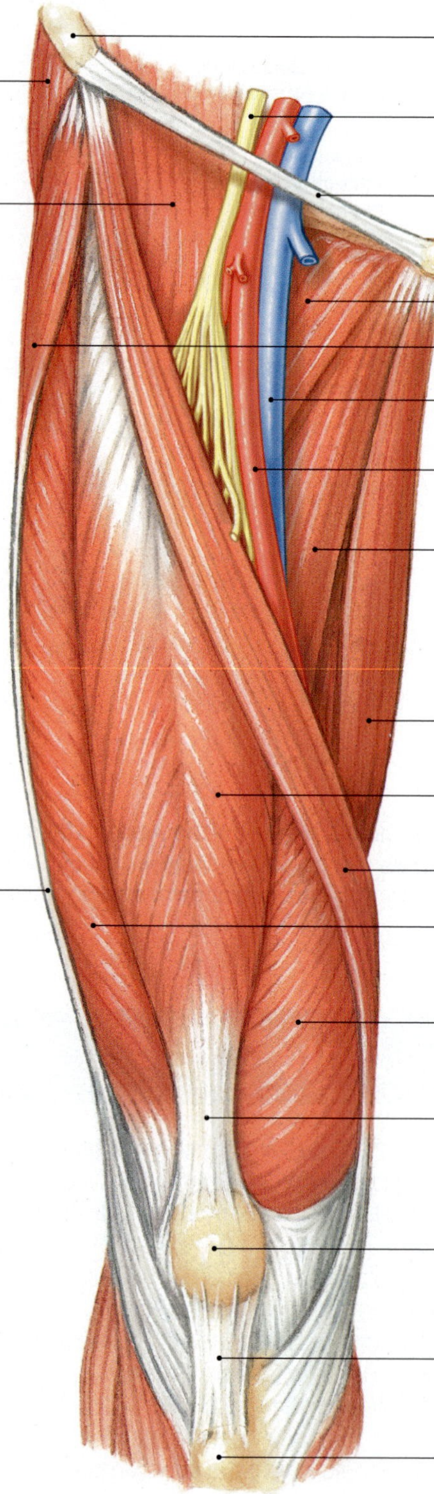

(b) Quadriceps and thigh muscles, anterior view

Figure 11.15 Muscles That Move the Leg, Part I
(a) Surface anatomy, anteromedial view, of the right thigh. **(b)** Diagrammatic anterior view of the superficial muscles of the right thigh. **(c)** Anterior view of a dissection of the muscles of the right thigh. **(d)** Transverse section of the right thigh. **(e)** Anterior view of the bones of the right lower limb showing the origins and insertions of selected muscles.

Muscles That Move the Leg [Figures 11.15 to 11.17 and Table 11.7]

Muscles that move the leg are detailed in Figures 11.15 to 11.17 and Table 11.7. As with our analysis of the muscles of the shoulder and hip muscles (pp. 290–292, 304–305), the relationships between the action lines and the axis of the knee joint can be used to predict the actions of the various muscles and muscle groups. However, the anterior/posterior orientation of the muscles that move the leg is reversed. This is related to the rotation of the limb during embryological development (*see Chapter 28, Embryology and Human Development*). As a result:

- Muscles that have action lines that pass anterior to the axis of the knee joint, such as the quadriceps femoris, are extensors of the knee.
- Muscles that have action lines that pass posterior to the axis of the knee joint, such as the hamstrings, are flexors of the knee.

Most of the extensor muscles originate on the femoral surface and extend along the anterior and lateral surfaces of the thigh (Figures 11.15 and 11.16). Flexor muscles originate on the pelvic girdle and extend along the posterior and medial surfaces of the thigh (Figure 11.17). Collectively the knee extensors (Figures 11.15 and 11.16) are called the *quadriceps muscles* or the *quadriceps femoris.* The three **vastus muscles** (**vastus lateralis**, **vastus medialis**, and **vastus intermedius**) originate along the body of the femur, and they cradle the **rectus femoris muscle** the way a bun surrounds a hot dog. All four muscles insert upon the tibial tuberosity via the quadriceps tendon, patella, and patellar ligament. The rectus femoris muscle originates on the anterior inferior iliac spine,

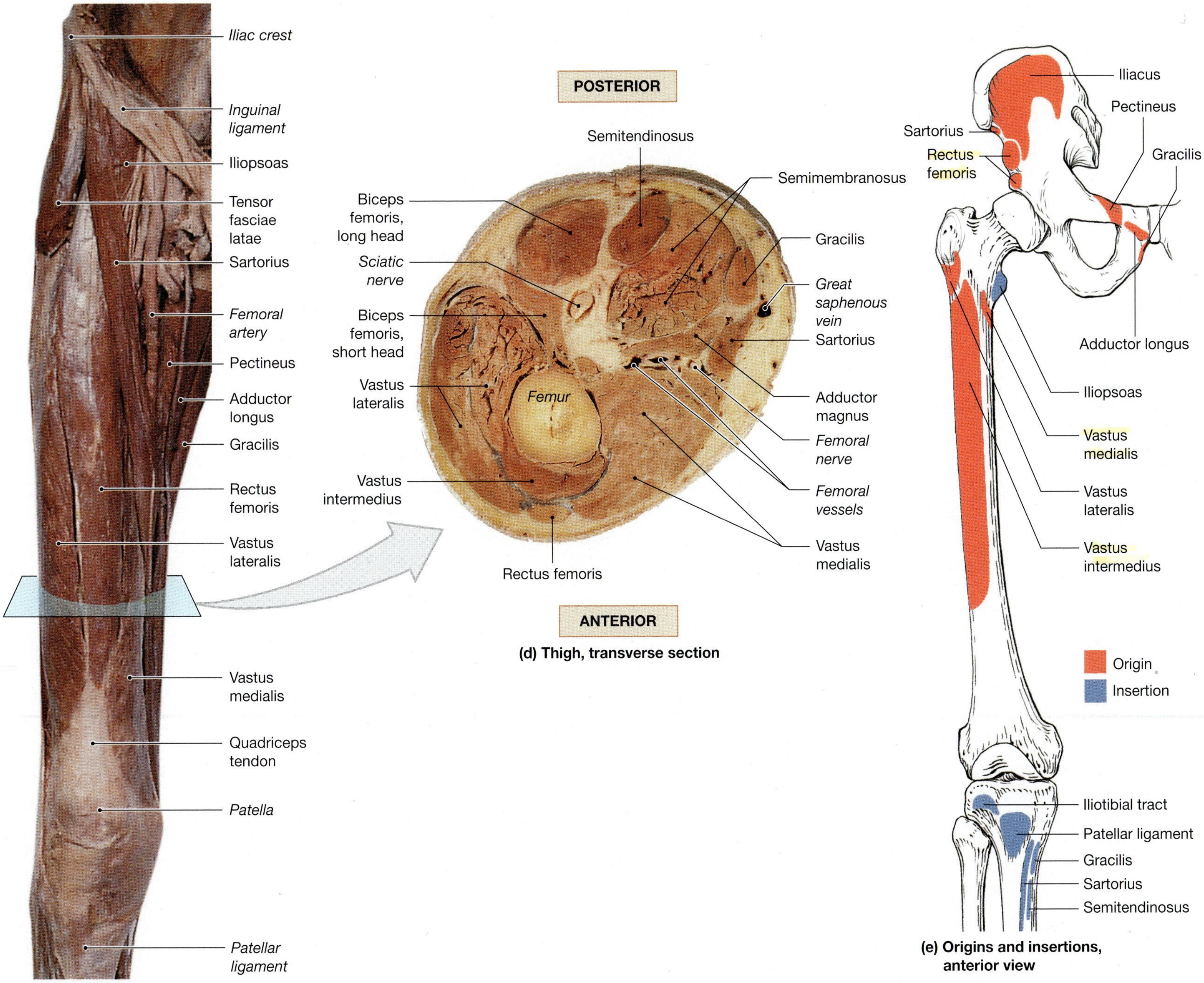

(c) Anterior view

(d) Thigh, transverse section

(e) Origins and insertions, anterior view

Figure 11.15 ***(continued)***

TABLE 11.7 Muscles That Move the Leg

Muscle	Origin	Insertion	Action	Innervation
FLEXORS OF THE KNEE				
Biceps femoris	Ischial tuberosity and linea aspera of femur	Head of fibula, lateral condyle of tibia	Flexion at knee; extension and lateral rotation at hip	Sciatic nerve; tibial portion (S_1–S_3 to long head) and common fibular branch (L_5–S_2 to short head)
Semimembranosus	Ischial tuberosity	Posterior surface of medial condyle of tibia	Flexion at knee; extension and medial rotation at hip	Sciatic nerve (tibial portion L_5–S_2)
Semitendinosus	As above	Proximal, medial surface of tibia near insertion of gracilis	As above	As above
Sartorius	Anterior superior iliac spine	Medial surface of tibia near tibial tuberosity	Flexion at knee; abduction, flexion, and lateral rotation at hip	Femoral nerve (L_2–L_3)
Popliteus	Lateral condyle of femur	Posterior surface of proximal tibial shaft	Medial rotation of tibia (or lateral rotation of femur) at knee; flexion at knee	Tibial nerve (L_4–S_1)
EXTENSORS OF THE KNEE				
Rectus femoris	Anterior inferior iliac spine and superior acetabular rim of ilium	Tibial tuberosity via quadriceps tendon, patella, and patellar ligament	Extension at knee; flexion at hip	Femoral nerve (L_2–L_4)
Vastus intermedius	Anterolateral surface of femur and linea aspera (distal half)	As above	Extension at knee	As above
Vastus lateralis	Anterior and inferior to greater trochanter of femur and along linea aspera (proximal half)	As above	As above	As above
Vastus medialis	Entire length of linea aspera of femur	As above	As above	As above

TABLE 11.8 Extrinsic Muscles That Move the Foot and Toes

Muscle	Origin	Insertion	Action	Innervation
ACTION AT THE ANKLE				
DORSIFLEXORS				
Tibialis anterior	Lateral condyle and proximal shaft of tibia	Base of first metatarsal bone and medial cuneiform	Dorsiflexion at ankle; inversion of foot	Deep fibular nerve (L_4–S_1)
PLANTAR FLEXORS				
Gastrocnemius	Femoral condyles	Calcaneus via calcaneal tendon	Plantar flexion at ankle; flexion at knee	Tibial nerve (S_1–S_2)
Fibularis brevis	Midlateral margin of fibula	Base of fifth metatarsal bone	Eversion of foot and plantar flexion at ankle	Superficial fibular nerve (L_4–S_1)
Fibularis longus	Head and proximal shaft of fibula	Base of first metatarsal bone and medial cuneiform	Eversion of foot and plantar flexion at ankle; supports ankle; supports longitudinal and transverse arches	As above
Plantaris	Lateral supracondylar ridge	Posterior portion of calcaneus	Plantar flexion at ankle; flexion at knee	Tibial nerve (L_4–S_1)
Soleus	Head and proximal shaft of fibula, and adjacent posteromedial shaft of tibia	Calcaneus via calcaneal tendon (with gastrocnemius)	Plantar flexion at ankle; postural muscle when standing	Sciatic nerve, tibial branch (S_1–S_2)
Tibialis posterior	Interosseous membrane and adjacent shafts of tibia and fibula	Navicular, all three cuneiforms, cuboid, second, third, and fourth metatarsal bones	Inversion of foot; plantar flexion at ankle	As above
ACTION AT THE TOES				
DIGITAL FLEXORS				
Flexor digitorum longus	Posteromedial surface of tibia	Inferior surface of distal phalanges, toes 2–5	Flexion of joints of toes 2–5; plantar flexes ankle	Tibial branch (L_5–S_1)
Flexor hallucis longus	Posterior surface of fibula	Inferior surface, distal phalanx of great toe	Flexion at joints of great toe; plantar flexes ankle	As above
DIGITAL EXTENSORS				
Extensor digitorum longus	Lateral condyle of tibia, anterior surface of fibula	Superior surfaces of phalanges, toes 2–5	Extension of toes 2–5; dorsiflexes ankle	Deep fibular nerve (L_5, S_1)
Extensor hallucis longus	Anterior surface of fibula	Superior surface, distal phalanx of great toe	Extension at joints of great toe; dorsiflexes ankle	As above

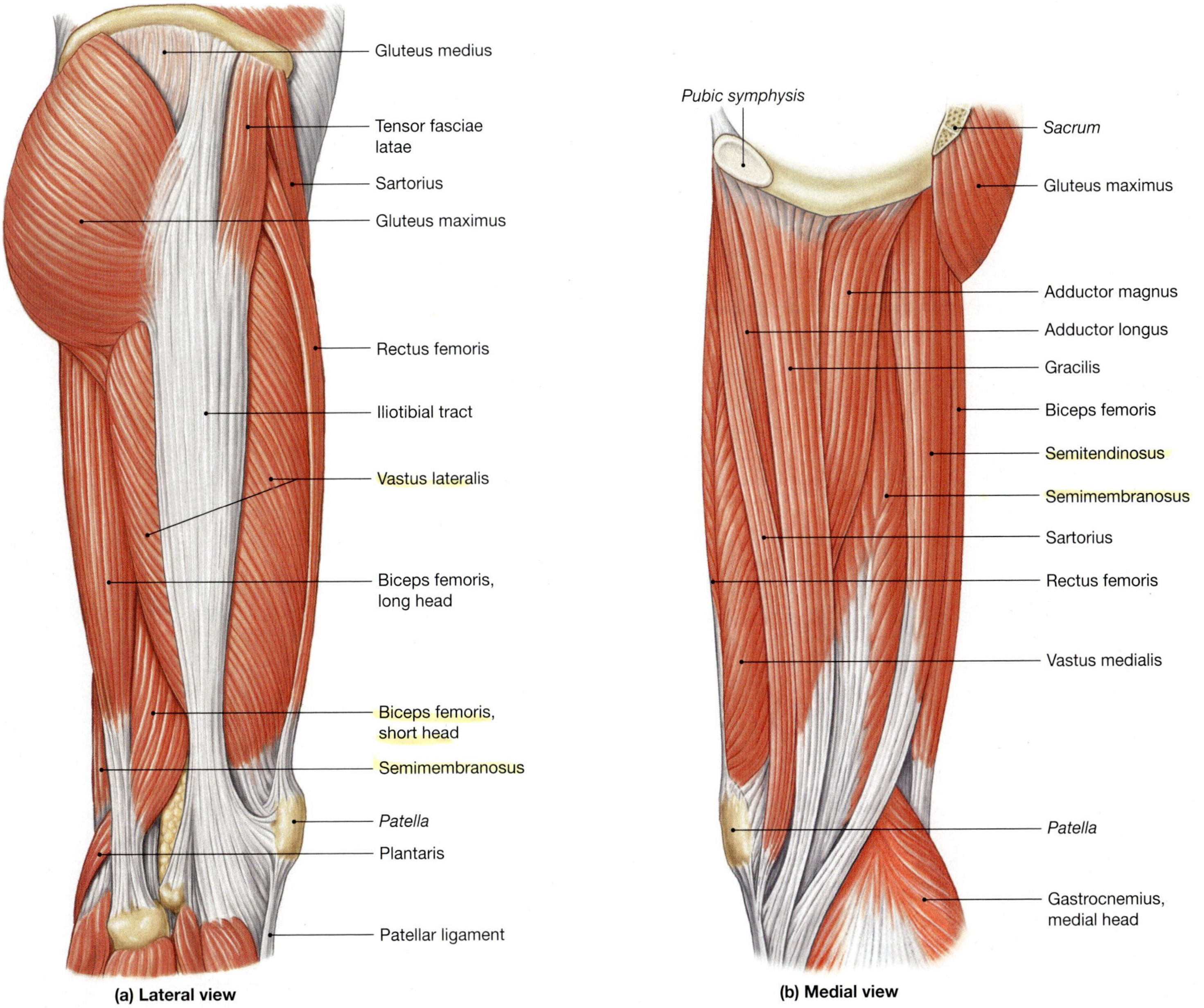

Figure 11.16 Muscles That Move the Leg, Part II
(a) Lateral view of the muscles of the right thigh. **(b)** Medial view of the muscles of the right thigh.

so in addition to producing extension of the knee, it can assist in flexion of the hip.

The flexors of the knee include the **biceps femoris**, **semimembranosus** (sem-ē-mem-bra-NŌ-sus), **semitendinosus** (sem-ē-ten-di-NŌ-sus), and **sartorius** (sar-TOR-ē-us) **muscles** (Figures 11.15a, 11.16a,b, and 11.17). These muscles originate along the edges of the pelvis and insert upon the tibia and fibula. Their contractions produce flexion at the knee. Because the biceps femoris, semimembranosus, and semitendinosus muscles originate on the pelvis inferior and posterior to the acetabulum, their contractions also produce extension at the hip. These muscles are often called the *hamstrings.*

The sartorius muscle is the only knee flexor that originates superior to the acetabulum, and its insertion lies along the medial aspect of the tibia. When it contracts, it produces flexion, abduction, and lateral rotation at the hip, as when crossing the legs. In Chapter 8 we noted that the knee joint can be locked at full extension by a slight lateral rotation of the tibia. p. 225 The small **popliteus** (pop-LI-tē-us) **muscle** originates on the femur near the lateral condyle and inserts on the posterior tibial shaft (Figure 11.18). When knee flexion is initiated, this muscle contracts to produce a slight medial rotation of the tibia that unlocks the joint. Figure 11.17d shows the surface anatomy of the posterior surface of the thigh and the landmarks associated with some of the knee flexors.

Muscles That Move the Foot and Toes

Extrinsic Muscles of the Foot [Figures 11.18 to 11.21a,b and Table 11.8]

Extrinsic muscles of the foot that move the foot and toes (Figures 11.18 to 11.21a,b) are detailed in Table 11.8. Most of the muscles that move the ankle produce the plantar flexion involved with walking and running movements.

The large **gastrocnemius** (gas-trok-NĒ-mē-us; *gaster*, stomach + *kneme*, knee) **muscle** of the calf is an important plantar flexor, but the slow muscle fibers of the underlying **soleus** (SŌ-lē-us) **muscle** make this the

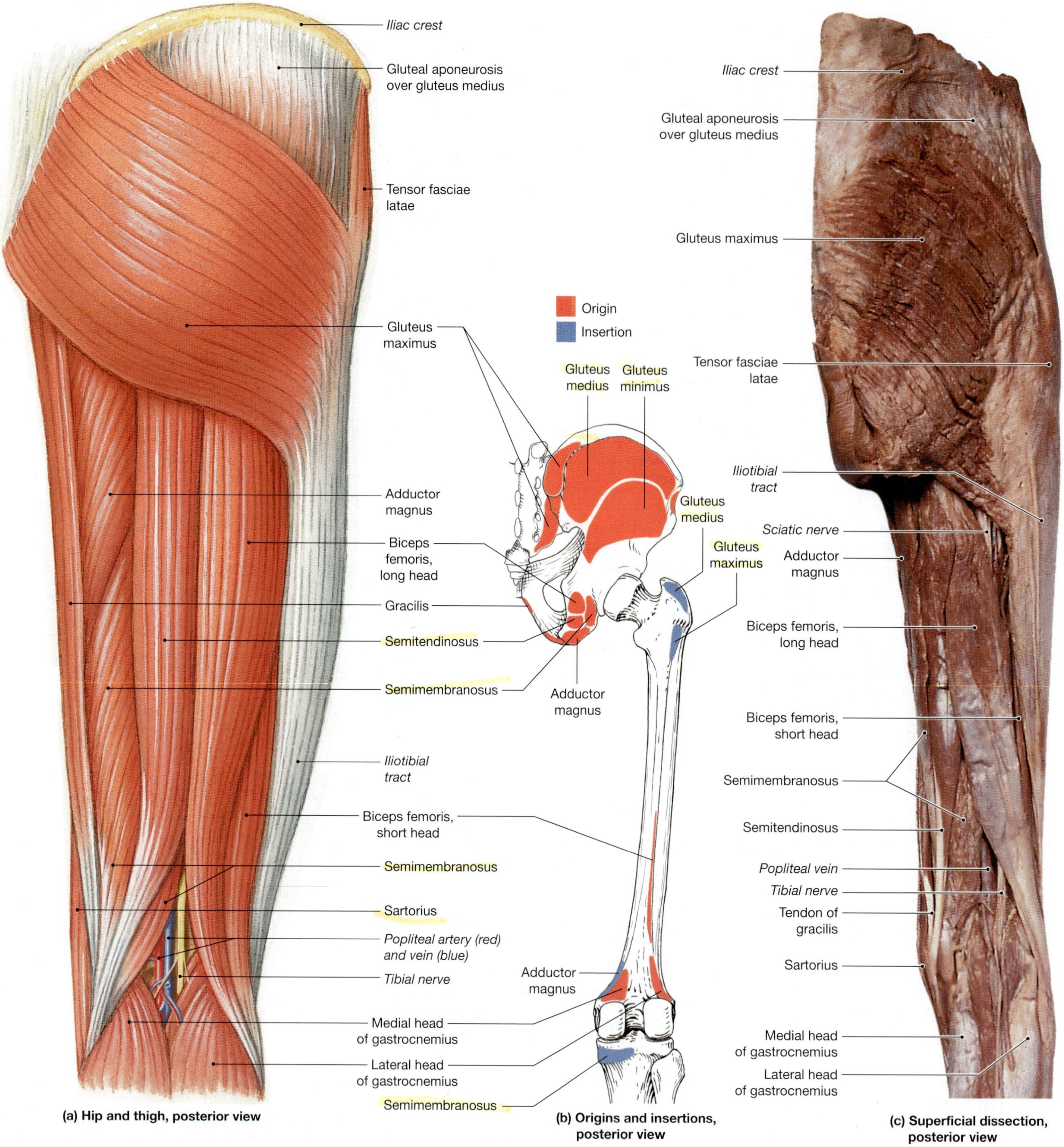

Figure 11.17 Muscles That Move the Leg, Part III

(a) Posterior view of superficial muscles of the right thigh. **(b)** Posterior view of the bones of the right hip, thigh, and proximal leg, showing the origins and insertions of selected muscles. **(c)** Posterior view of a dissection of the muscles of the thigh and proximal leg (part 1). **(d)** Surface anatomy of the right thigh, posterior view. **(e)** Deep muscles of the posterior thigh. **(f)** Posterior view of the bones of the right hip, thigh, and proximal leg, showing the origins and insertions of selected muscles (part 2).

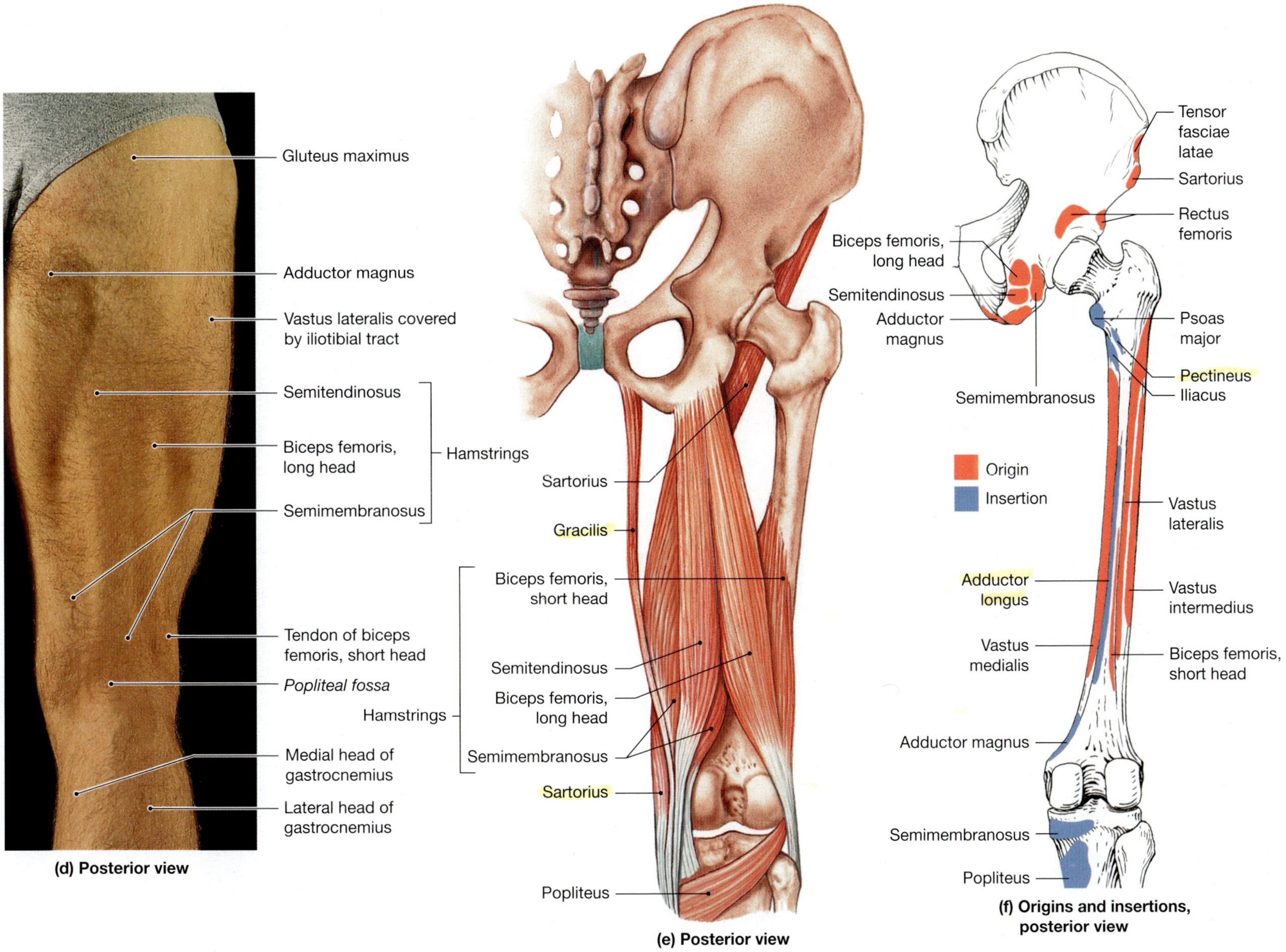

Figure 11.17 ***(continued)***

more powerful muscle. These muscles are best seen from the posterior and lateral views (**Figures 11.18** and **11.19b,c**). The gastrocnemius muscle arises from two tendons attached to the medial and lateral condyles and adjacent portions of the femur. A sesamoid bone, the *fabella*, is usually found within the gastrocnemius muscle. The gastrocnemius and soleus muscles share a common tendon, the **calcaneal tendon**. This tendon may also be called the *calcanean tendon* or the *Achilles tendon*.

The two **fibularis muscles** are partially covered by the gastrocnemius and soleus muscles (**Figure 11.18b,c,d**). These muscles, also known as the *peroneus muscles*, produce eversion of the foot as well as plantar flexion of the ankle. Inversion of the foot is caused by contraction of the **tibialis** (tib-e-A-lis) **muscle**; the large **tibialis anterior muscle** opposes the gastrocnemius muscle and dorsiflexes the ankle (**Figures 11.19** and **11.20**).

Important muscles that move the toes originate on the surface of the tibia, the fibula, or both (**Figures 11.18** to **11.20**). Large tendon sheaths surround the tendons of the tibialis anterior, extensor digitorum longus, and extensor hallucis longus muscles where they cross the ankle joint. The positions of these sheaths are stabilized by the **superior** and **inferior extensor retinacula** (**Figures 11.19**, **11.20a**, and **11.21a**).

Intrinsic Muscles of the Foot [Figure 11.21 and Table 11.9]

The small intrinsic muscles that move the toes originate on the bones of the tarsus and foot (**Figure 11.21** and Table 11.9). Some of the flexor muscles originate at the anterior border of the calcaneus; their muscle tone contributes to maintenance of the longitudinal arch of the foot.

As in the hand, the small interossei muscles (singular, *interosseus*) originate on the lateral and medial surfaces of the metatarsal bones. The four **dorsal interossei muscles** abduct the metatarsophalangeal joints of toes 3 and 4, while the three **plantar interossei muscles** adduct the metatarsophalangeal joints of toes 3–5.

Three intrinsic muscles of the foot move the great toe. The **flexor hallucis brevis muscle** flexes the great toe, while the **adductor hallucis muscle** adducts and the **abductor hallucis muscle** abducts the great toe.

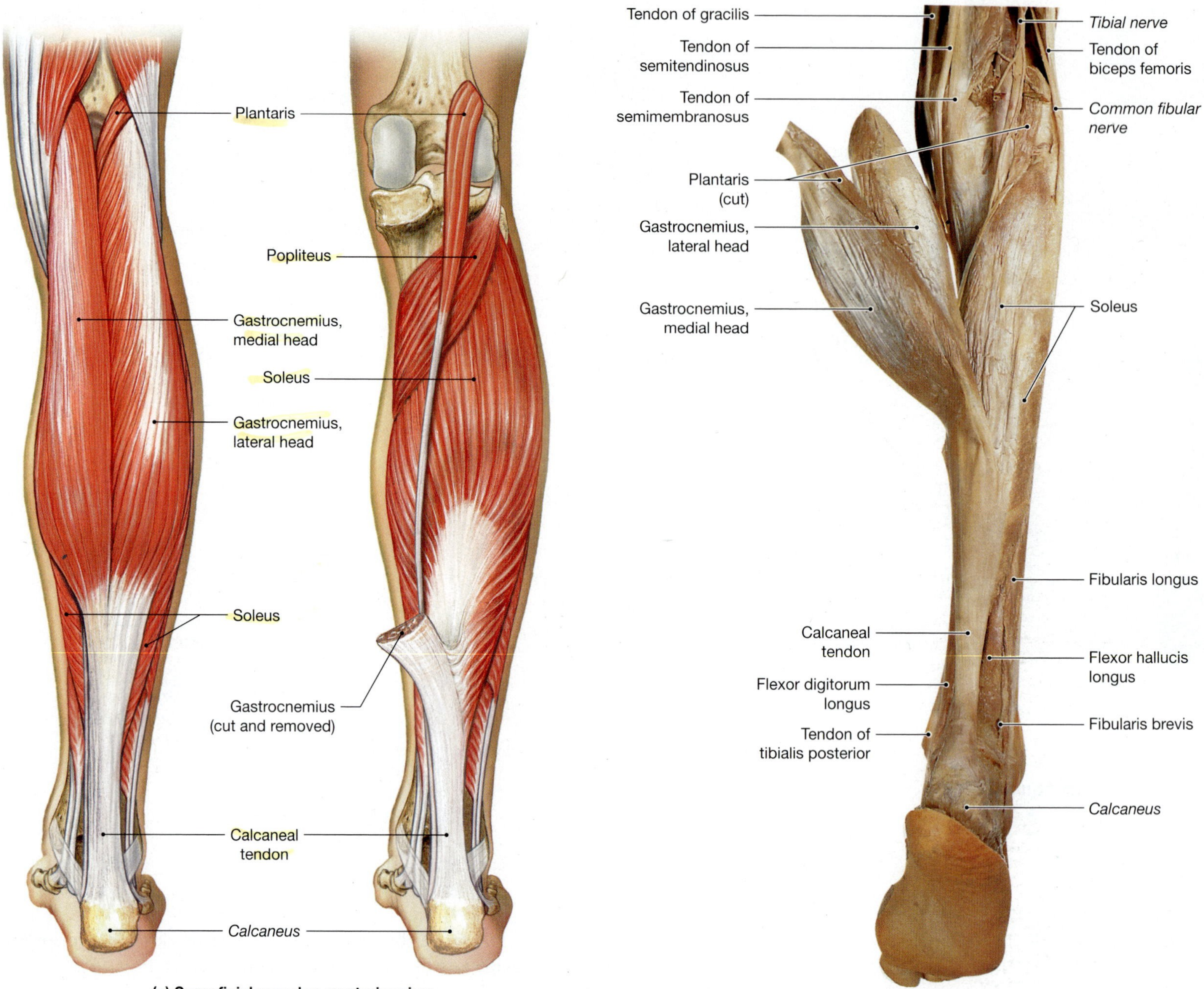

(a) Superficial muscles, posterior view

(b) Posterior view

Figure 11.18 Extrinsic Muscles That Move the Foot and Toes, Part I
(a) Superficial muscles of the posterior surface of the legs; these large muscles are primarily responsible for plantar flexion. **(b)** Posterior view of a dissection of the superficial muscles of the right leg. **(c)** Posterior view of deeper muscles of the leg. **(d)** A posterior view of the bones of the right leg and foot, showing the origins and insertions of selected muscles. For sectional views of the leg, see *Figure 11.24c,d*.

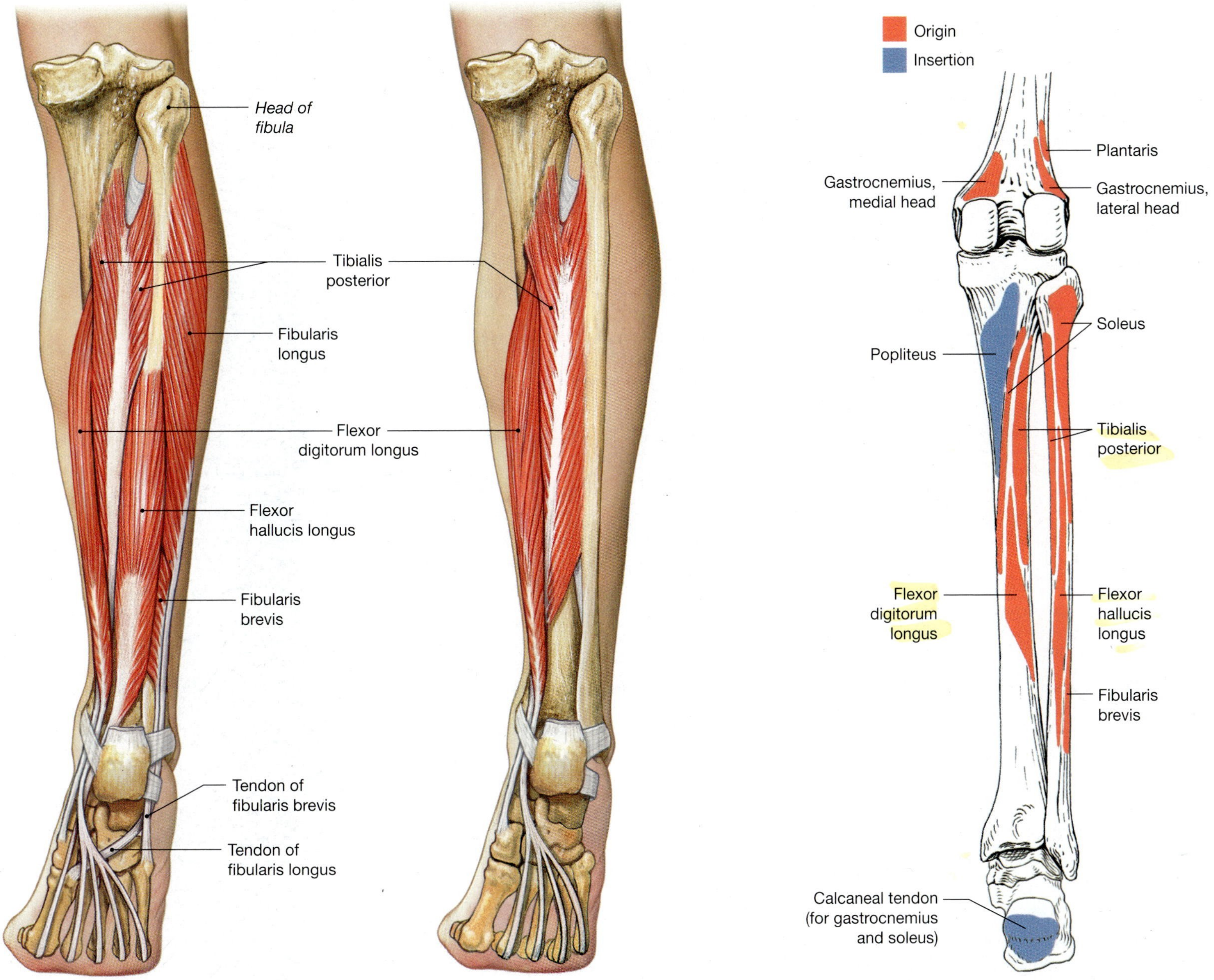

(c) Deep muscles, posterior view

(d) Origins and insertions, posterior view

Figure 11.18 ***(continued)***

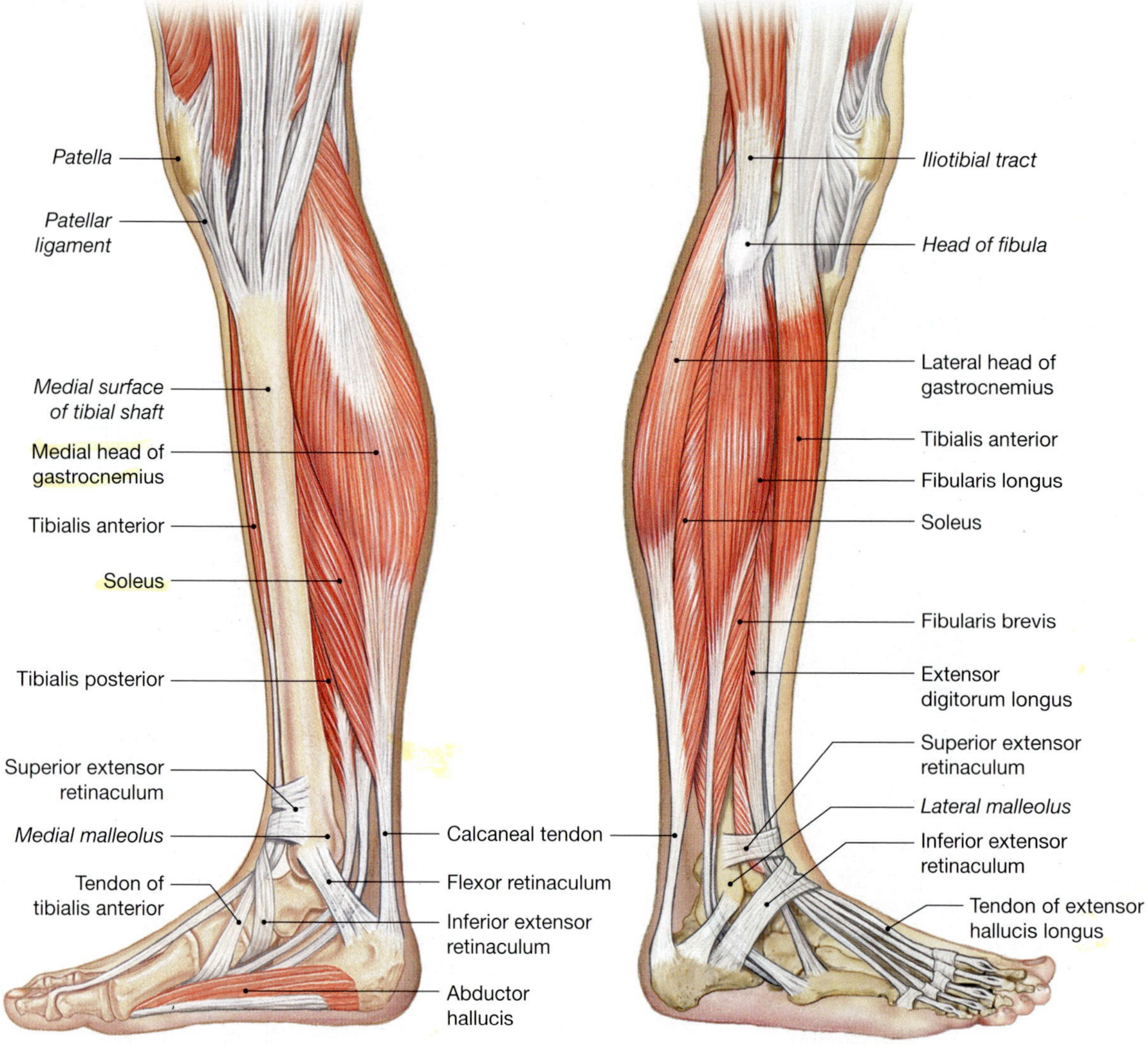

(a) Medial view **(b) Lateral view**

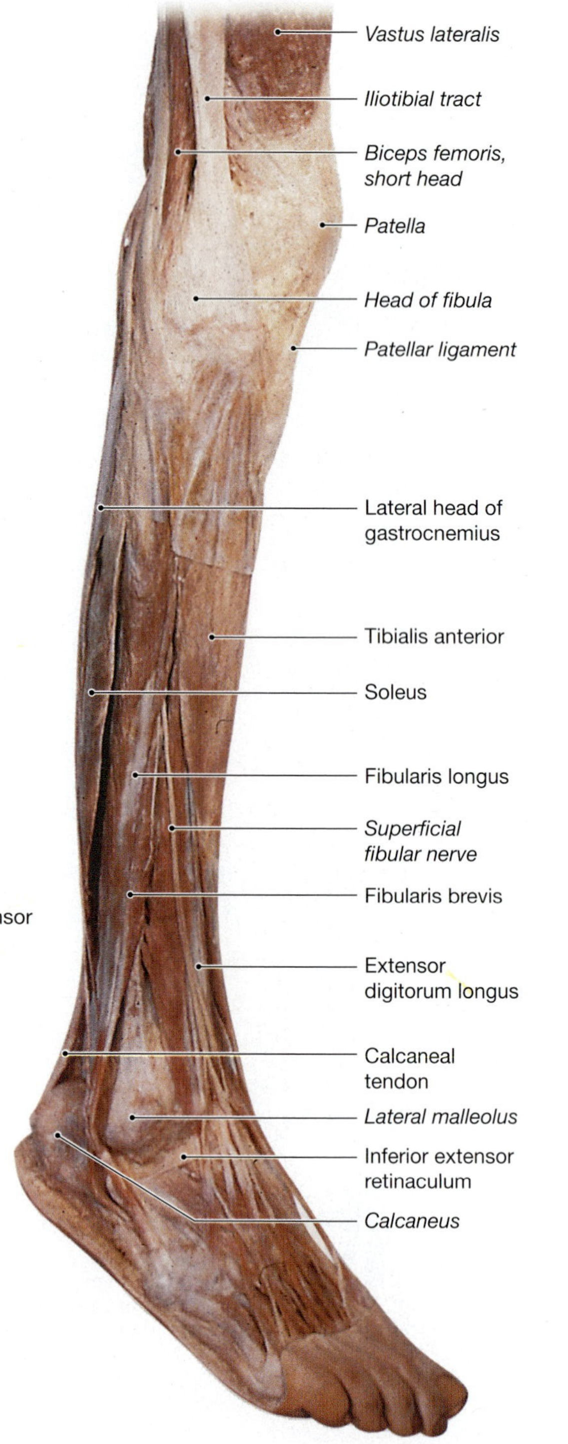

(c) Right lateral view, superficial muscles

Figure 11.19 Extrinsic Muscles That Move the Foot and Toes, Part II
(a) Medial view of the superficial muscles of the left leg. **(b)** Lateral view of the superficial muscles of the right leg. **(c)** Lateral view of a dissection of the superficial muscles of the right leg.

More intrinsic muscles participate in flexion of joints at the toes than participate in extension. The **flexor digitorum brevis muscle**, the **quadratus plantae muscles**, and the four **lumbrical muscles** are responsible for flexion at joints of toes 2–5. The **flexor digiti minimi brevis muscle** is responsible for flexion of toe 5. Extension of the toes is accomplished by the **extensor digitorum brevis muscle**. This muscle assists the extensor hallucis longus muscle in extension of the great toe, and also assists the extensor digitorum longus muscle (see Table 11.8) in extension of toes 2–4. It is the only intrinsic muscle found on the dorsum of the foot.

CONCEPT CHECK

1. What leg movement would be impaired by injury to the obturator muscles?
2. Often one hears of athletes suffering a "pulled hamstring." Describe the muscles in such an injury.
3. To which group of muscles do the pectineus and gracilis belong?
4. What is the collective name for the knee extensors?

See blue "Answers" tab at back of book.

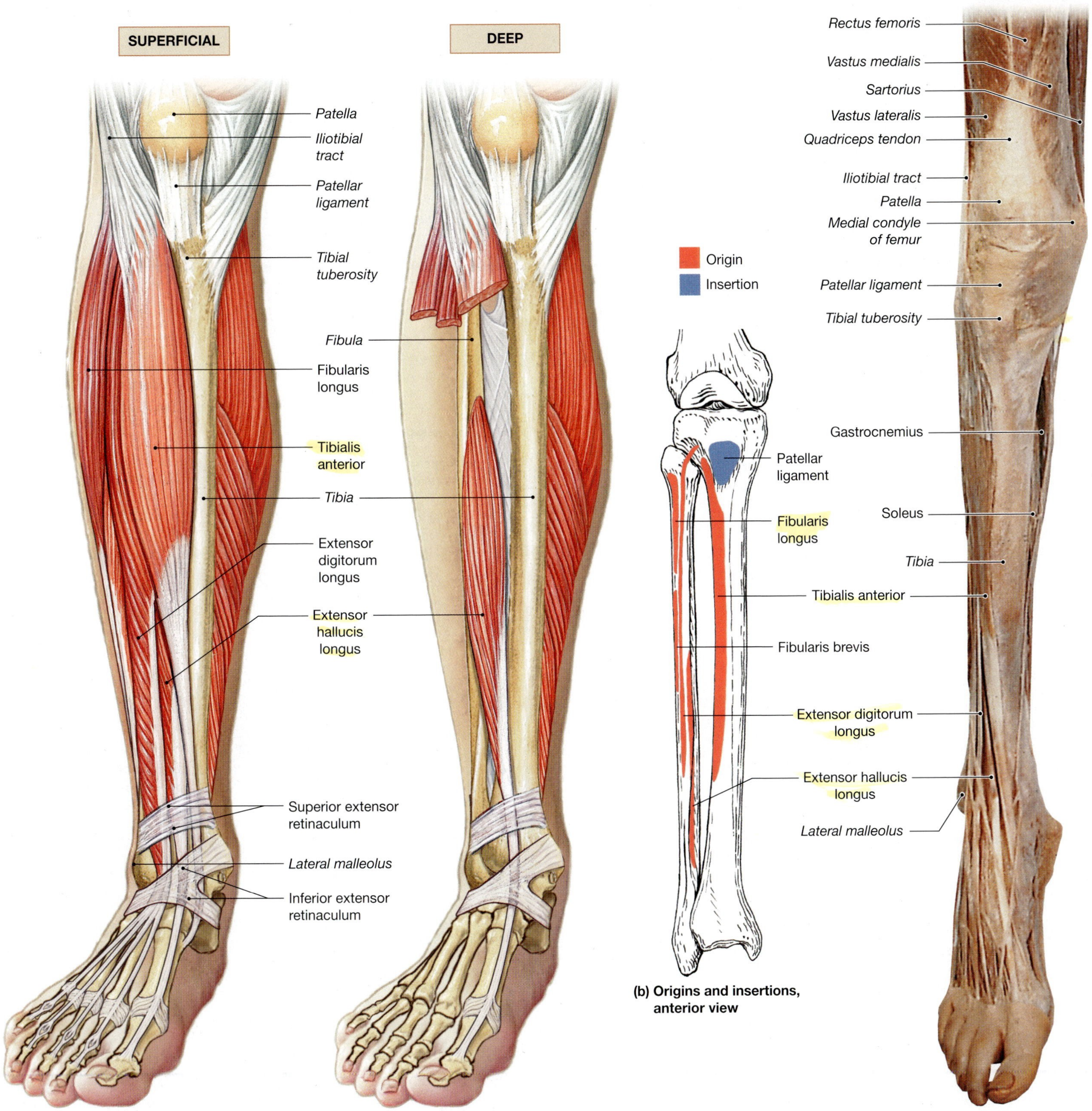

(a) Anterior view

(b) Origins and insertions, anterior view

(c) Anterior view

Figure 11.20 Extrinsic Muscles That Move the Foot and Toes, Part III
(a) Anterior views showing superficial and deep muscles of the right leg. **(b)** Anterior view of the bones of the right leg, showing the origins and insertions of selected muscles. **(c)** Anterior view of a dissection of the superficial muscles of the right leg.

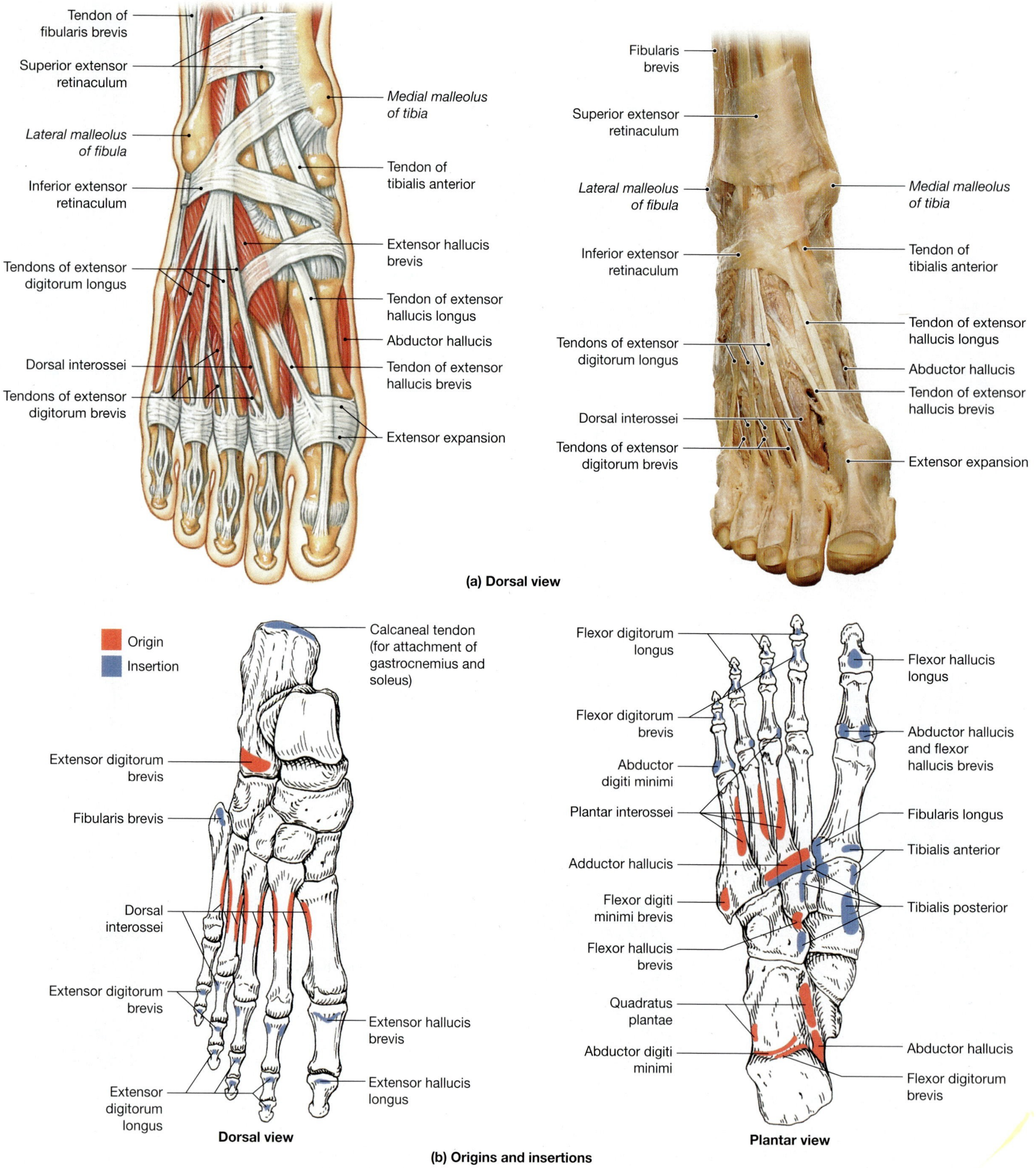

Figure 11.21 Intrinsic Muscles That Move the Foot and Toes
(a) Dorsal views of the right foot. **(b)** Dorsal (superior) and plantar (inferior) views of the bones of the right foot, showing the origins and insertions of selected muscles. **(c)** Right foot, sectional view through the metatarsal bones. **(d)** Plantar (inferior) view, superficial layer of the right foot. **(e)** Plantar (inferior) view, deep layer of the right foot. **(f)** Plantar (inferior) view, deepest layer of the right foot.

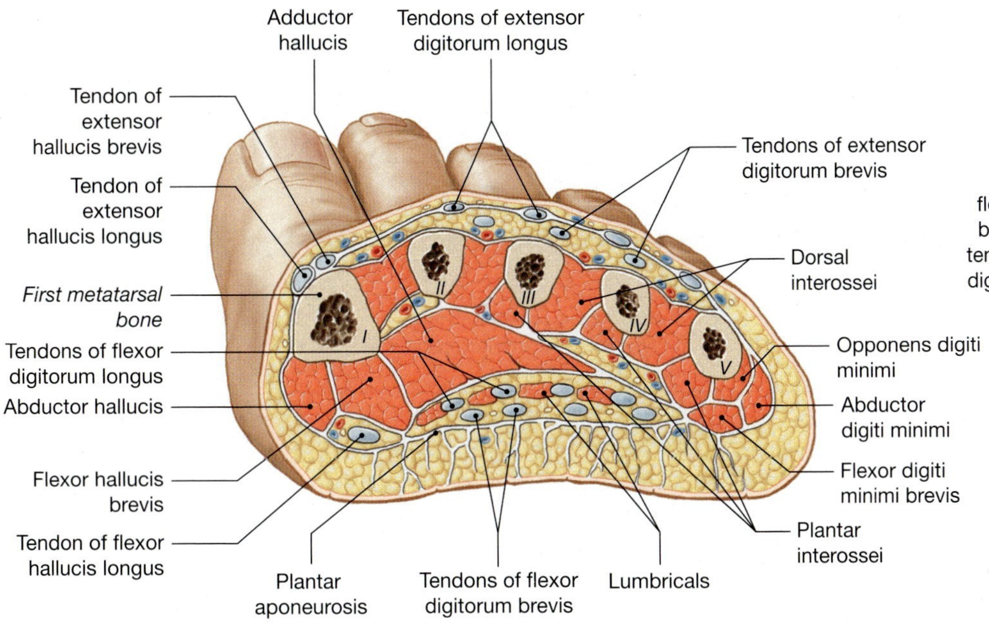

(c) Right foot, sectional view through the metatarsal bones

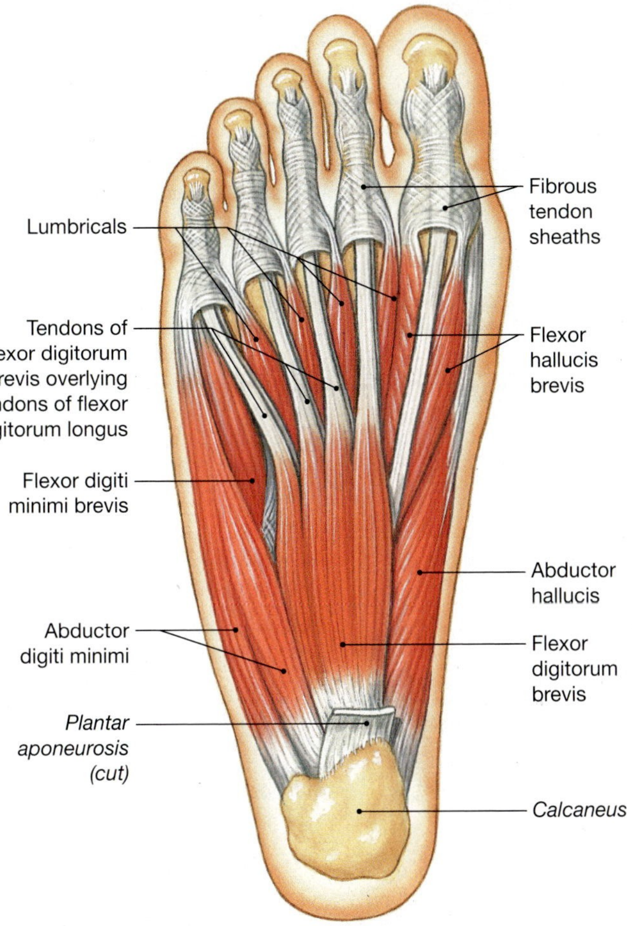

(d) Plantar view, superficial layer

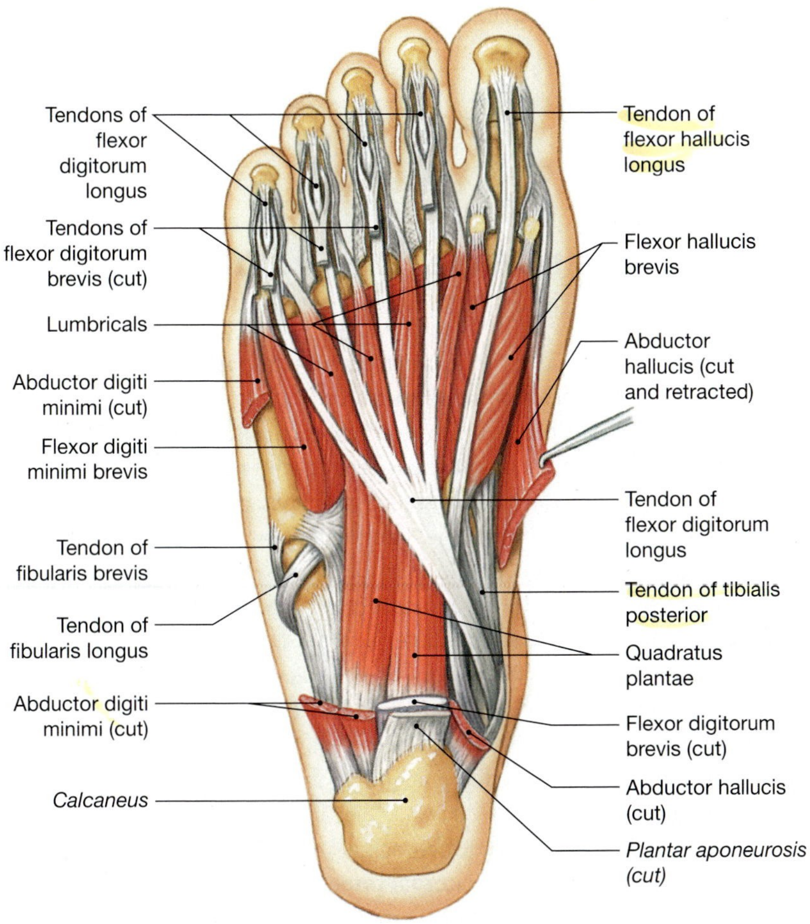

(e) Plantar view, deep layer

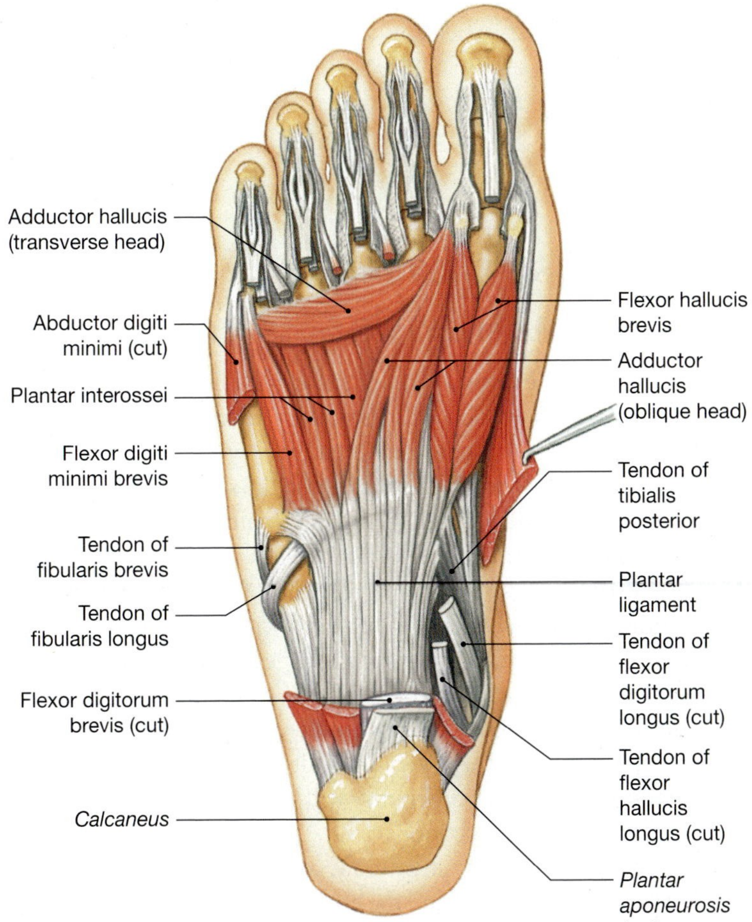

(f) Plantar view, deepest layer

Figure 11.21 ***(continued)***

TABLE 11.9 Intrinsic Muscles of the Foot

Muscle	Origin	Insertion	Action	Innervation
Extensor digitorum brevis	Calcaneus (superior and lateral surfaces)	Dorsal surface of toes 1–4	Extension at metatarsophalangeal joints of toes 1–4	Deep fibular nerve (S_1, S_2)
Abductor hallucis	Calcaneus (tuberosity on inferior surface)	Medial side of proximal phalanx of great toe	Abduction at metatarsophalangeal joint of great toe	Medial plantar nerve (S_2, S_3)
Flexor digitorum brevis	As above	Sides of middle phalanges, toes 2–5	Flexion of proximal interphalangeal joints of toes 2–5	As above
Abductor digiti minimi	As above	Lateral side of proximal phalanx, toe 5	Abduction and flexion at metatarsophalangeal joint of toe 5	Lateral plantar nerve (S_2, S_3)
Quadratus plantae	Calcaneus (medial, inferior surfaces)	Tendon of flexor digitorum longus	Flexion at joints of toes 2–5	As above
Lumbricals (4)	Tendons of flexor digitorum longus	Insertions of extensor digitorum longus	Flexion at metatarsophalangeal joints; extension at interphalangeal joints of toes 2–5	Medial plantar nerve (1), lateral plantar nerve (2–4)
Flexor hallucis brevis	Cuboid and lateral cuneiform	Proximal phalanx of great toe	Flexion at metatarsophalangeal joint of great toe	Medial plantar nerve (L_4–S_5)
Adductor hallucis	Bases of metatarsal bones II–IV and plantar ligaments	As above	Adduction and flexion at metatarsophalangeal joint of great toe	Lateral plantar nerve (S_1–S_2)
Flexor digiti minimi brevis	Base of metatarsal bone V	Lateral side of proximal phalanx of toe 5	Flexion at metatarsophalangeal joint of toe 5	As above
Dorsal interossei (4)	Sides of metatarsal bones	Medial and lateral sides of toe 2; lateral sides of toes 3 and 4	Abduction at metatarsophalangeal joints of toes 3 and 4; flexion of metatarsophalangeal joints and extension at the interphalangeal joints of toes 2 through 4	As above
Plantar interossei (3)	Bases and medial sides of metatarsal bones	Medial sides of toes 3–5	Adduction of metatarsophalangeal joints of toes 3–5; flexion of metatarsophalangeal joints and extension at interphalangeal joints	As above

Fascia, Muscle Layers, and Compartments

Chapter 3 introduced the various types of fascia in the body and the way these dense connective tissue layers provide a structural framework for the soft tissues of the body. p. 74 There are three basic types of fasciae: (a) the *superficial fascia*, a layer of areolar tissue deep to the skin; (2) the *deep fascia*, a dense fibrous layer bound to capsules, periostea, epimysia, and other fibrous sheaths surrounding internal organs; and (3) the *subserous fascia*, a layer of areolar tissue separating a serous membrane from adjacent structures.

The connective tissue fibers of the deep fasciae support and interconnect adjacent skeletal muscles but permit independent movement. In general, the more similar two adjacent muscles are in orientation, action, and range of movement, the more extensively they are interconnected by the deep fascia. This can make them very difficult to separate on dissection. If their orientations and actions differ, they will be less tightly interconnected and easier to separate on dissection.

In the limbs, however, the situation is complicated by the fact that the muscles are packed together around the bones and the interconnections between the superficial fascia, the deep fascia, and the periostea are quite substantial. The deep fascia extends between the bones and the superficial fascia and separates the soft tissues of the limb into separate **compartments**.

Compartments of the Upper Limb [Figures 11.22/11.23 and Table 11.10]

The deep fascia of the arm creates an **anterior compartment**, or *flexor compartment*, and a **posterior compartment**, or *extensor compartment* (Figures 11.22 and 11.23). The biceps brachii, coracobrachialis, and brachialis muscles are in the anterior compartment; the triceps brachii muscle fills the posterior compartment. The major blood vessels, lymphatics, and nerves of both compartments run along the boundaries between the two.

The separation between the anterior and posterior compartments becomes more pronounced where the deep fascia forms thick fibrous sheets, the **lateral** and **medial intermuscular septa** (Figure 11.23a,b). The lateral intermuscular septum extends along the lateral aspect of the humeral shaft from the lateral epicondyle to the deltoid tuberosity. The medial intermuscular septum is a bit shorter, extending along the medial aspect of the humeral shaft from the medial epicondyle to the insertion of the coracobrachialis muscle (Figure 11.23e).

The deep fascia and the antebrachial interosseous membrane divides the forearm into a **superficial compartment**, a **deep compartment**, and an **extensor compartment** (Figures 11.22 and 11.23c,d,e). Smaller fascial partitions further subdivide these compartments and separate muscle groups with differing functions. The components of the compartments of the upper limb are indicated in Table 11.10.

Clinical Note

Compartment Syndrome Blood vessels and nerves traveling to specific muscles within the limb enter and branch within the appropriate muscular compartments (Figures 11.22 and 11.23). When a crushing injury, severe contusion, or strain occurs, the blood vessels within one or more compartments may be damaged. When damaged, these compartments become swollen with tissue, fluid, and blood that has leaked from damaged blood vessels. Because the connective tissue partitions are very strong, the accumulated fluid cannot escape, and pressures rise within the affected compartments. Eventually compartment pressures may become so high that they compress the regional blood vessels and eliminate the circulatory supply to the muscles and nerves of the compartment. This compression produces a condition of **ischemia** (is-KĒ-mē-a), or "blood starvation," known as **compartment syndrome**. Slicing into the compartment along its longitudinal axis or implanting a drain are emergency measures used to relieve the pressure. If such steps are not taken, the contents of the compartment will suffer severe damage. Nerves in the affected compartment will be destroyed after 2–4 hours of ischemia, although they can regenerate to some degree if the circulation is restored. After 6 hours or more, the muscle tissue will also be destroyed, and no regeneration will occur. The muscles will be replaced by scar tissue, and shortening of the connective tissue fibers may result in *contracture*, a permanent reduction in muscle length.

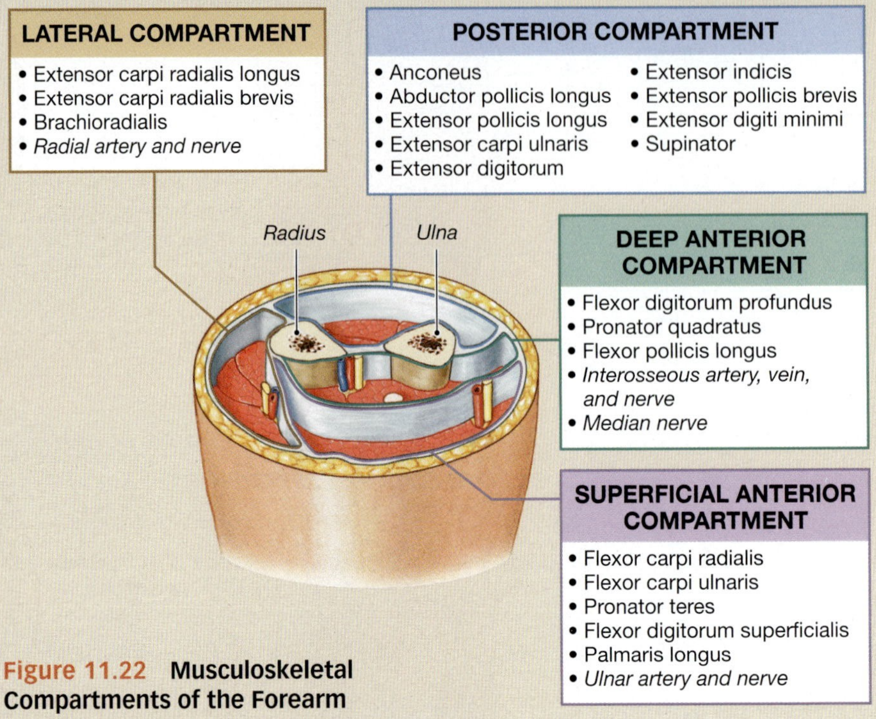

Figure 11.22 Musculoskeletal Compartments of the Forearm
The three-dimensional arrangement of septa and fascial boundaries within the right forearm.

TABLE 11.10 Compartments of the Upper Limb

Compartment	Muscles	Blood Vessels*,†	Nerves‡
ARM			
Anterior Compartment	Biceps brachii Brachialis Coracobrachialis	Brachial artery Inferior ulnar collateral artery Superior ulnar collateral artery Brachial veins	Median nerve Musculocutaneous nerve Ulnar nerve
Posterior Compartment	Triceps brachii	Deep brachial artery	Radial nerve
FOREARM			
Anterior Compartment			
Superficial	Flexor carpi radialis Flexor carpi ulnaris Flexor digitorum superficialis Palmaris longus Pronator teres	Radial artery Ulnar artery	Median nerve Ulnar nerve
Deep	Flexor digitorum profundus Flexor pollicis longus Pronator quadratus	Anterior interosseous artery Anterior ulnar recurrent artery Posterior ulnar recurrent artery	Anterior interosseous nerve Ulnar nerve Median nerve
Lateral Compartment§	Brachioradialis Extensor carpi radialis brevis Extensor carpi radialis longus	Radial artery	Radial nerve
Posterior Compartment	Abductor pollicis longus Anconeus Extensor carpi ulnaris Extensor digitorum Extensor digiti minimi Extensor indicis Extensor pollicis brevis Extensor pollicis longus Supinator	Posterior interosseous artery Posterior ulnar recurrent artery	Posterior interosseous nerve

*Cutaneous vessels are not listed. †Only large, named vessels are listed. ‡Cutaneous nerves are not listed. §Contains what is sometimes called the radial, or antero-external, group of muscles.

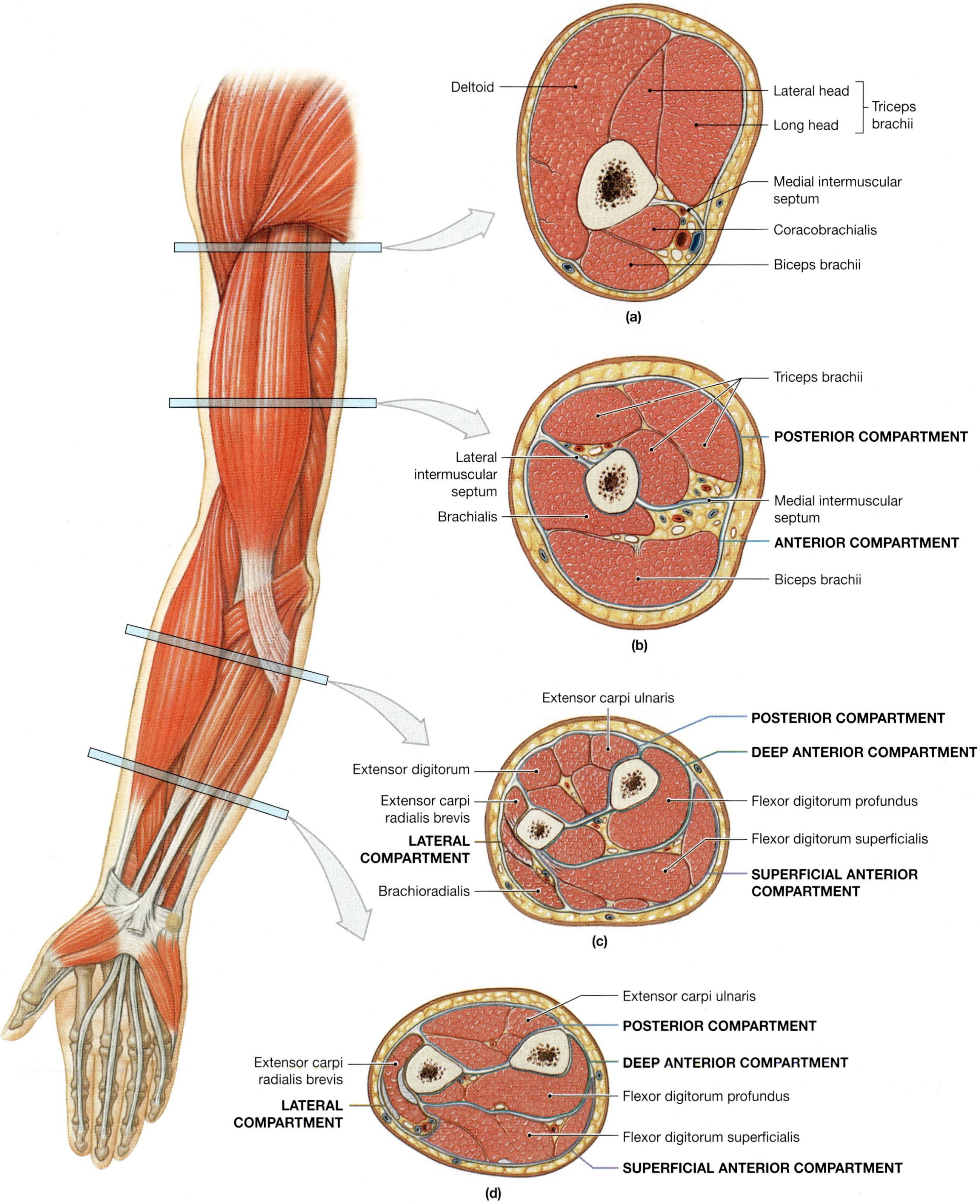

Figure 11.23 Musculoskeletal Compartments of the Upper Limb
(a), (b) Diagrammatic horizontal sections through the proximal and distal portions of the right arm, showing selected muscles. **(c), (d)** Diagrammatic horizontal sections through the proximal and distal portions of the right forearm, showing selected muscles. **(e)** Anterior view of the humerus showing the locations of the medial and lateral intermuscular septa.

Figure 11.23 *(continued)*

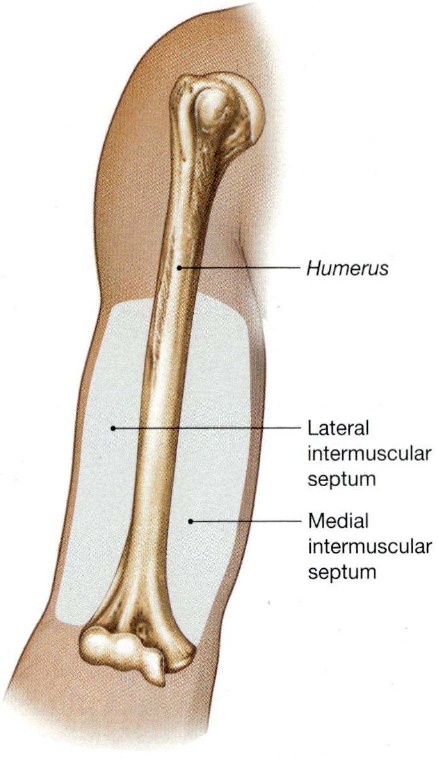

(e)

Compartments of the Lower Limb [Figure 11.24 and Table 11.11]

The thigh contains **medial** and **lateral intermuscular septa** that extend outward from the femur, as well as several smaller fascial partitions that separate adjacent muscle groups. In general, the thigh can be divided into **anterior**, **posterior**, and **medial compartments** (Figure 11.24a,b). The anterior compartment contains the tensor fasciae latae, sartorius, and the quadriceps group. The posterior compartment contains the hamstrings, and the medial compartment contains the gracilis, pectineus, obturator externus, adductor longus, adductor brevis, and adductor magnus (Table 11.11).

The tibia and fibula, crural interosseous membrane, and septa in the leg create four major compartments: an **anterior compartment**, a **lateral compartment**, and **superficial** and **deep posterior compartments** (Figure 11.24c,d). The anterior compartment contains muscles that dorsiflex the ankle, extend the toes, and invert/evert the ankle. The muscles of the lateral compartment evert and plantar flex the ankle. The superficial muscles of the posterior compartment plantar flex the ankle, while those of the deep posterior compartment plantar flex the ankle in addition to their specific actions on the joints of the foot and the toes. The muscles and other structures within these compartments are indicated in Table 11.11.

TABLE 11.11 Compartments of the Lower Limb

Compartment	Muscles	Blood Vessels	Nerves
THIGH			
Anterior Compartment	Iliopsoas	Femoral artery	Femoral nerve
	Iliacus	Femoral vein	Saphenous nerve
	Psoas major	Deep femoral artery	
	Psoas minor	Lateral circumflex femoral artery	
	Quadriceps femoris		
	Rectus femoris		
	Vastus intermedius		
	Vastus lateralis		
	Vastus medialis		
	Sartorius		
Medial Compartment	Pectineus		
	Adductor brevis	Obturator artery	Obturator nerve
	Adductor longus	Obturator vein	
	Adductor magnus	Deep femoral artery	
	Gracilis	Deep femoral vein	
	Obturator externus		
Posterior Compartment	Biceps femoris	Deep femoral artery	Sciatic nerve
	Semimembranosus	Deep femoral vein	
	Semitendinosus		
LEG			
Anterior Compartment	Extensor digitorum longus	Anterior tibial artery	Deep fibular nerve
	Extensor hallucis longus	Anterior tibial vein	
	Fibularis tertius		
	Tibialis anterior		
Lateral Compartment	Fibularis brevis		Superficial fibular nerve
	Fibularis longus		
Posterior Compartment			
Superficial	Gastrocnemius		
	Plantaris		
	Soleus		
Deep	Flexor digitorum longus	Posterior tibial artery	Tibial nerve
	Flexor hallucis longus	Fibular artery	
	Popliteus	Fibular vein	
	Tibialis posterior	Posterior tibial vein	

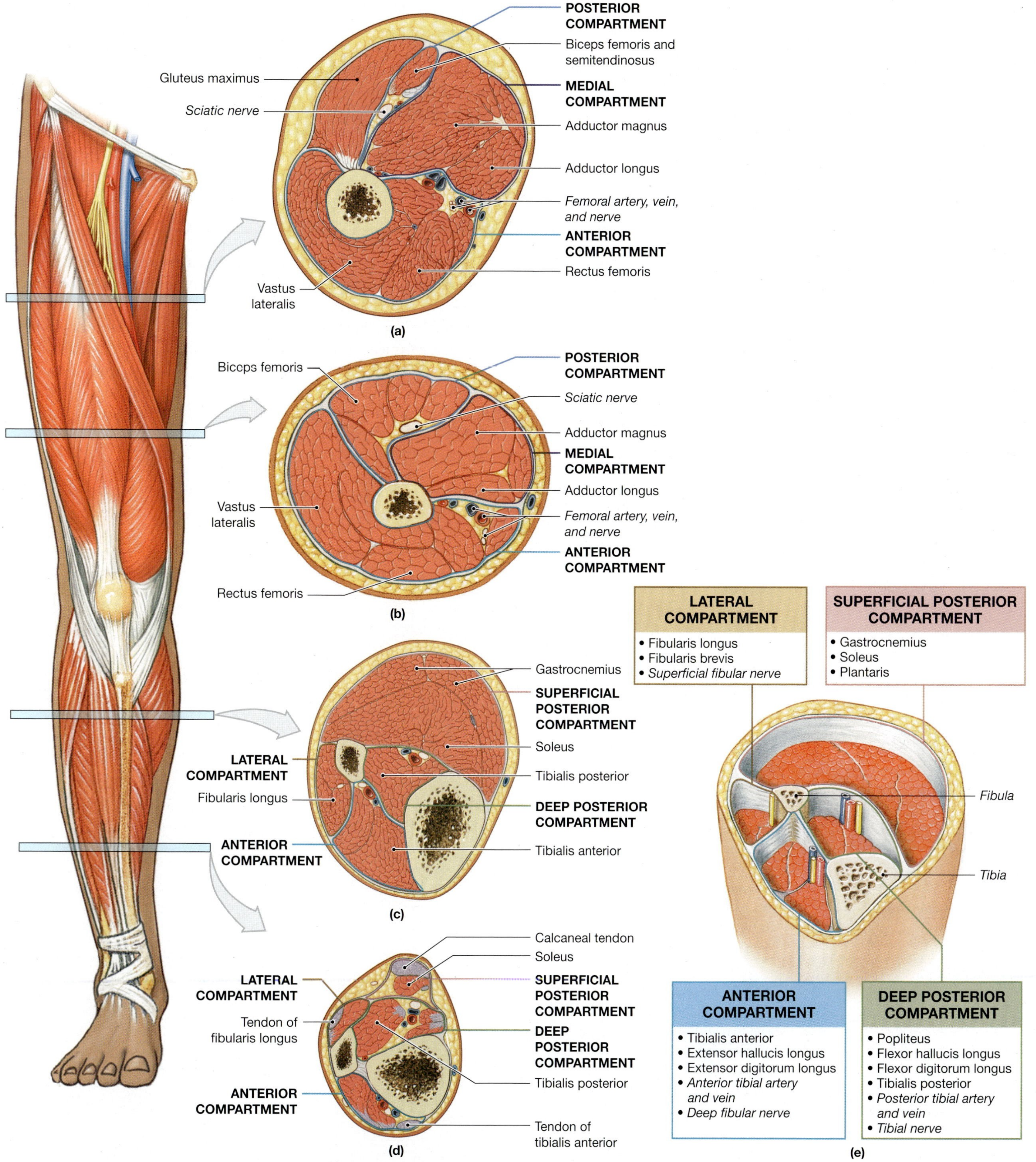

Figure 11.24 Musculoskeletal Compartments of the Lower Limb
(a), (b) Diagrammatic horizontal sections through the proximal and distal portions of the right thigh, showing selected muscles. **(c), (d)** Diagrammatic horizontal sections through the proximal and distal portions of the right leg, showing selected muscles. **(e)** Anterior view of the leg showing intermuscular septae and the four compartments of the leg.

Clinical Case

THE MUSCULAR SYSTEM

GRANDMA'S HIP

You stop to see your 75-year-old grandmother during your weekly visit to her apartment to set out her medications for the coming week. As you enter her apartment, you find her lying on her back in severe pain. She is confused and does not recognize you when you enter the room. In addition, she is unable to tell you how she came to be lying on the floor.

You try to help her up off the floor, but she immediately complains of significant pain in the groin area. You dial 911 and an ambulance arrives. As the paramedics make their initial assessment and transfer her to the gurney, they note that the right lower limb is laterally rotated and noticeably shorter than her left lower limb. An attending resident does the initial assessment upon admission to the ER.

Initial Examination and Laboratory Results

The resident does the initial assessment of your grandmother and the following is noted:

- The right lower limb is noticeably shorter than the left.
- The right thigh is externally rotated, and the patient is unable to change the limb's position without considerable pain.
- On palpation, the groin region is tender, but there is no obvious swelling.
- Passive movement of the hip causes extreme pain, especially upon external and internal rotation.
- White Blood Cell count (WBC) is 20,000 mm^3.
- Hemoglobin (Hgb) is 9.8 g/dl.
- Although confused, your grandmother repeatedly states that she was lying on the floor of her apartment for a long time prior to being found.

The resident is concerned that the time lag between the injury and being discovered and transported to the hospital may have caused complications. As a result, he is not sure about how treatment should proceed. He administers a painkiller to make your grandmother more comfortable and then pages the orthopedic surgeon on call for a consult.

The attending orthopedic surgeon arrives and immediately suggests intravenous fluid replacement to alleviate the dehydration caused by the time between injury and discovery. As fluids and electrolytes come back into balance, your grandmother informs the physician that she tripped on the throw rug in her apartment two days before you found her, and that she had been unable to crawl to the telephone for help.

In addition, the orthopedic surgeon confirms the facts from the resident's physical examination. She immediately orders anteroposterior and lateral radiographs of the hip region.

Follow-up Examination

Upon examination the orthopedic surgeon notes the following:

- The patient appears to be in a rather poor nutritional state.
- Initially she seemed to be mentally confused, but I.V. fluid and electrolyte replacement caused a significant improvement in her condition.
- The right lower limb is externally rotated and the patient is unable to lift her right heel from the stretcher.
- The right lower limb is shorter, which is confirmed by measuring the distance between the anterior, superior iliac spine and the distal tip of the medial malleolus of the tibia, and comparing the results with those of the left lower limb (after passive rotation by the surgeon).
- The greater trochanter on the right side also appears to be higher and more prominent than that of the left side.
- Palpation yields tenderness in the femoral triangle on the anterior surface of the hip joint.

Points to Consider

As you examine the information presented above, review the material covered in Chapters 5 through 11, and determine what anatomical information will enable you to sort through the information given to you about your grandmother and her particular problems.

1. What are the anatomical characteristics of the bones of the lower limb?
2. What anatomical landmarks are mentioned in the problem? Where would you find these landmarks on the hip bones, femur, and tibia?
3. What are the anatomical characteristics of the hip joint?
4. The patient's lower limb is externally rotated and she is unable to lift her right heel from the stretcher. Would this condition be the result of axial or appendicular muscles? What specific muscles would be involved in the external rotation of the hip? What muscles would be involved in flexion of the hip?

Analysis and Interpretation

1. The anatomical characteristics of the bones of the lower limb may be found in Chapter 7. pp. 193–198
2. The following anatomical landmarks are mentioned in this problem:
   - groin
   - anterior, superior iliac spine
   - distal tip of the medial malleolus of the tibia
   - greater trochanter of the femur

   These landmarks may be found in Chapter 7. pp. 188–197
3. The anatomical characteristics of the hip joint may be found in Chapter 8. pp. 223–225
4. The muscles involved in the positioning of your grandmother's lower limb would all be appendicular muscles. The muscles involved in externally (laterally) rotating the hip and flexing the hip may be found in Table 11.6 on p. 304.

CLINICAL CASE TERMS

I.V. fluid and electroylte replacement: The intravenous administration of an isotonic fluid to eliminate dehydration and to bring sodium, calcium, and potassium plasma levels back to normal physiological levels.

Clinical Case *continued*

Diagnosis

Your grandmother is 75 years old, and her skeleton is undergoing several anatomical changes as a result of the aging process. pp. 125–126 Your grandmother has a displaced, subcapital fracture of the femur. The angle between the head and neck of the femur is decreased, and the neck and shaft are externally rotated. The pelvic bones and femur have a high probability of marked osteoporosis. p. 128 This condition increases the likelihood of fractures in elderly individuals, and also lengthens the time required for the repair of a fracture. pp. 124–126

The position of your grandmother's lower limb is due to tightening of the external rotators (piriformis, superior and inferior gemelli, and obturator externus muscles). pp. 302–305 Her right lower limb is shorter than the left due to (a) the fracture of the hip and (b) contraction of the hip flexors and extensors (Table 11.6, p. 304). Her hip will probably require surgery. Although there are several procedures that might be used, removal of the head of the femur (pp. 193–197) and replacement with a prosthesis is a common procedure. The chosen prosthesis would replace the head of the femur and would also possess a long stem that would be inserted into the medullary cavity of the bone and extended almost halfway down the femoral shaft to anchor the head into place(Figure 11.25). The stem of the prosthesis would be designed with holes through it, and bits of spongy bone (pp. 113–117) would be inserted into the holes to serve as bone grafts. Another procedure commonly followed is cementing the prosthesis into place, which might be more likely for your grandmother considering her advanced age and reduced level of activity. ■

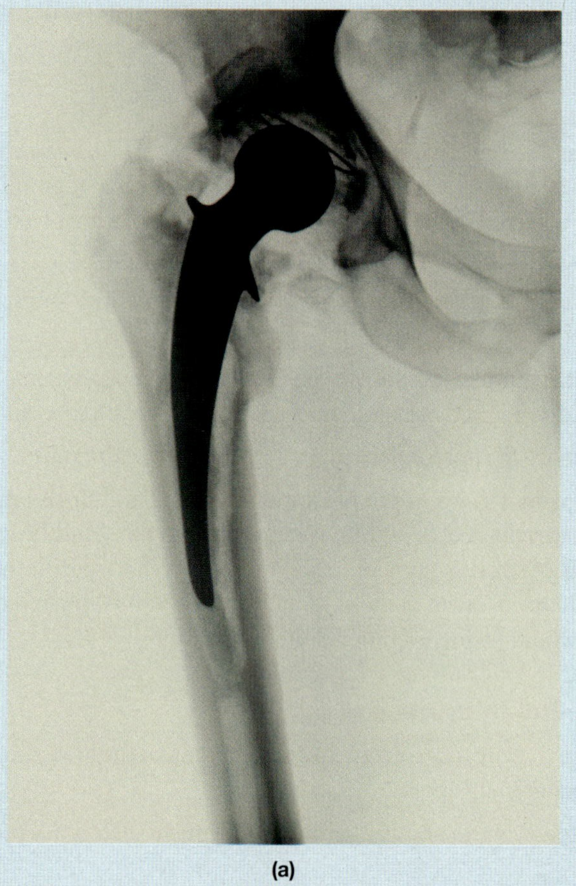

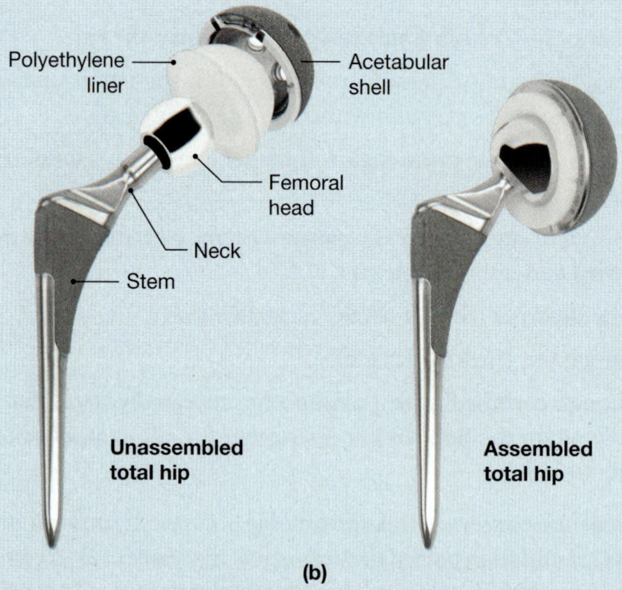

Figure 11.25 X-Ray of the Hip After Surgery
(a) X-ray of an individual with a surgically implanted hip prosthesis. **(b)** Diagram of hip prosthesis.

CLINICAL TERMS

bone bruise: Bleeding within the periosteum of a bone.

bursitis: Inflammation of the bursae around one or more joints.

carpal tunnel syndrome: An inflammation within the sheath surrounding the flexor tendons of the palm.

compartment syndrome: Ischemia resulting from accumulated blood and fluid trapped within a musculoskeletal compartment.

displaced, subcapital fracture: An injury that involves fracture to a bone inferior to the head, and simultaneous dislocation of the fractured bone from a joint.

ischemia (is-KĒ-mē-a): A condition of "blood starvation" resulting from compression of regional blood vessels.

muscle cramps: Prolonged, involuntary, painful muscular contractions.

rotator cuff: The muscles that surround the shoulder joint; a frequent site of sports injuries.

sprains: Tears or breaks in ligaments or tendons.

strains: Tears or breaks in muscles.

stress fractures: Cracks or breaks in bones subjected to repeated stress or trauma.

tendinitis: Inflammation of the connective tissue surrounding a tendon.

STUDY OUTLINE

Introduction 285

1. The **appendicular musculature** is responsible for stabilizing the pectoral and pelvic girdles and for moving the upper and lower limbs.

Factors Affecting Appendicular Muscle Function 285

1. A muscle of the appendicular skeleton may cross one or more joints between its origin and insertion. The position of the muscle as it crosses a joint will help in determining the action of that muscle. *(see Figure 11.1)*
2. Many complex actions involve more than one joint of the appendicular skeleton. Muscles that cross only one joint typically act as prime movers, while muscles that cross more than one joint typically act as synergists.

Muscles of the Pectoral Girdle and Upper Limbs 286

1. Four groups of muscles are associated with the pectoral girdle and upper limbs: (1) *muscles that position the pectoral girdle*, (2) *muscles that move the arm*, (3) *muscles that move the forearm and hand*, and (4) *muscles that move the hand and fingers.*

Muscles That Position the Pectoral Girdle 286

2. The **trapezius muscles** cover the back and parts of the neck, to the base of the skull. The trapezius muscle affects the position of the pectoral (shoulder) girdle, head, and neck. *(see Figures 11.2 to 11.5 and Table 11.1)*
3. Deep to the trapezius, the **rhomboid muscles** adduct the scapula, and the **levator scapulae muscle** elevates the scapula. Both insert on the scapula. *(see Figures 11.2 to 11.5 and Table 11.1)*
4. The **serratus anterior muscle**, which abducts the scapula and swings the shoulder anteriorly, originates along the ventrosuperior surfaces of several ribs. *(see Figures 11.2 to 11.5 and Table 11.1)*
5. Two deep chest muscles arise along the ventral surfaces of the ribs. Both the **subclavius** and the **pectoralis minor muscles** depress and protract the shoulder. *(see Figures 11.4/11.5 and Table 11.1)*

Muscles That Move the Arm 288

6. The action line of a muscle could be used to predict the muscle's action. *Figure 11.7* shows the positions of the biceps brachii, triceps brachii, and deltoid muscles in relation to the shoulder joint; it also summarizes the rules used to predict the action of a muscle.
7. Muscles that move the arm are best remembered when they are grouped by primary actions.
8. The **deltoid** and the **supraspinatus muscles** produce abduction at the shoulder. The **subscapularis** and the **teres major muscles** rotate the arm medially, whereas the **infraspinatus** and **teres minor muscles** rotate the arm laterally. The supraspinatus, infraspinatus, subscapularis, and teres minor are known as the muscles of the **rotator cuff**. The **coracobrachialis muscle** produces flexion and adduction at the shoulder. *(see Figures 11.2/11.5/11.6 and Table 11.2)*
9. The **pectoralis major muscle** flexes the shoulder, while the **latissimus dorsi muscle** extends it. Additionally, both adduct and medially rotate the arm. *(see Figures 11.2/11.5/11.6 and Table 11.2)*

Muscles That Move the Forearm and Hand 293

10. The primary actions of the **biceps brachii muscle** and the **triceps brachii muscle** (*long head*) affect the elbow joint. The biceps brachii flexes the elbow and supinates the forearm, while the triceps brachii extends the elbow. Additionally, both have a secondary effect on the pectoral girdle.
11. The **brachialis** and **brachioradialis muscles** flex the elbow. This action is opposed by the **anconeus muscle** and the **triceps brachii muscle**. The **flexor carpi ulnaris**, the **flexor carpi radialis**, and the **palmaris longus muscles** are superficial muscles of the forearm that cooperate to flex the wrist. Additionally, the flexor carpi ulnaris muscle adducts the wrist, while the flexor carpi radialis muscle abducts it. Extension of the wrist is provided by the **extensor carpi radialis muscle**, which also abducts the wrist, and the **extensor carpi ulnaris muscle**, which also adducts the wrist. The **pronator teres** and **pronator quadratus muscles** pronate the forearm without flexion or extension at the elbow; their action is opposed by the **supinator muscle**. *(see Figures 11.5/11.6/11.8/11.9 and Table 11.3)*

Muscles That Move the Hand and Fingers 295

12. Extrinsic muscles of the hand provide strength and crude control of the fingers. Intrinsic muscles provide fine control of the fingers and hand.
13. Muscles that perform flexion and extension of the finger joints are illustrated in *Figures 11.8 to 11.11* and detailed in *Tables 11.4/11.5.*

Muscles of the Pelvic Girdle and Lower Limbs 302

1. As with our analysis of the shoulder muscles (p. 000), the relationships between the action lines and the axis of the hip joint can be used to predict the actions of the various muscles and muscle groups. *(see Figure 11.14)*
2. Three groups of muscles are associated with the pelvis and lower limbs: (1) *muscles that move the thigh*, (2) *muscles that move the leg*, and (3) *muscles that move the foot and toes.*

Muscles That Move the Thigh 302

3. Muscles originating on the surface of the pelvis and inserting on the femur produce characteristic movements determined by their position relative to the acetabulum. *(see Figure 11.13 and Table 11.6)*
4. **Gluteal muscles** cover the lateral surface of the ilium. The largest is the **gluteus maximus muscle**, which produces extension and lateral rotation at the hip. It shares an insertion with the **tensor fasciae latae muscle**, which produces flexion, abduction, and medial rotation at the hip. Together these muscles pull on the **iliotibial tract** to provide a lateral brace for the knee. *(see Figures 11.2/11.5/11.13 to 11.17 and Table 11.6)*
5. The **piriformis** and the **obturator muscles** are the most important lateral rotators.
6. The **adductor group** (**adductor magnus**, **adductor brevis**, **adductor longus**, **pectineus**, and **gracilis muscles**) produce adduction at the hip. Individually, they can produce various other movements, such as medial or lateral rotation and flexion or extension at the hip. *(see Figures 11.13 to 11.17 and Table 11.6)*
7. The **psoas major** and the **iliacus** merge to form the **iliopsoas muscle**, a powerful flexor of the hip. *(see Figures 11.13/11.14 and Table 11.6)*

Muscles That Move the Leg 307

8. *Extensor muscles of the knee* are found along the anterior and lateral surfaces of the thigh; flexor muscles lie along the posterior and medial surfaces of the thigh. Flexors and adductors originate on the pelvic girdle, whereas most extensors originate at the femoral surface.
9. Collectively, the *knee extensors* are known as the **quadriceps femoris**. This group includes the **vastus intermedius**, **vastus lateralis**, and **vastus medialis muscles** and the **rectus femoris muscle**. *(see Figures 11.15/11.16 and Table 11.7)*
10. The *flexors of the knee* include the **biceps femoris**, **semimembranosus**, and **semitendinosus muscles** (together they also produce extension of the hip and are termed "hamstrings"), and the **sartorius muscle**. The **popliteus muscle** medially rotates the tibia (or laterally rotates the femur) to unlock the knee joint. *(see Figures 11.16/11.17 and Table 11.7)*

Muscles That Move the Foot and Toes 309

11. Extrinsic and intrinsic muscles that move the foot and toes are illustrated in *Figures 11.18 to 11.21* and listed in *Tables 11.8 and 11.9.*

12. The **gastrocnemius** and **soleus muscles** produce plantar flexion. The large **tibialis anterior muscle** opposes the gastrocnemius and dorsiflexes the ankle. A pair of **fibularis muscles** produce eversion as well as plantar flexion. *(see Figures 11.19/11.20 and Table 11.8)*
13. Smaller muscles of the calf and shin position the foot and move the toes. Precise control of the phalanges is provided by muscles originating on the tarsal and metatarsal bones. *(see Figure 11.21 and Table 11.9)*

Fascia, Muscle Layers, and Compartments 318

1. In addition to the functional approach utilized in this chapter, many anatomists also study the muscles of the upper and lower limbs in groups determined by their position within **compartments**.

Compartments of the Upper Limb 319

2. The arm has **medial** and **lateral compartments**; the forearm has **anterior**, **posterior**, and **lateral compartments**. *(see Figures 11.22/11.23 and Table 11.10)*

Compartments of the Lower Limb 321

3. The thigh has **anterior**, **medial**, and **posterior compartments**; the leg has **anterior**, **posterior**, and **lateral compartments**. *(see Figure 11.24 and Table 11.11)*

CHAPTER REVIEW

For answers to the Concept Check and Chapter Review questions, go to the blue "Answers" tab at the back of the book.

Level 1 Reviewing Facts and Terms

Match each numbered item with the most closely related lettered item. Use letters for answers in the spaces provided.

Column A	Column B
___ 1. rhomboid muscles	a. abducts the toes
___ 2. latissimus dorsi	b. flexes hip and/or lumbar spine
___ 3. infraspinatus	c. adduct (retract) scapula
___ 4. brachialis	d. connective tissue bands
___ 5. supinator	e. plantar flexion at ankle
___ 6. flexor retinaculum	f. origin—surface of ilium
___ 7. gluteal muscles	g. flexes elbow
___ 8. iliacus	h. dorsiflexes ankle and inverts foot
___ 9. gastrocnemius	i. lateral rotation of humerus at shoulder
___ 10. tibialis anterior	j. supinates forearm
___ 11. interossei	k. extends, adducts, medially rotates humerus at shoulder

12. The powerful extensors of the knee are the
    (a) hamstrings (b) quadriceps
    (c) iliopsoas (d) tensor fasciae latae
13. Which of the following is not a muscle of the rotator cuff?
    (a) supraspinatus (b) subclavius
    (c) subscapularis (d) teres minor
14. Which of the following does not originate on the humerus?
    (a) anconeus (b) biceps brachii
    (c) brachialis (d) triceps brachii, lateral head
15. Which of the following muscles is a flexor of the elbow?
    (a) biceps brachii (b) brachialis
    (c) brachioradialis (d) all of the above
16. The muscle that causes opposition of the thumb is the
    (a) adductor pollicis (b) extensor digitorum
    (c) abductor pollicis (d) opponens pollicis

Level 2 Reviewing Concepts

1. Damage to the pectoralis major muscle would interfere with the ability to
    (a) extend the elbow (b) abduct the humerus
    (c) adduct the humerus (d) elevate the scapula
2. Which of the following muscles produces abduction at the hip?
    (a) pectineus (b) psoas
    (c) obturator internus (d) piriformis
3. The tibialis anterior is a dorsiflexor of the foot. Which of the following muscles would be an antagonist to that action?
    (a) flexor digitorum longus (b) gastrocnemius
    (c) flexor hallucis longus (d) all of the above
4. If you bruised your gluteus maximus muscle, you would expect to experience discomfort when performing
    (a) flexion at the knee (b) extension at the hip
    (c) abduction at the hip (d) all of the above
5. The biceps brachii exerts actions upon three joints. What are these joints and what are the actions?
6. What muscle supports the knee laterally and becomes greatly enlarged in ballet dancers because of the need for flexion and abduction at the hip?
7. When a dancer is stretching the muscles of a leg by placing the heel over a barre, which groups of muscles are stretched?
8. What is the function of the intrinsic muscles of the hand?
9. How does the tensor fasciae latae muscle act synergistically with the gluteus maximus muscle?
10. What are the main functions of the flexor and extensor retinacula of the wrist and ankle?

Level 3 Critical Thinking

1. Describe how the hand muscles function in holding a pen or pencil in writing or drawing.
2. While playing soccer, Jerry pulls his hamstring muscle. As a result of the injury, he has difficulty flexing and medially rotating his thigh. Which muscle(s) of the hamstring group did he probably injure?
3. While unloading her car trunk, Linda pulls a muscle and, as a result, has difficulty moving her arm. The doctor in the emergency room tells her that she pulled her pectoralis major muscle. Linda tells you that she thought the pectoralis major was a chest muscle and doesn't understand what that has to do with her arm. What would you tell her?

12

Surface Anatomy and Cross-Sectional Anatomy

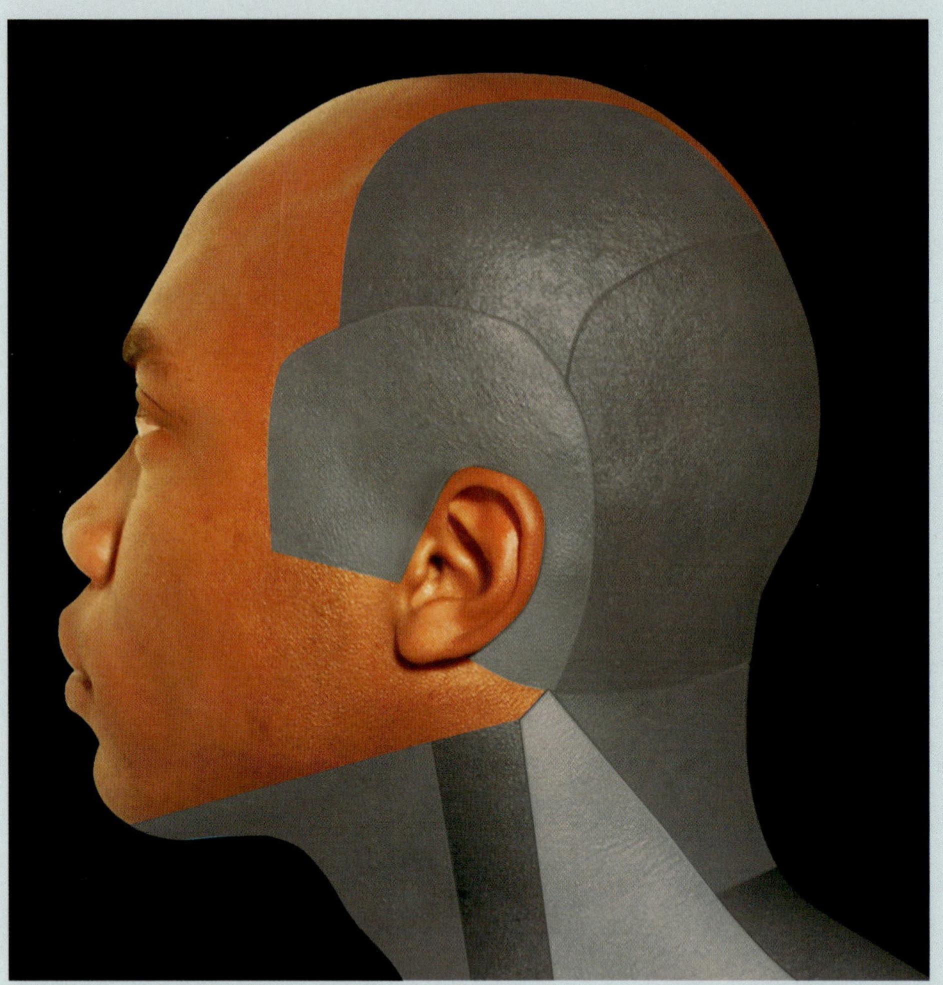

CHAPTER OBJECTIVES

1. Define surface anatomy and describe its importance in the clinical setting.
2. Examine through visual observation and palpation the surface anatomy of the head and neck, using the labeled photos for reference.
3. Examine through visual observation and palpation the surface anatomy of the thorax, using the labeled photos for reference.
4. Examine through visual observation and palpation the surface anatomy of the abdomen, using the labeled photos for reference.
5. Examine through visual observation and palpation the surface anatomy of the upper limb, using the labeled photos for reference.
6. Examine through visual observation and palpation the surface anatomy of the pelvis and lower limb, using the labeled photos for reference.
7. Describe the importance of cross-sectional anatomy in the development of a three-dimensional understanding of anatomical concepts.
8. Visualize the relative positions and orientation of major structures of the head and neck, using the labeled sectional images for reference.
9. Visualize the relative positions and orientation of major structures of the thoracic cavity, using the labeled sectional images for reference.
10. Visualize the relative positions and orientation of major structures of the abdominal cavity, using the labeled sectional images for reference.
11. Visualize the relative positions and orientation of major structures of the pelvic cavity, using the labeled sectional images for reference.

The first portion of this chapter focuses attention on anatomical structures that can be identified from the body surface. **Surface anatomy** is the study of anatomical landmarks on the exterior of the human body. The photographs in this chapter survey the entire body, providing a visual tour that highlights skeletal landmarks and muscle contours. Chapter 1 provided an overview of surface anatomy. pp. 3, 14–15 Now that you are familiar with the basic anatomy of the skeletal and muscular systems, a detailed examination of surface anatomy will help demonstrate the structural and functional relationships between those systems. Many of the figures in earlier chapters included views of surface anatomy; those figures will be referenced throughout this chapter.

Surface anatomy has many practical applications. For example, an understanding of surface anatomy is crucial to medical examination in a clinical setting. In the laboratory, a familiarity with surface anatomy is essential for both invasive and noninvasive laboratory procedures.

A Regional Approach to Surface Anatomy

Surface anatomy is best studied using a regional approach. The regions are the *head and neck, thorax, abdomen, upper limb,* and *lower limb.* This information is presented in pictorial fashion, using photographs of the living human body. These models have well-developed muscles and very little body fat. Because many anatomical landmarks can be hidden by a layer of subcutaneous fat, you may not find it as easy to locate these structures on your own body. In practice, anatomical observation often involves estimating the location and then palpating for specific structures. In the sections that follow, identify through visual observation and palpation the surface anatomy of the regions of the body, using the labeled photographs for reference.

The Head and Neck [Figure 12.1]

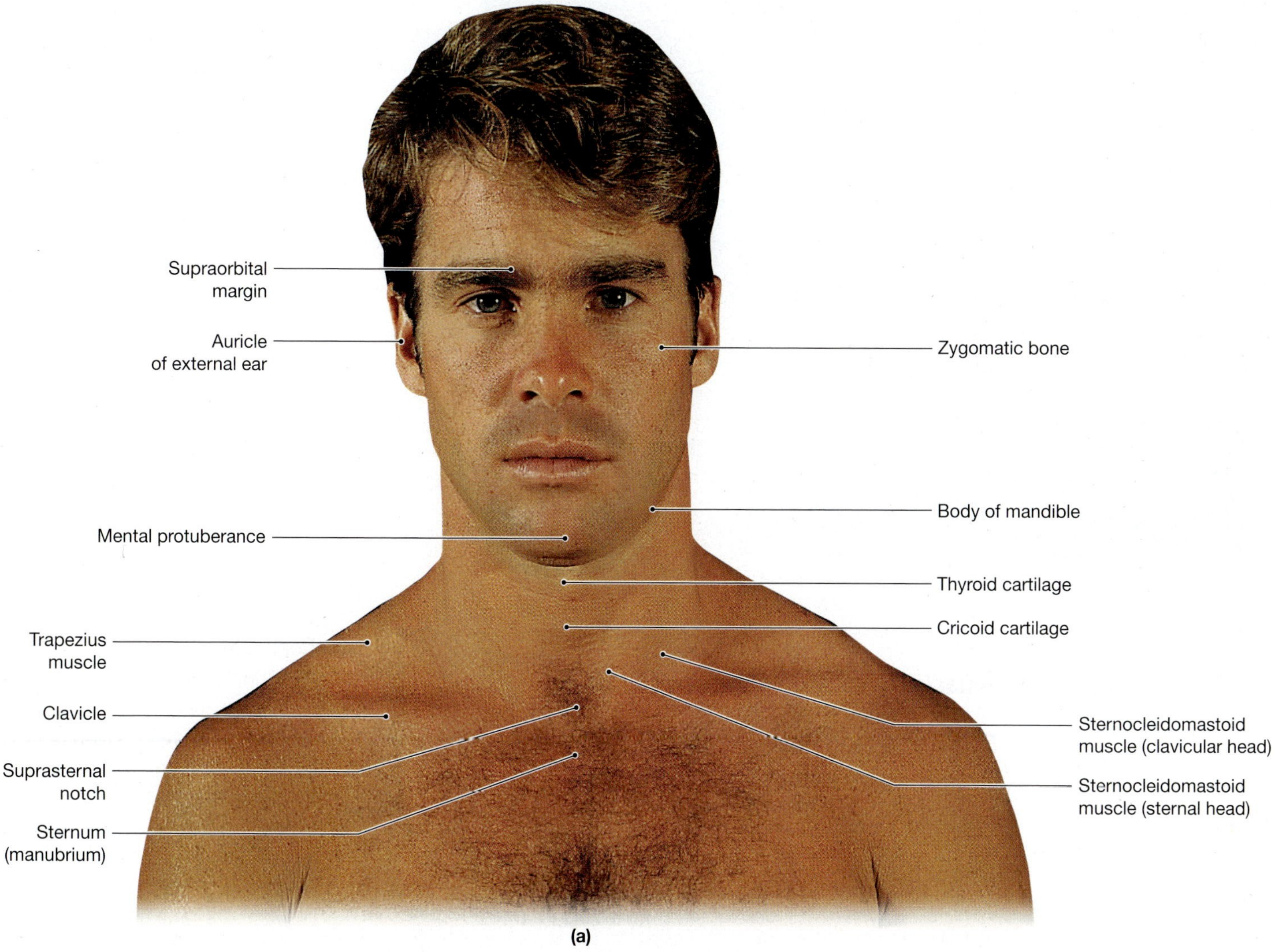

Figure 12.1 The Head and Neck
(a) Anterior view. *For details concerning the musculature of this region, see Figures 10.3 and 10.4, pp. 264–265.* The **anterior cervical triangle** (parts b and c) extends from the anterior midline to the anterior border of the sternocleidomastoid muscle. The **posterior cervical triangle** (part b) extends between the posterior border of the sternocleidomastoid and the anterior border of the trapezius.

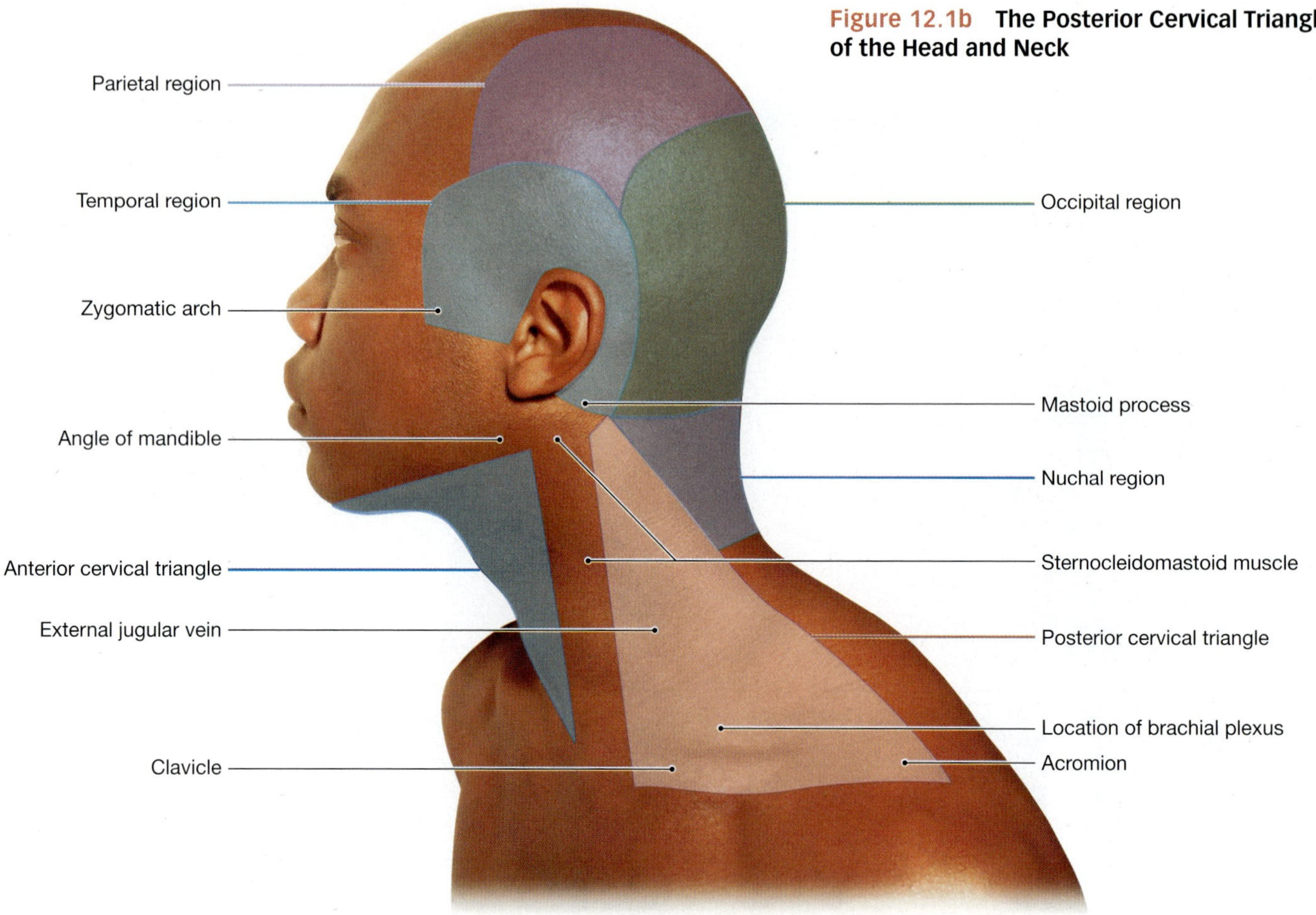

Figure 12.1b **The Posterior Cervical Triangles and the Larger Regions of the Head and Neck**

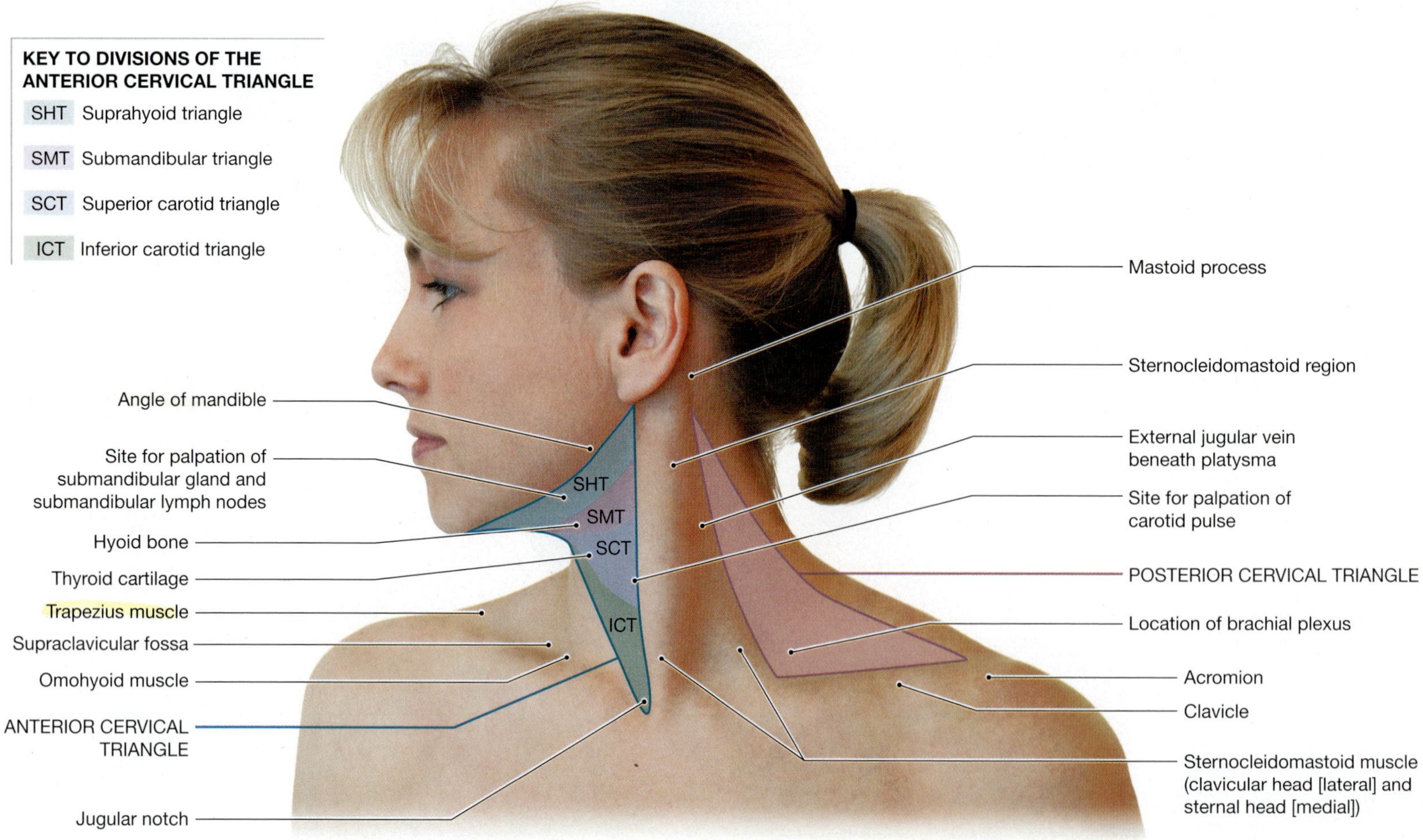

Figure 12.1c **The Subdivisions of the Anterior Cervical Triangle**

The Thorax [Figure 12.2]

Figure 12.2a The Anterior Thorax

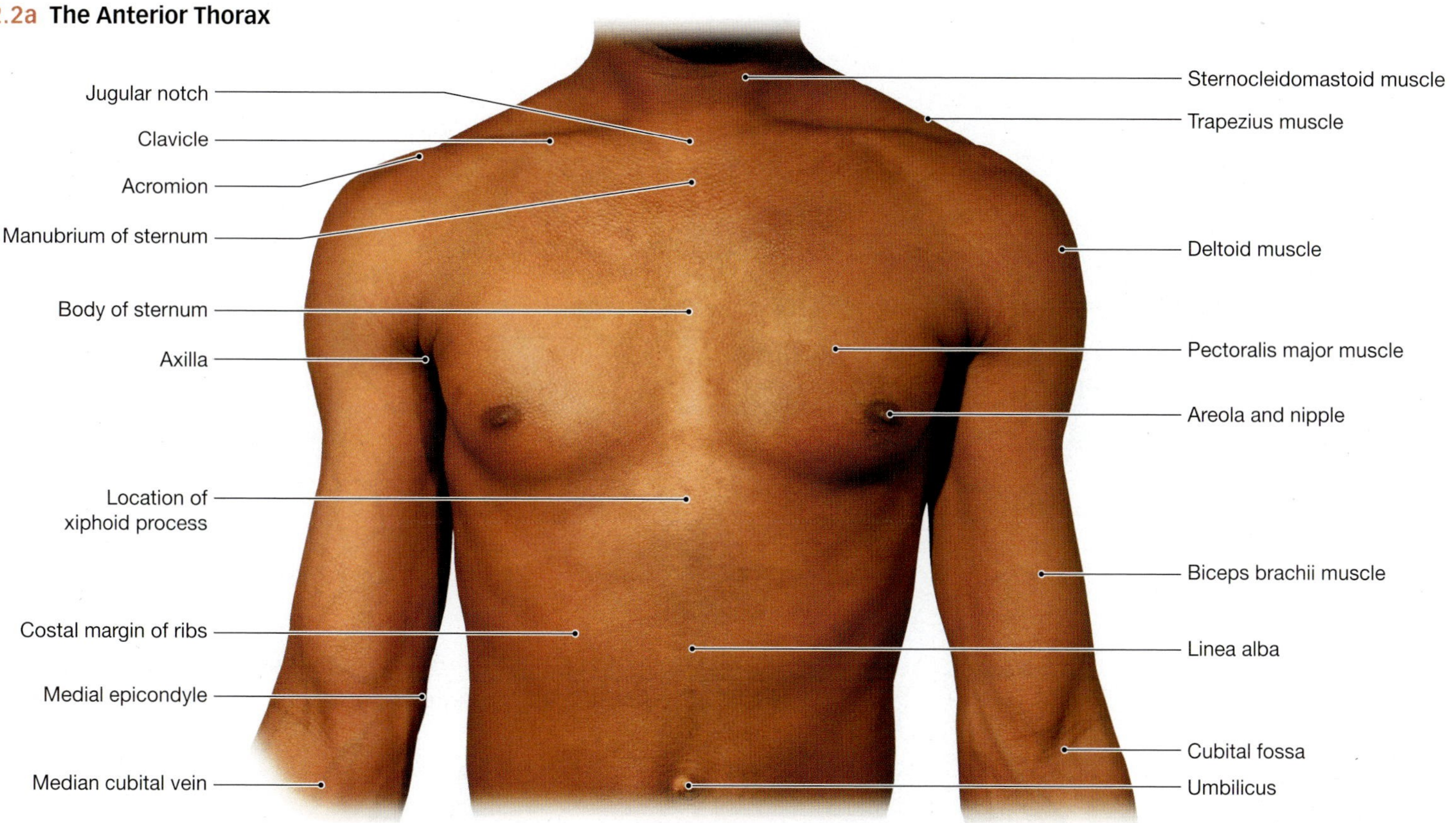

Figure 12.2b The Back and Shoulder Regions

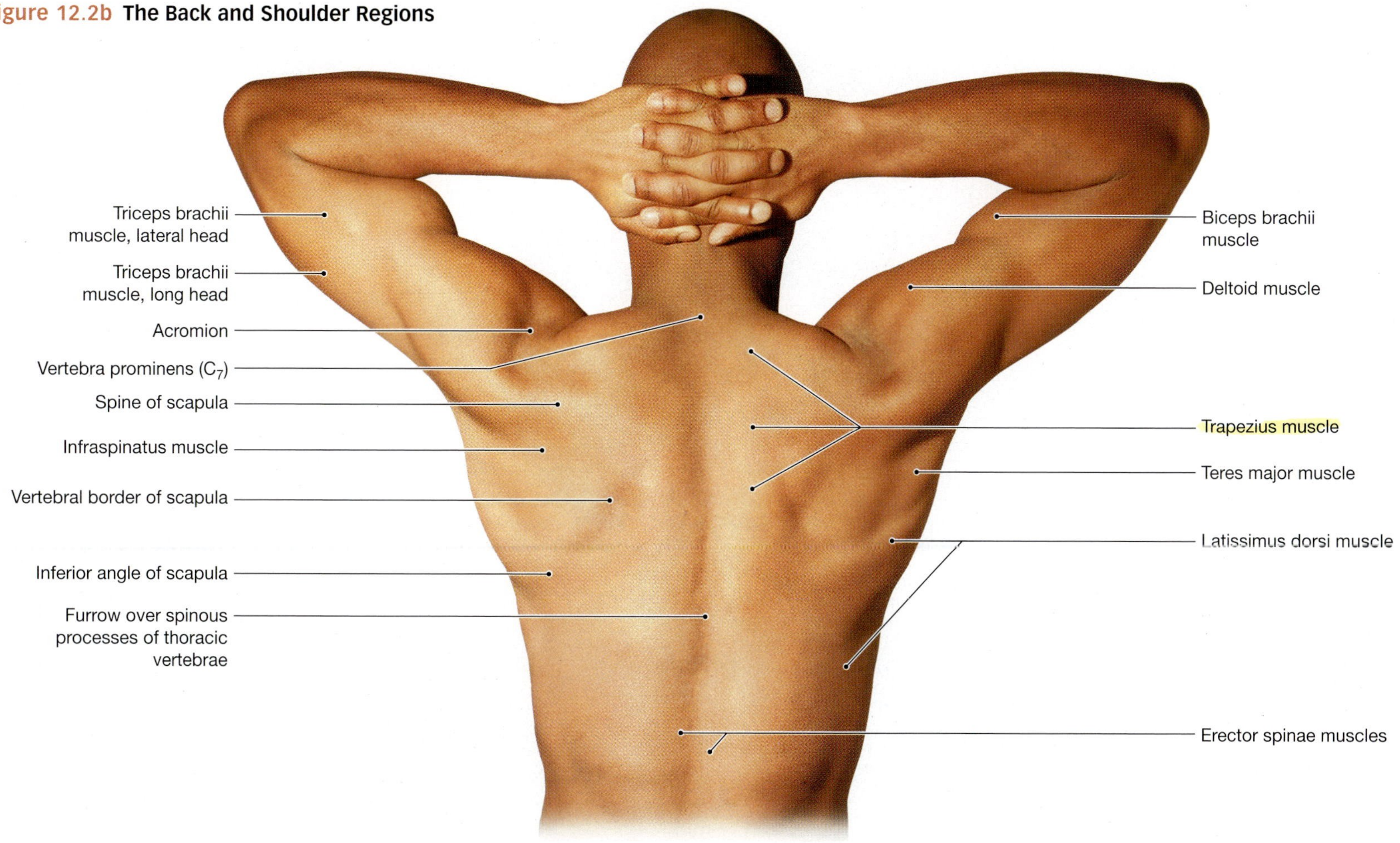

Figure 12.2 The Thorax

The Abdomen [Figure 12.3]

Figure 12.3a The Anterior Abdominal Wall

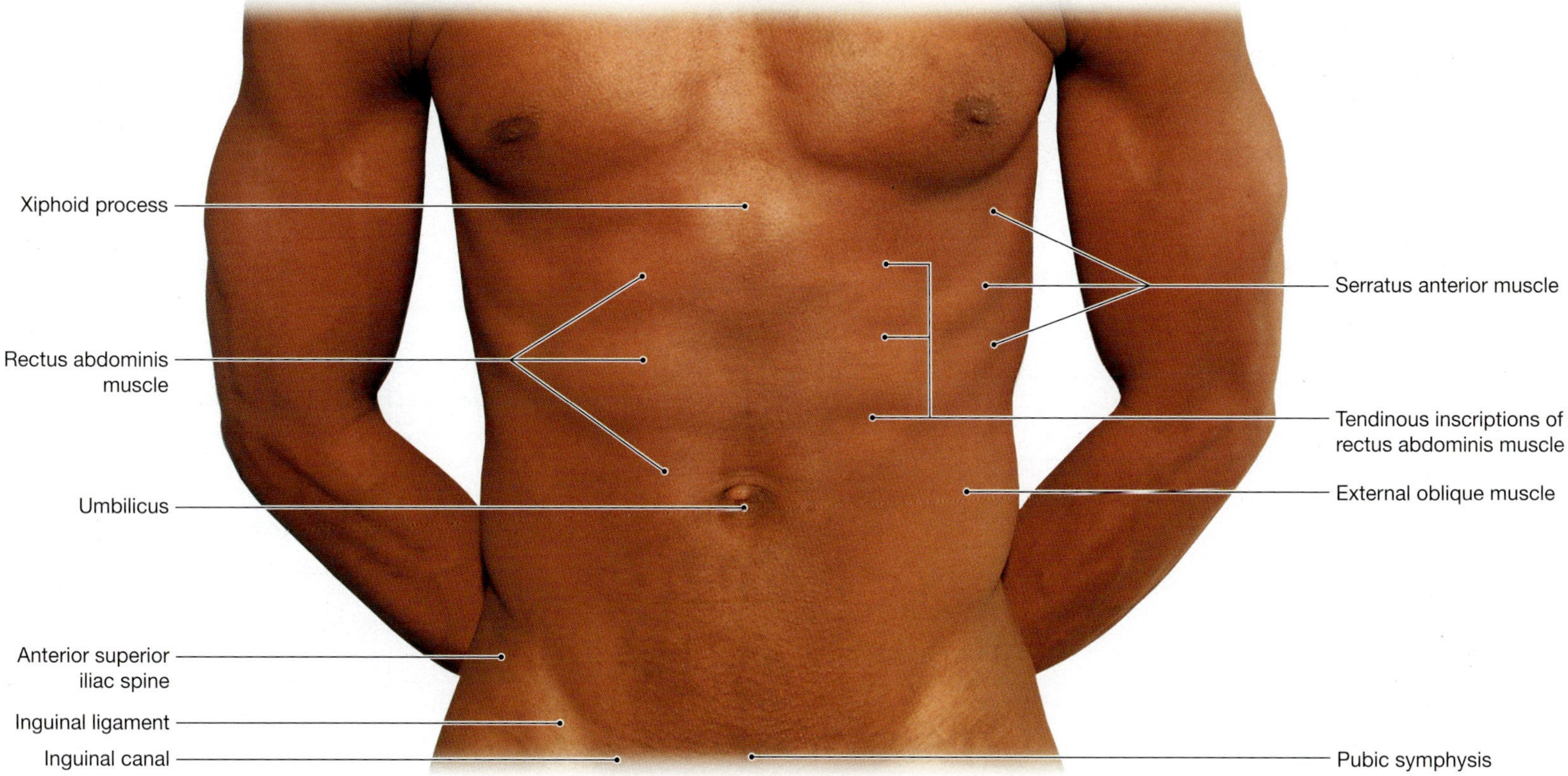

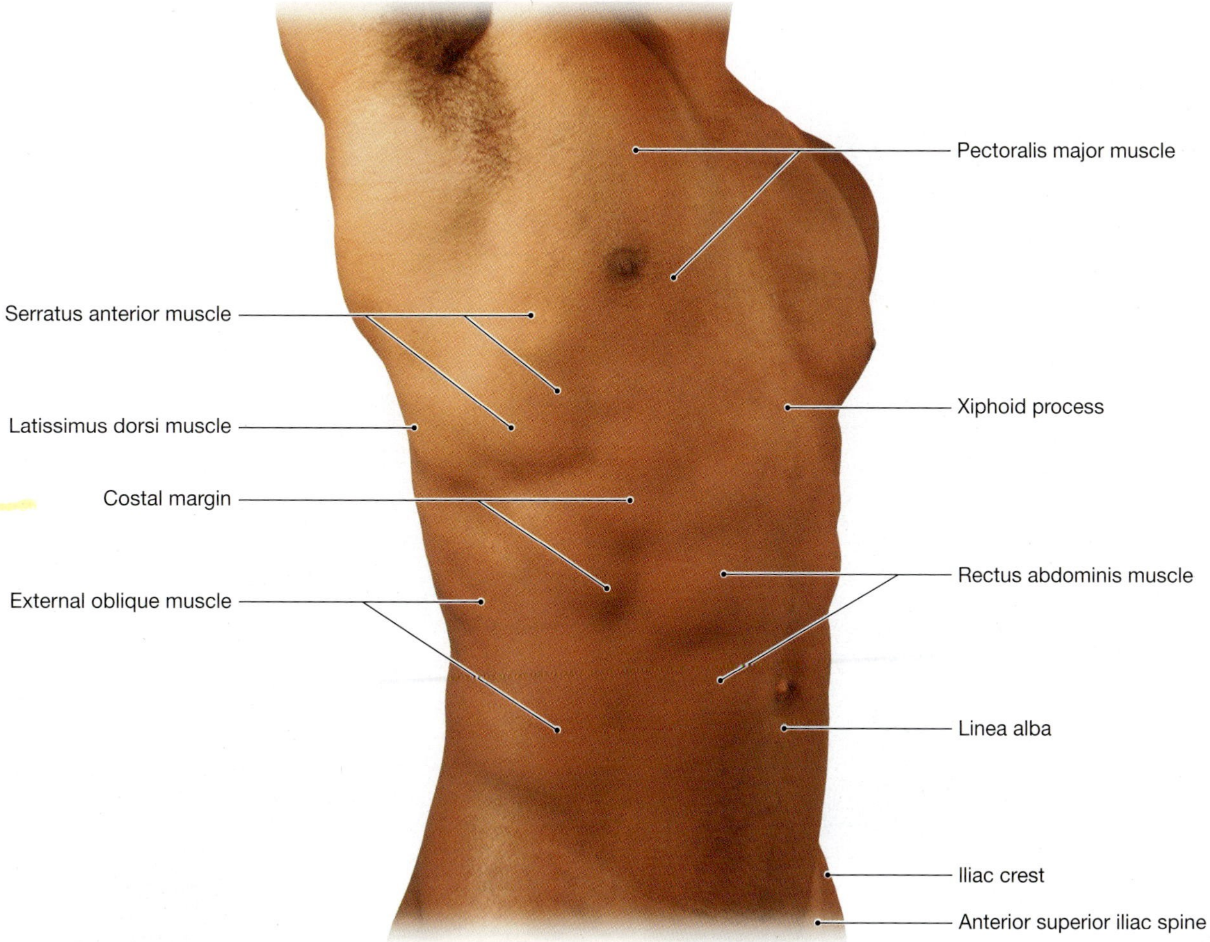

Figure 12.3b Anterolateral View of the Abdominal Wall

Figure 12.3 The Abdominal Wall
For additional details of the abdominal wall, see Figure 10.13, p. 277.

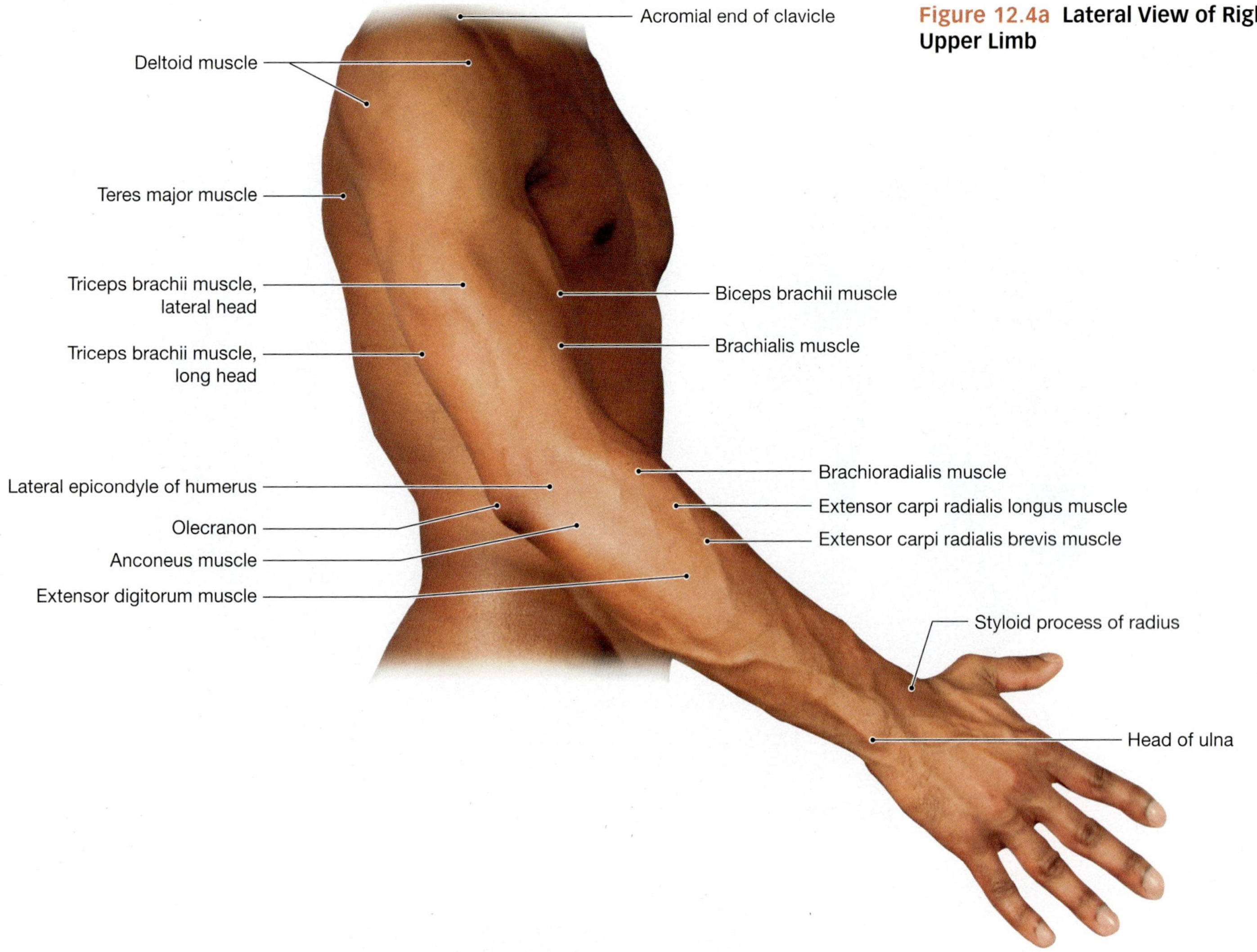

Figure 12.4a Lateral View of Right Upper Limb

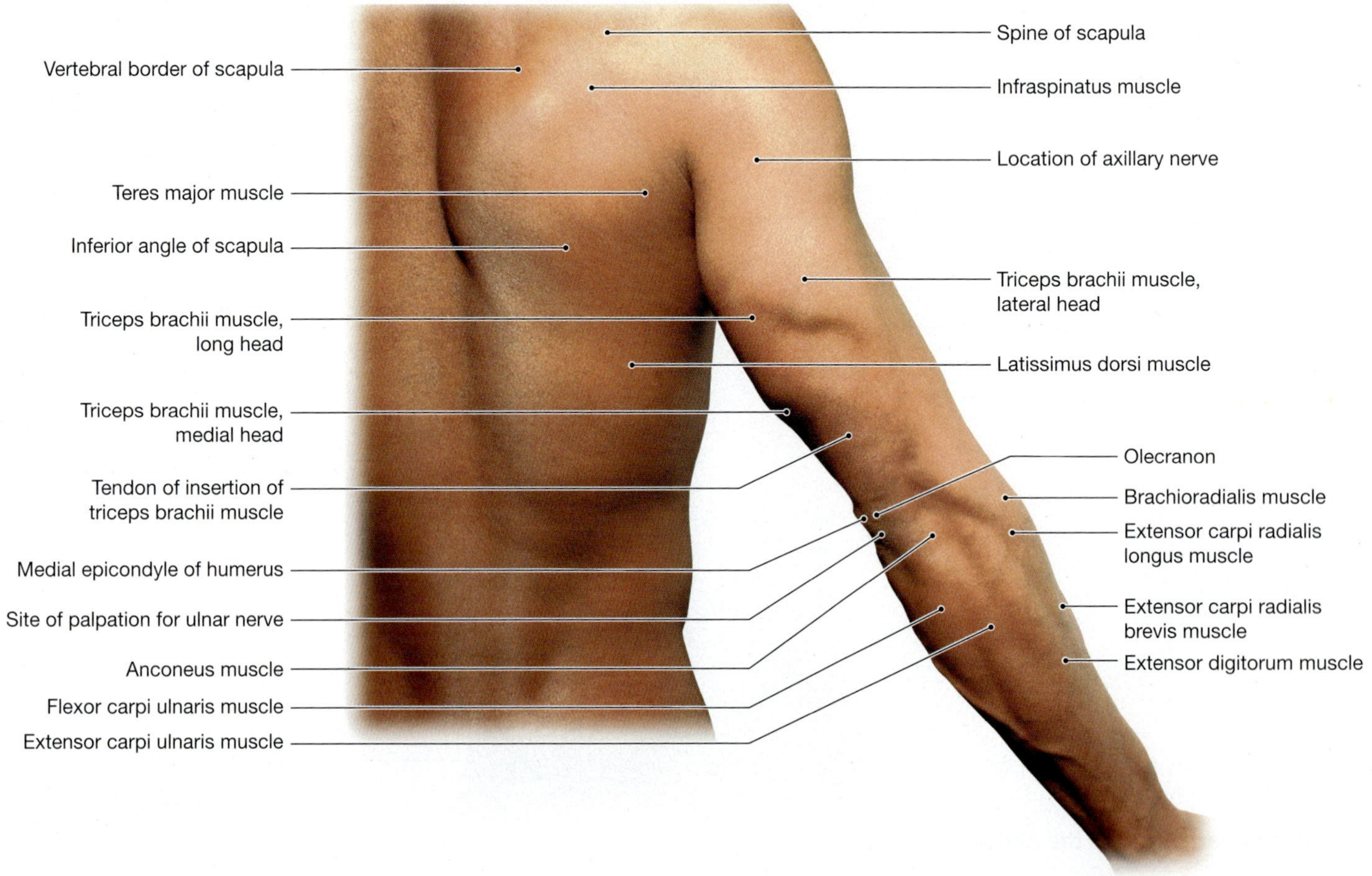

Figure 12.4b Posterior View of Thorax and Right Upper Limb

Figure 12.4 The Upper Limb

For additional details of the arm and forearm, see Figures 11.8 and 11.9, pp. 294–297.

The Arm, Forearm, and Wrist [Figure 12.5]

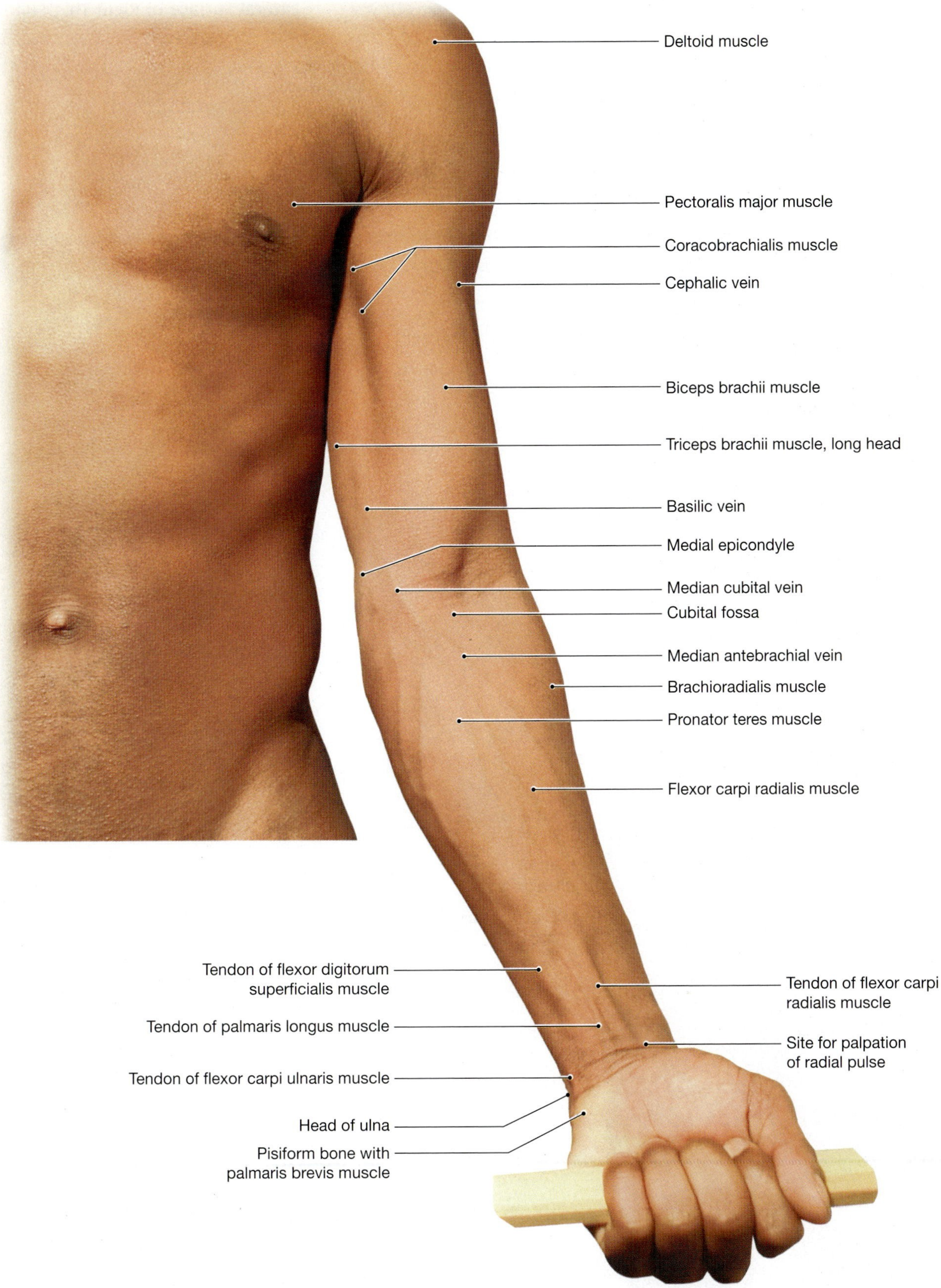

Figure 12.5 The Arm, Forearm, and Wrist
Anterior view of the left arm, forearm, and wrist. *For additional details of the arm and forearm, see Figures 11.5, 11.6, 11.8, and 11.9, pp. 289, 291, 294–295, 296–297.*

The Pelvis and Lower Limb [Figure 12.6]

Figure 12.6a Anterior Surface of Right Thigh

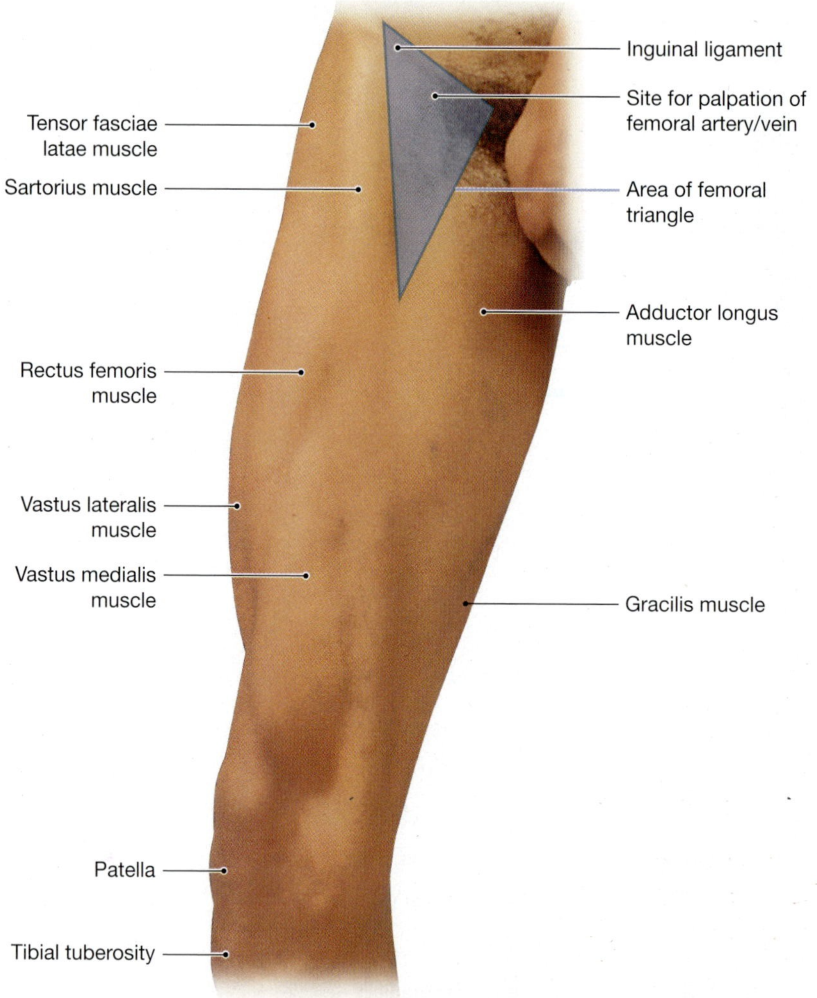

Figure 12.6b Lateral Surface of Right Thigh and Gluteal Region

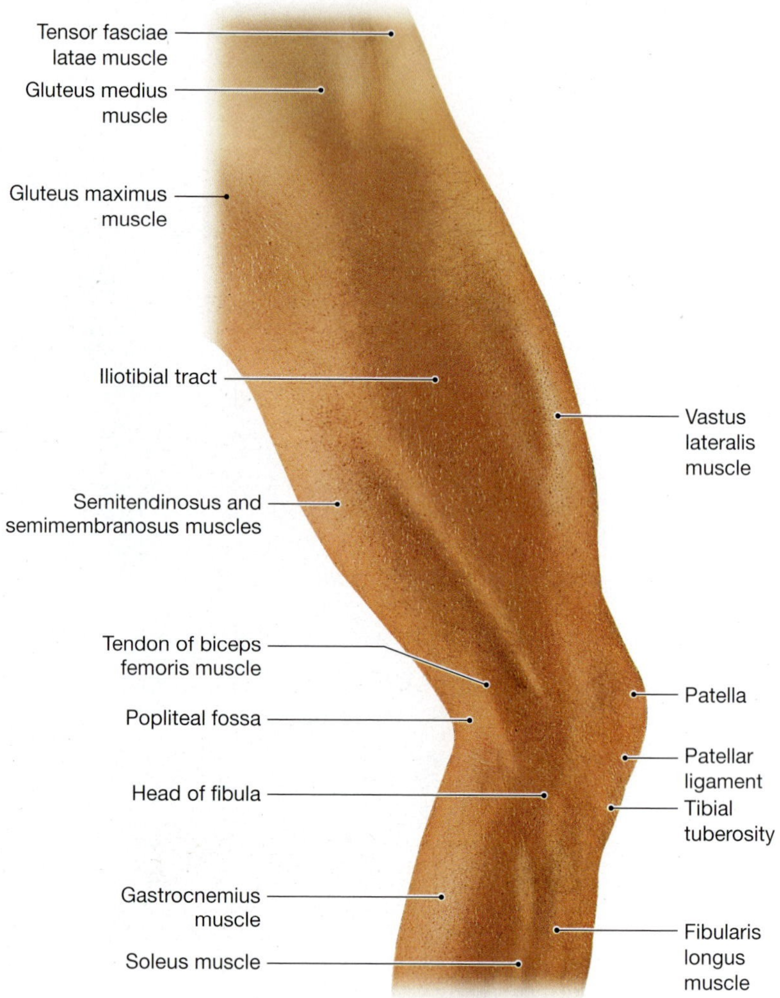

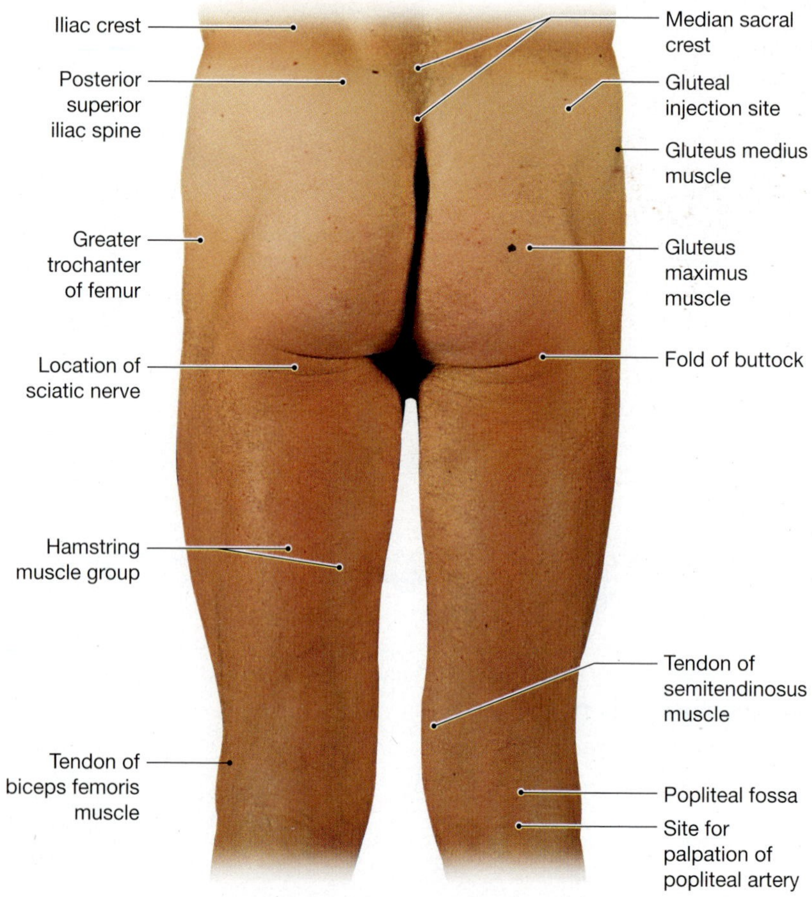

Figure 12.6c Posterior Surface of Right Thigh and Gluteal Region

Figure 12.6 The Pelvis and Lower Limb
The boundaries of the *femoral triangle* are the inguinal ligament, medial border of the sartorius muscle, and lateral border of the adductor longus muscle. *For additional details of the thigh, see Figures 11.12 to 11.17, pp. 302–303, 305–307, 309–311.*

The Leg and Foot [Figure 12.7]

Figure 12.7a Right Knee and Leg, Anterior View

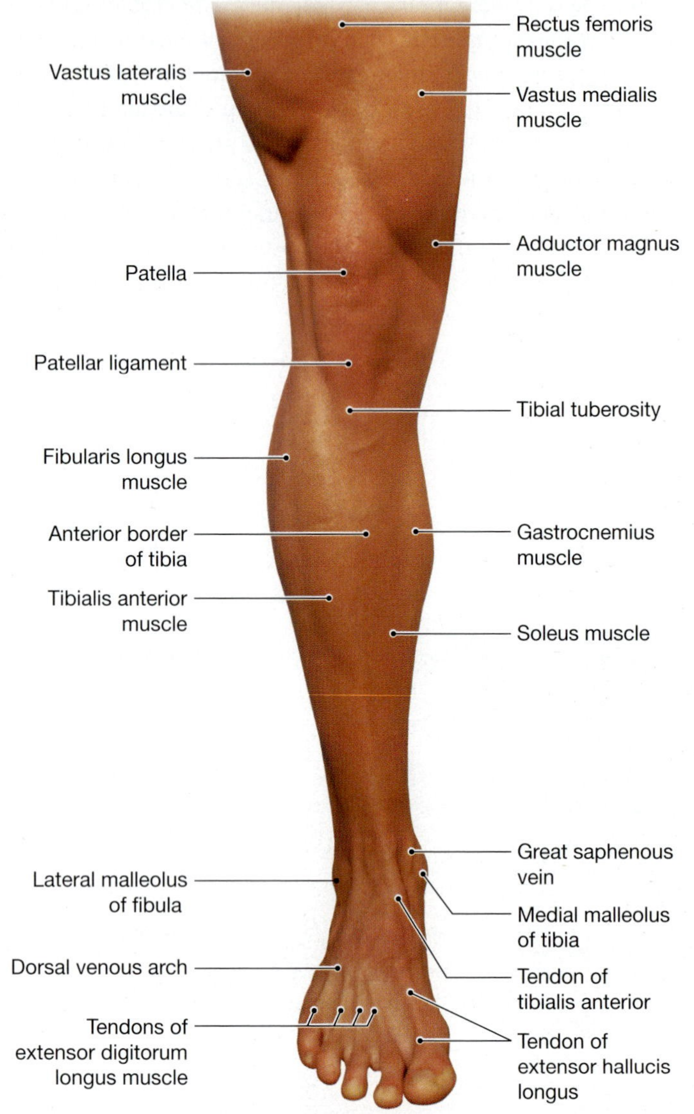

Figure 12.7b Right Knee and Leg, Posterior View

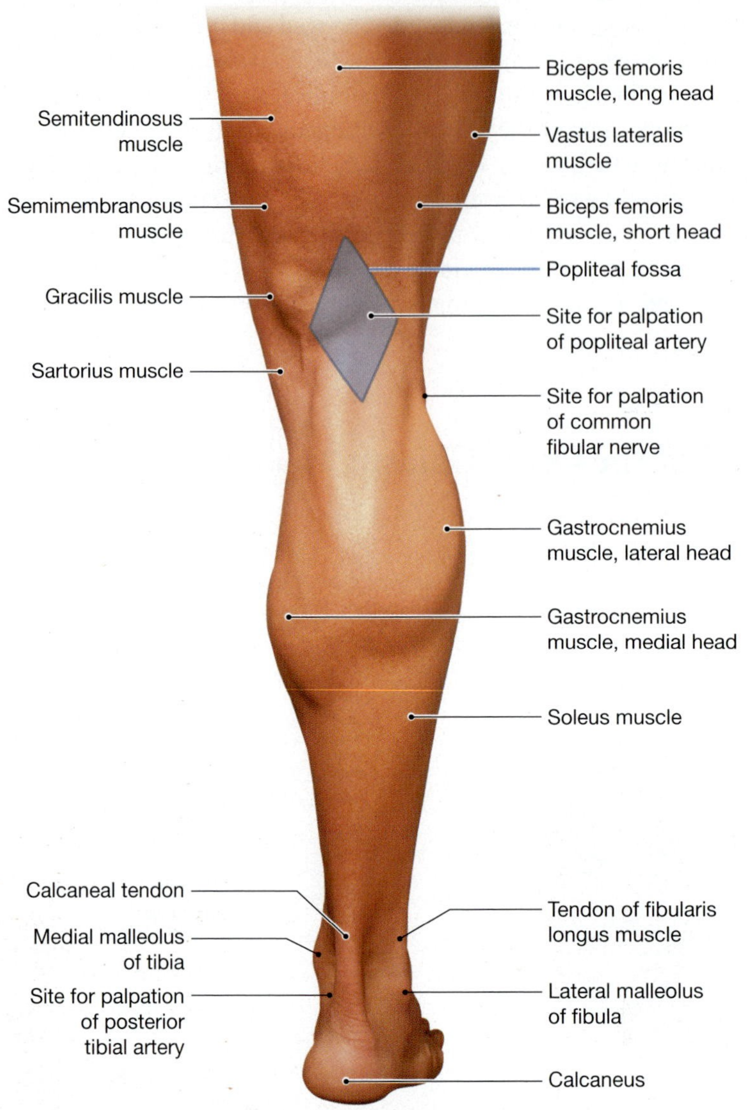

Figure 12.7c Right Ankle and Foot, Anterior View

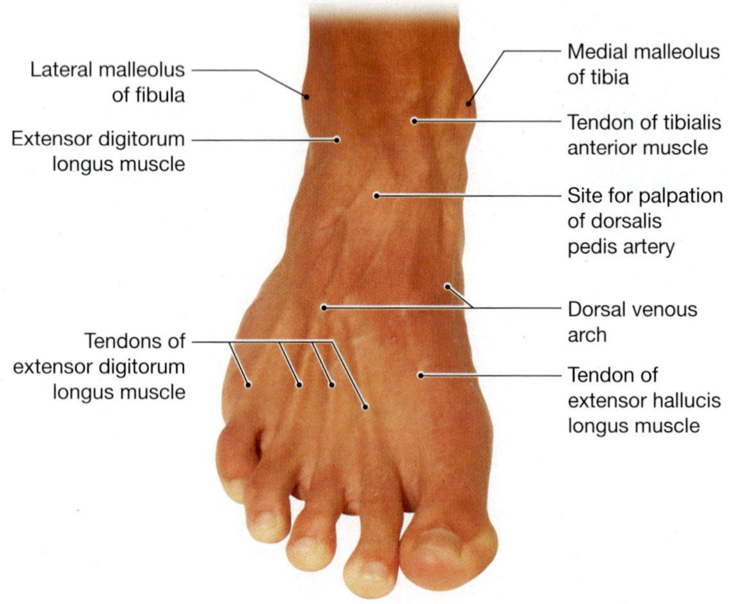

Figure 12.7d Right Ankle and Foot, Posterior View

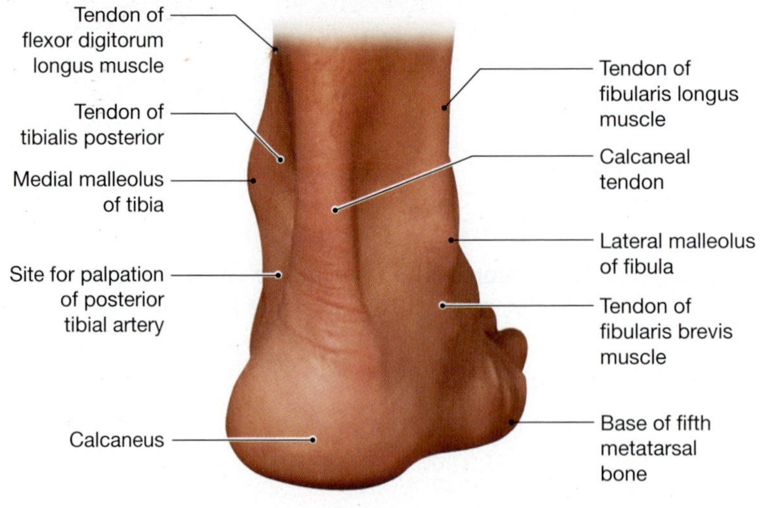

Figure 12.7 The Leg and Foot

For other views of the ankle and foot, see Figures 7.15 to 7.18, pp. 196–200, and Figures 11.15 to 11.21, pp. 306–307, 309–317.

Cross-Sectional Anatomy

The methodology utilized to view anatomical structures has changed dramatically within the last 10–20 years. Therefore, the demands placed on students of human anatomy have also changed and increased. Today's students of anatomy must now know how to visualize and understand the three-dimensional relationships of anatomical structures in a wider variety of formats. One of the most intriguing and challenging ways to visualize the human body is in cross section. A variety of technological methods may be used to view the body in cross section (∞ pp. 22–23). One of the most ambitious projects undertaken to further the understanding of human cross-sectional anatomy was *The Visible Human Project®* (∞ pp. 17–18). This project resulted in over 1800 cross-sectional images of the human body, and has contributed significantly to the understanding of the human body.

This section of the chapter provides several cross-sectional images obtained from The National Library of Medicine's *The Visible Human Project®*. As you view these cross-sectioned images, the following process will assist you in interpreting and understanding the anatomical relationship for each section: (1) The cross sections in this chapter are all inferior-view images. In other words, they are viewed as if you are standing at the individual's feet and looking toward the head. This is the standard method of presentation for all clinical images. (2) The same standard places the anterior surface at the top of the image, and the posterior surface at the bottom. This method of presentation means that structures on the right side of the body will appear on the left side of the image.

Level of the Optic Chiasm [Figure 12.8]

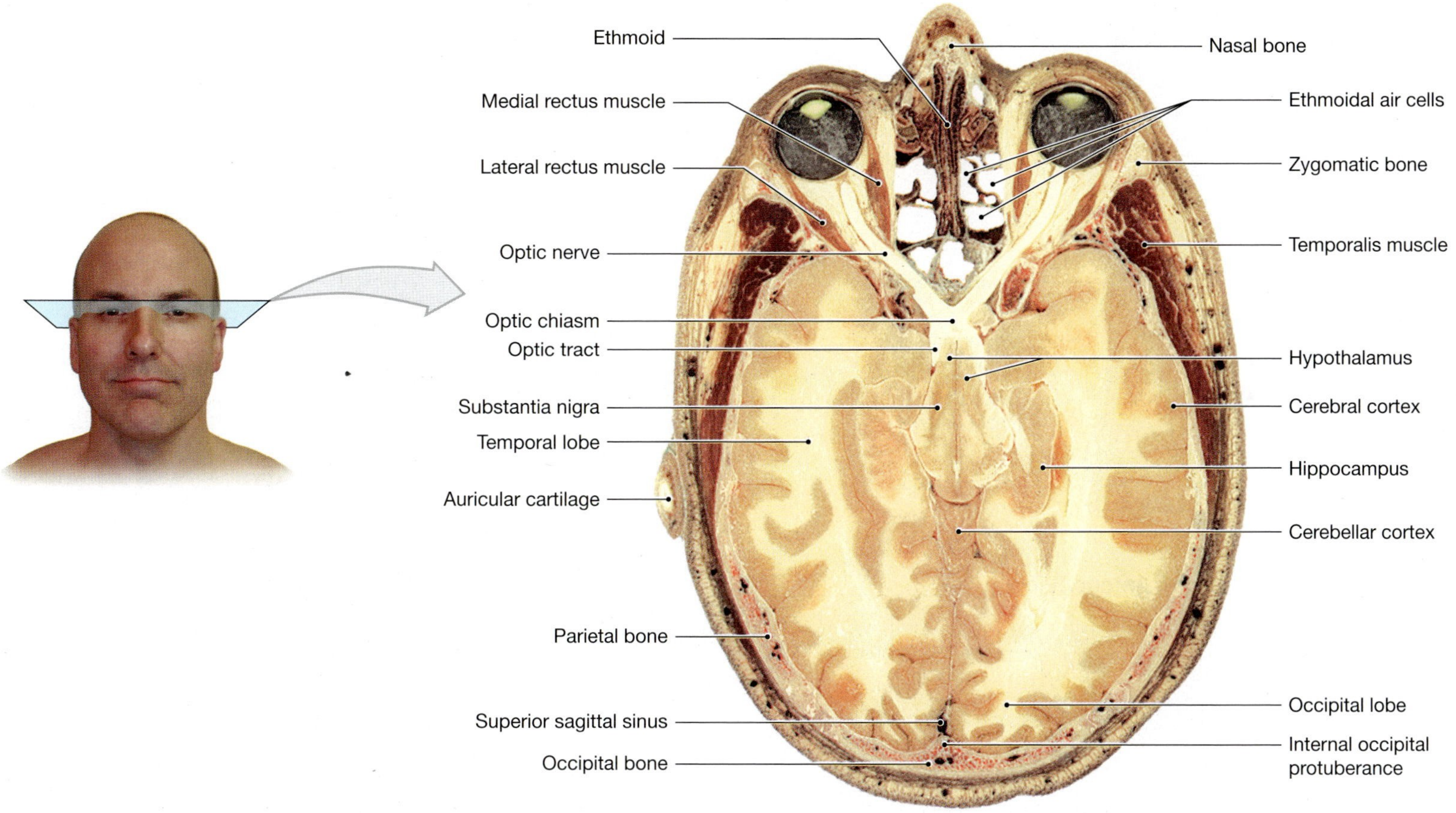

Figure 12.8 Cross Section of the Head at the Level of the Optic Chiasm
For other views of the brain, see Figures 15.13 and 15.21, pp. 405, 417.

Cross Section of the Head at the Level of C_2 [Figure 12.9]

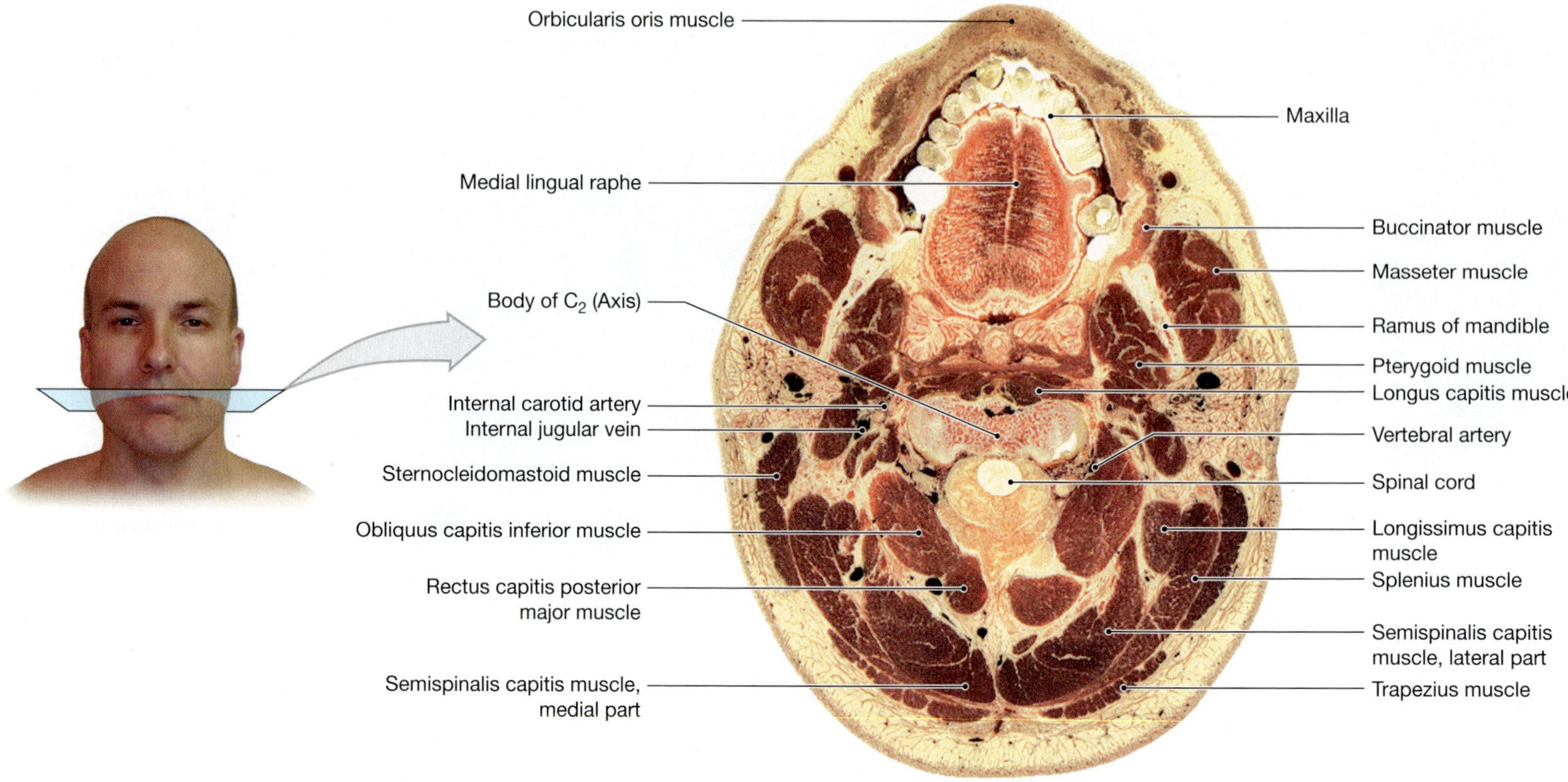

Figure 12.9 Cross Section of the Head at the Level of Vertebra C_2
For another view of the muscles of the vertebral column, see Figure 10.12, pp. 273–274.

Cross Section at the Level of Vertebra T_2 [Figure 12.10]

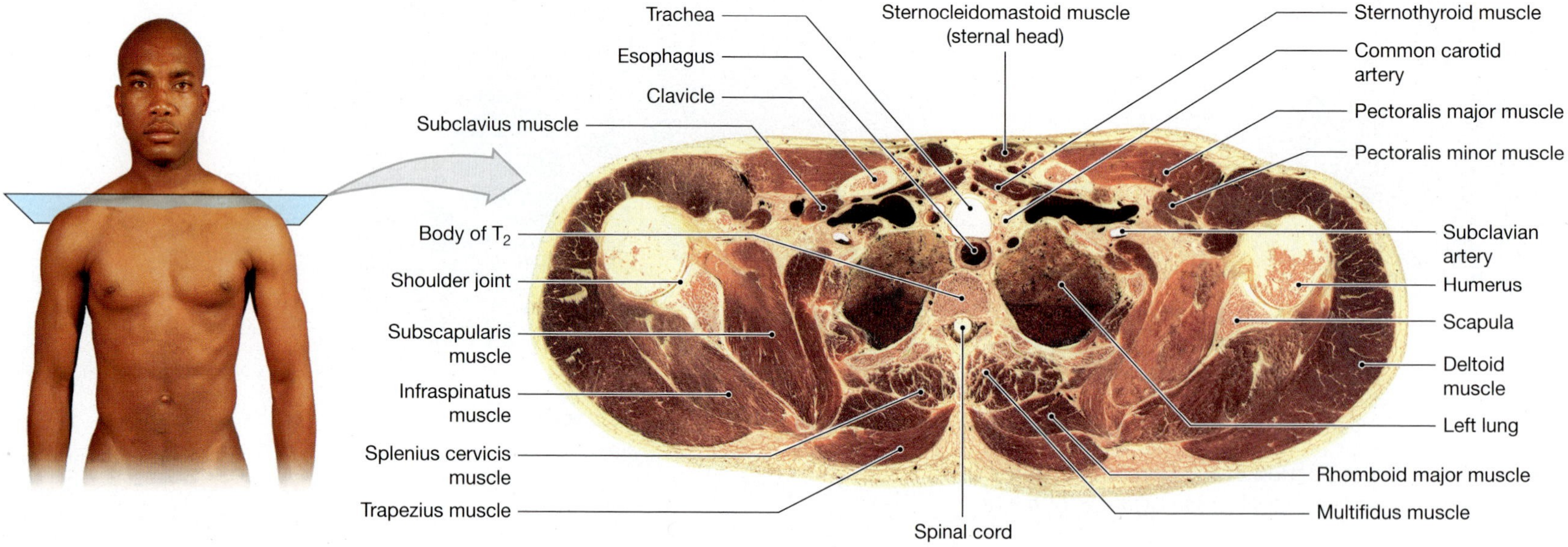

Figure 12.10 Cross Section at the Level of Vertebra T_2
For another view of the location of the heart within the thoracic cavity, see Figure 21.2, p. 549.

Cross Section at the Level of Vertebra T_8 [Figure 12.11]

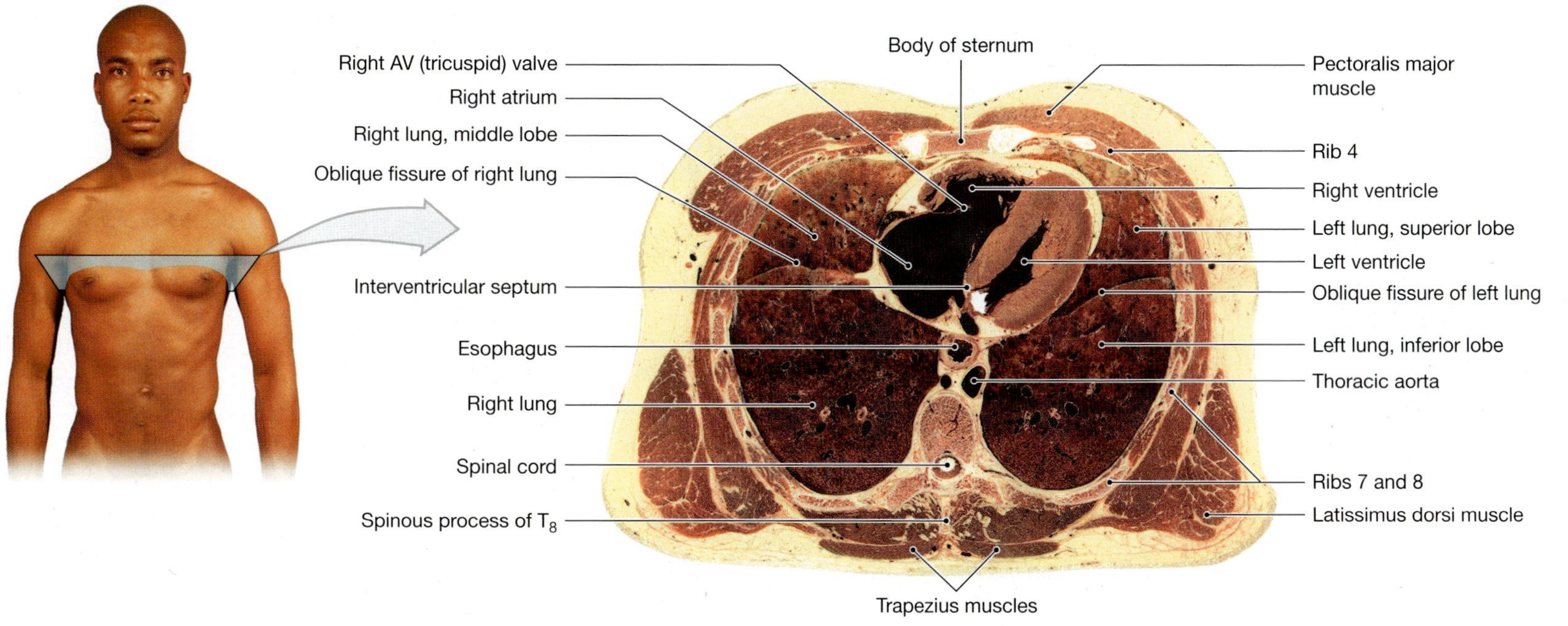

Figure 12.11 Cross Section at the Level of Vertebra T_8
For other views of the stomach and liver, see Figures 25.10, 25.11 and 25.20 on pp. 669–670, 682–683.

Cross Section at the Level of Vertebra T_{10} [Figure 12.12]

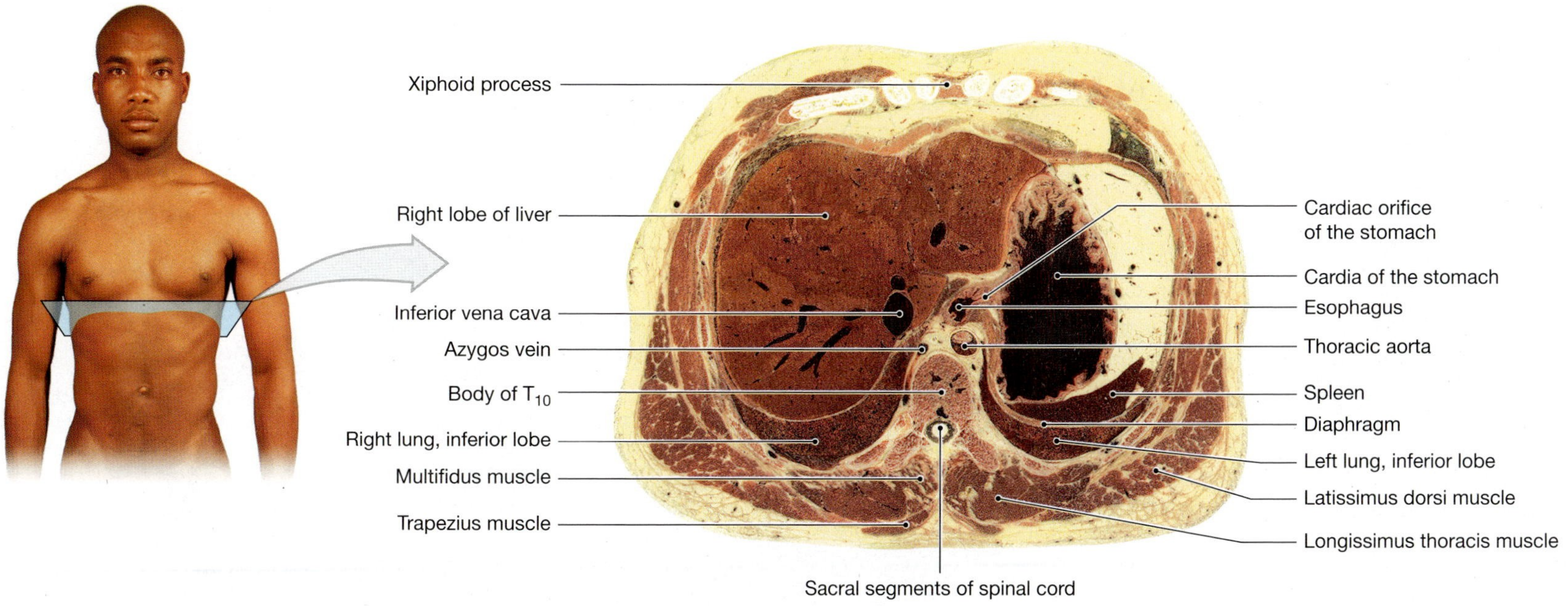

Figure 12.12 Cross Section at the Level of Vertebra T_{10}
For other views of the large intestine, see Figure 25.17, p. 678.

Cross Section at the Level of Vertebra T_{12} [Figure 12.13]

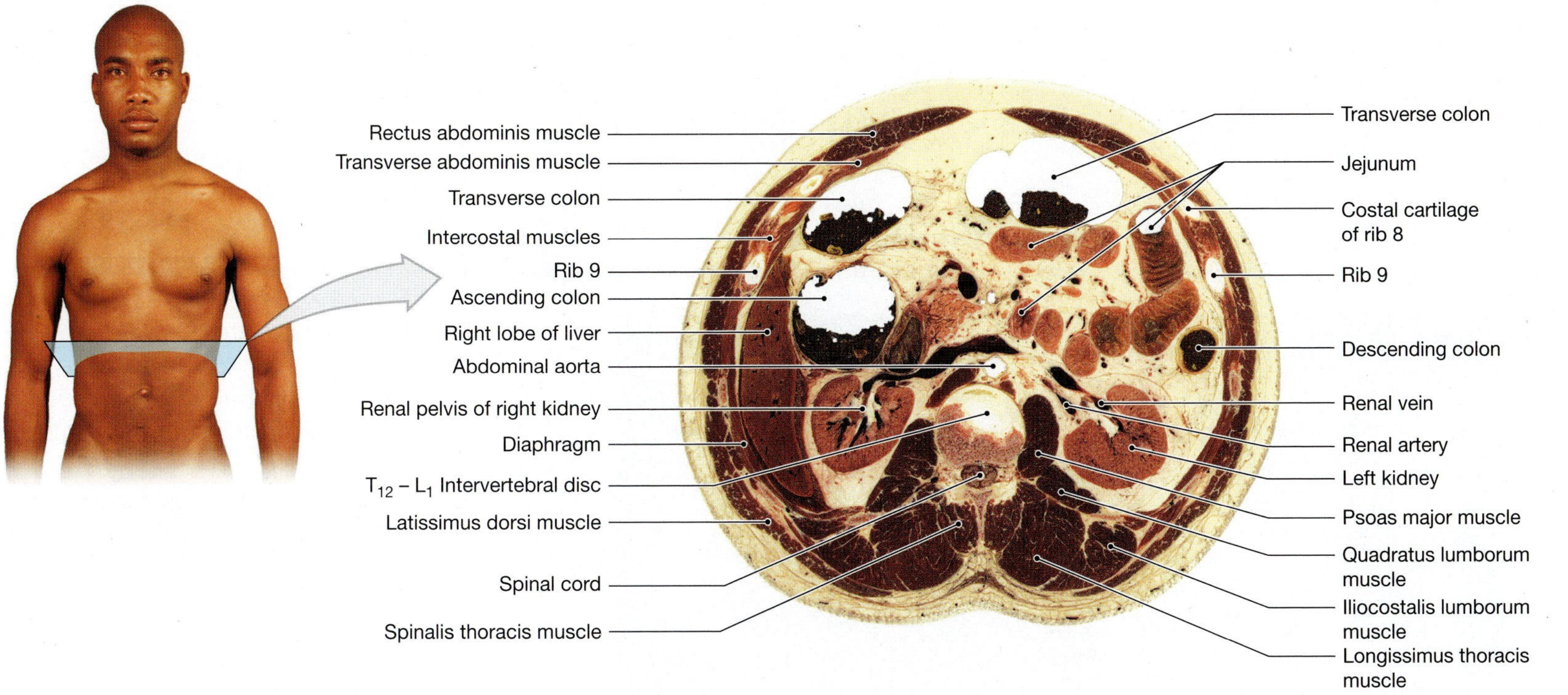

Figure 12.13 **Cross Section at the level of Vertebra T_{12}**
For other views of the kidney, see Figures 26.1 and 26.3, pp. 695 and 697.

Cross Section at the Level of Vertebra L_5 [Figure 12.14]

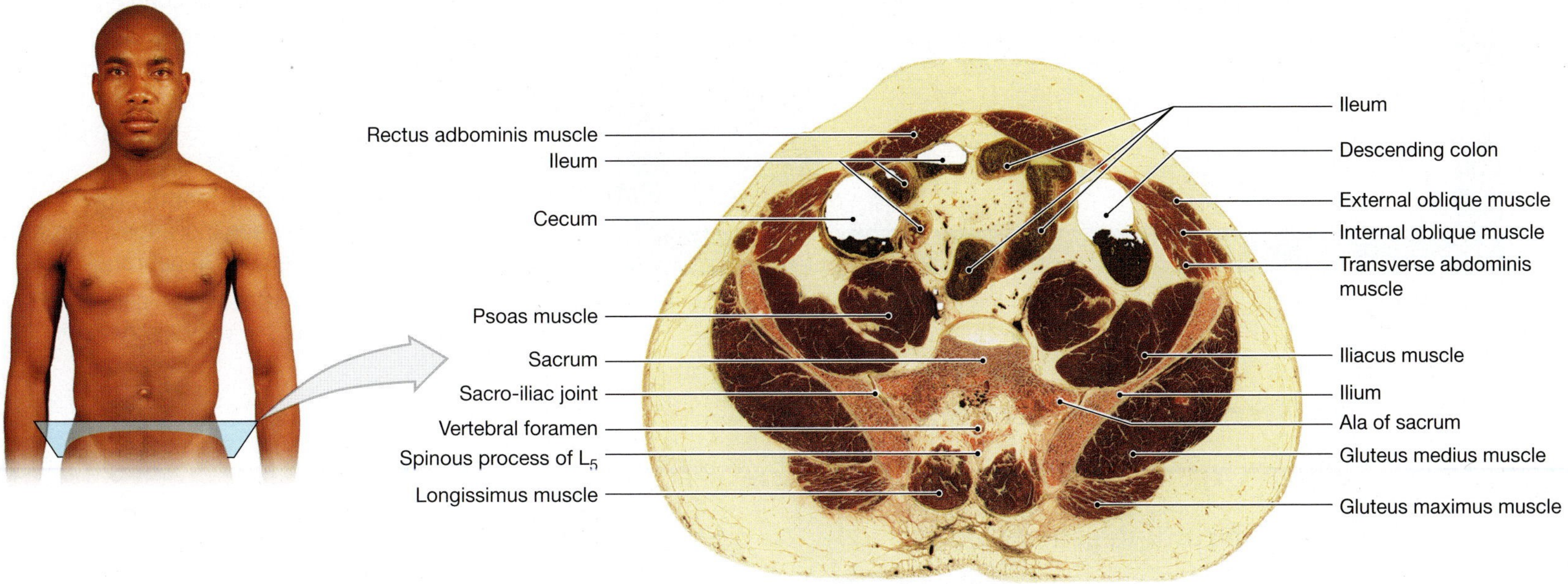

Figure 12.14 **Cross Section at the Level of Vertebra L_5**

13

The Nervous System

Neural Tissue

CHAPTER OBJECTIVES

1. Discuss the anatomical organization and general functions of the nervous system.
2. Compare and contrast the anatomical subdivisions of the nervous system.
3. Distinguish between neuroglia and neurons.
4. Describe the different types of neuroglia and compare their structures and functions.
5. Describe the structure and function of the myelin sheath and differences between its formation in the CNS and the PNS.
6. Describe the structure of a typical neuron and understand the basis for the structural and functional classification of neurons.
7. Describe the process of peripheral nerve regeneration after injury to an axon.
8. Describe the significance of excitability in muscle and nerve cell membranes.
9. Identify the factors that determine the speed of nerve impulse conduction.
10. Describe the microanatomy of a synapse, summarize the events that occur during synaptic transmission, and describe the effects of a typical neurotransmitter, ACh.
11. Discuss the possible methods of interaction between individual neurons or groups of neurons in neuronal pools.
12. Describe the basic anatomical organization of the nervous system.

The *nervous system* is among the smallest of organ systems in terms of body weight, yet it is by far the most complex. Although it is often compared to a computer, the nervous system is much more complicated and versatile than any electronic device. Yet, as in a computer, the rapid flow of information and high processing speed depend on electrical activity. Unlike a computer, however, portions of the brain can rework their electrical connections as new information arrives—that's part of the learning process.

Along with the *endocrine system*, discussed in Chapter 19, the nervous system controls and adjusts the activities of other systems. These two systems share important structural and functional characteristics. Both rely on some form of chemical communication with targeted tissues and organs, and they often act in a complementary fashion. The nervous system usually provides relatively swift but brief responses to stimuli by temporarily modifying the activities of other organ systems. The response may appear almost immediately—in a few milliseconds—but the effects disappear almost as quickly after neural activity ceases. In contrast, endocrine responses are typically slower to develop than neural responses, but they often last much longer—even as long as hours, days, or years. The endocrine system adjusts the metabolic activity of other systems in response to changes in nutrient availability and energy demands. It also coordinates processes that continue for extended periods (months to years), such as growth and development. Chapters 13–18 detail the various components and functions of the nervous system. This chapter begins the series by considering the structure and function of neural tissue and the basic principles of neural function. Subsequent chapters will build on this foundation as they explore the functional organization of the brain, spinal cord, higher-order functions, and sense organs.

An Overview of the Nervous System [Figures 13.1/13.2 and Table 13.1]

The **nervous system** includes all of the **neural tissue** in the body. p. 77 Table 13.1 provides an overview of the most important concepts and terms introduced in this chapter.

The nervous system has two anatomical subdivisions: the *central nervous system* and the *peripheral nervous system* (Figure 13.1). The **central nervous system (CNS)** consists of the *brain* and *spinal cord*. The CNS is responsible for integrating, processing, and coordinating sensory input and motor output. It is also the seat of higher functions, such as intelligence, memory, learning, and emotion. Early in development, the CNS begins as a mass of neural tissue organized into a hollow tube. As development continues, the central cavity decreases in relative size, but the thickness of the walls and the diameter of the enclosed space vary from one region to another. The narrow central cavity that persists within the spinal cord is called the *central canal*; the *ventricles* are expanded chambers, continuous with the central canal, found in specific regions of the brain. *Cerebrospinal fluid (CSF)* fills the central canal and ventricles and surrounds the CNS.

The **peripheral nervous system (PNS)** includes all of the neural tissue outside the CNS. The PNS provides sensory information to the CNS and carries motor commands from the CNS to peripheral tissues and systems. The PNS is subdivided into two divisions (Figure 13.2). The **afferent division** of the PNS brings sensory information to the CNS, and the **efferent division** carries motor commands to muscles and glands. The afferent division begins at **receptors** that monitor specific characteristics of the environment. A receptor may be a *dendrite* (a sensory process of a neuron), a specialized cell or cluster of cells, or a complex sense organ (such as the eye). Whatever its structure, the stimulation of a receptor provides information that may be carried to the CNS. The efferent division begins inside the CNS and ends at an **effector**: a muscle cell, gland cell, or other cell

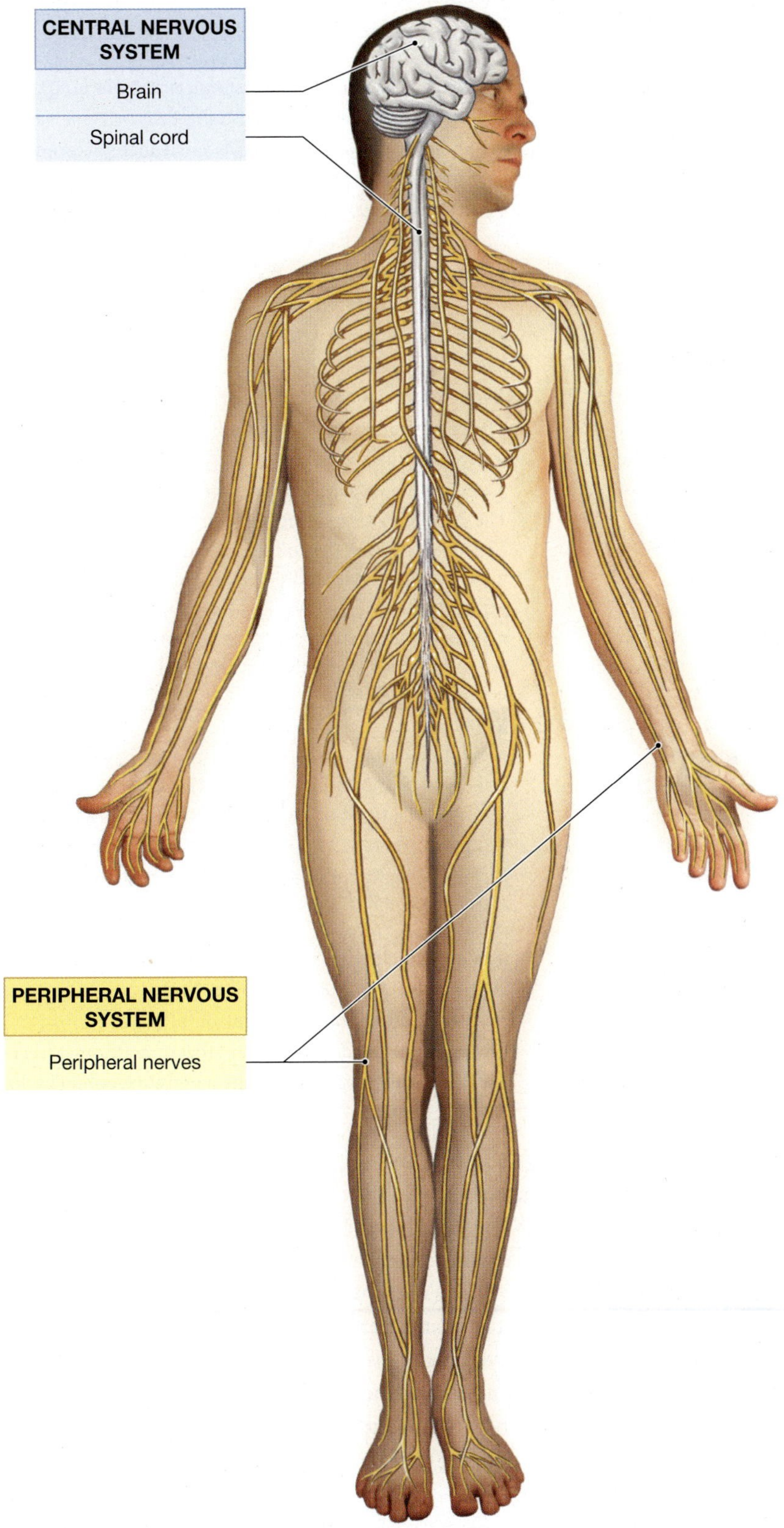

Figure 13.1 The Nervous System
The nervous system includes all of the neural tissue in the body. Its components include the brain, the spinal cord, sense organs such as the eye and ear, and the nerves that interconnect those organs and link the nervous system with other systems.

TABLE 13.1 An Introductory Glossary for the Nervous System

MAJOR ANATOMICAL AND FUNCTIONAL DIVISIONS	
Central Nervous System (CNS)	The brain and spinal cord, which contain control centers responsible for processing and integrating sensory information, planning and coordinating responses to stimuli, and providing short-term control over the activities of other systems.
Peripheral Nervous System (PNS)	Neural tissue outside the CNS whose function is to link the CNS with sense organs and other systems.
Autonomic Nervous System (ANS)	Components of the CNS and PNS that are concerned with the control of visceral functions.
GROSS ANATOMY	
Nucleus:	A CNS center with discrete anatomical boundaries (p. 357).
Center:	A group of neuron cell bodies in the CNS that share a common function (p. 357).
Tract:	A bundle of axons within the CNS that share a common origin, destination, and function (p. 357).
Column:	A group of tracts found within a specific region of the spinal cord (p. 357).
Pathways:	Centers and tracts that connect the brain with other organs and systems in the body (p. 357).
Ganglia:	An anatomically distinct collection of sensory or motor neuron cell bodies within the PNS (p. 346).
Nerve:	A bundle of axons in the PNS (p. 346).
HISTOLOGY	
Gray Matter:	Neural tissue dominated by neuron cell bodies (p. 345).
White Matter:	Neural tissue dominated by myelinated axons (p. 345).
Neural Cortex:	A layer of gray matter at the surface of the brain (p. 357).
Neuron:	The basic functional unit of the nervous system; a highly specialized cell; a nerve cell (pp. 341–342).
Sensory Neuron:	A neuron whose axon carries sensory information from the PNS toward the CNS (p. 351).
Motor Neuron:	A neuron whose axon carries motor commands from the CNS toward effectors in the PNS (p. 351).
Soma:	The cell body of a neuron (p. 344).
Dendrites:	Neuronal processes that are specialized to respond to specific stimuli in the extracellular environment (p. 344).
Axon:	A long, slender cytoplasmic process of a neuron; axons are capable of conducting nerve impulses (action potentials) (p. 344).
Myelin:	A membranous wrapping, produced by glial cells, that coats axons and increases the speed of action potential propagation; axons coated with myelin are said to be *myelinated* (p. 345).
Neuroglia or Glial Cells:	Supporting cells that interact with neurons and regulate the extracellular environment, provide defense against pathogens, and perform repairs within neural tissue (p. 344).
FUNCTIONAL CATEGORIES	
Receptor:	A specialized cell, dendrite, or organ that responds to specific stimuli in the extracellular environment and whose stimulation alters the level of activity in a sensory neuron (pp. 341, 351).
Effector:	A muscle, gland, or other specialized cell or organ that responds to neural stimulation by altering its activity and producing a specific effect (p. 341).
Reflex:	A rapid, stereotyped response to a specific stimulus.
Somatic:	Pertaining to the control of skeletal muscle activity (*somatic motor*) or sensory information from skeletal muscles, tendons, and joints (*somatic sensory*) (pp. 342, 351).
Visceral:	Pertaining to the control of functions, such as digestion, circulation, etc. (*visceral motor*) or sensory information from visceral organs (*visceral sensory*) (pp. 342, 351).
Voluntary:	Under direct conscious control (p. 342).
Involuntary:	Not under direct conscious control (p. 342).
Subconscious:	Pertaining to centers in the brain that operate outside a person's conscious awareness (p. 342).
Action Potentials:	Sudden, transient changes in the membrane potential that are propagated along the surface of an axon or sarcolemma (p. 353).

specialized to perform specific functions. Both divisions have *somatic* and *visceral* components. The afferent division carries information from **somatic** sensory receptors, which monitor skeletal muscles, joints, and the skin, and from **visceral** sensory receptors, which monitor other internal tissues such as smooth muscle, cardiac muscle, and glands. The afferent division also delivers information provided by special sense organs, such as the eye and ear. The efferent division includes the **somatic nervous system (SNS)**, which controls skeletal muscle contractions, and the **autonomic nervous system (ANS)**, or *visceral motor system*, which regulates smooth muscle, cardiac muscle, and glandular activity.

The activities of the somatic nervous system may be *voluntary* or *involuntary*. Voluntary contractions of our skeletal muscles are under conscious control; you exert voluntary control over your arm muscles as you raise a full glass of water to your lips. Involuntary contractions are directed outside your awareness; if you accidentally place your hand on a hot stove, it will be withdrawn immediately, usually before you even notice the pain. The activities of the autonomic nervous system are usually outside our awareness or control.

The organs of the CNS and PNS are complex, with numerous blood vessels and layers of connective tissue that provide physical protection and mechanical support. Nevertheless, all of the varied and essential functions of the nervous system are performed by individual neurons that must be kept safe, secure, and fully functional. Our discussion of the nervous system will begin at the cellular level, with the histology of neural tissue.

Cellular Organization in Neural Tissue [Figure 13.3]

Neural tissue contains two distinct cell types: nerve cells, or *neurons*, and supporting cells, or *neuroglia*. **Neurons** (*neuro*, nerve) are responsible for the transfer and processing of information in the nervous system. Neuron structure was

Figure 13.2 A Functional Overview of the Nervous System
This diagram shows the relationship between the CNS and PNS and the functions and components of the afferent and efferent divisions.

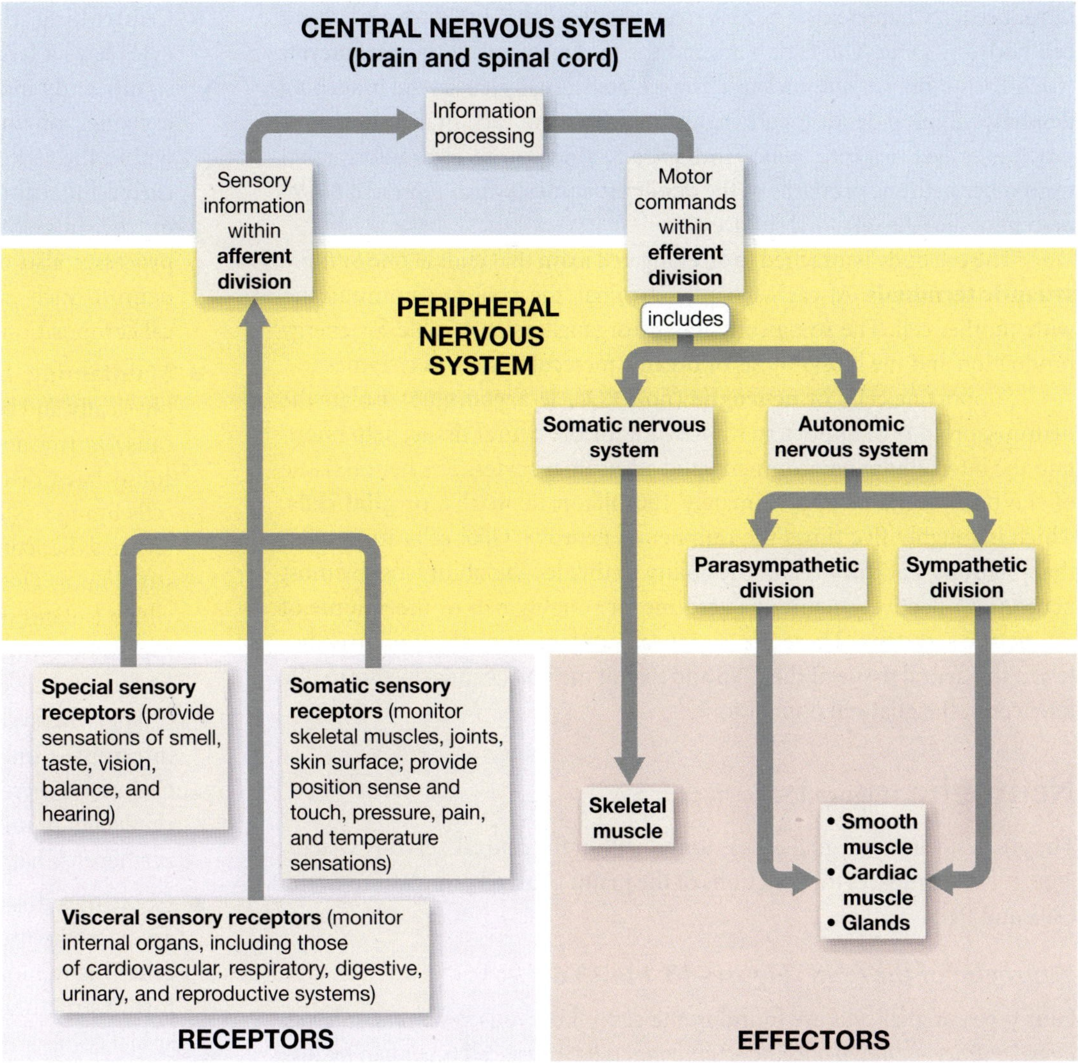

Clinical Note

The Symptoms of Neurological Disorders When homeostatic regulatory mechanisms break down under the stress of genetic or environmental factors, infection, or trauma, symptoms of neurological disorders appear. Because the nervous system has varied and complex functions, the symptoms of neurological disorders are equally diverse. However, a few symptoms accompany a wide variety of disorders:

- Headache seems to be a universal experience, with 70 percent of people reporting at least one headache each year. Almost everyone has experienced a headache at one time or another. Most headaches do not merit a visit to a neurologist. The majority are *tension-type headaches* with moderate pain that is pressing or tightening, poorly localized, and thought to be due to muscle tension, such as tight neck muscles. The trigger for tension-type headaches probably involves a combination of factors, but sustained contractions of the neck and facial muscles are most commonly implicated. Tension headaches can last for days or can occur daily over longer periods. Some tension headaches may accompany severe depression or anxiety. Tension-type headaches do not have the associated features that define *migraine headaches*: throbbing, often unilateral severe pain, light sensitivity, and nausa or vomiting. Migraine headaches have both neurological and cardiovascular origins. These conditions are rarely associated with life-threatening problems. Other headaches develop secondarily due to the following problems:
  1. CNS disorders, such as infections (meningitis, encephalitis, rabies) or brain tumors
  2. Trauma, such as a blow to the head
  3. Cardiovascular disorders, such as a stroke
  4. Metabolic disturbances, such as low blood sugar
- **Muscle weakness.** Muscle weakness can have an underlying neurological basis. The examiner must determine the primary cause of the symptom to select the most effective treatment. Myopathies (muscle disease) must be differentiated from neurological diseases such as demyelinating disorders, neuromuscular synapse dysfunction, and peripheral nerve damage.
- **Paresthesias.** Loss of feeling, numbness, or tingling sensations may develop after damage to (1) a sensory nerve (cranial or spinal nerve) or (2) sensory pathways in the central nervous system (CNS). The effects can be temporary or permanent. For example, *pressure palsy* may last a few minutes, whereas the paresthesia that develops distal to an area of severe spinal cord damage will probably be permanent.

introduced in Chapter 3. p. 77 A representative neuron (Figure 13.3) has a **cell body,** or *soma.* The region around the nucleus is called the **perikaryon** (per-i-KAR-ē-on; *karyon,* nucleus). The cell body usually has several branching **dendrites.** Typical dendrites are highly branched, and each branch bears fine processes called *dendritic spines.* In the CNS, a neuron receives information from other neurons primarily at the **dendritic spines,** which represent 80–90 percent of the neuron's total surface area.

The cell body is attached to an elongated **axon** that ends at one or more **synaptic terminals.** At each synaptic terminal, the neuron communicates with another cell. The soma contains the organelles responsible for energy production and the biosynthesis of organic molecules, such as enzymes.

Supporting cells, or **neuroglia** (noo-ROG-lē-a; *glia,* glue), isolate the neurons, provide a supporting framework for the neural tissue, help maintain the intercellular environment, and act as phagocytes. The neural tissue of the body contains approximately 100 billion neuroglia, or **glial cells,** which is roughly five times the number of neurons. Glial cells are smaller than neurons, and they retain the ability to divide—an ability lost by most neurons. Collectively, neuroglia account for roughly half of the volume of the nervous system. There are significant organizational differences between the neural tissue of the CNS and that of the PNS, primarily due to differences in the glial cell populations.

Neuroglia [Figure 13.4]

The greatest variety of glial cells is found within the central nervous system. Figure 13.4 compares the functions of the major glial cell populations in the CNS and PNS.

Neuroglia of the CNS [Figures 13.4 to 13.6]

Four types of glial cells are found in the central nervous system: *astrocytes, oligodendrocytes, microglia,* and *ependymal cells.* These cell types can be distinguished on the basis of size, intracellular organization, and the presence of specific cytoplasmic processes (Figures 13.4 to 13.6).

Astrocytes [Figures 13.4/13.5] The largest and most numerous glial cells are the **astrocytes** (AS-trō-sīts; *astro-,* star + *cyte,* cell) (Figures 13.4 and 13.5). Astrocytes have a variety of functions, but many are poorly understood. These functions can be summarized as follows:

- **Controlling the interstitial environment:** Structurally, astrocytes have a large number of cytoplasmic processes. These processes significantly increase the surface area of the cell, which facilitates the exchange of ions and other molecules with the extracellular fluid within the CNS. This exchange of ions and other molecules with the extracellular fluid enables astrocytes to control the chemical content of the interstitial environment of the CNS. These cytoplasmic processes also contact neuronal surfaces, often enclosing the entire neuron. Such enclosures isolate neurons from changes in the chemical composition of the interstitial space within the CNS.
- **Maintaining the blood–brain barrier:** Neural tissue must be physically and biochemically isolated from the general circulation because hormones or other chemicals normally present in the blood could have disruptive effects on neuron function. The endothelial cells lining CNS capillaries have very restricted permeability characteristics that control the chemical exchange between blood and interstitial fluid. They are responsible for the **blood–brain barrier (BBB),** which isolates the CNS from the general circulation. Many of the cytoplasmic processes of astrocytes, termed astrocyte "feet," contact the surface and cover most of the surface of the capillaries within the central nervous system. This cytoplasmic blanket around the capillaries is interrupted only where other glial cells contact the capillary walls. Chemicals secreted by astrocytes are essential for the *maintenance of the blood–brain barrier.* (The blood–brain barrier will be discussed further in Chapter 15.)
- **Creating a three-dimensional framework for the CNS:** Astrocytes are packed with microfilaments that extend across the breadth of the cell. This reinforcement provides mechanical strength, and astrocytes form a structural framework that supports the neurons of the brain and spinal cord.
- **Performing repairs in damaged neural tissue:** After damage to the CNS, astrocytes make structural repairs that stabilize the tissue and prevent further injury by producing scar tissue at the injury site.
- **Guiding neuron development:** In the embryonic brain, astrocytes appear to be involved in directing the growth and interconnection of developing neurons through the secretion of chemicals known as *neurotropic factors.*

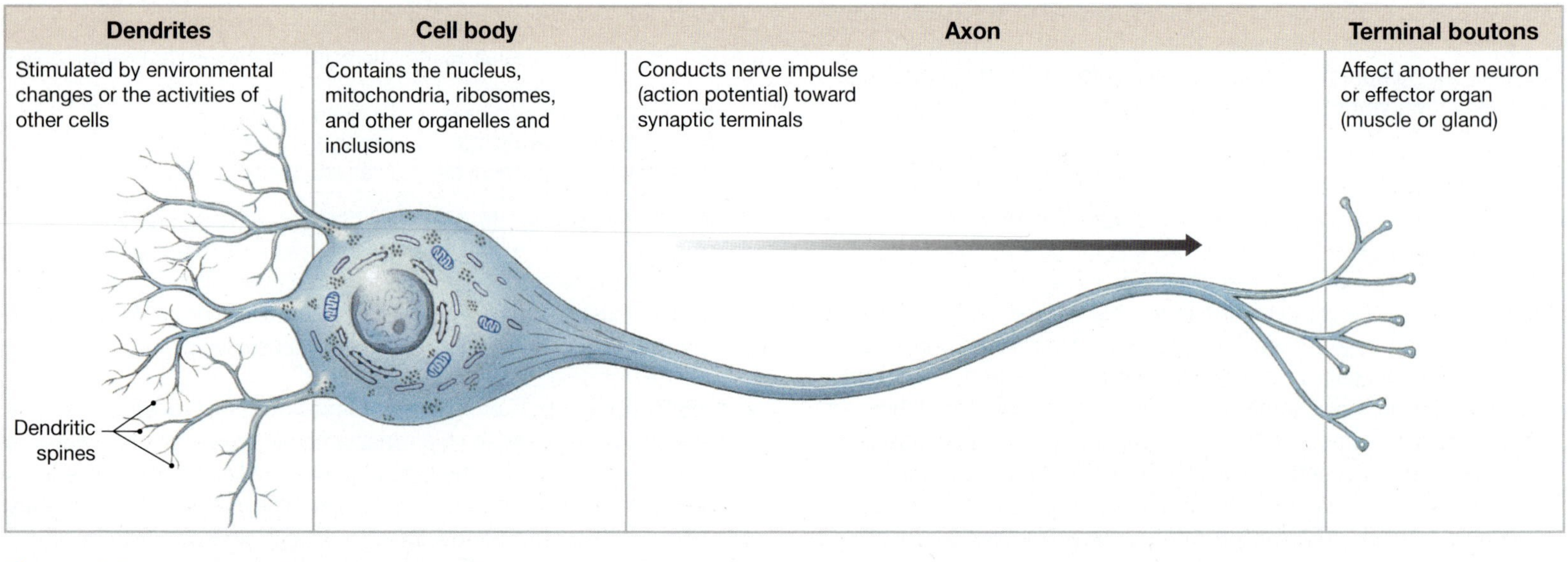

Figure 13.3 A Review of Neuron Structure
The relationship of the four parts of a neuron (dendrites, cell body, axon, and synaptic terminals); the functional activities of each part and the normal direction of action potential conduction are shown.

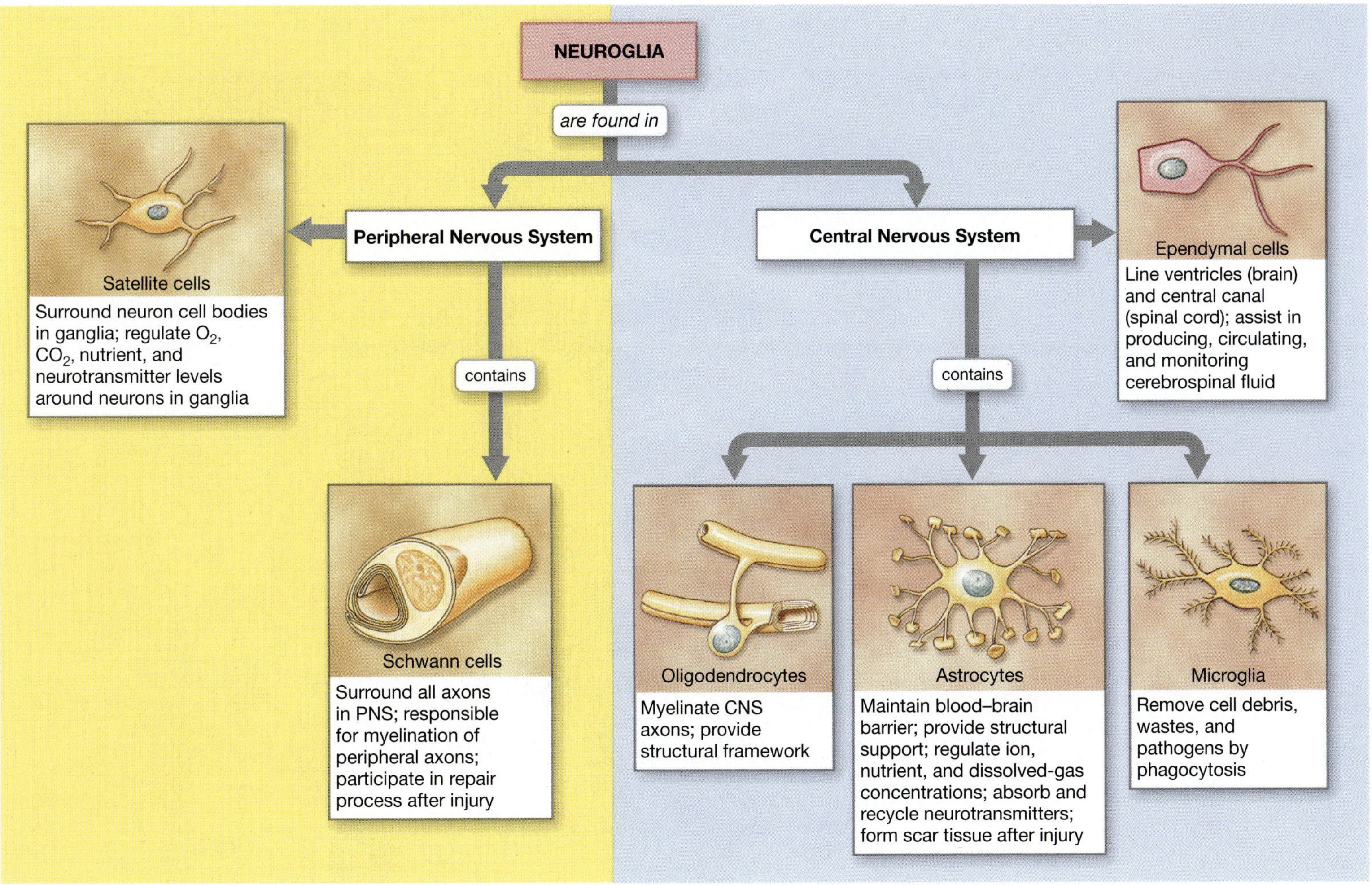

Figure 13.4 The Classification of Neuroglia
The categories and functions of the various glial cell types are summarized in this flowchart.

Oligodendrocytes [Figures 13.4/13.5] A second glial cell found within the CNS is the **oligodendrocyte** (ōl-i-gō-DEN-drō-sīt; *oligo*, few). This cell resembles an astrocyte only in that they both possess slender cytoplasmic extensions. However, oligodendrocytes have smaller cell bodies and fewer and shorter cytoplasmic processes (Figures 13.4 and 13.5). Oligodendrocyte processes usually contact the axons or cell bodies of neurons. Oligodendrocyte processes tie clusters of axons together and improve the functional performance of neurons by wrapping axons in *myelin*, a material with insulating properties. The functions of processes ending at the cell bodies have yet to be determined.

Many axons in the CNS are completely sheathed by the processes of oligodendrocytes. Near the tip of each process, the plasmalemma expands to form a flattened pad that wraps around the axon (Figure 13.5). This creates a multilayered membrane sheath composed primarily of phospholipids. This membranous coating is called **myelin** (MĪ-e-lin), and the axon is said to be **myelinated**. Myelin improves the speed at which an action potential, or *nerve impulse*, is conducted along an axon. Not all axons in the CNS are myelinated. In the CNS, **unmyelinated** axons may be incompletely covered by glial oligodendrocyte processes.

Many oligodendrocytes cooperate in the formation of the myelin sheath along the entire length of a myelinated axon. The relatively large areas wrapped in myelin are called **internodes** (*inter*, between). Small gaps, called **myelin sheath gaps**, or the *nodes of Ranvier* (rahn-vē-Ā), exist between the myelin sheaths produced by adjacent oligodendrocytes. When dissected, myelinated axons appear a glossy white, primarily because of the lipids present. Regions dominated by myelinated axons constitute the **white matter** of the CNS. In contrast, regions dominated by neuron cell bodies, dendrites, and unmyelinated axons are called **gray matter** because of their dusky gray color.

Microglia [Figures 13.4/13.5] The smallest of the glial cells possess slender cytoplasmic processes with many fine branches (Figures 13.4 and 13.5). These cells, called **microglia** (mī-KRŌ-glē-a), appear early in embryonic development through the division of mesodermal stem cells. The stem cells that produce microglia are related to those that produce tissue macrophages and monocytes of the blood. The microglia migrate into the CNS as it forms, and thereafter they remain within the neural tissue, acting as a roving security force. Microglia are the phagocytic cells of the CNS, engulfing cellular debris, waste products, and pathogens. In times of infection or injury, the number of microglia increases dramatically. Roughly 5 percent of the CNS glial cells are microglia, but in times of infection or injury this percentage increases dramatically.

Ependymal Cells [Figures 13.4/13.5/13.6] The ventricles of the brain and central canal of the spinal cord are lined by a cellular layer called the **ependyma** (ep-EN-di-mah) (Figures 13.4 and 13.5). These chambers and passageways are filled with **cerebrospinal fluid (CSF)**. This fluid, which also surrounds the brain and spinal cord, provides a protective cushion and transports dissolved gases, nutrients, wastes, and other materials. The composition, formation, and circulation of CSF will be discussed in Chapter 15.

Ependymal cells are cuboidal to columnar in form. Unlike typical epithelial cells, ependymal cells have slender processes that branch extensively

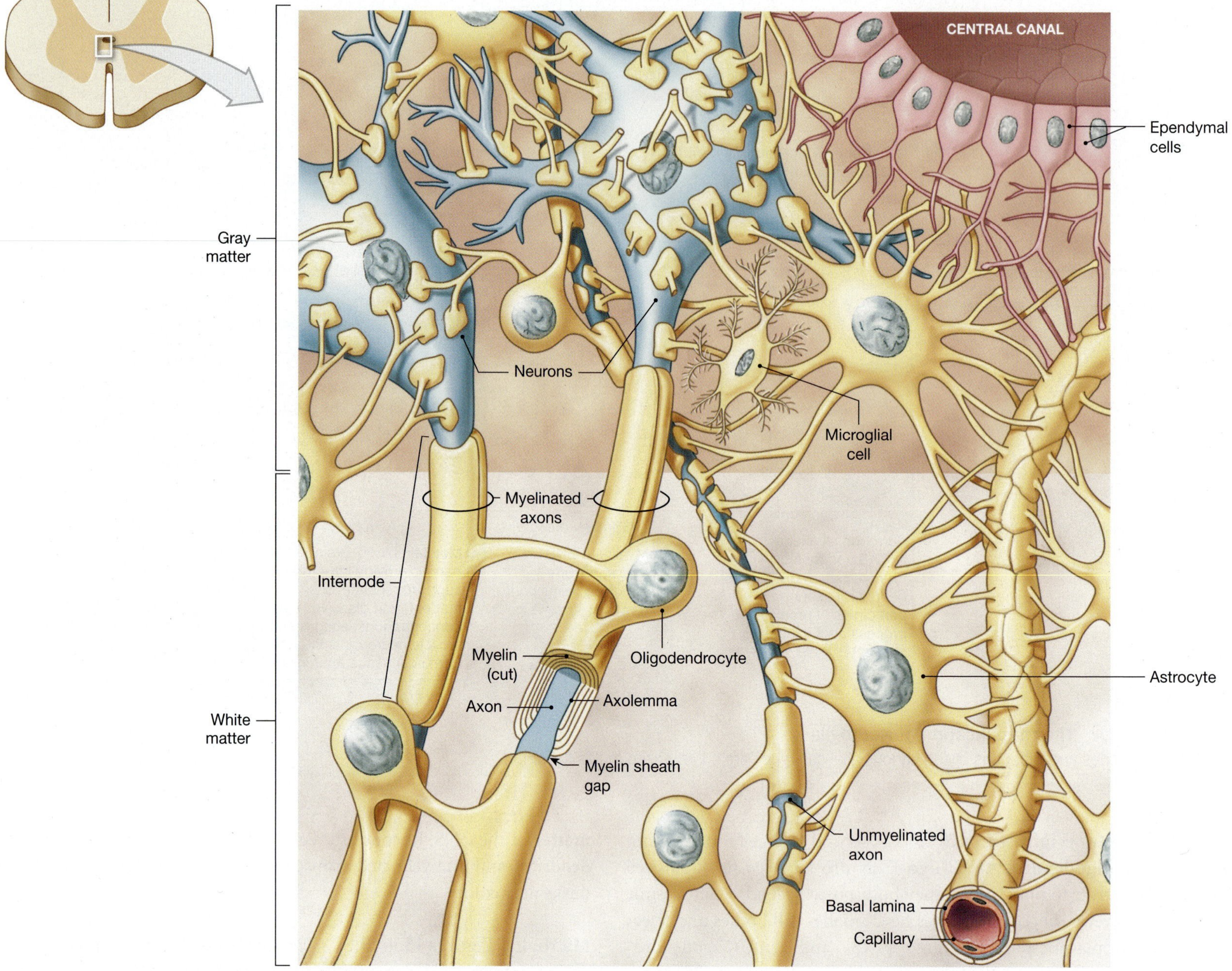

Figure 13.5 Histology of Neural Tissue in the CNS
A diagrammatic view of neural tissue in the spinal cord, showing relationships between neurons and glial cells.

and make direct contact with glial cells in the surrounding neural tissue (Figure 13.6a). Experimental evidence suggests that ependymal cells may act as receptors that monitor the composition of the CSF. During development and early childhood, the free surfaces of ependymal cells are covered with cilia. In the adult, cilia may persist on ependymal cells lining the ventricles of the brain (Figure 13.6b), but the ependyma elsewhere usually has only scattered microvilli. Ciliated ependymal cells may assist in the circulation of CSF. Within the ventricles, specialized ependymal cells participate in the secretion of cerebrospinal fluid.

Neuroglia of the PNS

Neuron cell bodies in the PNS are usually clustered together in masses called **ganglia** (singular, *ganglion*). Axons are bundled together and wrapped in connective tissue, forming **peripheral nerves**, or simply *nerves*. All neuron cell bodies and axons in the PNS are completely insulated from their surroundings by the processes of glial cells. The two glial cell types involved are called *satellite cells* and *Schwann cells*.

Satellite Cells [Figure 13.7] Neuron cell bodies in peripheral ganglia are surrounded by **satellite cells** (Figure 13.7). Satellite cells regulate the exchange of nutrients and waste products between the neuron cell body and the extracellular fluid. They also help isolate the neuron from stimuli other than those provided at synapses.

Schwann Cells [Figures 13.4/13.8] Every peripheral axon, whether it is unmyelinated or myelinated, is covered by **Schwann cells**, or *neurolemmocytes*. The plasmalemma of an axon is called the **axolemma** (*lemma*, husk); the superficial cytoplasmic covering provided by the Schwann

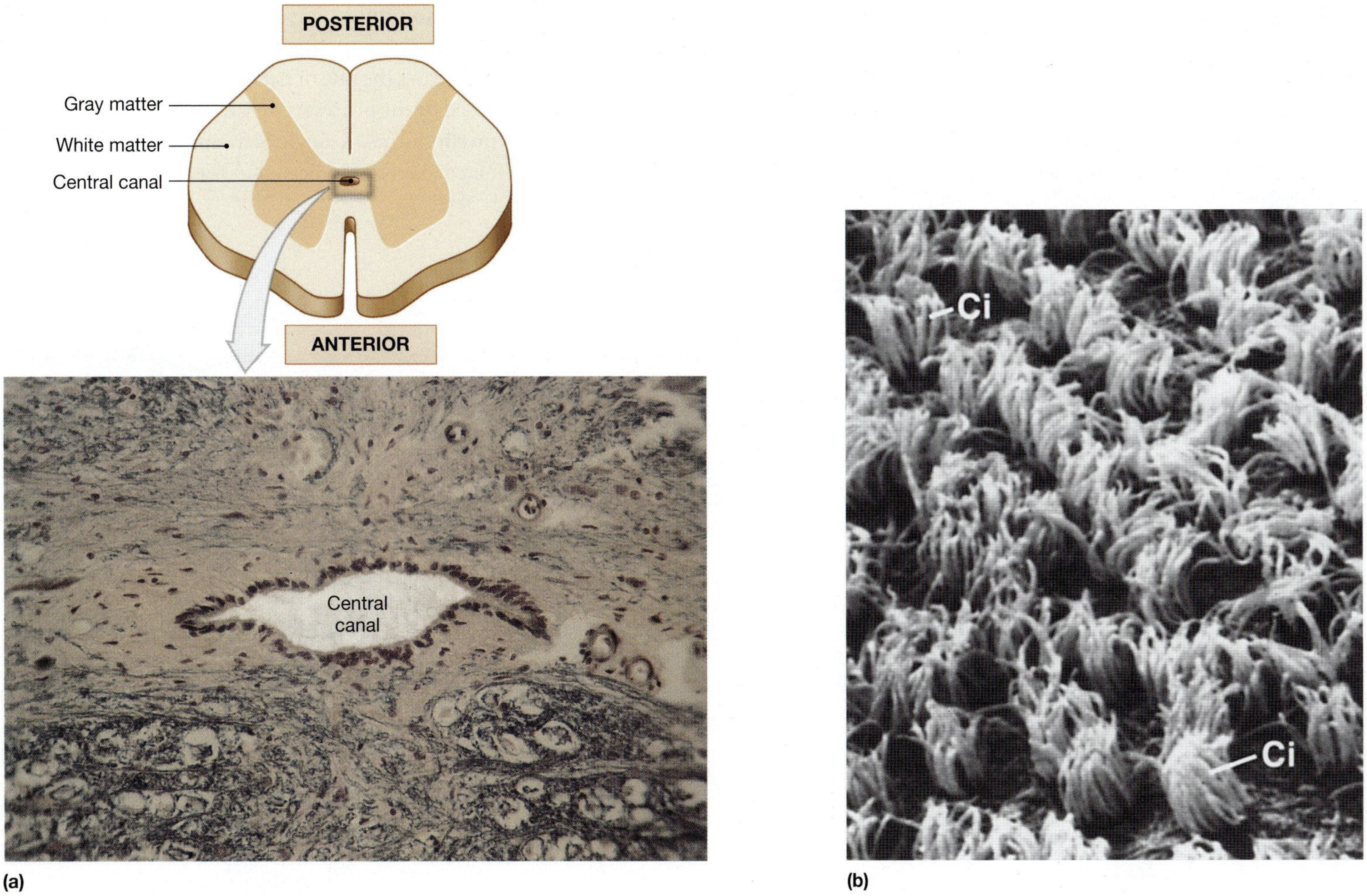

Figure 13.6 The Ependyma
The ependyma is a cellular layer that lines brain ventricles and the central canal of the spinal cord. **(a)** Light micrograph showing the ependymal lining of the central canal. (LM × 257) The diagrammatic view of ependymal organization is based on information provided by electron microscopy. **(b)** An SEM of the ciliated surface of the ependyma from one of the ventricles. (Ci = cilia; SEM × 1825) [© R. G. Kessel and R. H. Kardon, "Tissues and Organs: A Text-Atlas of Scanning Electron Microscopy," W. H. Freeman & Co., 1979. All Rights Reserved.]

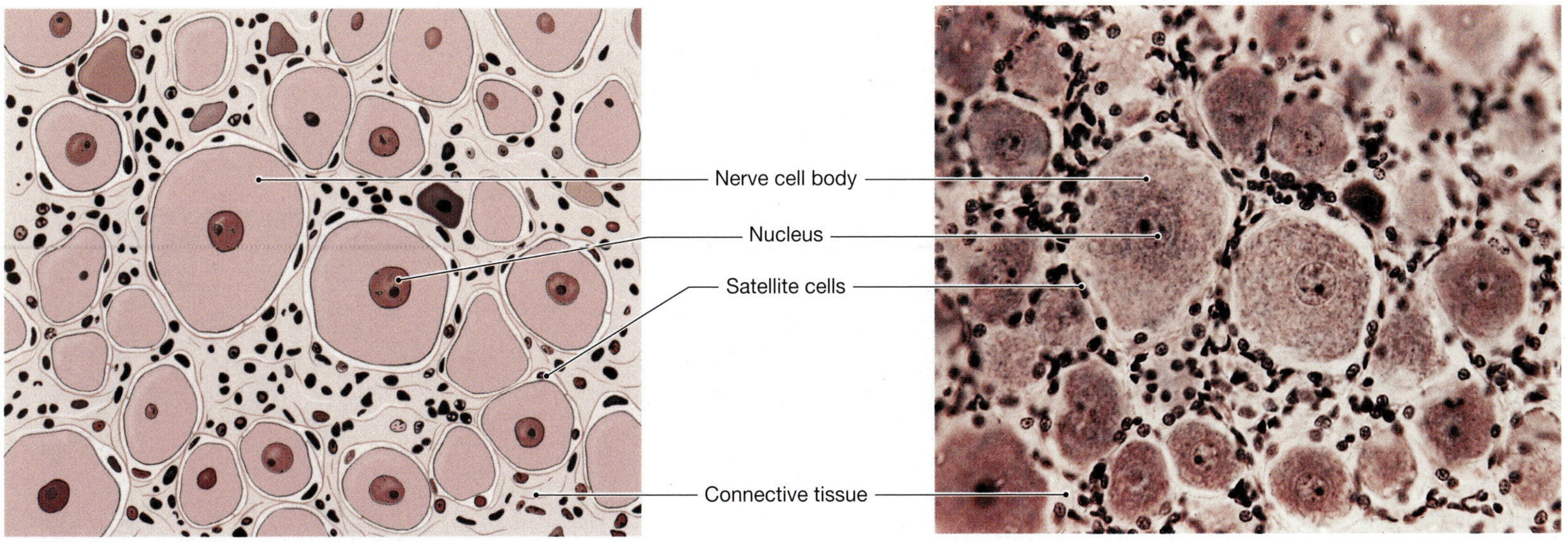

Figure 13.7 Satellite Cells and Peripheral Neurons
Satellite cells surround neuron cell bodies in peripheral ganglia. (LM × 20)

cells is known as the **neurilemma** (noor-i-LEM-a). The physical relationship between a Schwann cell and a myelinated peripheral axon differs from that of an oligodendrocyte and a myelinated axon in the CNS. A Schwann cell can myelinate only about 1 mm along the length of a single axon. In contrast, an oligodendrocyte can myelinate portions of several axons (compare Schwann cells, **Figure 13.8a**, with oligodendrocytes, **Figure 13.5**, p. 346). Although the mechanism of myelination differs, myelinated axons in both the CNS and PNS have myelin sheath gaps and internodes, and the presence of myelin—however formed—increases the rate of nerve impulse conduction. Unmyelinated axons are enclosed by the processes of Schwann cells, but the relationship is simple and no myelin forms. A single Schwann cell may surround several different unmyelinated axons, as indicated in **Figure 13.8b**.

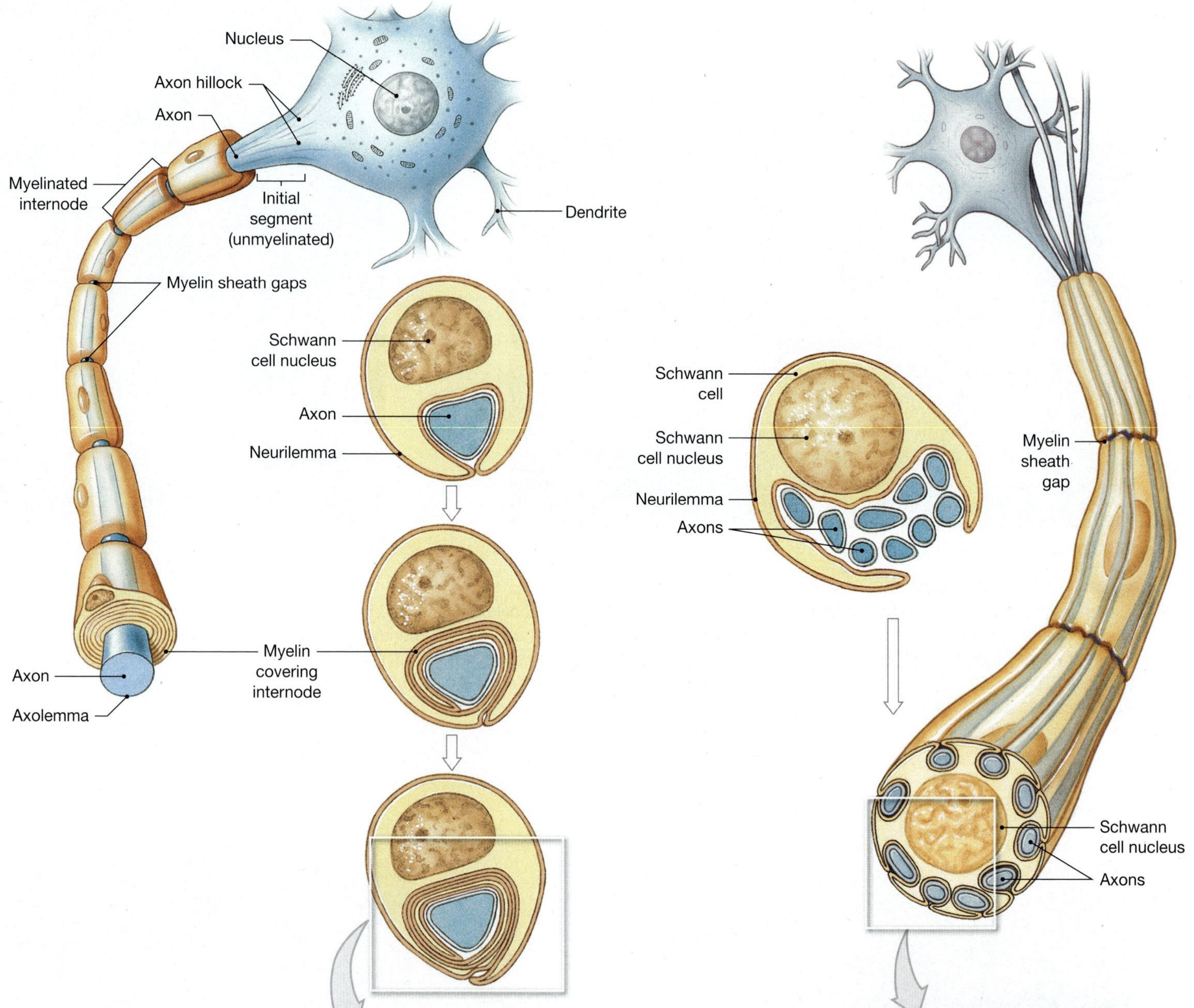

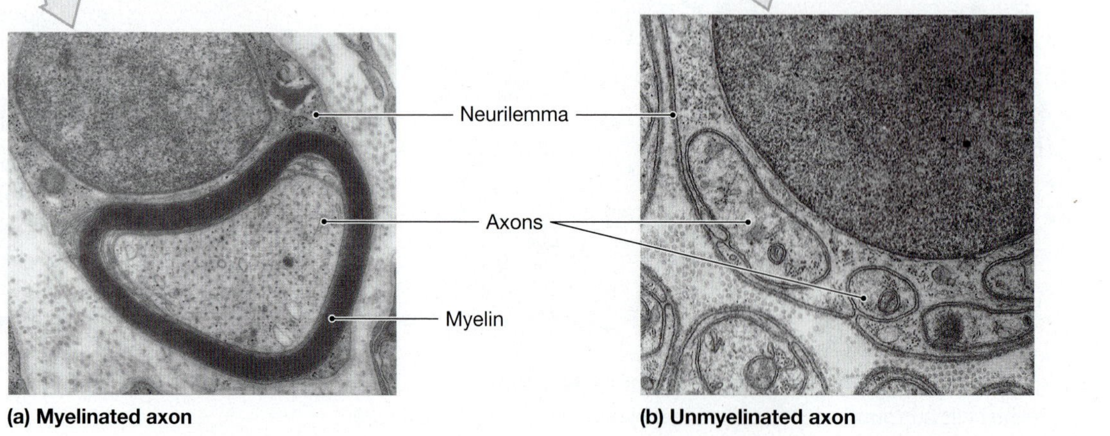

Figure 13.8 Schwann Cells and Peripheral Axons
Schwann cells ensheath every peripheral axon. **(a)** A single Schwann cell forms the myelin sheath around a portion of a single axon. This situation differs from the way myelin forms inside the CNS. *Compare with Figure 13.5*. (TEM × 20,603) **(b)** A single Schwann cell can encircle several unmyelinated axons. Unlike the situation inside the CNS, every axon in the PNS has a complete neurilemmal sheath. (LM × 27,627)

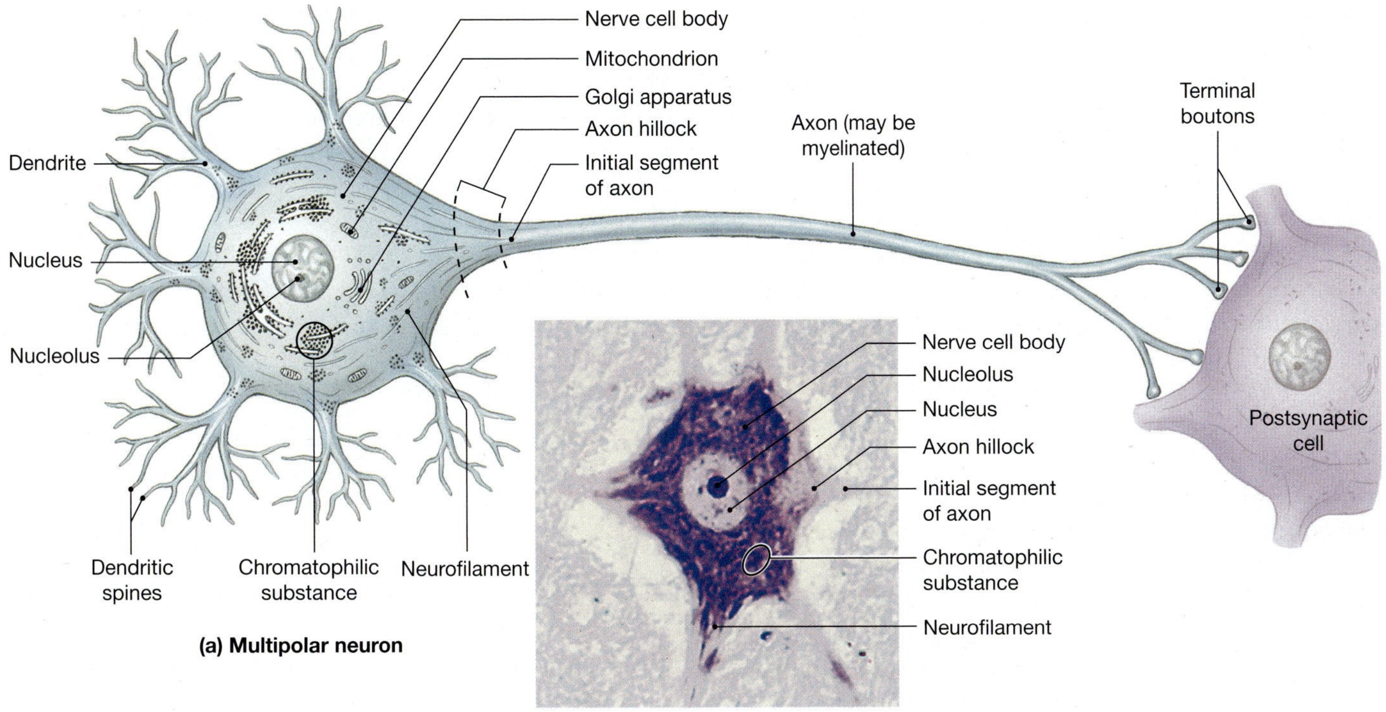

CONCEPT CHECK

1. Identify the two anatomical subdivisions of the nervous system.
2. What two terms are used to refer to the supporting cells in neural tissue?
3. Specifically, what cells help maintain the blood–brain barrier?
4. What is the name of the membranous coating formed around axons by oligodendrocytes?
5. Identify the cells in the peripheral nervous system that form a covering around axons.

See blue "Answers" tab at back of book.

Neurons [Figure 13.9]

The cell body of a representative neuron contains a relatively large, round nucleus with a prominent nucleolus (Figure 13.9a). The surrounding cytoplasm constitutes the *perikaryon* (per-i-KAR-ē-on; *karyon*, nucleus). The cytoskeleton of the perikaryon contains **neurofilaments** and **neurotubules**. Bundles of neurofilaments, called **neurofibrils**, are cytoskeletal elements that extend into the dendrites and axon.

The perikaryon contains organelles that provide energy and perform biosynthetic activities. The numerous mitochondria, free and fixed ribosomes, and membranes of the rough endoplasmic reticulum (RER) give the perikaryon a coarse, grainy appearance. Mitochondria generate ATP to meet the high energy demands of an active neuron. The ribosomes and RER synthesize peptides and proteins. Groups of fixed and free ribosomes are present in large numbers. These ribosomal clusters are called *chromatophilic substance* or *Nissl bodies.* The chromatophilic substance accounts for the gray color of areas that contain neuron cell bodies—the *gray matter* seen in gross dissection of the brain or spinal cord.

Most neurons lack the *centrosome* complex. pp. 36–37 In other cells, the centrioles of the centrosome form the spindle fibers that move chromosomes during cell division. Neurons usually lose their centrioles during differentiation,

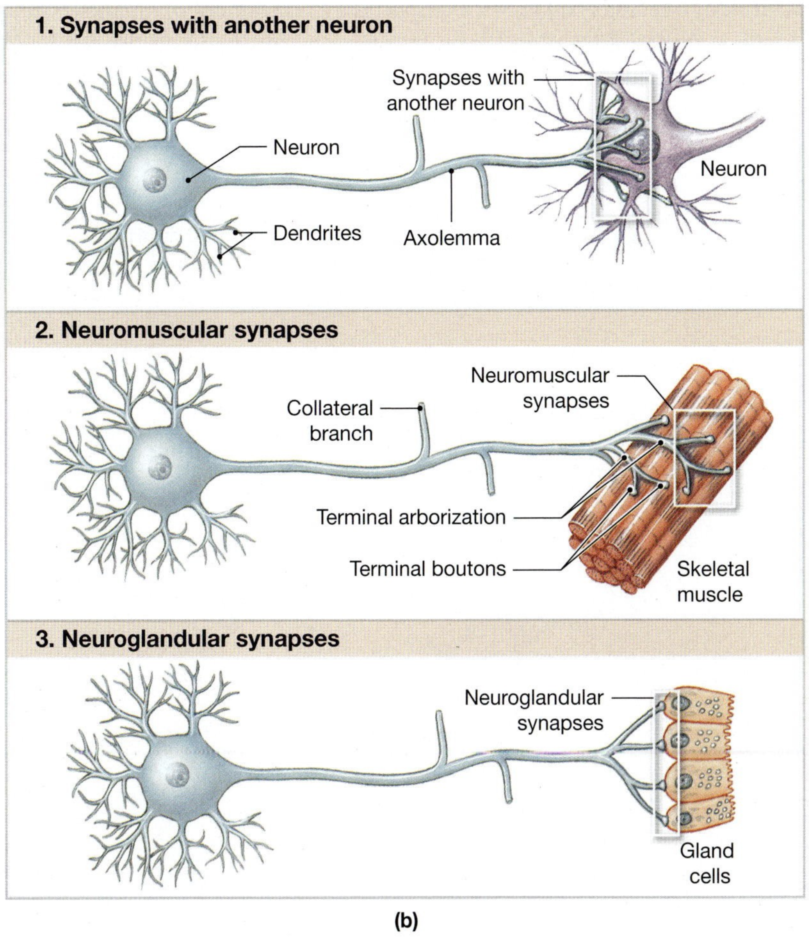

Figure 13.9 Anatomy of a Representative Neuron
A neuron has a cell body (soma), some branching dendrites, and a single axon. **(a)** Diagrammatic organization of the neuron. (LM × 1600) **(b)** A neuron may innervate (1) other neurons, (2) skeletal muscle fibers, or (3) gland cells. Synapses are shown in boxes for each example. A single neuron would not innervate all three.

and they become incapable of undergoing cell division. If these specialized neurons are later lost to injury or disease, they cannot be replaced.

The neurilemma permeability of the dendrites and cell body can be changed by exposure to chemical, mechanical, or electrical stimuli. One of the primary functions of glial cells is to limit the number or types of stimuli affecting individual neurons. Glial cell processes cover most of the surfaces of the cell body and dendrites, except where synaptic terminals exist or where dendrites function as sensory receptors, monitoring conditions in the extracellular environment. Exposure to appropriate stimuli can produce a localized change in the transmembrane potential and lead to the generation of an action potential at the axon. The *transmembrane potential* is a property resulting from the unequal distribution of ions across the neurilemma. We will examine transmembrane potentials and action potentials later in this chapter.

An axon, or *nerve fiber*, is a long cytoplasmic process capable of propagating an action potential. In a multipolar neuron, a specialized region, the **axon hillock**, connects the **initial segment** of the axon to the soma. The **axoplasm** (AK-sō-plazm), or cytoplasm of the axon, contains neurofibrils, neurotubules, numerous small vesicles, lysosomes, mitochondria, and various enzymes. An axon may branch along its length, producing side branches called **collaterals**. The main trunk and the collaterals end in a series of fine terminal extensions, called **terminal arborizations** or *telodendria* (tel-ō-DEN-drē-a; *telo-*, end + *dendron*, tree) (**Figure 13.9b**). The terminal arborizations end in a **synaptic terminal**, where the neuron contacts another neuron or effector. *Axoplasmic transport* is the movement of organelles, nutrients, synthesized molecules, and waste products between the cell body and the synaptic terminals. This is a complex process that consumes energy and relies on movement along the neurofibrils of the axon and its branches.

Each synaptic terminal is part of a **synapse**, a specialized site where the neuron communicates with another cell (**Figure 13.9b**). The structure of the synaptic terminal varies with the type of postsynaptic cell. A relatively simple, round **terminal bouton**, or *synaptic knob*, is found where one neuron synapses on another. The synaptic terminal found at a *neuromuscular synapse,* or *neuromuscular junction,* where a neuron contacts a skeletal muscle fiber, is much more complex. pp. 239, 246 Synaptic communication most often involves the release of specific chemicals called **neurotransmitters**. The release of these chemicals is triggered by the arrival of a nerve impulse; additional details are provided in a later section.

Neuron Classification

The billions of neurons in the nervous system are quite variable in form. Neurons may be classified based on (1) structure or (2) function.

Structural Classification of Neurons [Figure 13.10] The structural classification is based on the number of processes that project from the cell body (**Figure 13.10**).

- **Anaxonic** (an-ak-SON-ik) **neurons** are small, and there are no anatomical clues to distinguish dendrites from axons (**Figure 13.10a**). Anaxonic neurons are found only in the CNS and in special sense organs, and their functions are poorly understood.
- **Bipolar neurons** have a number of fine dendrites that fuse to form a single dendrite. The cell body lies between this dendrite and a single axon (**Figure 13.10b**). Bipolar neurons are relatively rare but play an important role in relaying sensory information concerning sight, smell, and hearing. Their axons are not myelinated.

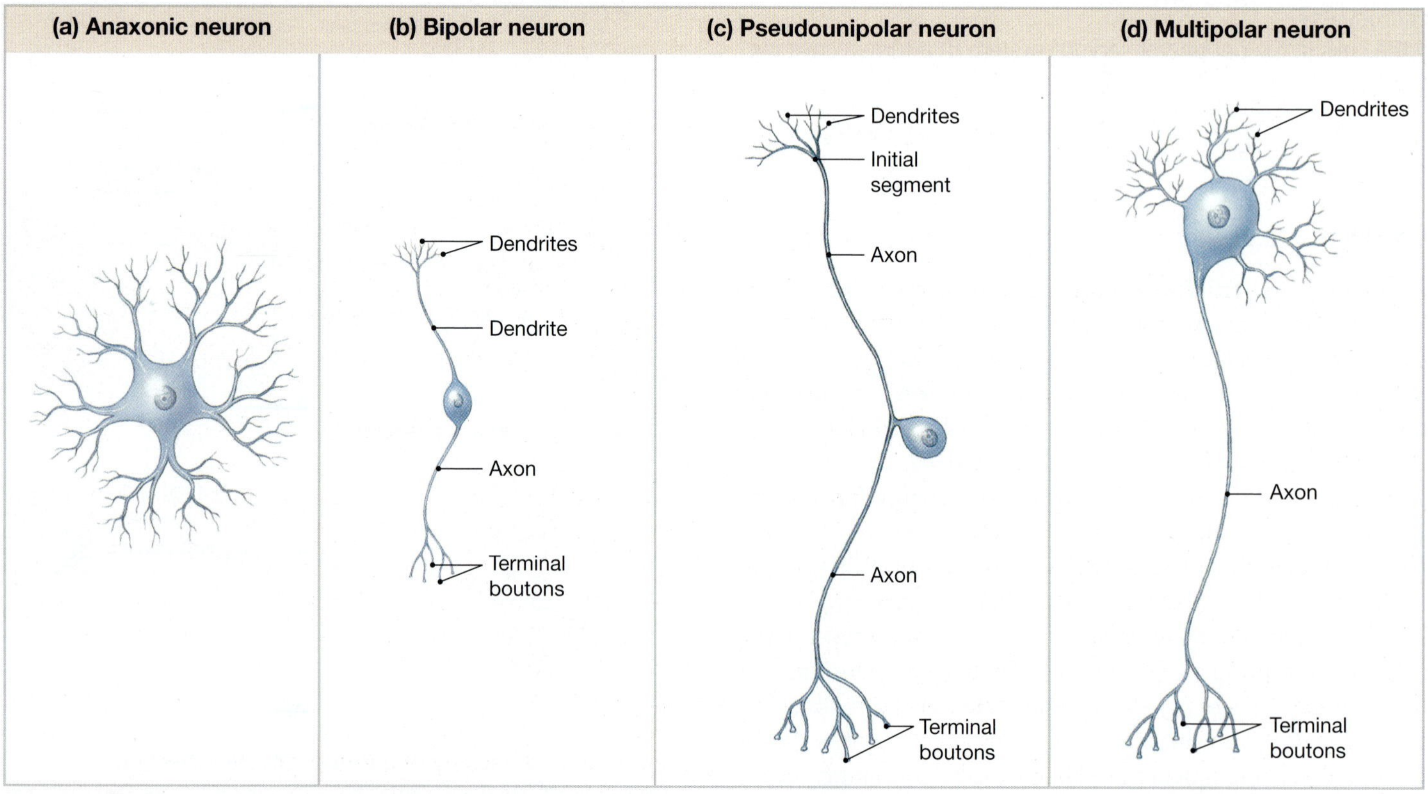

Figure 13.10 A Structural Classification of Neurons
This classification is based on the placement of the cell body and the number of associated processes. **(a)** Anaxonic neurons have more than two processes, but axons cannot be distinguished from dendrites. **(b)** Bipolar neurons have two processes separated by the cell body. **(c)** Pseudounipolar neurons have a single elongate process, with the cell body situated to one side. **(d)** Multipolar neurons have more than two processes; there is a single axon and multiple dendrites.

- **Pseudounipolar neurons** have continuous dendritic and axonal processes, and the cell body lies off to one side. In these neurons, the initial segment lies at the base of the dendritic branches (Figure 13.10c), and the rest of the process is considered an axon on both structural and functional grounds. Sensory neurons of the peripheral nervous system are usually pseudounipolar, and their axons may be myelinated.
- **Multipolar neurons** have several dendrites and a single axon that may have one or more branches (Figure 13.10d). Multipolar neurons are the most common type of neuron in the CNS. For example, all of the motor neurons that control skeletal muscles are multipolar neurons with myelinated axons.

Functional Classification of Neurons [Figure 13.11] Neurons can be categorized into three functional groups: (1) *sensory neurons*, (2) *motor neurons*, and (3) *interneurons*. Their relationships are diagrammed in Figure 13.11.

Almost all **sensory neurons** are pseudounipolar neurons with their cell bodies located outside the CNS in peripheral sensory ganglia. They form the *afferent division* of the PNS. Their function is to deliver information to the CNS. The axons of sensory neurons, called **afferent fibers**, extend between a sensory receptor and the spinal cord or brain. Sensory neurons collect information concerning the external or internal environment. There are about 10 million sensory neurons. **Somatic sensory neurons** transmit information about the outside world and our position within it. **Visceral sensory neurons** transmit information about internal conditions and the status of other organ systems.

Receptors may be either the processes of specialized sensory neurons or cells monitored by sensory neurons. Receptors are broadly categorized as follows:

- **Exteroceptors** (*extero-*, outside) provide information about the external environment in the form of touch, temperature, and pressure sensations and the more complex *special senses* of sight, smell, and hearing.
- **Proprioceptors** (prō-prē-ō-SEP-torz) monitor the position and movement of skeletal muscles and joints.
- **Interoceptors** (*intero-*, inside) monitor the digestive, respiratory, cardiovascular, urinary, and reproductive systems and provide sensations of deep pressure and pain as well as taste, another special sense.

Data from exteroceptors and proprioceptors are carried by somatic sensory neurons. Interoceptive information is carried by visceral sensory neurons.

Multipolar neurons that form the efferent division of the nervous system are **motor neurons**. A motor neuron stimulates or modifies the activity of a peripheral tissue, organ, or organ system. About half a million motor neurons are found in the body. Axons traveling away from the CNS are called **efferent fibers**. The two efferent divisions of the PNS—the somatic nervous system (SNS) and the autonomic nervous system (ANS)—differ in the way they innervate peripheral effectors. The SNS includes all of the somatic motor neurons that innervate skeletal muscles. The cell bodies of these motor neurons lie inside the CNS, and their axons extend to the neuromuscular synapses that control skeletal muscles. Most of the activities of the SNS are consciously controlled.

The autonomic nervous system includes all the **visceral motor neurons** that innervate peripheral effectors other than skeletal muscles. There are two groups of visceral motor neurons—one group has cell bodies inside the CNS, and the other has cell bodies in peripheral ganglia. The neurons inside the CNS control the neurons in the peripheral ganglia, and these neurons in turn control the peripheral effectors. Axons extending from the CNS to a ganglion are called **preganglionic fibers**. Axons connecting the ganglion cells with the peripheral effectors are known as **postganglionic fibers**. This arrangement clearly distinguishes the autonomic (visceral motor) system

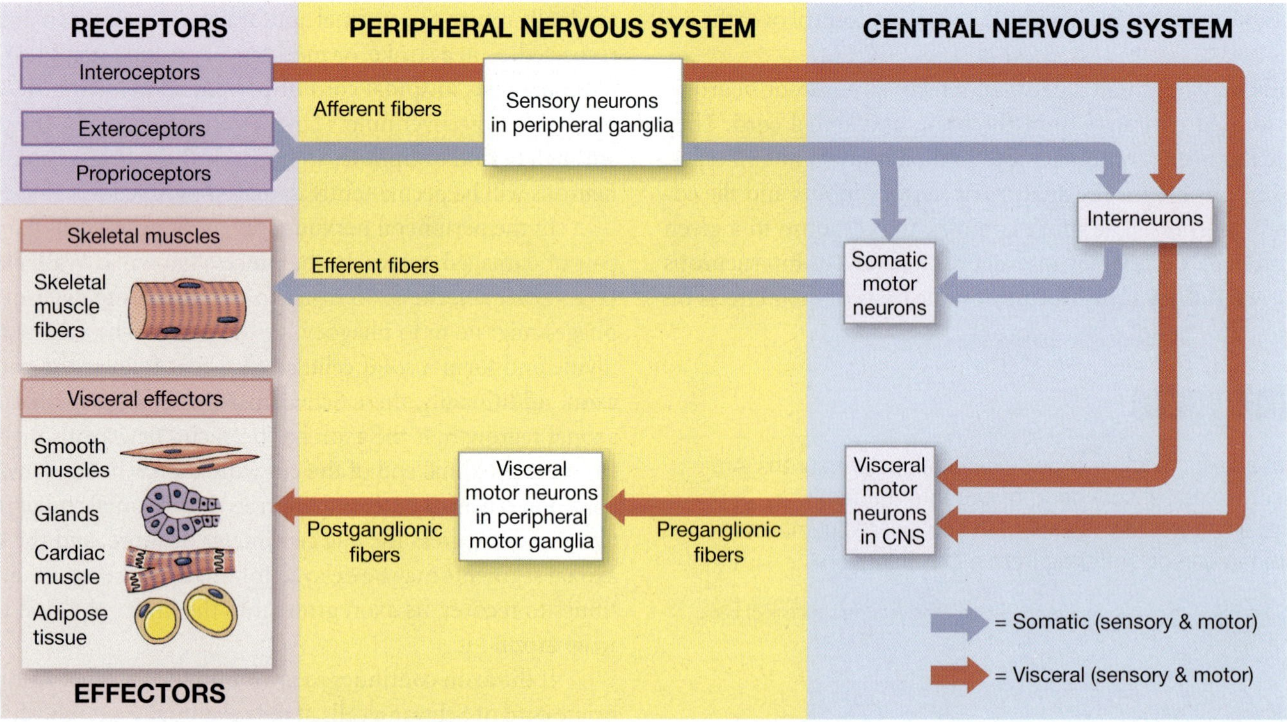

Figure 13.11 A Functional Classification of Neurons
Neurons are classified functionally into three categories: (1) sensory neurons that detect stimuli in the PNS and send information to the CNS, (2) motor neurons to carry instructions from the CNS to peripheral effectors, and (3) interneurons in the CNS that process sensory information and coordinate motor activity.

Clinical Note

Demyelination Disorders Demyelination disorders are linked by a common symptom: the destruction of myelinated axons in the CNS and peripheral nervous system (PNS). The mechanism responsible for this loss differs in each disorder. We will examine only the major categories:

- **Heavy-metal poisoning.** Chronic exposure to heavy-metal ions, such as arsenic, lead, and mercury, can lead to damage of neuroglia and to demyelination. As demyelination occurs, the affected axons deteriorate and the condition becomes irreversible. Historians note several examples of heavy-metal poisoning with widespread impact. For example, the contamination of drinking water with lead has been cited as one factor in the decline of the Roman Empire. Well into the 19th century, mercury used in the preparation of felt presented a serious occupational hazard for those employed in the manufacture of stylish hats. Over time, mercury absorbed through the skin and across the lungs accumulated in the CNS, producing neurological damage that affected both physical and mental functioning. (This effect is the source of the expression "mad as a hatter.") In the 1950s, Japanese fishermen and their families working in Minamata Bay, Japan, collected and consumed seafood contaminated with mercury discharged from a nearby chemical plant. Levels of mercury in their systems gradually rose to the point at which clinical symptoms appeared in hundreds of people. Pregnant women who consumed the mercury-contaminated fish had babies with severe, crippling birth defects. Less severe problems have affected children born to mothers in the midwestern United States who ate large amounts of fish during pregnancy. As a result, pregnant women are now advised to limit fish consumption. (For unknown reasons, the flesh of some species of fish contains relatively high levels of mercury.)
- **Diphtheria.** Diphtheria (dif-THĒ-rē-uh; *diphthera*, leather + *-ia*, disease) is a disease that results from a bacterial infection mainly of the respiratory tract and occasionally the skin. In the case of respiratory infections, in addition to restricting airflow and damaging the respiratory surfaces, the bacteria produce a powerful toxin that injures the kidneys and suprarenal glands, among other tissues. In the nervous system, diphtheria toxin damages Schwann cells and destroys myelin sheaths in the PNS. This demyelination leads to sensory and motor problems that can ultimately produce a fatal paralysis. The toxin also affects cardiac muscle cells by creating problems with the heart's conducting system. This causes permanent abnormal heartbeats, which may lead to heart failure. The fatality rate for untreated cases ranges from 35 to 90 percent, depending on the site of infection and the subspecies of bacterium. Because an effective vaccine (which is frequently combined with the tetanus vaccine) exists, cases are relatively rare in countries with adequate health care.
- **Multiple sclerosis.** Multiple sclerosis (skler-Ō-sis; *sklerosis*, hardness), or MS, is a disease characterized by recurrent incidents of demyelination that affects axons in the optic nerve, brain, and spinal cord. Common symptoms include partial loss of vision and problems with speech, balance, and general motor coordination, including bowel and urinary bladder control. The time between incidents and the degree of recovery vary from case to case. In about one-third of all cases, the disorder is progressive, and each incident leaves a greater degree of functional impairment. The average age at the first attack is 30–40 years; the incidence among women is 1.5 times that among men. In some patients, corticosteroid or interferon injections have slowed the progression of the disease.

from the somatic motor system. We have little conscious control over the activities of the ANS.

Interneurons may be situated between sensory and motor neurons. Interneurons are located entirely within the brain and spinal cord. They outnumber all other neurons combined both in total number and in types. Interneurons are responsible for the analysis of sensory inputs and the coordination of motor outputs. The more complex the response to a given stimulus, the greater the number of interneurons involved. Interneurons can be classified as **excitatory** or **inhibitory** on the basis of their effects on the postsynaptic membranes of other neurons.

CONCEPT CHECK

1. Examination of a tissue sample shows pseudounipolar neurons. Are these more likely to be sensory neurons or motor neurons?
2. What type of glial cell would you expect to find in large numbers in brain tissue from a person suffering from a CNS infection?

See blue "Answers" tab at back of book.

Neural Regeneration [Figure 13.12]

A neuron has a very limited ability to recover after an injury. Within the cell body, the chromatophilic substance disappears and the nucleus moves away from its centralized location. If the neuron regains normal function, it will gradually return to a normal appearance. If the oxygen or nutrient supply is restricted, as in a stroke, or mechanical pressure is applied to the neuron, as often happens in spinal cord or peripheral nerve injuries, the neuron may be unable to recover unless circulation is restored or the pressure removed within a period of minutes to hours. If these stresses continue, the affected neurons will be permanently damaged or killed.

In the peripheral nervous system, Schwann cells participate in the repair of damaged nerves. In the process known as **Wallerian degeneration** (Figure 13.12), the axon distal to the injury site deteriorates, and macrophages migrate in to phagocytize the debris. The Schwann cells in the area divide and form a solid cellular cord that follows the path of the original axon. Additionally, these Schwann cells release growth factors to promote axonal regrowth. If the axon has been cut, new axons may begin to emerge from the proximal end of the cut within a few hours. However, in the more common crushing or tearing injuries the proximal end of the damaged axon will die and regress for one centimeter or more, and the sprouting of new axonal segments may be delayed for one or more weeks. As the neuron continues to recover, its axon grows into the injury site, and the Schwann cells wrap around it.

If the axon continues to grow into the periphery alongside the appropriate cord of Schwann cells, it may eventually reestablish its normal synaptic contacts. If it stops growing, or wanders off in some new direction, normal function will not return. The growing axon is most likely to arrive at its appropriate destination if the damaged proximal and distal stumps remain in contact after the injury. When an entire peripheral nerve is dam-

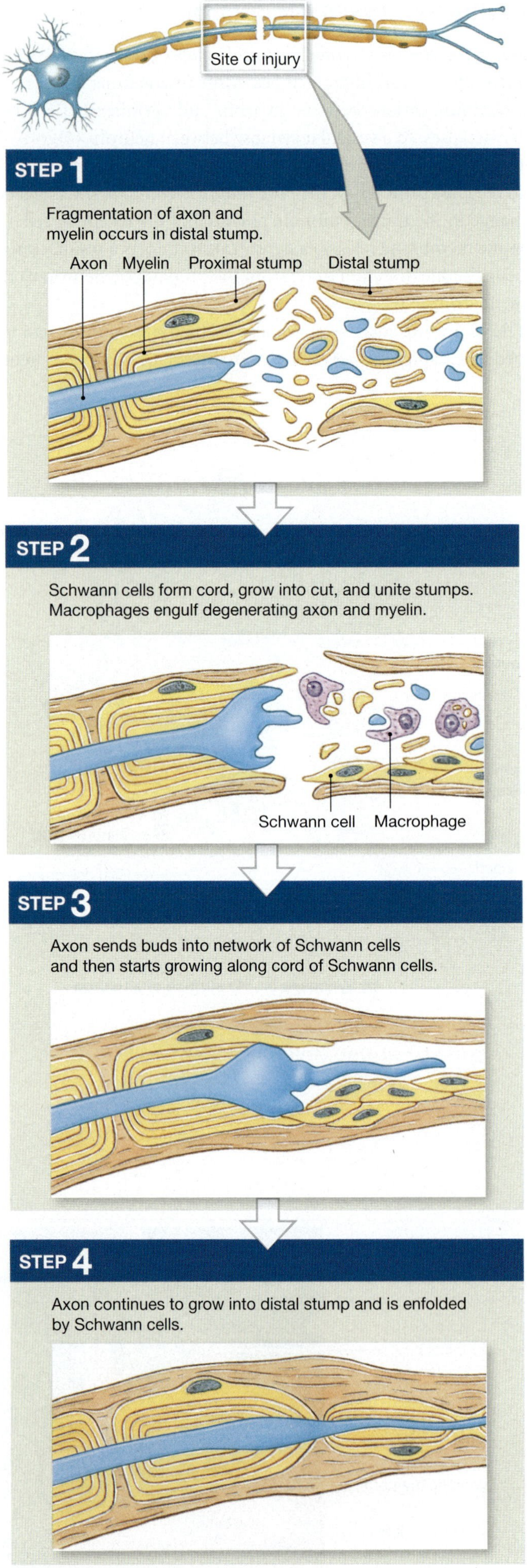

Figure 13.12 Nerve Regeneration after Injury
Steps involved in the repair of a peripheral nerve by the process of Wallerian degeneration.

aged, only a relatively small number of axons will successfully reestablish normal synaptic contacts. As a result, nerve function will be permanently impaired.

Limited regeneration can occur inside the central nervous system, but the situation is more complicated because (1) many more axons are likely to be involved, (2) astrocytes produce scar tissue that can prevent axon growth across the damaged area, and (3) astrocytes release chemicals that block the regrowth of axons. Additional information concerning neural regeneration and surgical repairs will be presented in the next chapter.

The Nerve Impulse

Excitability is the ability of a plasmalemma to conduct electrical impulses. Plasmalemmae of skeletal muscle fibers, cardiac muscle cells, some gland cells, and the axolemma of most neurons (including all multipolar and pseudounipolar neurons) are examples of excitable membranes. An electrical impulse, or **action potential**, develops after the plasmalemma is stimulated to a level known as the *threshold*. After the threshold level has been reached, the membrane permeability to sodium and potassium ions changes. The ion movements that result produce a sudden change in the transmembrane potential, and this change constitutes an action potential. The permeability changes are temporary and initially confined to the point of stimulation. However, the change in ion distribution almost immediately triggers changes in the permeability of adjacent portions of the plasmalemma. In this way, the action potential is conducted along the membrane surface. For example, in a skeletal muscle fiber, action potentials begin at the neuromuscular synapse and sweep across the entire surface of the sarcolemma. p. 246 In the nervous system, action potentials traveling along axons are known as **nerve impulses**.

Before a nerve impulse can occur, a stimulus of sufficient strength must be applied to the membrane of the neuron. Once initiated, the rate of impulse conduction depends on the properties of the axon, specifically:

1. *The presence or absence of a myelin sheath:* A myelinated axon conducts impulses five to seven times faster than an unmyelinated axon.
2. *The diameter of the axon:* The larger the diameter, the more rapidly the impulse will be conducted.

The largest myelinated axons, with diameters ranging from 4 to 20 μm, conduct nerve impulses at speeds of up to 140 m/s (300 mph). In contrast, small unmyelinated fibers (less than 2 μm in diameter) conduct impulses at speeds below 1 m/s (2 mph).

CONCEPT CHECK

1. What effect would cutting the axon have on transmitting the action potential?
2. Two axons are tested for conduction velocities. One conducts action potentials at 50 m/s, the other at 1 m/s. Which axon is myelinated?
3. Define excitability.
4. What term is used to identify conducted changes in transmembrane potential?

See blue "Answers" tab at back of book.

Synaptic Communication [Figure 13.9b]

A synapse between neurons may involve a synaptic terminal and (1) a dendrite (*axodendritic*), (2) the cell body (*axosomatic*), or (3) an axon (*axoaxonic*). A synapse may also permit communication between a neuron and another cell type; such synapses are called **neuroeffector junctions**. The *neuromuscular synapse* described in Chapter 9 was an example of a neuroeffector junction. pp. 239, 246 Neuroeffector junctions involving other cell types are shown in Figure 13.9b, p. 349.

At a synaptic terminal, a nerve impulse triggers events at a synapse that transfers the information either to another neuron or to an effector cell. A synapse may be *chemical*, involving the passage of a neurotransmitter substance between cells, or *electrical*, with communicating (gap) junctions permitting ion flow between the cells. p. 44

Vesicular Synapses [Figure 13.13]

Vesicular synapses, also termed *chemical synapses*, are by far the most abundant; there are several different types. Most interactions between neurons and all communications between neurons and peripheral effectors involve vesicular synapses. At a vesicular synapse between neurons (Figure 13.13), a neurotransmitter released at the *presynaptic membrane* of a terminal bouton binds to receptor proteins on the *postsynaptic membrane* and triggers a transient change in the transmembrane potential of the receptive cell. Only the presynaptic membrane releases a neurotransmitter. As a result, communication occurs in one direction only: from the presynaptic neuron to the postsynaptic neuron.

The neuromuscular synapse, also termed a *neuromuscular junction*, described in Chapter 9 is a vesicular synapse that releases the neurotrans-

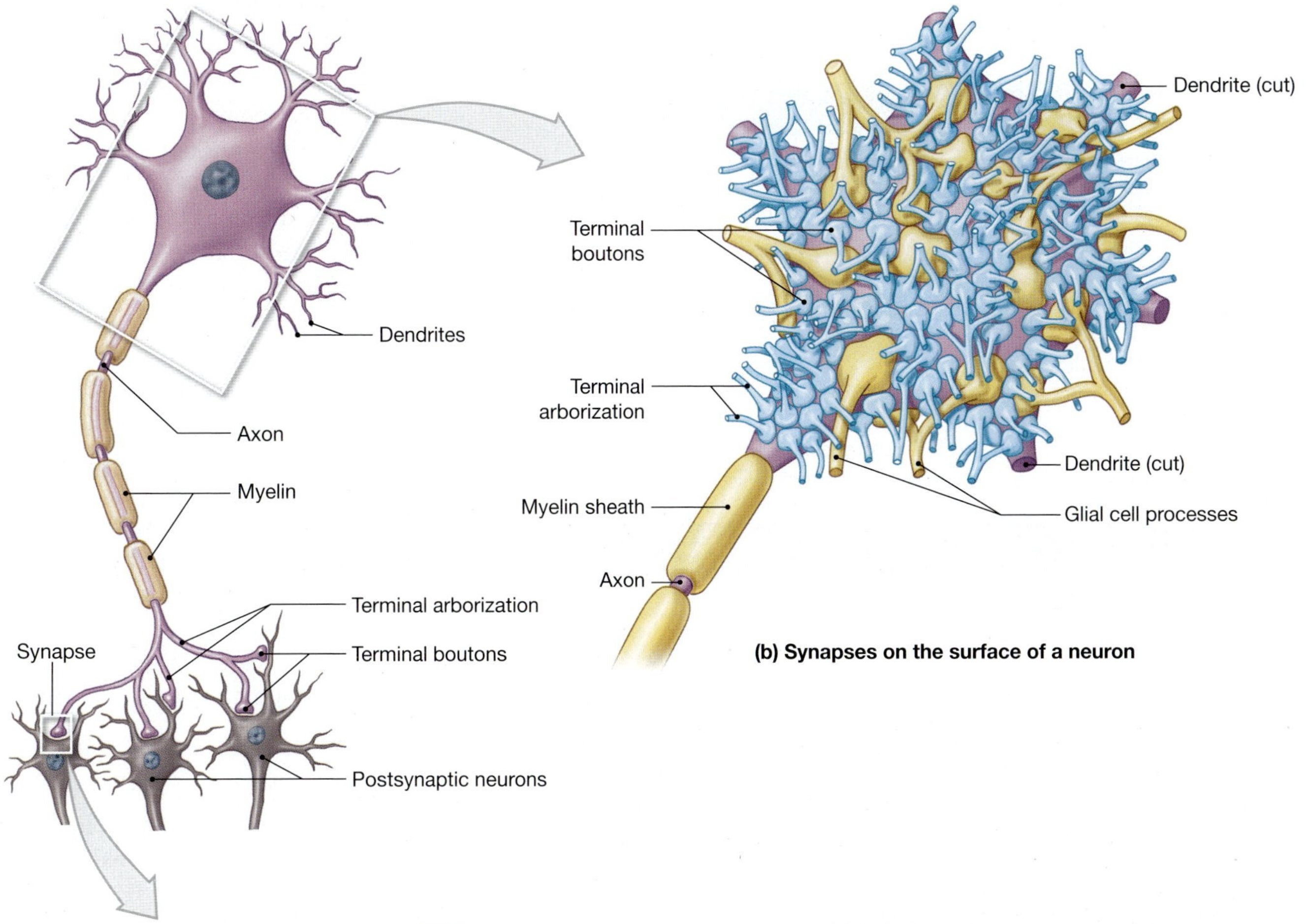

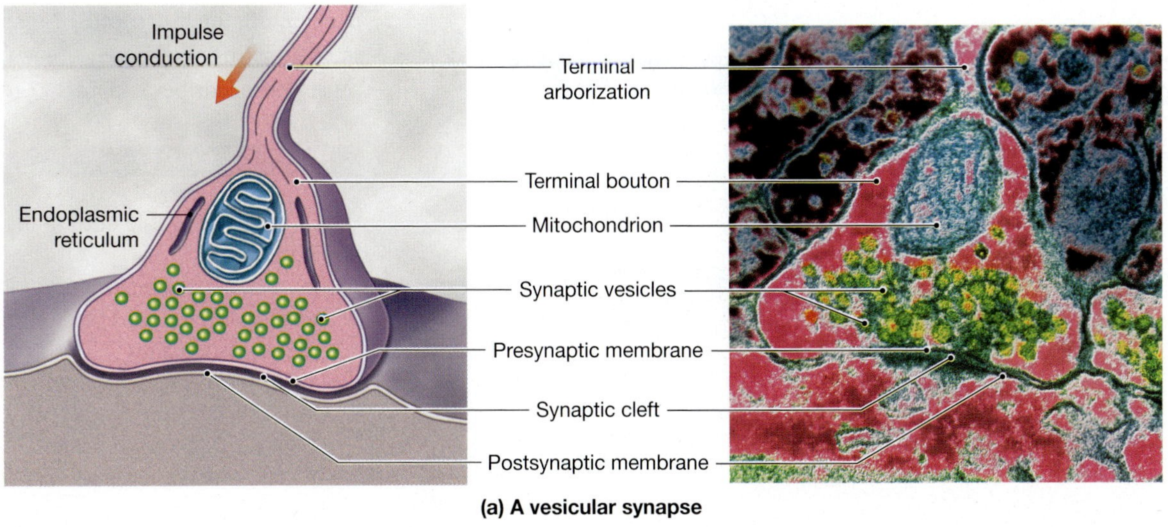

Figure 13.13 The Structure of a Synapse
A synapse is the site of communication between a neuron and another cell. **(a)** Diagrammatic view of a vesicular synapse between two neurons, paired with a color-enhanced TEM of a vesicular synapse. (TEM × 186,480) **(b)** There may be thousands of vesicular synapses on the surface of a single neuron. Many of these synapses may be active at any one moment.

mitter *acetylcholine* (*ACh*). p. 246 More than 50 different neurotransmitters have been identified, but ACh is the best known. All somatic neuromuscular synapses utilize ACh; it is also released at many vesicular synapses in the CNS and PNS. The general sequence of events is similar, regardless of the location of the synapse or the nature of the neurotransmitter.

- Arrival of the action potential at the terminal bouton triggers release of neurotransmitter from secretory vesicles, through exocytosis at the presynaptic membrane.
- The neurotransmitter diffuses across the synaptic cleft and binds to receptors on the postsynaptic membrane.
- Receptor binding results in a change in the permeability of the postsynaptic cell membrane. Depending on the identity and abundance of the receptor proteins on the postsynaptic membrane, the result may be excitatory or inhibitory. In general, excitatory effects promote the generation of action potentials, whereas inhibitory effects reduce the ability to generate an action potential.
- If the degree of excitation is sufficient, receptor binding may lead to the generation of an action potential in the axon (if the postsynaptic cell is a neuron) or sarcolemma (if the postsynaptic cell is a skeletal muscle fiber).
- The effects of one action potential on the postsynaptic membrane are short-lived because the neurotransmitter molecules are either enzymatically broken down or reabsorbed. To prolong or enhance the effects, additional action potentials must arrive at the synaptic terminal, and additional molecules of ACh must be released into the synaptic cleft.

Examples of neurotransmitters other than ACh will be presented in later chapters. There may be thousands of synapses on the cell body of a single neuron (Figure 13.13b). Many of these will be active at any given moment, releasing a variety of different neurotransmitters. Some will have excitatory effects, others inhibitory effects. The activity of the receptive neuron depends on the sum of all of the excitatory and inhibitory stimuli influencing the axon hillock at any given moment.

Nonvesicular Synapses

Vesicular synapses dominate the nervous system. **Nonvesicular synapses**, also termed *electrical synapses*, are found between neurons in both the CNS and PNS, but they are relatively rare. At a nonvesicular synapse, the presynaptic and postsynaptic membranes are tightly bound together, and *communicating (gap) junctions* permit the passage of ions between the cells. p. 44 Because the two cells are linked in this way, they function as if they shared a common membrane, and the nerve impulse crosses from one neuron to the next without delay. In contrast to vesicular synapses, nonvesicular synapses can convey nerve impulses in either direction.

Neuron Organization and Processing [Figure 13.14]

Neurons are the basic building blocks of the nervous system. The billions of interneurons within the CNS are organized into a much smaller number of **neuronal pools**. A neuronal pool is a group of interconnected neurons with specific functions. Neuronal pools are defined on the basis of function rather than on anatomical grounds. A pool may be diffuse, involving neurons in several different regions of the brain, or localized, with all of the neurons restricted to one specific location in the brain or spinal cord. Estimates concerning the actual number of neuronal pools range between a few hundred and a few thousand. Each has a limited number of input sources and output destinations, and the pool may contain both excitatory and inhibitory neurons.

The basic "wiring pattern" found in a neuronal pool is called a *neural circuit*. A neural circuit may have one of the following functions:

1. **Divergence** is the spread of information from one neuron to several neurons, as in Figure 13.14a, or from one pool to multiple pools. Divergence permits the broad distribution of a specific input. Considerable divergence occurs when sensory neurons bring information into the CNS, for the information is distributed to neuronal pools throughout the spinal cord and brain.

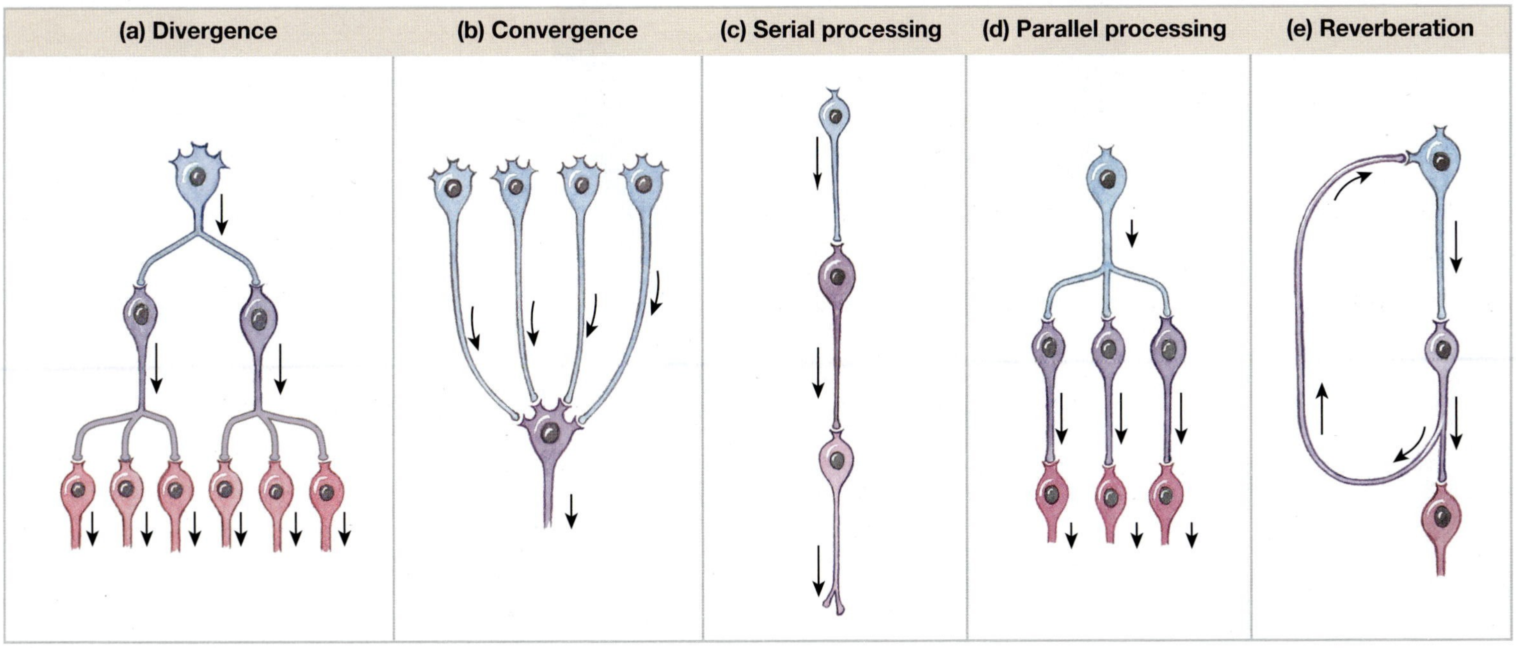

Figure 13.14 Organization of Neuronal Circuits
(a) Divergence, a mechanism for spreading stimulation to multiple neurons or neuronal pools in the CNS. **(b)** Convergence, a mechanism providing input to a single neuron from multiple sources. **(c)** Serial processing, in which neurons or pools work in a sequential manner. **(d)** Parallel processing, in which individual neurons or neuronal pools process information simultaneously. **(e)** Reverberation, a feedback mechanism that may be excitatory or inhibitory.

2. In **convergence**, several neurons synapse on the same postsynaptic neuron (Figure 13.14b). Several different patterns of activity in the presynaptic neurons can have the same effect on the postsynaptic neuron. Convergence permits the variable control of motor neurons by providing a mechanism for their voluntary and involuntary control. For example, the movements of your diaphragm and ribs are now being controlled by respiratory centers in the brain that operate outside your awareness. But the same motor neurons also can be controlled voluntarily, as when you take a deep breath and hold it. Two different neuronal pools are involved, both synapsing on the same motor neurons.
3. Information may be relayed in a stepwise sequence, from one neuron to another or from one neuronal pool to the next. This pattern, called **serial processing**, is shown in Figure 13.14c. Serial processing occurs as sensory information is relayed from one processing center to another in the brain.
4. **Parallel processing** occurs when several neurons or neuronal pools are processing the same information at one time (Figure 13.14d). Thanks to parallel processing, many different responses occur simultaneously. For example, stepping on a sharp object stimulates sensory neurons that distribute the information to a number of neuronal pools. As a result of parallel processing, you might withdraw your foot, shift your weight, move your arms, feel the pain, and shout, "Ouch!" all at the same time.
5. Some neural circuits utilize positive feedback to produce **reverberation**. In this arrangement, collateral axons extend back toward the source of an impulse and further stimulate the presynaptic neurons. Once a reverberating circuit has been activated, it will continue to function until synaptic fatigue or inhibitory stimuli break the cycle. As with convergence or divergence, reverberation can occur within a single neuronal pool, or it may involve a series of interconnected pools. An example of reverberation is shown in Figure 13.14e; much more complex examples of reverberation between neuronal pools in the brain may be involved in the maintenance of consciousness, muscular coordination, and normal breathing patterns. We will discuss these and other "wiring patterns" as we consider the organization of the spinal cord and brain in subsequent chapters.

Anatomical Organization of the Nervous System [Figure 13.15 and Table 13.1]

The functions of the nervous system depend on the interactions between neurons in neuronal pools, with the most complex neural processing steps occurring in the spinal cord and brain (CNS). The arriving sensory information and the outgoing motor commands are carried by the peripheral nervous system (PNS). Axons and cell bodies in the CNS and PNS are not randomly scattered. Instead, they form masses or bundles with distinct anatomical boundaries. The anatomical organization of the nervous system is depicted in Figure 13.15 and summarized in Table 13.1, p. 342.

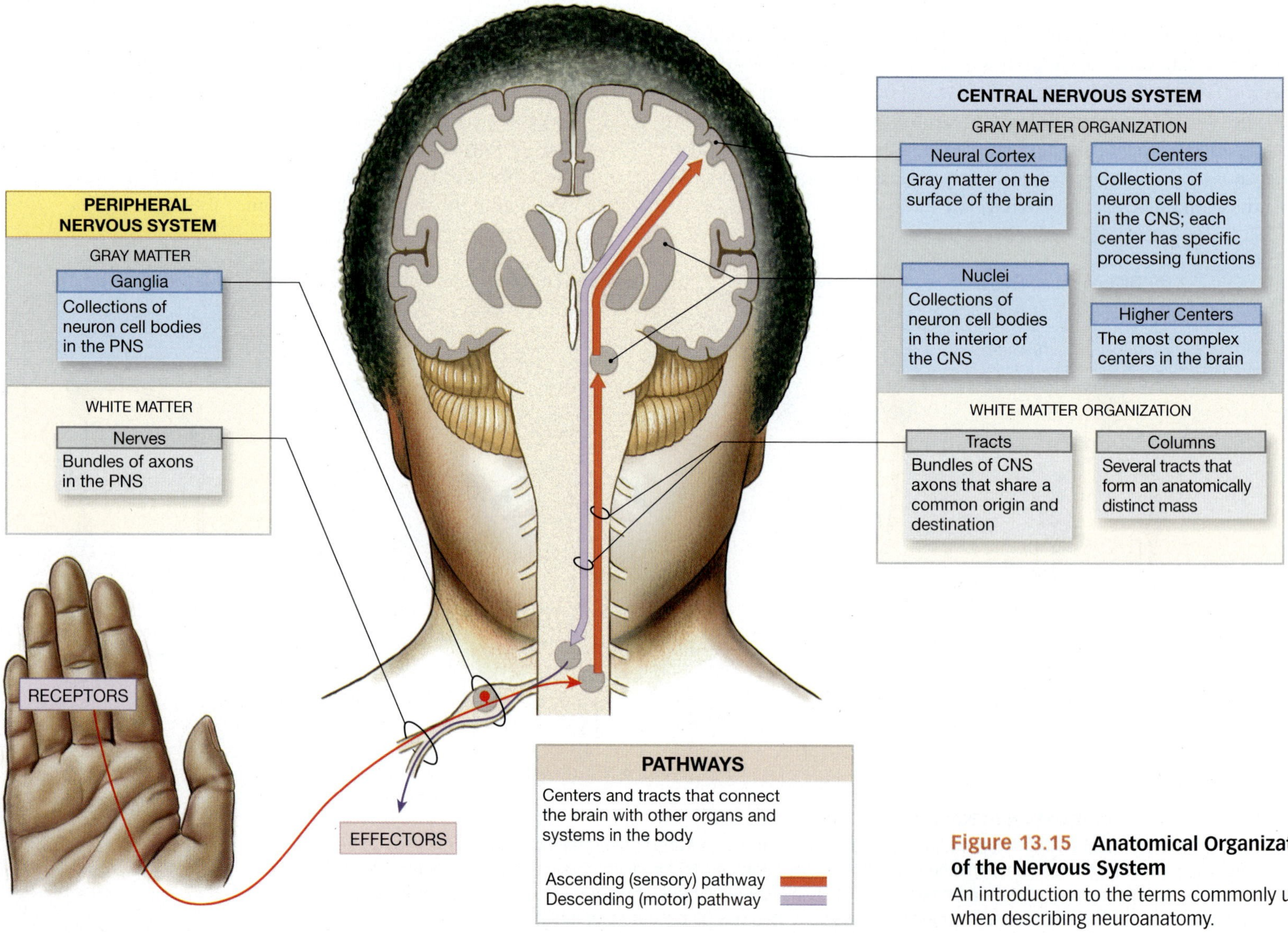

Figure 13.15 Anatomical Organization of the Nervous System
An introduction to the terms commonly used when describing neuroanatomy.

In the PNS:

- The cell bodies of sensory neurons and visceral motor neurons are found in *ganglia*.
- Axons are bundled together in nerves, with *spinal nerves* connected to the spinal cord and *cranial nerves* connected to the brain.

In the CNS:

- A collection of neuron cell bodies with a common function is called a **center**. A center with a discrete anatomical boundary is called a **nucleus**. Portions of the brain surface are covered by a thick layer of gray matter, called the **neural cortex**. The term *higher centers* refers to the most complex integration centers, nuclei, and cortical areas of the brain.
- The white matter of the CNS contains bundles of axons that share common origins, destinations, and functions. These bundles are called **tracts**. Tracts in the spinal cord form larger groups, called **columns**.
- The centers and tracts that link the brain with the rest of the body are called **pathways**. For example, **sensory pathways**, or *ascending pathways*, distribute information from peripheral receptors to processing centers in the brain, and **motor pathways**, or *descending pathways*, begin at CNS centers concerned with motor control and end at the effectors they control.

CONCEPT CHECK

1. Identify the two types of synapses.
2. In general, how do excitatory and inhibitory synapses differ?
3. Distinguish between a neuronal pool whose function is divergence and a neuronal pool whose function is convergence.
4. Describe the following anatomical structures that occur within the central nervous system: center, tract, and pathway.

See blue "Answers" tab at back of book.

Embryology Summary

For a summary of the development of the nervous system, see Chapter 28 (Embryology and Human Development).

CLINICAL TERMS

demyelination: The progressive destruction of myelin sheaths in the CNS and PNS, leading to a loss of sensation and motor control. Demyelination is associated with *heavy metal poisoning, diphtheria, multiple sclerosis*, and *Guillain-Barré syndrome*.

rabies: An acute viral disease of the central nervous system usually transmitted by the bite of an infected mammal. The virus reaches the CNS by transport along the axons of neurons innervating the region of the bite.

STUDY OUTLINE

Introduction 341

1. Two organ systems—the nervous and endocrine systems—coordinate and direct the activities of other organ systems. The nervous system provides swift, brief responses to stimuli; the endocrine system adjusts metabolic operations and directs long-term changes.

An Overview of the Nervous System 341

1. The **nervous system** encompasses all the **neural tissue** in the body. Its anatomical subdivisions are the **central nervous system (CNS)** (the brain and spinal cord) and the **peripheral nervous system (PNS)** (all of the neural tissue outside the CNS).
2. Functionally, the nervous system is subdivided into an **afferent division**, which transmits sensory information from somatic and visceral receptors to the CNS, and an **efferent division**, which carries motor commands to muscles and glands.
3. The efferent division includes both the **somatic nervous system (SNS)** (voluntary control over skeletal muscle contractions) and the **autonomic nervous system (ANS)** (automatic, involuntary regulation of smooth muscle, cardiac muscle, and glandular activity). *(see Figures 13.1/13.2 and Table 13.1)*

Cellular Organization in Neural Tissue 342

1. There are two types of cells in neural tissue: **neurons**, which are responsible for information transfer and processing, and **neuroglia**, or **glial cells**, which are supporting cells in the nervous system. A typical neuron has a **cell body (soma)**, an **axon**, and several **dendrites**. *(see Figures 13.3/13.4)*

Neuroglia 344

2. There are four types of neuroglia in the CNS: (1) *astrocytes*, (2) *oligodendrocytes*, (3) *microglia*, and (4) *ependymal cells*. *(see Figures 13.4 to 13.8)*
3. **Astrocytes** are the largest, most numerous glial cells. They maintain the blood–brain barrier to isolate the CNS from the general circulation, provide structural support for the CNS, regulate ion and nutrient concentrations, and perform repairs to stabilize the tissue and prevent further injury. *(see Figures 13.4/13.5/13.6)*
4. **Oligodendrocytes** wrap CNS axons in a membrane sheath termed **myelin**. Gaps between the myelin wrappings along an axon are called **myelin sheath gaps** (or *nodes of Ranvier*), whereas the large areas wrapped in myelin are called **internodes**. Regions primarily containing myelinated axons appear glossy white and are termed **white matter**. *(see Figures 13.4/13.5)*
5. **Microglia** are small cells with many fine cytoplasmic processes. These are phagocytic cells that engulf cellular debris, waste products, and pathogens. They increase in number as a result of infection or injury. *(see Figures 13.4/13.5)*
6. **Ependymal cells** are atypical epithelial cells that line chambers and passageways filled with **cerebrospinal fluid (CSF)** in the brain and spinal cord. They assist in producing, circulating, and monitoring CSF. *(see Figures 13.4 to 13.6)*
7. Neuron cell bodies in the PNS are clustered into **ganglia**, and their axons form **peripheral nerves**. *(see Figures 13.7/13.8)*
8. The PNS glial cell types are *satellite cells* and *Schwann cells*. *(see Figures 13.7/13.8)*
9. **Satellite cells** enclose neuron cell bodies in ganglia. *(see Figure 13.7)*
10. **Schwann cells** *(neurolemmocytes)* cover all peripheral axons, whether myelinated or unmyelinated. *(see Figure 13.8)*

Neurons 349

11. The **perikaryon** of a neuron is the cytoplasm surrounding the nucleus. It contains organelles, including **neurofilaments, neurotubules**, and bundles of neurofilaments, termed **neurofibrils**, which extend into the dendrites and axon. The **axon hillock** is a specialized region of an axon. It connects the **initial segment** of the axon to the cell body. The cytoplasm of the axon, the **axoplasm**, contains numerous organelles. *(see Figure 13.9)*
12. **Collaterals** are side branches from an axon. **Terminal arborizations** are a series of fine, terminal extensions branching from the axon tip. *(see Figure 13.9)*
13. Terminal arborizations end at *synaptic terminals.* A **synapse** is a site of intercellular communication between a neuron and another cell. A **terminal bouton** is located where one neuron synapses on another. Synaptic communication usually involves the release of specific chemicals, called neurotransmitters. *(see Figure 13.9)*
14. Structurally, neurons may be classified on the basis of the number of processes that project from the cell body: (1) **anaxonic** (no distinguishable axon); (2) **bipolar** (one dendrite and one axon); (3) **pseudounipolar** (dendrite and axon are continuous at one side of cell body); and (4) **multipolar** (several dendrites and one axon). *(see Figure 13.10)*
15. There are three functional categories of neurons: *sensory neurons, motor neurons*, and *interneurons* (association neurons). *(see Figure 13.11)*
16. **Sensory neurons** form the afferent division of the PNS and deliver information from sensory receptors to the CNS. Receptors are categorized as **exteroceptors** (provide information from external environment), **proprioceptors** (monitor position and movement of joints), and **interoceptors** (monitor digestive, respiratory, cardiovascular, urinary, and reproductive systems). *(see Figure 13.11)*
17. **Motor neurons** form the efferent pathways that stimulate or modify the activity of a peripheral tissue, organ, or organ system. **Somatic motor neurons** innervate skeletal muscle. **Visceral motor neurons** innervate all peripheral effectors other than skeletal muscles. Axons of visceral motor neurons from the CNS (**preganglionic fibers**) synapse on neurons in ganglia; these ganglion cells project axons (**postganglionic fibers**) to control the peripheral effectors. *(see Figure 13.11)*
18. **Interneurons (association neurons)** may be located between sensory and motor neurons; they analyze sensory inputs and coordinate motor outputs. Interneurons are classified as **excitatory** or **inhibitory** on the basis of their effects on postsynaptic neurons. *(see Figure 13.11)*

Neural Regeneration 352

1. Neurons have a very limited ability to regenerate after an injury. When an entire peripheral nerve is severed, only a relatively small number of axons within the nerve will successfully reestablish normal synaptic contacts. As a result, complete nerve function is impaired permanently. *(see Figure 13.12)*
2. Schwann cells participate in the repair of damaged peripheral nerves. This process is known as **Wallerian degeneration**. *(see Figure 13.12)*
3. Limited regeneration can occur inside the central nervous system, but the situation is more complicated because (1) many more axons are likely to be involved, (2) astrocytes produce scar tissue that can prevent axon growth across the damaged area, and (3) astrocytes release chemicals that block the regrowth of axons. *(see Figure 13.12)*

The Nerve Impulse 353

1. **Excitability** is the ability of a cell membrane to conduct electrical impulses; the cell membranes of skeletal muscle fibers and most neurons are excitable.
2. The conducted changes in the transmembrane potential that occur as a result of changes in the flow of sodium and potassium ions when the membrane *threshold* is reached and are called **action potentials**. An action potential traveling along an axon is called a **nerve impulse**.
3. The rate of impulse conduction depends on the properties of the axon, specifically the presence or absence of a myelin sheath (a myelinated axon conducts impulses five to seven times faster than an unmyelinated axon) and the diameter of the axon (the larger the diameter, the faster the rate of conduction).

Synaptic Communication 354

1. Synapses occur on dendrites, the cell body, or along axons. Synapses permit communication between neurons and other cells at **neuroeffector junctions**. *(see Figure 13.9b)*
2. A synapse may be **vesicular** (*chemical*) involving a neurotransmitter, or **nonvesicular** (*electrical*), with direct contact between cells. Vesicular synapses are more common. *(see Figure 13.13a)*

Vesicular Synapses 354

3. At a **vesicular synapse** between two neurons, a special relationship is established. Only the *presynaptic membrane* releases a neurotransmitter, which binds to receptor proteins on the *postsynaptic membrane*, causing a change in the transmembrane potential of the receptive cell. Thus, communication can occur in only one direction across a synapse: from the presynaptic neuron to the postsynaptic neuron. *(see Figure 13.13)*
4. More than 50 neurotransmitters have been identified. All neuromuscular synapses utilize ACh as a neurotransmitter; ACh is also released at many vesicular synapses in both the CNS and PNS.
5. The general sequence of events at a vesicular synapse is as follows: (1) Neurotransmitter release is triggered by the arrival of an action potential at the terminal bouton of the presynaptic membrane; (2) the neurotransmitter binds to receptors on the postsynaptic membrane after it diffuses across the synaptic cleft; (3) binding of the neurotransmitter causes a change in the permeability of the postsynaptic cell membrane, resulting in either excitatory or inhibitory effects, depending on the identity and abundance of receptor proteins; (4) the initiation of an action potential depends on the degree of excitation; and (5) the effects on the postsynaptic membrane fade rapidly as the neurotransmitter molecules are degraded by enzymes.
6. A single neuron may have thousands of synapses on its cell body. The activity of the neuron depends on the summation of all of the excitatory and inhibitory stimuli arriving at any given moment at the axon hillock.

Nonvesicular Synapses 355

7. **Nonvesicular synapses** (also termed *electrical synapses*) are found between neurons in the CNS and PNS, although they are rare. At these synapses, the neurolemmae of the presynaptic and postsynaptic cells are tightly bound together and the cells function as if they shared a common neurolemma. Nonvesicular synapses transmit information more rapidly than vesicular synapses. Nonvesicular synapses may also be bidirectional.

Neuron Organization and Processing 355

1. The roughly 20 billion interneurons can be classified into **neuronal pools**. The neural circuits of these neuronal pools may show (1) *divergence*, (2) *convergence*, (3) *serial processing*, (4) *parallel processing*, and (5) *reverberation. (see Figure 13.14)*
2. **Divergence** is the spread of information from one neuron to several neurons or from one pool to several pools. This facilitates the widespread distribution of a specific input. *(see Figure 13.14a)*
3. **Convergence** is the presence of synapses from several neurons on one postsynaptic neuron. It permits the variable control of motor neurons. *(see Figure 13.14b)*
4. **Serial processing** is a pattern of stepwise information processing, from one neuron to another or from one neuronal pool to the next. This is the way sensory information is relayed between processing centers in the brain. *(see Figure 13.14c)*
5. **Parallel processing** is a pattern that processes information by several neurons or neuronal pools at one time. Many different responses occur at the same time. *(see Figure 13.14d)*
6. **Reverberation** occurs when neural circuits utilize positive feedback to continue the activity of the circuit. Collateral axons establish a circuit to continue to stimulate presynaptic neurons. *(see Figure 13.14e)*

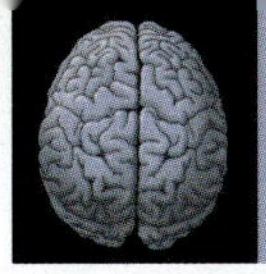

Anatomical Organization of the Nervous System 356

1. Nervous system functions depend on interactions between neurons in neuronal pools. Almost all complex processing steps occur inside the brain and spinal cord. *(see Figure 13.15)*
2. Neuronal cell bodies and axons in both the PNS and CNS are organized into masses or bundles with distinct anatomical boundaries. *(see Figure 13.15)*
3. In the PNS, *ganglia* contain the cell bodies of sensory and visceral motor neurons. Axons in nerves occur within *spinal nerves* to the spinal cord and *cranial nerves* to the brain. *(see Figure 13.11)*
4. In the CNS, cell bodies are organized into **centers**; a center with discrete boundaries is called a **nucleus**. The **neural cortex** is the gray matter that covers portions of the brain. It is called a *higher center* to reflect its involvement in complex activities. White matter has bundles of axons called **tracts.** Tracts organize into larger units, called **columns.** The centers and tracts that link the brain and body are **pathways**. Sensory *(ascending)* pathways carry information from peripheral receptors to the brain; motor *(descending)* pathways extend from CNS centers concerned with motor control to the associated skeletal muscles. *(see Figure 13.15)*

CHAPTER REVIEW

For answers to the Concept Check and Chapter Review questions, go to the blue "Answers" tab at the back of the book.

Level 1 Reviewing Facts and Terms

Match each numbered item with the most closely related lettered item. Use letters for answers in the spaces provided.

Column A	Column B
___ 1. afferent division	a. positive feedback
___ 2. effector	b. connects initial segment to soma
___ 3. astrocyte	c. sensory information
___ 4. oligodendrocyte	d. monitor position/movement of joints
___ 5. axon hillock	e. myelin
___ 6. collaterals	f. one dendrite
___ 7. bipolar neurons	g. neuron cell bodies in PNS
___ 8. proprioceptors	h. blood–brain barrier
___ 9. reverberation	i. side branches of axons
___ 10. ganglia	j. skeletal muscle cells

11. Which of the following is not a function of the neuroglia?
(a) support
(b) information processing
(c) secretion of cerebrospinal fluid
(d) phagocytosis

12. Glial cells found surrounding the cell bodies of peripheral neurons are
(a) astrocytes (b) ependymal cells
(c) microglia (d) satellite cells

13. The most important function of the soma of a neuron is to
(a) allow communication with another neuron
(b) support the neuroglial cells
(c) generate an electrical charge
(d) house organelles that produce energy and synthesize organic molecules

14. Axons terminate in a series of fine extensions known as
(a) terminal arborization (b) synapses
(c) collaterals (d) hillocks

15. Which of the following activities or sensations are not monitored by interoceptors?
(a) urinary activities (b) digestive system activities
(c) visual activities (d) cardiovascular activities

16. Neurons in which dendritic and axonal processes are continuous and the cell body lies off to one side are called
(a) anaxonic (b) pseudounipolar
(c) bipolar (d) multipolar

17. The structures at the ends of the terminal arborizations that form the synaptic terminals are the
(a) axons (b) terminal boutons
(c) collaterals (d) axon hillocks

18. Neurotransmitter is released by
(a) a postsynaptic membrane
(b) an effector organ
(c) all areas of the nerve cell
(d) a presynaptic membrane only

19. In neuron pools, parallel processing occurs when
(a) several neurons synapse on the same postsynaptic neuron
(b) information is relayed stepwise from one neuron to another
(c) several neurons process the same information at the same time
(d) neurons utilize positive feedback

20. A column is a
(a) collection of neuron cell bodies
(b) group of tracts in the spinal cord
(c) bundle of white matter with a common origin and destination
(d) none of the above

Level 2 Reviewing Concepts

1. Patterns of interactions between neurons include which of the following?
(a) divergence (b) parallel processing
(c) reverberation (d) all of the above

2. Which neuronal tissue cell type is likely to be malfunctioning if the blood–brain barrier is no longer adequately protecting the brain?
(a) ependymal cells (b) astrocytes
(c) oligodendrocytes (d) microglia

3. Developmental problems in the growth and interconnections of neurons in the brain reflect problems with the
(a) afferent neurons (b) microglia
(c) astrocytes (d) efferent neurons

4. What purpose do collaterals serve in the nervous system?
5. How does exteroceptor activity differ from interoceptor activity?
6. What is the purpose of the blood–brain barrier?
7. Differentiate between CNS and PNS functions.
8. Distinguish between the somatic nervous system and the autonomic nervous system.
9. Why is a nonvesicular synapse more efficient than a vesicular synapse? Why is it less versatile?
10. Differentiate between serial and parallel processing.

Level 3 Critical Thinking

1. In multiple sclerosis, there is progressive and intermittent damage to the myelin sheath of peripheral nerves. This results in poor motor control of the affected area. Why does destruction of the myelin sheath affect motor control?
2. An 8-year-old girl was cut on the elbow when she fell into a window while skating. This injury caused only minor muscle damage but partially severed a nerve in her arm. What is likely to happen to the severed axons of this nerve, and will the little girl regain normal function of the nerve and the muscles it controls?
3. Eve is diagnosed with spinal meningitis. Her attending physician informs her father that high doses of antibiotics will be needed to treat Eve's condition. Her father assumes this is due to the severity of the disease. Is he correct? If not, why are such high doses required to treat Eve's condition?

14

The Nervous System

The Spinal Cord and Spinal Nerves

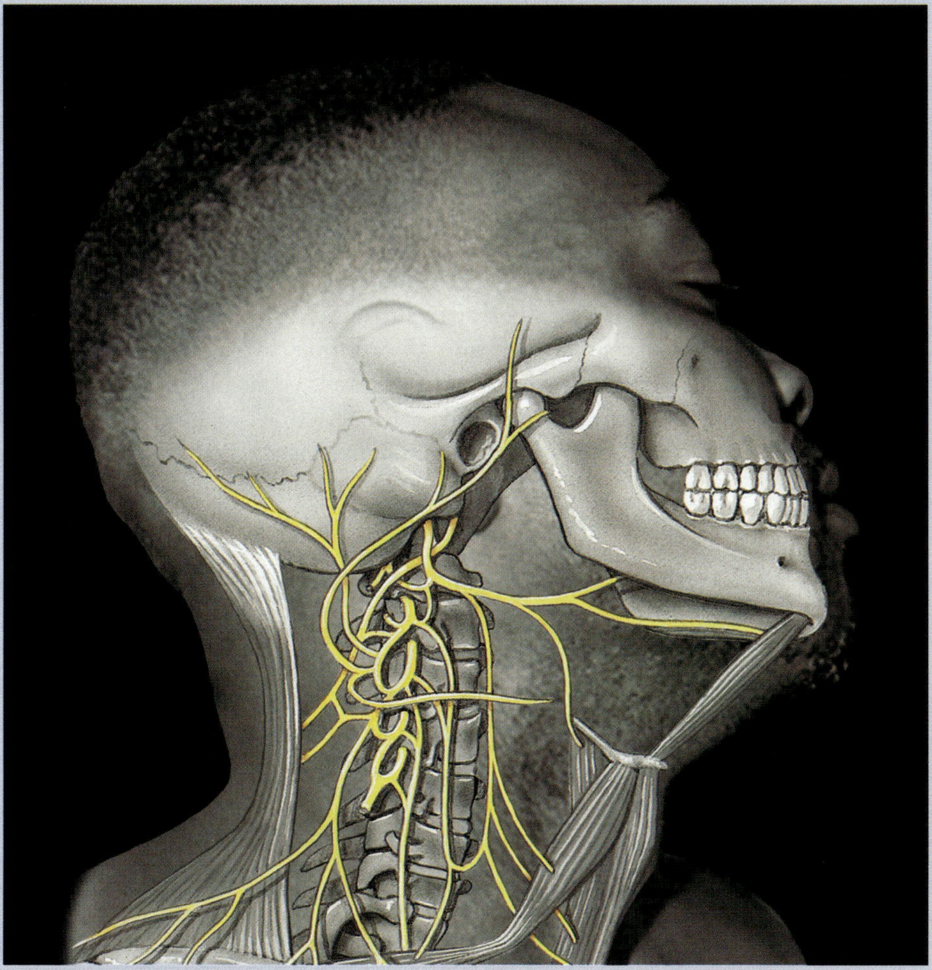

CHAPTER OBJECTIVES

1. Discuss the structure and functions of the spinal cord.
2. Locate the spinal meninges, describe their structure, and list their functions.
3. Discuss the structure and location of gray matter and white matter, and describe the roles of both in processing and relaying sensory and motor information.
4. Identify the regional groups of spinal nerves.
5. Describe the connective tissue layers associated with a spinal nerve.
6. Describe the various branches of a representative spinal nerve.
7. Define dermatomes and explain their significance.
8. Define *nerve plexus* and identify the four main spinal nerve plexuses.
9. Identify the spinal nerves originating at the four major nerve plexuses, list their major branches, and indicate their primary functions.
10. Describe the structures and steps involved in a neural reflex, classify reflexes, and identify their structural components.
11. Give examples of the types of motor responses produced by spinal reflexes.

The **central nervous system (CNS)** consists of the *spinal cord* and *brain.* Despite the fact that the two are anatomically connected, the spinal cord and brain show significant degrees of functional independence. The spinal cord is far more than just a highway for information traveling to or from the brain. Although most sensory data is relayed to the brain, the spinal cord also integrates and processes information on its own. This chapter describes the anatomy of the spinal cord and examines the integrative activities that occur in this portion of the CNS.

Gross Anatomy of the Spinal Cord [Figures 14.1 to 14.3]

The adult spinal cord (Figure 14.1a) measures approximately 45 cm (18 in.) in length and extends from the foramen magnum of the skull to the inferior border of the first lumbar vertebra (L_1). The dorsal surface of the spinal cord bears a shallow longitudinal groove, the **posterior median sulcus**. The deep crease along the ventral surface is the **anterior median fissure** (Figure 14.1d). Each region of the spinal cord (cervical, thoracic, lumbar, and sacral) contains tracts involved with that particular segment and those associated with it. Figure 14.1d provides a series of sectional views that demonstrate the variations in the relative mass of gray matter versus white matter along the length of the spinal cord.

The amount of gray matter is increased substantially in segments of the spinal cord concerned with the sensory and motor innervation of the limbs. These areas contain interneurons responsible for relaying arriving sensory information and coordinating the activities of the somatic motor neurons that control the complex muscles of the limbs. These areas of the spinal cord are expanded to form the **enlargements** of the spinal cord seen in Figure 14.1a. The **cervical enlargement** supplies nerves to the pectoral girdle and upper limbs; the **lumbosacral enlargement** provides innervation to structures of the pelvis and lower limbs. Inferior to the lumbosacral enlargement, the spinal cord tapers to a conical tip called the **conus medullaris**, at or inferior to the level of the first lumbar vertebra. A slender strand of fibrous tissue, the **filum terminale** ("terminal thread"), extends from the inferior tip of the conus medullaris along the length of the vertebral canal as far as the dorsum of the coccyx (Figure 14.1a,c). There it provides longitudinal support to the spinal cord as a component of the *coccygeal ligament.*

The entire spinal cord can be divided into 31 segments. Each segment is identified by a letter and number designation. For example, C_3 is the third cervical segment (Figure 14.1a).

Every spinal segment is associated with a pair of **dorsal root ganglia** that contain the cell bodies of sensory neurons. These sensory ganglia lie between the pedicles of adjacent vertebrae. ∞ p. 161 On either side of the spinal cord, a typical **dorsal root** contains the axons of the sensory neurons in the dorsal root ganglion (Figure 14.1b,c). Anterior to the dorsal root, a **ventral root** leaves the spinal cord. The ventral root contains the axons of somatic motor neurons and, at some levels, visceral motor neurons that control peripheral effectors. The dorsal and ventral roots of each segment enter and leave the vertebral canal between adjacent vertebrae at the *intervertebral foramina.* ∞ p. 162 The dorsal roots are usually thicker than the ventral roots.

Distal to each dorsal root ganglion, the sensory and motor fibers form a single **spinal nerve** (Figures 14.1d, 14.2c, and 14.3). Spinal nerves are classified as **mixed nerves** because they contain both afferent (sensory) and efferent (motor) fibers. Figure 14.3 shows the spinal nerves as they emerge from intervertebral foramina.

The spinal cord continues to enlarge and elongate until an individual is approximately 4 years old. Up to that time, enlargement of the spinal cord keeps pace with the growth of the vertebral column, and the segments of the spinal cord are aligned with the corresponding vertebrae. The ventral and dorsal roots are short, and leave the vertebral canal through the adjacent intervertebral foramina. After age 4 the vertebral column continues to grow, but the spinal cord does not. This vertebral growth carries the dorsal root ganglia and spinal nerves farther and farther away from their original position relative to the spinal cord. As a result, the dorsal and ventral roots gradually elongate. The adult spinal cord extends only to the level of the first or second lumbar vertebra; thus spinal cord segment S_2 lies at the level of vertebra L_1 (Figure 14.1a).

When seen in gross dissection, the filum terminale and the long ventral and dorsal roots that extend caudal to the conus medullaris reminded early anatomists of a horse's tail. With this in mind the complex was called the **cauda equina** (KAW-da ek-WĪ-na; *cauda*, tail + *equus*, horse) (Figure 14.1a,c).

Spinal Meninges [Figures 14.1b,c/14.2/14.4]

The vertebral column and its surrounding ligaments, tendons, and muscles isolate the spinal cord from the external environment. ∞ p. 215 The delicate neural tissues also must be protected against damaging contacts with the surrounding bony walls of the vertebral canal. Specialized membranes, collectively known as the **spinal meninges** (men-IN-jēz), provide protection, physical stability, and shock absorption (Figure 14.1b,c). The spinal meninges cover the spinal cord and surround the spinal nerve roots (Figure 14.2). Blood vessels branching within these layers also deliver oxygen and nutrients to the spinal cord. There are three meningeal layers: the *dura mater*, the *arachnoid mater*, and the *pia mater*. At the foramen magnum of the skull, the spinal meninges are continuous with the **cranial meninges** that surround the brain. (The cranial meninges, which have the same three layers, will be described in Chapter 15.)

The Dura Mater [Figures 14.1b,c/14.2]

The tough, fibrous **dura mater** (DOO-ra MĀ-ter; *dura*, hard + *mater*, mother) forms the outermost covering of the spinal cord and brain (Figure 14.1b,c). The dura mater of the spinal cord consists of a layer of dense irregular connective tissue whose outer and inner surfaces are covered by a simple squamous epithelium. The outer epithelium is not bound to the bony walls of the vertebral canal, and the intervening **epidural space** contains areolar tissue, blood vessels, and adipose tissue (Figure 14.2d).

Localized attachments of the dura mater to the edge of the foramen magnum of the skull, the second and third cervical vertebrae, the sacrum, and to the posterior longitudinal ligament, serve to stabilize the spinal cord within the vertebral canal. Caudally, the spinal dura mater tapers from a sheath to a dense cord of collagen fibers that ultimately blend with components of the filum terminale to form the **coccygeal ligament**. The coccygeal ligament extends along the sacral canal and is interwoven into the periosteum of the sacrum and coccyx. The cranial and sacral attachments provide longitudinal stability. Lateral support is provided by the connective tissues within the epidural space and by the extensions of the dura mater that accompany the spinal nerve roots as they pass through the intervertebral foramina. Distally, the connective tissue of the spinal dura mater is continuous with the connective tissue sheath that surrounds each spinal nerve (Figure 14.2a,c,d).

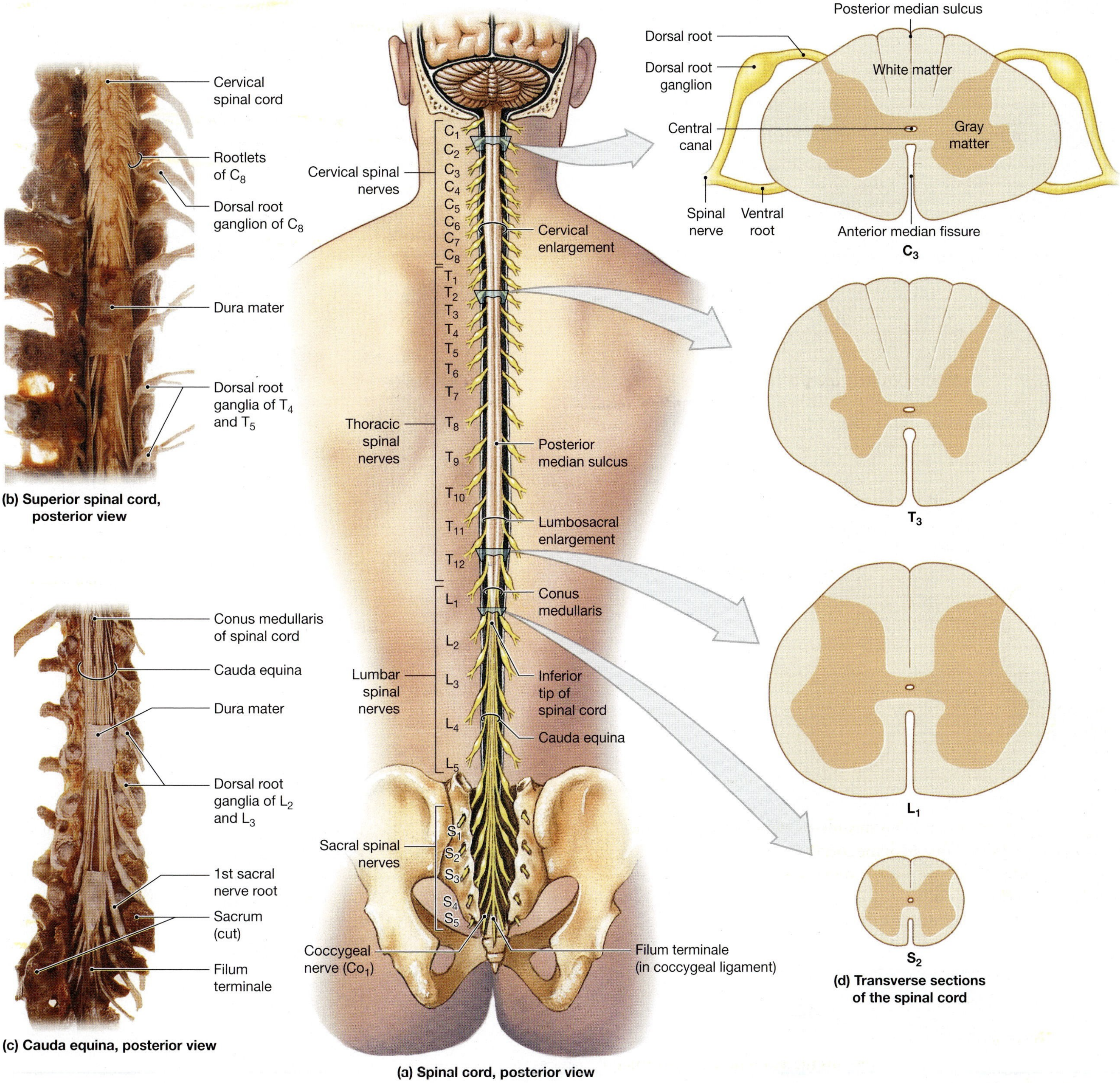

Figure 14.1 Gross Anatomy of the Spinal Cord

The spinal cord extends inferiorly from the base of the brain along the vertebral canal. **(a)** Superficial anatomy and orientation of the adult spinal cord. The numbers to the left identify the spinal nerves and indicate where the nerve roots leave the vertebral canal. The spinal cord, however, extends from the brain only to the level of vertebrae L_1–L_2. **(b)** Posterior view of a dissection of the cervical spinal cord. **(c)** Posterior view of a dissection of the conus medullaris, cauda equina, filum terminale, and associated spinal nerve roots. **(d)** Inferior views of cross sections through representative segments of the spinal cord, showing the arrangement of gray and white matter.

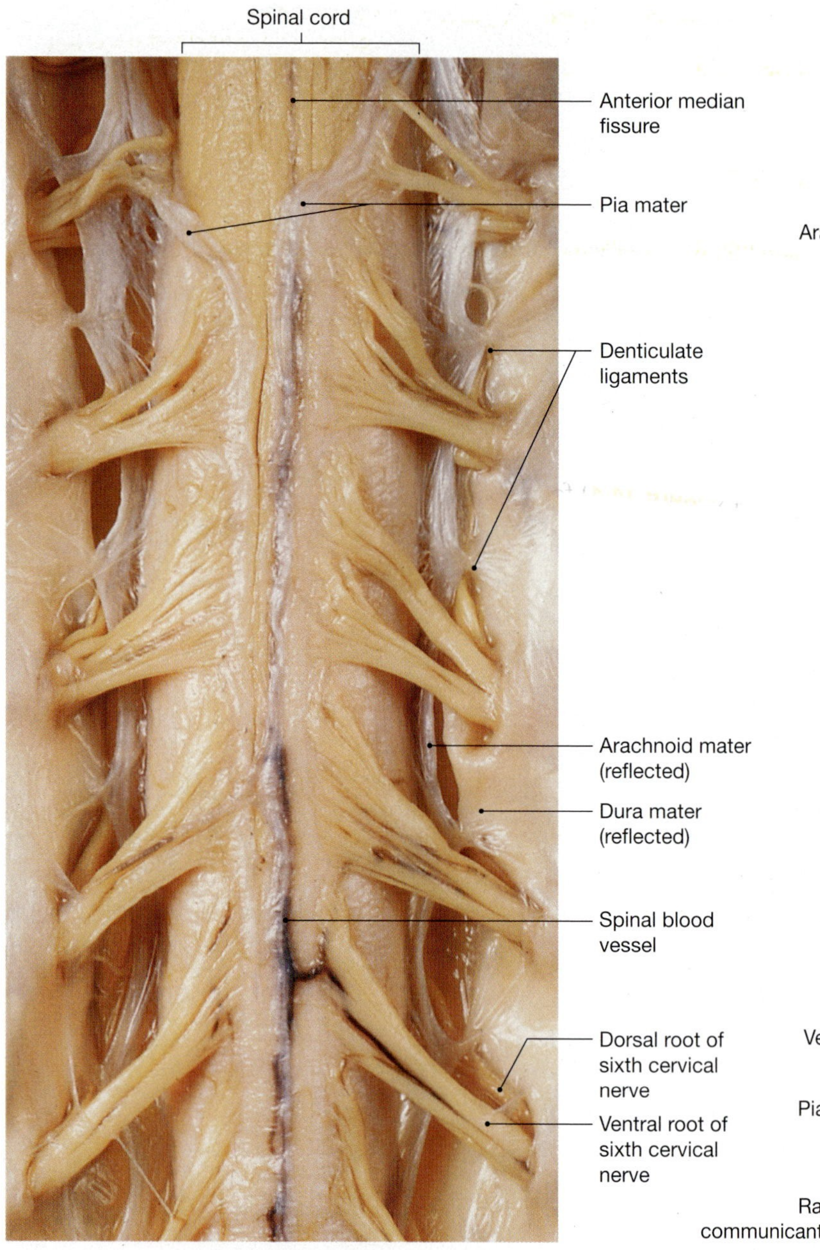

(a) Anterior view

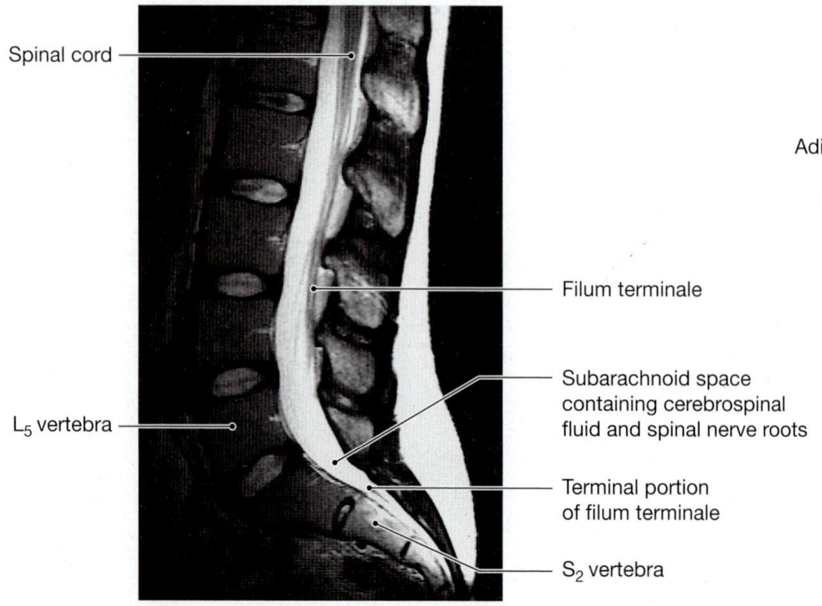

(b) MRI, sectional view

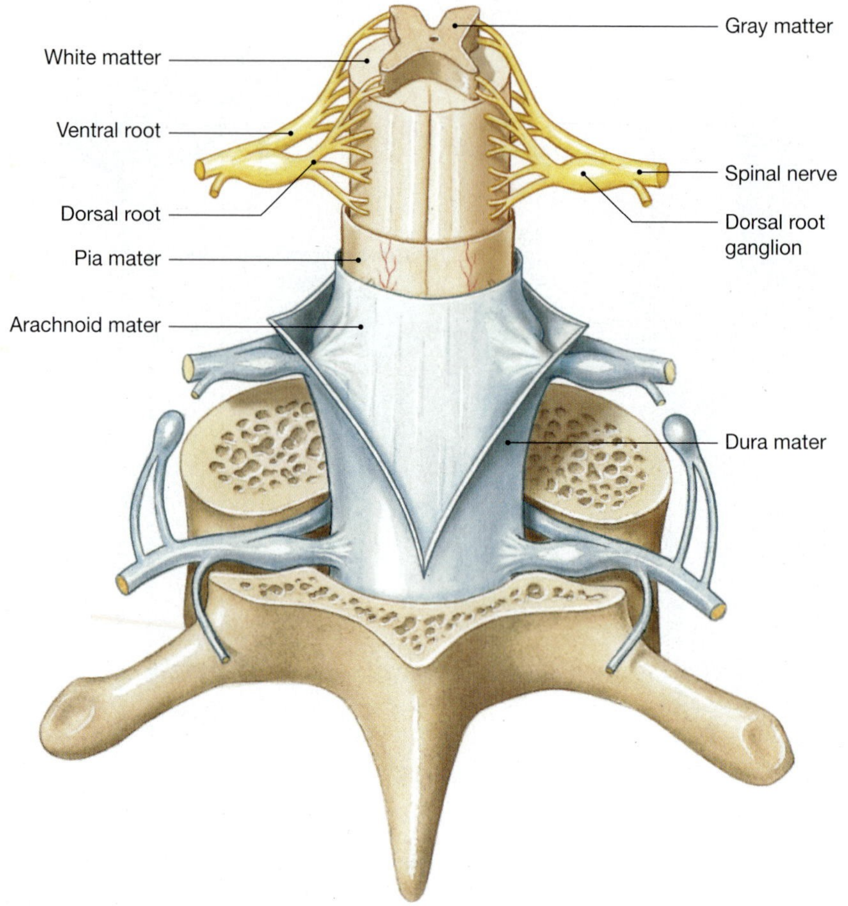

(c) Posterior view

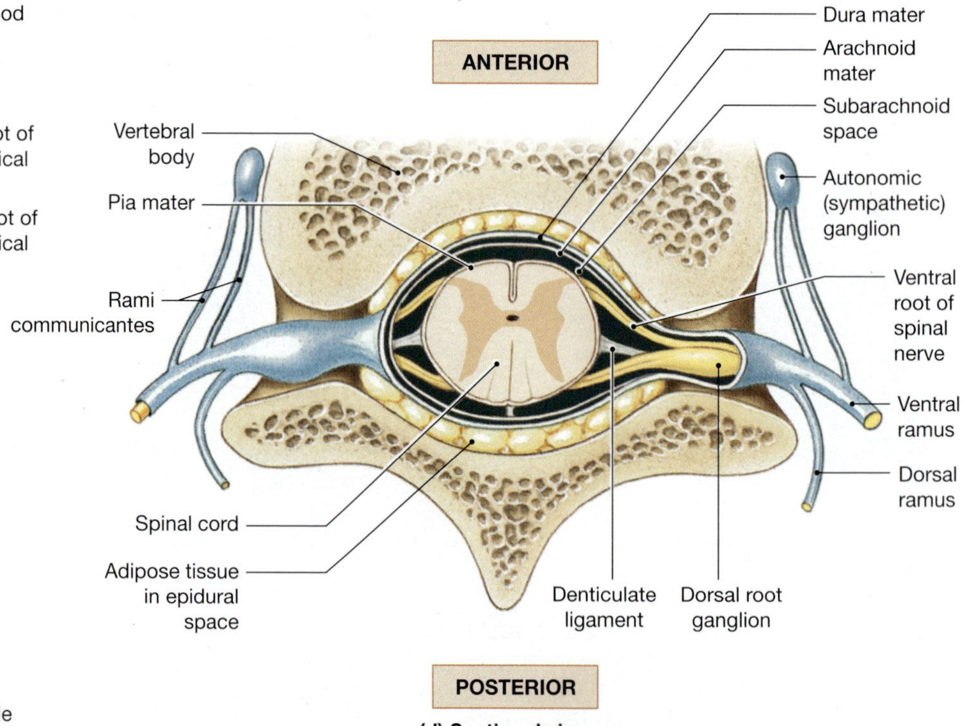

(d) Sectional view

Figure 14.2 The Spinal Cord and Spinal Meninges
(a) Anterior view of spinal cord showing meninges and spinal nerves. For this view, the dura and arachnoid membranes have been cut longitudinally and retracted (pulled aside); notice the blood vessels that run in the subarachnoid space, bound to the outer surface of the delicate pia mater. **(b)** An MRI scan of the inferior portion of the spinal cord, showing its relationship to the vertebral column. **(c)** Posterior view of the spinal cord, showing the meningeal layers, superficial landmarks, and distribution of gray and white matter. **(d)** Sectional view through the spinal cord and meninges, showing the peripheral distribution of the spinal nerves.

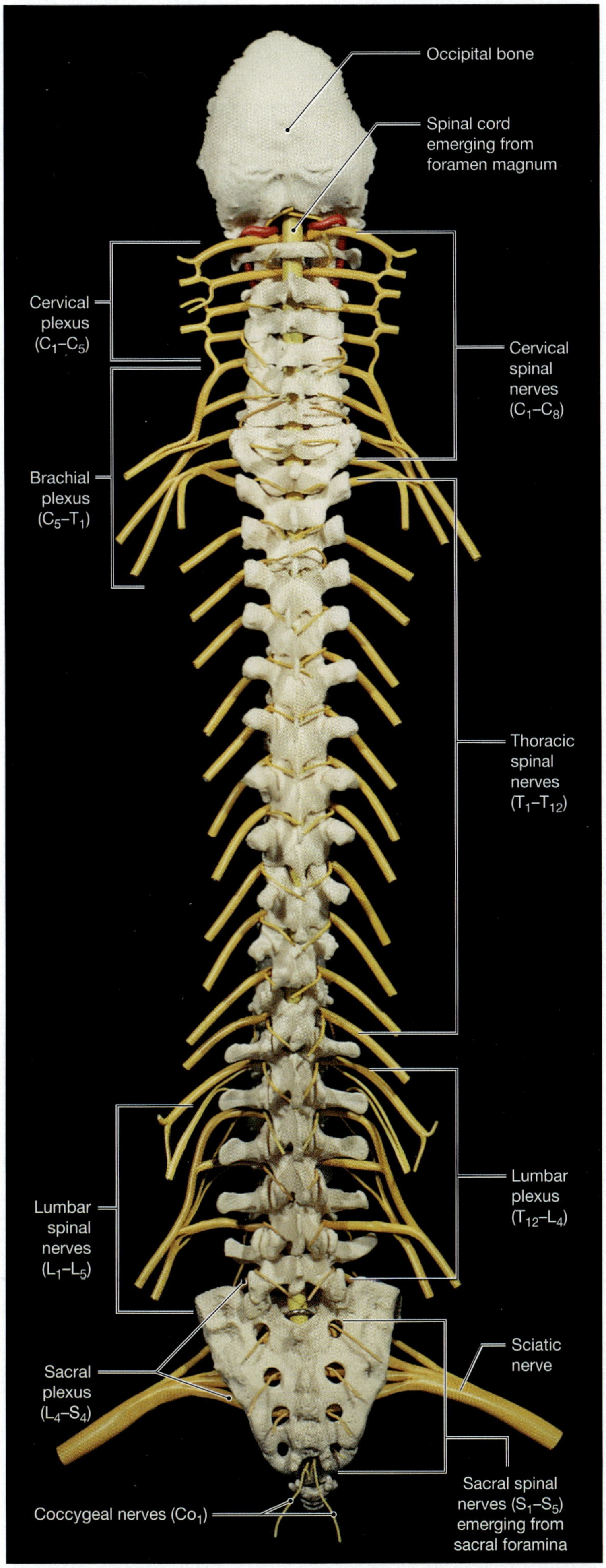

Figure 14.3 Posterior View of Vertebral Column and Spinal Nerves

The Arachnoid Mater [Figures 14.2a,c,d/14.4]

In most anatomical and histological preparations, a narrow **subdural space** separates the dura mater from deeper meningeal layers. It is likely, however, that in life no such space exists, and the inner surface of the dura is in contact with the outer surface of the **arachnoid** (a-RAK-noyd; *arachne*, spider) **mater** (Figure 14.2a,c). The arachnoid mater, the middle meningeal layer, consists of a simple squamous epithelium. It is separated from the innermost layer, the *pia mater*, by the **subarachnoid space**. This space contains **cerebrospinal fluid (CSF)** that acts as a shock absorber as well as a diffusion medium for dissolved gases, nutrients, chemical messengers, and waste products. The cerebrospinal fluid flows through a meshwork of collagen and elastin fibers produced by modified fibroblasts. Bundles of fibers, known as *arachnoid trabeculae*, extend from the inner surface of the arachnoid mater to the outer surface of the pia mater. The subarachnoid space and the role of cerebrospinal fluid will be discussed in Chapter 15. The subarachnoid space of the spinal meninges can be accessed easily between L_3 and L_4 (Figure 14.4) for the clinical examination of cerebrospinal fluid or for the administration of anesthetics.

The Pia Mater [Figure 14.2]

The subarachnoid space bridges the gap between the arachnoid epithelium and the innermost meningeal layer, the **pia mater** (*pia*, delicate + *mater*, mother) as seen in Figure 14.2a,c,d. The elastic and collagen fibers of the pia mater are interwoven with those of the arachnoid trabeculae. The blood vessels supplying the spinal cord are found here. The pia mater is firmly bound to the underlying neural tissue, conforming to its bulges and fissures. The surface of the spinal cord consists of a thin layer of astrocytes, and cytoplasmic extensions of these glial cells lock the collagen fibers of the spinal pia mater in place.

Along the length of the spinal cord, paired **denticulate ligaments** are extensions of the spinal pia mater that connect the pia mater and spinal arachnoid mater to the dura mater (Figure 14.2a,d). These ligaments originate along either side of the spinal cord, between the ventral and dorsal roots. They begin at the foramen magnum of the skull, and collectively they help prevent side-to-side movement and inferior movement of the spinal cord. The connective tissue fibers of the spinal pia mater continue from the inferior tip of the conus medullaris as the filum terminale. As noted earlier, the filum terminale blends into the coccygeal ligament; this arrangement prevents superior movement of the spinal cord.

The spinal meninges surround the dorsal and ventral roots within the intervertebral foramina. As seen in Figure 14.2c,d, the meningeal membranes are continuous with the connective tissues surrounding the spinal nerves and their peripheral branches.

✓ CONCEPT CHECK

1. Damage to which root of a spinal nerve would interfere with motor function?
2. Identify the location of the cerebrospinal fluid that surrounds the spinal cord.
3. What are the two spinal enlargements? Why are these regions of the spinal cord increased in diameter?
4. What is found within a dorsal root ganglion?

See blue "Answers" tab at back of book.

Clinical Note

Spinal Taps, Myelography, Spinal Anesthesia, and Caudal Anesthesia Tissue samples, or *biopsies*, are taken from many organs to assist in diagnosis. For example, when a liver or skin disorder is suspected, small plugs of tissue or tissue fluid are removed and examined for signs of cell damage or are used to identify the microorganisms causing an infection. Unlike many other tissues, however, neural tissue consists largely of cells rather than extracellular fluids or fibers. Tissue samples are seldom removed for analysis because any extracted or damaged neurons will not be replaced. Instead, small volumes of cerebrospinal fluid (CSF) are collected and analyzed. CSF is intimately associated with the neural tissue of the CNS, and pathogens, cell debris, and metabolic wastes in the CNS are detectable in the CSF.

The withdrawal of cerebrospinal fluid, known as a **spinal tap**, must be done with care to avoid injuring the spinal cord. The adult spinal cord extends only as far as vertebra L_1 or L_2. Between vertebra L_2 and the sacrum, the meningeal layers remain intact, but they enclose only the relatively sturdy components of the cauda equina and a significant quantity of CSF. With the vertebral column flexed, a needle can be inserted between the lower lumbar vertebrae and into the subarachnoid space with minimal risk to the cauda equina. In this procedure, known as a **lumbar puncture (LP)**, 3–9 ml of fluid are taken from the subarachnoid space between vertebrae L_3 and L_4 (Figure 14.4a). Spinal taps are performed when CNS infection is suspected or when diagnosing severe headaches, disc problems, some types of strokes, and other altered mental states.

Myelography involves the introduction of radiopaque dyes into the CSF of the subarachnoid space. Because the dyes are opaque to x-rays, the CSF appears white on an x-ray photograph (Figure 14.4b).

Any tumors, inflammation, or adhesions that distort or divert CSF circulation will be shown in silhouette. Pain medication and/or local anesthetics can be injected into the subarachnoid space. In the event of severe infection, inflammation, or leukemia (cancer of the white blood cells), antibiotics, steroids, or anticancer drugs can be injected as well.

Anesthetics can be used to control the functioning of spinal nerves in specific locations. Injecting a local anesthetic around a spinal nerve produces a temporary blockage of sensory and motor nerve function. This procedure can be done peripherally, as when skin lacerations are sewn up, or at sites around the spinal cord to obtain more widespread anesthetic effects. An *epidural block*—the injection of an anesthetic into the epidural space of the spinal cord—has the advantage of (1) affecting only the spinal nerves in the immediate area of the injection, and (2) providing mainly sensory anesthesia. If a catheter is left in place, continued injection allows sustained anesthesia. Epidural anesthesia can be difficult to achieve in the upper cervical and midthoracic regions, where the epidural space is extremely narrow. It is more effective in the lower lumbar region, inferior to the conus medullaris, because the epidural space is somewhat broader.

Caudal anesthesia involves the introduction of anesthetics into the epidural space of the sacrum. Injection at this site paralyzes and anesthetizes lower abdominal and perineal structures. Caudal anesthesia can be used to control pain during labor and delivery, but lumbar epidural anesthesia is often preferred.

Local anesthetics can also be introduced as a single dose into the subarachnoid space of the spinal cord. This procedure is commonly called "spinal anesthesia." However, the effects include both temporary muscle paralysis and sensory loss that tends to spread as the movement of cerebrospinal fluid distributes the anesthetic along the spinal cord. Problems with overdosing are seldom serious because controlling the patient's position during administration can limit the distribution of the drug to a degree. Moreover, because the diaphragmatic breathing muscles are controlled by upper cervical spinal nerves, respiration continues even if all thoracic and abdominal segments have been paralyzed.

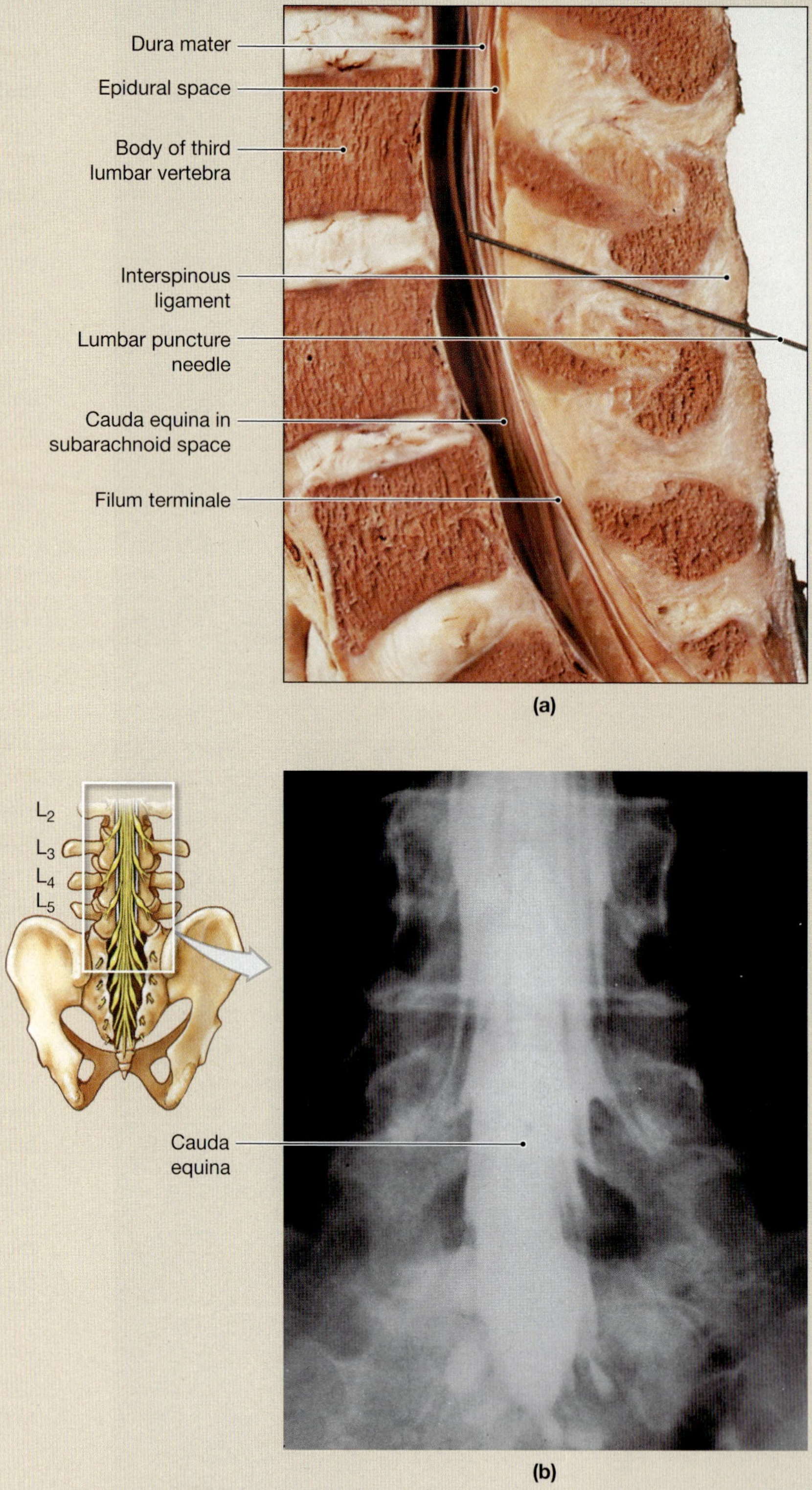

Figure 14.4 Spinal Taps and Myelography
(a) The position of the lumbar puncture needle is in the subarachnoid space, near the nerves of the cauda equina. The needle has been inserted in the midline between the third and fourth lumbar vertebral spines, pointing at a superior angle toward the umbilicus. Once the needle correctly punctures the dura and enters the subarachnoid space, a sample of CSF may be obtained. **(b)** A myelogram—an x-ray photograph of the spinal cord after introduction of a radiopaque dye into the CSF—showing the cauda equina in the lower lumbar region.

Sectional Anatomy of the Spinal Cord [Figure 14.5]

The anterior median fissure and the posterior median sulcus are longitudinal landmarks that follow the division between the left and right sides of the spinal cord (Figure 14.5). There is a central, H-shaped mass of **gray matter**, dominated by the cell bodies of neurons and glial cells. The gray matter surrounds the narrow **central canal**, which is located in the horizontal bar of the H. The projections of gray matter toward the outer surface of the spinal cord are called **horns** (Figure 14.5a,b). The peripherally situated **white matter** contains large numbers of myelinated and unmyelinated axons organized in *tracts* and *columns*. p. 345

Organization of Gray Matter [Figure 14.5b,c]

The cell bodies of neurons in the gray matter of the spinal cord are organized into groups, called *nuclei*, with specific functions. **Sensory nuclei** receive and relay sensory information from peripheral receptors, such as touch receptors located in the skin. **Motor nuclei** issue motor commands to peripheral effectors, such as skeletal muscles (Figure 14.5b). Sensory and motor nuclei may extend for a considerable distance along the length of the spinal cord. A frontal section along the axis of the central canal separates the sensory (dorsal) nuclei from the motor (ventral) nuclei. The **posterior** (dorsal) **gray horns** contain somatic and visceral sensory nuclei, whereas the **anterior** (ventral) **gray horns** contain neurons concerned with somatic motor control. **Lateral gray horns** (*intermediate horns*), found between segments T_1 and L_2, contain visceral motor neurons. The **gray commissures** (*commissura*, a joining together) contain axons crossing from one side of the cord to the other before reaching a destination within the gray matter (Figure 14.5b). There are two gray commissures, one posterior to and one anterior to the central canal.

Figure 14.5b shows the relationship between the function of a particular nucleus (sensory or motor) and its relative position within the gray matter of the spinal cord. Sensory nuclei are arranged within the white matter such that fibers entering the spinal cord more inferiorly (such as from the leg or hip) are located more medially than fibers entering at a higher level (trunk or arm). The nuclei within each gray horn are also highly organized. Motor nuclei are organized such that nerves innervating skeletal muscles of more proximal structures (such as the trunk and shoulder) would be located more medially within the gray matter than nuclei innervating the skeletal muscles of more distal structures (forearm and hand). Figure 14.5b,c illustrates the distribution of somatic motor nuclei in the anterior gray horns of the cervical enlargement. The size of the anterior horns varies with the number of skeletal muscles innervated by that segment. Thus, the anterior horns are largest in cervical and lumbar regions, which control the muscles associated with the limbs.

Organization of White Matter [Figure 14.5]

The white matter can be divided into regions, or **columns** (*funiculi*, singular, *funiculus*) (Figure 14.5c). The **posterior white columns** are sandwiched between the posterior gray horns and the posterior median sulcus. The **anterior white columns** lie between the anterior gray horns and the anterior median fissure; they are interconnected by the **anterior white commissure**. The white matter on either side between the anterior and posterior columns represents the **lateral white columns**.

Each column contains **tracts**, or *fasciculi*, whose axons share functional and structural characteristics (specific tracts are detailed in Chapter 16). A specific tract conveys either sensory information or motor commands, and the axons within a tract are relatively uniform with respect to diameter, myelination, and conduction speed. All of the axons within a tract relay information in the same direction. Small commissural tracts carry sensory or motor signals between segments of the spinal cord; other, larger tracts connect the spinal cord with the brain. **Ascending tracts** carry sensory information toward the brain, and **descending tracts** convey motor commands into the spinal cord. Within each column, the tracts are segregated according to the destination of the motor information or the source of the sensory information being carried. As a result, the tracts show a regional organization comparable to that found in the nuclei of the gray matter (Figure 14.5b,c). The identities of the major CNS tracts will be discussed when we consider sensory and motor pathways in Chapter 16.

Clinical Note

Spinal Cord Injuries Injuries affecting the spinal cord produce symptoms of sensory loss or motor paralysis that reflect the specific nuclei and tracts involved. At the outset, any severe injury to the spinal cord produces a period of sensory and motor paralysis termed **spinal shock**. The skeletal muscles become flaccid; neither somatic nor visceral reflexes function; and the brain no longer receives sensations of touch, pain, heat, or cold. The location and severity of the injury determine the extent and duration of these symptoms and how much recovery takes place.

Violent jolts, such as those associated with blows or gunshot wounds, may cause **spinal concussion** without visibly damaging the spinal cord. Spinal concussion produces a period of spinal shock, but the symptoms are only temporary and recovery may be complete in a matter of hours. More serious injuries, such as whiplash or falls, usually involve physical damage to the spinal cord. In a **spinal contusion**, hemorrhages occur in the meninges and within the spinal cord, pressure rises in the cerebrospinal fluid, and the white matter of the spinal cord may degenerate at the site of injury. Gradual recovery over a period of weeks may leave some functional losses. Recovery from a **spinal laceration** by vertebral fragments or other foreign bodies will usually be far slower and less complete. **Spinal compression** occurs when the spinal cord becomes physically squeezed or distorted within the vertebral canal. In a **spinal transection** the spinal cord is completely severed. Current surgical procedures cannot repair a severed spinal cord, but experimental techniques have restored partial function in laboratory rats.

Spinal injuries often involve some combination of compression, laceration, contusion, and partial transection. Relieving pressure and stabilizing the affected area through surgery may prevent further damage and allow the injured spinal cord to recover as much as possible. Extensive damage at or above the fourth or fifth cervical vertebra will eliminate sensation and motor control of the upper and lower limbs. The extensive paralysis produced is called **quadriplegia**. If the damage extends from C_3 to C_5, the motor paralysis will include all of the major respiratory muscles, and the patient will usually need mechanical assistance in breathing. **Paraplegia**, the loss of motor control of the lower limbs, may follow damage to the thoracic vertebrae and spinal cord. Injuries to the inferior lumbar vertebrae may compress or distort the elements of the cauda equina, causing problems with peripheral nerve function.

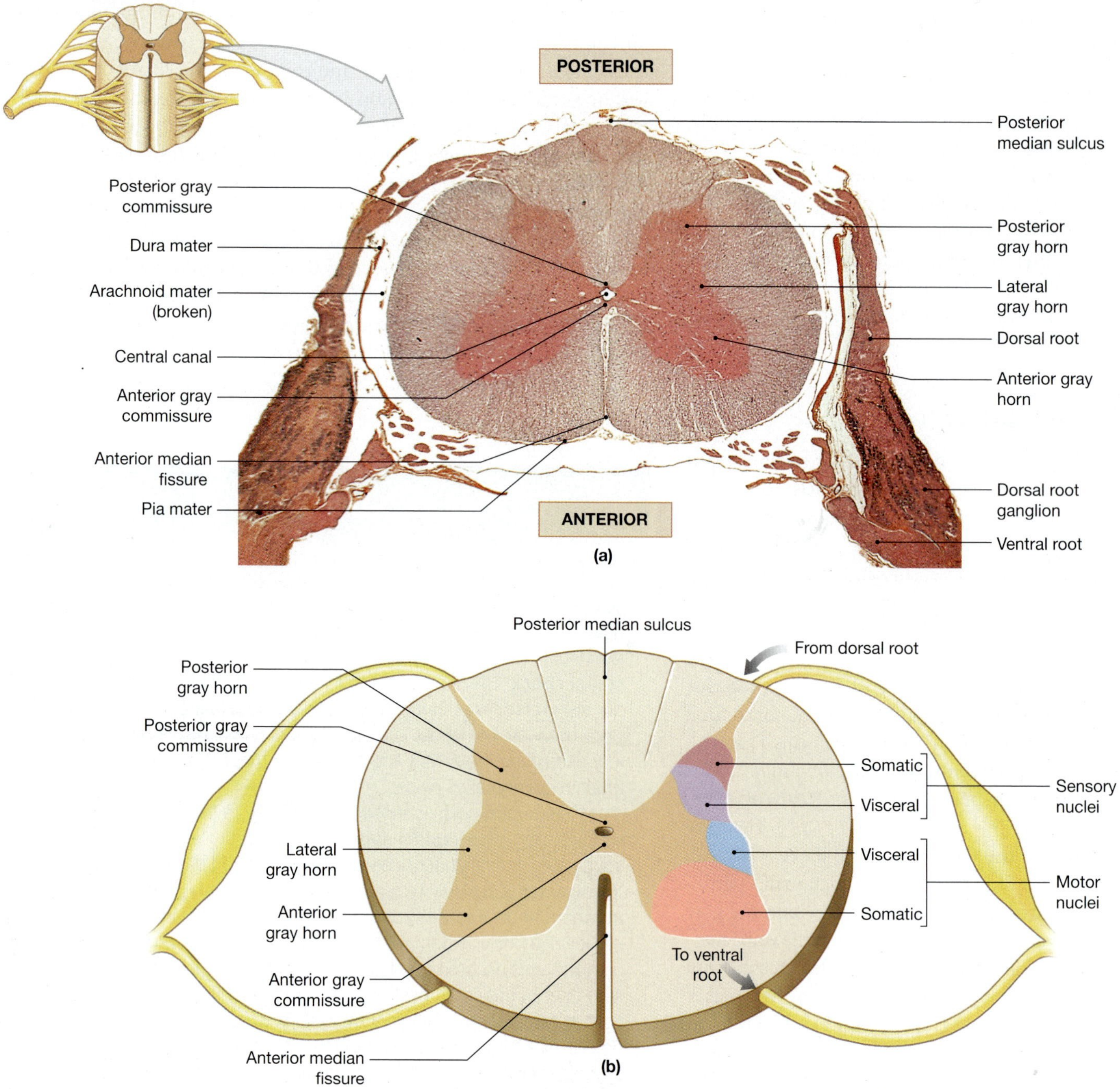

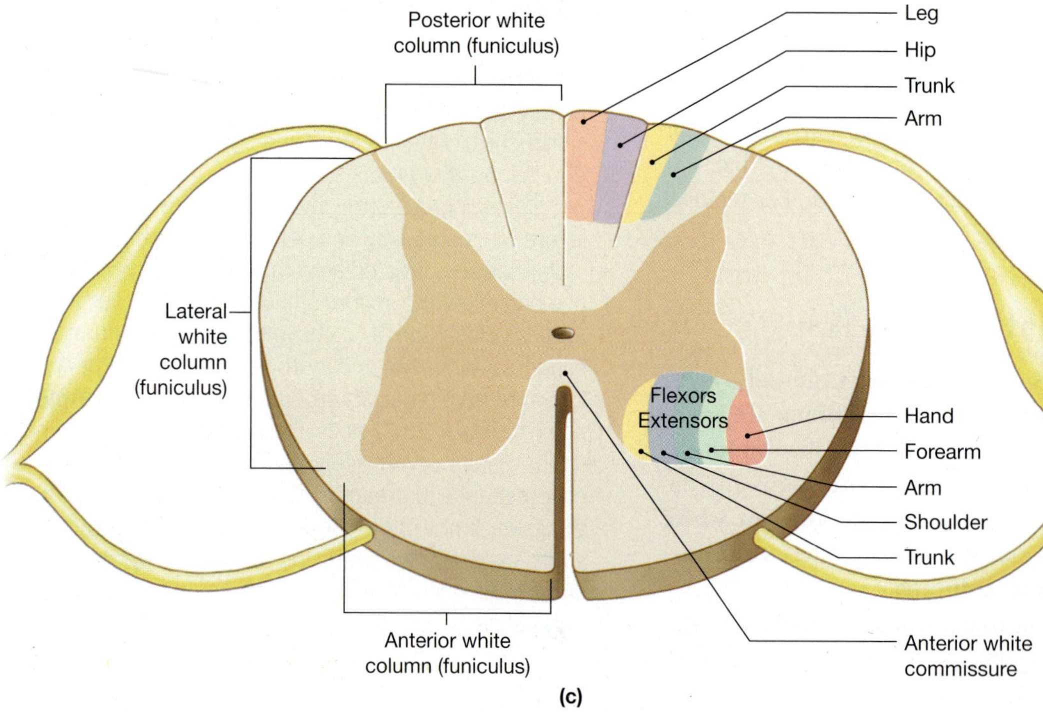

Figure 14.5 Sectional Organization of the Spinal Cord
(a) Histology of the spinal cord, transverse section. **(b)** The left half of this sectional view shows important anatomical landmarks; the right half indicates the functional organization of the gray matter in the anterior, lateral, and posterior gray horns. **(c)** The left half of this sectional view shows the major columns of white matter. The right half indicates the anatomical organization of sensory tracts in the posterior white column for comparison with the organization of motor nuclei in the anterior gray horn. Note that both sensory and motor components of the spinal cord have a definite regional organization.

CONCEPT CHECK

1. A patient with polio has lost the use of his leg muscles. In what area of the spinal cord would you expect to locate the virally infected motor neurons in this individual?
2. How is white matter organized within the spinal cord?
3. What is the term used to describe the projections of gray matter toward the outer surface of the spinal cord?
4. What is the difference between ascending tracts and descending tracts in the white matter?

See blue "Answers" tab at back of book.

Spinal Nerves [Figures 14.1/14.6]

There are 31 pairs of spinal nerves: 8 cervical spinal nerves, 12 thoracic, 5 lumbar, 5 sacral, and 1 coccygeal spinal nerve. Each can be identified by its association with adjacent vertebrae. Every spinal nerve has a regional number, as indicated in **Figure 14.1**, p. 363.

In the cervical region the first pair of spinal nerves, C_1 exits between the skull and the first cervical vertebra. For this reason, cervical nerves take their names from the vertebra immediately *following* them. In other words, cervical nerve C_2 *precedes* vertebra C_2, and the same system is used for the rest of the cervical spinal nerves. The transition from this identification method occurs between the last cervical and first thoracic vertebrae. The spinal nerve lying between these two vertebrae has been designated C_8 and is shown in **Figure 14.1b**. Thus, there are seven cervical vertebrae but *eight* cervical nerves. Spinal nerves caudal to the first thoracic vertebra take their names from the vertebra immediately *preceding* them. Thus, the spinal nerve T_1 emerges immediately caudal to vertebra T_1, spinal nerve T_2 follows vertebra T_2, and so forth.

Each peripheral nerve has three layers of connective tissue: an outer *epineurium*, a central *perineurium*, and an inner *endoneurium* (**Figure 14.6**). These are comparable to the connective tissue layers associated with skeletal muscles. p. 238 The **epineurium** is a tough fibrous sheath that forms the outermost layer of a peripheral nerve. It consists of dense irregular connective tissue primarily composed of collagen fibers and fibrocytes. At each intervertebral foramen, the epineurium of a spinal nerve becomes continuous with the dura mater of the spinal cord.

The **perineurium** is composed of collagenous fibers, elastic fibers, and fibrocytes. The perineurium divides the nerve into a series of compartments that contain bundles of axons. A single bundle of axons is known as a **fascicle**, or **fasciculus**.

Peripheral nerves must be isolated and protected from the chemical components of the interstitial fluid and the general circulation. The *blood–nerve barrier*, formed by the connective tissue fibers and fibrocyte cells of the epineurium, serves as this diffusion barrier.

The **endoneurium** consists of loose, irregularly arranged connective tissue composed of delicate collagenous and elastic connective tissue fibers and a few isolated fibrocytes that surround individual axons. Capillaries leaving the perineurium branch in the endoneurium and provide oxygen and nutrients to the axons and Schwann cells of the nerve.

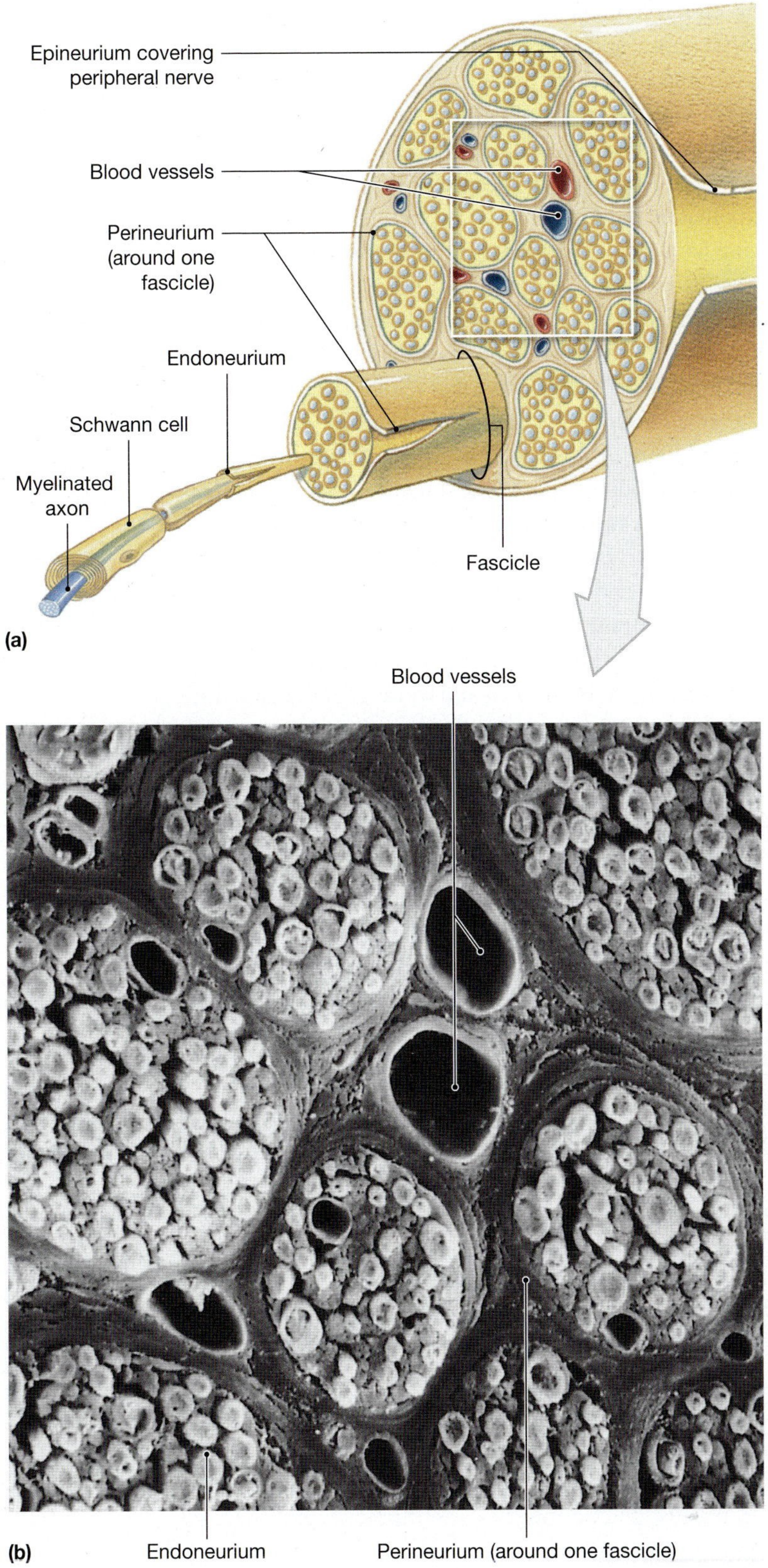

Figure 14.6 Anatomy of a Peripheral Nerve
A peripheral nerve consists of an outer epineurium enclosing a variable number of fascicles (bundles of nerve fibers). The fascicles are wrapped by the perineurium, and within each fascicle the individual axons, which are ensheathed by Schwann cells, are surrounded by the endoneurium. **(a)** A typical peripheral nerve and its connective tissue wrappings. **(b)** A scanning electron micrograph showing the various layers in great detail. (SEM × 425) [© R. G. Kessel and R. H. Kardon, "Tissues and Organs: A Text-Atlas of Scanning Electron Microscopy," W. H. Freeman & Co., 1979. All Rights Reserved.]

Peripheral Distribution of Spinal Nerves
[Figures 14.2a,c,d/14.7/14.8]

Each spinal nerve forms through the fusion of dorsal and ventral nerve roots as those roots pass through an intervertebral foramen; the only exceptions are at C_1 and Co_1, where some people lack dorsal roots (**Figure 14.2a,c,d,** p. 364). Distally, the spinal nerve divides into several branches. All spinal nerves form two branches, a *dorsal ramus* and a *ventral ramus*. For spinal nerves T_1 to L_2 there are four branches: a white ramus and a gray ramus, collectively known as the *rami communicantes* ("communicating branches"), a dorsal ramus, and a ventral ramus (Figure 14.7). The rami communicantes carry visceral motor fibers to and from a nearby **autonomic ganglion** associated with the *sympathetic division* of the ANS. (We will examine this division in Chapter 17.) Because preganglionic axons are myelinated, the branch carrying those fibers to the ganglion has a light color, and it is known as the **white ramus** (*ramus*, branch). Two groups of unmyelinated postganglionic fibers leave the ganglion. Those innervating glands and smooth muscles in the body wall or limbs form a second branch, the **gray ramus**, that rejoins the spinal nerve. The gray ramus is typically proximal to the white ramus. Preganglionic or postganglionic fibers that innervate internal organs do not rejoin the spinal nerves. Instead, they form a series of separate autonomic nerves, such as the *splanchnic nerves*, involved with regulating the activities of organs in the abdominopelvic cavity.

The **dorsal ramus** of each spinal nerve provides sensory innervation from, and motor innervation to, a specific segment of the skin and muscles of the neck and back. The region innervated resembles a horizontal band that begins at the origin of the spinal nerve. The relatively large **ventral ramus** supplies the ventrolateral body surface, structures in the body wall, and the limbs.

The distribution of the sensory fibers within the dorsal and ventral rami illustrates the segmental division of labor along the length of the spinal cord (Figure 14.7b). Each pair of spinal nerves monitors a specific region of the body surface, an area known as a **dermatome** (Figure 14.8). Dermatomes are clinically important because damage to either a spinal nerve or dorsal root ganglion will produce a characteristic loss of sensation in specific areas of the skin.

Nerve Plexuses [Figures 14.3/14.7 and 14.9]

The distribution pattern illustrated in Figure 14.7 applies to spinal nerves T_1–L_2. White and gray rami communicantes are found only in these segments; however, gray rami, dorsal rami, and ventral rami are characteristic of all spinal nerves. The dorsal rami provide roughly segmental sensory innervation, as evidenced by the pattern of dermatomes. The segmental alignment isn't exact, because the boundaries are imprecise, and there is some overlap between adjacent dermatomes. But in segments controlling the skeletal musculature of the neck and the upper and lower limbs, the peripheral distribution of the ventral rami does not proceed directly to their peripheral targets. Instead, the ventral rami of adjacent spinal nerves blend their fibers to produce a series of compound nerve trunks. Such a complex interwoven network of nerves is called a **nerve plexus** (PLEK-sus, "braid"). Nerve plexuses form during development as small skeletal muscles fuse with their neighbors to form larger muscles with compound origins. Although the anatomical boundaries between the embryonic muscles

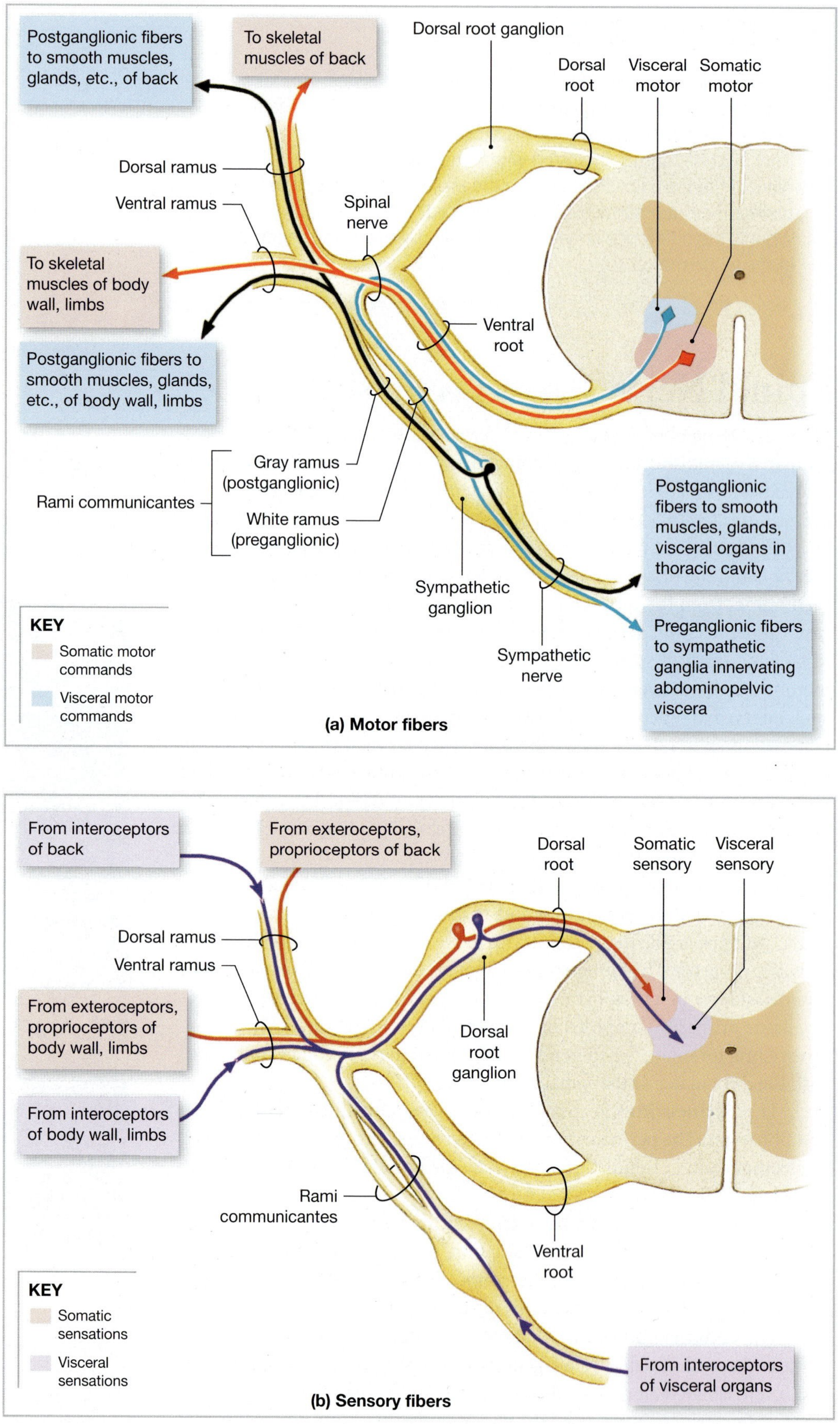

Figure 14.7 Peripheral Distribution of Spinal Nerves
Diagrammatic view illustrating the distribution of fibers in the major branches of a representative thoracic spinal nerve. **(a)** The distribution of motor neurons in the spinal cord and motor fibers within the spinal nerve and its branches. Although the gray ramus is typically proximal to the white ramus, this simplified diagrammatic view makes it easier to follow the relationships between preganglionic and postganglionic fibers. **(b)** A comparable view, detailing the distribution of sensory neurons and sensory fibers.

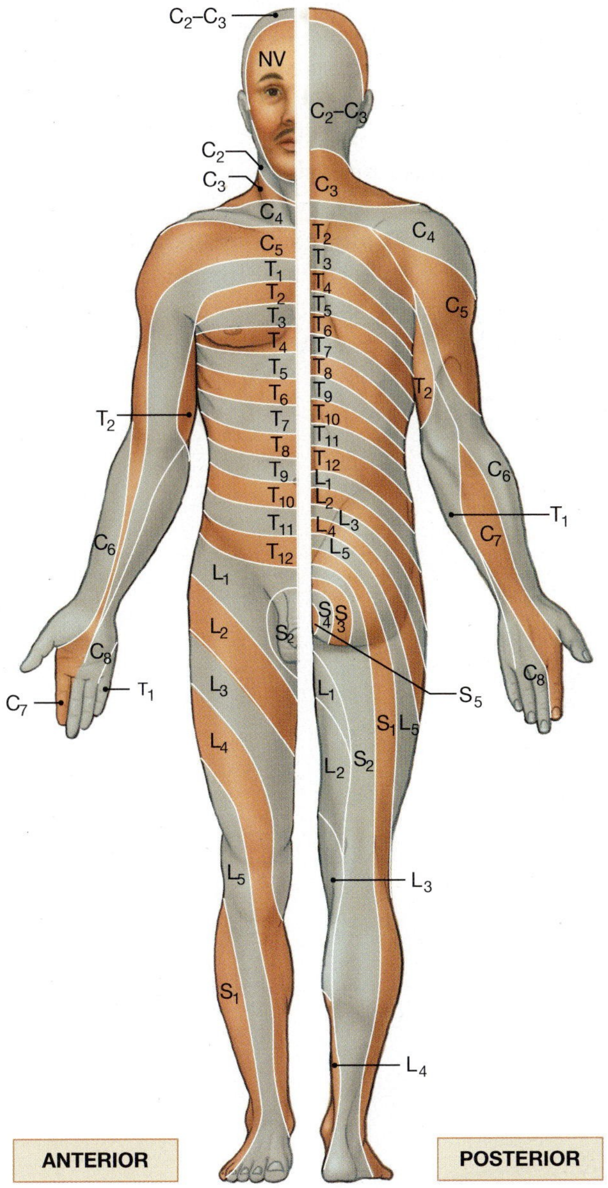

Figure 14.8 Dermatomes
Anterior and posterior distribution of dermatomes; the related spinal nerves are indicated for each dermatome.

disappear, the original pattern of innervation remains intact. Thus the "nerves" that innervate these compound muscles in the adult contain sensory and motor fibers from the ventral rami that innervated the embryonic muscles. Nerve plexuses exist where ventral rami are converging and branching to form these compound nerves. The four major nerve plexuses are the *cervical plexus*, *brachial plexus*, *lumbar plexus*, and *sacral plexus* (**Figures 14.3**, p. 365, and **14.9**).

Figure 14.9 Peripheral Nerves and Nerve Plexuses

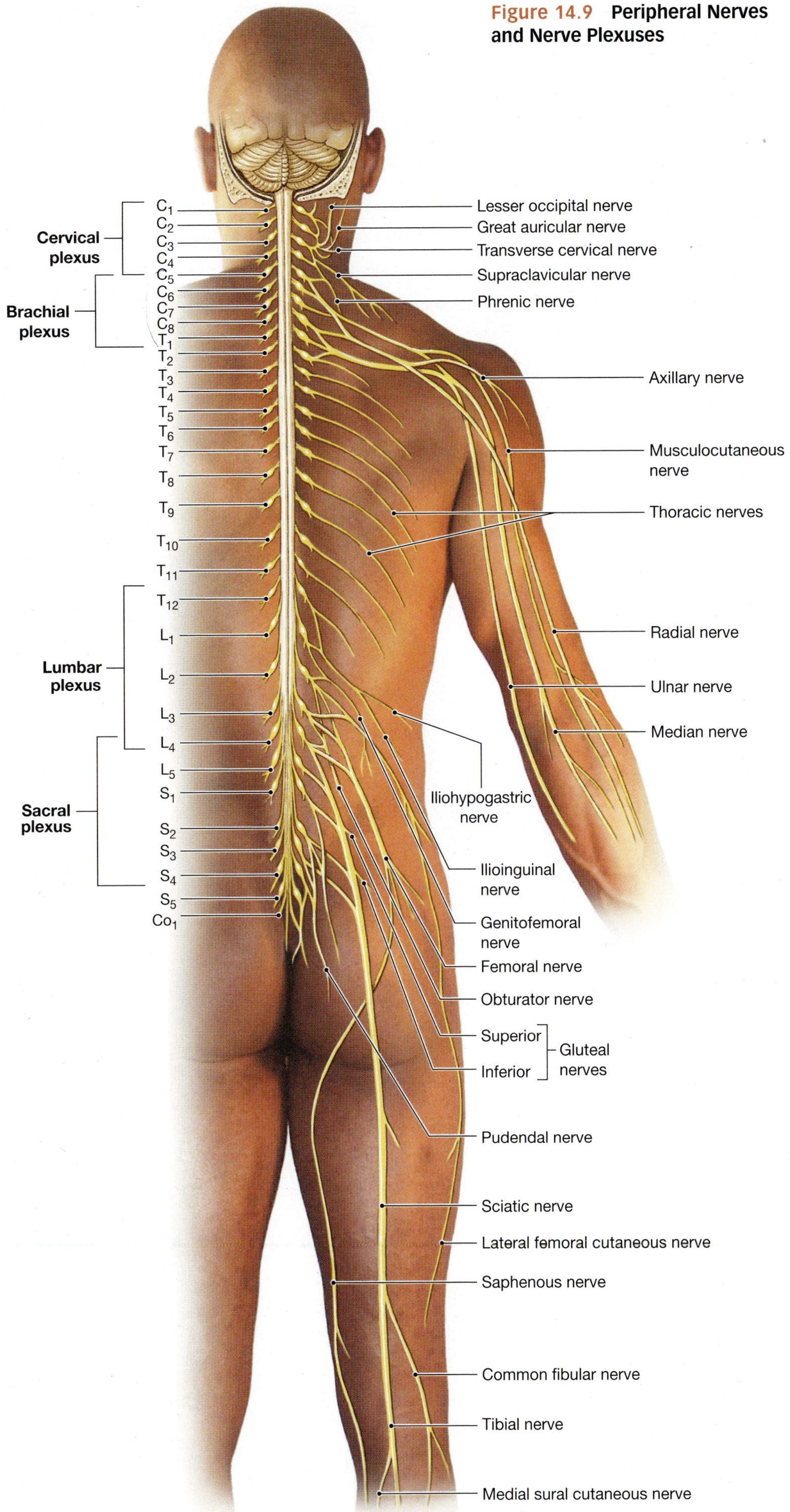

TABLE 14.1 The Cervical Plexus

Spinal Segments	Nerves	Distribution
C_1–C_4	Ansa cervicalis (superior and inferior branches)	Five of the extrinsic laryngeal muscles (sternothyroid, sternohyoid, omohyoid, geniohyoid, and thyrohyoid) by way of N XII
C_2–C_3	Lesser occipital, transverse cervical, supraclavicular, and great auricular nerves	Skin of upper chest, shoulder, neck, and ear
C_3–C_5	Phrenic nerve	Diaphragm
C_1–C_5	Cervical nerves	Levator scapulae, scalenes, sternocleidomastoid, and trapezius muscles (with N XI)

The Cervical Plexus [Figures 14.9/14.10 and Table 14.1]

The **cervical plexus** (Figures 14.9 and 14.10) consists of cutaneous and muscular branches in the ventral rami of spinal nerves C_1–C_4 and some nerve fibers from C_5. The cervical plexus lies deep to the sternocleidomastoid muscle (p. 271), and anterior to the middle scalene and levator scapulae muscles. p. 274–276, 286 The cutaneous branches of this plexus innervate areas on the head, neck, and chest. The muscular branches innervate the omohyoid, sternohyoid, geniohyoid, thyrohyoid, and sternothyroid muscles of the neck (p. 272), the sternocleidomastoid, scalene, levator scapulae, and trapezius muscles of the neck and shoulder (pp. 272, 276, 287), and the diaphragm. p. 276 The **phrenic nerve**, the major nerve of this plexus, provides the entire nerve supply to the diaphragm. Figures 14.9 and 14.10 identify the nerves responsible for the control of axial and appendicular skeletal muscles considered in Chapters 10 and 11.

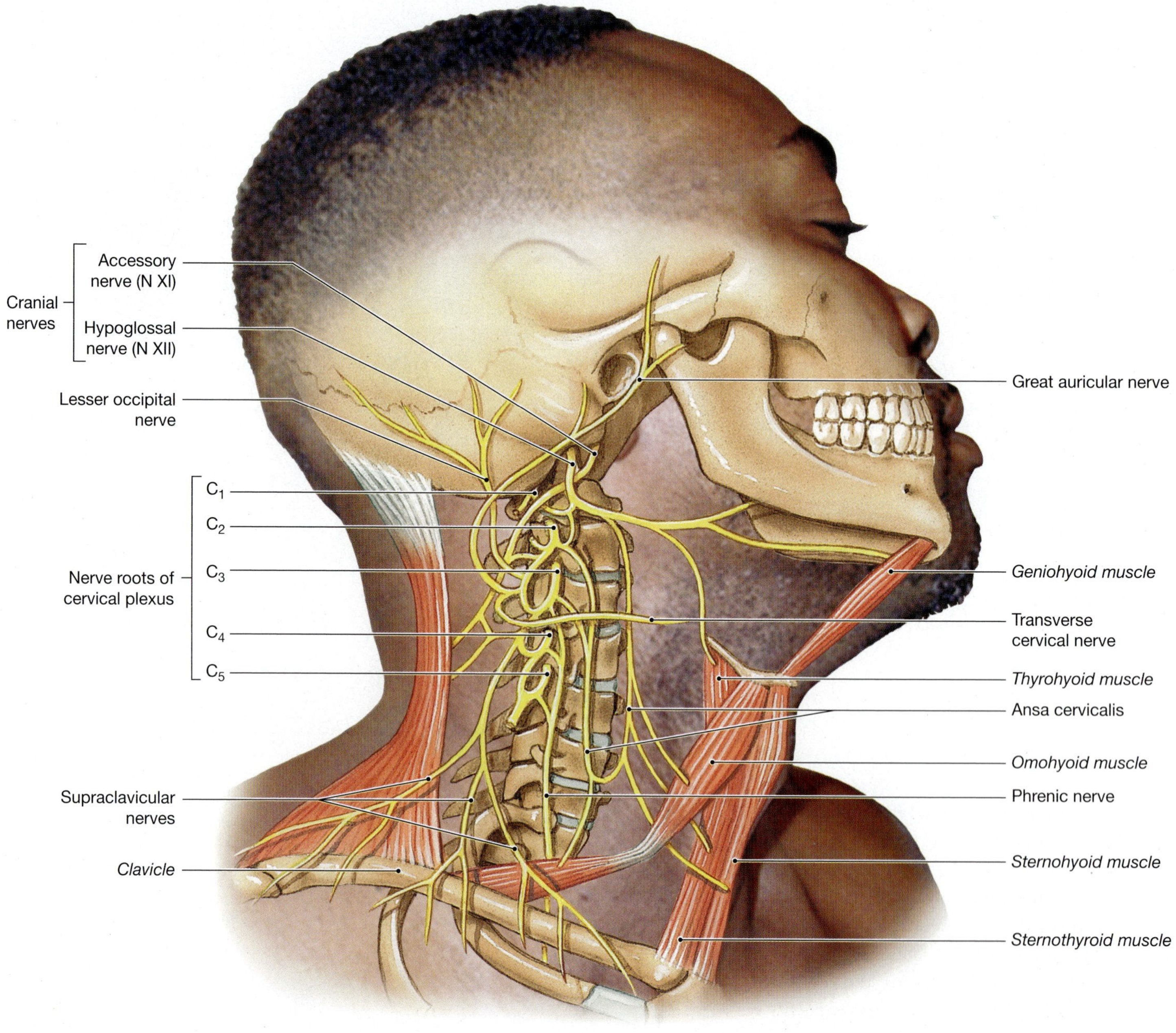

Figure 14.10 The Cervical Plexus

The Brachial Plexus [Figures 14.9/14.11/14.12 and Table 14.2]

The **brachial plexus** is larger and more complex than the cervical plexus. It innervates the pectoral girdle and upper limb. The brachial plexus is formed by the ventral rami of spinal nerves C_5–T_1 (Figures 14.9, 14.11a,b, and 14.12). The ventral rami converge to form the **superior**, **middle**, and **inferior trunks**. Each of these trunks then divides into an **anterior division** and a **posterior division**. All three posterior divisions will unite to form the **posterior cord**, while the anterior divisions of the superior and middle trunks unite to form the **lateral cord**. The **medial cord** is formed by a continuation of the anterior division of the inferior trunk. The nerves of the brachial plexus arise from one or more trunks or cords whose names indicate their positions relative to the axillary artery, a large artery supplying the upper limb. The lateral cord forms the **musculocutaneous nerve** exclusively and, together with the medial cord, contributes to the **median nerve**. The **ulnar nerve** is the other major nerve of the medial cord. The posterior cord gives rise to the **axillary nerve** and the **radial nerve**. Figures 14.9 and 14.11 identify these nerves as well as the smaller nerves responsible for the control of axial and appendicular skeletal muscles considered in Chapters 10 and 11. p. 275, 276, 290, 293 Table 14.2 provides further information about these and other major nerves of the brachial plexus.

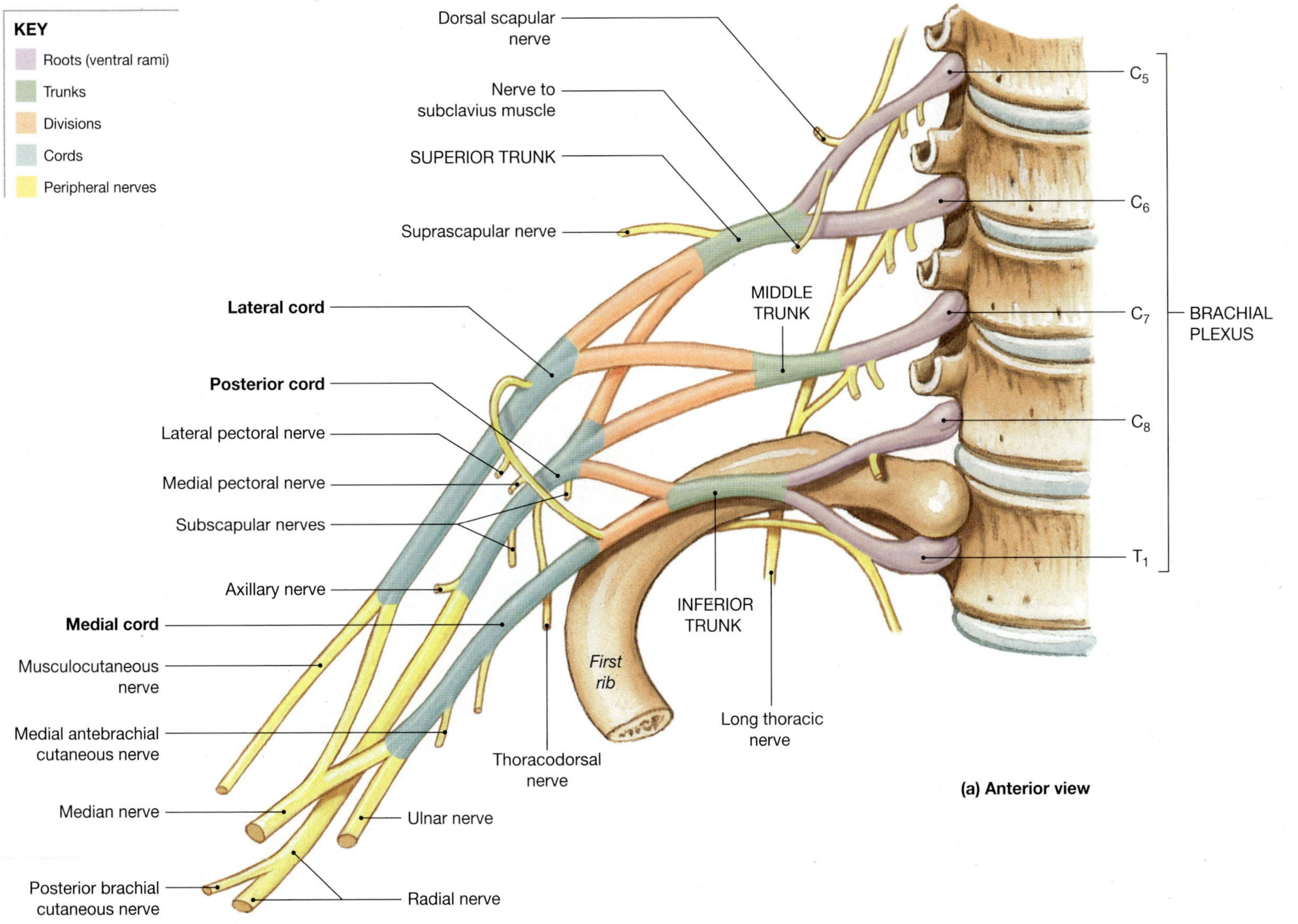

Figure 14.11 The Brachial Plexus
(a) The trunks and cords of the brachial plexus. **(b)** Anterior view of the brachial plexus and upper limb, showing the peripheral distribution of major nerves. **(c)** Posterior view of the brachial plexus and the innervation of the upper limb.

Figure 14.11 ***(continued)***

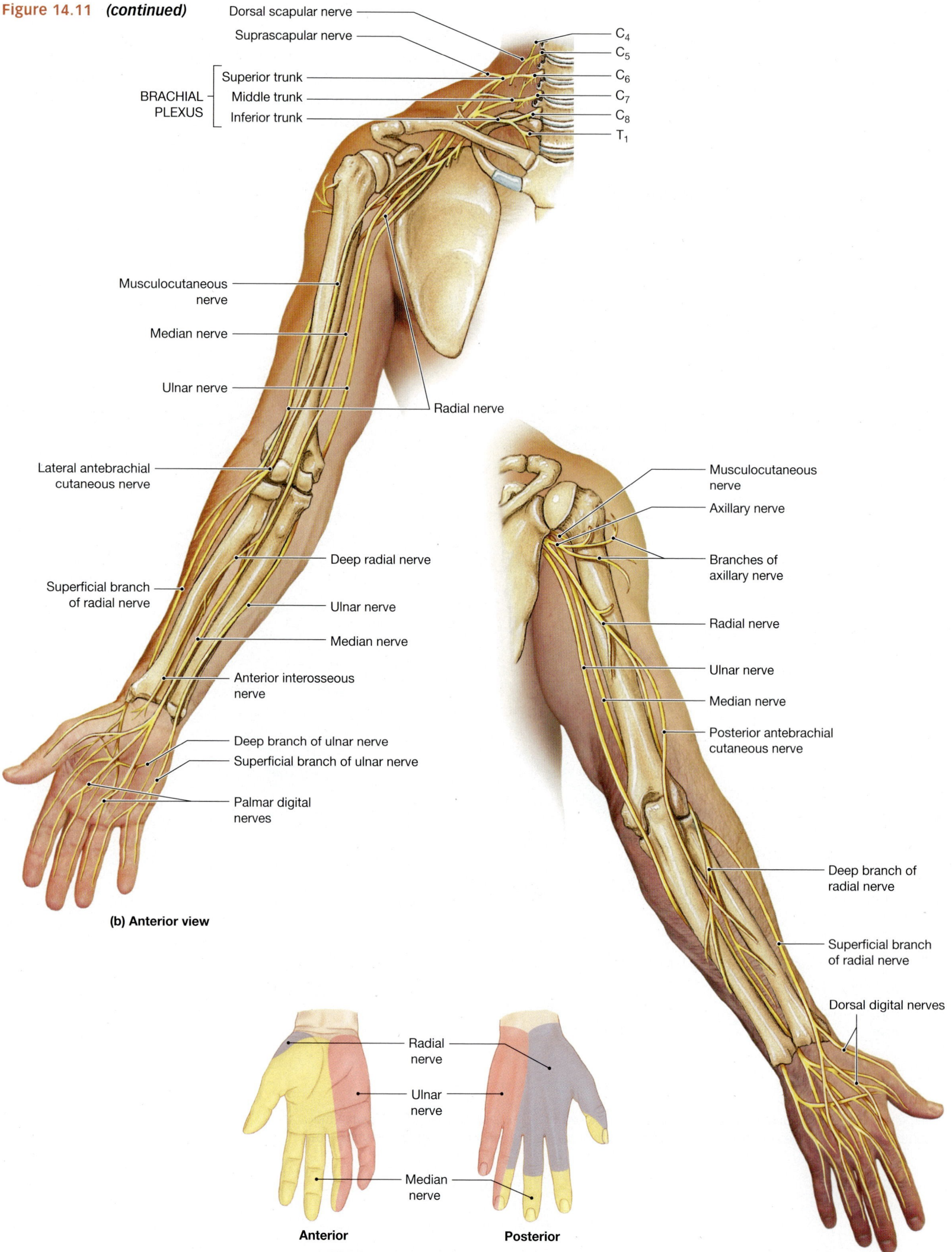

(b) Anterior view

Distribution of cutaneous nerves

(c) Posterior view

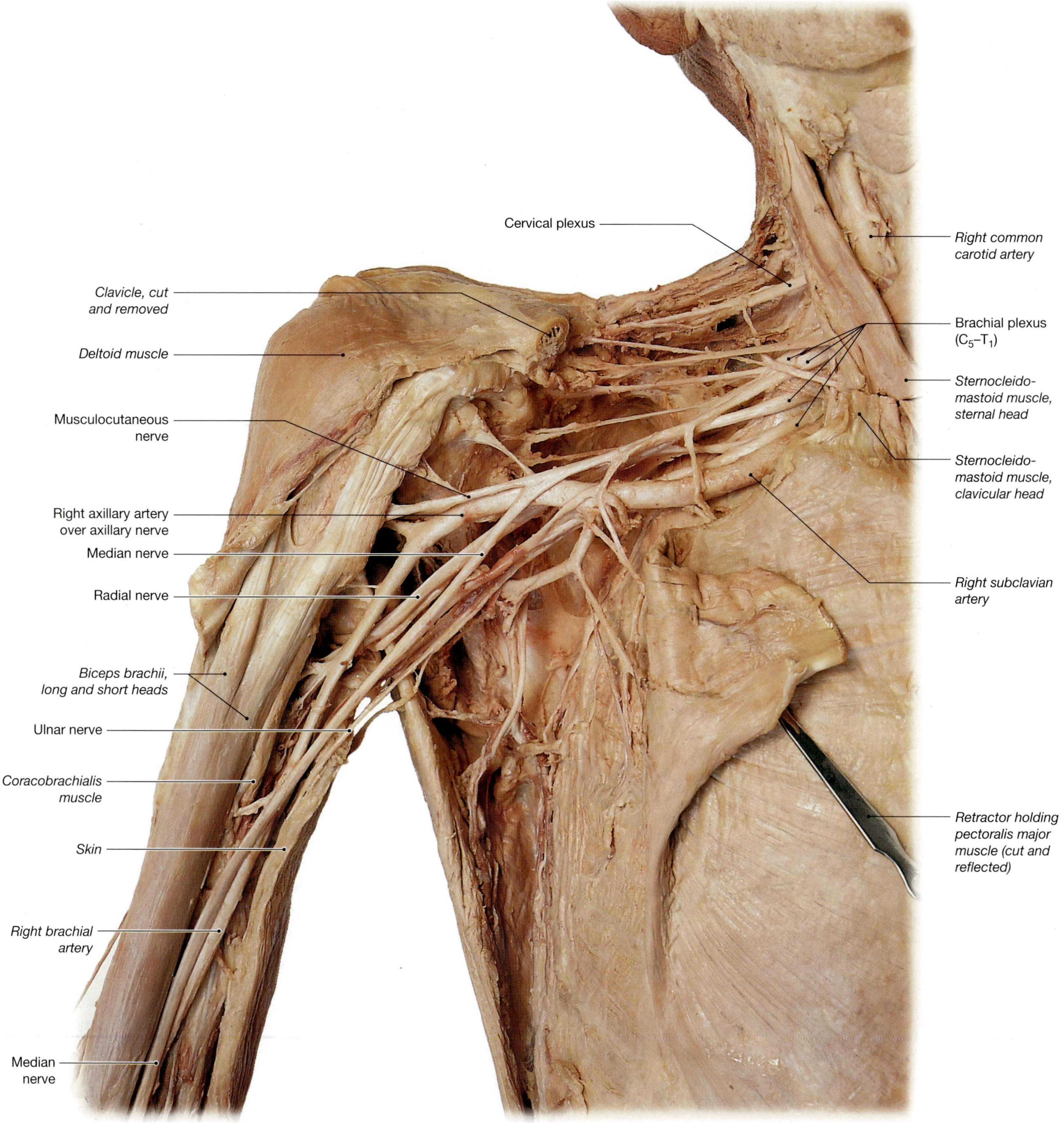

Figure 14.12 The Cervical and Brachial Plexuses
This dissection shows the major nerves arising from the cervical and brachial plexuses.

TABLE 14.2 The Brachial Plexus

Spinal Segments	Nerve(s)	Distribution
C_4–C_6	Nerve to subclavius	Subclavius muscle
C_5	Dorsal scapular nerve	Rhomboid and levator scapulae muscles
C_5–C_7	Long thoracic nerve	Serratus anterior muscle
C_5, C_6	Suprascapular nerve	Supraspinatus and infraspinatus muscles; sensory from shoulder joint and scapula
C_5–T_1	Pectoral nerves (medial and lateral)	Pectoralis muscles
C_5, C_6	Subscapular nerves	Subscapularis and teres major muscles
C_6–C_8	Thoracodorsal nerve	Latissimus dorsi muscle
C_5, C_6	Axillary nerve	Deltoid and teres minor muscles; sensory from skin of shoulder
C_8–T_1	Medial antebrachial cutaneous nerve	Sensory from skin over anterior, medial surface of arm and forearm
C_5–T_1	Radial nerve	Many extensor muscles on the arm and forearm (triceps brachii, anconeus, extensor carpi radialis, extensor carpi ulnaris, and brachioradialis muscles); supinator muscle, digital extensor muscles, and abductor pollicis muscle via the *deep branch;* sensory from skin over the posterolateral surface of the limb through the *posterior brachial cutaneous nerve* (arm), *posterior antebrachial cutaneous nerve* (forearm), and the *superficial branch* (radial portion of hand)
C_5–C_7	Musculocutaneous nerve	Flexor muscles on the arm (biceps brachii, brachialis, and coracobrachialis muscles); sensory from skin over lateral surface of the forearm through the *lateral antebrachial cutaneous nerve*
C_6–T_1	Median nerve	Flexor muscles on the forearm (flexor carpi radialis and palmaris longus muscles); pronator quadratus and pronator teres muscles; radial half of flexor digitorum profundus muscle, digital flexors (through the *anterior interosseous nerve*); sensory from skin over anterolateral surface of the hand
C_8, T_1	Ulnar nerve	Flexor carpi ulnaris muscle, ulnar half of flexor digitorum profundus muscle, adductor pollicis muscle, and small digital muscles through the *deep branch*; sensory from skin over medial surface of the hand through the *superficial branch*

The Lumbar and Sacral Plexuses [Figures 14.9/14.13/14.14 and Table 14.3]

The **lumbar plexus** and the **sacral plexus** arise from the lumbar and sacral segments of the spinal cord. The ventral rami of these nerves supply the pelvis and lower limb (**Figures 14.9,** p. 371, and **14.13**). Because the ventral rami of both plexuses are distributed to the lower limb, they are often collectively referred to as the *lumbosacral plexus.* The nerves that form the lumbar and sacral plexuses are detailed in Table 14.3.

The lumbar plexus is formed by the ventral rami of T_{12}–L_4. The major nerves of the lumbar plexus are the **genitofemoral nerve**, **lateral femoral cutaneous nerve**, and **femoral nerve**. The sacral plexus contains the ventral rami from spinal nerves L_4–S_4. The ventral rami of L_4 and L_5 form the **lumbosacral trunk**, which contributes to the sacral plexus along with the ventral rami of S_1–S_4 (**Figure 14.13a,b**). The major nerves of the sacral plexus are the **sciatic nerve** and the **pudendal nerve**. The sciatic nerve passes posterior to the femur and deep to the long head of the biceps femoris muscle. As it approaches the popliteal fossa, the sciatic nerve divides into two branches: the **common fibular nerve** and the **tibial nerve** (**Figures 14.9,** p. 371, and **14.14**). **Figures 14.9,** p. 371, **14.13,** and **14.14** show these nerves as well as the smaller nerves responsible for controlling the axial and appendicular muscles detailed in Chapters 10 and 11.

Although dermatomes can provide clues to the location of injuries along the spinal cord, the loss of sensation at the skin does not provide precise information concerning the site of injury, because the boundaries of dermatomes are not precise, clearly defined lines. More exact conclusions can be drawn from the loss of motor control on the basis of the origin and distribution of the peripheral nerves originating at nerve plexuses. In the assessment of motor performance, a distinction is made between the conscious ability to control motor activities and the performance of automatic, involuntary motor responses. These latter, programmed motor patterns, called *reflexes*, will be described now.

CONCEPT CHECK

1. Injury to which of the nerve plexuses would interfere with the ability to breathe?
2. Describe in order, from outermost to innermost, the three connective tissue layers surrounding each peripheral nerve.
3. Distinguish between a white ramus and a gray ramus.
4. Which nerve plexus may have been damaged if motor activity in the arm and forearm are affected by injury?

See blue "Answers" tab at back of book.

TABLE 14.3 The Lumbar and Sacral Plexuses

Spinal Segment(s)	Nerve(s)	Distribution
LUMBAR PLEXUS		
T_{12}–L_1	Iliohypogastric nerve	Abdominal muscles (external and internal oblique muscles, transverse abdominis muscles); skin over inferior abdomen and buttocks
L_1	Ilioinguinal nerve	Abdominal muscles (with *iliohypogastric nerve*); skin over superior, medial thigh and portions of external genitalia
L_1, L_2	Genitofemoral nerve	Skin over anteromedial surface of thigh and portions of external genitalia
L_2, L_3	Lateral femoral cutaneous nerve	Skin over anterior, lateral, and posterior surfaces of thigh
L_2–L_4	Femoral nerve	Anterior muscles of thigh (sartorius muscle and quadriceps group); adductors of hip (pectineus and iliopsoas muscles); skin over anteromedial surface of thigh, medial surface of leg and foot
L_2–L_4	Obturator nerve	Adductors of hip (adductors magnus, brevis, and longus); gracilis muscle; skin over medial surface of thigh
L_2–L_4	Saphenous nerve	Skin over medial surface of leg
SACRAL PLEXUS		
L_4–S_2	Gluteal nerves:	
	Superior	Abductors of hip (gluteus minimus, gluteus medius, and tensor fasciae latae)
	Inferior	Extensor of hip (gluteus maximus)
S_1–S_3	Posterior femoral cutaneous nerve	Skin of perineum and posterior surface of thigh and leg
L_4–S_3	Sciatic nerve:	Two of the hamstrings (semimembranosus and semitendinosus); adductor magnus (with *obturator nerve*)
	Tibial nerve	Flexors of knee and extensors (plantar flexors) of ankle (popliteus, gastrocnemius, soleus, and tibialis posterior muscles and long head of the biceps femoris muscle); flexors of toes; skin over posterior surface of leg; plantar surface of foot
	Fibular nerve	Short head of biceps femoris muscle; fibularis (brevis and longus) and tibialis anterior muscles; extensors of toes; skin over anterior surface of leg and dorsal surface of foot; skin over lateral portion of foot (through the *sural nerve*)
S_2–S_4	Pudendal nerve	Muscles of perineum, including urogenital diaphragm and external anal and urethral sphincter muscles; skin of external genitalia and related skeletal muscles (bulbospongiosus and ischiocavernosus muscles)

Clinical Note

Peripheral Neuropathies **Peripheral neuropathies**, or *peripheral nerve palsies*, are characterized by regional losses of sensory and motor function as a result of nerve trauma or compression. **Brachial palsies** result from injuries to the brachial plexus or its branches.

The pressure palsies are especially interesting; a familiar, but mild, example is the experience of having an arm or leg "fall asleep." The limb becomes numb, and afterward an uncomfortable "pins-and-needles" sensation, or **paresthesia**, accompanies the return to normal function. These incidents are seldom clinically significant, but they provide graphic examples of the effects of more serious palsies that can last for days to months. In **radial nerve palsy**, pressure on the back of the arm interrupts the function of the radial nerve, so the extensors of the wrist and fingers are paralyzed. This condition is also known as "Saturday night palsy," because falling asleep on a couch with your arm over the seat back (or beneath someone's head) can produce the right combination of pressures. Students may also be familiar with **ulnar palsy**, which can result from prolonged contact between an elbow and a desk. The ring finger and little finger lose sensation, and the fingers cannot be adducted. *Carpal tunnel syndrome* is a neuropathy resulting from compression of the median nerve at the wrist, where it passes deep to the flexor retinaculum with the flexor tendons. Repetitive flexion/extension at the wrist can irritate these tendon sheaths, the swelling that results is what compresses the median nerve.

Crural palsies involve the nerves of the lumbosacral plexus. Persons who carry large wallets in their hip pockets may develop symptoms of **sciatic compression** after they drive or sit in one position for extended periods. As nerve function declines, the individuals notice lumbar or gluteal pain, numbness along the back of the leg, and weakness in the leg muscles. Similar symptoms result from the compression of nerve roots that form the sciatic nerve by a distorted lumbar intervertebral disc. This condition is termed **sciatica**, and one or both lower limbs may be affected, depending on the site of compression. Finally, sitting with your legs crossed can produce symptoms of a **fibular palsy** (peroneal palsy). Sensory losses from the top of the foot and side of the leg are accompanied by a decreased ability to dorsiflex ("foot drop") or evert the foot.

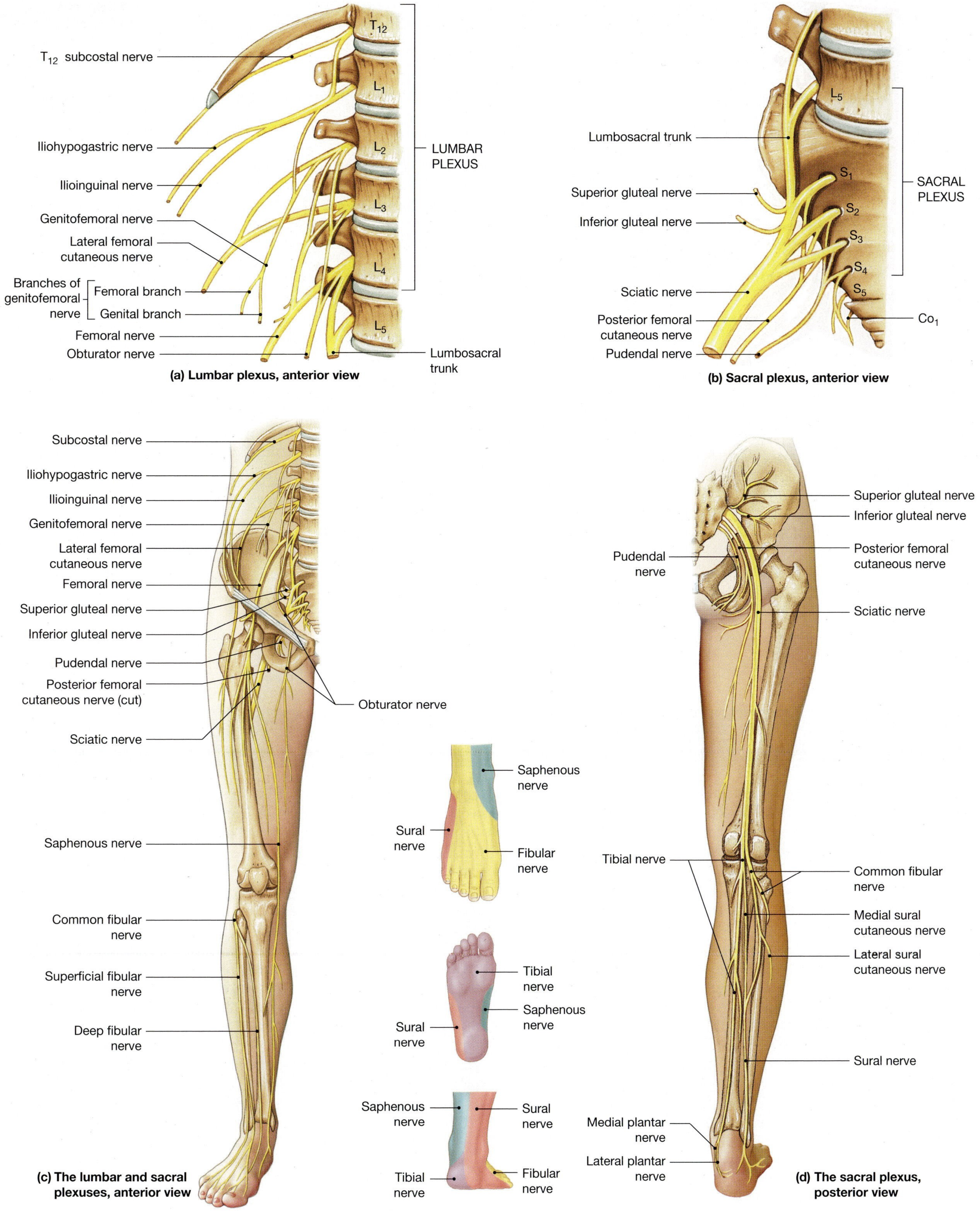

Figure 14.13 The Lumbar and Sacral Plexuses, Part I

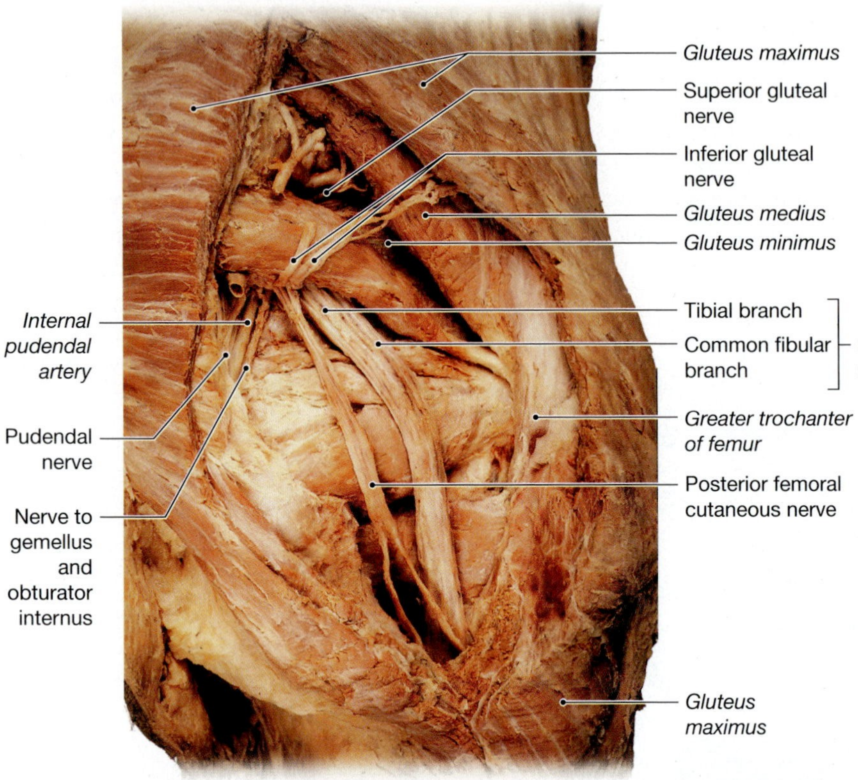

(a) Posterior gluteal region

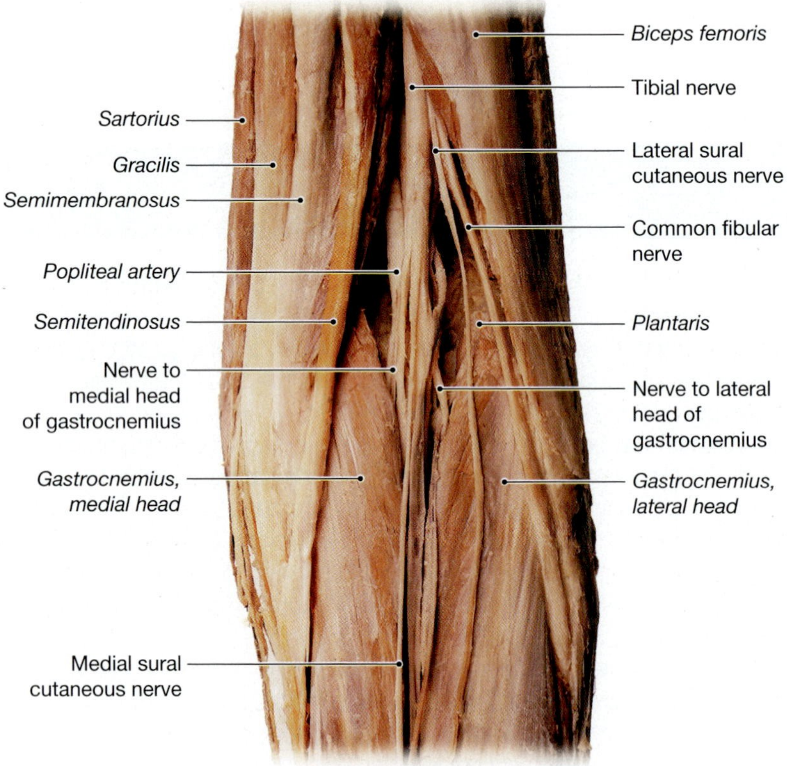

(b) Popliteal region

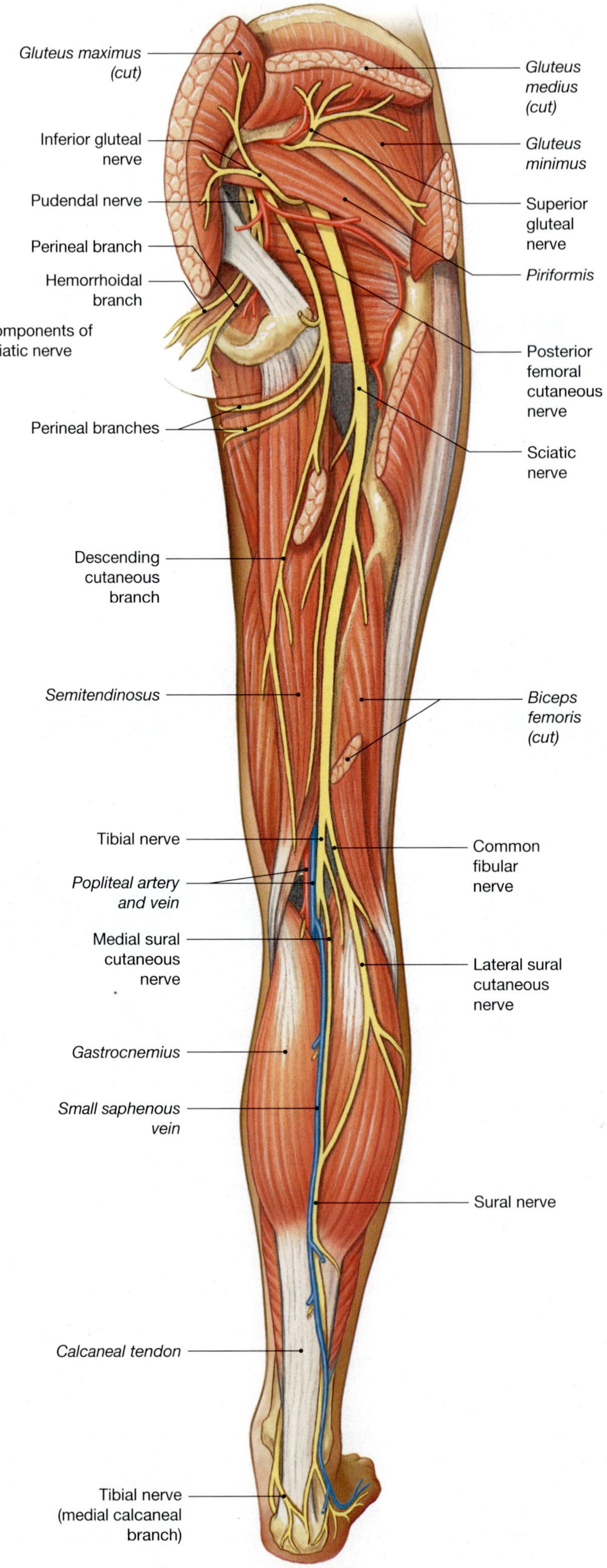

(c) Posterior view

Figure 14.14 The Lumbar and Sacral Plexuses, Part II
Posterior views of lumbar and sacral plexuses and distribution of peripheral nerves. Major nerves are seen in **(a)** a dissection of the right gluteal region and **(b)** a dissection of the popliteal fossa. **(c)** A diagrammatic posterior view of the right hip and lower limb, detailing the distribution of peripheral nerves.

Reflexes [Figures 14.15 to 14.18]

Conditions inside or outside the body can change rapidly and unexpectedly. A **reflex** is an immediate involuntary motor response to a specific stimulus (Figures 14.15 to 14.18). Reflexes help preserve homeostasis by making rapid adjustments in the function of organs or organ systems. The response shows little variability—activation of a particular reflex always produces the same motor response. The neural "wiring" of a single reflex is called a **reflex arc**. A reflex arc begins at a receptor and ends at a peripheral effector, such as a muscle or gland cell. Figure 14.15 illustrates the five steps involved in a neural reflex:

STEP 1. ***Arrival of a Stimulus and Activation of a Receptor.*** There are many types of sensory receptors, and general categories were introduced in Chapter 13. p. 351 Each receptor has a characteristic range of sensitivity; some receptors, such as pain receptors, respond to almost any stimulus. These receptors, the dendrites of sensory neurons, are stimulated by pressure, temperature extremes, physical damage, or exposure to abnormal chemicals. Other receptors, such as those providing visual, auditory, or

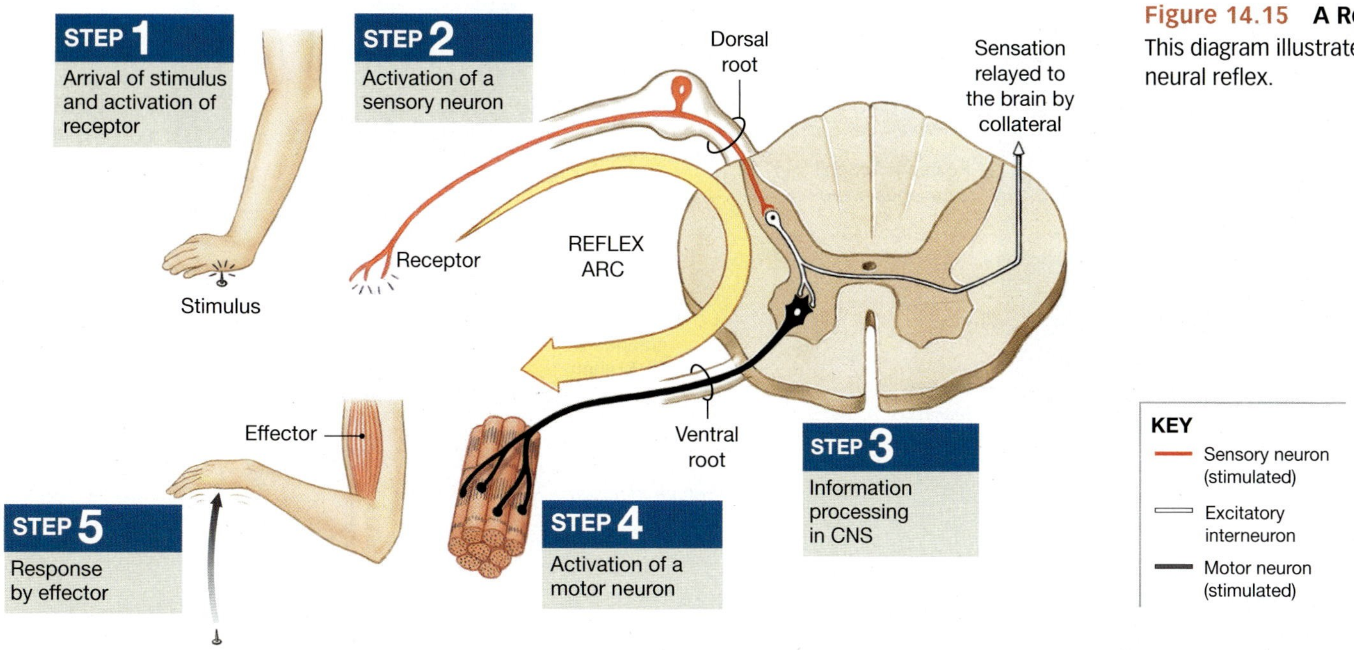

Figure 14.15 A Reflex Arc
This diagram illustrates the five steps involved in a neural reflex.

Clinical Note

Disorders of the Spinal Cord and Spinal Nerves Damage to spinal tracts produces losses of sensation and/or motor control. The nature of the sensory and motor deficit depends on the site of damage and the specific tracts involved.

Multiple sclerosis (MS) is a disease that produces muscular paralysis and sensory losses through demyelination. The initial symptoms—frequently involving some combination of paresthesias (altered sensations), clumsiness, and problems with vision and bladder control—appear as the result of myelin degeneration within the white matter of the lateral and posterior columns of the spinal cord, within the optic nerves, or along tracts within the brain. For example, spinal cord involvement can produce weakness, tingling sensations, and a loss of "position sense" for the limbs. For most patients, improvement occurs, but during subsequent attacks the effects become more widespread. The cumulative sensory and motor losses may eventually lead to a generalized muscular paralysis, with 50 percent of patients requiring help walking within 15 years after the initial occurrence of symptoms.

Current research suggests that this condition is linked to problems in the immune system, caused by a combination of genetic and environmental factors, that result in the production of antibodies that attack myelin sheaths. Individuals with MS have lymphocytes that do not respond normally to foreign proteins. Because several viral proteins have amino acid sequences similar to those of normal myelin, it has been proposed that MS results from a case of mistaken identity. It has been suggested that individuals who develop MS may have an inherited susceptibility to a virus and that this susceptibility is exaggerated by environmental conditions. The yearly incidence in the United States averages around 50 cases for every 100,000 people in the population. Improvement has been noted in some MS patients treated with drugs that affect the immune system, or "immunomodulators" such as beta interferon (a peptide secreted by cells of the immune system) and glatiramer (a synthetic polypeptide similar to myelin basic protein). Immunosuppression with corticosteroid treatment can reduce the severity of relapses, and one anticancer drug has been approved by the FDA for advanced chronic cases of MS.

Spinal trauma results from physical damage to the spinal cord such as a severe auto crash, causing permanent paralysis because the damaged tracts seldom undergo repair. Extensive damage to the spinal cord causes loss of motor and sensory function below the level of injury. Damage superior to the fifth cervical vertebra eliminates motor control (paralysis) and sensation of the upper and lower limbs, a condition termed *quadriplegia*. *Paraplegia*, the loss of motor control of the lower limbs, may follow damage to the thoracic spinal cord. Less-severe injuries affecting the spinal cord or cauda equina produce symptoms of sensory loss or motor paralysis that reflect the specific nuclei, tracts, or spinal nerves involved.

taste sensations, are specialized cells that respond to only a limited range of stimuli.

STEP 2. ***Relay of Information to the CNS.*** Information is carried in the form of action potentials along an afferent fiber. In this case, the axon conducts the action potentials into the spinal cord via one of the dorsal roots (Figure 14.17).

STEP 3. ***Information Processing.*** Information processing begins when a neurotransmitter released by synaptic terminals of the sensory neuron reaches the postsynaptic membrane of either a motor neuron or an interneuron. p. 354 In the simplest reflexes, such as the one diagrammed in Figure 14.15, this processing is performed by the motor neuron that controls peripheral effectors. In more complex reflexes, several pools of interneurons are interposed between the sensory and motor neurons, and both serial and parallel processing occur. pp. 355–356 The goal of this information processing is the selection of an appropriate motor response through the activation of specific motor neurons.

STEP 4. ***Activation of a Motor Neuron.*** A motor neuron stimulated to threshold conducts action potentials along its axon into the periphery, in this example, through the ventral root of a spinal nerve.

STEP 5. ***Response of a Peripheral Effector.*** Activation of the motor neuron causes a response by a peripheral effector, such as a skeletal muscle or gland. In general, this response is aimed at removing or counteracting the original stimulus. Reflexes play an important role in opposing potentially harmful changes in the internal or external environment.

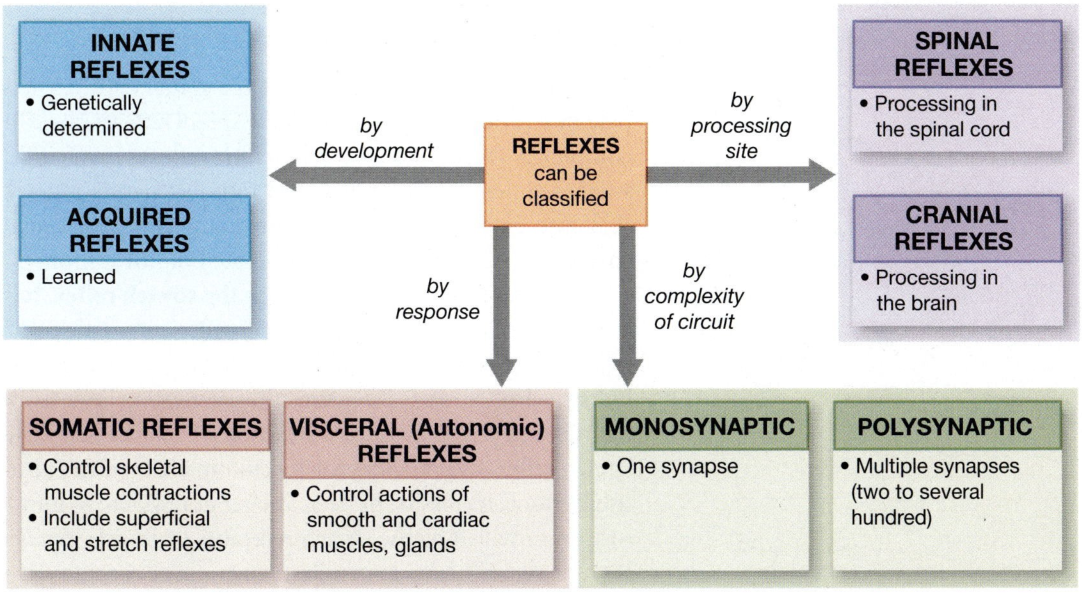

Figure 14.16 The Classification of Reflexes
Four different methods are used to classify reflexes.

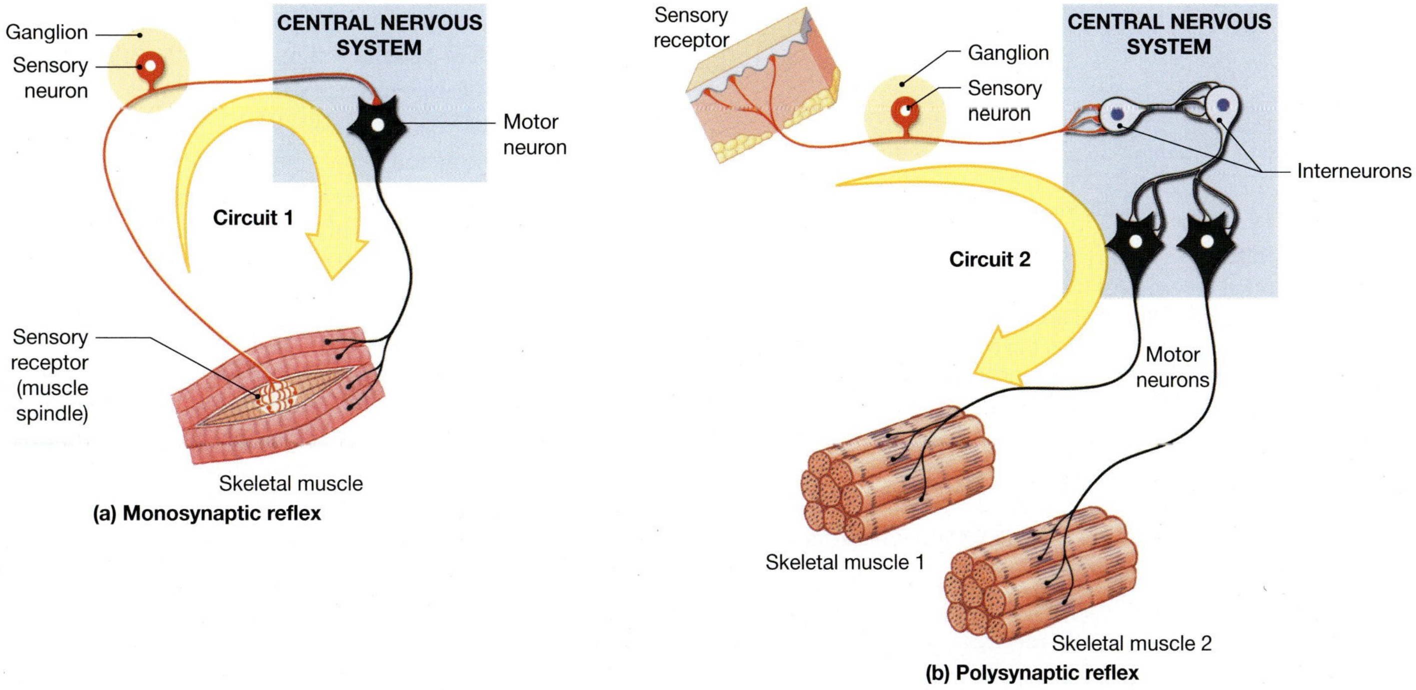

Figure 14.17 Neural Organization and Simple Reflexes
A comparison of monosynaptic and polysynaptic reflexes. **(a)** A monosynaptic reflex circuit involves a peripheral sensory neuron and a central motor neuron. In this example, stimulation of the receptor will lead to a reflexive contraction in a skeletal muscle. **(b)** A polysynaptic reflex circuit involves a sensory neuron, interneurons, and motor neurons. In this example, the stimulation of the receptor leads to the coordinated contractions of two different skeletal muscles.

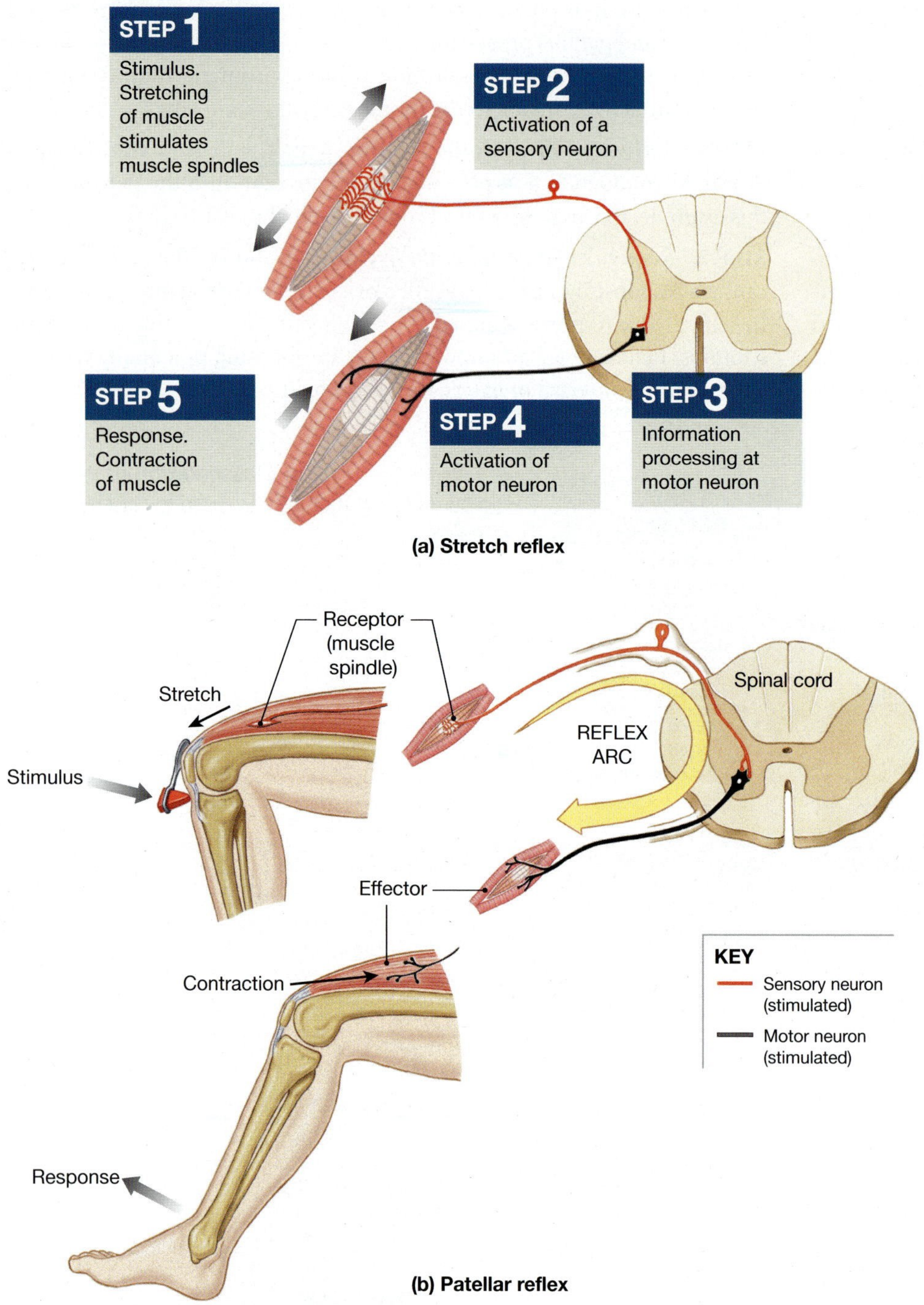

Figure 14.18 Stretch Reflexes
(a) Steps common to all stretch reflexes. **(b)** The patellar reflex is controlled by muscle spindles in the quadriceps group. The stimulus is a reflex hammer striking the muscle tendon, stretching the spindle fibers. This results in a sudden increase in the activity of the sensory neurons, which synapse on spinal motor neurons. The response occurs upon the activation of motor units in the quadriceps group, which produces an immediate increase in muscle tone and a reflexive kick.

Classification of Reflexes [Figures 14.16/14.17]

Reflexes can be classified according to (1) their development (**innate** and **acquired reflexes**), (2) the site where information processing occurs (**spinal** and **cranial reflexes**), (3) the nature of the resulting motor response (**somatic** and **visceral**, or **autonomic reflexes**), or (4) the complexity of the neural circuit involved (*monosynaptic* and *polysynaptic reflexes*). These categories, presented in Figure 14.16, are not mutually exclusive; they represent different ways of describing a single reflex.

In the simplest reflex arc, a sensory neuron synapses directly on a motor neuron. Such a reflex is termed a **monosynaptic reflex** (Figure 14.17a). Transmission across a vesicular synapse always involves a synaptic delay, but with only one synapse, the delay between stimulus and response is minimized.

Polysynaptic reflexes (Figure 14.17b) have a longer delay between stimulus and response, the length of the delay being proportional to the number of synapses involved. Polysynaptic reflexes can produce far more complicated responses because the interneurons can control several different muscle groups. Many of the motor responses are extremely complicated; for example, stepping on a sharp object not only causes withdrawal of the foot, but triggers all of the muscular adjustments needed to prevent a fall. Such complicated responses result from the interactions between multiple interneuron pools.

Spinal Reflexes [Figures 14.17/14.18]

The neurons in the gray matter of the spinal cord participate in a variety of reflex arcs. These *spinal reflexes* range in complexity from simple monosynaptic reflexes involving a single segment of the spinal cord to polysynaptic reflexes that integrate motor output from many different spinal cord segments to produce a coordinated motor response.

The best-known spinal reflex is the **stretch reflex**. It is a simple monosynaptic reflex that provides automatic regulation of skeletal muscle length (Figure 14.18a). The stimulus stretches a relaxed muscle, thus activating a sensory neuron and triggering the contraction of that muscle. The stretch reflex also provides for the automatic adjustment of muscle tone, increasing or decreasing it in response to information provided by the stretch receptors of *muscle spindles* (Figure 14.17a). Muscle spindles, which will be considered in Chapter 18, consist of specialized muscle fibers whose lengths are monitored by sensory neurons.

The most familiar stretch reflex is probably the *knee jerk*, or **patellar reflex**. In this reflex, a sharp rap on the patellar ligament stretches muscle spindles in the quadriceps muscles (Figure 14.18b). With so brief a stimulus, the reflexive contraction occurs unopposed and produces a noticeable kick. Physicians often test this reflex to check the status of the lower segments of the spinal cord. A normal patellar reflex indicates that spinal nerves and spinal segments L_1–L_4 are undamaged.

The stretch reflex is an example of a **postural reflex**, a reflex that maintains normal upright posture. Postural muscles usually have a firm muscle tone and extremely sensitive stretch receptors. As a result, very fine adjustments are continually being made, and you are not aware of the cycles of contraction and relaxation that occur.

Higher Centers and Integration of Reflexes

Reflexive motor activities occur automatically, without instructions from higher centers in the brain. However, higher centers can have a profound effect on reflex performance. For example, processing centers in the brain can enhance or suppress spinal reflexes via descending tracts that synapse on interneurons and motor neurons throughout the spinal cord. Motor control therefore involves a series of interacting levels. At the lowest level are monosynaptic reflexes that are rapid but stereotyped and relatively inflexible. At the highest level are centers in the brain that can modulate or build on reflexive motor patterns.

Embryology Summary

For a summary of the development of the spinal cord and spinal nerves, see Chapter 28 (Embryology and Human Development).

CONCEPT CHECK

1. What is a reflex?
2. In order, list the five steps in a reflex arc.
3. Distinguish between a monosynaptic and polysynaptic reflex.
4. What are the four methods of classifying reflexes?

See blue "Answers" tab at back of book.

CLINICAL TERMS

areflexia (ā-re-FLEK-sē-a): The lack of normal reflex responses to stimuli.

Babinski sign (positive Babinski reflex): A spinal reflex in infants, consisting of a fanning of the toes, produced by stroking the foot on the side of the sole; in adults, a sign of CNS injury.

caudal anesthesia: Injection of anesthetics into the epidural space of the sacrum to paralyze and reduce sensation of lower abdominal and perineal structures.

epidural block: Regional anesthesia produced by the injection of an anesthetic into the epidural space near targeted spinal nerve roots.

functional electrical stimulation (FES): A technique for stimulating specific muscles and muscle groups using electrodes controlled by a computer.

hyperreflexia: Exaggerated reflex responses that may develop in some pathological states or following stimulation of spinal and cranial nuclei by higher centers.

hyporeflexia: A condition in which normal spinal reflexes are present but weak.

lumbar puncture: A spinal tap performed between adjacent lumbar vertebrae.

meningitis: An inflammation of the meningeal membranes.

multiple sclerosis (skle-RŌ-sis) **(MS):** A disease of the nervous system characterized by recurrent, often progressive incidents of demyelination affecting tracts in the brain and/or spinal cord. Common symptoms include partial loss of vision and problems with speech, balance, and general motor coordination.

myelography: A diagnostic procedure in which a radiopaque dye is introduced into the cerebrospinal fluid in order to obtain an x-ray of the spinal cord.

nerve graft: Insertion of an intact section from a different peripheral nerve to bridge the gap between the cut ends of a damaged nerve and to provide a route for axonal regeneration.

paraplegia: Paralysis involving loss of motor control of the lower limbs.

patellar reflex: The "knee jerk" reflex; often used to provide information about the related spinal segments.

quadriplegia: Paralysis involving loss of sensation and motor control of the upper and lower limbs.

spinal shock: A period of sensory and motor paralysis following any severe injury to the spinal cord.

spinal tap: A procedure in which fluid is extracted from the subarachnoid space through a needle inserted between the vertebrae.

STUDY OUTLINE

Introduction 362

1. The **central nervous system (CNS)** consists of the *spinal cord* and *brain*. Although they are connected, they have some functional independence. The spinal cord integrates and processes information on its own, in addition to relaying information to and from the brain.

Gross Anatomy of the Spinal Cord 362

1. The adult spinal cord has a **posterior median sulcus** (shallow) and an **anterior median fissure** (wide). It includes localized **enlargements** (*cervical* and *lumbar*), which are expanded regions where there is increased gray matter to provide innervation of the limbs. *(see Figures 14.1 to 14.3)*
2. The adult spinal cord extends from the foramen magnum to L_1. The spinal cord tapers to a conical tip, the **conus medullaris**. The **filum terminale** (a strand of fibrous tissue) originates at this tip and extends through the vertebral canal to the second sacral vertebra, ultimately becoming part of the *coccygeal ligament. (see Figures 14.1 to 14.4)*
3. The spinal cord has 31 segments, each associated with a pair of **dorsal root ganglia** (containing sensory neuron cell bodies), and pairs of **dorsal roots** and **ventral roots**. The first cervical and first coccygeal nerves represent exceptions, in that the dorsal roots are absent in many individuals. *(see Figures 14.1 to 14.3)*
4. Sensory and motor fibers unite as a single **spinal nerve** distal to each dorsal root ganglion. Spinal nerves emerge from **intervertebral foramina** and are **mixed nerves** since they contain both sensory and motor fibers. *(see Figures 14.1 to 14.3)*
5. The **cauda equina** is the inferior extension of the ventral and dorsal roots and the filum terminale in the vertebral canal. *(see Figures 14.1/14.4)*

Spinal Meninges 362

1. The **spinal meninges** are a series of specialized membranes that provide physical stability and shock absorption for neural tissues of the spinal cord; the **cranial meninges** are membranes that surround the brain (Chapter 15). There are three meningeal layers: the *dura mater*, the *arachnoid mater*, and the *pia mater. (see Figure 14.2)*

The Dura Mater 362

2. The spinal **dura mater** is the tough, fibrous outermost layer that covers the spinal cord; caudally it forms the **coccygeal ligament** with the filum terminale. The **epidural space** separates the dura mater from the inner walls of the vertebral canal. *(see Figures 14.1b,c/14.2/14.4a)*

The Arachnoid Mater 365

3. Internal to the inner surface of the dura mater is the **subdural space**. When present it separates the dura mater from the middle meningeal layer, the **arachnoid mater**. Internal to the arachnoid mater is the **subarachnoid space**, which has a network of collagen and elastic fibers, the *arachnoid trabeculae.* This space also contains **cerebrospinal fluid**, which acts as a shock

absorber and a diffusion medium for dissolved gases, nutrients, chemical messengers, and waste products. *(see Figures 14.2/14.4)*

The Pia Mater 365

4. The **pia mater** is the innermost meningeal layer. It is bound firmly to the underlying neural tissue. Paired **denticulate ligaments** are supporting fibers extending laterally from the spinal cord surface, binding the spinal pia mater and arachnoid mater to the dura mater to prevent either side-to-side or inferior movement of the spinal cord. *(see Figure 14.2)*

Sectional Anatomy of the Spinal Cord 367

1. The central **gray matter** surrounds the **central canal** and contains cell bodies of neurons and glial cells. The gray matter projections toward the outer surface of the spinal cord are called **horns**. The peripheral **white matter** contains myelinated and unmyelinated axons in *tracts* and *columns. (see Figure 14.5)*

Organization of Gray Matter 367

2. Neuron cell bodies in the spinal cord gray matter are organized into groups, termed *nuclei.* The **posterior gray horns** contain somatic and visceral sensory nuclei, while nuclei in the **anterior gray horns** are involved with somatic motor control. The **lateral gray horns** contain visceral motor neurons. The **gray commissures** are posterior and anterior to the central canal. They contain the axons of interneurons that cross from one side of the cord to the other. *(see Figure 14.5)*

Organization of White Matter 367

3. The white matter can be divided into six **columns** (*funiculi*), each of which contains **tracts** *(fasciculi).* **Ascending tracts** relay information from the spinal cord to the brain, and **descending tracts** carry information from the brain to the spinal cord. *(see Figure 14.5)*

Spinal Nerves 369

1. There are 31 pairs of spinal nerves; each is identified through its association with an adjacent vertebra (*cervical, thoracic, lumbar,* and *sacral*). *(see Figures 14.1/14.3)*
2. Each spinal nerve is ensheathed by a series of connective tissue layers. The outermost layer, the **epineurium**, is a dense network of collagen fibers; the middle layer, the **perineurium**, partitions the nerve into a series of bundles *(fascicles)* and forms the *nerve–blood barrier*; and the inner layer, the **endoneurium**, is composed of delicate connective tissue fibers that surround individual axons. *(see Figure 14.6)*

Peripheral Distribution of Spinal Nerves 369

3. The first branch of each spinal nerve in the thoracic and upper lumbar regions is the **white ramus**, which contains myelinated axons going to an **autonomic ganglion**. Two groups of unmyelinated fibers exit this ganglion: a **gray ramus**, carrying axons that innervate glands and smooth muscles in the body wall or limbs back to the spinal nerve, and an autonomic nerve carrying fibers to internal organs. Collectively, the white and gray rami are termed the **rami communicantes**. *(see Figures 14.2/14.7)*
4. Each spinal nerve has both a **dorsal ramus** (provides sensory/motor innervation to the skin and muscles of the back) and a **ventral ramus** (supplies ventrolateral body surface, body wall structures, and limbs). Each pair of spinal nerves monitors a region of the body surface, an area called a **dermatome**. *(see Figures 14.2/14.7/14.8)*

Nerve Plexuses 370

5. A complex, interwoven network of nerves is called a **nerve plexus**. The four major plexuses are the *cervical plexus,* the *brachial plexus,* the *lumbar plexus,* and the *sacral plexus. (see Figures 14.3/14.9 to 14.14 and Tables 14.1 to 14.3)*
6. The **cervical plexus** consists of the ventral rami of C_1–C_4 and some fibers from C_5. Muscles of the neck are innervated; some branches extend into the thoracic cavity to the diaphragm. The **phrenic nerve** is the major nerve in this plexus. *(see Figures 14.3/14.9/14.10/14.12 and Table 14.1)*
7. The **brachial plexus** innervates the pectoral girdle and upper limbs by the ventral rami of C_5–T_1. The nerves in this plexus originate from cords or trunks: **superior**, **middle**, and **inferior trunks** give rise to the **lateral cord**, **medial cord**, and **posterior cord**. *(see Figures 14.3/14.9/14.11/14.12 and Table 14.2)*
8. Collectively the **lumbar plexus** and **sacral plexus** originate from the posterior abdominal wall and ventral rami of nerves supplying the pelvic girdle and lower limb. The lumbar plexus contains fibers from spinal segments T_{12}–L_4 and the sacral plexus contains fibers from spinal segments L_4–S_4. *(see Figures 14.3/14.9/14.13/14.14 and Table 14.3)*

Reflexes 380

1. A neural **reflex** is a rapid, automatic, involuntary motor response to stimuli. Reflexes help preserve homeostasis by rapidly adjusting the functions of organs or organ systems. *(see Figure 14.15)*
2. A **reflex arc** is the neural "wiring" of a single reflex. *(see Figure 14.15)*
3. A *receptor* is a specialized cell that monitors conditions in the body or external environment. Each receptor has a characteristic range of sensitivity.
4. There are five steps involved in a neural reflex: (1) arrival of a stimulus and activation of a receptor; (2) relay of information to the CNS; (3) information processing; (4) activation of a motor neuron; and (5) response by a peripheral effector. *(see Figure 14.15)*

Classification of Reflexes 382

5. Reflexes are classified by (1) their development *(innate, acquired)*; (2) where information is processed *(spinal, cranial)*; (3) motor response (*somatic, visceral [autonomic]*); and (4) complexity of the neural circuit *(monosynaptic, polysynaptic). (see Figure 14.16)*
6. **Innate reflexes** are genetically determined. **Acquired reflexes** are learned following repeated exposure to a stimulus. *(see Figure 14.16)*
7. Reflexes processed in the brain are **cranial reflexes.** In a **spinal reflex** the important interconnections and processing occur inside the spinal cord. *(see Figure 14.16)*
8. **Somatic reflexes** control skeletal muscle contractions, and **visceral** *(autonomic)* **reflexes** control the activities of smooth and cardiac muscles and glands. *(see Figure 14.16)*
9. A **monosynaptic reflex** is the simplest reflex arc. A sensory neuron synapses directly on a motor neuron that acts as the processing center. **Polysynaptic reflexes** have at least one interneuron placed between the sensory afferent and the motor efferent. Thus, they have a longer delay between stimulus and response. *(see Figures 14.16/14.17)*

Spinal Reflexes 382

10. **Spinal reflexes** range from simple monosynaptic reflexes (involving only one segment of the cord) to more complex polysynaptic reflexes (in which many segments of the cord interact to produce a coordinated motor response). *(see Figure 14.17)*
11. The **stretch reflex** is a monosynaptic reflex that automatically regulates skeletal muscle length and muscle tone. The sensory receptors involved are stretch receptors of *muscle spindles. (see Figure 14.18a)*
12. A **patellar reflex** is the familiar *knee jerk,* wherein a tap on the patellar ligament stretches the **muscle spindles** in the quadriceps muscles. *(see Figure 14.18b)*
13. A **postural reflex** is a stretch reflex that maintains normal upright posture.

Higher Centers and Integration of Reflexes 382

14. Higher centers in the brain can enhance or inhibit reflex motor patterns based in the spinal cord.

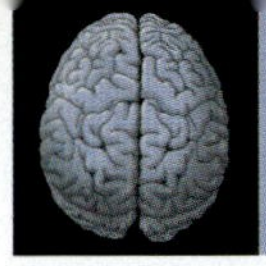

CHAPTER REVIEW

For answers to the Concept Check and Chapter Review questions, go to the blue "Answers" tab at the back of the book.

Level 1 Reviewing Facts and Terms

Match each numbered item with the most closely related lettered item. Use letters for answers in the spaces provided.

Column A	Column B
___ 1. ventral root	a. tracts and columns
___ 2. epidural space	b. specific region of body surface
___ 3. white matter	c. cervical plexus
___ 4. fascicle	d. motor neuron axons
___ 5. dermatome	e. sacral plexus
___ 6. phrenic nerve	f. lumbar plexus
___ 7. brachial plexus	g. single bundle of axons
___ 8. obturator nerve	h. involuntary motor response
___ 9. reflex	i. loose connective tissue, adipose tissue
___ 10. pudendal nerve	j. pectoral girdle/upper extremity

11. The ________________________ is a strand of fibrous tissue that provides longitudinal support as a component of the coccygeal ligament.
    (a) conus medullaris (b) filum terminale
    (c) cauda equina (d) dorsal root

12. Axons crossing from one side of the spinal cord to the other within the gray matter are found in the
    (a) anterior gray horns (b) white commissures
    (c) gray commissures (d) lateral gray horns

13. The paired structures that contain cell bodies of sensory neurons and are associated with each segment of the spinal cord are the
    (a) dorsal rami (b) ventral rami
    (c) dorsal root ganglia (d) ventral root ganglia

14. The deep crease on the ventral surface of the spinal cord is the
    (a) posterior median sulcus
    (b) posterior median fissure
    (c) anterior median sulcus
    (d) anterior median fissure

15. Sensory and motor innervations of the skin of the lateral and ventral surfaces of the body are provided by the
    (a) white rami communicantes
    (b) gray rami communicantes
    (c) dorsal ramus
    (d) ventral ramus

16. The brachial plexus
    (a) innervates the shoulder girdle and the upper extremity
    (b) is formed from the ventral rami of spinal nerves C_5–T_1
    (c) is the source of the musculocutaneous, radial, median, and ulnar nerves
    (d) all of the above

17. The middle layer of connective tissue that surrounds each peripheral nerve is the
    (a) epineurium (b) perineurium
    (c) endoneurium (d) endomysium

18. The expanded area of the spinal cord that supplies nerves to the pectoral girdle and upper limbs is the
    (a) conus medullaris
    (b) filum terminale
    (c) lumbosacral enlargement
    (d) cervical enlargement

19. Spinal nerves are called mixed nerves because
    (a) they contain sensory and motor fibers
    (b) they exit at intervertebral foramina
    (c) they are associated with a pair of dorsal root ganglia
    (d) they are associated with dorsal and ventral roots

20. The gray matter of the spinal cord is dominated by
    (a) myelinated axons only
    (b) cell bodies of neurons and glial cells
    (c) unmyelinated axons only
    (d) Schwann cells and satellite cells

Level 2 Reviewing Concepts

1. What nerve is likely to transmit pain when a person receives an intramuscular injection into the deltoid region of the arm?
   (a) ulnar nerve
   (b) radial nerve
   (c) intercostobranchial nerve
   (d) upper lateral cutaneous nerve of the arm

2. Which of the following actions would be compromised if a person suffered an injury to lumbar spinal segments L_3 and L_4?
   (a) a plié (shallow knee bend) in ballet
   (b) sitting cross-legged (lateral side of the foot on the medial side of opposite thigh) to form the lotus position
   (c) riding a horse
   (d) all of the above

3. Tingling and numbness in the palmar region of the hand could be caused by
   (a) compression of the median nerve in the carpal tunnel
   (b) compression of the ulnar nerve
   (c) compression of the radial artery
   (d) irritation of the structures that form the superficial arterial loop

4. What is the role of the meninges in protecting the spinal cord?

5. How does a reflex differ from a voluntary muscle movement?

6. If the dorsal root of the spinal cord were damaged, what would be affected?

7. Why is response time in a monosynaptic reflex much faster than the response time in a polysynaptic reflex?

8. Why are there eight cervical spinal nerves but only seven cervical vertebrae?

9. What prevents side-to-side movements of the spinal cord?

10. Why is it important that a spinal tap be done between the third and fourth lumbar vertebrae?

Level 3 Critical Thinking

1. The incision that allows access to the abdominal cavity involves cutting the sheath of the rectus abdominis muscle. This muscle is always retracted laterally, never medially. Why?

2. Cindy is in an automobile accident and injures her spinal cord. She has lost feeling in her right hand, and her doctor tells her that it is the result of swelling compressing a portion of her spinal cord. Which part of her cord is likely to be compressed?

3. Karen falls down a flight of stairs and suffers spinal cord damage due to hyperextension of the cord during the fall. The injury results in edema of the spinal cord with resulting compression of the anterior horn cells of the spinal region. What symptoms would you expect to observe as a result of this injury?

15

The Nervous System

The Brain and Cranial Nerves

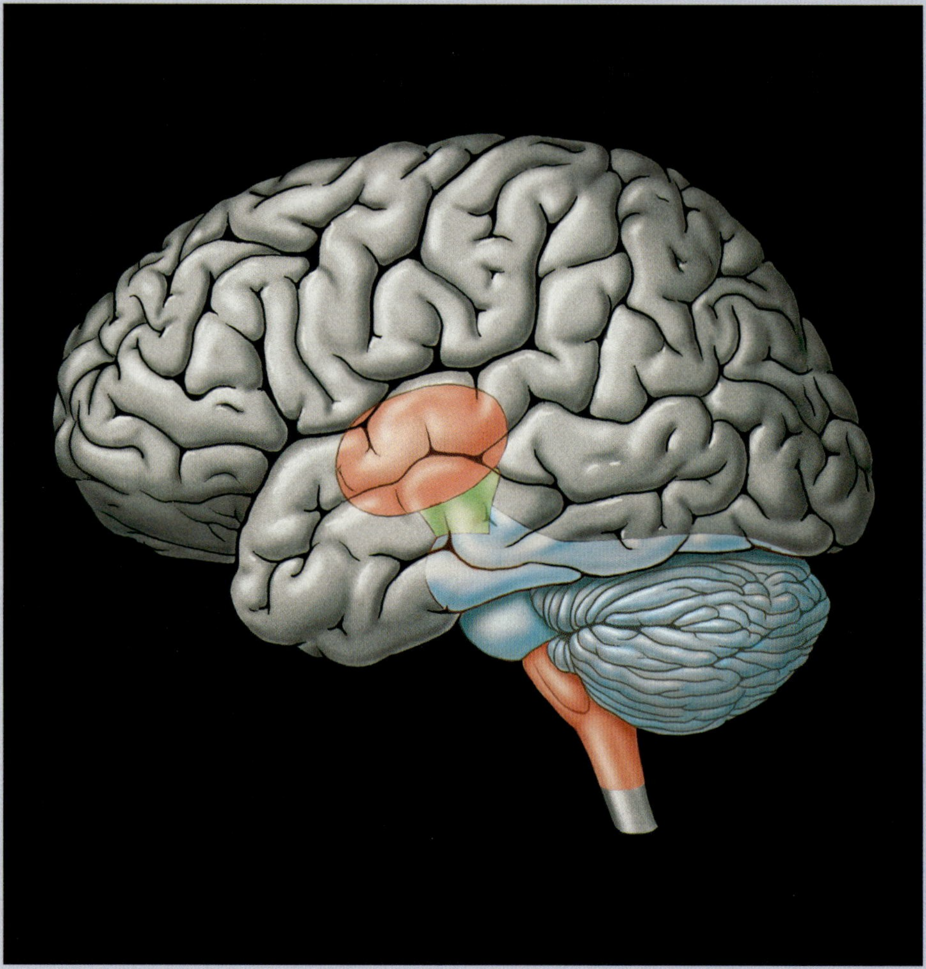

CHAPTER OBJECTIVES

1. Name the major regions of the brain and describe their functions.
2. Identify and describe the ventricles of the brain.
3. Identify and describe the structures that protect and support the brain.
4. Describe the structures that constitute the blood–brain barrier and indicate their functions.
5. Describe the structural and functional characteristics of the choroid plexus and the role played in the origin, function, and circulation of cerebrospinal fluid.
6. Identify the anatomical structures of the cerebrum and list their functions.
7. Identify three different types of white matter in the brain and list their functions.
8. Distinguish among motor, sensory, and association areas of the cerebral cortex.
9. Identify the anatomical structures that make up the limbic system and describe its functions.
10. Identify the anatomical structures that form the thalamus and hypothalamus and list their functions.
11. Identify major features of the mesencephalon and describe its functions.
12. Identify the components of the cerebellum and describe their functions.
13. Identify the anatomical structures of the medulla oblongata and describe their functions.
14. Identify and describe the 12 cranial nerves.

The brain is probably the most fascinating organ in the body. It has a complex three-dimensional structure and performs a bewildering array of functions. Often the brain is likened to an organic computer, with its nuclei and individual neurons compared to silicon "chips" and "switches." Like the brain, a computer receives enormous amounts of incoming information, files and processes this information, and directs appropriate output responses. However, any direct comparison between your brain and a computer is misleading, because even the most sophisticated computer lacks the versatility and adaptability of a single neuron. One neuron may process information from up to 200,000 different sources at the same time, and there are tens of billions of neurons in the nervous system. Rather than continuing to list the number of activities that can be performed by the brain, it is more appropriate to appreciate that this incredibly complex organ is the source of all of our dreams, passions, plans, memories, and behaviors. Everything we do and everything we are results from its activity.

The brain is far more complex than the spinal cord, and it can respond to stimuli with greater versatility. That versatility results from the tremendous number of neurons and neuronal pools in the brain and the complexity of their interconnections. The brain contains roughly 20 billion neurons, each of which may receive information across thousands of synapses at one time. Excitatory and inhibitory interactions among the extensively interconnected neuronal pools ensure that the response can vary to meet changing circumstances. But adaptability has a price: A response cannot be immediate, precise, and adaptable all at the same time. Adaptability requires multiple processing steps, and every synapse adds to the delay between stimulus and response. One of the major functions of spinal reflexes is to provide an *immediate* response that can be fine-tuned or elaborated on by more versatile but slower processing centers in the brain.

We now begin a detailed examination of the brain. This chapter focuses attention on the major structures of the brain and their relationships with the cranial nerves.

An Introduction to the Organization of the Brain [Figure 15.1]

The adult human brain (**Figure 15.1**) contains almost 95 percent of the neural tissue in the body. An average adult brain weighs 1.4 kg (3 lb) and has a volume of 1350 cc (82 in.^{3}). There is considerable individual variation, and the brains of males are on average about 10 percent larger than those of females, owing to differences in average body size. Its relatively unimpressive external appearance gives few clues to its real complexity and importance. An adult brain can be held easily in both hands. A freshly removed brain is gray externally, and its internal tissues are tan to pink. Overall, the brain has the consistency of medium-firm tofu or chilled gelatin.

Early in development, the brain resembles the spinal cord—hollow, and with a narrow central passageway filled with cerebrospinal fluid. As development proceeds, this simple passageway becomes subdivided, and in several regions it expands to form enlarged chambers called *ventricles*. We will consider the anatomy of these ventricles in a later section.

Embryology of the Brain [Table 15.1]

The development of the brain is detailed in Chapter 28. However, a brief overview will help you understand adult brain structure and organization. The central nervous system begins as a hollow *neural tube*, with a fluid-filled internal cavity called the *neurocoel*. In the fourth week of development, three areas in the cephalic portion of the neural tube enlarge rapidly through expansion of the neurocoel. This enlargement creates three prominent **primary brain vesicles** named for their relative positions: the **prosencephalon** (prōs-en-SEF-a-lon; *proso*, forward + *enkephalos*, brain), or "forebrain"; the **mesencephalon** (mez-en-SEF-a-lon; *mesos*, middle), or "midbrain"; and the **rhombencephalon** (rom-ben-SEF-a-lon), or "hindbrain."

The fate of the three primary divisions of the brain is summarized in Table 15.1. The prosencephalon and rhombencephalon are subdivided further, forming **secondary brain vesicles**. The prosencephalon forms the **telencephalon** (tel-en-SEF-a-lon; *telos*, end) and the *diencephalon*. The telencephalon forms the *cerebrum*, the paired cerebral hemispheres that dominate the superior and lateral surfaces of the adult brain. The hollow diencephalon has a roof (the *epithalamus*), walls (the left and right *thalamus*), and a floor (the *hypothalamus*). By the time the posterior end of the neural tube closes, secondary bulges, the *optic vesicles*, have extended laterally from the sides of the diencephalon. Additionally, the developing brain bends, forming creases that mark the boundaries between the ventricles. The mesencephalon does not subdivide, but its walls thicken and the neurocoel becomes a relatively narrow passageway with a diameter comparable to that of the central canal of the spinal cord. The portion of the rhombencephalon closest to the mesencephalon forms the **metencephalon** (met-en-SEF-a-lon; *meta*, after). The ventral portion of the metencephalon develops into the *pons*, and the dorsal portion becomes the *cerebellum*. The portion of the rhombencephalon closer to the spinal cord becomes the **myelencephalon** (mī-el-en-SEF-a-lon; *myelon*, spinal cord), which will form the *medulla oblongata*. We will now examine each of these structures in the adult brain.

Major Regions and Landmarks [Figure 15.1]

There are six major divisions in the adult brain: (1) the *cerebrum*, (2) the *diencephalon*, (3) the *mesencephalon*, (4) the *pons*, (5) the *cerebellum*, and (6) the *medulla oblongata*. Refer to **Figure 15.1** as we provide an overview of each division.

The Cerebrum

The **cerebrum** (ser-Ē-brum or SER-e-brum) is the largest part of the brain. It is divided into large, paired **cerebral hemispheres** separated by the **longitudinal fissure**. The surface of the cerebrum, the cerebral *cortex*, is composed of gray matter. The cerebral cortex is convoluted by furrows, termed *sulci*. These sulci separate the intervening ridges, termed *gyri*. The cerebrum is conveniently divided into *lobes* by a number of the larger sulci, and the names of the lobes are derived from the bones of the cranium under which they lie.

Conscious thought processes, intellectual functions, memory storage and retrieval, and complex motor patterns originate in the cerebrum.

The Diencephalon

The deep portion of the brain attached to the cerebrum is called the **diencephalon** (dī-en-SEF-a-lon; *dia*, through). The diencephalon has three subdivisions, and their functions can be summarized as follows:

- The **epithalamus** contains the hormone-secreting *pineal gland*, an endocrine structure.
- The right **thalamus** and left thalamus (THAL-a-mus; plural, *thalami*) are sensory information relay and processing centers.
- The floor of the diencephalon is the **hypothalamus** (*hypo-*, below), a visceral control center. A narrow stalk connects the hypothalamus to the **pituitary gland**, or *hypophysis* (*phyein*, to generate). The hypothalamus contains centers involved with emotions, autonomic nervous system function, and hormone production. It is the primary link between the nervous and endocrine systems.

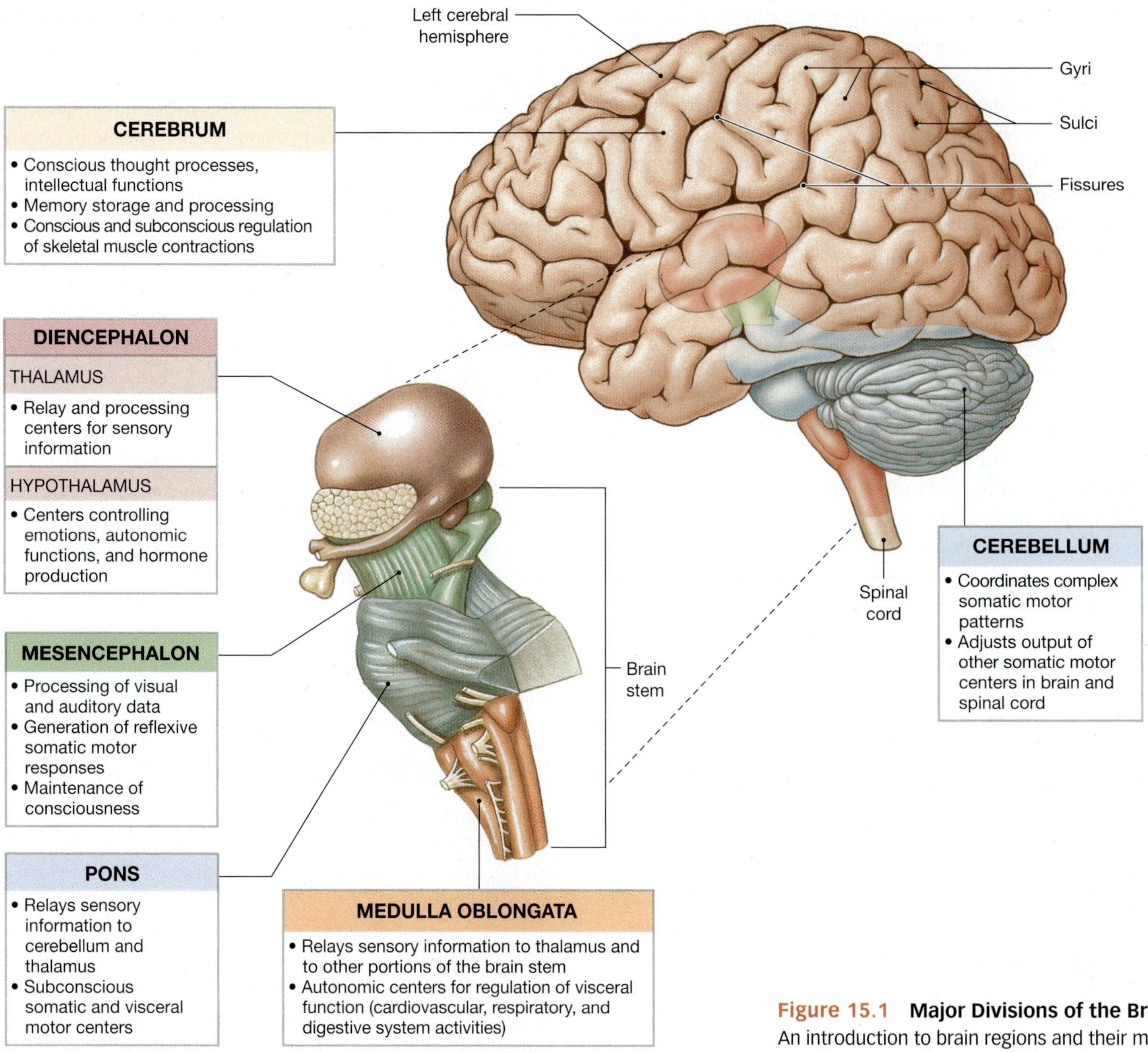

Figure 15.1 Major Divisions of the Brain
An introduction to brain regions and their major functions.

TABLE 15.1 Development of the Human Brain *(See also Chapter 28, pp. 747–798 for embryological summary)*

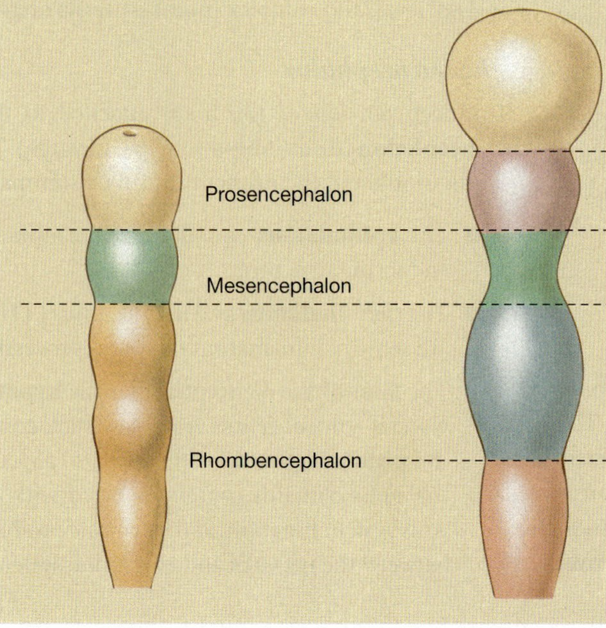

Primary Brain Vesicles (3 week embryo)	Secondary Brain Vesicles (6 week embryo)	Brain Regions at Birth
Prosencephalon	Telencephalon	Cerebrum
	Diencephalon	Diencephalon
Mesencephalon	Mesencephalon	Mesencephalon
Rhombencephalon	Metencephalon	Cerebellum and Pons
	Myelencephalon	Medulla oblongata

To visualize the relationships among these structures, you can compare the diencephalon to an empty shoebox: The lid is the *epithalamus*, the left and right sides are the *thalami*, the bottom is the *hypothalamus*, and the enclosed space is a ventricle.

The remaining regions of the brain are collectively known as the *brain stem*. The **brain stem** consists of the mesencephalon, pons, and medulla oblongata.[1] The brain stem contains important processing centers and also relays information to or from the cerebrum or cerebellum. Refer to Figure 15.1 as we describe the structure of the brain stem.

The Mesencephalon

Nuclei in the **mesencephalon**, or midbrain, process visual and auditory information and coordinate and direct reflexive somatic motor responses to these stimuli. This region also contains centers involved with the maintenance of consciousness.

The Pons and Cerebellum

The **pons** is immediately inferior to the mesencephalon. It contains nuclei involved with both somatic and visceral motor control. The term *pons* refers to a bridge, and the pons connects the cerebellum to the brain stem. The relatively small hemispheres of the **cerebellum** (ser-e-BEL-um) lie posterior to the pons and inferior to the cerebral hemispheres. The cerebellum automatically adjusts motor activities on the basis of sensory information and memories of learned patterns of movement.

The Medulla Oblongata

The spinal cord connects to the brain stem at the **medulla oblongata**. The superior portion of the medulla oblongata has a thin, membranous roof, whereas the inferior portion resembles the spinal cord. The medulla oblongata relays sensory information to the thalamus and to other brain stem centers. In addition, it contains major centers concerned with the regulation of autonomic function, such as heart rate, blood pressure, and digestive activities.

Gray Matter and White Matter Organization

The general distribution of gray matter in the brain stem resembles that in the spinal cord; there is an inner region of gray matter surrounded by tracts of white matter. The gray matter surrounds the fluid-filled ventricles and passageways that correspond to the central canal of the spinal cord. The gray matter forms *nuclei*—spherical, oval, or irregularly shaped clusters of neuron cell bodies. p. 367 Although tracts of white matter surround these nuclei, the arrangement is not as predictable as it is in the spinal cord. For example, the tracts may begin, end, merge, or branch as they pass around or through nuclei in their path. In the cerebrum and cerebellum the white matter is covered by the **neural cortex** (*cortex*, rind), a superficial layer of gray matter.

The term *higher centers* refers to nuclei, centers, and cortical areas of the cerebrum, cerebellum, diencephalon, and mesencephalon. Output from these processing centers modifies the activities of nuclei and centers in the lower brain stem and spinal cord. The nuclei and cortical areas of the brain can receive sensory information and issue motor commands to peripheral effectors indirectly, through the spinal cord and spinal nerves, or directly through the cranial nerves.

[1] Some sources consider the brain stem to include the diencephalon. We will use the more restrictive definition here.

The Ventricles of the Brain [Figure 15.2]

Ventricles (VEN-tri-kls) are fluid-filled cavities within the brain. They are filled with cerebrospinal fluid and lined by ependymal cells. p. 315 There are four ventricles in the adult brain: one within each cerebral hemisphere, a third within the diencephalon, and a fourth that lies between the pons and cerebellum and extends into the superior portion of the medulla oblongata. Figure 15.2 shows the position and orientation of the ventricles.

The ventricles in the cerebral hemispheres have a complex shape. A thin medial partition, the **septum pellucidum**, separates this pair of **lateral ventricles**. The *body* of each lateral ventricle lies within the parietal lobe, with an *anterior horn* extending into the frontal lobe. The body of each lateral ventricle also communicates with a *posterior horn*, which projects into the occipital lobe, and an *inferior horn* which curves laterally within the temporal lobe. There is no direct connection between the two lateral ventricles, but each communicates with the ventricle of the diencephalon through an **interventricular foramen** (*foramen of Monro*). Because there are two lateral ventricles (first and second), the cavity within the diencephalon is called the **third ventricle**.

The mesencephalon has a slender canal known as the **aqueduct of the midbrain** (*aqueduct of Sylvius* or *cerebral aqueduct*). This passageway connects the third ventricle with the **fourth ventricle**, which begins between the pons and cerebellum. In the inferior portion of the medulla oblongata, the fourth ventricle narrows and becomes continuous with the central canal of the spinal cord. There is a circulation of cerebrospinal fluid from the ventricles and central canal into the subarachnoid space through foramina in the roof of the fourth ventricle. However, before you can understand the origin and circulation of cerebrospinal fluid, you will need to know more about the organization of the cranial meninges and how they differ from the spinal meninges introduced in Chapter 14. p. 362

CONCEPT CHECK

1. List the six major divisions in the adult brain.
2. What are the three major structures of the brain stem?
3. What are the ventricles? What type of epithelial cell lines them?
4. List the secondary brain vesicles and the brain regions associated with each at birth.

See blue "Answers" tab at back of book.

Protection and Support of the Brain

The human brain is an extremely delicate organ that must be protected from injury yet remain in touch with the rest of the body. It also has a high demand for nutrients and oxygen and thus an extensive blood supply, yet it must be isolated from compounds in the blood that could interfere with its complex operations. Protection, support, and nourishment of the brain involves (1) the bones of the skull, which were detailed in Chapter 6. 135–154 (2) the cranial meninges, (3) the cerebrospinal fluid, and (4) the blood–brain barrier.

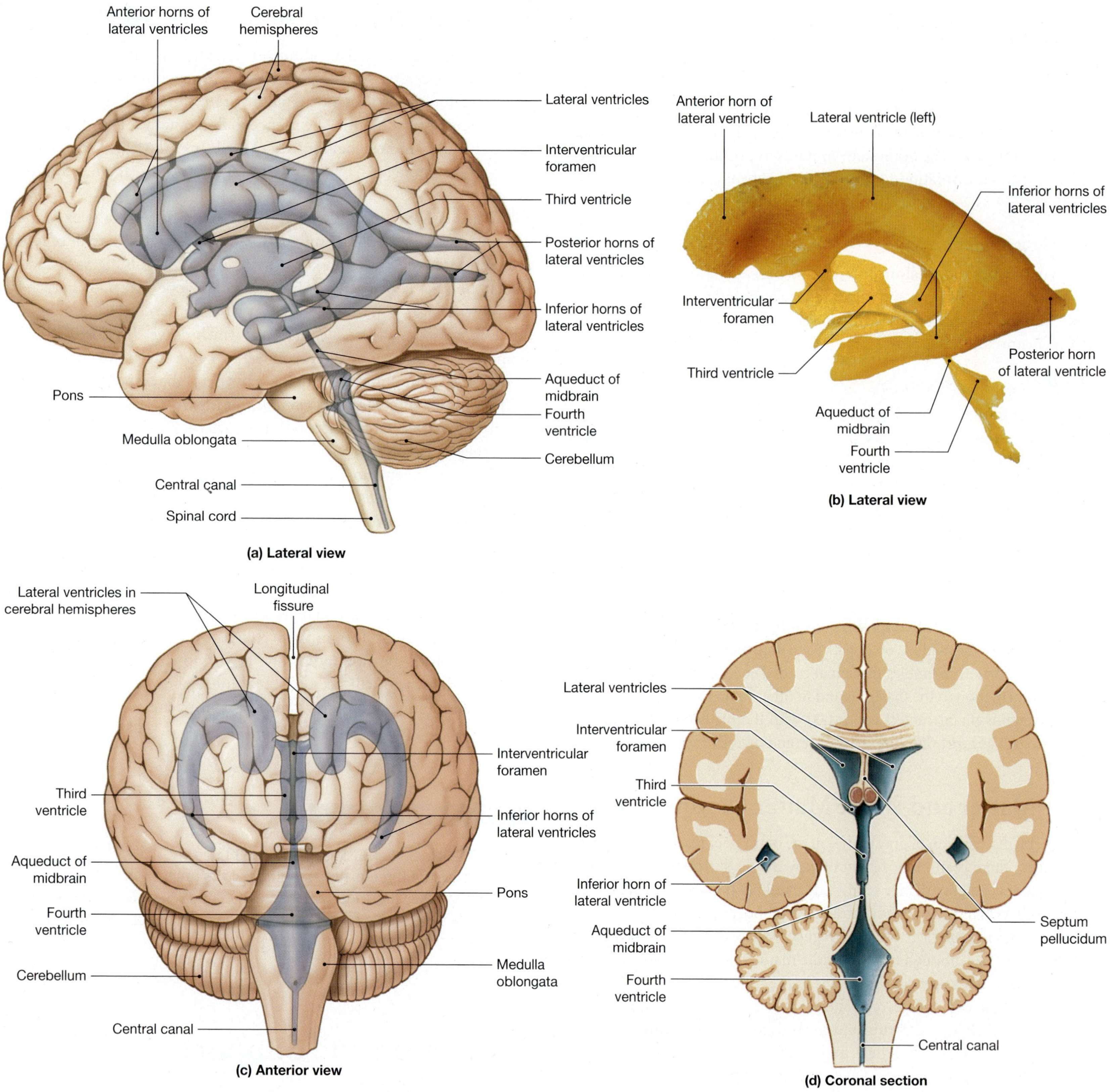

Figure 15.2 Ventricles of the Brain
The ventricles contain cerebrospinal fluid, which transports nutrients, chemical messengers, and waste products. **(a)** Orientation and extent of the ventricles as seen in a lateral view of a transparent brain. **(b)** Lateral view of a plastic cast of the ventricles. **(c)** Anterior view of the ventricles as if seen through a transparent brain. **(d)** Diagrammatic coronal section, showing the interconnections between the ventricles.

Clinical Note

Traumatic Brain Injuries *Traumatic brain injury (TBI)* may result from harsh contact between the head and another object or from a severe jolt. Head injuries account for more than half the deaths attributed to trauma. Every year roughly 1.5 million cases of TBI occur in the United States. Approximately 50,000 people die, and another 80,000 have long-term disability.

Concussions may accompany even minor head injuries. A concussion may involve transient confusion with abnormal mental status, temporary loss of consciousness, and some degree of amnesia. Physicians examine concussed individuals quite closely and may x-ray or CT-scan the skull to check for fractures or cranial bleeding. Mild concussions produce a brief interruption of consciousness and little memory loss. Severe concussions produce extended periods of unconsciousness and abnormal neurological functions. Severe concussions are typically associated with contusions (bruises), hemorrhages, or lacerations (tears) of the brain tissue; the possibilities for recovery vary with the areas affected. Extensive damage to the reticular formation can produce a permanent state of unconsciousness, and damage to the lower brain stem generally proves fatal.

Wearing helmets during activities such as bike, horse, skateboard, or motorcycle riding; contact sports such as football and hockey; and when batting and base running in baseball provides protection for the brain. Seat belts give similar protection in the event of a motor vehicle accident. If a concussion does occur, restricted activities, including delay in return to the activity that led to the injury, is recommended.

The Cranial Meninges [Figure 15.3]

The brain lies cradled within the cranium of the skull, and there is an obvious correspondence between the shape of the brain and that of the cranial cavity (**Figure 15.3**). The massive cranial bones provide mechanical protection, but they also pose a threat. The brain is like a person driving a car. If the car hits a tree, the car protects the driver from contact with the tree, but serious injury will occur unless a seat belt or airbag protects the driver from contact with the car.

Within the cranial cavity, the **cranial meninges** that surround the brain provide this protection, acting as shock absorbers that prevent contact with surrounding bones (**Figure 15.3a**). The cranial meninges are continuous with the spinal meninges, and they have the same three layers: *dura mater* (outermost), *arachnoid mater* (middle), and *pia mater* (innermost). However, the cranial meninges have distinctive specializations and functions.

The Dura Mater [Figures 15.3/15.4]

The cranial **dura mater** consists of two fibrous layers. The outermost layer, or *endosteal layer*, is fused to the periosteum lining the cranial bones (**Figure 15.3a**). The innermost layer is called the *meningeal layer*; in many areas the endosteal and meningeal layers are separated by a slender gap that contains interstitial fluid and blood vessels, including the large veins known as **dural sinuses**. The veins of the brain open into these sinuses, which in turn deliver that blood to the *internal jugular vein* of the neck.

At four locations, folds of the meningeal layer of the cranial dura mater extend deep into the cranial cavity. These septa subdivide the cranial cavity and provide support for the brain, limiting movement of the brain (**Figures 15.3b** and **15.4**):

- The **falx cerebri** (falks ser-Ē-brē; *falx*, curving, or sickle-shaped) is a fold of dura mater that projects between the cerebral hemispheres in the longitudinal fissure. Its inferior portions attach to the crista galli (anteriorly) and the internal occipital crest and *tentorium cerebelli* (posteriorly). Two large venous sinuses, the **superior sagittal sinus** and the **inferior sagittal sinus**, travel within this dural fold.
- The **tentorium cerebelli** (ten-TO-rē-um ser-e-BEL-ē; *tentorium*, covering) supports and protects the two occipital lobes of the cerebrum. It also separates the cerebellar hemispheres from those of the cerebrum. It extends across the cranium at right angles to the falx cerebri. The **transverse sinus** lies within the tentorium cerebelli.
- The **falx cerebelli** extends in the midsagittal line inferior to the tentorium cerebelli, dividing the two cerebellar hemispheres. Its posterior margin, which is locked in position, contains the *occipital sinus*.
- The **diaphragma sellae** is a continuation of the dural sheet that lines the sella turcica of the sphenoid (**Figure 15.3b**). The diaphragma sellae anchors the dura mater to the sphenoid and ensheathes the base of the pituitary gland.

The Arachnoid Mater [Figure 15.4]

The cranial **arachnoid mater** is a delicate membrane covering the brain and lying between the superficial dura mater and the pia mater that is in contact with the neural tissue of the brain. In most anatomical preparations, a narrow **subdural space** separates the opposing epithelia of the dura mater and the cranial arachnoid mater. It is likely, however, that in life no such space exists. The cranial arachnoid mater provides a smooth surface that does not follow the underlying neural convolutions or *sulci*. Deep to the arachnoid mater is the **subarachnoid space**, which contains a delicate, weblike meshwork of collagen and elastic fibers that link the arachnoid mater to the underlying pia mater. Externally, along the axis of the superior sagittal sinus, fingerlike extensions of the cranial arachnoid mater penetrate the dura mater and project into the venous sinuses. At these projections, called **arachnoid granulations**, cerebrospinal fluid flows past bundles of fibers (the *arachnoid trabeculae*), crosses the arachnoid mater, and enters the venous circulation (**Figure 15.4b,c**). The cranial arachnoid mater acts as a roof over the cranial blood vessels, and the underlying pia mater forms a floor. Cerebral arteries and veins are supported by the arachnoid trabeculae and surrounded by cerebrospinal fluid. Blood vessels, surrounded and suspended by arachnoid trabeculae, penetrate the substance of the brain within channels lined by pia mater.

The Pia Mater [Figure 15.4]

The cranial **pia mater** is tightly attached to the surface contours of the brain, following its contours and lining the sulci. The pia is anchored to the surface of the brain by the processes of astrocytes. pp. 344–345 The cranial pia mater is a highly vascular membrane that acts as a floor to support the large cerebral blood vessels as they branch over the surface of the brain, invading the neural contours to supply superficial areas of neural cortex (**Figure 15.4**). An extensive blood supply is vital, because the brain requires a constant supply of nutrients and oxygen.

The Blood–Brain Barrier

Neural tissue in the CNS has an extensive blood supply, yet it is isolated from the general circulation by the **blood–brain barrier (BBB)**. This barrier provides a means to maintain a constant environment, which is necessary for both control and proper functioning of CNS neurons.

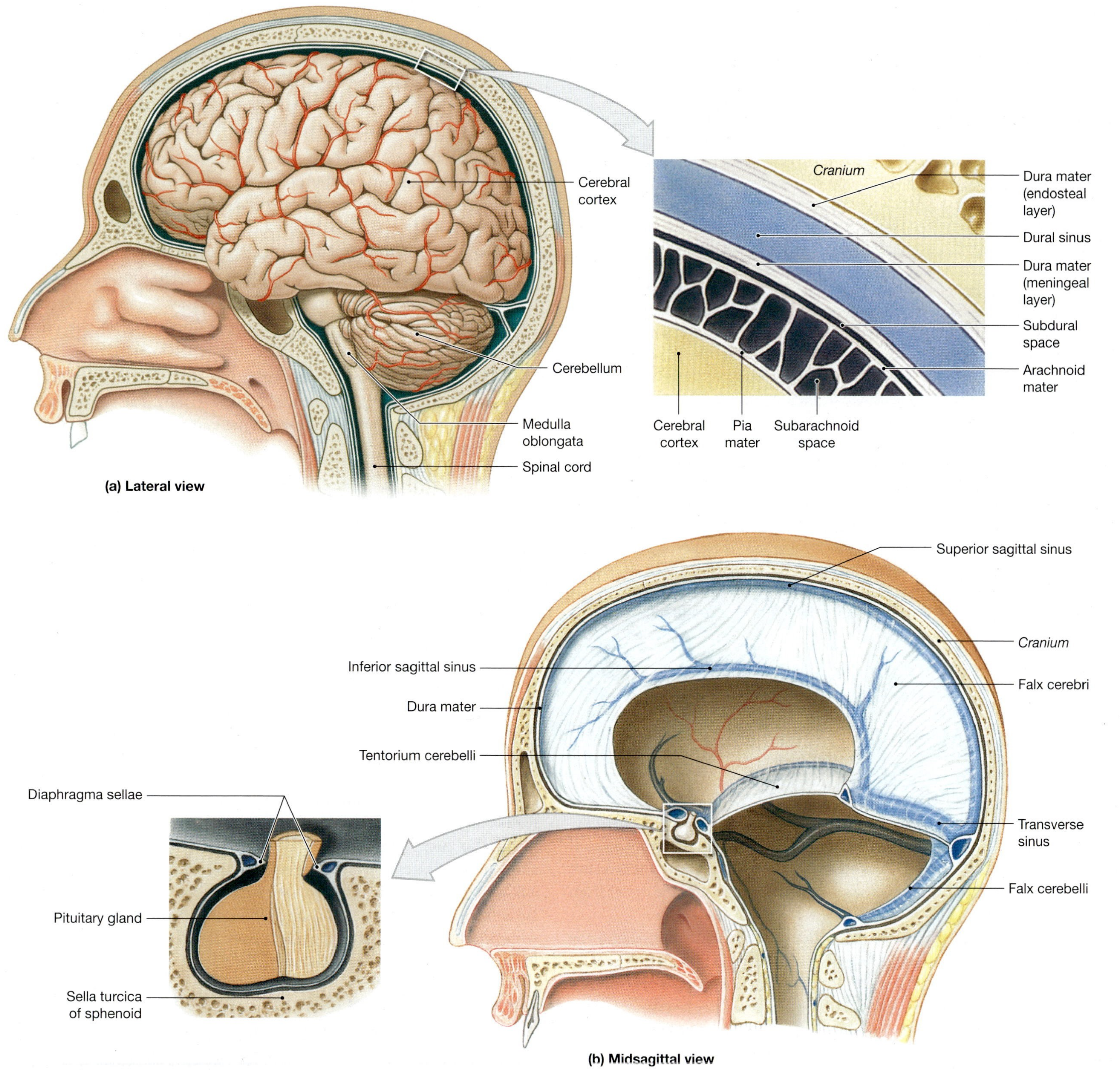

Figure 15.3 Relationships among the Brain, Cranium, and Meninges
(a) Lateral view of the brain, showing its position in the cranium and the organization of the meningeal coverings.
(b) A corresponding view of the cranial cavity with the brain removed, showing the orientation and extent of the falx cerebri and tentorium cerebelli.

The barrier exists because of the specific anatomy and transport characteristics of the endothelial cells lining the capillaries of the CNS. These endothelial cells are extensively interconnected by tight junctions, which prevent the diffusion of materials between adjacent endothelial cells. As a result, only lipid-soluble compounds can diffuse across the endothelial plasmalemmae and into the interstitial fluid of the brain and spinal cord. In addition, the endothelial cells of these capillaries exhibit very few pinocytotic vesicles, thereby limiting the movement of large-molecular-weight compounds into the CNS. Water-soluble compounds can cross the capillary walls only through passive or active transport mechanisms. Many different transport proteins are involved, and their activities are quite specific. For example, the transport system that handles

Figure 15.4 The Cranial Meninges
(a) A superior view of a dissection of the cranial meninges. **(b)** Organization and relationship of the cranial meninges to the brain. **(c)** A detailed view of the arachnoid membrane, the subarachnoid space, and the pia mater. Note the relationship between the cerebral vein and the subarachnoid space.

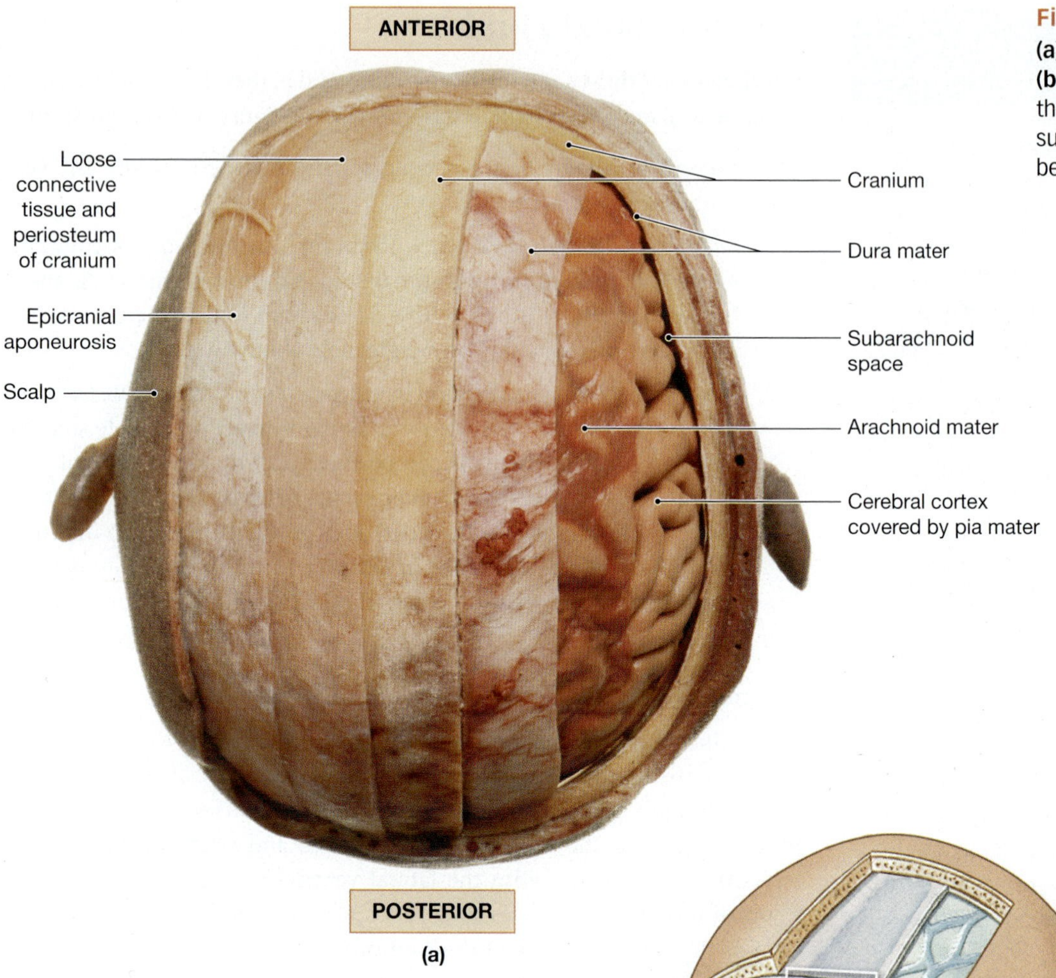

(a)

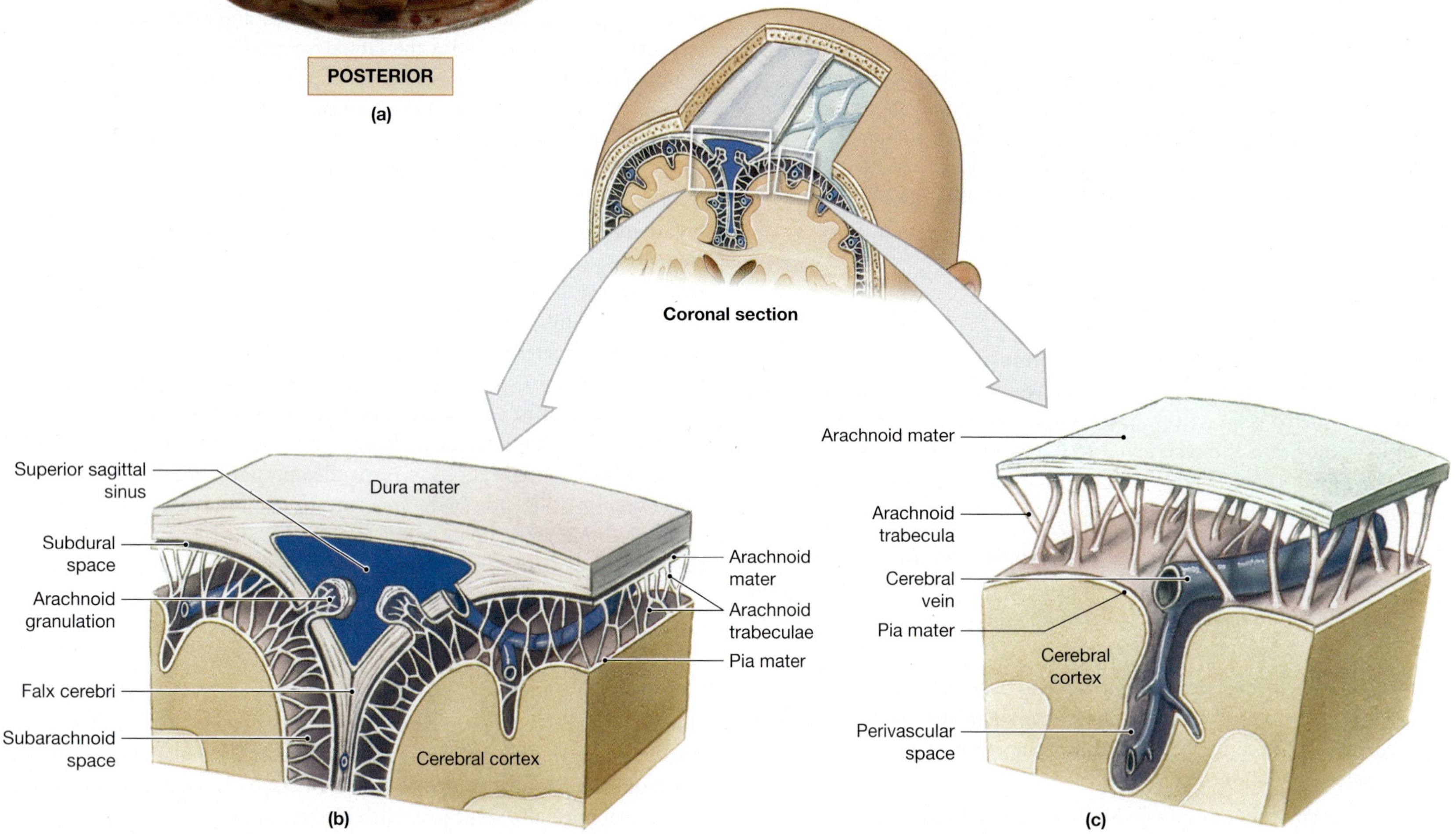

(b) (c)

glucose is different from those transporting large amino acids. The restricted permeability characteristics of the endothelial lining of brain capillaries are in some way dependent on chemicals secreted by astrocytes. These cells, which are in close contact with CNS capillaries, were described in Chapter 13. p. 344

Endothelial transport across the blood–brain barrier is selective and directional. Neurons have a constant need for glucose that must be met regardless of the relative concentrations in the blood and interstitial fluid. Even when circulating glucose levels are low, endothelial cells continue to transport glucose from the blood to the interstitial fluid of the brain. In

Clinical Note

Epidural and Subdural Hemorrhages A severe head injury may damage meningeal vessels and cause bleeding into the epidural or subdural spaces. The most common cases of epidural bleeding, or **epidural hemorrhage**, involve an arterial break. The arterial blood pressure rapidly forces considerable quantities of blood into the epidural space, distorting the underlying soft tissues of the brain. The individual loses consciousness from minutes to hours after the injury, and death follows in untreated cases.

An epidural hemorrhage involving a damaged vein does not produce massive symptoms immediately, and the individual may become unconscious from several hours to several days or even weeks after the original incident. Consequently, the problem may not be noticed until the nervous tissue has been severely damaged by distortion, compression, and secondary hemorrhaging. Epidural hemorrhages are rare, occurring in fewer than 1 percent of head injuries. This rarity is rather fortunate, for the mortality rate is 100 percent in untreated cases and more than 50 percent even after removal of the blood pool and closure of the damaged vessels.

The term **subdural hemorrhage** is somewhat misleading, because blood actually enters the inner layer of the dura, flowing beneath the epithelium that contacts the arachnoid membrane. Subdural hemorrhages are roughly twice as common as epidural hemorrhages. The most common source of blood is a small vein or one of the dural sinuses. Because the blood pressure is somewhat lower than in a typical epidural hemorrhage, the extent and effects of the condition may be quite variable. The hemorrhage produces a mass of clotted and partially clotted blood; this mass is called a *hematoma* (hē-ma-TŌ-ma). *Acute subdural hematomas* become symptomatic in minutes to hours after injury. *Chronic subdural hematomas* may produce symptoms weeks, months, or even years after a head injury.

contrast, the amino acid *glycine* is a neurotransmitter, and its concentration in neural tissue must be kept much lower than that in the circulating blood. Endothelial cells actively absorb this compound from the interstitial fluid of the brain and secrete it into the blood.

The blood–brain barrier remains intact throughout the CNS, with three noteworthy exceptions:

1. In portions of the hypothalamus, the capillary endothelium has an increased permeability, which both exposes hypothalamic nuclei in the anterior and tuberal regions to circulating hormones and permits the diffusion of hypothalamic hormones into the circulation.
2. Capillaries in the *pineal gland* are also very permeable. The pineal gland, an endocrine structure, is located in the roof of the diencephalon. The capillary permeability allows pineal secretions into the general circulation.
3. In the membranous roof of both the third and fourth ventricles, the pia mater supports extensive capillary networks that project into the ventricles of the brain. These capillaries are unusually permeable. However, substances do not have free access to the CNS because the capillaries are covered by modified ependymal cells that are interconnected by tight junctions. This complex, the *choroid plexus*, is the site of cerebrospinal fluid production.

Cerebrospinal Fluid

Cerebrospinal fluid completely surrounds and bathes the exposed surfaces of the central nervous system. It has several important functions, including:

1. *Preventing contact* between delicate neural structures and the surrounding bones.
2. *Supporting the brain:* In essence, the brain is suspended inside the cranium, floating in the cerebrospinal fluid. A human brain weighs about 1400 g in air, but it is only a little denser than water; when supported by the cerebrospinal fluid, it weighs only about 50 g.
3. *Transporting nutrients, chemical messengers, and waste products:* Except at the choroid plexus, the ependymal lining is freely permeable, and the CSF is in constant chemical communication with the interstitial fluid of the CNS. Because free exchange occurs between the interstitial fluid and CSF, changes in CNS function may produce changes in the composition of the CSF. As noted in Chapter 14, a spinal tap can provide useful clinical information concerning CNS injury, infection, or disease. p. 366

Formation of CSF [Figure 15.5]

All of the ventricles contain a **choroid plexus** (*choroid*, vascular coat + *plexus*, network), which consists of a combination of specialized ependymal cells and highly permeable capillaries. Two extensive folds of the choroid plexus originate in the roof of the third ventricle and extend through the interventricular foramina into the lateral ventricles. These folds cover the floors of the lateral ventricles (**Figure 15.5a**). In the lower brain stem, a region of the choroid plexus in the roof of the fourth ventricle projects between the cerebellum and the pons.

The choroid plexus is responsible for the production of cerebrospinal fluid (CSF). The capillaries are fenestrated and highly permeable, but large, highly specialized ependymal cells cover the capillaries and prevent free exchange between those capillaries and the CSF of the ventricles. The ependymal cells use both active and passive transport mechanisms to secrete cerebrospinal fluid into the ventricles. The regulation of CSF composition involves transport in both directions, and the choroid plexus removes waste products from the CSF and fine-tunes its composition over time. There are many differences in composition between cerebrospinal fluid and blood plasma (blood with the cellular elements removed). For example, the blood contains high concentrations of suspended proteins, but the CSF does not. There are also differences in the concentrations of individual ions and in the levels of amino acids, lipids, and waste products (**Figure 15.5b**). Thus, although CSF is derived from plasma, it is not merely a simple filtrate of blood.

Circulation of CSF [Figures 14.4a/15.4b/15.6]

The choroid plexus produces CSF at a rate of about 500 ml/day. The total volume of CSF at any given moment is approximately 150 ml. This means that the entire volume of CSF is replaced roughly every eight hours. Despite this rapid turnover, the composition of CSF is closely regulated, and the rate of removal normally keeps pace with the rate of production.

CSF produced in the lateral ventricles flows into the third ventricle through the *interventricular foramen.* From there, CSF flows into the *aqueduct of the midbrain.* Most of the CSF reaching the fourth ventricle enters the subarachnoid space by passing through the paired **lateral apertures** and a single **median aperture** in its membranous roof. (A relatively small quantity of cerebrospinal fluid circulates between the fourth ventri-

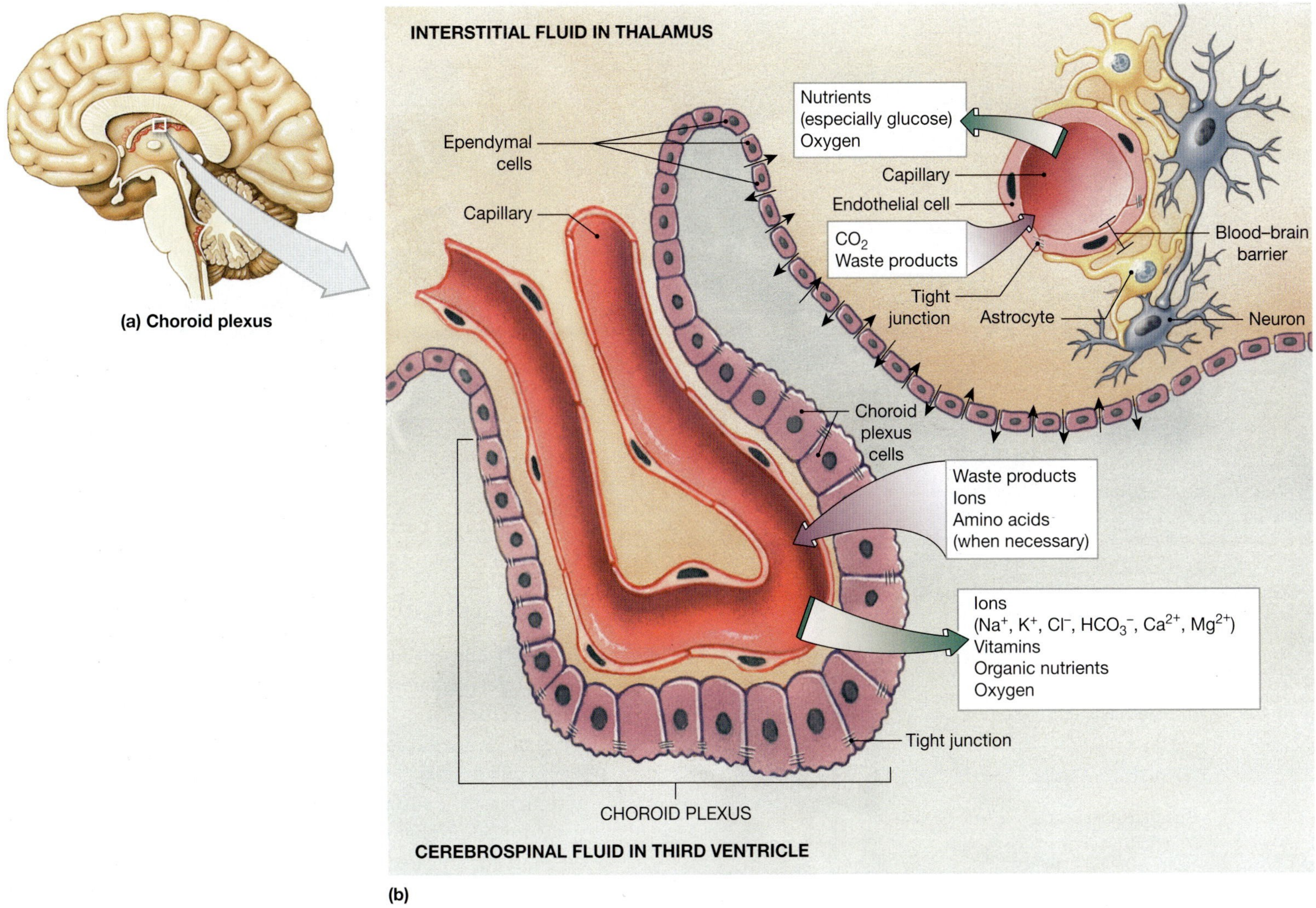

Figure 15.5 The Choroid Plexus and Blood–Brain Barrier
(a) The location of the choroid plexus in each of the four ventricles of the brain. **(b)** The structure and function of the choroid plexus. The ependymal cells are a selective barrier, actively transporting nutrients, vitamins, and ions into the CSF. When necessary, these cells also actively remove ions or compounds from the CSF to stabilize its composition.

cle and the central canal of the spinal cord.) CSF continuously flows through the subarachnoid space surrounding the brain, and movements of the vertebral column move it around the spinal cord and cauda equina (Figure 14.4a). p. 366 Cerebrospinal fluid eventually reenters the circulation through the **arachnoid granulations** (Figures 15.4b and 15.6). If the normal circulation of CSF is interrupted, a variety of clinical problems may appear.

The Blood Supply to the Brain [Figures 22.13/22.22]

Neurons have a high demand for energy while lacking energy reserves in the form of carbohydrates or lipid. In addition, neurons are lacking myoglobin and have no way to store oxygen reserves. Therefore their energy demands must be met by an extensive vascular supply. Arterial blood reaches the brain through the *internal carotid arteries* and the *vertebral arteries*. Most of the venous blood from the brain leaves the cranium in the *internal jugular veins*, which drain the dural sinuses. The arteries supplying blood to the brain, as well as the veins leaving the brain, will be discussed in Chapter 22. A head injury that damages the cerebral blood vessels may cause bleeding into the dura mater, either near the dural epithelium or between the outer layer of the dura mater and the bones of the skull. These are serious conditions, because the blood entering these spaces compresses and distorts the relatively soft tissues of the brain.

Cerebrovascular diseases are circulatory disorders that interfere with the normal blood supply to the brain. The particular distribution of the vessel involved determines the symptoms, and the degree of oxygen or nutrient starvation determines the severity. A **cerebrovascular accident (CVA)**, or *stroke*, occurs when the blood supply to a portion of the brain is shut off. Affected neurons begin to die in a matter of minutes.

CONCEPT CHECK

1. Identify the four extensions of the innermost layer of the dura mater into the cranial cavity that provide stabilization and support to the brain.
2. Discuss the structure and function of the pia mater.
3. What is the function of the blood–brain barrier?
4. What is the function of the cerebrospinal fluid? Where is it formed?

See blue "Answers" tab at back of book.

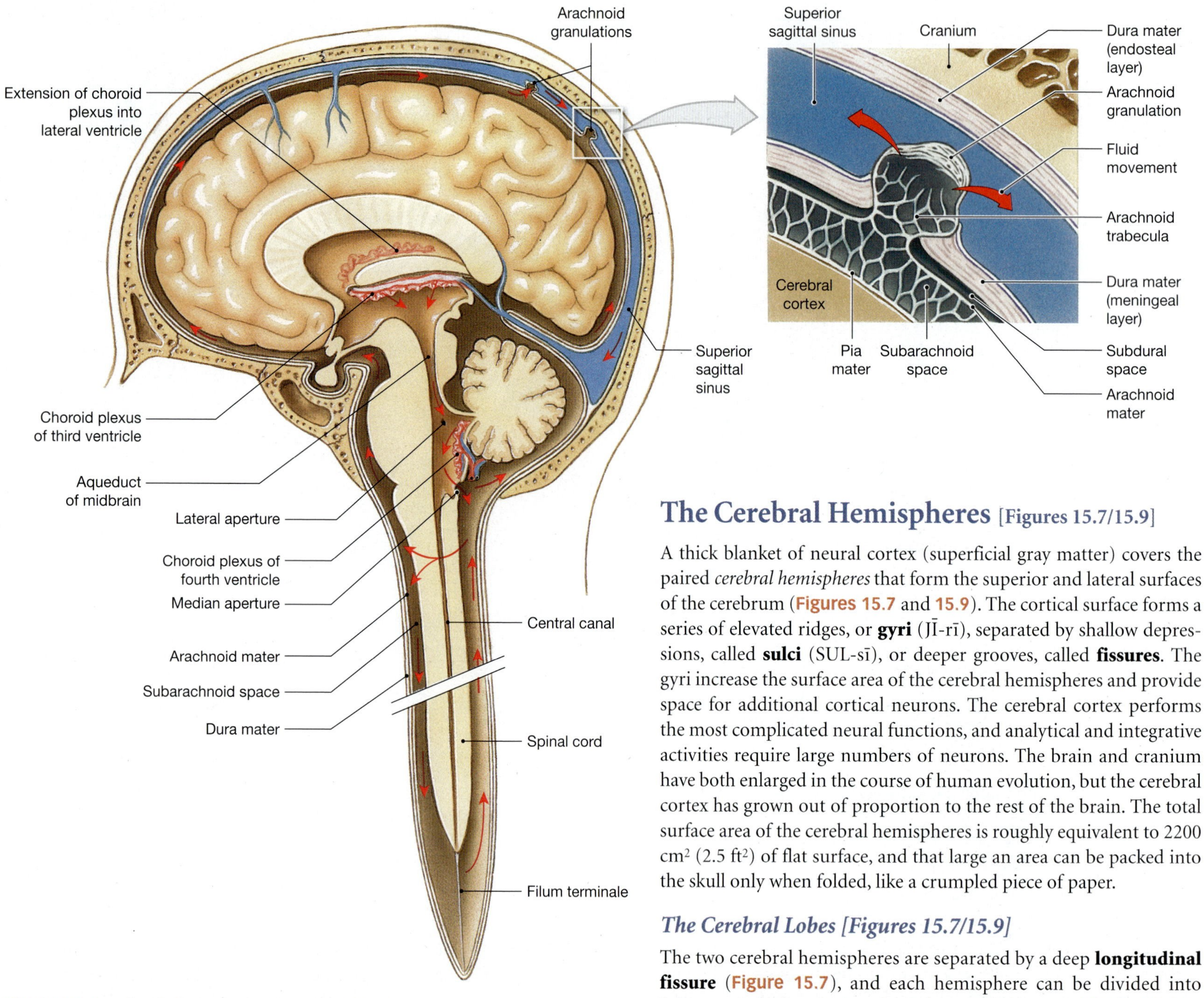

Figure 15.6 Circulation of Cerebrospinal Fluid
Sagittal section indicating the sites of formation and the routes of circulation of cerebrospinal fluid.

The Cerebrum [Figures 15.1/15.7/15.9]

The cerebrum is the largest region of the brain. It consists of the paired *cerebral hemispheres*, which rest on the diencephalon and brain stem. Conscious thought processes and all intellectual functions originate in the cerebral hemispheres. Much of the cerebrum is involved in the processing of somatic sensory and motor information. Somatic sensory information relayed to the cerebrum reaches our conscious awareness, and cerebral neurons exert direct (voluntary) or indirect (involuntary) control over somatic motor neurons. Most visceral sensory processing and visceral motor (autonomic) control occur at centers elsewhere in the brain, usually outside our conscious awareness. Figures 15.1, p. 388, 15.7, and 15.9 provide additional perspective on the cerebrum and its relationships with other regions of the brain.

The Cerebral Hemispheres [Figures 15.7/15.9]

A thick blanket of neural cortex (superficial gray matter) covers the paired *cerebral hemispheres* that form the superior and lateral surfaces of the cerebrum (Figures 15.7 and 15.9). The cortical surface forms a series of elevated ridges, or **gyri** (JĪ-rī), separated by shallow depressions, called **sulci** (SUL-sī), or deeper grooves, called **fissures**. The gyri increase the surface area of the cerebral hemispheres and provide space for additional cortical neurons. The cerebral cortex performs the most complicated neural functions, and analytical and integrative activities require large numbers of neurons. The brain and cranium have both enlarged in the course of human evolution, but the cerebral cortex has grown out of proportion to the rest of the brain. The total surface area of the cerebral hemispheres is roughly equivalent to 2200 cm^2 (2.5 ft^2) of flat surface, and that large an area can be packed into the skull only when folded, like a crumpled piece of paper.

The Cerebral Lobes [Figures 15.7/15.9]

The two cerebral hemispheres are separated by a deep **longitudinal fissure** (Figure 15.7), and each hemisphere can be divided into **lobes** named after the overlying bones of the skull (Figure 15.9a). There are differences in the appearance of the sulci and gyri of each individual brain, but the boundaries between lobes are reliable landmarks. A deep groove, the **central sulcus**, extends laterally from the longitudinal fissure. The area anterior to the central sulcus is the **frontal lobe**, and the **lateral sulcus** marks its inferior border. The region inferior to the lateral sulcus is the **temporal lobe**. Reflecting this lobe to the side (Figure 15.9b) exposes the **insula** (IN-sū-la), an "island" of cortex that is otherwise hidden. The **parietal lobe** extends posteriorly from the central sulcus to the **parieto-occipital sulcus**. The region posterior to the parieto-occipital sulcus is the **occipital lobe**.

Each lobe contains functional regions whose boundaries are less clearly defined. Some of these functional regions process sensory information, while others are responsible for motor commands. Three points about the cerebral lobes should be kept in mind:

1. *Each cerebral hemisphere receives sensory information from and generates motor commands to the opposite side of the body.* The left

TABLE 15.2 The Cerebral Cortex	
Region (Lobe)	**Functions**
FRONTAL LOBE **Primary motor cortex**	Conscious control of skeletal muscles
PARIETAL LOBE **Primary sensory cortex**	Conscious perception of touch, pressure, vibration, pain, temperature, and taste
OCCIPITAL LOBE **Visual cortex**	Conscious perception of visual stimuli
TEMPORAL LOBE **Auditory cortex and olfactory cortex**	Conscious perception of auditory and olfactory stimuli
ALL LOBES **Association areas**	Integration and processing of sensory data; processing and initiation of motor activities

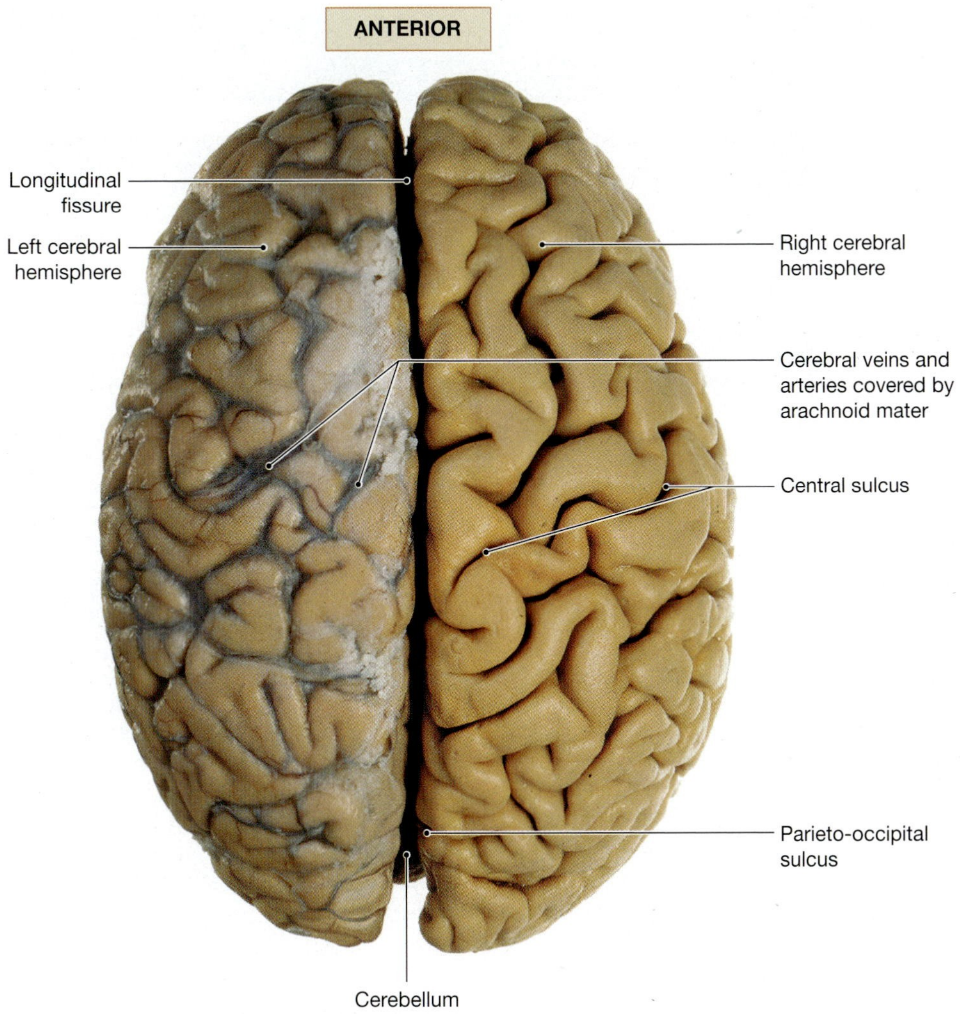

(a) Superior view

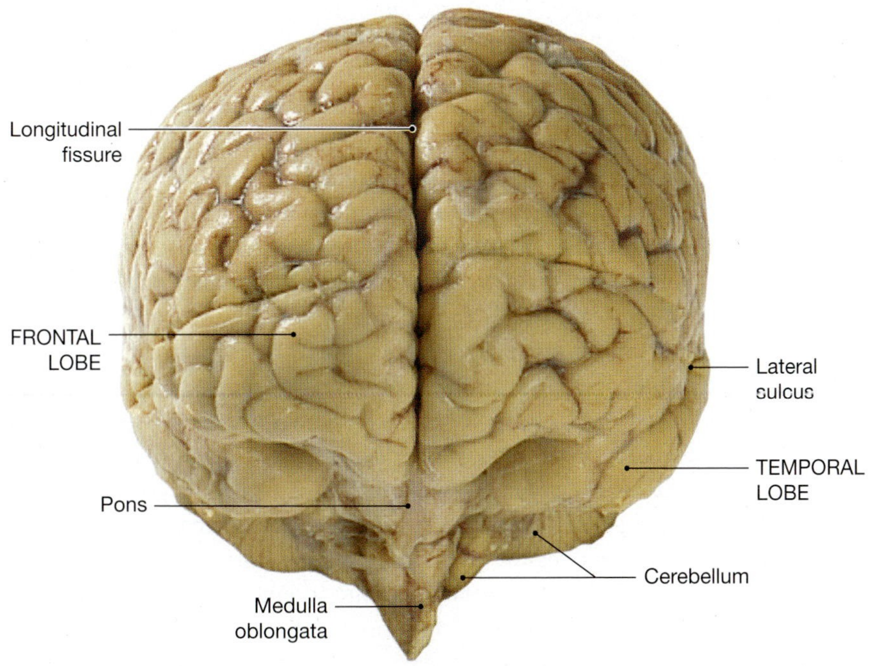

(b) Anterior view

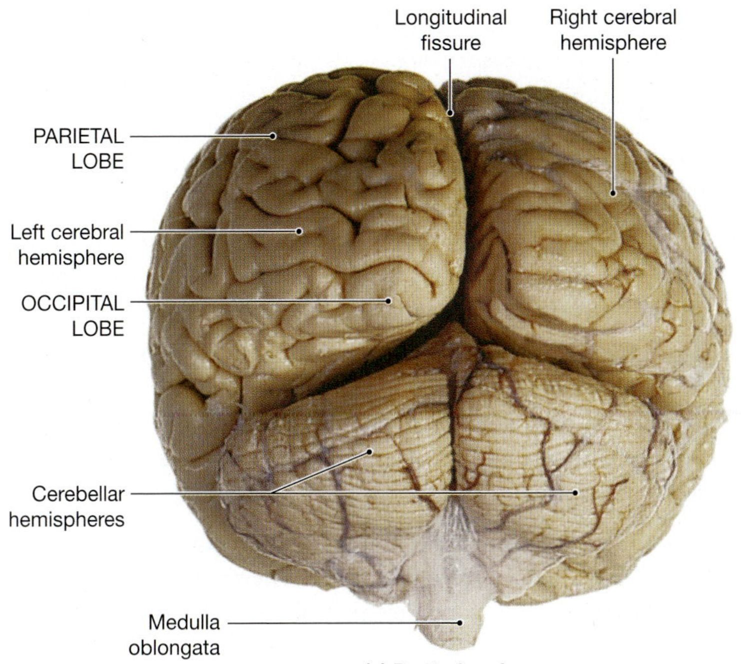

(c) Posterior view

Figure 15.7 The Cerebral Hemispheres, Part I
The cerebral hemispheres are the largest part of the adult brain. **(a)** Superior view. **(b)** Anterior view. **(c)** Posterior view. Note the relatively small size of the cerebellar hemispheres.

Clinical Note

Hydrocephalus The adult brain is surrounded by the inflexible bones of the cranium. The cranial cavity contains two fluids—blood and cerebrospinal fluid—and the relatively soft tissues of the brain. Because the total volume cannot change, when the volume of blood or CSF increases, the volume of the brain must decrease. In a subdural or epidural hemorrhage, the fluid volume increases as blood collects within the cranial cavity. The rising intracranial pressure compresses the brain, leading to neural dysfunction that often ends in unconsciousness and death.

Any alteration in the rate of cerebrospinal fluid production is normally matched by an increase in the rate of removal at the arachnoid granulations. If this equilibrium is disturbed, clinical problems appear as the intracranial pressure changes. The volume of cerebrospinal fluid will increase if the rate of formation accelerates or the rate of removal decreases. In either event the increased fluid volume leads to compression and distortion of the brain. Increased rates of formation may accompany head injuries, but the most common problems arise from masses, such as tumors or abscesses, or from developmental abnormalities. These conditions have the same effect: They restrict the normal circulation and reabsorption of CSF. Because CSF production continues, the ventricles gradually expand, distorting the surrounding neural tissues and causing the deterioration of brain function.

Infants are especially sensitive to alterations in intracranial pressure, because the arachnoid granulations do not appear until roughly 3 years of age. (Over the interim, CSF is reabsorbed into small vessels within the subarachnoid space and underlying the ependyma.) As in an adult, if intracranial pressure becomes abnormally high, the ventricles will expand. But in an infant, the cranial sutures have yet to fuse, and the skull can enlarge to accommodate the extra fluid volume. This enlargement produces an enormously expanded skull, a condition called **hydrocephalus**, or "water on the brain." Infant hydrocephalus (Figure 15.8) often results from some interference with normal CSF circulation, such as blockage of the aqueduct of the midbrain or constriction of the connection between the subarachnoid spaces of the cranial and spinal meninges. Untreated infants often suffer some degree of mental retardation. Successful treatment usually involves the installation of a **shunt**, a tube that either bypasses the blockage site or drains the excess cerebrospinal fluid. In either case, the goal is reduction of the intracranial pressure. The shunt may be removed if (1) further growth of the brain eliminates the blockage or (2) the intracranial pressure decreases following the development of the arachnoid granulations at 3 years of age.

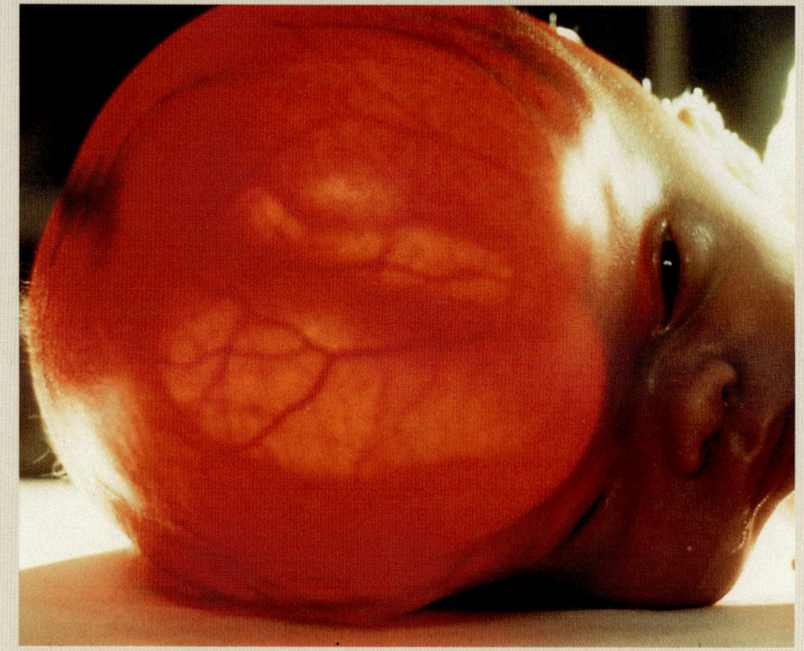

Figure 15.8 Hydrocephalus
This infant has severe hydrocephalus, a condition usually caused by impaired circulation and removal of cerebrospinal fluid. CSF buildup leads to distortion of the brain and enlargement of the cranium.

hemisphere controls the right side, and the right hemisphere controls the left side. This crossing over has no known functional significance.

2. *The two hemispheres have some functional differences, although anatomically they appear to be identical.* These differences affect primarily higher-order functions, a topic that will be discussed in Chapter 16.
3. *The assignment of a specific function to a specific region of the cerebral cortex is imprecise.* Because the boundaries are indistinct, with considerable overlap, any one region may have several different functions. Some aspects of cortical function, such as consciousness, cannot easily be assigned to any single region.

Our understanding of brain function is still incomplete, and not every anatomical feature has a known function. However, it is clear from studies on metabolic activity and blood flow that all portions of the brain are used in a normal individual.

Motor and Sensory Areas of the Cerebral Cortex [Figure 15.9b and Table 15.2]

Conscious thought processes and all intellectual functions originate in the cerebral hemispheres. However, much of the cerebrum is involved with the processing of somatic sensory and motor information. The major motor and sensory regions of the cerebral cortex are detailed in Figure 15.9b and Table 15.2. The central sulcus separates the motor and sensory portions of the cortex. The **precentral gyrus** of the frontal lobe forms the anterior margin of the central sulcus. The surface of this gyrus is the **primary motor cortex**. Neurons of the primary motor cortex direct voluntary movements by controlling somatic motor neurons in the brain stem and spinal cord. The neurons of the primary motor cortex are called **pyramidal cells**, and the pathway that provides voluntary motor control is known as the **corticospinal pathway** or *pyramidal system*, which will be discussed further in Chapter 16.

The **postcentral gyrus** of the parietal lobe forms the posterior margin of the central sulcus, and its surface contains the **primary sensory cortex**. Neurons in this region receive somatic sensory information from touch, pressure, pain, taste, and temperature receptors. We are consciously aware of these sensations because the sensory information has been relayed to the primary sensory cortex. At the same time, collaterals deliver information to the basal nuclei and other centers. As a result, sensory information is monitored at both conscious and unconscious levels.

Sensory information concerning sensations of sight, sound, and smell arrives at other portions of the cerebral cortex. The **visual cortex** of

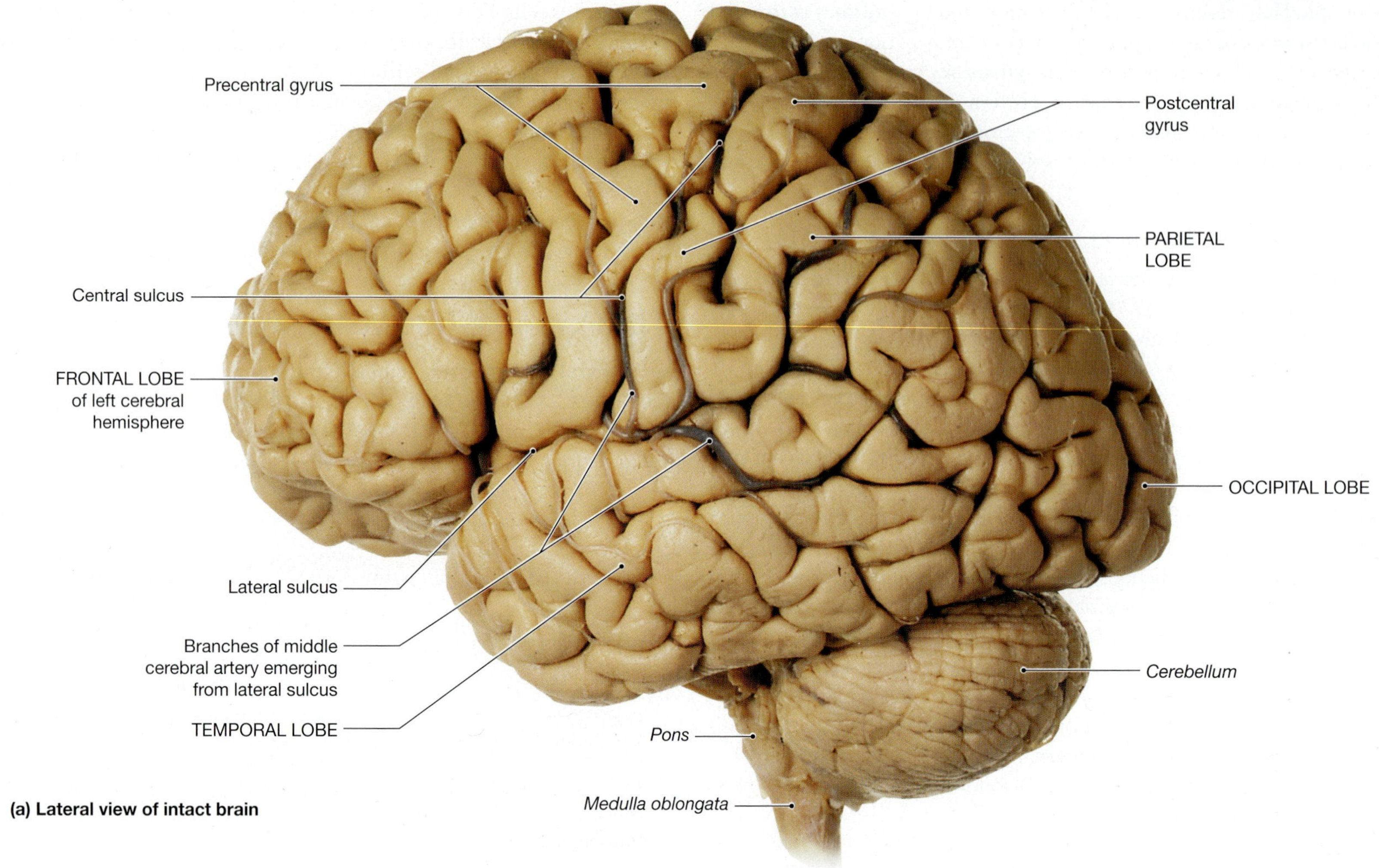

(a) Lateral view of intact brain

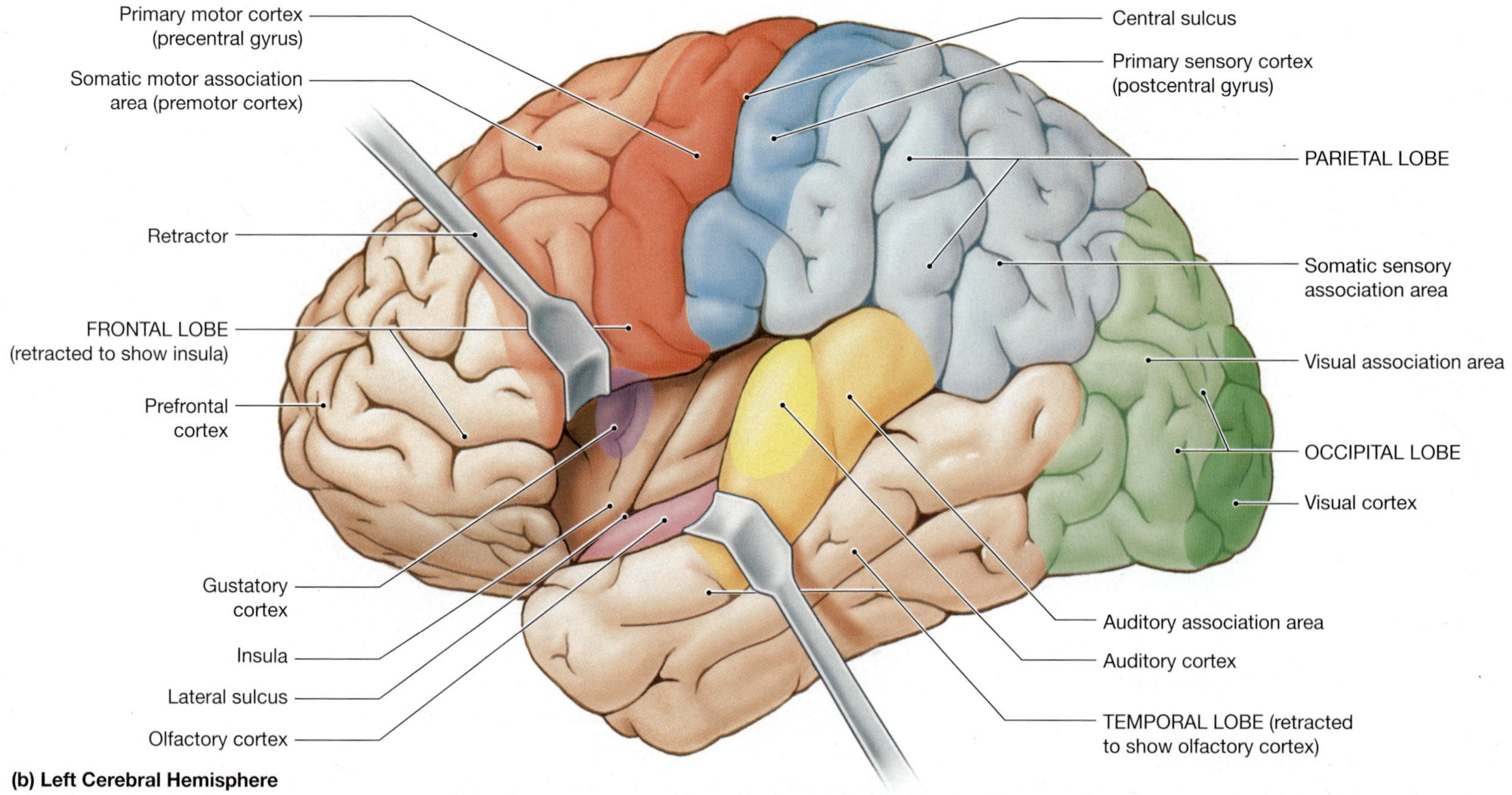

(b) Left Cerebral Hemisphere

Figure 15.9 The Cerebral Hemispheres, Part II

Lobes and functional regions. **(a)** Lateral view of intact brain after removal of the dura mater and arachnoid mater, showing superficial surface anatomy of the left hemisphere. **(b)** Major anatomical landmarks on the surface of the left cerebral hemisphere. Association areas are colored. To expose the insula, the lateral sulcus has been pulled open.

the occipital lobe receives visual information, and the **auditory cortex** and **olfactory cortex** of the temporal lobe receive information concerned with hearing and smelling, respectively. The **gustatory cortex** lies in the anterior portion of the insula and adjacent portions of the frontal lobe. This region receives information from taste receptors of the tongue and pharynx. The regions of the cerebral cortex involved with special sensory information are shown in Figure 15.9b.

Association Areas [Figure 15.9b]

Each of the sensory and motor regions of the cortex is connected to a nearby **association area** (Figure 15.9b). The term association area is used for regions of the cerebrum involved with the integration of sensory or motor information. These areas do not receive sensory information directly, nor do they generate motor commands. Instead, they interpret sensory input arriving elsewhere in the cerebral cortex, and they plan, prepare for, and help coordinate motor output. For example, the **somatic sensory association area** allows you to comprehend the size, form, and texture of an object, and the **somatic motor association area**, or *premotor cortex*, uses memories of learned movement patterns to coordinate motor activities.

The functional distinctions between the sensory and motor association areas are most evident after localized brain damage. For example, an individual with a damaged **visual association area** may see letters quite clearly, but be unable to recognize or interpret them. This person would scan the lines of a printed page and see rows of clear symbols that convey no meaning. Someone with damage to the area of the premotor cortex concerned with coordination of eye movements can understand written letters and words but cannot read, because his or her eyes cannot follow the lines on a printed page.

Integrative Centers [Figure 15.9b]

Integrative centers receive and process information from many different association areas. These regions direct extremely complex motor activities and perform complicated analytical functions. For example, the **prefrontal cortex** of the frontal lobe (Figure 15.9b) integrates information from sensory association areas and performs abstract intellectual functions, such as predicting the consequences of possible responses.

These lobes and cortical areas are found on both cerebral hemispheres. Higher-order integrative centers concerned with complex processes, such as speech, writing, mathematical computation, and understanding spatial relationships, are restricted to the left or right hemisphere. These centers and their functions are described in Chapter 16.

The Central White Matter [Figure 15.10 and Table 15.3]

The **central white matter** is covered by the gray matter of the cerebral cortex (Figure 15.10). It contains myelinated fibers that form bundles that extend from one cortical area to another or that connect areas of the cortex to other regions of the brain. These bundles include (1) *association fibers*,

TABLE 15.3 White Matter of the Cerebrum

Fibers/Tracts	Functions
Association fibers	Interconnect cortical areas within the same hemisphere
Arcuate fibers	Interconnect gyri within a lobe
Longitudinal fasciculi	Interconnect the frontal lobe with other cerebral lobes
Commissural fibers (anterior commissure and corpus callosum)	Interconnect corresponding lobes of different hemispheres
Projection fibers	Connect cerebral cortex to diencephalon, brain stem, cerebellum, and spinal cord

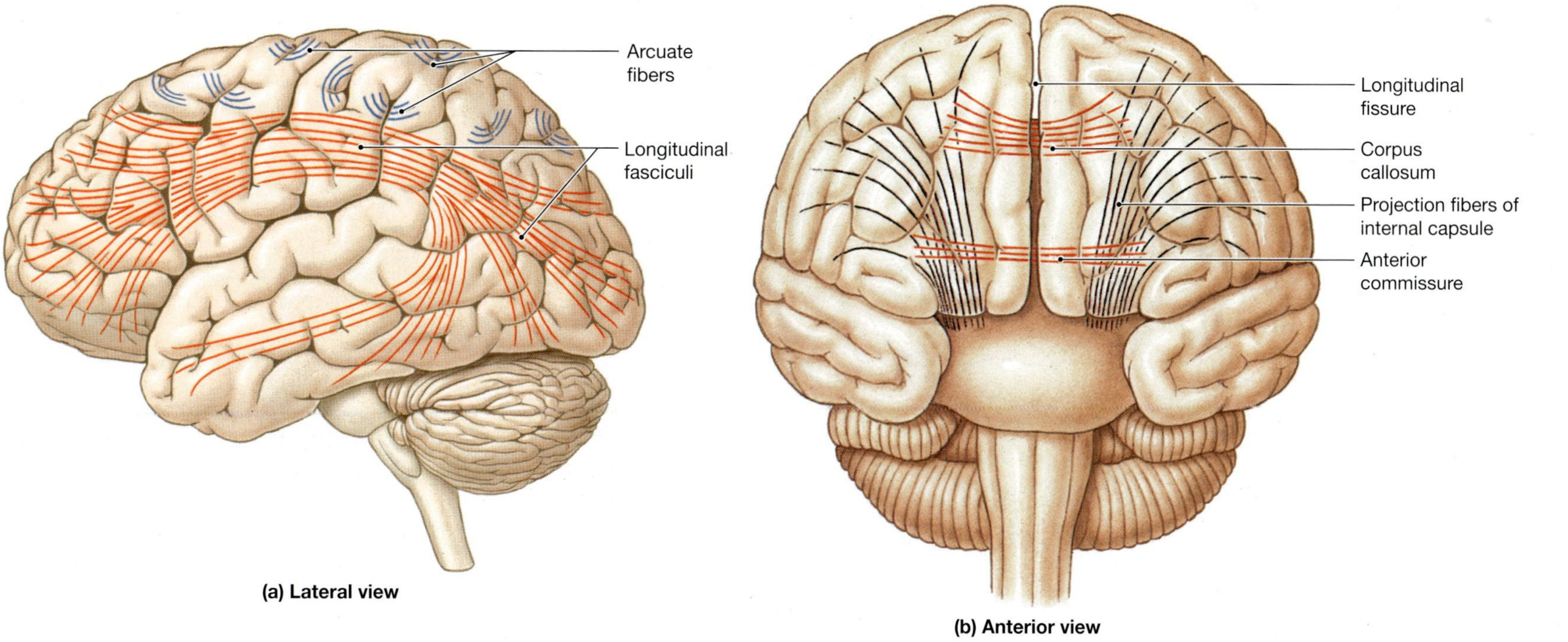

Figure 15.10 The Central White Matter
Shown are the major groups of axon fibers and tracts of the central white matter. **(a)** Lateral aspect of the brain, showing arcuate fibers and longitudinal fasciculi. **(b)** Anterior view of the brain, showing orientation of the commissural and projection fibers.

tracts that interconnect areas of neural cortex within a single cerebral hemisphere; (2) *commissural fibers*, tracts that connect the two cerebral hemispheres; and (3) *projection fibers*, tracts that link the cerebrum with other regions of the brain and the spinal cord. The names and functions of these groups are summarized in Table 15.3.

Association fibers interconnect portions of the cerebral cortex within the same cerebral hemisphere. The shortest association fibers are called **arcuate** (AR-kū-āt) **fibers** because they curve in an arc to pass from one gyrus to another. The longer association fibers are organized into discrete bundles. The **longitudinal fasciculi** connect the frontal lobe to the other lobes of the same hemisphere.

A dense band of **commissural** (kom-I-sūr-al; *commissura*, a crossing over) **fibers** permits communication between the two hemispheres. Prominent commissural bundles linking the cerebral hemispheres include the **corpus callosum** and the **anterior commissure**.

Projection fibers link the cerebral cortex to the diencephalon, brain stem, cerebellum, and spinal cord. All ascending and descending axons must pass through the diencephalon on their way to or from sensory, motor, or association areas of the cerebral cortex. In gross dissection the afferent fibers and efferent fibers look alike, and the entire collection of fibers is known as the **internal capsule**.

The Basal Nuclei [Figure 15.11 and Table 15.4]

The **basal nuclei** are paired masses of gray matter within the cerebral hemispheres.[2] These nuclei lie within each hemisphere inferior to the floor of the lateral ventricle (Figure 15.11). They are embedded within the central white matter, and the radiating projection and commissural fibers travel around or between these nuclei.

The **caudate nucleus** has a massive head and a slender, curving tail that follows the curve of the lateral ventricle. At the tip of the tail is a separate nucleus, the **amygdaloid** (ah-MIG-da-loyd; *amygdale*, almond) **body**. Three masses of gray matter lie between the bulging surface of the insula and the lateral wall of the diencephalon. These are the **claustrum** (KLAWS-trum), the **putamen** (pū-TĀ-men), and the **globus pallidus** (GLŌ-bus PAL-i-dus; pale globe).

Several additional terms are used to designate specific anatomical or functional subdivisions of the basal nuclei. The putamen and globus pallidus are often considered subdivisions of a larger **lentiform** (lens-shaped) **nucleus**, for when exposed on gross dissection, they form a rather compact, rounded mass (Figure 15.11b,c,d). The term *corpus striatum* is sometimes used to refer to the caudate *and* lentiform nuclei or to the caudate nucleus and the putamen. Table 15.4 summarizes these relationships and the functions of the basal nuclei.

Functions of the Basal Nuclei

The basal nuclei are involved with (1) the subconscious control and integration of skeletal muscle tone; (2) the coordination of learned movement patterns; and (3) the processing, integration, and relay of information from the cerebral cortex to the thalamus. Under normal conditions, these nuclei do not initiate particular movements. But once a movement is under way, the basal nuclei provide the general pattern and rhythm, especially for movements of the trunk and proximal limb muscles. (This system will be discussed further in Chapter 16.) Some functions assigned to specific basal nuclei are detailed next.

[2] These have also been called the cerebral nuclei or the basal ganglia.

TABLE 15.4 The Basal Nuclei

Nuclei	Functions
Amygdaloid body	Component of limbic system
Claustrum	Plays a role in the subconscious processing of visual information
Caudate nucleus **Lentiform nucleus (putamen and globus pallidus)**	Subconscious adjustment and modification of voluntary motor commands

Caudate Nucleus and Putamen When a person is walking, the caudate nucleus and putamen control the cycles of arm and leg movements that occur between the time the decision is made to "start walking" and the time the "stop" order is given.

Claustrum and Amygdaloid Body The claustrum appears to be involved in the processing of visual information at the subconscious level. Evidence suggests that it focuses attention on specific patterns or relevant features. The amygdaloid body is an important component of the *limbic system* and will be considered in the next section. The functions of other basal nuclei are poorly understood.

Globus Pallidus The globus pallidus controls and adjusts muscle tone, particularly in the appendicular muscles, to set body position in preparation for a voluntary movement. For example, when you decide to pick up an object, the globus pallidus positions the shoulder and stabilizes the arm as you consciously reach and grasp with the forearm, wrist, and hand.

The Limbic System [Figures 15.11/15.12/15.15 and Table 15.5]

The **limbic** (LIM-bik; *limbus*, border) **system** includes nuclei and tracts along the border between the cerebrum and diencephalon. The functions of the limbic system include (1) establishment of emotional states and related behavioral drives; (2) linking the conscious, intellectual functions of the cerebral cortex with the unconscious and autonomic functions of other portions of the brain; and (3) facilitating memory storage and retrieval. This system is a functional grouping rather than an anatomical one, and the limbic system includes components of the cerebrum, diencephalon, and mesencephalon (Table 15.5).

The amygdaloid body (Figures 15.11a,d and 15.12) appears to act as an integration center between the limbic system, the cerebrum, and various sensory systems. The **limbic lobe** of the cerebral hemisphere consists of the gyri and deeper structures that are adjacent to the diencephalon. The **cingulate** (SIN-gū-lāt; *cingulum*, girdle or belt) **gyrus** sits superior to the corpus callosum. The **dentate gyrus** and the adjacent **parahippocampal** (pa-ra-hip-ō-KAM-pal) **gyrus** conceal an underlying nucleus, the **hippocampus**, which lies deep in the temporal lobe (see Figures 15.11b and 15.12a,b). Early anatomists thought this nucleus resembled a seahorse (*hippocampus*); it plays an essential role in learning and the storage of long-term memories.

The **fornix** (FŌR-niks, arch) (Figure 15.15) is a tract of white matter that connects the hippocampus with the hypothalamus. From the hippocampus, the fornix curves medially and superiorly, inferior to the corpus callosum, and then forms an arch that curves anteriorly, ending in the hypothalamus. Many of the fibers end in the **mamillary** (MAM-i-lar-ē;

Figure 15.11 The Basal Nuclei
(a) Lateral view showing the relative positions of the basal nuclei. **(b)** Diagrammatic view of the brain dissected to show the orientation of cerebral and thalamic structures. Compare the three-dimensional representation seen in (a) with the horizontal section **(c)** and the frontal sections **(d,e)** of the brain.

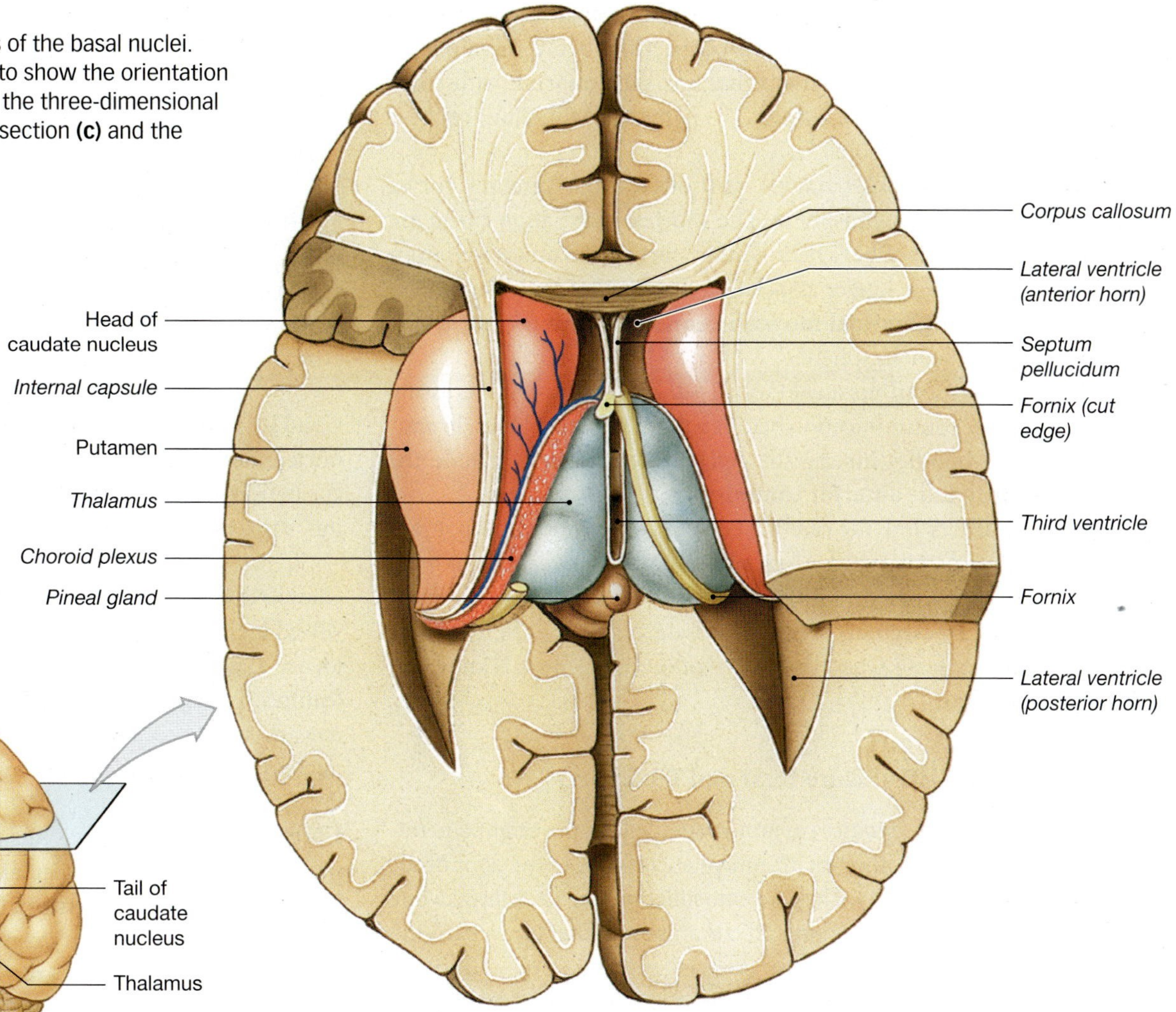

(b) Horizontal section, dissected

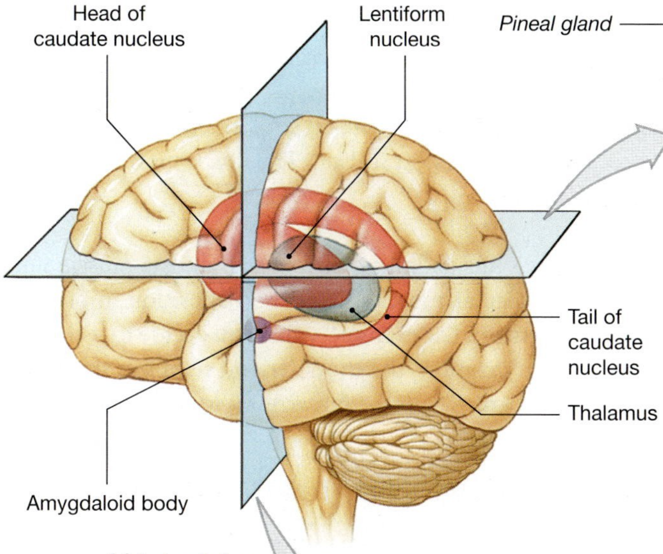

(a) Lateral view

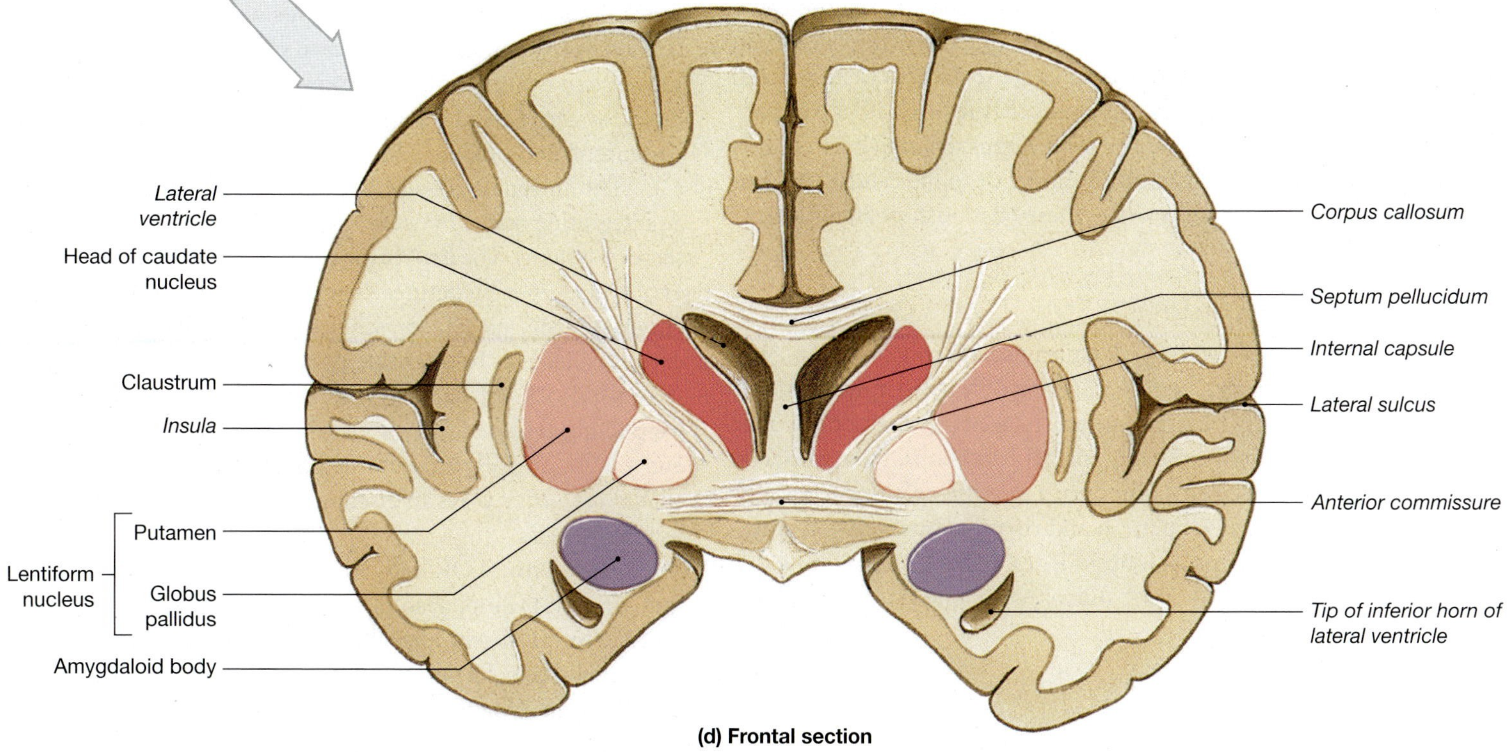

(d) Frontal section

Figure 15.11 ***(continued)***

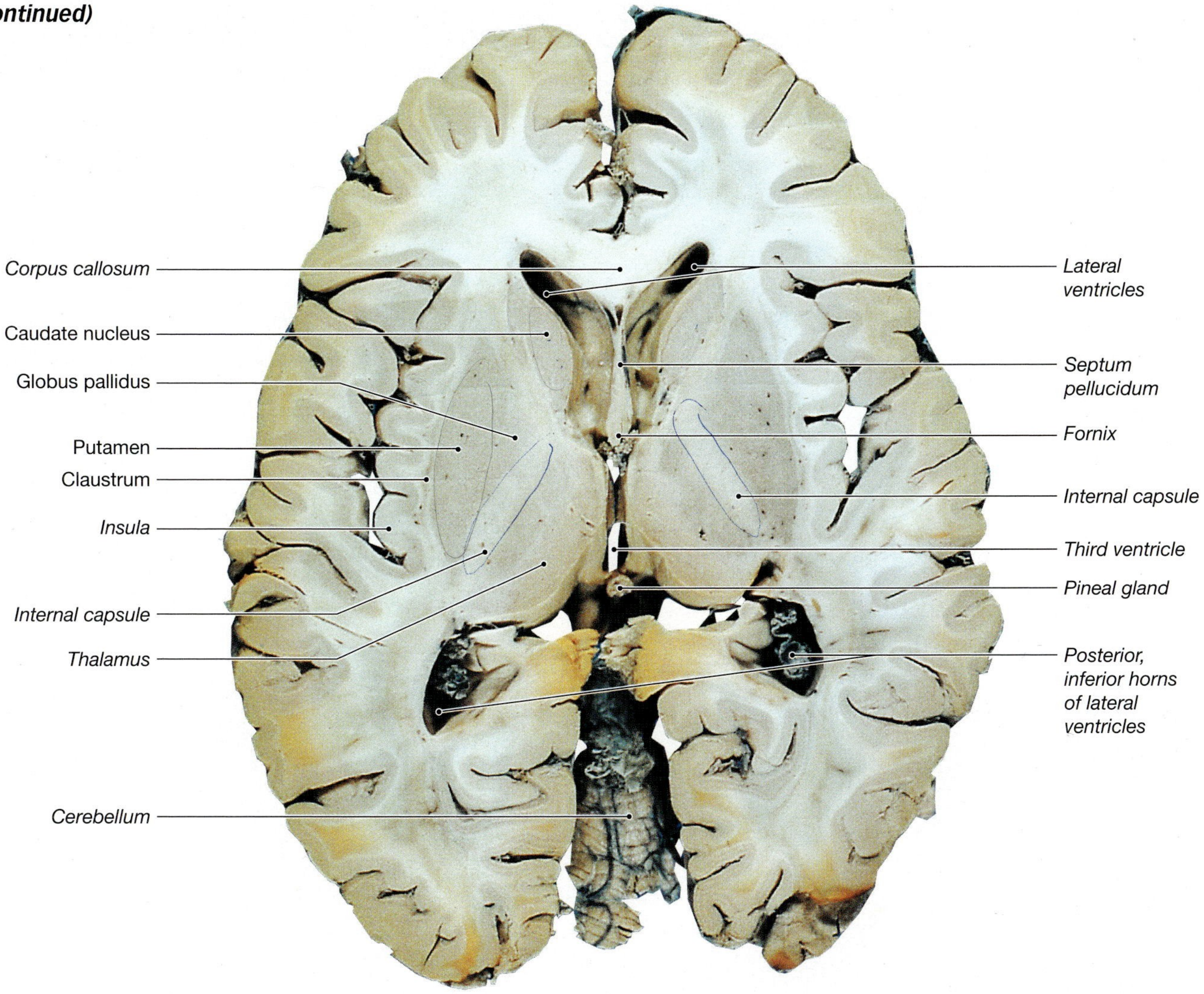

(c) Horizontal section

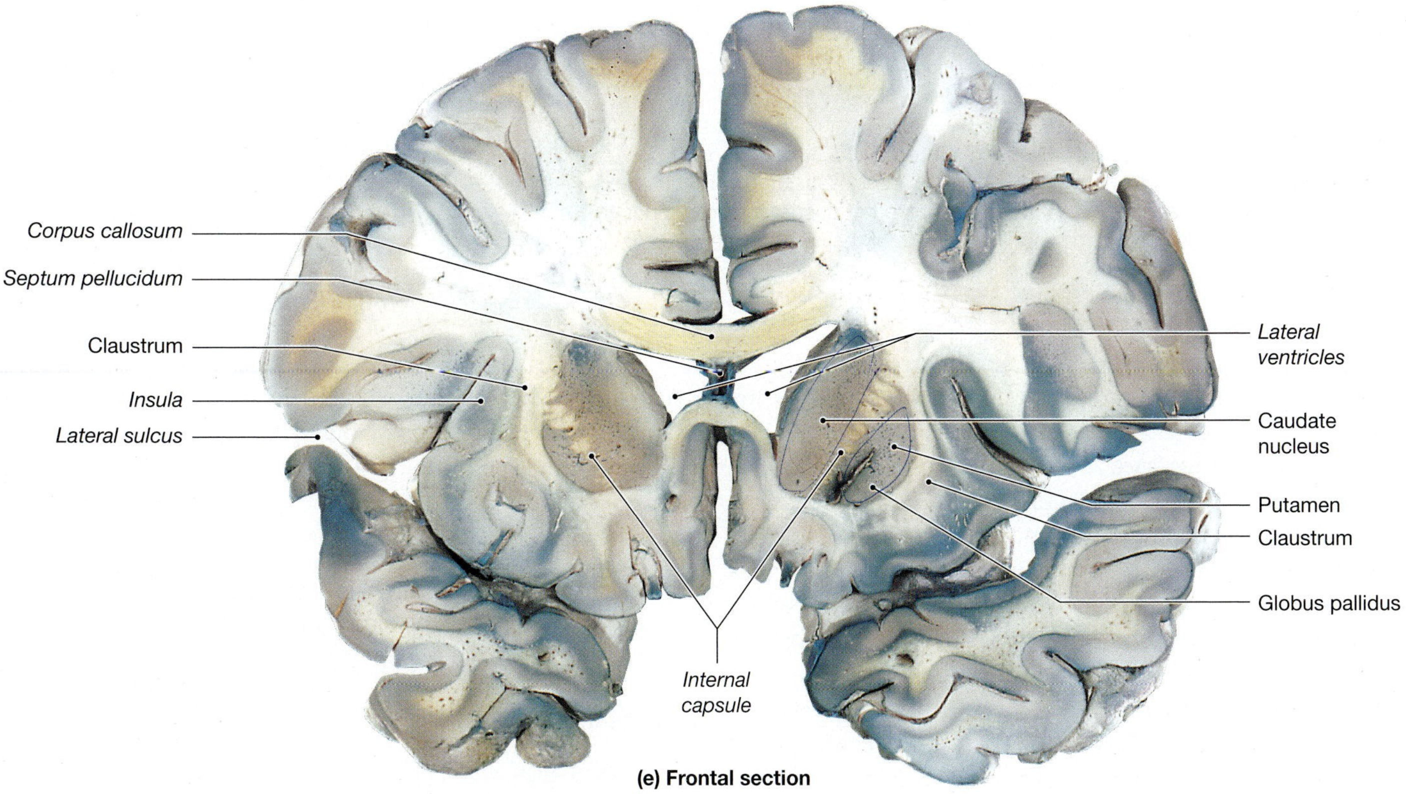

(e) Frontal section

TABLE 15.5 The Limbic System

FUNCTIONS	Processing of memories, creation of emotional states, drives, and associated behaviors
CEREBRAL COMPONENTS	
Cortical areas	Limbic lobe (cingulate gyrus, dentate gyrus, and parahippocampal gyrus)
Nuclei	Hippocampus, amygdaloid body
Tracts	Fornix
DIENCEPHALIC COMPONENTS	
Thalamus	Anterior nuclear group
Hypothalamus	Centers concerned with emotions, appetites (thirst, hunger), and related behaviors *(Table 15.7)*
OTHER COMPONENTS	
Reticular formation	Network of interconnected nuclei throughout brain stem

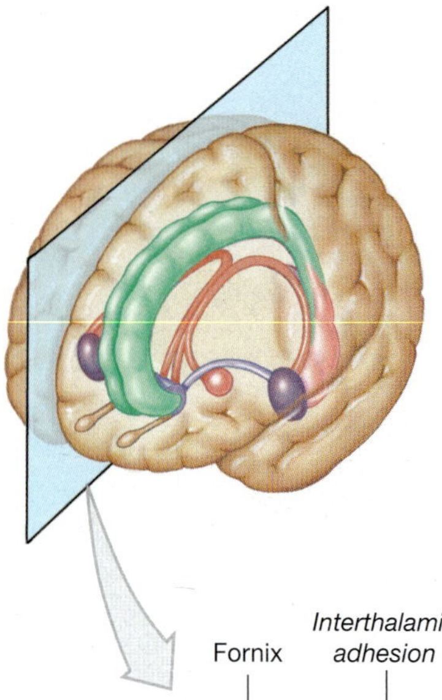

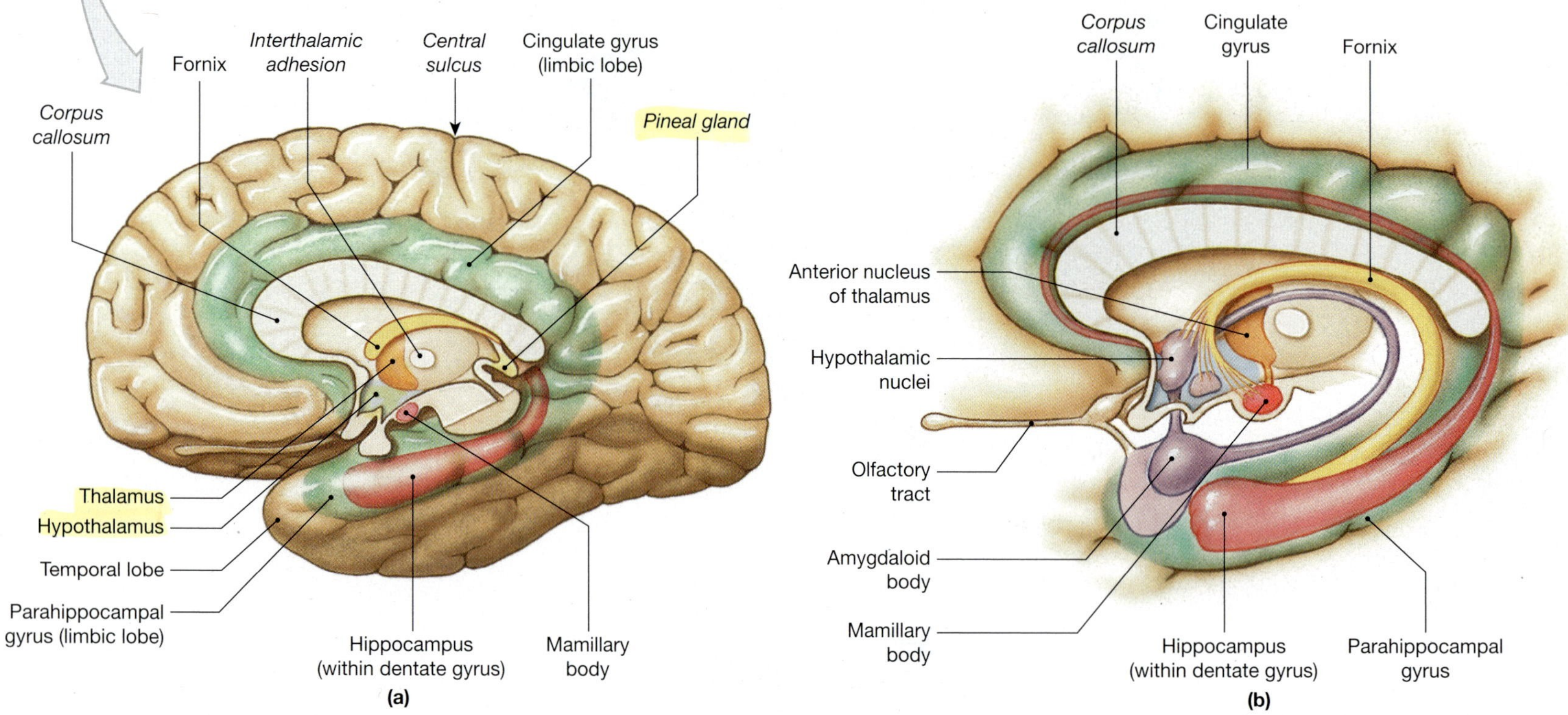

Figure 15.12 The Limbic System
(a) Sagittal section through the cerebrum, showing the cortical areas associated with the limbic system. The parahippocampal and dentate gyri are shown as if transparent so that deeper limbic components can be seen. **(b)** Additional details concerning the three-dimensional structure of the limbic system.

mamilla or *mammilla*, breast) **bodies**, prominent nuclei in the floor of the hypothalamus. The mamillary bodies contain motor nuclei that control reflex movements associated with eating, such as chewing, licking, and swallowing.

Several other nuclei in the wall (thalamus) and floor (hypothalamus) of the diencephalon are components of the limbic system. Among its other functions, the **anterior nucleus** of the thalamus relays visceral sensations from the hypothalamus to the cingulate gyrus. Experimental stimulation of the hypothalamus has localized a number of important centers responsible for the emotions of rage, fear, pain, sexual arousal, and pleasure.

Stimulation of the hypothalamus can also produce heightened alertness and a generalized excitement. This response is caused by widespread stimulation of the **reticular formation**, an interconnected network of brain stem nuclei whose dominant nuclei lie within the mesencephalon. Stimulation of adjacent portions of the hypothalamus or thalamus will depress reticular activity, resulting in generalized lethargy or actual sleep.

CONCEPT CHECK

1. Each cerebral hemisphere is subdivided into lobes. Identify the lobes and their general functions.
2. What are gyri and sulci?
3. List and describe the three major groups of axons in central white matter.

See blue "Answers" tab at back of book.

The Diencephalon [Figures 15.1/15.11b,c/15.12/15.15/15.16]

The diencephalon connects the cerebral hemispheres to the brain stem. It consists of the *epithalamus*, the left and right *thalamus*, and the *hypothalamus*. Figures 15.1, 15.11b,c, 15.12, and 15.15 show the position of the diencephalon and its relationship to other landmarks in the brain.

The Epithalamus [Figure 15.15a]

The *epithalamus* is the roof of the third ventricle (Figure 15.15a). Its membranous anterior portion contains an extensive area of choroid plexus that extends through the interventricular foramina into the lateral ventricles. The posterior portion of the epithalamus contains the **pineal gland**, an endocrine structure that secretes the hormone **melatonin**. Melatonin is involved in the regulation of day-night cycles, with possible secondary effects on reproductive function. (The role of melatonin will be described in Chapter 19.)

The Thalamus [Figures 15.11b/15.12/15.13/15.15]

Most of the neural tissue in the diencephalon is concentrated in the left thalamus and right thalamus. These two egg-shaped bodies form the walls of the diencephalon and surround the third ventricle (Figures 15.11b and 15.15). The thalamic nuclei provide the switching and relay centers for both sensory and motor pathways. Ascending sensory information from the spinal cord (other than information from the spinocerebellar tracts) and cranial nerves (other than the olfactory nerve) is processed in the thalamic nuclei before the information is relayed to the cerebrum or brain stem. The thalamus is thus the final relay point for ascending sensory information that will be projected to the primary sensory cortex. It acts as an information filter, passing on only a small portion of the arriving sensory information. The thalamus also acts as a relay station that coordinates motor activities at the conscious and subconscious levels.

The two thalami are separated by the third ventricle. Viewed in midsagittal section, the thalamus extends from the anterior commissure to the inferior base of the pineal gland (Figure 15.15a). A medial projection of gray matter, the **interthalamic adhesion**, or *massa intermedia*, extends into the ventricle from the thalamus on either side (Figure 15.12a). In roughly 70 percent of the population, the two intermediate masses fuse in the midline, interconnecting the two thalami.

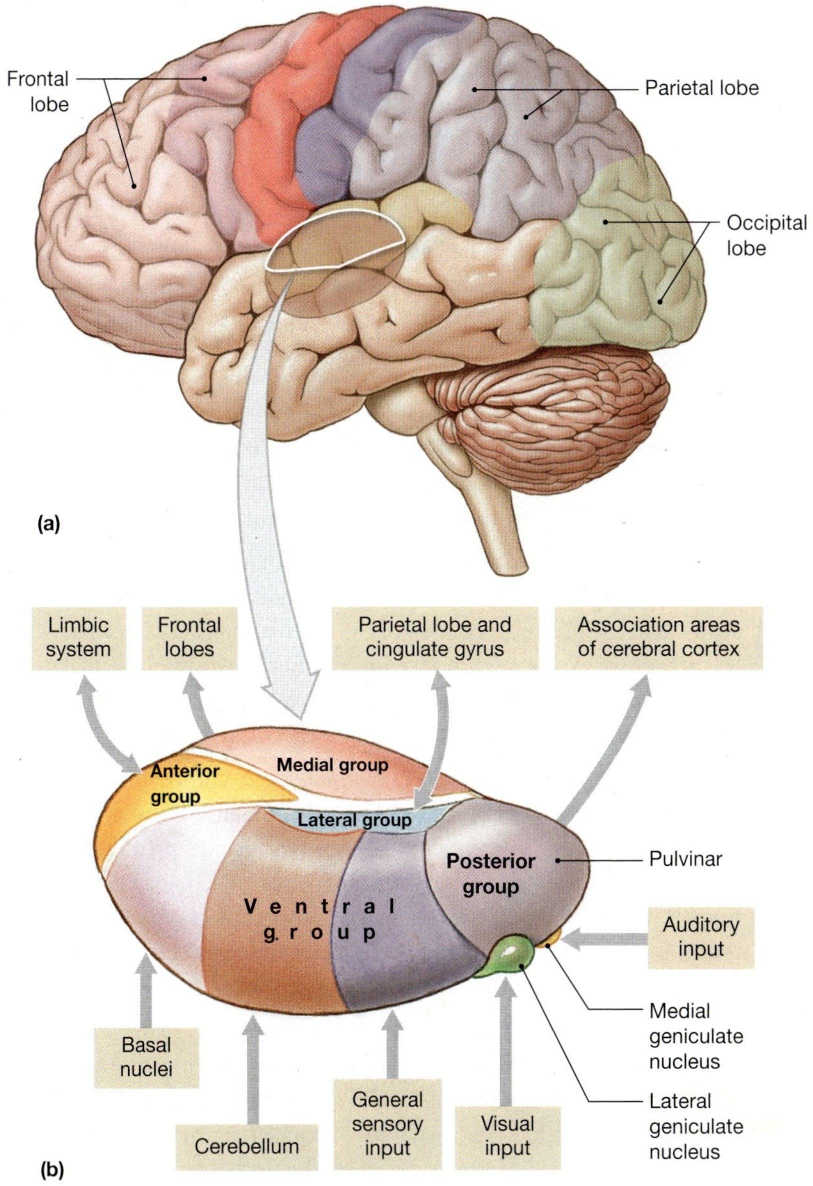

Figure 15.13 The Thalamus
(a) Lateral view of the brain, showing the positions of the major thalamic structures. Functional areas of cerebral cortex are also indicated, with colors corresponding to those of the associated thalamic nuclei. **(b)** Enlarged view of the thalamic nuclei of the left side. The color of each nucleus or group of nuclei matches the color of the associated cortical region. The boxes either provide examples of the types of sensory input relayed to the basal nuclei and cerebral cortex or indicate the existence of important feedback loops involved with emotional states, learning, and memory.

TABLE 15.6 The Thalamus

Structure/Nuclei	Functions
ANTERIOR GROUP	Part of the limbic system
MEDIAL GROUP	Integrates sensory information and other data arriving at the thalamus and hypothalamus for projection to the frontal lobes of the cerebral hemispheres
VENTRAL GROUP	Projects sensory information to the primary sensory cortex of the parietal lobe; relays information from cerebellum and basal nuclei to motor areas of cerebral cortex
POSTERIOR GROUP	
Pulvinar	Integrates sensory information for projection to association areas of cerebral cortex
Lateral geniculate nuclei	Projects visual information to the visual cortex of occipital lobe
Medial geniculate nuclei	Projects auditory information to the auditory cortex of temporal lobe
LATERAL GROUP	Form feedback loops involving the cingulate gyrus (emotional states) and the parietal lobe (integration of sensory information)

The thalamus on each side bulges laterally, away from the third ventricle, and anteriorly toward the cerebrum (Figures 15.11b,c, 15.12, 15.14, and 15.15b). The lateral border of each thalamus is established by the fibers of the internal capsule. Embedded within each thalamus is a rounded mass composed of several interconnected *thalamic nuclei.*

Functions of Thalamic Nuclei [Figure 15.13 and Table 15.6]

The thalamic nuclei are concerned primarily with the relay of sensory information to the basal nuclei and cerebral cortex. The five major groups of thalamic nuclei, detailed in Figure 15.13 and Table 15.6, are (1) the *anterior group*, (2) the *medial group*, (3) the *ventral group*, (4) the *posterior group*, and (5) the *lateral group.*

1. The **anterior nuclei** are part of the limbic system, and they play a role in emotions, memory, and learning. They relay information from the hypothalamus and hippocampus to the cingulate gyrus.
2. The **medial nuclei** provide a conscious awareness of emotional states by connecting the basal nuclei and emotional centers in the hypothalamus with the prefrontal cortex of the cerebrum. These nuclei also integrate sensory information arriving at other portions of the thalamus for relay to the frontal lobes.
3. The **ventral nuclei** relay information to and from the basal nuclei and cerebral cortex. Two of the nuclei (*ventral anterior* and *ventral lateral*) relay information concerning somatic motor commands from the basal nuclei and cerebellum to the primary motor cortex and premotor cortex. They are part of a feedback loop that helps plan a movement and then fine-tunes it. The *ventral posterior nuclei* relay sensory information concerning touch, pressure, pain, temperature, and proprioception from the spinal cord and brain stem to the primary sensory cortex of the parietal lobe.
4. The **posterior nuclei** include the *pulvinar* and the *geniculate nuclei.* The **pulvinar** integrates sensory information for projection to the association areas of the cerebral cortex. The **lateral geniculate** (je-NIK-ū-lāt; *genicula*, little knee) **nucleus** of each thalamus receives visual information from the eyes, brought by the optic tract. Efferent fibers project to the visual cortex and descend to the mesencephalon. The **medial geniculate nuclei** relay auditory information to the auditory cortex from the specialized receptors of the inner ear.
5. The **lateral nuclei** are relay stations in feedback loops that adjust activity in the cingulate gyrus and parietal lobe. They thus have an impact on emotional states and the integration of sensory information.

The Hypothalamus [Figures 15.14/15.15a]

The hypothalamus contains centers involved with emotions and visceral processes that affect the cerebrum as well as other components of the brain stem. It also controls a variety of autonomic functions and forms the link between the nervous and endocrine systems. The hypothalamus, which forms the floor of the third ventricle, extends from the area superior to the **optic chiasm**, where the *optic tracts* from the eyes arrive at the brain, to the posterior margins of the mamillary bodies (Figure 15.14). (The mamillary bodies were introduced in the discussion of the limbic system on p. 401.) Posterior to the optic chiasm, the **infundibulum** (in-fun-DIB-ū-lum; *infundibulum*, funnel) extends inferiorly, connecting the hypothalamus to the pituitary gland. In life, the diaphragma sellae (p. 391) surrounds the infundibulum as it enters the hypophyseal fossa of the sphenoid.

Viewed in midsagittal section (Figures 15.14 and 15.15a), the floor of the hypothalamus between the infundibulum and the mamillary bodies is the **tuberal area** (*tuber*, swelling). The tuberal area contains nuclei involved with the control of pituitary gland function.

Functions of the Hypothalamus [Figure 15.14b and Table 15.7]

The hypothalamus contains a variety of important control and integrative centers, in addition to those associated with the limbic system. These centers and their functions are summarized in Figure 15.14b and Table 15.7. Hypothalamic centers are continually receiving sensory information from the cerebrum, brain stem, and spinal cord. Hypothalamic neurons detect and respond to changes in the CSF and interstitial fluid composition; they also respond to stimuli in the circulating blood because of the high permeability of capillaries in this region. Hypothalamic functions include:

1. *Subconscious control of skeletal muscle contractions:* By stimulation of appropriate centers in other portions of the brain, hypothalamic nuclei direct somatic motor patterns associated with the emotions of rage, pleasure, pain, and sexual arousal.
2. *Control of autonomic function:* Hypothalamic centers adjust and coordinate the activities of autonomic centers in other parts of the brain stem concerned with regulating heart rate, blood pressure, respiration, and digestive functions.
3. *Coordination of activities of the nervous and endocrine systems:* Much of the regulatory control is exerted through inhibition or stimulation of endocrine cells within the pituitary gland.
4. *Secretion of hormones:* The hypothalamus secretes two hormones: (1) *Antidiuretic hormone*, produced by the **supraoptic nucleus**, restricts water loss at the kidneys, and (2) *oxytocin*, produced by the **paraventricular nucleus**, stimulates smooth muscle contractions in the uterus and prostate gland, and myoepithelial cell contractions in the mammary glands. Both hormones are transported along axons down the infundibulum for release into the circulation at the posterior portion of the pituitary gland.
5. *Production of emotions and behavioral drives:* Specific hypothalamic centers produce sensations that lead to changes in voluntary or involuntary behavior patterns. For example, stimulation of the **thirst center** produces the desire to drink.
6. *Coordination between voluntary and autonomic functions:* When you are facing a stressful situation, your heart rate and respiratory rate go up and your body prepares for an emergency. These autonomic adjustments are made because cerebral activities are monitored by the hypothalamus. The autonomic nervous system (ANS) is a division of the peripheral nervous system. ∞ p. 341 The ANS consists of two divisions: (1) *sympathetic* and (2) *parasympathetic.* The sympathetic division stimulates tissue metabolism, increases alertness, and prepares the body to respond to emergencies; the parasympathetic division promotes sedentary activities and conserves body energy. These divisions and their relationships will be discussed in Chapter 17.
7. *Regulation of body temperature:* The **preoptic area** of the hypothalamus controls physiological responses to changes in body temperature. In doing so, it coordinates the activities of other CNS centers and regulates other physiological systems.
8. *Control of circadian rhythms:* The **suprachiasmatic nucleus** coordinates daily cycles of activity that are linked to the day-night cycle. This nucleus receives direct input from the retina of the eye, and its output adjusts the activities of other hypothalamic nuclei, the pineal gland, and the reticular formation.

Figure 15.14 The Hypothalamus
(a) Midsagittal section through the brain, showing major features of the diencephalon and adjacent portions of the brain stem. **(b)** Enlarged view of the hypothalamus, showing the locations of major nuclei and centers. Functions for these centers are summarized in *Table 15.7*.

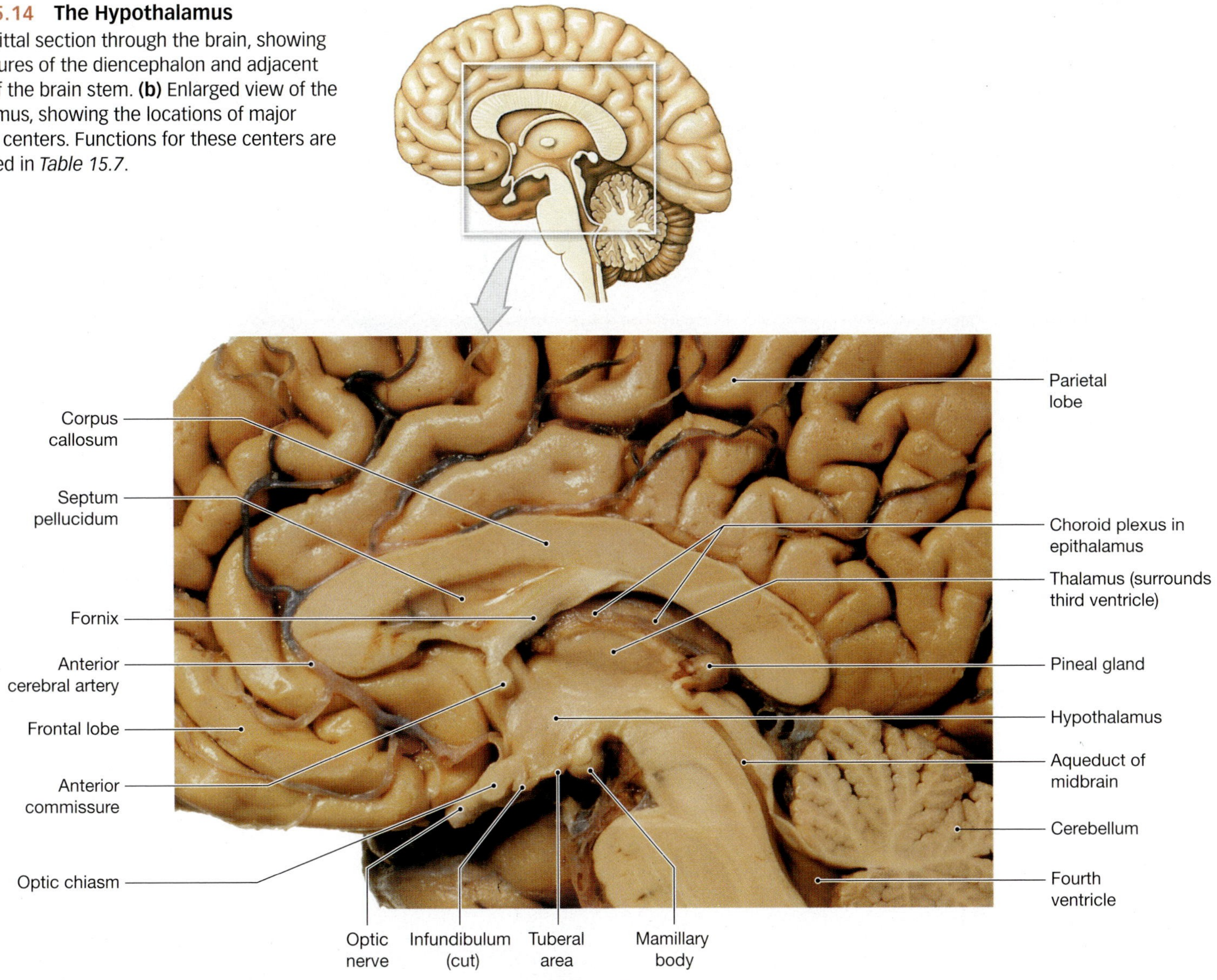

(a) Midsagittal section

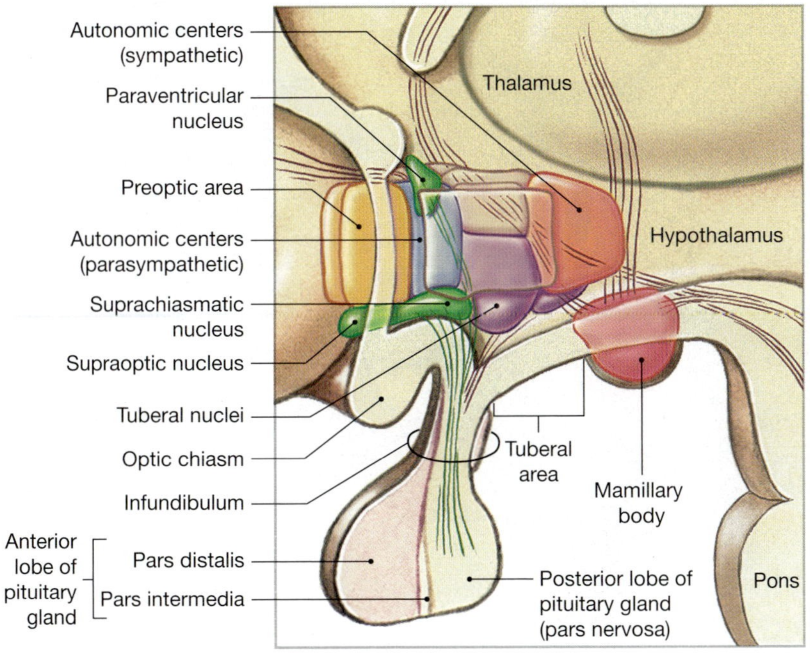

(b) Hypothalamus

TABLE 15.7 The Hypothalamus

Region/Nucleus	Functions
Hypothalamus in general	Controls autonomic functions; sets appetitive drives (thirst, hunger, sexual desire) and behaviors; sets emotional states (with limbic system); integrates with endocrine system *(see Chapter 19)*
Supraoptic nucleus	Secretes antidiuretic hormone, restricting water loss at the kidneys
Suprachiasmatic nucleus	Regulates daily (circadian) rhythms
Paraventricular nucleus	Secretes oxytocin, stimulating smooth muscle contractions in uterus and mammary glands
Preoptic area	Regulates body temperature via control of autonomic centers in the medulla oblongata
Tuberal area	Produces inhibitory and releasing hormones that control endocrine cells of the anterior lobe of the pituitary gland
Autonomic centers	Control heart rate and blood pressure via regulation of autonomic centers in the medulla oblongata
Mamillary bodies	Control feeding reflexes (licking, swallowing, etc.)

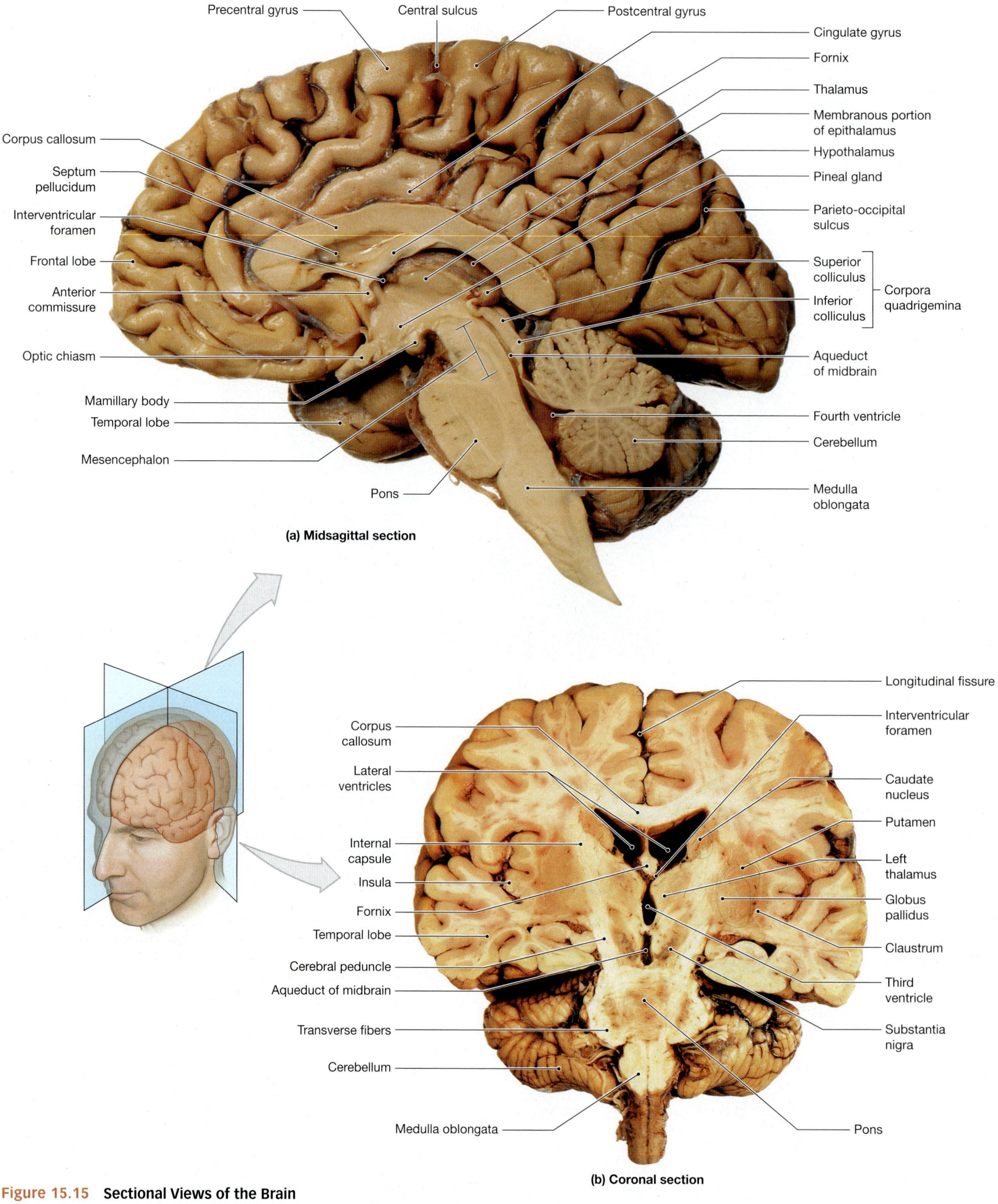

Figure 15.15 Sectional Views of the Brain
(a) A sagittal section through the brain. **(b)** A coronal section through the brain.

Figure 15.16 The Diencephalon and Brain Stem
(a) Diagrammatic view of the diencephalon and brain stem, seen from the left side. **(b)** Sagittal view of the brain stem, with a portion of the cerebellum sectioned and removed. **(c)** Posterior diagrammatic view of the diencephalon and brain stem. **(d)** Brain stem, posterior view.

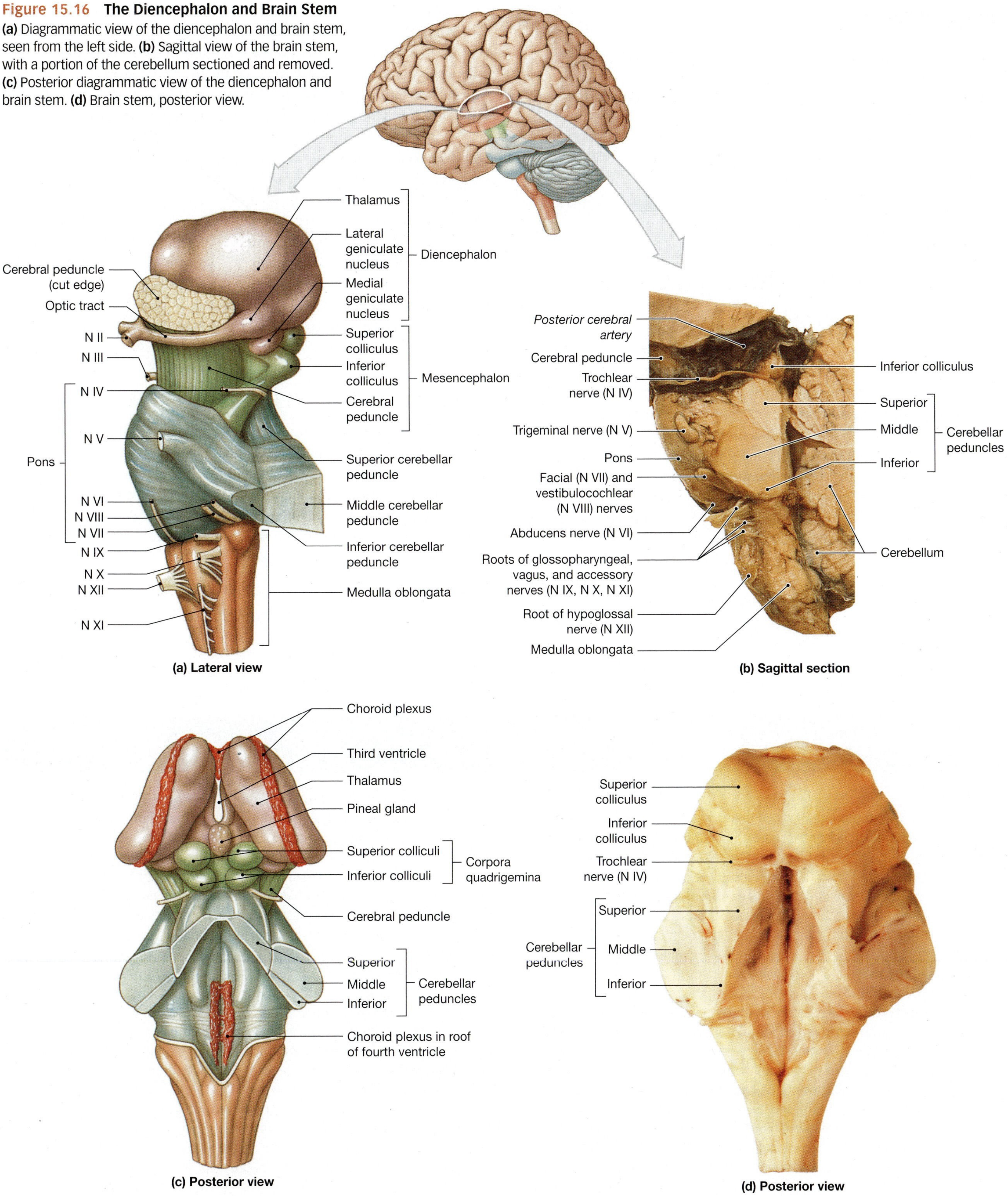

CONCEPT CHECK

1. What area of the diencephalon is stimulated by changes in body temperature?
2. Which region of the diencephalon helps coordinate somatic motor activities?
3. What endocrine structure in the diencephalon secretes melatonin?
4. What hormones are produced by the hypothalamus and released at the pituitary gland?

See blue "Answers" tab at back of book.

The Mesencephalon [Figures 15.1/15.15/15.16/15.17 and Table 15.8]

The mesencephalon, or midbrain, contains nuclei that process visual and auditory information and generate reflexive responses to these stimuli. The external anatomy of the mesencephalon can be seen in Figure 15.16, and the major nuclei are detailed in Figure 15.17 and Table 15.8. The surface of the midbrain posterior to the aqueduct of the midbrain is called the roof, or **tectum**, of the mesencephalon. This region contains two pairs of sensory nuclei known collectively as the **corpora quadrigemina** (KOR-pō-ra-qua-dri-JEM-i-na). These nuclei are relay stations concerned with the processing of visual and auditory sensations. Each **superior colliculus** (ko-LIK-ū-lus; *colliculus*, small hill) receives visual input from the lateral geniculate of the thalamus on that side. The **inferior colliculus** receives auditory data from nuclei in the medulla oblongata; some of this information may be forwarded to the medial geniculate on the same side.

The mesencephalon also contains the major nuclei of the reticular formation. Specific patterns of stimulation in this region can produce a variety of involuntary motor responses. Each side of the mesencephalon contains a pair of nuclei, the *red nucleus* and the *substantia nigra* (Figure 15.17). The **red nucleus** is provided with numerous blood vessels, giving it a rich red coloration. This nucleus integrates information from the cerebrum and cerebellum and issues involuntary motor commands concerned with the maintenance of muscle tone and limb position. The **substantia nigra** (NĪ-grah, "black") lies lateral to the red nucleus. The gray matter in this region contains darkly pigmented cells, giving it a black color. The substantia nigra plays an important role in regulating the motor output of the basal nuclei.

The nerve fiber bundles on the ventrolateral surfaces of the mesencephalon (Figures 15.16 and 15.17b) are the **cerebral peduncles** (*peduncles*, little feet). They contain (1) ascending fibers that synapse in the thalamic nuclei and (2) descending fibers of the corticospinal pathway that carry voluntary motor commands from the primary motor cortex of each cerebral hemisphere.

The Pons [15.15/15.16/15.18 and Table 15.9]

The pons extends inferiorly from the mesencephalon to the medulla oblongata. It forms a prominent bulge on the anterior surface of the brain stem. The cerebellar hemispheres lie posterior to the pons; the two are partially separated by the fourth ventricle. On either side, the pons is attached to the cerebellum by three *cerebellar peduncles*. Important features and regions are indicated in Figures 15.15, 15.16, and 15.18; structures are detailed in Table 15.9. The pons contains:

- **Sensory and motor nuclei for four cranial nerves.** (N V, N VI, N VII, and N VIII). These cranial nerves innervate the jaw muscles, the ante-

Clinical Note

The Substantia Nigra and Parkinson's Disease The basal nuclei contain two discrete populations of neurons. One group stimulates motor neurons by releasing acetylcholine (ACh), and the other inhibits motor neurons by the release of the neurotransmitter *gamma-aminobutyric acid*, or *GABA*. Under normal conditions, the excitatory neurons remain inactive, and the descending tracts are responsible primarily for inhibiting motor neuron activity. The excitatory neurons are quiet because they are continually exposed to the inhibitory effects of the neurotransmitter *dopamine*. This compound is manufactured by neurons in the substantia nigra and transported along axons to synapses in the basal nuclei. If the ascending tract or the dopamine-producing neurons are damaged, this inhibition is lost, and the excitatory neurons become increasingly active. This increased activity produces the motor symptoms of **Parkinson's disease**, or *paralysis agitans*.

Parkinson's disease is characterized by a pronounced increase in muscle tone. Voluntary movements become hesitant and jerky, for a movement cannot occur until one muscle group manages to overpower its antagonists. Individuals with Parkinson's disease show **spasticity** during voluntary movement and a continual **tremor** when at rest. A tremor represents a tug of war between antagonistic muscle groups that produces a background shaking of the limbs. Individuals with Parkinson's disease also have difficulty starting voluntary movements. Even changing one's facial expression requires intense concentration, and the individual acquires a blank, static expression. Finally, the positioning and preparatory adjustments normally performed automatically no longer occur. Every aspect of each movement must be voluntarily controlled, and the extra effort requires intense concentration that may prove tiring and extremely frustrating. In the late stages of this condition, other CNS effects, such as depression and hallucinations, often appear.

Providing the basal nuclei with dopamine can significantly reduce the symptoms for two-thirds of Parkinson's patients. Dopamine cannot cross the blood–brain barrier, and the most common treatment involves the oral administration of the drug L-DOPA (*levodopa*), a related compound that crosses the cerebral capillaries and is converted to dopamine. Surgery to control Parkinson's symptoms focuses on the destruction of large areas within the basal nuclei or thalamus to control the motor symptoms of tremor and rigidity. Transplantation of tissues that produce dopamine or related compounds directly into the basal nuclei is one method attempted as a cure. The transplantation of fetal brain cells into the basal nuclei of adult brains has slowed or even reversed the course of the disease in a significant number of patients, although problems with involuntary muscle contractions developed later in many cases.

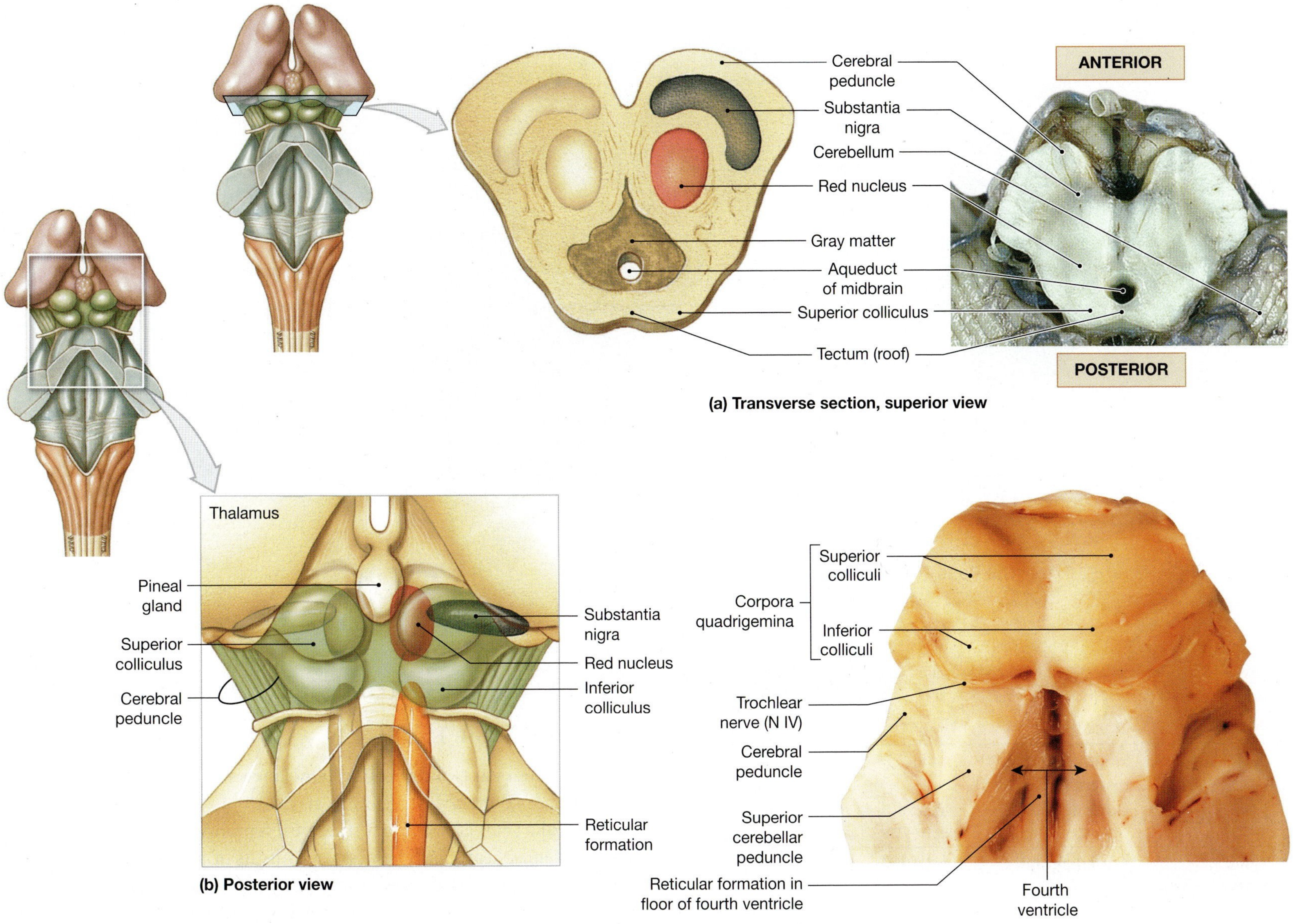

Figure 15.17 The Mesencephalon
(a) Diagrammatic view and sectioned brain stem, with the sections taken at the level indicated in the icon. **(b)** Diagrammatic and posterior views of the diencephalon and brain stem. The diagrammatic view is drawn as if transparent, to show the positions of important nuclei.

TABLE 15.8 The Mesencephalon

Subdivision	Region/Nucleus	Functions
GRAY MATTER		
Tectum (roof)	**Superior colliculi**	Integrate visual information with other sensory input; initiate reflex responses to visual stimuli
	Inferior colliculi	Relay auditory information to medial geniculate nuclei; initiate reflex responses to auditory stimuli
Walls and floor	**Red nuclei**	Involuntary control of background muscle tone and limb position
	Substantia nigra	Regulates activity in the basal nuclei
	Reticular formation	Automatic processing of incoming sensations and outgoing motor commands; can initiate motor responses to stimuli; helps maintain consciousness
	Other nuclei/centers	Nuclei associated with two cranial nerves (N III, N IV)
WHITE MATTER	**Cerebral peduncles**	Connect primary motor cortex with motor neurons in brain and spinal cord; carry ascending sensory information to thalamus

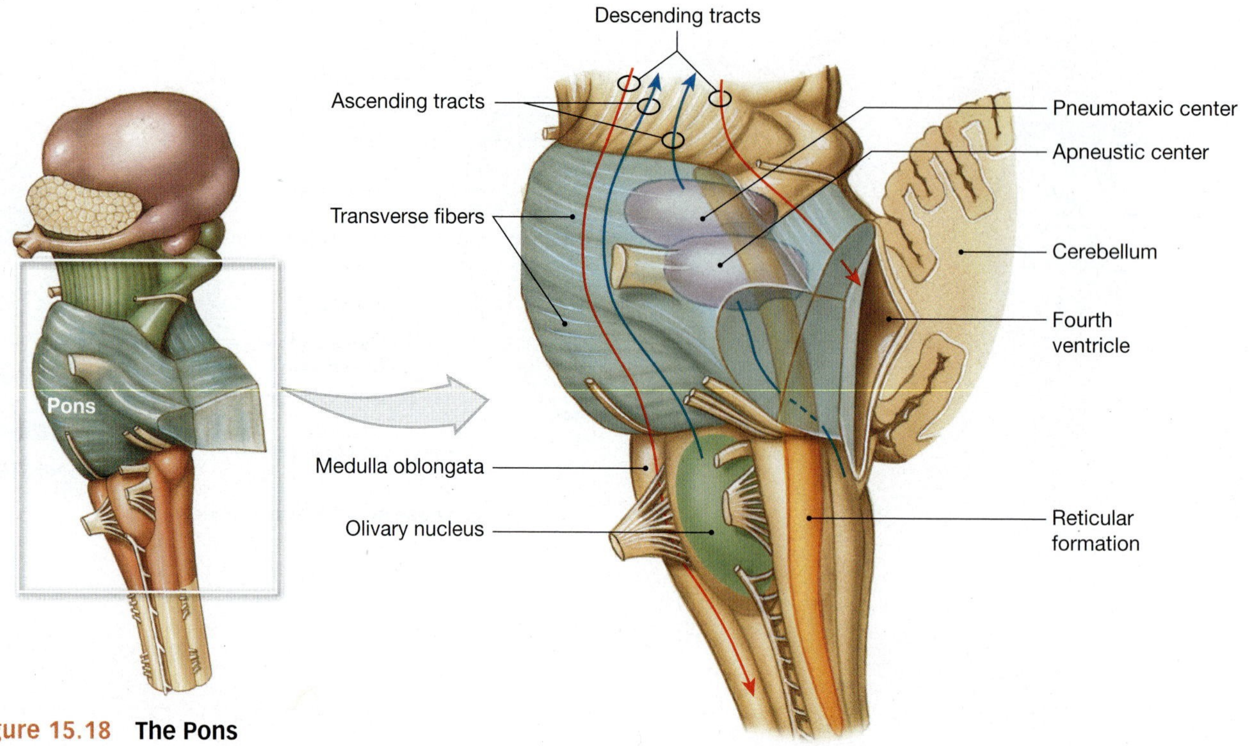

Figure 15.18 **The Pons**

TABLE 15.9 The Pons		
Subdivision	**Region/Nucleus**	**Functions**
Gray matter	**Respiratory centers**	Modify output of respiratory centers in the medulla oblongata
	Other nuclei/ centers	Nuclei associated with four cranial nerves and cerebellum
White matter	**Ascending and descending tracts**	Interconnect other portions of CNS
	Transverse fibers	Interconnect cerebellar hemispheres; interconnect pontine nuclei with the cerebellar hemispheres on the opposite side

rior surface of the face, one of the extra-ocular muscles (the lateral rectus), and organs of hearing and equilibrium in the inner ear.

- **Nuclei concerned with the involuntary control of respiration.** On each side of the brain, the reticular formation in this region contains two respiratory centers, the *apneustic center* and the *pneumotaxic center*. These centers modify the activity of the *respiratory rhythmicity center* in the medulla oblongata.
- **Nuclei that process and relay cerebellar commands arriving over the middle cerebellar peduncles.** The middle cerebellar peduncles are connected to the **transverse fibers** of the pons that cross its anterior surface.
- **Ascending, descending, and transverse tracts.** The longitudinal tracts interconnect other portions of the CNS. The anterior cerebellar peduncles contain efferent tracts arising at cerebellar nuclei. These fibers permit communication between the cerebellar hemispheres of opposite sides. The inferior cerebellar peduncles contain both afferent and efferent tracts that connect the cerebellum with the medulla oblongata.

The Cerebellum [Figures 15.8/15.15/15.16/15.19 and Table 15.10]

The cerebellum has two **cerebellar hemispheres**, each with a highly convoluted surface composed of neural cortex (Figures 15.8 and 15.19). These folds, or **folia** (FŌ-lē-a), of the surface are less prominent than the gyri of the cerebral hemispheres. Each hemisphere consists of two **lobes**, **anterior** and **posterior**, which are separated by the **primary fissure**. Along the midline a narrow band of cortex known as the **vermis** (VER-mis; worm) separates the cerebellar hemispheres. Slender **flocculonodular** (flok-ū-lō-NOD-ū-lar) **lobes** lie anterior and inferior to the cerebellar hemisphere. The anterior and posterior lobes assist in the planning, execution, and coordination of limb and trunk movements. The flocculonodular lobe is important in the maintenance of balance and the control of eye movements. The structures of the cerebellum and their functions are summarized in Table 15.10.

The cerebellar cortex contains huge, highly branched **Purkinje** (pur-KIN-jē) **cells** (Figure 15.19b). Purkinje cells have massive pear-shaped cell bodies that have large, numerous dendrites fanning out into the gray matter (neural cortex) of the cerebellar cortex. Axons project from the basal portion of the cell into the white matter to reach the cerebellar nuclei. Internally, the white matter of the cerebellum forms a branching array that in sectional view resembles a tree. Anatomists call it the **arbor vitae**, or "tree of life." The cerebellum receives proprioceptive information, indicating body position (position sense) from the spinal cord and monitors all proprioceptive, visual, tactile, balance, and auditory sensations received by the brain. Information concerning motor commands issued by the cerebral cortex reaches the cerebellum indirectly, relayed from nuclei in the pons. A relatively small portion of the afferent fibers synapse within **cerebellar nuclei** before projecting to the cerebellar cortex. Most axons carrying sensory information do not synapse in the cerebellar nuclei but pass through the deeper layers of the cerebellar cortex to end near the cortical surface. There they synapse with the dendritic processes of the Purkinje cells. Tracts containing the axons

Figure 15.19 The Cerebellum
(a) Superior surface of the cerebellum, showing major anatomical landmarks and regions. **(b)** Sagittal view of the cerebellum, showing the arrangement of gray matter and white matter. Purkinje cells are seen in the photograph; these large neurons are found in the cerebellar cortex. (LM × 120)

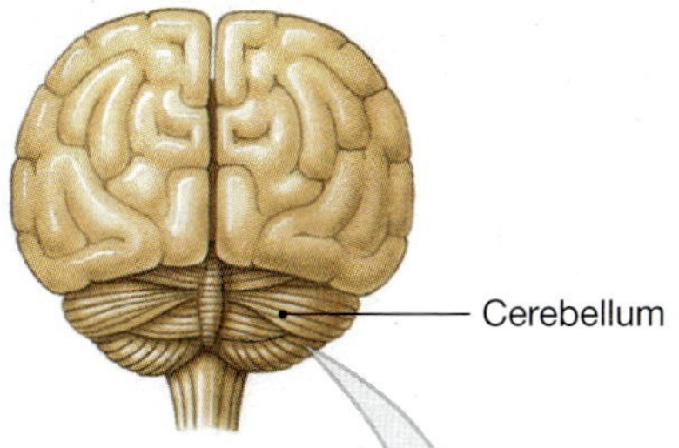

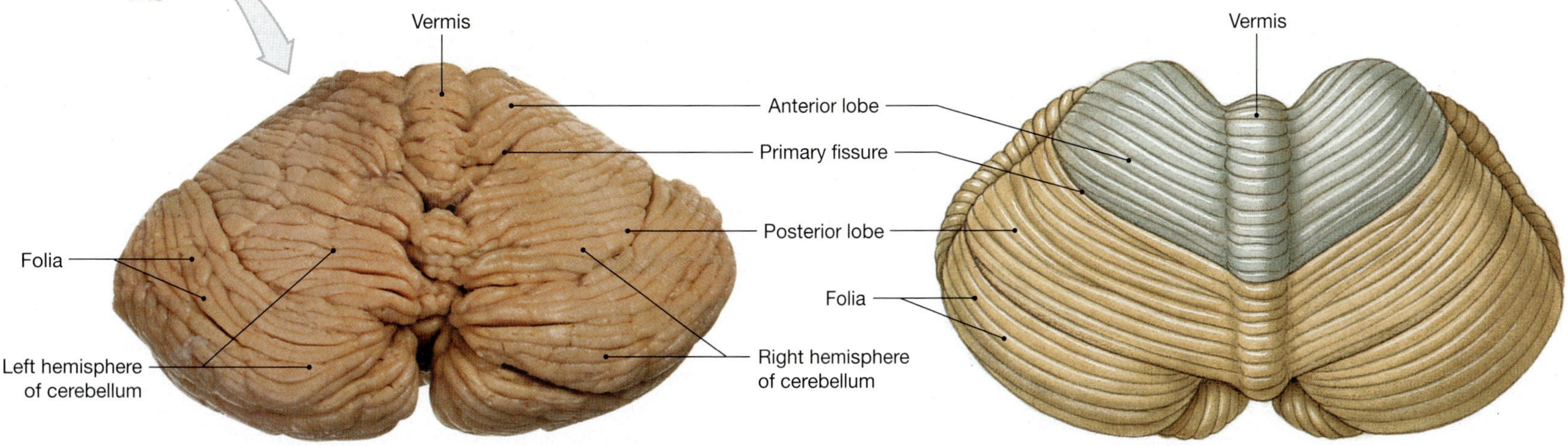

(a) Posterior, superior surface

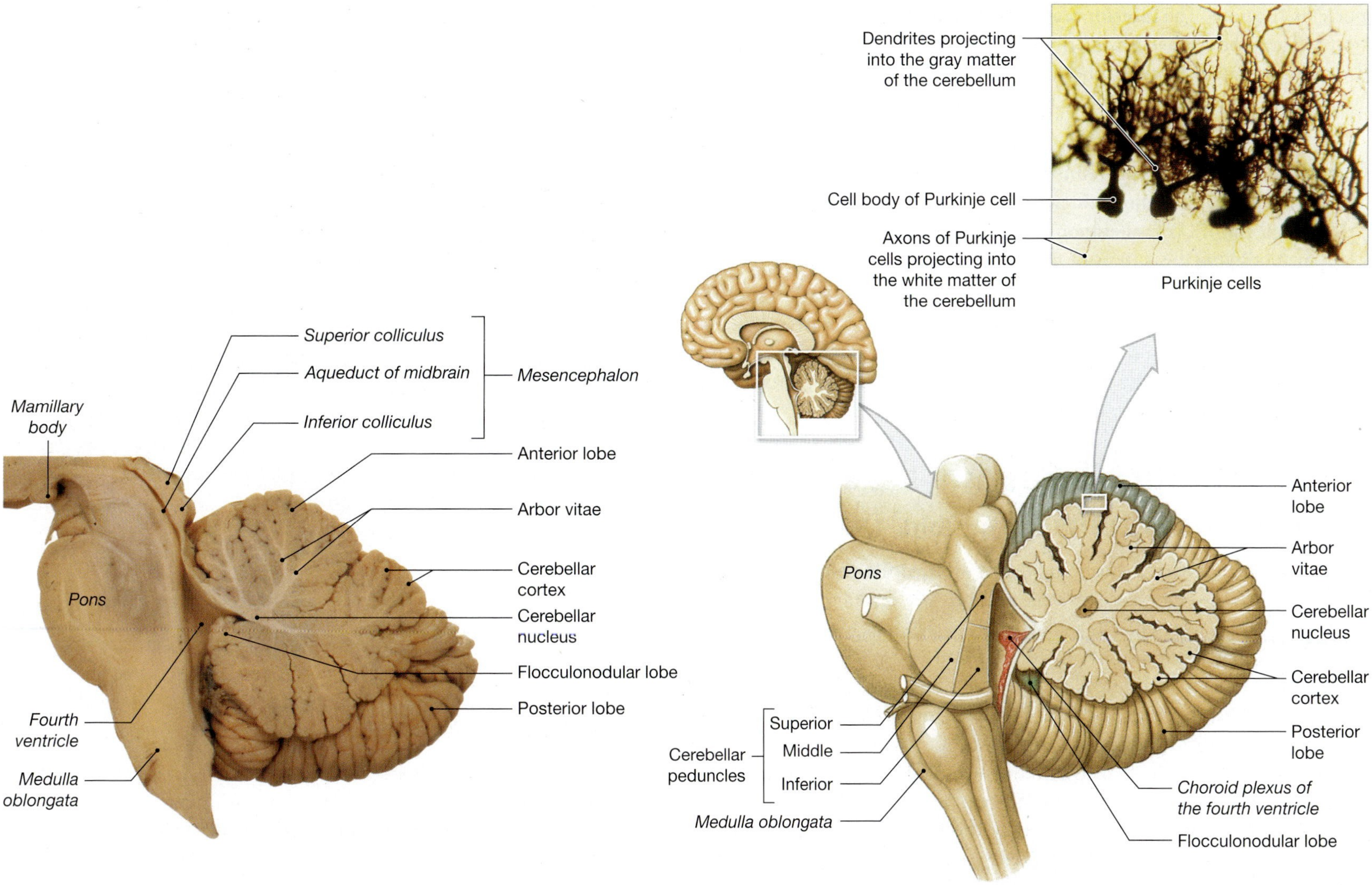

(b) Sagittal section

TABLE 15.10 The Cerebellum

Subdivision	Region/Nucleus	Functions
Gray matter	Cerebellar cortex	Subconscious coordination and control of ongoing movements of body parts
	Cerebellar nuclei	As above
White matter	Arbor vitae	Connects cerebellar cortex and nuclei with cerebellar peduncles
	Cerebellar peduncles	
	Superior	Link the cerebellum with mesencephalon, diencephalon, and cerebrum
	Middle	Contain transverse fibers and carry communications between the cerebellum and pons
	Inferior	Link the cerebellum with the medulla oblongata and spinal cord

of Purkinje cells then relay motor commands to nuclei within the cerebrum and brain stem.

Tracts that link the cerebellum with the brain stem, cerebrum, and spinal cord leave the cerebellar hemispheres as the *superior, middle,* and *inferior cerebellar peduncles* (Figures 15.15a, 15.16, and 15.19b). The **superior cerebellar peduncles** link the cerebellum with nuclei in the mesencephalon, diencephalon, and cerebrum. The **middle cerebellar peduncles** are connected to a broad band of fibers that cross the ventral surface of the pons at right angles to the axis of the brain stem. The middle cerebellar peduncles also connect the cerebellar hemispheres with sensory and motor nuclei in the pons. The **inferior cerebellar peduncles** permit communication between the cerebellum and nuclei in the medulla oblongata and carry ascending and descending cerebellar tracts from the spinal cord.

The cerebellum is an automatic processing center that has two primary functions:

- **Adjusting the postural muscles of the body:** The cerebellum coordinates rapid, automatic adjustments that maintain balance and equilibrium. These alterations in muscle tone and position are made by modifying the activity of the red nucleus.
- **Programming and fine-tuning voluntary and involuntary movements:** The cerebellum stores memories of learned movement patterns. These functions are performed indirectly, by regulating activity along motor pathways involving the cerebral cortex, basal nuclei, and motor centers in the brain stem.

The Medulla Oblongata [Figures 15.9/15.15/15.16/15.18/15.20 and Table 15.11]

The spinal cord connects to the brain stem at the **medulla oblongata**, which corresponds to the embryonic myelencephalon. The medulla oblongata, or *medulla,* is continuous with the spinal cord. The external appearance of the medulla oblongata is shown in Figures 15.9a and 15.16. The important nuclei and centers are diagrammed in Figure 15.20 and detailed in Table 15.11.

Figure 15.15a shows the medulla oblongata in midsagittal section. The caudal portion resembles the spinal cord in having a rounded shape and a narrow central canal. Closer to the pons, the central canal becomes enlarged and continuous with the fourth ventricle.

The medulla oblongata physically connects the brain with the spinal cord, and many of its functions are directly related to this connection. For example, all communication between the brain and spinal cord involves tracts that ascend or descend through the medulla oblongata.

Clinical Note

Cerebellar Dysfunction Cerebellar function can be altered permanently by trauma or a stroke or temporarily by drugs such as alcohol. The alterations can produce disturbances in motor control. In severe ataxia, balance problems are so great that the individual cannot sit or stand upright. Less-severe conditions cause an obvious unsteadiness and irregular patterns of movement. The individual typically watches his or her feet to see where they are going and controls ongoing movements by intense concentration and voluntary effort. Reaching for something becomes a major exertion, because the only information available must be gathered by sight or touch while the movement is taking place. Without the cerebellar ability to adjust movements while they are occurring, the individual becomes unable to anticipate the course of a movement over time. Most commonly, a reaching movement ends with the hand overshooting the target. This inability to anticipate and stop a movement precisely is called **dysmetria** (dis-MET-rē-uh; *dys-*, bad + *metron*, measure). In attempting to correct the situation, the person usually overshoots again, this time in the opposite direction, and so on. The hand oscillates back and forth until either the object can be grasped or the attempt is abandoned. This oscillatory movement is known as an *intention tremor*.

Clinicians check for ataxia by watching an individual walk in a straight line; the usual test for dysmetria involves touching the tip of the index finger to the tip of the nose or the examiner's fingertip. Because many drugs impair cerebellar performance, the same tests are used by police officers to check drivers suspected of driving while under the influence of alcohol or other drugs.

Nuclei in the medulla oblongata may be (1) relay stations along sensory or motor pathways, (2) sensory or motor nuclei associated with cranial nerves connected to the medulla oblongata, or (3) nuclei associated with the autonomic control of visceral activities.

1. *Relay stations:* Ascending tracts may synapse in sensory or motor nuclei that act as relay stations and processing centers. For example, the **nucleus gracilis** and the **nucleus cuneatus** pass somatic sensory information to the thalamus. The **olivary nuclei** relay information from the spinal cord, the cerebral cortex, diencephalon, and brain stem to the cerebellar cortex. The bulk of the olivary nuclei create the

15. The anterior nuclei of the thalamus
    (a) are part of the limbic system
    (b) are connected to the pituitary gland
    (c) produce the hormone melatonin
    (d) receive impulses from the optic nerve

16. The cortex inferior to the lateral sulcus is the
    (a) parietal lobe (b) temporal lobe
    (c) frontal lobe (d) occipital lobe

17. Lying within each hemisphere inferior to the floor of the lateral ventricles are the
    (a) anterior commissures (b) motor association areas
    (c) auditory cortex (d) basal nuclei

18. Nerve fiber bundles on the ventrolateral surface of the mesencephalon are the
    (a) tegmenta (b) corpora quadrigemina
    (c) cerebral peduncles (d) superior colliculi

19. Efferent tracts from the hypothalamus
    (a) control involuntary motor activities
    (b) control autonomic function
    (c) coordinate activities of the nervous and endocrine systems
    (d) all of the above

20. The diencephalic components of the limbic system include the
    (a) limbic lobe and hippocampus
    (b) fornix
    (c) amygdaloid body and parahippocampal gyrus
    (d) thalamus and hypothalamus

Level 2 Reviewing Concepts

1. Swelling of the jugular vein as it leaves the skull could compress which of the following cranial nerves?
   (a) N I, IV, V (b) N IX, X, XI
   (c) N II, IV, VI (d) N VIII, IX, XII

2. The condition of dysmetria often indicates damage to which brain region?
   (a) cerebellum (b) frontal lobes of cerebrum
   (c) pons (d) medulla oblongata

3. If damaged or diseased, which part of the brain would make a person unable to control and regulate the rate of respiratory movements?
   (a) the pneumotaxic center of the pons
   (b) the respiratory rhythmicity center of the medulla
   (c) the olivary nucleus of the medulla oblongata
   (d) the cerebral peduncles of the mesencephalon

4. Which lobe and specific area of the brain would be affected if one could no longer cut designs from construction paper?

5. Impulses from proprioceptors must pass through specific nuclei before arriving at their destination in the brain. What are the nuclei, and what is the destination of this information?

6. Which nuclei are more likely involved in the coordinated movement of the head in the direction of a loud noise?

7. Which cranial nerves are responsible for all aspects of eye function?

8. If an individual has poor emotional control and difficulty in remembering past events, what area of the brain might be damaged or have a lesion?

9. Which region of the brain provides links between the cerebellar hemispheres and the mesencephalon, diencephalon, cerebrum, and spinal cord?

10. Why is the blood–brain barrier less intact in the hypothalamus?

Level 3 Critical Thinking

1. Shortly after birth, the head of an infant begins to enlarge rapidly. What is occurring, why, and is there a clinical explanation and solution to this problem?

2. Rose awakened one morning and discovered that her face was paralyzed on the left side and she had no sensation of taste from the anterior two-thirds of the tongue on the same side. What is the cause of these symptoms, and what can be done to help Rose with this situation?

3. If a person who has sustained a head injury passes out several days after the incident occurred, what would you suspect to be the cause of the problem, and how serious might it be?

The Medulla Oblongata 414

1. The medulla oblongata connects the brain to the spinal cord. It contains the **nucleus gracilis** and the **nucleus cuneatus**, which are processing centers, and the **olivary nuclei**, which relay information from the spinal cord, cerebral cortex, and brain stem to the cerebellar cortex. Its **reflex centers**, including the **cardiovascular centers** and the **respiratory rhythmicity centers**, control or adjust the activities of peripheral systems. *(see Figures 15.1/15.8/15.15/15.16/15.18 and Table 15.11)*

The Cranial Nerves 416

1. There are 12 pairs of cranial nerves. Each nerve attaches to the brain near the associated sensory or motor nuclei on the ventrolateral surface of the brain. *(see Figure 15.21)*

The Olfactory Nerve (N I) 418

2. The **olfactory tract** (nerve) (N I) carries sensory information responsible for the sense of smell. The olfactory afferents synapse within the **olfactory bulbs**. *(see Figure 15.22)*

The Optic Nerve (N II) 419

3. The **optic nerve** (N II) carries visual information from special sensory receptors in the eyes. *(see Figure 15.23)*

The Oculomotor Nerve (N III) 420

4. The **oculomotor nerve** (N III) is the primary source of innervation for the extra-ocular muscles that move the eyeball. *(see Figure 15.24)*

The Trochlear Nerve (N IV) 420

5. The **trochlear nerve** (N IV), the smallest cranial nerve, innervates the superior oblique muscle of the eye. *(see Figure 15.24)*

The Trigeminal Nerve (N V) 421

6. The **trigeminal nerve** (N V), the largest cranial nerve, is a mixed nerve with **ophthalmic, maxillary**, and **mandibular branches**. *(see Figure 15.25)*

The Abducens Nerve (N VI) 422

7. The **abducens nerve** (N VI) innervates the sixth extrinsic oculomotor muscle, the lateral rectus. *(see Figure 15.24)*

The Facial Nerve (N VII) 422

8. The **facial nerve** (N VII) is a mixed nerve that controls muscles of the scalp and face. It provides pressure sensations over the face and receives taste information from the tongue. *(see Figure 15.26)*

The Vestibulocochlear Nerve (N VIII) 423

9. The **vestibulocochlear nerve** (N VIII) contains the **vestibular nerve**, which monitors sensations of balance, position, and movement, and the **cochlear nerve**, which monitors hearing receptors. *(see Figure 15.27)*

The Glossopharyngeal Nerve (N IX) 424

10. The **glossopharyngeal nerve** (N IX) is a mixed nerve that innervates the tongue and pharynx and controls the action of swallowing. *(see Figure 15.28)*

The Vagus Nerve (N X) 424

11. The **vagus nerve** (N X) is a mixed nerve that is vital to the autonomic control of visceral function and has a variety of motor components. *(see Figure 15.29)*

The Accessory Nerve (N XI) 425

12. The **accessory nerve** (N XI) has an **internal branch**, which innervates voluntary swallowing muscles of the soft palate and pharynx, and an **external branch**, which controls muscles associated with the pectoral girdle. *(see Figure 15.30)*

The Hypoglossal Nerve (N XII) 426

13. The **hypoglossal nerve** (N XII) provides voluntary motor control over tongue movements. *(see Figure 15.30)*

A Summary of Cranial Nerve Branches and Functions 426

14. The branches and functions of the cranial nerves are summarized in *Table 15.12.*

CHAPTER REVIEW

For answers to the Concept Check and Chapter Review questions, go to the blue "Answers" tab at the back of the book.

Level 1 Reviewing Facts and Terms

Match each numbered item with the most closely related lettered item. Use letters for answers in the spaces provided.

Column A	Column B
C 1. mesencephalon	a. visual cortex
H 2. myelencephalon	b. learned motor patterns
J 3. tentorium cerebelli	c. midbrain
F 4. abducens nerve	d. motor, tongue movements
___ 5. diencephalon E-thalamus	e. third ventricle
a 6. occipital lobe A	f. motor, eye movements
d 7. hypoglossal nerve	g. sensory information relay
g 8. basal nuclei B	h. medulla oblongata
e 9. thalamus G	i. Purkinje cells
b 10. cerebellum I	j. separate cerebrum/cerebellum

11. In contrast with those of the brain, responses of the spinal reflexes
    (a) are fine-tuned
    (b) are immediate
    (c) require many processing steps
    (d) are stereotyped
12. The primary link between the nervous and the endocrine systems is the
    (a) hypothalamus (b) pons
    (c) mesencephalon (d) medulla oblongata
13. Cranial blood vessels pass through the space directly deep to the
    (a) dura mater (b) pia mater
    (c) arachnoid granulations (d) arachnoid mater
14. The only cranial nerves that are attached to the cerebrum are the
    (a) optic (b) oculomotor
    (c) trochlear (d) olfactory

The Ventricles of the Brain 389

9. The central passageway of the brain expands to form chambers called **ventricles**. *Cerebrospinal fluid (CSF)* continually circulates from the ventricles and central canal of the spinal cord into the subarachnoid space of the meninges that surround the CNS. *(see Figures 15.2/15.13)*

Protection and Support of the Brain 389

The Cranial Meninges 391

1. The **cranial meninges**—the **dura mater**, **arachnoid mater**, and **pia mater**—are continuous with the same spinal meninges that surround the spinal cord. However, they have anatomical and functional differences. *(see Figures 15.3/15.4)*
2. Folds of dura mater stabilize the position of the brain within the cranium and include the **falx cerebri**, **tentorium cerebelli**, **falx cerebelli**, and **diaphragma sellae**. *(see Figures 15.3/15.4)*

The Blood–Brain Barrier 391

3. The **blood–brain barrier** isolates neural tissue from the general circulation.
4. The blood–brain barrier remains intact throughout the CNS except in portions of the hypothalamus, in the pineal gland, and at the choroid plexus in the membranous roof of the diencephalon and medulla.

Cerebrospinal Fluid 394

5. Cerebrospinal fluid (CSF) (1) cushions delicate neural structures, (2) supports the brain, and (3) transports nutrients, chemical messengers, and waste products.
6. The **choroid plexus** is the site of cerebrospinal fluid production. *(see Figure 15.5)*
7. Cerebrospinal fluid reaches the subarachnoid space via the **lateral apertures** and a **median aperture**. Diffusion across the **arachnoid granulations** into the **superior sagittal sinus** returns CSF to the venous circulation. *(see Figures 15.4/15.6)*
8. The blood–brain barrier isolates neural tissue from the general circulation.

The Blood Supply to the Brain 395

9. Arterial blood reaches the brain through the *internal carotid arteries* and the *vertebral arteries*. Venous blood leaves primarily in the *internal jugular veins*.

The Cerebrum 396

The Cerebral Hemispheres 396

1. The cortical surface contains **gyri** (elevated ridges) separated by **sulci** (shallow depressions) or deeper grooves (**fissures**). The **longitudinal fissure** separates the two **cerebral hemispheres**. The **central sulcus** marks the boundary between the **frontal lobe** and the **parietal lobe**. Other sulci form the boundaries of the **temporal lobe** and the **occipital lobe**. *(see Figures 15.1/15.8/15.9)*
2. Each cerebral hemisphere receives sensory information from and generates motor commands to the opposite side of the body. There are significant functional differences between the two; thus, the assignment of a specific function to a specific region of the cerebral cortex is imprecise.
3. The **primary motor cortex** of the **precentral gyrus** directs voluntary movements. The **primary sensory cortex** of the **postcentral gyrus** receives somatic sensory information from touch, pressure, pain, taste, and temperature receptors. *(see Figure 15.9 and Table 15.2)*
4. **Association areas**, such as the **visual association area** and **somatic motor association area** (**premotor cortex**), control our ability to understand sensory information. "Higher-order" integrative centers receive information from many different association areas and direct complex motor activities and analytical functions. *(see Figure 15.9 and Table 15.2)*

The Central White Matter 400

5. The **central white matter** contains three major groups of axons: (1) **association fibers** (tracts that interconnect areas of neural cortex within a single cerebral hemisphere); (2) **commissural fibers** (tracts connecting the two cerebral hemispheres); and (3) **projection fibers** (tracts that link the cerebrum with other regions of the brain and spinal cord). *(see Figure 15.10 and Table 15.3)*

The Basal Nuclei 401

6. The **basal nuclei** within the central white matter include the **caudate nucleus**, **amygdaloid body**, **claustrum**, **putamen**, and **globus pallidus**. The basal nuclei control muscle tone and the coordination of learned movement patterns and other somatic motor activities. *(see Figure 15.11 and Table 15.4)*

The Limbic System 401

7. The **limbic system** includes the amygdaloid body, **cingulate gyrus**, **dentate gyrus**, **parahippocampal gyrus**, **hippocampus**, and **fornix**. The **mamillary bodies** control reflex movements associated with eating. The functions of the limbic system involve emotional states and related behavioral drives. *(see Figures 15.12/15.15 and Table 15.5)*
8. The **anterior nucleus** relays visceral sensations, and stimulating the **reticular formation** produces heightened awareness and a generalized excitement.

The Diencephalon 405

1. The diencephalon provides the switching and relay centers necessary to integrate the sensory and motor pathways. *(see Figures 15.12/15.15)*

The Epithalamus 405

2. The epithalamus forms the roof of the diencephalon. It contains the hormone-secreting *pineal gland.*

The Thalamus 405

3. The thalamus is the principal and final relay point for ascending sensory information and coordinates voluntary and involuntary somatic motor activities. *(see Figures 15.11b/15.12/15.13/15.15b and Table 15.6)*

The Hypothalamus 406

4. The hypothalamus contains important control and integrative centers. It can (1) control involuntary somatic motor activities; (2) control autonomic function; (3) coordinate activities of the nervous and endocrine systems; (4) secrete hormones; (5) produce emotions and behavioral drives; (6) coordinate voluntary and autonomic functions; (7) regulate body temperature; and (8) control circadian cycles of activity. *(see Figures 15.12/15.13/15.14/15.15a and Table 15.7)*

The Mesencephalon 410

1. The **tectum** (roof) of the mesencephalon contains two pairs of nuclei, the **corpora quadrigemina**. On each side, the **superior colliculus** receives visual inputs from the thalamus, and the **inferior colliculus** receives auditory data from the medulla oblongata. The **red nucleus** integrates information from the cerebrum and issues involuntary motor commands related to muscle tone and limb position. The **substantia nigra** regulates the motor output of the basal nuclei. The **cerebral peduncles** contain ascending fibers headed for thalamic nuclei and descending fibers of the corticospinal pathway that carry voluntary motor commands from the primary motor cortex of each cerebral hemisphere. *(see Figures 15.15/15.16/15.17b and Table 15.8)*

The Pons 410

1. The pons contains: (1) sensory and motor nuclei for four cranial nerves; (2) nuclei concerned with involuntary control of respiration; (3) nuclei that process and relay cerebellar commands arriving over the middle cerebellar peduncles; and (4) ascending, descending, and transverse tracts. *(see Figures 15.1/15.15/15.16/15.18 and Table 15.9)*

The Cerebellum 412

1. The cerebellum oversees the body's postural muscles and programs and tunes voluntary and involuntary movements. The **cerebellar hemispheres** consist of neural cortex formed into folds, or **folia**. The surface can be divided into the **anterior** and **posterior lobes**, the **vermis**, and the **flocculonodular lobes**. *(see Figures 15.1/15.8/15.9/15.15/15.19 and Table 15.10)*

Clinical Note

Cranial Reflexes **Cranial reflexes** are reflex arcs that involve the sensory and motor fibers of cranial nerves. Examples of cranial reflexes are discussed in later chapters, and this section will simply provide an overview and general introduction.

Table 15.13 lists representative examples of cranial reflexes and their functions. These reflexes are clinically important because they provide a quick and easy method for observing the condition of cranial nerves and specific nuclei and tracts in the brain.

Cranial somatic reflexes are seldom more complex than the somatic reflexes of the spinal cord. This table includes four somatic reflexes: the *corneal reflex*, the *tympanic reflex*, the *auditory reflex*, and the *vestibulo-ocular reflex*. These reflexes are often used to check for damage to the cranial nerves or processing centers involved. The brain stem contains many reflex centers that control visceral motor activity. Many of these reflex centers are in the medulla oblongata, and they can direct very complex visceral motor responses to stimuli. These visceral reflexes are essential to the control of respiratory, digestive, and cardiovascular functions.

CONCEPT CHECK

1. John is experiencing problems in moving his tongue. His doctor tells him the problems are due to pressure on a cranial nerve. Which cranial nerve is involved?
2. What symptoms would you associate with damage to the abducens nerve (N VI)?
3. A blow to the head has caused Julie to lose her balance. Which cranial nerve and what branch of that nerve are probably involved?
4. Bruce has lost the ability to detect tastes on the tip of his tongue. What cranial nerve is involved?

See blue "Answers" tab at back of book.

Embryology Summary

For a summary of the development of the brain and cranial nerves, see Chapter 28 (Embryology and Human Development).

CLINICAL TERMS

ataxia: A disturbance of balance that in severe cases leaves the individual unable to stand without assistance; caused by problems affecting the cerebellum.

Bell's palsy: A condition resulting from an inflammation of the facial nerve; symptoms include paralysis of facial muscles on the affected side and loss of taste sensations from the anterior two-thirds of the tongue.

cranial trauma: A head injury resulting from violent contact with another object. Cranial trauma may cause a **concussion**, a condition characterized by a temporary loss of consciousness and a variable period of amnesia.

dysmetria (dis-MET-rē-a): An inability to stop a movement at a precise, predetermined position; it often leads to an *intention tremor* in the affected individual; usually reflects cerebellar dysfunction.

epidural hemorrhage: A condition involving bleeding into the epidural spaces.

hydrocephalus: Also known as "water on the brain"; a condition in which the skull expands to accommodate extra fluid.

Parkinson's disease (paralysis agitans): A condition characterized by a pronounced increase in muscle tone, resulting from loss of inhibitory control over neurons in the basal nuclei.

spasticity: A condition characterized by hesitant, jerky, voluntary movements and increased muscle tone.

subdural hemorrhage: A condition in which blood accumulates between the dura and the arachnoid mater.

tic douloureux (doo-loo-ROO), or **trigeminal neuralgia:** A disorder of the maxillary and mandibular branches of N V characterized by severe, almost totally debilitating pain triggered by contact with the lip, tongue, or gums.

tremor: A background shaking of the limbs resulting from a "tug of war" between antagonistic muscle groups.

STUDY OUTLINE

Introduction 387

1. The brain is far more complex than the spinal cord; its complexity makes it adaptable but slower in response than spinal reflexes.

An Introduction to the Organization of the Brain 387

Embryology of the Brain 387

1. The brain forms from three swellings at the superior tip of the developing neural tube: the **prosencephalon**, **mesencephalon**, and **rhombencephalon**. *(see Table 15.1 and Embryology Summary, pp. 388, 777–778)*

Major Regions and Landmarks 387

2. There are six regions in the adult brain: the cerebrum, the diencephalon, the mesencephalon, the pons, the cerebellum, and the medulla oblongata. *(see Figure 15.1)*
3. Conscious thought, intellectual functions, memory, and complex motor patterns originate in the **cerebrum**. *(see Figure 15.1)*
4. The roof of the **diencephalon** is the **epithalamus**; the walls are the **thalami**, which contain relay and processing centers for sensory data. The floor is the **hypothalamus**, which contains centers involved with emotions, autonomic function, and hormone production. *(see Figure 15.1)*
5. The **mesencephalon** processes visual and auditory information and generates involuntary somatic motor responses. *(see Figure 15.1)*
6. The **pons** connects the cerebellum to the brain stem and is involved with somatic and visceral motor control. The **cerebellum** adjusts voluntary and involuntary motor activities on the basis of sensory data and stored memories. *(see Figure 15.1)*
7. The spinal cord connects to the brain at the **medulla oblongata**, which relays sensory information and regulates autonomic functions. *(see Figure 15.1)*

Gray Matter and White Matter Organization 389

8. The brain contains extensive areas of **neural cortex**, a layer of gray matter on the surfaces of the cerebrum and cerebellum that covers underlying white matter.

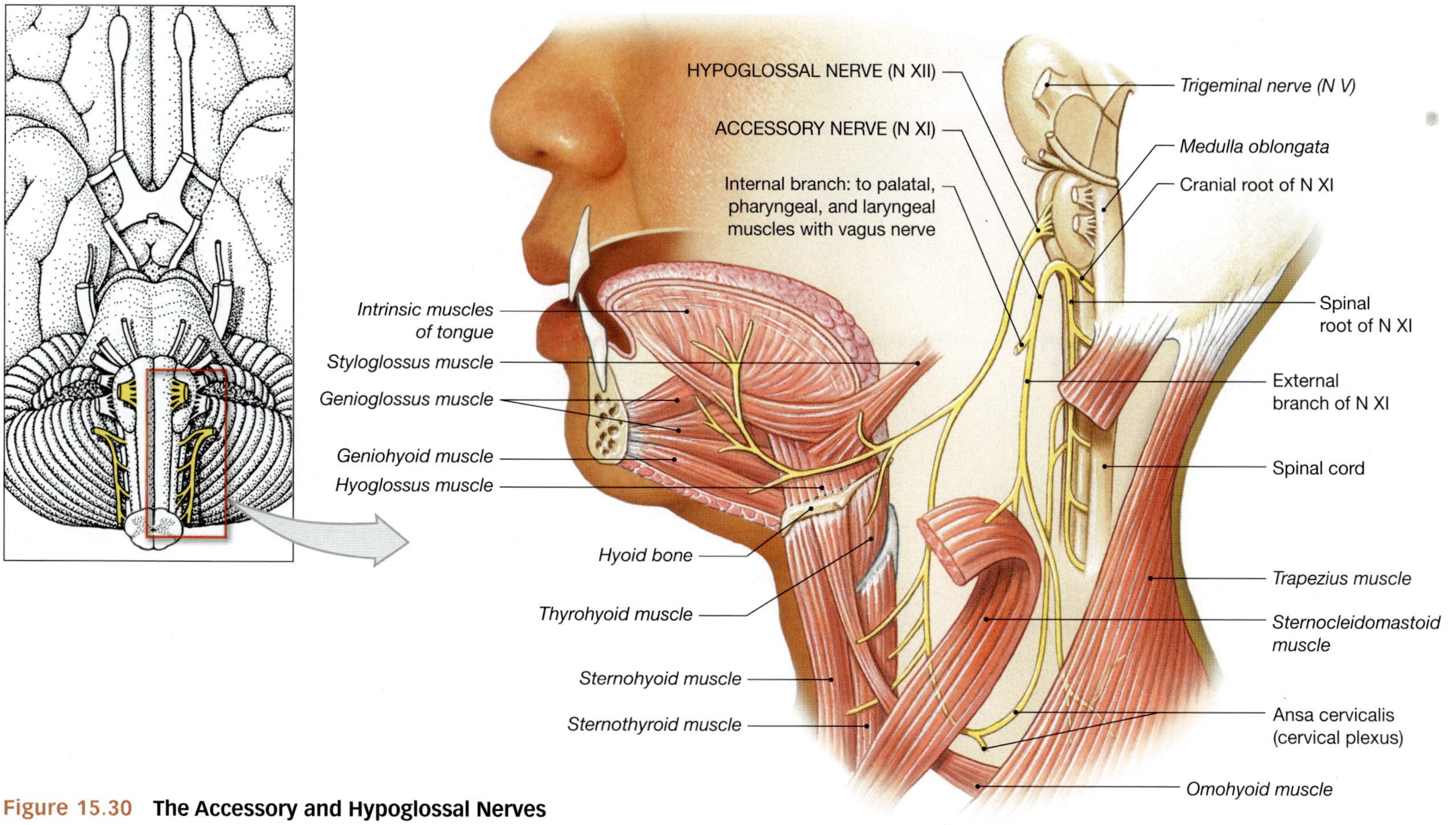

Figure 15.30 The Accessory and Hypoglossal Nerves

The Hypoglossal Nerve (N XII) [Figures 15.21/15.30]

Primary function: Motor, tongue movements

Origin: Motor nuclei of the medulla oblongata

Passes through: Hypoglossal canal of occipital bone p. 149

Destination: Muscles of the tongue p. 269

The **hypoglossal** (hī-po-GLOS-al) **nerve** leaves the cranium through the hypoglossal canal of the occipital bone. It then curves inferiorly, anteriorly, and then superiorly to reach the skeletal muscles of the tongue (Figures 15.21 and 15.30). This nerve provides voluntary motor control over movements of the tongue.

A Summary of Cranial Nerve Branches and Functions

Few people are able to remember the names, numbers, and functions of the cranial nerves without a struggle. Mnemonic devices may prove useful. The most famous and oft-repeated is *On Old Olympus Towering Top A Finn And German Viewed Some Hops.* (The *And* refers to the acoustic nerve, an alternative name for N VIII, and the *Some* refers to the spinal accessory nerve, an alternative name for N XI.) A more modern one, *Oh, Once One Takes The Anatomy Final, Very Good Vacations Are Heavenly,* may be a bit easier to remember. A summary of the basic distribution and function of each cranial nerve is detailed in Table 15.12.

TABLE 15.13 Cranial Reflexes

Reflex	Stimulus	Afferents	Central Synapse	Efferents	Response
SOMATIC REFLEXES					
Corneal reflex	Contact with corneal surface	N V (trigeminal)	Motor nuclei for N VII (facial nerve)	N VII	Blinking of eyelids
Tympanic reflex	Loud noise	N VIII (vestibulocochlear)	Inferior colliculi (midbrain)	N VII	Reduced movement of auditory ossicles
Auditory reflexes	Loud noise	N VIII	Motor nuclei of brain stem and spinal cord	N III, IV, VI, VII, X, cervical nerves	Eye and/or head movements triggered by sudden sounds
Vestibulo-ocular reflexes	Rotation of head	N VIII	Motor nuclei controlling extra-ocular muscles	N III, IV, VI	Opposite movement of eyes to stabilize field of vision
VISCERAL REFLEXES					
Direct light reflex	Light striking photoreceptors	N II (optic)	Superior colliculi (midbrain)	N III (oculomotor)	Constriction of ipsilateral pupil
Consensual light reflex	Light striking photoreceptors	N II	Superior colliculi	N III	Constriction of contralateral pupil

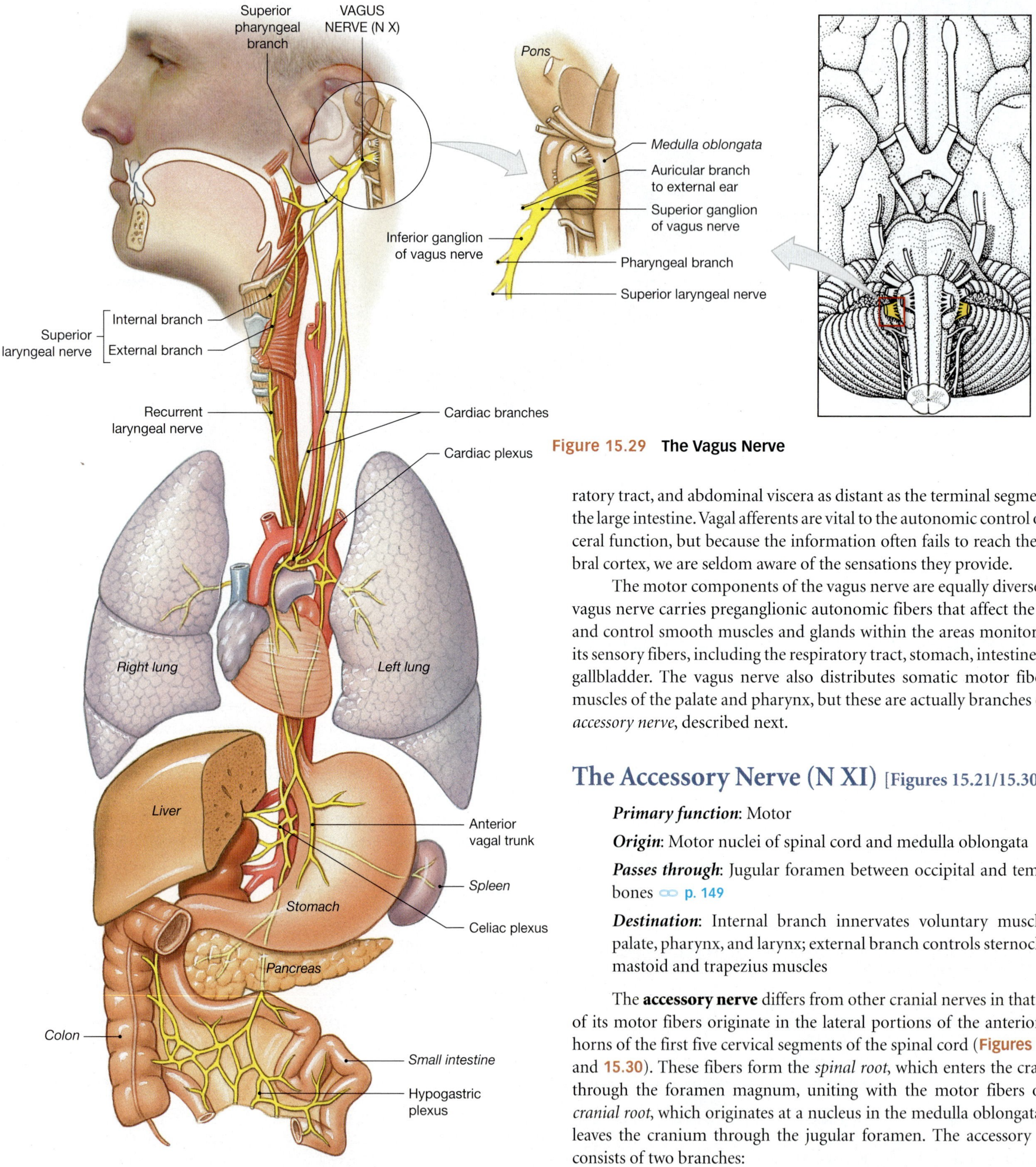

Figure 15.29 The Vagus Nerve

Sensory neurons are located within the **superior ganglion**, or *jugular ganglion*, and the **inferior ganglion**, or *nodose ganglion*. The vagus nerve provides somatic sensory information concerning the external acoustic meatus, a portion of the ear, the diaphragm, and special sensory information from pharyngeal taste receptors. But the majority of the vagal afferents provide visceral sensory information from receptors along the esophagus, respiratory tract, and abdominal viscera as distant as the terminal segments of the large intestine. Vagal afferents are vital to the autonomic control of visceral function, but because the information often fails to reach the cerebral cortex, we are seldom aware of the sensations they provide.

The motor components of the vagus nerve are equally diverse. The vagus nerve carries preganglionic autonomic fibers that affect the heart and control smooth muscles and glands within the areas monitored by its sensory fibers, including the respiratory tract, stomach, intestines, and gallbladder. The vagus nerve also distributes somatic motor fibers to muscles of the palate and pharynx, but these are actually branches of the *accessory nerve*, described next.

The Accessory Nerve (N XI) [Figures 15.21/15.30]

Primary function: Motor

Origin: Motor nuclei of spinal cord and medulla oblongata

Passes through: Jugular foramen between occipital and temporal bones p. 149

Destination: Internal branch innervates voluntary muscles of palate, pharynx, and larynx; external branch controls sternocleidomastoid and trapezius muscles

The **accessory nerve** differs from other cranial nerves in that some of its motor fibers originate in the lateral portions of the anterior gray horns of the first five cervical segments of the spinal cord (Figures 15.21 and 15.30). These fibers form the *spinal root*, which enters the cranium through the foramen magnum, uniting with the motor fibers of the *cranial root*, which originates at a nucleus in the medulla oblongata, and leaves the cranium through the jugular foramen. The accessory nerve consists of two branches:

1. The **internal branch** joins the vagus nerve and innervates the voluntary swallowing muscles of the soft palate and pharynx and the intrinsic muscles that control the vocal cords.
2. The **external branch** controls the sternocleidomastoid and trapezius muscles of the neck and back. pp. 271, 286 The motor fibers of this branch originate in the anterior gray horns of C_1 to C_5.

The Glossopharyngeal Nerve (N IX)

[Figures 15.21/15.28]

Primary function: Mixed (sensory and motor)

Origin: Sensory from posterior one-third of the tongue, part of the pharynx and palate, the carotid arteries of the neck; motor from motor nuclei of medulla oblongata

Passes through: Jugular foramen between occipital and temporal bones p. 149

Destination: Sensory fibers to sensory nuclei of medulla oblongata

Somatic motor: pharyngeal muscles involved in swallowing

Visceral motor: parotid salivary gland, after synapsing in the otic ganglion

In addition to the vestibular nucleus of N VIII, the medulla oblongata contains the sensory and motor nuclei for the ninth, tenth, eleventh, and twelfth cranial nerves. The **glossopharyngeal** (glos-ū-fah-RIN-jē-al; *glossum*, tongue) **nerve** innervates the tongue and pharynx. The glossopharyngeal nerve passes through the cranium through the jugular foramen in company with N X and N XI (**Figures 15.21** and **15.28**).

The glossopharyngeal is a mixed nerve, but sensory fibers are most abundant. The sensory neurons are in the **superior ganglion** (*jugular ganglion*) and the **inferior ganglion** (*petrosal ganglion*).[3] The afferent fibers carry general sensory information from the lining of the pharynx and the soft palate to a nucleus in the medulla oblongata. The glossopharyngeal nerve also provides taste sensations from the posterior third of the tongue and has special receptors monitoring the blood pressure and dissolved-gas concentrations within major blood vessels.

The somatic motor fibers control the pharyngeal muscles involved in swallowing. Visceral motor fibers synapse in the *otic ganglion*, and postganglionic fibers innervate the parotid salivary gland of the cheek.

[3] The names of the ganglia associated with N IX and N X vary from reference to reference. N IX has a *superior ganglion*, also called the *jugular ganglion*, and an *inferior ganglion*, also called the *petrosal* (or *petrous*) *ganglion*. N X also has two major ganglia, a *superior ganglion*, or *jugular ganglion*, and an *inferior ganglion*, or *nodose ganglion*. *Superior* and *inferior* are the names recommended by the Terminologia Anatomica.

The Vagus Nerve (N X) [Figures 15.21/15.29]

Primary function: Mixed (sensory and motor)

Origin: *Visceral sensory* from pharynx (part), auricle, external acoustic meatus, diaphragm, and visceral organs in thoracic and abdominopelvic cavities

Visceral motor from motor nuclei in the medulla oblongata

Passes through: Jugular foramen between occipital and temporal bones p. 149

Destination: Sensory fibers to sensory nuclei and autonomic centers of medulla oblongata

Somatic motor to muscles of the palate and pharynx

Visceral motor to respiratory, cardiovascular, and digestive organs in the thoracic and abdominal cavities

The **vagus** (VĀ-gus) **nerve** arises immediately inferior to the glossopharyngeal nerve (**Figure 15.21**). Many small rootlets contribute to its formation, and developmental studies indicate that this nerve probably represents the fusion of several smaller cranial nerves during our evolution. As its name suggests (*vagus*, wanderer), the vagus nerve branches and radiates extensively. **Figure 15.29** shows only the general pattern of distribution.

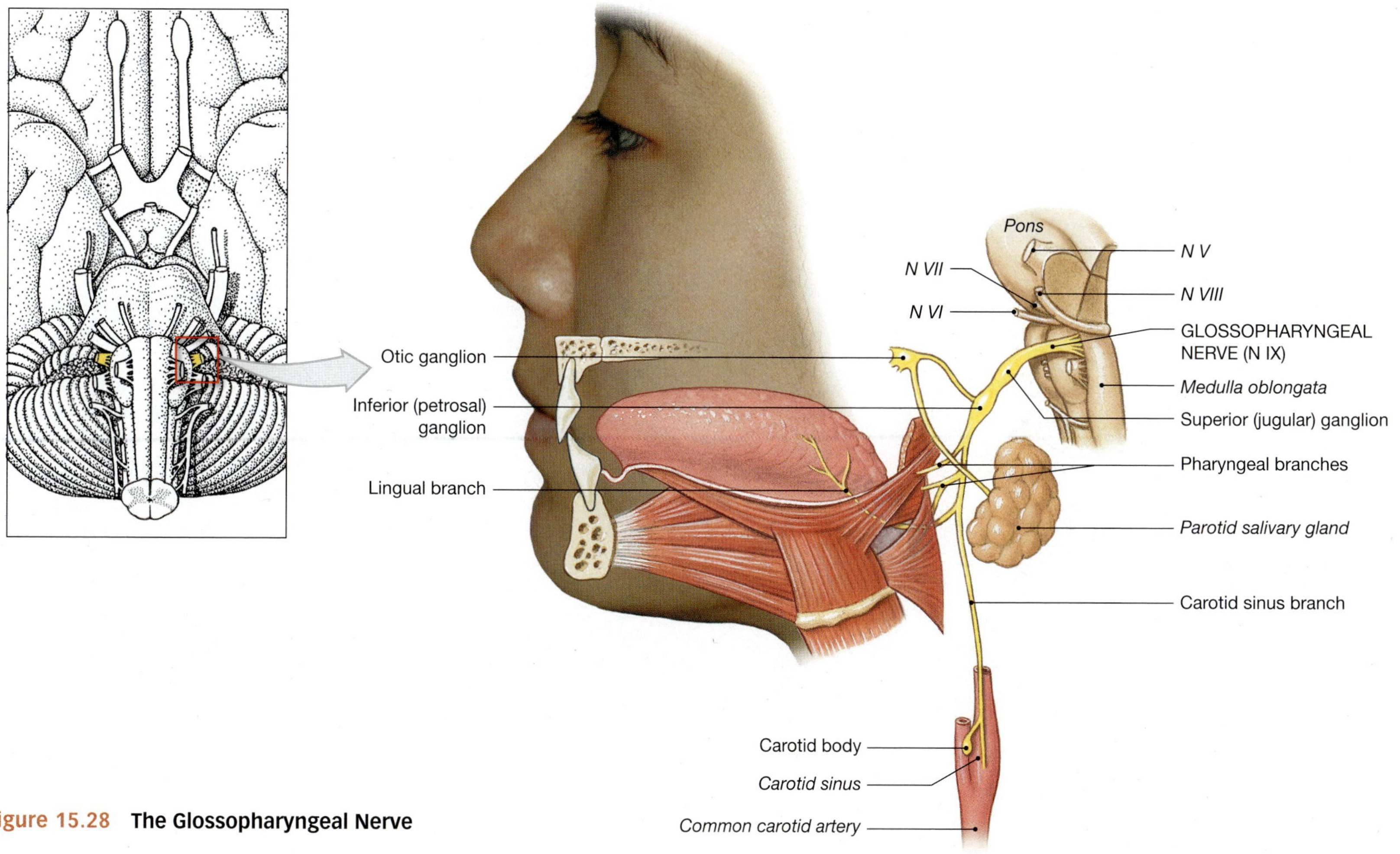

Figure 15.28 The Glossopharyngeal Nerve

Visceral motor: lacrimal (tear) gland and nasal mucous glands via pterygopalatine ganglion; submandibular and sublingual salivary glands via submandibular ganglion

The **facial nerve** is a mixed nerve. The cell bodies of the sensory neurons are located in the **geniculate ganglion**, and the motor nuclei are in the pons (Figure 15.21). The sensory and motor roots combine to form a large nerve that passes through the internal acoustic meatus of the temporal bone (Figure 15.26). The nerve then passes through the facial canal to reach the face through the stylomastoid foramen. p. 139 The sensory neurons monitor proprioceptors in the facial muscles, provide deep pressure sensations over the face, and receive taste information from receptors along the anterior two-thirds of the tongue. Somatic motor fibers control the superficial muscles of the scalp and face and deep muscles near the ear.

The facial nerve carries preganglionic autonomic fibers to the pterygopalatine and submandibular ganglia.

- **Pterygopalatine ganglion:** The *greater petrosal nerve* innervates the pterygopalatine ganglion. Postganglionic fibers from this ganglion innervate the lacrimal gland and small glands of the nasal cavity and pharynx.
- **Submandibular ganglion:** To reach the submandibular ganglion, autonomic fibers leave the facial nerve and travel along the mandibular branch of the trigeminal nerve. Postganglionic fibers from this ganglion innervate the *submandibular* and *sublingual* (*sub*, under + *lingua*, tongue) *salivary glands*.

Clinical Note

Bell's Palsy **Bell's palsy** results from an inflammation of the facial nerve that is probably related to viral infection. Involvement of the facial nerve (N VII) can be deduced from symptoms of paralysis of facial muscles on the affected side and loss of taste sensations from the anterior two-thirds of the tongue. The individual does not show prominent sensory deficits, and the condition is usually painless. In most cases, Bell's palsy "cures itself" after a few weeks or months but this process can be accelerated by early treatment with corticosteroids and antiviral drugs.

The Vestibulocochlear Nerve (N VIII)

[Figures 15.21/15.27]

Primary function: Special sensory: balance and equilibrium (vestibular branch) and hearing (cochlear branch)

Origin: Receptors of the inner ear (vestibule and cochlea)

Passes through: Internal acoustic meatus of the temporal bone p. 149

Destination: Vestibular and cochlear nuclei of pons and medulla oblongata pp. 410, 515

The **vestibulocochlear nerve** is also known as the *acoustic nerve* and the *auditory nerve*. We will use the term vestibulocochlear because it indicates the names of its two major branches: the *vestibular branch* and the *cochlear branch*. The vestibulocochlear nerve lies lateral to the origin of the facial nerve, straddling the boundary between the pons and the medulla oblongata (Figures 15.21 and 15.27). This nerve reaches the sensory receptors of the inner ear by entering the internal acoustic meatus in company with the facial nerve. There are two distinct bundles of sensory fibers within the vestibulocochlear nerve. The **vestibular nerve** (*vestibulum*, cavity) is the larger of the two bundles. It originates at the receptors of the *vestibule*, the portion of the inner ear concerned with balance sensations. The sensory neurons are located within an adjacent sensory ganglion, and their axons target the **vestibular nuclei** of the medulla oblongata. These afferents convey information concerning position, movement, and balance. The **cochlear** (KOK-lē-ar; *cochlea*, snail shell) **nerve** monitors the receptors in the cochlea that provide the sense of hearing. The nerve cells are located within a peripheral ganglion, and their axons synapse within the **cochlear nuclei** of the medulla oblongata. Axons leaving the vestibular and cochlear nuclei relay the sensory information to other centers or initiate reflexive motor responses. Balance and the sense of hearing will be discussed in Chapter 18.

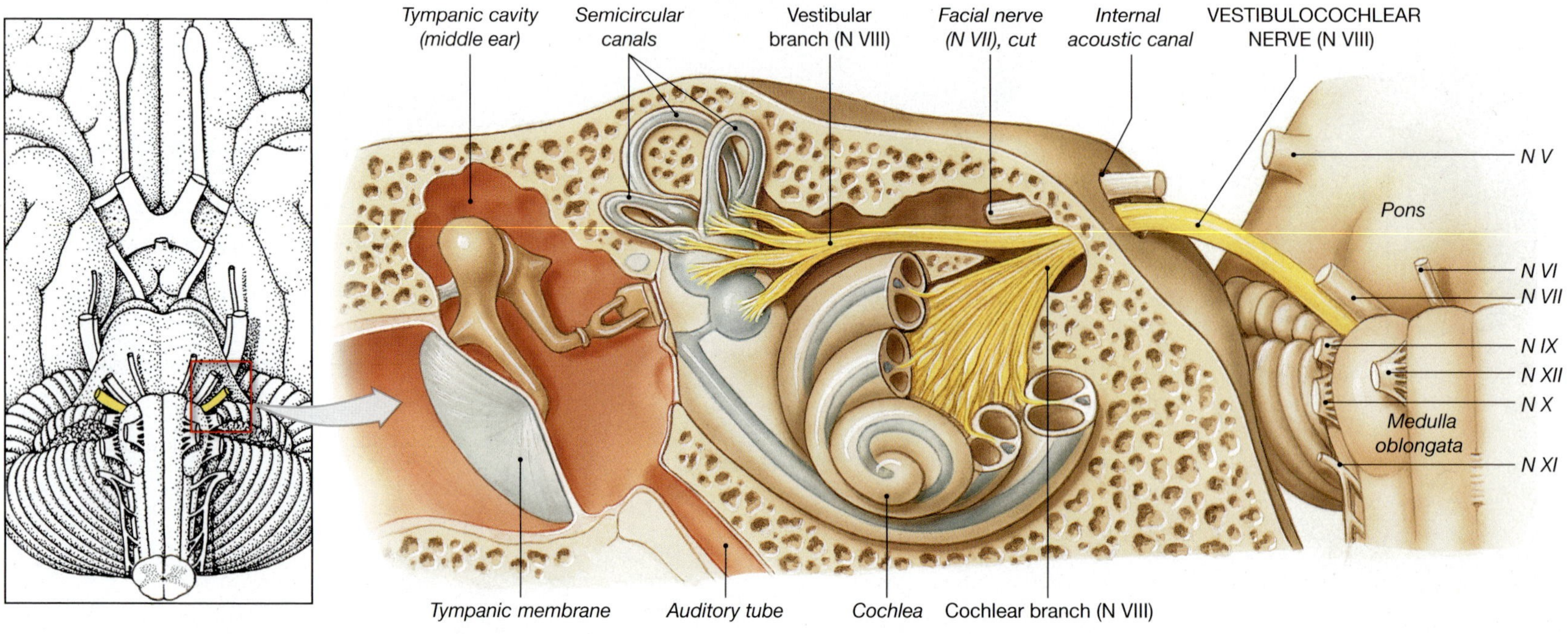

Figure 15.27 **The Vestibulocochlear Nerve**

vate the ganglion, and the postganglionic autonomic fibers may then travel with the trigeminal nerve to peripheral structures. The ciliary ganglion was discussed earlier (p. 420), and the other ganglia will be detailed shortly, with the branches of the *facial nerve* (N VII).

Clinical Note

Tic Douloureux **Tic douloureux** (doo-loo-ROO; *douloureux*, painful) affects one individual out of every 25,000. Sufferers complain of severe, almost totally debilitating pain triggered by contact with the lip, tongue, or gums. The pain arrives with a sudden, shocking intensity and then disappears. Usually only one side of the face is involved. Another name for this condition is **trigeminal neuralgia**, for it is the maxillary and mandibular branches of N V that innervate the sensitive areas. This condition usually affects adults over age 40; the cause is unknown. The pain can often be temporarily controlled by drug therapy, but surgical procedures may eventually be required. The goal of the surgery is the destruction of the sensory nerves carrying the pain sensations. They can be destroyed by actually cutting the nerve, a procedure called a **rhizotomy** (*rhiza*, root), or by injecting chemicals such as alcohol or phenol into the nerve at the foramina ovale and rotundum. The sensory fibers may also be destroyed by inserting an electrode and cauterizing the sensory nerve trunks as they leave the semilunar ganglion.

The Abducens Nerve (N VI) [Figures 15.21/15.24]

Primary function: Motor, eye movements

Origin: Pons

Passes through: Superior orbital fissure of sphenoid p. 149

Destination: Lateral rectus muscle p. 267

The **abducens** (ab-DŪ-senz) **nerve** innervates the lateral rectus, the sixth of the extrinsic eye muscles. Innervation of this muscle makes lateral movements of the eyeball possible. The nerve emerges from the inferior surface of the brain at the border between the pons and the medulla oblongata (Figure 15.21). It reaches the orbit through the superior orbital fissure in company with the oculomotor and trochlear nerves (Figure 15.24).

The Facial Nerve (N VII) [Figures 15.21/15.26]

Primary function: Mixed (sensory and motor)

Origin: Sensory from taste receptors on anterior two-thirds of tongue; motor from motor nuclei of pons

Passes through: Internal acoustic meatus of temporal bone, along facial canal to reach stylomastoid foramen p. 149

Destination: *Sensory* to sensory nuclei of pons;

Somatic motor: muscles of facial expression p. 264

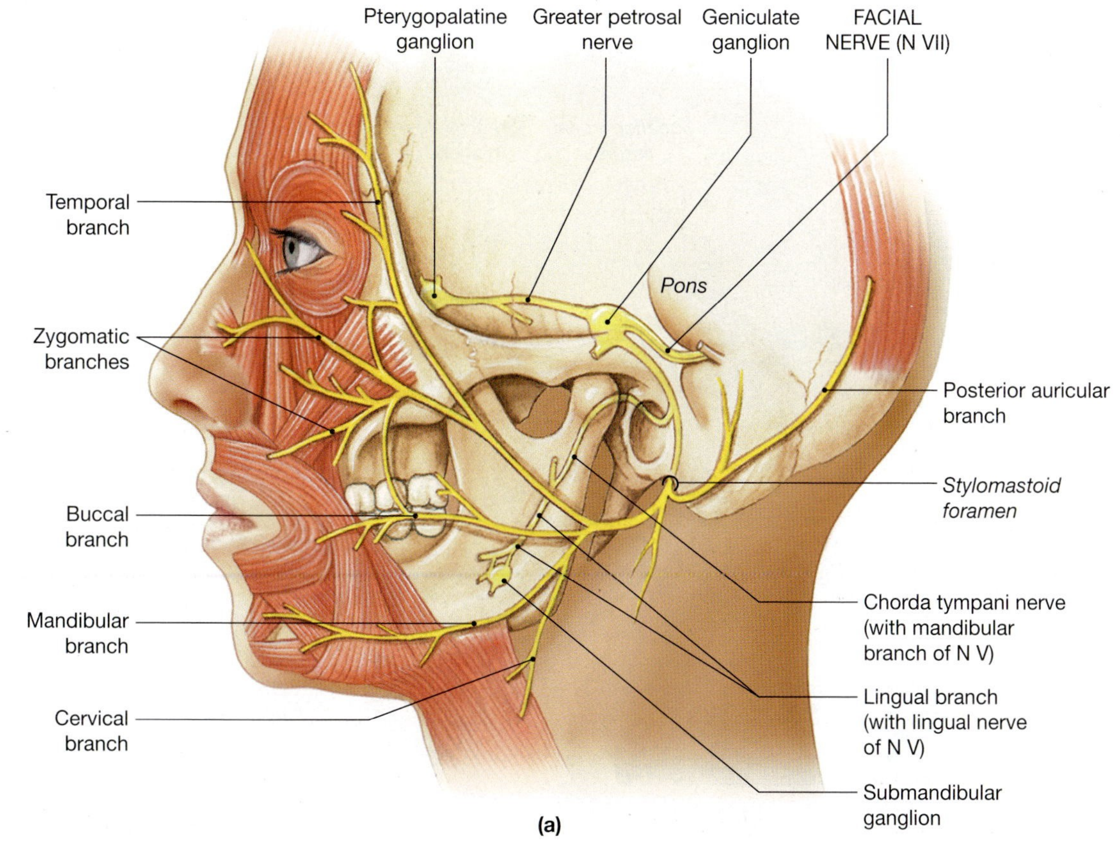

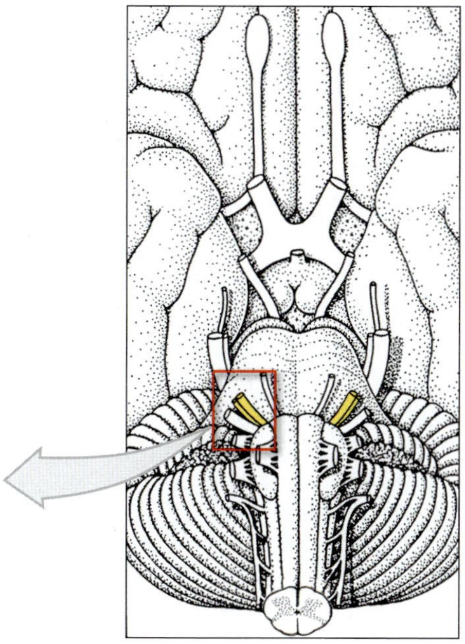

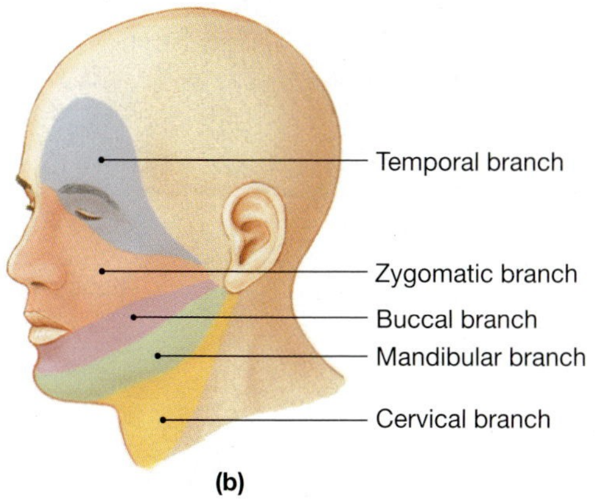

Figure 15.26 The Facial Nerve
(a) Origin and branches of the facial nerve. **(b)** The superficial distribution of the five major branches of the facial nerve.

The Trigeminal Nerve (N V) [Figures 15.21/15.25]

Primary function: Mixed (sensory and motor); ophthalmic and maxillary branches sensory, mandibular branch mixed

Origin: *Ophthalmic branch* (sensory): orbital structures, nasal cavity, skin of forehead, superior eyelid, eyebrow, and part of the nose

Maxillary branch (sensory): inferior eyelid, upper lip, gums, and teeth; cheek; nose, palate, and part of the pharynx

Mandibular branch (mixed): sensory from lower gums, teeth, and lips; palate and tongue (part); motor from motor nuclei of pons (Figure 15.21)

Passes through: Ophthalmic branch through superior orbital fissure, maxillary branch through foramen rotundum, mandibular branch through foramen ovale ∞ p. 149

Destination: Ophthalmic, maxillary, and mandibular branches to sensory nuclei in the pons; mandibular branch also innervates muscles of mastication ∞ p. 268

The pons contains the nuclei associated with three cranial nerves (N V, N VI, and N VII) and contributes to the control of a fourth (N VIII). The **trigeminal** (trī-JEM-i-nal) **nerve** (Figure 15.25) is the largest cranial nerve. This mixed nerve provides sensory information from the head and face and motor control to the muscles of mastication. Sensory (dorsal) and motor (ventral) roots originate on the lateral surface of the pons. The sensory branch is larger, and the enormous **semilunar ganglion** (*trigeminal ganglion*) contains the cell bodies of the sensory neurons. As the name implies, the trigeminal has three major branches; the relatively small motor root contributes to only one of the three.

Branch 1. The **ophthalmic branch** of the trigeminal nerve is purely sensory. This nerve innervates orbital structures, the nasal cavity and sinuses, and the skin of the forehead, eyebrows, eyelids, and nose. It leaves the cranium through the superior orbital fissure, then branches within the orbit.

Branch 2. The **maxillary branch** of the trigeminal nerve is also purely sensory. It supplies the lower eyelid, upper lip, cheek, and nose. Deeper sensory structures of the upper gums and teeth, the palate, and portions of the pharynx are also innervated by the maxillary nerve branch. The maxillary branch leaves the cranium at the foramen rotundum, entering the floor of the orbit through the inferior orbital fissure. A major branch of the maxillary, the *infraorbital nerve*, passes through the infraorbital foramen to supply adjacent portions of the face.

Branch 3. The **mandibular branch** is the largest branch of the trigeminal nerve, and it carries all of the motor fibers. This branch exits the cranium through the foramen ovale. The motor components of the mandibular nerve innervate the muscles of mastication. The sensory fibers carry proprioceptive information from those muscles and monitor: (1) the skin of the temples; (2) the lateral surfaces, gums, and teeth of the mandible; (3) the salivary glands; and (4) the anterior portions of the tongue.

The trigeminal nerve branches are associated with the *ciliary*, *pterygopalatine*, *submandibular*, and *otic ganglia*. These are autonomic ganglia whose neurons innervate structures of the face. The trigeminal nerve does not contain visceral motor fibers, and all of its fibers pass through these ganglia without synapsing. However, branches of other cranial nerves, such as the *facial nerve*, can be bound to the trigeminal nerve; these branches may inner-

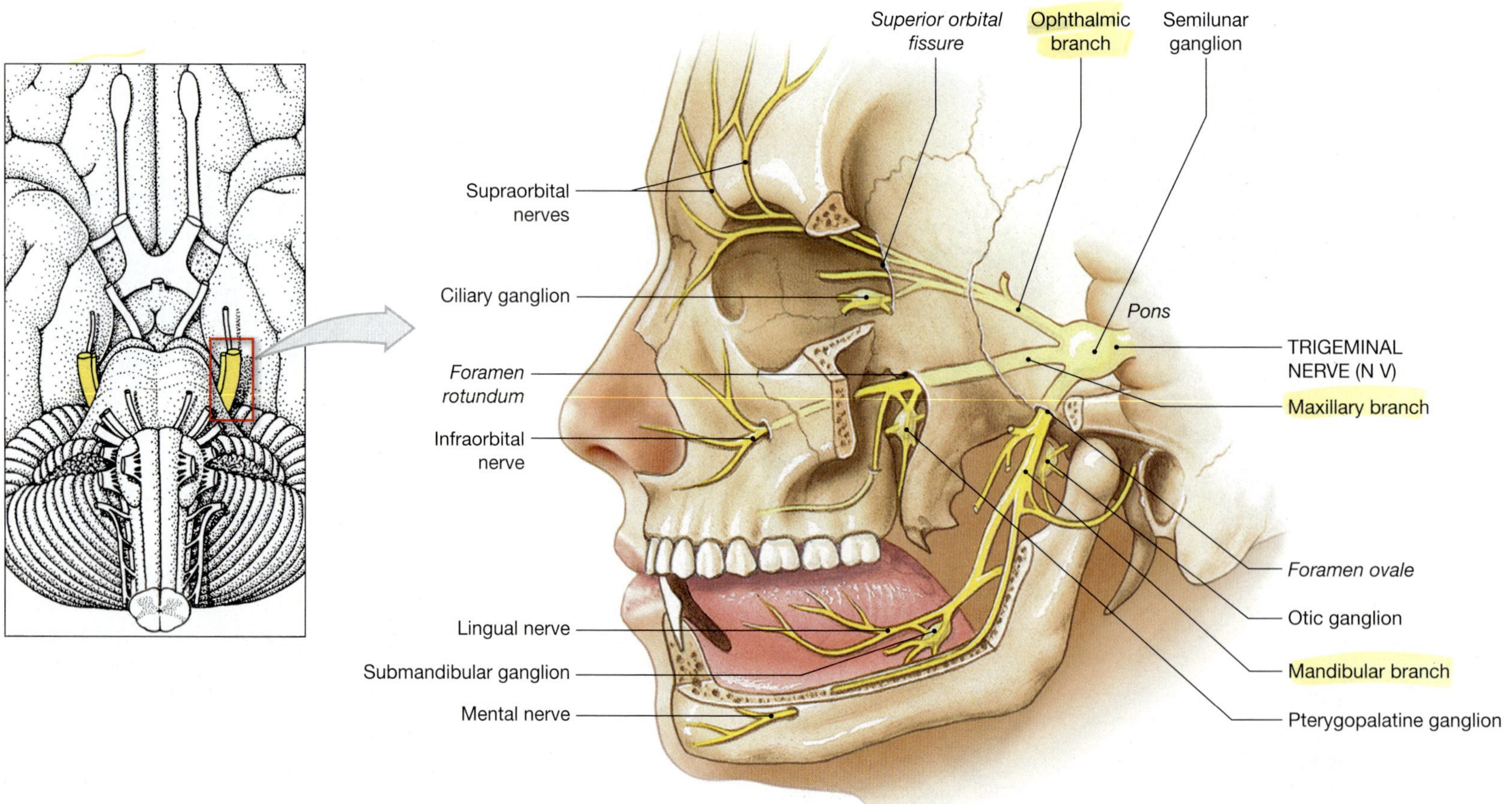

Figure 15.25 The Trigeminal Nerve

The Oculomotor Nerve (N III) [Figures 15.21/15.24]

Primary function: Motor, eye movements

Origin: Mesencephalon

Passes through: Superior orbital fissure of sphenoid ∞ p. 149

Destination: *Somatic motor:* superior, inferior, and medial rectus muscles; the inferior oblique muscle; the levator palpebrae superioris muscle ∞ p. 267

Visceral motor: intrinsic eye muscles

The mesencephalon contains the motor nuclei controlling the third and fourth cranial nerves. The **oculomotor nerves (N III)** emerge from the ventral surface of the mesencephalon (Figure 15.21) and penetrate the posterior orbital wall at the superior orbital fissure. The oculomotor nerve (Figure 15.24) controls four of the six extra-ocular muscles and the levator palpebrae superioris muscle, which raises the upper eyelid.

The oculomotor nerve also delivers preganglionic autonomic fibers to neurons of the **ciliary ganglion**. The ganglionic neurons control intrinsic eye muscles. These muscles change the diameter of the pupil, adjusting the amount of light entering the eye, and change the shape of the lens to focus images on the retina.

The Trochlear Nerve (N IV) [Figures 15.21/15.24]

Primary function: Motor, eye movements

Origin: Mesencephalon

Passes through: Superior orbital fissure of sphenoid ∞ p. 149

Destination: Superior oblique muscle ∞ p. 267

The **trochlear** (TRŌK-lē-ar; *trochlea*, pulley) **nerve**, smallest of the cranial nerves, innervates the superior oblique muscle of the eye (Figure 15.24). The motor nucleus lies in the ventrolateral portion of the mesencephalon, but the fibers emerge from the surface of the tectum to enter the orbit through the superior orbital fissure (Figure 15.21). The name *trochlear nerve* should remind you that the innervated muscle passes through a ligamentous sling, or *trochlea*, on its way to its insertion on the superior surface of the eye.

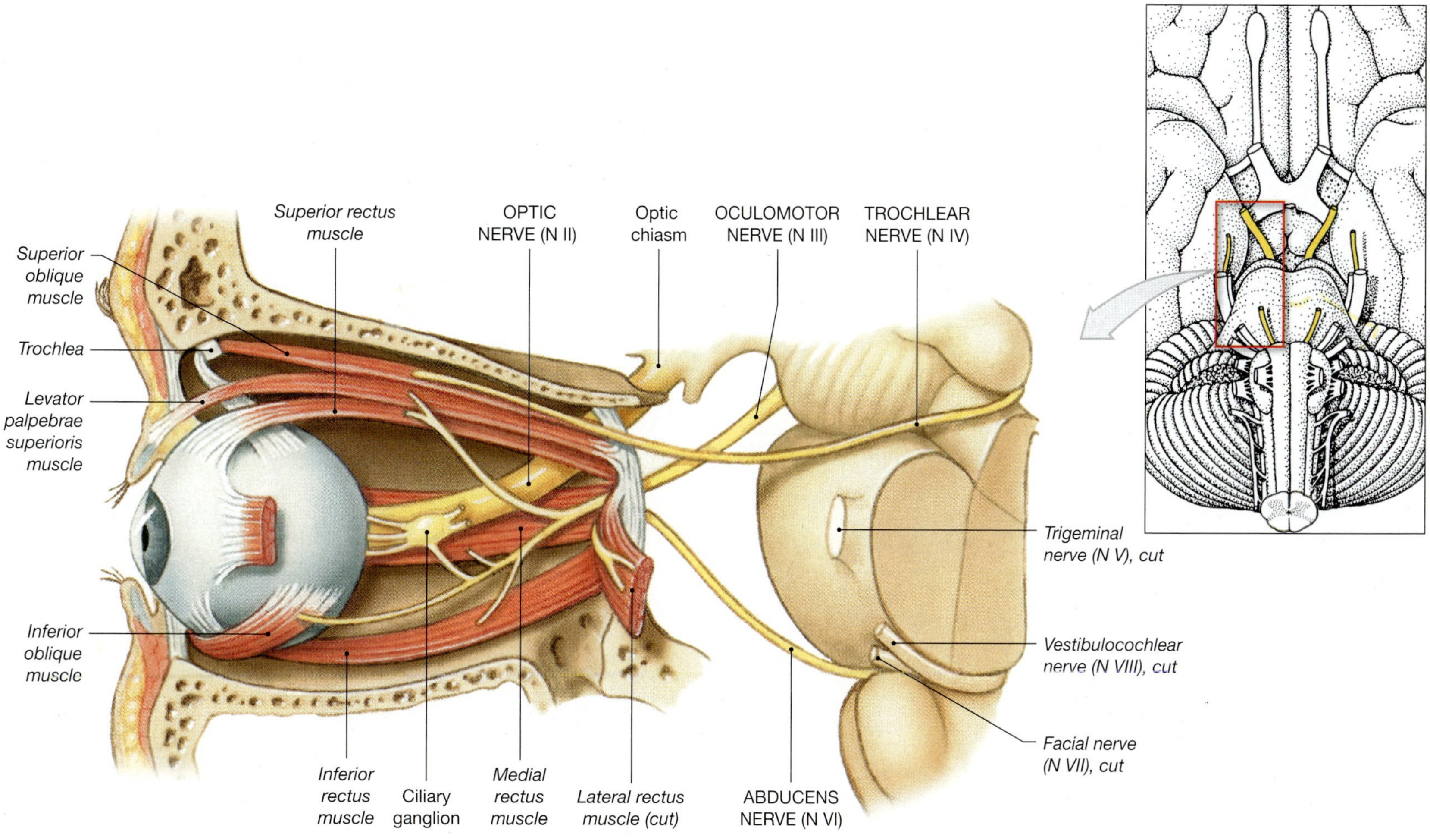

Figure 15.24 Cranial Nerves Controlling the Extra-Ocular Muscles

The Optic Nerve (N II) [Figures 15.21/15.23]

Primary function: Special sensory (vision)

Origin: Retina of eye

Passes through: Optic canal of sphenoid p. 149

Destination: Diencephalon by way of the optic chiasm

The **optic nerves (N II)** carry visual information from special sensory ganglia in the eyes. These nerves, diagrammed in Figure 15.23, contain about 1 million sensory nerve fibers. They pass through the optic canals of the sphenoid before converging at the ventral and anterior margin of the diencephalon, at the **optic chiasm** (*chiasma*, a crossing). At the optic chiasm, the medial fibers from each optic nerve cross over to the opposite, or contralateral, side of the brain, while the lateral fibers from each tract stay on the same, or ipsilateral, side of the brain. The reorganized axons continue toward the lateral geniculate nuclei of the thalamus as the **optic tracts** (Figures 15.21 and 15.23). After synapsing in the lateral geniculate nuclei, projection fibers deliver the information to the occipital lobe of the brain. This arrangement results in each cerebral hemisphere receiving visual information from the lateral half of the retina of the eye on that side and from the medial half of the retina of the eye on the opposite side. A relatively small number of axons in the optic tracts bypass the lateral geniculate nuclei and synapse in the superior colliculi of the mesencephalon. This pathway will be considered in Chapter 18.

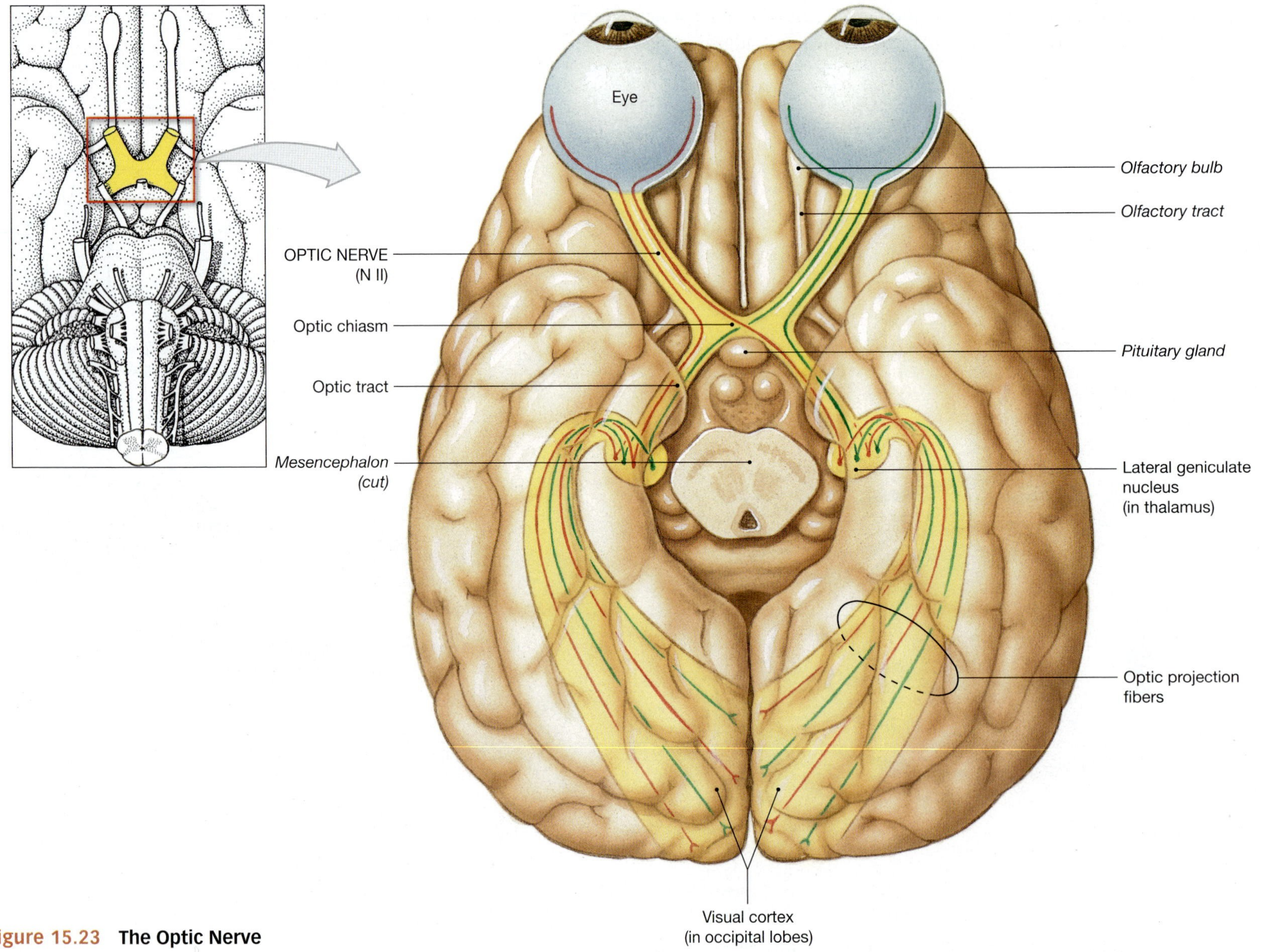

Figure 15.23 The Optic Nerve

16

The Nervous System

Pathways and Higher-Order Functions

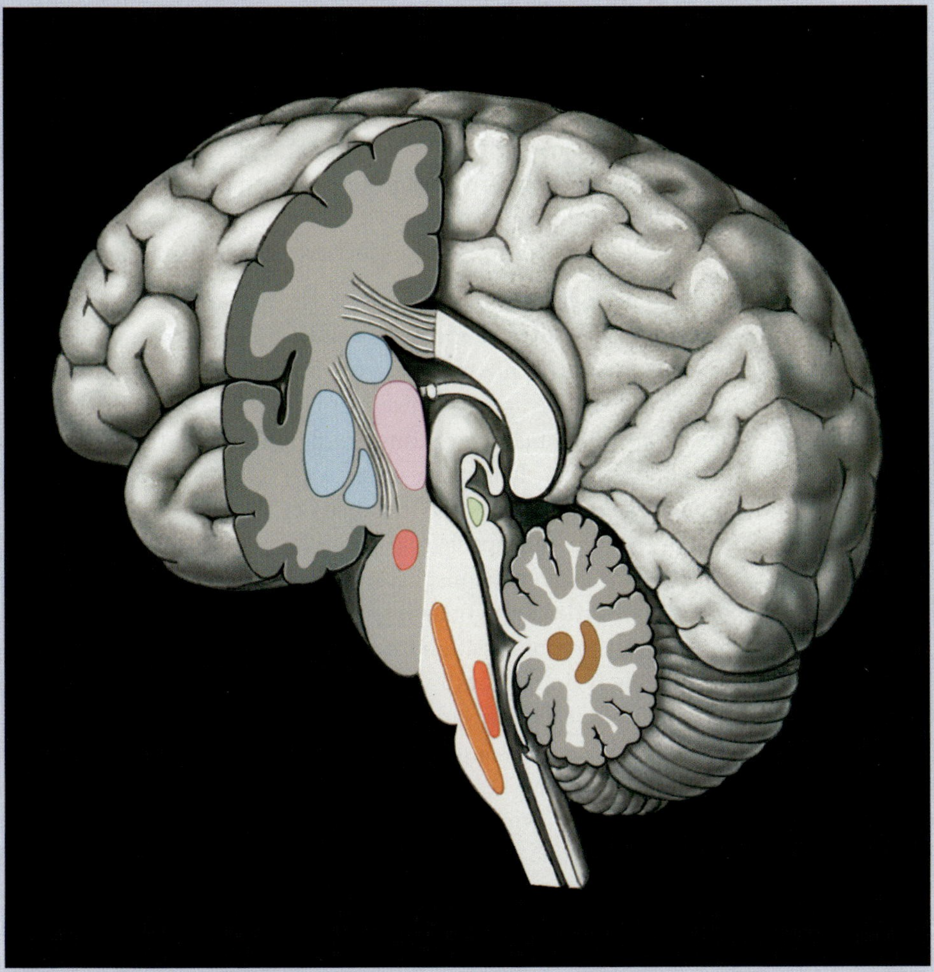

CHAPTER OBJECTIVES

1. Describe the functions of first-, second-, and third-order neurons.
2. Identify and describe the principal sensory pathways.
3. Identify and describe the corticospinal, medial, and lateral pathways.
4. Describe the anatomical structures that allow us to distinguish among sensations that originate in different areas of the body.
5. Identify the centers in the brain that interact to determine somatic motor output.
6. Identify and describe the integrative areas of the cerebral cortex and give their general functions.
7. Describe the significant functional differences between the left and right cerebral hemispheres.
8. Identify and describe the regions and structures of the brain involved in memory storage and recall.
9. Explain the structure of the reticular activating system and how it maintains consciousness.
10. Summarize the effects of aging on the nervous system.

There is a saying that "big cities never sleep." In Chicago or Los Angeles at 3:00 a.m., shops are open, deliveries are made, people are on the streets, and traffic moves briskly. The central nervous system is much more complex than any city, and far busier. There is a continuous flow of information between the brain, spinal cord, and peripheral nerves. At any given moment, millions of sensory neurons are delivering information to processing centers in the CNS, and millions of motor neurons are controlling or adjusting the activities of peripheral effectors. This process continues around the clock, whether we are awake or asleep. Your conscious mind may sleep soundly, but many brain stem centers are active throughout our lives, performing vital autonomic functions at the subconscious level.

Many subtle forms of interaction, feedback, and regulation link higher centers with the various components of the brain stem. Only a few are understood in any detail. In this chapter, we will focus on the anatomical design that allows neural structures to perform sensory and motor operations as well as higher-order brain functions, such as learning and memory.

Sensory and Motor Pathways

Communication between the CNS, the PNS, and peripheral organs and systems involves pathways that relay sensory and motor information between the periphery and higher centers of the brain. Each ascending (sensory) or descending (motor) pathway consists of a chain of tracts and associated nuclei. Processing usually occurs at several points along a pathway, wherever synapses relay signals from one neuron to another. The number of synapses varies from one pathway to another. For example, a sensory pathway ending in the cerebral cortex involves three neurons, whereas a sensory pathway ending in the cerebellum involves two neurons. Our attention will focus on pathways involving the major sensory and motor tracts of the spinal cord. In general, (1) these tracts are paired (bilaterally and symmetrically along the spinal cord) and (2) the axons within each tract are grouped according to the body region innervated. All tracts involve both the brain and spinal cord, and a tract name often indicates its origin and destination. If the name begins with *spino-*, the tract must *start* in the spinal cord and *end* in the brain; it must therefore carry sensory information. The last part of the name indicates a major nucleus or region of the brain near the end of the pathway. For example, the *spinocerebellar tract* begins in the spinal cord and ends in the cerebellum. If the name ends in *-spinal*, the tract must *start* in the brain and *end* in the spinal cord; it carries motor commands. Once again, the start of the name usually indicates the origin of the tract. For example, the *vestibulospinal tract* starts in the vestibular nucleus and ends in the spinal cord.

Sensory Pathways [Figures 16.1/16.2 and Table 16.1]

Sensory receptors monitor conditions both inside the body and in the external environment. When stimulated, a receptor passes information to the central nervous system. This information, called a **sensation**, arrives in the form of action potentials in an afferent (sensory) fiber. The complexity of the response to a particular stimulus depends in part on where processing occurs and where the motor response is initiated. For example, processing in the spinal cord can produce a very rapid, stereotyped motor response, such as a stretch reflex. ∞ p. 382 However, processing of sensory information within the brain stem may result in more complex motor activities, such as coordinated changes in the position of the eyes, head, neck, or trunk. Most of the processing of sensory information occurs in the spinal cord, thalamus, or brain stem; only about 1 percent of the information provided by afferent fibers reaches the cerebral cortex and our conscious awareness. However, the information arriving at the sensory cortex is organized so that we can determine the source and nature of the stimulus with great precision. Chapter 17 describes the distribution of visceral sensory information and considers reflexive responses to visceral sensations. Chapter 18 examines the origins of sensations and the pathways involved in relaying special sensory information, such as olfaction (smell) or vision, to conscious and subconscious processing centers in the brain.

We will describe three sensory pathways that deliver somatic sensory information to the sensory cortex of the cerebral or cerebellar hemispheres. These pathways involve a chain of neurons.

- A **first-order neuron** is the sensory neuron that delivers the sensations to the CNS; its cell body is in a dorsal root ganglion or a cranial nerve ganglion.
- A **second-order neuron** is an interneuron upon which the axon of the first-order neuron synapses. The second-order neuron's cell body may be located in either the spinal cord or the brain stem.
- In pathways ending at the cerebral cortex, the second-order neuron synapses on a **third-order neuron** in the thalamus. The axon of the third-order neuron carries the sensory information from the thalamus to the appropriate sensory area of the cerebral cortex.

In most cases, the axon of either the first-order or second-order neuron crosses over to the opposite side of the spinal cord or brain stem as it ascends. As a result of this crossover, or *decussation*, sensory information from the left side of the body is delivered to the right side of the brain, and vice versa. The functional or evolutionary significance of this decussation is unknown. In two of the sensory pathways (the *posterior column pathway* and the *spinothalamic pathway*), the axons of the third-order neurons ascend within the internal capsule to synapse on neurons of the primary sensory cortex of the cerebral hemisphere. Because decussation occurred at the level of the first-order or second-order neurons, the right cerebral hemisphere receives sensory information from the left side of the body, and vice versa.

Table 16.1 identifies and summarizes the three major somatic sensory pathways, also called *somatosensory pathways*: (1) the *posterior column pathway*, (2) the *spinothalamic pathway*, and (3) the *spinocerebellar pathway*. Figure 16.1 indicates their relative positions in the spinal cord. For clarity, the figure dealing with spinal pathways (Figure 16.2) shows how sensations originating on one side of the body are relayed to the cerebral cortex. Keep in mind, however, that these pathways are present on *both* sides of the body.

The Posterior Column Pathway [Figure 16.2a]

The **posterior column pathway**, or *medial lemniscal pathway* (Figure 16.2a), carries highly localized information from the skin and musculoskeletal system about proprioceptive (position), fine-touch, pressure, and vibration sensations. This pathway also carries information about the type of stimulus, the exact site of stimulation, and when the stimulus starts and stops. Therefore this pathway also provides you with information about "what," "where," and "when" for these sensations.

The axons of the first-order neurons reach the CNS through the dorsal roots of spinal nerves and the sensory roots of cranial nerves. Axons from the dorsal roots of spinal nerves ascend within the **fasciculus gracilis** or the **fasciculus cuneatus**, synapsing at the nucleus gracilis or the nucleus cuneatus in the medulla oblongata. The second-order neurons then relay the information to the thalamus of the opposite side of the brain along a tract called the **medial lemniscus** (*lemniskos*, ribbon). The decussation occurs as the axons of the second-order neurons leave the nuclei to enter the medial lemniscus. As it travels toward the thalamus, the medial lemniscus incorporates the same classes of sensory information (fine touch, pressure, and vibration) collected by cranial nerves V, VII, IX, and X.

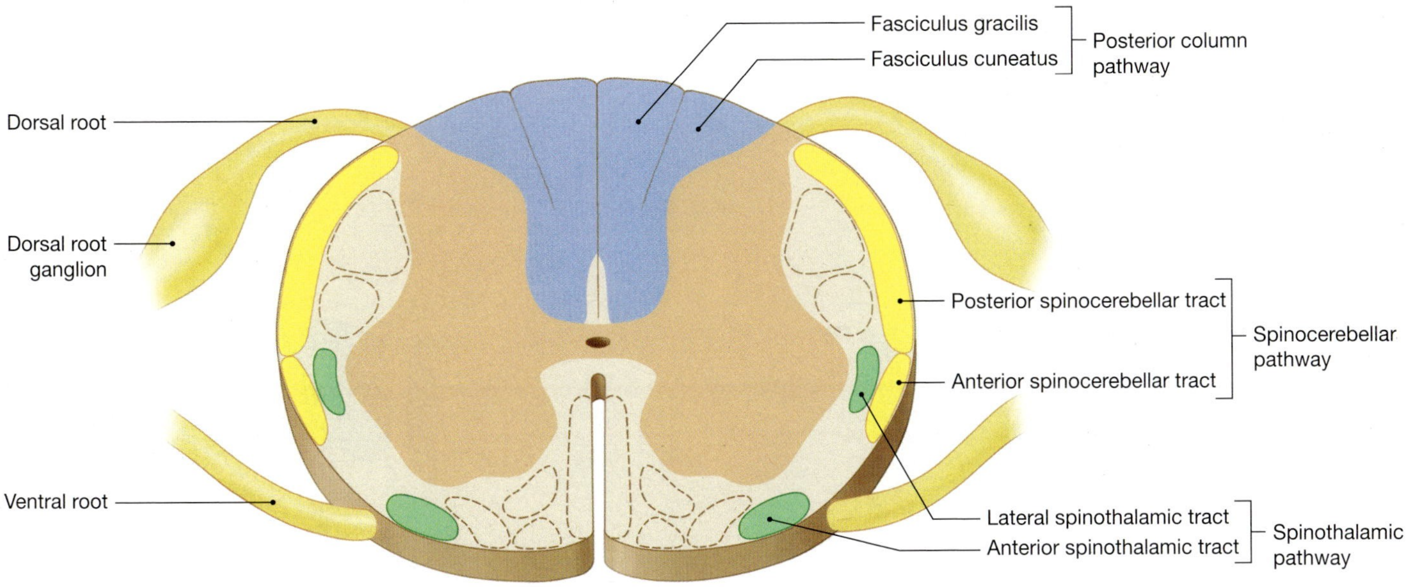

Figure 16.1 Ascending (Sensory) Pathways and Tracts in the Spinal Cord
A cross-sectional view indicating the locations of the major ascending (sensory) tracts in the spinal cord. For information about these tracts, *see Table 16.1*. Descending (motor) tracts are shown in dashed outline; these tracts are identified in *Figure 16.4*.

TABLE 16.1 Principal Ascending (Sensory) Pathways and the Sensory Information They Provide

Pathway/Tract	Sensations	Location of Neuron Cell Bodies: First-Order	Second-Order	Third-Order	Final Destination	Site of Crossover
POSTERIOR COLUMN PATHWAY						
Fasciculus gracilis	Proprioception, fine touch, pressure, and vibration from the inferior half of the body	Dorsal root ganglia of lower body; axons enter CNS in dorsal roots and ascend within fasciculus gracilis	Nucleus gracilis of medulla oblongata; axons cross over before entering medial lemniscus	Ventral posterolateral nucleus of thalamus	Primary sensory cortex on side opposite stimulus	Axons of second-order neurons, before joining medial lemniscus
Fasciculus cuneatus	Proprioception, fine touch, pressure, and vibration from the superior half of the body	Dorsal root ganglia of upper body; axons enter CNS in dorsal roots and ascend within fasciculus cuneatus	Nucleus cuneatus of medulla oblongata; axons cross over before entering medial lemniscus	Ventral posterolateral nucleus of thalamus	As above	As above
SPINOTHALAMIC PATHWAY						
Lateral spinothalamic tracts	Pain and temperature sensations	Dorsal root ganglia; axons enter CNS in dorsal roots and enter posterior gray horn	In posterior gray horn; axons enter lateral spinothalamic tract	Ventral posterolateral nucleus of thalamus	Primary sensory cortex on side opposite stimulus	Axons of second-order neurons, at level of entry
Anterior spinothalamic tracts	Crude touch and pressure sensations	As above	In posterior gray horn; axons enter anterior spinothalamic tract on opposite side	As above	As above	As above
SPINOCEREBELLAR PATHWAY						
Posterior spinocerebellar tracts	Proprioception	Dorsal root ganglia; axons enter CNS in dorsal roots	In posterior gray horn; axons enter posterior spinocerebellar tract on same side	Not present	Cerebellar cortex on side of stimulus	None
Anterior spinocerebellar tracts	Proprioception	As above	In same spinal segment; axons enter anterior spinocerebellar tract on same or opposite side	Not present	Cerebellar cortex, primarily on side of stimulus	Axons of most second-order neurons cross before entering tract and then cross again within cerebellum

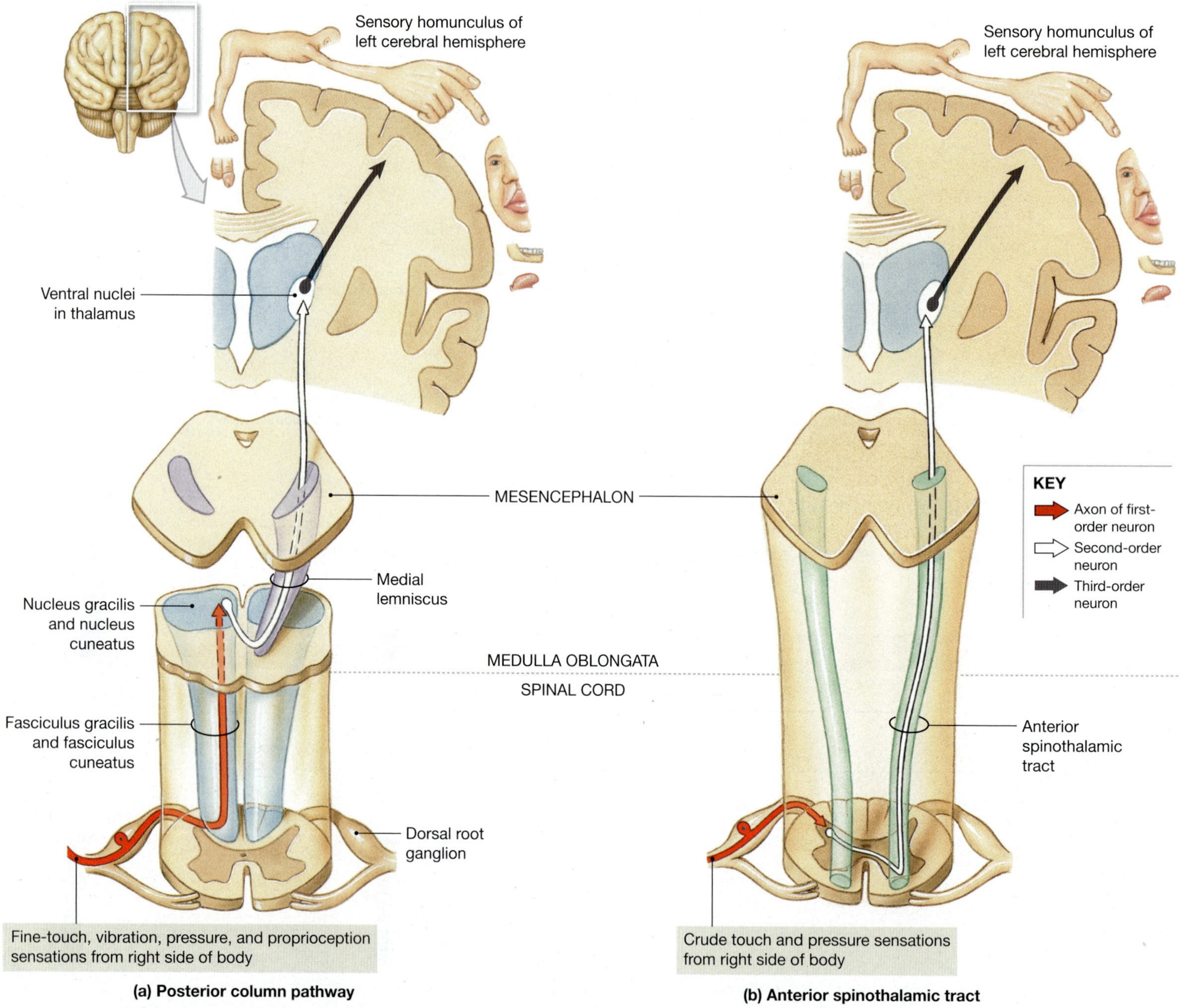

Figure 16.2 The Posterior Column, Spinothalamic, and Spinocerebellar Sensory Pathways
Diagrammatic comparison of first-, second-, and third-order neurons in ascending pathways. For clarity, this figure shows only the pathway for sensations originating on the right side of the body. **(a)** The posterior column pathway delivers fine-touch, vibration, and proprioception information to the primary sensory cortex of the cerebral hemisphere on the opposite side of the body. The crossover occurs in the medulla, after a synapse in the nucleus gracilis or nucleus cuneatus. **(b)** The anterior spinothalamic tract carries crude touch and pressure sensations to the primary sensory cortex on the opposite side of the body. The crossover occurs in the spinal cord at the level of entry. **(c)** The lateral spinothalamic tract carries sensations of pain and temperature to the primary sensory cortex on the opposite side of the body. The crossover occurs in the spinal cord, at the level of entry. **(d)** The spinocerebellar pathway carries proprioceptive information to the cerebellum. (Only one tract is detailed on each side, although each side has both tracts.)

Ascending sensory information maintains a strict regional organization along the pathway from center to center. p. 367 Sensory information entering the spinal cord inferior to T_6 travels to the medulla oblongata within the fasciculus gracilis, while sensory information entering the spinal cord at or superior to T_6 travels to the medulla oblongata within the fasciculus cuneatus. Sensory information in the posterior column pathway is integrated by the ventral posterolateral nucleus of the thalamus, which sorts data according to the region of the body involved and projects it to specific regions of the primary sensory cortex. The axons carrying the information from the thalamus to the sensory cortex are collectively known as *projection fibers*. The sensations arrive with sensory information from the toes at one end of the primary sensory cortex and information from the head at the other.

The individual "knows" the nature of the stimulus and its location because the information has been projected to a specific portion of the primary sensory cortex. If it is relayed to another part of the sensory cortex, the sensation will be perceived as having originated in a different part of the body. For example, the pain of a heart attack is often felt in the left arm; this is an example of referred pain, a topic addressed in Chapter 18. Our perception of a given sensation as touch, rather than as temperature or pain, depends on processing in the thalamus. If the cerebral cortex were damaged

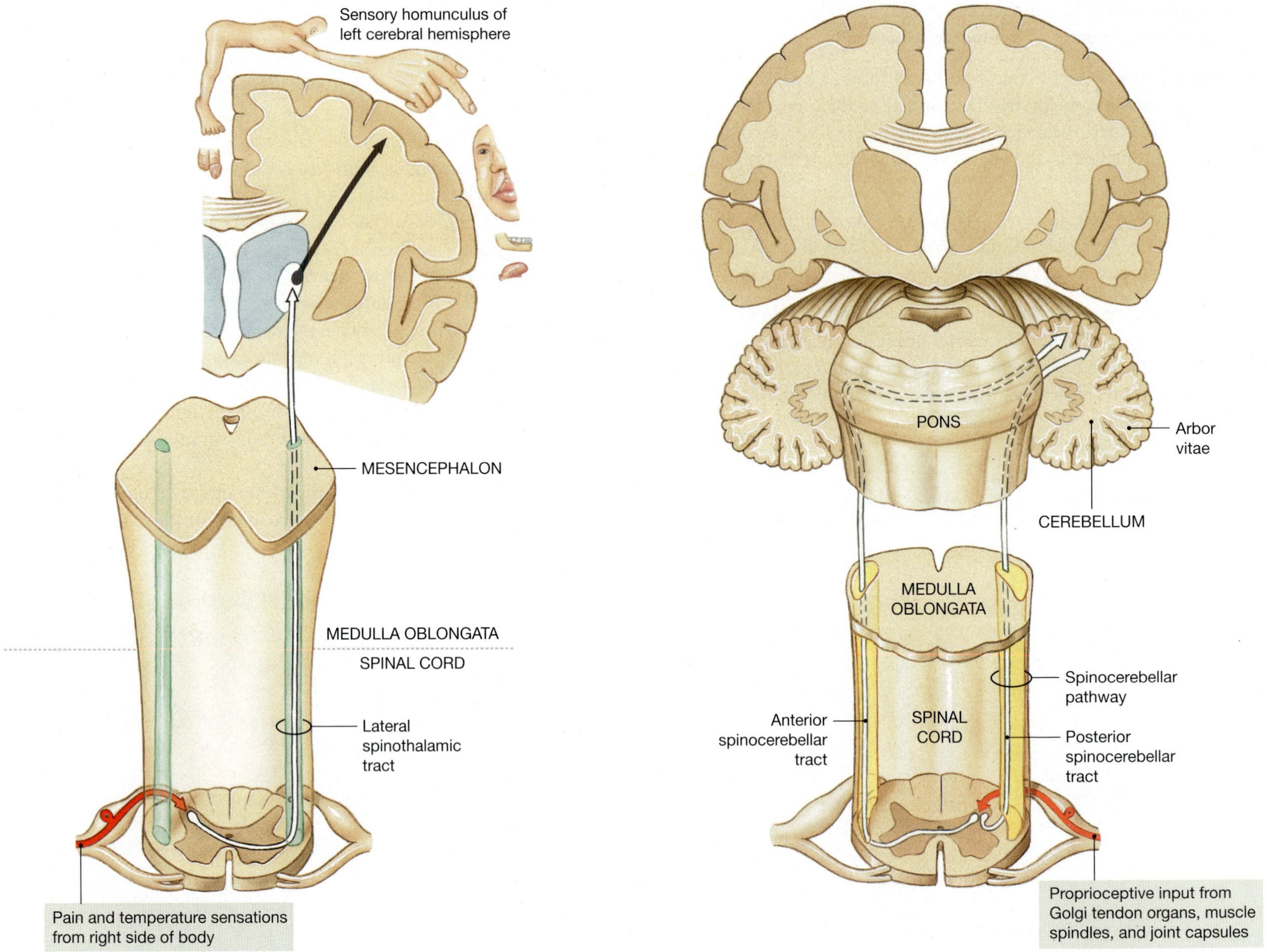

(c) Lateral spinothalamic tract

(d) Spinocerebellar pathway

Figure 16.2 ***(continued)***

or the projection fibers cut, a person could still be aware of a light touch because the thalamic nuclei remain intact. The individual, however, would be unable to determine its source, because localization is provided by the primary sensory cortex.

If a site on the primary sensory cortex is electrically stimulated, the individual reports feeling sensations in a specific part of the body. By electrically stimulating the cortical surface, investigators have been able to create a functional map of the primary sensory cortex (Figure 16.2a). This sensory map is called a **sensory homunculus** ("little man"). The proportions of the homunculus are obviously very different from those of the individual. For example, the face is huge and distorted, with enormous lips and tongue, whereas the back is relatively tiny. These distortions occur because the area of sensory cortex devoted to a particular region is proportional not to its absolute size but rather to *the number of sensory receptors* the region contains. In other words, it takes many more cortical neurons to process sensory information arriving from the tongue, which has tens of thousands of taste and touch receptors, than it does to analyze sensations originating on the back, where touch receptors are few and far between.

The Spinothalamic Pathway [Figure 16.2b,c]

The **spinothalamic pathway** (Figure 16.2b,c) carries sensations of pain, temperature, and "crude" sensations of touch and pressure. First-order spinothalamic neurons enter the spinal cord and synapse within the posterior gray horns. The axons of the second-order neurons cross to the opposite side of the spinal cord before ascending within the **anterior** and **lateral spinothalamic tracts**. These tracts converge on the ventral posterolateral nuclei of the thalamus. Projection fibers of third-order neurons then carry the information to the primary sensory cortex. Table 16.1 summarizes the origin and destination of these tracts and the associated sensations. For clarity, Figure 16.2 shows the distribution route for crude touch and pressure sensations and pain and temperature sensations from the right side of the body. However, both sides of the spinal cord have anterior and lateral spinothalamic tracts.

The Spinocerebellar Pathway [Figure 16.2d]

The **spinocerebellar pathway** carries proprioceptive information concerning the position of muscles, tendons, and joints to the cerebellum, which is responsible for fine coordination of body movements. The axons

of first-order sensory neurons synapse on second-order neurons in the posterior gray horns of the spinal cord. The axons of these neurons ascend in the **anterior** and **posterior spinocerebellar tracts** (Figure 16.2d).

- Axons that cross over to the opposite side of the spinal cord enter the anterior spinocerebellar tract and ascend to the cerebellar cortex by way of the superior cerebellar peduncle. These fibers then decussate a second time within the cerebellum to terminate in the ipsilateral cerebellum.[1]
- The posterior spinocerebellar tract carries axons that do not cross over to the opposite side of the spinal cord. These axons ascend to the cerebellar cortex by way of the inferior cerebellar peduncle.

Because the neurons of the spinocerebellar pathway do not synapse within the thalamus, this pathway carries proprioceptive information that will be processed at the subconscious level, as compared to the information carried to the cerebral cortex by the posterior column pathway.

Table 16.1 summarizes the origin and destination of these tracts and the associated sensations.

[1] The anterior spinocerebellar tract also contains relatively small numbers of uncrossed axons as well as axons that cross over and terminate in the contralateral cerebellum.

Motor Pathways [Figures 16.3/16.4]

The central nervous system issues motor commands in response to information provided by sensory systems. These commands are distributed by the somatic nervous system and the autonomic nervous system. The *somatic nervous system (SNS)* issues somatic motor commands that direct the contractions of skeletal muscles. The *autonomic nervous system (ANS)*, or *visceral motor system*, innervates visceral effectors, such as smooth muscles, cardiac muscle, and glands.

The motor neurons of the SNS and ANS are organized in different ways. Somatic motor pathways (Figure 16.3a) always involve at least two motor neurons: an **upper motor neuron**, whose cell body lies in a CNS processing center, and a **lower motor neuron** located in a motor nucleus of the brain stem or spinal cord. Activity in the upper motor neuron can excite or inhibit the lower motor neuron, but only the axon of the lower motor neuron extends to skeletal muscle fibers. Destruction of or damage to a lower motor neuron produces a flaccid paralysis of the innervated motor unit. Damage to an upper motor neuron may produce muscle rigidity, flaccidity, or uncoordinated contractions.

At least two neurons are involved in autonomic nervous system (ANS) pathways, and one of them is always located in the periphery (Figure 16.3b).

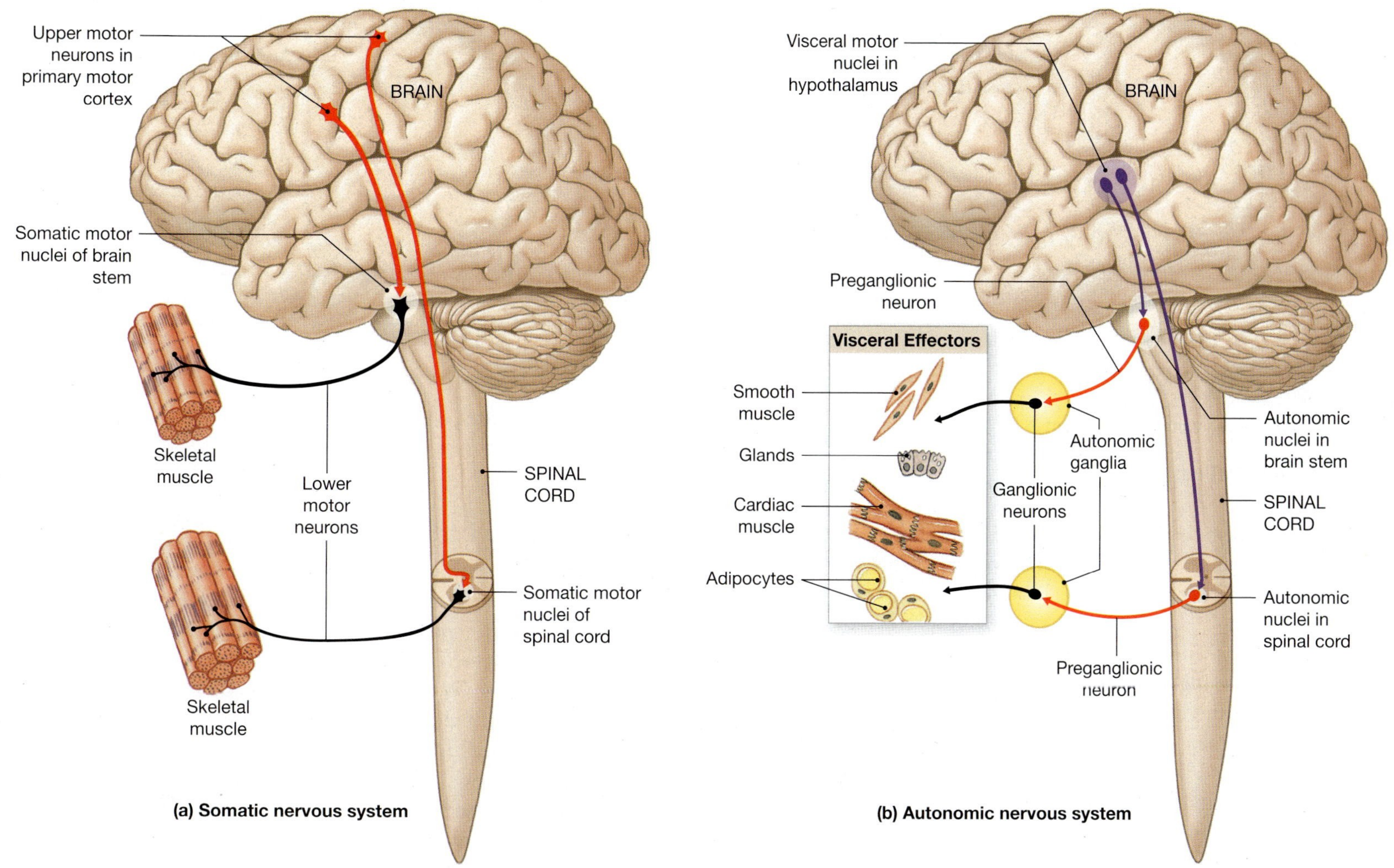

Figure 16.3 Motor Pathways in the CNS and PNS
Organization of the somatic and autonomic nervous systems. **(a)** In the SNS, an upper motor neuron in the CNS controls a lower motor neuron in the brain stem or spinal cord. The axon of the lower motor neuron has direct control over skeletal muscle fibers. Stimulation of the lower motor neuron always has an excitatory effect on the skeletal muscle fibers. **(b)** In the ANS, the axon of a preganglionic neuron in the CNS controls ganglionic neurons in the periphery. Stimulation of the ganglionic neurons may lead to excitation or inhibition of the visceral effector innervated.

Autonomic motor control involves a **preganglionic neuron** whose cell body lies within the CNS and a **ganglionic neuron** in a peripheral ganglion. Higher centers in the hypothalamus and elsewhere in the brain stem may stimulate or inhibit the preganglionic neuron. Motor pathways of the ANS will be described in Chapter 17.

Conscious and subconscious motor commands control skeletal muscles by traveling over three integrated motor pathways: the *corticospinal pathway*, the *medial pathway*, and the *lateral pathway*. Figure 16.4 indicates the positions of the associated motor tracts in the spinal cord. Activity within these motor pathways is monitored and adjusted by the basal nuclei and cerebellum. Their input stimulates or inhibits the activity of either (1) motor nuclei or (2) the primary motor cortex.

The Corticospinal Pathway [Figure 16.4]

The **corticospinal pathway**, sometimes called the *pyramidal system* (Figure 16.4a), provides voluntary control over skeletal muscles. This system begins at the *pyramidal cells* of the primary motor cortex. The axons of these upper motor neurons descend into the brain stem and spinal cord to synapse on lower motor neurons that control skeletal muscles. In general, the corticospinal pathway is direct: The upper motor neurons synapse directly on the lower motor neurons. However, the corticospinal pathway also works indirectly, as it innervates centers of the medial and lateral pathways.

The corticospinal pathway contains three pairs of descending tracts: (1) the *corticobulbar tracts*, (2) the *lateral corticospinal tracts*, and (3) the *anterior corticospinal tracts*. These tracts enter the white matter of the internal capsule, descend into the brain stem, and emerge on either side of the mesencephalon as the *cerebral peduncles*. p. 410

The Corticobulbar Tracts [Figure 16.4a and Table 16.2] Axons in the **corticobulbar** (kor-ti-kō-BUL-bar; *bulbar*, brain stem) **tracts** (Figure 16.4a and Table 16.2) synapse on lower motor neurons in the motor nuclei of cranial nerves III, IV, V, VI, VII, IX, XI, and XII. The corticobulbar tracts provide conscious control over skeletal muscles that move the eye, jaw, and face and some muscles of the neck and pharynx. The corticobulbar tracts also innervate the motor centers of the medial and lateral pathways. p. 416

The Corticospinal Tracts [Figure 16.4 and Table 16.2] Axons in the **corticospinal tracts** (Figure 16.4) synapse on lower motor neurons in the anterior gray horns of the spinal cord. As they descend, the corticospinal tracts are visible along the ventral surface of the medulla oblongata as a pair of thick bands, the **pyramids.** Along the length of the pyramids, roughly 85 percent of the axons cross the midline (decussate) to enter the descending **lateral corticospinal tracts** on the contralateral side of the spinal cord. The lateral corticospinal tract synapses on lower motor neurons in the anterior

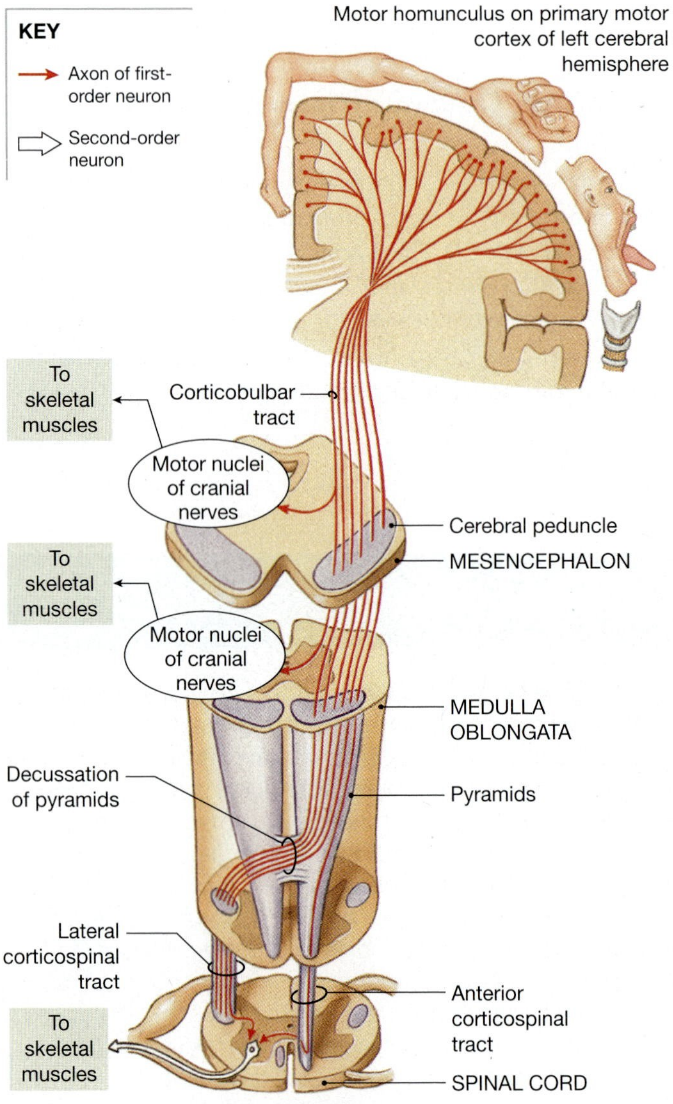

(a) Corticospinal pathway

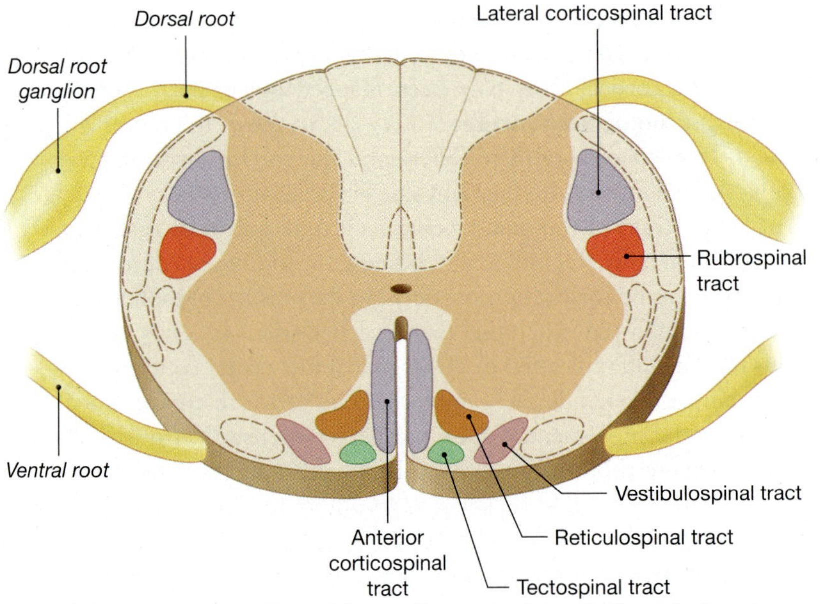

(b) Cross-sectional view of descending motor tracts in the spinal cord

Figure 16.4 The Corticospinal Pathway and Descending Motor Tracts in the Spinal Cord
(a) The corticospinal pathway originates at the primary motor cortex. The corticobulbar tracts end at the motor nuclei of cranial nerves on the opposite side of the brain. Most fibers in this pathway cross over in the medulla and enter the lateral corticospinal tracts; the rest descend in the anterior corticospinal tracts and cross over after reaching target segments in the spinal cord.
(b) A cross-sectional view indicating the locations of the major descending motor tracts that contain the axons of upper motor neurons. The origins and destinations of these tracts are listed in *Table 16.2*. Sensory tracts (*shown in Figure 16.1*) appear in dashed outline.

TABLE 16.2 Principal Descending (Motor) Pathways and the General Functions of the Associated Nuclei in the Brain

Pathway/Tract	Location of Upper Motor Neuron	Destination	Site of Crossover	Action
CORTICOSPINAL PATHWAY				
Corticobulbar tracts	Primary motor cortex (cerebral hemisphere)	Lower motor neurons of cranial nerve nuclei in brain stem	Brain stem	Conscious motor control of skeletal muscles
Lateral corticospinal tracts	As above	Lower motor neurons of anterior gray horns of spinal cord	Pyramids of medulla oblongata	As above
Anterior corticospinal tracts	As above	As above	Level of lower motor neuron	As above
MEDIAL PATHWAY				
Vestibulospinal tracts	Vestibular nucleus (at border of pons and medulla oblongata)	As above	None (uncrossed)	Subconscious regulation of balance and muscle tone
Tectospinal tracts	Tectum (mesencephalon: superior and inferior colliculi)	Lower motor neurons of anterior gray horns (cervical spinal cord only)	Brain stem (mesencephalon)	Subconscious regulation of eye, head, neck, and upper limb position in response to visual and auditory stimuli
Reticulospinal tracts	Reticular formation (network of nuclei in brain stem)	Lower motor neurons of anterior gray horns of spinal cord	None (uncrossed)	Subconscious regulation of reflex activity
LATERAL PATHWAY				
Rubrospinal tracts	Red nuclei of mesencephalon	As above	Brain stem (mesencephalon)	Subconscious regulation of upper limb muscle tone and movement

gray horns at all levels of the spinal cord. The other 15 percent continue uncrossed along the spinal cord as the **anterior corticospinal tracts**. At the spinal segment it targets, an axon in the anterior corticospinal tract decussates to the contralateral side of the spinal cord in the anterior white commissure. The upper motor neuron then synapses on lower motor neurons in the anterior gray horns of the cervical and superior thoracic regions of the spinal cord. Information concerning these tracts and their associated functions is summarized in Table 16.2.

The Motor Homunculus The activity of pyramidal cells in a specific portion of the primary motor cortex will result in the contraction of specific peripheral muscles. The identities of the stimulated muscles depend on the region of motor cortex that is active. As in the primary sensory cortex, the primary motor cortex corresponds point by point with specific regions of the body. The cortical areas have been mapped out in diagrammatic form, creating a **motor homunculus**. Figure 16.4a shows the motor homunculus of the left cerebral hemisphere and the corticospinal pathway controlling skeletal muscles on the right side of the body.

The proportions of the motor homunculus are quite different from those of the actual body (Figure 16.4a), because the motor area devoted to a specific region of the cortex is proportional to the number of motor units involved in the region's control rather than its actual size. As a result, the homunculus provides an indication of the degree of fine motor control available. For example, the hands, face, and tongue, all of which are capable of varied and complex movements, appear very large, whereas the trunk is relatively small. These proportions are similar to those of the sensory homunculus (Figure 16.2a, p. 434). The sensory and motor homunculi differ in other respects because some highly sensitive regions, such as the sole of the foot, contain few motor units, and some areas with an abundance of motor units, such as the eye muscles, are not particularly sensitive.

The Medial and Lateral Pathways [Figures 16.4b/16.5 and Table 16.2]

Several centers in the cerebrum, diencephalon, and brain stem may issue somatic motor commands as a result of processing performed at a subconscious level. pp. 397, 410, 414 These centers and their associated tracts were long known as the *extrapyramidal system (EPS)*, because it was thought that they operated independent of, and in parallel to, the *pyramidal system* (corticospinal pathway). This classification scheme is both inaccurate and misleading, because motor control is integrated at all

Clinical Note

Cerebral Palsy The term **cerebral palsy** refers to a number of disorders affecting voluntary motor performance that appear during infancy or childhood and persist throughout the life of the affected individual. The cause may be CNS trauma associated with premature or unusually stressful birth; maternal exposure to drugs, including alcohol; or a genetic defect that causes the improper development of motor pathways. Problems with labor and delivery may cause compression or interruption of placental circulation or oxygen supplies. If the oxygen concentration in fetal blood declines significantly for as little as 5–10 minutes, CNS function can be permanently impaired. The cerebral cortex, cerebellum, basal nuclei, hippocampus, and thalamus are particularly sensitive, and abnormalities in motor skills, posture and balance, memory, speech, and learning abilities can result.

levels through extensive feedback loops and interconnections. It is more appropriate to group these nuclei and tracts in terms of their primary functions: The components of the **medial pathways** help control gross movements of the trunk and proximal limb muscles, whereas those of the **lateral pathways** help control the distal limb muscles that perform more-precise movements.

The medial and lateral pathways can modify or direct skeletal muscle contractions by stimulating, facilitating, or inhibiting lower motor neurons. It is important to note that the axons of upper motor neurons in the medial and lateral pathways synapse on the same lower motor neurons innervated by the corticospinal pathway. This means that the various motor pathways interact not only within the brain, through interconnections between the primary motor cortex and motor centers in the brain stem, but also through excitatory or inhibitory interactions at the level of the lower motor neurons.

The Medial Pathway Control of muscle tone and gross movements of the neck, trunk, and proximal limb muscles is primarily transmitted by the medial pathway. The upper motor neurons of the medial pathway are located in the *vestibular nuclei*, the *superior* and *inferior colliculi*, and the *reticular formation* (**Figure 16.5**).

The vestibular nuclei receive information, over the vestibulocochlear nerve (N VIII), from receptors in the inner ear that monitor the position and movement of the head. These nuclei respond to changes in the orientation of the head, sending motor commands that alter the muscle tone, extension, and position of the neck, eyes, head, and limbs. The primary goal is to maintain posture and balance. The descending fibers in the spinal cord constitute the **vestibulospinal tracts** (**Figure 16.4b**).

The superior and inferior colliculi are located in the *tectum*, or roof, of the mesencephalon. p. 410 The colliculi receive visual (superior) and auditory (inferior) sensations, and these nuclei are involved in coordinating or directing reflexive responses to these stimuli. The superior colliculi receive auditory information relayed from the inferior colliculus, as well as collateral somatosensory information. The axons of upper motor neurons located in the superior colliculi descend in the **tectospinal tracts**. These axons cross to the opposite side immediately, before descending to synapse on lower motor neurons in the brain stem or spinal cord. Axons in the tectospinal tracts direct reflexive changes in the position of the head, neck, and upper limbs in response to bright lights, sudden movements, or loud noises.

The reticular formation is a loosely organized network of neurons that extends throughout the brain stem. The reticular formation receives input from almost every ascending and descending pathway. It also has extensive interconnections with the cerebrum, the cerebellum, and brain stem nuclei. Axons of upper motor neurons in the reticular formation descend in the **reticulospinal tracts** without crossing to the opposite side. The effects of reticular formation stimulation are determined by the region stimulated. For example, the stimulation of upper motor neurons in one portion of the reticular formation produces eye movements, whereas the stimulation of another portion activates respiratory muscles.

The Lateral Pathway Control of muscle tone and the movements of distal portions of the upper limbs is the primary information transmitted by the lateral pathway. The commands carried by the lateral pathway typically facilitate flexor muscles and inhibit extensor muscles. The upper motor neurons of the lateral pathway lie within the *red nuclei* of the mesencephalon. p. 410 Axons of upper motor neurons in the red nuclei cross to the opposite side of the brain and descend into the spinal cord in the **rubrospinal tracts** (*ruber*, red). In humans, the rubrospinal tracts are small and extend only to the cervical spinal cord. There they provide motor control over distal muscles of the upper limbs; normally, their role is insignificant as compared with that of the lateral corticospinal tracts. However, the rubrospinal tracts can be important in maintaining motor control and muscle tone in the upper limbs if the lateral corticospinal tracts are damaged.

Table 16.2 reviews the major motor tracts we discussed in this section.

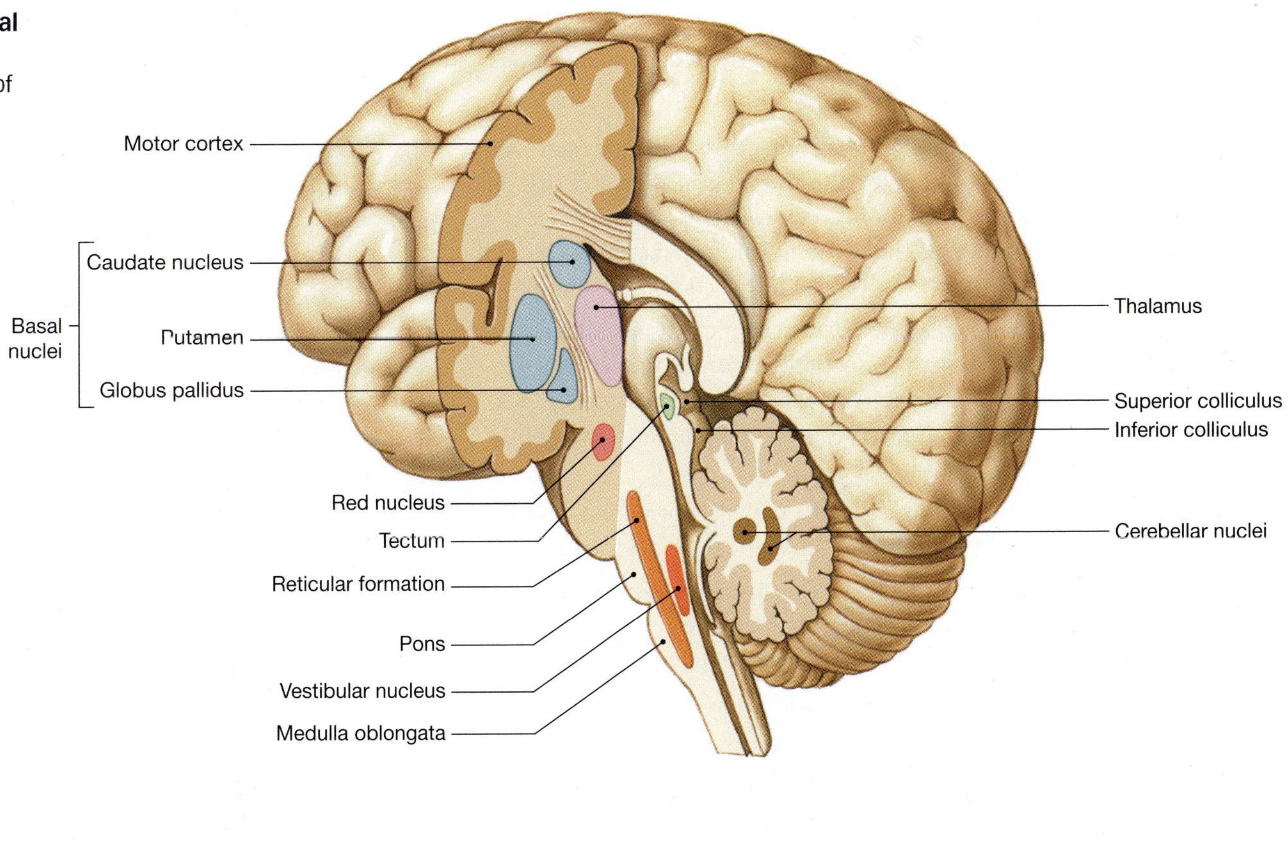

Figure 16.5 Nuclei of the Medial and Lateral Pathways
Cutaway view showing the location of major nuclei whose motor output is carried by the medial and lateral pathways. *See also Figure 15.11 and Table 15.4.*

Clinical Note

Amyotrophic Lateral Sclerosis Demyelinating disorders affect both sensory and motor neurons, producing losses in sensation and motor control. *Amyotrophic lateral sclerosis (ALS)* is a progressive disease that affects specifically motor neurons, leaving sensory neurons intact. As a result, individuals with ALS experience a loss of motor control, but have no loss of sensation or intellectual function. Motor neurons throughout the CNS are destroyed. Neurons involved with the innervation of skeletal muscles are the primary targets.

Symptoms of ALS generally do not appear until the individual is over age 40. ALS occurs at an incidence of three to five cases per 100,000 population worldwide. The disorder is somewhat more common among males than females. The pattern of symptoms varies with the specific motor neurons involved. When motor neurons in the cerebral hemispheres of the brain are the first to be affected, the individual experiences difficulty in performing voluntary movements and has exaggerated stretch reflexes. If motor neurons in other portions of the brain and the spinal cord are targeted, the individual experiences weakness, initially in one limb, but gradually spreading to other limbs and ultimately the trunk. When the motor neurons innervating skeletal muscles degenerate, a loss of muscle tone occurs. Over time, the skeletal muscles atrophy. The disease progresses rapidly, and the average survival after diagnosis is just three to five years. Because intellectual functions remain unimpaired, a person with ALS remains alert and aware throughout the course of the disease. This is one of the most disturbing aspects of the condition. Among well-known people who have developed ALS are baseball player Lou Gehrig and physicist Stephen Hawking.

The primary cause of ALS is uncertain; only 5–10 percent of ALS cases appear to have a genetic basis, with 5 percent of these genetic cases caused by a mutation in a gene that codes for an enzyme that protects the cell from harmful chemicals generated during metabolism. At the cellular level, it appears that the underlying problem is at the postsynaptic membranes of motor neurons. Treatment with riluzole, a drug that suppresses the release of glutamate (a neurotransmitter), has delayed the onset of respiratory paralysis and extended the life of ALS patients. The Food and Drug Administration (FDA) has approved this drug for clinical use.

The Basal Nuclei and Cerebellum [Figure 16.5]

The basal nuclei are clusters of gray matter within the cerebrum lateral to the thalamus (**Figure 16.5**). The basal nuclei and cerebellum are responsible for coordination and feedback control over muscle contractions, whether those contractions are consciously or subconsciously directed.

The Basal Nuclei Background patterns of movement involved in voluntary motor activities are provided by the basal nuclei. For example, they may control muscles that determine the background position of the trunk and limbs, or they may direct rhythmic cycles of movement, as in walking or running. The basal nuclei do not exert direct control over lower motor neurons; instead, they adjust the activities of upper motor neurons in the various motor pathways. The basal nuclei receive input from all portions of the cerebral cortex as well as from the substantia nigra.

The basal nuclei use four major pathways to adjust or establish patterns of movement:

1. One group of axons synapses on thalamic neurons, which then send their axons to the premotor cortex, the motor association area that directs activities of the primary motor cortex. This arrangement creates a feedback loop that changes the sensitivity of the pyramidal cells and alters the pattern of instructions carried by the corticospinal tracts.
2. The second group of axons synapses on thalamic neurons, which then send their axons to widespread association areas of the cerebral cortex. This arrangement creates a circuit whereby various association areas of the cerebral cortex can exert an effect upon motor activity of the cerebral cortex.
3. A third group of axons synapses in the reticular formation, altering the excitatory or inhibitory output of the reticulospinal tracts.
4. The fourth group of axons synapses on the superior colliculi of the mesencephalon and various areas of the cerebral cortex that control eye movements. This neural circuit affects rapid eye movements.

Two distinct populations of neurons exist: one that stimulates neurons by releasing acetylcholine (ACh) and another that inhibits neurons by the release of gamma aminobutyric acid (GABA). Under normal conditions, the excitatory interneurons are kept inactive and the tracts leaving the basal nuclei have an inhibitory effect on upper motor neurons. In *Parkinson's disease*, the excitatory neurons become more active, leading to problems with the voluntary control of movement. p. 410

If the primary motor cortex is damaged, the individual loses the ability to exert fine control over skeletal muscles. However, some voluntary movements can still be controlled by the basal nuclei. In effect, the medial and lateral pathways function as they usually do, but the corticospinal pathway cannot fine-tune the movements. For example, after damage to the primary motor cortex, the basal nuclei can still receive information about planned movements from the prefrontal cortex and can perform preparatory movements of the trunk and limbs. But, because the corticospinal pathway is inoperative, precise movements of the forearms, wrists, and hands cannot occur. An individual in this condition can stand, maintain balance, and even walk, but all movements are hesitant, awkward, and poorly controlled.

The Cerebellum Monitoring proprioceptive (position) sensations, visual information from the eyes, and vestibular (balance) sensations from the inner ear as movements are under way is one function of the cerebellum. pp. 412–414 Axons relaying proprioceptive information reach the cerebellar cortex in the spinocerebellar tracts. Visual information is relayed from the superior colliculi, and balance information is relayed from the vestibular nuclei. The output of the cerebellum affects upper motor neuron activity in the corticospinal, medial, and lateral pathways.

All motor pathways send information to the cerebellum when motor commands are issued. As the movement proceeds, the cerebellum monitors proprioceptive and vestibular information and compares the arriving sensations with those experienced during previous movements. It then adjusts the activities of the upper motor neurons involved. In general, any voluntary movement begins with the activation of far more motor units than are required—or even desirable. The cerebellum provides the necessary inhibition, reducing the number of motor commands to an efficient minimum. As the movement proceeds, the pattern and degree of inhibition change, producing the desired result.

The patterns of cerebellar activity are learned by trial and error, over many repetitions. Many of the basic patterns are established early in life; examples include the fine balancing adjustments you make while standing and walking. The ability to fine-tune a complex pattern of movement improves with practice, until the movements become fluid and automatic. Consider the relaxed, smooth movements of acrobats, golfers, and sushi chefs. These people move without thinking about the details of their movements. This ability is important, because when you concentrate on voluntary control, the rhythm and pattern of the movement usually fall apart as your primary motor cortex starts overriding the commands of the basal nuclei and cerebellum.

Levels of Somatic Motor Control [Figure 16.6]

Ascending information is relayed from one nucleus or center to another in a series of steps. For example, somatic sensory information from the spinal cord goes from a nucleus in the medulla oblongata to a nucleus in the thalamus before it reaches the primary sensory cortex. Information processing occurs at each step along the way. As a result, conscious awareness of the stimulus may be blocked, reduced, or heightened.

These processing steps are important, but they take time. Every synapse means another delay, and between conduction time and synaptic delays it takes several milliseconds to relay information from a peripheral receptor to the primary sensory cortex. Additional time will pass before the primary motor cortex orders a voluntary motor response.

This delay is not dangerous, because interim motor commands are issued by relay stations in the spinal cord and brain stem. While the conscious mind is still processing the information, neural reflexes provide an immediate response that can later be "fine-tuned." For example, if you touch a hot stove top, in the few milliseconds it takes for you to become consciously aware of the danger, you could be severely burned. But that doesn't happen, because your response (withdrawing your hand) occurs almost immediately, through a withdrawal reflex coordinated in the spinal cord. Voluntary motor responses, such as shaking the hand, stepping back, and crying out, occur somewhat later. In this case the initial reflexive response, directed by neurons in the spinal cord, was supplemented by a voluntary response controlled by the cerebral cortex. The spinal reflex provided a rapid, automatic, preprogrammed response that preserved homeostasis. The cortical response was more complex, but it required more time to prepare and execute.

Nuclei in the brain stem also are involved in a variety of complex reflexes. Some of these nuclei receive sensory information and generate appropriate motor responses. These motor responses may involve direct control over motor neurons or the regulation of reflex centers in other parts of the brain. **Figure 16.6** illustrates the various levels of somatic motor control from simple spinal reflexes to complex patterns of movement.

All of the levels of somatic motor control affect the activity of lower motor neurons. Reflexes coordinated in the spinal cord and brain stem are the simplest mechanisms of motor control. Higher levels perform more elaborate processing; as one moves from the medulla oblongata to the cerebral cortex, the motor patterns become increasingly complex and variable. For example, the respiratory rhythmicity center of the medulla oblongata sets a basic breathing rate. Centers in the pons adjust that rate in response to commands received from the hypothalamus (subconscious) or cerebral cortex (conscious).

The basal nuclei, cerebellum, mesencephalon, and hypothalamus control the most complicated involuntary motor patterns. Examples include motor patterns associated with eating and reproduction (hypothalamus), walking and body positioning (basal nuclei), learned movement patterns (cerebellum), and movements in response to sudden visual or auditory stimuli (mesencephalon).

Clinical Note

Anencephaly Although it may sound strange, physicians usually take a newborn infant into a dark room and shine a light against the skull. They are checking for **anencephaly** (an-en-SEF-a-lē), a rare condition in which the brain fails to develop at levels above the mesencephalon or lower diencephalon. The cranium typically does not develop at all, making diagnosis easy; if the cranial vault does develop, it is empty and translucent enough to transmit light.

Unless the condition is discovered right away, the parents may take the infant home, totally unaware of the problem. All the normal behavior patterns expected of a newborn are present, including suckling, stretching, yawning, crying, kicking, sticking fingers in the mouth, and tracking movements with the eyes. However, death will occur naturally over a period of days to months.

This tragic condition provides a striking demonstration of the role of the brain stem in controlling complex involuntary motor patterns. During normal development these patterns become incorporated into variable and versatile behaviors as control and analytical centers appear in the cerebral cortex.

As these events occur, cortical neurons continue to establish new interconnections that will have a long-term effect on the functional capabilities of the individual.

At the highest level are the complex, variable, and voluntary motor patterns dictated by the cerebral cortex. Motor commands may be given to specific motor neurons directly, or they may be given indirectly by altering the activity of a reflex control center. **Figure 16.6b,c** provides a simple diagram of the steps involved in the planning and execution of a voluntary movement.

During development, the control levels appear in sequence, beginning with the spinal reflexes. More complex reflexes develop as the neurons grow and interconnect. The process proceeds relatively slowly, as billions of neurons establish trillions of synaptic connections. At birth neither the cerebral nor the cerebellar cortex is fully functional, and their abilities take years to mature. A number of anatomical factors, noted in earlier chapters, contribute to this maturation:

1. Cortical neurons continue to increase in number until at least age 1.
2. The brain grows in size and complexity until at least age 4.
3. Myelination of CNS axons continues at least until age 1–2; peripheral myelination may continue through puberty.

CONCEPT CHECK

1. As a result of pressure on her spinal cord, Jill cannot feel touch or pressure on her legs. What spinal tract is being compressed?
2. What is the anatomical reason for the left side of the brain controlling motor function on the right side of the body?
3. An injury to the superior portion of the motor cortex would affect what part of the body?
4. Through which of the motor tracts would the following commands travel: (a) reflexive change of head position due to bright lights, (b) automatic alterations in limb position to maintain balance?

See blue "Answers" tab at back of book.

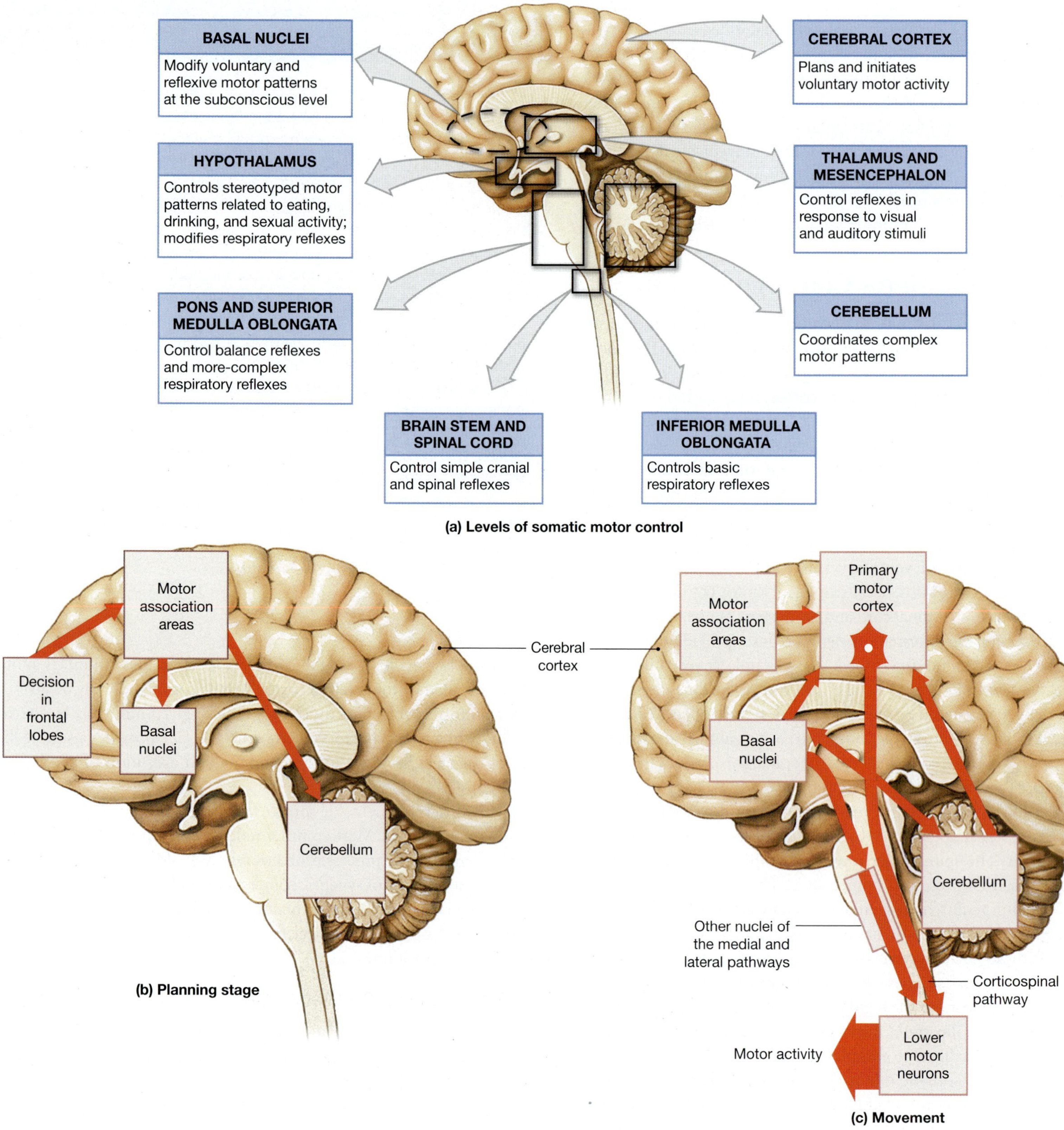

Figure 16.6 Somatic Motor Control
(a) Somatic motor control involves a series of levels, with simple spinal and cranial reflexes at the bottom and complex voluntary motor patterns at the top. **(b)** The planning stage: When a conscious decision is made to perform a specific movement, information is relayed from the frontal lobes to motor association areas. These areas in turn relay the information to the cerebellum and basal nuclei. **(c)** Movement: As the movement begins, the motor association areas send instructions to the primary motor cortex. Feedback from the basal nuclei and cerebellum modifies those commands, and output along the medial and lateral pathways directs involuntary adjustments in position and muscle tone.

Higher-Order Functions

Higher-order functions have the following characteristics:

1. They are performed by the cerebral cortex.
2. They involve complex interconnections and communication between areas within the cerebral cortex and between the cerebral cortex and other areas of the brain.
3. They involve both conscious and unconscious information processing.
4. They are not part of the programmed "wiring" of the brain; therefore, the functions are subject to modification and adjustment over time.

Our discussion of higher-order functions begins by identifying the cortical areas involved and considering functional differences between the left and right cerebral hemispheres. We will then briefly consider the mechanisms of memory, learning, and consciousness.

Integrative Regions of the Cerebral Cortex [Figure 16.7]

The sensory, motor, and association areas of the cerebral hemispheres were introduced in Chapter 15. ∞ p. 397 **Figure 16.7a** reviews the major cortical regions of the left cerebral hemisphere. Scanning data, electrical monitoring, and clinical observation have shown that several cortical areas integrate complex sensory stimuli and motor responses. These centers (**Figure 16.7b**) include the *general interpretive area*, the *speech center*, and the *prefrontal cortex*.

The General Interpretive Area

The **general interpretive area**, or *gnostic area*, receives information from all the sensory association areas. This analytical center is present in only one hemisphere, usually the left. Damage to the general interpretive area affects the ability to interpret what is read or heard, even though the words

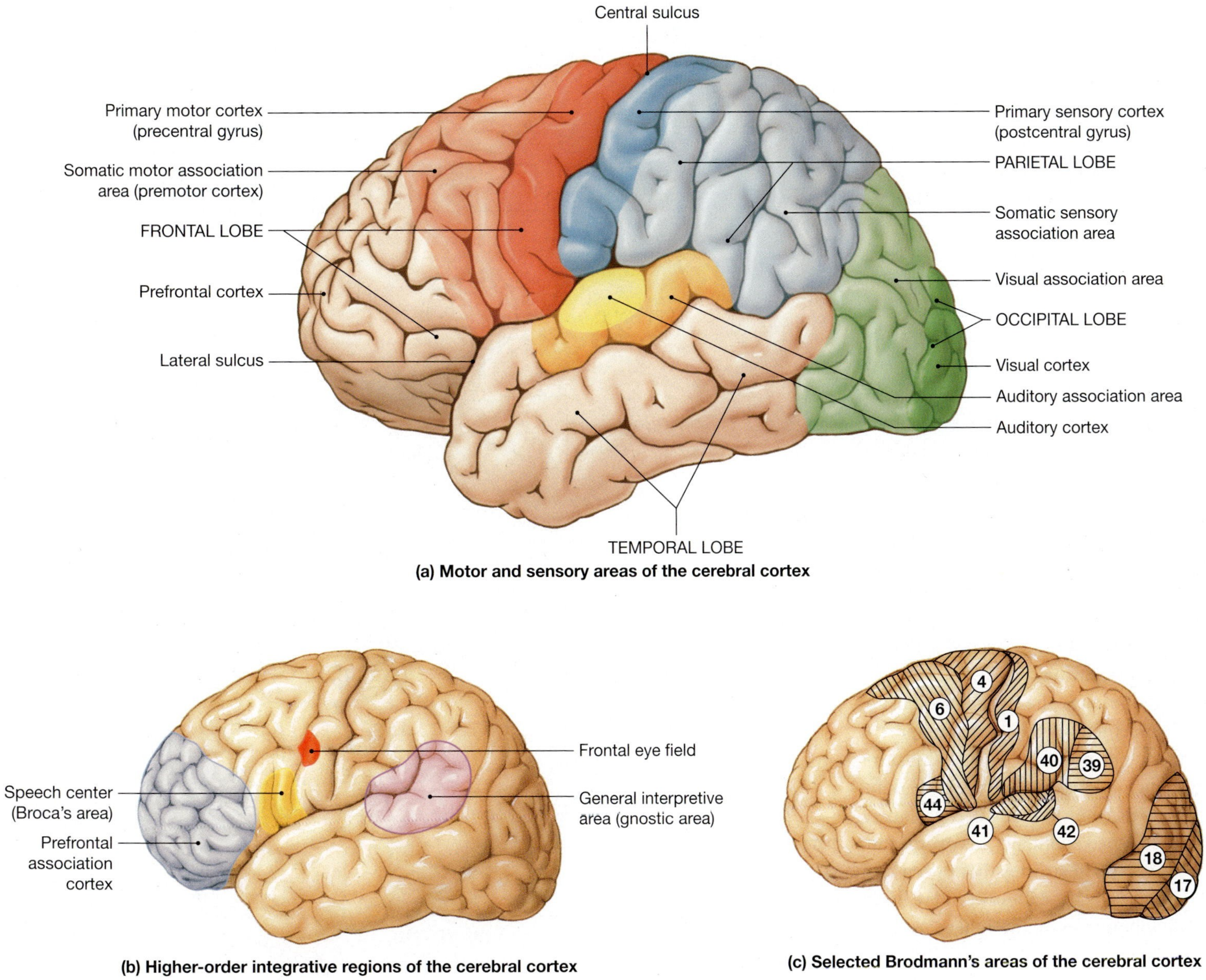

Figure 16.7 Functional Areas of the Cerebral Cortex
(a) Motor, sensory, and special sensory areas of the cerebral cortex that are found in both cerebral hemispheres. **(b)** The left hemisphere usually contains the general interpretive area and the speech center. Other specializations of the two cerebral hemispheres are shown in *Figure 16.8*. **(c)** These are some of the Brodmann areas of the cerebral cortex, each characterized by a distinctive pattern of cellular organization. Compare these anatomical regions with the functional zones shown in parts (a) and (b).

are understood as individual entities. For example, an individual might understand the meaning of the words *sit* and *here* but be totally bewildered by a request to "sit here."

The Speech Center

Efferents from the general interpretive area target the **speech center**, or *Broca's area.* This center lies along the edge of the premotor cortex in the same hemisphere as the general interpretive area. The speech center is a motor center that regulates the patterns of breathing and vocalization needed for normal speech. The corresponding regions on the opposite hemisphere are not "inactive," but their functions are less well defined. Damage to the speech center can manifest itself in various ways. Some individuals have difficulty speaking, although they know exactly what words to use; others talk constantly but use all the wrong words.

The Prefrontal Cortex

The **prefrontal cortex**, or *prefrontal association area*, of the frontal lobe is the most complex brain area. It has extensive connections with other cortical areas and with other portions of the brain, such as the limbic system. The prefrontal cortex performs complicated learning and reasoning functions. Through its interconnections with the limbic system, it also provides emotional context and motivation. The prefrontal cortex performs such abstract intellectual functions as predicting the future consequences of events or actions. Damage to the prefrontal cortex leads to difficulties in estimating the temporal relationships between events; questions such as "How long ago did this happen?" or "What happened first?" become difficult to answer.

Feelings of frustration, tension, and anxiety are generated at the prefrontal cortex as it interprets ongoing events and makes predictions about future situations or consequences. If the connections between the prefrontal cortex and other brain regions are severed, the tensions, frustrations, and anxieties are removed. Through the mid-twentieth century, this rather drastic procedure, called a **prefrontal lobotomy**, was used to "cure" a variety of mental illnesses, especially those associated with violent or antisocial behavior.

After a lobotomy, the patient would no longer be concerned about what had previously been a major problem, whether psychological (hallucinations) or physical (severe pain). However, the individual was often equally unconcerned about tact, decorum, and toilet training. Now that drugs have been developed to target specific pathways and regions of the CNS, lobotomies are no longer used to control behavior.

Brodmann Areas and Cortical Function [Figure 16.7c]

In the early 1900s, several attempts were made to describe and classify regional differences in the histological organization of the cerebral

Clinical Note

Damage to the Integrative Centers **Aphasia** (*a-*, without + *phasia*, speech) is a disorder affecting the ability to speak or read. Extreme aphasia, or **global aphasia**, results from extensive damage to the general interpretive area or to the associated sensory tracts. Affected individuals are totally unable to speak, to read, or to understand or interpret the speech of others. Recovery is possible when the condition results from edema or hemorrhage, but the process often takes months or even years.

Dyslexia (*lexis*, diction) is a disorder affecting the comprehension of written words. **Developmental dyslexia** affects children; there are estimates that up to 15 percent of children in the United States suffer from some degree of dyslexia. These children have difficulty reading and writing, although their other intellectual functions may be normal or above normal. Their writing looks uneven and disorganized, with letters reversed or written in the wrong order more frequently than in the writing of unaffected children. Recent evidence suggests that at least some forms of dyslexia result from problems in processing and sorting visual information in the occipital and temporal lobes.

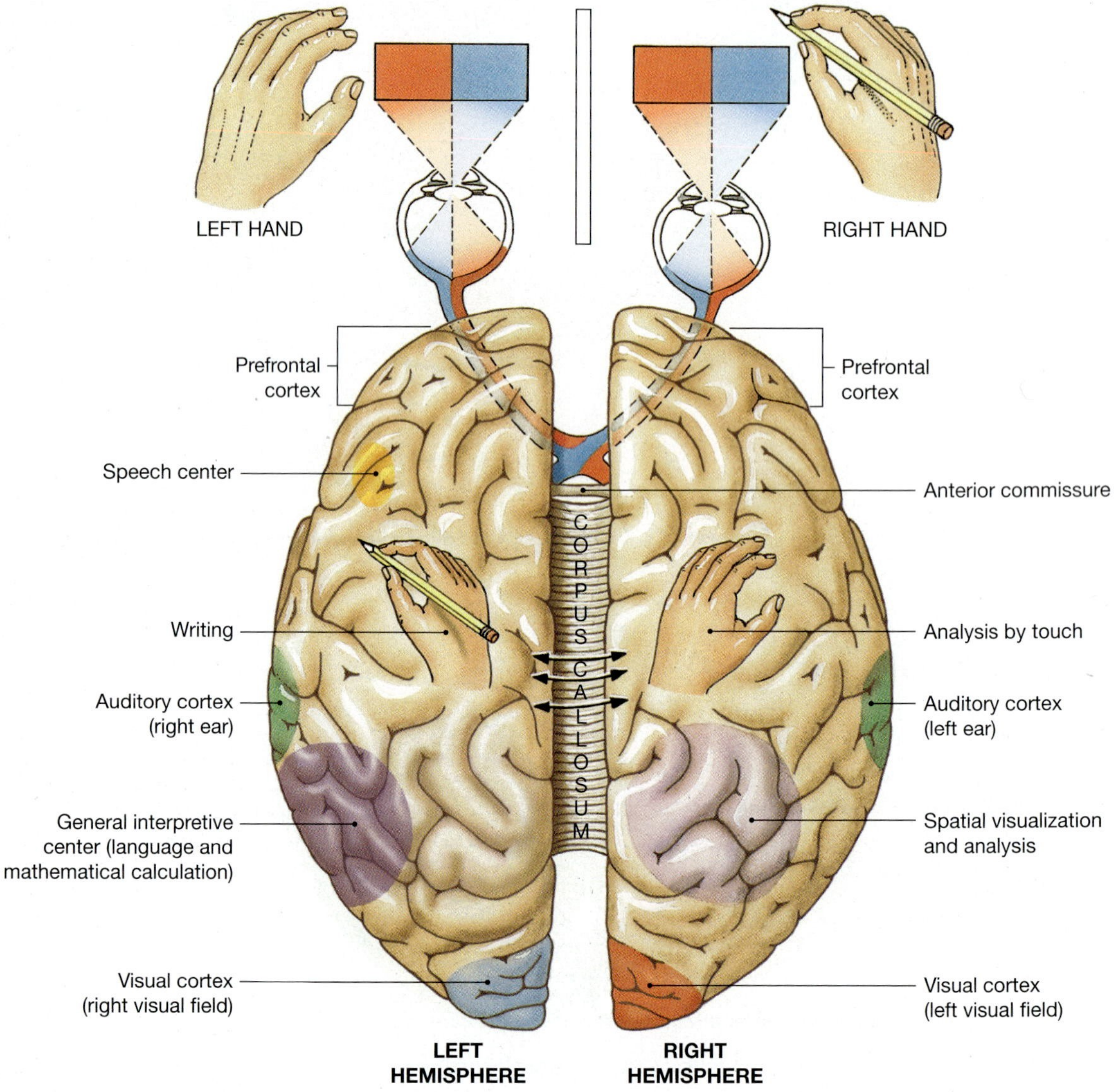

Figure 16.8 Hemispheric Specialization
Functional differences between the left and right cerebral hemispheres. Notice that special sensory information is relayed to the cerebral hemisphere on the opposite side of the body. Chapter 18 will provide additional details on these pathways.

cortex. It was hoped that the patterns of cellular organization could be correlated to specific sensory, motor, and integrative functions. By 1919, at least 200 different patterns had been described, and most of the classification schemes have since been abandoned. However, the cortical map prepared by Brodmann in 1909 has proved useful to neuroanatomists. Brodmann described 47 different patterns of cellular organization in the cerebral cortex. Several of these *Brodmann areas* are shown in **Figure 16.7c**. Some correspond to known functional areas. For example, Brodmann's area 44 corresponds to the motor speech center, and area 4 follows the contours of the primary motor cortex. In other cases, the correspondence is less precise. For example, Brodmann's area 1 lies within the primary sensory cortex.

Hemispheric Specialization [Figures 16.7a/16.8]

The regions seen in **Figure 16.7a** are present on both hemispheres, but the higher-order functions are not equally distributed. **Figure 16.8** indicates the major functional differences between the hemispheres. Higher-order centers in the left and right hemispheres have different but complementary functions. Some motor functions and capabilities primarily reflect the activities of one of the two cerebral hemispheres. For example, the speech center and the general interpretive center are usually in the same cerebral hemisphere, which is known as the **categorical hemisphere**. This hemisphere is also called the *dominant hemisphere* because it usually determines handedness as well; the left hemisphere is the categorical hemisphere in most right-handed people.

In contrast, spatial perception, the recognition of faces, the emotional context of language, and the appreciation of music are characteristic of the **representational hemisphere**, or *nondominant hemisphere.* The right cerebral hemisphere analyzes sensory information and relates the body to the sensory environment. Interpretive centers in this hemisphere permit identification of familiar objects by touch, smell, taste, or feel.

Interestingly, there may be a link between being right- or left-handed and sensory and spatial abilities. An unusually high percentage of musicians and artists are left-handed; the complex motor activities performed by these individuals are directed by the primary motor cortex and association areas on the right (representational) hemisphere.

Hemispheric specialization does not mean that the two hemispheres are independent, merely that certain centers have evolved to process information gathered by the system as a whole. The intercommunication occurs over commissural fibers, especially those of the corpus callosum. p. 401 The corpus callosum alone contains more than 200 million axons, carrying an estimated 4 billion impulses per second!

Memory

Memory is a higher-order function that involves considerable interaction between the cerebral cortex and other areas of the brain. Memory is the process of accessing stored bits of information gathered through experience; these bits of information are called *memories*, or *memory engrams.* Some memories can be retrieved voluntarily and expressed verbally, as when you recall and recite a phone number. Other memories are retrieved subconsciously; for example, when hungry, you may salivate at the smell of food. There are *short-term memories* that last seconds to hours, and *long-term memories* that can last for years. Each type of memory involves different anatomical structures. The conversion from a short-term to a long-term memory is called *memory consolidation.*

Two components of the limbic system, the amygdaloid body and the hippocampus, are essential to memory consolidation. pp. 401–404 Damage to either of those areas will interfere with normal memory consolidation. Damage to the hippocampus leads to an immediate loss of short-term memory, although long-term memories remain intact and accessible. Tracts leading from the amygdaloid body to the hypothalamus may link memories to specific emotions. A cerebral nucleus near the diencephalon, the *nucleus basalis*, plays an uncertain role in memory storage and retrieval. Tracts connect this nucleus with the hippocampus, the amygdaloid body, and all areas of the cerebral cortex. Damage to this nucleus is associated with changes in emotional states, memory, and intellectual function. (See the discussion of Alzheimer's disease later in this chapter.)

Long-term memories are stored in the cerebral cortex. Conscious motor and sensory memories are referred to the appropriate association areas. For example, visual memories are stored in the visual association area, and memories of voluntary motor activity are stored in the premotor cortex. Special portions of the occipital and temporal lobes retain memories of facial images, sounds of voices, and pronunciation of words.

Amnesia refers to the loss of memory from disease or trauma. The type of memory loss depends on the specific regions of the brain affected. Damage to sensory association areas produces memory loss of sensations arriving at the adjacent sensory cortex. Damage to thalamic and limbic structures, especially the hippocampus, will affect memory storage and consolidation. Amnesia may occur suddenly or progressively, and recovery may be complete, partial, or nonexistent, depending on the nature of the problem.

In retrograde amnesia (retro-, behind), the individual loses memories of past events. Some degree of retrograde amnesia commonly follows a head injury; after a car wreck or a fall, many victims are unable to remember the moments preceding the accident. In anterograde amnesia (antero-, ahead), an individual may be unable to store additional memories, but earlier memories remain intact and accessible. The problem appears to involve an inability to generate long-term memories. Some degree of anterograde amnesia is a common sign of senility, a condition discussed further on p. 447.

Clinical Note

Disconnection Syndrome Communication across the corpus callosum permits the integration of sensory information and motor commands. Yet the two hemispheres are significantly different in terms of their ongoing processing activities. Otherwise untreatable seizures may sometimes be "cured" by severing the corpus callosum. This surgery produces symptoms of **disconnection syndrome**. In this condition the two hemispheres function independently, each remaining "unaware" of stimuli or motor commands involving its counterpart. The result is a number of rather interesting changes in the individual's abilities. For example, objects touched by the left hand can be recognized but not verbally identified, because the sensory information arrives at the right hemisphere and the speech center is on the left. The object can be verbally identified if felt with the right hand, but the person will not be able to say whether it is the same object previously touched with the left hand. This problem with cross-referencing sensory information applies to all incoming sensations.

Two years after a surgical sectioning of the corpus callosum, the most striking behavioral abnormalities have disappeared, and the individual may test normally. In addition, individuals born without a functional corpus callosum do not show obvious sensory or motor deficits. In some way, the CNS adapts to the situation, probably by increasing the amount of information transferred across the anterior commissure.

CONCEPT CHECK

1. After suffering a head injury in an automobile accident, David has difficulty comprehending what he hears or reads. This problem might indicate damage to what portion of the brain?
2. Kyle has difficulty speaking; he talks continuously, but uses incorrect words. What center or area of the brain is probably involved?
3. What is memory consolidation?
4. Gina cannot perform abstract intellectual functions such as predicting the future consequences of her actions. What part of her brain is affected?

See blue "Answers" tab at back of book.

Consciousness: The Reticular Activating System [Figure 16.9 and Table 16.3]

A conscious individual is alert and attentive; an unconscious individual is not. The difference is obvious, but there are many gradations of both the conscious and unconscious states (Table 16.3). The state of consciousness experienced by an individual is determined by complex interactions between the brain stem and the cerebral cortex. One of the most important brain stem components is the **reticular activating system (RAS)**, a poorly defined network in the reticular formation. The RAS extends from the mesencephalon to the medulla oblongata (Figure 16.9). The output of the RAS projects throughout the cerebral cortex. When the RAS is inactive, so is the cerebral cortex; stimulation of the RAS produces a widespread activation of the cerebral cortex. The primary function of this activation is to keep the individual alert and conscious; if the level of cortical activity starts declining, the person gradually becomes increasingly lethargic and eventually becomes unconscious.

The mesencephalic portion of the RAS appears to be the control center of the system, and stimulation of this area produces the most pronounced and long-lasting effects on the cerebral cortex. Stimulating other portions of the RAS seems to have an effect only insofar as it changes the activity of the mesencephalic region. The greater the stimulation to the mesencephalic region of the RAS, the more alert and attentive the individual will be to incoming sensory information. Associated nuclei in the thalamus play a supporting role by focusing attention on specific mental processes.

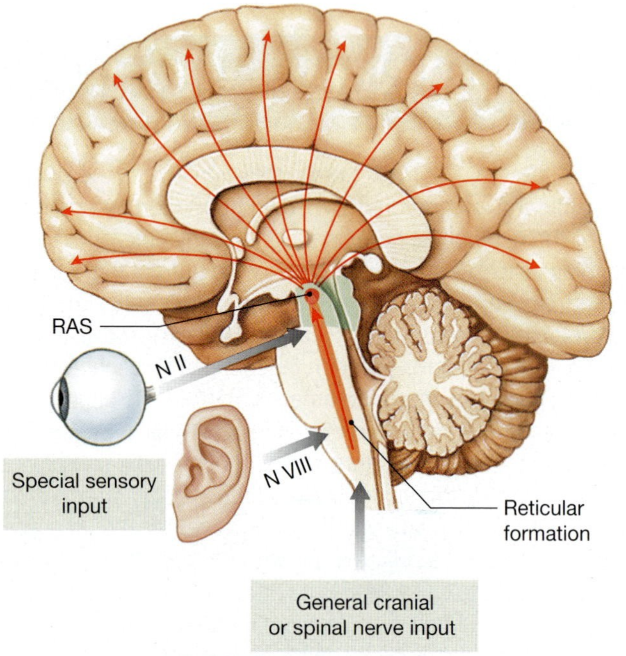

Figure 16.9 The Reticular Activating System
The mesencephalic control center of the reticular formation is the reticular activating system (RAS). It receives collateral inputs from a variety of sensory pathways. Stimulation of this region produces arousal and heightened states of attentiveness.

Clinical Note

Levels of Consciousness Normal individuals cycle between the alert, conscious state and the asleep state each day. For reference purposes, Table 16.3 indicates the entire range of conscious and unconscious states, ranging from *delirium* through *coma*. It is important to realize that these states are external indications of the level of ongoing CNS activity. When CNS function becomes abnormal, the state of consciousness can be affected. As a result, clinicians are quick to note any abnormalities in the state of consciousness in their patients.

TABLE 16.3 States of Awareness

Level or State	Description
CONSCIOUS STATES	
Delirium	Disorientation, restlessness, confusion, hallucinations, agitation, alternating with other conscious states; develops quickly
Dementia	Progressive decline in spatial orientation, memory, behavior, and language
Confusion	Reduced awareness, easily distracted, easily startled by sensory stimuli, alternates between drowsiness and excitability; resembles minor form of delirium state
Normal consciousness	Aware of self and external environment, well-oriented, responsive
Somnolence	Extreme drowsiness, but will respond normally to stimuli
Chronic vegetative state	Conscious but unresponsive, no evidence of cortical function
UNCONSCIOUS STATES	
Asleep	Can be aroused by normal stimuli (light touch, sound, etc.)
Stupor	Can be aroused by extreme and/or repeated stimuli
Coma	Cannot be aroused and does not respond to stimuli (coma states can be further subdivided according to the effect on reflex responses to stimuli)

Aging and the Nervous System

The aging process affects all bodily systems, and the nervous system is no exception. Anatomical changes begin shortly after maturity (probably by age 30) and accumulate over time. Although an estimated 85 percent of the elderly (above age 65) lead relatively normal lives, there are noticeable changes in mental performance and CNS functioning.

Common, age-related anatomical changes in the nervous system include the following:

1. *A reduction in brain size and weight:* This reduction results primarily from a decrease in the volume of the cerebral cortex. The brains of elderly individuals have narrower gyri and wider sulci than those of young people, and the subarachnoid space and ventricles are enlarged.
2. *A reduction in the number of neurons:* Reduced brain size has been linked to a loss of cortical neurons. However, neuronal loss occurs neither to the same degree in all individuals nor in all brain stem nuclei.
3. *A decrease in blood flow to the brain:* With age, fatty deposits gradually accumulate in the walls of blood vessels and reduce the rate of arterial blood flow. (This process, called *atherosclerosis*, may affect arteries throughout the body; it is described further in Chapter 22.) Reduced blood flow does not cause a cerebral crisis, but it does increase the probability that the individual will suffer a stroke.
4. *Changes in synaptic organization of the brain:* The number of dendritic branches and interconnections appears to decrease. As synaptic connections are lost, the rate of neurotransmitter production declines.
5. *Intracellular and extracellular changes in CNS neurons:* Many neurons in the brain begin accumulating abnormal intracellular deposits. *Plaques* are extracellular accumulations of an unusual fibrillar protein, *amyloid*, surrounded by abnormal dendrites and axons. *Neurofibrillary tangles* are masses of neurofibrils that form dense mats inside the soma. The significance of these cellular and extracellular

Clinical Note

Alzheimer's Disease **Alzheimer's disease** is a chronic, progressive illness characterized by memory loss and impairment of higher-order cerebral functions including abstract thinking, judgment, and personality. It is the most common cause of *senile dementia*, or *senility*. Symptoms may appear at age 50–60 or later, although the disease occasionally affects younger individuals. Alzheimer's disease has widespread impact. An estimated 4 million people in the United States have Alzheimer's—including roughly 3 percent of those from age 65 to 70, with the number doubling for every five years of aging until nearly 50 percent of those over age 85 have some form of the condition. Over 230,000 victims require nursing home care, and Alzheimer's disease causes more than 53,000 deaths each year.

Most cases of Alzheimer's disease are associated with large concentrations of neurofibrillary tangles and plaques in the nucleus basalis, hippocampus, and parahippocampal gyrus. These brain regions are directly associated with memory processing. It remains to be determined whether these deposits cause Alzheimer's disease or are secondary signs of ongoing metabolic alterations with an environmental, hereditary, or infectious basis.

In Down syndrome and in some inherited forms of Alzheimer's disease, mutations affecting genes on either chromosome 21 or a small region of chromosome 14 lead to increased risk of the early onset of the disease. Other genetic factors certainly play a major role. The late-onset form of Alzheimer's disease has been traced to a gene on chromosome 19 that codes for proteins involved in cholesterol transport.

Diagnosis involves excluding metabolic and anatomical conditions that can mimic dementia, a detailed history and physical, and an evaluation of mental functioning. Initial symptoms are subtle: moodiness, irritability, depression, and a general lack of energy. These symptoms are often ignored, overlooked, or dismissed. Elderly relatives are viewed as eccentric or irascible and are humored whenever possible.

As the condition progresses, however, it becomes more difficult to ignore or accommodate. An individual with Alzheimer's disease has difficulty making decisions, even minor ones. Mistakes—sometimes dangerous ones—are made, through either bad judgment or forgetfulness. For example, the person might light the gas burner, place a pot on the stove, and go into the living room. Two hours later, the pot, still on the stove, melts and starts a fire.

As memory losses continue, the problems become more severe. The individual may forget relatives, his or her home address, or how to use the telephone. The memory loss commonly starts with an inability to store long-term memories, followed by the loss of recently stored memories. Eventually, basic long-term memories, such as the sound of the individual's own name, are forgotten. The loss of memory affects both intellectual and motor abilities, and a person with severe Alzheimer's disease has difficulty performing even the simplest motor tasks. Although by that time victims are relatively unconcerned about their mental state or motor abilities, the condition can continue to have devastating emotional effects on the immediate family.

Individuals with Alzheimer's disease show a pronounced decrease in the number of cortical neurons, especially in the frontal and temporal lobes. This loss is correlated with inadequate ACh production in the nucleus basalis of the cerebrum. Axons leaving that region project throughout the cerebral cortex; when ACh production declines, cortical function deteriorates.

There is no cure for Alzheimer's disease, but a few medications and supplements slow its progress in many patients and reduce the need for nursing home care. The antioxidants vitamin E and ginkgo biloba and the B vitamins of folate, B_6, and B_{12} help some patients and may delay or prevent the disease. Drugs that increase glutamate levels (a neurotransmitter in the brain) also give some additional benefit. Various toxicities and side effects determine what combination of drugs is used. In mice, a vaccine has reduced tangles and plaques in the brain and improved maze-running ability. A preliminary trial of a human vaccine was stopped because cases of immune encephalitis developed in some treated patients. Modification of the vaccine may eliminate this problem, allowing further study of this new approach.

abnormalities remains to be determined. There is evidence that they appear in all aging brains, but when present in excess, they seem to be associated with clinical abnormalities.

These anatomical changes are linked to a series of functional alterations. In general, neural processing becomes less efficient. For example, memory consolidation often becomes more difficult, and the sensory systems of the elderly—notably hearing, balance, vision, smell, and taste—become less acute. Light must be brighter, sounds louder, and smells stronger before they are perceived. Reaction times are slowed, and reflexes—even some monosynaptic reflexes—become weaker or even disappear. There is a decrease in the precision of motor control, and it takes longer to perform a given motor pattern than it did 20 years earlier. For the majority of the elderly population, these changes do not interfere with their abilities to function in society. But for as yet unknown reasons, many elderly individuals become incapacitated by progressive CNS changes. By far the most common such incapacitating condition is *Alzheimer's disease.*

CONCEPT CHECK

1. What would happen to a sleeping individual if his or her reticular activating system (RAS) were suddenly stimulated?
2. Which major anatomical structures in the CNS are affected by aging?

See blue "Answers" tab at back of book.

Clinical Note

Cerebrovascular Diseases **Cerebrovascular diseases** are cardiovascular disorders that interfere with the normal circulatory supply to the brain. The particular distribution of the vessel involved will determine the symptoms, and the degree of oxygen or nutrient starvation will determine their severity. A stroke, or **cerebrovascular accident (CVA)**, occurs when the blood supply to a portion of the brain is shut off by a vascular blockage or hemorrhage. Affected neurons begin to die in a matter of minutes.

The symptoms of a stroke provide an indication of the vessel and region of the brain involved. For example, the carotid artery enters the skull via the carotid canal. One major branch of the carotid, the *middle cerebral artery*, is the most common site of a stroke. Superficial branches deliver blood to the temporal lobe and to large portions of the frontal and parietal lobes; deep branches supply the basal nuclei and portions of the thalamus. If a stroke blocks the middle cerebral artery on the left side of the brain, aphasia and a sensory and motor paralysis of the right side result. In a stroke affecting the middle cerebral artery on the right side, the individual experiences a loss of sensation and motor control over the left side and has difficulty drawing or interpreting spatial relationships. Strokes affecting vessels supplying the brain stem also produce distinctive symptoms; those affecting the lower brain stem are often fatal. (Further information on the causes, diagnosis, and treatment of strokes will be found in Chapter 22.)

CLINICAL TERMS

Alzheimer's disease: A progressive disorder marked by the loss of higher-order cerebral functions.

amnesia: The temporary or permanent loss of memory from disease or trauma.

anencephaly (an-en-SEF-a-lē): A rare condition in which the brain fails to develop at levels above the mesencephalon or lower diencephalon.

aphasia: A disorder affecting the ability to speak or read.

cerebral palsy: A number of disorders affecting voluntary motor performance that appear during infancy or childhood and persist throughout the life of the affected individual.

cerebrovascular accident (CVA): A condition in which the blood supply to a portion of the brain is blocked off.

cerebrovascular diseases: Vascular disorder that interferes with the arterial supply to the brain.

delirium: A conscious state involving confusion and wild oscillations in the level of consciousness.

dementia: A chronic state of consciousness characterized by deficits in memory, spatial orientation, language, or personality.

disconnection syndrome: Syndrome caused by severing the corpus callosum and separating the two cerebral hemispheres. Each hemisphere continues to function independently, and the right hand literally doesn't know what the left hand is doing.

dyslexia: A disorder affecting the comprehension and use of words.

Tay-Sachs disease: A disease resulting from a genetic abnormality involving the metabolism of *gangliosides.* Affected infants seem normal at birth, but the progress of symptoms typically includes muscular weakness, blindness, seizures, and death, usually before age 4.

STUDY OUTLINE

Introduction 432

1. Information passes continually between the brain, spinal cord, and peripheral nerves. Sensory information is delivered to CNS processing centers, and motor neurons control and adjust peripheral effector activities.

Sensory and Motor Pathways 432

1. Pathways relay sensory and motor information between the CNS, the PNS, and peripheral organs and systems. Ascending (sensory) and descending (motor) pathways contain a chain of tracts and associated nuclei.

Sensory Pathways 432

2. Sensory receptors detect changes in the body or external environment and pass this information to the CNS. This information, called a **sensation**, arrives as action potentials in an afferent *(sensory)* fiber. The response to the stimulus depends on where the processing occurs.
3. Sensory neurons that deliver the sensations to the CNS are termed **first-order neurons. Second-order neurons** are the CNS neurons on which the first-order neurons synapse. These neurons synapse on a **third-order neuron** in the thalamus. The axon of either the first-order or second-order neuron crosses to the opposite side of the CNS, in a process called **decussation**. Thus, the right cerebral hemisphere receives sensory information from the left side of the body, and vice versa. *(see Table 16.1)*

4. The **posterior column pathway** carries fine-touch, pressure, and proprioceptive (position) sensations. The axons ascend within the **fasciculus gracilis** and **fasciculus cuneatus** and synapse in the nucleus gracilis and nucleus cuneatus within the medulla oblongata. This information is then relayed to the thalamus via the **medial lemniscus**. Decussation occurs as the second-order neurons enter the medial lemniscus. *(see Figures 16.1/16.2 and Table 16.1)*
5. The nature of any stimulus and its location is known because the information projects to a specific portion of the primary sensory cortex. Perceptions of sensations such as touch depend on processing in the thalamus. The precise localization is provided by the primary sensory cortex. A functional map of the primary sensory cortex is called the **sensory homunculus**. *(see Figure 16.2)*
6. The **spinothalamic pathway** carries poorly localized sensations of touch, pressure, pain, and temperature. The axons of the second-order neurons decussate in the spinal cord and ascend in the **anterior** and **lateral spinothalamic tracts** to the ventral posterolateral nuclei of the thalamus. *(see Figure 16.2 and Table 16.1)*
7. The **spinocerebellar pathway**, including the **posterior** and **anterior spinocerebellar tracts**, carries sensations to the cerebellum concerning the position of muscles, tendons, and joints. *(see Figures 16.1/16.2 and Table 16.1)*

Motor Pathways 436

8. Motor commands from the CNS are issued in response to sensory system information. These commands are distributed by either the *somatic nervous system (SNS)* for skeletal muscles or the *autonomic nervous system (ANS)* for visceral effectors. *(see Figure 16.3)*
9. Somatic motor pathways always involve an **upper motor neuron** (whose cell body lies in a CNS processing center) and a **lower motor neuron** (located in a motor nucleus of the brain stem or spinal cord). Autonomic motor control requires a **preganglionic neuron** (in the CNS) and a **ganglionic neuron** (in a peripheral ganglion). *(see Figures 16.3 to 16.5)*
10. The neurons of the primary motor cortex are **pyramidal cells**; the **corticospinal pathway** provides a rapid, direct mechanism for voluntary skeletal muscle control. The corticospinal pathway consists of three pairs of descending motor tracts: (1) the *corticobulbar tracts,* (2) the *lateral corticospinal tracts,* and (3) the *anterior corticospinal tracts.* A functional map of the primary motor cortex is called the **motor homunculus**. *(see Figure 16.4 and Table 16.2)*
11. The **corticobulbar tracts** end at the motor nuclei of cranial nerves controlling eye movements, facial muscles, tongue muscles, and neck and superficial back muscles. *(see Figure 16.4a)*
12. The **corticospinal tracts** synapse on motor neurons in the anterior gray horns of the spinal cord and control movement in the neck and trunk and some coordinated movements in the axial skeleton. They are visible along the ventral side of the medulla oblongata as a pair of thick elevations, the **pyramids**, where most of the axons decussate to enter the descending **lateral corticospinal tracts**. The remaining axons are uncrossed here and enter the **anterior corticospinal tracts**. These fibers will cross inside the anterior gray commissure before they synapse on motor neurons in the anterior gray horns. *(see Figure 16.4 and Table 16.2)*
13. The **medial** and **lateral pathways** consist of several centers that may issue motor commands as a result of processing performed at an unconscious, involuntary level. These pathways can modify or direct somatic motor patterns. Their outputs may descend in (1) the *vestibulospinal,* (2) the *tectospinal,* (3) the *reticulospinal,* or (4) the *rubrospinal tracts. (see Figures 16.4/16.5 and Table 16.2)*
14. The vestibular nuclei receive sensory information from inner ear receptors through N VIII. These nuclei issue motor commands to maintain posture and balance. The fibers descend through the **vestibulospinal tracts**. *(see Figure 16.5 and Table 16.2)*
15. Commands carried by the **tectospinal tracts** change the position of the eyes, head, neck, and arms in response to bright lights, sudden movements, or loud noises. *(see Figure 16.5 and Table 16.2)*
16. Motor commands carried by the **reticulospinal tracts** vary according to the region stimulated. The reticular formation receives inputs from almost all ascending and descending pathways and from numerous interconnections with the cerebrum, cerebellum, and brain stem nuclei. *(see Figure 16.5 and Table 16.2)*
17. Basal nuclei, the cerebellum, and the reticular formation give inputs to the red nucleus. The **rubrospinal tracts** carry motor commands to lower motor neurons that provide supplemental control over distal muscles of the upper limbs. In humans these tracts are small and of little significance under normal circumstances. *(see Figure 16.5 and Table 16.2)*
18. The **basal nuclei** adjust the motor commands issued in other processing centers. They do not initiate specific movements, but provide a background pattern once movement is initiated. *(see Figure 16.5 and Table 16.2)*
19. The **cerebellum** regulates the activity along both conscious (corticospinal) and subconscious (medial and lateral) pathways. The integrative activities performed by neurons in the cerebellar cortex and cerebellar nuclei are essential for precise control of voluntary and involuntary movements. After voluntary movement is initiated, the cerebellum triggers inhibition of unnecessary motor units to complete the pattern of activity. *(see Figure 16.6)*

Levels of Somatic Motor Control 441

20. Ascending sensory information is relayed from one nucleus or center to another in a series of steps. Information processing occurs at each step along the way. Processing steps are important but time-consuming. Nuclei in the spinal cord, brain stem, and the cerebrum work together in various complex reflexes. *(see Figure 16.6)*

Higher-Order Functions 443

1. Higher-order functions have certain characteristics; they (1) are performed by the cerebral cortex; (2) involve complex fiber connections between areas of the cerebral cortex and between the cortex and other areas of the brain; (3) involve conscious and unconscious information processing; and (4) are subject to modification and adjustment over time. *(see Figures 16.7 to 16.9)*

Integrative Regions of the Cerebral Cortex 443

2. Several cortical areas act as higher-order integrative centers for complex sensory stimuli and motor responses. These centers include (1) the *general interpretive area,* (2) the *speech center,* and (3) the *prefrontal cortex. (see Figure 16.7)*
3. The **general interpretive area** *(gnostic area)* receives information from all the sensory association areas. It is present in only one hemisphere, usually the left. *(see Figures 16.7b/16.8)*
4. The **speech center** (*Broca's area*) regulates the patterns of breathing and vocalization needed for normal speech. *(see Figure 16.7b)*
5. The **prefrontal cortex** coordinates information from the secondary and special association areas of the entire cortex and performs abstract intellectual functions. *(see Figure 16.7b)*
6. Many functional areas of the cerebral cortex show a characteristic pattern of cellular organization, as described by Brodmann. *(see Figure 16.7c)*

Hemispheric Specialization 445

7. The left hemisphere is usually the **categorical hemisphere**; it contains the general interpretive and speech centers and is responsible for language-based skills. The right hemisphere, or **representational hemisphere**, is concerned with spatial relationships and analysis. *(see Figures 16.7/16.8)*

Memory 445

8. **Memory** is the process of accessing stored bits of information gathered through experience. It involves considerable interaction between the cerebral cortex and other areas of the brain. *Short-term memories* last for seconds to hours; *long-term memories* can last for years. Conversion of short-term memory to a long-term memory is called *memory consolidation.* The amygdaloid body and the hippocampus are essential to memory consolidation.

Consciousness: The Reticular Activating System 446

9. Consciousness is determined by interactions between the brain stem and cerebral cortex. One of the most important brain stem components is a network in the reticular formation called the **reticular activating system (RAS)**. *(see Figure 16.9 and Table 16.3)*

Aging and the Nervous System 447

1. Age-related changes in the nervous system include (1) *reduction in brain size and weight,* (2) *reduction in number of neurons,* (3) *decrease in blood flow to the brain,* (4) *changes in synaptic organization of the brain,* and (5) *intracellular and extracellular changes in CNS neurons.*

CHAPTER REVIEW

For answers to the Concept Check and Chapter Review questions, go to the blue "Answers" tab at the back of the book.

Level 1 Reviewing Facts and Terms

Match each numbered item with the most closely related lettered item. Use letters for answers in the spaces provided.

Column A	Column B
___ 1. decussation	a. second-order
___ 2. sensory	b. pain, temperature, crude touch, pressure
___ 3. interneuron	c. voluntary-control skeletal muscle
___ 4. posterior column	d. general interpretive
___ 5. spinothalamic	e. afferent
___ 6. spinocerebellar	f. proprioceptive information
___ 7. corticospinal system	g. speech
___ 8. tectospinal tracts	h. crossover
___ 9. medial pathway	i. position change—noise related
___10. gnostic area	j. subconscious motor command
___11. Broca's area	k. fasciculi gracilis and cuneatus

12. Axons ascend the posterior column to reach the
    (a) nucleus gracilis and nucleus cuneatus
    (b) ventral nucleus of the thalamus
    (c) posterior lobe of the cerebellum
    (d) medial nucleus of the thalamus

13. Which of the following is true of the spinothalamic pathway?
    (a) its neurons synapse in the anterior gray horn of the spinal cord
    (b) it carries sensations of touch, pressure, and temperature from the brain to the periphery
    (c) it transmits sensory information to the brain, where crossing over occurs in the thalamus
    (d) none of the above are correct

14. Which of the following is a spinal tract within the medial or lateral pathways?
    (a) vestibulospinal tracts
    (b) tectospinal tracts
    (c) reticulospinal tracts
    (d) all of the above are correct

15. Axons of the corticospinal tract synapse at
    (a) motor nuclei of cranial nerves
    (b) motor neurons in the anterior horns of the spinal cord
    (c) motor neurons in the posterior horns of the spinal cord
    (d) motor neurons in ganglia near the spinal cord

16. Which pair of terms is correctly associated?
    (a) lobotomy—ability to interpret what is read or heard
    (b) Broca's area—speech center
    (c) prefrontal cortex—insula lobe
    (d) general interpretive area—extensive connections to the limbic system

17. The cerebellum adjusts voluntary and involuntary motor activity in response to each of the following except
    (a) proprioceptive data
    (b) visual information
    (c) information from the cerebral cortex
    (d) information from the "vital centers"

18. The conscious state depends on proper functioning of the
    (a) prefrontal lobes
    (b) general interpretive area
    (c) reticular activating system
    (d) limbic system

19. Which of the following is essential for memory consolidation?
    (a) Brodmann's area 4 (b) basal nuclei
    (c) hippocampus (d) prefrontal lobe

20. Each of the following describes some aspect of Alzheimer's disease except
    (a) it is the most common cause of senile dementia
    (b) it occurs more frequently in patients with a CVA
    (c) it is associated with the formation of plaques and neurofibrillary tangles in regions of the brain that are involved with memory
    (d) it is characterized by a progressive loss of memory

Level 2 Reviewing Concepts

1. Dysfunction of which neurological components causes a person who has imbibed too much alcohol to stagger when attempting to walk?
   (a) cerebellar nuclei (b) rubrospinal tracts
   (c) parietal lobes (d) tectospinal tracts

2. In what region of the brain would you expect to find a problem in a dyslexic person?
   (a) cerebral nuclei (b) tectospinal tract
   (c) Broca's area (d) occipital lobes

3. What symptoms would you associate with damage to the nucleus gracilis on the right side of the medulla oblongata?
   (a) inability to perceive fine touch from the left lower limb
   (b) inability to perceive fine touch from the right lower limb
   (c) inability to direct fine motor activities involving the left shoulder
   (d) inability to direct fine motor activities involving the right shoulder

4. In the brains of left-handed people who have extremely good mathematical skills
   (a) the analytical region is in the right hemisphere more often than in right-handed individuals
   (b) the analytical region of the brain is in the left hemisphere in approximately 90 percent of cases
   (c) the analytical interpretive area is always in the right cerebral hemisphere
   (d) the corpus callosum is unusually large

5. Describe the function of first-order neurons in the CNS.

6. Why do the proportions of the sensory homunculus differ from those of the body?

7. What is the primary role of the cerebral nuclei in the function of the medial and lateral pathways?

8. How does the cerebellum influence overall motor activities in the body?

9. Where is the speech center and what are its functions?

10. Compare the actions directed by motor commands in the vestibulospinal tracts with those in the reticulospinal tracts.

Level 3 Critical Thinking

1. Cindy has a biking accident and injures her back. She is examined by a doctor who notices that Cindy cannot feel pain sensations (a pinprick) from her left hip and lower limb, but she has normal sensation elsewhere and has no problems with the motor control of her limbs. The physician tells Cindy that he thinks a portion of the spinal cord may be compressed and that this is responsible for her symptoms. Where might the problem be located?

2. A person is admitted to the hospital with symptoms of aphasia and sensory and motor paralysis of the right side of the body. What has probably happened to this individual, and what anatomic structures are most likely to have been involved?

17

The Nervous System

Autonomic Division

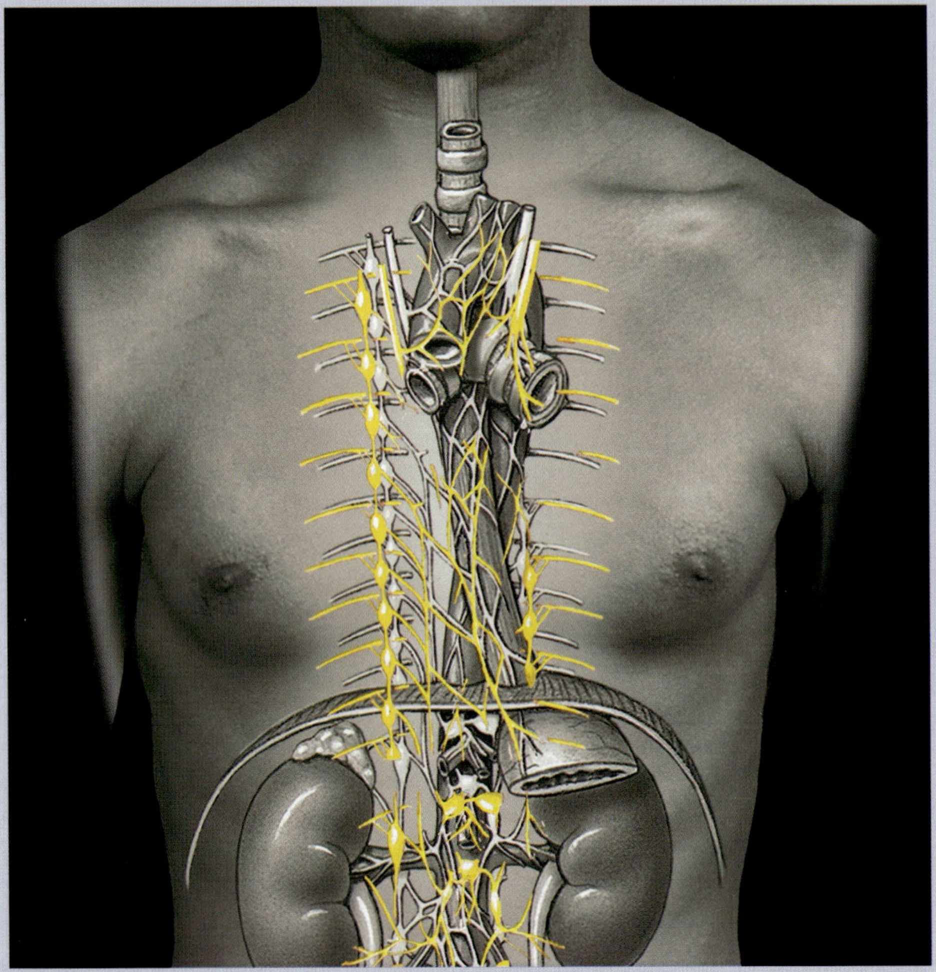

CHAPTER OBJECTIVES

1. Identify the principal structures of the ANS and compare the two functional divisions of the autonomic nervous system.
2. Describe the anatomy of the sympathetic division and its relationship to the spinal cord and spinal nerves.
3. Discuss the mechanisms of neurotransmitter release by the sympathetic nervous system.
4. Describe the anatomy of the parasympathetic division and its relationship to the brain, cranial nerves, and sacral spinal cord.
5. Discuss the relationship between the sympathetic and parasympathetic divisions and explain the implications of dual innervation.
6. Describe the levels of integration and control of the autonomic system.

Our conscious thoughts, plans, and actions represent only a tiny fraction of the activities of the nervous system. If all consciousness was eliminated, vital physiological processes would continue virtually unchanged—a night's sleep is not a life-threatening event. Longer, deeper states of unconsciousness are not necessarily more dangerous, as long as nourishment is provided. People who have suffered severe brain injuries have survived in a coma for decades. Survival under these conditions is possible because routine adjustments in physiological systems are made by the autonomic nervous system (ANS) outside our conscious awareness. The ANS regulates body temperature and coordinates cardiovascular, respiratory, digestive, excretory, and reproductive functions. In doing so, it adjusts internal water, electrolyte, nutrient, and dissolved-gas concentrations in body fluids.

This chapter examines the anatomical structure and subdivisions of the autonomic nervous system. Each subdivision has a characteristic anatomical and functional organization. Our examination of the ANS will begin with a description of the sympathetic and parasympathetic divisions. Then we will briefly examine the way these divisions maintain and adjust various organ systems to meet the body's ever-changing physiological needs.

A Comparison of the Somatic and Autonomic Nervous Systems

[Figures 16.3/17.1]

It is useful to compare the organization of the autonomic nervous system (ANS), which innervates visceral effectors, with the somatic nervous system (SNS), which was discussed in Chapter 16. The axons of lower motor neurons of the somatic nervous system extend from the CNS to contact and exert direct control over skeletal muscles. p. 436 The ANS, like the SNS, has afferent and efferent neurons. Like the SNS, the afferent sensory information of the ANS is processed in the central nervous system, and then efferent impulses are sent to effector organs. However, in the ANS, the afferent pathways originate in visceral receptors, and the efferent pathways connect to visceral effector organs.

In addition to the difference in receptor and effector organ location, the autonomic nervous system differs from the somatic nervous system in the arrangement of the neurons connecting the central nervous system to the effector organs (**Figure 16.3**). p. 436 In the ANS, the axon of a visceral motor neuron within the CNS innervates a second neuron located in a peripheral ganglion. This second neuron controls the peripheral effector. Visceral motor neurons in the CNS, known as **preganglionic neurons**, send their axons, called *preganglionic fibers,* to synapse on **ganglionic neurons**, whose cell bodies are located outside the CNS, in autonomic ganglia. Axons that leave the autonomic ganglia are relatively small and unmyelinated. These axons are called *postganglionic fibers* because they carry impulses away from the ganglion (for this reason some sources call the neurons *postganglionic,* although their cell bodies are within ganglia). Postganglionic fibers innervate peripheral tissues and organs, such as cardiac and smooth muscle, adipose tissue, and glands.

Subdivisions of the ANS [Figure 17.1]

The ANS contains two major subdivisions, the *sympathetic division* and the *parasympathetic* division (**Figure 17.1**). Most often, the two divisions have opposing effects; if the sympathetic division causes excitation, the parasympathetic division causes inhibition. However, this is not always the case because (1) the two divisions may work independently, with some structures innervated by only one division, and (2) the two divisions may work together, each controlling one stage of a complex process. In general, the parasympathetic division predominates under resting conditions, and the sympathetic division "kicks in" during times of exertion, stress, or emergency.

The ANS also includes a third division that most people have never heard of—*the enteric nervous system (ENS),* an extensive network of neurons and nerve networks located in the walls of the digestive tract. Although the activities of the enteric nervous system are influenced by the sympathetic and parasympathetic divisions, many complex visceral reflexes are initiated and coordinated locally, without instructions from the CNS. Altogether, the ENS has roughly 100 million neurons—at least as many as the spinal cord—and all of the neurotransmitters found in the brain. In this chapter, we focus on the sympathetic and parasympathetic divisions that integrate and coordinate visceral functions throughout the body. We will consider the activities of the enteric nervous system when we discuss visceral reflexes later in this chapter, and when we examine the control of digestive functions in Chapter 25.

Sympathetic (Thoracolumbar) Division [Figure 17.1]

Preganglionic fibers from both the thoracic and upper lumbar spinal segments synapse in ganglia near the spinal cord. These axons and ganglia are part of the **sympathetic division**, or **thoracolumbar** (thor-a-kō-LUM-bar) **division** of the ANS (**Figure 17.1**). This division is often called the "fight or flight" system because an increase in sympathetic activity generally stimulates tissue metabolism, increases alertness, and prepares the body to deal with emergencies.

Parasympathetic (Craniosacral) Division [Figure 17.1]

Preganglionic fibers originating in either the brain stem (cranial nerves III, VII, IX, and X) or the sacral spinal cord are part of the **parasympathetic division**, or **craniosacral** (krā-nē-ō-SĀ-kral) **division** of the ANS (**Figure 17.1**). The preganglionic fibers synapse on neurons of **terminal ganglia**, located close to the target organs, or **intramural ganglia** (*murus,* wall), within the tissues of the target organs. This division is often called the "rest and repose" system because it conserves energy and promotes sedentary activities, such as digestion.

Innervation Patterns

The sympathetic and parasympathetic divisions of the ANS affect their target organs through the controlled release of neurotransmitters by postganglionic fibers. Target organ activity may be either stimulated or inhibited, depending on the response of the plasmalemma receptor to the presence of the neurotransmitter. Three general statements describe ANS neurotransmitters and their effects:

1. All preganglionic autonomic fibers release acetylcholine (ACh) at their synaptic terminals. The effects are always stimulatory.
2. Postganglionic parasympathetic fibers also release ACh, but the effects may be either stimulatory or inhibitory, depending on the nature of the receptor.
3. Most postganglionic sympathetic terminals release the neurotransmitter **norepinephrine (NE)**. The effects are usually stimulatory.

CONCEPT CHECK

1. Describe the difference(s) between preganglionic and ganglionic neurons.
2. List the two subdivisions of the autonomic nervous system. What common name or term is applied to each?
3. What neurotransmitter is released by most postganglionic sympathetic terminals?
4. What organs are innervated by postganglionic fibers of the autonomic nervous system?

See blue "Answers" tab at back of book.

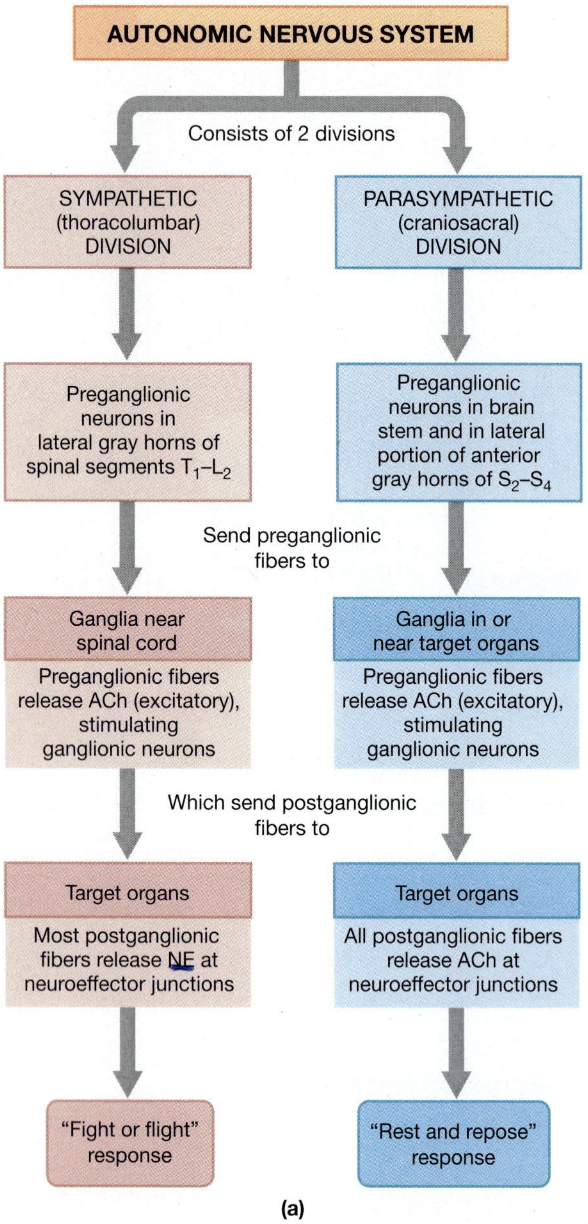

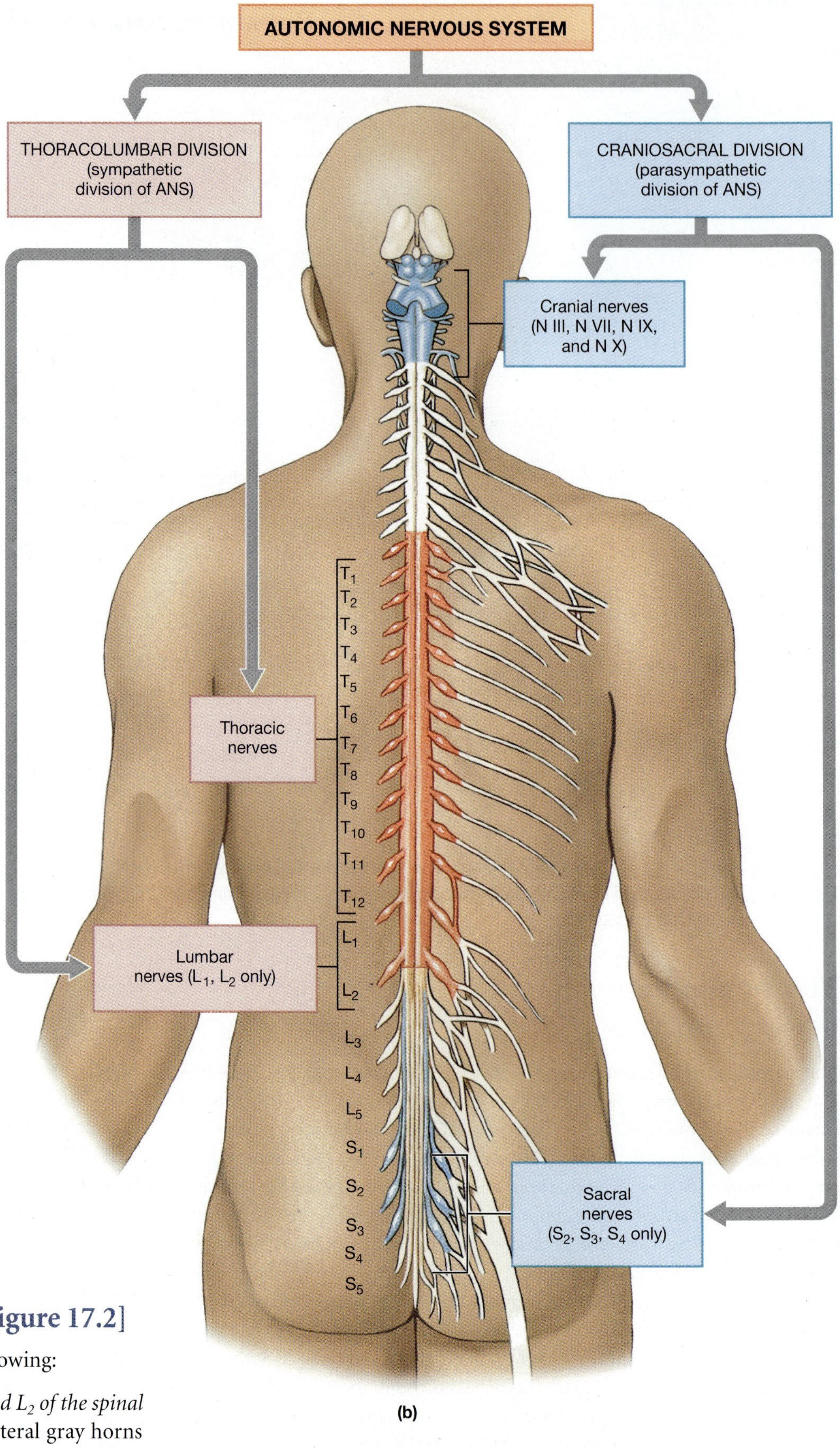

Figure 17.1 Components and Anatomic Subdivisions of the ANS
(a) Functional components. **(b)** Anatomical subdivisions. At the thoracic and lumbar levels, the visceral efferent fibers that emerge form the sympathetic division, *detailed in Figure 17.4.* At the cranial and sacral levels, the visceral efferent fibers from the CNS form the parasympathetic division, *detailed in Figure 17.8.*

The Sympathetic Division [Figure 17.2]

The sympathetic division (**Figure 17.2**) consists of the following:

1. *Preganglionic neurons located between segments T_1 and L_2 of the spinal cord:* The cell bodies of these neurons occupy the lateral gray horns between T_1 and L_2, and their axons enter the ventral roots of those segments.
2. *Ganglionic neurons in ganglia near the vertebral column:* There are two types of ganglia in the sympathetic division:
   - *Sympathetic chain ganglia,* also called *paravertebral,* or *lateral, ganglia,* lie lateral to the vertebral column on each side. Neurons in these ganglia control effectors in the body wall, head and neck, and limbs, and inside the thoracic cavity.
   - *Collateral ganglia,* also known as *prevertebral ganglia,* lie anterior to the vertebral column. Neurons in these ganglia innervate effectors in the abdominopelvic cavity.
3. *Specialized neurons in the interior of the suprarenal gland:* The center of each suprarenal gland, an area known as the *suprarenal medulla,* is a modified sympathetic ganglion. The ganglionic neurons here have very short axons and, when stimulated, release neurotransmitters into the bloodstream for distribution throughout the body as hormones.

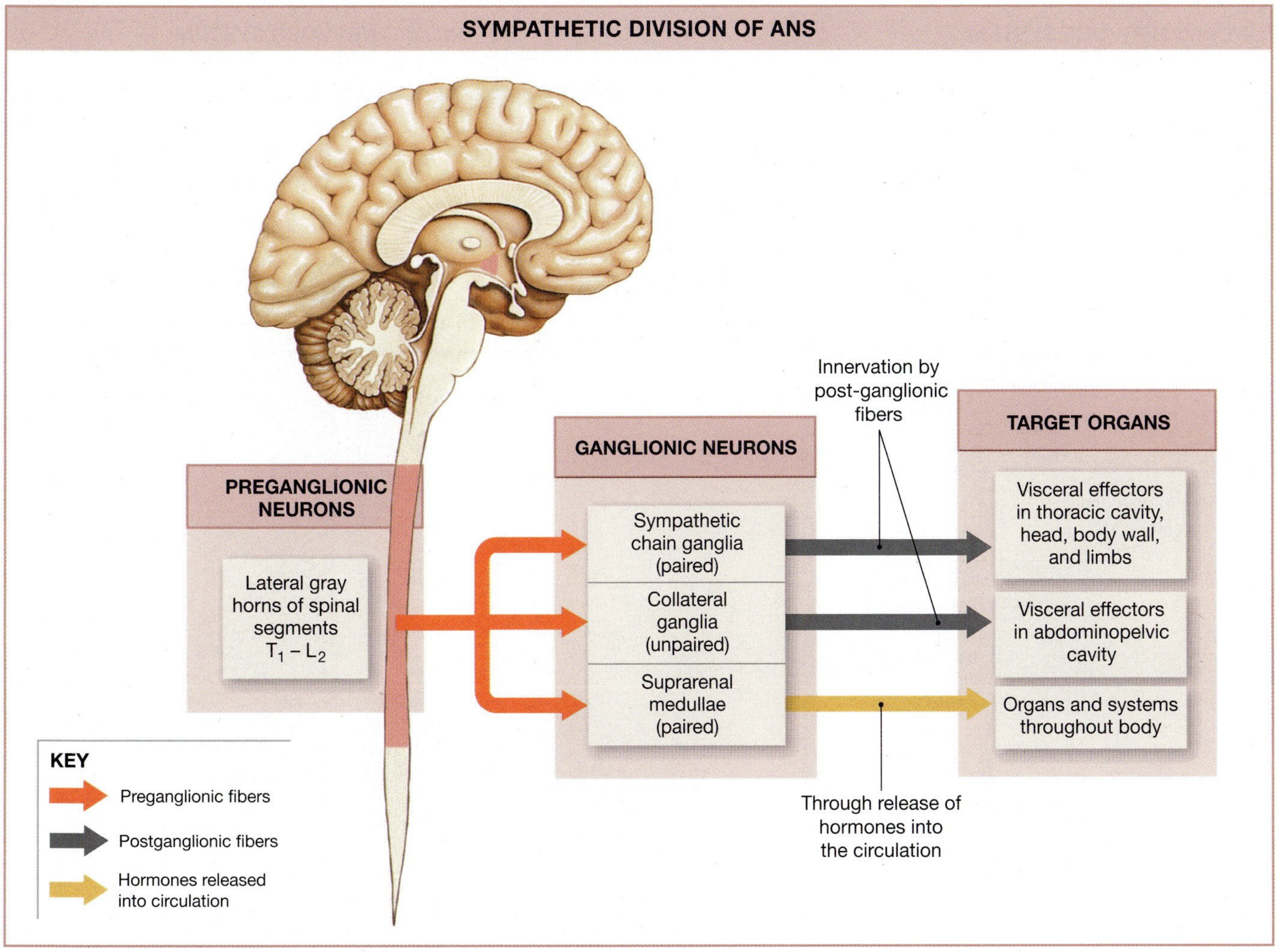

Figure 17.2 Organization of the Sympathetic Division of the ANS
This diagram highlights the relationships between preganglionic and ganglionic neurons and between ganglionic neurons and target organs.

The Sympathetic Chain Ganglia

[Figures 17.1a/17.2/17.3]

The ventral roots of spinal segments T_1 to L_2 contain sympathetic preganglionic fibers. The basic pattern of sympathetic innervation in these regions was described in **Figure 17.1a**. Each ventral root joins the corresponding dorsal root, which carries afferent sensory fibers, to form a spinal nerve that passes through an intervertebral foramen. p. 362 As it clears the foramen, a *white ramus,* or *white ramus communicans,* branches from the spinal nerve (**Figure 17.3a**). The white ramus carries myelinated preganglionic fibers into a nearby sympathetic chain ganglion. Fibers entering a sympathetic chain ganglion may have one of three destinations: (1) They may synapse within the sympathetic chain ganglion at the level of entry (**Figure 17.3a**); (2) they may ascend or descend within the sympathetic chain and synapse with a ganglion at a different level; or (3) they may pass through the sympathetic chain without synapsing and proceed to one of the collateral ganglia (**Figure 17.3b**) or the suprarenal medullae (**Figure 17.3c**). Extensive divergence occurs in the sympathetic division, with one preganglionic fiber synapsing on as many as 32 ganglionic neurons. Preganglionic fibers projecting between the sympathetic chain ganglia interconnect them, making the chain resemble a string of beads. Each ganglion in the sympathetic chain innervates a particular body segment or group of segments.

If a preganglionic fiber carries motor commands that target structures in the body wall or the thoracic cavity, it will synapse in one or more of the sympathetic chain ganglia. Unmyelinated postganglionic fibers then leave the sympathetic chain and proceed to their peripheral targets within spinal nerves and sympathetic nerves. Postganglionic fibers that innervate structures in the body wall, such as the sweat glands of the skin or the smooth muscles in superficial blood vessels, enter the *gray ramus* (*gray ramus communicans*) and return to the spinal nerve for subsequent distribution. However, spinal nerves do not provide motor innervation to structures in the ventral body cavities. Postganglionic fibers innervating visceral organs in the thoracic cavity, such as the heart and lungs, proceed directly to their peripheral targets as sympathetic nerves. These nerves are usually named after their primary targets, as in the case of the *cardiac nerves* and *esophageal nerves.*

Functions of the Sympathetic Chain [Figure 17.3a]

The primary results of increased activity along the postganglionic fibers leaving the sympathetic chain ganglia within spinal nerves and sympathetic nerves are summarized in **Figure 17.3a**. In general, the target cell responses help prepare the individual for a crisis that will require sudden, intensive physical activity.

Anatomy of the Sympathetic Chain [Figure 17.4]

Each sympathetic chain has 3 cervical, 11–12 thoracic, 2–5 lumbar, 4–5 sacral sympathetic ganglia, and 1 coccygeal sympathetic ganglion. Numbers may vary because adjacent ganglia may fuse. For example, the coccygeal ganglia from both sides usually fuse to form a single median ganglion, the *ganglion impar,* while the inferior cervical and first thoracic ganglia from both sides occasionally fuse to form a *stellate ganglion.* Preganglionic sympathetic

(a) SYMPATHETIC CHAIN GANGLIA

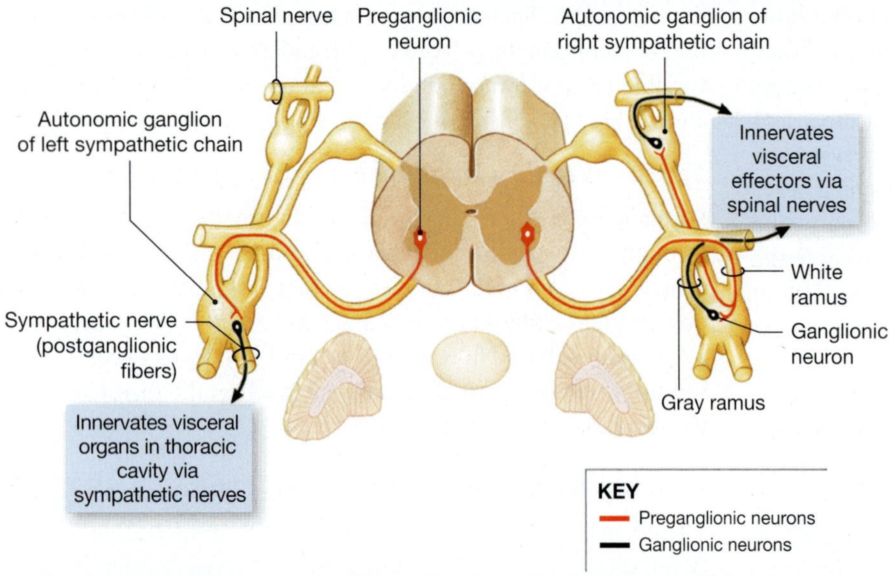

Major effects produced by sympathetic postganglionic fibers in spinal nerves:

- Constriction of cutaneous blood vessels, reduction in circulation to the skin and to most other organs in the body wall
- Acceleration of blood flow to skeletal muscles and brain
- Stimulation of energy production and use by skeletal muscle tissue
- Release of stored lipids from subcutaneous adipose tissue
- Stimulation of secretion by sweat glands
- Stimulation of arrector pili
- Dilation of the pupils and focusing for distant objects

Major effects produced by postganglionic fibers entering the thoracic cavity in sympathetic nerves:

- Acceleration of heart rate and increasing the strength of cardiac contractions
- Dilation of respiratory passageways

(b) COLLATERAL GANGLIA

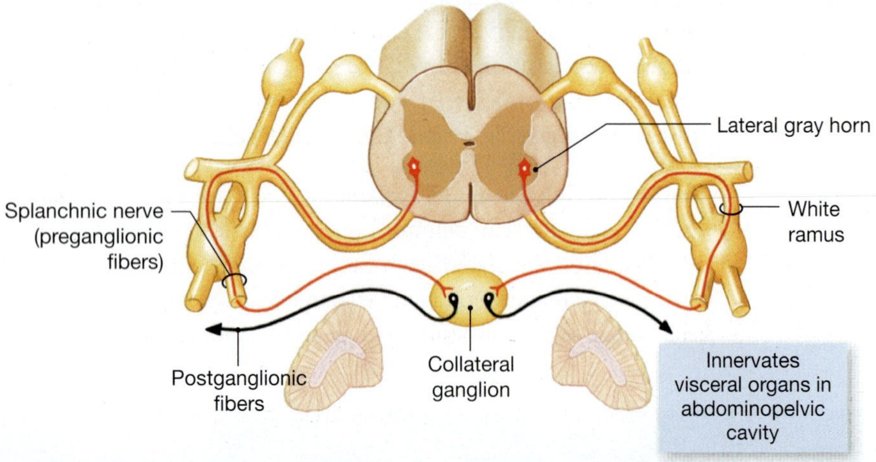

Major effects produced by preganglionic fibers innervating the collateral ganglia:

- Constriction of small arteries and reduction in the flow of blood to visceral organs
- Decrease in the activity of digestive glands and organs
- Stimulation of the release of glucose from glycogen reserves in the liver
- Stimulation of the release of lipids from adipose tissue
- Relaxation of the smooth muscle in the wall of the urinary bladder
- Reduction of the rate of urine formation at the kidneys
- Control of some aspects of sexual function, such as ejaculation in males

(c) THE SUPRARENAL MEDULLAE

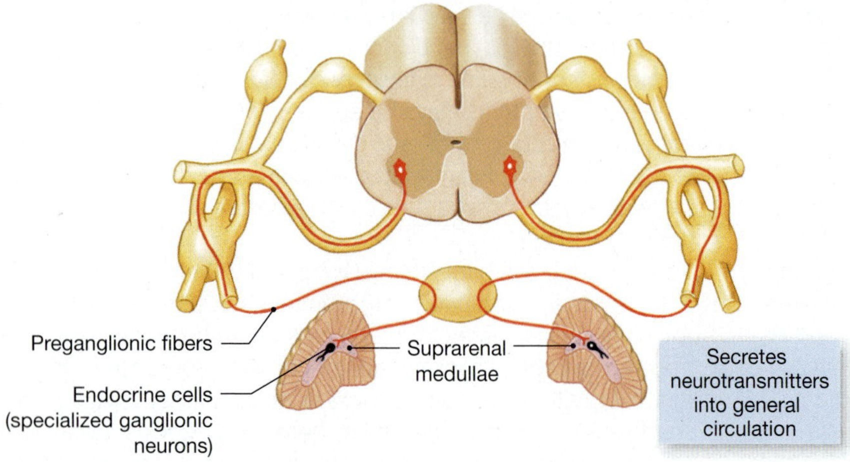

Major effect produced by preganglionic fibers innervating the suprarenal medullae:

- Release of epinephrine and norepinephrine into the general circulation

Figure 17.3 Sympathetic Pathways and Their General Functions
Preganglionic fibers leave the spinal cord in the ventral roots of spinal nerves. They synapse on ganglionic neurons in **(a)** sympathetic chain ganglia, **(b)** collateral ganglia, or **(c)** the suprarenal medullae. These sections are seen in inferior view, the standard format for radiographic scans and sectional views of the nervous system.

neurons are limited to segments T_1–L_2 of the spinal cord, and the spinal nerves of these segments have both white rami (preganglionic fibers) and gray rami (postganglionic fibers). The neurons in the cervical, inferior lumbar, and sacral sympathetic chain ganglia are innervated by preganglionic fibers extending along the axis of the chain. In turn, these chain ganglia provide postganglionic fibers, through the gray rami, to the cervical, lumbar, and sacral spinal nerves. *Every spinal nerve has a gray ramus that carries sympathetic postganglionic fibers.* About 8 percent of the axons in each spinal nerve are sympathetic postganglionic fibers. The dorsal and ventral rami of the spinal nerves provide extensive sympathetic innervation to structures in the body wall and limbs. In the head, postganglionic fibers leaving the cervical chain ganglia supply the regions and structures innervated by cranial nerves N III, N VII, N IX, and N X (Figure 17.4).

In summary: (1) Only the thoracic and superior lumbar ganglia receive preganglionic fibers from the white rami; (2) the cervical, inferior lumbar, and sacral chain ganglia receive preganglionic innervation from the thoracic and superior lumbar segments through preganglionic fibers that ascend or descend along the sympathetic chain; and (3) every spinal nerve receives a gray ramus from a ganglion of the sympathetic chain.

This anatomical arrangement has interesting functional consequences. If the ventral roots of thoracic spinal nerves are damaged, there will be no sympathetic motor function on the affected side of the head, neck, and trunk. Yet damage to the ventral roots of cervical spinal nerves will produce voluntary muscle paralysis on the affected side, *but leave sympathetic function intact* because the preganglionic fibers innervating the cervical ganglia originate in the white rami of thoracic segments, which are undamaged.

Collateral Ganglia [Figures 17.3b/17.4]

Preganglionic fibers that regulate the activities of the abdominopelvic viscera originate at preganglionic neurons in the inferior thoracic and superior lumbar segments of the spinal cord. These fibers pass through the sympathetic chain without synapsing, and converge to form the **greater**, **lesser**, and **lumbar splanchnic** (SPLANK-nik) **nerves** in the dorsal wall of the abdominal cavity. Splanchnic nerves from both sides of the body converge on the collateral ganglia (Figures 17.3b and 17.4). Collateral ganglia, which are variable in appearance, are located anterior and lateral to the descending aorta. These ganglia are most often single, rather than paired, structures.

Functions of the Collateral Ganglia [Figure 17.3b]

Postganglionic fibers that originate within the collateral ganglia extend throughout the abdominopelvic cavity, innervating visceral tissues and organs. A summary of the effects of increased sympathetic activity along these postganglionic fibers is included in Figure 17.3b. The general pattern is (1) a reduction of blood flow, energy use, and activity by visceral organs that are not important to short-term survival (such as the digestive tract), and (2) the release of stored energy reserves.

Anatomy of the Collateral Ganglia [Figures 17.4/17.9]

The splanchnic nerves (greater, lesser, lumbar, and sacral) innervate three collateral ganglia. Preganglionic fibers from the seven inferior thoracic segments end at the **celiac** (SĒ-lē-ak) **ganglion** and the **superior mesenteric ganglion**. These ganglia are embedded in an extensive, weblike network of nerve fibers termed an *autonomic plexus.* Preganglionic fibers from the lumbar segments form splanchnic nerves that end at the **inferior mesenteric ganglion**. These ganglia are diagrammed in Figure 17.4 and detailed in Figure 17.9, p. 463. The sacral splanchnic nerves end in the *hypogastric plexus,* an autonomic network supplying pelvic organs and the external genitalia.

The Celiac Ganglion Postganglionic fibers from the celiac ganglion innervate the stomach, duodenum, liver, gallbladder, pancreas, and spleen. The celiac ganglion is variable in appearance. It most often consists of a pair of interconnected masses of gray matter situated at the base of the *celiac trunk.* The celiac ganglion may also form a single mass of many small, interwoven masses.

Clinical Note

Hypersensitivity and Sympathetic Function Two interesting clinical conditions result from the disruption of normal sympathetic functions. In **Horner's syndrome**, the sympathetic postganglionic innervation to one side of the face becomes interrupted. The interruption may be the result of an injury, a tumor, or some progressive condition such as multiple sclerosis. The affected side of the face becomes flushed as vascular tone decreases. Sweating stops in the region, and the pupil on that side becomes markedly constricted. Other symptoms include a drooping eyelid and an apparent retreat of the eye into the orbit.

Primary Raynaud's phenomenon, also called **Raynaud's disease**, most commonly affects young women. In this condition, for unknown reasons, the sympathetic system temporarily orders excessive peripheral vasoconstriction of small arteries, usually in response to cold temperatures. The hands, feet, ears, and nose become deprived of their normal blood circulation and the skin in these areas changes color, becoming initially pale and then developing blue tones. A red color ends the cycle as normal blood flow returns. The symptoms may spread to adjacent areas as the disorder progresses. Most cases do not cause tissue damage, although in rare cases prolonged decreased blood flow may distort the skin and nails, even progressing to skin ulcers or the more extensive tissue death of dry gangrene.

Behavioral changes such as avoiding cold environments or wearing mittens and other protective clothing can usually reduce the frequency of occurrence. Stopping smoking and avoiding drugs that can cause vasoconstriction may also be beneficial. Drugs that prevent vasoconstriction (vasodilators) can be used if preventive steps prove ineffective.

Trauma such as frostbite or the cumulative damage caused by the chronic use of vibrating machinery can cause symptoms of Raynaud's syndrome. Symptoms may also appear in individuals with arterial diseases and in connective tissue disorders such as scleroderma, rheumatoid arthritis, and systemic lupus erythematosus (SLE). These secondary forms of Raynaud's syndrome usually improve with treatment of the underlying disorder.

A regional sympathectomy (sim-path-EK-to-mē), cutting the fibers that provide sympathetic innervation to the affected area, may occasionally be beneficial. Under normal conditions, sympathetic tone provides the effectors with a background level of stimulation. After the elimination of sympathetic innervation, peripheral effectors may become extremely sensitive to norepinephrine and epinephrine. This hypersensitivity can produce extreme alterations in vascular tone and other functions after stimulation of the suprarenal medullae. If the sympathectomy involves cutting the postganglionic fibers, hypersensitivity to circulating norepinephrine and epinephrine may eliminate the beneficial effects. The prognosis improves if the preganglionic fibers are transected, because the ganglionic neurons will continue to release small quantities of neurotransmitter across the neuromuscular or neuroglandular synapses. This release keeps the peripheral effectors from becoming hypersensitive.

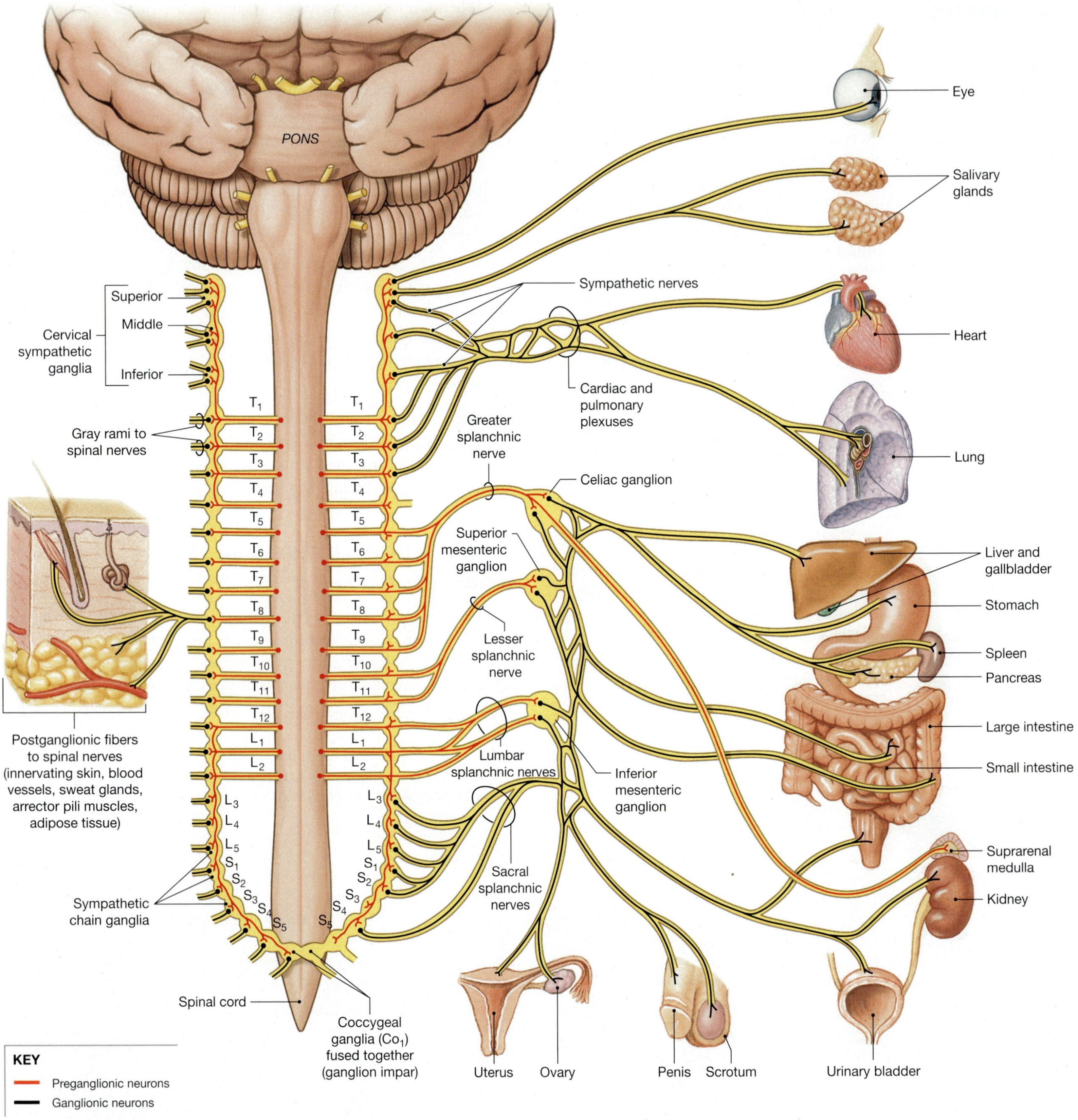

Figure 17.4 Anatomical Distribution of Sympathetic Postganglionic Fibers
The left side of this figure shows the distribution of sympathetic postganglionic fibers through the gray rami and spinal nerves. The right side shows the distribution of preganglionic and postganglionic fibers innervating visceral organs. However, *both* innervation patterns are found on *each* side of the body.

The Superior Mesenteric Ganglion Located near the base of the *superior mesenteric artery* is the superior mesenteric ganglion. Postganglionic fibers leaving the superior mesenteric ganglion innervate the small intestine and the initial segments of the large intestine.

The Inferior Mesenteric Ganglion Located near the base of the *inferior mesenteric artery* is the inferior mesenteric ganglion. Postganglionic fibers from this ganglion provide sympathetic innervation to the terminal portions of the large intestine, the kidney and bladder, and the sex organs.

The Suprarenal Medullae [Figures 17.3c/17.4/17.5]

Some preganglionic fibers originating between T_5 and T_8 pass through the sympathetic chain and the celiac ganglion without synapsing and proceed to the **suprarenal medulla** (Figures 17.3c, 17.4, and 17.5). There, these preganglionic fibers synapse on modified neurons that perform an endocrine function. These neurons have very short axons. When stimulated, they release the neurotransmitters *epinephrine* (E) and *norepinephrine* (NE) into an extensive network of capillaries (Figure 17.5). The neurotransmitters then function as hormones, exerting their effects in other regions of the body. Epinephrine, also called *adrenaline*, accounts for 75–80 percent of the secretory output; the rest is norepinephrine (*noradrenaline*).

The circulating blood then distributes these hormones throughout the body. This causes changes in the metabolic activities of many different cells. In general, the effects resemble those produced by the stimulation of sympathetic postganglionic fibers. But they differ in two respects: (1) Cells not innervated by sympathetic postganglionic fibers are affected by circulating levels of epinephrine and norepinephrine if they possess receptors for these molecules; and (2) the effects last much longer than those produced by direct sympathetic innervation because the released hormones continue to diffuse out of the circulating blood for an extended period.

Effects of Sympathetic Stimulation

The sympathetic division can change tissue and organ activities both by releasing norepinephrine at peripheral synapses and by distributing epinephrine and norepinephrine throughout the body in the bloodstream. The motor fibers that target specific effectors, such as smooth muscle fibers in blood vessels of the skin, can be activated in reflexes that do not involve other peripheral effectors. In a crisis, however, the entire division responds. This event, called **sympathetic activation**, affects peripheral tissues and alters CNS activity. Sympathetic activation is controlled by sympathetic centers in the hypothalamus.

When sympathetic activation occurs, an individual experiences the following:

1. Increased alertness, through stimulation of the reticular activating system, causing the individual to feel "on edge."
2. A feeling of energy and euphoria, often associated with a disregard for danger and a temporary insensitivity to painful stimuli.
3. Increased activity in the cardiovascular and respiratory centers of the pons and medulla oblongata, leading to increased heart rate and contraction strength, elevations in blood pressure, breathing rate, and depth of respiration.
4. A general elevation in muscle tone through stimulation of the extrapyramidal system, so that the person *looks* tense and may even begin to shiver.
5. The mobilization of energy reserves, through the accelerated breakdown of glycogen in muscle and liver cells and the release of lipids by adipose tissues.

These changes, coupled with the peripheral changes already noted, complete the preparations necessary for the individual to cope with stressful and potentially dangerous situations. We will now consider the cellular basis for the general effects of sympathetic activation on peripheral organs.

Sympathetic Activation and Neurotransmitter Release [Figure 17.6]

When they are active, sympathetic preganglionic fibers release ACh at their synapses with ganglionic neurons. These are *cholinergic* synapses. ∞ pp. 354–355 The ACh released always stimulates the ganglionic neurons. This stimulation of ganglionic neurons usually leads to the release of norepinephrine at neuroeffector junctions. These sympathetic terminals are called

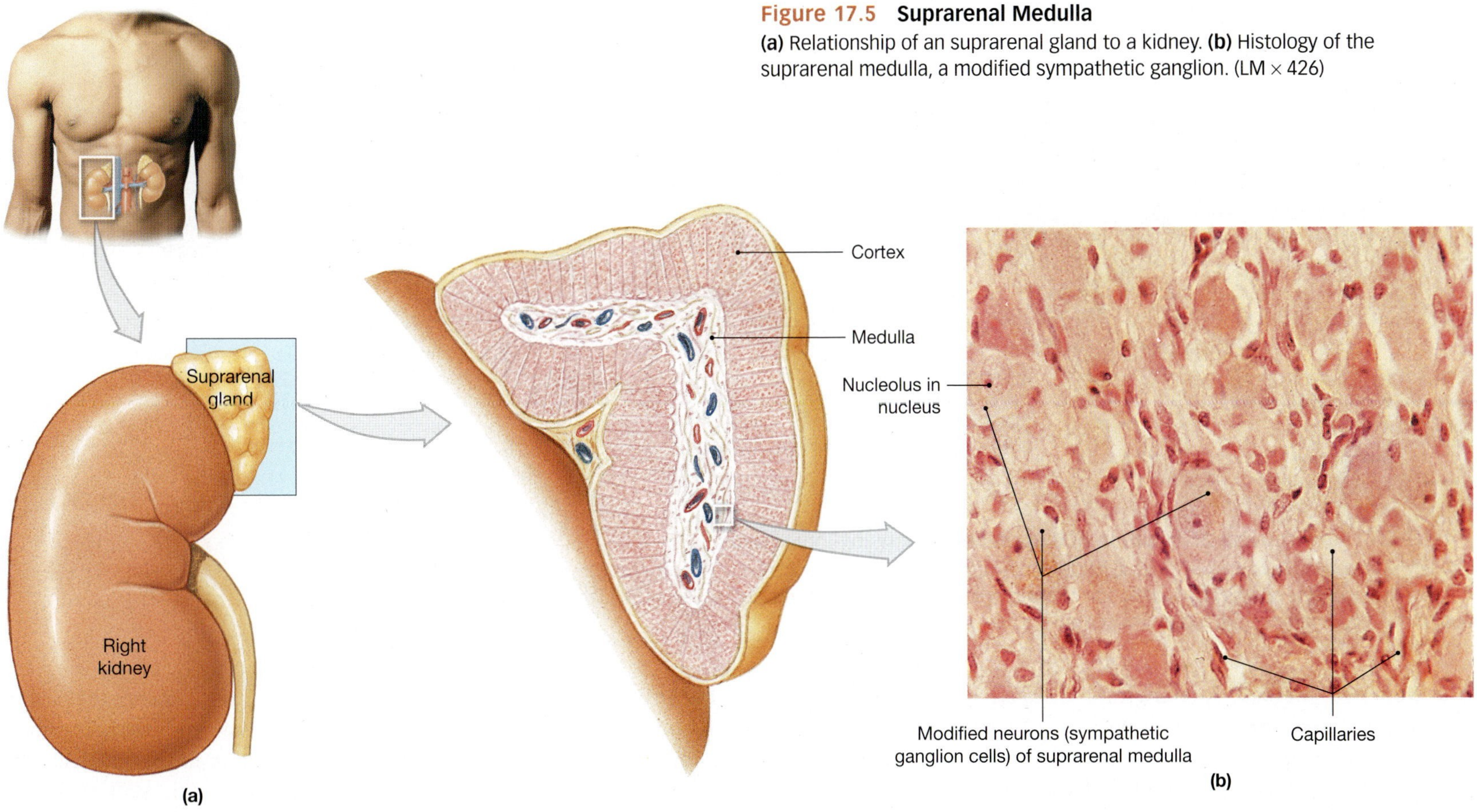

Figure 17.5 Suprarenal Medulla
(a) Relationship of an suprarenal gland to a kidney. **(b)** Histology of the suprarenal medulla, a modified sympathetic ganglion. (LM × 426)

adrenergic. The sympathetic division also contains a small but significant number of ganglionic neurons that release ACh, rather than NE, at their neuroeffector junctions. For example, ACh is released at sympathetic neuroeffector junctions in the body wall, in the skin, and within skeletal muscles.

Figure 17.6 details a representative sympathetic neuroeffector junction. Rather than ending at a single synaptic bouton, the telodendria form an extensive branching network. Each branch resembles a string of pop-beads, and each bead, or **varicosity**, is packed with mitochondria and neurotransmitter vesicles. These varicosities pass along or near the surfaces of many effector cells. A single axon may supply 20,000 varicosities that can affect dozens of surrounding cells. Receptor proteins are scattered across most plasmalemmae, and there are no specialized postsynaptic plasmalemmae.

The effects of neurotransmitter released by varicosities persist for at most a few seconds before the neurotransmitter is reabsorbed, broken down by enzymes, or removed by diffusion into the bloodstream. In contrast, the effects of the E and NE secreted by the suprarenal medullae are considerably longer in duration because (1) the bloodstream does not contain the enzymes that break down epinephrine or norepinephrine, and (2) most tissues contain relatively low concentrations of these enzymes. As a result, the suprarenal stimulation causes widespread effects that continue for a relatively long time. For example, tissue concentrations of epinephrine may remain elevated for as long as 30 seconds, and the effects may persist for several minutes.

Plasmalemma Receptors and Sympathetic Function

The effects of sympathetic stimulation result primarily from interactions with plasmalemma receptors sensitive to epinephrine and norepinephrine. (A few sympathetic neuroeffector junctions release ACh; these will be detailed shortly.) There are two classes of sympathetic receptors sensitive to E and NE: *alpha receptors* and *beta receptors.* Each of these classes of receptors has two or three subtypes. The diversity of receptors and their presence alone or in combination accounts for the variability of target organ responses to sympathetic stimulation. In general, epinephrine stimulates both classes of receptors, while norepinephrine primarily stimulates alpha receptors.

Alpha and Beta Receptors

Stimulation of **alpha receptors** on the surfaces of smooth muscle cells causes constriction of peripheral blood vessels and the closure of sphincters along the digestive tract. **Beta receptors** are found in many organs, including skeletal muscles, the smooth muscle surrounding respiratory airways, the heart, and the liver. Stimulation of these beta receptors triggers changes in the metabolic activity of the target cells. The effects depend on which enzymes are involved. The most common response is an increase in metabolic activity. In skeletal and cardiac muscles, beta receptor stimulation does not cause their contraction. However, skeletal muscles use energy at a faster rate, and the heart contracts faster and stronger. In other target organs E and NE have an inhibitory effect. For example, the dilation of blood vessels supplying skeletal muscles and the enlargement of the respiratory passageways—two important responses to sympathetic activation—result from the relaxation of smooth muscle cells. This relaxation follows the stimulation of beta receptors on their plasmalemmae.

Sympathetic Stimulation and ACh

Although the vast majority of sympathetic postganglionic fibers release NE and are adrenergic, a few postganglionic fibers are cholinergic. Activation of these sympathetic fibers stimulates sweat gland secretion and blood vessel dilation in skeletal muscle. Visceral effectors in both the body wall and skeletal muscles are innervated by the sympathetic division of the ANS only. Thus, the distribution of sympathetic, postganglionic cholinergic fibers provides a method for regulating sweat gland secretion and selectively controlling blood flow to skeletal muscles, while norepinephrine released by adrenergic terminals reduces the blood flow to other tissues in the body wall.

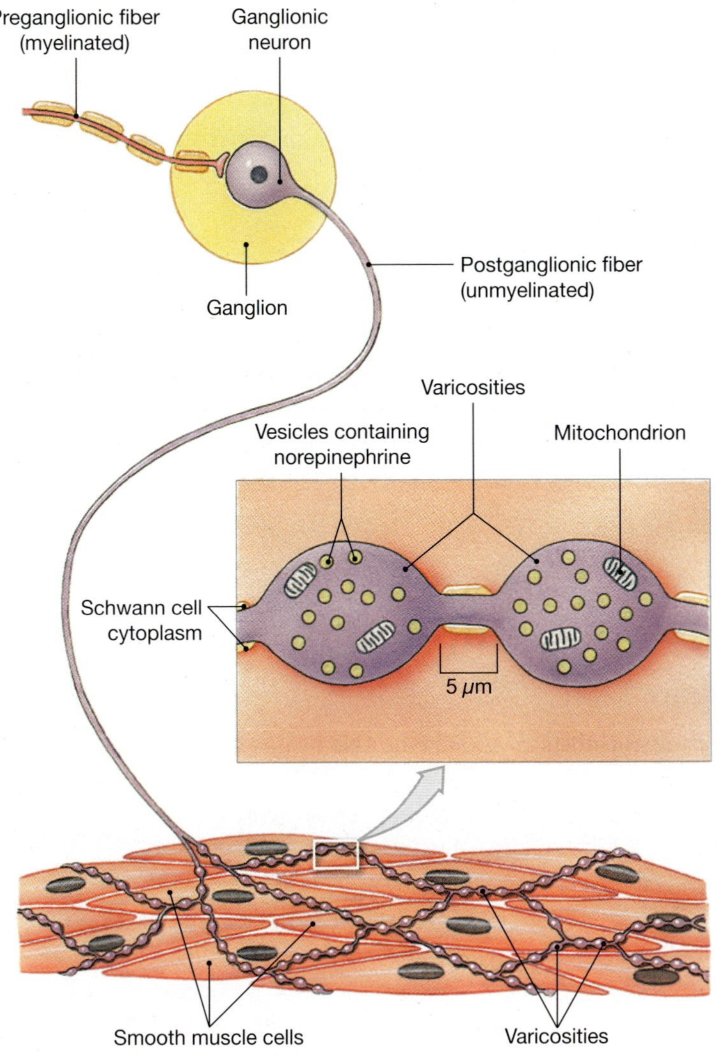

Figure 17.6 Sympathetic Postganglionic Nerve Endings
A diagrammatic view of sympathetic neuroeffector junctions.

A Summary of the Sympathetic Division [Table 17.1]

1. The sympathetic division of the ANS includes two sympathetic chains resembling a string of beads, one on each side of the vertebral column; three collateral ganglia anterior to the spinal column; and two suprarenal medullae.
2. Preganglionic fibers are short because the ganglia are close to the spinal cord. The postganglionic fibers are relatively long and extend a considerable distance before reaching their target organs. (In the case of the suprarenal medullae, very short axons from modified ganglionic neurons end at capillaries that carry their secretions to the bloodstream.)
3. The sympathetic division shows extensive divergence; a single preganglionic fiber may innervate as many as 32 ganglionic neurons in several different ganglia. As a result, a single sympathetic motor neuron inside the CNS can control a variety of peripheral effectors and produce a complex and coordinated response.
4. All preganglionic neurons release ACh at their synapses with ganglionic neurons. Most of the postganglionic fibers release norepinephrine, but a few release ACh.

5. The effector response depends on the function of the plasmalemma receptor activated when epinephrine or norepinephrine binds to either alpha or beta receptors.

Table 17.1 (p. 464) summarizes the characteristics of the sympathetic division of the ANS.

CONCEPT CHECK

1. Where do the nerve fibers that synapse in the collateral ganglia originate?
2. Individuals with high blood pressure may be given a medication that blocks beta receptors. How would this medication help their condition?
3. What are the two types of sympathetic ganglia and where are they located?

See blue "Answers" tab at back of book.

The Parasympathetic Division [Figure 17.7]

The parasympathetic division of the ANS (**Figure 17.7**) includes the following:

1. *Preganglionic neurons located in the brain stem and in sacral segments of the spinal cord:* In the brain, the mesencephalon, pons, and medulla oblongata contain autonomic nuclei associated with cranial nerves III, VII, IX, and X. In the sacral segments of the spinal cord, the autonomic nuclei lie in spinal segments S_2–S_4.
2. *Ganglionic neurons in peripheral ganglia located very close to—or even within—the target organs:* As noted earlier (p. 452), ganglionic neurons in the parasympathetic division are found in terminal ganglia (near the target organs) or intramural ganglia (within the tissues of the target organs). The preganglionic fibers of the parasympathetic division do not diverge as extensively as do those of the sympathetic division. A typical preganglionic fiber synapses on six to eight ganglionic neurons. These neurons are all located in the same ganglion, and their postganglionic fibers influence the same target organ. As a result, *the effects of parasympathetic stimulation are more specific and localized than those of the sympathetic division.*

Organization and Anatomy of the Parasympathetic Division [Figure 17.8]

Parasympathetic preganglionic fibers leave the brain in cranial nerves III (oculomotor), VII (facial), IX (glossopharyngeal), and X (vagus) (**Figure 17.8**). The

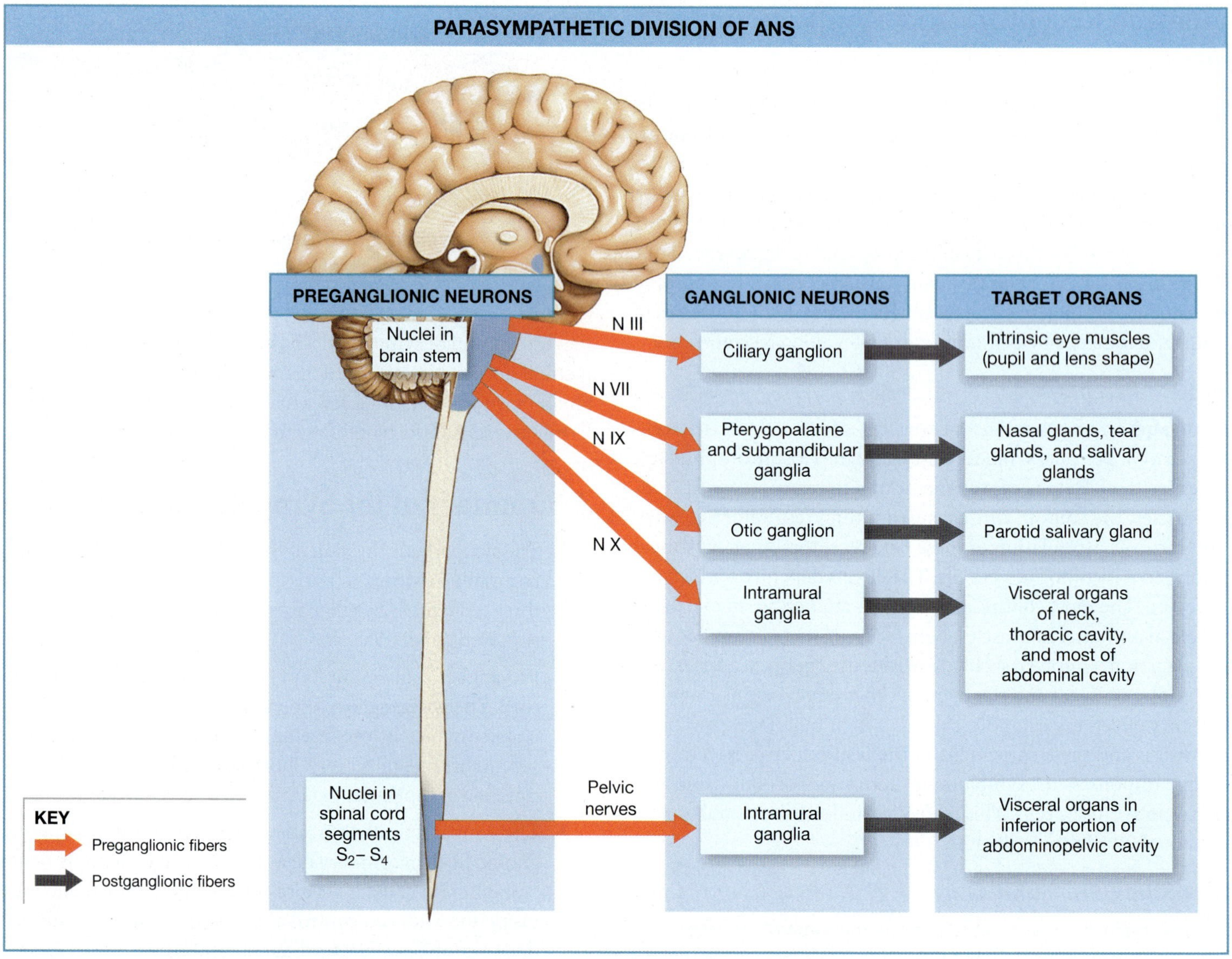

Figure 17.7 Organization of the Parasympathetic Division of the ANS
This diagram summarizes the relationships between preganglionic and ganglionic neurons and between ganglionic neurons and target organs.

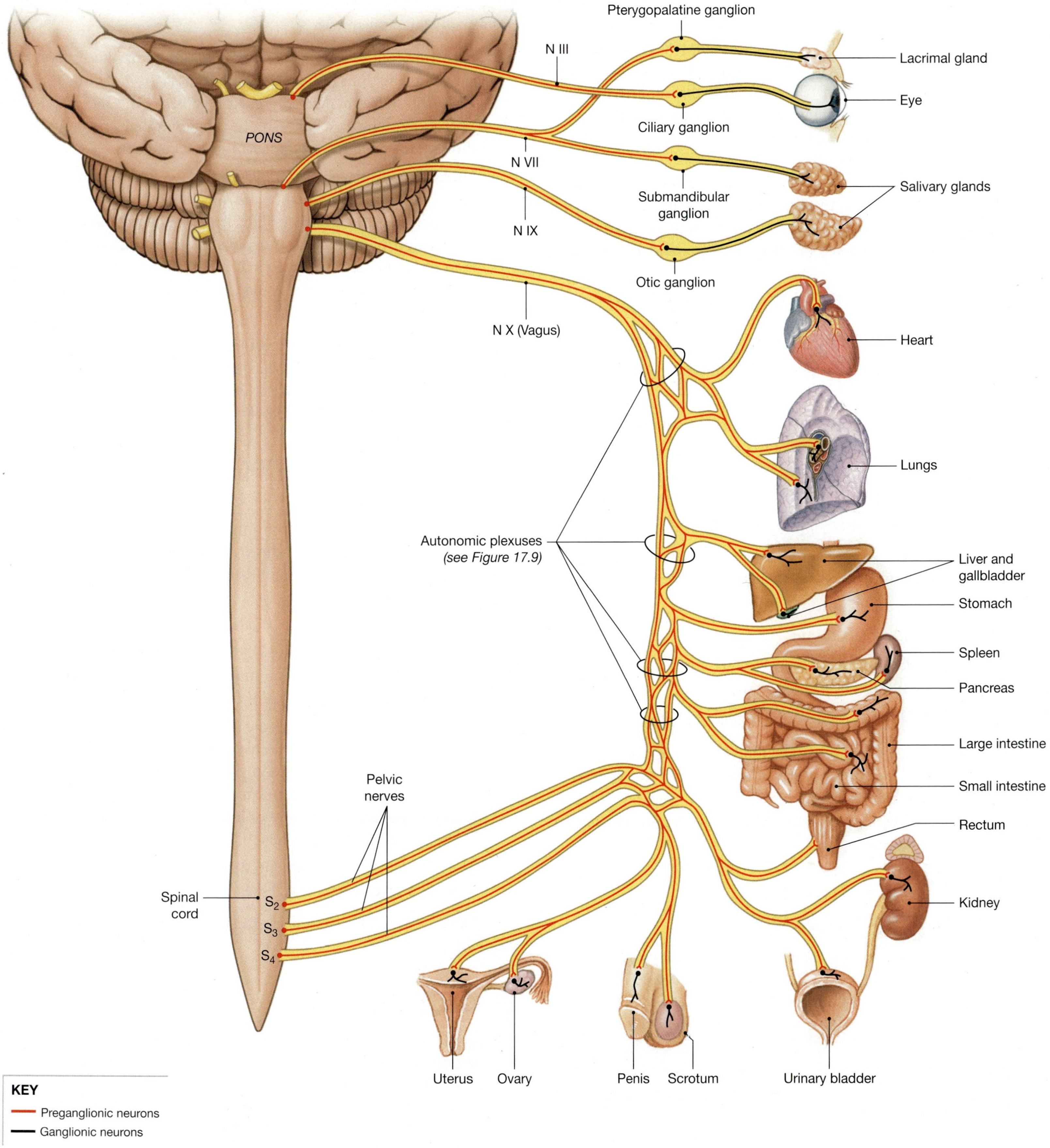

Figure 17.8 Anatomical Distribution of the Parasympathetic Output
Preganglionic fibers exit the CNS through either cranial nerves or pelvic nerves. The pattern of target-organ innervation is similar on each side of the body although only nerves on the left side are illustrated.

fibers in N III, N VII, and N IX help control visceral structures in the head. These preganglionic fibers synapse in the **ciliary**, **pterygopalatine**, **submandibular**, and **otic ganglia**. pp. 420–424 Short postganglionic fibers then continue to their peripheral targets. The vagus nerve provides preganglionic parasympathetic innervation to intramural ganglia within structures in the thoracic cavity and in the abdominopelvic cavity as distant as the last segments of the large intestine. The vagus nerve alone provides roughly 75 percent of all parasympathetic outflow.

The sacral parasympathetic outflow does not join the ventral rami of the spinal nerves. pp. 369, 461 Instead, the preganglionic fibers form distinct **pelvic nerves** that innervate intramural ganglia in the kidney and urinary bladder, the terminal portions of the large intestine, and the sex organs.

General Functions of the Parasympathetic Division

A partial listing of the major effects produced by the parasympathetic division includes the following:

1. Constriction of the pupils to restrict the amount of light entering the eyes; assists in focusing on nearby objects.
2. Secretion by digestive glands, including salivary glands, gastric glands, duodenal and other intestinal glands, the pancreas, and the liver.
3. Secretion of hormones that promote nutrient absorption by peripheral cells.
4. Increased smooth muscle activity along the digestive tract.
5. Stimulation and coordination of defecation.
6. Contraction of the urinary bladder during urination.
7. Constriction of the respiratory passageways.
8. Reduction in heart rate and force of contraction.
9. Sexual arousal and stimulation of sexual glands in both sexes.

These functions center on relaxation, food processing, and energy absorption. The effects of the parasympathetic division lead to a general increase in the nutrient content of the blood. Cells throughout the body respond to this increase by absorbing nutrients and using them to support growth and other anabolic activities.

Parasympathetic Activation and Neurotransmitter Release

All of the preganglionic and postganglionic fibers in the parasympathetic division release ACh at their synapses and neuroeffector junctions. The neuroeffector junctions are small, with narrow synaptic clefts. The effects of stimulation are short-lived, because most of the ACh released is inactivated by acetylcholinesterase within the synapse. Any ACh diffusing into the surrounding tissues is deactivated by the enzyme *tissue cholinesterase.* As a result, the effects of parasympathetic stimulation are quite localized, and they last a few seconds at most.

Plasmalemma Receptors and Responses

Although all the synapses (neuron-to-neuron) and neuroeffector junctions (neuron-to-effector) of the parasympathetic division use the same transmitter, acetylcholine, two different types of ACh receptors are found on the postsynaptic plasmalemmae:

1. **Nicotinic** (nik-ō-TIN-ik) **receptors** are found on the surfaces of all ganglionic neurons of both the parasympathetic and sympathetic divisions, as well as at neuromuscular synapses of the SNS. Exposure to ACh always causes excitation of the ganglionic neuron or muscle fiber through the opening of plasmalemma ion channels.
2. **Muscarinic** (mus-ka-RIN-ik) **receptors** are found at all cholinergic neuroeffector junctions in the parasympathetic division, as well as at the few cholinergic neuroeffector junctions in the sympathetic division. Stimulation of muscarinic receptors produces longer-lasting effects than does stimulation of nicotinic receptors. The response, which reflects the activation or inactivation of specific enzymes, may be either excitatory or inhibitory.

The names *nicotinic* and *muscarinic* indicate the chemical compounds that stimulate these receptor sites. Nicotinic receptors bind *nicotine,* a powerful component of tobacco smoke. Muscarinic receptors are stimulated by *muscarine,* a toxin produced by some poisonous mushrooms.

A Summary of the Parasympathetic Division [Table 17.1]

1. The parasympathetic division includes visceral motor nuclei in the brain stem associated with four cranial nerves (III, VII, IX, and X). In sacral segments S_2–S_4, autonomic nuclei lie in the lateral portions of the anterior gray horns.
2. The ganglionic neurons are situated in intramural ganglia or in ganglia closely associated with their target organs.
3. The parasympathetic division innervates structures in the head and organs in the thoracic and abdominopelvic cavities.
4. All parasympathetic neurons are cholinergic. Release of ACh by preganglionic neurons stimulates nicotinic receptors on ganglionic neurons, and the effect is always excitatory. The release of ACh at neuroeffector junctions stimulates muscarinic receptors, and the effects may be either excitatory or inhibitory, depending on the nature of the enzymes activated when ACh binds to the receptor.
5. The effects of parasympathetic stimulation are usually brief and restricted to specific organs and sites.

Table 17.1 summarizes the characteristics of the parasympathetic division of the ANS.

CONCEPT CHECK

1. Identify the neurotransmitter released by preganglionic fibers and by the postganglionic fibers in the parasympathetic division of the autonomic nervous system.
2. What are the two different ACh receptors found on postsynaptic plasmalemmae in the parasympathetic division?
3. What are intramural ganglia?
4. Why does sympathetic stimulation have such widespread effects?

See blue "Answers" tab at back of book.

Relationships between the Sympathetic and Parasympathetic Divisions

The sympathetic division has widespread impact, reaching visceral organs as well as tissues throughout the body. The parasympathetic division modifies the activity of structures innervated by specific cranial nerves and pelvic nerves. This includes the visceral organs within the thoracic and abdominopelvic cavities. Although some of these organs are innervated by only one autonomic division, most vital organs receive **dual innervation**—that is, they receive instructions from both the sympathetic and parasympathetic divisions. Where dual innervation exists, the two divisions often have opposing or antagonistic effects. Dual innervation is most prominent in the digestive tract, the heart, and the lungs. For example, sympathetic stimulation decreases digestive tract motility, whereas parasympathetic stimulation increases its motility.

Anatomy of Dual Innervation [Figure 17.9]

In the head, parasympathetic postganglionic fibers from the ciliary, pterygopalatine, submandibular, and otic ganglia accompany the cranial nerves to their peripheral destinations. The sympathetic innervation reaches the same structures by traveling directly from the superior cervical ganglia of the sympathetic chain.

In the thoracic and abdominopelvic cavities, the sympathetic postganglionic fibers mingle with parasympathetic preganglionic fibers at a series of plexuses (**Figure 17.9**). These are the *cardiac plexus,* the *pulmonary*

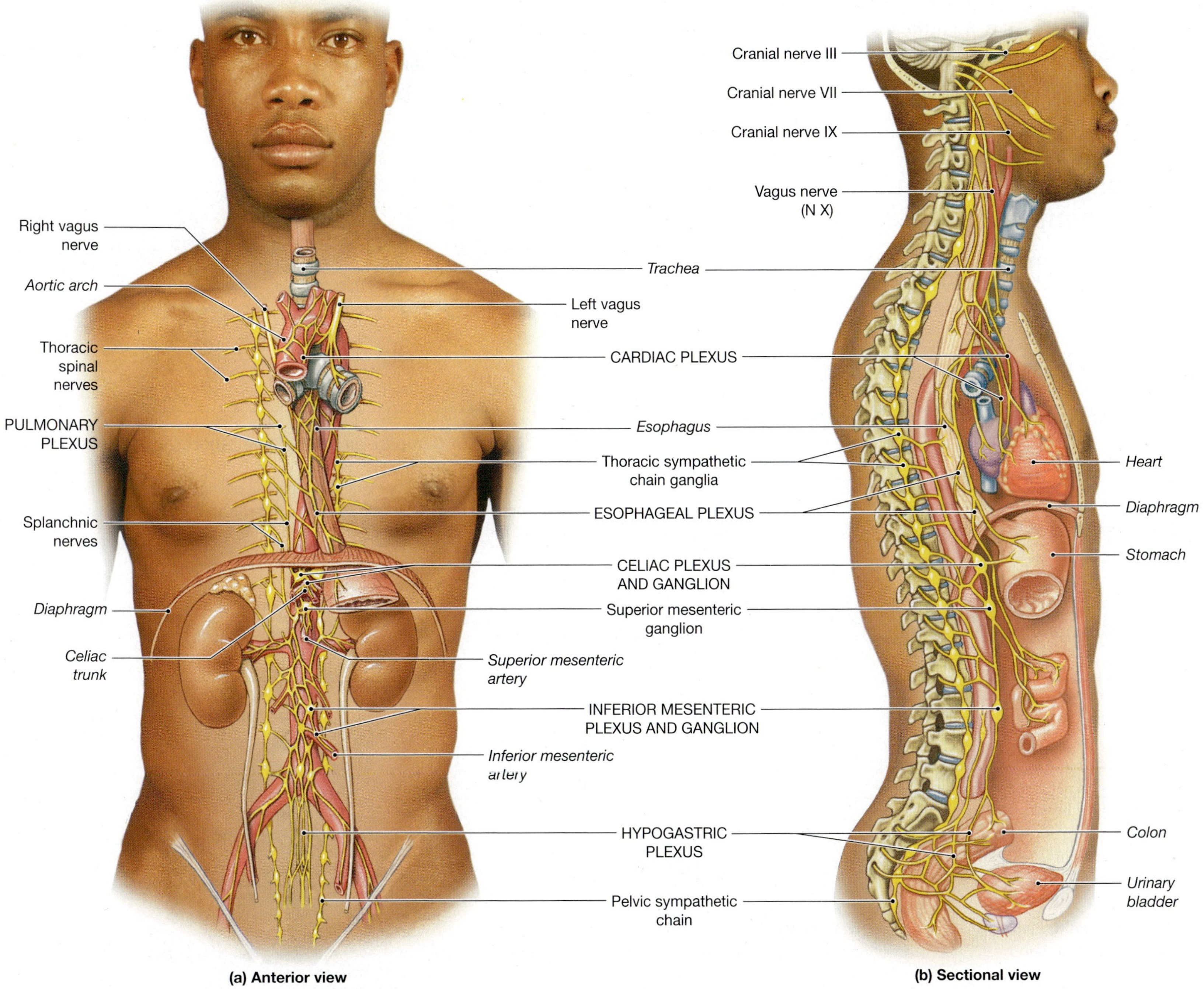

Figure 17.9 The Peripheral Autonomic Plexuses
(a) This is a diagrammatic view of the distribution of ANS plexuses in the thoracic cavity (cardiac, esophageal, and pulmonary plexuses) and the abdominopelvic cavity (celiac, inferior mesenteric, and hypogastric plexuses). **(b)** A sectional view of the autonomic plexuses.

plexus, the *esophageal plexus*, the *celiac plexus*, the *inferior mesenteric plexus*, and the *hypogastric plexus*. Nerves leaving these plexuses travel with the blood vessels and lymphatics that supply visceral organs.

Autonomic fibers entering the thoracic cavity intersect at the **cardiac plexus** and the **pulmonary plexus**. These plexuses contain both sympathetic and parasympathetic fibers bound for the heart and lungs, respectively, as well as the parasympathetic ganglia whose output affects those organs. The **esophageal plexus** contains descending branches of the vagus nerve and splanchnic nerves leaving the sympathetic chain on either side.

Parasympathetic preganglionic fibers of the vagus nerve enter the abdominopelvic cavity with the esophagus. There they join the network of the **celiac plexus**, also called the *solar plexus*. The celiac plexus and an associated smaller plexus, the **inferior mesenteric plexus**, innervate viscera down to the initial segments of the large intestine. The **hypogastric plexus** contains the parasympathetic outflow of the pelvic nerves, sympathetic postganglionic fibers from the inferior mesenteric ganglion, and sacral splanchnic nerves from the sympathetic chain. The hypogastric plexus innervates the digestive, urinary, and reproductive organs of the pelvic cavity.

A Comparison of the Sympathetic and Parasympathetic Divisions

Figure 17.10 and Table 17.1 compare key features of the sympathetic and parasympathetic divisions of the ANS.

Integration and Control of Autonomic Functions

The ANS, like the somatic nervous system (SNS), is organized into a series of interacting levels. At the first level you find the visceral motor neurons that participate in cranial and spinal *visceral reflexes*. The cell bodies of these motor neurons are located in the spinal cord and lower brain stem.

Visceral Reflexes [Figure 17.11 and Table 17.2]

Visceral reflexes (Figure 17.11) are the simplest functional units in the autonomic nervous system. They provide automatic motor responses that can be modified, facilitated, or inhibited by higher centers, especially those of the hypothalamus. All visceral reflexes are polysynaptic. p. 382 Each

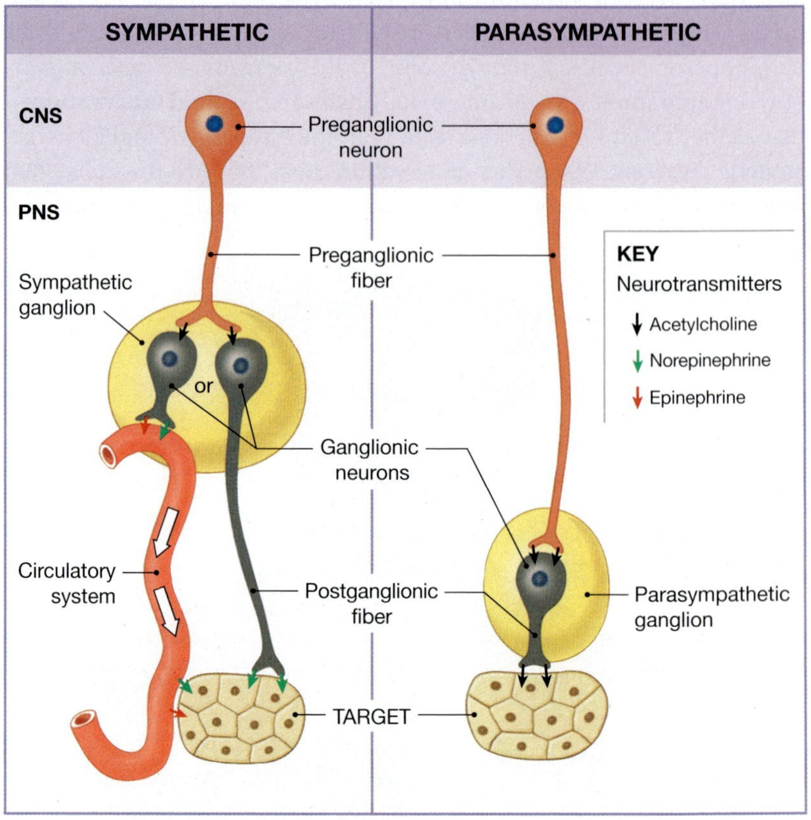

Figure 17.10 A Comparison of the Sympathetic and Parasympathetic Divisions
This diagram compares fiber length (preganglionic and postganglionic), the general location of ganglia, and the primary neurotransmitter released by each division of the autonomic nervous system.

TABLE 17.1 A Comparison of the Sympathetic and Parasympathetic Divisions of the ANS

Characteristic	Sympathetic Division	Parasympathetic Division
Location of CNS Visceral Motor Neurons	Lateral gray horns of spinal segments T_1–L_2	Brain stem and spinal segments S_2–S_4
Location of PNS Ganglia	Paravertebral sympathetic chain; collateral ganglia (celiac, superior mesenteric, and inferior mesenteric) located anterior and lateral to the descending aorta	Intramural or terminal
Preganglionic Fibers:		
Length	Relatively short, myelinated	Relatively long, myelinated
Neurotransmitter released	Acetylcholine	Acetylcholine
Postganglionic Fibers:		
Length	Relatively long, unmyelinated	Relatively short, unmyelinated
Neurotransmitter released	Usually norepinephrine	Always acetylcholine
Neuroeffector Junction	Varicosities and enlarged terminal knobs that release transmitter near target cells	Neuroeffector junctions that release transmitter to special receptor surface
Degree of Divergence from CNS to Ganglion Cells	Approximately 1:32	Approximately 1:6
General Functions	Stimulate metabolism, increase alertness, prepare for emergency "fight or flight" response	Promote relaxation, nutrient uptake, energy storage ("rest and repose")

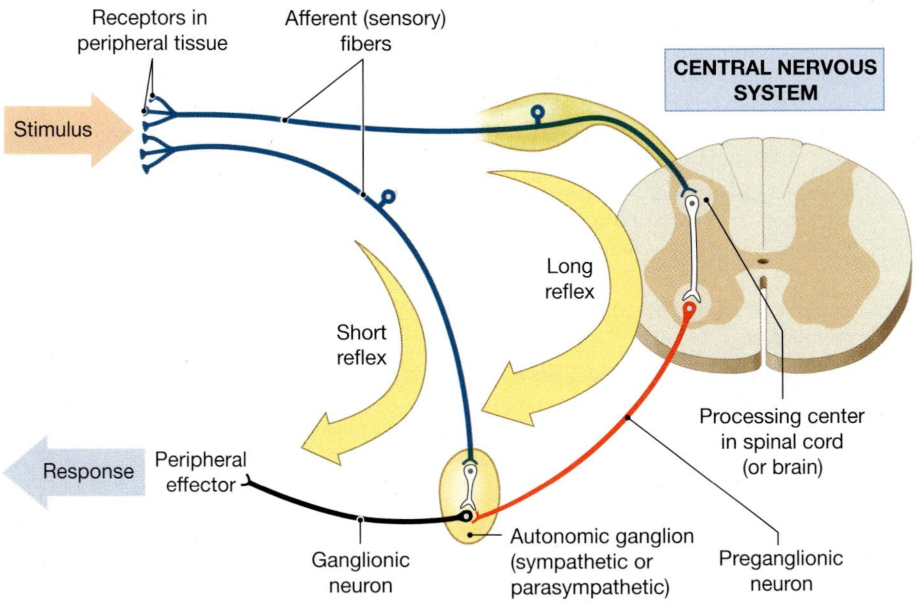

Figure 17.11 Visceral Reflexes
Visceral reflexes have the same basic components as somatic reflexes, but all visceral reflexes are polysynaptic.

visceral reflex arc (Figure 17.11) consists of a receptor, a sensory nerve, a processing center (interneuron or motor neuron), and two visceral motor neurons (preganglionic and ganglionic). Sensory nerves deliver information to the CNS along spinal nerves, cranial nerves, and the autonomic nerves that innervate peripheral effectors. For example, shining a light in the eye triggers a visceral reflex (the *consensual light reflex*) that constricts the pupils of both eyes. p. 382 In total darkness, the pupils dilate. The motor nuclei directing pupillary constriction or dilation are also controlled by hypothalamic centers concerned with emotional states. For example, when you are queasy or nauseated, your pupils constrict; when you are sexually aroused, your pupils dilate.

Visceral reflexes may be either *long reflexes* or *short reflexes.* **Long reflexes** are the autonomic equivalents of the polysynaptic reflexes introduced in Chapter 13. p. 382 Visceral sensory neurons deliver information to the CNS along the dorsal roots of spinal nerves, within the sensory branches of cranial nerves, and within the autonomic nerves that innervate visceral effectors. The processing steps involve interneurons within the CNS, and the motor neurons involved are located within the brain stem or spinal cord. The ANS carries the motor commands to the appropriate visceral effectors, after a synapse within a peripheral autonomic ganglion.

Short reflexes bypass the CNS entirely; they involve sensory neurons and interneurons whose cell bodies are located within autonomic ganglia. The interneurons synapse on ganglionic neurons, and the motor commands are then distributed by postganglionic fibers. Short reflexes control very simple motor responses with localized effects. In general, short reflexes may control patterns of activity in one small part of a target organ, whereas long reflexes coordinate the activities of the entire organ.

In most organs, long reflexes are most important in regulating visceral activities, but this is not the case with the digestive tract and its associated glands. The ganglia in the walls of the digestive tract contain the cell bodies of visceral sensory neurons, interneurons, and visceral motor neurons. Although parasympathetic innervation of the visceral motor neurons can stimulate and coordinate various digestive activities, the digestive system is quite capable of controlling its own functions independent of the central nervous system. For this reason it has been called the *enteric nervous system (ENS);* we shall consider its functions further in Chapter 25.

As we examine other body systems, many examples of autonomic reflexes involved in respiration, cardiovascular function, and other visceral activities will be examined. Table 17.2 summarizes information concerning important visceral reflexes. Note that the parasympathetic division participates in reflexes that affect individual organs and systems, reflecting the relatively specific and restricted pattern of innervation. In contrast, there are fewer sympathetic reflexes. This division is typically activated as a whole, in part because of the degree of divergence and in part because the release of hormones by the suprarenal medullae also produces widespread peripheral effects.

Higher Levels of Autonomic Control

[Figure 17.12]

The levels of activity in the sympathetic and parasympathetic divisions are controlled by centers in the brain stem concerned with specific visceral functions. Figure 17.12 diagrams the levels of autonomic control. As in the SNS, simple reflexes based in the spinal cord provide relatively rapid and automatic responses to stimuli. More complex sympathetic and parasympathetic reflexes are coordinated by processing centers in the medulla oblongata. In addition to the cardiovascular centers, the medulla oblongata contains centers and nuclei involved with respiration, digestive secretions, peristalsis, and urinary function. These medullary centers are in turn subject to regulation by the hypothalamus. In general, centers in the posterior and lateral hypothalamus are concerned with the coordination and regulation of sympathetic function, and portions of the anterior and medial hypothalamus control the parasympathetic division. p. 406

The term *autonomic* was originally applied to the visceral motor system because it was thought that the regulatory centers functioned without regard for other CNS activities. This view has been revised drastically in light of subsequent research. We now know that the hypothalamus interacts

Clinical Note

Diabetic Neuropathy and the ANS In the condition *diabetes mellitus,* blood glucose levels are elevated yet most cells are unable to absorb and use the glucose as an energy source. A variety of physiological problems result; these will be discussed further in Chapter 19. People with chronic, untreated, or poorly managed cases of diabetes mellitus often develop peripheral nerve problems. Peripheral nerve dysfunction, a condition known as *diabetic neuropathy,* has widespread effects. We will defer considering specifics until Chapter 19, except to note that diabetic neuropathy has multiple effects on the ANS. Most notably, it interferes with normal visceral reflexes (Table 17.2). Symptoms often include delayed gastric emptying; reduced sympathetic control of the cardiovascular system, leading to a slow heart rate and low blood pressure when standing; difficulty with urination; and impotence.

TABLE 17.2 Representative Visceral Reflexes

Reflex	Stimulus	Response	Comments
PARASYMPATHETIC REFLEXES			
Gastric and intestinal reflexes *(see Chapter 25)*	Pressure and physical contact with food materials	Smooth muscle contractions that propel food materials and mix food with secretions	Mediated by the vagus nerve (N X)
Defecation *(see Chapter 25)*	Distention of rectum	Relaxation of internal anal sphincter	Requires voluntary relaxation of external anal sphincter
Urination *(see Chapter 26)*	Distention of urinary bladder	Contraction of urinary bladder walls, relaxation of internal urethral sphincter	Requires voluntary relaxation of external urethral sphincter
Direct light and Consensual light reflexes *(see Chapter 18)*	Bright light shining in eye(s)	Constriction of pupils of both eyes	
Swallowing reflex *(see Chapter 25)*	Movement of food and drink into superior pharynx	Smooth muscle and skeletal muscle contractions	Coordinated by swallowing center in medulla oblongata
Vomiting reflex *(see Chapter 25)*	Irritation of digestive tract lining	Reversal of normal smooth muscle action to eject contents	Coordinated by vomiting center in medulla oblongata
Coughing reflex *(see Chapter 24)*	Irritation of respiratory tract lining	Sudden explosive ejection of air	Coordinated by coughing center in medulla oblongata
Baroreceptor reflex *(see Chapter 21)*	Sudden rise in blood pressure in carotid artery	Reduction in heart rate and force of contraction	Coordinated in cardiac center in medulla oblongata
Sexual arousal *(see Chapter 27)*	Erotic stimuli (visual or tactile)	Increased glandular secretions, sensitivity	
SYMPATHETIC REFLEXES			
Cardioacceleratory reflex *(see Chapter 21)*	Sudden decline in blood pressure in carotid artery	Increase in heart rate and force of contraction	Coordinated in cardiac center in medulla oblongata
Vasomotor reflexes *(see Chapter 22)*	Changes in blood pressure in major arteries	Changes in diameter of peripheral blood vessels	Coordinated in vasomotor center in medulla oblongata
Pupillary reflex *(see Chapter 18)*	Low light level reaching visual receptors	Dilation of pupil	
Emission and ejaculation (in males) *(see Chapter 27)*	Erotic stimuli (tactile)	Contraction of seminal glands and prostate, and skeletal muscle contractions that eject semen	Ejaculation involves the contractions of the bulbospongiosus muscles

Figure 17.12 Levels of Autonomic Control

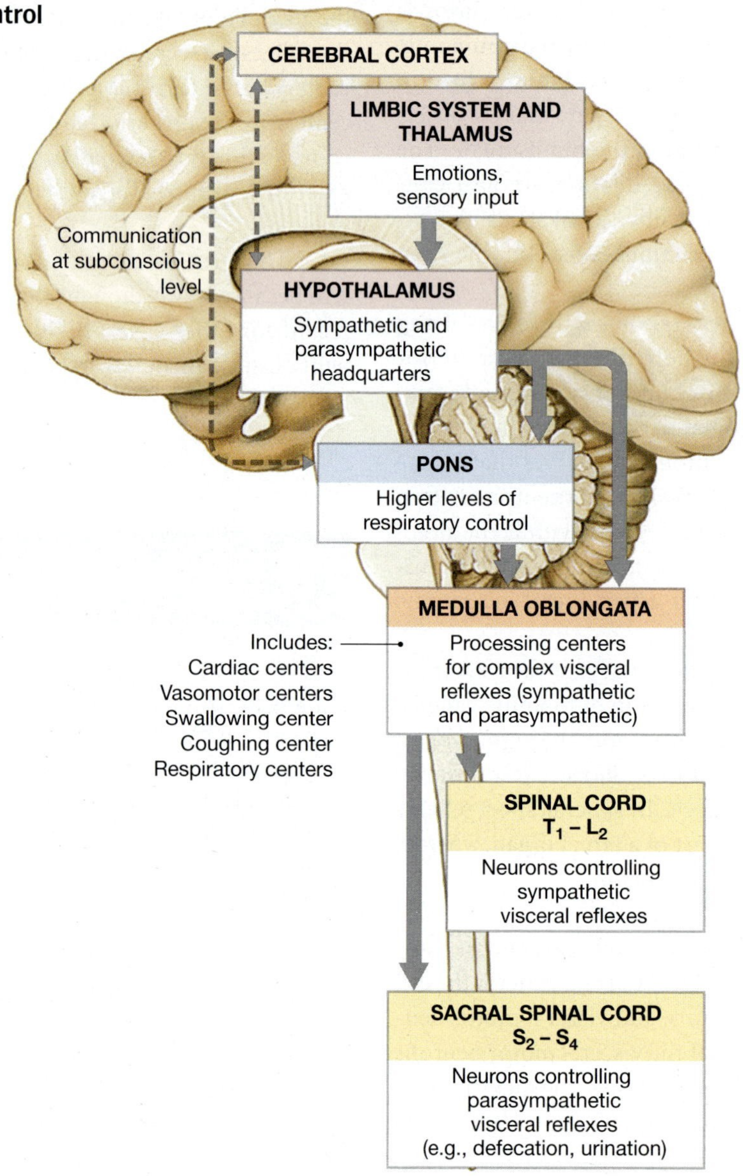

with all other portions of the brain, and that activity in the limbic system (memories, emotional states), thalamus (sensory information), or cerebral cortex (conscious thought processes) can have dramatic effects on autonomic function. Interconnections between the limbic system and the hypothalamus provide a direct link between emotional states and hypothalamic activity. For example, when you become angry, your heart rate accelerates and your blood pressure rises.

CONCEPT CHECK

1. What is meant by dual innervation?
2. What are visceral reflexes?
3. Name three plexuses in the abdominopelvic cavity.

See blue "Answers" tab at back of book.

CLINICAL TERMS

diabetic neuropathy: A degenerative neurological disorder that may develop in people with *diabetes mellitus.*

Horner's syndrome: A condition characterized by unilateral loss of sympathetic innervation to the face.

Raynaud's disease: A condition of unknown cause that results from excessive peripheral sympathetic vasoconstriction in response to cold stimuli.

STUDY OUTLINE

Introduction 452

1. The **autonomic nervous system (ANS)** regulates body temperature and coordinates cardiovascular, respiratory, digestive, excretory, and reproductive functions. Routine physiological adjustments to systems are made by the autonomic nervous system operating at the subconscious level.

A Comparison of the Somatic and Autonomic Nervous Systems 452

1. The autonomic nervous system, like the somatic nervous system, has afferent and efferent neurons. However, in the ANS, the afferent pathways originate in visceral receptors, and the efferent pathways connect to visceral effector organs.
2. In addition to the difference in receptor and effector organ location, the ANS differs from the SNS in the arrangement of the neurons connecting the central nervous system to the effector organs. Visceral motor neurons in the CNS, termed **preganglionic neurons**, send axons (*preganglionic fibers*) to synapse on **ganglionic**, or *postganglionic* **neurons**, whose cell bodies are located in autonomic ganglia outside the CNS. The axon of the ganglionic neuron is a **postganglionic fiber** that innervates peripheral organs. *(see Figure 17.1)*

Subdivisions of the ANS 452

3. There are two major subdivisions in the ANS: the *sympathetic division* and the *parasympathetic division. (see Figure 17.1)*
4. Visceral efferents from the thoracic and lumbar segments form the **thoracolumbar (sympathetic) division** ("fight or flight" system) of the ANS. Generally, it stimulates tissue metabolism, increases alertness, and prepares the body to deal with emergencies. Visceral efferents leaving the brain stem and sacral segments form the **craniosacral (parasympathetic) division** ("rest and repose" system). Generally, it conserves energy and promotes sedentary activities. *(see Figure 17.1)*
5. Both divisions affect target organs via neurotransmitters. Plasmalemma receptors determine whether the response will be stimulatory or inhibitory. Generally, neurotransmitter effects are as follows: (1) All preganglionic terminals release **acetylcholine (ACh)** and are excitatory; (2) all postganglionic parasympathetic terminals release ACh and effects may be excitatory or inhibitory; and (3) most postganglionic sympathetic terminals release **norepinephrine (NE)** and effects are usually excitatory.

The Sympathetic Division 453

1. The **sympathetic division** consists of preganglionic neurons between spinal cord segments T_1 and L_2; ganglionic neurons in ganglia near the vertebral column; and specialized neurons within the suprarenal gland. *(see Figures 17.1a to 17.4/17.10)*
2. There are two types of sympathetic ganglia: **sympathetic chain ganglia** (*paravertebral ganglia* or *lateral ganglia*) and **collateral ganglia** (*prevertebral ganglia*).

The Sympathetic Chain Ganglia 454

3. Between spinal segments T_1 and L_2 each ventral root gives off a *white ramus* with preganglionic fibers to a **sympathetic chain ganglion**. These preganglionic fibers tend to undergo extensive divergence before they synapse with the ganglionic neuron. The synapse occurs within the sympathetic chain ganglia, within one of the collateral ganglia, or within the suprarenal medullae. Preganglionic fibers run between the sympathetic chain ganglia and interconnect them. Postganglionic fibers targeting visceral effectors in the body wall enter the *gray ramus* to return to the spinal nerve for distribution, whereas those that target thoracic cavity structures form autonomic nerves that go directly to their visceral destination. *(see Figures 17.1a,b/17.3)*
4. There are 3 cervical, 11–12 thoracic, 2–5 lumbar, and 4–5 sacral ganglia, and 1 coccygeal sympathetic ganglion in each sympathetic chain. *Every spinal nerve has a gray ramus that carries sympathetic postganglionic fibers.* In summary: (1) Only thoracic and superior lumbar ganglia receive preganglionic fibers by way of white rami; (2) the cervical, inferior lumbar, and sacral chain ganglia receive preganglionic innervation from collateral fibers of sympathetic neurons; and (3) every spinal nerve receives a gray ramus from a ganglion of the sympathetic chain. *(see Figure 17.4)*

Collateral Ganglia 456

5. The abdominopelvic viscera receive sympathetic innervation via preganglionic fibers that pass through the sympathetic chain to synapse within collateral ganglia. The preganglionic fibers that innervate the collateral ganglia form the **splanchnic nerves** (*greater, lesser, lumbar,* and *sacral*). *(see Figures 17.3b/17.4/17.9)*
6. The splanchnic nerves innervate the hypogastric plexus and three collateral ganglia: (1) the *celiac ganglion,* (2) the *superior mesenteric ganglion,* and (3) the *inferior mesenteric ganglion. (see Figures 17.4/17.9)*
7. The **celiac ganglion** innervates the stomach, liver, pancreas, and spleen; the **superior mesenteric ganglion** innervates the small intestine and initial segments of the large intestine; and the **inferior mesenteric ganglion** innervates the kidney, bladder, sex organs, and terminal portions of the large intestine. *(see Figures 17.3b/17.4/17.9)*

The Suprarenal Medullae 458

8. Some preganglionic fibers do not synapse as they pass through both the sympathetic chain and collateral ganglia. Instead, they enter one of the

suprarenal glands and synapse on modified neurons within the **suprarenal medulla**. These cells release *norepinephrine (NE)* and *epinephrine (E)* into the circulation, causing a prolonged sympathetic innervation effect. *(see Figures 17.3c/17.4/17.5)*

Effects of Sympathetic Stimulation 458

9. In a crisis, the entire division responds, an event called **sympathetic activation.** Its effects include increased alertness, a feeling of energy and euphoria, increased cardiovascular and respiratory activity, general elevation in muscle tone, and mobilization of energy reserves.

Sympathetic Activation and Neurotransmitter Release 458

10. Stimulation of the sympathetic division has two distinctive results: the release of norepinephrine (or in some cases acetylcholine) at neuroeffector junctions and the secretion of epinephrine and norepinephrine into the general circulation. *(see Figure 17.6)*

Plasmalemma Receptors and Sympathetic Function 459

11. There are two classes of sympathetic receptors which are stimulated by both norepinephrine and epinephrine: **alpha receptors** (which respond to stimulation by depolarizing the plasmalemma) and **beta receptors** (which respond to stimulation by changing metabolic activity of the cells).
12. Most postganglionic fibers release norepinephrine (adrenergic), but a few release acetylcholine (cholinergic). Postganglionic fibers innervating sweat glands of the skin and blood vessels to skeletal muscles release ACh.

A Summary of the Sympathetic Division 459

13. The sympathetic division has the following characteristics: (1) Two segmentally arranged sympathetic chains lateral to the vertebral column, three collateral ganglia anterior to the vertebral column, and two suprarenal medullae; (2) preganglionic fibers are relatively short, except for those of the suprarenal medullae, while postganglionic fibers are quite long; (3) extensive divergence typically occurs, with a single preganglionic fiber synapsing with many ganglionic neurons in different ganglia; (4) all preganglionic fibers release ACh, while most postganglionic fibers release NE; and (5) effector response depends on the nature and activity of the receptor. *(see Table 17.1)*

The Parasympathetic Division 460

1. The parasympathetic division consists of (1) preganglionic neurons in the brain stem and in sacral segments of the spinal cord and (2) ganglionic neurons in peripheral ganglia located within or immediately next to target organs. *(see Figures 17.7/17.8 and Table 17.1)*

Organization and Anatomy of the Parasympathetic Division 460

2. Preganglionic fibers leave the brain in cranial nerves III (oculomotor), VII (facial), IX (glossopharyngeal), and X (vagus). *(see Figures 17.7/17.8)*
3. Parasympathetic fibers in the oculomotor, facial, and glossopharyngeal nerves help control visceral structures in the head, and they synapse in the **ciliary**, **pterygopalatine**, **submandibular**, and **otic ganglia**. Fibers in the vagus nerve supply preganglionic parasympathetic innervation to intramural ganglia within structures in the thoracic and abdominopelvic cavity. *(see Figures 17.7/17.8)*
4. Preganglionic fibers leaving the sacral segments form **pelvic nerves** that innervate intramural ganglia in the kidney, bladder, latter parts of the large intestine, and sex organs. *(see Figure 17.8)*

General Functions of the Parasympathetic Division 462

5. The effects produced by the parasympathetic division include (1) pupil constriction, (2) digestive gland secretion, (3) hormone secretion for nutrient absorption, (4) increased digestive tract activity, (5) defecation activities, (6) urination activities, (7) respiratory passageway constriction, (8) reduced heart rate, and (9) sexual arousal. These general functions center on relaxation, food processing, and energy absorption.

Parasympathetic Activation and Neurotransmitter Release 462

6. All the parasympathetic preganglionic and postganglionic fibers release ACh at synapses and neuroeffector junctions. The effects are short-lived because of the actions of enzymes at the postsynaptic plasmalemma and in the surrounding tissues.
7. Two different types of ACh receptors are found in postsynaptic plasmalemmae. **Nicotinic receptors** are located on ganglion cells of both divisions of the ANS and at neuromuscular synapses. Exposure to ACh causes excitation by opening plasmalemma channels. **Muscarinic receptors** are located at neuroeffector junctions in the parasympathetic division and those cholinergic neuroeffector junctions in the sympathetic division. Stimulation of muscarinic receptors produces a longer-lasting effect than does stimulation of nicotinic receptors.

A Summary of the Parasympathetic Division 462

8. The parasympathetic division has the following characteristics: (1) It includes visceral motor nuclei associated with cranial nerves III, VII, IX, and X and sacral segments S_2–S_4; (2) ganglionic neurons are located in terminal or intramural ganglia near or within target organs, respectively; (3) it innervates areas serviced by cranial nerves and organs in the thoracic and abdominopelvic cavities; (4) all parasympathetic neurons are cholinergic. The postganglionic neurons are also cholinergic and are further subdivided as being either muscarinic or nicotinic receptors; and (5) effects are usually brief and restricted to specific sites. *(see Figure 17.10 and Table 17.1)*

Relationships between the Sympathetic and Parasympathetic Divisions 463

1. The sympathetic division has widespread influence, reaching visceral and somatic structures throughout the body. *(see Figure 17.4 and Table 17.1)*
2. The parasympathetic division innervates only visceral structures serviced by cranial nerves or lying within the thoracic and abdominopelvic cavity. Organs with **dual innervation** receive instructions from both divisions. *(see Figure 17.10 and Table 17.1)*

Anatomy of Dual Innervation 463

3. In body cavities the parasympathetic and sympathetic nerves intermingle to form a series of characteristic nerve plexuses (nerve networks), which include the **cardiac**, **pulmonary**, **esophageal**, **celiac**, **inferior mesenteric**, and **hypogastric plexuses**. *(see Figure 17.9)*

A Comparison of the Sympathetic and Parasympathetic Divisions 464

4. Review *Figure 17.10* and *Table 17.1.*

Integration and Control of Autonomic Functions 464

Visceral Reflexes 464

1. **Visceral reflexes** are the simplest functions of the ANS. They provide automatic motor responses that can be modified, facilitated, or inhibited by higher centers, especially in the hypothalamus. *(see Figure 17.11 and Table 17.2)*

Higher Levels of Autonomic Control 465

2. In general, higher brain centers in the posterior and lateral hypothalamus are concerned with the coordination and regulation of sympathetic function, and portions of the anterior and medial hypothalamus control the parasympathetic division. *(see Figure 17.12)*

CHAPTER REVIEW

For answers to the Concept Check and Chapter Review questions, go to the blue "Answers" tab at the back of the book.

Level 1 Reviewing Facts and Terms

Match each numbered item with the most closely related lettered item. Use letters for answers in the spaces provided.

Column A	Column B
___ 1. preganglionic	a. all preganglionic fibers
___ 2. thoracolumbar	b. preganglionic fibers to collateral ganglia
___ 3. parasympathetic	c. first neuron
___ 4. prevertebral	d. collateral ganglia
___ 5. paravertebral	e. suprarenal medulla
___ 6. acetylcholine	f. sympathetic activation
___ 7. epinephrine	g. sympathetic division
___ 8. sympathetic	h. terminal ganglia
___ 9. splanchnic	i. sympathetic chain
___ 10. crisis	j. long postganglionic fiber

11. Visceral motor neurons in the CNS
    (a) are ganglionic neurons
    (b) are in the dorsal root ganglion
    (c) have unmyelinated axons except in the lower thoracic region
    (d) send axons to synapse on peripherally located ganglionic neurons

12. Splanchnic nerves
    (a) are formed by parasympathetic postganglionic fibers
    (b) include preganglionic fibers that go to collateral ganglia
    (c) control sympathetic function of structures in the head
    (d) connect one chain ganglion with another

13. Which of the following ganglia belong to the sympathetic division of the ANS?
    (a) otic ganglion (b) sphenopalatine ganglion
    (c) paravertebral ganglia (d) all of the above are correct

14. Preganglionic fibers of the ANS sympathetic division originate in the
    (a) cerebral cortex of the brain
    (b) medulla oblongata
    (c) brain stem and sacral spinal cord
    (d) thoracolumbar spinal cord

15. The neurotransmitter at all synapses and neuroeffector junctions in the parasympathetic division of the ANS is
    (a) epinephrine (b) cyclic-AMP
    (c) norepinephrine (d) acetylcholine

16. The large cells in the suprarenal medulla, which resemble neurons in sympathetic ganglia,
    (a) are located in the suprarenal cortex
    (b) release acetylcholine into blood capillaries
    (c) release epinephrine and norepinephrine into blood capillaries
    (d) have no endocrine functions

17. Sympathetic preganglionic fibers are characterized as
    (a) being short in length and unmyelinated
    (b) being short in length and myelinated
    (c) being long in length and myelinated
    (d) being long in length and unmyelinated

18. All preganglionic autonomic fibers release __________ at their synaptic terminals, and the effects are always __________.
    (a) norepinephrine; inhibitory (b) norepinephrine; excitatory
    (c) acetylcholine; excitatory (d) acetylcholine; inhibitory

19. Postganglionic fibers of autonomic neurons are usually
    (a) myelinated
    (b) unmyelinated
    (c) larger than preganglionic fibers
    (d) located in the spinal cord

20. The white ramus communicans
    (a) carries the postganglionic fibers to the effector organs
    (b) arises from the dorsal root of the spinal nerves
    (c) has fibers that do not diverge
    (d) carries the preganglionic fibers into a nearby sympathetic chain ganglion

Level 2 Reviewing Concepts

1. Cutting the ventral root of the spinal nerve at L_2 would interrupt the transmission of what type of information?
   (a) voluntary motor output (b) ANS motor output
   (c) sensory input (d) a and b are correct

2. Damage to the ventral roots of the first five thoracic spinal nerves on the right side of the body would interfere with
   (a) the ability to dilate the right pupil
   (b) the ability to dilate the left pupil
   (c) the ability to contract the right biceps brachii muscle
   (d) the ability to contract the left biceps brachii muscle

3. What anatomical mechanism is involved in causing a person to blush?
   (a) blood flow to the skin is increased by parasympathetic stimulation
   (b) sympathetic stimulation relaxes vessel walls, increasing blood flow to the skin
   (c) parasympathetic stimulation decreases skin muscle tone, allowing blood to pool at the surface
   (d) sympathetic stimulation increases respiratory oxygen uptake, making the blood brighter red

4. If the visceral signal from the small intestine does not reach the spinal cord, which structures might be damaged?
   (a) preganglionic neurons (b) white rami communicantes
   (c) gray rami communicantes (d) none of the above is correct

5. The effects of epinephrine and norepinephrine released by the suprarenal glands last longer than those of either chemical when released at neuroeffector junctions. Why?

6. Why are the effects of parasympathetic stimulation more specific and localized than those of the sympathetic division?

7. How is sweat gland function regulated by sympathetic activity?

8. How do sympathetic chain ganglia differ from both collateral ganglia and intramural ganglia?

9. Compare the general effects of the sympathetic and parasympathetic divisions of the ANS.

10. Describe the general organization of the pathway for visceral motor output.

Level 3 Critical Thinking

1. In some severe cases, a person suffering from stomach ulcers may need to have surgery to cut the branches of the vagus nerve that innervates the stomach. How would this help the problem?

2. What alterations in ANS function would lead a clinician to diagnose a condition of Horner's syndrome?

3. Kassie is stung on the neck by a wasp. Because she is allergic to wasp venom, her throat begins to swell and her respiratory passages constrict. Would acetylcholine or epinephrine be more helpful in relieving her symptoms? Why?

18

The Nervous System

General and Special Senses

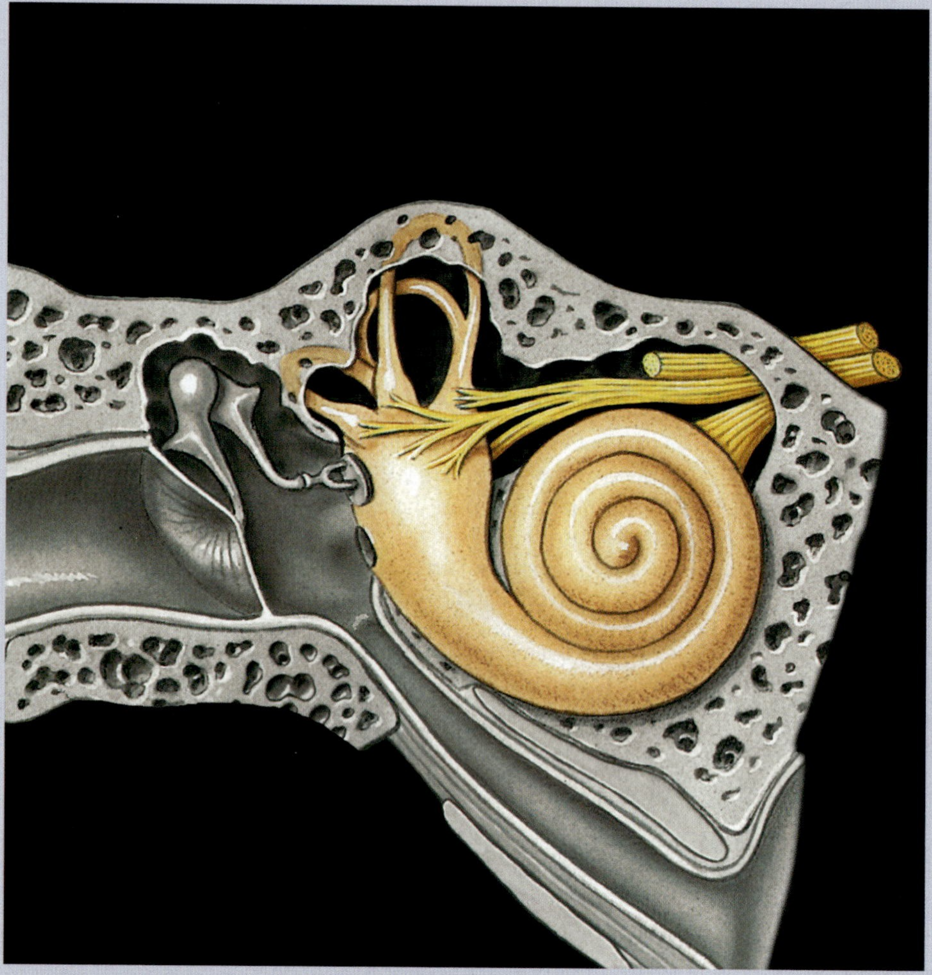

CHAPTER OBJECTIVES

1. Define sensation and discuss the origins of sensations.
2. Distinguish between the general and special senses.
3. Explain why receptors respond to specific stimuli and how the structure of a receptor affects its sensitivity.
4. Distinguish between phasic and tonic receptors.
5. Identify the receptors for the general senses and briefly describe how they function.
6. Classify receptors according to the stimulus detected, body location, and histological structure.
7. Identify, describe, and discuss the receptors and neural pathways involved in the sense of smell.
8. Identify, describe, and discuss the receptors and neural pathways involved in the sense of taste.
9. Identify and describe the structures of the ear and their roles in the processing of equilibrium sensations and describe the mechanism by which we maintain equilibrium.
10. Identify and describe the structures of the ear that collect, amplify, and conduct sound and the structures along the auditory pathway.
11. Describe pathways taken by auditory and equilibrium information traveling to the brain.
12. Identify and describe the layers of the eye and the functions of the structures within each layer.
13. Explain how light is focused by the eye.
14. Identify the structures of the visual pathway.

Every plasmalemma functions as a receptor for the cell, because it responds to changes in the extracellular environment. Plasmalemmae differ in their sensitivities to specific electrical, chemical, and mechanical stimuli. For example, a hormone that stimulates a neuron may have no effect on an osteocyte, because the plasmalemmae of neurons and osteocytes contain different receptor proteins. A **sensory receptor** is a specialized cell or cell process that monitors conditions in the body or the external environment. Stimulation of the receptor directly or indirectly alters the production of action potentials in a sensory neuron. p. 351

The sensory information arriving at the CNS is called a **sensation**; a **perception** is a conscious awareness of a sensation. The term **general senses** refers to sensations of temperature, pain, touch, pressure, vibration, and proprioception (body position). General sensory receptors are distributed throughout the body. These sensations arrive at the primary sensory cortex, or *somatosensory cortex*, via pathways previously described. p. 432

The **special senses** are smell (*olfaction*), taste (*gustation*), balance (*equilibrium*), hearing, and vision. The sensations are provided by specialized receptor cells that are structurally more complex than those of the general senses. These receptors are localized within complex **sense organs**, such as the eye or ear. The information is provided to centers throughout the brain.

Sensory receptors represent the interface between the nervous system and the internal and external environments. The nervous system relies on accurate sensory data to control and coordinate relatively swift responses to specific stimuli. This chapter begins by summarizing receptor function and basic concepts in sensory processing. We will then apply this information to each of the general and special senses as we discuss their structure.

Receptors [Figure 18.1]

Each receptor has a characteristic sensitivity. For example, a touch receptor is very sensitive to pressure but relatively insensitive to chemical stimuli. This concept is called **receptor specificity**. Specificity results from the structure of the receptor cell itself or from the presence of accessory cells or structures that shield it from other stimuli. The simplest receptors are the dendrites of sensory neurons, called **free nerve endings**. They can be stimulated by many different stimuli. For example, free nerve endings that provide the sensation of pain may be responding to chemical stimulation, pressure, temperature changes, or physical damage. In contrast, the receptor cells of the eye are surrounded by accessory cells that normally prevent their stimulation by anything other than light. The area monitored by a single receptor cell is its **receptive field** (Figure 18.1). Whenever a sufficiently strong stimulus arrives in the receptive field, the CNS receives the information. The larger the receptive field, the poorer our ability to localize a stimulus. For example, a touch receptor on the general body surface may have a receptive field 7 cm (2.5 in.) in diameter. As a result, a light touch can be described only generally, as affecting an area of about this size. On the tongue, where the receptive fields are less than a millimeter in diameter, we can be very precise about the location of a stimulus.

An arriving stimulus can take many different forms—it may be a physical force, such as pressure; a dissolved chemical; a sound; or a beam of light. Regardless of the nature of the stimulus, however, sensory information must be sent to the CNS in the form of action potentials, which are electrical events. The arriving information is processed and interpreted by the CNS at the conscious and subconscious levels.

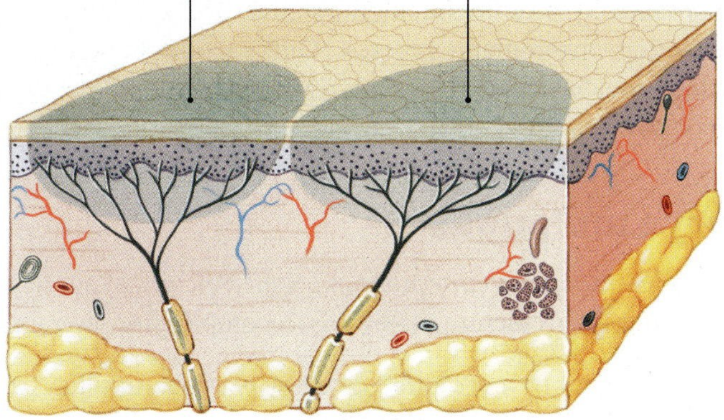

Figure 18.1 Receptors and Receptive Fields
Each receptor monitors a specific area known as the receptive field.

Interpretation of Sensory Information

When sensory information arrives at the CNS, it is routed according to the location and nature of the stimulus. Along the sensory pathways discussed in Chapter 16, axons relay information from point A (the receptor) to point B (a neuron at a specific site in the cerebral cortex). The connection between receptor and cortical neuron is called a **labeled line**. Each labeled line carries information concerning a specific sensation (touch, pressure, vision, and so forth) from receptors in a specific part of the body. The identity of the active labeled line indicates the location and nature of the stimulus. *All other characteristics of the stimulus are conveyed by the pattern of action potentials in the afferent fibers.* This **sensory coding** provides information about the strength, duration, variation, and movement of the stimulus.

Some sensory neurons, called **tonic receptors**, are always active. The photoreceptors of the eye and various receptors that monitor body position are examples of tonic receptors. Other receptors are normally inactive, but become active for a short time whenever there is a change in the conditions they are monitoring. These are **phasic receptors** and provide information on the intensity and rate of change of a stimulus. Many touch and pressure receptors in the skin are examples of phasic receptors. Receptors that combine phasic and tonic coding convey extremely complicated sensory information; receptors that monitor the positions and movements of joints are in this category.

Central Processing and Adaptation

Adaptation is a reduction in sensitivity in the presence of a constant stimulus. **Peripheral (sensory) adaptation** occurs when the receptors or sensory neurons alter their levels of activity. The receptor responds strongly at first, but thereafter the activity along the afferent fiber gradually declines, in part because of synaptic fatigue. This response is characteristic of phasic receptors, which are also called **fast-adapting receptors**. Tonic receptors show little peripheral adaptation and so are called **slow-adapting receptors**.

Adaptation also occurs inside the CNS along the sensory pathways. For example, a few seconds after exposure to a new smell, conscious awareness of the stimulus virtually disappears, although the sensory neurons are still quite active. This process is known as **central adaptation**. Central adaptation usually involves the inhibition of nuclei along a sensory pathway.

At the subconscious level, central adaptation further restricts the amount of detail arriving at the cerebral cortex. Most of the incoming sensory information is processed in centers along the spinal cord or brain stem, potentially triggering involuntary reflexes. Only about 1 percent of the information provided by afferent fibers reaches the cerebral cortex and our conscious awareness.

Sensory Limitations

Our sensory receptors provide a constant detailed picture of our bodies and our surroundings. This picture is, however, incomplete for several reasons:

1. Humans do not have receptors for every possible stimulus.
2. Our receptors have characteristic ranges of sensitivity.
3. A stimulus must be interpreted by the CNS. Our perception of a particular stimulus is an interpretation and not always a reality.

This discussion has introduced basic concepts of receptor function and sensory processing. We can now describe and discuss the receptors responsible for the general senses.

CONCEPT CHECK

1. What different types of stimuli may activate free nerve endings?
2. Contrast tonic and phasic receptors.
3. What is a sensation?
4. Which sensations are grouped under the banner "general senses"?

See blue "Answers" tab at back of book.

The General Senses

Receptors for the general senses are scattered throughout the body and are relatively simple in structure. A simple classification scheme divides them into *exteroceptors*, *proprioceptors*, and *interoceptors*. **Exteroceptors** provide information about the external environment, **proprioceptors** monitor body position, and **interoceptors** monitor conditions inside the body.

A more detailed classification system divides the general sensory receptors into four types according to the nature of the stimulus that excites them:

1. **Nociceptors** (nō-sē-SEP-torz; *noceo*, hurt) respond to a variety of stimuli usually associated with tissue damage. Receptor activation causes the sensation of pain.
2. **Thermoreceptors** respond to changes in temperature.
3. **Mechanoreceptors** are stimulated or inhibited by physical distortion, contact, or pressure on their plasmalemmae.
4. **Chemoreceptors** monitor the chemical composition of body fluids and respond to the presence of specific molecules.

Each class of receptors has distinct structural and functional characteristics. You will find that some tactile receptors and mechanoreceptors are identified by eponyms (commemorative names). Contemporary anatomists have proposed differing alternatives for these names, and as yet no standardization or consensus exists. More significantly, *none* of the alternative names has been widely accepted in the primary literature (professional, technical, or clinical journals or reports). To avoid later confusion, this chapter will use eponyms whenever there is no generally accepted or widely used alternative.

Nociceptors [Figures 18.2/18.3a]

Nociceptors, or pain receptors, are especially common in the superficial portions of the skin (**Figure 18.3a**), in joint capsules, within the periostea of bones, and around the walls of blood vessels. There are few nociceptors in other deep tissues or in most visceral organs. Pain receptors are free nerve endings with large receptive fields. As a consequence, it is often difficult to determine the exact origin of a painful sensation.

There are three types of nociceptors: (1) receptors sensitive to extremes of temperature, (2) receptors sensitive to mechanical damage, and (3) receptors sensitive to dissolved chemicals, such as those released by injured cells. However, very strong temperature, pressure, or chemical stimuli will excite all three receptor types.

Sensations of **fast pain**, or *prickling pain*, are produced by deep cuts or similar injuries. These sensations reach the CNS very quickly, where they often trigger somatic reflexes. They are also relayed to the primary sensory cortex and so receive conscious attention. Painful sensations cease only after tissue damage has ended. However, central adaptation may reduce *perception* of the pain while the pain receptors are still stimulated.

Sensations of **slow pain**, or *burning and aching pain*, result from the same types of injuries as fast pain sensations. However, sensations of slow pain begin later and persist longer than sensations of fast pain. For example, a cut on the hand would produce an immediate awareness of fast pain, followed somewhat later by the ache of slow pain. Slow pain sensations

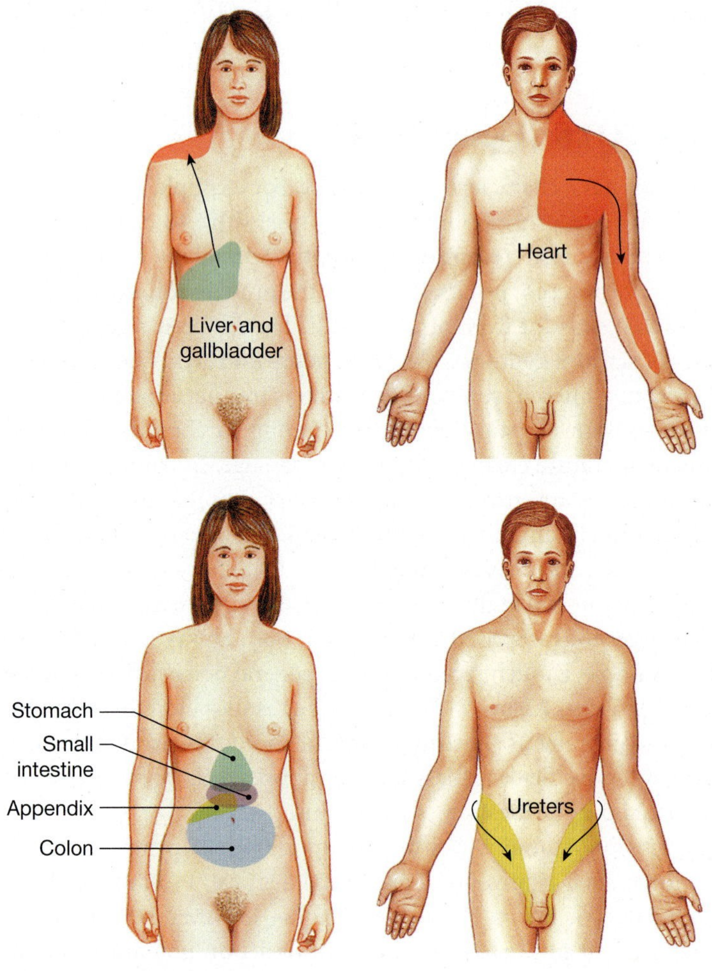

Figure 18.2 Referred Pain
Pain sensations originating in visceral organs are often perceived as involving specific regions of the body surface innervated by the same spinal nerves.

cause a generalized activation of the reticular formation and thalamus. The individual is aware of the pain but has only a general idea of the area affected. A person experiencing slow pain sensations will often palpate the area in an attempt to locate the source of the pain.

Pain sensations from visceral organs are carried by sensory nerves that reach the spinal cord with the dorsal roots of spinal nerves. These visceral pain sensations are often perceived as originating in more superficial regions that are innervated by these same spinal nerves. The precise mechanism responsible for this **referred pain** remains to be determined, but several clinical examples are shown in Figure 18.2. Cardiac pain, for example, is often perceived as originating in the upper chest and left arm.

Thermoreceptors

Temperature receptors are found in the dermis of the skin, in skeletal muscles, in the liver, and in the hypothalamus. Cold receptors are three or four times more numerous than warm receptors. The receptors are free nerve endings, and there are no known structural differences between cold and warm thermoreceptors.

Temperature sensations are conducted along the same pathways that carry pain sensations. They are sent to the reticular formation, the thalamus, and (to a lesser extent) the primary sensory cortex. Thermoreceptors are phasic receptors. They are very active when the temperature is changing, but they quickly adapt to a stable temperature. When you enter an air-conditioned classroom on a hot summer day or a warm lecture hall on a brisk fall evening, the temperature seems unpleasant at first, but the discomfort fades as adaptation occurs.

Mechanoreceptors

Mechanoreceptors are sensitive to stimuli that stretch, compress, twist, or distort their plasmalemmae. There are three classes of mechanoreceptors: (1) *tactile receptors* provide sensations of touch, pressure, and vibration; (2) *baroreceptors* (bar-ō-rē-SEP-torz; *baro-*, pressure) detect pressure changes in the walls of blood vessels and in portions of the digestive, reproductive, and urinary tracts; and (3) *proprioceptors* monitor the positions of joints and muscles and are the most complex of the general sensory receptors.

Tactile Receptors [Figure 18.3/Table 18.1]

Tactile receptors range in structural complexity from the simple free nerve endings to specialized sensory complexes with accessory cells and supporting structures. **Fine touch** and **pressure receptors** provide detailed information about a source of stimulation, including its exact location, shape, size, texture, and movement. These receptors are extremely sensitive and have relatively narrow receptive fields. **Crude touch** and **pressure receptors** provide poor localization and little additional information about the stimulus.

Figure 18.3 shows six different types of tactile receptors in the skin. They can be subdivided into two groups: *unencapsulated receptors* (free nerve endings, tactile disc, and root hair plexus) and *encapsulated receptors* (tactile corpuscle, Ruffini corpuscle, and lamellated corpuscle).

Clinical Note

Acute and Chronic Pain Painful sensations can result from tissue damage or sensory nerve irritation. The pain can originate where it is perceived, be referred from another location, or represent a false signal generated along the sensory pathway. The treatment differs in each case, and an accurate diagnosis is an essential first step.

Acute pain is the result of tissue injury; the cause is apparent, and local treatment of the injury is typically effective in relieving the pain. The most effective solution is to stop the damage, end the stimulation, and suppress the painful sensations at the site of injury. Tissue injury results in damage to cell membranes. A fatty acid called arachidonic acid escapes from injured membranes and stimulates nociceptors in the area. Pain sensations are suppressed when topical or locally injected anesthetics inactivate nociceptors in the immediate area. Analgesic drugs can also be administered.

Chronic pain is more difficult to categorize and treat. It includes (1) injury-related pain that persists after tissue structure has been repaired; (2) pain from a chronic disease; and (3) pain without any apparent cause. Complex psychological and physiological components are also involved. Chronic pain can be helped by antidepressants and antiseizure medicines. Counseling and increasing the level of physical activity often help the person focus attention outward rather than inward. The outward focus can lessen the perceived level of pain and reduce the amount of pain medication required.

In some cases, chronic pain and severe acute pain can be suppressed by inhibition of the central pain pathway. Analgesics related to morphine reduce pain by mimicking the action of endorphins. The perception of pain may be altered, although the pain remains. For example, patients on morphine report being aware of painful sensations, but they are not distressed by them. Surgical steps can be taken to control severe pain. For instance, (1) the sensory innervation of an area can be destroyed by an electrical current, (2) the dorsal roots carrying the painful sensations can be cut (a *rhizotomy*), (3) the ascending tracts in the spinal cord can be severed (a *tractotomy*), or (4) thalamic or limbic centers can be stimulated or destroyed. These options are used only when other methods of pain control have failed to provide relief.

When used to control pain, the Chinese technique of acupuncture involves the insertion of fine needles at specific locations. These needles are either heated or twirled by the therapist. Theories suggest that the pain relief may follow the release of endorphins. It is not known how acupuncture stimulates endorphin release; the acupuncture points do not correspond to the distribution of any of the major peripheral nerves.

Many other aspects of pain generation and control remain a mystery. Up to 30 percent of patients who receive nonfunctional medication subsequently experience a significant reduction of pain. It has been suggested that this *placebo effect* results from endorphin release triggered by the expectation of pain relief. Although the medication has no direct effect, the indirect effect can be quite significant and complicates the evaluation of analgesic medications.

Unencapsulated Receptors [Figure 18.3a–c] *Free nerve endings* are common in the papillary layer of the dermis (Figure 18.3a). In sensitive areas, the dendritic branches penetrate the epidermis and contact *Merkel cells* in the stratum germinativum. p. 91 Each Merkel cell communicates with a sensory neuron across a vesicular synapse that involves an expanded nerve terminal known as a **tactile disc** (also called a *Merkel's* [MER-kelz] *disc*) (Figure 18.3b). Merkel cells are sensitive to fine touch and pressure. They are tonically active and extremely sensitive and have narrow receptive fields. Free nerve endings are also associated with hair follicles.

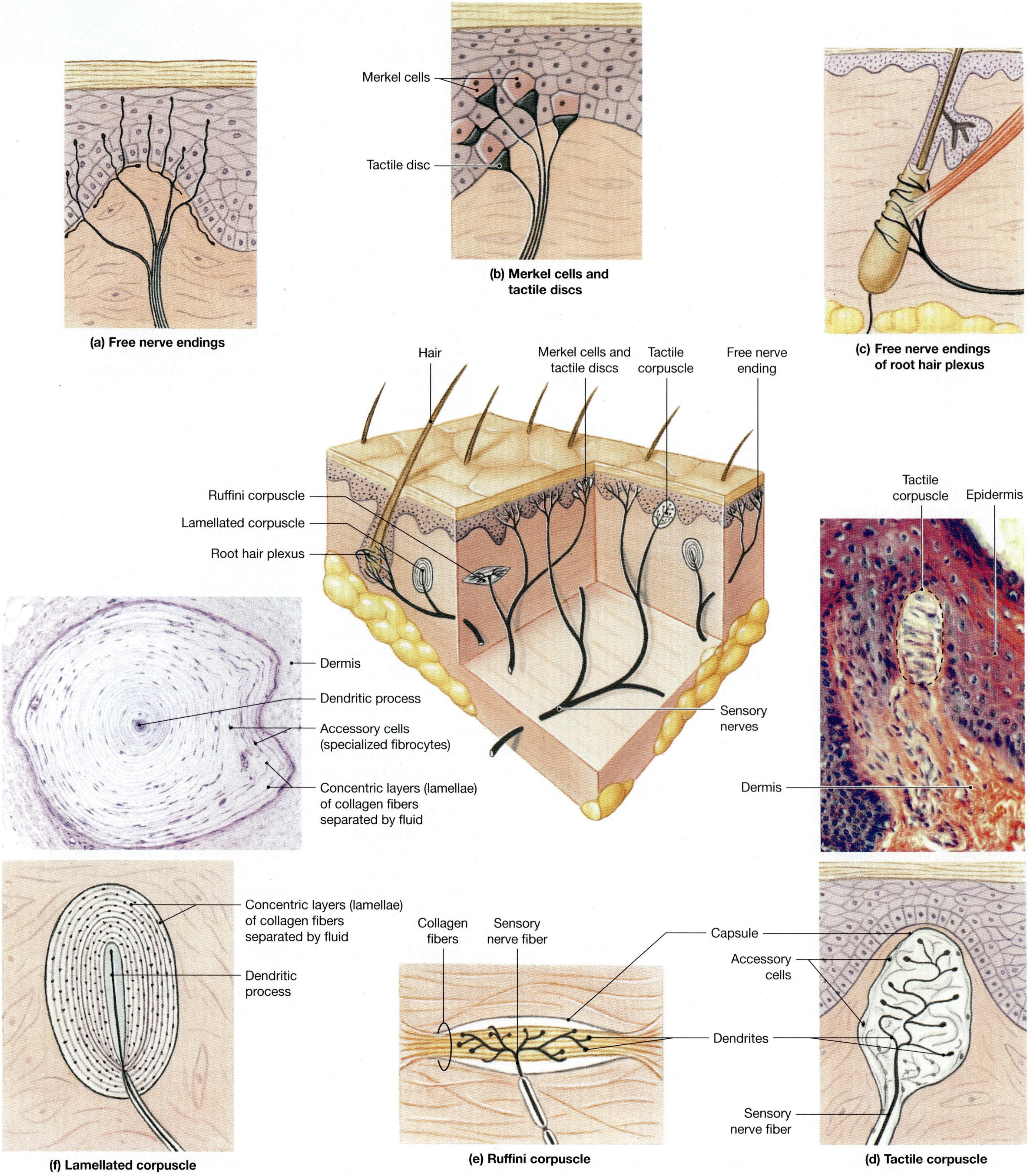

Figure 18.3 Tactile Receptors in the Skin

The location and general histological appearance of six important tactile receptors. **(a)** Free nerve endings. **(b)** Merkel cells and tactile discs. **(c)** Free nerve endings of root hair plexus. **(d)** Tactile corpuscle; the capsule boundary in the micrograph is indicated by a dashed line. (LM × 550) **(e)** Ruffini corpuscle. **(f)** Lamellated corpuscle. (LM × 125)

The free nerve endings of the **root hair plexus** monitor distortions and movements across the body surface (Figure 18.3c). When the hair is displaced, the movement of the follicle distorts the sensory dendrites and produces action potentials in the afferent fiber. These receptors adapt rapidly, so they are best at detecting initial contact and subsequent movements. For example, most people feel their clothing only when they move or when they consciously focus attention on tactile sensations from their skin.

Encapsulated Receptors [Figure 18.3d–f and Table 18.1] Large, oval **tactile corpuscles** (also called *Meissner's* [MĪS-nerz] *corpuscles*) are found where tactile sensitivities are extremely well developed (Figure 18.3d). They are especially common at the eyelids, lips, fingertips, nipples, and external genitalia. The dendrites are highly coiled and interwoven, and they are surrounded by modified Schwann cells. A fibrous capsule surrounds the entire complex and anchors it within the dermis. Tactile corpuscles detect light touch, movement, and vibration; they adapt to stimulation within a second after contact.

Ruffini (ru-FĒ-nē) **corpuscles**, located in the dermis, are also sensitive to pressure and distortion of the skin, but they are tonically active and show little if any adaptation. The capsule surrounds a core of collagen fibers that are continuous with those of the surrounding dermis. Dendrites within the capsule are interwoven around the collagen fibers (Figure 18.3e). Any tension or distortion of the dermis tugs or twists the fibers within the capsule, and this change stretches or compresses the attached dendrites and alters the activity in the myelinated afferent fiber.

Lamellated corpuscles (also called *pacinian* [pa-SIN-ē-an] *corpuscles*) are considerably larger encapsulated receptors (Figure 18.3f). The dendritic process lies within a series of concentric cellular layers. These layers shield the dendrite from virtually every source of stimulation other than direct pressure. Lamellated corpuscles respond to deep pressure but are most sensitive to pulsing or vibrating stimuli. Although both lamellated corpuscles and Ruffini corpuscles respond to pressure, the lamellated corpuscles adapt rapidly while the Ruffini corpuscles adapt quite slowly. These receptors are scattered throughout the dermis, notably in the fingers, breasts, and external genitalia. They are also encountered in the superficial and deep fasciae, in periostea and joint capsules, in mesenteries, in the pancreas, and in the walls of the urethra and urinary bladder.

Table 18.1 summarizes the functions and characteristics of the six tactile receptors discussed. The distribution of tactile sensations inside the CNS is via the posterior column and spinothalamic pathways. p. 432 Tactile sensitivities may be altered by peripheral infection, disease processes, and damage to sensory afferents or central pathways, and there are important clinical tests that evaluate tactile sensitivity.

CONCEPT CHECK

1. When the nociceptors in your hand are stimulated, what sensation do you perceive?
2. What would happen to an individual if the information from proprioceptors in the lower limbs were blocked from reaching the CNS?
3. What are the three classes of mechanoreceptors?

See blue "Answers" tab at back of book.

TABLE 18.1 Touch and Pressure Receptors

Sensation	Receptor	Responds to
Fine touch	Free nerve ending	Light contact with skin
	Tactile disc	As above
	Root hair plexus	Initial contact with hair shaft
Pressure and vibration	Tactile corpuscle	Initial contact and low-frequency vibrations
	Lamellated corpuscle	Initial contact (deep) and high-frequency vibrations
Deep pressure	Ruffini corpuscle	Stretching and distortion of the dermis

Baroreceptors [Figure 18.4]

Baroreceptors are stretch receptors that monitor changes in pressure. The receptor consists of free nerve endings that branch within the elastic tissues in the wall of a hollow organ, a blood vessel, or the respiratory, digestive, or urinary tract. When the pressure changes, the elastic walls of these tubes or organs stretch or recoil. These changes in shape distort the dendritic branches and alter the rate of action-potential generation. Baroreceptors respond immediately to a change in pressure.

Baroreceptors monitor blood pressure in the walls of major vessels, including the carotid artery (at the *carotid sinus*) and the aorta (at the *aortic sinus*). The information provided by these baroreceptors plays a major role in regulating cardiac function and adjusting blood flow to vital tissues. Baroreceptors in the lungs monitor the degree of lung expansion. This information is relayed to the respiratory rhythmicity center, which sets the pace of respiration. Baroreceptors in the urinary and digestive tracts trigger a variety of visceral reflexes, such as urination. Figure 18.4 provides examples of baroreceptor locations and functions.

Proprioceptors

Proprioceptors monitor the position of joints, the tension in tendons and ligaments, and the state of muscular contraction. Generally, proprioceptors do not adapt to constant stimulation. *Muscle spindles* are proprioceptors that monitor the length of skeletal muscles. p. 249 **Golgi tendon organs** monitor the tension in tendons during muscle contraction. Joint capsules are richly supplied with free nerve endings that detect tension, pressure, and movement at the joint. Your sense of body position results from the integration of information from these proprioceptors with information from the inner ear.

Chemoreceptors [Figure 18.5]

Chemoreceptors are specialized neurons that can detect small changes in the concentration of specific chemicals or compounds. In general, chemoreceptors respond only to water-soluble and lipid-soluble substances that are dissolved in the surrounding fluid.

The locations of important chemosensory receptors are indicated in Figure 18.5. Neurons within the respiratory centers of the brain respond to the concentration of hydrogen ions (pH) and carbon dioxide (P_{CO_2}) in the cerebrospinal fluid. Chemoreceptive neurons are found within the **carotid bodies**, near the origin of the internal carotid arteries on each side of the neck, and in the **aortic bodies** between the major branches of the aortic arch. These receptors monitor the carbon dioxide (P_{CO_2}) and oxygen (P_{O_2}) concentration of arterial blood. The afferent fibers leaving the carotid and aortic bodies reach the respiratory centers by traveling along the ninth (glossopharyngeal) and tenth (vagus) cranial nerves. These chemoreceptors play an important role in the reflexive control of respiration and cardiovascular function.

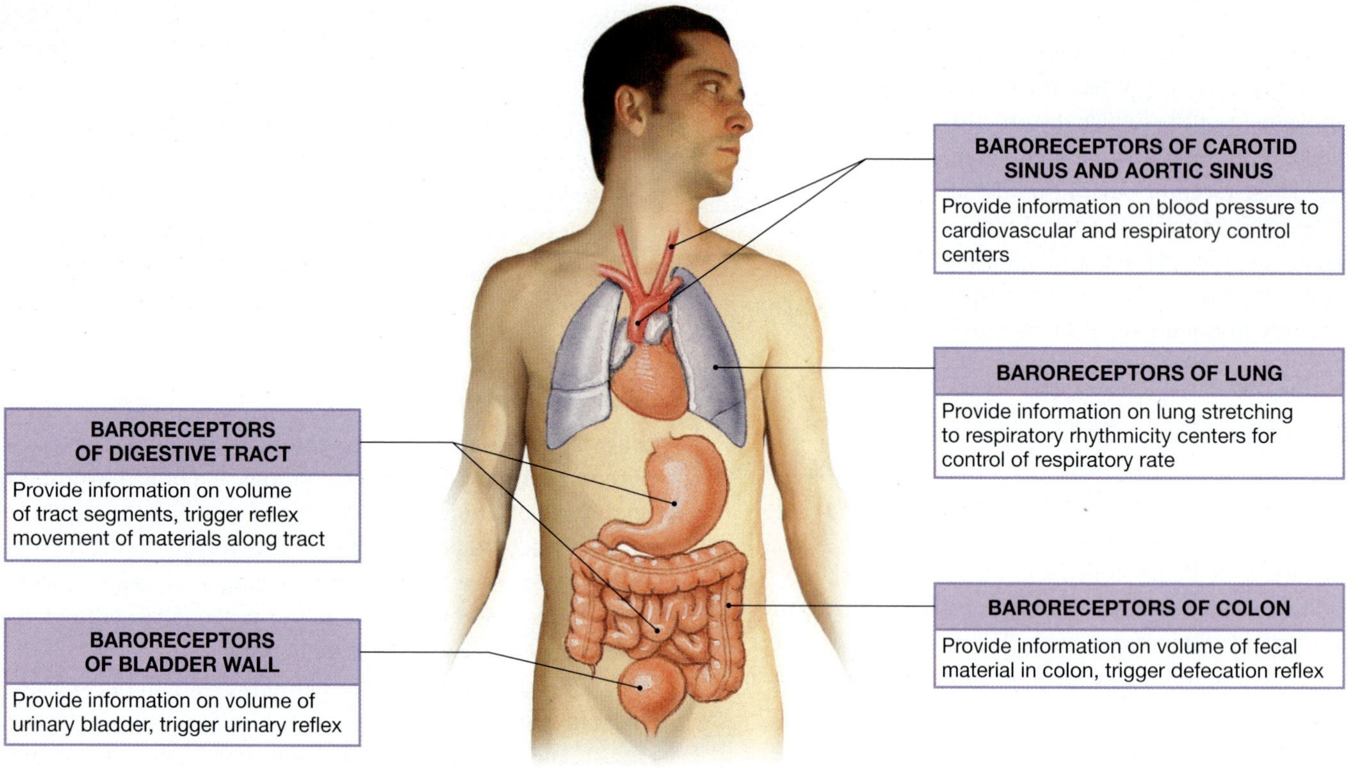

Figure 18.4 Baroreceptors and the Regulation of Autonomic Functions
Baroreceptors provide information essential to the regulation of autonomic activities, including respiration, digestion, urination, and defecation.

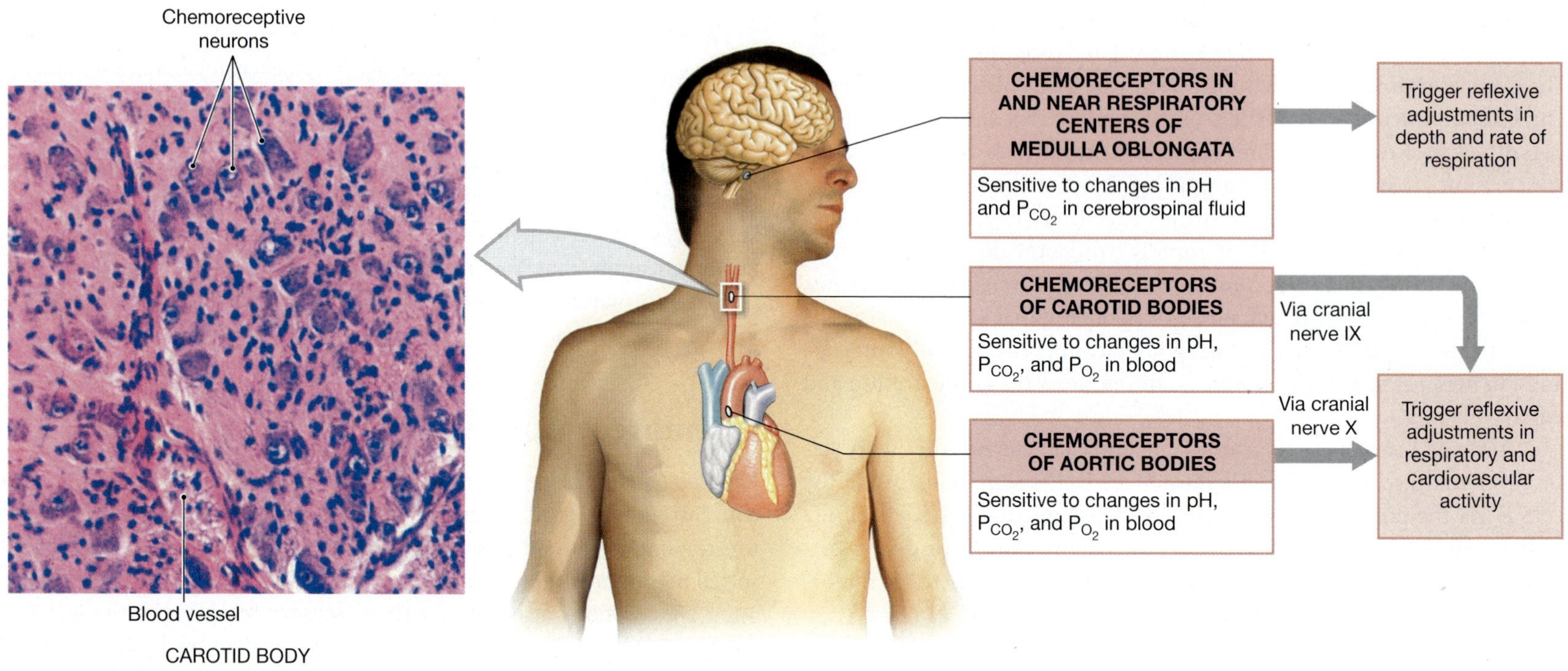

Figure 18.5 Chemoreceptors
Chemoreceptors are found both inside the CNS, on the ventrolateral surfaces of the medulla oblongata, and in the aortic and carotid bodies. These receptors are involved in the autonomic regulation of respiratory and cardiovascular function. The micrograph shows the histological appearance of the chemoreceptive neurons in the carotid body. (LM × 1500)

Olfaction (Smell) [Figure 18.6]

The sense of smell, more precisely called **olfaction**, is provided by paired **olfactory organs**. These organs are located in the nasal cavity on either side of the nasal septum. The olfactory organs (Figure 18.6) consist of the following:

- A specialized neuroepithelium, the **olfactory epithelium**, which contains the bipolar **olfactory receptors**, **supporting cells**, and **basal cells** (*stem cells*).
- An underlying layer of loose connective tissue known as the *lamina propria*. This layer contains (1) **olfactory glands**, also called *Bowman's glands*, which produce a thick, pigmented mucus; (2) blood vessels; and (3) nerves.

The olfactory epithelium covers the inferior surface of the cribriform plate and the superior portions of the nasal septum and superior nasal conchae of the ethmoid. ∞ p. 147 When air is drawn in through the nose, the nasal conchae produce turbulent airflow that brings airborne compounds into contact with the olfactory organs. A normal, relaxed inhalation provides a small sample of the inhaled air (around 2 percent) to the olfactory organs. Sniffing repeatedly increases the flow of air across the olfactory epithelium, intensifying the stimulation of the olfactory receptors. Once compounds have reached the olfactory organs, water-soluble and lipid-soluble materials must diffuse into the mucus before they can stimulate the olfactory receptors.

Olfactory Receptors [Figure 18.6b]

The olfactory receptor cells are highly modified neurons. The apical, dendritic portion of each receptor cell forms a prominent knob that projects beyond the epithelial surface and into the nasal cavity (Figure 18.6b). That projection provides a base for up to 20 cilia that extend into the surrounding mucus, exposing their considerable surface area to the dissolved chemical compounds. Somewhere between 10 and 20 million olfactory receptor cells are packed into an area of roughly 5 cm^2. Olfactory reception occurs on the surface of an olfactory cilium, through binding to specific membrane receptors. When the odorous substance binds to its receptor, the receptor membrane depolarizes. This may trigger an action potential in the axon of the olfactory receptor.

Olfactory Pathways [Figure 18.6]

The olfactory system is very sensitive. As few as four molecules of an odorous substance can activate an olfactory receptor. However, the activation of an afferent fiber does not guarantee a conscious awareness of the stimulus. Considerable convergence occurs along the olfactory pathway, and inhibition at the intervening synapses can prevent the sensations from reaching the cerebral cortex.

Axons leaving the olfactory epithelium collect into 20 or more bundles that penetrate the cribriform plate of the ethmoid bone to synapse on neurons within the olfactory bulbs (Figure 18.6). This collection of nerve bundles constitutes the first cranial nerve (N I). The axons of the second-order neurons in the olfactory bulb travel within the olfactory tract to reach the olfactory cortex, the hypothalamus, and portions of the limbic system.

Olfactory sensations are the only sensations that reach the cerebral cortex without first synapsing in the thalamus. The extensive limbic and hypothalamic connections help explain the profound emotional and behavioral responses that can be produced by certain smells, such as perfumes.

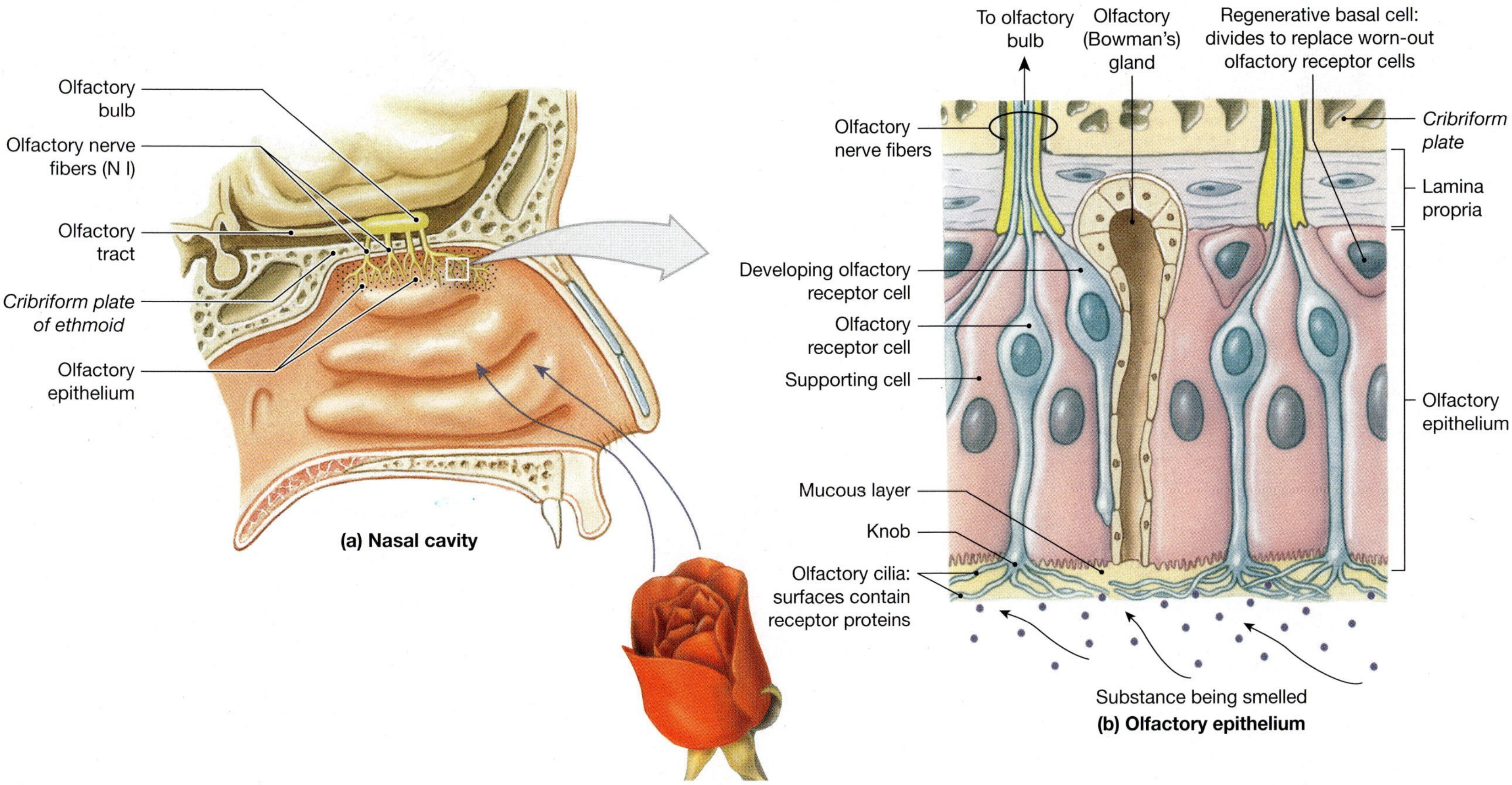

Figure 18.6 The Olfactory Organs
(a) The distribution of the olfactory receptors on the left side of the nasal septum is shown by the shading. **(b)** A detailed view of the olfactory epithelium.

Olfactory Discrimination

The olfactory system can make subtle distinctions between thousands of chemical stimuli. We know that there are at least 50 different "primary smells." No apparent structural differences exist among the olfactory cells, but the epithelium as a whole contains receptor populations with distinctly different sensitivities. The CNS interprets the smell on the basis of the particular pattern of receptor activity.

The olfactory receptor cells are the best-known examples of neuronal replacement in the adult human. (Neuron replacement can also occur in the hippocampus, but the regulatory mechanisms are unknown.) Despite ongoing replacement, the total number of olfactory receptors declines with age, and the remaining receptors become less sensitive. As a result, elderly individuals have difficulty detecting odors in low concentrations. This decline in the number of receptors accounts for Grandmother's tendency to apply perfume in excessive quantities and explains why Grandfather's aftershave seems so overdone; they must apply more to be able to smell it themselves.

Gustation (Taste) [Figure 18.7a]

Gustation, or taste, provides information about the foods and liquids that we consume. The **gustatory** (GUS-ta-tōr-ē) **receptors** (taste receptors) are distributed over the dorsal surface of the tongue (**Figure 18.7a**) and adjacent portions of the pharynx and larynx. By adulthood the taste receptors on the epithelium of the pharynx and larynx have decreased in importance, and the *taste buds* of the tongue are the primary gustatory receptors.

Taste buds lie along the sides of epithelial projections called **papillae** (pa-PIL-ē; *papilla*, nipple-shaped mound). There are three types of papillae on the human tongue: **filiform** (*filum*, thread), **fungiform** (*fungus*, mushroom), and **circumvallate** (sir-kum-VAL-āt; *circum*-, around + *vallum*, wall). There are regional differences in the distribution of the papillae (**Figure 18.7a**).

Gustatory Receptors [Figure 18.7b,c]

The taste receptors are clustered within individual **taste buds** (**Figure 18.7b,c**). Each taste bud contains around 40 slender receptors, called **gustatory cells**.

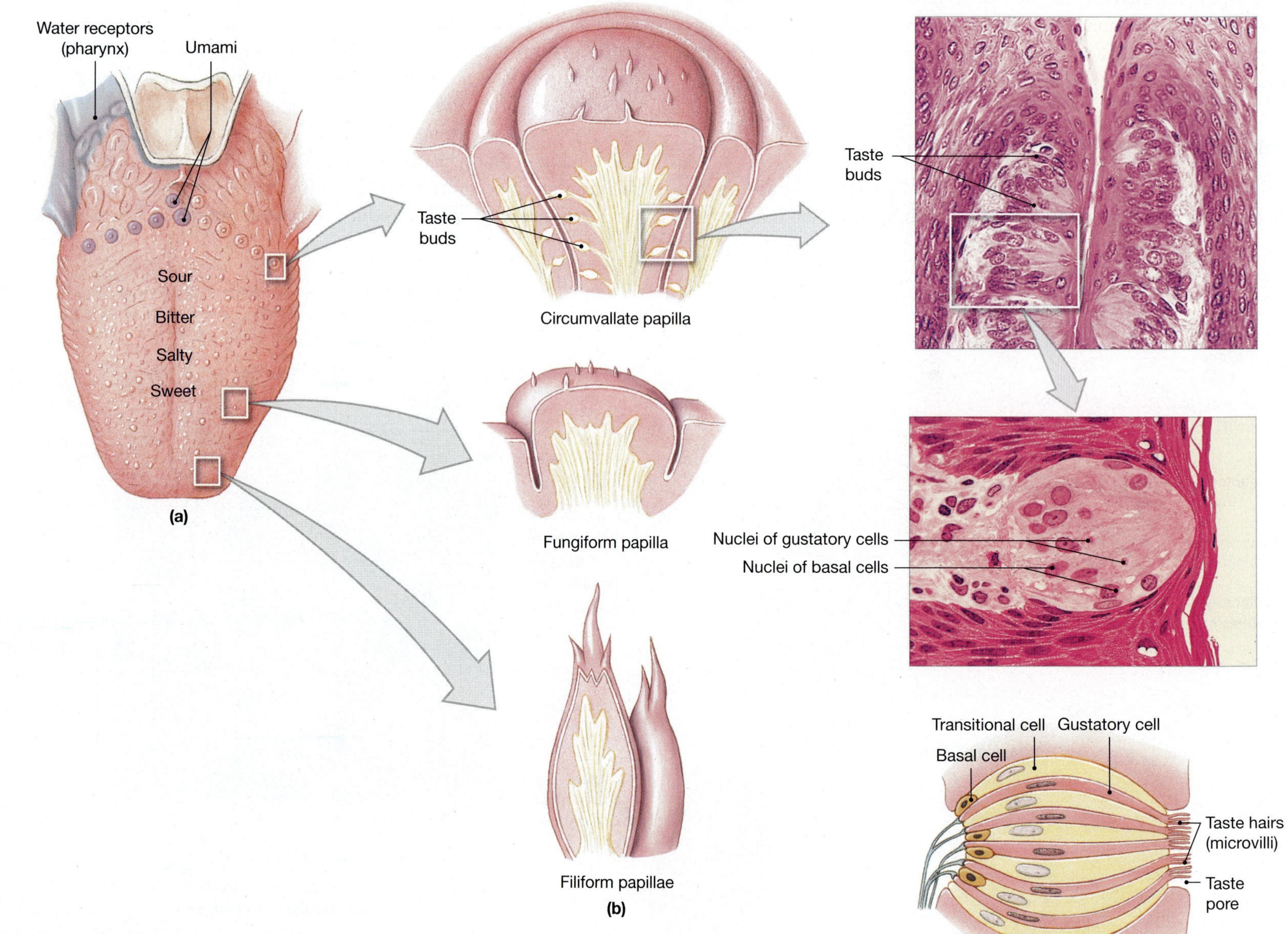

Figure 18.7 Gustatory Reception
(a) Gustatory receptors are found in taste buds that form pockets in the epithelium of the fungiform and circumvallate papillae. **(b)** Papillae on the surface of the tongue. **(c)** Histology of a taste bud, showing receptor cells and supporting cells. The diagrammatic view shows details of the taste pore not visible in the light micrograph. (LMs × 280 [upper] and × 650 [lower])

Each taste bud contains at least three different gustatory cell types, plus *basal cells* that are probably stem cells. A typical gustatory cell remains intact for only 10–12 days. Taste buds are recessed into the surrounding epithelium and isolated from the relatively unprocessed oral contents. Each gustatory cell extends slender microvilli, sometimes called *taste hairs*, into the surrounding fluids through a narrow opening, the **taste pore**.

The small fungiform papillae each contain about five taste buds, while the large circumvallate papillae, which form a V shape near the posterior margin of the tongue, contain as many as 100 taste buds per papilla. The typical adult has more than 10,000 taste buds.

The mechanism of gustatory reception appears to parallel that of olfaction. Dissolved chemicals contacting the taste hairs provide the stimulus that produces a change in the transmembrane potential of the taste cell. Stimulation of the gustatory cell results in action potentials in the afferent fiber.

Gustatory Pathways [Figure 18.8]

Taste buds are monitored by cranial nerves VII (facial), IX (glossopharyngeal), and X (vagus) (Figure 18.8). The sensory afferents synapse within the **nucleus solitarius** of the medulla oblongata; the axons of the postsynaptic neurons then enter the medial lemniscus. p. 432 After another synapse in the thalamus, the information is projected to the appropriate regions of the gustatory cortex.

A conscious perception of taste involves correlating the information received from the taste buds with other sensory data. Information concerning the general texture of the food, together with taste-related sensations of "peppery" or "burning hot," is provided by sensory afferents in the trigeminal nerve (N V). In addition, the level of stimulation from the olfactory receptors plays an overwhelming role in taste perception. We are several thousand times more sensitive to "tastes" when our olfactory organs are fully functional. When you have a cold, airborne molecules cannot reach the olfactory receptors, and meals taste dull and unappealing. This reduction in taste perception will occur even though the taste buds may be responding normally.

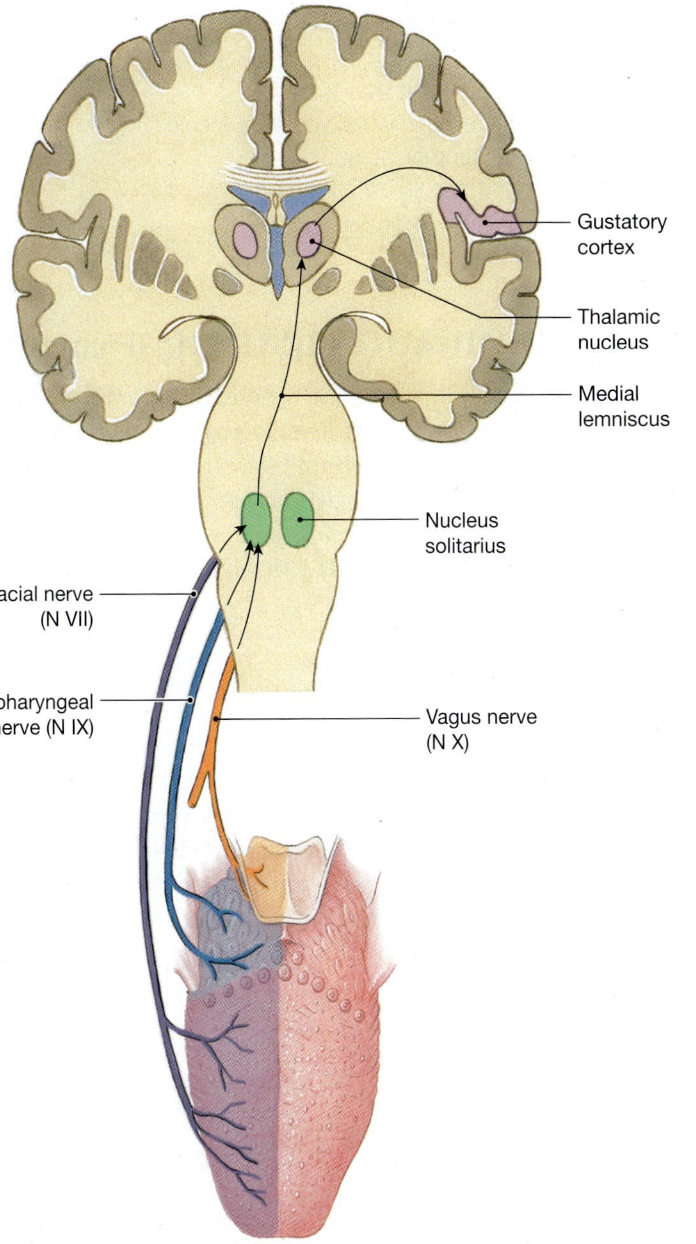

Figure 18.8 Gustatory Pathways
Three cranial nerves (VII, IX, and X) carry gustatory information to the gustatory cortex of the cerebrum.

Gustatory Discrimination

Many people are familiar with four **primary taste sensations**: sweet, salty, sour, and bitter. Although these do indeed represent distinct perceptions that are generally agreed on, they do not begin to describe the full range of perceptions experienced. For example, in describing a particular taste people may use terms like *fatty*, *starchy*, *metallic*, *pungent*, or *astringent*. Moreover, other cultures consider other tastes to be "primary." However, two additional tastes have recently been described in humans:

- **Umami.** **Umami** (oo-MAH-mē) is a pleasant taste that is characteristic of beef broth and chicken broth. This taste is produced by receptors sensitive to the presence of amino acids, especially glutamate, small peptides, and nucleotides. The distribution of these receptors is not known in detail, but they are present in taste buds of the circumvallate papillae.
- **Water.** Most people say that water has no flavor. However, research on humans and other vertebrates has demonstrated the presence of **water receptors**, especially in the pharynx. Their sensory output is processed in the hypothalamus and affects several systems that deal with water balance and the regulation of blood pressure.

One of the limiting factors in studying gustatory reception is that it is very difficult to quantify tastes scientifically. Gustatory cells that provide each of the primary sensations have been identified, and their plasmalemma characteristics and permeabilities differ. How what appears to be a relatively small number of receptor types provides such a rich and diverse sensory experience remains to be determined.

The threshold for receptor stimulation varies for each of the primary taste sensations, and the taste receptors respond most readily to unpleasant rather than to pleasant stimuli. For example, we are almost a thousand times more sensitive to acids, which give a sour taste, than to either sweet or salty chemicals, and we are a hundred times more sensitive to bitter compounds than to acids. This sensitivity has survival value, for acids can damage the mucous membranes of the mouth and pharynx, and many potent biological toxins produce an extremely bitter taste.

Our tasting abilities change with age. We begin life with more than 10,000 taste buds, but the number begins declining dramatically by age 50. The sensory loss becomes especially significant because aging individuals also experience a decline in the population of olfactory receptors. As a result, many elderly people find that their food tastes bland and unappetizing, whereas children often find the same foods too spicy.

CONCEPT CHECK

1. What are the primary taste sensations?
2. Why does food taste bland when you have a cold?
3. Where are taste receptors located?
4. List the three types of papillae on the tongue.

See blue "Answers" tab at back of book.

Equilibrium and Hearing [Figure 18.9]

The ear is divided into three anatomical regions: the *external ear*, the *middle ear*, and the *inner ear* (**Figure 18.9**). The external ear is the visible portion of the ear, and it collects and directs sound waves to the *eardrum*. The *middle ear* is a chamber located within the petrous portion of the temporal bone. Structures within the middle ear amplify sound waves and transmit them to an appropriate portion of the inner ear. The *inner ear* contains the sensory organs for equilibrium and hearing.

The External Ear [Figures 18.9/18.10a,b]

The **external ear** includes the flexible **auricle**, or *pinna*, which is supported by elastic cartilage. The auricle of the ear surrounds the **external acoustic meatus**. The auricle protects the external acoustic meatus and provides directional sensitivity to the ear by blocking or facilitating the passage of sound to the eardrum, also called the **tympanic membrane**, or **tympanum** (**Figures 18.9** and **18.10a**). The tympanic membrane is a thin, semitransparent connective tissue sheet (**Figure 18.10b**) that separates the external ear from the middle ear.

The tympanic membrane is very delicate. The auricle and the narrow external acoustic meatus provide some protection from accidental injury to the tympanic membrane. In addition, **ceruminous glands** distributed along the external acoustic meatus secrete a waxy material, and many small, outwardly projecting hairs help deny access to foreign objects or insects. The waxy secretion of the ceruminous glands, called **cerumen**, also slows the growth of microorganisms in the external acoustic meatus and reduces the chances of infection.

The Middle Ear [Figures 18.9/18.10]

The **middle ear** consists of an air-filled space, the **tympanic cavity**, which contains the *auditory ossicles* (**Figures 18.9** and **18.10**). The tympanic cavity is separated from the external acoustic meatus by the tympanic membrane, but it communicates with the nasopharynx through the auditory tube and with the mastoid sinuses through a number of small and variable connections. p. 146 The **auditory tube** is also called the *pharyngotympanic tube* or the *Eustachian tube*. This tube, about 4.0 cm in length, penetrates the petrous part of the temporal bone within the *musculotubal canal*. The connection to the tympanic cavity is relatively narrow and supported by elastic cartilage. The opening into the nasopharynx is relatively broad and funnel-shaped. The auditory tube serves to equalize the pressure in the middle ear cavity with external, atmospheric pressure. Pressure must be equal on both sides of the tympanic membrane or there will be a painful distortion of the membrane. Unfortunately, the auditory tube can also allow microorganisms to travel from the nasopharynx into the tympanic cavity, resulting in an "ear infection." Such infections are especially common in children, because their auditory tubes are relatively short and broad, as compared to those of adults.

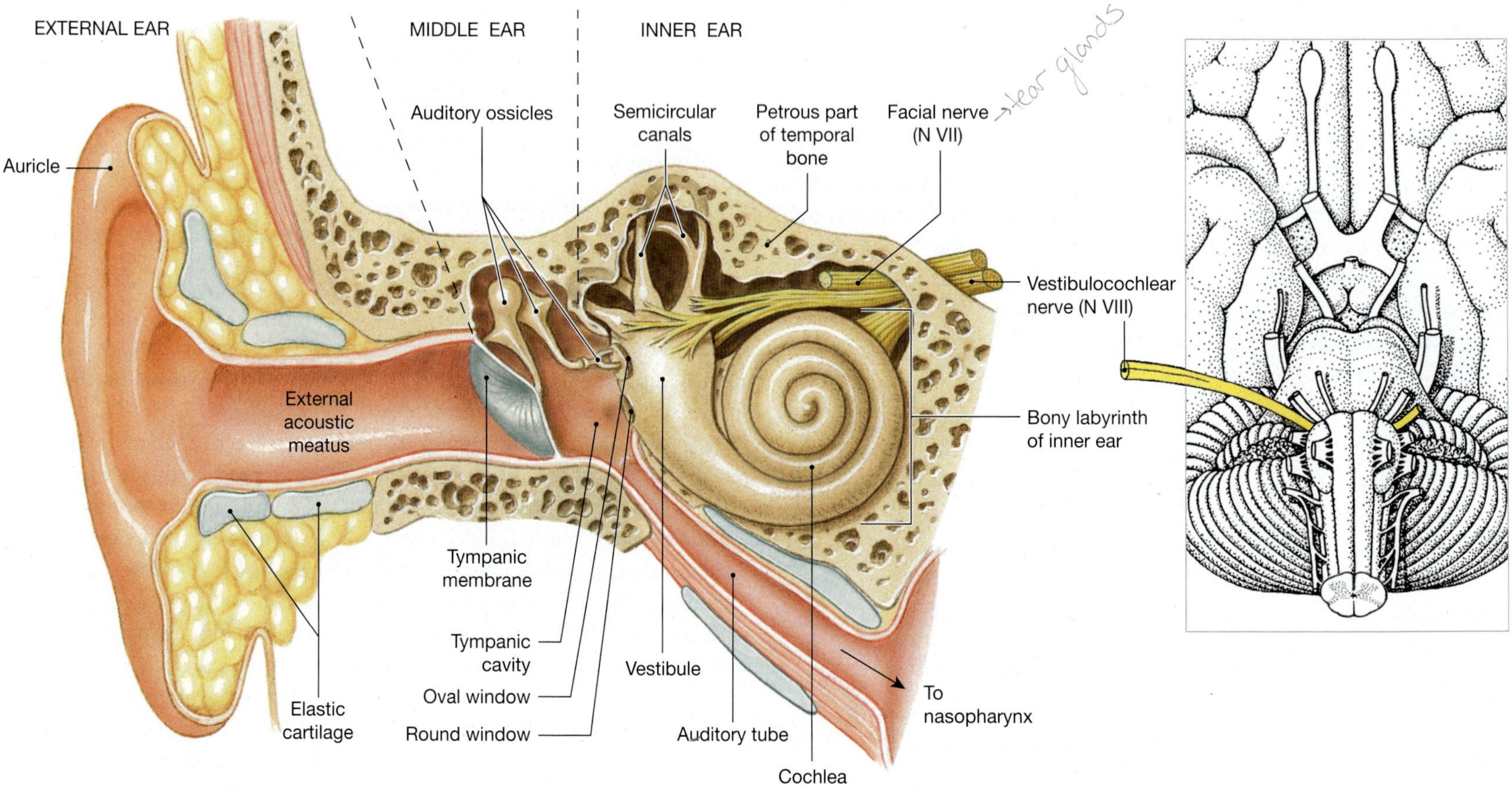

Figure 18.9 Anatomy of the Ear
A general orientation to the external, middle, and inner ear.

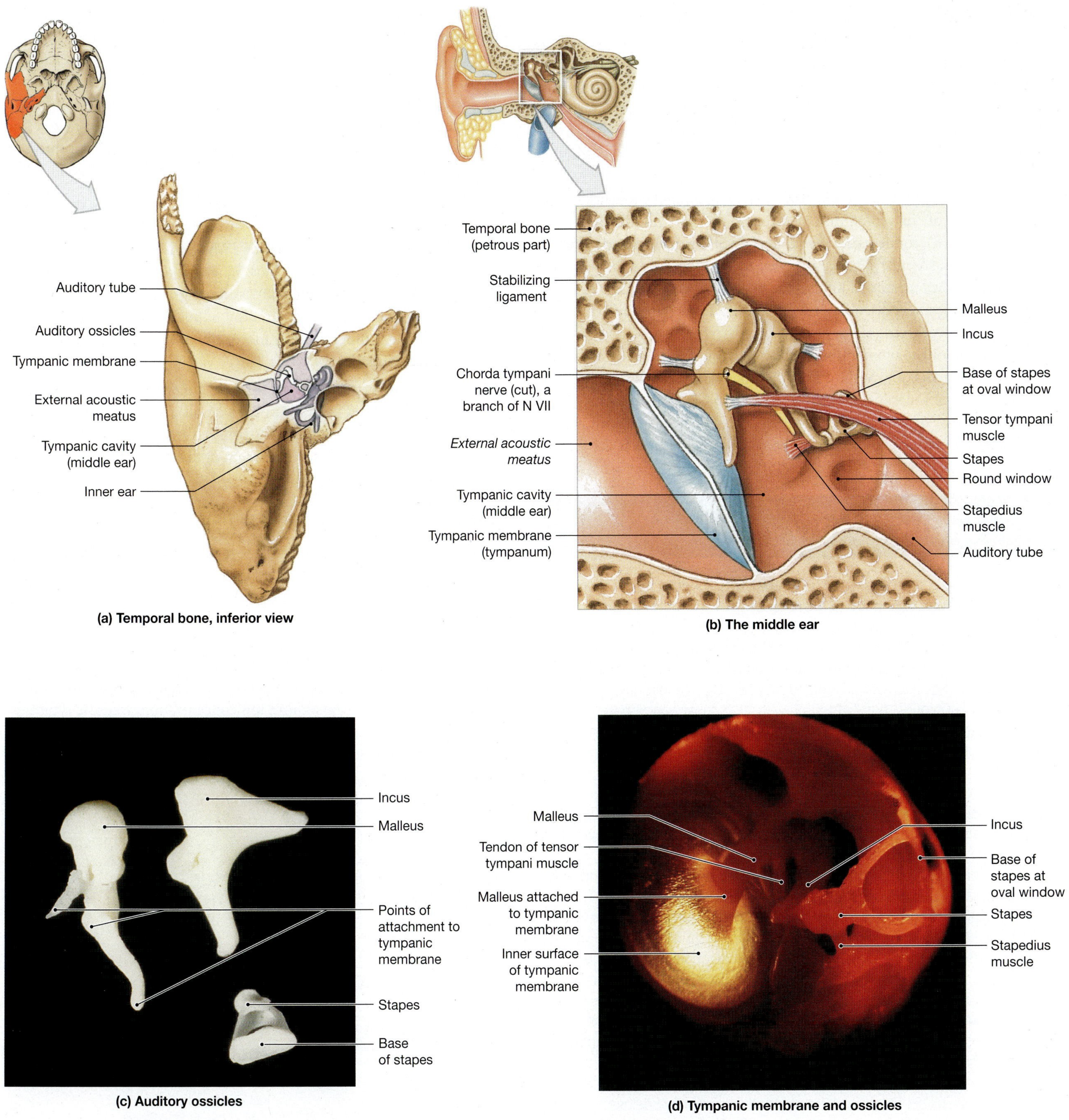

Figure 18.10 The Middle Ear

(a) Inferior view of the right temporal bone, drawn as if transparent, to show the location of the middle and inner ear. **(b)** Structures within the middle ear cavity. **(c)** The isolated auditory ossicles. **(d)** The tympanic membrane and auditory ossicles as seen through a fiber-optic tube inserted along the auditory canal and into the middle ear cavity.

The Auditory Ossicles [Figures 18.9/18.10]

The tympanic cavity contains three tiny ear bones collectively called **auditory ossicles.** ∞ p. 146 These ear bones, the smallest bones in the body, connect the tympanic membrane with the receptor complex of the inner ear (**Figures 18.9** and **18.10**). The three auditory ossicles are the *malleus*, the *incus*, and the *stapes*. These bones act as levers that transfer sound vibrations from the tympanum to a fluid-filled chamber within the inner ear.

The lateral surface of the **malleus** (*malleus*, hammer) attaches to the interior surface of the tympanum at three points. The middle bone, the **incus** (*incus*, anvil), connects the medial surface of the malleus to the **stapes** (STĀ-pēz; *stapes*, stirrup). The *base*, or *footplate*, of the stapes almost completely fills the *oval window*, a hole in the bony wall of the middle ear cavity. An *annular ligament* extends between the base of the stapes and the bony margins of the oval window.

Vibration of the tympanum converts arriving sound waves into mechanical movements. The auditory ossicles then conduct those vibrations, and movement of the stapes sets up vibrations in the fluid contents of the inner ear. Because of the way these ossicles are connected, an in-out movement of the tympanic membrane produces a rocking motion at the stapes.

The tympanic membrane is 22 times as large as the oval window, and the amount of force applied increases proportionally from the tympanic membrane to the oval window. This amplification process produces a relatively powerful deflection of the stapes at the oval window.

Because this amplification occurs, we can hear very faint sounds. But this degree of magnification can be a problem if we are exposed to very loud noises. Within the tympanic cavity, two small muscles serve to protect the eardrum and ossicles from violent movements under very noisy conditions.

- The **tensor tympani** (TEN-sor tim-PAN-ē) **muscle** is a short ribbon of muscle whose origin is the petrous part of the temporal bone, within the musculotubal canal, and whose insertion is on the "handle" of the malleus (**Figure 18.10b,d**). When the tensor tympani contracts, the malleus is pulled medially, stiffening the tympanum. This increased stiffness reduces the amount of possible movement. The tympani muscle is innervated by motor fibers of the mandibular branch of the trigeminal nerve (N V).
- The **stapedius** (sta-PĒ-dē-us) **muscle**, innervated by the facial nerve (N VII), originates from the posterior wall of the tympanic cavity and inserts on the stapes (**Figure 18.10b,d**). Contraction of the stapedius pulls the stapes, reducing movement of the stapes at the oval window.

Clinical Note

Otitis Media and Mastoiditis **Acute otitis media** is an infection of the middle ear, frequently of bacterial origin. It commonly occurs in infants and children and is occasionally seen in adults. The middle ear, usually a sterile, air-filled cavity, becomes infected by pathogens that arrive via the auditory tube, often during an upper respiratory infection. If caused by a virus, otitis media may resolve in a few days without use of antibiotics. This "watchful waiting" is most appropriate where medical care is readily available; the pain is reduced by analgesics, and the use of decongestants helps drain the stagnant clear mucus produced in response to mucosal swelling.

If bacteria become involved, symptoms worsen and the mucus becomes cloudy with the bacteria and active or dead neutrophils. Severe otitis media must be promptly treated with antibiotics. As pus accumulates in the middle ear cavity, the tympanic membrane becomes painfully distorted, and in untreated cases it will often rupture, producing a characteristic drainage from the external acoustic canal. The infection may also spread to the mastoid air cells. **Chronic mastoiditis**, accompanied by drainage through a perforated eardrum and scarring around the auditory ossicles, is a common cause of hearing loss in areas of the world without access to medical treatment. In developed countries, it is rare for otitis media to progress to the stage at which rupture of the tympanic membrane or infection of the adjacent mastoid bone occurs. *Serous otitis media (SOM)* involves the accumulation of clear, thick, gluelike fluid in the middle ear. The condition, which can follow acute otitis media or can result from chronic nasal infection and allergies, causes hearing loss. Affected toddlers may have delayed speech development as a result. Treatment involves decongestants, antihistamines, and, in some cases, prolonged antibiotic treatment. Nonresponsive cases and recurrent otitis media may be treated by myringotomy (drainage of the middle ear through a surgical opening in the tympanic membrane) and the placement of a temporary tube in the membrane. As toddlers grow, the auditory tube enlarges, allowing better drainage during upper respiratory infections, so both forms of otitis media become less common.

The Inner Ear [Figures 18.9 to 18.13]

The senses of equilibrium and hearing are provided by the receptors of the **inner ear** (**Figures 18.9** and **18.11**). The receptors are housed within a collection of fluid-filled tubes and chambers known as the **membranous labyrinth** (*labyrinthos*, network of canals). The membranous labyrinth contains a fluid called **endolymph** (EN-dō-limf). The receptor cells of the inner ear can function only when exposed to the unique ionic composition of the endolymph. (Endolymph has a relatively high potassium ion concentration and a relatively low sodium ion concentration, whereas typical extracellular fluids have high sodium and low potassium ion concentrations.)

The **bony labyrinth** is a shell of dense bone that surrounds and protects the membranous labyrinth. Its inner contours closely follow the contours of the membranous labyrinth (**Figure 18.12**), while its outer walls are

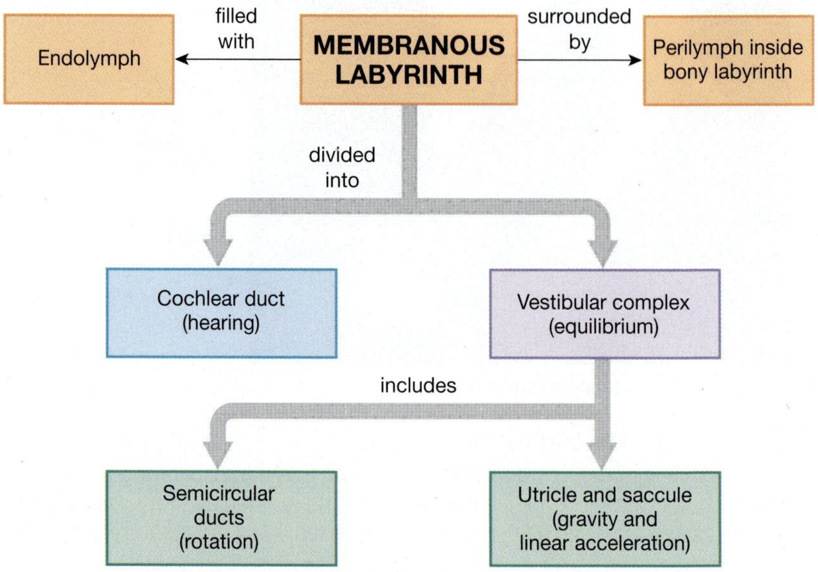

Figure 18.11 Structural Relationships of the Inner Ear
Flowchart showing inner ear structures and spaces, their contained fluids, and what stimulates these receptors.

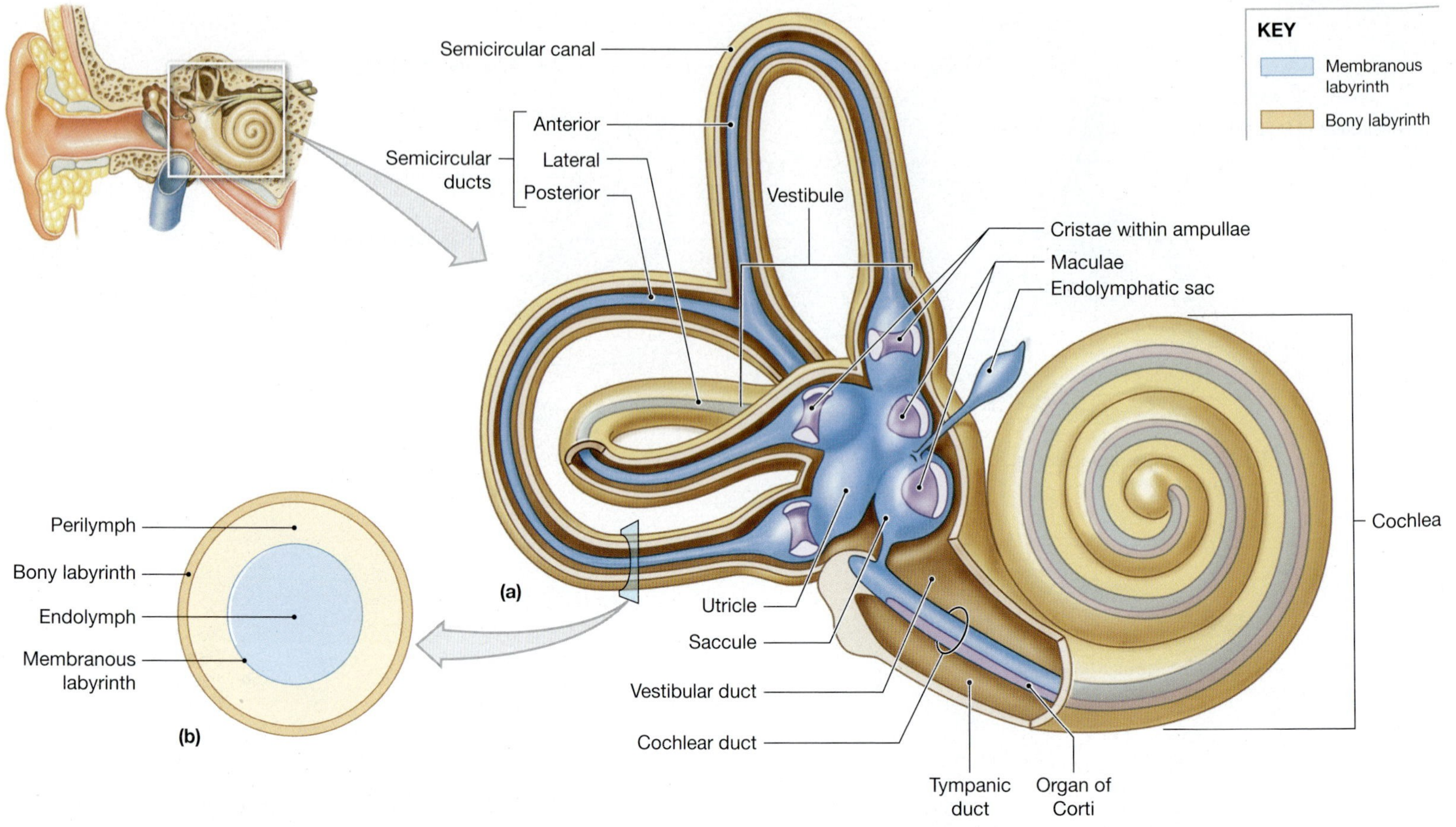

Figure 18.12 Semicircular Canals and Ducts
The orientation of the bony labyrinth within the petrous part of each temporal bone. **(a)** Anterior view of the bony labyrinth, cut away to show the semicircular canals and the enclosed semicircular ducts of the membranous labyrinth. **(b)** Cross section of a semicircular canal to show the orientation of the bony labyrinth, perilymph, membranous labyrinth, and endolymph.

fused with the surrounding temporal bone. p. 145 Between the bony and membranous labyrinths flows the **perilymph** (PER-i-limf), a liquid whose properties closely resemble those of cerebrospinal fluid.

The bony labyrinth can be subdivided into the **vestibule** (VES-ti-būl), the **semicircular canals**, and the **cochlea** (KOK-lē-a; *cochlea*, snail shell) as seen in Figures 18.9 and 18.12a. The structures and air spaces of the external ear and middle ear function in the capture and transmission of sound to the cochlea.

The vestibule and semicircular canals together are called the *vestibular complex*, because the fluid-filled chambers of the vestibule are broadly continuous with those of the semicircular canals. The cavity within the vestibule contains a pair of membranous sacs, the **utricle** (Ū-tre-kl) and the **saccule** (SAK-ūl), or the *utriculus* and *sacculus*. Receptors in the utricle and saccule provide sensations of gravity and linear acceleration. Those in the semicircular canals are stimulated by rotation of the head.

The cochlea contains a slender, elongated portion of the membranous labyrinth known as the **cochlear duct** (Figure 18.12a). The cochlear duct sits sandwiched between a pair of perilymph-filled chambers, and the entire complex makes turns around a central bony hub. In sectional view the spiral arrangement resembles that of a snail shell, or *cochlea* in Latin.

The outer walls of the perilymphatic chambers consist of dense bone everywhere except at two small areas near the base of the cochlear spiral. The **round window**, or *cochlear window*, is the more inferior of the two openings. A thin, flexible membrane spans the opening and separates the perilymph in one of the cochlear chambers from the air in the middle ear (Figure 18.9). The **oval window** is the more superior of the two openings in the cochlear wall (Figure 18.10b,c,d). The base of the stapes almost completely fills the oval window. The annular ligament, which extends between the edges of the base and the margins of the oval window, completes the seal. When a sound vibrates the tympanum, the movements are conducted to the perilymph of the inner ear by the movements of the stapes. This process ultimately leads to the stimulation of receptors within the cochlear duct, and we "hear" the sound.

The sensory receptors of the inner ear are called **hair cells** (Figure 18.13d). These receptor cells are surrounded by **supporting cells** and are monitored by sensory afferent fibers. The free surface of each hair cell supports 80–100 long *stereocilia*. p. 53 Hair cells are highly specialized mechanoreceptors sensitive to the distortion of their stereocilia. Their ability to provide equilibrium sensations in the vestibule and hearing in the cochlea depends on the presence of accessory structures that restrict the sources of stimulation. The importance of these accessory structures will become apparent as we consider hair cell function in the next section.

The Vestibular Complex and Equilibrium

The **vestibular complex** is the part of the inner ear that provides equilibrium sensations by detecting rotation, gravity, and acceleration. It consists of the semicircular canals, the utricle, and the saccule.

The Semicircular Canals [Figures 18.12/18.13/18.14] The **anterior**, **posterior**, and **lateral semicircular canals** are continuous with the vestibule (Figures 18.12a and 18.13a). Each semicircular canal surrounds a **semicircular duct**. The duct contains a swollen region, the **ampulla**, which contains the sensory receptors. These receptors respond to rotational movements of the head.

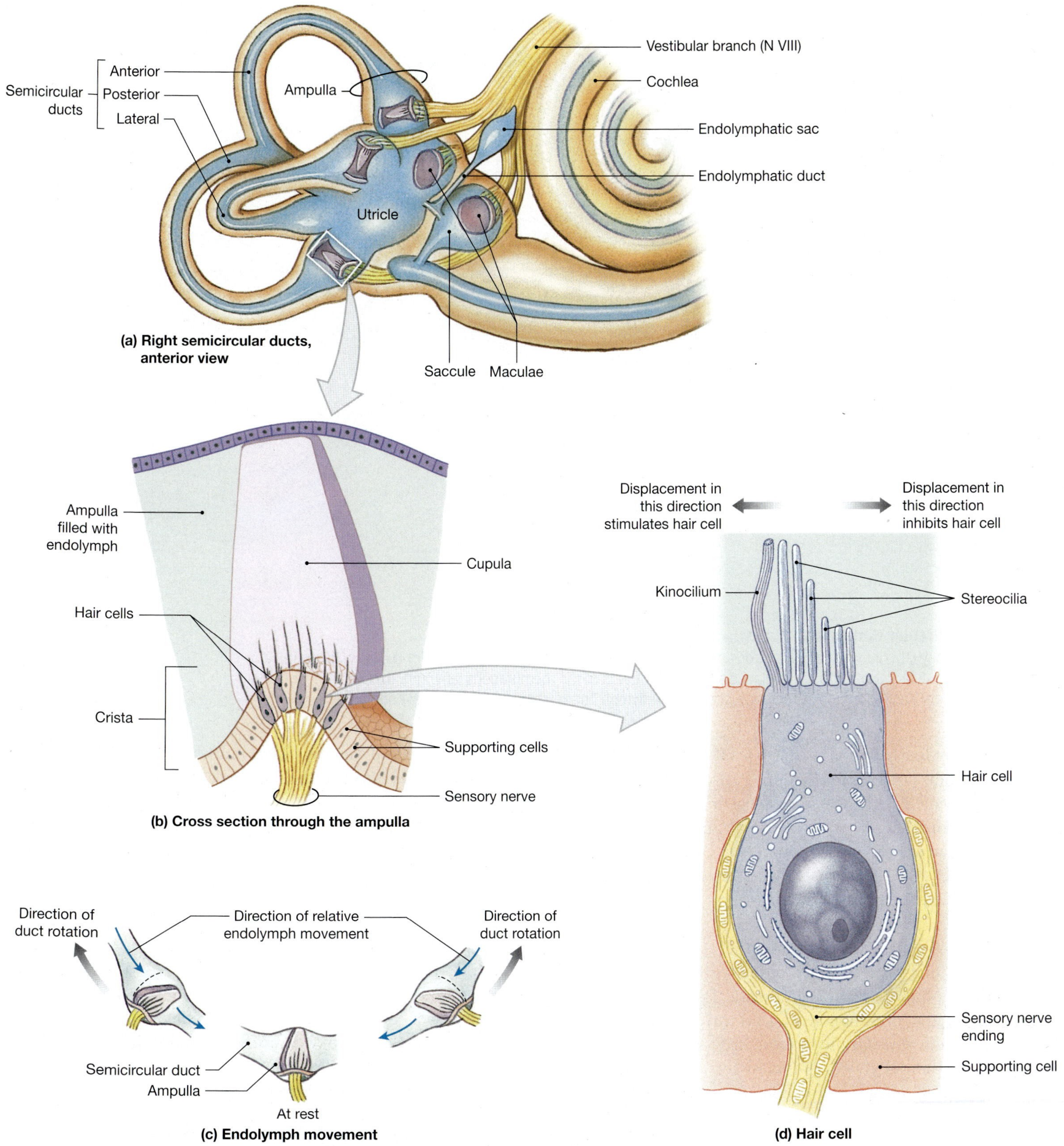

Figure 18.13 The Function of the Semicircular Ducts, Part I
(a) Anterior view of the maculae and semicircular ducts of the right side. **(b)** A section through the ampulla of a semicircular duct. **(c)** Endolymph movement along the length of the duct moves the cupula and stimulates the hair cells. **(d)** Structure of a typical hair cell, showing details revealed by electron microscopy. Bending the stereocilia toward the kinocilium depolarizes the cell and stimulates the sensory neuron. Displacement in the opposite direction inhibits the sensory neuron.

Hair cells attached to the wall of the ampulla form a raised structure known as a **crista** (Figures 18.12a and 18.13). In addition to its stereocilia, each hair cell in the vestibule also contains a **kinocilium**, a single large cilium (Figure 18.13d). Hair cells do not actively move their kinocilia and stereocilia. However, when an external force pushes against these processes, the distortion of the plasmalemma alters the rate of chemical transmitter released by the hair cell.

The kinocilia and stereocilia of the hair cells are embedded in a gelatinous structure, the **cupula** (KŪ-pū-la). Because the cupula has a density very close to that of the surrounding endolymph, it essentially "floats" above

the receptor surface, nearly filling the ampulla. When the head rotates in the plane of the duct, movement of the endolymph along the duct axis pushes the cupula and distorts the receptor processes (**Figure 18.13c**). Fluid movement in one direction stimulates the hair cells, and movement in the opposite direction inhibits them. When the endolymph stops moving, the elastic nature of the cupula makes it "bounce back" to its normal position.

Even the most complex movement can be analyzed in terms of motion in three rotational planes. The receptors within each semicircular duct respond to one of these rotational movements (**Figure 18.14**). A horizontal rotation, as in shaking the head "no," stimulates the hair cells of the lateral semicircular duct. Nodding "yes" excites the anterior duct, while tilting the head from side to side activates the receptors in the posterior duct.

The Utricle and Saccule [Figures 18.13a/18.15] A slender passageway continuous with the narrow **endolymphatic duct** connects the utricle and saccule (**Figure 18.13a**). The endolymphatic duct ends in a blind pouch, the **endolymphatic sac**, that projects through the dura mater lining the temporal bone and into the subdural space. Portions of the cochlear duct continually secrete endolymph, and at the endolymphatic sac, excess fluids return to the general circulation.

The hair cells of the utricle and saccule are clustered in the oval **maculae** (MAK-ū-lē; *macula*, spot) (**Figures 18.13a** and **18.15**). As in the ampullae, the hair cell processes are embedded in a gelatinous mass. However, the surface of this gelatinous material contains densely packed calcium carbonate crystals known as **statoconia** (stat-ō-KŌ-nē-a; *conia*, dust). The complex as a whole (gelatinous matrix and statoconia), called an **otolith** (Ō-tō-lith; *oto-*, ear + *lithos*, stone), can be seen in **Figure 18.15b**.

When the head is in the normal, upright position, the otoliths rest atop the maculae. Their weight presses down on the macular surfaces, pushing the sensory hairs down rather than to one side or another. When the head is tilted, the pull of gravity on the otoliths shifts them to the side. This shift distorts the sensory hairs, and the change in receptor activity tells the CNS that the head is no longer level (**Figure 18.15c**).

For example, when an elevator starts its downward plunge, we are immediately aware of it because the otoliths no longer push so forcefully against the surface of the receptor cells. Once they catch up, we are no longer aware of any movement until the elevator brakes to a halt. As the body slows down, the otoliths press harder against the hair cells, and we "feel" the force of gravity increase. A similar mechanism accounts for our perception of linear acceleration in a car that speeds up suddenly. The otoliths lag behind, distorting the sensory hairs and changing the activity in the sensory neurons.

Clinical Note

Nystagmus Automatic eye movements occur in response to sensations of motion (whether real or illusory) under the direction of the *superior colliculi*. p. 410 These movements attempt to keep the gaze focused on a specific point in space. When you spin around, your eyes fix on one point for a moment, then jump ahead to another, in a series of short, rhythmic, jerky movements. These eye movements may appear in normal stationary individuals with extreme lateral gaze and after damage to or stimulation of the brain stem or inner ear. This condition is called **nystagmus**. Physicians often check for nystagmus by asking the subject to watch a small penlight as it is moved across the field of vision.

Pathways for Vestibular Sensations [Figure 18.16] Hair cells of the vestibule and semicircular ducts are monitored by sensory neurons located in adjacent **vestibular ganglia**. Sensory fibers from each ganglion form the **vestibular branch** of the vestibulocochlear nerve (N VIII). These fibers synapse on neurons within the vestibular nuclei at the boundary between the pons and medulla oblongata. The two vestibular nuclei

1. integrate the sensory information concerning balance and equilibrium arriving from each side of the head;
2. relay information from the vestibular apparatus to the cerebellum;
3. relay information from the vestibular apparatus to the cerebral cortex, providing a conscious sense of position and movement; and
4. send commands to motor nuclei in the brain stem and spinal cord.

The reflexive motor commands issued by the vestibular nucleus are distributed to the motor nuclei for cranial nerves involved with eye, head, and neck movements (N III, N IV, N VI, and N XI). Descending instructions along the **vestibulospinal tracts** of the spinal cord adjust peripheral muscle tone to complement the reflexive movements of the head or neck. p. 439 These pathways are illustrated in **Figure 18.16**.

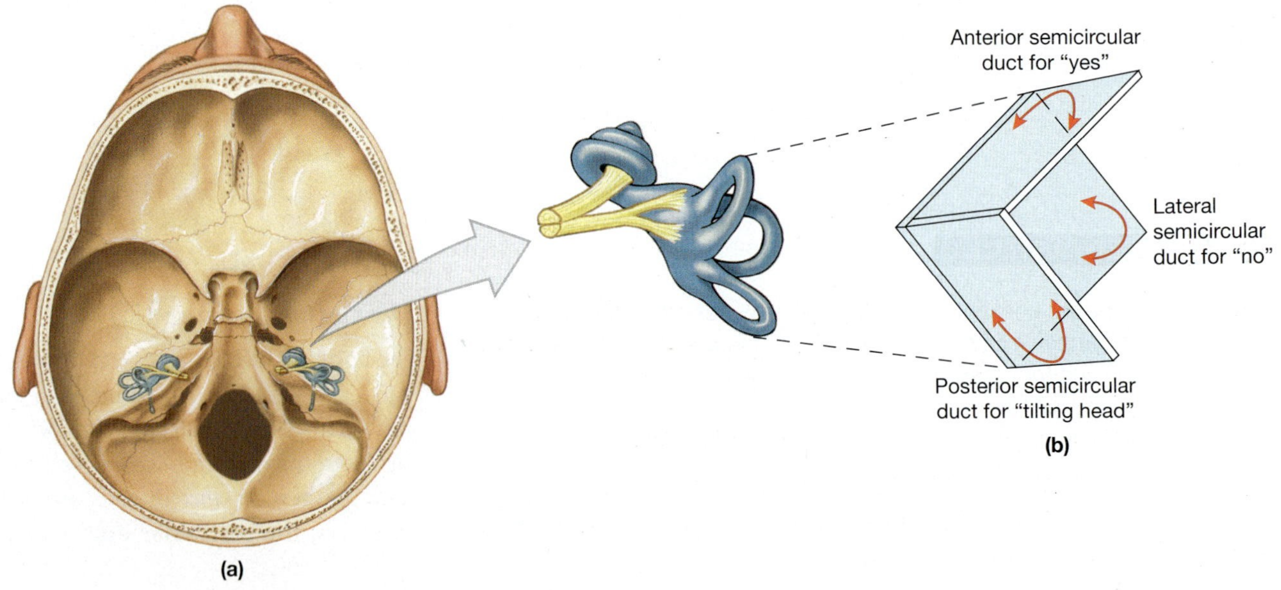

Figure 18.14 The Function of the Semicircular Ducts, Part II **(a)** Location and orientation of the membranous labyrinth within the petrous parts of the temporal bones. **(b)** A superior view showing the planes of sensitivity for the semicircular ducts.

Figure 18.15 The Maculae of the Vestibule
(a) Detailed structure of a sensory macula. **(b)** A scanning electron micrograph showing the crystalline structure of otoliths. **(c)** Diagrammatic view of changes in otolith position during tilting of the head.

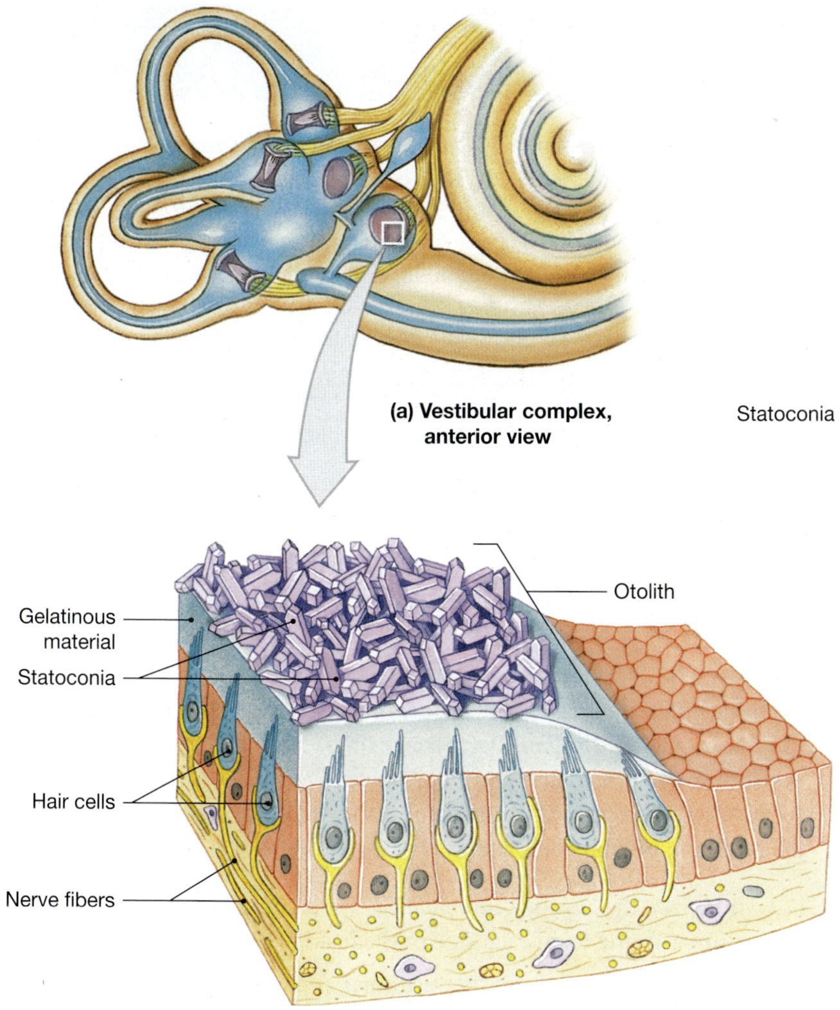

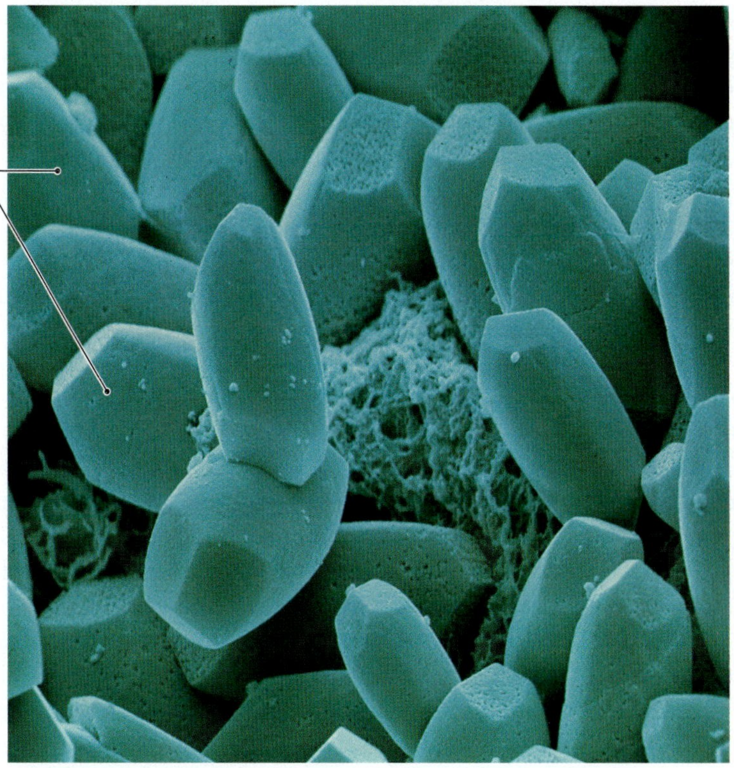

(b) Structure of a macula

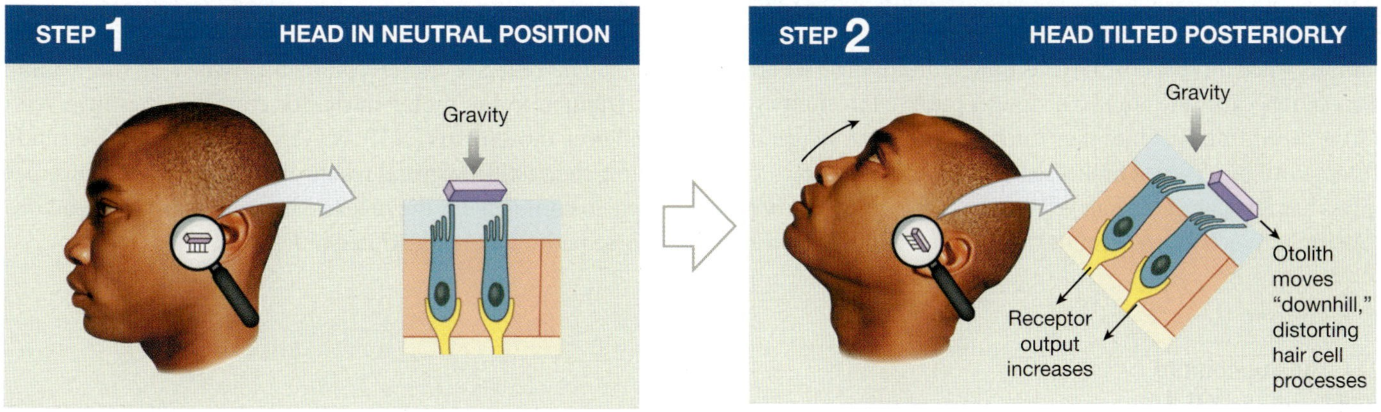

(c) Macular function

✓ CONCEPT CHECK

1. You are exposed unexpectedly to very loud noises. What happens within the tympanic cavity to protect the tympanum from damage?
2. Identify the auditory ossicles and describe their functions.
3. What is perilymph? Where is it located?
4. As you shake your head "no," you are aware of this head movement. How are these sensations detected?

See blue "Answers" tab at back of book.

Hearing

The Cochlea [Figure 18.17]

The bony cochlea (**Figure 18.17**) coils around a central hub, or **modiolus** (mō-DĪ-ō-lus). There are usually 2.5 turns in the cochlear spiral. The modiolus encloses the **spiral ganglion**, which contains the cell bodies of the sensory neurons that monitor the receptors in the cochlear duct. In sectional view, the *cochlear duct,* or *scala media,* lies between a pair of perilymphatic chambers, the **vestibular duct** (*scala vestibuli*) and the **tympanic duct**

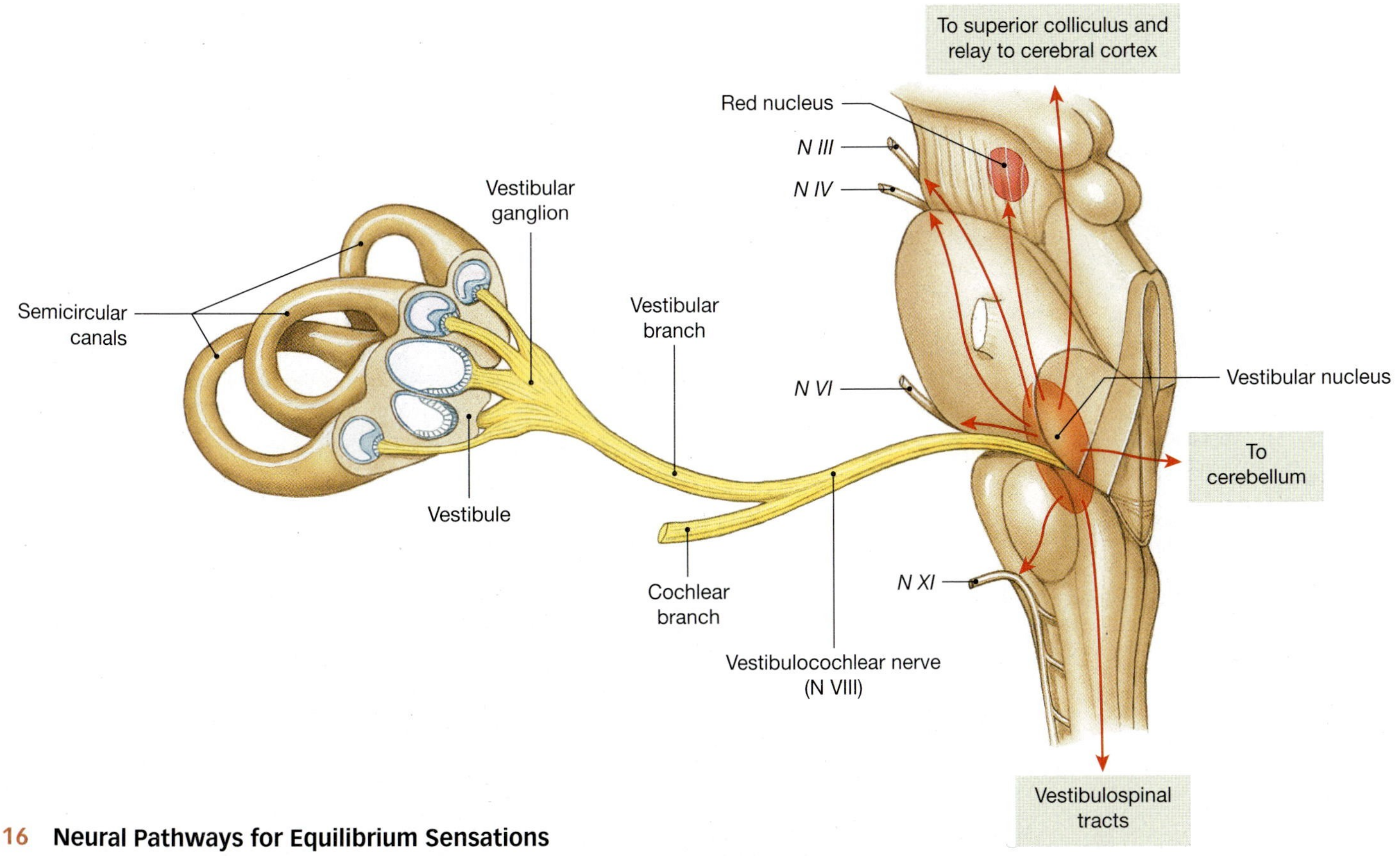

Figure 18.16 **Neural Pathways for Equilibrium Sensations**

Clinical Note

Vertigo, Motion Sickness, and Ménière's Disease The term **vertigo** describes an inappropriate sense of motion, usually a spinning sensation. This meaning distinguishes it from "dizziness," a sensation of light-headedness and disorientation. Vertigo can result from abnormal conditions in or stimulation of the inner ear or from problems elsewhere along the sensory pathway that carries equilibrium sensations. It can accompany CNS or other infections, and many people experience vertigo when they have a high fever.

Any event that sets endolymph in motion can stimulate the equilibrium receptors and produce vertigo. Placing an ice pack on the area over the mastoid process of the temporal bone or flushing the external acoustic meatus with cold water may chill the endolymph in the outermost portions of the labyrinth and establish a temperature-related circulation of fluid. A mild and temporary vertigo is the result. The consumption of excessive quantities of alcohol or exposure to certain drugs can also produce vertigo by changing the composition of the endolymph or disturbing the hair cells of the inner ear.

Other causes of vertigo include viral infection of the vestibular nerve and damage to the vestibular nucleus or its tracts. Acute vertigo can also result from damage caused by abnormal endolymph production, as in Ménière's disease. Probably the most common cause of vertigo is *motion sickness*.

The exceedingly unpleasant signs and symptoms of **motion sickness** include headache, sweating, flushing of the face, nausea, vomiting, and various changes in mental perspective. (Sufferers may go from a state of giddy excitement to almost suicidal despair in a matter of moments.) It is possible that the condition results when central processing areas, such as the tectum of the mesencephalon, receive conflicting visual and equilibrium information. Why these conflicting reports result in nausea, vomiting, and other symptoms is not known. Sitting belowdecks on a moving boat or reading in a car tends to provide the necessary conditions. Your eyes report that your position in space is not changing, but your semicircular ducts report that your body is lurching and turning. To counter this effect, seasick sailors watch the horizon rather than their immediate surroundings, so that their eyes will provide visual confirmation of the movements detected by their inner ears. It is not known why some individuals are almost immune to motion sickness, whereas others find travel by boat or car almost impossible.

Drugs commonly administered to prevent motion sickness include dimenhydrinate (*Dramamine*®), scopolamine, and promethazine. These compounds appear to depress activity at the vestibular nuclei. Sedatives, such as prochlorperazine (*Compazine*®), may also be effective. Scopolamine can be administered across the skin surface by using an adhesive patch (*Transderm Scop*®).

In **Ménière's disease**, distortion of the membranous labyrinth of the inner ear by high fluid pressures may rupture the membranous wall and mix endolymph and perilymph. The receptors in the vestibule and semicircular canals then become highly stimulated. The individual may be unable to start a voluntary movement (e.g., walking) because he or she is experiencing intense spinning or rolling sensations. In addition to the vertigo, the person may "hear" unusual sounds as the cochlear receptors are activated.

Figure 18.17 The Cochlea and Organ of Corti
(a) Structure of the cochlea in partial section. **(b)** Structure of the cochlea within the temporal bone as seen in section, showing the turns of the vestibular duct, cochlear duct, and tympanic duct. **(c)** Histology of the cochlea showing many of the structures in part (b).

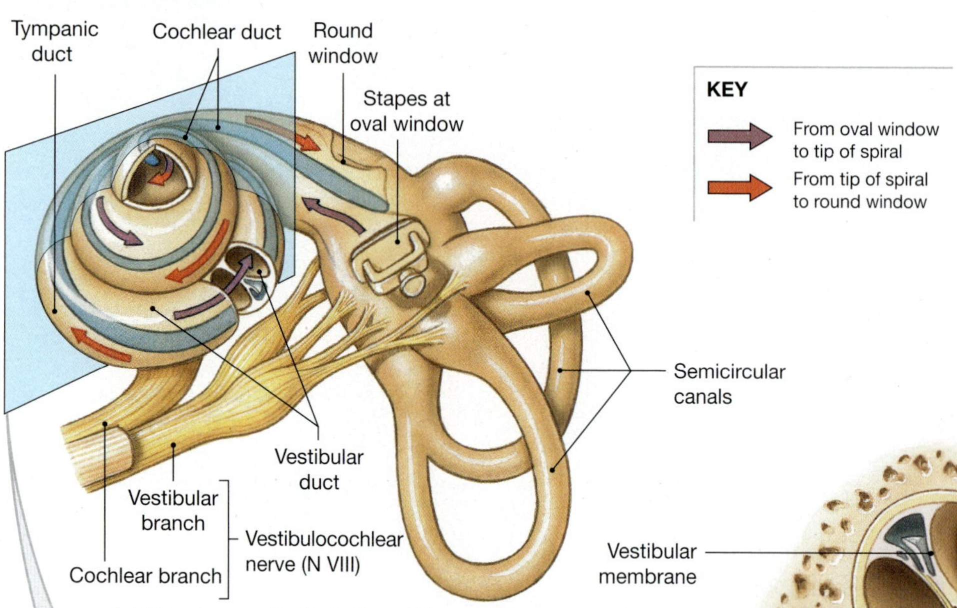

(a) Structure and orientation of the cochlea

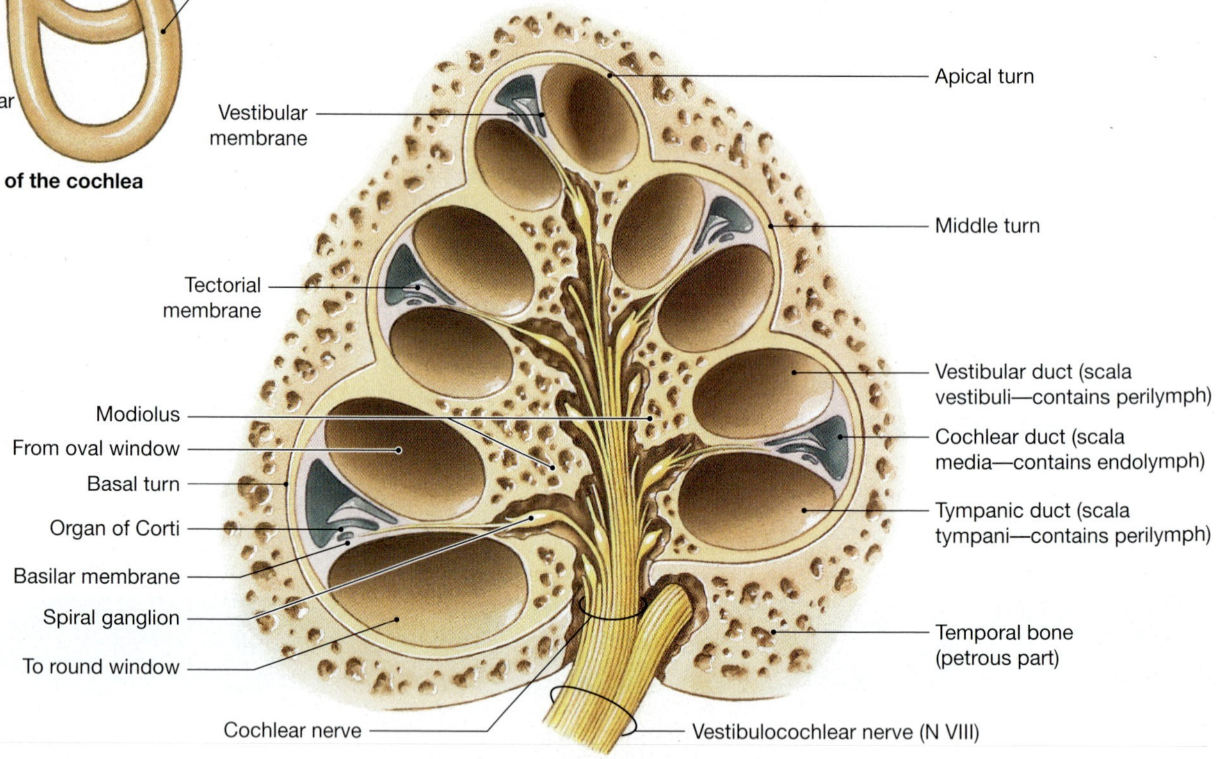

(b) Cochlear section, diagrammatic

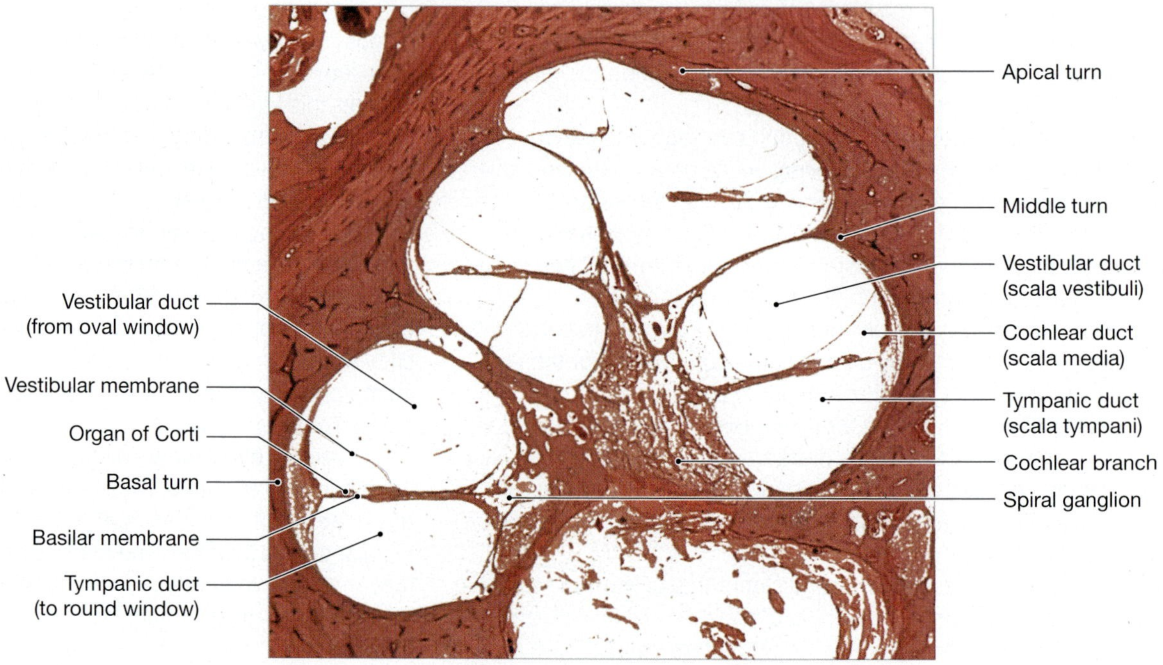

(c) Cochlear section, photomicrograph

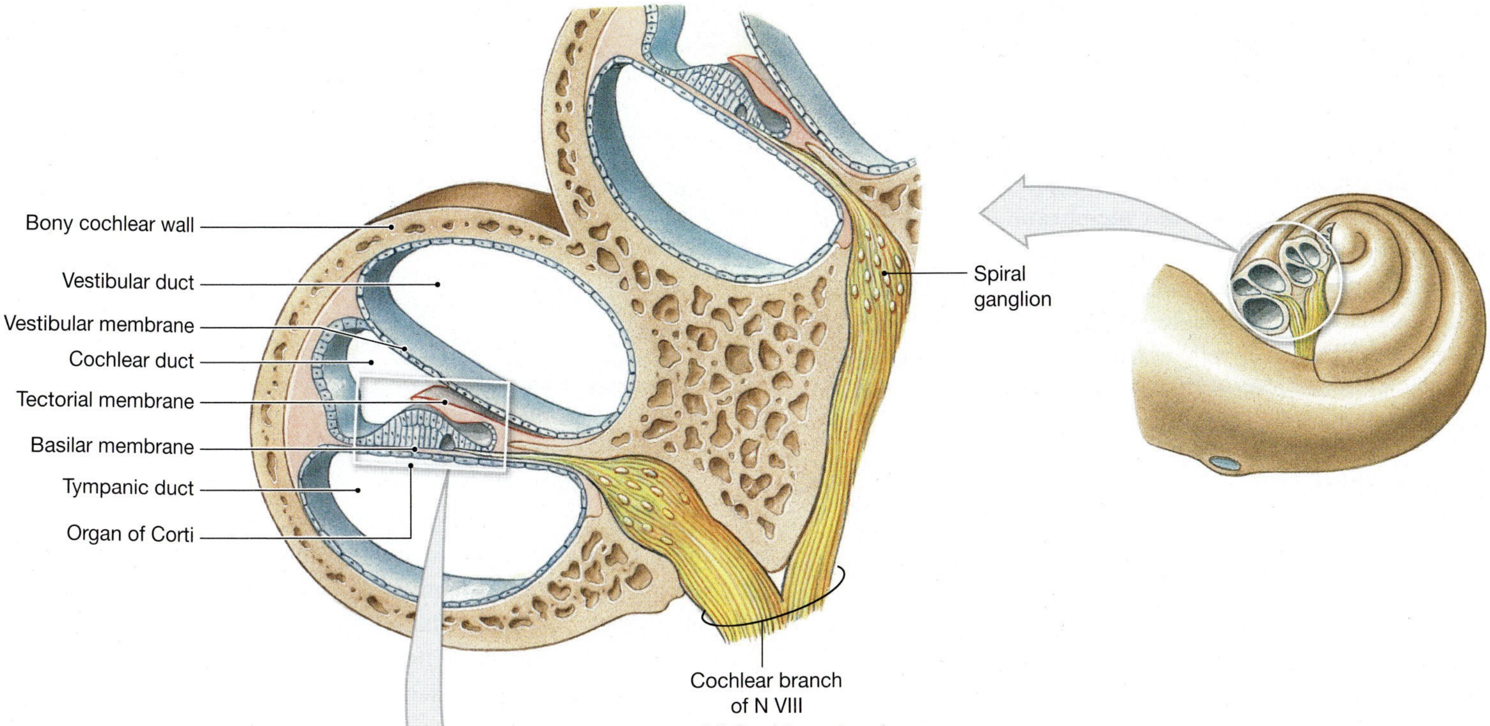

(d) Cochlear chambers

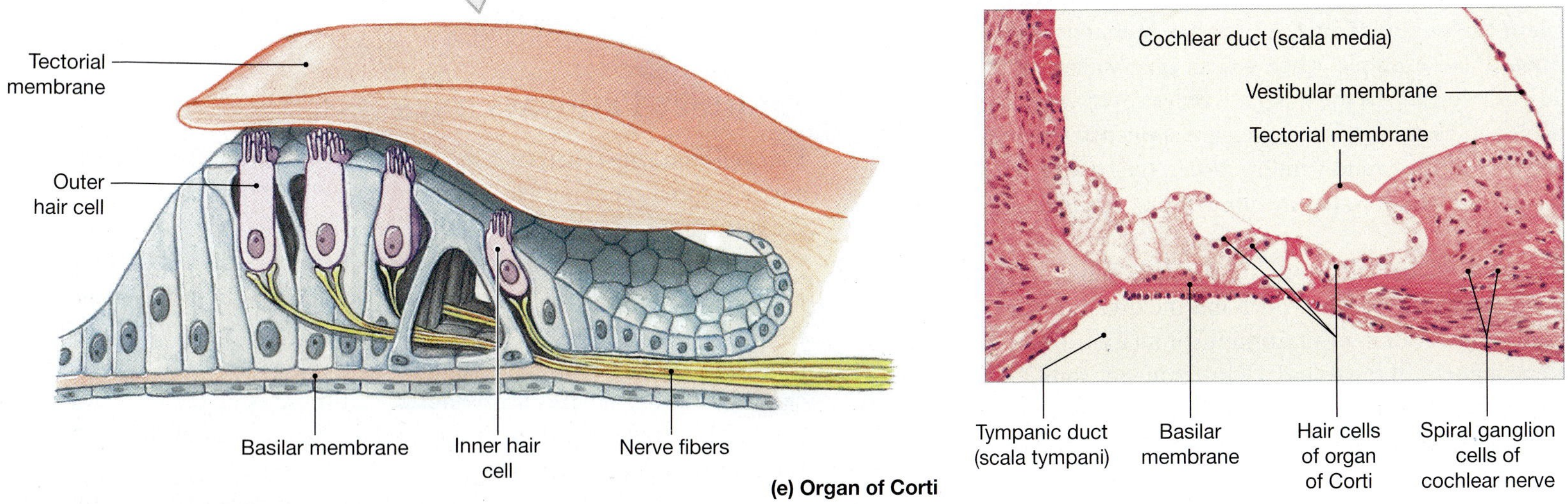

(e) Organ of Corti

(f) The receptor surface of the organ of Corti SEM × 1320

Figure 18.17 ***(continued)***
(d) Three-dimensional section showing the detail of the cochlear chambers, tectorial membrane, and organ of Corti. **(e)** Diagrammatic and histological sections through the receptor hair cell complex of the organ of Corti. (LM × 2022) **(f)** A color-enhanced SEM showing a portion of the receptor surface of the organ of Corti.

(*scala tympani*). The two perilymphatic chambers are interconnected at the tip of the cochlear spiral. The oval window is at the base of the vestibular duct, and the round window is at the base of the tympanic duct.

The Organ of Corti [Figure 18.17b–e] The hair cells of the cochlear duct are found in the **organ of Corti**, or **spiral organ** (Figure 18.17b–e). This sensory structure rests on the **basilar membrane** that separates the cochlear duct from the tympanic duct. The hair cells are arranged in inner and outer longitudinal rows. These hair cells lack kinocilia, and their stereocilia are in contact with the overlying **tectorial** (tek-TOR-ē-al; *tectum*, roof) **membrane**. This membrane is firmly attached to the inner wall of the cochlear duct. When a portion of the basilar membrane bounces up and down, the stereocilia of the hair cells are distorted.

Sound Detection [Table 18.2]

Hearing is the detection of sound, which consists of pressure waves conducted through air or water. Sound waves enter the external acoustic meatus and travel toward the tympanum. The tympanum provides the surface for sound collection, and it vibrates in response to sound waves with frequencies between approximately 20 and 20,000 Hz; this is the range in a young child, but with age the range decreases. As previously mentioned, the auditory ossicles transfer these vibrations in modified form to the oval window.

Movement of the stapes at the oval window applies pressure to the perilymph of the vestibular duct. A property of liquids is their inability to be compressed. For example, when you sit on a waterbed, you know that when you push down *here*, the waterbed bulges over *there*. Because the rest of the cochlea is sheathed in bone, pressure applied at the oval window can be relieved only at the round window. When the base of the stapes moves inward at the oval window, the membrane that spans the round window bulges outward.

Movement of the stapes sets up pressure waves in the perilymph. These waves distort the cochlear duct and the organ of Corti, stimulating the hair cells. The location of maximum stimulation varies depending on the frequency (pitch) of the sound. High-frequency sounds affect the basilar membrane near the oval window; the lower the frequency of the sound, the farther away from the oval window the distortion will be.

Clinical Note

Hearing Loss **Conductive deafness** results from conditions in the middle ear that block the normal transfer of vibration from the tympanic membrane to the oval window. An external acoustic meatus plugged by accumulated wax or trapped water may cause a temporary hearing loss. Scarring or perforation of the tympanum, fluid in the middle ear chamber, and immobilization of one or more of the auditory ossicles are more serious examples of conduction deafness.

In **nerve deafness** the problem lies within the cochlea or somewhere along the auditory pathway. The vibrations are reaching the oval window, but either the receptors cannot respond or their response cannot reach its central destinations. Also, certain drugs entering the endolymph may kill the receptors, and infections may damage the hair cells or affect the cochlear nerve. Hair cells can also be damaged by exposure to high doses of aminoglycoside antibiotics, such as neomycin or gentamicin; this potential side effect must be balanced against the severity of infection before these drugs are prescribed.

TABLE 18.2 Steps in the Production of an Auditory Sensation

1. Sound waves arrive at the tympanic membrane.
2. Movement of the tympanic membrane causes displacement of the auditory ossicles.
3. Movement of the stapes at the oval window establishes pressure waves in the perilymph of the vestibular duct.
4. The pressure waves distort the basilar membrane on their way to the round window of the tympanic duct.
5. Vibration of the basilar membrane causes vibration of hair cells against the tectorial membrane, resulting in hair cell stimulation and neurotransmitter release.
6. Information concerning the region and intensity of stimulation is relayed to the CNS over the cochlear branch of N VIII.

The actual amount of movement at a given location depends on the amount of force applied to the oval window. This relationship provides a mechanism for detecting the intensity (volume) of the sound. Very high-intensity sounds can produce hearing losses by breaking the stereocilia off the surfaces of the hair cells. The reflex contraction of the tensor tympani and stapedius in response to a dangerously loud noise occurs in less than 0.1 second, but this may not be fast enough to prevent damage and related hearing loss. Table 18.2 summarizes the steps involved in translating a sound wave into an auditory sensation.

Auditory Pathways [Figure 18.18]

Hair cell stimulation activates sensory neurons whose cell bodies are in the adjacent spiral ganglion. Their afferent fibers form the **cochlear branch** of the vestibulocochlear nerve (N VIII). These axons enter the medulla oblongata and synapse at the **cochlear nucleus** on the same side of the brain. The axons of the second-order neurons cross to the opposite side of the brain and ascend to the inferior colliculus of the midbrain (Figure 18.18). This processing center coordinates a number of responses to acoustic stimuli, including auditory reflexes involving skeletal muscles of the head, face, and trunk. These reflexes automatically change the position of the head in response to a sudden loud noise.

Before reaching the cerebral cortex and our conscious awareness, ascending auditory sensations synapse in the thalamus. Projection fibers then deliver the information to the auditory cortex of the temporal lobe. In effect, the auditory cortex contains a map of the organ of Corti. High-frequency sounds activate one portion of the cortex, and low-frequency sounds affect another. If the auditory cortex is damaged, the individual will respond to sounds and have normal acoustic reflexes, but sound interpretation and pattern recognition will be difficult or impossible. Damage to the adjacent association area does not affect the ability to detect the tones and patterns, but produces an inability to comprehend their meaning.

CONCEPT CHECK

1. If the membrane spanning the round window were not able to bulge out with increased pressure in the perilymph, how would sound perception be affected?
2. How would loss of stereocilia from the hair cells of the organ of Corti affect hearing?
3. Distinguish between the cochlear and tympanic ducts.
4. What structure stimulates hair cells in the organ of Corti?

See blue "Answers" tab at back of book.

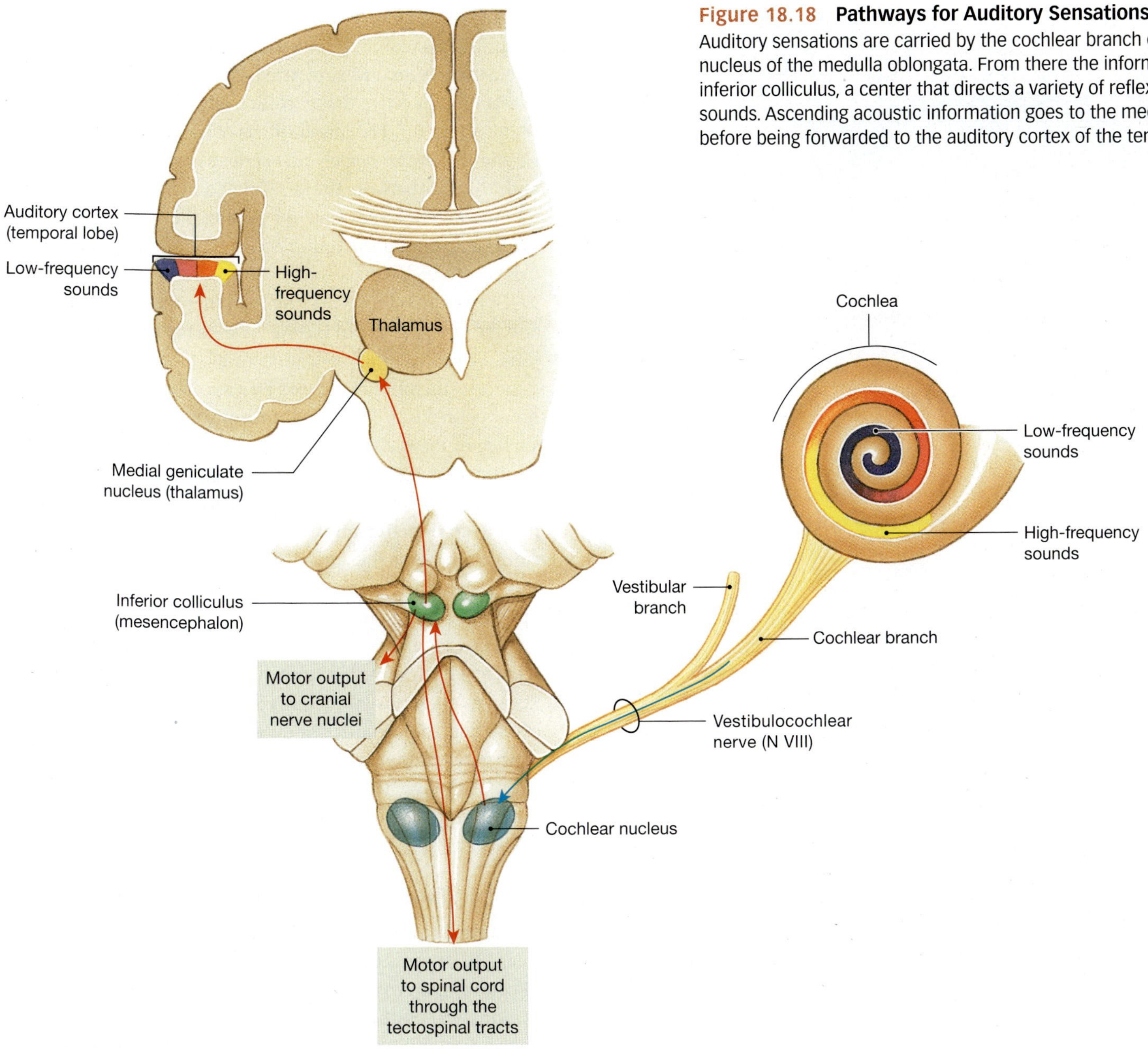

Figure 18.18 Pathways for Auditory Sensations
Auditory sensations are carried by the cochlear branch of N VIII to the cochlear nucleus of the medulla oblongata. From there the information is relayed to the inferior colliculus, a center that directs a variety of reflexive motor responses to sounds. Ascending acoustic information goes to the medial geniculate nucleus before being forwarded to the auditory cortex of the temporal lobe.

Vision [Figure 18.19]

Humans rely more on vision than on any other special sense, and the visual cortex is several times larger than the cortical areas devoted to other special senses. Our visual receptors are contained in elaborate structures, the eyes, which enable us not only to detect light but to create detailed visual images. We will begin our discussion with the *accessory structures* of the eye that provide protection, lubrication, and support. The superficial anatomy of the eye and the major accessory structures are illustrated in Figure 18.19.

Accessory Structures of the Eye

The **accessory structures** of the eye include the eyelids, the superficial epithelium of the eye, and the structures associated with the production, secretion, and removal of tears.

Eyelids [Figures 18.19/18.20/18.21b,e]

The eyelids, or **palpebrae** (pal-PĒ-brē) are a continuation of the skin. The eyelids act like windshield wipers; their continual blinking movements keep the surface lubricated and free from dust and debris. They can also close firmly to protect the delicate surface of the eye. The free margins of the upper and lower eyelids are separated by the **palpebral fissure**, but the two are connected at the **medial canthus** (KAN-thus) and the **lateral canthus** (Figure 18.19). The **eyelashes** along the palpebral margins are very robust hairs. Each of the eyelashes is monitored by a root hair plexus, and displacement of the hair triggers a blinking reflex. This response helps prevent foreign matter and insects from reaching the surface of the eye.

The eyelashes are associated with large sebaceous glands, the *glands of Zeis* (ZĪS). **Tarsal glands**, or *Meibomian* (mī-BŌ-mē-an) *glands*, along the inner margin of the lid secrete a lipid-rich product that helps keep the eyelids from sticking together. At the medial canthus, glands within the **lacrimal caruncle** (KAR-un-kul) (Figure 18.19a) produce the thick secretions that contribute to the gritty deposits occasionally found after a good night's sleep. These various glands are subject to occasional invasion and infection by bacteria. A cyst, or *chalazion* (kah-LĀ-zē-on; "small lump"), usually results from the infection of a tarsal gland. An infection in a sebaceous gland of an eyelash, a tarsal gland, or one of the many sweat glands that open to the surface between the follicles of the eyelashes produces a painful localized swelling known as a *sty*.

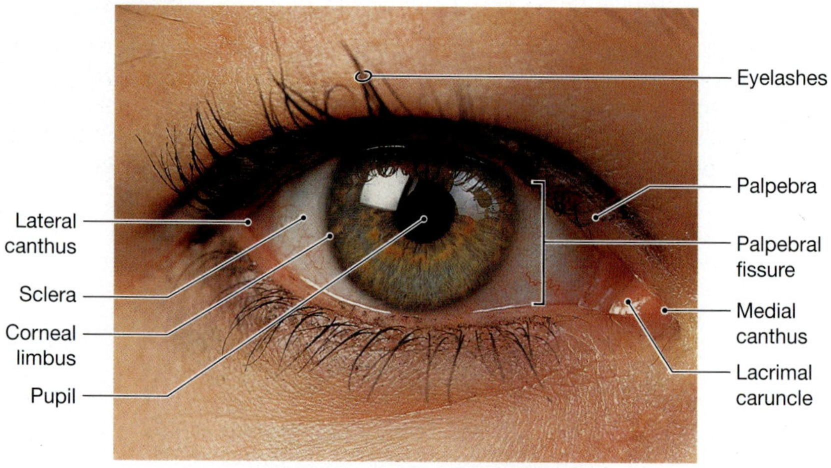

(a) Right eye, accessory structures

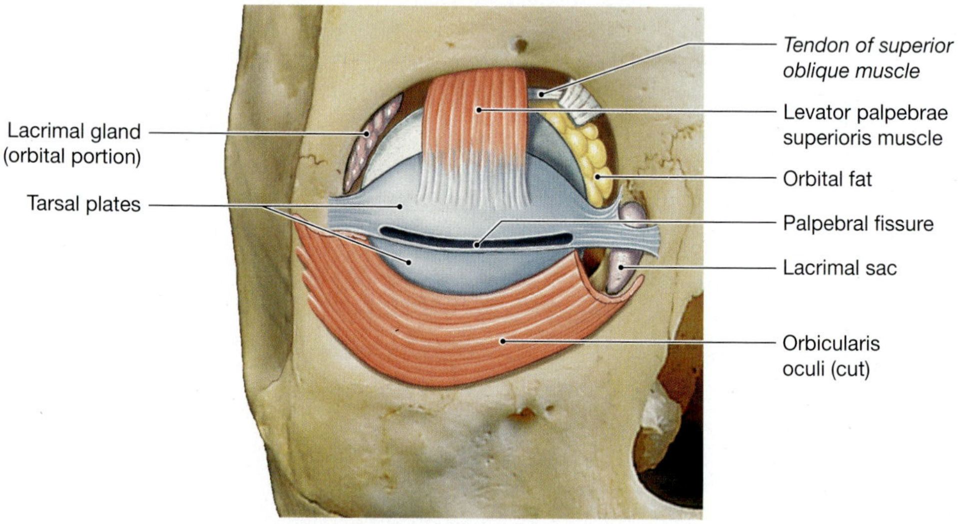

(b) Superficial dissection of right orbit

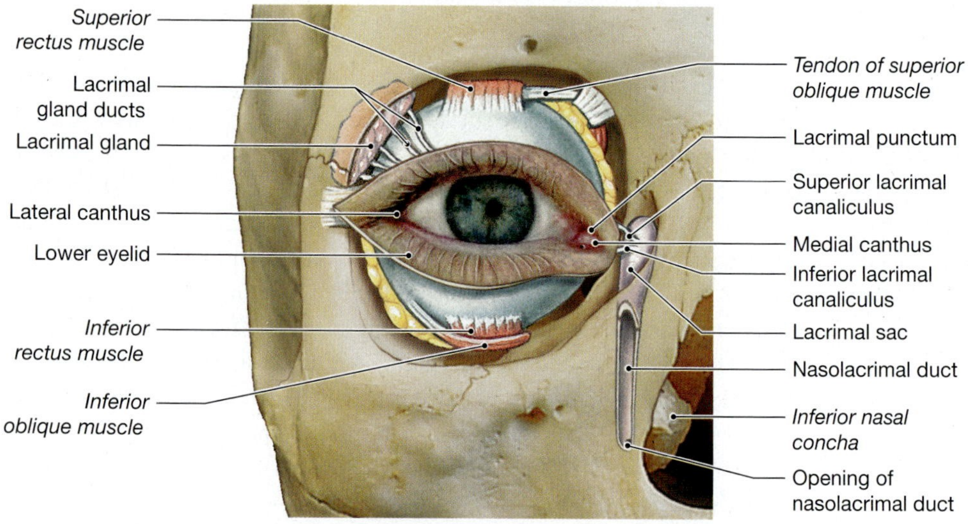

(c) Deep dissection of right orbit

Figure 18.19 Accessory Structures of the Eye, Part I
(a) Superficial anatomy of the right eye and its accessory structures. **(b)** Diagrammatic representation of a superficial dissection of the right orbit. **(c)** Diagrammatic representation of a deeper dissection of the right eye showing its position within the orbit and its relationship to accessory structures, especially the lacrimal apparatus.

The visible surface of the eyelid is covered by a thin layer of stratified squamous epithelium. Deep to the subcutaneous layer, the eyelids are supported and strengthened by broad sheets of connective tissue, collectively called the **tarsal plate** (Figure 18.19b). The muscle fibers of the *orbicularis oculi muscle* and the *levator palpebrae superioris muscle* (Figures 18.19b and 18.20) lie between the tarsal plate and the skin. These skeletal muscles are responsible for closing the eyelids (orbicularis oculi) and raising the upper eyelid (levator palpebrae superioris). ∞ p. 266

The epithelium covering the inner surface of the eyelids and the outer surface of the eye is called the **conjunctiva** (kon-junk-TĪ-va; "uniting" or "connecting") (Figure 18.21b,e). It is a mucous membrane covered by a specialized stratified squamous epithelium. The **palpebral conjunctiva** covers the inner surface of the eyelids, and the **ocular conjunctiva**, or **bulbar conjunctiva**, covers the anterior surface of the eye. A continuous supply of fluid washes over the surface of the eyeball, keeping the conjunctiva moist and clean. Goblet cells within the epithelium assist the various accessory glands in providing a superficial lubricant that prevents friction and drying of the opposing conjunctival surfaces.

Over the transparent **cornea** (KOR-nē-a) of the eye, the relatively thick stratified epithelium changes to a very thin and delicate squamous epithelium 5–7 cells thick. Near the edges of the lids, the conjunctiva develops a more robust stratified squamous epithelium characteristic of exposed bodily surfaces. Although there are no specialized sensory receptors monitoring the surface of the eye, there are abundant free nerve endings with very broad sensitivities.

The Lacrimal Apparatus [Figures 18.19b,c/18.20]

A constant flow of tears keeps conjunctival surfaces moist and clean. Tears reduce friction, remove debris, prevent bacterial infection, and provide nutrients and oxygen to portions of the conjunctival epithelium. The **lacrimal apparatus** produces, distributes, and removes tears. The lacrimal apparatus of each eye consists of (1) a *lacrimal gland,* (2) *superior* and *inferior lacrimal canaliculi,* (3) a *lacrimal sac,* and (4) a *nasolacrimal duct* (Figures 18.19b,c and 18.20).

The pocket created where the conjunctiva of the eyelid connects with that of the eye is known as the **fornix** (FŌR-niks). The lateral portion of the superior fornix receives 10–12 ducts from the **lacrimal gland**, or tear gland. The lacrimal gland is about the size and shape of an almond, measuring roughly 12–20 mm (0.5–0.75 in.). It nestles within a depression in the frontal bone, within the orbit and superior and lateral to the eyeball (Figure 18.20). ∞ p. 151

The lacrimal gland normally provides the key ingredients and most of the volume of the tears that bathe the conjunctival surfaces. Its secretions are watery and slightly alkaline and contain the enzyme **lysozyme**, which attacks microorganisms.

The lacrimal gland produces tears at a rate of around 1 ml/day. Once the lacrimal secretions have reached the ocular surface, they mix with the products of accessory glands and the oily secretions of the tarsal glands and glands of Zeis. The latter contributions produce a superficial "oil slick" that assists in lubrication and slows evaporation.

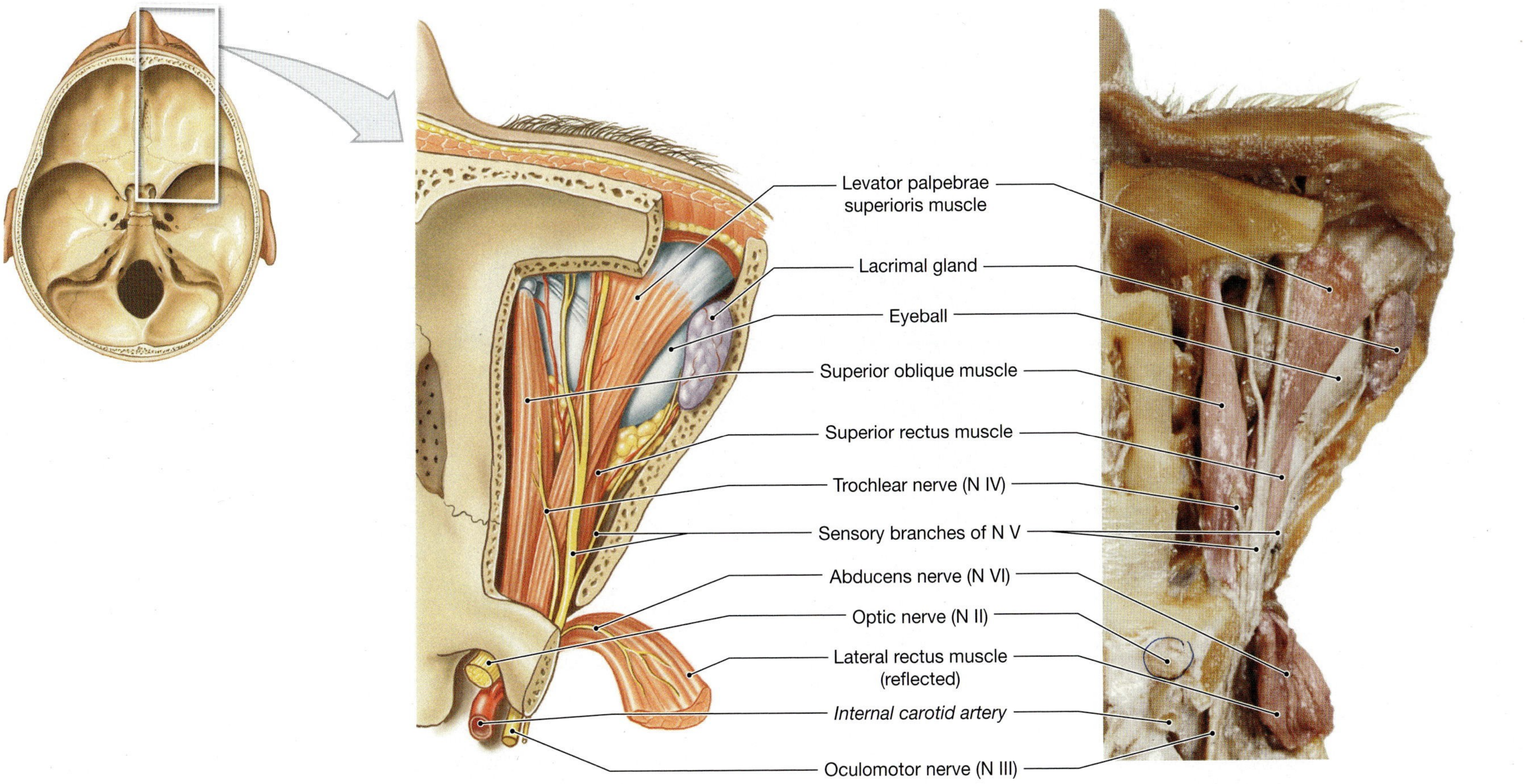

Figure 18.20 Accessory Structures of the Eye, Part II
A superior view of structures within the right orbit.

The blinking of the eye sweeps the tears across the ocular surface, and they accumulate at the medial canthus in an area known as the *lacus lacrimalis*, or "lake of tears." Two small pores, the **superior** and **inferior lacrimal puncta** (singular, *punctum*), drain the lacrimal lake, emptying into the **lacrimal canaliculi** that run along grooves in the surface of the lacrimal bone. These passageways lead to the **lacrimal sac**, which fills the lacrimal groove of the lacrimal bone. From there the **nasolacrimal duct** extends along the nasolacrimal canal formed by the lacrimal bone and the maxilla to deliver the tears to the inferior meatus on that side of the nasal cavity. p. 151

Blockage of the lacrimal puncta or oversecretion of the lacrimal glands can produce "watery eyes" that are constantly overflowing. Inadequate tear production, a more common condition, produces "dry eyes." Lubricating "artificial tears" in the form of eyedrops are the usual answer, but more serious cases may be treated by surgically closing the lacrimal puncta.

The Eye [Figures 18.20/18.21a,e,f]

The eyes are slightly irregular spheroids with an average diameter of 24 mm (almost 1 in.), slightly smaller than a Ping-Pong ball. Each eye weighs around 8 g (0.28 oz). The eyeball shares space within the orbit with the extra-ocular muscles, the lacrimal gland, and the cranial nerves and blood vessels that supply the eye and adjacent portions of the orbit and face (Figures 18.20 and 18.21e,f). A mass of **orbital fat** provides padding and insulation.

The wall of the eye contains three distinct layers, or tunics (Figure 18.21a): an outer *fibrous tunic*, an intermediate *vascular tunic*, and an inner *neural tunic*. The eyeball is hollow, and the interior is divided into two *cavities*. The large **posterior cavity** is also called the *vitreous chamber*, because it contains the gelatinous *vitreous body*. The smaller **anterior cavity** is subdivided into two chambers, *anterior* and *posterior*. The shape of the eye is stabilized in part by the vitreous body and the clear *aqueous humor* that fills the anterior cavity.

The Fibrous Tunic [Figures 18.20/18.21a,b,d,e]

The **fibrous tunic**, the outermost layer of the eye, consists of the *sclera* and the *cornea* (Figure 18.21a,b,d,e). The fibrous tunic: (1) provides mechanical support and some degree of physical protection, (2) serves as an attachment site for the extra-ocular muscles, and (3) contains structures that assist in the focusing process.

Most of the ocular surface is covered by the **sclera** (SKLER-a). The sclera, or "white of the eye," consists of a dense, fibrous connective tissue containing both collagen and elastic fibers. This layer is thickest at the posterior portion of the eye, near the exit of the optic nerve, and thinnest over the anterior surface. The six extra-ocular muscles insert on the sclera, and the collagen fibers of their tendons are interwoven into the collagen fibers of the outer tunic (Figure 18.20).

The anterior surface of the sclera contains small blood vessels and nerves that penetrate the sclera to reach internal structures. The network of small vessels that lie deep to the ocular conjunctiva usually does not carry enough blood to lend an obvious color to the sclera, but is visible, on close inspection, as red lines against the white background of collagen fibers. The transparent cornea of the eye is part of the fibrous tunic, and it is continuous with the sclera. The corneal surface is covered by a delicate stratified squamous epithelium continuous with the ocular conjunctiva. Deep to that epithelium, the cornea consists primarily of a dense matrix containing multiple layers of collagen fibers. The transparency of the cornea results from

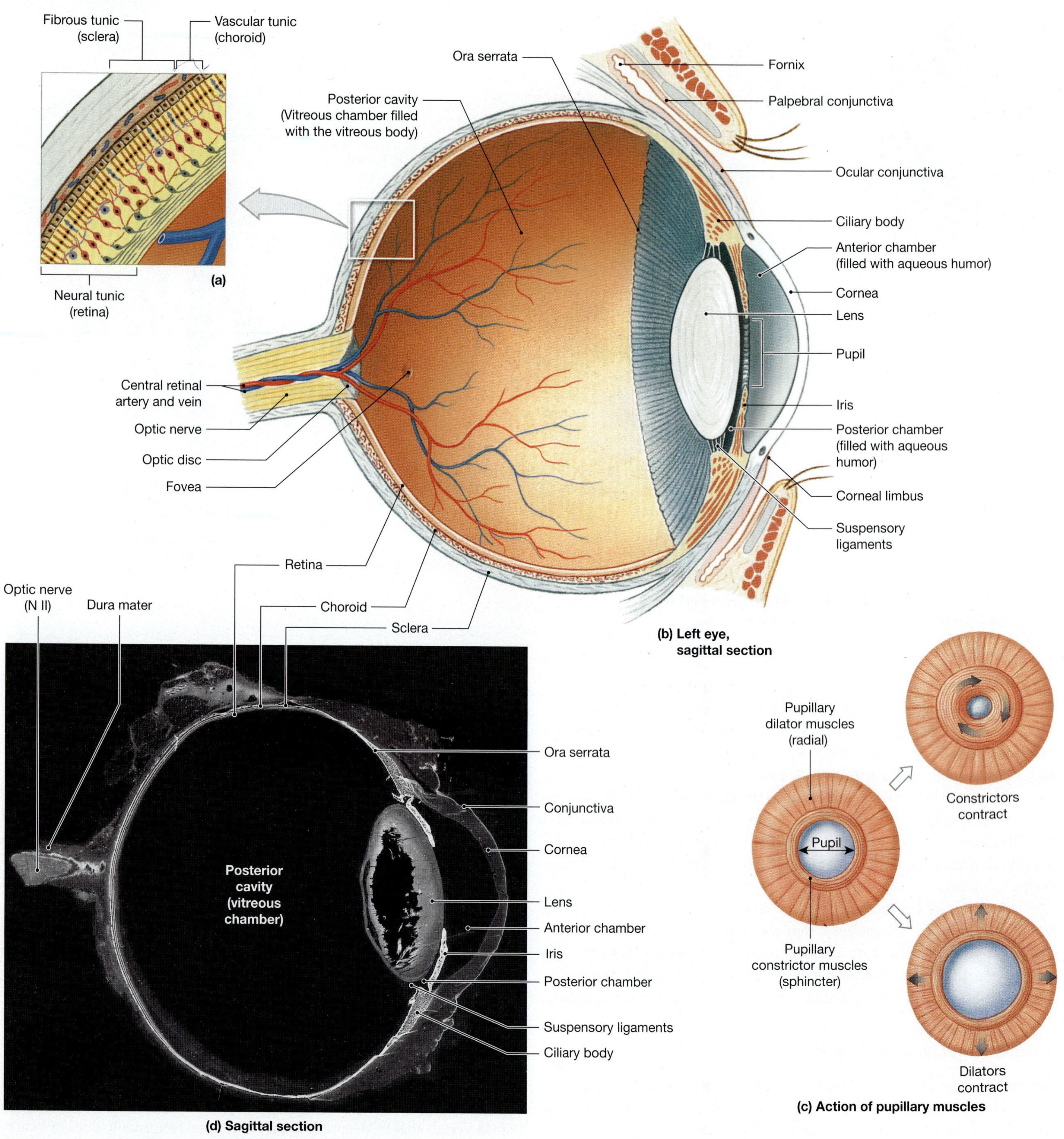

Figure 18.21 Sectional Anatomy of the Eye
(a) The three layers, or *tunics*, of the eye. **(b)** Major anatomical landmarks and features in a diagrammatic view of the left eye. **(c)** The action of pupillary muscles and changes in pupillary diameter. **(d)** Sagittal section through the eye. **(e)** Horizontal section through right eye. **(f)** Horizontal section through the superior portion of the right eye and orbit.

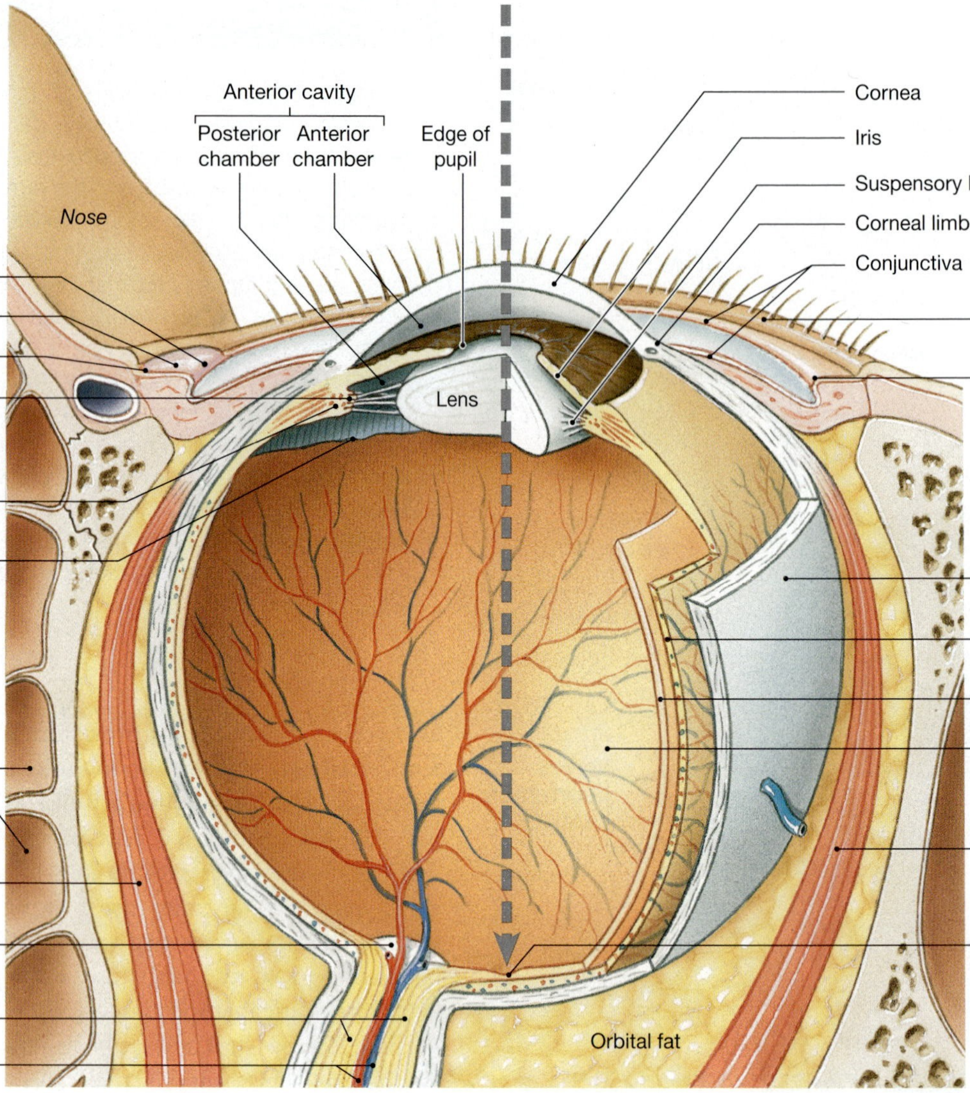

(e) Horizontal dissection of right eye

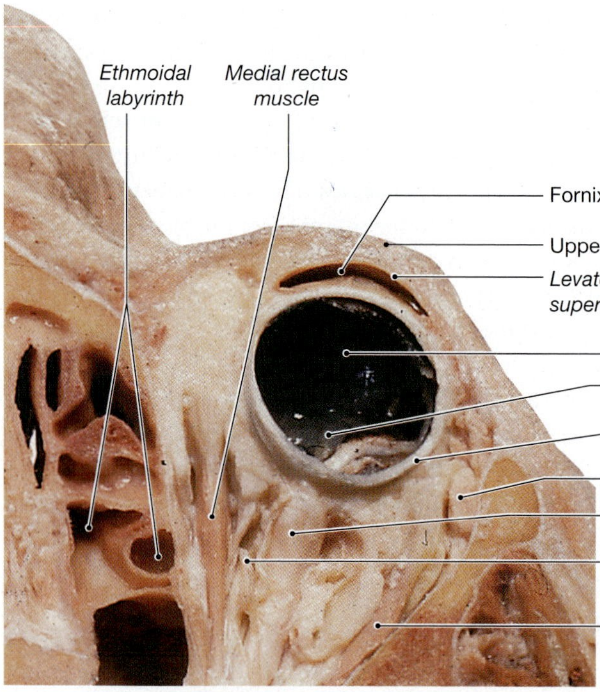

(f) Horizontal section, superior view

Figure 18.21 ***(continued)***

the precise alignment of the collagen fibers within these layers. A simple squamous epithelium separates the innermost layer of the cornea from the anterior chamber of the eye.

The cornea is structurally continuous with the sclera; the **corneal limbus** is the border between the two. The cornea is avascular, and there are no blood vessels between the cornea and the overlying conjunctiva. As a result, the superficial epithelial cells must obtain oxygen and nutrients from the tears that flow across their free surfaces while the innermost epithelial layer receives its nutrients from the aqueous humor within the anterior chamber. There are numerous free nerve endings in the cornea, and this is the most sensitive portion of the eye. This sensitivity is important because corneal damage will cause blindness even though the rest of the eye—photoreceptors included—is perfectly normal.

The Vascular Tunic [Figures 18.21a,b,d,e/18.22]

The **vascular tunic** contains numerous blood vessels, lymphatics, and the intrinsic eye muscles. The functions of this layer include (1) providing a route for blood vessels and lymphatics that supply tissues of the eye, (2) regulating the amount of light entering the eye, (3) secreting and reabsorbing the *aqueous humor* that circulates within the eye, and (4) controlling the shape of the lens, an essential part of the focusing process. The vascular tunic includes the *iris*, the *ciliary body*, and the *choroid* (**Figures 18.21a,b,d,e** and **18.22**).

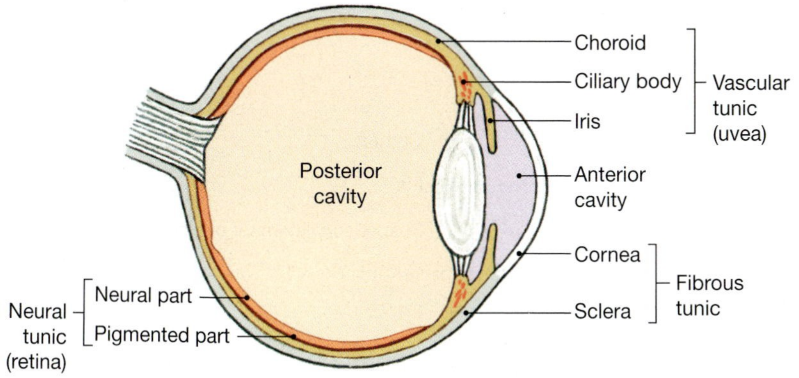

(a) Horizontal section of right eye

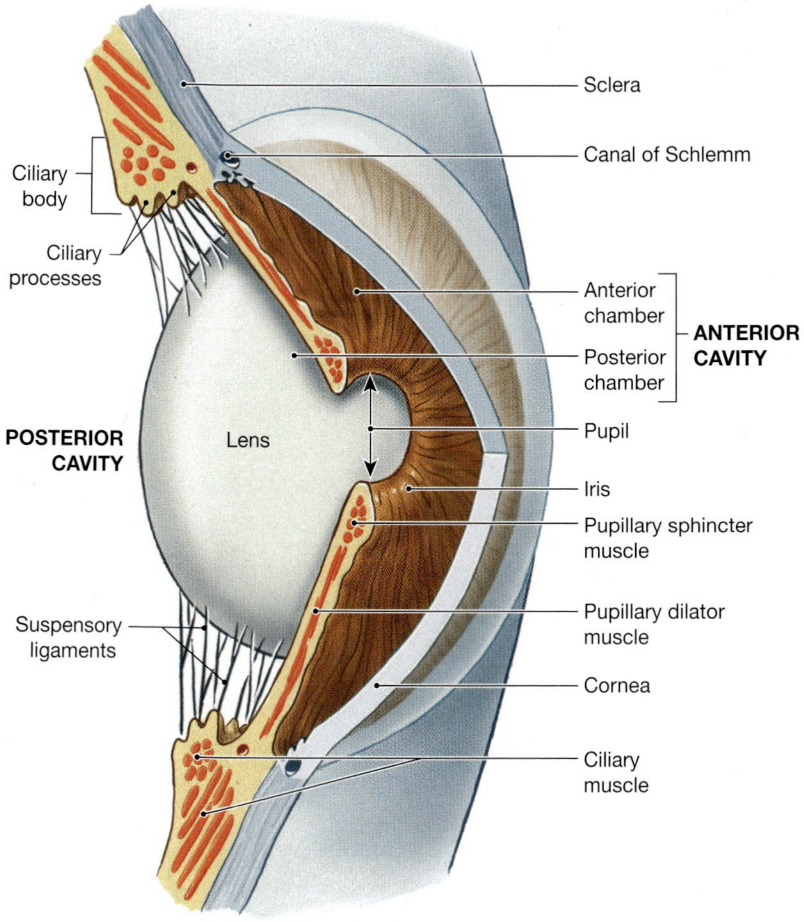

(b) Cavities of the eye

Figure 18.22 The Lens and Chambers of the Eye
(a) The lens is suspended between the posterior cavity and the posterior chamber of the anterior cavity. **(b)** Its position is maintained by the suspensory ligaments that attach the lens to the ciliary body.

The Iris [Figures 18.21/18.22] The **iris** can be seen through the transparent corneal surface. The iris contains blood vessels, pigment cells, and two layers of smooth muscle cells that are part of the *intrinsic eye muscles.* Contraction of these muscles changes the diameter of the central opening of the iris, the **pupil**. One group of smooth muscle fibers forms a series of concentric circles around the pupil (Figure 18.21c). The diameter of the pupil decreases when these **pupillary sphincter muscles** contract. A second group of smooth muscles extends radially from the edge of the pupil. Contraction of these **pupillary dilator muscles** enlarges the pupil. These antagonistic muscle groups are controlled by the autonomic nervous system; parasympathetic activation causes pupillary constriction, and sympathetic activation causes pupillary dilation. p. 266

The body of the iris consists of a connective tissue whose posterior surface is covered by an epithelium containing pigment cells. Pigment cells may also be present in the connective tissue of the iris and in the epithelium covering its anterior surface. Eye color is determined by the density and distribution of pigment cells. When there are no pigment cells in the body of the iris, light passes through it and bounces off the inner surface of the pigmented epithelium. The eye then appears blue. Individuals with gray, brown, and black eyes have more pigment cells, respectively, in the body and surface of the iris.

The Ciliary Body [Figures 18.21b,d,e/18.22b] At its periphery the iris attaches to the anterior portion of the ciliary body. The **ciliary body** begins at the junction between the cornea and sclera and extends posteriorly to the **ora serrata** (Ō-ra ser-RĀ-ta; "serrated mouth") (Figures 18.21b,d,e and 18.22b). The bulk of the ciliary body consists of the **ciliary muscle**, a muscular ring that projects into the interior of the eye. The epithelium is thrown into numerous folds, called **ciliary processes**. The **suspensory ligaments**, or *zonular fibers*, of the lens attach to the tips of these processes. These connective tissue fibers hold the lens posterior to the iris and centered on the pupil. As a result, any light passing through the pupil and headed for the photoreceptors will pass through the lens.

The Choroid [Figure 18.21] Oxygen and nutrients are delivered to the outer portion of the retina by an extensive capillary network contained within the **choroid**. It also contains scattered melanocytes, which are especially dense in the outermost portion of the choroid adjacent to the sclera (Figure 18.21a,b,d,e). The innermost portion of the choroid attaches to the outer retinal layer.

The Neural Tunic [Figures 18.21/18.23]

The **neural tunic**, or **retina**, consists of two distinct layers, an outer **pigmented layer** and an inner **neural layer**, called the **neural retina**, which contains the visual receptors and associated neurons (Figures 18.21 and 18.23). The pigment layer absorbs light after it passes through the

Clinical Note

Conjunctivitis Conjunctivitis, or "pinkeye," results from damage to and irritation of the conjunctival surface. The most obvious symptom results from dilation of the blood vessels deep to the conjunctival epithelium. The term *conjunctivitis* is more useful as the description of a symptom than as a name for a specific disease. A great variety of pathogens, including bacteria, viruses, and fungi can cause conjunctivitis, and a temporary form of the condition may be produced by allergic, chemical, or physical irritation (including even such mundane experiences as prolonged crying or peeling an onion).

Chronic conjunctivitis, or *trachoma*, results from bacterial or viral invasion of the conjunctiva. Many of these infections are highly contagious, and severe cases may scar the corneal surface and affect vision. The bacterium most often involved is *Chlamydia trachomatis*. Trachoma is a relatively common problem in southwestern North America, North Africa, and the Middle East. The condition must be treated with topical and systemic antibiotics to prevent corneal damage and vision loss.

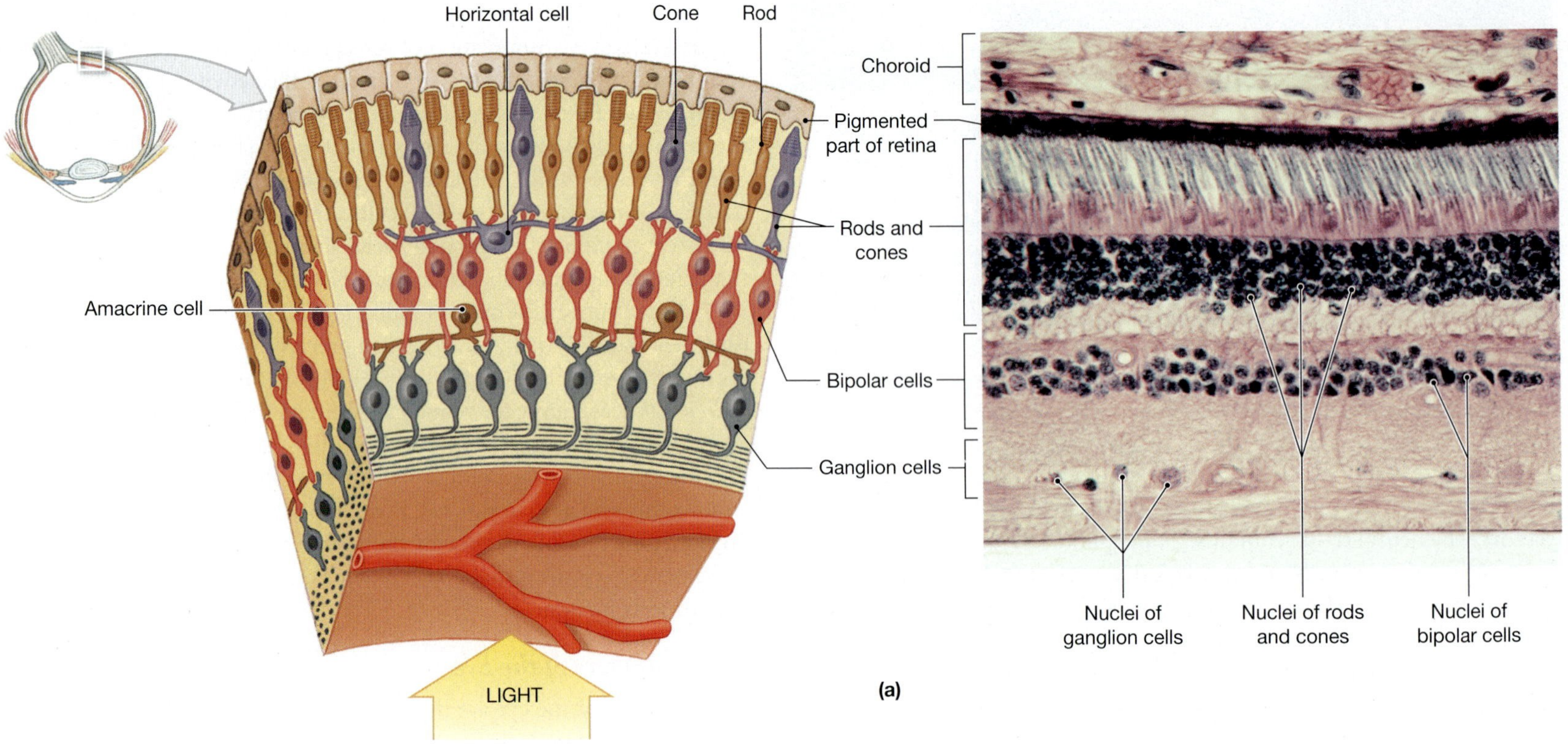

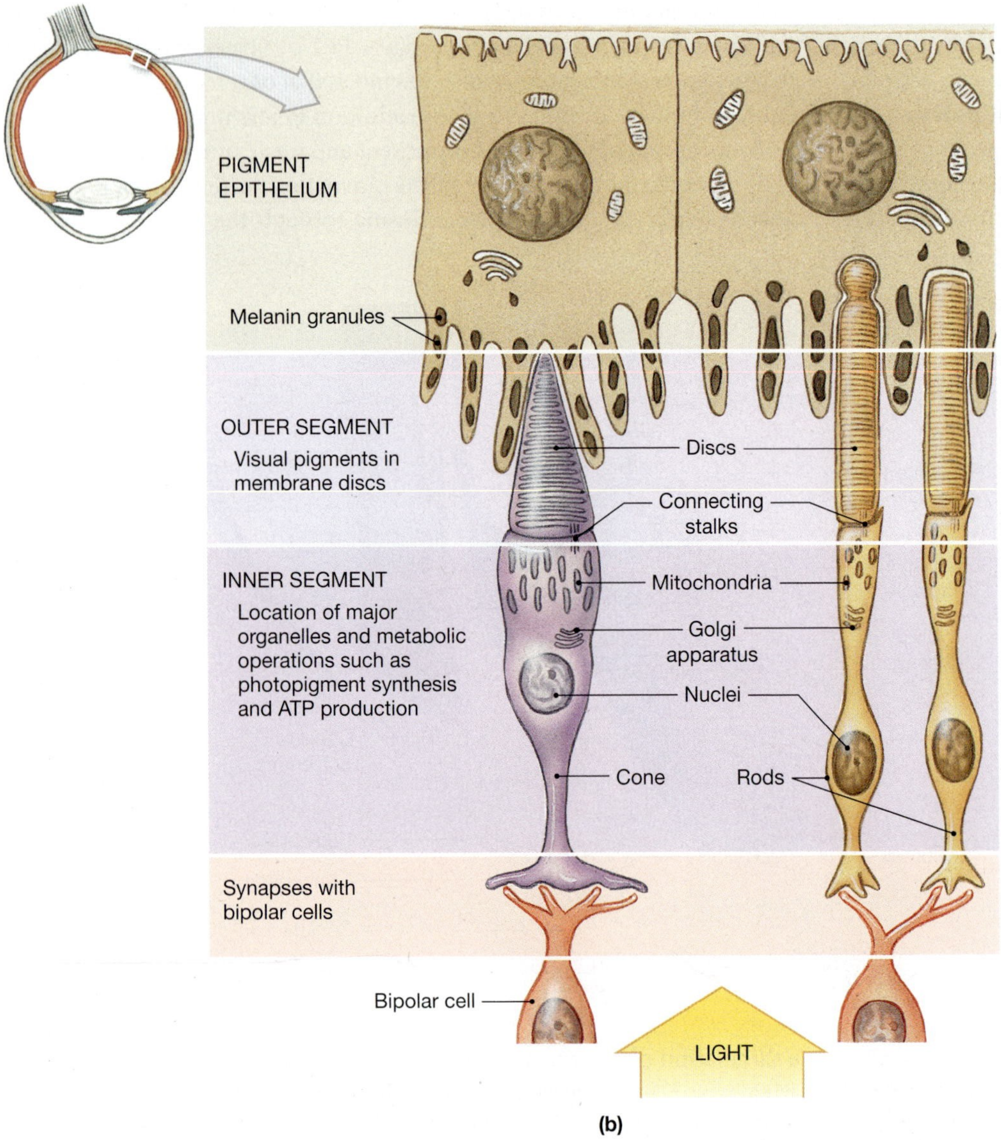

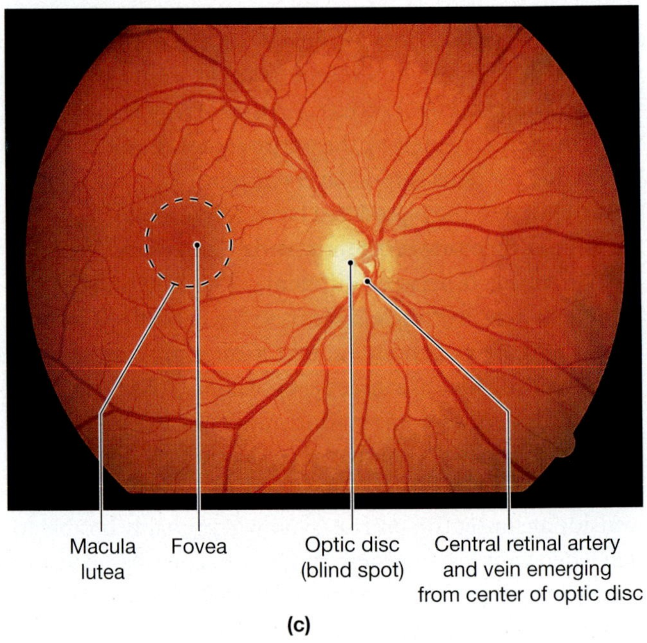

Figure 18.23 Retinal Organization
(a) Histological organization of the retina. Note that the photoreceptors are located closest to the choroid rather than near the vitreous chamber. (LM × 73) **(b)** Diagrammatic view of the fine structure of rods and cones, based on data from electron microscopy. **(c)** A photograph taken through the pupil of the eye, showing the retinal blood vessels, the origin of the optic nerve, and the optic disc.

Clinical Note

Corneal Transplants The cornea has a very restricted ability to repair itself, so corneal injuries must be treated immediately to prevent serious vision loss. To restore vision after corneal scarring, it is usually necessary to replace the cornea through a *corneal transplant*. Corneal replacements are probably the most common form of transplant surgery. They can be performed between unrelated individuals because there are no corneal blood vessels, and white blood cells that would otherwise reject the graft are unlikely to enter the area. Corneal tissues must be removed within five hours after the donor's death.

retina and has important biochemical interactions with retinal photoreceptors. The neural retina contains (1) the photoreceptors that respond to light, (2) supporting cells and neurons that perform preliminary processing and integration of visual information, and (3) blood vessels supplying tissues lining the posterior cavity.

The neural retina and pigmented layers are normally very close together, but not tightly interconnected. The pigmented layer continues over the ciliary body and iris, although the neural retina extends anteriorly only as far as the ora serrata. The neural retina thus forms a cup that establishes the posterior and lateral boundaries of the posterior cavity (Figure 18.21b,d,e,f).

Retinal Organization [Figures 18.21b,e/18.23] There are approximately 130 million photoreceptors in the retina, each monitoring a specific location on the retinal surface. A visual image results from the processing of information provided by the entire receptor population. In sectional view, the retina contains several layers of cells (Figure 18.23a,b). The outermost layer, closest to the pigmented layer, contains the visual receptors. There are two types of **photoreceptors**: **rods** and **cones**. Rods do not discriminate between different colors of light. They are very light-sensitive and enable us to see in dimly lit rooms, at twilight, or in pale moonlight. Cones provide us with color vision. There are three types of cones, and their stimulation in various combinations provides the perception of different colors. Cones give us sharper, clearer images, but they require more intense light than rods. If you sit outside at sunset (or sunrise), you will probably be able to tell when your visual system shifts from cone-based vision (clear images in full color) to rod-based vision (relatively grainy images in black and white).

Rods and cones are not evenly distributed across the outer surface of the retina. Approximately 125 million rods form a broad band around the periphery of the retina. The posterior retinal surface is dominated by the presence of roughly 6 million cones. Most of these are concentrated in the area where a visual image arrives after passing through the cornea and lens. There are no rods in this region, which is known as the **macula lutea** (LOO-tē-a; "yellow spot"). The highest concentration of cones is found in the central portion of the macula lutea, at the **fovea** (FŌ-vē-a; "shallow depression"), or *fovea centralis*. The fovea is the site of sharpest vision; when you look directly at an object, its image falls upon this portion of the retina (Figures 18.21b,e and 18.23c).

The rods and cones synapse with roughly 6 million **bipolar cells** (Figure 18.23a,b). Stimulation of rods and cones alters their rates of neurotransmitter release, and this in turn alters the activity of the bipolar cells. **Horizontal cells** at this same level form a network that inhibits or facilitates communication between the visual receptors and bipolar cells. Bipolar cells in turn synapse within the layer of **ganglion cells** that faces the vitreous chamber. **Amacrine** (AM-a-krin) **cells** at this level modulate communication between bipolar and ganglion cells. The ganglion cells are the only cells in the retina that generate action potentials to the brain.

Axons from an estimated 1 million ganglion cells converge on the **optic disc**, penetrate the wall of the eye, and proceed toward the diencephalon as the optic nerve (N II) (Figure 18.21b,e). The *central retinal artery* and *central retinal vein* that supply the retina pass through the center of the optic nerve and emerge on the surface of the optic disc (Figure 18.23c). There are no photoreceptors or other retinal structures at the optic disc. Because light striking this area goes unnoticed, it is commonly called the **blind spot**. You do not "notice" a blank spot in the visual field, because involuntary eye movements keep the visual image moving and allow the brain to fill in the missing information.

The Chambers of the Eye

The chambers of the eye are the *anterior*, *posterior*, and *vitreous chambers*. The anterior and posterior chambers are filled with *aqueous humor*.

Aqueous Humor [Figure 18.24] **Aqueous humor** forms continuously as interstitial fluids pass between the epithelial cells of the ciliary processes and enter the posterior chamber (Figure 18.24). The epithelial cells appear to regulate its composition, which resembles that of cerebrospinal fluid. The aqueous humor circulates so that in addition to forming a fluid cushion, it provides an important route for nutrient and waste transport.

Aqueous humor returns to the circulation in the anterior chamber near the edge of the iris. After diffusing through the local epithelium, it

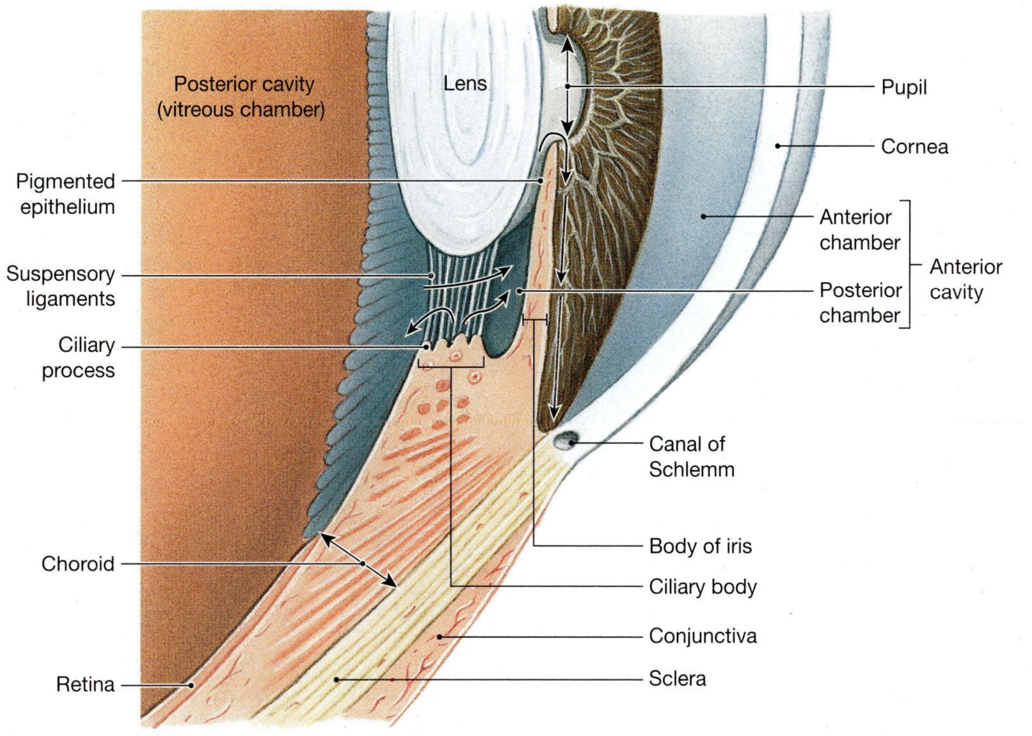

Figure 18.24 The Circulation of Aqueous Humor
Aqueous humor secreted at the ciliary body circulates through the posterior and anterior chambers as well as into the posterior cavity (arrows) before it is reabsorbed through the canal of Schlemm.

Clinical Note

Glaucoma Glaucoma affects roughly 2 percent of the population over 40. In this condition aqueous humor no longer has free access to the canal of Schlemm. The primary factors responsible cannot be determined in 90 percent of all cases. Although drainage is impaired, production of aqueous humor continues, and the intra-ocular pressure begins to rise. The fibrous scleral coat cannot expand significantly, so the increasing pressures begin to push against the surrounding intra-ocular soft tissues. When intra-ocular pressures have risen to roughly twice normal levels, distortion of the nerve fibers begins to affect visual perception. If this condition is not corrected, blindness eventually results.

Most eye exams include a glaucoma test. Intraocular pressure is tested by bouncing a tiny blast of air off the surface of the eye and measuring the deflection produced. Glaucoma may be treated by application of drugs that constrict the pupil and tense the edge of the iris, making the surface more permeable to aqueous humor. Surgical correction involves perforating the wall of the anterior chamber to encourage drainage and is now performed by laser surgery on an outpatient basis.

passes into the **canal of Schlemm**, or *scleral venous sinus*, which communicates with the veins of the eye.

The **lens** lies posterior to the cornea, held in place by the suspensory ligaments that originate on the ciliary body of the choroid (Figure 18.24). The lens and its attached suspensory ligaments form the anterior boundary of the vitreous chamber. This chamber contains the **vitreous body**, a gelatinous mass sometimes called the *vitreous humor*. The vitreous body helps maintain the shape of the eye, support the posterior surface of the lens, and give physical support to the retina by pressing the neural layer against the pigment layer. Aqueous humor produced in the posterior chamber freely diffuses through the vitreous body and across the retinal surface.

The Lens [Figures 18.21/18.24]

The primary function of the lens is to focus the visual image on the retinal photoreceptors. It accomplishes this by changing its shape. The lens consists of concentric layers of cells that are precisely organized (Figures 18.21b,d,e and 18.24). A dense, fibrous capsule covers the entire lens.

Many of the capsular fibers are elastic, and unless an outside force is applied, they will contract and make the lens spherical. Around the edges of the lens, the capsular fibers intermingle with those of the suspensory ligaments.

At rest, tension in the suspensory ligaments overpowers the elastic capsule and flattens the lens. In this position the eye is focused for distant vision. When the ciliary muscles contract, the ciliary body moves toward the lens. This movement reduces the tension in the suspensory ligaments, and the elastic lens assumes a more spherical shape, which focuses the eye on nearby objects.

Visual Pathways [Figures 18.25/18.26]

Each rod and cone cell monitors a specific receptive field. A visual image results from the processing of information provided by the entire receptor population. A significant amount of processing occurs in the retina before the information is sent to the brain, because of interactions between the various cell types.

The two optic nerves, one from each eye, reach the diencephalon at the optic chiasm (Figure 18.25). From this point, a partial decussation occurs: Approximately half of the fibers proceed toward the lateral geniculate nucleus of

Clinical Note

Cataracts The transparency of the lens depends on a precise combination of structural and biochemical characteristics. When that balance becomes disturbed, the lens loses its transparency and changes shape, becoming harder and flatter. The abnormal lens is known as a **cataract**. It acts like a fogged-up or frosty window, distorting and obscuring the image that reaches the retina.

Cataracts may be congenital or result from drug reactions, injuries, or radiation, but **senile cataracts**, a normal consequence of aging, are the most common form. As aging proceeds, the lens becomes less elastic, and the individual has difficulty focusing on nearby objects. (The person becomes "farsighted.") Over this period, a cataract may develop slowly and without pain. Initially, the cloudiness may affect only a small part of the lens, and the individual may not be aware of any vision loss.

Over time, the lens takes on a yellowish hue, and eventually it begins to lose its transparency. As the lens becomes "cloudy," the individual needs brighter reading lights, higher contrast, and larger type. Visual clarity begins to fade. Light from the sun, lamps or oncoming automobile headlights may seem too bright. Often glare and halos around lights may make driving uncomfortable and dangerous. Eyestrain and repetitive blinking may become more common. In addition, colors don't appear as vivid, or may even seem to have a yellowish tint.

If the lens becomes completely opaque, the person will be functionally blind, even though the retinal receptors are normal. Modern surgical procedures involve removing the lens, either intact or in pieces, after shattering it with high-frequency sound. The missing lens can be replaced by an artificial one placed behind the iris. Vision can then be fine-tuned with glasses or contact lenses.

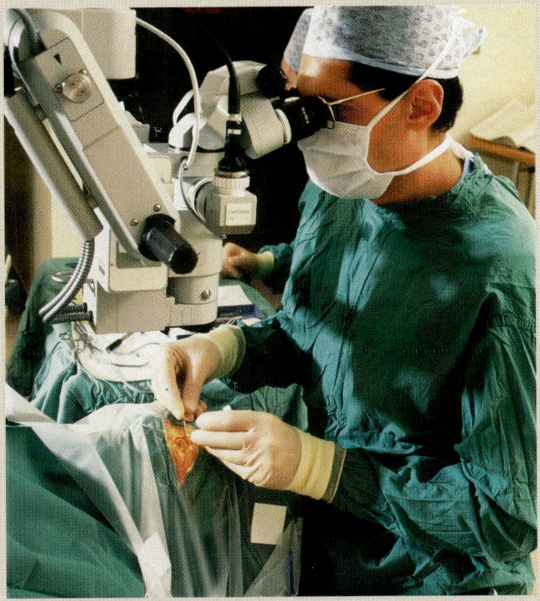

the same side of the brain, while the other half cross over to reach the lateral geniculate nucleus of the opposite side (Figure 18.26). Visual information from the left half of each retina arrives at the lateral geniculate nucleus of the left side; information from the right half of each retina goes to the right side. The lateral geniculate nuclei act as a switching center that relays visual information to reflex centers in the brain stem as well as to the cerebral cortex. The reflexes that control eye movement are triggered by information that bypasses the lateral geniculate nuclei to synapse in the superior colliculi.

Cortical Integration [Figure 18.26]

The sensation of vision arises from the integration of information arriving at the visual cortex of the occipital lobes of the cerebral hemispheres. The visual cortex contains a sensory map of the entire field of vision. As in the case of the primary sensory cortex, the map does not faithfully duplicate the relative areas within the sensory field.

Each eye also receives a slightly different image, because (1) their foveae are 2–3 inches apart, and (2) the nose and eye socket block the view of the opposite side. The association and integrative areas of the cortex compare the two perspectives (Figure 18.26) and use them to provide us with depth perception. The partial crossover that occurs at the optic chiasm ensures that the visual cortex receives a *composite* picture of the entire visual field.

The Brain Stem and Visual Processing [Figure 18.26]

Many centers in the brain stem receive visual information, either from the lateral geniculate nuclei or via collaterals from the optic tracts. Collaterals that bypass the lateral geniculate nuclei synapse in the superior colliculus or hypothalamus (Figure 18.26b). The superior colliculus of the midbrain issues motor commands controlling subconscious eye, head, or neck movements in response to visual stimuli. Visual inputs to the **suprachiasmatic** (soo-pra-kī-az-MA-tic) **nucleus** of the hypothalamus and the endocrine cells of the *pineal gland* affect the function of other brain stem nuclei. These nuclei establish a daily pattern of visceral activity that is tied to the day-night cycle. This **circadian rhythm** (*circa*, about + *dies*, day) affects metabolic rate, endocrine function, blood pressure, digestive activities, the awake-asleep cycle, and other physiological processes.

CONCEPT CHECK

1. What layer of the eye would be the first to be affected by inadequate tear production?
2. If the intra-ocular pressure becomes abnormally high, which structures of the eye are affected and how are they affected?
3. Would a person born without cones in her eyes be able to see? Explain.
4. In anatomy laboratory, your partner asks, "What are ciliary processes and what do they do?" How do you answer?

See blue "Answers" tab at back of book.

Embryology Summary

For a summary of the development of the special organs see Chapter 28 (Embryology and Human Development).

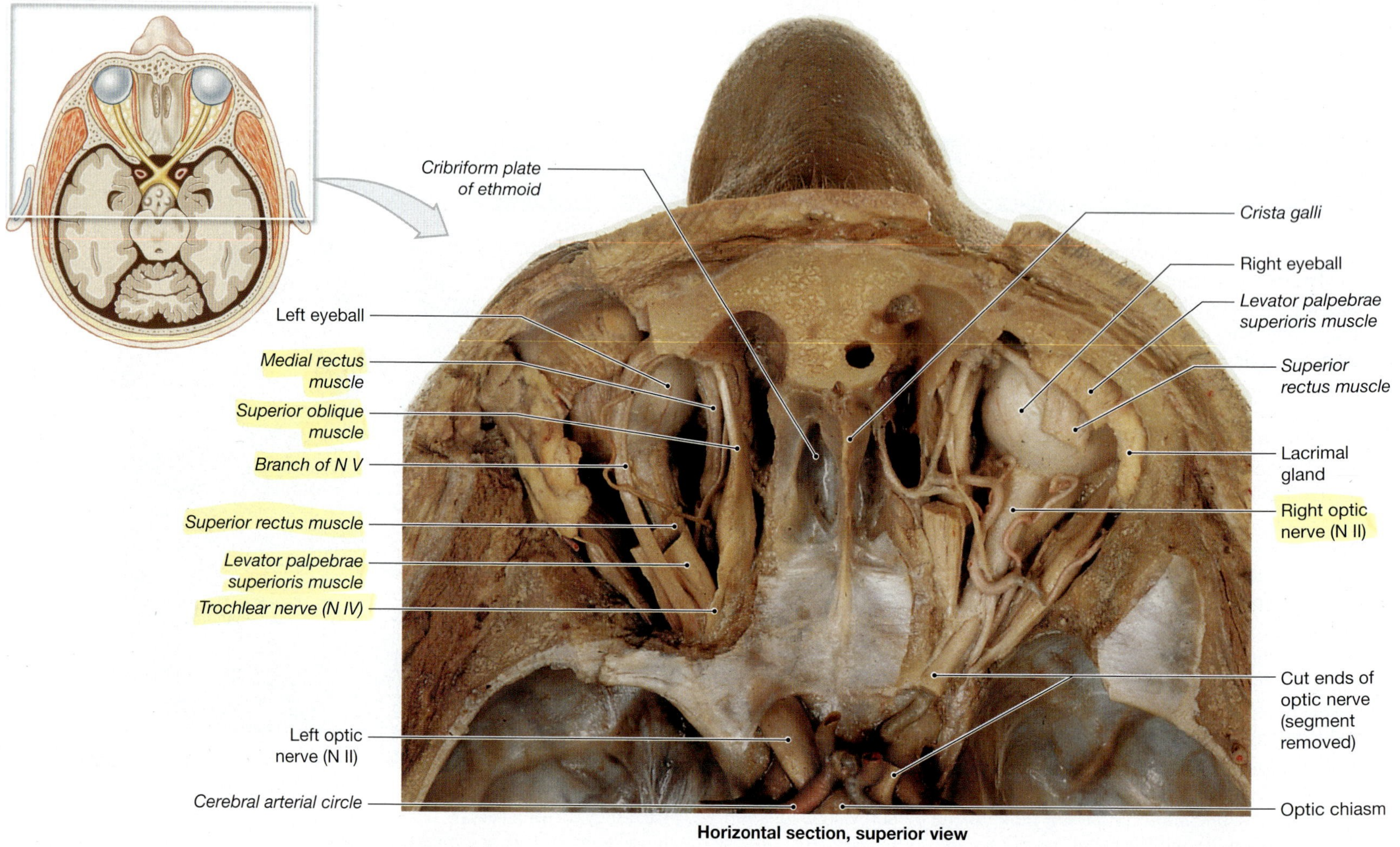

Figure 18.25 Anatomy of the Visual Pathways, Part I
A superior view of a horizontal section through the head at the level of the optic chiasm.

Figure 18.26 Anatomy of the Visual Pathways, Part II
(a) An inferior view of the brain. Much of the brain stem has been removed. Portions of the cerebral hemispheres have been dissected away to show the optic tract. **(b)** At the optic chiasm, a partial crossover of nerve fibers occurs. As a result, each hemisphere receives visual information from the lateral half of the retina of the eye on that side and from the medial half of the retina of the eye on the opposite side. Visual association areas integrate this information to develop a composite picture of the entire visual field.

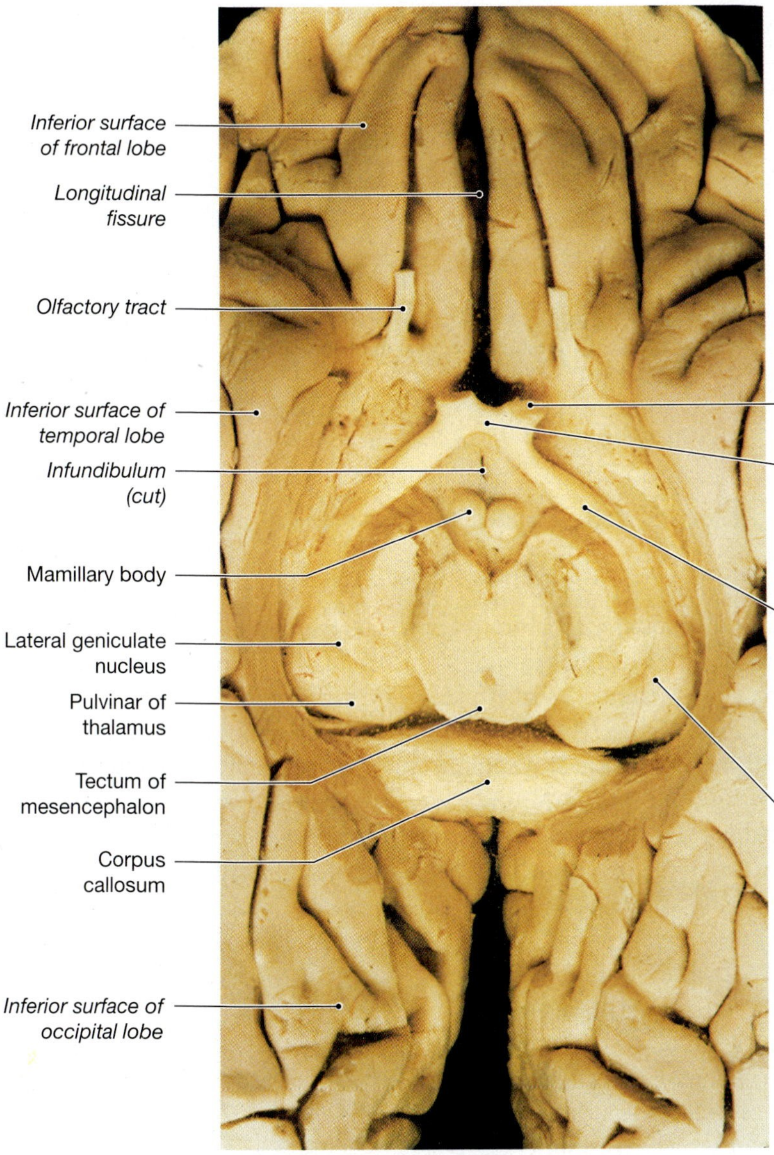

(a) Inferior view of the brain

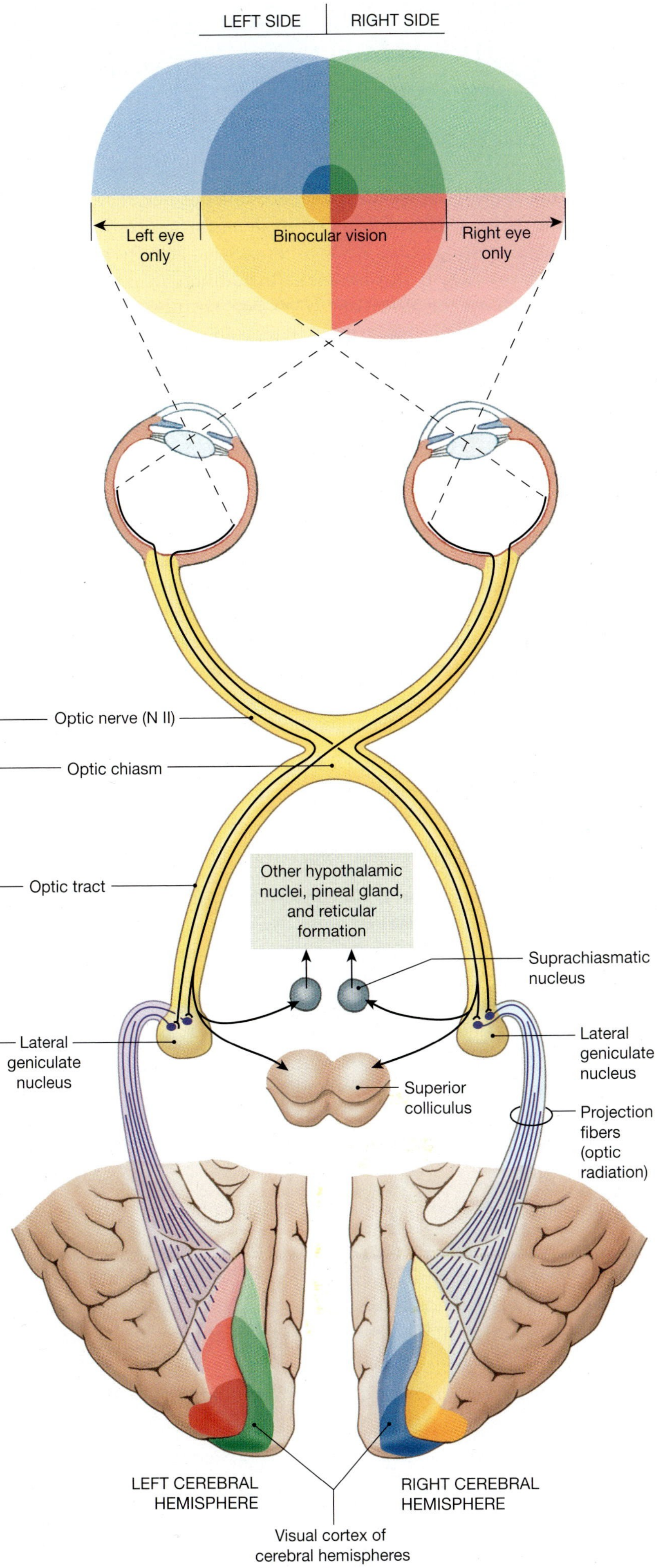

(b) Visual pathways

Clinical Case

NERVOUS SYSTEM

WHAT DID YOU SAY, DOC?

Juan Angleman, a 41-year-old machinist, visits the factory employees' health clinic to see the doctor with complaints of difficulty hearing in the right ear. This problem began about three months ago, and he thinks it is getting worse. His wife noticed that he turns his left ear toward her in order to hear her speak. In addition, Juan has noticed that he has to use the phone on his left side. He informs the doctor that he has also been a bit unsteady, but he attributes this to getting older. Juan states that he usually wears his protective earplugs when working.

Initial Examination

The physician examines him and finds that he cannot hear a high-pitched tuning fork with the right ear as well as he can with the left. He is referred to an audiologist.

The audiologist performs a formal assessment at a follow-up appointment the next day. The audiologist's examination confirms severe loss of high- and medium-pitched tones in both ears and moderate loss of low-pitched tones. As Juan has worked in a very noisy factory environment, he is presumed to have the common condition of noise-induced, high-frequency hearing loss. No formal patient history is conducted.

The audiologist recommends the following:

- Juan should immediately start utilizing a different form of protective ear covers that will block out a higher percentage of the factory machinery noise.
- Juan should also consider being fitted for hearing aids.

Juan returns to the doctor at his employer's health clinic two months later. In spite of wearing the new protective ear covers his hearing problems have worsened. In addition, he is also complaining of facial numbness and clumsiness of the right hand. He has also noticed frequent problems with his right leg when walking. The employee health doctor refers Juan to a neurologist.

Follow-up Examination

The neurologist reviews the results of the exams conducted by the factory doctor and the audiologist. She also conducts her own physical exam of Juan.

- Juan is found to have nystagmus, which is noticeably worse when he looks to the right.
- The neurologist asks Juan to do the following simple task:
  1. With one elbow flexed at 90 degrees and the hand supinated so that the palm is up and parallel to the ground, Juan places his other hand on the supinated palm.
  2. Juan is then asked to quickly pronate and supinate the second hand above his palm.

This task tests his ability to perform "rapid alternating movements."

- The neurologist then asks Juan to do another task:
  1. With most of his weight on one leg, Juan moves his other foot such that he taps it on the ground heel-toe as rapidly as possible.
  2. The neurologist has Juan repeat the motions using the other side of his body. The neurologist notes that Juan is extremely clumsy and unable to complete these tasks on one side.

The neurologist orders a CT scan. The results of the scan are negative for lesions. However, because a CT scan does not adequately visualize the posterior cranial fossa of the skull, an MRI is also ordered.

Points to Consider

As you examine the information presented above, review the material covered in Chapters 11 through 17 and determine what anatomical information will enable you to sort through the information given to you about Juan and his condition.

1. What structures are involved in the perception of sound?
2. Outline the cochlear pathway that is involved in the transmission of action potentials from the inner ear to the cerebral cortex.

Analysis and Interpretation

The information below answers the questions raised in the "Points to Consider" section. To review the material, refer to the pages referenced below.

1. The structures involved in the perception of sound include the structures of the external, middle, and internal ear (pp. 475–483).
2. The cochlear pathway is outlined on page 482.

Diagnosis

Juan is diagnosed with a tumor known as a vestibular schwannoma of cranial nerve VIII. This tumor is causing a lateral compression of the brain stem. Examples of such a lesion are found in **Figure 18.27a,b**.

Cranial nerve VIII (∞ pp. 416–417, 423) is a special sensory nerve dealing with balance and equilibrium (vestibular branch) and hearing (cochlear branch). A tumor such as this would disrupt the transmission of information to the brain from the auditory and vestibular portions of the inner ear. This disruption would result in a reduction in hearing ability as well as a disruption in equilibrium, both of which would account for many of Juan's symptoms.

A vestibular schwannoma is a benign (noncancerous) tumor caused by an increased cellular growth within the endoneurium of cranial nerve VIII. This type of tumor will result in disturbances in balance and hearing (often resulting in a ringing in the ear termed *tinnitus*) due to its effect on cranial nerve VIII. In addition, due to the location of the tumor in Juan's case, the

CLINICAL CASE TERMS

audiologist (aw-dē-OL-ojist): A specialist in the evaluation and rehabilitation of individuals whose communication disorders stem in whole or part from a hearing impairment.

nystagmus (nis-TAG-mus): An involuntary rhythmic movement of the eyeballs.

pin prick test: A test conducted whereby a pin is touched gently against the skin in various locations in order to determine a region's neurological sensitivity to various types of touch and pain.

Clinical Case *continued*

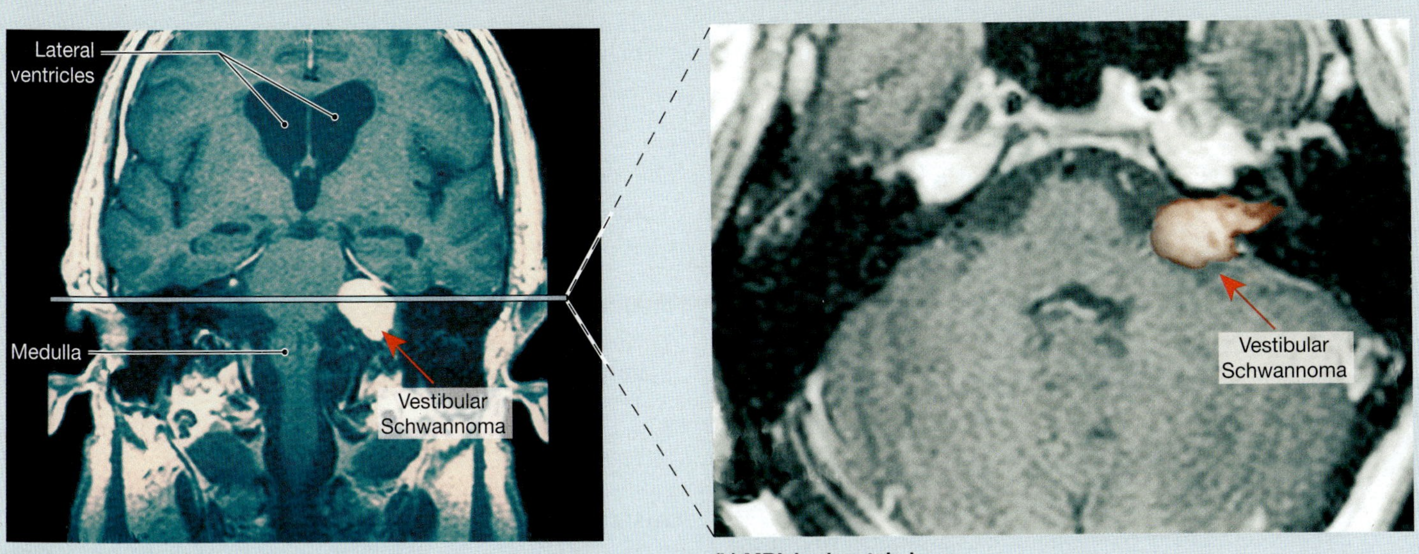

(a) MRI, frontal plane

(b) MRI, horizontal plane

Figure 18.27 Vestibular Schwannoma
(a) MRI in the horizontal plane demonstrating a vestibular schwannoma. **(b)** MRI in the frontal plane demonstrating a vestibular schwannoma.

vestibular schwannoma may cause pressure on the brain stem and cerebellum. As a result, the normal functioning of these two subdivisions of the brain would be disrupted. Although this tumor is benign, it is life threatening because the tumor often results in an increased intracranial pressure. This increased pressure within the cranium surrounding the brain results in disturbances in brain stem functioning, which can be fatal if not treated. ■

CLINICAL TERMS

audiogram: A graphical record of a subject's performance during a hearing test.

bone conduction test: A test for conductive deafness, usually involving placement of a vibrating tuning fork against the skull.

cataract: An abnormal lens that has lost its transparency.

cochlear implant: Insertion of electrodes into the cochlear nerve to provide external stimulation that provides some sensitivity to sounds in the absence of a functional organ of Corti.

conductive deafness: Deafness resulting from conditions in the middle ear that block the transfer of vibrations from the tympanic membrane to the oval window.

mastoiditis: Infection and inflammation of the mastoid air cells.

Ménière's disease: Acute vertigo caused by the rupture of the wall of the membranous labyrinth.

myringotomy: Drainage of the middle ear through a surgical opening in the tympanum.

nerve deafness: Deafness resulting from problems within the cochlea or along the auditory pathway.

nystagmus: Short, jerky eye movements that sometimes appear after damage to the brain stem or inner ear.

referred pain: Pain sensations from visceral organs, often perceived as originating in more superficial areas innervated by the same spinal nerves.

scotomas: Abnormal blind spots that are fixed in position.

vertigo: An inappropriate sense of motion.

STUDY OUTLINE

Introduction 471

1. The **general senses** are temperature, pain, touch, pressure, vibration, and proprioception; receptors for these sensations are distributed throughout the body. Receptors for the **special senses** (**olfaction**, **gustation**, **equilibrium**, **hearing**, and **vision**) are located in specialized areas, or **sense organs**. A **sensory receptor** is a specialized cell that when stimulated sends a **sensation** to the CNS.

Receptors 471

1. **Receptor specificity** allows each receptor to respond to particular stimuli. The simplest receptors are **free nerve endings**; the area monitored by a single receptor cell is the **receptive field**. *(see Figure 18.1)*

Interpretation of Sensory Information 471

2. **Tonic receptors** are always sending signals to the CNS; **phasic receptors** become active only when the conditions that they monitor change.

Central Processing and Adaptation 471

3. **Adaptation** (a reduction in sensitivity in the presence of a constant stimulus) may involve changes in receptor sensitivity (**peripheral**, or **sensory, adaptation**) or inhibition along the sensory pathways (**central adaptation**). **Fast-adapting receptors** are phasic; **slow-adapting receptors** are tonic.

Sensory Limitations 472

4. The information provided by our sensory receptors is incomplete because (1) we do not have receptors for every stimulus; (2) our receptors have limited ranges of sensitivity; and (3) a stimulus produces a neural event that must be interpreted by the CNS.

The General Senses 472

1. Receptors are classified as **exteroceptors** if they provide information about the external environment and **interoceptors** if they monitor conditions inside the body.

Nociceptors 472

2. **Nociceptors** respond to a variety of stimuli usually associated with tissue damage. There are two types of these painful sensations: **fast** (*prickling*) **pain** and **slow** (*burning and aching*) **pain**. *(see Figures 18.2/18.3a)*

Thermoreceptors 473

3. **Thermoreceptors** respond to changes in temperature. They conduct sensations along the same pathways that carry pain sensations.

Mechanoreceptors 473

4. **Mechanoreceptors** respond to physical distortion, contact, or pressure on their cell membranes: **tactile receptors** to touch, pressure, and vibration; **baroreceptors** to pressure changes in the walls of blood vessels and the digestive, reproductive, and urinary tracts; and **proprioceptors** (*muscle spindles*) to positions of joints and muscles. *(see Figures 18.3/18.4)*
5. **Fine touch** and **pressure receptors** provide detailed information about a source of stimulation; **crude touch** and **pressure receptors** are poorly localized. Important tactile receptors include **free nerve endings**, the **root hair plexus, tactile discs** (*Merkel's discs*), **tactile corpuscles** (*Meissner's corpuscles*), **Ruffini corpuscles**, and **lamellated corpuscles** (*pacinian corpuscles*). *(see Figure 18.3)*
6. **Baroreceptors** (stretch receptors) monitor changes in pressure; they respond immediately but adapt rapidly. Baroreceptors in the walls of major arteries and veins respond to changes in blood pressure. Receptors along the digestive tract help coordinate reflex activities of digestion. *(see Figure 18.4)*
7. **Proprioceptors** monitor the position of joints, tension in tendons and ligaments, and the state of muscular contraction.

Chemoreceptors 475

8. In general, **chemoreceptors** respond to water-soluble and lipid-soluble substances that are dissolved in the surrounding fluid. They monitor the chemical composition of body fluids. *(see Figure 18.5)*

Olfaction (Smell) 477

1. The **olfactory organs** contain the **olfactory epithelium** with **olfactory receptors** (neurons sensitive to chemicals dissolved in the overlying mucus), **supporting cells**, and **basal** (*stem*) **cells**. Their surfaces are coated with the secretions of the **olfactory glands**. *(see Figure 18.6)*

Olfactory Receptors 477

2. The olfactory receptors are modified neurons. *(see Figure 18.6b)*

Olfactory Pathways 477

3. The olfactory system has extensive limbic and hypothalamic connections that help explain the emotional and behavioral responses that can be produced by certain smells. *(see Figure 18.6b)*

Olfactory Discrimination 478

4. The olfactory system can make subtle distinctions between thousands of chemical stimuli; the CNS interprets the smell.
5. The olfactory receptor population shows considerable turnover and is the only known example of neuronal replacement in the adult human. The total number of receptors declines with age.

Gustation (Taste) 478

1. **Gustation**, or taste, provides information about the food and liquids that we consume.

Gustatory Receptors 478

2. **Gustatory receptors** are clustered in **taste buds**, each of which contains **gustatory cells**, which extend *taste hairs* through a narrow **taste pore**. *(see Figure 18.7b,c)*
3. Taste buds are associated with epithelial projections (**papillae**). *(see Figure 18.7a)*

Gustatory Pathways 479

4. The taste buds are monitored by cranial nerves VII, IX, and X. The afferent fibers synapse within the **nucleus solitarius** before proceeding to the thalamus and cerebral cortex. *(see Figure 18.8)*

Gustatory Discrimination 479

5. The **taste sensations** are sweet, salty, sour, bitter, umami, and water.
6. There are individual differences in the sensitivity to specific tastes. The number of taste buds and their sensitivity decline with age. *(see Figure 18.8)*

Equilibrium and Hearing 480

The External Ear 480

1. The **external ear** includes the **auricle**, which surrounds the entrance to the **external acoustic meatus** that ends at the **tympanic membrane (tympanum)**, or eardrum. *(see Figures 18.9/18.10)*

The Middle Ear 480

2. In the **middle ear**, the **tympanic cavity** encloses and protects the **auditory ossicles**, which connect the tympanic membrane with the receptor complex of the inner ear. The tympanic cavity communicates with the nasopharynx via the **auditory tube**. *(see Figures 18.9/18.10)*
3. The **tensor tympani** and **stapedius muscles** contract to reduce the amount of motion of the tympanum when very loud sounds arrive. *(see Figures 18.9/18.10b,d)*

The Inner Ear 482

4. The senses of equilibrium and hearing are provided by the receptors of the **inner ear** (housed within fluid-filled tubes and chambers known as the **membranous labyrinth**). Its chambers and canals contain **endolymph**. The **bony labyrinth** surrounds and protects the membranous labyrinth. The bony labyrinth can be subdivided into the **vestibule** and **semicircular canals** (providing the sense of equilibrium) and the **cochlea** (providing the sense of hearing). *(see Figures 18.9/18.11 to 18.17)*
5. The vestibule includes a pair of membranous sacs, the **utricle** and **saccule**, whose receptors provide sensations of gravity and linear acceleration. The cochlea contains the **cochlear duct**, an elongated portion of the membranous labyrinth. *(see Figure 18.12)*
6. The basic receptors of the inner ear are **hair cells** whose surfaces support stereocilia. Hair cells provide information about the direction and strength of varied mechanical stimuli.
7. The **anterior, posterior**, and **lateral semicircular ducts** are continuous with the utricle. Each contains an **ampulla** with sensory receptors. Here the cilia contact a gelatinous **cupula**. *(see Figures 18.13/18.14)*
8. The utricle and saccule are connected by a passageway continuous with the **endolymphatic duct**, which terminates in the **endolymphatic sac**. In

the saccule and utricle, hair cells cluster within **maculae**, where their cilia contact **otoliths** consisting of densely packed mineral crystals (**statoconia**) in a gelatinous matrix. When the head tilts, the mass of each otolith shifts, and the resulting distortion in the sensory hairs signals the CNS. *(see Figure 18.15)*

9. The vestibular receptors activate sensory neurons of the **vestibular ganglia**. The axons form the **vestibular branch** of the vestibulocochlear nerve (N VIII), synapsing within the **vestibular nuclei**. *(see Figure 18.16)*

Hearing 486

10. Sound waves travel toward the tympanum, which vibrates; the auditory ossicles conduct the vibrations to the base of the stapes at the oval window. Movement at the oval window applies pressure first to the perilymph of the **vestibular duct**. This pressure is passed on to the perilymph in the **tympanic duct**. *(see Figure 18.17)*
11. Pressure waves distort the **basilar membrane** and push the hair cells of the **organ of Corti (spiral organ)** against the **tectorial membrane**. *(see Figure 18.17* and *Table 18.2)*

Auditory Pathways 490

12. The sensory neurons for hearing are located in the **spiral ganglion** of the cochlea. Their afferent fibers form the **cochlear branch** of the vestibulocochlear nerve (N VIII), synapsing at the **cochlear nucleus**. *(see Figure 18.18)*

Vision 491

Accessory Structures of the Eye 491

1. The **accessory structures** of the eye include the **palpebrae** (eyelids), which are separated by the **palpebral fissure**. The **eyelashes** line the palpebral margins. **Tarsal glands**, which secrete a lipid-rich product, line the inner margins of the eyelids. Glands at the **lacrimal caruncle** produce other secretions. *(see Figure 18.19)*
2. The secretions of the **lacrimal gland** bathe the conjunctiva; these secretions are slightly alkaline and contain **lysozymes** (enzymes that attack bacteria). Tears collect in the *lacus lacrimalis*. The tears reach the inferior meatus of the nose after passing through the **lacrimal puncta**, the **lacrimal canaliculi**, the **lacrimal sac**, and the **nasolacrimal duct**. Collectively, these structures constitute the **lacrimal apparatus**. *(see Figures 18.19 to 18.21)*

The Eye 493

3. The eye has three layers: an outer *fibrous tunic*, a *vascular tunic*, and an inner *neural tunic*.
4. The **fibrous tunic** includes most of the ocular surface, which is covered by the **sclera** (a dense, fibrous connective tissue of the fibrous tunic); the **corneal limbus** is the border between the sclera and the cornea. *(see Figure 18.21)*
5. An epithelium called the **conjunctiva** covers most of the exposed surface of the eye; the **bulbar**, or **ocular**, **conjunctiva** covers the anterior surface of the eye, and the **palpebral conjunctiva** lines the inner surface of the eyelids. The **cornea** is transparent. *(see Figure 18.21)*
6. The **vascular tunic** includes the **iris**, the **ciliary body**, and the **choroid**. The iris forms the boundary between the anterior and posterior chambers. The ciliary body contains the **ciliary muscle** and the **ciliary processes**, which attach to the **suspensory ligaments** (*zonular fibers*) of the lens. *(see Figures 18.21/18.23)*
7. The **neural tunic (retina)** consists of an outer **pigmented layer** and an inner **neural retina**; the latter contains visual receptors and associated neurons. *(see Figures 18.21 to 18.23)*
8. There are two types of **photoreceptors** (visual receptors of the retina). **Rods** provide black-and-white vision in dim light; **cones** provide color vision in bright light. Cones are concentrated in the **macula lutea**; the **fovea** (*fovea centralis*) is the area of sharpest vision. *(see Figures 18.21/18.23)*
9. The direct line to the CNS proceeds from the photoreceptors to **bipolar cells**, then to **ganglion cells**, and to the brain via the optic nerve. **Horizontal cells** and **amacrine cells** modify the signals passed between other retinal components. *(see Figure 18.23a)*
10. The **aqueous humor** continuously circulates within the eye and reenters the circulation after diffusing through the walls of the anterior chamber and into the **canal of Schlemm** (*scleral venous sinus*). *(see Figure 18.24)*
11. The **lens**, held in place by the suspensory ligaments, lies posterior to the cornea and forms the anterior boundary of the vitreous chamber. This chamber contains the **vitreous body**, a gelatinous mass that helps stabilize the shape of the eye and support the retina. *(see Figures 18.21/18.24)*
12. The lens focuses a visual image on the retinal receptors.

Visual Pathways 499

13. Each photoreceptor monitors a specific receptive field. The axons of ganglion cells converge on the **optic disc** and proceed along the optic tract to the optic chiasm. *(see Figures 18.21b,e/18.23/18.25/18.26)*
14. From the optic chiasm, after a partial decussation, visual information is relayed to the lateral geniculate nuclei. From there the information is sent to the visual cortex of the occipital lobes. *(see Figure 18.26)*
15. Visual inputs to the **suprachiasmatic nucleus** and the pineal gland affect the function of other brain stem nuclei. These nuclei establish a visceral **circadian rhythm** that is tied to the day-night cycle and affects other metabolic processes. *(see Figure 18.26b)*

CHAPTER REVIEW

For answers to the Concept Check and Chapter Review questions, go to the blue "Answers" tab at the back of the book.

Level 1 Reviewing Facts and Terms

Match each numbered item with the most closely related lettered item. Use letters for answers in the spaces provided.

Column A	Column B
___ 1. monitored area	a. lost transparency
___ 2. physical distortion	b. receptive field
___ 3. olfactory	c. similar to CSF
___ 4. gustatory	d. mechanoreceptors
___ 5. ceruminous glands	e. Bowman's glands
___ 6. perilymph	f. cochlear duct
___ 7. ampulla	g. anterior cavity
___ 8. organ of Corti	h. taste buds
___ 9. aqueous humor	i. semicircular duct
___10. cataract	j. external acoustic meatus

11. The anterior, transparent part of the fibrous tunic is known as the
    (a) cornea (b) sclera
    (c) iris (d) fovea

12. A receptor that is especially common in the superficial layers of the skin, and which responds to pain, is a
    (a) proprioceptor (b) baroreceptor
    (c) nociceptor (d) mechanoreceptor

13. Fine touch and pressure receptors provide detailed information about
    (a) the source of the stimulus (b) the shape of the stimulus
    (c) the texture of the stimulus (d) all of the above are correct

14. Receptors in the saccule and utricle provide sensations of
    (a) balance and equilibrium (b) hearing
    (c) vibration (d) gravity and linear acceleration

15. Deep to the subcutaneous layer, the eyelids are supported by broad sheets of connective tissues, collectively termed the
    (a) palpebrae (b) tarsal plate
    (c) chalazion (d) medial canthus

16. The neural tunic
    (a) consists of three distinct layers
    (b) contains the photoreceptors
    (c) forms the iris
    (d) all of the above are correct

17. The semicircular canals include which of the following?
    (a) dorsal and ventral
    (b) lateral, middle, and medial
    (c) anterior, posterior, and lateral
    (d) spiral, upright, and reverse

18. Mechanoreceptors that detect pressure changes in the walls of blood vessels as well as in portions of the digestive, reproductive, and urinary tracts are
    (a) tactile receptors (b) baroreceptors
    (c) proprioceptors (d) free nerve receptors

19. Pupillary muscle groups are controlled by the ANS. Parasympathetic activation causes pupillary ________, and sympathetic activation causes ________.
    (a) dilation; constriction
    (b) dilation; dilation
    (c) constriction; dilation
    (d) constriction; constriction

20. Auditory information about the region and intensity of stimulation is relayed to the CNS over the cochlear branch of cranial nerve
    (a) N IV (b) N VI
    (c) N VIII (d) N X

Level 2 Reviewing Concepts

1. Why is a more severe burn less painful initially than is a less serious burn of the skin?
    (a) the skin's nociceptors are burned away and cannot transmit pain sensations to the CNS
    (b) a severe burn overwhelms the nociceptors, and they adapt rapidly so no more pain is felt
    (c) a mild skin burn registers pain from pain receptors and many other types simultaneously
    (d) a severe burn is out of the range of sensitivity of most pain receptors

2. How do the tensor tympani and stapedius muscles affect the functions of the ear?
    (a) they do not affect hearing, but play an important role in equilibrium
    (b) they increase the cochlea's sensitivity to vibration produced by incoming sound waves
    (c) they regulate the opening and closing of the pharyngotympanic tube
    (d) they dampen excessively loud sounds that could harm sensitive auditory hair cells

3. A person salivates when anticipating eating a tasty confection. Would this physical response enhance taste or olfaction? If so, why?
    (a) no, it would not enhance either taste or olfaction
    (b) salivation permits foods to slide through the oral cavity more easily; it has no effect on taste or smell
    (c) additional moisture would enhance the ability of molecules to be dissolved to enter the taste pores more readily and thus enhance taste; similar changes would enhance olfaction
    (d) only the sense of taste would be enhanced

4. What is receptor specificity? What causes it?

5. What could stimulate the release of an increased quantity of neurotransmitter by a hair cell into the synapse with a sensory neuron?

6. What are the functions of hair cells in the inner ear?

7. What is the functional role of sensory adaptation?

8. What type of information about a stimulus does sensory coding provide?

9. What would be the consequence of damage to the lamellated corpuscles of the arm?

10. What is the structural relationship between the bony labyrinth and the membranous labyrinth?

Level 3 Critical Thinking

1. Beth has surgery to remove some polyps (growths) from her sinuses. After she heals from the surgery, she notices that her sense of smell is not as keen as it was before the surgery. Can you suggest a reason for this?

2. Jared is 10 months old, and his pediatrician diagnoses him with otitis media. What does the physician tell his mother?

3. What happens to reduce the effectiveness of your sense of taste when you have a cold?

19

The Endocrine System

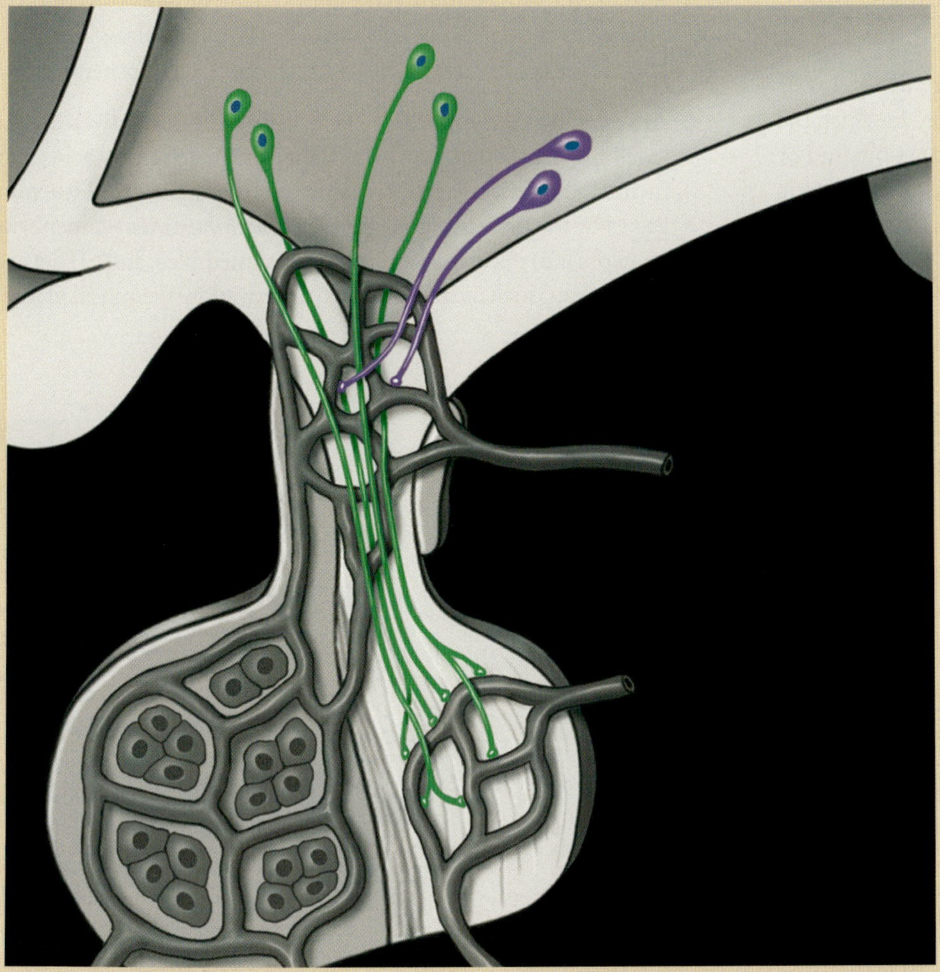

CHAPTER OBJECTIVES

1. Compare the basic organization and functions of the endocrine system and the nervous system.
2. Define a hormone, describe the major chemical classes of hormones, and explain how hormones control their target cells.
3. Describe the structural and functional relationships between the hypothalamus and the neurohypophysis.
4. Describe the structure of the neurohypophysis of the pituitary gland and the functions of the hormones it releases.
5. Describe the hypothalamic control of the adenohypophysis.
6. Discuss the structure of the adenohypophysis and the functions of its hormones.
7. Describe the manufacture, storage, and secretion of thyroid hormones.
8. Describe the structure of the parathyroid gland and the function of parathyroid hormones.
9. Describe the location and structure of the thymus and the functions of the hormones it produces.
10. Describe the structure of the suprarenal cortex and medulla and discuss the hormones produced in each region.
11. List and identify the function of the hormones produced by the kidneys, the heart, and the pancreas and other endocrine tissues of the digestive system.
12. List the hormones produced by the male and female gonads and discuss their functions.
13. Discuss the location and structure of the pineal gland, and describe the functions of pineal hormones.
14. Briefly describe the effects of aging on the endocrine system.
15. Discuss the results of abnormal hormone production.

Homeostatic regulation involves coordinating the activities of organs and systems throughout the body. At any given moment, the cells of both the nervous and endocrine systems are working together to monitor and adjust the body's physiological activities. The activities of these two systems are coordinated closely, and their effects are typically complementary. In general, the nervous system produces short-term (usually a few seconds) but very specific responses to environmental stimuli. In contrast, endocrine gland cells release chemicals into the bloodstream for distribution throughout the body. p. 59 These chemicals, called **hormones** (meaning "to excite"), alter the metabolic activities of many different tissues and organs simultaneously. The hormonal effects may not be apparent immediately, but when they appear, they often persist for days. This response pattern makes the endocrine system particularly effective in regulating ongoing processes such as growth and development.

At first glance, the nervous and endocrine systems are easily distinguished. Yet when they are viewed in detail, there are instances in which the two systems are difficult to separate either anatomically or functionally. For example, the suprarenal (suprarenal) medulla is a modified sympathetic ganglion whose neurons secrete epinephrine and norepinephrine into the blood. p. 458 The suprarenal medulla is thus an endocrine structure that is functionally and developmentally part of the nervous system, whereas the hypothalamus, which is anatomically part of the brain, secretes a variety of hormones. Although this chapter describes the components and functions of the endocrine system, the discussion will of necessity consider its interactions with the nervous system.

An Overview of the Endocrine System [Figure 19.1]

The **endocrine system** includes all of the endocrine cells and tissues of the body (Figure 19.1).

Endocrine cells are glandular secretory cells that release hormones directly into the interstitial fluids, lymphoid system, or blood. In contrast, secretions from exocrine glands are released onto an epithelial surface. p. 59

Hormones are organized into four groups based on chemical structure:

- **Amino acid derivatives:** The **amino acid derivatives** are relatively small molecules that are structurally similar to amino acids. Examples include (1) derivatives of tyrosine, such as the **thyroid hormones** released by the thyroid gland and the **catecholamines** (epinephrine, norepinephrine) released by the suprarenal medullae, and (2) derivatives of tryptophan, such as **melatonin** synthesized by the pineal gland.

KEY TO PITUITARY HORMONES

ACTH	Adrenocorticotropic hormone
TSH	Thyroid-stimulating hormone
GH	Growth hormone
PRL	Prolactin
FSH	Follicle-stimulating hormone
LH	Luteinizing hormone
MSH	Melanocyte-stimulating hormone
ADH	Antidiuretic hormone

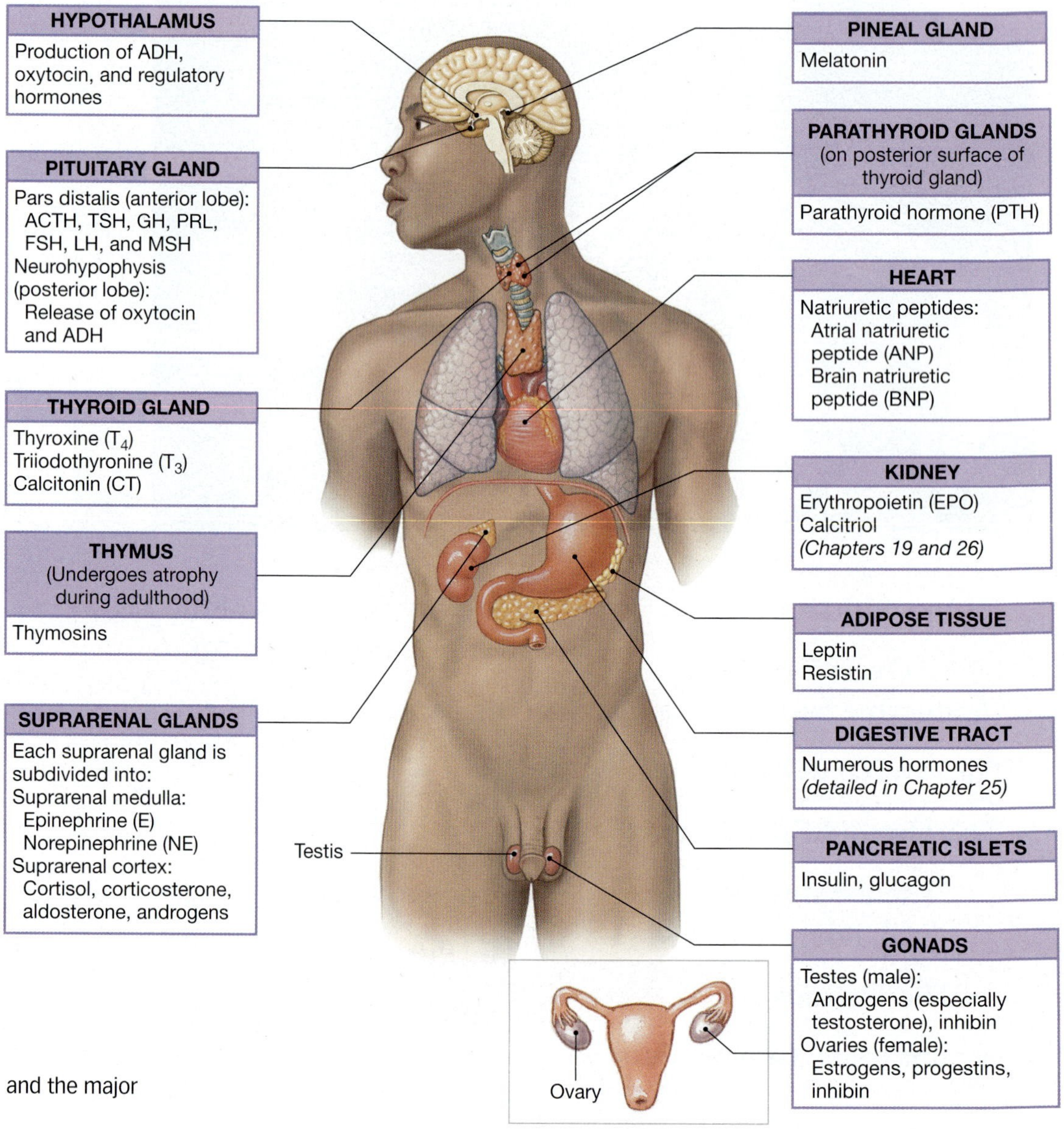

Figure 19.1 The Endocrine System
Location of endocrine glands and endocrine cells, and the major hormones produced by each gland.

- **Peptide hormones: Peptide hormones** are chains of amino acids. This is the largest group of hormones; all pituitary gland hormones are peptide hormones.
- **Steroid hormones: Steroid hormones**, derived from cholesterol, are released by the reproductive organs and the suprarenal glands.
- **Eicosanoids: Eicosanoids** are small molecules with a five-carbon ring at one end and are released by most body cells. These compounds coordinate cellular activities and affect enzymatic processes (such as blood clotting) that occur in extracellular fluids.

Enzymes control all cellular activities and metabolic reactions. Hormones influence cellular operations by changing the *types*, *activities*, or *quantities* of key cytoplasmic enzymes. In this way, a hormone can regulate the metabolic operations of its **target cells**—peripheral cells that respond to its presence.

Endocrine activity is controlled by **endocrine reflexes** that are triggered by (1) *humoral stimuli* (changes in the composition of the extracellular fluid), (2) *hormonal stimuli* (arrival or removal of a specific hormone), or (3) *neural stimuli* (the arrival of neurotransmitters at neuroglandular junctions). In most cases, endocrine reflexes are regulated by some form of negative feedback. In direct negative feedback control, (1) the endocrine cell responds to a disturbance in homeostasis (such as a change in the concentration of a substance in the extracellular fluid) by releasing its hormone into the circulatory system, (2) the released hormone stimulates a target cell, and (3) the target cell response restores homeostasis and eliminates the source of stimulation of the endocrine cell. One example noted in Chapter 5 was the control of calcium levels by parathyroid hormone. p. 124 When circulating calcium levels decline, parathyroid hormone is released and the responses of target cells (osteoclasts) elevate blood calcium levels. As calcium levels climb, the level of parathyroid stimulation declines and so does its rate of hormone secretion.

More complex endocrine reflexes involve one or more intermediary steps and often two or more hormones. These complicated chains of events may be controlled by complex negative feedback loops or, rarely, through positive feedback. Complex negative feedback loops are the most common regulatory mechanisms. In these cases the secretion of one hormone, such as the thyroid-stimulating hormone from the adenohypophysis (anterior lobe), triggers the secretion of a second hormone, such as the thyroid hormones produced by the thyroid gland. The second hormone may have multiple effects, one of which always includes the suppression of the release of the first hormone.

Hormone regulation through positive feedback is restricted to processes that must be rushed to completion. In these instances, the secretion of a hormone produces an effect that further stimulates hormone release. For example, the release of oxytocin during labor and delivery causes smooth muscle contractions in the uterus, and the uterine contractions further stimulate oxytocin release.

The Hypothalamus and Endocrine Regulation [Figure 19.2]

Coordinating centers in the hypothalamus regulate the activities of the nervous and endocrine systems by three different mechanisms (Figure 19.2):

1. The hypothalamus secretes **regulatory hormones**, or *regulatory factors*, that control the activities of endocrine cells in the adenohypophysis (anterior lobe) of the pituitary gland. There are two classes of regulatory hormones. (1) **Releasing hormones (RH)** stimulate production of one or more hormones at the adenohypophysis, whereas (2) **inhibiting hormones (IH)** prevent the synthesis and secretion of specific pituitary hormones.
2. The hypothalamus acts as an endocrine organ, releasing the hormones *ADH* and *oxytocin* into the circulation at the neurohypophysis (posterior lobe).
3. The hypothalamus contains autonomic centers that exert direct neural control over the endocrine cells of the suprarenal medullae. p. 406 When the sympathetic division is activated, the suprarenal medullae release hormones into the bloodstream.

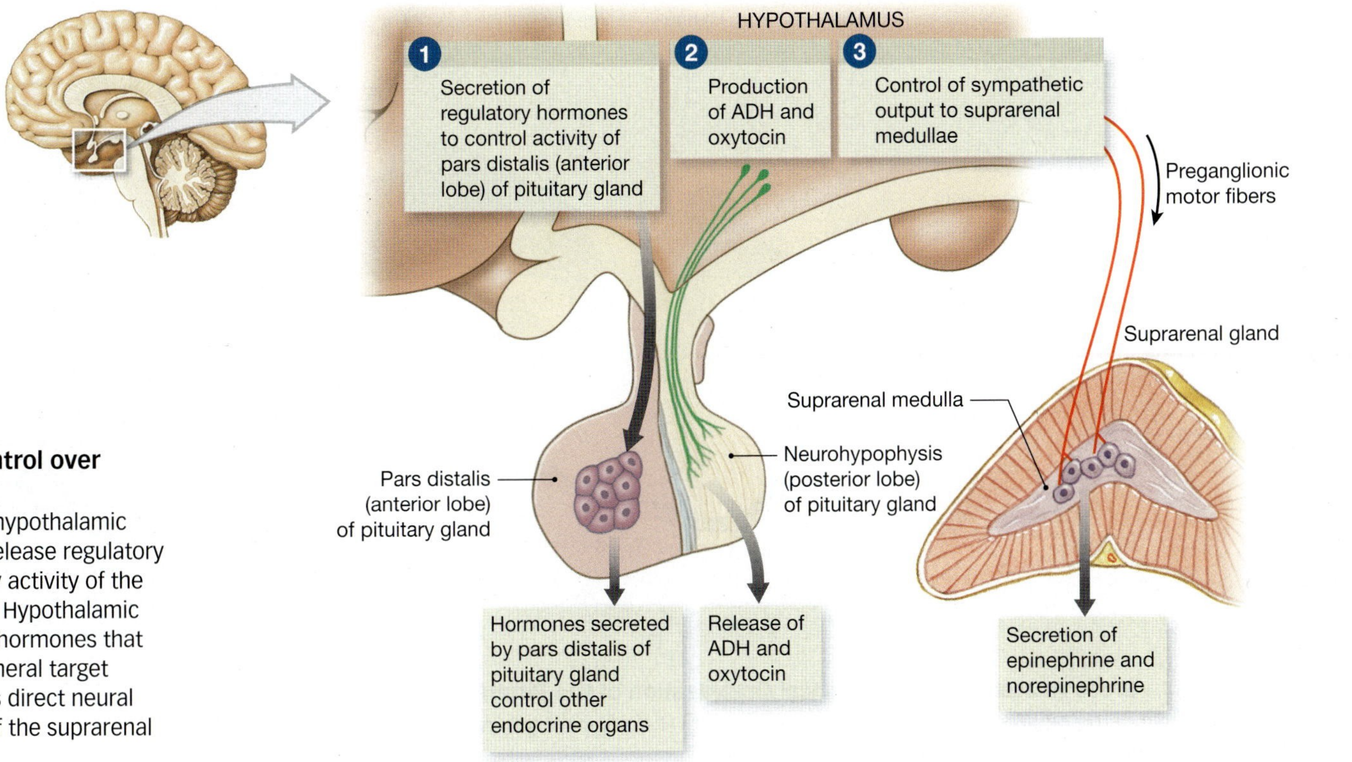

Figure 19.2 Hypothalamic Control over Endocrine Organs
A comparison of the three types of hypothalamic control. **(1)** Hypothalamic neurons release regulatory hormones that control the secretory activity of the adenohypophysis (anterior lobe). **(2)** Hypothalamic neurons secrete ADH and oxytocin, hormones that produce specific responses in peripheral target organs. **(3)** The hypothalamus exerts direct neural control over the secretory activity of the suprarenal (renal) medullae.

The Pituitary Gland [Figures 19.3/19.4 and Table 19.1]

The **pituitary gland**, or **hypophysis** (hī-POF-i-sis), weighs one-fifth of an ounce (~ 6 g) and is the most compact chemical factory in the body. This small, oval gland, about the size and weight of a small grape, lies inferior to the hypothalamus within the *sella turcica*, a depression in the sphenoid. pp. 146–147 The **infundibulum** (in-fun-DIB-ū-lum) extends from the hypothalamus inferiorly to the posterior and superior surfaces of the pituitary gland (Figure 19.3a). The *diaphragma sellae* encircles the stalk of the infundibulum and holds the pituitary gland in position within the sella turcica. p. 392

The pituitary gland has two lobes based on anatomical and developmental grounds: the *adenohypophysis*, or *anterior lobe*, and the *neurohypophysis*, or *posterior lobe*. (Figure 19.3). Nine important peptide hormones are released by the pituitary gland, two by the *neural lobe* of the neurohypophysis and seven by the *pars distalis* and *pars intermedia* of the adenohypophysis. Table 19.1 summarizes information about the pituitary gland hormones and their targets; representative target organs are diagrammed in Figure 19.4.

The Neurohypophysis [Figures 19.3 to 19.5/Table 19.1]

The **neurohypophysis** (noor-ō-hī-POF-i-sis) (Figure 19.3) is also called the **posterior lobe** of the pituitary gland. It contains the axons and axon terminals of roughly 50,000 hypothalamic neurons whose cell bodies are in either the **supraoptic** or **paraventricular nuclei** (Figure 19.5 and Table 19.1). The axons extend from these nuclei through the infundibulum and end in synaptic terminals in the *neural lobe* or *pars nervosa* ("nervous part") of the neurohypophysis. The hypothalamic neurons manufacture ADH (supraoptic nuclei) and oxytocin (paraventricular nuclei). ADH and oxytocin are called *neurosecretions* because they are produced and released by neurons. Once released, these hormones enter local capillaries supplied by the **inferior hypophyseal artery** (Figure 19.5). From there they will be transported into the general circulation.

Hormones released by the posterior lobe (Figure 19.4) include the following:

1. *ADH:* **Antidiuretic hormone**, or *vasopressin*, is released in response to a variety of stimuli, most notably to a rise in the concentration of electrolytes in the blood or a fall in blood volume or pressure. The primary function of ADH is to decrease the amount of water lost at the kidneys. ADH also causes the constriction of peripheral blood vessels, which helps to elevate blood pressure.
2. *Oxytocin:* The functions of **oxytocin** (ok-sē-TŌ-sin; *oxy-*, quick + *tokos*, childbirth) are best known in women, where it stimulates the contractions of smooth muscle cells in the uterus and contractile (myoepithelial) cells surrounding the secretory cells of the mammary glands. The stimulation of uterine muscles by oxytocin in the last stage of pregnancy is required for normal labor and childbirth. After birth, the sucking of an infant at the breast stimulates the release of oxytocin into the blood. Oxytocin then stimulates contraction of the myoepithelial cells in the mammary glands, causing the discharge of milk from the nipple. In the human male, oxytocin causes smooth muscle contractions in the prostate gland.

The Adenohypophysis [Figure 19.3 and Table 19.1]

The **adenohypophysis** (ad-e-nō-hī-POF-i-sis) (also called the **anterior lobe** of the pituitary gland) contains five different cell types (Table 19.1). The adenohypophysis can be subdivided into three regions: (1) a large **pars distalis** (dis-TA-lis; "distal part"), which represents the major portion of the pituitary gland; (2) a slender **pars intermedia** (in-ter-MĒ-dē-a; "intermediate

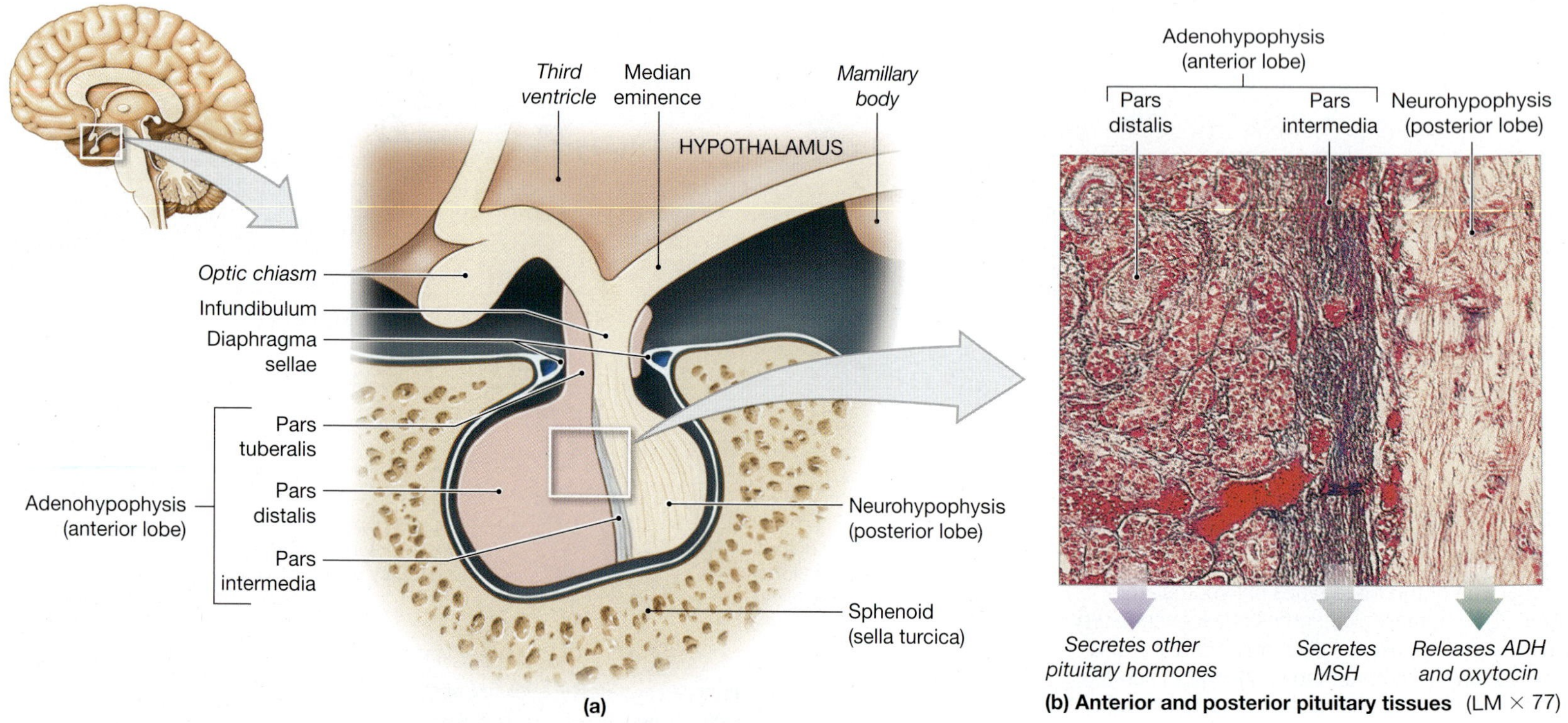

Figure 19.3 Gross Anatomy and Histological Organization of the Pituitary Gland and Its Subdivisions
(a) Relationship of the pituitary gland to the hypothalamus. **(b)** Histological organization of pituitary gland showing adenohypophysis and neurohypophysis.

TABLE 19.1 The Pituitary Hormones

Region/Area	Hormone	Targets	Hormonal Effects
ADENOHYPOPHYSIS (ANTERIOR LOBE)			
Pars distalis	Thyroid-stimulating hormone (TSH)	Thyroid gland	Secretion of thyroid hormones
	Adrenocorticotropic hormone (ACTH)	Suprarenal cortex (zona fasciculata)	Glucocorticoid secretion
	Gonadotropins:		
	Follicle-stimulating hormone (FSH)	Follicle cells of ovaries in female	Estrogen secretion, follicle development
		Nurse cells of testes in male	Stimulation of sperm maturation
	Luteinizing hormone (LH)	Follicle cells of ovaries in female	Ovulation, formation of corpus luteum, progesterone secretion
		Interstitial cells of testes in male	Testosterone secretion
	Prolactin (PRL)	Mammary glands in female	Production of milk
	Growth hormone (GH)	All cells	Growth, protein synthesis, lipid mobilization and catabolism
Pars intermedia (not active in normal adults)	Melanocyte-stimulating hormone (MSH)	Melanocytes	Increased melanin synthesis in epidermis
NEUROHYPOPHYSIS (POSTERIOR LOBE)			
Neural Lobe (Pars nervosa)	Antidiuretic hormone (ADH or vasopressin)	Kidneys	Reabsorption of water; elevation of blood volume and pressure
	Oxytocin (OT)	Uterus, mammary glands (females)	Labor contractions, milk ejection
		Ductus deferens and prostate gland (males)	Contractions of ductus deferens and prostate gland; ejection of secretions

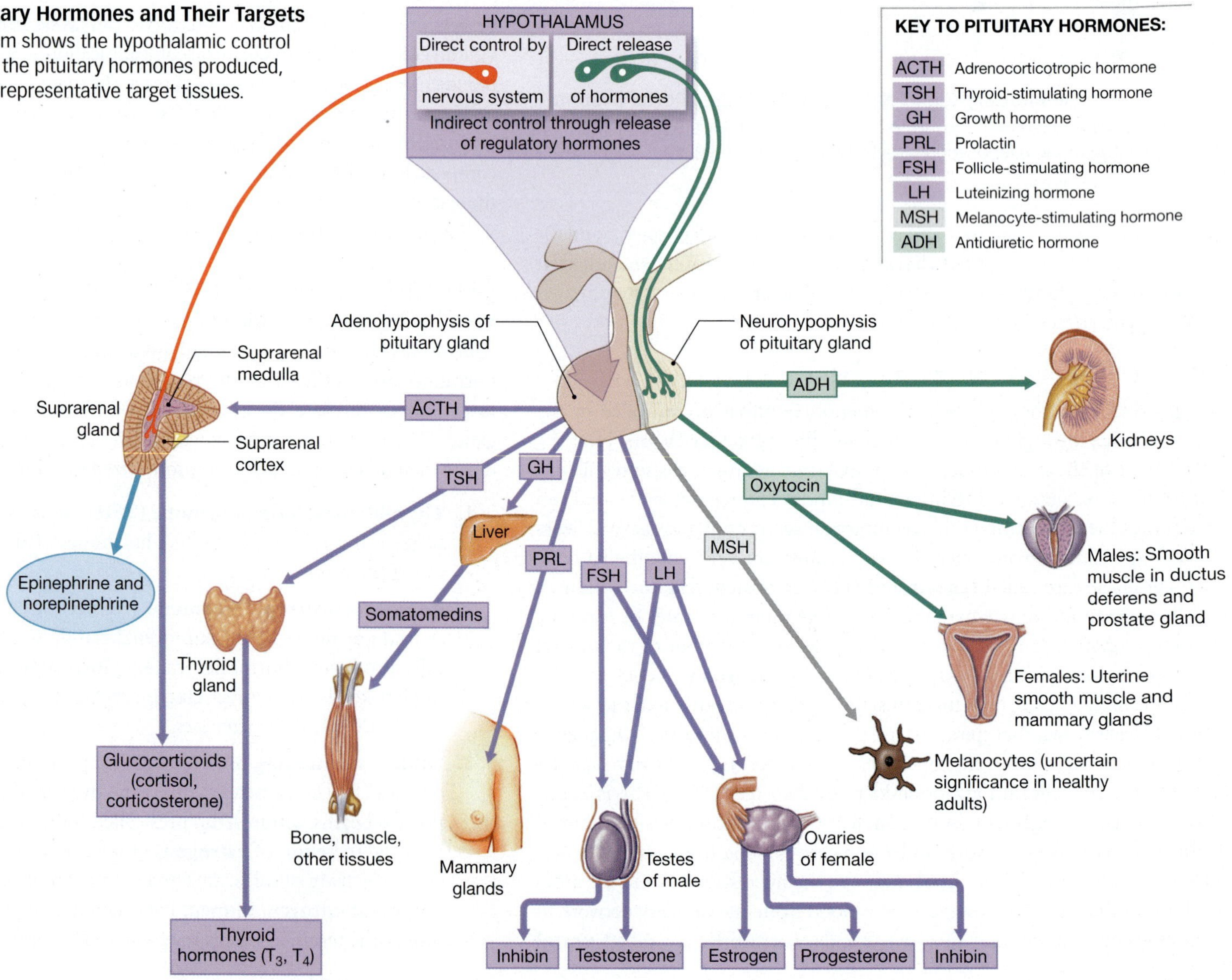

Figure 19.4 Pituitary Hormones and Their Targets This schematic diagram shows the hypothalamic control of the pituitary gland, the pituitary hormones produced, and the responses of representative target tissues.

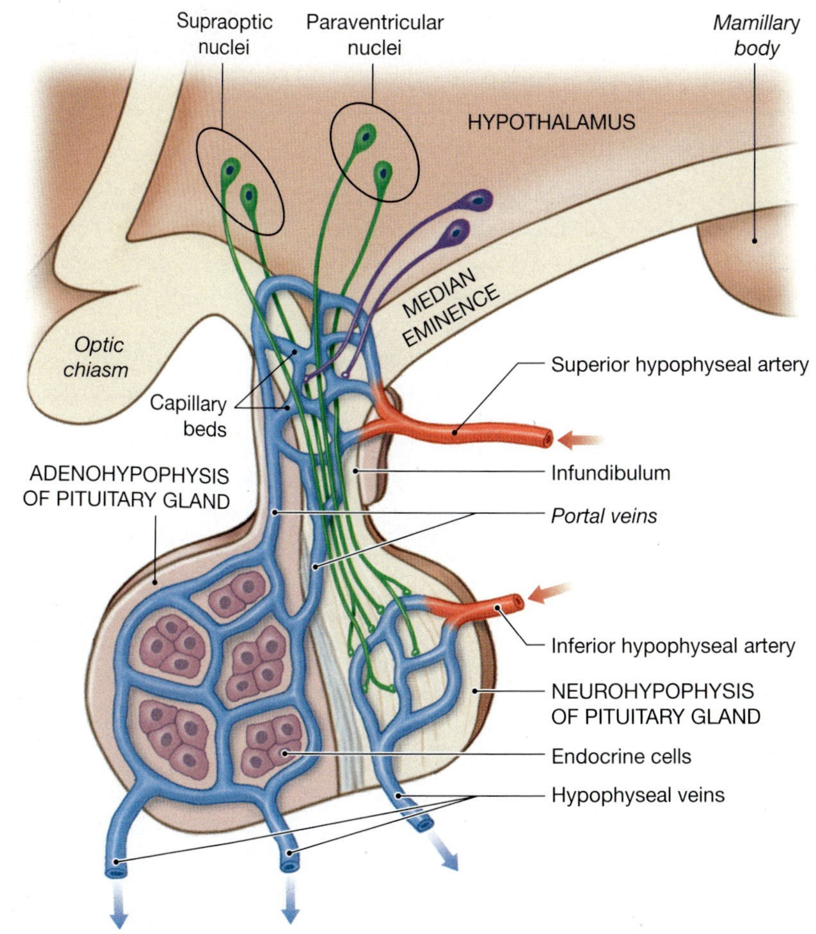

Figure 19.5 The Pituitary Gland and the Hypophyseal Portal System This circulatory arrangement forms the hypophyseal portal system, which permits control of the adenohypophysis by hypothalamic regulatory hormones.

part"), which forms a narrow band adjacent to the neurohypophysis; and (3) an extension called the **pars tuberalis**, which wraps around the adjacent portion of the infundibulum (Figure 19.3). The entire adenohypophysis is richly vascularized with an extensive capillary network.

The Hypophyseal Portal System [Figure 19.5]

The production of hormones in the adenohypophysis is controlled by the hypothalamus through the secretion of specific regulatory factors. Near the attachment of the infundibulum, hypothalamic neurons release regulatory factors into the surrounding interstitial fluids. The regulatory factors can easily enter the circulation in this region because the capillaries have a "Swiss cheese" appearance, with open spaces between adjacent endothelial cells. Such capillaries are called **fenestrated** (FEN-es-trā-ted; *fenestra*, window), and they are found only where relatively large molecules enter or leave the circulatory system. This *primary capillary plexus* in the floor of the tuberal area receives blood from the **superior hypophyseal artery** (Figure 19.5).

Before leaving the hypothalamus, the capillary network unites to form a series of larger vessels that spiral around the infundibulum to reach the adenohypophysis. Once within this lobe, these vessels form a *secondary capillary plexus*, which branches among the endocrine cells (Figure 19.5). This is an unusual vascular arrangement, in that an artery typically conducts blood from the heart to a capillary network, and a vein carries blood from a capillary network back to the heart. The vessels between the hypothalamus and the anterior lobe of the pituitary, however, carry blood from one capillary network to another. Blood vessels that link two capillary networks are called **portal vessels**, and the entire complex is termed a **portal system**. Portal systems provide an efficient means of chemical communication by ensuring that all of the blood entering the portal vessels will reach the intended target cells before returning to the general circulation. The communication is strictly one-way, however, because any chemicals released by the cells "downstream" must do a complete tour of the cardiovascular system before reaching the capillaries at the start of the portal system. Portal vessels are named after their destinations, so this particular network of vessels is the **hypophyseal portal system**.

Clinical Note

Diabetes Insipidus There are several different forms of diabetes, all characterized by excessive urine production (polyuria). Although diabetes can be caused by physical damage to the kidneys, most forms are the result of endocrine abnormalities. The two most important forms are *diabetes insipidus*, considered here, and *diabetes mellitus*, considered later.

Diabetes insipidus develops when the neurohypophysis, or posterior lobe of the pituitary gland, no longer releases adequate amounts of antidiuretic hormone (ADH). Water conservation at the kidneys is impaired, and excessive amounts of water are lost in the urine. As a result, an individual with diabetes insipidus is constantly thirsty, but the fluids consumed are not retained by the body. Mild cases may not require treatment, as long as fluid and electrolyte intake keep pace with urinary losses. In severe diabetes insipidus the fluid losses can reach 10 liters per day, and a fatal dehydration will occur unless treatment is provided. Administering a synthetic form of ADH, desmopressin acetate (DDAVP), in a nasal spray concentrates the urine and reduces urine volume. The drug enters the bloodstream after diffusing through the nasal epithelium. It is also an effective treatment for bedwetting if used at bedtime.

Hormones of the Adenohypophysis [Figure 19.4 and Table 19.1]

We will restrict our discussion to the seven hormones whose functions and control mechanisms are reasonably well understood. All but one of these hormones are produced by the pars distalis of the adenohypophysis, and five of them regulate the production of hormones by other endocrine glands. These hormones are termed *tropic* (*tropos*, turning). Their names indicate their activities; details are summarized in Table 19.1 and Figure 19.4.

1. **Thyroid-stimulating hormone (TSH)** targets the thyroid gland and triggers the release of thyroid hormones. TSH is secreted by cells called *thyrotropes.*
2. **Adrenocorticotropic hormone (ACTH)** stimulates the release of steroid hormones by the suprarenal gland. ACTH specifically targets cells producing hormones called **glucocorticoids (GC)** (gloo-kō-KOR-ti-koyds) that affect glucose metabolism. The cells that secrete ACTH are called *corticotropes.*
3. **Follicle-stimulating hormone (FSH)** promotes the development of oocytes (female gametes) within the ovaries of mature women. The process begins within structures called follicles, and FSH also stimulates the secretion of **estrogens** (ES-trō-jens) by follicle cells. Estrogens, which are steroids, are female sex hormones; *estradiol* is the most important estrogen. In men, FSH secretion supports sperm production in the testes. The cells that secrete FSH are called *gonadotropes.*

4. **Luteinizing** (LOO-tē-in-ī-zing) **hormone (LH)** induces ovulation in women and promotes the ovarian secretion of **progestins** (prō-JES-tinz), steroid hormones that prepare the body for possible pregnancy. *Progesterone* is the most important progestin. In men, LH stimulates the production of male sex hormones called **androgens** (AN-drō-jenz; *andros*, man) by the interstitial cells of the testes. *Testosterone* is the most important androgen. Because they regulate the activities of the male and female sex organs (gonads), FSH and LH are called **gonadotropins** (gō-nad-ō-TRŌ-pinz; *tropos*, turning). These hormones are produced by cells called *gonadotropes.*
5. **Prolactin** (prō-LAK-tin; *pro-*, before + *lac*, milk) **(PRL)** stimulates the development of the mammary glands and the production of milk. PRL exerts the dominant effect on the glandular cells, but the mammary glands are regulated by the interaction of a number of other hormones, including estrogen, progesterone, growth hormone, glucocorticoids, and hormones produced by the placenta. The functions of prolactin in males are poorly understood. PRL is secreted by cells called *lactotropes.*
6. **Growth hormone (GH)**, also called *human growth hormone (HGH)* or *somatotropin* (*soma*, body), stimulates cell growth and replication by accelerating the rate of protein synthesis. GH is secreted by cells called *somatotropes.* Although virtually every tissue responds to some degree, growth hormone has a particularly strong effect on skeletal and muscular development. Liver cells respond to GH by synthesizing and releasing somatomedins, which are peptide hormones. Somatomedins stimulate protein synthesis and cell growth in skeletal muscle fibers, cartilage cells, and other target cells. Children unable to produce adequate concentrations of growth hormone have *pituitary growth failure*, sometimes called *pituitary dwarfism.* The steady growth and maturation that normally precede and accompany puberty do not occur in these individuals.
7. **Melanocyte-stimulating hormone (MSH)** is the only hormone released by the pars intermedia. As the name indicates, MSH stimulates the melanocytes of the skin, increasing their rates of melanin production and distribution. MSH is secreted by *corticotropes* (also termed *ACTH cells*) only during fetal development, in young children, in pregnant women, and in some disease states.

CONCEPT CHECK

1. Which brain region controls production of hormones in the pituitary gland?
2. What is a target cell? What is the relationship between a hormone and its target cell?
3. Identify the two regions of the pituitary gland and describe how hormone release is controlled for each.

See blue "Answers" tab at back of book.

The Thyroid Gland [Figure 19.6a]

The **thyroid gland** curves across the anterior surface of the trachea (windpipe), just inferior to the **thyroid** ("shield-shaped") **cartilage** that dominates the anterior surface of the larynx (Figure 19.6a). Because of its location, the thyroid gland can easily be felt with the fingers; when something goes wrong with the gland, it may even become prominent. The size of the thyroid gland is quite variable, depending on heredity, environment, and nutritional factors, but the average weight is about 34 g (1.2 oz). The gland has a deep red coloration because of the large number of blood vessels supplying the glandular cells. On each side, the blood supply to the gland is from two sources: (1) a *superior thyroid artery*, which is a branch from the external carotid artery, and (2) an *inferior thyroid artery*, a branch of the thyrocervical trunk. Venous drainage of the gland is through the *superior* and *middle thyroid veins*, which end in the internal jugular veins, and the *inferior thyroid veins*, which deliver blood to the brachiocephalic veins.

The thyroid gland has a butterfly-like appearance and consists of two main **lobes**. The superior portion of each lobe extends over the lateral surface of the trachea toward the inferior border of the thyroid cartilage. Inferiorly, the lobes of the thyroid gland extend to the level of the second or third ring of cartilage in the trachea. The two lobes are united by a slender connection, the **isthmus** (IS-mus). The thyroid gland is anchored to the tracheal rings by a thin capsule that is continuous with connective tissue partitions that segment the glandular tissue and surround the *thyroid follicles.*

Thyroid Follicles and Thyroid Hormones [Figures 19.6b,c/19.7 and Table 19.2]

Thyroid follicles manufacture, store, and secrete thyroid hormones. Individual follicles are spherical, resembling miniature tennis balls. Thyroid follicles are typically lined by a simple cuboidal epithelium composed of *T thyrocytes* (also termed follicular cells) (Figure 19.6b,c). The type of epithelium is determined by the gland's activity, ranging from simple squamous in an inactive gland to simple columnar in a highly active gland. The T thyrocytes surround a **follicle cavity**, which contains **colloid**, a viscous fluid containing large quantities of suspended proteins. A network of capillaries surrounds each follicle, delivering nutrients and regulatory hormones to the follicular cells and accepting their secretory products and metabolic wastes.

The follicular cells have abundant mitochondria and an extensive rough endoplasmic reticulum. As you would expect from that description, these cells are actively synthesizing proteins. Follicular cells synthesize a globular protein called **thyroglobulin** (thī-rō-GLOB-ū-lin) and secrete it into the colloid of the thyroid follicle. Thyroglobulin contains molecules of tyrosine, and some of these amino acids will be modified into thyroid hormones inside the follicle, through the attachment of iodine. The T thyrocytes actively transport iodide ions (I^-) into the cell from the interstitial fluid. The iodine is converted to a special ionized form (I^+) and attached to the tyrosine molecules of thyroglobulin by enzymes on the luminal surfaces of the follicle cells. Two thyroid hormones—**thyroxine** (thī-ROK-sēn), also called **TX**, $\mathbf{T_4}$, or tetraiodothyronine, and **triiodothyronine** ($\mathbf{T_3}$)—are created in this way, and while in the colloid they remain part of the structure of the thyroglobulin. The thyroid is the only endocrine gland that stores its hormone product extracellularly.

The major factor controlling the rate of thyroid hormone release is the concentration of thyroid-stimulating hormone (TSH) in the circulating blood (Figure 19.7). Under the influence of **thyrotropin-releasing hormone (TRH)** from the hypothalamus, the adenohypophysis releases TSH. T thyrocytes respond by removing thyroglobulin from the lumen of the follicles by endocytosis. They next break down the protein through lysosomal activity, which releases molecules of both T_3 and T_4. These hormones then leave the cell, primarily by diffusion, and enter the circulation. Thyroxine (T_4)

Figure 19.6 Anatomy and Histological Organization of the Thyroid Gland
(a) Location and anatomy of the thyroid gland. **(b)** Histological organization of the thyroid. **(c)** Histological details of the thyroid gland showing thyroid follicles and both of the cell types in the follicular epithelium.

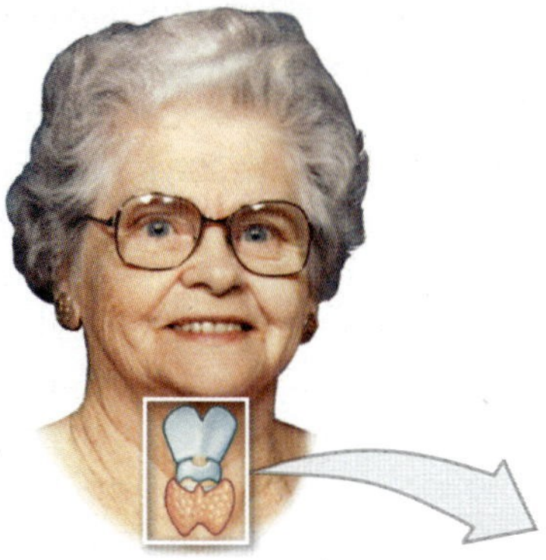

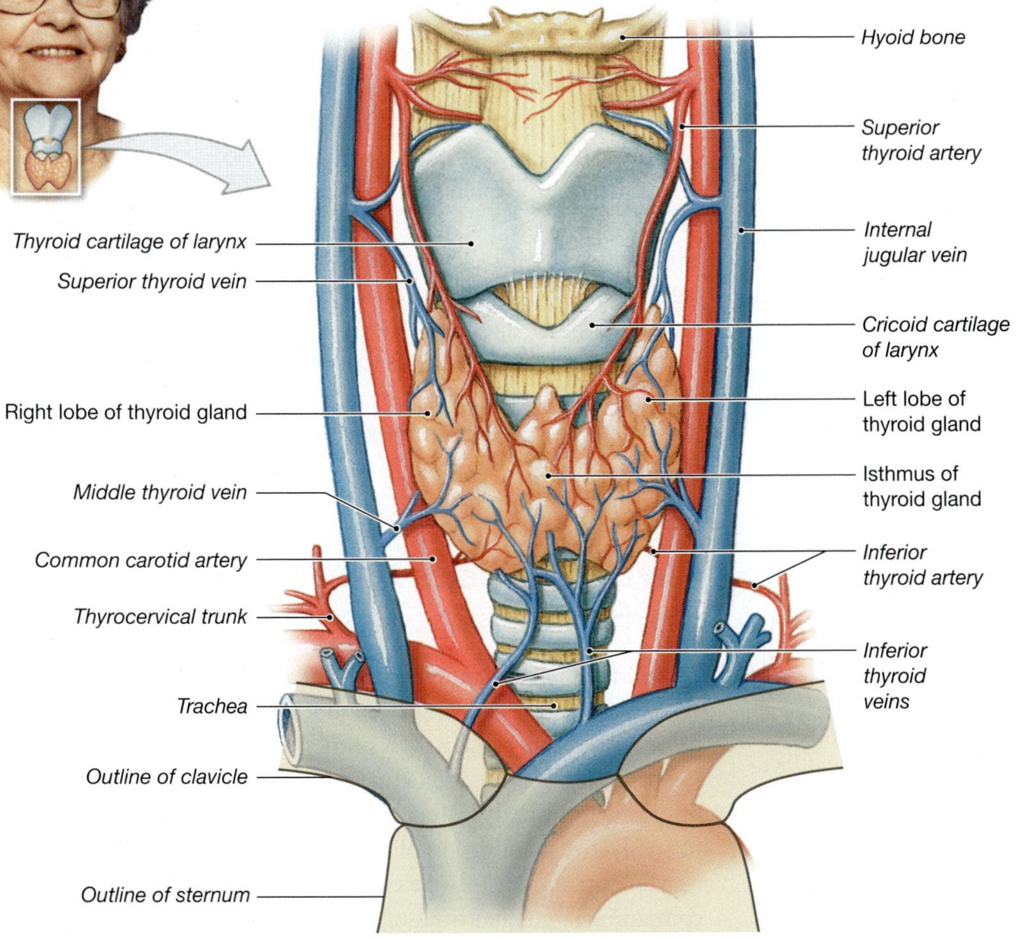

(a) Location of thyroid gland, anterior view

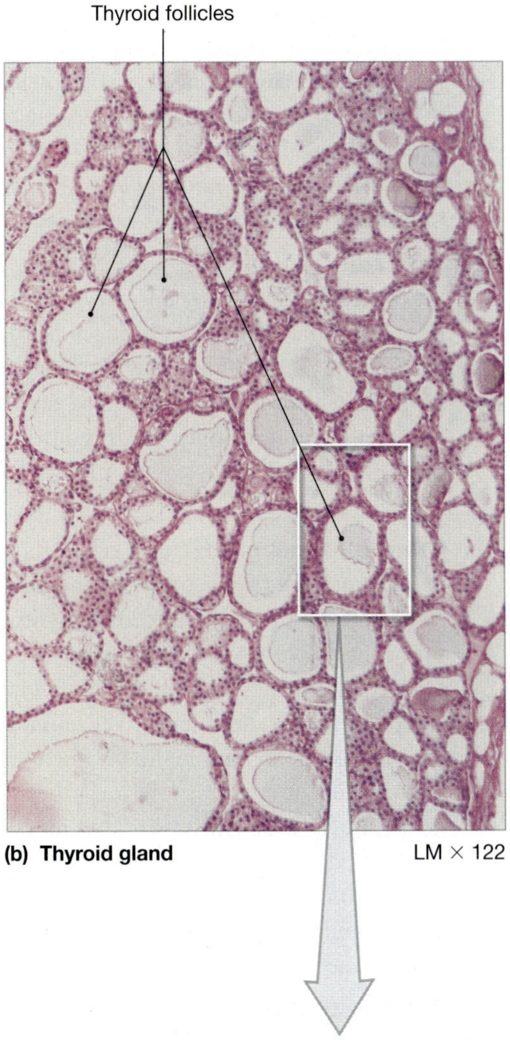

(b) Thyroid gland LM × 122

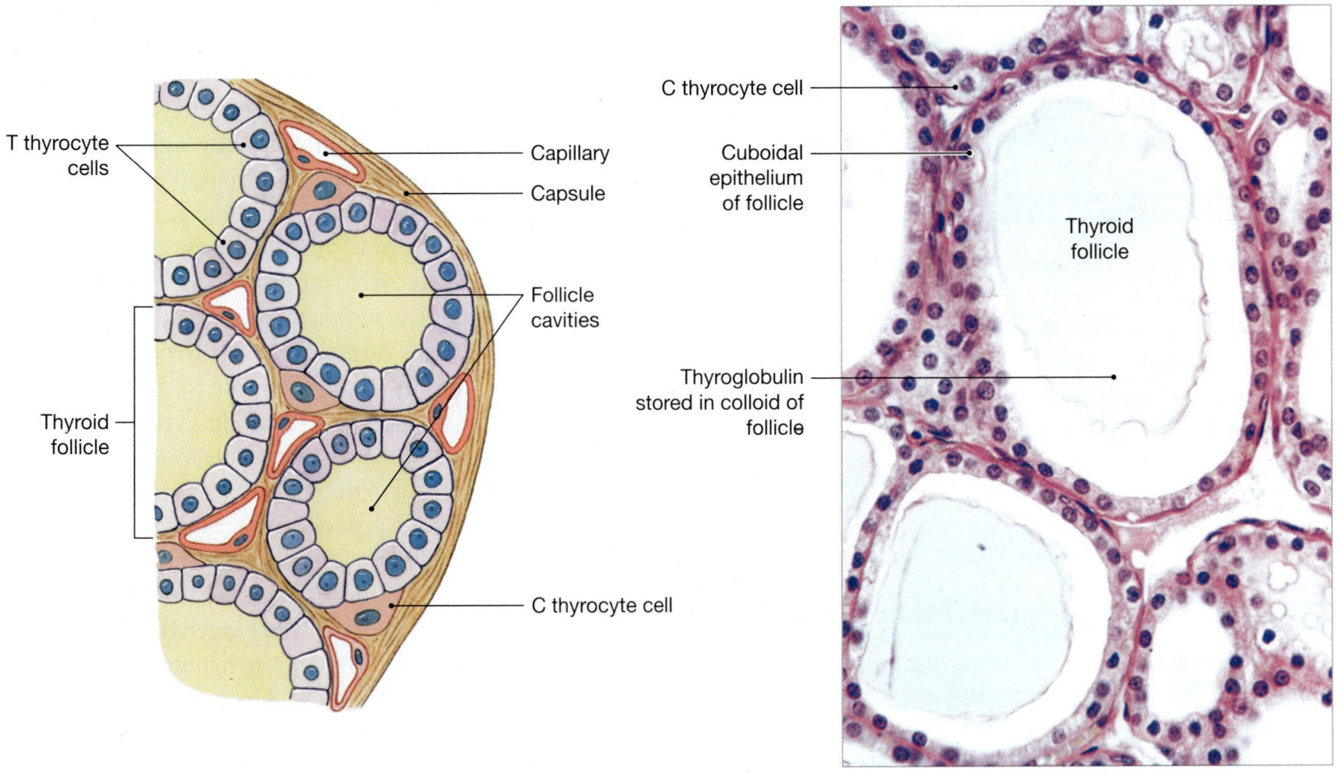

(c) Thyroid follicles LM × 260

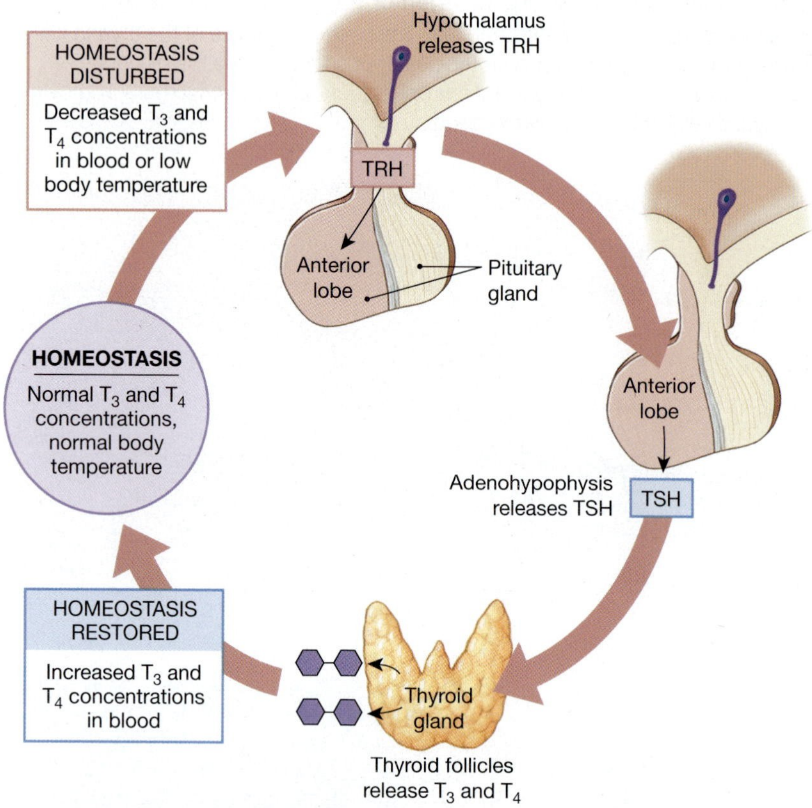

Figure 19.7 The Regulation of Thyroid Secretion
This negative feedback loop is responsible for the homeostatic control of thyroid hormone release. TRH = thyrotropin-releasing hormone; TSH = thyroid-stimulating hormone.

accounts for roughly 90 percent of all thyroid secretions. The two thyroid hormones, which have complementary effects, increase the rate of cellular metabolism and oxygen consumption in almost every cell in the body. These hormones are included in Table 19.2.

The C Thyrocytes of the Thyroid Gland [Figure 19.6c]

A second type of endocrine cell lies among the cuboidal follicle cells of the thyroid. Although in contact with the basal lamina, these cells do not reach the lumen. These are the **C thyrocytes**, or *parafollicular cells.* C thyrocytes occur singly or in small groups. They are larger than the cuboidal follicular cells and do not stain as clearly (Figure 19.6c). C thyrocytes produce the hormone **calcitonin** (kal-si-TŌ-nin) **(CT)**. Calcitonin assists in the regulation of calcium ion concentrations in body fluids, especially (1) during childhood when it stimulates bone growth and mineral deposition in the skeleton and (2) under physiological stresses such as starvation or pregnancy. Calcitonin lowers calcium ion concentrations by (1) inhibiting osteoclasts and (2) stimulating calcium ion excretion at the kidneys. The actions of calcitonin are opposed by those of *parathyroid hormone*, produced by the parathyroid glands.

The Parathyroid Glands

[Figures 19.6a/19.8]

There are typically four pea-sized, reddish brown **parathyroid glands** located on the posterior surfaces of the thyroid gland (Figure 19.8a). The glands usually are attached at the surface of the thyroid gland by the thyroid capsule. Like the thyroid gland, the parathyroid glands are surrounded by a connective tissue capsule that invades the interior of the gland, forming separations and small irregular *lobules.* Blood is supplied to the superior pair of parathyroid glands by the *superior thyroid arteries* and to the inferior pair by the *inferior thyroid arteries* (Figure 19.6a). The venous drainage is the same as that of the thyroid. All together the four parathyroid glands weigh a mere 1.6 g.

There are two types of cells in the parathyroid gland. The **parathyroid cells** (also termed **chief cells** or **principal cells**) (Figure 19.8b,c) are glandular cells that produce the hormone **parathyroid hormone (PTH)**; the other major cell types (*oxyphil cells* and *transitional cells*) are probably immature or inactive principal cells. Like the C thyrocytes of the thyroid, the parathyroid cells monitor the circulating concentration of calcium ions. When the calcium concentration falls below normal, the parathyroid cells secrete parathyroid hormone. PTH stimulates osteoclasts and osteoblasts (although osteoclast effects predominate), and reduces urinary excretion of calcium ions. It also stimulates the production of *calcitriol*, a kidney hormone that promotes intestinal absorption of calcium. PTH levels remain elevated until blood Ca^{2+} concentrations return to normal. PTH has been shown to be effective in reducing the progress of osteoporosis in the elderly.

The Thymus [Figure 19.1 and Table 19.2]

The **thymus** is embedded in a mass of connective tissue inside the thoracic cavity, usually just posterior to the sternum (Figure 19.1, p. 508). In newborn infants and young children, the thymus is relatively large, often extending from the base of the neck to the superior border of the heart. Although its relative size decreases as a child grows, the thymus continues to enlarge slowly, reaching its maximum size just before puberty, at a weight of around 40 g. After puberty it gradually diminishes in size; by age 50 the thymus may weigh less than 12 g.

The thymus produces several hormones important to the development and maintenance of normal immunological defenses (Table 19.2).

TABLE 19.2 Hormones of the Thyroid Gland, Parathyroid Glands, and Thymus

Gland/Cells	Hormones	Targets	Effects
THYROID			
T thyrocytes	Thyroxine (T_4), triiodothyronine (T_3)	Most cells	Increase energy utilization, oxygen consumption, growth, and development
C thyrocytes	Calcitonin (CT)	Bone and kidneys	Decreases calcium ion concentrations in body fluids; uncertain significance in healthy nonpregnant adults
PARATHYROIDS			
Parathyroid cells	Parathyroid hormone (PTH)	Bone and kidneys	Increases calcium ion concentrations in body fluids; increases bone mass
Thymus	"Thymosins" *(see Chapter 23)*	Lymphocytes	Maturation and functional competence of immune system

Figure 19.8 Anatomy and Histological Organization of the Parathyroid Glands
There are usually four separate parathyroid glands bound to the posterior surface of the thyroid gland. **(a)** The location and size of the parathyroid glands on the posterior surface of the thyroid lobes. **(b)** This photomicrograph shows both parathyroid and thyroid tissues. **(c)** A photomicrograph showing parathyroid cells and oxyphil cells of the parathyroid gland.

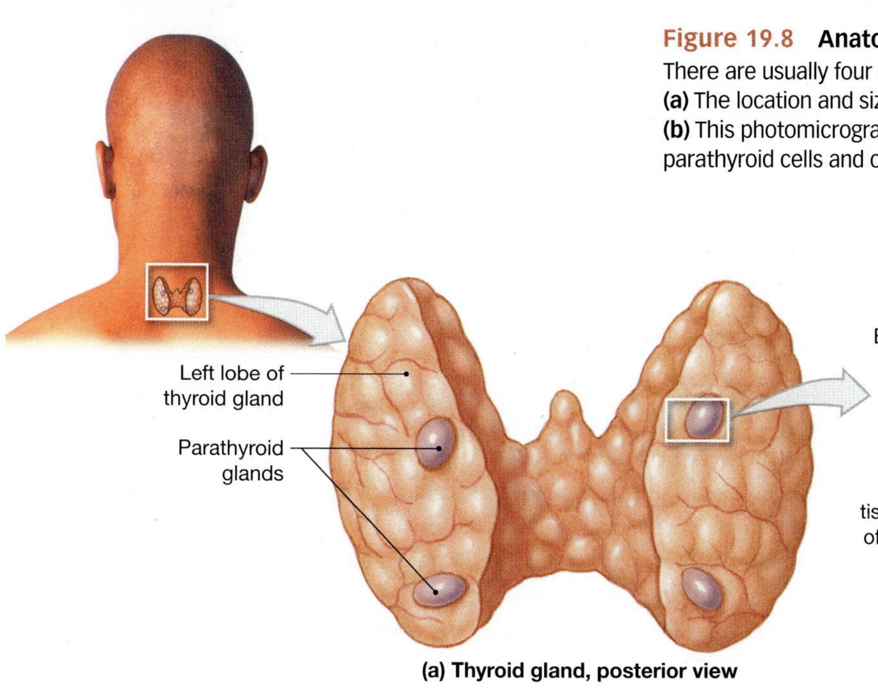

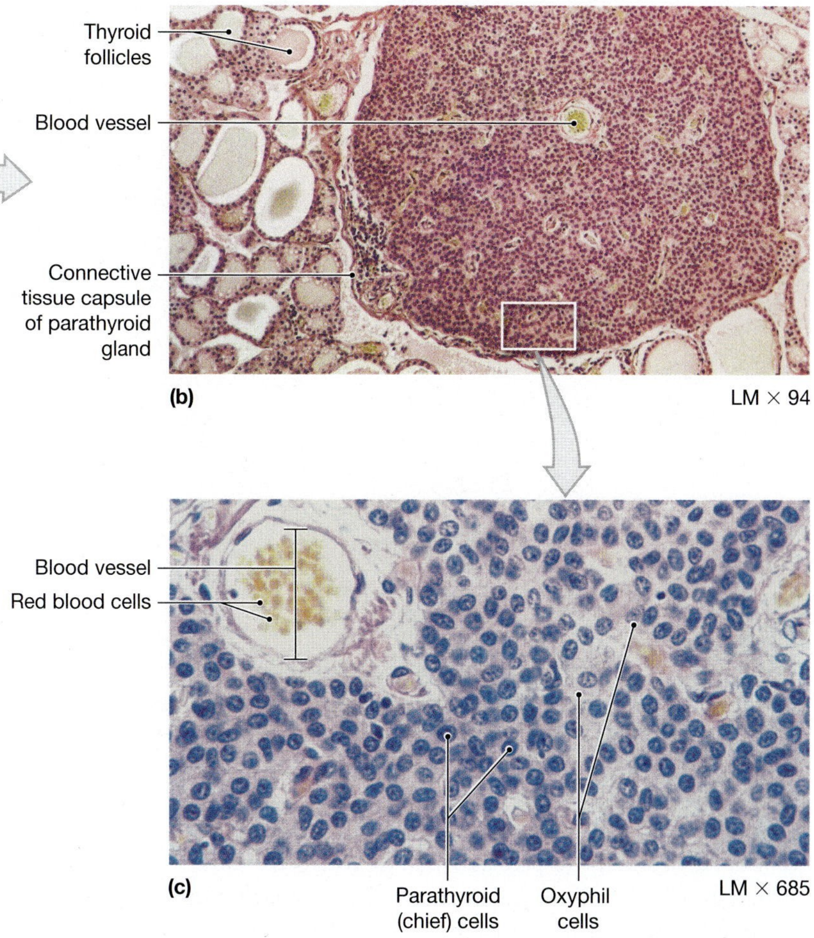

Thymosin (thī-MŌ-sin) was the name originally given to a thymic extract that promoted the development and maturation of lymphocytes and thus increased the effectiveness of the immune system. It has since become apparent that "thymosin" is a blend of several different, complementary hormones (thymosin-1, thymopoietin, thymopentin, thymulin, thymic humoral factor, and IGF-1).

It has been suggested that the gradual decrease in the size and secretory abilities of the thymus may make the elderly more susceptible to disease. The histological organization of the thymus and the functions of the various "thymosins" will be discussed further in Chapter 23.

The Suprarenal Glands [Figure 19.9]

A yellow, pyramid-shaped **suprarenal gland** (soo-pra-RĒ-nal; *supra-*, above + *renes*, kidneys), or **adrenal gland**, is firmly attached to the superior border of each kidney by a dense, fibrous **capsule** (Figure 19.9a). The suprarenal gland on each side nestles between the kidney, the diaphragm, and the major arteries and veins running along the dorsal wall of the abdominopelvic cavity. These glands are retroperitoneal, posterior to the peritoneal lining. Like the other endocrine glands, the suprarenal glands are highly vascularized. Branches of the *renal artery*, the *inferior phrenic artery*, and a direct branch from the aorta (the *middle suprarenal artery*) supply blood to each suprarenal gland. The *suprarenal veins* carry blood away from the suprarenal glands.

A typical suprarenal gland weighs about 7.5 g. It is generally heavier in men than in women, but the size can vary greatly as secretory demands change. Structurally and functionally, the suprarenal gland can be divided into two regions, each secreting different hormone types, but both aiding in managing stress: a superficial **cortex** and an inner **medulla** (Figure 19.9b,c).

The Cortex of the Suprarenal Gland [Figure 19.9c and Table 19.3]

The yellowish color of the cortex of the suprarenal gland is due to the presence of stored lipids, especially cholesterol and various fatty acids. The cortex produces more than two dozen different steroid hormones, collectively called **adrenocortical steroids**, or simply **corticosteroids**. These hormones are vital; if the suprarenal glands are destroyed or removed, corticosteroids must be administered or the person will not survive. The corticosteroids exert their effects on metabolic operations by determining which genes are transcribed in their target cells, and at what rates.

Deep to the capsule there are three distinct regions, or *zones*, in the cortex: (1) an outer *zona glomerulosa*; (2) a middle *zona fasciculata*; and (3) an inner *zona reticularis* (Figure 19.9c). Although each zone synthesizes different steroid hormones (Table 19.3), all of the cortical cells have an extensive smooth ER for the manufacture of lipid-based steroids. This is in marked contrast to the abundant rough ER characteristic of protein-secreting gland cells, such as those of the adenohypophysis or thyroid gland.

The Zona Glomerulosa [Figure 19.9c]

The **zona glomerulosa** (glō-mer-ū-LŌ-sa), the outermost cortical region, accounts for about 15 percent of the cortical volume (Figure 19.9c). This zone extends from the capsule to the radiating cords of the underlying zona fasciculata. A *glomerulus* is a little ball or knot, and here the endocrine cells form densely packed clusters.

The zona glomerulosa produces **mineralocorticoids (MC)**, steroid hormones that affect the electrolyte composition of body fluids. **Aldosterone** (al-DOS-ter-ōn) is the principal mineralocorticoid and targets kidney cells that regulate the ionic composition of the urine. It causes

Figure 19.9 Anatomy and Histological Organization of the Suprarenal Gland
(a) Anterior view of the kidney and suprarenal gland. Note the sectional plane for part (b). **(b)** A suprarenal gland cut to show both the cortex and the medulla. Note the orientation of the section for part (c). **(c)** Histology of the suprarenal gland showing identification of the major regions.

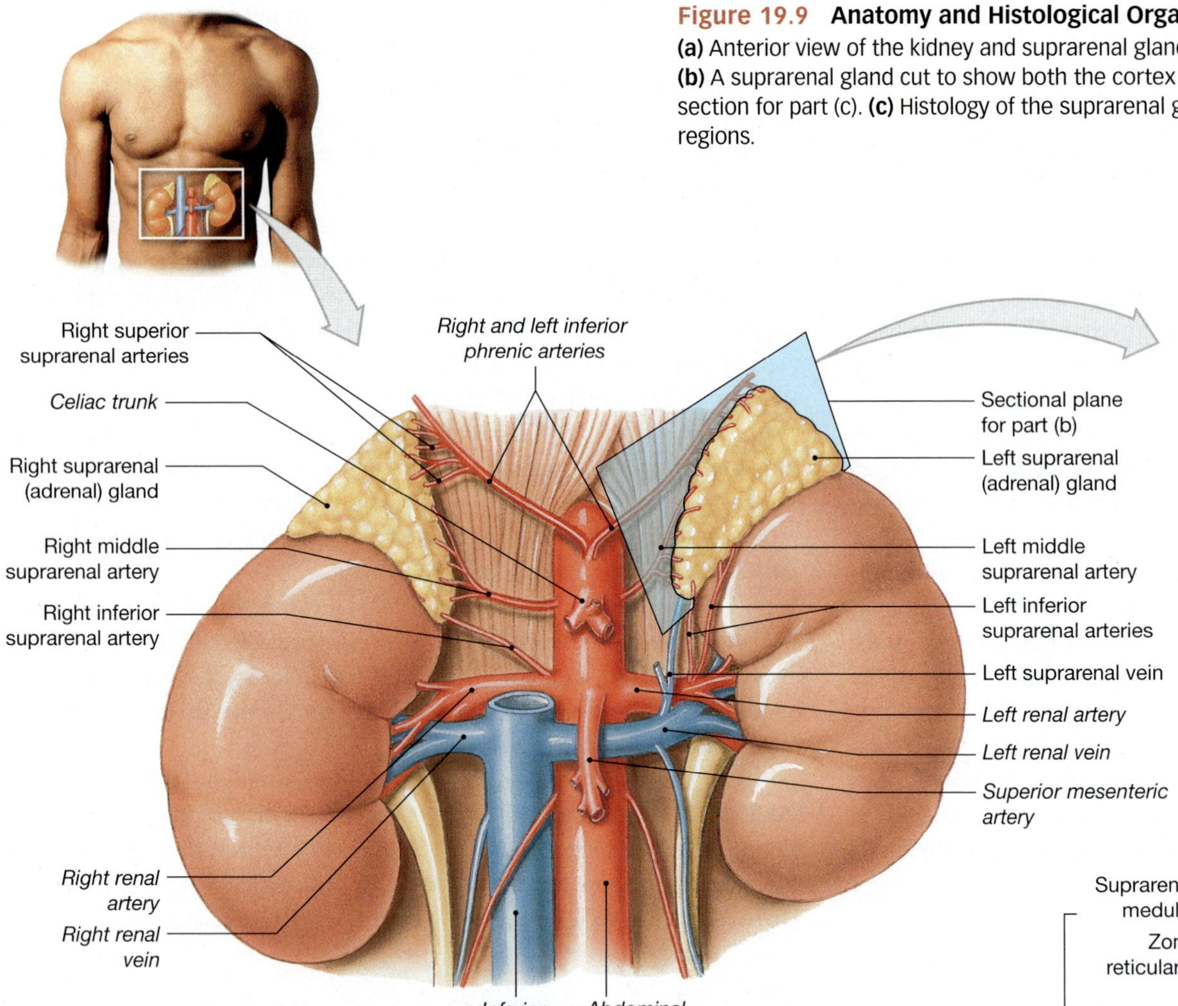

(a) Suprarenal glands and kidneys, anterior view

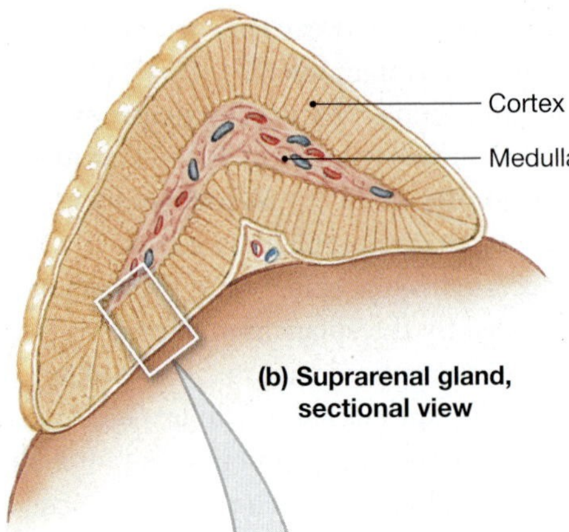

(b) Suprarenal gland, sectional view

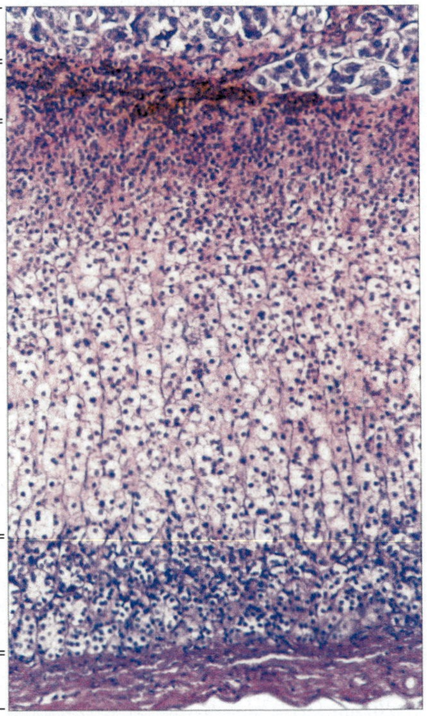

(c) Histology of suprarenal gland LM × 140

the retention of sodium ions (Na^+) and water, thereby reducing fluid losses in the urine. Aldosterone also reduces sodium and water losses at the sweat glands and salivary glands and along the digestive tract. It also promotes the loss of potassium ions (K^+) in the urine and at other sites as well. Aldosterone secretion occurs when the zona glomerulosa is stimulated by a fall in blood Na^+ levels, a rise in blood K^+ levels, or arrival of the hormone *angiotensin II* (*angeion*, vessel + *teinein*, to stretch).

The Zona Fasciculata [Figure 19.9c]

The **zona fasciculata** (fa-sik-ū-LA-ta; *fasciculus*, little bundle) begins at the inner border of the zona glomerulosa and extends toward the medulla (**Figure 19.9c**). It represents about 78 percent of the cortical volume. The cells are larger and contain more lipids than those of the zona glomerulosa, and the lipid droplets give the cytoplasm a pale, foamy appearance. The cells of the zona fasciculata form cords that radiate like a sunburst from the zona reticularis. Adjacent cords are separated by flattened vessels with fenestrated walls.

Steroid production in the zona fasciculata is stimulated by ACTH from the anterior lobe of the pituitary gland. This zone produces steroid hormones collectively known as *glucocorticoids (GC)* because of their effects on glucose metabolism. **Cortisol** (KOR-ti-sol; also called *hydrocortisone*) and **corticosterone** (kor-ti-KOS-ter-ōn) are the most important glucocorticoids secreted by the suprarenal cortex; the liver converts some of the circulating cortisol to **cortisone**, another active glucocorticoid. These hormones speed up the rates of glucose synthesis and glycogen formation, especially within the liver.

The Zona Reticularis [Figure 19.9c]

The **zona reticularis** (re-tik-ū-LAR-is; *reticulum*, network) forms a narrow band between the zona fasciculata and the outer border of the suprarenal medulla (**Figure 19.9c**). The cells of the zona reticularis are much smaller than those of the medulla, and this makes the boundary relatively easy to distinguish. In total, the zona reticularis accounts for only around 7 percent of the total cell volume of the suprarenal cortex. The endocrine cells of the zona reticularis form a folded, branching network with an extensive capillary supply. The zona reticularis normally secretes small amounts of sex hormones called *androgens*. Suprarenal androgens stimulate the development of pubic hair in boys and girls before puberty. While not important in adult men,

whose testes produce androgens in relatively large amounts, in adult women suprarenal androgens promote muscle mass, stimulate blood cell formation, and support the libido.

The Medulla of the Suprarenal Gland

[Figure 19.9b,c and Table 19.3]

The boundary between the cortex and medulla of the suprarenal gland does not form a straight line (Figure 19.9b,c), and the supporting connective tissues and blood vessels are extensively interconnected. The medulla has a reddish brown coloration due in part to the many blood vessels in this area. **Chromaffin cells**, or **pheochromocytes**, are large, rounded cells of the medulla that resemble the neurons in sympathetic ganglia. These cells are innervated by preganglionic sympathetic fibers; sympathetic activation, provided by the splanchnic nerves, triggers the secretory activity of these modified ganglionic neurons. p. 458

The suprarenal medulla contains two populations of endocrine cells—one secreting epinephrine (adrenaline), and the other norepinephrine (noradrenaline). The medulla secretes roughly three times as much epinephrine as norepinephrine. p. 458 Their secretion triggers cellular energy utilization and the mobilization of energy reserves. This combination increases muscular strength and endurance (Table 19.3). The metabolic changes that follow catecholamine release are at their peak 30 seconds after suprarenal stimulation, and they linger for several minutes thereafter. As a result, the effects produced by stimulation of the suprarenal medulla outlast the other signs of sympathetic activation.

CONCEPT CHECK

1. When a person's thyroid gland is removed, signs of decreased thyroid hormone concentration do not appear until about one week later. Why?
2. Removal of the parathyroid glands would result in a decrease in the blood of what important mineral?
3. A disorder of the suprarenal gland prevents Bill from retaining sodium ions in body fluids. Which region of the gland is affected, and what hormone is deficient?

See blue "Answers" tab at back of book.

Endocrine Functions of the Kidneys and Heart

The kidneys and heart produce several hormones, and most of them are involved with the regulation of blood pressure and blood volume. The kidneys produce *renin*, an enzyme (often called a hormone), and two hormones: *erythropoietin*, a peptide, and *calcitriol*, a steroid. Once in the circulation, **renin** converts circulating **angiotensinogen**, an inactive protein produced by the liver, to **angiotensin I**. In capillaries of the lungs, this compound is converted to **angiotensin II**, the hormone that stimulates the secretion of aldosterone by the suprarenal cortex. **Erythropoietin** (e-rith-rō-POY-e-tin) **(EPO)** stimulates red blood cell production by the bone marrow. This hormone is released when either blood pressure or blood oxygen levels in the kidneys decline. EPO stimulates red blood cell production and maturation, thus increasing the blood volume and its oxygen-carrying capacity.

Calcitriol is a steroid hormone secreted by the kidney in response to the presence of parathyroid hormone (PTH). Calcitriol synthesis is dependent on the availability of a related steroid, *cholecalciferol* (vitamin D_3), which may be synthesized in the skin or absorbed from the diet. Cholecalciferol from either source is absorbed from the bloodstream by the liver and converted to an intermediary product that is released into the circulation and absorbed by the kidneys for conversion to calcitriol. The term *vitamin D* is used to indicate the entire group of related steroids, including calcitriol, cholecalciferol, and various intermediaries.

The best-known function of calcitriol is the stimulation of calcium and phosphate ion absorption along the digestive tract. PTH stimulates the release of calcitriol, and in this way, PTH has an indirect effect on intestinal calcium absorption. The effects of calcitriol on the skeletal system and kidney are not well understood.

Cardiac muscle cells in the heart produce **atrial natriuretic peptide (ANP)** and **brain natriuretic peptide (BNP)** in response to increased blood pressure or blood volume. ANP and BNP suppress the release of ADH and aldosterone and stimulate water and sodium ion loss at the kidneys. These effects gradually reduce both blood pressure and blood volume.

The Pancreas and Other Endocrine Tissues of the Digestive System

The pancreas, the lining of the digestive tract, and the liver produce various exocrine secretions that are essential to the normal digestion of food. Although the pace of digestive activities can be affected by the autonomic nervous system, most digestive processes are controlled locally by the individual organs. The various digestive organs communicate with one another using hormones detailed in Chapter 25. This section focuses attention on one digestive organ, the pancreas, which produces hormones that affect metabolic operations throughout the body.

The Pancreas [Figure 19.10 and Table 19.4]

The **pancreas** is a mixed gland with both exocrine and endocrine activities. It lies within the abdominopelvic cavity in the J-shaped loop between the stomach and small intestine (Figure 19.10a). It is a slender, pink organ with

TABLE 19.3 The Suprarenal Hormones

Region/Zone	Hormones	Targets	Effects
CORTEX			
Zona glomerulosa	Mineralocorticoids (MC), primarily aldosterone	Kidneys	Increase renal reabsorption of sodium ions and water (especially in the presence of ADH) and accelerates urinary loss of potassium ions
Zona fasciculata	Glucocorticoids (GC): cortisol (hydrocortisone), corticosterone; cortisol converted to cortisone and released by the liver	Most cells	Release amino acids from skeletal muscles, lipids from adipose tissues; promote formation of liver glycogen and glucose; promote peripheral utilization of lipids (glucose-sparing); anti-inflammatory effects
Zona reticularis	Androgens		Uncertain significance under normal conditions
MEDULLA	Epinephrine, norepinephrine	Most cells	Increased cardiac activity, blood pressure, glycogen breakdown, blood glucose; release of lipids by adipose tissue *(see Chapter 17)*

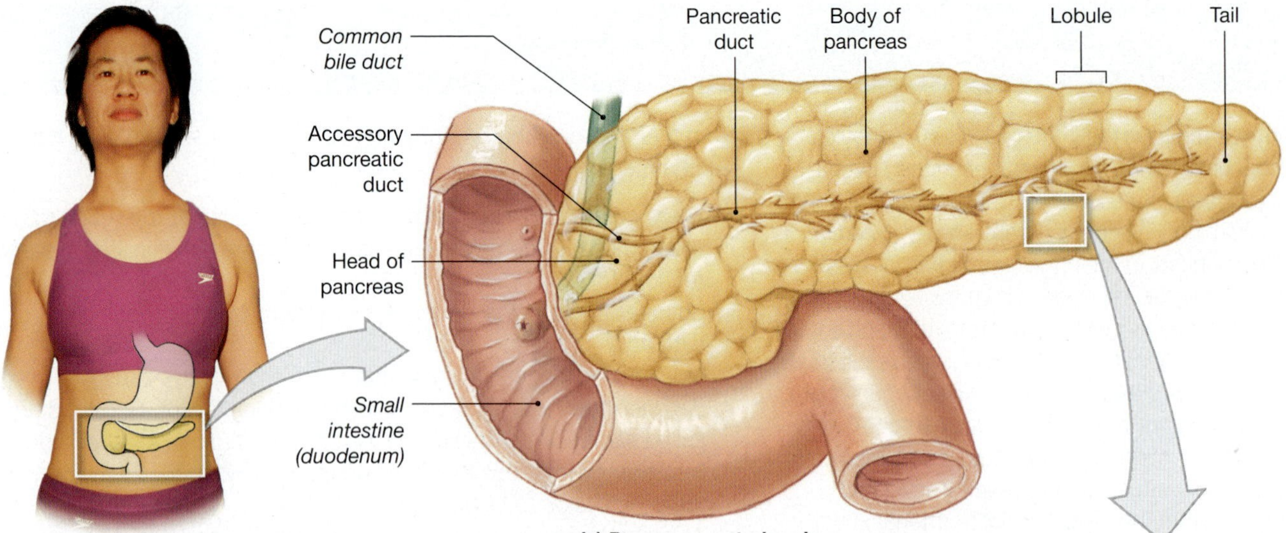

(a) Pancreas, anterior view

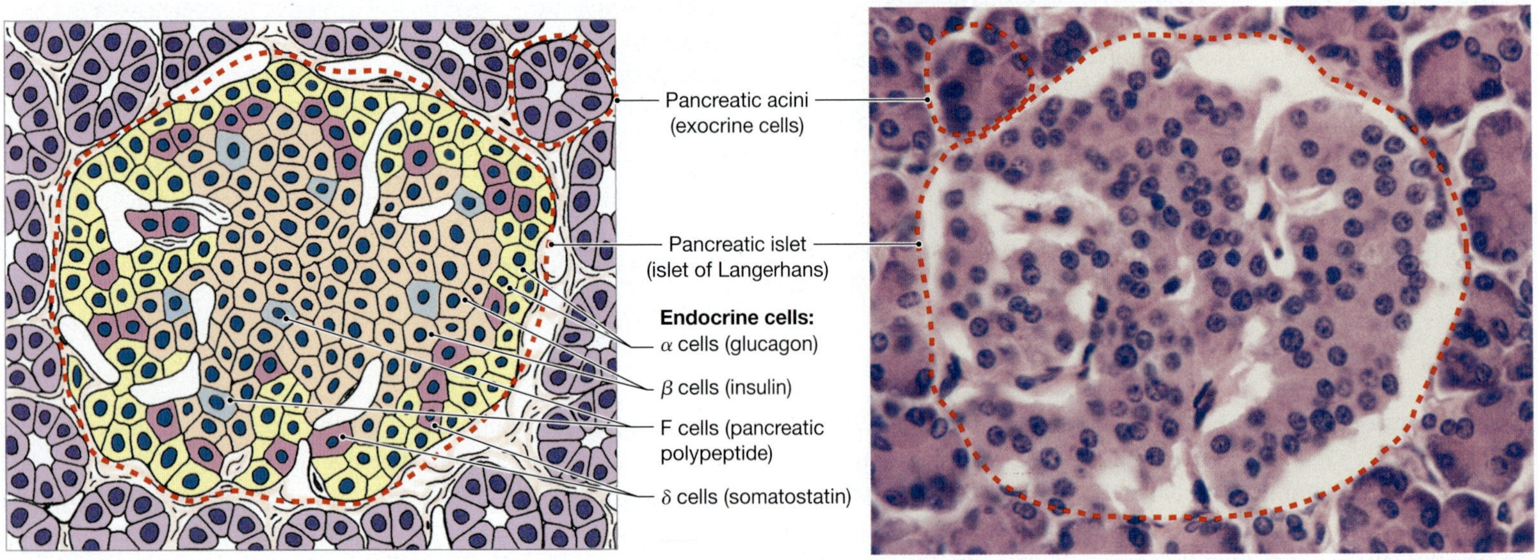

(b) Pancreatic islet LM × 400

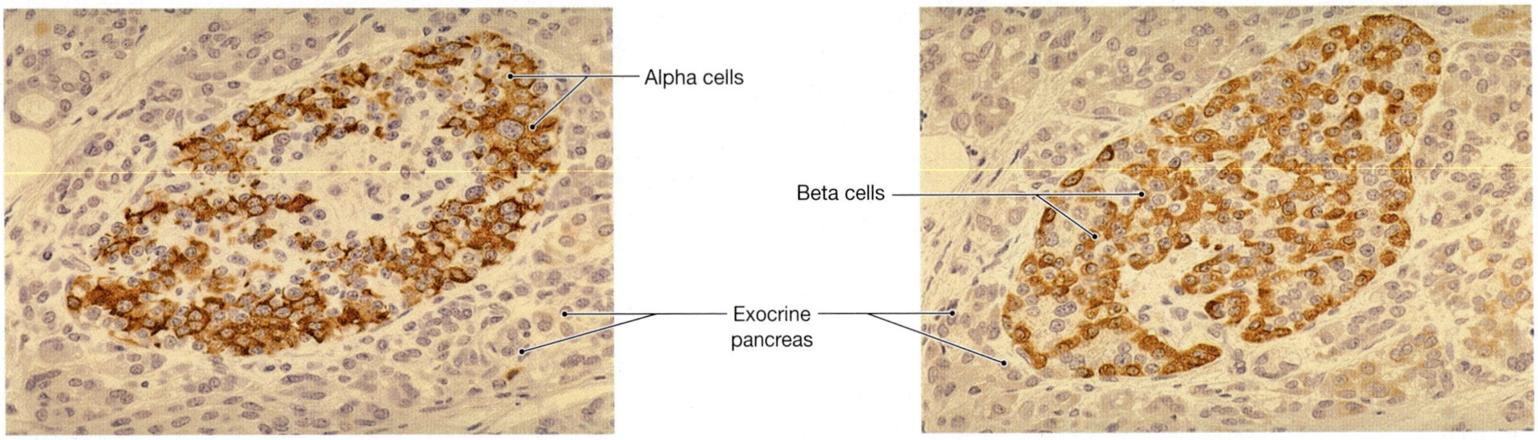

(c) Alpha cells LM × 184

(d) Beta cells LM × 184

Figure 19.10 Anatomy and Histological Organization of the Pancreas
This organ, which is dominated by exocrine cells, contains clusters of endocrine cells known as the pancreatic islets. **(a)** The gross anatomy of the pancreas. **(b)** General histology of the pancreatic islets. **(c)** and **(d)** Special histological staining techniques can be used to differentiate between alpha cells (c) and beta cells (d) in pancreatic islets.

Clinical Note

Diabetes Mellitus **Diabetes mellitus** (MEL-i-tus; *mellitum*, honey) is characterized by glucose concentrations that are high enough to overwhelm the reabsorption capabilities of the kidneys. (The presence of abnormally high glucose levels in the blood in general is called *hyperglycemia* [hī-per-glī-SĒ-mē-ah].) Glucose appears in the urine (*glycosuria;* glī-kō-SOO-rē-a), and urine production generally becomes excessive (*polyuria*).

Diabetes mellitus can be caused by genetic abnormalities, and some of the genes responsible have been identified. Mutations that result in inadequate insulin production, the synthesis of abnormal insulin molecules, or the production of defective receptor proteins produce comparable symptoms. Under these conditions, obesity accelerates the onset and severity of the disease. Diabetes mellitus can also result from other pathological conditions, injuries, immune disorders, or hormonal imbalances. There are two major types of diabetes mellitus: **insulin-dependent (type 1) diabetes** and **non-insulin-dependent (type 2) diabetes**. Type 1 diabetes can be controlled with varying success through the administration of insulin by injection or infusion by an insulin pump. Dietary restrictions are most effective in treating type 2 diabetes.

Probably because glucose levels cannot be stabilized adequately, even with treatment, individuals with diabetes mellitus commonly develop chronic medical problems. These problems arise because the tissues involved are experiencing an energy crisis—in essence, most of the tissues are responding as they would during chronic starvation, breaking down lipids and even proteins because they are unable to absorb glucose from their surroundings. Among the most common examples of diabetes-related medical disorders are the following:

- The proliferation of capillaries and hemorrhaging at the retina may cause partial or complete blindness. This condition is called *diabetic retinopathy*.
- Changes occur in the clarity of the lens of the eye, producing cataracts.
- Small hemorrhages and inflammation at the kidneys cause degenerative changes that can lead to kidney failure. This condition, called *diabetic nephropathy*, is the primary cause of kidney failure. Treatment with drugs that improve blood flow to the kidneys can slow the progression to kidney failure.
- A variety of neural problems appear, including peripheral neuropathies and abnormal autonomic function. These disorders, collectively termed *diabetic neuropathy*, are probably related to disturbances in the blood supply to neural tissues. p. 465
- Degenerative changes in cardiac circulation can lead to early heart attacks. For a given age group, heart attacks are three to five times more likely in diabetic individuals than in nondiabetic people.
- Other changes in the vascular system can disrupt normal blood flow to the distal portions of the limbs. For example, a reduction in blood flow to the feet can lead to tissue death, ulceration, infection, and loss of toes or a major portion of one or both feet.

a nodular or lumpy consistency. The adult pancreas ranges between 20 and 25 cm (8 and 10 in.) in length and weighs about 80 g (2.8 oz). Chapter 25 considers the detailed anatomy of the pancreas, because the **exocrine pancreas**, roughly 99 percent of the pancreatic volume, produces large quantities of a digestive enzyme–rich fluid that enters the digestive tract through a prominent secretory duct.

The **endocrine pancreas** consists of small groups of cells scattered throughout the gland, each group surrounded by exocrine cells. The groups, known as **pancreatic islets**, or the *islets of Langerhans* (LAN-ger-hanz), account for only about 1 percent of the pancreatic cell population (Figure 19.10b). Nevertheless, there are roughly 2 million islets in the normal pancreas.

Like other endocrine tissue, the islets are surrounded by an extensive, fenestrated capillary network that carries its hormones into the circulation. Two major arteries supply blood to the pancreas, the *pancreaticoduodenal arteries* and *pancreatic arteries*. Venous blood returns to the *hepatic portal vein*. (Circulation to and from major organs will be considered in Chapter 22.) The islets are also innervated by the autonomic nervous system, through branches from the *celiac plexus*. p. 456

Each islet contains four major cell types:

1. **Alpha cells** produce the hormone **glucagon** (GLOO-ka-gon), which raises blood glucose levels by increasing the rates of glycogen breakdown and glucose release by the liver (Figure 19.10b).
2. **Beta cells** produce the hormone **insulin** (IN-su-lin), which lowers blood glucose by increasing the rate of glucose uptake and utilization by most body cells (Figure 19.10b).
3. **Delta cells** produce the hormone **somatostatin** *(growth-hormone-inhibiting hormone)*, which inhibits the production and secretion of glucagon and insulin and slows the rates of food absorption and enzyme secretion along the digestive tract.
4. **F cells** produce the hormone **pancreatic polypeptide (PP)**. It inhibits gallbladder contractions and regulates the production of some pancreatic enzymes; it may help control the rate of nutrient absorption by the digestive tract.

Pancreatic alpha and beta cells are sensitive to blood glucose concentrations, and their regulatory activities are not under the direct control of other endocrine or nervous components. Yet because the islet cells are extremely sensitive to variations in blood glucose levels, any hormone that affects blood glucose concentrations will affect the production of insulin and glucagon indirectly. The major hormones of the pancreas are summarized in Table 19.4.

Endocrine Tissues of the Reproductive System

The endocrine tissues of the reproductive system are restricted primarily to the male and female gonads—the testes and ovaries, respectively. The anatomy of the reproductive organs will be described in Chapter 27.

Testes [Table 19.5]

In the male, the **interstitial cells** of the testes produce androgens. The most important androgen is **testosterone** (tes-TOS-ter-ōn). This hormone promotes the production of functional sperm, maintains the secretory glands of the male reproductive tract, influences secondary sexual characteristics,

TABLE 19.4 Hormones of the Pancreas

Structure/Cells	Hormones	Primary Targets	Effects
PANCREATIC ISLETS			
Alpha cells	Glucagon	Liver, adipose tissues	Mobilization of lipid reserves; glucose synthesis and glycogen breakdown in liver; elevation of blood glucose concentrations
Beta cells	Insulin	All cells except those of brain, kidneys, digestive tract epithelium, and RBCs	Facilitation of uptake of glucose by cells; stimulation of lipid and glycogen formation and storage; decrease in blood glucose concentrations
Delta cells	Somatostatin	Alpha and beta cells, digestive epithelium	Inhibition of secretion of insulin and glucagon
F cells	Pancreatic polypeptide (PP)	Gallbladder and pancreas, possibly gastrointestinal tract	Inhibits gallbladder contractions; regulates production of some pancreatic enzymes; may control nutrient absorption

TABLE 19.5 Hormones of the Reproductive System

Structure/Cells	Hormones	Primary Targets	Effects
TESTES			
Interstitial cells	Androgens	Most cells	Support functional maturation of sperm; protein synthesis in skeletal muscles; male secondary sex characteristics and associated behaviors
Nurse cells	Inhibin	Anterior lobe of pituitary gland	Inhibits secretion of FSH
OVARIES			
Follicular cells	Estrogens (especially estradiol)	Most cells	Support follicle maturation; female secondary sex characteristics and associated behaviors
	Inhibin	Anterior lobe of pituitary gland	Inhibits secretion of FSH
Corpus luteum	Progestins (especially progesterone)	Uterus, mammary glands	Prepare uterus for implantation; prepare mammary glands for secretory functions
	Relaxin	Pubic symphysis, uterus, mammary glands	Loosens pubic symphysis; relaxes uterine (cervical) muscles; stimulates mammary gland development

and stimulates muscle growth (Table 19.5). During embryonic development, the production of testosterone affects the anatomical development of the hypothalamic nuclei of the CNS.

Nurse cells (also termed **sustentacular cells**), which are directly associated with the formation of functional sperm, secrete an additional hormone, called **inhibin** (in-HIB-in). Inhibin production, which occurs under FSH stimulation, depresses the secretion of FSH by the anterior lobe of the pituitary gland. Throughout adult life, these two hormones interact to maintain sperm production at normal levels.

Ovaries [Table 19.5]

In the ovaries, oocytes begin their maturation into female gametes (sex cells) within specialized structures called **follicles**. The maturation process starts in response to stimulation by FSH. Follicle cells surrounding the oocytes produce estrogens, especially the hormone **estradiol**. These steroid hormones support the maturation of the oocytes and stimulate the growth of the uterine lining (Table 19.5). Under FSH stimulation, active follicles secrete inhibin, which suppresses FSH release through a feedback mechanism comparable to that described for males.

After ovulation has occurred, the remaining follicular cells reorganize into a **corpus luteum** (LOO-tē-um) that releases a mixture of estrogens and progestins, especially **progesterone** (prō-JES-ter-ōn). Progesterone accelerates the movement of the oocyte along the uterine tube and prepares the uterus for the arrival of the developing embryo. A summary of information concerning the reproductive hormones can be found in Table 19.5.

The Pineal Gland [Figure 19.1]

The small, red, pinecone–shaped **pineal gland**, or *epiphysis* (e-PIF-e-sis) *cerebri*, (**Figure 19.1**, p. 508) is part of the epithalamus. p. 405 The pineal gland contains neurons, glial cells, and special secretory cells called **pinealocytes** (PIN-ē-al-ō-sīts). Pinealocytes synthesize the hormone **melatonin** (mel-a-TŌN-in), which is derived from molecules of the neurotransmitter *serotonin*. Melatonin slows the maturation of sperm, oocytes, and reproductive organs by inhibiting the production of a hypothalamic releasing factor that stimulates FSH and LH secretion. Collaterals from the visual pathways enter the pineal gland and affect the rate of melatonin production. Melatonin production rises at night and declines during the day. This cycle is apparently important in regulating *circadian rhythms*, our natural awake-asleep cycles. pp. 405, 408 This hormone is also a powerful antioxidant that may help protect CNS tissues from toxins generated by active neurons and glial cells.

Embryology Summary

For a summary of the development of the endocrine system, see Chapter 28 (Embryology and Human Development).

Clinical Note

Endocrine Disorders Endocrine disorders may develop for a variety of reasons, including abnormalities in the endocrine gland, the endocrine or neural regulatory mechanisms, or the target tissues. For example, a hormone level may rise because its target organs are becoming less responsive, because a tumor has formed among the gland cells, or because something has interfered with the normal feedback control mechanism. When naming endocrine disorders, clinicians use the prefix *hyper-* when referring to excessive hormone production and *hypo-* when referring to inadequate hormone production.

Most endocrine disorders are the result of problems within the endocrine gland itself. The typical result is hyposecretion, the production of inadequate levels of a particular hormone. Hyposecretion may be caused by the following:

- **Metabolic factors.** Hyposecretion may result from a deficiency in some key substrate needed to synthesize the hormone in question. For example, hypothyroidism can be caused by inadequate dietary iodine levels or by exposure to drugs that inhibit iodine transport or utilization at the thyroid gland.
- **Physical damage.** Any condition that interrupts the normal circulatory supply or that physically damages the endocrine cells may cause them to become inactive immediately or after an initial surge of hormone release. If the damage is severe, the gland can become permanently inactive. For instance, temporary or permanent hypothyroidism can result from infection or inflammation of the gland (thyroiditis), from the interruption of normal blood flow, or from exposure to radiation as part of treatment for cancer of the thyroid gland or adjacent tissues. The thyroid gland can also be damaged in an autoimmune disorder that results in the production of antibodies that attack and destroy normal follicle cells.
- **Congenital disorders.** An individual may be unable to produce normal amounts of a particular hormone because (1) the gland itself is too small, (2) the required enzymes are abnormal, (3) the receptors that trigger secretion are relatively insensitive, or (4) the gland cells lack the receptors normally involved in stimulating secretory activity.

Endocrine abnormalities can also be caused by the presence of abnormal hormonal receptors in target tissues. In such a case, the gland involved and the regulatory mechanisms are normal, but the peripheral cells are unable to respond to the circulating hormone. The best example of this type of abnormality is type 2 diabetes, in which peripheral cells do not respond normally to insulin.

Many of these disorders produce distinctive anatomical features or abnormalities that are evident on a physical examination (Figure 19.11 and Table 19.6).

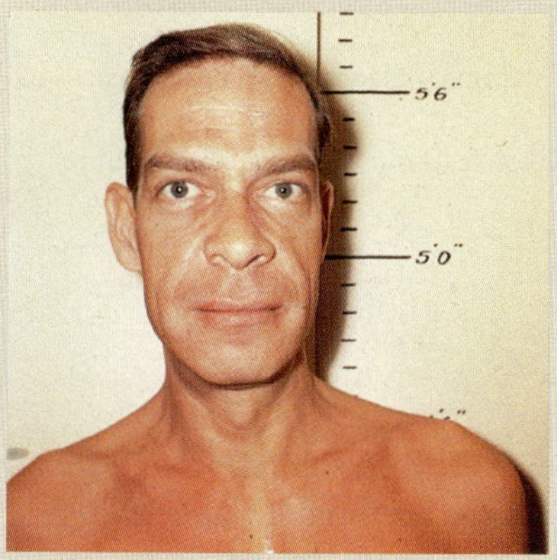

(a) *Acromegaly* results from the over-production of growth hormone after the epiphyseal plates have fused. Bone shapes change and cartilaginous areas of the skeleton enlarge. Note the broad facial features and the enlarged lower jaw.

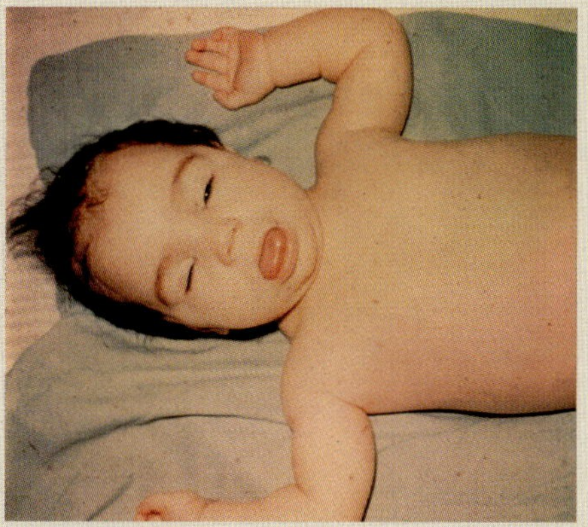

(b) *Cretinism* results from thyroid hormone insufficiency in infancy.

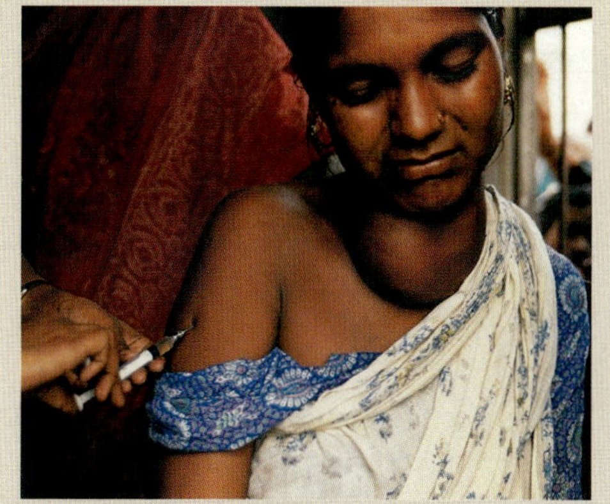

(c) An enlarged thyroid gland, or *goiter*, is usually associated with thyroid hyposecretion due to nutritional iodine insufficiency.

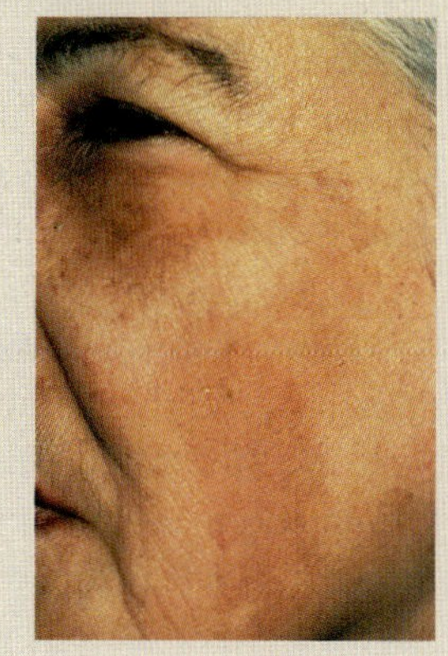

(d) *Addison's disease* is caused by hyposecretion of corticosteroids, especially glucocorticoids. Pigment changes result from stimulation of melanocytes by ACTH, which is structurally similar to MSH.

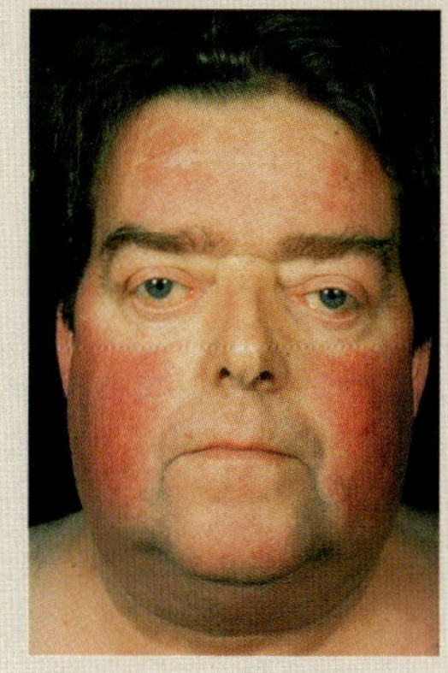

(e) *Cushing's disease* is caused by hypersecretion of glucocorticoids. Lipid reserves are mobilized, and adipose tissue accumulates in the cheeks and at the base of the neck.

Figure 19.11 Endocrine Abnormalities
Representative examples of anatomical features characteristic of specific endocrine disorders.

Clinical Note *(continued)*

TABLE 19.6 Clinical Implications of Endocrine Malfunctions

Hormone	Underproduction Syndrome	Principal Symptoms	Overproduction Syndrome	Principal Symptoms
Growth hormone (GH)	Pituitary growth failure (children)	Retarded growth, abnormal fat distribution, low blood glucose hours after a meal	Giantism (children), acromegaly (adults)	Excessive growth in stature of a child or in face and hands in an adult
Antidiuretic hormone (ADH)	Diabetes insipidus	Polyuria	SIADH (syndrome of inappropriate ADH secretion)	Increased body water content and hyponatremia
Thyroxine (T_3, T_4)	Myxedema, cretinism	Low metabolic rate, body temperature; impaired physical and mental development	Graves' disease	High metabolic rate, body temperature; tachycardia; weight loss
Parathyroid hormone (PTH)	Hypoparathyroidism	Muscular weakness, neurological problems, tetany due to low blood calcium concentrations	Hyperparathyroidism	Neurological, mental, muscular problems due to high blood calcium concentrations; weak and brittle bones
Insulin	Diabetes mellitus	High blood glucose, impaired glucose utilization, dependence on lipids for energy, glucosuria, ketosis	Excess insulin production or administration	Low blood glucose levels, possibly causing coma
Mineralocorticoids (MC)	Hypoaldosteronism	Polyuria, low blood volume, high blood potassium concentrations	Aldosteronism	Increased body weight due to water retention, low blood potassium concentrations
Glucocorticoids (GC)	Addison's disease	Inability to tolerate stress, mobilize energy reserves, maintain normal blood glucose concentrations	Cushing's disease	Excessive breakdown of tissue proteins and lipid reserves, impaired glucose metabolism
Epinephrine (E), norepinephrine (NE)	None identified		Pheochromocytoma	High metabolic rate, body temperature, and heart rate; elevated blood glucose levels; other symptoms comparable to those of excessive autonomic stimulation
Estrogens (female)	Hypogonadism	Sterility, lack of secondary sexual characteristics	Androgenital syndrome	Overproduction of androgens by zona reticularis of suprarenal cortex leads to masculinization
			Precocious puberty	Early production of developing follicles and estrogen secretion
	Menopause	Cessation of ovulation		
Androgens (male)	Hypogonadism, eunuchoidism	Sterility, lack of secondary sexual characteristics	Gynecomastia	Abnormal production of estrogens, sometimes due to suprarenal or intestinal cell tumors, leads to breast enlargement
			Precocious puberty	Early production of androgens, leading to premature physical development and behavioral changes

Hormones and Aging

The endocrine system shows relatively few functional changes with advancing age. The most dramatic exceptions are (1) the changes in reproduction hormone levels at puberty and (2) the decline in the concentration of reproductive hormones at menopause in women. It is interesting to note that age-related changes in other tissues affect their abilities to respond to hormonal stimulation. As a result, most tissues may become less responsive to circulating hormones, even though hormone concentrations remain normal.

CONCEPT CHECK

1. Where are the islets of Langerhans located? Name the hormones produced here.
2. What is the function of inhibin, and where is it produced?
3. Which hormone(s) of the endocrine system show the most dramatic decline in concentration as a result of aging?

See blue "Answers" tab at back of book.

Clinical Case

THE ENDOCRINE SYSTEM

WHY CAN'T I KEEP UP ANYMORE?

Joan is a 35-year-old college professor. She is a regular runner, averaging 35–40 miles per week. Joan has always been interested in running, and she continued to improve throughout high school and college. Her running career peaked when Joan earned cross-country all-American honors during her third and fourth years of intercollegiate running at the University of Wisconsin–Madison. Since joining the faculty at her college five years ago, Joan has enjoyed running during the week and on weekends with several of the male faculty members. She has always taken pride in the fact that she can, and does, run much faster than her male counterparts. For the past six months, however, Joan has noticed that it has become increasingly difficult to sustain her normal running tempo and pace, even on runs as short as 2–3 miles. This, combined with frequent muscle cramps, joint pains, cold-like symptoms, and chronic fatigue has forced her to think of herself as an "old runner" and someone who can't keep up with her normal running partners any more. Joan finally decides to make an appointment with her family physician when she is turned down as a blood donor due to anemia and elevated total cholesterol and triglyceride levels.

Initial Examination

Joan is examined by her family physician. The physical examination yields the following information:

- cold symptoms and a hoarse voice that have persisted for 2–3 weeks
- frequent problems with constipation
- yellow coloration to the skin, but no scleral involvement
- cool, dry, rough, and scaly skin
- presence of a puffy face and periorbital edema
- thickened and brittle nails
- slight, diffuse hair loss involving the scalp and the lateral third of the eyebrows
- blood pressure 110/80 mm Hg
- diminished deep tendon reflexes with prolonged muscle relaxation as observed by the Achilles tendon reflex
- slightly enlarged thyroid gland that is rubbery to palpation without any tenderness

Joan's physician orders the following laboratory tests:

- complete blood count (CBC)
- lipid profile
- urine test
- TSH levels
- free T_4 levels

Follow-up Examination

Joan and her physician meet the next week to discuss the results of her lab tests. The test results demonstrate the following:

- CBC is consistent with iron deficiency anemia.
- Lipid profile confirms high total cholesterol, high low-density lipoprotein, and high triglyceride levels.
- Plasma TSH levels are 20 mU/L.
- Free T_4 levels are 0.6 ng/dl.

CLINICAL CASE TERMS

anemia: Any condition in which the number of red blood cells or the concentration of hemoglobin is clinically reduced.

autoimmune disease: A condition in which an individual's lymphoid system produces cells and/or antibodies against the individual's own tissues.

cholesterol: The most abundant steroid in animal tissues, especially in bile, and present in food, especially food rich in animal fat.

complete blood count: Count of all the red and white blood cells and platelets found within a specific amount of blood.

deep tendon reflexes *(myotatic reflex)*: A contraction of muscles in response to a stretching force resulting from stimulation of proprioceptors.

lipid profile: A lab test that examines the concentrations and chemical characteristics of the lipids suspended within the blood of an individual.

periorbital edema: An accumulation of an excessive amount of watery fluid in the interstitial spaces of the skin surrounding the eyes.

sclera: A portion of the fibrous layer forming the outer layer of the eyeball; the white of the eye.

triglyceride: Fatty acid linked to glycerol; the most important form of lipid in the body. Also known as triacylglycerol.

Clinical Case *continued*

Points to Consider

Every system of the body, at one time or another, plays an important role in presenting signs or symptoms, thereby enabling a physician to piece together the various clues that will, ideally, lead to a correct diagnosis of the patient. Both the patient's presenting symptoms and the physician's analysis and interpretation of the symptoms contribute to the detective work.

To consider the meaning of the information presented in the case above, you need to review the anatomical material covered in Chapter 19 on the Endocrine System. The questions below will guide you in your review. Think about and answer each one, referring back to Chapter 19 if you need help.

1. At first glance, all of Joan's symptoms seem to be random and unrelated. What do all of these symptoms have in common?
2. Why did Joan's symptoms develop slowly over such a long period of time?
3. Why would Joan's lipid profile confirm high total cholesterol, high low-density lipoprotein, and high triglyceride levels?

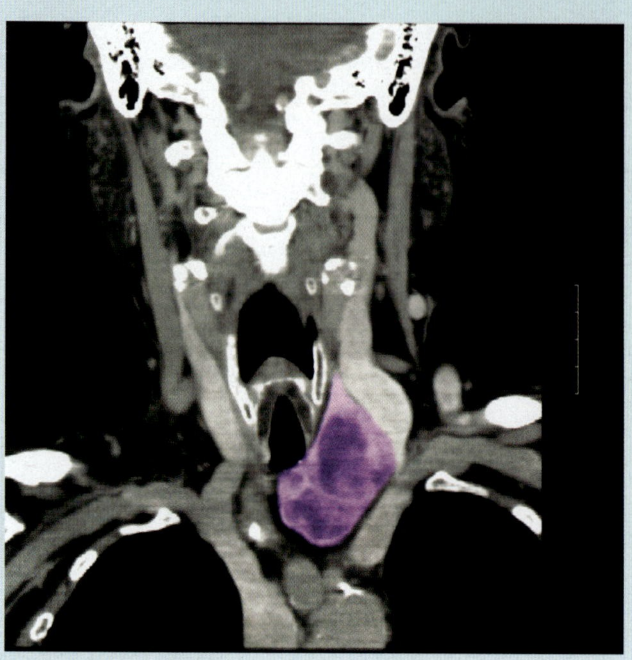

Figure 19.12 **Joan's MRI**

Analysis and Interpretation

The information below answers the questions raised in the "Points to Consider" section. To review the material, refer to the pages referenced below.

1. Many of the hormones secreted by the endocrine system have widespread metabolic effects. All of Joan's symptoms are related to her overall cellular metabolic level and rate of oxygen consumption (pp. 513–515).
2. The follicular cavities within the follicles of the thyroid gland store thyroxine (T_4) and triiodothyronine (T_3) (p. 513). The release of these hormones will slowly decrease as Joan's condition worsens—hence the slow development of her symptoms.
3. Joan's lipid profile, high total cholesterol, high low-density lipoprotein, and high triglyceride levels are the result of a decreased metabolic rate and the decreased absorption of lipids by peripheral tissues. Many of the hormones secreted by the endocrine system affect various aspects of the body's metabolism (pp. 518–521).

Diagnosis

After further testing for anti-thyroid antibodies and an MRI (**Figure 19.12**), Joan is diagnosed with an autoimmune disease: **Hashimoto thyroiditis**. This disease is characterized by the slow destruction of the thyroid cells by various cell- and antibody-mediated immune processes. The result of this autoimmune disease is inadequate thyroid hormone synthesis and release. However, the symptoms of this disease develop slowly over time due to the "leakage" of previously formed thyroxine and triiodothyronine from the thyroid follicles slowly being damaged by the autoimmune disease.

Hashimoto thryoiditis is the most common cause of hypothyroidism in residents of the United States over 6 years of age. World-wide, the most common cause of hypothyroidism is iodine deficiency. However, Hashimoto thyroiditis is the most common cause of spontaneous hypothyroidism worldwide in areas with adequate dietary iodine intake.

Joan's physician used her knowledge of the individual endocrine organs and their functions to predict the symptoms of specific endocrine disorders. For example, Joan's symptoms, as unrelated as they might have appeared initially, indicated to the physician that Joan's metabolism was not normal. Thyroid hormones increase basal metabolic rate, body heat production, perspiration, and heart rate. An elevated metabolic rate, increased body temperature, weight loss, nervousness, excessive perspiration, and an increased or irregular heartbeat are symptoms of hyperthyroidism. Conversely, a low metabolic rate, decreased body temperature, weight gain, lethargy, dry skin, and a reduced heart rate typically accompany hypothyroidism. However, many signs and symptoms related to endocrine disorders are less definitive. For example, polyuria, or increased urine production, can result from hyposecretion of ADH (diabetes insipidus) or the hyperglysuria caused by diabetes mellitus; a symptom such as hypertension (high blood pressure) can be caused by a variety of cardiovascular or endocrine problems. In these instances, many diagnostic decisions are based on blood and other tests, which can confirm the presence of an endocrine disorder by detecting abnormal levels of circulating hormones or metabolic products resulting from hormone action. Follow-up tests can determine whether the primary cause of the problem lies with the endocrine gland, the regulatory mechanism(s), or the target tissues. Often, a pattern of several different test results leads to the diagnosis. Table 19.6 provides a clinical overview of endocrine malfunctions, and Table 19.7 outlines some anatomical tests used in the diagnosis of endocrine disorders such as Joan's. ■

Clinical Case *continued*

TABLE 19.7 Representative Diagnostic Procedures for Disorders of the Endocrine System

Diagnostic Procedure	Method and Result	Representative Uses
Thyroid Gland		
Thyroid scanning	A dose of radionucleotide accumulates in the thyroid, giving off detectable radiation to create an image of the thyroid	Determines size, shape, and abnormalities of the thyroid gland; detects presence of nodules and/or tumors; may detect hyperactive or hypoactive areas; may determine cause of a mass in the neck.
Ultrasound examination of thyroid	Sound waves reflected off internal structures are used to generate a computer image	Detects thyroid cysts or tumors, enlarged lymph nodes, or abnormalities in the shape or size of the thyroid gland
Radioactive iodine uptake (RAIU) test	Radioactive iodine is ingested and trapped by the thyroid; detector determines the amount of radioiodine taken up over a period of time	Determines hyperactivity or hypoactivity of the thyroid gland; frequently done at the same time as thyroid scan
Pituitary Gland		
Wrist and hand x-ray film	Standard x-rays of epiphyseal cartilages for estimation of "bone age," based on the time of closure of epiphyseal cartilages	Compares a child's bone age and chronological age; a bone age greater than two years behind the chronological age suggests possible growth hormone deficiency with hypopituitarism or pituitary growth failure
X-ray study of sella turcica	Standard x-ray of the sella turcica, which houses the pituitary gland	Determines (with increasing accuracy and cost) the size of the pituitary gland; detects pituitary tumors
CT scan of pituitary gland	Standard cross-sectional CT; contrast media may be used	
MRI of pituitary gland	Standard MRI	
Parathyroid Glands		
Ultrasound examination of parathyroid glands	Standard ultrasound	Determines structural abnormalities of the parathyroid gland, such as enlargement
Suprarenal Glands		
Ultrasound of suprarenal gland	Standard ultrasound	Determines abnormalities in suprarenal gland size or shape; may detect tumors
CT scan of suprarenal gland	Standard cross-sectional CT	Determines abnormalities in suprarenal gland size or shape; may detect tumor
Suprarenal angiography	Injection of radiopaque dye for examination of the vascular supply to the suprarenal gland	Detects tumors and hyperplasia

CLINICAL TERMS

diabetes insipidus: A disorder that develops when the posterior lobe of the pituitary gland no longer releases adequate amounts of ADH.

diabetes mellitus (MEL-i-tus): A disorder characterized by glucose concentrations high enough to overwhelm the kidneys' reabsorption capabilities.

exophthalmos (ek-sof-THAL-mos): Protrusion of the eyes, a symptom of hyperthyroidism.

goiter: A diffuse enlargement of the thyroid gland.

insulin-dependent diabetes mellitus (IDDM) (also known as **type 1 diabetes** or **juvenile-onset diabetes**): A type of diabetes mellitus; the primary cause is inadequate insulin production by the beta cells of the pancreatic islets.

ketoacidosis: A condition in which large numbers of ketone bodies in the blood lead to a dangerously low blood pH.

myxedema (mik-se-DĒ-ma): Symptoms of severe hypothyroidism, which include subcutaneous swelling, dry skin, hair loss, low body temperature, muscular weakness, and slowed reflexes.

non-insulin-dependent diabetes mellitus (NIDDM) (also known as **type 2 diabetes** or **maturity-onset diabetes**): A type of diabetes mellitus in which insulin levels are normal or elevated but peripheral tissues no longer respond normally.

thyrotoxic crisis: A period when a subject with acute hyperthyroidism experiences an extremely high fever, rapid heart rate, and the malfunctioning of a variety of physiological systems.

STUDY OUTLINE

Introduction 508

1. The nervous and endocrine systems work together in a complementary way to monitor and adjust physiological activities for the regulation of homeostasis.
2. In general, the nervous system performs short-term "crisis management," while the endocrine system regulates longer-term, ongoing metabolic processes. *Endocrine cells* release chemicals called **hormones** that alter the metabolic activities of many different tissues and organs simultaneously.

An Overview of the Endocrine System 508

1. The endocrine system consists of all endocrine cells and tissues. They release their secretory products into interstitial fluids. *(see Figure 19.1)*
2. Hormones can be divided into four groups based on chemical structure: *amino acid derivatives, peptide hormones, steroids,* and *eicosanoids.*
3. Cellular activities and metabolic reactions are controlled by enzymes. Hormones exert their effects by modifying the activities of **target cells** (cells that are sensitive to that particular hormone).
4. Negative feedback control usually regulates endocrine activity. In this control, (1) the endocrine cell releases its hormone in response to changes in the composition of the extracellular fluid, (2) the target cell is stimulated, and (3) the target cell restores homeostasis. This response eliminates the source of stimulation of the endocrine cell.
5. Endocrine activity can be controlled by (1) neural activity, (2) positive feedback (rare), or (3) complex negative feedback mechanisms.

The Hypothalamus and Endocrine Regulation 509

6. The hypothalamus regulates endocrine and neural activities. It (1) controls the output of the suprarenal (suprarenal) medulla, an endocrine component of the sympathetic division of the ANS; (2) produces two hormones of its own (ADH and oxytocin), which are released from the neurohypophysis (posterior lobe); and (3) controls the activity of the adenohypophysis (anterior lobe) through the production of **regulatory hormones** (**releasing hormones**, or **RH**, and **inhibiting hormones**, or **IH**). *(see Figure 19.2)*

The Pituitary Gland 510

1. The **pituitary gland (hypophysis)** releases nine important peptide hormones. Two are synthesized in the hypothalamus and released at the neurohypophysis and seven are synthesized in the adenohypophysis. *(see Figures 19.3/19.4* and *Table 19.1)*

The Neurohypophysis 510

2. The **neurohypophysis (posterior lobe)** contains the axons of some hypothalamic neurons. Neurons within the **supraoptic** and **paraventricular nuclei** manufacture **antidiuretic hormone (ADH)** and **oxytocin**, respectively. ADH decreases the amount of water lost at the kidneys. It is released in response to a rise in the concentration of electrolytes in the blood or a fall in blood volume. In women, oxytocin stimulates smooth muscle cells in the uterus and contractile cells in the mammary glands. It is released in response to stretched uterine muscles and/or suckling of an infant. In men, it stimulates prostatic smooth muscle contractions. *(see Figures 19.3 to 19.5* and *Table 19.1)*

The Adenohypophysis 510

3. The **adenohypophysis (anterior lobe)** can be subdivided into the large **pars distalis**, the slender **pars intermedia**, and the **pars tuberalis**. The entire adenohypophysis is highly vascularized.
4. In the floor of the hypothalamus in the tuberal area, neurons release regulatory factors into the surrounding interstitial fluids. Endocrine cells in the adenohypophysis are controlled by releasing factors, inhibiting factors (hormones), or some combination of the two. These secretions enter the circulation through **fenestrated** capillaries that contain open spaces between their epithelial cells. Blood vessels, called **portal vessels**, form an unusual vascular arrangement that connects the hypothalamus and anterior lobe of the pituitary gland. This complex is the **hypophyseal portal system**. It ensures that all of the blood entering the portal vessels will reach the intended target cells before returning to the general circulation. *(see Figures 19.3/19.5)*
5. Important hormones released by the pars distalis include (1) **thyroid-stimulating hormone (TSH)**, which triggers the release of thyroid hormones; (2) **adrenocorticotropic hormone (ACTH)**, which stimulates the release of **glucocorticoids** by the suprarenal gland; (3) **follicle-stimulating hormone (FSH)**, which stimulates **estrogen** secretion (*estradiol*) and egg development in women and sperm production in men; (4) **luteinizing hormone (LH)**, which causes ovulation and production of **progestins** (*progesterone*) in women and **androgens** (*testosterone*) in men (together, FSH and LH are called **gonadotropins**); (5) **prolactin (PRL)**, which stimulates the development of the mammary glands and the production of milk; and (6) **growth hormone (GH**, or **somatotropin)**, which stimulates cells' growth and replication. *(see Figures 19.3/19.4)*
6. **Melanocyte-stimulating hormone (MSH)**, released by the pars intermedia, stimulates melanocytes to produce melanin. *(see Figure 19.4)*

The Thyroid Gland 513

1. The **thyroid gland** lies inferior to the **thyroid cartilage** of the larynx. It consists of two **lobes** connected by a narrow **isthmus**. *(see Figure 19.6a)*

Thyroid Follicles and Thyroid Hormones 513

2. The thyroid gland contains numerous **thyroid follicles**. Cells of the follicles manufacture **thyroglobulin** and store it within the **colloid** (a viscous fluid containing suspended proteins) in the **follicle cavity**. The cells also transport iodine from the extracellular fluids into the cavity, where it complexes with tyrosine residues of the thyroglobulin molecules to form thyroid hormones. *(see Figure 19.6b,c and Table 19.2)*
3. When stimulated by TSH, the follicular cells reabsorb the thyroglobulin, break down the protein, and release the thyroid hormones, **thyroxine** (TX or T_4) and **triiodothyronine** (T_3) into the circulation. *(see Figure 19.7)*

The C Thyrocytes of the Thyroid Gland 515

4. The **C thyrocytes** of the thyroid follicles produce **calcitonin (CT)**, which helps lower calcium ion concentrations in body fluids by inhibiting osteoclast activities and stimulating calcium ion excretion at the kidneys. *(see Figure 19.6c)*
5. Actions of calcitonin are opposed by those of the *parathyroid hormone* produced by the parathyroid glands. *(see Table 19.2)*

The Parathyroid Glands 515

1. Four **parathyroid glands** are embedded in the posterior surface of the thyroid gland. The **parathyroid (chief) cells** of the parathyroid produce **parathyroid hormone (PTH)** in response to lower-than-normal concentrations of calcium ions. Oxyphil cells of the parathyroid have no known function. *(see Figure 19.8 and Table 19.2)*
2. PTH (1) stimulates osteoclast activity, (2) stimulates osteoblast activity to a lesser degree, (3) reduces calcium loss in the urine, and (4) promotes calcium absorption in the intestine (by stimulating calcitriol production). *(see Table 19.2)*
3. The parathyroid glands and the C thyrocytes of the thyroid gland maintain calcium ion levels within relatively narrow limits. *(see Figure 19.8c and Table 19.2)*

The Thymus 515

1. The **thymus**, embedded in a connective tissue mass in the thoracic cavity, produces several hormones that stimulate the development and maintenance of normal immunological defenses. *(see Figure 19.1)*

2. **Thymosins** produced by the thymus promote the development and maturation of lymphocytes.

The Suprarenal Glands 516

1. A single **suprarenal** (*suprarenal*) **gland** rests on the superior border of each kidney. Each suprarenal gland is surrounded by a fibrous **capsule** and is subdivided into a superficial **cortex** and an inner **medulla**. *(see Figure 19.9)*

The Cortex of the Suprarenal Gland 516

2. The cortex of the suprarenal gland manufactures steroid hormones called **adrenocortical steroids (corticosteroids)**. The cortex can be subdivided into three separate areas: (1) The outer **zona glomerulosa** releases **mineralocorticoids (MC)**, principally **aldosterone**, which restrict sodium and water losses at the kidneys, sweat glands, digestive tract, and salivary glands. The zona glomerulosa responds to the presence of the hormone angiotensin II, which appears after the enzyme renin has been secreted by kidney cells exposed to a decline in blood volume and/or blood pressure. (2) The middle **zona fasciculata** produces **glucocorticoids (GC)**, notably **cortisol** and **corticosterone**. All of these hormones accelerate the rates of both glucose synthesis and glycogen formation, especially in liver cells. (3) The inner **zona reticularis** produces small amounts of sex hormones called androgens. The significance of the small amounts of androgens produced by the suprarenal glands remains uncertain. *(see Figure 19.9c and Table 19.3)*

The Medulla of the Suprarenal Gland 518

3. Each medulla of the suprarenal gland contains clusters of **chromaffin cells**, which resemble sympathetic ganglia neurons. They secrete either epinephrine (75–80 percent) or norepinephrine (20–25 percent). These catecholamines trigger cellular energy utilization and the mobilization of energy reserves (see Chapter 17). *(see Figure 19.9b,c* and *Table 19.3)*

Endocrine Functions of the Kidneys and Heart 518

1. Endocrine cells in both the kidneys and heart produce hormones that are important for the regulation of blood pressure and blood volume, blood oxygen levels, and calcium and phosphate ion absorption.
2. The kidney produces the enzyme *renin* and the peptide hormone *erythropoietin* when blood pressure or blood oxygen levels in the kidneys decline, and it secretes the steroid hormone *calcitriol* when parathyroid hormone is present. **Renin** catalyzes the conversion of circulating **angiotensinogen** to **angiotensin I**. In lung capillaries, it is converted to **angiotensin II**, the hormone that stimulates the production of aldosterone in the suprarenal cortex. **Erythropoietin (EPO)** stimulates red blood cell production by the bone marrow. **Calcitriol** stimulates the absorption of both calcium and phosphate in the digestive tract.
3. Specialized muscle cells of the heart produce **atrial natriuretic peptide (ANP)** and **brain natriuretic peptide (BNP)** when blood pressure or blood volume becomes excessive. These hormones stimulate water and sodium ion loss at the kidneys, eventually reducing blood volume.

The Pancreas and Other Endocrine Tissues of the Digestive System 518

1. The lining of the digestive tract, the liver, and the pancreas produce exocrine secretions that are essential to the normal breakdown and absorption of food.

The Pancreas 518

2. The **pancreas** is a nodular organ occupying a space between the stomach and small intestine. It contains both exocrine and endocrine cells. The **exocrine pancreas** secretes an enzyme-rich fluid into the lumen of the digestive tract. Cells of the **endocrine pancreas** form clusters called **pancreatic islets** (*islets of Langerhans*). Each islet contains four cell types: **Alpha cells** produce **glucagon** to raise blood glucose levels; **beta cells** secrete **insulin** to lower blood glucose levels; **delta cells** secrete **somatostatin (growth-hormone–inhibiting hormone)** to inhibit the production and secretion of glucagon and insulin; and **F cells** secrete **pancreatic polypeptide (PP)** to inhibit gallbladder contractions and regulate the production of some pancreatic enzymes. PP may also help control the rate of nutrient absorption by the GI tract. *(see Figure 19.10 and Table 19.4)*
3. Insulin lowers blood glucose by increasing the rate of glucose uptake and utilization by most body cells; glucagon raises blood glucose levels by increasing the rates of glycogen breakdown and glucose synthesis in the liver. Somatostatin reduces the rates of hormone secretion by alpha and beta cells and slows food absorption and enzyme secretion in the digestive tract. *(see Table 19.4)*

Endocrine Tissues of the Reproductive System 520

Testes 520

1. The **interstitial cells** of the male testes produce androgens. **Testosterone** is the most important androgen. It promotes the production of functional sperm, maintains reproductive-tract secretory glands, influences secondary sexual characteristics, and stimulates muscle growth. *(see Table 19.5)*
2. The hormone **inhibin**, produced by **nurse (sustentacular) cells** in the testes, interacts with FSH from the anterior lobe of the pituitary gland to maintain sperm production at normal levels.

Ovaries 521

3. Oocytes develop in **follicles** in the female ovary; follicle cells surrounding the oocytes produce estrogens, especially **estradiol**. Estrogens support the maturation of the oocytes and stimulate the growth of the uterine lining. Active follicles secrete inhibin, which suppresses FSH release by negative feedback. *(see Table 19.5)*
4. After ovulation, the follicle cells remaining within the ovary reorganize into a **corpus luteum**, which produces a mixture of estrogens and progestins, especially **progesterone**. Progesterone facilitates the movement of a fertilized egg through the uterine tube to the uterus and stimulates the preparation of the uterus for implantation. *(see Table 19.5)*

The Pineal Gland 521

1. The **pineal gland** (*epiphysis cerebri*) contains secretory cells called **pinealocytes**, which synthesize **melatonin**. Melatonin slows the maturation of sperm, eggs, and reproductive organs by inhibiting the production of FSH- and LH-releasing factors from the hypothalamus. Additionally, melatonin may establish circadian rhythms. *(see Figure 19.1)*

Hormones and Aging 523

1. The endocrine system shows relatively few functional changes with advancing age. The most dramatic endocrine changes are the rise in reproductive hormone levels at puberty and the decline in reproductive hormone levels at menopause.

CHAPTER REVIEW

For answers to the Concept Check and Chapter Review questions, go to the blue "Answers" tab at the back of the book.

Level 1 Reviewing Facts and Terms

Match each numbered item with the most closely related lettered item. Use letters for answers in the spaces provided.

Column A	Column B
___ 1. target cells	a. unknown function
___ 2. hypothalamus	b. stimulates milk production
___ 3. ADH	c. regulated by hormones
___ 4. prolactin	d. pineal gland
___ 5. FSH	e. norepinephrine release
___ 6. colloid	f. decreases water loss
___ 7. oxyphil	g. lymphocyte maturation
___ 8. thymosin	h. stimulates estrogen secretion
___ 9. chromaffin cells	i. produces releasing hormone
___ 10. melatonin	j. viscous fluid with stored hormones

11. The hormone that targets the thyroid gland and triggers the release of thyroid hormone is
    (a) follicle-stimulating hormone (FSH)
    (b) thyroid-stimulating hormone (TSH)
    (c) adrenocorticotropic hormone (ACTH)
    (d) luteinizing hormone (LH)

12. When a catecholamine or peptide hormone binds to receptors on the surface of a cell,
    (a) the hormone receptor complex moves into the cytoplasm
    (b) the plasmalemma becomes depolarized
    (c) a second messenger appears in the cytoplasm
    (d) the hormone is transported to the nucleus to alter DNA activity

13. Blood vessels that supply or drain the thyroid gland include which of the following?
    (a) superior thyroid artery
    (b) inferior thyroid artery
    (c) superior, inferior, and middle thyroid veins
    (d) all of the above are correct

14. How does aging affect the function of the endocrine system?
    (a) it is relatively much less affected than most other systems
    (b) hormone production increases to offset diminished response by receptors
    (c) endocrine function of the reproductive system is the most affected by increasing age
    (d) hormone production by the thyroid gland suffers the greatest decline with age

15. Endocrine organs can be controlled by
    (a) hormones from other endocrine glands
    (b) direct neural stimulation
    (c) changes in the composition of extracellular fluid
    (d) all of the above are correct

16. Reduced fluid losses in the urine due to retention of sodium ions and water are a result of the action of
    (a) antidiuretic hormone
    (b) calcitonin
    (c) aldosterone
    (d) cortisone

17. When blood glucose levels fall,
    (a) insulin is released
    (b) glucagon is released
    (c) peripheral cells quit taking up glucose
    (d) aldosterone is released to stimulate these cells

18. Hormones released by the kidneys include
    (a) calcitriol and erythropoietin
    (b) ADH and aldosterone
    (c) epinephrine and norepinephrine
    (d) cortisol and cortisone norepinephrine

19. The element required for normal thyroid function is
    (a) magnesium (b) potassium
    (c) iodine (d) calcium

20. A structure known as the corpus luteum secretes
    (a) testosterone (b) progesterone
    (c) aldosterone (d) cortisone

Level 2 Reviewing Concepts

1. Exophthalmos is a major symptom of
   (a) Cushing's disease (b) hyperthyroidism
   (c) hyperpituitarism (d) Graves' disease

2. If a person has too few or defective lymphocytes, which gland might be at fault?
   (a) thyroid (b) thymus
   (c) pituitary (d) pineal

3. Reductions in cardiac activity, blood pressure, ability to process glycogen, blood glucose level, and release of lipids by adipose tissues are collectively symptoms of a defective
   (a) pituitary gland (b) suprarenal cortex
   (c) pancreas (d) suprarenal medulla

4. Discuss the functional differences between the endocrine and the nervous systems.

5. Hormones can be divided into four groups on the basis of chemical structure. What are these four groups?

6. Describe the primary targets and effects of testosterone.

7. What effects do thyroid hormones have on body tissues?

8. Why is normal parathyroid function essential in maintaining normal calcium ion levels?

9. Describe the role of melatonin in regulating reproductive function.

10. What is the significance of the capillary network within the hypophysis?

Level 3 Critical Thinking

1. How could a pituitary tumor result in the production of excess amounts of growth hormone?

2. Endocrine abnormalities rarely, if ever, result in only a single change in a person's metabolism. What two endocrine abnormalities would result in excessive thirst *and* excessive urination?

3. Hypothyroidism (insufficient thyroid hormone production by the thyroid gland) can be caused by a problem at the level of the hypothalamus and pituitary gland or at the level of the thyroid. Explain how this is medically possible.

4. How do kidney and heart hormones regulate blood pressure and volume?

20
The Cardiovascular System
Blood

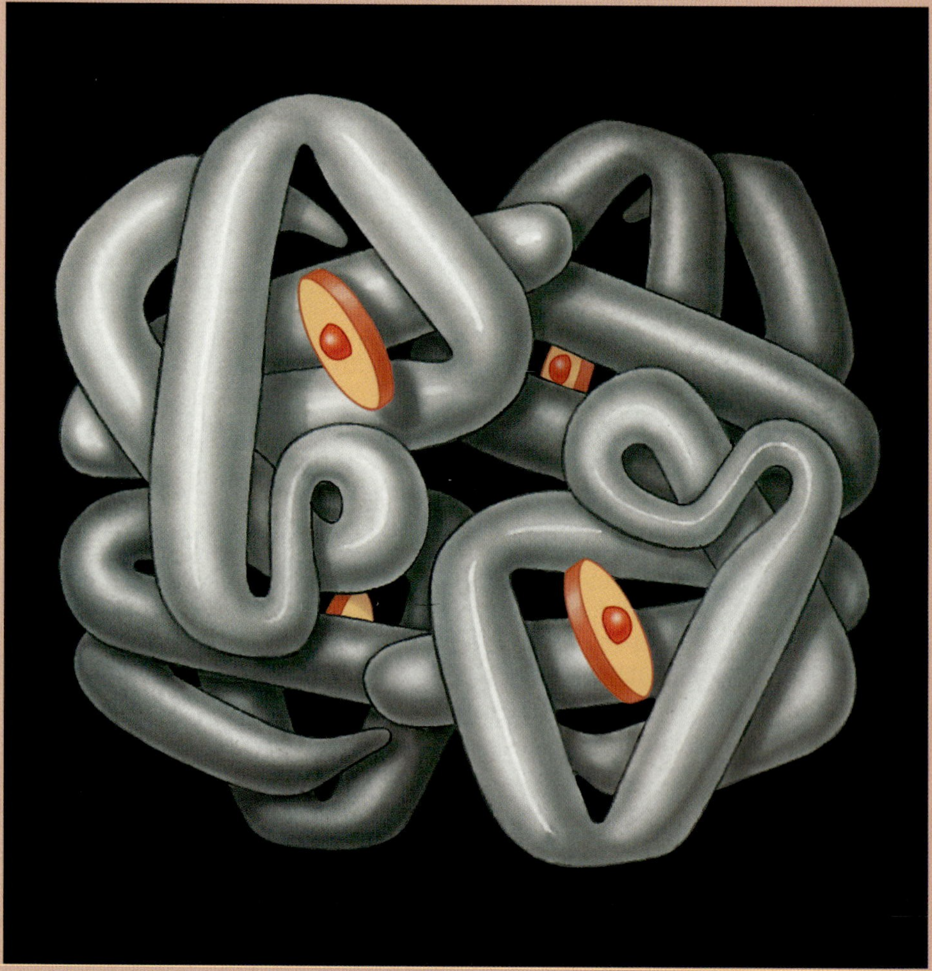

CHAPTER OBJECTIVES

1. List and describe the functions of the blood.
2. Discuss the composition of blood and the physical characteristics of plasma.
3. List the structural characteristics and functions of red blood cells.
4. Explain what determines a person's blood type and why blood types are important.
5. Categorize the various white blood cells on the basis of their structures and functions and describe how white blood cells fight infection.
6. Discuss the function of platelets.
7. Discuss the differentiation and life cycles of blood cells.
8. Identify the locations where the components of blood are produced and discuss the factors that regulate their production.

The living body is in constant chemical communication with its external environment. Nutrients are absorbed across the lining of the digestive tract, gases diffuse across the delicate epithelium of the lungs, and wastes are excreted in the feces and urine as well as in saliva, bile, sweat, and other exocrine secretions. These chemical exchanges occur at specialized sites or organs because all parts of the body are linked by the *cardiovascular system (CVS)*. The cardiovascular system can be compared to the cooling system of a car. The basic components include a circulating fluid (blood), a pump (the heart), and an assortment of conducting pipes (a network of blood vessels). The three chapters on the cardiovascular system examine those components individually: Chapter 20 discusses the nature of the circulating blood, Chapter 21 considers the structure and function of the heart, and Chapter 22 examines the network of blood vessels and the integrated functioning of the cardiovascular system. You will then be ready for Chapter 23, which considers the *lymphoid system*, whose vessels and organs are structurally and functionally linked to the CVS.

Functions of the Blood [Table 20.1]

Blood is a specialized fluid connective tissue (∞ p. 68) that (1) distributes nutrients, oxygen, and hormones to each of the roughly 75 trillion cells in the human body; (2) carries metabolic wastes to the kidneys for excretion; and (3) transports specialized cells that defend peripheral tissues from infection and disease. Table 20.1 contains a detailed listing of the functions of the blood. The services performed by the blood are absolutely essential; any body cells or region completely deprived of circulation may die in a matter of minutes.

Composition of the Blood [Figure 20.1 and Table 20.2]

Blood is a fluid connective tissue normally confined to the circulatory system. It has a characteristic and unique composition (Figure 20.1 and Table 20.2). Blood consists of two components:

1. **Plasma** (PLAZ-mah), the liquid matrix of blood, has a density only slightly greater than that of water. It contains dissolved proteins, rather than the network of insoluble fibers found in loose connective tissues or cartilage, and numerous dissolved solutes.
2. **Formed elements** are blood cells and cell fragments that are suspended in the plasma. These elements are present in great abundance and are

Clinical Note

Transfusions In a transfusion, blood components are provided to an individual whose blood volume has been reduced or whose blood is deficient in some way. Transfusions of whole blood are most often used to restore blood volume after massive hemorrhaging has occurred. In an **exchange transfusion**, most of the blood volume of an individual is removed and simultaneously replaced with whole blood from another source. This may be necessary to treat acute drug poisoning or *hemolytic disease of the newborn* (p. 544).

The blood is obtained under sterile conditions from carefully screened donors. It is tested for infectious bacteria and viruses and discarded if pathogens are detected. Whole blood is treated to prevent clotting and stabilize the red blood cells, and refrigerated. Chilled whole blood remains usable for around 3.5 weeks. For longer storage the blood must be fractionated. The red blood cells are separated from the plasma, and if necessary they may be frozen after treatment with a special antifreeze solution. The plasma can then be stored chilled, frozen, or freeze-dried. This procedure permits long-term storage of rare blood types that might not otherwise be available for emergency use.

Fractionated blood has many uses. **Packed red blood cells (PRBCs)**, with most of the plasma removed, are preferred for cases of anemia, in which the volume of blood may be close to normal but its oxygen-carrying capabilities have been reduced. Plasma may be administered when massive fluid losses are occurring, such as after severe burns.

Some 6 million units (3 million liters) of blood are used each year in the United States alone, and the demand for blood or blood components often exceeds the supply. Moreover, there has been increasing concern over the danger that transfusion recipients will become infected with hepatitis viruses or HIV (the virus that causes AIDS) from contaminated blood. The result has been a number of changes in transfusion practices over recent years. In general, fewer units of blood are now administered. There has also been an increase in **autologous transfusion**, in which blood is removed from a patient (or potential patient), stored, and later transfused back into the original donor when needed, such as after a surgical procedure. Moreover, new technology permits the reuse of blood "lost" during surgery. The blood is collected and filtered; the platelets are removed, and the remainder of the blood is reinfused into the patient.

TABLE 20.1 Functions of the Blood

1. *Transport of dissolved gases*, bringing oxygen from the lungs to the tissues and carrying carbon dioxide from the tissues to the lungs.
2. *Distribution of nutrients* absorbed from the digestive tract or released from storage in adipose tissue or the liver.
3. *Transport of metabolic wastes* from peripheral tissues to sites of excretion, especially the kidneys.
4. *Delivery of enzymes and hormones* to specific target tissues.
5. *Stabilization of the pH and electrolyte composition of interstitial fluids* throughout the body. By absorbing, transporting, and releasing ions as it circulates, blood helps prevent regional variations in the ion concentrations of body tissues. An extensive array of buffers enables the bloodstream to deal with the acids generated by tissues, such as the lactic acid produced by skeletal muscles.
6. *Prevention of fluid losses* through damaged vessels or at other injury sites. The **clotting reaction** seals the breaks in the vessel walls, preventing changes in blood volume that could seriously affect blood pressure and cardiovascular function.
7. *Defense against toxins and pathogens*. Blood transports *white blood cells*, specialized cells that migrate into peripheral tissues to fight infections or remove debris, and delivers *antibodies*, special proteins that attack invading organisms or foreign compounds. The blood also collects toxins, such as those produced by infection, and delivers them to the liver and kidneys, where they can be inactivated or excreted.
8. *Stabilization of body temperature* by absorbing and redistributing heat. Active skeletal muscles and other tissues generate heat, and the bloodstream carries it away. When body temperature is too high, blood flow to the skin increases, as does the rate of heat loss across the skin surface. When body temperature is too low, warm blood is directed to the most temperature-sensitive organs. These changes in circulatory flow are controlled and coordinated by the *cardiovascular centers* in the medulla oblongata. ∞ p. 414

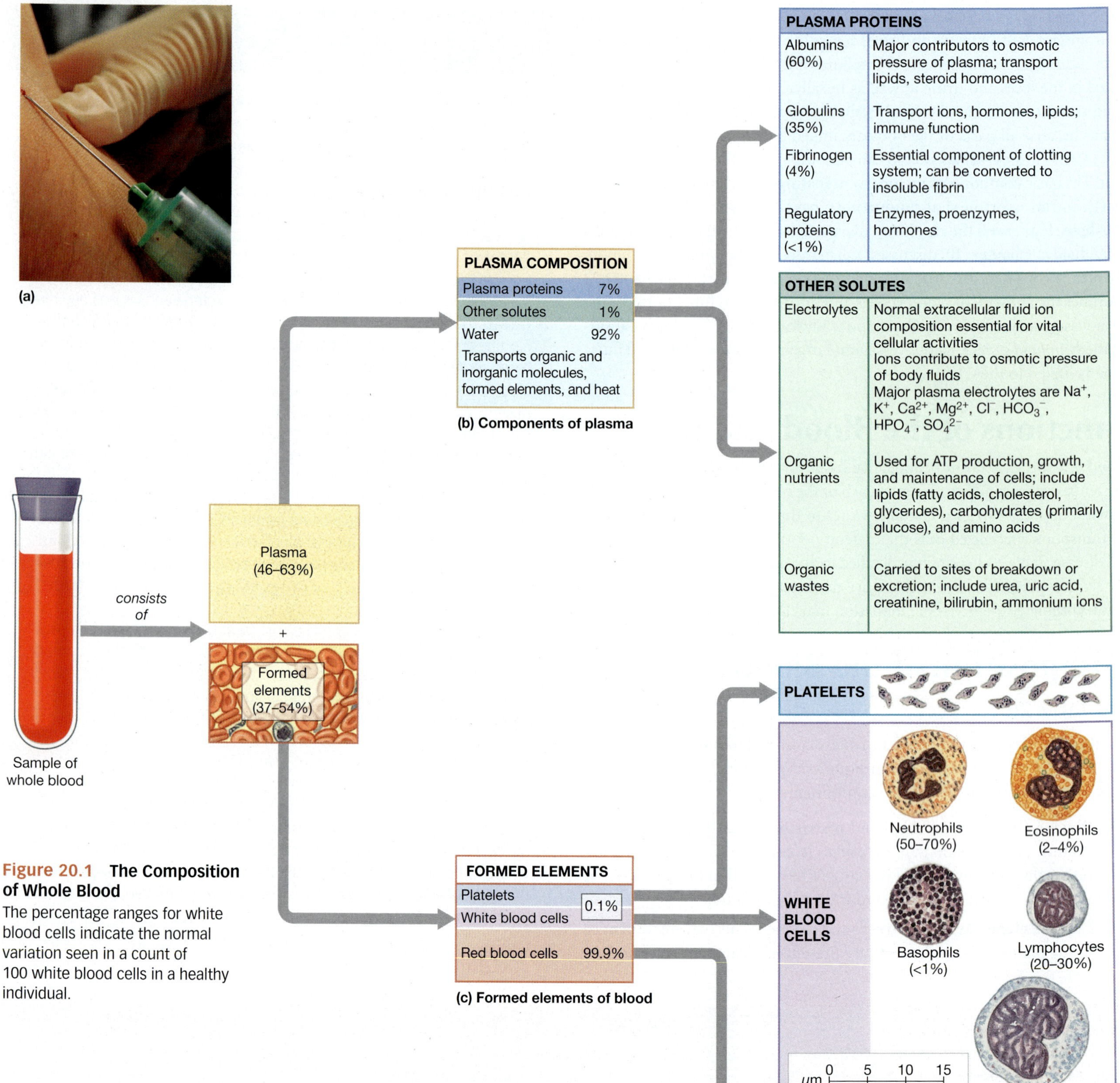

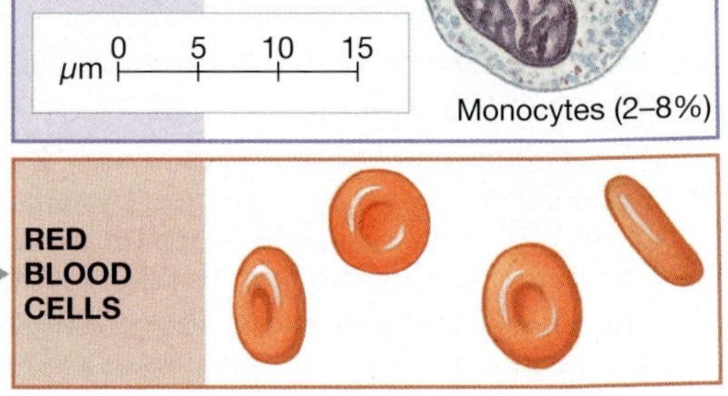

Figure 20.1 The Composition of Whole Blood The percentage ranges for white blood cells indicate the normal variation seen in a count of 100 white blood cells in a healthy individual.

highly specialized. **Red blood cells (RBCs)** transport oxygen and carbon dioxide. The less numerous **leukocytes**, or **white blood cells (WBCs)**, are components of the immune system. **Platelets** (PLĀT-lets) are small, membrane-enclosed packets of cytoplasm that contain enzymes and other factors essential for *blood clotting.*

Whole blood is a mixture of plasma and formed elements. Its components may be separated, or **fractionated**, for clinical purposes. Whole blood is sticky, cohesive, and resistant to flow, characteristics that determine the **viscosity** of a solution. Solutions are usually compared with pure water, which has a viscosity of 1.0. Plasma has a viscosity of 1.5, but the viscosity of whole blood is much greater (about 5.0) because of interactions between water molecules and the formed elements.

On average there are 5–6 liters of whole blood in the cardiovascular system of an adult man, and 4–5 liters in an adult woman. The blood has an alkaline pH (range of 7.35 to 7.45) and a temperature slightly higher than core body temperature (38°C vs. 37°C, or 100.4°F vs. 98.6°F). Clinicians use

TABLE 20.2 Composition of Whole Blood

Component	Significance
PLASMA	
Water	Dissolves and transports organic and inorganic molecules, distributes blood cells, and transfers heat
Electrolytes	Normal extracellular fluid ion composition essential for vital cellular activities
Nutrients	Used for energy production, growth, and maintenance of cells
Organic wastes	Carried to sites of breakdown or excretion
Proteins	
Albumins	Major contributor to osmotic concentration of plasma; transport some lipids
Globulins	Transport ions, hormones, lipids
Fibrinogen	Essential component of clotting system; can be converted to insoluble fibrin
FORMED ELEMENTS	
Red blood cells	Transport gases (oxygen and carbon dioxide)
White blood cells	Defend body against pathogens; remove toxins, wastes, and damaged cells
Platelets	Participate in clotting response

the terms **hypovolemic** (hī-pō-vō-LĒ-mik), **normovolemic** (nor-mō-vō-LĒ-mik), and **hypervolemic** (hī-per-vō-LĒ-mik) to refer to low, normal, or excessive blood volumes, respectively. Low or high blood volumes are potentially dangerous—for example, a hypervolemic condition can place a severe stress on the heart (for example, hypertension or "high blood pressure"), which must push the extra fluid around the circulatory system.

Plasma [Figure 20.1 and Table 20.2]

Plasma contributes approximately 55 percent of the volume of whole blood, and water accounts for 92 percent of the plasma volume. These are average values, and the actual concentrations vary depending on the region of the cardiovascular system or area of the body sampled and the ongoing activity within that particular region. Information concerning the composition of plasma is summarized in Figure 20.1 and Table 20.2.

Differences between Plasma and Interstitial Fluid

In many respects, plasma resembles interstitial fluid. For example, the ion concentrations in plasma are similar to those of interstitial fluid but very different from the ion concentrations in cytoplasm. The principal differences between plasma and interstitial fluid involve the concentrations of dissolved gases and proteins.

1. *Concentrations of dissolved oxygen and carbon dioxide:* The dissolved oxygen concentration in plasma is higher than that of interstitial fluid. As a result, oxygen diffuses out of the bloodstream and into peripheral tissues. The carbon dioxide concentration in interstitial fluid is much higher than that of plasma, so carbon dioxide diffuses out of the tissues and into the bloodstream.
2. *Concentration of dissolved proteins:* Plasma contains significant quantities of dissolved proteins, whereas interstitial fluid does not. The large size and globular shapes of most plasma proteins prevent them from crossing capillary walls, and they remain trapped within the cardiovascular system.

The Plasma Proteins [Figure 20.1/20.7]

Plasma proteins account for approximately 7 percent of the plasma composition (Figure 20.1). One hundred milliliters of human plasma normally contain 6–7.8 g of soluble proteins. There are three major classes of plasma proteins: *albumins* (al-BŪ-minz), *globulins* (GLOB-ū-linz), and *fibrinogen* (fī-BRIN-ō-jen).

1. **Albumins** constitute roughly 60 percent of the plasma proteins. As the most abundant proteins, they are major contributors to the osmotic pressure of the plasma. They are also important in the transport of fatty acids, steroid hormones, and other substances. Albumins are the smallest of the major plasma proteins.
2. **Globulins** account for approximately 35 percent of the plasma protein population. Globulins include both *immunoglobulins* and *transport globulins*. **Immunoglobulins** (im-ū-nō-GLOB-ū-linz), also called **antibodies**, attack foreign proteins and pathogens. **Transport globulins** bind small ions, hormones, or compounds that either are insoluble or might be filtered out of the blood at the kidneys.
3. **Fibrinogen** accounts for about 4 percent of all the plasma proteins. This protein, the largest of the plasma proteins, is essential for normal blood clotting. Under certain conditions fibrinogen molecules interact, forming large, insoluble strands of *fibrin* (FĪ-brin). These fibers provide the basic framework for a blood clot (Figure 20.7, p. 541). If steps are not taken to prevent clotting, the conversion of fibrinogen to fibrin will occur in a sample of plasma. This conversion removes the clotting proteins, leaving a fluid known as **serum**.

Both albumins and globulins can attach to lipids, such as triglycerides, fatty acids, or cholesterol, that are not water-soluble. These protein-lipid combinations, called **lipoproteins** (līp-ō-PRŌ-tēnz), readily dissolve in plasma, and this is how insoluble lipids are delivered to peripheral tissues.

The liver synthesizes and releases more than 90 percent of the plasma proteins. Because the liver is the primary source of plasma proteins, liver disorders can alter the composition and functional properties of the blood. For example, some forms of liver disease can lead to uncontrolled bleeding, caused by inadequate synthesis of fibrinogen and other plasma proteins involved in the clotting response.

Clinical Note

Plasma Expanders Plasma expanders are solutions that can be used to increase blood volume temporarily, over a period of hours, while preparing for a transfusion of whole blood. Plasma expanders contain large carbohydrate molecules, rather than dissolved proteins, to maintain proper osmolarity. Although these carbohydrates are not metabolized, they are gradually removed from circulation by phagocytes, and the blood volume steadily declines. Plasma expanders are easily stored, and their sterile preparation ensures that there are no problems with viral or bacterial contamination. Although they provide a temporary solution to hypovolemia (low blood volume), plasma expanders fail to increase the amount of oxygen delivered to peripheral tissues.

CONCEPT CHECK

1. How would a slow blood flow affect the stability of your body's temperature?
2. If a person is diagnosed as being hypovolemic, how would blood pressure be affected?
3. Why does whole blood have such a high viscosity?

See blue "Answers" tab at back of book.

Formed Elements [Table 20.3]

The major cellular components of blood are *red blood cells* and *leukocytes.* There are two major classes of leukocytes: *granular* (with granules) and *agranular* (without granules). In addition, blood contains noncellular formed elements called *platelets* that function in the clotting response. Table 20.3 summarizes information concerning the formed elements of the blood.

Red Blood Cells (RBCs) [Figure 20.1]

Red blood cells (RBCs), or **erythrocytes** (e-RITH-rō-sīts; *erythros,* red) account for slightly less than half of the total blood volume (Figure 20.1). The **hematocrit** (hē-MA-tō-krit) value indicates the percentage of whole blood contributed by formed elements. The normal hematocrit in adult men averages 45 (range: 40–54); the average for adult women is 42 (range: 37–47). Because whole blood contains roughly 1000 red blood cells for each white blood cell, the hematocrit closely approximates the volume of erythrocytes. As a result, hematocrit values are often reported as the **volume of packed red cells (VPRC)**, or, simply, the **packed cell volume (PCV)**.

The number of erythrocytes in the blood of a normal individual staggers the imagination. One microliter(μl), or cubic millimeter (mm^3), of whole blood from a man contains, on average, 5.4 million erythrocytes; a microliter of blood from a woman contains approximately 4.8 million erythrocytes. There are approximately 260 million red blood cells in a single drop of whole blood, and 25 trillion (2.5×10^{13}) RBCs in the blood of an average adult.

Structure of RBCs [Figure 20.2]

Erythrocytes transport both oxygen and carbon dioxide within the bloodstream. They are among the most specialized cells of the body, and their anatomical specializations are apparent when RBCs are compared with "typical" body cells. p. 29 Figure 20.2a,b indicates the significant differences detected with light and electron microscopy. Each red blood cell is a biconcave disc that has a thin central region and a thick outer margin (Figure 20.2c). The diameter of a typical erythrocyte measured in a standard blood smear is 7.7 μm; it has a maximum thickness of about 2.85 μm, although the center narrows to about 0.8 μm.

This unusual biconcave shape, which provides strength and flexibility, also gives each RBC a disproportionately large surface area for a cell its size. The large surface area permits rapid diffusion between the RBC cytoplasm and surrounding plasma. As blood circulates from the capillaries of the lungs to the capillaries in peripheral tissues and then back to the lungs, respiratory gases are absorbed and released by RBCs. The total surface area of

TABLE 20.3 A Review of the Formed Elements of the Blood

Formed Elements	Abundance (per μl*)	Characteristics	Functions	Remarks
RED BLOOD CELLS	5.2 million (range: 4.4–6.0 million)	Biconcave disc without a nucleus, mitochondria, or ribosomes; red color due to presence of hemoglobin molecules	Transport oxygen from lungs to tissues, and carbon dioxide from tissues to lungs	120-day life expectancy; amino acids and iron recycled; produced in bone marrow
WHITE BLOOD CELLS	7000 (range: 6000–9000)			
Granulocytes				
Neutrophils	4150 (range: 1800–7300) differential count: 57%	Round cell; nucleus resembles a series of beads; cytoplasm contains large, pale inclusions	Phagocytic; engulf pathogens or debris in tissues	Survive minutes to days, depending on activity; produced in bone marrow
Eosinophils	165 (range: 0–700) differential count: 2.4%	Round cell; nucleus usually in two lobes; cytoplasm contains large granules that stain bright orange-red with acid dyes	Attack anything that is labeled with antibodies; important in fighting parasitic infections; suppress inflammation	Produced in bone marrow
Basophils	44 (range: 0–150) differential count: 0.6%	Round cell; nucleus usually cannot be seen because of dense, purple-blue granules in cytoplasm	Enter damaged tissues and release histamine and other chemicals	Assist mast cells of tissues in producing inflammation; produced in bone marrow
Agranulocytes				
Monocytes	456 (range: 200–950) differential count: 6.5%	Very large, kidney bean–shaped nucleus; abundant pale cytoplasm	Enter tissues to become free macrophages; engulf pathogens or debris	Primarily produced in bone marrow
Lymphocytes	2185 (range: 1500–4000) differential count: 30%	Slightly larger than RBC; round nucleus; very little cytoplasm	Cells of lymphoid system, providing defense against specific pathogens or toxins	T cells attack directly; B cells form plasmocytes that secrete antibodies; produced in bone marrow and lymphoid tissues
PLATELETS	350,000 (range: 150,000–500,000)	Cytoplasmic fragments; contain enzymes and proenzymes; no nucleus	Hemostasis: clump together and stick to vessel wall (platelet phase); activate intrinsic pathway of coagulation phase	Produced by megakaryocytes in bone marrow

*Values reported are averages. Differential count: percentage of circulating white blood cells.

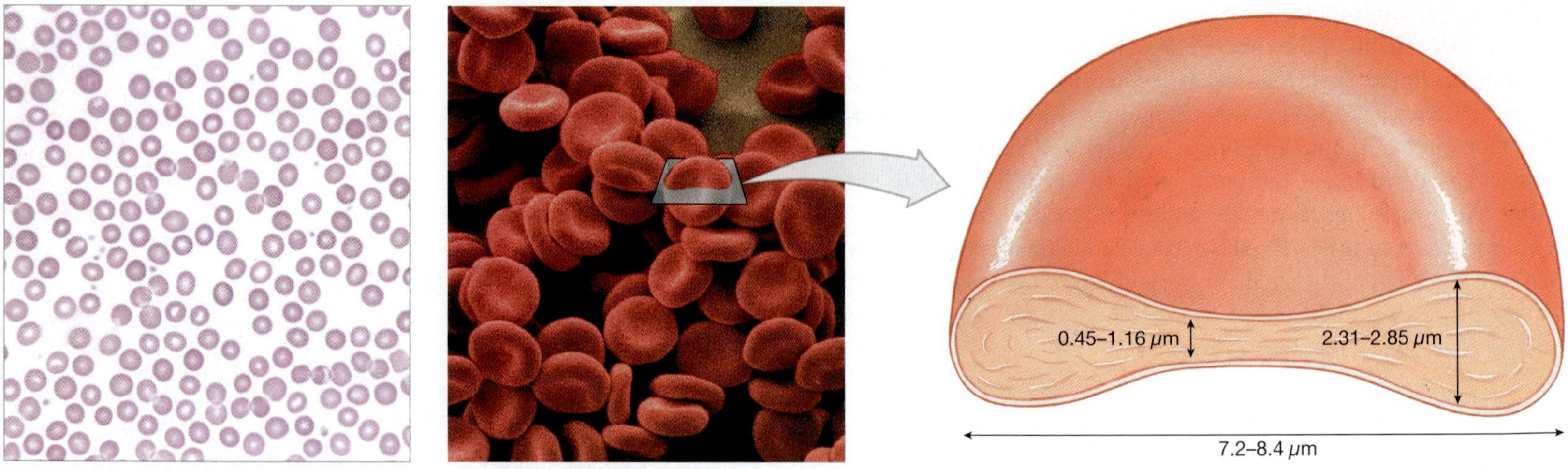

(a) Blood smear **(b) SEM of RBCs** **(c) Sectional view of RBC**

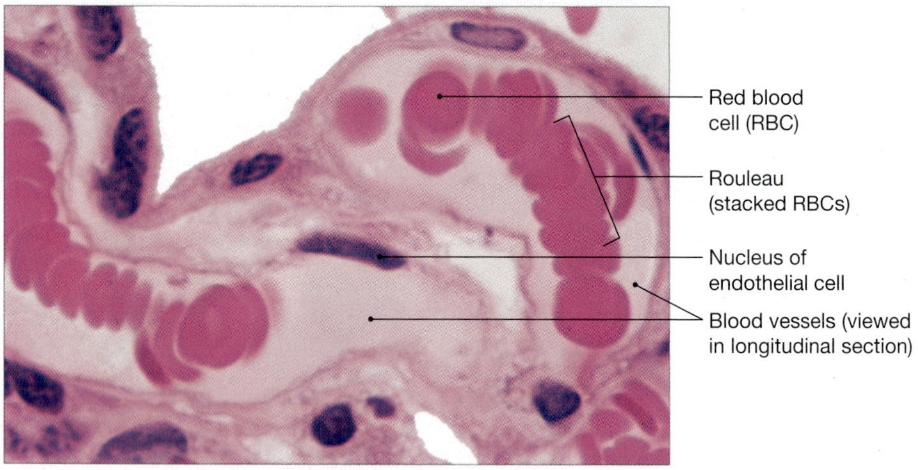

(d) Sectional view of capillaries

Figure 20.2 Histology of Red Blood Cells
(a) When viewed in a standard histological blood smear, red blood cells appear as two-dimensional objects because they are flattened against the surface of the slide. (LM × 477) **(b)** A scanning electron micrograph of red blood cells reveals their three-dimensional structure quite clearly. (SEM × 1838) **(c)** A sectional view of a red blood cell. **(d)** When traveling through relatively narrow capillaries, erythrocytes may stack like dinner plates, forming rouleaux. (LM × 1430)

the red blood cells in the blood of a typical adult is roughly 3800 m^2, 2000 times the total surface area of the body.

The biconcave shape also enables them to form stacks, like dinner plates. These stacks, called **rouleaux** (roo-LŌ; "little rolls," singular, *rouleau*), form and dissociate repeatedly without affecting the cells involved. One rouleau can pass along a blood vessel little larger than the diameter of a single erythrocyte (Figure 20.2d), whereas individual cells would bump the walls, band together, and form logjams that could block the vessel. Finally, the slender profile of an erythrocyte gives the cell considerable flexibility; erythrocytes can bend and flex with apparent ease, and by changing their shape, individual red blood cells can squeeze through small-diameter, distorted, or compressed capillaries.

RBC Life Span and Circulation

During their differentiation and maturation, red blood cells lose most of their organelles, retaining only an extensive cytoskeleton. As a result, circulating RBCs lack mitochondria, endoplasmic reticulum, ribosomes, and nuclei. (The process of RBC formation will be described in a later section.) Without mitochondria, these cells can obtain energy only through anaerobic metabolism, and they rely on glucose obtained from the surrounding plasma. This mechanism ensures that absorbed oxygen will be carried to peripheral tissues, not "stolen" by mitochondria in the RBCs. The lack of a nucleus or ribosomes means that protein synthesis cannot occur; thus, an RBC cannot replace damaged enzymes or structural proteins.

Clinical Note

Anemia and Polycythemia **Anemia** (a-NĒ-mē-a) exists when the oxygen-carrying capacity of the blood is reduced, diminishing the delivery of oxygen to peripheral tissues. Such a reduction causes a variety of symptoms, including premature muscle fatigue, weakness, lethargy, and a general lack of energy. Anemia may exist because the hematocrit is abnormally low or because the amount of hemoglobin in the RBCs is reduced. Standard laboratory tests can be used to differentiate between the various forms of anemia on the basis of the number, size, shape, and hemoglobin content of red blood cells.

An elevated hematocrit with a normal blood volume constitutes **polycythemia** (pol-ē-sī-THĒ-mē-a). There are several different types of polycythemia. **Erythrocytosis** (e-rith-rō-sī-TŌ-sis), a polycythemia affecting only red blood cells, will be considered later in the chapter. **Polycythemia vera** ("true polycythemia") results from an increase in the numbers of all types of blood cells. Many if not all of the blood cells develop from one abnormal hematopoietic stem cell. The hematocrit may reach 80–90, at which point the tissues become oxygen-starved because red blood cells are blocking the smaller vessels. This condition seldom strikes young people; most cases involve people age 60–80. There are several treatment options, but none cures the condition. The cause of polycythemia vera is unknown, although there is some evidence that the condition is linked to radiation exposure.

This is a serious problem because an erythrocyte is exposed to severe stresses. A single circuit of the circulatory system usually takes less than 30 seconds. In this time a single RBC stacks in rouleaux, contorts and squeezes through capillaries, and then joins its comrades in a headlong rush back to the heart for another round. With all this wear and tear and no repair mechanisms, a typical red blood cell has a relatively short life span of about 120 days. After traveling about 700 miles in 120 days, either the plasmalemma ruptures or the aged cell is detected and destroyed by phagocytic cells. About 1 percent of the circulating erythrocytes are replaced each day, and in the process approximately 3 million new erythrocytes enter the circulation *each second*!

RBCs and Hemoglobin [Figure 20.3]

A developing erythrocyte loses all intracellular components not directly associated with its primary functions: oxygen and carbon dioxide transport. A mature red blood cell consists of a plasmalemma surrounding cytoplasm containing water (66 percent) and proteins (about 33 percent). **Hemoglobin** (HĒ-mō-glō-bin) (**Hb**) molecules account for more than 95 percent of the erythrocyte's proteins. Hemoglobin is responsible for the cell's ability to transport oxygen and carbon dioxide. Hemoglobin is a red pigment; its presence gives blood its characteristic red color. Oxygenated hemoglobin has a bright red color, whereas deoxygenated hemoglobin has a deep red color. This accounts for the color difference between arterial (oxygen-rich) and venous (oxygen-poor) blood.

Each hemoglobin molecule has a complex shape. The molecule is composed of four polypeptide subunits: two *alpha (α) chains* and *two beta (β) chains*. Each subunit contains a single molecule of **heme** (Figure 20.3). Each heme unit holds an iron ion in such a way that it can interact with an oxygen molecule. The iron-oxygen interaction is very weak, and the two separate easily without damage to either the hemoglobin or the oxygen molecule. There are approximately 280 million molecules of hemoglobin in each normal red blood cell, and because a hemoglobin molecule contains four heme units, each erythrocyte potentially can carry more than a billion molecules of oxygen. Hemoglobin also carries about 23 percent of the carbon dioxide transported in the blood. Carbon dioxide binds to amino acids of the globin subunits rather than competing with oxygen for binding with iron. The binding of carbon dioxide to a globin subunit is just as reversible as the binding of oxygen to heme.

As red blood cells circulate through capillaries in the lungs, oxygen enters and carbon dioxide leaves the plasma by diffusion. As plasma oxygen levels climb, oxygen diffuses into RBCs and binds to hemoglobin; as plasma carbon dioxide levels fall, hemoglobin releases CO_2 that diffuses into the plasma. In other words, the red blood cells absorb oxygen and release carbon dioxide. In the peripheral tissues, the conditions reverse because active cells are consuming oxygen and producing carbon dioxide. As blood flows through these tissues, oxygen diffuses out of the plasma and carbon dioxide diffuses in. The RBCs then release oxygen and absorb CO_2.

Blood Types [Figure 20.4 and Table 20.4]

An individual's **blood type** is determined by the presence or absence of specific components in erythrocyte plasmalemmae. A typical red blood plasmalemma contains a number of **surface antigens**, or *agglutinogens* (a-gloo-TIN-ō-jenz), exposed to the plasma. These surface antigens are glycoproteins or glycolipids whose characteristics are genetically determined. At least 50 different kinds of surface antigens have been localized on the surfaces of RBCs. Three of particular importance have been designated surface antigens **A**, **B**, and **D** (**Rh**).

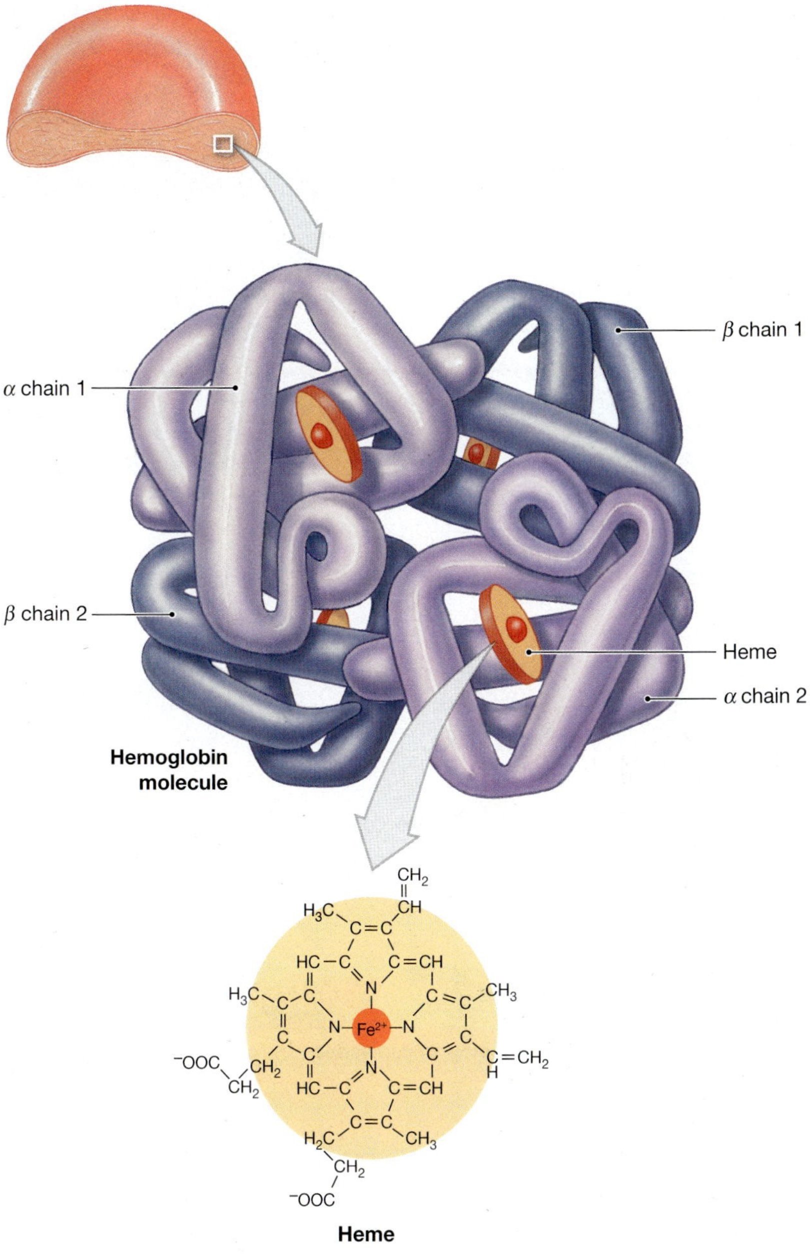

Figure 20.3 The Structure of Hemoglobin
Hemoglobin consists of four globular protein subunits. Each subunit contains a single molecule of heme, a porphyrin ring surrounding a single ion of iron. It is the iron ion that reversibly binds to an oxygen molecule.

Clinical Note

Elevating Hemoglobin Levels Blood for transfusion is a limited resource, and transfusions are not without risk. In an attempt to develop a lower-risk alternative, genetic engineering procedures are now being used to synthesize one of the subunits of normal human hemoglobin, which can be introduced into the circulation to increase oxygen transport and total blood volume. An alternative strategy involves removing hemoglobin molecules from red cells and attaching them to inert carrier molecules that will prevent their loss at the kidneys. Still a third approach draws on natural but nonhuman sources. The FDA recently approved testing of a blood substitute called *Hemopure* that contains purified hemoglobin from cattle. Because the hemoglobin is removed from erythrocytes and infused without plasma, cross-reactions are not expected to occur.

Clinical Note

Sickle Cell Anemia *Sickle cell anemia (SCA)* results from a mutation affecting the amino acid sequence of the beta chains of the hemoglobin molecule. When blood contains abundant oxygen, the Hb molecules and the RBCs that carry them appear normal. But when the defective hemoglobin gives up enough of its bound oxygen, the adjacent Hb molecules cluster into rods, and the cells become stiff and curved. This "sickling" makes the RBCs fragile and easily damaged. Moreover, even though RBCs that have folded to squeeze into a narrow capillary deliver their oxygen to the surrounding tissue, the cells can become stuck as sickling occurs. A circulatory blockage results, and nearby tissues become starved for oxygen. Today, sickle cell anemia affects approximately 0.2 percent of the African-American population, and from 0.07 to 0.1 percent of Hispanic Americans.

An individual with sickle cell anemia carries two copies of the abnormal gene—one from each parent. If only one copy is present, the individual has a *sickling trait.* One African-American in 12 carries the sickling trait. These genes are also present in some people of Mediterranean, Middle Eastern, and East Indian ancestry.

In an individual with the sickling trait, most of the hemoglobin is of the normal form, and the RBCs function normally. But the presence of the abnormal hemoglobin gives the individual some ability to resist the parasitic infection that causes **malaria**, a mosquito-borne illness. Malaria parasites enter the bloodstream when an individual is bitten by an infected mosquito. The microorganisms invade, and reproduce within, the RBCs. But when they enter the RBC of a person with the sickling trait, the cell responds by sickling. Either the sickling itself kills the parasite, or the sickling attracts the attention of a phagocyte that engulfs the RBC and kills the parasite. In either event, the individual better tolerates the parasitic infection, whereas individuals without the sickling trait are more likely to sicken and die of malaria.

When sickled RBCs get stuck in small capillaries and obstruct blood flow, they cause pain and eventually damage to a variety of organs and systems, depending on the location and duration of the obstructions. In addition, the trapped RBCs die and break down, producing a characteristic hemolytic anemia. A normal RBC stays in circulation 120 days; sickled cells are gone in 10–20 days. This rapid loss of RBCs damages the spleen and exceeds the maximum rate of RBC production. Transfusions of normal blood can temporarily prevent additional complications, and treatment of affected infants with antibiotics reduces deaths due to infections. The food additive butyrate, found in butter and other foods, appears to be effective in promoting the synthesis of fetal hemoglobin. In clinical trials, it has been effective in treating sickle cell anemia and other conditions caused by abnormal hemoglobin structure, such as beta-thalassemia.

The red blood cells of each person have a characteristic combination of surface antigens (Figure 20.4). For example, **Type A** blood has antigen A, **Type B** has antigen B, **Type AB** has both, and **Type O** has neither. The average values for the U.S. population are Type O, 46 percent, Type A, 40 percent, Type B, 10 percent, and Type AB, 4 percent. These values may differ among different racial and ethnic groups (Table 20.4).

The presence of the D or Rh antigen, sometimes called the *Rh factor*, is indicated by the terms **Rh-positive** (present) or **Rh-negative** (absent). In recording the complete blood type, the term Rh is usually omitted, and the data are reported as O-negative, A-positive, and so forth.

TABLE 20.4 Differences in Blood Group Distribution

	Percentage with Each Blood Type				
Population	**O**	**A**	**B**	**AB**	**Rh$^+$**
U. S. (average)	46	40	10	4	85
Caucasian	45	40	11	4	85
African-American	49	27	20	4	95
Chinese	42	27	25	6	100
Japanese	31	39	21	10	100
Korean	32	28	30	10	100
Filipino	44	22	29	6	100
Hawaiian	46	46	5	3	100
Native North American	79	16	4	<1	100
Native South American	100	0	0	0	100
Australian Aborigines	44	56	0	0	100

Antibodies and Cross-Reactions [Figure 20.4] You probably know that your blood type must be checked before you give or receive blood. The surface antigens on your own red blood cells are ignored by your immune system. (This ability to recognize your own body cells will be examined in Chapter 23.) However, your plasma contains antibodies (immunoglobulins) that will attack "foreign" surface antigens. These antibodies are known as *agglutinins* (a-GLOO-ti-ninz). The blood of a Type A, Type B, or Type O individual always contains antibodies that will attack foreign surface antigens (Figure 20.4a). For example, if you have Type A blood, your plasma contains circulating anti-B antibodies that will attack Type B erythrocytes (Figure 20.4b). If you are Type B, your plasma contains anti-A antibodies. In a Type O individual the red blood cells lack surface antigens A and B, and the plasma contains both anti-A and anti-B antibodies. At the other extreme, the plasma of a Type AB individual contains neither anti-A nor anti-B antibodies.

Even if a Type A person has never been exposed to Type B blood, the individual will still have anti-B antibodies in the plasma. In contrast, the plasma of an Rh-negative individual does not always contain anti-Rh antibodies. These antibodies are present only if the individual has been **sensitized** by previous exposure to Rh-positive erythrocytes. Such exposure may occur accidentally, during a transfusion, but it also may accompany a seemingly normal pregnancy involving an Rh-negative mother and an Rh-positive fetus.

When an antibody meets its specific surface antigen, a **cross-reaction** occurs (Figure 20.4b). Initially the red blood cells clump together, a process called **agglutination** (a-gloo-ti-NĀ-shun), and they may also **hemolyze**, or rupture. Clumps and fragments of red blood cells under attack form drifting masses that can plug small vessels in the kidneys, lungs, heart, or brain, damaging or destroying the tissues deprived of circulation. Such reactions can be avoided by ensuring that the blood types of the donor and the recipient are **compatible**. In practice, this procedure involves choosing a donor whose blood cells will not undergo cross-reaction with the plasma of the recipient.

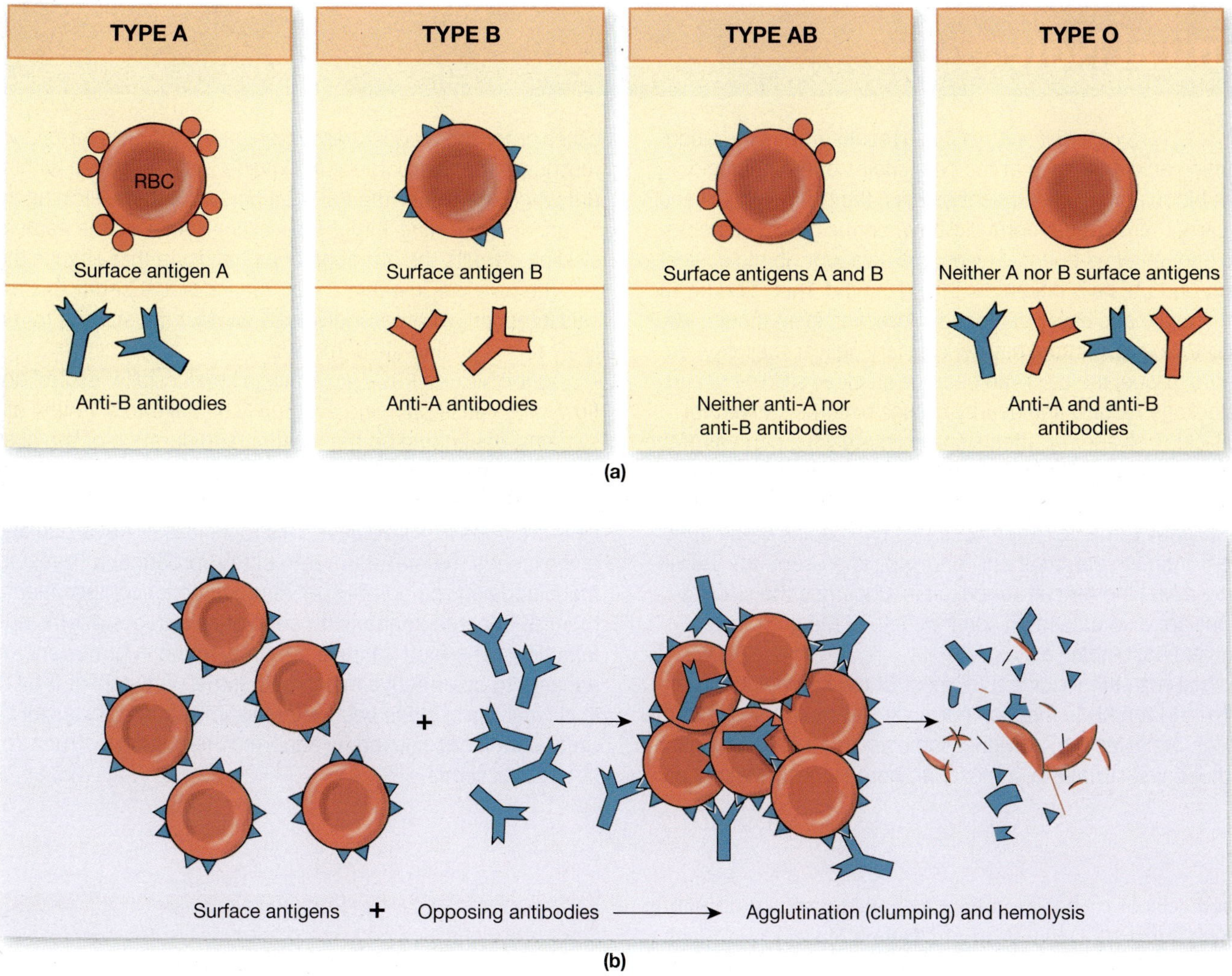

Figure 20.4 Blood Typing
The blood type depends on the presence of surface antigens on RBCs. The plasma contains antibodies that will react with foreign surface antigens. The relative frequencies of each blood type in the U.S. population are indicated in *Table 20.4*.

CONCEPT CHECK

1. If the hematocrit value of a woman is 42, what is the percentage of red blood cells present in her blood?
2. How does the shape of red blood cells aid in blood flow and the diffusion of oxygen?
3. Red blood cells have neither nuclei nor ribosomes. What effect does this have on their life span?
4. A person with Type AB blood can receive blood of any other blood type. Why?

See blue "Answers" tab at back of book.

Leukocytes [Figure 20.5 and Table 20.3]

Leukocytes (LOO-kō-sīts; *leukos*, white), or white blood cells (WBCs), are scattered throughout peripheral tissues. Circulating leukocytes represent only a small fraction of their total population; most of the leukocytes in the body are found in peripheral tissues. White blood cells help defend the body against invasion by pathogens and remove toxins, wastes, and abnormal or damaged cells. WBCs contain nuclei of characteristic sizes and shapes (**Figure 20.5**). All WBCs are as large as or larger than RBCs. There are two major classes of leukocytes: (1) **granular leukocytes**, or **granulocytes** (GRAN-ū-lō-sīts), which have large granular inclusions in their cytoplasm, and (2) **agranular leukocytes**, or **agranulocytes**, which do not possess cytoplasmic granules visible with the light microscope. Representative granular and agranular leukocytes are shown in **Figure 20.5**.

A typical microliter of blood contains 6000–9000 WBCs. The term **leukopenia** (loo-kō-PĒ-nē-a; *penia*, poverty) indicates inadequate numbers of leucokytes; a count of less than 2500 per μl usually indicates a serious disorder. **Leukocytosis** (loo-kō-sī-TŌ-sis) refers to excessive numbers of leukocytes; a count of more than 30,000 per μl usually indicates a serious disorder. A stained blood smear provides a **differential count** of the white blood cell population. The values obtained indicate the number of each type of cell encountered in a sample of 100 white blood cells. The normal range for each cell type is indicated in Table 20.3. The endings *-penia* and *-osis* can also be used to indicate low or high numbers, respectively, of specific types of white blood cells. For example, *lymphopenia* means too few lymphocytes and *lymphocytosis* means an unusually high number.

Leukocytes have a very short life span, typically only a few days. In instances of injury or invasion of an area by a foreign organism, a leukocyte can migrate across the endothelial lining of a capillary by squeezing between adjacent endothelial cells. This process is known as **diapedesis**. The bloodstream provides rapid transportation for WBCs to these injured sites, where they are attracted to the chemical signs of inflammation or infection

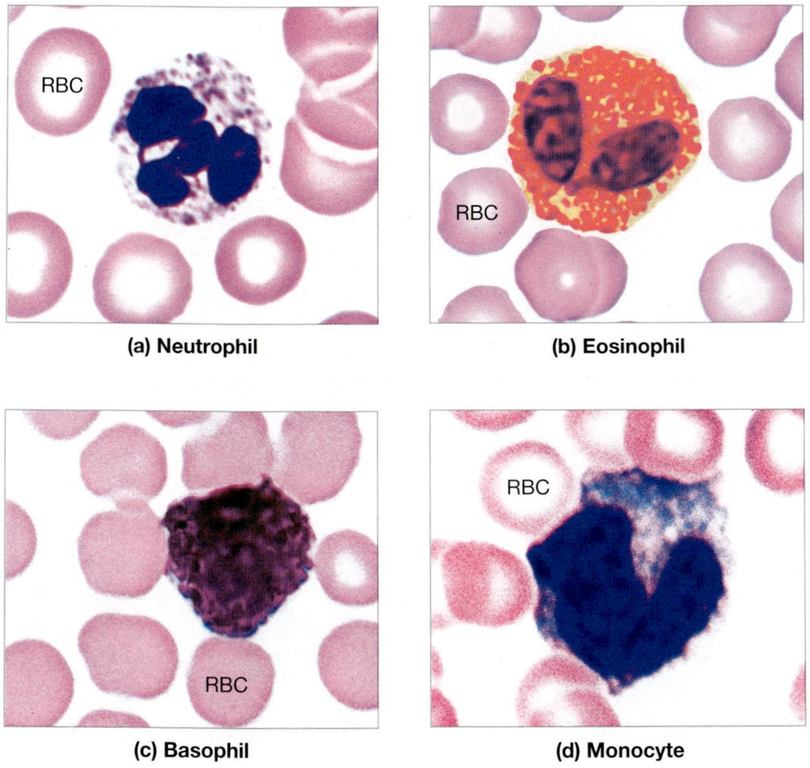

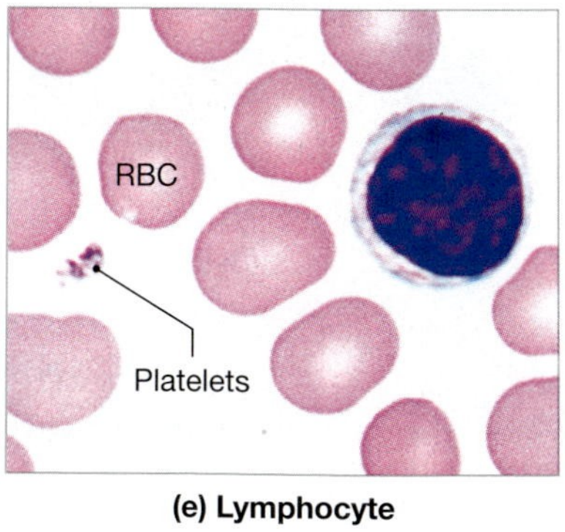

Figure 20.5 Histology of White Blood Cells
Histological comparison of leukocytes as seen in blood smears.
(a) Neutrophil. **(b)** Eosinophil.
(c) Basophil. **(d)** Monocyte.
(e) Lymphocyte. Platelets are visible in part (e) as small cellular fragments between the RBCs.
(LM × 1500)

in the adjacent interstitial fluids. This attraction to specific chemical stimuli, called **chemotaxis**, draws them to invading pathogens, damaged tissues, and white blood cells already in the damaged tissues.

Granular Leukocytes

Granular leukocytes are subdivided on the basis of their staining characteristics into *neutrophils*, *eosinophils*, and *basophils*. Neutrophils and eosinophils are important phagocytic cells that participate in the immune response.

Neutrophils [Figure 20.5a] From 50 to 70 percent of the circulating white blood cells are **neutrophils** (NOO-trō-filz). They are called neutrophils because their cytoplasm is packed with pale, neutral-staining granules containing lysosomal enzymes and bactericidal (bacteria-killing) compounds. Each mature neutrophil (Figure 20.5a) has a diameter of 12–15 μm, nearly twice that of a red blood cell. A neutrophil has a very dense, contorted nucleus that may be condensed into a series of lobes like beads on a string. This attribute has given these cells another name, **polymorphonuclear leukocytes** (pol-ē-mor-fō-NŪ-klē-ar; *poly*, many + *morphe*, form), or **PMNs**.

Neutrophils are highly mobile and are usually the first of the WBCs to arrive at an injury site. They are very active phagocytes, specializing in attacking and digesting bacteria. Neutrophils usually have a short life span, surviving for about 12 hours. After actively engulfing debris or pathogens, a neutrophil dies, but its breakdown releases some chemicals that attract other neutrophils to the site, and others that have a broad antibiotic activity against the pathogens.

Eosinophils [Figure 20.5b] **Eosinophils** (ē-ō-SIN-ō-filz), also called **acidophils** (a-SID-ō-fils), are so named because their granules stain with *eosin*, an acidic red dye. Eosinophils are similar in size to neutrophils and represent 2–4 percent of the circulating WBCs. These cells have both deep red granules and a bilobed (two-lobed) nucleus, making an eosinophil relatively easy to identify (Figure 20.5b). Eosinophils are phagocytic cells attracted to foreign compounds that have reacted with circulating antibodies. Eosinophil numbers increase dramatically during an allergic reaction or a parasitic infection. Eosinophils also are attracted to injury sites, where they release enzymes that reduce the degree of inflammation and control its spread to adjacent tissues.

Basophils [Figure 20.5c] **Basophils** (BĀ-sō-filz) are so named because they have numerous granules that stain with basic dyes. These inclusions stain a deep purple or blue with the stains used in a standard blood smear (Figure 20.5c). Basophils are relatively rare, accounting for less than 1 percent of the leukocyte population. They migrate to sites of injury and cross the capillary endothelium to accumulate within the damaged tissues, where they discharge their granules into the interstitial fluids. The granules contain histamine, which dilates blood vessels, and heparin, a compound that prevents blood from clotting. Release of these chemicals increases the inflammation response at the injury site by increasing capillary and venule permeability. Basophils also release chemicals that stimulate mast cells and attract basophils and other white blood cells to the area.[1]

Agranular Leukocytes

Circulating blood contains two types of agranular leukocytes: *monocytes* and *lymphocytes*. They differ both structurally and functionally.

Monocytes [Figure 20.5d] The largest WBC is the **monocyte** (MON-ō-sīt). It is 16–20 μm in diameter, two to three times the diameter of a typical RBC. These cells account for 2–8 percent of the WBC population. They are normally almost spherical, and, when flattened in a blood smear, they appear even larger; they are relatively easy to identify by their size and the shape of their nucleus. Each cell has a large oval or kidney bean–shaped nucleus (Figure 20.5d). Monocytes circulate for just a few days before entering peripheral tissues. Outside the bloodstream, monocytes are called *free macrophages*, to distinguish them from the immobile *fixed macrophages* found in many connective tissues. pp. 62–63 Free macrophages are highly mobile, phagocytic cells. They usually arrive at the injury site shortly after the first neutrophils. While phagocytizing, free and fixed macrophages release chemicals that attract and stimulate other monocytes and other phagocytic cells. Active macrophages also secrete substances that lure fibroblasts into the region. The fibroblasts begin producing a dense network of collagen fibers around the site. This *scar tissue*

[1] Histamine and other chemicals are also found in the granules of mast cells, connective tissue cells introduced in Chapter 3, p. 63, and the mast cells in damaged connective tissues also release their granules. However, the two cells are separate and distinct.

may eventually wall off the injured area. Monocytes are one component of the **monocyte-macrophage system** that includes related cell types, such as fixed macrophages and more specialized cells such as the microglia of the CNS, the Langerhans cells of the skin, and phagocytic cells in the liver, spleen, and lymph nodes.

Lymphocytes [Figure 20.5e] Typical **lymphocytes** (LIM-fō-sīts) have very little cytoplasm, with just a thin halo around a relatively large, round, purple-staining nucleus (Figure 20.5e). Lymphocytes are usually slightly larger than RBCs and account for 20–30 percent of the WBC population. Blood lymphocytes represent a minute segment of the entire lymphocyte population, for lymphocytes are the primary cells of the **lymphoid system**, a network of special vessels and organs distinct from, but connected to, those of the cardiovascular system.

Lymphocytes are responsible for *specific immunity*: the ability of the body to mount a counterattack against invading pathogens or foreign proteins *on an individual basis*. Lymphocytes respond to such threats in three ways. One group of lymphocytes, called **T cells**, enters peripheral tissues and attacks foreign cells directly. Another group of lymphocytes, the **B cells**, differentiates into plasmocytes (plasma cells) that secrete antibodies that attack foreign cells or proteins in distant portions of the body. T cells and B cells cannot be distinguished with the light microscope. **NK cells**, a third group, sometimes known as *large granular lymphocytes*, are responsible for *immune surveillance*, the destruction of abnormal tissue cells. These cells are important in preventing cancer. (The lymphoid system and immunity are discussed in Chapter 23.)

Platelets [Figures 20.5e/20.6/20.7]

Platelets are flattened, membrane-enclosed packets, which are round when viewed from above (Figure 20.5e) and spindle-shaped in section. Platelets were once thought to be cells that had lost their nuclei, because similar functions in vertebrates other than mammals are performed by small nucleated blood cells. Histologists called all of these cells **thrombocytes** (THROM-bō-sīts; *thrombos*, clot). The term is still in use, although in mammals the term *platelet* is more suitable because these are membrane-enclosed enzyme packets, not individual cells.

Normal red bone marrow contains a number of very unusual cells, called **megakaryocytes** (meg-a-KAR-ē-ō-sīts; *mega-*, big + *karyon*, nucleus + *cyte*, cell). As the name suggests, these are enormous cells (up to 160 μm in diameter) with large nuclei (Figure 20.6). The dense nucleus may be lobed or ring-shaped, and the surrounding cytoplasm contains Golgi apparatus, ribosomes, and mitochondria in abundance. The plasmalemma communicates with an extensive membrane network that radiates throughout the peripheral cytoplasm.

During their development and growth, megakaryocytes manufacture structural proteins, enzymes, and membranes. They then begin shedding cytoplasm in small membrane-enclosed packets. These packets are the platelets that enter the circulation. A mature megakaryocyte gradually loses all of its cytoplasm, producing around 4000 platelets before the nucleus is engulfed by phagocytes and broken down for recycling.

Platelets are continually replaced, and an individual platelet circulates for 10–12 days before being removed by phagocytes. A microliter of circulating blood contains an average of 350,000 platelets. About one-third of the platelets in the body at any moment are held in the spleen and other vascular organs rather than in the circulating blood. These reserves

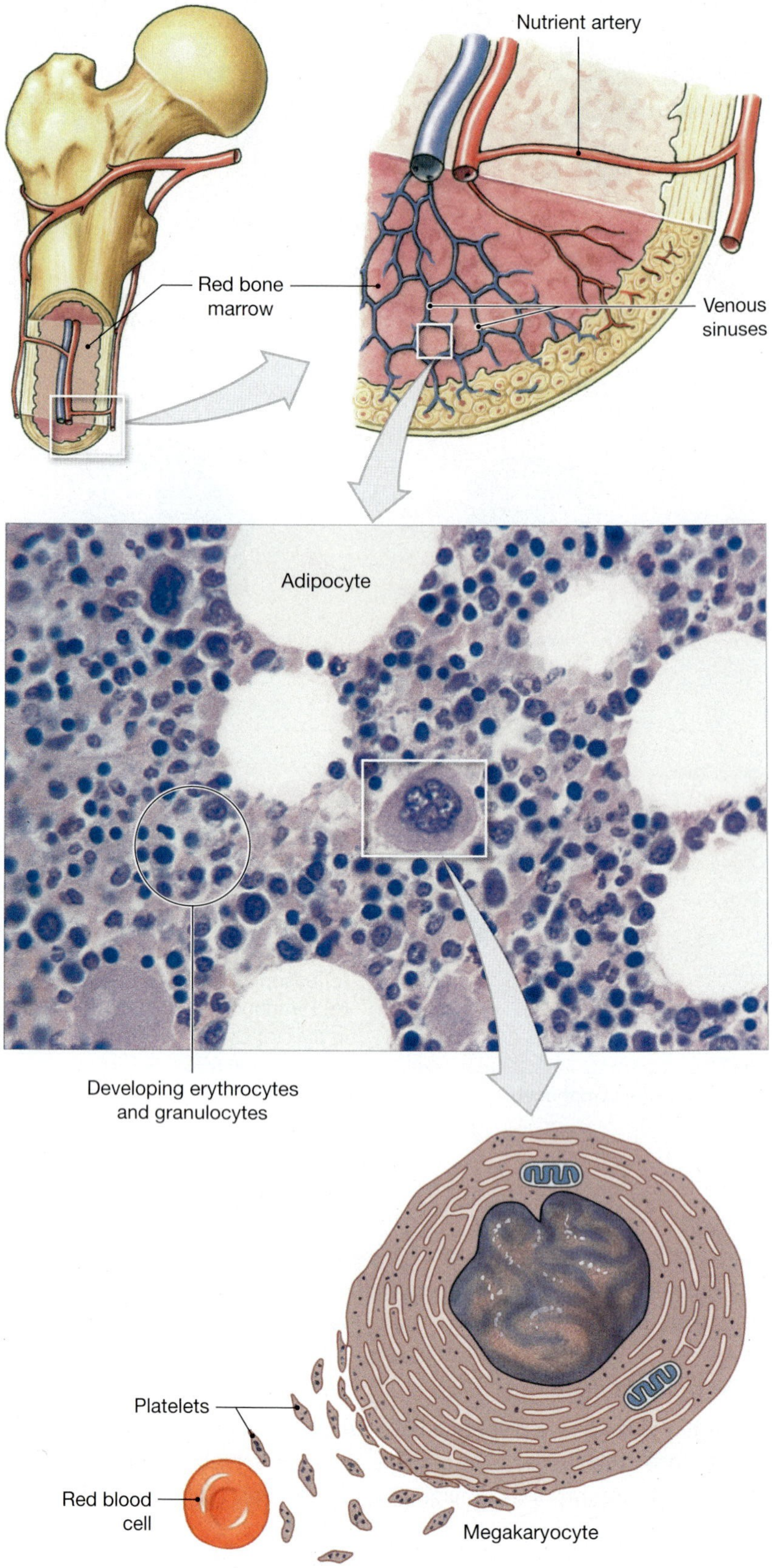

Figure 20.6 Histology of Megakaryocytes and Platelet Formation
Histologically, megakaryocytes stand out in bone marrow sections because of their enormous size and the unusual shape of their nuclei. These cells are continually shedding chunks of cytoplasm that enter the circulation as platelets. (LM × 673)

Clinical Note

Hemophilia **Hemophilia** (hē-mō-FĒL-ē-a) is one of many inherited disorders characterized by inadequate production of clotting factors. The incidence of this condition in the general population is about 1 in 10,000, with males accounting for 80–90 percent of those affected. In hemophilia A, production of a single clotting factor is reduced; the severity of the condition depends on the degree of reduction. In severe cases extensive bleeding accompanies the slightest mechanical stresses, and hemorrhages occur spontaneously at joints and around muscles.

Transfusions of clotting factors can often reduce or control the symptoms of hemophilia, but plasma samples from many individuals must be pooled (combined) to obtain adequate amounts of clotting factors. Pooling is very expensive and increases the risk of infection with blood-borne infections such as hepatitis or AIDS. Gene-splicing techniques have been used to manufacture the clotting factor most often involved (factor VIII). Although supplies are now limited, this procedure should eventually provide a safer method of treatment.

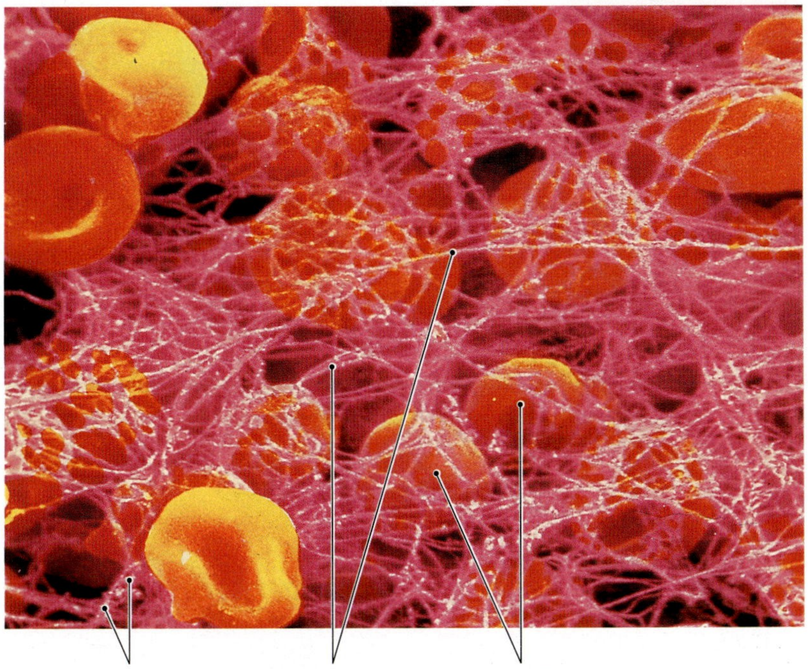

Figure 20.7 Structure of a Blood Clot
A colorized scanning electron micrograph showing the network of fibers that forms the framework of the clot. Red blood cells trapped in the clot add to its mass and give it a red color. (SEM × 4625)

can be mobilized when a circulatory crisis occurs, such as severe bleeding. An abnormally low platelet count (80,000 per μl, or less) is known as **thrombocytopenia** (throm-bō-sī-tō-PĒ-nē-a) and indicates excessive platelet destruction or inadequate platelet production. Symptoms include bleeding along the digestive tract, bleeding within the skin, and occasional bleeding inside the CNS. Platelet counts in **thrombocytosis** (throm-bō-sī-TŌ-sis) may exceed 1,000,000 per μl, which usually results from accelerated platelet formation in response to infection, inflammation, or cancer.

Platelets are one participant in a vascular *clotting system* that also includes plasma proteins and the cells and tissues of the circulatory network. The process of **hemostasis** (*haima*, blood + *stasis*, halt) prevents the loss of blood through the walls of damaged vessels. In doing so, it both restricts blood loss and establishes a framework for tissue repairs. A portion of a blood clot is shown in Figure 20.7.

Hemostasis involves a complex chain of events, and a disorder that affects any one step can disrupt the entire process. In addition, there are general requirements—for example, a deficiency of calcium ions or vitamin K will interfere with virtually all aspects of hemostasis.

The functions of platelets include the following:

1. *Transport of chemicals important to the clotting process:* By releasing enzymes and other factors at the appropriate times, platelets help initiate and control the clotting process.
2. *Formation of a temporary patch in the walls of damaged blood vessels:* Platelets clump together at an injury site, forming a *platelet plug* that can slow the rate of blood loss while clotting occurs.
3. *Active contraction after clot formation has occurred:* Platelets contain filaments of actin and myosin that can interact to produce contractions that shorten them. After a blood clot has formed, the contractions of platelets reduces the size of the clot and pulls together the cut edges of the vessel wall.

CONCEPT CHECK

1. What type of white blood cells would you expect to find in the greatest number in an infected cut?
2. What is thrombocytosis, and when does it occur?
3. If you have an allergic reaction, which white blood cell type would increase dramatically?
4. What is the function of the granules in basophils?

See blue "Answers" tab at back of book.

Hemopoiesis [Figure 20.8]

The process of blood cell formation is called **hemopoiesis** or (hēm-ō-poy-Ē-sis). Blood cells appear in the circulation during the third week of embryonic development. These cells divide repeatedly, increasing their numbers. As other organ systems appear, some of the embryonic blood cells move out of the circulation and into the liver, spleen, thymus, and bone marrow (Figure 20.8). These embryonic cells differentiate into stem cells that produce blood cells by their divisions. As the skeleton enlarges, the bone marrow becomes increasingly important; in the adult it is the primary site of blood cell formation.

Stem cells, called **pluripotential stem cells (PPSC)**, or *hemocytoblasts*, ultimately give rise to all blood cells, but the process occurs in a series of separate steps. Pluripotential stem cells give rise to two multipotential stem cells: **multipotential myeloid stem cells** (or **myeloid stem cell**) and **multipotential lymphoid stem cells** (or **lymphoid stem cell**). The myeloid stem cell will divide to form five different types of stem cells, each with relatively restricted functions. Two of these stem cells are responsible for the production of red blood cells and megakaryocytes, while the other three stem

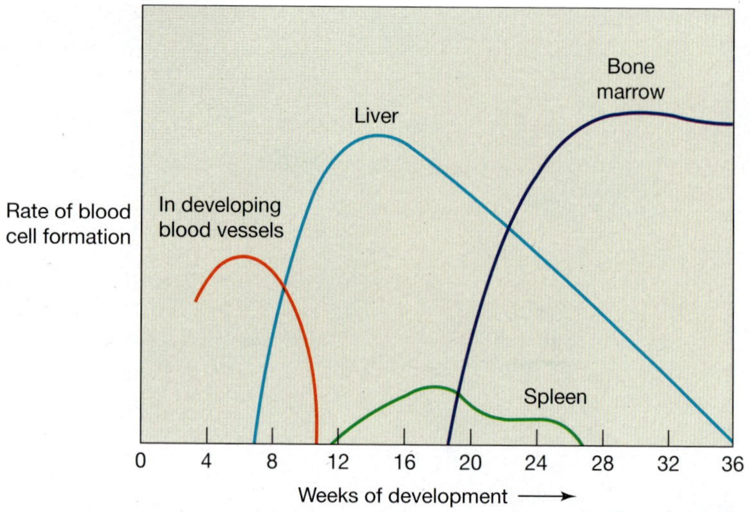

Figure 20.8 The Origins and Differentiation of Formed Elements Pluripotential stem cells give rise to both myeloid and lymphoid stem cells. Myeloid stem cells produce progenitor cells, which divide to produce the various classes of blood cells. The graph indicates the primary locations of blood cell formation during embryonic and fetal development.

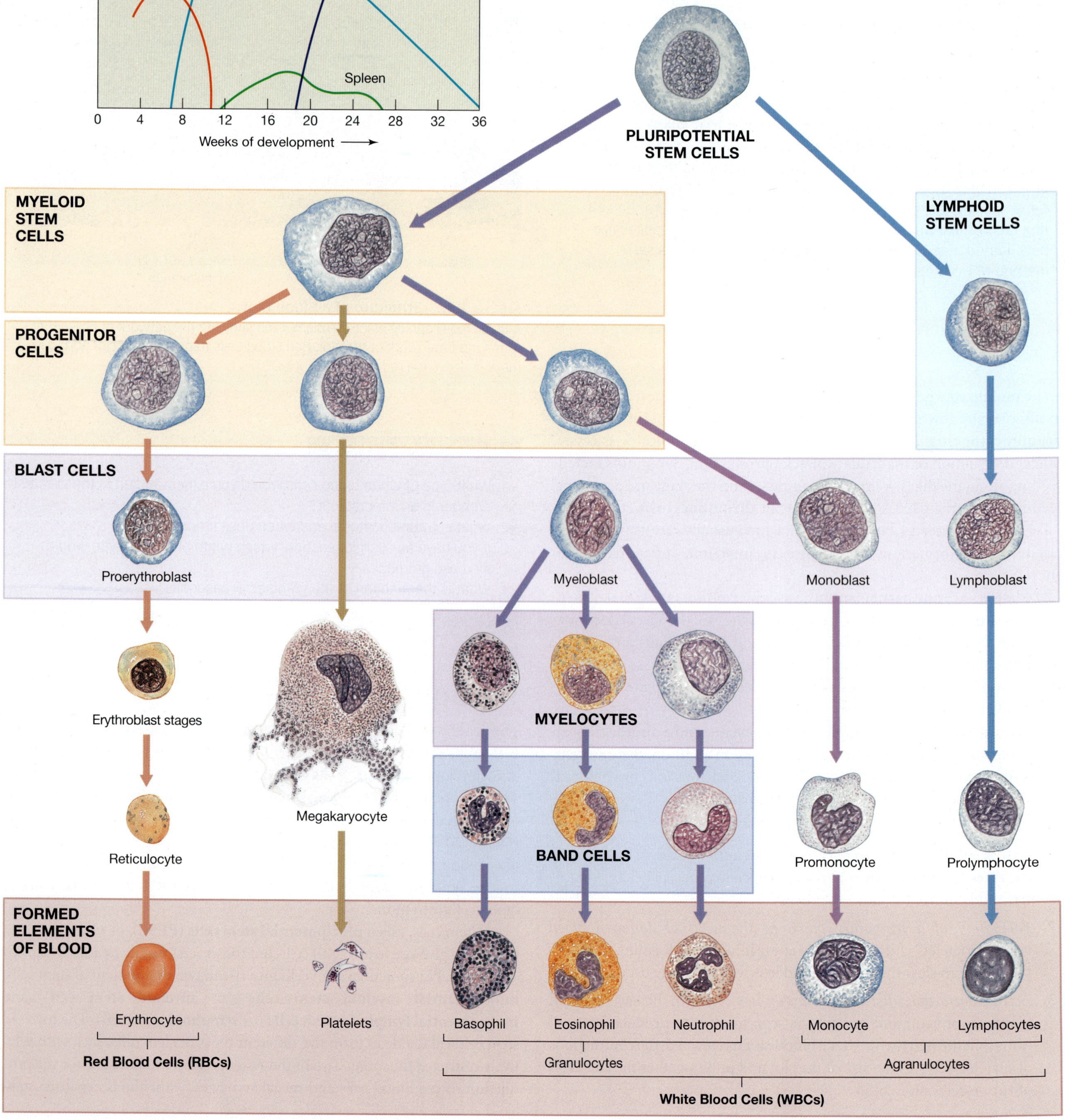

cells are responsible for forming the various forms of leukocytes (Figure 20.8). The lymphoid stem cell will divide to form two different types of stem cells. These two have relatively restricted functions, with one stem cell ultimately forming plasmocytes and the other stem cell forming T cells.

Erythropoiesis [Figure 20.8/20.6]

Erythropoiesis (e-rith-rō-poy-Ē-sis) refers specifically to the formation of erythrocytes (Figure 20.8). The red bone marrow is the primary site of blood cell formation in the adult (Figure 20.6). Red marrow is found in portions of the vertebrae, sternum, ribs, skull, scapulae, pelvis, and proximal limb bones. Under extreme conditions the fatty **yellow marrow** found in other bones can be converted to red marrow. For example, this conversion may occur after a severe and sustained blood loss, thereby increasing the rate of red blood cell formation. For erythropoiesis to proceed normally, the myeloid tissues must receive adequate supplies of amino acids, iron, and **vitamin B_{12}**, a vitamin obtained from dairy products and meat.

Erythropoiesis is regulated by **erythropoiesis-stimulating hormone**, or **erythropoietin (EPO)**, which was introduced in Chapter 19. p. 113

Erythropoietin is produced and secreted under hypoxic (low-oxygen) conditions, primarily in the kidneys. Erythropoietin has two major effects:

- It stimulates increased rates of cell division in erythroblasts and in the stem cells that produce erythroblasts; and
- It speeds up the maturation of RBCs, primarily by accelerating the rate of hemoglobin synthesis. Under maximum EPO stimulation, the bone marrow can increase the rate of red blood cell formation tenfold, to around 30 million per second.

Stages in RBC Maturation [Figure 20.8]

A maturing red blood cell passes through a series of developmental stages. **Hematologists** (hē-ma-TOL-ō-jists), specialists in blood formation and function, have given specific names to key stages (Figure 20.8). **Erythroblasts** are very immature red blood cells that are actively synthesizing hemoglobin. After shedding their nuclei, these cells become **reticulocytes** (re-TIK-ū-lō-sīts), the last step in the maturation process. Reticulocytes enter the circulation and gradually develop the appearance of mature erythrocytes. Maturing reticulocytes normally account for about 0.8 percent of the RBC population.

Leukopoiesis [Figure 20.8]

Stem cells responsible for the production of white blood cells (**leukopoiesis**) originate in the bone marrow (Figure 20.8). Granulocytes complete their development in bone marrow; monocytes begin their differentiation in the bone marrow, enter the circulation, and complete their development when they become free macrophages in peripheral tissues. Stem cells responsible for the production of lymphocytes, a process called **lymphopoiesis**, also originate in the bone marrow, but many of them subsequently migrate to the thymus. The bone marrow and thymus are called *primary lymphoid organs* because the divisions of undifferentiated stem cells at these sites produce daughter cells destined to become specialized lymphocytes. Immature B cells and NK cells are produced in the bone marrow, and immature T cells are produced in the thymus. These cells may subsequently migrate to *secondary lymphoid structures*, such as the spleen, tonsils, or lymph nodes. Although they retain the ability to divide, their divisions always produce cells of the same type—a dividing T cell produces daughter T cells and not NK or B cells. We will consider formation of lymphocytes in more detail in Chapter 23.

Factors that regulate lymphocyte maturation are as yet incompletely understood; however, prior to maturity, hormones of the thymus gland promote the differentiation and maintenance of T cell populations. Several hormones, collectively called **colony-stimulating factors (CSFs)**, are involved in the regulation of other white blood cell populations. Commercially available CSFs are now used to stimulate the production of WBCs in individuals undergoing cancer chemotherapy.

Clinical Note

Synthetic Blood Despite improvements in transfusion technology, shortages of blood and anxieties over safety persist. In addition, some people may be unable or unwilling to accept transfusions for medical or religious reasons. Thus there has been widespread interest in a number of recent attempts to develop synthetic blood components.

Whole blood substitutes are highly experimental solutions still undergoing clinical evaluation. In addition to the osmotic agents found in plasma expanders, these solutions contain small clusters of synthetic molecules built of carbon and fluorine atoms. The mixtures, known as **perfluorochemical (PFC) emulsions**, can carry roughly 70 percent of the oxygen of whole blood. Animals have been kept alive after an exchange transfusion that completely replaced their circulating blood with a PFC emulsion.

PFC solutions have the same advantages of other plasma expanders, plus the added benefits of transporting oxygen. Because there are no RBCs involved, the PFC emulsions can carry oxygen to regions whose capillaries have been partially blocked by fatty deposits or blood clots. Unfortunately, PFCs do not absorb oxygen as effectively as normal blood. To ensure that the PFCs deliver adequate oxygen to peripheral tissues, the individual must breathe air rich in oxygen, usually through an oxygen mask. In addition, phagocytes appear to engulf the PFC clusters. These problems have limited the use of PFC emulsions on humans. However, one PFC solution, *Fluosol*, has been used to enhance oxygen delivery to cardiac muscle during heart surgery.

Another approach involves the manufacture of miniature erythrocytes by enclosing small bundles of hemoglobin in a lipid membrane. These **neohematocytes** (nē-Ō-hēm-AT-ō-sīts) are spherical, with a diameter of less than 1 μm, and they can easily pass through narrow or partially blocked vessels. The major problem with this technique is that phagocytes treat neohematocytes like fragments of normal erythrocytes, so they remain in circulation for only about 5 hours.

CONCEPT CHECK

1. What are the two main effects of erythropoietin?
2. What is the function of pluripotential stem cells?
3. The ejection of the nucleus marks which stage of red blood cell maturation?
4. What cell sheds cytoplasmic packets to produce platelets?

See blue "Answers" tab at back of book.

Clinical Note

Blood Doping The practice of **blood doping** in various forms has become widespread among competitive athletes involved with endurance sports such as cycling. One procedure entails removing whole blood from the athlete in the weeks before an event. The packed red cells are separated from the plasma and stored. By the time of the race, the competitor's bone marrow will have replaced the lost blood. Immediately before the event, the packed red cells are reinfused, increasing the hematocrit. The objective is to elevate the oxygen-carrying capacity of the blood, and so increase endurance. The consequence is that the athlete's heart is placed under a tremendous strain. The long-term effects are unknown, but the practice carries a significant risk of stroke or heart attack; it has recently been banned in amateur sports. Training at high altitudes is a safer and currently acceptable alternative.

Because it is now being synthesized using recombinant DNA techniques, EPO can be obtained by individuals attempting to circumvent these rules. Although use of this drug will be difficult for officials to detect, individuals using it are taking the same risks as those who practice blood doping. Over the last five to ten years, the deaths of 18 European cyclists and the disqualification of several Olympic competitors during the 2002 Winter Olympics apparently resulted from blood doping, EPO abuse, or both.

CLINICAL TERMS

anemia (a-NĒ-mē-a): A condition in which the oxygen-carrying capacity of the blood is reduced, because of low hematocrit or low blood hemoglobin concentrations.

aplastic anemia: Anemia caused by failure of the bone marrow, leading to a low hematocrit and a low reticulocyte count.

bone marrow transplant: A transfusion of bone marrow cells, including stem cells, that can be used to repopulate the bone marrow after radiation exposure, chemotherapy, or aplastic anemia.

embolism: A condition in which a drifting blood clot becomes stuck in a blood vessel, blocking circulation to the area downstream.

hemolytic disease of the newborn (HDN): An anemia in the newborn usually caused by an incompatibility between the maternal (Rh^-) and fetal (Rh^+) blood types.

hemophilia: One of many inherited disorders characterized by inadequate production of clotting factors.

hemorrhagic anemia: Anemia caused by severe bleeding, typified by a low hematocrit and a low hemoglobin but normal RBCs.

normochromic: The condition in which red blood cells contain normal amounts of hemoglobin.

normocytic: A term referring to red blood cells of normal size.

normovolemic (nor-mō-vō-LĒ-mik): The condition of having normal blood volume.

packed red blood cells (PRBCs): Red blood cells from which most of the plasma has been removed.

plaque: An abnormal area within a blood vessel where large quantities of lipids accumulate.

polycythemia (pol-ē-sī-THĒ-mē-a): A blood condition showing an elevated hematocrit with a normal blood volume.

thrombus: A blood clot.

transfusion: A procedure in which blood components are given to someone whose blood volume has been reduced or whose blood is deficient in some components.

STUDY OUTLINE

Introduction 531

1. The cardiovascular system provides a mechanism for the rapid transport of nutrients, waste products, and cells within the body.

Functions of the Blood 531

1. **Blood** is a specialized connective tissue. Its functions include (1) transporting dissolved gases; (2) transporting and distributing nutrients; (3) transporting metabolic wastes; (4) transporting and delivering enzymes and hormones; (5) stabilizing the pH and electrolyte composition of interstitial fluids; (6) restricting fluid losses through damaged vessels or injuries via the **clotting reaction**; (7) defending the body against toxins and pathogens; and (8) stabilizing body temperature by absorbing and redistributing heat. *(see Table 20.1)*

Composition of the Blood 531

1. Blood consists of two components: **plasma**, the liquid matrix of blood, and **formed elements**, which include **red blood cells (RBCs)**, **leukocytes** or **white blood cells (WBCs)**, and **platelets**. The plasma and formed elements constitute **whole blood**, which can be **fractionated** for analytical or clinical purposes. *(see Figure 20.1 and Table 20.2)*
2. There are 4–6 liters of whole blood in an average adult. The terms *hypovolemic, normovolemic,* and *hypervolemic* refer to low, normal, or excessive blood volume, respectively.

Plasma 532

3. Plasma accounts for about 55 percent of the volume of blood; roughly 92 percent of plasma is water. *(see Figure 20.1 and Table 20.2)*
4. Plasma differs from interstitial fluid because it has a higher dissolved oxygen concentration and large numbers of dissolved proteins. There are three classes of plasma proteins: *albumins, globulins,* and *fibrinogen. (see Table 20.2)*
5. **Albumins** constitute about 60 percent of plasma proteins. **Globulins** constitute roughly 35 percent of plasma proteins: They include **immunoglobulins (antibodies)**, which attack foreign proteins and pathogens, and **transport globulins**, which bind ions, hormones, and other compounds. **Fibrinogen** molecules function in the clotting reaction by interacting to form *fibrin*; removing fibrinogen from plasma leaves a fluid called **serum**. *(see Table 20.2)* When albumins or globulins become attached to lipids, they form lipoproteins, which are carried in the circulatory system until the lipids are delivered to the tissues.

Formed Elements 534

Red Blood Cells (RBCs) 534

1. Red blood cells (RBCs), or **erythrocytes**, account for slightly less than half the blood volume. The **hematocrit** value indicates the percentage of whole blood occupied by cellular elements. Since blood contains about 1000 RBCs for each WBC, this value closely approximates the volume of RBCs. *(see Figures 20.2 to 20.4)*

2. RBCs transport oxygen and carbon dioxide within the bloodstream. They are highly specialized cells with large surface-to-volume ratios. Each RBC is a biconcave disc. This shape gives RBCs a large surface area, allowing for rapid diffusion of gases and the ability to form stacks (called **rouleaux**) that can pass easily through small vessels.
3. Because RBCs lack mitochondria, ribosomes, and nuclei, they are unable to perform normal maintenance operations, so they usually degenerate after about 120 days in the circulation. Damaged or dead RBCs are recycled by phagocytes. *(see Figure 20.2 and Table 20.3)*
4. Molecules of **hemoglobin (Hb)** account for more than 95 percent of the RBCs' proteins. Hemoglobin gives RBCs the ability to transport oxygen and carbon dioxide. Hemoglobin is a globular protein formed from four subunits. Each subunit contains a single molecule of **heme**, which holds an iron ion that can reversibly bind an oxygen molecule *(see Figure 20.3)*. At the lungs, carbon dioxide diffuses out of the blood and oxygen diffuses into the blood. In the peripheral tissues, the opposite occurs: oxygen diffuses out of the blood and carbon dioxide diffuses into the blood.
5. One's **blood type** is determined by the presence or absence of specific **surface antigens** *(agglutinogens)* in the RBC plasmalemmae: **A**, **B**, and **D (Rh)**. Type A blood has surface antigen A, Type B blood has surface antigen B, Type AB has both, and Type O has neither. Rh-positive blood has the Rh surface antigen, and Rh-negative does not. **Antibodies** specific to these surface antigens are called *agglutinins*. Antibodies within a person's plasma will react with RBCs bearing foreign surface antigens, causing a cross-reaction. *(see Figure 20.4 and Table 20.4)*

Leukocytes 538

6. White blood cells (WBCs), or **leukocytes**, defend the body against pathogens and remove toxins, wastes, and abnormal or damaged cells *(see Figure 20.5)*. The two classes of WBCs are granular leukocytes (granulocytes) and agranular leukocytes (agranulocytes).
7. A stained blood smear provides a differential count of the white blood cell population. The word endings *-penia* and *-osis* are used to indicate low or high numbers, respectively, of specific types of white blood cells.
8. Leukocytes show **chemotaxis** (the attraction to specific chemicals) and **diapedesis** (the ability to move through vessel walls).
9. **Granular leukocytes** (**granulocytes**) are subdivided into **neutrophils**, **eosinophils** (**acidophils**), and **basophils**. Fifty to 70 percent of circulating WBCs are neutrophils, which are highly mobile phagocytes. The much less common eosinophils are phagocytic cells, which are attracted to foreign compounds that have reacted with circulating antibodies. The relatively rare basophils migrate to damaged tissues and release histamines, aiding the inflammation response. *(see Figure 20.5 and Table 20.3)*
10. **Agranular leukocytes** are subdivided into **monocytes** and **lymphocytes**. Monocytes migrating into peripheral tissues become free macrophages, which are highly mobile, phagocytic cells. Lymphocytes, the primary cells of the **lymphoid system**, include **T cells** (which enter peripheral tissues and attack foreign cells directly), **B cells** (which produce antibodies), and **NK cells** (which destroy abnormal tissue cells). *(see Figure 20.5 and Table 20.3)*

Platelets 540

11. Platelets are sometimes called **thrombocytes**; they are not cells but are membrane-enclosed packets of cytoplasm.
12. **Megakaryocytes** are enormous cells in the bone marrow that release packets of cytoplasm (platelets) into the circulating blood. The functions of platelets include (1) transporting chemicals important to the clotting process; (2) forming a temporary patch in the walls of damaged blood vessels; and (3) causing contraction after a clot has formed in order to reduce the size of the break in the vessel wall. *(see Figures 20.6/20.7 and Table 20.3)*

Hemopoiesis 541

1. **Hemopoiesis** is the process of blood cell formation. **Stem cells** called **pluripotential stem cells** divide to form all of the blood cells. *(see Figure 20.8)*

Erythropoiesis 543

2. **Erythropoiesis**, the formation of erythrocytes, occurs mainly within the **myeloid tissue** (red bone marrow) in adults. RBC formation increases under the influence of **erythropoiesis-stimulating hormone (erythropoietin, EPO)**. Stages in RBC development include **erythroblasts** and **reticulocytes**. *(see Figure 20.8)*

Leukopoiesis 543

3. **Leukopoiesis**, the formation of white blood cells, begins in bone marrow. Granulocytes and monocytes are produced by stem cells in the bone marrow. Stem cells responsible for **lymphopoiesis** (production of lymphocytes) also originate in the bone marrow, but many migrate to peripheral lymphoid tissues. *(see Figure 20.8)*
4. The bone marrow and the thymus are called *primary lymphoid organs*. *Secondary lymphoid structures*, such as the spleen, tonsils, and lymph nodes, contain white blood cells that divide to produce cells of the same type.
5. Factors that regulate lymphocyte maturation are not completely understood. Several **colony-stimulating factors (CSFs)** are involved in regulating other WBC populations.

CHAPTER REVIEW

For answers to the Concept Check and Chapter Review questions, go to the blue "Answers" tab at the back of the book.

Level 1 Reviewing Facts and Terms

Match each numbered item with the most closely related lettered item. Use letters for answers in the spaces provided.

Column A	Column B
___ 1. basophils	a. stem cell source of all blood cells
___ 2. embolism	b. low blood volume
___ 3. lymphocyte	c. granular white blood cell
___ 4. leukopoiesis	d. clotting protein
___ 5. hemostasis	e. agranular white blood cell
___ 6. erythroblasts	f. process of white blood cell production
___ 7. fibrinogen	g. process of preventing blood loss
___ 8. immunoglobulins	h. clot in a blood vessel
___ 9. pluripotential stem cells	i. antibodies
___10. hypovolemic	j. immature red blood cells

11. Functions of the blood include
    (a) transport of nutrients and waste
    (b) regulation of pH and electrolyte concentrations
    (c) restricting fluid loss
    (d) all of the above are correct
12. The most common formed elements in the blood are the
    (a) platelets (b) white blood cells
    (c) proteins (d) red blood cells
13. The most abundant proteins in blood are
    (a) globulins (b) albumins
    (c) fibrinogens (d) lipoproteins
14. The major classes of white blood cells include
    (a) erythrocytes and platelets
    (b) granular and agranular cells
    (c) fibrinogens and collagen fibers
    (d) macromolecules and colloids

15. Stem cells responsible for the production of white blood cells originate in the
    (a) liver (b) thymus
    (c) spleen (d) bone marrow
16. Each of the following statements concerning red blood cells (RBCs) is true except
    (a) RBCs are biconcave discs
    (b) RBCs lack mitochondria
    (c) RBCs have a large nucleus
    (d) RBCs can form stacks called rouleaux
17. The primary function of hemoglobin is to
    (a) store iron
    (b) transport glucose
    (c) give RBCs their color
    (d) carry oxygen to peripheral tissues
18. People with Type A blood have
    (a) A surface antigens on their red blood cells
    (b) B surface antigens in their plasma
    (c) anti-A antibodies in their plasma
    (d) anti-O antibodies in their plasma
19. The white blood cells that increase in number during an allergic reaction or in response to parasitic infections are the
    (a) neutrophils (b) eosinophils
    (c) basophils (d) monocytes
20. Platelets are
    (a) large cells that lack a nucleus
    (b) small cells that lack a nucleus
    (c) fragments of cells
    (d) small cells with an irregular-shaped nucleus

Level 2 Reviewing Concepts

1. How does the reaction of an Rh-positive or Rh-negative blood type differ from that of types A, B, and O?
    (a) there are no significant differences; these blood types react all the same way
    (b) the blood of an Rh-positive individual contains Rh-positive agglutinogens, and the blood of an Rh-negative individual contains Rh-negative agglutinogens
    (c) the blood of an Rh-negative individual contains anti-Rh agglutinogens only if he or she has been sensitized by previous exposure to Rh-positive erythrocytes
    (d) the response is greater in a manner inverse to the amount of different Rh blood administered to the individual
2. Hemostasis can be disrupted by which of the following?
    (a) a deficiency of calcium ions
    (b) a deficiency of potassium ions
    (c) a deficiency of hemoglobin
    (d) a deficiency of sodium ions
3. Why does the lack of mitochondria make an erythrocyte more efficient at transporting oxygen?
    (a) since an erythrocyte transports gases passively, mitochondria would be useless, occupying valuable space within the cell
    (b) mitochondria require a large amount of energy to function, and so an erythrocyte lacking them has more energy to transport oxygen
    (c) since an erythrocyte transports gases passively, ATP is not needed for active transport processes, and therefore mitochondria are not needed and the energy mitochondria require is used to transport oxygen
    (d) without mitochondria, the erythrocyte will not use the oxygen it absorbs and can therefore carry all of it to peripheral tissues
4. Iron deficiency would result in which of the following?
    (a) decreased leukocyte count
    (b) decreased monocyte count
    (c) anemia
    (d) polycythemia
5. What is the volume of packed red cells, and why is it sometimes called "packed cell volume"?
6. What is the function of the clotting reaction?
7. What is the fate of megakaryocytes?
8. Give some examples of secondary lymphoid structures.
9. What are lipoproteins, and what is their function in the blood?
10. Can a person with Type O blood receive Type AB blood? Why or why not?

Level 3 Critical Thinking

1. Several months prior to the start of a competition, why do athletes often move to elevations higher than those at which they will compete?
2. Mononucleosis is a disease that can cause an enlarged spleen because of increased numbers of phagocytic and other cells. Common symptoms include pale complexion, a tired feeling, and a lack of energy sometimes to the point of not being able to get out of bed. What might cause these symptoms?
3. Almost half of our vitamin K is synthesized by bacteria that inhabit our large intestine. Based on this information, why would taking a broad-spectrum antibiotic (antibiotics are chemical agents that selectively kill microorganisms) produce frequent nosebleeds?

21

The Cardiovascular System

The Heart

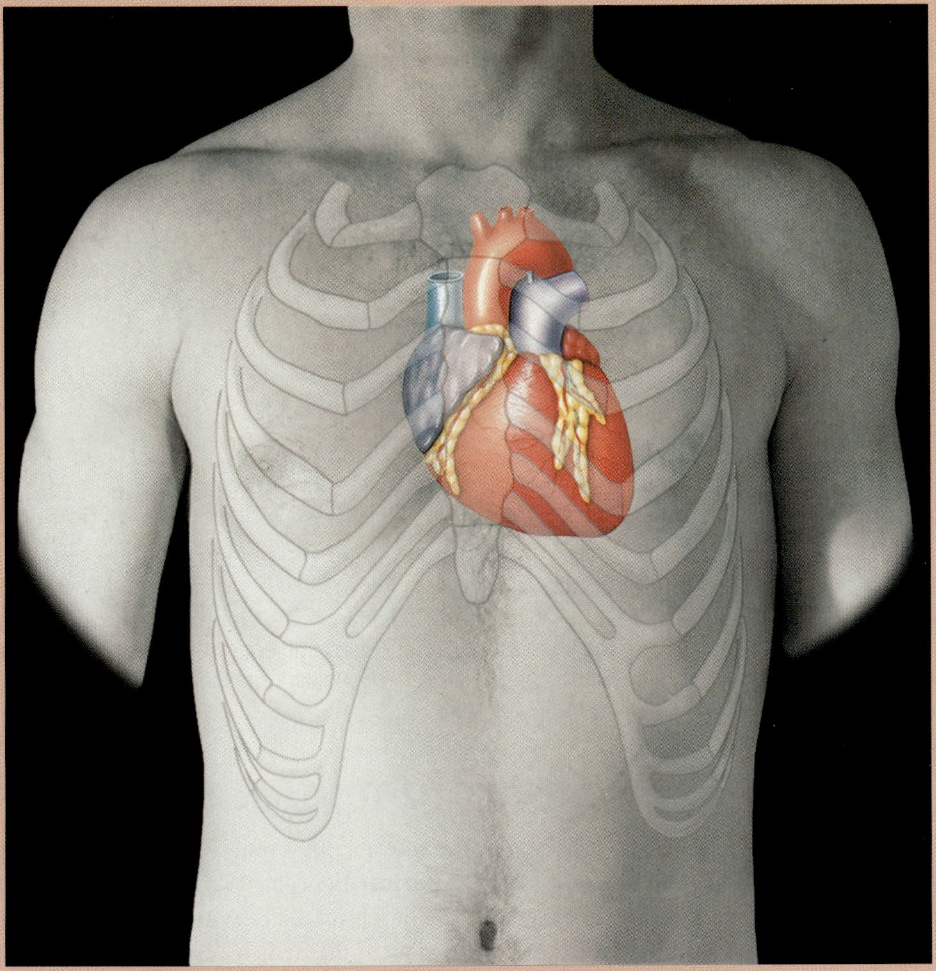

CHAPTER OBJECTIVES

1. Describe the basic design of the cardiovascular system and the function of the heart.
2. Describe the structure of the subdivisions of the pericardium and discuss its functions.
3. Identify and describe the epicardium, myocardium, and endocardium of the heart.
4. Identify important differences between cardiac muscle tissue and skeletal muscle tissue.
5. Discuss the structure and function of the fibrous skeleton of the heart.
6. Identify and describe the external form and surface features of the heart.
7. Describe the structural and functional specializations of each chamber of the heart.
8. Identify the major arteries and veins of the pulmonary and systemic circuits that are connected to the heart.
9. Trace the path of blood flow through the heart.
10. Describe the structure and function of each of the heart valves.
11. Locate the coronary blood vessels and identify their origins and major branches.
12. Name and trace the components of the conduction pathway of the heart.
13. Describe the function of the conduction pathway.
14. Discuss the events that take place during the cardiac cycle.
15. Describe the cardiac centers and discuss their functions in regulating the heart.

Every living cell relies on the surrounding interstitial fluid as a source of oxygen and nutrients and as a place for the disposal of wastes. Levels of gases, nutrients, and waste products in the interstitial fluid are kept stable through continuous exchange between the interstitial fluid and the circulating blood. The blood must stay in motion to maintain homeostasis. If blood stops flowing through a tissue, its oxygen and nutrient supplies are exhausted quickly, its capacity to absorb wastes is soon reached, and neither hormones nor white blood cells can get to their intended targets. Thus, all of the functions of the cardiovascular system ultimately depend on the heart, because it is the heart that keeps blood moving. This muscular organ beats approximately 100,000 times each day, propelling blood through the blood vessels. Each year the heart pumps more than 1.5 million gallons of blood, enough to fill 200 train tank cars.

For a practical demonstration of the heart's pumping abilities, turn on the faucet in the kitchen and open it all the way. To deliver an amount of water equal to the volume of blood pumped by the heart in an average lifetime, that faucet would have to be left on for at least 45 years. Equally remarkable, the volume of blood pumped by the heart can vary widely, between 5 and 30 liters per minute. The performance of the heart is closely monitored and finely regulated by the nervous system to ensure that gas, nutrient, and waste levels in the peripheral tissues remain within normal limits, whether one is sleeping peacefully, reading a book, or involved in a vigorous racquetball game.

We begin this chapter by examining the structural features that enable the heart to perform so reliably, even in the face of widely varying physical demands. We will then consider the mechanisms that regulate cardiac activity to meet the body's ever-changing needs.

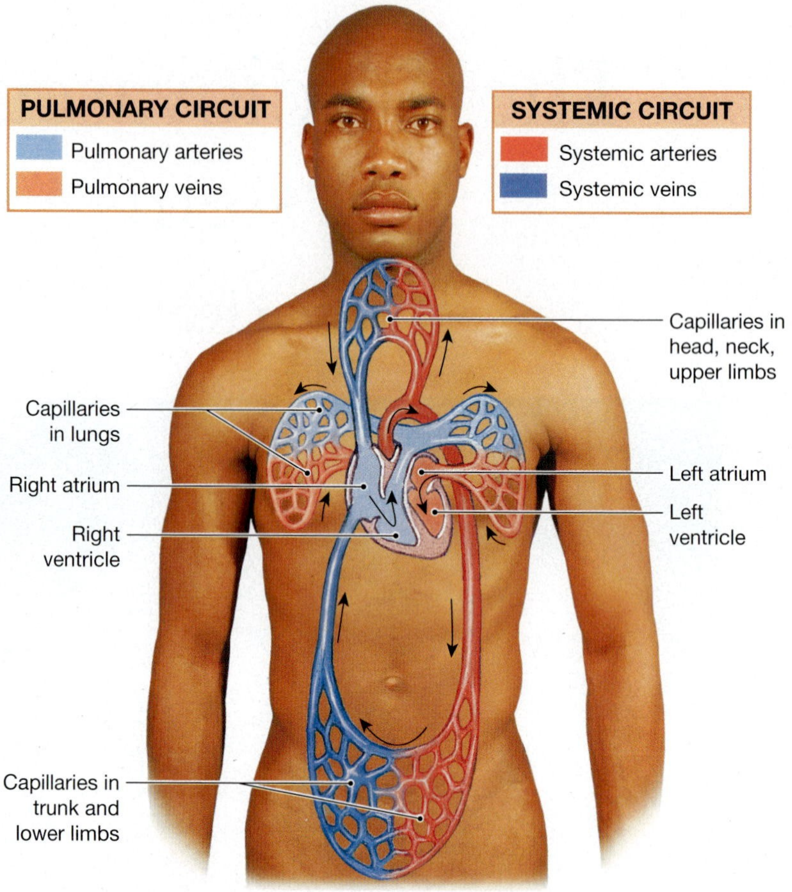

Figure 21.1 A Generalized View of the Pulmonary and Systemic Circuits
Blood flows through separate pulmonary and systemic circuits, driven by the pumping of the heart. Each circuit begins and ends at the heart and contains arteries, capillaries, and veins. Arrows indicate the direction of blood flow within each circuit.

An Overview of the Cardiovascular System [Figure 21.1]

Despite its impressive workload, the heart is a small organ; your heart is roughly the size of your clenched fist. The heart's four muscular chambers, the right and left **atria** (Ā-trē-a; singular, *atrium*; "chamber") and right and left **ventricles** (VEN-tri-kls; "little belly"), work together to pump blood through a network of blood vessels between the heart and the peripheral tissues. The network can be subdivided into two circuits: the **pulmonary circuit**, which carries carbon dioxide-rich blood from the heart to the gas-exchange surfaces of the lungs and returns oxygen-rich blood to the heart; and the **systemic circuit**, which transports oxygen-rich blood from the heart to the rest of the body's cells, returning carbon dioxide-rich blood back to the heart. The right atrium receives blood from the systemic circuit, and the right ventricle discharges blood into the pulmonary circuit. The left atrium collects blood from the pulmonary circuit, and the left ventricle ejects blood into the systemic circuit. When the heart beats, the atria contract first, followed by the ventricles. The two ventricles contract at the same time and eject equal volumes of blood into the pulmonary and systemic circuits.

Each circuit begins and ends at the heart. **Arteries** transport blood away from the heart; **veins** return blood to the heart (Figure 21.1). Blood travels through these circuits in sequence. For example, blood returning to the heart in the systemic veins must complete the pulmonary circuit before reentering the systemic arteries. **Capillaries** are small, thin-walled vessels that interconnect the smallest arteries and veins. Capillaries are called **exchange vessels** because their thin walls permit exchange of nutrients, dissolved gases, and waste products between the blood and surrounding tissues.

The Pericardium [Figure 21.2]

The heart is located near the anterior chest wall (Figure 21.2a), directly posterior to the sternum in the **pericardial** (per-i-KAR-dē-al) **cavity**, a portion of the ventral body cavity. The pericardial cavity is situated between the pleural cavities, in the mediastinum, which also contains the thymus, esophagus, and trachea. p. 19 The position of the heart relative to other structures in the mediastinum is shown in Figure 21.2c,d.

The **pericardium** is the serous membrane lining the pericardial cavity. To visualize the relationship between the heart and the pericardial cavity, imagine pushing your fist toward the center of a large balloon (Figure 21.2b). The wall of the balloon corresponds to the pericardium, and your fist is the heart. The pericardium is divided into the **visceral pericardium** (the part of the balloon in contact with your fist) and the **parietal pericardium** (the rest of the balloon). Your wrist, where the balloon folds back upon itself, corresponds to the *base* of the heart (so named because it is where the heart is attached to the major vessels and bound to the mediastinum).

The loose connective tissue of the visceral pericardium, or *epicardium*, is bound to the cardiac muscle tissue of the heart. The serous membrane of the parietal pericardium is reinforced by an outer layer of dense, irregular connective tissue containing abundant collagen fibers. This reinforcing layer is known as the **fibrous pericardium**. Together, the parietal pericardium and the fibrous pericardium form the tough **pericardial sac**. At the base of the heart, the collagen fibers of the fibrous pericardium stabilize

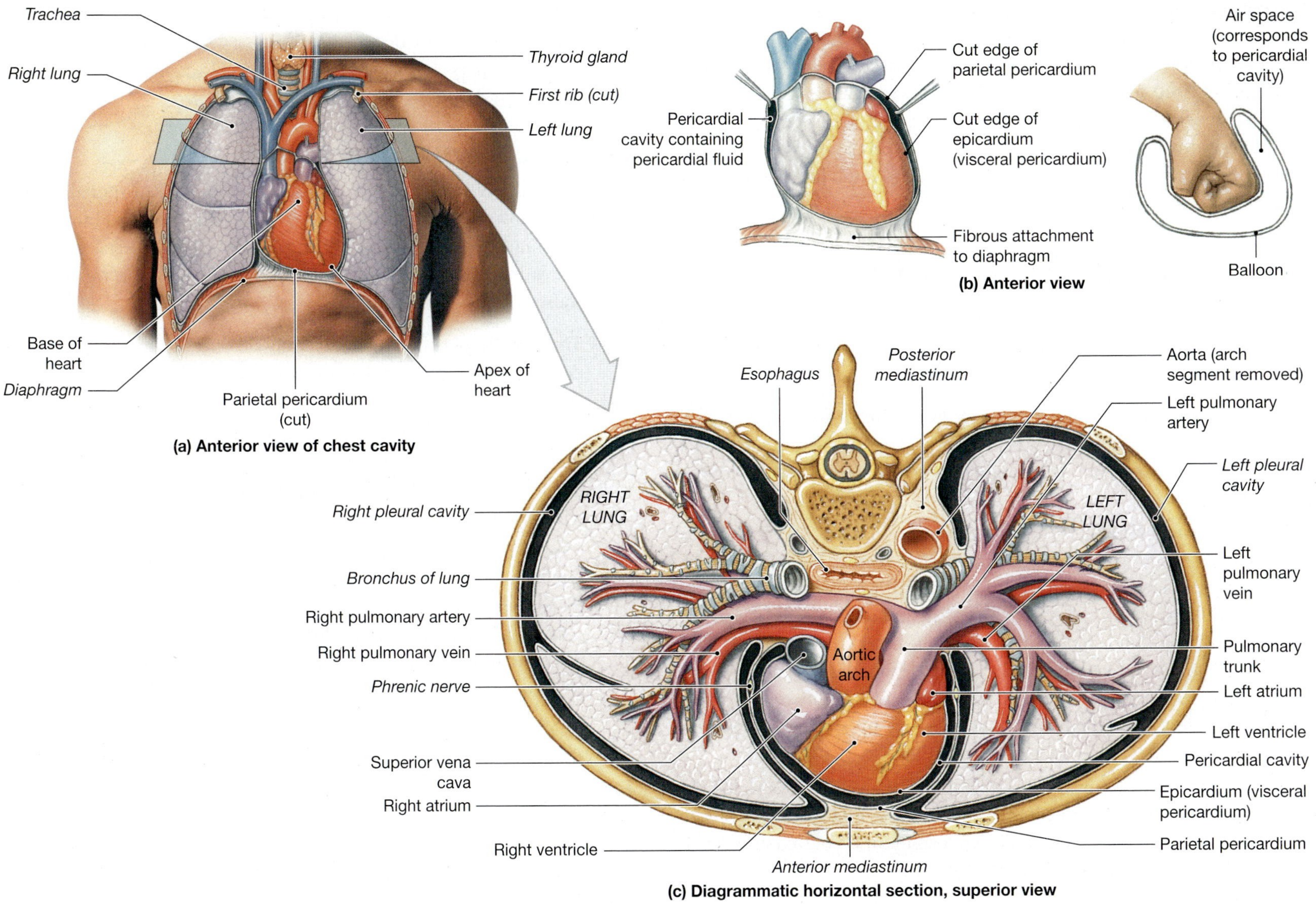

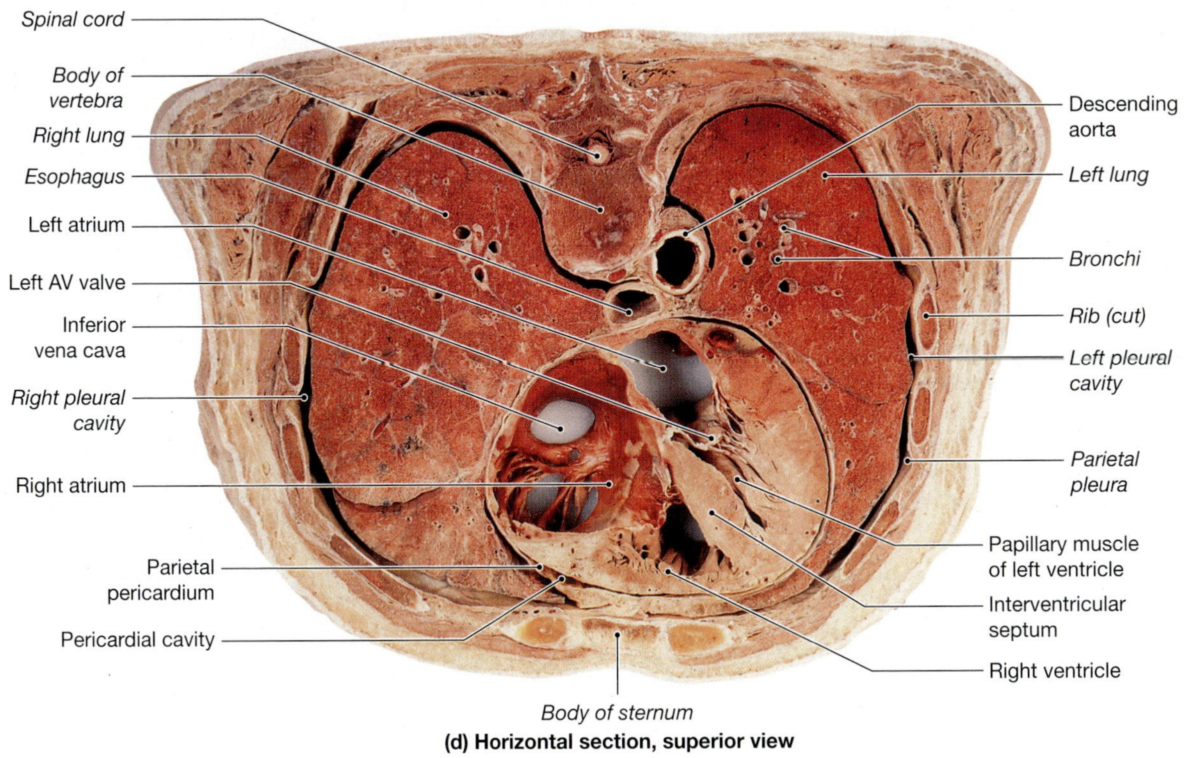

Figure 21.2 Location of the Heart in the Thoracic Cavity
The heart is situated within the middle portion of the mediastinum, immediately posterior to the sternum. **(a)** Anterior view of the open chest cavity, showing the position of the heart and major vessels relative to the lungs. The sectional plane indicates the orientation of part (c). **(b)** Relationships between the heart and the pericardial cavity. The pericardial cavity surrounds the heart like the balloon surrounds the fist (right). **(c)** Diagrammatic view showing the position of the heart and the location of other organs within the mediastinum. In this sectional view, the heart is shown intact so you can see the orientation of the major vessels. **(d)** Superior view of a horizontal section through the trunk at the level of vertebra T_8.

the positions of the pericardium, heart, and associated vessels in the mediastinum. The slender gap between the opposing parietal and visceral surfaces is the pericardial cavity. This cavity normally contains 10–20 ml of **pericardial fluid** secreted by the pericardial membranes. Pericardial fluid acts as a lubricant, reducing friction between the opposing surfaces. The moist pericardial lining prevents friction as the heart beats, and the collagen fibers binding the base of the heart to the mediastinum limit movement of the major vessels during a contraction.

Structure of the Heart Wall [Figure 21.3]

A section through the wall of the heart (Figure 21.3a,b) reveals three distinct layers: (1) an outer *epicardium* (visceral pericardium), (2) a middle *myocardium*, and (3) an inner *endocardium*.

1. The **epicardium** is the visceral pericardium; it forms the external surface of the heart. The epicardium is a serous membrane consisting of a mesothelium covering a supporting layer of areolar connective tissue.
2. The **myocardium** consists of multiple, interlocking layers of cardiac muscle tissue, with associated connective tissues, blood vessels, and nerves. The relatively thin atrial myocardium contains layers that form figure-eights as they pass from atrium to atrium. The ventricular myocardium is much thicker, and the muscle orientation changes from layer to layer. Superficial ventricular muscles wrap around both ventricles; deeper muscle layers spiral around and between the ventricles from the attached *base* toward the free tip, or *apex*, of the heart (Figure 21.3a–c).
3. The inner surfaces of the heart, including the valves, are covered by a simple squamous epithelium, known as the **endocardium** (en-dō-KAR-dē-um; *endo-*, inside). The endocardium is continuous with the endothelium of the attached blood vessels.

Cardiac Muscle Tissue [Figure 21.3b–e]

The unusual histological characteristics of cardiac muscle tissue give the myocardium its unique functional properties. Cardiac muscle tissue was introduced in Chapter 3, and its properties were briefly compared with those of other muscle types. p. 75 Cardiac muscle cells, or *cardiocytes*, are relatively small, averaging 10–20 μm in diameter and 50–100 μm in length. A typical cardiocyte has a single, centrally placed nucleus (Figure 21.3b–d).

Although they are much smaller than skeletal muscle fibers, cardiac muscle cells resemble skeletal muscle fibers in that each cardiac muscle cell contains organized myofibrils, and the alignment of their sarcomeres produces striations. However, cardiac muscle cells differ from skeletal muscle fibers in several important respects:

1. Cardiac muscle cells are almost totally dependent on aerobic respiration to obtain the energy needed to continue contracting. The sarcoplasm of a cardiac muscle cell thus contains hundreds of mitochondria and abundant reserves of myoglobin (to store oxygen). Energy reserves are maintained in the form of glycogen and lipid inclusions.
2. The relatively short T-tubules of cardiac muscle cells do not form triads with the sarcoplasmic reticulum.
3. The circulatory supply of cardiac muscle tissue is more extensive even than that of red skeletal muscle tissue. p. 250
4. Cardiac muscle cells contract without instructions from the nervous system; their contractions will be discussed later in this chapter.
5. Cardiac muscle cells are interconnected by specialized cell junctions called *intercalated discs* (Figure 21.3c–e).

The Intercalated Discs [Figure 21.3b–e]

Cardiac muscle cells are connected to neighboring cells at specialized cell junctions known as **intercalated** (in-TER-ka-lā-ted) **discs**. Intercalated discs are unique to cardiac muscle tissue (Figure 21.3b–e). The jagged appearance is due to the extensive interlocking of opposing sarcolemmal membranes. At an intercalated disc,

1. The sarcolemmae of two cardiac muscle cells are bound together by desmosomes (maculae adherens). p. 45 This locks the cells together and helps maintain the three-dimensional structure of the tissue.
2. Myofibrils in these muscle cells anchor firmly to the sarcolemma at the intercalated disc. The intercalated disc thus ties together the myofibrils of adjacent cells. As a result, the two muscle cells "pull together" with maximum efficiency.
3. Cardiac muscle cells are also connected by gap junctions. pp. 44, 75 Ions and small molecules can move between cells at gap junctions, thereby creating a direct electrical connection between the two muscle cells. As a result, the stimulus for contraction—an action potential—can move from one cardiac muscle cell to another as if the sarcolemmae were continuous.

Because cardiac muscle cells are mechanically, chemically, and electrically connected to one another, cardiac muscle tissue functions like a single, enormous muscle cell. The contraction of any one cell will trigger the contraction of several others, and the contraction will spread throughout the myocardium. For this reason, cardiac muscle has been called a *functional syncytium* (sin-SISH-ē-um; "fused mass of cells").

The Fibrous Skeleton [Figures 21.3b/21.7]

The connective tissues of the heart include large numbers of collagen and elastic fibers (Figure 21.3b). Each cardiac muscle cell is wrapped in a strong but elastic sheath, and adjacent cells are tied together by fibrous cross-links, or "struts." In turn, each muscle layer has a fibrous wrapping, and fibrous sheets separate the superficial and deep muscle layers. These connective tissue layers are continuous with dense bands of fibroelastic tissue that encircle (1) the bases of the pulmonary trunk and aorta and (2) the valves of the heart. This extensive connective tissue network is called the **fibrous skeleton** of the heart (Figure 21.7).

The fibrous skeleton has the following functions:

1. Stabilizing the positions of the muscle cells and valves in the heart.
2. Providing physical support for the cardiac muscle cells and for the blood vessels and nerves in the myocardium.
3. Distributing the forces of contraction.
4. Reinforcing the valves and helping prevent overexpansion of the heart.
5. Providing elasticity that helps return the heart to its original shape after each contraction.
6. Physically isolating the atrial muscle cells from the ventricular muscle cells; as you will see in a later section, this isolation is vital for the coordination of cardiac contractions.

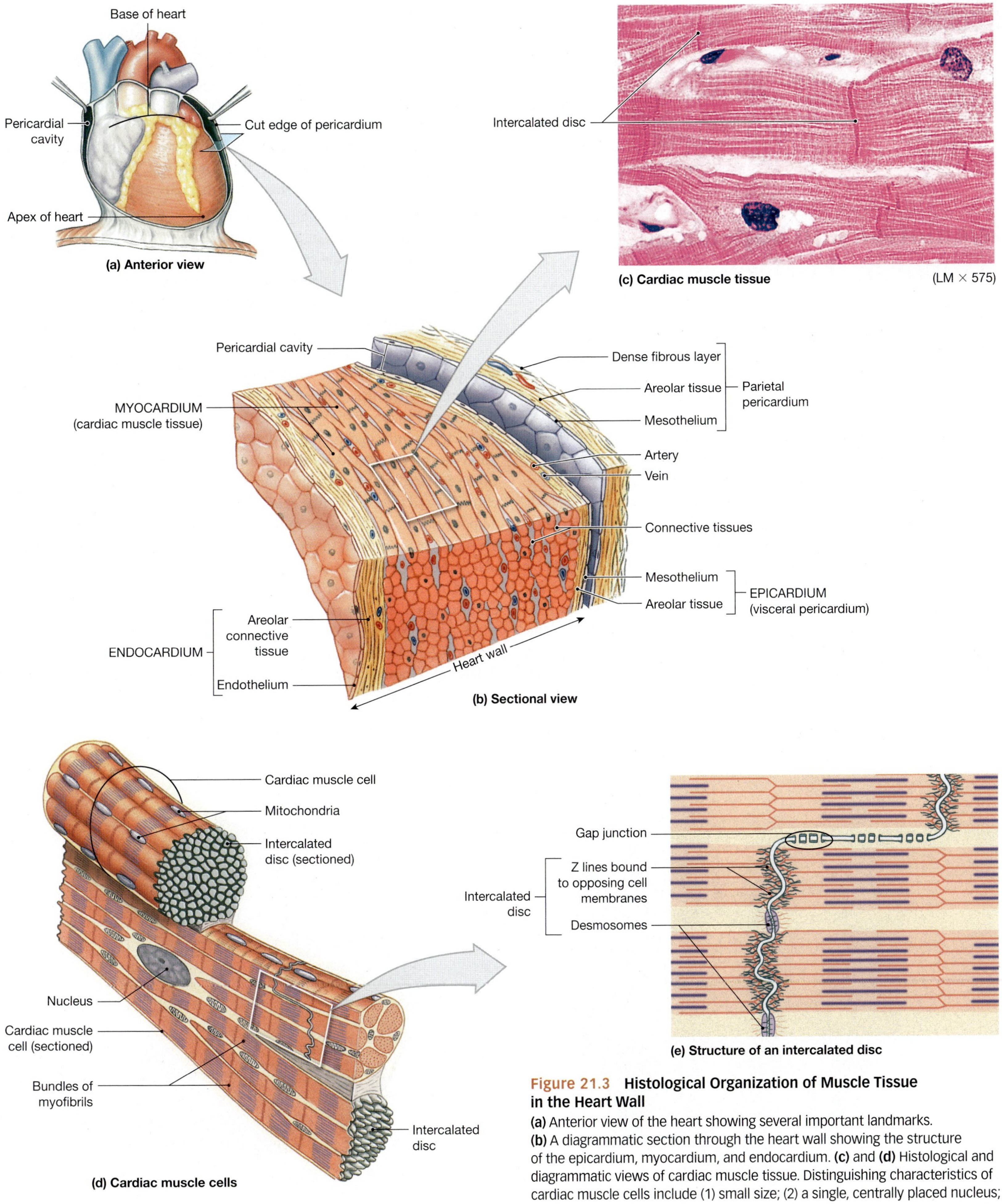

Figure 21.3 Histological Organization of Muscle Tissue in the Heart Wall
(a) Anterior view of the heart showing several important landmarks. **(b)** A diagrammatic section through the heart wall showing the structure of the epicardium, myocardium, and endocardium. **(c)** and **(d)** Histological and diagrammatic views of cardiac muscle tissue. Distinguishing characteristics of cardiac muscle cells include (1) small size; (2) a single, centrally placed nucleus; (3) branching interconnections between cells; and (4) the presence of intercalated discs. **(e)** The structure of an intercalated disc.

CONCEPT CHECK

1. How could you distinguish a sample of cardiac muscle tissue from a sample of skeletal muscle tissue?
2. What is the pericardial cavity?
3. How are cardiac muscle cells connected to their neighbors?
4. Why is cardiac muscle called a functional syncytium?

See blue "Answers" tab at back of book.

Orientation and Superficial Anatomy of the Heart

[Figures 21.2b/21.4/21.5]

Although advertisements and cartoons often show the heart at the center of the chest, a midsagittal section would not cut the heart in half. This is because the heart (1) lies slightly to the left of the midline, (2) sits at an angle to the longitudinal axis of the body, and (3) is rotated toward the left side.

1. *The heart lies slightly to the left of the midline:* The heart is located within the mediastinum, between the two lungs. Because the heart lies slightly to the left of the midline, the notch within the medial surface of the left lung is considerably deeper than the corresponding notch in the medial surface of the right lung. The **base** is the broad superior portion of the heart, where the heart is attached to the major arteries and veins of the systemic and pulmonary circuits. The base of the heart includes both the origins of the major vessels and the superior surfaces of the two atria. In terms of our balloon analogy, the base corresponds to the wrist (Figure 21.2b). The base sits posterior to the sternum at the level of the third costal cartilage, centered about 1.2 cm (0.5 in.) to the left side (Figure 21.4). The **apex** (Ā-peks) is the inferior, rounded tip of the heart, which points laterally at an oblique angle. A typical adult heart measures approximately 12.5 cm (5 in.) from the attached base to the apex. The apex reaches the fifth intercostal space approximately 7.5 cm (3 in.) to the left of the midline.
2. *The heart sits at an oblique angle to the longitudinal axis of the body:* The base forms the **superior border** of the heart. The **right border** of the heart is formed by the right atrium; the **left border** is formed by the left ventricle and a small portion of the left atrium. The left border extends to the apex, where it meets the **inferior border**. The inferior border is formed mainly by the inferior wall of the right ventricle.
3. *The heart is rotated slightly toward the left:* As a result of this rotation, the anterior surface, or **sternocostal** (ster-nō-KOS-tal) **surface**, consists primarily of the right atrium and right ventricle (Figure 21.5a). The posterior and inferior wall of the left ventricle forms much of the sloping posterior surface, or **diaphragmatic surface**, that extends between the base and the apex of the heart (Figure 21.5b).

The four internal chambers of the heart are associated with grooves or *sulci* visible on its external surface (Figure 21.5). A shallow *interatrial groove* separates the two atria, while the deeper **coronary sulcus** marks the border between the atria and the ventricles. The division between the left and right ventricles is indicated by linear depressions on the anterior surface (the **anterior interventricular sulcus**) and the posterior surface (the **posterior interventricular sulcus**). The connective tissue of the epicardium at the coronary and interventricular sulci usually contains substantial amounts of adipose tissue that must be removed to expose the underlying grooves. These sulci also contain the arteries and veins that supply blood to the cardiac muscle of the heart.

The atria and the ventricles have very different functions—the atria receive venous blood that must continue on to the ventricles, whereas the ventricles must propel blood around the systemic and pulmonary circuits. These functional differences are of course linked to external and internal structural differences. Examine Figure 21.5, which details the superficial anatomy of the heart, and note the distinguishing characteristics of the atria and ventricles.

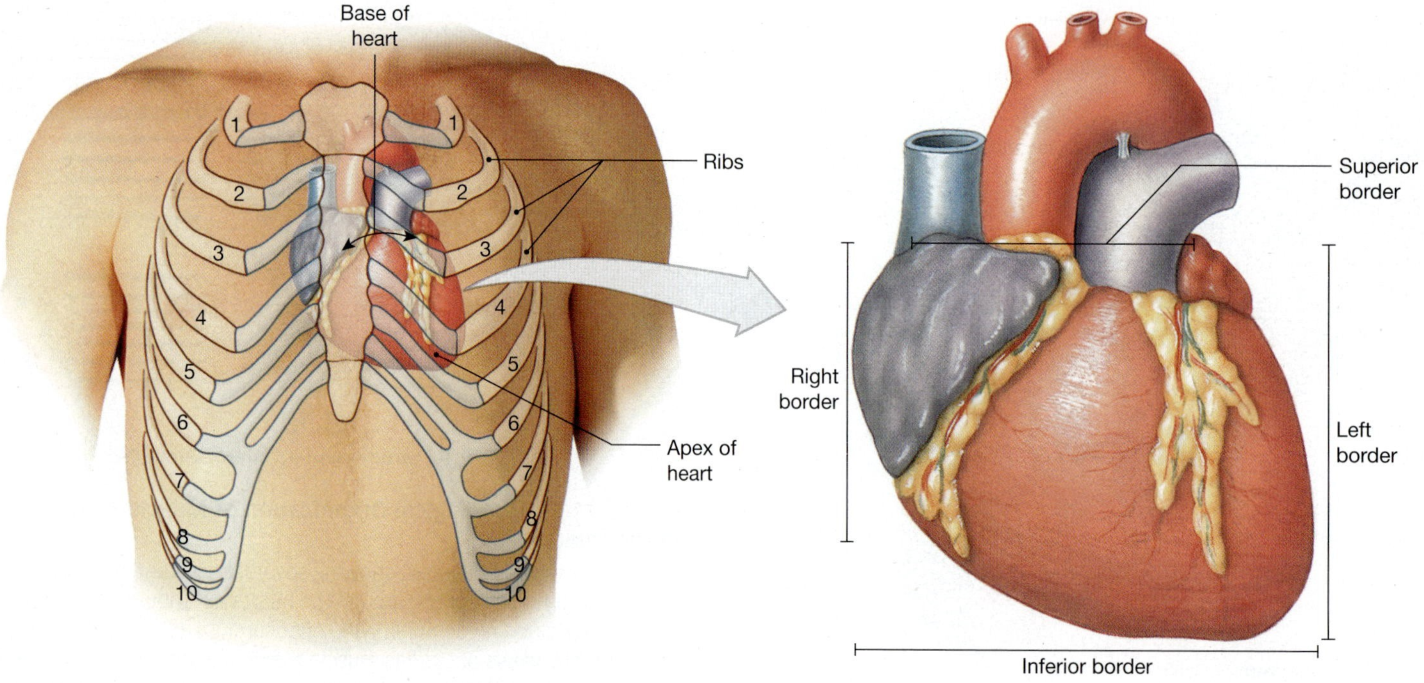

Figure 21.4 Position and Orientation of the Heart
The location of the heart within the thoracic cavity and the borders of the heart.

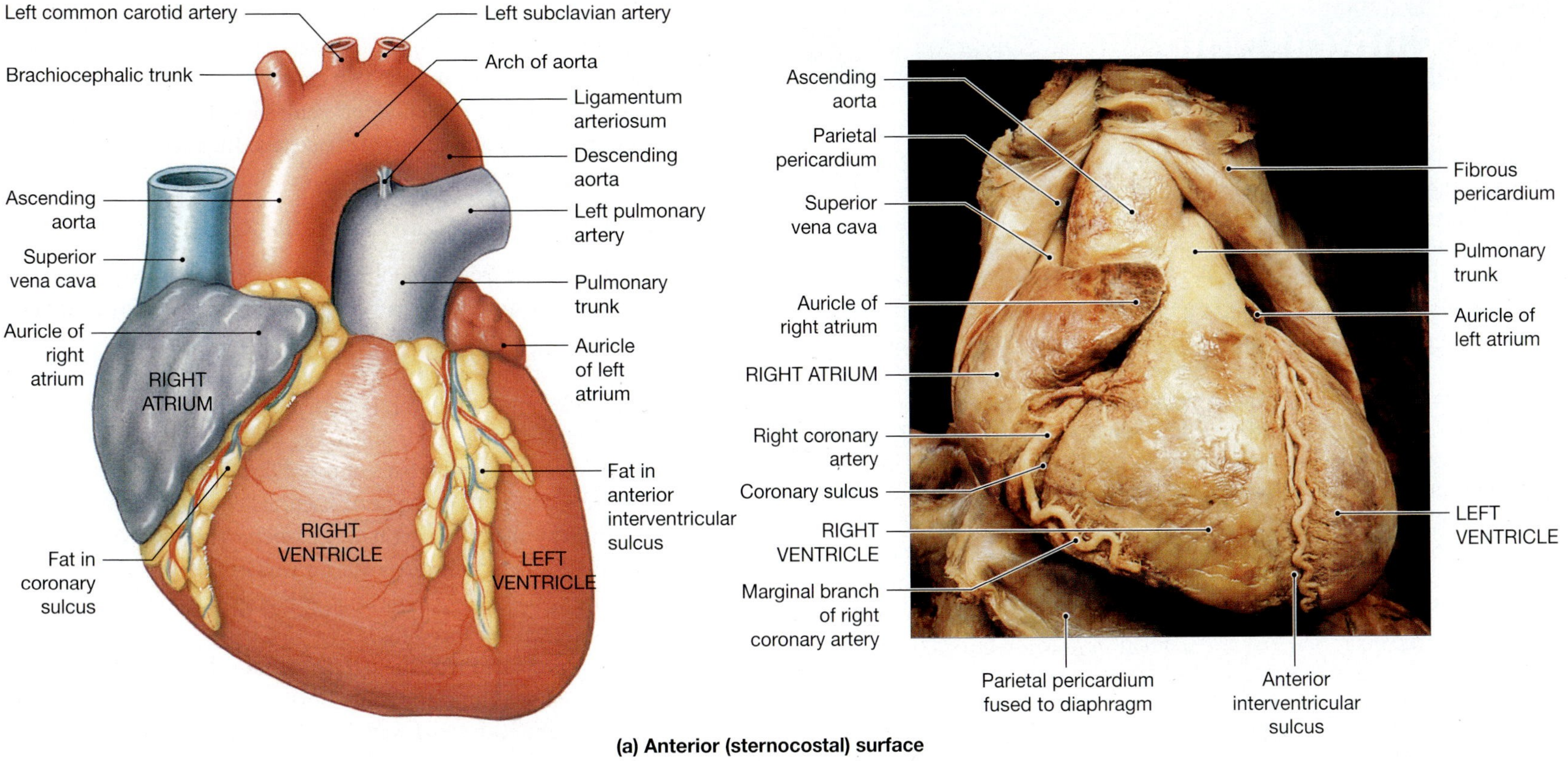

(a) Anterior (sternocostal) surface

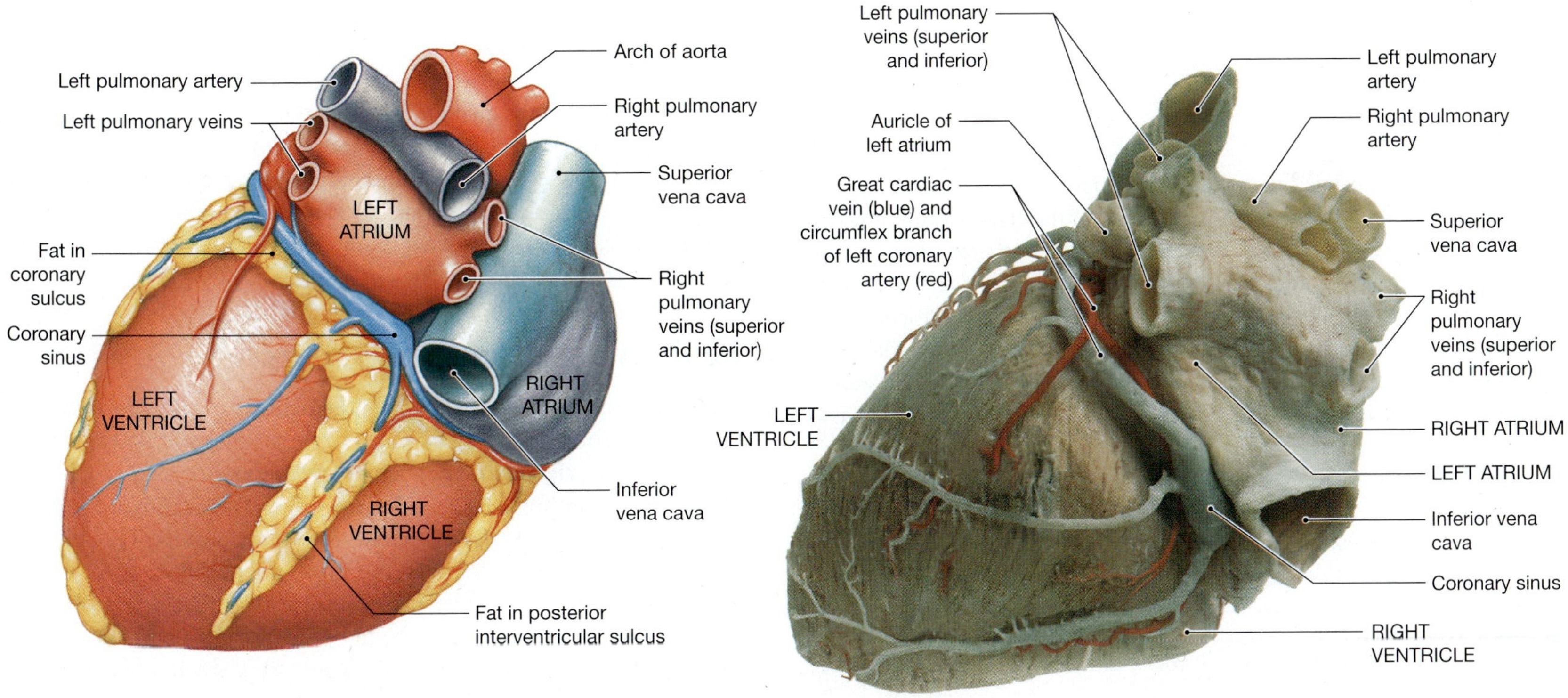

(b) Posterior (diaphragmatic) surface

Figure 21.5 Superficial Anatomy of the Heart
(a) Anterior view of the heart and great vessels. In the photo, the pericardial sac has been cut and reflected to expose the heart and great vessels. **(b)** Posterior view of the heart and great vessels; the coronary vessels have been injected with colored latex *(see Figure 21.8)*.

Clinical Note

Infection and Inflammation of the Heart Many different microorganisms may infect heart tissue, leading to serious cardiac abnormalities. **Carditis** (kar-DĪ-tis) is a general term for inflammation of the heart. Clinical conditions resulting from cardiac infection are usually identified by the primary site of the infection. For example, infections that affect the endocardium produce symptoms of *endocarditis*, a condition that damages primarily the chordae tendineae and heart valves; the mortality rate may reach 21–35 percent. The most severe complications of endocarditis result from the formation of blood clots on the damaged surfaces. These clots subsequently break free, entering the bloodstream as drifting emboli that may cause strokes, heart attacks, or kidney failure. The destruction of heart valves by the infection may lead to valve leakage, heart failure, and death.

Myocarditis, inflammation of the heart muscle, can be caused by bacteria, viruses, protozoans, or fungal pathogens that either attack the myocardium directly or produce toxins that damage the myocardium. The sarcolemma of infected heart muscle cells become facilitated, and the heart rate may rise dramatically. Over time, abnormal contractions may appear and the heart muscle weakens; these problems may eventually prove fatal.

If the pericardium becomes inflamed or infected, fluid may accumulate around the heart (**cardiac tamponade**), or the elasticity of the pericardium may be reduced (*constrictive pericarditis*). In both conditions, the expansion of the heart is restricted and cardiac output is reduced. Treatment includes draining the excess fluid or cutting a window in the pericardial sac.

The right atrium is situated anterior, inferior, and to the right of the left atrium. The left atrium extends posterior to the right atrium; it forms most of the posterior surface of the heart superior to the coronary sulcus. Both atria have relatively thin muscular walls and, as a result, they are highly distensible. When not filled with blood, the outer portion of each atrium deflates and becomes a rather lumpy and wrinkled flap. This expandable extension of an atrium is called an **auricle** (AW-ri-kel; *auris*, ear) because it reminded early anatomists of the external ear. The auricle is also known as an *atrial appendage*.

The ventricles lie inferior to the coronary sulcus (Figure 21.5). The right ventricle makes up a large percentage of the sternocostal surface of the heart. The left ventricle extends from the coronary sulcus to the apex or tip of the heart, forming the left and diaphragmatic surfaces of the heart.

Internal Anatomy and Organization of the Heart [Figure 21.6]

Figure 21.6 details the internal anatomy and functional organization of the atria and ventricles. The atria are separated by the *interatrial septum* (*septum*, a wall), and the *interventricular septum* separates the ventricles (Figure 21.6a,c). Each atrium communicates with the ventricle of the same side. **Valves** are folds of endocardium that extend into the openings between the atria and ventricles. These valves open and close to prevent backflow, thereby maintaining a one-way flow of blood from the atria into the ventricles. (Valve structure and function will be described under a separate heading.)

An atrium functions to collect blood returning to the heart and deliver it to the attached ventricle. The functional demands placed on the right and left atria are very similar, and the two chambers look almost identical. The demands placed on the right and left ventricles are very different, and there are significant structural differences between the two.

The Right Atrium [Figures 21.5/21.6a,c]

The right atrium receives oxygen-poor venous blood from the systemic circuit through the **superior vena cava** (VĒ-na CĀ-va) and the **inferior vena cava** (Figures 21.5 and 21.6a,c). The superior vena cava, which opens into the posterior, superior portion of the right atrium, delivers venous blood from the head, neck, upper limbs, and chest. The inferior vena cava, which opens into the posterior and inferior portion of the right atrium, delivers venous blood from the tissues and organs of the abdominal and pelvic cavities, and the lower limbs. The veins of the heart itself, called *coronary veins*, collect blood from the heart wall and deliver it to the *coronary sinus* (Figure 21.5b). This collecting vessel opens into the posterior wall of the right atrium, inferior to the opening of the inferior vena cava. (The coronary blood vessels will be described under a separate heading.)

Prominent muscular ridges, the **pectinate muscles** (*pectin*, comb), or *musculi pectinati*, extend along the inner surface of the right auricle and across the adjacent anterior atrial wall. The **interatrial septum** separates the right and left atria. From the fifth week of embryonic development until birth, there is an oval opening, the **foramen ovale**, in this septum. (*See Embryology Summaries* in Chapter 28.) The foramen ovale permits blood flow directly from the right atrium to the left atrium while the lungs are developing and nonfunctional. At birth the lungs begin functioning and the foramen ovale closes; after 48 hours it is permanently sealed. A small depression, the **fossa ovalis**, persists at this site in the adult heart. Occasionally the foramen ovale does not close, and it remains *patent* (open). As a result, blood recirculates into the pulmonary circuit, reducing the efficiency of systemic circulation and elevating blood pressure in the pulmonary vessels. This can lead to cardiac enlargement, fluid buildup in the lungs, and eventual heart failure.

The Right Ventricle [Figures 21.5/21.6]

Oxygen-poor venous blood travels from the right atrium into the right ventricle through a broad opening bounded by three fibrous flaps. These flaps, or **cusps**, form the **right atrioventricular (AV) valve**, or *tricuspid valve* (trī-KUS-pid; *tri*, three) (Figure 21.6). The free edges of the cusps are attached to bundles of collagen fibers, the *chordae tendineae* (KOR-dē TEN-di-nē-ē; "tendinous cords"). These bundles arise from the **papillary** (PAP-i-ler-ē) **muscles**, cone-shaped muscular projections of the inner ventricular surface. The chordae tendineae limit the movement of the cusps and prevent backflow of blood from the right ventricle into the right atrium; the mechanism will be detailed in a later section.

The internal surface of the ventricle contains a series of irregular muscular folds, the **trabeculae carneae** (tra-BEK-ū-lē CAR-nē-ē; *carneus*, fleshy). The **moderator band** is a band of ventricular muscle that extends from the **interventricular septum**, a thick, muscular partition that separates the two ventricles, to the anterior wall of the right ventricle and the bases of the papillary muscles.

The superior end of the right ventricle tapers to a smooth-walled, cone-shaped pouch, the **conus arteriosus**, which ends at the **pulmonary valve** *(pulmonary semilunar valve)*. This valve consists of three thick semilunar (half moon–shaped) cusps. As blood is ejected from the right ventricle, it passes

Figure 21.6 Sectional Anatomy of the Heart
(a) Diagrammatic frontal section through the relaxed heart, showing major landmarks and the path of blood flow through the atria and ventricles (arrows).
(b) Photograph of papillary muscles and chordae tendineae supporting the right AV valve. The picture was taken inside the right ventricle, looking toward a light shining from the right atrium.
(c) Anterior view of a frontally sectioned heart, showing internal features and valves. The cardiac arteries and veins have been injected with latex; the arteries are red, the veins blue.
(d) Horizontal section through the heart at the level of vertebra T_8.

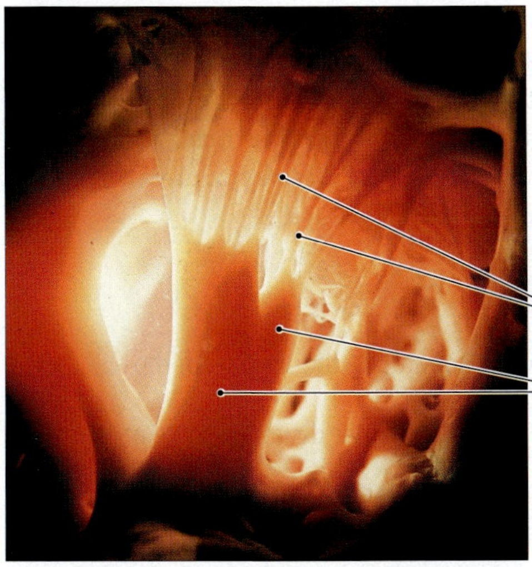

(b) Interior view, right ventricle

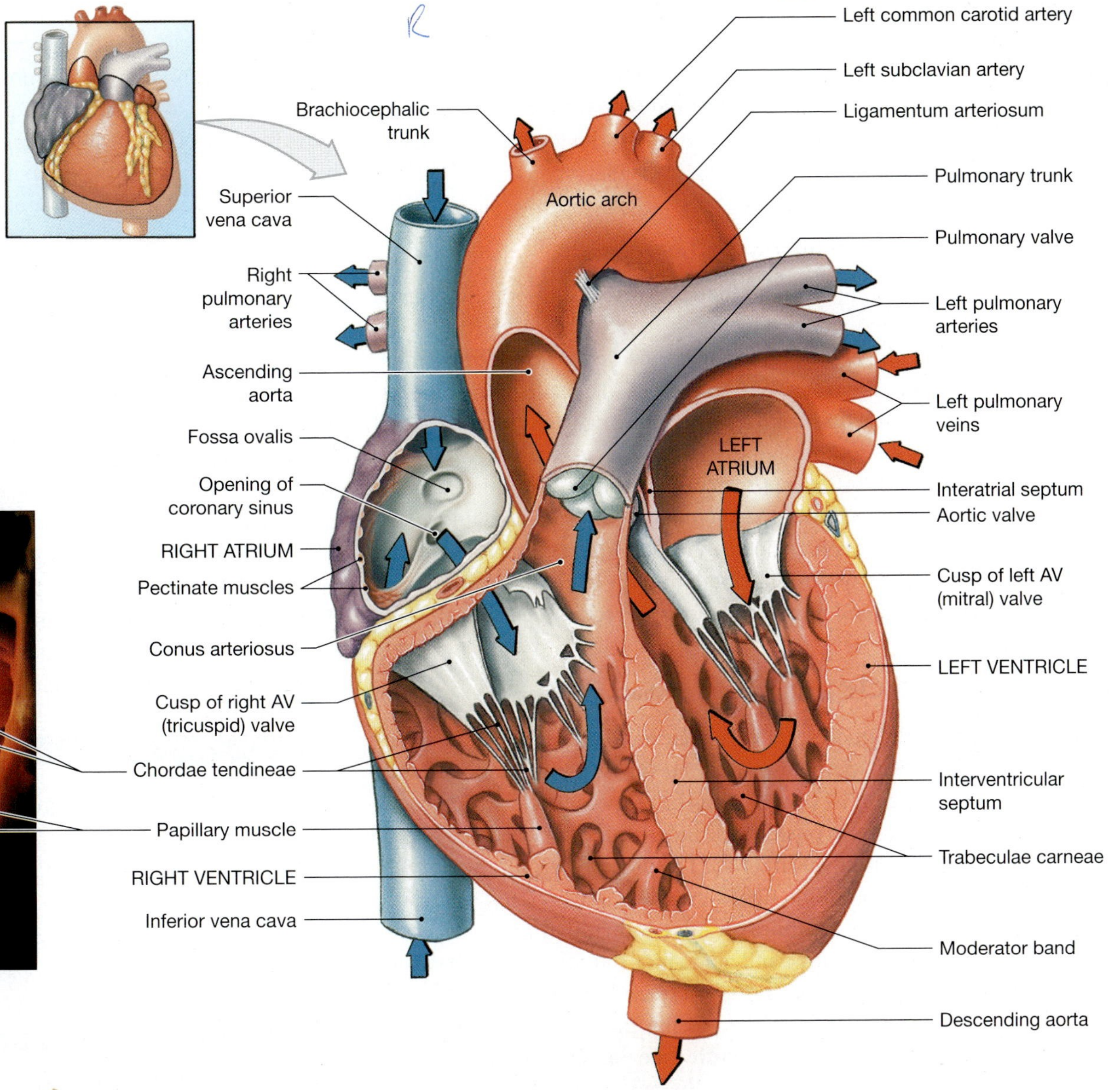

(a) Frontal section, anterior view

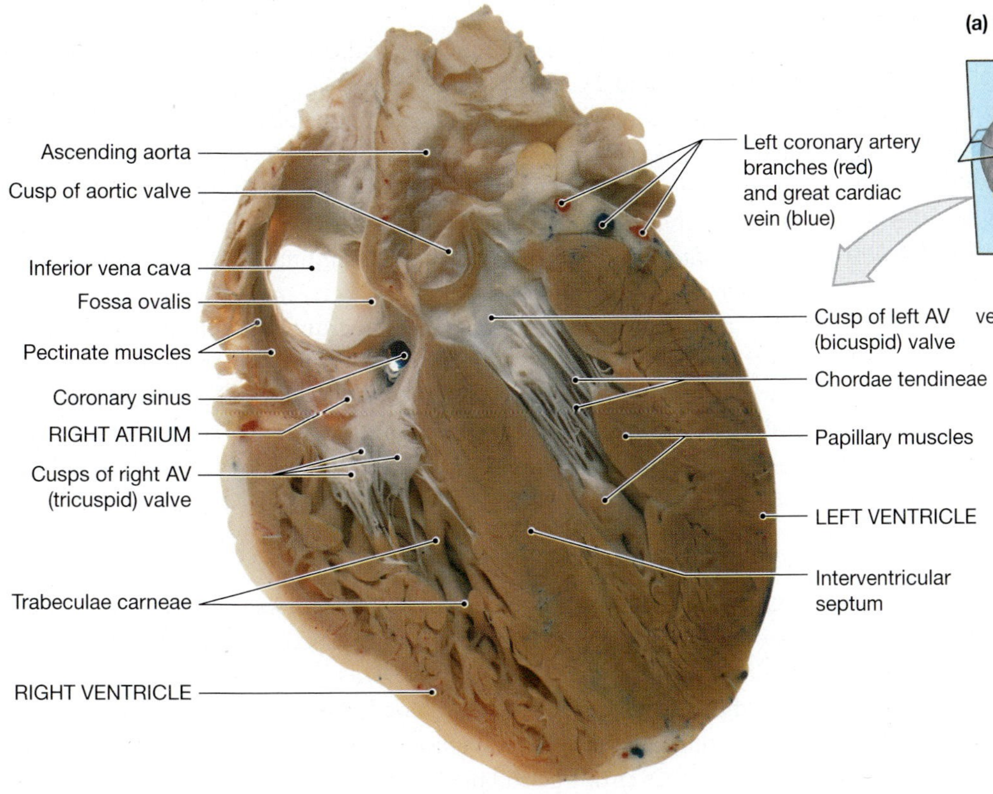

(c) Frontal section, anterior view

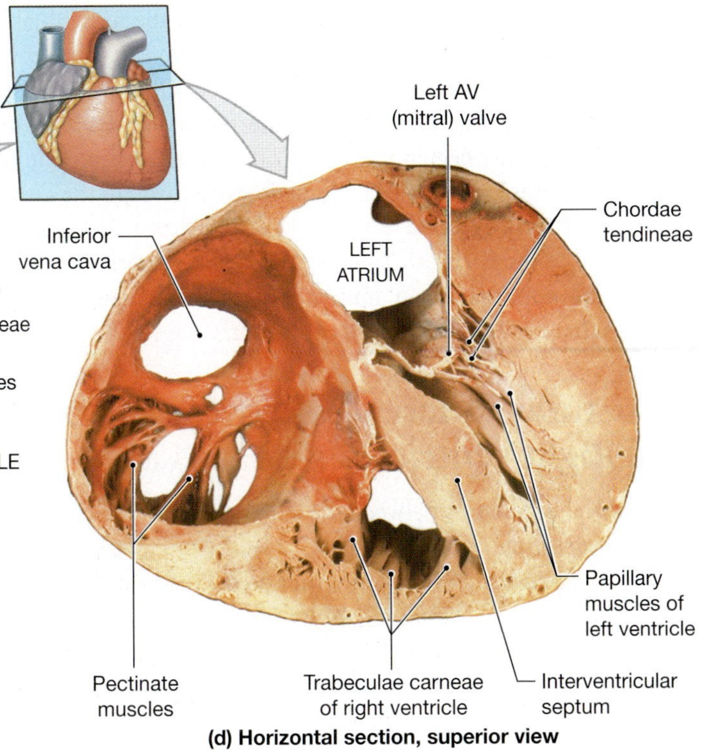

(d) Horizontal section, superior view

through this valve to enter the **pulmonary trunk**, the start of the pulmonary circuit. The arrangement of cusps in this valve prevents the backflow of blood into the right ventricle when that chamber relaxes. From the pulmonary trunk, blood flows into both the **left** and **right pulmonary arteries** (Figures 21.5 and 21.6). These vessels branch repeatedly within the lungs before supplying the pulmonary capillaries, where gas exchange occurs.

The Left Atrium [Figures 21.5/21.6a]

From the pulmonary capillaries, the blood, now oxygen-rich, flows into small veins that ultimately unite to form four pulmonary veins, two from each lung. These **left** and **right pulmonary veins** empty into the posterior portion of the left atrium (Figures 21.5 and 21.6a). The left atrium lacks pectinate muscles, but it has an auricle. Blood flowing from the left atrium into the left ventricle passes through the **left atrioventricular (AV) valve**, also known as the *mitral* (MĪ-tral; *mitre*, a bishop's hat) *valve* or the *bicuspid* (bī-KUS-pid) *valve.* As the name *bicuspid* implies, this valve contains a pair of cusps (*bi-*, two) rather than a trio (*tri-*, three). The left atrioventricular valve permits the flow of oxygen-rich blood from the left atrium into the left ventricle, but prevents blood flow in the reverse direction.

The Left Ventricle [Figures 21.5/21.6a,c,d]

The left ventricle has the thickest wall of any heart chamber. The extra-thick myocardium enables it to develop enough pressure to force blood around the entire systemic circuit; by comparison the right ventricle, which has a relatively thin wall, must push blood to the lungs and then back to the heart, a total distance of only about 30 cm (1 ft). The internal organization of the left ventricle resembles that of the right ventricle (Figure 21.6a,c,d). However, the trabeculae carneae are more prominent than they are in the right ventricle, there is no moderator band, and since the mitral valve has two cusps, there are two large papillary muscles rather than three.

Blood leaves the left ventricle by passing through the **aortic valve** *(aortic semilunar valve)* into the **ascending aorta**. The arrangement of cusps in the aortic valve is the same as in the pulmonary semilunar valve. Saclike dilations of the base of the ascending aorta occur adjacent to each cusp. These sacs, called **aortic sinuses**, prevent the individual cusps from sticking to the wall of the aorta when the valve opens. The *right* and *left coronary arteries*, which deliver blood to the myocardium, originate at the aortic sinus. The aortic valve prevents the backflow of blood into the left ventricle once it has been pumped out of the heart and into the systemic circuit. From the ascending aorta, blood flows on through the **aortic arch** and into the **descending aorta** (Figures 21.5 and 21.6a). The pulmonary trunk is attached to the aortic arch by the *ligamentum arteriosum*, a fibrous band that is the remnant of an important fetal blood vessel. Cardiovascular changes that occur at birth are described in Chapter 22.

Structural Differences between the Left and Right Ventricles [Figure 21.6a,c,d]

Anatomical differences between the left and right ventricles are best seen in three-dimensional or sectional views (Figure 21.6a,c,d). The lungs partially enclose the pericardial cavity, and the base of the heart lies between the left and right lungs. As a result, the pulmonary arteries and veins are relatively short and wide, and the right ventricle normally does not need to push very hard to propel blood through the pulmonary circuit. The wall of the right ventricle is relatively thin, and in sectional view it resembles a pouch attached to the massive wall of the left ventricle. When the right ventricle contracts, it moves toward the wall of the left ventricle. This compresses the blood within the right ventricle, and the rising pressure forces the blood through the pulmonary valve and into the pulmonary trunk. This mechanism moves blood very efficiently at relatively low pressures, which are all that one needs to move blood around the pulmonary circuit. Higher pressures would actually be dangerous, because the pulmonary capillaries are very delicate. Pressures as high as those found in systemic capillaries would both damage the pulmonary vessels and force fluid into the alveoli of the lungs.

A comparable pumping arrangement would not be suitable for the left ventricle, because six to seven times as much force must be exerted to propel blood through the systemic circuit. The left ventricle, which has an extremely thick muscular wall, is round in cross section. When the left ventricle contracts, two things happen: The distance between the base and apex decreases, and the diameter of the ventricular chamber decreases. If you imagine the effects of simultaneously squeezing and rolling up the end of a toothpaste tube, you will get the idea. The forces generated are quite powerful, more than enough to force open the aortic valve and eject blood into the ascending aorta. As the powerful left ventricle contracts, it also bulges into the right ventricular cavity. This intrusion improves the efficiency of the right ventricle's efforts. Individuals whose right ventricular musculature has been severely damaged may continue to survive because of the extra push provided by the contraction of the left ventricle.

CONCEPT CHECK

1. What is the name of the groove separating the atria from the ventricles?
2. What are some external characteristics that distinguish the atria from the ventricles?

See blue "Answers" tab at back of book.

The Structure and Function of Heart Valves [Figures 21.6/21.7]

Details of the structure and function of the four heart valves are shown in Figures 21.6 and 21.7.

The *atrioventricular (AV) valves* are situated between the atria and the ventricles. Each AV valve has four components: (1) a ring of connective tissue that attaches to the fibrous skeleton of the heart; (2) connective tissue *cusps*, which function to close the opening between the heart chambers; and (3) *chordae tendineae* that attach the margins of the cusps to (4) the *papillary muscles* of the heart wall.

There are two **semilunar valves** guarding the outflow from the two ventricles. These valves get their names from the shape of their three valvules or cusps, which resemble half moon–shaped pockets. The **pulmonary valve** is found at the exit of the pulmonary trunk from the right ventricle, while the **aortic valve** is found at the exit of the aorta from the left ventricle.

Valve Function during the Cardiac Cycle

The chordae tendineae and papillary muscles associated with the AV valves play an important role in the normal function of the AV valves during the cardiac cycle. During the period of ventricular relaxation (*ventricular diastole*) the ventricles are filling with blood, the papillary muscles are relaxed, and the open AV valve offers no resistance to the flow of blood from atrium to ventricle. Over this period the semilunar valves are closed; the semilunar valves do not need chordae tendineae because the relative positions of the

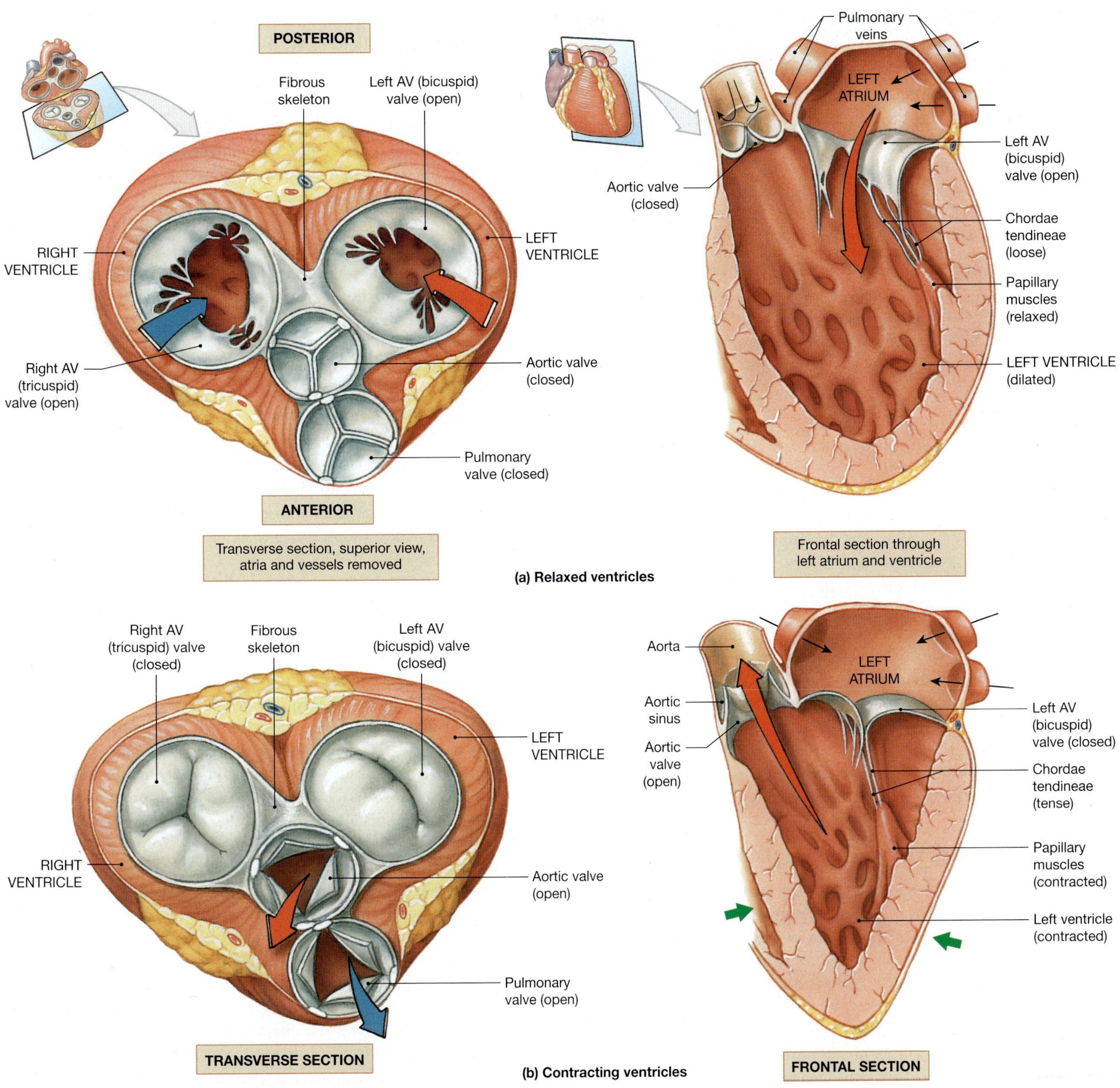

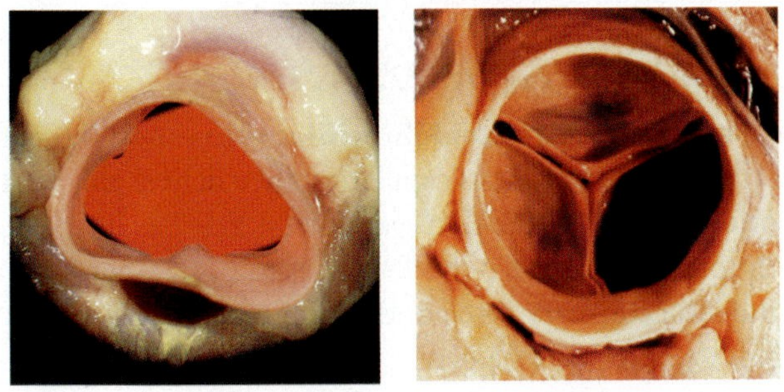

Figure 21.7 Valves of the Heart

Red (oxygenated) and blue (deoxygenated) arrows indicate blood flow into or out of a ventricle; black arrows, blood flow into an atrium; and green arrows, ventricular contraction. **(a)** When the ventricles are relaxed, the AV valves are open and the semilunar valves are closed. The chordae tendineae are loose, and the papillary muscles are relaxed. **(b)** When the ventricles are contracting, the AV valves are closed and the semilunar valves are open. In the frontal section notice the attachment of the left AV valve to the chordae tendineae and papillary muscles. **(c)** The aortic valve in the open (left) and closed (right) positions. The individual cusps brace one another in the closed position.

Clinical Note

Mitral Valve Prolapse Minor abnormalities in valve shape are relatively common. For example, an estimated 10 percent of normal individuals age 14–30 have some degree of **mitral valve prolapse (MVP)**. In this condition the mitral valve cusps do not close properly. The problem may involve abnormally long (or short) chordae tendineae or malfunctioning papillary muscles. Because the valve does not work perfectly, some regurgitation may occur during left ventricular systole. The surges, swirls, and eddies that occur during regurgitation create a rushing, gurgling sound known as a **heart murmur**. Most of these individuals are completely asymptomatic, and they live normal, healthy lives unaware of any circulatory malfunction. However, regurgitation may increase the risk of valve infection after dental (or some medical) procedures.

cusps are stable, and the three symmetrical cusps support one another like the legs of a tripod.

When the period of ventricular contraction *(ventricular systole)* begins, blood leaving the ventricles opens the semilunar valves, while blood moving back toward the atria swings the cusps of the AV valves together. Tension in the papillary muscles and chordae tendineae keeps the cusps from swinging farther and opening into the atria. Thus, the chordae tendineae and papillary muscles are essential to prevent the backflow, or *regurgitation*, of blood into the atria each time the ventricles contract.

Serious valvular abnormalities can interfere with cardiac function; the timing and intensity of the related heart sounds can provide useful diagnostic information. Physicians use an instrument called a **stethoscope** (STETH-ō-scōp) to listen to normal and abnormal heart sounds. Valve sounds may be muffled as they pass through the pericardium, surrounding tissues, and the chest wall. As a result, the stethoscope placement does not always correspond to the position of the valve under review.

Coronary Blood Vessels [Figure 21.8]

The heart works continuously, and cardiac muscle cells require reliable supplies of oxygen and nutrients. The **coronary circulation** supplies blood to the muscle tissue of the heart. During maximum exertion, the oxygen demand rises considerably, and the blood flow to the heart may increase to nine times that of resting levels.

The coronary circulation (Figure 21.8) includes an extensive network of coronary blood vessels. The left and right **coronary arteries** originate at the base of the ascending aorta, within the aortic sinus, as the first branches of this vessel. Blood pressure here is the highest found anywhere in the systemic circuit, and this pressure ensures a continuous flow of blood to meet the demands of active cardiac muscle tissue.

The Right Coronary Artery [Figure 21.8]

The **right coronary artery** (RCA) branches off the ascending aorta, turns to the right, and passes between the right auricle and the pulmonary trunk. It then continues within the coronary sulcus. Although many variations may occur, the branches of the right coronary artery typically supply blood to (1) the right atrium, (2) a portion of the left atrium, (3) the interatrial septum, (4) the entire right ventricle, (5) a variable portion of the left ventricle, (6) the posteroinferior one-third of the interventricular septum, and (7) portions of the conducting system of the heart. The major branches are shown in Figure 21.8.

1. *Atrial branches:* As it curves across the anterior surface of the heart, the right coronary artery gives rise to **atrial branches** that supply the myocardium of the right atrium and a portion of the left atrium.
2. *Ventricular branches:* Near the right border of the heart, the right coronary artery usually gives rise to the **right marginal branch** that extends toward the apex along the anterior surface of the right ventricle. It then continues across the posterior surface of the heart, supplying the **posterior interventricular branch**, or *posterior descending artery*, which runs toward the apex within the posterior interventricular sulcus. This branch supplies blood to the interventricular septum and adjacent portions of the ventricles.
3. *Branches to the conducting system:* A small branch near the base of the right coronary artery penetrates the atrial wall to reach the *sinoatrial (SA) node*, also known as the *cardiac pacemaker*. A small branch to the *atrioventricular (AV) node*, another part of the conducting system of the heart, originates from the right coronary artery near the posterior interventricular branch. These nodes and their role in the regulation of the heartbeat will be the topic of a later section.

The Left Coronary Artery [Figure 21.8]

The **left coronary artery** commonly supplies blood to (1) most of the left ventricle, (2) a narrow slip of the right ventricle, (3) most of the left atrium, and (4) the anterior two-thirds of the interventricular septum. As it reaches the anterior surface of the heart, it gives rise to a *circumflex branch* and an *anterior interventricular branch* (Figure 21.8). The **circumflex branch** curves to the left within the coronary sulcus, giving rise to one or more diagonal branches as it curves toward the posterior surface of the heart. It usually gives rise to a **left marginal branch**, and on reaching the posterior surface of the heart it forms a **posterior left ventricular branch**. The distal portions of the circumflex artery often meet and fuse with small branches of the right coronary artery. The much larger **anterior interventricular branch**, or *left anterior descending branch*, runs along the anterior surface within the anterior interventricular sulcus. This artery supplies the anterior ventricular myocardium and the anterior two-thirds of the interventricular septum. Small branches from the anterior interventricular branch of the left coronary artery are continuous with those of the posterior interventricular branch of the right coronary artery. Such interconnections between arteries are called **anastomoses** (a-nas-tō-MŌ-ses; *anastomosis*, outlet). Because the arteries are interconnected in this way, the blood supply to the ventricular muscle remains relatively constant, regardless of pressure fluctuations within the left and right coronary arteries.

The Cardiac Veins [Figures 21.5b/21.8a,b]

The **great cardiac vein** and **middle cardiac vein** collect blood from smaller veins draining the myocardial capillaries; they deliver this venous blood to the **coronary sinus**, a large thin-walled vein that lies in the posterior portion of the coronary sulcus (Figures 21.5b and 21.8a,b). As noted earlier in the chapter, the coronary sinus drains into the right atrium inferior to the opening of the inferior vena cava.

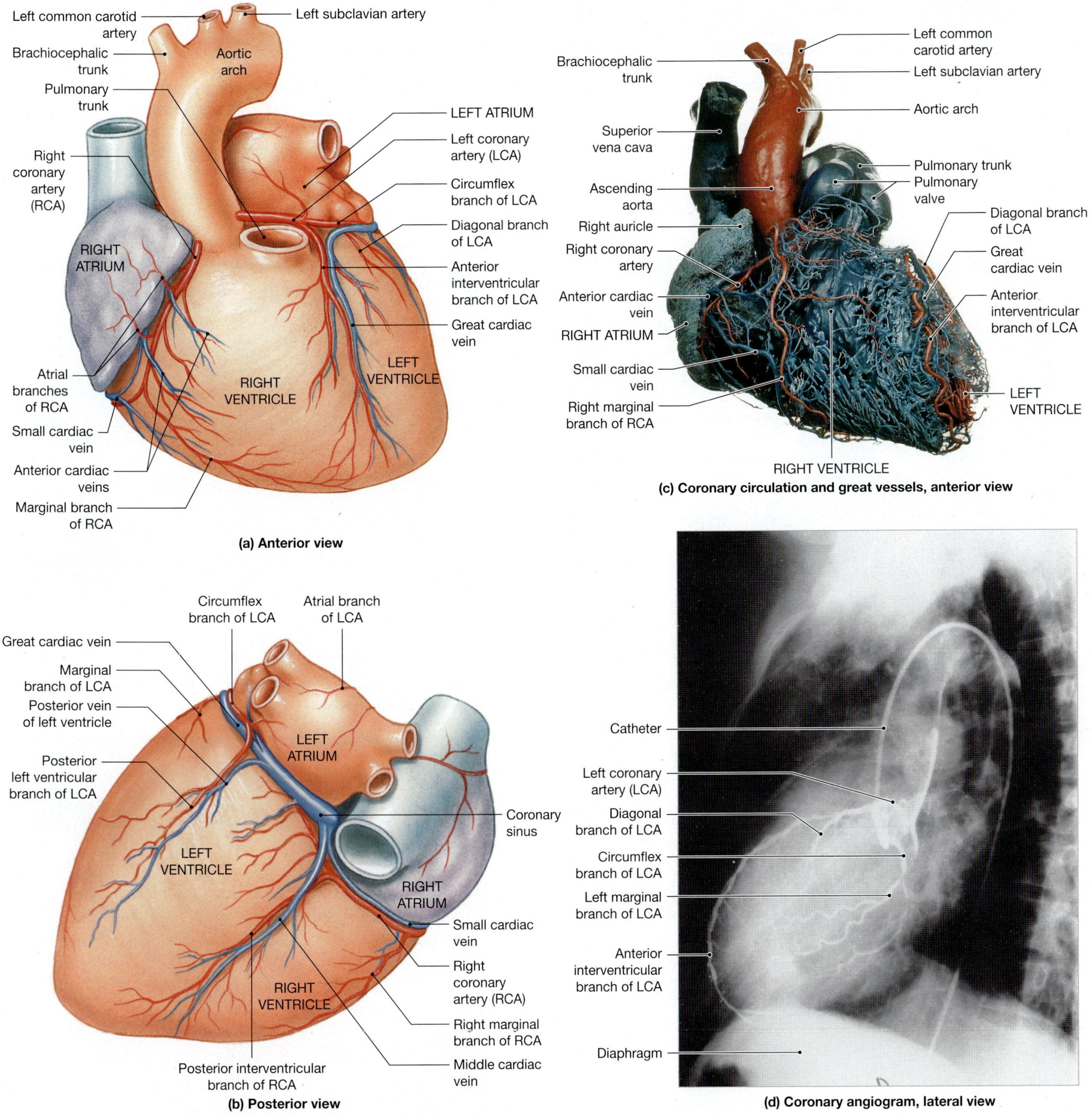

Figure 21.8 Coronary Circulation

(a) Coronary vessels supplying the anterior surface of the heart. **(b)** Coronary vessels supplying the posterior surface of the heart. **(c)** A cast of the coronary vessels, showing the complexity and extent of the coronary circulation. Coronary vessels are also seen in *Figure 21.5*. **(d)** Coronary angiogram showing the coronary arteries, left lateral projection.

Clinical Note

Coronary Artery Disease The term **coronary artery disease (CAD)** refers to degenerative changes in the coronary circulation. Cardiac muscle fibers need a constant supply of oxygen and nutrients, and any reduction in coronary circulation produces a corresponding reduction in cardiac performance. Such reduced circulatory supply, known as **coronary ischemia** (is-KĒ-mē-a), usually results from partial or complete blockage of the coronary arteries. The usual cause is the formation of a fatty deposit, or *plaque*, in the wall of a coronary vessel. The plaque, or an associated thrombus, then narrows the passageway and reduces or stops blood flow. Spasms in the smooth muscles of the vessel wall can further decrease blood flow or even stop it altogether. A variety of imaging procedures can be used to visualize coronary circulation, including **coronary angiography** (Figure 21.8d) and DSA (Digital Subtraction Angiography) scans (Figure 21.9a,b).

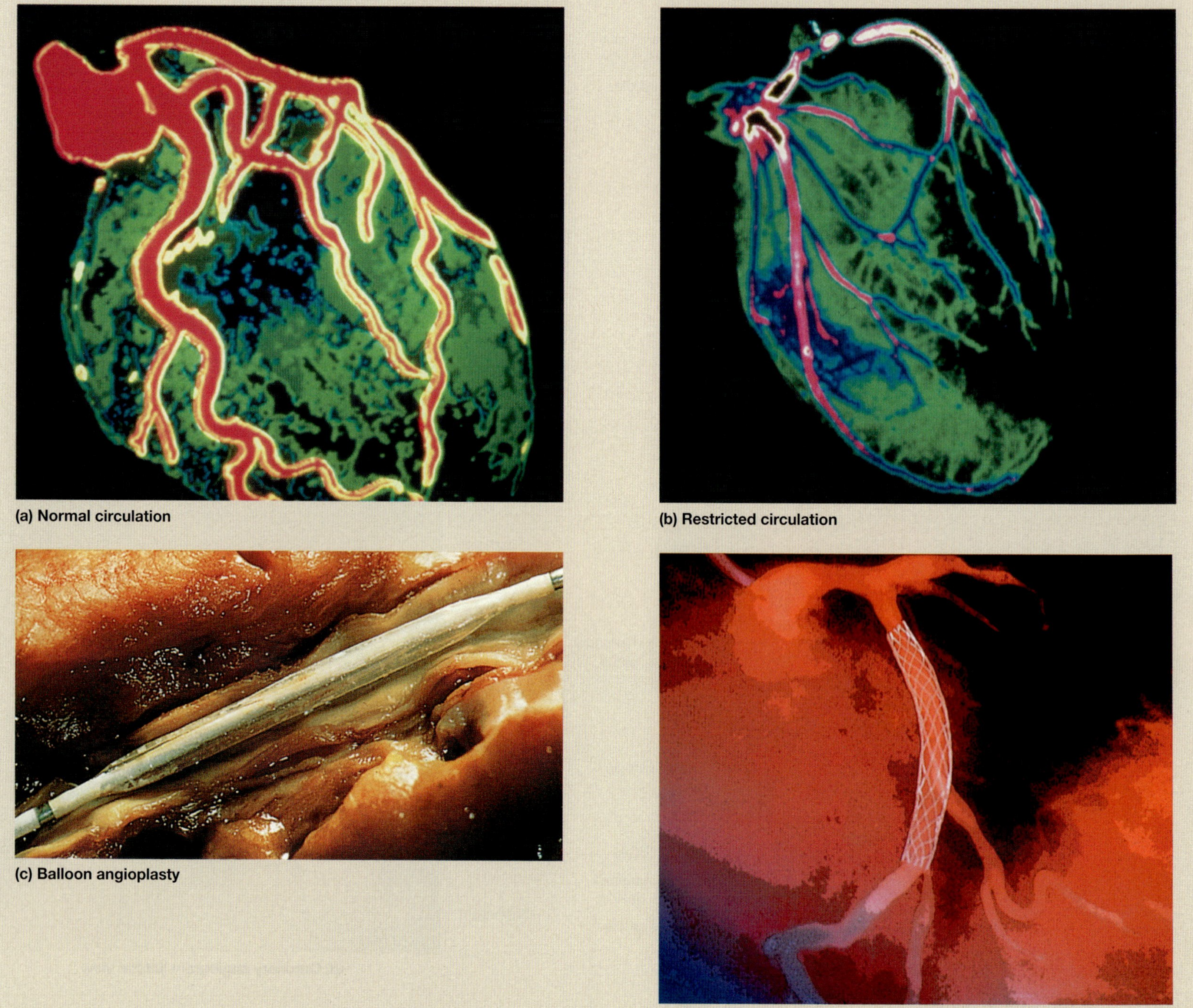

(a) Normal circulation

(b) Restricted circulation

(c) Balloon angioplasty

(d) Coronary stent

Figure 21.9 Coronary Circulation and Clinical Testing
(a) A color-enhanced DSA image of a healthy heart. The ventricular walls have an extensive circulatory supply. (The atria are not shown.) **(b)** A color-enhanced DSA image of a damaged heart. Most of the ventricular myocardium is deprived of circulation. **(c)** Balloon angioplasty can sometimes be used to remove a circulatory blockage. The catheter is guided through the coronary arteries to the site of blockage and inflated to press the soft plaque against the vessel wall. **(d)** A stent is often inserted after balloon angioplasty to help prevent plaques from recurring. This scan shows a stent in the anterior interventricular branch of the left coronary artery.

Clinical Note *(continued)*

One of the first symptoms of CAD is often **angina pectoris** (an-JĪ-na PEK-tor-is; *angina*, pain spasm + *pectoris*, of the chest). In the most common form of angina, temporary insufficiency of oxygen delivery and ischemia develop when the workload of the heart increases. Although the individual may feel comfortable at rest, any unusual exertion or emotional stress can produce a sensation of pressure, chest constriction, and pain that may radiate from the sternal area to the arms, back, and neck.

Angina can often be controlled by a combination of drug treatment and changes in lifestyle. Lifestyle changes to combat angina include (1) limiting activities known to trigger angina attacks, such as strenuous exercise, and avoiding stressful situations while doing moderate, regular exercise within tolerated limits; (2) stopping smoking; and (3) modifying the diet to lower fat consumption. Medications useful for controlling angina include drugs that block sympathetic stimulation (*propranolol* or *metoprolol*); vasodilators, such as *nitroglycerin* (nī-trō-GLIS-er-in) or *atrial natriuretic peptide*; or drugs that block calcium movement into the cardiac muscle fibers *(calcium channel blockers)*. Drugs that lower cholesterol and lipid levels in the blood may prevent plaque growth or even cause plaque regression.

Angina can also be treated surgically. A single, soft plaque may be removed with the aid of a slender, elongated **catheter** (KATH-e-ter). The catheter, a small-diameter tube, is inserted into a large artery (generally the femoral) and guided to the plaque in a coronary artery. A variety of different surgical tools can be slid into the catheter, and the plaque can then be removed with laser beams or chewed to pieces by a miniature version of the Roto-Rooter machine. Debris created during plaque destruction is sucked up by the catheter, preventing blockage of smaller vessels.

In **balloon angioplasty** (AN-jē-ō-plas-tē; *angeion*, vessel), the catheter tip contains an inflatable balloon. Once in position, the balloon is inflated, compressing the plaque against the vessel walls (Figure 21.9c). This procedure works best on small (under 10 mm), soft plaques. Because *restenosis*, or repeated narrowing, may develop, metal *stents*, or sleeves, can often be put into the artery to hold it open (Figure 21.9d).

Coronary bypass surgery involves taking a small section from either a small artery (often the *internal thoracic artery*) or a peripheral vein, such as a branch of the femoral vein, and using it to create a detour around the obstructed portion of a coronary artery. As many as four coronary arteries can be rerouted this way during a single operation. The procedures are named according to the number of vessels repaired, so one speaks of single, double, triple, or quadruple coronary bypass operations. Current recommendations are that coronary bypass surgery should be reserved for cases of severe angina that do not respond to other treatment.

Cardiac veins that empty into the great cardiac vein or the coronary sinus include (1) the **posterior vein of the left ventricle**, draining the area served by the circumflex artery; (2) the **middle cardiac vein**, draining the area supplied by the posterior interventricular artery; and (3) the **small cardiac vein**, which receives blood from the posterior surfaces of the right atrium and ventricle. The **anterior cardiac veins**, which drain the anterior surface of the right ventricle, empty directly into the right atrium.

CONCEPT CHECK

1. What would happen if there were no valves between the atria and ventricles?
2. What three major veins open into the right atrium?
3. Trace the path of blood from the left ventricle to the respiratory surfaces of the lungs.
4. What prevents the AV valves from opening back into the atria?

See blue "Answers" tab at back of book.

The Cardiac Cycle [Figure 21.10]

The period between the start of one heartbeat and the beginning of the next is a single cardiac cycle. The cardiac cycle therefore includes alternate periods of contraction and relaxation. For any one chamber in the heart, the cardiac cycle can be divided into two phases. During contraction, or **systole** (SIS-tō-lē), a chamber ejects blood either into another heart chamber or into an arterial trunk. Systole is followed by the second phase, one of relaxation, or **diastole** (dī-AS-tō-lē). During diastole a chamber fills with blood and prepares for the start of the next cardiac cycle. The events of the cardiac cycle are summarized in Figure 21.10.

The Coordination of Cardiac Contractions [Figure 21.11]

The function of any pump is to develop pressure and move a particular volume of fluid in a specific direction at an acceptable speed. The heart works in cycles of contraction and relaxation, and the pressure within each chamber alternately rises and falls. The AV and semilunar valves help ensure a one-way flow of blood despite these pressure oscillations. Blood will flow out of an atrium only as long as the AV valve is open and atrial pressure exceeds ventricular pressure. Similarly, blood will flow from a ventricle into an arterial trunk only as long as the semilunar valve is open and ventricular pressure exceeds the arterial pressure. The proper functioning of the heart thus depends on proper timing of atrial and ventricular contractions. The elaborate pacemaking and conduction systems normally provide the required timing.

Unlike skeletal muscle, cardiac muscle tissue contracts on its own, in the absence of neural or hormonal stimulation. This inherent ability to generate and conduct impulses is called *automaticity* or *autorhythmicity*. (Automaticity is also characteristic of some types of smooth muscle tissue discussed in Chapter 25.) Neural or hormonal stimuli can alter the basic rhythm of contraction, but even a heart removed for a heart transplant will continue to beat unless steps are taken to prevent it.

Each contraction follows a precise sequence: The atria contract first and then the ventricles. If the contractions follow another sequence, the normal pattern of blood flow is disturbed. For example, if the atria and ventricles contract at the same time, the closing of the AV valves prevents blood flow between the atria and ventricles. Cardiac contractions are coordinated by specialized *conducting cells*, cardiac muscle cells that are incapable of undergoing powerful contractions. There are two distinct populations of these

Figure 21.10 The Cardiac Cycle
Black arrows indicate movement of blood or valves; green arrows indicate myocardial contraction.

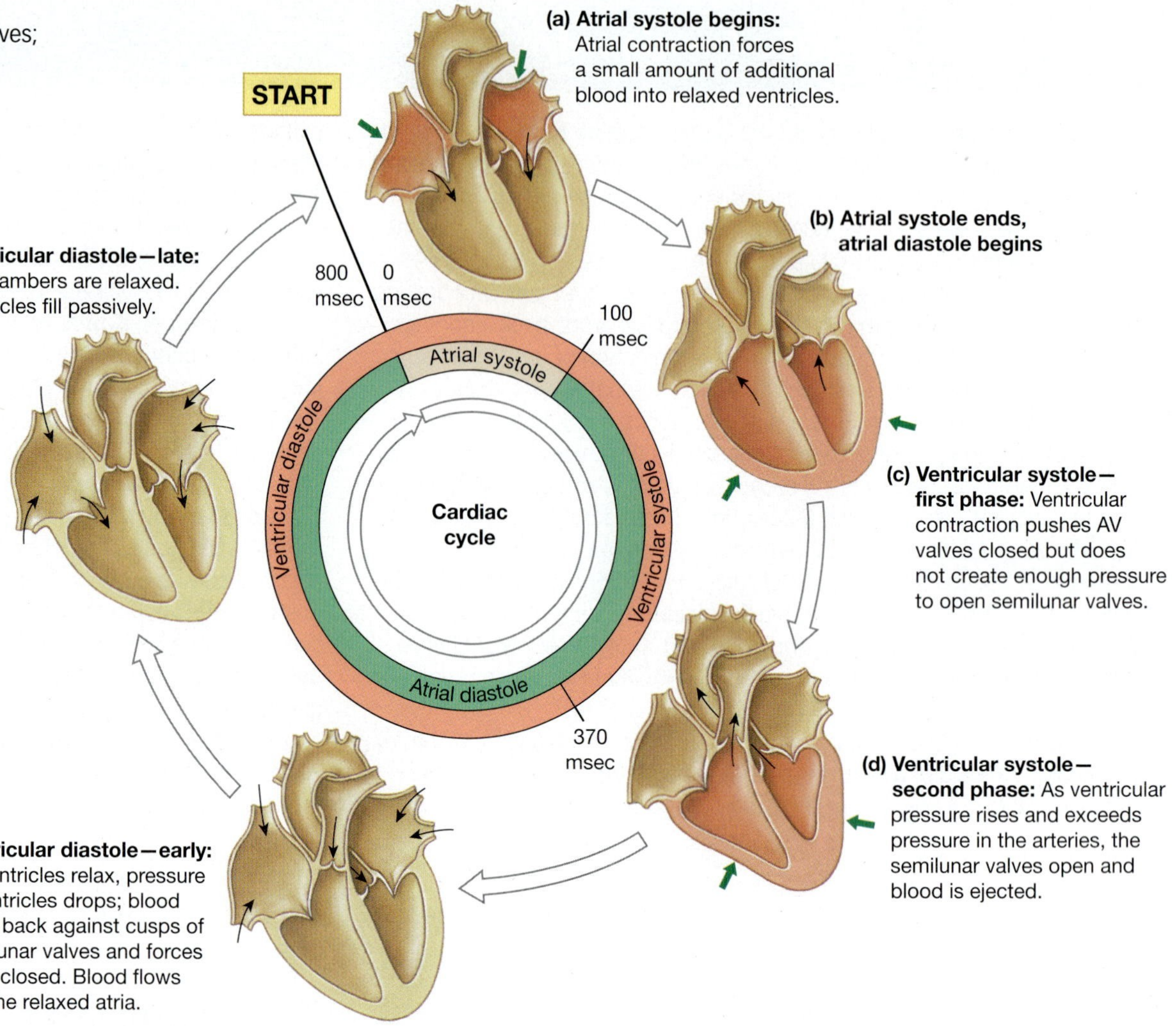

cells. **Nodal cells** are responsible for establishing the rate of cardiac contraction, and **conducting fibers** distribute the contractile stimulus to the general myocardium (**Figure 21.11**).

The Sinoatrial and Atrioventricular Nodes [Figure 21.11]

Nodal cells are unusual because their cell membranes spontaneously depolarize to threshold. Nodal cells are electrically coupled to one another, to conducting fibers, and to normal cardiac muscle cells. As a result, when an action potential appears in a nodal cell, it sweeps through the conducting system, reaching all of the cardiac muscle tissue and causing a contraction. In this way, nodal cells determine the heart rate.

Not all nodal cells depolarize at the same rate, and the normal rate of contraction is established by the nodal cells that reach threshold first; the impulse they produce will bring all other nodal cells to threshold. These rapidly depolarizing cells are called **pacemaker cells**. They are found in the **sinoatrial** (sī-nō-Ā-trē-al) **node (SA node)**, or **cardiac pacemaker**. The SA node is embedded in the posterior wall of the right atrium, near the entrance of the superior vena cava (**Figure 21.11**). Isolated pacemaker cells depolarize rapidly and spontaneously, generating 80–100 action potentials per minute.

Each time the SA node generates an impulse, it produces a heartbeat, so theoretically the resting heart rate would be 80–100 beats per minute (bpm). However, any factor that changes either the resting potential or the rate of spontaneous depolarization at the SA node will alter the heart rate. For example, nodal cell activity is affected by the activity of the autonomic nervous system. When acetylcholine (ACh) is released by parasympathetic neurons, it slows the rate of spontaneous depolarization and lowers the heart rate. In contrast, when norepinephrine (NE) is released by sympathetic neurons, the rate of depolarization increases, and the heart rate accelerates. Under normal resting conditions, parasympathetic activity reduces the heart rate from the inherent nodal rate of 80–100 impulses per minute to a more leisurely 70–80 beats per minute.

A number of clinical problems are the result of abnormal pacemaker function. **Bradycardia** (brād-ē-KAR-dē-a; *bradys*, slow) is the term used to indicate a heart rate that is slower than normal, whereas a faster-than-normal heart rate is termed **tachycardia** (tak-ē-KAR-dē-a; *tachys*, swift). Both terms are relative, and in clinical practice the definition varies depending on the normal resting heart rate and conditioning of the individual.

The Conducting System of the Heart [Figure 21.11]

The cells of the SA node are electrically connected to those of the larger **atrioventricular** (ā-trē-ō-ven-TRIK-ū-lar) **node (AV node)** through conducting fibers in the atrial walls (**Figure 21.11**). As the signal for contraction passes from the SA node to the AV node via the *internodal pathways*, the conducting fibers also pass the contractile stimulus to cardiac muscle cells of both atria. The action potential then spreads across the atrial sur-

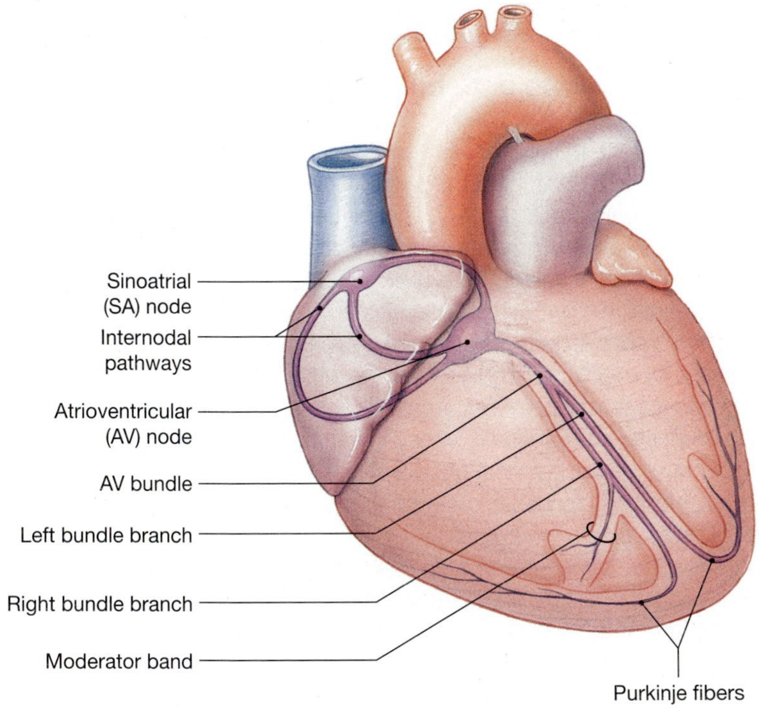

(a) Nodes and conducting fibers

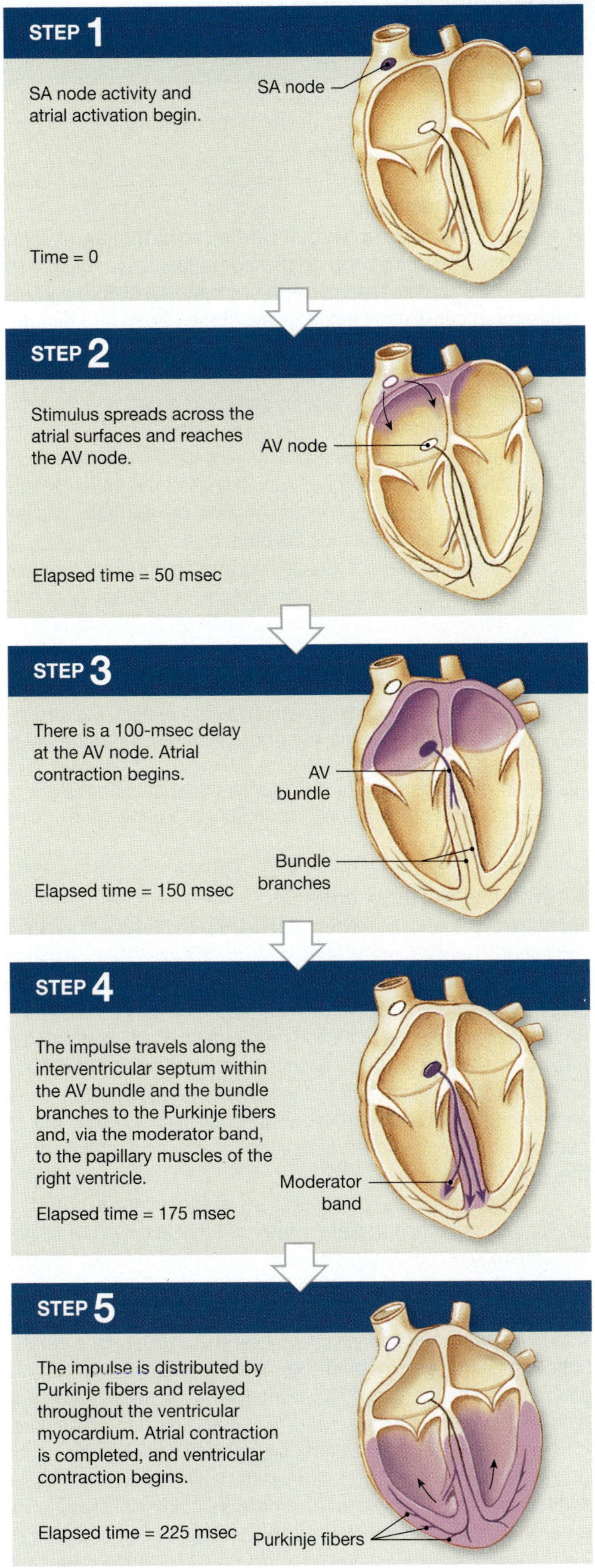

(b)

Figure 21.11 The Conducting System of the Heart
(a) The stimulus for contraction is generated by pacemaker cells at the SA node. From there, impulses follow three different paths through the atrial walls to reach the AV node. After a brief delay, the impulses are conducted to the bundle of His (AV bundle), and then on to the bundle branches, the Purkinje cells, and the ventricular myocardial cells. **(b)** The movement of the contractile stimulus through the heart is shown in **STEPS 1–5**.

faces through cell-to-cell contact. The stimulus affects only the atria, because the fibrous skeleton electrically isolates the atrial myocardium from the ventricular myocardium.

The AV node sits within the floor of the right atrium near the opening of the coronary sinus. Due to differences in the shape of the nodal cells, the impulse slows as it passes through the AV node. From there, the impulse travels to the **AV bundle**, also known as the *bundle of His* (HISS). This rather massive bundle of conducting fibers travels along the interventricular septum a short distance before dividing into a **right bundle branch** and a **left bundle branch** that extend toward the apex and then radiate across the inner surfaces of both ventricles. At this point, **Purkinje** (pur-KIN-jē) **cells** *(Purkinje fibers)* convey the impulses very rapidly to the contractile cells of the ventricular myocardium. The conducting fibers of the moderator band relay the stimulus to the papillary muscles, which tense the chordae tendineae before the ventricles contract.

The stimulus for a contraction is generated at the SA node, and the anatomical relationships among the contracting cells, the nodal cells, and the conducting fibers distribute the impulse so that (1) the atria contract together, before the ventricles, and (2) the ventricles contract together in a wave that begins at the apex and spreads toward the base. When the ventricles contract in this way, blood is pushed toward the base of the heart and out into the aortic and pulmonary trunks.

Embryology Summary

For a summary of the development of the cardiovascular system, see Chapter 28 (Embryology and Human Development).

Clinical Note

Cardiac Arrhythmias, Artificial Pacemakers, and Myocardial Infarctions

Cardiac Arrhythmias

There are many different types of **cardiac arrhythmias**, or abnormal cardiac rhythms, and they range from inconsequential to lethal. Many people have mild cardiac arrhythmias. For example, children and young adults commonly exhibit a quickening of their heart rate during inhalation, and a slowing during exhalation.

Healthy adults may occasionally have *premature atrial contractions (PACs)* that vary in duration and frequency. In a PAC, the normal atrial rhythm is momentarily interrupted by an "extra" atrial contraction. Stress, caffeine, and various drugs may increase the incidence of PACs, presumably by increasing the permeabilities of the SA pacemakers. The impulse spreads along the conduction pathway normally, and a typical ventricular contraction follows the atrial beat.

If arrhythmias are occasional and brief in duration, they are rarely of any importance. However, if an arrhythmia persists, or occurs frequently, it merits medical attention. In clinical diagnosis, arrhythmias are classified as:

1. Alterations in heart rate, with normal nodal and conducting pathway function. These conditions, which usually indicate abnormal function at the SA node and atria, are often relatively harmless and may go undetected.
2. Abnormal origination or distribution of the cardiac action potential within the ventricles. These conditions are dangerous and potentially lethal.

Alterations in Heart Rate

Tachycardia is usually defined as a heart rate of more than 100 beats per minute. Under some situations, as during exercise or excitement, tachycardia is quite normal. However chronic tachycardia, even at rest, indicates abnormal activity at the cardiac pacemaker. This type of arrhythmia increases the workload on the heart. Cardiac performance suffers at very high heart rates, because the ventricles do not have enough time to refill with blood before the next contraction occurs. Chronic or acute incidents of tachycardia may be controlled by drugs that affect the permeability of pacemaker membranes or block the effects of sympathetic stimulation.

In **paroxysmal** (par-ok-SIZ-mal) **atrial tachycardia**, or **PAT**, a premature atrial contraction triggers a flurry of atrial activity. The ventricles are still able to keep pace, and the heart rate jumps to about 180 beats per minute. In **atrial flutter**, the atria contract in a coordinated manner, but the contractions occur very frequently. During a bout of **atrial fibrillation** (fi-bri-LĀ-shun), the impulses move over the atrial surface at rates of perhaps 500 beats per minute. The atrial wall quivers instead of producing an organized contraction. The ventricular rate in atrial flutter or atrial fibrillation cannot follow the atrial rate and may remain within normal limits. Despite the fact that the atria are now essentially nonfunctional, the condition may go unnoticed, especially in older individuals who lead sedentary lives. In chronic atrial fibrillation, blood clots may form near the atrial walls. Pieces of the clot may break off, creating emboli and increasing the risk of stroke. As a result, most people diagnosed with this condition are placed on anticoagulant therapy. PACs, PAT, atrial flutter, and even atrial fibrillation are not considered very dangerous, unless they are prolonged or associated with some more serious indications of cardiac damage, such as coronary artery disease or valve problems.

Abnormal Origination or Conduction of Impulses

These conditions result in abnormal ventricular activity, which directly affects cardiac output. Many of these ventricular arrhythmias are potentially lethal. Because the conduction system functions in one direction only, from atria to ventricle, ventricular arrhythmias are not linked to atrial activities. **Premature ventricular contractions (PVCs)** occur when a Purkinje cell or ventricular myocardial cell depolarizes to threshold and triggers a premature contraction. The cell responsible for triggering the contraction is called an *ectopic pacemaker*. The frequency of PVCs can be increased by exposure to epinephrine, to other stimulatory drugs, or to ionic changes that depolarize cardiac muscle cell membranes. The abnormal ventricular contraction is strong, and after each abnormal beat, there is a pause before the next beat. Single PVCs are common and not dangerous, but they can be unsettling if they occur often enough that the individual starts noticing them.

Ectopic pacemaker activity, potentially enhanced by environmental factors, is probably responsible for periods of **ventricular tachycardia** (defined as four or more PVCs without intervening normal beats). This condition is also known as **VT** or *V-tach*. Multiple PVCs and VT often precede the most serious arrhythmia, **ventricular fibrillation (VF)**. During ventricular fibrillation, the cardiac muscle cells are overly sensitive to stimulation, and the impulses are traveling from cell to cell, around and around the ventricular walls. A normal rhythm cannot become established, because the ventricular muscle cells are stimulating one another at such a rapid rate. If untreated, death will occur within minutes; the condition is commonly called *cardiac arrest*.

Artificial Pacemakers

Bradycardia is usually defined as a heart rate of less than 50 beats per minute. As with tachycardia, bradycardia under certain conditions (deep sleep, for example) is not abnormal. But chronic bradycardia indicates that the heart is unable to respond to commands for increased cardiac output; when the body's need for oxygen goes up, the heart doesn't respond by working harder. Symptoms of severe bradycardia include weakness, fatigue, fainting, and confusion. Drug therapies are seldom helpful, but artificial pacemakers can be used with considerable success. Wires are run to the atria, the ventricles, or both, depending on the nature of the problem, and the unit delivers small electrical pulses to stimulate the myocardium. Internal pacemakers are surgically implanted, batteries and all (Figure 21.12). These units last seven to eight years or more before another operation is required to change the battery.

Significant technological advances have been made in artificial pacemakers in the past 10–15 years. Modern pacemakers improve the patient's quality of life by performing different functions under specific conditions, thanks to the introduction of microprocessors. New, more sophisticated "smart" pacemakers stimulate the atria and ventricles in sequence and may vary the rate of stimulation to adjust to changing circulatory demands, such as during exercise. Others are able to monitor cardiac activity and respond whenever the heart begins to function abnormally.

One type of smart pacemaker was implanted in Vice President Cheney during his term in office. This smart pacemaker is an automatic implantable cardioverter/defibrillator, which is commonly referred to as an AICD. An AICD is a device that continuously monitors the heart patient's cardiac rhythm. If the AICD detects an abnormally fast heart rhythm, it will automatically pace the heart electrically and attempt to slow the patient's heart rate. If the abnormal cardiac rhythm persists, the

Clinical Note *(continued)*

AICD will deliver a small electrical shock to the heart in an attempt to restore normal heart rhythm. The patient rarely feels the AICD rapidly pacing the heart in an attempt to return the cardiac rhythm to normal. However, if the electrical shock is used, it is felt as a strong jolt in the chest. The device is normally used for the instantaneous treatment of immediately life-threatening heart rhythms (i.e., ventricular tachycardia and ventricular fibrillation) that can't wait for treatment until an ambulance arrives.

An external defibrillator has two electrodes that are placed in contact with the chest, and a powerful electrical shock is administered. The electrical stimulus depolarizes the entire myocardium simultaneously. With luck, after repolarization, the SA node will be the first area of the heart to reach threshold. Thus, the primary goal of defibrillation is not just to stop the fibrillation, but to give the ventricles a chance to respond to normal SA commands.

Early defibrillation can result in dramatic recovery of an unconscious cardiac-arrest victim. Automatic external defibrillators (AEDs) are easily used, portable machines that can detect lethal ventricular rhythms in people who have collapsed and administer a defibrillating shock. These devices are increasingly being placed on planes, in airports, and in other public areas.

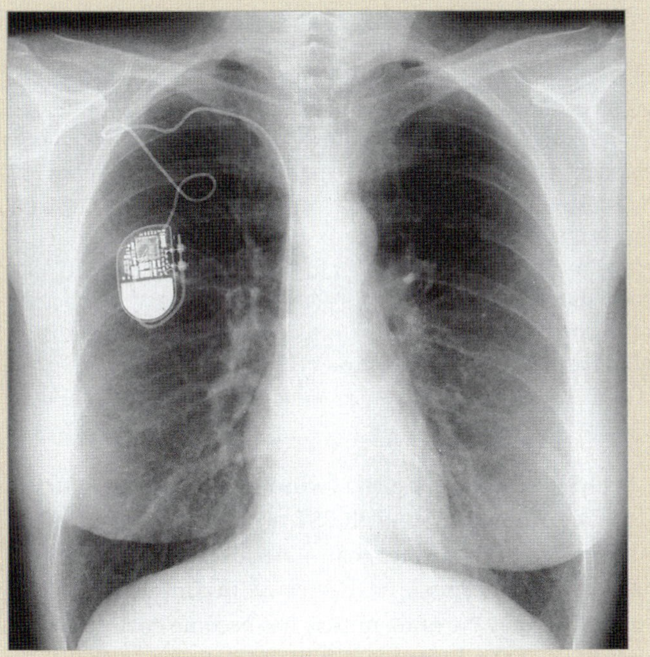

Figure 21.12 An artificial pacemaker.

Myocardial Infarction

In a **myocardial** (mī-ō-KAR-dē-al) **infarction (MI)**, or *heart attack*, the coronary circulation becomes blocked and the cardiac muscle cells die from lack of oxygen. The affected tissue then degenerates, creating a nonfunctional area known as an *infarct*. Heart attacks most often result from severe coronary artery disease. The consequences depend on the site and nature of the circulatory blockage. If it occurs near the base of one of the coronary arteries, the damage will be widespread and the heart will probably stop beating. If the blockage involves one of the smaller arterial branches, the individual may survive the immediate crisis, but there are many potential complications, all unpleasant. As scar tissue forms in the damaged area, the heartbeat may become irregular and less

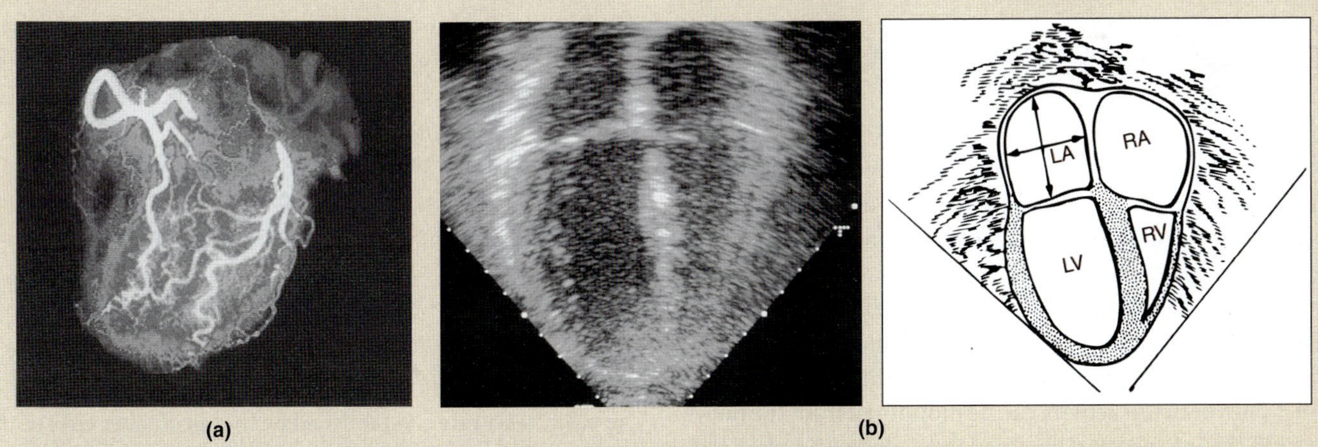

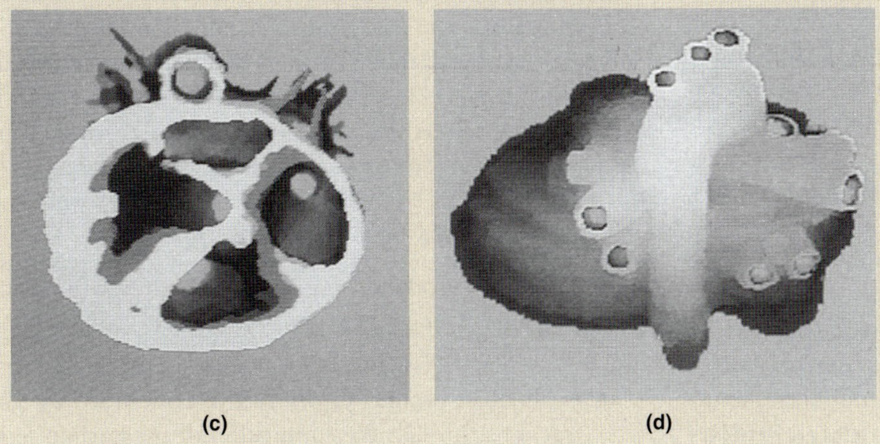

Figure 21.13 Monitoring the Heart
(a) A coronary angiogram. **(b)** An echocardium (left) with interpretive drawing (right). **(c)** A three-dimensional CT scan of an oblique section and **(d)** of a posterior-superior view of the heart and great vessels.

Clinical Note *(continued)*

effective as a pump, and other vessels can become constricted, creating additional cardiovascular problems such as angina.

Myocardial infarctions are most often associated with fixed blockages, such as those seen in CAD. When the crisis develops because of *thrombus* (stationary clot) formation at an area of plaque, the condition is called **coronary thrombosis**. A vessel already narrowed by plaque formation may also become blocked by a sudden spasm in the smooth muscles of the vascular wall. The individual then experiences intense pain, similar to that of an angina attack but persisting even at rest.

Roughly 25 percent of MI patients die before obtaining medical assistance, and 65 percent of MI deaths among those under age 50 occur within an hour after the initial infarct. The goals of treatment are to limit the size of the infarct and prevent additional complications by preventing irregular contractions, improving circulation with vasodilators, providing additional oxygen, reducing the cardiac workload, and, if possible, eliminating the cause of the circulatory blockage. Anticoagulants may help prevent the formation of additional thrombi. Chewing an aspirin early in the course of an MI is helpful, and clot-dissolving enzymes may reduce the extent of the damage if they are administered within 6 hours after the MI has occurred.

There are roughly 1.3 million MIs in the United States each year, and half of the victims die within a year of the incident. A number of factors have been identified that increase the risk of a heart attack. They include smoking, high blood pressure, high blood cholesterol levels, diabetes, and obesity. There are also hereditary factors that may predispose an individual to coronary artery disease. The presence of two risk factors more than doubles the risk, so eliminating as many risk factors as possible will improve one's chances of preventing or surviving a heart attack. For example, changes in eating habits to limit dietary cholesterol, exercise to lower weight, and seeking treatment for high blood pressure are relatively easy steps in the right direction, and the benefits are considerable.

Many techniques can be used to examine the structure and performance of the heart (Figure 21.13). No single diagnostic procedure provides the complete picture, so the test used will vary with the suspected nature of the problem.

CONCEPT CHECK

1. If the cells of the SA node were not functioning, what effect would this have on heart rate?
2. If norepinephrine is released at the heart, what is the effect on heart rate?
3. How do nodal cells coordinate cardiac muscle contractions?

See blue "Answers" tab at back of book.

The Electrocardiogram (ECG)

[Figure 21.14]

The electrical events associated with the depolarization and repolarization of the heart are powerful enough to be detected by electrodes placed on the body surface. A recording of these electrical activities constitutes an **electrocardiogram** (ē-lek-trō-KAR-dē-ō-gram), also called an **ECG** or **EKG.** During each cardiac cycle, a wave of depolarization radiates through the atria, reaches the AV node, travels down the interventricular septum to the apex, turns, and spreads through the ventricular myocardium toward the base (Figure 21.14). This electrical activity can be monitored from the body surface. By comparing the information obtained from electrodes placed at different locations, one can monitor the performance of specific nodal, conducting, and contractile components. For example, when a portion of the heart has been damaged, as after an MI, these cardiac muscle cells can no longer conduct action potentials, so an ECG will reveal an abnormal pattern of electrical conduction.

The appearance of the ECG tracing varies, depending on the placement of the monitoring electrodes, or *leads*. Figure 21.14 shows the important features of a representative electrocardiogram. The **P wave** accompanies the depolarization of the atria. The **QRS complex** appears as the ventricles depolarize. This electrical signal is relatively strong because the mass of the ventricular muscle is much larger than that of the atria. The smaller **T wave** indicates ventricular repolarization. You do not see a deflection corresponding to atrial repolarization because it occurs while the ventricles are depolarizing, and the electrical events are masked by the QRS complex.

Analysis of an ECG usually focuses on the size and duration of the P wave, the QRS complex, and the ST segment (between the QRS and T waves). For example, a smaller-than-normal electrical signal may mean that the mass of the heart muscle has decreased; in contrast, excessively large signals may mean that the heart muscle has become enlarged. Changes in the size and shape of the T wave may indicate a condition that slows ventricular repolarization.

Despite the variety of sophisticated equipment available to assess or visualize cardiac function, in the vast majority of cases, the electrocardiogram provides the first and most important diagnostic information. ECG analysis is especially useful in detecting and diagnosing *cardiac arrhythmias* (a-RITH-mē-az), abnormal patterns of cardiac activity. Clinical problems appear when the arrhythmias reduce the pumping efficiency of the heart. Serious arrhythmias may indicate damage to the myocardial musculature, injuries to the pacemakers or conduction pathways, or other factors.

Autonomic Control of Heart Rate [Figure 21.15]

The basic heart rate is established by the pacemaker cells of the SA node, but this intrinsic rate can be modified by the autonomic nervous system (ANS). The sympathetic and parasympathetic divisions of the ANS provide innervation to the heart through the cardiac plexus (anatomical details were presented in Chapter 17). p. 464 Both ANS divisions innervate the SA and AV nodes as well as the atrial and ventricular cardiac muscle cells and smooth muscle in the walls of the cardiac blood vessels (Figure 21.15).

The effects of NE and ACh on nodal tissues were detailed earlier in this chapter, and may be summarized as follows:

- NE release produces an increase in both heart rate and force of contractions through the stimulation of beta receptors on nodal cells and contractile cells;
- ACh release produces a decrease in both heart rate and force of contractions through the stimulation of muscarinic receptors of nodal cells and contractile cells.

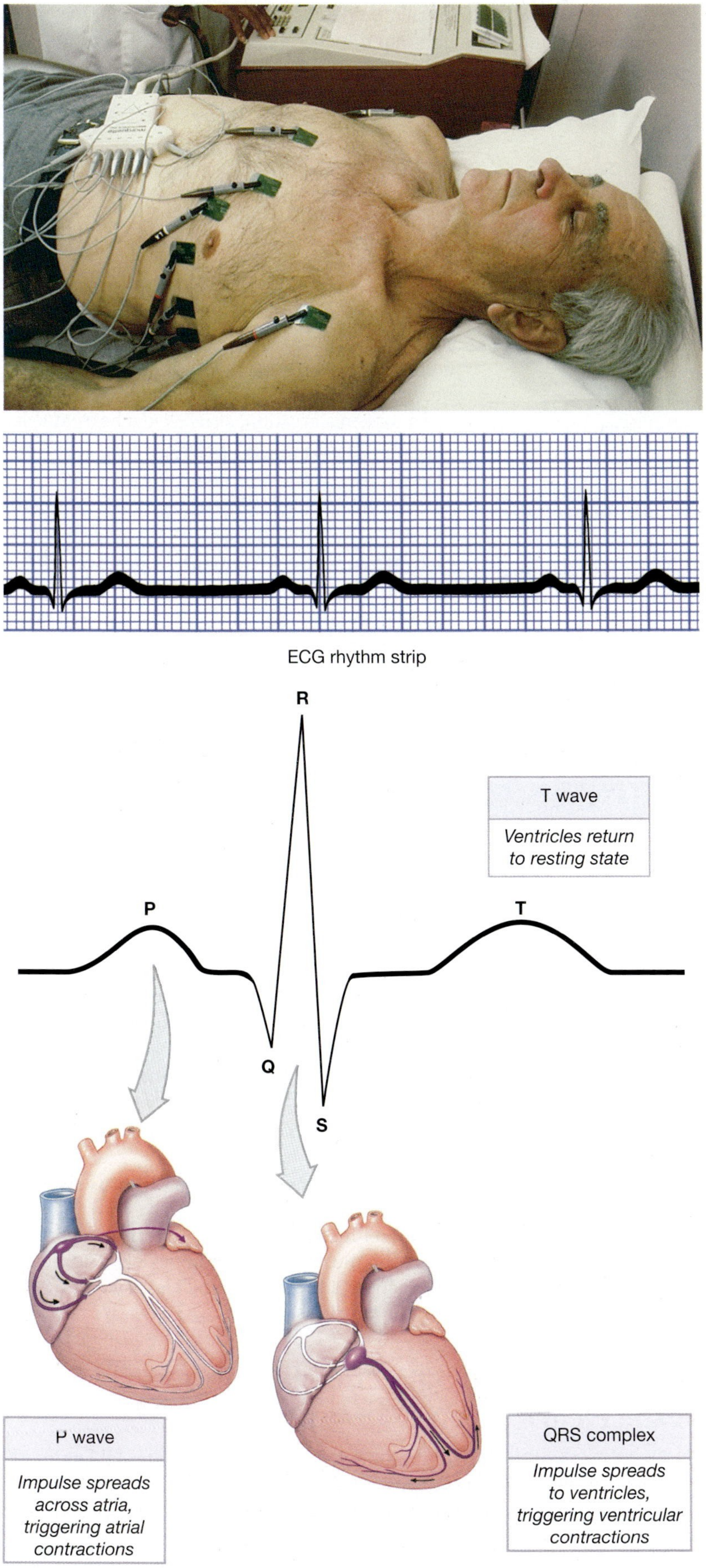

Figure 21.14 An Electrocardiogram
An ECG printout is a strip of graph paper containing a record of the electrical events monitored by electrodes attached to the body surface. The photo shows electrode locations for a standard ECG. The enlarged section indicates the major components of the ECG.

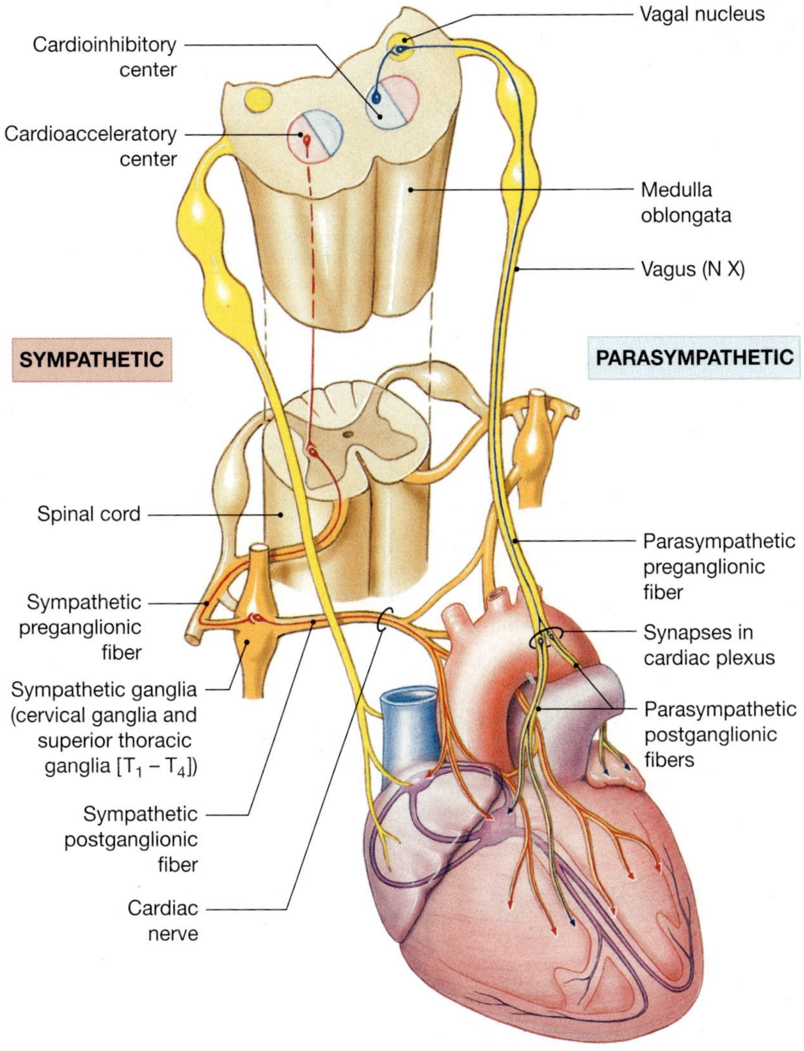

Figure 21.15 The Autonomic Innervation of the Heart
Cardiac centers in the medulla oblongata modify heart rate and cardiac output through the vagus nerve (parasympathetic) and through the cardiac nerves (sympathetic).

The cardiac centers of the medulla oblongata contain the autonomic centers for cardiac control. Stimulation of the **cardioacceleratory center** activates the necessary sympathetic neurons; the nearby **cardioinhibitory center** governs the activities of the parasympathetic neurons. The cardiac centers receive inputs from higher centers, especially from the parasympathetic and sympathetic headquarters in the hypothalamus. (These centers were described in Chapter 15.) p. 406

Information concerning the status of the cardiovascular system arrives at the cardiac centers from visceral sensory fibers that monitor baroreceptors sensitive to blood pressure and chemoreceptors sensitive to dissolved gas concentrations. These receptors are innervated by the glossopharyngeal (N IX) and vagus (N X) nerves. In response to this information, the cardiac centers adjust the cardiac performance to maintain adequate circulation to vital organs, such as the brain. These centers respond very quickly to changes in blood pressure and to the amount of dissolved oxygen and carbon dioxide in arterial blood. For example, a drop in blood pressure or an increase in carbon dioxide concentration usually indicates that the heart must work harder to meet the demands of peripheral tissues. The cardiac centers then respond by increasing the heart rate and force of contraction by activating the sympathetic nervous system.

CONCEPT CHECK

1. If the pressure in the ventricle remained equal to that in the atrium, what would happen to the blood flow?
2. The sympathetic and parasympathetic branches of the Autonomic Nervous System have different effects on nodal tissues within the heart. What are these effects?

See blue "Answers" tab at back of book.

CLINICAL TERMS

angina pectoris (an-JĪ-na PEK-tor-is): A condition in which exertion or stress can produce severe chest pain, resulting from temporary circulatory insufficiency and ischemia when the heart's workload increases.

bradycardia (brā-dē-KAR-dē-a): A heart rate that is slower than normal.

cardiac arrhythmias (a-RITH-mē-az): Abnormal patterns of cardiac contraction.

cardiac tamponade: A condition resulting from pericardial irritation and inflammation, in which fluid collects in the pericardial sac and restricts cardiac output.

cardiomyopathies (kar-dē-ō-mī-OP-a-thēz): A group of diseases characterized by the progressive, irreversible degeneration of the myocardium.

carditis (kar-DĪ-tis): A general term indicating inflammation of the heart.

coronary artery disease (CAD): Degenerative changes in the coronary circulation.

coronary thrombosis: A blockage due to the formation of a clot (thrombus) at a plaque in a coronary artery.

heart failure: A condition in which the heart weakens and peripheral tissues suffer from oxygen and nutrient deprivation.

heart murmur: A rushing, gurgling sound caused by blood regurgitation back through faulty heart valves.

mitral valve prolapse: A condition in which the mitral valve cusps do not close properly because of abnormally long (or short) chordae tendineae or malfunctioning papillary muscles.

myocardial (mī-ō-KAR-dē-al) **infarction (MI):** A condition in which the coronary circulation becomes blocked and the cardiac muscle cells die from oxygen starvation; also called a heart attack.

rheumatic heart disease (RHD): A disorder in which the heart valves become thickened and stiffen into a partially closed position, affecting the efficiency of the pumping action of the heart.

tachycardia (tak-e-KAR-dē-a): A heart rate that is faster than normal.

valvular stenosis (ste-NŌ-sis): A condition in which the opening between the heart valves is narrower than normal.

STUDY OUTLINE

Introduction 548

1. All of the tissues and fluids in the body rely on the cardiovascular system to maintain homeostasis. The proper functioning of the cardiovascular system depends on the activity of the **heart**, which can vary its pumping capacity depending on the needs of the peripheral tissues.

An Overview of the Cardiovascular System 548

1. The cardiovascular system can be subdivided into two closed circuits that occur in series. Each circuit functions individually in series, while the two circuits together function in parallel. The **pulmonary circuit** carries oxygen-poor blood from the heart to the lungs and back, and the **systemic circuit** transports oxygen-rich blood from the heart to the rest of the body and back. **Arteries** carry blood away from the heart; **veins** return blood to the heart. **Capillaries** are tiny vessels between the smallest arteries and veins. *(see Figure 21.1)*
2. The heart contains four chambers: the **right atrium** and **ventricle**, and the **left atrium** and **ventricle**. The atria collect blood returning to the heart, and the ventricles discharge blood into vessels to leave the heart.

The Pericardium 548

1. The heart is surrounded by the **pericardial cavity**, which is lined by the **pericardium** and contains a small amount of lubricating fluid, called the **pericardial fluid**. The **visceral pericardium (epicardium)** covers the heart's outer surface, and the **parietal pericardium** lines the inner surface of the **pericardial sac** that surrounds the heart. The heart lies in the anterior portion of the **mediastinum**. *(see Figure 21.2)*

Structure of the Heart Wall 550

1. The heart wall contains three layers: the **epicardium** (the visceral pericardium), the **myocardium** (the muscular wall of the heart), and the **endocardium** (the epithelium covering the inner surfaces of the heart). *(see Figure 21.3)*

Cardiac Muscle Tissue 550

2. The bulk of the heart consists of the muscular **myocardium**. Cardiac muscle cells (**cardiocytes**), which are smaller than skeletal muscle cells, are almost totally dependent on aerobic respiration. *(see Figure 21.3)*
3. Cardiocytes are interconnected by **intercalated discs**, which both convey the force of contraction from cell to cell and conduct action potentials. Intercalated discs join cardiac muscle cells through desmosomes, myofibrils, and gap junctions. Because cardiac muscle cells are connected in this way, they function like a single, enormous cell. *(see Figure 21.3d,e)*

The Fibrous Skeleton 550

4. The internal connective tissue of the heart is called the **fibrous skeleton**. *(see Figures 21.3b/21.7)*
5. The fibrous skeleton of the heart functions to stabilize the heart's contractile cells and valves; support the muscle cells, blood vessels, and nerves; distribute the forces of contraction; add strength and elasticity; and physically isolate the atria from the ventricles.

Orientation and Superficial Anatomy of the Heart 552

1. The division of the heart into four chambers produces external landmarks that are visible as grooves or *sulci* on the surface of the heart. The *interatrial groove* separates the two atria, while the **coronary sulcus** separates the atria from the ventricles.
2. The **auricle** (atrial appendage) is an expandable extension of the atrium. The *coronary sulcus* is the deep groove between the atria and the ventricles. Other shallower depressions include the **anterior interventricular sulcus** and the **posterior interventricular sulcus**.
3. The great vessels are connected to the superior end of the heart at the **base**. The inferior, pointed tip of the heart is the **apex**. *(see Figures 21.2b/21.4)*
4. The heart sits at an angle to the longitudinal axis of the body and presents the following **borders**: **superior**, **inferior**, **left**, and **right**. *(see Figure 21.4)*

5. The heart has the following surfaces: The **sternocostal surface** is formed by the anterior surfaces of the right atrium and ventricle; the **diaphragmatic surface** is formed primarily by the posterior, inferior wall of the left ventricle. *(see Figure 21.5)*

Internal Anatomy and Organization of the Heart 554

1. The atria are separated by the **interatrial septum**, and the ventricles are divided by the **interventricular septum.** The openings between the atria and ventricles contain folds of connective tissue covered by endocardium; these *valves* maintain a one-way flow of blood. *(see Figure 21.6)*

The Right Atrium 554

2. The right atrium receives blood from the systemic circuit through two great veins, the **superior vena cava** and **inferior vena cava.** The atrial walls contain prominent muscular ridges, the **pectinate muscles.** The **coronary veins** return blood to the *coronary sinus,* which opens into the right atrium. During embryonic development an opening called the **foramen ovale** penetrates the interatrial septum. This opening closes after birth, leaving a depression termed the **fossa ovalis.** *(see Figure 21.6)*

The Right Ventricle 554

3. Blood flows from the right atrium into the right ventricle through the **right atrioventricular (AV) valve,** or *tricuspid valve.* (This valve consists of three **cusps** of fibrous tissue braced by the tendinous **chordae tendineae** that are connected to **papillary muscles.**) *(see Figure 21.6a,c)*
4. Blood leaving the right ventricle enters the **pulmonary trunk** after passing through the **pulmonary valve.** The pulmonary trunk divides to form the **left** and **right pulmonary arteries.** *(see Figure 21.6)*

The Left Atrium 556

5. The left atrium receives oxygenated blood from the **left** and **right pulmonary veins**; it has thicker walls than those of the right atrium. *(see Figure 21.6a,c)*
6. Blood leaving the left atrium flows into the left ventricle through the **left atrioventricular (AV) valve** (*mitral* or *bicuspid valve*).

The Left Ventricle 556

7. The left ventricle is the largest and thickest of the four chambers because it must pump blood to the entire body. Blood leaving the left ventricle passes through the **aortic valve** and into the systemic circuit via the **ascending aorta.** Blood passes from the ascending aorta through the **aortic arch** and into the **descending aorta.** *(see Figure 21.6a,c)*

Structural Differences between the Left and Right Ventricles 556

8. The right ventricle has thin walls and develops low pressure when pumping into the pulmonary circuit to and from the adjacent lungs. Functionally, low pressure is necessary because the pulmonary capillaries at the gas-exchange surfaces of the lungs are very delicate. The left ventricle has a thick wall because it pumps blood throughout the systemic circuit. Anatomical differences between the left and right ventricles are shown in *Figure 21.6.*

The Structure and Function of Heart Valves 556

9. The *AV valves* have four components: (1) a ring of connective tissue attached to the fibrous skeleton of the heart, (2) cusps, (3) chordae tendineae, and (4) papillary muscles.
10. There are two *semilunar valves,* the **aortic valve** and the **pulmonary valve,** guarding the exits of the left and right ventricles. *(see Figures 21.6 and 21.7)*
11. Valves normally permit blood flow in only one direction, preventing the **regurgitation** (backflow) of blood.

Coronary Blood Vessels 558

12. The **coronary circulation** supplies blood to the muscles of the heart to meet the high oxygen and nutrient demands of cardiac muscle cells. The **coronary arteries** originate at the base of the ascending aorta, and each gives rise to two branches. The right coronary artery gives rise to both a **right marginal branch** and a **posterior interventricular branch.** The **left coronary artery** gives rise to both a **circumflex branch** and an **anterior interventricular branch.** Interconnections between arteries called **anastomoses** ensure a constant blood supply.
13. The **great** and **middle cardiac veins** carry blood from the coronary capillaries to the **coronary sinus.** *(see Figure 21.8)*
14. Other cardiac veins that empty into the great cardiac vein or the coronary sinus are the **posterior vein of the left ventricle**, draining the areas served by the circumflex branch of the LCA; the **middle cardiac vein**, draining the areas supplied by the posterior interventricular branch of the LCA; and the **small cardiac vein**, draining blood from the posterior surfaces of the right atrium and ventricle.
15. The **anterior cardiac veins** drain the anterior surface of the right ventricle and empty directly into the right atrium.

The Cardiac Cycle 561

1. The **cardiac cycle** consists of periods of **atrial** and **ventricular systole** (contraction) and atrial and ventricular **diastole** (relaxation/filling). *(see Figure 21.10)*

The Coordination of Cardiac Contractions 561

2. Cardiac muscle tissue contracts on its own, without neural or hormonal stimulation. This is called *automaticity* or *autorhythmicity.*
3. **Nodal cells** establish the rate of cardiac contraction, and **conducting fibers** distribute the contractile stimulus to the general myocardium. *(see Figure 21.11)*

The Sinoatrial and Atrioventricular Nodes 562

4. Nodal cells depolarize spontaneously and determine the heart rate.
5. **Pacemaker cells** found in the **sinoatrial (SA) node (cardiac pacemaker)** normally establish the rate of contraction. *(see Figure 21.11)*
6. From the SA node, the stimulus travels over the **internodal pathways** to the **atrioventricular (AV) node**, then to the **AV bundle**, which divides into a **right** and **left bundle branch**. From here **Purkinje cells** convey the impulses to the ventricular myocardium. *(see Figure 21.11)*

The Electrocardiogram (ECG) 566

1. A recording of electrical activities in the heart is an electrocardiogram (ECG or EKG). Important landmarks of an ECG include the P wave (atrial depolarization), QRS complex (ventricular depolarization) and T wave (ventricular repolarization). ECG analysis can detect cardiac arrhythmias, which are abnormal patterns of cardiac activity *(see Figure 21.14).*

Autonomic Control of Heart Rate 567

2. The basic heart rate is established by the pacemaker cells, but it can be modified by the ANS. Norepinephrine produces an increase in heart rate and force of contraction, while acetylcholine produces a decrease in heart rate and contraction.
3. The **cardioacceleratory center** in the medulla oblongata activates sympathetic neurons; the **cardioinhibitory center** governs the activities of the parasympathetic neurons. The cardiac centers receive inputs from higher centers and from receptors monitoring blood pressure and the concentrations of dissolved gases in the blood. *(see Figure 21.15)*

CHAPTER REVIEW

For answers to the Concept Check and Chapter Review questions, go to the blue "Answers" tab at the back of the book.

Level 1 Reviewing Facts and Terms

Match each numbered item with the most closely related lettered item. Use letters for answers in the spaces provided.

Column A	Column B
___ 1. cardiocytes	a. vein to the left atrium
___ 2. bradycardia	b. covers the outer surface of heart
___ 3. diastole	c. supplies blood to heart muscle
___ 4. coronary circulation	d. lines inner surface of pericardial sac
___ 5. visceral pericardium	e. slow heart rate
___ 6. systole	f. cardiac muscle cells
___ 7. myocardium	g. muscular wall of the heart
___ 8. right pulmonary vein	h. relaxation phase of the cardiac cycle
___ 9. superior vena cava	i. vein to the right atrium
___10. parietal pericardium	j. contraction phase of the cardiac cycle

11. The heart lies in the
    (a) pleural cavity (b) peritoneal cavity
    (c) abdominopelvic cavity (d) pericardial cavity
12. The atrioventricular valve that is located on the side of the heart that receives blood from the superior vena cava is the
    (a) mitral valve (b) bicuspid valve
    (c) tricuspid valve (d) aortic valve
13. The functions of the fibrous pericardium include
    (a) returning blood to the atria
    (b) pumping blood into circulation
    (c) anchoring the heart to surrounding structures
    (d) providing blood flow to the myocardium
14. All of the following are true of intercalated discs except
    (a) they provide additional strength from cells bound together by tight junctions
    (b) they have a smooth junction between the sarcolemmae of apposed muscle cells
    (c) they have the myofibrils of the interlocking muscle fibers anchored at the membrane
    (d) the cardiac muscle fibers at the intercalated discs are connected by gap junctions
15. The heart is innervated by
    (a) only parasympathetic nerves
    (b) only sympathetic nerves
    (c) both sympathetic and parasympathetic nerves
    (d) only splanchnic nerves
16. The pacemaker cells of the heart are located in
    (a) the SA node
    (b) the wall of the left ventricle
    (c) the Purkinje fibers
    (d) both the left and right ventricles
17. The muscle fibers of the atria are isolated physically from those of the ventricles
    (a) by the epicardium
    (b) by the fibrous skeleton of the heart
    (c) but not electrically, as they all contract at exactly the same time
    (d) by the coronary blood vessels
18. The two main branches of the right coronary artery are the
    (a) circumflex branch and the left marginal branch
    (b) anterior interventricular branch and the left anterior descending branch
    (c) right marginal branch and the posterior interventricular branch
    (d) great and middle cardiac veins
19. Analysis of ECG data is useful in the detection and diagnosis of
    (a) hypertension
    (b) cardiac arrhythmias
    (c) cerebrovascular accidents
    (d) all of the above
20. The mitral or bicuspid valve is located
    (a) in the opening of the aorta
    (b) between the left atrium and left ventricle
    (c) between the right atrium and right ventricle
    (d) in the opening of the pulmonary trunk

Level 2 Reviewing Concepts

1. If the sinoatrial node is damaged, what will happen to the heartbeat?
    (a) it will be generated by the bundle branches, at a much lower rate
    (b) the heart will stop
    (c) the atrioventricular node will take over setting the pace, at a speed somewhat slower than normal
    (d) the heartbeat will increase in rate, but not in forcefulness
2. If the papillary muscles fail to contract,
    (a) blood will not enter the atria
    (b) the ventricles will not pump blood
    (c) the AV valves will not close properly
    (d) the semilunar valves will not open
3. If there were damage to the sympathetic innervation to the heart, what would happen to the heart rate under the influence of the remaining autonomic nervous system stimulation?
    (a) it would increase
    (b) it would not change
    (c) it would decrease
    (d) it would first increase and then decrease
4. How is cardiac muscle similar to skeletal muscle?
5. Why do semilunar valves lack muscular braces like those found in AV valves?
6. Define a pacemaker cell, and list the group of cells that normally serve as the heart's pacemaker, as well as those other cells that have the potential to serve as a pacemaker.
7. What is the function of the pericardial fluid?
8. Which chamber of the heart has the thickest walls? Why are its walls so thick?
9. Why are nodal cells unique? What is their function?
10. What is the effect of NE release on cardiac function?

Level 3 Critical Thinking

1. Harvey has a heart murmur in his left ventricle that produces a loud "gurgling" sound at the beginning of systole. What do you suspect to be the cause of this sound?
2. Lee is brought to the emergency room of a hospital suffering from a cardiac arrhythmia. In the emergency room he begins to exhibit tachycardia and as a result loses consciousness. His wife asks you why he lost consciousness. What would you tell her?
3. If the cardiac centers detect an abundance of oxygen in the blood, what chemical is likely to be released?
4. If a child is diagnosed with rheumatic fever, what complications might be feared to occur up to as many as 10 to 20 years later?

22

The Cardiovascular System

Vessels and Circulation

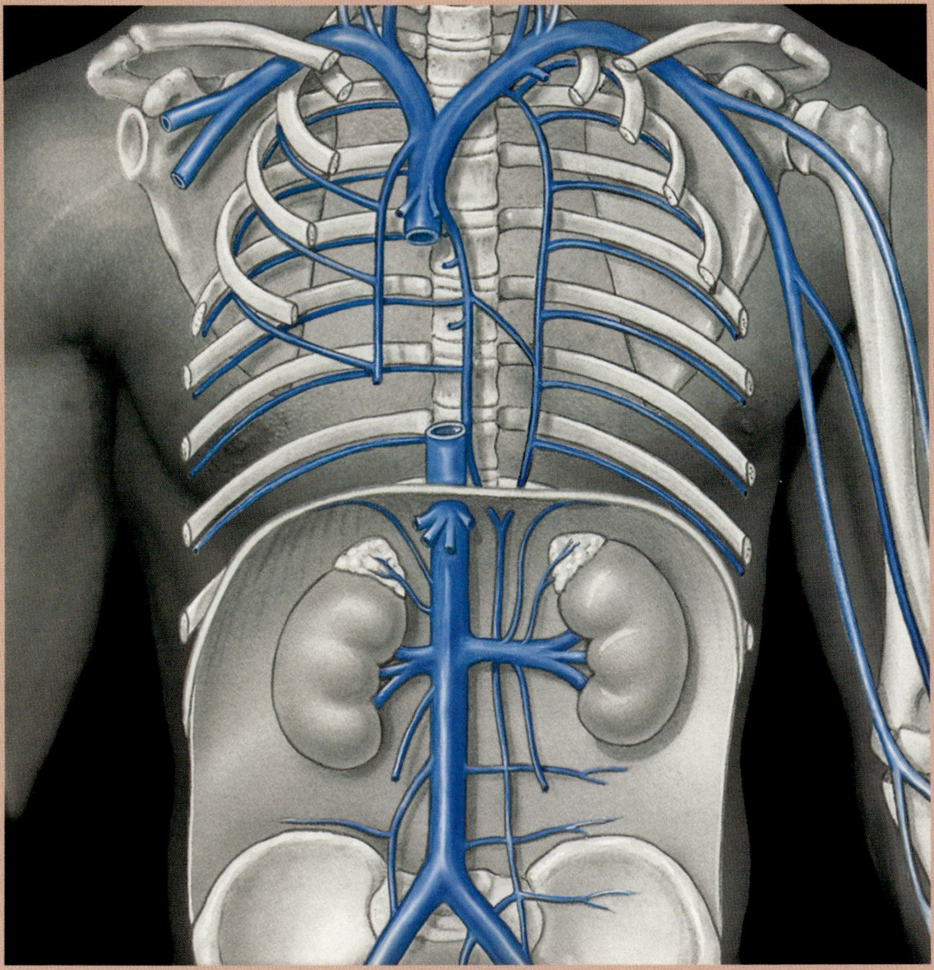

CHAPTER OBJECTIVES

1. Describe the general anatomical organization of the blood vessels and their relationship to the heart.
2. Identify and describe the various types of blood vessels based on their histological characteristics.
3. Describe how histological structure influences the function of each type of blood vessel.
4. Describe the structure, function, and permeability characteristics of capillaries, sinusoids, and capillary beds.
5. Describe the structure, function, and action of valves in veins.
6. Explain the distribution of blood in arteries, veins, and capillaries and discuss the function of blood reservoirs.
7. Identify and describe the vessels of the pulmonary circuit.
8. Identify the major vessels of the systemic circuit and the areas and organs supplied by each vessel.
9. Prepare a flowchart of arterial branches of the head, neck, chest, abdomen, and upper and lower limbs.
10. Describe the major cardiovascular changes that occur at birth and explain their functional significance.
11. Compare the prenatal pattern of blood flow with that of an infant.
12. Describe the age-related changes that occur in the cardiovascular system.

The cardiovascular system is a closed system that circulates blood throughout the body. There are two groups of blood vessels: one supplies the lungs (the *pulmonary circuit*), and the other supplies the rest of the body (the *systemic circuit*). Blood is pumped from the heart into both the pulmonary and systemic (aortic) trunks simultaneously. The relatively small pulmonary circuit begins at the pulmonary valve and ends at the entrance to the left atrium. Pulmonary arteries that branch from the pulmonary trunk carry blood to the lungs for gas exchange. The systemic circuit begins at the aortic valve and ends at the entrance to the right atrium. Systemic arteries branch from the aorta and distribute blood to all other organs for nutrient, gas, and waste exchange. The pulmonary trunk and the aorta each have a luminal diameter of around 2.5 cm (1 in.). These vessels branch to form numerous smaller vessels that supply individual regions and organs.

After entering the organs, further branching occurs, creating several hundred million tiny arteries that provide blood to more than 10 billion capillaries barely the diameter of a single red blood cell. These capillaries form extensive branching networks; estimates of the combined length of all of the capillaries in the body (placed end to end) range from 5000 to 25,000 miles. In other words, the capillaries in your body could at least cross the continental United States and perhaps circle the globe. All chemical and gaseous exchange between the blood and interstitial fluid takes place across capillary walls. Tissue cells rely on capillary diffusion to obtain nutrients and oxygen and to remove metabolic waste products. Blood leaving capillary networks enters a network of small veins that gradually merge to form larger vessels that ultimately supply either one of the pulmonary veins (pulmonary circuit) or the inferior or superior vena cava (systemic circuit).

Our discussion early in this chapter will focus attention on the histological and anatomical organization of arteries, capillaries, and veins. We will then proceed to identify the major blood vessels and circulatory routes of the cardiovascular system.

Histological Organization of Blood Vessels [Figure 22.1]

The walls of arteries and veins contain three distinct layers: (1) an inner *intima* (2) a middle *media*; and (3) an outer *adventitia*. View **Figure 22.1** as we examine the histological structure of arteries and veins.

- The **intima** is the innermost layer of a blood vessel. This layer includes the endothelial lining of the vessel and an underlying layer of connective tissue containing variable amounts of elastic fibers. In arteries the outer margin of the intima contains a thick layer of elastic fibers called the **internal elastic membrane**. In the largest arteries, the connective tissue is more extensive, and the intima is thicker than in smaller arteries.
- The **media** is the middle layer, and it contains concentric sheets of smooth muscle tissue in a framework of loose connective tissue. The smooth muscle fibers of the media encircle the lumen of the blood vessel. When stimulated by sympathetic activation, these smooth muscles constrict and reduce the diameter of the blood vessel, a process called **vasoconstriction**. Relaxation of the smooth muscles increases the diameter of the lumen, a process called **vasodilation** (vaz-ō-dī-LĀ-shun). These smooth muscles may contract or relax in response to local stimuli or under control of the sympathetic division of the ANS. Any resulting change in vessel diameter affects both blood pressure and blood flow through this tissue. Collagen fibers bind the media to both the intima and adventitia. Arteries have a thin band of elastic fibers, the **external elastic membrane**, located between the media and adventitia.
- The outer **adventitia** (ad-ven-TISH-a) forms a connective tissue sheath around the vessel. This layer is very thick, composed chiefly of collagen fibers, with scattered bands of elastic fibers. The fibers of the adventitia typically blend into those of adjacent tissues, stabilizing and anchoring the blood vessel. In veins this layer is usually thicker than the media.

Their layered walls give arteries and veins considerable strength. The combination of muscular and elastic components permits controlled alterations in diameter as blood pressure or blood volume changes. However, the vessel walls are too thick to allow diffusion between the bloodstream and surrounding tissues, or even between the blood and the tissues of the vessel itself. Instead, the walls of large vessels contain small arteries and veins that supply the smooth muscle fibers, fibroblasts, and fibrocytes of the media and adventitia. These blood vessels are called the **vasa vasorum** ("vessels of vessels").

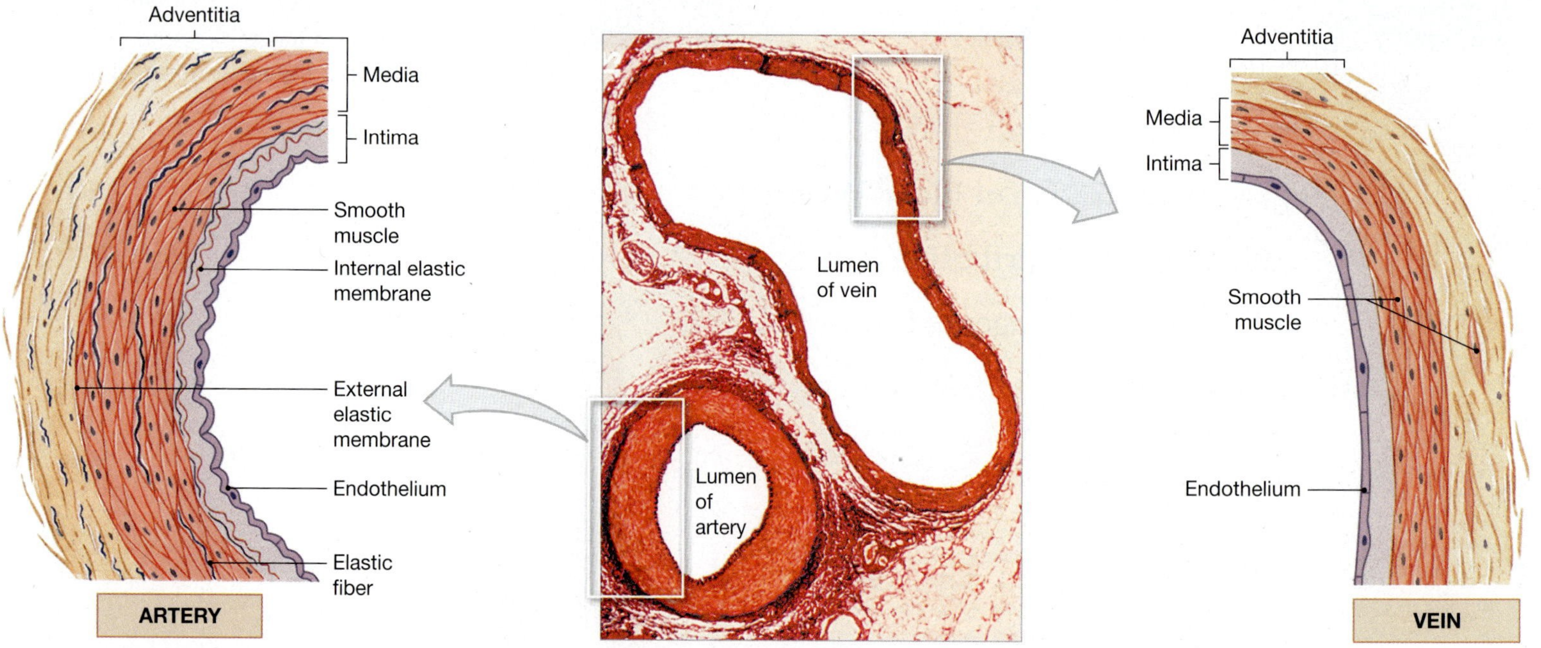

Figure 22.1 Histological Comparison of Typical Arteries and Veins
Light micrograph of an artery and vein. (LM × 60)

Distinguishing Arteries from Veins [Figure 22.1]

Arteries supplying and veins draining the same region typically lie side by side within a narrow band of connective tissue (**Figure 22.1**). Arteries and veins may be distinguished in histological sections by the following characteristics:

1. In general, when comparing two adjacent vessels, the walls of arteries are thicker than those of veins. The media of an artery contains more smooth muscle and elastic fibers than does that of a vein. These contractile and elastic components resist the pressure generated by the heart as it forces blood into the circuit.
2. When not opposed by blood pressure, arterial walls contract. Thus, when seen on dissection or in sectional view (**Figure 22.1**), arteries appear smaller than the corresponding veins. Because the walls of arteries are relatively thick and strong, they retain their circular shape in section. Cut veins tend to collapse, and in section they often look flattened or grossly distorted.
3. The endothelial lining of an artery cannot contract, so when an artery constricts, the endothelium is thrown into folds that give arterial sections a pleated appearance. The lining of a vein lacks these folds.

Arteries [Figure 22.2]

In traveling from the heart to peripheral capillaries, blood passes through a series of arteries of ever smaller diameter: *elastic arteries*, *muscular arteries*, and *arterioles* (**Figure 22.2**).

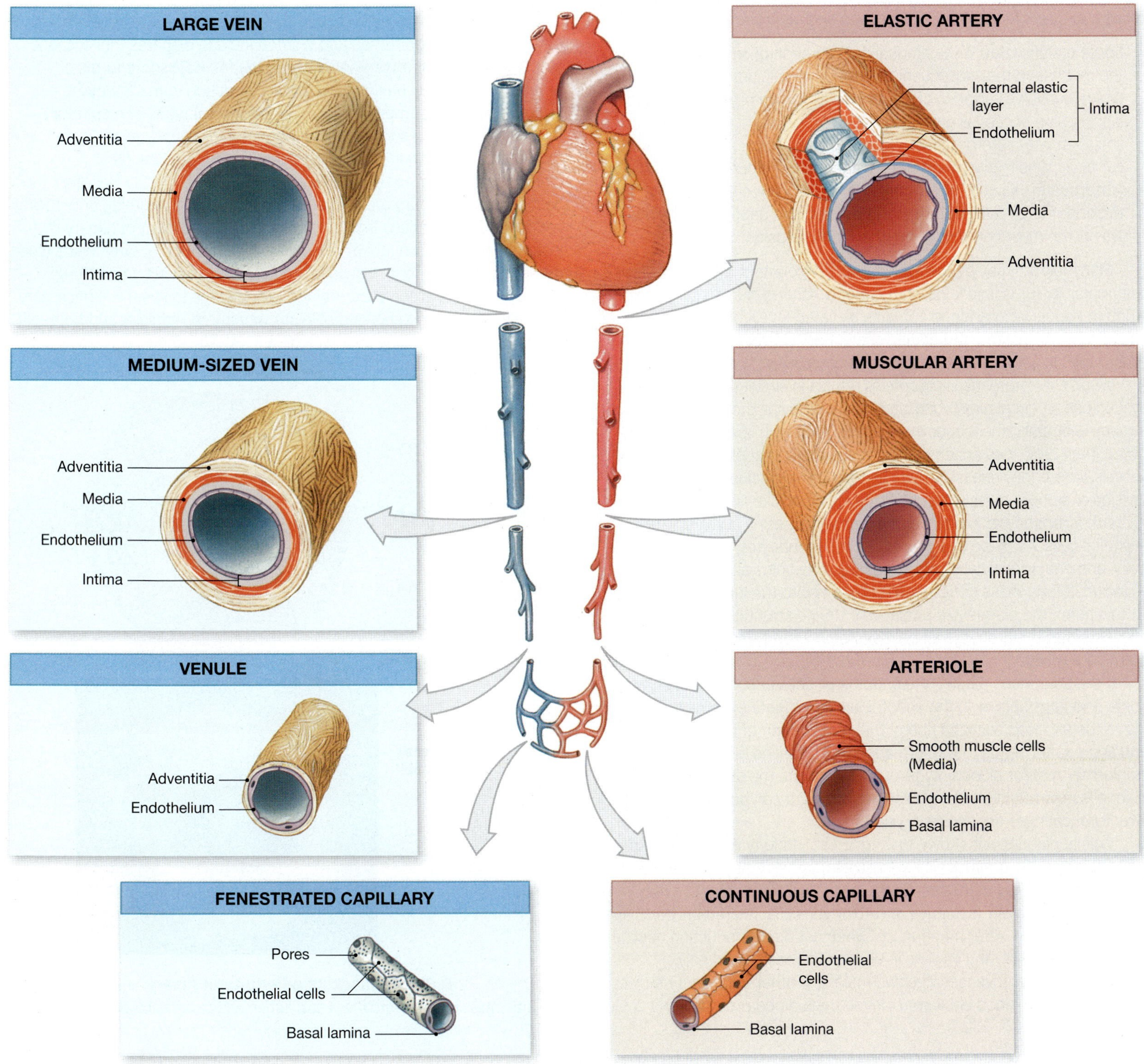

Figure 22.2 **Histological Structure of Blood Vessels**

Elastic Arteries [Figure 22.2]

Elastic arteries, or *conducting arteries*, are large vessels with diameters of up to 2.5 cm (1 in.). They transport large volumes of blood away from the heart. The pulmonary and aortic trunks and their major branches (the *pulmonary*, *common carotid*, *subclavian*, and *common iliac arteries*) are examples of elastic arteries. The walls of elastic arteries are not very thick relative to the vessel diameter, but they are extremely resilient. The media of these vessels contains a high density of elastic fibers and relatively few smooth muscle fibers (Figure 22.2). As a result, elastic arteries are able to tolerate the pressure changes that occur during the cardiac cycle. During

Clinical Note

Arteriosclerosis **Arteriosclerosis** (ar-tēr-ē-o-skler-Ō-sis) is a thickening and toughening of arterial walls. Complications related to arteriosclerosis account for roughly half of all deaths in the United States. There are many different forms of arteriosclerosis; one example is coronary artery disease (CAD), which was described in Chapter 21. p. 560 Arteriosclerosis takes two major forms: focal calcification and atherosclerosis.

- **Focal calcification** is the gradual degeneration of smooth muscle in the media and the subsequent deposition of calcium salts. This process typically involves arteries of the limbs and genital organs. Some focal calcification occurs as part of the aging process and may develop in association with atherosclerosis. Rapid and severe calcification may occur as a complication of diabetes mellitus, an endocrine disorder.
- **Atherosclerosis** (ath-er-ō-skler-Ō-sis) is associated with damage to the endothelial lining and the formation of lipid deposits in the media. This is the most common form of arteriosclerosis.

Many factors may be involved in the development of atherosclerosis. One major factor is lipid levels in the blood. Atherosclerosis tends to develop in people whose blood contains elevated levels of plasma lipids, specifically cholesterol. Circulating cholesterol is transported to peripheral tissues in *lipoproteins*, protein–lipid complexes.

When cholesterol-rich lipoproteins remain in circulation for an extended period, circulating monocytes begin removing them from the bloodstream. Eventually, the monocytes become filled with lipid droplets. Now called *foam cells*, they attach themselves to the endothelial walls of blood vessels, where they release growth factors. These cytokines stimulate the division of smooth muscle cells near the intima, thickening the vessel wall.

Other monocytes then invade the area, migrating between the endothelial cells. As these changes occur, the monocytes, smooth muscle cells, and endothelial cells begin phagocytizing lipids as well. The result is a *plaque*, a fatty mass of tissue that projects into the lumen of the vessel. At this point, the plaque has a relatively simple structure, and evidence suggests that the process can be reversed if appropriate dietary adjustments are made.

If the conditions persist, the endothelial cells become swollen with lipids, and gaps appear in the endothelial lining. Platelets now begin sticking to the exposed collagen fibers. The combination of platelet adhesion and aggregation leads to the formation of a localized blood clot, which will further restrict blood flow through the artery. The structure of the plaque is now relatively complex. Plaque growth can be halted, but the structural changes are generally permanent.

Typical plaques are shown in Figure 22.3. Elderly individuals, especially elderly men, are most likely to develop atherosclerotic plaques. Evidence suggests that estrogens may slow plaque formation; this may account for the lower incidence of CAD, myocardial infarctions (MIs), and strokes in women. After menopause, when estrogen production declines, the risk of CAD, MIs, and strokes in women increases markedly.

In addition to advanced age and male sex, other important risk factors include high blood cholesterol levels, high blood pressure, and cigarette smoking. Roughly 20 percent of middle-aged men have all three of these risk factors; these individuals are four times as likely to experience an MI or a cardiac arrest as are other men in their age group. Although fewer women develop atherosclerotic plaques, elderly women smokers with high blood cholesterol and high blood pressure are at much greater risk than are other women. Factors that can promote the development of atherosclerosis in both men and women include diabetes mellitus, obesity, and stress. Evidence also indicates that at least some forms of atherosclerosis may be linked to chronic infection with *Chlamydia pneumoniae*, a bacterium responsible for several types of respiratory infections, including some forms of pneumonia.

Potential treatments for atherosclerotic plaques include *catheterization*, *balloon angioplasty*, and *stents*. p. 561 However, the best approach is to try to avoid atherosclerosis by eliminating or reducing risk factors. Suggestions include (1) reducing the amount of dietary cholesterol and saturated fats by restricting consumption of fatty meats (such as beef, lamb, and pork), egg yolks, and cream; (2) giving up smoking; (3) checking your blood pressure and taking steps to lower it if necessary; (4) having your blood cholesterol levels monitored regularly and treated if necessary; (5) controlling your weight; and (6) exercising regularly.

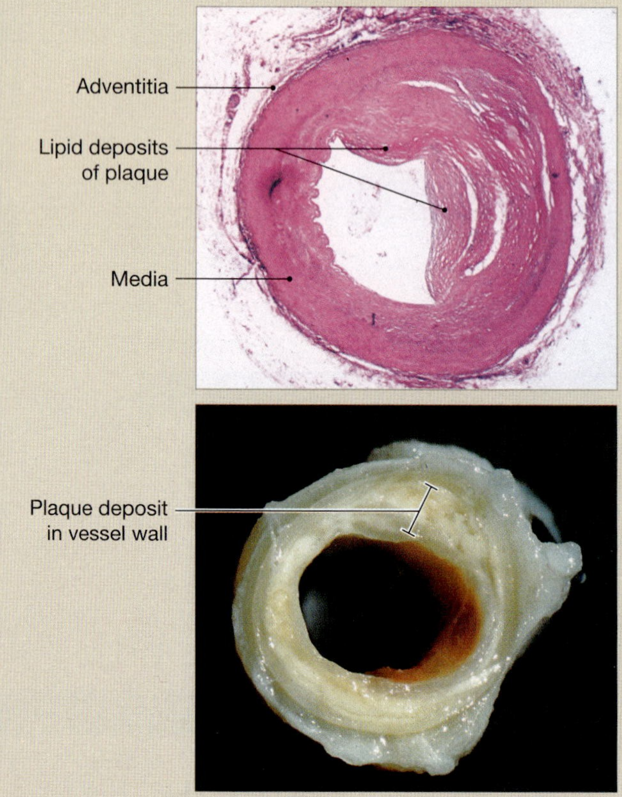

Figure 22.3 A Plaque Blocking a Peripheral Artery
The fatty mass extends into the vessel lumen and restricts blood flow. (LM × 28)

ventricular systole, pressures rise rapidly and the elastic arteries are stretched, whereas during ventricular diastole, blood pressure within the arterial system falls, and the elastic fibers recoil to their original dimensions. Their stretching cushions the sudden rise in pressure during ventricular systole, and their recoiling both slows the decline in pressure during ventricular diastole and forces blood onward toward the capillaries.

Muscular Arteries [Figures 22.1/22.2]

Muscular arteries, or *distribution arteries* (also known as *medium-sized arteries*), transport blood to the body's skeletal muscle and internal organs. A typical muscular artery has a diameter of approximately 0.4 cm (0.15 in.). Muscular arteries have a thicker media with a greater percentage of smooth muscle fibers than one finds in elastic arteries (Figures 22.1 and 22.2). The *external carotid artery* of the neck, the *brachial arteries* of the arms, the *femoral arteries* of the thighs, and the *mesenteric arteries* of the abdomen are examples of muscular arteries. The sympathetic division of the ANS can control the diameter of each of these arteries. By constricting *(vasoconstriction)* or relaxing *(vasodilation)* the smooth muscle in the media, the ANS can regulate the blood flow to each organ independently.

Arterioles [Figure 22.2]

Arterioles (ar-TĒR-ē-ōlz) are considerably smaller than muscular arteries. Arterioles have an average diameter of about 30μm. They have a poorly defined adventitia, and their media consists of scattered smooth muscle fibers that do not form a complete layer (Figure 22.2). The smaller muscular arteries and arterioles change their diameter in response to local conditions or to sympathetic or endocrine stimulation. For example, arterioles in most tissues vasoconstrict under sympathetic stimulation. p. 454 Arterioles control the blood flow between arteries and capillaries.

Elastic and muscular arteries are seamlessly interconnected, and vessel characteristics change gradually as the vessels get farther away from the heart. For example, the largest of the muscular arteries contain a considerable amount of elastic tissue, while the smallest resemble heavily muscled arterioles.

Capillaries [Figures 22.2/22.4]

Capillaries are the smallest and most delicate blood vessels (Figure 22.2). They are important functionally because they are the only blood vessels whose walls permit exchange between the blood and the surrounding interstitial fluids. Because the walls are relatively thin, the diffusion distances are small, and exchange can occur quickly. In addition, blood flows slowly through capillaries, allowing sufficient time for diffusion or active transport of materials across the capillary walls. Some substances cross the capillary walls by diffusing across the endothelial cell lining; other substances pass through gaps between adjacent endothelial cells. The fine structure of each capillary determines its ability to regulate the two-way exchange of substances between the blood and the interstitial fluid.

A typical capillary consists of an endothelial tube enclosed within a delicate basal lamina. The average internal diameter of a capillary is a mere 8 μm, very close to that of a single red blood cell.

Continuous capillaries are found in most regions of the body. In these capillaries, the endothelium is a complete lining, and the endothelial cells are connected by tight junctions and desmosomes (Figure 22.4a,b).

Fenestrated (FEN-es-trā-ted; *fenestra*, window) **capillaries** are capillaries that contain "windows," or pores in their walls, due to an incomplete or perforated endothelial lining (Figure 22.4).

A single endothelial cell may wrap all the way around the lumen of a continuous capillary (Figure 22.4c). The walls of a fenestrated capillary are far more permeable; they have a "Swiss cheese" appearance (Figure 22.4d), and the pores allow molecules as large as peptides and small proteins to pass into or out of the circulation. This type of capillary permits very rapid exchange of fluids and solutes. Examples of fenestrated capillaries noted in earlier chapters include the choroid plexus of the brain and the capillaries in a variety of endocrine organs, including the hypothalamus, the pituitary, the pineal, the suprarenals, and the thyroid gland. p. 394 Fenestrated capillaries are also found at filtration sites in the kidneys.

Sinusoids (SĪ-nu-soydz) resemble fenestrated capillaries except they have larger pores and a thinner basal lamina. (In some organs, such as the liver, there is no basal lamina.) Sinusoids are flattened and irregular and follow the internal contours of complex organs. They permit an extensive exchange of fluids and large solutes, including suspended proteins, between blood and interstitial fluid. Blood moves through sinusoids relatively slowly, maximizing the time available for absorption and secretion across the sinusoidal walls. Sinusoids are found in the liver, bone marrow, and suprarenal glands.

Four basic mechanisms are responsible for the exchange of materials across the walls of capillaries and sinusoids:

1. Diffusion across the capillary endothelial cells (lipid-soluble materials, gases, and water by osmosis).
2. Diffusion through gaps between adjacent endothelial cells (water and small solutes; larger solutes in the case of sinusoids).
3. Diffusion through the pores in fenestrated capillaries and sinusoids (water and solutes).
4. Vesicular transport by endothelial cells (endocytosis at luminal side, exocytosis at basal side), water, and specific bound and unbound solutes. pp. 32–33, 42

Capillary Beds [Figure 22.5]

Capillaries do not function as individual units. Each capillary is a part of an interconnected network called a **capillary bed**, or **capillary plexus** (Figure 22.5). A single arteriole usually gives rise to dozens of capillaries that empty into several venules. The entrance to each capillary is guarded by a band of smooth muscle, termed a **precapillary sphincter**. Contraction of the smooth muscle fibers constricts and narrows the diameter of the capillary entrance, thereby reducing or stopping the flow of blood. Relaxation of the sphincter dilates the opening, allowing blood to enter the capillary at a faster rate. Precapillary sphincters open when carbon dioxide levels rise; such a rise indicates that the tissue needs oxygen and nutrients. The sphincters close when carbon dioxide levels decline, or under sympathetic stimulation.

A capillary bed contains several relatively direct connections between arterioles and venules. The arteriolar segment of such a passageway contains smooth muscle cells capable of altering its diameter, and this region is often called a **metarteriole** (met-ar-TĒR-ē-ol) (Figure 22.5a). It is somewhat intermediate in structure between arterioles and capillaries. The rest of the passageway resembles a typical capillary, and it is called a **thoroughfare channel**.

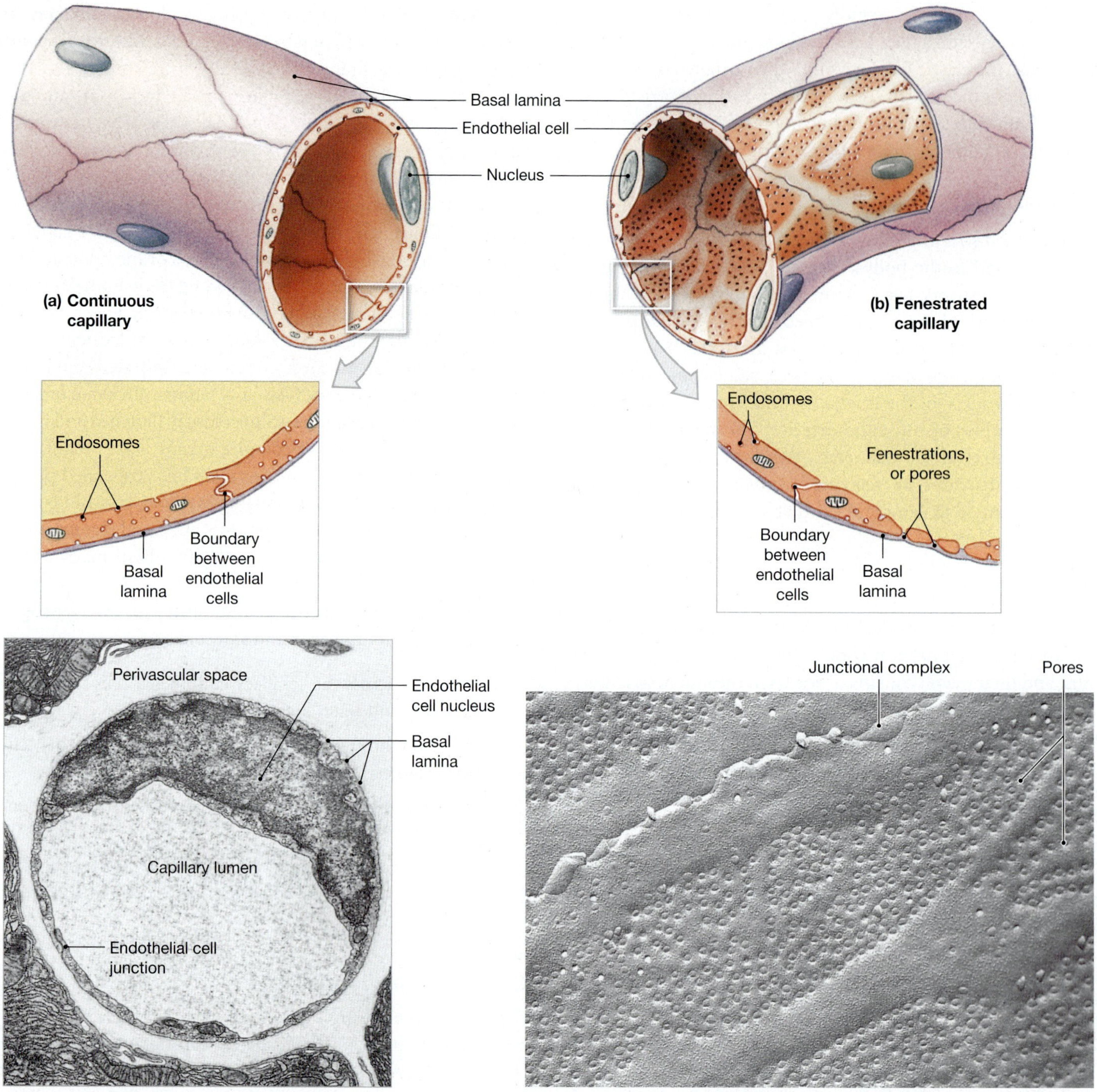

(c) TEM of continuous capillary

(d) SEM of fenestrated capillary

Figure 22.4 Structure of Capillaries

(a) This diagrammatic view of a continuous capillary shows the structure of its wall. **(b)** This diagrammatic view of a fenestrated capillary details the structure of the wall. **(c)** The TEM shows a cross section through a continuous capillary. A single endothelial cell forms a complete lining around this portion of the capillary. **(d)** A SEM shows the wall of a fenestrated capillary. The pores are gaps in the endothelial lining that permit the passage of large volumes of fluid and solutes. (SEM × 12,425)

Blood usually flows from the arterioles to the venules at a constant rate, but the blood flow within a single capillary can be quite variable. Each precapillary sphincter goes through cycles of alternately contracting and relaxing, perhaps a dozen times each minute. As a result, the blood flow within any one capillary occurs in a series of pulses rather than as a steady and constant stream. The net effect is that blood may reach the venules by one route now and by quite a different route later. This process, which is controlled at the tissue level, is called capillary **autoregulation**.

There are also mechanisms to modify the circulatory supply to the entire capillary complex. The capillary networks within an area are often supplied by more than one artery. The arteries, called **collaterals**, enter the region and fuse together rather than ending in a series of arterioles. The interconnection is an **arterial anastomosis**. Arterial anastomoses are found in the brain, heart, and stomach and in other organs or body regions with significant circulatory demands. Such an arrangement guarantees a reliable blood supply to the tissues; if one arterial supply becomes blocked, the

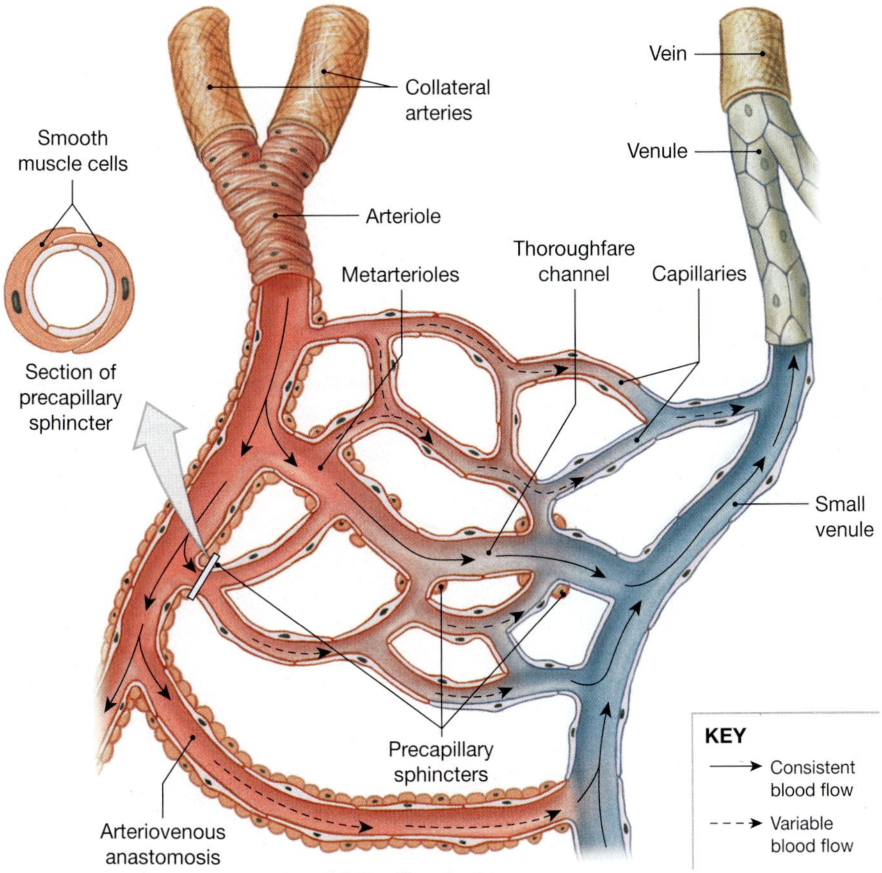

(a) Capillary bed

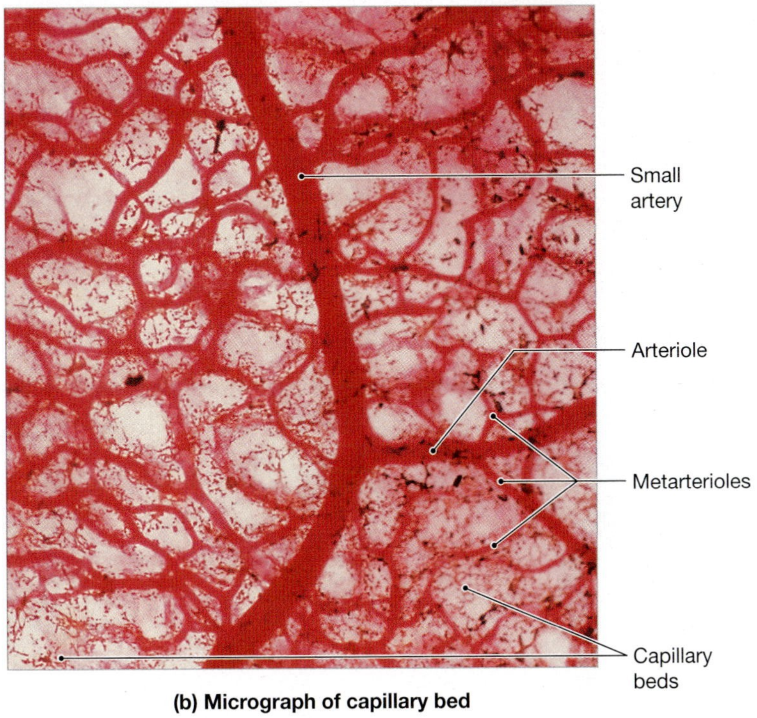

(b) Micrograph of capillary bed

Figure 22.5 Organization of a Capillary Bed
(a) Basic organization of a typical capillary bed. The pattern of blood flow changes continually in response to regional alterations in tissue oxygen demand. **(b)** Capillary bed as seen in living tissue.

other will supply blood to the capillary bed. **Arteriovenous** (ar-tēr-ē-ō-VĒ-nus) **anastomoses** are direct connections between arterioles and venules (Figure 22.5a). Arteriovenous anastomoses are common in visceral organs and joints where changes in body position could hinder blood flow through one vessel or another. Smooth muscles in the walls of these vessels can contract or relax to regulate the amount of blood reaching the capillary bed. For example, when the arteriovenous anastomoses are dilated, blood will bypass the capillary bed and flow directly into the venous circulation.

Veins [Figures 22.1/22.2]

Veins collect blood from all tissues and organs and return it to the heart. Following the pattern of blood flow, veins are discussed from smallest to largest (venule to medium-sized vein to large vein), whereas arteries were discussed from largest to smallest (elastic artery to muscular artery to arteriole). The walls of veins are thinner and less elastic than those of corresponding arteries because the blood pressure in veins is lower than that in arteries. Except for the smallest venules, all veins contain the same three layers in their walls that are found in arteries. However, veins show greater structural variation than arteries, and the histological structure of the wall of a particular vein may vary along its length.

Veins are classified on the basis of their size, and, in general, veins are larger in diameter than their corresponding arteries. Review Figures 22.1, p. 572, and 22.2, p. 573, to compare typical arteries and veins.

Venules

Venules, the smallest veins, collect blood from capillaries. They vary widely in size and character. The smallest venules resemble expanded capillaries, and venules smaller than 50 μm in total diameter lack a media altogether. An average venule has a luminal diameter of roughly 20 μm. The walls of venules larger than 50 μm contain all three layers, but the media is thin and dominated by connective tissue. The media of the very largest venules contain scattered smooth muscle cells.

Medium-Sized Veins

Medium-sized veins range from 2 to 9 mm in internal diameter and correspond in general size to medium-sized arteries. In these veins, the media is thin, and it contains relatively few smooth muscle fibers. The thickest layer of a medium-sized vein is the adventitia, which contains longitudinal bundles of elastic and collagen fibers.

Large Veins

Large veins include the *great veins*, the *superior* and *inferior venae cavae*, and their tributaries within the abdominopelvic and thoracic cavities. In veins, all of the layers are thickest in the large veins. The slender media is surrounded by a thick adventitia composed of a mixture of elastic and collagenous fibers.

Venous Valves [Figure 22.6]

The blood pressure in venules and medium-sized veins is too low to oppose the force of gravity. In the limbs, veins of this size contain one-way **valves** that are formed from infoldings of the intima (Figure 22.6). These valves act like the valves in the heart, preventing the backflow of blood. As long as the valves function normally, any movement that distorts or compresses a vein will push blood toward the heart. For example, when you are standing, blood returning from the foot must overcome the pull of gravity to ascend to the heart. Valves compartmentalize the blood within the veins, thereby

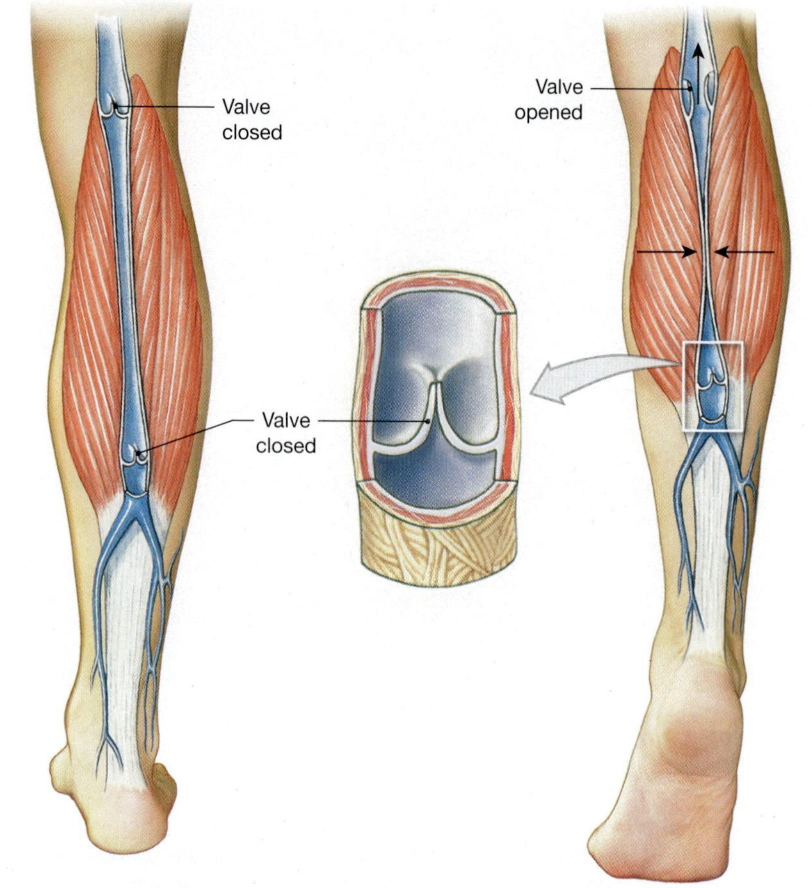

Figure 22.6 Function of Valves in the Venous System
Valves in the walls of medium-sized veins prevent the backflow of blood. Venous compression caused by the contraction of adjacent skeletal muscles creates pressure (shown by arrows) that assists in maintaining venous blood flow. Changes in body position and the thoracoabdominal pump may provide additional assistance.

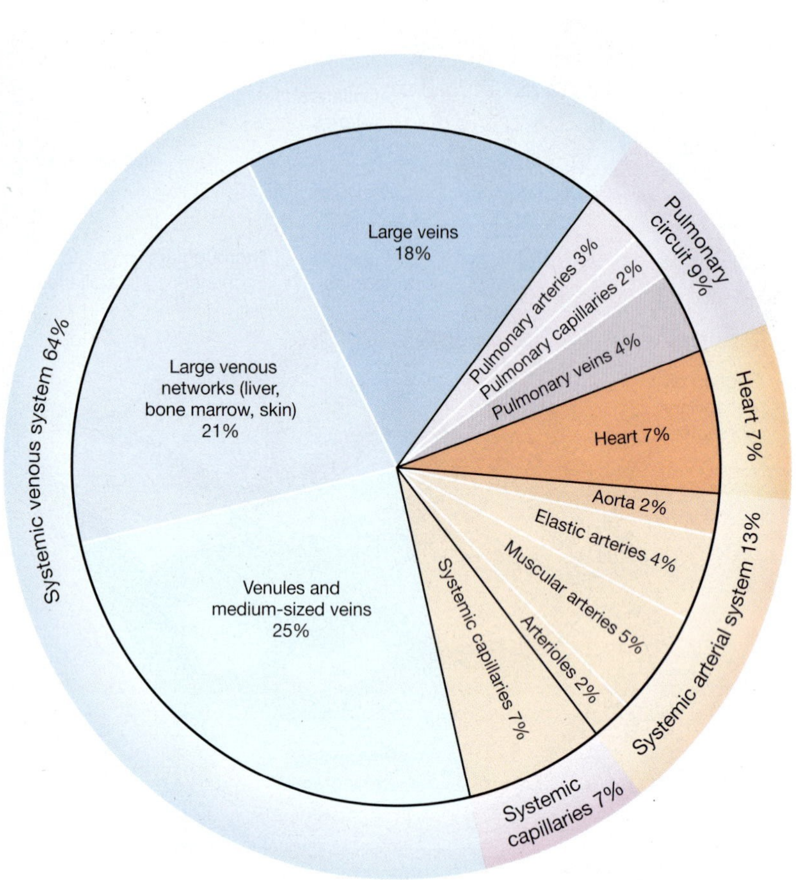

Figure 22.7 The Distribution of Blood in the Cardiovascular System

dividing the weight of the blood between the compartments. Any movement in the surrounding skeletal muscles squeezes the blood toward the heart. This mechanism is called a *skeletal muscle pump.* Large veins such as the vena cava do not have valves, but changes of pressure in the thoracic cavity assist in moving blood toward the heart. This mechanism, called the *thoracoabdominal pump*, will be considered further in Chapter 24.

The Distribution of Blood [Figure 22.7]

The total blood volume is unevenly distributed among arteries, veins, and capillaries (Figure 22.7). The heart, arteries, and capillaries normally contain 30–35 percent of the blood volume (roughly 1.5 L of whole blood), and the venous system contains the rest (65–70 percent or around 3.5 L).

Because their walls are thinner and contain a lower proportion of smooth muscle, veins are much more distensible than arteries. For a given rise in pressure, a typical vein will stretch about eight times as much as a corresponding artery. If the blood volume rises or falls, the elastic walls stretch or recoil, changing the volume of blood in the venous system.

If serious hemorrhaging occurs, the vasomotor center of the medulla oblongata stimulates sympathetic nerves innervating smooth muscle cells in the walls of medium-sized veins. When the smooth muscles in the walls contract, this **venoconstriction** (vē-nō-kon-STRIK-shun) reduces the volume of the venous system. In addition, blood enters the general circulation from venous networks in the liver, bone marrow, and skin. Reducing the amount of blood in the venous system can maintain the volume within the arterial system at near-normal levels despite a significant blood loss. The venous system therefore acts as a **blood reservoir**, with the liver acting as the primary reservoir; the change in volume constitutes the **venous reserve**. The venous reserve normally amounts to just more than 1 liter, 21 percent of the total blood volume.

CONCEPT CHECK

1. Examination of a section of tissue shows several small, thin-walled vessels with very little smooth muscle tissue in the media. What type of vessels are these?
2. Why are valves found in veins but not in arteries?
3. The femoral artery is an example of which type of artery?
4. Does gas exchange occur between the blood and surrounding tissues in arterioles?

See blue "Answers" tab at back of book.

Blood Vessel Distribution [Figure 22.8]

The blood vessels of the body can be divided into the pulmonary circuit and the systemic circuit. The pulmonary circuit is composed of arteries and veins that transport blood between the heart and the lungs, a relatively short distance. The arteries and veins of the systemic circuit transport oxygenated blood between the heart and all other tissues, a round-trip that involves much longer distances. There are some functional and structural differences between the vessels in these circuits. For example, blood pressure within the pulmonary circuit is relatively low, and the walls of pulmonary arteries are thinner than those of systemic arteries.

Figure 22.8 summarizes the primary circulatory routes within the pulmonary and systemic circuits. Three important functional patterns will emerge from the tables and figures that follow:

1. The peripheral distribution of arteries and veins on the left and right sides is usually identical except near the heart, where the largest vessels connect to the atria or ventricles.
2. A single vessel may have several different names as it crosses specific anatomical boundaries, making accurate anatomical descriptions possible when the vessel extends far into the periphery.
3. Arteries and veins often make anastomotic connections that reduce the impact of a temporary or even permanent occlusion (blockage) of a single vessel.

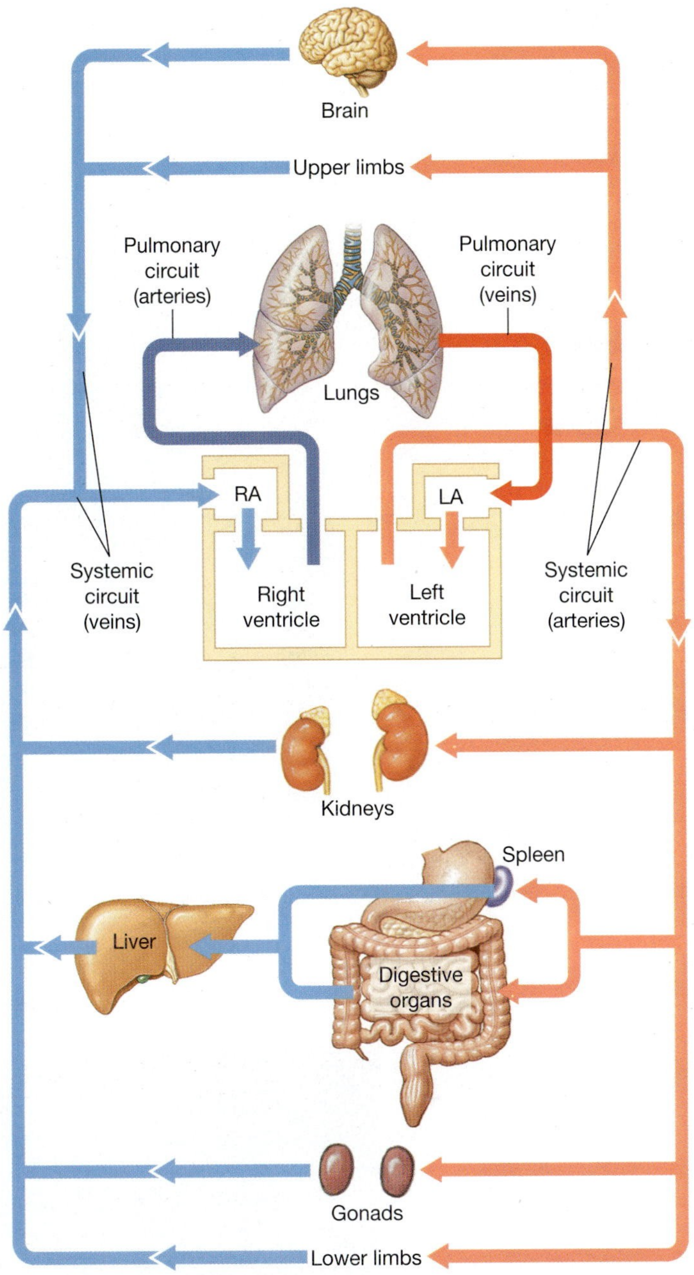

Figure 22.8 An Overview of the General Pattern of Circulation

The Pulmonary Circuit [Figure 22.9]

Blood entering the right atrium has just returned from capillary beds in peripheral tissues and the myocardium. While blood was in those capillary beds, oxygen was released and carbon dioxide absorbed. After traveling through the right atrium and right ventricle, blood enters the pulmonary trunk, the start of the pulmonary circuit. This circuit, which at any given moment contains about 9 percent of the total blood volume, begins at the pulmonary valve and ends at the entrance to the left atrium. In the pulmonary circuit (Figure 22.9a), oxygen will be replenished, carbon dioxide excreted, and the oxygenated blood returned to the heart for distribution to the body within the systemic circuit. Compared with the systemic circuit, the pulmonary circuit is relatively short; the base of the pulmonary trunk and the lungs are only about 15 cm (6 in.) apart.

The arteries of the pulmonary circuit differ from those of the systemic circuit in that they carry deoxygenated blood. (For this reason, color-coded diagrams usually show the pulmonary arteries in blue, the same color as systemic veins.) As the pulmonary trunk curves over the superior border of the heart, it gives rise to the **left** and **right pulmonary arteries**. These large arteries enter the lungs before branching repeatedly, giving rise to smaller and smaller arteries. The smallest branches, the *pulmonary arterioles*, provide blood to capillary networks that surround small air pockets, or **alveoli** (al-VĒ-ō-lī; *alveolus*, sac) in the lungs. The walls of alveoli are thin enough for gas exchange to occur between the capillary blood and inspired air. (Alveolar structure is described in Chapter 24.) As it leaves the alveolar capillaries, oxygenated blood enters venules that in turn merge to form larger vessels carrying blood toward the **pulmonary veins**. These four veins, two from each lung, empty into the left atrium, completing the pulmonary circuit (Figure 22.9a). Figure 22.9b is a coronary angiogram showing the vessels of the pulmonary circuit and their relationship to the heart and lungs in a living subject.

The Systemic Circuit

The systemic circuit begins at the aortic valve and ends at the entrance to the right atrium. It supplies the capillary beds in all parts of the body not supplied by the pulmonary circuit and, at any given moment, contains about 84 percent of the total blood volume.

Systemic Arteries [Figures 22.10 to 22.20]

Figure 22.10 is an overview of the arterial system. This figure indicates the relative locations of major systemic arteries. The detailed distribution of these

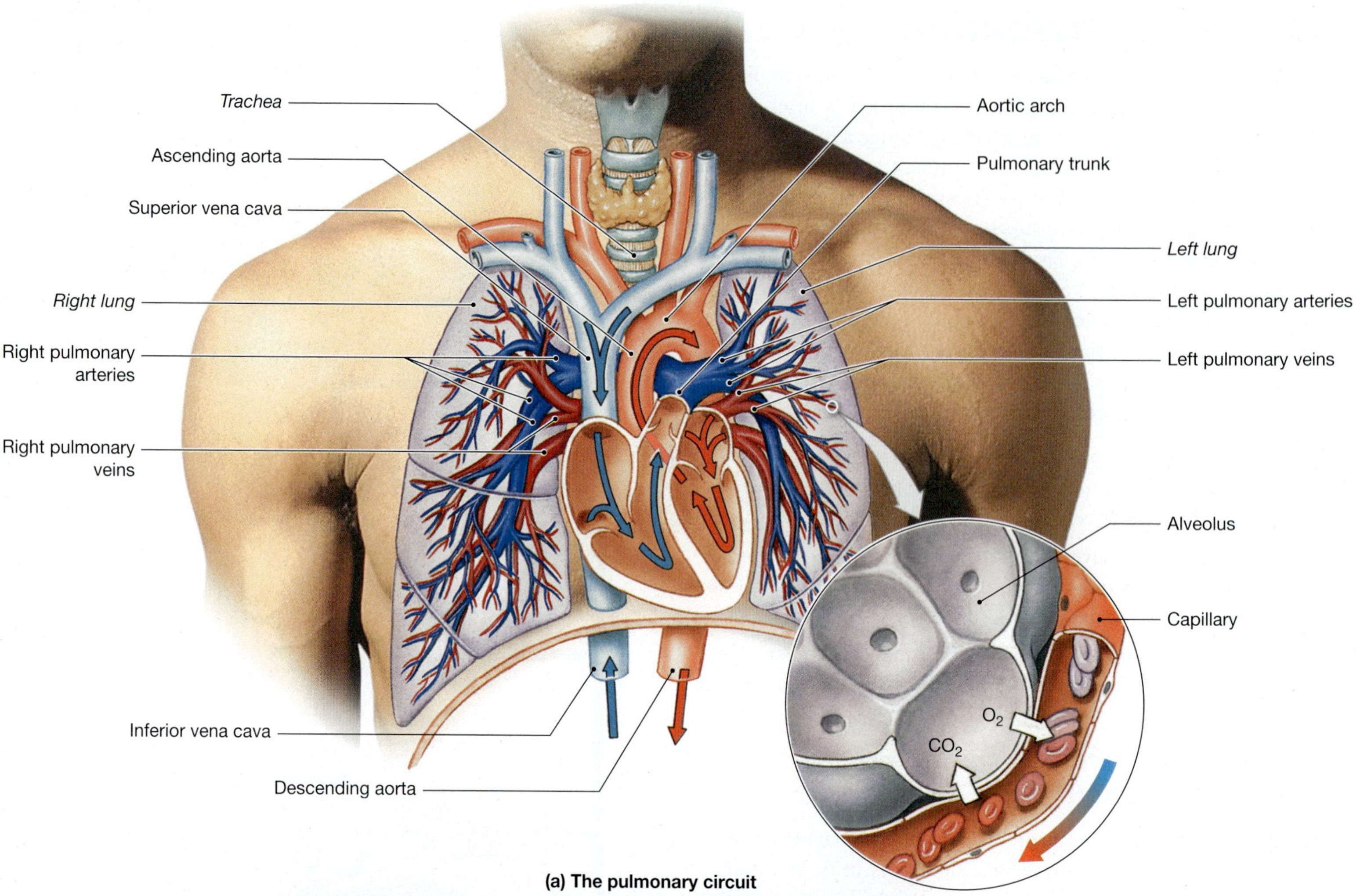

(a) The pulmonary circuit

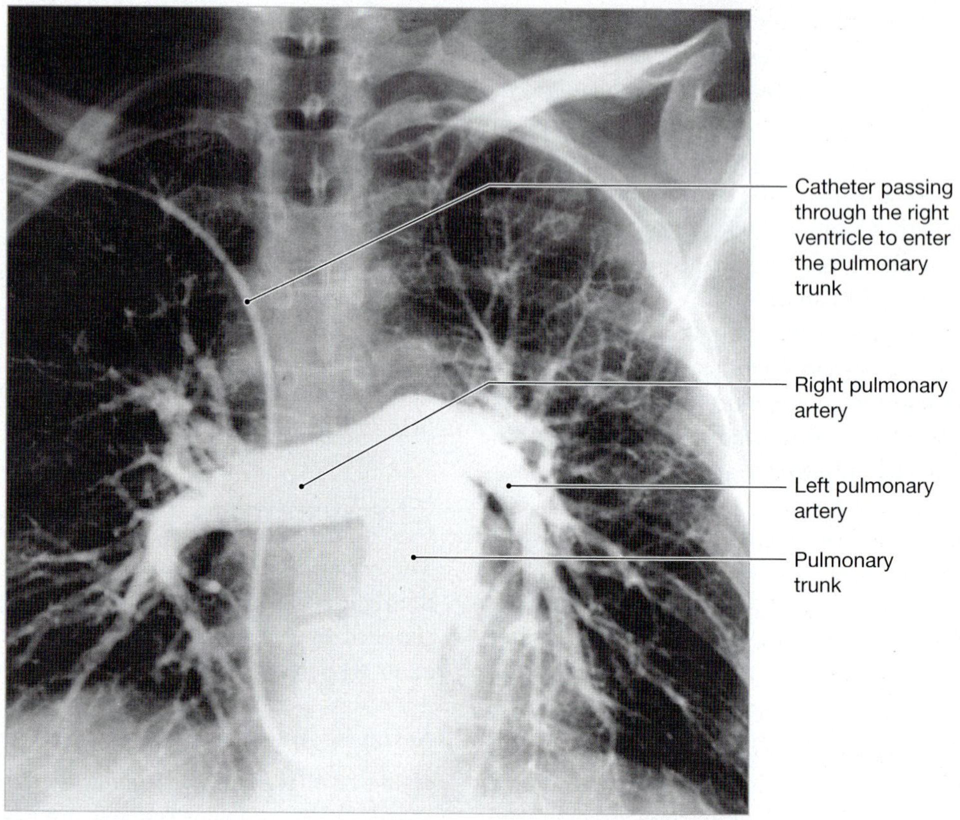

(b) Angiogram

Figure 22.9 The Pulmonary Circuit
(a) Anatomy of the pulmonary circuit. Blue arrows indicate the flow of deoxygenated blood; red arrows indicate the flow of oxygenated blood. The breakout shows the alveoli of the lung and the routes of gas diffusion into and out of the bloodstream across the walls of the alveolar capillaries. **(b)** Coronary angiogram, showing heart, vessels of the pulmonary circuit, diaphragm, and lungs.

arteries, supply the area around the elbow. At the cubital fossa, the brachial artery divides into the **radial artery**, which follows the radius, and the **ulnar artery**, which follows the ulna to the wrist. These arteries supply blood to the forearm. At the wrist, these arteries anastomose to form a **superficial palmar arch** and a **deep palmar arch** that respectively supply blood to the palm and to the **digital arteries** of the thumb and fingers.

The Carotid Arteries and the Blood Supply to the Brain [Figures 22.13 to 22.15] The common carotid arteries ascend deep in the tissues of the neck. A common carotid artery can usually be located by pressing gently along either side of the windpipe (trachea) until a strong pulse is felt. Each common carotid artery divides at the level of the larynx into an **external carotid artery** and an **internal carotid artery**. The **carotid sinus**, located at the base of the internal carotid artery, may extend along a portion of the common carotid artery (Figures 22.13a and 22.14). The carotid sinus contains baroreceptors and chemoreceptors involved in cardiovascular regulation. p. 475 The external carotid arteries supply blood to the structures of the neck, pharynx, esophagus, larynx, lower jaw, and face. The internal carotid arteries enter the skull through the *carotid canals* of the temporal bones, delivering blood to the brain. p. 139 Each internal carotid artery ascends to the level of the optic nerves, where it divides into three branches: (1) an **ophthalmic artery**, which supplies the eyes; (2) an **anterior cerebral artery**, which supplies the frontal and parietal lobes of the brain; and (3) a **middle cerebral artery**, which supplies the midbrain and lateral surfaces of the cerebral hemispheres (Figures 22.13 and 22.15).

The brain is extremely sensitive to changes in its circulatory supply. An interruption of circulation for several seconds will produce unconsciousness, and after 4 minutes there may be some permanent neural damage. Such circulatory crises are rare, because blood reaches the brain through the vertebral arteries as well as the internal carotid arteries. The vertebral arteries arise from the subclavian arteries and ascend within the *transverse foramina* of the cervical vertebrae. pp. 163–165 The vertebral arteries enter the cranium at the foramen magnum, where they fuse along the ventral surface of the medulla oblongata to form the **basilar artery**. The basilar artery continues on the ventral surface of the brain along the pons, branching many times before dividing into the **posterior cerebral arteries**. The **posterior communicating arteries** branch off the posterior cerebral arteries (Figures 22.13a and 22.15a,b).

The internal carotid arteries normally supply the arteries of the anterior half of the cerebrum, and the rest of the brain receives blood from the vertebral arteries. But this circulatory pattern can easily change, because the internal carotid arteries and the basilar artery are interconnected in a ring-shaped anastomosis, the **cerebral arterial circle**, or *circle of Willis*, that encircles the infundibulum of the pituitary gland (Figure 22.15a,b). With this arrangement, the brain can receive blood from either or both arterial sources, the carotids or the vertebrals, and the chances for a serious interruption of circulation are reduced.

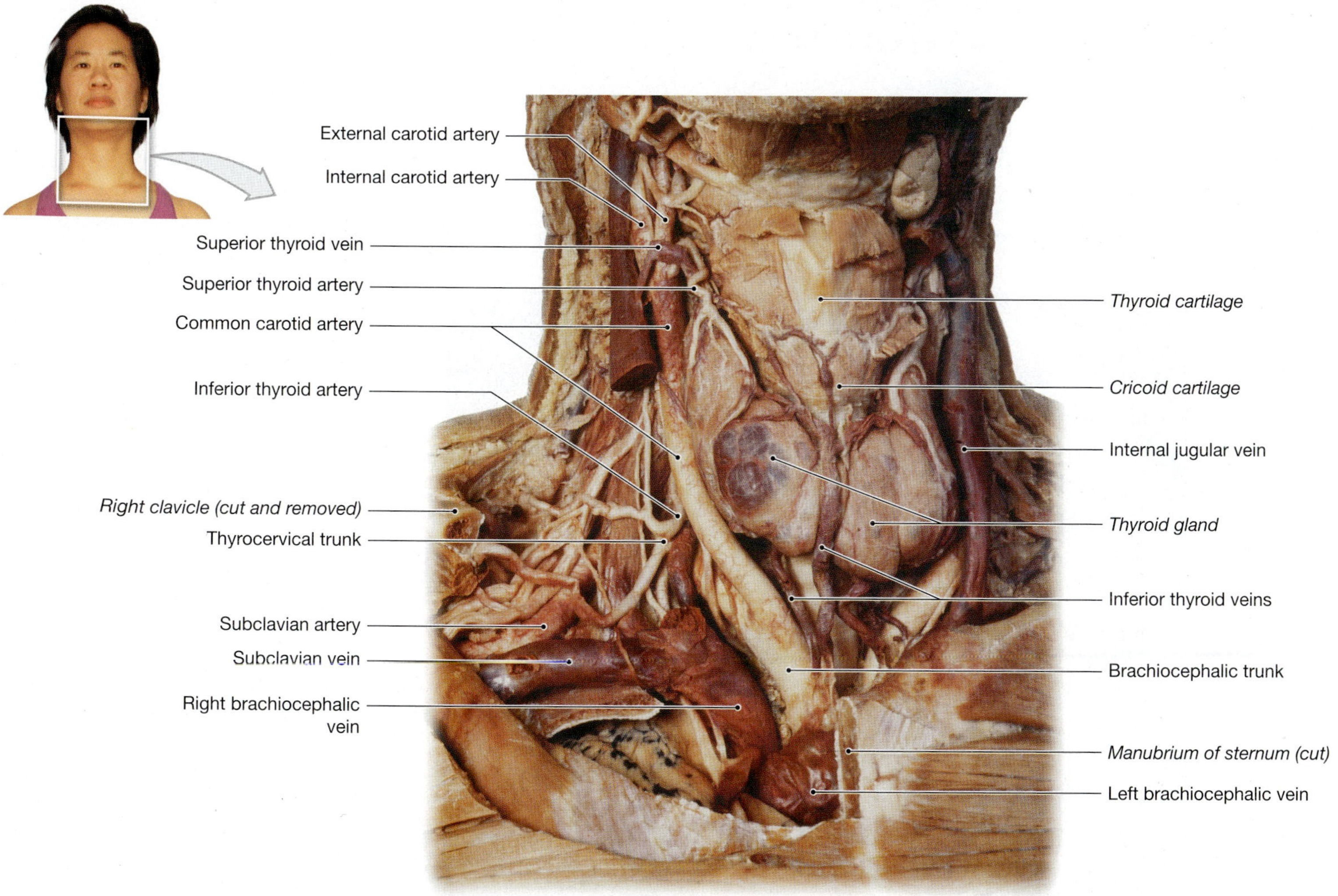

Figure 22.14 Major Arteries of the Neck
This dissection of the anterior neck shows the position and appearance of the major arteries in this region. In this dissection, part of the right clavicle, first rib, and manubrium of the sternum have been removed, along with the inferior portion of the right internal jugular vein.

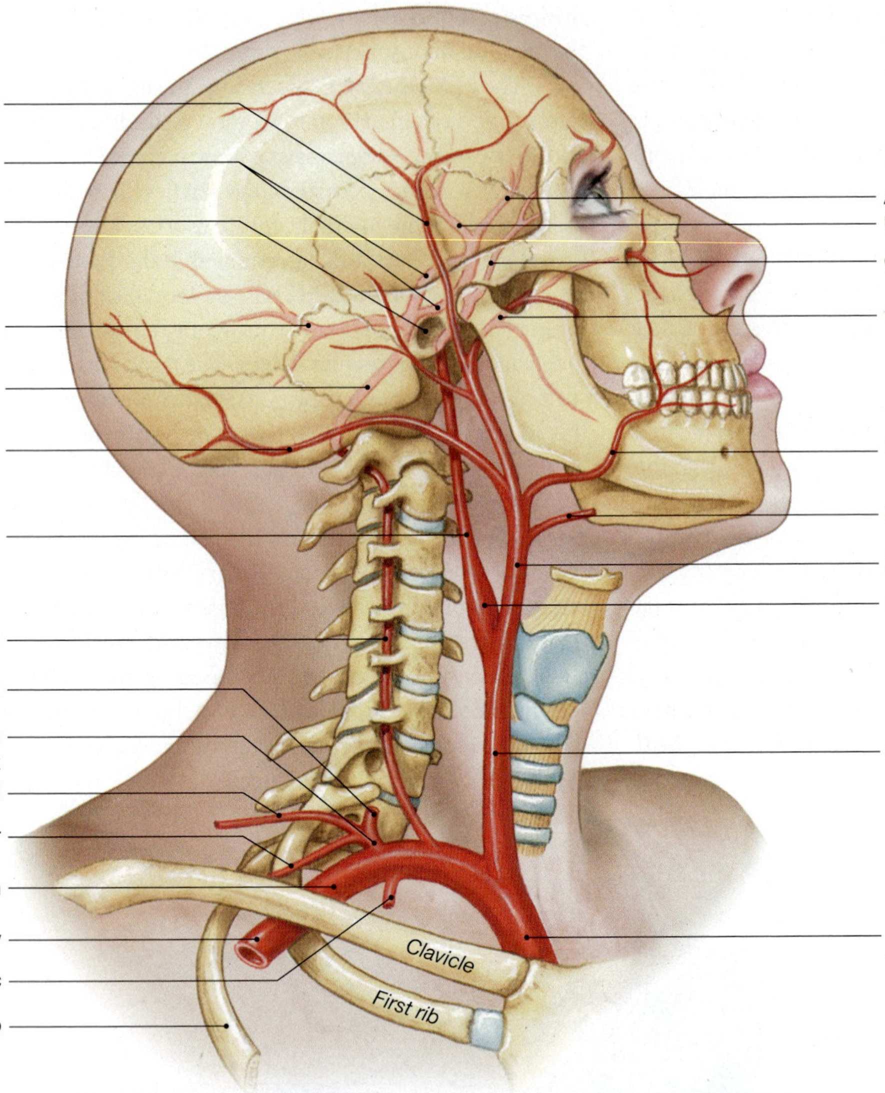

(a) Arteries of neck and head, an oblique lateral view from the right side

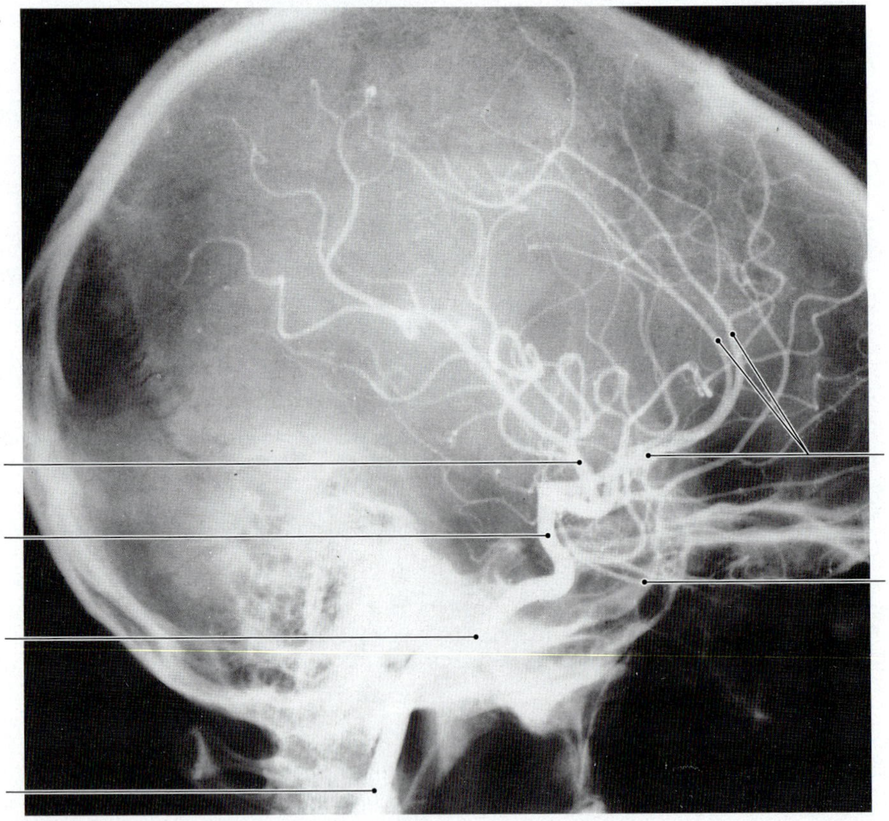

(b) Angiogram, lateral projection

Figure 22.13 Arteries of the Neck and Head
(a) General circulation pattern of arteries supplying the neck and superficial structures of the head; this is an oblique lateral view from the right side. **(b)** Angiogram showing the internal carotid arteries and their branches within the cranium.

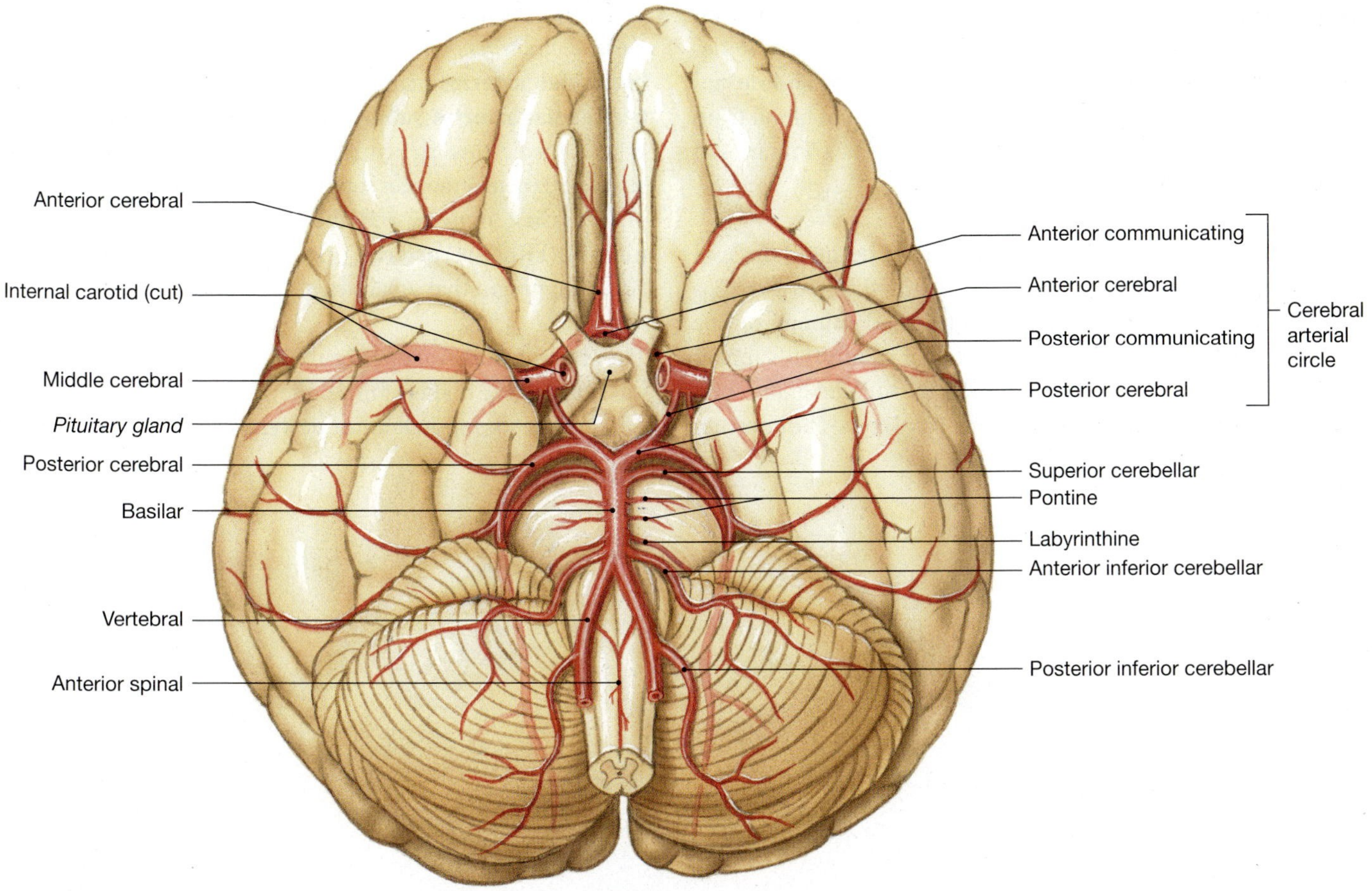

(a) Arteries of the brain, inferior view

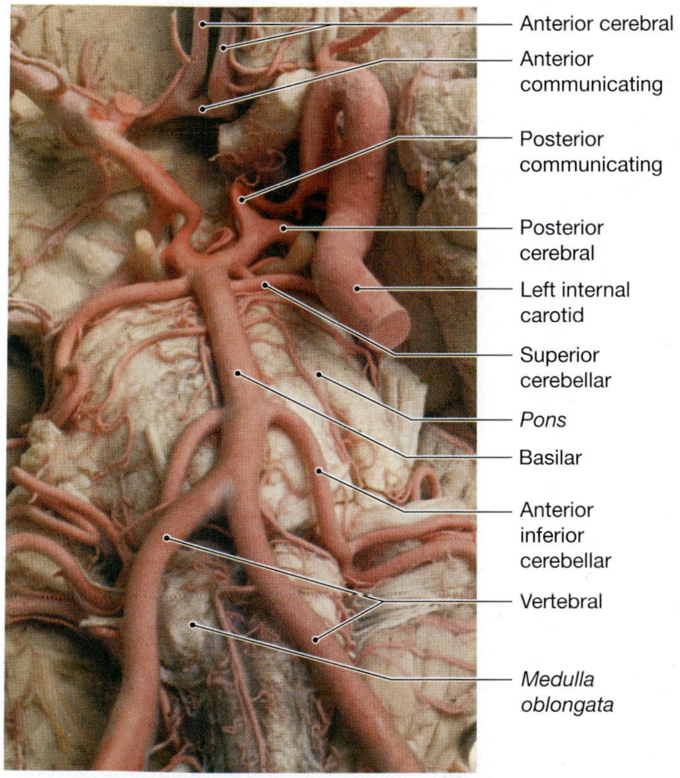

(b) Arteries injected to show cerebral arterial circle

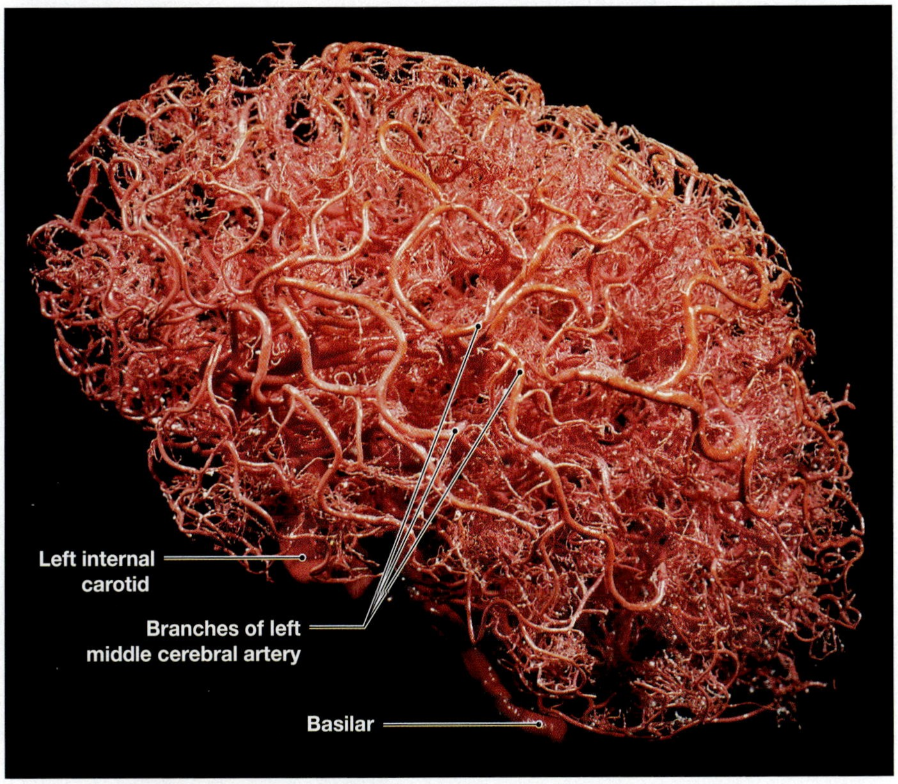

(c) Corrosion cast of cerebral arteries, left cerebral hemisphere

Figure 22.15 The Arterial Supply to the Brain
(a) An inferior view of the brain, showing the distribution of arteries. *See Figure 22.22b* for a comparable view of the veins on the inferior surface of the brain. **(b)** The arteries on the inferior surface of the brain; the vessels have been injected with red latex, making them easier to see. **(c)** A lateral view of the arteries supplying the brain. This is a corrosion cast: The vessels have been injected with latex, and then the brain tissue was dissolved and removed in an acid bath.

The Descending Aorta [Figures 22.10/22.16/22.20] Continuous with the aortic arch is the **descending aorta**. The diaphragm divides the descending aorta into a superior **thoracic aorta** and an inferior **abdominal aorta** (Figure 22.10, p. 581). A summary of the distribution of blood from the descending aorta is presented in Figure 22.20, p. 593. The tributaries of the thoracic aorta are shown in Figure 22.16.

The Thoracic Aorta [Figure 22.16] The thoracic aorta begins at the level of vertebra T_5 and penetrates the diaphragm at the level of vertebra T_{12} (Figure 22.16). The thoracic aorta travels within the mediastinum, on the dorsal thoracic wall, slightly to the left of the vertebral column. It supplies blood to branches servicing the viscera of the thorax, the muscles of the chest and the diaphragm, and the thoracic portion of the spinal cord. The branches of the thoracic aorta are grouped anatomically as either *visceral branches* or *parietal branches*. Visceral branches supply the organs of the chest: The **bronchial arteries** supply the conducting passageways of the lungs, **pericardial arteries** supply the pericardium, **mediastinal arteries** supply general mediastinal structures, and **esophageal arteries** supply the esophagus. The parietal branches supply the chest wall: The **intercostal arteries** supply the chest muscles and the vertebral column area, and the **superior phrenic** (FREN-ik) **arteries** deliver blood to the superior surface of the muscular diaphragm that separates the thoracic and abdominopelvic cavities.

The Abdominal Aorta [Figures 22.16/22.17] Beginning immediately inferior to the diaphragm is the abdominal aorta (Figures 22.16 and 22.17). The abdominal aorta descends slightly to the left of the vertebral

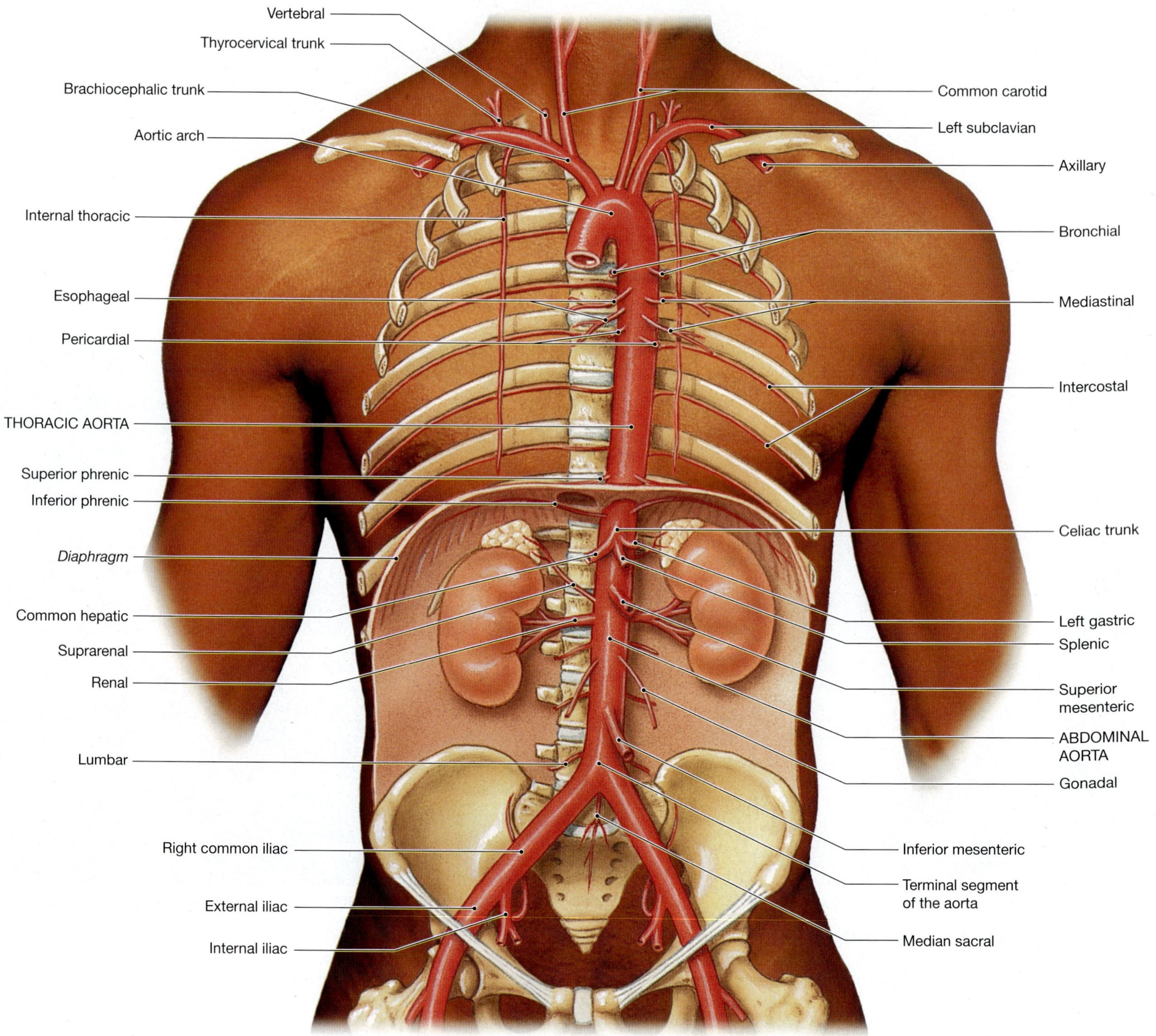

Figure 22.16 Major Arteries of the Trunk

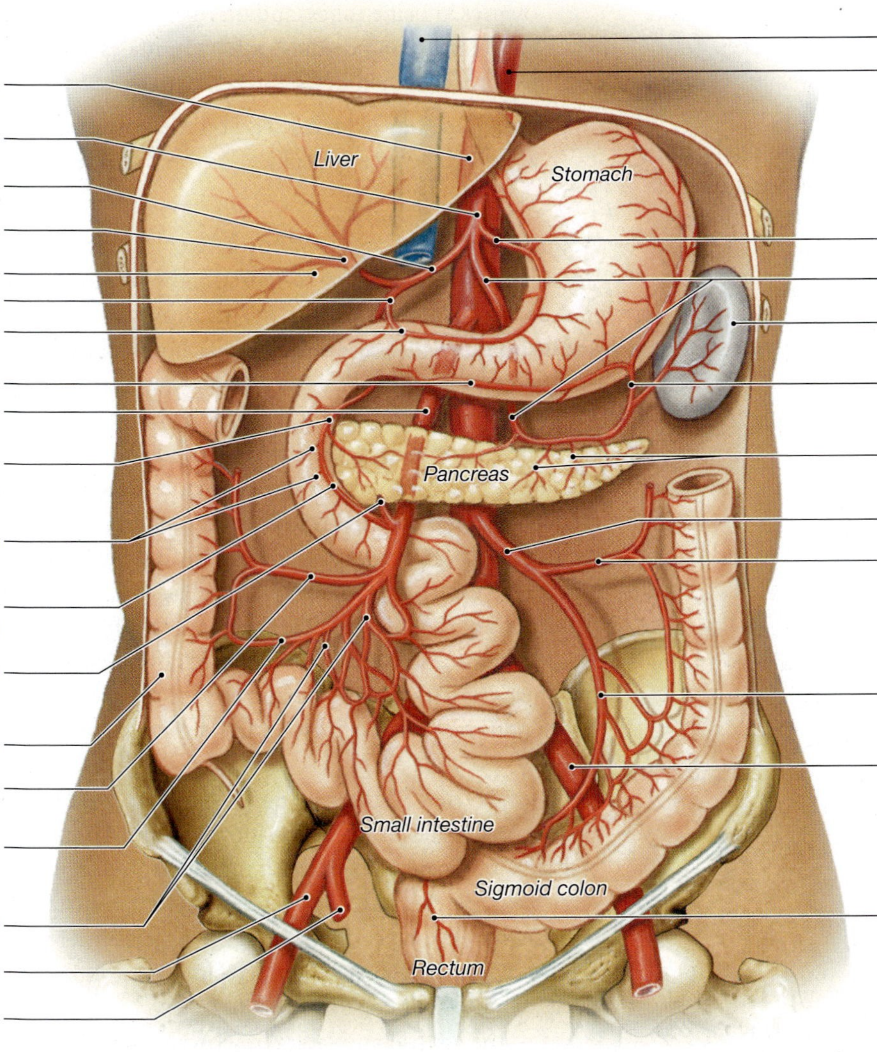

(a) Arteries supplying the abdominal organs (anterior view)

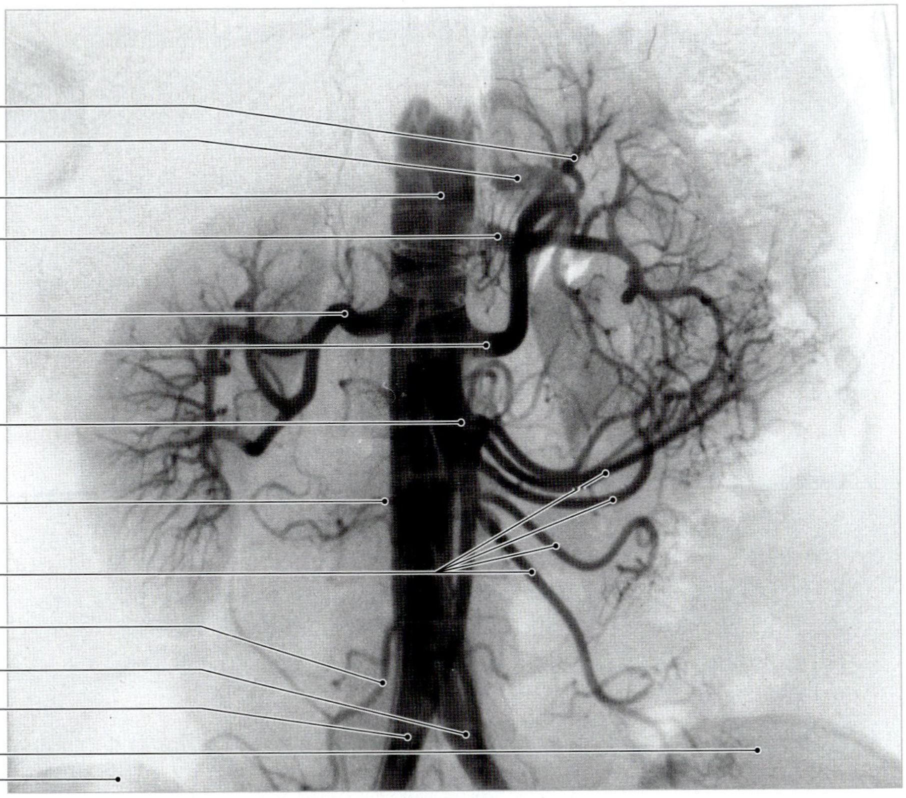

(b) Angiogram of the abdominal aorta

Figure 22.17 Arteries of the Abdomen
(a) Major arteries supplying the abdominal viscera. **(b)** Angiogram of the abdominal aorta, showing arteries to the viscera and to the kidneys (anterior/posterior projection).

column, but posterior to the peritoneal cavity; it is often surrounded by a cushion of adipose tissue. At the level of vertebra L_4, the abdominal aorta splits into the *right* and *left common iliac arteries*, which supply deep pelvic structures and the lower limbs. The region where the aorta splits is called the **terminal segment of the aorta**.

The abdominal aorta delivers blood to all of the abdominopelvic organs and structures. The major branches to visceral organs are unpaired, and they arise on the anterior surface of the abdominal aorta and extend into the mesenteries to reach the visceral organs. Branches to the body wall, the kidneys, and other structures outside the peritoneal cavity are paired, and they originate along the lateral surfaces of the abdominal aorta. Figure 22.16 shows the major arteries of the trunk, with the thoracic and abdominal organs removed.

There are three unpaired arteries: (1) the *celiac trunk*, (2) the *superior mesenteric artery*, and (3) the *inferior mesenteric artery* (Figures 22.16 and 22.17).

1. The **celiac** (SĒ-lē-ak) **trunk** delivers blood to the liver, stomach, esophagus, gallbladder, duodenum, pancreas, and spleen. The celiac artery divides into three branches:
   - the **left gastric artery**, which supplies the stomach and the inferior portion of the esophagus;
   - the **splenic artery**, which supplies the spleen and arteries to the stomach (*left gastroepiploic artery*) and pancreas (*pancreatic arteries*); and
   - the **common hepatic artery**, which supplies arteries to the liver (*hepatic artery proper*), stomach (*right gastric artery*), gallbladder (*cystic artery*), and duodenal area (*gastroduodenal, right gastroepiploic*, and *superior pancreaticoduodenal arteries*).
2. The **superior mesenteric** (mez-en-TER-ik) **artery** arises about 2.5 cm inferior to the celiac trunk to supply arteries to the pancreas and duodenum (*inferior pancreaticoduodenal artery*), small intestine (*intestinal arteries*), and most of the large intestine (*right colic, middle colic*, and *ileocolic arteries*).
3. The **inferior mesenteric artery** arises about 5 cm superior to the terminal segment of the aorta and delivers blood to the terminal portions of the colon (*left colic* and *sigmoid arteries*) and the rectum (*rectal arteries*).

There are five paired arteries: (1) the *inferior phrenics*, (2) the *suprarenals*, (3) the *renals*, (4) the *gonadals*, and (5) the *lumbars*.

1. The **inferior phrenic arteries** supply the inferior surface of the diaphragm and the inferior portion of the esophagus.
2. The **suprarenal arteries** originate on either side of the aorta near the base of the superior mesenteric artery. Each suprarenal artery supplies a suprarenal gland, which caps the superior part of a kidney.
3. The short (about 7.5 cm) **renal arteries** arise along the posterolateral surface of the abdominal aorta, about 2.5 cm inferior to the superior mesenteric artery, and travel posterior to the peritoneal lining to reach the suprarenal glands and kidneys. We shall discuss branches of the renal arteries in Chapter 26.
4. **Gonadal** (gō-NAD-al) **arteries** originate between the superior and inferior mesenteric arteries. In males, they are called *testicular arteries* and are long, thin arteries that supply blood to the testes and scrotum. In females, they are termed *ovarian arteries* and supply blood to the ovaries, uterine tubes, and uterus. The distribution of gonadal vessels (both arteries and veins) differs in males and females; the differences will be described in Chapter 27.
5. Small **lumbar arteries** arise on the posterior surface of the aorta and supply the vertebrae, spinal cord, and abdominal wall.

Arteries of the Pelvis and Lower Limbs [Figures 22.16/22.18/22.19] Near the level of vertebra L_4, the terminal segment of the abdominal aorta divides to form a pair of muscular arteries, the **right** and **left common iliac** (IL-ē-ak) **arteries** and the small **medial sacral artery**. These arteries carry blood to the pelvis and lower limbs (Figures 22.16, 22.18, and 22.19). As these arteries travel along the inner surface of the ilium, they descend posterior to the cecum and sigmoid colon and, at the level of the lumbosacral joint, each common iliac divides to form an **internal iliac artery** and an **external iliac artery**. The internal iliac arteries enter the pelvic cavity to supply the urinary bladder, the internal and external walls of the pelvis, the external genitalia, and the medial side of the thigh. The major tributaries of the internal iliac artery are the *superior gluteal, internal pudendal, obturator*, and *lateral sacral arteries*. In females, these vessels also supply the uterus and vagina. The external iliac arteries supply blood to the lower limbs, and they are much larger in diameter than the internal iliac arteries.

Arteries of the Thigh and Leg [Figures 22.18/22.19] The external iliac artery crosses the surface of the iliopsoas muscle and penetrates the abdominal wall midway between the anterior superior iliac spine and the pubic symphysis. It emerges on the anteromedial surface of the thigh as the **femoral artery** and roughly 5 cm distal to its emergence, the **deep femoral artery** branches off its lateral surface (Figure 22.18). The deep femoral artery, which gives rise to the *medial* and *lateral circumflex arteries*, supplies blood to the ventral and lateral regions of the skin and deep muscles of the thigh.

The femoral artery continues inferiorly and posterior to the femur. As it reaches the popliteal fossa, it gives off a branch, the **descending genicular artery**, which supplies the medial aspect of the knee. The femoral artery continues, and as it passes through the adductor magnus muscle it becomes the **popliteal** (pop-LIT-ē-al) **artery** (Figure 22.19). The popliteal artery crosses the popliteal fossa before branching to form the **posterior tibial artery** and the **anterior tibial artery**. The posterior tibial artery gives rise to the **fibular artery**, or *peroneal artery*, and continues inferiorly along the posterior surface of the tibia. The anterior tibial artery passes between the tibia and fibula, emerging on the anterior surface of the tibia. As it descends toward the foot, the anterior tibial artery provides blood to the skin and muscles of the anterior portion of the leg.

Arteries of the Foot [Figures 22.18/22.20] When the anterior tibial artery reaches the ankle, it becomes the **dorsalis pedis artery**. The dorsalis pedis branches repeatedly, supplying the ankle and dorsal portion of the foot (Figure 22.18).

As it reaches the ankle, the posterior tibial artery divides to form the **medial** and **lateral plantar arteries**, which supply blood to the plantar surface of the foot. The medial and lateral plantar arteries are connected to the dorsalis pedis artery by a pair of anastomoses. This connection links the **dorsal arch** (*arcuate arch*) to the **plantar arch**. Small arteries branching off these arches supply the distal portions of the foot and the toes.

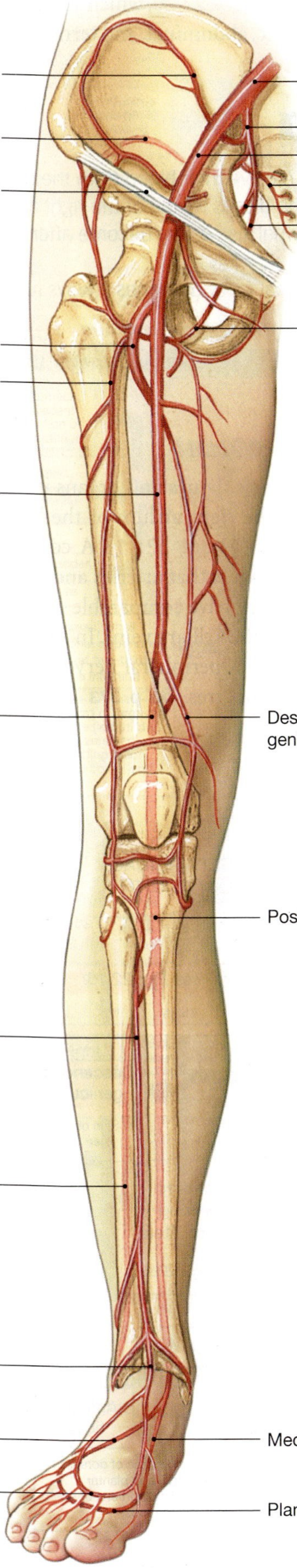

(a) Anterior view

(b) Femoral vessels

Figure 22.18 Major Arteries of the Lower Limb, Part I
(a) Anterior view of the arteries supplying the right lower limb. **(b)** Major arteries of the right thigh.

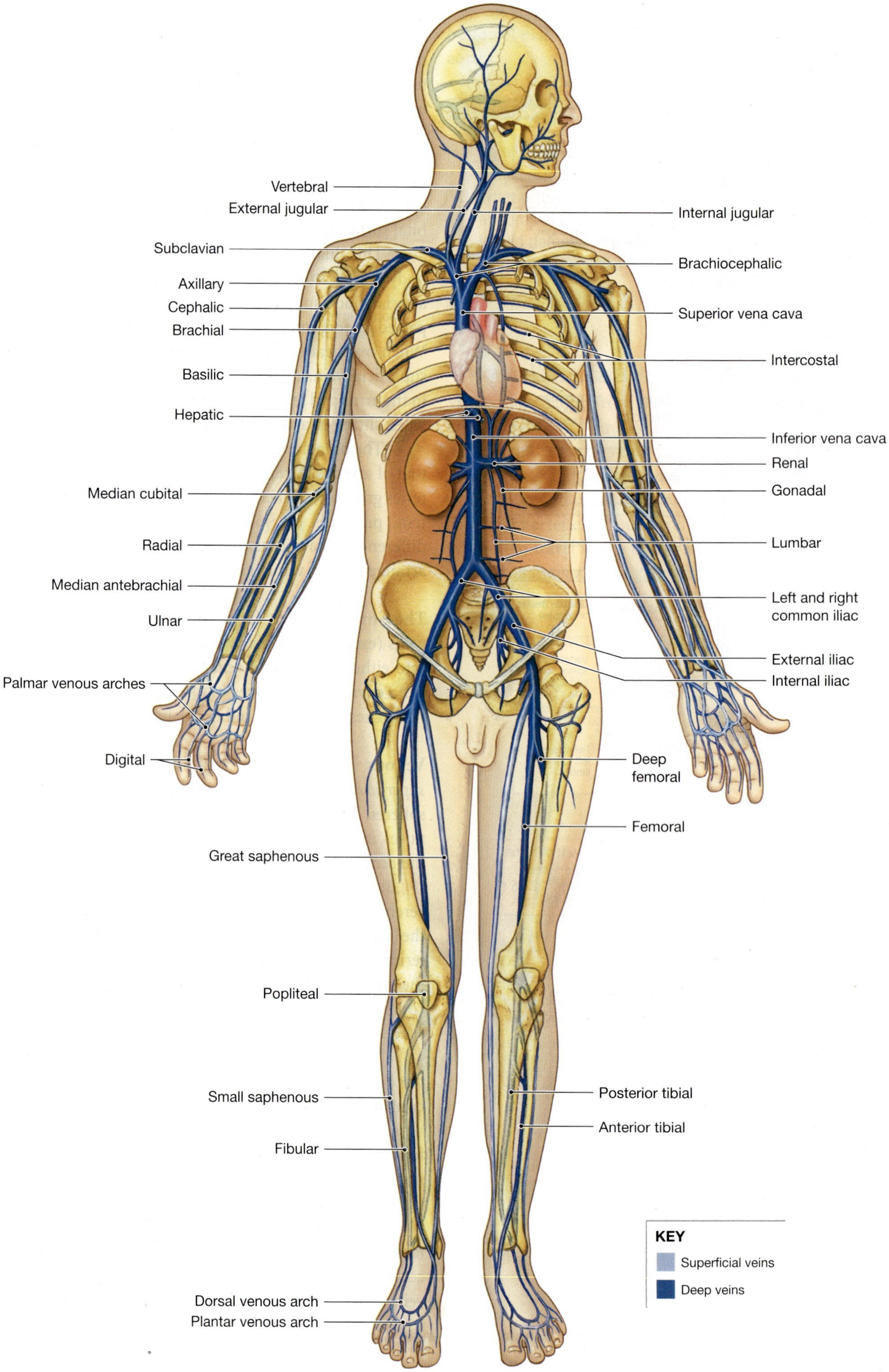

Figure 22.21 An Overview of the Systemic Venous System

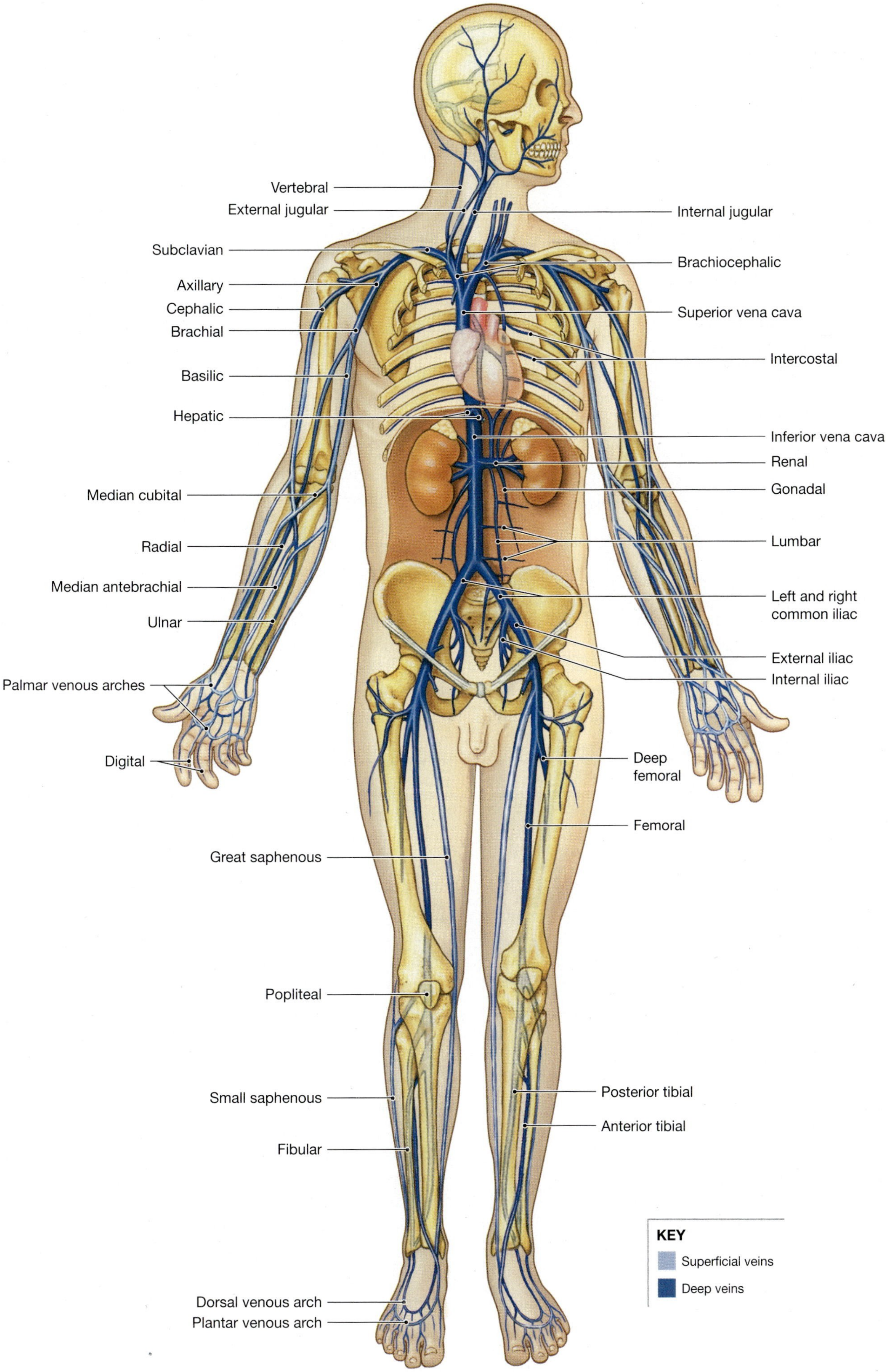

Figure 22.21 An Overview of the Systemic Venous System

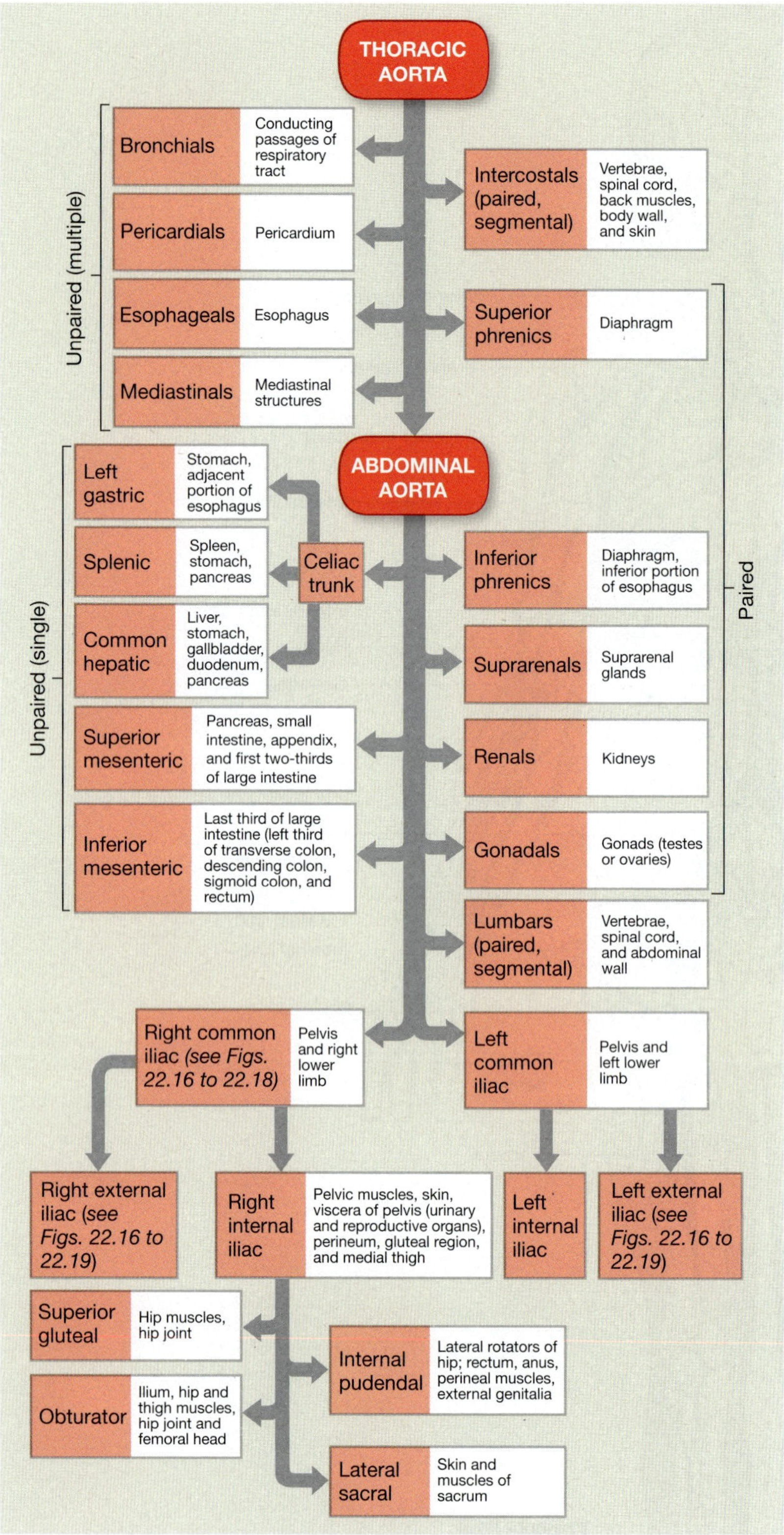

Figure 22.20 A Summary of the Arterial System
The distribution of blood from the aorta.

One significant difference between the arterial and venous systems concerns the distribution of major veins in the neck and limbs. Arteries in these areas are not found at the body surface; instead, they are deep, protected by bones and surrounding soft tissues. In contrast, the neck and limbs usually have two sets of peripheral veins, one superficial and the other deep. The superficial veins are so close to the surface that they can be seen quite easily. Because they are so close to the surface, they are easy targets for obtaining blood samples, and most blood tests are performed on venous blood collected from the superficial veins of the upper limb (usually the antecubital surface).

This dual venous drainage plays an important role in the control of body temperature. When body temperature becomes abnormally low, the arterial blood supply to the skin is reduced, and the superficial veins are bypassed. Blood enters the limbs, then returns to the trunk in the deep veins. When overheating occurs, the blood supply to the skin increases, and the superficial veins dilate. This mechanism is one reason why superficial veins in the arms and legs become prominent during periods of heavy exercise or when sitting in a sauna, hot tub, or steam bath.

The branching pattern of peripheral veins is much more variable than that of arteries. Arterial pathways are usually direct, because developing arteries grow toward active tissues. By the time blood reaches the venous system, pressures are low, and routing variations make little functional difference. The discussion that follows is based on the most common arrangement of veins.

The Superior Vena Cava [Figures 22.21/22.24a] All of the systemic veins (except the cardiac veins, which drain into the coronary sinus) drain into either the *superior vena cava* or the *inferior vena cava.* The **superior vena cava (SVC)** receives blood from the tissues and organs of the head, neck, chest, shoulders, and upper limbs (Figures 22.21 and 22.24a).

Venous Return from the Cranium [Figure 22.22] Numerous *superficial cerebral veins* and *internal cerebral veins* drain the cerebral hemispheres. The **superficial cerebral veins** empty into a network of dural sinuses, including the *superior* and *inferior sagittal sinuses,* the *petrosal sinuses,* the *occipital sinus,* the *left* and *right transverse sinuses,* and the *straight sinus* (Figure 22.22). The largest sinus, the **superior sagittal sinus,** is in the falx cerebri. p. 391 The majority of the **internal cerebral veins** collect inside the brain to form the **great cerebral vein,** which collects blood from the interior of the cerebral hemispheres and the choroid plexus and delivers it to the **straight sinus.** Other cerebral veins drain into the **cavernous sinus** in company with numerous small veins from the orbit. Blood from the cavernous sinus reaches the internal jugular vein through the **petrosal sinuses.**

The venous sinuses converge within the dura mater in the region of the lambdoid suture. The left and right transverse sinuses form at the **confluence of sinuses** near the base of the petrous part of the temporal bone, and each drains into a **sigmoid sinus,** which penetrates the jugular foramen and leaves the skull as the **internal jugular vein** on that side. The internal jugular vein descends parallel to the common carotid artery in the neck.

Vertebral veins drain the cervical spinal cord and the posterior surface of the skull. These vessels descend within the transverse foramina of the cervical vertebrae, in company with the vertebral arteries. The vertebral veins empty into the *brachiocephalic veins* of the chest.

Before proceeding, review **Figure 22.20**, which summarizes the distribution of blood from the thoracic, abdominal, and terminal portions of the aorta.

CONCEPT CHECK

1. What regions of the body receive their blood from the carotid arteries?
2. Which artery is found at the biceps region of the right arm?
3. What artery does the external iliac artery become after leaving the abdominal cavity?
4. Would damage to the internal carotid arteries always result in brain damage? Why or why not?

See blue "Answers" tab at back of book.

Systemic Veins [Figures 22.10/22.21]

Veins collect blood from the body's tissues and organs in an elaborate venous network that drains into the right atrium of the heart through the *superior* and *inferior venae cavae* (**Figure 22.21**). A comparison between **Figure 22.21** and **Figure 22.10** reveals that arteries and veins typically run side by side, and in many cases they have comparable names. For example, the axillary arteries run alongside the axillary veins. In addition, arteries and veins often travel in the company of peripheral nerves that have the same names and innervate the same structures. p. 373

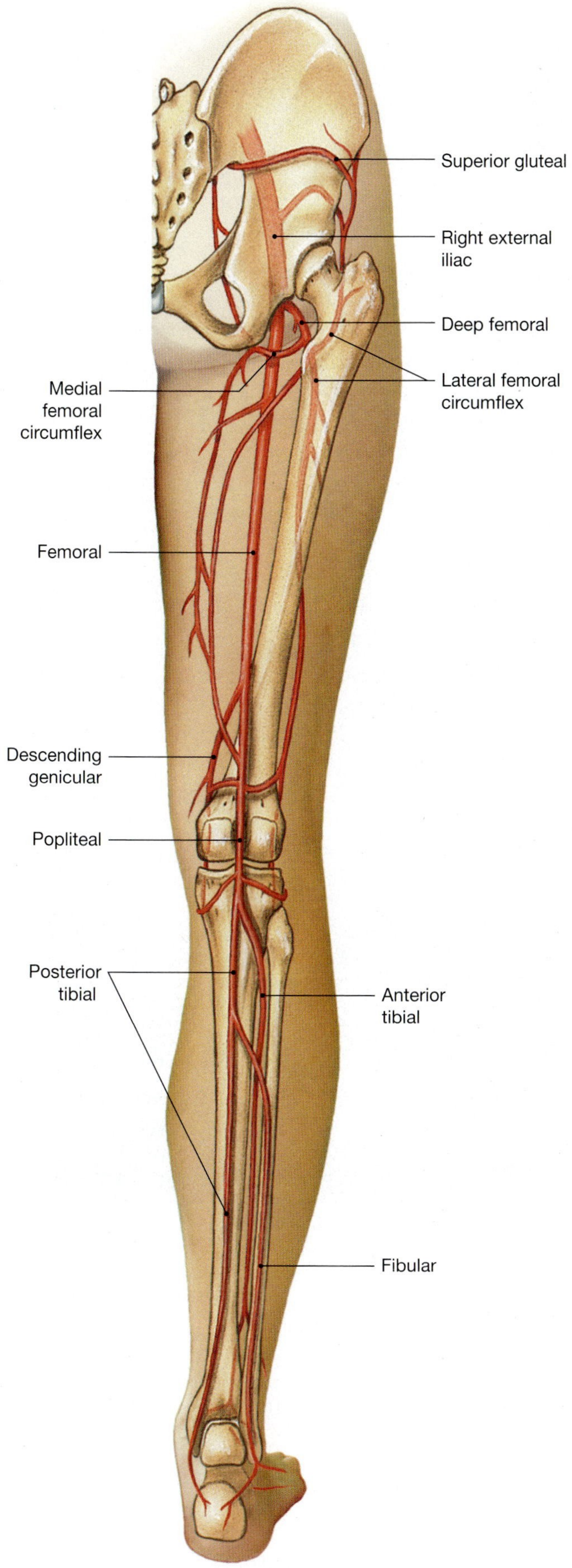

(a) Posterior view

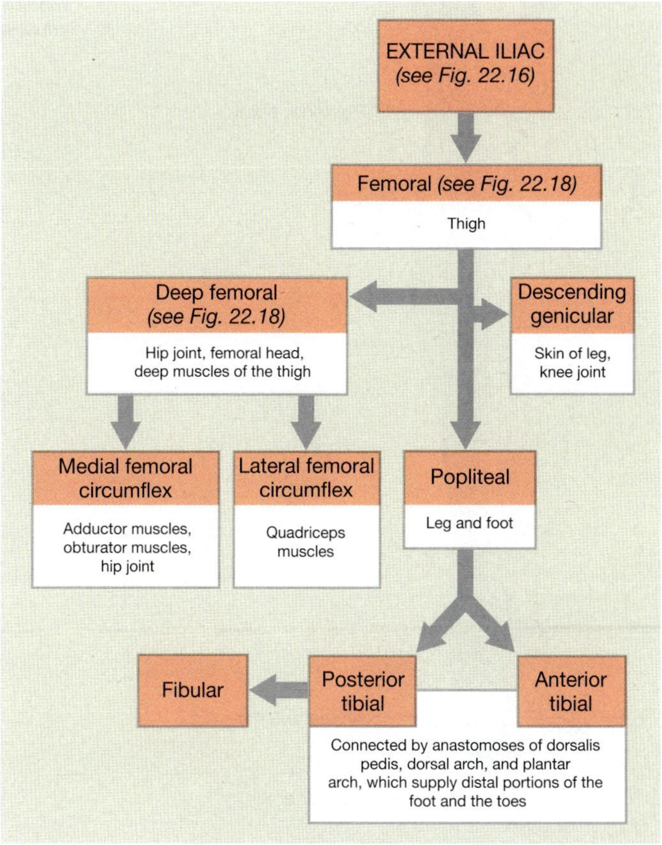

(b) Major arteries of the lower limb

Figure 22.19 Major Arteries of the Lower Limb, Part II
(a) Posterior view of the arteries supplying the right lower limb. **(b)** A summary of the major arteries of the lower limb.

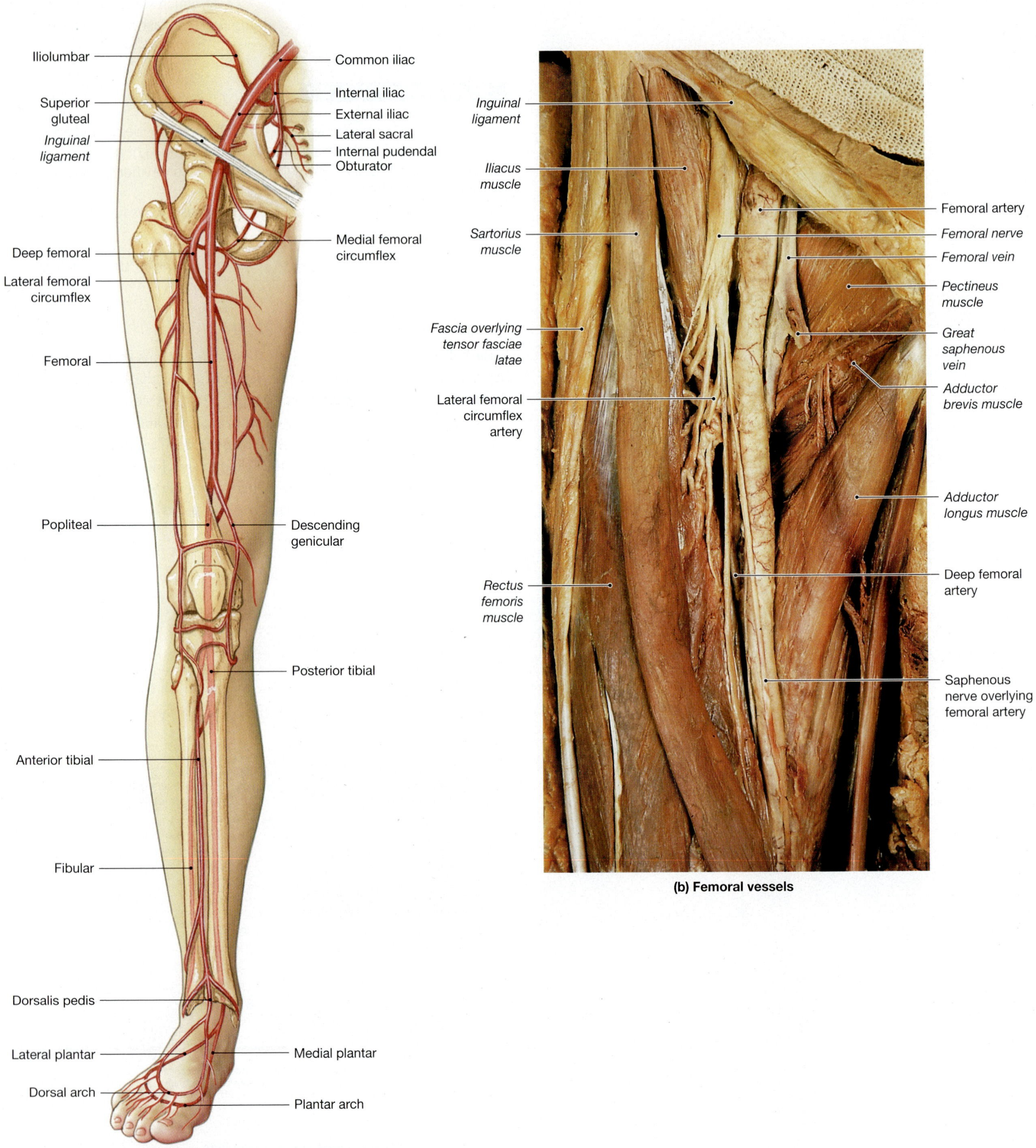

(a) Anterior view

(b) Femoral vessels

Figure 22.18 Major Arteries of the Lower Limb, Part I
(a) Anterior view of the arteries supplying the right lower limb. **(b)** Major arteries of the right thigh.

Figure 22.22 Major Veins of the Head and Neck
(a) An oblique lateral view of the head and neck, showing the major superficial and deep veins. **(b)** An inferior view of the brain, showing the major veins. Compare with the arterial supply to the brain shown in *Figure 22.15a*.

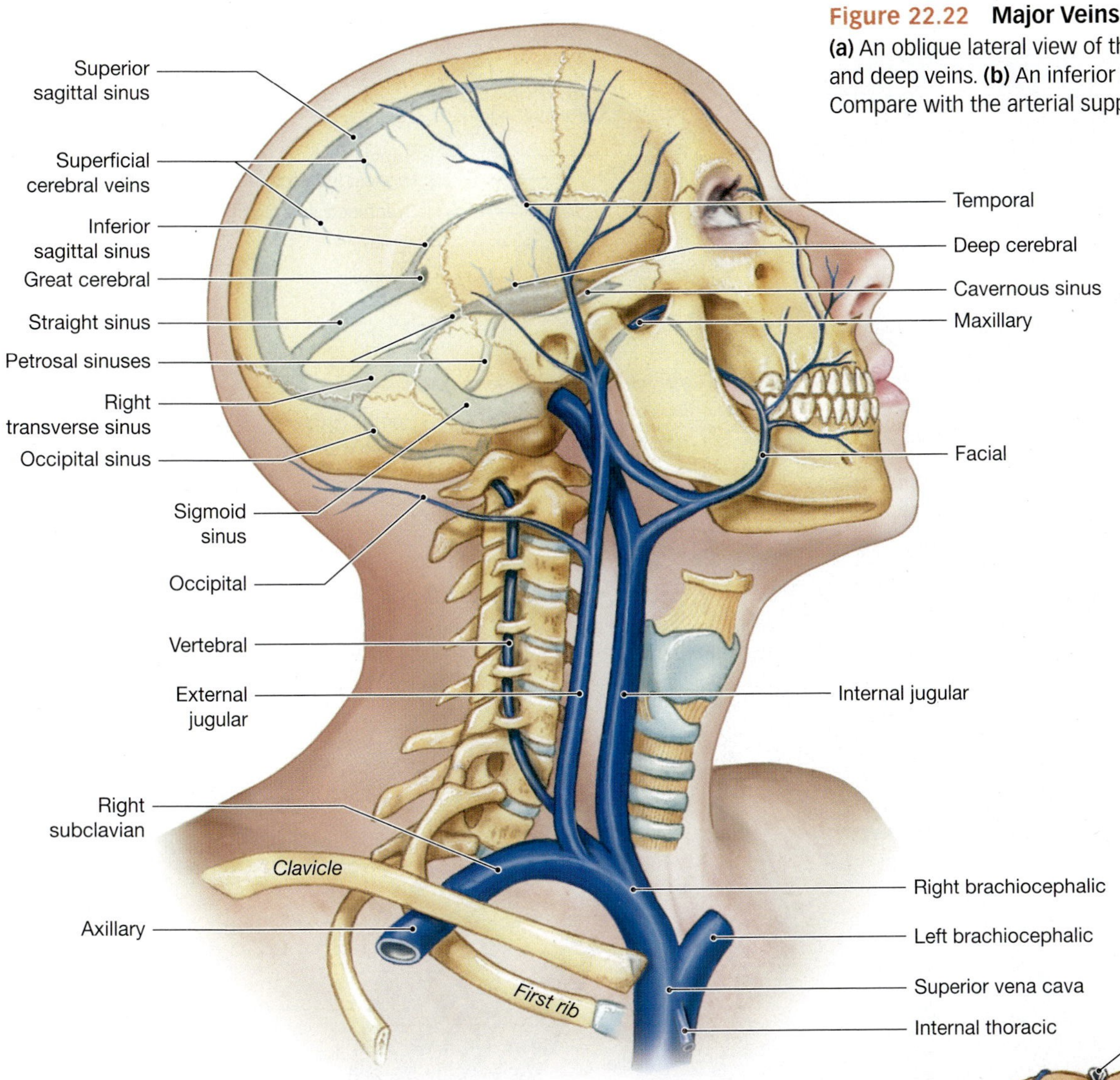

(a) Veins of the head and neck, lateral view

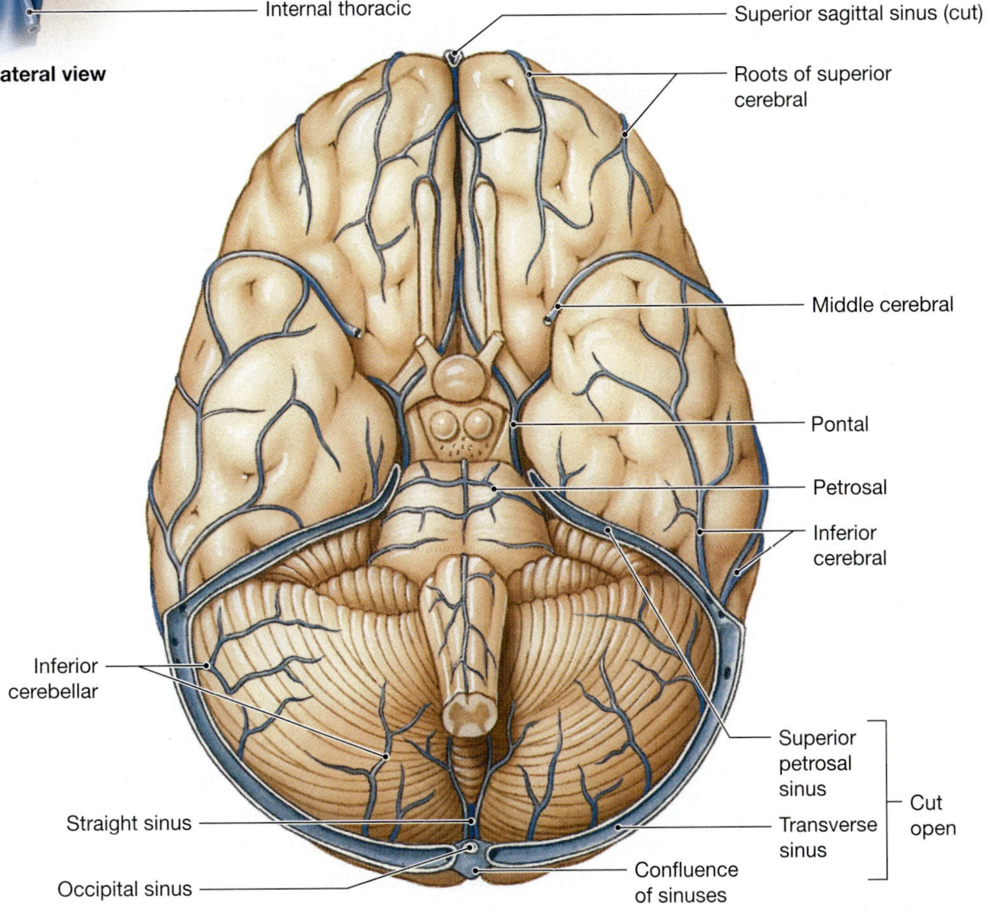

(b) Venous drainage of the brain, inferior view

Superficial Veins of the Head and Neck [Figure 22.22] Superficial veins of the head converge to form the **temporal**, **facial**, and **maxillary veins** (Figure 22.22). The temporal and maxillary veins drain into the **external jugular vein**. The facial vein drains into the internal jugular vein; a broad anastomosis between the external and internal jugular veins at the angle of the mandible provides dual venous drainage of the face, scalp, and cranium. The external jugular vein descends superficial to the sternocleidomastoid muscle. Posterior to the clavicle, the external jugular empties into the *subclavian vein*. In healthy individuals, the external jugular vein is easily palpable, and a *jugular venous pulse (JVP)* can sometimes be seen at the base of the neck.

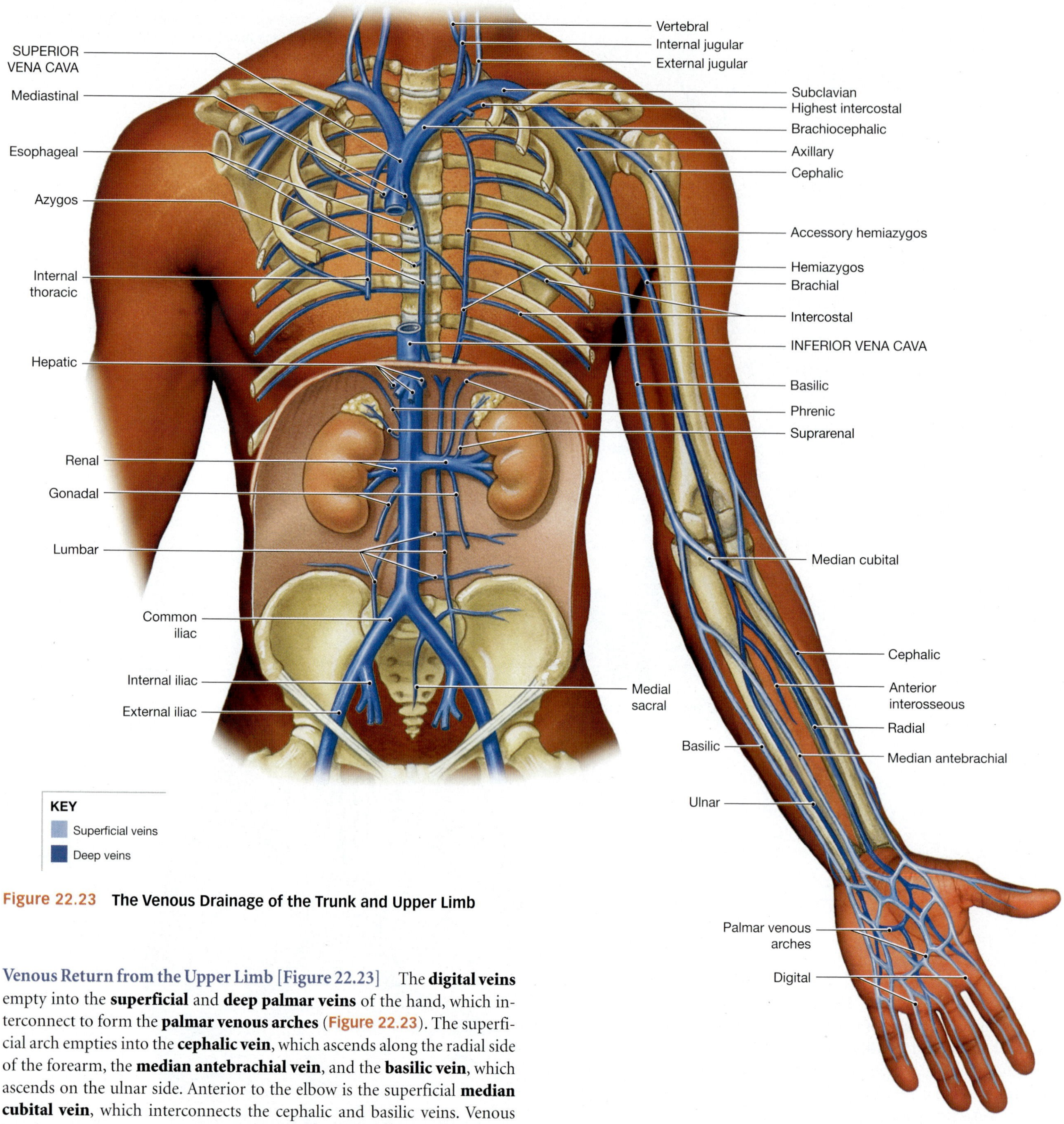

Figure 22.23 The Venous Drainage of the Trunk and Upper Limb

Venous Return from the Upper Limb [Figure 22.23] The **digital veins** empty into the **superficial** and **deep palmar veins** of the hand, which interconnect to form the **palmar venous arches** (Figure 22.23). The superficial arch empties into the **cephalic vein**, which ascends along the radial side of the forearm, the **median antebrachial vein**, and the **basilic vein**, which ascends on the ulnar side. Anterior to the elbow is the superficial **median cubital vein**, which interconnects the cephalic and basilic veins. Venous blood samples are typically collected from the median cubital vein.

From the elbow, the basilic vein passes superiorly along the medial surface of the biceps brachii muscle. As it approaches the axilla, the basilic vein joins the brachial vein to form the **axillary vein** (Figure 22.23).

The deep palmar veins drain into the **radial vein** and the **ulnar vein**. After crossing the elbow, these veins fuse with the *anterior crural interosseous vein* to form the **brachial vein**. The brachial vein lies parallel to the brachial artery. As the brachial vein continues toward the trunk, it receives blood from the basilic vein before entering the axilla as the axillary vein.

The Formation of the Superior Vena Cava [Figures 22.23/22.24] The cephalic vein joins the axillary vein on the outer surface of the first rib, forming the **subclavian vein**, which continues on to the chest. The subcla-

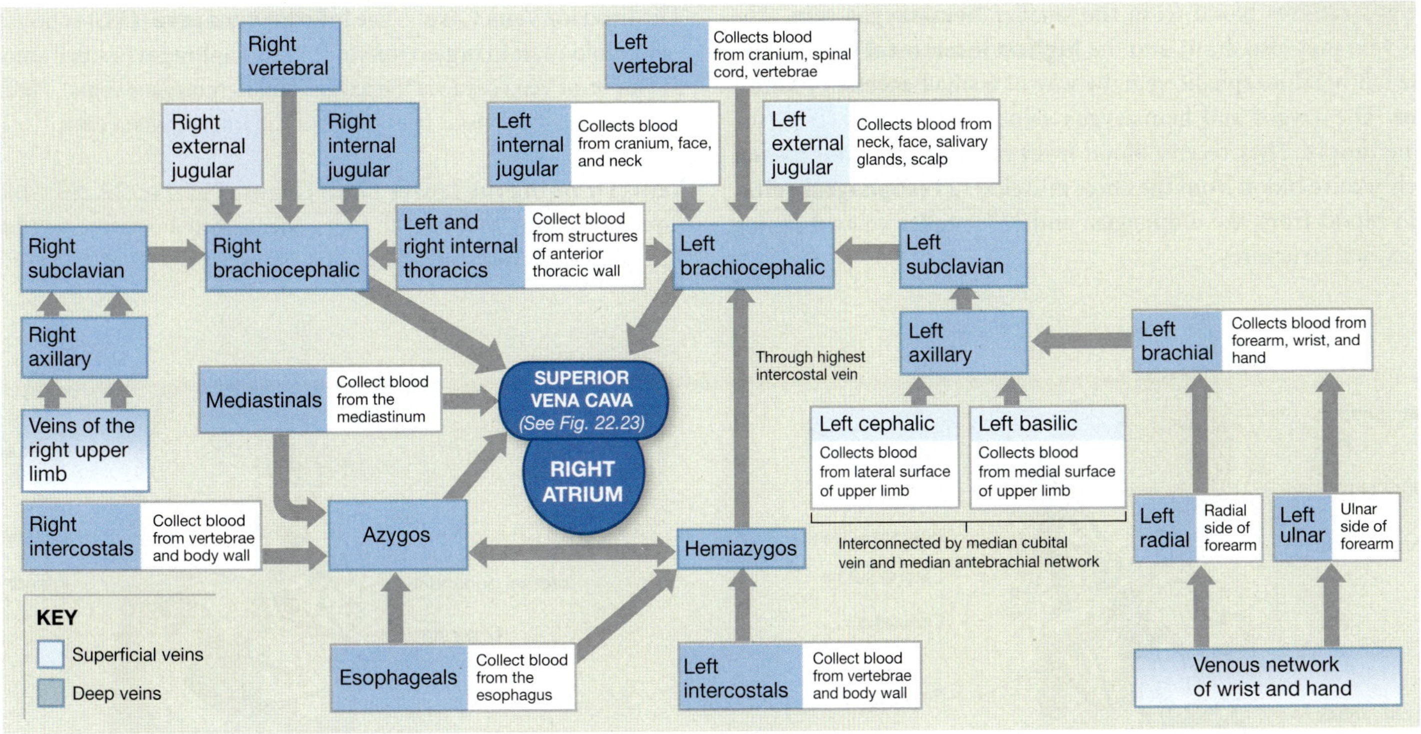

(a) Tributaries of the superior vena cava

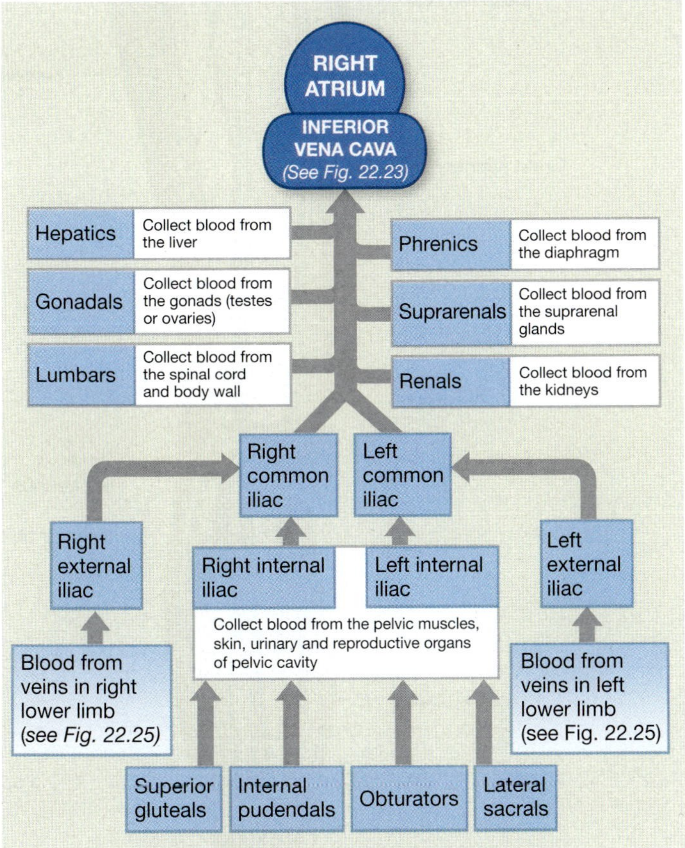

(b) Tributaries of the inferior vena cava

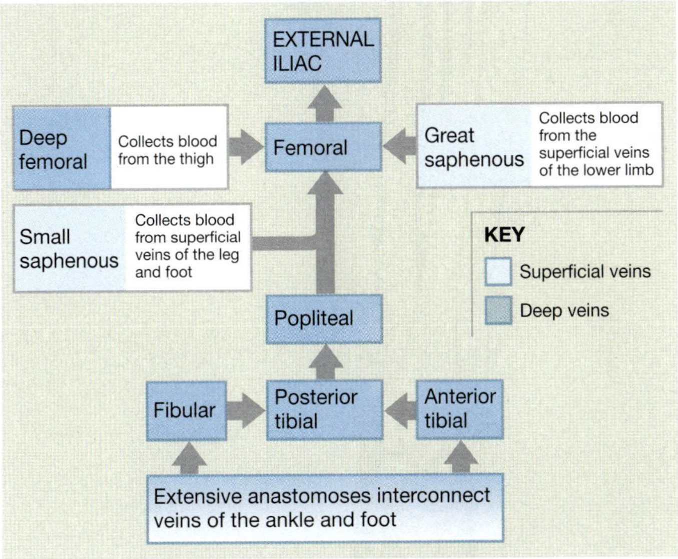

(c) Summary of the veins of the lower limb

Figure 22.24 A Summary Flowchart of the Venous System

vian vein passes over the superior surface of the first rib, along the clavicle, and into the thoracic cavity. The subclavian then merges with the external and internal jugular veins of that side. This creates the **brachiocephalic vein**, or *innominate vein* (Figure 22.23). The brachiocephalic vein receives blood from the *vertebral vein*, which drains the posterior portion of the skull and the spinal cord. At the level of the first and second ribs, the left and right brachiocephalic veins merge to form the **superior vena cava** (SVC). Close to the point of fusion, the **internal thoracic vein** empties into the left brachiocephalic vein. Figure 22.24a summarizes the venous tributaries of the superior vena cava.

The **azygos** (AZ-i-gos) **vein** is the major tributary of the superior vena cava. This vessel ascends from the lumbar region over the right side of the vertebral column to invade the thoracic cavity through the diaphragm. The azygos joins the superior vena cava at the level of vertebra

T_2. The azygos receives blood from the smaller **hemiazygos vein**. The hemiazygos vein may also drain into the **highest intercostal vein**, a tributary of the left brachiocephalic vein, by way of a small **accessory hemiazygos vein**. The azygos and hemiazygos veins are the chief collecting vessels of the thorax. They receive blood from (1) numerous **intercostal veins**, which receive blood from the chest muscles; (2) **esophageal veins**, which drain blood from the esophagus; and (3) smaller veins draining other mediastinal structures.

The Inferior Vena Cava The **inferior vena cava (IVC)** collects most of the venous blood from organs inferior to the diaphragm (a small amount reaches the superior vena cava via the azygos and hemiazygos veins). Figure 22.24b,c summarizes the venous tributaries of the inferior vena cava.

Veins Draining the Lower Limb [Figures 22.24c/22.25] Blood leaving capillaries in the sole of each foot collects into a network of **plantar veins**. The **plantar venous arch** provides blood to the deep veins of the leg: the

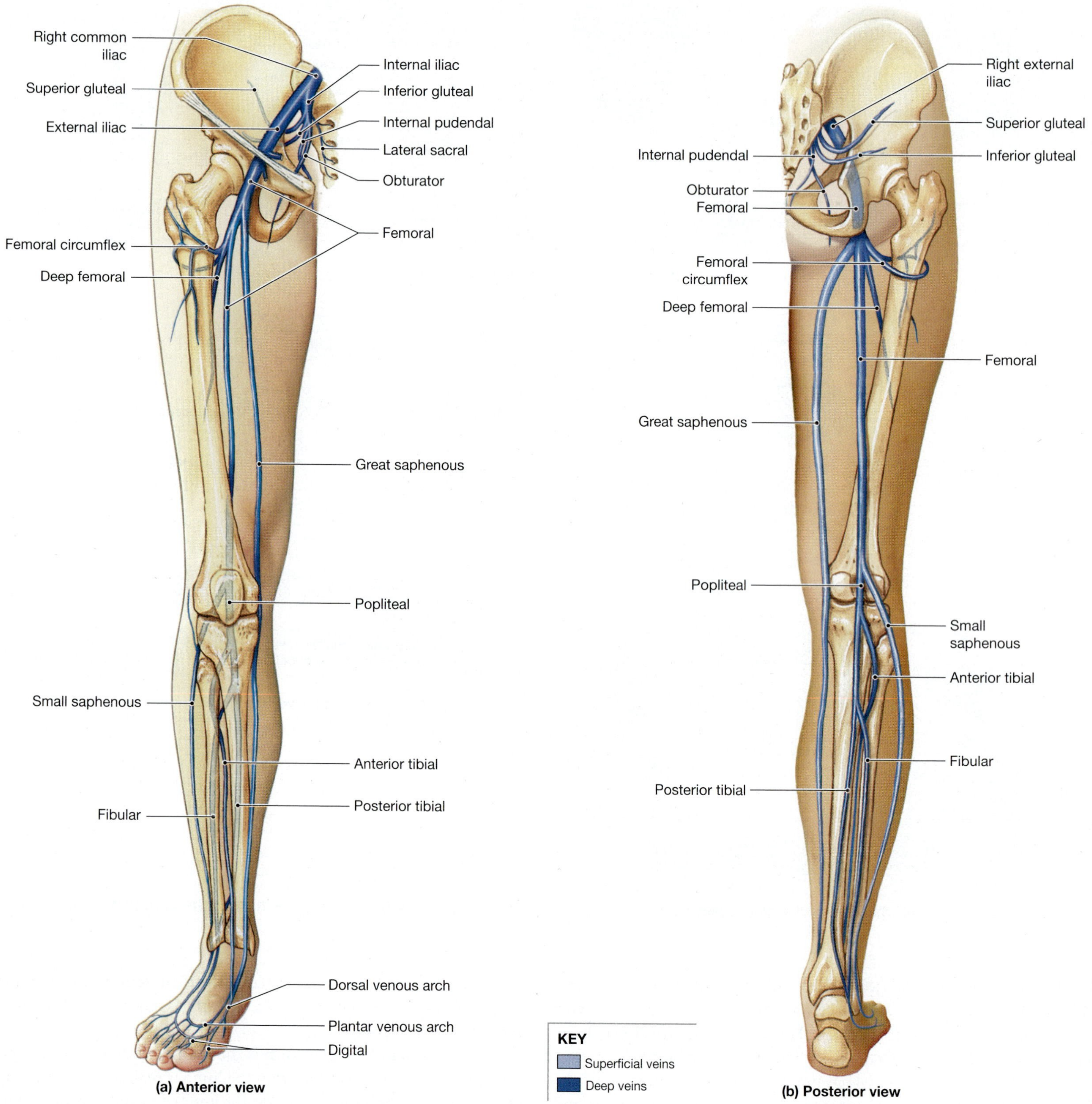

Figure 22.25 The Venous Drainage of the Lower Limb
(a) Anterior view, showing the veins of the right lower limb. **(b)** Posterior view, showing the veins of the right lower limb.

anterior tibial vein, the **posterior tibial vein**, and the **fibular vein**, or *peroneal vein* (Figures 22.24c and 22.25a). The **dorsal venous arch** collects blood from capillaries on the dorsal surface of the foot and the *digital veins* of the toes. There are extensive interconnections between the plantar arch and the dorsal arch, and the path of blood flow can easily shift from superficial to deep veins.

The dorsal venous arch is drained by two superficial veins, the **great saphenous** (sa-FĒ-nus; *saphenes*, prominent) **vein** and the **small saphenous vein**. The great saphenous vein is used in coronary bypass operations to replace blocked coronary vessels. It is the longest vein in the body; it ascends along the medial aspect of the leg and thigh, draining into the *femoral vein* near the hip joint. The small saphenous vein arises from the dorsal venous arch and ascends along the posterior and lateral aspect of the calf. It then enters the popliteal fossa, where it meets the **popliteal vein** formed by the union of the tibial and fibular veins. The popliteal vein may be easily palpated in the popliteal fossa adjacent to the adductor magnus muscle (Figure 22.25b). Once it reaches the femur, the popliteal vein becomes the **femoral vein**, which ascends along the thigh next to the femoral artery. Immediately before penetrating the abdominal wall, the femoral vein receives blood from (1) the great saphenous vein; (2) the **deep femoral vein**, which collects blood from deeper structures of the thigh; and (3) the **femoral circumflex vein**, which drains the area around the neck and head of the femur. The large vein that results penetrates the body wall and emerges in the pelvic cavity as the **external iliac vein**.

Veins Draining the Pelvis [Figures 22.23/22.25] The external iliac veins receive blood from the lower limbs, pelvis, and lower abdomen. As each external iliac vein travels across the inner surface of the ilium, it merges with the **internal iliac vein**, which drains the pelvic organs on that side. The internal iliac veins are formed by the fusion of the **gluteal**, **internal pudendal**, **obturator**, and **lateral sacral veins** (Figure 22.25). The union of the external and internal iliac veins forms the **common iliac vein**. The **medial sacral vein**, which drains the region supplied by the medial sacral artery, usually empties into the left common iliac (Figure 22.23). The left and right common iliac veins ascend at an oblique angle. Anterior to vertebra L_5, they unite to form the inferior vena cava.

Veins Draining the Abdomen [Figures 22.23/22.24] The abdominal wall, the gonads, the liver, the kidneys, the suprarenal glands, and the diaphragm are drained by the inferior vena cava. The visceral organs within the abdominal cavity are drained by the hepatic portal vein, which is discussed separately. The inferior vena cava ascends posterior to the peritoneal cavity, parallel to the aorta. Blood from the inferior vena cava flows into the right atrium, where it mixes with venous blood from the superior vena cava. This blood then enters the right ventricle and is pumped into the pulmonary circuit for oxygenation at the lungs. The abdominal portion of the inferior vena cava collects blood from six major veins (Figures 22.23 and 22.24).

1. **Lumbar veins** drain the lumbar portion of the abdomen. Superior branches of these veins are connected to the azygos vein (right side) and hemiazygos vein (left side), which empty into the superior vena cava.
2. **Gonadal** (*ovarian* or *testicular*) **veins** drain the ovaries or testes. The right gonadal vein empties into the inferior vena cava; the left gonadal usually drains into the left renal vein.
3. **Hepatic veins** leave the liver and empty into the inferior vena cava at the level of vertebra T_{10}.
4. **Renal veins** collect blood from the kidneys. These are the largest tributaries of the inferior vena cava.
5. **Suprarenal veins** drain the suprarenal glands. Usually only the right suprarenal vein drains into the inferior vena cava, and the left drains into the left renal vein.
6. **Phrenic veins** drain the diaphragm. Only the right phrenic vein drains into the inferior vena cava; the left drains into the left renal vein.

The Hepatic Portal System [Figure 22.26] The liver is the only digestive organ drained by the inferior vena cava. Instead of traveling directly to the inferior vena cava, blood leaving the capillary beds supplied by the celiac, superior mesenteric, and inferior mesenteric arteries flows into the veins of the **hepatic portal system**. You may recall from Chapter 19 a blood vessel connecting two capillary beds is called a *portal vessel*, and the network is a *portal system*. p. 512 In the hepatic portal system, venous blood that absorbs nutrients from the small intestine, parts of the large intestine, stomach, and pancreas flows directly to the liver for processing and storage.

Blood flowing in the hepatic portal system is therefore quite different from that in other systemic veins. For example, levels of blood glucose and amino acids in the hepatic portal vein often exceed those found anywhere else in the circulatory system. Additionally, at the same time that this oxygen-poor and nutrient-rich blood arrives at the liver from the digestive organs, the liver also receives oxygen-rich and nutrient-poor blood from the systemic circuit through the hepatic artery proper. This means that the liver receives mixed blood with respect to nutrients and oxygen.

The liver regulates the concentrations of nutrients, such as glucose or amino acids, in the circulating blood. During digestion, the stomach and intestines absorb high concentrations of nutrients, along with various wastes and even toxins. The hepatic portal system delivers these compounds directly to the liver for storage, metabolic conversion, or excretion by liver cells. After passing through the liver sinusoids, blood collects into the hepatic veins, which empty into the inferior vena cava (Figure 22.26). Because blood goes to the liver first, the composition of the blood in the general systemic circuit remains relatively stable, regardless of the digestive activities under way.

The hepatic portal system begins in the capillaries of the digestive organs and ends as the hepatic portal vein discharges blood into sinusoids in the liver. The tributaries of the hepatic portal vein include the following:

- The **inferior mesenteric vein** collects blood from capillaries along the inferior portion of the large intestine. Its tributaries include the **left colic vein** and the **superior rectal veins**, which drain the descending colon, sigmoid colon, and rectum.
- The **splenic vein** is formed by the union of the inferior mesenteric vein and veins from the spleen, the lateral border of the stomach *(left gastroepiploic vein)*, and the pancreas *(pancreatic veins)*.
- The **superior mesenteric vein** collects blood from veins draining the stomach *(right gastroepiploic vein)*, the small intestine *(intestinal* and *pancreaticoduodenal veins)*, and two-thirds of the large intestine *(ileocolic, right colic,* and *middle colic veins)*.

The hepatic portal vein forms through the fusion of the superior mesenteric and splenic veins. Of the two, the superior mesenteric vein normally contributes the greater volume of blood and most of the nutrients. As it proceeds toward the liver, the hepatic portal vein receives blood from the **gastric veins**, which drain the medial border of the stomach, and from the **cystic veins** from the gallbladder.

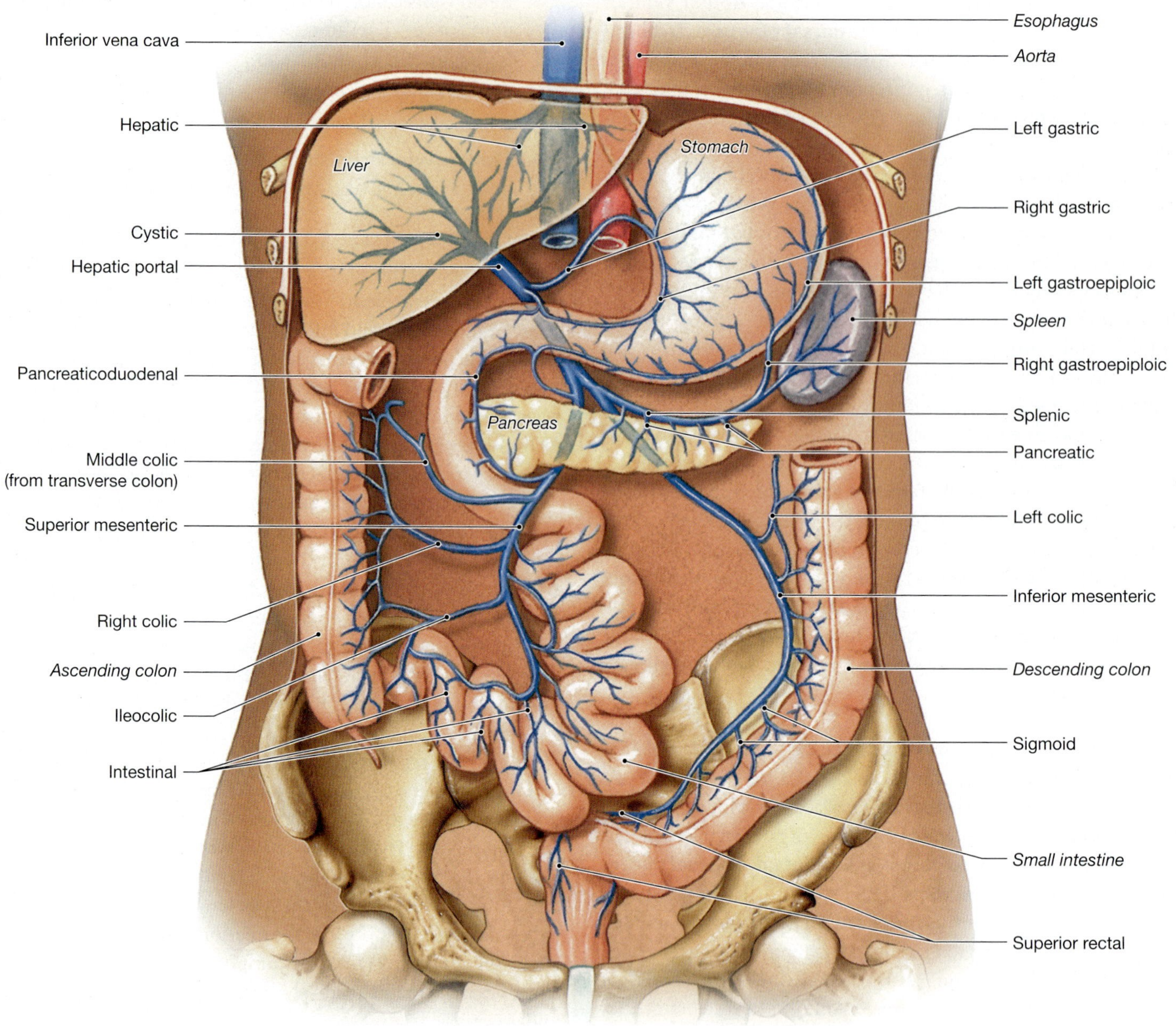

Figure 22.26 The Hepatic Portal System

CONCEPT CHECK

1. Diane is in an automobile accident and ruptures her celiac artery. What organs would be affected most directly by this injury?
2. It is 110°F outside, and you are very hot. What changes have occurred in your veins and why?
3. Which major vein receives the blood from the head, neck, chest, shoulders, and upper limbs?
4. Why does blood leaving the intestines first go to the liver?

See blue "Answers" tab at back of book.

Cardiovascular Changes at Birth [Figure 22.27]

There are significant differences between the fetal and adult cardiovascular systems that reflect differing sources of respiratory and nutritional support. The embryonic lungs are collapsed and nonfunctional, and the digestive tract has nothing to digest. All of the fetal nutritional and respiratory needs are provided by diffusion across the *placenta*, a complex organ that regulates exchange between the fetal and maternal bloodstreams. (We will discuss the structure of the placenta in Chapter 28.) Two **umbilical arteries** leave the internal iliac arteries of the fetus, enter the umbilical cord, and deliver blood to the placenta. Blood returns to the fetus from the placenta in the single **umbilical vein**, bringing oxygen and nutrients to the developing fetus. The umbilical vein drains into the **ductus venosus**, which is connected to an intricate network of veins within the developing liver. The ductus venosus collects the blood from the veins of the liver and from the umbilical vein and delivers it to the inferior vena cava (Figure 22.27a,c). When the placental connection is broken at birth, blood flow ceases along the umbilical vessels, and they soon degenerate.

Although the interatrial and interventricular septa develop early in fetal life, the interatrial partition remains functionally incomplete up to the time of birth. The interatrial opening, or *foramen ovale*, is associated with an elongated flap that acts as a valve. Blood can flow freely from the right atrium to the left atrium, but any backflow closes the valve and isolates the two chambers. Thus, blood can enter the heart at the right atrium and bypass the pulmonary circuit altogether. A second short circuit exists between the pulmonary and aortic trunks. This connection, the **ductus arteriosus**, consists of a short, muscular vessel.

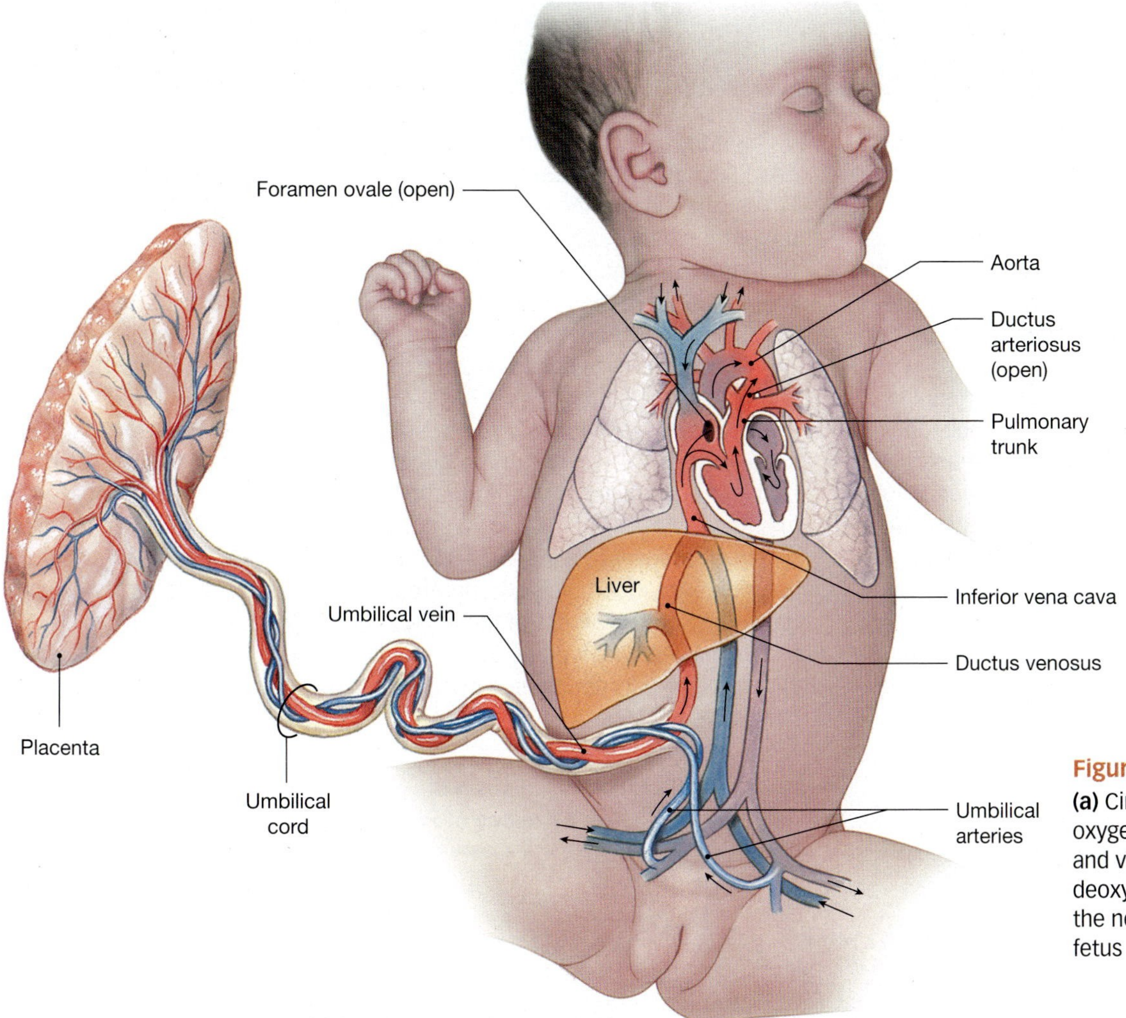

(a) Full-term fetus (before birth)

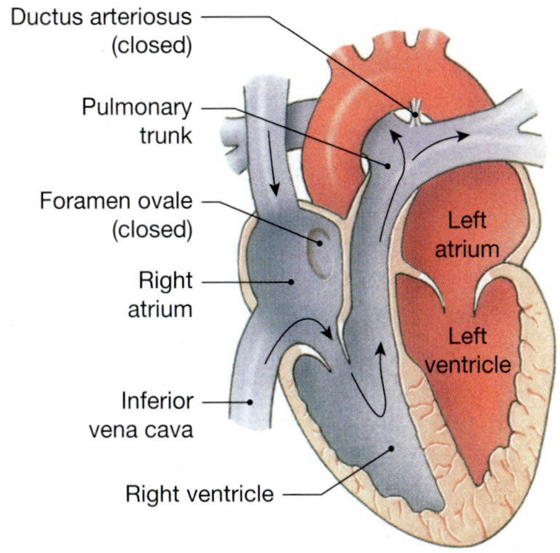

(b) After delivery

Figure 22.27 Changes in Fetal Circulation at Birth **(a)** Circulation pathways in a full-term fetus. Red indicates oxygenated blood, blue indicates deoxygenated blood, and violet indicates a mixture of oxygenated and deoxygenated blood. **(b)** Blood flow through the heart of the newborn. **(c)** Flowchart for circulatory patterns in the fetus and newborn infant.

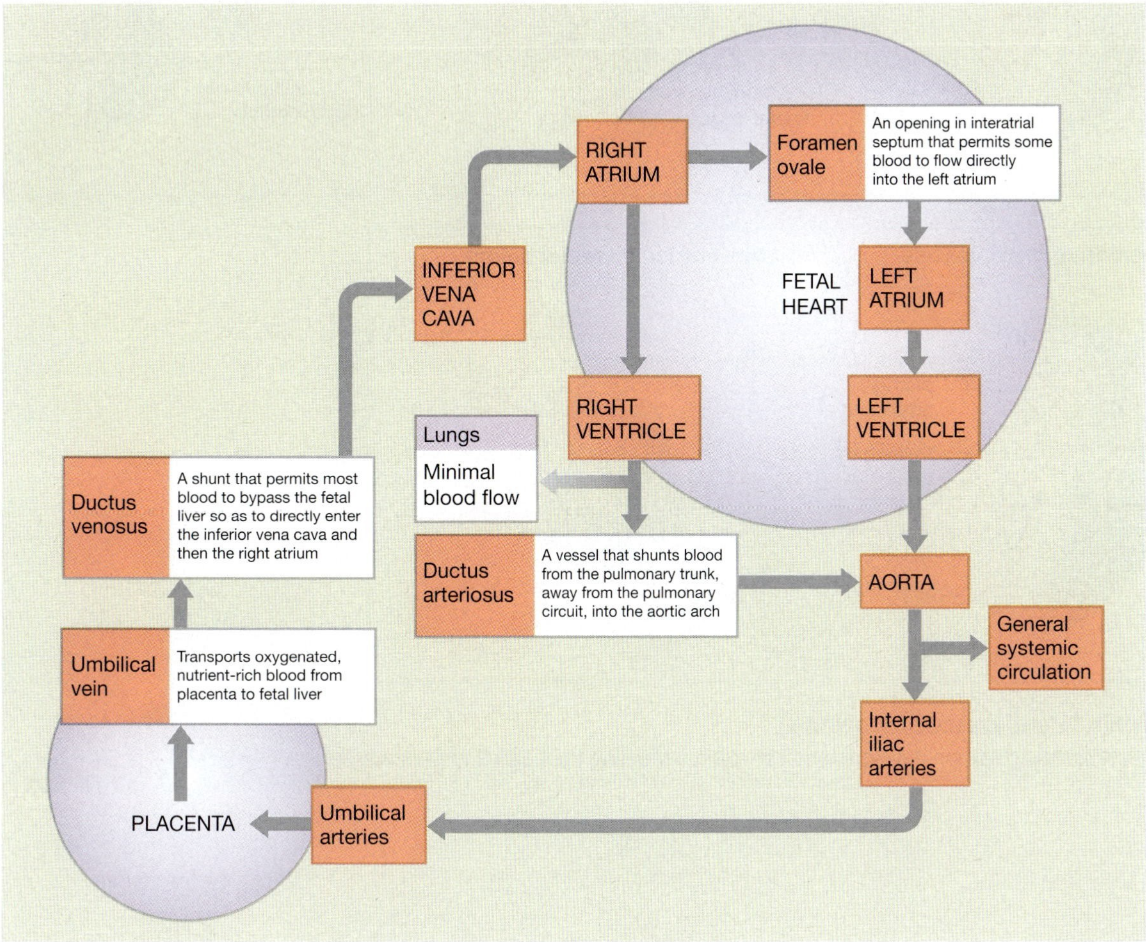

(c) Fetal circulatory pattern

Clinical Note

Congenital Cardiovascular Problems Congenital cardiovascular problems serious enough to represent a threat to homeostasis are relatively rare. They usually reflect abnormal formation of the heart or problems with the interconnections between the heart and the great vessels. Several examples of congenital cardiovascular defects are illustrated in Figure 22.28. Most of these conditions can be surgically corrected, although multiple surgeries may be required and life expectancy may be shortened in more severe defects.

The incomplete closure of the foramen ovale or ductus arteriosus (Figure 22.28a) results in the recirculation of blood into the pulmonary circuit. Pressures rise in the pulmonary circuit, leading to pulmonary edema and cardiac enlargement that can ultimately lead to heart failure.

Ventricular septal defects (Figure 22.28b) are the most common congenital heart problems, affecting 0.12 percent of newborn infants. The opening between the left and right ventricles has a similar effect to a connection between the atria: When it beats, the more powerful left ventricle ejects blood into the right ventricle and pulmonary circuit. Pulmonary hypertension, pulmonary edema, and cardiac enlargement may result.

The *tetralogy of Fallot* (fa-LŌ) (Figure 22.28c) is a complex group of heart and circulatory defects that affect 0.10 percent of newborn infants. In this condition (1) the pulmonary trunk is abnormally narrow, (2) the interventricular septum is incomplete, (3) the aorta originates where the interventricular septum normally ends, and (4) the right ventricle is enlarged. Because normal blood oxygenation does not occur, the circulating blood has a deep red color. The skin then develops the blue tones typical of cyanosis, a condition noted in Chapter 4, and the infant is known as a "blue baby."

In the *transposition of great vessels* (Figure 22.28d) the aorta is connected to the right ventricle, and the pulmonary artery is connected to the left ventricle. This malformation affects 0.05 percent of newborn infants.

In an *atrioventricular septal defect* (Figure 22.28e) the atria and ventricles are incompletely separated. The results are quite variable, depending on the extent of the defect and the effects on the atrioventricular valves. This type of defect most often affects infants with *Down syndrome*, a disorder caused by the presence of an extra copy of chromosome 21.

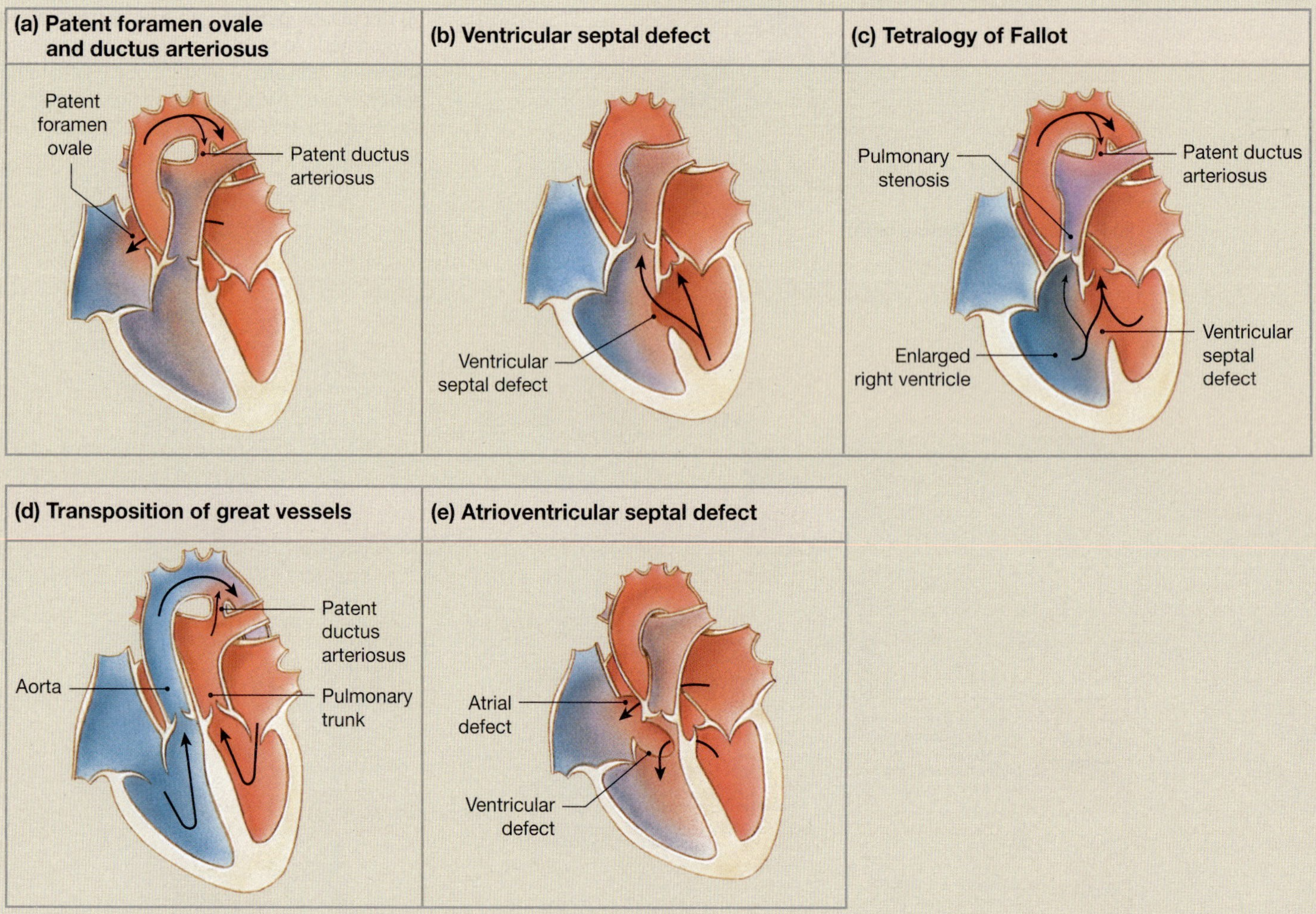

Figure 22.28 Congenital Cardiovascular Problems
Diagrams showing some relatively common developmental problems affecting the heart and great vessels.

With the lungs collapsed, the capillaries are compressed and little blood flows through the lungs. During diastole, blood enters the right atrium and flows into the right ventricle, but some also passes into the left atrium via the foramen ovale. About 25 percent of the blood arriving at the right atrium bypasses the pulmonary circuit in this way. In addition, more than 90 percent of the blood leaving the right ventricle passes through the ductus arteriosus and enters the systemic circuit, rather than continuing to the lungs.

At birth, dramatic changes occur. When the infant takes its first breath, the lungs expand, and so do the pulmonary vessels. The smooth muscles in the ductus arteriosus contract, isolating the pulmonary and aortic trunks, and blood begins flowing through the pulmonary circuit. As pressures rise in the left atrium, the valvular flap closes the foramen ovale and completes the cardiovascular remodeling. These alterations are diagrammed and summarized in Figure 22.27a,b. In the adult, the interatrial septum bears a shallow depression, the *fossa ovalis*, that marks the site of the original foramen ovale. The remnants of the ductus arteriosus persist as a fibrous cord, the **ligamentum arteriosum**. p. 556

If the proper circulatory changes do not occur at birth or shortly thereafter, problems will eventually develop. The severity of the problem varies, depending on which connection remains open and the size of the opening. Treatment may involve surgical closure of the foramen ovale or the ductus arteriosus or both. Other forms of congenital heart defects result from abnormal cardiac development or inappropriate connections between the heart and major arteries and veins.

Aging and the Cardiovascular System

The capabilities of the cardiovascular system gradually decline with age. The major changes are listed and summarized here, in the same sequence as the cardiovascular chapters: blood, heart, and vessels.

1. *Age-related changes in the blood* may include (1) decreased hematocrit; (2) constriction or blockage of peripheral veins by a **thrombus** (stationary blood clot); the thrombus can become detached, pass through the heart, and become wedged in a small artery, most often in the lungs, causing a **pulmonary embolism**; and (3) pooling of blood in the veins of the legs because valves are not working effectively.
2. *Age-related anatomical changes in the heart* include (1) a reduction in the maximum cardiac output, (2) a reduction in the elasticity of the fibrous skeleton, (3) progressive atherosclerosis that can restrict coronary circulation, and (4) replacement of damaged cardiac muscle fibers by scar tissue.
3. *Age-related changes in blood vessels* are often related to arteriosclerosis and include the following: (1) inelastic walls of arteries become less tolerant of sudden increases in pressure, which may lead to an **aneurysm** (AN-ū-rizm), causing a stroke, infarct, or massive blood loss, depending on the vessel involved; (2) calcium salts can deposit on weakened vascular walls, increasing the risk of a stroke or infarct; and (3) thrombi can form at atherosclerotic plaques.

CONCEPT CHECK

1. What major changes occur in the heart and major vessels of a newborn at birth?
2. What causes varicose veins?
3. Why is a reduction in elasticity of the arteries with age dangerous?

See blue "Answers" tab at back of book.

Embryology Summary

For a summary of the development of the cardiovascular system, see Chapter 28 (Embryology and Human Development).

Clinical Case — THE CARDIOVASCULAR SYSTEM

THE COMPLAINING POSTAL CARRIER

Tony is a 59-year-old rural postal worker who goes to see his family physician for an examination. Tony complains that he has been experiencing brief and unpredictable dizzy spells for the past 2–3 years. In addition to these symptoms, Tony has recently noticed occasional pain and numbness in his left arm. Exercise increases both the intensity of the pain and the duration of the numbness. Tony tells the physician that he made the appointment at the urging of his wife.

Initial Examination

The physician notes the following during his examination and discussion with Tony:

1. In addition to dizziness, symptoms include nausea, occasional fainting spells, and blurred vision.
2. The duration of these spells varies, ranging from a few seconds to several minutes.
3. The patient is robust and exercises regularly, playing tennis once or twice a week and running 20–25 miles per week at an 8-minute mile pace.
4. The patient reports that he carries his postal bag on his left shoulder 99 percent of the time.
5. Blood pressure is 180/95.
6. Pulse is 55/minute and strong.
7. The patient's family has a history of atherosclerosis.

The physician suspects that the pain and numbness in Tony's arm could be caused by the long-term effects of carrying the heavy postal bag on the same shoulder. He instructs Tony to carry the mailbag only on his right shoulder for 7 to 10 days. At the end of this time period Tony is to carry the bag by alternating shoulders, switching every 10–15 minutes, for an additional 7 to 10 days. Noting the elevated blood pressure, the physician prescribes a medication for hypertension. Tony is scheduled for a follow-up examination.

Clinical Case *continued*

Follow-up Examination

At the follow-up examination, Tony states that he has been carrying his postal bag as instructed. However, the symptoms have persisted and in some instances intensified. The physician now has time for a more extensive examination and finds that:

- the duration of the spells is increasing, with the average spell now lasting 4–6 minutes;
- the frequency of the spells has also increased, to every other day;
- the occasional pain and numbness in the left arm have increased in intensity and duration;
- exercise seems to intensify the symptoms, e.g. within the past week, the pain and numbness were such that Tony was not able to play tennis or run;
- blood pressure, as measured in the right arm, is 180/95;
- blood pressure, as measured in the left arm, is 93/70;
- pulse, as measured at the right wrist, is 55/minute and strong;
- pulse, as measured at the left wrist, is 55/minute but diminished in strength;
- bilateral carotid pulses are strong and symmetrical;
- there is diminished pulsation in the left supraclavicular fossa, accompanied by a systolic bruit;
- when asked to hold a light weight in his left hand and repeatedly lift it over his head, Tony complains of numbness and tingling in the arm, accompanied by lightheadedness and dizziness; and
- no such symptoms accompany the identical exercise when the weight is held in his right hand.

Points to Consider

A physician must piece together the various clues that lead to a correct diagnosis. Both the patient's symptoms, any physical signs, and the physician's interpretation are part of the detective work.

To consider the meaning of the information presented in the case above, you need to review the anatomical material covered in Chapters 20 through 23. The questions below will guide you in your review. Try to answer each one, referring back to the appropriate chapters if you need help.

1. Tony is experiencing dizziness, nausea, occasional fainting spells, and blurred vision. Which system of the body is likely implicated by these symptoms?
2. What is the vascular supply to the system that would be responsible for Tony's dizziness, nausea, occasional fainting spells, and blurred vision?
3. The physician noted a diminished strength in Tony's pulse at the left wrist. Is there a difference in the distribution of blood vessels serving the right and left wrists? If so, what is the anatomical difference? How does the finding of a diminished pulsation in the left supraclavicular fossa relate to this anatomical difference?
4. Tony's bilateral carotid pulses are strong and symmetrical. What is the significance of this finding?

Analysis and Interpretation

The information below answers the questions raised in the "Points to Consider" section. To review the material, refer to the pages and figures referenced in this discussion.

Analysis and Interpretation

The information below answers the questions raised in the "Points to Consider" section. To review the material, refer to the pages and figures referenced in this discussion.

1. Tony's dizziness, nausea, fainting spells, and blurred vision all point to some problem with the central nervous system, particularly those portions of the CNS involved with the inner ear and eye. pp. 487, 500
2. The brain is supplied with blood by branches of the right and left internal carotid arteries and branches of the right and left vertebral arteries. The vertebral arteries are branches of the subclavian artery (Figure 22.13,

CLINICAL CASE TERMS

atherosclerosis: A disease characterized by irregularly distributed lipid deposits in the intima of large and medium-sized arteries. These deposits cause a narrowing of the lumen.

bilateral carotid pulse: The pulse within both of the carotid arteries of the neck.

blood pressure: The pressure of the blood within the systemic arteries.

diminished pulsation: A reduction of the pulse within a blood vessel.

supraclavicular fossa: A depressed area above the middle of the clavicle, lateral to the sternocleidomastoid muscle.

systolic bruit: Any abnormal sound or murmur heard during systole of the cardiac cycle.

Clinical Case *continued*

p. 585). A reduction in blood flow through any of these major vessels could result in a temporary loss of consciousness (fainting).

3. Blood is supplied to the left upper limb by the left subclavian artery. This vessel branches directly off the arch of the aorta. Refer to Figure 22.12, pp. 583–584. The right upper limb is supplied with blood by the right subclavian artery. The right subclavian artery is a branch of the brachiocephalic trunk. The left subclavian artery can be palpated in the left supraclavicular fossa. A diminished pulsation in this region indicates diminished flow in the left subclavian artery.
4. The presence of strong bilateral carotid pulses indicates that the vascular problem is found in a segment of the arterial tree not involving the common carotid arteries (Figure 22.12, p. 583).

Diagnosis

Tony has a condition termed "Subclavian Steal Syndrome" involving the left subclavian artery. In this syndrome, the lumenal diameter of the left subclavian artery is reduced (Figure 22.29). This reduction in diameter reduces blood flow to the left upper limb and may also reduce blood flow to the left side of the brain. Tony complained of numbness and tingling in the arm, accompanied by lightheadedness and dizziness following exercise involving only the right upper limb. When the muscles of the left upper limb are working at peak levels, their metabolic demands increase and tissue oxygen and nutrient levels decline. This triggers peripheral vasodilation that would, under normal conditions, dramatically increase blood flow through the left subclavian artery. However, in Tony's case blood flow can only increase slightly, due to a narrowing of the left subclavian artery. That increase is inadequate for the demands of the exercising muscles and the sensory nerves in the limb, and this accounts for the numbness and tingling sensations. Meanwhile, as more of the blood that *does* enter the left subclavian artery flows into the limb, less flows into the left vertebral artery, a proximal branch of the left subclavian artery. It is this reduction in blood flow to the brain that produces the dizziness and vertigo. The flow in the vertebral artery decreases markedly due to the following anatomical relationships:

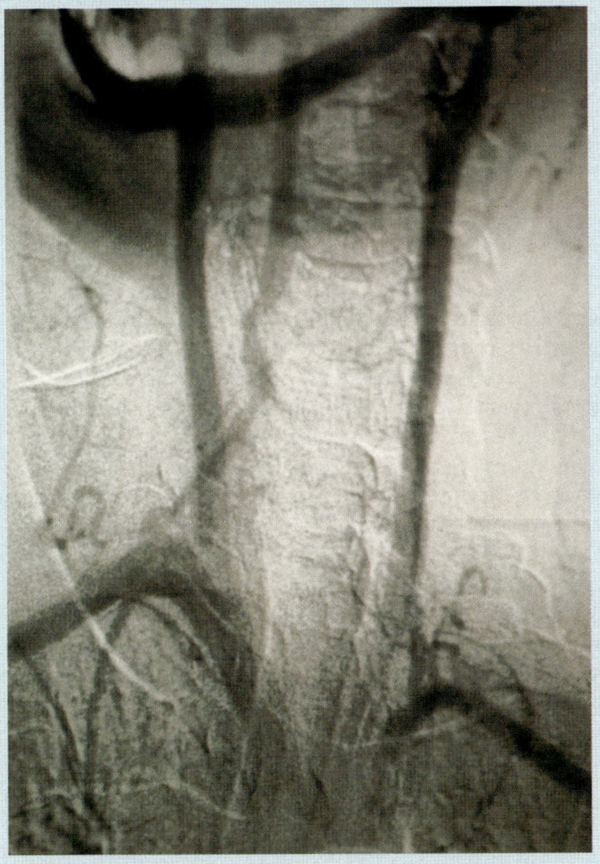

Figure 22.29 Radiograph of Tony's left subclavian artery showing decreased diameter.

1. The site of Tony's subclavian stenosis is at the root of the vessel, proximal to the origin of the vertebral artery (Figure 22.29).
2. The increased cardiovascular demands in the left upper limb during exercise causes vasodilation of the left subclavian artery and its distal branches. Due to the stenosis this exercise-induced vasodilation decreases the blood pressure within the subclavian artery and its branches, and this causes a reduction or even a reversal of blood flow within the vertebral artery.

CLINICAL TERMS

aneurysm (AN-ū-rizm): A bulge in the weakened wall of a blood vessel, usually an artery.

arteriosclerosis (ar-tēr-ē-ō-skler-Ō-sis): A thickening and toughening of arterial walls.

atherosclerosis (ath-er-ō-skler-Ō-sis): A type of arteriosclerosis characterized by changes in the endothelial lining and the formation of plaques.

hemorrhoids (HEM-ō-roidz): Varicose veins in the walls of the rectum and/or anus, often associated with pregnancy or frequent straining to force bowel movements.

pulmonary embolism: Circulatory blockage caused by the trapping of a freed thrombus in a pulmonary artery.

thrombus: A stationary blood clot within a blood vessel.

varicose (VAR-i-kōs) **veins:** Sagging, swollen veins distorted by gravity and the failure of the venous valves.

STUDY OUTLINE

Introduction 572

1. The cardiovascular system is a closed system with two circulatory patterns: a *pulmonary circuit* and a *systemic circuit.*
2. Blood flows through a network of arteries, veins, and capillaries. All chemical and gaseous exchange between the blood and interstitial fluid takes place across capillary walls.

Histological Organization of Blood Vessels 572

1. The walls of arteries and veins contain three layers: the **intima** (the innermost layer), the **media** (the middle layer), and the **adventitia** (the connective tissue sheath around the vessel). *(see Figure 22.1)*

Distinguishing Arteries from Veins 573

2. In general, the walls of arteries are thicker than those of veins. The endothelial lining of an artery cannot contract, so it is thrown into folds. Arteries constrict when blood pressure does not distend them; veins constrict very little. *(see Figure 22.1)*

Arteries 573

3. The arterial system includes the large **elastic arteries**, **muscular** or **medium-sized arteries**, and smaller **arterioles**. Elastic arteries, or *conducting arteries*, transport large volumes of blood away from the heart. They are able to stretch and recoil with pressure changes. Muscular arteries *(distribution arteries)* distribute blood to skeletal muscles and organs. Arterioles can change their diameter (*vasoconstriction or vasodilation*) in response to conditions in the body. As we proceed toward the capillaries, the number of vessels increases, but the diameters of the individual vessels decrease and the walls become thinner. *(see Figures 22.1* and *22.2)*

Capillaries 575

4. Capillaries are the smallest blood vessels and the only blood vessels whose walls permit exchange between blood and interstitial fluid. Capillaries may be **continuous** (the endothelium is a complete lining) or **fenestrated** (the endothelium contains "windows"). **Sinusoids** are specialized fenestrated capillaries found in selected tissues (such as the liver) that allow very slow blood flow. *(see Figure 22.4)*
5. Capillaries form interconnected networks called **capillary beds (capillary plexuses)**. A **precapillary sphincter** (a band of smooth muscle) adjusts the blood flow into each capillary. **Central**, or **preferred**, **channels** provide the means of arteriole-venule communication. A **metarteriole** is the arteriolar segment of the channel. The entire capillary plexus may be bypassed by blood flow through **arteriovenous anastomoses** or via central channels within the capillary plexus. *(see Figure 22.5)*

Veins 577

6. **Veins** collect deoxygenated blood from the tissues and organs and return it to the heart. **Venules** collect blood from the capillaries and merge into **medium-sized veins** and then **large veins**. The arterial system is a high-pressure system; blood pressure in veins is much lower. **Valves** in veins prevent the backflow of blood. *(see Figures 22.1/22.2/22.6)*

The Distribution of Blood 578

7. While the heart, arteries, and capillaries usually contain about 30–35 percent of the blood volume, most of the blood volume is in the venous system (65–70 percent). Peripheral **venoconstriction** helps maintain adequate blood volume in the arterial system after a hemorrhage. The **venous reserve**, which is the extra blood in the venous system that can be distributed within the arterial system, normally accounts for up to 21 percent of the total blood volume. *(see Figure 22.7)*

Blood Vessel Distribution 579

1. The blood vessels of the body can be divided into those of the **pulmonary circuit** (between the heart and lungs) and the **systemic circuit** (from the heart to all organs and tissues). *(see Figure 22.8)*

The Pulmonary Circuit 579

2. The arteries of the pulmonary circuit carry deoxygenated blood. The pulmonary circuit includes the **pulmonary trunk**, the **left** and **right pulmonary arteries**, and the **pulmonary veins**, which empty into the left atrium. *(see Figure 22.9)*

The Systemic Circuit 579

3. The **ascending aorta** gives rise to the coronary circulation. The **aortic arch** continues as the **descending aorta**. Three large arteries arise from the aortic arch to collectively supply the head, neck, shoulder, and upper limbs: the **brachiocephalic trunk**, the **left common carotid artery**, and the **left subclavian artery**. The detailed distribution of these blood vessels and their branches will be found in *Figures 22.10 to 22.20.*
4. The brachiocephalic trunk gives rise to the **right subclavian artery** and the **right common carotid artery**. These arteries supply the right upper limb and portions of the right shoulder, neck, and head. *(see Figures 22.12 to 22.14)*
5. Each subclavian artery exits the thoracic cavity to become the **axillary artery**, which enters the arm to become the **brachial artery**. The brachial arteries and their branches supply blood to the upper limbs. *(see Figure 22.12)*
6. Each common carotid artery divides into an **external carotid artery** and **internal carotid artery**. The external carotids and their branches supply blood to structures in the neck and face. The internal carotids and their branches enter the skull to supply blood to the brain and eyes. The brain also receives blood from the **vertebral arteries**. The vertebral arteries and the internal carotids form the **cerebral arterial circle** (or *circle of Willis*), which ensures the blood supply to the brain. *(see Figures 22.13 to 22.15)*
7. The descending aorta superior to the diaphragm is termed the **thoracic aorta** and inferior to it the **abdominal aorta**. The thoracic aorta and its branches supply blood to the thorax and thoracic viscera. The abdominal aorta and its branches supply blood to the abdominal wall, abdominal viscera, pelvic structures, and lower limbs. The three unpaired arteries are the **celiac trunk**, the **superior mesenteric artery**, and the **inferior mesenteric artery**. The celiac trunk divides into the **left gastric artery**, the **common hepatic artery**, and the **splenic artery**. Paired arteries include the **suprarenal arteries**, the **renal arteries**, the **lumbar arteries**, and the **gonadal arteries**. The detailed distribution of these blood vessels and their branches will be found in *Figures 22.10 to 22.18/22.20.*
8. Arteries in the neck and limbs are deep beneath the skin; in contrast, there are usually two sets of peripheral veins—one superficial and one deep. This dual venous drainage is important for controlling body temperature *(see Figures 22.10/22.21)*. Arteries of the pelvis and lower limbs include the **right** and **left common iliac arteries**, which branch to form the **external** and **internal iliac arteries**. The **femoral** and **deep femoral arteries** supply the lower limb (*see Figure 22.18*). The arteries of the foot can be seen in *Figures 22.18 and 22.20.*
9. The **superior vena cava (SVC)** receives blood from the head, neck, chest, shoulders, and upper limbs. The detailed distribution of these collecting vessels and their branches may be seen in *Figures 22.21 to 22.24.* The **inferior vena cava (IVC)** collects most of the venous blood from organs and structures inferior to the diaphragm that are not drained by the hepatic portal vein. The detailed distribution of these collecting vessels and their branches may be seen in *Figures 22.23 to 22.26.*
10. Any blood vessel connecting two capillary beds is called a *portal vessel*, and the network of blood vessels comprises a *portal system.*
11. Blood leaving the capillaries supplied by the celiac, superior, and inferior mesenteric arteries flows into the **hepatic portal system**. Blood in the hepatic portal system is unique compared to that of the other systemic veins, because portal blood contains high concentrations of nutrients. These substances are collected from the digestive organs through the vessels of the portal system and are transported directly to the liver for processing. *(see Figure 22.26b)*
12. The vessels that form the hepatic portal system are shown in *Figure 22.26.*

Cardiovascular Changes at Birth 600

1. During fetal development, the **umbilical arteries** carry blood to the placenta. It returns via the **umbilical vein** and enters a network of vascular sinuses in the liver. The **ductus venosus** collects this blood and returns it to the inferior vena cava *(see Figure 22.27 and Development of the Cardiovascular System in Chapter 28).*
2. At this time, the interatrial septum is incomplete and the **foramen ovale** allows the passage of blood from the right atrium to the left atrium. The **ductus arteriosus** also permits the flow of blood between the pulmonary trunk and the aortic arch. At birth or shortly thereafter, as the pulmonary circuit becomes functional, these connections normally close, forming a depression called the **fossa ovalis**, where the foramen ovale was, and the **ligamentum arteriosum**, where the ductus arteriosus used to be. *(see Figure 22.27 and Development of the Cardiovascular System in Chapter 28)*

Aging and the Cardiovascular System 603

1. Age-related changes in the blood can include: (1) decreased hematocrit, (2) constriction or blockage of peripheral veins by a **thrombus** (stationary blood clot), and (3) pooling of blood in the veins of the lower legs because valves are not working effectively.
2. Age-related anatomical changes in the heart include (1) a reduction in the maximum cardiac output, (2) a reduction in the elasticity of the fibrous skeleton, (3) progressive atherosclerosis that can restrict coronary circulation, and (4) replacement of damaged cardiac muscle fibers by scar tissue.
3. Age-related changes in blood vessels are often related to arteriosclerosis and include (1) inelastic walls of arteries being less tolerant of sudden increases in pressure, which may lead to an **aneurysm**; (2) calcium salts, which can deposit on weakened vascular walls, increasing the risk of a stroke or infarct; and (3) thrombi that form at atherosclerotic plaques.

CHAPTER REVIEW

For answers to the Concept Check and Chapter Review questions, see blue "Answers" tab at the back of the book.

Level 1 Reviewing Facts and Terms

Match each numbered item with the most closely related lettered item. Use letters for answers in the spaces provided.

Column A	Column B
___ 1. elastic arteries	a. deliver blood to the head
___ 2. thrombus	b. distribution arteries
___ 3. collaterals	c. conducting arteries
___ 4. renal veins	d. stationary blood clot
___ 5. iliac arteries	e. network of capillaries
___ 6. alveoli	f. arteries that supply a capillary network
___ 7. carotid arteries	g. supply blood to the upper limbs
___ 8. subclavian arteries	h. small air sacs
___ 9. capillary plexus	i. supply blood to the lower limbs
___ 10. muscular arteries	j. collect blood from the kidneys

11. Compared with arteries, veins
    (a) are more elastic
    (b) have thinner walls
    (c) have more smooth muscle in their media
    (d) have a pleated endothelium
12. Capillaries that have a complete lining are called
    (a) continuous capillaries (b) fenestrated capillaries
    (c) sinusoidal capillaries (d) sinusoids
13. The only blood vessels whose walls permit exchange between the blood and the surrounding interstitial fluids are the
    (a) arteries (b) arterioles
    (c) veins (d) capillaries
14. Blood flow through the capillaries is regulated by the
    (a) arterial anastomosis (b) central channel
    (c) vasa vasorum (d) precapillary sphincter
15. Blood from the brain returns to the heart by way of the
    (a) vertebral vein (b) internal jugular vein
    (c) external jugular vein (d) azygos vein
16. Branches off the aortic arch include
    (a) the left subclavian artery (b) the right subclavian artery
    (c) the right axillary artery (d) the right common carotid artery
17. During increased exercise
    (a) stroke volume decreases (b) cardiac output decreases
    (c) venous return increases (d) vasoconstriction occurs at the active skeletal muscles
18. In the leg, the femoral artery becomes the
    (a) popliteal artery (b) deep femoral artery
    (c) tibial artery (d) iliac artery
19. The fusion of the brachiocephalic veins forms the
    (a) azygos vein (b) superior vena cava
    (c) inferior vena cava (d) subclavian vein
20. Elderly individuals usually have
    (a) elevated hematocrits (b) stiff, inelastic arteries
    (c) increased venous return (d) decreased blood pressure

Level 2 Reviewing Concepts

1. A major difference between the arterial and venous systems is that
   (a) arteries are usually more superficial than veins
   (b) in the limbs there is dual venous drainage
   (c) veins are usually less branched than the arteries
   (d) veins exhibit a more orderly pattern of branching in the limbs
2. You would expect to find fenestrated capillaries in
   (a) the pancreas (b) skeletal muscles
   (c) cardiac muscle (d) the spleen
3. Why does the endothelial lining of a constricted artery appear to have pleats?
   (a) spaces between the endothelial cells allow the lining to sag when the artery is constricted
   (b) the endothelial lining cannot contract, so it is folded in pleats when the artery contracts
   (c) the expansion regions of the artery are folded when the artery constricts
   (d) the vasa vasorum contract irregularly
   (e) none of the above
4. What are some examples of elastic arteries?
5. Where are sinusoids found?
6. What are arteriovenous anastomoses?
7. What are the functions of venous valves in the limbs?
8. What three elastic arteries originate along the aortic arch?
9. From which regions of the body does the superior vena cava receive blood?
10. What is the function of the foramen ovale in a fetal heart?

Level 3 Critical Thinking

1. Why can it be dangerous for a person to squeeze pimples in the upper nasal and eyebrow region?
2. John loves to soak in hot tubs and whirlpools. One day he decides to raise the temperature in his hot tub as high as it will go. After a few minutes in the water, he feels faint, passes out, and nearly drowns. Luckily, he is saved by a bystander. Explain what happened.
3. Millie's grandfather suffers from congestive heart failure. When she visits him, she notices that his ankles and feet appear swollen. She asks you why this occurs. What would you tell her?

23

The Lymphoid System

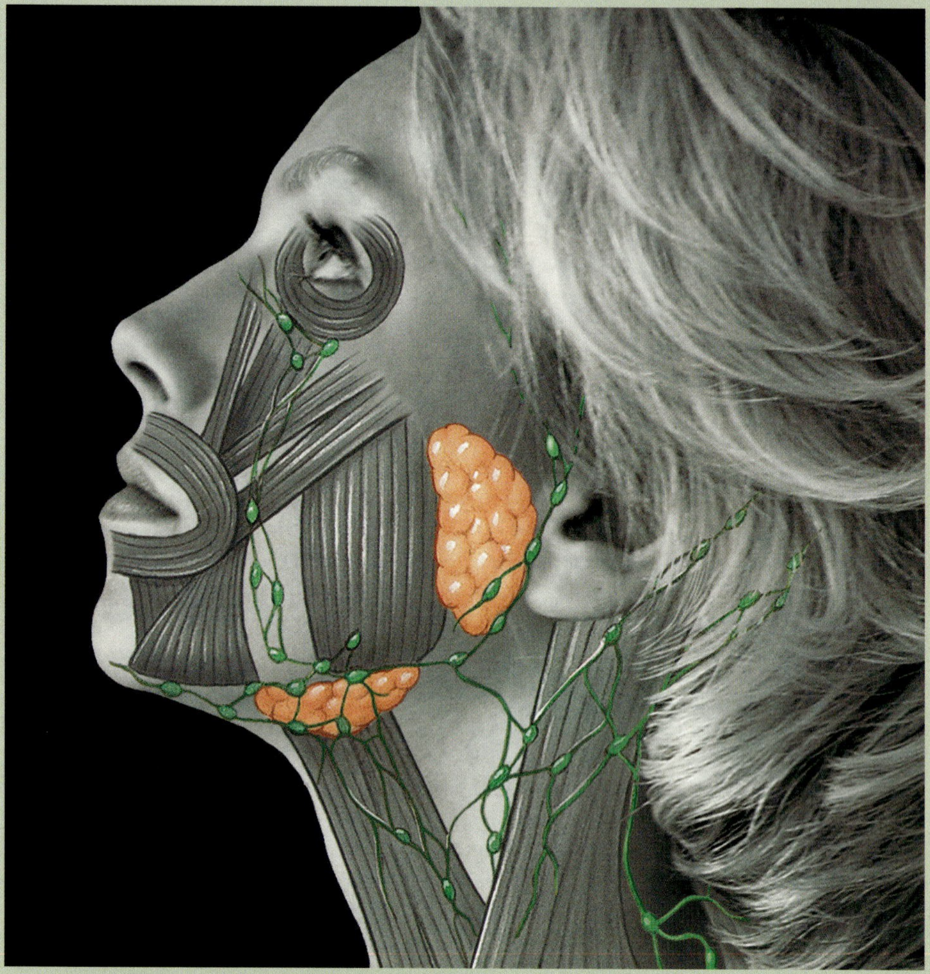

CHAPTER OBJECTIVES

1. Describe the role played by the lymphoid system in the body's defenses.
2. Identify the major components of the lymphoid system.
3. Describe the origin of lymph and its relationship with blood.
4. Contrast the structure of lymphatic vessels and veins.
5. Describe the location, structure, and function of lymphatic vessels.
6. Trace the pattern of lymph circulation.
7. Discuss the importance of lymphocytes and describe where they are found in the body.
8. Describe the activation of lymphocytes.
9. Briefly describe the role of the various lymphoid system components in the immune response.
10. Describe the anatomical and functional relationship between the lymphoid and cardiovascular systems, and relate lymphoid tissue structures to defense against disease.
11. Describe the location, structure, and function of the principal lymph nodes.
12. Describe the location, structure, and function of the thymus.
13. Describe the location, structure, and function of the spleen.
14. Describe the changes in the immune system that occur with aging.

The world is not always kind to the human body. Accidental collisions and interactions with objects in our environment produce bumps, cuts, and burns. The effects of an injury may be compounded by assorted viruses, bacteria, and other microorganisms that thrive in our environment. Some of these microorganisms normally live on the surface of and inside our bodies, but all have the potential to cause us great harm. Remaining alive and healthy involves a massive, combined effort involving many different organs and systems. In this ongoing struggle, the lymphoid system plays the primary role.

In this chapter we will describe the anatomical organization of the lymphoid system and consider how this system interacts with other systems and tissues to defend the body against infection and disease.

An Overview of the Lymphoid System [Figure 23.1]

The **lymphoid system**, or *lymphatic system*, has several components (**Figure 23.1**). *Lymph* is the fluid connective tissue transported and monitored by this system.* pp. 62, 68 The vessels that carry lymph are called *lymphatic vessels*, and the cells suspended within the liquid are known as *lymphocytes*. Specialized *lymphoid tissues* and *lymphoid organs* adjust the composition of lymph and produce lymphocytes of various kinds.

Lymphatic vessels originate in peripheral tissues and deliver lymph to the venous system. Lymph consists of (1) interstitial fluid, which resembles blood plasma, but with a lower concentration of proteins; (2) lymphocytes, cells responsible for the immune response; and (3) macrophages of various types. pp. 64–65 Lymphatic vessels often begin within or pass through lymphoid tissues and lymphoid organs, structures that contain large number of lymphocytes, macrophages, and (in many cases) lymphoid stem cells.

Functions of the Lymphoid System [Figure 23.2]

The primary functions of the lymphoid system are the following:

1. *Produce, maintain, and distribute lymphocytes:* Lymphocytes, which are essential to the normal defense mechanisms of the body, are produced and stored within lymphoid organs, such as the spleen, thymus, and bone marrow. Lymphoid tissues and organs are classified as either *primary* or *secondary*. *Primary lymphoid structures* contain stem cells that divide to produce daughter cells that differentiate into B, T, or NK cells. p. 540 The bone marrow and thymus of the adult are primary lymphoid structures. However, most immune responses begin in *secondary lymphoid structures*, where immature or activated lymphocytes divide to produce additional lymphocytes of the same type. For example, the divisions of activated B cells can produce the additional B cells needed to fight off an infection. Secondary lymphoid structures are located "at the front lines," where invading bacteria are first encountered. Examples include lymph nodes and tonsils.
2. *Maintain normal blood volume and eliminate local variations in the chemical composition of the interstitial fluid:* The blood pressure at the proximal end of a systemic capillary is approximately 35 mm Hg. The blood pressure tends to force water and solutes out of the plasma and into the interstitial fluid (**Figure 23.2**). There is a small net movement of fluid from the plasma into the interstitial fluid along every systemic capillary. The total volume is substantial—approximately 3.6 L, or 72

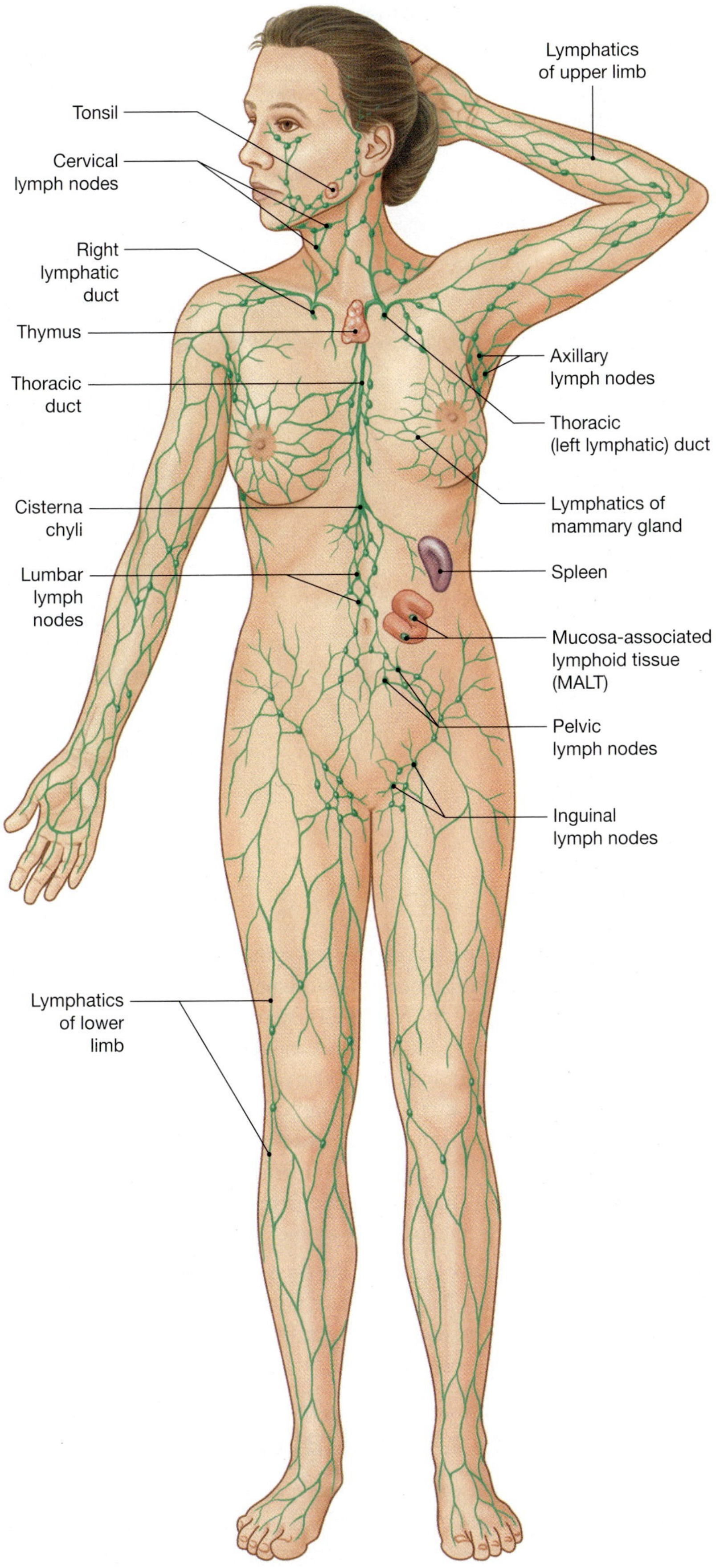

Figure 23.1 Lymphoid System
An overview of the arrangement of lymphatic vessels, lymph nodes, and lymphoid organs.

*The terms 'lymphoid' and 'lymphatic' have long been used interchangeably, and this synonymy is reflected in the terms endorsed by the Terminologia Anatomica.

Figure 23.2 Lymphatic Capillaries
Lymphatic capillaries are blind vessels that begin in areas of loose connective tissue. **(a)** A three-dimensional view of the association of blood capillaries and lymphatic capillaries. Arrows show the direction of blood, interstitial fluid, and lymph movement. **(b)** Sectional view through a cluster of lymphatic capillaries.

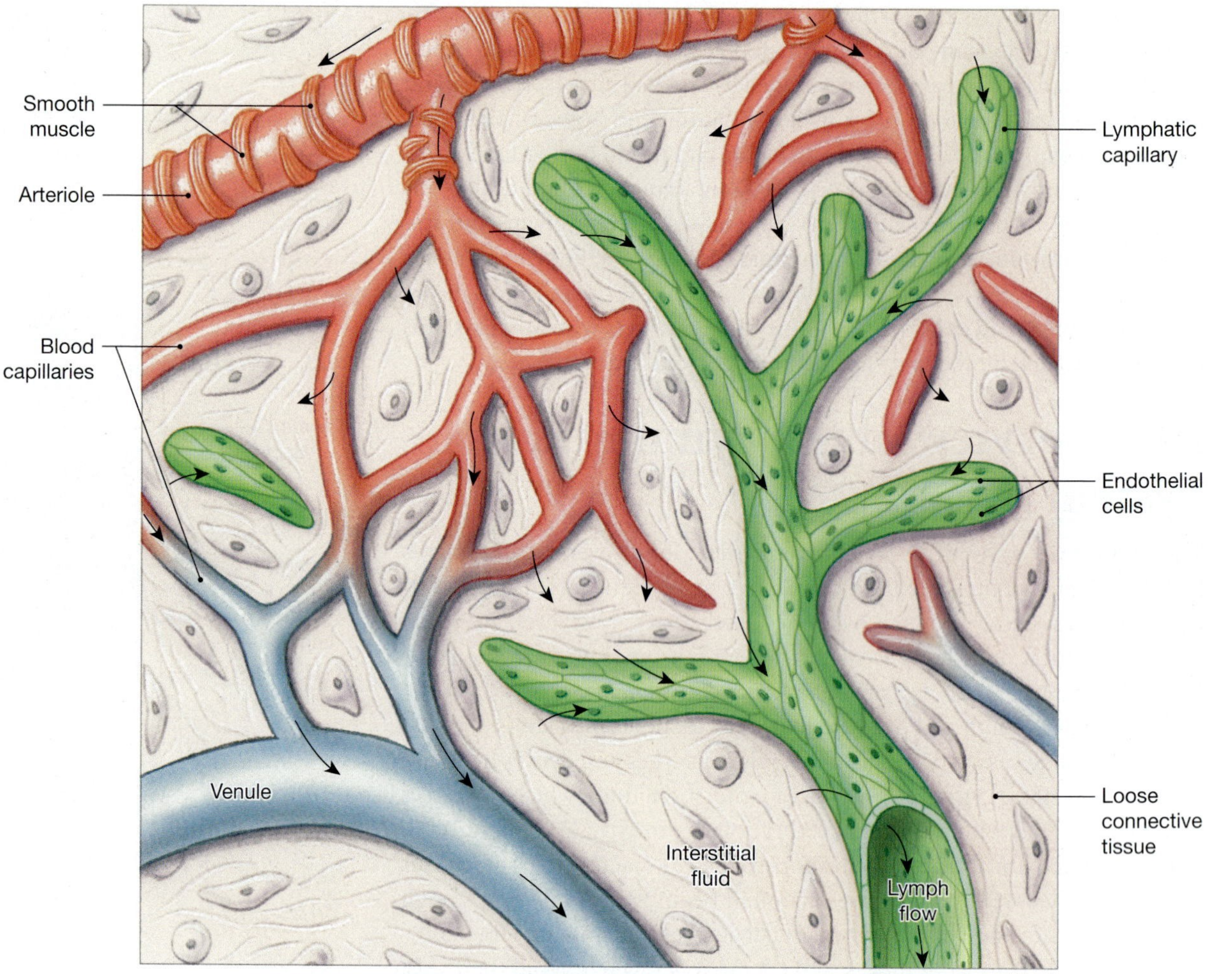

(a) Association of blood capillaries, tissue, and lymphatic capillaries

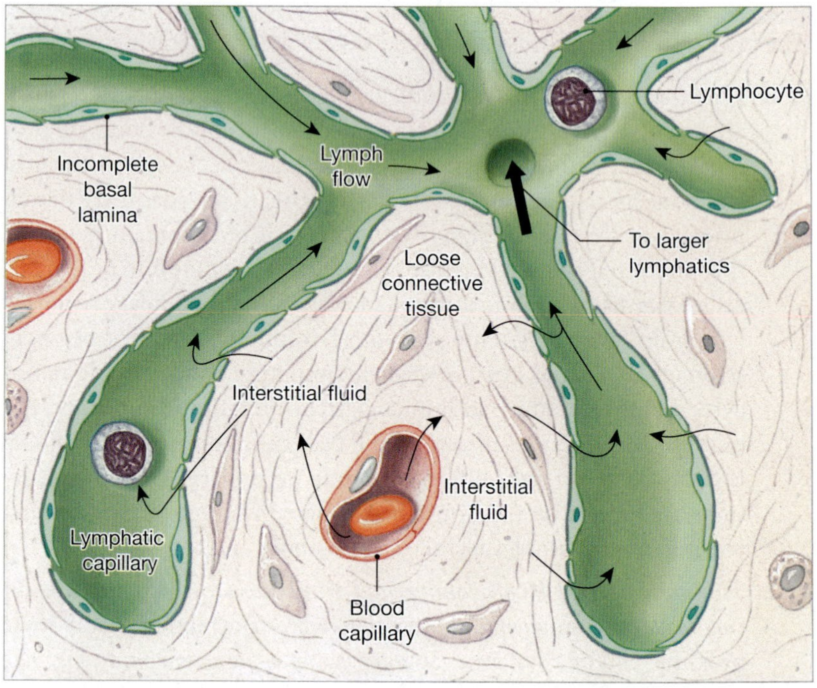

(b) Sectional view

percent of the total blood volume, enters the interstitial fluid each day. Under normal circumstances this movement goes unnoticed, because each day the vessels of the lymphoid system return an equal volume of interstitial fluid to the bloodstream. Consequently, there is a continual movement of fluid from the bloodstream into the tissues and then back to the bloodstream through lymphatic vessels. This circulation of fluid helps eliminate regional differences in the composition of interstitial fluid. Because so much fluid moves through the lymphoid system each day, a break in a major lymphatic vessel can cause a rapid and potentially fatal decline in blood volume.

3. *Provide an alternative route for the transport of hormones, nutrients, and waste products:* For example, certain lipids absorbed by the digestive tract are carried to the bloodstream by lymphatic vessels rather than by absorption across capillary walls.

Structure of Lymphatic Vessels

Lymphatic vessels, often called *lymphatics*, carry lymph from peripheral tissues to the venous system. As with blood vessels, the lymphatic vessels range in size from small-diameter *lymphatic capillaries* to large-diameter collecting vessels, called *lymphatic ducts*.

Lymphatic Capillaries [Figure 23.2]

The lymphatic network begins with the **lymphatic capillaries**, or *terminal lymphatics*, which form a complex network within peripheral tissues. Lymphatic capillaries differ from vascular capillaries in several ways: (1) Lymphatic capillaries are larger both in diameter and in sectional view; (2) they have thinner walls because their endothelial cells lack a continuous basal lamina; (3) they typically have a flat or irregular outline; (4) they have collagenous *anchoring filaments* that extend from the incomplete basal lamina to the surrounding connective tissue; these filaments help keep the passageways open when interstitial pressures increase; and (5) they have endothelial cells that overlap instead of being tightly bound to one another (**Figure 23.2**). The region of endothelial cell overlap acts as a one-way valve, permitting passage of interstitial fluid into the lymphatic capillary but preventing its escape (**Figure 23.2b**). The endothelial cells are often fenestrated, and with pores in the cells and gaps between cells there is little in the interstitial fluid that cannot find its way into a lymphatic capillary. The gaps between endothelial cells are large enough that the lymphatic capillaries absorb not only interstitial fluid and dissolved solutes but any viruses or other abnormal items, such as cell debris or bacteria, that are present in damaged or infected tissues. As a result, a lymphatic capillary contains chemical and physical evidence about the health of the surrounding tissues.

Lymphatic capillaries are especially numerous in the connective tissue deep to skin and mucous membranes, and in the mucosa and submucosa of the digestive tract. Prominent lymphatic capillaries in the small intestine, called *lacteals*, transport lipids absorbed by the digestive tract. Lymphatic capillaries are present in most tissues. However, they are absent in areas that lack a blood supply, such as the matrix of cartilage and the cornea of the eye, and there are no lymphatics in either bone marrow or the central nervous system.

Valves of Lymphatic Vessels [Figure 23.3]

From the lymphatic capillaries, lymph flows into larger lymphatic vessels that lead toward the lymphatic trunks in the abdominopelvic and thoracic cavities. The larger lymphatics are comparable to veins both in the layers in their walls and in the presence of internal valves. The valves are quite close together, and at each valve the lymphatic vessel bulges noticeably. This configuration gives large lymphatics a beaded appearance (**Figure 23.3**). Pressures within the lymphatic system are minimal; in fact, interstitial fluid pressure is lower than that of the venous system. The valves prevent the backflow of lymph within lymphatic vessels, especially those of the limbs. The larger lymphatic vessels have layers of smooth muscle in their walls. Rhythmic contractions of these vessels propel lymph toward the lymphatic ducts. Skeletal muscle contraction and respiratory movements work together to help move lymph through the lymphatic vessels. Contractions of skeletal muscles in the limbs compress the lymphatics and squeeze lymph toward the trunk; a comparable mechanism assists venous return. With each inhalation, pressure decreases inside the thoracic cavity, and lymph is pulled from smaller lymphatic vessels into the lymphatic ducts.

If a lymphatic vessel is compressed or blocked or its valves are damaged, lymph drainage slows or ceases in the affected area. When fluid continues to leave the vascular capillaries in that region but the lymphoid system is no longer able to remove it, the interstitial fluid volume and pressure gradually increase. The affected tissues become distended and swollen, and this condition is called *lymphedema*.

Lymphatic vessels are typically found in association with blood vessels. Note the differences in relative size, general appearance, and branching pattern that distinguish lymphatic vessels from arteries and veins (**Figure 23.3a,c**). There are also characteristic color differences that are apparent on examining living tissues. Arteries are usually a bright red, veins a dark red, and lymphatics a pale golden color.

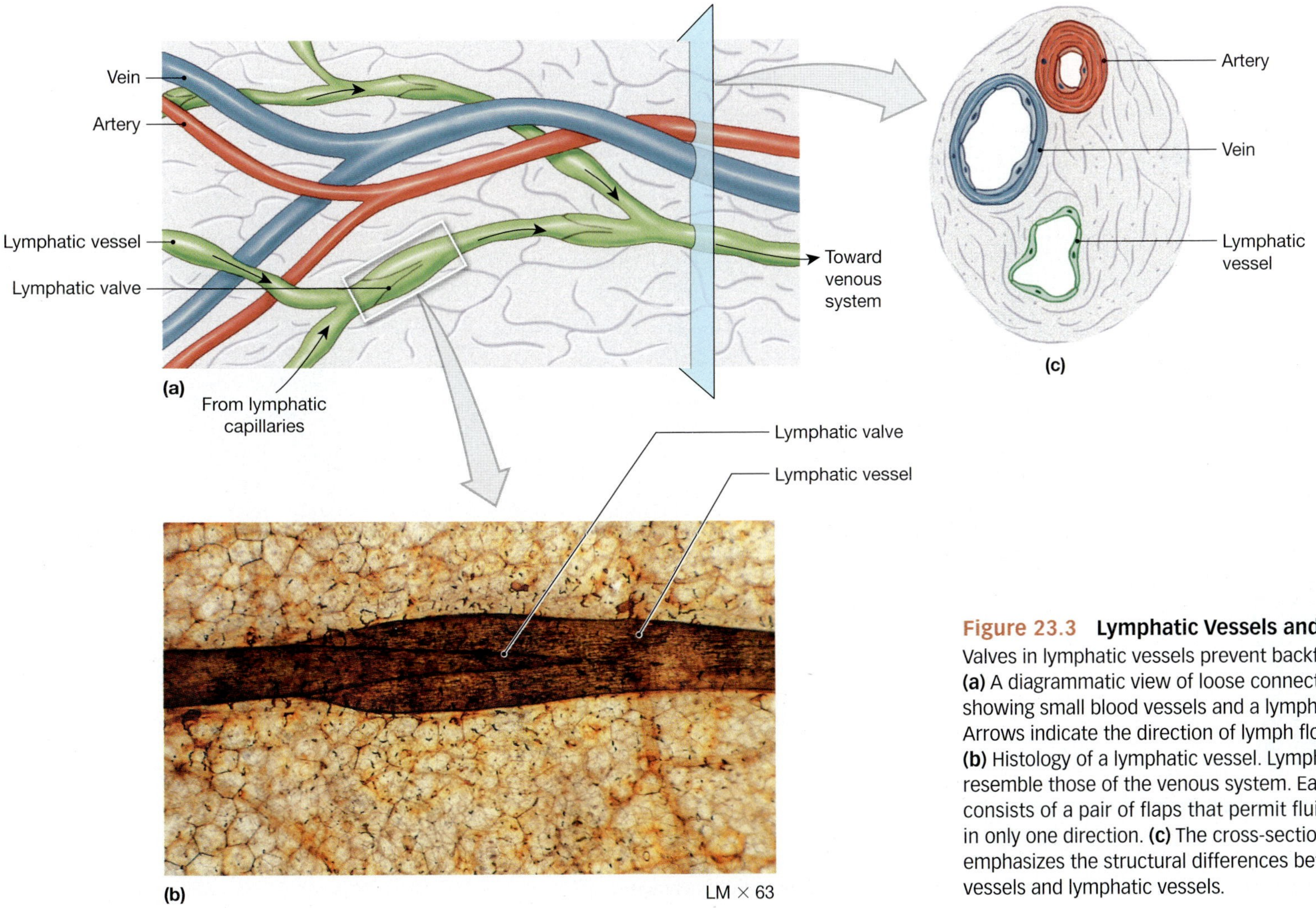

Figure 23.3 Lymphatic Vessels and Valves
Valves in lymphatic vessels prevent backflow of lymph. **(a)** A diagrammatic view of loose connective tissue, showing small blood vessels and a lymphatic vessel. Arrows indicate the direction of lymph flow. **(b)** Histology of a lymphatic vessel. Lymphatic valves resemble those of the venous system. Each valve consists of a pair of flaps that permit fluid movement in only one direction. **(c)** The cross-sectional view emphasizes the structural differences between blood vessels and lymphatic vessels.

Major Lymph-Collecting Vessels [Figure 23.4]

Two sets of lymphatic vessels, the superficial lymphatics and the deep lymphatics, collect lymph from the lymphatic capillaries. **Superficial lymphatics** travel with superficial veins and are found in the following locations:

- The subcutaneous layer next to the skin.
- The loose connective tissues of the mucous membranes lining the digestive, respiratory, urinary, and reproductive tracts.
- The loose connective tissues of the serous membranes lining the pleural, pericardial, and peritoneal cavities.

Deep lymphatics are large lymphatic vessels that accompany the deep arteries and veins. These lymphatic vessels collect lymph from skeletal muscles and other organs of the neck, limbs, and trunk, as well as visceral organs in the thoracic and abdominopelvic cavities.

Within the trunk, superficial and deep lymphatics converge to form larger vessels called **lymphatic trunks**. The lymphatic trunks include the (1) *lumbar trunks*, (2) *intestinal trunks*, (3) *bronchomediastinal trunks*, (4) *subclavian trunks*, and (5) *jugular trunks* (Figure 23.4). The lymphatic trunks in turn empty into two large collecting vessels, the **lymphatic ducts**, that deliver lymph to the venous circulation.

The Thoracic Duct [Figures 23.4/23.5]

The **thoracic duct** collects lymph from both sides of the body inferior to the diaphragm and from the left side of the body superior to the diaphragm. The thoracic duct begins inferior to the diaphragm at the level of vertebra L_2. The base of the thoracic duct is an expanded, saclike chamber, the **cisterna chyli** (KĪ-lē) (Figures 23.4 and 23.5). The cisterna chyli receives lymph from the inferior region of the abdomen, pelvis, and lower limbs through the *right* and *left lumbar trunks* and the *intestinal trunks*.

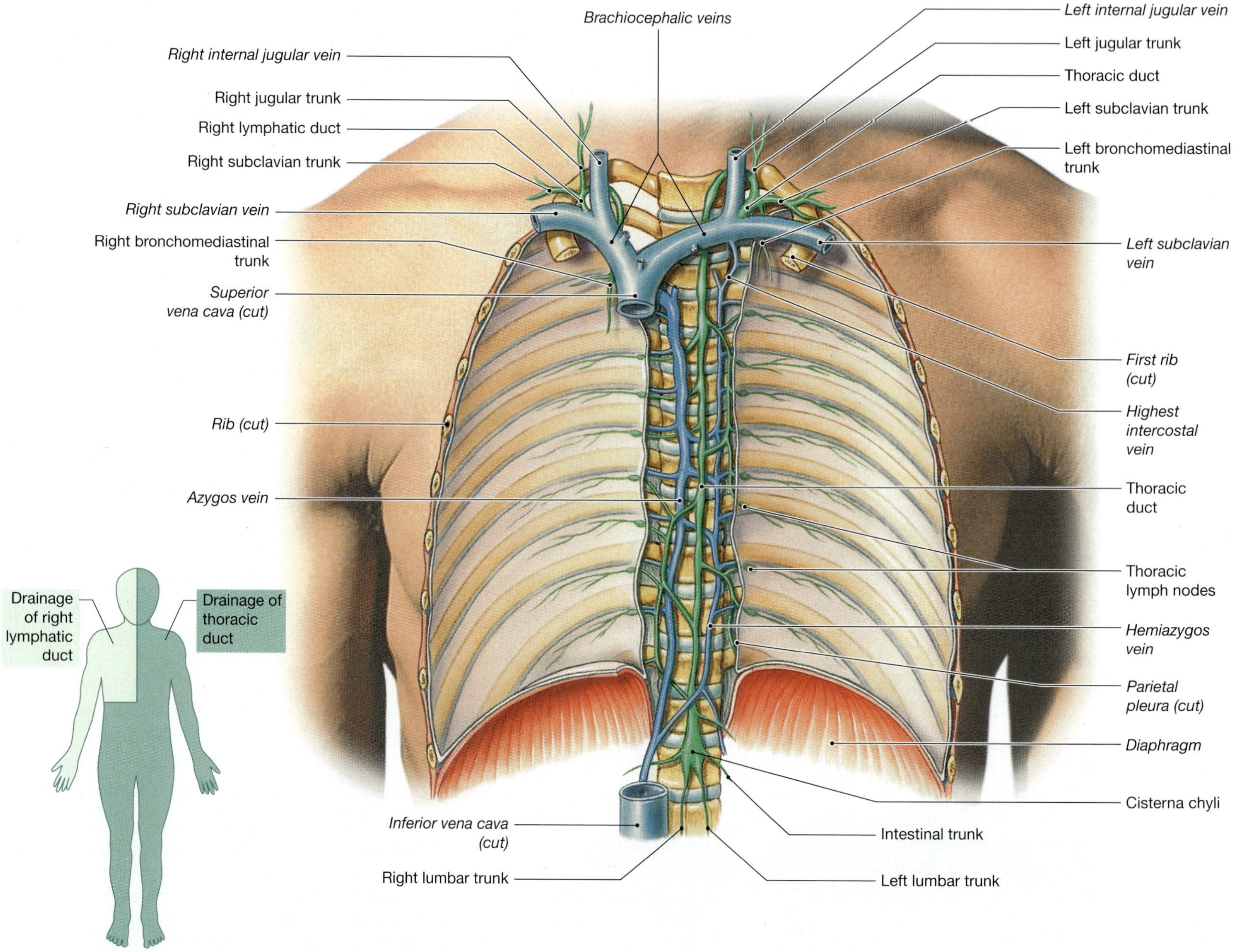

Figure 23.4 Lymphatic Ducts and Lymphatic Drainage
The collecting system of lymph vessels, lymph nodes, and major lymphatic collecting ducts and their relationship to the brachiocephalic veins. The thoracic duct collects lymph from tissues inferior to the diaphragm and from the left side of the upper body. The right lymphatic duct drains the right half of the body superior to the diaphragm.

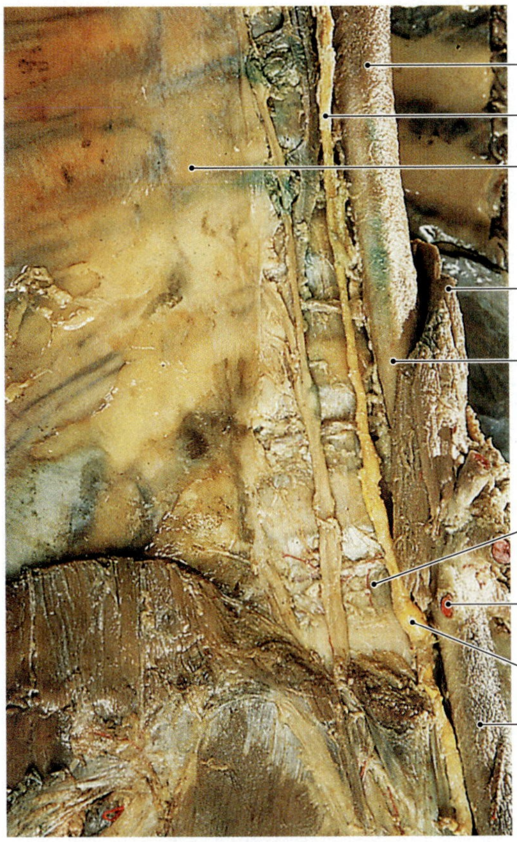

Figure 23.5 Major Lymphatic Vessels of the Trunk
Anterior view of a dissection of the thoracic duct and adjacent blood vessels. The thoracic and abdominopelvic organs have been removed.

The inferior segment of the thoracic duct lies anterior to the vertebral column. From its origin anterior to the second lumbar vertebra, it penetrates the diaphragm with the aorta, at an opening known as the *aortic hiatus*, and ascends along the left side of the vertebral column to the level of the left clavicle. After collecting lymph from the *left bronchomediastinal trunk*, the *left subclavian trunk*, and the *left jugular trunk*, it empties into the left subclavian vein near the base of the left internal jugular vein (Figure 23.4). Lymph collected from the left side of the head, neck, and thorax as well as lymph from the entire body inferior to the diaphragm reenters the venous system in this way.

The Right Lymphatic Duct [Figure 23.4]

The relatively small **right lymphatic duct** collects lymph from the right side of the body superior to the diaphragm. The right lymphatic duct receives lymph from smaller lymphatic vessels that converge in the region of the right clavicle. This duct empties into the venous system at or near the junction of the right internal jugular vein and right subclavian vein (Figure 23.4).

CONCEPT CHECK

1. What is the main function of the lymphoid system?
2. You are looking through a microscope at a cross section of two capillaries. Capillary number one is larger than number two and has a thinner wall. Capillary number two has a round shape, whereas capillary one has an irregular outline. Which capillary is probably a lymphatic capillary?
3. Would the rupture of a major lymphatic vessel be fatal? Why or why not?
4. Which lymphoid structures contain stem cells?

See blue "Answers" tab at back of book.

Lymphocytes

Lymphocytes are the primary cells of the lymphoid system, and they are responsible for specific immunity. p. 540 They respond to the presence of (1) invading organisms, such as bacteria and viruses; (2) abnormal body cells, such as virus-infected cells or cancer cells; and (3) foreign proteins, such as the toxins released by some bacteria. Lymphocytes attempt to eliminate these threats or render them harmless by a combination of physical and chemical attack. They travel throughout the body, circulating in the bloodstream, then moving through peripheral tissues and eventually returning to the bloodstream through the lymphoid system. The time spent within the lymphoid system varies; a lymphocyte may remain within a lymph node or other lymphoid organ for hours, days, or even years. When in peripheral tissues, lymphocytes may encounter invading pathogens or foreign proteins; while in the lymphoid system, they may be exposed to pathogens or proteins carried by lymph. Regardless of the source, lymphocytes respond by initiating an immune response.

Types of Lymphocytes

There are three different classes of lymphocytes in the blood: **T cells** (**t**hymus-dependent), **B cells** (**b**one marrow–derived), and **NK cells** (**n**atural **k**iller). Each type has distinctive biochemical and functional characteristics.

T Cells

Approximately 80 percent of circulating lymphocytes are classified as T cells. There are several types of T cells. **Cytotoxic T cells** attack foreign cells or body cells infected by viruses. Their attack often involves direct contact. These lymphocytes are responsible for providing **cell-mediated immunity**. **Helper T cells** and **suppressor T cells** assist in the regulation and coordination of the immune response; for this reason they are also called *regulatory T cells*. Regulatory T cells control both the activation and the activity of B cells. **Memory T cells** are produced by the division of activated T cells following exposure to a particular antigen. They are called memory cells because they remain "on reserve," becoming activated only if the same antigen appears in the body at a later date. This is not a complete list, as there are several other types of specialized T cells in the body.

B Cells

B cells account for 10–15 percent of circulating lymphocytes. When stimulated by exposure to an antigen, a B cell can differentiate into a **plasmocyte**. Plasmocytes are responsible for the production and secretion of **antibodies**. p. 537 These soluble proteins react with specific chemical targets called **antigens**. Antigens are usually associated with pathogens, parts or products of pathogens, or other foreign compounds. Most antigens are short peptide chains or short amino acid sequences along a complex protein, but some lipids, polysaccharides, and nucleic acids can also stimulate antibody production. When an antibody binds to its corresponding antigen, it starts a chain of events leading to the destruction, neutralization, or elimination of the antigen. Antibodies are also known as **immunoglobulins** (im-ū-nō-GLOB-ū-lins). Because the blood is the primary distribution route for immunoglobulins, B cells are said to be responsible for **antibody-mediated immunity**, or *humoral* ("liquid") *immunity*. **Memory B cells** are produced by the division of activated B cells; activation occurs following exposure to a particular antigen. Memory B cells become activated only if the antigen appears in the body at a later date.

Helper T cells promote the differentiation of plasmocytes and accelerate the production of antibodies. Suppressor T cells inhibit the formation of plasmocytes and reduce the production of antibodies by existing plasmocytes.

NK Cells

The remaining 5–10 percent of circulating lymphocytes are NK cells, also known as *large granular lymphocytes.* These lymphocytes attack foreign cells, normal cells infected with viruses, and cancer cells that appear in normal tissues. The continual policing of peripheral tissues by NK cells and activated macrophages has been called **immunological surveillance**.

Lymphocytes and the Immune Response [Figure 23.6]

The goal of the **immune response** is the destruction or inactivation of pathogens, abnormal cells, and foreign molecules such as toxins. The body has two different ways to do this:

1. Direct attack by activated T cells *(cell-mediated immunity)*;
2. Attack by circulating antibodies released by the *plasmocytes* derived from activated B cells *(antibody-mediated immunity).*

Figure 23.6 provides an overview of the immune response to bacterial infection and viral infection. After the appearance of an antigen, the first step in the immune response is often the phagocytosis of the antigen by a macrophage. The macrophage then displays pieces of the antigen in its cell membrane. In this way the macrophage "presents" the antigen to T cells, and the process is called *antigen presentation.* The T cells that respond are sensitive to that particular antigen and none other. These lymphocytes respond because their plasmalemmae contain receptors capable of binding that specific antigen. When binding occurs, the T cells undergo activation and begin to divide. Some daughter cells differentiate into cytotoxic T cells, others into helper T cells that will in turn activate B cells, and some become memory T cells that will differentiate further only if they encounter this antigen at a later date.

Your immune system has no way of anticipating which antigens it will actually encounter. Its protective strategy is to prepare for *any* antigen that might appear. During development, differentiation of cells in the lymphoid system produces an enormous number of lymphocytes with varied antigen sensitivities. The ability of a lymphocyte to recognize a specific antigen is called

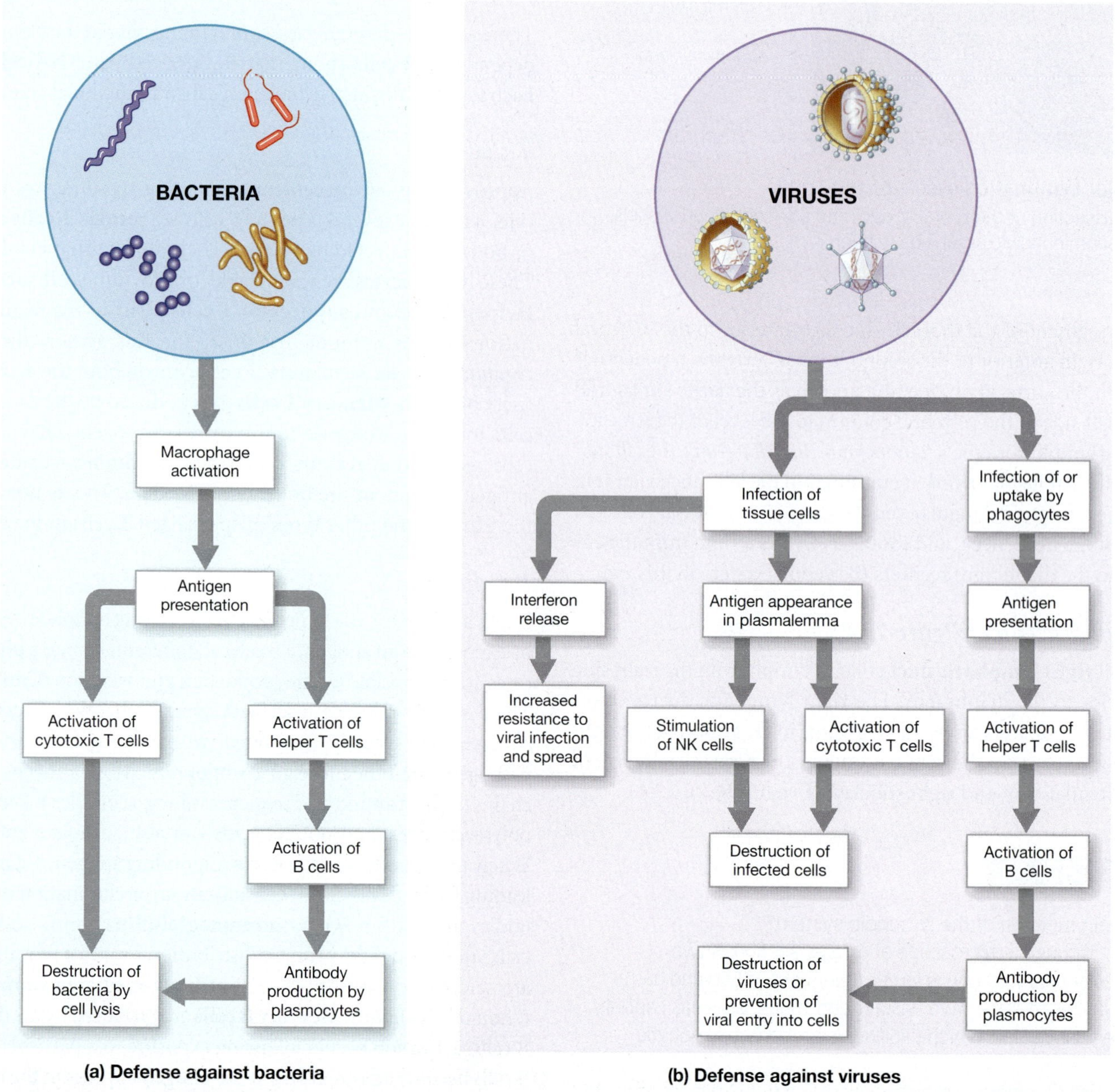

Figure 23.6 Lymphocytes and the Immune Response
(a) Defenses against bacterial pathogens are usually initiated by active macrophages. **(b)** Defenses against viruses are usually activated after the infection of normal cells. In each instance, B cells and T cells cooperate to produce a coordinated chemical and physical attack.

immunocompetence. Among the trillion or so lymphocytes in the human body are millions of different lymphocyte populations. Each population consists of several thousand cells that are prepared to recognize a specific antigen. When one of these lymphocytes binds an antigen, it becomes activated, dividing to produce more lymphocytes sensitive to that particular antigen. Some of the lymphocytes function immediately to eliminate the antigen, and others (the memory cells) will be ready if the antigen reappears at a later date. This mechanism provides an immediate defense and ensures an even more massive and rapid response if the antigen appears in the body at some later date.

Distribution and Life Span of Lymphocytes

The ratio of B cells to T cells varies depending on the tissue or organ considered. For example, B cells are seldom found in the thymus; in the blood, T cells outnumber B cells by a ratio of 8:1. This ratio changes to 1:1 in the spleen and 1:3 in the bone marrow.

The lymphocytes within these organs are visitors, not residents. Lymphocytes continually move throughout the body; they wander through a tissue and then enter a blood vessel or lymphatic vessel for transport to another site. T cells move relatively quickly. For example, a wandering T cell may spend about 30 minutes in the blood and 15–20 hours in a lymph node. B cells move more slowly; a typical B cell spends around 30 hours in a lymph node before moving to another location.

In general, lymphocytes have relatively long life spans, far longer than other formed elements in the blood. Roughly 80 percent survive for 4 years, and some last 20 years or more. Throughout life, normal lymphocyte populations are maintained by the process of *lymphopoiesis.*

Lymphopoiesis: Lymphocyte Production [Figure 23.7]

Lymphopoiesis occurs in the bone marrow and thymus. Figure 23.7 shows the relationships among bone marrow, thymus, and peripheral lymphoid tissues with respect to lymphocyte production, maturation, and distribution.

Pluripotential lymphoid stem cells in the bone marrow produce lymphocytic stem cells with two distinct fates. One group remains in the bone marrow. These stem cells divide to produce NK cells and B cells, which gain immunocompetence and migrate into peripheral tissues. The NK cells continuously circulate through peripheral tissues, whereas the B cells take up residence in lymph nodes, the spleen, and lymphoid tissues. The second group of stem cells migrates to the thymus. Under the influence of the thymic hormones (thymosin-1, thymopentin, thymulin, and others) these stem cells divide repeatedly, producing daughter cells that undergo functional maturation into T cells. These T cells subsequently migrate to the spleen, other lymphoid organs, and the bone marrow.

As a lymphocyte migrates through peripheral tissues, it retains the ability to divide. Its divisions produce daughter cells of the same type and with sensitivity to the same specific antigen. For example, a dividing B cell produces other B cells, not T cells or NK cells. The ability to increase the number of lymphocytes of a specific type is important to the success of the immune response. If that ability is compromised, the individual will be unable to mount an effective defense against infection and disease. For example, the disease *AIDS (acquired immune deficiency syndrome)* results from infection with a virus that selectively destroys T cells. Individuals with AIDS are likely to be killed by bacterial or viral infections that would be overcome easily by a normal immune system.

Figure 23.7 Derivation and Distribution of Lymphocytes
Pluripotential stem cell divisions produce lymphoid stem cells with two different fates. **(a)** One group remains in the bone marrow, producing daughter cells that mature into B cells and NK cells that enter peripheral tissues. **(b)** The second group of stem cells migrates to the thymus, where subsequent divisions produce daughter cells that mature into T cells. **(c)** Mature T cells leave the circulation to take temporary residence in peripheral tissues. All three types of lymphocytes circulate throughout the body in the bloodstream.

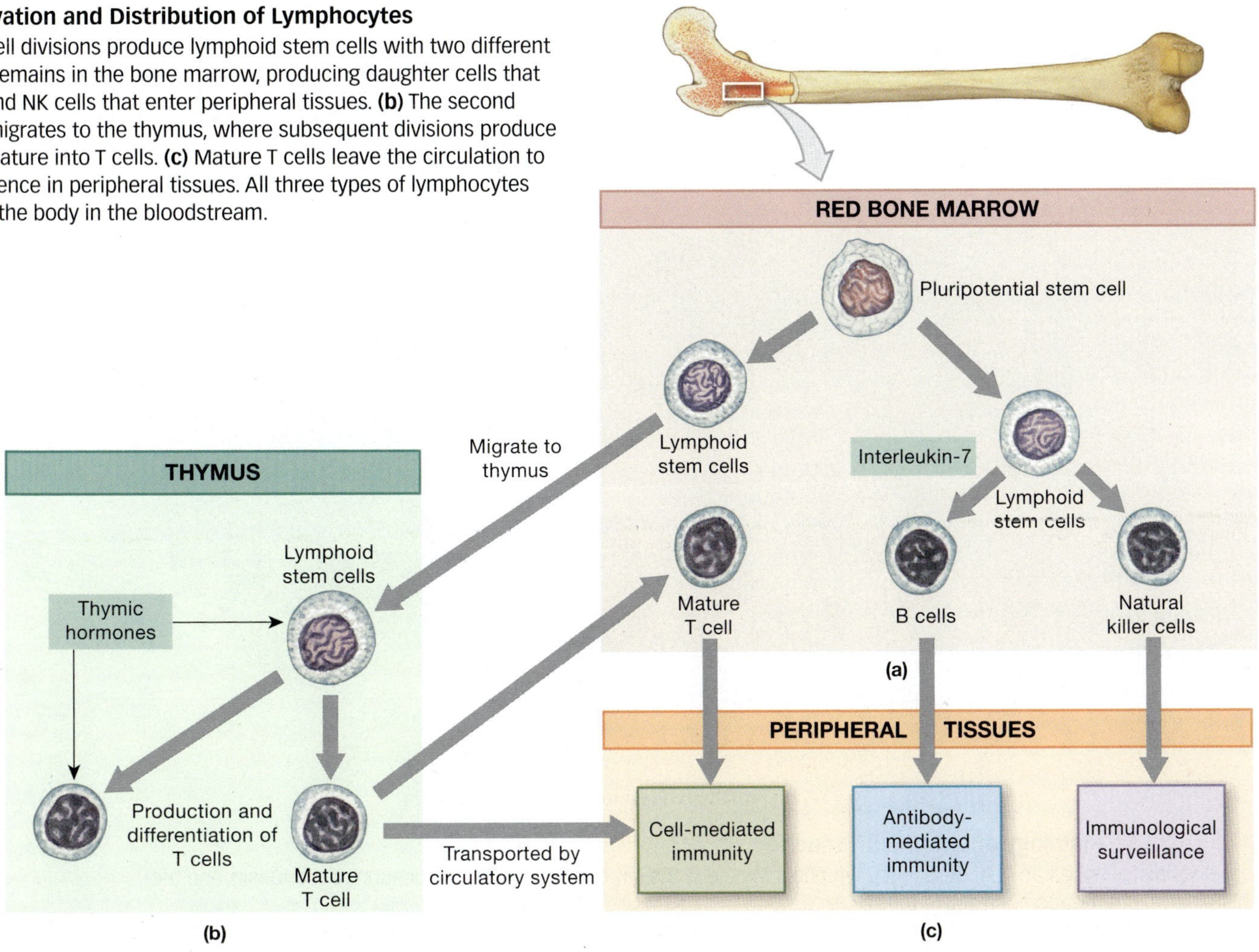

Lymphoid Tissues [Figure 23.8]

Lymphoid tissues are connective tissues dominated by lymphocytes. In **diffuse lymphoid tissue**, lymphocytes are loosely aggregated within connective tissue of the mucous membrane of the respiratory or urinary tracts. **Lymphoid nodules** are aggregations of lymphocytes contained within a supporting framework of reticular fibers. Lymphoid nodules are typically oval in shape, and are often found within the wall of various segments of the digestive tract, including the ileum and gallbladder (Figure 23.8a). Typical lymphoid nodules average around a millimeter in diameter, but the boundaries are indistinct because no fibrous capsule surrounds them. They often have a pale, central zone, called a **germinal center**, which contains activated, dividing lymphocytes (Figure 23.8b).

The digestive tract has an extensive array of lymphoid nodules collectively known as the **mucosa-associated lymphoid tissue (MALT)**. Large nodules in the wall of the pharynx are called **tonsils** (Figure 23.8b). The lymphocytes aggregated in tonsils gather and remove pathogens that enter the pharynx in either inspired air or food. There are usually five tonsils:

- a single **pharyngeal tonsil**, often called the *adenoids*, located in the posterior superior wall of the nasopharynx;
- a pair of **palatine tonsils**, located at the posterior margin of the oral cavity along the boundary of the pharynx to the soft palate; and
- a pair of **lingual tonsils**, which are not visible because they are located at the base of the tongue.

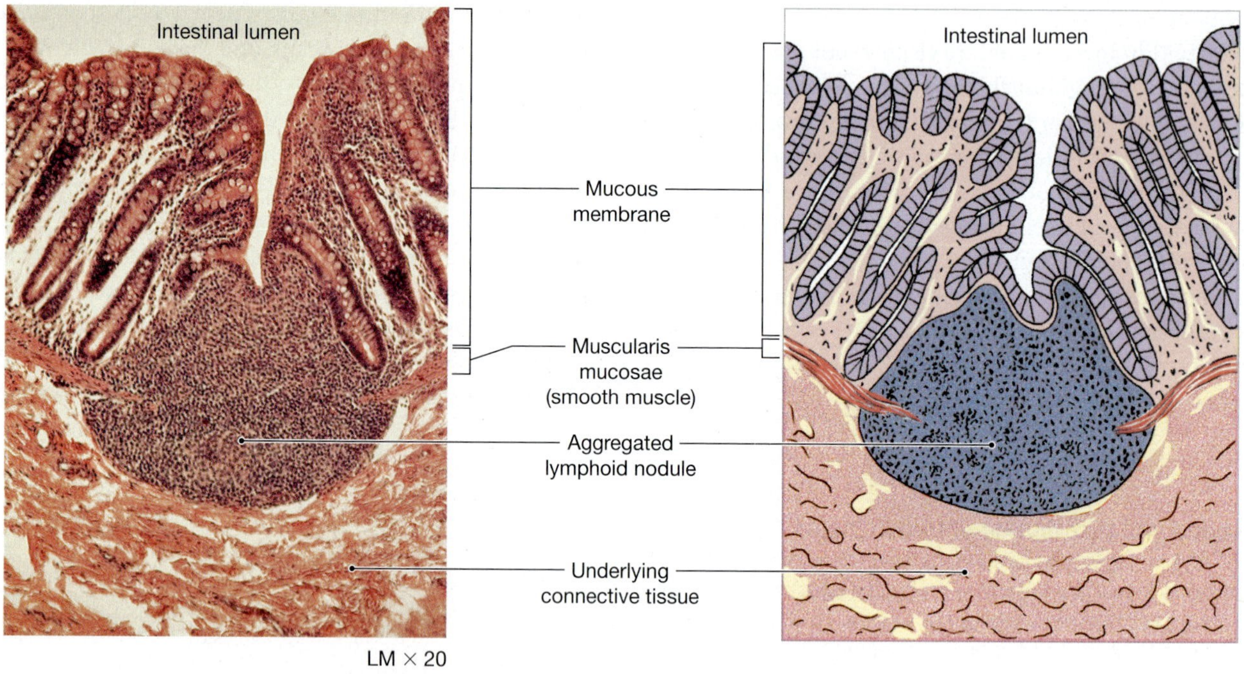

(a) Aggregated lymphoid nodule (intestinal tract)

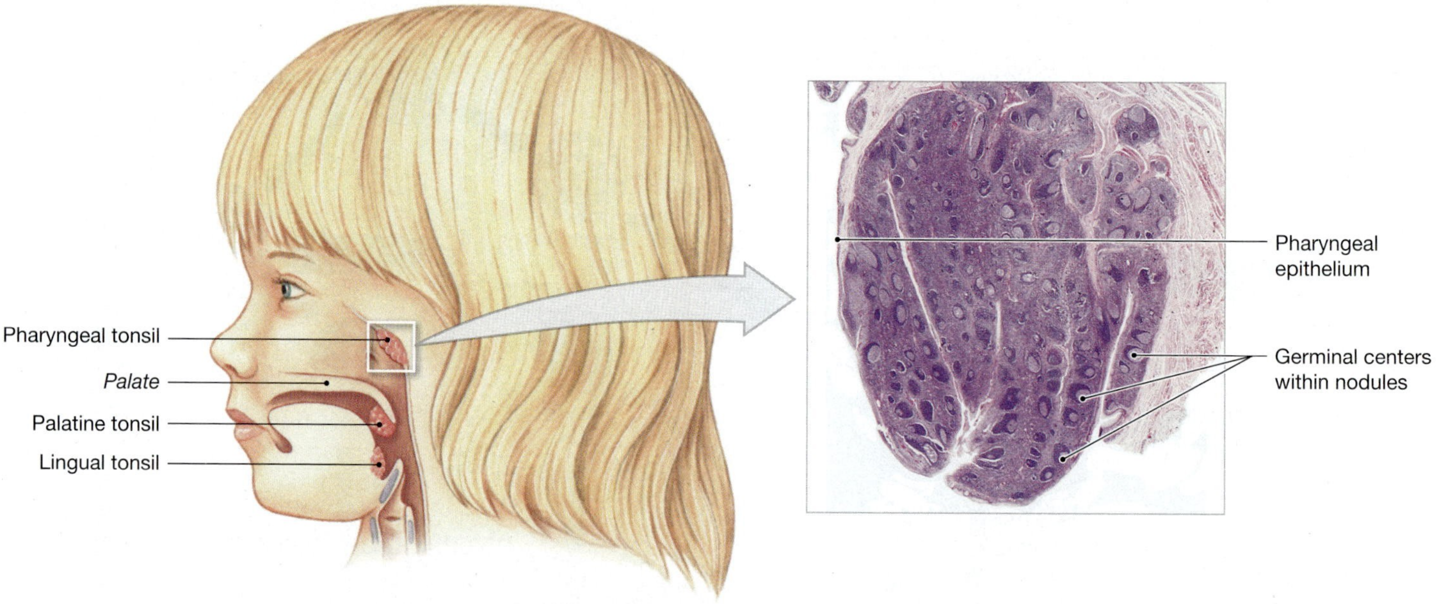

(b) Pharyngeal tonsil (respiratory tract)

Figure 23.8 Histology of Lymphoid Tissues
(a) Histological appearance of an isolated lymphoid nodule in the large intestine. **(b)** The location of the tonsils and the histological organization of a single tonsil.

Clinical Note

Infected Lymphoid Nodules Lymphoid nodules can be overwhelmed by a pathogenic invasion. The result is a localized infection accompanied by regional swelling and discomfort. The tonsils are a first line of defense against infection of the pharyngeal walls.

An individual with tonsillitis has infected tonsils. Symptoms include a sore throat, high fever, and often leukocytosis (an abnormally high white blood cell count). The affected tonsils (normally, the pharyngeal tonsils) become swollen and inflamed, sometimes enlarging enough to partially block the entrance to the trachea. Breathing then becomes difficult or, in severe cases, impossible. If the infection proceeds, abscesses may develop within the tonsillar or peritonsillar tissues. Bacteria may enter the bloodstream by passing through the lymphatic capillaries and vessels to the venous system.

In the early stages, antibiotics may control the infection, but once abscesses have formed, the best treatment involves surgical drainage of the abscesses and **tonsillectomy**, the removal of the tonsil. Tonsillectomy was once highly recommended prior to the development of antibiotics, in order to prevent recurring tonsillar infections. The procedure does reduce the incidence and severity of subsequent infections, but questions have arisen about the overall cost to the individual, especially now that antibiotics are available to treat severe infections.

Appendicitis generally follows an erosion of the epithelial lining of the vermiform appendix. Several factors may be responsible for the initial ulceration—notably, bacterial or viral pathogens. Bacteria that normally inhabit the lumen of the large intestine then cross the epithelium and enter the underlying tissues. Inflammation occurs, and the opening between the vermiform appendix and the rest of the intestinal tract may become constricted. Mucous secretion and pus formation accelerate, and the organ becomes increasingly distended. Eventually, the swollen and inflamed appendix may rupture, or *perforate.* If it does, bacteria will be released into the warm, dark, moist confines of the peritoneal space, where they can cause a life-threatening peritonitis. The most effective treatment for appendicitis is the surgical removal of the organ, a procedure known as an **appendectomy.**

Clusters of lymphoid nodules in the mucosal lining of the small intestine are known as **aggregated lymphoid nodules**, or *Peyer's patches.* In addition, the walls of the *appendix*, a blind pouch that originates near the junction between the small and large intestines, contain a mass of fused lymphoid nodules.

The lymphocytes within these lymphoid nodules are not always able to destroy bacterial or viral invaders that have crossed the epithelium of the digestive tract. An infection may then develop; familiar examples include *tonsillitis* and *appendicitis.*

CONCEPT CHECK

1. Which type of lymphocyte is the most common?
2. John becomes infected with a pathogen. A few months later, while relatively healthy, he is exposed to the same pathogen. Will he definitely get sick again? Why or why not?
3. Circulating lymphocytes retain the ability to divide. Why is this important?
4. What is the name given to the clusters of lymphoid nodules found in the mucosal lining of the small intestine?

See blue "Answers" tab at back of book.

Lymphoid Organs

Lymphoid organs are separated from surrounding tissues by a fibrous connective tissue capsule. These organs include the *lymph nodes*, the *thymus*, and the *spleen.*

Lymph Nodes [Figures 23.1/23.4/23.9 to 23.14]

Lymph nodes are small, oval lymphoid organs ranging in diameter from 1 to 25 mm (up to around 1 in.). The general pattern of lymph node distribution in the body can be seen in Figure 23.1, p. 609. Each lymph node is covered by a dense fibrous connective tissue capsule. Fibrous extensions from the capsule extend partway into the interior of the node. These fibrous extensions are called *trabeculae* (Figure 23.9).

Blood vessels and nerves attach to the lymph node at the indentation, or **hilum** (Figure 23.9). Each lymph node has two sets of lymphatic vessels: *afferent lymphatics* and *efferent lymphatics.* The afferent lymphatic vessels, which bring lymph to the node from peripheral tissues, penetrate the capsule on the side opposite the hilum. Lymph then flows slowly through the lymph node within a network of sinuses, which are open passageways with incomplete walls. Upon arriving at the node, lymph first enters the *subcapsular space*, which contains a meshwork of branching reticular fibers, macrophages, and *dendritic cells.* **Dendritic cells** collect antigens from the lymph and present them in their cell membranes. T cells encountering these bound antigens become activated, thus initiating an immune response. After passing through the subcapsular space, lymph flows through the **outer cortex** of the node. The outer cortex contains aggregated B cells with germinal centers similar to those of lymphoid nodules.

Lymph flow continues through lymph sinuses in the **deep cortex** *(paracortical area).* Here, circulating lymphocytes leave the bloodstream and enter the lymph node by crossing the walls of blood vessels within the deep cortex. The deep cortical area is dominated by T cells.

After flowing through the sinuses of the deep cortex, lymph continues into the core, or **medulla**, of the lymph node. The medulla contains B cells and plasmocytes organized into elongate masses known as **medullary cords.** Lymph enters the efferent lymphatics at the hilum after passing through a network of sinuses in the medulla.

The lymph nodes function like a kitchen water filter: They filter and purify lymph before it reaches the venous system. As lymph flows through a lymph node, at least 99 percent of the antigens present in the arriving lymph are removed. Fixed macrophages in the walls of the lymphatic sinuses engulf debris or pathogens in the lymph as it flows past. Antigens removed in this way are then processed by the macrophages and "presented" to nearby T cells. Other antigens stick to the surfaces of dendritic cells, where they can stimulate T cell activity.

The largest lymph nodes are found where peripheral lymphatics connect with the trunk (Figure 23.4, p. 612), in regions such as the base of the neck (Figure 23.10), the axillae (Figure 23.11), and the groin

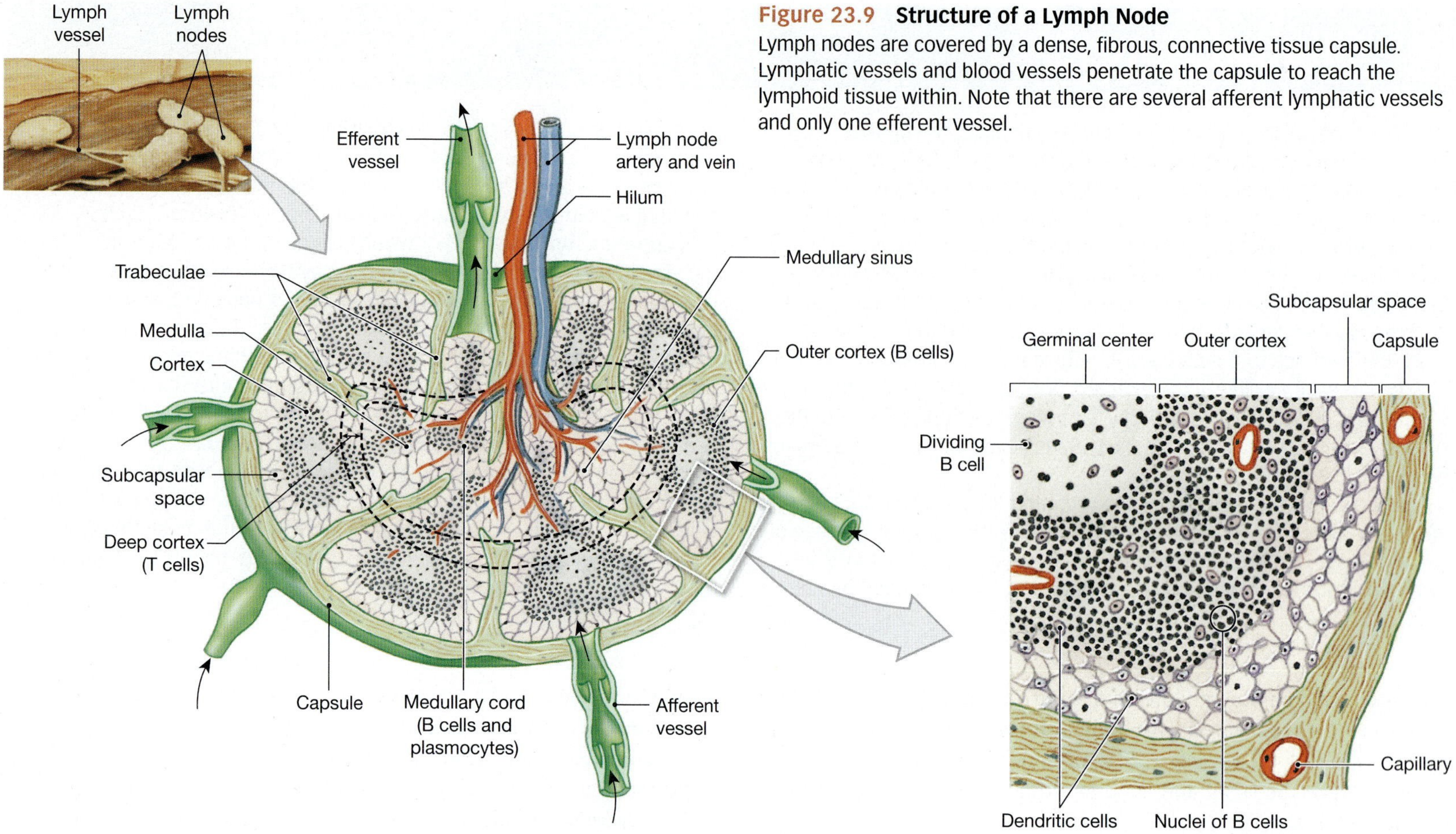

Figure 23.9 Structure of a Lymph Node
Lymph nodes are covered by a dense, fibrous, connective tissue capsule. Lymphatic vessels and blood vessels penetrate the capsule to reach the lymphoid tissue within. Note that there are several afferent lymphatic vessels and only one efferent vessel.

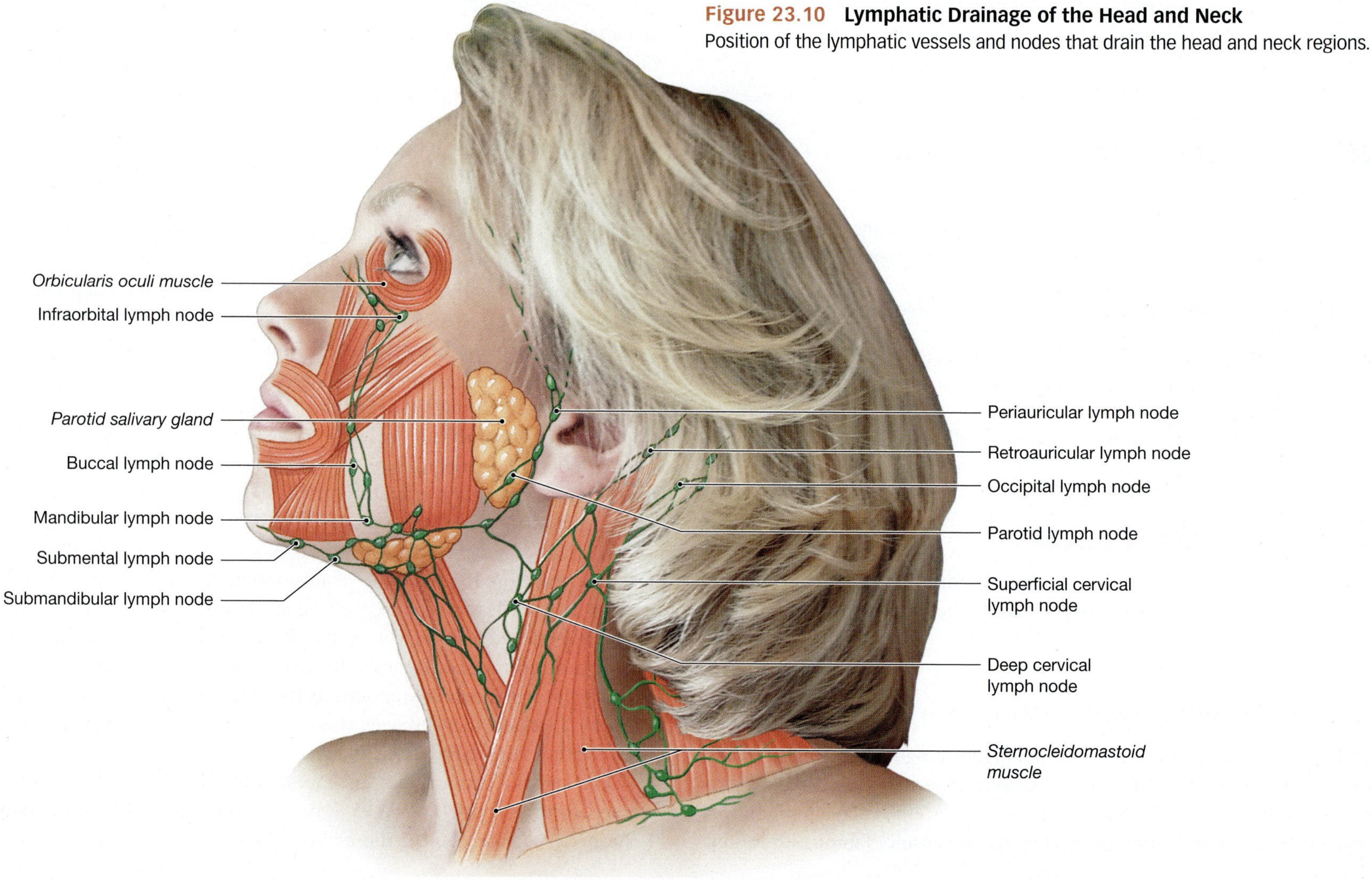

Figure 23.10 Lymphatic Drainage of the Head and Neck
Position of the lymphatic vessels and nodes that drain the head and neck regions.

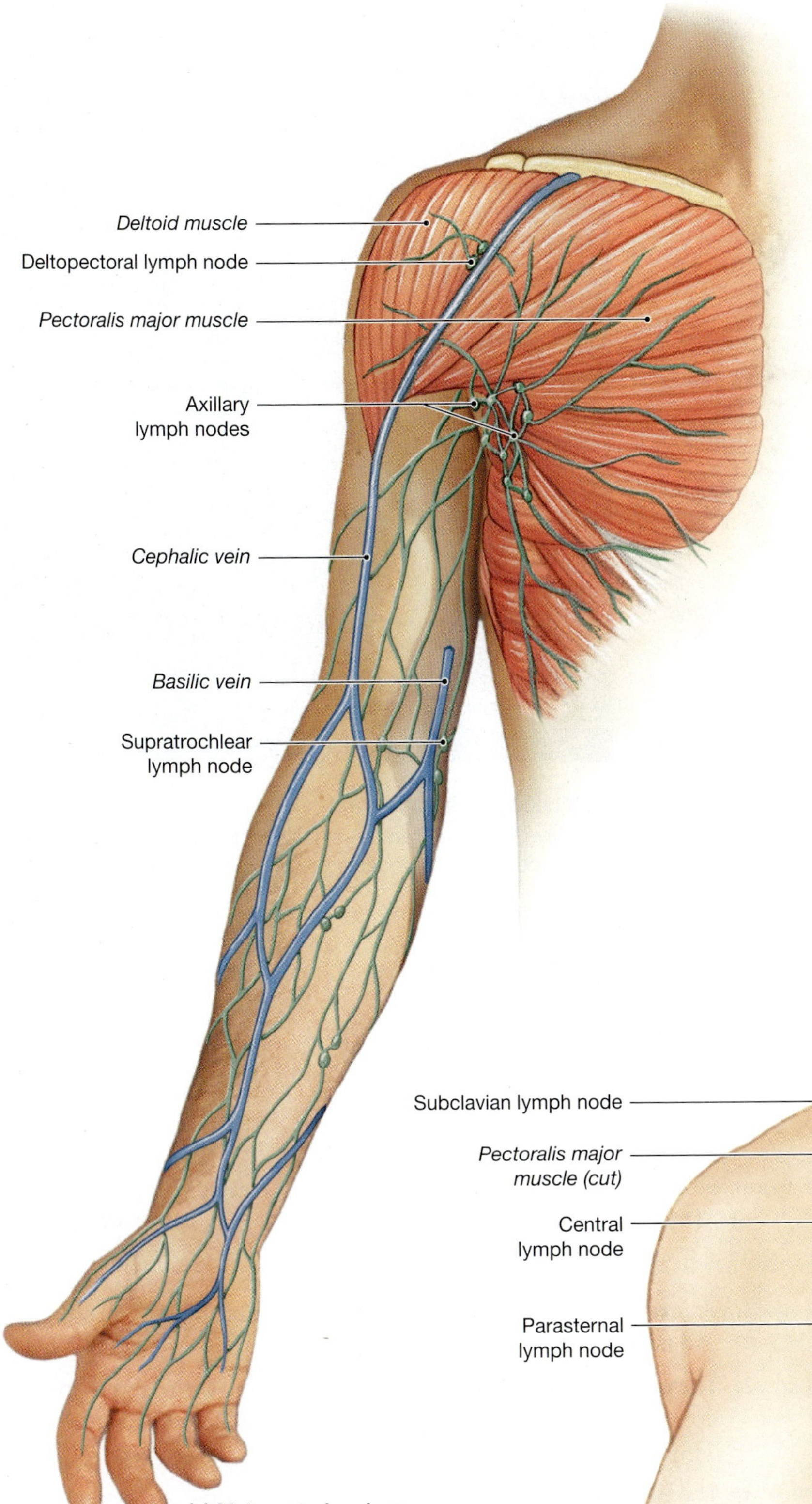

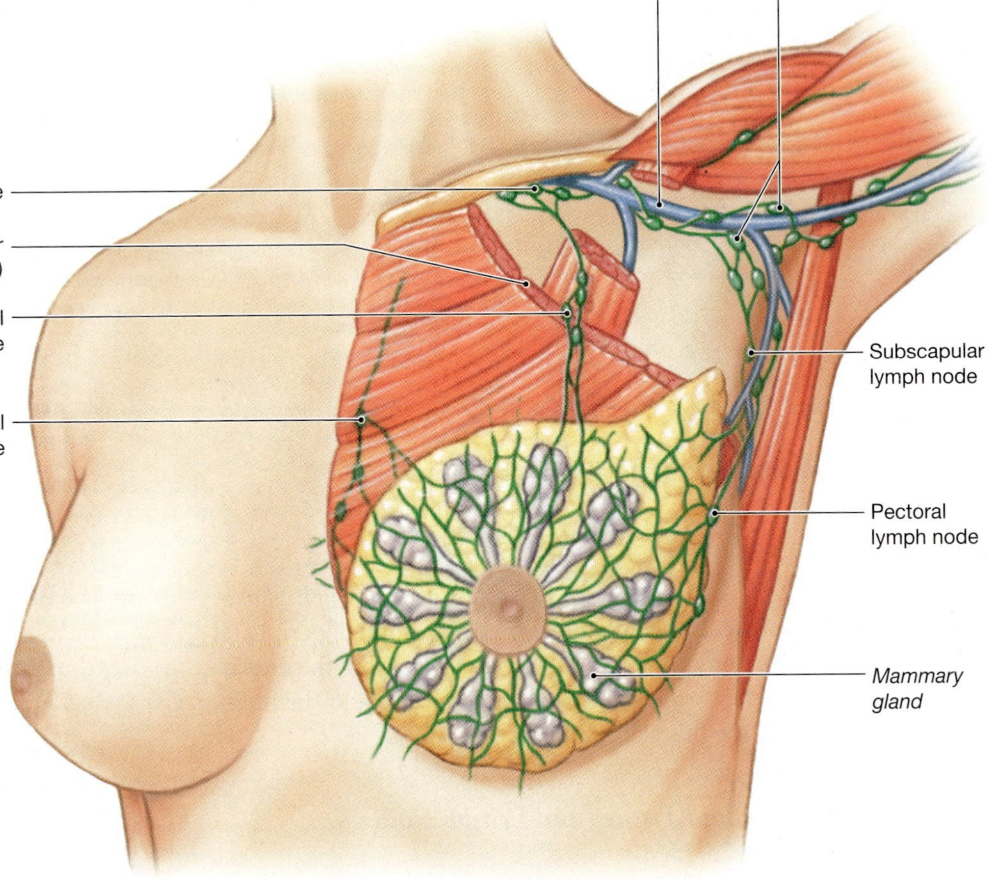

Figure 23.11 Lymphatic Drainage of the Upper Limb
(a) Superficial lymphatic vessels and nodes that drain the upper limb and chest of a male. **(b)** Superficial and deeper lymphatic vessels and nodes of the upper limb and chest of a female.

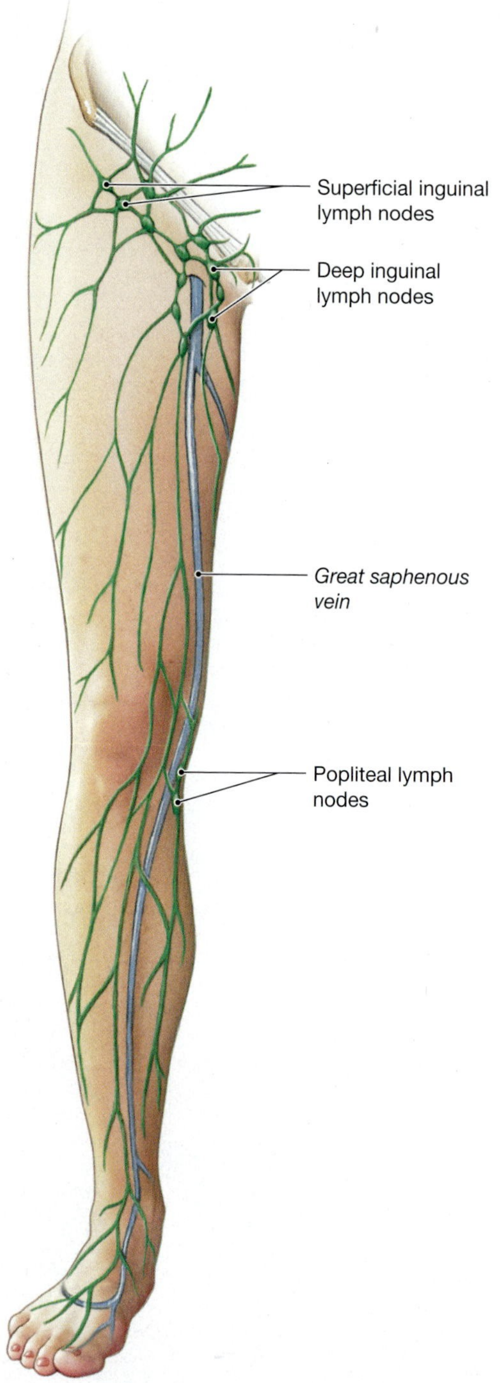

Figure 23.12 Lymphatic Drainage of the Lower Limb

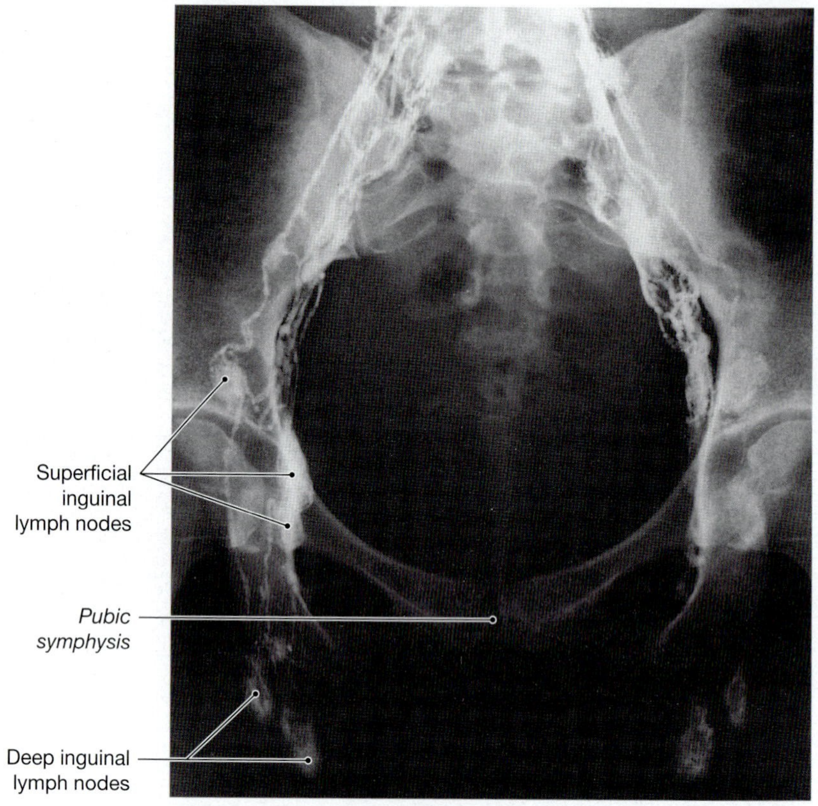

Figure 23.13 A Pelvic Lymphangiogram
The lymph vessels and lymph nodes can be visualized in a *lymphangiogram*, an x-ray taken after the introduction of a radiopaque dye into the lymphoid system.

(**Figures 23.12** to **23.14**). These nodes are often called *lymph glands.* "Swollen glands" usually indicate inflammation or infection of peripheral structures. Dense collections of lymph nodes also exist within the mesenteries of the gut, near the trachea and passageways leading to the lungs, and in association with the thoracic duct.

Distribution of Lymphoid Tissues and Lymph Nodes [Figures 23.4/23.10 to 23.15]

Lymphoid tissues and lymph nodes are distributed in areas particularly susceptible to injury or invasion. If we wanted to protect a house against intrusion, we might guard all doors and windows and perhaps keep a big dog indoors. The distribution of lymphoid tissues and lymph nodes is based on a similar strategy:

1. The **cervical lymph nodes** monitor lymph originating in the head and neck (**Figure 23.10**).
2. The **axillary lymph nodes** filter lymph arriving at the trunk from the upper limbs (**Figure 23.11a**). In women, the axillary nodes also drain lymph from the mammary glands (**Figure 23.11b**).
3. The **popliteal lymph nodes** filter lymph arriving at the thigh from the leg, and the **inguinal lymph nodes** monitor lymph arriving at the trunk from the lower limbs (**Figures 23.12** to **23.14**).
4. The **thoracic lymph nodes** receive lymph from the lungs, respiratory passageways, and mediastinal structures (**Figure 23.4**, p. 612).
5. The **abdominal lymph nodes** filter lymph arriving from the urinary and reproductive systems.
6. The lymphoid tissue of Peyer's patches, the **intestinal lymph nodes**, and the **mesenteric lymph nodes** receive lymph originating from the digestive tract (**Figure 23.15**).

Figure 23.14 Lymphatic Drainage of the Inguinal Region
(a) An anterior view of a dissection of the inguinal lymph nodes and vessels. **(b)** A superficial and deeper view of the inguinal region of a male, showing the distribution of lymph nodes and lymphatics.

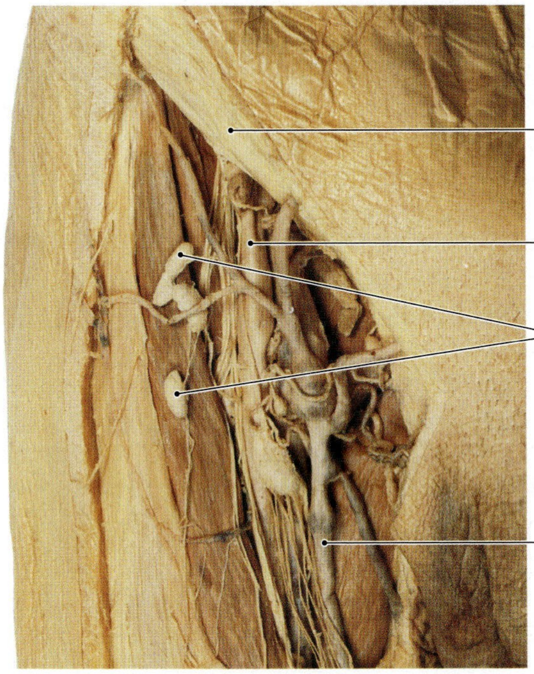

(a) Dissection of the upper right inguinal region in a male

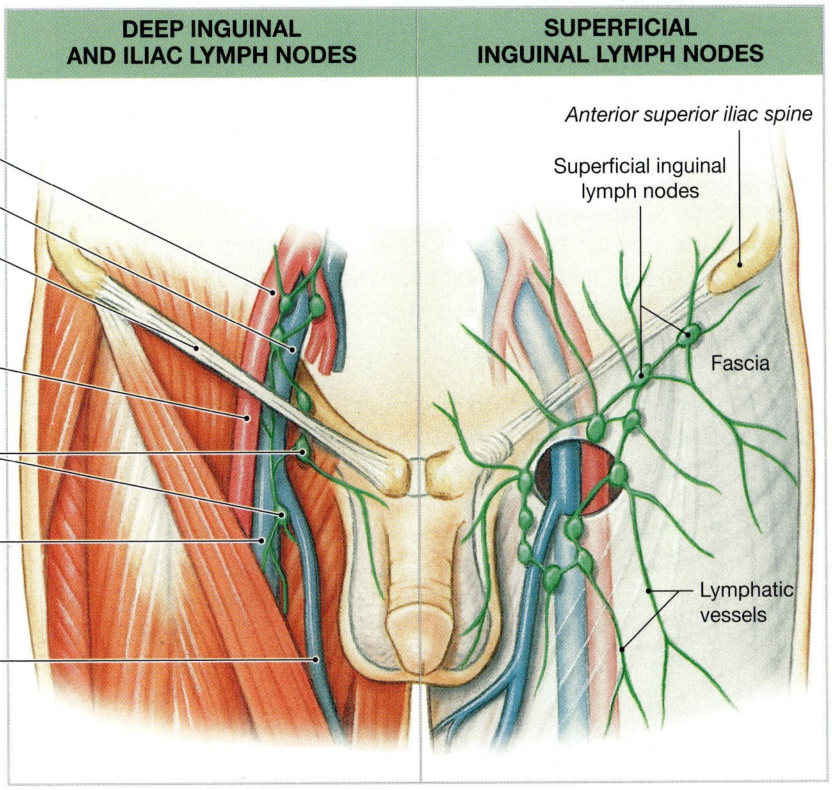

(b) Inguinal lymph nodes and vessels

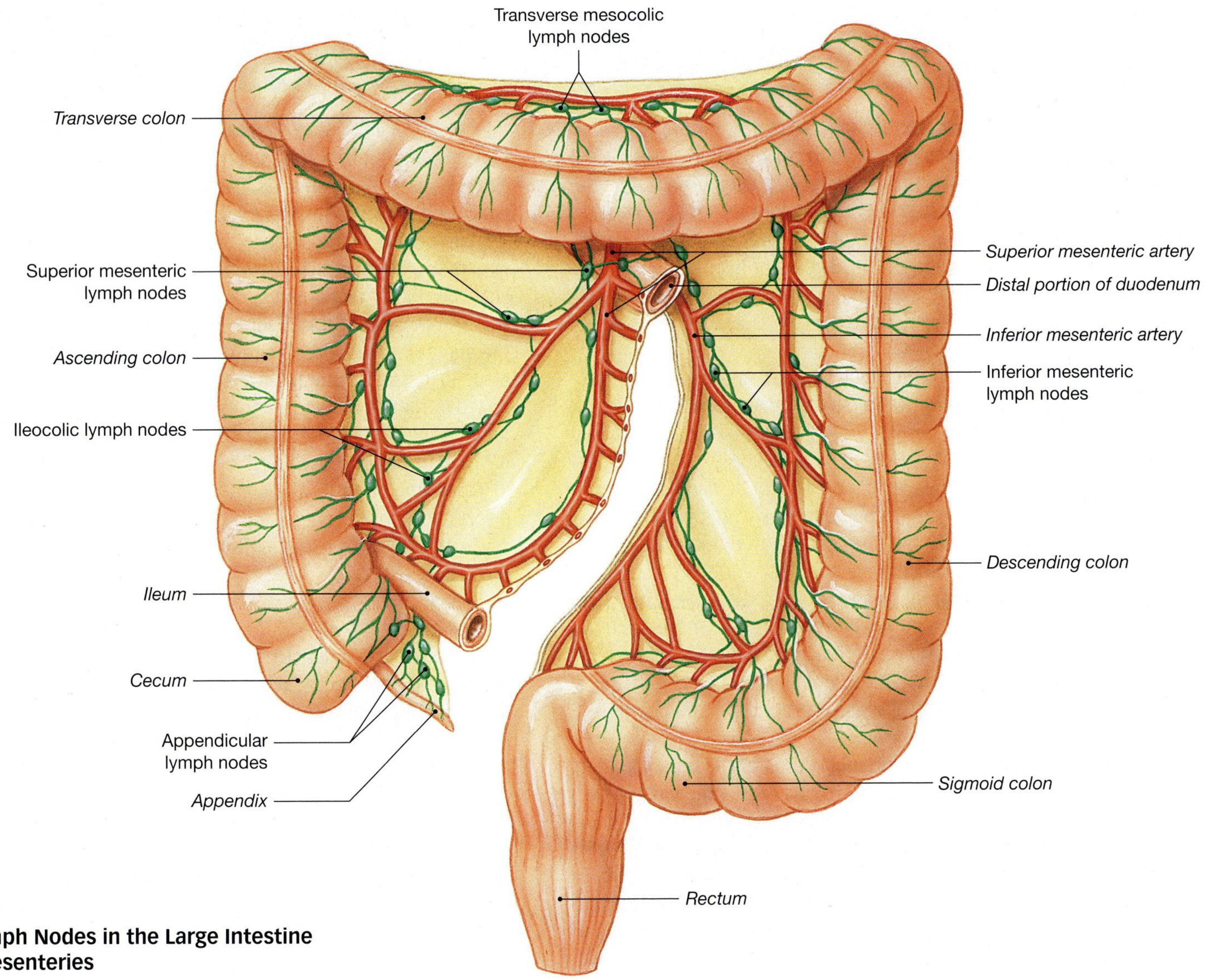

Figure 23.15 Lymph Nodes in the Large Intestine and Associated Mesenteries

Clinical Note

Lymphadenopathy and Metastatic Cancer A minor injury normally produces a slight enlargement of the nodes along the lymphatics draining the region. The enlargement usually results from an increase in the number of lymphocytes and phagocytes in the node, in response to a minor, localized infection. Chronic or excessive enlargement of lymph nodes constitutes **lymphadenopathy** (lim-fad-e-NOP-a-thē). This condition may occur in response to scarring of damaged lymphatic ducts; bacterial, viral, or parasitic infections; or cancer.

Lymphatics are found in most regions of the body, and lymphatic capillaries offer little resistance to the passage of cancer cells. As a result, metastasizing cancer cells often spread along the lymphatics. Under these circumstances the lymph nodes serve as way stations for migrating cancer cells. Thus, an analysis of lymph nodes can provide information on the spread of the cancer cells, and such information has a direct influence on the selection of appropriate therapies. One example is the classification of breast cancer or lymphomas by the degree of lymph node involvement.

The Thymus [Figure 23.16]

The **thymus** lies posterior to the manubrium of the sternum, in the superior portion of the mediastinum. It has a nodular consistency and a pinkish coloration. The thymus reaches its greatest size (relative to body size) in the first year or two after birth, and its maximum absolute size during puberty, when it weighs between 30 and 40 g. Thereafter, the thymus gradually decreases in size, and the functional cells are replaced by connective tissue fibers. This degenerative process is called *involution.*

The capsule that covers the thymus divides it into two **thymic lobes** (Figure 23.16a,b). Fibrous partitions, or **septa**, extend from the capsule to divide the lobes into **lobules** averaging 2 mm in width (Figure 23.16b,c). Each lobule consists of a dense outer **cortex** and a somewhat diffuse, paler central **medulla**. The cortex contains lymphoid stem cells that divide rapidly, producing daughter cells that mature into T cells and migrate into the medulla. During the maturation process, any T cells that are sensitive to normal tissue antigens are destroyed. The surviving T cells eventually enter one of the specialized blood vessels in that region. While they are within the thymus, T cells do not participate in the immune response; they remain inactive until they enter the general circulation. The capillaries of

Clinical Note

Lymphomas **Lymphomas** are malignant tumors consisting of cancerous lymphocytes or lymphocytic stem cells. About 61,000 cases of lymphoma are diagnosed in the United States each year. There are many types of lymphoma. One form, called *Hodgkin's disease (HD)*, accounts for roughly 13 percent of all lymphoma cases. Hodgkin's disease most commonly strikes individuals at age 15–35 years or over age 50. The reason for this pattern of incidence is unknown. Although the cause of the disease is uncertain, an infectious agent (probably a virus) may be involved.

Other types of lymphoma are usually grouped together under the heading of **non-Hodgkin's lymphoma (NHL)**. These lymphomas are extremely diverse. More than 85 percent of NHL cases are associated with chromosomal abnormalities of the tumor cells, typically involving translocations, in which sections of chromosomes have been swapped from one chromosome to another. The shifting of genes from one chromosome to another interferes with the normal regulatory mechanisms, and the cells grow uncontrollably (become cancerous). For example, one form, called **Burkitt's lymphoma**, develops only after genes from chromosome 8 have been translocated to chromosome 14. (There are at least three variations.) Burkitt's lymphoma normally affects male children in Africa and New Guinea who have been infected with the *Epstein–Barr virus (EBV).* This highly variable virus is also responsible for infectious mononucleosis.

EBV infects B cells, but under normal circumstances most infected cells are destroyed by the immune system. This virus affects many people, and childhood exposure generally produces lasting immunity. Children who develop Burkitt's lymphoma may have a genetic susceptibility to EBV infection. The first symptom usually associated with any lymphoma is a painless enlargement of lymph nodes. The involved nodes have a firm, rubbery texture. Because the nodes are pain free, the condition is typically overlooked until it has progressed far enough for secondary symptoms to appear. For example, patients seeking help for recurrent fevers, night sweats, gastrointestinal or respiratory problems, or weight loss may be unaware of any underlying lymph node changes. In the late stages of the disease, symptoms can include liver or spleen enlargement, central nervous system dysfunction, pneumonia, a variety of skin conditions, and anemia.

The most important factor influencing which treatment is selected is the stage of the disease. When the condition is diagnosed early (stage I or stage II), localized therapies may be effective. Few lymphomas are diagnosed in the early stages. For example, only 10–15 percent of NHL patients are diagnosed at stage I or stage II. For lymphomas at stages III and IV, most treatments involve chemotherapy. Combination chemotherapy, in which two or more drugs are administered simultaneously, is the most effective treatment.

A **bone marrow transplant**, or **hematologic stem cell transplant**, is a treatment option for acute, late-stage lymphoma. When suitable donor marrow stem cells are available, the patient receives whole-body irradiation, chemotherapy, or some combination of the two sufficient to kill tumor cells throughout the body. Unfortunately, this treatment also destroys normal bone marrow stem cells. Donor stem cells are then infused. Within two weeks, the donor cells colonize the bone marrow and begin producing new blood cells.

Potential complications of stem cell transplantation include the risk of infection and bleeding while the donor marrow is becoming established. For a person with stage I or stage II lymphoma without bone marrow involvement, bone marrow can be removed and stored (frozen) for more than 10 years. If other treatment options fail or if the person comes out of remission at a later date, an autologous marrow transplant can be performed.

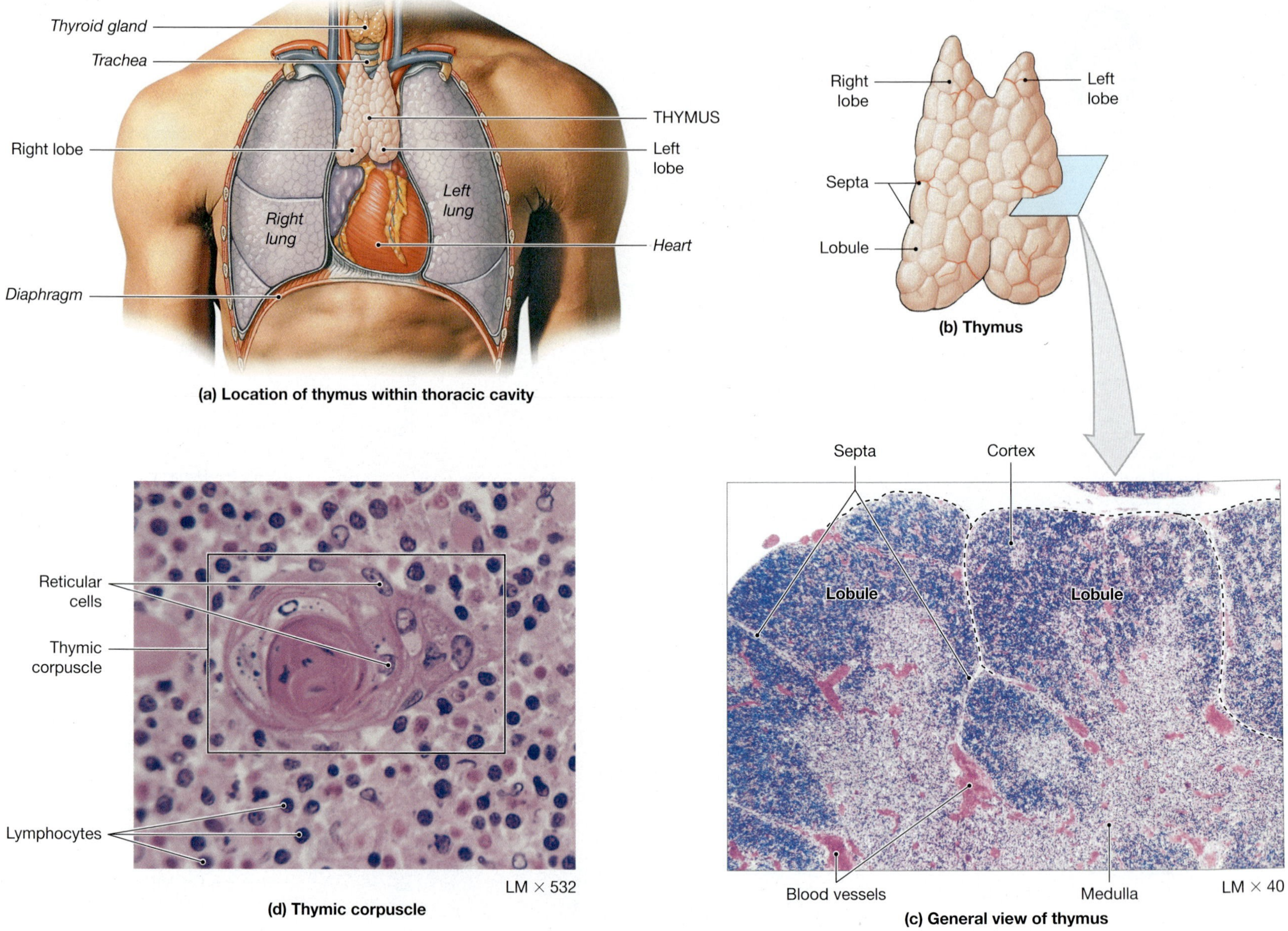

Figure 23.16 Anatomy and Histological Organization of the Thymus
(a) The location of the thymus on gross dissection; note the relationship to other organs in the chest. **(b)** Anatomical landmarks on the thymus. **(c)** Histology of the thymus. Note the fibrous septa that divide the thymic tissue into lobules resembling interconnected lymphoid nodules. The dashed line follows the edges of a single lobule. **(d)** Histology of the unusual structure of thymic corpuscles. The small cells in view are lymphocytes in various stages of development.

the thymus resemble those of the CNS in that they do not permit free exchange between the interstitial fluid and the circulation. This **blood–thymus barrier** prevents premature stimulation of the developing T cells by circulating antigens.

Reticular cells are scattered among the lymphocytes of the thymus. These cells are responsible for the production of thymic hormones that promote the differentiation of functional T cells. In the medulla, these cells cluster together in concentric layers, forming distinctive structures known as **thymic corpuscles** (Figure 23.16d), whose function remains unknown.

The Spleen [Figure 23.17a]

The **spleen** is the largest lymphoid organ in the body. It is around 12 cm (5 in.) long and weighs up to 160 g (5.6 oz). The spleen lies along the curving lateral border of the stomach, extending between the ninth and eleventh ribs on the left side. It is attached to the lateral border of the stomach by a broad mesenteric band, the **gastrosplenic ligament** (Figure 23.17a).

On gross dissection the spleen has a deep red color because of the blood it contains. The spleen performs functions for the blood comparable to those performed by the lymph nodes for lymph. The functions of the spleen include (1) the removal of abnormal blood cells and other blood components through phagocytosis, (2) the storage of iron recycled from broken down red blood cells, and (3) the initiation of immune responses by B cells and T cells in response to antigens in the circulating blood.

Surfaces of the Spleen [Figure 23.17]

The spleen has a soft consistency, and its shape primarily reflects its association with the structures around it. It lies wedged between the stomach, the left kidney, and the muscular diaphragm. The **diaphragmatic surface** (Figure 23.17a) is smooth and convex, conforming to the shape of the diaphragm and body wall. The **visceral surface** (Figure 23.17b) contains

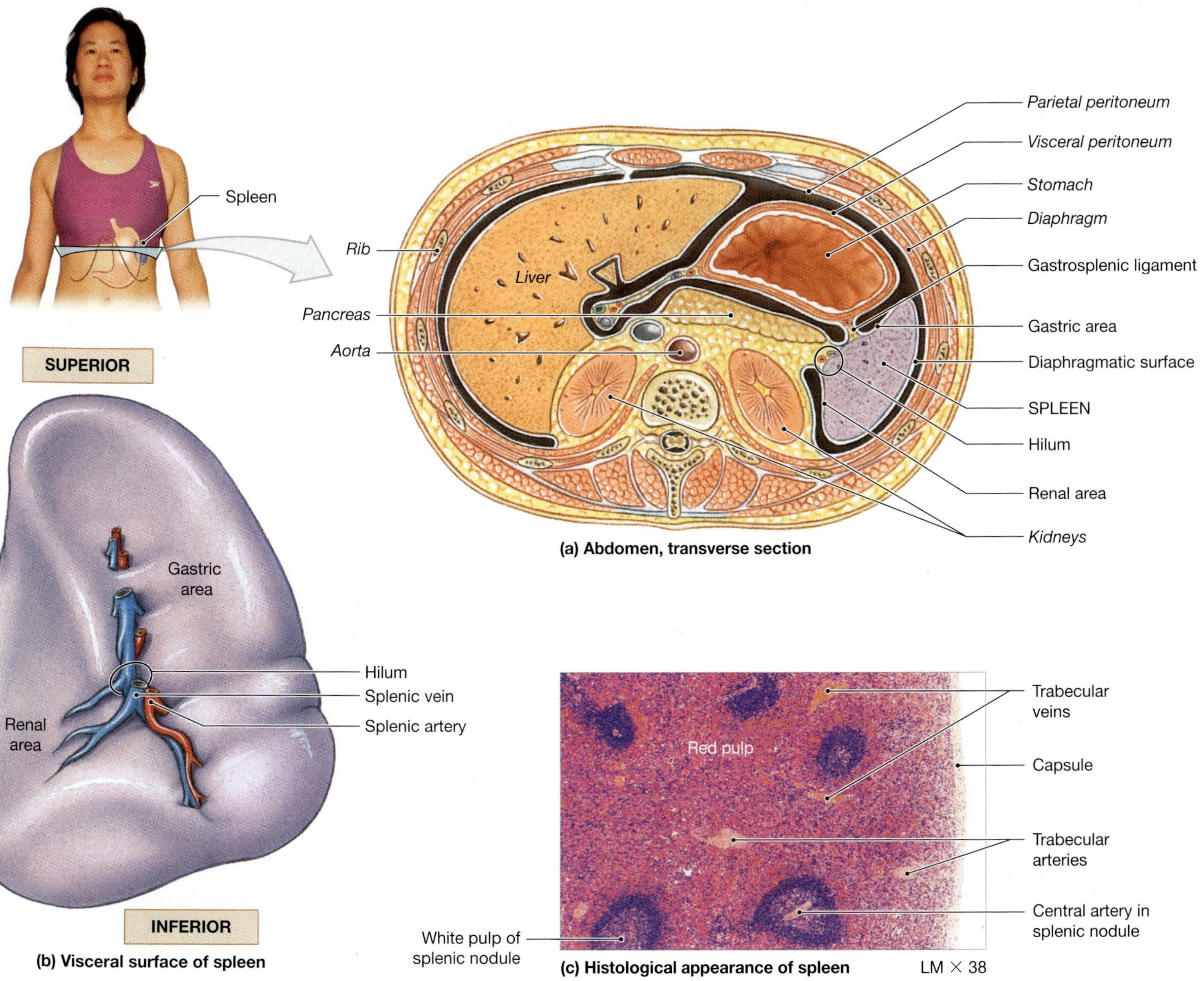

Figure 23.17 Anatomy and Histological Organization of the Spleen
(a) The shape of the spleen roughly conforms to the shapes of adjacent organs. This transverse section through the trunk shows the typical position of the spleen within the abdominopelvic cavity (inferior view). **(b)** External appearance of the visceral surface of the intact spleen, showing major anatomical landmarks. This view should be compared with that of part (a). **(c)** Histological appearance of the spleen. Areas of white pulp are dominated by lymphocytes; they appear blue or purple because the nuclei of the lymphocytes stain very darkly. Areas of red pulp contain a preponderance of red blood cells.

indentations that follow the shapes of the stomach (the **gastric area**) and kidney (the **renal area**). Splenic blood vessels and lymphatics communicate with the spleen on the visceral surface at the **hilum**, a groove marking the border between the gastric and renal areas. The **splenic artery**, the **splenic vein**, and the lymphatics draining the spleen are attached at the hilum.

Histology of the Spleen [Figure 23.17c]

The spleen is surrounded by a capsule containing collagen and elastic fibers. The cellular components within constitute the **pulp** of the spleen (Figure 23.17c). Areas of **red pulp** form *splenic cords*, which contain large quantities of red blood cells, whereas areas of **white pulp** form lymphoid nodules. The splenic artery enters at the hilum and branches to produce a number of arteries that radiate outward toward the capsule. These **trabecular arteries** branch extensively, and their arteriolar branches are surrounded by areas of white pulp. Capillaries then discharge the blood into the venous sinuses of the red pulp.

The cell population of the red pulp includes all of the normal components of the circulating blood, plus fixed and free macrophages. The structural framework of the red pulp consists of a network of reticular fibers. The blood passes through this meshwork and enters large sinusoids, also lined by fixed macrophages. The sinusoids empty into small veins, and these ultimately merge to form **trabecular veins**, which continue toward the hilum.

This circulatory arrangement gives the phagocytes of the spleen an opportunity to identify and engulf any damaged or infected cells in the circulating blood. Lymphocytes are scattered throughout the red pulp, and the region surrounding each area of white pulp has a high concentration of macrophages. Thus, any microorganisms or abnormal plasma components will quickly come to the attention of the splenic lymphocytes.

Embryology Summary

For a summary of the development of the lymphoid system, see Chapter 28 (Embryology and Human Development).

CONCEPT CHECK

1. Why is it important that lymph encounters T cells before B cells?
2. What is important about the placement of lymph nodes?
3. Why is there a blood–thymus barrier in the capillaries of the thymus?
4. Why do lymph nodes often enlarge during an infection?

See blue "Answers" tab at back of book.

Aging and the Lymphoid System

With advancing age, the lymphoid system becomes less effective at combating disease. T cells become less responsive to antigens; as a result, fewer cytotoxic T cells respond to an infection. Because the number of helper T cells is also reduced, B cells are less responsive, and antibody levels do not rise as quickly after antigen exposure. The net result is an increased susceptibility to viral and bacterial infection. For this reason, vaccinations for acute viral diseases, such as the flu (influenza), are strongly recommended for elderly individuals. The increased incidence of cancer in the elderly reflects the fact that surveillance by the lymphoid system declines, and tumor cells are not eliminated as effectively.

Clinical Case — THE LYMPHOID SYSTEM

I FEEL LIKE I AM GOING TO SUFFOCATE! WHAT'S HAPPENING TO ME?

Jan is a 46-year-old married mother of two living in Colorado. Her entire family loves the outdoors and does a considerable amount of biking and hiking on the weekends. Lately, she has noticed occasional difficulty keeping up on the family hikes in the mountains. She has also noticed an increased feeling of generalized fatigue, and an increased incidence of chest pains upon taking a really deep breath—particularly during exercise. At night, Jan feels as if she can't get a deep enough breath, and she often sits up to take a few deep breaths before going back to sleep. She mentioned this to her physician during her last yearly physical, but the physician found no abnormalities when listening to Jan's heart and lungs or when checking her pulse, blood pressure, and respiration. They discussed a chest x-ray, but with no history of smoking and no presence of wheezing or other abnormal breath sounds, Jan and her physician decided not to do an x-ray unless Jan developed progressive problems.

Several months later, Jan gets a respiratory infection with a runny nose and cough. Since she typically recovers in a few days with chicken soup and plenty of rest, Jan cuts down on her daily activities and waits to get better. Early Sunday morning, Jan awakens with chest pain and a sensation of near suffocation and fainting. Sitting up alleviates the problems slightly. Jan and her husband wait until the Urgent Care Clinic opens at 8 a.m. She is the first patient seen by the physician.

Initial Examination

The physician in the Urgent Care Clinic notes the following:

- Blood pressure, HDL and LDL levels are all within normal ranges as they have been for the last five years, including Jan's most recent physical.
- Current blood pressure is 112/76.
- An ECG (electrocardiogram) does not show evidence of myocardial ischemia or infarction.
- The patient has no family history of heart problems or stroke.
- The patient complains of generalized fatigue that has increased in duration and intensity over the last five months.
- The patient is experiencing generalized chest pain, and she reports a sensation of near suffocation and fainting.

The physician orders an anterior-posterior view chest x-ray. The x-ray reveals a widened mediastinum and an opacity in the anterior mediastinal area (Figure 23.18). Jan is immediately rushed to the local hospital for further examination.

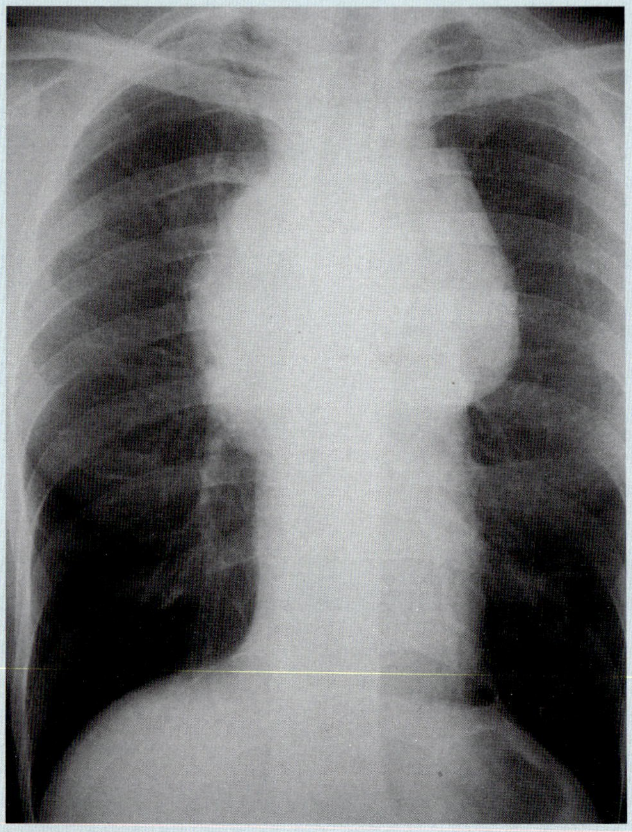

Figure 23.18 Jan's x-ray

Clinical Case *continued*

Follow-up Examination

The physician at the hospital reviews the clinical findings from the Urgent Care Clinic and orders an MRI. The MRI reveals the following.

- A large mass is present in the anterior mediastinum.
- The large mass appears to be pressing on Jan's heart and tracheal bifurcation.

Jan undergoes surgery, and a mass is removed from her anterior mediastinum.

Points to Consider

As you consider the case presented above, review the material covered in Chapter 23 on the lymphoid system. The questions below will guide you in your review. Think about and answer each one.

1. Where is the mediastinum located?
2. What anatomical structures are located within the mediastinum?
3. Jan's symptoms have worsened over the past year. What would account for these changes in her symptoms?

Analysis and Interpretation

The information below answers the questions raised in the "Points to Consider" section. To review the material, refer to the pages in the chapter indicated by the link icons.

1. The mediastinum extends from the superior thoracic aperture to the diaphragm, and from the sternum anteriorly to the thoracic vertebrae posteriorly. pp. 18–19
2. The mediastinum contains the trachea, esophagus, pericardial sac, heart and its major vessels, thymus, and thoracic lymph nodes. The mediastinum also serves as a passageway for structures such as the esophagus, thoracic duct, and components of the nervous system as they pass from the thoracic cavity into the abdominal cavity. pp. 18–20
3. As a mass in the mediastinum increases in size, it will press upon various structures within the mediastinum. The increased pressure upon the trachea, bronchi, and lungs would account for Jan's shortness of breath and sensation of suffocation, while pressure on the heart and great vessels of the thoracic cavity would cause her sensation of fainting.

Diagnosis

Jan is diagnosed as having a thoracic (mediastinal) lymphoma. A solid tumor growth of lymphocytes may result in a benign (noncancerous) lymphadenopathy, or a malignant lymphoma, a cancerous tumor involving one or more lymph nodes of the body. Malignant lymphoma tumors are classified as either **Hodgkin's disease (HD)** or **non-Hodgkin's lymphoma (NHL)**. The thoracic cavity is involved in 85 percent of all cases of HD, and 45 percent of all cases of NHL.

Non-Hodgkin's lymphoma is a term used to describe a variety of cancers. Non-Hodgkin's lymphomas are often classified by the type of cell that is involved in the formation of the malignant tumor, such as B or T cell lymphomas. In 2007, NHL accounts for approximately 4 percent of all newly diagnosed cancers in the United States. NHL incidence increases in patients taking immunosuppressive drugs and in those individuals with HIV infection. For unknown reasons, an increased incidence of NHL has been seen in women in the last 20 years. Advances in chemotherapy and radiation therapy have prolonged the survival time of all NHL patients, with the five-year relative survival rate now being 63 percent.

CLINICAL CASE TERMS

B cell lymphoma (B cell leukemia): A cancerous lymphoid tumor resulting from abnormal growth and multiplication of B lymphocytes.

ECG (electrocardiogram): A graphic record of the heart's action potentials obtained by placing recording electrodes on the skin of a patient.

HDL (high-density lipoproteins): A class of lipoproteins found in the blood whose main function is transporting cholesterol to the liver for excretion as bile.

LDL (low-density lipoproteins): A class of lipoproteins found in the blood whose main function is transporting cholesterol to tissues other than the liver.

leukemia: A form of cancer characterized by the progressive proliferation of abnormal leukocytes in bone marrow and other hemopoietic tissues, resulting in the increased number of abnormal leukocytes found in the blood and other tissues.

lymphadenopathy: Any disease affecting one or more lymph nodes.

T cell lymphoma (T cell leukemia): A cancerous lymphoid tumor resulting from abnormal growth and multiplication of T lymphocytes.

CLINICAL TERMS

acquired immune deficiency syndrome (AIDS): A disorder that develops after HIV infection, characterized by reduced T cell populations and depressed cellular immunity.

allergy: An inappropriate or excessive immune response to antigens.

appendicitis: Inflammation of the appendix, often requiring treatment in the form of an *appendectomy*.

autoimmune disorder: A disorder that develops when the immune response mistakenly targets normal body cells and tissues.

immunodeficiency disease: A disease in which either the immune system fails to develop normally or the immune response is somehow blocked.

lymphadenopathy (lim-fad-e-NOP-a-thē): Chronic or excessive enlargement of lymph nodes.

lymphomas: Malignant cancers consisting of abnormal lymphocytes or lymphocytic stem cells; include **Hodgkin's disease** and **non-Hodgkin's lymphoma**.

severe combined immunodeficiency disease (SCID): A congenital condition in which an individual fails to develop either cellular or humoral immunity because of a lack of normal B and T cells.

splenectomy (splē-NEK-tō-mē): Surgical removal of the spleen, usually after splenic rupture.

splenomegaly (splē-nō-MEG-a-lē): Enlargement of the spleen; often caused by infection, inflammation, or cancer.

systemic lupus erythematosus (LOO-pus e-rith-ē-ma-TŌ-sis) **(SLE):** A condition resulting from a generalized breakdown in the antigen-recognition mechanism.

tonsillectomy: The removal of an infected tonsil to remove symptoms of **tonsillitis**.

STUDY OUTLINE

Introduction 609

1. The cells, tissues, and organs of the *lymphoid system* play a central role in the body's defenses against viruses, bacteria, and other microorganisms.

An Overview of the Lymphoid System 609

1. The **lymphoid system** includes a network of lymphatic vessels that carry **lymph** (a fluid similar to plasma but with a lower concentration of proteins). A series of lymphoid organs and lymphoid tissues are interconnected by the lymphatic vessels. *(see Figures 23.1/23.2)*

Functions of the Lymphoid System 609

2. The lymphoid system produces, maintains, and distributes lymphocytes (cells that attack invading organisms, abnormal cells, and foreign proteins). The system also helps maintain blood volume and eliminate local variations in the composition of the interstitial fluid. Lymphoid structures can be classified as *primary* (containing stem cells) or *secondary* (containing immature or activated lymphocytes).

Structure of Lymphatic Vessels 610

Lymphatic Capillaries 610

1. **Lymphatic vessels**, or *lymphatics*, carry lymph from peripheral tissues to the venous system. Lymph flows along a network of lymphatics that originate in the **lymphatic capillaries** *(terminal lymphatics)*. The endothelial cells of a lymphatic capillary overlap to act as a one-way valve, preventing fluid from returning to the intercellular spaces. *(see Figure 23.2b)*

Valves of Lymphatic Vessels 611

2. Lymphatics contain numerous internal valves to prevent backflow of lymph.

Major Lymph-Collecting Vessels 612

3. Two sets of lymphatic vessels collect blood from the lymphatic capillaries: the **superficial lymphatics** and the **deep lymphatics**. The lymphatic vessels empty into the **thoracic duct** and the **right lymphatic duct**. *(see Figures 23.2 to 23.5)*

Lymphocytes 613

Types of Lymphocytes 613

1. There are three different classes of lymphocytes: **T cells** (thymus-dependent), **B cells** (bone marrow–derived), and **NK cells** (natural killer). *(see Figures 23.6/23.7)*
2. **Cytotoxic T cells** attack foreign cells or body cells infected by viruses; they provide **cell-mediated immunity**. *Regulatory T cells* (**helper** and **suppressor**) regulate and coordinate the immune response, while **memory T cells** remain "on reserve." *(see Figure 23.6)*
3. B cells can differentiate into **plasmocytes**, which produce and secrete *antibodies* that react with specific chemical targets, or **antigens**. Antibodies in body fluids are called **immunoglobulins**. B cells are responsible for **antibody-mediated immunity**. **Memory B cells** are activated if the antigen appears again at a later date. *(see Figure 23.6)*
4. NK cells (also called *large granular lymphocytes*) attack foreign cells, normal cells infected with viruses, and cancer cells. They provide **immunological surveillance**.

Lymphocytes and the Immune Response 614

5. The goal of the **immune response** is the destruction or inactivation of pathogens, abnormal cells, and foreign molecules such as toxins. Antigens are engulfed by macrophages, which then present the antigen to T cells so they can begin differentiating. The millions of different lymphocytes, which retain the ability to divide, allow the body to be prepared for any antigen. The ability to recognize antigens is called *immunocompetence. (see Figure 23.6)*

Distribution and Life Span of Lymphocytes 615

Lymphopoiesis: Lymphocyte Production 615

6. Lymphocytes continually migrate in and out of the blood through the lymphoid tissues and organs and, in general, have relatively long life spans. **Lymphopoiesis** (lymphocyte production) involves the bone marrow, thymus, and peripheral lymphoid tissues. *(see Figure 23.7)*

Lymphoid Tissues 616

1. **Lymphoid tissues** are connective tissues dominated by lymphocytes. In a **lymphoid nodule**, the lymphocytes are densely packed in an area of loose connective tissue. Important lymphoid nodules are **aggregated lymphoid nodules** beneath the lining of the intestine, the *appendix*, and the **tonsils** in the walls of the pharynx. *(see Figure 23.8)*

Lymphoid Organs 617

1. Important **lymphoid organs** include the *lymph nodes*, the *thymus*, and the *spleen. (see Figures 23.1/23.9 to 23.15)*

Lymph Nodes 617

2. **Lymph nodes** are encapsulated masses of lymphoid tissue. The **deep cortex** is dominated by T cells; the **outer cortex** and **medulla** contain B cells arranged into **medullary cords**. **Lymph glands** are the largest lymph nodes, found where peripheral lymphatics connect with the trunk. *(see Figures 23.1/23.9 to 23.15)*
3. Lymphoid tissues and nodes are located in areas particularly susceptible to injury or invasion by microorganisms.
4. The **cervical lymph nodes, axillary lymph nodes, popliteal lymph nodes, inguinal lymph nodes, thoracic lymph nodes, abdominal lymph nodes, intestinal lymph nodes**, and **mesenterial lymph nodes** serve to protect the vulnerable areas of the body. *(see Figures 23.4/23.5/23.10 to 23.15)*

The Thymus 622

5. The **thymus** lies posterior to the manubrium, in the superior mediastinum. **Epithelial cells** scattered among the lymphocytes produce thymic hormones. These hormones promote the differentiation of T cells. The **blood–thymus barrier** does not allow free exchange between the interstitial fluid and the circulation, protecting the T cells from being prematurely activated. After puberty the thymus gradually decreases in size, a process called *involution. (see Figure 23.16)*

The Spleen 623

6. The adult **spleen** contains the largest mass of lymphoid tissue in the body. The spleen performs the same functions for the blood that lymph nodes perform for the lymph. The **diaphragmatic surface** of the spleen lies against the diaphragm; the **visceral surface** is against the stomach and kidney and contains a groove called the **hilum**. The cellular components form the **pulp** of the spleen. **Red pulp** contains large numbers of red blood cells, and areas of **white pulp** resemble lymphoid nodules. Lymphocytes are scattered throughout the red pulp, and the region surrounding the white pulp has a high concentration of macrophages. *(see Figure 23.17)*

Aging and the Lymphoid System 625

1. With aging, the immune system becomes less effective at combating disease.

CHAPTER REVIEW

For answers to the Concept Check and Chapter Review questions, go to the blue "Answers" tab at the back of the book.

Level 1 Reviewing Facts and Terms

Match each numbered item with the most closely related lettered item. Use letters for answers in the spaces provided.

Column A	Column B
___ 1. plasmocytes	a. terminal lymphatics
___ 2. spleen	b. responsible for cell-mediated immunity
___ 3. thymus	c. produce antibodies
___ 4. cytotoxic T cells	d. aid in immunological surveillance
___ 5. antibodies	e. contains developing T cells
___ 6. NK cells	f. immunoglobulins
___ 7. lymphatic capillaries	g. responsible for antibody-mediated immunity
___ 8. cisterna chyli	h. production of lymphocytes
___ 9. lymphopoiesis	i. saclike chamber of the thoracic duct
___10. B cells	j. largest lymphoid organ in the body

11. The lymphoid system is composed of
    (a) lymphatic vessels (b) the spleen
    (c) lymph nodes (d) all of the above

12. Compared to blood capillaries, lymph capillaries
    (a) have a basal lamina
    (b) are smaller in diameter
    (c) have walls of a smooth endothelial lining
    (d) are frequently irregular in shape

13. Most of the lymph returns to the venous circulation by way of the
    (a) right lymphatic duct (b) cisterna chyli
    (c) hepatic portal vein (d) thoracic duct

14. Some cells known as lymphocytes
    (a) are actively phagocytic
    (b) destroy red blood cells
    (c) produce proteins called antibodies
    (d) are primarily found in red bone marrow

15. ____________________ are large lymphoid nodules located in the walls of the pharynx.
    (a) Tonsils (b) Lymph nodes
    (c) Thymus gland (d) Thymic corpuscles

16. Areas of the spleen that contain large numbers of lymphocytes are known as
    (a) white pulp (b) red pulp
    (c) adenoids (d) lymph nodes

17. The red pulp of the spleen contains large numbers of
    (a) macrophages (b) antibodies
    (c) neutrophils (d) lymphocytes

18. The cells responsible for the production of circulating antibodies are
    (a) NK cells (b) plasmocytes
    (c) helper T cells (d) cytotoxic T cells

19. The medullary cords of a lymph node contain
    (a) cytotoxic T cells (b) suppressor T cells
    (c) NK cells (d) B cells

20. Lymphocytes that attack foreign cells or body cells infected with viruses are
    (a) B cells (b) helper T cells
    (c) cytotoxic T cells (d) suppressor T cells

Level 2 Reviewing Concepts

1. If the thymus failed to produce the hormone thymosin, we would expect to see a decrease in the number of
   (a) B lymphocytes (b) NK cells
   (c) cytotoxic T cells (d) neutrophils

2. The human immunodeficiency virus (HIV) that causes the disease known as AIDS selectively infects
   (a) helper T cells (b) plasmocytes
   (c) cytotoxic T cells (d) suppressor T cells

3. Blocking the antigen receptors on the surface of lymphocytes would interfere with
   (a) phagocytosis of the antigen
   (b) that lymphocyte's ability to produce antibodies
   (c) antigen recognition
   (d) the ability of the lymphocyte to present antigen

4. What is the function of the blood–thymus barrier?

5. What major artery and vein pass through the hilum of the spleen?

6. From what areas of the body does the thoracic duct collect lymph?

7. Which type of lymphocyte is most common?

8. What is lymphedema?

9. What occurs in secondary lymphoid structures?

10. Where are aggregated lymphoid nodules, also termed Peyer's patches, found?

Level 3 Critical Thinking

1. Tom has just been exposed to the measles virus, and since he can't remember whether he has had measles before, he wonders whether he is going to come down with the disease. He asks you how he can tell whether he has been previously exposed or is going to get sick before it actually happens. What would you tell him?

2. Willy is allergic to ragweed pollen and tells you that he read about a medication that can help his condition by suppressing his immune response. Do you think that this treatment could help Willy? Explain.

3. Paula's grandfather is diagnosed as having lung cancer. His physician orders biopsies of several lymph nodes from neighboring regions of the body, and Paula wonders why, since the cancer is in his lungs. What would you tell her?

24

The Respiratory System

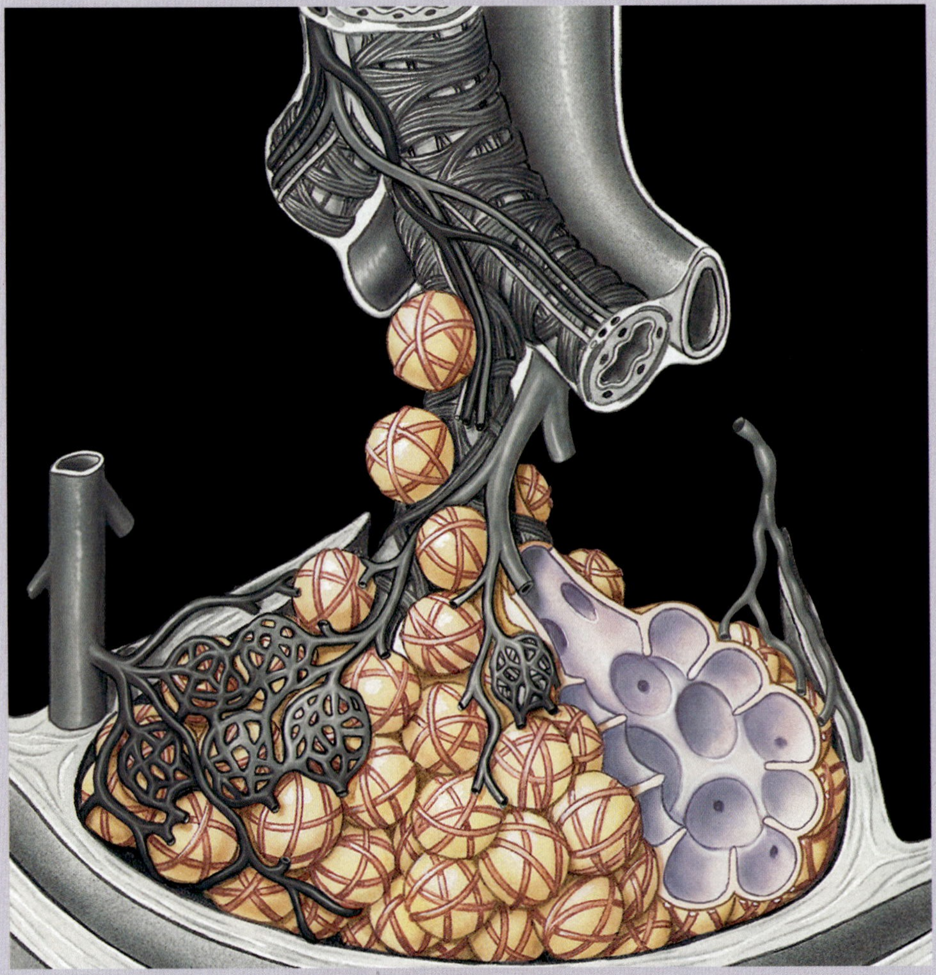

CHAPTER OBJECTIVES

1. Describe the primary functions of the respiratory system.
2. Describe the structural organization of the respiratory system and its major organs.
3. Distinguish between the conducting and respiratory portions of the respiratory tract.
4. Describe the histology and function of the respiratory epithelium.
5. Describe the functional anatomy of the components of the upper respiratory system.
6. Describe the functional anatomy of the larynx and explain its role in respiration and sound production.
7. Discuss the gross anatomical and histological specializations of the trachea.
8. Describe the histological specializations of the conducting and respiratory portions of the lower respiratory system.
9. Describe the functional anatomy of the bronchial tree and bronchopulmonary segments.
10. Describe the structure and function of the respiratory membrane.
11. Describe the pleural cavities and pleural membranes.
12. Identify the muscles of respiration and discuss the movements responsible for pulmonary ventilation.
13. Distinguish between the muscles involved in quiet respiration versus forced respiration.
14. Explain how muscular activity results in the movement of air to and from the alveoli.
15. Describe the changes that occur in the respiratory system at birth.
16. Identify the respiratory control centers, how they interact, and the function of the chemoreceptors and stretch receptors in the control of respiration.
17. Identify the reflexes that regulate respiration.
18. Describe the changes that occur in the respiratory system with age.

Cells obtain energy primarily through aerobic metabolism, a process that requires oxygen and produces carbon dioxide. For cells to survive, they must have a way to obtain that oxygen and eliminate the carbon dioxide. The cardiovascular system provides the link between the interstitial fluids around peripheral cells and the gas-exchange surfaces of the lungs. The respiratory system facilitates the exchange of gases between the air and the blood. As it circulates, blood carries oxygen from the lungs to peripheral tissues; it also accepts the carbon dioxide produced by these tissues and transports it to the lungs for elimination.

We begin our discussion of the respiratory system by describing the anatomical structures that conduct air from the external environment to the gas-exchange surfaces in the lungs. We will then discuss the mechanics of breathing and the neural control of respiration.

An Overview of the Respiratory System [Figure 24.1]

The **respiratory system** includes the nose, the nasal cavity and sinuses, the pharynx, the larynx (voice box), the trachea (windpipe), and smaller conducting passageways leading to the gas-exchange surfaces of the lungs. These structures are illustrated in Figure 24.1. The **respiratory tract** consists of the airways that carry air to and from these surfaces. The respiratory tract can be divided into a *conducting portion* and a *respiratory portion*. The conducting portion extends from the entrance to the nasal cavity to the smallest *bronchioles* of the lungs. The respiratory portion of the tract includes the *respiratory bronchioles* and the delicate air sacs, or **alveoli** (al-VĒ-ō-lī), where gas exchange occurs.

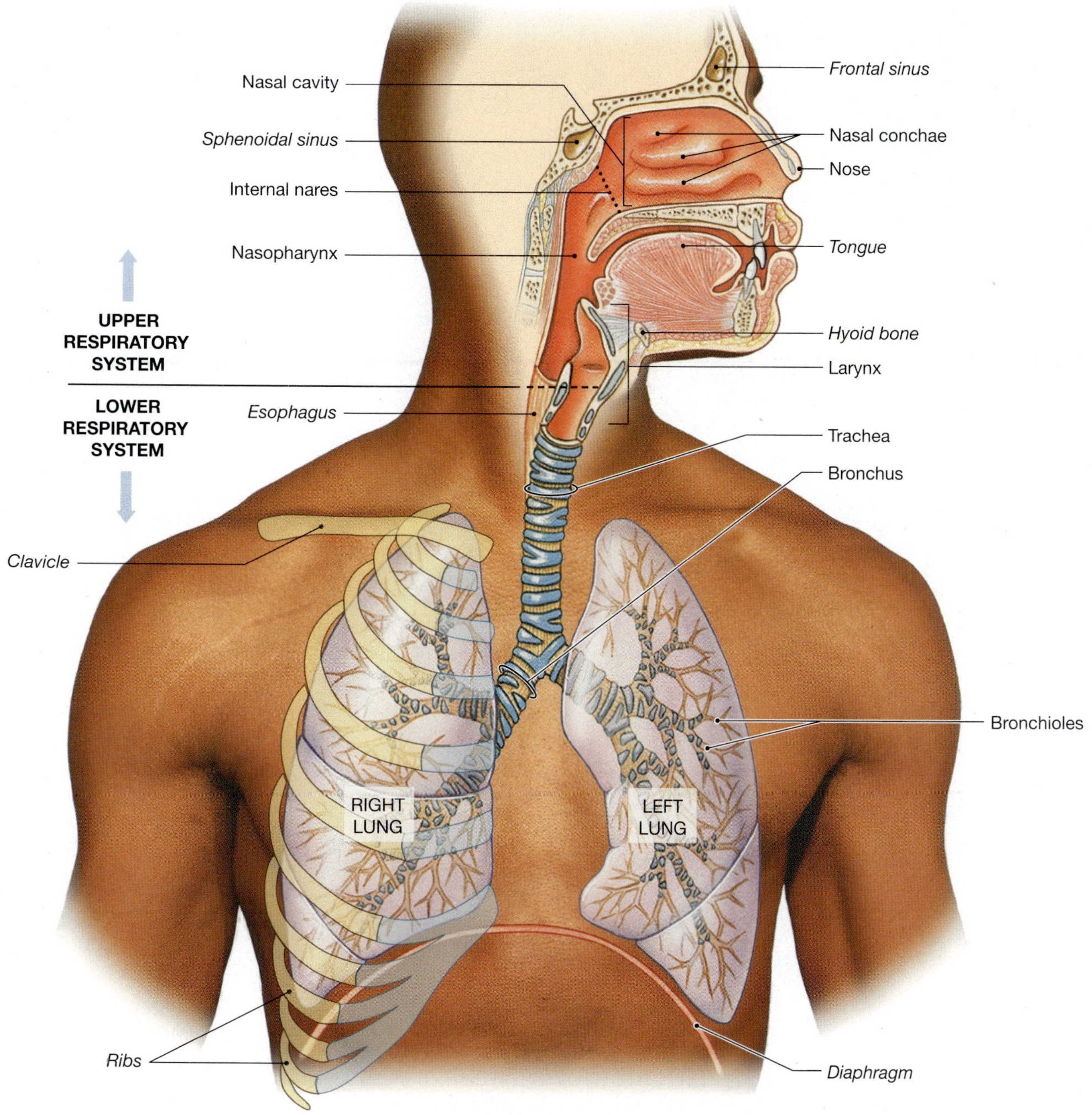

Figure 24.1 Structures of the Respiratory System

The respiratory system includes the respiratory tract and the associated tissues, organs, and supporting structures. The **upper respiratory system** consists of the nose, nasal cavity, paranasal sinuses, and pharynx. These passageways filter, warm, and humidify the air, protecting the more delicate conduction and exchange surfaces of the **lower respiratory system** from debris, pathogens, and environmental extremes. The lower respiratory system includes the larynx, trachea, bronchi, and lungs.

Filtering, warming, and humidification of the inhaled air begin at the entrance to the upper respiratory system and continue throughout the rest of the conducting system. By the time the air reaches lung alveoli, most foreign particles and pathogens have been removed, and the humidity and temperature are within acceptable limits. The success of this "conditioning process" is due primarily to the properties of the *respiratory epithelium*, discussed in a later section.

Functions of the Respiratory System

The functions of the respiratory system are:

1. Providing an extensive area for gas exchange between air and circulating blood;
2. Moving air to and from the exchange surfaces of the lungs;
3. Protecting respiratory surfaces from dehydration, temperature changes, and other environmental variations;
4. Defending the respiratory system and other tissues from invasion by pathogenic microorganisms;
5. Producing sounds involved in speaking, singing, or nonverbal communication;
6. Assisting in the regulation of blood volume, blood pressure, and the control of body fluid pH.

The respiratory system performs these functions with the cooperation of the cardiovascular and lymphoid systems, selected skeletal muscles, and the nervous system.

The Respiratory Epithelium [Figure 24.2]

The **respiratory epithelium** consists of a pseudostratified, ciliated, columnar epithelium with numerous mucous cells (Figure 24.2). The respiratory epithelium lines the entire respiratory tract except for the inferior portions of the pharynx, the smallest conducting passages, and the alveoli. A stratified

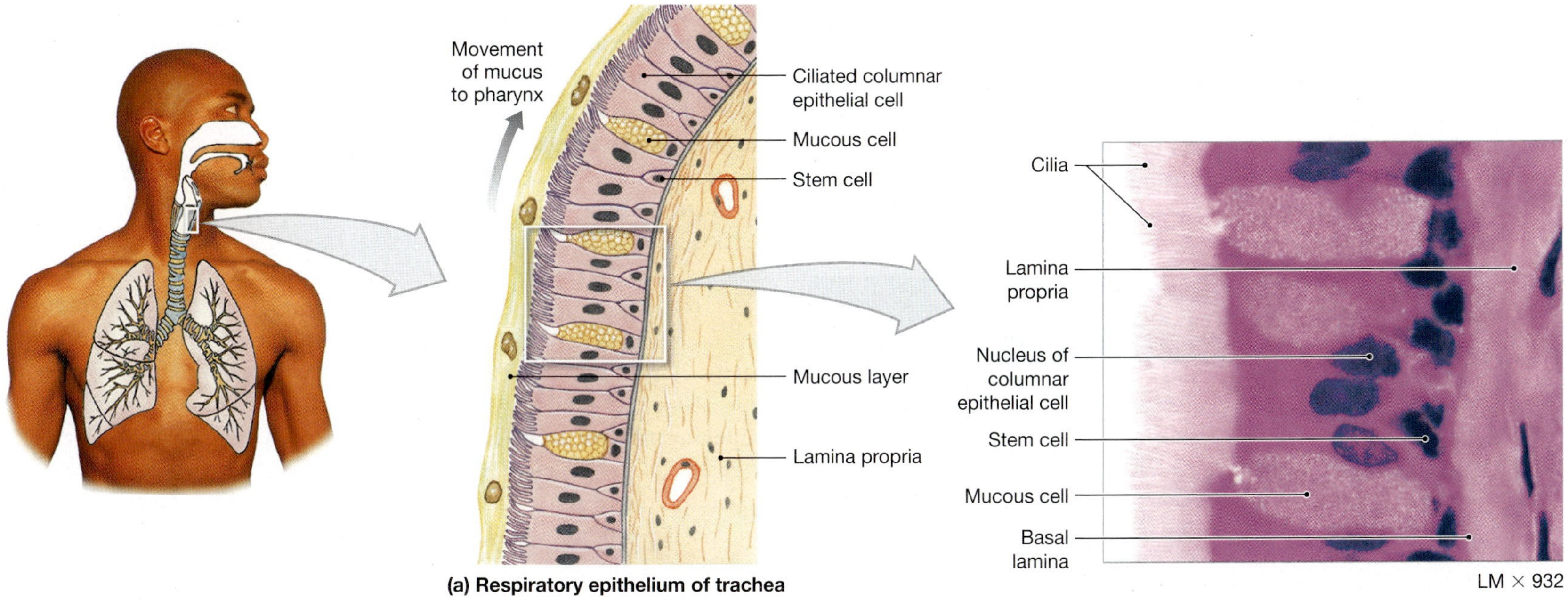

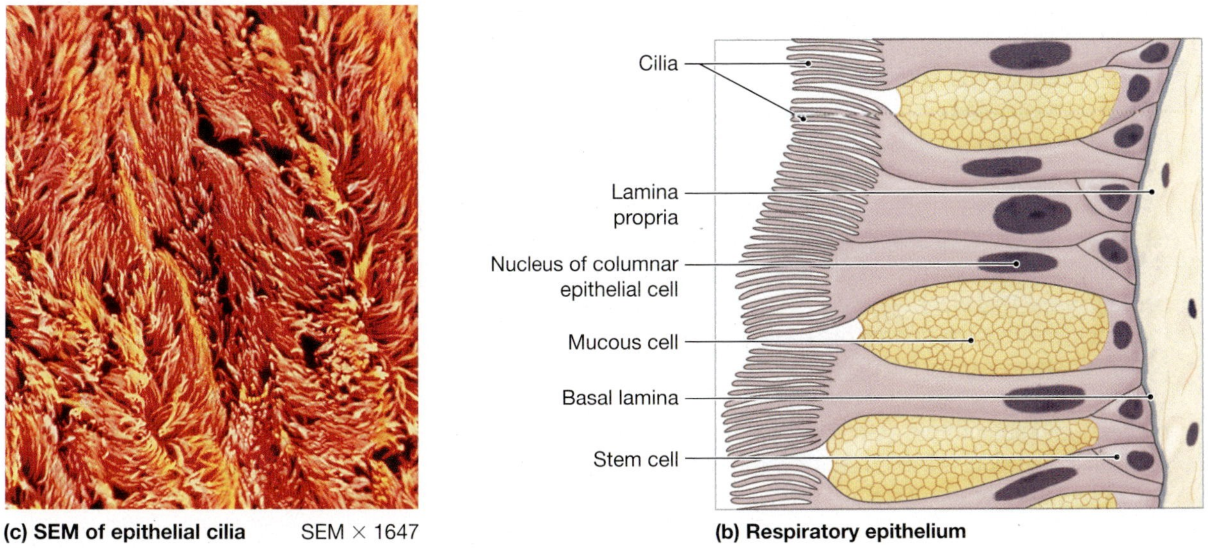

Figure 24.2 Histology of the Respiratory Epithelium
(a) Diagrammatic and histological views of the respiratory epithelium. **(b)** Histological appearance of respiratory epithelium. **(c)** A surface view of the epithelium, as seen with the scanning electron microscope. In this colorized image, the cilia of the epithelial cells form a dense layer that resembles a shag carpet. The movement of these cilia propels mucus across the epithelial surface.

squamous epithelium lines the inferior portion of the pharynx, protecting it from abrasion and chemical attack. This portion of the pharynx conducts air to the larynx and also conveys food to the esophagus.

Mucous cells in the epithelium and mucous glands deep to the respiratory epithelium in the lamina propria produce a sticky mucus that bathes the exposed surfaces. In the nasal cavity, cilia sweep any debris trapped in mucus or microorganisms toward the pharynx, where it will be swallowed and exposed to the acids and enzymes of the stomach. In lower portions of the respiratory tract, the cilia also beat toward the pharynx, creating a *mucus escalator* that cleans the respiratory passageways.

The delicate surfaces of the respiratory system can be severely damaged if the inspired air becomes contaminated with debris or pathogens. However, the air entering the respiratory system is filtered to remove these contaminants. The respiratory filtration mechanisms form the **respiratory defense system**. In the nasal cavity, virtually all particles larger than 10 μm are removed from the inspired air. Larger particles are removed by the stiff hairs, termed *vibrissae*, found within the nasal cavity. Smaller particles may be trapped by the mucus of the nasopharynx or secretions of the pharynx before proceeding farther along the conducting system. Exposure to unpleasant stimuli, such as noxious vapors, large quantities of dust and debris, allergens, and pathogens, usually causes a rapid increase in the rate of mucus production. (The familiar symptoms of the "common cold" result from the invasion of the respiratory epithelium by one of more than 200 viruses.)

Filtration, warming, and humidification of inhaled air occur throughout the conducting portion of the respiratory system, but the greatest changes occur within the nasal cavity. Breathing through the mouth eliminates much of the preliminary filtration, heating, and humidifying of the inspired air. Patients breathing on a respirator, or mechanical ventilator, receive air that is introduced directly into the trachea. That air must be externally filtered and humidified to prevent alveolar damage.

Clinical Note

Cystic Fibrosis **Cystic fibrosis (CF)** is the most common lethal inherited disease in the Caucasian population, occurring at a frequency of 1 birth in 3000. Each year approximately 2000 babies are born with this condition in the United States alone. Even with improved therapies, only 34 percent reach adulthood and fewer than 10 percent survive past age 30. Death is usually the result of a massive bacterial infection of the lungs and associated lung and heart failure.

The underlying problem involves an abnormality in a membrane transport protein responsible for the active transport of chloride ions. This membrane protein is abundant in exocrine cells that produce watery secretions. In people with CF, these cells cannot transport salts and water effectively, and the secretions produced are thick and gooey. Mucous glands of the respiratory tract and secretory cells of the pancreas, salivary glands, digestive tract, and reproductive tract are affected.

The most serious symptoms appear because the respiratory defense system cannot transport such dense mucus. The mucus escalator stops working, and mucus plugs block the smaller respiratory passageways. This blockage reduces the diameter of the airways, and the inactivation of the normal respiratory defenses leads to frequent bacterial infections.

The gene responsible for CF has been identified, and the structure of the membrane protein determined. Now that the structure of the gene is understood, research continues with the goal of correcting the defect by the insertion of normal genes.

The Upper Respiratory System

The Nose and Nasal Cavity [Figure 24.3]

The nose is the primary passageway for air entering the respiratory system. The bones, cartilages, and sinuses associated with the nose were introduced in Chapter 6. p. 138 Air normally enters the respiratory system through the paired **external nares** (NA-rēz), which open into the **nasal cavity**. The **nasal vestibule** (VES-ti-būl), the portion of the nasal cavity enclosed by the flexible tissues of the nose (Figure 24.3d), is supported by thin, paired *lateral cartilages* and two pairs of *alar cartilages* (Figure 24.3a). The epithelium of the nasal vestibule contains coarse hairs that extend across the external nares. Large airborne particles such as sand, sawdust, and even insects are trapped in these hairs and are prevented from entering the nasal cavity.

The *nasal septum* separates the right and left portions of the nasal cavity. The bony portion of the nasal septum is formed by the fusion of the perpendicular plate of the ethmoid and the plate of the vomer. The anterior portion of the nasal septum is formed of hyaline cartilage. This cartilaginous plate supports the bridge, or **dorsum of the nose**, and **apex** (tip) **of the nose**.

The maxillae, nasal and frontal bones, ethmoid, and sphenoid form the lateral and superior walls of the nasal cavity. The mucous secretions produced in the associated *paranasal sinuses* (p. 153), aided by tears draining through the nasolacrimal ducts, help keep the surface of the nasal cavity moist and clean. The superior portion, or *olfactory region*, of the nasal cavity includes the areas lined by olfactory epithelium (p. 147): (1) the inferior surface of the cribriform plate, (2) the superior nasal conchae of the ethmoid, and (3) the superior portion of the nasal septum. p. 147

The superior, middle, and inferior nasal conchae, or *turbinate bones*, project toward the nasal septum from the lateral walls of the nasal cavity. To pass from the nasal vestibule to the **internal nares**, or *choanae* (kō-ĀN-ē), air tends to flow between adjacent conchae, through the **superior**, **middle**, or **inferior meatuses** (mē-Ā-tus-es; *meatus*, passage) (Figure 24.3b,d). These are narrow grooves rather than open passageways, and the incoming air bounces off the conchal surfaces and churns around like water flowing over rapids. This turbulence serves a purpose: As the air eddies and swirls, small airborne particles are likely to come in contact with the mucus that coats the lining of the nasal cavity. In addition to promoting filtration, the turbulence allows extra time for warming and humidifying the incoming air.

A bony **hard palate**, formed by the maxillary and palatine bones, forms the floor of the nasal cavity and separates the oral and nasal cavities. A fleshy **soft palate** extends posterior to the hard palate, marking the boundary line between the superior *nasopharynx* and the rest of the pharynx (Figure 24.3c,d). The nasal cavity opens into the nasopharynx at the internal nares.

CONCEPT CHECK

1. If it is very cold outside, why is it hard on the lower respiratory system if you breathe only through your mouth?
2. What is the mucus escalator?
3. What is the function of the nasal conchae? How does this affect the lower respiratory system?

See blue "Answers" tab at back of book.

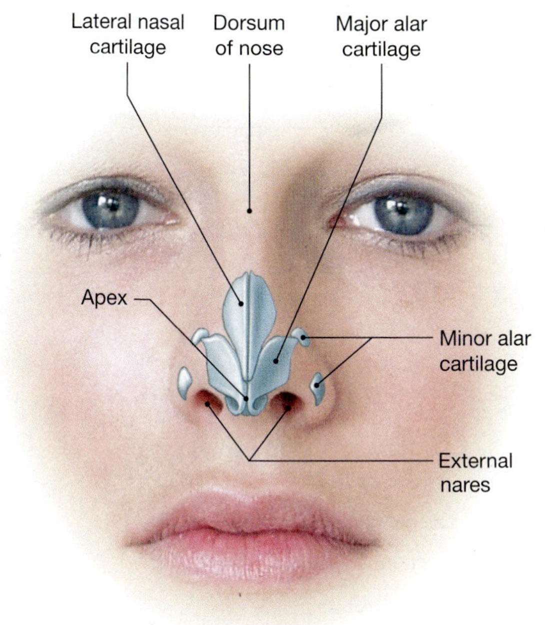

(a) Anterior view

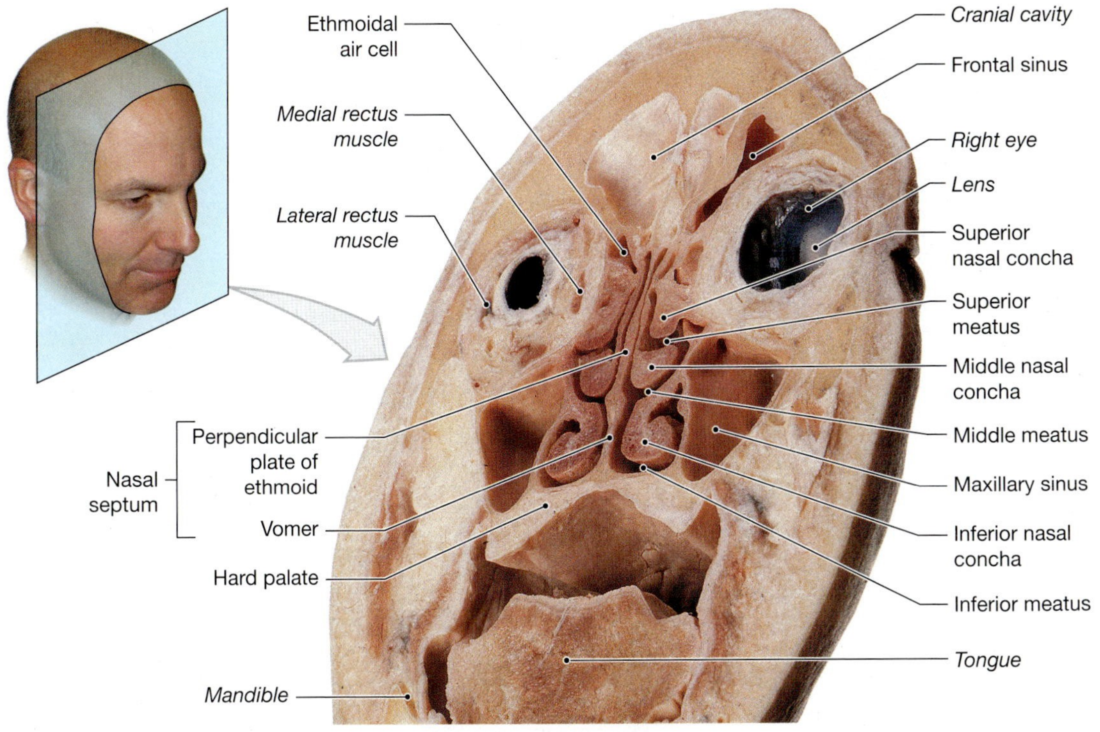

(b) Head, coronal section

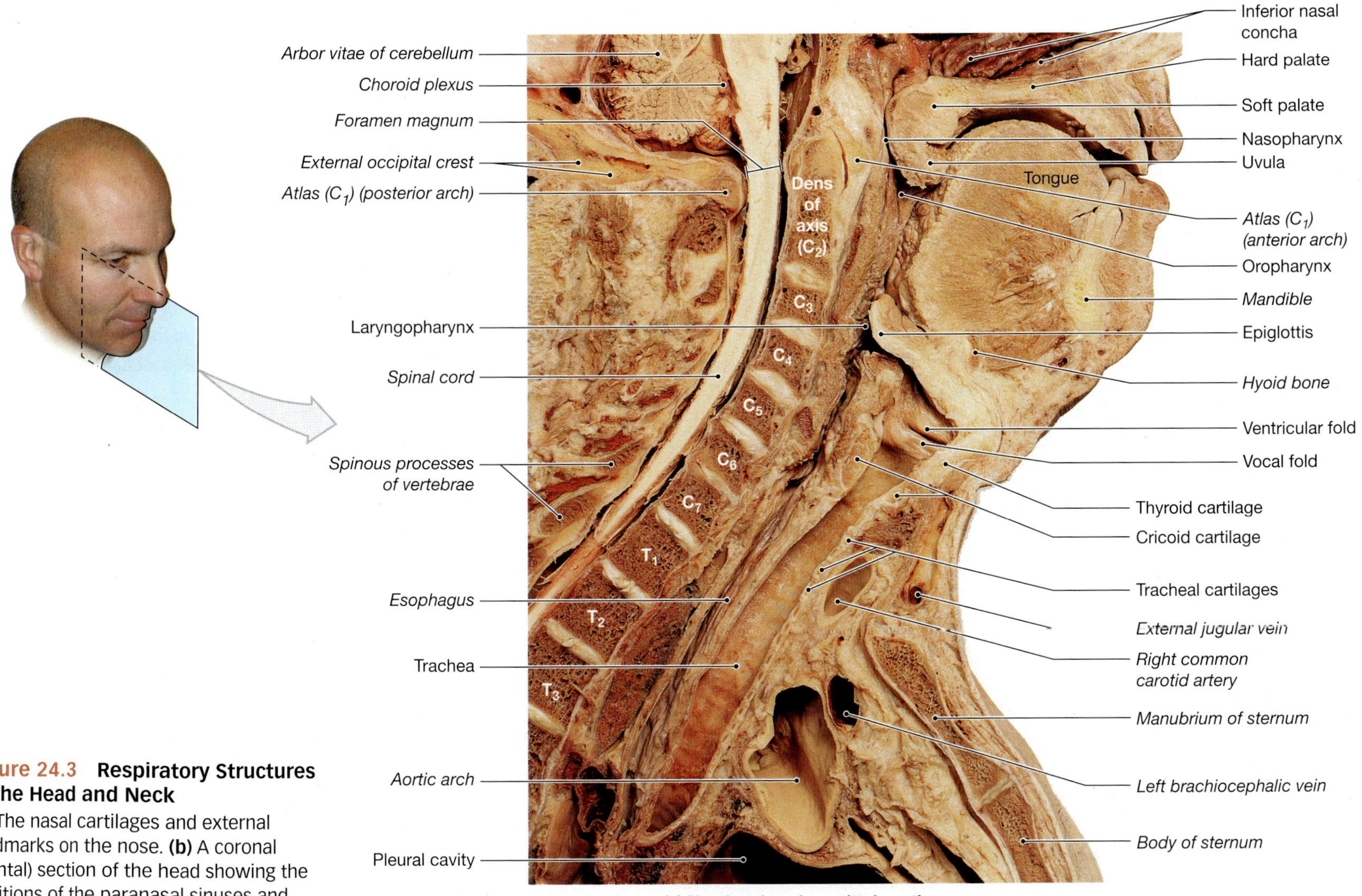

(c) Head and neck, sagittal section

Figure 24.3 Respiratory Structures in the Head and Neck
(a) The nasal cartilages and external landmarks on the nose. **(b)** A coronal (frontal) section of the head showing the positions of the paranasal sinuses and nasal structures. **(c)** The nasal cavity and pharynx as seen in a sagittal section of the head and neck.

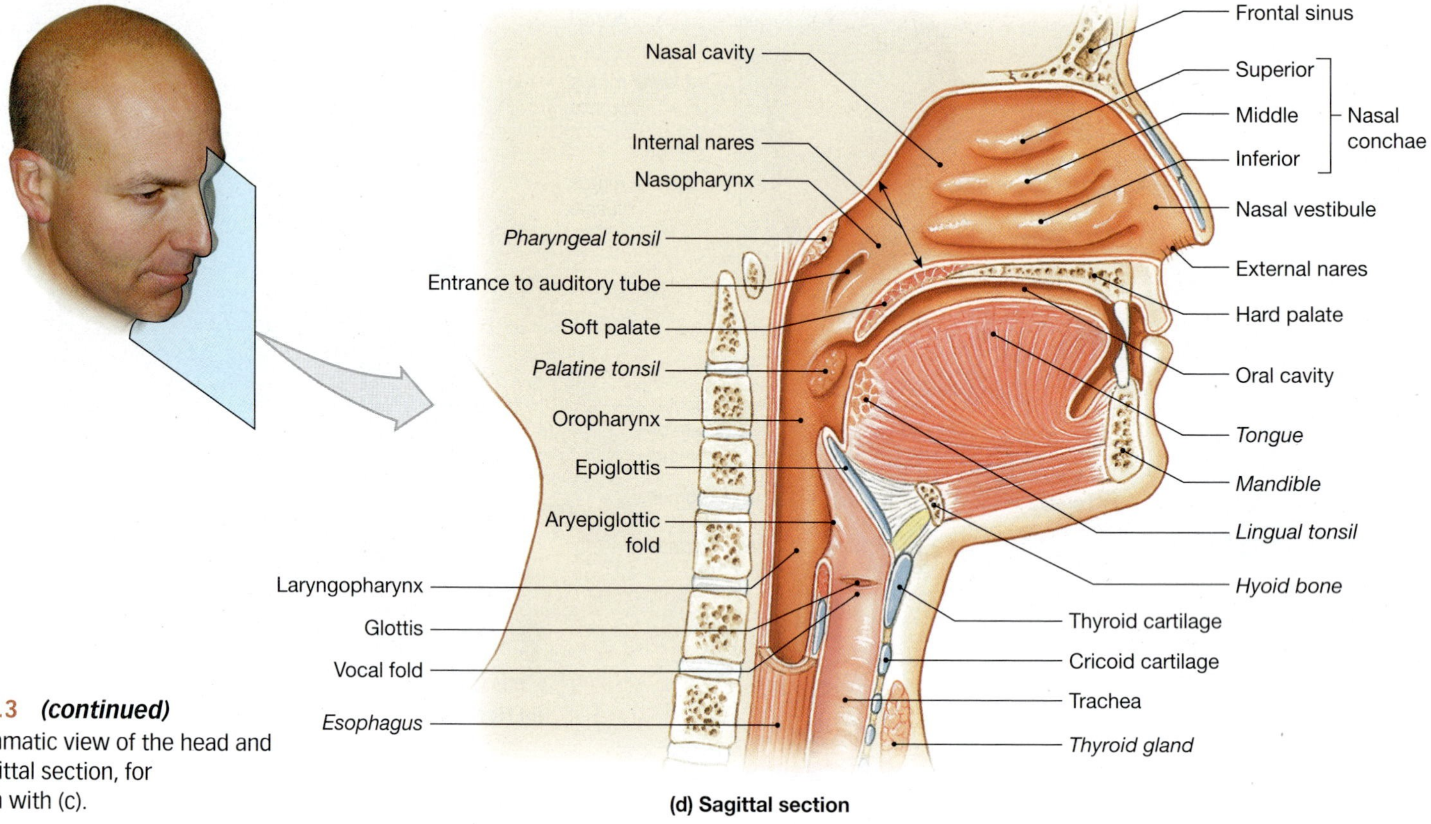

Figure 24.3 ***(continued)***
(d) Diagrammatic view of the head and neck in sagittal section, for comparison with (c).

The Pharynx [Figure 24.3c,d]

The nose, mouth, and throat connect to each other by a common passageway or chamber called the **pharynx** (FAR-inks). The pharynx is shared by the digestive and respiratory systems. It extends between the internal nares and the entrances to the trachea and esophagus. The curving superior and posterior walls are closely bound to the axial skeleton, but the lateral walls are quite flexible and muscular. The pharynx is divided into three regions (Figure 24.3c,d): the *nasopharynx*, the *oropharynx*, and the *laryngopharynx*.

The Nasopharynx [Figure 24.3c,d]

The **nasopharynx** (nā-zō-FAR-inks) is the superior portion of the pharynx. It is connected to the posterior portion of the nasal cavity via the internal nares, and is separated from the oral cavity by the soft palate (Figure 24.3c,d).

The nasopharynx is lined by typical respiratory epithelium. The *pharyngeal tonsil* is located on the posterior wall of the nasopharynx; the lateral walls contain the openings of the *auditory tubes* (Figure 24.3d).

The Oropharynx [Figure 24.3c,d/25.5a]

The **oropharynx** (ōr-ō-FAR-inks; *oris*, mouth) extends between the soft palate and the base of the tongue at the level of the hyoid bone. The posterior portion of the oral cavity communicates directly with the oropharynx, as do the posterior and inferior portions of the nasopharynx (Figure 24.3c,d). At the boundary between the nasopharynx and oropharynx, the epithelium changes from a pseudostratified ciliated columnar epithelium to a stratified squamous epithelium similar to that of the oral cavity.

The posterior margin of the soft palate supports the dangling **uvula** (Ū-vū-la) and two pairs of muscular **pharyngeal arches**. On either side a palatine tonsil lies between an anterior **palatoglossal** (pal-a-tō-GLOS-al) **arch** and a posterior **palatopharyngeal** (pal-a-tō-fa-RIN-jē-al) **arch** (Figure 25.5a). A curving line that connects the palatoglossal arches and uvula forms the boundaries of the **fauces** (FAW-sēz), the passageway between the oral cavity and the oropharynx.

The Laryngopharynx [Figure 24.3c,d]

The narrow **laryngopharynx** (la-RING-gō-far-inks) includes the region of the pharynx lying between the hyoid bone and the entrance to the esophagus (Figure 24.3c,d). The laryngopharynx is the most inferior part of the pharynx, and like the oropharynx it is lined by a stratified squamous epithelium that can resist mechanical abrasion, chemical attack, and pathogenic invasion.

The Lower Respiratory System

The Larynx [Figures 24.3d/24.4]

Inspired (inhaled) air leaves the pharynx by passing through a narrow opening, the **glottis** (GLOT-is) (Figure 24.3d). The **larynx** (LAR-inks) begins at the level of vertebra C_4 or C_5 and ends at the level of vertebra C_7. It is essentially a cylinder whose cartilaginous walls are stabilized by ligaments or skeletal muscles or both.

Cartilages of the Larynx [Figure 24.4]

Three large unpaired cartilages form the body of the larynx: the *thyroid cartilage*, the *cricoid cartilage*, and the *epiglottis* (Figure 24.4). The thyroid and cricoid cartilages are hyaline cartilages; the epiglottic cartilage is an elastic cartilage.

The Thyroid Cartilage [Figure 24.4a,b] The largest laryngeal cartilage is the **thyroid** ("shield-shaped") **cartilage**. It forms most of the anterior and lateral walls of the larynx (Figure 24.4a,b). The thyroid cartilage, when

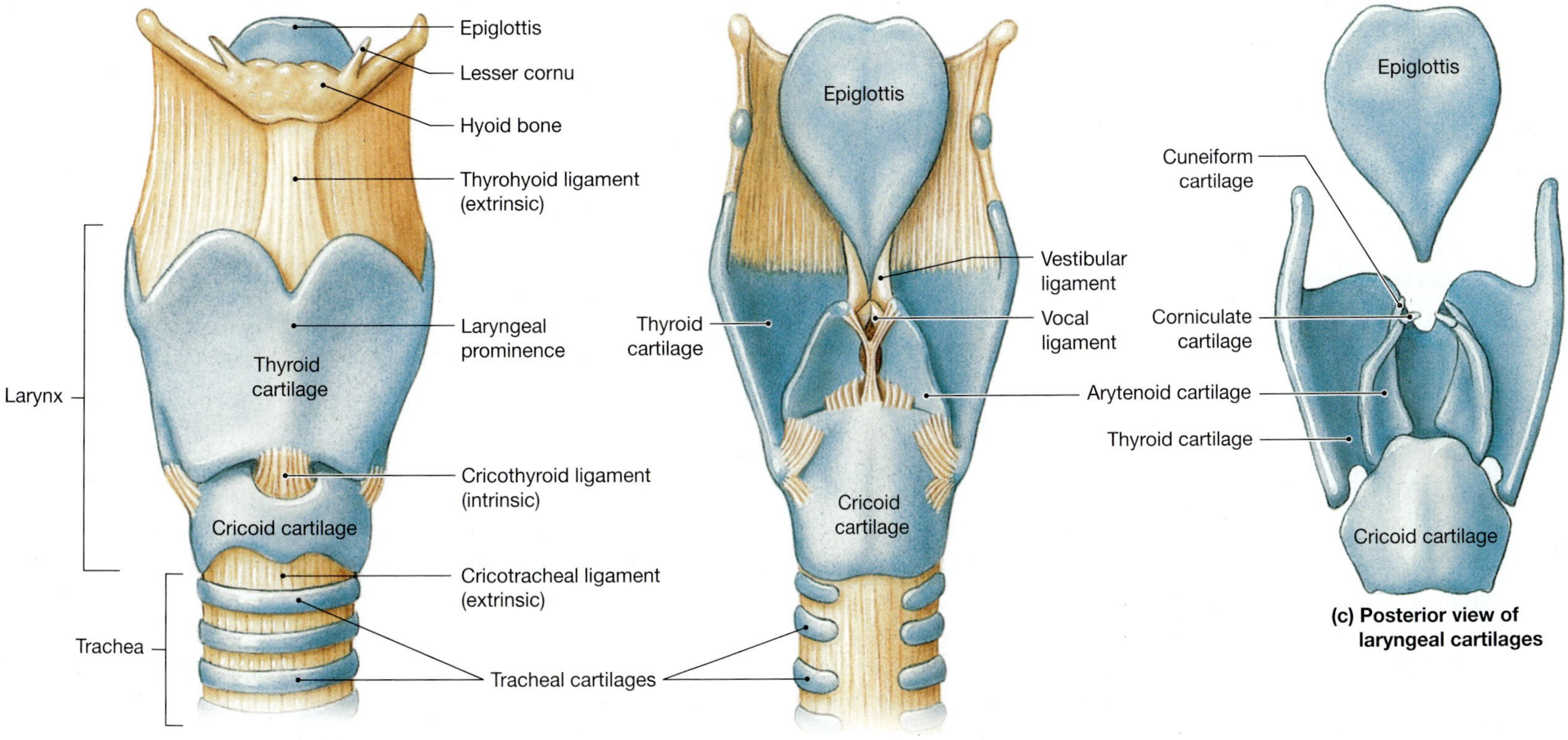

(a) Larynx, anterior view

(b) Larynx, posterior view

(c) Posterior view of laryngeal cartilages

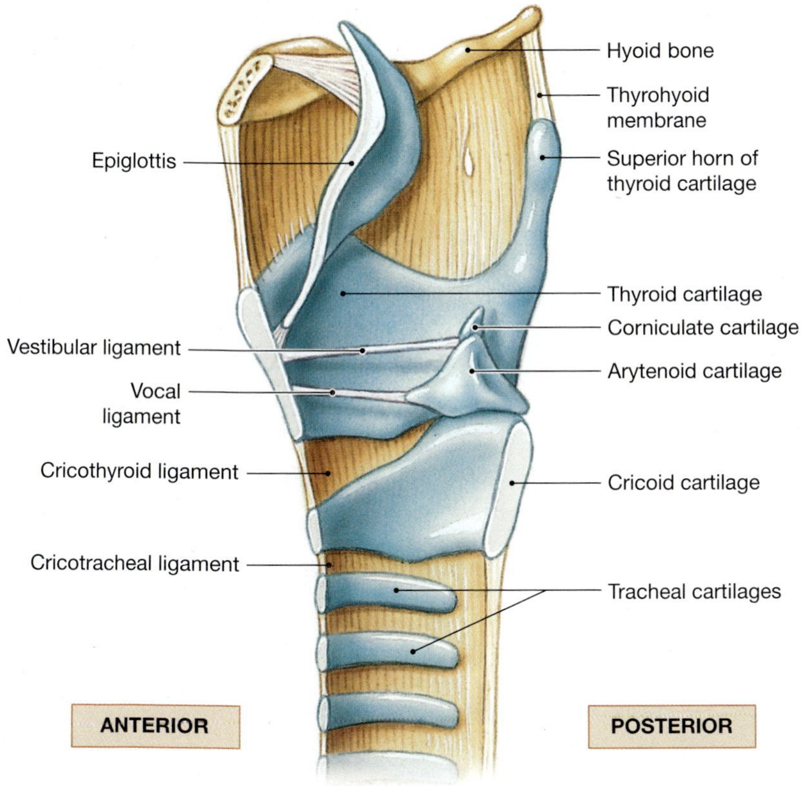

(d) Larynx, sagittal section

Figure 24.4 Anatomy of the Larynx
(a) Anterior view of the intact larynx. **(b)** Posterior view of the intact larynx. **(c)** Posterior view, showing the relationships among the individual laryngeal cartilages. **(d)** Sagittal section of the intact larynx.

viewed in sagittal section, is incomplete posteriorly. The anterior surface of this cartilage bears a thick ridge, the **laryngeal prominence**. This ridge is easily seen and felt, and the thyroid cartilage is commonly called the *Adam's apple*. During embryological development, the thyroid cartilage is formed by two pieces of cartilage that meet in the anterior midline to form the laryngeal prominence.

The inferior surface of the thyroid cartilage articulates with the cricoid cartilage; the superior surface has ligamentous attachments to the epiglottis and smaller laryngeal cartilages.

The Cricoid Cartilage [Figure 24.4a,c] The thyroid cartilage sits superior to the **cricoid** (KRĪ-koyd; "ring-shaped") **cartilage**. It is a complete ring whose posterior portion is greatly expanded, providing support in the absence of the thyroid cartilage. The cricoid and thyroid cartilages protect the glottis and the entrance to the trachea, and their broad surfaces provide sites for the attachment of important laryngeal muscles and ligaments. Ligaments attach the inferior surface of the cricoid cartilage to the first cartilage of the trachea (Figure 24.4a,c). The superior surface of the cricoid cartilage articulates with the small paired *arytenoid cartilages*.

The Epiglottis [Figures 24.3c,d/24.4b,c,d] The shoehorn-shaped **epiglottis** (ep-i-GLOT-is) projects superior to the glottis (Figures 24.3c,d and 24.4b,c,d). The *epiglottic cartilage* that supports it has ligamentous attachments to the anterior and superior borders of the thyroid cartilage and the hyoid bone. During swallowing, the larynx is elevated, and the epiglottis folds back over the glottis, preventing the entry of liquids or solid food into the respiratory passageways.

Paired Laryngeal Cartilages [Figures 24.4b–d/24.5] The larynx also contains three pairs of smaller cartilages: the *arytenoid*, *corniculate*, and *cuneiform cartilages*. The arytenoids and corniculates are hyaline cartilages; the cuneiforms are elastic cartilages.

- The paired **arytenoid** (ar-i-TĒ-noyd; "ladle-shaped") **cartilages** articulate with the superior border of the enlarged portion of the cricoid cartilage (Figure 24.4b–d).
- The **corniculate** (kor-NIK-ū-lāt; "horn-shaped") **cartilages** articulate with the arytenoid cartilages (Figures 24.4c,d and 24.5). The corniculate and arytenoid cartilages play a role in the opening and closing of the glottis and the production of sound.
- Elongate, curving **cuneiform** (kū-NĒ-i-form; "wedge-shaped") **cartilages** lie within the *aryepiglottic fold* that extends between the lateral aspect of each arytenoid cartilage and the epiglottis (Figures 24.4c and 24.5).

Laryngeal Ligaments [Figures 24.4a,b/24.5]

A series of **intrinsic ligaments** binds all nine cartilages together to form the larynx (Figure 24.4a,b). **Extrinsic ligaments** attach the thyroid cartilage to the hyoid bone and the cricoid cartilage to the trachea. The **vestibular ligaments** and the **vocal ligaments** extend between the thyroid cartilage and the arytenoids.

The vestibular and vocal ligaments are covered by folds of laryngeal epithelium that project into the glottis. The vestibular ligaments lie within the superior pair of folds, known as the **vestibular folds** (Figures 24.4b and 24.5). The vestibular folds, which are relatively inelastic, help prevent foreign objects from entering the glottis and provide protection for the more delicate **vocal folds**.

The vocal folds are highly elastic, because the vocal ligament is a band of elastic tissue. The vocal folds are involved with the production of sounds, and for this reason they are known as the **true vocal cords**. Because the vestibular folds play no part in sound production, they are often called the **false vocal cords**.

Sound Production Air passing through the glottis vibrates the vocal folds and produces sound waves. The pitch of the sound produced depends on the diameter, length, and tension in the vocal folds. The diameter and length are directly related to the size of the larynx. The tension is controlled by the contraction of voluntary muscles that change the relative positions of the thyroid and arytenoid cartilages. When the distance increases, the vocal folds tense and the pitch rises; when the distance decreases, the vocal folds relax and the pitch falls.

Children have slender, short vocal folds, and their voices tend to be high-pitched. At puberty the larynx of a male enlarges considerably more than that of a female. The true vocal cords of an adult male are thicker and longer, and they produce lower tones than those of an adult female.

The entire larynx is involved in sound production because its walls vibrate, creating a composite sound. Amplification and echoing of the sound occur within the pharynx, the oral cavity, the nasal cavity, and the paranasal sinuses. The final production of distinct sounds depends on voluntary movements of the tongue, lips, and cheeks.

The Laryngeal Musculature [Figure 24.6]

The larynx is associated with two different groups of muscles, the *intrinsic laryngeal muscles* and the *extrinsic laryngeal muscles*. The **intrinsic laryngeal muscles** have two major functions. One group regulates tension in the vocal folds, while a second set opens and closes the glottis. Those involved with the vocal folds insert upon the thyroid, arytenoid, and corniculate cartilages. Opening or closing the glottis involves rotational movements of the arytenoids that move the vocal folds apart or together.

The **extrinsic laryngeal musculature** positions and stabilizes the larynx. These muscles were considered in Chapter 10. p. 270

During swallowing, both extrinsic and intrinsic muscles cooperate to prevent food or drink from entering the glottis. Before you swallow, the material is crushed and chewed into a pasty mass known as a *bolus*. Extrinsic muscles then elevate the larynx, bending the epiglottis over the entrance to the glottis, so that the bolus can glide across the epiglottis, rather than falling into the larynx (Figure 24.6). While this movement is under way, intrinsic muscles close the glottis. Should any food particles or liquids touch the surfaces of the vestibular or vocal folds, the coughing reflex will be triggered. Coughing usually prevents the material from entering the glottis.

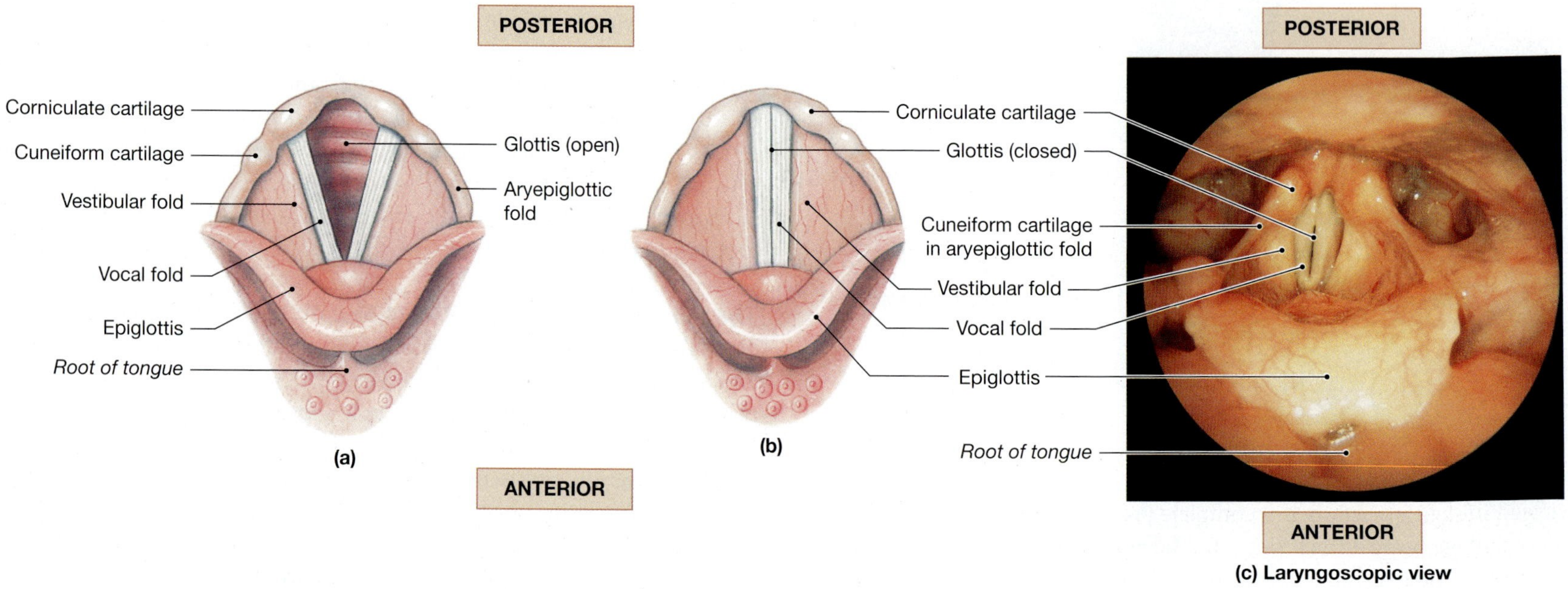

Figure 24.5 The Vocal Cords
The glottis is shown in the open position **(a)** and closed position **(b)**. The photograph **(c)** is a representative laryngoscopic view. For this view the camera is positioned within the oropharynx, just superior to the larynx.

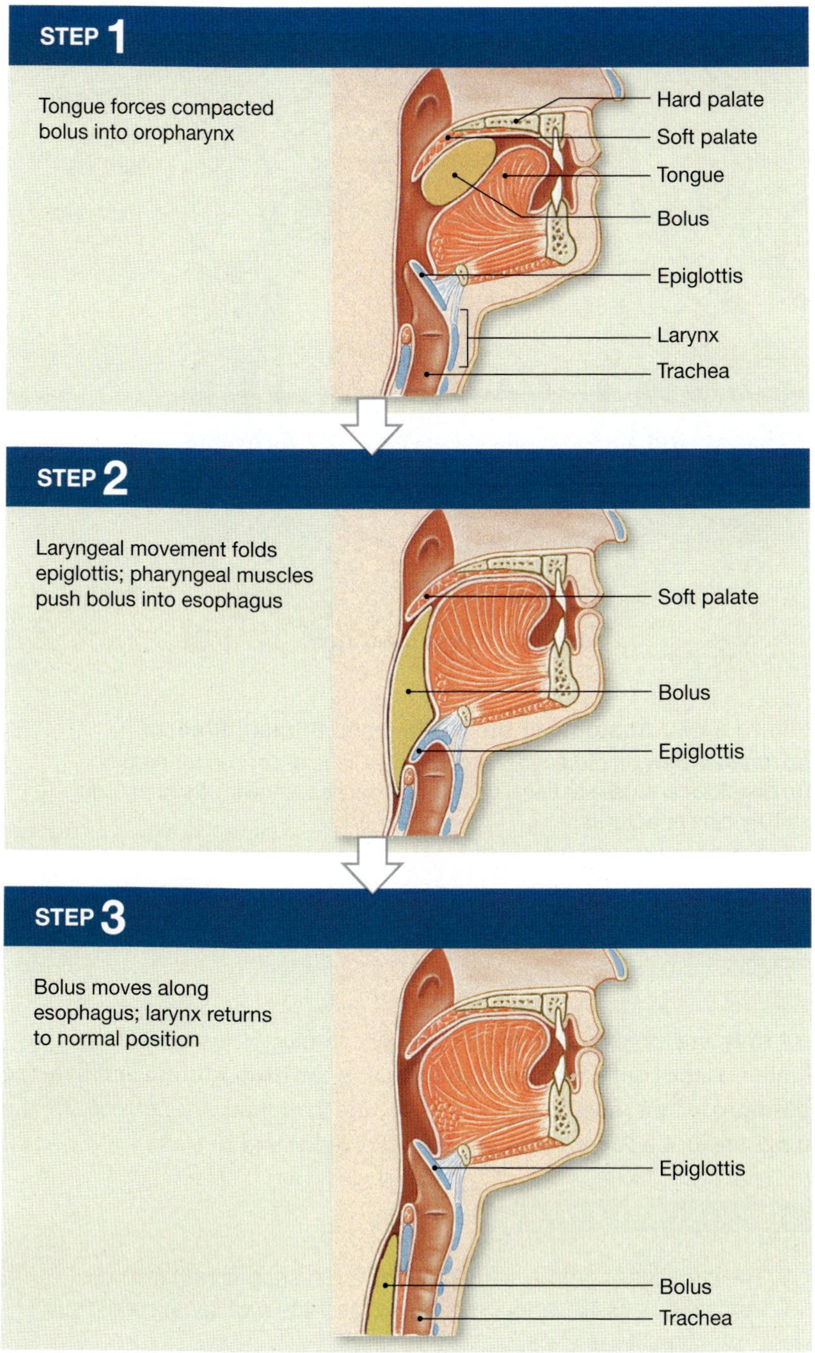

Figure 24.6 Movements of the Larynx during Swallowing
During swallowing the elevation of the larynx folds the epiglottis over the glottis, steering materials into the esophagus.

✓ CONCEPT CHECK

1. What are the functions of the thyroid cartilage?
2. What is the function of the epiglottis?
3. Laurel uses voluntary muscle contraction to shorten the distance between her thyroid and arytenoid cartilages. What is happening to the pitch of her voice?
4. How would the absence of intrinsic laryngeal muscles affect swallowing?

See blue "Answers" tab at back of book.

The Trachea [Figures 24.2a/24.3c/24.7]

The epithelium of the larynx is continuous with that of the **trachea** (TRĀ-kē-a), or "windpipe." The trachea is a tough, flexible tube with a diameter of about 2.5 cm (1 in.) and a length of approximately 11 cm (4.25 in.) (Figures 24.3c, p. 633, and 24.7). The trachea begins anterior to vertebra C_6 in a ligamentous attachment to the cricoid cartilage; it ends in the mediastinum, at the level of vertebra T_5, where it branches to form the *right* and *left primary*, or *main, bronchi.*

The lining of the trachea consists of respiratory epithelium overlying a layer of loose connective tissue called the **lamina propria** (LA-mi-na PRŌ-prē-a) (Figure 24.2a, p. 631). The lamina propria separates the respiratory epithelium from underlying cartilages. The epithelium and lamina propria are interdependent, and the combination is an example of a *mucous membrane*, or **mucosa** (mū-KŌ-sa). ∞ p. 72

A thick layer of connective tissue, the **submucosa** (sub-mū-KO-sa), surrounds the mucosa. The submucosa contains mucous glands that communicate with the epithelial surface through a number of secretory ducts.

Superficial to the submucosa, the trachea contains 15–20 **tracheal cartilages** (Figure 24.7). Each tracheal cartilage is bound to neighboring cartilages by elastic **annular ligaments**. The tracheal cartilages stiffen the tracheal walls and protect the airway. They also prevent its collapse or overexpansion as pressures change in the respiratory system.

Each tracheal cartilage is C-shaped. The closed portion of the C protects the anterior and lateral surfaces of the trachea. The open portions of the tracheal cartilages face posteriorly, toward the esophagus (Figure 24.7b). Because the cartilages do not continue around the trachea, the posterior tracheal wall can easily change shape during swallowing, permitting the passage of large masses of food along the esophagus.

Clinical Note

Tracheal Blockage Foreign objects, usually food, that become lodged in the larynx or trachea are usually expelled by coughing. If the individual can speak or make a sound, the airway is still open, and no emergency measures should be taken. If the victim can neither breathe nor speak, an immediate threat to life exists. Unfortunately, some victims become acutely embarrassed by this situation, fail to realize the danger, and rather than seek assistance, they run to the nearest restroom and quietly die there.

In the **Heimlich** (HĪM-lik) **maneuver**, or *abdominal thrust*, a rescuer applies compression to the abdomen just inferior to the diaphragm. Compression elevates the diaphragm forcefully and may generate enough pressure to remove the blockage. This maneuver must be performed properly to avoid damage to internal organs. Organizations such as the Red Cross, the local fire department, and other charitable groups usually hold brief training sessions throughout the year.

If the blockage remains, professionally qualified rescuers may perform a **tracheostomy** (trā-kē-OS-tō-mē). In this procedure an incision is made through the anterior tracheal wall and a tube is inserted. The tube bypasses the larynx and permits airflow directly into the trachea. A tracheostomy may also be required (1) when the larynx becomes blocked by a foreign object, inflammation, or sustained laryngeal spasms; (2) when a portion of the trachea has been crushed; or (3) when a portion of the trachea has been removed during treatment of laryngeal cancer.

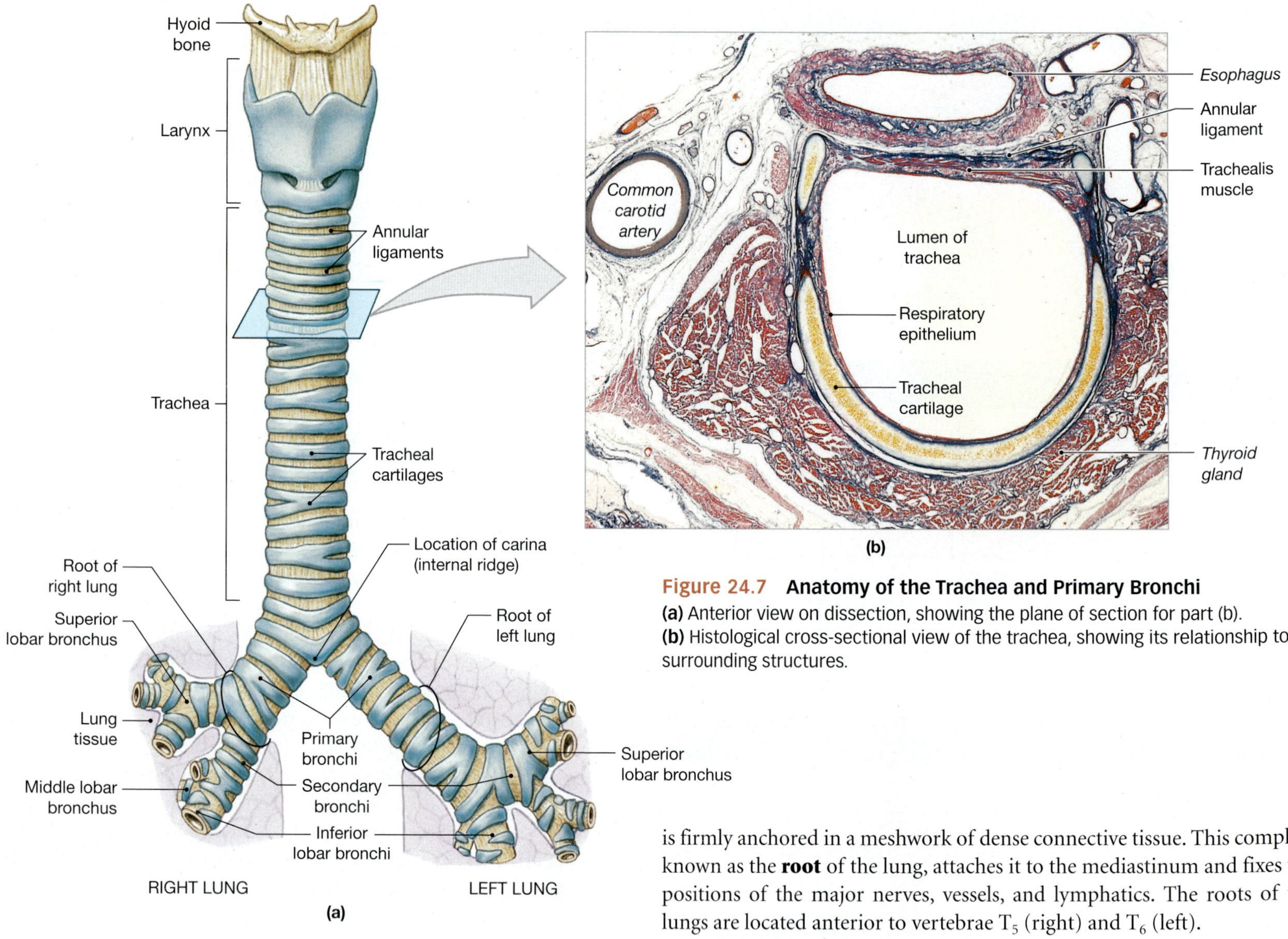

Figure 24.7 Anatomy of the Trachea and Primary Bronchi
(a) Anterior view on dissection, showing the plane of section for part (b).
(b) Histological cross-sectional view of the trachea, showing its relationship to surrounding structures.

An elastic ligament and a band of smooth muscle, the **trachealis**, connect the ends of each tracheal cartilage (Figure 24.7b). Contraction of the trachealis muscle alters the diameter of the tracheal lumen, changing the resistance to airflow. Sympathetic activation leads to the relaxation of the trachealis muscle, increasing the diameter of the trachea and making it easier to move large volumes of air along the respiratory passageways.

The Primary Bronchi [Figure 24.7a]

The trachea branches within the mediastinum, giving rise to the **right** and **left primary**, or *main*, **bronchi** (BRONG-kī; singular, bronchus). The left and right primary bronchi are outside the lungs and are called the **extrapulmonary bronchi**. An internal ridge, called the **carina** (ka-RĪ-na), lies between the entrances to the two primary bronchi (Figure 24.7a). The histological organization of the primary bronchi is the same as the trachea, with cartilaginous C-shaped supporting rings. The right primary bronchus supplies the right lung, and the left supplies the left lung. The right primary bronchus has a larger diameter than the left, and it descends toward the lung at a steeper angle. For these reasons foreign objects that enter the trachea usually become lodged in the right bronchus rather than the left.

Each primary bronchus travels to a groove along the medial surface of its lung before branching further. This groove, the **hilum** (HĪ-lum), also provides access for entry to pulmonary vessels and nerves. The entire array is firmly anchored in a meshwork of dense connective tissue. This complex, known as the **root** of the lung, attaches it to the mediastinum and fixes the positions of the major nerves, vessels, and lymphatics. The roots of the lungs are located anterior to vertebrae T_5 (right) and T_6 (left).

CONCEPT CHECK

1. The cartilages reinforcing the trachea are C-shaped rather than complete rings. How does this shape facilitate swallowing while still protecting the trachea?
2. What type of epithelium can be observed in the trachea?
3. How are tracheal cartilages involved in respiration?
4. How can you distinguish the right primary bronchus from the left primary bronchus?

See blue "Answers" tab at back of book.

The Lungs [Figure 24.8]

The left and right lungs (Figure 24.8) are situated in the left and right pleural cavities. Each lung is a blunt cone with the tip, or **apex**, pointing superiorly. The apex on each side extends into the base of the neck above the first rib. The broad concave inferior portion, or **base**, of each lung rests on the superior surface of the diaphragm.

Lobes of the Lungs [Figure 24.8]

The lungs have distinct **lobes** separated by deep fissures. The **right lung** has three lobes: **superior**, **middle**, and **inferior**. The *horizontal fissure* separates

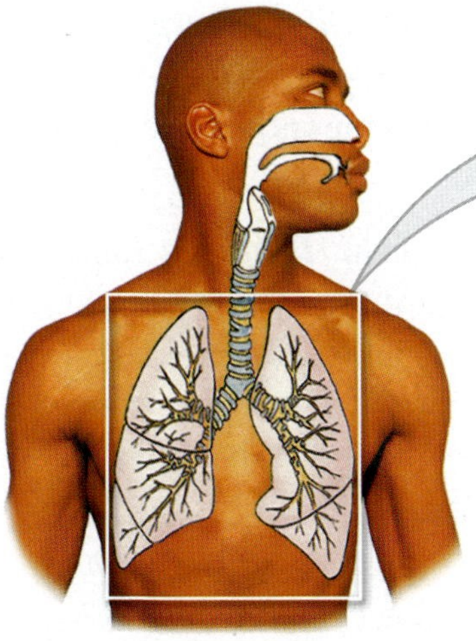

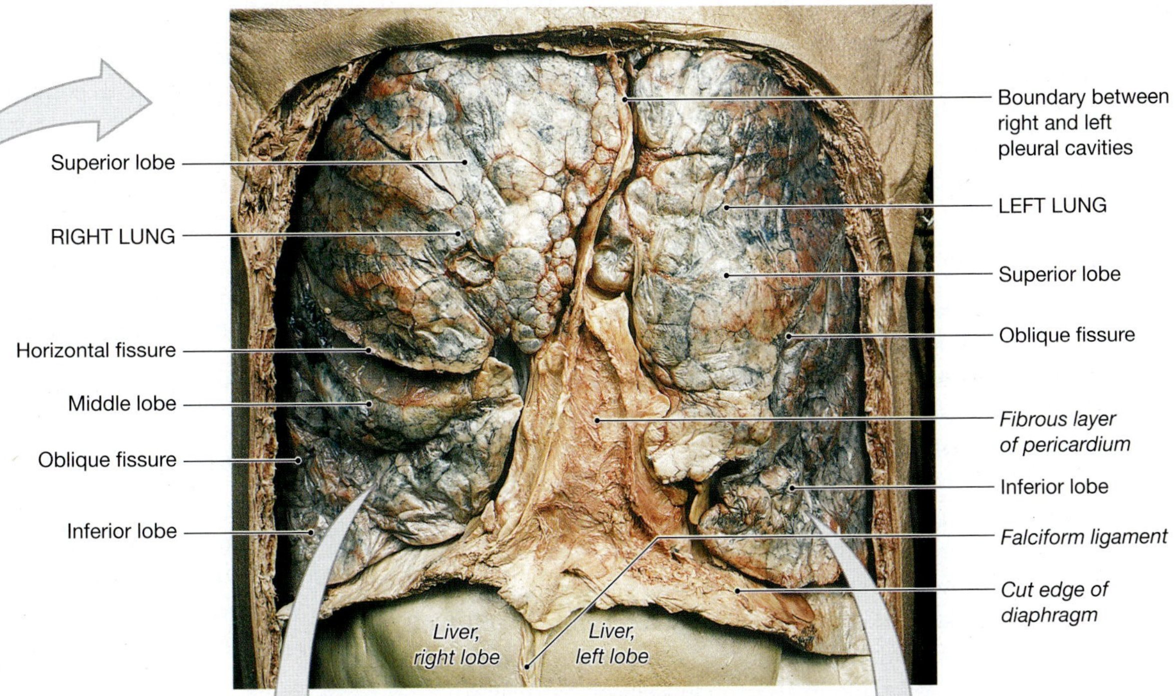

(a) Thoracic cavity, anterior view

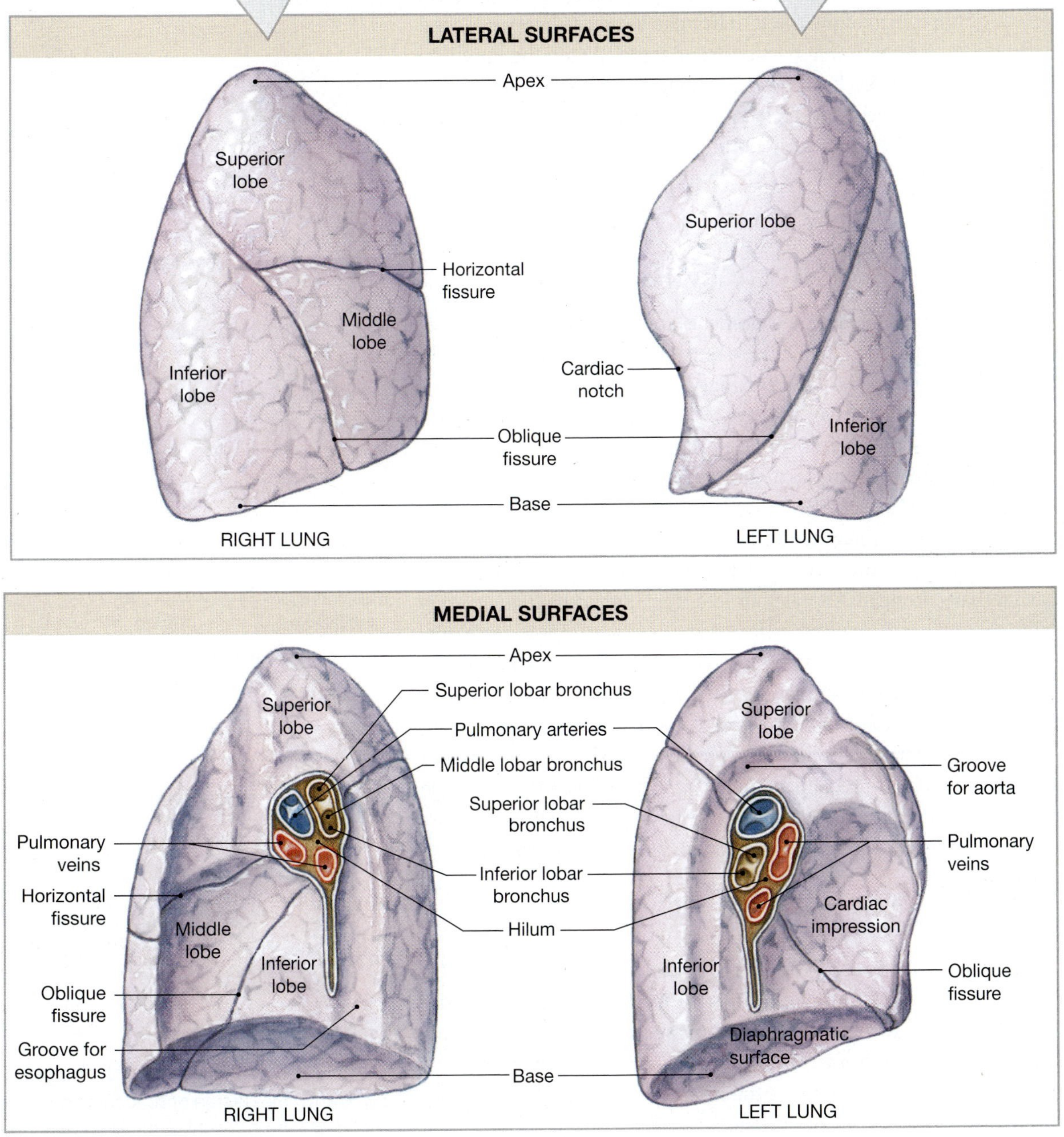

(b) The right and left lungs

Figure 24.8 Superficial Anatomy of the Lungs
(a) Anterior view of the opened chest, showing the relative positions of the left and right lungs and heart. **(b)** Diagrammatic views of the lateral and medial surfaces of the isolated right and left lungs.

the superior and middle lobes. The *oblique fissure* separates the superior and inferior lobes. The **left lung** has only two lobes, **superior** and **inferior**, separated by the *oblique fissure* (Figure 24.8). The right lung is broader than the left because most of the heart and great vessels project into the left pleural cavity. However, the left lung is longer than the right lung because the diaphragm rises on the right side to accommodate the mass of the liver.

Lung Surfaces [Figure 24.8]

The curving anterior portion of the lung that follows the inner contours of the rib cage is the **costal surface** (Figure 24.8a). The **mediastinal surface**, or *medial surface*, contains the hilum and has a more irregular shape (Figure 24.8b). The mediastinal surfaces of both lungs bear grooves that mark the positions of the great vessels and the heart. The heart is located to the left of the midline, and the left lung has a large *cardiac impression.* In anterior view, the medial margin of the right lung forms a vertical line, whereas the medial margin of the left lung bears a concavity, the **cardiac notch**.

The connective tissues of the root of each lung extend into its substance, or **parenchyma** (pa-RENG-ki-ma). These fibrous partitions, or **trabeculae**, contain elastic fibers, smooth muscles, and lymphatics. They branch repeatedly, dividing the lobes into smaller and smaller compartments. The branches of the conducting passageways, pulmonary vessels, and nerves of the lungs follow these trabeculae to reach their peripheral destinations. The terminal partitions, or **septa**, divide the lung into **lobules** (LOB-ūlz), each supplied by tributaries of the pulmonary arteries, pulmonary veins, and respiratory passageways. The connective tissues of the septa are in turn continuous with those of the visceral pleura. We will now follow the branching pattern of the bronchi from the hilum to the alveoli of each lung.

The Pulmonary Bronchi [Figures 24.7/24.9/24.10]

The primary bronchi and their branches form the *bronchial tree.* Because the left and right bronchi are outside the lungs, they are called *extrapulmonary bronchi.* As the primary bronchi enter the lungs, they divide to form smaller passageways (Figures 24.7, 24.9, and 24.10). Those branches are collectively called the *intrapulmonary bronchi.*

Each primary bronchus divides to form **secondary bronchi**, also known as **lobar bronchi**. Secondary bronchi in turn branch to form **tertiary bronchi**, or **segmental bronchi**. The branching pattern differs, depending on the lung considered; details are provided shortly. Each tertiary bronchus supplies air to a single *bronchopulmonary segment*, a specific region of one lung (Figure 24.10a,b). There are 10 tertiary bronchi (and 10 bronchopulmonary segments) in the right lung. The left lung also has 10 segments during development, but subsequent fusion usually reduces that number to 8 or 9. The walls of the primary, secondary, and tertiary bronchi contain progressively lesser amounts of cartilage. The walls of secondary and tertiary bronchi contain cartilage plates arranged around the lumen. These cartilages serve the same purpose as the rings of cartilage in the trachea and primary bronchi.

Branches of the Right Primary Bronchus [Figures 24.7/24.10]

The right lung has three lobes, and the right primary bronchus divides into three secondary bronchi: a **superior lobar bronchus**, a **middle lobar bronchus**, and an **inferior lobar bronchus**. The middle and inferior lobar bronchi branch from the right primary bronchus almost as soon as it enters the lung at the hilum (Figure 24.7). Each lobar branch delivers air to one of the lobes of the right lung (Figure 24.10).

Branches of the Left Primary Bronchus [Figures 24.7/24.9/24.10]

The left lung has two lobes, and the left primary bronchus divides into two secondary bronchi: a **superior lobar bronchus** and an **inferior lobar bronchus** (Figures 24.7, 24.9, and 24.10).

Branches of the Secondary Bronchi [Figure 24.10a,d]

The secondary bronchi in each lung divide to form tertiary bronchi. In the right lung three tertiary bronchi supply the superior lobe, two supply the middle lobe, and five supply the inferior lobe. The superior lobe of the left lung usually contains four tertiary bronchi, whereas the inferior lobe has five (Figure 24.10a,d). The tertiary bronchi deliver air to the bronchopulmonary segments of the lungs.

The Bronchopulmonary Segments [Figure 24.10a,b,d]

Each lobe of the lung can be divided into smaller units called **bronchopulmonary segments**. Each segment consists of the lung tissue associated with a single tertiary bronchus. The bronchopulmonary segments have names that correspond to those of the associated tertiary bronchi (Figure 24.10a,b,d).

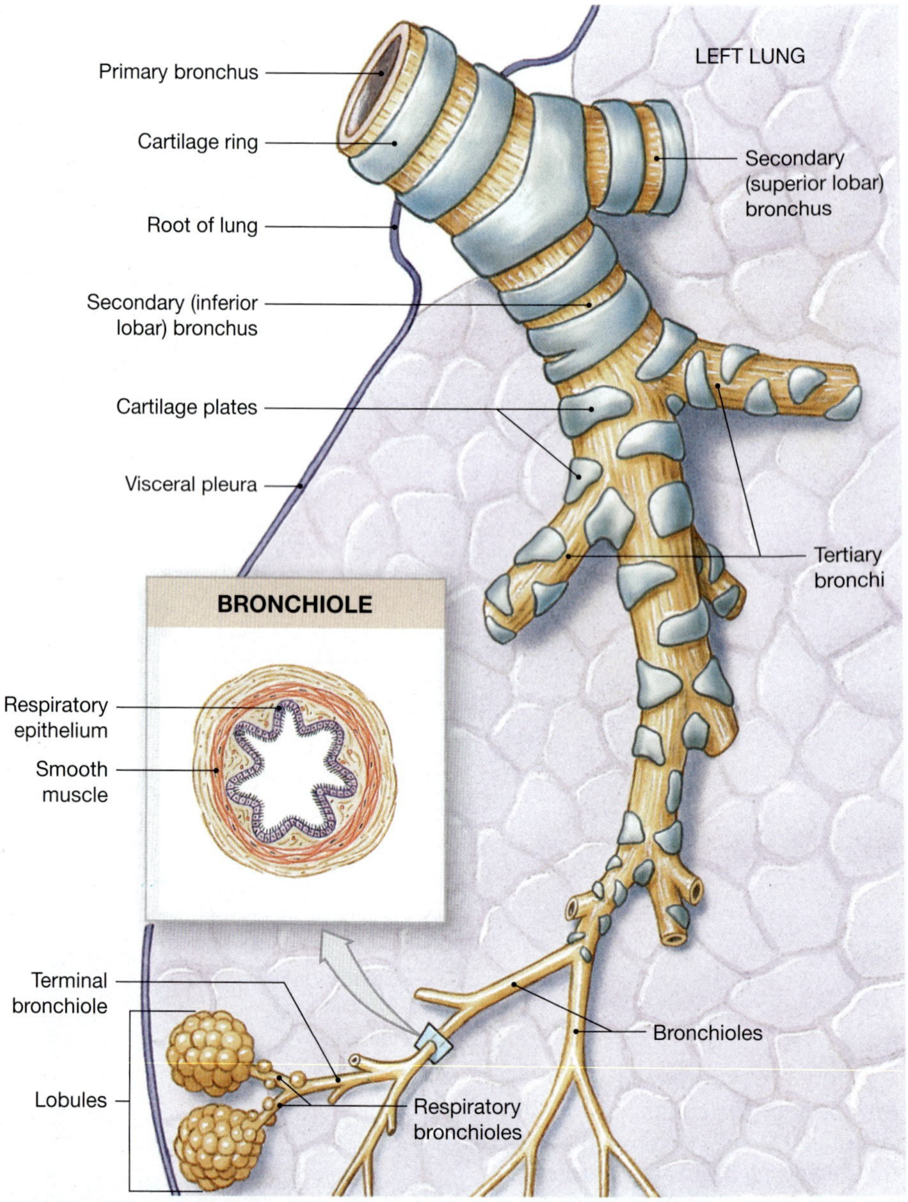

Figure 24.9 Bronchi and Bronchioles
For clarity, the degree of branching has been reduced; an airway branches approximately 23 times before reaching the level of a lobule.

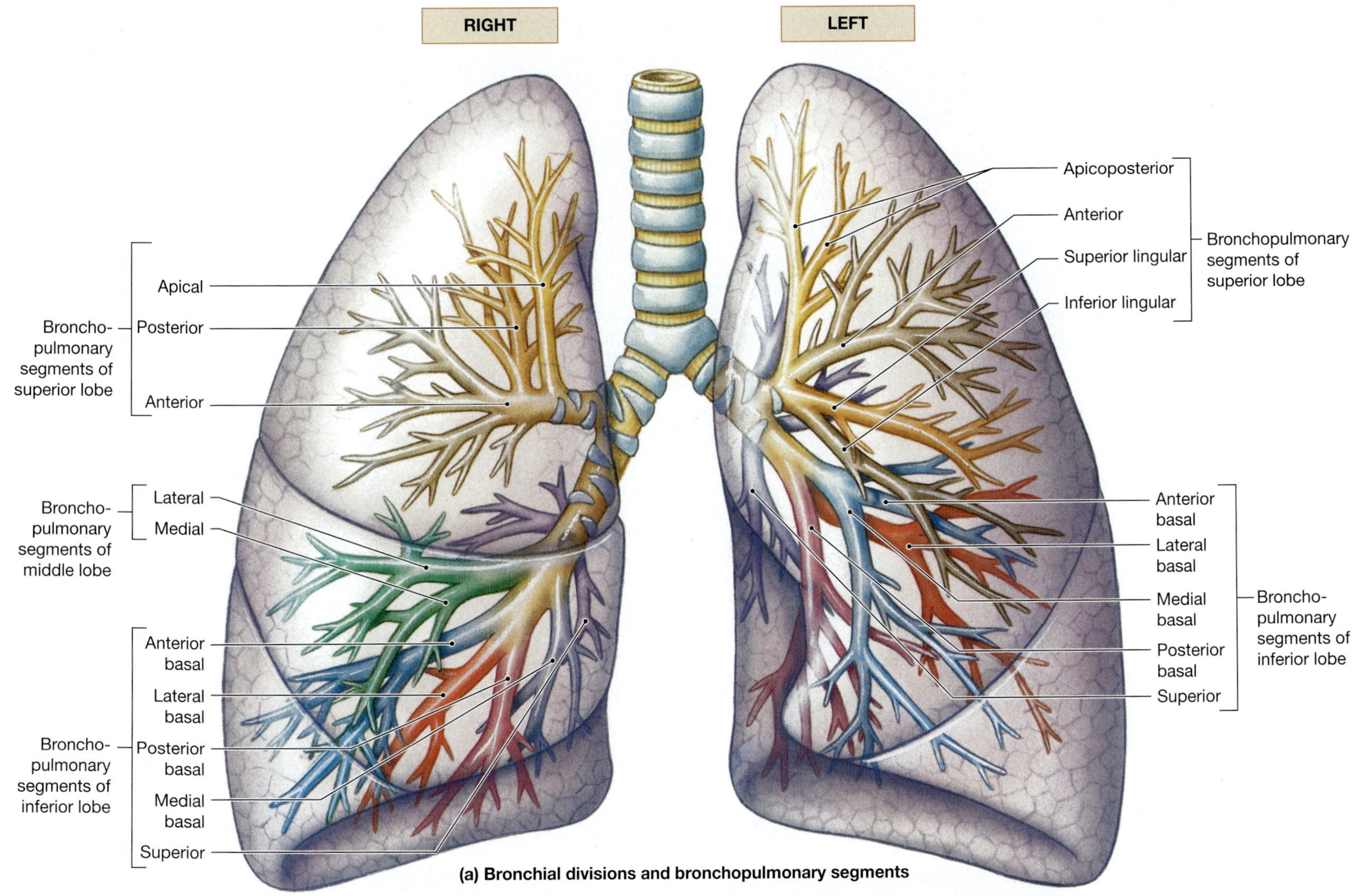

(a) Bronchial divisions and bronchopulmonary segments

(b) Bronchopulmonary segments of left and right lungs

Figure 24.10 The Bronchial Tree and Divisions of the Lungs
(a) Gross anatomy of the lungs, showing the bronchial tree and its divisions. **(b)** Isolated left and right lungs have been colored to show the distribution of the bronchopulmonary segments.

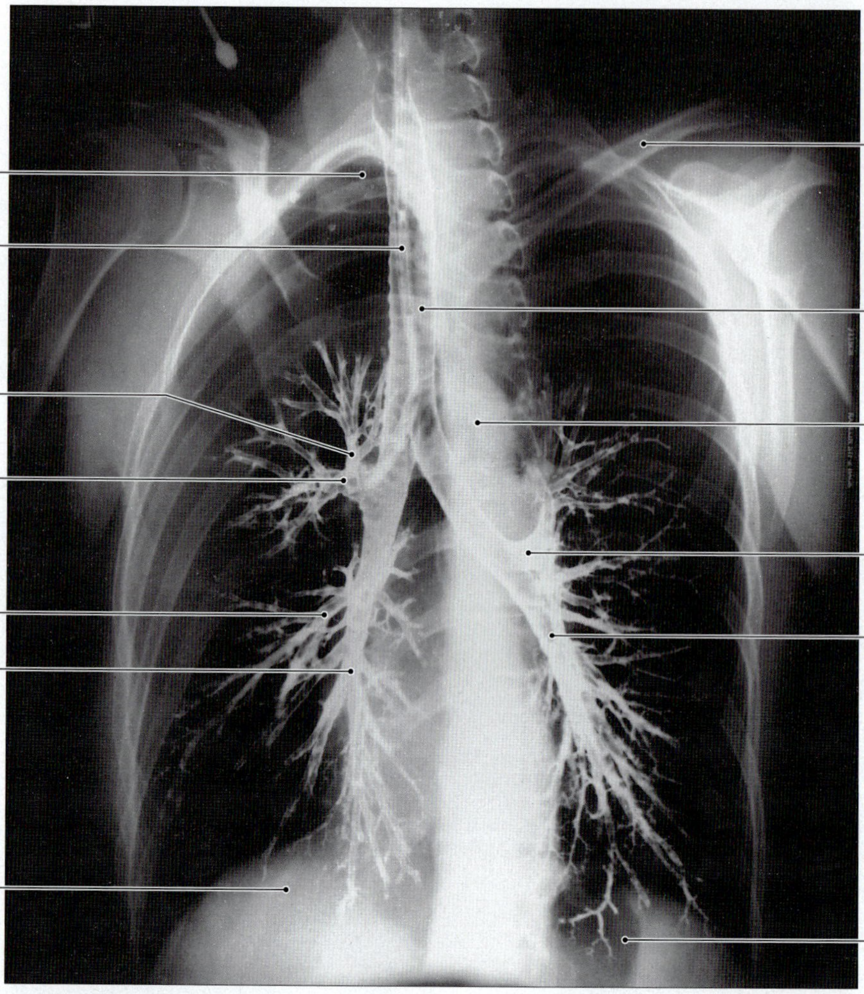

(c) Bronchogram

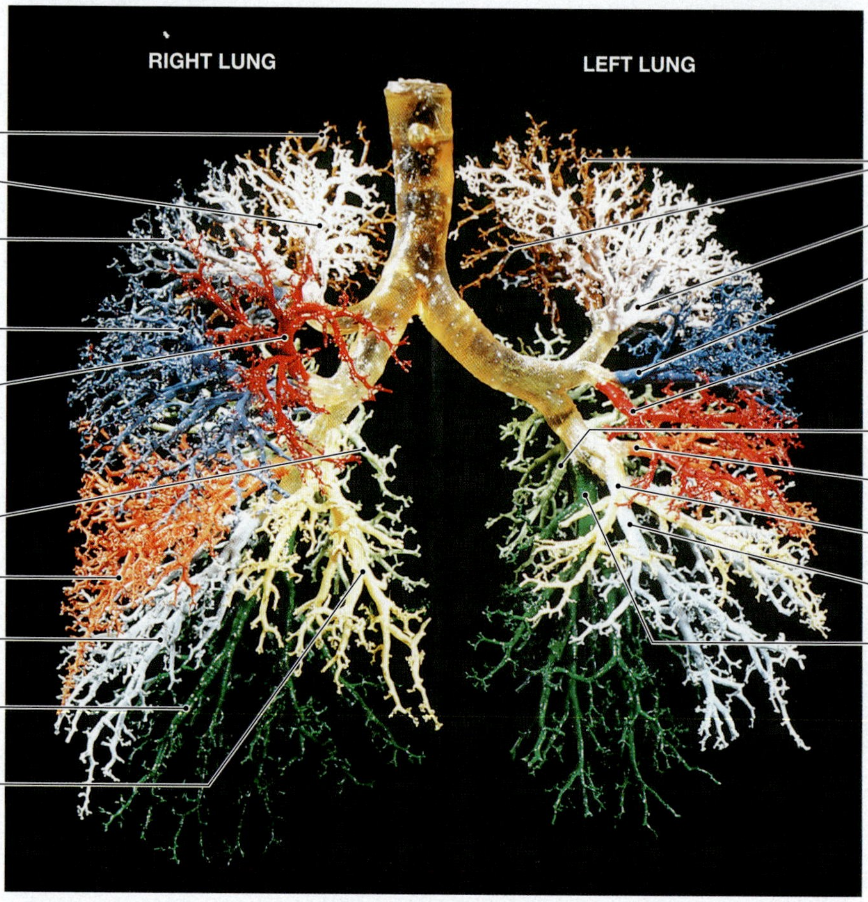

(d) The bronchial tree

Figure 24.10 ***(continued)***
(c) Colorized bronchogram of the bronchial tree, anteroposterior view. **(d)** Plastic cast of the adult bronchial tree. All of the branches in a given bronchopulmonary segment have been painted the same color.

Clinical Note

COPD: Asthma, Bronchitis, and Emphysema *Chronic obstructive pulmonary disease (COPD)* is a progressive disorder of the airways that restricts airflow and reduces alveolar ventilation. Three patterns of symptoms may appear in individuals with COPD. *Asthma*, or *asthmatic bronchitis*, is the term commonly applied when symptoms are acute and intermittent. The terms *bronchitis* and *emphysema* are used when symptoms are chronic and only slowly progressive toward an acute stage. However, because the symptoms and causes of these conditions overlap, the term COPD is being used in clinical practice to refer to all three disorders.

Asthma (AZ-ma) affects an estimated 3–6 percent of the U.S. population. Unusually sensitive and irritable air-conducting passageways respond to irritants by constricting, called a *bronchospasm*. In many cases, the trigger appears to be an immediate hypersensitivity reaction to an allergen in the inhaled air. Drug reactions, air pollution, chronic respiratory infections, exercise, and emotional stress can also induce an asthma attack in sensitive individuals.

The most obvious and potentially dangerous symptoms include (1) the constriction of smooth muscles all along the bronchial tree, (2) edema and swelling of the mucosa of the respiratory passageways, and (3) the accelerated production of mucus. The combination makes breathing very difficult. Exhalation is affected more than inhalation; the narrowed passageways often collapse before exhalation is completed. Although mucus production increases, mucus transport slows, so fluids accumulate along the passageways. Coughing and wheezing then develop. The bronchoconstriction and mucus production occur in a few minutes, in response to the release of histamine and prostaglandins by mast cells. Over a period of hours, neutrophils and eosinophils migrate into the area, which then becomes inflamed, further reducing airflow and damaging respiratory tissues. A severe attack reduces the functional capabilities of the respiratory system. Peripheral tissues become starved for oxygen, a condition that can prove fatal. The annual death rate from asthma in the United States is approximately four deaths per million population among those age 5–34. Mortality among asthmatic African Americans is twice that of Caucasian Americans.

The treatment of asthma involves the dilation of the respiratory passageways by administering **bronchodilators** (brong-kō-DĪ-lā-torz) (drugs that relax bronchial smooth muscle) and by reducing inflammation and swelling of the respiratory mucosa with anti-inflammatory medication. Important bronchodilators include *theophylline*, *epinephrine*, *albuterol*, and other beta-adrenergic drugs. Although the strongest beta-adrenergic drugs are quite useful in a crisis, they are effective only for brief periods, and overuse can reduce their efficiency.

Bronchitis (brong-KĪ-tis) is an inflammation and swelling of the bronchial lining, leading to overproduction of mucous secretions. The most characteristic symptom is frequent coughing with copious sputum production. An estimated 20 percent of adult males have chronic bronchitis, a condition most commonly related to cigarette smoking, but also caused by other environmental irritants. Over time, the increased mucus production can block smaller airways and reduce air exchange and respiratory efficiency. Chronic bacterial infections leading to more lung damage are common. Treatment involves stopping smoking and the administration of bronchodilators, antibiotics, and supplemental oxygen as necessary.

Emphysema (em-fi-SĒ-muh) is a chronic, progressive condition characterized by shortness of breath and an inability to tolerate physical exertion. The underlying problem is the destruction of respiratory exchange surfaces; respiratory bronchioles and alveoli are functionally eliminated. The alveoli gradually expand and capillaries deteriorate, leaving large nonfunctional cavities in the lungs where gas exchange is severely decreased or eliminated.

Unfortunately, the loss of alveoli and bronchioles in emphysema is irreversible. Further progression can be limited by the cessation of smoking. The only effective treatment for most severe cases is the administration of supplemental oxygen. Lung transplants and the surgical removal of nonfunctional lung tissue have helped some patients.

Two clinical patterns of advanced disease occur. People with emphysema tend to maintain near-normal arterial pressure. Their respiratory muscles work hard, and they use a lot of energy just breathing. As a result, they tend to be thin. Because their blood oxygenation is near normal, skin color in Caucasians in this group is pink. The combination of heavy breathing and pink coloration accounts for the descriptive term *pink puffers* for individuals with this condition. People with chronic bronchitis may have symptoms of heart failure, including widespread edema. Their blood oxygenation is low, and their skin may have a bluish color. The combination of widespread edema and bluish coloration explains the descriptive term *blue bloaters* for individuals with this condition.

The Bronchioles [Figures 24.9/24.11a,b]

Each tertiary bronchus branches several times within the bronchopulmonary segment, ultimately giving rise to 6500 smaller **terminal bronchioles**. Terminal bronchioles have a luminal diameter of 0.3–0.5 mm. The walls of terminal bronchioles, which lack cartilaginous support, are dominated by smooth muscle tissue (**Figures 24.9** and **24.11a,b**). The autonomic nervous system regulates the activity in the smooth muscle layer of the terminal bronchioles and thereby controls the diameter. Sympathetic activation and the release of epinephrine by the suprarenal medullae cause enlargement of the airways, or **bronchodilation**. Parasympathetic stimulation leads to **bronchoconstriction**. These changes alter the resistance to airflow toward or away from the respiratory exchange surfaces. Tension in the smooth muscles often throws the bronchiolar mucosa into a series of folds, and excessive stimulation, as in *asthma*, can almost completely prevent airflow along the terminal bronchioles.

Each terminal bronchiole delivers air to a single pulmonary lobule. Within the lobule, the terminal bronchiole branches to form several **respiratory bronchioles**. These are the thinnest and most delicate branches of the bronchial tree, and they deliver air to the exchange surfaces of the lungs. The preliminary filtration and humidification of the incoming air are completed before air leaves the terminal bronchioles. The epithelial cells of the respiratory bronchioles and the smaller terminal bronchioles are cuboidal. Cilia are rare, and there are no mucous cells or underlying mucous glands.

Alveolar Ducts and Alveoli [Figures 24.11/24.12]

Respiratory bronchioles are connected to individual alveoli and to multiple alveoli along regions called **alveolar ducts**. These passageways end at **alveolar sacs**, common chambers connected to several individual alveoli (**Figures 24.11** and **24.12a–c**). Each lung contains approximately 150 million alveoli, giving the lung an open, spongy appearance. An extensive

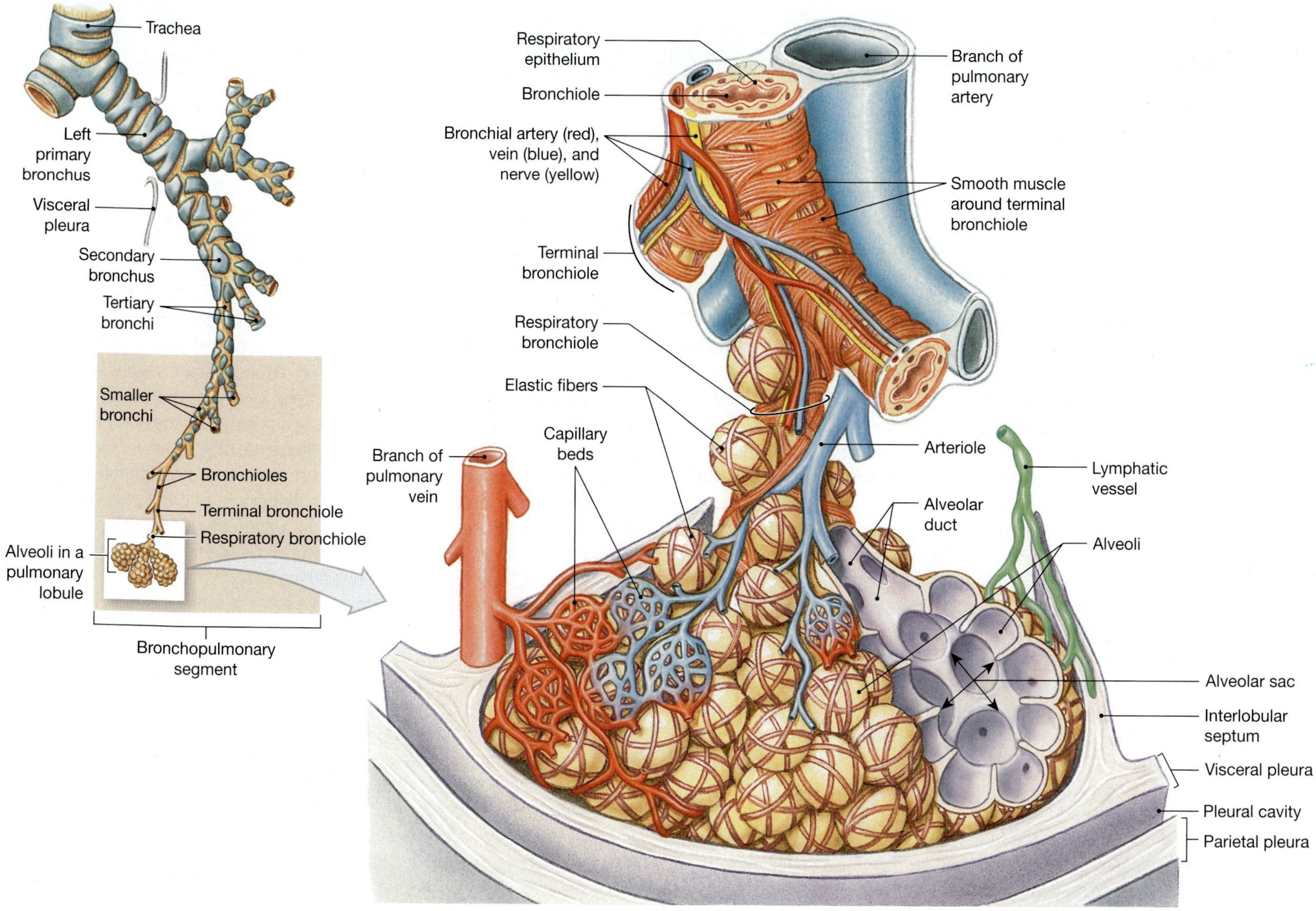

(a) Components of a lung lobule

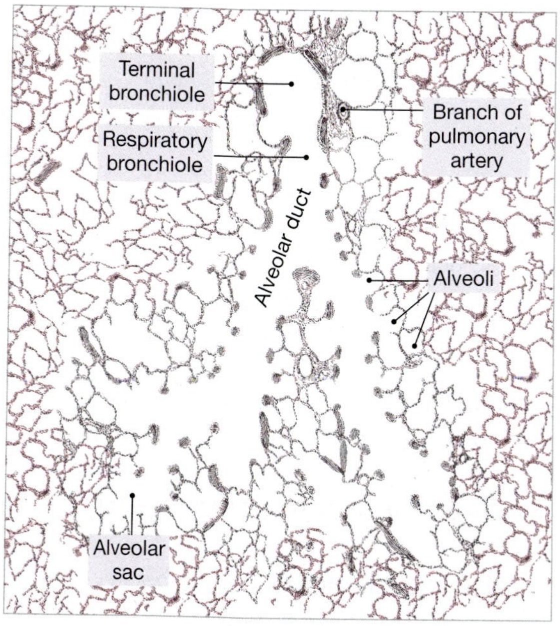

(b) Histology of the lung

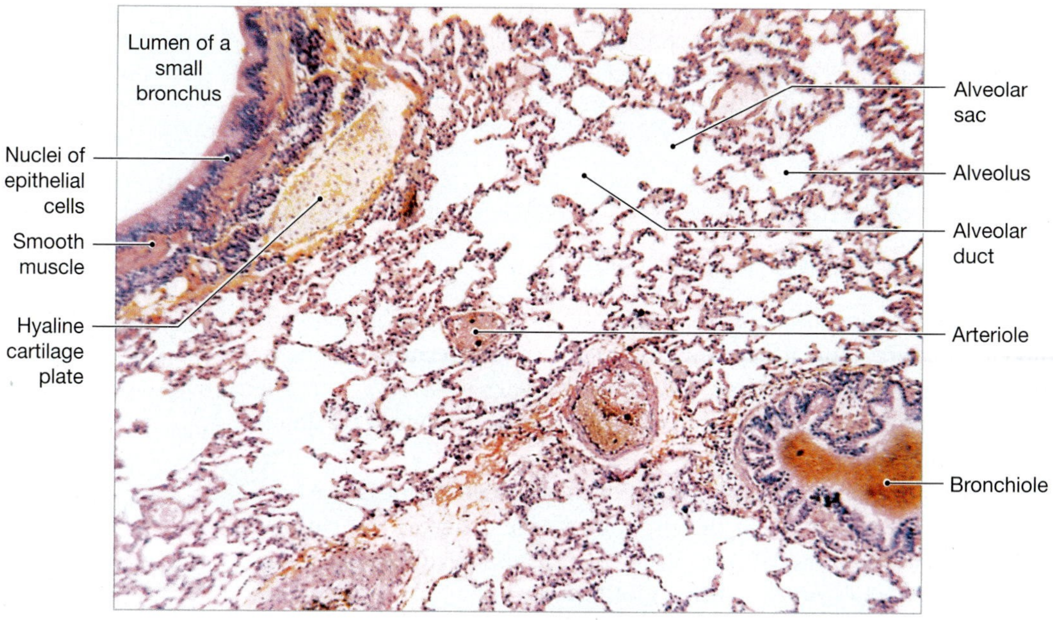

(c) Histology of the lung LM × 62

Figure 24.11 Bronchi and Bronchioles
(a) The structure of one portion of a single lobule. **(b)** and **(c)** Histological sections of the lung.

Figure 24.12 Alveolar Organization
(a) Basic structure of a lobule, cut to reveal the arrangement between the alveolar ducts and alveoli. A network of capillaries surrounds each alveolus. These capillaries are surrounded by elastic fibers. **(b)** SEM of lung tissue, showing the appearance and organization of the alveoli. **(c)** Diagrammatic sectional view of alveolar structure and the respiratory membrane. **(d)** The respiratory membrane.

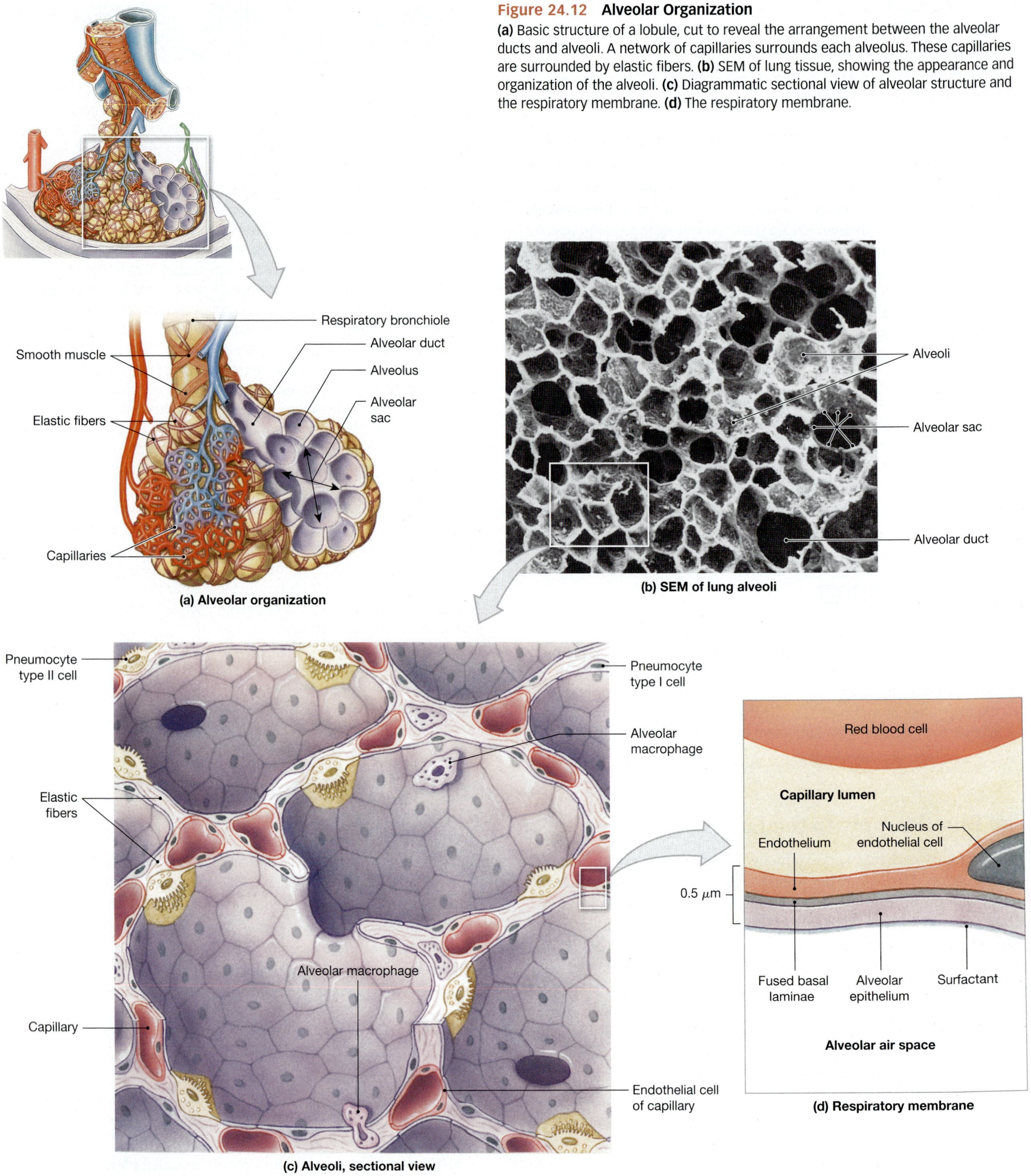

network of capillaries is associated with each alveolus (Figure 24.12c); the capillaries are surrounded by a network of elastic fibers. This elastic tissue helps maintain the relative positions of the alveoli and respiratory bronchioles. Recoil of these fibers during expiration reduces the size of the alveoli and assists in the process of expiration.

The Alveolus and the Respiratory Membrane [Figure 24.12c,d]

The alveolar epithelium consists primarily of simple squamous epithelium (Figure 24.12c). The squamous epithelial cells, called **pneumocyte type I cells**, or *type I alveolar cells*, are unusually thin and delicate. **Pneumocyte type II cells**, or *type II alveolar cells* are scattered among the squamous cells. These large cells produce an oily secretion containing a mixture of phospholipids. This secretion, termed **surfactant** (sur-FAK-tant), coats the inner surface of each alveolus and reduces surface tension in the fluid coating the alveolar surface. Without surfactant the alveoli would collapse. Roaming **alveolar macrophages** *(dust cells)* patrol the epithelium, phagocytizing any particulate matter that has eluded the respiratory defenses and reached the alveolar surfaces.

Gas exchange occurs in areas where the basal laminae of the alveolar epithelium and adjacent capillaries have fused (Figure 24.12d). In these areas the total distance separating the respiratory and circulatory systems can be as little as 0.1 μm. Diffusion across this **respiratory membrane** proceeds very rapidly because (1) the distance is small and (2) the gases are lipid soluble. The membranes of the epithelial and endothelial cells thus do not pose a barrier to the movement of oxygen and carbon dioxide between the blood and alveolar airspaces.

CONCEPT CHECK

1. Why do chronic smokers develop a hacking "smoker's cough"?
2. Chronic bronchitis involves the overproduction of mucus. Over time, how could this affect respiration?
3. Why are there almost no cilia and no mucous cells or mucous glands in the respiratory bronchiole?
4. What is the function of the surfactant produced by the alveolar cells?

See blue "Answers" tab at back of book.

The Blood Supply to the Lungs [Figure 24.11a]

The respiratory-exchange surfaces receive blood from arteries of the pulmonary circuit. The pulmonary arteries enter the lungs at the hilum and branch with the bronchi as they approach the lobules. Each lobule receives an arteriole and a venule, and a network of capillaries surrounds each alveolus directly beneath the respiratory membrane. In addition to providing a mechanism for gas exchange, the alveolar capillaries are the primary source of *angiotensin-converting enzyme*, which converts circulating angiotensin I to angiotensin II, a hormone involved with the regulation of blood volume and blood pressure. p. 518

Blood from the alveolar capillaries passes through the pulmonary venules and then enters the pulmonary veins that deliver it to the left atrium. The conducting portions of the respiratory tract receive blood from the *external carotid arteries* (nasal passages and larynx), the *thyrocervical trunk* (branches of the subclavian arteries that supply the inferior larynx and trachea), and the *bronchial arteries* (Figure 24.11a). The capillaries supplied by the bronchial arteries provide oxygen and nutrients to the conducting passageways of the lungs. The venous blood flows into the pulmonary veins, bypassing the rest of the systemic circuit and diluting the oxygenated blood leaving the alveoli.

Clinical Note

Lung Cancer Lung cancers now account for 13 percent of new cancer cases and 28 percent of all cancer deaths, making this condition the primary cause of cancer death in the U.S. population. It kills more people than colon, breast, and prostate cancer combined. Despite advances in the treatment of other forms of cancer, the survival statistics for lung cancer have not changed significantly.

Detailed statistical and experimental evidence has shown that *85–90 percent of all lung cancers are the direct result of cigarette smoking*. The incidence of lung cancer for nonsmokers is 3.4 per 100,000 population, whereas the incidence for smokers ranges from 59.3 per 100,000 for those who smoke between a half-pack and a pack per day, to 217.3 per 100,000 for those who smoke one to two packs per day. Before 1970, this disease affected primarily middle-aged men, but as the number of female smokers has increased (a trend that started in the 1940s), so has the number of women who die from lung cancer.

Smoking changes the quality of the inspired air, making it drier and contaminated with several carcinogenic compounds and particulate matter. The combination overloads the respiratory defenses and damages the epithelial cells throughout the respiratory system. The risk of developing lung cancer is related to the total cumulative exposure to the carcinogens. The more cigarettes smoked, the greater the risk, whether those cigarettes are smoked over a period of weeks or years. At any point before tumors form, the histological changes induced by smoking are reversible; a normal epithelium will return if the carcinogens are removed. At the same time, the statistical risks decline to significantly lower levels. Ten years after quitting, a former smoker stands only a 10 percent greater chance of developing lung cancer than does a nonsmoker.

The fact that cigarette smoking typically causes cancer is not surprising in view of the toxic chemicals contained in the smoke. What is surprising is that more smokers do not develop lung cancer. Evidence suggests that some smokers have a genetic predisposition to develop one form of lung cancer.

The Pleural Cavities and Pleural Membranes [Figures 24.8a/24.13]

The thoracic cavity has the shape of a broad cone. Its walls are the rib cage, and the muscular diaphragm forms the floor. The two *pleural cavities* are separated by the mediastinum (Figures 24.8a and 24.13). Each lung occupies a single pleural cavity, lined by a serous membrane, or **pleura** (PLOO-rah; plural, *pleurae*). The pleural membrane consists of two continuous layers. The **parietal pleura** covers the inner surface of the thoracic wall and extends over the diaphragm and mediastinum. The **visceral pleura** covers the outer surfaces of the lungs, extending into the fissures between the lobes. The space between the parietal and visceral pleurae is called the **pleural cavity**. Each pleural cavity actually represents a potential space rather than an open chamber, for the parietal and visceral layers are usually in close contact. A small amount of **pleural fluid** is secreted by both pleural membranes. Pleural fluid covers the opposing surfaces, and this moist, slippery coating reduces friction between the parietal and visceral surfaces during breathing.

Inflammation of the pleurae, a condition called **pleurisy**, may cause the membranes to produce and secrete excess amounts of pleural fluid, or the inflamed pleurae may adhere to one another, limiting relative movement. In either form of this disorder, breathing becomes difficult, and prompt medical attention is required.

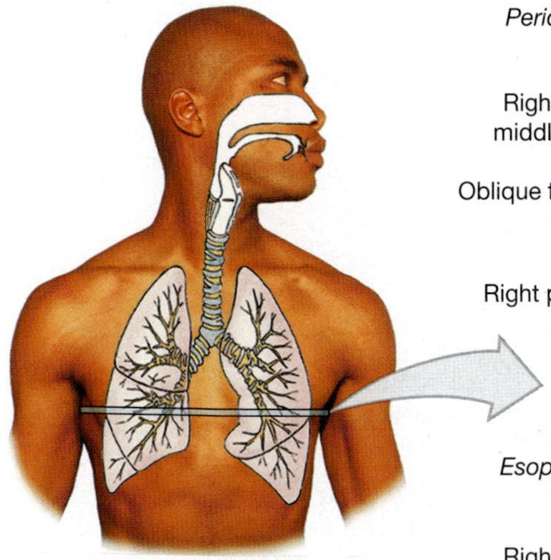
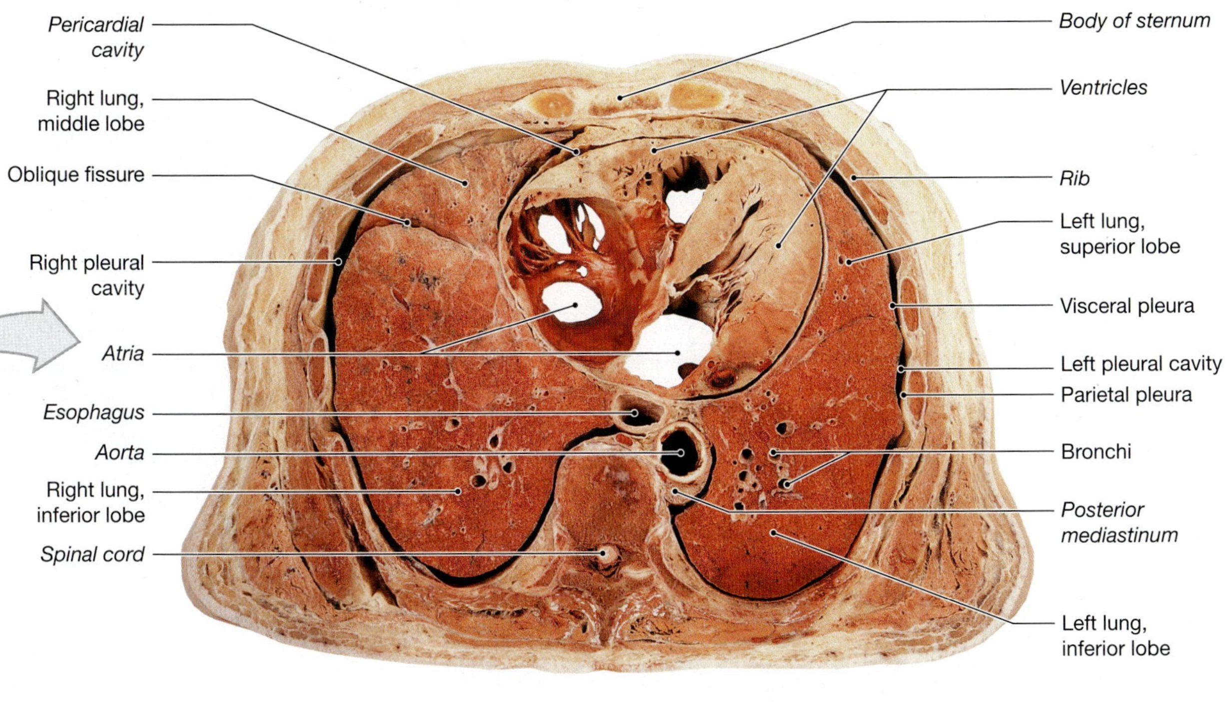

Figure 24.13 Anatomical Relationships in the Thoracic Cavity The relationships among thoracic structures are best seen in a horizontal section. This is an inferior view of a section taken at the level of T_8.

CONCEPT CHECK

1. If a pulmonary embolism involves a major pulmonary vessel, why can this cause heart failure?
2. What is the function of the pleural fluid?
3. What vessels supply the conducting portions of the respiratory tract?

See blue "Answers" tab at back of book.

Respiratory Muscles and Pulmonary Ventilation

Pulmonary ventilation, or breathing, refers to the physical movement of air into and out of the bronchial tree. The function of pulmonary ventilation is to maintain adequate *alveolar ventilation*, the movement of air into and out of the alveoli. Alveolar ventilation prevents the buildup of carbon dioxide in the alveoli and ensures a continual supply of oxygen that keeps pace with absorption by the bloodstream.

Respiratory Muscles [Figure 24.14]

The skeletal muscles involved in respiratory movements were introduced in Chapters 10 and 11. ∞ p. 582 Of these, the most important are the **diaphragm** and the **external** and **internal intercostal muscles**. The diaphragm tenses and flattens as it contracts, and this increases the volume of the thoracic cavity. When the diaphragm relaxes, it arches upward and reduces the volume of the thoracic cavity. Air is drawn into the lungs when the volume of the thoracic cavity increases, and air is expelled when the volume decreases. The external intercostal muscles may assist in inspiration by elevating the ribs. When the ribs are elevated, they swing anteriorly, and the width of the thoracic cage increases along its anterior-posterior axis. The internal intercostal muscles depress the ribs and reduce the width of the thoracic cavity, thereby contributing to expiration. These muscles and their actions are diagrammed in Figure 24.14.

Clinical Note

Respiratory Distress Syndrome (RDS) Pneumocyte type II cells among the lining cells of the alveoli begin producing surfactant at the end of the sixth fetal month. By the eighth month, surfactant production has risen to the level required for normal respiratory function. **Neonatal respiratory distress syndrome (NRDS)**, also known as *hyaline membrane disease (HMD)*, develops when surfactant production fails to reach normal levels. Although some forms of HMD are inherited, the condition most commonly accompanies premature delivery.

In the absence of surfactant, the alveoli tend to collapse during exhalation. Although the conducting passageways remain open, the newborn infant must then inhale with extra force to reopen the alveoli on the next breath. In effect, every breath must approach the power of the first, so the infant rapidly becomes exhausted. Respiratory movements become progressively weaker; eventually, the alveoli fail to expand and gas exchange ceases.

One method of treatment assists the infant by administering air under pressure so that the alveoli are held open. This procedure, known as **positive end-expiratory pressure (PEEP)**, can keep the newborn alive until surfactant production increases to normal levels. Surfactant administered in the form of a fine mist of surfactant droplets via the trachea on the first day of life has reduced the death rate from NRDS from nearly 100 percent to less than 10 percent.

Surfactant abnormalities can also develop in adults as the result of severe respiratory infections or pulmonary injuries. Alveolar collapse follows, producing a condition known as **adult respiratory distress syndrome (ARDS)**. The PEEP procedure maintains life until the underlying problem can be corrected, but at least 50–60 percent of ARDS cases result in fatalities.

The **accessory respiratory muscles** become active when the depth and frequency of respiration must be increased markedly. The sternocleidomastoid, serratus anterior, pectoralis minor, and scalene muscles assist the external intercostal muscles in elevating the ribs and performing inspiration.

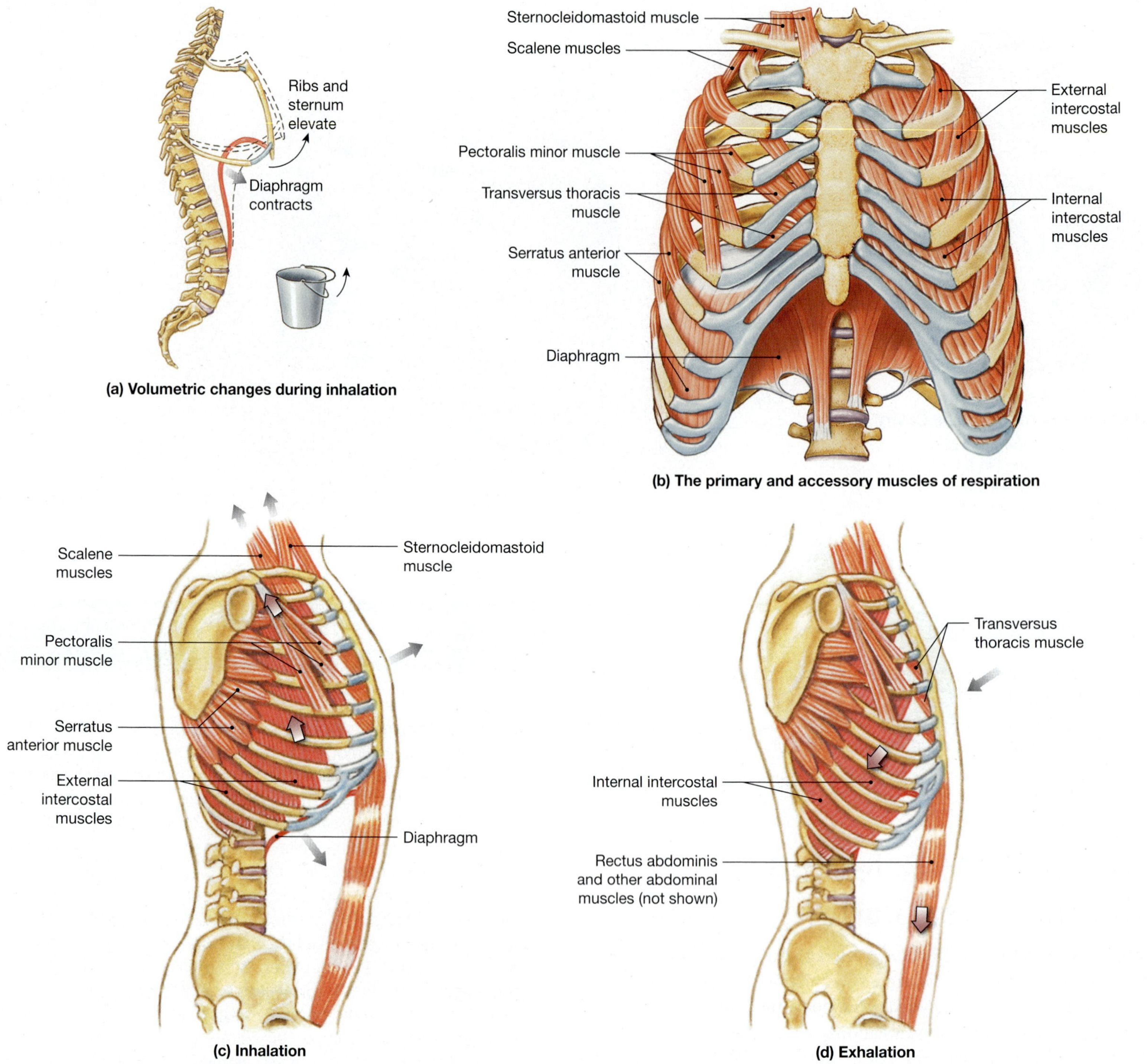

Figure 24.14 Respiratory Muscles
(a) As the ribs are elevated or the diaphragm is depressed, the volume of the thoracic cavity increases and air moves into the lungs. The outward movement of the ribs as they are elevated resembles the outward swing of a raised bucket handle. **(b)** Anterior view at rest, with no air movement. **(c) Inhalation**, showing the primary and accessory respiratory muscles that elevate the ribs and flatten the diaphragm. **(d) Exhalation**, showing the primary and accessory respiratory muscles that depress the ribs and elevate the diaphragm.

The transversus thoracis, oblique, and rectus abdominis muscles assist the internal intercostal muscles in expiration by compressing the abdominal contents, forcing the diaphragm upward, and further reducing the volume of the thoracic cavity.

Respiratory Movements

The respiratory muscles may be used in various combinations, depending on the volume of air that must be moved in or out of the lungs. Respiratory movements may be classified as *eupnea* or *hyperpnea*, based on whether expiration is passive or active.

Eupnea In **eupnea** (ūp-NĒ-a), or **quiet breathing**, inspiration involves muscular contractions, but expiration is a passive process. During quiet breathing, expansion of the lungs stretches their elastic fibers. In addition, elevation of the rib cage stretches opposing skeletal muscles and elastic fibers in the connective tissues of the body wall. When the inspiratory muscles relax, these elastic structures contract, returning the diaphragm or rib cage or both to their original positions.

Eupnea may involve *diaphragmatic breathing* or *costal breathing*.

- During **diaphragmatic breathing**, or **deep breathing**, contraction of the diaphragm provides the necessary change in thoracic volume. Air is drawn into the lungs as the diaphragm contracts, and exhalation occurs when the diaphragm relaxes.

- In **costal breathing**, or **shallow breathing**, the thoracic volume changes because the rib cage changes shape. Inhalation occurs when contraction of the external intercostal muscles elevates the ribs and enlarges the thoracic cavity. Exhalation occurs when these muscles relax. During pregnancy women increasingly rely on costal breathing as the uterus enlarges and pushes the abdominal viscera against the diaphragm.

Hyperpnea **Hyperpnea** (hī-perp-NĒ-a), or **forced breathing**, involves active inspiratory and expiratory movements. Forced breathing calls upon the accessory muscles to assist with inspiration, and expiration involves contraction of the transversus thoracis and internal intercostal muscles. When a person is breathing at absolute maximum levels, such as during vigorous exercise, the abdominal muscles are used in exhalation. Their contraction compresses the abdominal contents, pushing them up against the diaphragm and further reducing the volume of the thoracic cavity.

Respiratory Changes at Birth

There are several important differences between the respiratory system of a fetus and that of a newborn infant. Before delivery, pulmonary arterial resistance is high because the pulmonary vessels are collapsed. The rib cage is compressed, and the lungs and conducting passageways contain only small amounts of fluid and no air. At birth the newborn infant takes a truly heroic first breath through powerful contractions of the diaphragmatic and external intercostal muscles. The inspired air enters the passageways with enough force to push the contained fluids out of the way and inflate the entire bronchial tree and most of the alveoli. The same drop in pressure that pulls air into the lungs pulls blood into the pulmonary circulation; the changes in blood flow that occur lead to the closure of the *foramen ovale*, the embryonic interatrial connection, and the *ductus arteriosus*, the fetal connection between the pulmonary trunk and the aorta. p. 601

The exhalation that follows fails to completely empty the lungs, for the rib cage does not return to its former, fully compressed state. Cartilages and connective tissues keep the conducting passageways open, and the surfactant covering the alveolar surfaces prevents their collapse. Subsequent breaths complete the inflation of the alveoli.

CONCEPT CHECK

1. John breaks a rib that punctures the thoracic cavity on his left side. Which structures are potentially damaged, and what do you predict will happen to the lung as a result?
2. In emphysema, alveoli are replaced by large air spaces and elastic fibrous connective tissue. How do these changes affect the lungs?
3. Summarize the changes that occur in a newborn infant's cardiovascular and respiratory systems as a newborn infant starts to breathe.

See blue "Answers" tab at back of book.

Respiratory Centers of the Brain [Figure 24.15]

Under normal conditions, cellular rates of oxygen absorption and carbon dioxide generation are matched by the capillary rates of delivery and removal. When adjustments by the cardiovascular and respiratory systems are needed to meet the body's ever-changing demands for oxygen, these systems must be coordinated. The regulatory centers that integrate the responses by these systems are located in the pons and medulla oblongata.

The **respiratory centers** are three pairs of loosely organized nuclei in the reticular formation of the pons and medulla oblongata (Figure 24.15). These nuclei regulate the activities of the respiratory muscles by adjusting the frequency and depth of pulmonary ventilation.

The **respiratory rhythmicity center** sets the basic pace and depth of respiration. It can be subdivided into a **dorsal respiratory group (DRG)** and a **ventral respiratory group (VRG)**. The dorsal respiratory group, or *inspiratory center*, controls motor neurons innervating the external intercostal muscles and the diaphragm. This group functions in every respiratory cycle, whether quiet or forced. The ventral respiratory group functions only during forced respiration. It innervates motor neurons controlling accessory muscles involved in active exhalation and maximal inhalation. The neurons involved with active exhalation are sometimes said to form an *expiratory center*.

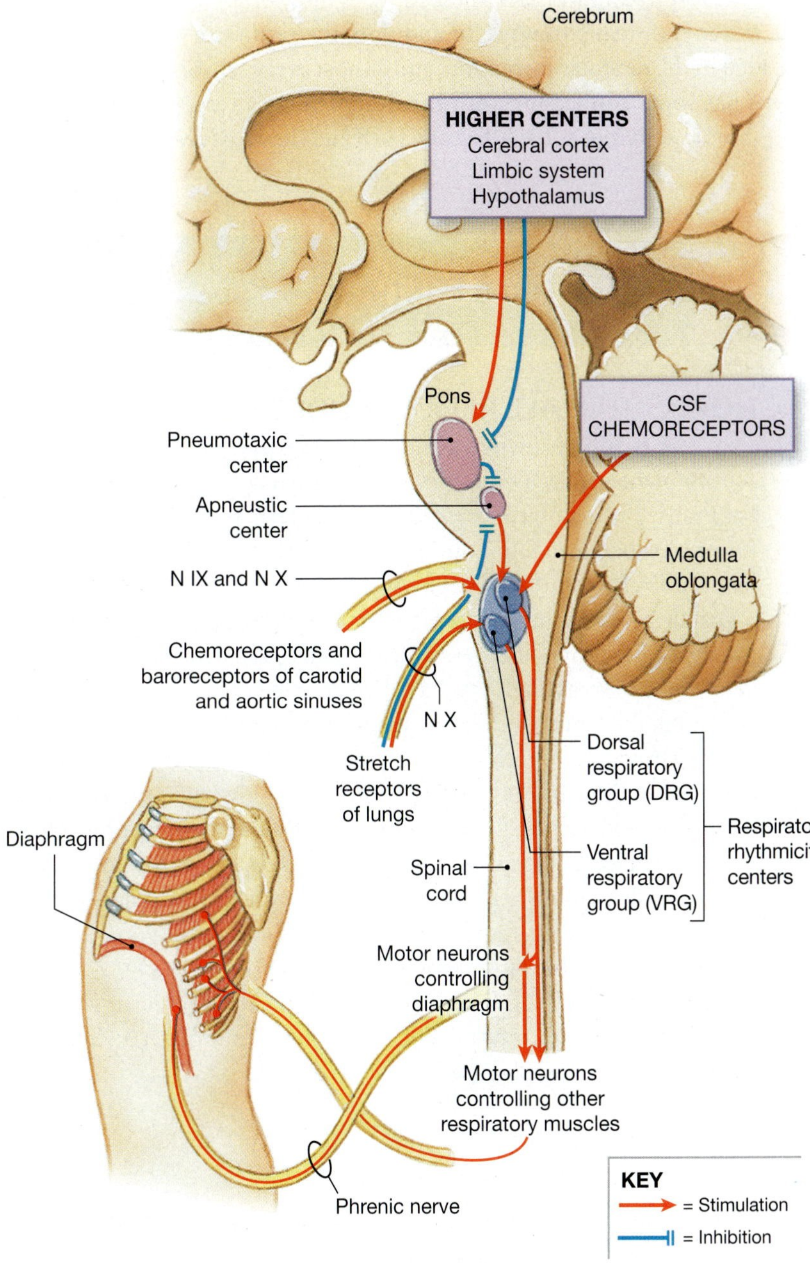

Figure 24.15 Respiratory Centers and Reflex Controls
The positions and relationships between the major respiratory centers and other factors important to respiratory control. Pathways for conscious control over respiratory muscles are not shown.

The **apneustic** (ap-NŪ-stik) and **pneumotaxic** (noo-mō-TAKS-ik) **centers** of the pons are paired nuclei that adjust the output of the rhythmicity center, thereby modifying the pace of respiration. Their activities adjust the respiratory rate and the depth of respiration in response to sensory stimuli or instructions from higher centers. The locations of the apneustic, pneumotaxic, and respiratory rhythmicity centers are reviewed in **Figure 24.15**.

Normal breathing occurs automatically, without conscious control. Three different reflexes are involved in the regulation of respiration: (1) *mechanoreceptor reflexes* that respond to changes in the volume of the lungs or to changes in arterial blood pressure; (2) *chemoreceptor reflexes* that respond to changes in the P_{CO_2}, pH, and P_{O_2} of the blood and cerebrospinal fluid; and (3) *protective reflexes* that respond to physical injury or irritation of the respiratory tract.

Higher centers influence respiration via inputs to the pneumotaxic center and by their direct influence on respiratory muscles. These higher centers are found in the cerebrum, especially the cerebral cortex, and in the hypothalamus. Although pyramidal output provides conscious control over the respiratory muscles, these muscles most often receive instructions via extrapyramidal pathways. In addition, the respiratory centers are embedded in the reticular formation, and almost every sensory and motor nucleus has some connection with this complex. As a result, emotional and autonomic activities often affect the pace and depth of respiration.

Aging and the Respiratory System

Many factors interact to reduce the efficiency of the respiratory system in elderly individuals. Three examples are particularly noteworthy:

1. With increasing age, elastic tissue deteriorates throughout the body. The primary impact on the respiratory system is a reduction in the lungs' ability to inflate and deflate.
2. Movements of the rib cage are restricted by arthritic changes in the rib articulations and by decreased flexibility at the costal cartilages. In combination with the changes noted in (1), the stiffening and reduction in chest movement effectively limit the respiratory volume. This restriction contributes to the reduction in exercise performance and capabilities with increasing age.
3. Some degree of emphysema is normally found in individuals age 50–70. On average, roughly 1 square foot of respiratory membrane is lost each year after age 30. However, the extent varies widely, depending on lifetime exposure to cigarette smoke and other respiratory irritants.

Embryology Summary

For an introduction to the development of the Respiratory System, see Chapter 28 (Embryology and Human Development).

Clinical Case — THE RESPIRATORY SYSTEM

HOW IS THIS ALL RELATED, DOC?

Dorothy is the co-owner, chief cook, and bartender at the small, family-owned Dew Drop Inn, located on Highway 12 just west of SakPrairie, a small farm town in southwestern Wisconsin. Dorothy is known for having a family-oriented restaurant and bar that serves the best hamburger west of the Wisconsin River.

Lately Dorothy hasn't been feeling like herself. She has been complaining of chronic shoulder, arm, and hand pain. Dorothy has also developed a chronic cough that has forced her to cut her daily 5- to 7-mile run along the banks of the Wisconsin River to only 3 or 4 miles.

On Thursday, Dorothy's run is especially difficult. It is a warm and windy morning, and her cough continues to give her trouble. At the completion of her run, Dorothy notices that she is sweating only on one side of her face. Later, as she applies her makeup, Dorothy notices that she is unable to open her right eye completely. Dorothy points this out to her husband John, and he recommends that Dorothy make an appointment to see the family physician.

On Monday, Dorothy sees her physician. The physician is mildly concerned about Dorothy's cough, but focuses most of her attention on Dorothy's other complaints.

Initial Examination

The physician notes the following:

- Dorothy is 35 years old and in excellent physical condition.
- Blood pressure is normal.
- CBC is normal.
- Chest sounds are normal.
- Dorothy has no history of smoking. However, the Dew Drop Inn has a smoking section that is consistently filled to capacity with patrons.
- Dorothy confirms that she has had severe pain in the right shoulder region radiating from the scapula toward the axilla and down along the inner aspect of her arm and hand.
- Examination by the physician notes some atrophy of muscles on the anterior, medial surface of the right forearm.
- Dorothy has diminished cutaneous sensitivity of the ring and little fingers of the right hand.
- The physician notes miosis of the right pupil.
- Dorothy has a negative ciliospinal reflex.
- When the lights in the examining room are dimmed, the right pupil dilates more slowly than the left pupil.
- The skin on the right side of the face is noticeably drier than that on the left side of the face.
- Palpation of the supraclavicular nodes on both sides demonstrates enlarged and asymmetrical lymph nodes on the right side.

After a discussion with the radiologist, the physician schedules Dorothy for a chest x-ray and an MRI.

Clinical Case *continued*

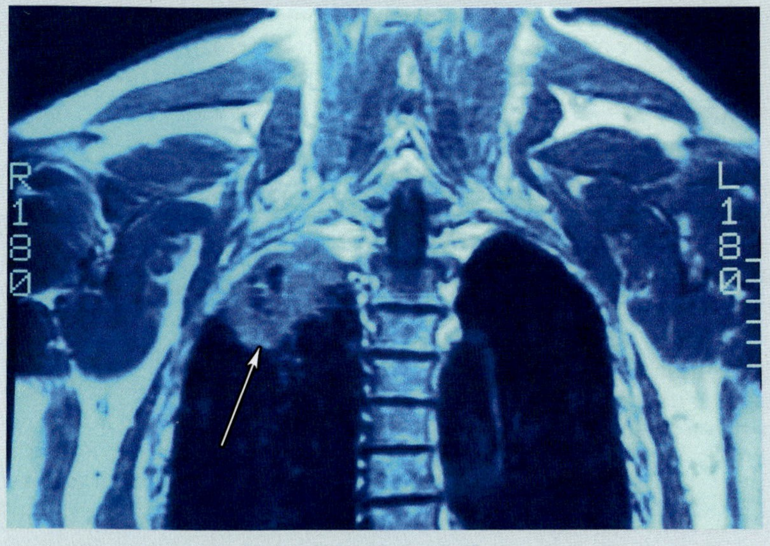

Figure 24.16 Results of Dorothy's MRI

Follow-up Examination

Upon examination of the MRI (**Figure 24.16**), the radiologist notes the following:

- Dorothy has stage IV tumor in the superior lobe of the right lung.
- The tumor appears to have invaded the posterior chest wall.

Points to Consider

At one time or another, every system of the body plays an important role in presenting signs or symptoms, thereby enabling a physician to piece together the various clues that will ideally lead to a correct diagnosis of the patient. Both the patient's presenting symptoms and the physician's analysis and interpretation of the symptoms contribute to the detective work.

To consider the meaning of the information presented in the case above, you need to review the anatomical material covered in this and previous chapters. The questions below will guide you in your review. Think about and answer each one, referring back to Chapter 24 if you need help.

1. What nerve innervates muscles of the anterior, medial surfaces of the right forearm?
2. What branch of the nervous system controls the activity of the sweat glands?
3. Dorothy is not sweating on one side of her face. What nerves innervate the sweat glands of the face?
4. Dorothy's right eye does not dilate properly. What muscles are responsible for dilation of the pupil of the eye? What nerves innervate these muscles?

Analysis and Interpretation

The information below answers the questions raised in the "Points to Consider" section. To review the material, refer to the pages in the chapter indicated by the link icons.

1. The ulnar nerve innervates the flexor carpi ulnaris muscle and the ulnar side of the flexor digitorum profundus muscle. pp. 373–376
2. The activity of the sweat glands is controlled by the sympathetic branch of the autonomic nervous system. pp. 454–455
3. The sympathetic branch of the autonomic nervous system innervates the sweat glands of the face. These ANS fibers originate from T_1. pp. 454–455
4. The dilator muscles of the iris of the eye are innervated by the sympathetic branch of the autonomic nervous system. These ANS fibers originate from T_1. pp. 464–466

Diagnosis

Dorothy is diagnosed with Horner's syndrome and lower brachial plexus involvement secondary to lung cancer. She has a Pancoast tumor within the superior lobe of the right lung. (Doctors Horner and Pancoast first described the pattern of symptoms and the anatomical lesions that produced them.) The overwhelming majority of cases of Pancoast tumors are non-small cell lung carcinoma, with more than 95 percent located in the superior lobe of the lung. A Pancoast tumor often grows posteriorly, pressing against the posterior thoracic wall. This pressure will cause disruption in peripheral nerve function.

Tumor pressure often affects the superior cervical ganglion of the sympathetic chain. This leads to the interruption of preganglionic and/or postganglionic neuron function, resulting in Horner's syndrome. In addition, damage to the afferent pain fibers of the sympathetic trunk will result in pain in the scapular, shoulder, and axillary regions.

Brachial plexus function (8th cervical and 1st thoracic spinal nerves) is often compromised as well. Tumor pressure on the lower brachial plexus causes compression of the motor and sensory components of the ulnar nerve, resulting in (1) muscular dysfunction and atrophy of the flexor carpi ulnaris muscle, (2) muscular dysfunction and atrophy of the ulnar component of the flexor digitorum profundus muscle, (3) muscular dysfunction and atrophy of many intrinsic hand muscles, and (4) loss of cutaneous sensitivity of the ring and little fingers and corresponding surfaces of the hand.

Patients with this form of lung cancer are often treated initially for the local musculoskeletal conditions, which trouble them more than any early respiratory symptoms. Initial patient diagnosis may include conditions such as bursitis and vertebral osteoarthritis. Symptoms may persist for several months before diagnosis of the lung cancer. ■

CLINICAL CASE TERMS

bursitis: Inflammation of a bursa.

ciliospinal reflex (pupillary-skin reflex): Dilation of the pupil following scratching of the skin of the neck.

pupil miosis: Pupil that is rounded and constricted.

vertebral osteoarthritis: Arthritis of the joints between two articulating vertebrae.

CLINICAL TERMS

asthma (AZ-ma): A condition characterized by unusually sensitive, irritable, inflamed conducting passageways.

atelectasis (at-e-LEK-ta-sis): A partially or completely collapsed lung.

bronchitis (brong-KĪ-tis): An inflammation of the bronchial lining.

cardiopulmonary resuscitation (CPR): Applying cycles of compression to the rib cage and mouth-to-mouth breathing to maintain circulatory and respiratory function.

cystic fibrosis (CF): A relatively common, lethal inherited disease in which mucous secretions in the lungs become too thick to be transported easily.

emphysema (em-fi-ZĒ-ma): A chronic, progressive condition characterized by shortness of breath and resulting from the destruction of respiratory exchange surfaces.

epistaxis (ep-i-STAK-sis): A nosebleed caused by trauma, infection, allergies, hypertension, or other factors.

Heimlich (HĪM-lik) **maneuver:** A method of applying abdominal pressure to force the expulsion of foreign objects lodged in the trachea or larynx.

laryngitis (lar-in-JĪ-tis): Infection or inflammation of the larynx.

lung cancer: A class of aggressive malignancies originating in the bronchial passageways or alveoli.

pleural effusion: An abnormal accumulation of fluid within the pleural cavities.

pneumonia (nū-MŌ-nē-a): A condition caused by an infection of the lobules of the lung and characterized by a decline in respiratory function due to fluid leakage into the alveoli and/or swelling and constriction of the respiratory bronchioles.

pneumothorax (noo-mō-THOR-aks): The entry of air into the pleural cavity.

pulmonary embolism: Blockage of a pulmonary artery by a blood clot, fat mass, or air bubble.

respiratory distress syndrome (RDS): A condition resulting from inadequate surfactant production; characterized by collapse of the alveoli and an inability to maintain adequate levels of gas exchange at the lungs.

silicosis (sil-i-KŌ-sis), **asbestosis** (as-bes-Tō-sis), and **anthracosis** (an-thra-Kō-sis): Serious clinical conditions caused by the inhalation of dust or other particulate matter in sufficient quantities to overload the respiratory defense system, resulting in lung scarring and a reduction in respiratory function.

thoracentesis: Removal of a sample of pleural fluid for diagnostic evaluation.

tracheostomy (trā-kē-OS-tō-mē): Insertion of a tube through an incision in the anterior tracheal wall to bypass a foreign body or damaged larynx.

tuberculosis (tū-ber-kū-Lō-sis) **(TB):** Infection of the lungs by the bacteria *Mycobacterium tuberculosis*. Symptoms are variable but usually include coughing and chest pain, with fever, night sweats, fatigue, and weight loss.

STUDY OUTLINE

Introduction 630

An Overview of the Respiratory System 630

1. The **respiratory system** includes the nose, nasal cavity and sinuses, pharynx, larynx, trachea, and conducting passageways leading to the exchange surfaces of the lungs. *(see Figure 24.1)*
2. The **upper respiratory system** consists of the nose, nasal cavity, paranasal sinuses, and pharynx. These structures begin the process of filtration and humidification of the incoming air. The **lower respiratory system** includes the larynx, trachea, lungs, bronchi, bronchioles, and alveoli.
3. The **respiratory tract** consists of a *conducting portion*, which extends from the entrance to the nasal cavity to the bronchioles, and a *respiratory portion*, which includes the *respiratory bronchioles* and the **alveoli**. *(see Figure 24.1)*

Functions of the Respiratory System 631

4. The respiratory system: (1) provides an area for gas exchange between air and circulating blood; (2) moves air to and from exchange surfaces; (3) protects respiratory surfaces; (4) defends the respiratory system and other tissues from pathogens; (5) permits vocal communication; and (6) helps regulate blood volume and pressure and body fluid pH.

The Respiratory Epithelium 631

5. The **respiratory epithelium** lines the conducting portions of the respiratory system down to the level of the smallest bronchioles.
6. The respiratory epithelium consists of a pseudostratified, ciliated, columnar epithelium with mucous cells. *(see Figure 24.2)*
7. The respiratory epithelium produces mucus that traps incoming particles. Underneath is the **lamina propria** (a layer of connective tissue); the combined respiratory epithelium and lamina propria form a **mucosa** (mucous membrane). *(see Figure 24.2)*
8. The **respiratory defense system** includes the *mucus escalator* (which washes particles toward the stomach), alveolar macrophages, hairs, and cilia.

The Upper Respiratory System 632

The Nose and Nasal Cavity 632

1. Air normally enters the respiratory system via the **external nares**, which open into the **nasal cavity**. The **vestibule** (entryway) of the nose is guarded by hairs that screen out large particles. *(see Figure 24.3)*
2. Incoming air flows through the **superior**, **middle**, or **inferior meatuses** (narrow grooves) and bounces off the conchal surfaces. *(see Figure 24.3b,d)*
3. The **hard palate** separates the oral and nasal cavities. The **soft palate** separates the superior *nasopharynx* from the oral cavity. The connections between the nasal cavity and nasopharynx represent the **internal nares**. *(see Figure 24.3)*

The Pharynx 634

4. The **pharynx** is a chamber shared by the digestive and respiratory systems. The **nasopharynx** is the superior part of the pharynx. The **oropharynx** is continuous with the oral cavity; the **laryngopharynx** includes the narrow zone between the hyoid and the entrance to the esophagus. *(see Figures 24.3c,d and 25.5a)*

The Lower Respiratory System 634

The Larynx 634

1. Inhaled air passes through the **glottis** en route to the lungs; the **larynx** surrounds and protects the glottis. The **epiglottis** projects into the pharynx. *(see Figures 24.3c,d/24.4/24.5)*
2. Two pairs of folds span the glottal opening: the relatively inelastic **vestibular folds** and the more delicate **vocal folds**. Air passing through the glottis vibrates the vocal folds and produces sound. *(see Figure 24.5)*
3. The **intrinsic laryngeal muscles** regulate tension in the vocal folds and open and close the glottis. The **extrinsic laryngeal musculature** positions and stabilizes the larynx. During swallowing, both sets of muscles help to prevent particles from entering the glottis. *(see Figure 24.6)*

The Trachea 637

1. The **trachea** ("windpipe") extends from the sixth cervical vertebra to the fifth thoracic vertebra. The **submucosa** contains C-shaped **tracheal cartilages** that stiffen the tracheal walls and protect the airway. The posterior tracheal wall can distort to permit large masses of food to move along the esophagus. *(see Figures 24.2a/24.3c/24.7)*

The Primary Bronchi 638

1. The trachea branches within the mediastinum to form the **right** and **left primary** *(main)* **bronchi.** The primary bronchi and their branches form the *bronchial tree.* Each bronchus enters a lung at the **hilum**. The **root** of the lung is a connective tissue mass including the bronchus, pulmonary vessels, and nerves. *(see Figures 24.7/24.8)*

The Lungs 638

Lobes of the Lungs 638

1. The **lobes** of the lungs are separated by fissures. The **right lung** has three lobes: **superior**, **middle**, and **inferior** with an *oblique fissure* separating superior and inferior and a *horizontal fissure* separating superior and middle. The right lung also has three secondary bronchi: the **superior lobar, middle lobar**, and **inferior lobar bronchi**. The **left lung** has two lobes: **superior** and **inferior** with an *oblique fissure* separating the lobes; and two secondary bronchi: **superior lobar** and **inferior lobar bronchi**. *(see Figure 24.8)*

Lung Surfaces 640

2. The **costal surface** of the lung follows the inner contours of the rib cage. The **mediastinal surface** contains a hilum, and the left lung bears the **cardiac impression**. *(see Figure 24.8)*
3. The connective tissues of the root extend into the **parenchyma** of the lung as a series of **trabeculae** (partitions). These branches form **septa** that divide the lung into **lobules**. *(see Figure 24.9)*

The Pulmonary Bronchi 640

4. *Extrapulmonary bronchi* (**left** and **right primary bronchi**) are outside the lung tissue. *Intrapulmonary bronchi* (branches within the lung) are surrounded by bands of smooth muscle. *(see Figures 24.7/24.9/24.10/24.11)*
5. Each lung is further divided into smaller units called **bronchopulmonary segments**. These segments are named according to the associated tertiary bronchi. The right lung contains 10 and the left lung usually contains 8–9 bronchopulmonary segments. *(see Figures 24.7/24.9/24.10)*

The Bronchioles 643

6. Within the bronchopulmonary segments each tertiary bronchus ultimately gives rise to 50–80 **terminal bronchioles** that supply individual lobules. *(see Figures 24.9/24.11)*

Alveolar Ducts and Alveoli 643

7. The **respiratory bronchioles** open into **alveolar ducts**; many alveoli are interconnected at each duct. *(see Figures 24.11/24.12)*
8. The **respiratory membrane** (alveolar lining) consists of a simple squamous epithelium of **pneumocyte type I cells** *(type I alveolar cells)*; **pneumocyte type II cells** *(type II alveolar cells)* scattered in it produce an oily secretion (**surfactant**) that keeps the alveoli from collapsing. **Alveolar macrophages** *(dust cells)* patrol the epithelium and engulf foreign particles. *(see Figure 24.12)*

The Blood Supply to the Lungs 646

9. The respiratory-exchange surfaces are extensively connected to the circulatory system via the vessels of the pulmonary circuit.

The Pleural Cavities and Pleural Membranes 646

1. Each lung occupies a single **pleural cavity** lined by a **pleura** (serous membrane). The two types of pleurae are the **parietal pleura**, covering the inner surface of the thoracic wall, and the **visceral pleura**, covering the lungs. **Pleural fluid** is secreted by both pleural membranes. *(see Figure 24.13)*

Respiratory Muscles and Pulmonary Ventilation 647

Respiratory Muscles 647

1. **Pulmonary ventilation** is the movement of air into and out of the lungs. The most important respiratory muscles are the **diaphragm** and the **external** and **internal intercostal muscles**. Contraction of the diaphragm increases the volume of the thoracic cavity; the external intercostals may assist in inspiration by elevating the ribs; the internal intercostals depress the ribs and reduce the width of the thoracic cavity, thereby contributing to expiration. The **accessory respiratory muscles** become active when the depth and frequency of respiration must be increased markedly. Accessory muscles include the sternocleidomastoid, serratus anterior, transversus thoracis, scalene, pectoralis minor, oblique, and rectus abdominis muscles. *(see Figure 24.14)*

Respiratory Changes at Birth 649

2. Before delivery the fetal lungs are fluid-filled and collapsed. At the first breath, the lungs inflate and never collapse completely thereafter.

Respiratory Centers of the Brain 649

3. The **respiratory centers** are three pairs of nuclei in the reticular formation of the pons and medulla. The **respiratory rhythmicity center** sets the pace for respiration. The **apneustic center** causes strong, sustained inspiratory movements, and the **pneumotaxic center** inhibits the apneustic center and the inspiratory center in the medulla oblongata. *(see Figure 24.15)*
4. Three different reflexes are involved in the regulation of respiration: (1) *Mechanoreceptor reflexes* respond to changes in the volume of the lungs or to changes in arterial blood pressure; (2) *chemoreceptor reflexes* respond to changes in the P_{CO_2}, pH, and P_{O_2} of the blood and cerebrospinal fluid; and (3) *protective reflexes* respond to physical injury or irritation of the respiratory tract. *(see Figure 24.15)*
5. Conscious and unconscious thought processes can also control respiratory activity by affecting the respiratory centers or controlling the respiratory muscles.

Aging and the Respiratory System 650

1. The respiratory system is generally less efficient in the elderly because (1) elastic tissue deteriorates, lowering the vital capacity of the lungs; (2) movements of the chest cage are restricted by arthritic changes and decreased flexibility of costal cartilages; and (3) some degree of emphysema is normal in the elderly.

CHAPTER REVIEW

For answers to the Concept Check and Chapter Review questions, go to the blue "Answers" tab at the back of the book.

Level 1 Reviewing Facts and Terms

Match each numbered item with the most closely related lettered item. Use letters for answers in the spaces provided.

Column A	Column B
___ 1. extrinsic laryngeal musculature	a. superior portion of the pharynx
___ 2. tertiary bronchi	b. bridge of the nose
___ 3. nasopharynx	c. nose, nasal cavity, paranasal sinuses
___ 4. vestibular folds	d. windpipe
___ 5. lower respiratory system	e. lobar bronchi
___ 6. trachea	f. surrounds and protects the glottis
___ 7. dorsum nasi	g. larynx, trachea, bronchi, lungs
___ 8. secondary bronchi	h. provide protection for the vocal folds
___ 9. upper respiratory system	i. positions and stabilizes the larynx
___10. larynx	j. segmental bronchi

11. Air entering the body is filtered, warmed, and humidified by the
    (a) upper respiratory tract (b) lower respiratory tract
    (c) lungs (d) alveoli
12. Surfactant
    (a) protects the surfaces of the lungs
    (b) phagocytizes small particulates
    (c) replaces mucus in the alveoli
    (d) helps prevent the alveoli from collapsing
13. The portion of the pharynx that receives both air and food is the
    (a) nasopharynx (b) oropharynx
    (c) vestibule (d) laryngopharynx
14. The portion of the nasal cavity contained within the flexible tissues of the external nose is the
    (a) nasopharynx (b) vestibule
    (c) internal chamber (d) glottis
15. What aspect of laryngeal function would be impaired if the arytenoid and corniculate cartilages were damaged?
    (a) the air would not be able to enter
    (b) the larynx would be unable to move up or downward during swallowing to ease the passing of a bolus
    (c) sound production would be impaired
    (d) the person would be likely to choke
16. What is the function of the uvula?
    (a) it has no known function
    (b) it catches food items that accidentally slip posteriorly prior to being properly masticated for swallowing and returns them to the oral cavity
    (c) it forms a seal between the oral cavity and the nasopharynx to prevent materials from entering the pharyngeal region prematurely
    (d) it is lymphoid tissue as are the nearby tonsils
17. The cartilage that serves as a base for the larynx is the
    (a) thyroid cartilage (b) cuneiform cartilage
    (c) corniculate cartilage (d) cricoid cartilage
18. The vocal folds are located in the
    (a) nasopharynx (b) oropharynx
    (c) larynx (d) trachea
19. The trachea
    (a) is lined by simple squamous epithelium
    (b) is reinforced with C-shaped cartilages
    (c) contains no mucous glands
    (d) does not alter its diameter
20. The cartilage blocks in the walls of the secondary and tertiary bronchi
    (a) have a completely different function than do those of the tracheal rings
    (b) support the bronchi and assist in keeping the lumens open
    (c) are unusual among cartilaginous tissues in that they are highly vascular
    (d) assist directly in gas exchange by acting as baffles to direct the airflow

Level 2 Reviewing Concepts

1. The epithelium of the vestibule
   (a) does not assist with filtration
   (b) contains many small short cilia
   (c) contains hairs that prevent only the smallest particles from entering the nasal passages
   (d) contains coarse hairs that guard the nasal opening from the entry of large particles and insects
2. Why does a person with a cold often have a stuffed-up nose?
   (a) the response of the nasal epithelium to irritants, such as those that cause the common cold, is to secrete greater amounts of mucus than normal to trap the virus particles
   (b) during the time that a person has a cold, air is easier to breathe if it is of much higher humidity than normal, and the presence of the cold viruses stimulates mucus production to increase that humidity
   (c) excess saliva is inhaled through the internal nares when a person sneezes and fills the nasal cavity
   (d) no known reason
3. How does deep breathing differ from costal breathing?
   (a) in deep breathing, the thoracic volume changes because the rib cage changes shape
   (b) it moves air into and out of the bronchial tree, which does not occur in costal breathing
   (c) the diaphragm contracts in deep breathing, while it does not contract in costal breathing
   (d) in deep breathing, muscles contract to assist in both inspiration and expiration
4. How many lobes does the right lung have?
5. What is bronchodilation?
6. What is the function of the alveolar macrophages?
7. What is the function of the septa?
8. What do the intrinsic laryngeal muscles do?
9. Which paired laryngeal cartilages are involved with the opening and closing of the glottis?
10. What portion of the pharynx does the laryngopharynx include?

Level 3 Critical Thinking

1. What is the condition called asthma, and how can the symptoms be explained in anatomical terms?
2. A newborn infant was found dead, abandoned by the road. Among the many questions that the police would like to have answered is whether the infant was born dead or alive. After an autopsy the medical examiner tells them that the infant was dead at birth. How could the medical examiner determine this?

25

The Digestive System

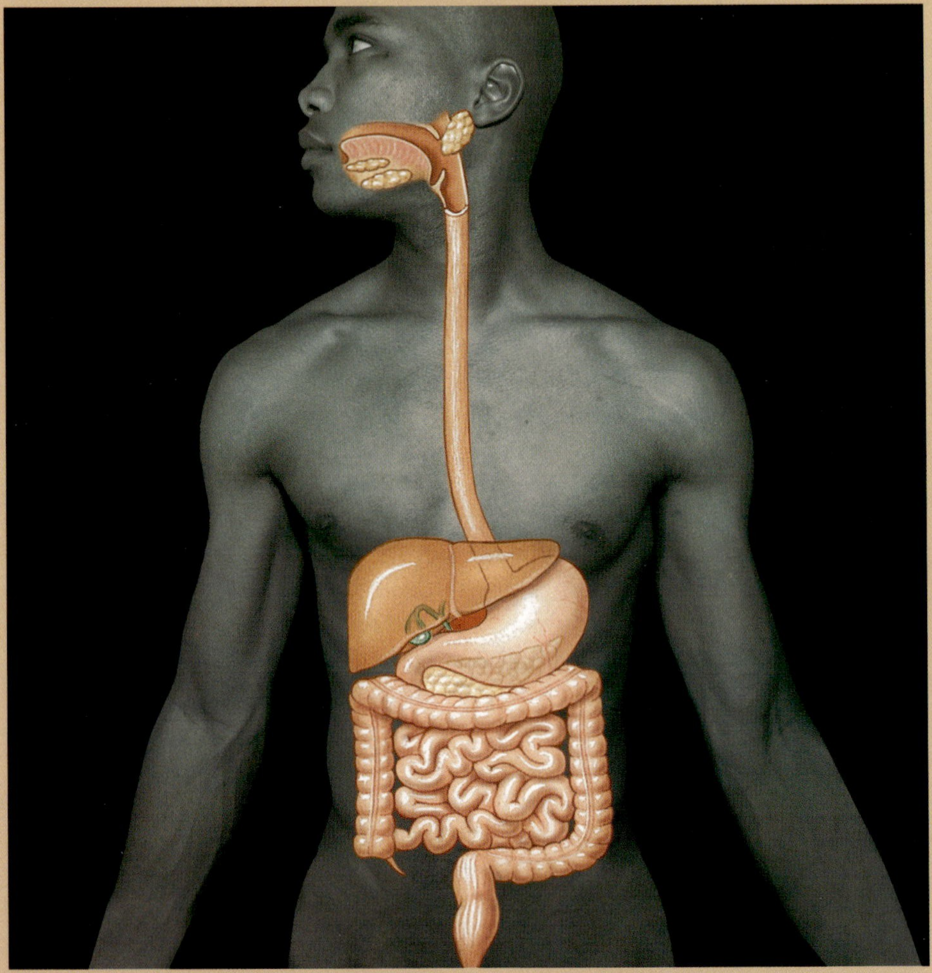

CHAPTER OBJECTIVES

1. Summarize the functions of the digestive system.
2. Locate the components of both the digestive tract and accessory organs and state the functions of each.
3. Describe the histological organization and general characteristics of the four layers of the digestive tract.
4. Explain how ingested food is propelled via the actions of smooth muscle through the digestive tract.
5. Describe the peritoneum and the locations and functions of the mesenteries.
6. Describe the gross and microscopic anatomical structure of the tongue, teeth, and salivary glands as well as their location and basic functions.
7. Describe the general structure and function of the pharynx and the swallowing process.
8. Describe the gross and microscopic anatomy, histology, and functions of the esophagus.
9. Describe the gross and microscopic anatomy of the stomach, its functions, and the hormones that regulate its activities.
10. Describe the gross and microscopic anatomy of the small intestine, its functions, and the hormones that regulate its activities.
11. Describe the gross and microscopic anatomy of the large intestine, its functions, and the hormones that regulate its activities.
12. Discuss the gross and microscopic anatomy of the liver, its functions, and the hormones that regulate its activities.
13. Discuss the gross and microscopic anatomy of the gallbladder, its functions, and the hormones that regulate its activities.
14. Describe the gross and microscopic anatomy of the pancreas and the hormones that regulate its activities.
15. Describe the changes in the digestive system that occur with aging.

Few of us give any serious thought to the digestive system unless it malfunctions. Yet each day we spend hours of conscious effort filling and emptying it. References to this system are part of our everyday language. We may have a "gut feeling," "want to chew on" something, or find an opinion "hard to swallow." When something does go wrong with the digestive system, even something minor, most of us seek treatment immediately. For this reason, television advertisements promote toothpaste and mouthwash, diet supplements, antacids, and laxatives.

The digestive system consists of a muscular tube, called the **digestive tract**, and various **accessory organs**. The *oral cavity* (mouth), *pharynx*, *esophagus*, *stomach*, *small intestine*, and *large intestine* make up the digestive tract. Accessory digestive organs include the teeth, tongue, and various *glandular organs*, such as the salivary glands, liver, and pancreas, which secrete into ducts emptying into the digestive tract. Food enters the digestive tract and passes along its length. On the way, the secretions of the glandular organs, which contain water, enzymes, buffers, and other components, assist in preparing organic and inorganic nutrients for absorption across the epithelium of the digestive tract. The digestive tract and accessory organs work together to perform the following functions:

1. *Ingestion:* Ingestion occurs when foods and liquids enter the digestive tract via the mouth.
2. *Mechanical processing:* Most ingested solids must undergo mechanical processing before they are swallowed. Squashing with the tongue and tearing and crushing with the teeth are examples of mechanical processing that occur before ingestion. Swirling, mixing, churning, and propulsive motions of the digestive tract continue to provide mechanical processing after swallowing.
3. *Digestion:* Digestion is the chemical and enzymatic breakdown of complex sugars, lipids, and proteins into small organic molecules that can be absorbed by the digestive epithelium.
4. *Secretion:* Digestion usually involves the action of acids, enzymes, and buffers produced by active secretion. Some of these secretions are produced by the lining of the digestive tract, but most are provided by the accessory organs, such as the pancreas.
5. *Absorption:* Absorption is the movement of organic molecules, electrolytes, vitamins, and water across the digestive epithelium and into the interstitial fluid of the digestive tract.
6. *Excretion:* Waste products are secreted into the digestive tract, primarily by the accessory glands (especially the liver).
7. *Compaction:* Compaction is the progressive dehydration of indigestible materials and organic wastes prior to elimination from the body. The compacted material is called **feces**; **defecation** (def-e-KĀ-shun) is the elimination of feces from the body.

The lining of the digestive tract also plays a defensive role by protecting surrounding tissues against (1) the corrosive effects of digestive acids and enzymes; (2) mechanical stresses, such as abrasion; and (3) pathogens that are either swallowed with food or reside within the digestive tract.

In summary, the organs of the digestive system mechanically and chemically process food that is introduced into the mouth and passed along the digestive tract. The purpose of these activities is to reduce the solid, complex chemical structures of food into small molecules that can be absorbed by the epithelium lining the digestive tract for transfer to the circulating blood.

An Overview of the Digestive System [Figure 25.1]

The major components of the digestive system are shown in Figure 25.1. Although several of the organs of the digestive system have overlapping functions, each has certain areas of specialization and shows distinctive histological characteristics. Before discussing these specializations and distinctions, we will consider the basic structural characteristics common to all portions of the digestive tract.

Histological Organization of the Digestive Tract [Figure 25.2]

The major layers of the digestive tract include (1) the *mucosa*, (2) the *submucosa*, (3) the *muscularis externa*, and (4) the *serosa*. Variations in the structure of these four layers occur along the digestive tract. These variations are related to the specific functions of each organ and region. Sectional and diagrammatic views of a representative region of the digestive tract are presented in Figure 25.2.

The Mucosa [Figure 25.2]

The inner lining, or **mucosa**, of the digestive tract is an example of a **mucous membrane**. Mucous membranes, introduced in Chapter 3, consist of a layer of loose connective tissue covered by an epithelium moistened by glandular secretions. p. 72 The **mucosal epithelium** may be stratified or simple, depending on the location and the stresses involved. For example, the oral cavity and esophagus are lined by a stratified squamous epithelium that can resist stress and abrasion, whereas the stomach, small intestine, and almost the entire large intestine have a simple columnar epithelium specialized for secretion and absorption. The mucosa of the digestive tract is often organized in transverse or longitudinal folds (Figure 25.2). The folds, called *plicae* (PLĪ-sē; singular, *plica* [PLĪ-ka]), resemble pleats. Plicae dramatically increase the surface area available for absorption. In some regions of the digestive tract, plicae are permanent features that involve both the mucosa and submucosa. In other regions, plicae are temporary features that disappear as the lumen fills, enabling expansion of the lumen after a large meal. Ducts opening onto the epithelial surfaces carry the secretions of gland cells located either in the mucosa and submucosa or within accessory organs.

The underlying layer of areolar tissue, called the **lamina propria**, contains blood vessels, sensory nerve endings, lymphatic vessels, smooth muscle fibers, and scattered areas of lymphoid tissue. The latter is part of the network of mucosa-associated lymphoid tissue, or MALT, introduced in Chapter 23. p. 616 In most regions of the digestive tract the outer portion of the mucosa, external to the lamina propria, is a narrow band of smooth muscle and elastic fibers. This band is called the **muscularis** (mus-kū-LA-ris) **mucosae**. The smooth muscle fibers in the muscularis mucosae are arranged in two thin concentric layers (Figure 25.2a). The inner layer encircles the lumen (the *circular layer*), and the outer layer contains muscle fibers oriented parallel to the long axis of the tract (the *longitudinal layer*). Contraction of these layers alters the shape of the lumen and moves the epithelial pleats and folds.

The Submucosa [Figure 25.2a]

The **submucosa** (sub-mū-KŌ-sa) is a layer of dense, irregular connective tissue that surrounds the muscularis mucosae. Large blood vessels and lym-

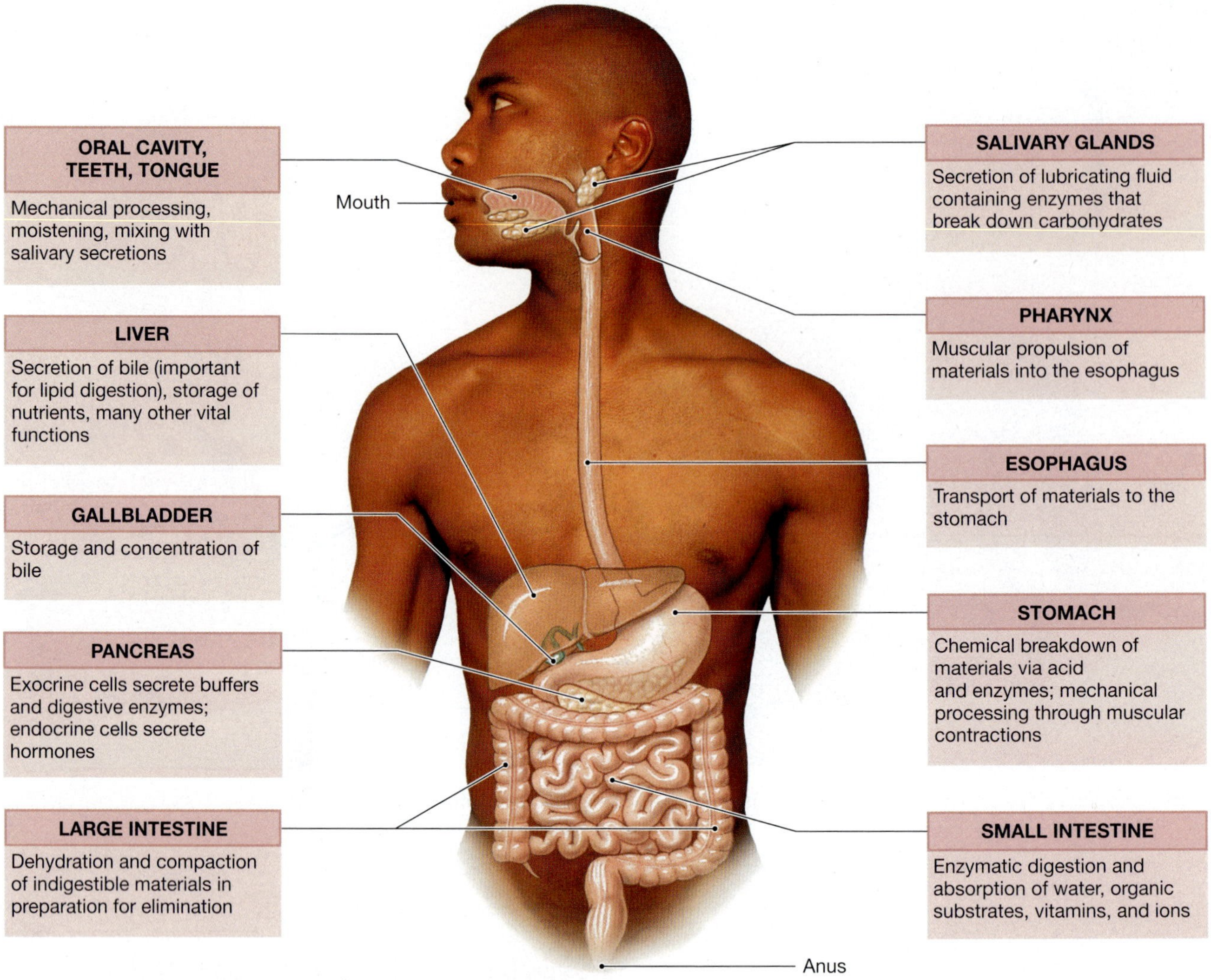

Figure 25.1 Components of the Digestive System
This figure introduces the major regions and accessory organs of the digestive tract, together with their primary functions.

phatics are found in this layer, and in some regions the submucosa also contains exocrine glands that secrete buffers and enzymes into the lumen. Along its outer margin, the submucosa contains a network of nerve fibers and scattered neuron cell bodies. This **submucosal plexus** *(plexus of Meissner)* innervates the mucosa; it contains sensory neurons, parasympathetic ganglia, and sympathetic postganglionic fibers (Figure 25.2a).

The Muscularis Externa [Figure 25.2]

The **muscularis externa**, which surrounds the submucosa, is a region dominated by smooth muscle fibers. These fibers are arranged in both circular (inner) and longitudinal (outer) layers (Figure 25.2). These layers of smooth muscle play an essential role in mechanical processing and in the propulsion of materials along the digestive tract. These movements are coordinated primarily by neurons of the **myenteric** (mī-en-TER-ik; *mys*, muscle + *enteron*, intestine) **plexus**, or *plexus of Auerbach*. This network of parasympathetic ganglia and sympathetic postganglionic fibers lies sandwiched between the circular and longitudinal muscle layers. Parasympathetic stimulation increases muscular tone and stimulates contractions, whereas sympathetic stimulation promotes inhibition of muscular activity and relaxation.

Additionally, at specific locations along the digestive tract, the muscularis externa forms sphincters, or *valves*, that help prevent materials from moving along the tract at an inappropriate time or in the wrong direction. These valves, which are thickened areas of the circular smooth muscle layer, constrict the lumen to restrict the flow of digestive material through the lumen.

The Serosa [Figure 25.2]

Along most regions of the digestive tract within the peritoneal cavity, the muscularis externa is covered by a *serous membrane* known as the **serosa** (Figure 25.2). There is no serosa, however, surrounding the muscularis externa of the oral cavity, pharynx, esophagus, and rectum. Instead, the muscularis externa is wrapped by a dense network of collagen fibers that firmly attaches the digestive tract to adjacent structures. This fibrous sheath is called the **adventitia** (ad-ven-TISH-a).

Muscularis Layers and the Movement of Digestive Materials

The digestive tract contains **visceral smooth muscle tissue**. A single smooth muscle cell ranges from 5 to 10 μm in diameter and from 30 to 200 μm in length. They are surrounded by connective tissue, but the collagen fibers do not form tendons or aponeuroses. The contractile proteins of these smooth muscle cells are not organized into sarcomeres, so the muscle cells are nonstriated, involuntary muscle. p. 75 Although they are nonstriated, their contractions are as strong as those of skeletal or cardiac muscle cells. In visceral smooth muscle tissue, many of the muscle cells have no motor innervation. The muscle cells are arranged in sheets or layers, and adjacent muscle cells are electrically connected by gap junctions. When one visceral smooth muscle cell contracts, the contraction spreads in a wave that travels throughout the tissue.

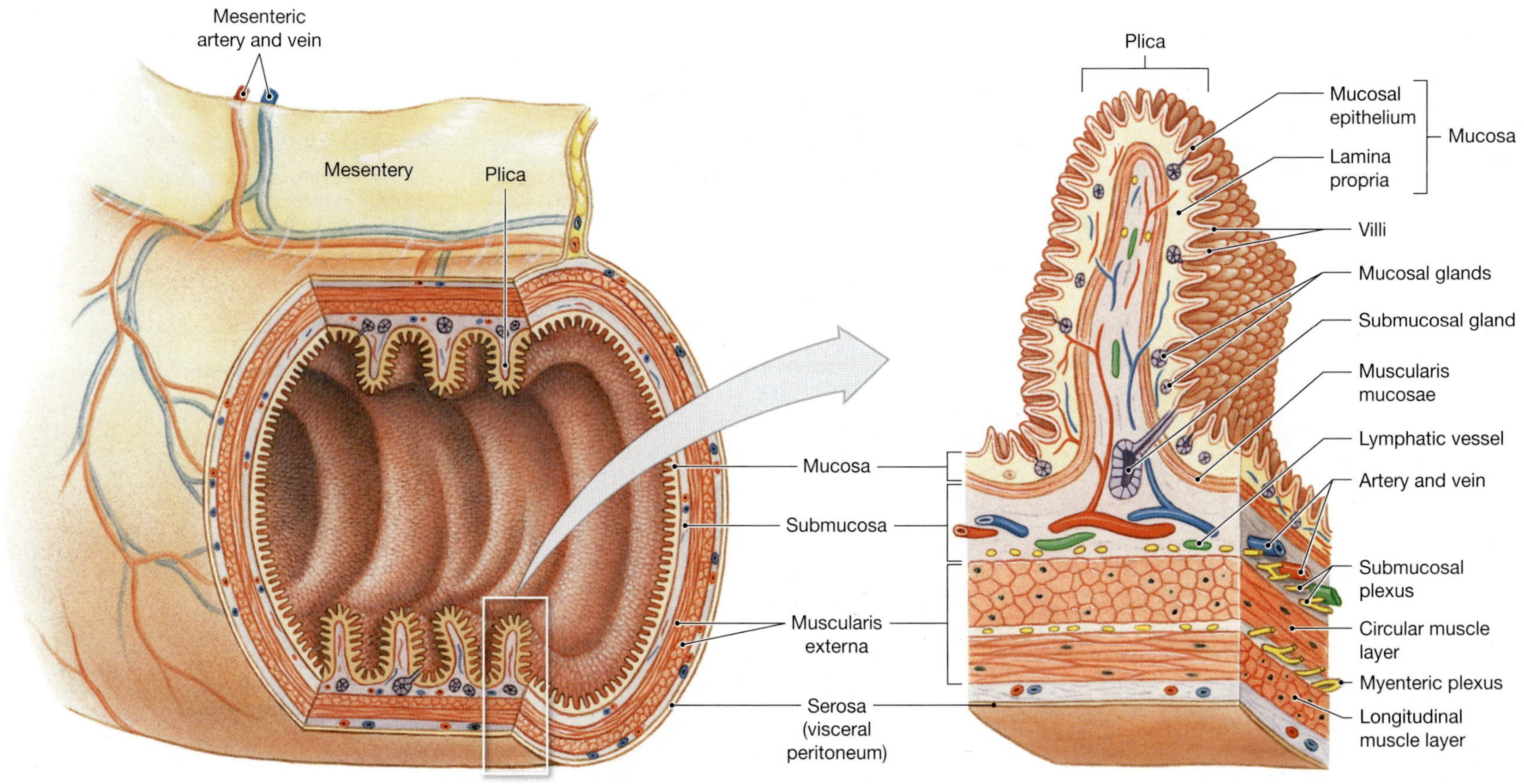

(a) Histological organization of the digestive tract

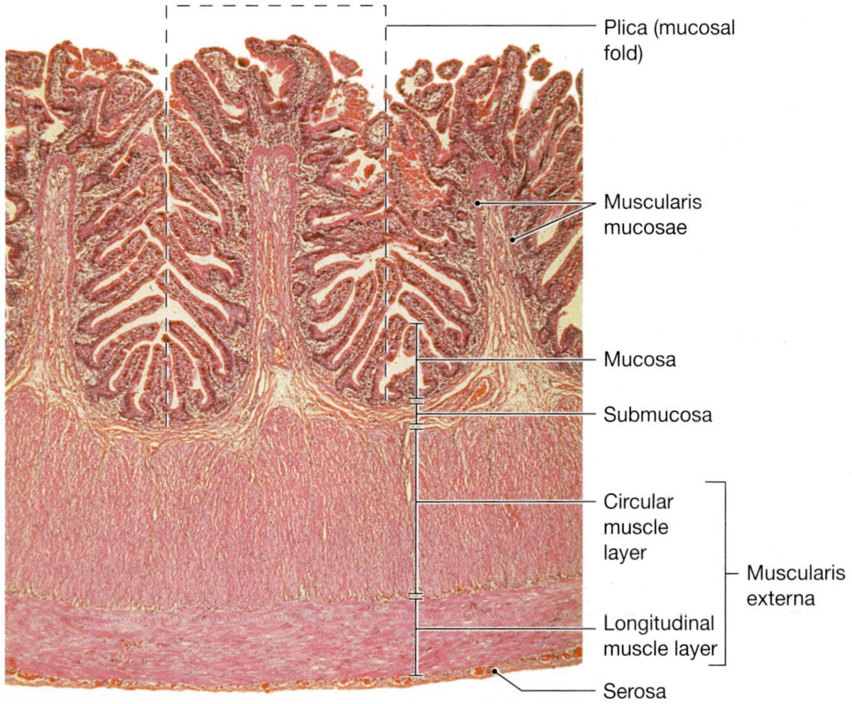

(b) Photomicrograph of ileum

Figure 25.2 Histological Structure of the Digestive Tract **(a)** Three-dimensional view of the histological organization of the general digestive tube. **(b)** Photomicrograph of the ileum, showing aspects of the histological organization of the small intestine.

The initial stimulus may be the activation of a motor neuron that contacts one of the smooth muscle cells in the region. It may also be a local response to chemicals, hormones, the concentrations of oxygen or carbon dioxide, or physical factors such as extreme stretching or irritation.

Because the contractile filaments of smooth muscle cells are not rigidly organized, a stretched smooth muscle cell soon adapts to its new length and retains the ability to contract on demand. This ability to tolerate extreme stretching is called *plasticity*. Plasticity is especially important for digestive organs that undergo great changes in volume, such as the stomach.

Smooth muscle in the digestive tract shows rhythmic cycles of activity because of the presence of **pacesetter cells**. Pacesetter cells are found in both the muscularis mucosae and muscularis externa. These smooth muscle cells undergo spontaneous depolarization, which triggers contractions leading to two types of movement events, *peristalsis* and *segmentation*.

These wavelike contractions spread through the entire muscular sheet and facilitate the propulsion and mixing of contents along the digestive tract.

Peristalsis [Figure 25.3a]

The muscularis externa propels materials from one region of the digestive tract to another through the contractions of **peristalsis** (per-i-STAL-sis). Peristalsis consists of waves of muscular contractions that move a *bolus* (a small oval mass of food) along the length of the digestive tract. During a **peristaltic wave**, the circular muscles contract behind the digestive contents. Longitudinal muscles contract next, shortening adjacent segments. A wave of contraction in the circular muscles then forces the materials in the desired direction (Figure 25.3a).

Segmentation [Figure 25.3b]

Most areas of the small intestine and some regions of the large intestine undergo contractions that produce **segmentation** (Figure 25.3b). These movements churn and fragment the digestive materials, mixing the contents with intestinal secretions. They do not produce net movement in any particular direction.

Segmentation and peristalsis may be triggered by pacesetter cells, hormones, chemicals, and physical stimulation. Peristaltic waves also can be initiated by afferent and efferent fibers within the glossopharyngeal, vagus, or pelvic nerves. Local peristaltic movements limited to a few centimeters of the digestive tract are triggered by sensory receptors in the walls of the digestive tract. These afferent fibers synapse within the myenteric plexus to

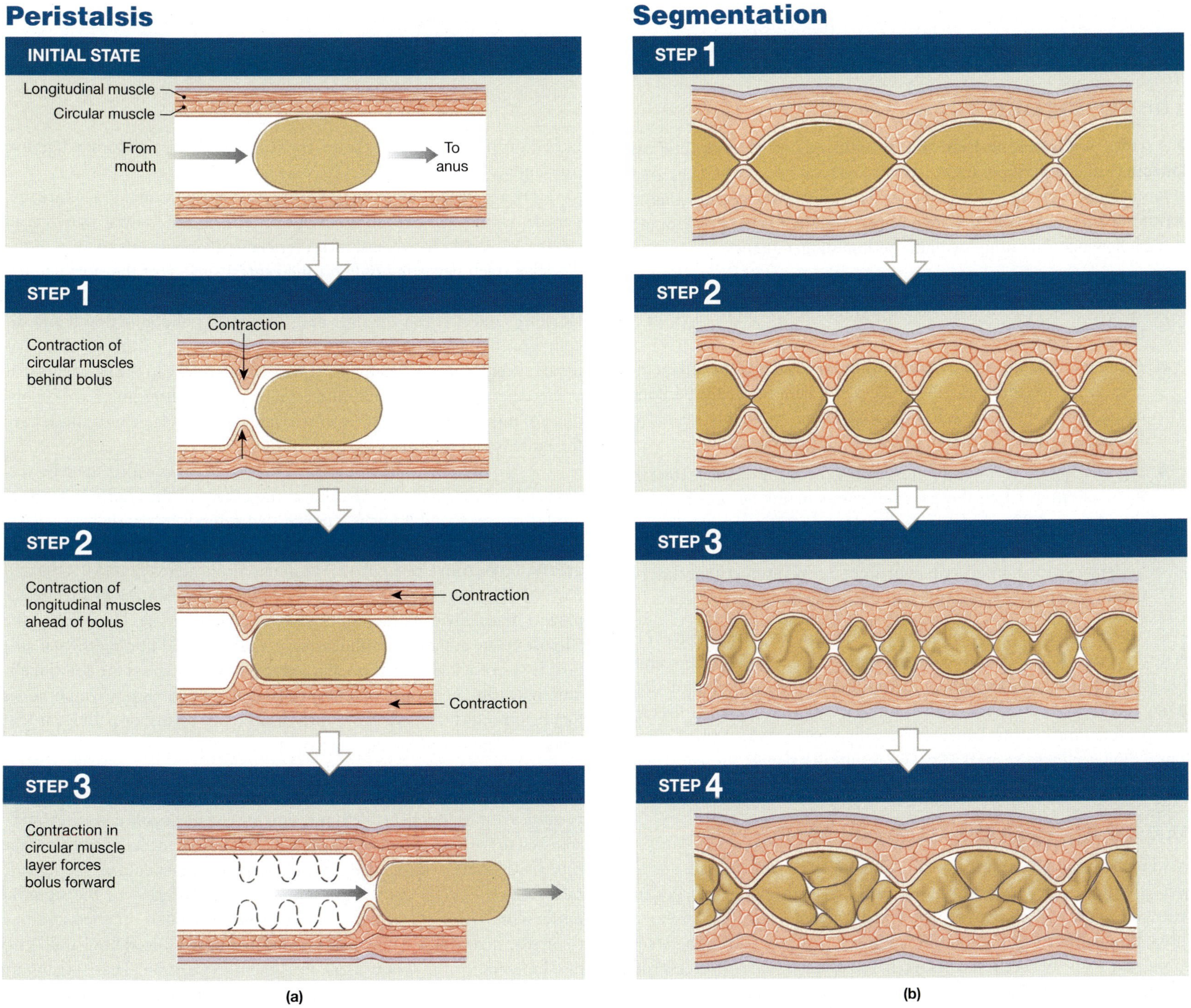

Figure 25.3 Peristalsis and Segmentation
(a) Peristalsis propels materials along the length of the digestive tract by coordinated contractions of the circular and longitudinal layers. **(b)** Segmentation movements involve primarily the circular muscle layers. These activities churn and mix the contents of the digestive tract, but do not produce net movement in a particular direction.

produce localized **myenteric reflexes**. These are short reflexes that do not involve the CNS. p. 465 The term *enteric nervous system* refers to the neural network that coordinates these reflexes.

In general, short reflexes control activities in one region of the digestive tract. This control may involve coordinating local peristalsis and triggering the secretion of digestive glands. Many neurons are involved—the enteric nervous system has roughly as many neurons and neurotransmitters as the spinal cord has.

Sensory information from receptors in the digestive tract is also distributed to the CNS, where it can trigger long reflexes. p. 465 Long reflexes, which involve interneurons and motor neurons in the CNS, provide a higher level of control over digestive and glandular activities. These reflexes generally control large-scale peristaltic waves that move materials from one region of the digestive tract to another. Long reflexes may involve motor fibers in the glossopharyngeal, vagus, or pelvic nerves that synapse in the myenteric plexus.

Clinical Note

Peritonitis Inflammation of the peritoneal membrane produces symptoms of **peritonitis** (per-i-tō-NĪ-tis), a painful condition that interferes with the normal functioning of the affected organs. Physical damage, chemical irritation, or bacterial invasion of the peritoneum can lead to severe and even fatal cases of peritonitis. Peritonitis due to bacterial infection is a potential complication of any surgery that involves opening the peritoneal cavity or any disease that perforates the walls of the stomach or intestines. Liver disease, kidney disease, or heart failure can cause an increase in the rate of fluid movement through the peritoneal lining. The accumulation of fluid, called **ascites** (a-SĪ-tēz), creates a characteristic abdominal swelling. Distortion of internal organs by the contained fluid can result in a variety of symptoms; heartburn, indigestion, and low back pain are common complaints.

The Peritoneum

The serosa, or **visceral peritoneum**, is continuous with the **parietal peritoneum** that lines the inner surfaces of the body wall. p. 19–20 The organs of the abdominal cavity are often described as lying *within* the abdominal and peritoneal cavities. Actually, abdominal organs may demonstrate one or more of the following relationships with the peritoneal membranes:

- *Intraperitoneal organs* lie within the peritoneal cavity, in that they are covered on all sides by the visceral peritoneum. Examples of intraperitoneal organs include the stomach, liver, and ileum.
- *Retroperitoneal organs* are covered by the visceral peritoneum on their anterior surface only, and the organ per se lies outside the peritoneal cavity. These organs typically do not develop from the embryonic gut. Examples include the kidneys, ureters, and abdominal aorta.
- *Secondarily retroperitoneal organs* are organs of the digestive tract that form as intraperitoneal organs but subsequently become retroperitoneal organs. The shift occurs during embryonic development as a portion of the associated visceral peritoneum fuses with the opposing parietal peritoneum. Examples of secondarily retroperitoneal organs include the pancreas and much of the duodenum.

The peritoneal lining continually produces a watery peritoneal fluid that lubricates the peritoneal surfaces. About 7 liters of fluid are secreted and reabsorbed each day, although the volume within the peritoneal cavity at any one time is very small. Under unusual conditions, such as liver disease, heart failure, or disturbances in electrolyte balance, the volume of peritoneal fluid can increase markedly. This results in a dangerous reduction in blood volume and distortion of visceral organs.

Mesenteries [Figures 25.2a/25.4/25.10a/25.11b]

Within the peritoneal cavity, most regions of the digestive tract are suspended by sheets of serous membrane that connect the parietal peritoneum with the visceral peritoneum. These **mesenteries** (MES-en-ter-ēz) are fused, double sheets of peritoneal membrane (**Figure 25.2a**). The areolar connective tissue between the mesothelial surfaces provides an access route for the passage of the blood vessels, nerves, and lymphatics to and from the digestive tract. Mesenteries also stabilize the relative positions of the attached organs and prevent the entanglement of intestines during digestive movements or sudden changes in body position.

During development, the digestive tract and accessory organs are suspended within the peritoneal cavity by dorsal and ventral mesenteries (**Figure 25.4a,b**). The ventral mesentery later disappears along most of the digestive tract, persisting only on the ventral surface of the stomach, between the stomach and liver (the **lesser omentum** [ō-MEN-tum; *omentum*, fat skin]) and between the liver and the anterior abdominal wall and diaphragm (the *falciform ligament*) (**Figure 25.4b,c,d**). (Although this peritoneal sheet is called a "ligament," it is not comparable to the ligaments that interconnect bones.) For additional information concerning the development of the digestive tract, accessory organs, and associated mesenteries, see the Embryology Summary in Chapter 28.

As the digestive tract elongates, it twists and turns within the relatively crowded peritoneal cavity. The dorsal mesentery of the stomach becomes greatly enlarged, and it forms a pouch that extends inferiorly between the body wall and the anterior surface of the small intestine. This pouch is the **greater omentum** (see **Figure 25.4b** and look ahead to **Figures 25.10a** and **25.11b**). The loose connective tissue within the mesentery of the greater omentum usually contains a thick layer of adipose tissue. The lipids in the adipose tissue are an important energy reserve. In addition, omental adipose tissue provides insulation that reduces heat loss across the anterior abdominal wall. The greater omentum also contains numerous lymph nodes that help protect the body from foreign proteins, toxins, or pathogens that evade the defenses of the digestive tract.

All but the first 25 cm of the small intestine is suspended by a thick *mesenterial sheet*, termed the **mesentery proper**, that provides stability but permits a degree of independent movement. The **mesocolon** is a mesentery attached to the large intestine. The middle portion of the large intestine (the *transverse colon*) is suspended by the **transverse mesocolon**. The *sigmoid colon*, which leads to the rectum and anus, is suspended by the **sigmoid mesocolon**. During development, the dorsal mesentery of the ascending colon, the descending colon, and rectum fuse to the dorsal body wall. This fused mesentery, the *fusion fascia*, fixes them in position. These organs are now secondarily retroperitoneal, and visceral peritoneum covers only their anterior surfaces and portions of their lateral surfaces (**Figure 25.4b–d**).

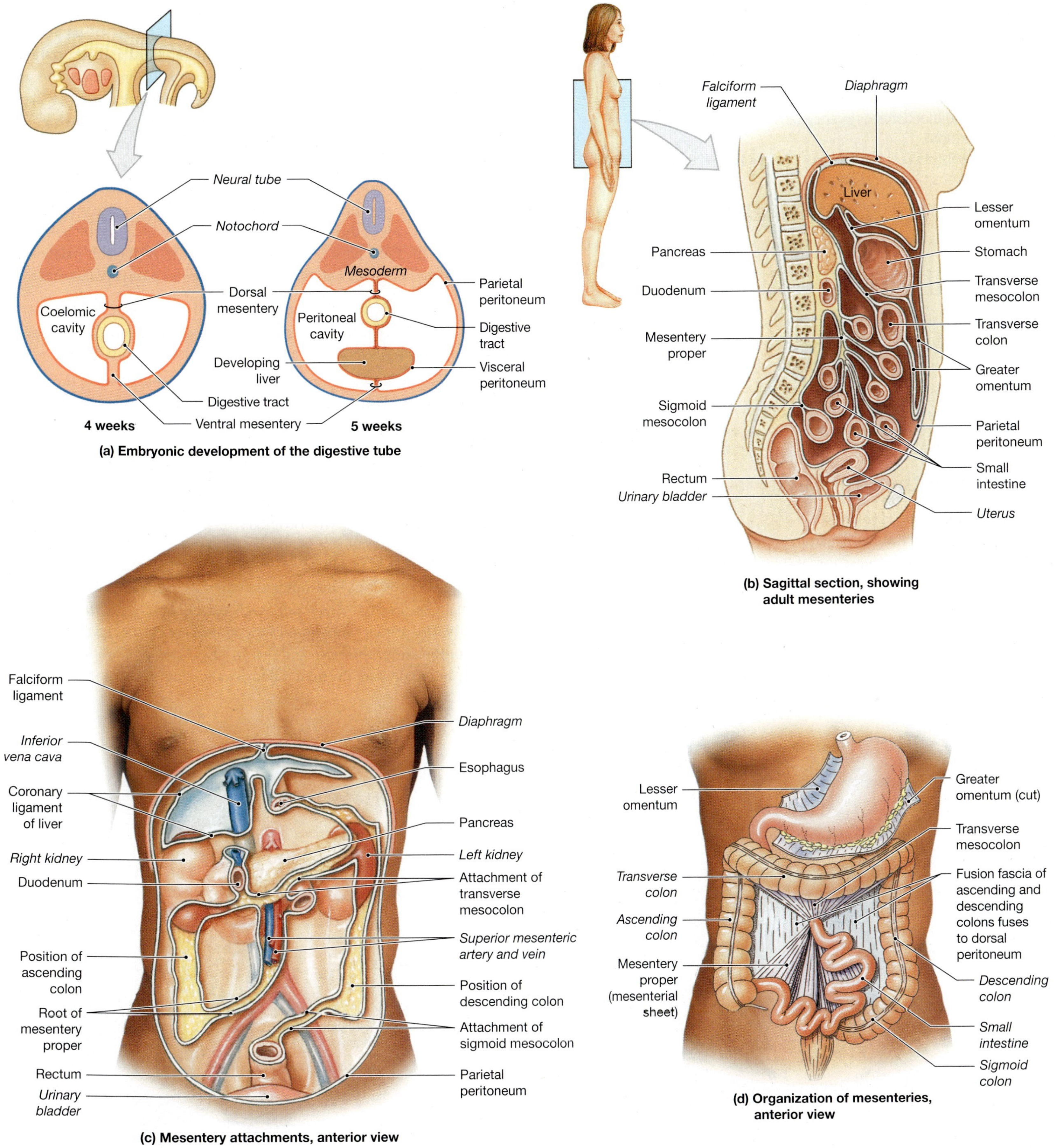

Figure 25.4 Mesenteries

(a) Diagrammatic view of early embryonic state, with dorsal and ventral mesenteries supporting the digestive tract (left). A slightly later stage, showing the development of the liver within the ventral mesentery (right). (*For further information, see the Embryology Summary in Chapter 28.*) **(b)** Mesenteries of the abdominopelvic cavity, as seen in a diagrammatic sagittal section. **(c)** Anterior view of the empty peritoneal cavity showing the attachment of mesenteries and visceral organs to the posterior wall of the abdominal cavity. **(d)** The organization of mesenteries in the adult. This is a simplified view; the length of the small intestine has been greatly reduced.

CONCEPT CHECK

1. What are the components and functions of the mucosa of the digestive tract?
2. What are the functions of mesenteries?
3. What is the functional difference between peristalsis and segmentation?
4. What is important about the lack of organization in the contractile filaments of smooth muscle cells?

See blue "Answers" tab at back of book.

The Oral Cavity

Our exploration of the digestive tract will follow the path of food from the mouth to the anus. The mouth opens into the *oral cavity*. The functions of the oral cavity include (1) *analysis* of material before swallowing; (2) *mechanical processing* through the actions of the teeth, tongue, and palatal surfaces; (3) *lubrication* by mixing with mucous and salivary secretions; and (4) limited *digestion* of carbohydrates by a salivary enzyme.

Anatomy of the Oral Cavity [Figure 25.5]

The **oral cavity**, or *buccal* (BUK-al) *cavity* (Figure 25.5), is lined by the **oral mucosa**, which has a stratified squamous epithelium that protects the mouth from abrasion during the ingestion of food. Unlike the stratified squamous epithelium of the skin, the oral epithelium does not undergo keratinization. The mucosa of the **cheeks**, or lateral walls of the oral cavity, are supported and formed by *buccal fat pads* and the *buccinator muscles.* p. 264 Anteriorly, the mucosa of the cheeks are continuous with the lips, or **labia** (LĀ-bē-a). The **vestibule** is the space between the cheeks, lips, and the teeth. A ridge of oral mucosa, the gums, or **gingivae** (JIN-ji-vē), surrounds the base of each tooth on the alveolar surfaces of the maxillary bone and mandible. pp. 148–152

The roof of the oral cavity is formed by the **hard** and **soft palates**, while the tongue dominates its floor. The hard palate separates the oral cavity from the nasal cavity. The soft palate separates the oral cavity from the nasopharynx and closes off the nasopharynx during swallowing. The finger-shaped **uvula** (Ū-vū-la), which dangles from the center of the posterior margin of the soft palate, helps to prevent food from entering the pharynx prematurely. Inferior to the tongue, the floor receives additional support from the *mylohyoid muscle.* p. 271 The hard palate is formed by the palatine process of the maxilla and the palatine bone. The soft palate lies posterior to the hard palate. The posterior margin of the soft palate supports the dangling uvula and two pairs of muscular *pharyngeal arches.*

1. The *palatoglossal arches* extend between the soft palate and the base of the tongue. Each arch consists of a mucous membrane and the underlying *palatoglossus muscle* and associated tissues. p. 269
2. The *palatopharyngeal arches* extend from the soft palate to the side of the pharynx. Each arch consists of a mucous membrane and the underlying *palatopharyngeus muscle* and associated tissues. p. 270

The palatine tonsils lie between the palatoglossal and palatopharyngeal arches. The posterior margin of the soft palate, including the uvula, the palatopharyngeal arches, and the base of the tongue, frames the **fauces** (FAW-sēz), the entrance to the oropharynx.

The Tongue [Figures 18.7/25.5/25.6a]

The **tongue** (Figure 25.5) manipulates materials inside the mouth and may occasionally be used to bring foods (such as ice cream or pudding) into the oral cavity. The primary functions of the tongue are (1) mechanical processing by compression, abrasion, and distortion; (2) manipulation to assist in chewing and to prepare the material for swallowing; (3) sensory analysis by

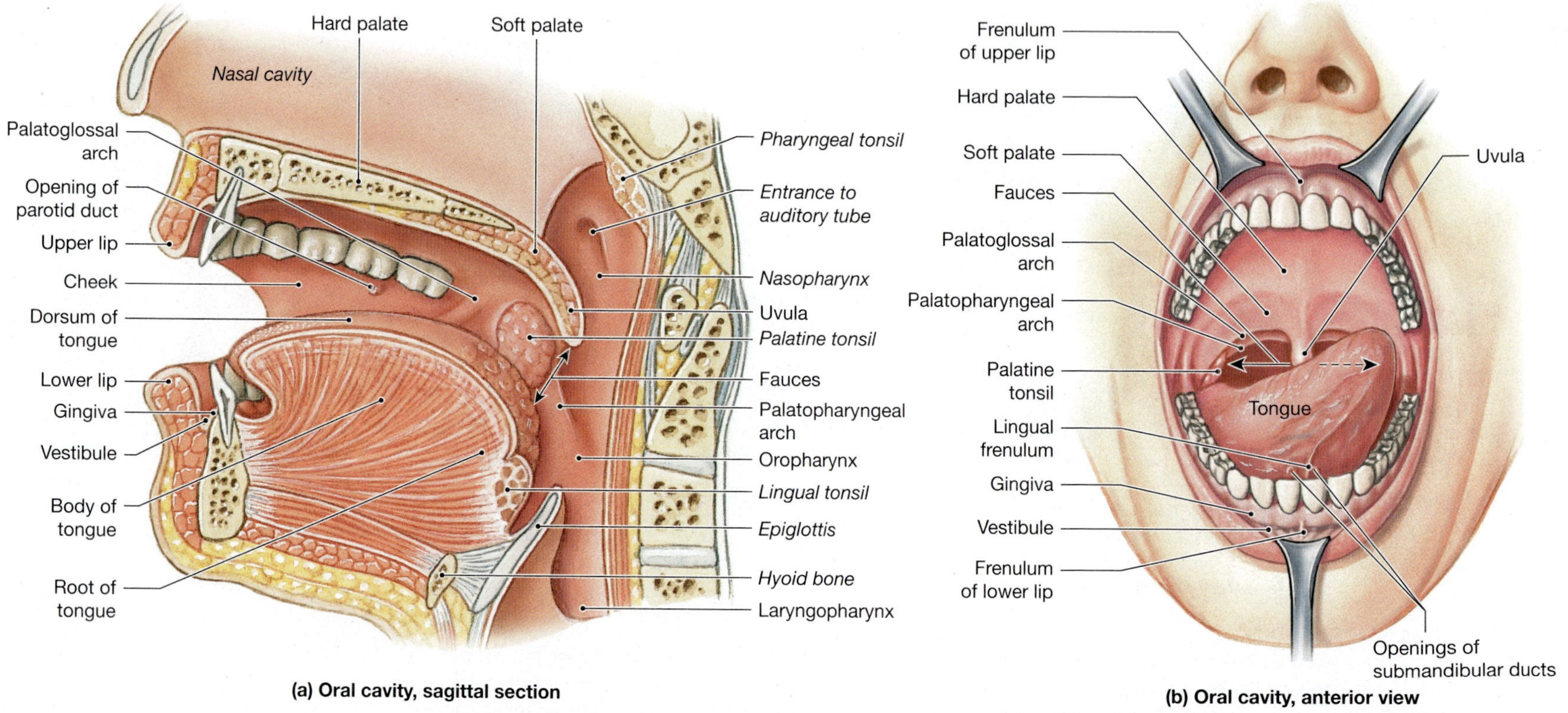

Figure 25.5 The Oral Cavity
(a) The oral cavity as seen in sagittal section. **(b)** An anterior view of the oral cavity, as seen through the open mouth.

touch, temperature, and taste receptors; and (4) secretion of mucins and an enzyme that aids in fat digestion.

The tongue can be divided into an anterior **body**, or *oral portion*, and a posterior **root**, or *pharyngeal portion*. The superior surface, or **dorsum**, of the body contains numerous fine projections called *papillae*. The thickened epithelium covering each papilla produces additional friction that assists in the movement of materials by the tongue. Additionally, taste buds are found along the edges of many papillae. Surface features and histological details of the tongue are shown in **Figure 18.7**. p. 478 A V-shaped line of circumvallate papillae roughly indicates the boundary between the body and the root of the tongue, which is situated in the pharynx.

The tongue's epithelium is flushed by the secretions of small glands that extend into the lamina propria of the tongue. These secretions contain water mucins and the enzyme *lingual lipase*. Lingual lipase begins the enzymatic breakdown of lipids, specifically triglycerides. The epithelium covering the inferior surface of the tongue is thinner and more delicate than that of the dorsum. Along the inferior midline a thin fold of mucous membrane, the **lingual frenulum** (FREN-ū-lum; *frenulum*, small bridle), connects the body of the tongue to the mucosa of the oral floor. Ducts from one of the salivary glands are visible as they open on either side of the lingual frenulum (**Figures 25.5b** and **25.6a**).

The lingual frenulum prevents extreme movements of the tongue. However, if the lingual frenulum is *too* restrictive, the individual cannot eat or speak normally. When properly diagnosed, this condition, called **ankyloglossia** (ang-ki-lō-GLOS-ē-a), can be corrected surgically.

The tongue contains two different groups of muscles, **intrinsic tongue muscles** and **extrinsic tongue muscles**. Both intrinsic and extrinsic tongue muscles are under the control of the hypoglossal nerve (N XII). The extrinsic muscles, discussed in Chapter 10, include the *hyoglossus*, *styloglossus*, *genioglossus*, and *palatoglossus muscles*. p. 269 All gross movements of the tongue are performed by the extrinsic muscles. The less massive intrinsic muscles alter the shape of the tongue and assist the extrinsic muscles during precise movements, as in speech.

Salivary Glands [Figures 25.5/25.6]

Three pairs of salivary glands secrete into the oral cavity (**Figure 25.6**). Each salivary gland is covered by a fibrous capsule. The saliva produced by the secretory cells of the gland is transported through a network of fine ducts to a single large drainage duct. This main duct penetrates the capsule and opens onto the surface of the oral mucosa. These salivary glands are described as follows:

1. The **parotid** (pa-ROT-id) **salivary glands** are the largest salivary glands, with an average weight of roughly 20 g. They are irregularly shaped, extending between the inferior surface of the zygomatic arch and the anterior margin of the sternocleidomastoid muscle, and from the mastoid process of the temporal bone anteriorly across the superficial surface of

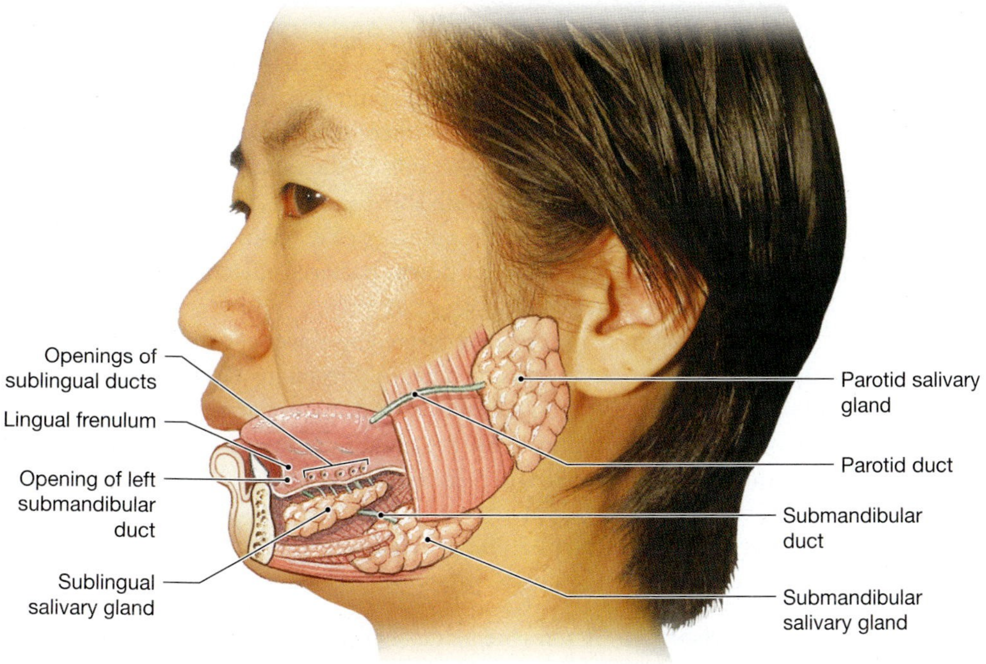

(a) Lateral view with left mandibular body and ramus removed

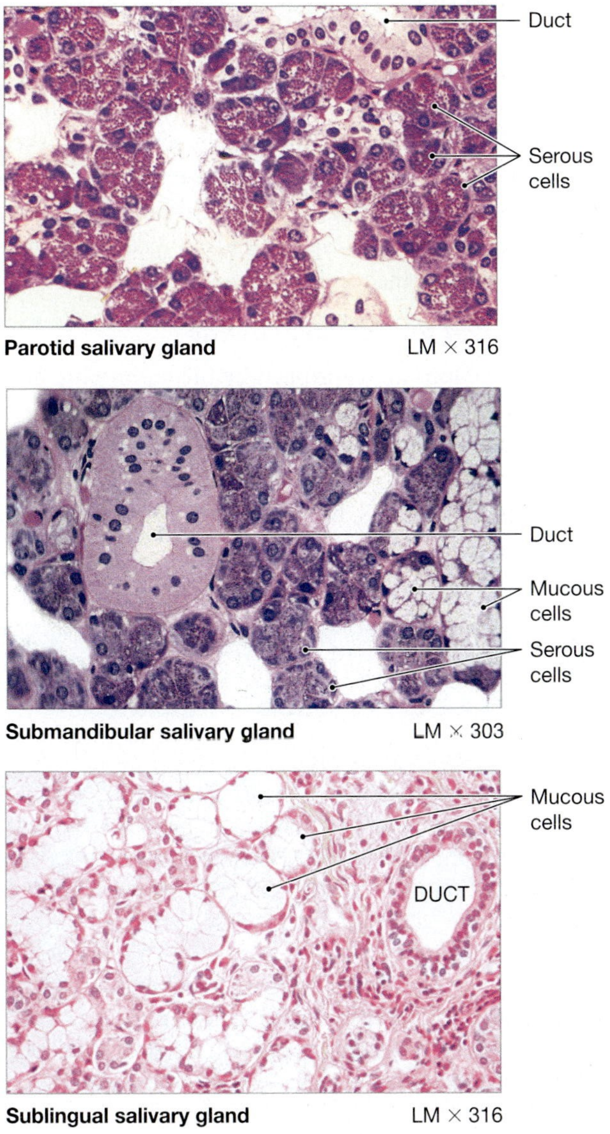

(b) Salivary gland histology

Figure 25.6 The Salivary Glands
(a) Lateral view, showing the relative positions of the salivary glands and ducts on the left side of the head. Much of the left half of the body and the left ramus of the mandible have been removed. For the positions of the ducts inside the oral cavity, *see Figure 25.5*. **(b)** Histological detail of the parotid, submandibular, and sublingual salivary glands. The parotid salivary gland produces saliva rich in enzymes. The gland is dominated by serous secretory cells. The submandibular salivary gland produces saliva containing enzymes and mucins, and it contains both serous and mucous secretory cells. The sublingual salivary gland produces saliva rich in mucins. This gland is dominated by mucous secretory cells.

the masseter muscle. The secretions of each gland are drained by a **parotid duct**, or *Stensen's duct*, which empties into the vestibule at the level of the second upper molar (Figure 25.5a).

2. The **sublingual** (sub-LING-gwal) **salivary glands** are covered by the mucous membrane of the floor of the mouth. Numerous **sublingual ducts**, or *ducts of Rivinus*, open along either side of the lingual frenulum (Figure 25.6a).
3. The **submandibular salivary glands** are found in the floor of the mouth along the medial surfaces of the mandible inferior of the *mylohyoid line.* p. 151 The **submandibular ducts**, or *Wharton's ducts*, open into the mouth on either side of the lingual frenulum immediately posterior to the teeth (Figure 25.5b). The histological appearance of the submandibular gland can be seen in Figure 25.6b.

Each of the salivary glands has a distinctive cellular organization and produces saliva with slightly different properties. For example, the parotid salivary glands produce a thick, serous secretion containing the digestive enzyme **salivary amylase**, which begins the chemical breakdown of complex carbohydrates. The saliva in the mouth is a mixture of glandular secretions; about 70 percent of the saliva originates in the submandibular salivary glands, 25 percent from the parotid salivary glands, and 5 percent from the sublingual salivary glands. Collectively the salivary glands produce 1.0–1.5 L of saliva each day, with a composition of 99.4 percent water, plus an assortment of ions, buffers, metabolites, and enzymes. Glycoproteins called *mucins* are primarily responsible for the lubricating effects of saliva. pp. 58–59

At mealtimes the production of large quantities of saliva lubricate the mouth, moisten the food, and dissolve chemicals that stimulate the taste buds. A continual background level of secretion flushes the oral surfaces and helps control populations of oral bacteria. A reduction or elimination of salivary secretions triggers a bacterial population explosion in the oral cavity. This proliferation rapidly leads to recurring infections and the progressive erosion of the teeth and gums.

Regulation of the Salivary Glands

Salivary secretions are controlled by the autonomic nervous system. Each salivary gland receives parasympathetic and sympathetic innervation. Any object placed within the mouth can trigger a salivary reflex by stimulating receptors monitored by the trigeminal nerve or by stimulating taste buds innervated by N VII, N IX, or N X. pp. 421, 479 Parasympathetic stimulation accelerates secretion by all of the salivary glands, resulting in the production of large amounts of watery saliva. In contrast, sympathetic activation results in the secretion of a small volume of viscous saliva containing high enzyme concentrations. The reduced volume produces the sensation of a dry mouth.

The Teeth [Figure 25.7a]

The movements of the tongue are important in passing food across the surfaces of the teeth. Teeth perform chewing, or **mastication** (mas-ti-KĀ-shun), of food. Mastication breaks down tough connective tissues and plant fibers and helps saturate the materials with salivary secretions and enzymes.

Figure 25.7a is a sectional view through an adult tooth. The bulk of each tooth consists of a mineralized matrix similar to bone. This material, called **dentine** (DEN-teen), or *dentin* (DEN-tin), differs from bone because it does not contain living cells. Instead, cytoplasmic processes extend into the dentine from cells in the central **pulp cavity**. The pulp cavity is spongy and highly vascular. It receives blood vessels and nerves via a narrow tunnel, the **root canal**, located at the base, or **root**, of the tooth. The **dental artery**, **dental vein**, and **dental nerve** enter the root canal through the **apical foramen** to service the pulp cavity.

The root of the tooth is anchored into a bony socket, or *alveolus*. Collagen fibers of the **periodontal** (per-ē-ō-DON-tal) **ligament** extend from the dentine of the root to the alveolar bone, creating a strong articulation known as a *gomphosis.* p. 206 A layer of **cement**, or *cementum*, (sē-MEN-tum) covers the dentine of the root, providing protection and firmly anchoring the periodontal ligament. The cement is very similar in histological structure to bone, and less resistant to erosion than dentine.

The **neck** of the tooth marks the boundary between the root and the **crown**. The crown is the visible portion of the tooth that projects above the soft tissue of the gingiva. Epithelial cells of the **gingival** (JIN-ji-val) **sulcus** form tight attachments to the tooth above the neck, preventing bacterial access to the lamina propria of the gingiva or the relatively soft cement of the root. If this attachment breaks down, bacterial infection of the gingiva, termed *gingivitis*, may occur.

The dentine of the crown is covered by a layer of **enamel**. Enamel contains densely packed crystals of calcium phosphate and is the hardest biologically manufactured substance. Adequate amounts of calcium, phosphates, and vitamin D during childhood are essential if the enamel coating is to be complete and resistant to decay.

Types of Teeth [Figure 25.7b,c] There are four types of teeth, each with specific functions (Figure 25.7b,c):

1. **Incisors** (in-SĪ-zerz) are blade-shaped teeth found at the front of the mouth. Incisors are useful for clipping or cutting, as when nipping off the tip of a carrot stick.
2. The **cuspids** (KUS-pidz), or *canines*, are conical with a sharp ridgeline and a pointed tip. They are used for tearing or slashing. A tough piece of celery might be weakened by the clipping action of the incisors, but it can then be moved to one side to take advantage of the shearing action provided by the cuspids. Incisors and cuspids each have a single root.
3. **Bicuspids** (bī-KUS-pidz), or *premolars*, have one or two roots. Premolars have flattened crowns with prominent ridges. They are used for crushing, mashing, and grinding.
4. **Molars** have very large flattened crowns with prominent ridges and typically have three or more roots. Molars also have flattened crowns for crushing and grinding.

Clinical Note

Mumps The **mumps** virus preferentially targets the salivary glands, most often the parotids, although other organs may also become infected. Infection most often occurs at age 5–9. The first exposure stimulates antibody production and usually confers permanent immunity; active immunity can be conferred by immunization. In postadolescent males, the mumps virus may also infect the testes and cause sterility. Infection of the pancreas by the mumps virus may produce temporary or permanent diabetes; other organ systems, including the CNS, may be affected in severe cases. An effective mumps vaccine is available; widespread distribution has almost eliminated this disease in the United States.

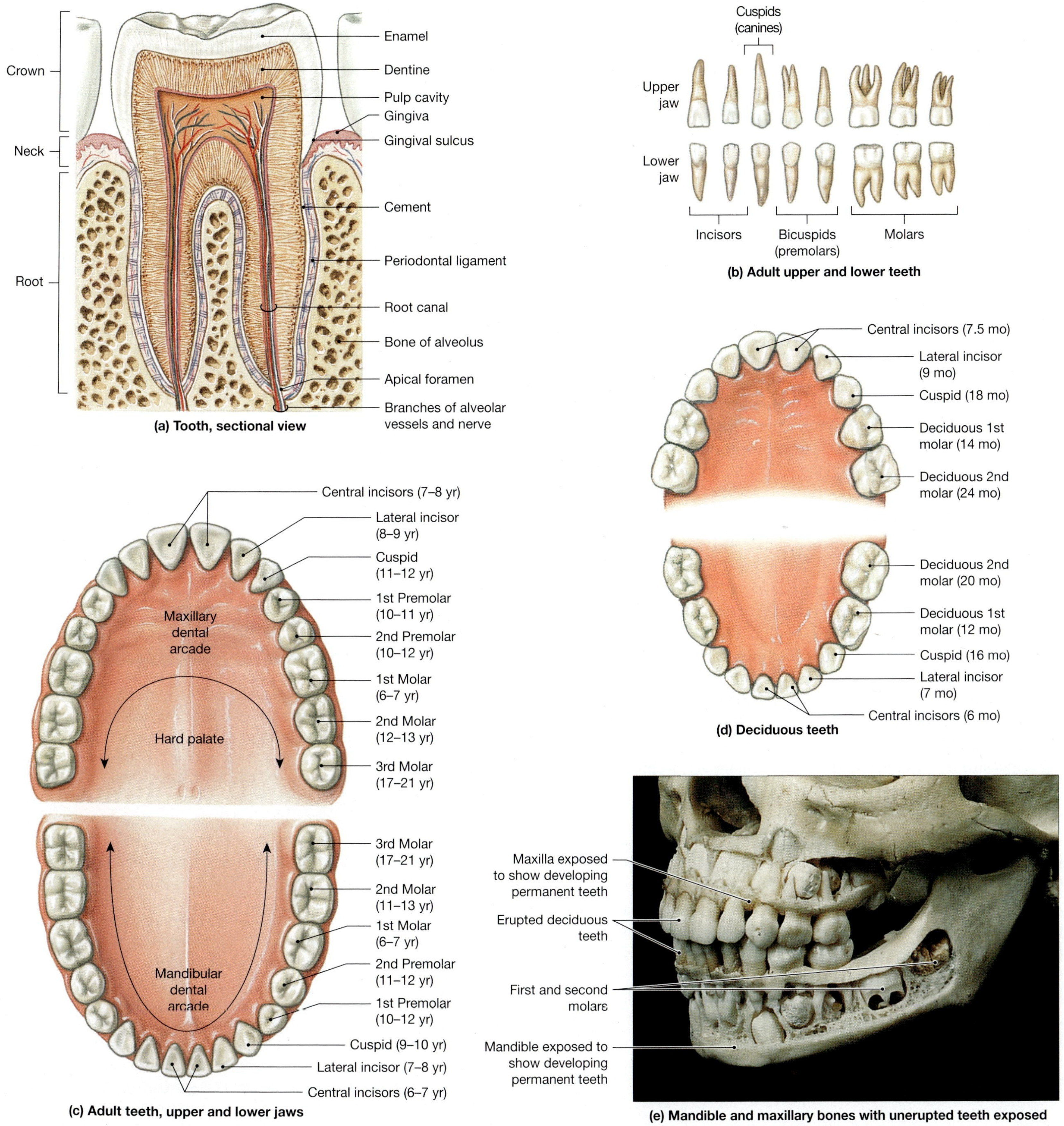

Figure 25.7 Teeth

Teeth perform chewing or mastication of food. **(a)** Diagrammatic section through a typical adult tooth. **(b)** The adult teeth. **(c)** The normal orientation of adult teeth. The normal range of ages at eruption for each tooth is shown in parentheses. **(d)** The deciduous teeth with the age at eruption given in months. **(e)** The skull of a 4-year-old child, with the maxillae and mandible cut away to expose the unerupted permanent teeth.

Dental Succession [Figure 25.7c,d,e] During development, two sets of teeth begin to form. The first to appear are the **deciduous** (dē-SID-ū-us; *deciduus*, falling off) **teeth**, also called the *primary teeth, milk teeth*, or *baby teeth*. These are the temporary teeth of the **primary dentition** (Figure 25.7d,e). There are usually 20 deciduous teeth, five on each side of the upper and lower jaws. The larger adult jaws can accommodate more than 20 permanent teeth, and three additional molars appear on each side of the upper and lower jaws as the individual ages. These teeth extend the length of the tooth rows posteriorly and bring the permanent tooth count to 32.

On each side of the upper or lower jaw, the primary dentition consists of two incisors, one cuspid, and a pair of deciduous molars. These are gradually replaced by the permanent dentition.

Figure 25.7c,d indicate the sequence of eruption of the primary dentition and the approximate ages at their replacement. In this process the periodontal ligaments and roots of the deciduous teeth are eroded away until they fall out or are pushed aside by the emergence, or **eruption**, of the secondary teeth. The adult premolars take the place of the deciduous molars, and the definitive adult molars extend the tooth row as the jaw enlarges. The third molars, or *wisdom teeth*, may not erupt before age 21, if they appear at all. Wisdom teeth often develop in inappropriate positions, and they may be unable to erupt properly.

A Dental Frame of Reference [Figure 25.7b,c] The upper and lower rows of the teeth form a curving **dental arcade**. Relative positions along the *arcade* are indicated by the use of special terms (Figure 25.7b,c). The term **labial** or **buccal** refers to the outer surface of the dental arcade, adjacent to the lips or cheeks. **Palatal** (upper) or **lingual** (lower) refers to the inner surface of the dental arcade. **Mesial** (MĒ-zē-al) or **distal** refers to the opposing surfaces between the teeth in a single dental arcade. The mesial surface is the side of a tooth that faces away from the last molar; the distal surface faces away from the first incisor. For example, the mesial surface of each canine faces the distal surface of the second incisor. The **occlusal** (ō-KLOO-zal; *occlusio*, closed) **surfaces** of the teeth face their counterparts on the opposing *dental arcade*. The occlusal surfaces perform the actual clipping, tearing, crushing, and grinding actions of the teeth.

Mastication The muscles of mastication close the jaws and slide or rock the lower jaw from side to side. ∞ p. 268 During mastication, food is forced back and forth between the vestibule and the rest of the oral cavity, crossing and recrossing the occlusal surfaces. This movement results in part from the action of the masticatory muscles, but control would be impossible without the aid of the buccal, labial, and lingual muscles. Once the material has been shredded or torn to a satisfactory consistency and moistened with salivary secretions, the tongue begins compacting the debris into a small oval mass, or **bolus**, that can be swallowed.

CONCEPT CHECK

1. What type of epithelium lines the oral cavity?
2. What are the functions of saliva?
3. What nutrient begins its chemical breakdown in the mouth?
4. Pretend you are eating an apple. Summarize the actions of the teeth involved.

See blue "Answers" tab at back of book.

The Pharynx

The pharynx serves as a common passageway for food, liquids, and air. The epithelial lining and divisions of the pharynx, the nasopharynx, the oropharynx, and the laryngopharynx were described and illustrated in Chapter 24. ∞ p. 634 Deep to the lamina propria of the mucosa lies a dense layer of elastic fibers, bound to the underlying skeletal muscles. The specific pharyngeal muscles involved in swallowing, summarized next, were detailed in Chapter 10. ∞ p. 269

- The *pharyngeal constrictors* (superior, middle, and inferior) push the bolus toward the esophagus.
- The *palatopharyngeus* and *stylopharyngeus muscles* elevate the larynx.
- The *palatal muscles* raise the soft palate and adjacent portions of the pharyngeal wall.

The pharyngeal muscles cooperate with muscles of the oral cavity and esophagus to initiate the swallowing process, or **deglutition** (dē-gloo-TISH-un).

The Swallowing Process [Figure 25.8]

Swallowing is a complex process whose initiation is voluntarily controlled, but it proceeds involuntarily once initiated. ∞ p. 269–270 It can be divided into *buccal, pharyngeal*, and *esophageal phases*. Key aspects of each phase are illustrated in Figure 25.8.

Clinical Note

Achalasia, Esophagitis, and GERD In the condition known as **achalasia** (ak-a-LĀ-zē-uh), a swallowed bolus descends along the esophagus relatively slowly as a result of abnormally weak peristaltic waves, and its arrival does not trigger the opening of the lower esophageal sphincter. Materials then accumulate at the base of the esophagus like cars at a stoplight. Secondary peristaltic waves may occur repeatedly, causing the individual discomfort. The most successful treatment involves weakening the lower esophageal sphincter muscle by either cutting the circular muscle layer at the base of the esophagus or expanding a balloon in the lower esophagus until the muscle layer tears.

Brief, limited reflux of stomach contents into the lower part of the esophagus often occurs after meals, and the incidence is increased with abdominal obesity, pregnancy, and reclining after large meals. A weakened or permanently relaxed sphincter can cause frequent, prolonged reflux, leading to **esophagitis** (ē-sof-a-JĪ-tis), or inflammation of the esophagus from contact with powerful stomach acids. The esophageal epithelium has few defenses against attack by acids and enzymes; inflammation, epithelial erosion, and intense discomfort result. Frequent episodes of backflow result in **gastroesophageal reflux disease (GERD)**, which causes the symptoms commonly known as heartburn. Simply elevating the head of one's bed reduces GERD symptoms as much as medication in many people. Some people with GERD may cough and suffer throat and lung problems, presumably from flow of stomach fluids up the esophagus and aspiration into the trachea. However, coughing may promote esophageal reflux, so the cause-and-effect link is uncertain.

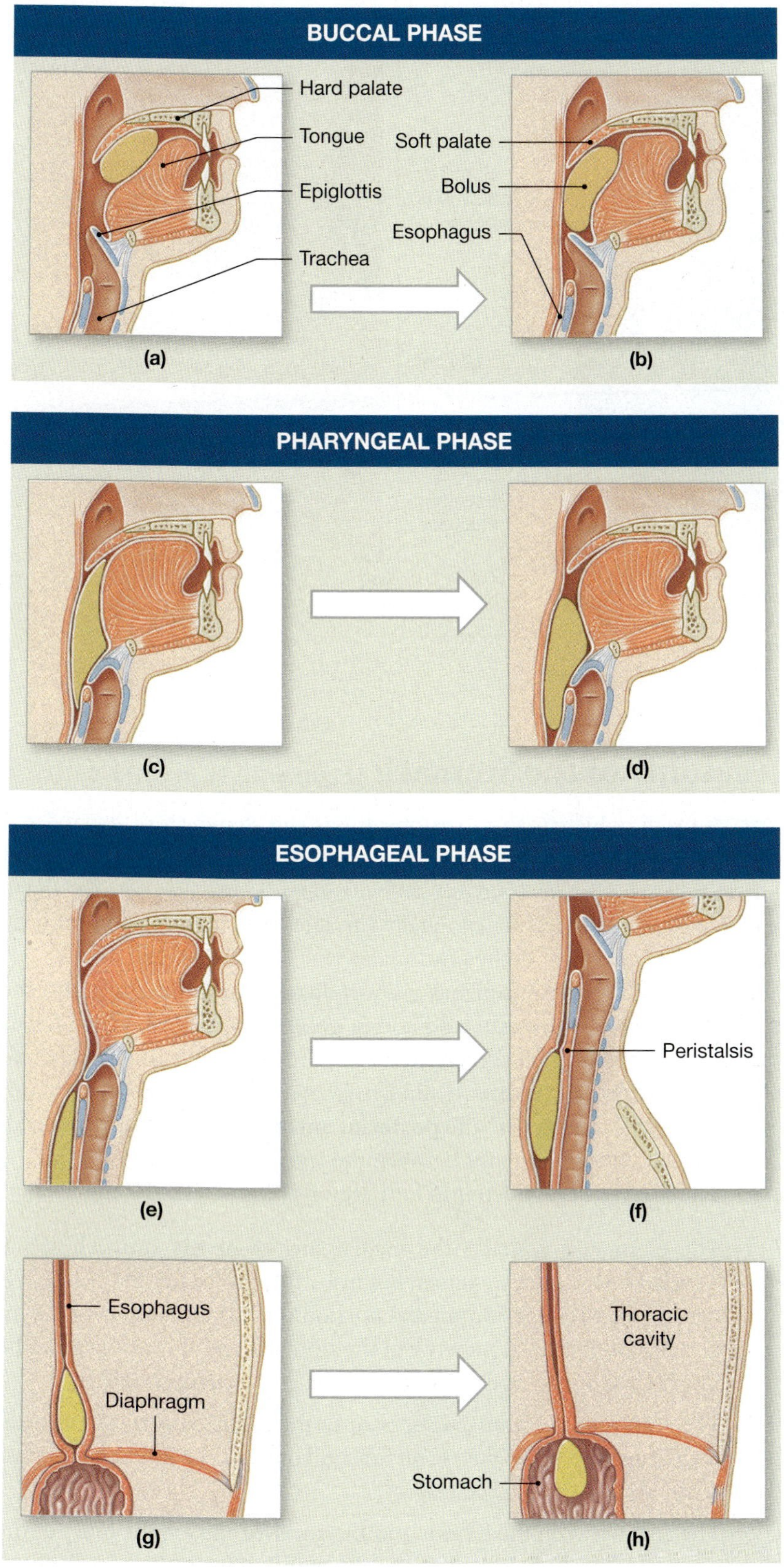

Figure 25.8 The Swallowing Process
This sequence, based on a series of x-rays, shows the stages of swallowing and the movement of materials from the mouth to the stomach: **(a, b)** buccal phase, **(c, d)** pharyngeal phase, and **(e–h)** esophageal phase.

1. The **buccal phase** begins with the compression of the bolus against the hard palate. Subsequent retraction of the tongue then forces the bolus into the pharynx and assists in the elevation of the soft palate by the palatal muscles, thereby isolating the nasopharynx (Figure 25.8a,b). The buccal phase is strictly voluntary. However, once the bolus enters the oropharynx, involuntary reflexes are initiated, and the bolus is moved toward the stomach.
2. The **pharyngeal phase** begins as the bolus comes in contact with the palatal arches, the posterior pharyngeal wall, or both (Figure 25.8c,d). Elevation of the larynx (by the palatopharyngeus and stylopharyngeus muscles) and folding of the epiglottis direct the bolus past the closed glottis. In less than a second, the pharyngeal constrictor muscles have propelled the bolus into the esophagus. During the time it takes for the bolus to travel through the pharynx and into the esophagus, the respiratory centers are inhibited and breathing ceases. p. 649
3. The **esophageal phase** of swallowing (Figure 25.8e–g) starts with the opening of the **upper esophageal sphincter**. After passing through the open sphincter, the bolus is pushed along the length of the esophagus by peristaltic waves. The approach of the bolus triggers the opening of the weak **lower esophageal sphincter**, and the bolus then continues into the stomach (Figure 25.8g,h).

The Esophagus [Figures 25.1/25.8]

The **esophagus** (Figure 25.1, p. 657) is a hollow muscular tube that transports foods and liquids to the stomach. Located posterior to the trachea (Figure 25.8), it passes along the dorsal wall of the mediastinum in the thoracic cavity and enters the peritoneal cavity through an opening in the diaphragm, the **esophageal hiatus** (hī-Ā-tus), before emptying into the stomach. p. 278 The esophagus is approximately 25 cm (1 ft) long and about 2 cm (0.75 in.) in diameter. It begins at the level of the cricoid cartilage anterior to vertebra C_6 and ends anterior to vertebra T_7.

The esophagus receives blood from the esophageal arteries and branches of (1) the *thyrocervical trunk* and *external carotid arteries* of the neck, (2) the *bronchial arteries* and *esophageal arteries* of the mediastinum, and (3) the *inferior phrenic artery* and *left gastric artery* of the abdomen. Venous blood from the esophageal capillaries collects into the *esophageal, inferior thyroid, azygos,* and *gastric veins.* The esophagus is innervated by the vagus and sympathetic trunks via the *esophageal plexus.* pp. 463, 588–589 Neither the upper nor the lower portion of the esophagus has a well-defined sphincter muscle comparable to those located elsewhere along the digestive tract. Nevertheless, the terms *upper esophageal sphincter* and *lower esophageal sphincter (cardiac sphincter)* are used to describe these regions because they are similar in function to other sphincters.

Histology of the Esophageal Wall [Figures 25.2/25.9]

The wall of the esophagus has mucosal, submucosal, and muscularis layers comparable to those described earlier (Figure 25.2, p. 658). There are several distinctive features of the esophageal wall, shown in Figure 25.9:

- The mucosa of the esophagus contains an abrasion-resistant stratified squamous epithelium.
- The mucosa and submucosa form large folds that run the length of the esophagus. These folds permit expansion during the passage of a large bolus; except during swallowing, muscle tone in the walls keeps the lumen closed.
- The smooth muscle layer of the muscularis mucosae may be very thin or absent near the pharynx, but it gradually thickens to 200–400 μm as it approaches the stomach.

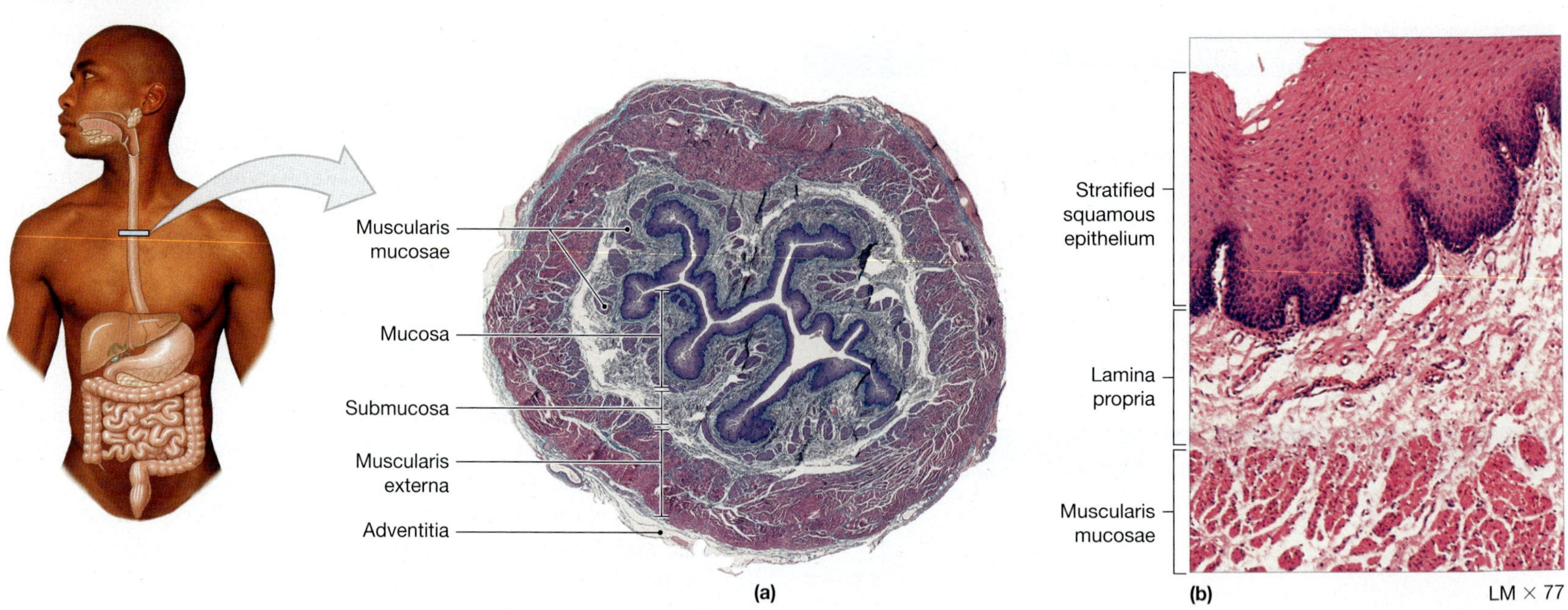

Figure 25.9 Histology of the Esophagus
(a) Low-power view of a section through the esophagus. **(b)** The esophageal mucosa.

- The submucosa contains scattered *esophageal glands.* These simple, branched, tubular glands produce a mucous secretion that lubricates the bolus and protects the epithelial surface.
- The muscularis externa has inner circular and outer longitudinal muscle layers. In the superior third of the esophagus both layers contain skeletal muscle fibers; in the middle third there is a mixture of skeletal and smooth muscle tissue; along the inferior third only smooth muscles are found. The skeletal muscle and smooth muscle in the esophagus are controlled by visceral reflexes, and you do not have voluntary control over these contractions.
- There is no serosa. A layer of connective tissue outside the muscularis externa anchors the esophagus in position against the dorsal body wall. This outer fibrous layer is called the *adventitia.* Over the 1–2 cm between the diaphragm and the stomach the esophagus is retroperitoneal, with peritoneum covering the anterior and left lateral surfaces.

CONCEPT CHECK

1. Where is the fauces?
2. What is occurring when the soft palate and larynx are elevated and the glottis closes?
3. Which stage of swallowing is voluntary?
4. When someone experiences heartburn, what is happening in the esophagus?

See blue "Answers" tab at back of book.

The Stomach

The stomach performs three major functions: (1) bulk storage of ingested food, (2) mechanical breakdown of ingested food, and (3) chemical digestion of ingested food through the disruption of chemical bonds by acids and enzymes. This mixing of ingested substances with the acids and enzymes secreted by the glands of the stomach produces a viscous, strongly acidic, soupy mixture called **chyme** (kīm).

Anatomy of the Stomach [Figures 25.10 to 25.12]

The stomach, which is intraperitoneal, has the shape of an expanded J (Figures 25.10 and 25.11). It occupies the *left hypochondriac, epigastric,* and portions of the *umbilical* and *left lumbar regions* (Figure 25.12). The shape and size of the stomach are extremely variable from individual to individual and from one meal to the next.

The J-shaped stomach has a short **lesser curvature**, forming the **medial surface** of the organ, and a long **greater curvature**, which forms the **lateral surface**. In an average stomach the lesser curvature has a length of approximately 10 cm (4 in.), and the greater curvature measures about 40 cm (16 in.). The **anterior** and **posterior surfaces** are smoothly rounded. The stomach typically extends between the levels of vertebrae T_7 and L_3.

The stomach is divided into four regions (Figures 25.10 and 25.11):

1. The esophagus contacts the medial surface of the stomach at the **cardia** (KAR-dē-a), so named because of its proximity to the heart. It consists of the superior, medial portion of the stomach within 3 cm (1.2 in.) of the junction between the stomach and the esophagus. The esophageal lumen opens into the cardia at the **cardiac orifice**.
2. The region of the stomach superior to the gastroesophageal junction is the **fundus** (FUN-dus). The fundus contacts the inferior and posterior surface of the diaphragm.
3. The area between the fundus and the curve of the J is the **body** of the stomach. The body is the largest region of the stomach; it functions as a mixing tank for ingested food and gastric secretions.
4. The **pylorus** (pī-LŌR-us) is the curve of the J. The pyloris is divided into the *pyloric antrum,* which is connected to the body of the stomach, and the *pyloric canal,* which is connected to the *duodenum,* the proximal segment of the small intestine. As mixing movements occur during digestion, the pylorus frequently changes shape. A muscular **pyloric sphincter** regulates the release of chyme from the **pyloric orifice** into the duodenum.

The volume of the stomach increases at mealtimes and decreases as chyme leaves the stomach and enters the small intestine. In the relaxed

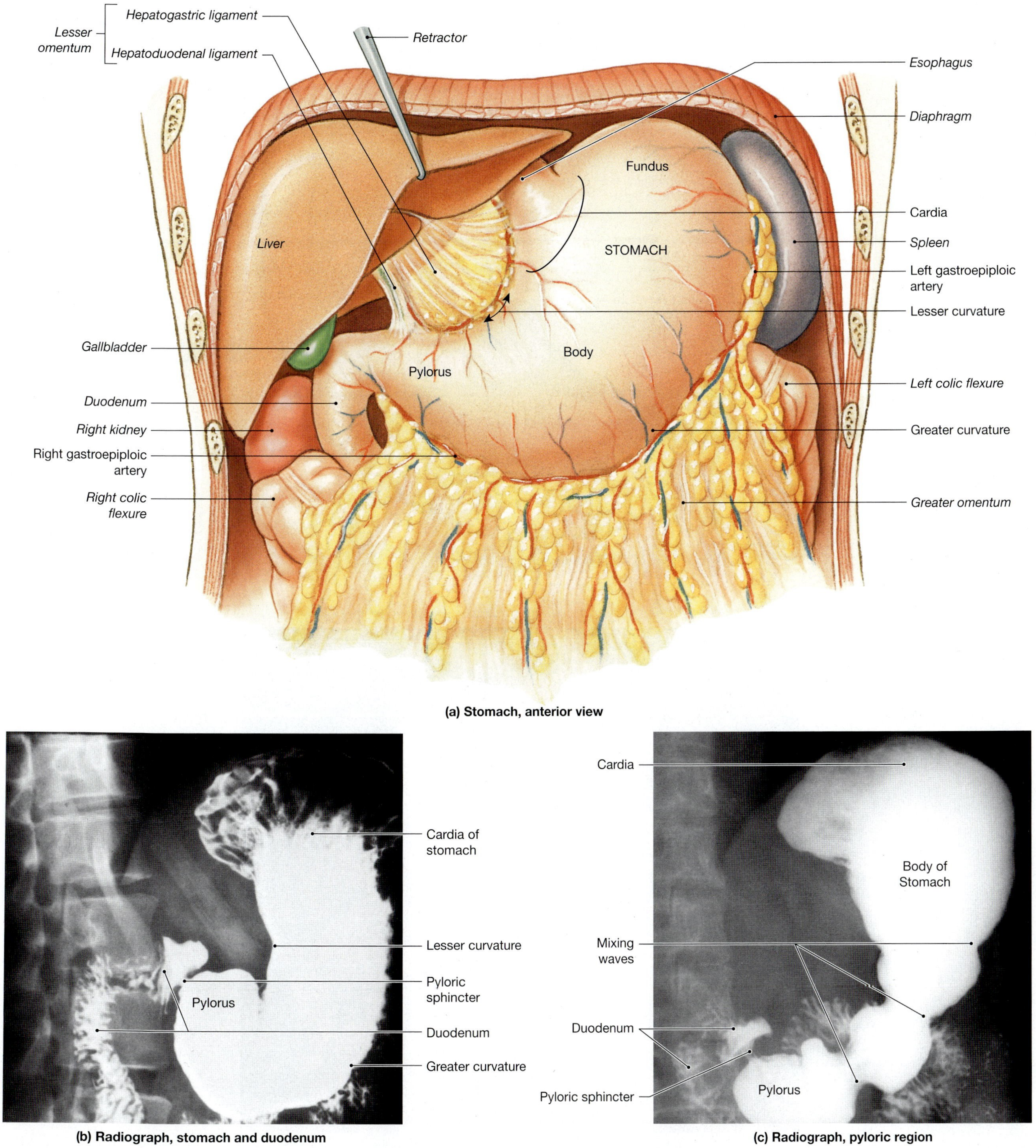

Figure 25.10 The Stomach and Omenta
(a) Surface anatomy of the stomach, showing blood vessels and relation to liver and intestines. **(b)** Radiograph of the stomach and duodenum, after swallowing a barium solution to increase contrast. **(c)** Radiograph of the pyloric region, pyloric valve, and duodenum.

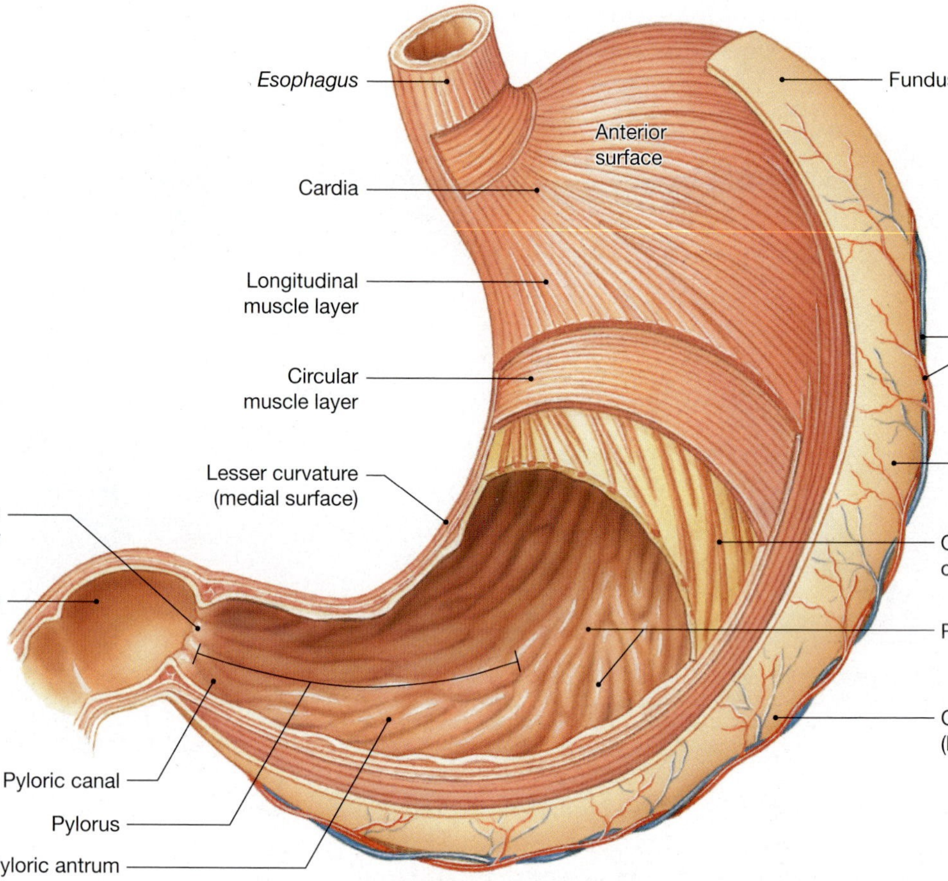

(a) Stomach, anterior view

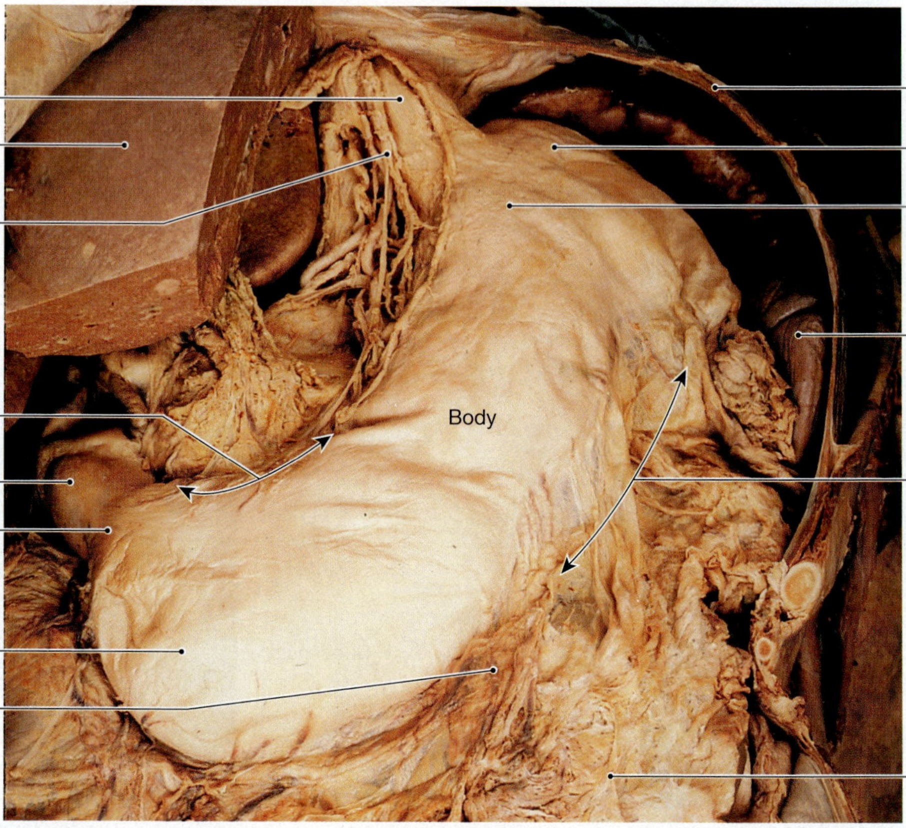

(b) Anterior view of the stomach and adjacent organs

Figure 25.11 Gross Anatomy of the Stomach
(a) External and internal anatomy of the stomach. **(b)** Anterior view of the superior portion of abdominal cavity after removal of the left lobe of the liver and the lesser omentum. Note the position and orientation of the stomach.

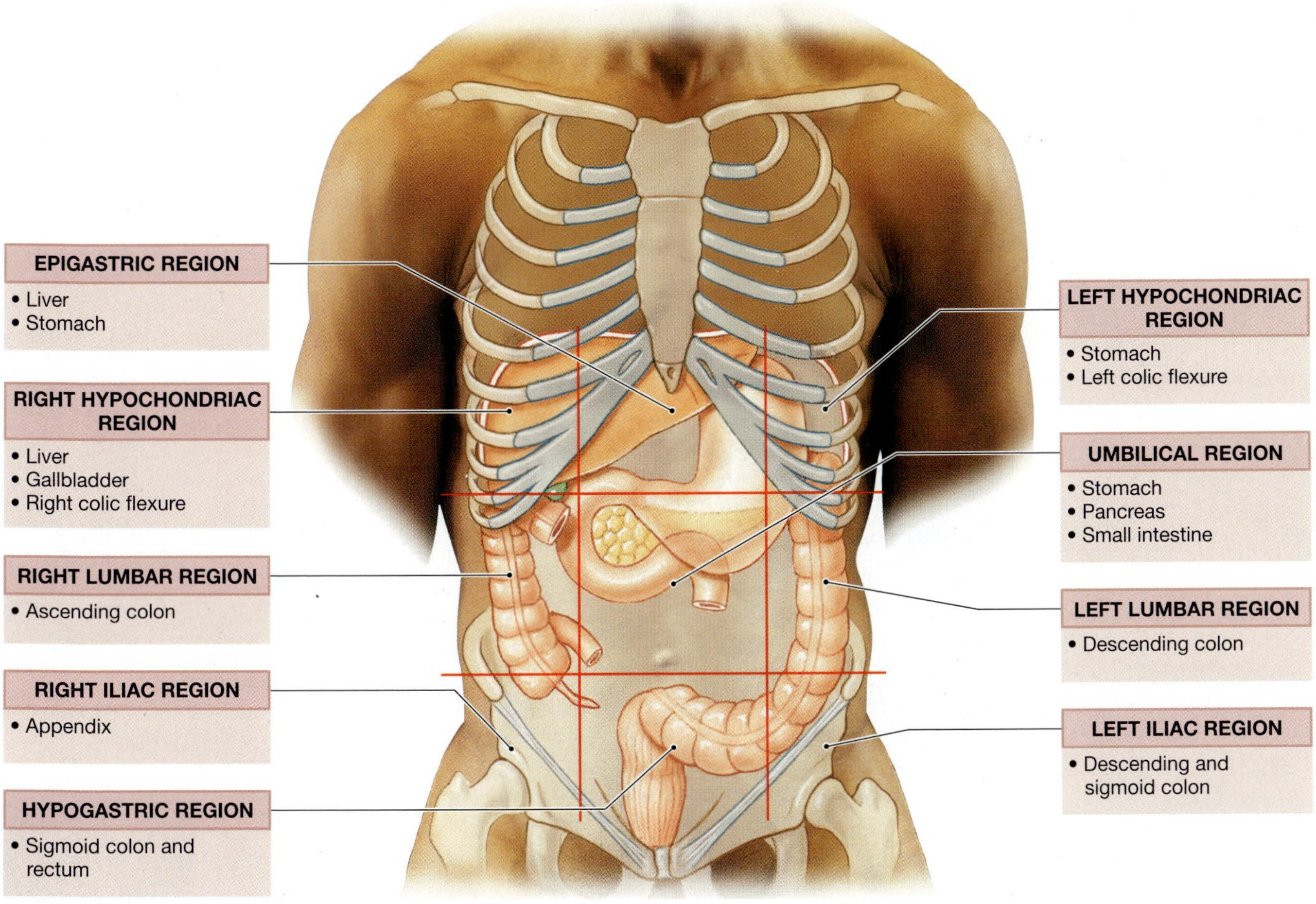

Figure 25.12 **Abdominal Regions and Planes**

(empty) stomach, the mucosa is thrown into a number of prominent longitudinal folds, called **rugae** (ROO-gē; "wrinkles") (Figure 25.11a). Rugae permit expansion of the gastric lumen. As expansion occurs, the epithelial lining, which cannot stretch, flattens out, and the rugae become less prominent. In a full stomach the rugae almost disappear.

Mesenteries of the Stomach [Figures 25.4/25.10a]

The visceral peritoneum covering the outer surface of the stomach is continuous with a pair of prominent mesenteries. The *greater omentum* forms a large pouch that hangs like an apron from the greater curvature of the stomach. The greater omentum lies posterior to the anterior abdominal wall and anterior to the abdominal viscera (Figures 25.4, p. 661, and 25.10a). Adipose tissue in the greater omentum conforms to the shapes of the surrounding organs; it provides padding and protects the anterior and lateral surfaces of the abdomen. The lipids in the adipose tissue represent an important energy reserve, and the greater omentum provides insulation that reduces heat loss across the anterior abdominal wall. The *lesser omentum* is a much smaller pocket in the ventral mesentery between the lesser curvature of the stomach and the liver. The lesser omentum stabilizes the position of the stomach and provides an access route for blood vessels and other structures entering or leaving the liver.

Blood Supply to the Stomach [Figures 22.17/22.26/25.10a]

The three branches of the celiac artery supply blood to the stomach (Figures 22.17, ∞ p. 589, and 25.10a):

- The *left gastric artery* supplies blood to the lesser curvature and cardia.
- The *splenic artery* supplies the fundus directly, and the greater curvature through the *left gastroepiploic artery*.
- The *common hepatic artery* supplies blood to the lesser and greater curvatures of the pylorus through the *right gastric artery*, the *right gastroepiploic artery*, and the *gastroduodenal artery*. *Gastric* and *gastroepiploic veins* drain blood from the stomach into the hepatic portal vein (Figure 22.26) ∞ p. 600.

Musculature of the Stomach [Figure 25.11a]

The muscularis mucosae and muscularis externa of the stomach contain extra layers of smooth muscle in addition to the usual *circular* and *longitudinal layers*. The muscularis mucosae usually contains an additional outer, circular layer of muscle fibers. The muscularis externa has an extra inner, *oblique layer* of smooth muscle (Figure 25.11a). The extra layers of smooth muscle strengthen the stomach wall and perform the mixing and churning activities essential to the formation of chyme.

Histology of the Stomach [Figure 25.13]

A simple columnar epithelium lines all regions of the stomach. The epithelium is a *secretory sheet* that produces a carpet of mucus that covers the luminal surfaces of the stomach. ∞ p. 72 The mucous layer protects the epithelium against the acids and enzymes in the gastric lumen. Shallow depressions, called **gastric pits**, open onto the gastric surface (Figure 25.13). The mucous cells at the base, or *neck*, of each gastric pit actively divide to replace superficial cells that are shed continuously into the chyme. The continual replacement of epithelial cells provides an additional defense against

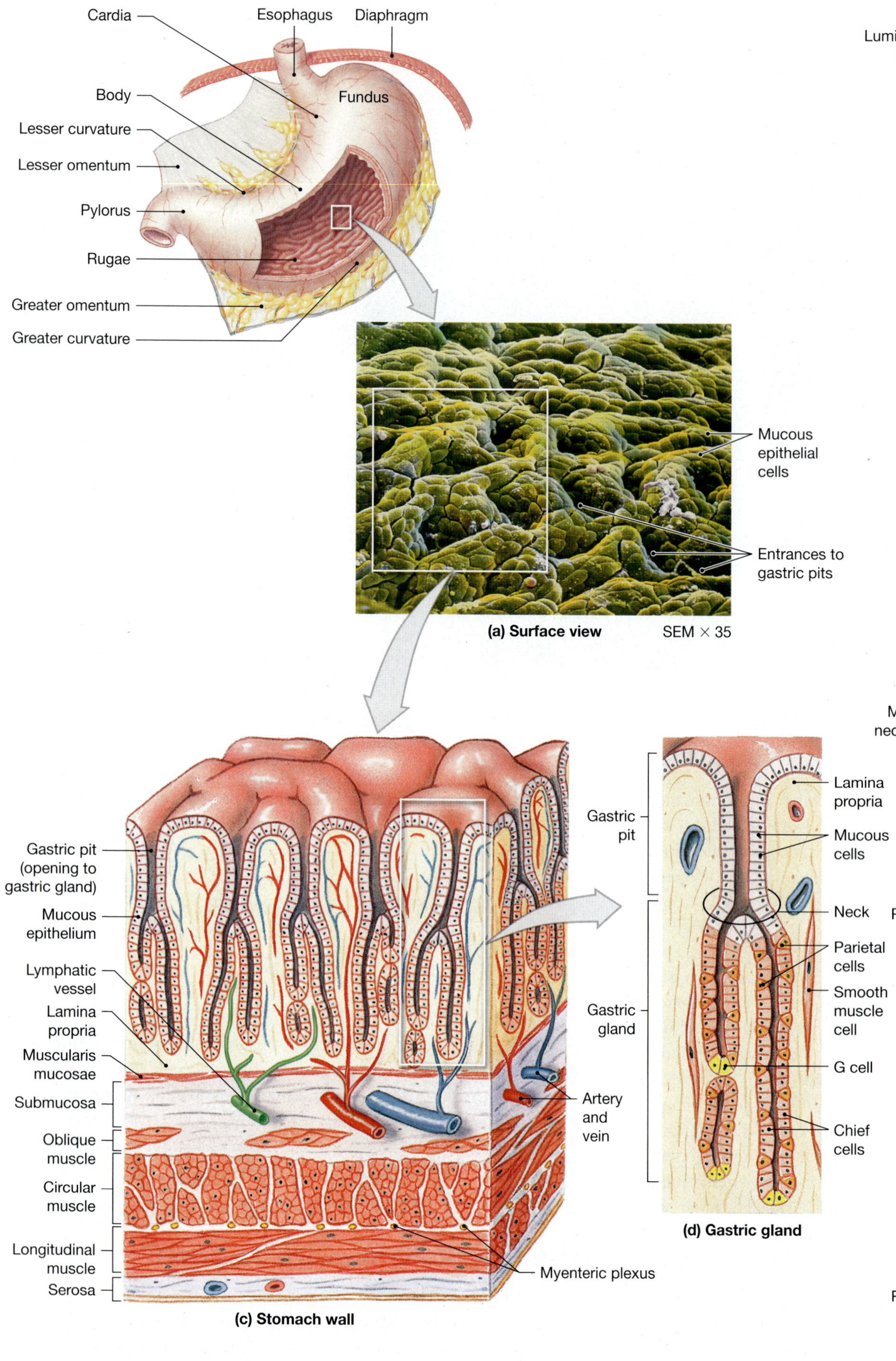

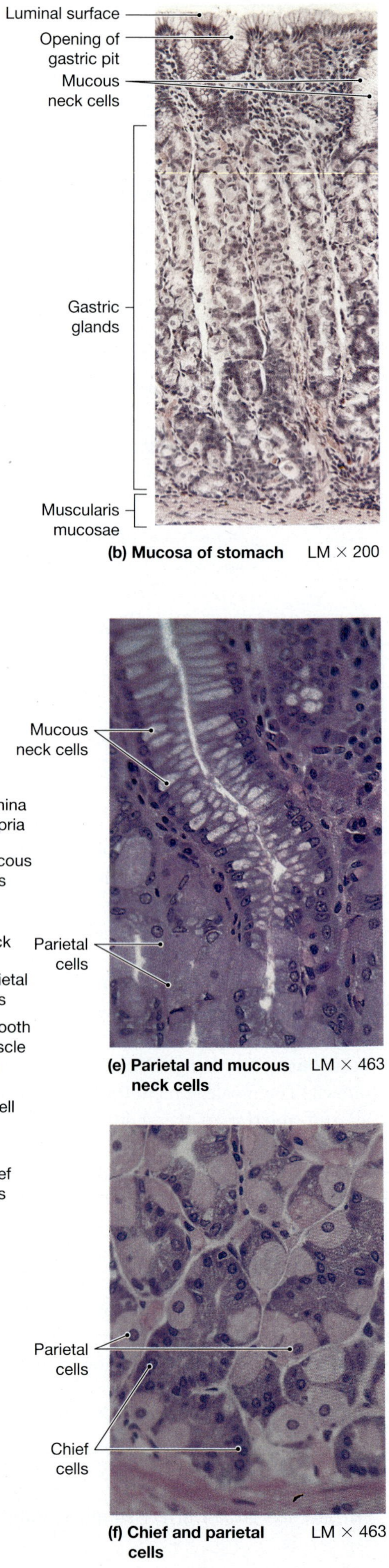

Figure 25.13 Histology of the Stomach Wall
(a) Diagrammatic view and colorized SEM of the gastric mucosa. **(b)** Micrograph of the gastric mucosa. **(c)** Diagrammatic view of the organization of the stomach wall. This corresponds to a sectional view through the area indicated by the box in part (a). **(d)** A gastric gland. **(e)** The parietal and mucous neck cells of the outer portion of a gastric gland. **(f)** Chief and parietal cells of the deepest portions of a gastric gland.

the gastric contents. If stomach acid and digestive enzymes penetrate the mucous layers, any damaged epithelial cells are quickly replaced.

Gastric Secretory Cells

In the fundus and body of the stomach, each gastric pit communicates with several **gastric glands** that extend deep into the underlying lamina propria. Gastric glands (Figure 25.13b) are simple branched tubular glands dominated by three types of secretory cells: *parietal cells, chief cells,* and *enteroendocrine cells* scattered between the other two cell types (Figure 25.13c–f). The parietal and chief cells work together to secrete about 1500 ml of **gastric juice** each day.

Parietal Cells Cells that secrete *intrinsic factor* and *hydrochloric acid* (HCl) are termed **parietal cells**, or *oxyntic cells.* They are especially common along the proximal portions of each gastric gland. **Intrinsic factor** facilitates the absorption of vitamin B_{12} across the intestinal lining. Vitamin B_{12} is necessary for normal erythropoiesis. p. 543 Hydrochloric acid lowers the pH of the gastric juice, kills microorganisms, breaks down cell walls and connective tissues in food, and activates the secretions of the chief cells.

Chief Cells **Chief cells**, or *zymogen cells*, are most abundant near the base of a gastric gland. These cells secrete **pepsinogen** (pep-SIN-ō-jen), which is converted by the acids in the gastric lumen to an active proteolytic (protein digesting) enzyme, **pepsin**. The stomachs of newborn infants (but not adults) also produce **rennin** and **gastric lipase**, enzymes important for the digestion of milk. Rennin coagulates milk proteins, and gastric lipase initiates the digestion of milk fats.

Enteroendocrine Cells Scattered among the parietal and chief cells are the **enteroendocrine** (en-ter-ō-EN-dō-krin) **cells**. These cells produce at least seven different secretions. **G cells**, for example, are enteroendocrine cells that are most abundant in the gastric pits of the pyloric region. They secrete the hormone **gastrin** (GAS-trin). Gastrin, which is released when food enters the stomach, stimulates the secretory activity of both parietal and chief cells. It also promotes smooth muscle activity in the stomach wall. This enhances mixing and churning activity.

Regulation of the Stomach

The production of acid and enzymes by the gastric mucosa can be directly controlled by the central nervous system and indirectly regulated by local hormones. CNS regulation involves both the vagus nerve (parasympathetic innervation) and branches of the celiac plexus (sympathetic innervation). The sight or thought of food triggers motor output in the vagus nerve. Postganglionic parasympathetic fibers innervate parietal cells, chief cells, and mucous cells of the stomach. Stimulation causes an increase in the production of acids, enzymes, and mucus. The arrival of food in the stomach stimulates stretch receptors in the stomach wall and chemoreceptors in the mucosa. Reflexive contractions occur in the muscularis layers of the stomach wall, and gastrin is released by enteroendocrine cells. Both parietal and chief cells respond to the presence of gastrin by accelerating their secretory activities. Parietal cells are especially sensitive to gastrin, so the rate of acid production increases more dramatically than the rate of enzyme secretion.

Sympathetic activation leads to the inhibition of gastric activity. In addition, the small intestine releases two hormones that inhibit gastric secretion. **Secretin** (se-KRĒ-tin) and **cholecystokinin** (kō-lē-sis-tō-KĪ-nin) stimulate secretion by both the pancreas and liver; the depression of gastric activity is a secondary, but complementary, effect.

Clinical Note

Gastritis and Peptic Ulcers Inflammation of the gastric mucosa causes **gastritis** (gas-TRĪ-tis), a superficial inflammation of the stomach lining. This condition may develop after swallowing drugs, including alcohol and aspirin. Gastritis may also appear after severe emotional or physical stress, bacterial infection of the gastric wall, or ingestion of strong acid or alkaline chemicals. Infections involving the bacterium *Helicobacter pylori* are an important factor in ulcer formation; an *ulcer* is a distinct, localized erosion of the stomach lining. These bacteria are able to survive long enough to penetrate the mucus that coats the epithelium. Once within the protective layer of mucus, they are safe from the action of gastric acids and enzymes. Over time, the infection damages the epithelial lining, with two major results: (1) erosion of the lamina propria by gastric juices and (2) entry and spread of the bacteria through the gastric wall and into the bloodstream.

A **peptic ulcer** develops when the digestive acids and enzymes manage to erode their way through the defenses of the stomach lining or proximal portions of the small intestine. The locations may be indicated by using the terms **gastric ulcer** (stomach) or **duodenal ulcer** (duodenum). Peptic ulcers result from the excessive production of acid or the inadequate production of the alkaline mucus that poses an epithelial defense. An estimated 50–80 percent of gastric ulcers and 95 percent of duodenal ulcers involve people infected with *H. pylori*.

Once gastric juices have destroyed the epithelial layers, the virtually defenseless lamina propria will be exposed to digestive attack. Sharp abdominal pain results, and bleeding can develop. The administration of antacids can often control peptic ulcers by neutralizing the acids and allowing time for the mucosa to regenerate. Several drugs inhibit acid production and secretion. Treatment with an intense two-week course of multiple antibiotics can eliminate *H. pylori* and cure most ulcers, although reinfection may occur. Dietary restrictions to limit the intake of acidic beverages and eliminate foods that promote acid production (caffeine) or damage unprotected mucosal cells (alcohol) also help. In severe cases the damage may provoke significant bleeding, and the acids may even erode their way through the wall of the digestive tract and enter the peritoneal cavity. This condition, called a **perforated ulcer**, requires immediate surgical correction.

CONCEPT CHECK

1. What are the functions of the greater omentum?
2. How do the cells that line the stomach keep from becoming damaged in such an acidic environment?
3. What do chief cells secrete?
4. What hormone stimulates the secretion of parietal and chief cells?

See blue "Answers" tab at back of book.

The Small Intestine [Figures 25.2a,b/25.10/25.12/25.14 to 25.16]

The **small intestine** plays the primary role in the digestion and absorption of nutrients. The small intestine averages 6 m (20 ft) in length (range, 5.0–8.3 m [5–25 ft]) and has a diameter ranging from 4 cm (1.6 in.) at the stomach to about 2.5 cm (1 in.) at the junction with the large intestine. It occupies all abdominal regions except the left hypochondriac and epigastric regions (**Figures 25.12**, p. 671, and **25.14**). Ninety percent of nutrient absorption occurs in the small intestine, and most of the rest occurs in the proximal portion of the large intestine.

The small intestine fills much of the peritoneal cavity. Its position is stabilized by mesenteries attached to the dorsal body wall. Movement of the small intestine during digestion is restricted by the stomach, the large intestine, the abdominal wall, and the pelvic girdle. **Figures 25.10**, p. 669, **25.12**, and **25.14** show the position of the small intestine relative to the other segments of the digestive tract.

The intestinal lining bears a series of transverse folds called **plicae circulares** (sir-kū-LAR-ēs) (**Figures 25.2a,b**, p. 658, **25.15a**, and **25.16b**). Unlike the rugae in the stomach, each plica is a permanent feature of the intestinal lining; plicae do not disappear as the small intestine fills. Roughly 800 plicae are found along the length of the small intestine, and their presence greatly increases the surface area available for absorption.

Regions of the Small Intestine [Figure 25.14]

The small intestine has three anatomical subdivisions: the *duodenum*, the *jejunum*, and the *ileum* (**Figure 25.14**).

The Duodenum [Figures 25.4b/25.10b,c/25.14]

The **duodenum** (doo-ō-DĒ-num) (**Figures 25.10b,c**, p. 669, and **25.14**) is the shortest and widest segment of the small intestine; it is approximately 25 cm (10 in.) long. The duodenum is connected to the pylorus of the stomach, and the interconnection is guarded by the pyloric sphincter. From its start at the pyloric sphincter, the duodenum curves in a C that encloses the pancreas. The proximal 2.5-cm (1-in.) portion is intraperitoneal, while the rest is secondarily retroperitoneal and located between vertebrae L_1 and L_4 (**Figure 25.4b**, p. 661).

The duodenum is a "mixing bowl" that receives chyme from the stomach and digestive secretions from the pancreas and liver. Almost all essential digestive enzymes enter the small intestine from the pancreas.

The Jejunum

A rather abrupt bend, the *duodenojejunal flexure*, marks the boundary between the duodenum and the **jejunum** (je-JOO-num). At this junction the small intestine reenters the peritoneal cavity, becoming intraperitoneal and supported by a sheet of mesentery. The jejunum is about 2.5 m (8 ft) long. The bulk of chemical digestion and nutrient absorption occurs in the jejunum.

The Ileum

The **ileum** (IL-ē-um), which is also intraperitoneal, is the third and last segment of the small intestine. It is also the longest, averaging 3.5 m (12 ft) in length. The ileum ends at a sphincter, the *ileocecal valve*, which controls the flow of materials from the ileum into the *cecum* of the large intestine. The ileocecal valve protrudes into the cecum.

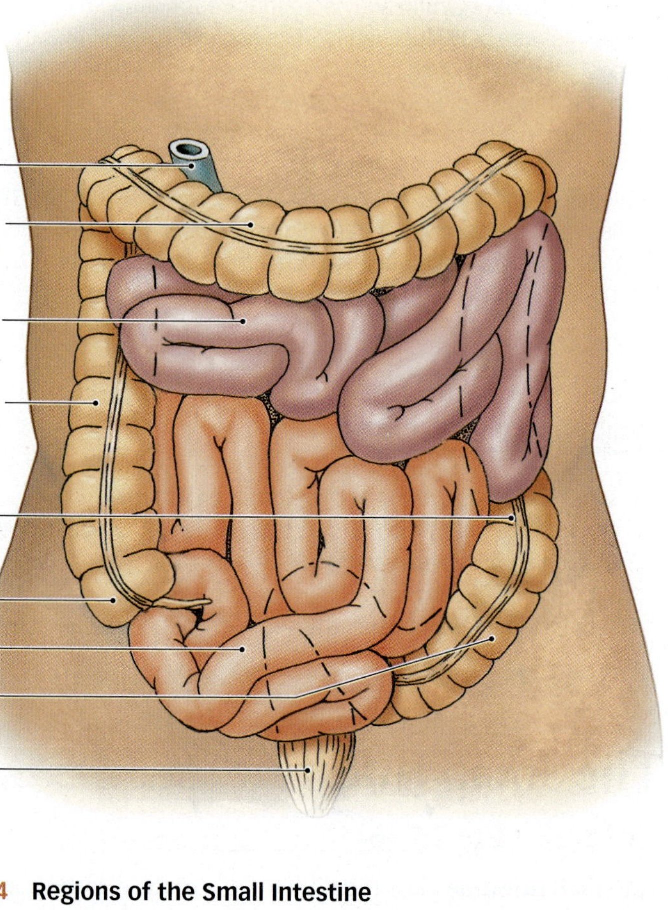

Figure 25.14 Regions of the Small Intestine
The color coding indicates the relative sizes and positions of the duodenum, jejunum, and ileum.

Support of the Small Intestine [Figures 22.17/22.26/25.4]

The duodenum has no supporting mesentery. The proximal 2.5 cm is movable, but the rest is secondarily retroperitoneal and fixed in position. The jejunum and ileum are supported by an extensive, fan-shaped mesentery known as the **mesentery proper** (**Figure 25.4**, p. 661). Blood vessels, lymphatics, and nerves reach these segments of the small intestine by passing through the connective tissue of the mesentery. The blood vessels involved are *intestinal arteries*, branches of the *superior mesenteric artery* and *superior mesenteric vein* (**Figures 22.17** and **22.26**). pp. 589, 600 Parasympathetic innervation is provided by the vagus nerve; sympathetic innervation involves postganglionic fibers from the superior mesenteric ganglion. p. 457

Histology of the Small Intestine

The Intestinal Epithelium [Figures 25.15/25.16]

The mucosa of the small intestine forms a series of fingerlike projections, the **intestinal villi** (**Figures 25.15** and **25.16**), that project into the lumen. Each villus is covered by a simple columnar epithelium. The apical surfaces of the epithelial cells are carpeted with microvilli, and the cells are often said to have a "brush border." If the small intestine was a simple tube with smooth walls, it would have a total absorptive area of roughly 0.33 m^2. Instead, the epithelium contains plicae circulares. Each plica supports a forest of villi, and each villus is covered by epithelial cells whose exposed surfaces contain microvilli. This arrangement increases the total area for absorption to more than 200 m^2.

Intestinal Crypts [Figure 25.15b,d]

Between the columnar epithelial cells, goblet cells eject mucins onto the intestinal surfaces. At the bases of the villi are the entrances to the **intestinal crypts**, or *crypts of Lieberkühn*. These pockets extend deep into the underlying lamina propria (**Figure 25.15b,d**). Near the base of each crypt, stem

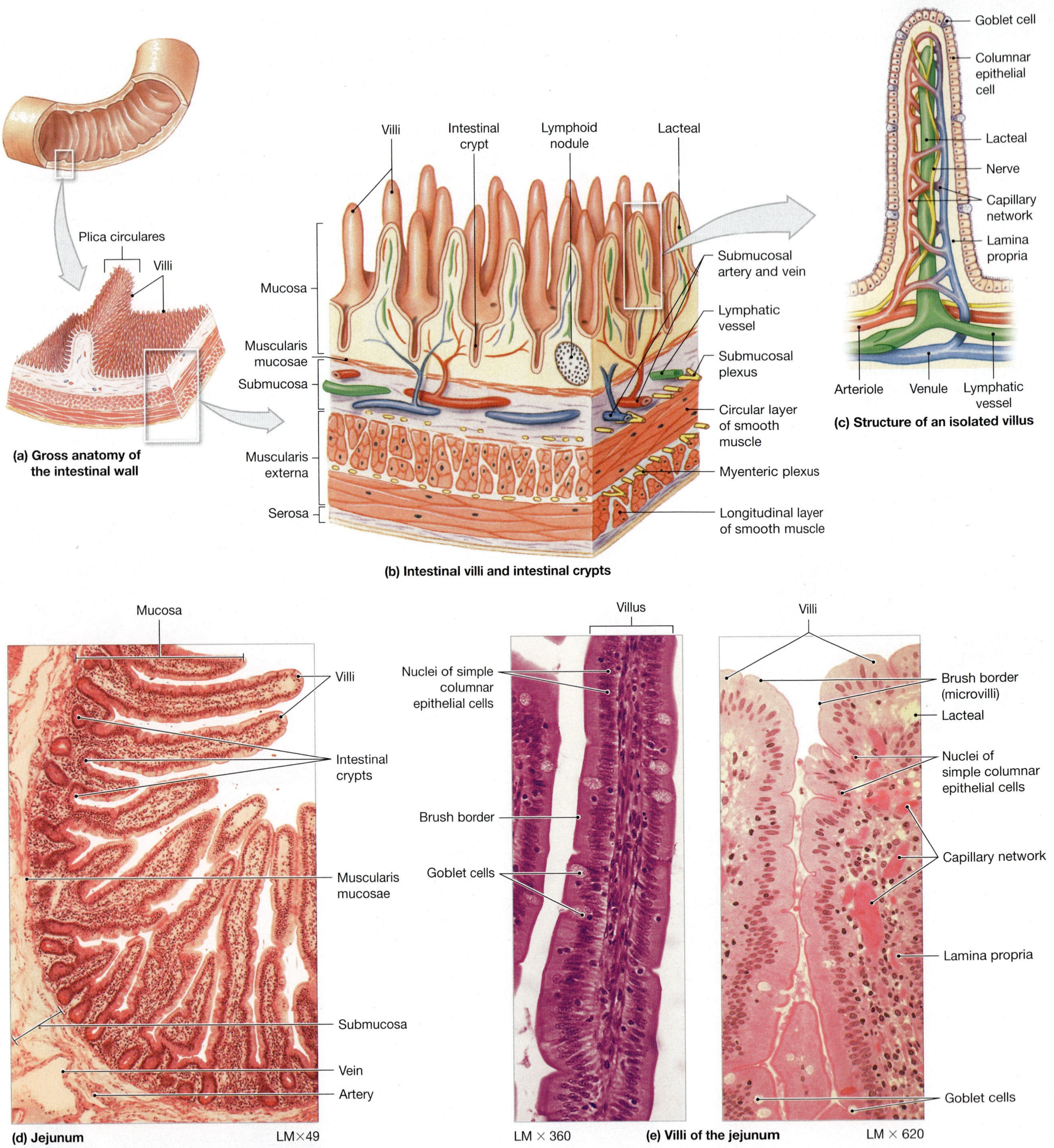

Figure 25.15 Histology of the Intestinal Wall
(a) Characteristic features of the intestinal lining. **(b)** The organization of villi and the intestinal crypts. **(c)** Diagrammatic view of a single villus, showing the capillary and lymphatic supply. **(d)** Panoramic view of the wall of the small intestine showing mucosa with characteristic villi, plica, submucosa, and muscularis layers. **(e)** Photomicrographs of villi from the jejunum.

cell divisions continually produce new generations of epithelial cells. These new cells are continually displaced toward the intestinal surface, and within a few days they will have reached the tip of a villus, where they are shed into the intestinal lumen. This ongoing process renews the epithelial surface and adds intracellular enzymes to the chyme.

Intestinal crypts also contain enteroendocrine cells responsible for the production of several intestinal hormones, including cholecystokinin and secretin, and enzymes with antibacterial activity.

The Lamina Propria [Figure 25.15b,c,e]

The lamina propria of each villus contains an extensive network of capillaries that absorbs and carries nutrients to the hepatic portal circulation. In addition to capillaries and nerve endings, each villus contains a terminal lymphatic called a **lacteal** (LAK-tē-al; *lacteus*, milky) (**Figure 25.15b,c,e**). Lacteals transport materials that cannot enter local capillaries. These materials, such as large lipid–protein complexes, ultimately reach the venous circulation by way of the thoracic duct. The name *lacteal* refers to the pale, milky appearance of lymph containing large quantities of lipids.

Regional Specializations [Figure 25.16]

The regions of the small intestine have histological specializations related to their primary functions. Representative sections from each region of the small intestine are presented in **Figure 25.16**.

The Duodenum [Figures 25.16/25.22b] The duodenum contains numerous mucous glands. In addition to the intestinal crypts, the submucosa contains **duodenal submucosal glands**, also known as *Brunner's glands*. These glands produce large quantities of mucus (**Figure 25.16**). The mucus produced by the intestinal and submucosal glands protects the epithelium from the acid chyme arriving from the stomach. The mucus also contains buffers that help elevate the pH of the chyme. Submucosal glands are most abundant in the proximal portion of the duodenum, and their numbers decrease approaching the jejunum. Over this distance the pH of the intestinal contents changes from 1–2 to 7–8; by the beginning of the jejunum, the extra mucus production is no longer needed.

Buffers and enzymes from the pancreas and bile from the liver enter the duodenum roughly halfway along its length. Within the duodenal wall,

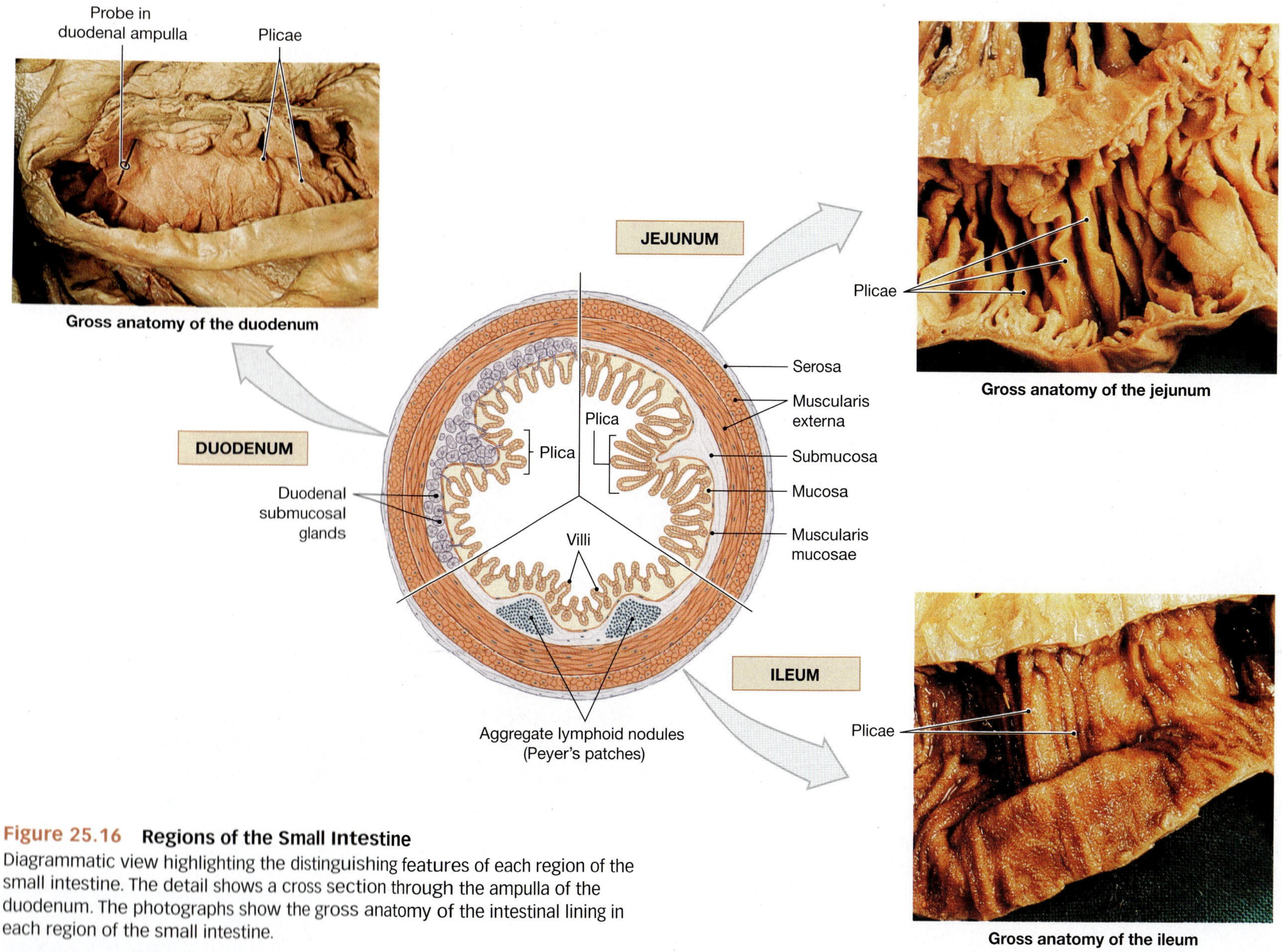

Figure 25.16 Regions of the Small Intestine
Diagrammatic view highlighting the distinguishing features of each region of the small intestine. The detail shows a cross section through the ampulla of the duodenum. The photographs show the gross anatomy of the intestinal lining in each region of the small intestine.

the *common bile duct* from the liver and gallbladder and the *pancreatic duct* from the pancreas come together at a muscular chamber called the **duodenal ampulla** (am-PŪL-la), or **hepatopancreatic ampulla**. This chamber opens into the duodenal lumen at a small mound known as the **duodenal papilla**, or, when an accessory pancreatic duct is present, the *greater duodenal papilla* (Figures 25.16 and 25.22b).

The Jejunum and Ileum [Figures 25.15d,e/25.16] Plicae and villi remain prominent over the proximal half of the jejunum (Figures 25.15d,e and 25.16). Most nutrient absorption occurs here. As one approaches the ileum, the plicae and villi become smaller and continue to diminish in size and number to the end of the ileum. This reduction parallels the reduction in absorptive activity; most nutrient absorption has occurred before materials reach the terminal portion of the ileum. The region adjacent to the large intestine lacks plicae altogether, and the scattered villi are stumpy and conical.

Bacteria, especially *E. coli*, are normal inhabitants within the lumen of the large intestine. These bacteria are nourished by the surrounding mucosa. The epithelial barriers (cells, mucus, and digestive juices) and underlying cells of the immune system protect the small intestine from bacteria migrating from the large intestine. Small, isolated, individual lymphoid nodules are present in the lamina propria of the jejunum. In the ileum the lymphoid nodules become more numerous, and they fuse together to form large masses of lymphoid tissue (Figure 25.16). These lymphoid centers, called **aggregated lymphoid nodules**, or *Peyer's patches*, may reach the size of cherries. ∞ p. 617 They are most abundant in the terminal portion of the ileum, near the entrance to the large intestine, which normally contains large numbers of potentially harmful bacteria.

Regulation of the Small Intestine

As absorption occurs, weak peristaltic contractions slowly move materials along the length of the small intestine. Movements of the small intestine are controlled primarily by neural reflexes involving the submucosal and myenteric plexuses. Stimulation of the parasympathetic system increases the sensitivity of these reflexes and accelerates peristaltic contractions and segmentation movements. These contractions and movements, which promote mixing of the intestinal contents, are usually limited to within a few centimeters of the original stimulus. Coordinated intestinal movements occur when food enters the stomach; these movements tend to move materials away from the duodenum and toward the large intestine. During these periods the ileocecal valve permits the passage of material into the large intestine.

Hormonal and CNS controls regulate the secretory output of the small intestine and accessory glands. The secretions of the small intestine are collectively called **intestinal juice**. Secretory activities are triggered by local reflexes and parasympathetic (vagal) stimulation. Sympathetic stimulation inhibits secretion. Duodenal enteroendocrine cells produce secretin and cholecystokinin, hormones that coordinate the secretory activities of the stomach, duodenum, liver, and pancreas.

CONCEPT CHECK

1. Which histological features of the small intestine facilitate the digestion and absorption of nutrients?
2. What is the function of plicae?
3. What are the functions of intestinal crypts?
4. Which section of the small intestine serves as a "mixing bowl"?

See blue "Answers" tab at back of book.

The Large Intestine [Figures 25.1/25.12/25.14/25.17]

The horseshoe-shaped **large intestine** begins at the end of the ileum and ends at the anus. The large intestine lies inferior to the stomach and liver and almost completely frames the small intestine (Figures 25.1, p. 657, 25.12, p. 671, and 25.14).

The large intestine, often called the **large bowel**, has an average length of about 1.5 m (5 ft) and a width of 7.5 cm (3 in.). It can be divided into three parts: (1) the *cecum*, the first portion of the large intestine, which appears as a pouch; (2) the *colon*, the largest portion of the large intestine; and (3) the *rectum*, the last 15 cm (6 in.) of the large intestine and the end of the digestive tract (Figure 25.17).

The major functions of the large intestine are (1) the *reabsorption of water and electrolytes*, and *compaction* of the intestinal contents into feces; (2) the *absorption of important vitamins* produced by bacterial action; and (3) the *storing of fecal material* before defecation.

The large intestine receives blood from tributaries of the *superior mesenteric* and *inferior mesenteric arteries*. Venous blood is collected from the large intestine by the *superior mesenteric* and *inferior mesenteric veins*. ∞ pp. 589, 600

The Cecum [Figure 25.17]

Materials arriving from the ileum first enter an expanded pouch called the **cecum** (SĒ-kum). The ileum attaches to the medial surface of the cecum and opens into the cecum at the **ileal papilla**. Muscles encircling the opening form the **ileocecal** (il-ē-ō-SĒ-kal) **valve** (Figure 25.17), which regulates the passage of materials into the large intestine. The cecum, which is intraperitoneal, collects and stores the arriving materials and begins the process of compaction. The slender, hollow **appendix**, or *vermiform appendix*, is attached to the posteromedial surface of the cecum. The appendix usually is approximately 9 cm (3.5 in.) long, but its size and shape are quite variable. A band of mesentery, the **mesoappendix**, connects the appendix to the ileum and cecum. The mucosa and submucosa of the appendix are dominated by lymphoid nodules, and its primary function as an organ of the lymphoid system is comparable to one of the tonsils. Inflammation of the appendix produces the symptoms of *appendicitis*.

The Colon [Figure 25.17]

The **colon** has a larger diameter and a thinner wall than the small intestine. Refer to Figure 25.17 as we describe several distinctive features of the colon:

1. The wall of the colon forms a series of pouches, or **haustra** (HAWS-tra; singular, *haustrum*), that permit considerable distension and elongation. Cutting into the intestinal lumen reveals that the creases between the haustra extend into the mucosal lining, producing a series of internal folds.
2. Three separate longitudinal ribbons of the smooth muscle, the **taeniae coli** (TĒ-nē-ē cō-lī; singular, *taenia*), are visible on the outer surfaces of the colon just beneath the serosa.
3. The serosa of the colon contains numerous teardrop-shaped sacs of fat, called the **omental appendices**, or *fatty appendices of the colon* (Figure 25.17a).

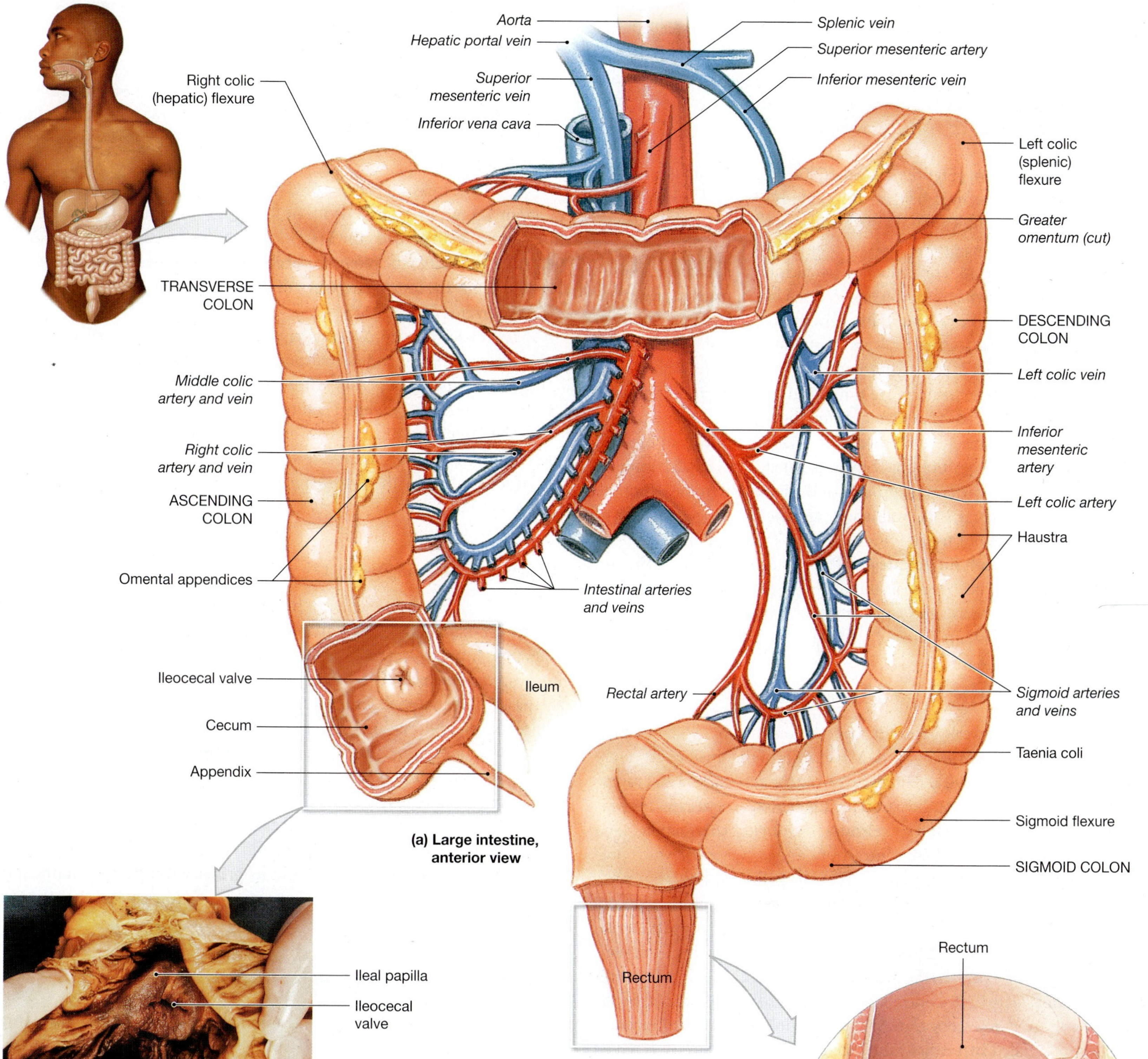

(a) Large intestine, anterior view

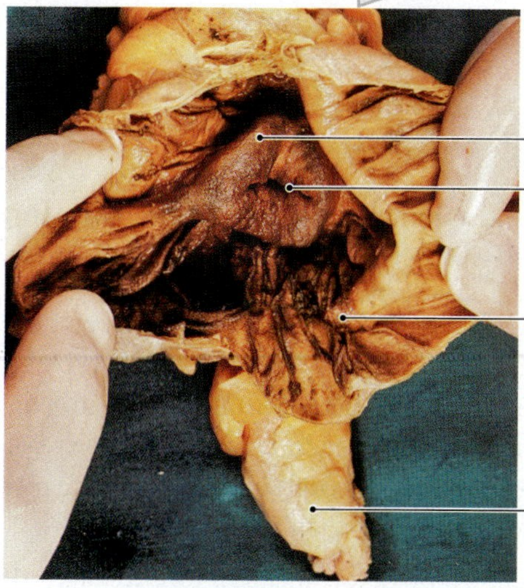

(b) Cecum and appendix

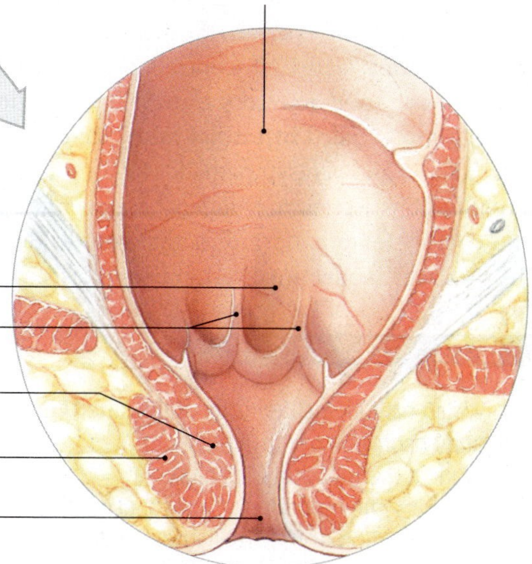

(c) Rectum, sectioned

Figure 25.17 The Large Intestine
(a) Gross anatomy and regions of the large intestine. **(b)** The cecum and appendix. **(c)** Detailed anatomy of the rectum and anus.

Regions of the Colon [Figures 25.17a/25.18]

The colon is subdivided into four regions: the *ascending colon*, the *transverse colon*, the *descending colon*, and the *sigmoid colon* (Figure 25.17a). The regions of the colon may be seen clearly in the radiograph in Figure 25.18.

The Ascending Colon [Figure 25.4c,d/25.17a] Beginning at the superior border of the cecum and ascending along the right lateral and posterior abdominal wall of the peritoneal cavity to the inferior surface of the liver is the **ascending colon**. At this point the colon turns to the left at the **right colic flexure**, or *hepatic flexure*. The right colic flexure marks the end of the ascending colon and the beginning of the *transverse colon*. The ascending colon is secondarily retroperitoneal; its lateral and anterior surfaces are covered by visceral peritoneum (Figures 25.4c,d, p. 661 and 25.17a).

The Transverse Colon At the right colic flexure, the **transverse colon** curves anteriorly and crosses the abdomen from right to left. As the transverse colon crosses the abdominal cavity, its peritoneal relationship changes. The initial segment is intraperitoneal, supported by the *transverse mesocolon* and separated from the anterior abdominal wall by the layers of the greater omentum. As the transverse colon reaches the left side, it passes inferior to the greater curvature of the stomach and becomes secondarily retroperitoneal.

The **gastrocolic ligament** attaches the transverse colon to the greater curvature of the stomach. Near the spleen, the colon makes a right-angle bend, termed the **left colic flexure**, or *splenic flexure*, and then proceeds caudally.

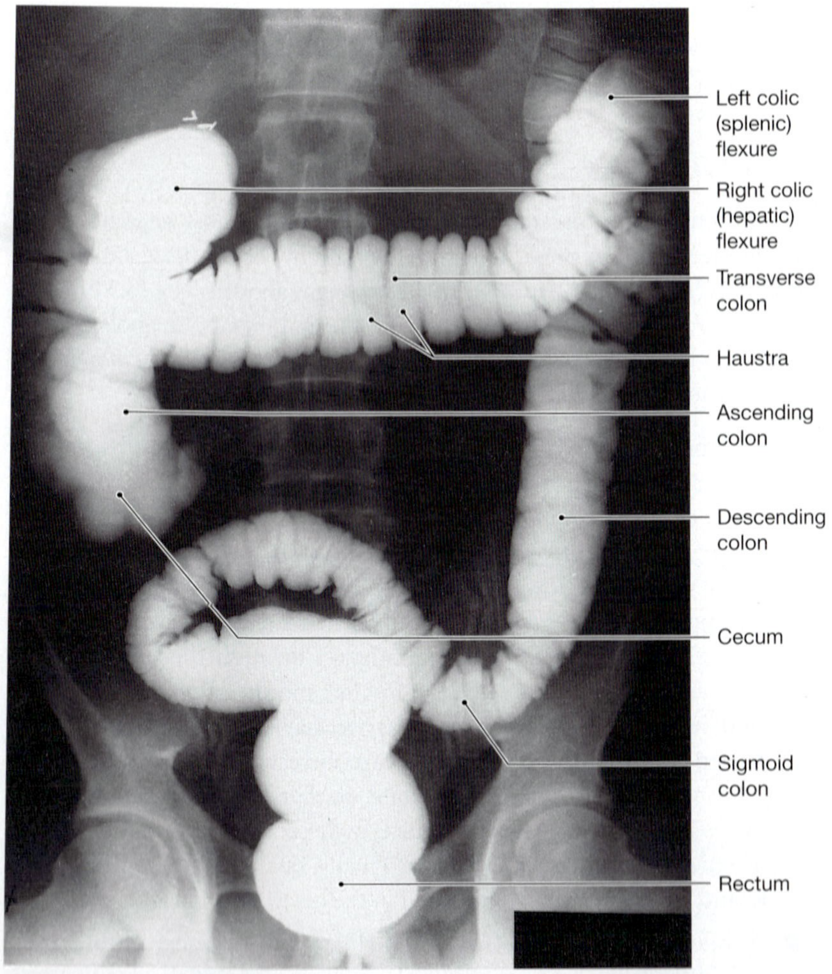

Figure 25.18 Anterior/Posterior Radiograph of the Colon

The Descending Colon The **descending colon** proceeds inferiorly along the left side of the abdomen. Because it is secondarily retroperitoneal, this portion of the colon is firmly attached to the abdominal wall. At the iliac fossa, the descending colon enters an S-shaped segment, the *sigmoid colon*.

The Sigmoid Colon [Figures 25.4/25.17a] The **sigmoid** (SIG-moyd; *sigmoides*, the Greek letter *S*) **colon** is an S-shaped segment of the large intestine that is only about 15 cm (6 in.) long. It begins at the **sigmoid flexure** and ends at the *rectum* (Figure 25.17a). The sigmoid colon is intraperitoneal, and as it curves posterior to the urinary bladder it is suspended by the *sigmoid mesocolon* (Figure 25.4, p. 661).

The Rectum [Figures 25.12/25.17a,c/25.18]

The sigmoid colon discharges fecal wastes into the *rectum*. The **rectum** (REK-tum) is a secondarily retroperitoneal segment that forms the last 15 cm (6 in.) of the digestive tract (Figures 25.12, p. 671, 25.17a,c, and 25.18). It is an expandable organ for the temporary storage of fecal material; movement of fecal materials into the rectum triggers the urge to defecate.

The last portion of the rectum, the **anal canal**, contains small longitudinal folds, the **anal columns**. The distal margins of the anal columns are joined by transverse folds that mark the boundary between the columnar epithelium of the proximal rectum and a stratified squamous epithelium similar to that found in the oral cavity. The anal canal ends at the **anus**, or *anal orifice*. Very close to the anus, the epidermis becomes keratinized and identical to the surface of the skin.

Veins in the lamina propria and submucosa of the anal canal occasionally become distended, producing *hemorrhoids*. The circular muscle layer of the muscularis externa in this region forms the **internal anal sphincter**. The smooth muscle fibers of the internal anal sphincter are not under voluntary control. The **external anal sphincter** encircles the distal portion of the anal canal. This sphincter, which consists of a ring of skeletal muscle fibers, is under voluntary control.

Histology of the Large Intestine [Figures 23.8a/25.19]

The histological characteristics that distinguish the large intestine from the small intestine are as follows:

- The wall of the large intestine is relatively thin. Although the diameter of the colon is roughly three times that of the small intestine, the wall is much thinner.
- The large intestine lacks villi, which are characteristic of the small intestine.
- Goblet cells are much more abundant than they are in the small intestine.
- The large intestine has distinctive intestinal crypts (Figure 25.19). The glands of the large intestine are deeper than those of the small intestine, and they are dominated by goblet cells. Secretion occurs as local stimuli trigger reflexes involving the local nerve plexuses, resulting in the production of copious amounts of mucus to promote lubrication as undigested waste is compacted.
- Large lymphoid nodules are scattered throughout the lamina propria and extend into the submucosa (Figure 23.8a). ∞ p. 616
- The muscularis externa differs from that of other intestinal regions because the longitudinal layer has been reduced to the muscular bands of the taeniae coli. However, the mixing and propulsive contractions of the colon resemble those of the small intestine.

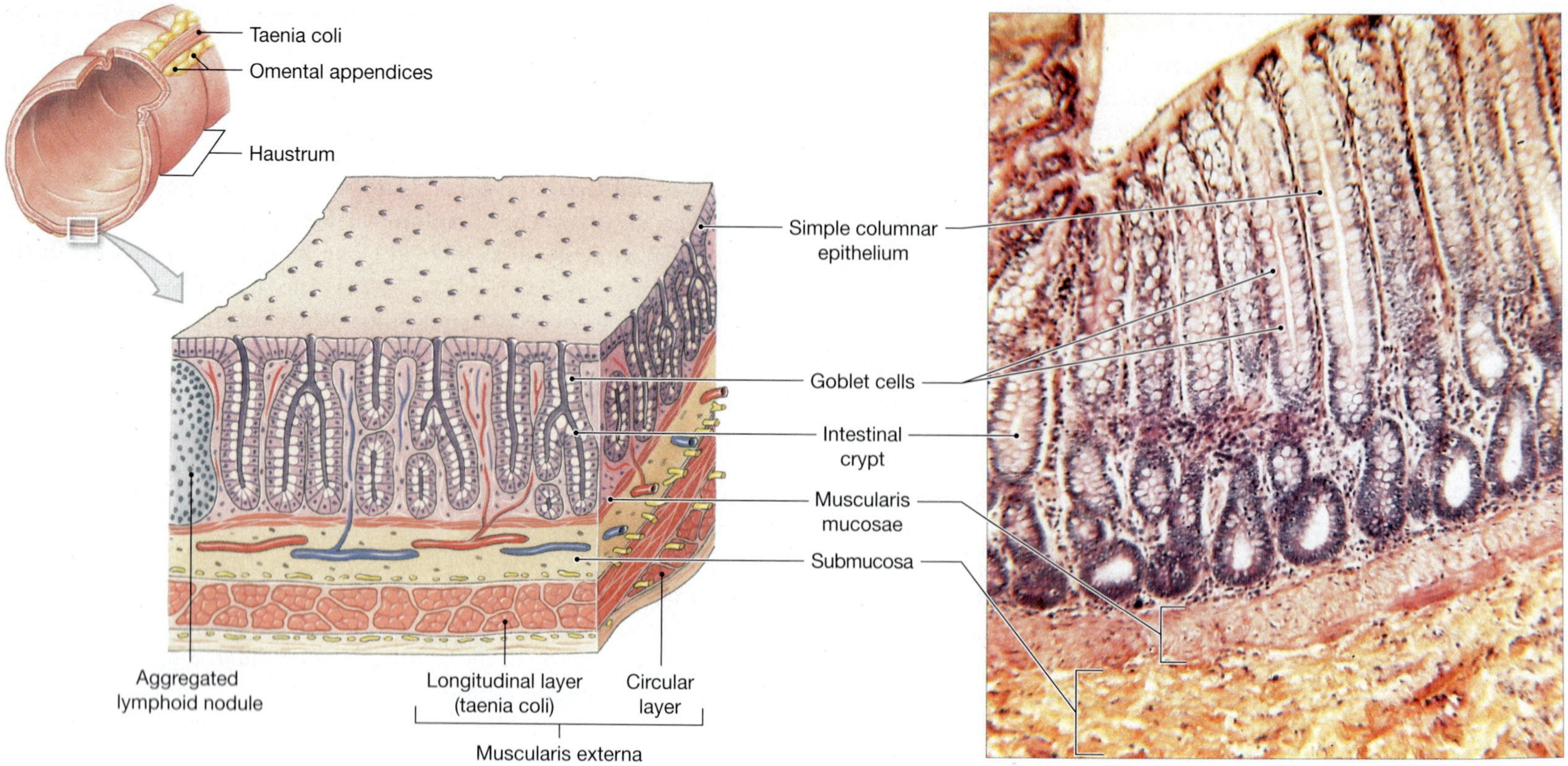

Figure 25.19 The Wall of the Large Intestine
(a) Three-dimensional and colonoscopic views of the colon wall. **(b)** Colon histology, showing detail of mucosal and submucosal layers.

Regulation of the Large Intestine

Movement of ingested materials from the cecum to the transverse colon occurs very slowly. It involves both peristaltic activity and *haustral churning*, the segmentation movements of the large intestine. The slow passage of materials along the large intestine allows time for the fecal material to be converted into a sludgy paste. Movement from the transverse colon through the rest of the large intestine results from powerful peristaltic contractions, called **mass movements**, that occur a few times each day. The stimulus is distension of the stomach and duodenum, and the commands are relayed over the intestinal nerve plexuses. The contractions force fecal materials into the rectum and produce the conscious urge to defecate.

The rectal chamber is usually empty except when one of those powerful mass movements forces fecal materials out of the sigmoid colon into the rectum. Distension of the rectal wall then stimulates the conscious urge to defecate. It also leads to the relaxation of the internal sphincter through the *defecation reflex*, and fecal material moves into the anal canal. ∞ p. 466 When the external anal sphincter is voluntarily relaxed, defecation can occur.

Accessory Glandular Digestive Organs

The accessory glandular organs of the digestive tract are the *salivary glands*, the *liver*, the *gallbladder*, and the *pancreas*. The glandular organs produce and store enzymes and buffers that are essential to normal digestive function. In addition to their roles in digestion, the salivary glands, liver, and pancreas have exocrine functions. The liver and pancreas have other vital functions in addition to their roles in the digestive process.

The Liver [Figure 25.12 and Table 25.1]

The **liver** is the largest visceral organ and it is one of the most versatile organs in the body. Most of its mass lies within the right hypochondriac and epigastric regions (Figure 25.12, p. 671). The liver weighs about 1.5 kg (3.3 lb). This large, firm, reddish-brown organ provides essential metabolic and synthetic services that fall into three basic categories: *metabolic regulation*, *hematological regulation*, and *bile production*.

- **Metabolic regulation:** The liver represents the central clearinghouse for metabolic regulation in the body. Circulating levels of carbohydrates, lipids, and amino acids are regulated by the liver. All blood leaving the absorptive surfaces of the digestive tract enters the hepatic portal system and flows into the liver. This arrangement gives liver cells the opportunity to extract absorbed nutrients or toxins from the blood before it reaches the systemic circulation through the hepatic veins. Liver cells, or *hepatocytes* (HEP-a-tō-sīts), monitor the circulating levels of metabolites and adjust them as necessary. Excess nutrients are removed and stored, and deficiencies are corrected by mobilizing stored reserves or performing appropriate synthetic activities. Circulating toxins and metabolic waste products are also removed for subsequent inactivation, storage, or excretion. Finally, fat-soluble vitamins (A, D, K, and E) are absorbed and stored in the liver.
- **Hematological regulation:** The liver is the largest blood reservoir in the body, and it receives about 25 percent of the cardiac out-

put. As blood passes through the liver sinusoids, (1) phagocytic cells in the liver remove old or damaged RBCs, cellular debris, and pathogens from the circulation; and (2) liver cells synthesize plasma proteins that contribute to the osmotic concentration of the blood, transport nutrients, and establish the clotting and complement systems.

- **Synthesis and secretion of bile:** **Bile** is synthesized by liver cells, stored in the gallbladder, and excreted into the lumen of the duodenum. Bile consists mostly of water, with minor amounts of ions, *bilirubin* (a pigment derived from hemoglobin), and an assortment of lipids collectively known as the *bile salts.* The water and ions assist in the dilution and buffering of acids in chyme as it enters the small intestine. Bile salts associate with lipids in the chyme and make it possible for enzymes to break down those lipids into fatty acids suitable for absorption.

To date, more than 200 different functions have been attributed to the liver. A partial listing of these functions is presented in Table 25.1. Any condition that severely damages the liver represents a serious threat to life. The liver has a limited ability to regenerate after injury, but liver function will not fully recover unless the normal vascular pattern returns.

Anatomy of the Liver [Figure 25.20a,b,c,d,f]

The liver is the largest intraperitoneal organ. Deep to the visceral peritoneal layer is a tough fibrous capsule. On the anterior surface, a ventral mesentery, the **falciform** (FAL-si-form) **ligament**, marks the division between the **left lobe** and **right lobe** of the liver (Figure 25.20a–c). A thickening in the inferior margin of the falciform ligament is the **round ligament**, or *ligamentum teres*, a fibrous band that marks the path of the degenerated fetal umbilical vein. The liver is suspended from the inferior surface of the diaphragm by the **coronary ligament**.

The shape of the liver conforms to its surroundings. The **anterior surface** follows the smooth curve of the body wall (Figure 25.20c). The **posterior surface** bears the impressions of the stomach, small intestine, right kidney, and large intestine (Figure 25.20d). The superior, anterior, and posterior surfaces of the liver are referred to as the *diaphragmatic surfaces* due to their relationship to the diaphragm. The inferior surface is referred to as the *visceral surface.*

The liver has classically been described as having four lobes (Figure 25.20d). The impression left by the inferior vena cava marks the division between the right lobe and the small **caudate** (KAW-dāt) **lobe**. Inferior to the caudate lobe lies the **quadrate lobe**, sandwiched between the left lobe and the gallbladder.

The classical description of four lobes was based on the superficial topography of the liver, and as such it has not met the needs of modern medical science, particularly surgery. As a result, a more comprehensive system for describing the structure of the liver has been developed. The new terminology is complex, but in essence it subdivides the lobes of the liver into segments based on the major subdivisions of the hepatic artery, portal vein, and hepatic ducts. Figure 25.20f indicates the approximate boundaries between the segments; the actual boundaries cannot be determined without dissection of the liver.

The Blood Supply to the Liver [Figures 22.17/22.26/25.17a/25.20d] The circulation to the liver was detailed in Chapter 22 and summarized in Figures 22.17 and 22.26. pp. 589, 600 Afferent blood vessels and other structures reach the liver by traveling within the connective tissue of the lesser omentum. They converge at a region known as the **porta hepatis** ("doorway to the liver").

Two blood vessels deliver blood to the liver, the **hepatic artery proper** and the **hepatic portal vein** (Figures 25.17a and 25.20d). Roughly one-third of the normal hepatic blood flow arrives via the hepatic artery, and the rest is provided by the hepatic portal vein. Blood returns to the systemic circuit through the **hepatic veins** that open into the inferior vena cava. The arterial supply provides oxygenated blood to the liver and the hepatic portal vein supplies nutrients and other chemicals absorbed from the intestine.

Histological Organization of the Liver [Figure 25.21]

Each lobe of the liver is divided by connective tissue into approximately 100,000 **liver lobules**, the basic functional units of the liver. The histological organization and structure of a typical liver lobule are shown in Figure 25.21.

The Liver Lobule [Figure 25.21] The liver cells, or **hepatocytes** (HEP-a-tō-sīts), in a liver lobule form a series of irregular plates arranged like the spokes of a wheel (Figure 25.21a,c). The plates are only one cell thick, and exposed hepatocyte surfaces are covered with short microvilli. Sinusoids between adjacent plates empty into the **central vein** (Figure 25.21b). The fenestrated walls of the sinusoids contain large openings that allow substances to pass out of the circulation and into the spaces surrounding the hepatocytes. In addition to typical endothelial cells, the sinusoidal lining includes a large number of **Kupffer** (KOOP-fer) **cells**, also known as *stellate reticuloendothelial cells.* These phagocytic cells are part of the monocyte–macrophage system, and they engulf pathogens, cell debris, and damaged blood cells. Kupffer cells also engulf and retain any heavy metals, such as tin or mercury, that are absorbed by the digestive tract.

Blood enters the liver sinusoids from small branches of the portal vein and hepatic artery. A typical lobule is hexagonal in cross section (Figure 25.21a,b). There are six **portal areas**, or *hepatic triads*, one at each of the six corners of the lobule. A portal area (Figure 25.21c) contains three

TABLE 25.1 Major Functions of the Liver

DIGESTIVE AND METABOLIC FUNCTIONS
Synthesis of somatomedins
Synthesis and secretion of bile
Storage of glycogen and lipid reserves
Maintenance of normal blood glucose, amino acid, and fatty acid concentrations
Synthesis and interconversion of nutrient types (e.g., transamination of amino acids, or conversion of carbohydrates to lipids)
Synthesis and release of cholesterol bound to transport proteins
Inactivation of toxins
Storage of iron reserves
Storage of fat-soluble vitamins
OTHER MAJOR FUNCTIONS
Synthesis of plasma proteins
Synthesis of clotting factors
Synthesis of the inactive hormone angiotensinogen
Phagocytosis of damaged red blood cells (by Kupffer cells)
Blood storage (major contributor to venous reserve)
Absorption and breakdown of circulating hormones (including insulin and epinephrine) and immunoglobulins
Absorption and inactivation of lipid-soluble drugs

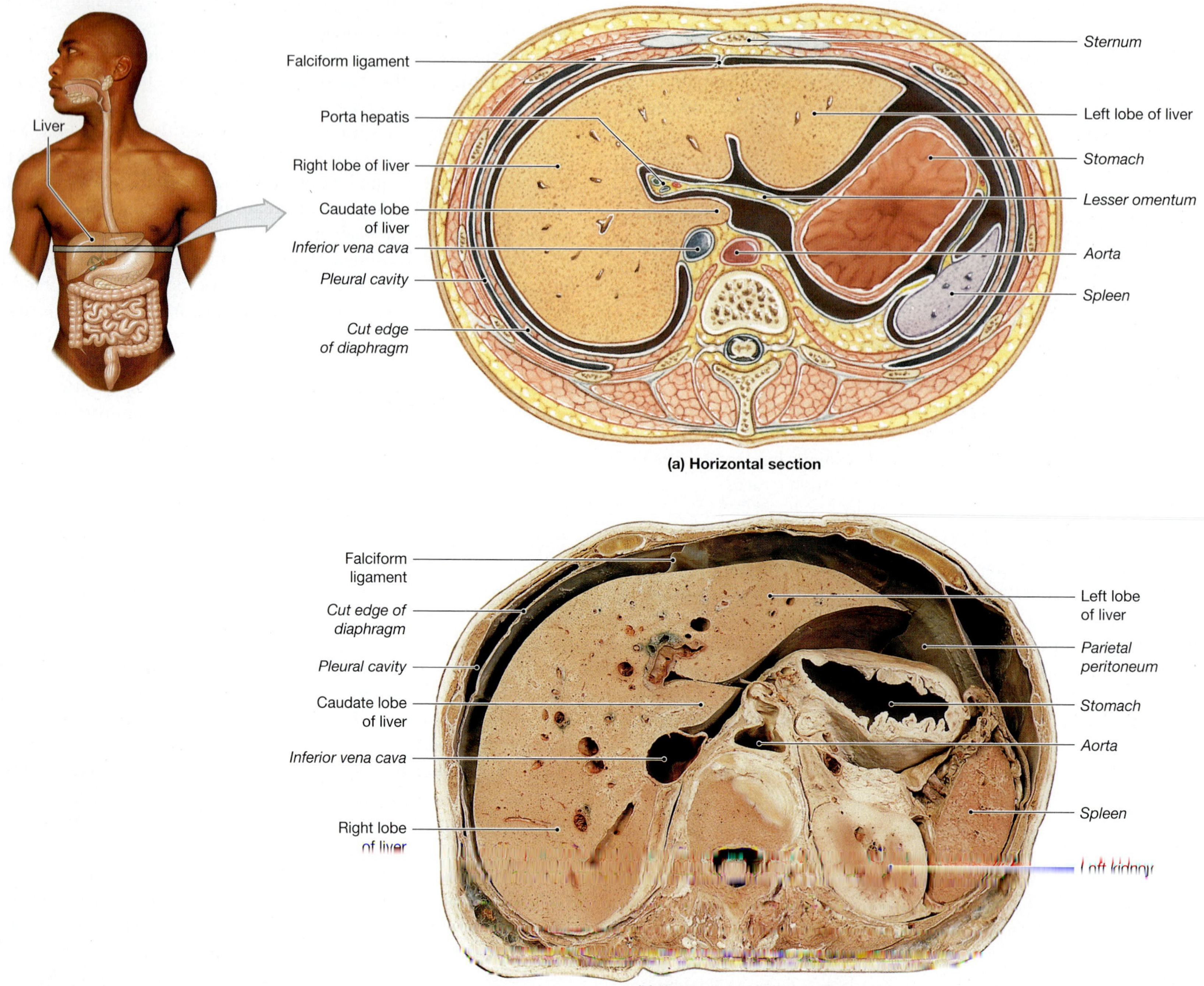

Figure 25.20 Anatomy of the Liver
(a) Horizontal section through the upper abdomen, showing the position of the liver relative to other visceral organs. **(b)** Horizontal section through the upper abdomen, showing structures illustrated in part (a). **(c)** Anatomical landmarks on the anterior surface of the liver. **(d)** The posterior surface of the liver. **(e)** Cast of the liver, showing gallbladder, biliary ducts, and associated blood vessels as seen from the inferior and posterior surfaces. **(f)** Approximate boundaries between the major segments of the liver.

structures: (1) a branch of the hepatic portal vein, (2) a branch of the hepatic artery proper, and (3) a small branch of the bile duct.

Branches from the arteries and veins deliver blood to the sinusoids of adjacent lobules (Figure 25.21a). As blood flows through the sinusoids, hepatocytes absorb and secrete materials into the bloodstream across their exposed surfaces. Blood then leaves the sinusoids and enters the central vein of the lobule. The central veins ultimately merge to form the hepatic veins that empty into the inferior vena cava.

Bile Secretion and Transport [Figures 25.21a/25.22] Bile is secreted into a network of narrow channels between the opposing membranes of adjacent liver cells. These small passageways, called **bile canaliculi**, extend outward through the liver lobule, away from the central vein. The canaliculi eventually connect with fine **bile ductules** (DUK-tūlz) that carry bile to a bile duct in the nearest portal area (Figure 25.21a). The **right** and **left hepatic ducts** collect bile from all of the bile ducts of the liver lobes. These ducts unite to form the **common hepatic duct** that leaves the liver. The bile within the common

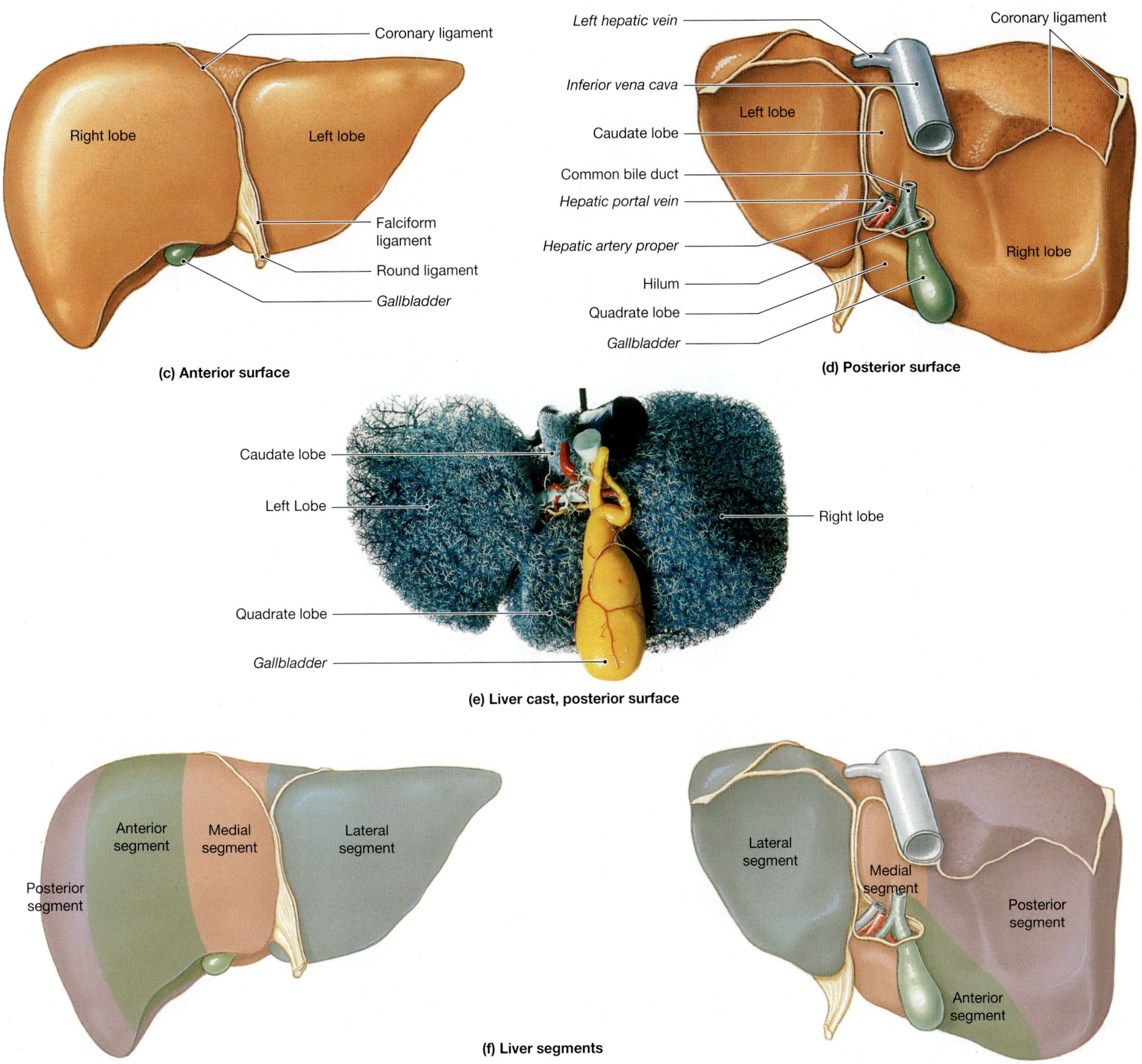

(c) Anterior surface

(d) Posterior surface

(e) Liver cast, posterior surface

(f) Liver segments

Figure 25.20 ***(continued)***

hepatic duct may either (1) flow into the *common bile duct* that empties into the duodenum or (2) enter the *cystic duct* that leads to the gallbladder. These structures are illustrated and shown in a radiograph in **Figure 25.22**.

The Gallbladder [Figures 25.16/25.22]

The **gallbladder** is a hollow, pear-shaped, muscular organ. The gallbladder is a muscular sac that stores and concentrates bile before its excretion into the small intestine. The gallbladder is located in a recess, or fossa, in the visceral surface of the right lobe. Like the liver, the gallbladder is intraperitoneal.

The gallbladder is divided into three regions: the **fundus**, the **body**, and the **neck** (**Figure 25.22a,c**). The **cystic duct** leads from the gallbladder toward the porta hepatis, where the common hepatic duct and the cystic duct unite to create the **common bile duct** (**Figure 25.22a**). At the duodenum, a muscular **hepatopancreatic sphincter**, or *sphincter of Oddi*, surrounds the lumen of the common bile duct and the duodenal ampulla (**Figures 25.16**, p. 676, and **25.22b**). The duodenal ampulla opens into the duodenum at the duodenal papilla, a small raised projection. Contraction of this sphincter seals off the passageway and prevents bile from entering the small intestine.

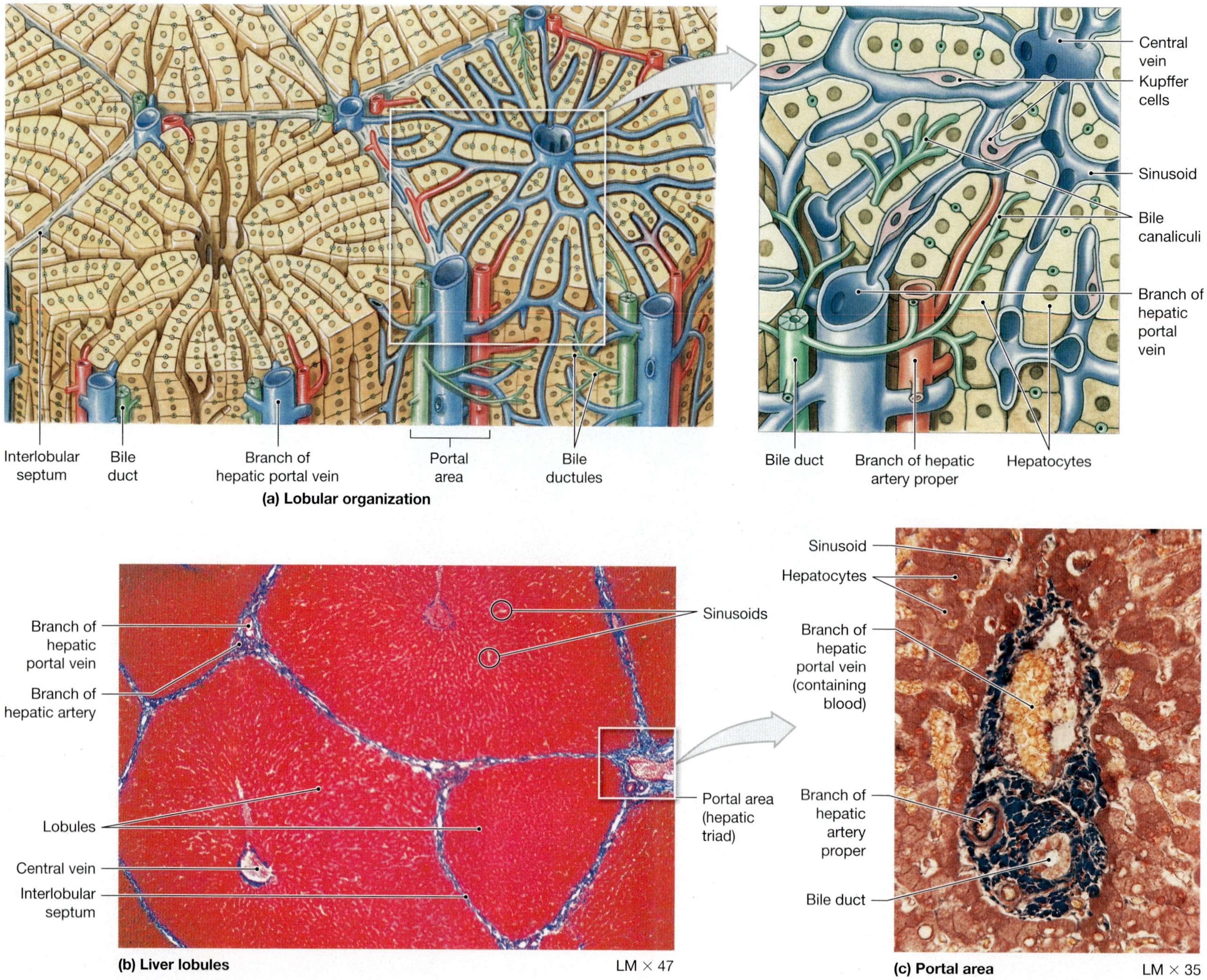

Figure 25.21 Liver Histology
(a) Diagrammatic view of lobular organization. **(b)** Light micrograph showing representative mammalian liver lobules. Human liver lobules lack a distinct connective tissue boundary, making them difficult to distinguish in histological section.
(c) Light micrograph showing histological detail of portal area (hepatic triad).

The gallbladder has two major functions, *bile storage* and *bile modification.* When the hepatopancreatic sphincter is closed, bile enters the cystic duct. In the interim, when bile cannot flow along the common bile duct, it enters the cystic duct for storage within the expandable gallbladder. When filled to capacity, the gallbladder contains 40–70 ml of bile. As bile remains in the gallbladder, its composition gradually changes. Water is absorbed from the bile, and the bile salts and other components of bile become increasingly concentrated.

Bile ejection occurs under stimulation of the hormone *cholecystokinin,* or *CCK.* Cholecystokinin is released into the bloodstream at the duodenum, when chyme arrives containing large amounts of lipids and partially digested proteins. CCK causes relaxation of the hepatopancreatic sphincter and contraction of the gallbladder.

The Pancreas [Figures 22.26/23.17a/25.22a/25.23]

The **pancreas** lies posterior to the stomach, extending laterally from the duodenum toward the spleen (**Figures 25.22a, 25.23,** and **23.17a**). p. 620 The pancreas is an elongate, pinkish-gray organ, approximately 15 cm (6 in.) long and around 80 g (3 oz). The broad **head** of the pancreas lies within the loop formed by the duodenum as it leaves the pylorus. The slender **body** extends transversely toward the spleen, and the **tail** is short and bluntly rounded. The pancreas is secondarily retroperitoneal, and it is firmly bound to the posterior wall of the abdominal cavity.

The surface of the pancreas has a lumpy, nodular texture. A thin, transparent connective tissue capsule wraps the pancreas. The pancreatic lobules, associated blood vessels, and excretory ducts can be seen through the anterior capsule and the overlying layer of peritoneum.

The pancreas is primarily an exocrine organ producing digestive enzymes and buffers, although it does serve an endocrine function as discussed in Chapter 19. p. 578 The large **pancreatic duct** (*duct of Wirsung*) delivers these secretions to the duodenal ampulla. A small **accessory pancreatic duct**, or *duct of Santorini*, may branch from the pancreatic duct before it leaves the pancreas (Figure 25.23a). When present, the accessory pancreatic duct typically empties into the duodenum at a separate papilla, the *lesser duodenal papilla*. This papilla lies a few centimeters proximal to the greater duodenal papilla.

Arterial blood reaches the pancreas through branches of the *splenic*, *superior mesenteric*, and *common hepatic arteries* (Figures 22.17 and 25.23a). p. 586 The **pancreatic arteries** and **pancreaticoduodenal arteries** (**superior** and **inferior**) are the major branches from these vessels. The *splenic vein* and its branches drain the pancreas (Figure 22.26). p. 600

Histological Organization of the Pancreas [Figure 25.23b,c]

Partitions of connective tissue divide the pancreatic tissue into distinct lobules (Figure 25.23b,c). The blood vessels and tributaries of the pancreatic ducts are found within these connective tissue septa. The pancreas is an example of a compound tubuloacinar gland. p. 60 Within each lobule, the ducts branch repeatedly before ending in blind pockets, the **pancreatic**

Clinical Note

Problems with Bile Storage and Secretion If bile becomes too concentrated, crystals of insoluble minerals and salts begin to appear. These deposits are called **gallstones**. Merely having them, a condition termed **cholelithiasis** (kō-lē-li-THĪ-a-sis; *chole*, bile), does not represent a problem as long as the stones remain very small. Small stones are normally flushed down the bile duct and excreted.

If gallstones enter and jam in the cystic or bile duct, the painful symptoms of **cholecystitis** (kō-lē-sis-TĪ-tis) appear. The gallbladder becomes swollen and inflamed, infections may develop, and if the blockage does not work its way down the common bile duct to the duodenum, it must be removed or destroyed. Small gallstones can be chemically dissolved. One chemical now under clinical review is *methyl tertbutyl ether* (MTBE). When introduced into the gallbladder, it dissolves gallstones in a matter of hours. Unfortunately, stones frequently recur. One's health and digestion seem totally unaffected by the removal of the gallbladder, so even asymptomatic individuals with gallstones are often advised to have their gallbladders removed. Surgery is usually required to remove large gallstones, and the gallbladder is removed at the same time to prevent recurrence. The procedure can be performed with a laparoscope inserted through several small incisions.

Another therapy for cholecystitis involves placing the individual in a water bath on a soft cushion and shattering the stones with focused sound waves. The apparatus used is called a *lithotripter*. The particles produced are then small enough to pass through the bile duct without difficulty.

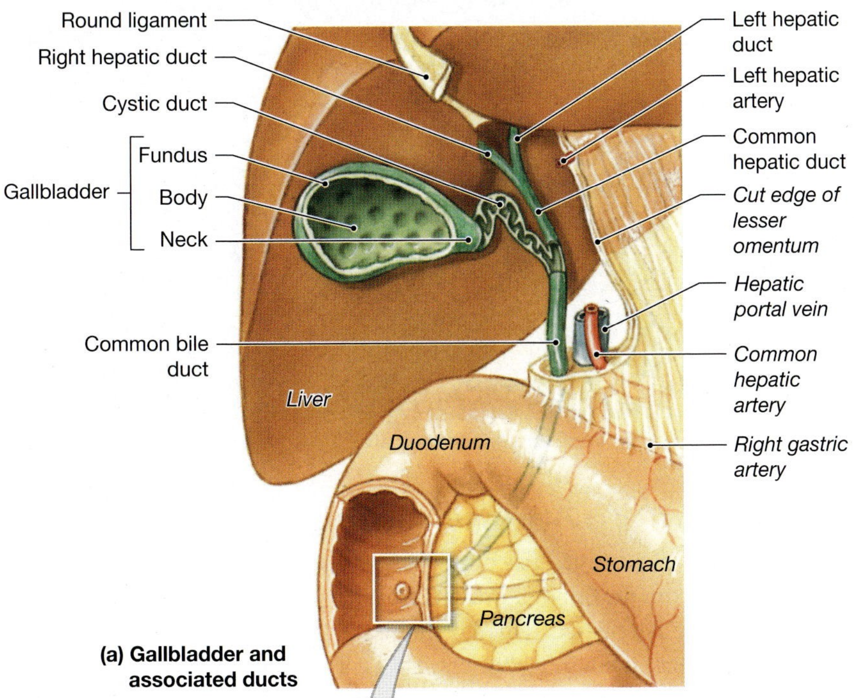

(a) Gallbladder and associated ducts

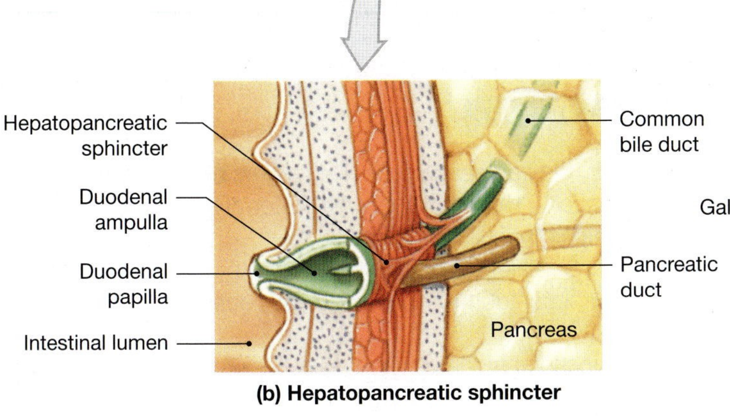

(b) Hepatopancreatic sphincter

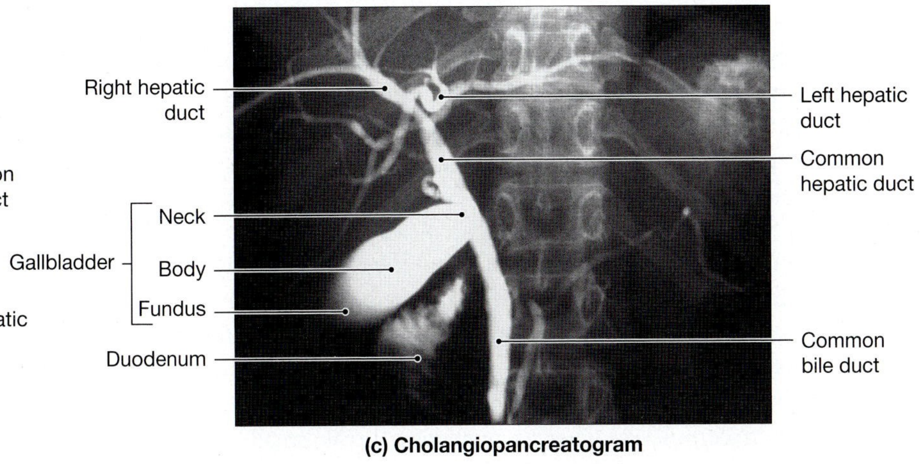

(c) Cholangiopancreatogram

Figure 25.22 The Gallbladder and Associated Bile Ducts
(a) A view of the inferior surface of the liver, showing the position of the gallbladder and ducts that transport bile from the liver to the gallbladder and duodenum. **(b)** A portion of the lesser omentum has been cut away to make it easier to see the relationships among the common bile duct, the hepatic duct, and the cystic duct. **(c)** A radiograph (cholangiopancreatogram, anterior-posterior view) of the gallbladder, biliary ducts, and pancreatic ducts.

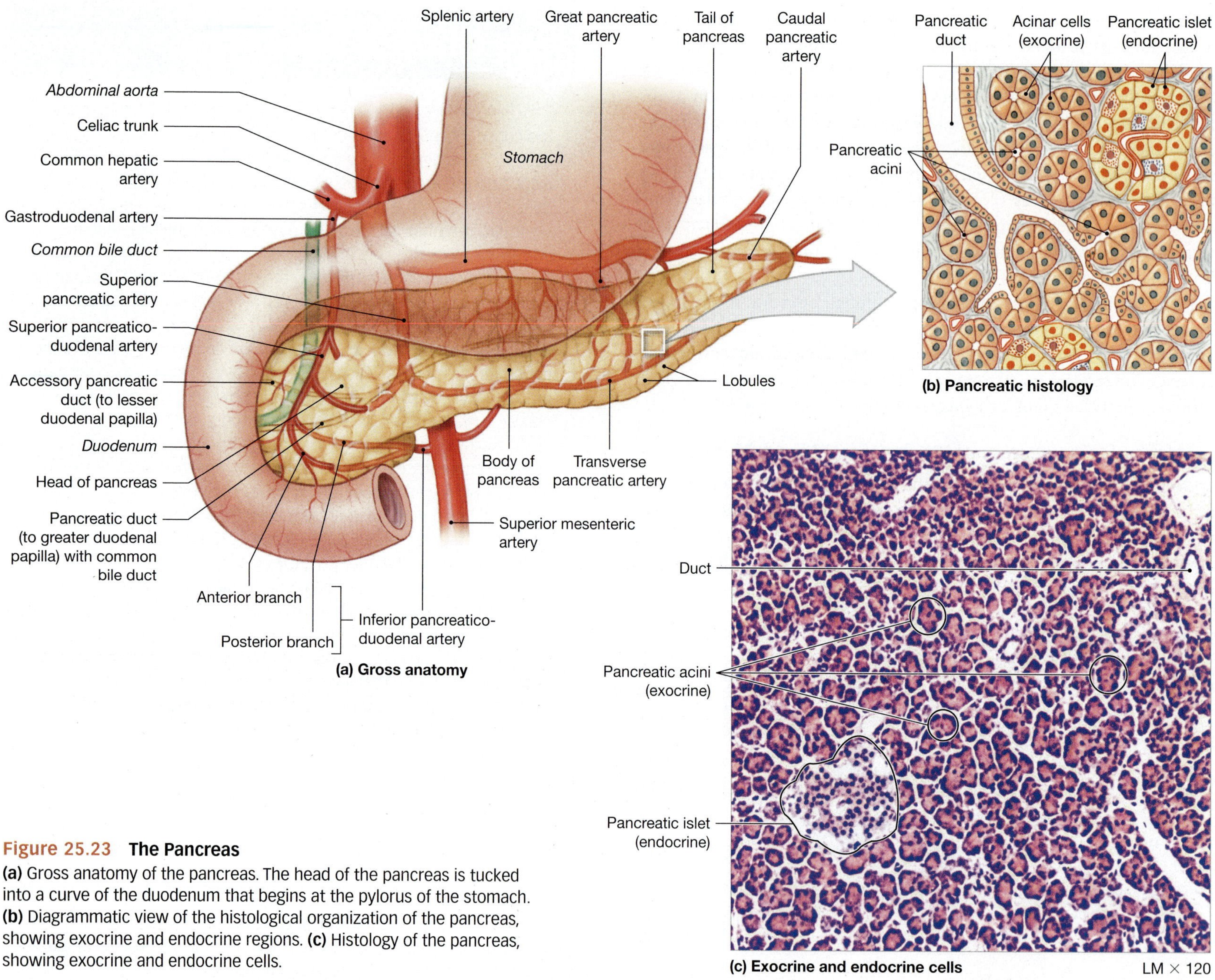

Figure 25.23 The Pancreas
(a) Gross anatomy of the pancreas. The head of the pancreas is tucked into a curve of the duodenum that begins at the pylorus of the stomach. **(b)** Diagrammatic view of the histological organization of the pancreas, showing exocrine and endocrine regions. **(c)** Histology of the pancreas, showing exocrine and endocrine cells.

acini (AS-i-nī). Each pancreatic acinus is lined by a simple cuboidal epithelium. *Pancreatic islets* are scattered between the acini, but they account for only around 1 percent of the cellular population of the pancreas.

The pancreatic acini secrete a mixture of water, ions, and pancreatic digestive enzymes into the duodenum. This secretion, called **pancreatic juice**, contains pancreatic enzymes. These enzymes do most of the digestive work in the small intestine, breaking down ingested materials into small molecules suitable for absorption. The pancreatic ducts secrete buffers (primarily sodium bicarbonate) in a watery solution. These secretions are important in neutralizing the acid in chyme and stabilizing the pH of the intestinal contents.

Pancreatic Enzymes

Pancreatic enzymes are classified according to their intended targets. **Lipases** (LĪ-pā-zez) digest lipids, **carbohydrases** (kar-bō-HĪ-drā-zez) such as *pancreatic amylase* digest sugars and starches, **nucleases** attack nucleic acids, and **proteolytic** (prō-tē-ō-LIT-ik) **enzymes** break proteins apart. Proteolytic enzymes include **proteinases** and **peptidases**. Proteinases break apart large protein complexes, whereas peptidases break small peptide chains into individual amino acids.

The Regulation of Pancreatic Secretion

Secretion of pancreatic juice occurs primarily in response to hormonal instructions from the duodenum. When acid chyme arrives in the small intestine, secretin is released. This hormone triggers the production of watery pancreatic juice containing buffers, especially sodium bicarbonate. Another duodenal hormone, cholecystokinin, stimulates the production and secretion of pancreatic enzymes.

CONCEPT CHECK

1. In cystic fibrosis, the pancreatic duct can become blocked with thickened secretions. This condition would interfere with the proper digestion of which group(s) of nutrients?
2. What are the three major functions of the liver?
3. What does contraction of the hepatopancreatic sphincter accomplish?
4. What are the functions of the pancreas?

See blue "Answers" tab at back of book.

Aging and the Digestive System

Essentially, normal digestion and absorption occur in elderly individuals. However, many changes in the digestive system parallel age-related changes already described for other systems.

1. *The rate of epithelial stem cell division declines:* The digestive epithelium becomes more susceptible to damage by abrasion, acids, or enzymes. Peptic ulcers therefore become more likely. Stem cells in the epithelium divide less frequently with age, so tissue repair is less efficient. In the mouth, esophagus, and anus the stratified epithelium becomes thinner and more fragile.
2. *Smooth muscle tone decreases:* General motility decreases, and peristaltic contractions are weaker. This change slows the rate of chyme movement and promotes constipation. Sagging of the walls of haustra in the colon can produce symptoms of *diverticulitis.* Straining to eliminate compacted fecal materials can stress the less resilient walls of blood vessels, producing *hemorrhoids.* Weakening of the cardiac sphincter can lead to *esophageal reflux* and frequent bouts of "heartburn."
3. *The effects of cumulative damage become apparent:* A familiar example is the gradual loss of teeth because of tooth decay or gingivitis. Cumulative damage can involve internal organs as well. Toxins such as alcohol, heavy metals, and other injurious chemicals that are absorbed by the digestive tract are transported to the liver for processing or storage. The liver cells are not immune to these compounds, and chronic exposure can lead to *cirrhosis* or other types of liver disease.
4. *Cancer rates increase:* Cancers are most common in organs where stem cells divide to maintain epithelial cell populations. p. 78 Rates of colon cancer and stomach cancer rise in the elderly; oral and pharyngeal cancers are particularly common in elderly smokers.
5. *Changes in other systems have direct or indirect effects on the digestive system:* For example, the reduction in bone mass and calcium content in the skeleton is associated with erosion of the tooth sockets and eventual tooth loss. The decline in olfactory and gustatory sensitivity with age can lead to dietary changes that affect the entire body.

Embryology Summary

For an introduction to the development of the Digestive System, see Chapter 28 (Embryology and Human Development).

Clinical Case — THE DIGESTIVE SYSTEM

CHINA WAS GREAT BUT ...

Bohdan is a microbiology professor at a small liberal arts college in the Midwest. For the past 10 years he has been developing an interest in China and infectious diseases that are specific to China. Finally, after a lot of planning and grant writing, Bohdan will be spending his sabbatical in Beijing. He will study infectious diseases at the Beijing Youan Hospital—a hospital known throughout China for its work on infectious diseases endemic to China. This will be Bohdan's first trip outside the United States, and he is very excited about everything—except for the food. Bohdan has a very touchy digestive tract and has been suffering from chronic, intermittent diarrhea for almost two months. In addition, almost any form of spicy food will set off a prolonged bout of gastrointestinal distress. Prior to his departure, several of Bohdan's friends accompany him to some local Chinese restaurants. They hope to "condition" Bohdan's GI tract to new and different foods. Over a three-week period, Bohdan experiments with numerous dishes from two of the local Chinese restaurants, always resulting in diarrhea and abdominal pain. Sichuan cooking, which is known for being spicy, is especially problematic and elicits the worst instances of gastrointestinal distress. Bohdan decides to stock up on Imodium prior to his departure for Beijing.

Once in Beijing Bohdan is pleasantly surprised that he seems to be adapting well to his new diet. His intermittent bouts with diarrhea haven't worsened, and he seems to be able to keep everything under control as long as he eats lots of rice, noodles, and yeast buns.

Three weeks into his sabbatical, Bohdan notices that he is more sluggish than usual. In addition, his bouts with diarrhea are becoming more chronic. His sabbatical sponsor, Dr. Xiaouyun Liu, suggests that Bohdan drink more fluids to prevent dehydration and that he have some tests run in the next few days at the hospital.

Clinical Case *continued*

Initial Examination

Dr. Xiaouyun Liu conducts a complete physical on Bohdan and notes the following:

- White blood cell (WBC) count is elevated ($13 \times 10^3/mm^3$).
- Platelet count is mildly elevated ($450{,}000/mm^3$).
- Mean corpuscular volume (MCV) is low (75 f/L).
- Temperature is 98.6°F (37°C) (normal).
- Abdominal pain is localized in the midline, between the xiphoid process and the umbilicus. No tenderness is noted in the same region.

Dr. Xiaouyun Liu is concerned that Bohdan might be experiencing chronic appendicitis or Irritable Bowel Syndrome. However, he asks Bohdan to do several stool tests, checking for bacterial and parasitic pathogens. The doctor also orders a 3-day hemacult test. Bohdan is informed that, depending on the results, he may need an abdominal x-ray and colonoscopy at the follow-up examination.

In the 3–4 days following his initial examination, Bohdan's diarrhea becomes almost constant. In addition, the abdominal pain intensifies. His stamina continues to decline. Bohdan takes his hemacult samples to the hospital and has additional blood tests, an abdominal x-ray, and a colonoscopy.

Follow-up Examination

The physician notes the following:

- The abdominal pain has intensified but has not changed location.
- Bohdan's temperature is still normal.
- The stool tests show no evidence of bacterial or parasite infections, but the hemacult tests are positive for trace blood loss in the bowel.
- Blood levels have continued to deteriorate. WBC count and platelet count continue to rise, MCV continues to fall, and the hematocrit (Hct) is low (38).
- Mean corpuscular hemoglobin concentration (MCHCV) is down (25 g/dL).
- Abdominal x-rays demonstrate segmental thickening of the colonic walls with an incomplete obstruction in the transverse colon, and the colonoscopy demonstrates an inflammation of the colon wall (**Figure 25.24**).

Points to Consider

At one time or another, every system of the body plays an important role in presenting signs or symptoms, thereby enabling a physician to piece together the various clues that will ideally lead to a correct diagnosis of the patient. Both the patient's presenting symptoms and the physician's analysis and interpretation of the symptoms contribute to the detective work.

To consider the meaning of the information presented in the case above, you need to review the anatomical material covered in Chapter 25.

1. The abdominal cavity is subdivided into various surface regions to facilitate the examination process. What regions would be located in the midline between the xiphoid process and the umbilicus?
2. What digestive system structures would be found in the midline between the xiphoid process and the umbilicus?
3. The physician initially thought that Bohdan might be in the early stages of appendicitis. In which region of the abdominal cavity is this structure found?

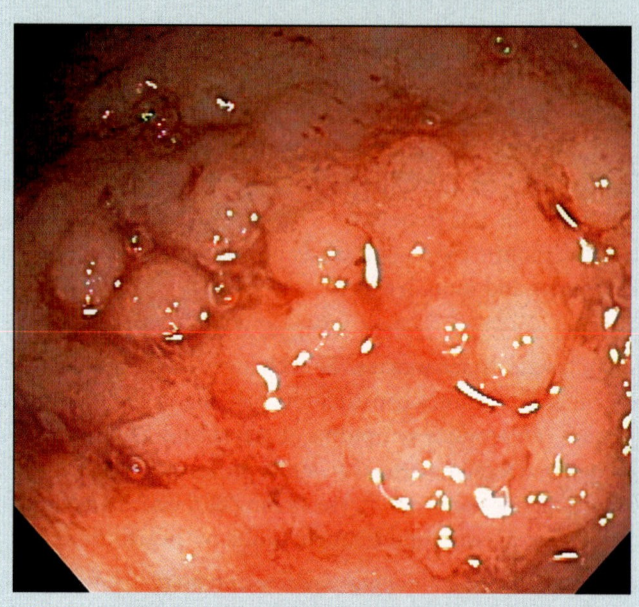

Figure 25.24 Inflammation of the colon, as seen by colonoscopy

Analysis and Interpretation

The information below answers the questions raised in the "Points to Consider" section. To review the material, refer to the page in the chapter indicated by the link icon.

1. The abdominal cavity is subdivided into nine surface regions. The epigastric and umbilical regions are located in the midline between the xiphoid process and the umbilicus. p. 15
2. The following digestive system structures would be found within the epigastric and umbilical regions of the abdomen: liver, esophagus, stomach, pancreas, duodenum, jejunum, and ileum, p. 671.
3. The appendix is found within the right iliac region of the abdomen, p. 671.

CLINICAL CASE TERMS

anemia: Any condition in which the number of red blood cells (RBCs) per mm^3, the volume of packed RBCs per 100 ml of blood, or the amount of hemoglobin in 100 ml of blood is reduced.

autoimmune disease: A disease in which an individual develops an immune reaction to his or her own body tissues. Such a disease results in the individual's own tissues being attacked by the lymphoid system, resulting in tissue destruction and failure.

chronic: Long-term or prolonged condition.

diarrhea: Abnormally frequent evacuation of watery stools.

hemacult: A fecal test that determines the presence of non-visible, or "occult" blood in the stool.

imodium: An over-the-counter antidiarrheal medicine.

leukocytosis: An abnormally large number of leukocytes per 100 ml of blood.

sedimentation rate: The rate at which RBCs settle to the bottom of a test tube in anticoagulated blood. Increased sedimentation rates are often associated with anemia or inflammatory conditions.

Clinical Case *continued*

Diagnosis

Based on his symptoms and laboratory results, Bohdan has a form of Inflammatory Bowel Disease (IBD). IBD is a disease of unknown origin. It is believed to be an autoimmune disease in which an individual develops an immune reaction to his or her own intestinal tract. Approximately one million individuals in the United States have IBD. Internationally, IBD is more common in individuals living in urban areas within developed countries than in individuals living in the rural portions of developing regions of the world. In addition, individuals living in colder climates have a higher incidence of IBD than do individuals living in warmer climates. The two major forms of IBD are ulcerative colitis and Crohn's disease. An individual with ulcerative colitis will develop ulcers within one or more segments of the colon, or large bowel. Crohn's disease typically affects only the distal segment of the ileum of the small intestine. The form of IBD with which Bohdan is diagnosed is Crohn's disease.

The lymphoid system causes inflammation of the lamina propria in Crohn's disease. This leads to macrophages attacking layers of the bowel wall from mucosa to serosa. As a result of this chronic inflammation in Crohn's disease, the bowel walls become markedly thickened and the lumen narrowed.

General features of Crohn's disease are fever, abdominal pain, diarrhea, and chronic fatigue. Weight loss is also common. Inflammation of the small intestine can lead to steady and localized pain in the right iliac region. Physical examination may reveal right iliac region tenderness with an associated fullness or mass. Patients may also have mild anemia, leukocytosis, and an increased erythrocyte sedimentation rate.

Intestinal obstruction occurring at narrowed areas of the bowel is a frequent complication. In the initial stage, obstruction from edema and inflammation (commonly in the ileum) is reversible. As the disease progresses, fibrosis develops, leading to decreasing diarrhea and more incidence of constipation and obstruction of the bowel. ■

CLINICAL TERMS

achalasia (ak-a-LĀ-zē-a): Blockage of the lower part of the esophagus due to weak peristalsis and malfunction of the lower esophageal sphincter.

cholecystitis (kō-lē-sis-TĪ-tis): A painful condition caused by blockage of the cystic or common bile duct by gallstones.

cholelithiasis (kō-lē-li-THĪ-a-sis): Presence of gallstones in the gallbladder.

cirrhosis: A condition caused by scarring of the liver following destruction of hepatocytes by drug exposure, viral infection, ischemia, or other factors.

colitis: Irritation of the colon, leading to abnormal bowel function.

colostomy: Attachment and opening of the colon to the abdominal wall, bypassing the distal portion of the large intestine.

constipation (kon-sti-PĀ-shun): Infrequent defecation of small, dry, hard feces, usually less than three times a week. Constipation occurs when fecal materials move through the colon so slowly that excessive reabsorption of water occurs. Inadequate dietary fiber and water and lack of exercise are common causes of constipation.

diarrhea (dī-a-RĒ-uh): Frequent, watery bowel movements. Bacterial, viral, or protozoan infection of the colon or small intestine can cause acute bouts of diarrhea lasting several days.

diverticulosis (dī-ver-tik-ū-LŌ-sis): A condition in which pockets *(diverticula)* form in the mucosa of the colon, usually in the sigmoid colon.

enteritis (en-ter-Ī-tis): Irritation of the small intestine by toxins or other irritants; causes diarrhea due to frequent peristalsis along the small intestine.

esophagitis (ē-sof-a-JĪ-tis): Inflammation of the esophagus due to erosion by gastric juices.

gastrectomy: Surgical removal of the stomach; a potential treatment for stomach cancer.

gastric stapling and gastric bypass: Surgical procedures to promote weight loss by blocking off a large portion of the gastric lumen.

gastritis (gas-TRĪ-tis): Inflammation of the gastric mucosa.

gastroenteritis: Vomiting and diarrhea caused by an extremely powerful irritating stimulus.

gastroscope: A fiber-optic instrument used to visualize the interior of the stomach.

Irritable Bowel Syndrome: A digestive disorder characterized by diarrhea, constipation, or an alternation between the two. When constipation is the primary problem, the condition is sometimes called a spastic colon, or spastic colitis.

mumps: A viral infection that most often affects the parotid salivary glands between ages 5 and 9.

pancreatitis (pan-krē-a-TĪ-tis): An inflammation of the pancreas due to blockage of the pancreatic ducts, bacterial or viral infections, or drug reactions.

peptic ulcer: A localized erosion of the gastric or duodenal mucosa by acids and enzymes in chyme.

periodontal disease: A progressive condition resulting from erosion of the connections between the necks of teeth and the gingiva.

peritonitis (per-i-tō-NĪ-tis): A painful condition resulting from inflammation of the peritoneal membrane.

plaque: A dense deposit of food particles and bacterial secretions on the surfaces of teeth.

STUDY OUTLINE

Introduction 656

1. The **digestive system** consists of the muscular **digestive tract** and various **accessory organs**. *(see Figure 25.1)*
2. Digestive functions include *ingestion, mechanical processing, digestion, secretion, absorption, compaction,* and *excretion.*

An Overview of the Digestive System 656

Histological Organization of the Digestive Tract 656

1. The **lamina propria** and epithelium form the **mucosa** (a **mucous membrane**) of the digestive tract. The major layers of the digestive tract are the **submucosa** (areolar tissue), the **muscularis externa** (a region of smooth

muscle fibers), and (in the peritoneal cavity) a serous membrane called the **serosa.** *(see Figure 25.2)*

2. The digestive tract is lined by a **mucosal epithelium** moistened by glandular secretions of the epithelial and accessory organs. The mucosal epithelium may be simple or stratified. The lining of the digestive tract contains pleats that allow for expansion. *(see Figure 25.2)*

Muscularis Layers and the Movement of Digestive Materials 657

3. The smooth muscle cells of the digestive tract are capable of plasticity, which is the ability to tolerate extreme stretching. The digestive system contains visceral smooth muscle tissue, in which the muscle cells are arranged in sheets and contain no motor innervation. The presence of **pacesetter cells** allows for rhythmic waves of contraction that spread through the entire muscular sheet.
4. The muscularis externa propels materials through the digestive tract through the contractions of **peristalsis. Segmentation** movements in areas of the small intestine churn digestive materials. *(see Figure 25.3)*

The Peritoneum 660

5. The serosa, also known as the **visceral peritoneum**, is continuous with the **parietal peritoneum** that lines the inner surfaces of the body wall.
6. Fused double sheets of peritoneal membrane called **mesenteries** suspend portions of the digestive tract. *(see Figure 25.2a)*
7. Organs of the abdominal cavity may have a variety of relationships with the peritoneum, including **intraperitoneal**, **retroperitoneal**, and **secondarily retroperitoneal.**
8. Important **mesenteries** include the **greater omentum**, **lesser omentum**, **mesentery proper**, **transverse mesentery**, and **sigmoid mesocolon**. The ascending colon, descending colon, duodenum, and pancreas are attached to the posterior wall of the abdominopelvic cavity; they are **retroperitoneal.** *(see Figures 25.4/25.10/25.11)*

The Oral Cavity 662

1. The functions of the oral cavity include (1) **analysis** of potential foods; (2) **mechanical processing** using the teeth, tongue, and palatal surfaces; (3) **lubrication** by mixing with mucus and salivary secretions; and (4) **digestion** by salivary enzymes. Structures of the oral cavity include the tongue, salivary glands, and teeth. *(see Figure 25.5)*

Anatomy of the Oral Cavity 662

2. The **buccal cavity** (oral cavity) is lined by a stratified squamous epithelium. The **hard** and **soft palates** form the roof of the oral cavity. Other important features can be seen in *Figure 25.5.*
3. The **tongue** aids in mechanical processing and manipulation of food as well as sensory analysis. The superior surface (**dorsum**) of the **body** of the tongue is covered with *papillae.* The inferior portion of the tongue contains a thin fold of mucous membrane called the **lingual frenulum. Intrinsic** and **extrinsic tongue muscles** are controlled by the hypoglossal nerve. *(see Figure 25.5).*
4. The **parotid**, **sublingual**, and **submandibular salivary glands** discharge their secretions into the oral cavity. The parotid salivary glands release **salivary amylase**, which begins the breakdown of carbohydrates. *(see Figures 25.5/25.6)*
5. **Saliva** lubricates the mouth, solubilizes food, dissolves chemicals, flushes the oral surfaces, and helps control bacteria. Salivation is usually controlled by the autonomic nervous system.
6. **Dentine** forms the basic structure of a tooth. The **crown** is coated with **enamel**, and the **root** with **cement**. The **neck** marks the boundary between the root and the crown. The **periodontal ligament** anchors the tooth in an alveolar socket. **Mastication** (chewing) occurs through the contact of the opposing **occlusal surfaces** of the teeth. *(see Figure 25.7)*
7. There are four types of teeth, each with specific functions: **incisors**, for cutting; **cuspids** (canines) for tearing; **bicuspids** (premolars), for crushing; and **molars**, for grinding. *(see Figure 25.7b,c)*
8. The first set of teeth to appear are called **deciduous teeth** (*primary*, *milk*, or *baby teeth*), the temporary teeth of the **primary dentition**. These are replaced by the adult **secondary dentition**, termed **permanent teeth**. The sequence of tooth eruption is presented in *Figure 25.7d.*
9. The upper rows of teeth form a **dental arcade** with **labial**, **palatal** (upper teeth) or **lingual** (lower teeth), **mesial**, and **distal surfaces.** *(see Figure 25.7c)*
10. **Mastication** forces the food across the surfaces of the teeth until it forms a **bolus** that can be swallowed easily.

The Pharynx 666

1. Skeletal muscles involved with swallowing include the *pharyngeal constrictor muscles* and the *palatopharyngeus*, *stylopharyngeus*, and *palatal muscles.*

The Swallowing Process 666

2. **Deglutition** (swallowing) has three phases. The **buccal phase** begins with the compaction of a **bolus** and its movement into the pharynx. The **pharyngeal phase** involves the elevation of the larynx, reflection of the epiglottis, and closure of the glottis. Finally, the **esophageal phase** involves the opening of the **upper esophageal sphincter** and peristalsis moving the bolus down the esophagus to the **lower esophageal sphincter**. *(see Figure 25.8)*

The Esophagus 667

1. The **esophagus** is a hollow muscular tube that transports food and liquid to the stomach, through the **esophageal hiatus**, an opening in the diaphragm.

Histology of the Esophageal Wall 667

2. The wall of the esophagus is formed by *mucosa*, *submucosa*, *muscularis*, and *adventitia* layers. *(see Figures 25.1/25.2/25.9)*

The Stomach 668

1. The **stomach** has three major functions: (1) *bulk storage of ingested matter*, (2) *mechanical breakdown of resistant materials*, and (3) *chemical digestion* through the disruption of chemical bonds using acids and enzymes.

Anatomy of the Stomach 668

2. The stomach is divided into four regions: the **cardia**, the **fundus**, the **body**, and the **pylorus**. The **pyloric sphincter** guards the exit from the stomach. The mucosa and submucosa are thrown into longitudinal folds, called **rugae.** The muscularis layer is formed of three bands of smooth muscle: a *longitudinal layer*, a *circular layer*, and an inner *oblique layer*. *(see Figures 25.4/25.10 to 25.13)*
3. The mesenteries of the stomach are the **greater omentum**, which hangs from the greater curvature, and the **lesser omentum**, which is attached to the lesser curvature.
4. Three branches of the **celiac trunk** supply blood to the stomach: the *left gastric artery*, the *splenic artery*, and the *common hepatic artery*. *(see Figures 22.17/22.26/25.10a)*

Histology of the Stomach 671

5. Simple columnar epithelia line all portions of the stomach. Shallow depressions, called **gastric pits**, contain the **gastric glands** of the fundus and body. **Parietal cells** secrete **intrinsic factor** and hydrochloric acid. **Chief cells** secrete **pepsinogen**, which acids in the gastric lumen convert to the enzyme **pepsin**. **G cells** of the stomach secrete the hormone **gastrin**. *(see Figure 25.13)*

Regulation of the Stomach 673

6. The production and secretion of **gastric juices** are directly controlled by the CNS (the vagus nerve [parasympathetic innervation] and the celiac plexus [sympathetic innervation]). The release of the local hormones **secretin** and **cholecystokinin** inhibits gastric secretion but stimulates secretion by the pancreas and liver.

The Small Intestine 673

Regions of the Small Intestine 674

1. The small intestine includes the **duodenum**, the **jejunum**, and the **ileum**.

Support of the Small Intestine 674

2. The *superior mesenteric artery* and *superior mesenteric vein* supply numerous branches to the segments of the small intestine. *(see Figures 22.17/22.26)*
3. The **mesentery proper** supports the branches of the superior mesenteric artery and vein, lymphatics, and nerves that supply the jejunum and ileum. *(see Figure 25.4)*

Histology of the Small Intestine 674

4. The intestinal mucosa bears transverse folds, called **plicae circulares**. The mucosa of the small intestine forms small projections, called **intestinal villi**, that increase the surface area for absorption. Each villus contains a terminal lymphatic called a **lacteal**. Pockets called **intestinal crypts** *(crypts of Lieberkühn)* house enteroendocrine, goblet, and stem cells. *(see Figures 25.4/25.10/25.12/25.14 to 25.16)*
5. The regions of the small intestine have histological specializations that determine their primary functions. The duodenum (1) contains **duodenal** (*Brunner's*) **glands** that aid the crypts in producing mucus and (2) receives the secretions of the common bile duct and pancreatic duct. The jejunum and ileum contain large groups of **aggregated lymphoid nodules** (*Peyer's patches*) within the lamina propria. *(see Figures 25.15/25.16)*

Regulation of the Small Intestine 677

6. **Intestinal juice** moistens the chyme, helps buffer acids, and dissolves digestive enzymes and the products of digestion.
7. *Secretin* and *cholecystokinin* (*CCK*) are two hormones important in the coordination of digestive activities. Parasympathetic (vagal) innervation stimulates digestive function; sympathetic stimulation inhibits activity along the digestive tract.

The Large Intestine 677

1. The **large intestine (large bowel)** begins as a pouch inferior to the terminal portion of the ileum and ends at the anus. The main functions of the large intestine are to: (1) *reabsorb water and compact feces*, (2) *absorb vitamins by bacteria*, and (3) *store fecal material* prior to defecation. *(see Figures 25.4/25.12/25.14/25.17 to 25.19)*
2. The large intestine is divided into three parts: the **cecum**, the **colon**, and the **rectum**.

The Cecum 677

3. The **cecum** collects and stores materials arriving from the ileum. The ileum opens into the cecum at the **ileal papilla**, with muscles encircling the opening forming the **ileocecal valve**. The **appendix** is attached to the cecum, and it functions as part of the lymphoid system. *(see Figure 25.17)*

The Colon 677

4. The **colon** has a larger diameter and a thinner wall than the small intestine. It bears **haustra** (pouches), the **taeniae coli** (longitudinal bands of muscle), and **omental appendices**, or *fatty appendices of the colon* (fat aggregations within the serosa). *(see Figures 25.17/25.18)*
5. The colon is subdivided into four regions: **ascending**, **transverse**, **descending**, and **sigmoid**. *(see Figures 25.4/25.17/25.18)*

The Rectum 679

6. The rectum terminates in the **anal canal** leading to the **anus**. **Internal** and **external anal sphincters** control the passage of fecal material to the anus. Distension of the rectal wall triggers the *defecation reflex*. *(see Figures 25.12/25.17/25.18)*

Histology of the Large Intestine 679

7. The major histological features of the colon are lack of villi, abundance of goblet cells, and distinctive mucus-secreting intestinal crypts. *(see Figure 25.19)*

Regulation of the Large Intestine 680

8. Movement from the cecum to the transverse colon occurs slowly via peristalsis and *haustral churning*. Movement from the transverse to the sigmoid colon occurs several times each day via **mass movements.**
9. Distention of the rectal wall from a mass movement may stimulate the conscious desire to relax internal and external anal sphincters to defecate.

Accessory Glandular Digestive Organs 680

The Liver 680

1. The **liver** performs metabolic and hematological regulation and produces **bile.** Its metabolic role is to regulate the concentrations of wastes and nutrients in the blood, and its hematological role is as a blood reservoir. *(see Figures 25.12/25.20/25.21 and Table 25.1)*
2. The classical topographical description of the liver has the organ divided into four lobes: **left**, **right**, **quadrate**, and **caudate**. The gallbladder is located in a fossa within the **posterior surface** of the right lobe. New terminology for the lobular structure for liver has recently been adopted, which is based upon subdivisions of the hepatic artery, portal vein, and hepatic ducts. *(see Figure 25.20a,b,c,d,f)*
3. The **hepatic artery proper** and **hepatic portal vein** supply blood to the liver. **Hepatic veins** drain blood from the liver and return it to the systemic circuit via the inferior vena cava. *(see Figures 22.17/22.26/ 25.20d)*
4. Liver cells are specialized epithelial cells, termed **hepatocytes**. **Kupffer cells**, or *stellate reticuloendothelial cells*, are phagocytic cells that reside in the sinusoidal lining. The **liver lobule** is the basic functional unit of the liver. Each lobule is hexagonal in cross section and contains six **portal areas**, or *hepatic triads*. A portal area consists of a branch of the hepatic portal vein, a branch of the hepatic artery proper, and a branch of the hepatic (bile) duct. **Bile canaliculi** carry bile to **bile ductules** that lead to portal areas. The bile ducts from each lobule unite to form the **left** and **right hepatic ducts**, which merge to form the **common hepatic duct**. *(see Figures 25.20 to 25.22)*

The Gallbladder 683

5. The **gallbladder** is a hollow muscular organ that stores and concentrates bile before excretion in the small intestine. **Bile salts** break apart large drops of lipids and make them accessible to digestive enzymes. Bile ejection occurs under stimulation of cholecytstokinin (CCK).
6. The gallbladder is divided into **fundus**, **body**, and **neck** regions. The **cystic duct** leads from the gallbladder to merge with the common hepatic duct to form the **common bile duct**. *(see Figures 25.16/25.20d/25.22)*

The Pancreas 684

7. The **pancreas** is divided into **head**, **body**, and **tail** regions. The **pancreatic duct** penetrates the wall of the duodenum. Within each lobule, ducts branch repeatedly before ending in the **pancreatic acini** (blind pockets). The **accessory pancreatic duct** (if present) and pancreatic duct perforate the wall of the duodenum to discharge **pancreatic juice** at the *lesser duodenal papilla* and *greater duodenal papilla*, respectively. *(see Figures 25.22/25.23)*
8. Pancreatic tissue consists of exocrine and endocrine portions. The bulk of the organ is exocrine in function, as the pancreatic acini secrete water, ions, and digestive enzymes into the small intestine. Pancreatic enzymes include **lipases**, **carbohydrases**, **nucleases**, and **proteolytic enzymes**. The major hormones produced by the endocrine portion are insulin and glucagon.
9. Regulation of the production of pancreatic juice is via the hormones cholecystokinin and secretin.

Aging and the Digestive System 687

1. Normal digestion and absorption occur in elderly individuals; however, changes in the digestive system reflect age-related changes in other body systems. These include a slowed rate of epithelial stem cell division, a decrease in smooth muscle tone, the appearance of cumulative damage, an increase in cancer rates, and numerous changes in other systems.

CHAPTER REVIEW

For answers to the Concept Check and Chapter Review questions, go to the blue "Answers" tab at the back of the book.

Level 1 Reviewing Facts and Terms

Match each numbered item with the most closely related lettered item. Use letters for answers in the spaces provided.

Column A	Column B
___ 1. segmentation	a. mesentery sheet suspending small intestine
___ 2. mesentery proper	b. propels materials through the digestive tract
___ 3. cuspids	c. churn and fragment digestive materials
___ 4. serosa	d. canines
___ 5. buccal fat pads	e. mechanical/chemical digestion of food
___ 6. mastication	f. serous membrane covering muscularis externa
___ 7. bicuspids	g. chewing
___ 8. digestive tract	h. premolars
___ 9. mesocolon	i. mesentery associated with the large intestine
___10. peristalsis	j. form the cheeks

11. The actions involved in the mechanical processing of food include all but which of the following?
    (a) absorption
    (b) squashing foods with the tongue
    (c) tearing or crushing foods with the teeth
    (d) churning or swirling of the foods by the stomach
12. Digestion refers to
    (a) the progressive dehydration of indigestible residue
    (b) the input of food into the digestive tract
    (c) the chemical breakdown of food
    (d) the absorption of nutrients into the gut
13. Most of the digestive tract is lined by
    (a) pseudostratified ciliated columnar epithelium
    (b) cuboidal epithelium
    (c) stratified squamous epithelium
    (d) simple columnar epithelium
14. The ______________________ are double sheets of peritoneal membrane that hold some of the visceral organs in their proper position.
    (a) serosa (b) adventitia
    (c) mesenteries (d) fibrosa
15. The activities of the digestive system are regulated by
    (a) hormones (b) parasympathetic neurons
    (c) sympathetic neurons (d) all of the above
16. Sandwiched between the layer of circular and longitudinal muscle in the muscularis externa is the
    (a) mucosa (b) submucosa
    (c) muscularis mucosa (d) myenteric plexus
17. The mesentery that suspends most of the small intestine is the
    (a) mesentery proper (b) transverse mesentery
    (c) lesser omentum (d) greater omentum
18. The passageway between the oral cavity and the pharynx is the
    (a) uvula (b) fauces
    (c) palatoglossal arch (d) palatopharyngeal arch
19. Plicae and intestinal villi
    (a) increase the surface area of the mucosa of the small intestine
    (b) carry digestion products that do not enter blood capillaries
    (c) produce new cells for the mucosa of the small intestine
    (d) secrete digestive enzymes
20. The ventral mesentery
    (a) becomes the main attachment point for digestive organs in the peritoneal cavity in the adult
    (b) is highly glandular, but not vascular
    (c) contains and forms a pathway for the hepatic portal vein and its tributaries
    (d) none of the above

Level 2 Reviewing Concepts

1. Which of the following does not apply to the entire small intestine?
   (a) it is the primary site of digestion and the absorption of approximately 80 percent of nutrients
   (b) it averages 6 meters in length
   (c) it is retroperitoneal
   (d) it bears a series of transverse folds called plicae circulares
2. In elderly individuals, the function of the digestive tract
   (a) changes in ways that parallel age-related changes of most other systems of the body
   (b) is independent of the changes that occur in other systems
   (c) can be determined by a study of liver function
   (d) improves in efficiency, but not in the rate of digestion
3. How would damage or removal of parts of the mesentery interfere with normal function of the small intestine?
   (a) it would cause an increase in peristalsis
   (b) hormone secretion would increase
   (c) the blood and nerve supply would suffer interference
   (d) the intestines would lose some of their motility
4. What is the function of the lipase from the pancreas?
5. What is the function of the hepatopancreatic sphincter?
6. What does the gallbladder do with bile?
7. What is the function of Kupffer cells?
8. What is the last region of the colon before it reaches the rectum?
9. What is the function of the lacteals in the small intestine?
10. What triggers the release of gastrin?

Level 3 Critical Thinking

1. A murder suspect claims to have had dinner with the victim 4 hours before the latter was killed. The forensic scientist who performed the autopsy states that the suspect is lying, as it is clear that the victim had not eaten in more than 10 hours. How does the forensic specialist know this?
2. From the oral cavity to the anus, what six sphincters control movement of materials through the digestive tract? Over which do you have conscious, voluntary control, and why?
3. From the lumen outward, what six histological layers form the wall of the digestive tube?

26

The Urinary System

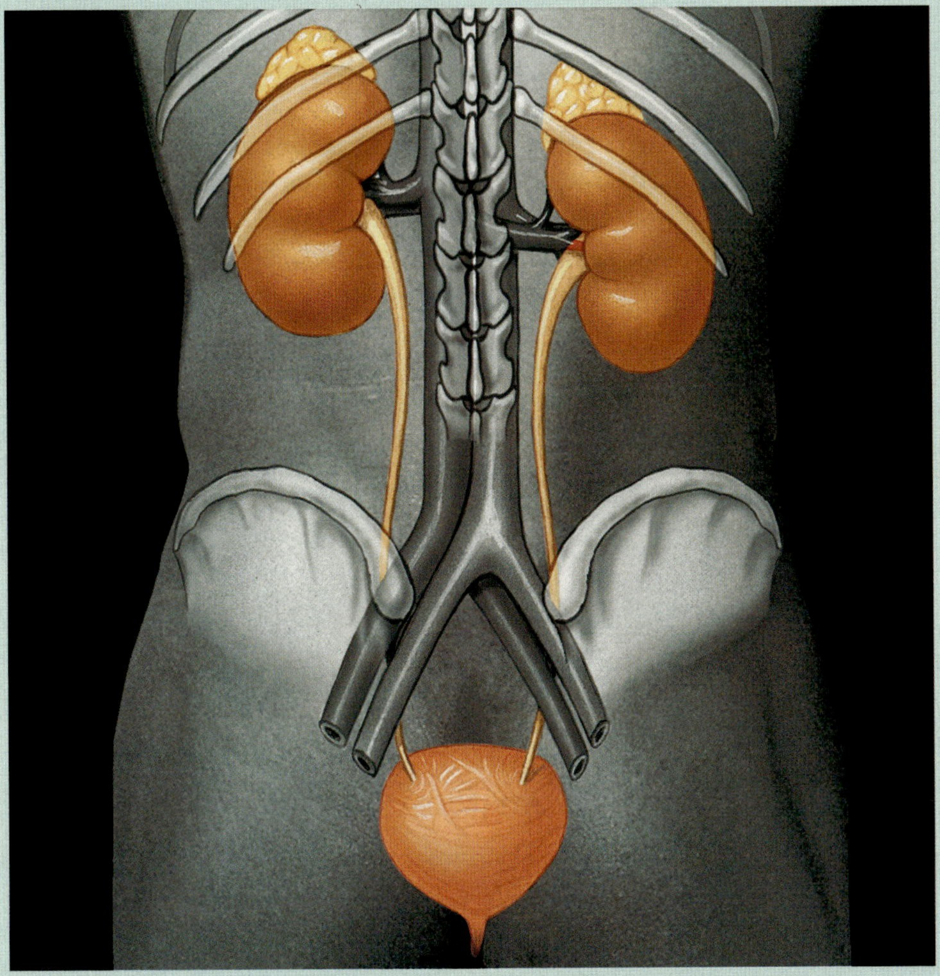

CHAPTER OBJECTIVES

1. Describe the functions of the urinary system and its relation to other excretory organs.
2. Identify the components of the urinary system and their functions.
3. Describe the location of the kidneys, their external features, and their relationships to adjacent tissues and organs.
4. Identify the structure and function of each gross anatomical feature of the kidneys.
5. Identify the blood vessels that supply blood to the nephrons.
6. Describe the unusual characteristics and properties of glomerular capillaries.
7. Describe the blood flow through and around the nephron.
8. Identify the innervation of the kidneys and the effects of innervation on renal function.
9. Describe the histological organization of the nephron and the functions of each segment.
10. Describe the location, gross anatomy, and histology of the ureters, urinary bladder, and urethra.
11. Identify the functions of the ureters, urinary bladder, and urethra.
12. Discuss the micturition reflex and its control.
13. Describe the effects of aging on the urinary system.

The coordinated activities of the digestive, cardiovascular, respiratory, and urinary systems prevent the development of "pollution" problems inside the body. The digestive tract absorbs nutrients from food, and the liver adjusts the nutrient concentration of the circulating blood. The cardiovascular system delivers these nutrients, along with oxygen from the respiratory system, to peripheral tissues. As blood leaves these tissues, it carries the carbon dioxide and other waste products generated by active cells to sites of excretion. The carbon dioxide is eliminated at the lungs. Most of the organic waste products, along with excess water and electrolytes, are removed and excreted by the urinary system, the focus of this chapter. Other systems assist the kidneys in the excretion of water and solutes. For example, the sweat produced by sweat glands contains water and solutes, and various digestive organs secrete waste products into the lumen of the digestive tract. However, the contribution of these organs is minor compared to that of the kidneys.

The **urinary system** performs vital excretory functions and eliminates the organic waste products generated by cells throughout the body. It also has a number of other essential functions that are often overlooked. A more complete list of urinary system functions includes:

1. *regulating plasma concentrations of sodium, potassium, chloride, calcium, and other ions* by controlling the quantities lost in the urine;
2. *regulating blood volume and blood pressure* by (a) adjusting the volume of water lost in the urine, (b) releasing erythropoietin, and (c) releasing renin; ∞ p. 518
3. *contributing to the stabilization of blood pH*;
4. *conserving valuable nutrients* by preventing their excretion in the urine;
5. *eliminating organic waste products*, especially nitrogenous wastes such as *urea* and *uric acid*, toxic substances, and drugs;
6. *synthesizing calcitriol*, a hormone derivative of vitamin D_3 that stimulates calcium ion absorption by the intestinal epithelium; and
7. *assisting the liver* in detoxifying poisons and, during starvation, deaminating amino acids so that other tissues can break them down.

All urinary system activities are carefully regulated to maintain the solute composition and concentration of the blood within acceptable limits. A disruption of any one of these functions will have immediate and potentially fatal consequences.

This chapter considers the functional organization of the urinary system and describes the major regulatory mechanisms that control urine production and concentration. The urinary system (**Figure 26.1a**) includes the *kidneys, ureters, urinary bladder*, and *urethra*. The excretory functions of this system are performed by a pair of **kidneys**. These organs produce **urine**, a fluid waste product containing water, ions, and small soluble compounds. Urine leaving the kidneys travels along the **urinary tract**, which consists of the paired **ureters** (ū-RĒ-terz) and the **urinary bladder**, where urine is temporarily stored. When **urination**, or **micturition** (mik-tū-RISH-un), occurs, contraction of the muscular urinary bladder forces urine through the **urethra** (ū-RĒ-thra) and out of the body.

The Kidneys [Figures 26.1/26.2]

The kidneys are located lateral to the vertebral column between the last thoracic and third lumbar vertebrae on each side (**Figure 26.2a**). The superior surface of the right kidney is often situated inferior to the superior surface of the left kidney (**Figures 26.1** and **26.2a**).

On gross dissection, the anterior surface of the right kidney is covered by the liver, the hepatic flexure of the colon, and the duodenum. The anterior surface of the left kidney is covered by the spleen, stomach, pancreas, jejunum, and splenic flexure of the colon. The superior surface of each kidney is capped by a suprarenal gland (**Figures 26.1a** and **26.2**). The kidneys, suprarenal glands, and ureters lie between the muscles of the dorsal body wall and the parietal peritoneum in a retroperitoneal position (**Figures 26.1c** and **26.2**).

The position of the kidneys in the abdominal cavity is maintained by (1) the overlying peritoneum, (2) contact with adjacent visceral organs, and (3) supporting connective tissues. Three concentric layers of connective tissue (**Figure 26.1c**) protect and stabilize each kidney:

1. A layer of collagen fibers covers the outer surface of the entire organ. This layer is known as the **fibrous capsule** of the kidney. It maintains the shape of the kidney and provides mechanical protection.
2. A layer of adipose tissue, the **perinephric fat** or *perirenal fat* (*peri-*, around + *renes*, kidneys), surrounds the fibrous capsule. This layer can be quite thick, and on dissection the perinephric fat usually obscures the outline of the kidney.
3. Collagen fibers extend outward from the inner fibrous capsule through the perinephric fat to a dense outer layer known as the **renal fascia**, which anchors the kidney to surrounding structures. Posteriorly the renal fascia is bound to the deep fascia surrounding the muscles of the body wall. A layer of *pararenal* (*para*, near) *fat* separates the posterior and lateral portions of the renal fascia from the body wall. Anteriorly the renal fascia is attached to the peritoneum and to the anterior renal fascia of the opposite side.

In effect, the kidney is suspended by collagen fibers from the renal fascia and is packed in a soft cushion of adipose tissue. This arrangement prevents the jolts and shocks of day-to-day existence from disturbing normal kidney function. If the suspensory fibers stretch, or body fat content declines, reducing the amount of adipose tissue padding, the kidneys may become more vulnerable to traumatic injury.

Superficial Anatomy of the Kidney [Figures 26.2/26.3]

Each brownish-red kidney has the shape of a kidney bean. A typical adult kidney (**Figures 26.2** and **26.3**) measures approximately 10 cm (4 in.) in length, 5.5 cm (2.2 in.) in width, and 3 cm (1.2 in.) in thickness. A single kidney averages around 150 g (5.25 oz). A prominent medial indentation, the **hilum**, is the entry point for the *renal artery* and the exit for the *renal vein* and *ureter*.

The fibrous capsule has inner and outer layers. In sectional view (**Figure 26.3a**), the inner layer folds inward at the hilum and lines the **renal sinus**, an internal cavity within the kidney. Renal blood vessels, lymphatic vessels, renal nerves, and the ureter that drains the kidney pass through the hilum and branch within the renal sinus. The thick, outer layer of the capsule extends across the hilum and stabilizes the position of these structures.

Sectional Anatomy of the Kidney [Figure 26.3]

The interior of each kidney contains a renal cortex, renal medulla, and renal sinus. The **renal cortex**, which is granular and reddish-brown in color, is the outer layer of the kidney. The cortex is in contact with the capsule (**Figure 26.3a**). The **renal medulla** is internal to the cortex, and is darker in color. It consists of 6–18 distinct conical or triangular structures, called

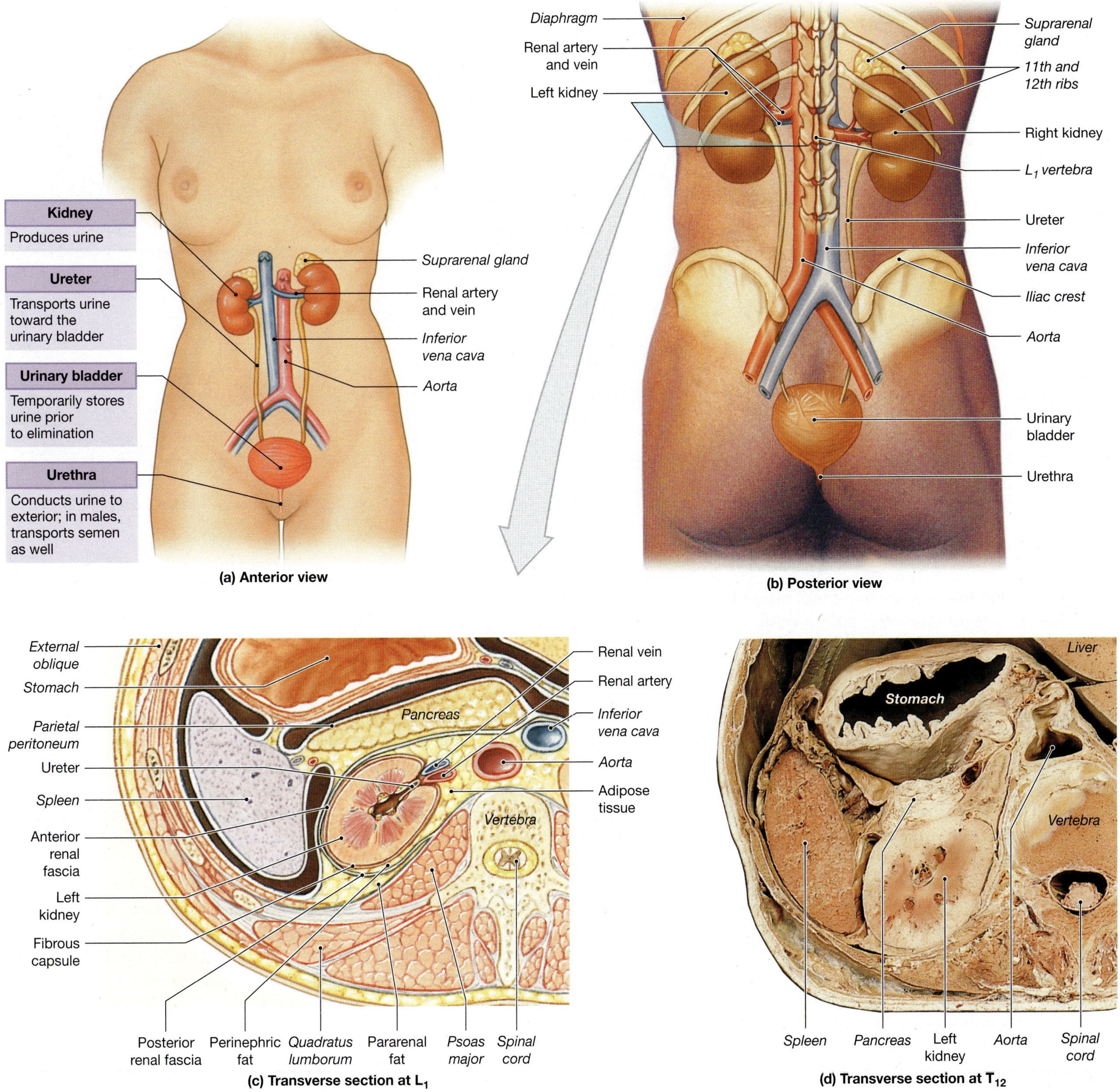

Figure 26.1 An Introduction to the Urinary System
(a) Anterior view, showing the components of the urinary system. **(b)** A posterior view of the trunk, showing the positions of the kidneys and other structures of the urinary system. **(c)** Diagrammatic sectional view at the level indicated in part (b). **(d)** Sectional view slightly superior to the plane of part (c). For surface anatomy *see also Figure 12.3*.

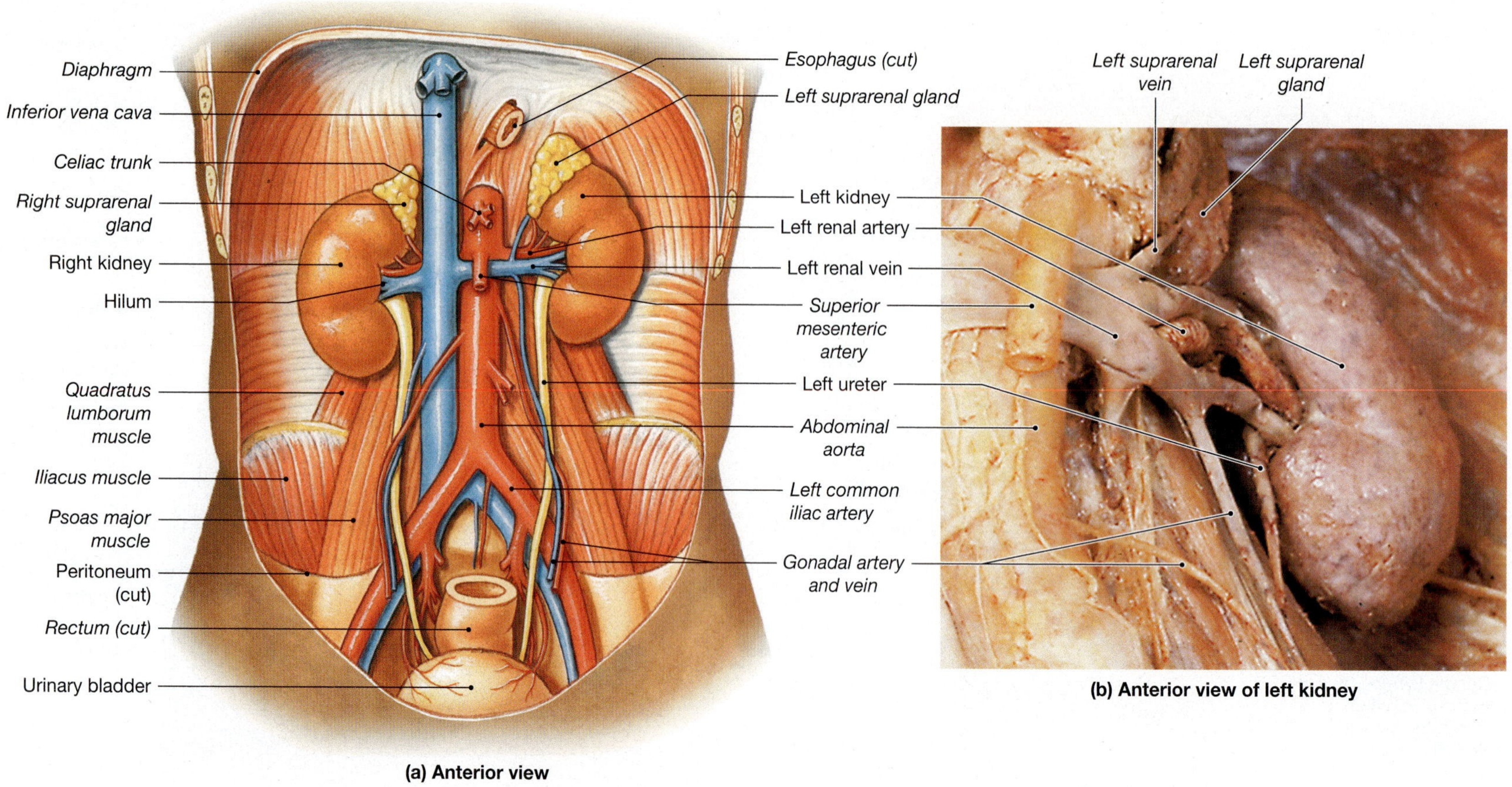

Figure 26.2 The Urinary System in Gross Dissection
(a) Diagrammatic anterior view of the abdominopelvic cavity showing the kidneys, suprarenal glands, ureters, urinary bladder, and blood supply to the kidneys. **(b)** Anterior view of the left kidney and associated structures.

renal pyramids. The base of each pyramid faces the cortex, and the tip, or **renal papilla**, projects into the renal sinus. Each pyramid has a series of fine grooves that converge at the papilla. Adjacent renal pyramids are separated by bands of cortical tissue, called **renal columns**. The columns have a distinctly granular texture, similar to that of the cortex. A **renal lobe** contains a renal pyramid, the overlying area of renal cortex, and adjacent tissues of the renal columns.

Urine production occurs in the renal lobes. Ducts within each renal papilla discharge urine into a cup-shaped drain, called a **minor calyx** (KĀ-liks). Four or five minor calyces (KĀL-i-sēz) merge to form a **major calyx**, and the major calyces combine to form a large, funnel-shaped chamber, the **renal pelvis**. The renal pelvis, which fills most of the renal sinus, is connected to the ureter at the hilum of the kidney.

Urine production begins in microscopic, tubular structures called **nephrons** (NEF-ronz) in the cortex of each renal lobe. Each kidney has roughly 1.25 million nephrons, with a combined length of about 145 km (85 miles).

The Blood Supply to the Kidneys

[Figures 22.16/26.4/26.5b/26.9b]

The kidneys receive 20–25 percent of the total cardiac output. In normal individuals, about 1200 ml of blood flows through the kidneys each minute. Each kidney receives blood from a **renal artery** that originates along the lateral surface of the abdominal aorta near the level of the superior mesenteric artery. p. 588 As the renal artery enters the renal sinus, it branches into the **segmental arteries** (Figure 26.4). Segmental arteries further divide into a series of **interlobar arteries** that radiate outward, penetrating the fibrous capsule and extending through the renal columns between the renal pyramids into the cortex. The interlobar arteries supply blood to the **arcuate** (AR-kū-āt) **arteries** that parallel the boundary between the cortex and medulla of the kidney. Each arcuate artery gives rise to a number of **cortical radiate arteries**, or *interlobular arteries*, which supply portions of the adjacent renal lobe. Numerous **afferent arterioles** branch from each cortical radiate artery to supply individual nephrons.

From the nephrons, blood enters a network of venules and small veins that converge on the **interlobular veins**. In a mirror image of the arterial distribution, the interlobular veins deliver blood to **arcuate veins** that empty into **interlobar veins**. The interlobar veins merge to form the **renal vein**; there are no segmental veins. Many of these blood vessels are visible in corrosion casts of the kidneys (Figure 26.5b) and in renal angiograms (Figure 26.9b).

Innervation of the Kidneys

Urine production in the kidneys is regulated in part through *autoregulation*, which involves reflexive changes in the diameters of the arterioles supplying the nephrons, thereby altering blood flow and filtration rates. Both hormonal and neural mechanisms can supplement or adjust the local responses. The kidneys and ureters are innervated by **renal nerves**.

Most of the nerve fibers involved are sympathetic postganglionic fibers from the superior mesenteric ganglion. p. 456 A renal nerve enters each kidney at the hilum and follows the branches of the renal artery to reach individual nephrons. Known functions of sympathetic innervation include (1) regulation of renal blood flow and pressure; (2) stimulation of renin release; and (3) direct stimulation of water and sodium ion reabsorption.

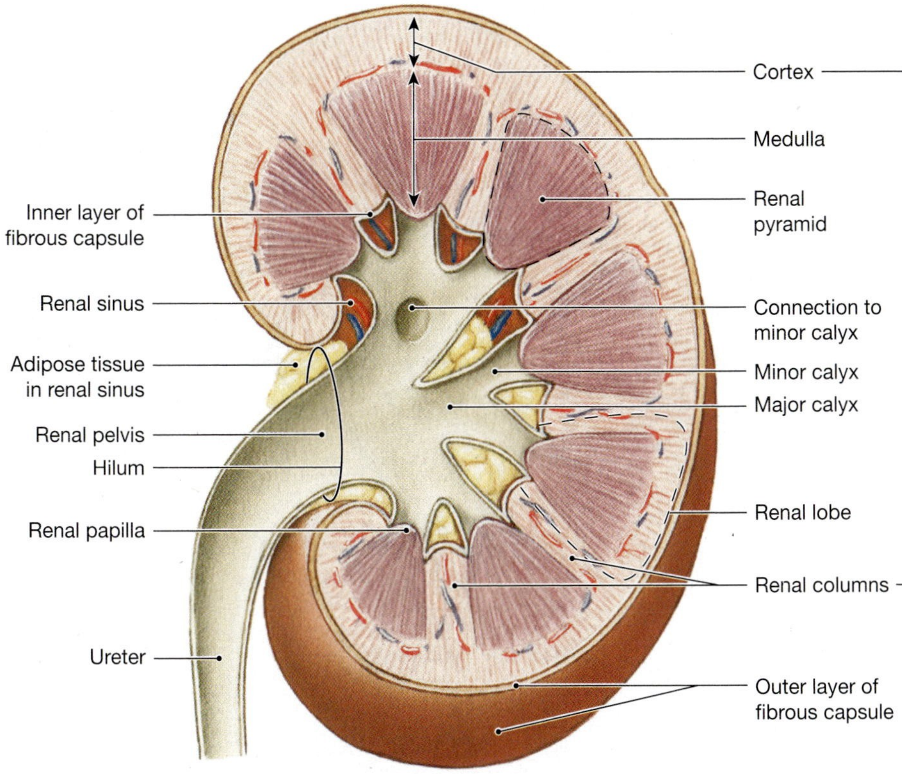

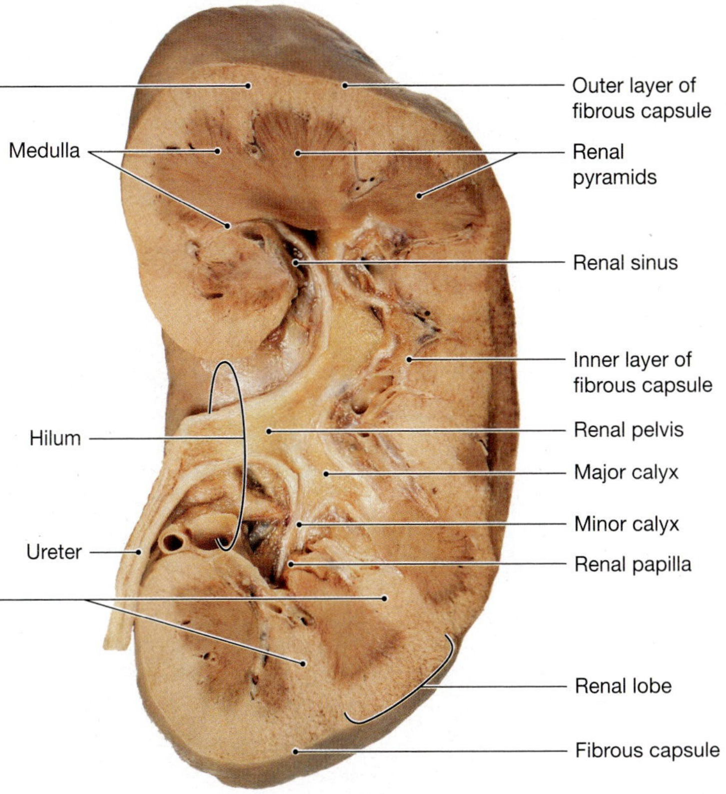

(a) Frontal section of left kidney, anterior view

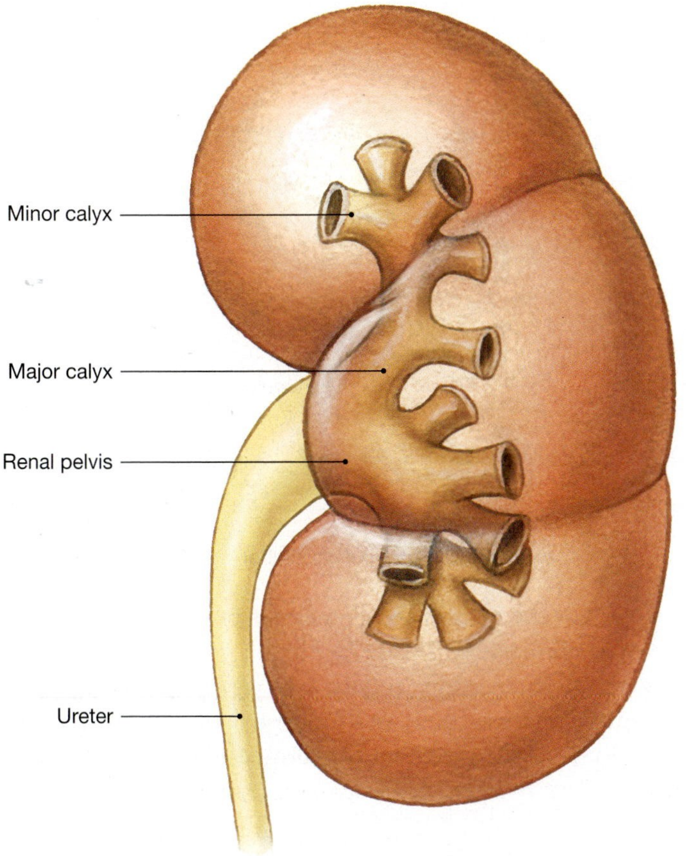

(b) Calyces and renal pelvis

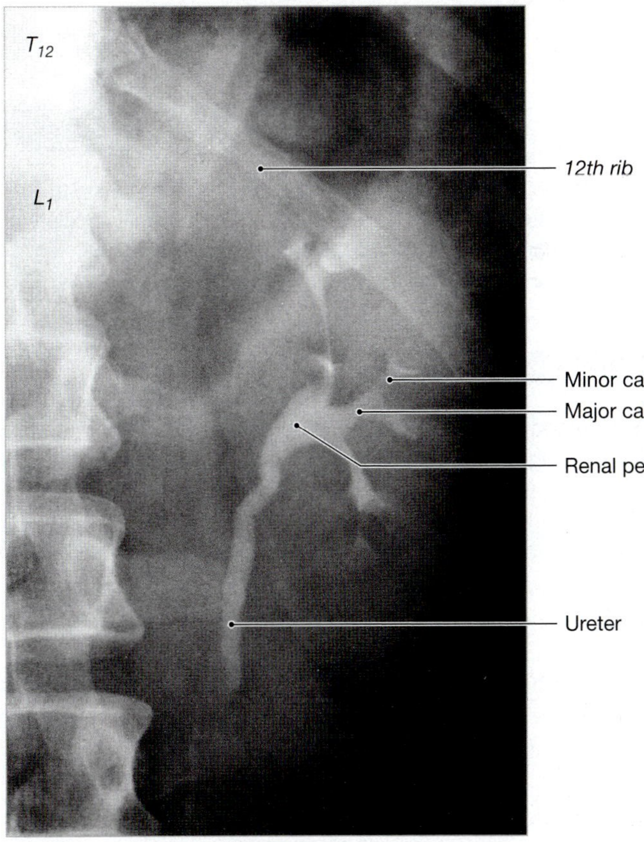

(c) Urogram

Figure 26.3 Structure of the Kidney
(a) Frontal section through the left kidney, showing major structures. The outlines of a renal lobe and a renal pyramid are indicated by dotted lines. **(b)** Shadow drawing to show the arrangement of the calyces and renal pelvis within the kidney. **(c)** Urogram of left kidney showing calyces, renal pelvis, and ureter.

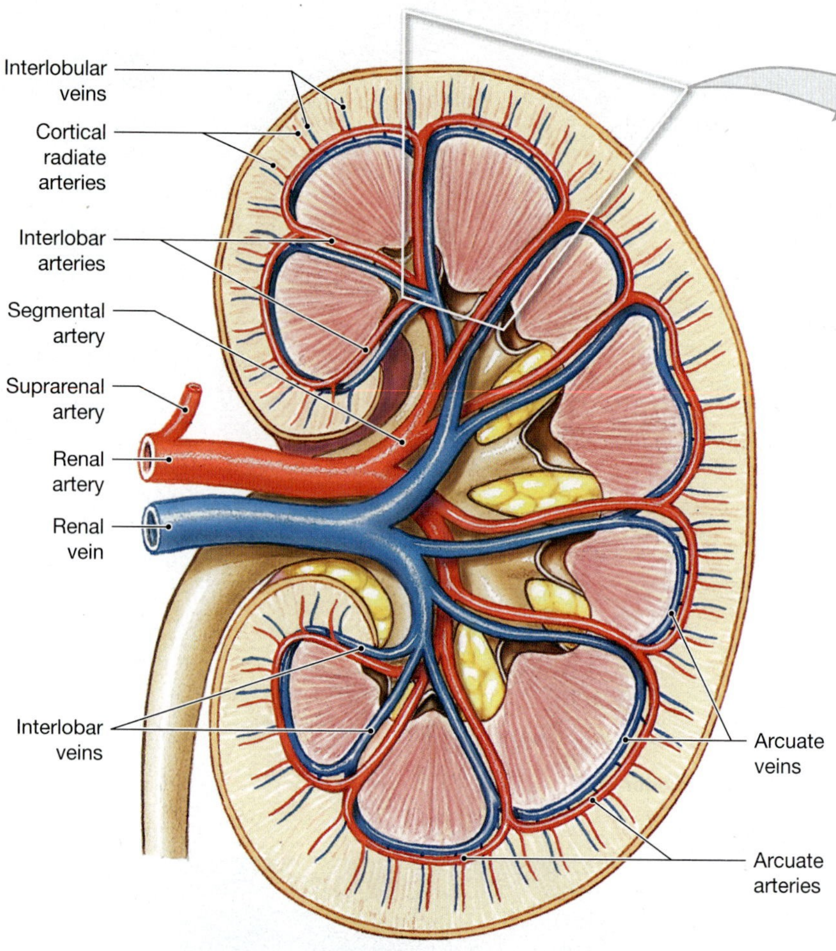

(a) Frontal section

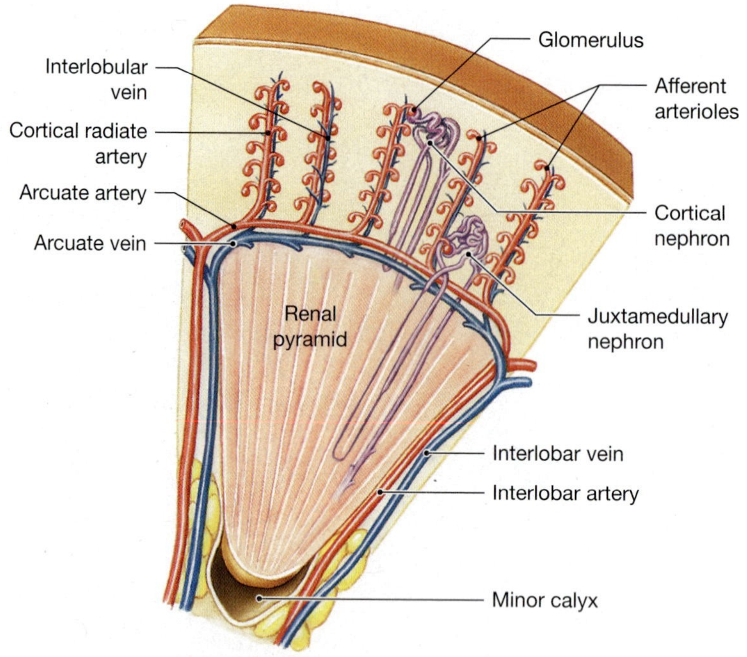

(b) Cortical circulation

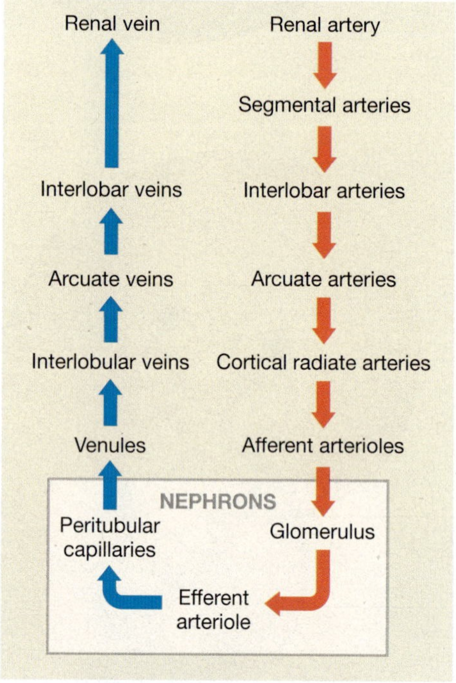

(c) Flowchart of renal circulation

Figure 26.4 Blood Supply to the Kidneys
(a) Sectional view, showing major arteries and veins; compare with *Figure 26.3* and *26.8*. **(b)** Circulation in the cortex. **(c)** Flowchart of renal circulation. The flowchart summarizes the pattern of renal circulation.

CONCEPT CHECK

1. If your blood pressure is low, what changes will you see in the kidneys?
2. After leaving the kidneys, where does the urine go?
3. What is the function of calcitriol?

See blue "Answers" tab at back of book.

Histology of the Kidney [Figure 26.6]

The *nephron*, the basic structural and functional unit of the kidney, can be viewed only with a microscope. For clarity, the nephron diagrammed in Figure 26.6 has been shortened and straightened out.

An Introduction to the Structure and Function of the Nephron [Figures 26.4c/26.6/26.7]

The **renal tubule**, a long tubular passageway, begins at the **renal corpuscle** (KOR-pus-ul), a cup-shaped chamber. The renal corpuscle is approximately 200 μm (0.2 mm) in diameter. It contains a capillary network called the **glomerulus** (glō-MER-ū-lus; plural, *glomeruli*), which consists of about 50 intertwining capillaries. Blood arrives at the glomerulus by way of an **afferent arteriole** and departs in an **efferent arteriole**. These structures of the nephron are shown in Figure 26.6.

Filtration across the walls of the glomerulus produces a protein-free solution known as **glomerular filtrate**, or simply *filtrate*. From the renal corpuscle, the filtrate enters a long tubular passageway that is subdivided into regions with varied structural and functional characteristics. Major subdivisions include (1) the **proximal convoluted tubule (PCT)**; (2) the **nephron loop**, or *loop of Henle* (HEN-lē); and (3) the **distal convoluted tubule (DCT)**.

Each nephron empties into the **collecting system**. A **connecting tubule** connected to the distal convoluted tubule carries the filtrate toward a nearby **collecting duct**. The collecting duct leaves the cortex and descends into the medulla, carrying fluid toward a **papillary duct** that drains into the renal pelvis.

Nephrons from different locations differ slightly in structure. Roughly 85 percent of all nephrons are **cortical nephrons**, located almost entirely within the superficial cortex of the kidney (Figure 26.7a,e). In a cortical

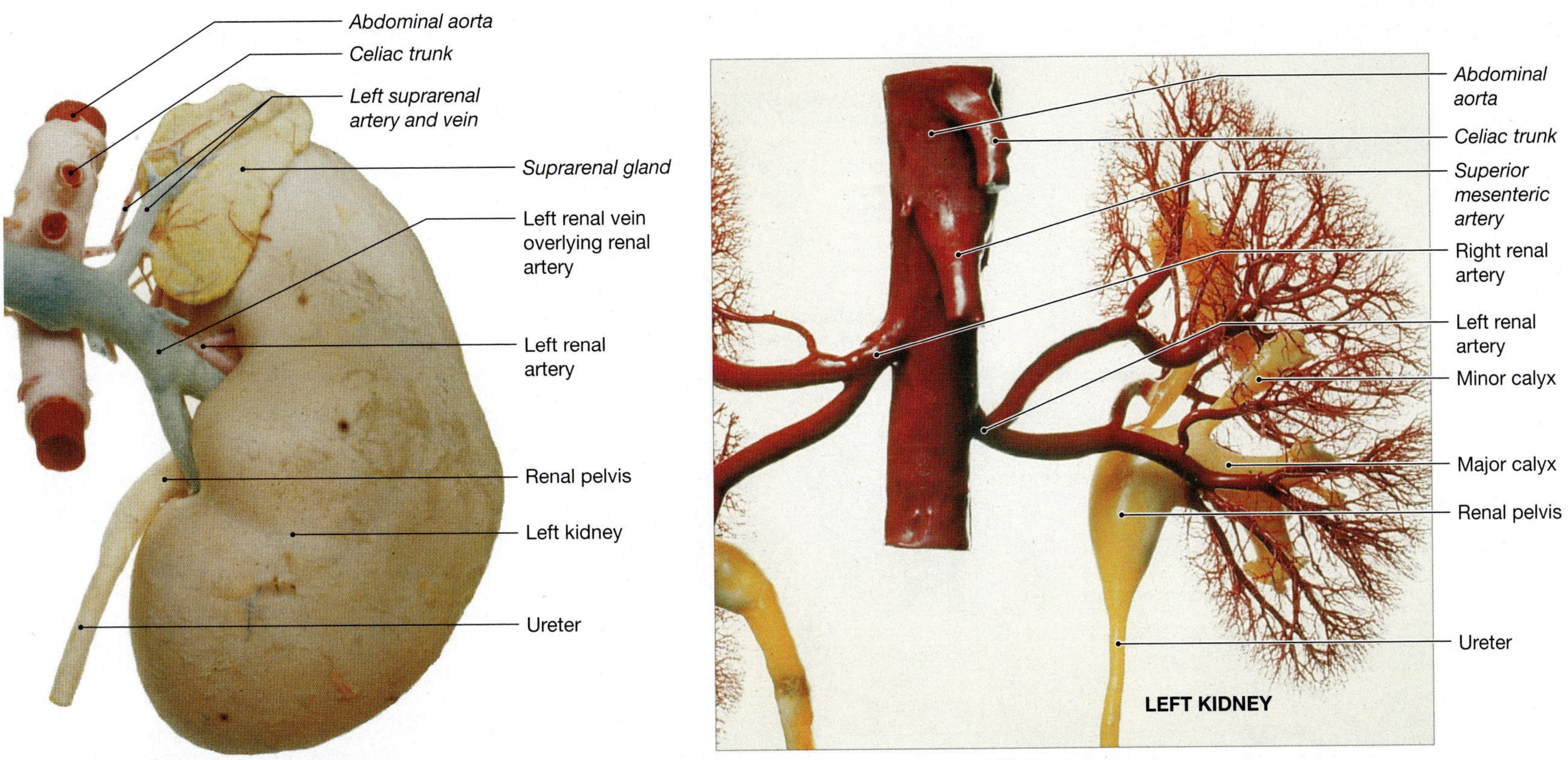

(a) Left kidney and related vessels, anterior view

(b) Corrosion cast

Figure 26.5 Renal Vessels and Blood Flow
(a) The left kidney, ureter, and associated vessels. The vessels have been injected with latex to make them easier to see.
(b) Corrosion cast of the circulation and conducting passageways of the kidneys.

nephron, the nephron loop is relatively short, and the efferent arteriole delivers blood to a network of **peritubular capillaries**, which surround the entire renal tubules. These capillaries drain into small venules that carry blood to the interlobular veins (Figure 26.4c). The remaining 15 percent of nephrons, termed **juxtamedullary** (juks-ta-MED-ū-lar-ē; *juxta*, near) **nephrons** are located closer to the medulla, and they have long nephron loops that extend deep into the renal pyramids (Figure 26.7a,f). Because they are more numerous than juxtamedullary nephrons, cortical nephrons perform most of the reabsorptive and secretory functions of the kidneys. However, the juxtamedullary nephrons create the conditions necessary for the production of a concentrated urine.

The urine arriving at the renal pelvis is very different from the filtrate produced at the renal corpuscle. The passive process of filtration promotes movement across a barrier based solely on solute size. A filter with pores large enough to permit the passage of organic waste products is unable to prevent the passage of water, ions, and other organic molecules, such as glucose, fatty acids, or amino acids. The other distal segments of the nephron are responsible for

- reabsorbing all of the useful organic substrates from the filtrate,
- reabsorbing more than 80 percent of the water in the filtrate, and
- secreting into the filtrate waste products that were missed by the filtration process.

We will now examine each of the segments of a juxtamedullary nephron in greater detail.

The Renal Corpuscle [Figure 26.6/26.8c–e]

The renal corpuscle has a diameter averaging 150–250 μm. It includes (1) the capillary knot of the glomerulus and (2) the expanded initial segment of the renal tubule, a region known as the **glomerular capsule**, or *Bowman's capsule.* The glomerulus projects into the glomerular capsule in the same way that the heart projects into the pericardial cavity (Figure 26.8c). The outer wall of the capsule is lined by a simple squamous **parietal** *(capsular)* **epithelium**, and this layer is continuous with the **visceral** *(glomerular)* **epithelium** that covers the glomerular capillaries. The visceral epithelium consists of large cells with complex processes that wrap around the glomerular capillaries. These specialized cells are called **podocytes** (PŌD-ō-sīts; *podos*, foot + *cyte*, cell) as seen in Figure 26.8c–e. The **capsular space** separates the parietal and visceral epithelia. The connection between the parietal and visceral epithelia lies at the **vascular pole** of the renal corpuscle. At the vascular pole, the glomerular capillaries are connected to the bloodstream. Blood arrives at these capillaries through the afferent arteriole and departs in the smaller-diameter efferent arteriole (Figure 26.8c). (This unusual circulatory arrangement will be discussed further in a later section.)

Filtration occurs as blood pressure forces fluid and dissolved solutes out of the glomerulus and into the capsular space. The resulting filtrate is very similar to plasma with the blood proteins removed. The filtration process involves passage across three physical barriers (Figure 26.8d):

1. *The capillary endothelium:* The glomerular capillaries are *fenestrated capillaries* with pores ranging from 60 to 100 nm (0.06–0.1 μm) in diameter. p. 575 These openings are small enough to prevent the passage of blood cells, but they are too large to restrict the diffusion of solutes, even those the size of plasma proteins.
2. *The basal lamina:* The basal lamina that surrounds the capillary endothelium has a dense layer several times the density and thickness of a typical basal lamina. The dense layer of the glomerulus restricts the passage of the larger plasma proteins but permits the movement of smaller plasma proteins, nutrients, and ions. Unlike basal laminae

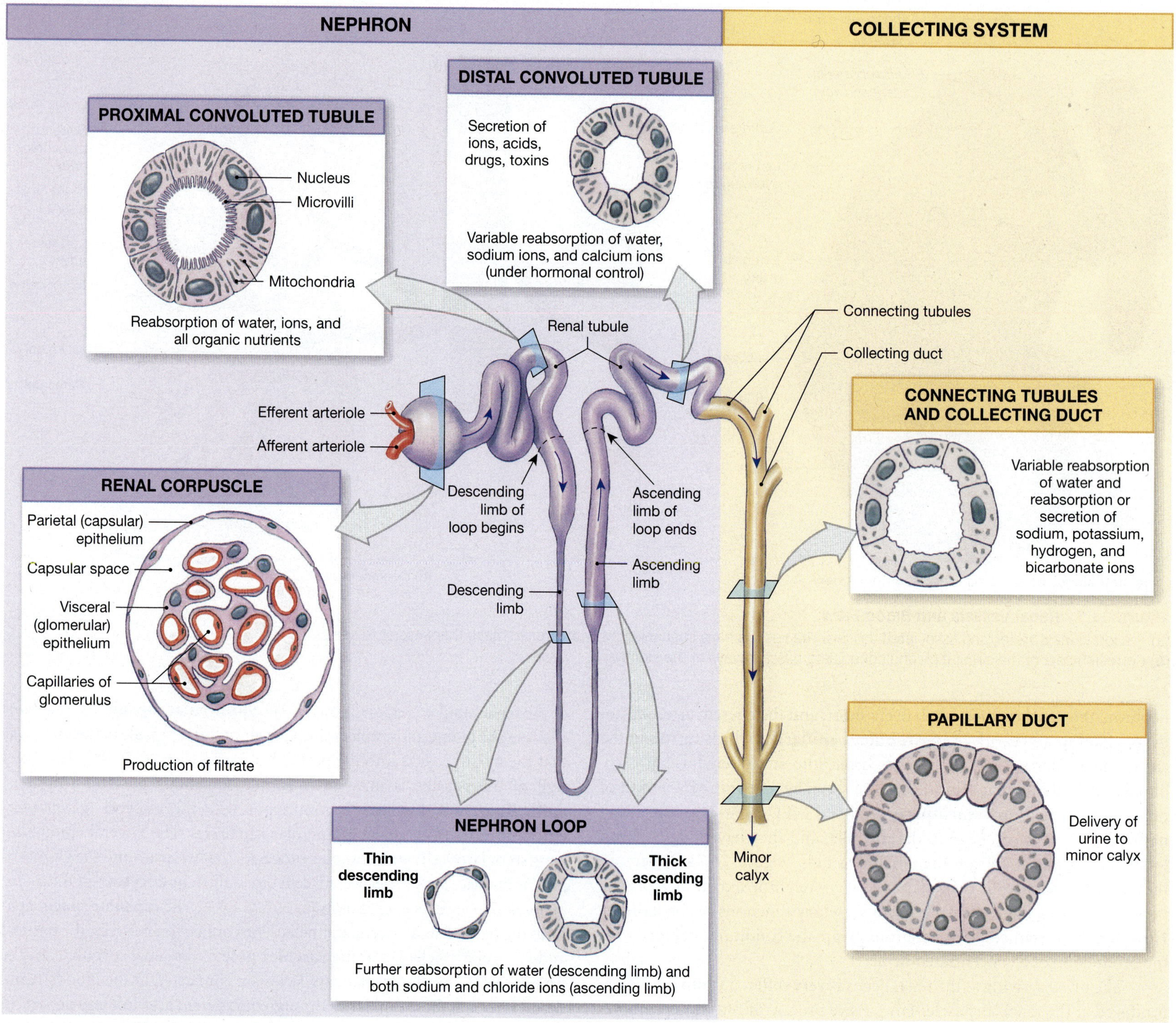

Figure 26.6 A Typical Nephron
A diagrammatic view showing the histological structure and the major functions of each segment of the nephron (violet) and collecting system (tan).

elsewhere in the body, the dense layer may encircle two or more capillaries. When it does, **mesangial cells** are situated between the endothelial cells of adjacent capillaries. Mesangial cells (1) provide physical support for the capillaries, (2) engulf organic materials that might otherwise clog the dense layer, and (3) regulate the diameters of the glomerular capillaries, and thus play a role in the regulation of glomerular blood flow and filtration.

3. *The glomerular epithelium:* The podocytes have long cellular processes that wrap around the outer surfaces of the basal lamina. These delicate "feet," or **secondary processes** (Figure 26.8d,e), are separated by narrow gaps called **filtration slits**. Because the filtration slits are very narrow, the filtrate entering the capsular space consists of water with dissolved ions, small organic molecules, and few if any plasma proteins.

In addition to metabolic wastes, the filtrate contains other organic compounds such as glucose, free fatty acids, amino acids, and vitamins. These potentially useful materials are reabsorbed by the proximal convoluted tubule.

The Proximal Convoluted Tubule [Figures 26.6/26.7a,b/26.8c]

The proximal convoluted tubule (PCT) is the first part of the renal tubule. Entry into the PCT lies almost directly opposite the vascular pole of the

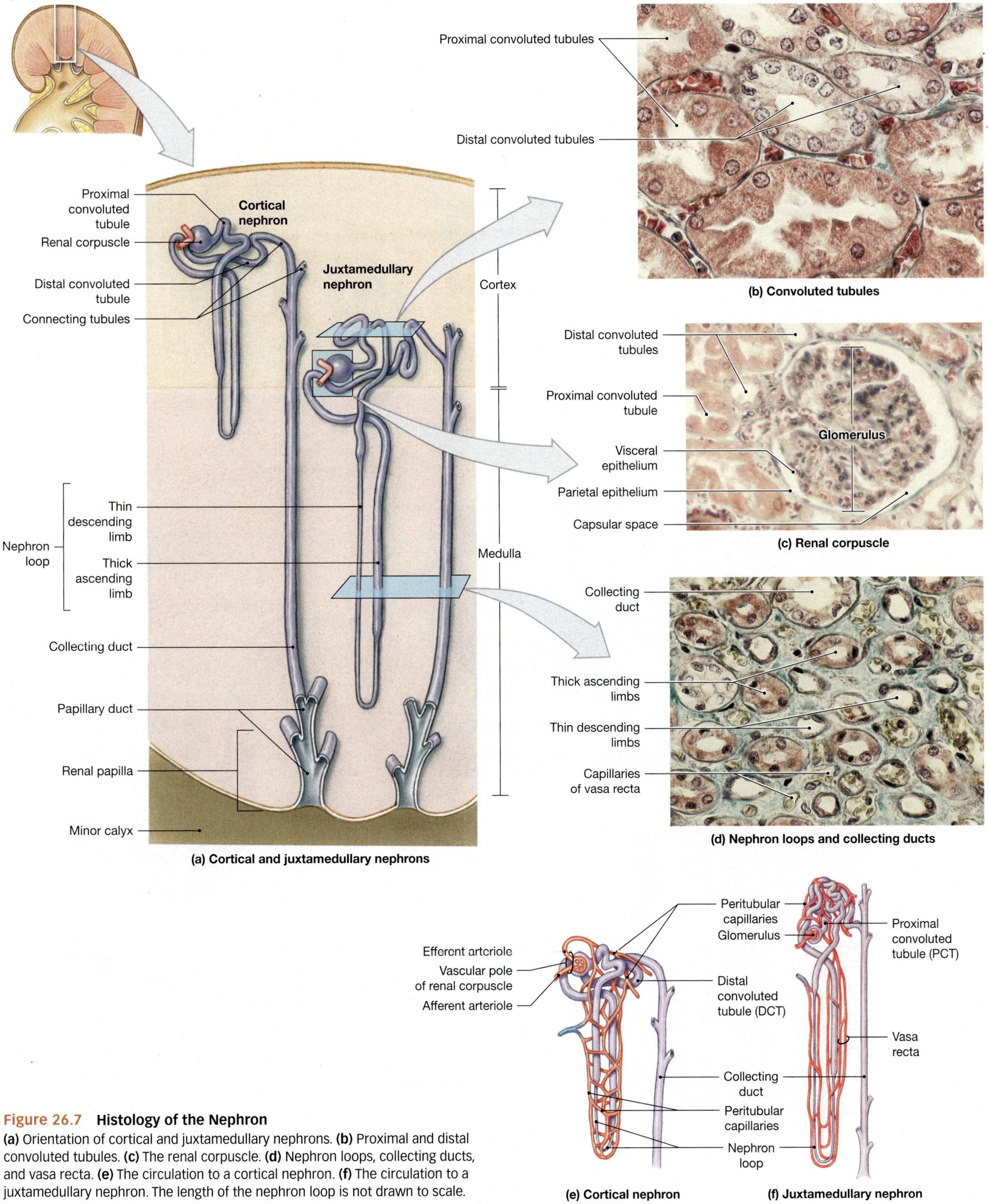

Figure 26.7 Histology of the Nephron
(a) Orientation of cortical and juxtamedullary nephrons. **(b)** Proximal and distal convoluted tubules. **(c)** The renal corpuscle. **(d)** Nephron loops, collecting ducts, and vasa recta. **(e)** The circulation to a cortical nephron. **(f)** The circulation to a juxtamedullary nephron. The length of the nephron loop is not drawn to scale.

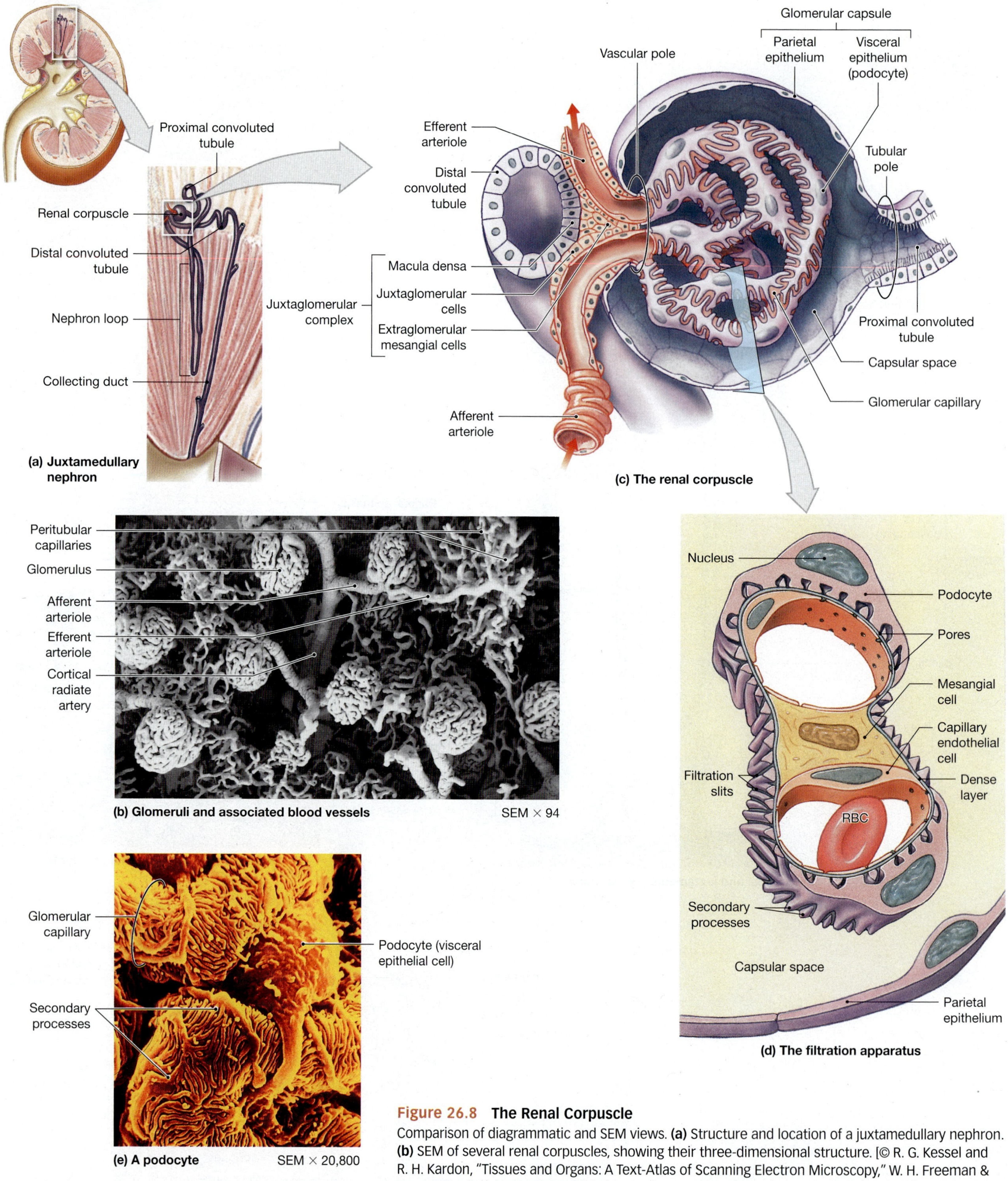

Figure 26.8 The Renal Corpuscle
Comparison of diagrammatic and SEM views. **(a)** Structure and location of a juxtamedullary nephron. **(b)** SEM of several renal corpuscles, showing their three-dimensional structure. [© R. G. Kessel and R. H. Kardon, "Tissues and Organs: A Text-Atlas of Scanning Electron Microscopy," W. H. Freeman & Co., 1979. All Rights Reserved] **(c)** The renal corpuscle. Arrows show the pathway of blood flow. **(d)** Diagrammatic view of the filtration apparatus. **(e)** Colorized SEM of the electron micrograph of the glomerular surface, showing individual podocytes and their foot processes and secondary processes.

renal corpuscle, at the **tubular pole** of the renal corpuscle (Figure 26.8c). The lining of the PCT consists of a simple cuboidal epithelium whose apical surfaces are blanketed with microvilli, increasing the surface area for reabsorption (Figures 26.6 and 26.7a,b). These cells actively absorb organic nutrients, ions, and plasma proteins (if any) from the filtrate as it flows along the PCT. As these solutes are absorbed, osmotic forces pull water across the wall of the PCT and into the surrounding interstitial fluid, which is called *peritubular fluid*. Absorption represents the primary function of the PCT. As tubular fluid passes along the PCT, the epithelial cells reabsorb virtually all of the organic nutrients and plasma proteins and 60 percent of the sodium ions, chloride ions, and water. The PCT also actively reabsorbs potassium, calcium, magnesium, bicarbonate, phosphate, and sulfate ions.

The Nephron Loop [Figures 26.6/26.7a,d]

The proximal convoluted tubule ends at an acute bend that turns the renal tubule toward the medulla. This bend marks the start of the nephron loop (Figure 26.7a,d). The nephron loop can be divided into a **descending limb** and an **ascending limb**. The descending limb travels in the medulla toward the renal pelvis, and the ascending limb returns toward the cortex. Each limb contains a **thick segment** and a **thin segment** (Figures 26.6 and 26.7a,d). (The terms *thick* and *thin* refer to the thickness of the surrounding epithelium, not to the diameter of the lumen.)

Thick segments are found closest to the cortex, whereas a thin squamous epithelium lines the thin segment within the deeper medullary portions. The thick ascending limb, which begins deep in the medulla, contains active transport mechanisms that pump sodium and chloride ions out of the tubular fluid. As a result of these transport activities, the medullary interstitial fluid contains an unusually high concentration of solutes. Solute concentration is usually expressed in terms of milliosmoles (mOsml). Near the base of the loop, in the deepest part of the medulla, the solute concentration of the interstitial fluid is roughly four times that of plasma (1200 mOsml versus 300 mOsml). The thin descending and ascending limbs are freely permeable to water, but relatively impermeable to ions and other solutes. The high osmotic concentration surrounding the nephron loop results in an osmotic flow of water out of the nephron. This water is absorbed by the slender capillaries of the **vasa recta**, which return the liquid to the general circulation.

The net effect is that the nephron loop reabsorbs an additional 25 percent of the water from the tubular fluid and an even higher percentage of the sodium and chloride ions. Reabsorption in the PCT and nephron loop normally reclaims all of the organic nutrients, 85 percent of the water, and more than 90 percent of the sodium and chloride ions. The remaining water, ions, and all of the organic wastes filtered at the glomerulus remain in the nephron loop and enter the distal convoluted tubule.

The Distal Convoluted Tubule [Figures 26.6/26.7b,c/26.8a,c,d]

The ascending limb of the nephron loop ends where it forms a sharp angle that places the tubular wall in close contact with the glomerulus and its accompanying vessels. The distal convoluted tubule (DCT) begins at that bend. The initial portion of the DCT crosses the vascular pole of the renal corpuscle, passing between the afferent and efferent arterioles (Figure 26.8a,c,d).

In sectional view (Figures 26.6 and 26.7b,c), the DCT differs from the PCT in that (1) the DCT has a smaller diameter, (2) the epithelial cells of the DCT lack microvilli, and (3) the boundaries between the epithelial cells in the DCT are distinct. These characteristics reflect the major differences in function between the two regions of convoluted tubules: The PCT is primarily involved in reabsorption, whereas the DCT is primarily involved in secretion.

The distal convoluted tubule is an important site for (1) the active secretion of ions, acids, and other materials; (2) the selective reabsorption of sodium and calcium ions from the tubular fluid; and (3) the selective reabsorption of water, which helps concentrate the tubular fluid. The sodium transport activities of the DCT are controlled by circulating levels of *aldosterone* secreted by the suprarenal cortex. p. 516

The Juxtaglomerular Complex [Figure 26.8c] The epithelial cells in the distal convoluted tubule immediately adjacent to the afferent arteriole at the vascular pole of the glomerulus are taller than those seen elsewhere along the DCT. This region of the DCT, detailed in Figure 26.8c, is called the **macula densa** (MAK-ū-la DEN-sa). These cells monitor electrolyte concentration (specifically sodium and chloride ions) in the tubular fluid. The cells of the macula densa are closely associated with unusual smooth muscle fibers in the wall of the afferent arteriole. These muscle fibers are known as **juxtaglomerular cells** (*juxta*, near). **Extraglomerular mesangial cells** occupy the space between the glomerulus, the afferent and efferent arterioles, and the DCT. Together the macula densa, juxtaglomerular cells, and extraglomerular mesangial cells form the **juxtaglomerular complex**, or juxtaglomerular apparatus, an endocrine structure that secretes two hormones, *renin* and *erythropoietin*, described in Chapter 19. p. 518 These hormones, released when renal blood pressure, blood flow, or local oxygen levels decrease, elevate blood volume, hemoglobin levels, and blood pressure, and restore normal rates of filtrate production.

The Collecting System [Figures 26.6/26.7a,d,e,f]

The distal convoluted tubule, the last segment of the nephron, opens into the collecting system, which consists of *connecting tubules*, *collecting ducts*, and *papillary ducts* (Figure 26.7a,d). Individual connecting tubules connect each nephron to a nearby collecting duct (Figure 26.7a,e,f). Each collecting duct receives fluid from many connecting tubules, draining both cortical and juxtamedullary nephrons. Several collecting ducts converge to empty into the larger papillary duct that empties into a minor calyx in the renal pelvis. The epithelium lining the collecting system begins as simple cuboidal cells in the connecting tubules and changes to a columnar epithelium in the collecting and papillary ducts (Figure 26.6).

In addition to transporting tubular fluid from the nephron to the renal pelvis, the collecting system makes final adjustments to its osmotic concentration and volume. The regulatory mechanism changes the permeability of the collecting ducts to water. This change is significant because the collecting ducts pass through the medulla, where the nephron loop has established very high solute concentrations in the interstitial fluids. If collecting duct permeability is low, most of the tubular fluid reaching the collecting duct will flow into the renal pelvis and the urine will be dilute. In contrast, if collecting duct permeability is high, the osmotic flow of water out of the duct into the medulla will be promoted. This results in a small amount of highly concentrated urine. ADH (antidiuretic hormone) is the hormone responsible for controlling the permeability of the collecting system. p. 510 The higher the levels of circulating ADH, the greater the amount of water reabsorbed, and the more concentrated the urine.

CONCEPT CHECK

1. Trace the path of a drop of blood from the renal artery to a glomerulus and back to a renal vein.
2. Trace the path taken by filtrate in traveling from a glomerulus to a minor calyx.
3. Explain why filtration alone is not sufficient for urine production.
4. What is the function of the nephron loop?

See blue "Answers" tab at back of book.

Clinical Note

Advances in the Treatment of Renal Failure One normal kidney is sufficient to filter the blood and maintain homeostasis. Renal failure will therefore not develop unless both kidneys are damaged. Management of chronic renal failure typically restricts the intake of water and salt, and minimizes dietary protein. This combination reduces strain on the urinary system by minimizing the volume of urine produced and preventing the generation of large quantities of nitrogenous wastes.

If drugs and dietary controls cannot stabilize blood composition, more drastic measures are taken. In **hemodialysis** (hē-mō-dī-AL-i-sis), a *dialysis machine* containing an artificial membrane is used to regulate the composition of blood. For temporary kidney dialysis, a silicone rubber tube called a *shunt* is inserted into a medium-sized artery and vein. (The typical location is the forearm, although the lower leg is sometimes used.) While connected to the dialysis machine, the individual sits quietly as blood circulates from the arterial shunt, through the machine, and back through the venous shunt. The patient's blood flows past a selectively permeable artifical *membrane*, which contains pores large enough to permit the diffusion of small ions, but small enough to prevent the loss of plasma proteins. On the other side of the membrane flows a special *dialysis fluid*. As diffusion occurs across the membrane, blood composition changes. Potassium ions, phosphate ions, sulfate ions, urea, creatinine, and uric acid diffuse across the membrane into the dialysis fluid. Bicarbonate ions and glucose diffuse into the bloodstream. In effect, diffusion across the dialysis membrane replaces normal glomerular filtration. The characteristics of the dialysis fluid can be modified for each patient to ensure that important metabolites remain in the bloodstream rather than diffusing across the membrane.

As an alternative to hemodialysis, **peritoneal dialysis** uses the peritoneal lining as a dialysis membrane. Dialysis fluid is introduced into the peritoneum through a catheter in the abdominal wall, and the fluid is removed and replaced at intervals. One procedure involves cycling 2 liters of fluid in an hour—15 minutes for infusion, 30 minutes for exchange, and 15 minutes for fluid reclamation. This procedure may be performed in a hospital or at home. In **continuous ambulatory peritoneal dialysis (CAPD)**, patients self-administer 2 liters of dialysis fluid through the catheter and then continue normal activity until four to six hours later, when the fluid is replaced with fresh dialysis fluid.

Probably the most satisfactory solution for overall quality of life is *kidney transplantation*: implantating a new kidney obtained from a living donor or a cadaver. The damaged kidney is removed and its blood supply is connected to the transplant. An arterial graft is inserted to carry blood from the iliac artery or the aorta to the transplant, which is placed in the pelvic or lower abdominal cavity. The success rate for kidney transplantation varies; the one-year success rate is now 85–95 percent. Using kidneys taken from close relatives significantly improves the chances that the transplant will succeed for five years or more. Immunosuppressive drugs are administered to reduce tissue rejection, but this treatment also lowers the individual's resistance to infection.

Structures for Urine Transport, Storage, and Elimination [Figure 26.9c]

Filtrate modification and urine production end when the fluid enters the minor calyx. The remaining parts of the urinary system (the *ureters*, *urinary bladder*, and *urethra*) are responsible for the transport, storage, and elimination of the urine. **Figure 26.9c** provides an orientation to the relative sizes and positions of these organs.

The minor and major calyces, the renal pelvis, the ureters, the urinary bladder, and the proximal portion of the urethra are lined by a *transitional epithelium* that can tolerate cycles of distension and contraction without damage. p. 57

The Ureters [Figures 26.1a,b/26.2/26.3/26.9c/26.10]

The ureters are a pair of muscular tubes that extend inferiorly from the kidneys for about 30 cm (12 in.) before reaching the urinary bladder (**Figure 26.1a,b**, p. 695). Each ureter begins as a continuation of the funnel-shaped renal pelvis through the hilum (**Figures 26.3**, p. 697 and **26.9c**). As the ureters extend to the urinary bladder, they pass inferiorly and medially over the psoas major muscles. The ureters are retroperitoneal, and they are firmly attached to the posterior abdominal wall (**Figure 26.2**, p. 696). The paths taken by the ureters as they approach the wall of the urinary bladder differ in men and women because of variations in the nature, size, and position of the reproductive organs (**Figure 26.10a,b**).

The ureters penetrate the posterior wall of the urinary bladder without entering the peritoneal cavity. They pass through the bladder wall at an oblique angle, and the **ureteral opening** is slit-like rather than rounded (**Figure 26.10c**). This shape helps prevent backflow of urine toward the ureter and kidneys when the urinary bladder contracts.

Histology of the Ureters [Figure 26.11a]

The wall of each ureter consists of three layers: (1) an inner mucosa lined by a transitional epithelium, (2) a middle muscular layer made up of longitudinal (inner) and circular (outer) bands of smooth muscle, and (3) an outer connective tissue layer (adventitia) that is continuous with the fibrous capsule and peritoneum (**Figure 26.11a**). Starting at the kidney, about every half-minute, peristaltic contractions of the muscular wall are triggered by stimulation of stretch receptors in the ureteral wall. These contractions "milk" urine out of the renal pelvis and along the ureter to the bladder.

The Urinary Bladder [Figure 26.10b,c]

The urinary bladder is a hollow muscular organ that functions as a temporary storage reservoir for urine. In the male, the base of the urinary bladder lies between the rectum and the symphysis pubis; in the female, the base of the urinary bladder sits inferior to the uterus and anterior to the vagina. The dimensions of the urinary bladder vary, depending on the state of distension, but the full urinary bladder can contain about a liter of urine.

The superior surfaces of the urinary bladder are covered by a layer of peritoneum; several peritoneal folds assist in stabilizing its position. The **median umbilical ligament** extends from the anterior and superior border toward the umbilicus (**Figure 26.10b,c**). The **lateral umbilical ligaments** pass along the sides of the bladder and also reach the umbilicus. These fibrous cords contain the vestiges of the two *umbilical arteries* that supplied blood to the placenta during embryonic and fetal development. p. 600 The posterior, inferior, and anterior surfaces of the urinary bladder lie outside the peritoneal cavity. In these areas, tough ligamentous bands anchor the bladder to the pelvic and pubic bones.

In sectional view (**Figure 26.10c**), the mucosa lining the urinary bladder is usually thrown into folds, or **rugae**, that disappear as the bladder

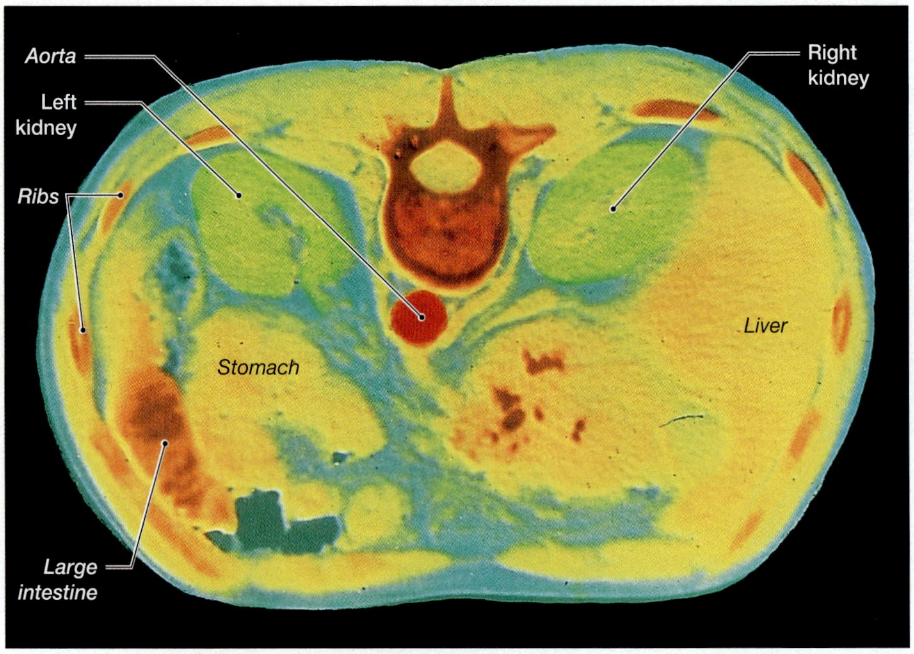

(a) Color-enhanced CT scan

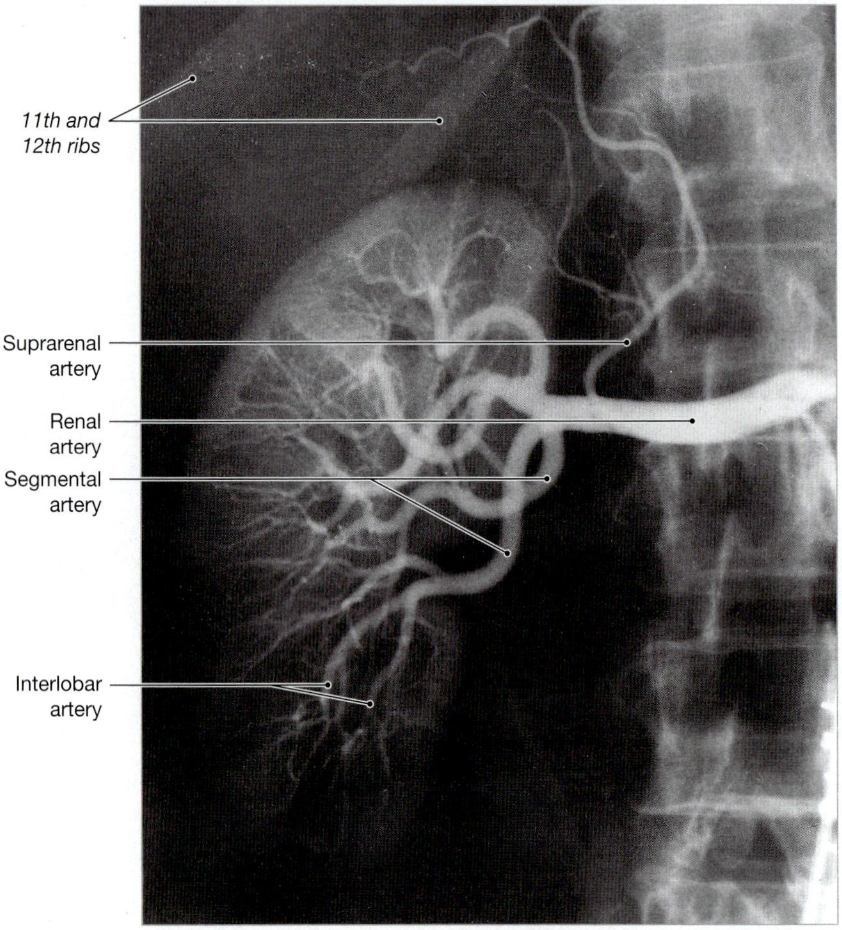

(b) Renal angiogram

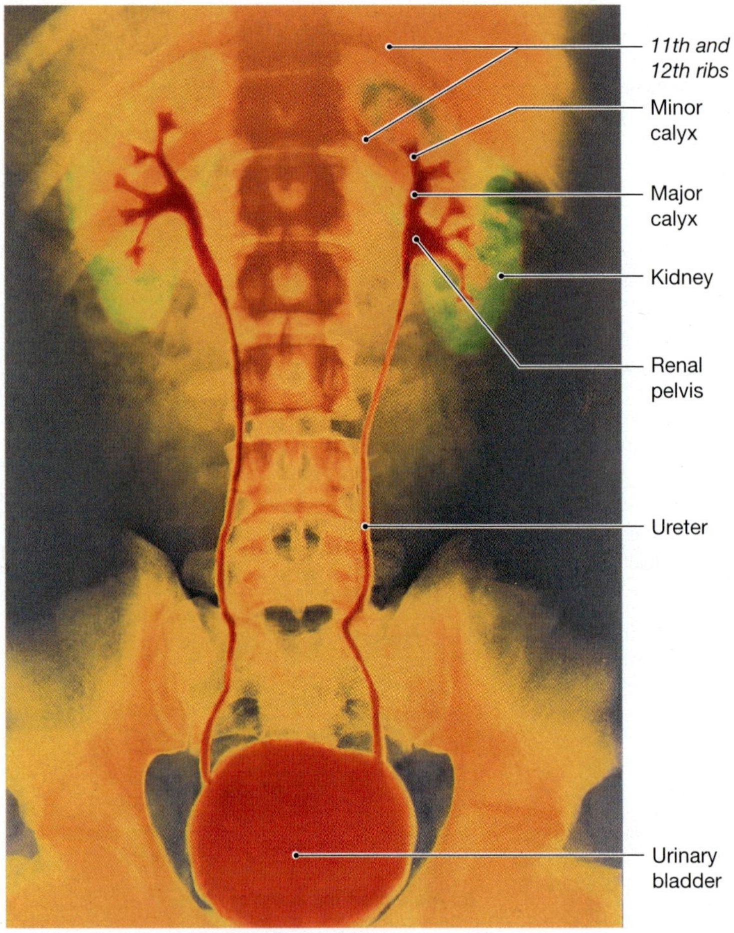

(c) Normal pyelogram

Figure 26.9 Images of the Urinary System
(a) A CT scan showing the position of the kidneys in a transverse section through the trunk as viewed from below. Such scans can provide useful information concerning localized abnormalities or masses. **(b)** An arteriogram of the right kidney. Arteriography involves the administration of a radiopaque compound that enables visualization of blood vessels in an x-ray. **(c)** This colorized x-ray was taken after the intravenous injection of a radiopaque dye that was filtered into the urine. The image is known as a *pyelogram*, and the procedure is often called an IVP (intravenous pyelography).

stretches and fills with urine. The triangular area bounded by the ureteral openings and the entrance to the urethra constitutes the **trigone** (TR Ī-gōn) of the urinary bladder. The mucosa here lacks rugae; it is smooth and very thick. The trigone acts as a funnel that channels urine into the urethra when the urinary bladder contracts.

The urethral entrance lies at the apex of the trigone, at the most inferior point in the bladder. The region surrounding the urethral opening, known as the **neck of the urinary bladder**, contains a muscular **internal urethral sphincter** (Figure 26.10b,c). The smooth muscle of the internal urethral sphincter provides involuntary control over the discharge of urine from the bladder. The urinary bladder is innervated by postganglionic fibers from ganglia in the *hypogastric plexus* and by parasympathetic fibers from intramural ganglia that are controlled by branches of the pelvic nerves. p. 463

Histology of the Urinary Bladder [Figure 26.11b]

The wall of the bladder contains a mucosa of transitional epithelium, a submucosa, and muscularis layers (Figure 26.11b). The muscularis layer consists of three layers: inner and outer longitudinal smooth muscle layers, with

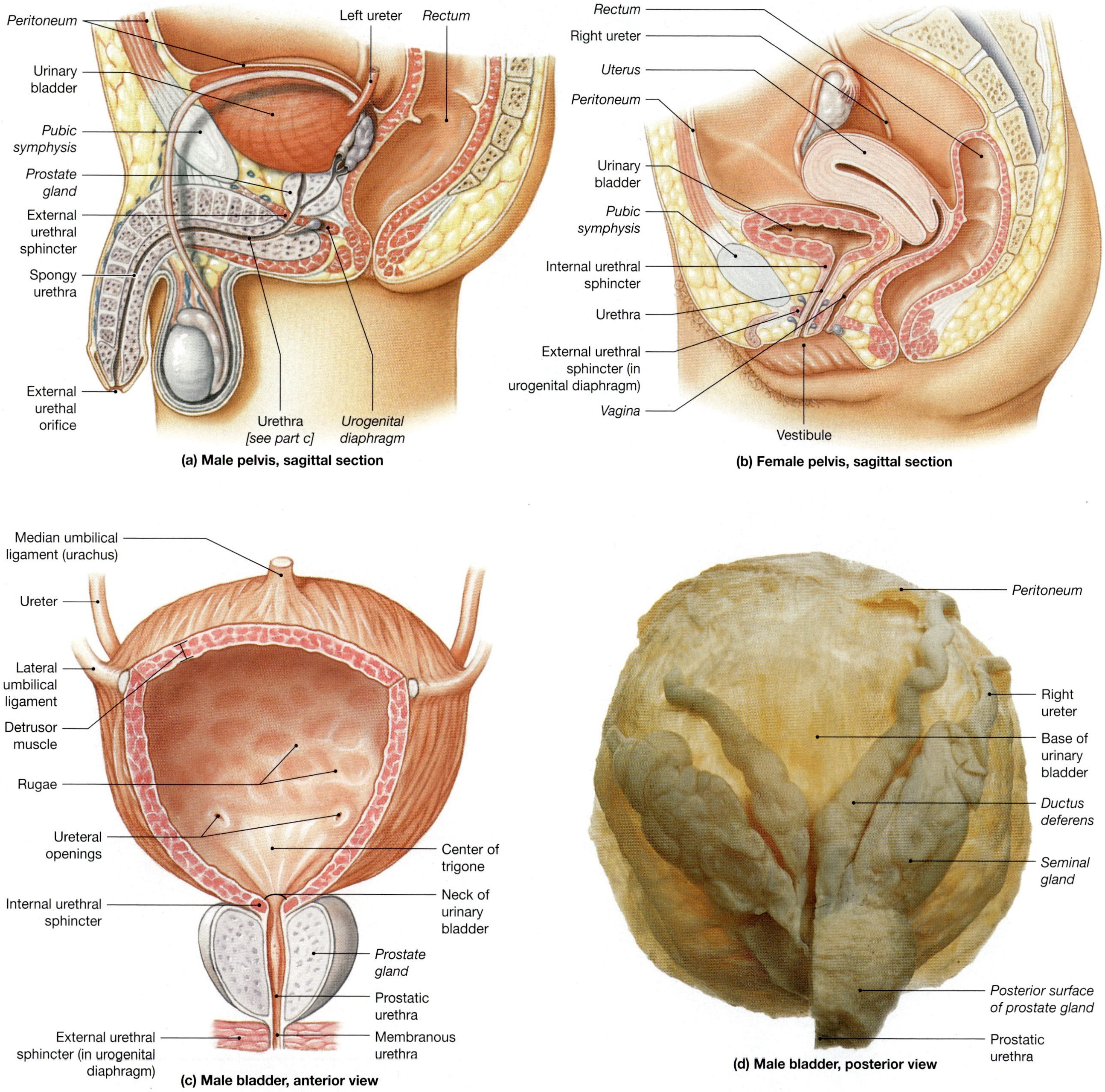

Figure 26.10 Organs Responsible for the Conduction and Storage of Urine
(a) Position of the ureter, urinary bladder, and urethra in the male. **(b)** Position of these organs in the female. **(c)** Anatomy of the urinary bladder in a male. **(d)** The male urinary bladder and accessory reproductive structures as seen in posterior view.

a layer of circular muscle sandwiched between. Collectively, these layers form the powerful **detrusor** (dē-TROO-sor) **muscle** of the urinary bladder. Contraction of this muscle compresses the urinary bladder and expels its contents into the urethra. A layer of serosa covers the superior surface of the urinary bladder.

The Urethra [Figure 26.10]

The urethra extends from the neck of the urinary bladder (Figure 26.10c) to the exterior. The female and male urethra differ in length and in function. In the female, the urethra is very short, extending 3–5 cm (1–1.5 in.)

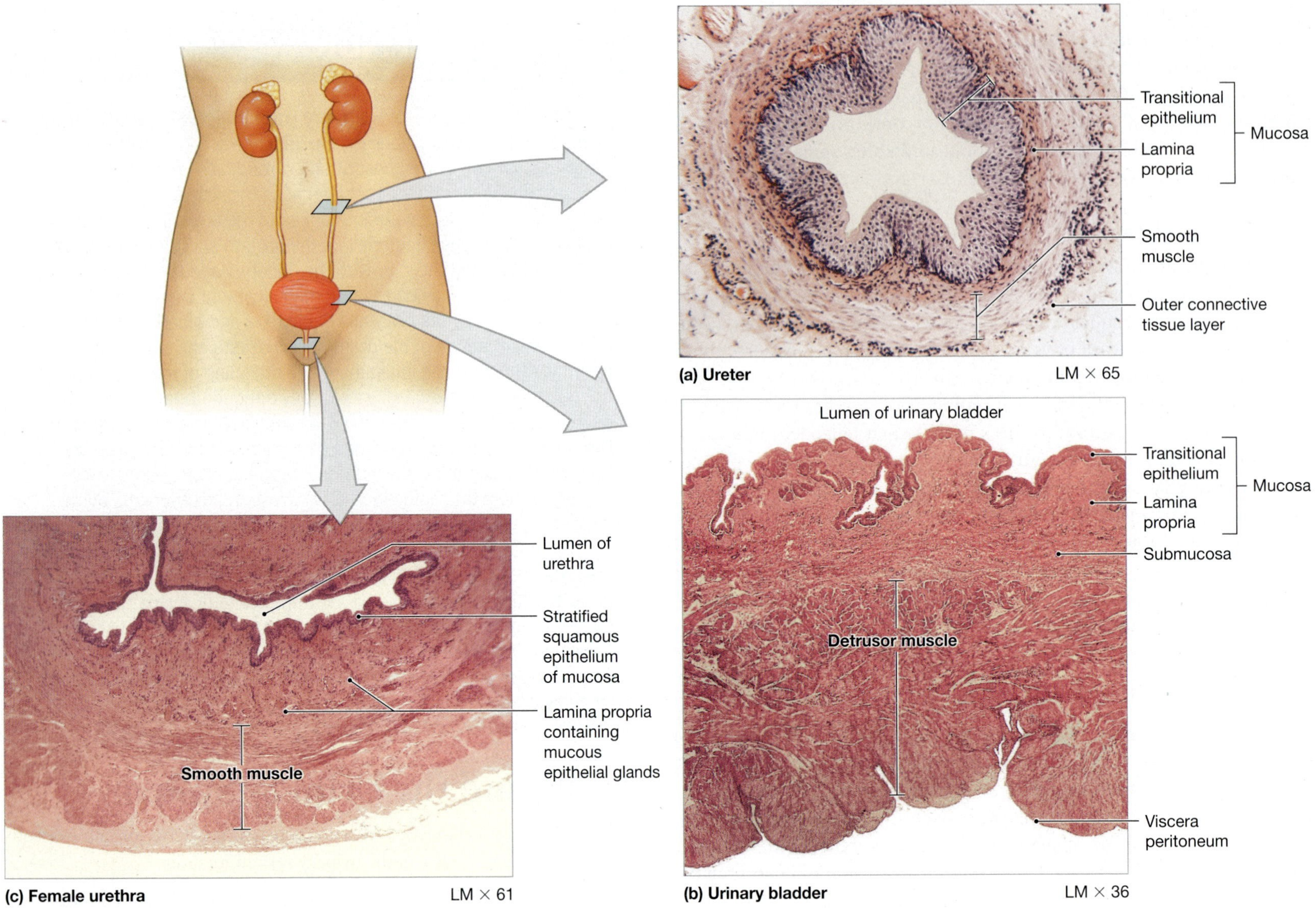

Figure 26.11 Histology of the Collecting and Transport Organs
(a) A ureter seen in transverse section. Note the thick layer of smooth muscle surrounding the lumen. (*See also Figure 3.5c.*)
(b) The wall of the urinary bladder. **(c)** A transverse section through the female urethra.

Clinical Note

Problems with the Conducting System Local blockages of the collecting tubules, collecting ducts, or ureters may result from the formation of small blood clots, epithelial cells, lipids, or other materials, collectively called **casts**. Casts are often excreted in the urine and visible in microscopic analysis of urine samples. **Calculi** (KAL-kū-lī), or "kidney stones," form from calcium deposits, magnesium salts, or crystals of uric acid, resulting in a condition called **nephrolithiasis** (nef-rō-li-THĪ-a-sis). The **urinary obstruction** caused by kidney stones or other factors, such as external compression, is a painful and serious problem because it reduces or eliminates filtration in the affected kidney. If peristalsis and fluid pressures cannot dislodge them, the stones must be surgically removed or destroyed. One nonsurgical alternative breaks kidney stones apart with a lithotripter, similar to the one used to destroy gallstones.

from the bladder to the vestibule (Figure 26.10b). The external urethral opening, or **external urethral orifice**, is situated near the anterior wall of the vagina.

In the male, the urethra extends from the neck of the urinary bladder to the tip of the penis, a distance that may be 18–20 cm (7–8 in.). The male urethra can be subdivided into three portions (Figure 26.10a,c,d): (1) the *prostatic urethra*, (2) the *membranous urethra*, and (3) the *spongy urethra*.

The **prostatic urethra** passes through the center of the prostate gland (Figure 26.10c). The **membranous urethra** includes the short segment that penetrates the urogenital diaphragm, the muscular floor of the pelvic cavity. pp. 280–281 The **spongy urethra**, or *penile* (PĒ-nīl) *urethra*, extends from the distal border of the urogenital diaphragm to the external urethral orifice at the tip of the penis (Figure 26.10a). The functional differences between these regions will be considered in Chapter 27.

In both sexes, as the urethra passes through the urogenital diaphragm, a circular band of skeletal muscle forms the **external urethral sphincter**. pp. 280–281 The contractions of both the external and internal urethral

sphincters are controlled by branches of the hypogastric plexus. Only the external urethral sphincter is under voluntary control, through the perineal branch of the pudendal nerve. ∞ p. 281 The sphincter has a resting muscle tone and usually must be voluntarily relaxed to permit urination. The autonomic innervation of the external sphincter becomes important only if voluntary control is lacking, as in infants or in adults after spinal cord injuries. (See the section on the micturition reflex.)

Histology of the Urethra [Figure 26.11c]

In females, the urethral lining is usually a transitional epithelium near the neck of the urinary bladder. The rest of the urethra is typically lined by a stratified squamous epithelium (**Figure 26.11c**). The lamina propria contains an extensive network of veins, and the entire complex is surrounded by concentric layers of smooth muscle.

In males, the histological organization of the urethra varies along its length. As one proceeds from the neck of the urinary bladder to the external urethral orifice, the epithelium changes from transitional to pseudostratified columnar or stratified columnar, and then to stratified squamous. The lamina propria is thick and elastic; the mucous membrane is thrown into longitudinal folds. Mucus-secreting cells are found in the epithelial pockets, and in the male the epithelial mucus glands may form tubules that extend into the lamina propria. Connective tissues of the lamina propria anchor the urethra to surrounding structures.

The Micturition Reflex and Urination

Urine reaches the urinary bladder by the peristaltic contractions of the ureters. The process of urination, which empties the urinary bladder, is coordinated by the **micturition reflex**. Stretch receptors in the wall of the urinary bladder are stimulated as it fills with urine. Afferent fibers in the pelvic nerves carry the impulses generated to the sacral spinal cord. Their increased level of activity (1) facilitates parasympathetic motor neurons in the sacral spinal cord, (2) stimulates contraction of the urinary bladder, and (3) stimulates interneurons that relay sensations to the cerebral cortex. As a result, we become consciously aware of the fluid pressure in the urinary bladder. The urge to urinate first develops when the urinary bladder contains approximately 200 ml of urine. Voluntary urination involves conscious relaxation of the external sphincter and subconscious facilitation of the micturition reflex. When the external urethral sphincter relaxes, feedback through the autonomic nervous system relaxes the internal urethral sphincter. Tensing of the abdominal and expiratory muscles increases abdominal pressures and assists in compressing the urinary bladder. At the end of a typical micturition, the urinary bladder contains less than 10 ml of urine. In the absence of voluntary relaxation of the external urethral sphincter, reflexive relaxation of both sphincters will eventually occur as the urinary bladder nears capacity.

CONCEPT CHECK

1. An obstruction of a ureter by a kidney stone would interfere with the flow of urine between what two points?
2. Explain how the lining of the urinary bladder allows the bladder to become distended.
3. Why are females more susceptible to urinary tract infections than males?
4. How is the urinary bladder held in place?

See blue "Answers" tab at back of book.

Clinical Note

Urinary Tract Infections **Urinary tract infections**, or **UTIs**, result from bacteria or fungi colonizing the urinary tract. The intestinal bacterium *Escherichia coli* is most often involved, and women are particularly susceptible to urinary tract infections because of the close proximity of the external urethral orifice to the anus. Sexual intercourse may also push bacteria into the urethra and, since the female urethra is relatively short, toward the urinary bladder.

The condition may be asymptomatic (without symptoms), but it can be detected by the presence of bacteria and blood cells in the urine. If inflammation of the urethral wall occurs, the condition is called **urethritis**, while inflammation of the lining of the urinary bladder represents **cystitis**. Many infections affect both regions to some degree. Urination becomes painful, a symptom known as **dysuria** (dis-Ū-rē-a), and the bladder becomes tender and sensitive to pressure. Despite the discomfort, the individual feels the urge to urinate frequently. Urinary tract infections usually respond to antibiotic therapies, although subsequent reinfections may occur.

In untreated cases, the bacteria may proceed along the ureters to the renal pelvis. The resulting inflammation of the walls of the renal pelvis produces **pyelitis** (pī-e-LĪ-tis). If the bacteria invade the renal cortex and medulla as well, **pyelonephritis** (pī-e-lō-ne-FRĪ-tis) results. Signs and symptoms of pyelonephritis include a high fever, intense pain on the affected side, vomiting, diarrhea, and the presence of blood cells and pus in the urine.

Aging and the Urinary System

In general, aging is associated with an increased incidence of kidney problems. Age-related changes in the urinary system include:

1. *A decline in the number of functional nephrons:* The total number of kidney nephrons drops by 30–40 percent between ages 25 and 85.
2. *A reduction in glomerular filtration:* This reduction results from decreased numbers of glomeruli, cumulative damage to the filtration apparatus in the remaining glomeruli, and reductions in renal blood flow.
3. *Reduced sensitivity to ADH:* With age the distal portions of the nephron and the entire collecting system become less responsive to ADH. With less reabsorption of water and sodium ions, urination becomes more frequent, and daily fluid requirements increase.
4. *Problems with the micturition reflex:* Several factors are involved in such problems:
   - **a.** The sphincter muscles lose muscle tone and become less effective at voluntarily retaining urine. This loss of tone leads to *incontinence*, a slow leakage of urine.
   - **b.** The ability to control micturition is often lost after a stroke, Alzheimer's disease, or other CNS problems affecting the cerebral cortex or hypothalamus.
   - **c.** In males, **urinary retention** may develop secondary to chronic inflammation of the prostate gland. In this condition swelling and distortion of prostatic tissues compress the prostatic urethra, restricting or preventing the flow of urine.

Embryology Summary

For an introduction to the development of the Urinary System, see Chapter 28 (Embryology and Human Development).

Clinical Case

THE URINARY SYSTEM

HOW COME SHE GOT REALLY SICK AND I DIDN'T?

Initial Examination

Julie is a third-year student on a small Midwestern college campus. It is "Sibling Weekend," and Julie has asked Danni, her 7-year-old sister, to stay with her on campus. She and Danni go the football game, the women's soccer match, and the movie on Saturday. Danni's greatest thrill, however, is going to Burrito Bob's for lunch. Burrito Bob's is a small, family-owned restaurant located in a small town 3 miles from Julie's college. Burrito Bob's became Danni's favorite restaurant when Julie first started college, and she always begs to eat there every time she travels with her parents to pick up Julie for semester break or drop her off afterward.

Two to three hours after lunch, both Danni and Julie start to feel nauseous and develop diarrhea. As the day progresses, their conditions worsen, prompting Julie to call home and ask for advice. At her father's urging, Julie drives Danni and herself to the emergency room around midnight. The emergency room physician examines Julie and Danni, and notes the following:

- Both have had loose bowel movements every 15 to 30 minutes for the past 5 to 6 hours.
- Julie has a temperature of 101°F (38°C); Danni's temperature is 101.5°F (38.5°C).
- Both have abdominal cramping.
- Stool samples are positive for blood.
- Complete blood count (CBC) demonstrates a white blood count (WBC) count in excess of 10,000 per mm^3.
- Stool samples from both individuals are sent for pathogenic bacterial culture.

The physician suspects bacterial food poisoning. Both patients are given IV fluid replacement in the ER and advice on oral fluids to consume at home. The physician will receive the results of the stool culture within 48–72 hours. The physician advises Julie and Danni about the proper way to handle food, including lettuce and undercooked meat.

He explains that improperly handled food may lead to increased bacterial growth in the food, which can overwhelm the gastrointestinal tract's defenses (such as stomach acidity) and cause food poisoning.

Three days later, Danni's parents are concerned. Although a telephone call to Julie confirms that she seems to be getting better, with no fever and reduced diarrhea, Danni, now back at home with her parents, still has a fever of 102°F (39°C) and persistent diarrhea. Danni has also developed widespread red spots in her skin, and she has become lethargic. They decide to call Danni's pediatrician, and he tells them to meet him at the emergency room immediately.

Follow-Up Examination

During the examination, the pediatrician explains to Danni's parents that he feels Danni might have developed a rare complication from the food poisoning that may, if not treated immediately, result in kidney failure. The physician notes the following:

- Fever of 102.1°F (39.5°C).
- Widespread petechiae.
- CBC confirms anemia, with hemoglobin of 7 g/dL.
- Urinalysis demonstrates proteinuria and the presence of WBCs, red blood cells (RBCs), and RBC casts in the urine.
- Blood urea nitrogen (BUN) and creatine are elevated.
- Renal ultrasound demonstrates the absence of any urinary obstruction.

Points to Consider

At one time or another, every system of the body plays an important role in presenting signs or symptoms, thereby enabling a physician to piece together the various clues that will ideally lead to a correct diagnosis of the patient. Both the patient's presenting symptoms and the physician's analysis and interpretation of the symptoms contribute to the detective work.

To consider the meaning of the information presented in the case above, you need to review the anatomical material covered in Chapter 26 on the urinary system. The questions below will guide you in your review. Think about and answer each one, referring back to Chapter 26 if you need help.

1. The nephron is composed of several parts, each with distinct functions in the formation of urine. Lab results of Danni's urine demonstrate the presence of several substances that are not found within the urine of a healthy individual. Are these substances normally found within the blood? If so, how could you account for their presence in Danni's urine?
2. The filtration process in the formation of urine involves three physical diffusion barriers. What are these barriers, and how do they accomplish their tasks?
3. Chapter 25 discussed the histological anatomy of the hollow organs of the digestive system. What histological layer of the large intestine must be damaged for blood to enter the lumen of the large intestine?

Clinical Case *continued*

Analysis and Interpretation

The information below answers the questions raised in the "Points to Consider" section. To review the material, refer to the pages in the chapter indicated by the link icons.

1. The nephron is composed of the renal corpuscle, the proximal convoluted tubule, the nephron loop (loop of Henle), the distal convoluted tubule, and the collecting system, pp. 698–703. The renal corpuscle filters blood, with the resulting filtrate containing metabolic wastes and other organic compounds. The main function of the proximal convoluted tubule is the reabsorption of organic nutrients, ions, and any plasma proteins that are present in the filtrate. The nephron loop is responsible for the reabsorption of water, sodium, and chloride. The distal convoluted tubule is an important site for the secretion of ions, acids, and other materials, as well as the reabsorption of sodium and calcium ions from the tubular fluids. The last segment of the nephron, the collecting system, is responsible for transporting the tubular fluid from the nephron to the renal pelvis, as well as making the final adjustments in osmotic pressure and volume, p. 703.
2. The filtration barrier within the renal corpuscle is composed of the capillary endothelium, the basal lamina, and the glomerular epithelium, pp. 699–703. The abnormal presence of plasma proteins and blood cells in Danni's urine may indicate damage to one or more components of this diffusion barrier.
3. The hollow organs of the digestive system are composed of the following layers: mucosa, submucosa, muscularis externa, and serosa. The inner lining, or mucosa, is composed of an epithelium moistened by glandular secretions. The underlying layer, the lamina propria, contains blood vessels, sensory nerve endings, lymphatic vessels, smooth muscle fibers, and scattered areas of lymphoid tissue. pp. 656, 675–679 If blood is entering the lumen of the hollow organs, the epithelial lining of the mucosa has been damaged.

Diagnosis

Danni is diagnosed with Hemolytic Uremic Syndrome, or HUS, the most common cause of acute renal failure in children. For unknown reasons, the number of cases in young adolescents and adults is significantly smaller than those in children age 2–7.

HUS is believed to result from damage to the endothelial cells in the renal corpuscle (Figure 26.12), causing plasma proteins, WBCs, RBCs, and RBC casts to be present in the urine in abnormal amounts.

In North America and Western Europe, 70 percent of HUS cases are secondary to a toxic strain of *Escherichia coli* bacterial infection, typically as a result of food poisoning. After the ingestion of the toxigenic type of *E. coli*, the bacteria adhere to the mucosal walls of the intestine. Research is ongoing to determine the reasons bacteria sometimes spread from the digestive tract to the glomerulus of the kidney. Following the adhesion of *E. coli* to the endothelial cells of the renal corpuscle, all components of the filtration barrier are damaged, presumably from bacterial toxins that target the vascular endothelium.

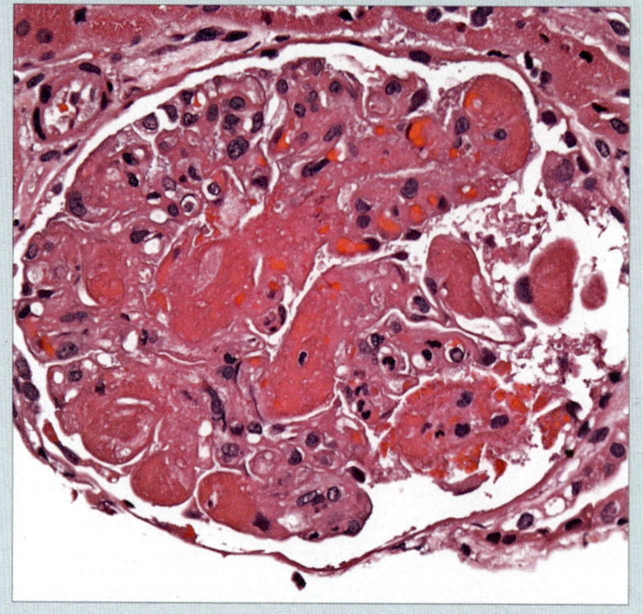

Figure 26.12 Histology of a Renal Glomerulus of a Patient with a Condition Similar to Danni's.

Successful treatment for HUS involves (1) rapid diagnosis of the condition; (2) maintenance of fluid volume and proper electrolyte balance; (3) appropriate treatment of the patient's anemia; and (4) observation and treatment, if needed, of any hypertension that might develop as a result of the syndrome. The use of antibiotics is not recommended because they have not been shown to improve recovery and because of the added strain they might pose to the kidney. Most young patients recover within 1–3 weeks following diagnosis. However, some patients do not recover, and acute renal failure progresses, ultimately resulting in kidney failure and the need for a kidney transplant. ■

CLINICAL CASE TERMS

blood urea nitrogen (BUN): Amount of nitrogen, in the form of urea, found in the blood.

creatine: The breakdown product of phosphocreatine.

diarrhea: Abnormally frequent evacuation of watery stools.

escherichia coli (esh-e-RIK-ē-a kō-lī): A bacteria normally found within the intestine of humans and other vertebrates; a cause of food poisoning and diarrhea.

petechiae (pe-TĒ-kē-ē; **petechia**, singular): Minute red, hemorrhagic spots on the skin of pinpoint size that do not lighten by pressure.

proteinuria: Presence of protein in the urine.

RBC casts: Clumps of red blood cells in various stages of degeneration that form in the nephron tubules; caused by glomerular bleeding and damage and found in the urine.

CLINICAL TERMS

automatic bladder: A clinical condition in which the micturition reflex remains intact, but voluntary control of the external urethral sphincter is lost due to CNS damage. Thus, the person cannot prevent the reflexive emptying of the urinary bladder.

calculi (KAL-kū-lī): "Kidney stones" formed from calcium deposits, magnesium salts, or crystals of uric acid.

cystitis: Inflammation of the urinary bladder lining, usually from infection.

dysuria (dis-Ū-rē-a): Painful urination.

hemodialysis (hē-mō-dī-AL-i-sis): A technique in which an artificial membrane is used to regulate the composition of the blood and remove waste products.

incontinence (in-KON-ti-nens): An inability to voluntarily control urination.

nephrolithiasis (nef-rō-li-THĪ-a-sis): The presence of kidney stones.

pyelogram (PĪ-el-ō-gram): An image obtained by taking an x-ray of the kidneys after a radiopaque compound has been administered.

urethritis: Inflammation of the urethral wall.

urinary obstruction: Blockage of the conducting system by a calculus or other factors.

urinary tract infection (UTI): Urinary tract inflammation caused by bacteria or fungal infection.

STUDY OUTLINE

Introduction 694

1. The functions of the urinary system include (1) regulating plasma concentrations of ions; (2) regulating blood volume and pressure by adjusting the volume of water lost and releasing erythropoietin and renin; (3) helping stabilize blood pH; (4) conserving nutrients; (5) eliminating organic wastes; and (6) synthesizing **calcitriol**.
2. The **urinary system** includes the **kidneys**, the **ureters**, the **urinary bladder**, and the **urethra**. The kidneys produce **urine** (a fluid containing water, ions, and soluble compounds); during **urination (micturition)** urine is forced out of the body. *(see Figure 26.1)*

The Kidneys 694

1. The kidneys are located on either side of the vertebral column between the last thoracic and third lumbar vertebrae. *(see Figures 26.1 and 26.2)*
2. The position of the kidneys in the abdominal cavity is maintained by (1) the overlying peritoneum, (2) contact with adjacent visceral organs, and (3) supporting connective tissues. The three concentric layers of connective tissue are the **fibrous capsule**, which covers the outer surface of the organ; the **perinephric fat**, which surrounds the fibrous capsule; and the **renal fascia**, which anchors the kidney to surrounding structures. *(see Figure 26.3)*

Superficial Anatomy of the Kidney 694

3. The ureter and renal blood vessels are attached to the **hilum** of the kidney. The inner layer of the fibrous capsule lines the **renal sinus**. *(see Figure 26.3)*

Sectional Anatomy of the Kidney 694

4. The kidney is divided into an outer **renal cortex**, a central **renal medulla**, and an inner **renal sinus**. The medulla contains 6–18 **renal pyramids**, whose tips, or **renal papillae**, project into the renal sinus. **Renal columns** composed of cortex separate adjacent pyramids. A **renal lobe** contains a renal pyramid, the overlying area of renal cortex, and adjacent tissues of the renal columns. *(see Figure 26.3a)*
5. The **minor calyces** are continuous with the **major calyces**. These spaces lead into the **renal pelvis**, which is continuous with the **ureter**. *(see Figure 26.3a–c)*

The Blood Supply to the Kidneys 696

6. The vasculature of the kidneys includes the **renal**, **segmental**, **interlobar**, **arcuate**, and **cortical radiate arteries** to the **afferent arterioles** that supply the nephrons. From the nephrons, blood flows into the **cortical radiate**, **arcuate**, **interlobar**, and **renal veins**. *(see Figures 26.4 and 26.5b)*

Innervation of the Kidneys 696

7. The kidneys and ureters are innervated by **renal nerves**. Sympathetic activation regulates glomerular blood flow and pressure, stimulates renin release, and accelerates sodium ion and water reabsorption.

Histology of the Kidney 698

8. The **nephron** (the basic functional unit in the kidney) consists of a **renal tubule** that empties into the **collecting system**. From the **renal corpuscle**, the **tubular fluid** travels through the **proximal convoluted tubule (PCT)**, the **nephron loop (loop of Henle)**, and the **distal convoluted tubule (DCT)**. It then flows through the **connecting tubule**, **collecting duct**, and **papillary duct** to reach the renal minor calyx. *(see Figure 26.6)*
9. Roughly 85 percent of the nephrons are **cortical nephrons** found within the cortex. The nephron loops are short, and the **efferent arteriole** provides blood to the **peritubular capillaries** that surround the renal tubules. The **juxtamedullary nephrons** are closer to the medulla, with their nephron loops extending deep into the renal pyramids. *(see Figures 26.4c,d/26.7a)*
10. Nephrons are responsible for (1) production of filtrate, (2) reabsorption of organic nutrients, and (3) reabsorption of water and ions. The **parietal epithelium** lines the outer wall of the renal corpuscle. Blood arrives via the relatively large **afferent arteriole** and departs in the relatively small **efferent arteriole**. *(see Figure 26.8c)*
11. The renal corpuscle contains the capillary knot of the **glomerulus** and **glomerular capsule**. At the glomerulus, **podocytes** of the visceral epithelium wrap their "feet" around the capillaries. The **secondary processes** of the podocytes are separated by narrow **filtration slits**. The **capsular space** separates the **parietal** and **visceral epithelia**. The glomerular capillaries are *fenestrated capillaries*. The dense layer of the basal lamina is unusually thick. Blood arrives at the **vascular pole** of the renal corpuscle via the afferent arteriole and departs in the **efferent arteriole**. From the efferent arteriole blood enters the peritubular capillaries and the **vasa recta** that follow the nephron loops in the medulla. *(see Figure 26.8)*
12. The proximal convoluted tubule (PCT) actively reabsorbs nutrients, ions, plasma proteins, and electrolytes from the tubular fluid. The nephron loop includes a **descending limb** and an **ascending limb**; each limb contains a **thick segment** and a **thin segment**. The ascending limb delivers fluid to the distal convoluted tubule (DCT), which actively secretes ions and reabsorbs sodium ions from the urine. Reabsorption in the PCT and the nephron loop reclaims all of the organic nutrients, 85 percent of the water, and more than 90 percent of the Na and Cl ions. *(see Figures 26.6 to 26.8)*
13. The **distal convoluted tubule** is an important site for the secretion of ions and other materials and the reabsorption of sodium ions. *(see Figures 26.6 to 26.8)*
14. The **juxtaglomerular complex** (*juxtaglomerular apparatus*) is composed of the **macula densa**, **juxtaglomerular cells**, and the **extraglomerular mesangial cells**. The juxtaglomerular complex secretes the hormones *renin* and *erythropoietin*. *(see Figure 26.8c)*
15. The DCT opens into the **collecting system**. The collecting system consists of *connecting tubules*, *collecting ducts*, and *papillary ducts*. In addition to transporting fluid from the nephron to the renal pelvis, the collecting system adjusts the osmotic concentrations and volume. *(see Figures 26.6 and 26.7a,d,e,f)*

Structures for Urine Transport, Storage, and Elimination 704

1. Tubular fluid modification and urine production end when the fluid enters the minor calyx in the renal sinus. The rest of the urinary system (the *ureters, urinary bladder,* and *urethra*) is responsible for transporting, storing, and eliminating the urine. *(see Figure 26.10)*

The Ureters 704

2. The ureters extend from the renal pelvis to the urinary bladder and are responsible for transporting urine to the bladder. The wall of each ureter consists of an inner mucosal layer, a middle muscular layer, and an outer connective tissue layer (adventitia). *(see Figures 26.1/26.2/26.3/26.9c/26.10)*

The Urinary Bladder 704

3. The **urinary bladder** is a hollow muscular organ that serves as a storage reservoir for urine. The bladder is stabilized by the **median umbilical ligament** and the **lateral umbilical ligaments.** Internal features include the **trigone,** the **neck,** and the **internal urethral sphincter.** The mucosal lining contains prominent **rugae** (folds). Contraction of the **detrusor muscle** compresses the urinary bladder and expels the urine into the urethra. *(see Figures 26.10/26.11)*

The Urethra 706

4. The urethra extends from the neck of the urinary bladder to the exterior. In the female, the urethra is short and ends in the **external urethral orifice** (external urethral opening), and in the male, the urethra has **prostatic, membranous,** and **penile** sections; the spongy urethra ends at the external urethral orifice. In both sexes, as the urethra passes through the urogenital diaphragm, a circular band of skeletal muscles forms the **external urethral sphincter,** which is under voluntary control.
5. The female urethral lining is usually a transitional epithelium near the urinary bladder; the rest is usually a stratified squamous epithelium. The urethral lining of males varies from a transitional epithelium at the urinary bladder, to a stratified columnar or a pseudostratified epithelium, and then to stratified squamous epithelium near the external urethral orifice. *(see Figures 26.10/26.11)*

The Micturition Reflex and Urination 708

6. The process of urination is coordinated by the **micturition reflex,** which is initiated by stretch receptors in the bladder wall. Voluntary urination involves coupling this reflex with the voluntary relaxation of the external urethral sphincter.

Aging and the Urinary System 708

1. Aging is usually associated with increased kidney problems. Age-related changes in the urinary system include (1) a declining number of functional nephrons, (2) reduced glomerular filtration, (3) reduced sensitivity to ADH, and (4) problems with the micturition reflex (**urinary retention** may develop in men whose prostate glands are enlarged).

CHAPTER REVIEW

For answers to the Concept Check and Chapter Review questions, go to the blue "Answers" tab at the back of the book.

Level 1 Reviewing Facts and Terms

Match each numbered item with the most closely related lettered item. Use letters for answers in the spaces provided.

Column A	Column B
___ 1. urination	a. muscle of the urinary bladder
___ 2. detrusor muscle	b. basic functional unit of a kidney
___ 3. macula densa	c. micturition
___ 4. medulla	d. fibrous tunic of the kidney
___ 5. hilum	e. kidney stones
___ 6. nephron	f. consists of 6–18 renal pyramids
___ 7. calculi	g. dense outer layer of the kidney
___ 8. vasa recta	h. series of capillaries
___ 9. fibrous capsule	i. region of the juxtaglomerular complex
___ 10. renal fascia	j. site of entry/exit for the renal artery and vein

11. Each kidney is protected/stabilized by the
    (a) fibrous capsule only
    (b) perinephric fat and fibrous capsule only
    (c) perinephric fat only
    (d) fibrous capsule, perinephric fat, and renal fascia

12. The urinary system does all of the following except
    (a) secrete excess glucose molecules
    (b) regulate blood volume
    (c) contribute to stabilizing blood pH
    (d) eliminate organic waste products

13. The renal sinus is
    (a) the innermost layer of kidney tissue
    (b) a conical structure located in the renal medulla
    (c) an internal cavity lined by the fibrous capsule and located inside the hilum
    (d) a large branch of the renal pelvis

14. Which vessels form the plexus that supplies the proximal and distal convoluted tubules?
    (a) segmental arteries (b) peritubular capillaries
    (c) cortical radiate arteries (d) arcuate arteries

15. The process of filtration occurs at the
    (a) proximal convoluted tubule
    (b) renal corpuscle
    (c) collecting duct
    (d) nephron loop

16. The ability to form concentrated urine depends on the functions of the
    (a) proximal convoluted tubule
    (b) distal convoluted tubule
    (c) collecting duct
    (d) nephron loop

17. The ureters and urinary bladder are lined by ______________________ epithelium.
   (a) stratified squamous (b) pseudostratified columnar
   (c) simple cuboidal (d) transitional

18. Each of the following is a normal component of urine except
   (a) hydrogen ions (b) urea
   (c) large proteins (d) salts

19. A ligament that extends from the anterior and superior border of the bladder to the umbilicus is the
   (a) round ligament
   (b) square ligament
   (c) median umbilical ligament
   (d) lateral umbilical ligaments

20. The portion of the nephron that attaches to the collecting duct is the
   (a) nephron loop (b) proximal convoluted tubule
   (c) distal convoluted tubule (d) collecting duct

Level 2 Reviewing Concepts

1. What is the significance of the slit-like, rather than rounded, openings of the entrance of the ureters into the bladder?
   (a) they can distort more easily to permit urine to move in or out
   (b) the shape prevents urine backflow toward the ureters when the urinary bladder contracts
   (c) the opening is compressed between the middle and lateral umbilical ligaments because these structures support this part of the ureter
   (d) there is no significance; the shape occurs because of the position only
2. Problems with the micturition reflex in older individuals include
   (a) increased tone in the sphincter muscles, preventing easy emptying of the urinary bladder
   (b) urinary retention in males because of prostate enlargement
   (c) increased sensitivity to ADH
   (d) increased retention of sodium ions
3. How will kidney function be altered in an individual who has more than one renal artery and vein per side, with the same overall volume of possible lumen space entering the kidney at the hilum?
   (a) these kidneys will be able to handle blood at higher pressures in this individual than in others
   (b) as long as the arteries and veins in the individual are normal, kidney function will be normal
   (c) greater blood flow will occur through these kidneys
   (d) these kidneys will be more flexible in the amounts of urine they can produce at any given time
4. Where is the glomerulus located in a nephron?
5. What is unique about the glomerular epithelium?
6. What does the juxtaglomerular complex secrete?
7. What is the trigone of the urinary bladder?
8. Which urethral sphincter is under voluntary control?
9. What is the primary function of the proximal convoluted tubule?
10. Identify the purpose of rugae in the urinary bladder.

Level 3 Critical Thinking

1. Although neural control of the external urethral sphincter does not completely develop until 2 to 3 years of age, the internal urethral sphincter is functional at birth. Why is premature toilet training often a fruitless and frustrating experience for both parents and child?
2. Jennifer was a champion marathon runner until renal failure forced her to retire from running. During her last two marathons, lab tests confirmed she experienced acute kidney dysfunction. How could long-distance running cause this condition?
3. Why does a pregnant woman have a greater need to urinate frequently than she does when she is not pregnant?

27

The Reproductive System

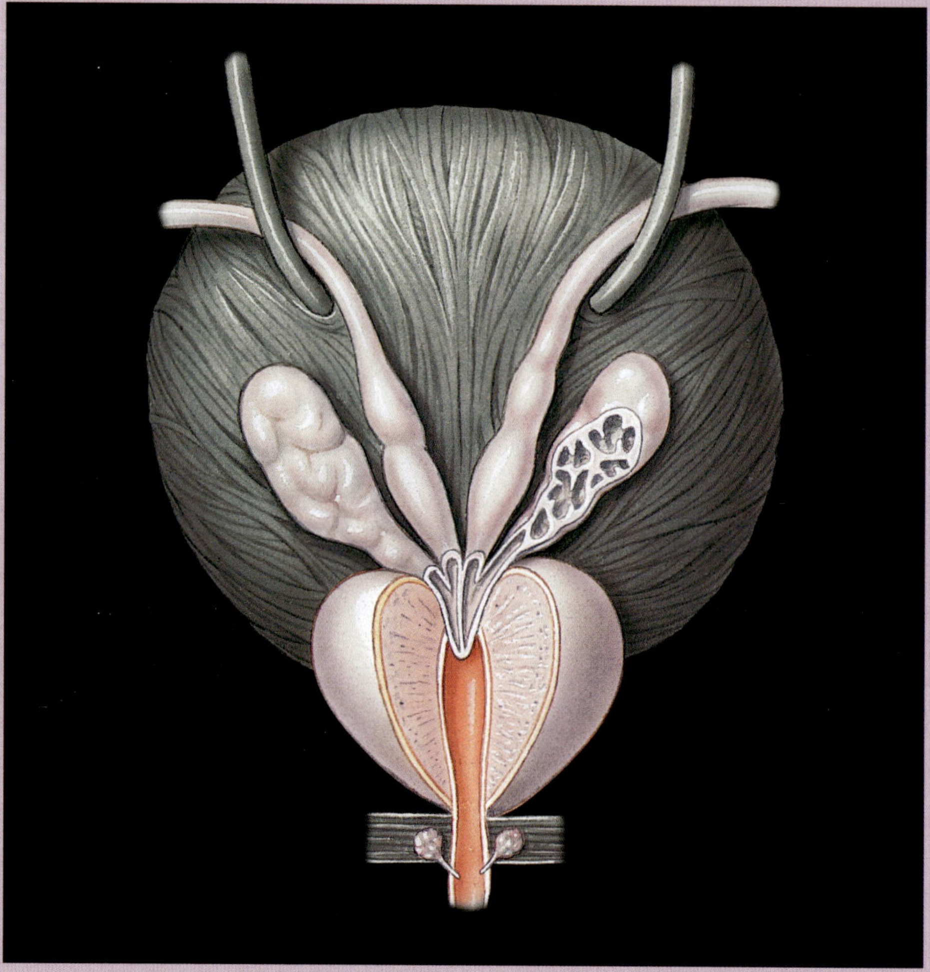

CHAPTER OBJECTIVES

1. Describe the function of the reproductive system.
2. Describe and compare the general organization of the male and female reproductive systems.
3. Identify and describe the location, gross anatomy, and functions of the principal structures of the male reproductive system.
4. Describe the histological features of the gonads, ducts, and accessory glands of the male reproductive system.
5. Distinguish between spermatogenesis and spermiogenesis and discuss the storage and transport of sperm cells.
6. Discuss the components and properties of semen.
7. Distinguish among the physiological processes of erection, emission, and ejaculation.
8. Identify and describe the location, gross anatomy, and functions of the principal structures of the female reproductive system.
9. Describe the histological features of the gonads, ducts, and accessory glands of the female reproductive system.
10. Describe the endometrial changes that accompany the uterine cycle.
11. Discuss oogenesis and ovulation and trace the path of oocytes following ovulation.
12. Describe the ovarian and uterine cycles and identify the hormones that regulate and coordinate these cycles.
13. Describe the gross anatomy and histology of the mammary glands.
14. Describe the anatomical and hormonal changes that accompany pregnancy.
15. Compare age-related changes in the male and female reproductive systems.

An individual's life span can be measured in decades, but the human species has survived for millions of years through the activities of the reproductive system. The human reproductive system produces, stores, nourishes, and transports functional male and female reproductive cells, or **gametes** (GAM-ēts). The combination of the genetic material provided by a **sperm** from the father and an immature **ovum** (Ō-vum) from the mother occurs shortly after **fertilization**, or *conception*. Fertilization produces a **zygote** (ZĪ-gōt), a single cell whose growth, development, and repeated divisions will, in approximately nine months, produce an infant who will grow and mature as part of the next generation. The reproductive system also produces sex hormones that affect the structure and function of all other systems.

This chapter will describe the structures and mechanisms involved in the production and maintenance of gametes and, in the female, the development and support of the developing embryo and fetus. Chapter 28, the last chapter in the text, will begin at fertilization and consider the process of development.

Organization of the Reproductive System

The reproductive system includes the following:

- Reproductive organs, or **gonads** (GŌ-nadz), which produce gametes and hormones.
- A reproductive tract, consisting of ducts that receive, store, and transport the gametes.
- Accessory glands and organs that secrete fluids into the ducts of the reproductive system or into other excretory ducts.
- Perineal structures associated with the reproductive system. These perineal structures are collectively known as the **external genitalia** (jen-i-TĀ-lē-a).

The male and female reproductive systems are functionally quite different. In the adult male, the gonads, called *testes* (TES-tēz; singular, *testis*), secrete sex hormones called *androgens*, principally *testosterone*, and produce one-half billion sperm per day. p. 520 After storage, mature sperm travel along a lengthy duct system where they are mixed with the secretions of accessory glands, forming the mixture known as *semen* (SĒ-men). During *ejaculation* (ē-jak-ū-LĀ-shun), the semen is expelled from the body.

In adult females the gonads, or *ovaries*, typically produce only one immature gamete, or *oocyte*, per month. The oocyte travels along short *uterine tubes* (*oviducts*) that open into the muscular *uterus* (Ū-ter-us). A short passageway, the *vagina* (va-JĪ-na), connects the uterus with the exterior. During intercourse, male ejaculation introduces semen into the vagina, and the sperm cells may ascend the female reproductive tract, where they may encounter an oocyte and begin the process of fertilization.

Anatomy of the Male Reproductive System [Figure 27.1]

The principal structures of the male reproductive system are shown in **Figure 27.1**. Sperm cells, or *spermatozoa* (sper-ma-tō-ZŌ-a), leave the testes and travel along a duct system that includes the *epididymis* (ep-i-DID-i-mus); the *ductus deferens* (DUK-tus DEF-e-renz), or *vas deferens*; the *ejaculatory* (ē-JAK-ū-la-tōr-ē) *duct*; and the *urethra* before leaving the body. Accessory organs, notably the *seminal* (SEM-i-nal) *glands*, the *prostate* (PROS-tāt) *gland*, and the *bulbo-urethral* (bul-bō-ū-RĒ-thral) *glands* secrete into the ejaculatory ducts and urethra. The external genitalia include the *scrotum* (SKRŌ-tum), which encloses the testes, and the *penis* (PĒ-nis), an erectile organ through which the distal portion of the urethra passes.

The Testes [Figures 27.1/27.3]

Each testis has the shape of a flattened egg roughly 5 cm (2 in.) long, 3 cm (1.2 in.) wide, and 2.5 cm (1 in.) thick. Each has a weight of 10–15 g (0.35–0.53 oz). The testes hang within the **scrotum**, a pouch of skin suspended inferior to the perineum and anterior to the anus. Note the location and relation of the testes in sagittal section (**Figure 27.1**) and in frontal section (**Figure 27.3**).

Descent of the Testes [Figure 27.2]

During development, the testes form inside the body cavity adjacent to the kidneys. The relative positions of these organs change as the fetus enlarges, resulting in a gradual movement of the testes inferiorly and anteriorly toward the anterior abdominal wall. The **gubernaculum testis** is a cord of connective tissue and muscle fibers that extends from the inferior part of each testis to the posterior wall of a small, inferior pocket of the peritoneum. As growth proceeds, the gubernacula do not elongate, and the testes are held in position (**Figure 27.2**). During the seventh developmental month (1) growth continues at a rapid pace, and (2) circulating hormones stimulate contraction of the gubernaculum testis. Over this period the relative position of the testes changes further, and they move through the abdominal musculature, accompanied by small pockets of the peritoneal cavity. This process is known as the **descent of the testes**.

As it moves through the body wall, each testis is accompanied by the ductus deferens, the testicular blood vessels, nerves, and lymphatics. Once the testes have descended, the ducts, vessels, nerves, and lymphatics remain bundled together within the *spermatic cords*.

The Spermatic Cords [Figure 27.3]

The **spermatic cords** consist of layers of fascia, tough connective tissue, and muscle enclosing the blood vessels, nerves, and lymphatics supplying the testes. Each spermatic cord begins at the *deep inguinal ring*, extends through the *inguinal canal*, exits at the *superficial inguinal ring*, and descends to the testes within the scrotum (**Figure 27.3**). The spermatic cords form during the descent of the testes. Each spermatic cord contains the ductus deferens, the **testicular artery**, the **pampiniform** (pam-PIN-i-form; *pampinus*, tendril + *forma*, form) **plexus** of the **testicular vein**, and the **ilioinguinal** and **genitofemoral nerves** from the lumbar plexus. pp. 378, 590

The narrow canals linking the scrotal chambers with the peritoneal cavity are called the **inguinal canals**. These passageways usually close, but the persistence of the spermatic cords creates weak points in the abdominal wall that remain throughout life. As a result, *inguinal hernias*, discussed in Chapter 10, are relatively common in males. p. 281 The inguinal canals in females are very small, containing only the ilioinguinal nerves and the round ligaments of the uterus. The abdominal wall is nearly intact, and inguinal hernias in women are rare.

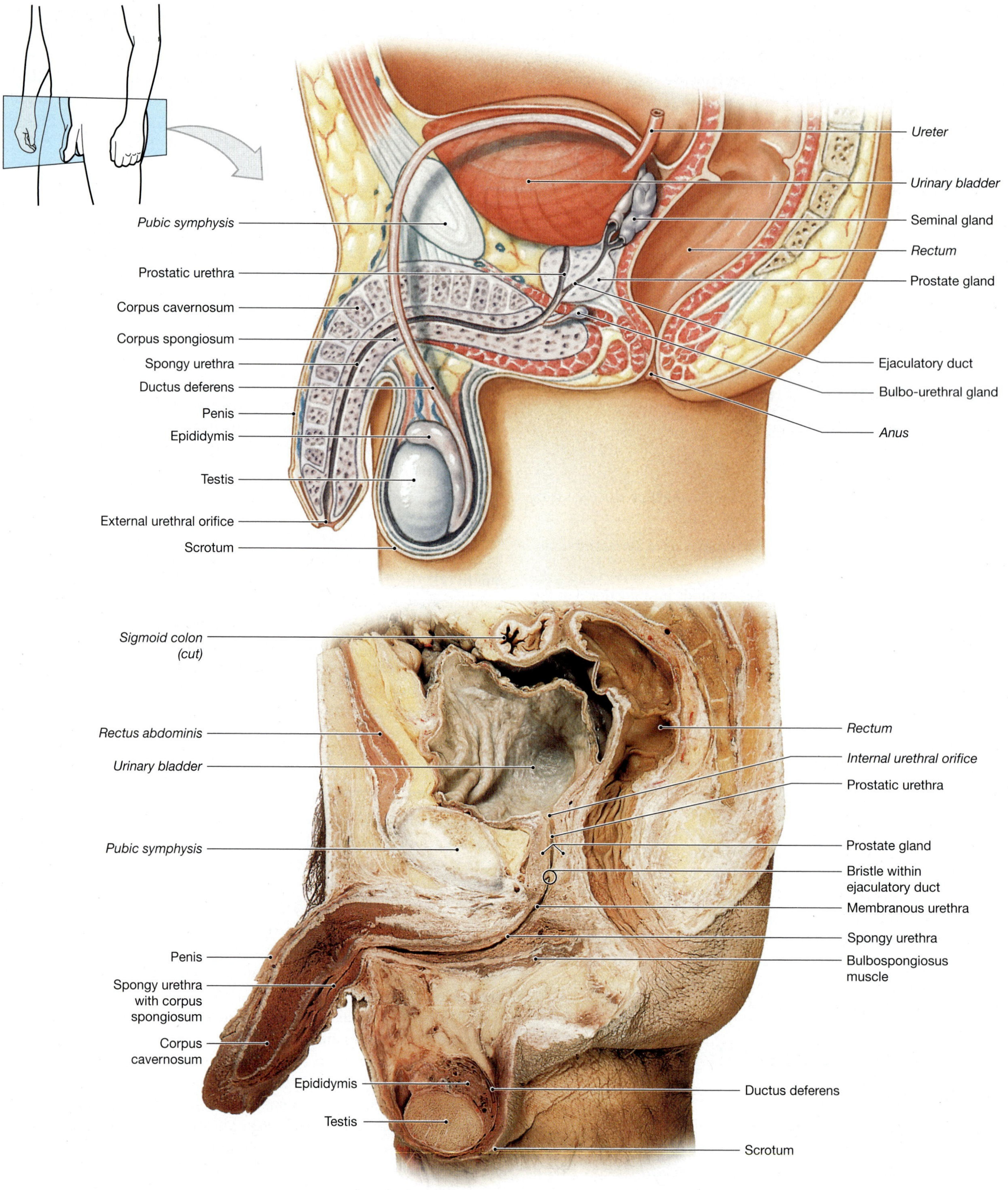

Figure 27.1 The Male Reproductive System, Part I

The male reproductive system as seen in sagittal section. The diagrammatic view shows several intact organs on the left side; this should help you to interpret the cadaver section.

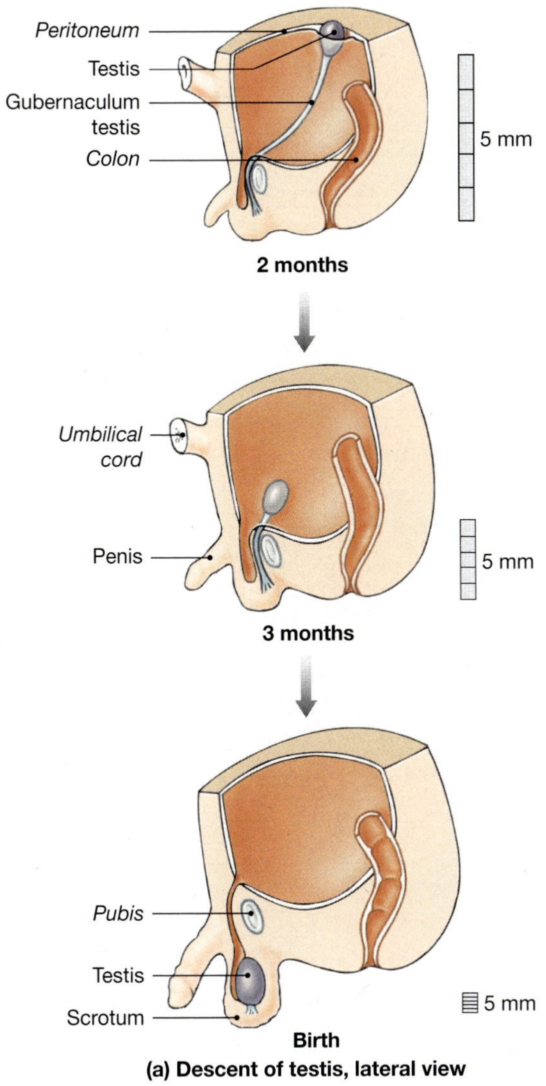

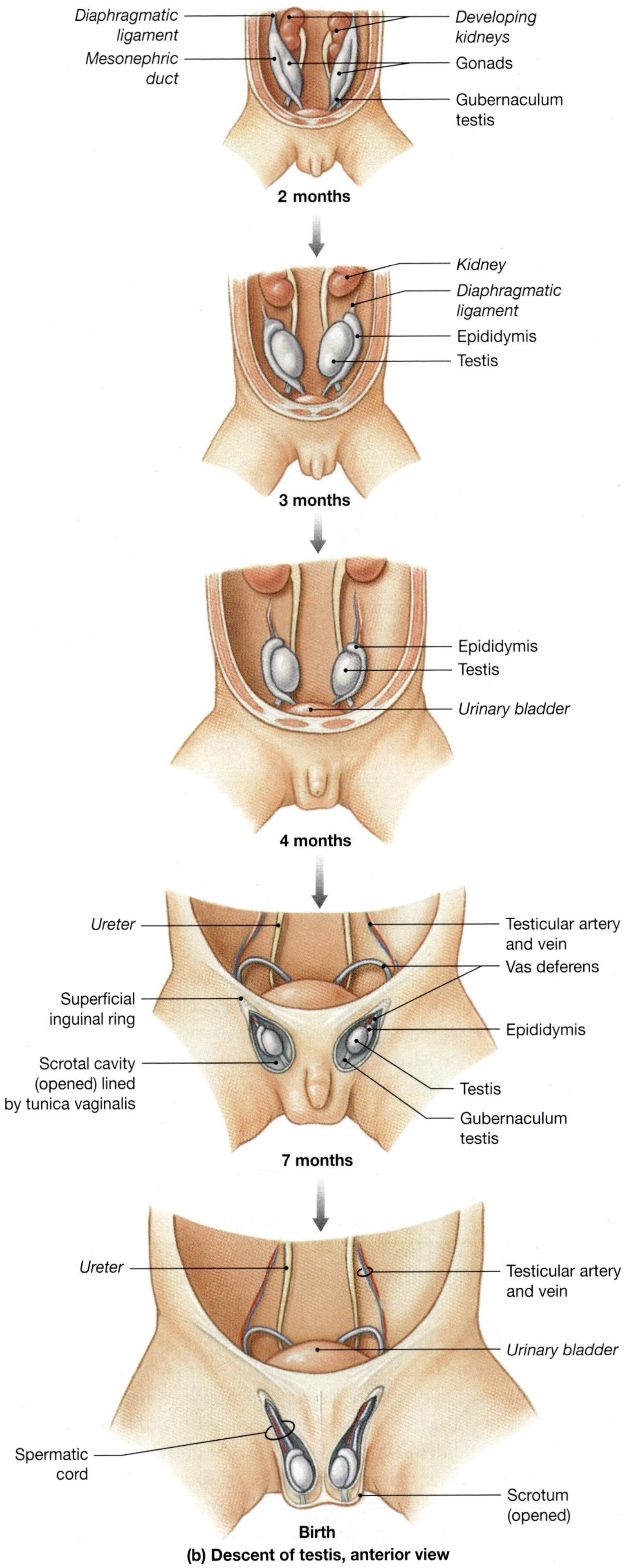

Figure 27.2 The Descent of the Testes
(a) Diagrammatic sectional views. Note the scale bar to the right of each image. **(b)** Anterior views of the opened abdomen at representative stages in the descent of the testes.

The Scrotum and the Position of the Testes [Figures 27.3/27.4a] The scrotum is divided internally into two separate chambers. The partition between the two is marked externally by a raised thickening in the scrotal surface, a continuation of the **perineal raphe** (RĀ-fē) that extends along the middle of the perineum from the anus, across the scrotum, and along the anterior surface of the penis (Figures 27.3 and 27.4a). Each testis occupies a separate compartment, or **scrotal cavity**, with a narrow space separating the inner surface of the scrotum from the outer surface of the testis. The **tunica vaginalis** (TOO-ni-ka vaj-i-NAL-is) is a serous membrane that covers the outside of each testis and lines the scrotal cavity. This membrane reduces friction between the opposing surfaces.

The scrotum consists of a thin layer of skin and the underlying superficial fascia. The dermis of the scrotum contains a layer of smooth muscle, the **dartos** (DAR-tōs) **muscle**. Its tonic contraction causes the characteristic wrinkling of the scrotal surface and assists in elevation of the testes. A layer of skeletal muscle, the **cremaster** (kre-MAS-ter) **muscle**, lies deep to the dermis. Contraction of the cremaster tenses the scrotum and pulls the testes closer to the body. These contractions are controlled by the *cremasteric reflex*. Contraction occurs during sexual arousal and in response

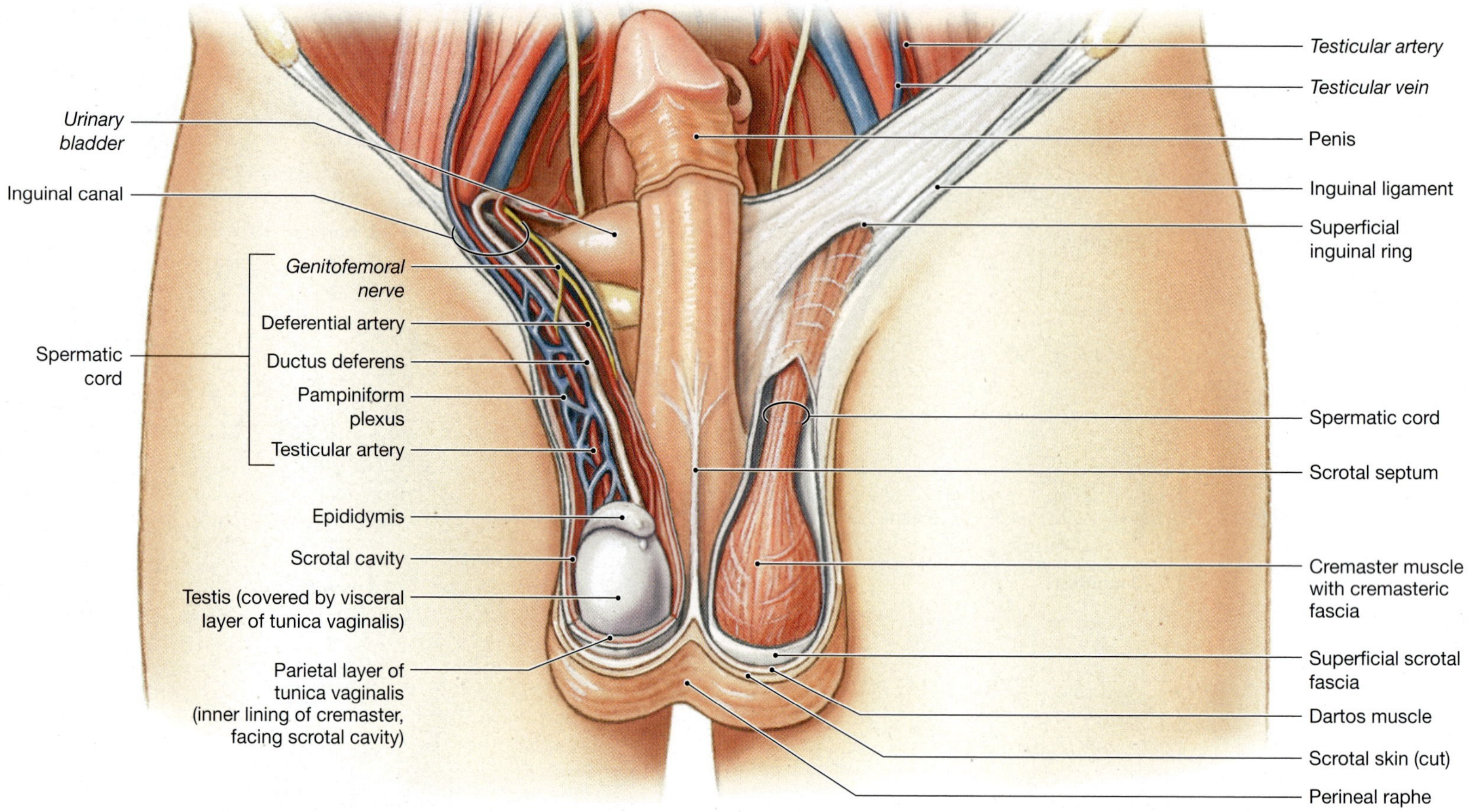

Figure 27.3 The Male Reproductive System, Part II
Diagrammatic anterior view of the gonads, external genitalia, and associated structures in a male.

to changes in temperature. Normal sperm development in the testes requires temperatures around 1.1°C (2°F) lower than those found elsewhere in the body. The cremaster moves the testes away from or toward the body as needed to maintain acceptable testicular temperatures. When air or body temperatures rise, the cremaster relaxes and the testes then move away from the body. Cooling the scrotum, as when entering a cold swimming pool, initiates the cremasteric reflex—cremasteric contractions that pull the testes closer to the body and keep testicular temperatures from falling.

The scrotum is richly supplied with sensory and motor nerves from the *hypogastric plexus* and branches of the *ilioinguinal nerves*, the *genitofemoral nerves*, and the *pudendal nerves*. p. 378 The vascular supply to the scrotum includes the **internal pudendal arteries** (supplied by the internal iliac arteries), the **external pudendal arteries** (supplied by the femoral arteries), and the *cremasteric branch* of the **inferior epigastric arteries** (supplied by the external iliac arteries). p. 591 The names and distributions of the veins follow those of the arteries.

Structure of the Testes [Figure 27.4]

The **tunica albuginea** (TOO-ni-ka al-bū-JIN-ē-a) is a dense fibrous layer that surrounds the testis and is covered by the tunica vaginalis. This fibrous capsule is rich in collagen fibers that are continuous with those surrounding the adjacent epididymis. The collagen fibers of the tunica albuginea also extend into the interior of the testis, forming fibrous partitions, or *septa* (Figure 27.4). These septa converge toward the **mediastinum** of the testis. The mediastinum supports the blood vessels and lymphatics supplying the testis and the ducts that collect and transport sperm into the epididymis.

Histology of the Testes [Figures 27.4/27.5c,d/27.7a]

The septa partition the testis into compartments called **lobules**. Roughly 800 slender, tightly coiled **seminiferous** (sem-i-NIF-er-us) **tubules** are distributed among the lobules (Figure 27.4). Each tubule averages around 80 cm (31 in.) in length, and a typical testis contains nearly one-half mile of seminiferous tubules. Sperm production occurs within these tubules.

Each seminiferous tubule is U-shaped and connected to a single **straight tubule** that enters the mediastinum of the testis (Figures 27.4a and 27.7a). Within the mediastinum, straight tubules are extensively interconnected, forming a maze of passageways known as the **rete** (RĒ-tē; *rete*, net) **testis**. Fifteen to 20 large **efferent ductules** connect the rete testis to the epididymis.

Because the seminiferous tubules are tightly coiled, histological preparations most often show them in transverse section. A delicate capsule surrounds each tubule, and loose connective tissue fills the external spaces between the tubules. Within those spaces are numerous blood vessels and large **interstitial cells** *(interstitial cells of Leydig)* (Figure 27.5c,d). Interstitial cells produce male sex hormones, called *androgens*. p. 520 *Testosterone* is the most important androgen. Testosterone functions to (1) stimulate spermatogenesis; (2) promote the physical and functional maturation of spermatozoa; (3) maintain the accessory organs of the male reproductive tract; (4) cause development of secondary sexual characteristics by influencing the development and maturation of nonreproductive structures such as the distribution of facial hair and adipose tissue, muscle mass, and total body size; (5) stimulate growth and metabolism throughout the body; and (6) influence brain development by stimulating sexual behaviors and sexual drive.

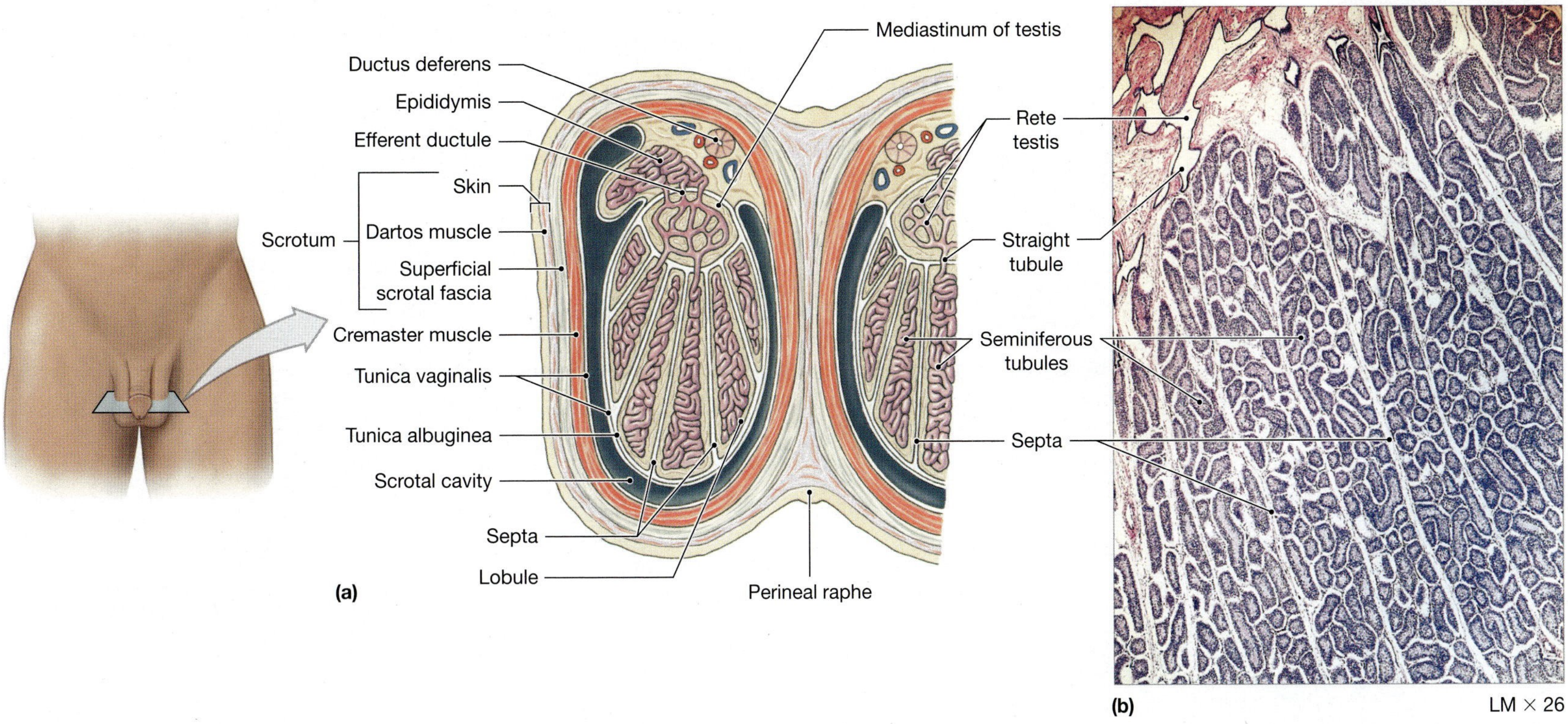

Figure 27.4 Structure of the Testes
(a) Diagrammatic horizontal section showing the anatomical relationships of the testes within the scrotal cavities. The connective tissues surrounding the seminiferous tubules and the rete testis are not shown. **(b)** General histological view of septae separating seminiferous tubules. (LM × 26)

Spermatogenesis and Meiosis [Figure 27.5]

Sperm cells, or spermatozoa, are produced through the process of **spermatogenesis** (sper-ma-tō-JEN-e-sis). Spermatogenesis begins at the outermost layer of cells in the seminiferous tubules. Stem cells called **spermatogonia** (sper-ma-tō-GŌ-nē-a) form during embryonic development but remain dormant until puberty. Beginning at sexual maturation, spermatogonia divide throughout the individual's reproductive years. As each division occurs, one of the daughter cells remains in the outer layer of the seminiferous tubule, as an undifferentiated stem cell, while the other cell is pushed toward the lumen. The latter cell differentiates into a **primary spermatocyte** (sper-MA-tō-sīt) that prepares to begin **meiosis** (mī-Ō-sis), a form of cell division that produces gametes containing half the normal number of chromosomes. Because they contain only one member of each pair of chromosomes, gametes are called **haploid** (HAP-loyd; *haplo*, single).

Meiosis is a special form of cell division that produces gametes. Mitosis and meiosis differ significantly in terms of the nuclear events. In mitosis a single division produces two identical daughter cells, each containing 23 pairs of chromosomes. In meiosis a pair of divisions produces four different, haploid gametes, each containing 23 individual chromosomes.

In the testes, the first step in meiosis is the division of a primary spermatocyte to produce a pair of **secondary spermatocytes**. Each secondary spermatocyte divides to produce a pair of **spermatids** (SPER-ma-tidz). As a result, four spermatids are produced for every primary spermatocyte that enters meiosis (**Figure 27.5a,b**). Spermatogonia, spermatocytes undergoing meiosis, and spermatids are depicted in **Figure 27.5c,d.**

Spermatogenesis is directly stimulated by testosterone and indirectly stimulated by FSH (follicle-stimulating hormone), as detailed shortly. Testosterone is produced by interstitial cells of the testis in response to LH (luteinizing hormone). ∞ p. 520

Spermiogenesis [Figure 27.5b–d]

Each spermatid matures into a single **spermatozoon** (sper-ma-tō-ZŌ-on), or sperm cell, by a maturation process called **spermiogenesis** (**Figure 27.5b–d**). During spermiogenesis, spermatids are embedded within the cytoplasm of large **nurse cells** *(Sertoli cells)*. Nurse cells are attached to the basal lamina at the tubular capsule and extend toward the lumen between the spermatocytes undergoing meiosis. As spermiogenesis proceeds, the spermatids gradually develop the appearance of mature spermatozoa. At *spermiation*, a spermatozoon becomes detached from the nurse cell and enters the lumen of the seminiferous tubule. This process marks the end of spermiogenesis. The entire process, from spermatogonial division to spermiation, takes approximately nine weeks.

Nurse Cells [Figure 27.5c,d]

Nurse cells have five important functions:

1. *Maintenance of the blood–testis barrier:* The seminiferous tubules are isolated from the general circulation by a **blood–testis barrier** (**Figure 27.5c,d**), comparable to the blood–brain barrier. ∞ p. 391 Tight junctions between extensions of nurse cells isolate the luminal portion of the seminiferous tubule from the surrounding interstitial fluid. Transport of materials across the nurse cells is tightly regulated, so that the environment surrounding the spermatocytes and spermatids remains very stable. The lumen of a seminiferous tubule contains a fluid very different from interstitial fluid; this tubular fluid is high in androgens, estrogens, potassium, and amino acids. The blood–testis barrier is essential to preserving these differences. In addition, developing spermatozoa contain sperm-specific antigens in their cell membranes. These antigens,

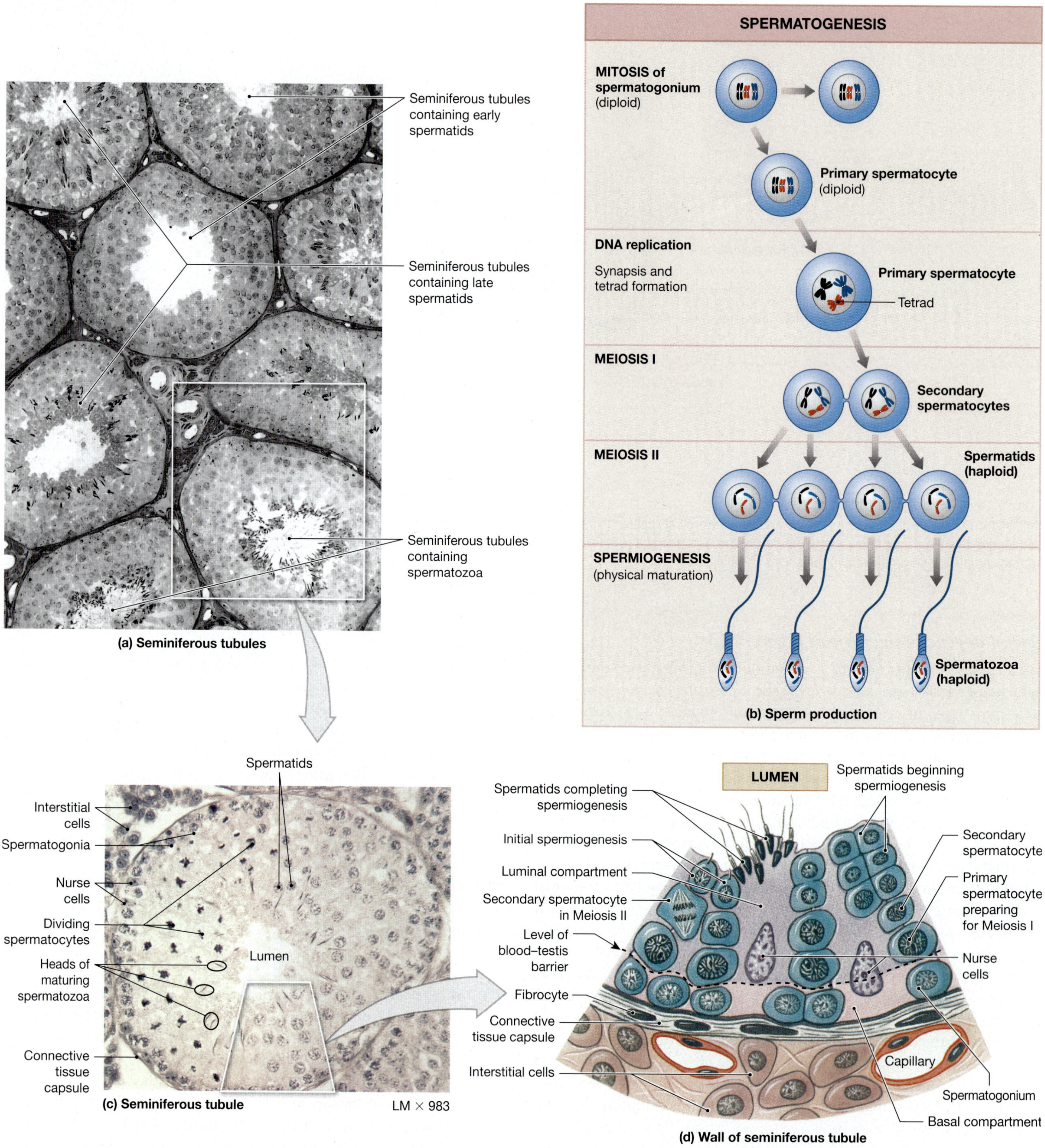

Figure 27.5 Histology of the Seminiferous Tubules
(a) Seminiferous tubules in sectional view. **(b)** Meiosis in the testes, showing the fates of three representative chromosomes. **(c)** Spermatogenesis within one segment of a seminiferous tubule. **(d)** The blood–testis barrier and the structure of the wall of a seminiferous tubule.

not found in somatic cell membranes, would be attacked by the immune system if the blood–testis barrier did not prevent their detection.

2. *Support of spermatogenesis:* Spermatogenesis depends on the stimulation of nurse cells by circulating FSH and testosterone. Stimulated nurse cells then support the division of spermatogonia and the meiotic divisions of spermatocytes.
3. *Support of spermiogenesis:* Spermiogenesis requires the presence of nurse cells. These cells surround and enfold the spermatids, providing nutrients and chemical stimuli that promote their development.
4. *Secretion of inhibin:* Nurse cells secrete a hormone called **inhibin** (in-HIB-in). Inhibin depresses the pituitary production of follicle-stimulating hormone (FSH) and gonadotropin-releasing hormone (GnRH). p. 521 The faster the rate of sperm production, the greater the amount of inhibin secreted.
5. *Secretion of androgen-binding protein:* **Androgen-binding protein (ABP)** binds androgens (primarily testosterone) in the fluid contents of the seminiferous tubules. This protein is thought to be important in elevating the concentration of androgens within the tubules and stimulating spermiogenesis.

Anatomy of a Spermatozoon [Figure 27.6]

There are three distinct regions to each spermatozoon: the *head*, the *middle piece*, and the *tail* (**Figure 27.6**).

- The **head** is a flattened oval containing densely packed chromosomes. The tip contains the **acrosomal** (ak-rō-SŌ-mal) **cap** or *acrosome*, a membrane-bound, vesicular compartment containing enzymes involved in the preliminary steps of fertilization.
- A short **neck** attaches the head to the **middle piece**. The neck contains both centrioles of the original spermatid. The microtubules of the distal centriole are continuous with those of the middle piece and tail. Mitochondria arranged in a spiral around the microtubules provide the energy needed to move the tail.
- The **tail** is the only example of a flagellum in the human body. p. 38 A **flagellum** moves a cell from one place to another. In contrast to cilia, which beat in a predictable, waving fashion, the flagellum of a spermatozoon has a complex, corkscrew motion. The microtubules of the flagellum are surrounded by a dense, fibrous sheath.

Unlike other, less specialized cells, a mature spermatozoon lacks an endoplasmic reticulum, Golgi apparatus, lysosomes, peroxisomes, inclusions, and many other intracellular structures. Because the cell does not contain glycogen or other energy reserves, it must absorb nutrients (primarily fructose) from the surrounding fluid.

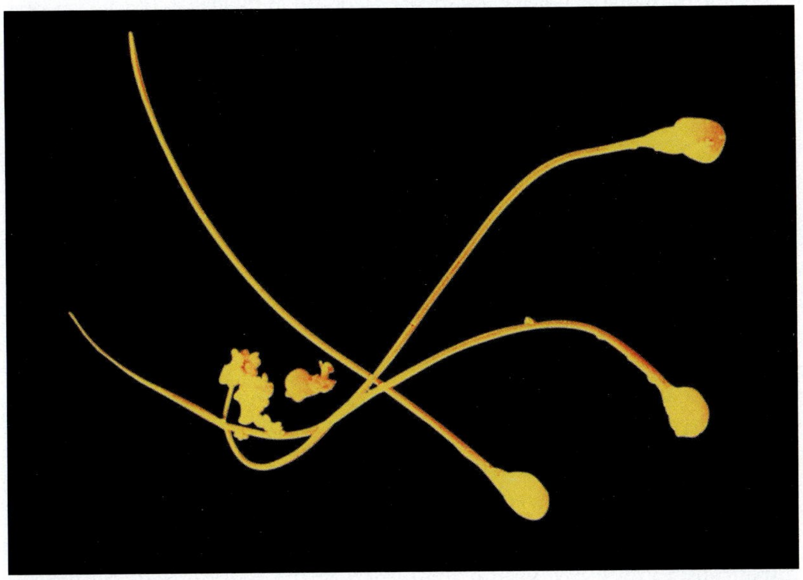

(b) Spermatozoa SEM × 1688

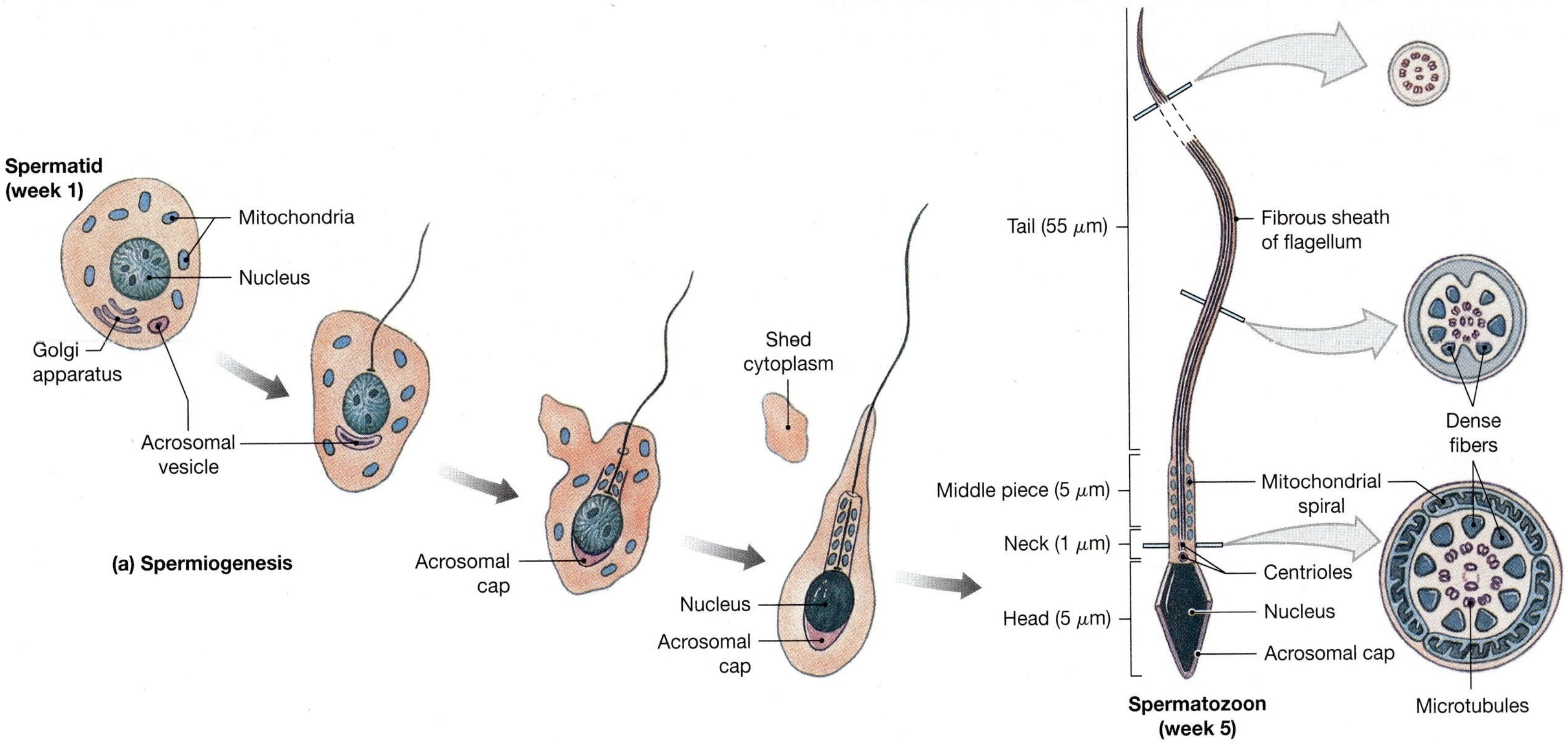

Figure 27.6 Spermiogenesis and Spermatozoon Histology
(a) Differentiation of a spermatid into a spermatozoon. **(b)** Histology of human spermatozoa.

Clinical Note

Testicular Cancer **Testicular cancer** occurs at a relatively low rate: approximately 8250 new cases are reported each year in the United States. However, testicular cancer is the most common cancer among males between the age of 15 and 34. Nine out of ten testicular cancers result from abnormal spermatogonia or spermatocytes. Treatment generally consists of a combination of orchiectomy and chemotherapy. Cyclist Lance Armstrong won the grueling Tour de France a record seven consecutive times after successful treatment for testicular cancer that had metastasized to his brain and lungs.

CONCEPT CHECK

1. What structures make up the body of the spermatic cord?
2. Why are inguinal hernias relatively common in males?
3. How is the location of the testes (outside the peritoneal cavity) important to the production of viable sperm?
4. What is the function of the blood–testis barrier?

See blue "Answers" tab at back of book.

The Male Reproductive Tract

The testes produce physically mature spermatozoa that are not yet capable of successful fertilization because they are not yet motile. The other regions of the male reproductive system are concerned with the functional maturation, nourishment, storage, and transport of spermatozoa.

The Epididymis [Figures 27.1/27.3/27.4/27.7]

Late in their development, the spermatozoa become detached from the nurse cells and are free within the lumen of the seminiferous tubule. Although they have most of the physical characteristics of mature sperm cells, they are still functionally immature and incapable of coordinated locomotion or fertilization. Fluid currents then transport the spermatozoa along the straight tubule, through the rete testis (Figure 27.7a), and into the epididymis. The lumen of the epididymis is lined by a distinctive pseudostratified columnar epithelium with long stereocilia (Figure 27.7b,c).

The **epididymis** lies along the posterior border of the testis (Figures 27.1, p. 716, 27.3, p. 718, 27.4, p. 719, and 27.7a). It has a firm texture and can be felt through the skin of the scrotum. The epididymis consists of a tubule almost 7 m (23 ft) long, coiled and twisted so as to take up very little space. The epididymis has a *head*, a *body*, and a *tail*.

- The superior **head** receives spermatozoa via the efferent ducts of the mediastinum of the testis.
- The **body** begins distal to the last efferent duct and extends inferiorly along the posterior margin of the testis.
- Near the inferior border of the testis, the number of convolutions decreases, marking the start of the **tail**. The tail reverses direction, and as it ascends, the tubular epithelium changes. The stereocilia disappear and the epithelium becomes indistinguishable from that of the attached ductus deferens. The tail of the epididymis is the principal region involved with sperm storage.

The epididymis has three major functions:

1. It *monitors and adjusts the composition of the fluid produced by the seminiferous tubules:* The pseudostratified columnar epithelial lining of the epididymis bears distinctive *stereocilia* (Figure 27.7b,c) that increase the surface area available for absorption and secretion into the tubular fluid.
2. It *acts as a recycling center for damaged spermatozoa:* Cellular debris and damaged spermatozoa are absorbed, and the products of enzymatic breakdown are released into the surrounding interstitial fluids for pickup by the epididymal circulation.
3. It *stores spermatozoa and facilitates their functional maturation:* It takes about 2 weeks for a spermatozoon to pass through the epididymis, and during this period it completes its functional maturation in a protected environment. Although spermatozoa leaving the epididymis are mature, they remain immobile. To become active, motile, and fully functional, the spermatozoa must undergo **capacitation**. This process normally occurs in two steps: (1) spermatozoa become motile when mixed with secretions of the seminal glands; and (2) they become capable of successful fertilization when, upon exposure to conditions inside the female reproductive tract, the permeability of the sperm plasmalemma changes. While the spermatozoa remain in the male reproductive tract, a secretory product of the epididymis prevents premature capacitation.

Transport along the epididymis involves some combination of fluid movement and peristaltic contractions of smooth muscle. Spermatozoa eventually leave the tail of the epididymis and enter the ductus deferens.

The Ductus Deferens [Figures 27.1/27.3/27.7a/27.8a,b]

The **ductus deferens**, also called the *deferential duct* or *vas deferens*, is 40–45 cm (16–18 in.) long. It begins at the end of the tail of the epididymis (Figure 27.7a) and ascends into the abdominopelvic cavity through the inguinal canal as part of the spermatic cord (Figure 27.3). Inside the abdominal cavity, the ductus deferens passes posteriorly, curving inferiorly along the lateral surface of the urinary bladder toward the superior and posterior margin of the prostate gland (Figure 27.1). Just before it reaches the prostate, the ductus deferens becomes enlarged, and the expanded portion is known as the **ampulla** (am-PŪL-la) (Figure 27.8a).

The wall of the ductus deferens contains a thick layer of smooth muscle (Figure 27.8b). Peristaltic contractions in this layer propel spermatozoa and fluid along the duct, which is lined by a columnar epithelium with stereocilia. In addition to transporting sperm, the ductus deferens can store spermatozoa for several months. During this time the spermatozoa remain in a state of suspended animation with low metabolic rates.

The junction of each ampulla with the base of a seminal gland marks the start of an **ejaculatory duct**. This relatively short passageway (2 cm, or less than 1 in.) penetrates the muscular wall of the prostate gland and empties into the urethra (Figure 27.1) near the ejaculatory duct from the other side.

The Urethra [Figures 27.1/27.9]

The urethra of the male extends from the urinary bladder to the tip of the penis, a distance of 15–20 cm (6–8 in.). It is divided into *prostatic*, *membranous*, and *spongy regions* (Figures 27.1 and 27.9). These subdivisions were considered in Chapter 26. ∞ p. 707 The urethra in the male is a passageway used by both the urinary and reproductive systems.

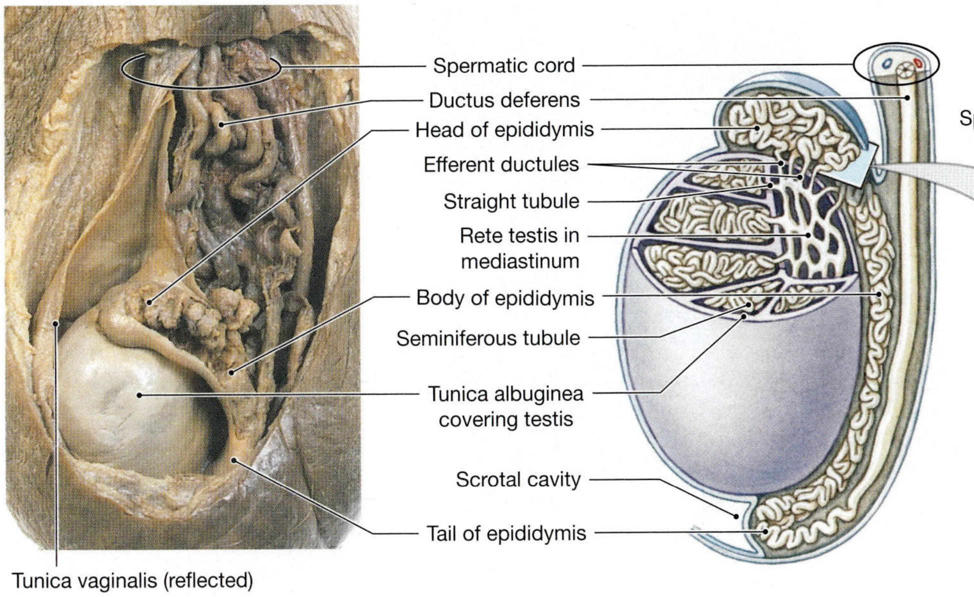

(a) Testis and epididymis

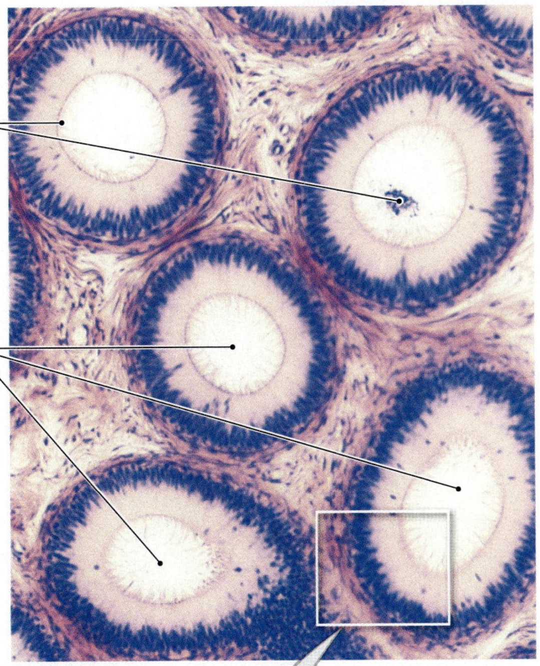

(b) Epididymis LM × 49

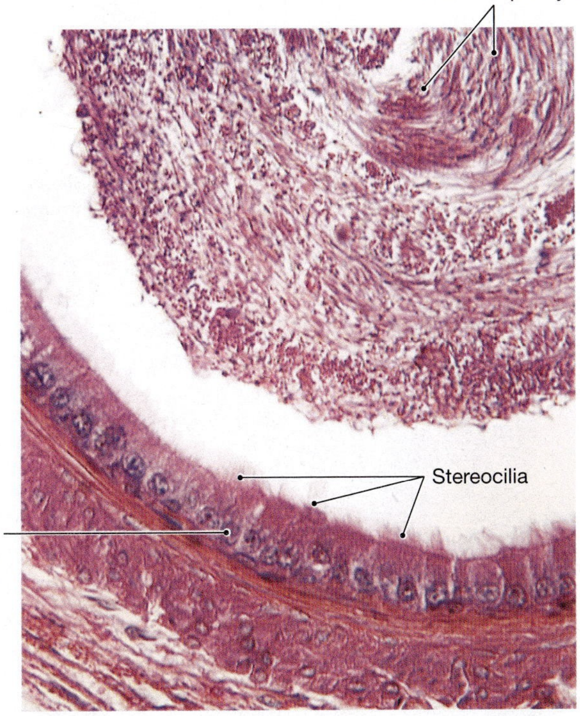

(c) Epididymis LM × 304

Figure 27.7 The Epididymis
(a) (Left) Appearance of the testis and epididymis on gross dissection. (Right) Diagrammatic view of the testis and epididymis, showing the sectional plane of part (b). **(b)** Histological organization of tubules within the head region and the surrounding connective tissues. **(c)** A light micrograph showing epithelial characteristics, especially the elongate stereocilia.

The Accessory Glands [Figures 27.1/27.8a]

The fluids contributed by the seminiferous tubules and the epididymis account for only about 5 percent of the final volume of semen. The seminal fluid is a mixture of the secretions from many different glands, each with distinctive biochemical characteristics. These glands include the *seminal glands*, the *prostate gland*, and the *bulbo-urethral glands* (Figures 27.1, p. 716, and 27.8a). Major functions of these glands include: (1) activating the spermatozoa, (2) providing the nutrients spermatozoa need for motility, and (3) producing buffers that counteract the acidity of the urethral and vaginal contents.

The Seminal Glands [Figures 27.1/27.8a,c/27.9a]

The ductus deferens ends at the junction between the ampulla and the duct draining the seminal gland. The **seminal glands**, or *seminal vesicles*, are embedded in connective tissue on either side of the midline, sandwiched between the posterior wall of the urinary bladder and the anterior wall of the rectum. Each seminal gland is a tubular gland, around 15 cm (6 in.) in length. Each tubule has many short side branches, and the entire assemblage is coiled and folded into a compact, tapered mass roughly 5 cm by 2.5 cm (2 in. by 1 in.). The location of the seminal glands can be seen in Figures 27.1, 27.8a, and 27.9a.

The seminal glands are extremely active secretory glands, with a pseudostratified, columnar or cuboidal epithelial lining (Figure 27.8c). These glands contribute about 60 percent of the volume of semen, and although the vesicular fluid usually has the same osmotic concentration as blood plasma, the composition is quite different. In particular, the secretion of the seminal glands contains prostaglandins, clotting proteins, and relatively high concentrations of fructose, which is easily metabolized by spermatozoa to produce ATP. ∞ p. 38 Seminal fluid is discharged into the ductus deferens at *emission*, when peristaltic contractions are under way in the ductus deferens, seminal glands, and prostate gland. These contractions are under the control of the sympathetic nervous system. ∞ p 466 When mixed with the secretions of the seminal glands, previously inactive but functional spermatozoa begin beating their flagella, becoming highly mobile.

The Prostate Gland [Figures 27.1/27.8a,e/27.9a]

The **prostate gland** is a small, muscular, rounded organ with a diameter of about 4 cm (1.6 in.). The prostate gland encircles the prostatic urethra as it leaves the urinary bladder (Figures 27.1, 27.8a, and 27.9a). The glandular tissue of the prostate consists of a cluster of 30–50 *compound tubuloalveolar glands* (Figure 27.8e). These glands are surrounded and wrapped in a thick

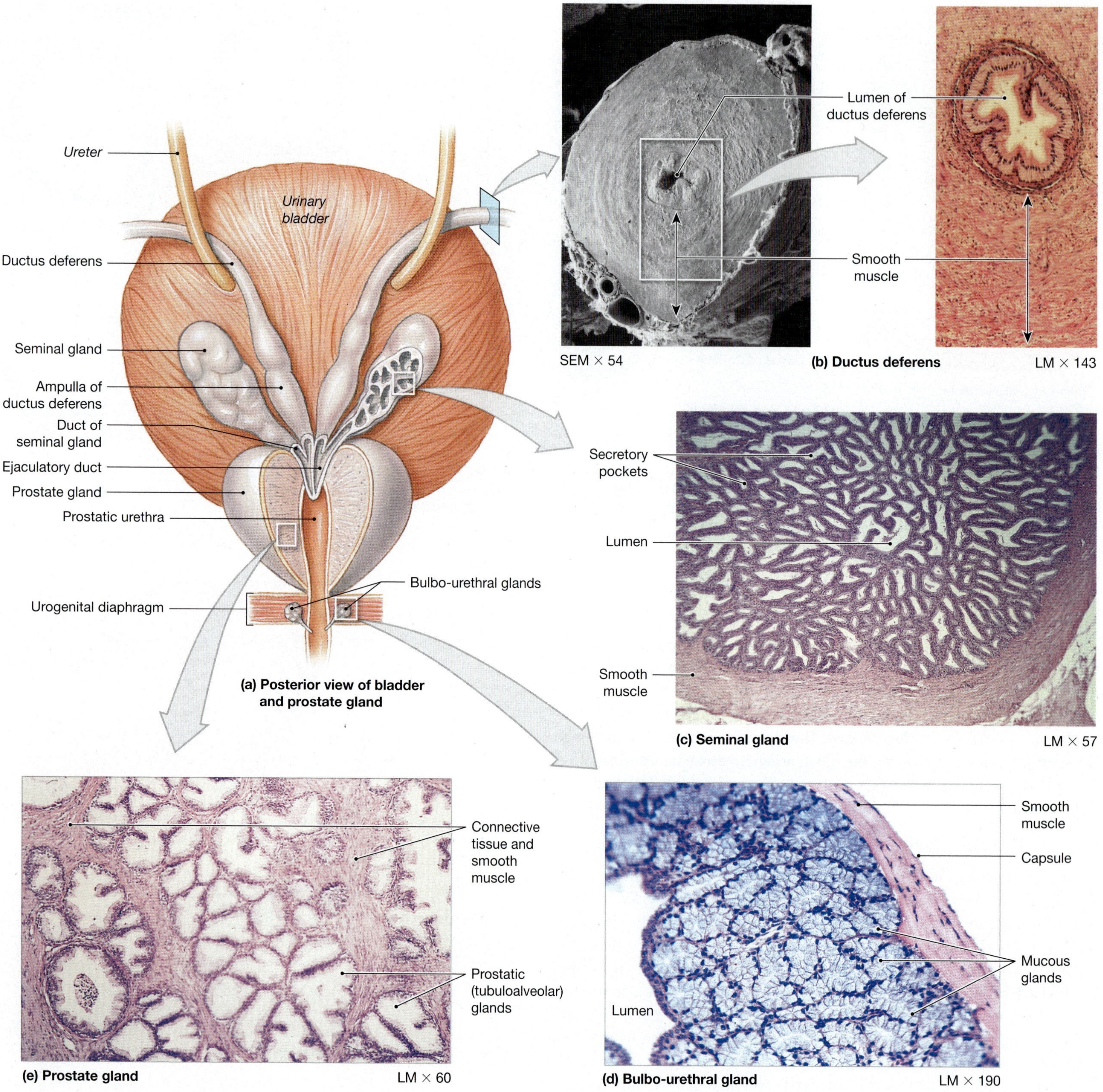

Figure 27.8 The Ductus Deferens and Accessory Glands
(a) A posterior view of the urinary bladder and prostate gland, showing subdivisions of the ductus deferens in relation to surrounding structures. **(b)** Light and scanning electron micrographs showing extensive layering with smooth muscle around the lumen of the ductus deferens. [SEM ©R. G. Kessel and R. H. Kardon, "Tissues and Organs: A Text-Atlas of Scanning Electron Microscopy," W. H. Freeman & Co., 1979. All Rights Reserved.] **(c)** Histology of the seminal glands. Note the extensive glandular surface area here; these organs produce most of the volume of seminal fluid. **(d)** Histology of the bulbo-urethral glands, which secrete a thick mucus into the spongy urethra. **(e)** Histological detail of the glands of the prostate. The tissue between the individual glandular units consists largely of smooth muscle. Contractions of this muscle tissue help move the secretions into the ejaculatory duct and urethra.

blanket of smooth muscle fibers. The epithelial lining typically varies from a simple to a pseudostratified columnar epithelium.

The prostatic glands produce **prostatic fluid**, a weakly acidic secretion that contributes 20–30 percent of the volume of semen. In addition to several other compounds of uncertain significance, prostatic secretions contain **seminalplasmin** (sem-i-nal-PLAZ-min), an antibiotic that may help prevent urinary tract infections in males. These secretions are ejected into the prostatic urethra by peristaltic contractions of the muscular wall.

The Bulbo-urethral Glands [Figures 27.1/27.8a,d/27.9a]

The paired **bulbo-urethral glands**, or *Cowper's glands*, are located at the base of the penis, covered by the fascia of the urogenital diaphragm (Figures 27.1, p. 716, 27.8a, and 27.9a). The bulbo-urethral glands are round, with diameters approaching 10 mm (less than 0.5 in.). The duct of each gland parallels the spongy urethra for 3–4 cm (1.2–1.6 in.) before emptying into the urethral lumen. The glands and ducts are lined by a simple columnar epithelium. These compound tubuloalveolar mucous glands (Figure 27.8d) secrete a thick, sticky, alkaline mucus. This secretion helps neutralize any urinary acids that may remain in the urethra and provides lubrication for the tip of the penis.

Semen

A typical ejaculation releases 2–5 ml of semen. This volume of fluid, called an **ejaculate**, contains the following:

1. *Spermatozoa:* A normal **sperm count** ranges from 20 to 100 million spermatozoa per milliliter of semen.
2. *Seminal fluid:* **Seminal fluid**, the fluid component of semen, is a mixture of glandular secretions with a distinctive ionic and nutrient composition. In terms of total volume, seminal fluid contains the combined secretions of the seminal glands (60 percent), the prostate (30 percent), the nurse cells and epididymis (5 percent), and the bulbo-urethral glands (5 percent).
3. *Enzymes:* Several important enzymes are present in the seminal fluid, including (1) a protease that may help dissolve mucous secretions in the vagina and (2) seminalplasmin, an antibiotic enzyme that kills a variety of bacteria, including *Escherichia coli.*

The Penis [Figures 27.1/27.9]

The **penis** is a tubular organ that contains the distal portion of the urethra (Figure 27.1). It conducts urine to the exterior and introduces semen into the female vagina during sexual intercourse. The penis (Figure 27.9a,c) is divided into three regions:

- The **root** of the penis is the fixed portion that attaches the penis to the rami of the ischia. This connection occurs within the urogenital triangle immediately inferior to the pubic symphysis. p. 280
- The **body (shaft)** of the penis is the tubular, movable portion. Masses of *erectile tissue* are found within the body.
- The **glans** of the penis is the expanded distal end that surrounds the *external urethral* orifice.

The skin overlying the penis is generally hairless and is generally more darkly pigmented than skin elsewhere on the body. The dermis contains a layer of smooth muscle, and the underlying loose connective tissue allows the thin skin to move without distorting underlying structures. The subcutaneous layer also contains superficial arteries, veins, and lymphatics but relatively few fat cells.

A fold of skin, the **prepuce** (PRĒ-pūs), or *foreskin*, surrounds the tip of the penis. The prepuce attaches to the relatively narrow **neck** of the penis and continues over the glans that surrounds the external urethral orifice. There are no hair follicles on the opposing surfaces, but **preputial** (prē-PŪ-she-al) **glands** in the skin of the neck and the inner surface of the prepuce secrete a waxy material known as **smegma** (SMEG-ma). Unfortunately, smegma can be an excellent nutrient source for bacteria. Mild inflammation and infections in this region are common, especially if the area is not washed thoroughly and frequently. One way of avoiding these problems is to perform a **circumcision** (ser-kum-SIZH-un) and surgically remove the prepuce. In Western societies (especially in the United States), this procedure is usually performed shortly after birth. Although controversial, continuation of this practice is supported by strong cultural biases and epidemiological evidence. Uncircumcised males have a higher incidence of urinary tract infections and are at greater risk for penile cancer than circumcised males.

Deep to the loose connective tissue that underlies the dermis, a dense network of elastic fibers encircles the internal structures of the penis. Most of the body of the penis consists of three parallel cylindrical columns of **erectile tissue** (Figure 27.9). Erectile tissue consists of a three-dimensional maze of vascular channels incompletely separated by partitions of elastic connective tissue and smooth muscle fibers. In the resting state, the arterial branches are constricted and the muscular partitions are tense. This combination reduces blood flow into the erectile tissue. Parasympathetic stimulation relaxes the smooth muscles in the arterial walls. When the muscles relax: (1) the vessels dilate, (2) blood flow increases, (3) the vascular channels become engorged with blood, and (4) **erection** of the penis occurs. The flaccid (non-erect) penis hangs inferior to the pubic symphysis anterior to the scrotum, but during erection the penis stiffens and assumes a more upright position.

On the anterior surface of the flaccid penis, the two cylindrical **corpora cavernosa** (KOR-pōr-a ka-ver-NŌ-sa) are separated by a thin septum and encircled by a dense collagenous sheath. At their bases the corpora cavernosa diverge, forming the **crura** (*crura*, legs; singular, *crus*) of the penis. Each crus is bound to the ramus of the ischium by tough connective tissue ligaments. The corpora cavernosa extend distally along the length of the penis as far as the glans, and each corpus cavernosum contains a **deep artery of the penis** (Figure 27.9a–c).

The **corpus spongiosum** (spon-jē-Ō-sum) surrounds the spongy urethra. This erectile body extends from the superficial fascia of the urogenital diaphragm to the tip of the penis, where it expands to form the glans. The sheath surrounding the corpus spongiosum contains more elastic fibers than does that of the corpora cavernosa, and the erectile tissue contains a pair of arteries. The **bulb** of the penis is the thickened, proximal end of the corpus spongiosum.

After erection has occurred, semen release involves a two-step process. During **emission** the sympathetic nervous system coordinates peristaltic contractions that in sequence sweep along the ductus deferens, the seminal glands, the prostate gland, and the bulbo-urethral glands. These contractions mix the fluid components of the semen within the male reproductive tract. **Ejaculation** then occurs, as powerful, rhythmic contractions begin in the *ischiocavernosus* and *bulbospongiosus muscles* of the pelvic floor. pp. 279–280 The ischiocavernosus muscles insert along the sides of the penis, and their contractions primarily serve to stiffen the organ. The bulbospongiosus wraps around the base of the penis, and its contraction

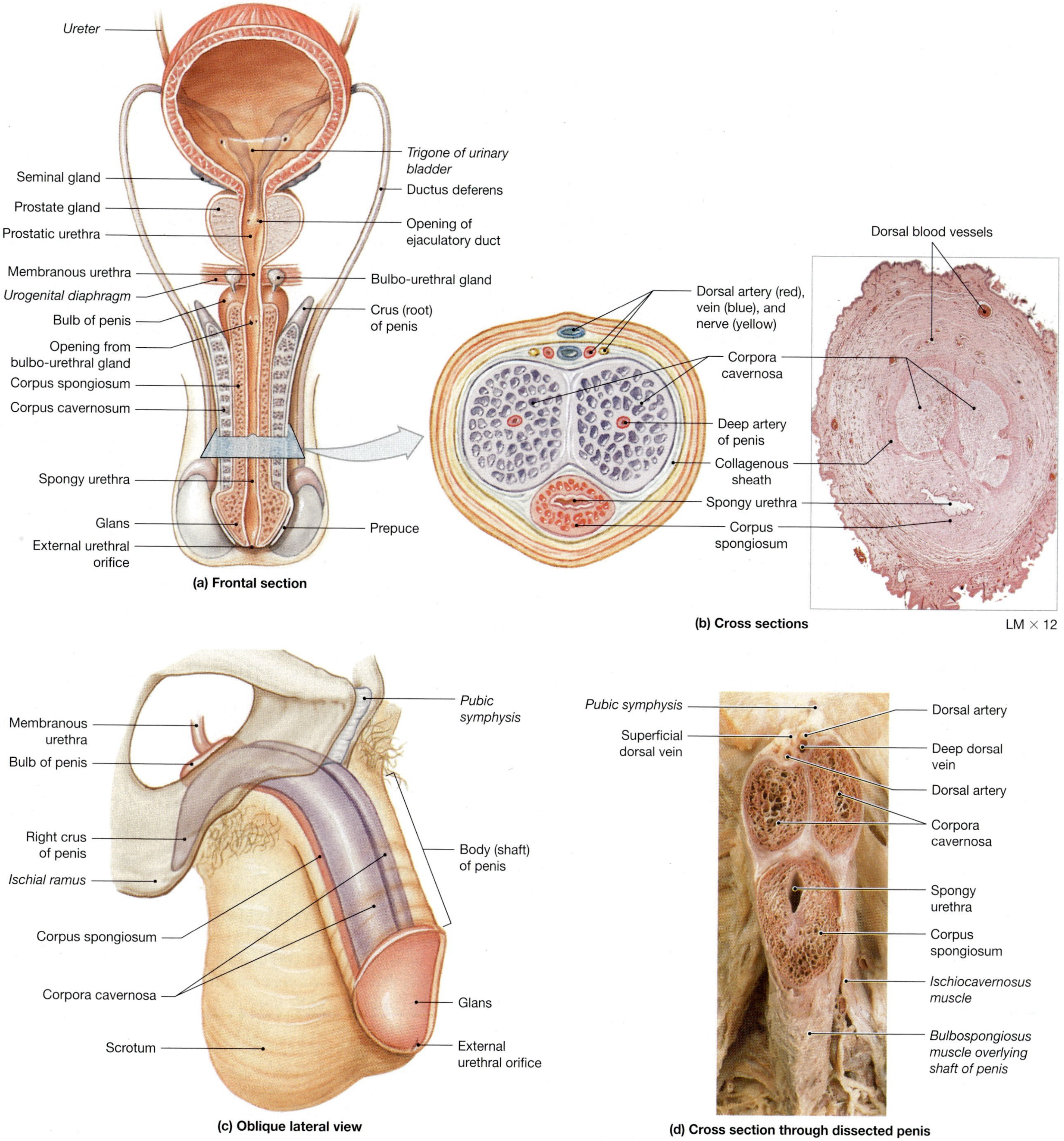

Figure 27.9 The Penis
(a) Frontal section showing the structures of the penis. **(b)** Cross sections of the penis, showing the histological relation of the urethra and three masses of erectile tissue. **(c)** Lateral and oblique view of the penis, showing the orientation of the erectile tissues. **(d)** A cross section through the shaft of the penis.

pushes semen toward the external urethral orifice. These contractions are controlled by reflexes involving the inferior lumbar and superior sacral segments of the spinal cord. pp. 457, 466

CONCEPT CHECK

1. What are the two steps of capacitation and where do they occur?
2. Trace the path of a developing sperm from the time it becomes detached from the nurse cells until it is released from the body.

See blue "Answers" tab at back of book.

Embryology Summary

For a summary of the development of the male reproductive system, see Chapter 28 (Embryology and Human Development).

Anatomy of the Female Reproductive System

[Figures 27.10/27.11/27.15]

A woman's reproductive system must produce functional gametes, protect and support a developing embryo, and nourish the newborn infant. The principal structures of the female reproductive system are shown in Figure 27.10. Female gametes leave the **ovaries**, travel along the **uterine tubes** *(Fallopian tubes* or *oviducts)*, where fertilization may occur, and eventually reach the **uterus**. The uterus opens into the **vagina**; the external opening of the vagina is surrounded by the female external genitalia. As in the male, a variety of accessory glands secrete into the reproductive tract.

The ovaries, uterine tubes, and uterus are enclosed within an extensive mesentery known as the **broad ligament** (Figures 27.11 and 27.15). The uterine tubes extend along the superior border of the broad ligament and open into the pelvic cavity lateral to the ovaries. The free edge of the broad ligament that attaches to each uterine tube is known as the **mesosalpinx** (mez-ō-SAL-pinks). A thickened fold of the broad ligament, the **mesovarium** (mez-ō-VA-rē-um), supports and stabilizes the position of each ovary.

The broad ligament attaches to the sides and floor of the pelvic cavity, where it becomes continuous with the parietal peritoneum. The broad ligament thus subdivides the pelvic cavity. The pocket formed between the posterior wall of the uterus and the anterior surface of the colon is the **rectouterine** (rek-tō-Ū-ter-in) **pouch**, while the pocket between the anterior wall of the uterus and the posterior wall of the urinary bladder is the **vesicouterine** (ves-i-kō-Ū-ter-in) **pouch** (Figures 27.10 and 27.11c). These subdivisions are most apparent in sagittal section.

Several other ligaments assist the broad ligament in supporting and stabilizing the position of the uterus and associated reproductive organs. These ligaments travel within the mesentery sheet of the broad ligament on the way to the ovaries or uterus. The broad ligament limits side-to-side movement and rotation, and the other ligaments (detailed in the next section) prevent superior-inferior movement.

The Ovaries [Figures 27.10/27.11/27.15]

The **ovaries** are small, paired organs located near the lateral walls of the pelvic cavity (Figures 27.10, 27.11, and 27.15). A typical ovary is a flattened oval that measures approximately 5 cm long, 2.5 cm wide, and 8 mm thick (2 in. × 1 in. × 0.33 in.). Each ovary weighs 6–8 g (roughly 0.25 oz). These organs are responsible for the production of ova and the secretion of hormones. The position of each ovary is stabilized by the mesovarium and by a pair of supporting ligaments: the *ovarian ligament* and the *suspensory ligament.* The **ovarian ligament** extends from the lateral wall of the uterus, near the attachment of the uterine tube, to the medial surface of the ovary. The **suspensory ligament** extends from the lateral surface of the ovary past the open end of the uterine tube to the pelvic wall. The major blood vessels, the **ovarian artery** and **ovarian vein**, travel to and from the ovary within the suspensory ligament. They extend through the mesovarium, along with nerves and lymphatic vessels, and are connected to the ovary at the **ovarian hilum** (Figure 27.11).

Each ovary has a pink or yellowish coloration and a nodular consistency that resembles cottage cheese or lumpy oatmeal. The visceral peritoneum covering the surface of each ovary is a single layer of cuboidal epithelium called the **germinal epithelium**. It overlies a layer of dense connective tissue called the **tunica albuginea**. The interior of the ovary can be divided into a superficial *cortex* and a deep *medulla* (Figure 27.11b). The production of gametes occurs in the ovarian cortex.

The Ovarian Cycle and Oogenesis [Figures 27.12/27.13]

The production of female gametes, a process called **oogenesis** (ō-ō-JEN-e-sis), begins before birth, remains dormant until puberty, and ends at *menopause.* At puberty, this usually occurs on a monthly basis as part of the **ovarian cycle**. Gamete development occurs in specialized structures called **ovarian follicles** (ō-VAR-ē-an FOL-i-klz). Unlike the situation in the male gonads, the stem cells, or **oogonia** (ō-ō-GŌ-nē-a), of the female complete their mitotic divisions before birth. There are roughly 2 million **primary oocytes** (Ō-ō-sīts) in the ovaries at birth; by puberty that number has declined to around 400,000 due to degeneration. This degenerative process,

Clinical Note

Ovarian Cancer **Ovarian cancer** is the third most common reproductive cancer among women. It has the highest mortality because it is seldom diagnosed in its early stages. A woman in the United States has a lifetime risk of one chance in 70 of developing ovarian cancer. Approximately 6 percent of all cancers in women are diagnosed as ovarian cancer, and it is the fourth leading cause of cancer-related deaths among women in the United States. The prognosis is relatively good for cancers that originate in the general ovarian tissues or from abnormal oocytes. These cancers respond well to some combination of chemotherapy, radiation, and surgery. However, 85 percent of ovarian cancers develop from epithelial cells, and sustained remission can be obtained in only about one-third of these cases. Early diagnosis greatly improves the chances of successful treatment, but as yet there is no standardized, effective screening procedure.

The treatment required at an early stage involves the unilateral removal of an ovary and uterine tube (a *salpingo-oophorectomy*). For more advanced cancer, a *bilateral salpingo-oophorectomy* (BSO) and *total hysterectomy* (removal of the uterus) are performed. Because stem cells in the bone marrow are destroyed by the chemicals used in aggressive chemotherapy, a bone marrow transplant may also be required. Some chemotherapy agents are introduced into the peritoneal cavity, where higher concentrations can be administered without the systemic effects that would accompany the infusion of these drugs into the bloodstream. This procedure is called *intraperitoneal therapy*.

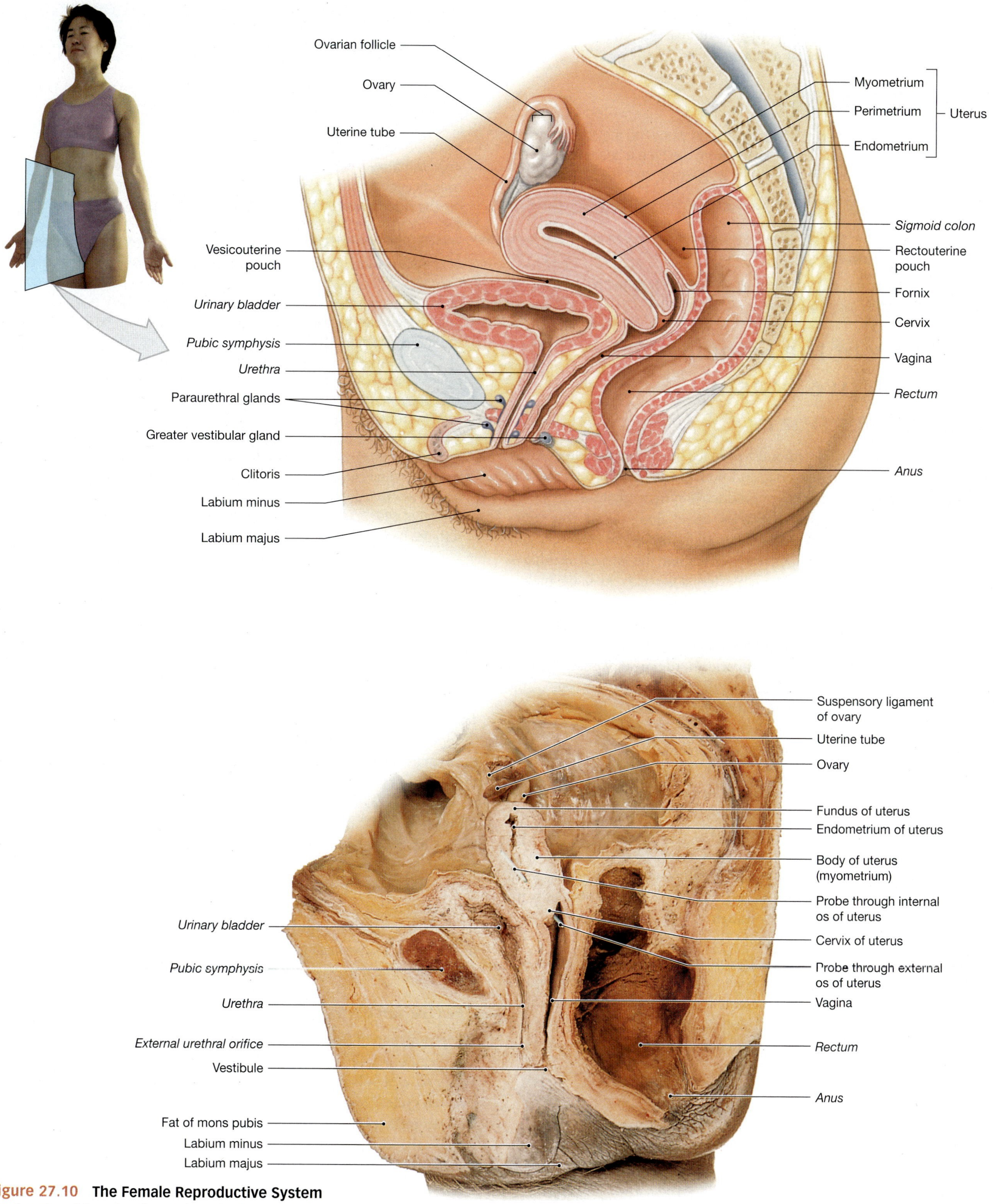

Figure 27.10 The Female Reproductive System
The female pelvis and perineum in sagittal section.

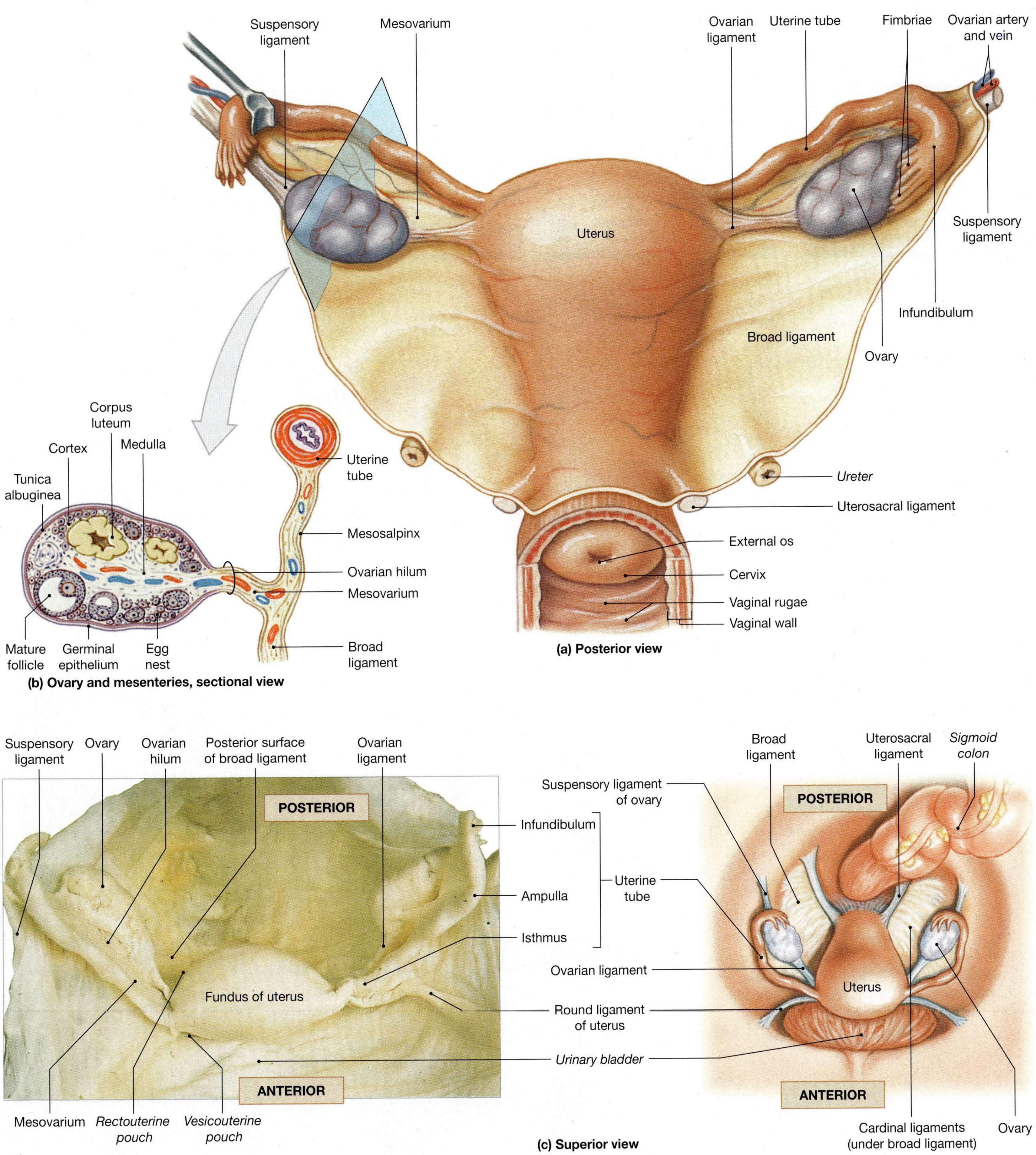

Figure 27.11 The Ovaries, Uterine Tubes, and Uterus
(a) Posterior view of the ovaries, uterine tubes, and uterus along with their supporting ligaments. **(b)** The ovary and associated mesenteries in sectional view. **(c)** Superior view of the female pelvic cavity, showing supporting ligaments of uterus and ovaries. In the photo, the urinary bladder cannot be seen because it is covered by peritoneum.

called **atresia** (a-TRĒ-zē-a), forms *atretic follicles.* The remaining primary oocytes are located in the outer portion of the ovarian cortex near the tunica albuginea, in clusters called **egg nests**. Each primary oocyte within an egg nest is surrounded by a layer of simple squamous follicular cells. Together, the primary oocyte and follicle cells constitute a **primordial** (prī-MOR-dē-al) **ovarian follicle**.

At puberty, rising levels of FSH trigger the start of the ovarian cycle, and each month thereafter some of the primordial follicles are stimulated to undergo further development. Important steps of this cycle are shown in **Figure 27.12**.

Step 1. ***Formation of Primary Ovarian Follicles.*** The ovarian cycle begins as activated primordial follicles develop into **primary follicles**. In a primary follicle, the follicular cells enlarge and undergo repeated cell divisions. As a result of these divisions, several layers of follicular cells develop around the oocyte. As the wall of the follicle thickens further, a space opens

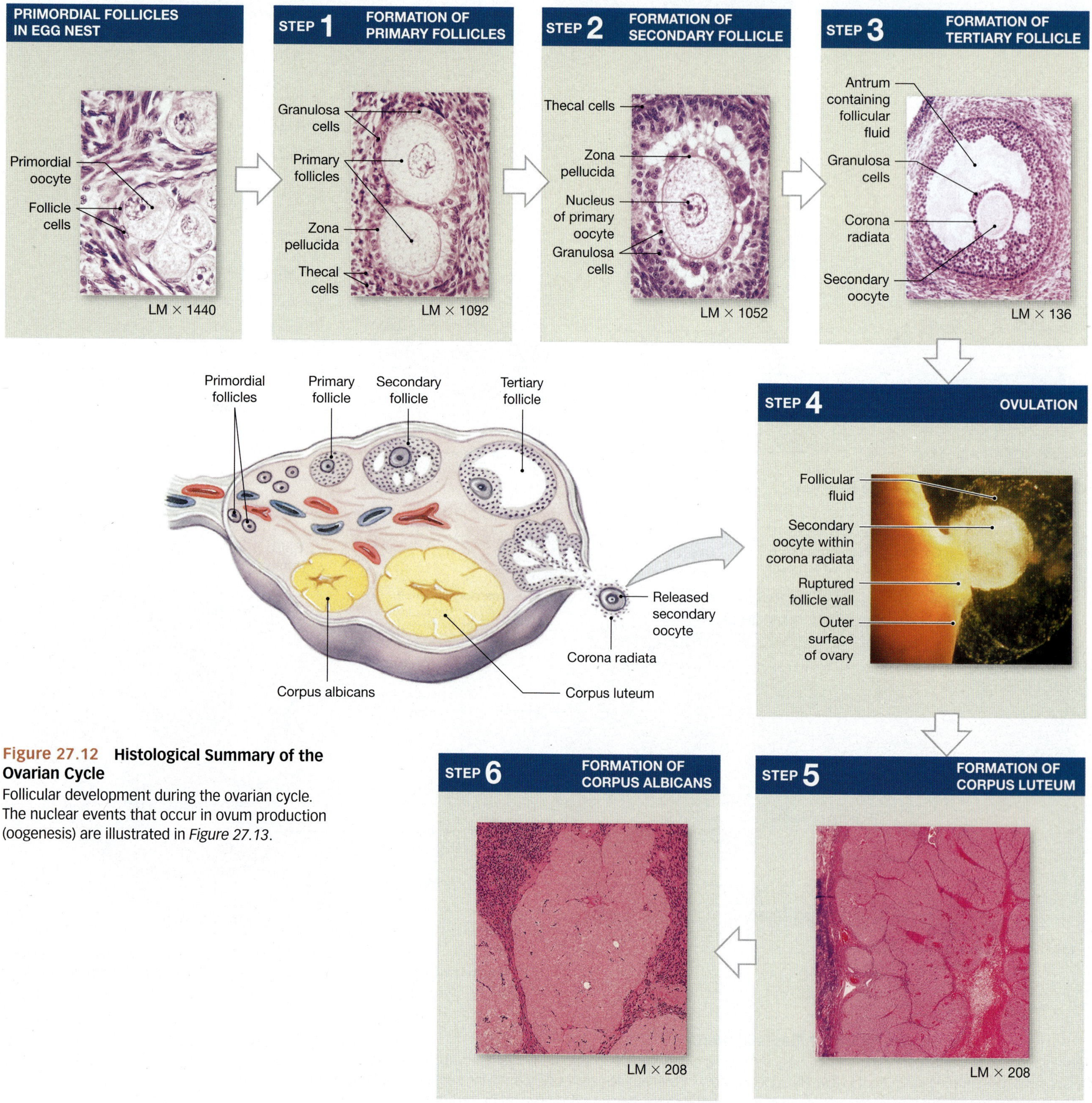

Figure 27.12 Histological Summary of the Ovarian Cycle
Follicular development during the ovarian cycle. The nuclear events that occur in ovum production (oogenesis) are illustrated in *Figure 27.13*.

up between the developing oocyte and the innermost follicular cells. This region, which contains interdigitating microvilli from the follicle cells and the oocyte, is called the **zona pellucida** (ZŌ-na pel-OO-si-da). Follicular cells continually provide the developing oocyte with nutrients. These follicle cells are called **granulosa cells**.

The development from primordial to primary follicles and subsequent follicular maturation occur under FSH stimulation. As the follicular cells enlarge and multiply, adjacent cells in the ovarian stroma form a layer of **thecal cells** around the follicle. Thecal cells and granulosa cells work together to release steroid hormones called *estrogens*. The hormone **estradiol** (es-tra-DĪ-ol) is the most important estrogen, and it is the dominant hormone prior to ovulation. Estrogens have several important functions, including (1) stimulating bone and muscle growth; (2) maintaining female secondary sex characteristics; (3) affecting CNS activity, including sex-related behaviors and drives; (4) maintaining the function of the reproductive glands and organs; and (5) initiating repair and growth of the uterine lining.

Step 2. ***Formation of Secondary Ovarian Follicles.*** Although many primordial follicles develop into primary follicles, only a few primary follicles develop into secondary follicles. The transformation begins as the wall of the follicle thickens and the deeper follicular cells begin secreting small amounts of fluid. This **follicular fluid**, or *liquor folliculi*, accumulates in small pockets that gradually expand and separate cells of the inner and outer layers of the follicle. At this stage the complex is known as a **secondary follicle**. Although the oocyte continues to grow at a slow pace, the follicle as a whole now enlarges rapidly because of this accumulation of fluid.

Step 3. ***Formation of a Tertiary Ovarian Follicle.*** Eight to 10 days after the start of the ovarian cycle, the ovaries usually contain only a single secondary follicle destined for further development. By the 10th to the 14th day of the cycle, it has developed into a **tertiary follicle**, or **mature ovarian follicle**, or *Graafian* (GRAF-ē-an) *follicle*, roughly 15 mm (0.6 in.) in diameter. This complex spans the entire width of the cortex and stretches the ovarian wall, creating a prominent bulge in the surface of the ovary. The oocyte projects into the expanded central chamber, or **antrum** (AN-trum), surrounded by a mass of granulosa cells.

Until this time, the primary oocyte has been suspended in prophase of the first meiotic division. That division is now completed. Although the nuclear events during oogenesis are identical to those in spermatogenesis, the cytoplasm of the primary oocyte is not evenly distributed (Figure 27.13). Instead of producing two secondary oocytes, the first meiotic division yields a **secondary oocyte** and a small, nonfunctional **polar body**. The secondary oocyte then proceeds to the metaphase stage of the second meiotic division, which will not be completed unless fertilization occurs. If fertilization does occur, the second meiotic division will be completed, producing an ovum and a nonfunctional polar body. Thus instead of producing four gametes, each of approximately equal size, oogenesis produces a single ovum containing most of the cytoplasm of the primary oocyte and polar bodies that are simply containers for the "extra" chromosomes.

Step 4. ***Ovulation.*** As the time of gamete release, or **ovulation** (ov-ū-LĀ-shun), approaches, the secondary oocyte and the surrounding follicular cells lose their connections with the follicular wall and drift free within the antrum. This event ideally occurs on day 14 of a 28-day cycle. The follicular cells surrounding the oocyte are now known as the **corona radiata** (kō-RŌ-na rā-dē-A-ta). The distended follicular wall then ruptures, releasing the follicular contents, including the oocyte, into the peritoneal cavity. The sticky follicular fluid usually keeps the corona radiata attached to the surface of the ovary, where either direct contact with the entrance to the uterine tube or fluid currents move the oocyte into the uterine tube.

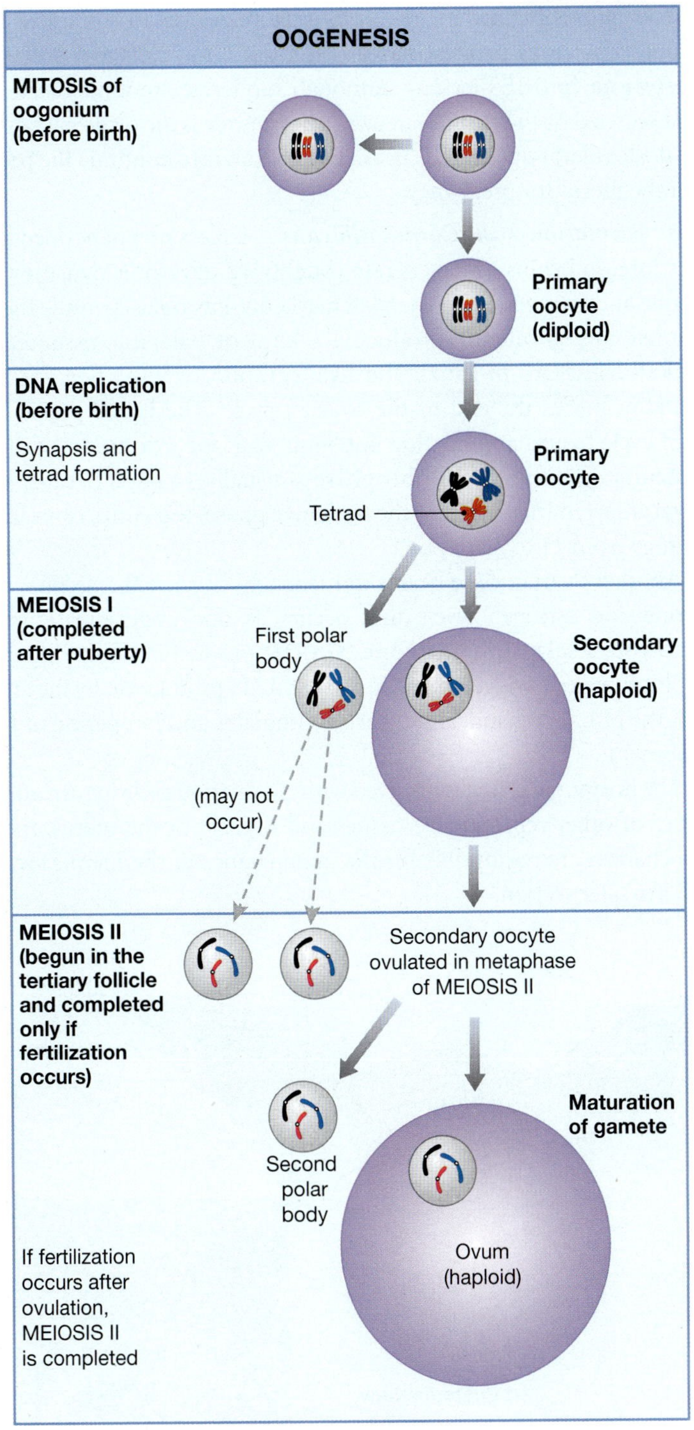

Figure 27.13 Meiosis and Ovum Production

The stimulus for ovulation is a sudden rise in LH levels that weakens the follicular wall. The surge in LH release coincides with, and is triggered by, a peak in estrogen levels as the tertiary follicle matures. The **follicular phase** of the ovarian cycle is the period between the start of the cycle and the completion of ovulation. The duration of this phase commonly varies from 7 to 28 days.

Step 5. ***Formation of the Corpus Luteum.*** The empty follicle initially collapses, and ruptured vessels bleed into its lumen. The remaining follicular cells then invade the area and proliferate to form a short-lived endocrine structure known as the **corpus luteum** (LOO-tē-um), named for its yellow color (*lutea*, yellow). The formation of the corpus luteum occurs under LH stimulation.

The lipids contained in the corpus luteum are used to synthesize steroid hormones known as **progestins** (prō-JES-tinz); the principal progestin is **progesterone** (prō-JES-ter-ōn). Although moderate amounts of estrogens are also secreted by the corpus luteum, progesterone is the principal hormone of the postovulatory period. Its primary function is to continue the preparation of the uterus for pregnancy.

Step 6. ***Formation of the Corpus Albicans.*** Unless pregnancy occurs, the corpus luteum begins to degenerate roughly 12 days after ovulation. Progesterone and estrogen levels then fall markedly. Fibroblasts invade the nonfunctional corpus luteum, producing a knot of pale scar tissue called a **corpus albicans** (AL-bi-kanz). The disintegration, or *involution*, of the corpus luteum marks the end of the ovarian cycle. The **luteal phase** of the ovarian cycle begins at ovulation and ends with the involution of the corpus luteum. The duration of this phase is usually 14 days. Because of the wide variation in the length of the follicular phase, the entire ovarian cycle may range from 21 to 35 days.

Another ovarian cycle begins immediately, because the decline in progesterone and estrogen levels that occurs as one cycle ends stimulates **gonadotropin-releasing hormone (GnRH)** production at the hypothalamus. This hormone triggers a rise in FSH and LH production by the anterior lobe of the pituitary gland, and this rise stimulates another period of follicle development.

The hormonal changes involved with the ovarian cycle in turn affect the activities of other reproductive tissues and organs. In the uterus, the hormonal changes are responsible for the maintenance of the *uterine cycle*, discussed in a later section.

Age and Oogenesis

Although many primordial follicles may have developed into primary ovarian follicles, and several primary follicles matured into secondary follicles, usually only a single secondary oocyte is released into the pelvic cavity at ovulation. The rest undergo atresia. At puberty there are approximately 200,000 primordial follicles in each ovary. Forty years later, few if any follicles remain, although only around 500 will have been ovulated over the interim.

The Uterine Tubes [Figures 27.10/27.11/27.14/27.15]

Each **uterine tube** is a hollow, muscular tube measuring roughly 13 cm (5 in.) in length (Figures 27.10, p. 728, 27.11, p. 729, 27.14, and 27.15). Each tube is divided into four regions:

1. *The infundibulum:* The end closest to the ovary forms an expanded funnel, or **infundibulum** (in-fun-DIB-ū-lum), with numerous fingerlike projections that extend into the pelvic cavity. The projections are called **fimbriae** (FIM-brē-ē). The cells lining the inner surface of the infundibulum have cilia that beat toward the middle segment of the uterine tube, the *ampulla.*
2. *The ampulla:* The **ampulla** is the intermediate portion of the uterine tube. The thickness of the smooth muscle layers in the wall of the ampulla greatly increases as it approaches the uterus.
3. *The isthmus:* The ampulla leads to the **isthmus** (IS-mus), a short segment adjacent to the uterine wall.

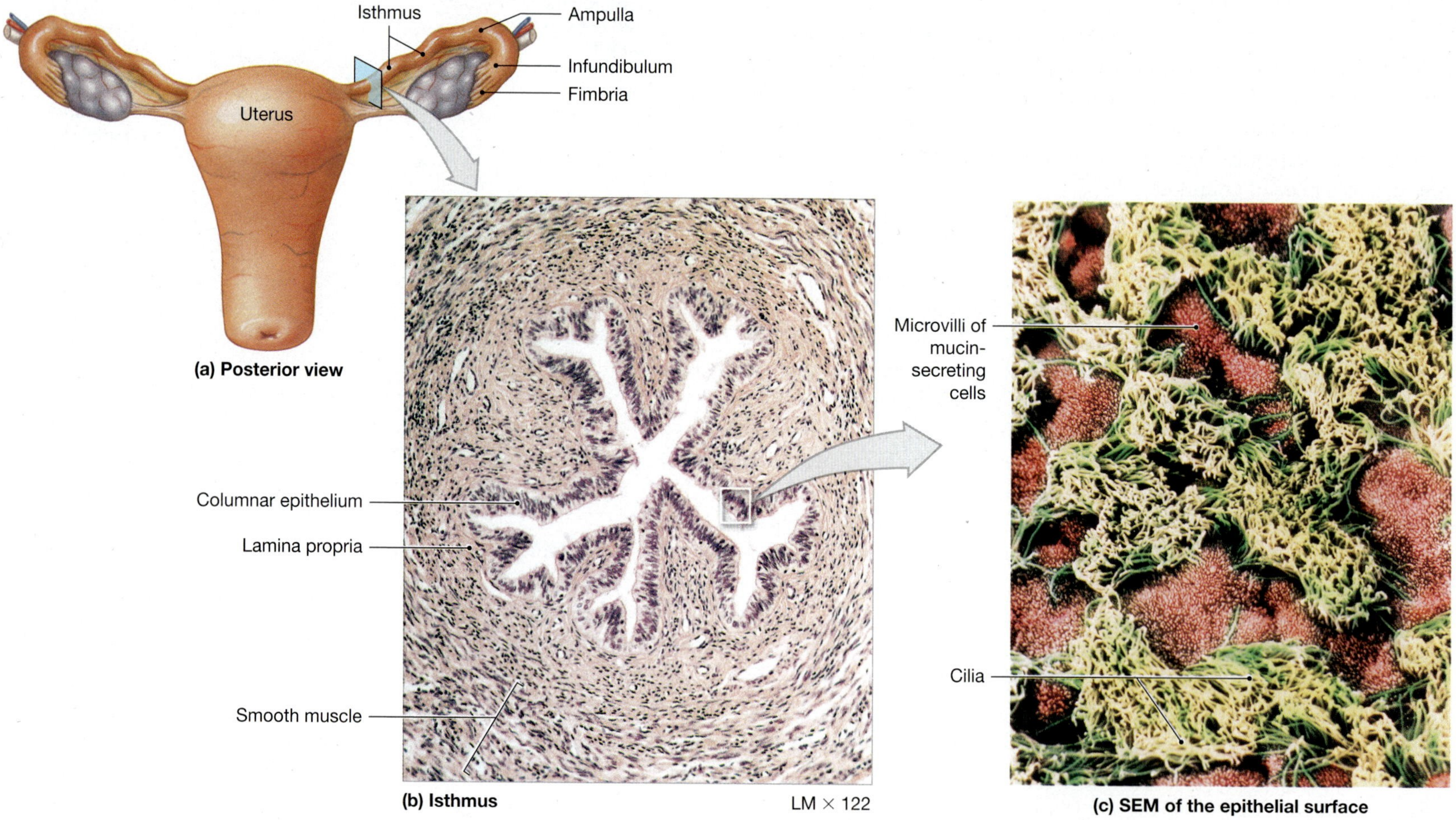

Figure 27.14 The Uterine Tubes
(a) Regions of the uterine tubes. **(b)** Histology of the isthmus as seen in sectional view. **(c)** A colorized SEM of the ciliated lining of the uterine tube.

4. *The uterine part:* The isthmus is continuous with the short **uterine part**, or *intramural* (in-tra-MŪ-ral) *part*, of the uterine tube. The uterine part opens into the uterine cavity.

Histology of the Uterine Tube [Figure 27.14b,c]

The epithelium lining the uterine tube has both ciliated and nonciliated simple columnar cells (Figure 27.14c). The mucosa is surrounded by concentric layers of smooth muscle (Figure 27.14b). Transport of the materials along the uterine tube involves a combination of ciliary movement and peristaltic contractions in the walls of the uterine tube. A few hours before ovulation, sympathetic and parasympathetic nerves from the hypogastric plexus "turn on" this beating pattern. The uterine tubes transport a secondary oocyte for final maturation and fertilization. It normally takes three to four days for an oocyte to travel from the infundibulum to the uterine chamber. *If fertilization is to occur, the secondary oocyte must encounter spermatozoa during the first 12–24 hours of its passage.* Fertilization typically occurs in the ampulla of the uterine tube.

Along with its transport function, the uterine tube also provides a rich, nutritive environment containing lipids and glycogen. This mixture provides nutrients to both spermatozoa and a developing pre-embryo. Unfertilized oocytes degenerate in the terminal portions of the uterine tubes or within the uterus.

CONCEPT CHECK

1. What are the functions of the follicular cells?
2. How could scarring of the uterine tubes cause infertility?

See blue "Answers" tab at back of book.

The Uterus [Figures 27.10/27.11/27.15]

The **uterus** (Ū-ter-us) provides mechanical protection, nutritional support, and waste removal for the developing embryo (weeks 1–8) and fetus (from week 9 to delivery). In addition, contractions in the muscular wall of the uterus are important in ejecting the fetus at the time of birth. The position of the uterus within the pelvic cavity and its relation to other pelvic organs can be seen in different views in Figures 27.10, p. 728, 27.11, p. 729, and 27.15.

The uterus is a small, pear-shaped organ about 7.5 cm (3 in.) long with a maximum diameter of 5 cm (2 in.). It weighs 30–40 g (1–1.4 oz). In its normal position, the uterus bends anteriorly near its base, a condition known as **anteflexion** (an-tē-FLEK-shun). In this position the body of the uterus lies across the superior and posterior surfaces of the urinary bladder (Figure 27.10). If instead the uterus bends backward toward the sacrum, the condition is termed **retroflexion** (re-trō-FLEK-shun). Retroflexion, which occurs in about 20 percent of adult women, has no clinical significance.

Suspensory Ligaments of the Uterus [Figures 27.11/27.15a]

In addition to the mesenteric sheet of the broad ligament, three pairs of suspensory ligaments stabilize the position of the uterus and limit its range of movement (Figures 27.11 and 27.15a). The **uterosacral** (ū-ter-ō-SĀ-kral) **ligaments** extend from the lateral surfaces of the uterus to the anterior face of the sacrum, keeping the *body* of the uterus from moving inferiorly and anteriorly. The **round ligaments** arise on the lateral margins of the uterus just inferior to the bases of the uterine tubes. They extend anteriorly, passing through the inguinal canal before ending in the connective tissues of the external genitalia. These ligaments primarily restrict posterior movement of the uterus. The **cardinal ligaments** extend from the base of the uterus and vagina to the lateral walls of the pelvis. These ligaments also tend to prevent the inferior movement of the uterus. Additional mechanical support is provided by the skeletal muscles and fascia of the pelvic floor.

Internal Anatomy of the Uterus [Figure 27.15]

The uterine **body**, or *corpus*, is the largest region of the uterus (Figure 27.15a). The **fundus** is the rounded portion of the body superior to the attachment of the uterine tubes. The body ends at a constriction known as the *isthmus* of the uterus. The **cervix** (SER-viks) of the uterus is the inferior portion that extends from the isthmus to the vagina.

The tubular cervix projects about 1.25 cm (0.5 in.) into the vagina. Within the vagina, the distal end of the cervix forms a curving surface surrounding the **external os** (*os*, opening or mouth), the external opening of the uterus. The external os leads into the **cervical canal**, a constricted passageway that opens into the **uterine cavity** of the body at the **internal os**, or internal opening (Figure 27.15). The mucus that fills the cervical canal and covers the external os helps prevent the passage of bacteria from the

Clinical Note

Uterine Cancers **Uterine cancers** affect approximately 6 women per 100,000. In 2006 in the United States, an estimated 40,770 new cases were reported, and 8200 women died from the disease. There are two types of uterine cancers: (1) *endometrial* and (2) *cervical*.

Endometrial cancer, an invasive cancer of the endometrium, most commonly affects women age 50–70. Estrogen therapy, used to treat osteoporosis in postmenopausal women, increases the risk of endometrial cancer by two- to ten-fold. Adding progesterone therapy to the estrogen therapy seems to reduce this risk. There is no perfect screening test for endometrial cancer. The most common symptom is irregular bleeding, and diagnosis typically involves examination of tissue from a biopsy of the endometrium. The treatment of early-stage endometrial cancer involves a hysterectomy, perhaps followed by localized radiation therapy. In advanced stages, more aggressive radiation treatment may be recommended. Chemotherapy has not been demonstrated to be a successful treatment for endometrial cancers, and only 30–40 percent of patients appear to benefit from this treatment approach.

Cervical cancer is the most common reproductive system cancer in women age 15–34. The primary risk factor for this cancer appears to be a history of multiple sexual partners. The cancer seems to develop after a genital viral infection by one of several different forms of human papillomaviruses (HPVs), which are transmitted through sexual contact. Most women with cervical cancer fail to develop symptoms until late in the disease. At that stage vaginal bleeding, especially after intercourse, pelvic pain, and vaginal discharge may occur. Treatment of more advanced cancers typically combines radiation therapy, **hysterectomy** (complete or partial removal of the uterus), lymph node removal, and chemotherapy.

Early detection is the key to reducing the mortality rate for cervical cancer. The standard screening test is the *Pap smear*, named for Dr. George Papanicolaou, an anatomist and cytologist. Because the cervical epithelium normally sheds its superficial cells, a sample of cells scraped or brushed from the epithelial surface can be examined for abnormal or cancerous cells. The American Cancer Society recommends yearly Pap tests at ages 20 and 21, followed by smears at one- to three-year intervals until age 65. Treatment of localized, noninvasive cervical cancer removes the affected portion of the cervix.

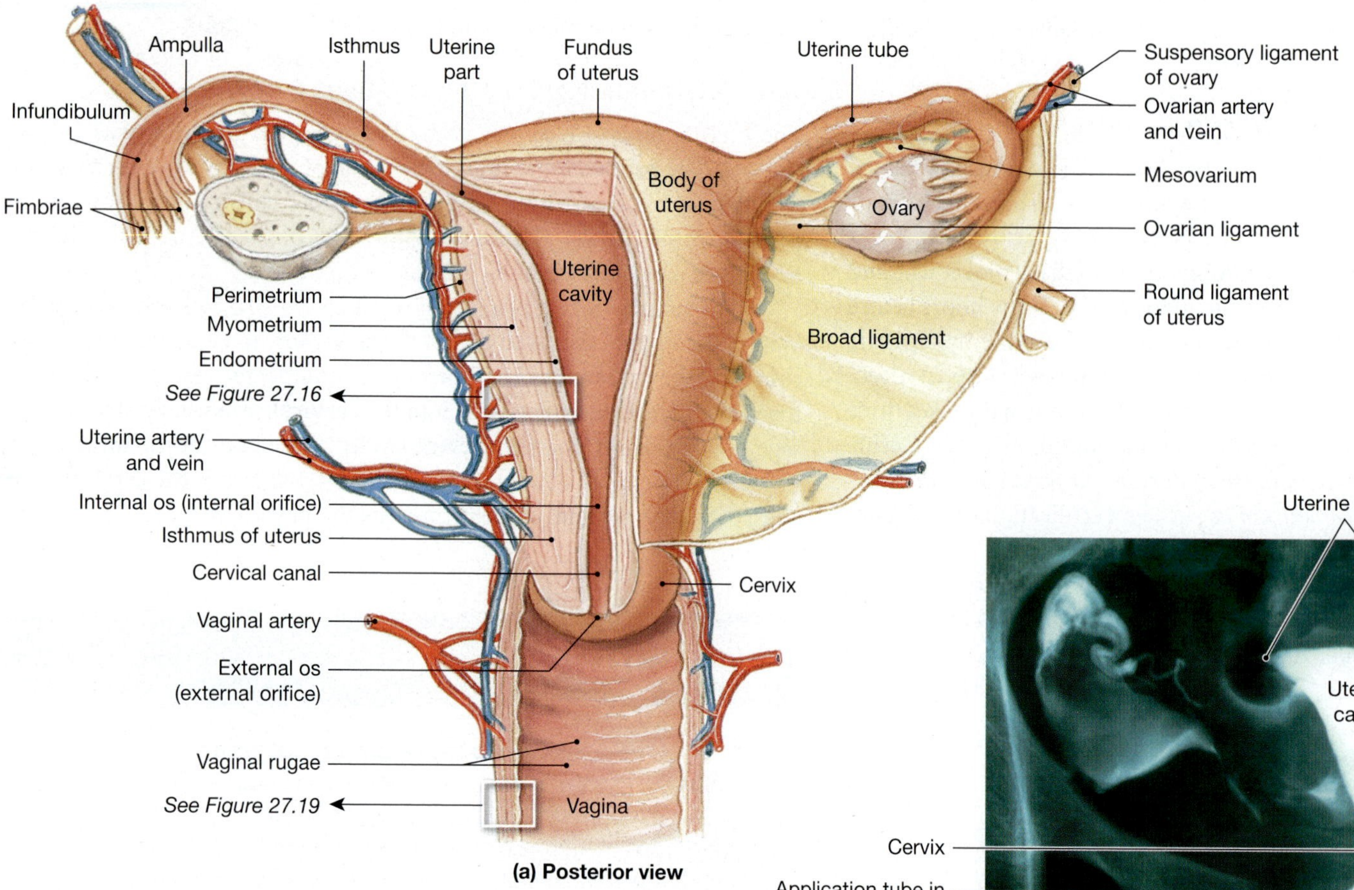

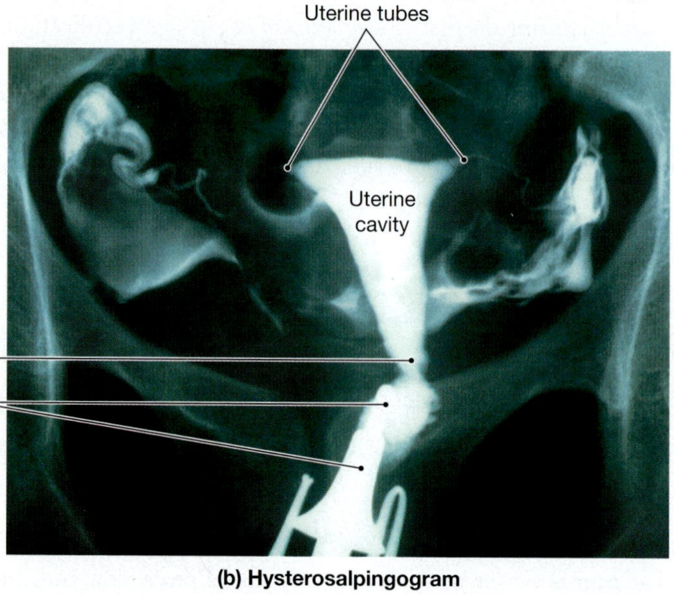

Figure 27.15 The Uterus
(a) Posterior view of the uterus and stabilizing ligaments within the pelvic cavity. **(b)** The uterine cavity and uterine lumen as seen in a hysterosalpingogram.

vagina into the cervical canal. As ovulation approaches, the mucus changes its consistency, becoming more watery. If the mucus remains viscous, sperm have a difficult time entering the uterus, and they may be unable to ascend the uterine tubes. This reduces the odds for successful fertilization. For this reason, treatment of female infertility may include drugs that reduce the viscosity of the cervical mucus.

The uterus is supplied with branches of the uterine and ovarian arteries and veins. Numerous lymphatic vessels also supply each portion of the uterus. The uterus is innervated by autonomic fibers from the hypogastric plexus (sympathetic nervous system) and sacral segments S_3 and S_4 (parasympathetic nervous system). Sensory afferents from the uterus enter the spinal cord in the dorsal roots of spinal nerves T_{11} and T_{12}

The Uterine Wall [Figures 27.15a/27.16]

The dimensions of the uterus are highly variable. In adult women of reproductive age who have not borne children, the uterine wall is about 1.5 cm (0.5 in.) thick. The uterine wall has an outer, muscular **myometrium** (mī-ō-MĒ-trē-um; *myo-*, muscle + *metra*, uterus) and an inner glandular **endometrium** (en-dō-MĒ-trē-um), or *mucosa*. The fundus and the anterior and posterior surfaces of the uterine body are covered by a serous membrane continuous with the peritoneal lining. This incomplete serosal layer is called the **perimetrium** (Figures 27.15a and 27.16).

The endometrium contributes about 10 percent to the mass of the uterus. Vast numbers of uterine glands open onto the endometrial surface. These glands extend deep into the lamina propria almost all the way to the myometrium. Under the influence of estrogen, the uterine glands, blood vessels, and endothelium change with the various phases of the monthly *uterine cycle*. The glandular and vascular tissues of the endometrium support the physiological demands of the growing fetus.

The myometrium is the thickest portion of the uterine wall, and it forms almost 90 percent of the mass of the uterus. Smooth muscle in the myometrium is arranged into longitudinal, circular, and oblique layers. The smooth muscle tissue of the myometrium provides much of the force needed to push a large fetus out of the uterus and into the vagina.

Blood Supply to the Uterus [Figure 27.15a]

The uterus receives blood from branches of the **uterine arteries** (Figure 27.15a), which arise from branches of the internal iliac arteries, and the **ovarian arteries**, which arise from the abdominal aorta inferior to the renal arteries. p. 588 There are extensive interconnections among the arteries to the uterus. This arrangement helps ensure a reliable flow of blood to the organ, despite changes in position and in uterine shape that accompany pregnancy.

Histology of the Uterus [Figure 27.16]

The endometrium can be subdivided into an inner **functional layer**, the layer closest to the uterine cavity, and an outer **basilar layer** adjacent to the myometrium. The functional layer contains most of the uterine glands and

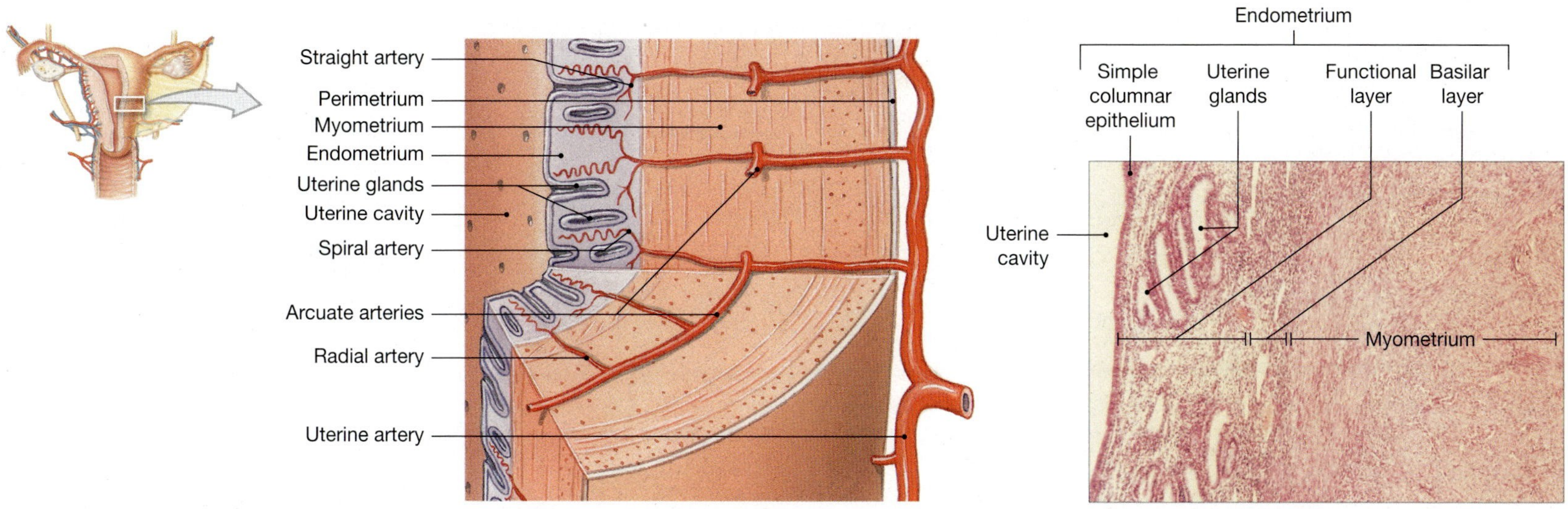

(a) Uterine wall, sectional view

(b) Uterine wall, histology LM × 32

Figure 27.16 The Uterine Wall
(a) A diagrammatic sectional view of the uterine wall, showing the endometrial regions and the arterial supply to the endometrium. **(b)** Basic histology of the uterine wall.

contributes most of the endometrial thickness. The basilar layer attaches the endometrium to the myometrium and contains the terminal branches of the tubular glands (Figure 27.16a).

Within the myometrium, branches of the uterine arteries form **arcuate arteries** that encircle the endometrium. **Radial arteries** branch from the arcuate arteries and supply both **straight arteries** that deliver blood to the basilar layer of the endometrium and **spiral arteries** that supply the functional layer (Figure 27.16b).

The structure of the basilar layer remains relatively constant over time, but the structure of the functional layer undergoes cyclical changes in response to sexual hormone levels. These alterations produce the characteristic histological features of the *uterine cycle.*

The Uterine Cycle [Figures 27.17/27.18]

The **uterine cycle**, or *menstrual* (MEN-stroo-al) *cycle*, averages 28 days in length, but it can range from 21 to 35 days in normal individuals. The three phases of the uterine cycle are (1) *menses*, (2) the *proliferative phase*, and (3) the *secretory phase*. The histological appearance of the endometrium during each phase is shown in Figure 27.17. The phases occur in response to hormones associated with the regulation of the ovarian cycle (Figure 27.18).

Menses [Figures 27.17a/27.18] The uterine cycle begins with the onset of **menses** (MEN-sēz), a period marked by the wholesale destruction of the functional layer of the endometrium. The arteries begin constricting, reducing blood flow to this region, and the secretory glands and tissues of the functional layer begin to die. Eventually the weakened arterial walls rupture, and blood pours into the connective tissues of the functional layer. Blood cells and degenerating tissues break away from the endometrium and enter the uterine lumen, and pass through the external os and into the vagina. This sloughing of tissue, which continues until the entire functional layer has been lost (Figure 27.17a), is called **menstruation** (men-stroo-Ā-shun). Menstruation usually lasts from one to seven days, and over this period roughly 35–50 ml of blood is lost. Painful menstruation, or **dysmenorrhea**, may result either from uterine inflammation and contraction or from conditions involving adjacent pelvic structures.

Menses occurs when progestin and estrogen concentrations decrease at the end of the ovarian cycle. It continues until the next group of follicles has developed to the point where estrogen levels rise once again (Figure 27.18).

The Proliferative Phase [Figures 27.17b/27.18] The basilar layer, including the basal portions of the uterine glands, survives menses because its circulatory supply remains constant. In the days following the completion of menses, and under the influence of circulating estrogens, the epithelial cells of the glands multiply and spread across the endometrial surface, restoring the integrity of the uterine epithelium (Figure 27.17b). Further growth and vascularization result in the complete restoration of the functional layer. As this reorganization proceeds, the endometrium is said to be in the **proliferative phase**. This restoration occurs at the same time as the enlargement of primary and secondary follicles in the ovary. The proliferative phase is stimulated and sustained by estrogen secreted by the developing follicles (Figure 27.18).

By the time ovulation occurs, the functional layer is several millimeters thick, and prominent mucous glands extend to the border with the basilar layer. At this time the endometrial glands are manufacturing a mucus rich in glycogen. The entire functional layer is highly vascularized, with small arteries spiraling toward the inner surface from larger trunks in the myometrium.

The Secretory Phase [Figures 27.17c/27.18] During the secretory phase of the uterine cycle, the endometrial glands enlarge, accelerating their rates of secretion, and the arteries elongate and spiral through the tissues of the functional layer (Figure 27.17c). This activity occurs under the combined stimulatory effects of progestins and estrogens from the corpus luteum (Figure 27.18). This phase begins at the time of ovulation and persists as long as the corpus luteum remains intact.

Secretory activities peak about 12 days after ovulation. Over the next day or two, the glandular activity declines, and the uterine cycle ends as the

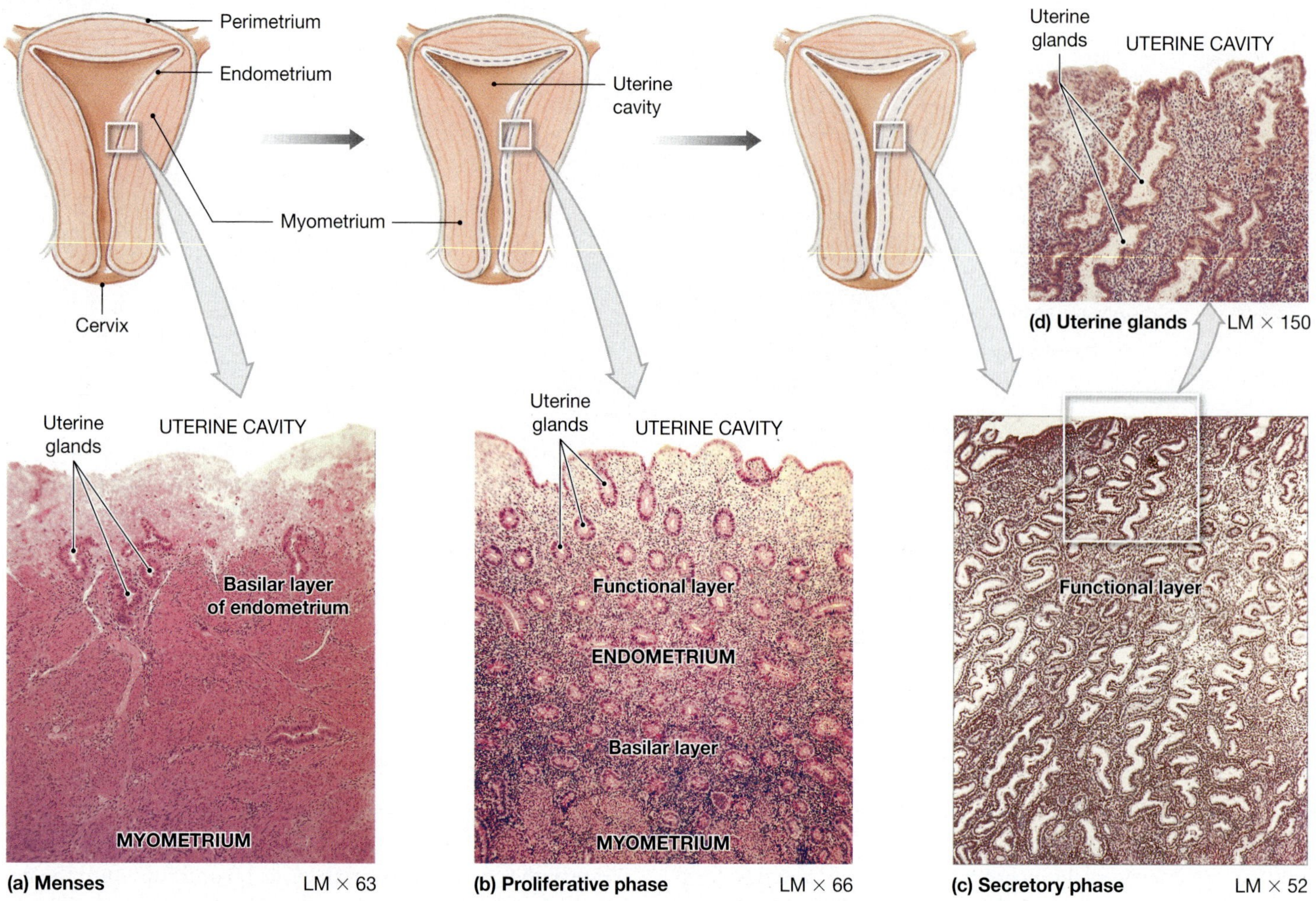

Figure 27.17 Histological Changes in the Uterine Cycle
(a) Menses. **(b)** Proliferative phase. **(c)** Secretory phase. The functional layer is now so thick that at a magnification comparable to that of part (a) or part (b) you cannot capture the entire width of the endometrium in one image. **(d)** Detail of uterine glands.

corpus luteum stops producing stimulatory hormones. A new cycle then begins with the onset of menses and the disintegration of the functional layer. The secretory phase usually lasts 14 days. As a result, the date of ovulation can be determined after the fact by counting backward 14 days from the first day of menses.

Menarche and Menopause The uterine cycle of events begins with the **menarche** (me-NAR-kē), or first uterine cycle at puberty, typically at age 11–12. The cycles continue until age 45–55, when **menopause** (MEN-ō-paws), the last uterine cycle, occurs. Over the intervening decades, the regular appearance of uterine cycles is interrupted only by unusual circumstances such as illness, stress, starvation, or pregnancy. Typically, irregular cycles are characteristic of the first two years after menarche and the last two years before menopause.

The Vagina [Figures 27.10/27.11a]

The *vagina* is an elastic, muscular tube extending from the cervix of the uterus to the *vestibule*, a space bounded by the external genitalia (Figures 27.10, p. 728, and 27.11a, p. 729). The vagina has an average length of 7.5–9 cm (3–3.5 in.), but because the vagina is highly distensible, its length and width are quite variable.

At the proximal end of the vagina, the cervix projects into the **vaginal canal**. The shallow recess surrounding the cervical protrusion is known as the **fornix** (FOR-niks). The vagina lies parallel to the rectum, and the two are in close contact posteriorly. Anteriorly, the urethra travels along the superior wall of the vagina as it travels from the urinary bladder to its opening into the vestibule. The primary blood supply of the vagina is via the **vaginal branches** of the internal iliac (or uterine) arteries and veins. Innervation is from the hypogastric plexus, sacral nerves S_2–S_4, and branches of the pudendal nerve.

The vagina has three major functions:

- It serves as a passageway for the elimination of menstrual fluids;
- It receives the penis during sexual intercourse and holds spermatozoa before they pass into the uterus.
- In childbirth, it forms the lower portion of the birth canal through which the fetus passes during delivery.

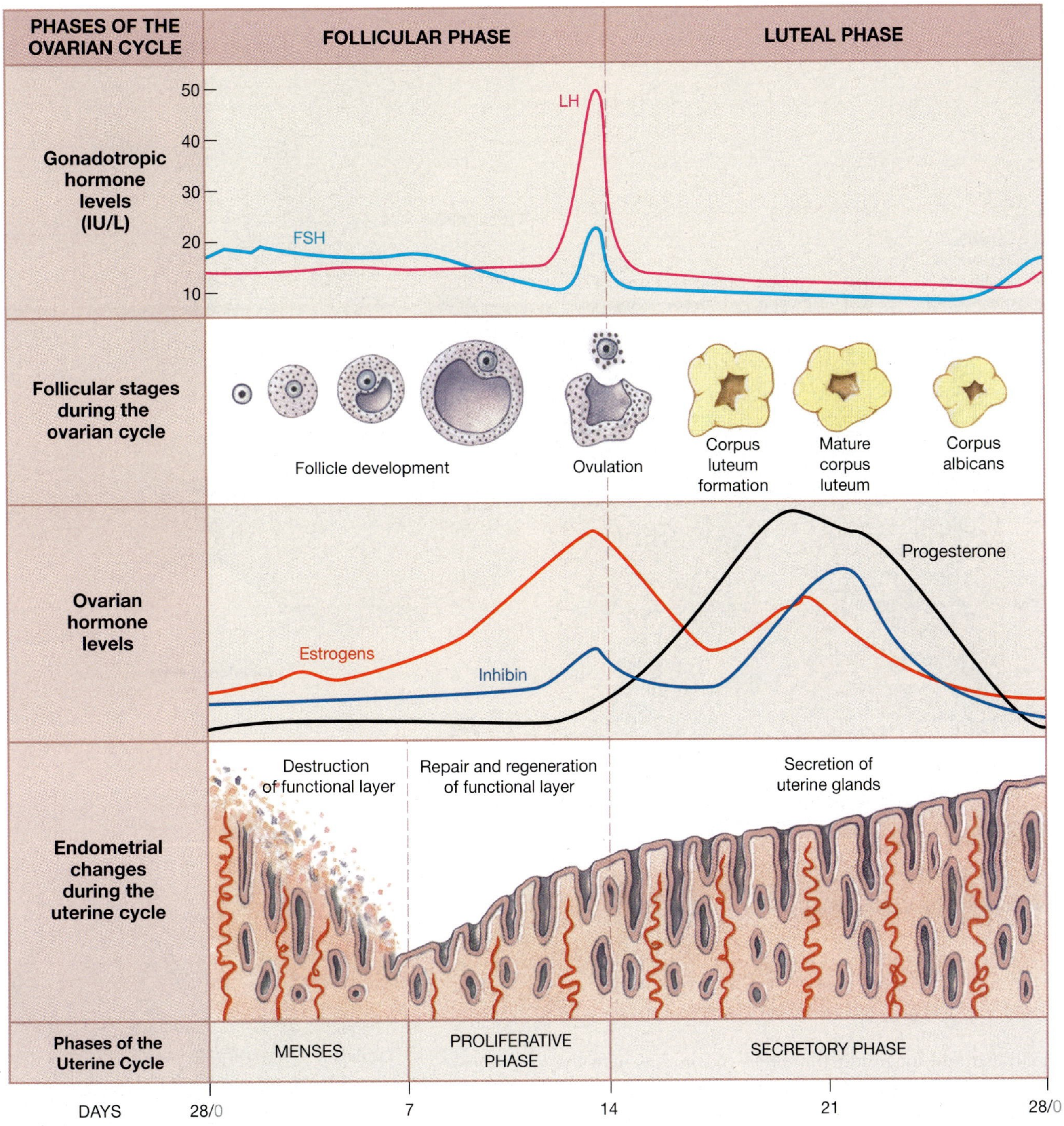

Figure 27.18 The Hormonal Regulation of Female Reproductive Function

Histology of the Vagina [Figures 27.15a/27.19/27.20b]

In sectional view, the lumen of the vagina appears constricted, roughly forming the shape of an H. The vaginal walls contain a network of blood vessels and layers of smooth muscle (**Figures 27.15a** and **27.19**), and the lining is moistened by the secretions of the cervical glands and by the movement of water across the permeable epithelium. The vagina and vestibule are separated by an elastic epithelial fold, the **hymen** (HĪ-men), which may partially or completely block the entrance to the vagina. The two bulbospongiosus muscles pass on either side of the vaginal orifice, and their contractions constrict the entrance. These muscles cover the *vestibular bulbs*, masses of erectile tissue that pass on either side of the vaginal entrance (**Figure 27.20b**). During development, the vestibular bulbs are derived from the same embryonic tissues as the corpus spongiosum of the male (see the Embryology Summary in Chapter 28). The vestibular bulbs and corpus spongiosum are called *homologous* (ho-MOL-ō-gus; *homo*, same + *logos*, relation) because they are similar in structure and origin; however, homologous structures can have very different functions.

The vaginal lumen is lined by a stratified squamous epithelium (**Figure 27.19**) that in the relaxed state is thrown into folds, called *rugae* (**Figure 27.15a**). The underlying lamina propria is thick and elastic, and it contains small blood vessels, nerves, and lymph nodes. The vaginal mucosa is surrounded by an elastic *muscularis layer*, with layers of smooth muscle

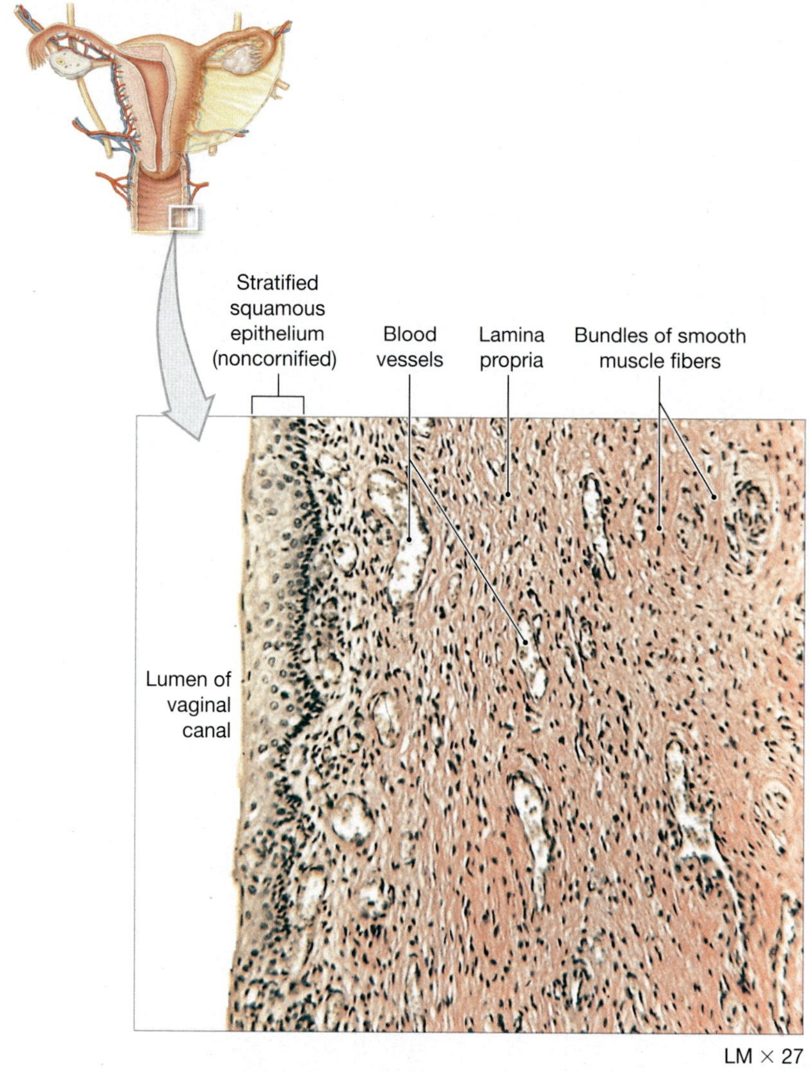

Figure 27.19 Histology of the Vaginal Wall

fibers arranged in circular and longitudinal bundles continuous with the uterine myometrium. The portion of the vagina adjacent to the uterus has a serosal covering continuous with the pelvic peritoneum; over the rest of the vagina the muscularis layer is surrounded by an *adventitia* of fibrous connective tissue.

The vagina contains a normal population of resident bacteria, supported by the nutrients found in the cervical mucus. The metabolic activity of these bacteria creates an acid environment, which restricts the growth of many pathogenic organisms. An acid environment also inhibits sperm motility, and for this reason the buffers contained in seminal fluid are important to successful fertilization.

The External Genitalia [Figures 27.10a/27.20a]

The region enclosing the female external genitalia is called the **vulva** (VUL-va), or *pudendum* (pū-DEN-dum) (Figure 27.20a). The vagina opens into the **vestibule**, a central space bounded by the **labia minora** (LĀ-bē-a mī-NOR-a; singular, *labium minus*). The labia minora are covered with a smooth, hairless skin. The urethra opens into the vestibule just anterior to the vaginal entrance. The **paraurethral glands**, or *Skene's glands*, discharge

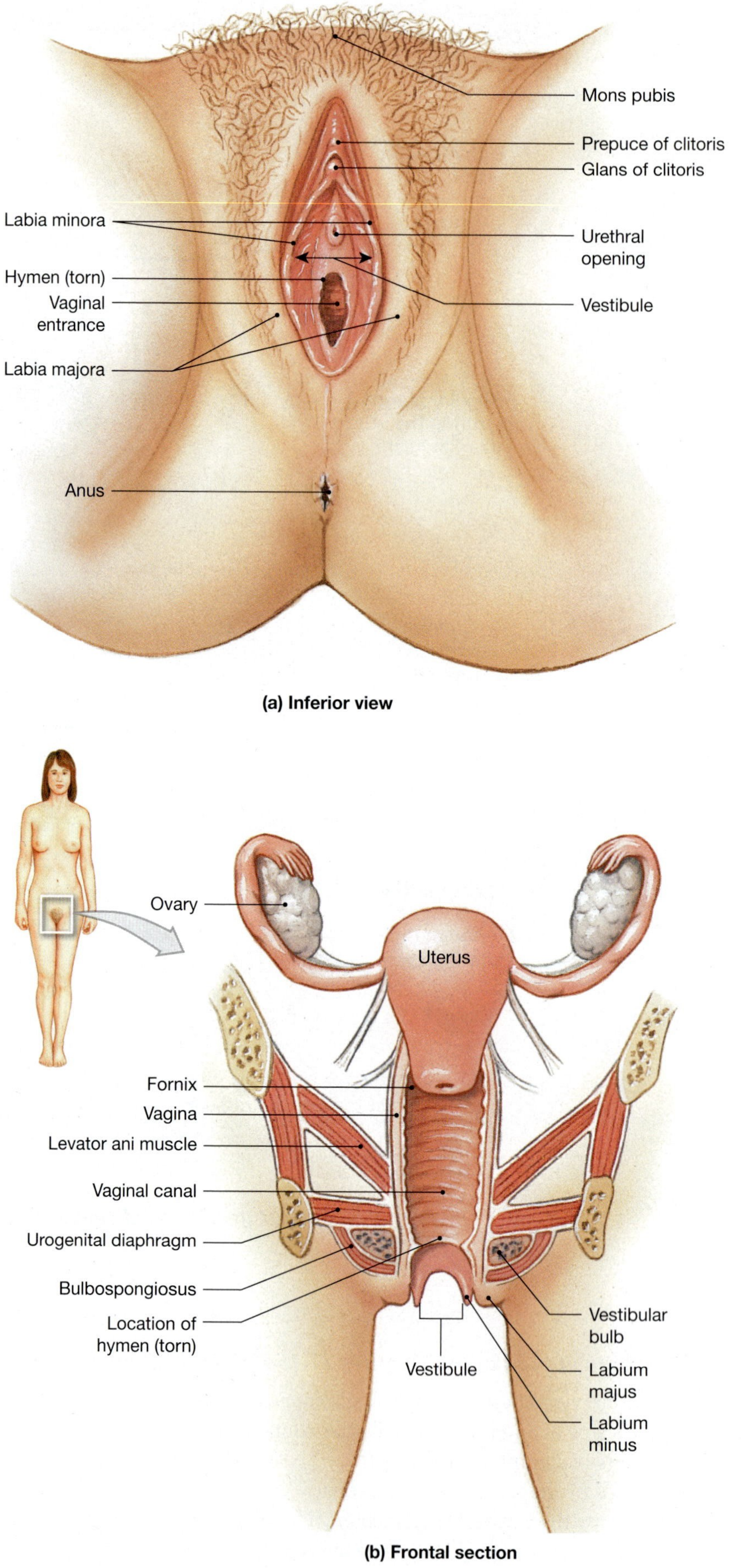

Figure 27.20 The Female External Genitalia
(a) An inferior view of the female perineum. **(b)** A diagrammatic frontal section, showing the relative positions of the internal and external reproductive structures.

into the urethra near the external urethral orifice. Anterior to the urethral opening, the **clitoris** (KLIT-ō-ris) projects into the vestibule. Internally the clitoris contains erectile tissue homologous with the corpora cavernosa in males (see the Embryology Summary in Chapter 28). The clitoris becomes engorged with blood during sexual arousal. A small erectile *glans* sits atop the organ, and extensions of the labia minora encircle the body of the clitoris, forming the **prepuce**, or *hood*, of the clitoris.

A variable number of small **lesser vestibular glands** discharge their secretions onto the exposed surface of the vestibule, keeping it moistened. During arousal, a pair of ducts discharges the secretions of the **greater vestibular glands** *(Bartholin's glands)* into the vestibule near the posterolateral margins of the vaginal entrance (Figure 27.10a, p. 728). These mucous glands resemble the bulbo-urethral glands of the male.

The outer limits of the vulva are established by the *mons pubis* and the *labia majora.* The prominent bulge of the **mons pubis** is formed by adipose tissue beneath the skin anterior to the pubic symphysis. Adipose tissue also accumulates within the fleshy **labia majora** (singular, *labium majus*), which are homologous to the scrotum of males. The labia majora encircle and partially conceal the labia minora and vestibular structures. The outer margins of the labia majora are covered with the same coarse hair that covers the mons pubis, but the inner surfaces are relatively hairless. Sebaceous glands and scattered apocrine sweat glands secrete onto the inner surface of the labia majora, moistening them and providing lubrication.

Embryology Summary

For a summary of the development of the female reproductive system, see Chapter 28 (Embryology and Human Development).

The Mammary Glands [Figure 27.21]

At birth, the newborn infant cannot fend for itself, and several key systems have yet to complete their development. Over the initial period of adjustment to an independent existence, the infant gains nourishment from the milk secreted by the maternal **mammary glands**. Milk production, or **lactation** (lak-TĀ-shun), occurs in the mammary glands of the breasts, specialized accessory organs of the female reproductive system.

The mammary glands lie on either side of the chest in the subcutaneous tissue of the **pectoral fat pad** deep to the skin (Figure 27.21a,b). Each breast bears a small conical projection, the **nipple**, where the ducts of underlying mammary glands open onto the body surface. The region of reddish-brown skin surrounding each nipple is known as the **areola** (a-RĒ-ō-la). The presence of large sebaceous glands in the underlying dermis gives the areolar surface a granular texture.

The glandular tissue of the breast consists of a number of separate lobes, each containing several secretory lobules (Figure 27.21a). Ducts leaving the lobules converge, giving rise to a single **lactiferous** (lak-TIF-e-rus) **duct** in each lobe (Figure 27.21a,c,d). Near the nipple, that lactiferous duct expands, forming an expanded chamber called a **lactiferous sinus**. Usually 15–20 lactiferous sinuses open onto the surface of each nipple. Dense connective tissue surrounds the duct system and forms partitions that extend between the lobes and lobules. These bands of connective tissue, known as the **suspensory ligaments of the breast**, originate in the dermis of the overlying skin. A layer of loose connective tissue separates the mammary complex from the underlying pectoralis muscles. Branches of the *internal thoracic artery* supply blood to each mammary gland. ∞ p. 583 The lymphatic drainage of the mammary gland was detailed in Chapter 23. ∞ p. 620

Clinical Note

Breast Cancer Breast cancer is the primary cause of death for women between ages 40 and 59. In general, the incidence of breast cancer becomes more common after age 50. In the United States roughly 212,000 new cases are reported each year. An estimated 1 in 8 women in the United States will develop breast cancer at some point in their lives. The incidence is highest among Caucasians, somewhat lower in African Americans, and lowest in Asians and Native Americans. Notable risk factors include (1) a family history of breast cancer, (2) a pregnancy after age 30, (3) an early menarche (first menstrual period), and (4) a late menopause (last menstrual period). Despite repeated studies, there are no proven links between breast cancer and oral contraceptive use, estrogen therapy, breast feeding, fat consumption, or alcohol use. Multiple factors are involved; most women never develop breast cancer, but women in families with a history of this disease have a greater probability.

Early detection of breast cancer is the key to reducing the death rate. Most breast cancers are found through self-examination, but clinical screening techniques have increased in recent years. **Mammography** uses x-rays to examine breast tissues; the radiation dosage can be restricted because only soft tissues must be penetrated. This test gives the clearest picture of conditions within the breast tissues (Figure 27.21b). Ultrasound can also provide some information, but the images lack the detail of standard mammograms.

For treatment to be successful the cancer must be identified while it is still relatively small and localized. Once it has grown larger than 2 cm (0.78 in.) the chances for long-term survival worsen. A poor prognosis also follows if the cancer cells have spread through the lymphoid system to the axillary lymph nodes. If the nodes are not yet involved, the chances of five-year survival are about 82 percent; but if four or more nodes are involved, the survival rate drops to 21 percent.

Treatment of breast cancer begins with the removal of the tumors and sampling of the axillary lymph nodes. Because the cancer cells usually begin spreading before the condition is diagnosed, surgical treatment requires the removal of part or all of the affected breast. A combination of chemotherapy, radiation treatments, and hormone treatments may be used to supplement the surgical procedures.

Development of the Mammary Glands during Pregnancy [Figure 27.21c,d]

Figure 27.21c,d compares the histological organization of the inactive and active mammary glands. The resting mammary gland is dominated by a duct system, rather than by active glandular cells. The size of the breast in a nonpregnant woman reflects primarily the amount of adipose tissue in the breast, rather than the amount of glandular tissue. The secretory apparatus does not develop until pregnancy occurs.

Further mammary gland development requires a combination of hormones, including *prolactin (PRL)* and *growth hormone (GH)* from the anterior lobe of the pituitary gland. ∞ p. 513 Under stimulation by these hormones, aided by **human placental lactogen** (LAK-tō-jen) **(HPL)** from the placenta, the mammary gland ducts become mitotically active, and gland cells begin to appear. By the end of the sixth month of pregnancy, the mammary glands are fully developed, and they begin producing secretions that are stored in the duct system. Milk is released when the infant begins to suck on the nipple. This stimulation causes the release of oxytocin by the posterior

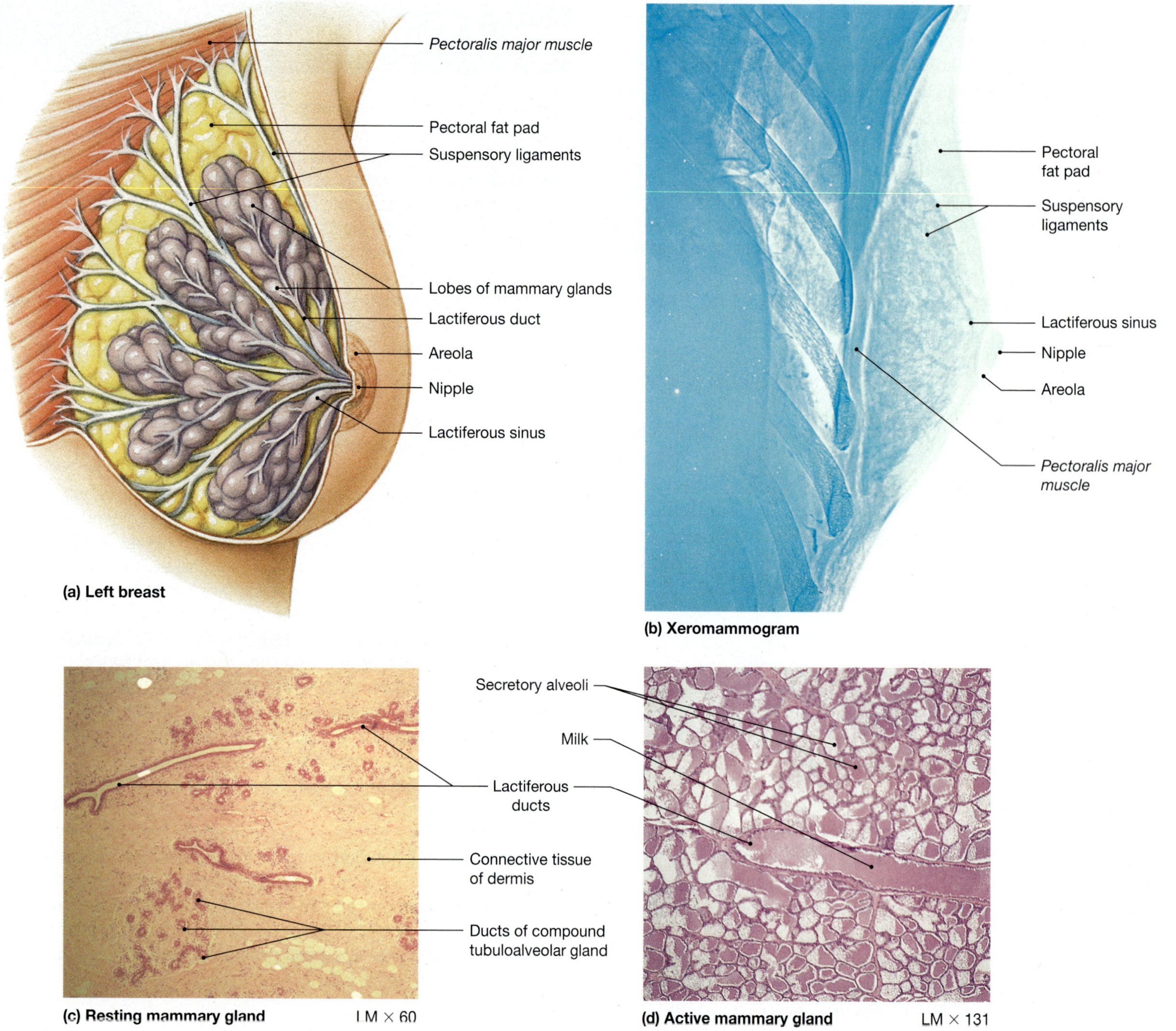

Figure 27.21 The Mammary Glands
(a) Gross anatomy of the breast. **(b)** Xeromammogram, a radiographic technique designed to show the tissue detail of the breast, mediolateral projection. **(c, d)** Histological comparison of resting and active mammary glands.

lobe of the pituitary gland. Oxytocin triggers the contraction of smooth muscles in the walls of the lactiferous ducts and sinuses, ejecting milk.

CONCEPT CHECK

1. During the proliferative phase of the uterine cycle, what activities occur in the ovarian cycle?
2. What marks the beginning of the secretory phase?
3. Would blockage of a single lactiferous sinus interfere with delivery of milk to the nipple? Explain.
4. What hormones stimulate lactation?

See blue "Answers" tab at back of book.

Pregnancy and the Female Reproductive System

If fertilization occurs, the zygote (fertilized egg) undergoes a series of cell divisions, forming a hollow ball of cells known as a **blastocyst** (BLAS-tō-sist). Upon arrival in the uterine cavity, the blastocyst initially obtains nutrients by absorbing the secretions of the uterine glands. Within a few days, it contacts the endometrial wall, erodes the epithelium, and buries itself in the endometrium. This process, known as **implantation** (im-plan-TĀ-shun), initiates the chain of events leading to the formation of a special organ, the **placenta** (pla-SEN-ta), that will support embryonic and fetal development over the next nine months.

The placenta provides a medium for the transfer of dissolved gases, nutrients, and waste products between the fetal and maternal bloodstreams. It also acts as an endocrine organ, producing hormones. The hormone **human chorionic** (kō-rē-ON-ik) **gonadotropin (HCG)** appears in the maternal bloodstream soon after implantation has occurred. The presence of HCG in blood or urine samples provides a reliable indication of pregnancy. In function, HCG resembles LH, for in the presence of HCG the corpus luteum does not degenerate. If it did, the pregnancy would end, for the functional layer of the endometrium would disintegrate.

In the presence of HCG, the corpus luteum persists for about three months before degenerating. Its departure does not trigger the return of menstrual periods, because by then the placenta is actively secreting both estrogen and progesterone. Over the following months, the placenta also synthesizes two additional hormones: **relaxin**, which increases the flexibility of the pelvis during delivery and causes dilation of the cervix during birth; and **human placental lactogen**, which helps prepare the mammary glands for milk production.

Aging and the Reproductive System

The aging process affects the reproductive systems of men and women. The most striking age-related changes in the female reproductive system occur at menopause, while changes in the male reproductive system occur more gradually and over a longer period of time.

Menopause

Menopause is usually defined as the time when ovulation and menstruation cease. Menopause typically occurs at age 45–55, but in the years preceding it, the regularity of the ovarian and menstrual cycles gradually fades. **Premature menopause** occurs before age 40. A shortage of primordial follicles is the underlying cause of premature menopause. Menopause is accompanied by a sharp and sustained rise in the production of GnRH, FSH, and LH, while circulating concentrations of estrogen and progesterone decline. The decline in estrogen levels leads to (1) a reduction in the size of the uterus, (2) a reduction in the size of the breasts, (3) a thinning of the urethral and vaginal walls, and (4) a weakening of the connective tissue supporting the ovaries, uterus, and vagina. The reduced estrogen concentrations have also been linked to the development of osteoporosis and a variety of cardiovascular and neural effects, including "hot flashes," anxiety, and depression.

The Male Climacteric

Changes in the male reproductive system occur more gradually, over a period known as the **male climacteric**. Circulating testosterone levels begin to decline between ages 50 and 60, coupled with increases in circulating levels of FSH and LH. Although sperm production continues (men can father children well into their eighties), there is a gradual reduction in sexual activity in older men, which may be linked to declining testosterone levels. Some clinicians are now suggesting the use of testosterone replacement therapy to enhance libido (sexual drive) in older men and women.

Clinical Case — THE URINARY AND REPRODUCTIVE SYSTEMS

IS THIS NORMAL FOR SOMEONE MY AGE?

Eleanor, an 88-year-old widow and mother of two, visits her local RediMed convenient-care clinic late on a Sunday afternoon. Because her family physician retired a few months ago and she does not yet have a "regular" physician, Eleanor decided to go to the convenient-care clinic. Eleanor's chief complaints to the physician on duty are the following:

- She has an increased urge to urinate, and a "slight" inability to control her urinary process.
- She has recurring bouts of pain upon urination.
- She is experiencing chronic backaches that do not respond to OTC pain medication.
- She reports a previous radical mastectomy.
- Eleanor also has mild hypertension, for which she is on regular medication.

Due to her lack of familiarity with the physician and embarrassment, Eleanor refuses to have a pelvic examination.

Initial Examination

The physician in the clinic notes the following:

- Blood pressure, while medicated, is 145/92.
- A urine specimen, tested by "dipstick," showed chemical signs of white blood cells.
- The patient mentions a mild "backache" pain localized to the regions of rib 11 and lower on the left side, and rib 12 and lower on the right.

The physician informs Eleanor that an inability to control the urinary sphincter is quite common among elderly patients, as are urinary tract infections. He then tells her that she has a urinary tract infection. He prescribes a sulfa drug and recommends that she select a new family physician and have a complete physical examination.

Two weeks later, the pain has recurred. In addition, Eleanor's symptoms have become more severe and slightly modified since her visit to the convenient-care clinic. Mary, her daughter-in-law, advises Eleanor to seek an appointment with Mary's gynecologist. Eleanor agrees, and Mary makes the appointment.

Follow-up Examination

Eleanor relates to the gynecologist the information presented to the physician at RediMed and also presents the following information:

- Whenever she coughs, sneezes, or carries something as light as a bag of groceries, she cannot avoid "wetting herself." This problem

Clinical Case *continued*

has been developing for months and has worsened in the last few weeks. The gynecologist notes "stress incontinence."

- She also complains of having to urinate as many as 10 times during the day and 5 or more times at night. This problem has also been developing for months and worsened in the last few weeks.
- She has difficulties with constipation.
- Her continuing backaches increase in severity by the end of the day.
- She feels a sensation that "something is coming down" her vagina when she is in the upright position, with a worsening of this sensation by the end of the day.
- Upon further questioning by the gynecologist, Eleanor indicates that the stress incontinence and increased frequency of urination have decreased as the sensation that "something is coming down" her vagina has intensified.

The gynecologist performs a pelvic examination and finds physical changes that assist in diagnosing Eleanor's problems.

Points to Consider

At one time or another, every system of the body plays an important role in presenting signs or symptoms, thereby enabling a physician to piece together the various clues that will ideally lead to a correct diagnosis of the patient. Both the patient's presenting symptoms and the physician's analysis and interpretation of the symptoms contribute to the detective work.

To consider the meaning of the information presented in the case above, you need to review the anatomical material covered in the chapters on the urinary and reproductive systems. The questions below will guide you in your review. Think about and answer each one, referring back to Chapters 26 and 27 if you need help.

1. What anatomical structures might be the source of Eleanor's pain?
2. Which specific pathological and/or age-related changes in anatomical structures might be contributing to Eleanor's pain?
3. Explain why Eleanor's complaint of constipation could be closely related to her other symptoms.

Analysis and Interpretation

The information below answers the questions raised in the "Points to Consider" section. To review the material, refer to the pages in the chapters indicated.

1. Eleanor is experiencing referred pain from the kidneys, probably due to the presence of a urinary tract infection. ∞ p. 472
2. The patient's age is an important factor in the physician's diagnosis. Incontinence is a common age-related problem of the urinary system. It is often caused by age-related functional disorders that prevent adequate control of the micturition reflex by the central nervous system. ∞ p. 708 There are several pieces of connective tissue that support the uterus and urinary bladder in a woman. Several factors, including multiple vaginal births and menopause and the accompanying reduction in the release of GnRH, FSH and LH, can weaken these supporting pieces of connective tissue, p. 733. ∞ p. 704
   - Tearing of the cardinal ligament results in a failure to support the superior aspect of the vagina and uterus over the pelvic diaphragm, p. 733.
   - The posterior ligament, or rectovaginal fold, is composed of peritoneum reflected from the posterior vaginal fornix on to the front of the rectum, forming the deep rectouterine pouch, p. 727. The rectouterine pouch is a pocket formed between the posterior wall of the uterus and the anterior surface of the colon. Tearing of the rectovaginal fold may allow the uterus to descend into the rectouterine pouch.
   - Menopause may also weaken the cervical ligaments, the uterosacral ligaments, and the pubocervical ligaments. The cervical ligaments provide important mechanical support for the uterus, pp. 727, 733. The uterosacral ligaments support the uterus, passing posteriorly from the cervix and uterine body on either side of the rectum, attaching to the sacrum. The pubocervical ligaments pass anteriorly from the anterior aspect of the uterus and upper vagina, passing around the urethra and attaching to the posterior aspects of the pubic bones. Weakening of any or all of these ligaments will allow the uterus to move inferiorly.
3. If the uterus is prolapsed into the pelvis it may partially block the entrance to the rectum. Childbirth may stretch and damage the anterior muscular layers of the rectal wall, resulting in less propulsive force when the urge to defecate occurs. The combination slows the passage of fecal material along the colon, and longer transit times means more time for water reabsorption. The result is constipation. Retained fecal material may press against a filled bladder, slowing urination, interfering with complete bladder evacuation, and promoting urinary tract infection. A self-perpetuating cycle may develop where pelvic laxity, uterine prolapse, constipation, and urinary incontinence are interrelated.

CLINICAL CASE TERMS

constipation: A condition in which bowel movements are incomplete or infrequent.

hypertension: Sustained blood pressure above 120/80 mm/hg. (Previously, blood pressure between 120–140/80–90 was termed pre-hypertension.)

OTC medication: Over-the-counter medication; medication that can be purchased without a prescription.

radical mastectomy: A surgical procedure involving the removal of the entire breast, including nipple, areola, overlying skin, and pectoral muscles, and the lymphatic tissue of the chest wall, axilla, and mammary chain.

stress incontinence Inability to keep the urinary sphincter closed during sudden muscular actions, such as sneezing, or abdominal compression while lifting heavy objects. Urinary leakage then occurs.

sulfa drug: An antibacterial drug, containing the sulfanilamide chemical group, commonly used to treat urinary tract infections.

Diagnosis

Eleanor is diagnosed with uterovaginal prolapse (Figure 27.22), which involves partial herniation of the uterus and/or portions of the bladder, urethra, and terminal rectum through the pelvic floor/diaphragm and muscular vaginal walls. Advanced age, menopause, and vaginal births of two or more children all increase the chance of a woman experiencing prolapse. ■

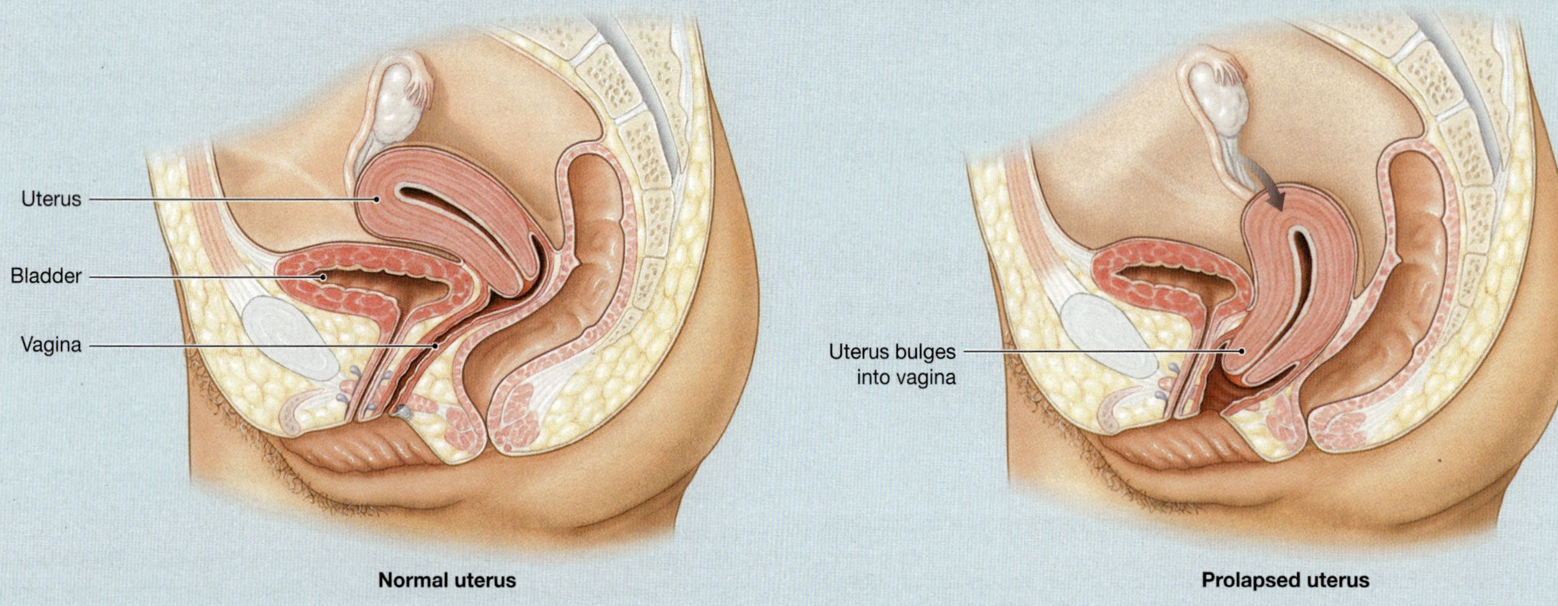

Figure 27.22 **Uterovaginal Prolapse**

CLINICAL TERMS

bacterial (nonspecific) vaginitis: A vaginal inflammation resulting from the combined action of several bacteria in extremely high numbers. The bacteria are normally present in small numbers in about 30 percent of adult women. In this form of vaginitis, the vaginal discharge contains epithelial cells and large numbers of bacteria. Antibiotics are often effective in controlling this condition.

candidiasis (kan-di-DĪ-a-sis): A vaginal inflammation resulting from a fungal (yeast) infection. The organism responsible is a component of the normal vaginal microbial population in 30–80 percent of healthy women. Symptoms include itching and burning sensations, and a lumpy white discharge may also be produced. Antifungal medications are used to treat this condition.

chlamydial infections: The bacterium *Chlamydia trachomatis* is responsible for the majority of pelvic inflammatory disease (PID) cases, and even asymptomatic infections may result in uterine tube blockage infertility.

cryptorchidism (krip-TOR-ki-dizm): Failure of one or both testes to descend into the scrotum by the time of birth.

endometrial polyps: Benign epithelial tumors of the uterine lining.

endometriosis (en-dō-mē-trē-Ō-sis): Growth of endometrial tissue outside of the uterus.

gonorrhea (gon-ō-RĒ-a): A sexually transmitted disease of the reproductive tract.

leiomyomas (LĪ-ō-mī-Ō-maz) or **fibroids:** Benign myometrial tumors that are the most common reproductive system tumors in women.

orchiectomy (or-kē-EK-tō-mē): Surgical removal of a testis.

pelvic inflammatory disease (PID): An infection of the uterine tubes.

prostate cancer: A malignant, metastasizing cancer that is the second most common cause of cancer deaths in males.

prostatectomy (pros-ta-TEK-tō-mē): Surgical removal of the prostate gland.

prostate-specific antigen (PSA): An antigen whose concentration in the blood increases in individuals with prostate cancer or other prostate diseases.

sexually transmitted diseases (STDs): Diseases transferred from one individual to another primarily or exclusively through sexual contact. Commons examples include: chlamydia, gonorrhea, syphilis, herpes, and AIDS.

syphilis (SIF-i-lis): A life-threatening STD that results from infection by the bacterium *Treponema pallidum.*

testicular torsion: Twisting of the spermatic cord and reduction in testicular blood flow resulting from rotation of the testis inside the scrotal cavity.

toxic shock syndrome (TSS): A serious vaginal infection by *Staphylococcus* bacteria. Symptoms include high fever, sore throat, vomiting, diarrhea, and a generalized rash; shock, respiratory distress, and kidney or liver failure may develop. The mortality rate is 10–15 percent, which makes this a very serious condition.

trichomoniasis (trik-ō-mō-NĪ-a-sis): An infection caused by the parasite *Trichomonas vaginalis.* The parasite is introduced by sexual contact with a carrier.

vaginitis (va-jin-Ī-tis): Infection of the vaginal canal by fungal or bacterial pathogens.

vasectomy (va-ZEK-tō-mē): Surgical removal of a segment of the ductus deferens, making it impossible for spermatozoa to reach the distal portions of the reproductive tract.

STUDY OUTLINE

Introduction 715

1. The human reproductive system produces, stores, nourishes, and transports functional **gametes** (reproductive cells). **Fertilization** is the fusion of a **sperm** from the male and an immature **ovum** from the female to form a **zygote** (fertilized egg).

Organization of the Reproductive System 715

1. The reproductive system includes **gonads**, ducts, accessory glands and organs, and the **external genitalia**.
2. In the male, the **testes** produce sperm, which are expelled from the body in **semen** during **ejaculation**. The **ovaries** (gonads) of a sexually mature female produce an egg that travels along **uterine tubes** to reach the **uterus**. The **vagina** connects the uterus with the exterior.

Anatomy of the Male Reproductive System 715

1. The **spermatozoa** travel along the **epididymis**, the **ductus deferens**, the **ejaculatory duct**, and the **urethra** before leaving the body. Accessory organs (notably the **seminal glands**, **prostate gland**, and **bulbo-urethral glands**) secrete into the ejaculatory ducts and urethra. The **scrotum** encloses the testes, and the **penis** is an erectile organ. *(see Figures 27.1 to 27.9)*

The Testes 715

2. The testes hang within the scrotum, and each measures about 2 in. long and 1 in. in diameter.
3. The **descent of the testes** through the inguinal canals occurs during development. Before this time, the testes are held in place by the **gubernaculum testis**. During the seventh developmental month, differential growth and contraction of the gubernaculum testis causes the testes to descend. *(see Figure 27.2)*
4. Layers of fascia, connective tissue, and muscle collectively form a sheath, the spermatic cord, which encloses the ductus deferens, the testicular artery and vein, the **pampiniform plexus**, and the **ilioinguinal** and **genitofemoral nerves**. *(see Figure 27.3)*
5. The testes remain connected to the abdominal cavity through the **spermatic cords**. The **perineal raphe** marks the boundary between the two chambers in the scrotum. Each testis lies in its own **scrotal cavity**. *(see Figures 27.1/27.2/27.4)*
6. Contraction of the **dartos muscle** gives the scrotum a wrinkled appearance; the **cremaster muscle** pulls the testes closer to the body. The **tunica vaginalis** is a serous membrane that covers the **tunica albuginea**, the fibrous capsule that surrounds each testis. Septa extend from the tunica albuginea to the **mediastinum**, creating a series of **lobules**. **Seminiferous tubules** within each lobule are the sites of sperm production. From there, sperm pass through a **straight tubule** to the **rete testis**. **Efferent ducts** connect the rete testis to the epididymis. Between the seminiferous tubules, **interstitial cells** secrete male sex hormones, *androgens*. Seminiferous tubules contain **spermatogonia**, stem cells involved in **spermatogenesis** (the production of sperm). *(see Figures 27.1 to 27.5)*
7. The spermatogonia produce **primary spermatocytes**, **diploid** cells ready to undergo **meiosis**. Four spermatids are produced for every primary spermatocyte. The spermatids remain embedded within **nurse cells** while they mature into a **spermatozoon**, a process called **spermiogenesis**. The nurse cells function to maintain the **blood–testis barrier**, support spermatogenesis, support spermiogenesis, secrete **inhibin**, and secrete **androgen-binding protein**.

Anatomy of a Spermatozoon 721

8. Each spermatozoon has a **head**, **neck**, **middle piece**, and **tail**. The tip of the head contains the **acrosomal cap** or (**acrosome**). The tail consists of a single **flagellum**. Lacking most intracellular structures, the spermatozoon must absorb nutrients from the environment. *(see Figure 27.6)*

The Male Reproductive Tract 722

9. After detaching from the nurse cells, the spermatozoa are carried along fluid currents into the epididymis, an elongate tubule with **head**, **body**, and **tail** regions. The epididymis monitors and adjusts the composition of the tubular fluid, serves as a recycling center for damaged spermatozoa, stores spermatozoa, and facilitates their functional maturation (a process called **capacitation**). *(see Figures 27.1/27.4/27.7)*
10. The **ductus deferens** *(vas deferens)* begins at the epididymis and passes through the inguinal canal as one component of the spermatic cord. Near the prostate, it enlarges to form the **ampulla**. The junction of the base of the seminal gland and the ampulla creates the **ejaculatory duct**, which empties into the urethra. The ductus deferens functions to transport and store spermatozoa. *(see Figures 27.1/27.7/27.8)*
11. The urethra extends from the urinary bladder to the tip of the penis. It can be divided into three regions: the *prostatic urethra, membranous urethra,* and *spongy urethra. (see Figures 27.1/27.9)*

The Accessory Glands 723

12. The accessory glands function to activate and provide nutrients to the spermatozoa and to produce buffers to neutralize the acidity of the urethra and vagina.
13. Each **seminal gland (seminal vesicle)** is an active secretory gland that contributes about 60 percent of the volume of semen; its secretions are high in fructose, which is easily used to produce ATP by spermatozoa. The spermatozoa become highly active after mixing with the secretions of the seminal glands. *(see Figures 27.1/27.8/27.9)*
14. The **prostate gland** secretes a weakly acidic fluid (**prostatic fluid**) that accounts for 20–30 percent of the volume of semen. These secretions contain an antibiotic, **seminalplasmin**, which may help prevent urinary tract infections in men. *(see Figures 27.1/27.8/27.9)*
15. Alkaline mucus secreted by the **bulbo-urethral glands** (*Cowper's glands*) has lubricating properties. *(see Figures 27.1/27.8/27.9)*

Semen 725

16. A typical ejaculation releases 2–5 ml of semen (an **ejaculate**), which contains a **sperm count** of 20 to 100 million sperm per milliliter. The **seminal fluid** is a specific mixture of secretions of the accessory glands and contains important enzymes.

The Penis 725

17. The **penis** can be divided into a **root**, **body (shaft)**, and **glans**. The skin overlying the penis resembles that of the scrotum. The **prepuce** *(foreskin)* surrounds the tip of the penis. **Preputial glands** on the inner surface of the prepuce secrete **smegma**. Most of the body of the penis consists of three masses of **erectile tissue**. Beneath the superficial fascia, there are two **corpora cavernosa** and a single **corpus spongiosum** that surrounds the urethra. When the smooth muscles in the arterial walls relax, the erectile tissue becomes engorged with blood, producing an **erection**. *(see Figures 27.1/27.2/27.9)*

Anatomy of the Female Reproductive System 727

1. Principal structures of the female reproductive system include the **ovaries**, **uterine tubes**, **uterus**, **vagina**, and external genitalia. *(see Figures 27.10 to 27.21)*
2. The ovaries, uterine tubes, and uterus are enclosed within the **broad ligament** (an extensive mesentery). The **mesovarium** supports and stabilizes each ovary. *(see Figures 27.10/27.11/27.15)*

The Ovaries 727

3. The ovaries are held in position by the **ovarian ligament** and the **suspensory ligament**. The **ovarian artery** and **vein** enter the ovary at the

ovarian hilum. Each ovary is covered by a **tunica albuginea.** *(see Figures 27.10/27.11/27.15)*

4. **Oogenesis** (gamete production) occurs monthly in **ovarian follicles** as part of the **ovarian cycle.** As **primordial ovarian follicles** develop into **primary ovarian follicles, thecal granulosa cells** surrounding the oocyte release estrogens, most importantly **estradiol. Follicular fluid** encourages rapid growth during the formation of only a few **secondary ovarian follicles.** Finally, one **tertiary (mature ovarian** or *Graafian*) **follicle** develops. The primary oocyte undergoes meiotic division, producing a secondary oocyte. At **ovulation,** a **secondary oocyte** surrounded by follicular cells (the **corona radiata**) is released through the ruptured ovarian wall. *(see Figure 27.12)*
5. The follicular cells remaining within the ovary form the **corpus luteum,** which produces **progestins,** mainly **progesterone.** If pregnancy does not occur, it degenerates into a **corpus albicans** of scar tissue. *(see Figure 27.12)*
6. The decline in progesterone and estrogen triggers the secretion of **GnRH,** which in turn triggers a rise in FSH and LH production, and the entire cycle begins again. *(see Figure 27.18)*

The Uterine Tubes 732

7. Each **uterine tube** has an expanded funnel, the **infundibulum,** with **fimbriae** (projections); an **ampulla;** an **isthmus;** and a **uterine part** that opens into the **uterine cavity.** *(see Figures 27.10/27.11/27.14/27.15)*
8. The uterine tube is lined with ciliated and nonciliated simple columnar epithelial cells, which aid in the transport of materials. For fertilization to occur, the ovum must encounter spermatozoa during the first 12–24 hours of its passage from the infundibulum to the uterus.

The Uterus 733

9. The **uterus** provides mechanical protection and nutritional support to the developing embryo. Normally the uterus bends anteriorly near its base *(anteflexion).* It is stabilized by the broad ligament, **uterosacral ligaments, round ligaments,** and the **cardinal ligaments.** *(see Figures 27.10/27.11/ 27.15)*
10. The gross divisions of the uterus include the **body** (the largest portion), **fundus, isthmus, cervix, external os, uterine cavity, cervical canal,** and **internal os.** The uterine wall can be divided into an inner **endometrium,** a muscular **myometrium,** and a superficial **perimetrium.** *(see Figures 27.15/27.16)*
11. The uterus receives blood from the **uterine arteries,** which then branch and form extensive interconnections.
12. A typical 28-day **uterine cycle** *(menstrual cycle)* begins with the onset of **menses** and the destruction of the functional layer of the endometrium. This process of **menstruation** continues from one to seven days. *(see Figures 27.17/27.18)*
13. After menses, the **proliferative phase** begins and the functional layer undergoes repair and thickens. Menstrual activity begins at **menarche** (first uterine cycle) and continues until **menopause.** *(see Figures 27.17/27.18)*

The Vagina 736

14. The **vagina** is an elastic, muscular tube extending between the uterus and external genitalia. The vagina serves as a passageway for menstrual fluids, receives the penis during sexual intercourse, and forms the lower portion of the birth canal. A thin epithelial fold, the **hymen,** partially blocks the entrance to the vagina. The vagina is lined by a stratified squamous epithelium which, when relaxed, forms *rugae* (folds). *(see Figures 27.10/27.11/27.19)*

The External Genitalia 738

15. The structures of the **vulva** *(pudendum)* include the **vestibule, labia minora, clitoris, prepuce** (hood), and **labia majora.** The **lesser** and **greater vestibular glands** keep the area moistened in and around the vestibule. The fatty **mons pubis** creates the outer limit of the vulva. *(see Figures 27.10/27.20)*

The Mammary Glands 739

16. The **mammary glands** lie in the subcutaneous layer beneath the skin of the chest and are the site of milk production, or **lactation.** The glandular tissue of the breast consists of secretory lobules. Ducts leaving the lobules converge into a single **lactiferous duct** and expand near the nipple, forming a **lactiferous sinus.** The ducts of underlying mammary glands open onto the body surface at the **nipple.** *(see Figure 27.21)*
17. Branches of the *internal thoracic artery* supply blood to each breast.
18. Mammary glands develop during pregnancy under the influence of *prolactin (PRL)* and *growth hormone (GH)* from the anterior pituitary, as well as **human placental lactogen (HPL)** from the placenta.

Pregnancy and the Female Reproductive System 740

19. If fertilization occurs, **implantation** of the **blastocyst** occurs in the endometrial wall. The **placenta** that develops functions as a temporary endocrine organ, producing several important hormones. **Human chorionic gonadotropin (HCG)** maintains the corpus luteum for several months. By the time the corpus luteum degenerates, the placenta is actively secreting both estrogen and progesterone. The placenta also produces **relaxin,** which is important for delivery, and human placental lactogen (HPL).

Aging and the Reproductive System 741

Menopause 741

1. **Menopause** (the time when ovulation and menstruation cease) typically occurs around age 50. **Premature menopause** occurs before age 40. Production of GnRH, FSH, and LH rises, while circulating concentrations of estrogen and progestins decline.

The Male Climacteric 741

2. The **male climacteric,** which occurs between ages 50 and 60, involves a decline in circulating testosterone levels and a rise in FSH and LH levels.

CHAPTER REVIEW

For answers to the Concept Check and Chapter Review questions, go to the blue "Answers" tab at the back of the book.

Level 1 Reviewing Facts and Terms

Match each numbered item with the most closely related lettered item. Use letters for answers in the spaces provided.

Column A	Column B
___ 1. interstitial cells	a. link from scrotal chamber to peritoneal cavity
___ 2. inguinal canals	b. stem cells that produce spermatozoa
___ 3. mammary glands	c. compartment of the scrotum containing a testis
___ 4. endometrium	d. site of lactation
___ 5. dartos	e. flagellum
___ 6. scrotal cavity	f. inner layer of the uterine wall
___ 7. spermatogonia	g. enlarged portion of the uterine tube
___ 8. estradiol	h. important estrogen hormone
___ 9. ampulla	i. responsible for the production of androgens
___10. spermatozoon tail	j. layer of smooth muscle in dermis of the scrotum

11. The reproductive system includes
 (a) gonads and external genitalia
 (b) ducts that receive and transport the gametes
 (c) accessory glands and organs that secrete fluids
 (d) all of the above

12. Accessory organs of the male reproductive system include all of the following except
 (a) seminal glands (b) scrotum
 (c) bulbo-urethral glands (d) prostate gland

13. Sperm production occurs in the
 (a) ductus deferens (b) seminiferous tubules
 (c) epididymis (d) seminal glands

14. The structure that carries sperm from the epididymis to the urethra is the
 (a) ductus deferens (b) epididymis
 (c) seminal gland (d) ejaculatory duct

15. The mediastinum of the testis
 (a) is ventrally located
 (b) supports the blood vessels and lymphatics supplying the testis
 (c) separates the left and right testis
 (d) forms part of the external testicular capsule

16. The structure that transports the ovum to the uterus is the
 (a) uterosacral ligament (b) vagina
 (c) uterine tube (d) infundibulum

17. Which of the following is not a supporting ligament of the uterus?
 (a) suspensory (b) cardinal
 (c) round (d) broad

18. During the proliferative phase of the menstrual cycle
 (a) ovulation occurs
 (b) a new functional layer is formed in the uterus
 (c) secretory glands and blood vessels develop in the endometrium
 (d) the old functional layer is sloughed off

19. The vagina is
 (a) a central space surrounded by the labia minora
 (b) the inner lining of the uterus
 (c) the inferior portion of the uterus
 (d) a muscular tube extending between the uterus and the external genitalia

20. The structure of the female reproductive system that is homologous to the scrotum of the male reproductive system is the
 (a) vagina (b) cervix
 (c) labia majora (d) uterine tube

Level 2 Reviewing Concepts

1. How will penile function be altered if the blood supply to the corpora cavernosa is impaired?
 (a) the erect penis will be unable to become flaccid
 (b) erection will not occur
 (c) erection can occur, but ejaculation cannot
 (d) the urethra will be occluded

2. What will happen to the function of the male reproductive tract if the testes fail to descend?
 (a) the testicular blood supply will not be adequate
 (b) the spermatic cord will herniate through the inguinal canal
 (c) excess amounts of male sex hormones will be secreted in the abdominal cavity
 (d) no viable spermatozoa will be produced

3. In some cases, a tumor of the breast can be detected by noticing a dimple in the skin over the area. Which breast structures are responsible for this phenomenon?
 (a) the tumor, in that it stimulates contraction of the smooth muscles of the skin
 (b) no breast structures are involved; only the pectoralis major and minor muscles
 (c) the breast lymph nodes, which the tumor causes to contract
 (d) the suspensory ligaments of the breast, which are connected to the tumor

4. Which region of the sperm cell contains chromosomes?

5. What is the function of the acrosomal cap?

6. Where is seminalplasmin produced, and what is its function?

7. How does follicular fluid benefit the development of a follicle?

8. Menstruation results in the loss of which layer of the endometrium?

9. What is the hormone that can be detected soon after implantation is complete?

10. When does descent of the testes normally begin?

Level 3 Critical Thinking

1. Jerry is in an automobile accident that severs his spinal cord at the L_3 level. After his recovery, he wonders if he will still be able to have an erection. What would you tell him?

2. In a condition known as endometriosis, endometrial cells proliferate within a uterine tube or within the peritoneal cavity. A major symptom of endometriosis is periodic pain. Why do you think this occurs?

3. Women are much more susceptible than men to both peritonitis and urinary tract infections as a result of sexual activity. Explain in terms of the differences in male and female anatomy why this can occur.

28

Embryology and Human Development

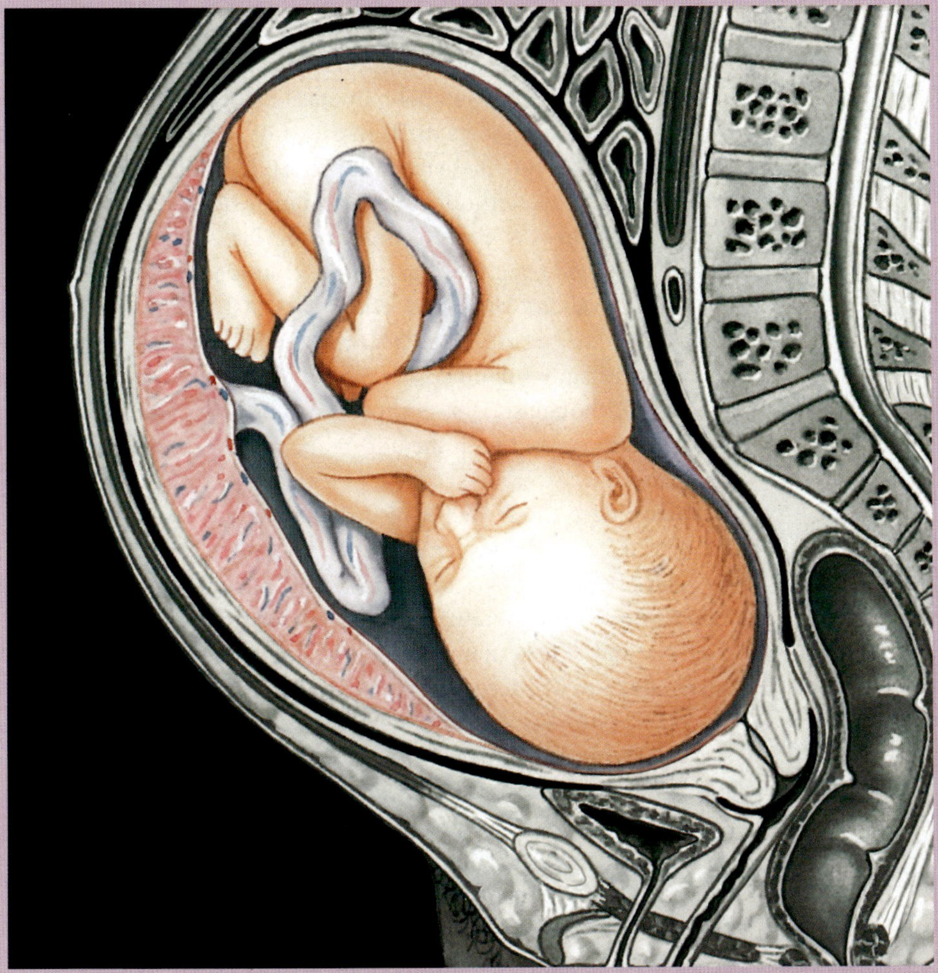

CHAPTER OBJECTIVES

1. Discuss conditions necessary for successful fertilization.
2. Describe the process of fertilization.
3. Discuss the stages of embryonic and fetal development.
4. Describe the process of cleavage and discuss where it occurs.
5. Distinguish among the pre-embryonic, embryonic, and fetal stages.
6. Describe the process of implantation.
7. Describe the events that take place in the first trimester and explain why they are vital to the survival of the embryo.
8. Describe the process of placentation and explain its significance.
9. Provide a summary of embryogenesis.
10. Summarize the events that occur in the second and third trimesters.
11. Explain the stages of labor and the events that occur immediately before and after delivery.
12. Identify the anatomical changes that occur as the fetus completes the transition to the newborn infant.

Development is the gradual modification of anatomical structures during the period from conception to maturity. The changes are truly remarkable—what begins as a single cell slightly larger than the period at the end of this sentence becomes a human body containing trillions of cells organized into tissues, organs, and organ systems. The formation of specialized cell types during development, called **differentiation**, occurs through selective changes in genetic activity. A basic appreciation of human development provides a framework for enhancing the understanding of anatomical structures. This discussion will focus on highlights of the developmental process. Embryology Summaries visualizing the development of specific body systems also appear in this chapter.

An Overview of Development

Development involves (1) the division and differentiation of cells, resulting in the formation of diverse cell types; and (2) reorganization of those cell types to produce or modify anatomical structures. Development produces a mature individual capable of reproduction. The process is a continuum that begins at **fertilization**, or **conception**, and can be separated into periods characterized by specific anatomical changes. **Prenatal development**, the period from conception to delivery, will be the primary focus of this chapter. The term **embryology** (em-brē-OL-ō-jē) refers to the study of the developmental events that occur during prenatal development. **Postnatal development** begins at birth and continues to maturity. We will briefly consider the *neonatal period* that immediately follows delivery, but other aspects of childhood and adolescent development were considered in earlier chapters dealing with specific systems.

The period of prenatal development can be further subdivided. **Pre-embryonic development** begins at fertilization and continues through *cleavage* (an initial series of cell divisions) and *implantation* (the movement of the pre-embryo into the uterine lining).

Pre-embryonic development is followed by **embryonic development**, which extends from implantation, typically occurring on the ninth or tenth day after fertilization, to the end of the eighth developmental week. **Fetal development** begins at the start of the ninth developmental week and continues up to the time of birth. We will now look at each of these processes in greater detail.

Fertilization [Figure 28.1a]

Fertilization involves the fusion of two haploid gametes, producing a diploid zygote containing the normal somatic number of chromosomes (46). pp. 45, 719 The functional roles and contributions of the spermatozoon and the ovum are very different. The spermatozoon simply delivers the paternal chromosomes to the site of fertilization, but the ovum must provide all of the nourishment and genetic programming to support the embryonic development for nearly a week after conception. The volume of the ovum is therefore much greater than that of the spermatozoon (Figure 28.1a).

Normal fertilization occurs in the ampulla of the uterine tube, usually within a day of ovulation. Over this period of time, the secondary oocyte has traveled a few centimeters, but the spermatozoa must cover the distance between the vagina and the ampulla. The sperm arriving in the vagina are already motile, but they cannot fertilize an oocyte until they have undergone capacitation within the female reproductive tract. p. 722

Contractions of the uterine musculature and ciliary currents in the uterine tubes are likely mechanisms for accelerating the movement of spermatozoa from the vagina to the fertilization site. The passage time may be from 30 minutes to two hours. Even with transport assistance and available nutrients, this is not an easy passage. Of the 200 million spermatozoa introduced into the vagina from a typical ejaculate, only around 10,000 enter the uterine tube, and fewer than 100 actually reach the ampulla. A male with a sperm count below 20 million per milliliter is functionally **sterile** because too few spermatozoa will survive to reach the secondary oocyte. One or two spermatozoa cannot accomplish fertilization, because of the condition of the secondary oocyte at ovulation.

The Oocyte at Ovulation [Figure 28.1b]

Ovulation occurs before the completion of oocyte maturation, and the secondary oocyte leaving the follicle is in metaphase of the second meiotic division (meiosis II). Metabolic operations have also been discontinued, and the secondary oocyte drifts in a sort of suspended animation, awaiting the stimulus for further development. If fertilization does not occur, it will disintegrate without completing meiosis.

Fertilization is complicated by the fact that when the secondary oocyte is ejected from the ovary, it is surrounded by a layer of follicle cells, the *corona radiata.* p. 731 The events that follow are diagrammed in Figure 28.1b. The corona radiata protects the secondary oocyte as it passes through the ruptured follicular wall and into the infundibulum of the uterine tube. Although the physical process of fertilization requires only a single sperm in contact with the oocyte membrane, that spermatozoon must first penetrate the corona radiata. The acrosomal cap of the sperm contains **hyaluronidase** (hī-el-yu-RA-ni-dāz), an enzyme that breaks down the intercellular cement between adjacent follicle cells in the corona radiata. Dozens of spermatozoa must release hyaluronidase before the connections between the follicular cells break down enough to permit fertilization. No matter how many spermatozoa slip through the gap, only a single spermatozoon will accomplish fertilization and activate the oocyte. When that spermatozoon passes through the zona pellucida and contacts the secondary oocyte, their cell membranes fuse, and the sperm enters the **ooplasm**, or cytoplasm of the oocyte. This membrane fusion triggers **oocyte activation**. Oocyte activation involves a series of changes in the metabolic activity of the secondary oocyte. The metabolic rate of the oocyte rises suddenly, and immediate changes in the plasmalemma prevent fertilization by additional sperm. (If more than one sperm does penetrate the oocyte membrane, an event called *polyspermy*, normal development cannot occur.) Perhaps the most dramatic change in the oocyte is the completion of meiosis.

Pronucleus Formation and Amphimixis [Figure 28.1b]

After oocyte activation and the completion of meiosis, the nuclear material remaining within the ovum reorganizes as the **female pronucleus** (Figure 28.1b). While these changes are under way, the nucleus of the spermatozoon swells, becoming the **male pronucleus**. The male pronucleus then migrates toward the center of the cell, and the two pronuclei fuse in a process called **amphimixis** (am-fi-MIK-sis). Fertilization is now complete, with the formation of a **zygote** containing the normal complement of 46 chromosomes. The zygote now prepares to begin dividing; these mitotic divisions will ultimately produce billions of specialized cells.

Figure 28.1 Fertilization and Preparation for Cleavage
(a) A secondary oocyte surrounded by spermatozoa. **(b)** Events at fertilization and immediately thereafter.

(a)

Prenatal Development

The time spent in prenatal development is known as the period of **gestation** (jes-TĀ-shun). For convenience, the gestation period is usually considered as three integrated **trimesters**, each three months in duration:

- The **first trimester** is the period of embryonic and early fetal development. During this period the rudiments of all the major organ systems appear.
- In the **second trimester** the organs and organ systems complete most of their development. The body proportions change, and by the end of the second trimester the fetus looks distinctively human.
- The **third trimester** is characterized by rapid fetal growth. Early in the third trimester most of the major organ systems become fully functional, and an infant born 1 month or even 2 months prematurely has a reasonable chance of survival.

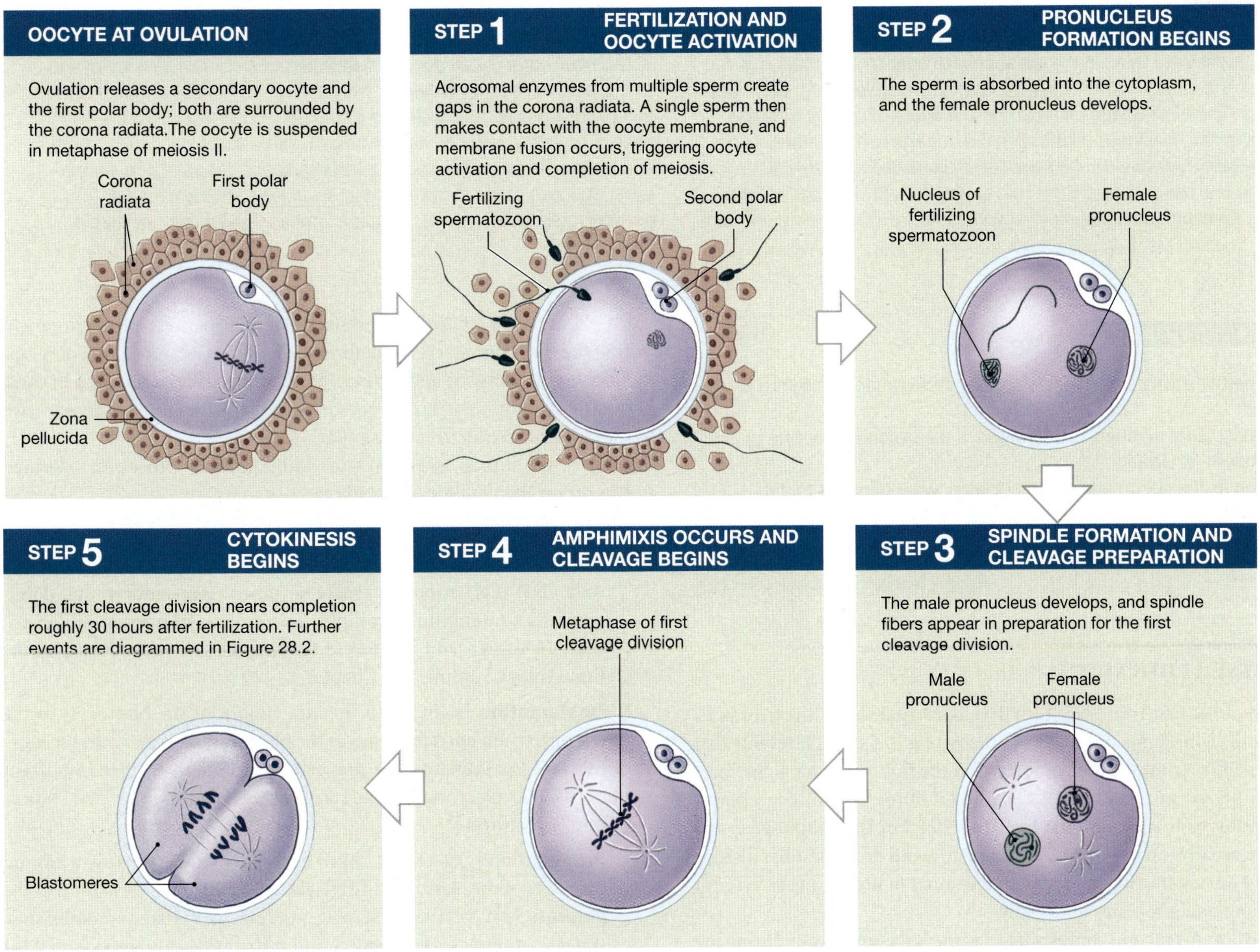

(b)

Clinical Note

Complexity and Perfection The expectation of prospective parents that every pregnancy will be idyllic and every baby will be perfect reflects deep-seated misconceptions about the nature of the developmental process. These misconceptions lead to the belief that when serious developmental errors occur, someone or something is at fault. Blame might be assigned to maternal habits (such as smoking, alcohol consumption, or poor diet), maternal exposure to toxins or prescription drugs, or the presence of other disruptive stimuli in the environment. The reality is, however, that even if every pregnant woman were packed in cotton and confined to bed from conception to delivery, developmental accidents and errors would continue to occur with regularity.

Spontaneous mutations result from random errors in replication; such incidents are relatively common. At least 10 percent of fertilizations produce zygotes with abnormal chromosomes. Because most spontaneous mutations fail to produce visible defects, the actual number of mutations must be far larger. Most of the affected zygotes die before completing development, and only about 0.5 percent of newborns show chromosomal abnormalities that result from spontaneous mutations.

Due to the nature of the regulatory mechanisms, prenatal development does not follow precise, predetermined pathways. For example, much variation exists in the pathways of blood vessels and nerves; it does not matter how blood or neural impulses get to their destinations, as long as they get there. If the variations fall outside acceptable limits, however, the embryo or fetus fails to complete development. Very minor changes in heart structure can result in the death of a fetus, whereas large variations in venous distribution are common and relatively harmless. Virtually everyone can be considered abnormal to some degree, because no one has characteristics that are statistically average in every respect. An estimated 20 percent of your genes are subtly different from those found in the majority of the population, and minor defects such as extra nipples or birthmarks are quite common.

As many as half of all conceptions produce zygotes that do not survive the cleavage stage. These zygotes disintegrate within the uterine tubes or uterine cavity; because implantation never occurs, there are no obvious signs of pregnancy. Preimplantation mortality is commonly associated with chromosomal abnormalities. Of those embryos that implant, roughly 20 percent fail to complete five months of development, with an average survival time of eight weeks. In most cases, severe problems affecting early embryogenesis or placenta formation are responsible.

Prenatal mortality tends to eliminate the most severely affected fetuses. Those with less extensive defects may survive, completing full-term gestation or premature delivery. **Congenital malformations** are structural abnormalities present at birth and affect major systems. Spina bifida, hydrocephalus, anencephaly, cleft lip, and Down syndrome are among the most common congenital malformations. The incidence of congenital malformations at birth averages about 6 percent, but only 2 percent are categorized as severe. Of these congenital problems, only 10 percent can be attributed to environmental factors in the absence of chromosomal abnormalities or genetic factors, including a family history of similar or related defects.

Medical technology continues to improve our abilities to understand and manipulate anatomical and physiological processes. Genetic analysis of potential parents can now provide estimates of the likelihood of specific problems, but the problems themselves remain outside our control. Even with a better understanding of the genetic mechanisms involved, we will probably never be able to control every aspect of development and thereby prevent spontaneous abortions and congenital malformations. Because prenatal development involves so many complex, interdependent steps, malfunctions of some kind are statistically inevitable.

CONCEPT CHECK

1. Can sperm arriving in the vagina perform fertilization immediately? Explain.
2. Why must large numbers of sperm reach the secondary oocyte to accomplish fertilization?
3. As soon as the sperm enters the ooplasm, what happens to the secondary oocyte?
4. What developments characterize the first trimester?

See blue "Answers" tab at back of book.

The First Trimester

By the end of the first trimester (12th developmental week), the fetus is almost 75 mm (3 in.) long and weighs perhaps 14 g (0.5 oz). The events that occur in the first trimester are complex, and the first trimester is the most dangerous period in prenatal life. Only about 40 percent of conceptions produce embryos that survive the first trimester. For this reason pregnant women are usually warned to take great care to avoid drugs or other disruptive stresses during the first trimester, in the hopes of preventing an error in the developmental processes under way.

Many important and complex developmental events occur during the first trimester. The Embryology Summaries presented in Chapter 3 provided an overview of two important sequential periods of development during the first trimester: (1) the formation of tissues and (2) the development of epithelial tissue and the origins of connective tissues. Each of these periods of development has unique characteristics that the reader may wish to review in further detail at this point. pp. 79–81

We will focus attention on four general processes: *cleavage*, *implantation*, *placentation*, and *embryogenesis*.

1. **Cleavage** (KLĒV-ej) is a sequence of cell divisions that begins immediately after fertilization and ends at the first contact with the uterine wall. Over this period the zygote becomes a **pre-embryo** that develops into a multicellular complex known as a **blastocyst** (BLAS-tō-sist). (Cleavage and blastocyst formation were introduced in the Embryology Summary in Chapter 3.) p. 79
2. **Implantation** begins with the attachment of the blastocyst to the endometrium and continues as the blastocyst burrows into the uterine wall. As implantation proceeds, a number of other important events take place that set the stage for the formation of vital embryonic structures.
3. **Placentation** (plas-en-TĀ-shun) begins as blood vessels form around the edges of the blastocyst. This is the first step in the formation of the **placenta** (pla-SEN-ta). The placenta links maternal and embryonic systems; it provides respiratory and nutritional support essential for further prenatal development.

4. **Embryogenesis** (em-brē-ō-JEN-e-sis) is the formation of a viable embryo. This process forms the body of the embryo and its internal organs.

Cleavage and Blastocyst Formation [Figure 28.2]

Cleavage (**Figure 28.2**) is a series of cell divisions that subdivides the cytoplasm of the zygote into smaller cells called **blastomeres** (BLAS-tō-mērz). The first cleavage division produces a pre-embryo consisting of two identical blastomeres. The first division is completed roughly 30 hours after fertilization, and subsequent cleavage divisions occur at intervals of 10–12 hours. During the initial cleavage divisions, all of the blastomeres undergo mitosis simultaneously, but as the number of blastomeres increases, the time interval between divisions becomes less predictable.

At this stage, the pre-embryo is a solid ball of cells, resembling a mulberry. This stage is called the **morula** (MOR-ū-la; "mulberry"). After five days of cleavage, the blastomeres form a hollow ball, the **blastocyst**, with an

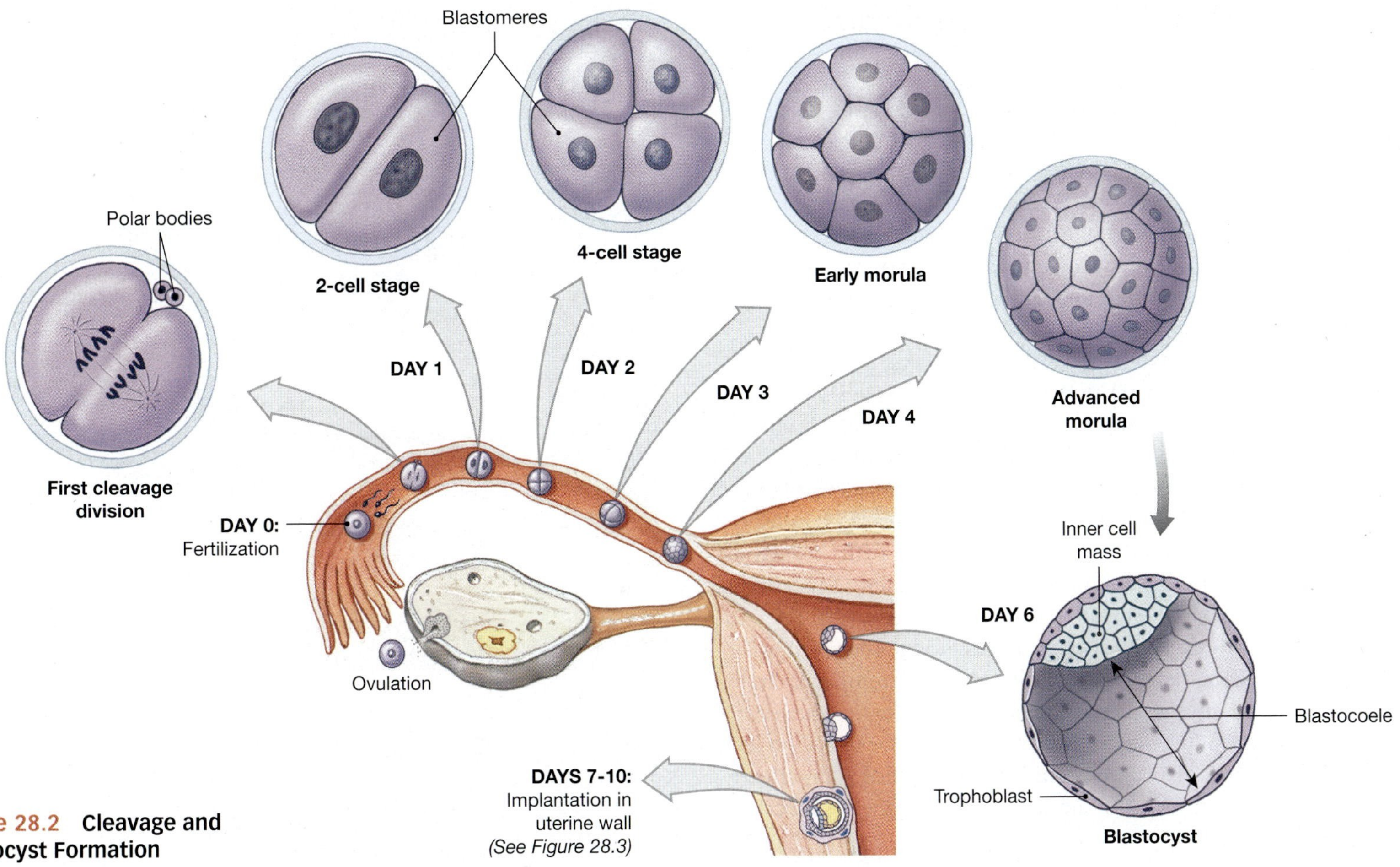

Figure 28.2 Cleavage and Blastocyst Formation

Clinical Note

Teratogens and Abnormal Development **Teratogens** (ter-A-tō-jenz) are stimuli that disrupt normal fetal development by damaging cells, altering their chromosomal structure, or interfering with normal induction. Pesticides, herbicides, and a number of prescription drugs, including certain antibiotics, tranquilizers, sedatives, steroid hormones, diuretics, anesthetics, and analgesics, can have teratogenic effects. Pregnant women should read the "Caution" label before using any drug without the advice of a physician. Most "natural" herbs and substances have not been tested, and their chemical composition may vary from source to source. Because their effects during pregnancy are unknown, they should not be considered uniformly safe to use during pregnancy.

Fetal alcohol syndrome (FAS) occurs when maternal alcohol consumption produces developmental defects in the fetus, such as skeletal deformation, cardiovascular defects, and neurological disorders. Fetal mortality rates can be as high as 17 percent, and the survivors are plagued by problems in later development. The most severe cases involve mothers who consume the alcohol content of at least 7 ounces of hard liquor, 10 beers, or two bottles of wine each day. However, because the effects produced are directly related to the degree of exposure, there is probably no level of alcohol consumption that can be considered completely safe. Fetal alcohol syndrome is the number one cause of mental retardation in the United States, affecting roughly 7500 infants each year.

Smoking presents another major risk to the developing fetus. In addition to introducing potentially harmful chemicals, such as nicotine, smoking lowers the P_{O_2} of maternal blood and reduces the amount of oxygen that reaches the placenta. A fetus carried by a smoking mother will not grow as rapidly as one carried by a nonsmoking mother, and smoking increases the risks of spontaneous abortion, prematurity, and fetal death. Infant mortality after delivery is also higher when the mother smokes, and postnatal development can be adversely affected as well.

inner cavity known as the **blastocoele** (BLAS-tō-sēl). At this stage you can begin to see differences between the cells of the blastocyst. The outer layer of cells, separating the external environment from the blastocoele, is called the **trophoblast** (TRŌ-fō-blast). The function is implied by the name: *trophos*, food + *blast*, precursor. These cells will be responsible for providing food to the developing embryo. Trophoblast cells are the only cells of the pre-embryo that contact the uterine wall. A second group of cells, the **inner cell mass**, lies clustered at one end of the blastocyst. These cells are exposed to the blastocoele but are insulated from contact with the outside environment by the trophoblast. The cells of the inner cell mass are the stem cells responsible for producing all of the cells and cell types of the body.

Implantation [Figure 28.3]

At fertilization the zygote is still four days away from the uterus. It arrives in the uterine cavity as a morula, and over the next two to three days, blastocyst formation occurs. During this period the cells are absorbing nutrients from the fluid within the uterine cavity. This fluid, rich in glycogen, is secreted by the endometrial glands. When fully formed, the blastocyst contacts the endometrium, usually in the fundus or body of the uterus, and implantation occurs. Stages in the implantation process are illustrated in Figure 28.3.

Implantation begins as the surface of the blastocyst closest to the inner cell mass touches and adheres to the uterine lining (see *Day 7*, Figure 28.3). At the point of contact, the trophoblast cells divide rapidly, making the trophoblast several layers thick. Near the endometrial wall, the cell membranes separating the trophoblast cells disappear, forming a layer of cytoplasm containing multiple nuclei *(Day 8)*. This outer layer, called the **syncytial** (sin-SISH-al) **trophoblast**, begins to erode a path through the uterine epithelium, by secreting the enzyme *hyaluronidase*. This enzyme breaks down the intercellular cement between adjacent epithelial cells, just as the hyaluronidase released by spermatozoa dissolved the connections between cells of the corona radiata. At first this erosion creates a gap in the uterine lining, but the migration and divisions of adjacent epithelial cells soon repair the surface. When the repairs are completed, the blastocyst loses contact with the uterine cavity and is completely embedded within the endometrium. Development hereafter occurs entirely within the functional layer of the endometrium.

As implantation proceeds, the syncytial trophoblast continues to enlarge and spread into the surrounding endometrium *(Day 9)*. This process results in the disruption and enzymatic digestion of uterine glands. The nutrients released are absorbed by the syncytial trophoblast and distributed by diffusion across the underlying **cellular trophoblast** to the inner cell mass. These nutrients provide the energy needed to support the early stages of embryo formation. Trophoblastic extensions grow around endometrial capillaries, and as the capillary walls are destroyed, maternal blood begins to percolate through trophoblastic channels called **lacunae**. Fingerlike **primary villi** extend away from the trophoblast into the surrounding endometrium; each primary villus consists of an extension of syncytial trophoblast with a core of cellular trophoblast. Over the next few days, the trophoblast begins breaking down larger endometrial veins and arteries, and blood flow through the lacunae increases.

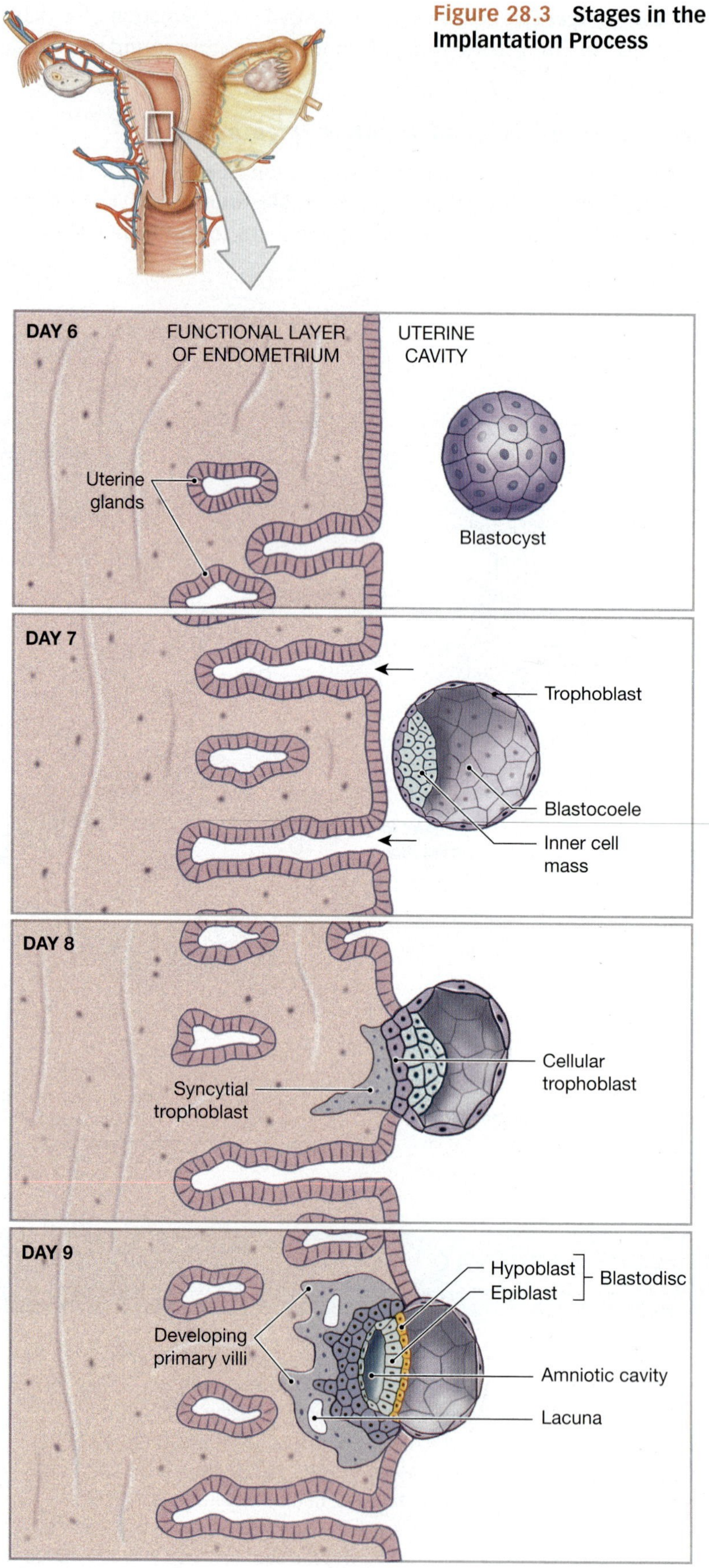

Figure 28.3 Stages in the Implantation Process

Formation of the Blastodisc [Figures 28.3/28.4] In the early blastocyst stage, the inner cell mass has little visible organization. But by the time of implantation, the inner cell mass has already started separating from the trophoblast. The separation gradually increases, creating a fluid-filled chamber called the **amniotic** (am-nē-OT-ik) **cavity**. The amniotic cavity can be seen in *Day 9* of Figure 28.3; additional details from *Days 10–12* are shown in Figure 28.4. At this stage the cells of the inner cell mass are organized into an oval sheet that is two cell layers thick. This oval, called a **blastodisc** (BLAS-tō-disk), initially consists of two epithelial layers: the **epiblast** (EP-i-blast), which faces the amniotic cavity, and the **hypoblast** (HĪ-pō-blast), which is exposed to the fluid contents of the blastocoele.

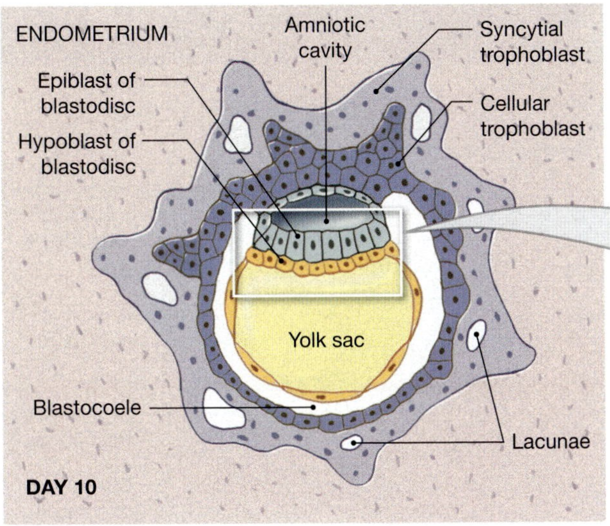

The blastodisc begins as two layers: the *epiblast*, facing the amniotic cavity, and the *hypoblast*, exposed to the blastocoele. Migration of epiblast cells around the amniotic cavity is the first step in the formation of the amnion. Migration of hypoblast cells creates a sac that hangs below the blastodisc. This is the first step in yolk sac formation.

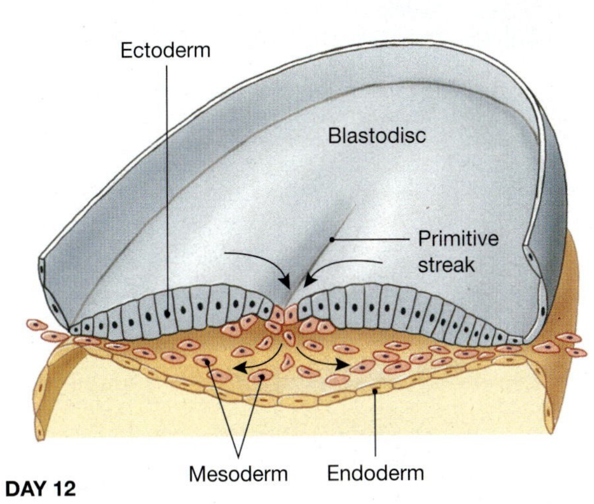

Migration of epiblast cells into the region between epiblast and hypoblast gives the blastodisc a third layer. From the time this process (gastrulation) begins, the epiblast is called *ectoderm*, the hypoblast *endoderm*, and the migrating cells *mesoderm*.

Figure 28.4 Blastodisc Organization and Gastrulation

Gastrulation and Germ Layer Formation [Figure 28.4 and Table 28.1] A few days later, a third layer begins forming through the process of **gastrulation** (gas-troo-LĀ-shun) (*see Day 12*, Figure 28.4). During gastrulation, cells in specific areas of the epiblast move toward the center of the blastodisc, toward a line known as the **primitive streak**. Once they arrive at the primitive streak, the migrating cells leave the surface and move between the epiblast and hypoblast. This movement creates three distinct embryonic layers with markedly different fates. Once gastrulation begins, the layer remaining in contact with the amniotic cavity is called the **ectoderm**, the hypoblast is known as the **endoderm**, and the new intervening layer is the **mesoderm**. The formation of the mesoderm and the developmental fates of these three **germ layers** were introduced in an Embryology Summary in Chapter 3. p. 79 Table 28.1 contains a more comprehensive listing of the contributions each germ layer makes to the body systems.

Formation of Extraembryonic Membranes [Figure 28.5] In addition to forming body structures and organs, germ layers also form four structures that extend outside the embryonic body. These structures, known as **extraembryonic membranes**, are (1) the *yolk sac* (endoderm and mesoderm), (2) the *amnion* (ectoderm and mesoderm), (3) the *allantois* (endoderm and mesoderm), and (4) the *chorion* (mesoderm and trophoblast). These membranes support embryonic and fetal development by maintaining a consistent, stable environment and by providing access to the oxygen and nutrients carried by the maternal bloodstream. Despite their importance during prenatal development, they leave few traces of their existence in adult systems. Figure 28.5 shows representative stages in the development of the extraembryonic membranes.

The Yolk Sac [Figures 28.4/28.5] The first of the extraembryonic membranes to appear is the **yolk sac** (Figures 28.4 and 28.5). The yolk sac begins as migrating hypoblast cells spread out around the outer edges of the blastocoele to form a complete pouch suspended below the blastodisc. This pouch is already visible 10 days after fertilization (Figure 28.4). As gastrulation proceeds, mesodermal cells migrate around this pouch and complete

TABLE 28.1 The Fates of the Primary Germ Layers
Ectodermal Contributions
Integumentary system: epidermis, hair follicles and hairs, nails, and glands communicating with the skin (apocrine and merocrine sweat glands, mammary glands, and sebaceous glands)
Skeletal system: pharyngeal cartilages and their derivatives in the adult (portion of sphenoid, the auditory ossicles, the styloid processes of the temporal bones, the horns and superior rim of the hyoid bone)*
Nervous system: all neural tissue, including brain and spinal cord
Endocrine system: pituitary gland and suprarenal medullae
Respiratory system: mucous epithelium of nasal passageways
Digestive system: mucous epithelium of mouth and anus, salivary glands
Mesodermal Contributions
Integumentary system: dermis, except for epidermal derivatives
Skeletal system: all components except some pharyngeal derivatives
Muscular system: all components
Endocrine system: suprarenal cortex and endocrine tissues of heart, kidneys, and gonads
Cardiovascular system: all components, including bone marrow
Lymphoid system: all components
Urinary system: the kidneys, including the nephrons and the initial portions of the collecting system
Reproductive system: the gonads and the adjacent portions of the duct systems
Miscellaneous: the lining of the body cavities (thoracic, pericardial, peritoneal) and the connective tissues supporting all organ systems
Endodermal Contributions
Endocrine system: thymus, thyroid, and pancreas
Respiratory system: respiratory epithelium (except nasal passageways) and associated mucous glands
Digestive system: mucous epithelium (except mouth and anus); exocrine glands (except salivary glands); liver, and pancreas
Urinary system: urinary bladder and distal portions of the duct system
Reproductive system: distal portions of the duct system; stem cells that produce gametes

*The neural crest is derived from ectoderm and contributes to the formation of the skull and the skeletal derivatives of the embryonic pharyngeal arches.

(a) WEEK 2

Migration of mesoderm around the inner surface of the trophoblast creates the chorion. Mesodermal migration around the outside of the amniotic cavity, between the ectodermal cells and the trophoblast, forms the amnion. Mesodermal migration around the endodermal pouch creates the yolk sac.

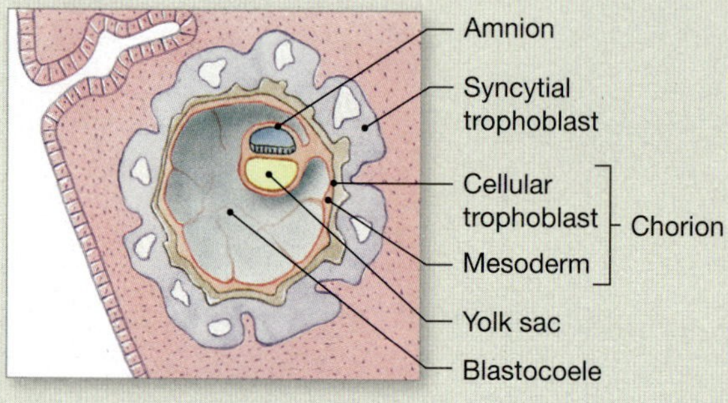

(b) WEEK 3

The embryonic disc bulges into the amniotic cavity at the head fold. The allantois, an endodermal extension surrounded by mesoderm, extends toward the trophoblast.

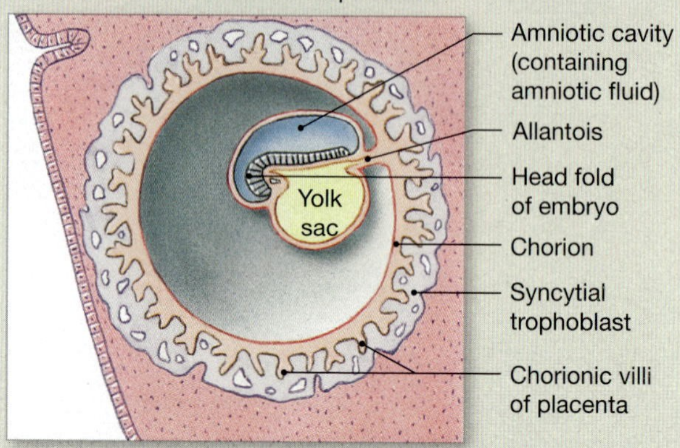

(c) WEEK 4

The embryo now has a head fold and a tail fold. Constriction of the connections between the embryo and the surrounding trophoblast narrows the yolk stalk and body stalk.

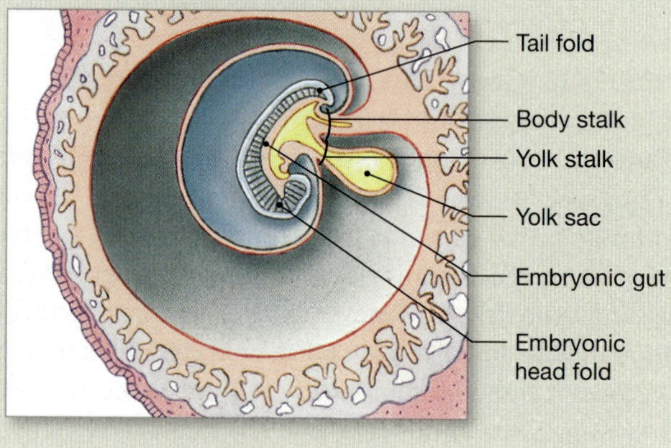

(d) WEEK 5

The developing embryo and extraembryonic membranes bulge into the uterine cavity. The trophoblast pushing out into the uterine lumen remains covered by endometrium but no longer participates in nutrient absorption and embryo support. The embryo moves away from the placenta, and the body stalk and yolk stalk fuse to form an umbilical stalk.

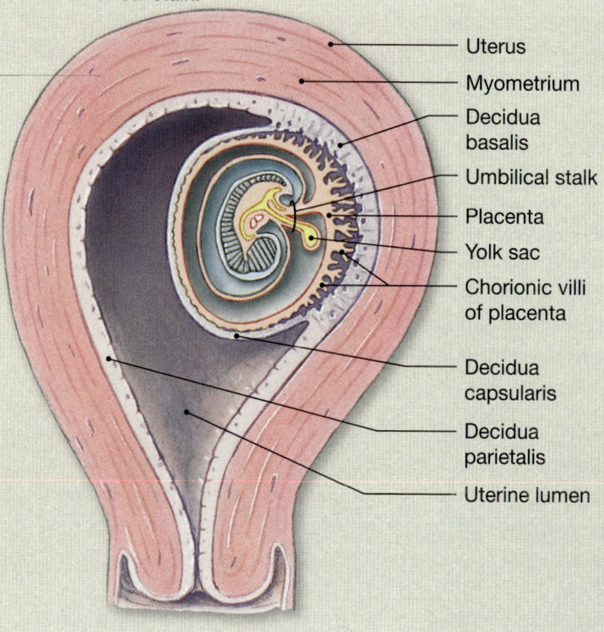

(e) WEEK 10

The amnion has expanded greatly, filling the uterine cavity. The fetus is connected to the placenta by an elongated umbilical cord that contains a portion of the allantois, blood vessels, and the remnants of the yolk stalk.

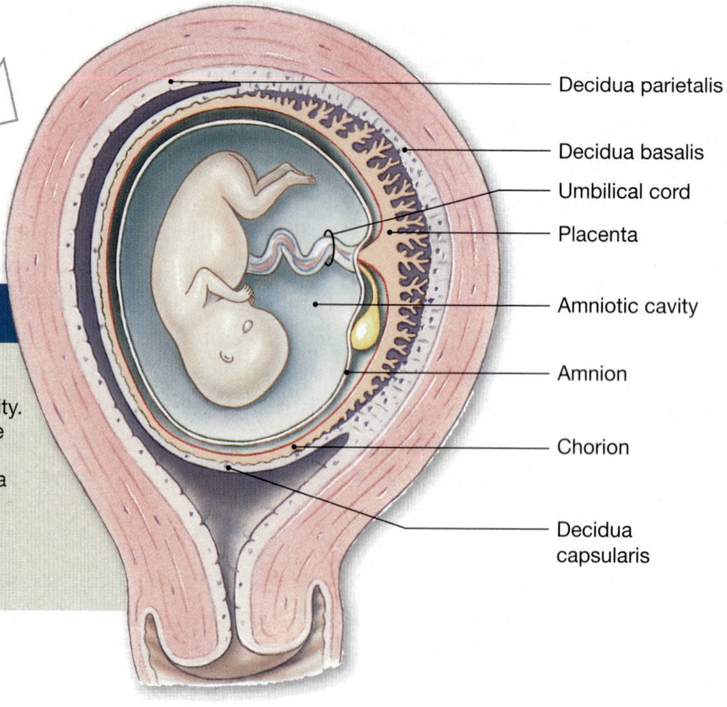

Figure 28.5 The Embryonic Membranes and Placenta Formation

the formation of the yolk sac. Blood vessels soon appear within the mesoderm, and the yolk sac becomes an important site of early blood cell formation.

The Amnion [Figure 28.5a,b,e] The ectodermal layer also undergoes an expansion, and ectodermal cells spread over the inner surface of the amniotic cavity. Mesodermal cells soon follow, creating a second, outer layer. This combination of ectoderm and mesoderm is the **amnion** (AM-nē-on) (Figure 28.5a,b). As the embryo, and later the fetus, enlarges this membrane continues to expand, increasing the size of the amniotic cavity. The amniotic cavity contains **amniotic fluid**, which surrounds and cushions the developing embryo or fetus (Figure 28.5b,e).

The Allantois [Figure 28.5b] The third extraembryonic membrane begins as an outpocketing of the endoderm near the base of the yolk sac (Figure 28.5b). The free endodermal tip then grows toward the wall of the blastocyst, surrounded by a mass of mesodermal cells. This sac of endoderm and mesoderm is the **allantois** (a-LAN-tō-is); its base later gives rise to the urinary bladder. The formation of the allantois and its relationship to the urinary bladder are illustrated later in this chapter in the Embryology Summary: The Development of the Urinary System.

The Chorion [Figure 28.5a,b] The mesoderm associated with the allantois spreads until it extends completely around the inside of the trophoblast, forming a mesodermal layer underneath the trophoblast. This combination of mesoderm and trophoblast is the **chorion** (KO-rē-on) (Figure 28.5a,b).

When implantation first occurs, the nutrients absorbed by the trophoblast can easily reach the blastodisc by simple diffusion. But as the embryo and the trophoblastic complex enlarge, the distance between the two increases, and diffusion alone can no longer keep pace with the demands of the developing embryo. The chorion solves this problem, for blood vessels developing within the mesoderm provide a rapid-transit system linking the embryo with the trophoblast. Circulation through those chorionic vessels begins early in the third week of development, when the heart starts beating.

Placentation [Figure 28.5b,c,d,e]

The appearance of blood vessels in the chorion is the first step in the formation of a functional placenta. By the third week of development (Figure 28.5b), mesoderm extends along the core of each of the trophoblastic villi, forming **chorionic villi** in contact with maternal tissues. These villi continue to enlarge and branch, forming an intricate network within the endometrium. Maternal blood vessels continue to be eroded, and maternal blood slowly percolates through lacunae lined by the syncytial trophoblast. Diffusion occurs between the maternal blood flowing through the lacunae and fetal blood flowing through vessels within the chorionic villi.

At first the entire blastocyst is surrounded by chorionic villi. The chorion continues to enlarge, expanding like a balloon within the endometrium, and by the fourth week, the embryo, amnion, and yolk sac are suspended within an expansive, fluid-filled chamber (Figure 28.5c). The connection between the embryo and chorion, known as the **body stalk**, contains the distal portions of the allantois and blood vessels carrying blood to and from the placenta. The narrow connection between the endoderm of the embryo and the yolk sac is called the **yolk stalk**. The formation of the yolk stalk and body stalk are illustrated later in this chapter in the Embryology Summary: The Development of the Digestive System.

The placenta does not continue to enlarge indefinitely. Regional differences in placental organization begin to develop as placental expansion forms a prominent bulge in the endometrial surface. The relatively thin portion of the endometrium that covers the embryo and separates it from the uterine cavity is called the **decidua capsularis** (dē-SID-ū-a kap-sū-LA-ris; *deciduus*, a falling off). This layer no longer participates in nutrient exchange, and the chorionic villi disappear in this region (Figure 28.5d). Placental functions are now concentrated in a disc-shaped area situated in the deepest portion of the endometrium, a region called the **decidua basalis** (ba-SA-lis). The rest of the endometrium, which has no contact with the chorion, is called the **decidua parietalis** (pa-rī-e-TAL-is). As the end of the first trimester approaches, the fetus moves farther away from the placenta (Figure 28.5d,e). It remains connected by the **umbilical cord**, or *umbilical stalk*, which contains the allantois, placental blood vessels, and the yolk stalk.

The developing fetus is totally dependent on maternal organ systems for nourishment, respiration, and waste removal. These functions must be performed by maternal systems in addition to their normal operations. For example, the mother must absorb enough oxygen, nutrients, and vitamins for herself and her fetus, and she must eliminate all of the generated wastes. Although this is not a burden over the initial weeks of gestation, the demands placed upon the mother become significant in subsequent trimesters, as the fetus grows larger. In practical terms the mother must breathe, eat, and excrete for two.

Placental Circulation [Figure 28.6] Figure 28.6a diagrams circulation at the placenta near the end of the first trimester. Blood flows from the fetus to the placenta through the paired **umbilical arteries** and returns in a single **umbilical vein**. The chorionic villi (Figure 28.6b) provide the surface area for active and passive exchange between the fetal and maternal bloodstreams. As noted in Chapter 27, the placenta also synthesizes important hormones that affect maternal as well as embryonic tissues. ∞ p. 741 Human chorionic gonadotropin (HCG) production begins within a few days of implantation; it stimulates the corpus luteum so that it continues to produce progesterone throughout the early stages of the pregnancy. During the second and third trimesters the placenta also releases progesterone, estrogens, human placental lactogen (HPL), and relaxin. These hormones are synthesized and released into the maternal circulation by the trophoblast.

Embryogenesis [Figures 28.5b,c/28.7 and Table 28.2]

Shortly after gastrulation begins, folding and differential growth of the embryonic disc produce a bulge that projects into the amniotic cavity (Figure 28.5b). This projection is known as the **head fold**; similar movements lead to the formation of a **tail fold** (Figure 28.5c). The **embryo** is now physically as well as developmentally separated from the rest of the blastodisc and the extraembryonic membranes. The definitive orientation of the embryo can now be seen, complete with dorsal and ventral surfaces and left and right sides. Many of these changes in proportions and appearance that occur between the fourth developmental week and the end of the first trimester are seen in Figure 28.7.

The first trimester is a critical period for development because events in the first 12 weeks establish the basis for organ formation, a process called **organogenesis**. Important developmental milestones of organogenesis in each organ system are detailed in Table 28.2.

✓ CONCEPT CHECK

1. What is the fate of the inner cell mass of the blastocyst?
2. What is the function of the syncytial trophoblast?
3. What systems does the mesodermal layer give rise to?
4. What are the functions of the placenta?

See blue "Answers" tab at back of book.

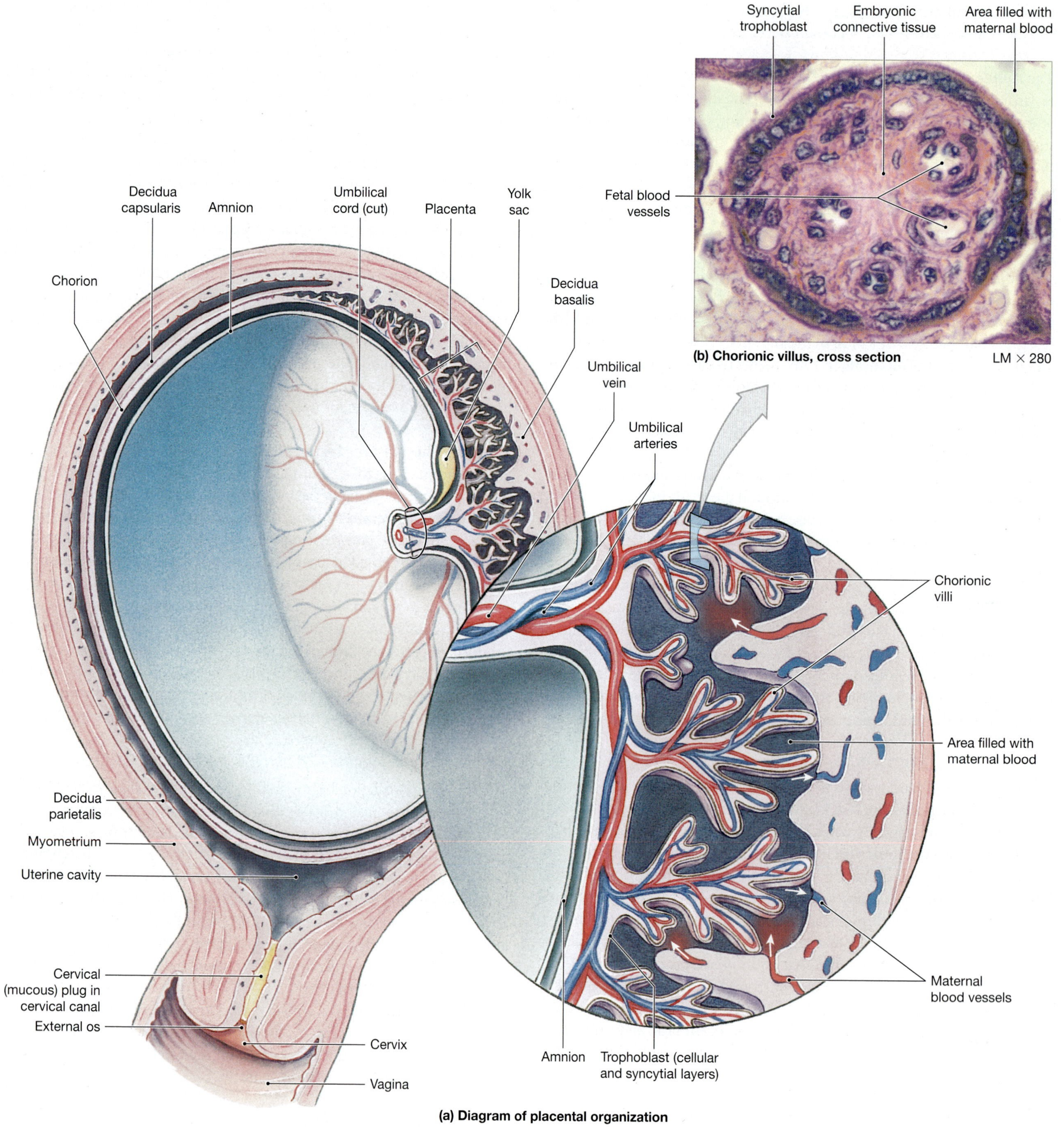

(b) Chorionic villus, cross section LM × 280

(a) Diagram of placental organization

Figure 28.6 A Three-Dimensional View of Placental Structure
(a) For clarity, the uterus is shown after the embryo has been removed and the umbilical cord cut. Blood flows into the placenta through ruptured maternal arteries. It then flows around chorionic villi, which contain fetal blood vessels. Fetal blood arrives through paired umbilical arteries and leaves through a single umbilical vein. Maternal blood reenters the venous system of the mother through the broken walls of small uterine veins. Maternal blood flow is shown by arrows; note that no actual mixing of maternal and fetal blood occurs. **(b)** Histology of a chorionic villus, cross section showing the syncytial trophoblast exposed to the maternal blood space.

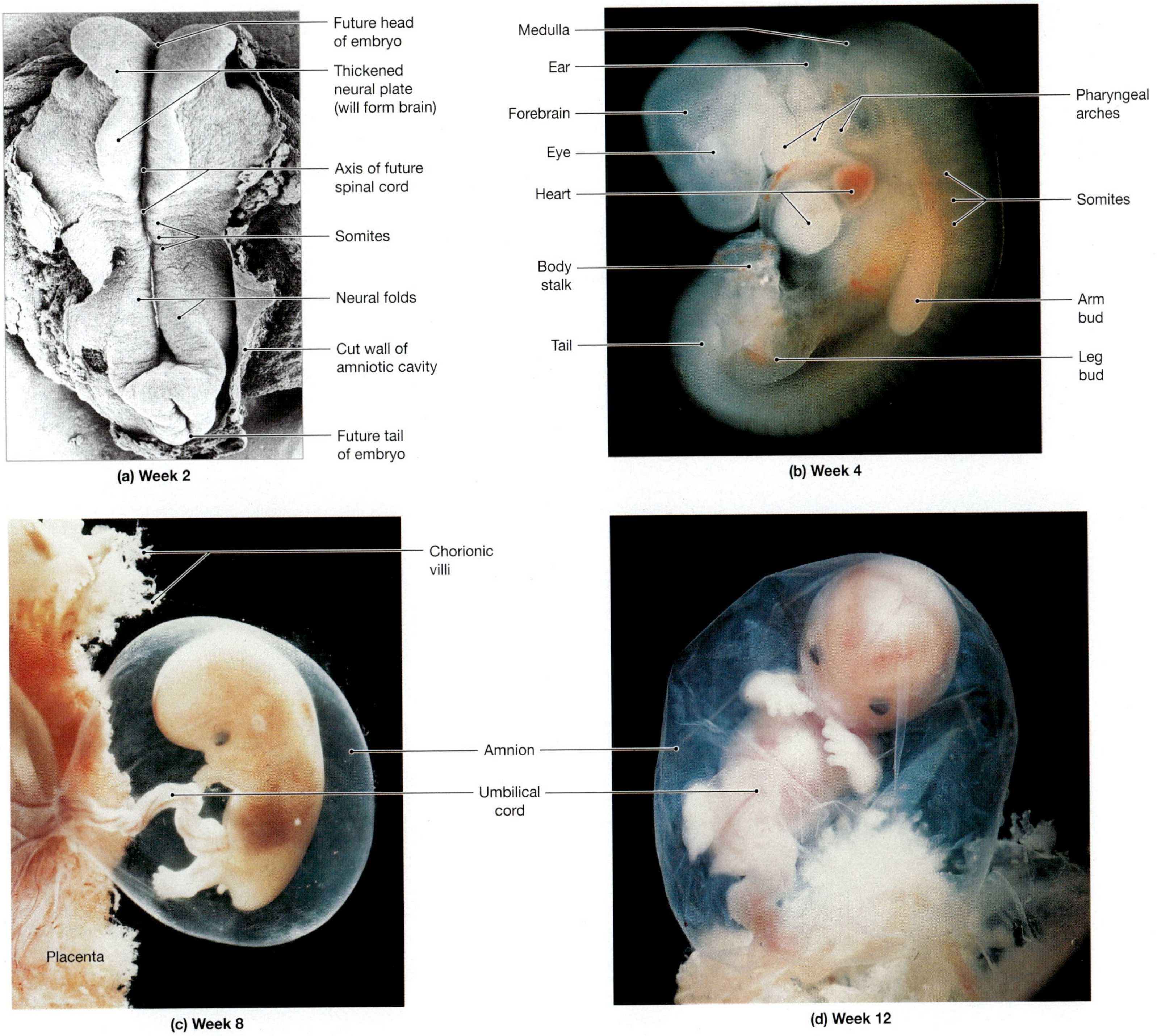

Figure 28.7 The First Trimester
(a) An SEM of the superior surface of a two-week embryo; neurulation (neural tube formation) is under way. **(b–d)** Fiber-optic views of human development in the first trimester.

The Second and Third Trimesters

[Figures 28.7d/28.8/28.9 and Table 28.2]

By the end of the first trimester (Figure 28.7d), the rudiments of all of the major organ systems have formed. Over the next three months, these systems will complete their functional development, and by the end of the second trimester, the fetus weighs around 0.64 kg (1.4 lb). During the second trimester the fetus, encircled by the amnion, grows faster than the surrounding placenta. Soon the mesodermal outer covering of the amnion fuses with the inner lining of the chorion. Figure 28.8 shows a four-month fetus as viewed with a fiber-optic endoscope and a six-month fetus as seen in ultrasound.

During the third trimester, all of the fetal organ systems become functional. The rate of growth begins to decrease, but in absolute terms this trimester sees the largest weight gain. In three months the fetus puts on around 2.6 kg (5.7 lb), reaching a full-term weight of somewhere near 3.2 kg (7 lb). Important events in organ system development in the second and third trimesters are detailed in the Embryology Summaries at the end of this chapter, and highlights are noted in Table 28.2.

TABLE 28.2 An Overview of Prenatal Development

Background Material in Chapter 3:
Formation of Tissues (p. 79)
Development of Epithelia (p. 80)
Origins of Connective Tissues (p. 81)
Development of Organ Systems (pp. 82–83)

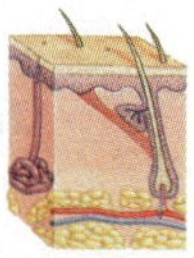

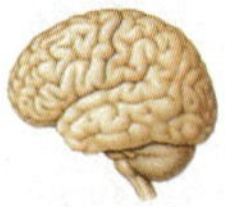
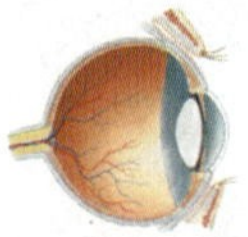

Gestational Age (months)	Size and Weight	Integumentary System	Skeletal System	Muscular System	Nervous System	Special Sense Organs
1	5 mm 0.02 g		(b) Somite formation	(b) Somite formation	(b) Neural tube formation	(b) Eye and ear formation
2	28 mm 2.7 g	(b) Formation of nail beds, hair follicles, sweat glands	(b) Formation of axial and appendicular cartilages	(c) Rudiments of axial musculature	(b) CNS, PNS organization, growth of cerebrum	(b) Formation of taste buds, olfactory epithelium
3	78 mm 26 g	(b) Epidermal layers appear	(b) Ossification centers spreading	(c) Rudiments of appendicular musculature	(c) Basic spinal cord and brain structure	
4	133 mm 150 g	(b) Formation of hair, sebaceous glands (c) Sweat glands	(b) Articulations (c) Facial and palatal organization	Fetus starts moving	(b) Rapid expansion of cerebrum	(c) Basic eye and ear structure (b) Peripheral receptor formation
5	185 mm 460 g	(b) Keratin production, nail production			(b) Myelination of spinal cord	
6	230 mm 823 g			(c) Perineal muscles	(b) CNS tract formation (c) Layering of cortex	
7	270 mm 1492 g	(b) Keratinization, nail formation, hair formation				(c) Eyelids open, retina sensitive to light
8	310 mm 2274 g		(b) Epiphyseal cartilage formation			(c) Taste receptors functional
9	346 mm 2912 g					
Postnatal development		Hair changes in consistency and distribution	Formation and growth of epiphyseal cartilages continue	Muscle mass and control increase	Myelination, layering, CNS tract formation continue	
Embryological Summaries by System		Development of the Integumentary System (pp. 764–765)	Development of the Skull (pp. 766–767) Development of the Vertebral Column (pp. 768–769) Development of the Appendicular Skeleton (pp. 770–771)	Development of the Muscular System (pp. 772–773)	Introduction to the Development of the Nervous System (p. 774) Development of the Spinal Cord and Spinal Nerves (pp. 775–776) Development of the Brain and Cranial Nerves (pp. 777–778)	Development of Special Sense Organs (pp. 779–780)

Note: (b) = begin formation;(c) = complete formation.

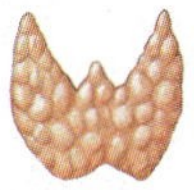
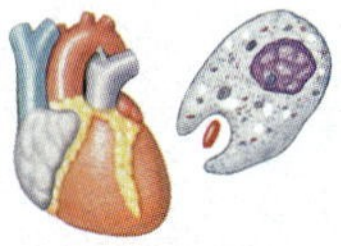
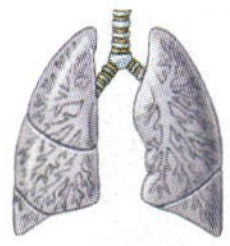
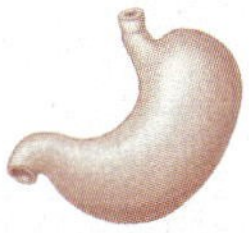
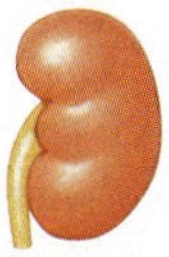
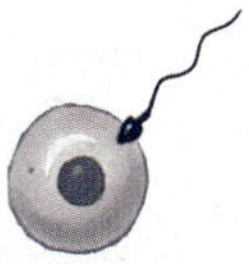

Endocrine System	Cardiovascular and Lymphoid Systems	Respiratory System	Digestive System	Urinary System	Reproductive System
	(b) Heartbeat	(b) Trachea and lung formation	(b) Formation of intestinal tract, liver, pancreas (c) Yolk sac	(c) Allantois	
(b) Formation of thymus, thyroid, pituitary, suprarenal glands	(c) Basic heart structure, major blood vessels, lymph nodes and ducts (b) Blood formation in liver	(b) Extensive bronchial branching into mediastinum (c) Diaphragm	(b) Formation of intestinal subdivisions, villi, salivary glands	(b) Kidney formation (adult form)	(b) Formation of mammary glands
(c) Thymus, thyroid gland	(b) Tonsils, blood formation in bone marrow		(c) Gallbladder, pancreas		(b) Formation of definitive gonads, ducts, genitalia
	(b) Migration of lymphocytes to lymphoid organs, blood formation in spleen			(b) Degeneration of embryonic kidneys	
	(c) Tonsils	(c) Nostrils open	(c) Intestinal subdivisions		
(c) Suprarenal glands	(c) Spleen, liver, bone marrow	(b) Alveolar formation	(c) Epithelial organization, glands		
(c) Pituitary gland			(c) Intestinal plicae		(b) Descent of testes
		Complete pulmonary branching and alveolar formation		Complete nephron formation at birth	Descent of testes complete at or near time of birth
	Cardiovascular changes at birth; lymphoid system gradually becomes fully operational				
Development of the Endocrine System (pp. 781–782)	Development of the Heart (p. 783) Development of the Cardiovascular System (pp. 784–785) Development of the Lymphoid System (p. 786)	Development of the Respiratory System (pp. 787–788)	Development of the Digestive System (pp. 789–790)	Development of the Urinary System (pp. 791–792)	Development of the Reproductive System (pp. 793–795)

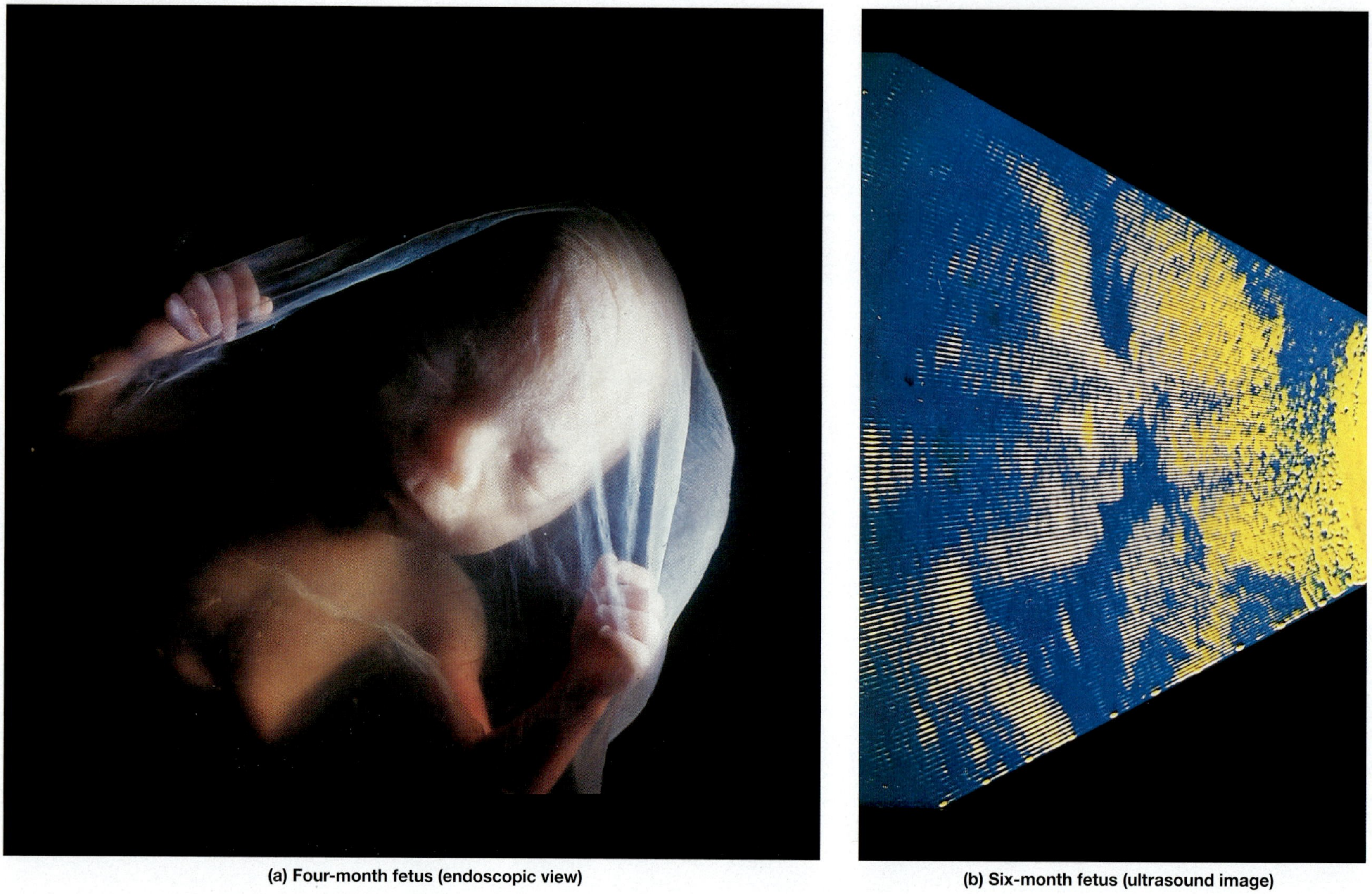

Figure 28.8 The Second and Third Trimesters
(a) A four-month fetus seen through a fiber-optic endoscope. **(b)** Head of a six-month fetus as seen in an ultrasound scan.

At the end of gestation, a typical uterus will have undergone a tremendous increase in size. It will grow from 7.5 cm (3 in.) to 30 cm (12 in.) long and will contain almost 5 L of fluid. The uterus and its contents weigh roughly 10 kg (22 lb). This remarkable expansion occurs through the enlargement and elongation of existing smooth muscle fibers. Figure 28.9 shows the position of the uterus, fetus, and placenta from 16 weeks to *full term* (nine months). When the pregnancy is at term, the uterus and fetus push many of the abdominal organs out of their normal positions (Figure 28.9c).

Labor and Delivery

The goal of labor is the expulsion of the fetus, a process known as **parturition** (par-tūr-ISH-un), or birth. Labor is triggered by the combination of increased oxytocin levels and increased uterine sensitivity to oxytocin. This combination stimulates *labor contractions* in the myometrium. During *true labor,* as opposed to the occasional uterine spasms of *false labor,* each labor contraction begins near the fundus of the uterus and sweeps in a wave toward the cervix. These contractions are strong and occur at regular intervals. As parturition approaches, the contractions increase in force and frequency, changing the position of the fetus and moving it toward the cervical canal.

Stages of Labor [Figure 28.10]

Labor is usually divided into three stages (Figure 28.10): the *dilation stage,* the *expulsion stage,* and the *placental stage.*

The Dilation Stage [Figure 28.10a]

The **dilation stage** (Figure 28.10a) begins with the onset of true labor, as the cervix dilates and the fetus begins to move down the cervical canal. This stage typically lasts eight or more hours, but during this period the labor contractions occur at intervals of once every 10–30 minutes. Late in the process, the amnion usually ruptures, an event sometimes referred to as "having the water break."

The Expulsion Stage [Figure 28.10b]

The **expulsion stage** (Figure 28.10b) begins as the cervix dilates completely, pushed open by the approaching fetus. Expulsion continues until the fetus has completed its emergence from the vagina, a period usually lasting less than two hours. The arrival of the newborn infant into the outside world represents birth, or **delivery**.

If the vaginal canal is too small to permit the passage of the fetus, and there is acute danger of perineal tearing, the passageway may be temporarily enlarged by making an incision through the perineal musculature. After

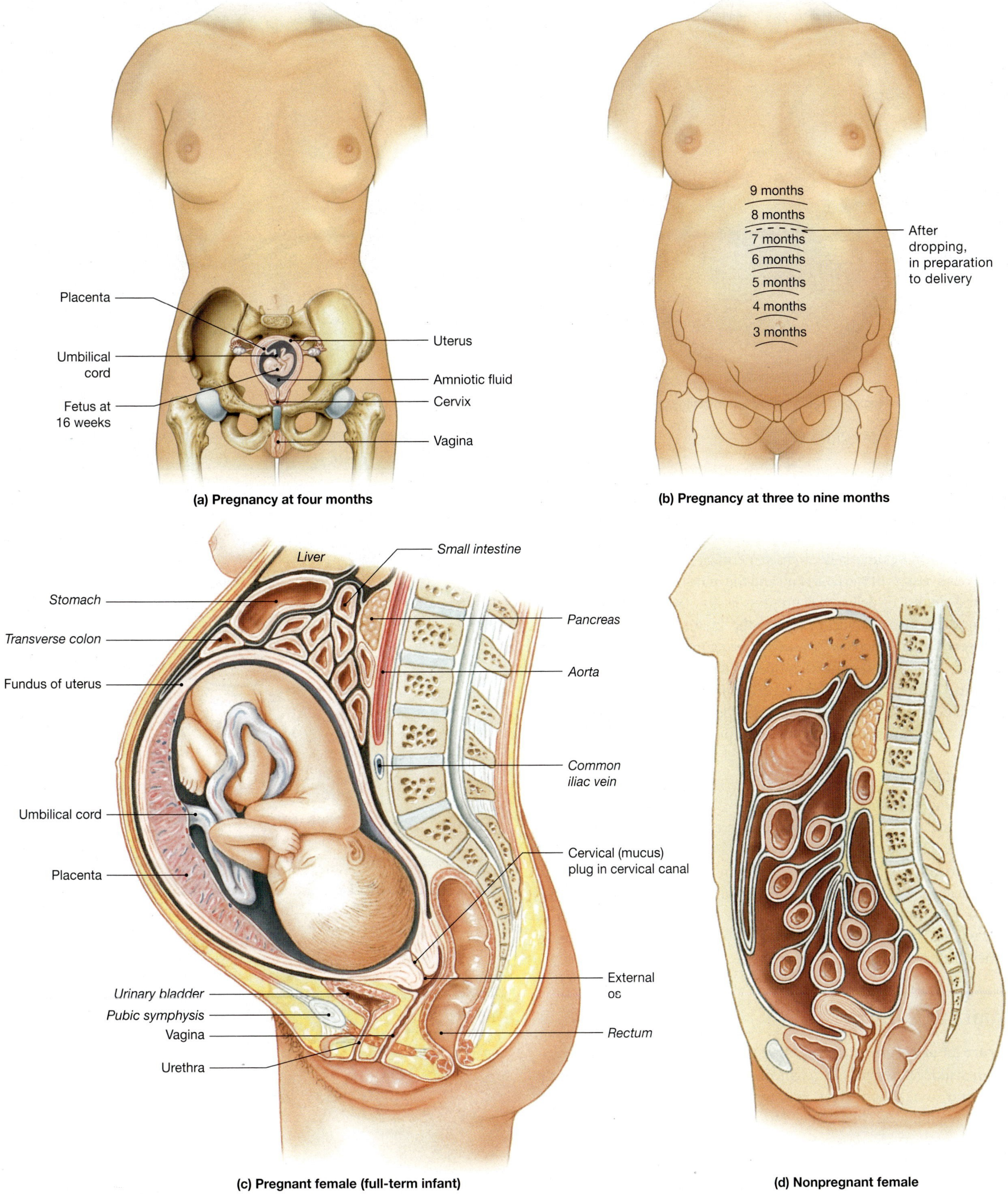

Figure 28.9 The Growth of the Uterus and Fetus
(a) Pregnancy at four months (16 weeks), showing the positions of the uterus, fetus, and placenta. **(b)** Changes in the size of the uterus during the second and third trimesters. **(c)** Pregnancy at full term. Note the position of the uterus and fetus and the displacement of abdominal organs relative to part (d). **(d)** Organ position and orientation in a nonpregnant female.

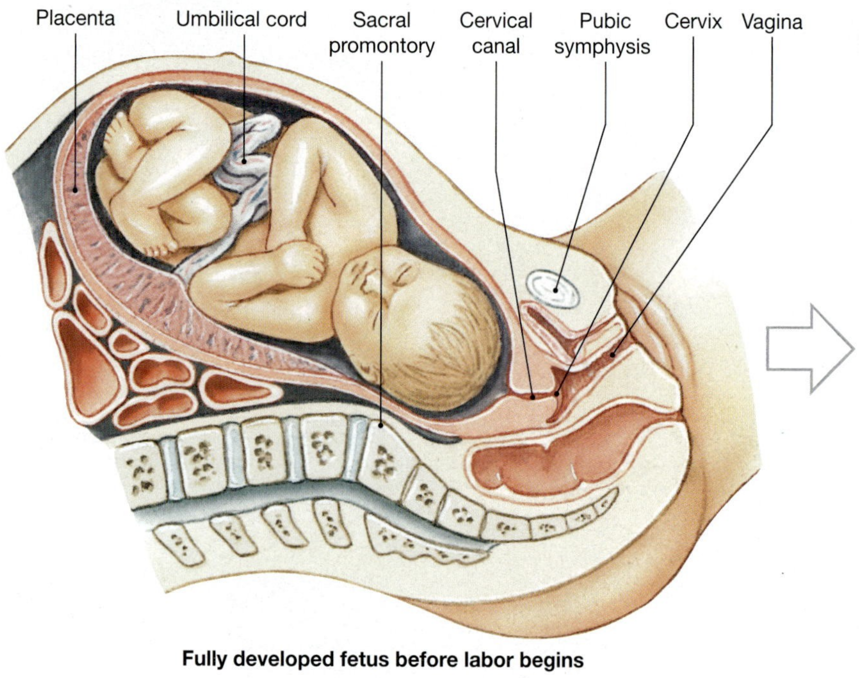

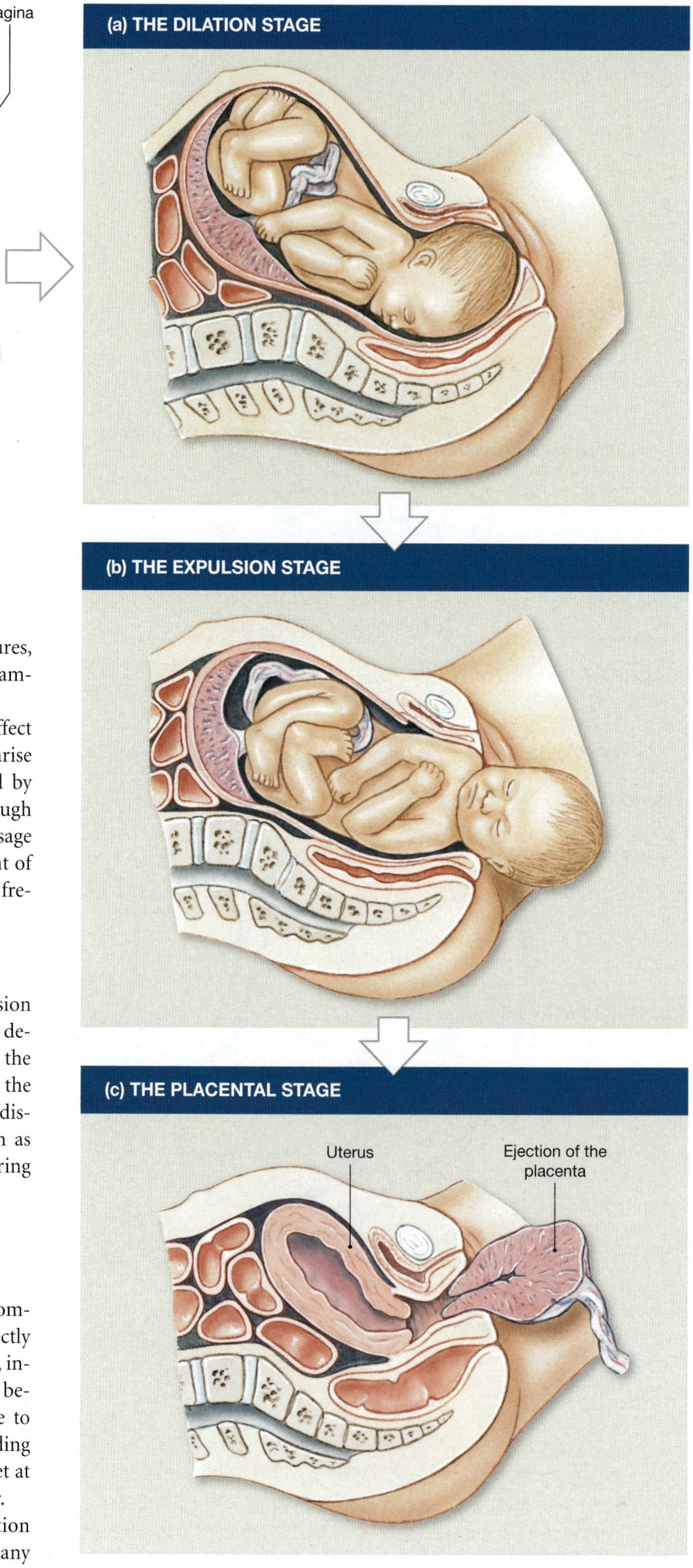

Figure 28.10 **The Stages of Labor**

delivery this **episiotomy** (e-pēz-ē-OT-ō-mē) can be repaired with sutures, a much simpler procedure than dealing with the bleeding and tissue damage associated with a potentially extensive perineal tear.

The relative sizes of the fetal skull and the maternal pelvic outlet affect the ease and success of delivery. If progress is slow or complications arise during the dilation or expulsion stages, the infant may be removed by **cesarean section**, or *"c-section."* In such cases an incision is made through the abdominal wall, and the uterus is opened just enough to allow passage of the infant's head. This procedure is performed during 15–25 percent of deliveries in the United States. Efforts are now being made to reduce the frequency of both episiotomies and cesarean sections.

The Placental Stage [Figure 28.10c]

During the **placental stage** of labor (Figure 28.10c), the muscle tension builds in the walls of the partially empty uterus, and the organ gradually decreases in size. This uterine contraction tears the connections between the endometrium and the placenta. Usually within an hour after delivery, the placental stage ends with the ejection of the placenta, or *afterbirth.* The disruption of the placenta is accompanied by a loss of blood (as much as 500–600 ml), but because the maternal blood volume has increased during pregnancy, the loss can be tolerated.

Premature Labor

Premature labor occurs when true labor begins before the fetus has completed normal development. The chances of newborn survival are directly related to body weight at delivery. Even with massive supportive efforts, infants born weighing less than 400 g (14 oz) will not survive, primarily because the respiratory, cardiovascular, and urinary systems are unable to support life without the aid of maternal systems. As a result, the dividing line between *spontaneous abortion* and **immature delivery** is usually set at 500 g (17.6 oz), the normal weight near the end of the second trimester.

Infants delivered before completing seven months of gestation (weight under 1 kg) have less than a 50/50 chance of survival, and many

Clinical Note

Forceps Deliveries and Breech Births In most pregnancies, by the end of gestation, the fetus has rotated within the uterus to transit the birth canal head first, facing the mother's sacrum. In about 6 percent of deliveries, the fetus faces the mother's pubis instead. These infants can be delivered normally, given enough time, but risks to infant and mother are reduced by a *forceps delivery.* The forceps resemble large, curved salad tongs that can be separated for insertion into the vaginal canal one side at a time. Once in place, they are reunited and used to grasp the head of the fetus. An intermittent pull is applied, so that the forces on the head resemble those of normal delivery.

In 3–4 percent of deliveries, the legs or buttocks of the fetus enter the vaginal canal first. Such deliveries are known as **breech births**. Risks to the infant are relatively higher in breech births because the umbilical cord may become constricted, and placental circulation cut off. Because the head is normally the widest part of the fetus, the cervix may dilate enough to pass the legs and body but not the head. Entrapment of the fetal head compresses the umbilical cord, prolongs delivery, and subjects the fetus to severe distress and potential damage. If the fetus cannot be repositioned manually, a cesarean section is usually performed.

survivors suffer from severe developmental abnormalities. A **premature delivery** produces a newborn weighing over 1 kg (35.2 oz), and its chances of survival range from fair to excellent, depending on the individual circumstances.

The Neonatal Period

Developmental processes do not cease at delivery, for the newborn infant has few of the anatomical, functional, or physiological characteristics of the mature adult. The **neonatal period** extends from the moment of birth to one month thereafter. A variety of physiological and anatomical alterations occurs as the fetus completes the transition to the status of a newborn infant, or **neonate**. Before delivery, transfer of dissolved gases, nutrients, waste products, hormones, and immunoglobulins occurred across the placental interface. At birth, the newborn infant must become relatively self-sufficient, with the processes of respiration, digestion, and excretion performed by its own specialized organs and organ systems. The transition from fetus to neonate may be summarized as follows:

1. The lungs at birth are collapsed and filled with fluid, and filling them with air involves a massive and powerful inhalation.
2. When the lungs expand, the pattern of cardiovascular circulation changes because of alterations in blood pressure and flow rates. The ductus arteriosus closes, isolating the pulmonary and systemic trunks, and the closure of the foramen ovale separates the atria of the heart, completing separation of the pulmonary and systemic circuits. These cardiovascular changes were discussed in Chapters 21 and 22.
3. Typical heart rates of 120–140 beats per minute and respiratory rates of 30 breaths per minute in neonates are normal, and considerably higher than those of adults.
4. Prior to birth, the digestive system remains relatively inactive, although it does accumulate a mixture of bile secretions, mucus, and epithelial cells. This collection of debris is excreted in the first few days of life. Over that period the newborn infant begins to nurse.
5. As waste products build up in the arterial blood, they are filtered into the urine at the kidneys. Glomerular filtration is normal, but the urine cannot be concentrated to any significant degree. As a result, urinary water losses are high, and neonatal fluid requirements are much greater than those of adults.

Clinical Note

Evaluating the Newborn Infant Each newborn infant is closely scrutinized after delivery. This procedure checks for the presence of anatomical and physiological abnormalities. It also provides baseline information useful in assessing postnatal development. In addition to general appearance, the pulse, respiratory rate, weight, length, and other physical dimensions are noted. Newborn infants are also screened for genetic and metabolic disorders, such as *phenylketonuria (PKU)* or congenital *hypothyroidism*.

The **Apgar rating** considers heart rate, respiratory rate, muscle tone, response to stimulation, and color at 1 and 5 minutes after birth. In each category the infant receives a score ranging from 0 (poor) to 2 (excellent), and the scores are then totaled. An infant's Apgar rating (0–10) has been shown to be an accurate predictor of newborn survival and the presence of neurological damage. For example, newborn infants with *cerebral palsy* usually have a low Apgar rating.

6. The neonate has little ability to control body temperature, particularly in the first few days after delivery. As the infant grows larger and increases the thickness of its insulating subcutaneous adipose "blanket," its metabolic rate also rises. Daily and even hourly alterations in body temperature continue throughout childhood.

CONCEPT CHECK

1. What embryonic changes are seen in the second trimester?
2. Which stage of labor usually takes the longest?
3. Why does a newborn infant have a much higher relative fluid intake than do adults?
4. What triggers the expulsion of the placenta?

See blue "Answers" tab at back of book.

The next section of this chapter summarizes important aspects of the embryological development of each of the organ systems. Table 28.2 on pages 758–759 provides an overview of the major developmental landmarks that occur in each trimester.

The Development of the Integumentary System

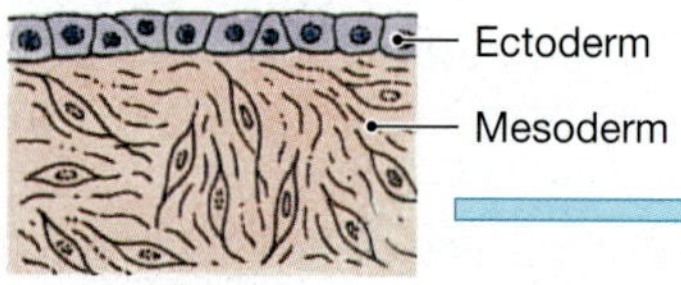

1 MONTH

At the start of the second month, the superficial ectoderm is a simple epithelium overlying loosely organized mesenchyme.

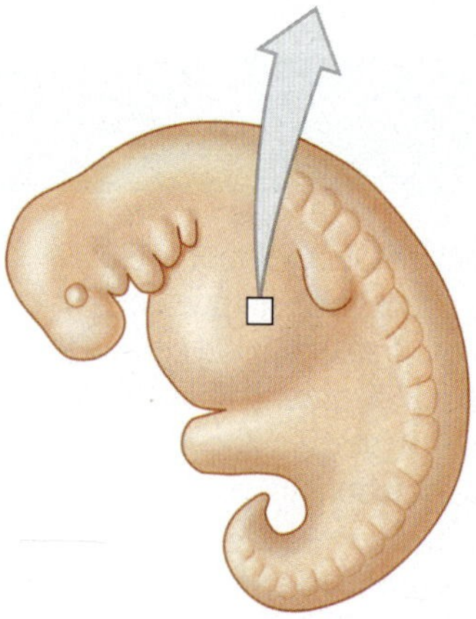

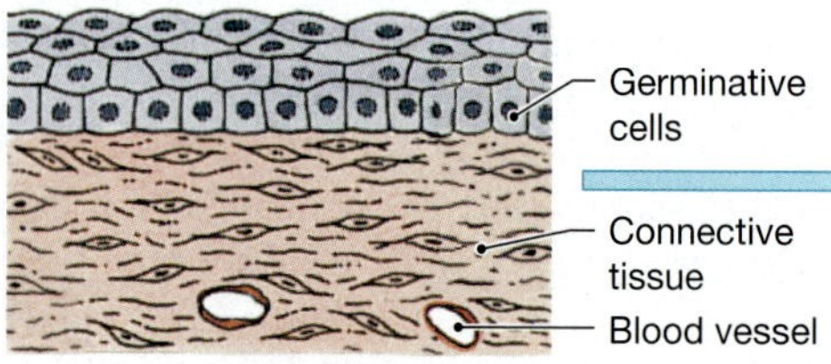

3 MONTHS

Over the following weeks, the epithelium becomes stratified through repeated divisions of the *basal* or *germinative cells*. The underlying mesenchyme differentiates into embryonic connective tissue containing blood vessels that bring nutrients to the region.

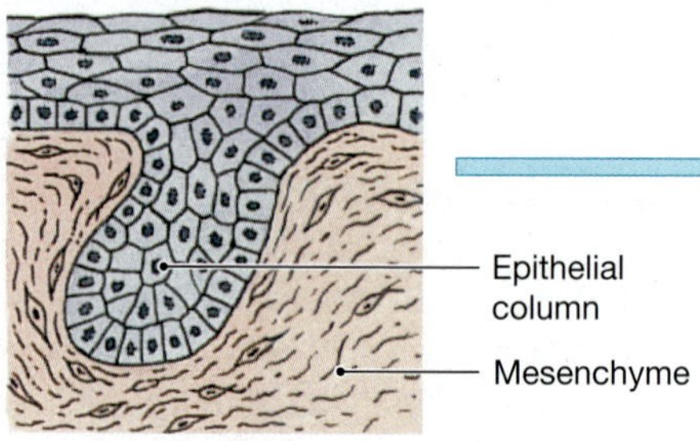

4 MONTHS

During the third and fourth months, small areas of epidermis undergo extensive divisions and form cords of cells that grow into the dermis. These are **epithelial columns**. Mesenchymal cells surround the columns as they extend deeper and deeper into the dermis. Hair follicles, sebaceous glands, and sweat glands develop from these columns.

SKIN

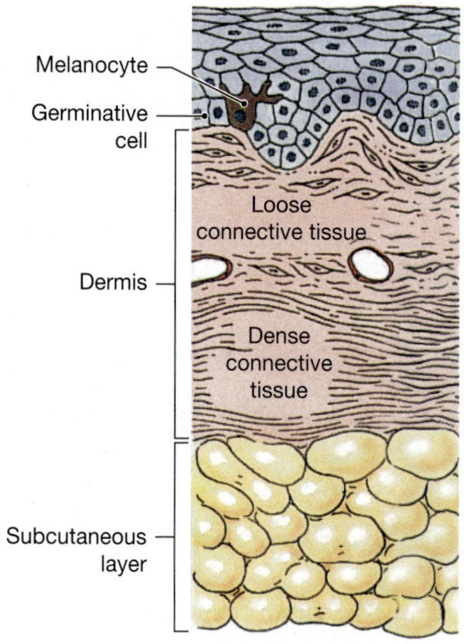

4 MONTHS

As basal cell divisions continue, the epithelial layer thickens and the basal lamina is thrown into irregular folds. Pigment cells called *melanocytes* migrate into the area and squeeze between the germinative cells. The epithelium now resembles the *epidermis* of the adult.

The embryonic connective tissue differentiates into the *dermis*. Fibroblasts and other connective tissue cells form from mesenchymal cells or migrate into the area. The density of fibers increases. Loose connective tissue extends into the ridges, but a deeper, less vascular region is dominated by a dense, irregular collagen fiber network. Below the dermis the embryonic connective tissue develops into the *subcutaneous layer*, a layer of loose connective tissue.

NAILS

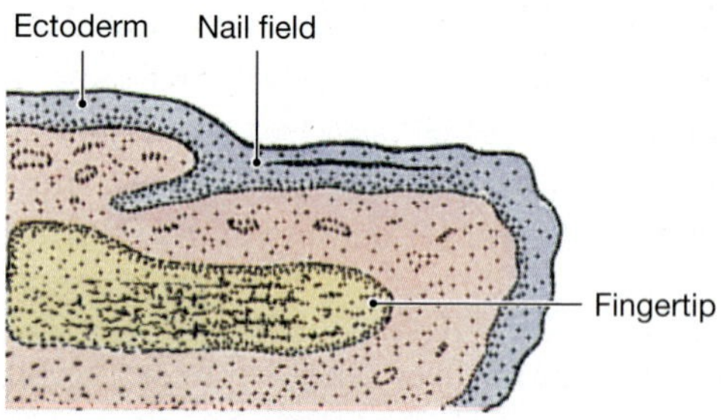

4 MONTHS

Nails begin as thickenings of the epidermis near the tips of the fingers and toes. These thickenings settle into the dermis, and the borderline with the general epidermis becomes distinct. Initially, nail production involves all of the germinative cells of the *nail field*.

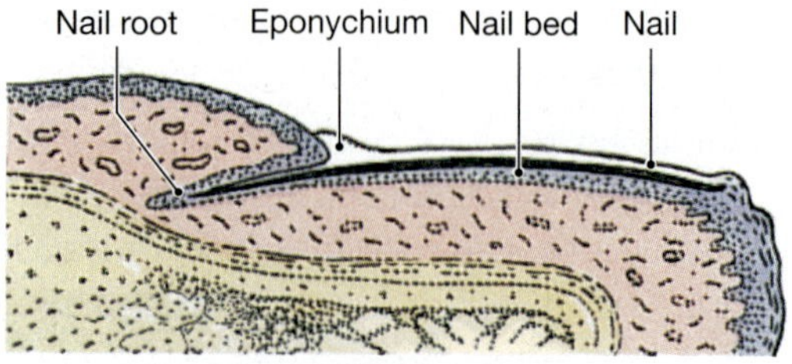

BIRTH

By the time of birth, nail production is restricted to the *nail root*.

HAIR FOLLICLES

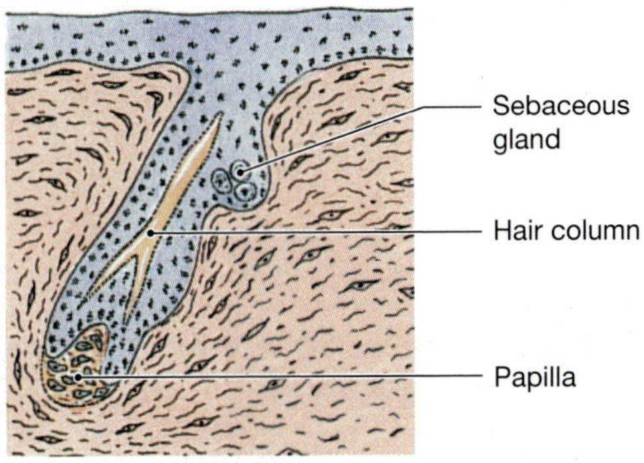

5 MONTHS

A hair follicle develops as a deep column surrounds a *papilla*, a small mass of connective tissue. Hair growth will occur in the epithelium covering the papilla. An outgrowth from the epithelial column forms a *sebaceous gland*.

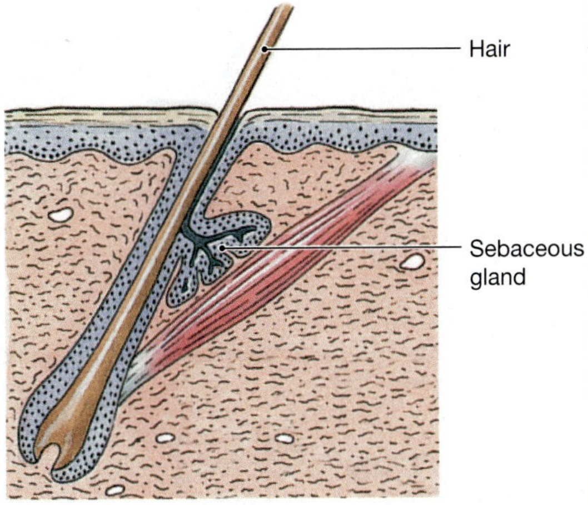

BIRTH

At birth a hair projects from the follicle, and the secretions of the sebaceous gland lubricate the hair shaft.

EXOCRINE GLANDS

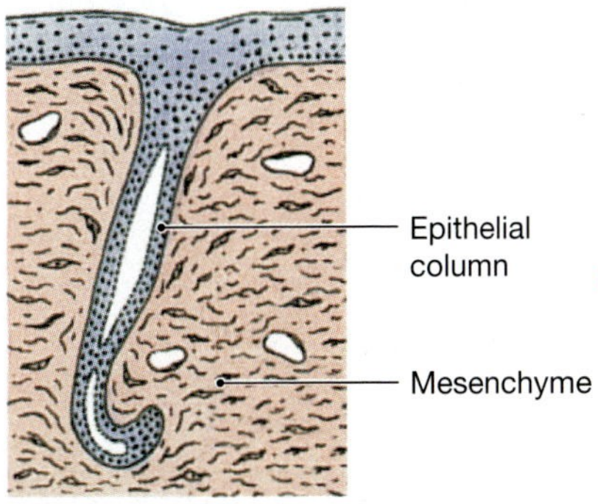

5 MONTHS

A sweat gland develops as an epithelial column elongates, coils, and becomes hollow.

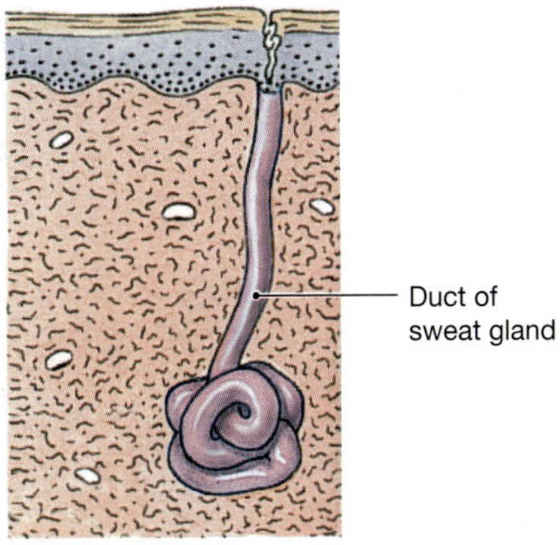

BIRTH

At birth, sweat gland ducts carry the secretions of the gland cells to the skin surface.

MAMMARY GLANDS

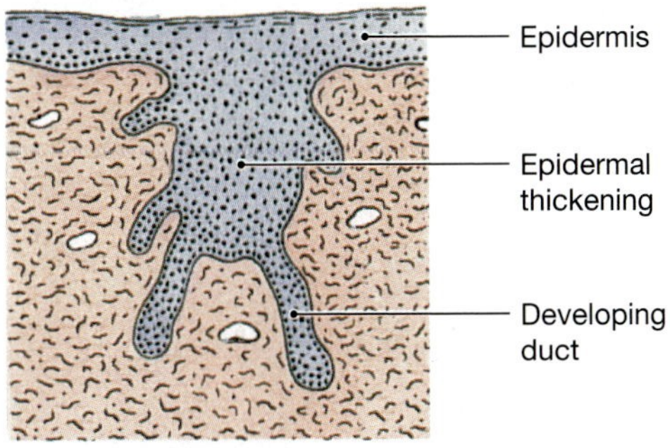

5 MONTHS

Mammary glands develop in a comparable fashion, but the epidermal thickenings are much broader and extensive branching occurs.

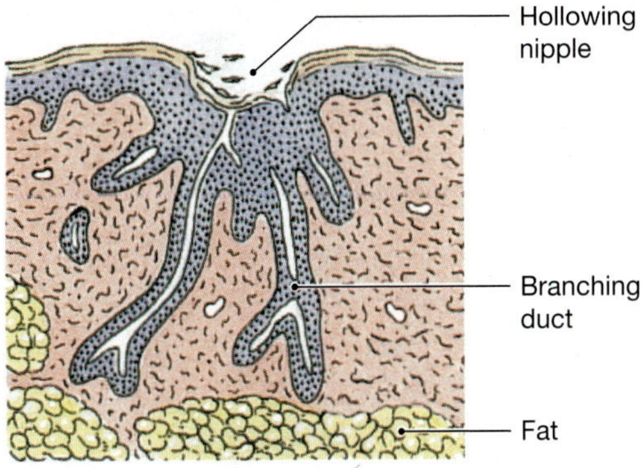

BIRTH

At birth, the mammary glands have not completed their development. In females, further elaboration of the duct and gland system occurs at puberty, but functional maturity does not occur until late in pregnancy.

The Development of the Skull

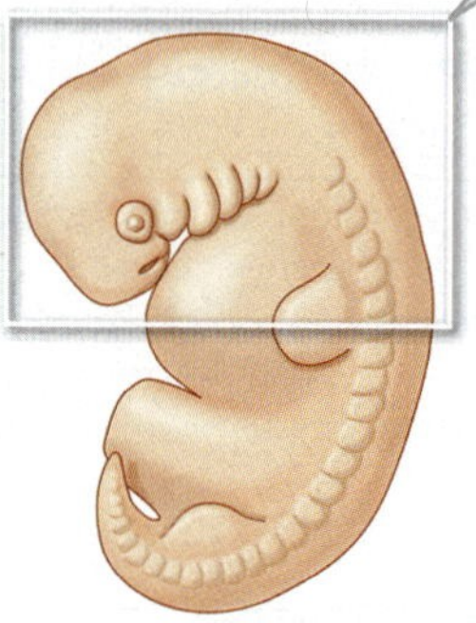

5-WEEK EMBRYO

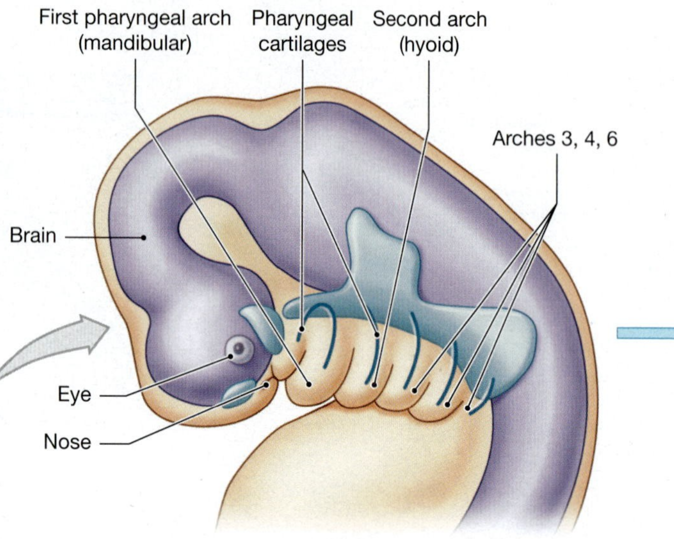

5 WEEKS

After 5 weeks of development, the central nervous system is a hollow tube that runs the length of the body. A series of cartilages appears in the mesenchyme of the head beneath and alongside the expanding brain and around the developing nose, eyes, and ears. These cartilages are shown in light blue. Five additional pairs of cartilages develop in the walls of the pharynx. These cartilages, shown in dark blue, are located within the **pharyngeal**, or **branchial, arches**. (*Branchial* refers to gills—in fish the caudal arches develop into skeletal supports for the gills.) The first arch, or **mandibular arch**, is the largest.

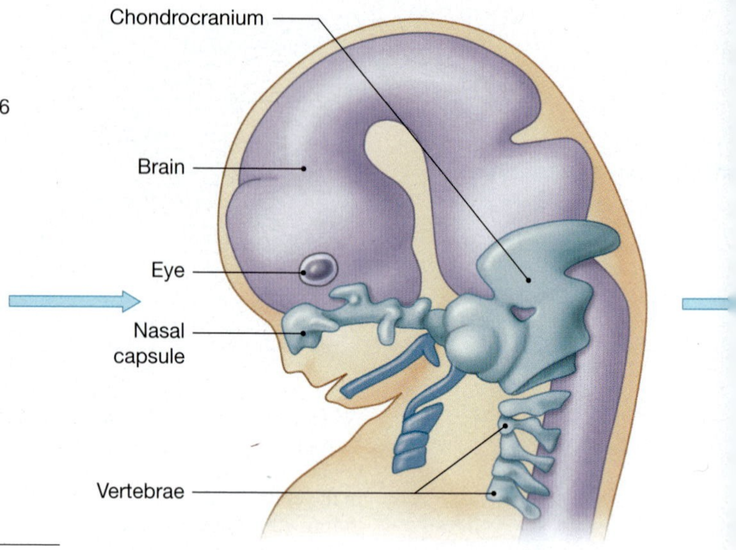

8 WEEKS

The cartilages associated with the brain enlarge and fuse, forming a cartilaginous **chondrocranium** (kon-drō-KRĀ-nē-um; *chondros*, cartilage + *cranium*, skull) that cradles the brain and sense organs. At 8 weeks its walls and floor are incomplete, and there is no roof.

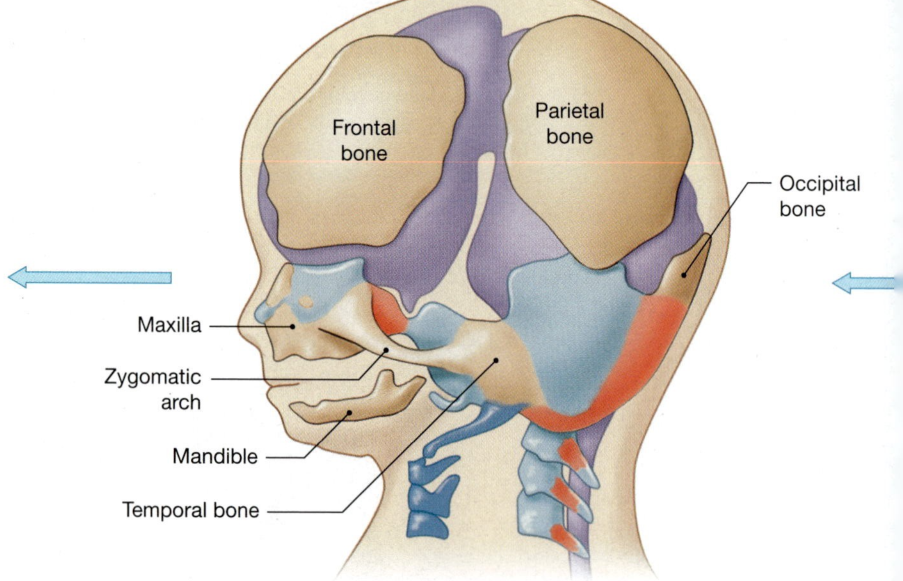

12 WEEKS

After 12 weeks ossification is well under way in the cranium and face. *Compare with Figure 5.6, p. 119.*

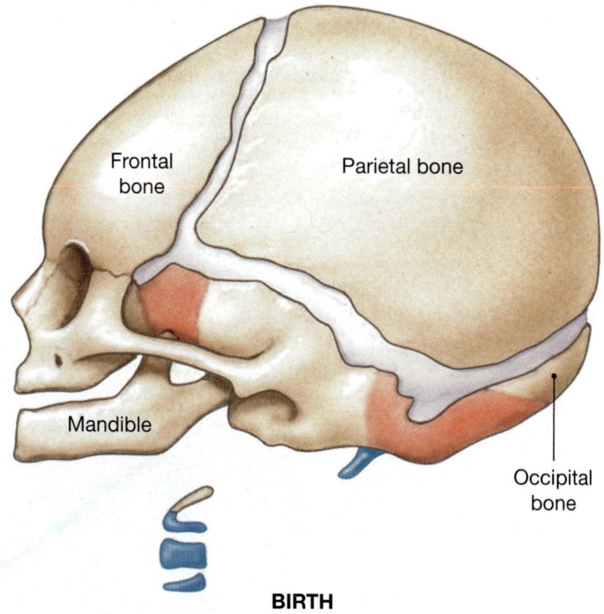

BIRTH

The skull at birth; compare with the situation at 12 weeks. Extensive fusions have occurred, but the cranial roof remains incomplete. (For further details, *see Figure 6.18, p. 159.*)

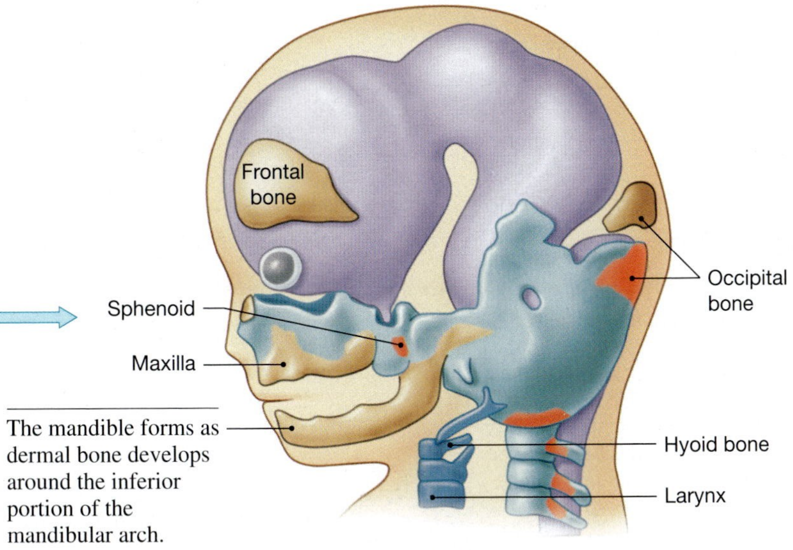

9 WEEKS

During the ninth week, numerous centers of endochondral ossification appear within the chondrocranium. These centers are shown in red. Gradually, the frontal and parietal bones of the cranial roof appear as intramembranous ossification begins in the overlying dermis. As these centers (beige) enlarge and expand, extensive fusions occur.

The dorsal portion of the mandibular arch fuses with the chondrocranium. The fused cartilages do not ossify; instead, osteoblasts begin sheathing them in dermal bone. On each side this sheath fuses with a bone developing at the entrance to the nasal cavity, producing the two maxillae. Ossification centers in the roof of the mouth spread to form the palatine processes and later fuse with the maxillae.

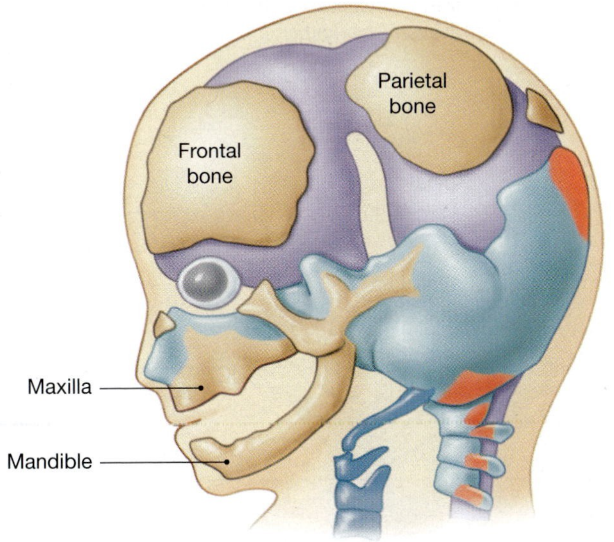

10 WEEKS

The second arch, or **hyoid arch**, forms near the temporal bones. Fusion of the superior tips of the hyoid with the temporals forms the styloid processes. The ventral portion of the hyoid arch ossifies as the hyoid bone. The third arch fuses with the hyoid, and the fourth and sixth arches form laryngeal cartilages.

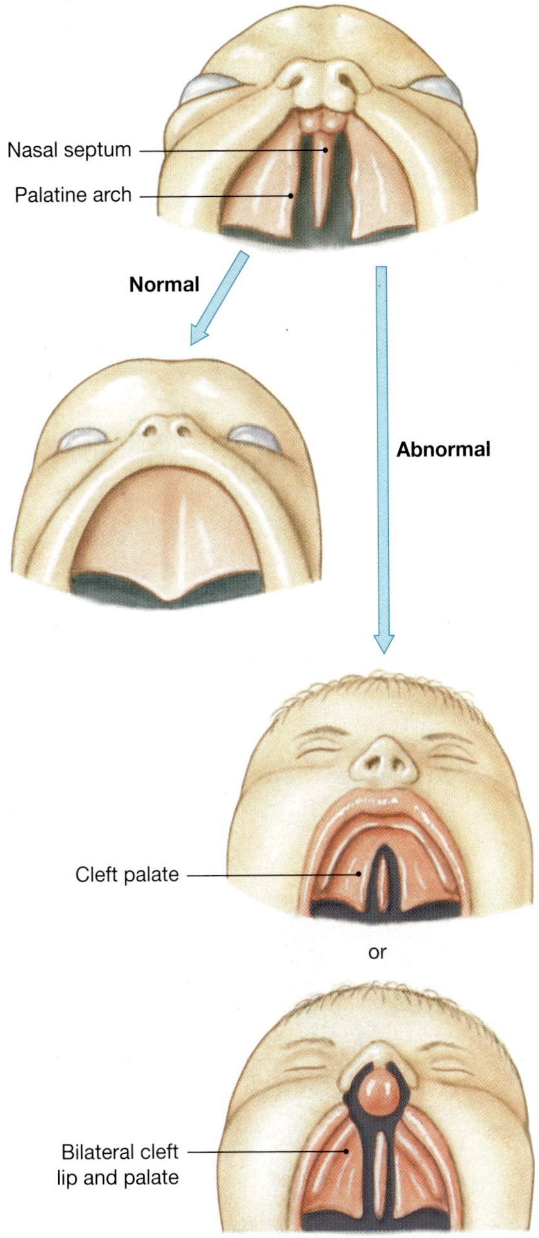

If the overlying skin does not fuse normally, the result is a **cleft lip**. Cleft lips affect roughly one birth in a thousand. A split extending into the orbit and palate is called a **cleft palate**. Cleft palates are half as common as cleft lips. Both conditions can be corrected surgically.

The Development of the Vertebral Column

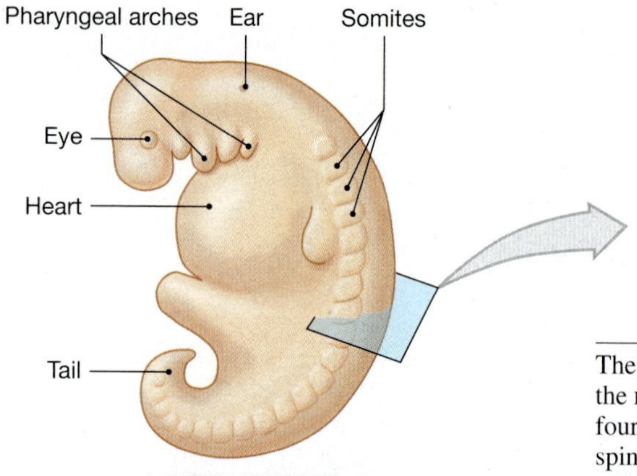

4-WEEK EMBRYO

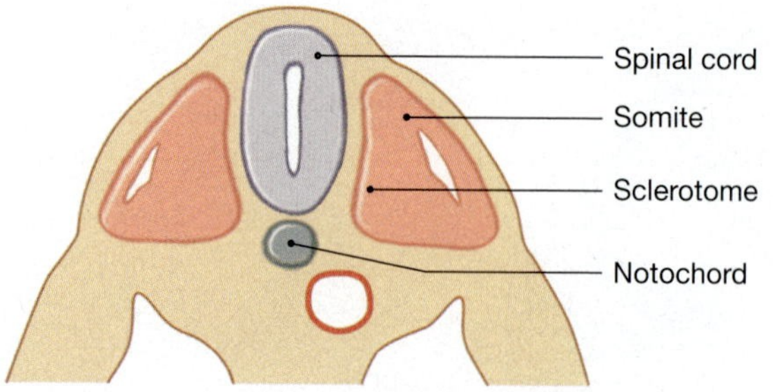

The developing spinal cord lies posterior to a longitudinal rod, the **notochord** (NŌ-tō-kōrd; *noton*, back + *chorde*, cord). In the fourth week of development, mesoderm on either side of the spinal cord and notochord forms a series of mesenchymal blocks called **somites** (SŌ-mīts). Mesenchyme in the medial portions of each somite, a region known as the **sclerotome** (SKLER-ō-tōme; *skleros*, hard), will produce the vertebral column and contribute to the floor of the cranium.

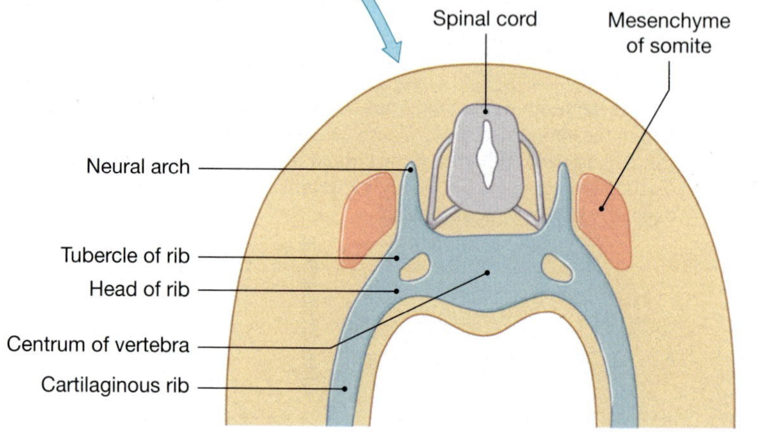

8 WEEKS

The cartilages of the vertebral centra grow around the spinal cord, creating a model of the complete vertebra. In the cervical, thoracic, and lumbar regions, articulations develop where adjacent cartilaginous blocks come into contact. In the sacrum and coccyx, the cartilages fuse together.

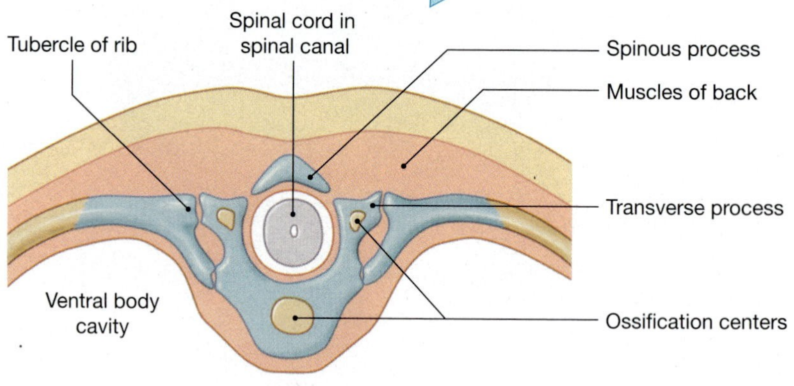

12 WEEKS

About the time the ribs separate from the vertebrae, ossification begins. Only the shortest ribs undergo complete ossification. In the rest, the distal portions remain cartilaginous, forming the costal cartilages. Several ossification centers appear in the sternum, but fusion gradually reduces the number.

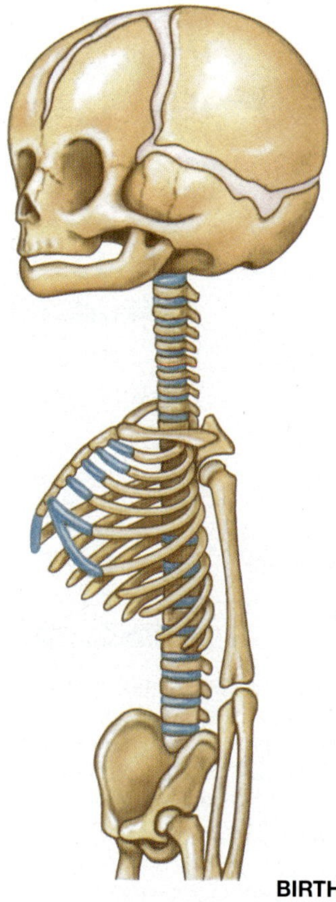

BIRTH

At birth, the vertebrae and ribs are ossified, but many cartilaginous areas remain. For example, the anterior portions of the ribs remain cartilaginous. Additional growth will occur for many years; in vertebrae, the bases of the neural arches enlarge until ages 3–6, and the spinal processes and vertebral bodies grow until ages 18–25.

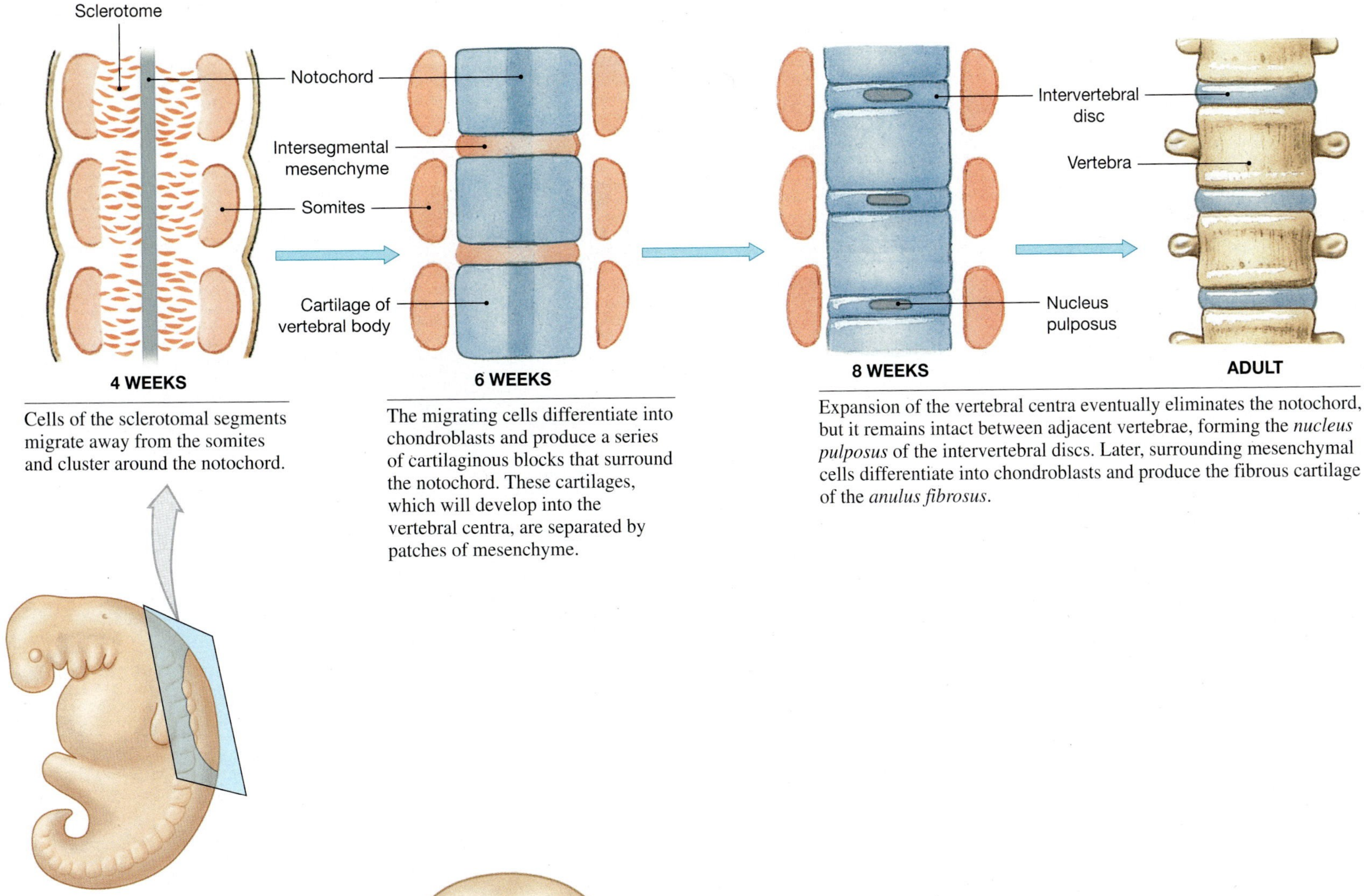

4 WEEKS

Cells of the sclerotomal segments migrate away from the somites and cluster around the notochord.

6 WEEKS

The migrating cells differentiate into chondroblasts and produce a series of cartilaginous blocks that surround the notochord. These cartilages, which will develop into the vertebral centra, are separated by patches of mesenchyme.

8 WEEKS / ADULT

Expansion of the vertebral centra eventually eliminates the notochord, but it remains intact between adjacent vertebrae, forming the *nucleus pulposus* of the intervertebral discs. Later, surrounding mesenchymal cells differentiate into chondroblasts and produce the fibrous cartilage of the *anulus fibrosus*.

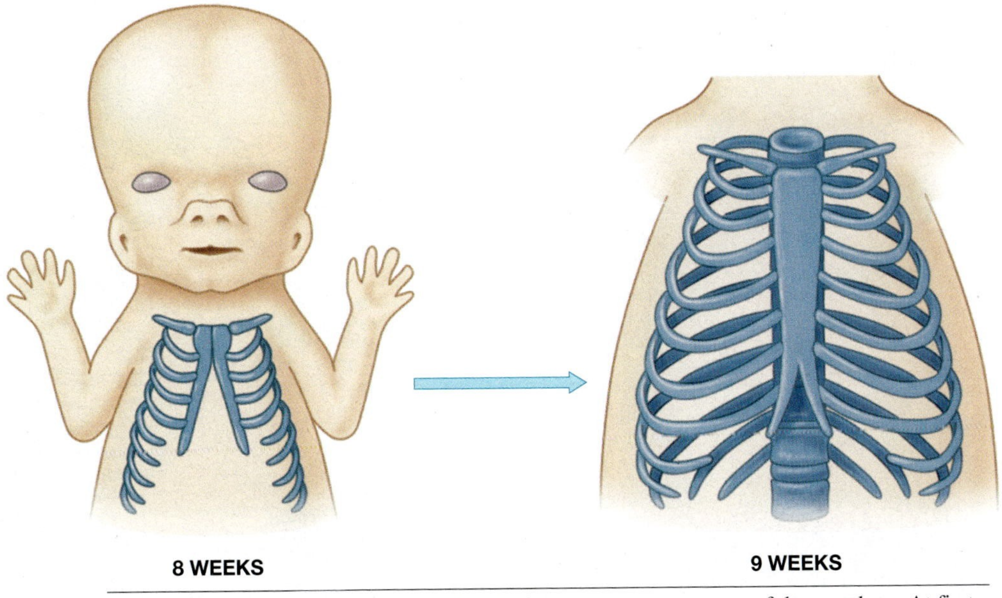

Rib cartilages expand away from the developing transverse processes of the vertebrae. At first they are continuous, but by week 8 the ribs have separated from the vertebrae. Ribs form at every vertebra, but in the cervical, lumbar, sacral, and coccygeal regions they remain small and later fuse with the growing vertebrae. The ribs of the thoracic vertebrae continue to enlarge, following the curvature of the body wall. When they reach the ventral midline, they fuse with the cartilages of the sternum.

The Development of the Appendicular Skeleton

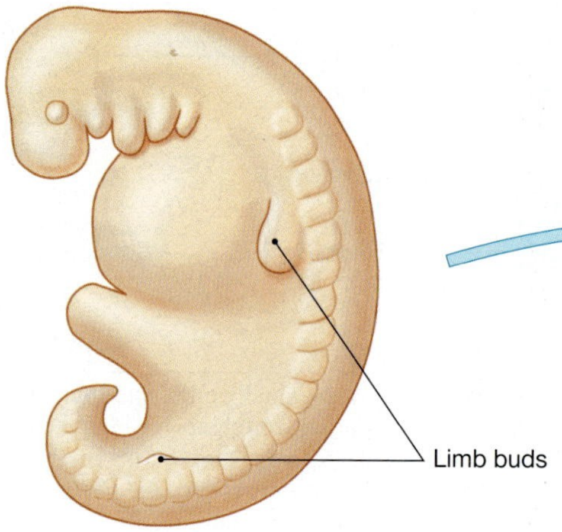

4 WEEKS

In the fourth week of development, ridges appear along the flanks of the embryo, extending from just behind the throat to just before the anus. These ridges form as mesodermal cells congregate beneath the ectoderm of the flank. Mesoderm gradually accumulates at the end of each ridge, forming two pairs of limb buds.

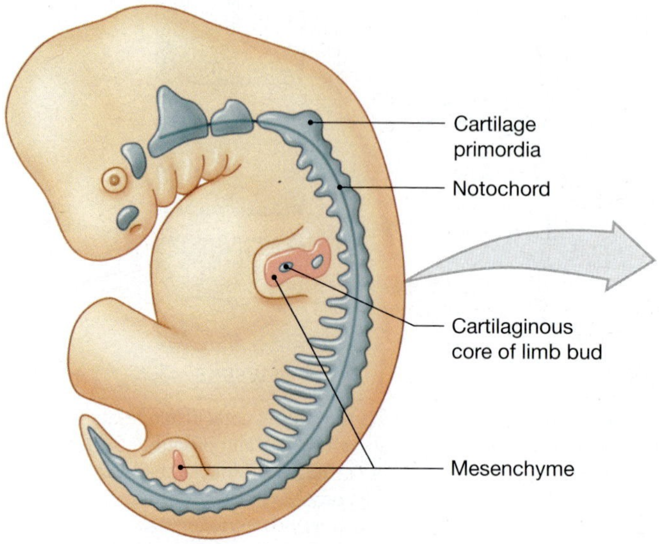

5 WEEKS

After 5 weeks of development, the pectoral limb buds have a cartilaginous core and scapular cartilages are developing in the mesenchyme of the trunk.

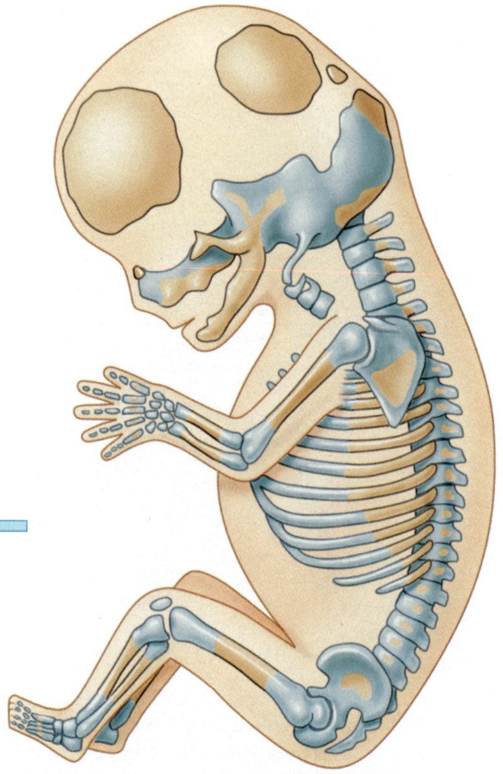

10 WEEKS

Ossification in the embryonic skeleton after approximately 10 weeks of development. The shafts of the limb bones are undergoing rapid ossification, but the distal bones of the carpus and tarsus remain cartilaginous.

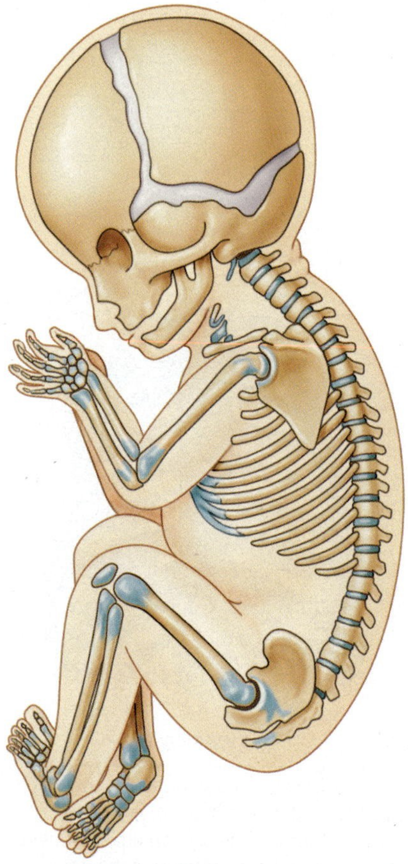

BIRTH

The skeleton of a newborn infant. Note the extensive areas of cartilage (blue) in the humeral head, in the wrist, between the bones of the palm and fingers, and in the hips. Notice the appearance of the axial skeleton, with reference to the two previous Embryology Summaries.

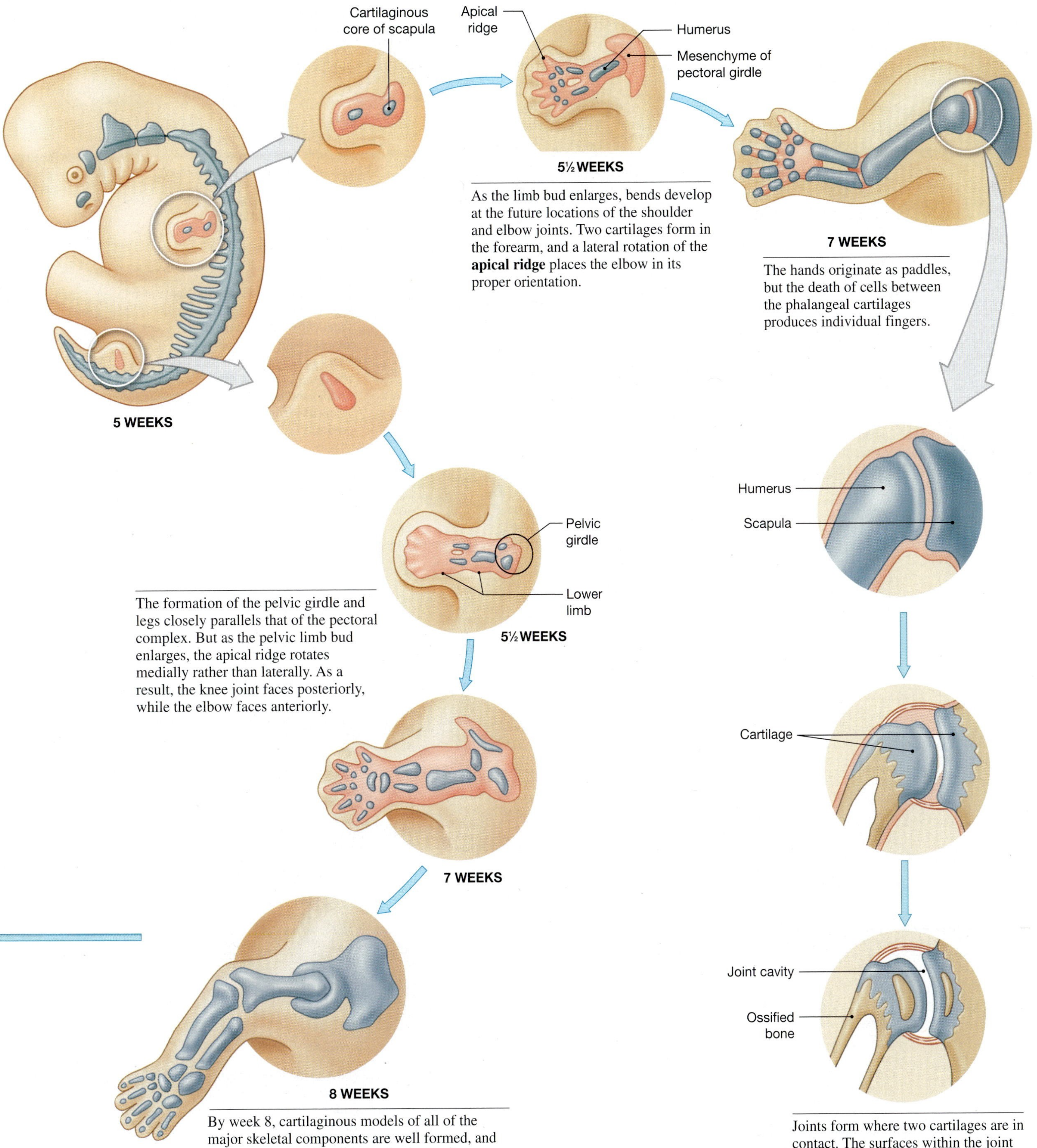

As the limb bud enlarges, bends develop at the future locations of the shoulder and elbow joints. Two cartilages form in the forearm, and a lateral rotation of the **apical ridge** places the elbow in its proper orientation.

The hands originate as paddles, but the death of cells between the phalangeal cartilages produces individual fingers.

The formation of the pelvic girdle and legs closely parallels that of the pectoral complex. But as the pelvic limb bud enlarges, the apical ridge rotates medially rather than laterally. As a result, the knee joint faces posteriorly, while the elbow faces anteriorly.

By week 8, cartilaginous models of all of the major skeletal components are well formed, and endochondral ossification begins in the future limb bones. Ossification of the hip bones begins at three separate centers that gradually enlarge.

Joints form where two cartilages are in contact. The surfaces within the joint cavity remain cartilaginous, while the rest of the bones undergo ossification.

The Development of the Muscles

Near the head, mesoderm forms skeletal muscle associated with the pharyngeal arches.

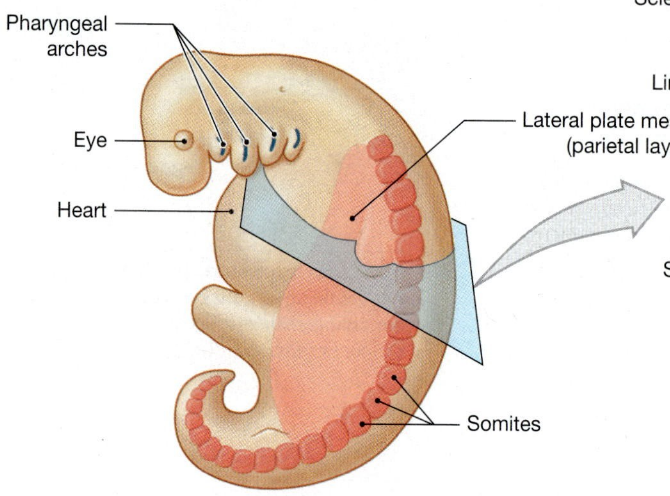

Mesoderm from the parietal portion of the lateral plate and the adjacent myotome forms the limb buds.

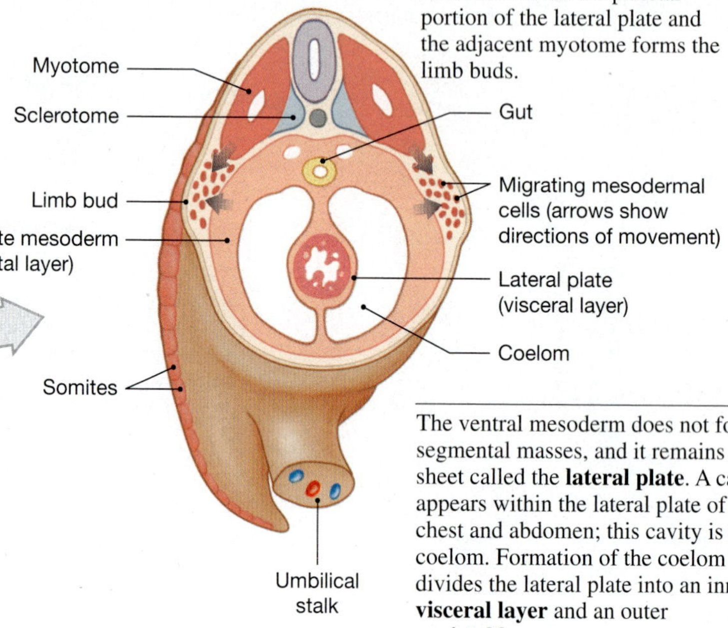

The ventral mesoderm does not form segmental masses, and it remains as a sheet called the **lateral plate**. A cavity appears within the lateral plate of the chest and abdomen; this cavity is the coelom. Formation of the coelom divides the lateral plate into an inner **visceral layer** and an outer **parietal layer**.

After 4 weeks of development, mesoderm on either side of the notochord has formed somites. The medial portion of each somite will form skeletal muscles; this region is called the **myotome**.

4 WEEKS

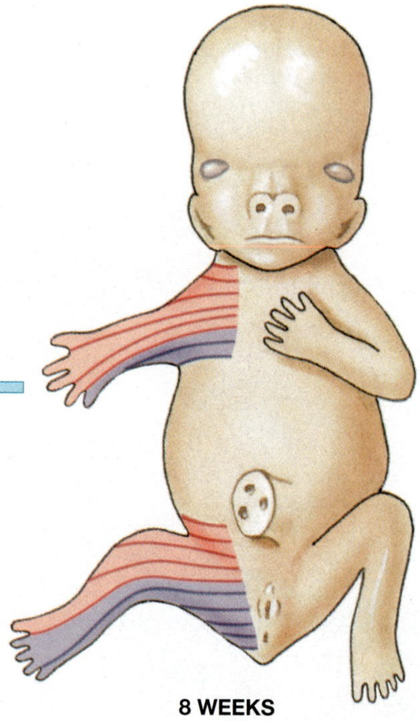

8 WEEKS

While the limb buds enlarge, additional myoblasts invade the limb from myotomal segments nearby. Lines indicate the boundaries between myotomes providing myoblasts to the limb.

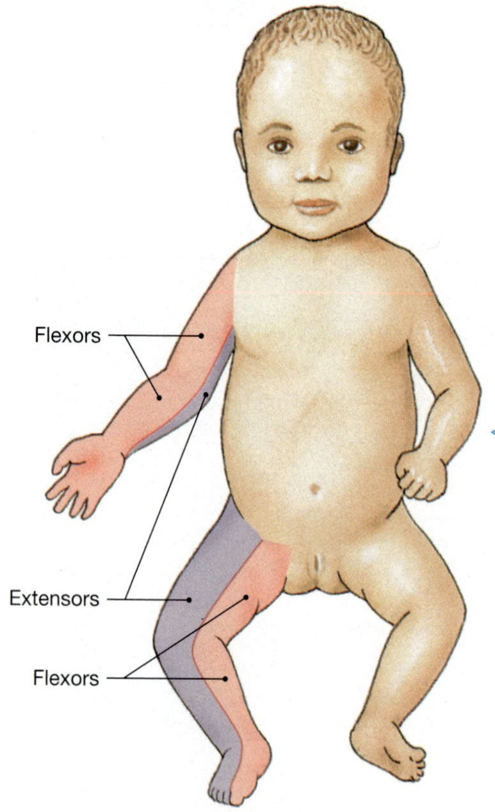

BIRTH

Rotation of the arm and leg buds produces a change in the position of these masses relative to the body axis.

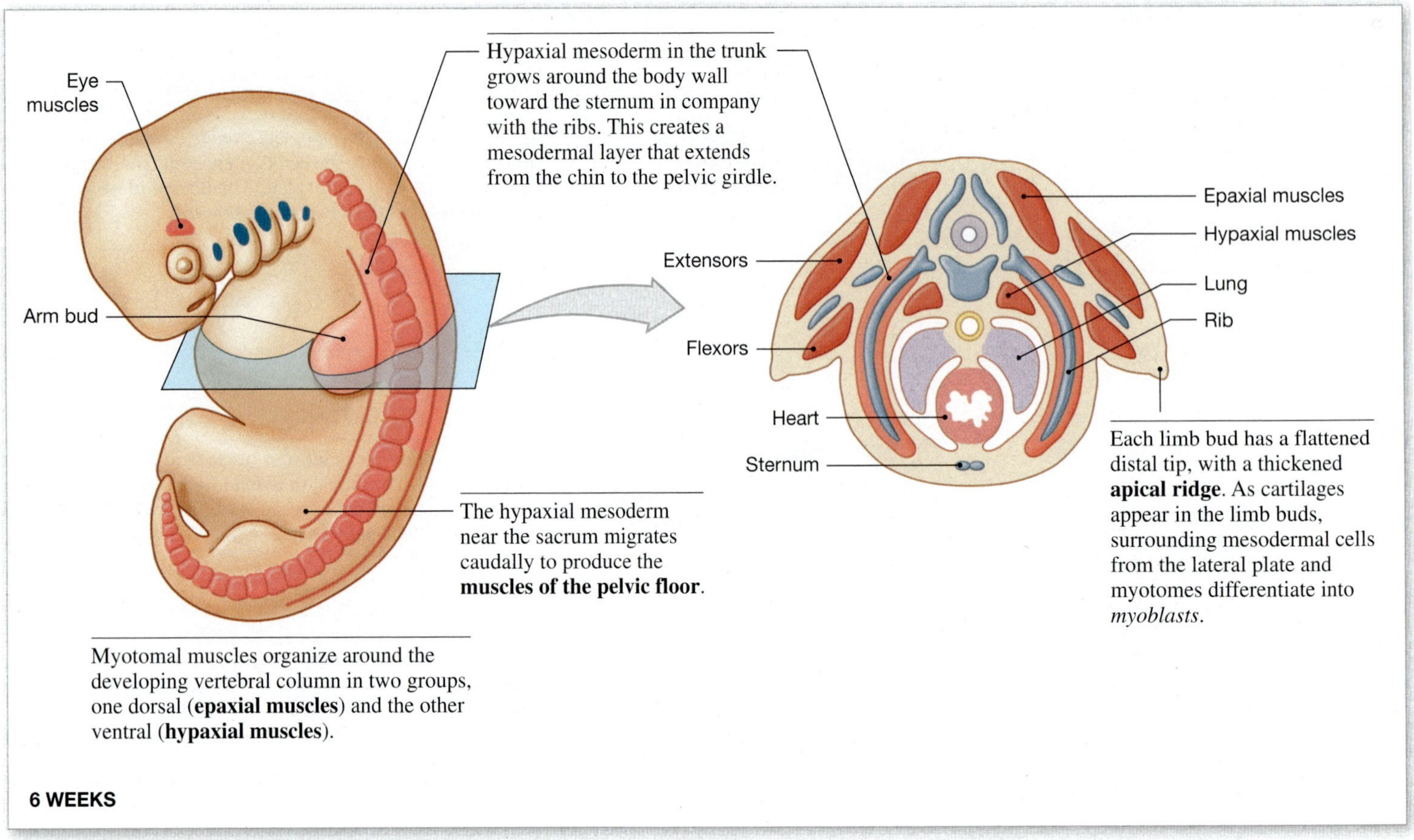
Eye muscles
Arm bud
Hypaxial mesoderm in the trunk grows around the body wall toward the sternum in company with the ribs. This creates a mesodermal layer that extends from the chin to the pelvic girdle.
Extensors
Flexors
Heart
Sternum
Epaxial muscles
Hypaxial muscles
Lung
Rib
Each limb bud has a flattened distal tip, with a thickened **apical ridge**. As cartilages appear in the limb buds, surrounding mesodermal cells from the lateral plate and myotomes differentiate into *myoblasts*.
The hypaxial mesoderm near the sacrum migrates caudally to produce the **muscles of the pelvic floor**.
Myotomal muscles organize around the developing vertebral column in two groups, one dorsal (**epaxial muscles**) and the other ventral (**hypaxial muscles**).
6 WEEKS

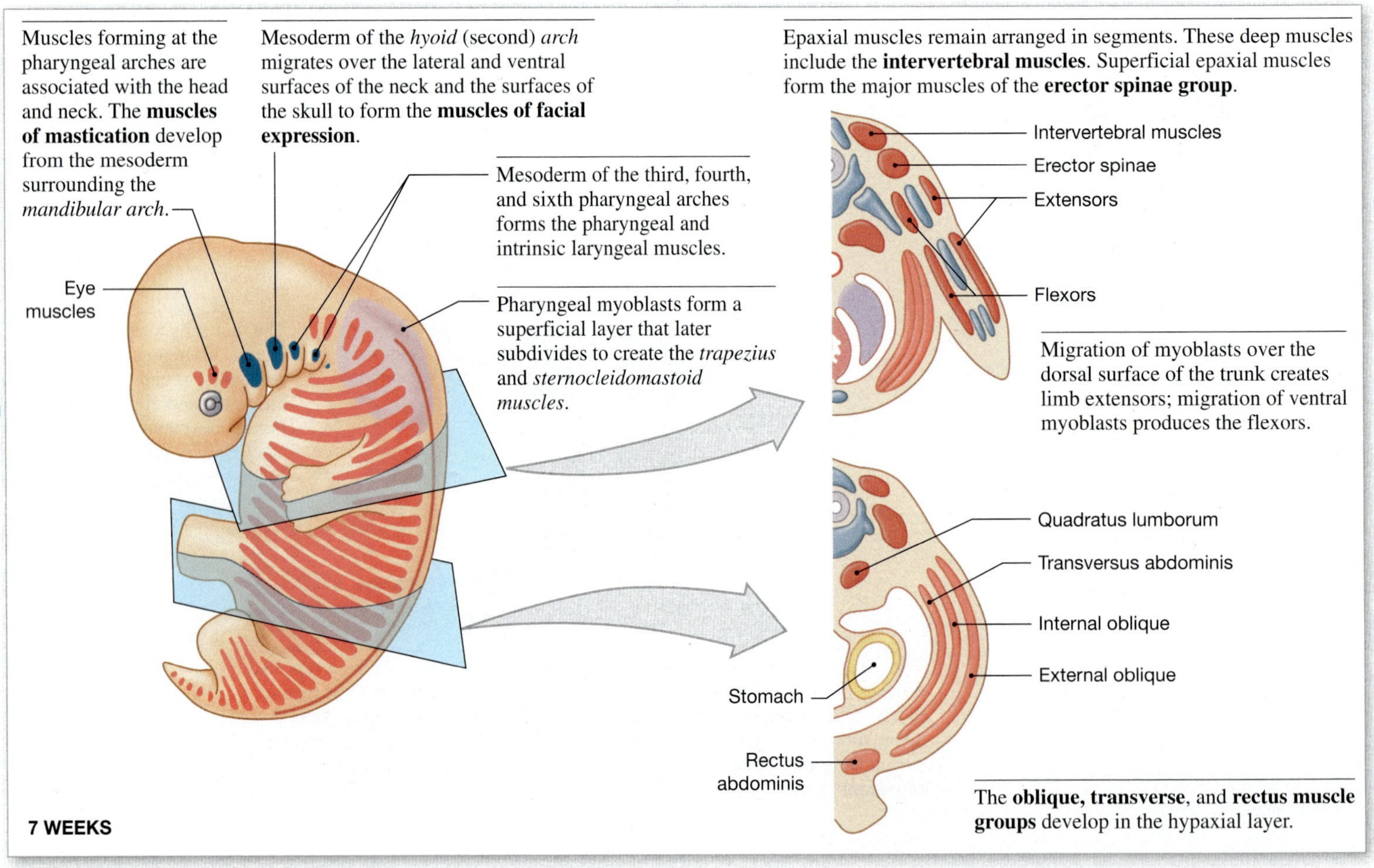
Muscles forming at the pharyngeal arches are associated with the head and neck. The **muscles of mastication** develop from the mesoderm surrounding the *mandibular arch*.
Mesoderm of the *hyoid* (second) *arch* migrates over the lateral and ventral surfaces of the neck and the surfaces of the skull to form the **muscles of facial expression**.
Mesoderm of the third, fourth, and sixth pharyngeal arches forms the pharyngeal and intrinsic laryngeal muscles.
Pharyngeal myoblasts form a superficial layer that later subdivides to create the *trapezius* and *sternocleidomastoid muscles*.
Eye muscles
Epaxial muscles remain arranged in segments. These deep muscles include the **intervertebral muscles**. Superficial epaxial muscles form the major muscles of the **erector spinae group**.
Intervertebral muscles
Erector spinae
Extensors
Flexors
Migration of myoblasts over the dorsal surface of the trunk creates limb extensors; migration of ventral myoblasts produces the flexors.
Quadratus lumborum
Transversus abdominis
Internal oblique
External oblique
Stomach
Rectus abdominis
The **oblique, transverse,** and **rectus muscle groups** develop in the hypaxial layer.
7 WEEKS

The Development of the Nervous System

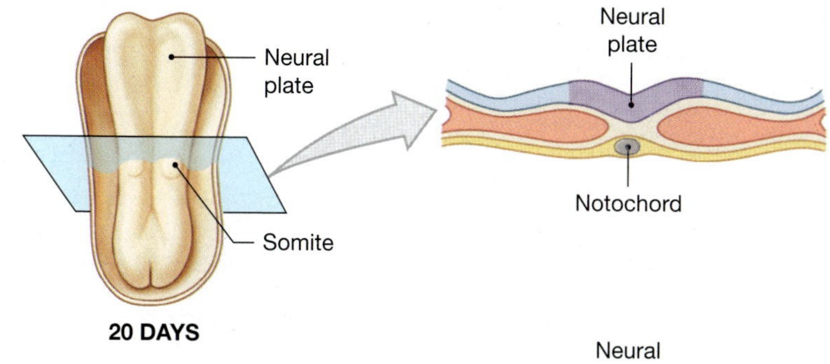

After two weeks of development, *somites* are appearing on either side of the *notochord*. The ectoderm near the midline thickens, forming an elevated neural plate. The **neural plate** is largest near the future head of the developing embryo.

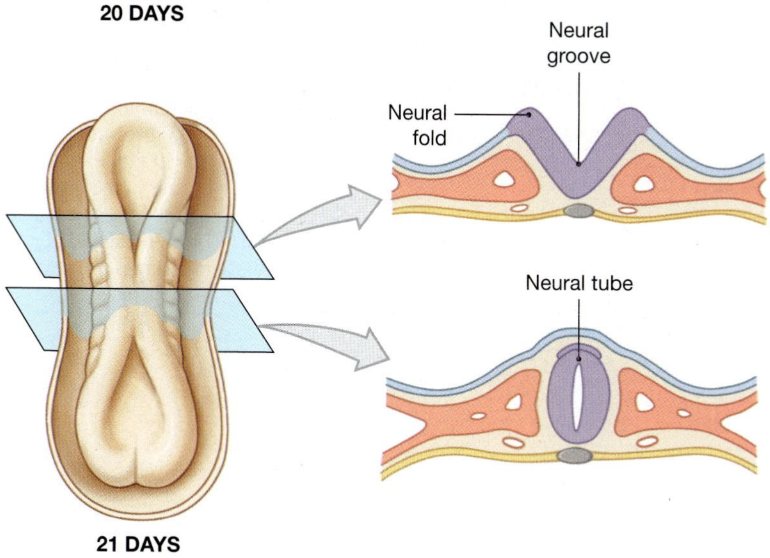

A crease develops along the axis of the neural plate, creating the **neural groove**. The edges, or **neural folds**, gradually move together. They first contact one another midway along the axis of the neural plate, near the end of the third week.

Where the neural folds meet, they fuse to form a cylindrical **neural tube** that loses its connection with the superficial ectoderm. The process of neural tube formation is called **neurulation**; it is completed in less than a week. The formation of the axial skeleton and that of the musculature around the developing neural tube were described on pages 768 and 773.

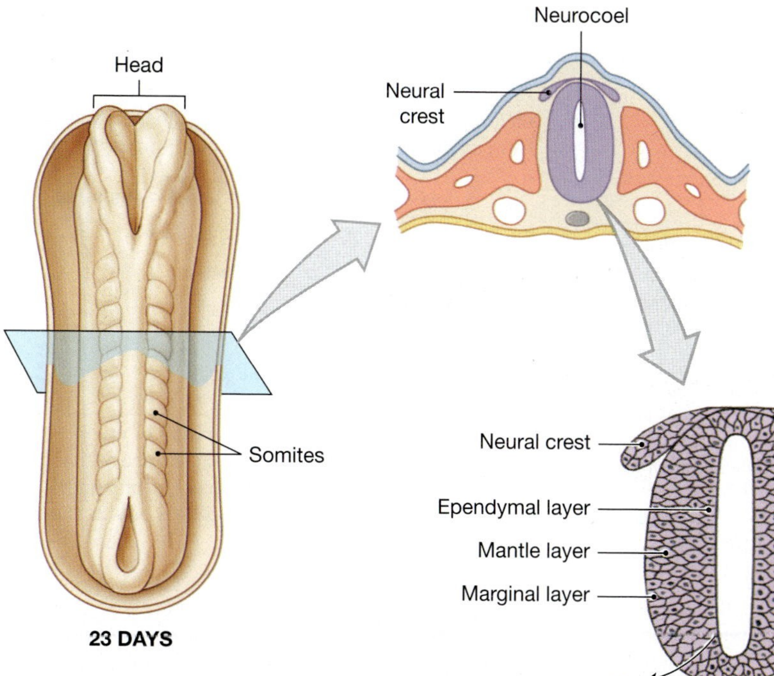

Cells at the tips of the neural folds do not participate in neural tube formation. These cells of the **neural crest** at first remain between the dorsal surface of the neural tube and the ectoderm, but they later migrate to other locations. The neural tube becomes the CNS. Axons from neurons within the neural tube and the axons of neural crest cells form the PNS.

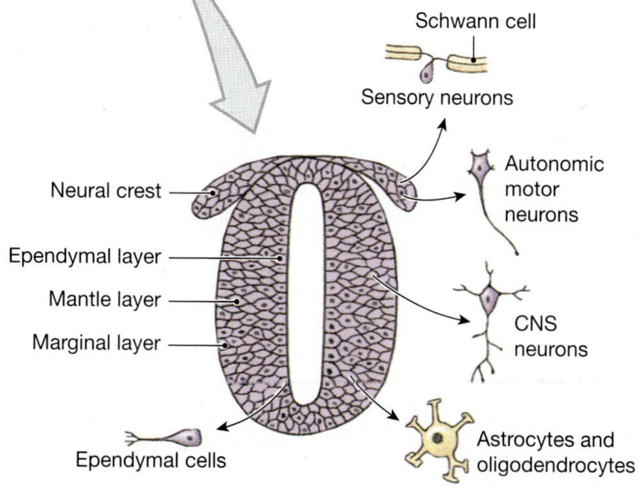

The first cells to appear in the mantle differentiate into neurons, while the last cells to arrive become astrocytes and oligodendrocytes. Further development of the CNS and PNS will be found in the Embryology Summaries later in this chapter.

The neural tube increases in thickness as its epithelial lining undergoes repeated mitoses. By the middle of the fifth developmental week, there are three distinct layers. The **ependymal layer** lines the enclosed cavity, or **neurocoel**. The ependymal cells continue their mitotic activities, and daughter cells create the surrounding **mantle layer**. Axons from developing neurons form a superficial **marginal layer**.

The Development of the Spinal Cord, Part I

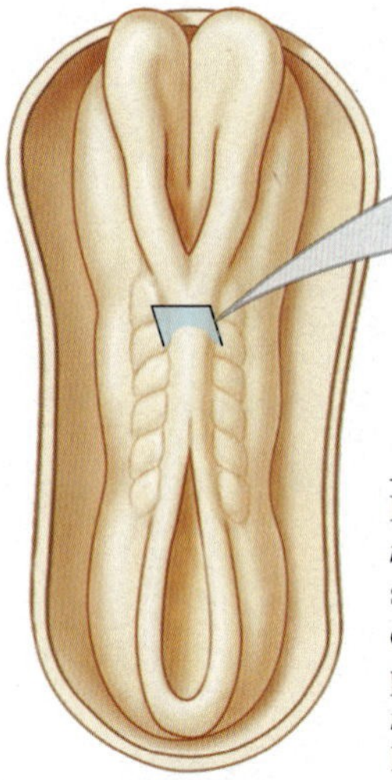

22 DAYS

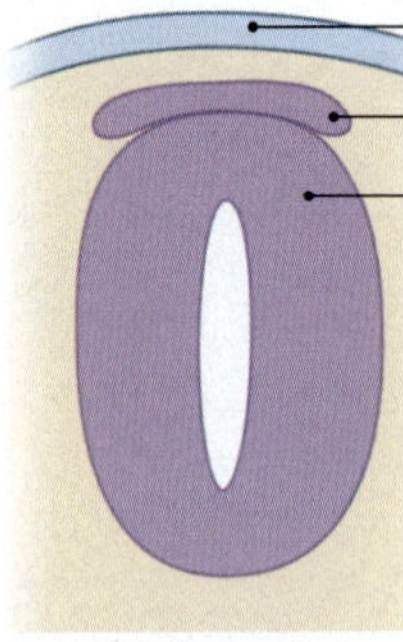

By the end of the fifth developmental week, the *neural tube* is almost completely closed. In the spinal cord the *mantle layer* that contains developing neurons and neuroglial cells will produce the gray matter that surrounds the *neurocoel*. As neurons develop in the mantle layer, their axons grow toward central or peripheral destinations. The axons leave the mantle layer and travel toward synaptic targets within a peripheral *marginal layer*.

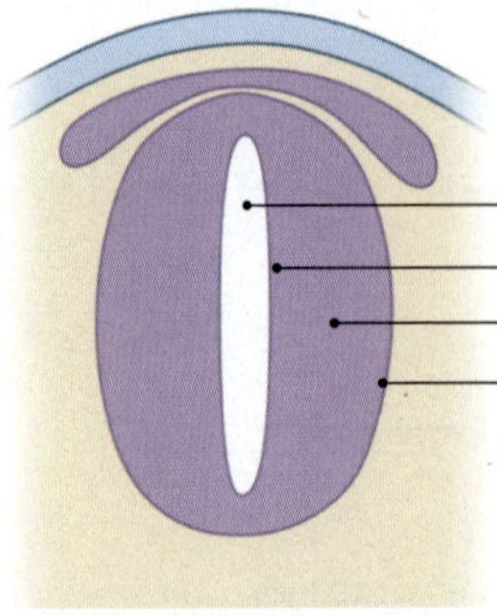

23 DAYS

Eventually, the growing axons will form bundles, or tracts, in the marginal layer, and these tracts will crowd together in the columns that form the white matter of the spinal cord.

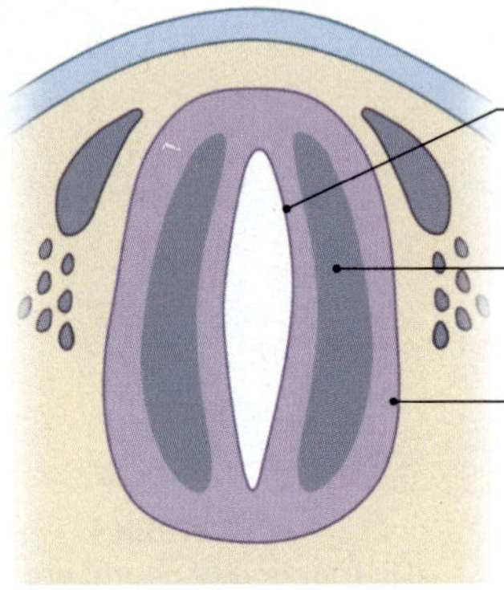

28 DAYS

By this time, cells of the *neural crest* have migrated to either side of the spinal cord and have formed the dorsal root ganglia. The neural crest cells become sensory neurons and glial cells (Schwann cells and satellite cells). Processes from these sensory neurons grow both into the periphery, to contact receptors, and into the CNS via the dorsal roots.

In each segment the axons of developing motor neurons form a pair of ventral roots that grow away from the spinal cord.

Distal to each dorsal root ganglion, the motor efferents of the ventral root and the sensory afferents of the dorsal root are bound together into a single spinal nerve. Along much of the spinal cord, these nerves share a stereotyped pattern of peripheral branches, and the pattern accounts for the distribution of dermatomes.

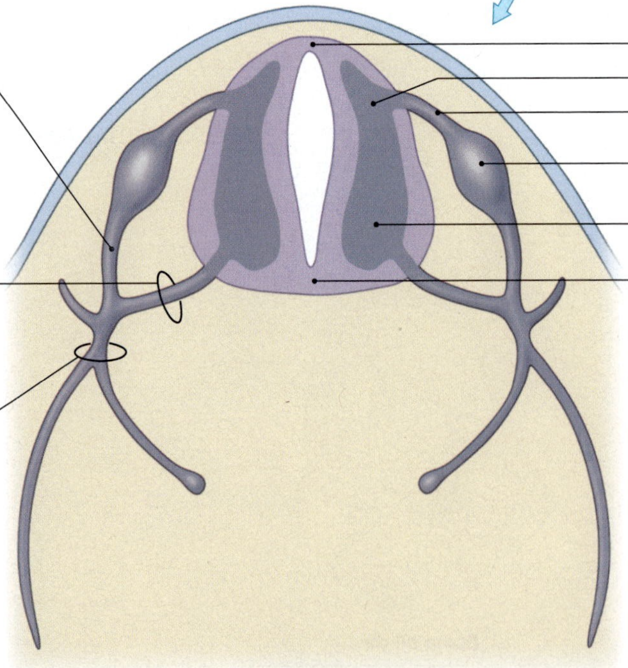

7 WEEKS

As the mantle enlarges, the neurocoel becomes laterally compressed and relatively narrow. The relatively thin **roof plate** and **floor plate** will not thicken substantially, but the **dorsolateral** and **ventrolateral plates** enlarge rapidly. Neurons developing within the dorsolateral plate will receive and relay sensory information, while those in the ventrolateral region will develop into motor neurons.

The Development of the Spinal Cord, Part II

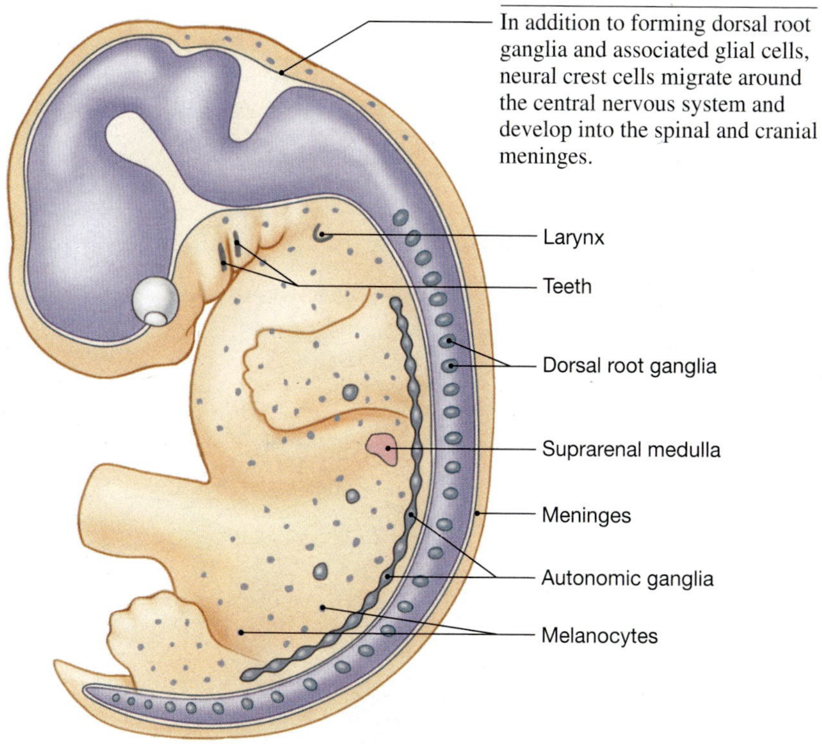

7 WEEKS
(Distribution of neural crest cells)

Neural crest cells aggregate to form autonomic ganglia near the vertebral column and in peripheral organs. Migrating neural crest cells contribute to the formation of teeth and form the laryngeal cartilages, melanocytes of the skin, the skull, connective tissues around the eye, the intrinsic muscles of the eye, Schwann cells, satellite cells, and the suprarenal medullae.

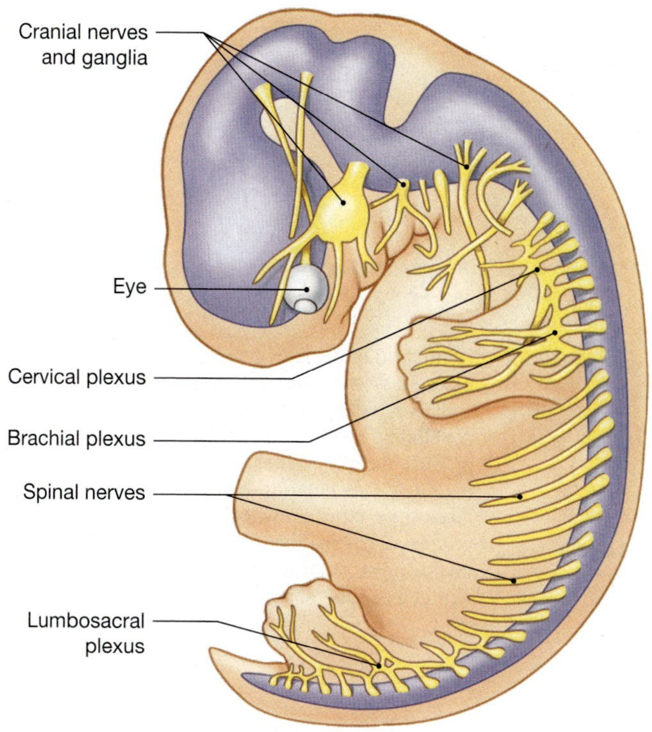

7 WEEKS
(Peripheral nerve distribution)

Several spinal nerves innervate each developing limb. When embryonic muscle cells migrate away from the myotome, the nerves grow right along with them. If a large muscle in the adult is derived from several myotomal blocks, connective tissue partitions will often mark the original boundaries, and the innervation will always involve more than one spinal nerve.

DEVELOPMENTAL ABNORMALITIES

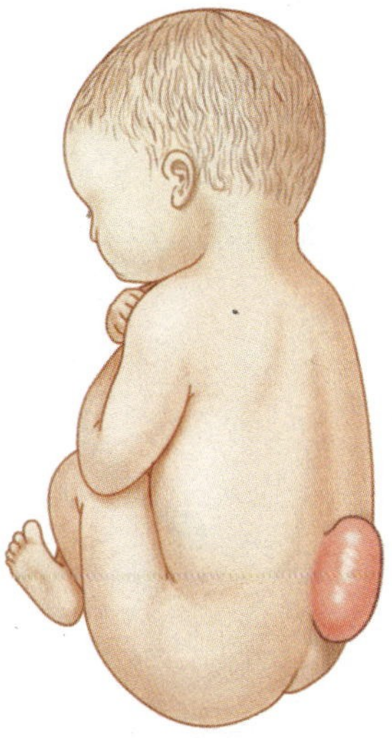

Spina bifida

Spina bifida (BI-fi-da) results when the developing vertebral laminae fail to unite due to abnormal neural tube formation at that site. The neural arch is incomplete, and the meninges bulge outward beneath the skin of the back. The extent of the abnormality determines the severity of the defects. In mild cases, the condition may pass unnoticed; extreme cases involve much of the length of the vertebral column.

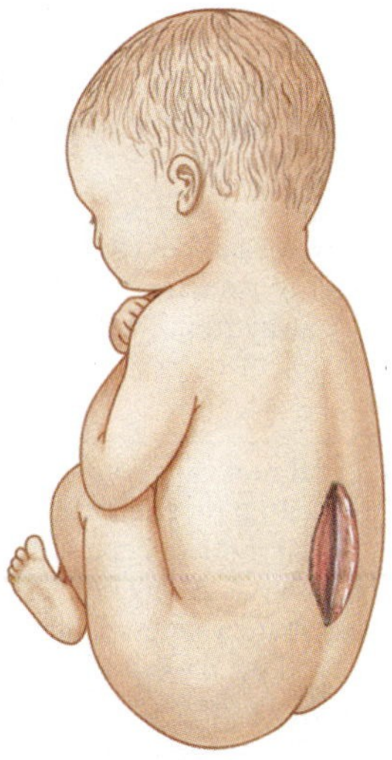

Neural tube defect

A **neural tube defect (NTD)** is a condition that is secondary to a developmental error in the formation of the spinal cord. Instead of forming a hollow tube, a portion of the spinal cord develops as a broad plate. This is often associated with spina bifida. Neural tube defects affect roughly one individual in 1000; prenatal testing can detect the existence of these defects with an 80–85 percent success rate.

The Development of the Brain, Part I

Before proceeding, briefly review the summaries of skull formation, vertebral column development, and development of the spinal cord in the previous Embryology Summaries.

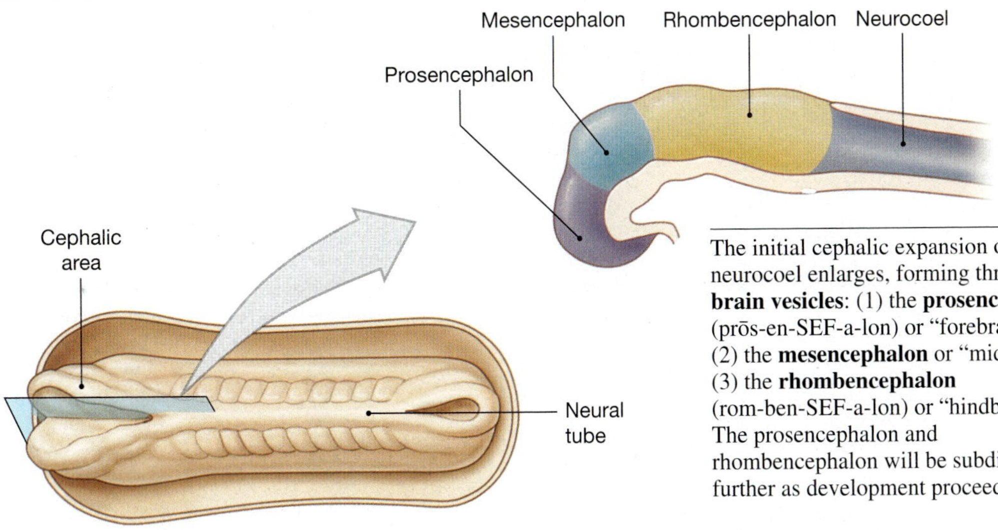

The initial cephalic expansion occurs as the neurocoel enlarges, forming three distinct **brain vesicles**: (1) the **prosencephalon** (prōs-en-SEF-a-lon) or "forebrain," (2) the **mesencephalon** or "midbrain," and (3) the **rhombencephalon** (rom-ben-SEF-a-lon) or "hindbrain." The prosencephalon and rhombencephalon will be subdivided further as development proceeds.

Even before **neural tube** formation has been completed, the cephalic portion begins to enlarge. Major differences in brain versus spinal cord development include (1) early breakdown of mantle (gray matter) and marginal (white matter) organization; (2) appearance of areas of neural cortex; (3) differential growth between and within specific regions; (4) appearance of characteristic bends and folds; and (5) loss of obvious segmental organization.

23 DAYS

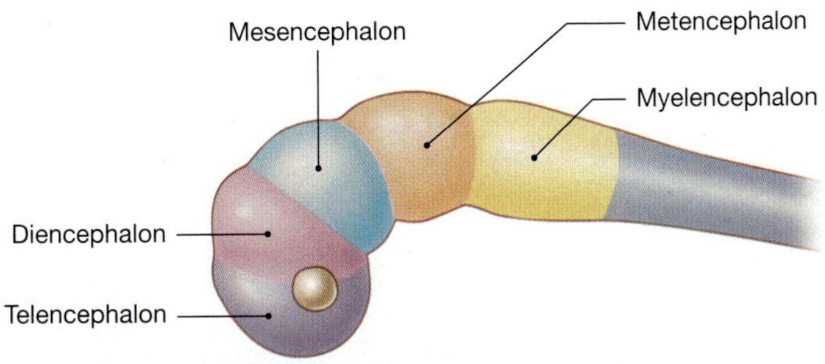

The rhombencephalon first subdivides into the **metencephalon** (met-en-SEF-a-lon; *meta*, after) and the **myelencephalon** (mī-el-en-SEF-a-lon; *myelon*, spinal cord).

The prosencephalon forms the **telecephalon** (tel-en-SEF-a-lon; *telos*, end + *enkephalos*, brain) and the **diencephalon**. The telencephalon begins as a pair of swellings near the rostral, dorsolateral border of the prosencephalon.

4 WEEKS

Cranial nerves develop as sensory ganglia and link peripheral receptors with the brain, and motor fibers grow out of developing cranial nuclei. Special sensory neurons of cranial nerves I, II, and VIII develop in association with the developing receptors. The somatic motor nerves III, IV, and VI grow to the eye muscles; the mixed nerves (V, VII, IX, and X) innervate the **pharyngeal arches** (page 766).

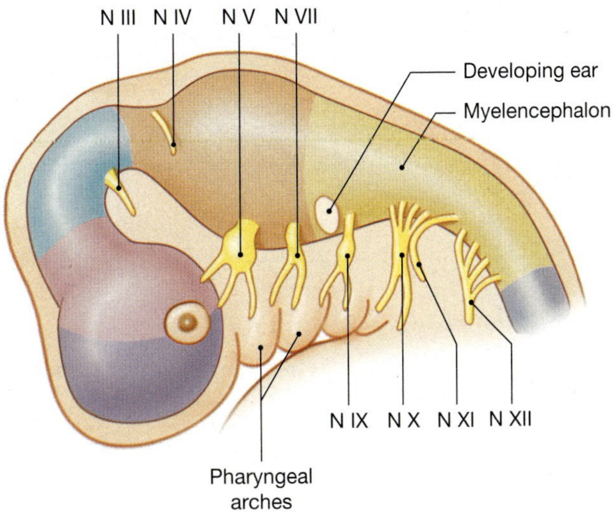

Development of the **mesencephalon** produces a small mass of neural tissue with a constricted neurocoel, the *aqueduct of the midbrain*.

As differential growth proceeds and the position and orientation of the embryo change, a series of bends, or **flexures** (FLEK-sherz), appears along the axis of the developing brain.

5 WEEKS

The Development of the Brain, Part II

The roofs of the diencephalon and myelencephalon fail to develop, leaving a thin ependymal layer in contact with the developing meninges. Blood vessels invading these regions create areas of the **choroid plexus**.

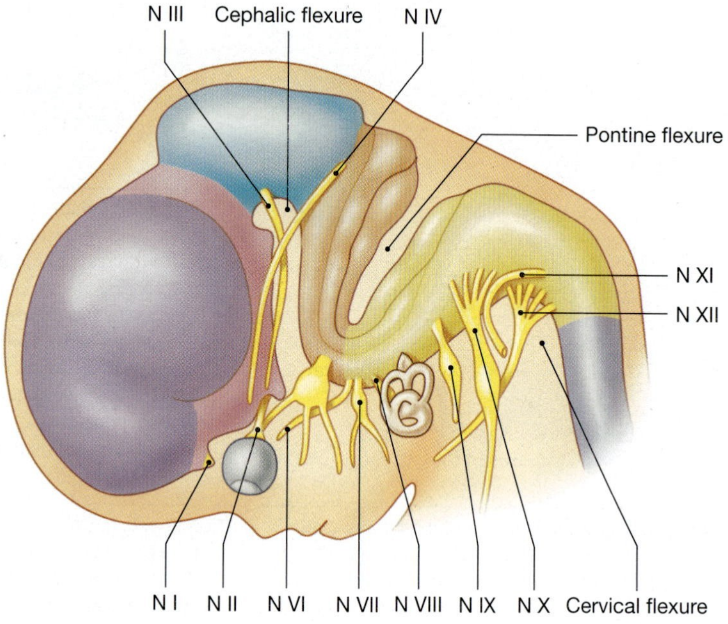

8 WEEKS

As growth continues and the pontine flexure develops, the brain becomes more compact. The expanding cerebral hemispheres now dominate the superior and lateral surfaces of the brain. Migrating neuroblasts create the cerebral cortex, and underlying masses of gray matter develop into the basal nuclei.

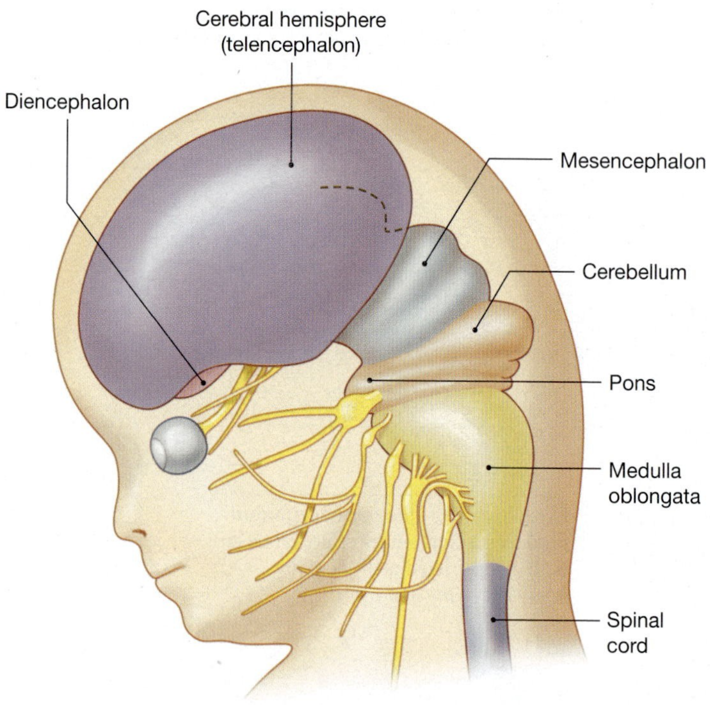

After 11 weeks, the expanding cerebral hemispheres have overgrown the diencephalon. At the metencephalon, cortical formation and expansion produce the cerebellum, which overlies the nuclei and tracts of the pons.

11 WEEKS

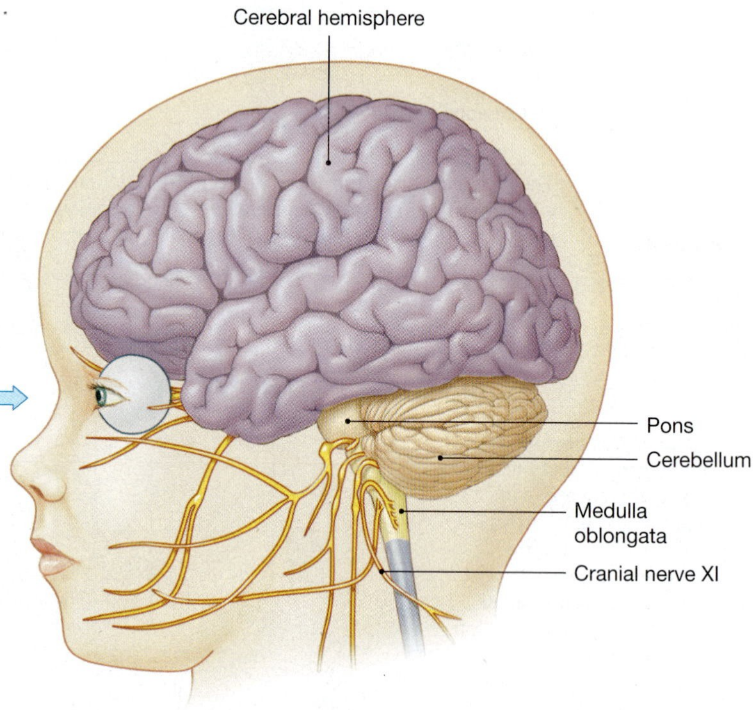

CHILD

The Development of Special Sense Organs, Part I

All special sense organs develop from the interaction between the epithelia and the developing nervous system of the embryo.

VISION

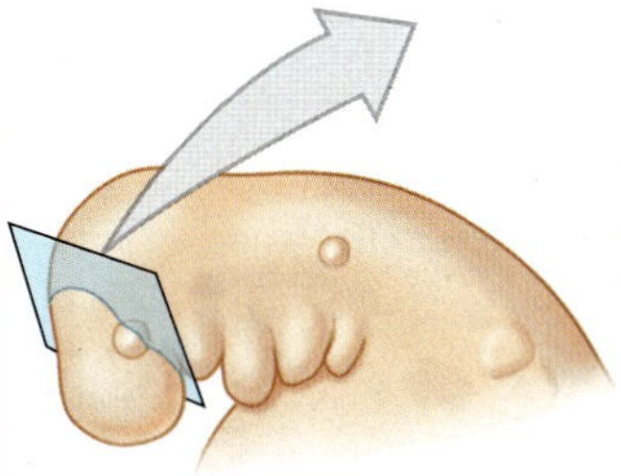

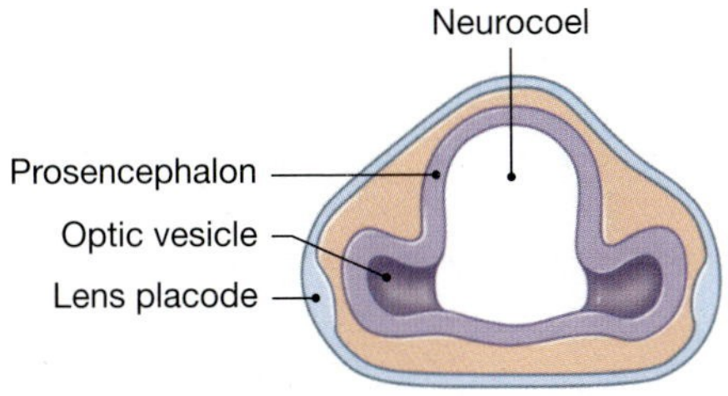

4 WEEKS

The first indication of optic development appears as a pair of bulges called **optic vesicles** in the lateral walls of the prosencephalon. These extend to either side like a pair of dumbbells, each containing a cavity continuous with the neurocoel.

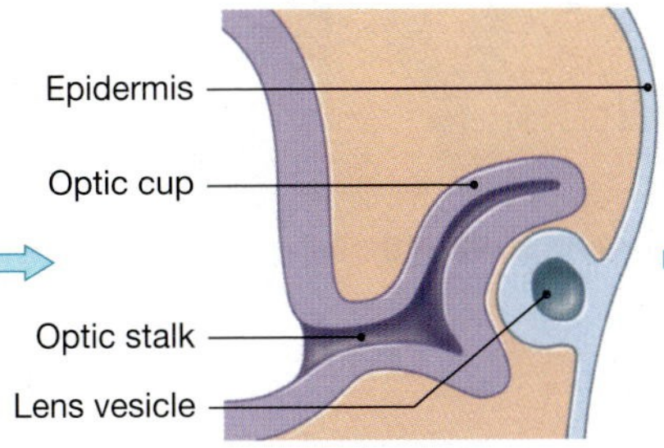

These bulges become indented, forming a pair of **optic cups**, which remain connected to the diencephalon by **optic stalks**. The epidermis overlying the optic cup responds by forming a **lens placode**, which thickens and creates another vesicle. This **lens vesicle** becomes the lens.

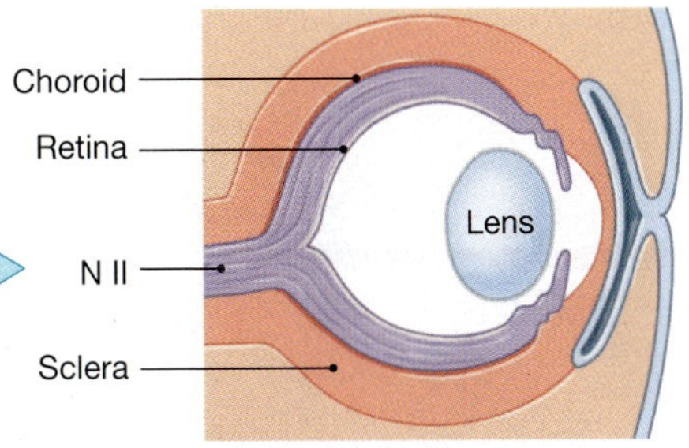

Mesoderm aggregating around this complex forms the choroid and scleral coats. The anterior and posterior chambers develop as cavities appear within the mesoderm.

OLFACTION

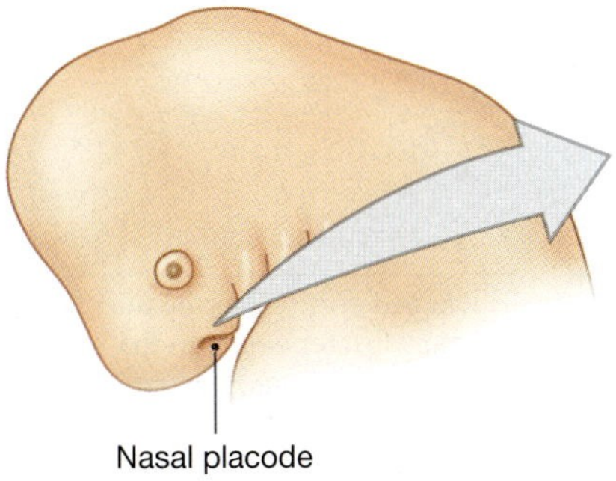

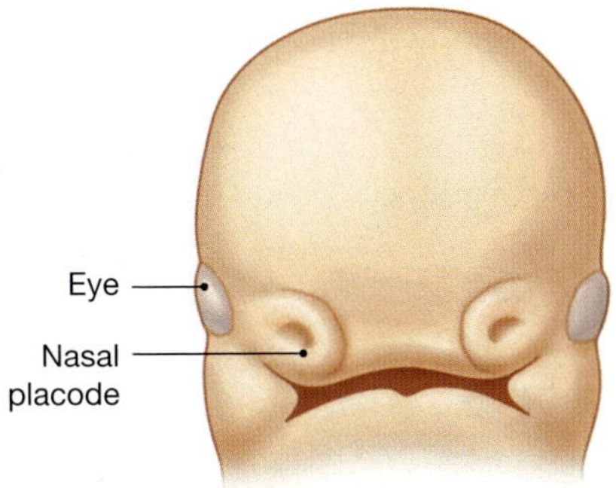

5 WEEKS

Olfactory receptors begin as a pair of thickened areas in front of the prosencephalon during the fifth developmental week. The thickenings are called **nasal placodes**.

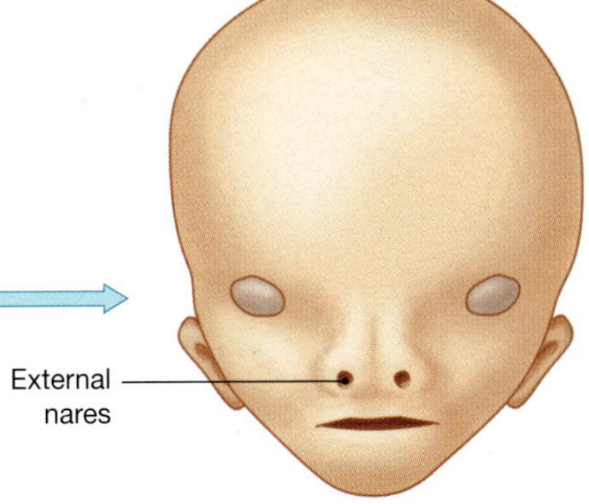

10 WEEKS

Over time, the nasal placodes are enfolded and protected by developing facial structures. (Development of the face was discussed in the previous Embryology Summary of the Skull.)

GUSTATION

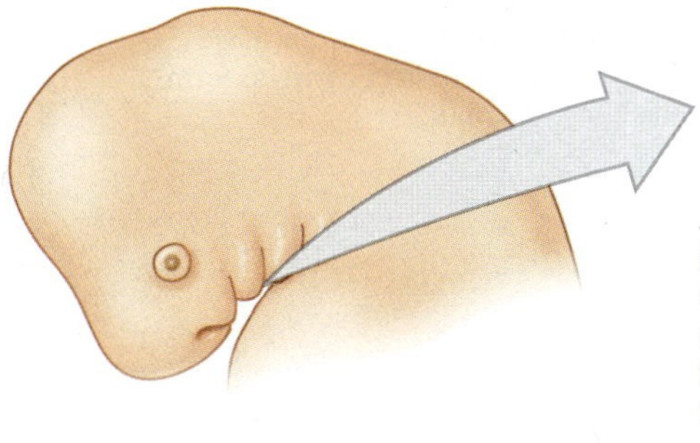

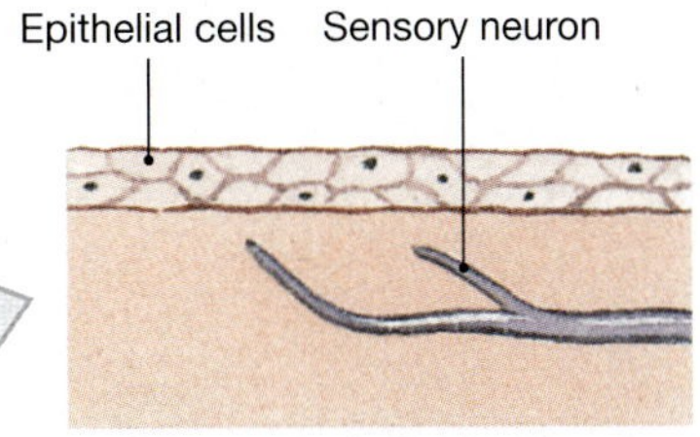

Gustatory receptors are the least specialized of any of the special sense organs. Taste buds develop as sensory fibers grow into the developing mouth and pharynx.

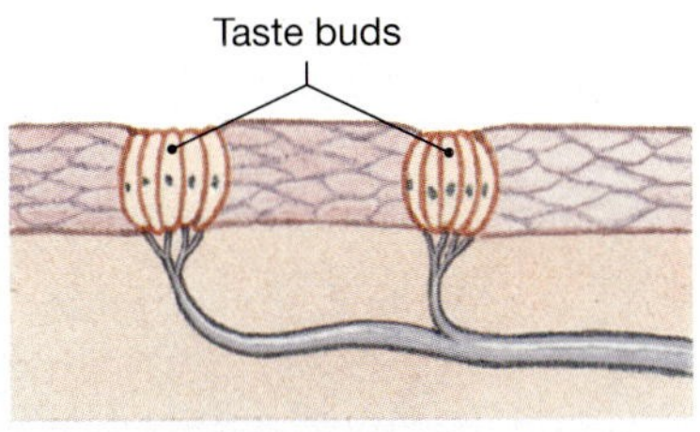

When the nerve endings contact epithelial cells, the epithelial cells differentiate into gustatory cells. If the sensory nerves are cut, the taste buds degenerate; if the sensory nerve is moved, it will stimulate the development of new taste buds at its new location.

The Development of Special Sense Organs, Part II

EQUILIBRIUM AND HEARING

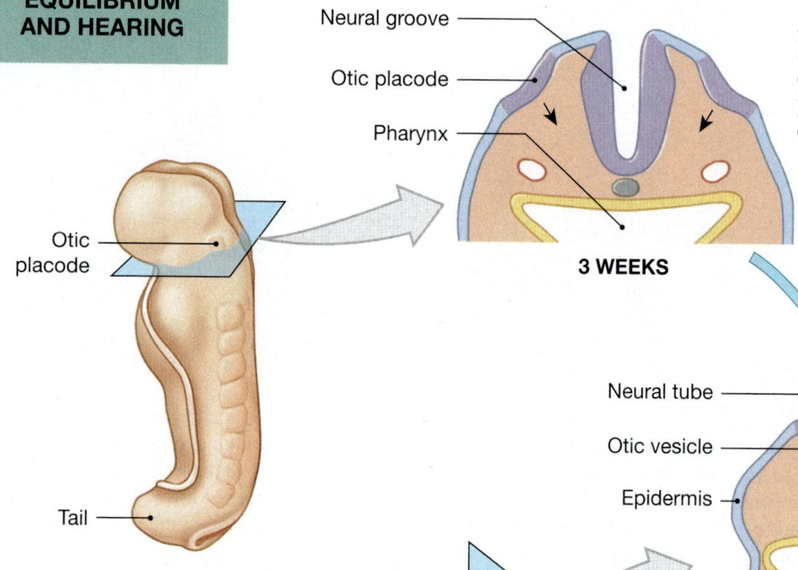

Late in the third week of development, a pair of **otic placodes** appears on either side of the rhombencephalon.

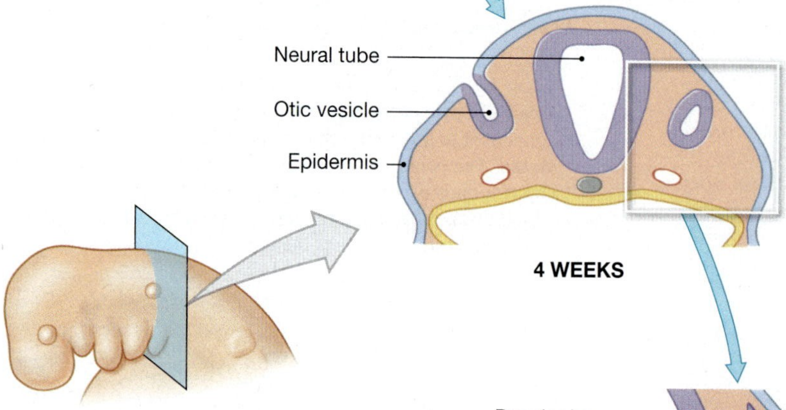

The otic placodes form deep pockets that subsequently lose their connection with the epidermis, creating hollow **otic vesicles**.

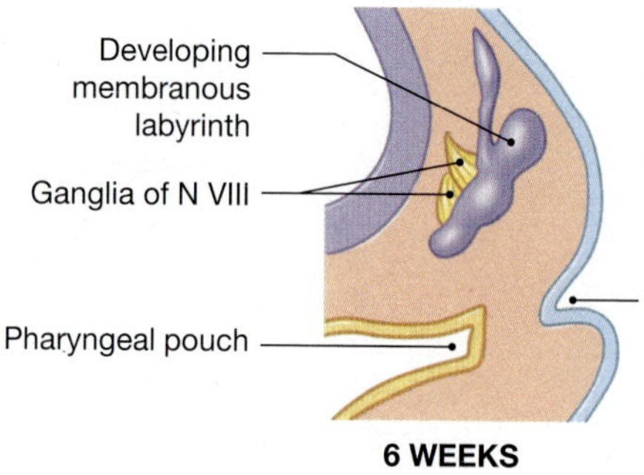

These vesicles gradually change shape, forming the membranous labyrinth. This process has essentially been completed by the end of the third developmental month.

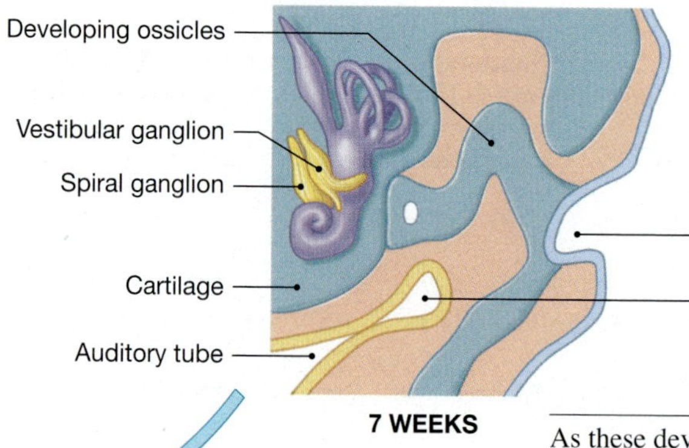

Thickened portions of the otic vesicles differentiate into the *spiral* and *vestibular ganglia*, and their sensory terminals grow toward the developing hair cells.

As these developments are under way, the surrounding mesenchyme begins to differentiate into cartilage. This cartilage will later ossify to form the bony labyrinth.

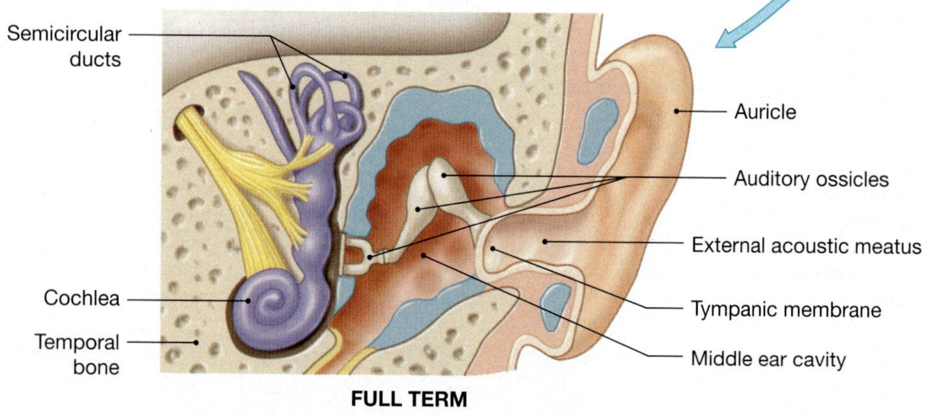

The Development of the Endocrine System, Part I

As noted in Chapter 3, all secretory glands, whether exocrine or endocrine, are derived from epithelia. Endocrine organs develop from epithelia (1) covering the outside of the embryo, (2) lining the digestive tract, and (3) lining the coelomic cavity.

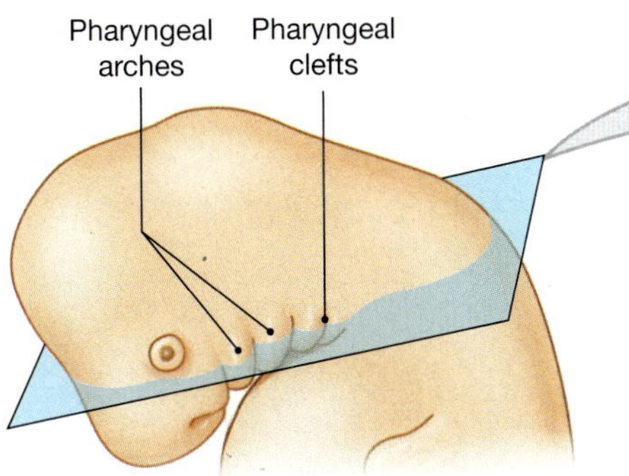

WEEK 5

The pharyngeal region of the embryo plays a particularly important role in endocrine development. After 4–5 weeks of development, the *pharyngeal arches* are well formed. Human embryos develop five or six pharyngeal arches, not all visible from the exterior. (Arch 5 may not appear or may form and degenerate almost immediately.) The five major arches (I–IV, VI) are separated by *pharyngeal clefts*, deep ectodermal grooves.

PARATHYROID GLANDS AND THYMUS

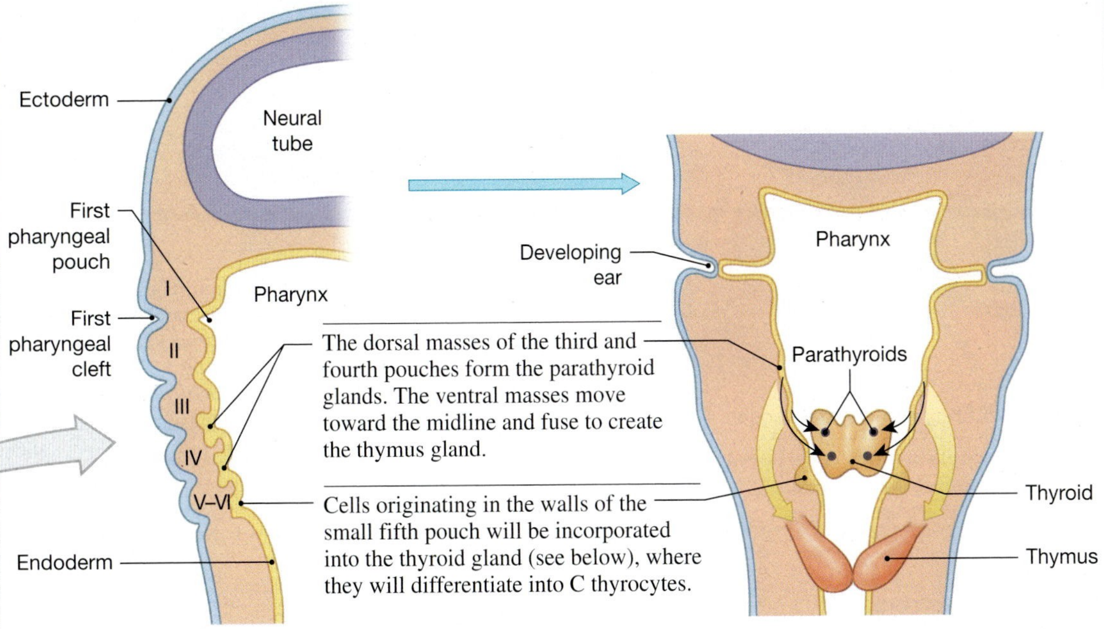

In sectional view, five **pharyngeal pouches** extend laterally toward the pharyngeal clefts. The first pouch lies caudal to the first (mandibular) arch. Pharyngeal pouches 5 and 6 are very small and are interconnected. Endoderm lining the third, fourth, and fifth pairs of pharyngeal pouches forms dorsal and ventral masses of cells that migrate beneath the endodermal epithelium.

THYROID GLAND

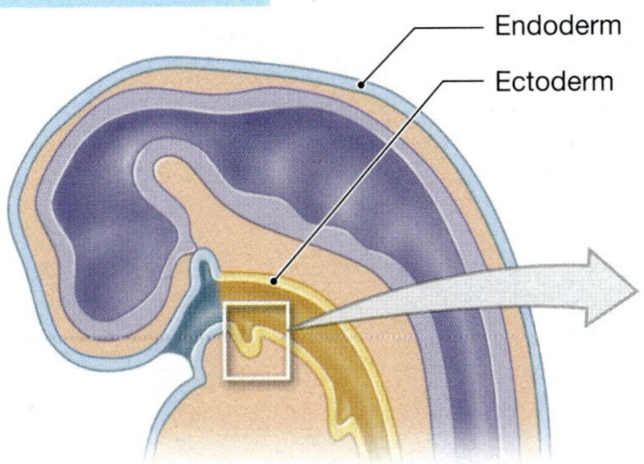

WEEK 5, Mid-sagittal section

The boundary between ectoderm and endoderm lies along the line formed by the circumvallate papillae of the tongue (*see Figure 18.7, p. 478*). This line roughly corresponds to the middle of the mandibular (first) arch. The thyroid gland forms here in the ventral midline.

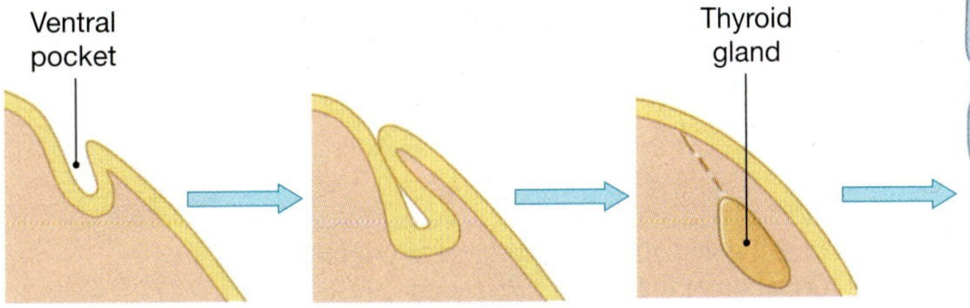

The thyroid gland begins as a pocket in the ventral midline. As this pocket branches slightly, its walls thicken, and the paired masses lose their connection with the surface.

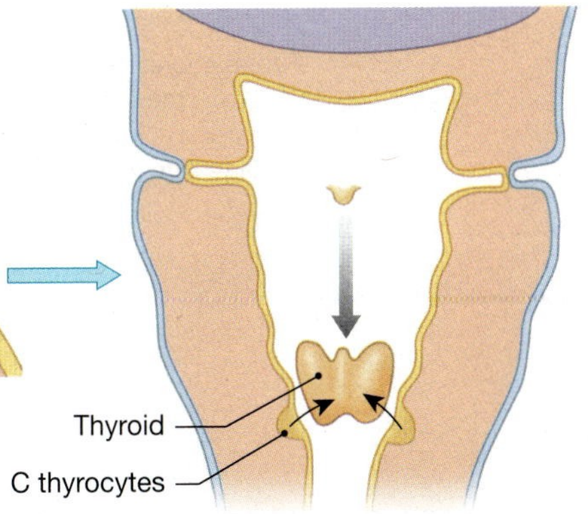

As the embryo enlarges and changes shape, the thyroid shifts caudally to a position near the thyroid cartilage of the larynx. On its way, the thyroid gland incorporates C thyrocytes from the walls of the fifth pouch.

The Development of the Endocrine System, Part II

PITUITARY GLAND

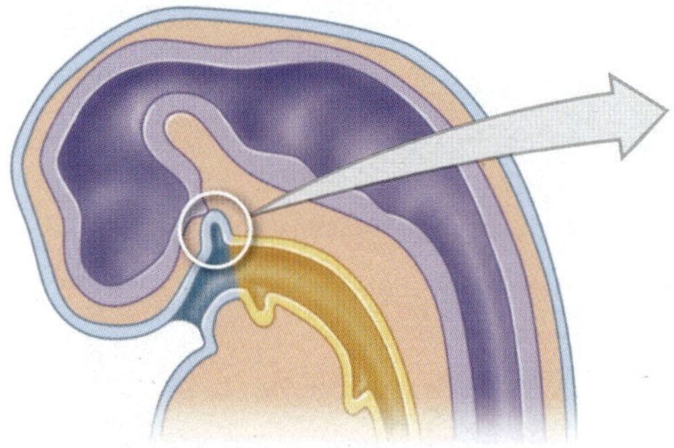

WEEK 5, Mid-sagittal section

The pituitary gland forms in the dorsal midline above the forming thyroid gland.

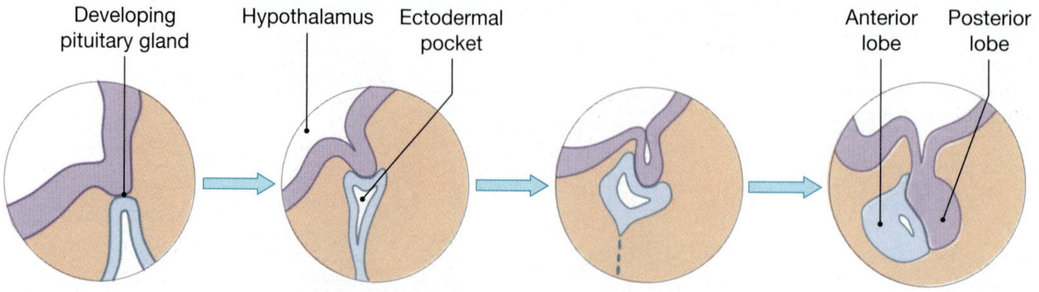

The pituitary gland has a compound origin. The first step is the formation of an ectodermal pocket in the dorsal midline of the pharynx. This pocket loses its connection to the pharynx, creating a hollow ball of cells that lies inferior to the floor of the diencephalon posterior to the optic chiasm.

As these cells undergo division, the central chamber gradually disappears. This endocrine mass will become the adenohypophysis (anterior lobe) of the pituitary gland. The neurohypophysis (posterior lobe) of the pituitary gland begins as a depression in the hypothalamic floor and grows toward the developing adenohypophysis.

SUPRARENAL GLANDS

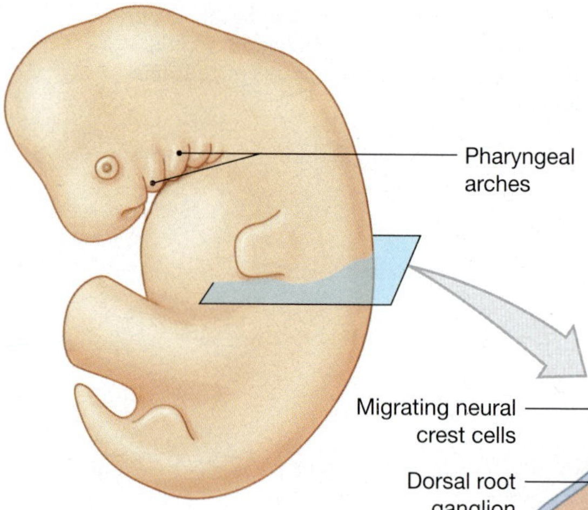

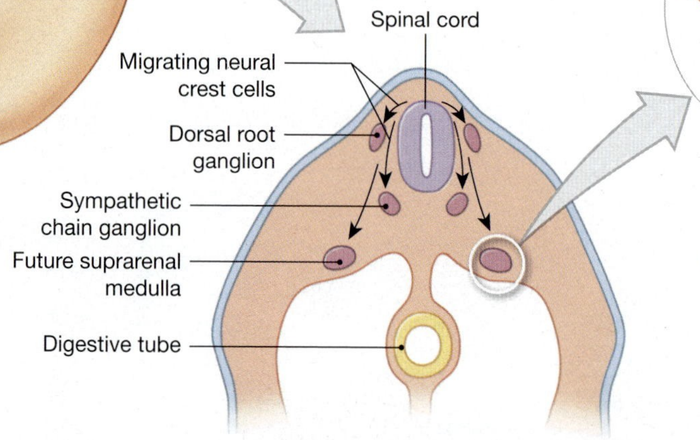

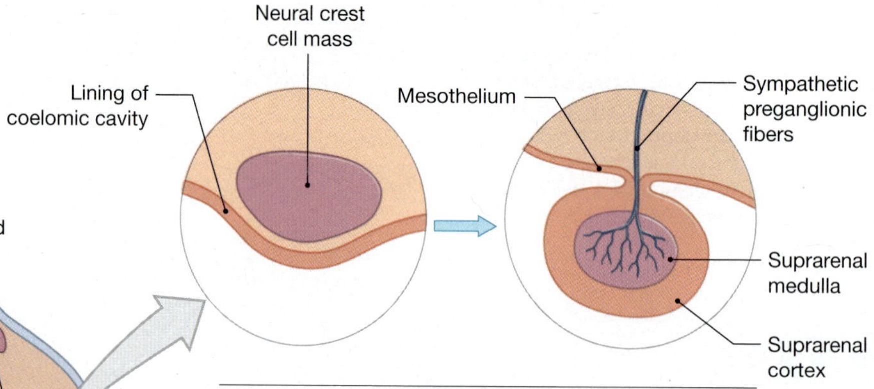

Overlying epithelial cells respond by undergoing division, and the daughter cells surround the neural crest cells to form a thick suprarenal cortex.

WEEK 5

Each suprarenal gland also has a compound origin. Shortly after the formation of the *neural tube*, neural crest cells migrate away from the CNS. This migration leads to the formation of the dorsal root ganglia and autonomic ganglia. On each side of the coelomic cavity, neural crest cells aggregate in a mass that will become a suprarenal medulla.

For additional details concerning the development of other endocrine organs, refer to the subsequent Embryology Summaries on the Lymphoid, Digestive, Urinary, and Reproductive systems.

The Development of the Heart

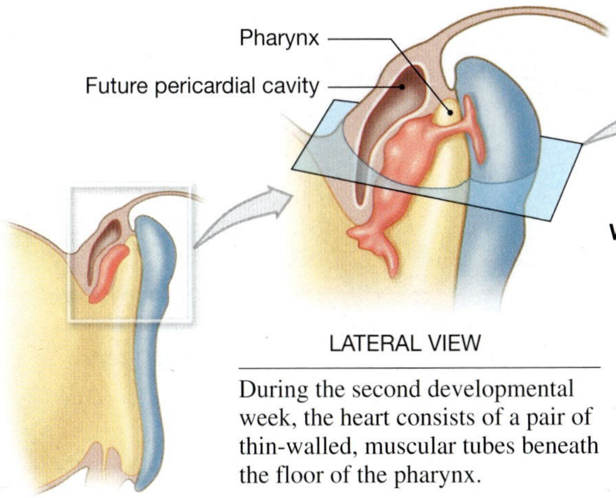

During the second developmental week, the heart consists of a pair of thin-walled, muscular tubes beneath the floor of the pharynx.

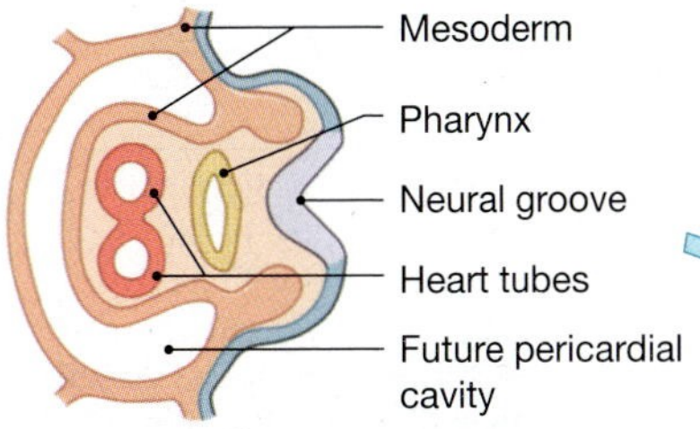

The lateral plate mesoderm in this region has already split into parietal and visceral layers, creating a space that will eventually form the pericardial cavity.

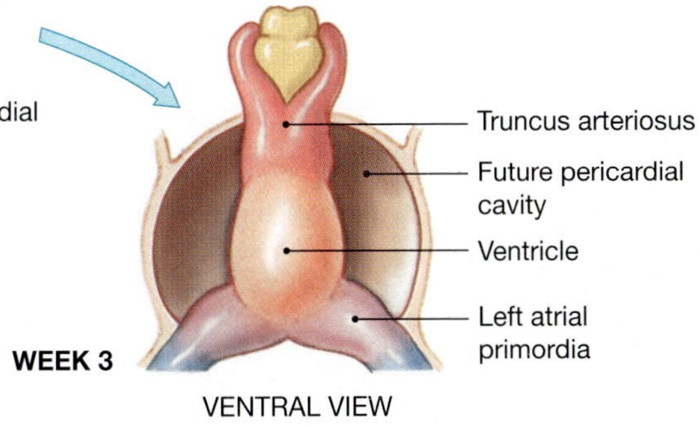

By the third week, the heart is pumping and circulating blood. The cardiac tubes have fused, producing a heart with a single central chamber. Two large veins bring blood to the heart, and a single large artery, the **truncus arteriosus**, carries blood to the general circulation.

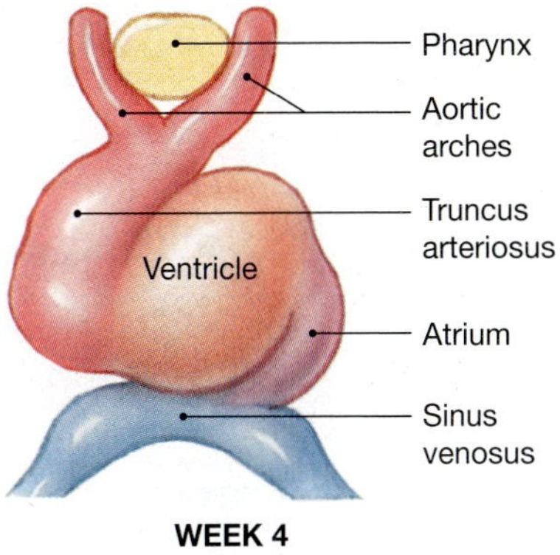

The heart elongates as the embryo grows larger. It curves back upon itself, forming an S-curve that gradually becomes more pronounced. The atrial and ventricular regions already differ in thickness.

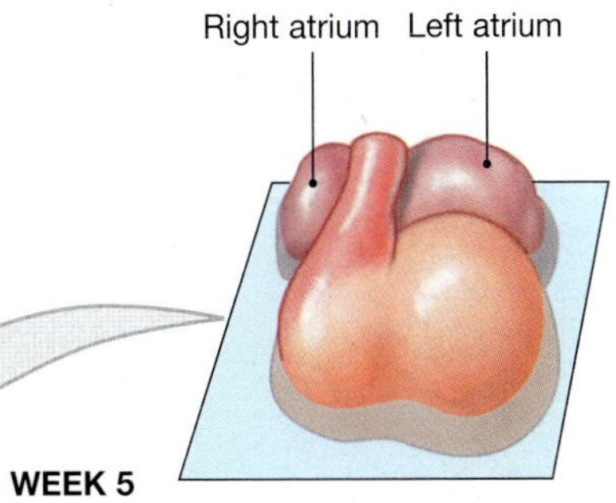

In week 5, the interatrial and interventricular septa begin to subdivide the interior of the heart.

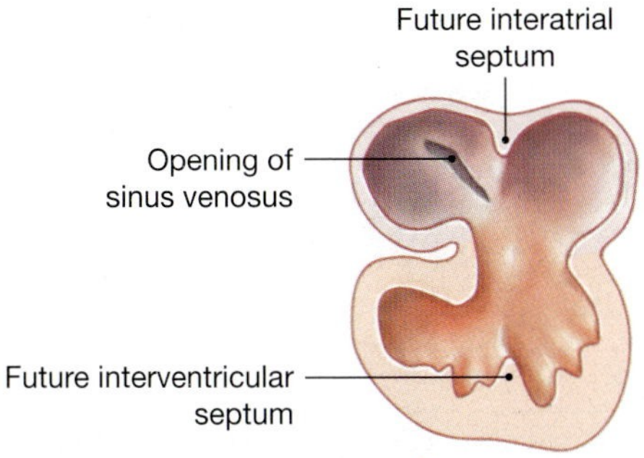

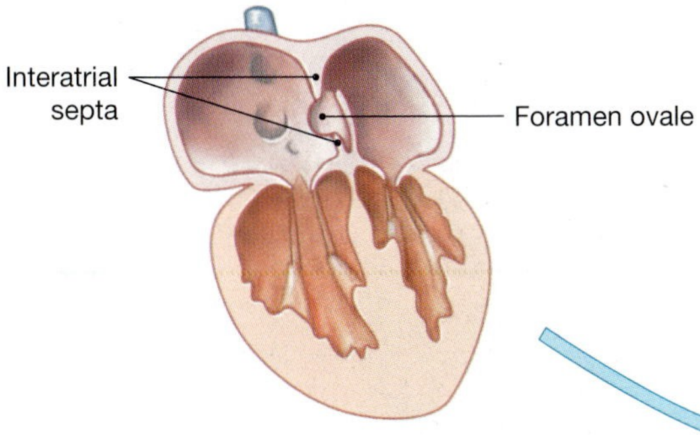

Two interatrial septa develop, one overlapping the other. A gap between the two, called the **foramen ovale**, permits blood flow from the right atrium to the left atrium. Backflow from left to right is prevented by a flap that acts as a one-way valve. Until birth, this atrial short circuit diverts blood from the pulmonary circuit.

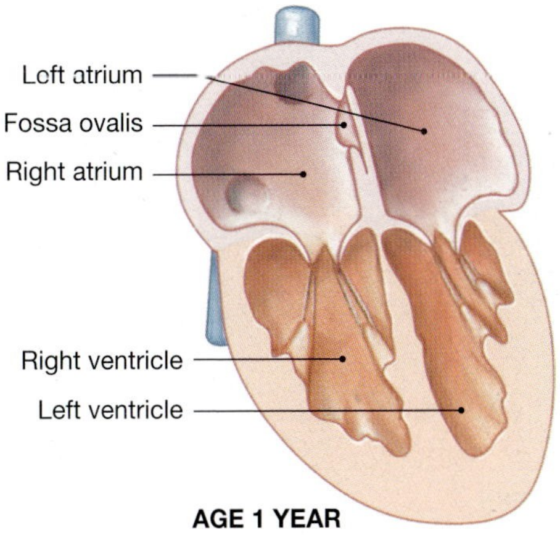

At birth, the foramen ovale closes, separating the pulmonary and systemic circuits in the heart. A shallow depression, the **fossa ovalis**, remains through adulthood at the site of the foramen ovale. (Other cardiovascular changes at birth are detailed in Figures 18.7, p. 478 and 22.8, p. 602.)

The Development of the Cardiovascular System

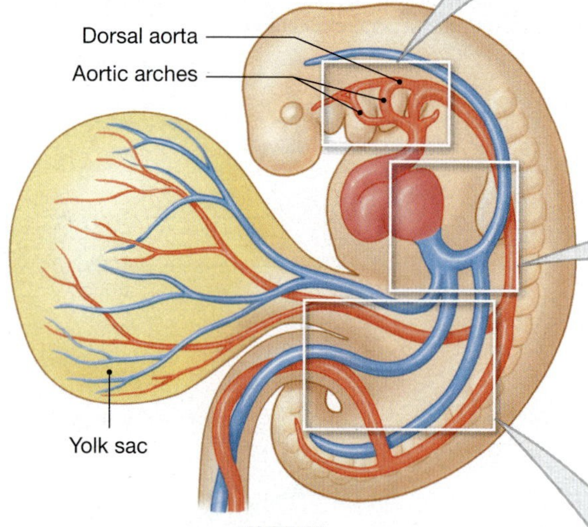

4 WEEKS

We will follow the development of three major vessel complexes: the aortic arch, the venae cavae, and the hepatic portal and umbilical systems. (Arteries are shown in red and veins in blue regardless of the oxygenation of the blood they carry.)

THE AORTIC ARCHES

An **aortic arch** carries arterial blood through each of the *pharyngeal arches*. In the dorsal pharyngeal wall, these vessels fuse to create the **dorsal aorta**, which distributes blood throughout the body. The arches are usually numbered from I to VI, corresponding to the pharyngeal arches.

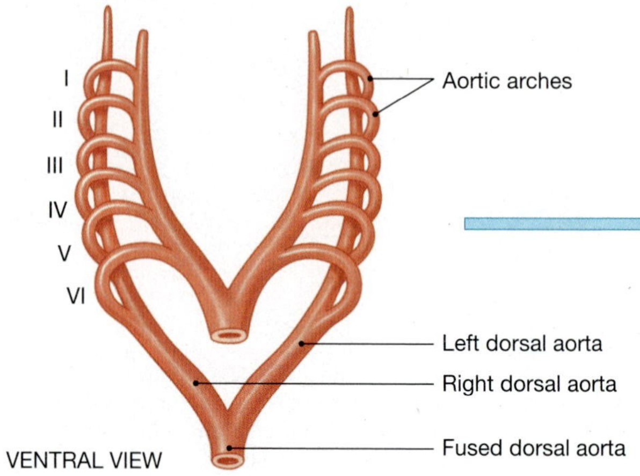

THE VENAE CAVAE

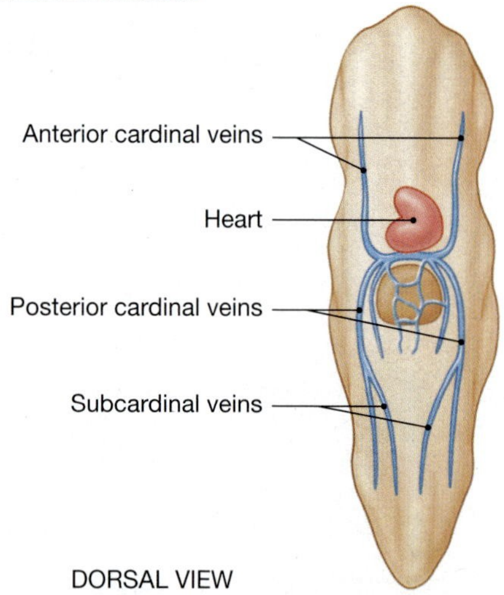

DORSAL VIEW

The early venous circulation draining the tissues of the body wall, limbs, and head centers around the paired **anterior cardinal veins, posterior cardinal veins**, and **subcardinal veins**.

THE HEPATIC PORTAL AND UMBILICAL VESSELS

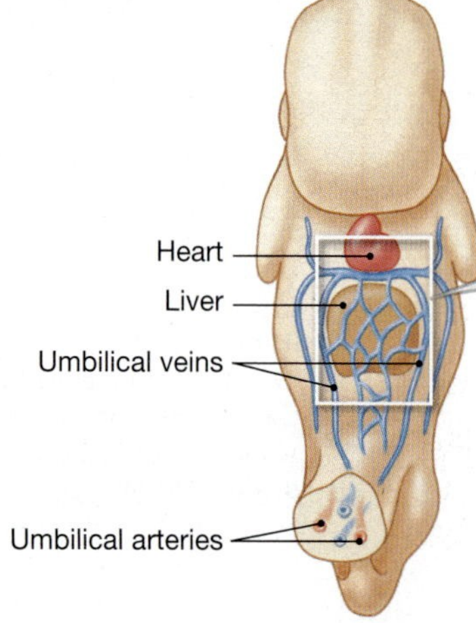

4 WEEKS

Paired **umbilical arteries** deliver blood to the placenta. At 4 weeks, paired **umbilical veins** return blood to capillary networks in the liver. Veins running along the length of the digestive tract have extensive interconnections.

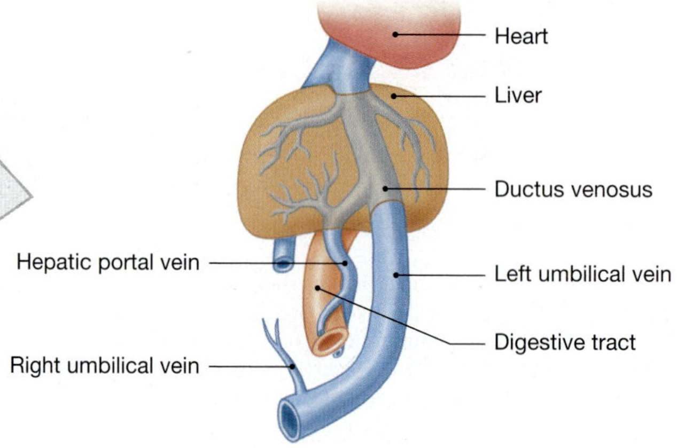

12 WEEKS

By week 12, the right umbilical vein disintegrates, and the blood from the placenta travels along a single umbilical vein. The **ductus venosus** allows some venous blood to bypass the liver. The veins draining the digestive tract have fused, forming the hepatic portal vein.

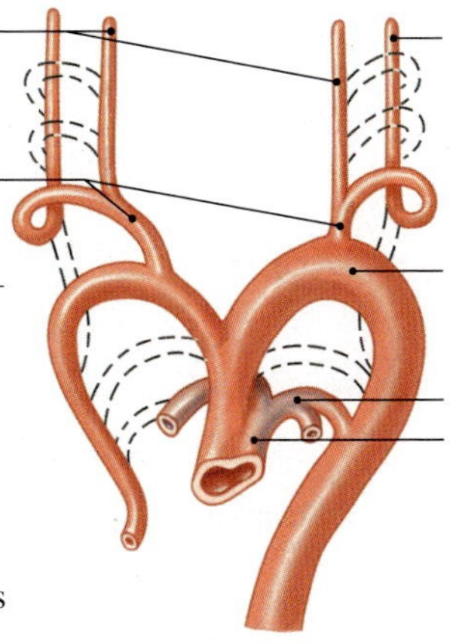

As development proceeds, some of these arches disintegrate. The **ductus arteriosus** provides an external short-circuit between the pulmonary and systemic circuits. Most of the blood entering the right atrium bypasses the lungs, passing instead through the ductus arteriosus or the **foramen ovale** in the heart.

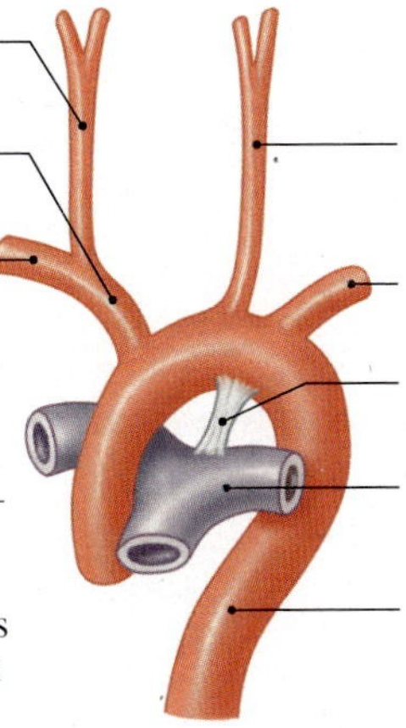

The left half of arch IV ultimately becomes the aortic arch, which carries blood away from the left ventricle.

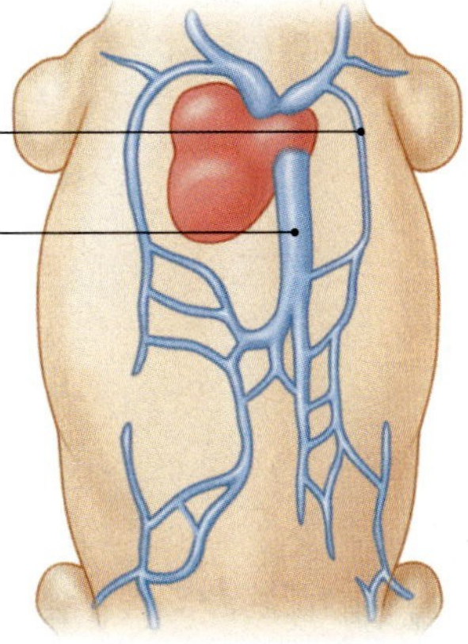

Interconnections form among these veins, and a combination of fusion and disintegration produces more-direct, larger-diameter connections to the right atrium.

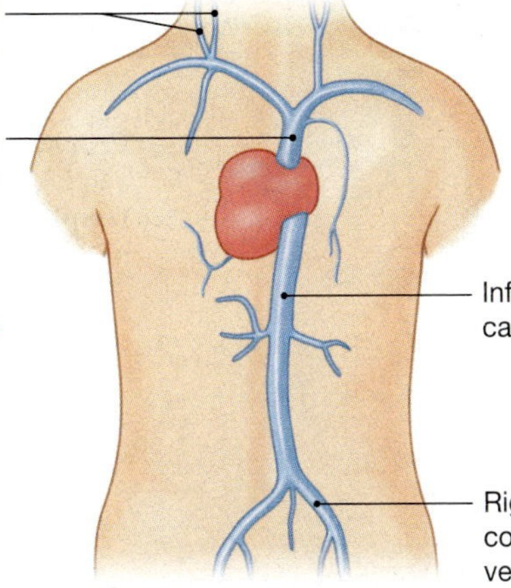

This process continues, ultimately producing the superior and inferior venae cavae.

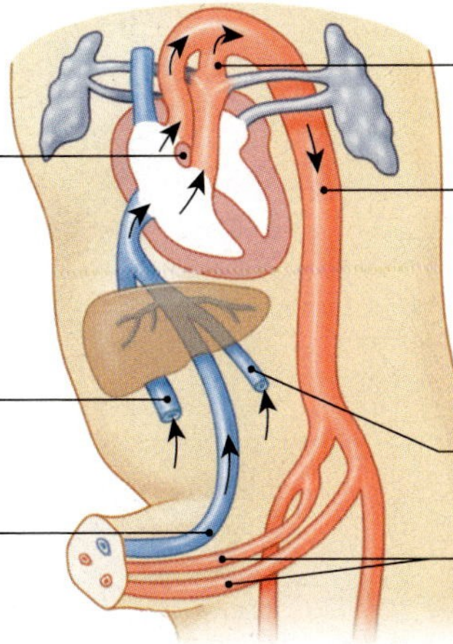

FULL TERM

Shortly before birth, blood returning from the placenta travels through the liver in the ductus venosus to reach the inferior vena cava. Much of the blood delivered by the venae cavae bypasses the lungs by traveling through the foramen ovale and the ductus arteriosus.

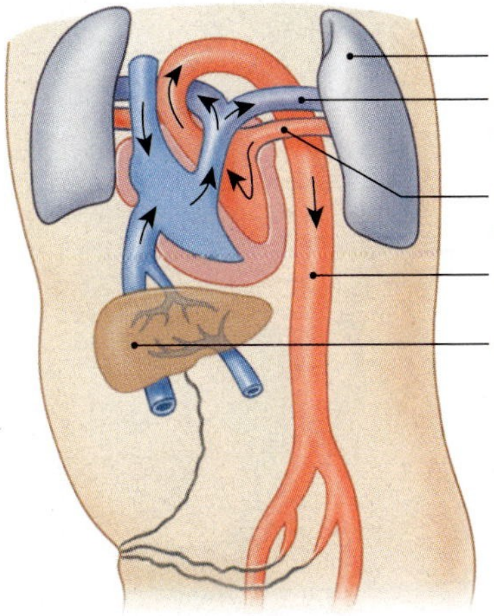

NEWBORN

At birth, pressures drop in the pleural cavities as the chest expands and the infant takes its first breath. The pulmonary vessels dilate, and blood flow to the lungs increases. Pressure falls in the right atrium, and the higher left atrial pressures close the valve that guards the foramen ovale. Smooth muscles contract the ductus arteriosus, which ultimately converts to the **ligamentum arteriosum**, a fibrous strand.

The Development of the Lymphoid System

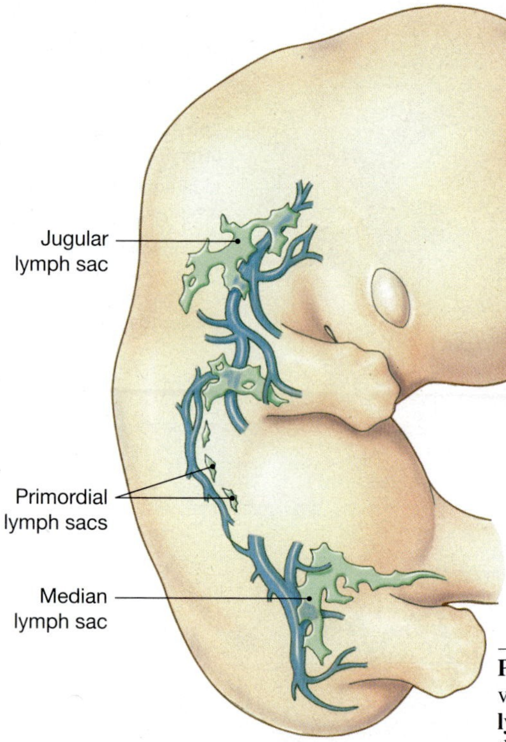

7 WEEKS

The development of the lymphatic vessels is closely tied to the formation of blood vessels. Paired **jugular lymph sacs** form from the fusion of small, endothelium-lined pockets in the mesoderm of the neck. By week 7, these sacs become connected to the venous system.

Primordial lymph sacs form parallel with veins of the trunk, and a large **median lymph** sac marks the future location of the cisterna chyli.

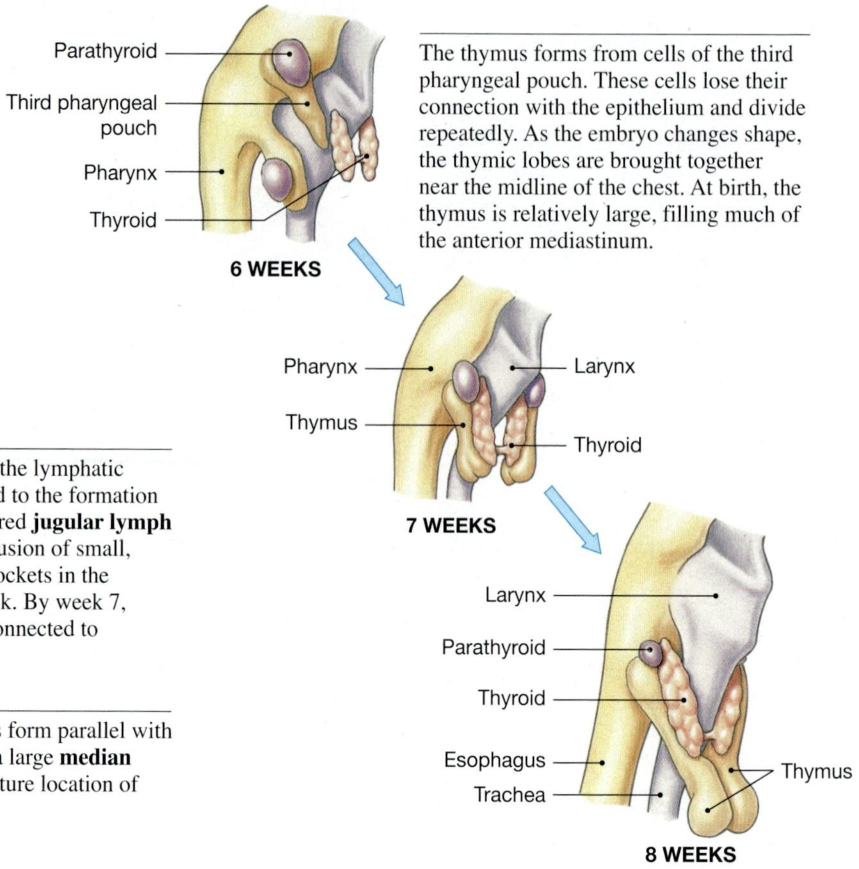

The thymus forms from cells of the third pharyngeal pouch. These cells lose their connection with the epithelium and divide repeatedly. As the embryo changes shape, the thymic lobes are brought together near the midline of the chest. At birth, the thymus is relatively large, filling much of the anterior mediastinum.

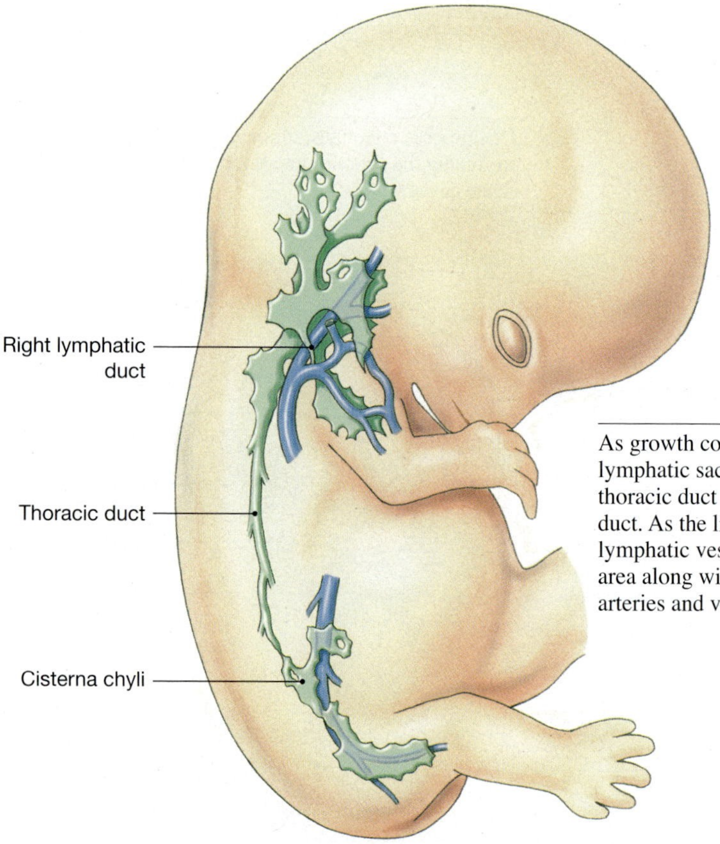

8 WEEKS

As growth continues, the isolated lymphatic sacs fuse, forming the thoracic duct and right lymphatic duct. As the limb buds enlarge, lymphatic vessels grow into the area along with developing arteries and veins.

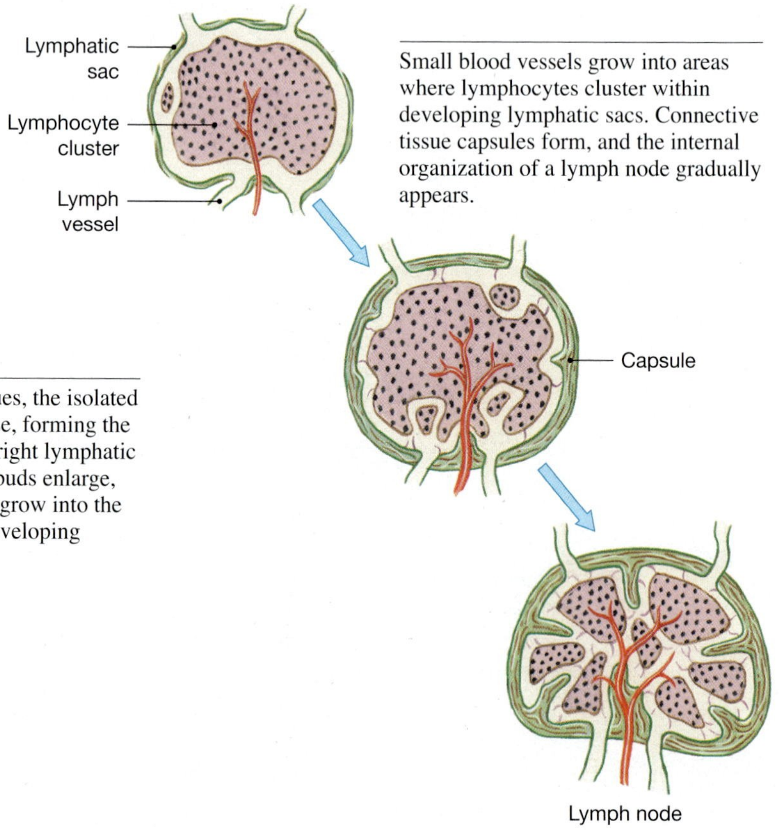

Small blood vessels grow into areas where lymphocytes cluster within developing lymphatic sacs. Connective tissue capsules form, and the internal organization of a lymph node gradually appears.

The Development of the Respiratory System, Part I

THE LUNGS

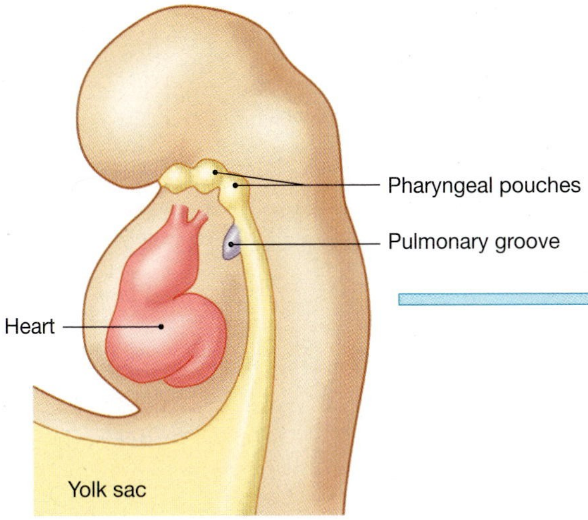

3 WEEKS

A shallow **pulmonary groove** appears in the midventral floor of the pharynx after roughly 3½ weeks of development. This groove, which lies near the level of the last pharyngeal arch, gradually deepens.

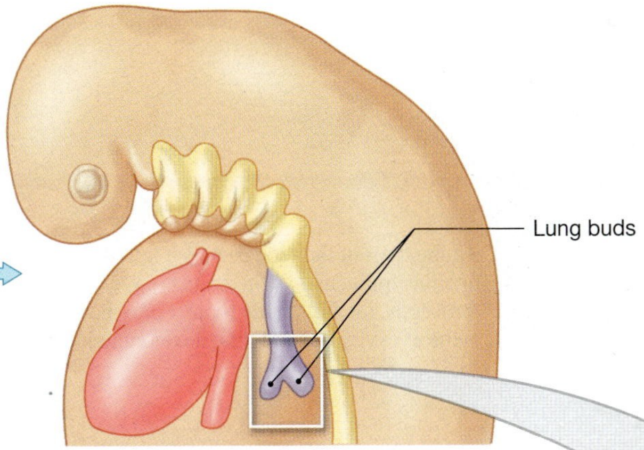

4 WEEKS

By week 4, the groove has become a blind pocket that extends caudally, anterior to the esophagus. This tube will become the trachea. At its tip, the tube branches, forming a pair of **lung buds**.

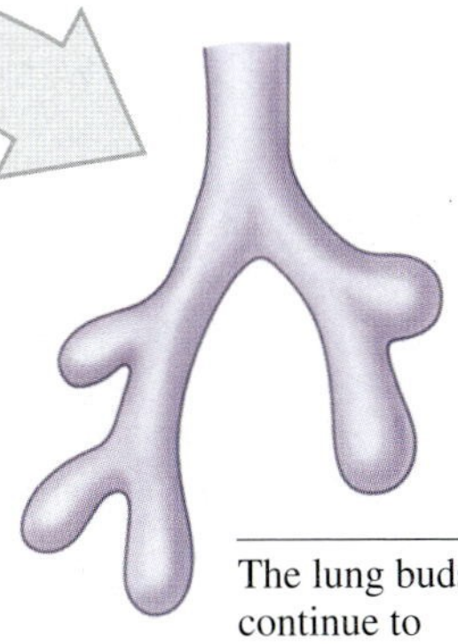

The lung buds continue to elongate and branch repeatedly.

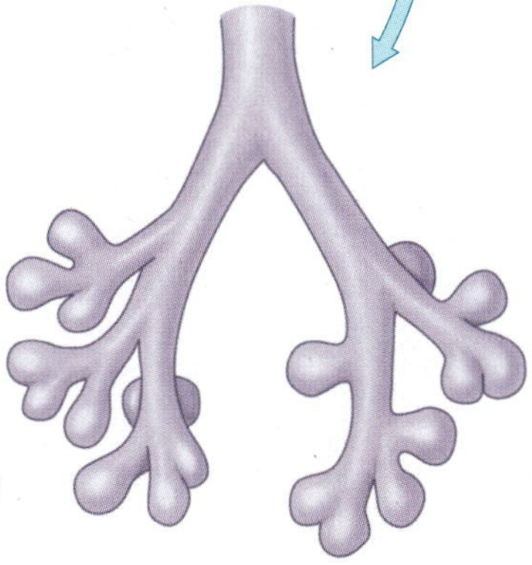

3 MONTHS

By the end of the sixth fetal month, there are around a million terminal branches, and the conducting passageways are complete to the level of the bronchioles.

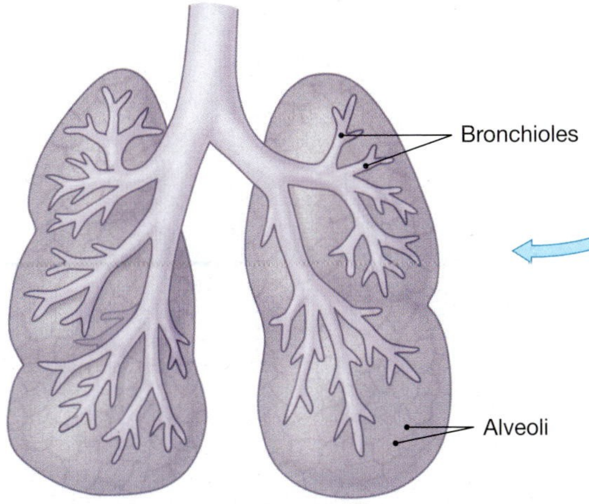

Over the next three months, each of the bronchioles gives rise to several hundred alveoli. This process continues for a variable period after birth.

The Development of the Respiratory System, Part II

THE PLEURAL CAVITIES

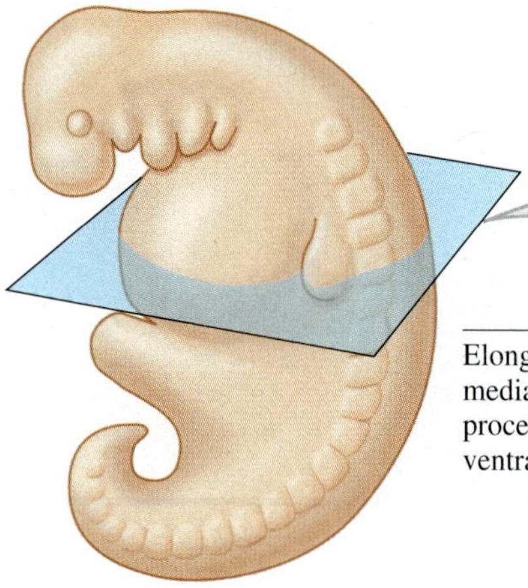

4 WEEKS

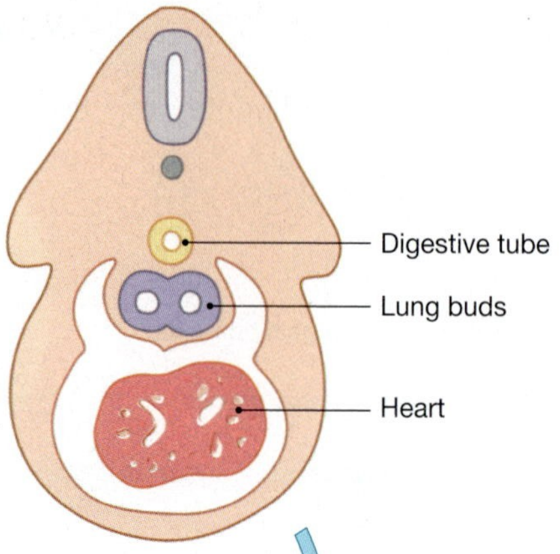

Elongation of the tube carries it into the mediastinum, and as the branching proceeds, the lung buds project into the ventral cavity dorsal to the developing heart.

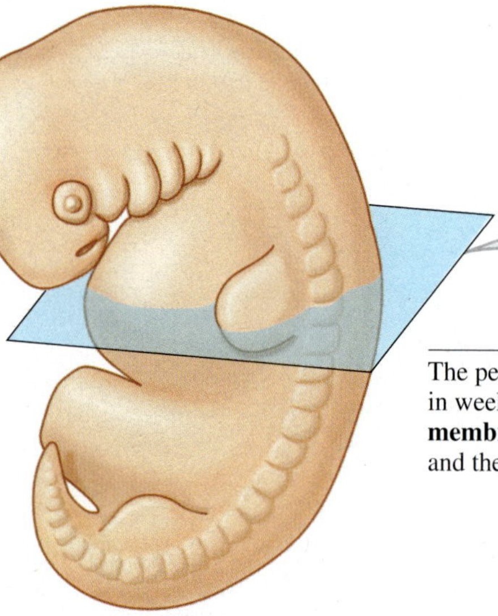

6 WEEKS

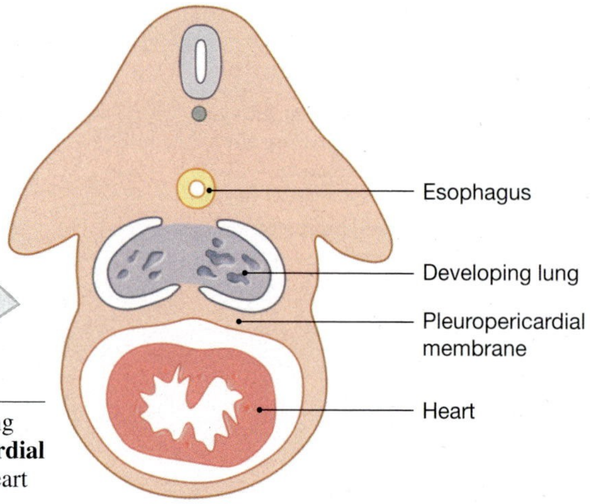

The pericardial sac begins forming in week 6 as a thin **pleuropericardial membrane** forms between the heart and the developing lungs.

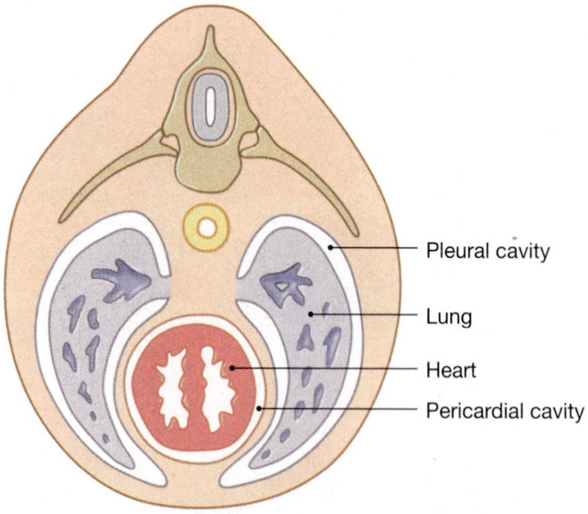

8 WEEKS

By week 8, the pericardial sac is complete and the pericardial cavity is isolated from the rest of the ventral body cavity. The diaphragm then completes its formation, attaching to the pericardial sac and tissues of the mediastinum. This attachment separates the abdominopelvic cavity from the pleural cavities.

By week 9, the diaphragm completes its formation, forming a transverse sheet superior to the liver.

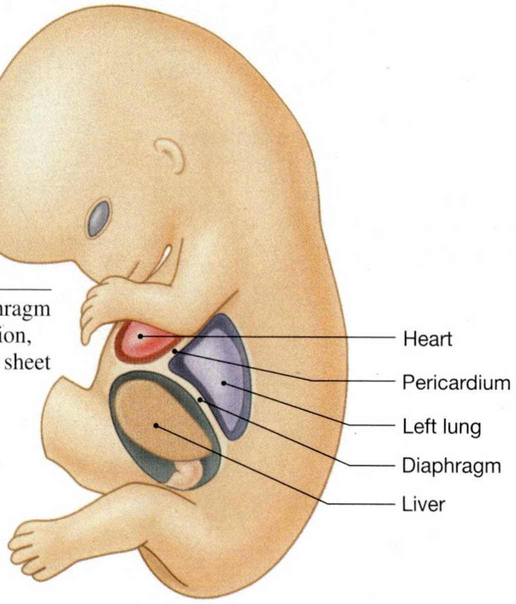

9 WEEKS

The Development of the Digestive System, Part I

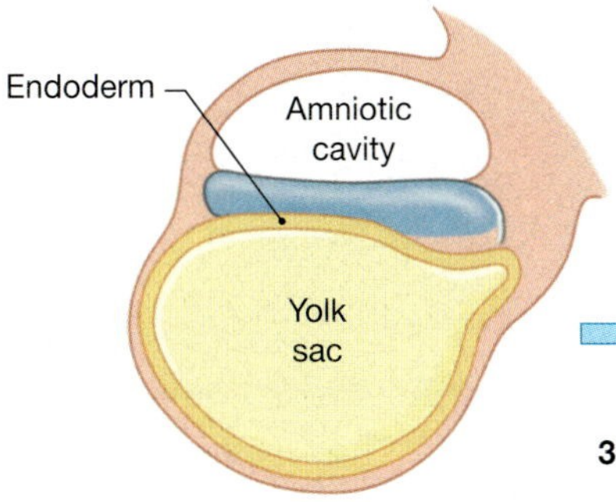

By week 3, endodermal cells have migrated around the inside of the *blastocyst*, completing a pouch known as the **yolk sac**.

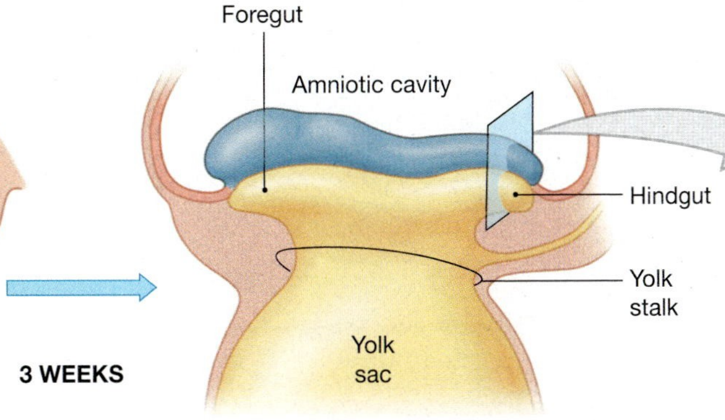

As the embryo forms on the *embryonic shield*, two pockets of endoderm are created: the **foregut** and **hindgut**. A broad connection between these pockets and the yolk sac remains within the **yolk stalk**.

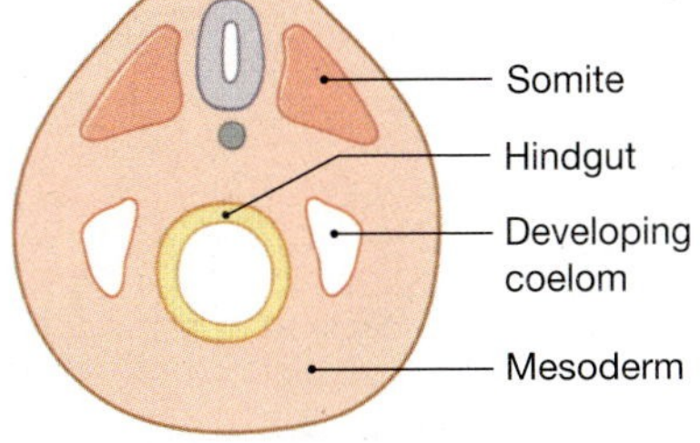

In sectional view, the embryonic gut is a simple endodermal tube surrounded by mesoderm. Cavities appearing within the mesoderm create the *coelom* (ventral body cavity).

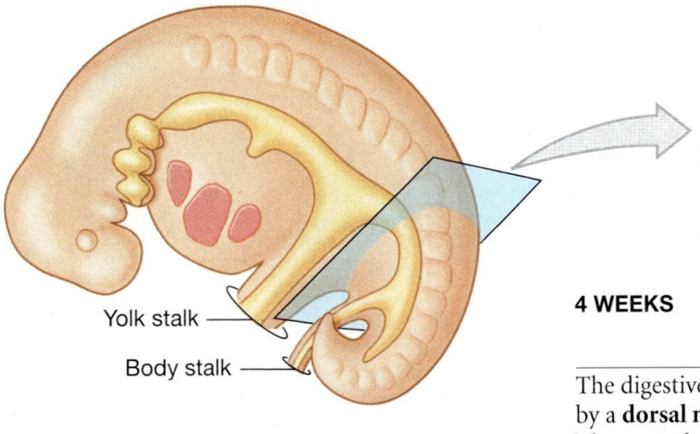

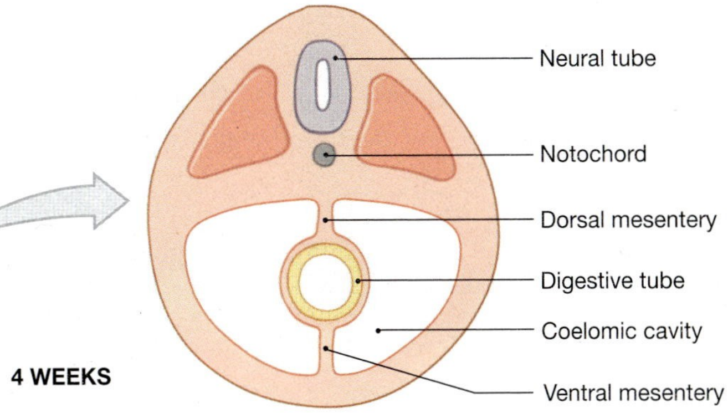

The digestive tube remains suspended in the coelom by a **dorsal mesentery** and a **ventral mesentery**. The ventral mesentery disintegrates everywhere except where major vessels or visceral organs have grown into it. It remains intact along the path of the *umbilical arteries* and where the *umbilical vein* and liver develop.

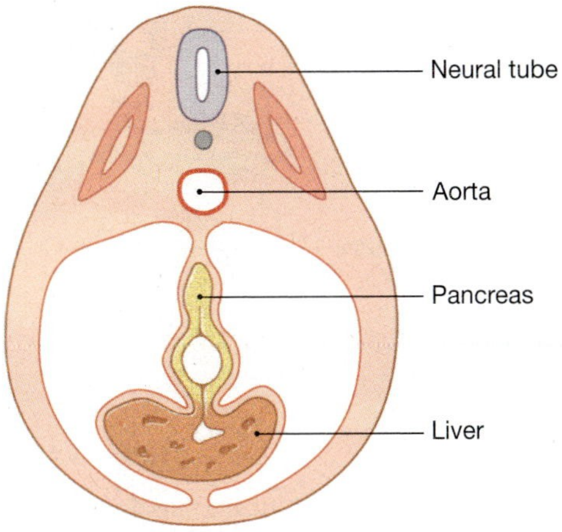

The pancreas and liver begin as epithelial pockets that grow away from the digestive tract and into the dorsal and ventral mesenteries, respectively.

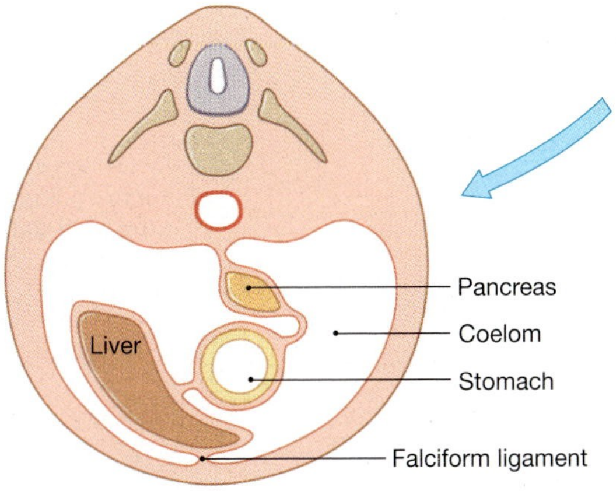

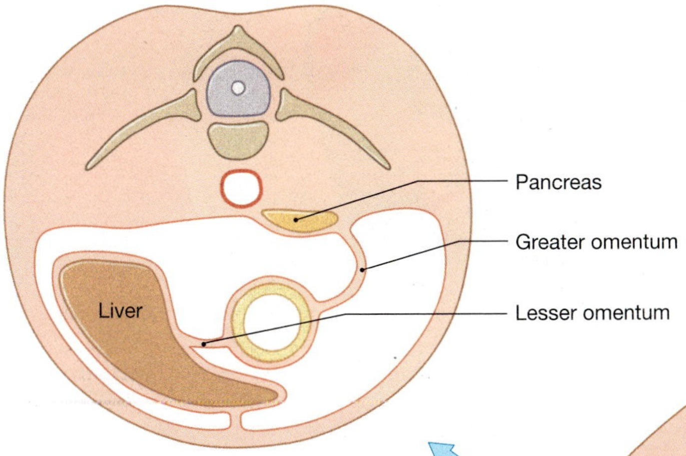

As the embryo enlarges, the stomach and liver rotate toward the right, creating two pockets. The mesenteries that form these pockets are the greater omentum and the lesser omentum.

The Development of the Digestive System, Part II

The intestines begin to elongate, and with the breakdown of the ventral mesentery, they push outward into the umbilical stalk. Further elongation and coiling occur ouside the body of the embryo.

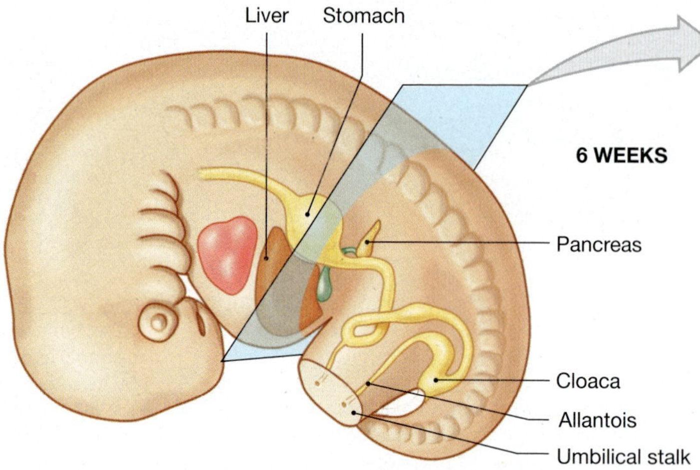

See sectional view at 4 weeks in Part I.

The hindgut extends into the tail, where it forms a large chamber, the **cloaca**. A tubular extension of the cloaca, the **allantois** (a-LAN-tō-is; *allantos*, sausage) projects away from the body and into the **body stalk.** Fusion of the yolk stalk and body stalk will create the **umbilical stalk**, also known as the *umbilical cord*.

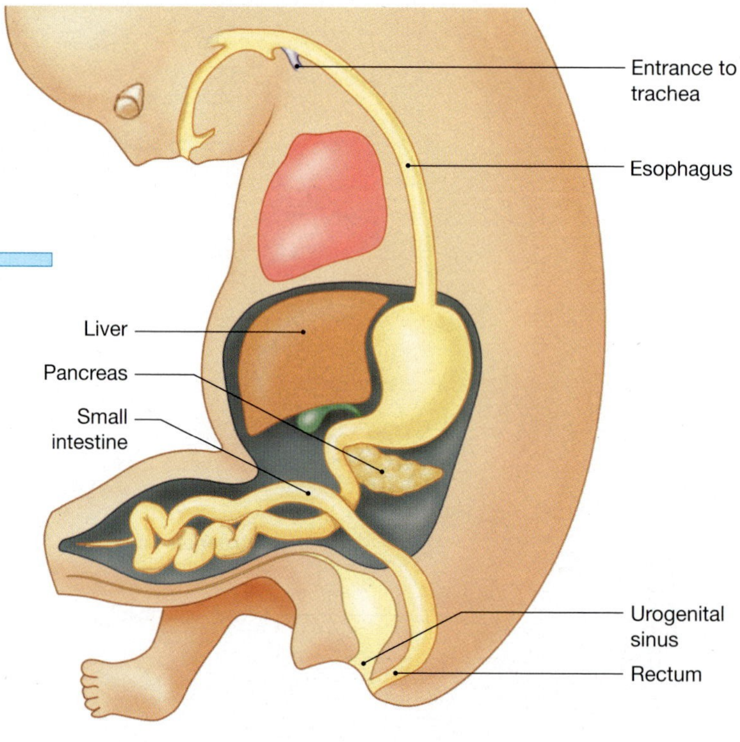

8 WEEKS

A partition grows across the cloaca, dividing it into a posterior rectum and an anterior **urogenital sinus** that retains a connection to the allantois.

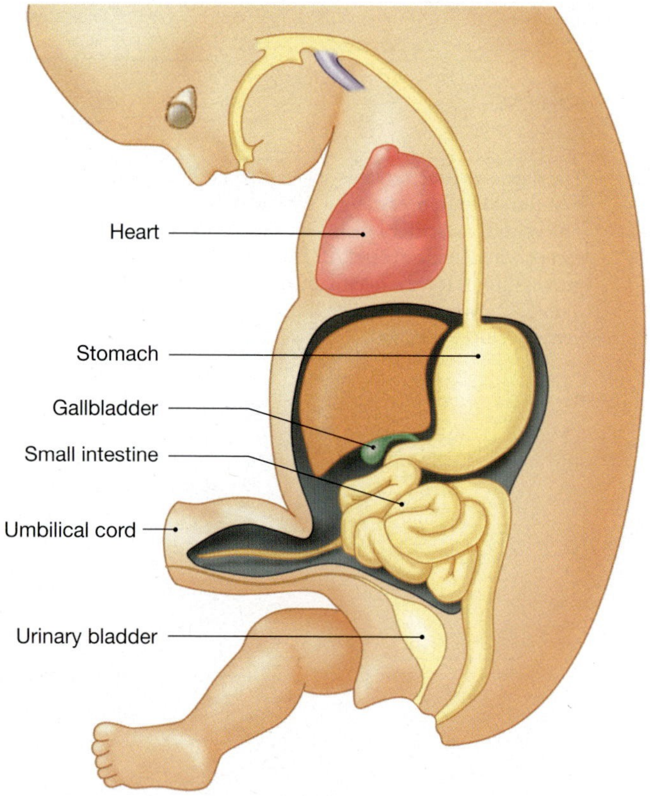

10 WEEKS

By week 10, the intestines have begun moving back into the coelomic cavity, although they continue to grow longer.

The Development of the Urinary System, Part I

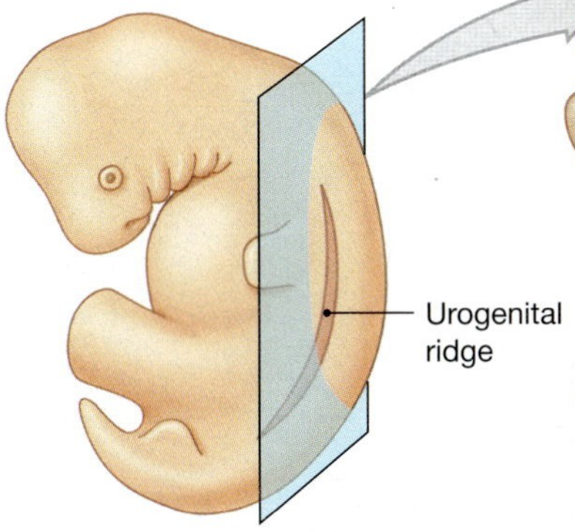

The kidneys develop in stages along the axis of the **urogenital ridge**, a thickened area beneath the dorsolateral wall of the coelomic cavity.

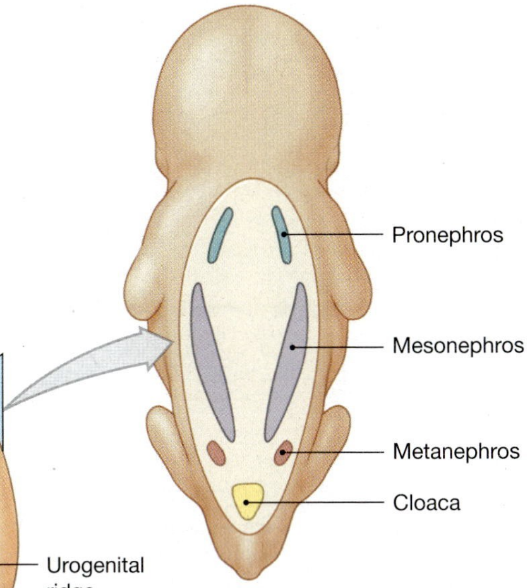

Kidney development proceeds along the cranial/caudal axis of this ridge, beginning with the formation of the **pronephros**, continuing along the **mesonephros**, and ending with the development of the **metanephros**.

The pronephros consists of a series of tubules (generally 7 pairs) that appears within the **nephrotome**, the narrow band of mesoderm between the somites and the lateral plate.

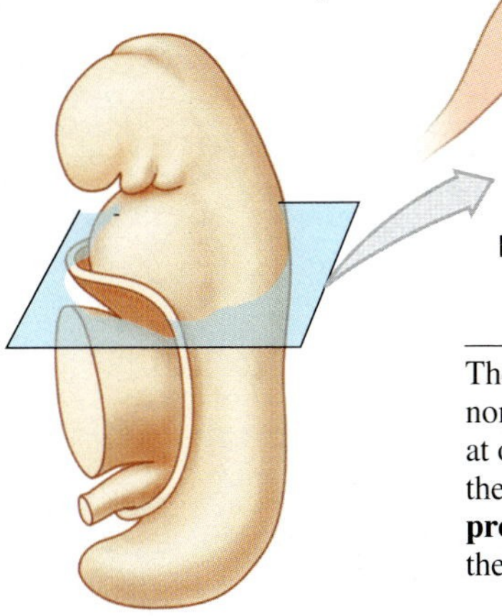

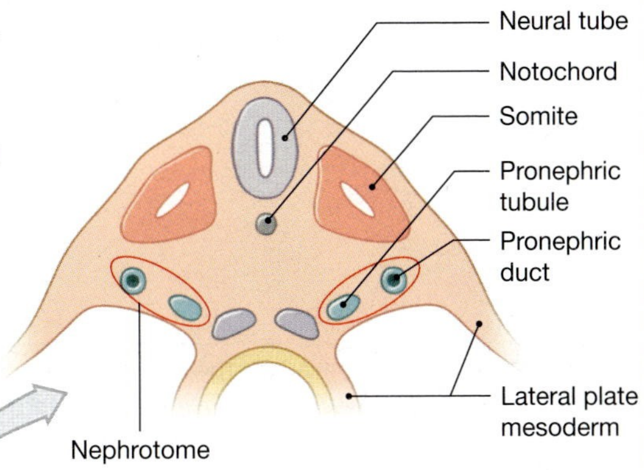

The pronephric tubules are very small and nonfunctional, and they disintegrate almost at once. The only significant contribution of the pronephros is the formation of a pair of **pronephric ducts** that grow caudally until they connect to the *cloaca*.

3½ WEEKS

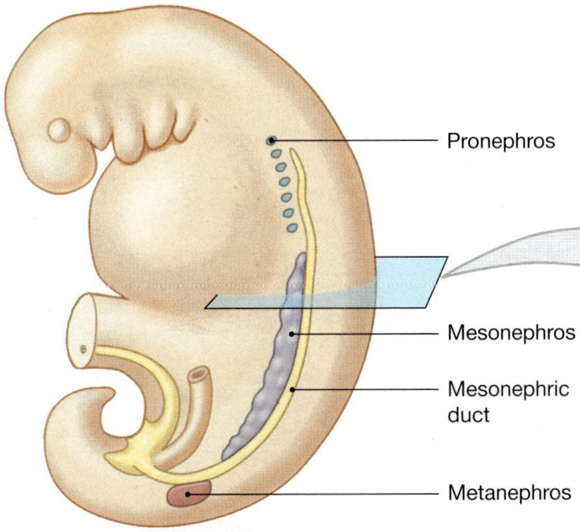

Nephrotomal mesoderm of the metanephros forms a dense mass without a trace of segmental organization. This will become the functional adult kidney.

4 WEEKS

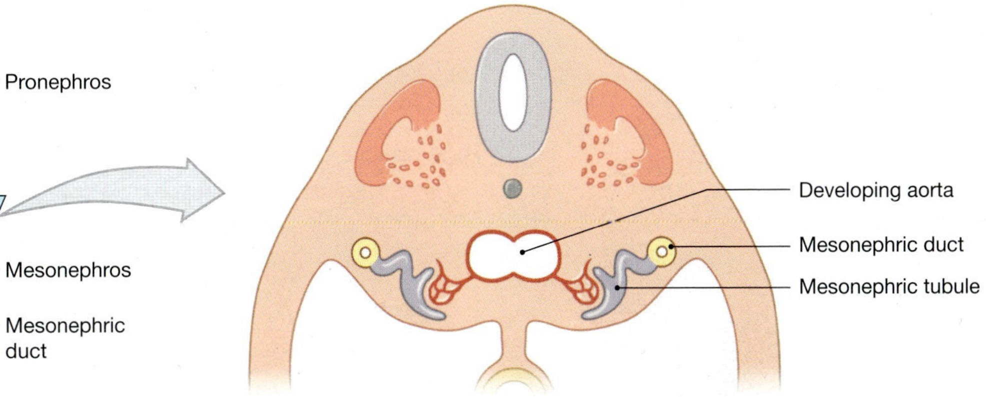

After approximately 4 weeks of development, the mesoderm midway along the urogenital ridge begins organizing into the mesonephros. On either side of the midline, approximately 70 tubules develop within these segments. These tubules grow toward the adjacent pronephric duct and fuse with it. From this moment on, the duct is called the **mesonephric duct**.

The Development of the Urinary System, Part II

A **ureteric bud**, or *metanephric diverticulum*, forms in the wall of each mesonephric duct, and this blind tube elongates and branches within the adjacent metanephros. Tubules developing within the metanephros then connect to the terminal branch of the ureteric bud.

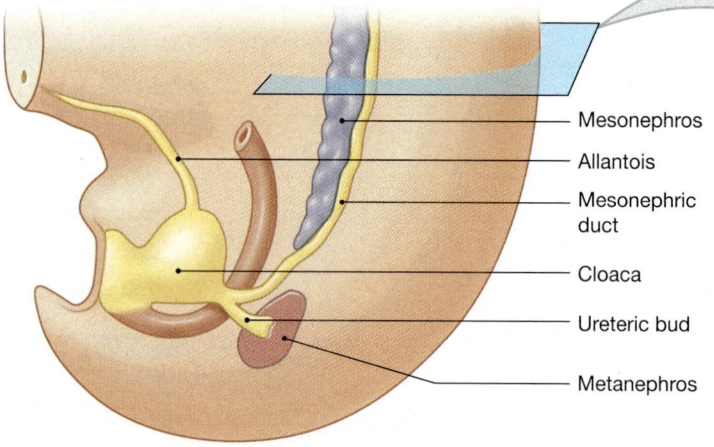

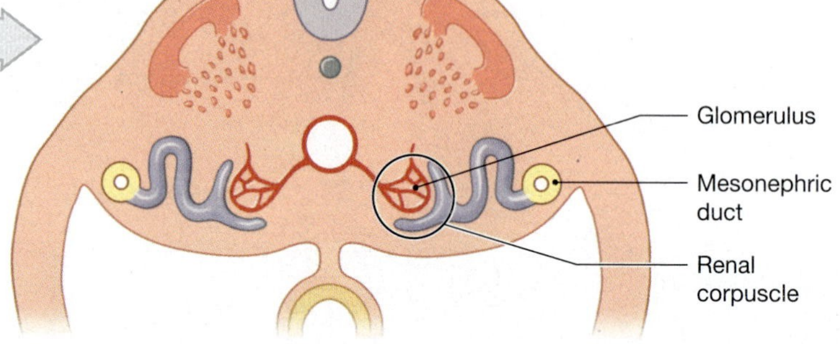

In each segment, a branch of the aorta grows toward the nephrotome, and the tubules form large nephrons with enormous glomeruli. Like the pronephros, the mesonephros does not persist, and when the last segments of the mesonephros are forming, the first are already beginning to degenerate.

Most of the metabolic wastes produced by the developing embryo are passed across the placenta to enter the maternal circulation. The small amount of urine produced by the kidneys accumulates within the cloaca and the *allantois*, an endoderm-lined sac that extends into the umbilical stalk.

6 WEEKS

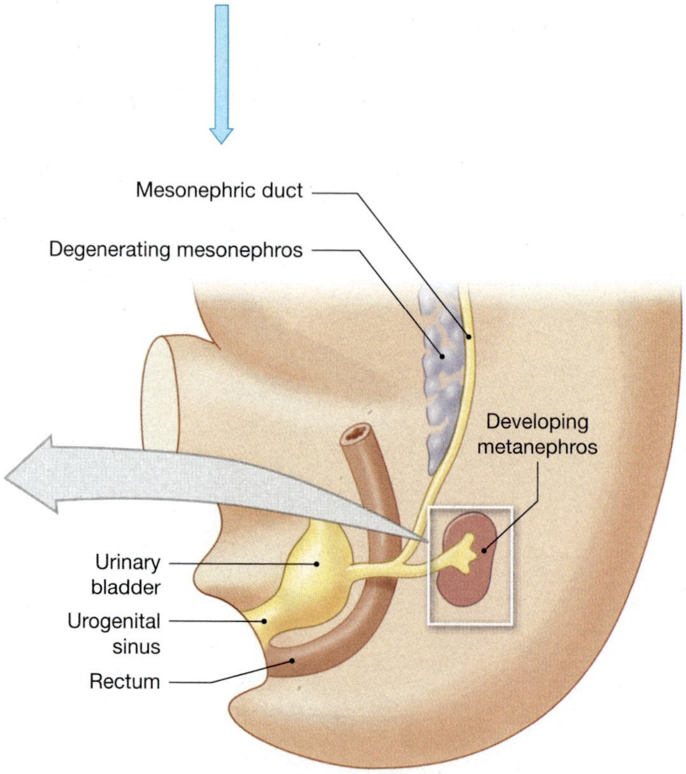

8 WEEKS

Near the end of the second developmental month, the cloaca is subdivided into a dorsal rectum and a ventral **urogenital sinus**. The proximal portions of the allantois persist as the **urinary bladder**, and the connection between the bladder and an opening on the body surface will form the **urethra**.

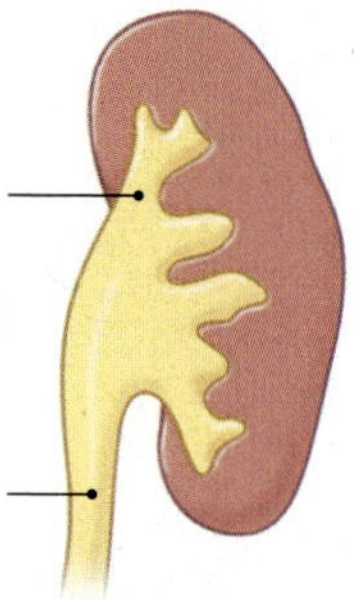

The ureteric bud branches within the metanephros, creating the calyces and the collecting system. The nephrons, which form within the mesoderm of the metanephros, tap into the collecting tubules.

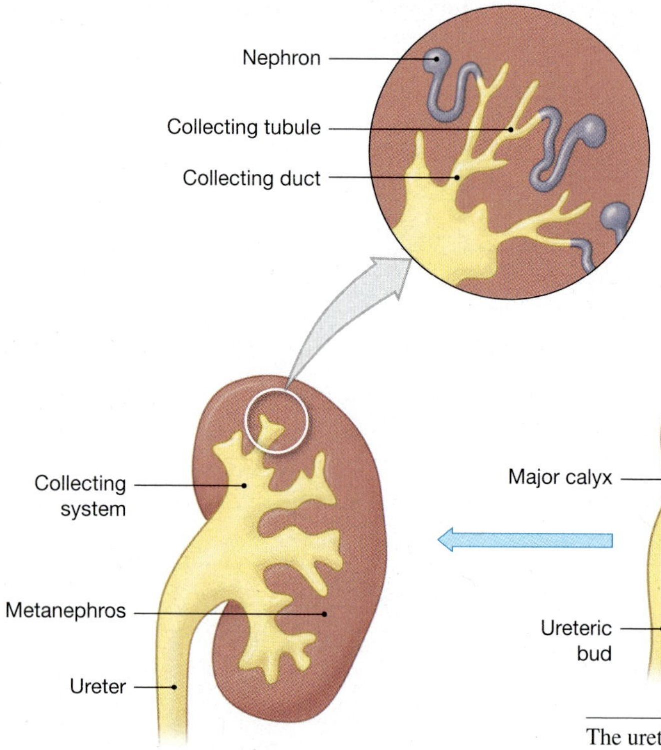

12 WEEKS

The kidneys begin producing filtrate by the third developmental month. The filtrate does not contain waste products, as they are excreted at the placenta for removal and elimination by the maternal kidneys. The sterile filtrate mixes with the amniotic fluid and is swallowed by the fetus and reabsorbed across the lining of the digestive tract.

The Development of the Reproductive System

SEXUALLY INDIFFERENT STAGES (WEEKS 3–6)

DEVELOPMENT OF THE GONADS

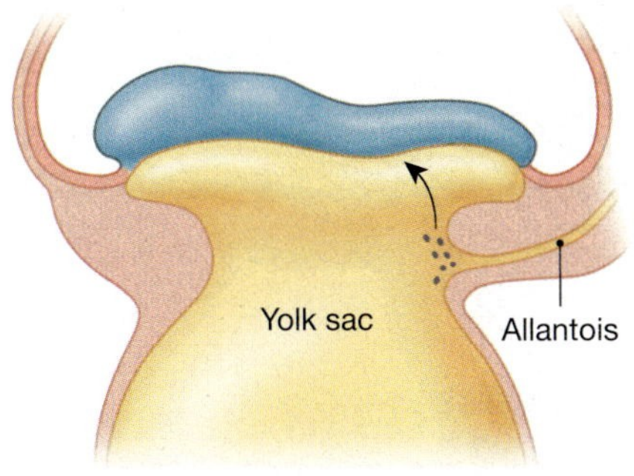

3 WEEKS

During the third week, endodermal cells migrate from the wall of the yolk sac near the allantois to the dorsal wall of the abdominal cavity. These primordial germ cells enter the **genital ridges** that parallel the mesonephros.

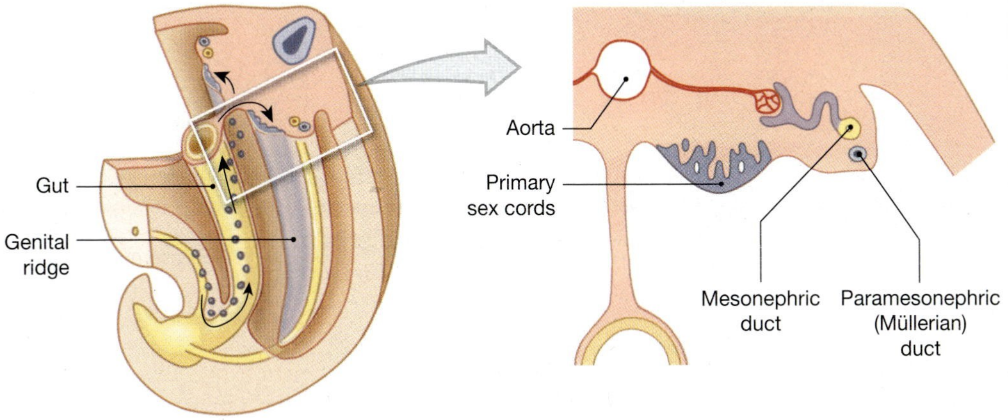

Each ridge has a thick epithelium continuous with columns of cells, the **primary sex cords**, that extend into the center (medulla) of the ridge. Anterior to each mesonephric duct, a duct forms that has no connection to the kidneys. This is the **paramesonephric** (*Müllerian*) **duct**; it extends along the genital ridge and continues toward the cloaca. At this sexually indifferent stage, male embryos cannot be distinguished from female embryos.

DEVELOPMENT OF DUCTS AND ACCESSORY ORGANS

Both sexes have mesonephric and paramesonephric ducts at this stage. Unless exposed to androgens, the embryo—regardless of its genetic sex—will develop into a female. In a normal male embryo, cells in the core (medulla) of the genital ridge begin producing testosterone sometime after week 6. Testosterone triggers the changes in the duct system and external genitalia that are detailed on the following page.

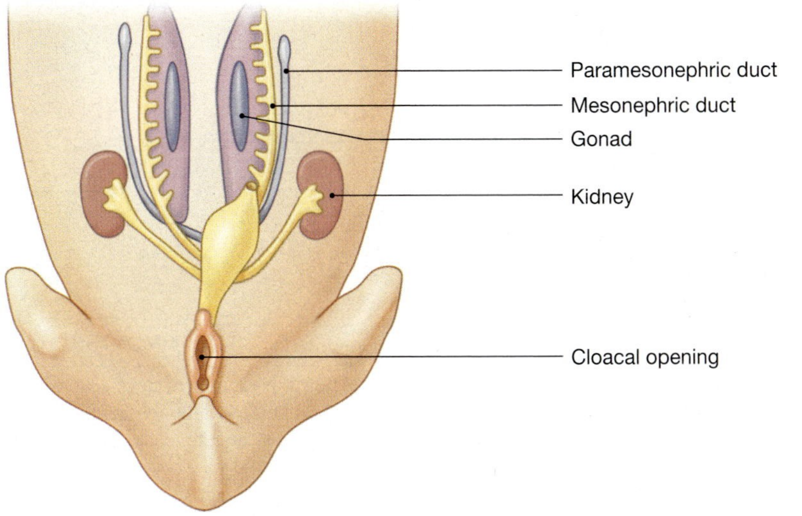

DEVELOPMENT OF EXTERNAL GENITALIA

4 WEEKS

After 4 weeks of development, there are mesenchymal swellings called **cloacal folds** around the **cloacal membrane** (the cloaca does not open to the exterior). The **genital tubercle** forms the glans of the penis in males and the clitoris in females.

6 WEEKS

Two weeks later, the cloaca has been subdivided, separating the cloacal membrane into a posterior *anal membrane*, bounded by the *anal folds*, and an anterior **urogenital membrane**, bounded by the **urethral folds**. A prominent **genital swelling** forms lateral to each urethral fold.

The Development of the Reproductive System

DEVELOPMENT OF THE MALE REPRODUCTIVE SYSTEM

DEVELOPMENT OF THE TESTES

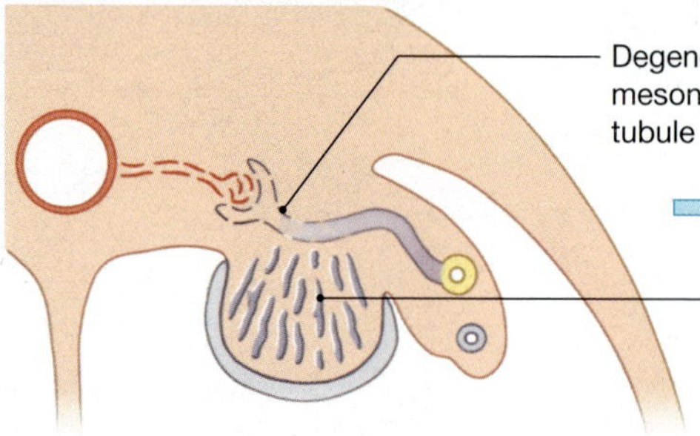

7 WEEKS

In the male, the primary sex cords proliferate and the germ cells migrate into the sex cords. The resulting **testis cords** will form the seminiferous tubules.

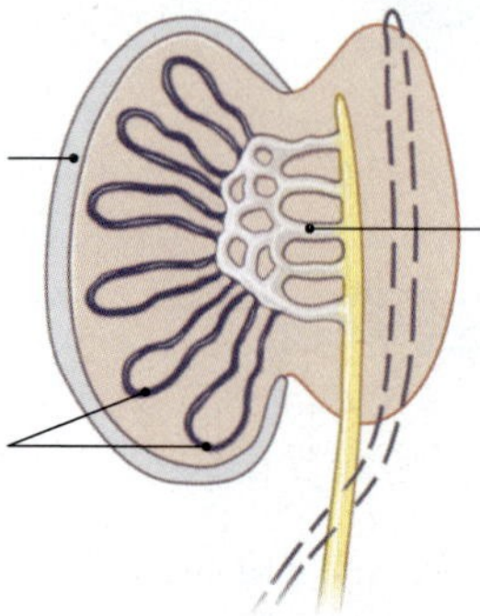

12 WEEKS

Connections form between the arching testis cords and the adjacent mesonephric nephrons. Although these nephrons later degenerate, the seminiferous tubules remain connected to the mesonephric duct.

DEVELOPMENT OF MALE DUCTS AND ACCESSORY ORGANS

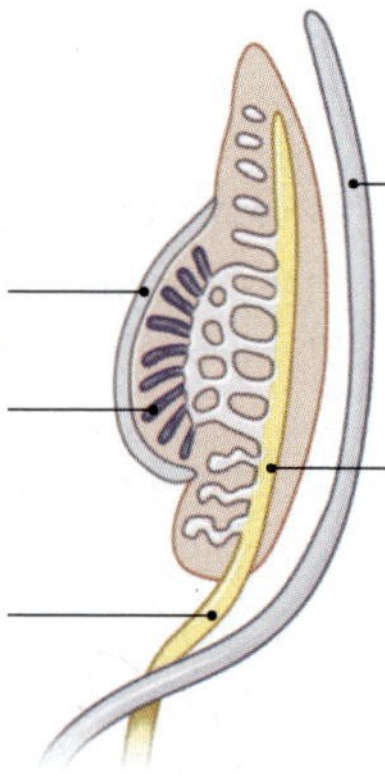

A view of the testis and ducts of the left side as seen in frontal section. Note the location and orientation of the mesonephros relative to the developing testis.

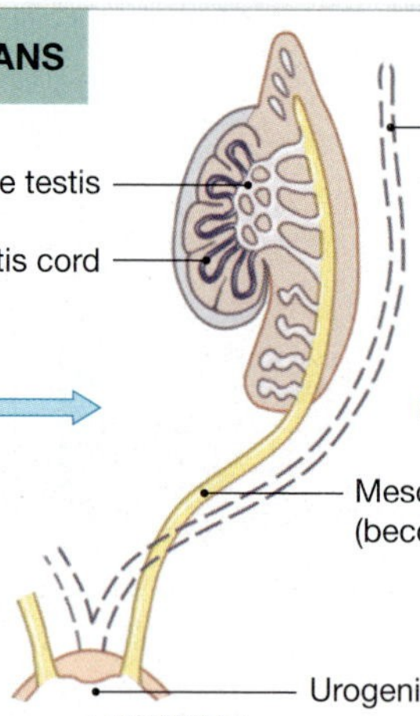

4 MONTHS

After four months of development, the testis cords are connected to the remnants of the mesonephric tubules by the rete testis. The paramesonephric (Müllerian) duct has degenerated.

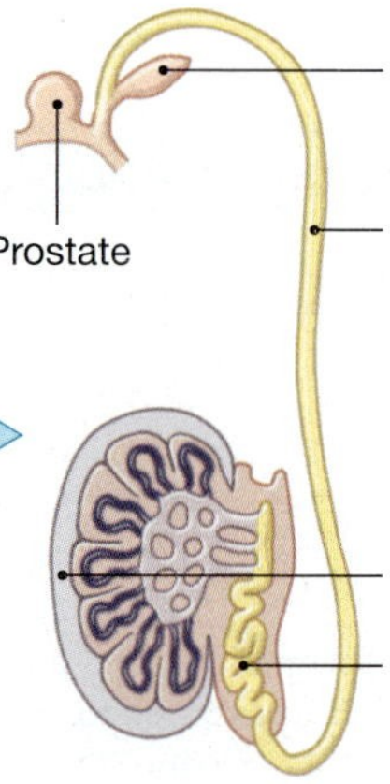

7 MONTHS

Definitive organization after the testis has descended into the scrotum (*see Figure 27.2, p. 717*). Note the relationships between the definitive sex organs and the embryonic structures.

DEVELOPMENT OF MALE EXTERNAL GENITALIA

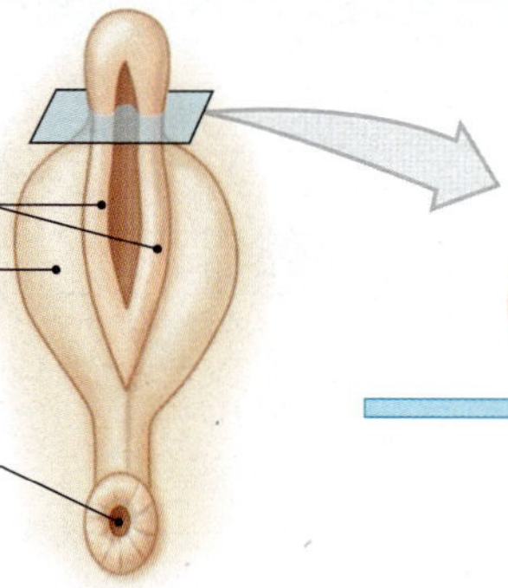

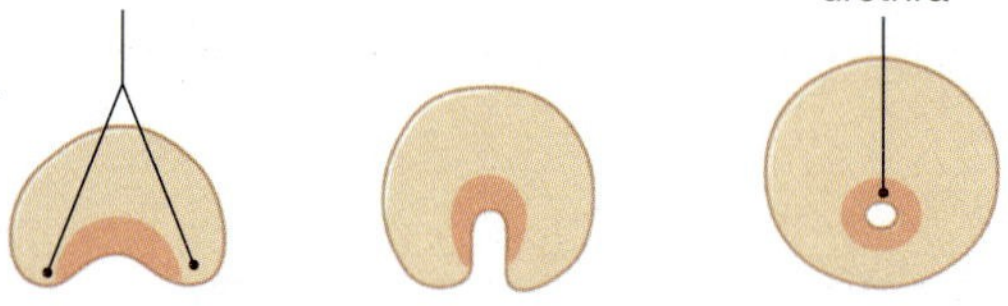

10 WEEKS

At 10 weeks, the **genital tubercle** has enlarged, the tips of the urethral folds are moving together to form the spongy urethra (see sectional views), and paired **scrotal swellings** have developed from the genital swellings.

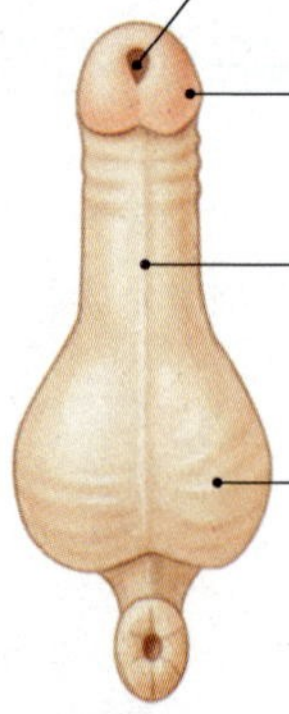

BIRTH

In the newborn male, the line of fusion between the urethral folds is quite evident.

DEVELOPMENT OF THE FEMALE REPRODUCTIVE SYSTEM

DEVELOPMENT OF THE OVARIES

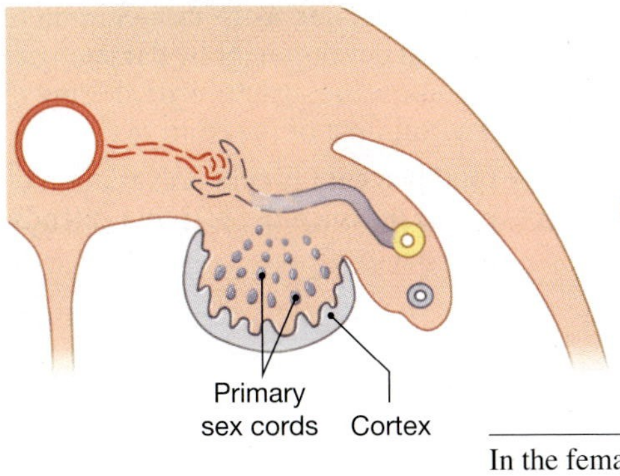

7 WEEKS

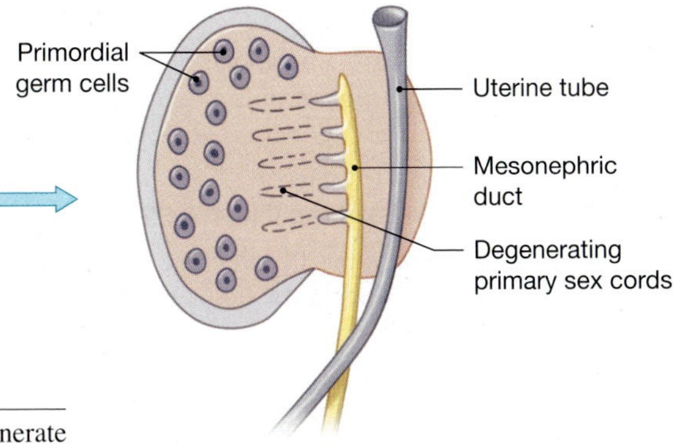

12 WEEKS

In the female embryo, the **primary sex cords** degenerate and the **primordial germ cells** migrate into the outer region (cortex) of the genital ridge.

DEVELOPMENT OF FEMALE DUCTS AND ACCESSORY ORGANS

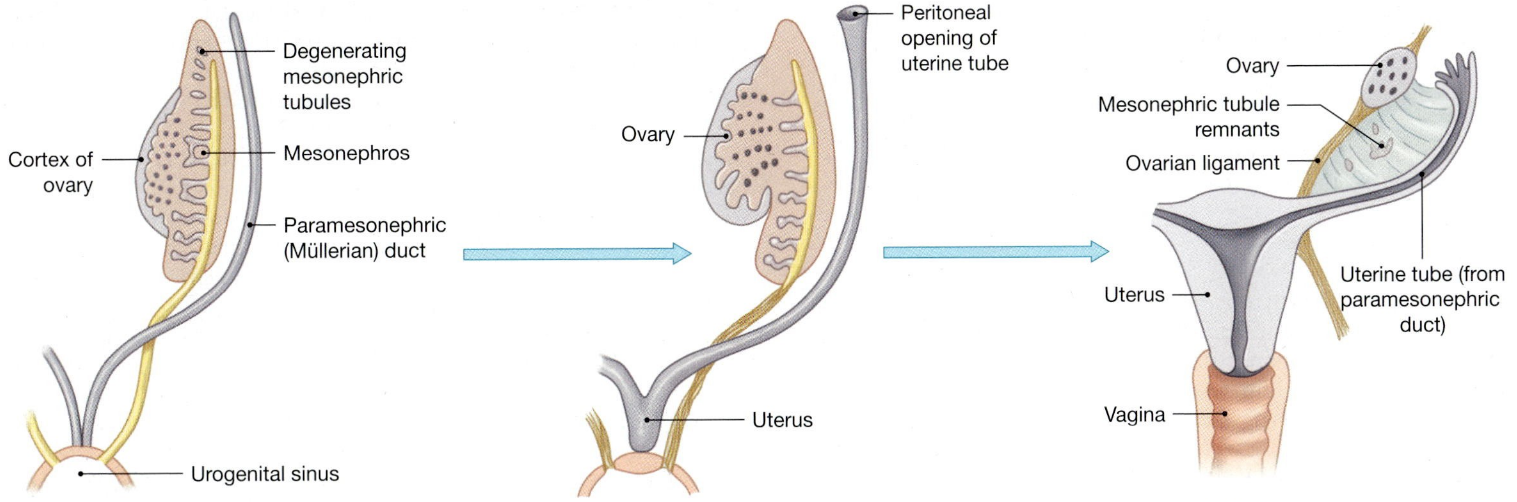

The mesonephric tubules and duct degenerate; the paramesonephric (Müllerian) duct develops a broad opening into the peritoneal cavity. Note the fusion of the ducts and the separation of the common chamber, which will form the uterus, from the urogenital sinus.

COMPARISON OF MALE AND FEMALE EXTERNAL GENITALIA

Males	Females
Penis	Clitoris
Corpora cavernosa	Erectile tissue
Corpus spongiosum	Vestibular bulbs
Proximal shaft of penis	Labia minora
Spongy urethra	Vestibule
Bulbo-urethral glands	Greater vestibular glands
Scrotum	Labia majora

DEVELOPMENT OF FEMALE EXTERNAL GENITALIA

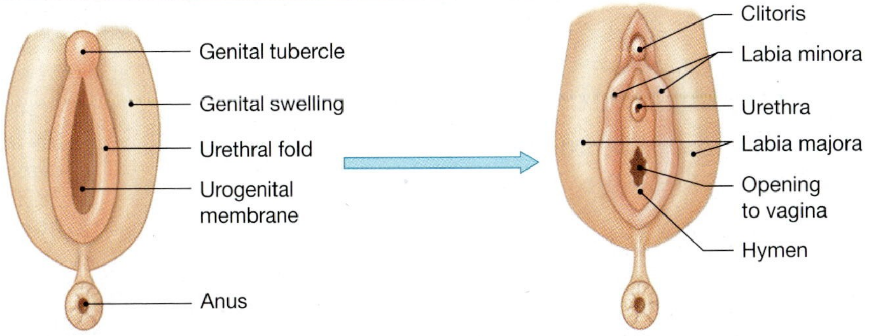

In the female, the urethral folds do not fuse; they develop into the labia minora. The genital swellings will form the labia majora. The genital tubercle develops into the clitoris. The urethra opens to the exterior immediately posterior to the clitoris. The hymen remains as an elaboration of the urogenital membrane.

CLINICAL TERMS

abruptio placentae (a-BRUP-shē-ō pla-SEN-tē): Tearing of the placenta sometime after the fifth gestational month.

amniocentesis: An analysis of fetal cells taken from a sample of amniotic fluid.

Apgar rating: A method of evaluating newborn infants; a test for developmental problems and neurological damage.

breech birth: A delivery wherein the legs or buttocks of the fetus enter the vaginal canal first.

chorionic villus sampling: An analysis of cells collected from the chorionic villi during the first trimester.

congenital malformation: A severe structural abnormality, present at birth, that affects major systems.

ectopic pregnancy: A pregnancy in which implantation occurs somewhere other than the uterus.

fetal alcohol syndrome (FAS): A neonatal condition resulting from maternal alcohol consumption; characterized by developmental defects often involving the skeletal, nervous, and/or cardiovascular systems.

placenta previa: A condition resulting from implantation in or near the cervix.

preeclampsia (prē-e-KLAMP-sē-uh): Development of hypertension with edema or proteinuria (protein in the urine) due to pregnancy or the influence of a recent pregnancy.

teratogens (ter-A-tō-jen): Stimuli that disrupt normal development by damaging cells, altering chromosome structure, or altering the chemical environment of the embryo.

total placenta previa: A variation of placenta previa in which the placenta extends across the internal os.

STUDY OUTLINE

Introduction 748

1. **Development** is the gradual modification of physical and physiological characteristics from conception to maturity. The creation of different cell types during development is called **differentiation**.

An Overview of Development 748

1. Development begins at **conception** (fertilization) and can be divided into **prenatal** (before birth) and **postnatal** (birth to maturity) **development**.

Fertilization 748

1. Fertilization normally occurs in the ampulla of the uterine tube within a day after ovulation. Sperm cannot fertilize an egg until they have undergone *capacitation.* Around 200 million sperm are ejaculated into the vagina, and only around 100 will reach the ampulla. A man with fewer than 20 million sperm per milliliter is functionally **sterile**.

The Oocyte at Ovulation 748

2. The acrosomal caps of the spermatozoa release **hyaluronidase**, an enzyme that separates cells of the corona radiata and exposes the oocyte membrane. When a single spermatozoon contacts that membrane, fertilization occurs and **oocyte activation** follows. *(see Figure 28.1)*

Pronucleus Formation and Amphimixis 748

3. During activation the secondary oocyte completes meiosis. The **female pronucleus** then fuses with the **male pronucleus**, a process called **amphimixis**. *(see Figure 28.1)*

Prenatal Development 749

1. The nine-month **gestation** period can be divided into three **trimesters**, each three months in duration.

The First Trimester 750

2. The **first trimester** is the most critical period in prenatal life. **Cleavage** subdivides the cytoplasm of the zygote in a series of mitotic divisions; the zygote becomes a **blastocyst**. During **implantation** the blastocyst burrows into the uterine endometrium. **Placentation** occurs as blood vessels form around the blastocyst and the **placenta** appears. **Embryogenesis** is the formation of a viable embryo.
3. The blastocyst consists of an outer **trophoblast** and an **inner cell mass**, which is clustered at one end next to a hollow cavity (the **blastocoele**). *(see Figure 28.2 and Table 28.1)*
4. When the blastocyst adheres to the uterine lining, the trophoblast next to the endometrium undergoes changes and becomes a **syncytial trophoblast**, which then erodes a path through the uterine epithelium. As the trophoblast enlarges and spreads, maternal blood flows through trophoblastic channels, or **lacunae**. The blastocyst organizes into layers and becomes a **blastodisc**. After **gastrulation** the blastodisc contains an embryo composed of **endoderm**, **ectoderm**, and an intervening **mesoderm**. These **germ layers** help form four **extraembryonic membranes**: the yolk sac, amnion, allantois, and chorion. *(see Figures 28.3 to 28.5 and Table 28.1)*
5. The **yolk sac** is an important site of blood cell formation. The **amnion** encloses fluid that surrounds and cushions the developing embryo. The base of the **allantois** later gives rise to the urinary bladder. Circulation within the vessels of the **chorion** provides a rapid-transit system linking the embryo with the trophoblast. *(see Figures 28.4/28.5)*
6. **Chorionic villi** extend outward into the maternal tissues, forming an intricate, branching network through which maternal blood flows. The **body stalk** and the **yolk stalk** connect the embryo with the chorion and the yolk sac, respectively. As development proceeds, the **umbilical cord** connects the fetus to the placenta. Blood flow occurs through the umbilical arteries and the umbilical vein, and exchange occurs at the chorionic villi. The placenta synthesizes HCG, estrogens, progestins, HPL, and relaxin. *(see Figures 28.5/28.6)*
7. The **embryo**, which has a **head fold** and a **tail fold**, will undergo critical changes in the first trimester. Events in the first 12 weeks establish the basis for **organogenesis** (organ formation). *(see Figures 28.5b,c/28.7 and Table 28.2)*
8. Organogenesis of all the body organ systems appears during the first trimester, with the development of fully functional fetal organ systems completed by the end of the third trimester. *(see Table 28.2 and Embryology Summaries)*

The Second and Third Trimesters 757

9. In the **second trimester**, the organ systems near functional completion and the fetus grows rapidly. During the **third trimester**, the organ systems become functional and the fetus undergoes its largest weight gain. *(see Figures 28.7 to 28.9, Table 28.2, and Embryology Summaries)*
10. By the end of gestation, the uterus will be about 12 inches long and contain almost 5 liters of fluid. *(see Figure 28.9)*

Labor and Delivery 760

1. The goal of *true labor* is **parturition**, the forcible expulsion of the fetus.

Stages of Labor 760

2. Labor can be divided into three stages: **dilation stage**, **expulsion stage**, and **placental stage**. The dilation stage, in which the cervix dilates, usually lasts

eight or more hours. The expulsion stage involves the birth (**delivery**) of the fetus. The placenta is ejected during the placental stage. *(see Figure 28.10)*

Premature Labor 762

3. **Premature labor** occurs before the fetus has completely developed. A **premature delivery** produces a newborn weighing over 1 kg, which may or may not survive.

The Neonatal Period 763

1. The **neonatal period** extends from birth to one month of age.
2. In the transition from fetus to **neonate**, the respiratory, circulatory, digestive, and urinary systems undergo tremendous changes as they begin functioning independently. The newborn must also begin thermoregulating.

CHAPTER REVIEW

For answers to the Concept Check and Review Questions, go to the blue "Answers" tab at the back of the book.

Level 1 Reviewing Facts and Terms

Match each numbered item with the most closely related lettered item. Use letters for answers in the spaces provided.

Column A	Column B
___ 1. corona radiata	a. begins with the onset of true labor
___ 2. hyaluronidase	b. begins as the cervix dilates completely
___ 3. second trimester	c. birth
___ 4. expulsion stage	d. characterized by rapid fetal growth
___ 5. ooplasm	e. incision through the perineal musculature
___ 6. third trimester	f. layer of follicular cells around the oocyte
___ 7. first trimester	g. enzyme in the acrosomal cap
___ 8. parturition	h. cytoplasm of the oocyte
___ 9. dilation stage	i. time of embryonic/early fetal development
___ 10. episiotomy	j. characterized by the continued development of organ systems

11. The egg is normally fertilized in the
    (a) uterus
    (b) ampulla of the uterine tube
    (c) cervix
    (d) vagina
12. During amphimixis
    (a) sperm become capacitated
    (b) the ovum finishes meiosis II
    (c) the male and female pronuclei fuse
    (d) meiosis occurs
13. During the first trimester of development,
    (a) the fetal lungs begin to process air
    (b) the rudiments of all of the major organ systems begin to appear
    (c) the organs and organ systems complete their development
    (d) the fastest period of fetal growth occurs
14. The process of cell division that occurs after fertilization is called
    (a) cleavage
    (b) implantation
    (c) placentation
    (d) embryogenesis
15. A blastocyst is a(n)
    (a) extraembryonic membrane that forms blood vessels
    (b) solid ball of cells
    (c) hollow ball of cells
    (d) portion of the placenta
16. During the second trimester, the most significant event that permits the mother to realize that she is carrying a new life within her body is that
    (a) the fetal brain begins to grow greatly
    (b) the fetus begins to move inside the uterus
    (c) eye and ear basic structures form
    (d) articulations between joints appear
17. The hormone that is the basis for pregnancy tests is
    (a) LH
    (b) progesterone
    (c) human chorionic gonadotropin (HCG)
    (d) human placental lactogen (HPL)
18. The first stage of labor is the ______________________ stage.
    (a) dilation
    (b) expulsion
    (c) placental
    (d) decidual
19. The extraembryonic membrane that forms the urinary bladder is the
    (a) yolk sac
    (b) allantois
    (c) amnion
    (d) chorion
20. During implantation, the
    (a) syncytial trophoblast erodes a path through the endometrium
    (b) inner cell mass begins to form the placenta
    (c) maternal blood vessels in the endometrium are walled off from the blastocyst
    (d) entire trophoblast becomes syncytial

Level 2 Reviewing Concepts

1. What would be the fate of an embryo if the chorion failed to form properly?
    (a) there would be an insufficient number of blood cells formed and the infant would need a transfusion at birth
    (b) there would be no effect; the allantois would assume the function
    (c) there would be no protective cushion of fluid surrounding the embryo, which would be subjected to injury within the uterus
    (d) the embryo would be unable to receive nutrients and oxygen in sufficient amounts, and the pregnancy might terminate spontaneously
2. What would be the effect of a direct connection between the blood supply of the chorionic villi and the decidua basalis of the placenta?
    (a) normal development, as this is usually what occurs
    (b) a possible incompatibility reaction that could damage or kill the fetus
    (c) fetal growth would be retarded
    (d) the fetus would grow faster than usual

3. Under what circumstances would you expect to find that two developing fetuses share a chorion and placenta but have separate amniotic sacs?
   (a) they are fraternal twins
   (b) they have serious developmental defects
   (c) they are identical twins
   (d) they are different genetically
4. What is cleavage and in which trimester does it occur?
5. What is the primitive streak?
6. Describe the effects of human chorionic gonadotropin. Where and when is it produced?
7. What occurs during amphimixis?
8. Which extraembryonic membrane is important for blood cell formation?
9. Describe the process of organogenesis.
10. Why is the first trimester considered a critical period?

Level 3 Critical Thinking

1. Joe and Jane desperately want to have children, and although they have tried for two years, they have not been successful. Finally, each of them consults a physician, and it turns out that Joe has oligospermia (low sperm count). He confides to you that he doesn't understand why this would interfere with his ability to have children since he remembers from biology class that it only takes one sperm to fertilize an egg. What would you tell him?
2. The virus that causes rubella, or "German measles," has been recognized for decades as a powerful teratogen. During which trimester of pregnancy would it be most dangerous for pregnant women to be exposed to this pathogen? Why?

Answers to Concept Check and Chapter Review Questions

CHAPTER 1

Concept Check

p. 4 1. A histologist investigates the structure and properties of tissue.

p. 4 2. A gross anatomist investigates organ systems and their relationships to the body as a whole.

p. 4 3. Regional anatomy considers all of the superficial and internal features in a specific area of the body, such as the head, neck, or trunk. Systemic anatomy considers the structure of major organ systems, such as the skeletal or muscular system.

p. 13 1. Integumentary system.

p. 13 2. Reproductive system of the female.

p. 13 3. The gradual appearance of characteristic cellular specializations during development, as the result of gene activation or repression.

p. 18 1. The two eyes would be separated by a midsagittal section.

p. 18 2. The fall would affect your forearm.

p. 18 3. Groin = inguen, buttock = gluteus, and hand = manus.

p. 20 1. Mesenteries are double sheets of serous membranes in the peritoneal cavity that provide support and stability for organs (stomach, small intestine, and parts of the large intestine) while permitting limited movement.

p. 20 2. The body cavity inferior to the diaphragm is the abdominopelvic cavity.

p. 20 3. (a) distal, (b) inferior

Chapter Review

Level 1 Reviewing Facts and Terms

1. F	**2.** E	**3.** G	**4.** H
5. B	**6.** D	**7.** C	**8.** A
9. C	**10.** D	**11.** B	**12.** C
13. D	**14.** B	**15.** B	

Level 2 Reviewing Concepts

1. A
2. All living organisms have the same basic functions: responsiveness, growth and differentiation, reproduction, movement, metabolism, and excretion.
3. The hand is distal to the arm of the upper limb.
4. B
5. B
6. In large organisms with specialized organ systems that perform absorption, respiration, and excretion in different regions of the body, there must be a means of internal transport for these products. Passive processes such as diffusion and osmosis would occur too slowly to permit the organism to function and remain alive.

Level 3 Critical Thinking

1. A disruption of cellular division process within the bone marrow will result in the production of too few red blood cells (anemia) or too many red blood cells (polycythemia) within the vessels of the cardiovascular system. Anemia will affect the amount of oxygen carried to peripheral tissues, thereby affecting overall metabolism. Polycythemia will produce altered peripheral metabolism due to the "clogging" of blood vessels by the increased number of cells attempting to get through peripheral capillaries.
2. The body systems affected would include: digestive, respiratory, and skeletal systems. The anatomical specialties involved include surface anatomy, regional anatomy studies, systemic anatomy, comparative anatomy, and developmental anatomy.

CHAPTER 2

Concept Check

p. 35 1. Plasmalemmae are selectively permeable.

p. 35 2. Diffusion is a general term that refers to the passive movement of materials from regions of high concentration to regions of low concentration. Osmosis is the diffusion of water across a membrane; water moves into the solution containing the higher solute concentration (the lower water concentration).

p. 35 3. There are three types of endocytosis: pinocytosis, phagocytosis, and receptor-mediated endocytosis. Pinocytosis is the formation of vesicles (pinosomes) filled with extracellular fluid. Phagocytosis produces vesicles (phagosomes) containing solid objects. Receptor-mediated endocytosis resembles pinocytosis but is very selective: The coated vesicles contain a specific target molecule in high concentrations bound to receptors on the membrane surface.

p. 35 4. The structures are called microvilli. Their function is to increase surface area for absorption.

p. 38 1. The lack of a flagellum would render the sperm cell immobile.

p. 38 2. The two divisions of the cytoplasm are (1) the cytosol, which is the intracellular fluid containing dissolved nutrients, ions, proteins and waste products; and (2) organelles, which are structures that perform specific functions within the cell.

p. 43 1. Mitochondria produce ATP. The number of mitochondria in a particular cell varies depending on the cell's energy demand. If a cell contains many mitochondria, the energy demands for the cell are very high.

p. 43 2. Cells in the ovaries and testes contain large amounts of smooth endoplasmic reticulum (SER). Here, the SER functions to synthesize steroid hormones.

p. 43 3. If lysosomes disintegrate in a damaged cell, they release active enzymes into the cytosol. These enzymes rapidly destroy the proteins and organelles of the cell, a process called autolysis.

p. 48 1. Cell division is a form of cellular reproduction that results in an increase in cell number.

p. 48 2. Mitosis is a process that occurs during the division of somatic cells. It is the accurate duplication of the cell's genetic material and the distribution of one copy to each of the two new daughter cells.

p. 48 3. Interphase can be divided into the G_1, S, and G_2 phases. In the G_1 phase, the cell manufactures organelles and cytosol to make two functional cells. During the S phase, the cell replicates its chromosomes. The G_2 phase is a time for last-minute protein synthesis before mitosis. An interphase cell in the G_0 phase is not preparing for mitosis, but is performing all other normal cell functions. Mitosis consists of four stages: prophase, metaphase, anaphase, and telophase. In prophase, the spindle fibers form and the nuclear membrane disappears; in metaphase, the chromatids line up along the metaphase plate; in anaphase, the chromatids separate and move to opposite poles of the spindle apparatus; and in telophase, the nuclear membrane reappears and chromosomes uncoil as the daughter cells separate through cytokinesis.

Chapter Review

Level 1 Reviewing Facts and Terms

1. E	**2.** G	**3.** H	**4.** B
5. D	**6.** I	**7.** C	**8.** F
9. A	**10.** B	**11.** C	**12.** B
13. B	**14.** D	**15.** D	**16.** B
17. A	**18.** C	**19.** C	**20.** B

Level 2 Reviewing Concepts

1. The nuclear membrane partially separates the nucleoplasm from the cytosol, which is necessary to permit and promote specific nuclear functions.
2. The three basic concepts of the cell theory are:
   (a) Cells are the structural "building blocks" of all plants and animals.
   (b) Cells are produced by the division of preexisting cells.
   (c) Cells are the smallest structural units that perform all vital functions.
3. The four passive processes by which substances get into and out of cells are diffusion, osmosis, filtration, and facilitated diffusion.
4. Similarities: Both processes utilize carrier proteins. Differences: In facilitated diffusion, substances move down their concentration gradients (from high to low concentration) and this process does not utilize energy obtained by the splitting of ATP. In active transport, substances move against their concentration gradients (low to high concentration), a process requiring the energy provided by the splitting of ATP.
5. Three major factors that determine whether a substance can diffuse across a plasmalemma are the size of the molecule, the concentration gradient across the membrane, and the solubility of the molecule.
6. Organelles are structures that perform specific functions within the cell. Organelles can be divided into two broad categories: (1) nonmembranous organelles, which are always in contact with the cytoplasm, and (2) membranous organelles, which are surrounded by membranes that isolate their contents from the cytosol.
7. The frequency of cell divisions can be estimated by the number of cells in mitosis at any given time. The longer the life expectancy of a cell, the slower the mitotic rate.
8. The stages of mitosis are:
   (a) Prophase—chromosomes (called chromatids) become visible; paired centrioles move apart; spindle fibers extend between centriole pairs; nuclear membrane disappears.
   (b) Metaphase—chromatids move to metaphase plate.
   (c) Anaphase—chromatid pairs separate; daughter chromosomes move toward opposite ends of the cell.
   (d) Telophase—"reverse of prophase": nuclear membranes form; nuclei enlarge; chromosomes gradually uncoil.
9. The general functions of the plasmalemma include:
   (a) physical isolation
   (b) regulation of exchange with the environment
   (c) sensitivity
   (d) structural support
10. Microfilaments have two major functions:
   (a) Microfilaments anchor the cytoskeleton to integral proteins of the plasmalemma.
   (b) Microfilaments can interact with other microfilaments or thick filaments to produce active movement of a portion of a cell.

Level 3 Critical Thinking

1. Your body tissues have a higher solute concentration than fresh water, so over time osmosis draws water into your skin, producing swelling and distortion.
2. Skin cells are tightly held together by abundant desmosomes, very strong cell junctions that can resist twisting and stretching or breaking apart.
3. The isolation of the internal contents of membranous organelles allows them to manufacture or store secretions, enzymes, or toxins that could adversely affect the cytoplasm in general. Another benefit is the increased efficiency of having specialized enzyme systems concentrated in one place. For example, mitochondria contain the concentration of enzymes necessary for energy production in the cell.
4. Since the transport of the molecule is against the concentration gradient (that is, from lower to higher concentration) and requires energy to move across the membrane, this type of transport is called active transport.

CHAPTER 3

Concept Check

p. 54 1. There are four primary tissue types: epithelial tissue, connective tissue, muscle tissue, and neural tissue.

p. 54 2. Characteristics of epithelia include cellularity, polarity, attachment, avascularity, and regeneration.

p. 54 3. Specializations of epithelial cells include production of secretions, movement of fluids over the surface, and movement of fluids through the epithelium itself.

p. 61 1. No. A simple squamous epithelium does not provide enough protection against infection, abrasion, and dehydration, and is not found in the skin surface.

p. 61 2. In holocrine secretion, the entire gland cell is destroyed during the secretory process. Further secretion by the gland requires regeneration of cells to replace those lost during secretion.

p. 61 3. During apocrine secretion, the secretory product and the apical portion of the cell cytoplasm are shed.

p. 61 4. A simple columnar epithelium provides protection and may be involved in both absorption and secretion.

p. 72 1. The three basic components of connective tissue are specialized cells, extracellular protein fibers, and a fluid called ground substance.

p. 72 2. Connective tissue proper refers to connective tissues with many types of cells and extracellular fibers in a syrupy ground substance. Supporting connective tissue (cartilage and bone) have a less diverse cell population and a matrix that contains closely packed fibers. The matrix is either gel-like (cartilage) or calcified (bone).

p. 72 3. The two types of cells in connective tissue proper are fixed cells and wandering cells. Fixed cells include fibroblasts, fibrocytes, fixed macrophages, adipocytes, mesenchymal cells, and sometimes melanocytes. Wandering cells include free macrophages, mast cells, lymphocytes, plasmocytes, eosinophils and neutrophils.

p. 72 4. Collagen fibers add strength to connective tissue. We would expect vitamin C deficiency to result in the production of connective tissue that is weaker and more prone to damage.

p. 75 1. Mucous membranes line passageways that communicate with the exterior. They form a barrier that resists the entry of pathogens; they must remain moist at all times.

p. 75 2. Another name for the superficial fascia is *subcutaneous layer* or *hypodermis*. It separates the skin from underlying tissues and organs. It provides insulation and padding and lets the skin or underlying structures move independently.

p. 75 3. The pericardium is a serous membrane that lines the pericardial cavity and covers the heart.

p. 75 4. The cutaneous membrane of the skin covers the surface of the body. It consists of a stratified squamous epithelium and an underlying layer of areolar tissue reinforced by a layer of dense connective tissue.

p. 77 1. Since both cardiac and skeletal muscle cells are striated (banded), this must be smooth muscle.

p. 77 2. Skeletal muscle cells have a banded or striated appearance because of the organization of actin and myosin filaments within the cells.

p. 77 3. Neural tissue.

Chapter Review

Level 1 Reviewing Facts and Terms

1. J	2. H	3. A	4. C
5. F	6. G	7. I	8. B
9. E	10. D	11. C	12. C
13. C	14. D	15. D	16. B
17. D	18. C	19. A	20. D

Level 2 Reviewing Concepts

1. A single cell is the unit of structure and function, whereas groups of cells work together as units called tissues (collections of special cells and cell products that perform limited functions).
2. B
3. D
4. A tendon is made of cords of dense regular connective tissue that attaches a skeletal muscle to a bone. The collagen fibers run along the long axis of the tendon and transfer the pull of the contracting muscle to the bone.
5. Exocrine secretions occur in ducts that lead onto surfaces; endocrine secretions occur in the interstitial fluid and then enter into blood vessels.

6. The presence of the cilia at the surface of the epithelium means that the mucous layer, which rests on the epithelium surface, will be kept moving and the respiratory surface will be kept clean (or clear).
7. The skin is separated from the muscles by a layer of loose connective tissue. The loose connective tissue provides padding and elastic properties that permit a considerable amount of independent movement of the two layers. Thus, pinching the skin does not affect the underlying muscle.
8. While a tendon is made of cords of dense regular connective tissue, an aponeurosis is made of a sheet or ribbon of connective tissue that resembles a flat tendon. Aponeuroses may cover the surface of muscles and assist superficial muscles in attaching to one another or to other structures.
9. Germinative cells are stem cells usually found in the deepest layer of the epithelium. They divide to replace cells lost or destroyed at the epithelial surface.

Level 3 Critical Thinking

1. The presence of DNA, RNA, and membrane components suggests that the cells were destroyed during the process of secretion. This is consistent with a holocrine type of secretion.
2. Skeletal muscle tissue would be made up of densely packed fibers running in the same direction, but since these fibers are composed of cells, they would have many nuclei and mitochondria. Skeletal muscle also has an obvious banding pattern or striations due to the arrangement of the actin and myosin filaments within the cell. The student is probably looking at a slide of tendon (dense regular connective tissue).
3. Mucus is produced by the respiratory epithelium in response to irritation from smoking. The cilia found on many cells of the respiratory system beat upward, thereby moving mucus produced by the respiratory epithelium up to the level of the esophagus, where it can be swallowed and eliminated. Destruction of the cilia prevents the elimination of this mucus. Therefore coughing is the only mechanism by which the mucus can be removed.
4. Like skeletal muscle fibers, cardiac muscle fibers are incapable of dividing. However, because cardiac muscle lacks the myosatellite cells that divide to repair skeletal muscle injured by ischemia, cardiac muscle fibers exposed to ischemia die, resulting in a heart attack, which is life-threatening.

CHAPTER 4

Concept Check

p. 92 1. Cells are shed constantly from the outer layers of the stratum corneum.

p. 92 2. The splinter is lodged in the stratum granulosum.

p. 92 3. The two major subdivisions of the integumentary system are the cutaneous membrane and the accessory structures. The cutaneous membrane has two parts: the superficial epidermis and the deeper dermis. The accessory structures include hair follicles, exocrine glands, and nails.

p. 92 4. Keratinization is the production of keratin by epidermal cells. It occurs in the stratum granulosum of the epidermis. Keratin fibers develop within cells of the stratum granulosum. As keratin fibers are produced, these cells become thinner and flatter, and their plasmalemmae become thicker and less permeable. As these cells die, they form the densely packed layers of the stratum lucidum and stratum corneum.

p. 94 1. These terms refer to the relative thickness of the epidermis, not to the integument as a whole. Thick skin occurs on the palms of the hands (epidermal thickness may be as much as 0.5 mm thick), whereas thin skin covers most of the body (epidermal thickness averages 0.08 mm).

p. 94 2. Sanding the tips of one's fingers will not permanently remove fingerprints. Since the epidermal ridges of the fingertips are formed in layers of the skin that are constantly regenerated, they will eventually reappear. The actual pattern of the ridges is determined by arrangement of tissue in the dermis, which is not affected by the sanding.

p. 94 3. The color of the epidermis is due to a combination of the dermal blood supply and variable quantities of two pigments: carotene and melanin.

p. 94 4. Epidermal ridges are formed by the deeper layers of the epidermis that extend into the dermis, increasing the contact area between the two regions. Dermal papillae are projections of the dermis that extend between adjacent ridges.

p. 100 1. When the dermis is stretched excessively, the elastic fibers are overstretched and are not able to recoil. The skin then forms folds or wrinkles, called stretch marks, in the affected areas.

p. 100 2. Contraction of the arrector pili pulls the hair follicle erect, depressing the area at the base of the hair and making the surrounding skin appear higher. The combined activity of the arrectores pilorum produces "goose bumps" or "goose pimples."

p. 100 3. Each hair has a medulla, produced by the central portion of the hair matrix, surrounded by a cortex and covered by a cuticle. The shaft of the hair begins where its internal organization is complete (roughly halfway toward the surface).

p. 103 1. Apocrine sweat glands produce a viscous, cloudy, and potentially odorous secretion. The secretion contains several kinds of organic compounds. Some of these have an odor, and others produce an odor when metabolized by skin bacteria. Deodorants are used to mask the resulting odor. Merocrine sweat glands produce a watery secretion that chiefly contains sodium chloride, metabolites, and waste products. Merocrine secretions are watery, and are generally known as sweat.

p. 103 2. Sensible perspiration is the sweat produced by merocrine sweat glands.

p. 103 3. Sebaceous and apocrine sweat glands can be collectively turned on or off by the autonomic nervous system, but no local or regional control is possible. The autonomic nervous system controls the amount of merocrine sweat gland secretion and the region of the body involved.

Chapter Review

Level 1 Reviewing Facts and Terms

1. E	2. F	3. D	4. G
5. C	6. H	7. B	8. I
9. A	10. D	11. A	12. D
13. D	14. B	15. B	16. B
17. B	18. C	19. A	20. A

Level 2 Reviewing Concepts

1. B
2. Fair-skinned individuals produce less melanin in their melanocytes, and are therefore less able to prevent the absorption of potentially damaging ultraviolet radiation. Since more UV radiation reaches the deeper skin layers, it may cause a greater amount of damage.
3. Mechanical stresses cause cells in the stratum germinativum to divide more rapidly, increasing the thickness of the epithelium.
4. If the skin stretches and then does not contract to its original size, it wrinkles and creases, creating a network of stretch marks.
5. Keratin is produced in large amounts in the stratum granulosum. Fibers of keratin interlock in the cells in this layer during the process of keratinization. The cells become thinner and flatter; subsequently, they dehydrate. The keratin is important in maintaining the structure of the outer part of the epidermis and participating in its water resistance. Additionally, keratin forms the basic structural component of hair and nails.
6. It has no vital organs.
7. These activities either reduce the amount of potentially odorous secretion on the surface of the skin or inhibit the activity of bacteria on these secretions.
8. An individual who is cyanotic has a sustained reduction in circulatory supply to the skin. As a result, the skin takes on a bluish coloration, called cyanosis.
9. In elderly people the blood supply to the dermis and the activity of sweat glands both decrease. This combination makes the elderly less able to lose body heat and less able to cool themselves when exposed to high temperatures.
10. D

Level 3 Critical Thinking

1. When the body temperature increases, more blood flow is directed to the vessels of the skin. The red pigment in the blood gives the skin a redder-than-usual color and accounts for the person's flushed appearance. The skin is dry because the sweat glands are not producing sweat (avoids further dehydration). Without evaporation cooling, not enough heat is dissipated from the skin, the skin is warm, and the body temperature rises.
2. Lines of cleavage are important because a cut that runs parallel to a cleavage line closes more easily, whereas a cut made at right angles to a cleavage line will sever elastic fibers in the skin and thus be pulled open as they recoil. A parallel cut will also heal faster and with less scarring than a cut at right angles to cleavage lines.

3. The palms of the hands and the soles of the feet have a thicker epidermis and an extra layer in the epidermis, the stratum lucidum. This thicker layer slows down the rate of diffusion of the medication and significantly decreases its effectiveness.

CHAPTER 5

Concept Check

p. 117 1. If the ratio of collagen to hydroxyapatite in a bone increased, the bone would be more flexible and less strong.

p. 117 2. Concentric layers of bone around a central canal are indicative of an osteon or Haversian system. Osteons are found in compact bone. Since the ends (epiphyses) of long bones are primarily cancellous (spongy) bone, this sample most likely came from the shaft (diaphysis) of a long bone.

p. 117 3. Since osteoclasts function in breaking down or demineralizing bone, the bone would have less mineral content and as a result would be weaker.

p. 117 4. Fracture repair would be impeded.

p. 124 1. Long bones of the body, like the femur, have an epiphyseal cartilage separating the epiphysis from the diaphysis, as long as the bone is still growing in length. An x-ray would indicate whether the epiphyseal cartilage is still present. If it is, then growth is still occurring, and if not, the bone has reached its adult length.

p. 124 2. (1) In a fibrous connective tissue, osteoblasts secrete matrix components in an ossification center. (2) Growth occurs outward from the ossification center in small struts called spicules. (3) Over time, the bone assumes the shape of spongy bone; subsequent remodeling can produce compact bone.

p. 124 3. The diameter of a bone enlarges through appositional growth at the outer surface. In this process, periosteal cells differentiate into osteoblasts and contribute to the growth of the bone matrix.

p. 124 4. The epiphyseal cartilage is a relatively narrow band of cartilage separating the epiphysis from the diaphysis. It is located at the metaphysis. The continued growth of chondrocytes at the epiphyseal side and their subsequent replacement by bone at the diaphyseal side allow for an increase in the length of a developing bone.

p. 126 1. Bones increase in thickness in response to physical stress. One common type of stress that is applied to a bone is that produced by muscles. We would expect the bones of an athlete to be thicker after the addition of the extra muscle mass because of the greater stress that the muscle would apply to the bone.

p. 126 2. Vitamin D plays an important role in normal calcium metabolism by stimulating the absorption and transport of calcium and phosphate ions into the blood. Calcitonin inhibits osteoclasts and increases the rate of calcium loss in the urine. Parathyroid hormone stimulates osteoclasts and osteoblasts, increases calcium absorption at the intestines (this action requires another hormone, calcitriol), and decreases the rate of urinary calcium loss. Vitamins A and C are also important, as are growth hormone and sex hormones.

p. 126 3. In a 15-year-old, the rate of bone formation would be expected to exceed the rate of bone reabsorption, whereas in the 30-year-old, these rates would be expected to be approximately the same.

p. 130 1. Bone markings are often palpable at the surface; they provide reference points for orientation on associated soft tissues. For pathologists, bone markings can be used to estimate the size, weight, sex, and general appearance of an individual on the basis of incomplete remains.

p. 130 2. A sesamoid bone is usually round, small, and flat. Irregular bones may have complex shapes with short, flat, notched, or ridged surfaces.

p. 130 3. Sutural bones, also called *Wormian bones*, are small, flat, oddly shaped bones found between the flat bones of the skull in the suture line.

Chapter Review

Level 1 Reviewing Facts and Terms

1. B	**2.** B	**3.** A	**4.** B
5. B	**6.** A	**7.** A	**8.** A
9. A	**10.** B		

Level 2 Reviewing Concepts

1. C
2. A
3. In intramembranous ossification, bone develops from mesenchyme or fibrous connective tissue. In endochondral ossification, bone replaces an existing cartilage model.
4. At maturity, the rate of epiphyseal cartilage growth slows down, while the rate of osteoblast production increases, narrowing the region of the epiphyseal plate. When the plate disappears, the epiphysis and diaphysis of the bone grow together, and elongation stops.
5. Spongy bone is found where bones receive stresses from many directions. In the expanded ends of the long bones, the epiphyses, the trabeculae in the spongy bone are extensively cross-braced to withstand stress applied from different directions.
6. A bone grows in diameter by appositional growth, wherein the outer surface of the bone grows as cells of the periosteum differentiate into osteoblasts that contribute to the bone matrix. Eventually, these cells become surrounded by matrix and differentiate into osteocytes. Additionally, the bone matrix is removed from the inner surface by osteoclasts to expand the medullary cavity.
7. The final repair is slightly thicker and stronger than the original bone.
8. A fractured bone requires a good supply of calcium and phosphate to manufacture new matrix. Therefore, a diet that is low in these minerals will hinder the rate at which a broken bone heals.
9. A sesamoid bone is usually small, round, and flat. It develops inside tendons and is most often encountered near joints at the knee, the hands, and the feet. Wormian (sutural) bones are small, flat, oddly shaped bones found between the flat bones of the skull in the suture line.
10. Ossification is the process of replacing other tissues with bone. Calcification refers to the deposition of calcium salts within a tissue.

Level 3 Critical Thinking

1. At the fracture point, bleeding into the area creates a fracture hematoma. An internal callus forms as a network of spongy bone unites the inner surfaces, and an external callus of cartilage and bone stabilizes the outer edges. Together, these are seen as the enlargement. A swelling initially marks the location of the fracture. Over time this region will be remodeled, and little evidence of the fracture will remain.
2. In children the long bones are relatively supple and easily deformed in that the relative proportion of collagenous fibers to ossified calcium and phosphate salts is higher. This makes a greenstick fracture more common in children than in adults. With increased age the proportion of collagenous fibers to ossified calcium and phosphate salts decreases, making the bones more brittle, thereby decreasing the frequency of greenstick fractures.
3. The patient most likely suffered the fracture due to osteoporosis, which has an increased incidence in postmenopausal women. Osteoporosis is a reduction in bone mass that compromises normal bone function. Increased activity of osteoclasts is responsible for the reduction in bone mass. Therapy may include estrogen replacement treatment, dietary changes to elevate calcium levels in the blood, and exercise that stresses bones and stimulates osteoblast activity.

CHAPTER 6

Concept Check

p. 148 1. Each internal jugular vein passes through the jugular foramen, an opening between the occipital bone and the temporal bone.

p. 148 2. The sella turcica is located in the sphenoid, and it contains the pituitary gland.

p. 148 3. Nerve fibers to the olfactory bulb, which is involved with the sense of smell, pass through the cribriform plate from the nasal cavity. If the cribriform plate failed to form, these sensory nerves could not reach the olfactory bulbs and the sense of smell (olfaction) would be lost.

p. 148 4. Eight bones of the skull form the cranium, or "braincase": the frontal bone, parietal bones (2), occipital bone, temporal bones (2), sphenoid, and ethmoid.

p. 158 1. The 14 facial bones are the maxillae (2), zygomatic bones (2), nasal bones (2), lacrimal bones (2), inferior nasal conchae (2), palatine bones (2), vomer, and mandible. These bones protect and support the entrances to the digestive and respiratory tracts and provide extensive areas for skeletal muscle attachment.

p. 158 2. The paranasal sinuses function to make some of the skull bones lighter, to produce mucus, and to resonate during sound production.

p. 158 3. The orbital complex consists of portions of seven bones: the palatine, zygomatic, frontal, and lacrimal bones and the maxillae, sphenoid, and ethmoid.

p. 170 1. The odontoid process, or dens, is found on the second cervical vertebra, or axis, which is located in the neck.

p. 170 2. Improper compression of the chest during CPR could result in a fracture of the ribs or sternum, especially at the xiphoid process.

p. 170 3. The vertebral column is divided into cervical, thoracic, lumbar, sacral, and coccygeal regions. Distinguishing features are as follows: cervical—triangular foramen, bifid spinous process, transverse foramina; thoracic—round foramen, heart-shaped body, transverse facets, costal facets; lumbar—triangular foramen, oval-shaped, large robust body; sacral—five fused vertebrae; coccygeal—three to five small fused vertebrae.

p. 170 4. The spinal curves from superior to inferior are the: (1) cervical curve, (2) thoracic curve, (3) lumbar curve, and (4) sacral curve.

Chapter Review

Level 1 Reviewing Facts and Terms

1. B	**2.** E	**3.** H	**4.** J
5. I	**6.** A	**7.** D	**8.** G
9. F	**10.** C	**11.** D	**12.** D
13. A	**14.** A	**15.** D	**16.** A
17. A	**18.** C	**19.** A	**20.** D

Level 2 Reviewing Concepts

1. D
2. The design of the atlas is such that it provides more free space for the spinal cord than any other vertebra. The extra space helps ensure that the spinal cord is not impinged on during the large amount of motion that occurs here.
3. A prominent central depression between the wings of the sphenoid bone cradles the pituitary gland just inferior to the brain. This depression is called the hypophyseal fossa, and the bony enclosure is called the sella turcica.
4. The shifting of weight over the legs helps to move the center of gravity anteriorly, which will provide a more stable base for standing and walking.
5. The ligamentum nuchae is a large elastic ligament that begins at the vertebra prominens and extends cranially to an insertion along the external occipital crest. Along the way it attaches to the spinous processes of the other cervical vertebrae. When the head is held upright, this ligament is like the string on a bow, maintaining the cervical curvature without muscular effort.
6. The mucous membrane of the paranasal sinuses responds to environmental stress by accelerating the production of mucus. The mucus flushes irritants off the walls of the nasal cavities. A variety of stimuli produce this result, including sudden changes in temperature or humidity, irritating vapors, and bacterial or viral infections.
7. The body of the lumbar vertebrae is largest because these vertebrae bear the most weight.
8. The thick petrous portion of the temporal bone houses the inner ear structures that provide information about hearing and balance.
9. The foramina in the cribriform plate permit passage of the olfactory nerves, providing the sense of smell.

Level 3 Critical Thinking

1. Women in later stages of pregnancy develop lower back pain because of changes in the lumbar curvature of the spine. The increased mass of the pregnant uterus shifts the center of gravity, and to compensate for this the lumbar curvature is exaggerated and more of the body weight is supported by the lumbar region than normal. This results in sore muscles and lower back pain.
2. Jeff probably has a deviated septum as a result of his broken nose. In a deviated septum, the cartilaginous portion of the septum is bent where it joins the bone. This condition often blocks the drainage of one or more sinuses, with resulting sinus headaches, infections, and sinusitis.
3. As a result of a cold or the flu, the teeth in the maxillae ache and the front of the head feels heavy. An inflammation of the paranasal sinuses' mucous membranes increases the production of mucus. The maxillary sinuses are often involved because gravity does little to assist mucus drainage from these sinuses. Congestion increases and the patient experiences headaches, a feeling of pressure in facial bones, and an ache in the teeth rooted in the maxillae.
4. The facial features referred to as cheekbones are made by the anterior processes of the temporal bones which articulate with the posterior processes of the zygomatic bones inferior to the orbit. These features are prominent in the face as they act as protection for the orbits superior to them. The model complimented on the large appearance of her eyes would have to have larger than normal regions housing larger than normal eyeballs to truly have larger eyes. In all probability, the appearance of her photogenic eyes has to do with the arrangement of her soft tissue structures and makeup more than because of an unusual arrangement of the bones of the face.

CHAPTER 7

Concept Check

p. 186 1. The clavicle attaches the scapula to the sternum and thus restricts the scapula's range of movement. If the clavicle is broken, the scapula will have a greater range of movement and will be less stable.

p. 186 2. The radius is in a lateral position when the forearm is in the anatomical position.

p. 186 3. The olecranon is the point of the elbow. During extension of the elbow, the olecranon swings into the olecranon fossa on the posterior surface of the humerus to prevent overextension.

p. 186 4. The clavicle articulates with the manubrium of the sternum, and this provides the only direct connection between the pectoral girdle and the axial skeleton.

p. 200 1. The three bones that make up the hip bone are the ilium, ischium, and pubic bones.

p. 200 2. Although the fibula is not part of the knee joint and does not bear weight, it is an important point of attachment for many leg muscles. When the fibula is fractured, these muscles cannot function properly to move the leg, and walking is difficult and painful. The fibula also helps stabilize the ankle joint.

p. 200 3. Mark has most likely fractured his calcaneus (heel bone).

p. 200 4. There are six differences that are adaptations for childbearing: an enlarged pelvic outlet; less curvature on the sacrum and coccyx, which in the male arc anteriorly into the pelvic outlet; a wider, more circular pelvic inlet; a relatively broad, low pelvis; ilia that project farther laterally, but do not extend as far superior to the sacrum; and a broader pubic arch, with the inferior angle between the pubic bones greater than 100°.

p. 200 5. During dorsiflexion, as when "digging in the heels," all of the body weight rests on the calcaneus. During plantar flexion and "standing on tiptoe," the talus and calcaneus transfer the weight to the metatarsal bones and phalanges through more anterior tarsal bones.

Chapter Review

Level 1 Reviewing Facts and Terms

1. B	**2.** E	**3.** G	**4.** J
5. C	**6.** I	**7.** F	**8.** A
9. H	**10.** D	**11.** B	**12.** C
13. C	**14.** A	**15.** D	**16.** B
17. C	**18.** C	**19.** C	**20.** C

Level 2 Reviewing Concepts

1. D
2. A
3. A
4. To determine the age of a skeleton, one would consider some or all of the following: the fusion of the epiphyseal plates, the amount of mineral content, the size and roughness of bone markings, teeth, bone mass of the mandible, and intervertebral disc size.
5. Weight transfer occurs along the longitudinal arch of the foot. Ligaments and tendons maintain this arch by tying the calcaneus to the distal portions of the metatarsal bones. The lateral, calcaneal side of the foot carries most of the weight of the body while standing normally. This portion of the arch has less curvature than the medial, talar portion.
6. Fractures of the medial portion of the clavicle are common because a fall on the palm of the hand of an outstretched upper limb produces compressive forces that are conducted to the clavicle and its articulation with the manubrium.
7. The tibia is part of the knee joint and is involved in the transfer of weight to the ankle and foot. The fibula is excluded from the knee joint and does not transfer weight to the ankle and foot.

8. The olecranon of the ulna is the point of the elbow. During extreme extension, this process swings into the olecranon fossa on the posterior surface of the humerus to prevent overextension of the forearm relative to the arm.
9. Body weight is passed to the metatarsal bones through the cuboid and the cuneiform bones.

Level 3 Critical Thinking

1. In osteoporosis, a decrease in the calcium content of the body leads to bones that are weak and brittle. Since the hip joint and leg bones must support the weight of the body, any weakening of these bones may result in insufficient strength to support the body mass, and as a result the bone will break under the great weight. The shoulder joint is not a load-bearing joint and is not subject to the same great stresses or strong muscle contractions as the hip joint. As a result, breaks in the bones of this joint occur less frequently.
2. The general appearance of the pelvis, the shape of the pelvic inlet, the depth of the iliac fossa, the characteristics of the ilium, the angle inferior to the pubic symphysis, the position of the acetabulum, the shape of the obturator foramen, and the characteristics of the ischium are all important in determining an individual's sex from a skeleton. Age can be determined by the size, degree of mineralization, and various markings on the bone. The individual's general appearance can be reconstructed by looking at the markings where muscles attach to the bones. This can indicate the size and shape of the muscles and thus the individual.
3. Many cranial characteristics would reveal the sex of the individual, but there are also characteristics in other skeletal elements, such as the robusticity of the bones, the angles at which the pubic bones meet, the width of the pelvis, the angles of the femurs, and many more.
4. The condition known as flatfeet is due to a lower-than-normal longitudinal arch in the foot. A weakness in the ligaments and tendons that attach the calcaneus to the distal ends of the metatarsals would most likely contribute to this condition.

CHAPTER 8

Concept Check

p. 208 1. No relative movement is permitted at a synarthrosis, whereas an amphiarthrosis permits slight movement.

p. 208 2. The main advantage is that it permits a broad range of motion without significant friction.

p. 208 3. Friction reduction and the distribution of dissolved gases, nutrients, and waste products.

p. 208 4. Bursae are pockets lined by a synovial membrane and filled with synovial fluid. They reduce friction between adjacent structures, such as tendons and bones or muscles.

p. 212 1. Originally, the joint is a type of syndesmosis. When the bones fuse, the bones along the suture represent a synostosis.

p. 212 2. (a) abduction, (b) supination, (c) flexion.

p. 221 1. Since the subscapular bursa is located in the shoulder joint, an inflammation of this structure (bursitis) would be found in the tennis player. The condition is associated with repetitive motion that occurs at the shoulder, such as swinging a tennis racket. The jogger would be more at risk for injuries to the knee joint.

p. 221 2. Mary has most likely fractured her ulna.

p. 228 1. The iliofemoral, pubofemoral, and ischiofemoral ligaments would all be found in the hip joint.

p. 228 2. Damage to the menisci in the knee joint would result in a decrease in the joint's stability. The individual would have a harder time locking the knee in place while standing and would have to use muscular contractions to stabilize the joint. When standing for long periods, the muscles would fatigue and the knee would "give out." We would also expect the individual to experience pain.

p. 228 3. The patellar ligament provides support to the anterior surface of the knee joint. Damage to the patellar ligament would affect this support.

p. 228 4. The tibial collateral ligament reinforces the medial surface of the knee joint, and the fibular collateral ligament reinforces the lateral surface. These ligaments tighten only at full extension, and in this position they act to stabilize the joint.

Chapter Review

Level 1 Reviewing Facts and Terms

1. I	2. D	3. H	4. C
5. G	6. B	7. F	8. A
9. E	10. D	11. D	12. B
13. C	14. D	15. B	16. A
17. C	18. B	19. A	20. A

Level 2 Reviewing Concepts

1. A
2. A joint cannot be both highly mobile and very strong. The greater the range of motion at a joint, the weaker it becomes, and vice versa. For example, a synarthrosis, which is the strongest type of joint, does not permit any movement.
3. Prior to fusion, the two parts of a single bone are united by a line of cartilage and are called a synchondrosis. Once the cartilaginous plate is obliterated, there is no more joint, and it becomes an immovable synostosis.
4. The tibiotalar joint, or ankle joint, involves the distal articular surface of the tibia, including the medial malleolus, the lateral malleolus of the fibula, and the trochlea and lateral articular facets of the talus. The malleoli, supported by ligaments of the ankle joint (the medial deltoid ligament and the three lateral ligaments) and associated fat pads, prevent the ankle bones from sliding from side to side.
5. Articular cartilages cover articulating surfaces of bones. They resemble hyaline cartilages elsewhere in the body, but they have no perichondrium, and the matrix contains more water than other cartilages have.
6. Factors that limit the range of movement of a joint include accessory ligaments and collagen fibers of the joint capsule, the shapes of the articulating surfaces that allow movement in some directions while preventing it in others, the tension in the tendons attached to the articulating bones, and the bulk of the muscles surrounding the joint.
7. The joint capsule that surrounds the entire synovial joint is continuous with the periostea of the articulating bones. Accessory ligaments are localized thickenings of the capsule. Extracapsular ligaments are on the outside of the capsule; intracapsular ligaments are found inside the capsule. In the humeroulnar joint, the capsule is reinforced by strong ligaments. The radial collateral ligament stabilizes the lateral surface of the joint. The annular ligament binds the proximal radial head to the ulna. The medial surface of the joint is stabilized by the ulnar collateral ligament.
8. The edges of the bones are interlocked and bound together at the suture by dense connective tissue. A different type of synarthrosis binds each tooth to the surrounding bony socket. This fibrous connection is the periodontal ligament.
9. The movement of the wrist and hand from palm-facing-front to palm-facing-back is called pronation. Circumduction is a special type of angular motion that encompasses all types of angular motion: flexion, extension, adduction, and abduction.
10. As one ages, the water content of the nucleus pulposus within each disc decreases. Loss of water by the discs causes shortening of the vertebral column.

Level 3 Critical Thinking

1. The term *whiplash* is used to describe an injury wherein the body suddenly changes position, as in a fall or during rapid acceleration or deceleration. The balancing muscles are not strong enough to stabilize the head. A dangerous partial or complete dislocation of the cervical vertebrae can result, with injury to muscles and ligaments and potential injury to the spinal cord. It is called whiplash because the movement of the head resembles the cracking of a whip.
2. In a sprain, a ligament is stretched to the point where some of the collagen fibers are torn. The ligament remains functional, and the structure and stability of the joint are not affected. In a more serious incident, the entire ligament may be torn apart, simply termed a torn ligament, or the connection between the ligament and the malleolus may be so strong that the bone breaks before the ligament. In general, a broken bone heals more quickly and effectively than a torn ligament does. A dislocation often accompanies such injuries.
3. When the knee is flexed, it is able to move in response to a hit from the inside or outside (medial or lateral surfaces). However, when the knee is "planted," the knee is in the

locked position. In this position the medial and lateral collateral ligaments and the anterior cruciate ligaments are taut, thereby increasing their chance of injury.

CHAPTER 9

Concept Check

p. 239 1. Skeletal muscle tissue moves the body by pulling on bones of the skeleton. The cardiac muscle tissue of the heart pushes blood through the arteries and veins of the cardiovascular system. Smooth muscle tissues push fluids and solids along the digestive tract and perform varied functions in other systems.

p. 239 2. The perimysium is the connective tissue partition that separates adjacent fasciculi in a skeletal muscle. The perimysium contains blood vessels and nerves that supply each individual fascicle.

p. 239 3. Tendons are collagenous bands that connect skeletal muscle to the skeleton. Aponeuroses are thick, flattened tendinous sheets.

p. 239 4. A myoneural junction (also called a neuromuscular synapse) is the site where the axon meets the muscle sarcolemma, or cell membrane. A motor end plate is the region of the sarcolemma at the neuromuscular synapse.

p. 244 1. Skeletal muscle appears striated when viewed under the microscope because it is composed of the myofilaments actin and myosin, which are arranged in such a way as to produce a banded appearance in the muscle.

p. 244 2. A myofibril is a cylindrical collection of myofilaments within a cardiac or skeletal muscle cell.

p. 244 3. Myofilaments consist primarily of actin and myosin, along with accessory proteins of the thin filament (tropomyosin and troponin).

p. 244 4. The functional unit of skeletal muscle is the sarcomere.

p. 244 5. The proteins tropomyosin and troponin help regulate the actin and myosin interactions.

p. 248 1. During contraction, the width of the A band remains the same and the I band gets smaller.

p. 248 2. Stimulation of a motor neuron triggers the release of chemicals at the neuromuscular synapse, which alter the transmembrane potential at the sarcolemma. This change sweeps across the surface of the sarcolemma and into the T tubules. The change in the transmembrane potential of the T tubules triggers the release of calcium ions by the sarcoplasmic reticulum. This release initiates the contraction, which proceeds as myosin heads go through repeated cycles of attach-pivot-detach-return.

p. 248 3. Terminal cisternae are expanded chambers of the sarcoplasmic reticulum—they store calcium ions, which are required to initiate contractile activities within skeletal muscle cells. Transverse tubules are sandwiched between terminal cisternae. A transverse tubule is an invagination of the sarcolemma, which conducts the stimulation into the interior of the cell. On arrival, it causes the release of calcium ions from the terminal cisternae, and this results in a muscle contraction.

p. 248 4. A neurotransmitter is a chemical compound released by one neuron to affect the transmembrane potential of another.

p. 251 1. The sprinter requires large amounts of energy for a relatively short burst of activity. To supply this demand for energy, the muscles switch to anaerobic metabolism. Anaerobic metabolism is not as efficient in producing energy as is aerobic metabolism, and the process also produces acidic waste products. The combination of less energy and the waste products contributes to fatigue. Marathon runners, on the other hand, derive most of their energy from aerobic metabolism, which is more efficient and does not produce the level of waste products that anaerobic metabolism does.

p. 251 2. Individuals who are naturally better at endurance types of activities such as cycling or marathon running have a higher percentage of slow-twitch muscle fibers, which are physiologically better adapted to this type of activity than the fast-twitch fibers, which are less vascular and fatigue faster.

p. 251 3. It depends on the number of branches in the motor neurons. A lesser number of branches (collaterals) results in the activation in only a few motor neurons.

p. 251 4. Recruitment is the smooth but steady increase in muscular tension produced by increasing the number of active motor units.

p. 256 1. This is a long muscle that flexes the joints of the finger.

p. 256 2. Each muscle begins at an origin, which typically remains stationary, and ends at an insertion, which is the part of the muscle that moves during a contraction.

p. 256 3. A synergist contracts to assist the prime mover in performing a specific action.

p. 256 4. *Major* is used to describe muscles that are bigger, whereas *minor* is used to describe muscles that are smaller.

Chapter Review

Level 1 Reviewing Facts and Terms

1. C	**2.** A	**3.** B	**4.** C
5. C	**6.** A	**7.** C	**8.** D
9. B	**10.** C		

Level 2 Reviewing Concepts

1. C
2. D
3. C
4. C
5. *Rectus* means "straight"; these muscles are parallel muscles whose fibers generally run along the long axis of the body. Muscles that are visible at the body surface are often called *externus*. A muscle whose name includes *flexor* indicates that flexion is a primary function of the muscle. The name *trapezius* indicates the shape of the muscle.
6. A nerve impulse arrives at the terminal bouton of the neuromuscular synapse and causes acetylcholine to be released into the synaptic cleft. The acetylcholine released then binds to receptors on the sarcolemma surface, initiating a change in the local transmembrane potential. This change results in the generation of electrical signals that sweep over the surface of the sarcolemma.
7. Connective tissues bind and attach skeletal muscles to other structures. There are three concentric layers of connective tissue. The outer layer, or epimysium, surrounds the entire muscle. The middle layer, or perimysium, divides the muscle into a series of internal compartments, each containing a bundle of muscle fibers. Each compartment is called a fascicle. The inner layer, or endomysium, surrounds each skeletal muscle fiber and binds each fiber to its neighbors.
8. A motor unit with 1500 fibers would be involved in powerful, gross movements. The greater the number of fibers in a motor unit, the more powerful the contraction, and the less fine control exhibited by the motor unit.
9. In the zone of overlap, the thin filaments pass between the thick filaments. It is in this region that interaction between thick and thin filaments occurs to form cross-bridges so that contraction may occur and tension may be generated.

Level 3 Critical Thinking

1. If a muscle is not stimulated by a motor neuron on a regular basis, the muscle will lose tone and mass and become weak (atrophy). During the time that Tom's leg was immobilized, it did not receive sufficient stimulation to maintain proper tone. It will take a while for the muscle to build back up to support his weight.
2. Weight lifting requires anaerobic endurance. The students would want to develop fast fibers for short-term maximum strength. This could be achieved by engaging in activities that involve frequent, brief but intensive workouts, such as with progressive-resistance machines. Repeated exhaustive stimulation will help the fast fibers develop more mitochondria and a higher concentration of glycolytic enzymes, as well as increase the size and strength of the muscle (hypertrophy).
3. Muscle biopsies are used to determine the relative percentage of red and white muscle fibers within the leg muscles. An individual with a higher percentage of white muscles has a greater chance of being a good sprinter than an individual with a higher percentage of red muscle. Conversely, an individual with a high percentage of red muscle has a greater chance of being a good distance runner than an individual with a higher percentage of white muscle.

CHAPTER 10

Concept Check

p. 271 1. The muscles of facial expression originate on the surface of the skull.

p. 271 2. The muscles of mastication move the mandible at the temporomandibular joint during chewing.

p. 271 3. The contraction of the extra-ocular muscles causes the eye to look up, look down, rotate laterally, rotate medially, roll and look up to the side, or roll and look down to the side.

p. 271 4. The pharyngeal muscles are important in the initiation of swallowing.

p. 281 1. Damage to the external intercostal muscles would interfere with the process of breathing.

p. 281 2. A blow to the rectus abdominis muscle would cause the muscle to contract forcefully, resulting in flexion of the torso. In other words, you would "double up."

p. 281 3. The muscles of the pelvic diaphragm have the following functions: (1) support the organs of the pelvic cavity, (2) flex the joints of the sacrum and coccyx, and (3) control the movement of materials through the urethra and anus.

p. 281 4. The diaphragm is a major muscle of respiration.

Chapter Review

Level 1 Reviewing Facts and Terms

1. H	**2.** D	**3.** A	**4.** I
5. F	**6.** B	**7.** J	**8.** E
9. C	**10.** G	**11.** B	**12.** B
13. A	**14.** B	**15.** C	**16.** A
17. C	**18.** B	**19.** A	**20.** D

Level 2 Reviewing Concepts

1. C
2. A
3. B
4. C
5. In addition to using the flexor muscles, the trunk can be assisted to move forward by gravity. The bulk of the mass of the body is anterior to the vertebral column, making the movement toward the anterior easier to make.
6. All of the extrinsic and intrinsic muscles of the tongue are involved in different aspects of the swallowing process. These muscles control the position of the food bolus on the tongue and position it correctly for swallowing to be initiated.
7. The contraction of the internal oblique effects the following activities: compresses the abdomen; depresses the ribs; and flexes, bends to the side, or rotates the spine.
8. The anterior muscles of the neck control the position of the larynx, depress the mandible, tense the floor of the mouth, and provide a stable foundation for muscles of the tongue and pharynx.
9. The diaphragm is a major muscle of respiration. It is included in the axial musculature because it is developmentally linked to the other muscles of the chest wall.
10. The muscles include the muscles of the erector spinae and multifidus groups, as well as the sternocleidomastoid. These muscles control the position of the head, both maintaining posture involuntarily and moving the head voluntarily.

Level 3 Critical Thinking

1. The muscles of the anal triangle form the posterior aspect of the perineum, a structure that has boundaries established by the inferior margins of the pelvis. A muscular sheet, the pelvic diaphragm, forms the foundation of the anal triangle and extends anteriorly superior to the urogenital diaphragm to attach anteriorly to the posterior aspect of the pubic symphysis. A sphincter muscle in this region surrounds the opening to the anus.
2. The contraction of the frontalis and procerus muscles cause Mary to raise her eyebrows and wrinkle her forehead (frontalis), and to move her nose and change the position and shape of the nostrils. The raising of the eyebrows and flaring of the nostrils show that she has some concern with this meeting.

CHAPTER 11

Concept Check

p. 290 1. The rotator cuff muscles include the supraspinatus, infraspinatus, subscapularis, and teres minor muscles. The tendons of these muscles help enclose and stabilize the shoulder joint.

p. 290 2. The fan-shaped muscle that inserts along the anterior margin of the vertebral border of the scapula is the serratus anterior muscle.

p. 290 3. The deltoid muscle is the major abductor at the shoulder joint.

p. 290 4. The teres major muscle and the latissimus dorsi muscle both produce extension, adduction, and medial rotation at the shoulder.

p. 297 1. Injury to the flexor carpi ulnaris muscle would prevent flexion and adduction at the wrist.

p. 297 2. The pronator teres and the supinator muscles arise on both the humerus and forearm. They rotate the radius without flexing or extending the elbow.

p. 297 3. The tendons that cross the dorsal and ventral surfaces of the wrist pass through tendon sheaths, elongated bursae that reduce friction.

p. 297 4. The thickened fascia of the forearm on the posterior surface of the wrist is the extensor retinaculum.

p. 314 1. Injury to the obturator muscles would interfere with your ability to perform lateral rotation at the hip.

p. 314 2. The hamstring refers to a group of three muscles that collectively function in flexing the knee. These muscles are the biceps femoris, semimembranosus, and semitendinosus muscles.

p. 314 3. The pectineus and the gracilis muscles belong to the adductor group of muscles that move the thigh.

p. 314 4. Collectively, knee extensors are known as the quadriceps femoris.

Chapter Review

Level 1 Reviewing Facts and Terms

1. C	**2.** K	**3.** I	**4.** G
5. J	**6.** D	**7.** F	**8.** B
9. E	**10.** H	**11.** A	**12.** B
13. B	**14.** B	**15.** D	**16.** D

Level 2 Reviewing Concepts

1. C
2. D
3. D
4. B
5. The biceps brachii exerts actions on the shoulder joint (flexion), elbow joint (flexion), and radioulnar joint (supination, also termed lateral or external rotation).
6. The muscle that becomes greatly enlarged in ballet dancers because of the need to flex and abduct the hip and that supports the knee laterally is the tensor fascia latae.
7. The muscles that are most involved are the adductors of the thigh, which are stretched as the leg is supported at the hip and calcaneal tendon. Other muscles that may also be stretched are the hamstring group at the rear of the thigh, especially if the dancer leans forward over the barre.
8. The intrinsic muscles of the hand are involved in fine control of hand and finger movement.
9. Both the tensor fasciae latae and the gluteus maximus pull on the iliotibial tract, a band of collagen fibers that provides a lateral brace for the knee. It is especially important when a person balances on one foot.
10. These sheets of connective tissue that encircle the wrist and ankle joint act as a bracelet and anklet and allow the tendons on the long hand and foot extensors and flexors to pass internal to them. These structures hold the tendons close to the surface of the limb and effectively change the position from which the tendons act to change the position of the hand and the foot.

Level 3 Critical Thinking

1. The intrinsic muscles of the hand allow use of the precision grip to make the small movements that are used to make lettering or precise marks with the writing implement. However, the large muscles of the arm maintain the proper position of the arm for writing or drawing.
2. Jerry probably injured the semimembranosus and/or the semitendinosus, since both of these muscles are primarily involved in the action with which he is having difficulty.
3. Although the pectoralis muscle is located across the chest, it inserts on the greater tubercle of the humerus, the large bone of the arm. When the muscle contracts, it contributes

to flexion, adduction, and medial rotation of the humerus at the shoulder joint. All of these arm movements would be partly impaired if the muscle were damaged.

CHAPTER 13

Concept Check

p. 349 1. The two anatomical subdivisions of the nervous system are the central nervous system and the peripheral nervous system.

p. 349 2. The supporting cells in neural tissue are called either glial cells or neuroglia.

p. 349 3. Astrocytes help maintain the blood–brain barrier.

p. 349 4. Oligodendrocytes produce a membranous coating that wraps around axons and is called myelin.

p. 349 5. In the peripheral nervous system, Schwann cells form a myelin covering around axons.

p. 352 1. Sensory neurons of the peripheral nervous system are usually pseudounipolar; thus, this tissue is most likely associated with a sensory organ.

p. 352 2. Microglial cells are small phagocytic cells that are found in increased numbers in damaged and diseased areas of the CNS.

p. 353 1. Cutting the axon of a neuron prevents the transmission of the nerve impulse along the length of the axon.

p. 353 2. Myelinated fibers conduct action potentials much faster than nonmyelinated fibers, so the axon conducting at 50 m/s is myelinated.

p. 353 3. Excitability is the ability of a cell membrane to conduct electrical impulses.

p. 353 4. The conducted changes in the transmembrane potential are called action potentials.

p. 357 1. A synapse may be either vesicular, involving a neurotransmitter substance, or nonvesicular, with gap junctions providing direct physical contact between the cells.

p. 357 2. Excitatory synapses promote the generation of nerve impulses in the postsynaptic cell, whereas inhibitory synapses oppose the generation of nerve impulses in the postsynaptic cell.

p. 357 3. Divergence is the spread of information from one neuron to several neurons, or from one pool to multiple pools. Convergence occurs when several neurons synapse on the same postsynaptic neuron, or several neuronal pools synapse on one neuronal pool.

p. 357 4. A center is a collection of neuron cell bodies with a common function. Bundles of axons in the CNS that share common origins, destinations, and functions are called tracts. The centers and tracts that link the brain with the rest of the body are called pathways.

Chapter Review

Level 1 Reviewing Facts and Terms

1. C	**2.** J	**3.** H	**4.** E
5. B	**6.** I	**7.** F	**8.** D
9. A	**10.** G	**11.** B	**12.** D
13. D	**14.** A	**15.** C	**16.** B
17. B	**18.** D	**19.** C	**20.** B

Level 2 Reviewing Concepts

1. D
2. B
3. C
4. Collaterals enable a single neuron to communicate with several other cells at the same time.
5. Exteroceptors provide information about the external environment in the form of touch, temperature, pressure, sight, smell, hearing, and taste. Interoceptors monitor the digestive, respiratory, cardiovascular, urinary, and reproductive systems and provide sensations of taste, deep pressure, and pain.
6. The blood–brain barrier is needed to isolate neural tissue from the general circulation because hormones or other chemicals normally present in the blood could have disruptive effects on neuron function.
7. The CNS is responsible for integrating, processing, and coordinating sensory data and motor commands. It is also the seat of higher functions, such as intelligence, memory, learning, and emotion. The PNS provides sensory information to the CNS and carries motor commands to peripheral tissues and systems.
8. The somatic nervous system controls skeletal muscle contractions, which may be voluntary or involuntary. The autonomic nervous system regulates smooth muscle, cardiac muscle, and glandular activity, usually outside our conscious awareness or control.
9. A nonvesicular synapse is a more efficient carrier of impulses than is a vesicular synapse because the two cells are linked by gap junctions, and they function as if they shared a common plasmalemma. However, vesicular synapses are more versatile because the neuron membrane can be influenced by excitatory and inhibitory stimuli simultaneously. The cell membrane at an nonvesicular synapse simply passes the signal from one cell to another, whereas a vesicular synapse integrates information arriving across multiple synapses.
10. In serial processing, information may be relayed in a stepwise sequence, from one neuron to another or from one neuronal pool to the next. Parallel processing occurs when several neurons or neuronal pools are processing the same information at one time.

Level 3 Critical Thinking

1. Action potentials travel faster along myelinated fibers than along unmyelinated fibers. Destruction of the myelin sheath slows the time it takes for motor neurons to communicate with their effector muscles. This delay in response results in varying degrees of uncoordinated muscle activity. The situation is very similar to that of a newborn; the infant cannot control its arms and legs very well because the myelin sheaths are still being laid down for the first year. Since not all motor neurons to the same muscle may be demyelinated to the same degree, some fibers are slow to respond while others respond normally, producing contractions that are erratic and poorly controlled.
2. In the process known as Wallerian degeneration, the axons distal to the injury site deteriorate, and macrophages migrate in to phagocytize the debris. The Schwann cells in the area divide and form a solid cellular cord that follows the path of the original axon. As the neuron recovers, its axon grows into the injury site, and the Schwann cells wrap around it. If the axon continues to grow into the periphery alongside the appropriate cord of Schwann cells, it may eventually reestablish normal synaptic contacts. If it stops growing or wanders off in some new direction, normal function will not return.
3. No, Eve's father is not totally correct. In order to treat Eve's disease, any medication utilized will have to pass through the blood–brain barrier. High doses of antibiotics will be needed in order to facilitate their passage through the blood–brain barrier.

CHAPTER 14

Concept Check

p. 365 1. The ventral root of a spinal nerve is composed of visceral and somatic motor fibers. Damage to this root would interfere with motor functions.

p. 365 2. The cerebrospinal fluid that surrounds the spinal cord is found in the subarachnoid space, which lies between the arachnoid mater and the pia mater.

p. 365 3. The two spinal enlargements are the cervical enlargement and the lumbosacral enlargement. These regions are increased in size because of the increase in neuron cell bodies in the gray matter here. These segments of the spinal cord are concerned with innervation of the limbs.

p. 365 4. Each dorsal root ganglion contains cell bodies of sensory neurons.

p. 369 1. Since the poliovirus would be located in the somatic motor neurons, we would find it in the anterior gray horns of the spinal cord where the cell bodies of these neurons are located.

p. 369 2. White matter is organized in columns (anterior, lateral, and posterior) around the periphery of the spinal cord.

p. 369 3. Projections of gray matter toward the surface of the spinal cord are called horns.

p. 369 4. Ascending tracts carry sensory information toward the brain. Descending tracts carry motor commands into the spinal cord.

p. 376 1. The phrenic nerves that innervate the diaphragm originate in the cervical plexus. Damage to this plexus or, more specifically, to the phrenic nerves, would greatly interfere with the ability to breathe and possibly result in death by suffocation.

p. 376 2. The outermost layer is called the epineurium. It surrounds the entire nerve. The middle layer, or perineurium, divides the nerve into a series of compartments that contain bundles of axons. A single bundle is called a fascicle. The endoneurium is the innermost layer, and it surrounds individual axons.

p. 376 3. The white and gray rami connect the spinal nerve to a nearby autonomic ganglion. The white ramus carries preganglionic axons that are myelinated from the nerve to the ganglion. The gray ramus carries postganglionic, unmyelinated axons from the ganglion back to the spinal nerve.

p. 376 4. The brachial plexus may have been damaged.

p. 383 1. A reflex is an immediate, involuntary motor response to a specific stimulus.

p. 383 2. (1) Arrival of a stimulus and activation of a receptor. (2) Relay of information to the CNS. (3) Information processing. (4) Activation of a motor neuron in the CNS. (5) Response of a peripheral effector.

p. 383 3. A monosynaptic reflex has a sensory neuron synapsing directly on a motor neuron. A polysynaptic reflex has more than one synapse between stimulus and response.

p. 383 4. Reflexes are classified according to (1) their development, (2) the site where information processing occurs, (3) the nature of the resulting motor response, or (4) the complexity of the neural circuit involved.

Chapter Review

Level 1 Reviewing Facts and Terms

1. D	**2.** I	**3.** A	**4.** G
5. B	**6.** C	**7.** J	**8.** F
9. H	**10.** E	**11.** B	**12.** C
13. C	**14.** D	**15.** D	**16.** D
17. B	**18.** D	**19.** A	**20.** B

Level 2 Reviewing Concepts

1. D
2. D
3. A
4. The meninges provide a tough protective covering, longitudinal physical stability, and a space for shock-absorbing fluid.
5. A reflex is an immediate involuntary response, whereas voluntary motor movement is under conscious control and is voluntary.
6. Incoming sensory information would be disrupted.
7. Transmission of information between neurons at synapses takes a finite amount of time. Thus, the more synapses in a reflex, the longer the delay between the stimulus and responses. In a monosynaptic reflex, there is only one synapse. It has the most rapid response time. In a polysynaptic reflex, there are multiple synapses, each contributing to the overall delay.
8. In the cervical region, the first pair of spinal nerves, C_1, exits between the skull and the first cervical vertebra. Thereafter, a numbered cervical spinal nerve exits after each cervical vertebra. For instance, nerve C_2 exits after vertebra C_1, nerve C_3 exits after vertebra C_2, and so on until nerve C_8 exits after vertebra C_7.
9. The denticulate ligaments prevent side-to-side movements of the spinal cord.
10. The adult spinal cord extends only as far as vertebra L_1 or L_2. Inferior to this point in the vertebral foramen, the meningeal layers enclose the relatively sturdy components of the cauda equina and a significant quantity of CSF.

Level 3 Critical Thinking

1. The rectus abdominis muscle is always retracted laterally, as it is innervated by T_7–T_{12}, entering through the posterior aspect along the lateral margin. If the muscle were to be retracted medially, the nerves would be torn, thereby paralyzing the muscle.
2. The part of the cord that is most likely compressed is an ascending tract.
3. The neurons for the anterior horn of the spinal cord are somatic motor neurons that direct the activity of skeletal muscles. The lumbar segments of the spinal cord control the skeletal muscles that are involved with the control of the muscles of the hip and lower limb. As a result of the injury, Karen would have poor control of most lower limb muscles, a problem with walking (if she could walk at all), and (if she could stand) problems maintaining balance.

CHAPTER 15

Concept Check

p. 389 1. The six major divisions in the adult brain are the cerebrum; the diencephalon; the mesencephalon or midbrain; the pons; the cerebellum; and the medulla oblongata.

p. 389 2. The three major structures of the brain stem are the mesencephalon, the pons, and the medulla oblongata.

p. 389 3. The ventricles are fluid-filled chambers inside the telencephalon, the diencephalon, the metencephalon, and the superior portion of the myelencephalon. The ventricles are lined by ependymal cells.

p. 389 4. The secondary brain vesicles and the brain regions associated with each at birth are the telencephalon (cerebrum), diencephalon (epithalamus, thalamus, and hypothalamus), mesencephalon (midbrain), metencephalon (cerebellum and pons), and myelencephalon (medulla oblongata).

p. 395 1. The four extensions of the dura mater are the falx cerebri, tentorium cerebelli, falx cerebelli, and diaphragma sellae.

p. 395 2. The pia mater is a highly vascular membrane composed primarily of areolar connective tissue. It acts as a floor to support the large cerebral blood vessels as they branch over the surface of the brain, invading the neural contours to supply superficial areas of neural cortex.

p. 395 3. The blood–brain barrier functions to isolate the CNS from the general circulation.

p. 395 4. Cerebrospinal fluid (CSF) has several functions: cushioning delicate neural structures; supporting the brain; and transporting nutrients, chemical messengers, and waste products. CSF is produced by the choroid plexus, a combination of specialized ependymal cells and permeable capillaries in the ventricle lining.

p. 404 1. The frontal lobe contains the primary motor cortex for voluntary muscular activities. Additionally, it contains the prefrontal cortex, which integrates information and performs abstract intellectual functions. The parietal lobe contains the primary sensory cortex, which receives somatic sensory information. The occipital lobe contains the visual cortex for conscious perception of visual stimuli. The temporal lobe contains the auditory cortex and olfactory cortex for the conscious perception of auditory and olfactory stimuli.

p. 404 2. Gyri are the elevated ridges on the surface of the cerebrum. Sulci are the shallow depressions that separate neighboring gyri.

p. 404 3. The three major groups of axons in the central white matter are (1) association fibers, tracts that interconnect areas of neural cortex within a single cerebral hemisphere; (2) commissural fibers, tracts that connect the two cerebral hemispheres; and (3) projection fibers, tracts that link the cerebrum with other regions of the brain and spinal cord.

p. 410 1. Changes in body temperature would stimulate the preoptic area of the hypothalamus, a division of the diencephalon.

p. 410 2. The thalamus coordinates somatic motor activities at the conscious and subconscious levels.

p. 410 3. The posterior epithalamus contains the pineal gland, which secretes melatonin.

p. 410 4. The hypothalamus produces and secretes two hormones: antidiuretic hormone, produced by the supraoptic nucleus, and oxytocin, produced by the paraventricular nucleus.

p. 415 1. The vermis and arbor vitae are structures associated with the cerebellum.

p. 415 2. The medulla oblongata is small, but it contains many vital reflex centers, including those that control breathing and regulate the heart and blood pressure. Damage to the medulla oblongata can result in a cessation of breathing, or changes in heart rate and blood pressure that are incompatible with life. In contrast, damage to a small region of the cerebrum may affect a specific area/function. It should not be fatal.

p. 415 3. These nuclei, collectively called the corpora quadrigemina, are relay stations concerned with the processing of visual and auditory sensations.

p. 415 4. Voluntary movements become hesitant and jerky. A continual tremor may occur during rest.

p. 427 1. The cranial nerve responsible for tongue movements is the hypoglossal nerve.

p. 427 2. Since the abducens (N VI) controls lateral movements of the eyes, we would expect an individual with damage to this nerve to be unable to move the eyes laterally.

p. 427 3. The vestibulocochlear nerve (N VIII) is concerned with balance. The branch would be the vestibular branch.

p. 427 4. The facial nerve (N VII) is involved with the sensory detection of taste.

Chapter Review

Level 1 Reviewing Facts and Terms

1. C	**2.** H	**3.** J	**4.** F
5. E	**6.** A	**7.** D	**8.** B
9. G	**10.** I	**11.** B	**12.** A
13. D	**14.** D	**15.** A	**16.** B
17. D	**18.** C	**19.** D	**20.** D

Level 2 Reviewing Concepts

1. B
2. A
3. B
4. Damage would have occurred in the premotor cortex of the frontal lobe.
5. Impulses from proprioceptors must pass through the olivary nuclei on their way to the cerebellum.
6. The nuclei involved in the coordinated movement of the head in the direction of a loud noise are the inferior colliculi.
7. The cranial nerves that collectively participate in eye function are II, III, IV, V, and VI.
8. The person might have a lesion in the limbic system.
9. The pons provides links between the cerebellar hemispheres and the mesencephalon, diencephalon, cerebrum, and spinal cord.
10. A less intact blood–brain barrier suggests that the endothelium is extremely permeable. This permeability exposes hypothalamic nuclei to circulating hormones and permits the diffusion of hypothalamic hormones into the circulation.

Level 3 Critical Thinking

1. The cerebrospinal fluid is accumulating inside the skull of the child, causing the bones of the skull, which have not yet fused, to expand somewhat at the sutures. Because the arachnoid villi, which usually serve to drain the CSF, do not develop until children reach age 3, a drain must be installed to reduce the amount of fluid retained within the skull. This drain is called a shunt and most commonly empties into the jugular veins.
2. The condition is Bell's palsy, and it is caused by inflammation of the facial nerve. The problem is easily distinguished from tic douloureux, as it is usually painless and disappears on its own within a few days to weeks.
3. The person might have an epidural hemorrhage, an extremely serious injury that occurs when an artery—one of the meningeal vessels—breaks and allows blood to leak into the epidural space. Depending on the size of the break, more or less blood may enter the space, and at different rates of speed. Such injuries cause death in 100 percent of untreated cases and in approximately 50 percent of treated cases, because the brain can be damaged by compression and starvation of the normal blood supply before the problem is discovered.

CHAPTER 16

Concept Check

p. 441 1. The fasciculus gracilis in the posterior column of the spinal cord is responsible for carrying information about touch and pressure from the lower part of the body to the brain.

p. 441 2. The anatomical basis for motor control occurring on the opposite side is that crossing over (decussation) occurs, and the corticospinal motor fibers innervate lower motor neurons on the opposite side of the body.

p. 441 3. The superior portion of the motor cortex controls the upper limb and superior portion of the lower limb. An injury to this area would affect the ability to control the muscles in those regions of the body.

p. 441 4. (a) tectospinal tracts, (b) vestibulospinal tracts.

p. 446 1. An inability to comprehend the written or spoken word indicates a problem with the general interpretive area of the brain, which in most individuals is located in the left temporal lobe of the cerebrum.

p. 446 2. Difficulty speaking indicates that the speech center, also called Broca's area, is involved.

p. 446 3. Memory consolidation is the conversion from short-term memory to long-term memory.

p. 446 4. The prefrontal cortex makes predictions about future events.

p. 448 1. The reticular activating system (RAS) is responsible for rousing the cerebrum to a state of consciousness. If a sleeping individual's RAS were stimulated, he or she would certainly wake up.

p. 448 2. The brain is affected by age. Some common age-related anatomical changes in the CNS are (1) reduction in brain size and weight, (2) loss of cortical neurons, (3) decrease in blood flow to the brain due to the accumulation of fatty deposits, (4) decrease in the number and organization of dendritic branching and synaptic connections, and (5) abnormal accumulation of intercellular deposits, including plaques, and neurofibrillary tangles.

Chapter Review

Level 1 Reviewing Facts and Terms

1. H	**2.** E	**3.** A	**4.** K
5. B	**6.** F	**7.** C	**8.** I
9. J	**10.** D	**11.** G	**12.** A
13. D	**14.** D	**15.** B	**16.** B
17. D	**18.** C	**19.** C	**20.** B

Level 2 Reviewing Concepts

1. A
2. D
3. B
4. B
5. The first-order neuron is the sensory neuron that delivers the sensations to the CNS.
6. The sensory homunculus is distorted because the area of sensory cortex devoted to a particular region is proportional not to its absolute size but rather to the number of sensory receptors the region contains.
7. The cerebral nuclei are processing centers that provide background patterns of movement involved in the performance of voluntary motor activities.
8. The pyramidal and extrapyramidal systems function effectively when their outputs are continually readjusted as movement occurs. The complex processing and integration of neural information from peripheral structures, visual information from the eyes, and equilibrium-related sensations from the inner ear is performed by the cerebellum.
9. The speech center, or Broca's area, lies along the edge of the premotor cortex in the same hemisphere (left) as the general interpretive area.
10. The vestibulospinal tracts direct the involuntary regulation of balance in response to sensations from the inner ear. The reticulospinal tracts direct the involuntary regulation of reflex activity and autonomic functions.

Level 3 Critical Thinking

1. The problem with Cindy's spinal cord is probably located in the lateral spinothalamic tract on the right side, somewhere around the level of spinal segment L_2. To figure this out, you would need to determine (1) what tract carries sensory information from the lower limb, (2) where it decussates, and (3) what spinal segments innervate the hip and lower limb, as detailed in the dermatome illustration in Chapter 14 (Figure 14.8).
2. The person in this question has had a stroke, or a cerebrovascular accident (CVA). The symptoms indicate that the artery damaged was the middle cerebral artery on the left side of the brain.

CHAPTER 17

Concept Check

p. 452 1. Preganglionic neurons have their cell bodies in the CNS, and their axons project to ganglia in the PNS; ganglionic neurons have their cell bodies in ganglia in the PNS, and their axons innervate effector cells.

p. 452 2. Sympathetic division (thoracolumbar division) and parasympathetic division (craniosacral division).

p. 452 3. Norepinephrine is the neurotransmitter released by most postganglionic sympathetic terminals.

p. 452 4. Cardiac muscle in the heart and the smooth muscle, glands, and adipose tissues in all peripheral organs.

p. 460 1. The neurons that synapse in the collateral ganglia originate in the inferior thoracic and superior lumbar regions of the spinal cord and pass through the sympathetic chain ganglia without synapsing before reaching the collateral ganglia.

p. 460 2. Blocking the beta receptors on cells would decrease or prevent sympathetic stimulation of those tissues. This would result in decreased heart rate and force of contraction, and relaxation of the smooth muscle in the walls; the combination would lower blood pressure.

p. 460 3. Sympathetic chain ganglia (paravertebral ganglia) are lateral to each side of the vertebral column. Collateral ganglia (prevertebral ganglia) are anterior to the vertebral column.

p. 462 1. The neurotransmitter is acetylcholine.

p. 462 2. Nicotinic receptors and muscarinic receptors.

p. 462 3. These ganglia are located in the tissues of their target organs.

p. 462 4. (1) The extensive divergence of preganglionic fibers in the sympathetic division distributes sympathetic output to many different visceral organs and tissues simultaneously; and (2) the release of E and NE by the suprarenal (adrenal) medullae affects tissues and organs throughout the body.

p. 467 1. Dual innervation means that most vital organs receive instructions from both the sympathetic and parasympathetic divisions.

p. 467 2. Visceral reflexes are the simplest functional units in the autonomic nervous system. They provide automatic motor responses that can be modified, facilitated, or inhibited by higher centers, especially those of the hypothalamus.

p. 467 3. The celiac plexus, the inferior mesenteric plexus, and the hypogastric plexus.

Chapter Review

Level 1 Reviewing Facts and Terms

1. C	**2.** G	**3.** H	**4.** D
5. I	**6.** A	**7.** E	**8.** J
9. B	**10.** F	**11.** D	**12.** B
13. C	**14.** D	**15.** D	**16.** C
17. B	**18.** C	**19.** B	**20.** D

Level 2 Reviewing Concepts

1. D
2. A
3. B
4. D
5. There are no enzymes to break down epinephrine and norepinephrine in the blood and very little in peripheral tissues.
6. The parasympathetic division innervates only visceral structures served by some cranial nerves or lying within the thoracic and/or abdominopelvic cavities. The sympathetic division has widespread impact due to extensive collateral branching of preganglionic fibers, which reach visceral organs and tissues throughout the body.
7. The distribution of sympathetic ganglionic cholinergic fibers provides a method for regulating sweat gland secretion in the skin.
8. Sympathetic chain ganglia are innervated by preganglionic fibers from the thoracolumbar regions of the spinal cord, and they are interconnected by preganglionic fibers and axons from each ganglion in the chain innervating a particular body segment. The collateral ganglia are part of the abdominal autonomic plexuses anterior to the vertebral column. Preganglionic sympathetic fibers innervate the collateral ganglia as splanchnic nerves. Intramural ganglia (also termed terminal ganglia) are part of the parasympathetic division. They are located near or within the tissues of the visceral organs.
9. The sympathetic division of the ANS stimulates metabolism, increases alertness, and prepares for emergency in "fight or flight." The parasympathetic division promotes relaxation, nutrient uptake, energy storage, and "rest and repose."
10. Visceral motor neurons, called preganglionic neurons, send their axons, called preganglionic fibers, from the CNS to synapse on ganglionic neurons, whose cell bodies are located in ganglia outside the CNS.

Level 3 Critical Thinking

1. Cutting off autonomic nervous system stimulation to the stomach through the vagus nerve decreases stimulation of digestive glands, thus reducing their secretion. This may diminish ulcers in the wall of the stomach.
2. Horner's syndrome is caused by damage to the sympathetic postganglionic innervation to one side of the face. Symptoms, typically limited to the affected side, include facial flushing, an inability to sweat, a markedly constricted pupil of the eye, drooping eyelids, and a sunken appearance of the eye.
3. Kassie should be treated with epinephrine. This would mimic sympathetic activation, which dilates air passageways in the lungs. The constriction of her respiratory passages would be alleviated.

CHAPTER 18

Concept Check

p. 472 1. Free nerve endings may be stimulated by chemical stimulation, pressure, temperature changes, or physical damage.

p. 472 2. Tonic receptors are always active, whereas phasic receptors are normally inactive, but become active for a short time.

p. 472 3. A sensation is the sensory information arriving at the CNS.

p. 472 4. The general senses refer to sensations of temperature, pain, touch, pressure, vibration, and proprioception.

p. 475 1. Since nociceptors are pain receptors, if they are stimulated, you perceive a pain sensation in your affected hand.

p. 475 2. Proprioceptors relay information about limb position and movement to the central nervous system, especially the cerebellum. Lack of this information would result in uncoordinated movements, and the individual would probably be unable to walk.

p. 475 3. The three classes of mechanoreceptors are tactile receptors, baroreceptors, and proprioceptors.

p. 480 1. There are four primary taste sensations: sweet, salty, sour, and bitter.

p. 480 2. When you have a cold, airborne molecules cannot reach the olfactory receptors, and meals taste dull and unappealing.

p. 480 3. Taste receptors are clustered in individual taste buds. Papillae on the tongue contain taste buds.

p. 480 4. The tongue has three types of papillae: filiform, fungiform, and circumvallate.

p. 486 1. Two small muscles contract to protect the eardrum and ossicles from violent movements. These are the tensor tympani and stapedius muscles.

p. 486 2. The auditory ossicles are the three tiny ear bones that are located within the middle ear. They act as levers that transfer sound vibrations from the tympanum to a fluid-filled chamber within the inner ear.

p. 486 3. Perilymph is a liquid whose properties closely resemble those of cerebrospinal fluid. It fills the space between the bony and membranous labyrinths.

p. 486 4. Shaking the head "no" stimulates the hair cells of the lateral semicircular duct. This stimulation is interpreted by the brain as a movement of the head.

p. 490 1. Without the movement of the membrane spanning the round window, the perilymph would be moved by the vibration of the stapes at the oval window, and there would be little or no perception of sound.

p. 490 2. Loss of stereocilia (as a result of constant exposure to loud noises, for instance) would reduce hearing sensitivity and could eventually result in deafness.

p. 490 3. The cochlear duct (scala media) is sandwiched between the vestibular (scala vestibuli) and tympanic ducts (scala tympani). The hair cells for hearing are located in the cochlear duct.

p. 490 4. The tectorial membrane overlies the hair cells in the organ of Corti. When the membrane containing these hair cells vibrates, the stereocilia of the hair cells are distorted and sound is detected.

p. 500 1. Inadequate tear production would affect the cornea first. Since the cornea is avascular, the cells of the cornea must obtain oxygen and nutrients from the tear fluid that passes over its surface.

p. 500 2. The two structures most affected by an abnormally high intra-ocular pressure are (1) the canal of Schlemm (the aqueous humor no longer has free access to this structure) and (2) the optic nerve (the nerve fibers of this structure are distorted, which affects visual perception).

p. 500 3. An individual born without cones would be able to see only in black and white (monochromatic) and would have very poor visual acuity.

p. 500 4. Ciliary processes are folds in the epithelium of the ciliary body. The ciliary body includes the ciliary muscle, which helps control the shape of the lens for near and far vision.

Chapter Review

Level 1 Reviewing Facts and Terms

1. B	2. D	3. E	4. H
5. J	6. C	7. I	8. F
9. G	10. A	11. A	12. C
13. D	14. A	15. B	16. B
17. C	18. B	19. C	20. C

Level 2 Reviewing Concepts

1. A
2. D
3. C
4. Each receptor has a characteristic sensitivity. For example, a touch receptor is very sensitive to pressure but relatively insensitive to chemical stimuli.
5. An increased quantity of neurotransmitter is released when the stereocilia of the hair cell are displaced toward the kinocilium.
6. The hair cells in the inner ear act as sensory receptors.
7. Sensory adaptation is a reduction in sensitivity in the presence of a constant stimulus. The receptor responds strongly at first, but thereafter the activity along the afferent fiber gradually declines, in part because of synaptic fatigue.
8. Sensory coding provides information about the strength, duration, variation, and movement of the stimulus.
9. An individual with damage to the lamellated corpuscles would have trouble feeling direct pressure, such as a pinch.
10. The bony labyrinth is a shell of dense bone. It surrounds and protects fluid-filled tubes and chambers known as the membranous labyrinth.

Level 3 Critical Thinking

1. In removing the polyps, some of the olfactory epithelium was probably damaged or destroyed. This would decrease the surface area available for the detection of odor molecules and thus the intensity of the stimulus. As a result, it would take a larger stimulus to provide the same level of smell after the surgery than before the surgery.
2. Jared has an infection of the middle ear, most often of bacterial origin, most commonly found in children and infants. Pathogens usually gain access to the middle ear cavity through the auditory tube, which is shorter and more horizontally oriented in infants and children than in adults, usually during an upper respiratory infection. As the infection progresses, the middle ear cavity can fill with pus. The increase in pressure in the middle ear cavity can eventually rupture the tympanum. This condition can be treated with antibiotics.
3. When a person has a cold, the mucous membranes of the nasal and oral cavities swell and may become plugged with mucus, preventing the molecules that form the odors of foods from reaching the olfactory epithelium at the superior aspect of the olfactory chamber. As much of what we perceive as taste is really olfaction, a reduced sense of smell decreases the appeal of foods.

CHAPTER 19

Concept Check

p. 513 1. The hypothalamus is the region of the brain responsible for regulating hormone secretion by the pituitary gland.

p. 513 2. It is a peripheral cell that responds to the presence of a specific hormone. Hormones change cellular metabolic activities.

p. 513 3. The neurohypophysis contains axon terminals of neurons whose cell bodies are in the hypothalamus. When these neurons are stimulated, their axon terminals release neurosecretions (oxytocin or ADH). Most endocrine cells of the adenohypophysis are controlled by the secretion of regulatory factors by the hypothalamus.

p. 518 1. Most of the thyroid hormone in the blood is bound to proteins called thyroid-binding globulins. This represents a large reservoir of thyroxine that guards against rapid fluctuations in the level of this important hormone. Because such a large amount is stored in this way, it takes several days to deplete the supply of hormone, even after the thyroid gland has been removed.

p. 518 2. Removal of the parathyroid glands would result in a decrease in the blood levels of calcium ions. This can be counteracted by increasing the amount of vitamin D and calcium in the diet.

p. 518 3. The region of the gland affected is the zona glomerulosa. The deficient hormone is aldosterone.

p. 523 1. The islets of Langerhans (also termed pancreatic islets) are located within the pancreas. The primary hormones released there are glucagon, insulin, and somatostatin.

p. 523 2. It depresses the secretion of FSH by the adenohypophysis as part of a negative-feedback control mechanism. Inhibin is produced by nurse cells of the testes and by follicular cells in the ovaries.

p. 523 3. The reproductive hormones.

Chapter Review

Level 1 Reviewing Facts and Terms

1. C	2. I	3. F	4. B
5. H	6. J	7. A	8. G
9. E	10. D	11. B	12. C
13. D	14. C	15. D	16. C
17. B	18. A	19. C	20. B

Level 2 Reviewing Concepts

1. B
2. B
3. D
4. The nervous system has localized, immediate, short-term effects on neurons, gland cells, muscle cells, and fat cells. The endocrine system has widespread, gradual, long-term effects on all tissues.
5. The four types of chemical structure of hormones are amino acid derivatives, peptide hormones, steroid hormones, and eicosanoids.
6. The primary targets are most cells in the body. The effects include supporting functional maturation of sperm, protein synthesis in skeletal muscles, male secondary sex characteristics, and associated behaviors.
7. Thyroid hormones increase energy utilization, oxygen consumption, and growth and development of cells.
8. Parathyroid glands produce parathyroid hormone (PTH) in response to low calcium concentrations. PTH increases calcium ion concentrations in body fluids by stimulating osteoclasts, inhibiting osteoblasts, reducing urinary excretion of calcium ions, and promoting intestinal absorption of calcium (through stimulation of calcitriol production by the kidneys) until blood calcium ion concentrations return to normal.
9. Melatonin slows the maturation of sperm, eggs, and reproductive organs by inhibiting the production of a hypothalamic-releasing hormone that stimulates FSH and LH secretion.
10. The capillary network is part of the hypophyseal portal system. Capillaries in the hypothalamus absorb regulatory secretions from hypothalamic nuclei, then unite as portal

vessels, which proceed to the anterior pituitary gland. Here the portal vessels branch into a second capillary network, where regulatory factors leave the vessels and stimulate endocrine cells in the anterior pituitary gland.

Level 3 Critical Thinking

1. Secretion of growth hormone (GH) by the pituitary gland is stimulated by growth hormone–releasing hormone (GHRH) and inhibited by GH release–inhibitory hormone or somatostatin (also termed somatotropin release–inhibitory factor or SRIF). Most pituitary tumors resulting in exaggerated growth patterns, such as acromegaly, are tumors that result in excess growth of the somatotrophs within the pituitary. This excessive growth of somatotrophs within the pituitary will result in elevated blood levels of GH.
2. The two disorders are (1) diabetes insipidus, and (2) diabetes mellitus. With diabetes insipidus the posterior pituitary no longer produces ADH; dehydration consequently occurs, and increased urination is an outcome. With diabetes mellitus, there is an inadequate production of insulin, which results in an elevation of blood glucose levels and an increase in urine production.
3. Either (1) the hypothalamus isn't secreting enough releasing hormone to stimulate adequate production of TSH by the adenohypophysis gland; (2) the adenohypophysis gland cannot produce normal levels of TSH under normal stimulation; or (3) the thyroid gland is unable to respond normally to TSH stimulation.
4. Two kidney hormones act indirectly to increase blood pressure and volume, opposed by a hormone from the heart. (1) Renin, released by kidney cells, converts angiotensinogen from the liver into angiotensin I, which is converted by the capillaries of the lungs into angiotensin II. Angiotensin II stimulates suprarenal production of aldosterone, which in turn causes the kidney to retain sodium ions and water, thereby reducing fluid loss in the urine and increasing blood volume and pressure. (2) Erythropoietin (EPO), a second kidney hormone, stimulates red blood cell production by bone marrow. Released when blood pressure or oxygen levels are low, EPO ultimately increases blood volume and its oxygen-carrying capacity. (3) When blood pressure or volume becomes excessive, cardiac muscle in the right atrium produces atrial natriuretic peptide (ANP). ANP suppresses the release of ADH and aldosterone, stimulating water and sodium loss at the kidneys and gradually reducing blood volume and pressure.

CHAPTER 20

Concept Check

p. 534 1. Blood carries heat away from areas that are warm and distributes it either to the skin when the body is too warm, or to vital organs when the body is cold; marked slowing of flow would disrupt the body's ability to cool or warm itself properly.

p. 534 2. A hypovolemic individual has a low blood volume and would therefore have abnormally low blood pressure.

p. 534 3. Whole blood contains significant numbers of formed elements, such as RBCs, WBCs, and platelets. These components of the blood make it thicker and more resistant to flow.

p. 538 1. The hematocrit value closely approximates the percentage of red blood cells; thus, red blood cells account for 42 percent of her blood volume.

p. 538 2. Red blood cells have the ability to stack and create a rouleau, which can pass through a tiny blood vessel more easily than could many separate red blood cells. In addition, red blood cells are flexible, which allows them to squeeze through small capillaries.

p. 538 3. Because RBCs do not have a nucleus or ribosomes, protein synthesis for repair and replacement cannot take place. As a result they have a shorter life span than most other cells; RBCs survive for only around 120 days in the circulation.

p. 538 4. Type AB blood has A and B surface antigens, so it has neither anti-A nor anti-B antibodies because the body's immune system ignores its own antigens.

p. 541 1. We would expect to find a large number of neutrophils in an infected cut.

p. 541 2. Thrombocytosis refers to unusually high numbers of platelets; this probably occurs in response to infection, inflammation, or cancer.

p. 541 3. Eosinophils.

p. 541 4. The granules contain histamine; its release exaggerates the inflammation response at the injury site.

p. 543 1. Erythropoietin increases the rate of both erythroblast cell division and stem cell division, and it speeds up the maturation of RBCs.

p. 543 2. Pluripotential stem cells produce all formed elements.

p. 543 3. The ejection of the nucleus transforms an erythroblast (normoblast) into a reticulocyte, which represents the final stage in RBC maturation.

p. 543 4. Megakaryocytes, which are derived from pluripotential stem cells, produce platelets.

Chapter Review

Level 1 Reviewing Facts and Terms

1. C	2. H	3. E	4. F
5. G	6. J	7. D	8. I
9. A	10. B	11. D	12. D
13. B	14. B	15. D	16. C
17. D	18. A	19. B	20. C

Level 2 Reviewing Concepts

1. C
2. A
3. D
4. C
5. The volume of packed cells is a hematocrit. It is expressed as a percentage and closely approximates the volume of erythrocytes in the blood sample. As a result, the hematocrit value is often called the volume of packed red cells or simply the packed cell volume.
6. The clotting reaction seals the breaks in blood vessel walls, preventing changes in blood volume that could seriously affect blood pressure and cardiovascular function.
7. A mature megakaryocyte begins to shed its cytoplasm in small membrane-enclosed packets called platelets.
8. Secondary lymphoid structures include the spleen, tonsils, and lymph nodes.
9. Lipoproteins are protein–lipid molecules that readily dissolve in plasma. Some lipoproteins transport insoluble lipids to peripheral tissues.
10. People with type O blood have anti-A and anti-B antibodies in their plasma. Thus, they could not receive blood from an AB donor because the RBCs in this blood type contain surface antigens A and B on their surface. A cross-reaction would occur.

Level 3 Critical Thinking

1. At higher elevations, each erythrocyte carries less oxygen because less oxygen is present in the atmosphere. This situation triggers erythrocytosis, the production of an increased number of erythrocytes in response to a large release of erythropoietin from oxygen-deprived tissues. The larger number of RBCs increases the total oxygen-carrying capacity of the blood to offset the lower saturation of each RBC. Thus, when the athlete moves back to a lower elevation, his or her blood can carry even more oxygen, increasing endurance and perhaps allowing better performance in competition.
2. A major function of the spleen is to destroy old, defective, and worn-out red blood cells. As the spleen increases in size, so does its capacity to eliminate red blood cells, and this produces anemia. The decreased number of red blood cells decreases the blood's ability to deliver oxygen to the tissues and thus the metabolism is slowed down. This would account for the tired feeling and lack of energy. Because there are fewer red blood cells than normal, the blood circulating through the skin is not as red, and so the person has a pale or white skin coloration.
3. Broad-spectrum antibiotics act to kill a wide range of bacteria, both pathogenic and nonpathogenic. When an individual takes such an antibiotic, it kills a large number of bacteria normally found in the intestine. Because these bacteria produce vitamin K, their elimination substantially decreases the amount of vitamin K that is available to the liver for the production of prothrombin, a procoagulant that is vital to clotting reactions. With decreased amounts of prothrombin in the blood, normal daily injuries such as breaks in the vessels in the nasal passageways, which are normally sealed off quickly by coagulation, do not seal off as quickly, producing the effect of nosebleeds.

CHAPTER 21

Concept Check

p. 552 1. The most obvious characteristic that differentiates cardiac muscle tissue from skeletal muscle tissue is that cardiac muscle cells are small with a centrally placed nucleus. Additionally, they are mechanically, chemically, and electrically connected to neighboring cells at intercalated discs.

p. 552 2. The pericardial cavity is a small space between the visceral surface of the heart and the parietal surface of the pericardial sac. It contains pericardial fluid, which acts as a lubricant, reducing friction between opposing surfaces.

p. 552 3. Cardiac muscle cells are connected to their neighbors at specialized junctional sites termed intercalated discs. At an intercalated disc, the membranes are bound together by desmosomes, myofibrils of the cells are anchored to the membrane, and gap junctions connect the cells.

p. 552 4. A syncytium is a single giant cell with multiple nuclei; it forms through the fusion of many small individual cells. Cardiac muscle tissue functions much like a single muscle cell. The contraction of one cardiac muscle cell triggers the contractions of several others, and so on, spreading throughout the myocardium.

p. 556 1. The groove between the atria and ventricles is the coronary sulcus.

p. 556 2. The atria have relatively thin, highly distensible muscular walls, and when not distended, the outer portion looks like a deflated, wrinkled flap (the auricle).

p. 561 1. The valves prevent backflow from the ventricles into the atria when the ventricles contract, so without them, the blood would rush back into the atria.

p. 561 2. The superior vena cava, the inferior vena cava, and the coronary sinus.

p. 561 3. Blood from the left ventricle passes through the aortic valve, travels through the systemic circuit, and enters the right atrium. From there it passes through the tricuspid valve and enters the right ventricle. Blood leaving the right ventricle passes through the pulmonary valve and enters the pulmonary trunk. Then it flows into the pulmonary arteries before arriving at the capillaries in the respiratory surfaces of the lungs.

p. 561 4. As the ventricles begin to contract, they force the AV valves to close, which in turn pull on the chordae tendineae. The chordae tendineae pull on the papillary muscles. The papillary muscles respond by contracting, opposing the force that is pushing the valves toward the atria.

p. 566 1. If these cells were not functioning, the heart would still continue to beat, but at a slower rate, following the pace set by the AV node.

p. 566 2. The heart rate is increased in response to norepinephrine.

p. 566 3. Because the plasmalemmae of nodal cells depolarize spontaneously and nodal cells are electrically connected to one another, to conducting fibers, and to cardiac muscle cells, contractions are able to sweep through the conducting system and trigger the contractions of cardiac muscle cells. The timing of contraction is controlled by the rate of propagation and the distribution of the contractile stimulus to the cardiac muscle tissue in the atria versus the ventricles.

p. 568 1. The flow of blood from one chamber to the next occurs only if the pressure is higher in the first chamber than in the second, so equal pressures would mean that the blood would not flow from the atrium to the ventricle.

p. 568 2. Norepinephrine (NE) release produces an increase in both heart rate and force of contractions through the stimulation of beta receptors on nodal cells and contractile cells. Acetylcholine (ACh) release produces a decrease in both heart rate and force of contractions through the stimulation of muscarinic receptors of nodal cells and contractile cells.

Chapter Review

Level I Reviewing Facts and Terms

1. F	**2.** E	**3.** H	**4.** C
5. B	**6.** J	**7.** G	**8.** A
9. I	**10.** D	**11.** D	**12.** C
13. C	**14.** B	**15.** C	**16.** A
17. B	**18.** C	**19.** C	**20.** B

Level 2 Reviewing Concepts

1. C

2. C

3. C

4. Cardiac muscle cells are like skeletal muscle fibers in that each cardiac muscle cell contains organized myofibrils, and the alignment of their sarcomeres gives the cardiocyte a striated appearance.

5. The semilunar valves do not require muscular braces because the arterial walls do not contract, and the relative positions of the cusps are stable.

6. A pacemaker cell is a cell that depolarizes spontaneously. The normal pacemaker cells (SA node) depolarize at the fastest rate. Other groups of cells that have the potential to serve as pacemaker cells are the atrioventricular node, AV bundle, right bundle branch, left bundle branch, and Purkinje fibers.

7. Pericardial fluid is secreted by pericardial membranes and acts as a lubricant, reducing friction between the opposing visceral and parietal pericardial surfaces.

8. The left ventricle has the thickest walls because it needs to exert so much force to push blood around the systemic circuit.

9. Nodal cells are unusual because their plasmalemmae depolarize spontaneously. Nodal cells are responsible for establishing the rate of cardiac contraction.

10. Norepinephrine release produces an increase in both heart rate and force of contractions through the stimulation of beta receptors on nodal cells and contractile cells.

Level 3 Critical Thinking

1. It would appear that Harvey has a regurgitating mitral valve. When an AV valve fails to close properly, the blood flowing back into the atrium produces the abnormal heart sound or murmur. If the sound is heard at the beginning of the systole, this would indicate the AV valve because this is the period when the valve is just closed and the blood in the ventricle is under increasing pressure; thus, the likelihood of backflow is the greatest. If the sound is heard at the end of systole or the beginning of diastole, it would indicate a regurgitating semilunar valve—in this case, the aortic semilunar valve.

2. During tachycardia, the heart beats at an abnormally fast rate. The faster the heart beats, the less time there is in between contractions for it to fill with blood again. As a result, over a period of time, the heart fills with less and less blood and thus pumps less blood out. The stroke volume decreases, as does the cardiac output. When the cardiac output decreases to the point where not enough blood reaches the central nervous system, loss of consciousness occurs.

3. Acetylcholine would be released, resulting in a decreased heart rate.

4. Rheumatic fever can cause carditis, an irritation of the myocardium and heart valves. Scar tissue can form gradually, eventually causing impairment of the function of the valves' leaflets, resulting in decreased efficiency of the heart. If not corrected, this condition continues to worsen and can lead to heart failure.

CHAPTER 22

Concept Check

p. 578 1. The blood vessels are veins. Arteries and arterioles have a relatively large amount of smooth muscle tissue in a thick, well-developed tunica media.

p. 578 2. Blood pressure in the arterial system pushes blood into the capillaries. Blood pressure on the venous side is very low, and other forces help keep the blood moving. Valves in the walls of venules and medium-sized veins permit blood flow in only one direction, toward the heart, preventing the backflow of blood toward the capillaries.

p. 578 3. The femoral artery is a muscular artery.

p. 578 4. No gas exchange occurs in arterioles.

p. 592 1. The carotid arteries supply blood to structures of the head and the neck, including the brain.

p. 592 2. The right brachial artery is the artery at the biceps region.

p. 592 3. The external iliac artery gives rise to the femoral artery in the thigh.

p. 592 4. Damage to the internal carotid arteries would not always result in brain damage, because the vertebral arteries also supply blood to the brain.

p. 600 1. Organs served by the celiac artery include the stomach, spleen, liver, and pancreas.

p. 600 2. The superficial veins are dilated to promote heat loss through the skin.

p. 600 3. The superior vena cava receives blood from the head, neck, chest, shoulders, and upper limbs.

p. 600 4. Blood from the intestines contains high amounts of glucose, amino acids, and other nutrients and toxins absorbed from the digestive tract. These are processed by the liver before the blood goes to the general systemic circuit in order to keep the composition of the blood in the body relatively stable.

p. 603 1. The major changes in the heart and the major vessels that occur at birth are as follows: (1) The pulmonary vessels expand; (2) the ductus arteriosus contracts, forcing blood to flow through the pulmonary circuit; and (3) the valvular flap closes the foramen ovale.

p. 603 2. The blood pools in the veins of the legs because the valves are not working effectively.

p. 603 3. The arteries must be able to expand with a sudden increase in pressure. A reduced ability to do so could result in a bulge or tear in the wall of the artery.

Chapter Review

Level 1 Reviewing Facts and Terms

1. C	**2.** D	**3.** F	**4.** J
5. I	**6.** H	**7.** A	**8.** G
9. E	**10.** B	**11.** B	**12.** A
13. D	**14.** D	**15.** B	**16.** A
17. C	**18.** A	**19.** B	**20.** B

Level 2 Reviewing Concepts

1. D
2. A
3. B
4. The pulmonary, common carotid, subclavian, and common iliac arteries are examples of elastic arteries.
5. Sinusoids are found in liver, bone marrow, and suprarenal glands.
6. They are direct connections between arterioles and venules.
7. They prevent backflow and aid in the flow of blood back to the heart by compartmentalizing it.
8. The brachiocephalic, left common carotid, and left subclavian are elastic arteries that originate on the aortic arch.
9. The superior vena cava receives blood from the head, neck, shoulders, and upper limbs.
10. Blood can flow directly from the right atrium to the left atrium, bypassing the pulmonary circuit.

Level 3 Critical Thinking

1. Emissary veins connect the superficial circulation to the deep circulation draining into the cranial venous sinuses. Infections from the superficial region in the area of the eyes can be transported inward to anterior cranial sinuses, which could lead to meningitis. Therefore, it is important not to spread infection from the superficial to the deep region.
2. In response to the high temperature of the water, John's body shunted more blood to the superficial veins to decrease body temperature. The dilation of the superficial veins caused a shift in blood to the arms and legs and resulted in a decreased venous return. Because of the decreased venous return, the cardiac output decreased and less blood with oxygen was delivered to the brain. This caused John to feel light-headed and faint and nearly caused his demise.
3. In heart failure, the heart is not able to produce enough force to circulate the blood properly. The blood tends to pool in the extremities and as more and more fluid accumulates in the capillaries, the blood hydrostatic pressure increases and the blood osmotic pressure decreases. The fluid accumulation exceeds the ability of the lymphatics to drain it, and, as a result, edema occurs and produces obvious swelling.

CHAPTER 23

Concept Check

p. 613 1. The lymphoid system produces, maintains, and distributes lymphocytes, which are essential to the defense of the body.

p. 613 2. Capillary number one.

p. 613 3. Because lymph delivers so much of the body's fluid back to the bloodstream, a break in a major lymphatic vessel could mean a potentially fatal decline in blood volume.

p. 613 4. Primary lymphoid structures carry stem cells.

p. 617 1. T cells account for about 80 percent of the body's circulating lymphocytes.

p. 617 2. Some B cells differentiate into memory B cells, which will become activated when the antigen appears again. Therefore, John's body will be able to mount an immune response faster and more effectively, possibly warding off any symptoms of illness.

p. 617 3. The body must be able to mount a rapid and powerful response to antigens, requiring the production of certain types of lymphocytes at certain times. Without this ability, the body's immune response would be slower and weaker and could fall victim to infection or disease.

p. 617 4. Aggregated lymphoid nodules (Peyer's patches).

p. 625 1. T cells regulate the activation or suppression of B cells and therefore manage the extent of the immune response.

p. 625 2. Lymph nodes are strategically placed throughout the body in areas susceptible to injury or invasion.

p. 625 3. The capillaries in the thymus do not allow free exchange between the interstitial fluid and the circulation. If they did, circulating antigens would prematurely stimulate the developing T cells.

p. 625 4. Lymph nodes enlarge during an infection due to increased numbers of lymphocytes and phagocytes within the active nodes.

Chapter Review

Level 1 Reviewing Facts and Terms

1. C	**2.** J	**3.** E	**4.** B
5. F	**6.** D	**7.** A	**8.** I
9. H	**10.** G	**11.** D	**12.** D
13. D	**14.** C	**15.** A	**16.** A
17. A	**18.** B	**19.** D	**20.** C

Level 2 Reviewing Concepts

1. C
2. C
3. B
4. The blood–thymus barrier prevents premature stimulation of developing T cells by circulating antigens.
5. The splenic artery and the splenic vein pass through the hilum of the spleen.
6. The thoracic duct collects lymph from areas of the body inferior to the diaphragm and from the left side of the body superior to the diaphragm.
7. T cells are the most common type of lymphocyte.
8. Lymphedema is swelling in the tissues as a result of damaged valves in lymphatic vessels or blocked lymphatic vessels.
9. Immature or activated lymphocytes divide to produce additional lymphocytes of the same type.
10. Aggregated lymphoid nodules (Peyer's patches) are found in the lamina propria, which lies internal to the epithelium that lines part of the small intestine.

Level 3 Critical Thinking

1. If Tom has previously had the measles, there should be a significant amount of IgG antibody in his blood shortly after the exposure, the result of an antibody-mediated immune response. If he has not previously had the disease and is in the early stages of a primary response, his blood might show an elevated level of antibodies.
2. Allergies occur when antigens called allergens bind to specific types of antibodies that are bound to the surface of mast cells and basophils. A person becomes allergic when he or she develops antibodies for a specific allergen. Theoretically, at least, a molecule that would bind to the specific antibodies for ragweed and prevent the allergen from binding should help to relieve the allergy.
3. Lymphatic capillaries are found in most regions of the body, and lymphatic capillaries offer little resistance to the passage of cancer cells, which often spread along them, using them as way stations.

CHAPTER 24

Concept Check

p. 632 1. The upper respiratory system warms and humidifies the air, which protects the lower respiratory system from extreme temperatures and dry conditions. Breathing through the mouth eliminates much of the filtration, humidification, and warming that must occur before the air reaches the sensitive tissues of the lungs.

p. 632 2. The mucus escalator is present in the lower regions of the respiratory tract, where the cilia of the respiratory epithelium beat toward the pharynx, cleaning the respiratory passageways.

p. 632 3. The conchae cause turbulence in the inspired air. This slows air movement and brings the air into contact with the moist, warm walls of the nasal cavity. Turbulent airflow is essential to the filtration, humidification, and warming of air; these processes protect more delicate regions of the lower respiratory system. If the nasal cavity were a tubular passageway with straight walls, turbulence would be minimal.

p. 637 1. The thyroid cartilage protects the glottis and the opening to the trachea.

p. 637 2. During swallowing, the epiglottis folds over the glottis, preventing food or liquids from entering the respiratory passageways.

p. 637 3. The pitch of her voice is getting lower.

p. 637 4. The glottis could not close without the intrinsic laryngeal muscles, so food could enter the respiratory passageways.

p. 638 1. The tracheal cartilages are C-shaped to allow room for esophageal expansion when large portions of food or liquid are swallowed.

p. 638 2. The trachea has a typical respiratory epithelium, which is pseudostratified, ciliated, columnar epithelial cells.

p. 638 3. Tracheal cartilages prevent the overexpansion or collapse of the airways during respiration, thereby keeping the airway open and functional.

p. 638 4. The right primary bronchus has a larger diameter, and it extends toward the lung at a steeper angle.

p. 646 1. Chronic smoking damages the lining of the air passageways. Cilia are seared off the surface of the cells by the heat, and the large number of particles that escape filtering are trapped in the excess mucus that is secreted to protect the irritated lining. This combination of circumstances creates a situation in which there is a large amount of thick mucus that is difficult to clear from the passages. The cough reflex is an attempt to remove this material from the airways.

p. 646 2. The overproduction of mucus can lead to the obstruction of smaller airways, causing a decrease in respiratory efficiency.

p. 646 3. Filtration and humidification are complete by the time air reaches this point, so the need for those structures is eliminated.

p. 646 4. The surfactant coats the inner surface of each alveolus and helps to reduce surface tension and avoid the collapse of the alveoli.

p. 647 1. This would place a great strain on the right ventricle as it continues to try to force blood through the blocked vessel. Over time, the strain can cause heart failure.

p. 647 2. Pleural fluid provides lubrication between the parietal and visceral surfaces during breathing.

p. 647 3. The conducting portions of the respiratory tract receive blood from the external carotid arteries, the thyrocervical trunk, and the bronchial arteries.

p. 649 1. Since the rib penetrates the chest wall, the thoracic cavity will be damaged, as well as the inner pleura. Atmospheric air will then enter the pleural cavity. This space is normally at a lower pressure than the outside air, so when the air enters, the natural elasticity of the lungs will not be compensated and the lung will collapse. The entry of air into the pleural cavity is called a pneumothorax; the resulting collapsed lung is called atelectasis.

p. 649 2. As a result of emphysema, the larger air spaces and lack of elasticity will reduce the efficiency of capillary exchange and pulmonary ventilation.

p. 649 3. During a baby's first breath, air is forced into the lungs due to the change in pressure. Fluids are pushed out of the way of the conducting passageways, and the alveoli immediately inflate with air. Pulmonary circulation becomes activated, and this closes the foramen ovale and the ductus arteriosus.

Chapter Review

Level I Reviewing Facts and Terms

1. I	**2.** J	**3.** A	**4.** H
5. G	**6.** D	**7.** B	**8.** E
9. C	**10.** F	**11.** A	**12.** D
13. B	**14.** B	**15.** C	**16.** C
17. D	**18.** C	**19.** B	**20.** B

Level 2 Reviewing Concepts

1. D
2. A
3. C
4. The right lung has three lobes.
5. Bronchodilation is the enlargement of the airway.
6. They phagocytize particulate matter.
7. The septa divide the lung into lobules.
8. One group regulates tension in the vocal folds, and the second group opens and closes the glottis.
9. The paired laryngeal cartilages involved with the opening and closing of the glottis are the corniculate and arytenoid cartilages.
10. It includes the portion lying between the hyoid bone and the entrance to the esophagus.

Level 3 Critical Thinking

1. Asthma occurs when the conducting respiratory passageways are unusually sensitive and irritable, usually as a result of exposure to an antigen in the inspired air. The most important symptoms are edema and swelling of the walls of the passageways; the constriction of the smooth muscles in the walls of the bronchial tree, reducing lumen size; and accelerated production of mucus. Together, all of these factors reduce the ability of the lungs to function normally in air exchange.
2. Unless the infant was suffocated immediately when it was born, the first breath that it took would start to inflate the lungs and some of the air would be trapped in the lungs. By placing the lungs in water to see if they float, the medical examiner can determine whether any air is in the lungs. Other measurements and tests could also be used to determine whether the infant had breathed at all (air in the lungs) or was dead at birth (lungs collapsed and a small amount of fluid).

CHAPTER 25

Concept Check

p. 662 1. The components of the mucosa are (1) the mucosal epithelium (depending on location, it may be simple columnar or stratified squamous); (2) the lamina propria, areolar tissue underlying the epithelium; and (3) the muscularis mucosae, bands of smooth muscle fibers arranged in concentric layers. The mucosa of the digestive tract is an example of a mucous membrane, serving both absorptive and secretory functions.

p. 662 2. Mesenteries provide an access route for the passage of blood vessels, nerves, and lymphatics to and from the digestive tract. They also stabilize the relative positions of the attached organs.

p. 662 3. Peristalsis is waves of muscular contractions that move substances the length of the digestive tube. Segmentation activities churn and mix the contents of the small and large intestines but do not produce net movement in a particular direction.

p. 662 4. This allows the stretched smooth muscle to adapt to its new shape and still have the ability to contract when necessary.

p. 666 1. The oral cavity is lined by the oral mucosa, which is composed of nonkeratinized stratified squamous epithelium.

p. 666 2. At mealtime, saliva lubricates the mouth and dissolves chemicals that stimulate the taste buds. Saliva contains the digestive enzyme salivary amylase, which begins the chemical breakdown of carbohydrates.

p. 666 3. Carbohydrates are broken down by salivary amylase in the mouth.

p. 666 4. The incisors cut away a section of the apple, which then enters the mouth. The cuspids tear at the rough skin and pulp of the apple. The apple then moves to the bicuspids and molars for thorough mashing and grinding before finally being swallowed.

p. 668 1. The fauces is the opening between the oral cavity and the pharynx.

p. 668 2. The process that is being described is deglutition, or swallowing.

p. 668 3. The buccal phase is the only voluntary phase of swallowing.

p. 668 4. When someone experiences heartburn their lower esophageal sphincter may not have closed completely, and powerful stomach acids are entering the lower esophagus, causing uncomfortable acid reflux.

p. 673 1. The greater omentum provides support to the surrounding organs, pads the organs from the surfaces of the abdomen, provides an important energy reserve, and provides insulation.

p. 673 2. The epithelium produces a carpet of mucus that covers the interior surfaces of the stomach, providing protection against the powerful acids and enzymes. Any cells that do become damaged are quickly replaced.

p. 673 3. Chief cells secrete pepsinogen. In infants, they also secrete rennin and gastric lipase.

p. 673 4. Gastrin, produced by enteroendocrine cells, stimulates the secretion of parietal and chief cells.

p. 677 1. The characteristic lining of the small intestine contains plicae circulares, which support intestinal villi. The villi are covered by a simple columnar epithelium whose apical surface is covered by microvilli. This arrangement increases the total area for digestion and absorption to more than 200 m^2.

p. 677 2. Plicae are folds in the lining of the intestine that greatly increase the surface area available for absorption.

p. 677 3. Intestinal crypts house the stem cells that produce new epithelial cells, which renew the epithelial surface and add intracellular enzymes to the chyme. In addition, intestinal crypts contain cells that produce several intestinal hormones.

p. 677 4. The duodenum acts as a mixing bowl for the chyme entering from the stomach.

p. 686 1. The condition of cystic fibrosis interferes with the digestion of sugars, starches, lipids, nucleic acids, and proteins.

p. 686 2. The liver acts as a metabolic regulator by extracting nutrients and toxins from the blood before it enters the bloodstream. It also regulates the blood, serving as a blood reservoir, phagocytizing old or damaged RBCs, and synthesizing plasma proteins. Finally, the liver synthesizes and secretes bile.

p. 686 3. Contraction of the hepatopancreatic sphincter seals off the passageway between the gallbladder and the small intestine and keeps bile from entering the small intestine.

p. 686 4. The pancreas produces digestive enzymes and buffers (exocrine functions) and hormones (endocrine functions).

Chapter Review

Level 1 Reviewing Facts and Terms

1. C	**2.** A	**3.** D	**4.** F
5. J	**6.** G	**7.** H	**8.** E
9. I	**10.** B	**11.** A	**12.** C
13. D	**14.** C	**15.** D	**16.** D
17. A	**18.** B	**19.** A	**20.** D

Level 2 Reviewing Concepts

1. C
2. A
3. C
4. Lipase attacks lipids.
5. The hepatopancreatic sphincter seals off the passageway between the gallbladder and the small intestine and prevents bile from entering the small intestine.
6. The gallbladder stores bile and concentrates it.
7. Kupffer cells engulf pathogens, cell debris, and damaged blood cells in the liver.
8. The last region of the colon before the rectum is the sigmoid colon.
9. Lacteals transport materials that could not enter local capillaries. These materials eventually reach the circulation via the thoracic duct.
10. Gastrin release is triggered by food entering the stomach.

Level 3 Critical Thinking

1. During the autopsy, the forensic scientist examined the stomach contents of the murder victim and found the stomach visually empty. As a full meal usually takes more than 4 hours to leave the stomach completely, it was obvious that the victim had not eaten dinner at the time indicated by the murder suspect.
2. The (1) upper esophageal, (2) lower esophageal, (3) pyloric, (4) ileocecal valve, (5) internal anal, and (6) external anal sphincters constrict the lumen of the digestive tract to control movement of materials through it. Only the last, the external anal sphincter, is composed of skeletal muscle with somatic motor innervation, and therefore is under conscious, voluntary control.
3. The following six histological layers form the wall of the digestive tube: (1) mucosal epithelium, (2) lamina propria, (3) muscularis mucosae, (4) submucosa, (5) muscularis externa, and (6) serosa or adventitia.

CHAPTER 26

Concept Check

p. 698 1. The kidneys will absorb more water, release erythropoietin, and release renin.

p. 698 2. The urine goes through the ureters to the urinary bladder, where it is stored until urination occurs. From there, it travels through the urethra before exiting the body.

p. 698 3. Calcitriol, released by the kidneys in response to low calcium levels in the blood, causes increased calcium absorption by the intestinal epithelium.

p. 703 1. The route blood must take from the renal artery to the glomerulus is as follows: renal artery → segmental arteries → interlobar arteries → arcuate arteries → cortical radiate arteries → afferent arterioles → glomerulus. The route blood must take from the glomerulus to the renal vein is as follows: glomerulus → efferent arterioles → peritubular capillaries/vasa recta → venules → interlobular veins → arcuate veins → interlobar veins → renal vein.

p. 703 2. Filtrate flows from glomerulus to a minor calyx via the following route: glomerulus → capsular space → PCT → descending limb of loop → nephron loop → ascending limb of loop → DCT → connecting tubule → collecting duct → papillary duct → minor calyx.

p. 703 3. Filtration, which is a passive process, allows ions and molecules to pass based on their size. This means that if the pores are big enough to allow the passage of organic wastes, they are also big enough to allow the passage of water, ions, and other important organic molecules. This is why some elements of the filtrate must be actively reabsorbed before the production of urine is complete.

p. 703 4. The loop absorbs additional water from the tubular fluid and an even higher percentage of the sodium and chloride ions. This results from the high osmotic concentration of its surroundings in the medulla.

p. 708 1. An obstruction of the ureters would interfere with the passage of urine from the renal pelvis to the urinary bladder.

p. 708 2. The mucosa lining of the urinary bladder is thrown into folds, called rugae, that allow the bladder to stretch when it is full.

p. 708 3. Females experience urinary tract infections, which are caused by bacteria, more often than do males because of the proximity of the urethra to the anus. In addition, the urethra is shorter in females, so the bacteria can more easily migrate to the urinary bladder.

p. 708 4. The urinary bladder is held in place by the median umbilical ligament extending from the anterior and superior border, and the lateral umbilical ligaments passing along the sides of the bladder.

Chapter Review

Level 1 Reviewing Facts and Terms

1. C	**2.** A	**3.** I	**4.** F
5. J	**6.** B	**7.** E	**8.** H
9. D	**10.** G	**11.** D	**12.** A
13. C	**14.** B	**15.** B	**16.** D
17. D	**18.** C	**19.** C	**20.** C

Level 2 Reviewing Concepts

1. B
2. B
3. B
4. The glomerulus is contained within the expanded chamber of the nephron (glomerular capsule).

5. It consists of large cells (podocytes) with "feet" that wrap around the glomerular capillaries.
6. The juxtaglomerular complex secretes two hormones—renin and erythropoietin.
7. The trigone is the triangular area of the urinary bladder bounded by the ureteral openings and the entrance to the urethra.
8. The external urethral sphincter is under voluntary control.
9. The primary function of the proximal convoluted tubule is absorption.
10. The rugae in the urinary bladder allow it to expand as it fills with urine.

Level 3 Critical Thinking

1. Since the external urethral sphincter provides the only conscious, voluntary control of micturition, it is physically impossible for a child to restrict urine release by choice until the neural control of the muscle matures. The internal urethral sphincter is not under voluntary, somatic nervous system control. Before age two successful toilet training usually amounts to little more that the parents' learning to anticipate the timing of the child's micturition reflex.
2. Strenuous exercise, such as long-distance running, causes sympathetic activation, which stimulates powerful vasoconstriction of the afferent arterioles in the kidneys. Because these vessels deliver blood to the renal corpuscles, their constriction decreases the rate of glomerular filtration. Blood flow to the kidneys declines further as dilated peripheral blood vessels shunt blood away from the kidneys and to skeletal muscle during running. As the passage of blood through the kidney continues to fall due to water loss during exercise, the potential for renal dysfunction increases as a result of the prolonged periods of exercise associated with running marathons.
3. The increased mass of the uterus, which is located superior and posterior to the urinary bladder in females, presses downward on the bladder, increasing the feeling of pressure and triggering the micturition reflex, even when the bladder is only partially full. Also, as a woman comes closer to delivery of her infant, the baby might kick her in the bladder, which would stimulate the micturition reflex.

CHAPTER 27

Concept Check

p. 722 1. The ductus deferens, testicular blood vessels, nerves, and lymphatics make up the body of the spermatic cord.

p. 722 2. The inguinal canals, which are narrow canals linking the scrotal chambers with the peritoneal cavity, usually close, but the presence of the spermatic cords leaves weak points in the abdominal wall.

p. 722 3. The temperature inside the peritoneal cavity is too high for the production of sperm cells, so the testes are located within the scrotal cavity, outside the peritoneal cavity, where temperatures are cooler.

p. 722 4. The blood–testis barrier isolates the inner portions of the seminiferous tubule from the surrounding interstitial fluid. Transport across the sustentacular cells is tightly regulated to maintain a very stable environment inside the tubule.

p. 727 1. Capacitation involves sperm becoming active, motile, and fully functional. It occurs when sperm are mixed with secretions of the seminal glands, and upon exposure to conditions within the female reproductive tract.

p. 727 2. After becoming detached from the sustentacular cells, the sperm lies within the lumen of the seminiferous tubule. It will then travel in fluid currents along the straight tubule, through the rete testis, and into the epididymis, where it will remain for about two weeks, completing its functional maturation. Upon leaving the epididymis, the sperm will enter the ductus deferens, where it can be stored for several months. The sperm then enters the ejaculatory duct, which enters the urethra for passage out of the body.

p. 733 1. The follicular cells provide the developing oocyte with nutrients and release estrogens. They stimulate the growth of the follicle by secreting follicular fluid. Once ovulation occurs, the remaining follicular cells in the empty follicle create the corpus luteum.

p. 733 2. Scarring in the uterine tubes can cause infertility by preventing the passage of a zygote to the uterus. This can be caused by pelvic inflammatory disease, which is an infection of the uterine tubes.

p. 740 1. Enlargement of the primary and secondary follicles in the ovary happens at the same time as the proliferative phase of the uterine cycle.

p. 740 2. Ovulation occurs at the beginning of the secretory phase.

p. 740 3. Blockage of a single lactiferous sinus would not interfere with milk moving to the nipple because each breast usually has between 15 and 20 lactiferous sinuses.

p. 740 4. Prolactin, growth hormone, and human placental lactogen stimulate the mammary glands to become mitotically active, producing the gland cells, which are necessary for lactation.

Chapter Review

Level 1 Reviewing Facts and Terms

1. I	2. A	3. D	4. F
5. J	6. C	7. B	8. H
9. G	10. E	11. D	12. B
13. B	14. A	15. B	16. C
17. A	18. B	19. D	20. C

Level 2 Reviewing Concepts

1. B
2. D
3. D
4. The head of the sperm cell contains a nucleus with the chromosomes.
5. The acrosomal cap contains enzymes involved in the primary steps of fertilization.
6. Seminalplasmin is produced by the prostate gland; it is an antibiotic that may help prevent UTIs in males.
7. Follicular fluid causes the follicle to enlarge rapidly.
8. During menstruation, the functional layer of the endometrium is lost.
9. Soon after implantation, human chorionic gonadotropin (hCG) can be detected.
10. The testes normally begin to descend at the seventh developmental month.

Level 3 Critical Thinking

1. Yes, he would still be able to have an erection. Forming an erection is a parasympathetic reflex that is controlled by the sacral region of the spinal cord (inferior to the injury). Tactile stimulation of the penis would initiate the parasympathetic reflex that controls erection. He would also be able to experience an erection by the sympathetic route, since this would be controlled in the T_{12}–L_2 area of the cord (superior to the injury). Stimulation by higher centers could produce a decreased sympathetic tone in the vessels to the penis, resulting in an erection.
2. The endometrial cells have receptors for the hormones estrogen and progesterone and respond to them the same as they would if the cells were in the body of the uterus. Under the influence of estrogen, the cells proliferate at the beginning of the menstrual cycle and begin to develop glands and blood vessels, which then further develop under the control of progesterone. This dramatic change in tissue size and characteristics interferes with neighboring tissues by pressing on them or interrupting their functions in other ways. This interference causes periodic painful sensations.
3. Sexually transmitted pathogens can pass through the vagina, uterus, and uterine tubes and directly into the peritoneal cavity of a woman to cause peritonitis; males have no such access route. Because the female urethra is relatively short and opens near the vagina and anus, microbial infections of the urethra (urethritis) and urinary bladder (cystitis) are often caused by normal microbial inhabitants of the perineum that are moved upward through the urethra as an indirect consequence of sexual intercourse. Because the male urethra is longer, urinary tract infection is less likely.

CHAPTER 28

Concept Check

p. 750 1. The sperm is not ready for fertilization until it undergoes capacitation, which occurs in the female reproductive tract.

p. 750 2. The oocyte is surrounded by a layer of follicular cells. The acrosomal cap of the spermatozoa contains hyaluronidase to break down the connections between adjacent follicular cells. One or two spermatozoa is not enough, however, because at least a hundred must release hyaluronidase in order for the connections to break down enough to allow fertilization.

p. 750 3. The oocyte undergoes oocyte activation, which includes a sudden rise in metabolism, a change in the cell membrane to prevent fertilization by other sperm, and the completion of meiosis.

p. 750 4. The first trimester involves the development of all the major organ systems.

p. 755 1. The inner cell mass of the blastocyst eventually develops into the embryo.

p. 755 2. The syncytial trophoblast erodes a path through the uterine epithelium. There is some digestion of uterine glands, which release nutrients that are absorbed by the syncytial trophoblast and distributed by diffusion to the inner cell mass.

p. 755 3. The mesodermal layer gives rise to the skeletal, muscular, endocrine, cardiovascular, lymphoid, urinary, and reproductive systems and the lining of body cavities; it also forms connective tissues.

p. 755 4. The placenta contains the maternal arteries and single umbilical vein, permits nutrient exchange at the chorionic villi, and synthesizes hormones that are important to the mother and to the embryo.

p. 763 1. The organ systems continue development, and the embryo grows rapidly, though more notably in height than in weight.

p. 763 2. The dilation stage, in which the cervix dilates and the fetus slides down the cervical canal, usually takes eight or more hours.

p. 763 3. The kidneys, while able to filter wastes, cannot yet concentrate the urine. This means that the newborn loses a large amount of water through urination and must take in a large amount of fluid to make up for the loss.

p. 763 4. During the placental stage, the empty uterus contracts and decreases in size, which breaks the connection between the endometrium and the placenta, causing the expulsion of the placenta.

Chapter Review

Level 1 Reviewing Facts and Terms

1. F	2. G	3. J	4. B
5. H	6. D	7. I	8. C
9. A	10. E	11. B	12. C
13. B	14. A	15. C	16. B
17. C	18. A	19. B	20. A

Level 2 Reviewing Concepts

1. D
2. B
3. C
4. Cleavage is a sequence of cell divisions that occur immediately after fertilization in the first trimester.
5. The primitive streak is the center line of the blastodisc where cells migrate and begin separating into germ layers.
6. Human chorionic gonadotropin is produced in the trophoblast cells shortly after implantation. It signals the corpus luteum to produce more progesterone.
7. Amphimixis is the fusion of the male and female pronuclei.
8. The yolk sac functions in the production of blood cells.
9. Organogenesis is the process of organ formation.
10. The first trimester is critical because events in the first 12 weeks establish the basis for organ formation.

Level 3 Critical Thinking

1. Although technically what Joe says is true—it takes only one sperm to fertilize an egg—the probability of this occurring if not enough sperm are deposited is very slim. Of the millions of sperm that enter the female reproductive tract, most are killed or disabled before they reach the uterus. The acid environment, temperature, and presence of immunoglobulins in the vaginal secretions are just a few of the factors responsible for the demise of so many sperm. Many sperm are not capable of making the complete trip. Once they arrive at the secondary oocyte, the sperm must penetrate the corona radiata, and this requires the combined enzyme contributions of a hundred or more sperm. If the ejaculate contains few sperm, it is likely that none will reach the oocyte, and fertilization will be impossible.
2. Because processes such as cleavage, gastrulation, and organogenesis occur during the first three months of pregnancy, embryonic development can be disrupted during the first trimester of pregnancy. Since each cell of the early embryo may give rise to multiple tissues, the earlier embryonic development is disrupted, the more structures are affected. Contraction of rubella during the first 10 weeks of pregnancy often causes congenital heart defects, eye cataracts, deafness, and mental retardation in the developing infant. By the end of the first trimester, the basis for the formation of all of the major organ systems has been established, so that disruptions after this time will more likely affect only specific organs or body systems.

Appendix

Weights and Measures

Accurate descriptions of physical objects would be impossible without a precise method of reporting the pertinent data. Dimensions such as length and width are reported in standardized units of measurement, such as centimeters or inches. These values can be used to calculate the volume of an object, a measurement of the amount of space it fills. **Mass** is another important physical property. The mass of an object is determined by the amount of matter it contains; on Earth the mass of an object determines its weight.

Most U.S. readers describe length and width in terms of inches, feet, or yards; volumes in pints, quarts, or gallons; and weights in ounces, pounds, or tons. These are units of the **U.S. system** of measurement. Table A.1 summarizes the familiar and unfamiliar terms used in the U.S. system. For reference purposes, this table also includes a definition of the "household units" popular in recipes and cookbooks. The U.S. system can be very difficult to work with because there is no logical relationship between the various units. For example, there are 12 inches in a foot, 3 feet in a yard, and 1760 yards in a mile. Without a clear pattern of organization, converting feet to inches or miles to feet can be confusing and time-consuming. The relationships between ounces, pints, quarts, and gallons, or ounces, pounds, and tons are no more logical.

In contrast, the **metric system** has a logical organization based on powers of 10, as indicated in Table A.2 For example, a **meter** (m) represents the basic unit for the measurement of size. When measuring larger objects, data can be reported in terms of **dekameters** (*deka*, ten), **hectometers** (*hekaton*, hundred), or **kilometers** (**km**; *chilioi*, thousand); for smaller objects, data can be reported in **decimeters** (**dm**; 0.1 m; *decem*, ten), **centimeters** (**cm** = 0.01 m; *centum*, hundred), **millimeters** (**mm** = 0.001 m; *mille*, thousand), and so forth. Notice that the same prefixes are used to report weights, based on the **gram (g)**, and volumes, based on the **liter (L)**. This text reports data in metric units, usually with U.S. equivalents. You should use this opportunity to become familiar with the metric system, because most technical sources report data only in metric units, and most of the rest of the world uses the metric system exclusively. Conversion factors are included in Table A.2.

Pharmacies at one time used the **apothecary system**, a relatively specialized system of measurement borrowed from England when America was still a colony. This system has been largely replaced by the metric system, and we will ignore apothecary units in this text. The apothecary system deals only with volumes and weights, and the volumetric units are comparable to those of the U.S. system. The two systems differ, however, in terms of the definitions of mass units.

The U.S. and metric systems also differ in their methods of reporting temperatures; in the United States, temperatures are usually reported in degrees Fahrenheit (°F), whereas scientific literature and individuals in most other countries report temperatures in degrees Centigrade or Celsius (°C). The relationship between temperatures in degrees Fahrenheit and those in degrees Centigrade has been indicated at the bottom of Table A.2.

TABLE A.1 The U.S. System of Measurement

Physical Property	Unit	Relationship to Other U.S. Units	Relationship to Household Units
Length	inch (in.)	1 in. = 0.083 ft	
	foot (ft)	1 ft = 12 in.	
		= 0.33 yd	
	yard (yd)	1 yd = 36 in.	
		= 3 ft	
	mile (mi)	1 mi = 5280 ft	
		= 1760 yd	
Volume	fluidram (fl dr)	1 fl dr = 0.125 fl oz	
	fluid ounce (fl oz)	1 fl oz = 8 fl dr	= 6 teaspoons (tsp)
		= 0.0625 pt	= 2 tablespoons (tbsp)
	pint (pt)	1 pt = 128 fl dr	= 32 tbsp
		= 16 fl oz	= 2 cups (c)
		= 0.5 qt	
	quart (qt)	1 qt = 256 fl dr	= 4 c
		= 32 fl oz	
		= 2 pt	
		= 0.25 gal	
	gallon (gal)	1 gal = 128 fl oz	
		= 8 pt	
		= 4 qt	
Mass	grain (gr)	1 gr = 0.002 oz	
	dram (dr)	1 dr = 27.3 gr	
		= 0.063 oz	
	ounce (oz)	1 oz = 437.5 gr	
		= 16 dr	
	pound (lb)	1 lb = 7000 gr	
		= 256 dr	
		= 16 oz	
	ton (t)	1 t = 2000 lb	

Table A.2 The Metric System of Measurement

Physical Property	Unit	Relationship to Standard Metric Units	Conversion to U.S. Units	
Length	nanometer (nm)	1 nm = 0.000000001 m (10^{-9})	= 4×10^{-8} in.	25,000,000 nm = 1 in.
	micrometer (μm)	1 μm = 0.000001 m (10^{-6})	= 4×10^{-5} in.	25,000 m = 1 in.
	millimeter (mm)	1 mm = 0.001 m (10^{-3})	= 0.0394 in.	25.4 mm = 1 in.
	centimeter (cm)	1 cm = 0.01 m (10^{-2})	= 0.394 in.	2. 54 cm = 1 in.
	decimeter (dm)	1 dm = 0.1 m (10^{-1})	= 3.94 in.	0.25 dm = 1 in.
	meter (m)	standard unit of length	= 39.4 in.	0.0254 m = 1 in.
			= 3.28 ft	0.3048 m = 1 ft
			= 1.09 yd	0.914 m = 1 yd
	dekameter (dam)	1 dam = 10 m		
	hectometer (hm)	1 hm = 100 m		
	kilometer (km)	1 km = 1000 m	= 3280 ft	
			= 1093 yd	
			= 0.62 mi	1.609 km = 1 mi
Volume	microliter (μl)	1 μl = 0.000001 L (10^{-6}) = 1 cubic millimeter (mm^3)		
	milliliter (ml)	1 ml = 0.001 L (10^{-3}) = 1 cubic centimeter (cm^3 or cc)	= 0.03 fl oz	5 ml = 1 tsp
				15 ml = 1 tbsp
				30 ml = 1 fl oz
	centiliter (cl)	1 cl = 0.01 L (10^{-2})	= 0.34 fl oz	3 cl = 1 fl oz
	deciliter (dl)	1 dl = 0.1 L (10^{-1})	= 3.38 fl oz	0.29 dl = 1 fl oz
	liter (L)	standard unit of volume	= 33.8 fl oz	0.0295 L = 1 fl oz
			= 2.11 pt	0.473 L = 1 pt
			= 1.06 qt	0.946 L = 1 qt
Mass	picogram (pg)	1 pg = 0.000000000001 g (10^{-12})		
	nanogram (ng)	1 ng = 0.000000001 g (10^{-9})		
	microgram (μg)	1 μg = 0.000001 g (10^{-6})	= 0.000015 gr	66,666 μg = 1 gr
	milligram (mg)	1 mg = 0.001 g (10^{-3})	= 0.015 gr	66.7 mg = 1 gr
	centigram (cg)	1 cg = 0.01 g (10^{-2})	= 0.15 gr	6.7 cg = 1 gr
	decigram (dg)	1 dg = 0.1 g (10^{-1})	= 1.5 gr	0.67 dg = 1 gr
	gram (g)	standard unit of mass	= 0.035 oz	28.35 g = 1 oz
			= 0.0022 lb	453.6 g = 1 lb
	dekagram (dag)	1 dag = 10 g		
	hectogram (hg)	1 hg = 100 g		
	kilogram (kg)	1 kg = 1000 g	= 2.2 lb	0.453 kg = 1 lb
	metric ton (kt)	1 kt = 1000 kg	= 1.1 t	
			= 2205 lb	0.907 kt = 1 t

Temperature	Centigrade	Fahrenheit
Freezing point of pure water	0°	32°
Normal body temperature	36.8°	98.6°
Boiling point of pure water	100°	212°
Conversion °C → °F:	°F = (1.8 × °C) + 32	°F → °C: °C = (°F – 32) × 0.56

APPENDIX

Foreign Word Roots, Prefixes, Suffixes, and Combining Forms

APPENDIX

Many of the words we use in everyday English have their roots in other languages, particularly Greek and Latin. This is especially true for anatomical terms, many of which were introduced into the anatomical literature by Greek and Roman anatomists. This list includes some of the foreign word roots, prefixes, suffixes, and combining forms that are part of many of the biological and anatomical terms you will see in this text.

a-, *a-*, without: avascular
ab-, ab, from: abduct
-ac,*-akos*, pertaining to: cardiac
ad-, *ad*, to, toward: adduct
aden-, **adeno-**, *adenos*, gland: adenoid
af-, *ad*, toward: afferent
-al, *-alis*, pertaining to: brachial
-algia, *algos*, pain: neuralgia
ana-, *ana*, up, back: anaphase
andro-, *andros*, male: androgen
angio-, *angeion*, vessel: angiogram
anti-, ant-, *anti*, against: antibiotic
apo-, apo, from: apocrine
arachn-, *arachne*, spider: arachnoid
arthro-, *arthros*, joint: arthroscopy
-asis, **-asia**, state, condition: homeostasis
astro-, *aster*, star: astrocyte
atel-, *ateles*, imperfect: atelectasis
baro-, *baros*, pressure: baroreceptor
bi-, bi-, two: bifurcate
blast-, **-blast**, *blastos*, precursor: blastocyst
brachi-, *brachium*, arm: brachiocephalic
brady-, *bradys*, slow: bradycardia
bronch-, *bronchus*, windpipe, airway: bronchial
cardi-, **cardio-**, **-cardia**, *kardia*, heart: cardiac
-centesis, *kentesis*, puncture: thoracocentesis
cerebro-, *cerebrum*, brain: cerebrospinal
chole-, *chole*, bile: cholecystitis
chondro-, *chondros*, cartilage: chondrocyte
chrom-, **chromo-**, *chroma*, color: chromatin
circum-, *circum*, around: circumduction
-clast, *klastos*, broken: osteoclast
coel-, **-coel**, *koila*, cavity: coelom
contra-, *contra*, against: contralateral
cranio-, *cranium*, skull: craniosacral
cribr-, *cribrum*, sieve: cribriform
-crine, *krinein*, to separate: endocrine
cyst-, **-cyst**, *kystis*, sac: blastocyst
desmo-, *desmos*, band: desmosome
di-, *dis*, twice: disaccharide
dia-, *dia*, through: diameter
diure-, *diourein*, to urinate: diuresis
dys-, dys-, painful: dysmenorrhea
-ectasis, *ektasis*, expansion: atelectasis
ecto-, *ektos*, outside: ectoderm
ef-, *ex*, away from: efferent
emmetro-, *emmetros*, in proper measure: emmetropia
encephalo-, *enkephalos*, brain: encephalitis
end-, **endo-**, *endos*, inside: endometrium
entero-, *enteron*, intestine: enteric
epi-, *epi*, on: epimysium
erythema-, *erythema*, flushed (skin): erythematosis
erythro-, *erythros*, red: erythrocyte
ex-, *ex*, out, away from: exocytosis
ferr-, *ferrum*, iron: transferrin
-gen, **-genic**, *gennan*, to produce: mutagen
genicula-, *geniculum*, kneelike structure: geniculate
genio-, *geneion*, chin: geniohyoid
glosso-, **-glossus**, *glossus*, tongue: hypoglossal
glyco-, *glykys*, sugar: glycogen
-gram, *gramma*, record: myogram
-graph, **-graphia**, *graphein*, to write, record: electroencephalograph
gyne-, **gyno-**, *gynaikos*, woman: gynecologist
hem-, **hemato-**, *haima*, blood: hemopoiesis
hemi-, hemi-, half: hemisphere
hepato-, *hepaticus*, liver: hepatocyte
hetero-, *heteros*, other: heterosexual
histo-, *histos*, tissue: histology
holo-, *holos*, entire: holocrine
homeo-, **homo-**, *homos*, same: homeostasis
hyal-, **hyalo-**, *hyalos*, glass: hyaline
hydro-, *hydros*, water: hydrolysis
hyo-, *hyoeides*, U-shaped: hyoid
hyper-, *hyper*, above: hyperpolarization
ili-, **ilio-**, *ilium:* iliac
infra-, *infra*, beneath: infraorbital
inter-, *inter*, between: interventricular
intra-, *intra*, within: intracapsular
ipsi-, *ipse*, itself: ipsilateral
iso-, *isos*, equal: isotonic
-itis, -itis, inflammation: dermatitis
karyo-, *karyon*, body: megakaryocyte
kerato-, *keros*, horn: keratin
kino-, **-kinin**, *kinein*, to move: bradykinin
lact-, **lacto-**, **-lactin**, *lac*, milk: prolactin
-lemma, *lemma*, husk: plasmalemma
leuko-, *leukos*, white: leukocyte
liga-, *ligare*, to bind together: ligase
lip-, **lipo-**, *lipos*, fat: lipoid
lyso-, **-lysis**, **-lyze**, *lysis*, dissolution: hydrolysis
mal-, *mal*, abnormal: malabsorption
mamilla-, *mamilla*, little breast: mamillary
mast-, **masto-**, *mastos*, breast: mastoid
mega-, *megas*, big: megakaryocyte
mero-, *meros*, part: merocrine
meso-, *mesos*, middle: mesoderm
meta-, *meta*, after, beyond: metaphase
mono-, *monos*, single: monocyte
morpho-, *morphe*, form: morphology
-mural, *murus*, wall: intramural
myelo-, *myelos*, marrow: myeloblast
myo-, *mys*, muscle: myofilament
natri-, *natrium*, sodium: natriuretic
neur-, **neuro-**, *neuron*, nerve: neuromuscular
oculo-, *oculus*, eye: oculomotor
oligo-, *oligos*, little, few: oligopeptide
-ology, *logos*, the study of: physiology
-oma,-oma, swelling: carcinoma
onco-, *onkos*, mass, tumor: oncology
-opia, *ops*, eye: optic
-osis,-osis, state, condition: neurosis
osteon, **osteo-**, *os*, bone: osteocyte
oto-, *otikos*, ear: otoconia
para-, *para*, beyond: paraplegia
patho-, **-path**, **-pathy**, *pathos*, disease: pathology
pedia-, *paidos*, child: pediatrician
peri-, *peri*, around: perineurium
-phasia, *phasis*, speech: aphasia
-phil, **-philia**, *philus*, love: hydrophilic
-phobe, **-phobia**, *phobos*, fear: hydrophobic
-phylaxis, *phylax*, a guard: prophylaxis
physio-, *physis*, nature: physiology
-plasia, *plasis*, formation: dysplasia
platy-, *platys*, flat: platysma
-plegia, *plege*, a blow, paralysis: paraplegia
-plexy, *plessein*, to strike: apoplexy
podo-, *podon*, foot: podocyte
-poiesis, *poiesis*, making: hemopoiesis
poly-, *polys*, many: polysaccharide
presby-, *presbys*, old: presbyopia
pro-, *pro*, before: prophase
pterygo-, *pteryx*, wing: pterygoid
pulp-, *pulpa*, flesh: pulpitis
retro-, *retro*, backward: retroperitoneal
-rrhea, *rhein*, flow, discharge: amenorrhea
sarco-, *sarkos*, flesh: sarcomere
scler-, **sclero-**, *skleros*, hard: sclera
semi-, *semis*, half: semitendinosus
-septic, *septikos*, putrid: antiseptic
-sis, state, condition: metastasis
som-, **-some**, *soma*, body: somatic
spino-, *spina*, spine, vertebral column: spinodeltoid
-stomy, *stoma*, mouth, opening: colostomy
stylo-, *stylus*, stake, pole: styloid
sub-, *sub*, below: subcutaneous
syn-, *syn*, together: synthesis
tachy-, *tachys*, swift: tachycardia
telo-, *telos*, end: telophase
therm-, **thermo-**, *therme*, heat: thermoregulation
-tomy, *temnein*, to cut: appendectomy
trans-, *trans*, through: transudate
-trophic, **-trophin**, **-trophy**, *trophikos*, nourishing: adrenocorticotropic
tropho-, *trophe*, nutrition: trophoblast
tropo-, *tropikos*, turning: troponin
uro-, **-uria**, *ouron*, urine: glycosuria

Eponyms in Common Use

Eponym	Equivalent Terms	Individual Referenced
THE CELLULAR LEVEL OF ORGANIZATION (CHAPTER 2)		
Golgi apparatus		Camillo Golgi (1844–1926), Italian histologist; shared Nobel Prize in 1906
Krebs cycle	Tricarboxylic or citric acid cycle	Hans Adolph Krebs (1900–1981), British biochemist; shared Nobel Prize in 1953
THE SKELETAL SYSTEM (CHAPTERS 5–8)		
Colles' fracture		Abraham Colles (1773–1843), Irish surgeon
Haversian canals	Central canals	Clopton Havers (1650–1702), English anatomist and microscopist
Haversian systems	Osteons	Clopton Havers (1650–1702), English anatomist and microscopist
Pott's fracture		Percivall Pott (1714–1788), English surgeon
Sharpey's fiber	Perforating fibers	William Sharpey (1802–1880), Scottish histologist and physiologist
Volkmann's canals	Perforating canals	Alfred Wilhelm Volkmann (1800–1877), German surgeon
Wormian bones	Sutural bones	Olas Worm (1588–1654), Danish anatomist
THE MUSCULAR SYSTEM (CHAPTERS 9–11)		
Achilles tendon	Calcaneal tendon	Achilles, hero of Greek mythology
Cori cycle		Carl Ferdinand Cori (1896–1984) and Gerty Theresa Cori (1896–1957), American biochemists; shared Nobel Prize in 1947
THE NERVOUS SYSTEM (CHAPTERS 13–17)		
Broca's center	Speech center	Pierre Paul Broca (1824–1880), French surgeon
Foramina of Luschka	Lateral foramina	Hubert von Luschka (1820–1875), German anatomist
Foramen of Magendie	Median foramen	François Magendie (1783–1855), French physiologist
Foramen of Munro	Interventricular foramen	John Cummings Munro (1858–1910), American surgeon
Nissl bodies	Chromatophilic substance	Franz Nissl (1860–1919), German neurologist
Purkinje cells		Johannes E. Purkinje (1787–1869), Czechoslovakian physiologist
Nodes of Ranvier	Myelin sheath gap	Louis Antoine Ranvier (1835–1922), French physiologist
Island of Reil	Insula	Johann Christian Reil (1759–1813), German anatomist
Fissure of Rolando	Central sulcus	Luigi Rolando (1773–1831), Italian anatomist
Schwann cells		Theodor Schwann (1810–1882), German anatomist
Aqueduct of Sylvius	Aqueduct of midbrain	Jacobus Sylvius (Jacques Dubois, 1478–1555), French anatomist
Sylvian fissure	Lateral sulcus	Franciscus Sylvius (Franz de le Boë, 1614–1672), Dutch anatomist
Pons varolii	Pons	Costanzo Varolio (1543–1575), Italian anatomist
SENSORY FUNCTION (CHAPTER 18)		
Organ of Corti		Alfonso Corti (1822–1888), Italian anatomist
Eustachian tube	Auditory tube	Bartolomeo Eustachio (1520–1574), Italian anatomist
Golgi tendon organs	Tendon organs	*See* Golgi apparatus *under* The Cellular Level (Chapter 2)
Hertz (Hz)		Heinrich Hertz (1857–1894), German physicist
Meibomian glands		Heinrich Meibom (1638–1700), German anatomist
Corpuscles of Meissner	Tactile corpuscles	Georg Meissner (1829–1905), German physiologist
Merkel's discs	Tactile discs	Friedrich Siegismund Merkel (1845–1919), German anatomist
Pacinian corpuscles	Lamellated corpuscles	Filippo Pacini (1812–1883), Italian anatomist
Ruffini's corpuscles		Angelo Ruffini (1864–1929), Italian anatomist
Canal of Schlemm	Scleral venous sinus	Friedrich S. Schlemm (1795–1858), German anatomist
Glands of Zeis		Edward Zeis (1807–1868), German ophthalmologist
THE ENDOCRINE SYSTEM (CHAPTER 19)		
Islets of Langerhans	Pancreatic islets	Paul Langerhans (1847–1888), German pathologist
Interstitial cells of Leydig	Interstitial cells	Franz von Leydig (1821–1908), German anatomist

Eponym	Equivalent Terms	Individual Referenced
THE CARDIOVASCULAR SYSTEM (CHAPTER 20–22)		
Bundle of His		Wilhelm His (1863–1934), German physician
Purkinje cells		*See under* The Nervous System (Chapters 13–17)
Starling's law		Ernest Henry Starling (1866–1927), English physiologist
Circle of Willis	Cerebral arterial circle	Thomas Willis (1621–1675), English physician
THE LYMPHOID SYSTEM (CHAPTER 23)		
Hassall's corpuscles	Thymic corpuscles	Arthur Hill Hassall (1817–1894), English physician
Kupffer cells	Stellate reticuloendothelial cells	Karl Wilhelm Kupffer (1829–1902), German anatomist
Langerhans cells		*See* Islets of Langerhans *under* The Endocrine System (Chapter 19)
Peyer's patches	Aggregated lymphoid nodules	Johann Conrad Peyer (1653–1712), Swiss anatomist
THE RESPIRATORY SYSTEM (CHAPTER 24)		
Adam's apple	Laryngeal prominence of thyroid cartilage	Biblical reference
Bohr effect		Cristian Bohr (1855–1911), Danish physiologist
Boyle's law		Robert Boyle (1621–1691), English physicist
Charles' law		Jacques Alexandre César Charles (1746–1823), French physicist
Dalton's law		John Dalton (1766–1844), English physicist
Henry's law		William Henry (1775–1837), English chemist
THE DIGESTIVE SYSTEM (CHAPTER 25)		
Plexus of Auerbach	Myenteric plexus	Leopold Auerbach (1827–1897), German anatomist
Brunner's glands	Duodenal submucosal glands	Johann Conrad Brunner (1653–1727), Swiss anatomist
Kupffer cells	Stellate reticuloendothelial cells	*See under* The Lymphoid System (Chapter 23)
Crypts of Lieberkuhn	Intestinal crypts (Intestinal glands)	Johann Nathaniel Lieberkuhn (1711–1756), German anatomist
Plexus of Meissner	Submucosal plexus	*See* Corpuscles of Meissner *under* Sensory Function (Chapter 18)
Sphincter of Oddi	Hepatopancreatic sphincter	Ruggero Oddi (1864–1913), Italian physician
Peyer's patches	Aggregated lymphoid nodules	*See under* The Lymphoid System (Chapter 23)
Duct of Santorini	Accessory pancreatic duct	Giovanni Domenico Santorini (1681–1737), Italian anatomist
Stensen's duct	Parotid duct	Niels Stensen (1638–1686), Danish physician/priest
Ampulla of Vater	Duodenal ampulla	Abraham Vater (1684–1751), German anatomist
Wharton's duct	Submandibular duct	Thomas Wharton (1614–1673), English physician
Foramen of Winslow	Epiploic foramen	Jacob Benignus Winslow (1669–1760), French anatomist
Duct of Wirsung	Pancreatic duct	Johann Georg Wirsung (1600–1643), German physician
THE URINARY SYSTEM (CHAPTER 26)		
Bowman's capsule	Glomerular capsule	Sir William Bowman (1816–1892), English physician
Loop of Henle	Nephron loop	Friedrich Gustav Jakob Henle (1809–1885), German histologist
Glands of Littre	Urethral glands	Alexis Littre (1658–1726), French surgeon
THE REPRODUCTIVE SYSTEM (CHAPTER 27–28)		
Bartholin's glands	Greater vestibular glands	Casper Bartholin, Jr. (1655–1738), Danish anatomist
Cowper's glands	Bulbo-urethral glands	William Cowper (1666–1709), English surgeon
Fallopian tube	Uterine tube/oviduct	Gabriele Falloppio (1523–1562), Italian anatomist
Graafian follicle	Tertiary follicle	Reijnier de Graaf (1641–1673), Dutch physician
Interstitial cells of Leydig	Interstitial cells	*See under* The Endocrine System (Chapter 19)
Sertoli cells	Nurse cells (Sustentacular cells)	Enrico Sertoli (1842–1910), Italian histologist

Glossary of Key Terms

abdomen: Region of trunk bounded by the diaphragm and pelvis.
abdominopelvic cavity: Portion of the ventral body cavity that contains abdominal and pelvic subdivisions.
abducens (ab-DŪ-senz): Cranial nerve VI; innervates the lateral rectus muscle of the eye.
abduction: Movement away from the midline.
abortion: Premature loss or expulsion of an embryo or fetus.
abscess: A localized collection of pus within a damaged tissue.
absorption: The active or passive uptake of gases, fluids, or solutes.
accommodation: Alteration in the curvature of the lens to focus an image on the retina; decrease in receptor sensitivity or perception following chronic stimulation.
acetabulum (a-se-TAB-ū-lum): Fossa on lateral aspect of pelvis that accommodates the head of the femur.
acetylcholine (ACh) (as-e-til-KŌ-lēn): Chemical neurotransmitter in the brain and PNS; dominant neurotransmitter in the PNS, released at neuromuscular synapses and synapses of the parasympathetic division.
acetylcholinesterase (AChE): Enzyme found in the synaptic cleft, bound to the postsynaptic membrane, and in tissue fluids; breaks down and inactivates ACh molecules.
achalasia (ak-a-LĀ-zē-a): Condition that develops when the lower esophageal sphincter fails to dilate, and ingested materials cannot enter the stomach.
Achilles tendon: Calcaneal tendon.
acid: A compound whose dissociation in solution releases a hydrogen ion and an anion; an acid solution has a pH below 7. 0 and contains an excess of hydrogen ions.
acinus/acini (A-si-nī): Histological term referring to a blind pocket, pouch, or sac.
acne: Condition characterized by inflammation of sebaceous glands and follicles; commonly affects adolescents and most often involves the face.
acoustic: Pertaining to sound or the sense of hearing.
acquired immune deficiency syndrome (AIDS): A disease caused by the **human immunodeficiency virus (HIV)**, characterized by destruction of helper T cells and a resulting severe impairment of the immune response.
acromegaly: Condition caused by overproduction of growth hormone in the adult, characterized by thickening of bones and enlargement of cartilages and other soft tissues.
acromion (a-KRŌ-mē-on): Continuation of the scapular spine that projects superior to the capsule of the shoulder joint.
acrosomal cap (ak-rō-SŌ-mal): Membranous sac at the tip of a sperm cell that contains hyaluronic acid.
actin: Protein component of microfilaments; forms thin filaments in skeletal muscles and produces contractions of all muscles through interaction with thick (myosin) filaments; *see* **sliding filament theory**.
action potential: A conducted change in the transmembrane potential of excitable cells, initiated by a change in the membrane permeability to sodium ions: *see* **nerve impulse**.
active transport: The ATP-dependent absorption or excretion of solutes across a cell membrane.
acute: Sudden in onset, severe in intensity, and brief in duration.
adaptation: Alteration of pupillary size in response to changes in light intensity; in CNS, often used as a synonym for accommodation: physiological responses that produce acclimatization.
Addison's disease: Condition resulting from hyposecretion of glucocorticoids, characterized by lethargy, weakness, hypotension, and increased skin pigmentation.
adduction: Movement toward the axis or midline of the body as viewed in the anatomical position.
adenine: A purine, one of the nitrogen bases in the nucleic acids RNA and DNA.
adenohypophysis (ad-e-nō-hī-POF-i-sis): The anterior lobe of the pituitary gland, also called the *anterior pituitary* or the **pars distalis**.
adenoid: The pharyngeal tonsil.
adenosine triphosphate (ATP): A high-energy compound consisting of adenosine with three phosphate groups attached; the third is attached by a high-energy bond.
adhesion: Fusion of two mesenteric layers following damage or irritation of their opposing surfaces.
adipocyte (AD-i-pō-sīt): A fat cell.
adipose tissue: Loose connective tissue dominated by adipocytes.
adrenocortical hormone: Any of the steroids produced by the adrenal cortex.
adrenocorticotropic hormone (ACTH): Hormone that stimulates the production and secretion of glucocorticoids by the zona fasciculata of the adrenal cortex; released by the anterior pituitary in response to CRF.
adventitia (ad-ven-TISH-a): Superficial layer of connective tissue surrounding an internal organ; fibers are continuous with those of surrounding tissues, providing support and stabilization.
afferent: Toward a central receiving area.
afferent arteriole: An arteriole bringing blood to the glomerulus of the kidney.
afferent fiber: Axons carrying sensory information to the CNS.
agglutination (a-gloo-ti-NĀ-shun): Aggregation of red blood cells due to interactions between surface agglutinogens and plasma agglutinins.
aggregated lymphoid nodules: Lymphoid nodules beneath the epithelium of the small intestine. Also called *Peyer's Patches.*
agonist: A muscle responsible for a specific movement.
agranular: Without granules; **agranular leukocytes** are monocytes and lymphocytes; the **agranular reticulum** is an intracellular organelle that synthesizes and stores carbohydrates and lipids.
AIDS: *See* **acquired immune deficiency syndrome**.
AIDS-related complex (ARC): Early symptoms of HIV infection, consisting chiefly of lymphadenopathy, fevers, and chronic nonfatal infections.
alba, albicans, albuginea (AL-bi-kanz) (al-bū-JIN-ē-a): White.
albinism: Absence of pigment in hair and skin caused by inability of body to produce melanin.
albumins (al-BŪ-minz): The smallest of the plasma proteins; function as transport proteins and important in contributing to plasma oncotic pressure.
aldosterone: A mineralocorticoid (steroid) produced by the zona glomerulosa of the adrenal cortex that stimulates sodium and water conservation at the kidneys; secreted in response to the presence of angiotensin II.
aldosteronism: Condition caused by the oversecretion of aldosterone, characterized by fluid retention, edema, and hypertension.
allantois (a-LAN-tō-is): One of the extraembryonic membranes; it provides vascularity to the chorion and is therefore essential to placenta formation; the proximal portion becomes the urinary bladder.
alpha cells: Cells in the pancreatic islets that secrete glucagon.
alpha receptors: Membrane receptors sensitive to norepinephrine or epinephrine; stimulation usually results in excitation of the target cell.
alveolar sac: An air-filled chamber that supplies air to several alveoli.
alveolus/alveoli (al-VĒ-ō-lī): Blind pockets at the end of the respiratory tree, lined by a simple squamous epithelium and surrounded by a capillary network; gas exchange with the blood occurs here.
Alzheimer's disease: Disorder resulting from degenerative changes in populations of neurons in the cerebrum, causing dementia characterized by problems with attention, short-term memory, and emotions.
amacrine cells (AM-a-krīn): Modified neurons in the retina that facilitate or inhibit communication between bipolar and ganglion cells.
amino acids: Organic compounds whose chemical structure can be summarized as R—$CHNH_2COOH$.
amnesia: Temporary or permanent memory loss.
amniocentesis: Sampling of amniotic fluid for analytical purposes; used to detect certain forms of genetic abnormalities.
amnion (AM-nē-on): One of the extraembryonic membranes; surrounds the developing embryo/fetus.
amniotic fluid (am-nē-OT-ik): Fluid that fills the amniotic cavity; provides cushioning and support for the embryo/fetus.
amphiarthrosis (am-fē-ar-THRŌ-sis): An articulation that permits a small degree of independent movement.
amphimixis (am-fi-MIK-sis): The fusion of male and female pronuclei following fertilization.
ampulla/ampullae (am-PŪL-la): A localized dilation in the lumen of a canal or passageway.
amygdala/amygdaloid nucleus (ah-MIG-da-loid): A basal nucleus that is a component of the limbic system and acts as an interface between that system, the cerebrum, and sensory systems.
amylase: An enzyme that breaks down polysaccharides, produced by the salivary glands and pancreas.
anabolism (a-NAB-ō-lizm): The synthesis of complex organic compounds from simpler precursors.
anal canal: The distal portion of the rectum that contains the anal columns and ends at the anus.
analgesia: Relief from pain.
anal triangle: The posterior subdivision of the perineum.
anaphase (AN-uh-fāz): Mitotic stage in which the paired chromatids separate and move toward opposite ends of the spindle apparatus.
anastomosis (a-nas-tō-MŌ-sis): The joining of two tubes, usually referring to a connection between two peripheral vessels without an intervening capillary bed.
anatomical position: An anatomical reference position, the body viewed from the anterior surface with the palms facing forward; supine.
anatomy (a-NAT-ō-mē): The study of the structure of the body.
anaxonic neuron (an-ak-SON-ik): A CNS neuron that has many processes but no apparent axon.
androgen (AN-drō-jen): A steroid sex hormone produced primarily by the interstitial cells of the testis, and manufactured in small quantities by the adrenal cortex in either sex.
anemia (a-NĒ-mē-a): Condition marked by a reduction in the hematocrit and/or hemoglobin content of the blood.
anencephaly (an-en-SEF-a-lē): Development defect characterized by incomplete development of cerebral hemispheres and cranium.

anesthesia: Total or partial loss of sensation from a region of the body.
aneurysm (AN-ū-rizm): A weakening and localized dilation in the wall of a blood vessel.
angiogram (AN-jē-ō-gram): An x-ray image of circulatory pathways.
angiography: X-ray examination of vessel distribution following the introduction of radiopaque substances into the bloodstream.
angiotensin I, II: Angiotensin II is a hormone that causes an elevation in systemic blood pressure, stimulates secretion of aldosterone, promotes thirst, and causes the release of ADH; a converting enzyme in the pulmonary capillaries converts angiotensin I to angiotensin II.
angiotensinogen: Blood protein produced by the liver that is converted to angiotensin I by the enzyme renin.
ankyloglossia (ang-ki-lō-GLOS-ē-a): Condition characterized by an overly robust and restrictive lingual frenulum.
annulus (AN-ū-lus): A cartilage or bone shaped like a ring.
anorexia nervosa: An eating disorder marked by a loss of appetite and pronounced weight loss.
anoxia (an-OK-sē-a): Tissue oxygen deprivation.
antagonist: A muscle that opposes the movement of an agonist.
antebrachium: The forearm.
anteflexion (an-tē-FLEK-shun): Normal position of the uterus, with the superior surface bent forward.
anterior: On or near the front or ventral surface of the body.
antibiotic: Chemical agent that selectively kills pathogenic microorganisms.
antibody (AN-ti-bod-ē): A globular protein produced by plasmocytes that will bind to specific antigens and promote their destruction or removal from the body.
anticoagulant: Compound that slows or prevents clot formation by interfering with the clotting system.
antidiuretic hormone (ADH) (an-tī-dī-ū-RET-ik): Hormone synthesized in the hypothalamus and secreted at the posterior pituitary; causes water retention at the kidneys and an elevation of blood pressure.
antigen: A substance capable of inducing the production of antibodies.
antrum (AN-trum): A chamber or pocket.
anuria (a-NŪ-rē-a): Cessation of urine production.
anus: External opening of the anal canal.
aorta: Large, elastic artery that carries blood away from the left ventricle and into the systemic circuit.
aortic reflex: Baroreceptor reflex triggered by increased aortic pressures; leads to a reduction in cardiac output and a fall in systemic pressure.
apex (Ā-peks): A pointed tip, usually referring to a triangular object and positioned opposite a broad base.
Apgar rating: A test used to assess the neurological status of a newborn infant.
aphasia: Inability to speak.
apnea (AP-nē-a): Cessation of breathing.
apneustic center (ap-NŪ-stik): Respiratory center whose chronic activation would lead to apnea at full inspiration.
apocrine secretion: Mode of secretion where the glandular cell sheds portions of its cytoplasm.
aponeurosis/aponeuroses (ap-ō-noo-RŌ-sēz): A broad tendinous sheet that may serve as the origin or insertion of a skeletal muscle.
appendicitis: Inflammation of the appendix.
appendicular: Pertaining to the upper or lower limbs.
appendix: A blind tube connected to the cecum of the large intestine.
appositional growth: Enlargement by the addition of cartilage or bony matrix to the outer surface.
aqueous humor: Fluid similar to perilymph or CSF that fills the anterior chamber of the eye.
arachnoid granulations: Processes of the arachnoid that project into the superior sagittal sinus; sites where CSF enters the venous circulation.
arachnoid mater (a-RAK-noyd): The middle meninges that enclose CSF and protect the central nervous system.
arbor vitae: Central, branching mass of white matter inside the cerebellum.
arcuate (AR-kū-āt): Curving.
areflexia (ā-re-FLEK-sē-a): Absence of normal reflex responses to stimulation.
areola (a-RĒ-ō-la): Pigmented area that surrounds the nipple of a breast.
areolar: Containing minute spaces, as in areolar connective tissue.
arrector pili (ar-REK-tor PĪ-lī): Smooth muscles whose contractions cause piloerection.
arrhythmias (a-RITH-mē-az): Abnormal patterns of cardiac contractions.
arteriole (ar-TĒ-rē-ōl): A small arterial branch that delivers blood to a capillary network.
artery: A blood vessel that carries blood away from the heart and toward a peripheral capillary.
arthritis (ar-THRĪ-tis): Inflammation of a joint.
arthroscope: Fiber-optic device intended for visualizing the interior of joints; may also be used for certain forms of joint surgery.
articular: Pertaining to a joint.
articular capsule: Dense collagen fiber sleeve that surrounds a joint and provides protection and stabilization.
articular cartilage: Cartilage pad that covers the surface of a bone inside a joint cavity.
articulation (ar-tik-ū-LĀ-shun): A joint; formation of words.
arytenoid cartilages (ar-i-TĒ-noyd): A pair of small cartilages in the larynx.
ascending tract: A tract carrying information from the spinal cord to the brain.
ascites (a-SĪ-tēz): Overproduction and accumulation of peritoneal fluid.
aseptic: Free from pathogenic contamination.
asphyxia: Unconsciousness due to oxygen deprivation at the CNS.
aspirate: To remove or obtain by suction; to inhale.
association areas: Cortical areas of the cerebrum responsible for integration of sensory inputs and/or motor commands.
asthma (AZ-ma): Reversible constriction of smooth muscles around respiratory passageways, frequently caused by an allergic response.
astigmatism: Visual disturbance due to an irregularity in the shape of the cornea.
astrocyte (AS-trō-sīt): One of the glial cells in the CNS.
atelectasis (at-e-LEK-ta-sis): Collapse of a lung or a portion of a lung.
atherosclerosis (ath-er-ō-skle-RŌ-sis): Formation of fatty plaques in the walls of arteries, leading to circulatory impairment.
atresia (a-TRĒ-zē-a): Closing of a cavity, or its incomplete development; used in the reproductive system to refer to the degeneration of developing ovarian follicles.
atria: Thin-walled chambers of the heart that receive venous blood from the pulmonary or systemic circuits.
atrial natriuretic peptide (nā-tre-ū-RET-ik): Hormone released by specialized atrial cardiocytes when they are stretched by an abnormally large venous return; promotes fluid loss and reductions in blood pressure and venous return.
atrioventricular (AV) node (ā-trē-ō-ven-TRIK-ū-lar): Specialized cardiocytes that relay the contractile stimulus to the bundle of His, the bundle branches, the Purkinje fibers, and the ventricular myocardium; located at the boundary between the atria and ventricles.
atrioventricular valve: One of the valves that prevent backflow into the atria during ventricular systole.
atrophy (AT-rō-fē): Wasting away of tissues from lack of use or nutritional abnormalities.
auditory ossicles: The bones of the middle ear: malleus, incus, and stapes.
auditory tube: A passageway that connects the nasopharynx with the middle ear cavity; *also called the Eustachian or pharyngotympanic tube.*
autoimmunity: Immune system sensitivity to normal cells and tissues, resulting in the production of autoantibodies.
autolysis: Destruction of a cell due to the rupture of lysosomal membranes in its cytoplasm.
automatic bladder: Reflex micturition following stimulation of stretch receptors in the bladder wall; seen in patients who have lost motor control of the lower body.
automaticity: Spontaneous depolarization to threshold, a characteristic of cardiac pacemaker cells.
autonomic ganglion: A collection of visceral motor neurons outside the CNS.
autonomic nerve: A peripheral nerve consisting of preganglionic or postganglionic autonomic fibers.
autonomic nervous system (ANS): Centers, nuclei, tracts, ganglia, and nerves involved in the unconscious regulation of visceral functions; includes components of the CNS and PNS.
autopsy: Detailed examination of a body after death, usually performed by a pathologist.
autoregulation: Alterations in activity that maintain homeostasis in direct response to changes in the local environment; does not require neural or endocrine control.
autosomal (aw-tō-SŌ-mal): Chromosomes other than the X or Y chromosomes that determine the genetic sex of an individual.
avascular (ā-VAS-kū-lar): Without blood vessels.
avulsion: An injury involving the violent tearing away of body tissues.
axilla: The armpit.
axolemma: The cell membrane of an axon, continuous with the cell membrane of the soma and dendrites and distinct from any glial cell coverings.
axon: Elongate extension of a neuron that conducts an action potential away from the soma and toward the synaptic terminals.
axon hillock: Portion of the neural cell body adjacent to the initial segment.
axoplasm (AK-sō-plazm): Cytoplasm within an axon.
Babinski sign: Reflexive dorsiflexion of the toes following stroking of the plantar surface of the foot; positive reflex (Babinski sign) is normal up to age 1.5 years; thereafter a positive reflex indicates damage to descending tracts.
bacteria: Single-celled microorganisms, some pathogenic, that are common in the environment.
baroreception: Ability to detect changes in pressure.
baroreceptor reflex: A reflexive change in cardiac activity in response to changes in blood pressure.
baroreceptors (bar-ō-rē-SEP-torz): Receptors responsible for baroreception.
basal nuclei: Nuclei of the cerebrum that are involved in the regulation of somatic motor activity at the subconcious level.
base: A compound whose dissociation releases a hydroxide ion (OH^-) or removes a hydrogen ion from the solution.
basement membrane: A layer of filaments and fibers that attach an epithelium to the underlying connective tissue.
basilar lamina: Membrane that supports the organ of Corti and separates the cochlear duct from the scala tympani in the inner ear.
basophils (BĀ-sō-filz): Circulating granulocytes (WBCs) similar in size and function to tissue mast cells.
B cells: Lymphocytes responsible for the production of antibodies, following their conversion to plasmocytes.
benign: Not malignant.

beta cells: Cells of the pancreatic islets that secrete insulin in response to elevated blood sugar concentrations.
beta receptors: Membrane receptors sensitive to epinephrine; stimulation may result in excitation or inhibition of the target cell.
bicarbonate ions: HCO_3^-; anion components of the bicarbonate buffer system.
bicuspid (bī-KUS-pid): A sharp, conical tooth, also called a canine tooth.
bifurcate: To branch into two parts.
bile: Exocrine secretion of the liver that is stored in the gallbladder and ejected into the duodenum.
bile salts: Steroid derivatives in the bile, responsible for the emulsification of ingested lipids.
bilirubin (bil-ē-ROO-bin): A reddish pigment, a product of hemoglobin catabolism.
biopsy: The removal of a small sample of tissue for pathological analysis.
bipennate muscle: A muscle whose fibers are arranged on either side of a common tendon.
bladder: A muscular sac that distends as fluid is stored and whose contraction ejects the fluid at an appropriate time; used alone, the term usually refers to the urinary bladder.
blastocoele (BLAS-tō-sēl): Fluid-filled cavity within a blastocyst.
blastocyst (BLAS-tō-sist): Early stage in the developing embryo, consisting of an outer trophoblast and an inner cell mass.
blastodisc (BLAS-tō-disk): Later stage in the development of the inner cell mass; it includes the cells that will form the embryo.
blastomere (BLAS-tō-mēr): One of the cells in the morula, a collection of cells produced by the division of the zygote.
blood–brain barrier: Isolation of the CNS from the general circulation; primarily the result of astrocyte regulation of capillary permeabilities.
blood clot: A network of fibrin fibers and trapped blood cells.
blood pressure: A force exerted against the vascular walls by the blood, as the result of the push exerted by cardiac contraction and the elasticity of the vessel walls. It is usually measured along one of the muscular arteries, with systolic pressure measured during ventricular systole, and diastolic pressure during ventricular diastole.
blood–testis barrier: Isolation of the seminiferous tubules from the general circulation, due to the activities of the nurse (Sertoli) cells.
boil: An abscess of the skin, usually involving a sebaceous gland.
bolus: A compact mass; usually refers to compacted ingested material on its way to the stomach.
bone: *See* **osseous tissue**.
bowel: The intestinal tract.
brachial: Pertaining to the arm.
brachial plexus: Network formed by branches of spinal nerves C_5–T_1 en route to innervate the upper limb.
brachium: The arm.
bradycardia (brā-dē-KAR-dē-a): An abnormally slow heart rate.
brain stem: The brain minus the cerebrum and cerebellum.
brevis: Short.
Broca's center: The speech center of the brain, usually found on the neural cortex of the left cerebral hemisphere.
bronchial tree: The trachea, bronchi, and bronchioles.
bronchitis (brong-KĪ-tis): Inflammation of the bronchial passageways.
bronchoscope: A fiber-optic instrument used to examine the bronchial passageways.
bronchus/bronchi: One of the branches of the bronchial tree between the trachea and bronchioles.
buccal (BUK-al): Pertaining to the cheeks.
buffer: A compound that stabilizes the pH of a solution by removing or releasing hydrogen ions.
bulbar: Pertaining to the brain stem.
bulbo-urethral glands (bul-bō-ū-RĒ-thral): Mucous glands at the base of the penis that secrete into the penile urethra; also called Cowper's glands.
bundle branches: Specialized conducting cells in the ventricles that carry the contractile stimulus from the bundle of His to the Purkinje fibers.
bundle of His (HISS): Specialized conducting cells in the interventricular septum that carry the contracting stimulus from the AV node to the bundle branches and then to the Purkinje fibers.
bursa: A small sac filled with synovial fluid that cushions adjacent structures and reduces friction.
bursectomy: The surgical removal of an inflamed bursa.
bursitis: Painful inflammation of one or more bursae.
calcaneal tendon: Large tendon that inserts on the calcaneus; tension on this tendon produces plantar flexion of the foot; also called the *Achilles tendon.*
calcaneus (kal-KĀ-nē-us): The heelbone, the largest of the tarsal bones.
calcification: The deposition of calcium salts within a tissue.
calcitonin (kal-si-TŌ-nin): Hormone secreted by thyrotropes, or C cells of the thyroid when calcium ion concentrations are abnormally high; restores homeostasis by increasing the rate of bone deposition and the renal rate of calcium loss, and inhibiting calcium uptake at the digestive tract.
calculus/calculi (KAL-kū-lī): Concretions of insoluble materials that form within body fluids, especially the gallbladder, kidneys, or urinary bladder.
callus: A localized thickening of the epidermis due to chronic mechanical stresses; a thickened area that forms at the site of a bone break as part of the repair process.
calvaria (kal-VAR-ē-a): The skullcap, formed of the frontal, parietal, and occipital bones.
calyx/calyces (KĀL-i-sēz): A cup-shaped division of the renal pelvis.
canaliculi (kan-a-LIK-ū-lē): Microscopic passageways between cells; bile canaliculi carry bile to bile ducts in the liver; in bone, canaliculi permit the diffusion of nutrients and wastes to and from osteocytes.
cancer: A malignant tumor that tends to undergo metastasis.
cannula: A tube that can be inserted into the body; often placed in blood vessels prior to transfusion or dialysis.
canthus, medial and lateral (KAN-thus): The angles formed at either corner of the eye between the upper and lower eyelids.
capacitation (ka-pas-i-TĀ-shun): Activation process that must occur before a spermatozoon can successfully fertilize an egg; occurs in the vagina following ejaculation.
capillaries: Small blood vessels, interposed between arterioles and venules, whose thin walls permit the diffusion of gases, nutrients, and wastes between the plasma and interstitial fluids.
capitulum (ka-PIT-ū-lum): General term for a small, elevated articular process; used to refer to the rounded distal surface of the humerus that articulates with the radial head.
caput: The head.
carbohydrase (kar-bō-HĪ-drāz): An enzyme that breaks down carbohydrate molecules.
carbohydrate (kar-bō-HĪ-drāt): Organic compound containing carbon, hydrogen, and oxygen in a ratio that approximates 1:2:1.
carbon dioxide: CO_2, a compound produced by the decarboxylation reactions of aerobic glycolysis.
carbonic anhydrase: An enzyme that catalyzes the reaction $H_2O + CO_2 \rightarrow H_2CO_3$; important in carbon dioxide transport, gastric acid secretion, and renal pH regulation.
carboxypeptidase (kar-bok-sē-PEP-ti-dāz): A protease that breaks down proteins and releases amino acids.
carcinogenic (kar-sin-ō-JEN-ik): Stimulating cancer formation in affected tissues.
cardia (KAR-dē-a): The area of the stomach surrounding its connection with the esophagus.
cardiac: Pertaining to the heart.
cardiac cycle: One complete heartbeat, including atrial and ventricular systole and diastole.
cardiac glands: Mucous glands characteristic of the cardia of the stomach.
cardiac output: The amount of blood ejected by the left ventricle each minute; normally about 5 liters.
cardiac tamponade: Compression of the heart due to fluid accumulation in the pericardial cavity.
cardiocyte (KAR-dē-ō-sīt): A cardiac muscle cell.
cardiomyopathy (kar-dē-ō-mī-OP-a-thē): A progressive disease characterized by damage to the cardiac muscle tissue.
cardiopulmonary resuscitation: Method of artificially maintaining respiratory and circulatory function.
cardiovascular: Pertaining to the heart, blood, and blood vessels.
cardiovascular centers: Poorly localized centers in the reticular formation of the medulla of the brain; includes cardioacceleratory, cardioinhibitory, and vasomotor centers.
cardium: The heart.
carina (ka-RĪ-na): A ridge on the inner surface of the base of the trachea that runs anteroposteriorly, between the two primary bronchi.
carotene (KAR-ō-tēn): A yellow-orange pigment found in carrots and in green and orange leafy vegetables; a compound that the body can convert to vitamin A.
carotid artery: The principal artery of the neck, servicing cervical and cranial structures; one branch, the internal carotid, represents a major blood supply for the brain.
carotid body: A group of receptors adjacent to the carotid sinus that are sensitive to changes in the carbon dioxide levels, pH, and oxygen concentrations of the arterial blood.
carotid sinus: A dilated segment of the internal carotid artery whose walls contain baroreceptors sensitive to changes in blood pressure.
carotid sinus reflex: Reflexive changes in blood pressure that maintain homeostatic pressures at the carotid sinus, stabilizing blood flow to the brain.
carpus/carpal: The wrist.
cartilage: A connective tissue with a gelatinous matrix and an abundance of fibers.
castration: Removal of the testes, also called bilateral orchiectomy.
catabolism (ka-TAB-ō-lizm): The breakdown of complex organic molecules into simpler components, accompanied by the release of energy.
cataract: A reduction in lens transparency that causes visual impairment.
catecholamines (kat-e-KŌL-am-inz): Epinephrine, norepinephrine, and related compounds.
catheter (KATH-e-ter): Surgical instrument; a tube inserted into a body cavity or along a blood vessel or excretory passageway for the collection of body fluids, blood pressure monitoring, or the introduction of medications or radiographic dyes.
cauda equina (KAW-da ek-WĪ-na): Spinal nerve roots distal to the tip of the adult spinal cord; they extend caudally inside the vertebral canal en route to lumbar and sacral segments.
caudal/caudally: Closest to or toward the tail (coccyx).
caudate nucleus (KAW-dāt): One of the basal nuclei, involved with the subconscious control of muscular activity.
cavernous tissue: Erectile tissue that can be engorged with blood; found in the penis and clitoris.
cecum (SĒ-kum): An expanded pouch at the start of the large intestine.

cell: The smallest living unit in the human body.
cell-mediated immunity: Resistance to disease through the activities of sensitized T cells that destroy antigen-bearing cells by direct contact or through the release of lymphotoxins; also called cellular immunity.
cellulitis (sel-ū-LĪ-tis): Diffuse inflammation, usually involving areas of loose connective tissue, such as the subcutaneous layer.
cement or **cementum (se-MEN-tum):** Bony material covering the root of a tooth, not shielded by a layer of enamel.
center of ossification: Site in a connective tissue where bone formation begins.
central canal: Longitudinal canal in the center of an osteon that contains blood vessels and nerves, also called the Haversian canal; a passageway along the longitudinal axis of the spinal cord that contains cerebrospinal fluid.
central nervous system (CNS): The brain and spinal cord.
central sulcus: Groove in the surface of a cerebral hemisphere, between the primary sensory and primary motor areas of the cortex.
centriole: A cylindrical intracellular organelle composed of nine groups of microtubules, three in each group; functions in mitosis or meiosis by forming the basis of the spindle apparatus.
centromere (SEN-trō-mēr): Localized region where two chromatids remain connected following chromosome replication; site of spindle fiber attachment.
centrosome: Region of cytoplasm containing a pair of centrioles oriented at right angles to one another.
centrum: The vertebral body.
cephalic: Pertaining to the head.
cerebellum (ser-e-BEL-um): Posterior portion of the metencephalon, containing the cerebellar hemispheres; includes the arbor vitae, cerebellar nuclei, and cerebellar cortex.
cerebral cortex: An extensive area of neural cortex covering the surfaces of the cerebral hemispheres.
cerebral hemispheres: Expanded portions of the cerebrum covered in neural cortex.
cerebral palsy: Chronic condition resulting from damage to motor areas of the brain during development or at delivery.
cerebral peduncle: Mass of nerve fibers on the ventrolateral surface of the mesencephalon; contains ascending tracts that terminate in the thalamus and descending tracts that originate in the cerebral hemispheres.
cerebrospinal fluid: Fluid bathing the internal and external surfaces of the CNS; secreted by the choroid plexus.
cerebrovascular accident (CVA): A stroke; occlusion of a blood vessel supplying a portion of the brain, resulting in damage to the dependent neurons.
cerebrum (SER-e-brum or **ser-Ē-brum):** The largest portion of the brain, composed of the cerebral hemispheres; includes the cerebral cortex, the basal nuclei, and the internal capsule.
cerumen: Waxy secretion of integumentary glands along the external acoustic meatus.
ceruminous glands (se-ROO-mi-nus): Integumentary glands that secrete cerumen.
cervical enlargement: Relative enlargement of the cervical portion of the spinal cord due to the abundance of CNS neurons involved with motor control of the arms.
cervix: The inferior part of the uterus.
cesarean section: Surgical delivery of an infant via an incision through the lower abdominal wall and uterus.
chalazion (kah-LĀ-zē-on): An inflammation and distension of a Meibomian gland on the eyelid; also called a sty.
chancre (SHANG-ker): A skin lesion that develops at the primary site of a syphilis infection.
charley horse: Soreness and stiffness in a strained muscle, usually involving the quadriceps group.
chemoreception: Detection of alterations in the concentrations of dissolved compounds or gases.
chemotaxis (kē-mō-TAK-sis): The attraction of phagocytic cells to the source of abnormal chemicals in tissue fluids.
chloride shift: Movement of plasma chloride ions into RBCs in exchange for bicarbonate ions generated by the intracellular dissociation of carbonic acid.
cholecystitis (kō-lē-sis-TĪ-tis): Inflammation of the gallbladder.
cholecystokinin (CCK) (kō-lē-sis-tō-KĪ-nin): Duodenal hormone that stimulates the contraction of the gallbladder and the secretion of enzymes by the exocrine pancreas; also called *pancreozymin.*
cholelithiasis (kō-lē-li-THĪ-a-sis): The formation or presence of gallstones.
cholesterol: A steroid component of cell membranes and a substrate for the synthesis of steroid hormones and bile salts.
choline: Chemical compound; a breakdown product or precursor of acetylcholine.
cholinergic synapse (kō-lin-ER-jik): Synapse where the presynaptic membrane releases ACh on stimulation.
cholinesterase (kō-li-NES-te-rās): Enzyme that breaks down and inactivates ACh.
chondrocyte (KON-drō-sīt): Cartilage cell.
chondroitin sulfate (kon-DROY-tin): The predominant proteoglycan in cartilage, responsible for the gelatinous consistency of the matrix.
chordae tendineae (KOR-dē TEN-di-nē-ē): Fibrous cords that brace the AV valves in the heart, stabilizing their position and preventing backflow during ventricular systole.
chorion/chorionic (KOR-ē-on) (kō-rē-ON-ik): An extraembryonic membrane, consisting of the trophoblast and underlying mesoderm, that forms the placenta.
choroid: Middle, vascular layer in the wall of the eye.
choroid plexus: The vascular complex in the roof of the third and fourth ventricles of the brain, responsible for CSF production.
chromatid (KRŌ-ma-tid): One complete copy of a DNA strand.
chromatin (KRŌ-ma-tin): Histological term referring to the grainy material visible in cell nuclei during interphase; the appearance of the DNA content of the nucleus when the chromosomes are uncoiled.
chromatophilic substance (krō-ma-tō-FIL-ik): The ribosomes, Golgi, RER, and mitochondria of the nerve cell body, or perikaryon, of a typical nerve cell; also termed *Nissl bodies.*
chromosomes: Dense structures, composed of tightly coiled DNA strands and associated histones, that become visible in the nucleus when a cell prepares to undergo mitosis or meiosis; normal human somatic cells contain 46 chromosomes apiece.
chronic: Habitual or long-term.
chylomicrons (kī-lō-MĪ-kronz): Relatively large droplets that may contain triglycerides, phospholipids, and cholesterol in association with proteins; synthesized and released by intestinal cells and transported to the venous blood via the lymphoid system.
chyme (KĪM): A semifluid mixture of ingested food and digestive secretions that is found in the stomach as digestion proceeds.
chymotrypsin (kī-mō-TRIP-sin): A protease found in the small intestine.
chymotrypsinogen: Inactive proenzyme secreted by the pancreas that is subsequently converted to chymotrypsin.
ciliary body: A thickened region of the choroid that encircles the lens of the eye; it includes the ciliary muscle and the ciliary processes that support the suspensory ligaments of the lens.
cilium/cilia: A slender organelle that extends above the free surface of an epithelial cell, and usually undergoes cycles of movement; composed of a basal body and microtubules in a 9×2 array.
circulatory system: The network of lymphatic and blood vessels involved in the circulation and recirculation of extracellular fluid.
circumduction (sir-kum-DUK-shun): A movement at a synovial joint where the distal end of the bone describes a circle, but the shaft does not rotate.
circumvallate papilla (sir-kum-VAL-āt pa-PIL-la): One of the large, dome-shaped papillae on the dorsum of the tongue that form the V that separates the body of the tongue from the root.
cirrhosis (sir-RŌ-sis): A liver disorder characterized by the degeneration of hepatocytes and their replacement by connective tissue.
cisterna (sis-TUR-na): An expanded chamber.
clavicle (KLAV-i-kul): The collarbone.
cleavage (KLĒV-ij): Mitotic divisions that follow fertilization of the ovum and lead to the formation of a blastocyst.
cleavage lines: Stress lines in the skin that follow the orientation of major bundles of collagen fibers in the dermis.
climacteric: Age-related cessation of gametogenesis in the male or female due to reduced sex hormone production.
clitoris (KLI-to-ris): A small erectile organ of the female that is the developmental equivalent of the male penis.
clone: The production of genetically identical cells.
clonus (KLŌ-nus): Rapid cycles of muscular contraction and relaxation.
clot: A network of fibrin fibers and trapped blood cells; also called a thrombus.
clotting factors: Plasma proteins synthesized by the liver that are essential to the clotting response.
clotting response: Series of events that result in the formation of a clot.
coccygeal ligament: Fibrous extension of the dura mater and filum terminale; provides longitudinal stabilization to the spinal cord.
coccyx (KOK-siks): Terminal portion of the vertebral column, consisting of relatively tiny, fused vertebrae.
cochlea (KOK-lē-a): Spiral portion of the bony labyrinth of the inner ear that surrounds the organ of hearing.
cochlear duct (KOK-lē-ar): Membranous tube within the cochlea that is filled with endolymph and contains the organ of Corti; also called the **scala media**.
codon (KŌ-don): A sequence of three nitrogen bases along an mRNA strand that will specify the location of a single amino acid in a peptide chain.
coelom (SĒ-lom): The ventral body cavity, lined by a serous membrane and subdivided during development into the pleural, pericardial, and abdominopelvic (peritoneal) cavities.
coenzymes (kō-EN-zīmz): Complex organic cofactors, usually structurally related to vitamins.
cofactors: Ions or molecules that must be attached to the active site before an enzyme can function; examples include mineral ions and several vitamins.
colectomy (kō-LEK-tō-mē): Surgical removal of part or all of the colon.
colitis: Inflammation of the colon.
collagen: Strong, insoluble protein fiber common in connective tissues.
collagenous tissues: (ko-LA-jin-us): Dense connective tissues in which collagen fibers are the dominant fiber type; includes dense regular and dense irregular connective tissues.
collateral ganglion (kō-LAT-er-al): A sympathetic ganglion situated in front of the spinal column and separate from the sympathetic chain.
Colles' fracture (KOL-lēz): Fracture of the distal end of the radius and possibly the ulna, with posterior and dorsal displacement of the distal bone fragments.
colliculus/colliculi (ko-LIK-ū-lus): A little mound; in the brain, used to refer to one of the cortical thickenings in the roof of the mesencephalon; the superior colliculus

GLOSSARY

is associated with the visual system, and the inferior colliculi with the auditory system.

colon: The large intestine.

colonoscope (kō-LON-ō-skōp): A fiber-optic device for examining the interior of the colon.

colostomy (kō-LOS-tō-mē): The surgical connection of a portion of the colon to the body wall, sometimes performed after a colectomy to permit the discharge of fecal materials.

colostrum (kō-LOS-trum): Secretion of the mammary glands at the time of childbirth and for a few days thereafter; contains more protein and less fat than the milk secreted later.

coma (KŌ-ma): An unconscious state from which the individual cannot be aroused, even by strong stimuli.

comedo (kō-MĒ-dō): An inflamed sebaceous gland.

comminuted: Broken or crushed into small pieces.

commissure: A crossing over from one side to another.

common bile duct: Duct formed by the union of the cystic duct from the gallbladder and the bile ducts from the liver; terminates at the duodenal ampulla, where it meets the pancreatic duct.

common pathway: In the clotting response, the events that begin with the appearance of thromboplastin and end with the formation of a clot.

compact bone: Dense bone containing parallel osteons.

compensation curvatures: The cervical and lumbar curves that develop to center the body weight over the legs.

complement: 11 plasma proteins that interact in a chain reaction following exposure to activated antibodies on the surfaces of certain pathogens, and which promote cell lysis, phagocytosis, and other defense mechanisms.

compliance: The ability of certain organs to tolerate changes in volume; a property that reflects the presence of elastic fibers and smooth muscles.

compound: A molecule containing two or more elements in combination.

concentration: Amount (in grams) or number of atoms, ions, or molecules (in moles) per unit volume.

conception: Fertilization.

concha/conchae (KON-kē): Three pairs of thin, scroll-like bones that project into the nasal cavities; the superior and medial conchae are part of the ethmoid, and the inferior conchae are separate bones.

concussion: A violent blow or shock; loss of consciousness due to a violent blow to the head.

condyle: A rounded articular projection on the surface of a bone.

cone: Retinal photoreceptor responsible for color vision.

congenital (kon-JEN-i-tal): Already present at the birth of an individual.

congestive heart failure (CHF): Failure to maintain adequate cardiac output due to circulatory problems or myocardial damage.

conjunctiva (kon-junk-TĪ-va): A layer of stratified squamous epithelium that covers the inner surfaces of the lids and the anterior surface of the eye to the edges of the cornea.

conjunctivitis: Inflammation of the conjunctiva.

connective tissue: One of the four primary tissue types; provides a structural framework for the body that stabilizes the relative positions of the other tissue types; includes connective tissue proper, cartilage, bone, and blood; always has cell products, cells, and ground substance.

contractility: The ability to contract, possessed by skeletal, smooth, and cardiac muscle cells.

contracture: A permanent contraction of an entire muscle following the atrophy of individual muscle cells.

contralateral reflex: A reflex that affects the side of the body opposite the stimulus.

conus medullaris: Conical tip of the spinal cord that gives rise to the filum terminale.

convergence: In the nervous system, the innervation of a single neuron by the axons from several neurons; this is most common along motor pathways.

coracoid process (KOR-a-koyd): A hook-shaped process of the scapula that projects above the anterior surface of the capsule of the shoulder joint.

Cori cycle: Metabolic exchange of lactic acid from skeletal muscle for glucose from the liver; performed during the recovery period following muscular exertion.

cornea (KOR-nē-a): Transparent portion of the fibrous tunic of the anterior surface of the eye.

corniculate cartilages (kor-NIK-ū-lāt): A pair of small laryngeal cartilages.

cornification: The production of keratin by a stratified squamous epithelium; also called **keratinization**.

cornu: A horn.

corona radiata (ko-RŌ-na rā-dē-A-ta): A layer of follicle cells surrounding an oocyte at ovulation.

coronoid (KOR-ō-noyd): Hooked or curved.

corpora quadrigemina (KOR-pō-ra quad-ri-JEM-i-na): The superior and inferior colliculi of the mesencephalic tectum (roof) in the brain.

corpus albicans: The scar tissue that remains after degeneration of the corpus luteum at the end of a uterine cycle.

corpus callosum: Bundle of axons linking centers in the left and right cerebral hemispheres.

corpus cavernosum (KOR-pus ka-ver-NŌ-sum): Masses of erectile tissue within the body of the penis (male) or clitoris (female).

corpus/corpora: Body.

corpus luteum (LOO-tē-um): Progestin-secreting mass of follicle cells that develops in the ovary after ovulation.

corpus spongiosum (spon-jē-Ō-sum): Mass of erectile tissue that surrounds the urethra in the penis and expands distally to form the glans.

cortex: Outer layer or portion of an organ.

Corti, organ of: The spiral organ; a receptor complex in the scala media of the cochlea that includes the inner and outer hair cells, supporting cells and structures, and the tectorial membrane; provides the sensation of hearing.

corticobulbar tracts (kor-ti-kō-BUL-bar): Descending tracts that carry information/commands from the cerebral cortex to nuclei and centers in the brain stem.

corticospinal tracts: Descending tracts that carry motor commands from the cerebral cortex to the anterior gray horns of the spinal cord.

corticosteroid: A steroid hormone produced by the adrenal cortex.

corticosterone (kor-ti-KOS-te-rōn): One of the corticosteroids secreted by the zona fasciculata of the adrenal cortex; a glucocorticoid.

corticotropin: *See* **adrenocorticotropic hormone** (ACTH).

corticotropin-releasing hormone (CRH): Releasing hormone secreted by the hypothalamus that stimulates secretion of ACTH by the anterior pituitary.

cortisol (KOR-ti-sol): One of the corticosteroids secreted by the zona fasciculata of the adrenal cortex; a glucocorticoid.

costa/costae: A rib.

cotransport: Membrane transport of a nutrient, such as glucose, in company with the movement of an ion, usually sodium; transport requires a carrier protein but does not involve direct ATP expenditure and can occur regardless of the concentration gradient for the nutrient.

countercurrent multiplication: Active transport between two limbs of a loop that contains a fluid moving in one direction; responsible for the concentration of the urine in the kidney tubules.

cranial: Pertaining to the head.

cranial nerves: Peripheral nerves originating at the brain.

craniosacral division (krā-nē-ō-SA-kral): *See* **parasympathetic division**.

craniostenosis (krā-nē-ō-sten-Ō-sis): Skull deformity caused by premature closure of the cranial sutures.

cranium: The braincase; the skull bones that surround the brain.

creatine: A nitrogenous compound synthesized in the body that can bind a high-energy phosphate and serve as an energy reserve.

creatine phosphate: A high-energy compound present in muscle cells; during muscular activity the phosphate group is donated to ADP, regenerating ATP.

creatinine: A breakdown product of creatine metabolism.

crenation: Cellular shrinkage due to an osmotic movement of water out of the cytoplasm.

cribriform plate: Portion of the ethmoid of the skull that contains the foramina used by the axons of olfactory receptors en route to the olfactory bulbs of the cerebrum.

cricoid cartilage (KRĪ-koyd): Ring-shaped cartilage forming the inferior margin of the larynx.

crista/cristae: A ridge-shaped collection of hair cells in the ampulla of a semicircular canal; the crista and cupula form a receptor complex sensitive to movement along the plane of the canal.

cross-bridge: Myosin head that projects from the surface of a thick filament, and that can bind to an active site of a thin filament in the presence of calcium ions.

cruciate ligaments: A pair of intracapsular ligaments (anterior and posterior) in the knee.

cryptorchidism (kript-OR-ki-dizm): The failure of the testes to descend into the inguinal canal during late fetal development.

cryptorchid testis: An undescended testis that is in the abdominopelvic cavity rather than the scrotum.

cuneiform cartilages (kū-NĒ-i-form): A pair of small cartilages in the larynx.

cupula (KŪ-pū-la): A gelatinous mass that sits in the ampulla of a semicircular canal in the inner ear, and whose movement stimulates the hair cells of the crista.

Cushing's disease: Condition caused by oversecretion of adrenal steroids.

cuspids (KUS-pids): Conical upper teeth with sharp ridges, located in the upper jaw on either side posterior to the second incisor.

cutaneous membrane: The epidermis and papillary layer of the dermis.

cuticle: Layer of dead, cornified cells surrounding the shaft of a hair; for nails, *see* **eponychium**.

cutis: The skin.

cyanosis: Bluish coloration of the skin due to the presence of deoxygenated blood in vessels near the body surface.

cyst: A fibrous capsule containing fluid or other material.

cystic duct: A duct that carries bile between the gallbladder and the common bile duct.

cystitis: Inflammation of the urinary bladder.

cytokinesis (sī-tō-kī-NĒ-sis): The cytoplasmic movement that separates two daughter cells at the completion of mitosis.

cytology (sī-TOL-ō-jē): The study of cells.

cytoplasm: The material between the cell membrane and the nuclear membrane.

cytoskeleton: A network of microtubules and microfilaments in the cytoplasm.

cytosol: The fluid portion of the cytoplasm.

cytotoxic: Poisonous to living cells.

cytotoxic T cells: Lymphocytes of the cellular immune response that kill target cells by direct contact or through the secretion of lymphotoxins; also called killer T cells.

daughter cells: Genetically identical cells produced by mitosis.

decerebrate: Lacking a cerebrum.

decomposition reaction: A chemical reaction that breaks a molecule into smaller fragments.

decubitis ulcers: Ulcers that form where chronic pressure interrupts circulation to a portion of the skin.

decussate: To cross over to the opposite side, usually referring to the crossover of the pyramidal tracts on the ventral surface of the medulla oblongata.

defecation (def-e-KĀ-shun): The elimination of fecal wastes.

deglutition (de-gloo-TISH-un): Swallowing.
delta cell: A pancreatic islet cell that secretes somatostatin.
dementia: Loss of mental abilities.
demyelination: The loss of the myelin sheath of an axon, usually due to chemical or physical damage to Schwann cells or oligodendrocytes.
dendrite (DEN-drīt): A sensory process of a neuron.
denticulate ligaments: Supporting fibers that extend laterally from the surface of the spinal cord, tying the pia mater to the dura mater and providing lateral support for the spinal cord.
dentine or **dentin (DEN-tin):** Bonelike material that forms the body of a tooth; it differs from bone in lacking osteocytes and osteons.
deoxyribonucleic acid (DNA) (dē-ok-sē-rī-bō-nū-KLĀ-ik): DNA strand: a nucleic acid consisting of a chain of nucleotides containing the sugar deoxyribose and the nitrogen bases adenine, guanine, cytosine, and thymine. DNA molecule: two DNA strands wound in a double helix and held together by weak bonds between complementary nitrogen base pairs.
depolarization: A change in the transmembrane potential that moves it from a negative value toward 0 millivolts (mV).
depression: Inferior (downward) movement of a body part.
dermatitis: Inflammation of the skin.
dermatome: A sensory region monitored by the dorsal rami of a single spinal segment.
dermis: The connective tissue layer beneath the epidermis of the skin.
desmosomes (DEZ-mō-sōmz): A cell junction consisting of a thin proteoglycan layer reinforced by a network of intermediate filaments that lock the two cells together.
detrusor muscle (dē-TROO-sor): Smooth muscle in the wall of the urinary bladder.
detumescence (dē-tū-MES-ens): Loss of a penile erection in the male.
development: Growth and the acquisition of increasing structural and functional complexity; includes the period from conception to maturity.
diabetes insipidus: Polyuria due to inadequate production of ADH.
diabetes mellitus (mel-LĪ-tus): Polyuria and glycosuria, most often due to inadequate production of insulin with resulting elevation of blood glucose levels.
dialysis: Diffusion between two solutions of differing solute concentrations across a semipermeable membrane containing pores that permit the passage of some solutes and not others.
diapedesis (dī-a-pe-DĒ-sis): Movement of white blood cells through the walls of blood vessels by migration between adjacent endothelial cells.
diaphragm (DĪ-a-fram): Any muscular partition; often used to refer to the respiratory muscle that separates the thoracic cavity from the abdominopelvic cavity.
diaphysis (dī-AF-i-sis): The shaft of a long bone.
diarrhea (dī-a-RĒ-uh): Abnormally frequent defecation, associated with the production of unusually fluid feces.
diarthrosis (dī-ar-THRŌ-sis): A synovial joint.
diastole (dī-AS-tō-lē): A period of relaxation; may refer to either the atria or the ventricles.
diastolic pressure: Pressure measured in the walls of a muscular artery when the left ventricle is in diastole.
diencephalon (dī-en-SEF-a-lon): A division of the brain that includes the epithalamus, thalamus, and hypothalamus.
differential count: The determination of the relative abundance of each type of white blood cell, based on a random sampling of 100 WBCs.
differentiation: The gradual appearance of characteristic cellular specializations during development, as the result of gene activation or repression.
diffusion: Passive molecular movement from an area of relatively high concentration to an area of relatively low concentration.
digestion: The chemical breakdown of ingested materials into simple molecules that can be absorbed by the cells of the digestive tract.
digestive system: The digestive tract and associated glands.
digestive tract: An internal passageway that begins at the mouth and ends at the anus.
dilate: To increase in diameter; to enlarge or expand.
diploë (DIP-lō-ē): A layer of spongy bone between the internal and external tables of a flat bone.
dislocation: Forceful displacement of an articulating bone to an abnormal position, usually accompanied by damage to tendons, ligaments, the articular capsule, or other structures.
distal: Movement away from the point of attachment or origin; for a limb, away from its attachment to the trunk.
distal convoluted tubule: Portion of the nephron closest to the collecting tubule and duct; an important site of active secretion.
diuresis: Fluid loss at the kidneys; the production of urine.
divergence: In neural tissue, the spread of excitation from one neuron to many neurons; an organizational pattern common along sensory pathways of the CNS.
diverticulitis (dī-ver-tik-ū-LĪ-tis): Inflammation of a diverticulum.
diverticulosis (dī-ver-tik-ū-LŌ-sis): The formation of diverticula.
diverticulum: A sac or pouch in the wall of the colon or other organ.
dizygotic twins (dī-zī-GOT-ik): Twins that result from the fertilization of two different ova.
dopamine (DŌ-pah-mēn): An important neurotransmitter in the CNS.
dorsal: Toward the back, posterior.
dorsal root ganglion: PNS ganglion containing the cell bodies of sensory neurons.
dorsiflexion: Elevation of the superior surface of the foot.
Down syndrome: A genetic abnormality resulting from the presence of three copies of chromosome 21; individuals with this condition have characteristic physical and intellectual deficits.
duct: A passageway that delivers exocrine secretions to an epithelial surface.
ductus arteriosus (DUK-tus ar-tē-rē-Ō-sus): Vascular connection between the pulmonary trunk and the aorta that functions throughout fetal life; normally closes at birth or shortly thereafter, and persists as the ligamentum arteriosum.
ductus deferens (DUK-tus DEF-e-renz): A passageway that carries sperm from the epididymis to the ejaculatory duct.
duodenal ampulla: Chamber that receives bile from the common bile duct and pancreatic secretions from the pancreatic duct.
duodenal glands: *See* **submucosal glands**.
duodenal papilla: Conical projection from the inner surface of the duodenum that contains the opening of the duodenal ampulla.
duodenum (doo-o-DĒ-num): The proximal 1 ft of the small intestine that contains short villi and submucosal glands.
dura mater (DOO-ra MĀ-ter): Outermost component of the meninges that surround the brain and spinal cord.
dynamic equilibrium: Maintenance of normal body orientation as sudden changes in position (rotation, acceleration, etc.) occur.
dyslexia: Impaired ability to comprehend written words.
dysmenorrhea: Painful menstruation.
dysuria (dis-Ū-rē-a): Painful urination.
eccrine glands (EK-rin): Sweat glands of the skin that produce a watery secretion.
echocardiography (ek-ō-kar-dē-OG-ra-fē): Examination of the heart using modified ultrasound techniques.
ectoderm: One of the three primary germ layers; covers the surface of the embryo and gives rise to the nervous system, the epidermis and associated glands, and a variety of other structures.
ectopic (ek-TOP-ik): Outside of its normal location.
effector: A peripheral gland or muscle cell innervated by a motor neuron.
efferent: Away from a central receiving area.
efferent arteriole: An arteriole carrying blood away from the glomerulus of the kidney.
efferent fiber: An axon that carries impulses away from the CNS.
ejaculation (ē-jak-ū-LĀ-shun): The ejection of semen from the penis as the result of muscular contractions of the bulbocavernosus and ischiocavernosus muscles.
ejaculatory duct (ē-JAK-ū-la-tō-rē): Short ducts that pass within the walls of the prostate and connect the ductus deferens with the prostatic urethra.
elastase (ē-LAS-tāz): A pancreatic enzyme that breaks down elastin fibers.
elastin: Connective tissue fibers that stretch and rebound, providing elasticity to connective tissues.
electrocardiogram (ECG, EKG) (ē-lek-trō-KAR-dē-ō-gram): Graphic record of the electrical activities of the heart, as monitored at specific locations on the body surface.
electroencephalogram (EEG): Graphic record of the electrical activities of the brain.
electrolytes (ē-LEK-trō-līts): Soluble inorganic compounds whose ions will conduct an electric current in solution.
electron: One of the three fundamental particles; a subatomic particle that bears a negative charge and normally orbits around the protons of the nucleus.
elephantiasis (el-e-fan-TĪ-a-sis): A lymphedema caused by infection and blockage of lymphatics by mosquito-borne parasites.
elevation: Movement in a superior, or upward, direction.
embolism (EM-bō-lizm): Obstruction or closure of a vessel by an embolus.
embolus (EM-bō-lus): An air bubble, fat globule, or blood clot drifting in the circulation.
embryo (EM-brē-ō): Developmental stage beginning at fertilization and ending at the start of the third developmental month.
embryogenesis (em-brē-ō-JEN-e-sis): The process of embryo formation.
embryology (em-brē-OL-ō-jē): The study of embryonic development, focusing on the first 2 months after fertilization.
emesis (EM-e-sis): Vomiting.
emmetropia: Normal vision.
emulsification (ē-mul-si-fi-KĀ-shun): The physical breakup of fats in the digestive tract, forming smaller droplets accessible to digestive enzymes; normally the result of mixing with bile salts.
enamel: Crystalline material similar in mineral composition to bone, but harder and without osteocytes, that covers the exposed surfaces of the teeth.
encephalitis: Inflammation of the brain.
endocarditis: Inflammation of the endocardium of the heart.
endocardium (en-dō-KAR-dē-um): The simple squamous epithelium that lines the heart and is continuous with the endothelium of the great vessels.
endochondral ossification (en-dō-KON-dral): The conversion of a cartilaginous model to bone; the characteristic mode of formation for skeletal elements other than the bones of the cranium, the clavicles, and sesamoid bones.
endocrine gland: A gland that secretes hormones into the blood.
endocrine system: The endocrine glands of the body.
endocytosis (en-dō-sī-TŌ-sis): The movement of relatively large volumes of extracellular material into the cytoplasm via the formation of a membranous vesicle at the cell surface; includes pinocytosis and phagocytosis.

endoderm: One of the three primary germ layers; the layer on the undersurface of the embryonic disc that gives rise to the epithelia and glands of the digestive system, the respiratory system, and portions of the urinary system.
endogenous: Produced within the body.
endolymph (EN-dō-limf): Fluid contents of the membranous labyrinth (the saccule, utricle, semicircular ducts, and cochlear duct) of the inner ear.
endometrial glands: Secretory glands of the endometrium.
endometrium (en-dō-MĒ-trē-um): The mucous membrane lining the uterus.
endomysium (en-dō-MĪS-ē-um): A delicate network of connective tissue fibers that surrounds individual muscle cells.
endoneurium: A delicate network of connective tissue fibers that surrounds individual nerve fibers.
endoplasmic reticulum (en-dō-PLAZ-mik re-TIK-ū-lum): A network of membranous channels in the cytoplasm of a cell that function in intracellular transport, synthesis, storage, packaging, and secretion.
endorphins (en-DOR-finz): Neuromodulators produced in the CNS that inhibit activity along pain pathways.
endosteum: An incomplete cellular lining found on the inner (medullary) surfaces of bones.
endothelium (en-dō-THĒ-lē-um): The simple squamous epithelium that lines blood and lymphatic vessels.
enkephalins (en-KEF-a-linz): Neuromodulators produced in the CNS that inhibit activity along pain pathways.
enteritis (en-ter-Ī-tis): Inflammation of the intestinal tract.
enterocrinin: A hormone secreted by the duodenal lining when exposed to acid chyme; stimulates the secretion of the duodenal glands.
enteroendocrine cells (en-ter-ō-EN-dō-krin): Endocrine cells scattered among the epithelial cells lining the digestive tract.
enterogastric reflex: Reflexive inhibition of gastric secretion initiated by the arrival of acid chyme in the small intestine.
enterohepatic circulation: Excretion of bile salts by the liver, followed by absorption of bile salts by intestinal cells for return to the liver via the hepatic portal vein.
enterokinase: An enzyme in the lumen of the small intestine that activates the proenzymes secreted by the pancreas.
enzyme: A protein that catalyzes a specific biochemical reaction.
eosinophils (ē-ō-SIN-ō-filz): A granulocyte (WBC) with a lobed nucleus and red-staining granules; participates in the immune response and is especially important during allergic reactions.
ependyma (ep-EN-di-mah): Layer of cells lining the ventricles and central canal of the CNS.
epiblast (EP-i-blast): The layer of the inner cell mass facing the amniotic cavity prior to gastrulation.
epicardium: Serous membrane covering the outer surface of the heart; also called the *visceral pericardium.*
epidermis: The epithelium covering the surface of the skin.
epididymis (ep-i-DID-i-mus): Coiled duct that connects the rete testis to the ductus deferens; site of functional maturation of spermatozoa.
epidural block: Anesthesia caused by the elimination of sensory inputs from dorsal nerve roots following the introduction of drugs into appropriate regions of the epidural space.
epidural space: Space between the spinal dura mater and the walls of the vertebral foramen; contains blood vessels and adipose tissue; a frequent site of injection for regional anesthesia.
epiglottis (ep-i-GLOT-is): Blade-shaped flap of tissue, reinforced by cartilage, that is attached to the dorsal and superior surface of the thyroid cartilage; it folds over the entrance to the larynx during swallowing.
epimysium (ep-i-MĪS-ē-um): A dense investment of collagen fibers that surrounds a skeletal muscle, and is continuous with the tendons/aponeuroses of the muscle and with the perimysium.
epineurium: A dense investment of collagen fibers that surrounds a peripheral nerve.
epiphyseal cartilage (e-pi-FI-sē-al): Cartilaginous region between the epiphysis and diaphysis of a growing bone.
epiphysis (e-PIF-i-sis): The end of a long bone.
epistaxis (ep-i-STAK-sis): Nosebleed.
epithelium (e-pi-THĒ-lē-um): One of the four primary tissue types; a layer of cells that forms a superficial covering or an internal lining of a body cavity or vessel.
eponychium (ep-ō-NIK-ē-um): A narrow zone of stratum corneum that extends across the surface of a nail at its exposed base; also called the **cuticle**.
equational division: The second meiotic division.
equilibrium (ē-kwi-LIB-rē-um): A dynamic state where two opposing forces or processes are in balance.
erection: Stiffening of the penis prior to copulation due to the engorgement of the erectile tissues of the corpora cavernosa and the corpus spongiosum.
erythema (er-i-THĒ-ma): Redness and inflammation at the surface of the skin.
erythrocyte (e-RITH-rō-sīt): A red blood cell; an anucleate blood cell containing large quantities of hemoglobin.
erythrocytosis (e-rith-rō-sī-TŌ-sis): An abnormally large number of erythrocytes in the circulating blood.
erythropoiesis (e-rith-rō-poy-Ē-sis): Red blood cell formation.
erythropoietin (e-rith-rō-POY-e-tin): Hormone released by tissues, especially the kidneys, exposed to low oxygen concentrations; stimulates hematopoiesis in bone marrow.
Escherichia coli: Normal bacterial resident of the large intestine.
esophagus: A muscular tube that connects the pharynx to the stomach.
estradiol (es-tra-DĪ-ol): The primary estrogen secreted by ovarian follicles.
estrogens (ES-trō-jenz): The dominant sex hormones in females; notably estradiol.
eupnea (ūp-NĒ-a): Normal quiet breathing.
eversion (ē-VER-shun): A turning outward.
excitable membranes: Membranes that conduct action potentials, a characteristic of muscle and nerve cells.
excretion: Elimination from the body.
exocrine gland: A gland that secretes onto the body surface or into a passageway connected to the exterior.
exocytosis (eks-ō-sī-TŌ-sis): The ejection of cytoplasmic materials by fusion of a membranous vesicle with the cell membrane.
expiration: Exhalation; breathing out.
expiratory reserve: The amount of additional air that can be voluntarily moved out of the respiratory tract after a normal tidal expiration.
extension: An increase in the angle between two articulating bones; the opposite of flexion.
extensor retinaculum (ret-i-NAK-ū-lum): A thickening of the fascia of the forearm at the wrist or the leg at the ankle, forming a band of dense connective tissue that holds extensor muscle tendons in place.
external acoustic meatus: Passageway in the temporal bone that leads to the tympanic membrane.
external ear: The auricle, external acoustic meatus, and tympanic membrane.
external nares: The nostrils; the external openings into the nasal cavity.
exteroceptors: Sensory receptors in the skin, mucous membranes, and special sense organs that provide information about the external environment and our position within it.
extracellular fluid: All body fluid other than that contained within cells; includes plasma and interstitial fluid.
extraembryonic membranes: The yolk sac, amnion, chorion, and allantois.
extrafusal fibers: Contractile muscle fibers, as opposed to the sensory intrafusal fibers (muscle spindles).
extrinsic pathway: Clotting pathway that begins with damage to blood vessels or surrounding tissues and ends with the formation of tissue thromboplastin.
fabella: A sesamoid bone often found in the tendon of the lateral head of the gastrocnemius muscle.
facilitated diffusion: Passive movement of a substance across a cell membrane via a protein carrier.
facilitation: Depolarization of a neuron cell membrane toward threshold, or making the cell more sensitive to depolarizing stimuli.
falciform ligament (FAL-si-form): A sheet of mesentery that contains the ligamentum teres, the fibrous remains of the umbilical vein of the fetus.
falx (falks): Sickle-shaped.
falx cerebri (falks ser-Ē-brē): Curving sheet of dura mater that extends between the two cerebral hemispheres; encloses the superior sagittal sinus.
fascia (FASH-a): Connective tissue fibers, primarily collagenous, that form sheets or bands beneath the skin to attach, stabilize, enclose, and separate muscles and other internal organs.
fasciculus (fa-SIK-ū-lus): A small bundle, usually referring to a collection of nerve axons or muscle fibers.
fatty acids: Hydrocarbon chains ending in a carboxyl group.
fauces (FAW-sēz): The passage from the mouth to the pharynx, bounded by the palatal arches, the soft palate, and the uvula.
feces: Waste products eliminated by the digestive tract at the anus; contain indigestible residue, bacteria, mucus, and epithelial cells.
fenestra: An opening.
fenestrated (FEN-es-trāt-ed): Having multiple openings; used when referring to very permeable capillaries whose endothelial cells are penetrated by pores of varying sizes.
fertilization: Fusion of egg and sperm to form a zygote.
fetus: Developmental stage lasting from the start of the third developmental month to delivery.
fibrillation (fi-bri-LĀ-shun): Uncoordinated contractions of individual muscle cells that impair or prevent normal function.
fibrin (FĪ-brin): Insoluble protein fibers that form the basic framework of a blood clot.
fibrinogen (fī-BRIN-ō-jen): Plasma proteins that can be converted by the action of enzymes into insoluble strands of fibrin that form the basis for a blood clot.
fibrinolysis (fī-brin-OL-i-sis): The breakdown of the fibrin strands of a blood clot by a proteolytic enzyme.
fibroblasts (FĪ-brō-blasts): Cells of connective tissue proper that are responsible for the production of extracellular fibers and the secretion of the organic compounds of the extracellular matrix.
fibrocytes (FĪ-brō-sīt): Cells of connective tissue proper that are responsible for the maintenance of the extracellular fibers and ground substance of the extracellular matrix.
fibrous cartilage: Cartilage containing an abundance of collagen fibers; found around the edges of joints, in the intervertebral discs, the menisci of the knee, etc. Also termed *fibrocartilage.*
fibrous tunic: The outermost layer of the eye, composed of the sclera and cornea.
fibula (FIB-ū-la): The lateral, relatively small bone of the lower leg.
filariasis (fil-a-RĪ-a-sis): Condition resulting from infection by mosquito-borne parasites; may cause elephantiasis.
filiform papillae: Slender conical projections from the dorsal surface of the anterior two-thirds of the tongue.
filtrate: Fluid produced by filtration at a glomerulus in the kidney.
filtration: Movement of a fluid across a membrane whose pores restrict the passage of solutes on the basis of size.

filum terminale: A fibrous extension of the spinal cord that extends from the conus medullaris to the coccygeal ligament.
fimbriae (FIM-brē-ē): A fringe; used to describe the fingerlike processes that surround the entrance to the uterine tube.
fissure: An elongated groove or opening.
fistula: An abnormal passageway between two organs or from an internal organ or space to the body surface.
flaccid: Limp, soft, flabby; a muscle without muscle tone.
flagellum/flagella (fla-JEL-ah): An organelle structurally similar to a cilium, but used to propel a cell through a fluid.
flatus: Intestinal gas.
flexion (FLEK-shun): A movement at a joint that reduces the angle between two articulating bones; the opposite of extension.
flexor: A muscle that produces flexion.
flexor reflex: A reflex contraction of the flexor muscles of a limb in response to an unpleasant stimulus.
flexure: A bending.
fluoroscope: An instrument that permits the examination of the body with x-rays in real time, rather than via fixed images on photographic plates.
folia (FŌ-lē-a): Leaflike folds; used in reference to the slender folds in the surface of the cerebellar cortex.
follicle (FOL-i-kl): A small secretory sac or gland.
follicle-stimulating hormone (FSH): A hormone secreted by the anterior pituitary; stimulates oogenesis (female) and spermatogenesis (male).
folliculitis (fo-lik-ū-LĪ-tis): Inflammation of a follicle, such as a hair follicle of the skin.
fontanel (fon-tah-NEL): A relatively soft, flexible, fibrous region between two flat bones in the developing skull.
foramen: An opening or passage through a bone.
forearm: Distal portion of the upper limb between the elbow and wrist.
forebrain: The cerebrum.
fornix (FOR-niks): An arch, or the space bounded by an arch; in the brain, an arching tract that connects the hippocampus with the mamillary bodies; in the eye, a slender pocket found where the epithelium of the ocular conjunctiva folds back upon itself as the palpebral conjunctiva.
fossa: A shallow depression or furrow in the surface of a bone.
fourth ventricle: An elongate ventricle of the metencephalon (pons and cerebellum) and the myelencephalon (medulla) of the brain; the roof contains a region of choroid plexus.
fovea (FŌ-vē-a): Portion of the retina providing the sharpest vision, with the highest concentration of cones; also called the **macula lutea**.
fracture: A break or crack in a bone.
frenulum (FREN-ū-lum): A bridle; *see* **lingual frenulum**.
frontal plane: A sectional plane that divides the body into anterior and posterior portions.
fructose: A hexose (simple sugar containing six carbons) found in foods and in semen.
fundus (FUN-dus): The base of an organ.
fungiform papillae: Mushroom-shaped papillae on the dorsal and dorsolateral surfaces of the tongue.
furuncle (FŪR-ung-kl): A boil, resulting from the invasion and inflammation of a hair follicle or sebaceous gland.
gallbladder: Pear-shaped reservoir for the bile secreted by the liver.
gametes (GAM-ēts): Reproductive cells (sperm or eggs) that contain one-half of the normal chromosome complement.
gametogenesis (ga-mē-tō-JEN-e-sis): The formation of gametes.
gamma aminobutyric acid (GABA) (GAM-ma a-MĒ-nō-bū-TIR-ik): A neurotransmitter of the CNS whose effects are usually inhibitory.
gamma motor neurons: Motor neurons that adjust the sensitivities of muscle spindles (intrafusal fibers).
ganglion/ganglia: A collection of nerve cell bodies outside the CNS.
gap junctions: Connections between cells that permit electrical coupling.
gaster (GAS-ter): The stomach; the body or belly of a skeletal muscle.
gastrectomy (gas-TREK-tō-mē): Partial or total surgical removal of the stomach.
gastric: Pertaining to the stomach.
gastric glands: Tubular glands of the stomach whose cells produce acid, enzymes, intrinsic factor, and hormones.
gastrin (GAS-trin): Hormone produced by enteroendocrine cells of the stomach, when exposed to mechanical stimuli or vagal stimulation, and the duodenum, when exposed to chyme containing undigested proteins.
gastritis (gas-TRĪ-tis): Inflammation of the stomach.
gastroenteric reflex (gas-trō-en-TER-ik): An increase in peristalsis along the small intestine triggered by the arrival of food in the stomach.
gastroileal reflex (gas-trō-IL-ē-al): Peristaltic movements that shift materials from the ileum to the colon, triggered by the arrival of food in the stomach.
gastrointestinal (GI) tract: An internal passageway that begins at the mouth, ends at the anus, and is lined by a mucous membrane; also known as the digestive tract.
gastroscope: A fiber-optic instrument that permits visual inspection of the stomach lining.
gastrulation (gas-troo-LĀ-shun): The movement of cells of the inner cell mass that creates the three primary germ layers of the embryo.
gene: A portion of a DNA strand that functions as a hereditary unit and is found at a particular locus on a specific chromosome.
genetic engineering: Research and experiments involving the manipulation of the genetic makeup of an organism.
genetics: The study of mechanisms of heredity.
geniculate (je-NIK-ū-lāt): Like a little knee; the medial geniculate nuclei and the lateral geniculate nuclei are thalamic nuclei in the walls of the thalamus of the brain.
genitalia (jen-i-TĀ-lē-a): Reproductive organs.
genotype (JĒN-ō-tīp): The genetic complement of a particular individual.
germinal centers: Pale regions in the interior of lymphoid tissues or nodules, where mitoses are under way.
gestation (jes-TĀ-shun): The period of intrauterine development.
gingivae (JIN-ji-vē): The gums.
gingivitis: Inflammation of the gums.
gland: Cells that produce exocrine or endocrine secretions, derived from epithelia.
glans penis: Expanded tip of the penis that surrounds the urethra meatus; continuous with the corpus spongiosum.
glaucoma: Eye disorder characterized by rising intraocular pressures due to inadequate drainage of aqueous humor at the canal of Schlemm.
glenoid cavity: A rounded depression that forms the articular surface of the scapula at the shoulder joint.
glial cells (GLĒ-al): Supporting cells in the neural tissue of the CNS and PNS.
globular proteins: Proteins whose tertiary structure makes them rounded and compact.
globulins (GLOB-ū-linz): Globular plasma proteins with a variety of important functions.
glomerular capsule: Expanded initial portion of the nephron that surrounds the glomerulus.
glomerulonephritis (glō-mer-ū-lō-nef-RĪ-tis): Inflammation of the glomeruli of the kidneys.
glomerulus (glō-MER-ū-lus): A ball or knot; in the kidneys, a knot of capillaries that projects into the enlarged, proximal end of a nephron; the site where filtration occurs, the first step in the production of urine.
glossopharyngeal nerve (glos-ō-fah-RIN-jē-al): Cranial nerve IX.
glottis (GLOT-is): The passage from the pharynx to the larynx.
glucagon (GLOO-ka-gon): Hormone secreted by the alpha cells of the pancreatic islets; elevates blood glucose concentrations.
glucocorticoids (gloo-kō-KOR-ti-kōyds): Hormones secreted by the zona fasciculata of the adrenal cortex to modify glucose metabolism; cortisol and corticosterone are important examples.
glucose (GLOO-kōs): A six-carbon sugar, $C_6H_{12}O_6$; the preferred energy source for most cells and the only energy source for neurons under normal conditions.
glucose-dependent insulinotropic hormone (GIP): A duodenal hormone released when the arriving chyme contains large quantities of carbohydrates; triggers the secretion of insulin and a slowdown in gastric activity.
glycerides: Lipids composed of glycerol bound to 1–3 fatty acids.
glycogen (GLI-kō-jen): A polysaccharide that represents an important energy reserve; a polymer consisting of a long chain of glucose molecules.
glycolipids (glī-cō-LIP-idz): Compounds created by the combination of carbohydrate and lipid components.
glycoprotein (glī-kō-PRŌ-tēn): A compound containing a relatively small carbohydrate group attached to a large protein.
glycosuria (glī-cō-SŪ-rē-a): The presence of glucose in the urine.
goblet cell: A goblet-shaped, mucus-producing, unicellular gland found in certain epithelia of the digestive tract.
goiter: Enlargement of the thyroid gland.
Golgi apparatus (GŌL-jē): Cellular organelle consisting of a series of membranous plates that give rise to lysosomes and secretory vesicles.
Golgi tendon organ (GOL-jē): *See* **tendon organ**.
gomphosis (gom-FŌ-sis): A fibrous synarthrosis that binds a tooth to the bone of the jaw; *see* **periodontal ligament**.
gonadotropic hormones: FSH and LH, hormones that stimulate gamete development and sex hormone secretion.
gonadotropin-releasing hormone (GnRH) (gō-nad-ō-TRŌ-pin): Hypothalamic releasing hormone that causes the secretion of FSH and LH by the anterior pituitary gland.
gonadotropins (gō-nad-ō-TRŌ-pinz): Hormones that stimulate the gonads (testes or ovaries).
gonads (GŌ-nadz): Organs that produce gametes and hormones.
gout: Clinical condition resulting from elevated uric acid concentrations in the blood and peripheral tissues.
granulocytes (GRAN-ū-lō-sīts): White blood cells containing granules visible with the light microscope; includes eosinophils, basophils, and neutrophils; also called granular leukocytes.
gray matter: Areas in the central nervous system dominated by nerve cell bodies, glial cells, and unmyelinated axons.
gray ramus: A bundle of postganglionic sympathetic nerve fibers that go to a spinal nerve for distribution to effectors in the body wall, skin, and extremities.
greater omentum: A large fold of the dorsal mesentery of the stomach that hangs in front of the intestines.
greater vestibular glands: Mucous glands in the vaginal walls that secrete into the vestibule; the equivalent of the bulbo-urethral glands of the male.
greenstick fracture: A fracture most often affecting the long bones of young children.
groin: The inguinal region.
gross anatomy: The study of the structural features of the human body without the aid of a microscope.
growth hormone (GH): Anterior pituitary hormone that stimulates tissue growth and anabolism when nutrients are abundant, and restricts tissue glucose dependence when nutrients are in short supply.

gustation (gus-TĀ-shun): Taste.
gynecologists (gī-ne-KOL-ō-jists): Physicians specializing in the pathology of the female reproductive system.
gyrus (JĪ-rus): A prominent fold or ridge of neural cortex on the surfaces of the cerebral hemispheres.
hair: A keratinous strand produced by epithelial cells of the hair follicle.
hair cells: Sensory cells of the inner ear.
hair follicle: An accessory structure of the integument; a tube lined by a stratified squamous epithelium that begins at the surface of the skin and ends at the hair papilla.
hair root: A thickened, conical structure consisting of a connective tissue papilla and the overlying matrix; a layer of epithelial cells that produces the hair shaft.
hallux: The great toe.
haploid (HAP-loid): Possessing one-half of the normal number of chromosomes; a characteristic of gametes.
hard palate: The bony roof of the oral cavity, formed by the maxillary and palatine bones.
haustra (HAWS-tra): Saclike pouches along the length of the large intestine that result from tension in the taeniae coli.
Haversian system: *See* **osteon**.
heart block: A cardiac arrhythmia due to conduction delays that affect communication between the atria and ventricles.
Heimlich maneuver (HĪM-lik): A technique for removing an airway blockage by external compression of the abdomen and forceful elevation of the diaphragm.
helper T cells: Lymphocytes (T cells) whose secretions and other activities coordinate the cellular and humoral immune responses.
hematocrit (hē-MA-tō-krit): Percentage of the volume of whole blood contributed by cells; also called the packed cell volume (PCV) or the volume of packed red cells (VPRC).
hematologists (hē-ma-TOL-ō-jists): Specialists in disorders of the blood and blood-forming tissues.
hematoma: A tumor or swelling filled with blood.
hematuria (hē-ma-TŪ-rē-a): The presence of abnormal numbers of red blood cells in the urine.
heme (hēm): A porphyrin ring containing a central iron atom that can reversibly bind oxygen molecules; a component of the hemoglobin molecule.
hemiplegia: Paralysis affecting one side of the body (arm, trunk, and leg).
hemodialysis (hē-mō-dī-AL-i-sis): Dialysis of the blood.
hemoglobin (HĒ-mō-glō-bin): Protein composed of four globular subunits, each bound to a single molecule of heme; the protein found in red blood cells that gives them the ability to transport oxygen in the blood.
hemolysis: Breakdown (lysis) of red blood cells.
hemophilia (hē-mō-FĒL-ē-a): A congenital condition resulting from the inadequate synthesis of one of the clotting factors.
hemopoiesis (hē-mō-poy-Ē-sis): Blood cell formation and differentiation.
hemorrhage: Blood loss.
hemorrhoids (HEM-ō-roidz): Swollen, varicose veins that protrude from the walls of the rectum and/or anal canal.
hemostasis: The cessation of bleeding.
hemothorax: The entry of blood into one of the pleural cavities.
heparin (HEP-a-rin): An anticoagulant released by activated basophils and mast cells.
hepatic duct: Duct carrying bile away from the liver lobes and toward the union with the cystic duct.
hepatic portal vein: Vessel that carries blood between the intestinal capillaries and the sinusoids of the liver.
hepatitis (hep-a-TĪ-tis): Inflammation of the liver, resulting from exposure to toxic chemicals, drugs, or viruses.
hepatocyte (he-PAT-ō-sīt): A liver cell.
hernia: The protrusion of a loop or portion of a visceral organ through the abdominopelvic wall or into the thoracic cavity.
herniated disc: Rupture of the connective tissue sheath of the nucleus pulposus of an intervertebral disc.
heterotopic: Ectopic; outside of its normal location.
heterozygous (het-er-ō-ZĪ-gus): Possessing two different alleles at corresponding loci on a chromosome pair; the individual's phenotype may be determined by one or both of the alleles.
hexose: A six-carbon simple sugar.
hiatus (hī-Ā-tus): A gap, cleft, or opening.
hilum (HĪ-lum) or **hilus (HĪ-lus):** A localized region where blood vessels, lymphatics, nerves, and/or other anatomical structures are attached to an organ.
hippocampus: A portion of the limbic system that is concerned with the organization and storage of memories.
hirsutism (HER-sut-izm): Excessive hair growth in women that follows the distribution pattern typical of adult males; sometimes caused by the overproduction of androgens.
histamine (HIS-ta-mēn): Chemical released by stimulated mast cells or basophils to initiate or enhance an inflammatory response.
histology (his-TOL-ō-jē): The study of tissues.
histones: Proteins associated with the DNA of the nucleus, and around which the DNA strands are wound.
holocrine secretion (HŌL-ō-krin): Form of exocrine secretion where the secretory cell becomes swollen with vesicles and then ruptures.
homeostasis (hō-mē-ō-STĀ-sis): The maintenance of a relatively constant internal environment.
homologous chromosomes (hō-MOL-ō-gus): The members of a chromosome pair, each containing the same gene loci.
homozygous (hō-mō-ZĪ-gus): Having the same gene for a particular character on two homologous chromosomes.
hormone: A compound secreted by one cell that travels through the circulatory system to affect the activities of cells in another portion of the body.
human chorionic gonadotropin (HCG): Placental hormone that maintains the corpus luteum for the first 3 months of pregnancy.
human immunodeficiency virus (HIV): The infectious agent that causes **acquired immune deficiency syndrome (AIDS)**.
human leukocyte antigen (HLA): Antigens on cell surfaces important to foreign antigen recognition and that play a role in the coordination and activation of the immune response.
human placental lactogen (HPL): Placental hormone that stimulates the functional development of the mammary glands.
humoral immunity: Immunity resulting from the presence of circulating antibodies produced by plasmocytes.
hyaline cartilage (HĪ-a-lin): The most common type of cartilage; the matrix contains collagen fibers. Examples include the connections between the ribs and sternum, the tracheal and bronchial cartilages, and synovial cartilages.
hyaluronic acid or **hyaluronan:** A proteoglycan in the matrix of many connective tissues that gives the matrix a viscous consistency; also functions as intercellular cement.
hyaluronidase (hī-a-lūr-ON-a-dāz): An enzyme that breaks down hyaluronic acid; produced by some bacteria and found in the acrosomal cap of a sperm cell.
hydrocephalus: Condition resulting from excessive production or inadequate drainage of cerebrospinal fluid.
hydrostatic pressure: Fluid pressure.
hymen: A membrane that forms during development, covering the entrance to the vagina.
hypercapnia (hī-per-KAP-nē-a): High plasma carbon dioxide concentrations, often the result of hypoventilation or inadequate tissue perfusion.
hyperglycemia: Elevated plasma glucose concentrations.
hyperopia: The farsighted condition, characterized by an inability to focus on objects close by.
hyperplasia: Abnormal enlargement of an organ due to an increase in the number of cells.
hyperpnea (hī-perp-NĒ-a): Abnormal increases in the rate and depth of respiration.
hyperreflexia: Abnormally exaggerated reflex responses to stimulation.
hypersecretion: Overactivity of glands that produce exocrine or endocrine secretions.
hypertension: Abnormally high blood pressure.
hyperthermia: Excessively high body temperature.
hyperthyroidism: Excessive production of thyroid hormones.
hypertonic: When comparing two solutions, used to refer to the solution with the higher osmolarity.
hypertrophy (hī-PER-trō-fē): Increase in the size of tissue without cell division.
hyperventilation (hī-per-ven-ti-LĀ-shun): A rate of respiration sufficient to reduce the plasma P_{CO_2} to levels below normal.
hypoblast (HĪ-pō-blast): The undersurface of the inner cell mass that faces the blastocoele of the early embryo.
hypocapnia: Abnormally low plasma P_{CO_2} usually the result of hyperventilation.
hypodermic needle: A needle inserted through the skin to introduce drugs into the subcutaneous layer.
hypodermis: The subcutaneous layer, a region of loose connective tissue also called the **superficial fascia**.
hypoesthesia: Abnormally decreased sensitivity to stimuli.
hypoglossal nerve: N XII, the cranial nerve responsible for the control of the muscles that move the tongue.
hyponychium (hī-pō-NIK-Ē-um): A thickening in the epidermis beneath the free edge of a nail.
hypophyseal portal system (hī-pō-FIZ-ē-al): Network of vessels that carry blood from capillaries in the hypothalamus to capillaries in the anterior lobe of the pituitary gland (hypophysis).
hypophysis (hī-POF-i-sis): The anterior lobe of the pituitary gland, which can be further subdivided into the pars distalis and the pars intermedia.
hyporeflexia: Abnormally depressed reflex responses to stimuli.
hyposecretion: Abnormally low rates of exocrine or endocrine secretion.
hypothalamus: The floor of the diencephalon; region of the brain containing centers involved with the unconscious regulation of visceral functions, emotions, drives, and the coordination of neural and endocrine functions.
hypotonic: When comparing two solutions, used to refer to the one with the lower osmolarity.
hypoventilation: A respiratory rate insufficient to keep plasma P_{CO_2} within normal levels.
hypovolemic (hī-pō-vō-LĒ-mik): An abnormally low blood volume.
hypoxia (hī-POKS-ē-a): Low tissue oxygen concentrations.
ileocecal valve (il-ē-ō-SĒ-kal): A fold of mucous membrane that guards the connection between the ileum and the cecum.
ileostomy (il-ē-OS-tō-mē): Surgical creation of an opening into the ileum; the opening created when the ileum is surgically attached to the abdominal wall.
ileum (IL-ē-um): The last 8 ft of the small intestine.
ilium (IL-ē-um): The largest of the three bones whose fusion creates a coxa.
immunity: Resistance to injuries and diseases caused by foreign compounds, toxins, and pathogens.
immunization: Developing immunity by the deliberate exposure to antigens under conditions that prevent the development of illness but stimulate the production of memory B cells.
immunoglobulin (i-mū-nō-GLOB-ū-lin): A circulating antibody.

implantation (im-plan-TĀ-shun): The erosion of a blastocyst into the uterine wall.
impotence: Inability to obtain or maintain an erection in the male.
incisors (in-SĪ-zerz): Two pairs of flattened, bladelike teeth located at the front of the dental arches in both the upper and lower jaws.
inclusions: Aggregations of insoluble pigments, nutrients, or other materials in the cytoplasm.
incontinence (in-KON-ti-nens): Inability to voluntarily control micturition (or defecation).
incus (IN-kus): The central auditory ossicle, situated between the malleus and the stapes in the middle ear cavity.
infarct: An area of dead cells resulting from an interruption of circulation.
infection: Invasion and colonization of body tissues by pathogenic organisms.
inferior: A directional reference meaning below.
inferior vena cava: The vein that carries blood from the parts of the body below the heart to the right auricle.
infertility: Inability to conceive.
inflammation: A nonspecific defense mechanism that operates at the tissue level, characterized by swelling, redness, warmth, pain, and some loss of function.
inflation reflex: A reflex mediated by the vagus nerve that prevents overexpansion of the lungs.
infundibulum (in-fun-DIB-ū-lum): A tapering, funnel-shaped structure; in the nervous system, refers to the connection between the pituitary gland and the hypothalamus; the infundibulum of the uterine tube is the entrance bounded by fimbriae that receives the ova at ovulation.
ingestion: The introduction of materials into the digestive tract via the mouth.
inguinal canal: A passage through the abdominal wall that marks the path of testicular descent, and that contains the testicular arteries, veins, and ductus deferens.
inguinal region: The area near the junction of the trunk and the thighs that contains the external genitalia.
inhibin (in-HIB-in): A hormone produced by the sustentacular cells that inhibits the pituitary secretion of FSH.
initial segment: The proximal portion of the axon, adjacent to the axon hillock, where an action potential first appears.
injection: Forcing of fluid into a body part or organ.
inner cell mass: Cells of the blastocyst that will form the body of the embryo.
inner ear: *See* **internal ear**.
innervation: The distribution of sensory and motor nerves to a specific region or organ.
insertion: Point of attachment of a muscle that is more movable.
insoluble: Incapable of dissolving in solution.
insomnia: Sleep disorder characterized by an inability to fall asleep.
inspiration: Inhalation; the movement of air into the respiratory system.
inspiratory reserve: The maximum amount of air that can be drawn into the lungs over and above the normal tidal volume.
insula (IN-sū-la): A region of the temporal lobe that is visible only after opening the lateral sulcus.
insulin (IN-su-lin): Hormone secreted by the beta cells of the pancreatic islets; causes a reduction in plasma glucose concentrations.
integument (in-TEG-ū-ment): The skin and associated organs (hair, glands, receptors, etc.).
intercalated discs (in-TER-ka-lā-ted): Regions where adjacent cardiocytes interlock and where gap junctions permit electrical coupling between the cells.
intercellular cement: Proteoglycans, containing the polysaccharide hyaluronic acid, found between adjacent epithelial cells.
intercellular fluid: *See* **interstitial fluid**.
interdigitate: To interlock.
interferons (in-ter-FĒR-ons): Peptides released by virally infected cells, especially lymphocytes, that make other cells more resistant to viral infection and slow viral replication.
interleukins (in-ter-LOO-kins): Peptides released by activated monocytes and lymphocytes that assist in the coordination of the cellular and humoral immune responses.
internal capsule: Term given to the appearance of the white matter of the cerebral hemispheres on gross dissection of the brain.
internal ear: The membranous labyrinth that contains the organs of hearing and equilibrium.
internal nares: The entrance to the nasopharynx from the nasal cavity.
internal respiration: Diffusion of gases between the blood and interstitial fluid.
interneuron: Neurons inside the CNS that are interposed between sensory and motor neurons.
internode: *See* **myelin sheath gap**. Area between adjacent glial cells where the myelin covering of an axon is incomplete. Also termed a *node of Ranvier.*
interoceptors: Sensory receptors monitoring the functions and status of internal organs and systems.
interosseous membrane: Fibrous connective tissue membrane between the shafts of the tibia and fibula or the radius and ulna; an example of a fibrous amphiarthrosis.
interphase: Stage in the life of a cell during which the chromosomes are uncoiled and all normal cellular functions except mitosis are under way.
intersegmental reflex: A reflex that involves several segments of the spinal cord.
interstitial cell-stimulating hormone: An alternative name for LH in the male; stimulates androgen production by the interstitial cells of the testes.
interstitial fluid (in-ter-STISH-al): Fluid in the tissues that fills the spaces between cells.
interstitial growth: Form of cartilage growth through the growth, mitosis, and secretion of chondrocytes inside the matrix.
interventricular foramen: The opening that permits fluid movement between the lateral and third ventricles.
intervertebral disc: Fibrous cartilage pad between the centra of successive vertebrae that acts as a shock absorber.
intestinal crypt: A tubular epithelial pocket lined by secretory cells and opening into the lumen of the digestive tract; also called an intestinal gland.
intestine: Tubular organ of the digestive tract.
intracellular fluid: The cytosol.
intrafusal fibers: Muscle spindle fibers.
intramembranous ossification (in-tra-MEM-bra-nus): The formation of bone within a connective tissue without the prior development of a cartilaginous model.
intramuscular injection: Injection of medication into the bulk of a skeletal muscle.
intraocular pressure: The hydrostatic pressure exerted by the aqueous humor of the eye.
intrapleural pressure: The pressure measured in a pleural cavity; also called the intrathoracic pressure.
intrapulmonary pressure (in-tra-PUL-mō-ner-ē): The pressure measured in an alveolus; also called the intra-alveolar pressure.
intrauterine: Within the uterus; used to refer to the period of prenatal development.
intrinsic factor: Glycoprotein secreted by the parietal cells of the stomach that facilitates the intestinal absorption of vitamin B_{12}.
inversion: A turning inward.
in vitro: Outside of the body, in an artificial environment.
in vivo: In the living body.
involuntary: Not under conscious control.
ion: An atom or molecule bearing a positive or negative charge due to the acceptance or donation of an electron.
ipsilateral: A reflex response affecting the same side as the stimulus; referring to the same side of the body.
iris: A contractile structure made up of smooth muscle that forms the colored portion of the eye.
ischemia (is-KĒ-mē-a): Inadequate blood supply to a region of the body.
ischium (IS-kē-um): One of the three bones whose fusion creates the coxa.
islets of Langerhans: *See* **pancreatic islets**.
isometric contraction: A muscular contraction characterized by rising tension production but no change in length.
isotonic: A solution having an osmolarity that does not result in water movement across cell membranes; of the same contractive strength.
isotonic contraction: A muscular contraction during which tension climbs and then remains stable as the muscle shortens.
isthmus (IS-mus): A narrow band of tissue connecting two larger masses.
jaundice (JAWN-dis): Condition characterized by yellowing of connective tissues due to elevated tissue bilirubin levels; usually associated with damage to the liver or biliary system.
jejunum (je-JOO-num): The middle portion of the small intestine.
joint: An area where adjacent bones interact; an articulation.
juxtaglomerular cells: Modified smooth muscle cells in the walls of the afferent and efferent arterioles adjacent to the glomerulus and the macula densa.
juxtaglomerular complex or **juxtaglomerular apparatus:** The macula densa, mesangial, and juxtaglomerular cells; a complex responsible for the release of renin and erythropoietin.
juxtamedullary nephrons: The 15 percent of nephrons whose nephron loops, or loops of Henle, extend into the medulla; these nephrons are responsible for creating the osmotic gradient within the medulla.
karyotyping (KAR-ē-ō-tī-ping): The determination of the chromosomal characteristics of an individual or cell.
keratin (KER-a-tin): Tough, fibrous protein component of nails, hair, calluses, and the general integumentary surface.
keratinization (KER-a-tin-ī-zā-shun): The production of keratin by epithelial cells.
keratinized (KER-a-tin-īz'd): Containing large quantities of keratin.
keratohyalin (ker-a-tō-HĪ-a-lin): A protein within maturing keratinocytes.
ketone bodies: Keto acids produced during the catabolism of lipids and ketogenic amino acids; specifically acetone, acetoacetate, and beta-hydroxybutyrate.
kidney: A component of the urinary system; an organ functioning in the regulation of plasma composition, including the excretion of wastes and the maintenance of normal fluid and electrolyte balance.
killer T cells: *See* **cytotoxic T cells**.
Kupffer cells (KOOP-fer): Stellate cells of the liver; phagocytic cells of the liver sinusoids.
kyphosis (kī-FŌ-sis): Exaggerated thoracic curvature.
labia (LĀ-bē-a): Lips; labia majora and minora are components of the female external genitalia.
labrum: A lip or rim.
labyrinth: A maze of passageways; usually refers to the structures of the inner ear.
lacrimal gland (LAK-ri-mal): Tear gland on the dorsolateral surface of the eye.
lactase: An enzyme that breaks down a disaccharide (lactose) in milk.
lactation (lak-TĀ-shun): The production of milk by the mammary glands.
lacteal (LAK-tē-al): A terminal lymphatic within an intestinal villus.

lactic acid: Compound produced from pyruvic acid during glycolysis.

lactiferous duct (lak-TIF-e-rus): Duct draining one lobe of the mammary gland.

lactiferous sinus: An expanded portion of a lactiferous duct adjacent to the nipple of a breast.

lacuna (la-KOO-na): A small pit or cavity.

lambdoid suture (lam-DOYD): Synarthrotic articulation between the parietal and occipital bones of the cranium.

lamellae (la-MEL-lē): Concentric layers of bone within an osteon.

lamellated corpuscle: Receptor sensitive to vibration; also called a *pacinian corpuscle.*

lamina (LA-mi-na): A thin sheet or layer.

lamina propria (PRŌ-prē-a): A layer of loose connective tissue situated immediately beneath the epithelium of a mucous membrane.

laminectomy: Removal of the spinous processes of a vertebra to gain access to and treat a herniated disc.

Langerhans cells (LAN-ger-hanz): Cells in the epithelium of the skin and digestive tract that participate in the immune response by presenting antigens to T cells.

laparoscope (LAP-a-rō-skōp): Fiber-optic instrument used to visualize the contents of the abdominopelvic cavity.

large intestine: The terminal portions of the intestinal tract, consisting of the colon, the rectum, and the anal canal.

laryngopharynx (la-RING-gō-far-inks): Division of the pharynx inferior to the epiglottis and superior to the esophagus.

larynx (LAR-inks): A complex cartilaginous structure that surrounds and protects the glottis and vocal cords; the superior margin is bound to the hyoid bone and the inferior margin is bound to the trachea.

lateral: Pertaining to the side.

lateral apertures: Openings in the roof of the fourth ventricle that permit the circulation of CSF into the subarachnoid space.

lateral ventricle: Fluid-filled chamber within one of the cerebral hemispheres.

laxatives: Compounds that promote defecation via increased peristalsis or an increase in the water content and volume of the feces.

lens: The transparent body lying behind the iris and pupil and in front of the vitreous humor.

lesion: A localized abnormality in tissue organization.

lesser omentum: A small pocket in the mesentery that connects the lesser curvature of the stomach to the liver.

leukemia (loo-KĒ-mē-ah): A malignant disease of the blood-forming tissues.

leukocyte (LOO-kō-sīt): A white blood cell.

leukocytosis (loo-kō-sī-TŌ-sis): Abnormally high numbers of circulating white blood cells.

leukopenia (loo-kō-PĒ-nē-a): Abnormally low numbers of circulating white blood cells.

leukopoiesis (loo-kō-poy-Ē-sis): White blood cell formation.

ligament (LIG-a-ment): Dense band of connective tissue fibers that attach one bone to another.

ligamentum arteriosum: The fibrous strand found in the adult that represents the remains of the ductus arteriosus of the fetus.

ligamentum nuchae (NOO-kā): An elastic ligament that extends between the vertebra prominens and the external occipital crest.

ligamentum teres: The fibrous strand in the falciform ligament that represents the remains of the umbilical vein of the fetus.

ligate: To tie off.

limbic system (LIM-bik): Group of nuclei and centers in the cerebrum and diencephalon that are involved with emotional states, memories, and behavioral drives.

limbus (LIM-bus): The edge of the cornea, marked by the transition from the corneal epithelium to the ocular conjunctiva.

liminal stimulus: A stimulus sufficient to depolarize the transmembrane potential of an excitable membrane to threshold, and produce an action potential.

linea alba: Tendinous band that runs along the midline of the rectus abdominis.

lingual: Pertaining to the tongue.

lingual frenulum: An epithelial fold that attaches the inferior surface of the tongue to the floor of the mouth.

lipase (LĪ-pāz): A pancreatic enzyme that breaks down triglycerides.

lipemia (lip-Ē-mē-a): Elevated concentration of lipids in the circulation.

lipid: An organic compound containing carbons, hydrogens, and oxygens in a ratio that does not approximate 1:2:1; includes fats, oils, and waxes.

lipogenesis (lī-pō-JEN-e-sis): Synthesis of lipids from nonlipid precursors.

lipolysis: The catabolism of lipids as a source of energy.

lipoprotein (lī-pō-PRŌ-tēn): A compound containing a relatively small lipid bound to a protein.

liver: An organ of the digestive system with varied and vital functions that include the production of plasma proteins, the excretion of bile, the storage of energy reserves, the detoxification of poisons, and the interconversion of nutrients.

lobule (LOB-ūl): A small lobe or subdivision of a lobe; the basic organizational unit of the liver at the histological level.

loose connective tissue: A loosely organized, easily distorted connective tissue containing several different fiber types, a varied population of cells, and a viscous ground substance.

lordosis (lor-DŌ-sis): An exaggeration of the lumbar curvature.

lumbar: Pertaining to the lower back.

lumen: The central space within a duct or other internal passageway.

lungs: Paired organs of respiration, situated in the left and right pleural cavities.

luteinizing hormone (LH) (LOO-tē-in-ī-zing): Anterior pituitary hormone that in the female assists FSH in follicle stimulation, triggers ovulation, and promotes the maintenance and secretion of the endometrial glands; in the male, stimulates spermatogenesis; also known as **interstitial cell-stimulating hormone**.

luxation (luks-Ā-shun): Dislocation of a joint.

lymph: Fluid contents of lymphatic vessels, similar in composition to interstitial fluid.

lymphadenopathy (lim-fad-e-NOP-a-thē): Pathological enlargement of the lymph nodes.

lymphatics: Vessels of the lymphoid system.

lymphedema (lim-fe-DĒ-ma): Swelling of peripheral tissues due to excessive lymph production or inadequate drainage.

lymph nodes: Lymphoid organs that monitor the composition of lymph.

lymphocyte (LIM-fō-sīt): A cell of the lymphoid system that participates in the immune response.

lymphokines: Chemicals secreted by activated lymphocytes.

lymphopoiesis: The production of lymphocytes.

lymphotoxin (lim-fō-TOK-sin): A secretion of lymphocytes that kills the target cells.

lysis (LĪ-sis): The destruction of a cell through the rupture of its cell membrane.

lysosome (LĪ-sō-sōm): Intracellular vesicle containing digestive enzymes.

lysozyme: An enzyme present in some exocrine secretions that has antibiotic properties.

macrophage: A phagocytic cell of the monocyte-macrophage system.

macula (MAK-ū-la): A receptor complex in the saccule or utricle that responds to linear acceleration or gravity.

macula densa (MAK-ū-la DEN-sa): A group of specialized secretory cells in a portion of the distal convoluted tubule adjacent to the glomerulus and the juxtaglomerular cells; a component of the juxtaglomerular apparatus.

macula lutea (LOO-tē-a): The fovea.

malignant cancer: A form of cancer characterized by rapid cellular growth and the spread of cancer cells throughout the body.

malleus (MAL-ē-us): The first auditory ossicle, bound to the tympanic membrane and the incus.

mamillary bodies (MAM-i-lar-ē): Nuclei in the hypothalamus concerned with feeding reflexes and behaviors; a component of the limbic system.

mammary glands: Milk-producing glands of the female breast.

manubrium: The broad, roughly triangular, superior element of the sternum.

manus: The hand.

marrow: A tissue that fills the internal cavities in a bone; may be dominated by hemopoietic cells (red marrow) or adipose tissue (yellow marrow).

mass peristalsis: Powerful peristaltic contraction that moves fecal materials along the colon and into the rectum.

mass reflex: Hyperreflexia in an area innervated by spinal cord segments distal to an area of injury.

mast cell: A connective tissue cell that when stimulated releases histamine, serotonin, and heparin, initiating the inflammatory response.

mastectomy: Surgical removal of part or all of a mammary gland.

mastication (mas-ti-KĀ-shun): Chewing.

mastoid sinus: Air-filled spaces in the mastoid process of the temporal bone.

matrix: The ground substance of a connective tissue.

maxillary sinus (MAK-si-ler-ē): One of the paranasal sinuses; an air-filled chamber lined by a respiratory epithelium that is located in a maxilla and opens into the nasal cavity.

meatus (mē-Ā-tus): An opening or entrance into a passageway.

mechanoreception: Detection of mechanical stimuli, such as touch, pressure, or vibration.

medial: Toward the midline of the body.

mediastinum (mē-dē-as-TĪ-num): A septum between two parts of an organ or a cavity such as the central tissue mass that divides the thoracic cavity into two pleural cavities; includes the aorta and other great vessels, the esophagus, trachea, thymus, the pericardial cavity and heart, and a host of nerves, small vessels, and lymphatics.

medulla: Inner layer or core of an organ.

medulla oblongata: The most caudal of the five brain regions, also known as the **myelencephalon**.

medullary cavity: The space within a bone that contains the marrow.

medullary rhythmicity center: Center in the medulla oblongata that sets the background pace of respiration; includes inspiratory and expiratory centers.

megakaryocytes (meg-a-KAR-ē-ō-sīts): Bone marrow cells responsible for the formation of platelets.

meiosis (mī-Ō-sis): Cell division that produces gametes with half of the normal somatic chromosome complement.

melanin (MEL-a-nin): Yellow-brown pigment produced by the melanocytes of the skin.

melanocyte (me-LAN-ō-sīt): Specialized cell found in the deeper layers of the stratified squamous epithelium of the skin, responsible for the production of melanin.

melanocyte-stimulating hormone (MSH): Hormone of the pars intermedia of the anterior pituitary that stimulates melanin production.

melanomas (mel-a-NŌ-maz): Dangerous malignant skin cancers that involve melanocytes.

melatonin (mel-a-TŌ-nin): Hormone secreted by the pineal gland; inhibits secretion of MSH and gonadotropins.

membrane: Any sheet or partition; a layer consisting of an epithelium and the underlying connective tissue.

membrane flow: The movement of sections of membrane surface to and from the cell surface and components of the endoplasmic reticulum, the Golgi apparatus, and vesicles.

membranous labyrinth: Endolymph-filled tubes of the inner ear that enclose the receptors of the inner ear.

menarche (me-NAR-kē): The beginning of menstrual function.

meninges (men-IN-jēz): Three membranes that surround the surfaces of the CNS; the dura mater, the pia mater, and the arachnoid mater.

meningitis: Inflammation of the spinal or cranial meninges.

meniscectomy: Removal of a meniscus.

meniscus (men-IS-kus): A fibrous cartilage pad between opposing surfaces in a joint.

menopause (MEN-ō-paws): The cessation of uterine cycles as a consequence of the aging process and exhaustion of viable follicles.

menses (MEN-sēz): The first menstrual period that normally occurs at puberty.

menstrual (MEN-stroo-al) cycle: *See* **uterine cycle.**

menstruation (men-stroo-Ā-shun): The sloughing of blood and endometrial tissue at menses.

merocrine (MER-ō-krin): A method of secretion where the cell ejects materials through exocytosis.

mesencephalic aqueduct: Passageway that connects the third ventricle (diencephalon) with the fourth ventricle (metencephalon).

mesencephalon (mez-en-SEF-a-lon): The midbrain.

mesenchyme (MEZ-en-kīm): Embryonic/fetal connective tissue.

mesentery (MES-en-ter-ē): A double layer of serous membrane that supports and stabilizes the position of an organ in the abdominopelvic cavity and provides a route for the associated blood vessels, nerves, and lymphatics.

mesoderm: The middle germ layer that lies between the ectoderm and endoderm of the embryo.

mesothelium (mez-ō-THĒ-lē-um): A simple squamous epithelium that lines one of the divisions of the ventral body cavity.

messenger RNA (mRNA): RNA formed at transcription to direct protein synthesis in the cytoplasm.

metabolism (me-TAB-ō-lizm): The sum of all of the biochemical processes underway within the human body at a given moment; includes anabolism and catabolism.

metabolites (me-TAB-ō-līts): Compounds produced in the body as the result of metabolic reactions.

metacarpals (met-a-KAR-pals): The five bones of the palm of the hand.

metalloproteins (me-tal-ō-PRŌ-tenz): Plasma proteins that transport metal ions.

metaphase (MET-a-fāz): A stage of mitosis wherein the chromosomes line up along the equatorial plane of the cell.

metaphysis (me-TAF-i-sis): The region of a long bone between the epiphysis and diaphysis, corresponding to the location of the epiphyseal cartilage of the developing bone.

metarteriole (met-ar-TĒ-rē-ōl): A vessel that connects an arteriole to a venule and that provides blood to a capillary plexus. Also termed a *precapillary arteriole.*

metastasis (me-TAS-ta-sis): The spread of a disease from one organ to another.

metatarsal: One of the five bones of the foot that articulate with the tarsals (proximally) and the phalanges (distally).

metencephalon (met-en-SEF-a-lon): The pons and cerebellum of the brain.

micelle (mī-SEL): A spherical aggregation of bile salts, monoglycerides, and fatty acids in the lumen of the intestinal tract.

microcephaly (mī-krō-SEF-a-lē): An abnormally small cranium, due to premature closure of one or more fontanels.

microfilaments: Fine protein filaments visible with the electron microscope; components of the cytoskeleton.

microglia (mī-KRŌ-glē-a): Phagocytic glial cells in the CNS, derived from the monocytes of the blood.

microphages: Neutrophils and eosinophils.

microtubules: Microscopic tubules that are part of the cytoskeleton and are found in cilia, flagella, the centrioles, and spindle fibers.

microvilli: Small, fingerlike extensions of the exposed cell membrane of an epithelial cell.

micturition (mik-tū-RI-shun): Urination.

midbrain: The mesencephalon.

middle ear: Space between the external and internal ear that contains auditory ossicles.

midsagittal plane: A plane passing through the midline of the body that divides it into left and right halves.

mineralocorticoids: Corticosteroids produced by the zona glomerulosa of the adrenal cortex; steroids such as aldosterone that affect mineral metabolism.

miscarriage: Spontaneous abortion.

mitochondrion (mī-tō-KON-drē-on): An intracellular organelle responsible for generating most of the ATP required for cellular operations.

mitosis (mī-TŌ-sis): The division of a single cell that produces two identical daughter cells; the primary mechanism of tissue growth.

mitral valve (MĪ-tral): The left AV, or bicuspid, valve of the heart.

mixed gland: A gland that contains exocrine and endocrine cells, or an exocrine gland that produces serous and mucous secretions.

mixed nerve: A peripheral nerve that contains sensory and motor fibers.

modiolus (mō-DĪ-ō-lus): The bony central hub of the cochlea.

mole: A quantity of an element or compound having a mass in grams equal to its atomic or molecular weight.

molecular weight: The sum of the atomic weights of the atoms in a molecule.

molecule: A compound containing two or more atoms that are held together by chemical bonds.

monocytes (MON-ō-sīts): Phagocytic agranulocytes (white blood cells) in the circulating blood.

monoglyceride (mon-ō-GLI-se-rīd): A lipid consisting of a single fatty acid bound to a molecule of glycerol.

monokines: Secretions released by activated cells of the monocyte-macrophage system to coordinate various aspects of the immune response.

monosaccharide (mon-ō-SAK-ah-rīd): A simple sugar, such as glucose or ribose.

monosynaptic reflex: A reflex where the sensory afferent synapses directly on the motor efferent.

monozygotic twins: Twins produced through the splitting of a single fertilized egg (zygote).

morula (MOR-ū-la): A mulberry-shaped collection of cells produced through the mitotic divisions of a zygote.

motor unit: All of the muscle cells controlled by a single motor neuron.

mucins (MŪ-sins): Proteoglycans responsible for the lubricating properties of mucus.

mucosa (mū-KŌ-sa): A mucous membrane; the epithelium plus the lamina propria.

mucous: An adjective referring to the presence or production of mucus.

mucous cell: A mucus-producing, unicellular gland found in certain epithelia of the respiratory system.

mucous membrane: *See* **mucosa.**

mucus: Lubricating secretion produced by unicellular and multicellular glands along the digestive, respiratory, urinary, and reproductive tracts.

multipennate muscle: A muscle whose internal fibers are organized around several different tendons.

multipolar neuron: A neuron with many dendrites and a single axon, the typical form of a motor neuron.

multiunit smooth muscle: Smooth muscle tissue whose muscle cells are innervated in motor units.

muriatic acid: Hydrochloric acid (HCl).

muscarinic receptors (mus-kar-IN-ik): Membrane receptors sensitive to acetylcholine (ACh) and to muscarine, a toxin produced by certain mushrooms; found at all parasympathetic neuroeffector junctions and at a few sympathetic neuroeffector junctions.

muscle: A contractile organ composed of muscle tissue, blood vessels, nerves, connective tissues, and lymphatics.

muscle tissue: A tissue characterized by the presence of cells capable of contraction; includes skeletal, cardiac, and smooth muscle tissue.

muscularis externa (mus-kū-LAR-is): Concentric layers of smooth muscle responsible for peristalsis.

muscularis mucosae: Layer of smooth muscle beneath the lamina propria responsible for moving the mucosal surface.

mutagens (MŪ-ta-jenz): Chemical agents that induce mutations and may be carcinogenic.

myalgia (mī-AL-jē-a): Muscle pain.

myasthenia gravis (mī-as-THĒ-nē-a GRA-vis): Muscular weakness due to a reduction in the number of ACh receptor sites on the sarcolemmal surface; suspected to be an autoimmune disorder.

myelencephalon (mī-el-en-SEF-a-lon): The medulla oblongata.

myelin (MĪ-e-lin): Insulating sheath around an axon consisting of multiple layers of glial cell membrane; significantly increases conduction rate along the axon.

myelination: The formation of myelin.

myelin sheath gap: Area between adjacent glial cells where the myelin covering an axon is incomplete. Also termed a *node of Ranvier* or *internode.*

myenteric plexus (mī-en-TER-ik): Parasympathetic motor neurons and sympathetic postganglionic fibers located between the circular and longitudinal layers of the muscularis externa.

myocardial infarction (mī-ō-KAR-dē-al): Heart attack; damage to the heart muscle due to an interruption of regional coronary circulation.

myocarditis: Inflammation of the myocardium.

myocardium: The cardiac muscle tissue of the heart.

myofibrils: Organized collections of myofilaments in skeletal and cardiac muscle cells.

myofilaments: Fine protein filaments, composed of the proteins actin (thin filaments) and myosin (thick filaments).

myoglobin (MĪ-ō-glō-bin): An oxygen-binding pigment especially common in slow skeletal and cardiac muscle fibers.

myogram: A recording of the tension produced by muscle fibers on stimulation.

myometrium (mī-ō-MĒ-trē-um): The thick layer of smooth muscle in the wall of the uterus.

myopia: Nearsightedness; an inability to accommodate for distant vision.

myosepta: Connective tissue partitions that separate adjacent skeletal muscles.

myosin: Protein component of the thick myofilaments.

myositis (mī-ō-SĪ-tis): Inflammation of muscle tissue.

nail: Keratinous structure produced by epithelial cells of the nail root.

narcolepsy: A sleep disorder characterized by falling asleep at inappropriate moments.

nares, external (NA-rēz): The entrance from the exterior to the nasal cavity.

nares, internal: The entrance from the nasal cavity to the nasopharynx.

nasal cavity: A chamber in the skull bounded by the internal and external nares.

nasolacrimal duct: Passageway that transports tears from the nasolacrimal sac to the nasal cavity.

nasolacrimal sac: Chamber that receives tears from the nasolacrimal ducts.

nasopharynx (nā-zō-FAR-inks): Region posterior to the internal nares, superior to the soft palate, and ending at the oropharynx.

necrosis (NEK-rō-sis): Death of cells or tissues from disease or injury.
negative feedback: Corrective mechanism that opposes or negates a variation from normal limits.
neonate: A newborn infant, or baby.
neoplasm: A tumor, or mass of abnormal tissue.
nephritis (nef-RĪ-tis): Inflammation of the kidney.
nephrolithiasis (nef-rō-li-THĪ-a-sis): Condition resulting from the formation of kidney stones.
nephron (NEF-ron): Basic functional unit of the kidney.
nephron loop: The segment of the nephron between the proximal and distal convoluted tubules. Also termed the *loop of Henle.*
nerve impulse: An action potential in a nerve cell membrane.
neural cortex: An area where gray matter is found at the surface of the CNS.
neurilemma (noo-ri-LEM-ma): The outer surface of a glial cell that encircles an axon.
neuroeffector junction: A synapse between a motor neuron and a peripheral effector, such as a muscle cell or gland cell.
neurofibrils: Microfibrils in the cytoplasm of a neuron.
neurofilaments: Microfilaments in the cytoplasm of a neuron.
neuroglandular junction: A specific type of neuroeffector junction.
neuroglia (noo-ROG-lē-a): Nonneural cells of the CNS and PNS that support and protect the neurons.
neurohypophysis (noo-rō-hī-POF-i-sis): The posterior lobe of the pituitary gland or *pars nervosa.*
neuromuscular synapse: A specific type of neuroeffector junction. Also termed a *neuromuscular junction.*
neuron (NOO-ron): A nerve cell.
neurotransmitter: Chemical compound released by one neuron to affect the transmembrane potential of another.
neurotubules: Microtubules in the cytoplasm of a neuron.
neurulation: The embryological process responsible for the formation of the CNS.
neutropenia: An abnormally low number of neutrophils in the circulating blood.
neutrophil (NOO-trō-fil): A phagocytic microphage (granulocyte, WBC) that is very numerous and usually the first of the mobile phagocytic cells to arrive at an area of injury or infection.
nicotinic receptors (nik-ō-TIN-ik): ACh receptors found on the surfaces of sympathetic and parasympathetic ganglion cells, that will also respond to the compound nicotine.
nipple: An elevated epithelial projection on the surface of the breast, containing the openings of the lactiferous sinuses.
nitrogenous wastes: Organic waste products of metabolism that contain nitrogen, such as urea, uric acid, and creatinine.
NK cells (natural killer cells): Lymphocytes responsible for immune surveillance, the detection and destruction of cancer cells.
nociception (nō-sē-SEP-shun): Pain perception.
nodose ganglion (NŌ-dōs): A sensory ganglion of cranial nerve X.
nonvesicular synapse: A synapse found between neurons of the CNS and PNS. Also termed an *electrical synapse.*
noradrenaline: Catecholamine secreted by the adrenal medulla, released at most sympathetic neuroeffector junctions, and at certain synapses inside the CNS; also called **norepinephrine**.
norepinephrine (nor-ep-i-NEF-rin): A catecholamine neurotransmitter in the PNS and CNS, and a hormone secreted by the adrenal medulla; also called **noradrenaline**.
normovolemic (nor-mō-vō-LĒ-mik): Having a normal blood volume.
nucleic acid (noo-KLĒ-ik): A polymer of nucleotides containing a pentose sugar, a phosphate group, and one of four nitrogenous bases that regulate the synthesis of proteins and make up the genetic material in cells.
nucleolus (noo-KLĒ-ō-lus): Dense region in the nucleus that represents the site of RNA synthesis.
nucleoplasm: Fluid content of the nucleus.
nucleoproteins: Proteins of the nucleus that are generally associated with the DNA.
nucleus: Cellular organelle that contains DNA, RNA, and proteins; a mass of gray matter in the CNS.
nucleus pulposus (pul-PŌ-sus): The gelatinous core of an intervertebral disc.
nurse cell: Cells attached to the basal lamina of the seminiferous tubule capsule. During spermeogensis developing spermatids are embedded within the cytoplasm of these cells. Also termed *Sertoli cells.*
nutrient: An organic compound that can be broken down in the body to produce energy.
nystagmus: Involuntary, continual movement of the eyes as if to adjust to constant motion.
obesity: Body weight 10–20 percent above standard values, as the result of body fat accumulation.
occlusal surface (o-KLOO-zal): The opposing surfaces of the teeth that come into contact when processing food.
ocular: Pertaining to the eye.
oculomotor nerve (ok-ū-lō-MŌ-ter): Cranial nerve III that controls the extra-ocular muscles other than the superior oblique and the lateral rectus.
olecranon: The proximal end of the ulna that forms the prominent point of the elbow.
olfaction: The sense of smell.
olfactory bulb (ol-FAK-tor-ē): Two olfactory nerves that lie beneath the frontal lobe of the cerebrum.
olfactory tract: Tract over which nerve impulses from the retina are transmitted between the optic chiasma and the thalamus.
oligodendrocytes (ol-i-gō-DEN-drō-sīts): CNS glial cells responsible for maintaining cellular organization in the gray matter and providing a myelin sheath in areas of white matter.
oncogene (ON-kō-jēn): A gene that can turn a normal cell into a cancer cell.
oncologists (on-KŌL-ō-jists): Physicians specializing in the study and treatment of tumors.
oocyte (Ō-ō-sīt): A cell whose meiotic divisions will produce a single ovum and three polar bodies.
oogenesis (ō-ō-JEN-e-sis): Ovum production.
oogonia (ō-ō-GŌ-nē-a): Stem cells in the ovaries whose divisions give rise to oocytes.
oophorectomy (ō-of-ō-REK-tō-mē): Surgical removal of the ovaries.
oophoritis (ō-of-ō-RĪ-tis): Inflammation of the ovaries.
ooplasm: The cytoplasm of the ovum.
opsin: A protein, one structural component of the visual pigment rhodopsin.
opsonization: An effect of coating an object with antibodies; the attraction and enhancement of phagocytosis.
optic chiasma (OP-tik kī-AZ-ma): Crossing point of the optic nerves.
optic nerve: Nerve that carries signals from the eye to the optic chiasma.
ora serrata (Ō-ra ser-RA-ta): The anterior edge of the neural retina.
orbit: Bony cavity of the skull that contains the eyeball.
orchiectomy (or-kē-EK-tō-mē): Surgical removal of one or both testes.
orchitis: Inflammation of the testes.
organelle (or-gan-EL): An intracellular structure that performs a specific function or group of functions.
organic compound: A compound containing carbon, hydrogen, and usually oxygen.
organogenesis: The formation of organs during embryological and fetal development.
organ of Corti: *See* **Corti, organ of.**
organs: Combinations of tissues that perform complex functions.
origin: Point of attachment of a muscle that is less movable.
oropharynx (or-ō-FAR-inks): The middle portion of the pharynx, bounded superiorly by the nasopharynx, anteriorly by the oral cavity, and inferiorly by the laryngopharynx.
os coxa/coxae: The bones of the hip.
osmolarity (oz-mō-LAR-i-tē): The total concentration of dissolved materials in a solution, regardless of their specific identities, expressed in terms of moles.
osmoreceptor: A receptor sensitive to changes in the osmolarity of the plasma.
osmosis (oz-MŌ-sis): The movement of water across a semipermeable membrane toward a solution containing a relatively high solute concentration.
osmotic pressure: The force of osmotic water movement; the pressure that must be applied to prevent osmotic movement across a membrane.
osseous tissue: A strong connective tissue containing specialized cells and a mineralized matrix of crystalline calcium phosphate and calcium carbonate.
ossicles: Small bones.
ossification: The formation of bone.
osteoblasts (OS-tē-ō-blasts): Cells that produce bone within connective tissue (intramembranous ossification) or cartilage (endochondral ossification); may differentiate into osteocytes.
osteoclast (OS-tē-ō-klast): A cell that dissolves the fibers and matrix of bone.
osteocyte (OS-tē-ō-sīt): A bone cell responsible for the maintenance and turnover of the mineral content of the surrounding bone.
osteogenesis (os-tē-ō-JEN-e-sis): Bone production.
osteogenic layer (os-tē-ō-JEN-ik): The inner cellular layer of the periosteum that participates in bone growth and repair.
osteoid (OS-tē-oyd): The organic components of the bone matrix, produced by osteoblasts and osteocytes.
osteolysis (os-tē-OL-i-sis): The breakdown of the mineral matrix of bone.
osteon (OS-tē-on): The basic histological unit of compact bone, consisting of osteocytes organized around a central canal and separated by concentric lamellae.
osteopenia (os-tē-ō-PĒ-nē-a): The condition of inadequate bone production in the adult, leading to a loss in bone mass and strength.
osteoporosis (os-tē-ō-pō-RŌ-sis): A reduction in bone mass and strength sufficient to compromise normal bone function.
osteoprogenitor cells: Stem cells that give rise to osteoblasts.
otic: Pertaining to the ear.
otitis media: Inflammation of the middle ear cavity.
oval window: Opening in the bony labyrinth where the stapes attaches to the membranous wall of the scala vestibuli.
ovarian cycle (ō-VAR-ē-an): Monthly cycle of gamete development in the ovaries, associated with cyclical changes in the production of sex hormones (estrogens and progestins).
ovary: Female reproductive gland.
ovulation (ov-ū-LĀ-shun): The release of a secondary oocyte, surrounded by cells of the corona radiata, following the rupture of the wall of a tertiary follicle.
ovum/ova (Ō-vum): A gamete produced by the reproductive system of a female; an egg.
oxytocin (ok-sē-TŌ-sin): Hormone produced by hypothalamic cells and secreted into capillaries at the posterior pituitary; stimulates smooth muscle contractions of the uterus or mammary glands in the female, but has no known function in males.
pacemaker cells: Cells of the SA node that set the pace of cardiac contraction.
palate: Horizontal partition separating the oral cavity from the nasal cavity and nasopharynx; can be divided into

an anterior bony (hard) palate and a posterior fleshy (soft) palate.
palatine: Pertaining to the palate.
palpate: To examine by touch.
palpebrae (pal-PĒ-brē): Eyelids.
pancreas: Digestive organ containing exocrine and endocrine tissues; exocrine portion secretes pancreatic juice; endocrine portion secretes hormones, including insulin and glucagon.
pancreatic duct: A tubular duct that carries pancreatic juice from the pancreas to the duodenum.
pancreatic islets: Aggregations of endocrine cells in the pancreas.
pancreatic juice: A mixture of buffers and digestive enzymes that is discharged into the duodenum under the stimulation of the enzymes secretin and cholecystokinin.
pancreatitis (pan-krē-a-TĪ-tis): Inflammation of the pancreas.
Papanicolaou (Pap) test: Test for the detection of malignancies of the female reproductive tract, especially the cervix and uterus.
papilla (pa-PIL-la): A small, conical projection.
paralysis: Loss of voluntary motor control over a portion of the body.
paranasal sinuses: Bony chambers lined by respiratory epithelium that open into the nasal cavity; include the frontal, ethmoidal, sphenoid, and maxillary sinuses.
parapalegia: Paralysis of the upper limbs.
parasagittal: A section or plane that parallels the midsagittal plane but does not pass along the midline.
parasympathetic division: One of the two divisions of the autonomic nervous system; also known as the craniosacral division; generally responsible for activities that conserve energy and lower the metabolic rate.
parathyroid glands: Four small glands embedded in the posterior surface of the thyroid; responsible for parathyroid hormone secretion.
parathyroid hormone: Hormone secreted by the parathyroid gland when plasma calcium levels fall below the normal range; causes increased osteoclast activity, increased intestinal calcium uptake, and decreased calcium ion loss at the kidneys.
parenchyma (pa-RENG-ki-ma): The cells of a tissue or organ that are responsible for fulfilling its functional role.
paresthesia: Sensory abnormality that produces a tingling sensation.
parietal: Referring to the body wall or outer layer.
parietal cell: Cells of the gastric glands that secrete HCl and intrinsic factor.
Parkinson's disease: Progressive motor disorder due to degeneration of the cerebral nuclei.
parotid glands (pa-ROT-id): Large salivary glands that secrete a saliva containing high concentrations of salivary (alpha) amylase.
pars distalis (dis-TAL-is): The large, anterior portion of the adenohypophysis, or anterior lobe of the pituitary gland.
pars intermedia (in-ter-MĒ-dē-a): The portion of the anterior lobe of the pituitary gland immediately adjacent to the posterior pituitary and the infundibulum.
pars nervosa or **neurohypophysis (noor-ō-hī-POF-i-sis):** The posterior pituitary gland.
parturition (par-tū-RISH-un): Childbirth, delivery.
patella (pa-TEL-a): The sesamoid bone of the kneecap.
pathogenic: Disease-causing.
pathologist (pa-THOL-ō-jist): An M.D. specializing in the identification of diseases based on characteristic structural and functional changes in tissues and organs.
pedicel (PED-i-sel): A slender process of a podocyte that forms part of the filtration apparatus of the kidney glomerulus.
pedicles (PED-i-kls): Thick bony struts that connect the vertebral body with the articular and spinous processes.
pelvic cavity: Inferior subdivision of the abdominopelvic (peritoneal) cavity; encloses the urinary bladder, the sigmoid colon and rectum, and male or female reproductive organs.
pelvis: A bony complex created by the articulations between the coxae, the sacrum, and the coccyx.
penis (PĒ-nis): Component of the male external genitalia; a copulatory organ that surrounds the urethra and serves to introduce semen into the female vagina.
pepsin: Proteolytic enzyme secreted by the chief cells of the gastric glands in the stomach.
pepsinogen (pep-SIN-ō-jen): The inactive proenzyme that is secreted by chief cells of the gastric pits; after secretion it is converted to the proteolytic enzyme pepsin.
peptidases: Enzymes that split peptide bonds and release amino acids.
perforating canal: A passageway in compact bone that runs at right angles to the axes of the osteons, between the periosteum and endosteum.
perfusion: The blood flow through a tissue.
pericardial cavity (per-i-KAR-dē-al): The space between the parietal pericardium and the epicardium (visceral pericardium) that covers the outer surface of the heart.
pericarditis: Inflammation of the pericardium.
pericardium (per-i-KAR-dē-um): The fibrous sac that surrounds the heart, and whose inner, serous lining is continuous with the epicardium.
perichondrium (per-ē-KON-drē-um): Layer that surrounds a cartilage, consisting of an outer fibrous and an inner cellular region.
perikaryon (per-i-KAR-ē-on): The cytoplasm that surrounds the nucleus in the soma of a nerve cell. Also termed the *nerve cell body.*
perilymph (PER-i-limf): A fluid similar in composition to cerebrospinal fluid; found in the spaces between the bony labyrinth and the membranous labyrinth of the inner ear.
perimysium (per-i-MIS-ē-um): Connective tissue partition that separates adjacent fasciculi in a skeletal muscle.
perineum (per-i-NĒ-um): The pelvic floor and associated structures.
perineurium: Connective tissue partition that separates adjacent bundles of nerve fibers in a peripheral nerve.
periodontal ligament (per-ē-ō-DON-tal): Collagen fibers that bind the cement, or cementum, of a tooth to the periosteum of the surrounding alveolus.
periosteum (per-ē-OS-tē-um): Layer that surrounds a bone, consisting of an outer fibrous and inner cellular region.
peripheral nervous system (PNS): All neural tissue outside the CNS.
peristalsis (per-i-STAL-sis): A wave of smooth muscle contractions that propels materials along the axis of a tube such as the digestive tract, the ureters, or the ductus deferens.
peritoneal cavity: *See* **abdominopelvic cavity**.
peritoneum (per-i-tō-NĒ-um): The serous membrane that lines the peritoneal (abdominopelvic) cavity.
peritonitis (per-i-tō-NĪ-tis): Inflammation of the peritoneum.
peritubular capillaries: A network of capillaries that surrounds the proximal and distal convoluted tubules of the kidneys.
permeability: Ease with which dissolved materials can cross a membrane; if freely permeable, any molecule can cross the membrane; if impermeable, nothing can cross; most biological membranes are selectively permeable.
peroxisome: A membranous vesicle containing enzymes that break down hydrogen peroxide (H_2O_2).
pes: The foot.
petrosal ganglion: Sensory ganglion of the glossopharyngeal nerve (N IX).
petrous: Stony; usually used to refer to the thickened portion of the temporal bone that encloses the inner ear.
Peyer's patches (PĪ-erz): *See* **aggregated lymphoid nodules**.
pH: The negative exponent of the hydrogen ion concentration, in moles per liter.
phagocyte: A cell that performs phagocytosis.
phagocytosis (FA-gō-sī-TŌ-sis): The engulfing of extracellular materials or pathogens; movement of extracellular materials into the cytoplasm by enclosure in a membranous vesicle.
phalanx/phalanges (fa-LAN-jēz): Digits; the bones of the fingers and toes.
pharmacology: The study of drugs, their physiological effects, and their clinical uses.
pharynx (FAR-inks): The throat; a muscular passageway shared by the digestive and respiratory tracts.
phasic response: A pattern of response to stimulation by sensory neurons that are normally inactive; stimulation causes a burst of neural activity that ends when the stimulus either stops or stops changing in intensity.
phenotype (FĒN-ō-tīp): Physical characteristics that are genetically determined.
phonation (fō-NĀ-shun): Sound production at the larynx.
phosphate group: PO_4^{3-}.
phospholipid (fos-fō-LIP-id): An important membrane lipid whose structure includes hydrophilic and hydrophobic regions.
phosphorylation (fos-for-i-LĀ-shun): The addition of a phosphate group to a molecule.
photoreception: Sensitivity to light.
physiology (fiz-ē-OL-ō-jē): The study of function; considers the ways living organisms perform vital activities.
pia mater: The delicate inner meningeal layer that is in direct contact with the neural tissue of the CNS.
pigment: A compound with a characteristic color.
piloerection: "Goosebumps" effect produced by the contraction of the arrector pili muscles of the skin.
pineal gland: Neural tissue in the posterior portion of the roof of the diencephalon, responsible for the secretion of melatonin.
pinealocytes (PĪN-ē-a-lō-sīts): Secretory cells of the pineal gland.
pinna: The expanded, projecting portion of the external ear that surrounds the external auditory meatus.
pinocytosis (PIN-ō-sī-TŌ-sis): The introduction of fluids into the cytoplasm by enclosing them in membranous vesicles at the cell surface.
pituitary gland: The "master gland," situated in the sella turcica of the sphenoid bone and connected to the hypothalamus by the infundibulum; includes the posterior lobe (pars nervosa) and the anterior lobe (pars intermedia and pars distalis).
placenta (pla-SENT-a): A complex structure in the uterine wall that permits diffusion between the fetal and maternal circulatory systems; also called the afterbirth.
placentation (pla-sen-TĀ-shun): Formation of a functional placenta following implantation of a blastocyst in the endometrium.
plantar: Referring to the sole of the foot.
plasma (PLAZ-mah): The fluid ground substance of whole blood; what remains after the cells have been removed from a sample of whole blood.
plasmalemma (plaz-ma-LEM-a): Cell membrane.
plasmocyte: Activated B cells that secrete antibodies. Also termed a *plasma cell.*
platelets (PLĀT-lets): Small packets of cytoplasm that contain enzymes important in the clotting response; manufactured in the bone marrow by cells called **megakaryocytes**.
pleura (PLOO-rah): The serous membrane lining the pleural cavities.
pleural cavities: Subdivisions of the thoracic cavity that contain the lungs.

pleuritis (ploor-Ī-tis): Inflammation of the pleura.
plexus (PLEK-sus): A complex interwoven network of peripheral nerves or blood vessels.
plica (PLĪ-ka): A permanent transverse fold in the wall of the small intestine.
pluripotential stem cells: Stem cells that ultimately give rise to all blood cells. Also termed *hemocytoblasts*.
pneumotaxic center (nū-mō-TAKS-ik): A center in the reticular formation of the pons that regulates the activities of the apneustic and respiratory rhythmicity centers to adjust the pace of respiration.
pneumothorax (nū-mō-THŌR-aks): The introduction of air into the pleural cavity.
podocyte (POD-ō-sīt): A cell whose processes surround the glomerular capillaries and assist in the filtration process.
polar body: A nonfunctional packet of cytoplasm containing chromosomes eliminated from an oocyte during meiosis.
pollex (POL-eks): The thumb.
polycythemia (po-lē-sī-THĒ-mē-a): An unusually high hematocrit due to the presence of excess numbers of formed elements, especially RBCs.
polymorph: Polymorphonuclear leukocyte; a neutrophil.
polypeptide: A chain of amino acids strung together by peptide bonds; those containing more than 100 peptides are called proteins.
polysaccharide (pol-ē-SAK-ah-rīd): A complex sugar, such as glycogen or a starch.
polysynaptic reflex: A reflex with interneurons interposed between the sensory fiber and the motor neuron(s).
polyuria (pol-ē-Ū-rē-a): Excessive urine production.
pons: The portion of the metencephalon anterior to the cerebellum.
popliteal (pop-LIT-ē-al): Pertaining to the back of the knee.
porphyrins (POR-fi-rinz): Ring-shaped molecules that form the basis for important respiratory and metabolic pigments, including heme and the cytochromes.
porta hepatis: A region of mesentery between the duodenum and liver that contains the hepatic artery, the hepatic portal vein, and the common bile duct.
positive feedback: Mechanism that increases a deviation from normal limits following an initial stimulus.
postcentral gyrus: The primary sensory cortex, where touch, vibration, pain, temperature, and taste sensations arrive and are consciously perceived.
posterior: Toward the back; dorsal.
postganglionic neuron: An autonomic neuron in a peripheral ganglion, whose activities control peripheral effectors.
postovulatory phase: The secretory phase of the menstrual cycle.
precentral gyrus: The primary motor cortex on a cerebral hemisphere, located rostral to the central sulcus.
prefrontal cortex: Rostral portion of each cerebral hemisphere thought to be involved with higher intellectual functions, predictions, calculations, and so forth.
preganglionic neuron: Visceral motor neuron inside the CNS whose output controls one or more ganglionic motor neurons in the PNS.
premolars: Bicuspids; teeth with flattened occlusal surfaces located anterior to the molar teeth.
premotor cortex: Motor association area between the precentral gyrus and the prefrontal area.
preoptic nucleus: Hypothalamic nucleus that coordinates thermoregulatory activities.
preovulatory phase: A portion of the menstrual cycle; period of estrogen-induced repair of the functional zone of the endometrium through the growth and proliferation of epithelial cells in the glands not lost during menses.
prepuce (PRĒ-pus): Loose fold of skin that surrounds the glans penis (males) or the clitoris (females).
preputial glands (prē-PŪ-shal): Glands on the inner surface of the prepuce that produce a viscous, odorous secretion called **smegma**.
presbyopia: Farsightedness; an inability to accommodate for near vision.
prevertebral ganglion: *See* **collateral ganglion**.
prime mover: A muscle that performs a specific action.
proenzyme: An inactive enzyme secreted by an epithelial cell.
progesterone (prō-JES-ter-ōn): The most important progestin secreted by the corpus luteum following ovulation.
progestins (prō-JES-tinz): Steroid hormones structurally related to cholesterol.
prognosis: A prediction concerning the possibility or time course of recovery from a specific disease.
projection fibers: Axons carrying information from the thalamus to the cerebral cortex.
prolactin (prō-LAK-tin): Hormone that stimulates functional development of the mammary gland in females; secreted by the anterior lobe of the pituitary gland.
prolapse: The abnormal descent or protrusion of a portion of an organ, such as the vagina or anorectal canal.
proliferative phase: *See* **preovulatory phase**.
pronation (prō-NĀ-shun): Rotation of the forearm that makes the palm face posteriorly.
pronucleus: Enlarged egg or sperm nucleus that forms after fertilization but before amphimixis.
properdin: Complement factor that prolongs and enhances non-antibody-dependent complement binding to bacterial cell walls.
prophase (PRŌ-fāz): The initial phase of mitosis, characterized by the appearance of chromosomes, breakdown of the nuclear membrane, and formation of the spindle apparatus.
proprioception (prō-prē-ō-SEP-shun): Awareness of the positions of bones, joints, and muscles.
prostaglandin (pros-tah-GLAN-din): Lipoid secreted by one cell that alters the metabolic activities or sensitivities of adjacent cells; sometimes called *local hormones*.
prostate gland (PROS-tāt): Accessory gland of the male reproductive tract, contributing roughly one-third of the volume of semen.
prostatectomy (pros-ta-TEK-tō-mē): Surgical removal of the prostate.
prostatitis (pros-ta-TĪ-tis): Inflammation of the prostate.
prosthesis: An artificial substitute for a body part.
protease: *See* **proteinase**.
protein: A large polypeptide with a complex structure.
proteinase: An enzyme that breaks down proteins into peptides and amino acids.
proteinuria (prō-tēn-ŪR-ē-a): Abnormal amounts of protein in the urine.
proteoglycan (prō-tē-ō-GLĪ-kan): Compound containing a large polysaccharide complex attached to a relatively small protein; examples include hyaluronic acid and chondroitin sulfate.
prothrombin: Circulating proenzyme of the common pathway of the clotting system; converted to thrombin by the enzyme thromboplastin.
proton: A fundamental particle bearing a positive charge.
protraction: Movement anteriorly in the horizontal plane.
proximal: Toward the attached base of an organ or structure.
proximal convoluted tubule: The portion of the nephron between Bowman's capsule and the nephron loop; the major site of active reabsorption from the filtrate.
pruritis (proo-RĪ-tus): Itching.
pseudopodia (soo-dō-PŌ-dē-a): Temporary cytoplasmic extensions typical of mobile or phagocytic cells.
pseudostratified epithelium: An epithelium containing several layers of nuclei, but whose cells are all in contact with the underlying basement membrane.
psoriasis (sō-RĪ-a-sis): Skin condition characterized by excessive keratin production and the formation of dry, scaly patches on the body surface.
psychosomatic condition: An abnormal physiological state with a psychological origin.
puberty: Period of rapid growth, sexual maturation, and the appearance of secondary sexual characteristics; usually occurs at ages 10–15.
pubic symphysis: Fibrocartilaginous amphiarthrosis between the pubic bones of the coxae.
pubis (PŪ-bis): The anterior, inferior component of the coxa.
pudendum (pū-DEN-dum): The external genitalia.
pulmonary circuit: Blood vessels between the pulmonary semilunar valve of the right ventricle and the entrance to the left atrium; the blood circulation through the lungs.
pulmonary ventilation: Movement of air in and out of the lungs.
pulp cavity: Internal chamber in a tooth, containing blood vessels, lymphatics, nerves, and the cells that maintain the dentin.
pulpitis (pul-PĪ-tis): Inflammation of the tissues of the pulp cavity.
pupil: The opening in the center of the iris through which light enters the eye.
purine: An N compound with a ring-shaped structure; examples include adenine and guanine, two nitrogen bases common in nucleic acids.
Purkinje cell (pur-KIN-jē): Large, branching neuron of the cerebellar cortex.
Purkinje fibers: Specialized conducting cardiocytes in the ventricles.
pus: An accumulation of debris, fluid, dead and dying cells, and necrotic tissue.
putamen (pū-TĀ-men): Thalamic nucleus involved in the integration of sensory information prior to projection to the cerebral hemispheres.
P wave: Deflection of the ECG corresponding to atrial depolarization.
pyelogram (PĪ-el-ō-gram): A radiographic image of the kidneys and ureters.
pyelonephritis (pī-e-lō-nef-RĪ-tis): Inflammation of the kidneys.
pyloric sphincter (pī-LOR-ic): Sphincter of smooth muscle that regulates the passage of chyme from the stomach to the duodenum.
pylorus (pī-LŌR-us): Gastric region between the body of the stomach and the duodenum; includes the pyloric sphincter.
pyrexia (pī-REK-sē-a): A fever.
pyrimidine: An N compound with a ring-shaped structure; examples include cytosine, thymine, and uracil, nitrogen bases common in nucleic acids.
pyruvic acid (pī-RŪ-vik): Three-carbon compound produced by glycolysis.
quadriplegia: Paralysis of the upper and lower limbs.
radiodensity: Relative resistance to the passage of x-rays.
radiographic techniques: Methods of visualizing internal structures using various forms of radiational energy.
radiopaque: Having a relatively high radiodensity.
rami communicantes: Axon bundles that link the spinal nerves with the ganglia of the sympathetic chain.
ramus: A branch.
raphe (RĀ-fē): A seam.
receptor field: The area monitored by a single sensory receptor.
recessive gene: An allele that will affect the phenotype only when the individual is homozygous for that trait.
rectal columns: Longitudinal folds in the walls of the anorectal canal.
rectouterine pouch (rek-tō-Ū-te-rin): Peritoneal pocket between the anterior surface of the rectum and the posterior surface of the uterus.
rectum (REK-tum): The last 15 cm (6 in.) of the digestive tract.

rectus: Straight.
red blood cell: *See* **erythrocyte**.
reduction: The gain of hydrogen atoms or electrons, or the loss of an oxygen molecule.
reductional division: The first meiotic division, which reduces the chromosome number from 46 to 23.
reflex: A rapid, automatic response to a stimulus.
reflex arc: The receptor, sensory neuron, motor neuron, and effector involved in a particular reflex; interneurons may or may not be present, depending on the reflex considered.
refraction: The bending of light rays as they pass from one medium to another.
refractory period: Period between the initiation of an action potential and the restoration of the normal resting potential; over this period the membrane will not respond normally to stimulation.
relaxation phase: The period following a contraction when the tension in the muscle fiber returns to resting levels.
relaxin: Hormone that loosens the pubic symphysis; a hormone secreted by the placenta.
renal: Pertaining to the kidneys.
renal corpuscle: The initial portion of the nephron, consisting of an expanded chamber that encloses the glomerulus.
renin: Enzyme released by the juxtaglomerular cells when renal blood pressure or P_{O_2} declines; converts angiotensinogen to angiotensin I.
rennin: Gastric enzyme that breaks down milk proteins.
replication: Duplication.
repolarization: Movement of the transmembrane potential away from positive millivolt (mV) values and toward the resting potential.
residual volume: Amount of air remaining in the lungs after maximum forced expiration.
respiration: Exchange of gases between living cells and the environment; includes pulmonary ventilation, external respiration, internal respiration, and cellular respiration.
respiratory minute volume: The amount of air moved in and out of the respiratory system each minute.
resting potential: The transmembrane potential of a normal cell under homeostatic conditions.
rete (RĒ-tē): An interwoven network of blood vessels or passageways.
reticular activating center: Mesencephalic portion of the reticular formation responsible for arousal and the maintenance of consciousness.
reticular formation: Diffuse network of gray matter that extends the entire length of the brain stem.
reticulocytes (re-TIK-ū-lō-sīts): The last stage in the maturation of red blood cells; normally the youngest red blood cells present in the blood.
reticulospinal tracts: Descending tracts that carry involuntary motor commands issued by neurons of the reticular formation.
retina: The innermost layer of the eye, lining the vitreous chamber; also known as the neural tunic.
retinene (RET-i-nēn): Visual pigment derived from vitamin A.
retraction: Movement posteriorly in the horizontal plane.
retroflexion (re-trō-FLEK-shun): A posterior tilting of the uterus that has no clinical significance.
retrograde flow (RET-rō-grād): Transport of materials from the terminal arborization to the soma of a neuron.
retroperitoneal (re-trō-per-i-tō-NĒ-al): Situated behind or outside of the peritoneal cavity.
reverberation: Positive feedback along a chain of neurons, so that they remain active once stimulated.
rheumatism (ROO-muh-tizm): A condition characterized by pain in muscles, tendons, bones, or joints.
Rh factor: Agglutinogen that may be present (Rh-positive) or absent (Rh-negative) from the surfaces of red blood cells.
rhizotomy: Surgical transection of a dorsal root, usually performed to relieve pain.
rhodopsin (rō-DOP-sin): The visual pigment found in the membrane discs of the distal segments of rods.
rhythmicity center: Medullary center responsible for the basic pace of respiration; includes inspiratory and expiratory centers.
ribonucleic acid (RNA) (rī-bō-nū-KLĀ-ik): A nucleic acid consisting of a chain of nucleotides that contain the sugar ribose and the nitrogen bases adenine, guanine, cytosine, and uracil.
ribosome: An organelle containing rRNA and proteins that is essential to mRNA translation and protein synthesis.
right lymphatic duct: Lymphatic vessel delivering lymph from the right side of the head, neck, and chest to the venous system via the right subclavian vein.
rigor mortis: Extended muscular contraction and rigidity that occurs after death, as the result of calcium ion release from the SR and the exhaustion of cytoplasmic ATP reserves.
rod: Photoreceptor responsible for vision under dimly lit conditions.
rostral: Toward the nose; used when referring to relative position inside the skull.
rough endoplasmic reticulum (RER): A membranous organelle that is a site of protein synthesis and storage.
rouleau/rouleaux (roo-LŌ): A stack of red blood cells.
round window: An opening in the bony labyrinth of the inner ear that exposes the membranous wall of the scala tympani to the air of the middle ear cavity.
rubrospinal tracts: Descending tracts that carry involuntary motor commands issued by the red nucleus of the mesencephalon.
Ruffini corpuscles (ru-FĒ-nē): Receptors sensitive to tension and stretch in the dermis of the skin.
rugae (ROO-gē): Mucosal folds in the lining of the empty stomach that disappear as gastric distension occurs.
saccule (SAK-ūl): A portion of the vestibular apparatus of the inner ear, responsible for static equilibrium.
sagittal plane: Sectional plane that divides the body into left and right portions.
salivatory nucleus (SAL-i-va-tōr-ē): Medullary nucleus that controls the secretory activities of the salivary glands.
saltatory conduction: Relatively rapid conduction of a nerve impulse between successive nodes of a myelinated axon.
sarcolemma: The cell membrane of a muscle cell.
sarcoma (sar-KŌ-ma): A tumor of connective tissues.
sarcomere: The smallest contractile unit of a striated muscle cell.
sarcoplasm: The cytoplasm of a muscle cell.
scala media: The central, endolymph-filled chamber of the inner ear; *see* **cochlear duct**.
scala tympani: The perilymph-filled chamber of the inner ear below the basilar membrane; pressure changes here distort the round window.
scala vestibuli: The perilymph-filled chamber of the inner ear above the vestibular membrane; pressure changes here result from distortions of the oval window.
scapula (SKAP-ū-la): The shoulder blade.
scar tissue: Thick, collagenous tissue that forms at an injury site.
Schlemm, canal of: Passageway that delivers aqueous humor from the anterior chamber of the eye to the venous circulation.
Schwann cells: Glial cells responsible for the neurilemma that surrounds axons in the PNS.
sciatica (sī-AT-i-ka): Pain resulting from compression of the roots of the sciatic nerve.
sciatic nerve (sī-AT-ik): Nerve innervating the posteromedial portions of the thigh and lower leg.
sclera (SKLER-a): The fibrous, outer layer of the eye forming the white area of the anterior surface; a portion of the fibrous tunic of the eye.
sclerosis: A hardening and thickening that often occurs secondary to tissue inflammation.
scoliosis (skō-lē-Ō-sis): An abnormal, exaggerated lateral curvature of the spine.
scrotum (SKRŌ-tum): Loose-fitting, fleshy pouch that encloses the testes of the male.
sebaceous glands (se-BĀ-shus): Glands that secrete sebum, usually associated with hair follicles.
sebum (SĒ-bum): A waxy secretion that coats the surfaces of hairs.
secondary sex characteristics: Physical characteristics that appear at puberty in response to sex hormones, but are not involved in the production of gametes.
secretin (sē-KRĒ-tin): Duodenal hormone that stimulates pancreatic buffer secretion and inhibits gastric activity.
semen (SĒ-men): Fluid ejaculate containing spermatozoa and the secretions of accessory glands of the male reproductive tract.
semicircular ducts: Tubular components of the vestibular apparatus responsible for dynamic equilibrium.
semilunar valve: A three-cusped valve guarding the exit from one of the cardiac ventricles; includes the pulmonary and aortic valves.
seminal glands (SEM-i-nal): Glands of the male reproductive tract that produce roughly 60 percent of the volume of semen. Also known as *seminal vesicles*.
seminiferous tubules (sem-in-IF-er-us): Coiled tubules where sperm production occurs in the testis.
senescence: Aging.
septae (SEP-tē): Partitions that subdivide an organ.
serosa: *See* **serous membrane**.
serotonin (ser-ō-TŌ-nin): A neurotransmitter in the CNS; a compound that enhances inflammation, released by activated mast cells and basophils.
serous cell: A cell that produces a watery secretion containing high concentrations of enzymes.
serous membrane: A squamous epithelium and the underlying loose connective tissue; the lining of the pericardial, pleural, and peritoneal cavities.
serum: Blood plasma from which clotting agents have been removed.
sesamoid bone: A bone that forms in a tendon.
sigmoid colon (SIG-moid): The S-shaped 8-inch portion of the colon between the descending colon and the rectum.
sign: A clinical term for objective evidence of the presence of a disease.
simple epithelium: An epithelium containing a single layer of cells above the basement membrane.
sinus: A chamber or hollow in a tissue; a large, dilated vein.
sinusitis: Inflammation of a nasal sinus.
sinusoid (SĪ-nus-oid): An extensive network of vessels found in the liver, adrenal cortex, spleen, and pancreas; similar in histological structure to capillaries.
skeletal muscle: A contractile organ of the muscular system.
skeletal muscle tissue: Contractile tissue dominated by skeletal muscle fibers; characterized as striated, voluntary muscle.
sliding filament theory: The concept that a sarcomere shortens as the thick and thin filaments slide past one another.
small intestine: The duodenum, jejunum, and ileum; the digestive tract between the stomach and large intestine.
smegma (SMEG-ma): Secretion of the preputial glands of the penis or clitoris.
smooth endoplasmic reticulum: Membranous organelle where lipid and carbohydrate synthesis and storage occur.
smooth muscle tissue: Muscle tissue found in the walls of many visceral organs; characterized as nonstriated, involuntary muscle.
soft palate: Fleshy posterior extension of the hard palate, separating the nasopharynx from the oral cavity.
sole: The inferior surface of the foot.

solute: Material dissolved in a solution.
solution: A fluid containing dissolved materials.
solvent: The fluid component of a solution.
soma (SŌ-ma): Body.
somatic (sō-MAT-ik): Pertaining to the body.
somatic nervous system: System of nerve fibers that run from the central nervous system to the muscles of the skeleton.
somatomedins: Compounds stimulating tissue growth, released by the liver following GH secretion.
somatostatin: GH-IH, a hypothalamic regulatory hormone that inhibits GH secretion by the anterior pituitary.
somatotropin: Growth hormone produced by the anterior pituitary in response to GH-RH.
sperm: *See* **spermatozoon/spermatozoa**.
spermatic cords: Spermatic vessels, nerves, lymphatics, and the ductus deferens, extending between the testes and the proximal end of the inguinal canal.
spermatids (SPER-ma-tidz): The product of meiosis in the male, cells that differentiate into spermatozoa.
spermatocyte (sper-MAT-ō-sīt): Cells of the seminiferous tubules that are engaged in meiosis.
spermatogenesis (sper-ma-tō-JEN-e-sis): Sperm production.
spermatogonia (sper-ma-tō-GŌ-nē-a): Stem cells whose mitotic divisions give rise to other stem cells and spermatocytes.
spermatozoon/spermatozoa (sper-ma-tō-ZŌ-on): A sperm cell, the male gamete.
spermicide: Compound toxic to sperm cells, sometimes used as a contraceptive method.
spermiogenesis: The process of spermatid differentiation that leads to the formation of physically mature spermatozoa.
sphincter (SFINK-ter): Muscular ring that contracts to close the entrance or exit of an internal passageway.
spina bifida (SPĪ-na BI-fi-da): A developmental abnormality in which the vertebral laminae fail to unite at the midline; the entire vertebral column and skull may be affected in severe cases.
spinal meninges (men-IN-jēz): Specialized membranes that line the vertebral canal and provide protection, stabilization, nutrition, and shock absorption to the spinal cord.
spinal nerve: One of 31 pairs of nerves that originate on the spinal cord from anterior and posterior roots.
spindle apparatus: A muscle spindle (intrafusal fiber) and its sensory and motor innervation.
spinocerebellar tracts: Ascending tracts carrying sensory information to the cerebellum.
spinothalamic tracts: Ascending tracts carrying poorly localized touch, pressure, pain, vibration, and temperature sensations to the thalamus.
spinous process: Prominent posterior projection of a vertebra, formed by the fusion of two laminae.
splanchnic nerves: Preganglionic (myelinated) sympathetic nerves that end in one of the collateral ganglia.
spleen: Lymphoid organ important for red blood cell phagocytosis, immune response, and lymphocyte production.
splenectomy (splē-NEK-tō-mē): Surgical removal of the spleen.
spongy bone: Trabecular bone, composed of a network of bony struts. Also termed *cancellous* (KAN-se-lus) *bone.*
sprain: Forceful distortion of an articulation that produces damage to the capsule, ligaments, or tendons but not dislocation.
sputum (SPŪ-tum): Viscous mucus ejected from the mouth after transport to the pharynx by the mucus escalator of the respiratory tract.
squama: A broad, flat surface.
squamous (SKWĀ-mus): Flattened.
squamous epithelium: An epithelium whose superficial cells are flattened and platelike.
stapedius (sta-PĒ-dē-us): A muscle of the middle ear whose contraction tenses the auditory ossicles and reduces the forces transmitted to the oval window.
stapes (STĀ-pēz): The auditory ossicle attached to the tympanic membrane.
statoconia (otoliths) (sta-tō-KŌ-nē-a): Aggregations of calcium carbonate crystals in a gelatinous membrane that sits above one of the maculae of the vestibular apparatus.
stenosis (ste-NŌ-sis): A constriction or narrowing of a passageway.
stereocilia: Elongate microvilli characteristic of the epithelium of the epididymis and portions of the ductus deferens.
steroid: A ring-shaped lipid structurally related to cholesterol.
stimulus: An environmental alteration that produces a change in cellular activities; often used to refer to events that alter the transmembrane potentials of excitable cells.
stratified: Containing several layers.
stratum (STRĀ-tum): Layer.
stratum corneum (KOR-nē-um): Layers of flattened, dead, keratinized cells covering the epidermis of the skin.
stretch receptors: Sensory receptors that respond to stretching of the surrounding tissues.
stroma: The connective tissue framework of an organ, as distinguished from the functional cells (parenchyma) of that organ.
subarachnoid space: Meningeal space containing CSF; the area between the arachnoid mater and the pia mater.
subclavian (sub-KLĀ-vē-an): Pertaining to the region under the clavicle.
subcutaneous layer: The layer of loose connective tissue below the dermis; also called the **hypodermis** or **superficial fascia.**
sublingual salivary glands (sub-LING-gwal): Mucus-secreting salivary glands situated under the tongue.
subluxation (sub-luks-Ā-shun): A partial dislocation of a joint.
submandibular salivary glands: Salivary glands nestled in depressions on the medial surfaces of the mandible; salivary glands that produce a mixture of mucins and enzymes (salivary amylase).
submucosa (sub-mū-KŌ-sa): Region between the muscularis mucosae and the muscularis externa.
submucosal glands: Mucous glands in the submucosa of the duodenum.
subserous fascia: Loose connective tissue layer beneath the serous membrane lining the ventral body cavity.
substantia nigra: A nucleus in the midbrain that is responsible for negative feedback control of the basal nuclei.
substrate: A participant (product or reactant) in an enzyme-catalyzed reaction.
sulcus (SUL-kus): A groove or furrow.
summation: Temporal or spatial addition of stimuli.
superficial fascia: *See* **subcutaneous layer**.
superior: Directional reference meaning above.
superior vena cava: The vein that carries blood from the parts of the body above the heart to the right atrium.
supination (su-pi-NĀ-shun): Rotation of the forearm so that the palm faces anteriorly.
supine (soo-PĪN): Lying face up, with palms facing anteriorly.
suppressor T cells: Lymphocytes that inhibit B cell activation and plasmocyte secretion of antibodies.
suprarenal cortex: Superficial portion of adrenal gland that produces steroid hormones; also called the *adrenal cortex.*
suprarenal gland: Small endocrine gland secreting steroids and catecholamines, located superior to each kidney; also called the *adrenal gland.*
suprarenal medulla: Core of the adrenal gland (also called the *adrenal medulla*); a modified sympathetic ganglion that secretes catecholamines into the blood following sympathetic activation.
surfactant (sur-FAK-tant): Lipid secretion that coats alveolar surfaces and prevents their collapse.
sustentacular cells (sus-ten-TAK-ū-lar): Supporting cells of the seminiferous tubules of the testis, responsible for the differentiation of spermatids, the maintenance of the blood–testis barrier, and the secretion of inhibin.
sutural bones: Irregular bones that form in fibrous tissue between the flat bones of the developing cranium; also called **Wormian bones.**
suture: Fibrous joint between flat bones of the skull.
sympathectomy (sim-path-EK-tō-mē): Transection of the sympathetic innervation to a region.
sympathetic division: Division of the autonomic nervous system responsible for "fight or flight" reactions; concerned primarily with the elevation of metabolic rate and increased alertness.
symphysis: A fibrous amphiarthrosis, such as those between adjacent vertebrae or between the pubic bones of the coxae.
symptom: Clinical term for an abnormality of function due to the presence of disease.
synapse (SIN-aps): Site of communication between a nerve cell and some other cell; if the other cell is not a neuron, the term *neuroeffector junction* is often used.
synarthrosis (sin-ar-THRŌ-sis): A joint that does not permit relative movement between the articulating elements.
synchondrosis (sin-kon-DRŌ-sis): A cartilaginous synarthrosis, such as the articulation between the epiphysis and diaphysis of a growing bone.
syncope: A sudden, transient loss of consciousness; a faint.
syncytial trophoblast (sin-SISH-al): Multinucleate cytoplasmic layer that covers the blastocyst; the layer responsible for uterine erosion and implantation.
syncytium: A multinucleate mass of cytoplasm, produced by the fusion of cells or repeated mitoses without cytokinesis.
syndesmosis (sin-dez-MŌ-sis): A fibrous amphiarthrosis.
syndrome: A discrete set of symptoms that occur together.
syneresis (si-NER-ē-sis): Clot retraction.
synergist (SIN-er-jist): A muscle that assists a prime mover in performing its primary action.
synostosis (sin-os-TŌ-sis): A synarthrosis formed through the fusion of the articulating elements.
synovial cavity (sin-Ō-vē-al): Fluid-filled chamber in a diarthrotic joint.
synovial fluid: Substance secreted by synovial membranes that lubricates joints.
synovial membrane: An incomplete layer of fibroblasts confronting the synovial cavity, plus the underlying loose connective tissue.
synthesis (SIN-the-sis): Manufacture; anabolism.
system: An interacting group of organs that performs one or more specific functions.
systemic circuit: Vessels between the aortic semilunar valve and the entrance to the right atrium; the circulatory system other than vessels of the pulmonary circuit.
systole (SIS-tō-lē): The period of cardiac contraction.
systolic pressure: Peak arterial pressure measured during ventricular systole.
tachycardia (tak-ē-KAR-dē-a): An abnormally rapid heart rate.
tactile: Pertaining to the sense of touch.
tactile corpuscles: Touch receptors located within dermal papillae adjacent to the basement membrane of the epidermis; also called *Meissner's corpuscles.*
tactile discs: Sensory nerve endings that contact special receptors called Merkel cells, located within the deeper layers of the epidermis; also called *Merkel's discs.*
taenia coli (TĒ-nē-a KŌ-lī): Three longitudinal bands of smooth muscle in the muscularis externa of the colon.
tarsus: The ankle.
T cells: Lymphocytes responsible for cellular immunity, and for the coordination and regulation of the immune response; include regulatory T cells (helpers and suppressors) and cytotoxic (killer) T cells.

tears: Fluid secretions of the lacrimal glands that bathe the anterior surfaces of the eyes.
tectorial membrane (tek-TŌR-ē-al): Gelatinous membrane suspended over the hair cells of the organ of Corti.
tectospinal tracts: Descending extrapyramidal tracts carrying involuntary motor commands issued by the colliculi.
tectum: The roof of the mesencephalon of the brain.
telencephalon (tel-en-SEF-a-lon): The forebrain or cerebrum, including the cerebral hemispheres, the internal capsule, and the cerebral nuclei.
telophase (TEL-ō-fāz): The final stage of mitosis, characterized by the disappearance of the spindle apparatus, the reappearance of the nuclear membrane and the disappearance of the chromosomes, and the completion of cytokinesis.
temporal: Pertaining to time (temporal summation) or pertaining to the temples (temporal bone).
tendinitis: Painful inflammation of a tendon.
tendon: A collagenous band that connects a skeletal muscle to an element of the skeleton.
tendon organ: Receptor sensitive to tension in a tendon.
tentorium cerebelli (ten-TŌR-ē-um ser-e-BEL-ē): Dural partition that separates the cerebral hemispheres from the cerebellum.
teratogen (TER-a-tō-jen): Stimulus that causes developmental defects.
teres: Long and round.
terminal: Toward the end.
terminal arborizations: Terminal axonal branches that end in terminal boutons; also termed *telodendria.*
terminal bouton: A structure found where one neuron synapses with another. Also termed a *synaptic knob.*
tertiary follicle: A mature ovarian follicle containing a large, fluid-filled chamber.
testes (TES-tēz): The male gonads, sites of gamete production and hormone secretion.
testosterone (tes-TOS-ter-ōn): The principal androgen produced by the interstitial cells of the testes.
tetanic contraction: Sustained skeletal muscle contraction due to repeated stimulation at a frequency that prevents muscle relaxation.
tetanus: A tetanic contraction; also used to refer to a disease state resulting from the stimulation of muscle cells by bacterial toxins.
tetrad (TET-rad): Paired, duplicated chromosomes visible at the start of meiosis I.
tetraiodothyronine (tet-ra-ī-ō-dō-THĪ-rō-nēn): T_4, or thyroxine, a thyroid hormone.
thalamus: The walls of the diencephalon.
thalassemia (thal-ah-SĒ-mē-uh): A hereditary disorder affecting hemoglobin synthesis and producing anemia.
theory: A hypothesis that makes valid predictions, as demonstrated by evidence that is testable, unbiased, and repeatable.
therapy: Treatment of disease.
thermogenesis (ther-mō-JEN-e-sis): Heat production.
thermography: Diagnostic procedure involving the production of an infrared image.
thermoreception: Sensitivity to temperature changes.
thermoregulation: Homeostatic maintenance of body temperature.
thick filament: A myosin filament in a skeletal or cardiac muscle cell.
thin filament: An actin filament in a skeletal or cardiac muscle cell.
thoracoabdominal pump (thō-ra-kō-ab-DOM-i-nal): Changes in the intrapleural pressures during the respiratory cycle that assist the venous return to the heart.
thoracolumbar division (thor-a-kō-LUM-bar): The sympathetic division of the ANS.
thorax: The chest.
threshold: The transmembrane potential at which an action potential begins.
thrombin (THROM-bin): Enzyme that converts fibrinogen to fibrin.
thrombocytes (THROM-bō-sīts): *See* **platelets.**
thrombocytopenia (throm-bō-sī-tō-PĒ-nē-a): Abnormally low platelet count in the circulating blood.
thromboembolism (throm-bō-EM-bō-lizm): Occlusion of a blood vessel by a drifting blood clot.
thromboplastin: Enzyme that converts prothrombin to thrombin; enzyme formed by the intrinsic or extrinsic clotting pathways.
thrombus: A blood clot.
thymic corpuscles: Aggregations of epithelial cells in the thymus whose functions are unknown. Also termed *Hassall's corpuscles.*
thymine: A pyrimidine found in DNA.
thymosin (thī-MŌ-sin): Thymic hormone essential to the development and differentiation of T cells.
thymus: Lymphoid organ, site of T cell formation.
thyroglobulin (thī-rō-GLOB-ū-lin): Circulating transport globulin that binds thyroid hormones.
thyroid gland: Endocrine gland whose lobes sit lateral to the thyroid cartilage of the larynx.
thyroid hormones: Thyroxine (T_4) and triiodothyronine (T_3), hormones of the thyroid gland; hormones that stimulate tissue metabolism, energy utilization, and growth.
thyroid-stimulating hormone (TSH): Anterior pituitary hormone that triggers the secretion of thyroid hormones by the thyroid gland.
thyroxine (TX) (thī-ROKS-ēn): A thyroid hormone (T_4).
tibia (TIB-ē-a): The large, medial bone of the leg.
tidal volume: The volume of air moved in and out of the lungs during a normal quiet respiratory cycle.
tissue: A collection of specialized cells and cell products that perform a specific function.
tonsil: A lymphoid nodule beneath the epithelium of the pharynx; includes the palatine, pharyngeal, and lingual tonsils.
topical: Applied to the body surface.
trabecula (tra-BEK-ū-la): A connective tissue partition that subdivides an organ.
trabeculae carneae (tra-BEK-ū-lē CAR-nē-ē): Muscular ridges projecting from the walls of the ventricles of the heart.
trachea (TRĀ-kē-a): The windpipe, an airway extending from the larynx to the primary bronchi.
tracheal ring: C-shaped supporting cartilage of the trachea.
tracheostomy (trā-kē-OS-tō-mē): Surgical opening of the anterior tracheal wall to permit airflow.
trachoma: An infectious disease of the conjunctiva and cornea.
tract: A bundle of axons inside the CNS.
tractotomy: The surgical transection of a tract, sometimes used to relieve pain.
transcription: The encoding of genetic instructions on a strand of mRNA.
transdermal medication: Administration of medication by absorption through the skin.
transection: To sever or cut in the transverse plane.
transfusion: Transfer of blood from a donor directly into the bloodstream of another person.
transient ischemic attack: A temporary loss of consciousness due to the occlusion of a small blood vessel in the brain.
translation: The process of peptide formation using the instructions carried by an mRNA strand.
transmembrane potential: The potential difference, in millivolts, measured across the cell membrane; a potential difference that results from the uneven distribution of positive and negative ions across a cell membrane.
transudate (TRANS-ū-dāt): Fluid that diffuses across a serous membrane and lubricates opposing surfaces.
treppe (TREP-ē): "Staircase" increase in tension production following repeated stimulation of a muscle, even though the muscle is allowed to complete each relaxation phase.
triad (liver): The combination of branches of the hepatic duct, the hepatic portal vein, and the hepatic artery, found at each corner of a liver lobule.
triad (muscle cell): The combination of a T tubule and two cisternae of the sarcoplasmic reticulum.
tricuspid valve (trī-KUS-pid): The right atrioventricular valve that prevents backflow of blood into the right atrium during ventricular systole.
trigeminal nerve (trī-JEM-i-nal): Cranial nerve V, responsible for providing sensory information from the lower portions of the face, including the upper and lower jaws, and delivering motor commands to the muscles of mastication.
triglyceride (trī-GLIS-e-rīd): A lipid composed of a molecule of glycerol attached to three fatty acids.
trigone (TRĪ-gōn): Triangular region of the bladder bounded by the exits of the ureters and the entrance to the urethra.
triiodothyronine: T_3, one of the thyroid hormones.
trisomy: The abnormal possession of three copies of a chromosome; trisomy 21 is responsible for Down syndrome.
trochanters (trō-KAN-terz): Large processes near the head of the femur.
trochlea (TRŌK-lē-a): A pulley.
trochlear nerve (TRŌK-lē-ar): Cranial nerve IV, controlling the superior oblique muscle of the eye.
trophoblast (TRŌ-fō-blast): Superficial layer of the blastocyst that will be involved with implantation, hormone production, and placenta formation.
troponin/tropomyosin (TRŌ-pō-nin) (trō-pō-MĪ-ō-sin): Proteins on the thin filaments that mask the active sites in the absence of free calcium ions.
trunk: The thoracic and abdominopelvic regions.
trypsin (TRIP-sin): One of the pancreatic proteases.
trypsinogen: The inactive proenzyme secreted by the pancreas and converted to trypsin in the duodenum.
T tubules: Transverse, tubular extensions of the sarcolemma that extend deep into the sarcoplasm to contact cisternae of the sarcoplasmic reticulum.
tuberculum (too-BER-kū-lum): A small, localized elevation on a bony surface.
tuberosity: A large, roughened elevation on a bony surface.
tubulin: Protein subunit of microtubules.
tumor: A tissue mass formed by the abnormal growth and replication of cells.
tunica (TŪ-ni-ka): A layer or covering; in blood vessels: t. externa, the outermost layer of connective tissue fibers that stabilizes the position of the vessel; t. intima, the innermost layer, consisting of the endothelium plus an underlying elastic membrane; t. media, a middle layer containing collagen, elastin, and smooth muscle fibers in varying proportions.
turbinates: *See* **concha/conchae.**
T wave: Deflection of the ECG corresponding to ventricular repolarization.
twitch: A single contraction/relaxation cycle in a skeletal muscle.
tympanic membrane (tim-PAN-ik): Membrane that separates the external acoustic meatus from the middle ear; membrane whose vibrations are transferred to the auditory ossicles and ultimately to the oval window; the "eardrum."
ulcer: An area of epithelial sloughing associated with damage to the underlying connective tissues and vasculature.
ultrasound: Diagnostic visualization procedure that uses high-frequency sound waves.
umbilical cord (um-BIL-i-kal): Connecting stalk between the fetus and the placenta; contains the allantois, the umbilical arteries, and the umbilical vein.
umbilicus: The navel.
unicellular gland: Goblet cell; mucous cell.

unipennate muscle: A muscle whose fibers are all arranged on one side of the tendon.
unipolar neuron: A sensory neuron whose soma lies in a dorsal root ganglion or a sensory ganglion of a cranial nerve.
unmyelinated axon: Axon whose neurilemma does not contain myelin, and where continuous conduction occurs.
urachus (Ū-ra-kus): The middle umbilical ligament.
uracil: One of the pyrimidines characteristic of RNA.
uremia (ū-RĒ-mē-a): Abnormal condition caused by impaired kidney function, characterized by the retention of wastes and the disruption of many other organ systems.
ureters (ū-RĒ-terz): Muscular tubes, lined by transitional epithelium, that carry urine from the renal pelvis to the urinary bladder.
urethra (ū-RĒTH-ra): A muscular tube that carries urine from the urinary bladder to the exterior.
urethritis: Inflammation of the urethra.
urinalysis: Analysis of the physical and chemical characteristics of urine.
urinary bladder: Muscular, distensible sac that stores urine prior to micturition.
urination: The voiding of urine; micturition.
uterine (menstrual) cycle: Cyclical changes in the uterine lining that occur in reproductive-age women. Each uterine cycle, which occurs in response to circulating hormones (*see* **ovarian cycle**), lasts 21–35 days.
uterus (Ū-ter-us): Muscular organ of the female reproductive tract where implantation, placenta formation, and fetal development occur.
utricle (Ū-tre-kl): The largest chamber of the vestibular apparatus; contains a macula important for static equilibrium.
uvea: The vascular tunic of the eye.
uvula (Ū-vū-la): A dangling, fleshy extension of the soft palate.
vagina (va-JĪ-na): A muscular tube extending between the uterus and the vestibule.
vagus nerve: N X, the cranial nerve responsible for most (75 percent) of the parasympathetic preganglionic output from the CNS.
varicose veins (VAR-i-kōs): Distended superficial veins.
vasa vasorum: Blood vessels that supply the walls of large arteries and veins.
vascular: Pertaining to blood vessels.
vascularity: The blood vessels in a tissue.
vascular spasm: Contraction of the wall of a blood vessel at an injury site, a process that may slow the rate of blood loss.
vasoconstriction: A reduction in the diameter of arterioles due to contraction of smooth muscles in the media of a blood vessel; an event that elevates peripheral resistance, and that may occur in response to local factors, through the action of hormones, or from stimulation of the vasomotor center.
vasodilation (vaz-ō-dī-LĀ-shun): An increase in the diameter of arterioles due to the relaxation of smooth muscles in the media of a blood vessel; an event that reduces peripheral resistance, and that may occur in response to local factors, through the action of hormones, or following decreased stimulation of the vasomotor center.
vasomotion: Alterations in the pattern of blood flow through a capillary bed in response to changes in the local environment.
vasomotor center: Medullary center whose stimulation produces vasoconstriction and an elevation in peripheral resistance.
vein: Blood vessel carrying blood from a capillary bed toward the heart.
venae cavae (VĒ-nē CĀ-vē): The major veins delivering systemic blood to the right atrium.
ventilation: Air movement in and out of the lungs.
ventilatory rate: The respiratory rate.
ventral: Pertaining to the anterior surface.
ventricle (VEN-tri-kl): One of the large, muscular pumping chambers of the heart that discharges blood into the pulmonary or systemic circuits.
venules (VEN-ūlz): Thin-walled veins that receive blood from capillaries.
vermis (VER-mis): Midsagittal band of neural cortex on the surface of the cerebellum.
vertebral canal: Passageway that encloses the spinal cord, a tunnel bounded by the neural arches of adjacent vertebrae.
vertebral column: The cervical, thoracic, and lumbar vertebrae, the sacrum, and the coccyx.
vertebrochondral ribs: Ribs 8–10, false ribs connected to the sternum by shared cartilaginous bars.
vertebrosternal ribs: Ribs 1–7, true ribs connected to the sternum by individual cartilaginous bars.
vertigo: Dizziness.
vesicle: A membranous sac in the cytoplasm of a cell.
vesicular synapse: The most abundant neuronal synapse. Also termed a *chemical synapse.*
vestibular folds: Mucosal folds in the laryngeal walls that do not play a role in sound production; the false vocal cords.
vestibular membrane: The membrane that separates the scala media from the scala vestibuli of the inner ear.
vestibular nucleus: Processing center for sensations arriving from the vestibular apparatus; located near the border between the pons and medulla oblongata.
vestibule (VES-ti-bul): A chamber; in the inner ear, the term refers to the utricle, saccule, and semicircular ducts; also refers to (1) a region of the female external genitalia, (2) the space within the fleshy portion of the nose between the nostrils and the external nares, and (3) the space between the ventricular folds and the vocal folds of the larynx.
vestibulospinal tracts: Descending tracts of the extrapyramidal system, carrying involuntary motor commands issued by the vestibular nucleus to stabilize the position of the head.
villus: A slender projection of the mucous membrane of the small intestine.
virus: A pathogenic microorganism.
viscera: Organs in the ventral body cavity.
visceral: Pertaining to viscera or their outer coverings.
visceral smooth muscle tissue: Smooth muscle tissue forming sheets or layers in the walls of visceral organs; the cells may not be innervated, and the layers often show automaticity (rhythmic contractions).
viscosity: The resistance to flow exhibited by a fluid, due to molecular interactions within the fluid.
viscous: Thick, syrupy.
vital capacity: The maximum amount of air that can be moved in or out of the respiratory system; the sum of the inspiratory reserve, the expiratory reserve, and the tidal volume.
vitamin: An essential organic nutrient that functions as a coenzyme in vital enzymatic reactions.
vitreous humor: Gelatinous mass in the vitreous chamber of the eye.
vocal folds: Folds in the laryngeal wall containing elastic ligaments whose tension can be voluntarily adjusted; the true vocal cords, responsible for phonation.
voluntary: Controlled by conscious thought processes.
vulva (VUL-va): The female pudendum (external genitalia).
Wallerian degeneration: Disintegration of an axon and its myelin sheath distal to an injury site.
white blood cells: Leukocytes; the granulocytes and agranulocytes of the blood.
white matter: Regions inside the CNS that are dominated by myelinated axons.
white ramus: A nerve bundle containing the myelinated preganglionic axons of sympathetic motor neurons en route to the sympathetic chain or a collateral ganglion.
Wormian bones: *See* **sutural bones**.
xiphoid process (ZĪ-foyd): Slender, inferior extension of the sternum.
Y chromosome: The sex chromosome whose presence indicates that the individual is a genetic male.
yolk sac: One of the three extraembryonic membranes, composed of an inner layer of endoderm and an outer layer of mesoderm.
Zeis, glands of (zīs): Enlarged sebaceous glands on the free edges of the eyelids.
zona fasciculata (ZŌ-na fa-sik-ū-LA-ta): Region of the adrenal cortex responsible for glucocorticoid secretion.
zona glomerulosa (glō-mer-ū-LŌ-sa): Region of the adrenal cortex responsible for mineralocorticoid secretion.
zona pellucida (pel-LOO-si-da): Region between a developing oocyte and the surrounding follicular cells of the ovary.
zona reticularis (re-tik-ū-LAR-is): Region of the adrenal cortex responsible for androgen secretion.
zygote (ZĪ-gōt): The fertilized ovum prior to the start of cleavage.

Photo Credits

Visible Human Data courtesy of the Library of Medicine and the Visible Human Project.

Chapter 1
1.7 The New Yorker Collection 1990 Ed Fisher from cartoonbank.com. All Rights Reserved
1.9 Custom Medical Stock Photo, Inc.
1.13d Ralph T. Hutchings
1.15aL Omikron/Photo Researchers, Inc.
1.15aR AGFA/Photo Researchers, Inc.
1.15bL Photo Researchers, Inc.
1.15bR Custom Medical Stock Photo, Inc.
1.16b Frederic H. Martini, Inc.
1.16c CNSI/Photo Researchers, Inc.
1.16d Frederic H. Martini, Inc.
1.17a Philips Medical Systems
1.17b Alexander Tsiaras/Photo Researchers, Inc.

Chapter 2
2.1a Todd Derksen
2.1b David M. Phillips/Visuals Unlimited
2.1c Todd Derksen
2.7a M. Sahliwa/Visuals Unlimited
2.9b Fawcett, Hirikawa, Heuser/Photo Researchers, Inc.
2.9c M. Sahliwa/Visuals Unlimited
2.10a Fawcett, de Harven, Kalnins/Photo Researchers, Inc.
2.11a Frederic H. Martini, Inc.
2.12 CNRI/Photo Researchers, Inc.
2.13a Don W. Fawcett, M.D., Harvard Medical School
2.13b Biophoto Associates/Photo Researchers, Inc.
2.15R Bollender & Don W. Fawcett/Visuals Unlimited
2.16 Biophoto Associates/Photo Researchers, Inc.
2.17b Dr. Birgit H. Satir
2.22a,b Ed Reschke/Peter Arnold, Inc.
2.22c James Solliday/Biological Photo Service
2.22d,e,f Ed Reschke/Peter Arnold, Inc.
2.22g Centers for Disease Control and Prevention (CDC)

Chapter 3
3.2b P. Motta/Custom Medical Stock Photo
3.3c C. P. Leblond and A. Rambourg, McGill University
3.4a Ward's Natural Science Establishment, Inc.
3.4b Frederic H. Martini, Inc.
3.5a Pearson Benjamin Cummings
3.5b Gregory N. Fuller, M. D. Anderson Cancer Center, Houston, TX
3.6a Frederic H. Martini, Inc.
3.6b Gregory N. Fuller, M. D. Anderson Cancer Center, Houston, TX
3.7a,b Frederic H. Martini, Inc.
3.8a S. Elem/Visuals Unlimited
3.8b Frederic H. Martini, Inc.
3.10 Carolina Biological Supply Company/Phototake
3.12b Ward's Natural Science Establishment, Inc.
3.13a,b Project Masters, Inc./The Bergman Collection
3.14a Biophoto Associates/Photo Researchers, Inc.
3.14b Frederic H. Martini, Inc.
3.14c Ward's Natural Science Establishment, Inc.
3.15a John D. Cunningham/Visuals Unlimited
3.15b Bruce Iverson/Visuals Unlimited
3.15c Frederic H. Martini, Inc.
3.17a Frederic H. Martini, Inc.
3.18a Robert Brons/Biological Photo Service
3.18b Photo Researchers, Inc.
3.18c Ed Reschke/Peter Arnold, Inc.
3.19 Frederic H. Martini, Inc.
3.22a G. W. Willis, MD/Visuals Unlimited
3.22b Phototake NYC
3.22c Pearson Benjamin Cummings
3.23b Pearson Benjamin Cummings

Chapter 4
4.3 John D. Cunningham/Visuals Unlimited
4.4b,c Frederic H. Martini, Inc.
4.5 R. G. Kessel and R. H. Kardon/Visuals Unlimited
4.6 Pearson Benjamin Cummings
4.7a R. G. Kessel and R. H. Kardon/Visuals Unlimited
4.7b David Scharf Photography
4.7c P. Motta/SPL/Photo Researchers, Inc.
4.9b Manfred Kage/Peter Arnold, Inc.
4.10b John D. Cunningham/Visuals Unlimited
4.13; 4.14a,b Frederic H. Martini, Inc.
4.16 PhotoDisc/Getty Images
4.U01 Joe McNally/Getty Images
4.17 Custom Medical Stock Photo

Chapter 5
5.1b R. G. Kessel and R. H. Kardon/Visuals Unlimited
5.1c,d Pearson Benjamin Cummings
5.2d; 5.3a,b,c Ralph T. Hutchings
5.4c; 5.5 Frederic H. Martini, Inc.
5.6a,b Ralph T. Hutchings
5.7b Pearson Benjamin Cummings
5.8a,b Project Masters, Inc./The Bergman Collection
5.12a,b P. Motta/SPL/Photo Researchers, Inc.
5.U01; 5.U02 Southern Illinois University/Visuals Unlimited
5.U03 Frederic H. Martini, Inc.
5.U04 Southern Illinois University/Peter Arnold, Inc.
5.U05 Custom Medical Stock Photo, Inc.
5.U06 Scott Camazine/Photo Researchers, Inc.
5.U07 Frederic H. Martini, Inc.
5.U08 Southern Illinois University/Visuals Unlimited
5.U09 Project Master, Inc./The Bergman Collection

Chapter 6
6.1b; 6.3a,b,c,d,e; 6.4; 6.5; 6.6a,b,c; 6.7a,b,c; 6.8a,c,d Ralph T. Hutchings
6.8b Michael J. Timmons
6.9a; 6.10a,c; 6.11b; 6.12a; 6.13b,c; 6.14a,b; 6.15; 6.16a,c; 6.17b Ralph T. Hutchings
6.18c Michael J. Timmons
6.18d; 6.19b Ralph T. Hutchings
6.19c Siemens Medical Systems, Inc.
6.20a Science Photo Library/Custom Medical Stock Photos, Inc.
6.20b National Medical Slide/Custom Medical Stock Photos, Inc.
6.20c Princess Margaret Rose Orthopaedic Hospital, Edinburgh, Scotland/Science Photo Library/Photo Researchers, Inc.
6.22a,b,c,d; 6.23a,b,c,d,e; 6.24a,b,c,d; 6.25a,b; 6.26a,b,c; 6.27a,b,c,d Ralph T. Hutchings

Chapter 7
7.1a,b; 7.2a Ralph T. Hutchings
7.2b Bates/Custom Medical Stock Photo, Inc.
7.3a,b; 7.4a; 7.5d,e,f; 7.6a,b,c,d; 7.7a,b,c,d,e,f; 7.8.a,b,c; 7.9a Ralph T. Hutchings
7.9b Custom Medical Stock Photo, Inc.
7.10a,b; 7.11a,b; 7.14a,b,c,d,e,f; 7.15a,b; 7.16a,b,c,d; 7.17b; 7.18a,b Ralph T. Hutchings

Chapter 8
8.3aB,bB,cL,cR,d; 8.4M; 8.5a,b,c,d,e,fL,fR; 8.9; 8.10; 8.11d; 8.12b,e Ralph T. Hutchings
8.14d Patrick M. Timmons
8.16c Ralph T. Hutchings
8.17d Frederic H. Martini, Inc.
8.18b,c Ralph T. Hutchings
8.19 SIU Biomed Comm/Custom Medical Stock Photo, Inc.
8.20a Ralph T. Hutchings
8.20b Eugene C. Wasson, III and staff of Maui Radiology Consultants, Maui Memorial Hospital
8.21b,e Ralph T. Hutchings
8.22a,b Marko Krpan
8.U03 AP Photos

Chapter 9
9.2a Fred Hossler/Visuals Unlimited
9.2b Don W. Fawcett/Photo Researchers, Inc.
9.3b Ward's Natural Science Establishment, Inc.
9.4b Don W. Fawcett/Photo Researchers, Inc.
9.7 J.J. Head/Carolina Biological Supply Company/Phototake NYC
9.13a Comack, D. (ed): HAM'S HISTOLOGY, 9th ed. Philadelphia: J. B. Lippincott, 1987. By Permission.
9.13bT,bB Frederic H. Martini, Inc.

Chapter 10
10.4 Ralph T. Hutchings
10.11a Mentor Networks Inc.
10.11b Ralph T. Hutchings
10.13c Mentor Networks Inc.
10.13d; 10.14c Ralph T. Hutchings

Chapter 11
11.8d Ralph T. Hutchings
11.9a Mentor Networks Inc.
11.9d; 11.11f,g; 11.13b,c Ralph T. Hutchings
11.15a Custom Medical Stock Photo, Inc.
11.15c,d; 11.17c Ralph T. Hutchings
11.17d Mentor Networks Inc.
11.18b; 11.19c; 11.20c; 11.21aR Ralph T. Hutchings
11.25a Image Source Limited/Phototake
11.25b Zimmer, Inc.

Chapter 12
12.1a Mentor Networks Inc.
12.6a Custom Medical Stock Photo, Inc.
12.6c; 12.7a Mentor Networks Inc.
12.8; 12.9; 12.10; 12.11; 12.12; 12.13; 12.14 National Library of Medicine, Visual Human Project

Chapter 13
13.6a Frederic H. Martini, Inc.
13.6b R. G. Kessel and R. H. Kardon/Visuals Unlimited
13.7 John D. Cunningham/Visuals Unlimited
13.8a Biophoto Associates/Photo Researchers, Inc.
13.8b Photo Researchers, Inc.
13.9a Pearson Benjamin Cummings
13.13a David Scott/Phototake NYC

Chapter 14
14.1b,c; 14.2a Ralph T. Hutchings
14.3 Patrick M. Timmons

14.4a Ralph T. Hutchings
14.4b Hinerfeld/Custom Medical Stock Photo, Inc.
14.5a Michael J. Timmons
14.6b R. G. Kessel and R. H. Kardon/Visuals Unlimited
14.11b,c Mentor Networks Inc.
14.12 Ralph T. Hutchings
14.14a,b Ralph T. Hutchings

Chapter 15
15.2b; 15.3c; 15.4a Ralph T. Hutchings
15.7 SIU/Visuals Unlimited
15.8a,b,c; 15.9a Ralph T. Hutchings
15.11c Pat Lynch/Photo Researchers, Inc.
15.11e Michael J. Timmons
15.14a; 15.15a,b; 15.16b,d Ralph T. Hutchings
15.17a Daniel P. Perl, Mount Sinai School of Medicine
15.17b; 15.19a,b Ralph T. Hutchings
15.19bT Ward's Natural Science Establishment, Inc.
15.21a,c Ralph T. Hutchings

Chapter 17
17.5b Ward's Natural Science Establishment, Inc.

Chapter 18
18.3d,f; 18.5 Frederic H. Martini, Inc.
18.7cT Pearson Benjamin Cummings
18.7cB G. W. Willis/Visuals Unlimited
18.10c Ralph T. Hutchings
18.10d; 18.15b Lennart Nilsson/Albert Bonniers Forlag AB
18.17c Michael J. Timmons
18.17e Ward's Natural Science Establishment, Inc.
18.17f P. Motta/SPL/Photo Researchers, Inc.
18.19a; 18.20 Ralph T. Hutchings
18.21d Michael J. Timmons
18.21f Ralph T. Hutchings
18.23a Ed Reschke/Peter Arnold, Inc.
18.23c Custom Medical Stock Photo, Inc.
18.25; 18.26a Ralph T. Hutchings
18.27a,b ISM/Phototake
18.U01 Geoff Thompkins/Science Photo Library/Photo Researchers Inc.

Chapter 19
19.3b Manfred Kage/Peter Arnold, Inc.
19.6b,c; 19.8b,c Frederic H. Martini, Inc.
19.9c; 19.10b Ward's Natural Science Establishment, Inc.
19.10c,d Michael S. Ballo, Duke University Medical Center
19.11a,b Project Masters, Inc./The Bergman Collection
19.11c John Paul Kay/Peter Arnold, Inc.
19.11d Custom Medical Stock Photo, Inc.
19.11e Biophoto Associates/Photo Researchers, Inc.
19.12 Neil Borden/Photo Researchers, Inc.

Chapter 20
20.1a Martin M. Rotker
20.2a David Scharf/Peter Arnold, Inc.
20.2b Dennis Kunkel/CNRI/Phototake NYC
20.2d; 20.5a,b,c,d,e Ed Reschke/Peter Arnold, Inc.
20.6 Frederic H. Martini, Inc.
20.7 Custom Medical Stock Photo, Inc.

Chapter 21
21.2d Ralph T. Hutchings
21.3c Ed Reschke/Peter Arnold, Inc.
21.5a,b Ralph T. Hutchings
21.6b Lennart Nilsson/Albert Bonniers Forlag AB
21.6c,d Ralph T. Hutchings
21.7cL Science Photo Library/Photo Researchers, Inc.
21.7cR Biophoto Associates/Photo Researchers, Inc.
21.8c Ralph T. Hutchings
21.8d Frederic H. Martini, Inc.
21.9a,b Howard Sochurek/Medichrome/The Stock Shop, Inc.
21.9c Peter Arnold, Inc.
21.9d ISM/Phototake
21.12 Jim Wehtje/Getty Images, Inc.-Photodisc
21.13a Science Photo Library/Photo Researchers, Inc.
21.13b Darryl Torckler/Getty Images Inc./Stone Allstock
21.13c,d Philips Medical Systems
21.14 Larry Mulvehill/Photo Researchers, Inc.

Chapter 22
22.1 Biophoto Associates/Photo Researchers, Inc.
22.3T William Ober/Visuals Unlimited
22.3B B & B Photos/Custom Medical Stock Photo, Inc.
22.4c,d BAILEY'S TEXTBOOK OF MICROSCOPIC ANATOMY by Kelly, Wood, & Enders. Copyright 1984, Williams & Wilkins.
22.5b Biophoto Associates/Photo Researchers, Inc.
22.11 E. L. Lansdown/University of Toronto
22.12b,c; 22.14; 22.15b,c Ralph T. Hutchings
22.17b Frederic H. Martini, Inc.
22.18b Ralph T. Hutchings
22.29 Custom Medical Stock Photo

Chapter 23
23.3b Frederic H. Martini, Inc.
23.5 Ralph T. Hutchings
23.8a David M. Phillips/Visuals Unlimited
23.8b Biophoto Associates/Photo Researchers, Inc.
23.9 Ralph T. Hutchings
23.13 Frederic H. Martini, Inc.
23.14a Ralph T. Hutchings
23.16c,d; 23.17c Frederic H. Martini, Inc.

Chapter 24
24.2a Frederic H. Martini, Inc.
24.2c Photo Researchers, Inc.
24.3b,c Ralph T. Hutchings
24.5c Phototake NYC
24.7b John D. Cunningham/Visuals Unlimited
24.8a; 24.10b,c,d Ralph T. Hutchings
24.11c Ward's Natural Science Establishment, Inc.
24.12b Don W. Fawcett. Micrograph by P. Gehr
24.13 Ralph T. Hutchings
24.16 James Cavallini/Photo Researchers

Chapter 25
25.2 G. W. Willis/Visuals Unlimited
25.6.bT,bM,bB Frederic H. Martini, Inc.
25.7e Ralph T. Hutchings
25.9a Alfred Pasieka/Peter Arnold, Inc.
25.9b Astrid and Hanns-Frieder Michler/SPL/Photo Researchers, Inc.
25.10b NetAnatomy.com
25.10c ISM/PhototakeUSA
25.11b Ralph T. Hutchings
25.13a P. Motta/SPL/Photo Researchers, Inc.
25.13b John D. Cunningham/Visuals Unlimited
25.13e,f Frederic H. Martini, Inc.
25.15d John D. Cunningham/Visuals Unlimited
25.15eL Michael J. Timmons
25.15eR G. W. Willis/Visuals Unlimited
25.16; 25.17b Ralph T. Hutchings
25.18 Custom Medical Stock Photo, Inc.
25.19b Ward's Natural Science Establishment, Inc.
25.20b,e Ralph T. Hutchings
25.21b Ward's Natural Science Establishment, Inc.
25.21c Michael J. Timmons
25.22c; 25.23 Frederic H. Martini, Inc.
25.24 David Musher/Photo Researcher
25.U01 Bob Tallitsch

Chapter 26
26.1d; 26.2; 26.3a Ralph T. Hutchings
26.3c Mentor Networks Inc.
26.5a,b Ralph T. Hutchings
26.7b,c,d Pearson Benjamin Cummings
26.8b R. G. Kessel and R. H. Kardon/Visuals Unlimited
26.8e David M. Phillips/Visuals Unlimited
26.9a Photo Researchers, Inc.
26.9b E. L. Lansdown
26.9c Photo Researchers, Inc.
26.10d Ralph T. Hutchings
26.11a Ward's Natural Science Establishment, Inc.
26.11b,c Frederic H. Martini, Inc.
26.12 Courtesy of Samih Nasr, M.D., Columbia University Medical Center, New York
26.U01 Bob Tallitsch

Chapter 27
27.1 Ralph T. Hutchings
27.4b Frederic H. Martini, Inc.
27.5a Don W. Fawcett, Harvard Medical School
27.5c Ward's Natural Science Establishment, Inc.
27.6b David M. Phillips/Visuals Unlimited
27.7a Ralph T. Hutchings
27.7b,c Frederic H. Martini, Inc.
27.8bT Ward's Natural Science Establishment, Inc.
27.8bM R. G. Kessel and R. H. Kardon/Visuals Unlimited
27.8c,d,e Frederic H. Martini, Inc.
27.9b Ward's Natural Science Establishment, Inc.
27.9d; 27.10; 27.11c Ralph T. Hutchings
27.12a,b,c,d Frederic H. Martini, Inc.
27.12e C. Edelmann/La Villete/Photo Researchers, Inc.
27.12f,g G. W. Willis/Visuals Unlimited
27.14b Frederic H. Martini, Inc.
27.14c Custom Medical Stock Photo, Inc.
27.15b CNRI/SPL/Photo Researchers, Inc.
27.16 Ward's Natural Science Establishment, Inc.
27.17a,b Frederic H. Martini, Inc.
27.17c Michael J. Timmons
27.17d Frederic H. Martini, Inc.
27.19 Michael J. Timmons
27.21b Ralph T. Hutchings
27.21c Fred E. Hossler/Visuals Unlimited
27.21d Frederic H. Martini, Inc.

Chapter 28
28.1a Francis Leroy/Photo Researchers, Inc.
28.6b Frederic H. Martini, Inc.
28.7a Arnold Tamarin
28.7b,c,d; 28.8a Lennart Nilsson/Albert Bonniers Forlag AB
28.8b Photo Researchers, Inc.

Index

INDEX

INDEX

INDEX

INDEX

INDEX

G

INDEX

INDEX

INDEX

P

INDEX

INDEX

T

U

V

INDEX

W

X

Y

Z

stin, my grandson—keep those electrons flowing.

ry of Congress Cataloging-in-Publication Data

Ronald A.
lectronic project design and fabrication / Ronald A. Reis.— 5th ed.
p. cm.
SBN 0–13–019565–0
. Electronic apparatus and appliances—Design and construction. 2. Prototypes,
gineering. 3. Science projects—Design and construction. I. Title.
7870.R425 2002
.381′078—dc21

2001018523

President and Editor in Chief: Stephen Helba
tant Vice President and Publisher: Charles E. Stewart, Jr.
tant Editor: Delia Uherec
uction Editor: Alexandrina Benedicto Wolf
uction Coordinator: Karen Fortgang, *bookworks*
gn Coordinator: Robin G. Chukes
r Designer: Rod Harris
r Image: Stone Images
luction Manager: Matthew Ottenweller

book was set in Century Schoolbook by The Clarinda Company. It was printed and bound by Courier /
dallville, Inc. The cover was printed by The Lehigh Press, Inc.

10 9 8 7 6 5 4 3 2 1

ISBN: 0-13-019565-0

Prentice Hall

Electronic Project Design and Fabrication

Fifth Edition

RONALD A. REIS
Los Angeles Valley College

Prentice Hall

Upper Saddle River, New Jersey
Columbus, Ohio

Preface

Electronic Project Design and Fabrication, Fifth Edition, offers a complete experience in the design and fabrication of electronic prototype projects. Whether you are enrolled in a traditional lecture and laboratory class or a fabrication course devoted entirely to the subject, this book provides the hands-on experience in project building and documentation every prospective electronics technician requires.

A project, however, is not all you will be developing as you progress through the text. You will also be building confidence in your ability to construct electronic devices. The know-how to take a project from an initial concept through to final construction with support documentation is sure to give you pride and self-assurance as you enter the electronics industry. *Electronic Project Design and Fabrication* will prepare you for that exciting moment.

Think of yourself as a technician on the job. Your supervisor presents you with a project idea designed to fill a need or to solve a problem. You must determine if the idea is feasible and, if so, build a working prototype project and develop an accompanying Project Report.

The project should resemble the final, mass-produced product. You must design the cicuit, breadboard it, design and fabricate a printed circuit board, and then enclose the project in a functional and attractive case. The Project Report is to include appropriate written and graphic documentation. It delineates various troubleshooting and test procedures, summarizes project developments, and contains the 10-drawing set used to construct the prototype project.

In project construction, you have a choice of three approaches. In the first approach, you choose to build the Sample Project—the Variable Power Supply. This project progresses from chapter to chapter, starting with the two-step design process and ending with a completely packaged and tested prototype project, along with necessary documentation.

The Exercise Project, the 3-Channel Color Organ, is at a slightly higher level of difficulty. Because less help is provided in building this project, you'll have to do a bit of digging and developing on your own. The Exercise Project also is carried from chapter to chapter.

Finally, 30 Elective Projects are presented in Part III. Only Concepts and Requirements Documents and circuit design sketches are provided. Here you will need to develop specific project design and fabrication details on your own.

Although the project construction and documentation motivate you to progress from one chapter to the next, *Electronic Project Design and Fabrication* is more than a project book. The fundamentals of prototype project design, fabrication, and documentation are a part of every chapter. Even if you elect not to construct a project (a most unlikely occurrence), you will gain a firmer understanding of electronic device fabrication after studying the book.

The fifth edition of *Electronic Project Design and Fabrication* represents an up-to-date revision of a well-received text. New material has been added, including the following:

- ☐ "Something to Think About" minisections have been added at the end of every section. Students will find these suggestions for further inquiry inspiring.

- ☐ Chapter summaries have been updated to better lead into the material to come.
- ☐ Searching for electronic component sources has become easier, via the Internet. In Chapter 3 we explain how best to do this.
- ☐ In Chapter 7, a section has been added on PC board trace-width spacing.
- ☐ Electronics Workbench material in Chapter 3 has been revised to include a discussion of MultiSim V6.2.
- ☐ Material on computer-aided design (CAD), in Chapter 11, has been revised.
- ☐ Five new elective projects have been added in Chapter 17.
- ☐ Two new appendices have been added: Appendix J lists electronic kit sources, and Appendix K lists electronic project design and fabrication web sites to visit. In addition, Appendix G has been revised to include additional published sources for technical writers.
- ☐ New terms have been added to the glossary.

I hope you will find the fifth edition of *Electronic Project Design and Fabrication* a great tool as you design and create new electronic products.

ACKNOWLEDGMENTS

Many people at Prentice Hall have provided me with invaluable assistance in the preparation of this new edition. In particular, I want to thank Charles Stewart, Assistant Vice President and Publisher, who has given me technical assistance, patient encouragement, and most importantly, enthusiastic encouragement.

I would like to thank the following reviewers for their valuable feedback: Mark Highum, Bay de Noc Community College, MI; Jon Speer, Northwest State Community College, OH; and David Ward, Southern Utah University, UT.

Ronald A. Reis
Los Angeles Valley College

Contents

Appendices

PART I

Project Design and Fabrication

1 An Overview—Making It in Electronics

OBJECTIVES

In this chapter you will learn

- ☐ How an electronics design and fabrication experience can enhance skill level in a traditional "lecture and laboratory" classroom.
- ☐ Just what it is that electronics technicians do.
- ☐ About a new career path for technicians with fabrication experience.
- ☐ What the five-stage design and fabrication process is all about.
- ☐ How the three-tier project approach provides maximum flexibility for project design and fabrication.
- ☐ How the drawings and written documentation come together in the Project Report.
- ☐ What drafting tools are required for making the 10-drawing set contained in the Project Report.
- ☐ How CAD is replacing traditional drafting equipment.
- ☐ What tools are necessary for the mechanical and electrical fabrication of the prototype projects.

"You built that? I didn't know you could do such things, that you were so into electronics. How smart and clever!" Has anyone ever said something like that to you? And have you ever experienced the glow, the sense of pride, accomplishment, and satisfaction that comes when others compliment you on something you have built? Actually, you don't need to hear praise from someone else—although that's always nice. As you lean back from your workbench, surveying your new project, an inner voice tells you: "I did it; I made it myself"—and that sense of accomplishment feels great.

If you haven't quite reached that nirvana yet, don't despair—you will be there soon enough. Why? Because that's what electronics design and fabrication is all about: building—taking a project from the concept and design stage all the way to a finished, working prototype. And, in addition to getting the practical exposure actually needed to work as an electronics technician, the electronics design and fabrication experience will give you that all-important sense of accomplishment. After all, the completed project is the culmination of all you have been doing and learning. For the prospective technician, theory and laboratory exercises are a means to an end. And that end is the fabricated project: the device you will learn to develop and build.

In this chapter we first look at the traditional electronics course and see how the electronics design and fabrication experience can be made a part of it. We then explore this process, from the design and drawing stages on through experimenting, prototyping, testing, troubleshooting, and documenting the working project. Finally, we examine the "tools of the trade," on the board, at the computer, and on the bench. We will see what tools and equipment you will need to "make it" in electronics.

1.1 ELECTRONICS DESIGN AND FABRICATION IN THE SCHOOL LABORATORY

This section examines the traditional electronics course with its "lecture and lab" approach to learning. You will then see how your knowledge can be expanded by supplementing such a method with an electronics design and fabrication experience.

The Traditional Electronics Course

Let's review what is done in the standard lecture and lab class and, where it exists, the separate electronics design and fabrication course.

Lecture and Lab Class

Most electronics courses taught at the college or technical school level are organized around the lecture and lab structure. During the lecture portion, students listen to the professor speak, take notes, enter into discussions, and read the textbook. This aspect of the course is known as the "theory" part.

Lectures on the subject matter are supplemented by laboratory experience. In addition to familiarizing the student with the type of equipment he or she will use in industry, the lab experience is designed to verify, or "prove out," the theoretical concepts discussed in the classroom. For example, you learn in the lecture that the output frequency of a 555 IC oscillator is determined by its R/C (resistance/capacitance) time constant. To "prove" it, you go to the lab, run a simulation, using a simulation software program, and construct, that is, breadboard, the actual circuit (Figure 1–1). Building such circuits, as every student knows, is an extremely important part of any electronics learning experience.

Yet this experimenting in the lab is often the only hands-on experience the electronics student is likely to get. In the traditional course, students do not ordinarily build permanent, working *prototype projects,* that is, projects that are hand-assembled to resemble as much as possible the final, mass-produced equipment (Figure 1–2). Nonetheless, building such projects is an experience every electronics student should have.

Separate Electronics Design and Fabrication Course

In a separate electronics design and fabrication course, students often build a complete project, taking it from the design stage to a finished prototype. Such a course usually involves printed circuit board design and manufacture, chassis and enclosure construction, project packaging, and the necessary documentation. It is likely to be a popular course, for all of the obvious reasons. Students are building the types of electronic devices they will assemble on the job. They are doing what technicians do.

We believe that students who are unable to take a separate electronics design and fabrication course should be building prototype projects in their lecture and lab classes. This book is written for use in *both* types of courses. Before we examine how it can be used in such courses, let's see why electronics fabrication is such an important part of what students should be doing.

FIGURE 1–1
Experimenting in the laboratory

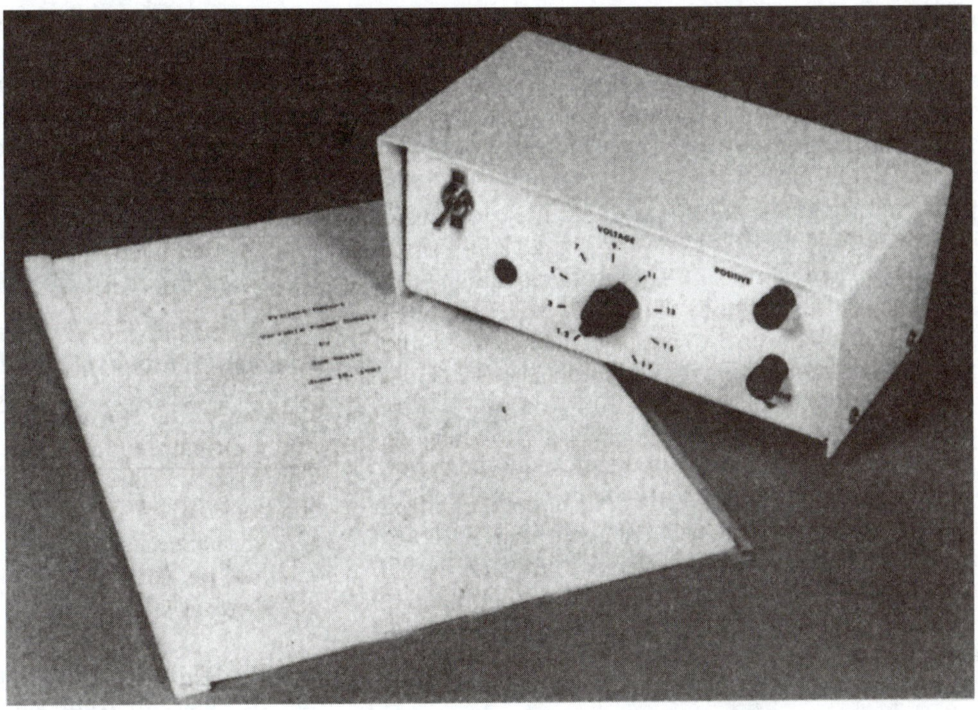

FIGURE 1–2
Finished prototype project and Project Report

The Need for an Electronics Design and Fabrication Experience

In order to appreciate why, as future electronics technicians, you need to have an electronics design and fabrication background, let's examine briefly just what it is that technicians do. Let's see how the familiar "learning by doing" concept fits nicely into the activities that lie ahead and examine the possibility of a new career path, that of fabrication technologist.

What Electronics Technicians Actually Do

Electronics technicians build, repair, test, modify, and install electronic devices and equipment. That is, they do electronics fabrication. They are a hands-on group. If electronic theory is your overriding interest, perhaps you should strive to be an engineer rather than a technician. But if you want to "do" as well as "know," produce with your hands as well as your head, then working with the actual hardware is where you need to be. A soldering iron, rather than a hand calculator, will be your primary tool.

As a working technician, you may not do all the things covered in this book. For example, you may never actually design a printed circuit board, but you will undoubtedly work (or "interface") with those who do. You need to appreciate their concerns and problems and be able to provide technical input when required. In addition, although you may rarely make a printed circuit board yourself, you will certainly treat the boards with greater respect if you are familiar with the process. The point is, as an electronics technician, you will be working with a variety of people in the long chain of the design and fabrication process. Thus, even as a student, you will want to know about and experience that process.

Learning by Doing

If your background in electronics is limited, or if the field is new to you, you may be reluctant to plunge right into electronics design and fabrication. Don't be. Learning by doing is not hard; in fact, it can be downright enjoyable. Think a moment. You probably got interested in electronics because it seemed like a field in which you could get paid for doing the fun and interesting things you always wanted to do. If you have been an electronics hobbyist or enthusiast for some time, you are already familiar with the basics of electronics fabrication and are that much farther ahead. If signing up for an electronics course is your first experience, don't worry; this book will show you all you need to know to get started.

Fabrication Technologist: A New Career Path?

Ordinarily, the electronics technician is expected to do it all: installation, maintenance, testing, troubleshooting, repair, and prototyping. Whether in medical, communications, industrial, computer, military, or consumer electronics (to name but a few specialties), the technician deals with all aspects of the equipment, except perhaps its initial design. This is particularly true, for instance, with regard to troubleshooting and repair, two areas that are often seen as merging into one. Until recently, if you could find the problem (diagnosis), repair was just a simple follow-up: grab some solder, a soldering iron, a couple of additional hand tools, and the repair was quick and easy. With just a little training almost anyone could do it!

Increasingly, this is no longer the case. In many situations, prototyping and repair have become so complex, sophisticated, and demanding of special skills that the typical generalist electronics technician cannot be expected to do them well, if at all. Rising to meet the challenge, fortunately, is the *fabrication technologist,* a skilled technician specializing in the prototyping, rework, and repair of electronic devices.

It is true in most cases, especially in small and medium-sized firms, that an electronics technician is still required to handle routine repairs and do an occasional prototype. However, today's rapid trend toward microminiaturized components and multilayered circuit boards has created a host of specialized problems in repair, rework, and prototyping. The fabrication technologist is emerging to deal with this new reality.

As a fabrication technologist (F.T.), you will need to become highly proficient in three areas: rework, repair, and prototyping.

> *Rework* involves reestablishing a device's functional and physical characteristics without deviating from the original manufacturer's specifications.
>
> *Repair* means reestablishing the functionality, quality, and reliability of an assembly that has failed or has been damaged. It may require deviations from the original manufacturer's specifications, however.
>
> *Prototyping,* of course, involves the creation of a hand-assembled project that will resemble as much as possible the final, mass-produced equipment.

Although the skills necessary to produce a quality prototype differ somewhat from those required for circuit repair and rework, there is, as you would expect, considerable commonality among the three areas. Circuit board fabrication, component assembly, sheet metal cutting and bending, the application of external finishes and rub-on lettering—all these techniques are necessary for project repair, rework, and prototyping. The knowledge and skills acquired in your fabrication course should go a long way in helping you to become a unique kind of electronics technician—a fabrication technologist.

> ***Something to Think About***
>
> *With virtual electronics a reality, do we need to actually prototype anything? What will the term* hands-on *come to mean in the near future?*

1.2 THE ELECTRONICS DESIGN AND FABRICATION PROCESS

Let's examine the five stages of electronics design and fabrication, from thought to finished project, and see how these stages are covered in the book. Keep in mind that when you have completed the process involved, you will have both a finished **prototype project** and a completed **Project Report** (Figure 1–2).

From Thought to Finished Prototype: A Five-Stage Process

This book explores the five stages required to design and fabricate a working prototype project: design; drawing; experimenting; prototyping; and testing, troubleshooting, and final documentation. What follows is a brief look at each stage, defining what the stage is and explaining why it is needed.

Doing It All: From Design to Documentation

Figure 1–3 illustrates the five-stage design and fabrication process and how it relates to the written and graphics documentation of the Project Report. At each stage, the project progresses, as does the documentation for it. The figure also gives the individual chapters in which these stages are discussed. You will probably refer to Figure 1–3 often. Now let's see what each stage comprises.

Design Stage. The project design is usually, but not always, done by the electronics engineer. The technician, however, is often intimately involved. At the very least, the technician is expected to spot errors and inconsistencies in design, particularly when they concern product packaging, testing, installation, and maintenance.

FIGURE 1–3
Five-stage electronics design and fabrication process to produce a working prototype and Project Report

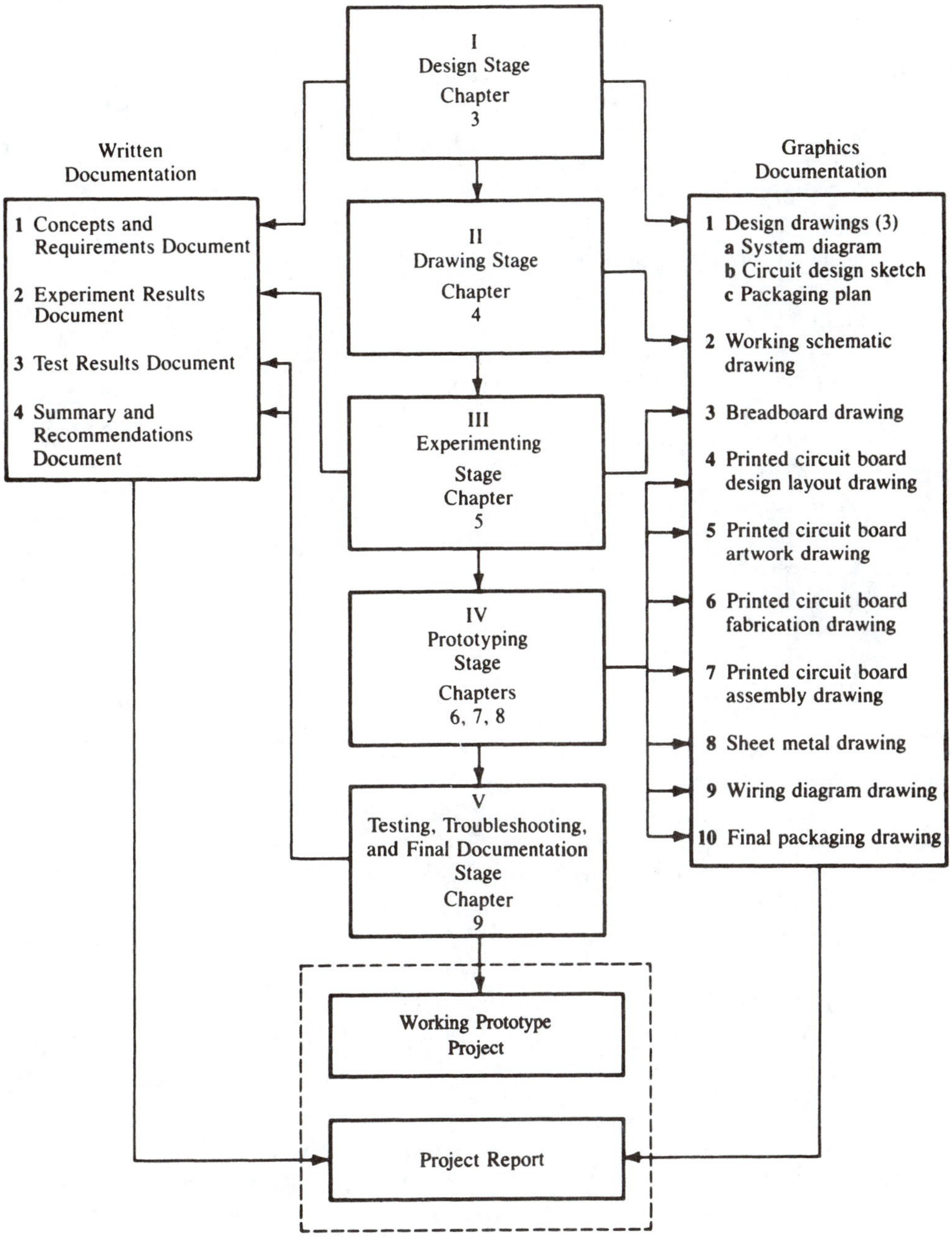

At this stage, a two-step design process takes place. It involves producing a Concepts and Requirements Document and a set of three design drawings. One of these drawings, the circuit design sketch (schematic), is often difficult to read and incomplete in this beginning stage, especially with regard to component identification. This sketch must be finished and cleaned up, at a later time, before any serious work on the project can begin.

If, in the design stage, you are preparing computer-generated circuit simulations, using CircuitMaker or Multisim, for example, you will, of course, want to include your graphic results as part of your design drawing set. Such a set will thus contain at least four drawings instead of three.

Drawing Stage. A group of 10 drawings (including the design drawing set) is required to explain graphically how the project will be built. A working schematic, breadboard drawing, printed circuit board design layout and artwork, and fabrication and assembly drawings must be produced.

Furthermore, a sheet metal layout, wiring diagram, and packaging illustration will be necessary. Although all these drawings are eventually completed and become part of the Project Report, only the design drawing set and working schematic drawing will actually be done before proceeding to the experimenting stage.

Experimenting Stage. This stage, often referred to as the *breadboarding* stage, is essential in proving out the design; that is, to see if the circuit actually works. Various quick and easy circuit assembly methods, the most popular of which involves the use of engineering solderless circuit board, have been developed specifically for use in the experimenting stage. With solderless circuit board, circuits can be assembled and altered in very little time, in many cases, without requiring any soldering at all. More permanent methods of circuit assembly involving cut-slash-and-hook and wire wrapping are also extensively used. A breadboard drawing and Experiment Results Document are produced at this time.

Prototyping Stage. It is here that a permanent, working project is actually built. Prototype devices are almost always made with **printed circuit boards,** circuits in which the interconnecting wires have been replaced by conductive strips etched onto an insulating board. The design and manufacture of printed circuit boards are a major part of the entire fabrication process. All the remaining drawings are completed at this stage.

Testing, Troubleshooting, and Final Documentation Stage. Once the prototype is completed, it must be tested. Does it meet the design requirements? Does it work under adverse environmental conditions? Often extensive laboratory and field testing is needed to determine the answers. If the device does not work correctly, it must be fixed. Troubleshooting becomes a very necessary part of this stage. The Test Results and Summary and Recommendations Documents are now produced. Finally, all the documentation must come together. The Project Report, with its written and graphics documentation, is assembled at this time.

These, then, are the five stages required to produce a working prototype project and Project Report. Of course, there is, strictly speaking (when overall product development and manufacturing is considered), a sixth stage. It is the production stage, in which the project is mass-produced. Because assemblers, rather than technicians, are usually involved here, this book does not cover production in any great detail.

But I'm an Electronics Technician!

Why, you ask, does an *electronics* technician need to know about drafting, sheet metal fabrication, and rub-on lettering techniques? The answer is simple: the problems a technician encounters on the job are not exclusively electronic. The technician works with mechanical assemblies, enclosures, and systems. Often, the most sought-after technicians are those with an electromechanical background. At the very least, the technician is required to read mechanical drawings, assemble and disassemble enclosures, and do minor mechanical adjustments and calibrations. This situation is especially true at small- and medium-sized companies, where the technician is expected to do it all. As a student preparing to be such a technician, you will want to gain as broad a design and fabrication experience as possible—now.

The Electronics Design and Fabrication Process and This Book

Let's look at the five-stage design and fabrication process as it is discussed in individual chapters, see how student projects form an integral part of the book, and investigate the role of the Project Report.

Five Stages—Seven Chapters

Except for this overview chapter, Chapter 2 (on safety), and the concluding chapter (on computer-aided design, or CAD), Part I of this text is devoted to exploring the five stages of electronics design and fabrication.

1. **Design Stage**—Chapter 3. This chapter, in addition to reviewing basic electronic principles, introduces concepts of electronics design and looks at how we think up problems to be solved.
2. **Drawing Stage**—Chapter 4. Chapter 4 introduces an important language of engineering—the drawing—and examines the 10-drawing set that you will develop throughout the book. The working schematic is also produced at this stage.
3. **Experimenting Stage**—Chapter 6. In this chapter the different methods used to assemble projects in order to test out their design are studied. Various experimenting systems, including cut-slash-and-hook, are reviewed.
4. **Prototyping Stage**—Chapters 7, 8, and 9. Chapters 7 and 8 cover the design and manufacture of printed circuit boards. Chapter 9 deals

with printed circuit board assembly, project packaging, and final assembly.

5. **Testing, Troubleshooting, and Final Documentation Stage**—Chapter 10. Here, the testing and troubleshooting of the completed prototype project are investigated. Preliminary testing and troubleshooting, at the project experimentation level, will already have taken place. Also, here is where all the necessary documentation that has been produced in the appropriate chapters is pulled together in the final Project Report.

As you can see, the design and fabrication of an electronics prototype project means producing two items: a Project Report, consisting of written and graphics documentation, and the finished working prototype project. Both items are developed concurrently as you move back and forth between the drawing board, or computer screen, and the workbench.

Student Construction Projects

Although the seven chapters just reviewed contain miniexercises designed to help you become familiar with the various processes discussed, it is through the building of either a Sample or Exercise Project, one of the 30 projects in the Elective Projects group, or one of the three Surface Mount Technology Projects in Appendix E that you will derive the greatest benefit from this book (Figure 1–4). Let's see how project building fits into the learning scheme.

A Sample Project, a regulated Variable Power Supply, is carried from chapter to chapter, starting with the two-step design process and ending with a completely packaged and tested prototype. All documentation is brought together in the Project Report, presented in Part III. With this Sample Project, you see a real project develop before your eyes as you proceed through the chapters. You may wish to recreate this project, along with its documentation, as your class project.

An Exercise Project, a 3-Channel Color Organ, is also developed in the appropriate chapters. However, the information presented for this project is not as complete as that for the Sample Project. This situation, of course, is what is intended. If you choose to build the Exercise Project, you will be challenged at a slightly higher level because less assistance is provided. Nonetheless, since the 3-Channel Color Organ parallels, in design and construction difficulty, the Variable Power Supply, you will find the exercise well suited for a first construction project. Furthermore, if you wish to refer

Sample Project

Variable Power Supply

Step-by-step construction details are provided, along with a complete project report.

or

Exercise Project

3-Channel Color Organ

Step-by-step construction hints and suggestions are given, along with a complete project report.

or

Elective Projects (30)

- ☐ Adjustable Dual Power Supply
- ☐ Attic Fan Actuator
- ☐ Audible Logic Probe
- ☐ Burglar Alarm
- ☐ Carport Night-Light Controller
- ☐ Clap-On/Clap-Off Switch
- ☐ Contestant Lockout Game
- ☐ Digital Thermometer
- ☐ Emergency Strobe Light
- ☐ Events Timer
- ☐ Flashing Brake Light
- ☐ Gas Detector
- ☐ Intercom
- ☐ Laser Pointer Remote Control
- ☐ LED Attention-Getter
- ☐ LED Logic Probe
- ☐ Light-Controlled Switch
- ☐ Photoelectric Counter
- ☐ "Poor Person's" Function Generator
- ☐ Push-Button Combination Lock
- ☐ Reaction Timing Tester
- ☐ Siren
- ☐ Sound-Activated Switch
- ☐ Symbol Animator
- ☐ Telephone Line Monitor with Hold Button
- ☐ Telephone Recording Beeper
- ☐ Turn-Signal Reminder
- ☐ 2-W Stereo Amplifier
- ☐ Variable Strobe Light
- ☐ Wireless Microphone

No special construction details are provided, and only the Concepts and Requirements Document is included for each project. (See Appendix E for Surface Mount Technology Projects.)

FIGURE 1–4
Student construction projects

to it, a completed Project Report for the 3-Channel Color Organ is provided in Part III.

Also in Part III are an additional 30 Elective Projects to choose from. Only the Concepts and Requirements Document and the three design drawings are provided for each project. You must take it from there.

As you can see, then, you are given a choice, at three different levels, of appropriate projects to build, or "fabricate."

Project Report

Along with actually fabricating a project, you must produce the proper documentation. It is true that for the Variable Power Supply and 3-Channel Color Organ Projects, complete documentation is already provided (Part III). But to gain the full benefit and experience in the design and fabrication process, you will need to complete the appropriate graphics and written documentation, regardless of which project you construct.

With respect to drawings, you can simply redo the 10-drawing set for the Sample Project. With the Exercise Project, you can copy the drawings from the Project Report in Part III, or preferably, draw your own set. If you choose a project from the Elective Projects group, however, you will have to produce all but the design drawings yourself.

In addition to the graphics documentation, the Project Report requires written certification in the form of Concepts and Requirements, Experiment Results, Test Results, and Summary and Recommendations Documents. Such paperwork is not extensive; in some cases just a page or two is all that is needed. However, it must be done, and it must be concise and complete.

If all this sounds a bit like work, well, it is. But when you bring that completed project, along with its Project Report, to your first job interview, you will know it has all been worthwhile.

Beginning at the Beginning

Although electronics design and fabrication involves effort, this book is not going to make you run before you walk—or crawl. It is going to take you through the process step by step and keep it simple. You will learn the basics—not everything there is to know about electronics design and fabrication. There is nothing to be gained by cluttering up your mind with a description of a dozen types of soldering lugs, for example. Although consistency with industry standards is needed, the main concern is to provide the instruction that will enable electronics design and fabrication to take place in the typical school setting. The purpose of this book is to get you started in the right direction; the "bells and whistles" can come later.

To design and fabricate electronic projects requires four things. You will need *tools* for building and repairing; *plans* in the form of drawings and written documentation; *materials* such as hardware and electronic components; and the *knowledge* and *skills* necessary to complete the task. Because we promised to take first things first, let's now turn our attention to the tools of the trade, both on the board and on the bench.

> **Something to Think About**
>
> *Why not add to the list of elective projects? Searching magazines, books, and, of course, the Internet, see if you can come up with additional, interesting, yet relatively simple, projects to include.*

1.3 TOOLS OF THE TRADE: ON THE BOARD

The tools needed to design an electronic project are of two types: traditional and computer-based. With the former, often referred to as drafting tools, or board tools, any of the drawings in the 10-drawing set can be made. Although the same is literally true for a computer-aided design (CAD) system, for our purposes, CAD is best used to make two critical drawings: the working schematic and the printed circuit board artwork drawing.

In this section we list each traditional drafting tool needed and explain what it does. Discussion of tool use, however, comes later, in chapters where the applicable drawing procedure is described. In the next section, we look at the CAD drawing process.

The Drafting Table

There are two types of drawing tables: the permanent table mounted on "all fours" (or at least twos) and the portable drawing table, one that literally can go anywhere.

Sturdy and Smooth

When it comes to a "stay-in-one-place" drafting table, four legs are usually better than two (Figure 1–5). Simply put, such tables are more stable, and less likely to wobble while you are trying to draw a

FIGURE 1–5
Standard drafting table

straight line. A smooth surface to draw on is a must. This surface is ordinarily obtained in one of two ways: either by coating the table with a roll of Borco, a vinyl-like material especially formulated to provide a smooth drawing surface, or by using a *drawing board.* A drawing board is made of seasoned, straight-grained soft woods and is designed to be used with a T-square and triangles.

Although some drafters prefer to stand at their table, most usually sit. Above all, the chair you choose should be comfortable. Chairs with an adjustable seat height and back support—the ideal choice—are available from many commercial sources.

You should choose lighting with great care. The key factor here is to provide direct, as well as indirect, illumination. Drafting lamps with articulated support arms are available. They can accommodate a 100-watt (W) bulb, have an adjustable arm, and include a clamp so that they can be mounted on the edge of the drawing table.

Portable Drafting Tables

Various portable drafting tables are available that make drawing convenient and inexpensive for the part-time or on-the-go drafter (Figure 1–6). Many of these units consist of far more than a drafting table. A number of them contain a small drafting machine, an instrument that allows you to quickly draw straight lines at designated lengths and angles. If you are primarily interested in electronics fabrication, the economy of the portable drafting table would be its main attraction. But before you make a decision, read on. An even more preferable solution, the mini-drafting machine, may be your answer.

Drafting Equipment

Here, both new and traditional drafting equipment are discussed, as well as printed circuit board design and artwork materials. (Additional drafting materials, as they pertain specifically to surface mount technology design, are discussed in Chapter 13.)

Equipment for Drawing Straight Lines

The standard drafting machine is large and expensive, and its cost is rarely justified for the part-time electronics drafter. A much better way to go is to buy a traditional package of drafting tools consisting of a T-square, two triangles (30°/60°, and 45°), protractor, scale, and drawing board—all that is necessary to draw straight lines at any particular length or angle (Figure 1–7).

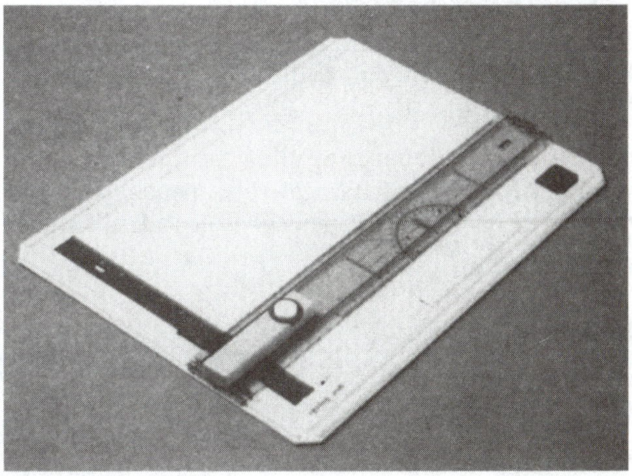

FIGURE 1–6
Portable drafting table

FIGURE 1–7
Traditional drafting tools

You can, however, combine all these features in a fascinating product known as a mini-drafting machine that sells for less than $12. These machines, one of which is illustrated in Figure 1–8, are made of durable plastic and contain two pairs of knurled rollers that contact the paper surface. No special table or paper is required. With just a few minutes' practice, you will be making penciled or inked lines just like a professional.

Pencils, Paper, and Things

Whether you use basic drafting equipment or a drafting machine, you will still need additional "bits and pieces" (Figure 1–9).

- ☐ **Pencils.** Because they allow for the interchanging of leads, mechanical refill pencils are preferred over wood pencils. The lead itself comes in a variety of grades: from very hard (7H and 6H), which draws a light line, to extremely soft (HB down to 7B), which lays a dark line on the paper. Select a 4H for drawing dimension and hidden lines; use a 2H or H for object lines.
- ☐ **Paper.** For the 10-drawing set you will be producing, graph paper with a 0.100″ × 0.100″ cross-sectional grid is required. It is available in $8\frac{1}{2}$″ × 11″ (A size) sheets of vellum or layout bond paper. The grid should be printed in nonreproducible blue. This means that the grid pattern will not reproduce when the drawing is copied.
- ☐ **Compass and Circle Guides.** Compass and circle guides are used to draw circles and arcs. For circles greater than $1\frac{1}{2}$″ in diameter, the compass should be used. For small circles, rounds, or fillets, the circle guide is ideal.

FIGURE 1–8
Mini-drafting machine

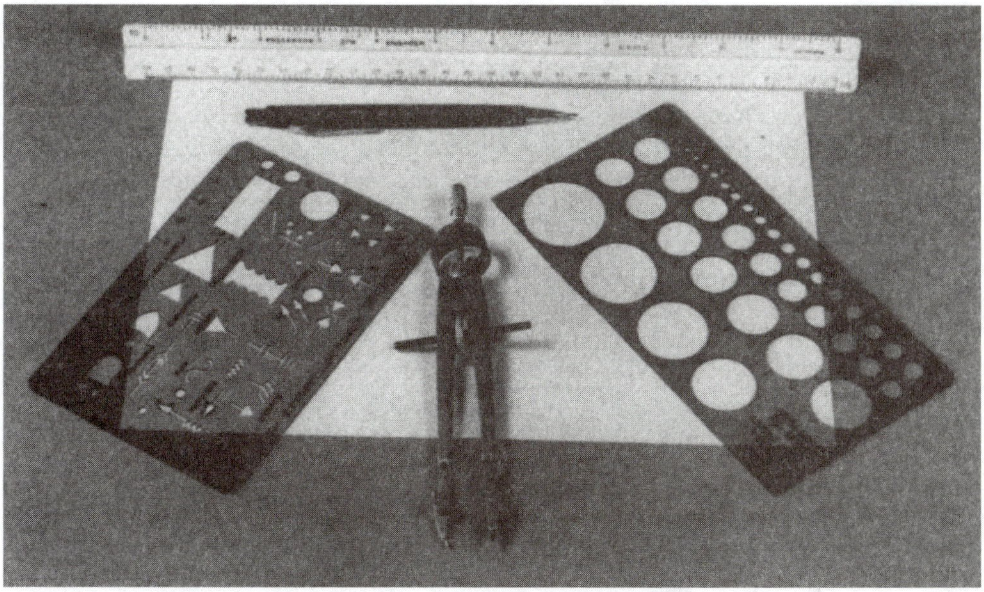

FIGURE 1–9
Pencils, paper, and things

- ☐ **Drafting Templates.** Templates save time and effort. You will need two types: one to aid in making schematic symbols, the other for creating printed circuit board design layouts. The latter should be chosen in the full, or 1× scale.
- ☐ **Scale.** You are going to need a scale. Avoid the ones available at the local drugstore; quality is of the utmost importance here. A mechanical engineer's scale, graduated in 0.02″ divisions, is required. It doesn't really matter whether it's triangular or flat, as long as it is of good quality.

There are a few additional items: pencil sharpener, eraser, erasing shield, drafting tape, lettering guides, and so forth. Your local stationery or drafting supply center will help you with these supplemental supplies.

Printed Circuit Board Design Layout and Tape-up Equipment

In addition to the printed circuit layout template, you are going to need colored pencils, an X-Acto knife, acetate sheets, tape-up materials, and possibly a light table (Figure 1–10). Let's take them in order:

- ☐ **Colored Pencils.** A set of colored pencils comes in handy when you are producing the printed circuit board design layout. A half-dozen different colors are all that is required.
- ☐ **X-Acto Knife.** An X-Acto knife holder accepts a variety of blade shapes. Because the blade will be used to cut layout tape or to position stick-on pads, a #16 blade is the ideal choice. Blades should be changed frequently, so purchase a package with at least five blades.
- ☐ **Acetate Sheets.** You will use these thin, clear, plasticlike sheets as a base for your printed circuit artwork. They are available in individual or packaged sheets and in an assortment of sizes. You will want $8\frac{1}{2}''$ × 11″ sheets, 0.005″ or 0.007″ thick.
- ☐ **Artwork Materials.** Materials for artwork consist of the component mounting configurations and the rolls of opaque tape you will be using to tape up your printed circuit design layout. (See Chapter 7 for a discussion of these materials.)
- ☐ **Light Table.** A light table is useful but certainly not required. Printed circuit tape-up is easier when light shines up through the design layout, drawn on graph paper, to the acetate sheet placed on top of it. A light table gives you this advantage. If you use one, be sure that the work surface is flooded with completely diffused, shadow-free light.

A Note on Quality

Drafting instruments and tools should last you a lifetime. In fact, much of the equipment available from top manufacturers is guaranteed for the life of the owner. Look for tools that are sturdy and fit together well. To find such equipment, your best bet is to seek out only quality, name-brand manufacturers. Avoid cheap goods; they will wind up costing you much more in the end.

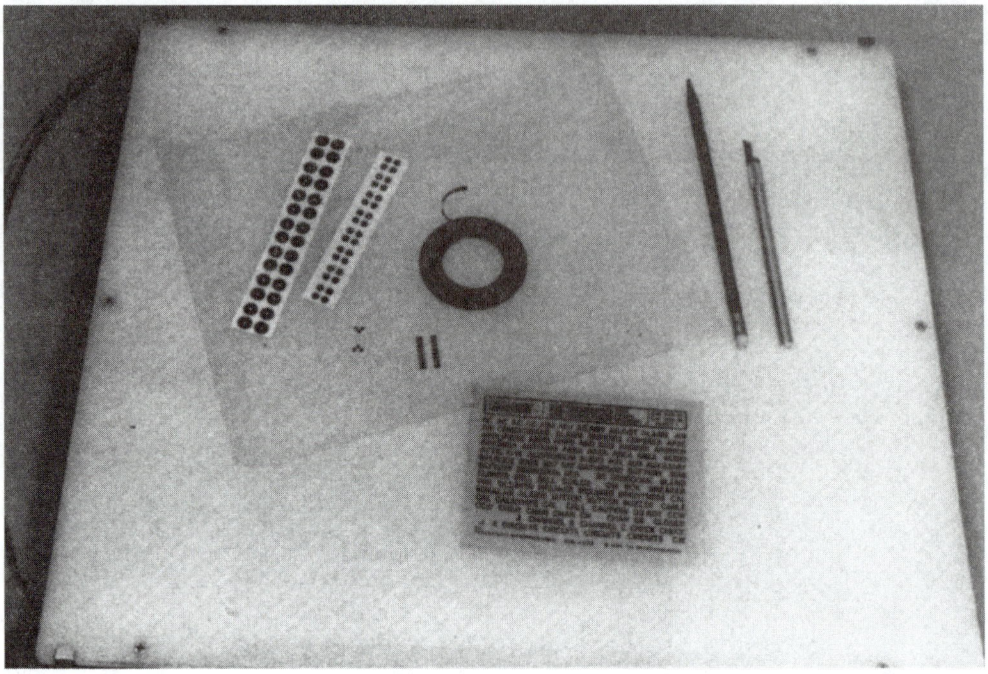

FIGURE 1–10
Printed circuit (PC) design layout and artwork materials on a light table

> ***Something to Think About***
>
> *Drafting equipment rarely wears out. A quality triangle is good for a lifetime. With a whole generation of mechanical engineers now in retirement, you might be able to purchase a complete set of drafting tools at a garage sale down the block. It's worth looking into.*

1.4 TOOLS OF THE TRADE: AT THE COMPUTER

In creating a prototype project there is a design stage and a drafting stage. In design, new ideas are formulated; in drafting, these ideas are documented on paper in the form of drawings. Computers can help with both phases. With a sophisticated CAD (known both as computer-aided design *and* computer-aided drafting) system, every drawing in the Project Report can be entirely produced with the aid of a computer. Let's see what CAD is and then examine the computer hardware necessary to produce computer-generated drawings.

The What and Why of CAD

CAD does for graphics documentation what word processing does for written documentation. A written document is much easier to create, store, alter, produce, and transmit with a word processor than on an electric typewriter. We are about to see how, with CAD, we can do all these same things for graphics documentation as well.

CAD: What Is It?

In the beginning, the early 1960s, there was just computer-aided drafting. It was run on a large mainframe computer, it was slow, and it was very, very costly. At the latter end of the decade, computer-aided design came along. It, too, was available only on the large machines. But with the advent of fast, memory-filled microcomputers in the late 1980s and early 1990s, both computer-aided design and drafting are now within the reach of practically everyone who needs them.

CAD uses a computer as a design and drafting tool (Figure 1–11). With it, you can design new or modify old circuits and create finished working drawings. The result is a product that is less expensive, more accurate, of higher quality, of greater consistency, and easier to store, alter, and transmit than would be possible without a computer. The discussion in this chapter is confined to electronic schematic and PC board drawings, but keep in mind that any type of drawing in the mechanical, architectural, civil engineering, and aerospace fields can also be produced with a powerful enough CAD system.

FIGURE 1–11
A computer used to produce CAD drawings

Why Use CAD? Beyond the T-Square

CAD is not just a drawing aid but a design assistant. With a powerful computer-aided design program, you can save yourself a great deal of bench time and breadboarding. Many software packages allow you to do waveform analysis and troubleshooting without ever handling an electronic component. At the touch of a keyboard or stroke of a light pen, design modifications and improvements can easily be made. In addition, circuit simulations allow real-world circuit operations to be performed. You can also play "what if" games. Change one circuit parameter—for example, a transistor value—and the program will tell you what effect that change has on the entire circuit operation.

CAD really comes into its own as a drafting aid. Actually, creating a drawing for the first time with a CAD system is probably no faster than with the paper-and-pencil method. Where CAD shines is when changes, modifications, and updates are required. It's similar to what happens in word processing. I could probably write this text just as fast on an IBM Selectric typewriter as I can on an IBM-PC. But when using the Selectric, if I make a few mistakes, or want to insert a paragraph here, delete one there, the whole chapter will probably need to be retyped. Not so with the computer. With the PC, I just correct mistakes and insert or delete text right on the video display terminal. When I am satisfied with the results, I call for a print operation, lean back, sip a cup of coffee, and watch my printer turn out the document at roughly four pages a minute.

The concept behind computer-aided drafting is the same as the one behind word processing. You create a drawing on the screen and store it in the computer's memory. When you need modifications, you just make the necessary changes on the video display terminal and then ask the printer or plotter to make a new drawing. The work is done neatly, quickly, and accurately. The old-fashioned way requires laborious redrawing (often in ink) by hand—a wasteful, messy, inaccurate process at best.

There are other advantages in using CAD to create drawings. Because all the information about the drawing (what components are located where, for example) is stored in the computer in digital bits, the drawing can be transmitted across town, or around the world, more or less instantaneously. Furthermore, drawings produced with CAD are much more consistent in lettering, line weight, and symbol configuration (Figure 1–12). Finally, think of the savings in storage space that result from keeping a drawing on a tiny section of floppy disk rather than on a large sheet of paper.

Computer Systems/CAD Systems

A CAD system is, naturally, a computer system. So what's a computer system? That's the logical first question that we need to answer before we can go on to see how computers are configured specifically for CAD.

A Basic Computer System

A computer is an electronic device that performs arithmetic and logic functions. In so doing, it manipulates numbers, letters, and practically any other graphics symbols. All these symbols are converted into binary 1s and 0s (high and low voltages) that, under software control, are processed inside the computer. This processing takes place in what is called the CPU, the central processing unit. The CPU, made up of the ALU (arithmetic logic unit), a few registers, and control circuitry, forms a computer (Figure 1–13a). The CPU is not, however, a computer system.

To create a **computer system,** we must, as with any electronic system (see Chapter 3), in addition to providing a circuit (CPU), include at least one input and one output device, or transducer. A computer system (Figure 1–13b) is made up of a CPU (and associated circuitry), where electrical

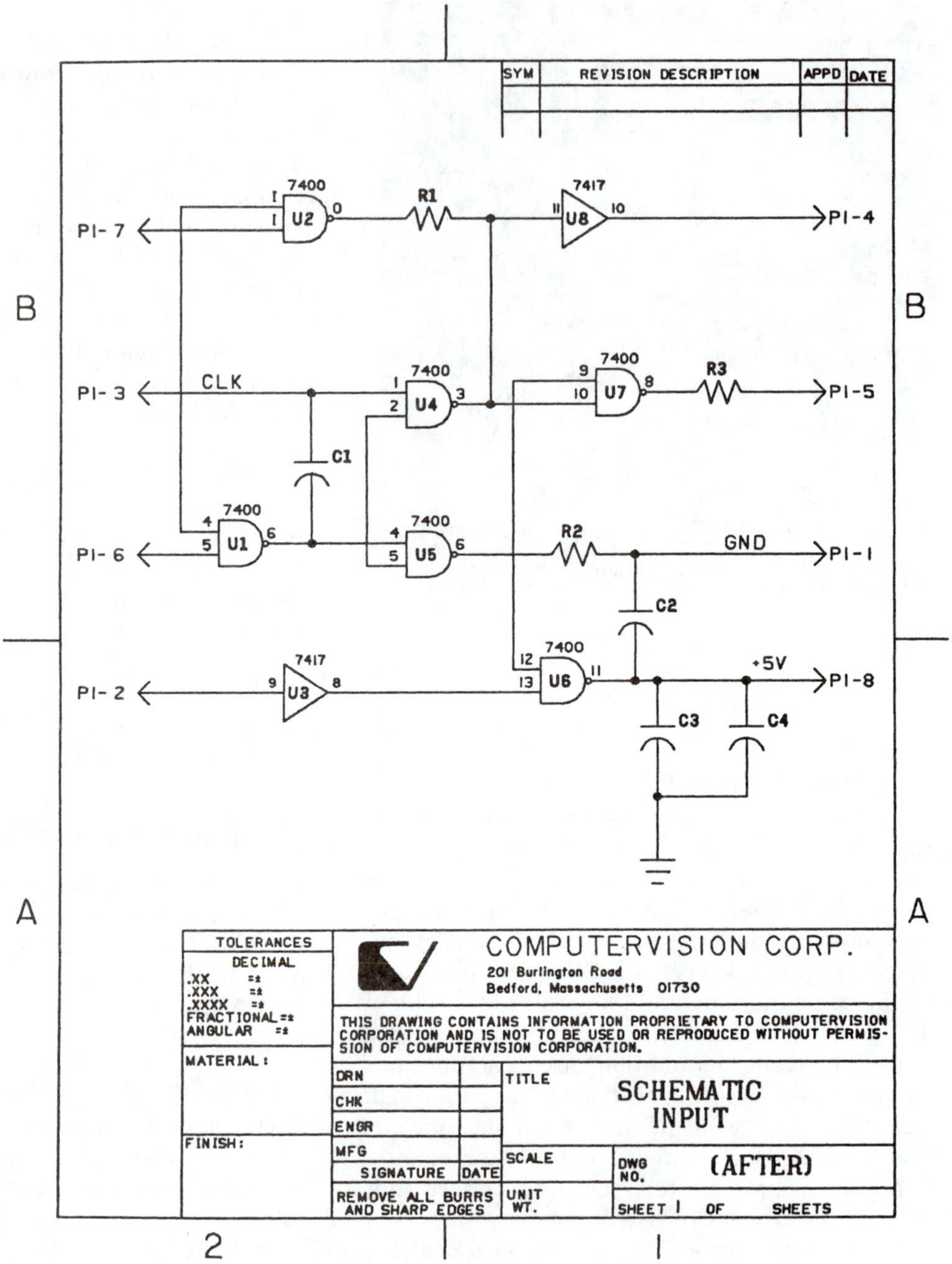

FIGURE 1–12
CAD drawing
Courtesy Computervision Corp.

signals are manipulated digitally, with memory, and various input and output transducers, called *peripherals*.

A functional diagram of a typical computer system is shown in Figure 1–14. The keyboard is the input peripheral, used to enter data into the computer. The video display terminal (VDT) displays the data as they are being entered or after they have been manipulated (processed). The printer produces a hard copy of what appears on the screen.

But the computer won't accept or manipulate anything unless it is told specifically what to do. The instructions come in the form of a *program*, known as *software*. The program, with its lines of code, or instructions, is stored in the computer's memory, as are the results of any data processing.

A Basic CAD System

Let's examine a basic computer system configured to do computer-aided design.

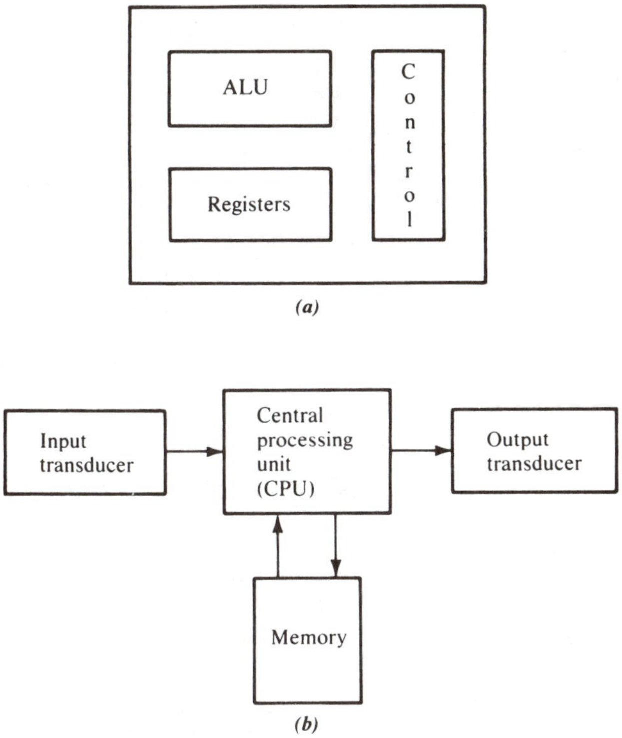

FIGURE 1–13
Computer and computer system

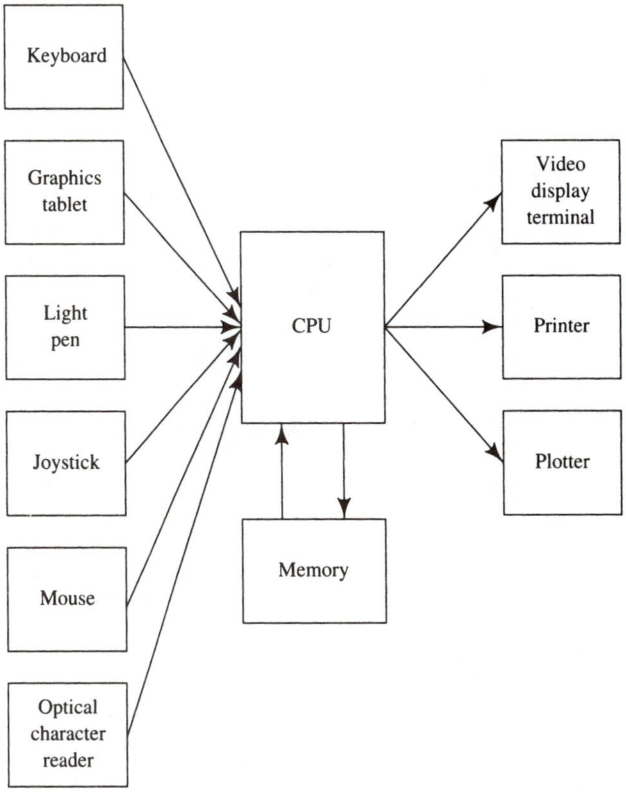

FIGURE 1–15
CAD system

In Figure 1–15 we see a functional diagram of a CAD computer system, in Figure 1–16, an illustration of representative hardware. Like any computer system, it contains a CPU, along with memory to store a program and the results of data manipulation. What makes the CAD system different, at least from a hardware standpoint, are the input and output peripherals. These devices are used primarily to enter and display graphic symbols—lines, geometric shapes, schematic symbols, and so forth. Let's examine the more common types of peripherals used for CAD generation.

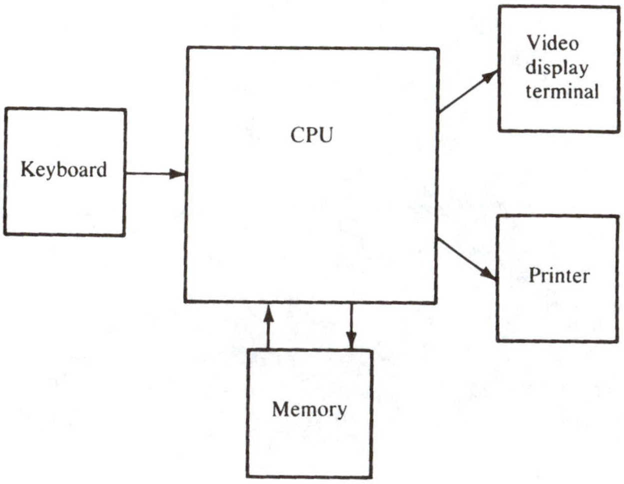

FIGURE 1–14
Computer system as word processor

Included among the input peripherals are such devices as the keyboard, graphics tablet (digitizer), light pen, joystick, mouse, and optical character reader (OCR).

Keyboard. The keyboard was mentioned earlier; for entering numbers, letters, and basic computer commands, it can't be beat.

Graphics Tablet. The graphics tablet is used for inputting graphics with a stylus. Diagrams or freehand drawings can be created and appear instantly on a video display terminal. The typical tablet consists of a grid of wires partially embedded in a thin substrate. When the tablet is touched by a stylus, the wires are brought into electrical contact. The result is a pulse that enables the computer to register the position of the stylus. With a sketch placed atop the tablet, practically any shape can be digitized, stored, and displayed in the computer.

FIGURE 1–16
CAD hardware

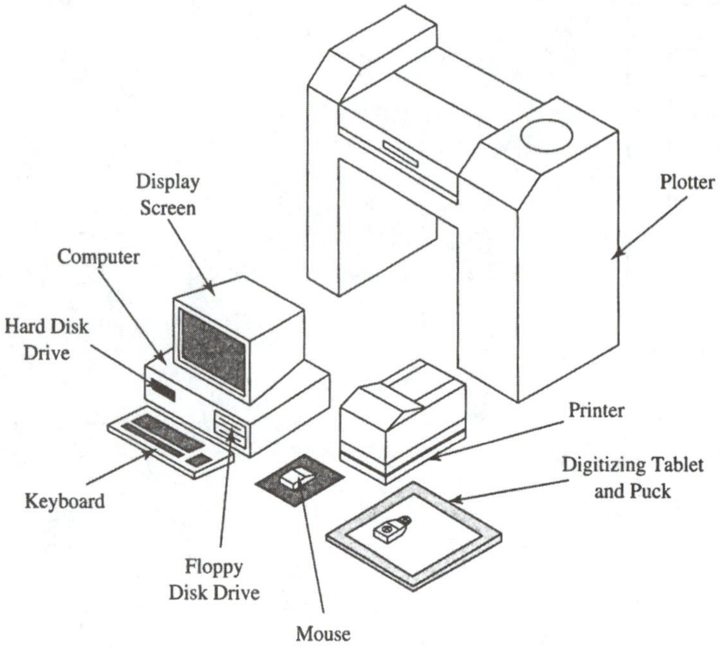

Light Pen. The light pen is an electronic stylus. It contains a light sensor that, when aimed at the video screen, specifies a position on the screen.

Joystick. The joystick, an upgraded version of the type used with video games, is a lever whose motions control the movement of a cursor (small square of light) on the VDT. It can also be used to draw diagrams and geometric shapes.

Mouse. Probably the most popular input peripheral for graphics generation, the mouse is moved by an operator over the surface of a mouse pad, graphics tablet, or table. Its position is recorded by the computer. The mouse is used to move text and illustrations about on the screen. It is also used to enter various commands into the computer.

Optical Character Reader (OCR). An optical character reader is most often a handheld device that is pulled over printed material, both text and graphics (Figure 1–17). It "recognizes" what it "sees" and stores the information in a computer data file for later manipulation.

Included among the output peripherals are the video display terminal, the printer, and the plotter.

Video Display Terminal. For CAD work, a video display terminal should be a video color monitor with at least a 14″ screen. Its VGA (video graphics array) card should be capable of presenting a video resolution of at least 1024 by 768 pixels—with up to 256 colors displayed simultaneously.

Printer. Although an ink-jet printer can produce acceptable schematic drawings and PC board artwork, for truly professional results, a laser printer is a must. Such a printer should have a minimum resolution of 300 dpi (dots per inch), with 400 dpi being better, and 600 dpi being the best. (Although some laser printers are capable of 2400 dpi, they are beyond the price range of most students, hobbyists, and technicians.)

FIGURE 1–17
Optical character reader (OCR)

Plotter. The plotter is a true wonder of printing technology. Most use an ink pen, often more than one (each of a different color), that is driven on X-Y axes. The plotter rapidly and tirelessly draws the most intricate illustrations with perfect precision and consistency. With what seems like a mind of its own, the plotter produces drawings with a quality no human being could match.

> ***Something to Think About***
>
> *New, improved CAD systems are constantly coming on the market. Now is the time to gather vendor literature on what's available. Why not contact product manufacturers and distributors to start building a file?*

1.5 TOOLS OF THE TRADE: ON THE BENCH

Like tools for the drawing board, tools for the workbench must be chosen for their quality. As a working technician, you will be judged by the tools you keep. Your reputation is at stake; select tools that will give you pride of ownership.

In this section the workbench and the tools for mechanical and electrical assembly that go with it are examined. In Chapter 10, the basic instruments needed to test and troubleshoot electronic projects are briefly introduced. (Additional tools and equipment, necessary to work with surface mount devices, are discussed in Chapter 13.)

The Bench: More Than the Kitchen Table

Whether selecting a workbench for the home, school, or workplace, the basic criteria for its selection are the same. You must be concerned with its location within a given setting, its structure and storage features, and lighting and power requirements (Figure 1–18).

Location and Structure

Ideally, the workbench should be located in an area that will provide a minimum of distractions. Such a location will increase the likelihood that the bench will be used only for its intended purpose, electronics fabrication. If you must use a common area, such as the kitchen table, assemble your project on a large plywood board that can be moved. In that way hardware, components, and small tools will remain undisturbed.

The workbench area should remain relatively clean. The dirt and mess associated with normal mechanical assembly (such as is found in the typical auto shop) is incompatible with modern electronics fabrication. Electronic assembly is considered a "light industry"—light and clean.

FIGURE 1–18
Workbench

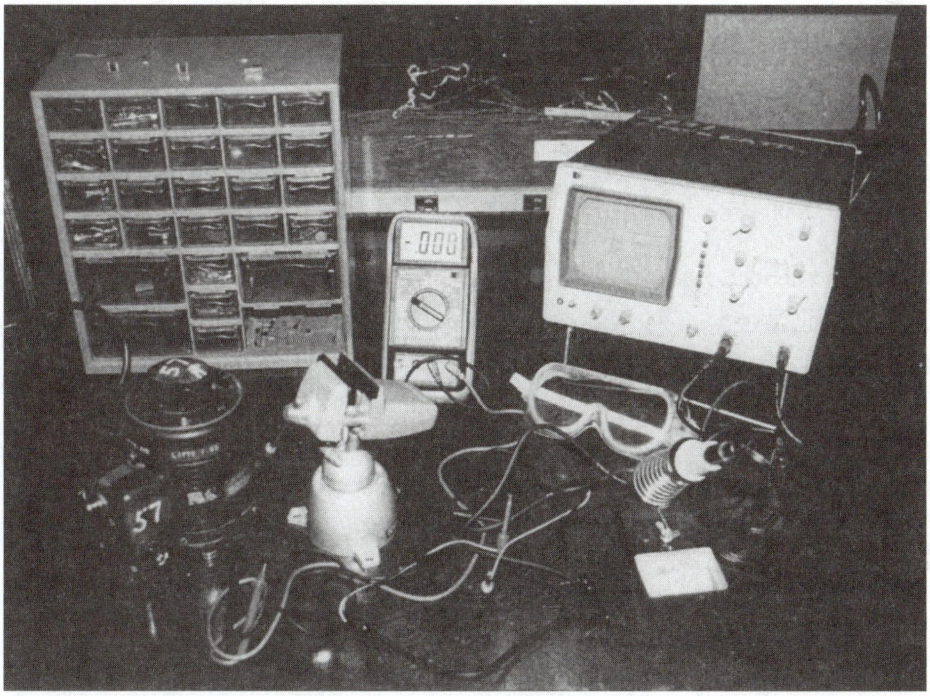

In terms of structure, the workbench must provide comfort to lessen fatigue. It should have a solid, nonmetallic surface and be of such height that you can rest your elbows comfortably on the surface.

Adequate storage must also be provided. Shelves should be placed immediately in front of the work area to house test equipment. For storing electronic components and small hardware items, modular plastic drawers are ideal. An alternative approach is to arrange a baker's dozen of boxes or drawers. Twelve of the boxes contain the dozen basic electronic components used in electronics: resistors, capacitors, transistors, and the like. The thirteenth box is labeled "miscellaneous." Nothing should remain in this particular junk box too long; if you can't file something within a few days, it probably isn't worth keeping.

Lighting and Power Requirements

The workbench should be bathed in direct and indirect light. You might not think this lighting is necessary, but when you are working with tiny circuits and minute letters and numbers printed on small components, you will need all the brightness you can muster. A drafting lamp (Figure 1–19) can provide a concentrated direct beam of light. An even better choice is a swivel lamp with an illuminated magnifier. Such lamps are particularly useful when you are inspecting or assembling printed circuit boards (Figure 1–20).

Obviously, power outlets are a must. Your workbench should have at least six, all fused (or provided with a circuit breaker) and rated at 20–25 amperes (A). Of course, they should be of the three-conductor, or grounded socket, type. Bench-mounted power distribution strips can be expensive (from $20 to $50), especially the individually fused or switched units, but the protection to equipment and projects they provide is worth the cost. Finally, an isolation transformer will provide the optimum in safety, since it totally isolates the incoming line voltage from the project in use. No complete test bench should be without one.

Tools for the Workbench

Now it's time to take a look at the tools that go on the workbench. The discussion divides them into two broad categories: those used for *mechanical work* and those required for *electrical work.* However, keep in mind that the distinction between the two is not always clear-cut. A needle nose pliers is useful both for holding small pieces of hardware and for bending wire.

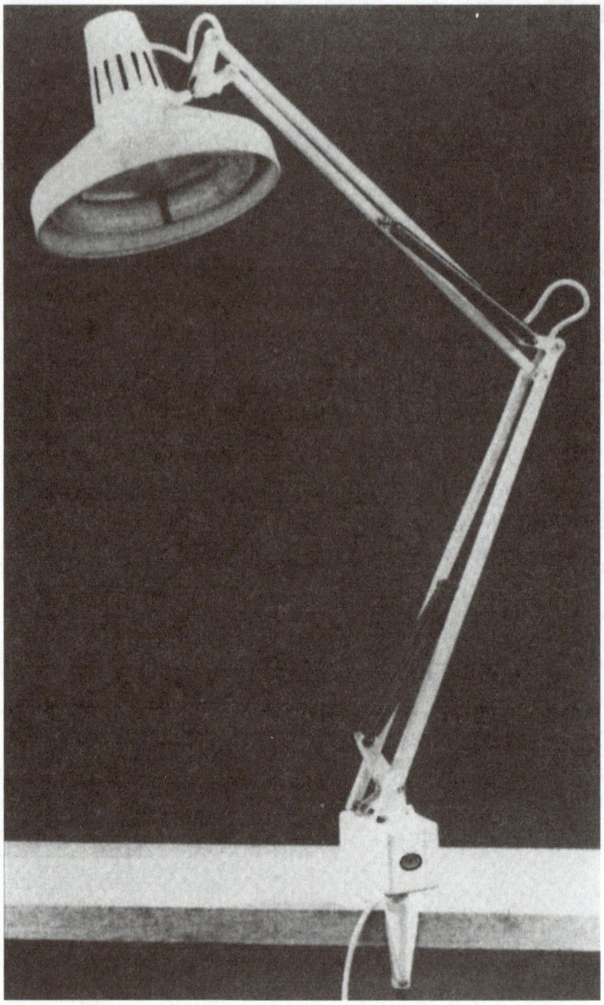

FIGURE 1–19
Drafting lamp

Tools for Mechanical Work

What follows is a list of must-have tools, those that are essential to the mechanical fabrication associated with project building.

1. Drivers. There are two types of *drivers:* screwdrivers and nutdrivers. The former are used to turn screws; the latter, to twist nuts. You will need a set of both (Figure 1–21).

Screwdrivers are either *blade* or *Phillips head.* The blade type has a chisel-shaped head that mates with straight-slotted screws. Phillips screwdrivers are designed to fit screws with star-shaped holes in their heads. Sets of each type are available in two packaging styles: one containing individual screwdrivers, the other having a handle into which any of several driver shafts can be inserted.

FIGURE 1–20
Magnifier lamp

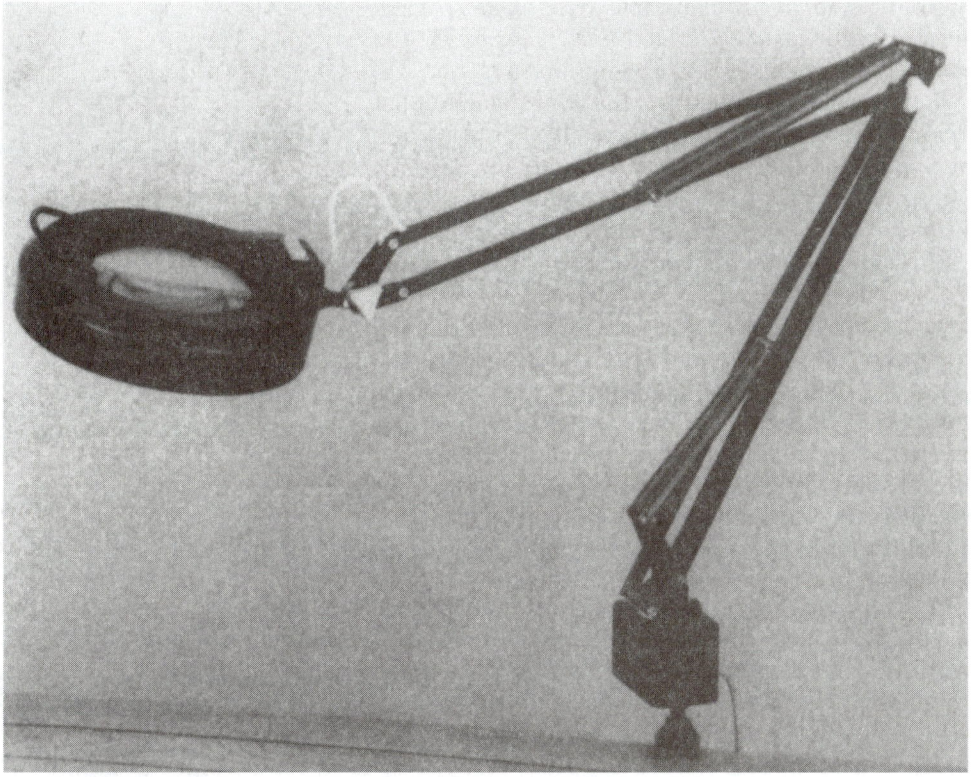

FIGURE 1–21
Drivers: both screw and nut

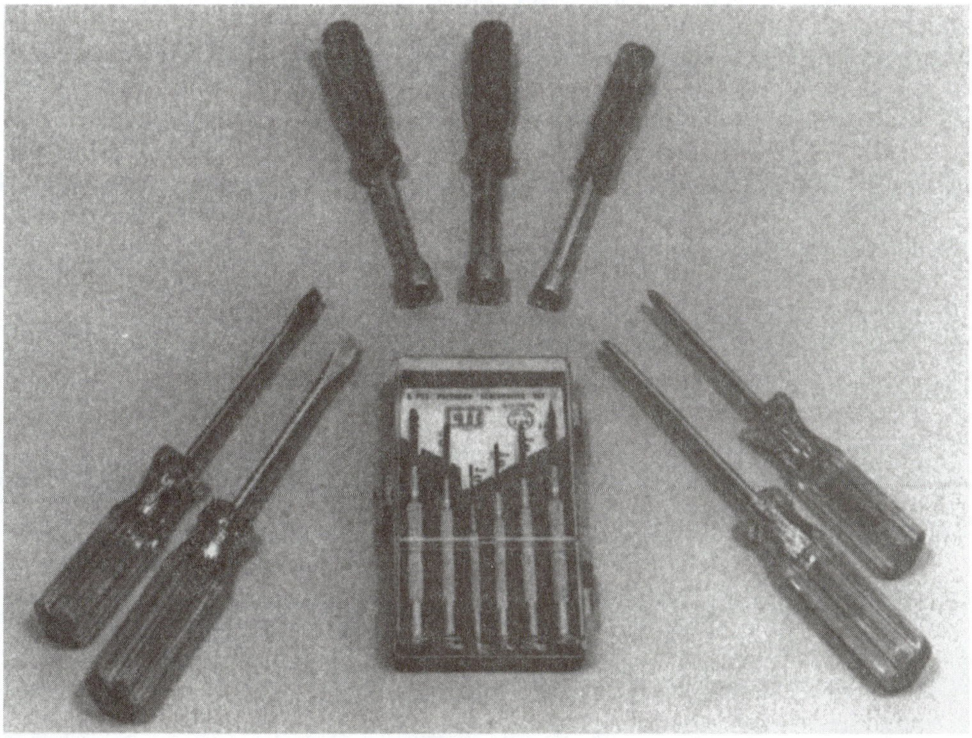

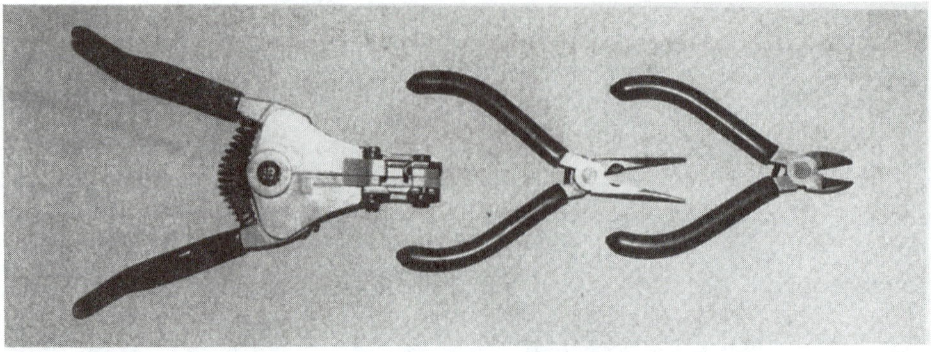

FIGURE 1–22
Wire stripper, pliers, and diagonal cutter

A set of inexpensive *jeweler's screwdrivers* also is useful in electronic assembly. They are necessary to turn the tiny setscrews holding shaft couplers and control knobs.

Nutdrivers are almost as indispensable as screwdrivers. They, too, come individually or as a set with driver shafts that plug into a common handle. Choose those with a hollow shaft. This type allows you to keep a grip on the nut even though the screw on which the nut is mounted is protruding.

2. Pliers, Cutters, and Wire Strippers. *Pliers* are small pincers with long, jagged jaws. They are used for holding small objects or for bending and cutting wire (Figure 1–22). In electronics fabrication, two types are required: *slip-joint* pliers handle the bulk of heavy mechanical assembly; for holding wires in place during soldering and for acting as a heat sink, *needle nose* (or long-nose) pliers are the logical choice. At the start, all you will need is one of each.

Diagonal cutters, also called *dykes,* are used to cut wires or component leads. A diagonal cutter should be made of high-quality tool steel, and its jaws should be well aligned. With a little practice, you can also use diagonal cutters to strip wire. A better approach, however, is to purchase an inexpensive *wire stripper,* either the simple plier type or a compound unit that automatically adjusts to wire size, specifically designed to do the job. With such a tool, the possibility of nicking or gouging a wire is greatly reduced.

3. Wrenches. A *wrench*—a tool with adjustable jaws, lugs, or sockets at one or both ends—is used for holding, twisting, or turning a bolt or nut. One type, of particular interest to us, is the *Allen wrench,* consisting of an L-shaped hexagonal bar of hardened steel either end of which fits the socket of a screw or bolt (Figure 1–23). The Allen wrench is used to install or remove control knobs with small Allen setscrews. A complete set, with a dozen or more wrenches, sells for just a few dollars. No technician should be without one.

4. Metalworking Tools. The more common metalworking tools needed by the electronics technician are shown in Figure 1–24. A *hacksaw* for cutting metal, a *center punch* for marking the center of

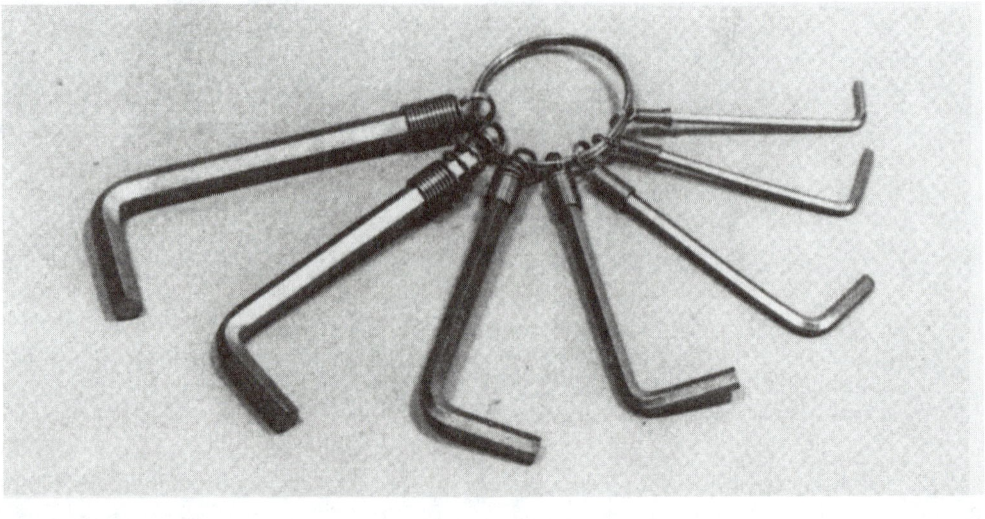

FIGURE 1–23
An Allen wrench has many uses.

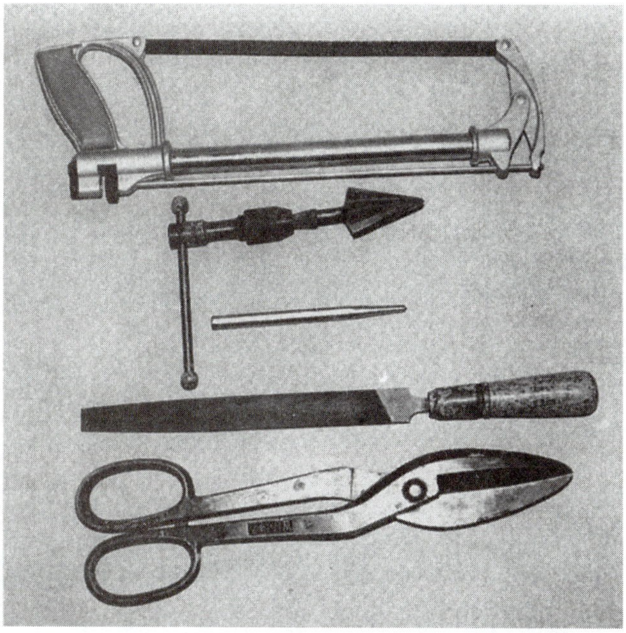

FIGURE 1–24
Metalworking tools

holes to be drilled, a *reamer* to enlarge or shape a hole, a *tin snip* to cut sheet metal, and a set of *files* for forming or smoothing metal surfaces are all tools likely to be familiar to the electronics enthusiast. Two metalworking tools designed to punch and cut holes in sheet metal, however, may require an introduction.

A set of *chassis punches* (Figure 1–25) makes cutting large holes in chassis for sockets, meters, panel lights, and so forth, a breeze. They make neat, clean holes. Choose a set that provides the hole sizes you are likely to use. Keep in mind, though, that you can add individual punches as the need arises.

Another handy chassis cutter is the *nibbling tool,* also shown in Figure 1–25. With it, bite-size chunks of metal are taken out of the chassis in the process of forming practically any shape hole of any required size. A nibbler can be purchased for less than $10. It is an excellent investment.

5. Drills and Drill Bits. Two types of drills need to be considered. The *power hand drill* is indispensable for general drilling in wood, plastic, and metal (Figure 1–26). Select one that has a variable speed control, a chuck capacity of $\frac{1}{4}$ inch or $\frac{3}{8}$ inch, and either a grounded three-conductor cord or a two-conductor cord with double-insulated plastic body. Drill bits, which actually do the cutting, should be of high-speed steel, not carbon steel, as high-speed steel bits have the superior cutting and wearing characteristics required in electronics fabrication. Buy a set that has bits ranging in size from $\frac{3}{32}$ inch to $\frac{3}{8}$ inch.

A drill particularly adaptable for printed circuit board work is the *Dremel Moto Tool,* a high-speed drill and grinder (Figure 1–26). This drill, which can be held comfortably in one hand, accepts drill bits ranging in size from #80 to #30 (the larger number being the smaller bit size). The Dremel Moto Tool can be converted into an excellent printed circuit board drill press by mounting it in one of the many *drill stands* designed specifically to accommodate it (Figure 1–26). A Dremel Moto-Tool

FIGURE 1–25
Sheet metal hole cutters. Left: chassis punch; right: nibbler

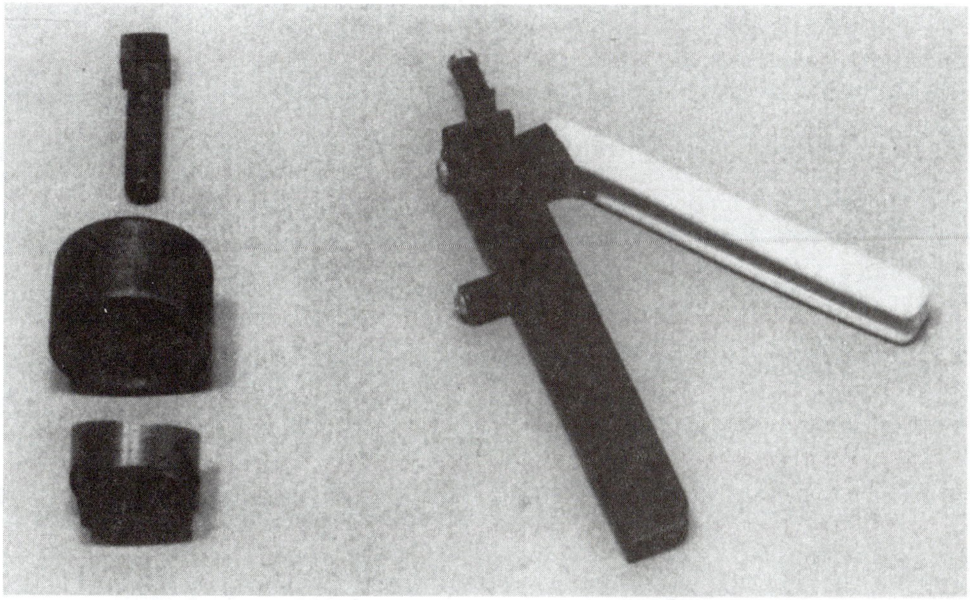

FIGURE 1–26
Drills and drill bits

is essential for those wanting to manufacture their own printed circuit boards.

Tools for Electrical Work

Tools for use in electrical work are needed to secure connections between conductors. Because most connections are still made with solder, soldering and desoldering equipment is emphasized in this book. Nonetheless, wire-wrapping materials and solderless breadboards are also explored.

1. Soldering Equipment. Soldering is the process of joining metal leads, wires, and terminals by melting an alloy of tin and lead (solder) over them. To heat the connection, a *soldering iron* is used (Figure 1–27). Soldering irons come in two basic configurations: guns and pencils. *Guns* are basically used to supply heat to large electrical connections and metal chassis. For general electronics fabrication, only a soldering *pencil* should be used.

Soldering irons have a wattage rating that measures how quickly they transfer heat. A 25- to 35-W iron is a good choice, particularly for printed circuit board fabrication. It should have a well-insulated handle (your hand should be kept cool) and, preferably, a grounded tip to protect static-sensitive components (such as CMOS ICs and JFET transistors). Although controlled temperature and cordless soldering irons are also available, the former (Figure 1–27) are quite expensive (often more than

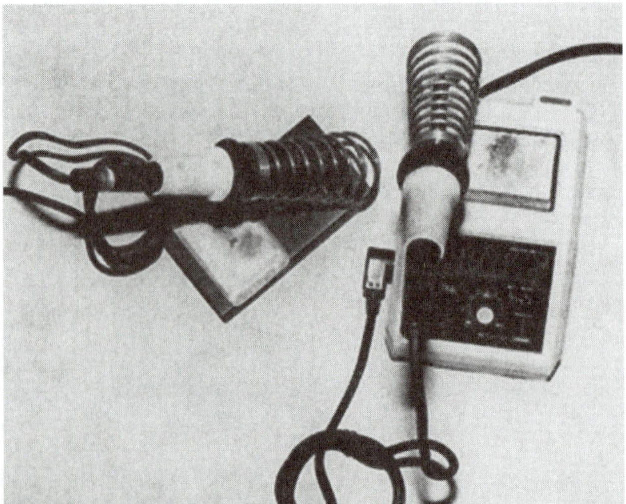

FIGURE 1–27
Soldering equipment

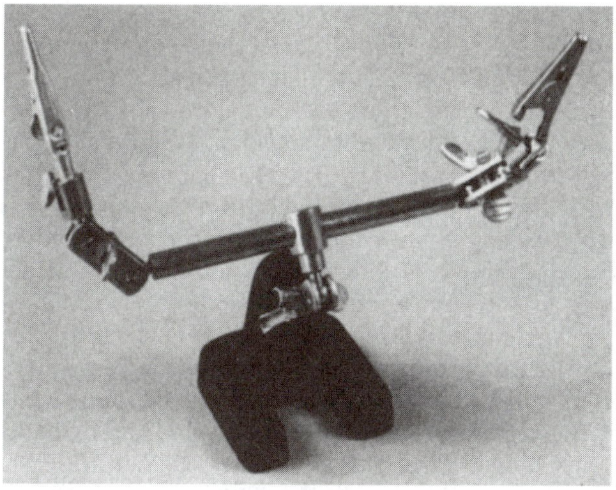

FIGURE 1–28
Third hand

$100) and the latter are used only rarely. As a beginner, you should perhaps stick to the basics, a good-quality solder pencil.

When purchasing solder, choose a 60/40 or 63/37 rosin core solder with a #21 gauge (0.031 inch). You may also wish to buy a "third hand" soldering aid to hold the circuit board during project assembly (Figure 1–28). Such a unit is quite helpful and inexpensive (often less than $6).

The *soldering tip,* the element that actually transfers heat to the connection, is available in two materials and three basic configurations. You can purchase raw copper or nickel-plated copper tips. Choose the plated type; they last up to 10 times as long. Tip shape is, to a large extent, a matter of personal preference. Blunt chisel, pyramid, and needlelike tips are the most popular. For printed circuit board soldering, the needlelike tip is the preferred choice.

2. Desoldering Equipment. Unfortunately, what is often assembled sometimes must be disassembled. When it is necessary to desolder connections, special (though inexpensive) implements are required (Figure 1–29). The rubber suction *bulb* with a Teflon tip draws up molten solder that has been reheated with a soldering iron. A combination bulb and soldering iron is also available. The *desoldering pump* (also known as a solder sucker) uses the action of a spring-loaded plunger to suck up, in one quick action, melted solder from a connection. Finally, there is the *desoldering wick,* a braided copper material that uses capillary action to pull up the hot solder. Any of these tools will do the job of removing solder from an electrical connection. Their selection is based both on the particular job to be done and on personal preference.

3. Wire-Wrapping Equipment. In wire wrapping the stripped ends of a thin wire are tightly wrapped around a square or rectangular terminal post. No soldering is involved in making the connection. Wire wrapping as a breadboarding method is discussed in Chapter 6. Here, we just want to alert you to the tools and materials necessary to do the job, should you choose to use this construction approach at the breadboarding stage.

FIGURE 1–29
Desoldering equipment

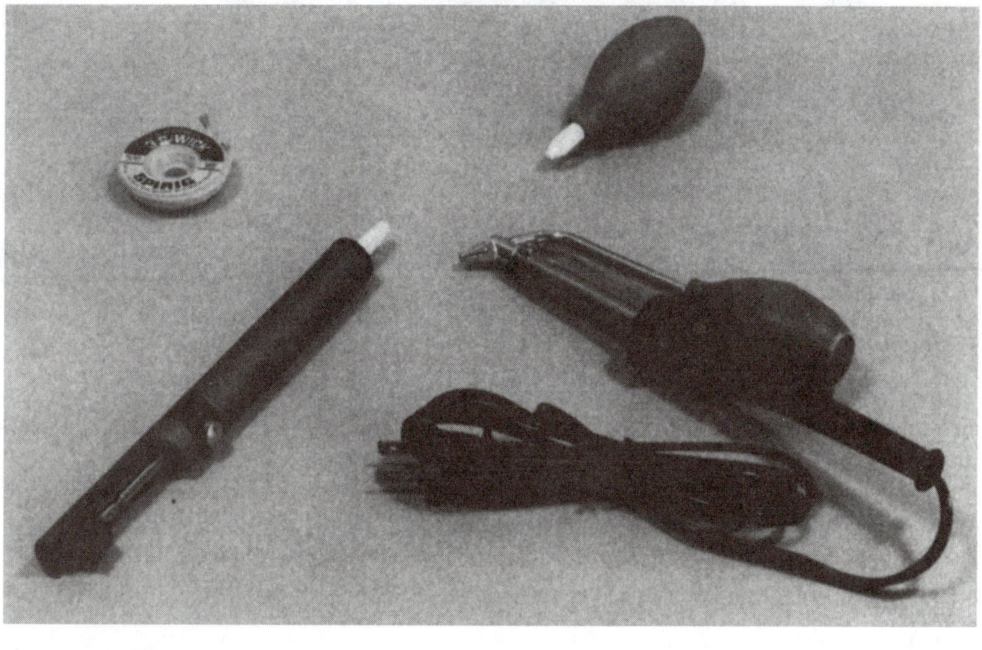

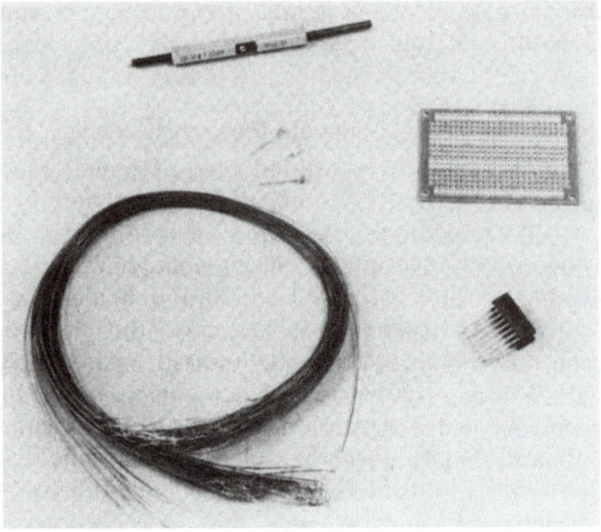

FIGURE 1–30
Wire-wrapping materials

You are going to need a *wire-wrapping/unwrapping/stripping tool* (often referred to simply as a wire-wrap tool). The type shown in Figure 1–30 is available for less than $10. The *wire* you will use is #30 gauge and comes in spools or individually prestripped lengths in five popular colors: red, blue, white, black, and yellow. Special *wire-wrap sockets* are needed when connecting integrated circuits. The pins must be longer than those on the solder type socket and they must be square, not round or flat. Various *terminal posts,* designed specifically for wire wrapping, are also necessary. Component leads will be attached to the non-wire-wrapped side of the terminal post, usually by soldering. Finally, you will need a special *perforated board* on which to mount the sockets and pins. The board is a phenolic material, $\frac{1}{16}''$ thick, with holes spaced 0.10″ apart.

Wire-wrapping equipment is available from a number of sources. OK Machine & Tool Corporation and Vector Electronics Company, Inc. are the leading manufacturers.

4. Solderless Circuit Board. In the early stage of breadboarding, when the circuit design

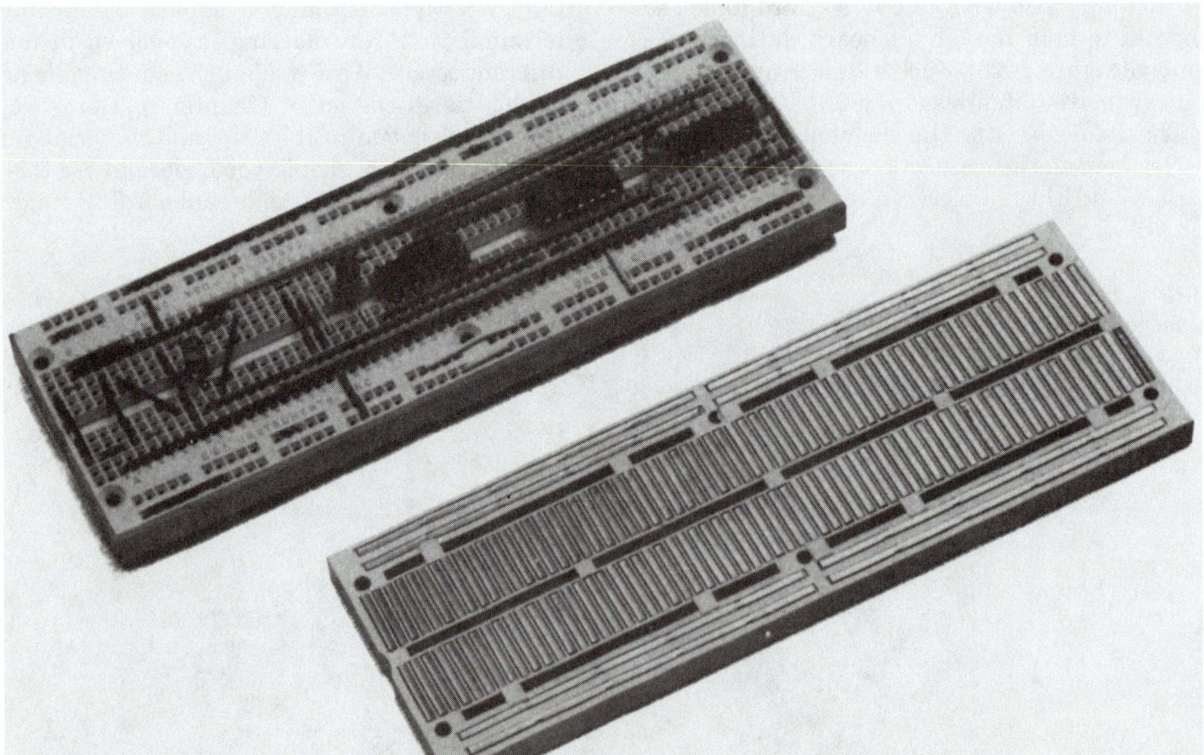

FIGURE 1–31
Solderless circuit board

may be undergoing frequent changes, a quick and easy system of circuit assembly is required. Solderless circuit board provides that method (Figure 1–31). The board consists of a plastic block with arrays of holes spaced 0.10″ apart. Electrical conductors interconnect adjacent rows or columns of holes. The board readily accepts IC pins and the leads of other electronic components. Thus the technician can build up a circuit with reliable connections without having to resort to soldering or wire wrapping.

Some solderless circuit boards are designed with interlocking ridges so that any number can be snapped together to expand the total breadboarding area. You can start out with a piece 2″ × 5″ and as your needs and budget permit, add additional units. In no time you will have a very professional setup for serious experimenting and breadboarding.

One final note: There are a number of tool kits, or caddies, on the market that provide an essential assortment of hand tools in a convenient carrying case. One such kit, from Graymark International, Inc., is shown in Figure 1–32. Prices range from $25 to $50 for the less expensive units.

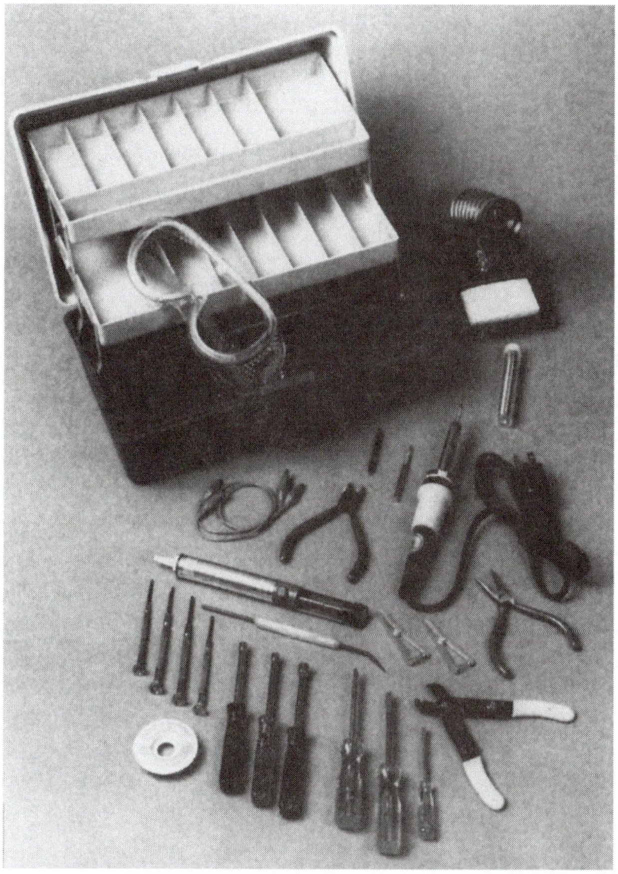

FIGURE 1–32
Tool kit

Additional Tools for Modern Electronic Circuits

Before the advent of printed circuit technology, the tools required for electronics fabrication were basic and few. Today, a screwdriver, needle nose pliers, and soldering iron just aren't enough. The basic tools you will need have been discussed, along with a few of the more specialized ones. But there are other tools and instruments you will want to keep an eye out for. You don't have to rush out and buy them all now; as we move through the fabrication process, we will identify and discuss specific ones. Then you can make the major "buy/borrow/forget it" decision on acquiring them.

> ***Something to Think About***
>
> *Tool catalogs are available for the asking, from manufacturers and distributors alike. Why not begin a collection now? When you receive a new catalog, look through it slowly and carefully, studying the description of each tool. Such catalogs can be an education in themselves.*

SUMMARY

In this chapter the traditional electronics course and how the lecture and lab approach to learning can be supplemented with an electronics fabrication experience were discussed. By examining just what it is electronics technicians do, an appreciation of the need for learning how to design, build, troubleshoot, and document a complete prototype project was gained.

Next, the five-stage design and fabrication process was investigated by probing the features of the (1) design; (2) drawing; (3) experimenting; (4) prototyping; and (5) testing, troubleshooting, and final documentation stages. We then saw how this book is structured around those five stages. We discussed the three-tier project building experience and looked into the Project Report, a summary containing all the necessary written and graphics documentation for the prototype project.

The tools of the trade, on the board, at the computer, and on the bench, were explored. We examined the drafting table, along with the materials that go with it. The basic equipment necessary to make schematic and assembly drawings was described, as well as what is needed to produce the design layout and artwork for printed circuit board fabrication. We probed the outlines of a computer-aided design (CAD) system. Finally, we considered the workbench and its requirements in terms of space, size, construction, and lighting and power needs. We concluded with an inventory of the tools required for mechanical and electronics fabrication.

Before you go on to that actual fabrication, however, you need to be sure that you can protect both your project and yourself. To do that, we examine lab safety, the subject of Chapter 2.

QUESTIONS

1. Most of the electronics courses taught at the college or trade school level are organized around the ____________ and ____________ structure.
2. Electronics ____________ build, repair, test, modify, and install electronic devices and equipment.
3. A project that is hand-assembled to resemble as much as possible the final, mass-produced equipment is known as a ____________.
4. Name the five stages in producing a working prototype project. ____________, ____________, ____________, ____________, ____________.
5. The ____________ ____________ contains all the written and graphics documentation that will accompany the prototype project.
6. Many portable drafting tables have an instrument called a drafting ____________ that allows you to quickly draw straight lines at designated lengths and angles.
7. List three input and three output peripheral devices used with a CAD system.

Input	Output
a. ____________	a. ____________
b. ____________	b. ____________
c. ____________	c. ____________

8. Both the drawing table (board) and the workbench must be bathed in direct and indirect ____________.
9. Although diagonal cutters can be used for stripping wire, a better choice is a ____________ stripper, specifically designed for the job.
10. For general soldering work, a soldering ____________ should never be used, only a soldering ____________.

2 Safety—It's Your Life

OBJECTIVES

In this chapter you will learn

- ☐ Why employers are so safety conscious and why you should be, too.
- ☐ How your eyes, ears, nose, throat, and skin are susceptible to harm from laboratory accidents.
- ☐ What electrical shock is, and how it can affect your heart.
- ☐ How today's solid-state circuits are safer than those of the vacuum tube era.
- ☐ How to avoid danger while working on electrical circuits.
- ☐ How to handle toxic and hazardous chemicals safely.
- ☐ How hand tools can be more dangerous than power tools.
- ☐ How to avoid safety problems when working with power tools.
- ☐ How to protect your voltage-sensitive projects from the "static electricity monster."
- ☐ What first-aid steps to take if an accident occurs in the laboratory.
- ☐ About environmental concerns with regard to product design and development.

Congratulations!

What for? For reading, or at least starting to read, this chapter. There are those who would just as soon skip this chapter and get right to the hands-on material. But hold on a moment; have a little patience—"safety first," as the saying goes.

To protect both yourself and the project you build, you need to become thoroughly familiar with basic electronics laboratory safety procedures. If you want to become an accomplished electronics technician, then now, while you are still in school, is the time to obtain the knowledge and develop the effective safety habits necessary to succeed on the job. We want you to have that success and, along with it, a safe and satisfying experience with electronics.

In this chapter you will see why safety is so essential, so important to you and your colleagues, whether they be students in school or coworkers at the plant. We'll examine why practicing good safety is considered an essential job requirement. We will investigate how exposure to hazardous conditions affects various parts of the human body, and how to minimize the risks arising from electrical shock, contact with toxic chemicals, and the misuse of hand and power tools. We will also analyze how you, by storing static electricity, can be the source of danger, destroying the projects around you. In Appendix A is a comprehensive *electronics safety test.* Be sure you take, and pass, that safety test immediately after reading this chapter.

2.1 SAFETY: WHO CARES?

Who cares about safety? Well, your employer for sure and, we hope, you too. For your employer, safety is primarily an economic and legal issue; for you, it is a personal and, when your colleagues are involved, a moral concern.

Safety as a Part of Your Job Description

Companies take safety very seriously. On the firm's entrance examination, you are just as likely to be asked a question on the safe handling of etching solutions as one on Ohm's law. The reason is the bottom line: Accidents cost money. Let's look at the economic and legal issues from the employer's standpoint and then consider why you should also be sharing this concern for a safe working environment.

Economic and Legal Issues

As an electronics technician, you will be required to perform such tasks as soldering, operating complex test equipment, building and repairing electronic devices, using hand and power tools, and possibly handling toxic and hazardous materials. You will be expected not only to do these assignments well but to do them in such a way that minimizes the danger to equipment, to yourself, and to others around you. In today's electronics environment, it is not uncommon to find printed circuit boards populated with dozens of sensitive integrated circuits that together cost hundreds of dollars. A bolt of static electricity, discharged from you or your clothing, could render the entire circuit mute. In some sophisticated laboratories, oscilloscopes and related pieces of test equipment can cost as much as a new automobile.

But much more serious than damage to equipment is injury to people. The lost hours due to accidents are costing U.S. industry billions of dollars a year. Although accidents will happen, try not to be "accident prone." You can be sure that any company you work for is keenly aware of problems arising from accident litigation. No matter how good you are at troubleshooting complex digital circuits or building sophisticated prototype projects, your value to the company will be seriously diminished if you are costing them money by being a safety risk. Simply stated: Practicing good safety habits makes good economic sense.

Personal and Moral Issues

Being a safety risk to yourself is one thing, but endangering fellow students and coworkers is quite another. No one wants to be around a person with a reputation for accidents; they might be injured, too. And if no one will work with you, how can you keep your job?

You have a responsibility to watch out for your safety and that of others around you. It's like driving a car. Every time you get behind the wheel, the lives of other drivers and pedestrians are in your hands. They are counting on you to stay to the right of a center line and stop at a red light. You and your colleagues in electronics are depending on each other, too. Everyone needs to be part of the safety solution, not the safety problem.

Body Parts Susceptible to Damage

The human body is a fragile thing. It is easily cut, bruised, burned, irritated, shocked, and poisoned. External organs associated with our five senses and internal organs vital to our very lives are susceptible to injury in the school or workplace.

Covering Your Five Senses

Although bionics is the current rage, and electronics has contributed mightily to its development, most would agree that the real thing is still the best. To keep our eyes, ears, nose, throat, and skin safe from harm, we must first see how they can be hurt when exposed to hazardous conditions.

Injury to the *eyes* can cause permanent blindness. Small objects, such as clipped component leads and flying solder balls, can stab and burn sensitive parts of the eye. Furthermore, a splash of acid or the spray from a cleaning solvent can, at the very least, irritate; at the worst, it can destroy the entire eye. Even a bright flash of light from a xenon strobe tube, for example, can cause a serious accident. Even if you are only momentarily blinded, it may be enough to make you susceptible to other forms of injury.

Loud sounds and high-pitched tones can be very irritating to the *ears*. In extreme cases they may cause temporary or even permanent hearing loss. It isn't just heavy metal rock bands that can produce such noises. They can be found right in the electronics laboratory.

You may not think your *nose* is vulnerable to dangers found in the laboratory, yet toxic fumes can be irritating to the membranes lining the nasal passages. More importantly, the nose is one entry leading to the lungs. Damage there can be very serious, as it may affect your ability to breathe properly.

Your mouth, or *throat,* can also be an opening for foreign and hazardous particles. Of course, you wouldn't knowingly put any acid solution or solder wire (which is 40 percent lead) in your mouth. But if acid gets under your fingernails, and you bite your nails, you could be in trouble. Also, inadvertent chewing on a strip of solder is not unheard of. The greatest danger, however, lies in using your mouth as a temporary vise to hold small pieces of hardware, tiny transistors, and short strips of wire.

FIGURE 2–1
Current flow

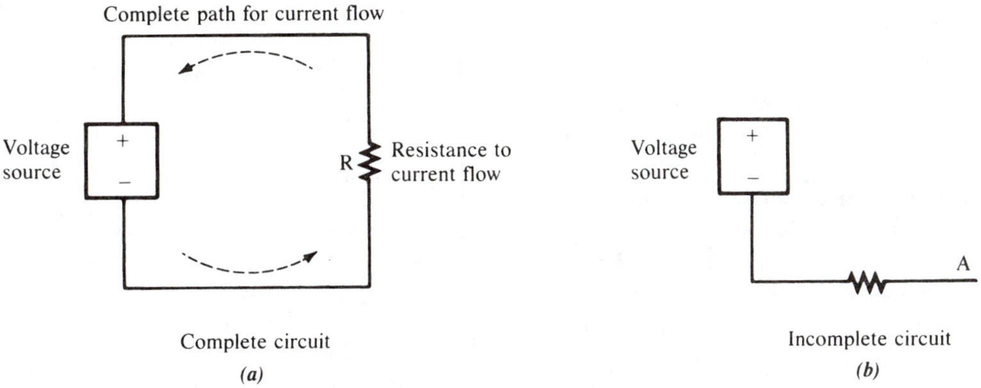

Accidental swallowing, or a friendly slap on the back from your lab partner, and presto—it's time to have your stomach pumped.

Then there is the *skin,* the outer layer designed to protect the entire body. Destruction of nerve endings as a result of electrical shock, burns from soldering irons and hot components, acid irritations, and, of course, common cuts, bruises, and abrasions can occur in an environment where safety is lax.

Clearly, your entire body is subject to harm. However, there is no cause for alarm, only a healthy concern. Shortly, you will see how you can eliminate most of these dangers by taking simple precautions and following commonly accepted safety practices.

At the Heart of the Matter

Of all the internal organs, the *heart* is certainly the most vital. If it stops, even for only 4 to 6 minutes, death can result. Many factors can cause the heart to stop beating. Here, however, only the most relevant one—**electrocution**, or **electrical shock**—is considered. Let's see just what electrical shock is and how it can destroy the heart.

Electrical shock is the passage of current through the body. Current flows through the human body, as it does anywhere else, when a complete circuit exists. Such a circuit is shown in Figure 2–1a. A source of voltage and a conducting path (shown in the figure as having a given amount of resistance) are all that is required. Note, however, that the path for current flow must be complete. In Figure 2–1b no current flows to point A. The reason is that although it has a place to come from (in this case, the battery's negative terminal), it has no place to go (in this case, the battery's positive terminal).

The same is true when the human body is the conducting path. As illustrated in Figure 2–2a, even though the person is touching the positive terminal of the voltage source, he is in no danger. As long as he is wearing insulated boots, current can find no path through him to the negative, or ground, terminal of the battery. However, if he completes the circuit by, for instance, touching the negative battery terminal with the other hand (possibly through a

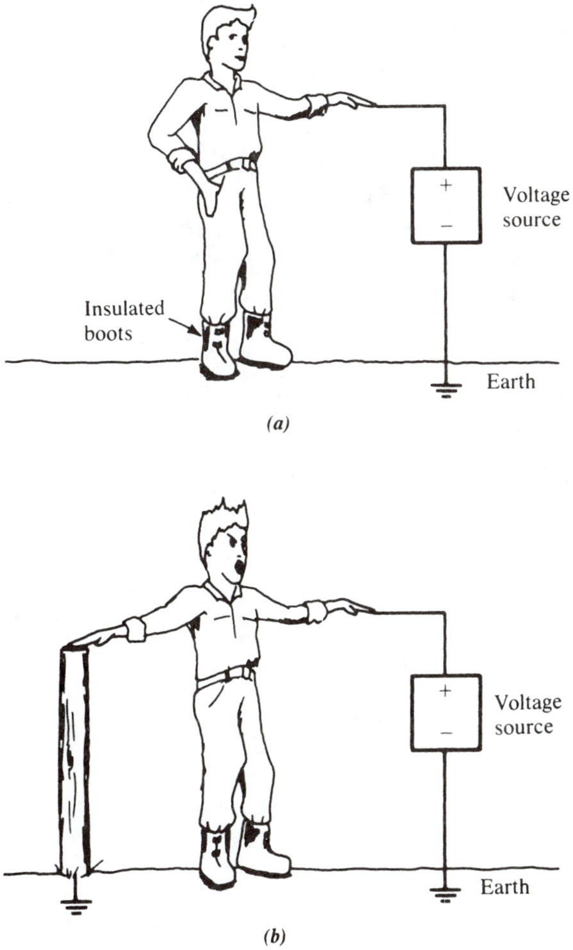

FIGURE 2–2
The human body as a conducting path

ground connection), current will indeed flow, as in Figure 2–2b. Just how much current depends on a number of factors.

One way to increase current flow is to reduce circuit resistance. Body resistance may be quite high if skin moisture is low and there are no cuts or abrasions at the point of electrical contact. In such cases, little current will flow and only a mild shock may result. Nonetheless, if any of these factors is reversed, resistance will be lowered and large amounts of current can result. If the path for current flow is through the chest, the heart can receive a lethal dose of current, an electrical shock. The heart will then most likely go into fibrillation (rapid, irregular muscle contraction) and stop beating.

How much current is enough to kill? Although the amount varies widely and especially depends on the organs that current passes through, it is less than you probably think. Figure 2–3 gives the effects of even mild doses of current. A mere 1 to 20 milliamperes (mA) can cause a painful sensation; at 30 mA, breathing may stop; and 100 to 300 mA is enough to cause electrocution. Clearly, even small amounts of unwanted current through the body can be very dangerous to your health.

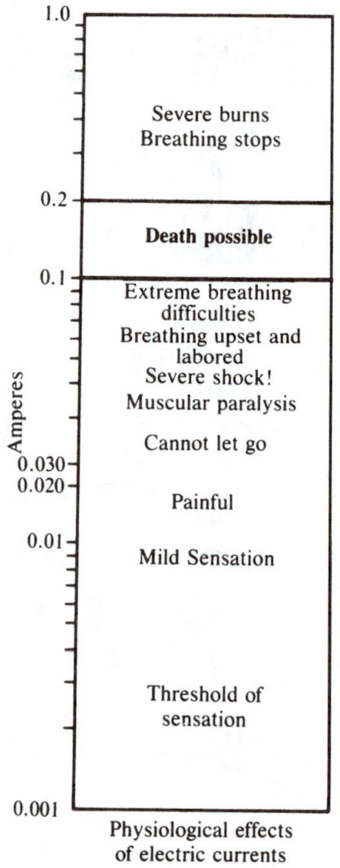

FIGURE 2–3
How much current is enough to kill?

> ***Something to Think About***
>
> *The amount of current flow is equal to the voltage divided by the resistance—Ohm's law. Using an analog or digital multimeter, why not measure the current flowing between your hands by grabbing the meter's probes? Are you surprised at the results?*

2.2 WHERE THE DANGER LIES

It is time to look at where in the school laboratory or workplace the danger to your safety lies. Problem areas and practical solutions will be identified. Although specific advice in the form of "do's and don't's" will be given, keep in mind that maintaining a safe working environment isn't complicated. It involves just four simple rules:

1. Keep your work area neat and orderly. Being able to see what you have and what you are doing will eliminate many problems.
2. Be alert and attentive at all times. Distractions of any kind can only leave you open to risk.
3. Know the correct safety procedures. If you are not sure how to operate safely a piece of test equipment, a tool, or any machinery, ask your instructor. There is a safe way to do everything. Learn what it is—and do it.
4. If an accident does occur, know what action to take. Be familiar with the basic first-aid measures that could mean the difference between a quick recovery and a serious medical complication.

Electricity: The Tingle That Hurts

Let's examine how you can get into trouble when working with electricity, how to avoid major problems, and what few simple first-aid steps you should take if an accident does occur.

The Problem—The Solution

The problem is that there's both good news and bad news. The good news is that today's electronic devices, many of which are solid state and battery powered, are much safer than their predecessors of the vacuum tube era. Instead of circuits with voltages in the hundreds and currents in amperes, we now have equipment operating on 5 to 12 volts (V) dc and drawing currents of less than 50 to 100 mA. The bad news is that many systems, even though employing solid-state circuitry, do not get their power directly from a battery but rather from the ac line. Any electronic project that is plugged into the wall outlet is a potential death trap.

The problem with ac is twofold. An ordinary wall outlet supplies up to 25 A of current, certainly enough under many conditions to kill you. In addition, ac tends to "hang on." The victim can be prevented from releasing the source of voltage, thus increasing the damage to the body.

However, circuits powered from an ac line are not the only problem. A serious shock can be had from many circuits, dc or ac, containing charged capacitors, faulty wiring, or shorted components. Treat every electronic circuit as potentially hazardous. Electricity, though not to be unduly feared, must certainly be respected.

The solution to being safe while working with electricity is to follow some basic "do's and don't's." Here are the more important ones:

The Do's

- ☐ *Do* work with one hand behind your back while testing live circuits. In that way if you complete the path for current flow, at least it won't be through your heart.
- ☐ *Do* use an isolation transformer while working on ac-powered equipment. This device isolates the powered equipment from the power source, adding a strong measure of safety.
- ☐ *Do* make sure that all capacitors (components that store an electrical charge) are discharged before beginning troubleshooting. Use an insulated screwdriver to short out capacitor leads.
- ☐ *Do* use three-conductor grounded line cords and polarized plugs with ac-operated equipment. Both items reduce the danger from short-circuited chassis.
- ☐ *Do* keep your fingers out of live chassis. Test all circuits with a voltmeter or specially designed test lamps.

The Don't's

- ☐ *Don't* install or remove any electronic components while the circuit is connected to a power source. Following this procedure will protect you as well as the component.
- ☐ *Don't* overfuse. Using a fuse with a higher rating than is recommended only defeats the fuse's purpose.
- ☐ *Don't* work with wet hands. As noted earlier, if body resistance goes down, current flow goes up. Even sweat can moisten the hands enough to cause excessive current flow.
- ☐ *Don't* cut wires carrying electricity. Again, it isn't just the ac line cord that is lethal. Assume all wires carry enough current to harm you.
- ☐ *Don't* disconnect electrical devices from the wall outlet by pulling on the line cord; pull the plug handle.

First Aid

With severe electrical shock, you must think not only of the victim but of yourself as well. You don't want to become part of the problem. After sending for help, immediately turn off the source of power. If that can't be done, do not attempt to pull the victim away; you will only get shocked yourself. Use a nonconducting material, such as a two-by-four piece of lumber, to remove the victim from the circuit. Once the victim is free and lying down, check for signs of breathing. If there are none, begin artificial respiration. If a heartbeat cannot be detected, and you are trained to do so, apply cardiopulmonary resuscitation (CPR).

In less traumatic cases, where electrical shock is not life-threatening, keep the victim calm and send for expert medical help.

Exposure to Toxic and Hazardous Chemicals

Let's examine the problems associated with potentially dangerous chemicals and how best to protect yourselves when working around various sprays and liquids, and what first-aid procedures to take if something goes wrong.

The Problem—The Solution

With toxic and hazardous chemicals, you should be concerned about inhaling vapors, swallowing liquids, acid burns on the skin, contact with the eyes, and the overall danger of fire and explosion. Chemicals such as etching solutions, spray paints, component cleaners, glues, photographic developing solutions, and general household solvents, all of which are likely to be found in the electronics laboratory, can cause health hazards if improperly used or stored. To minimize risks, here are some do's and don't's:

The Do's

- ☐ *Do* read the labels on all the chemicals you use. Pay particular attention to printed warnings.
- ☐ *Do* work in well-ventilated areas. This is particularly important when using paint and chemical sprays.

- ☐ *Do* wear eye protection when working around hazardous chemicals.
- ☐ *Do* wear rubber gloves when working with acid solutions. Be sure they are washed or thrown away when work is done.
- ☐ *Do* hold printed circuit boards securely with tongs when placing them in or removing them from an acid solution.
- ☐ *Do* immediately clean all tools that have come in contact with hazardous chemicals. This will prevent someone from inadvertently touching the toxic substances.

The Don'ts

- ☐ *Don't* pour solvents, paints, or acids down the drain. In addition to being a health hazard, in many localities it is illegal.
- ☐ *Don't* transfer chemicals to unlabeled containers.
- ☐ *Don't* inhale fumes from soldering paste. Such fumes can be harmful to your lungs.
- ☐ *Don't* leave any chemicals in open containers where they can be splashed or spilled. Put all unused chemicals safely away, preferably in a locked metal cabinet.
- ☐ *Don't* place any chemicals near sparks or open flames. Assume that all chemicals are highly combustible.

First Aid

In an emergency, follow all first-aid directions printed on the label of the chemical you have been using. Read the label before use so that you won't be confused if trouble develops. For example, some instructions tell you to induce vomiting if the substance is swallowed; others tell you not to. Do what the label says and call a physician immediately.

More specifically, in the case of acid burns and eye irritations, wash and flush thoroughly with cold running water. If your lab is equipped with an *eyewash station,* be sure you understand its proper use. When exposure to vapors has occurred, get the victim outside in the open air.

Safety Hazards Caused by the Misuse of Hand Tools

In this section hand tool safety is discussed. For convenience hand tools are defined as those that are held in the hand and are not powered by electricity.

The Problem—The Solution

Hand tools can be more dangerous than power tools. Why? Because they are used more often and we tend to dismiss their risk. Do not be deceived. A slip of a hacksaw blade or the launching of a loose hammerhead can maim you—or someone else—for life. Whether it's a puncture from a file tang, a gash from a saw blade, or a slit from a knife, hand tools can do plenty of damage. To avoid the obvious dangers, consider this list of important do's and don't's:

The Do's

- ☐ *Do* keep hands free of dirt, grease, or oil when using hand tools.
- ☐ *Do* keep hand tools sharp. A dull tool is more dangerous than a sharp one because with a dull tool you tend to apply more pressure, increasing the likelihood of slippage.
- ☐ *Do* cut away from your body, not toward it.
- ☐ *Do* secure all small pieces of work in a vise or with appropriate clamps.
- ☐ *Do* put sharp tools away when not in use. Leaving knives, awls, and punches lying around for someone to lean on is extremely dangerous.

The Don'ts

- ☐ *Don't* carry hand tools in your pockets; they may injure you or someone else.
- ☐ *Don't* use a file without a handle. An exposed file tang can easily puncture your hand or wrist.
- ☐ *Don't* toss any hand tools to a neighbor. Flying objects of any kind are never to be seen in the electronics laboratory.
- ☐ *Don't* run your hands over the edges of sheet metal. These edges are sharp and can cause severe cuts.

First Aid

Injury from hand tools usually results in a cut or burn. What specific action to take when a laceration occurs depends on its severity. In all cases, clean the wound, apply direct pressure, and elevate the injured body part. With regard to burns, flush the affected area with cold water (do not apply ice directly) and cover with a clean cloth, then seek medical aid.

Safety Hazards Caused by the Misuse of Power Tools

Power tools are defined as those that use electricity, usually in the form of ac from the wall outlet. Let's look at the problems and solutions for this area, the do's and don't's, and the appropriate first-aid procedures.

The Problem—The Solution

Power tools can burn, cut, scrape, and even hit you with flying objects. Because most of them plug directly into the wall outlet, they can also give you a nasty electrical shock. Injuries from power tools occur when long hair or unsuitable clothing gets caught in a revolving machine, when small objects fly out of a drill press vise, when guards or safety devices are removed, or when a hot soldering iron is left where someone can lean against it. To prevent such injuries, practice the correct safety procedures as outlined by your instructor, and follow these do's and don't's:

The Do's

- ☐ *Do* turn on and off all power tools yourself. Do not allow others to do it for you.
- ☐ *Do* make sure all objects being drilled or cut are securely fastened. Small objects, and especially sheet metal, should be held in a vise, clamp, or suitable gripping tool such as pliers or vise grips.
- ☐ *Do* see to it that all implements and adjusting tools are removed from the work area.
- ☐ *Do* remove the chuck key from a drill press before turning on the machine. A flying chuck key is a frequent cause of injury in the laboratory.
- ☐ *Do* ease up on the drill pressure as you break through the work. This will reduce the possibility of the material's "grabbing."
- ☐ *Do* grasp a soldering iron only by the handle. Don't reach for a falling soldering iron—let it fall.
- ☐ *Do* return a soldering iron to its holder. It should be in one of two places: your hand or the holder.

The Don't's

- ☐ *Don't* ever leave power tools unattended. If the tool is on, stay with it until it is off—and until all parts have stopped moving.
- ☐ *Don't* wear clothing or accessories (jewelry) that can get tangled in revolving machine parts.
- ☐ *Don't* distract others while they are using power tools. If distractions cause problems with hand tools, the same is doubly true for power equipment.
- ☐ *Don't* stand in the direct "throw" of any machine. Don't line yourself up with a revolving saw blade or spinning grinding wheel.
- ☐ *Don't* remove guards or safety devices from power tools. They have been installed for a good reason; keep them in place.
- ☐ *Don't* put your face too close to moving machinery. Metal chips and oil spray can cause eye and skin injury.
- ☐ *Don't* test a soldering iron with your hand. Assume that all soldering irons are hot. Test them by attempting to melt a piece of solder.
- ☐ *Don't* hand a soldering iron directly to another person. Instead, return it to its holder. The other person can take it from there.

First Aid

Injuries resulting from misuse of power tools are similar to those that occur with hand tools, so the first-aid procedures are essentially the same. The accident itself, however, may be more severe. Send for help immediately, then follow the appropriate first-aid measures.

Project Safety

Although electronic circuits can do you harm, you can also damage them; you can zap as well as be zapped. In this section we will see how **static electricity** can destroy the projects we build. We will examine how this monster is created, what its effects are, and how we can cure its most troublesome characteristics by attempting to keep it in its place. Practicing good safety isn't just for us; it's also for our projects.

The Static Electricity Monster

Static electricity is a stationary charge. As such, it is a potential (voltage) waiting to go somewhere (Figure 2–4). If that charge gets to a sensitive circuit, it can destroy the circuit. In the normal course of your work, it is possible to build up a static charge of more than 50,000 V. But today's solid-state circuits don't need anything like that kind of voltage to render them useless. In some cases, less than a few volts of static electricity is all that it takes.

You have felt the effects of a static charge many times. When you walk across a shaggy carpet on a dry, winter day, electrons are literally torn off the rug and deposited all over your body. You become a walking reservoir of negative (static) charges. When you reach for a metal doorknob, which is neutral with regard to potential, the electrons on your hand jump to the knob (Figure 2–5a). An instant before the jump, the air is ionized and a spark is created. You don't have to see the spark to know that there has been a transfer of charged particles—the pain in your fingertips lets you know. That jump of electrical charges, from a more negative source (you) to a relatively neutral source, can damage sensitive circuits. If you reach for a CMOS (complementary metal-oxide semiconductor) integrated circuit instead of a doorknob, both you and the IC may feel the pain (Figure 2–5b)—in the circuit's case, perhaps enough to destroy it.

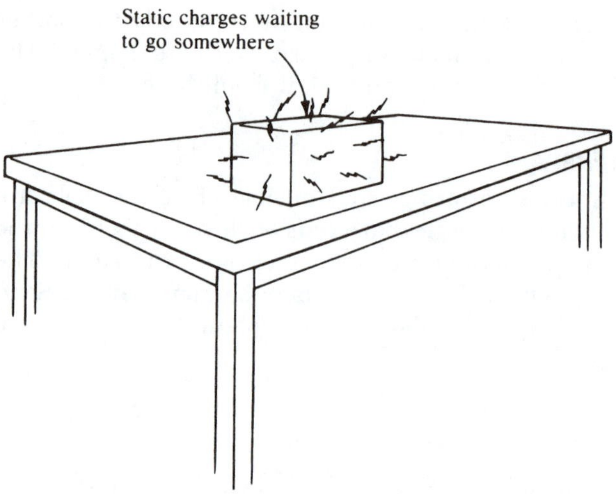

FIGURE 2–4
Static charge

How the Static Charge Is Created

The most common way of creating a static charge is through friction, in which electrons are torn off one surface and accumulate on another. Any time objects are rubbed together, friction is created. If the substances are dissimilar materials, the accumulated charge can be considerable. If one or both of the elements are nonconducting, the charge remains for a long time. It has no place to go. On the other hand, if both materials are good conductors, the charges will leak off quickly, and little danger exists. The solution, then, is either to keep charged insulating materials away from sensitive circuits or to make sure the charge is bled away before it can do any damage.

Materials Susceptible to Damage

Any integrated circuit in the MOS (metal-oxide semiconductor) family can easily be destroyed by static discharge. In addition, many transistors

FIGURE 2–5
Static charge

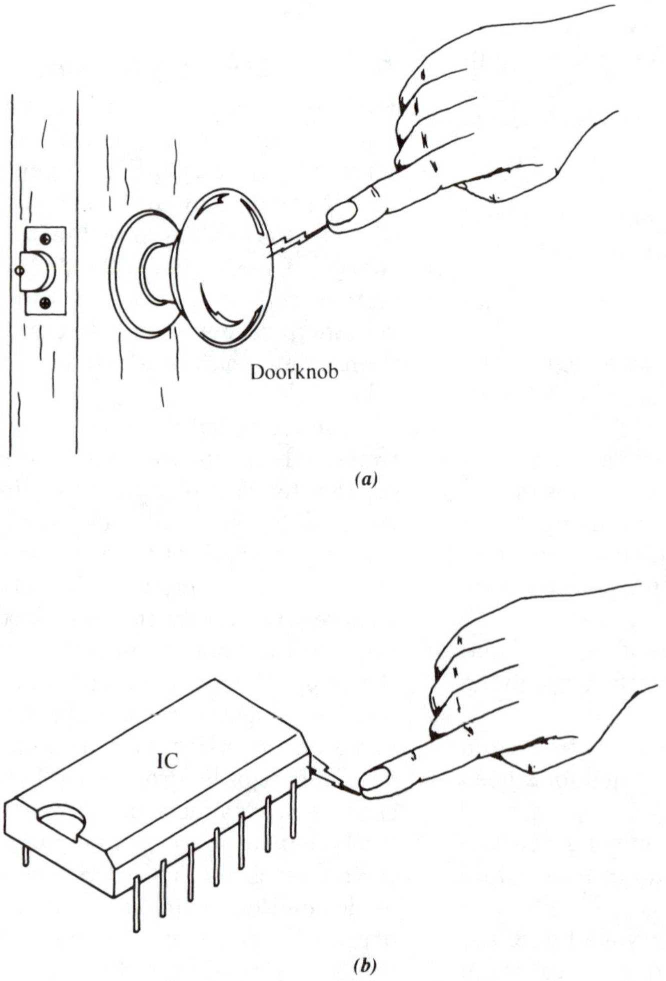

(FETs, for example) are subject to the same effect. If it's a solid-state circuit (and what isn't today?), assume that the circuit is susceptible to damage from static electricity. This will not be true in all cases, but it is best to proceed as though it were. Following basic electrostatic discharge (ESD) safety procedures for all circuits is not difficult. Get in the habit of doing it.

Protecting Your Circuits

One way to reduce the risk from static electricity is to keep the room's humidity high. With high humidity there is a greater conducting path, and thus an electrostatic buildup will leak away much more easily.

The key to protecting circuits, however, is to try to bring everything around you to a common potential. If there is no difference in charge, there is no voltage, and therefore no static buildup. For example, if you're grounded and the integrated circuits you are working with are grounded, there is no difference in charge between you and them. There is no problem (Figure 2–6). Here is a list of what you can do to keep you and the circuits you're working on at the same potential:

- ☐ Be sure all MOS-type integrated circuits remain packaged in antistatic materials until used. These materials consist of specially coated plastic carriers, conductive foam, or aluminum foil. The idea is to keep all pins of an IC shorted together and thus at the same potential. In that way no charge can build up between them.
- ☐ When handling MOS components, avoid touching the pins. That will keep any charge you might have accumulated off the component leads, which are, of course, connected to the solid-state material within the IC package.
- ☐ Never install or remove integrated circuits while power is still applied to the circuit. The sudden voltage jolt that could result may damage them.
- ☐ If possible, use an antistatic wrist strap. The strap brings you to ground potential. Assuming your components are there too, no charge can build up.
- ☐ Use a soldering iron with a grounded tip. In that way no static charge will transfer to sensitive components while they are being soldered in the circuit.

The idea is to prevent a static buildup in the first place. If that is not possible, at least make sure that any such charge has a path to leak away. Doing that will ensure safe operation for your projects.

FIGURE 2–6
Common potential

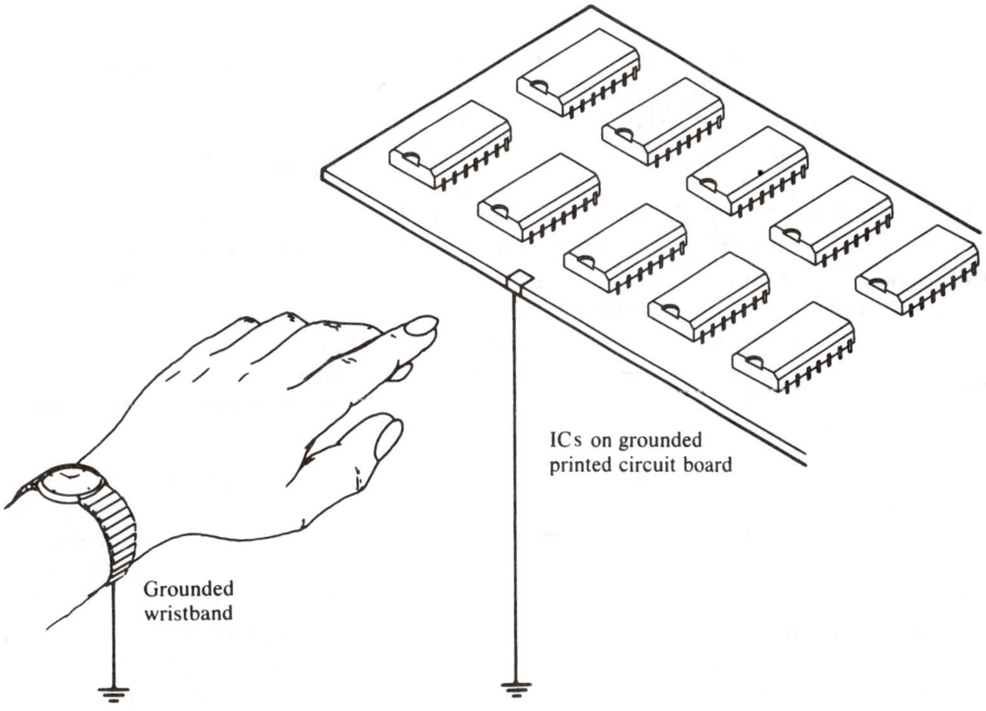

Environmental Concerns

A moment ago we discussed exposure to toxic and hazardous chemicals. We saw how handling such materials can, if one is not vigilant, have a detrimental effect on those working in a school laboratory or industrial setting. Broader issues of environmental concern have begun to surface, however, and will assume greater significance for the electronics industry and those employed in it, in the decades to come. In this concluding section you need to see why you, the prototype electronics technician, should be interested in such matters and what your role might be in workplace environmental protection.

Why You Should Be Concerned

There are at least two significant reasons why you must become familiar with and concerned about your company's role in environmental protection. *First,* the entire electronics industry is "going green," and for good reasons. Companies such as Intel, Tektronix, and 3M, to name but a few, are spending millions of dollars a year disposing of everyday toxic waste—the chemicals and other substances used to manufacture semiconductors, printed circuit boards, and other products. In some cases, with certain solvents and metals, it costs more to dispose of them than to buy them. Ways have to be found to either reduce the demand for such materials or recycle them more efficiently. Every employee at an electronics firm, whether it be a large or small enterprise, has to be part of that solution. As an electronics design and fabrication technician involved in prototyping, you're at the front end of the chain of production, and you will be expected to do your part in dealing with the company's environmental problems.

There is a *second,* and perhaps more relevant, reason why you in particular will be involved with environmental issues, most notably those of waste generation. Emphasis is now shifting from waste disposal on the back end to toxin use up front. In other words, environmental concerns are becoming firmly entrenched in product design and production. For example, Texas Instruments was planning to make a device with a mercury switch. Even though safeguards had been incorporated to deal with the mercury, the firm decided to redo the design using steel balls instead. The point is that you, working with the design and fabrication of prototype projects, will need to involve yourself with "green design," electronic products that are environmentally friendly from the start.

Your Role in the "Greening" of Your Company

As we have seen, your role here is primarily up front, at the design end. It is simply no longer good enough to clean up the mess—it shouldn't be generated in the first place. As the mercury switch example indicates, you want to be aware of components, materials, and fabrication processes that are environmentally sensitive—and help design these materials and processes into the products your company creates.

How do you learn about such matters? First, you adopt a positive attitude about environmental concerns—that is, don't fight the revolution, join it. Second, read all you can on the subject, in newspapers, magazines, trade journals, and books. Third, talk to coworkers and others who share your interest and concern. Network and exchange information.

If all this seems a bit overwhelming for you and your industry, understand that those in electronics are used to rapid change and development. Fortunately, our industry is better positioned than most, in temperament, outlook, and experience, to deal with the new environmental concerns.

> **Something to Think About**
>
> *If your school laboratory does not already have a posted listing of safety do's and don't's, why not create one? Distill the list of do's and don't's presented in Chapter 2 to create the poster.*

SUMMARY

Congratulations again—assuming, of course, that you did indeed read this chapter on safety. We dealt in general terms, discussing first just why it is so important to care about safety. Then, after looking at what body parts are susceptible to harm, we focused on where the dangers lie. We examined the risks related to electrical shock, toxic and hazardous chemicals, the misuse of hand and power tools, the dangers of static electricity to projects, and industrywide environmental concerns. In the chapters to come you will be reminded of what is presented here. You will also read about additional safety precautions when specific pieces of equipment and construction procedures are introduced. Now, before you rush on to Chapter 3, don't forget to take the safety test in Appendix A.

In Chapter 3, after first looking at design and designers, we examine the fundamentals of an electronic system. We explore the two-step design process while delving into the workings of the Sample and Exercise Projects. We conclude with a look at computer-based circuit design, simulation, and analysis.

QUESTIONS

1. As an electronics technician you will be required to perform your tasks in such a way as to minimize the ____________ to equipment, to yourself, and to others around you.
2. Even a bright flash of light from a xenon strobe tube can cause ____________ blindness.
3. Toxic ____________ can irritate the membranes lining the nasal passages of your nose.
4. Electrical shock is the passage of ____________ through the body.
5. Any electronic project that is plugged into the wall outlet is a potential ____________ ____________.
6. When testing "live" circuits, you should work with one ____________ behind your back.
7. With toxic and hazardous ____________, we are concerned about inhaling vapors, swallowing liquids, acid burns on the skin, contact with the eyes, and the overall danger of fire and explosion.
8. Hand tools can be more dangerous than power tools because they are used more often and we tend to ____________ their risk.
9. Don't ever reach for a falling ____________ ____________—let it fall.
10. An integrated circuit in the MOS family can easily be destroyed by a strong ____________ ____________.

3 The Design Process—An Idea Is Born

OBJECTIVES

In this chapter you will learn

- ☐ How electronic products and services are created to solve a particular need.
- ☐ What personality characteristics and technical background make for a good electronics designer.
- ☐ How design problems and solutions are classified for easy identification and better understanding.
- ☐ How electronic circuits combine with input and output transducers to form electronic systems.
- ☐ How the four active components—vacuum tubes, transistors, integrated circuits, and microprocessors—switch or regulate current flow.
- ☐ How passive components, such as resistors, capacitors, diodes, coils, and transformers, help the active components do their job.
- ☐ How to select and acquire electronic components.
- ☐ About Total Quality Management (TQM).
- ☐ What a Concepts and Requirements Document does to explain the project goals, objectives, and responsibilities.
- ☐ What design drawings are required to illustrate system operation, circuit function, and packaging concept.
- ☐ How the Concepts and Requirements Document and design drawings are produced for the Exercise and Sample Projects.
- ☐ The theory of operation for the Variable Power Supply and 3-Channel Color Organ.
- ☐ How computer-based design tools allow us to design, simulate, and analyze electronic circuits.
- ☐ How **Electronics Workbench, Multisim V6.2**, works as a virtual laboratory to aid in the design process.

"What will they think of next?" We are all a bit awed by the explosion of new electronic products and services. Just how did microwave ovens, VCRs, ATMs, handheld wireless devices, personal GPS devices, and digital this, digital that, come about? Did the idea just pop into someone's head, or was there a perceived need for the product or service? How, in other words, is electronics design done?

In this chapter, we find out. After all, we can't build something if we don't know what to build. We first have to have an idea for a new product or service, then we have to refine that idea by specifying exactly what we want and how we intend to develop it. This chapter looks at how this is done by examining electronics design: what it is, the type of people who do it, and the basic methodology involved. We will analyze the **systems approach** to electronics design by studying the fundamentals of electronics design and by outlining the two-step design process. We will look at the important issue of Total Quality Management (TQM). Then, we will introduce the Sample Project, the Variable Power Supply, and the Exercise Project, the 3-Channel Color Organ. These projects, which are carried from chapter to chapter as the subject of electronics design and fabrication unfolds, will provide practical examples of the electronics design process.

Finally, since it is possible to both design a circuit and simulate its operation on a computer, we look at a software package that does just that—**Electronics Workbench, Multisim V6.2**. Using this program as an example, we see what computer-based circuit design, simulation, and analysis is all about.

3.1 ELECTRONICS DESIGN: PROBLEMS IN SEARCH OF SOLUTIONS

In this section we give some examples of electronics design and the kind of people who are involved in it. We will also explore a design methodology that is based on the identification of certain problem and solution categories.

Design and Designers

First, let's see how electronic products and services are created to solve a particular need and then look at the creators themselves.

Creating Products and Services

Why are our homes, offices, and factories, along with our vast communications and transportation systems, filled with electronic devices? Could it be because many of today's problems demand solutions in the form of electronic products and services? Clearly, this must be so. Let's look at some examples:

- Burglaries have increased dramatically in your neighborhood. What can you do? You can begin a neighborhood watch, hire a patrol service, or buy a kennel of guard dogs. But consider electronics. Electronic burglar alarm products, from the simple latch-buzzer type to sophisticated intrusion-detection systems, can be installed to discourage would-be robbers. Electronics clearly has a role to play in solving this problem.
- You want to know how fast you're traveling while out on your daily bike ride. You need a bicycle attachment that will monitor the bike's speed. Mechanical speedometers have been doing that reasonably well for years. Today, however, you can buy electronic versions that will not only give speed in miles per hour but, at the push of a button, tell you the elapsed time of travel, projected time of arrival, distance traveled, distance to go, and, of course, time of day.
- Your local bank wants to provide its customers with 24-hour basic banking services. What are the options? The bank could remain open 24 hours a day, or it could set up minibanks at gas stations that are open around the clock. However, banks all over the world discovered a better solution when they developed the computerized electronic automated teller machine (ATM). After all, computers can work unattended any time, night or day.
- You own a medium-sized stationery store and you want instant inventory information. You could hire more personnel to monitor every item that comes in and goes out of the store. At the end of the day they would tally up what items were still on hand. Even if you were willing to hire the necessary extra workers, though, it is doubtful that they could provide the instant information you demand. An electronic cash register with computerized inventory control is the product and service you are looking for.

Electronics can't solve all our problems, and, as we know, it can create a few difficulties of its own; but in a great many cases, the electronic solution is the best solution. For the foreseeable future, countless new electronic products and services will need to be designed and produced. Let's take a look at the people who will be doing the creating.

The Designer

Who designs or creates electronic products and services? Are they engineers, designers, technicians, or just plain tinkerers? Actually, designers can be any of the above. You don't have to be an electronics engineer with a degree in electrical engineering to do design. Although it helps to have formal course work, anyone who creates something may qualify as a designer. Technicians, for example, are constantly modifying, improving on, and creating new projects. Because they, of all the electronics personnel, are closest to the actual working device, technicians are often in the best position to see what changes and improvements need to be made, and given their electronics training and experience, they can usually come up with an actual design to solve the problem.

The key to electronics design is taking the **systems approach**. This means knowing about electronic circuitry, the role of input and output transducers, and the fundamentals of good product packaging. It also means understanding and respecting the users' needs. We'll look at these and other design aspects more closely later in the chapter.

For now, it is enough to understand that being an electronics designer does not mean crossing some invisible barrier, some magic line that separates the hobbyist and technician from the college-trained engineer. Given the right attitude (always questioning, wanting to improve things, constantly fiddling and dabbling) and technical experience, you, or anyone else, can do electronics design work.

The Design Methodology

In addition to having the appropriate attitude and technical expertise, you must familiarize yourself with electronics design methodologies. One such design method involves identifying *problem* and *solution categories.* As a result, you often gain clearer insight into the overall design effort. Let's see what this means.

Identifying the Problem Category

Usually, design problems can be put into one of three categories: (1) a need in search of a product or service; (2) a product or service in search of a need; or (3) improvement on an existing product. Obviously, the differences among these three categories are not that well defined. You can't always be sure if you have a problem in search of a solution, or the reverse. Nonetheless, an attempt at classifying each design project into one of these three categories is bound to help you conceptualize the design problem.

In the first instance we often find ourselves saying, "We have this problem. Can electronics help us with the solution?" Illustrations of this type of thinking are endless. Suppose you are constantly "bugged" by mosquitoes at the company's annual picnic. You have tried everything, from gallons of insecticide to gas-powered flyswatters. But what about an ultrasonic electronic oscillator that drives mosquitoes batty? Small battery-powered units that actually claim to do just that are available at your local sporting goods store. Or do you constantly misplace the car keys, searching frantically for them on the mantle, between the couch pillows, or in your jacket pocket? Well, someone has come up with an electronic solution: a small circuit attached to the key chain that lets out a high-pitched audio tone when you clap your hands. Now, retrieving your lost keys is as easy as snapping your fingers.

These, and the other examples mentioned earlier, have one thing in common: first there was a need or problem, then came the solution.

It doesn't always work that way. Often we think of the product or service first and then look to see if there is a real need for it. If there is, does a product or service already exist to satisfy that need? What about a string of small dc lights that "dance" to the music? Such a color organ can be designed and built easily, but has someone already done it? If not, and you create such a product, would anyone buy it? How about an emergency strobe light that campers could carry into the outback? If lost, they could use it to signal search crews. Again, designing and building such a product isn't difficult, but is there a market for it? In these examples, first the product came quickly to mind; the need had yet to be determined.

Sometimes we just want to improve on what we already have. This could be as simple as adding an on-off indicator light to a power supply, or as complex as upgrading an analog (needle-type) tachometer to a digital version. The latter, of course, could be considered a brand-new product, not just an upgrade.

The idea behind identifying a problem category is simply to help formulate the design effort. Once the problem is clear, you can move on to singling out the best type of solution.

Identifying the Solution Category

Regardless of how the problem is categorized, one of three solution approaches is usually taken: (1) we see if the product or service already exists; (2) we see if we can modify an existing item that is close to what we want; or (3) if the first two methods don't work, we design a new product from scratch. Let's briefly examine each procedure.

Why waste time, money, and tremendous design effort if what you want already exists? Why reinvent the wheel? It is, in part, the designer's responsibility to know what's out there and whether a particular design is "common property," to be used freely by all. True, your company may still find it more advantageous to design and make its own version of a particular item, but, at the very least, the option to choose what is already available should be there.

Perhaps what you are looking for already exists, and only a slight modification is all that is needed. Designers spend a great deal of time poring over data sheets of circuit schematics that are very close to what they require. An extra stage of amplification, the addition of a variable speed control, slightly more filtering at the output—make these kinds of small modifications and you could have a custom-designed project that exactly meets your needs.

However, if you can't find it or modify it when you do, then starting from scratch is the only solution. Naturally, this approach involves the greatest effort. But at least this way you should get very close to exactly what you want—and, of course, it will be all yours.

> ***Something to Think About***
>
> *Why not talk to a few designers and engineers? Identify a company, contact the engineering department, and request to speak with an electronics engineer or designer, then ask if you can make an appointment to conduct a half-hour "information interview." Believe me, they will be flattered you asked. Who knows where this could lead?*

3.2 ELECTRONICS DESIGN: THE SYSTEMS APPROACH

To do electronics design, you must be able to recognize the complete electronic system and understand how it functions. We'll look at the systems approach first. In today's industrial environment you also need to be familiar with the concept of Total Quality Management (TQM). We'll examine TQM, and your role in it, next. It's then on to an exploration of the important two-step design process. We will also find out about some basic sketching techniques useful in the design stage.

The Fundamentals of Electronics Design

Here we explore the fundamentals of electronics design by defining the term *electronic system.* Then we go on to discuss electronic components: their function, description, packaging styles, and selection and acquisition. In addition to providing insight into the design process, this procedure also allows us to review some important principles of electronics.

An Electronic System Defined

Your friend enthusiastically invites you over to see his brand-new 200-W stereo amplifier. You arrive to find it sitting on the dining room table, plugged in, and producing absolutely nothing: no sound, no hum, no nothing! It's a great amplifier, assembled using the latest solid-state circuitry, but by itself it is useless. An electronic circuit is only part of the picture: "An electronic circuit does not a system make."

The amplifier needs a signal to amplify. It gets that signal from what is called an electrical **input transducer**, a component that changes some form of energy into electricity. In a stereo system that component could be a microphone, tape head, CD laser, or tuner. The amplified signal needs somewhere to go—to a component known as an electrical **output transducer**. This component—an earphone or speaker—changes electricity into another form of energy, the reverse of what the input transducer does. Together, the input transducer, electronic circuit, and output transducer make up an electronic system—in this case, a stereo system (Figure 3–1).

All electronic systems first take a form of energy, such as heat, light, or sound (movement of a microphone's diaphragm), and convert it into electricity. The circuit then manipulates the electrical current, by switching or regulating it, and sends it to an output transducer. Here it is converted into another form of energy, one we find useful, such as mechanical motion (the movement of a speaker cone), light, or heat (Figure 3–2).

To understand better this systems approach, let's look at electronic components, which combine to form electronic circuits, which must then be coupled to input and output transducers to make up the electronic system (Figure 3–3).

Electronic Component Function

Electronic components can be classified as either active or passive. **Active** components control electrons by switching or regulating them; **passive** components help the active components carry out these functions.

A giant leap from the electrical to the electronic age occurred in 1906, with the invention of the first active component, the **vacuum tube** (Figure 3–4). (We are talking here about the triode, not the diode, vacuum tube. The diode, although an active component, only rectified but did not regulate current flow.) Now, for the first time, electrons were all alone. These minute particles, traveling between the vacuum tube's cathode and plate, could be controlled by a tiny grid of wire with a negative charge placed on it. The result? Switching speeds in the hundreds of thousands of cycles per second and amplification factors on the order of a million or more.

When this first active component was combined in various ways, the electronic computer was born, as were radio, television, and a host of other twentieth-century electronic wonders. Clearly, the vacuum tube is one of the most important inventions of all time.

Amazing as it was, the vacuum tube had its shortcomings. It was relatively large, easily breakable, generally unreliable, hungry for power, and had a limited life expectancy. A more efficient replacement was needed.

In 1947 the **transistor** emerged from the laboratory, as a second-generation active compo-

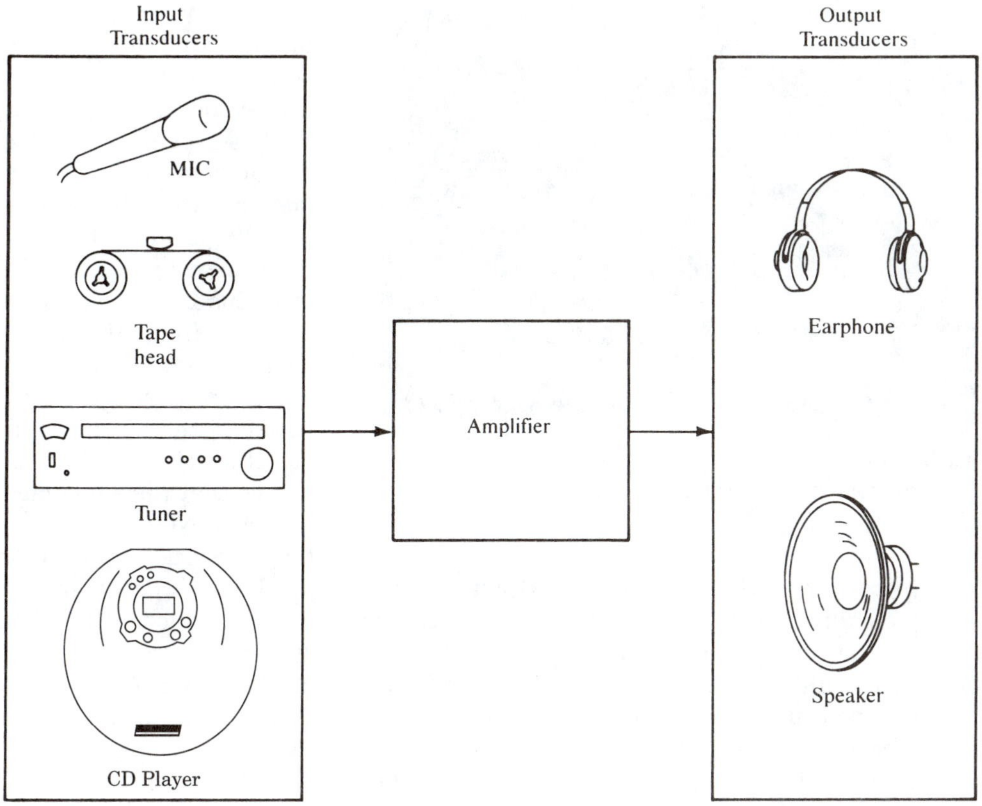

FIGURE 3–1
Electronic stereo system

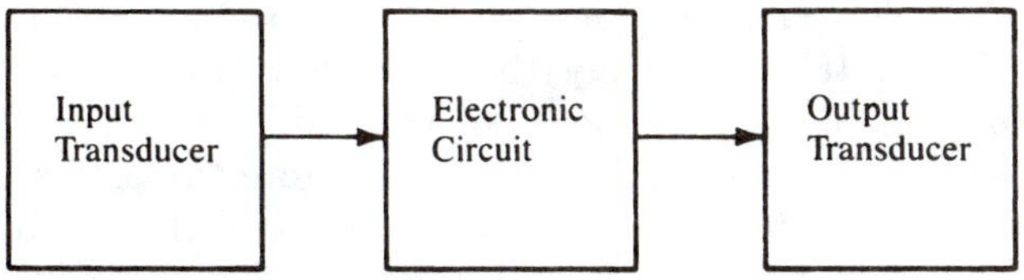

FIGURE 3–2
A complete electronic system

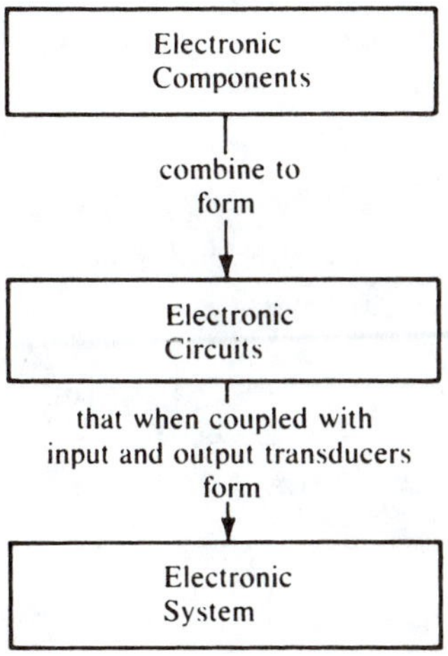

FIGURE 3–3
Electronic components, circuits, system

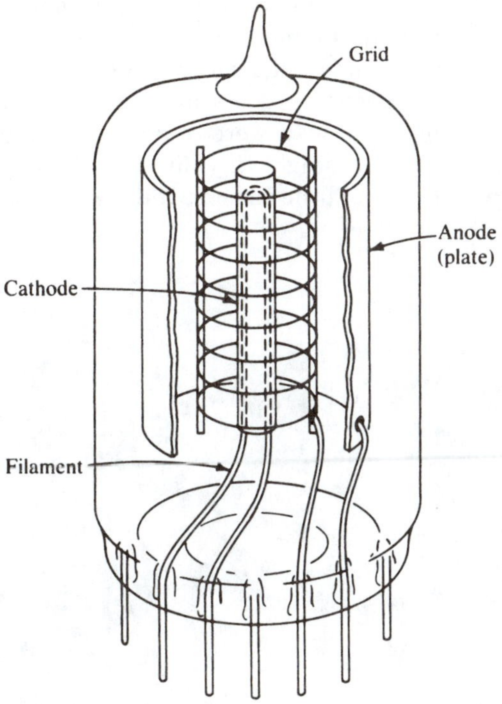

FIGURE 3–4
Vacuum tube

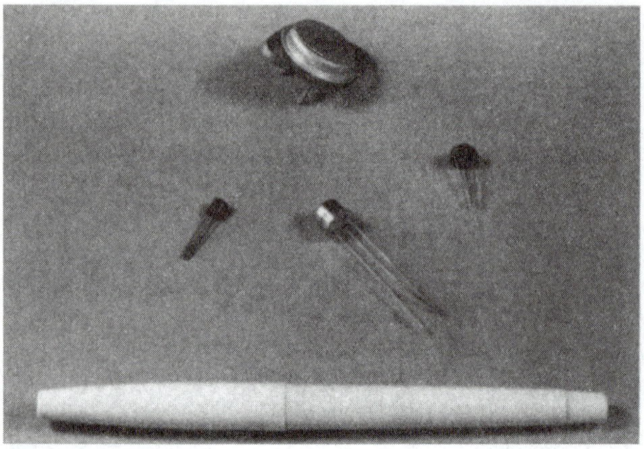

FIGURE 3–5
The transistor, an active component

nent, to challenge the vacuum tube (Figure 3–5). The new transistor did everything its predecessor did, only better. It was smaller, highly reliable, consumed milliwatts instead of watts of power, and could be counted on to last at least as long as any other component in the circuit. In addition, once mass production opened up, transistor costs plummeted to only pennies per unit, while the average vacuum tube still sold for more than $2.

But even with the transistor, improvements were called for. Using basic transistor technology, engineers at Fairchild developed a tiny component, no bigger than an infant's fingernail, that contained dozens of transistor elements. These transistors, along with various resistors and capacitors fabricated in the same way, were combined to form entire circuits on a single tiny sliver of silicon. The year was 1958, and the **integrated circuit** had arrived (Figure 3–6).

Today, integrated circuits (ICs) containing hundreds of thousands of transistor elements are being mass-produced for just a few dollars. This third-generation active component has all the advantages of discrete (individual) transistors, plus the added benefit of much greater circuit density and, surprisingly, even lower power consumption.

We are not through yet. Although the **microprocessor** is a type of integrated circuit, many feel that this device, developed in 1972, is so radically different from its predecessors that it deserves its own identity as an active component (Figure 3–7). The microprocessor, of which there are now more in use than there are people on earth, is programmable. It is software that determines its function. This means that the same microprocessor can be used in a microwave oven, a videocassette recorder, an automobile cruise control, or a personal computer, depending on the program that controls it. This component, which is the heart of all computer-based systems, has revolutionized the design of electronic products and services. Now, the electronics designer must know about computer software as well as computer hardware.

The passive components (Figure 3–8)—resistors, capacitors, inductors, and transformers—help the active components manipulate electrical current. The **resistor** limits current flow and drops voltage. It is probably the most abundant of all components; rarely does an electronic circuit not contain at least one resistor. The **capacitor** acts as a temporary battery to store an electrical charge. It is used in timing circuits, tuners, and filters. The **inductor** (coil), which stores electrical energy in a magnetic field, acts as a choke (a device used to limit or suppress the flow of alternating current) and, along with a capacitor, as a tuner. The **trans-**

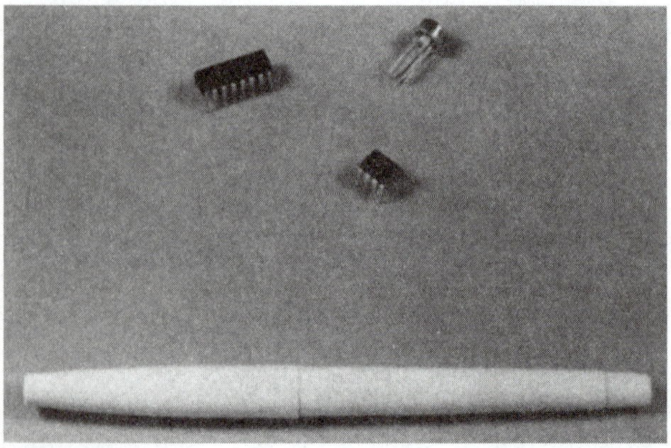

FIGURE 3–6
Integrated circuit

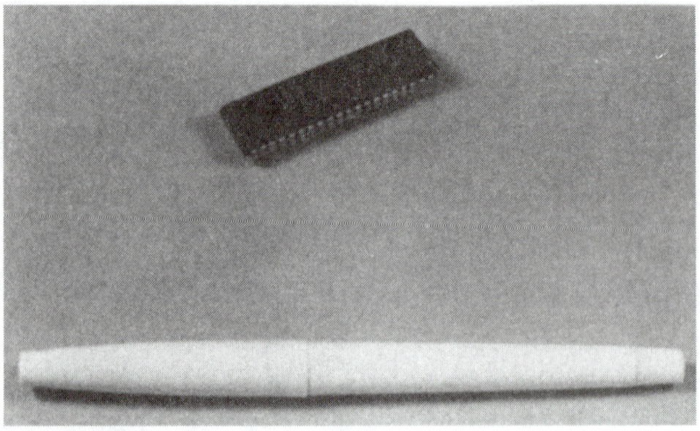

FIGURE 3–7
Microprocessor

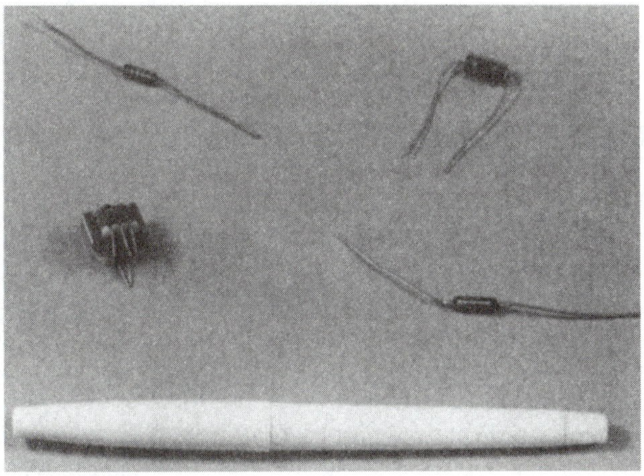

FIGURE 3–8
Passive components

former steps up or down incoming voltage. It is found in power supplies and as an energy-matching component in amplifiers and oscillators.

Electronic Component Description

Let's take a moment to examine more closely the most widely used active and passive electronic components. These components are found extensively in the projects discussed in Part III.

Diodes. A diode is a two-element (cathode and anode) component that allows current to flow through it in one direction only. The schematic symbol and pictorial presentation for a typical silicon diode are shown in Figure 3–9a. The diode conducts current when forward-biased (its cathode negative, its anode positive). It blocks current flow when reversed-biased (its cathode positive, its anode negative). Thus, the diode acts as a one-way valve. It is used primarily for switching, although it also operates as a rectifier to change ac to dc.

Diodes are rated with regard to current- and voltage-handling ability. For example, a 1N4001 diode is rated at 1 A/50 V. That is, it will carry *up to* 1 ampere while handling *up to* 50 volts. The question is, Could such a diode work in a circuit requiring only 500 mA at 25 V? Yes, it could.

As noted in Figure 3–9a, the cathode end of a diode is identified by an atypical marking, usually a band, a chamfer, or "-" symbol.

Transistors. A transistor is a semiconductor component that can both switch and amplify. It consists of three terminals: emitter (E), base (B), and collector (C). There are two configurations, NPN and PNP. There are also two broad types, classified according to current-handling ability: general-purpose and power transistors. The schematic symbols for NPN and PNP transistors, along with typical packaging styles, are shown in Figure 3–9b.

A transistor is operated as an amplifier or as a switch. As an amplifier, a small varying signal

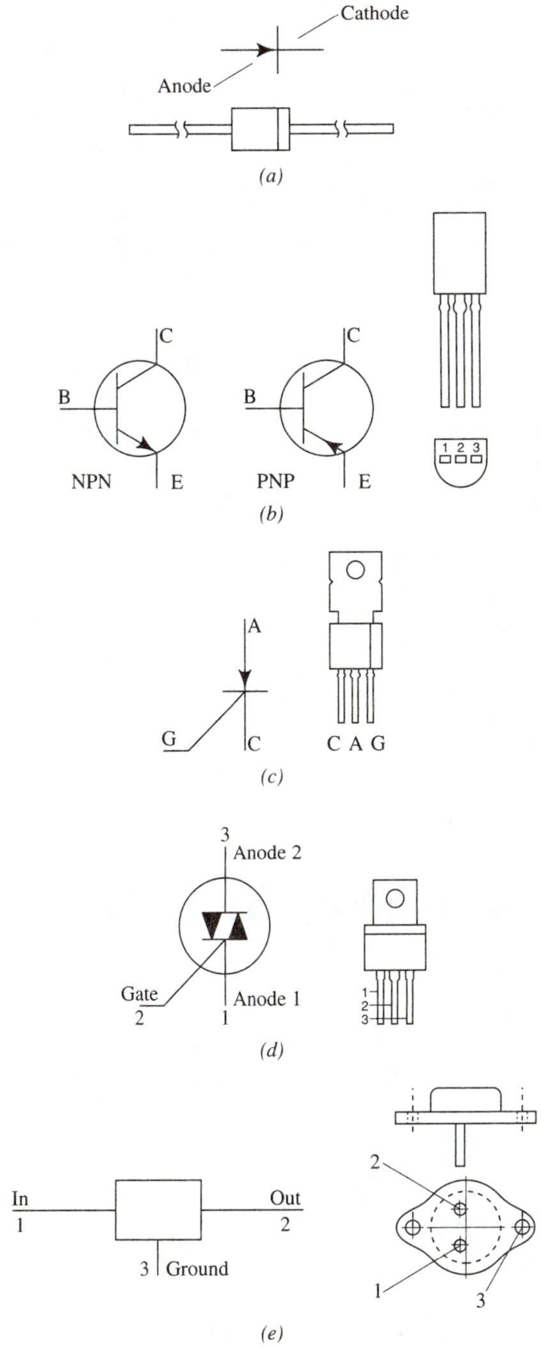

FIGURE 3–9
Active electronic components

placed on the base causes a much larger varying signal to flow from collector to emitter. When a transistor is operated as a switch, it is either at cutoff (no collector–emitter current is allowed to flow) or saturation (maximum collector–emitter current flows).

The transistor as an amplifier finds extensive use in audio- and radio-frequency equipment. As a switch it is used to activate and deactivate a wide variety of circuit loads.

Silicon Controlled Rectifiers (SCRs). The SCR is a three-terminal solid-state latching switch. It conducts current from the cathode to the anode when the gate receives a positive voltage. Once the conduction takes place, it continues even when the control voltage to the gate is removed. The SCR ceases conducting only when the anode voltage is removed, reduced, or reversed. Thus, we have a latching switch, designed to operate primarily in a dc circuit.

In Figure 3–9c we see the schematic symbol and typical packaging for an SCR. SCRs are rated in current- and voltage-handling ability. For example, a 1-A/200-V SCR conducts *up to* 1 ampere while handling *up to* 200 volts. Will such an SCR work in a circuit delivering 500 mA at 6 V? Yes, of course. SCRs are used extensively in burglar alarms, color organs, strobe lights, and industrial control applications where dc is involved—anywhere, that is, where a solid-state latch is required.

Triacs. A triac is a back-to-back SCR (Figure 3–9d). It functions as an electrically controlled switch for ac loads. Like an SCR, the triac is rated in terms of current- and voltage-handling ability. The former ranges from 1 to over 40 A; the latter, from 200 to 600 V. Triacs are used to control high-current, high-voltage ac loads. In dc circuits we use the SCR; in ac circuits, where current and voltage tend to be higher, the triac is the choice.

Voltage Regulators. A voltage regulator is a circuit that holds an output voltage at a predetermined value regardless of normal input voltage changes or changes in the load impedance. There are fixed and variable voltage regulators. The former have a fixed output, such as 5.0, 6.0, 10.0, and 18.0 V. The latter hold their output voltage steady within a predetermined range. For example, the LM317 is a 1.2–17-V regulator. When set to any voltage within that range (usually with a potentiometer), it holds the output at the selected voltage.

Many voltage regulators come in a three-terminal package. They have only one input terminal, one output terminal, and one ground terminal, as shown in Figure 3–9e. Such regulators are chosen primarily to satisfy the voltage and current requirements of the load. For example, the LM7805 is a fixed 5-V/1-A voltage regulator. It holds the output voltage at 5 V while the load draws up to 1 A. If the load exceeds 1 A, the voltage regulator automatically shuts down. It resumes operation when the load requirement is reduced below 1 A.

Voltage regulators are a must for any dc power supply. Considering their simplicity and low cost (in many cases under $1), there is no reason why they shouldn't be designed into every power-supply project.

Resistors. A resistor is a passive electronic component that acts to oppose current flow and drop voltage. The schematic symbol and physical characteristics of a fixed carbon-composition resistor (the most popular type) are shown in Figure 3–10a. Note the colored band, which we will discuss in a moment.

Resistors have two ratings. They have a resistance value, measured in *ohms* (Ω), and a heat-dissipation factor, measured in *watts.* The ohm is just a measurement of resistance, or opposition, to current flow. The more ohms, the more resistance. Standard carbon-composition resistors range in value from less than 1 ohm to over 100 million ohms.

A resistor's wattage rating is a measurement of how much heat it will get rid of. The larger its physical size, the greater its wattage rating. Common ratings are $\frac{1}{4}$, $\frac{1}{2}$, 1, and 2 W.

Carbon resistors use a color code to display their value in ohms. Four colored bands surround the resistor body. (See Appendix H for a discussion of five-band resistor color codes.) Each color is assigned a numeric value, as shown in Figure 3–11. Black is 0; brown, 1; red, 2; and so on. The first three bands (the first, or number one, band being closest to the edge) give the value in ohms, the fourth band the tolerance in percent of nominal value. Furthermore, the first two bands represent numerals, while the third band designates the number of zeros to be added to the numeric value.

It's really not that complicated. For example, a resistor color-coded *brown*, *red*, *orange*, *silver* would have an ohmic value of 12,000 ohms and a tolerance of plus or minus (±) 10%, meaning the resistor could be plus or minus 10% of the numeric value of 12,000 ohms. Its actual value could fall between 10,800 and 13,200 ohms. (For a more in-depth discussion of the resistor color code, consult a standard dc/ac textbook such as Thomas Floyd's *Electronics*

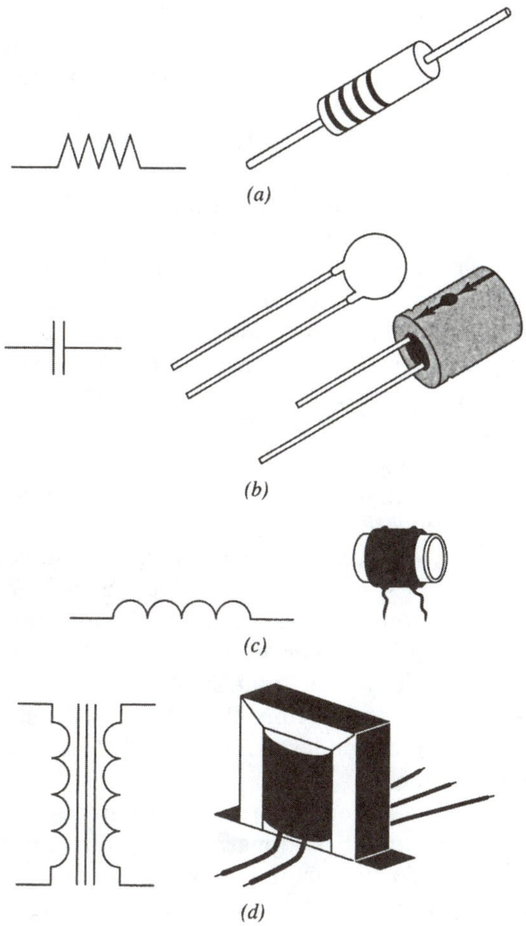

FIGURE 3–10
Passive electronic components

Fundamentals, published by Prentice Hall Career and Technology.)

Resistors find application in virtually every circuit. They are the most popular of all electronic components, active or passive.

Capacitors. A capacitor is a passive component that stores electricity. It consists of two metal plates separated by a dielectric, or insulator. There are two types of fixed capacitors: polarized and nonpolarized. The former have a positive and a negative lead. Also known as electrolytic capacitors, polarized capacitors must be installed in a circuit in the correct direction. Nonpolarized capacitors can be installed in either direction.

The schematic symbols and body styles for two types of capacitors are shown in Figure 3–10b. Note that the positive lead of an electrolytic capacitor is identified by physical characteristics in one of two ways: In radial leads (those protruding from the same side), the positive lead is the longer of the two. In axial leads (those extending like the axle of an automobile), the positive lead emerges from the side where the cylinder indents.

Capacitor values are given in microfarads (μF) and picofarads (pF). Values up to 1 μF are nonpolarized; beyond 1 μF the capacitor is almost always polarized. Capacitors have a voltage rating, too, for example, 47 μF/50 V. This capacitor should not be placed in a circuit where more than 50 V would be impressed across its leads.

Capacitors are used as filters in power supplies, in tuning circuits for radios, and as part of resistance/capacitance (R/C) networks in timing circuits.

Inductors. An inductor, or coil, stores energy in a magnetic field. It consists of a coil of wire wound on an air or iron core. The schematic symbol and case styles for a typical coil are shown in Figure 3–10c. Inductors are nonpolarized, that is, they can be installed in either direction within the circuit. Inductor values are given in millihenries (mH) or microhenries (μH). They have no voltage rating. Coils are used in motors, antennas, tuners, relays, and solenoids.

Transformers. A transformer looks very much like a coil. That is because a transformer consists of two or more windings wrapped around a common core. It's really just two or more coils using the same core.

A transformer steps ac voltage up or down. Its primary coil receives the incoming voltage. Through magnetic induction, the voltage is induced into the secondary winding. If the secondary winding has more turns than the primary, the incoming voltage is stepped up. If the number of windings in the secondary coil is less than that of the primary, the incoming voltage is reduced.

Transformers are classified as power, audio, and radio frequency (RF). The former are the largest, the latter the smallest. The schematic symbol and physical characteristics of a typical

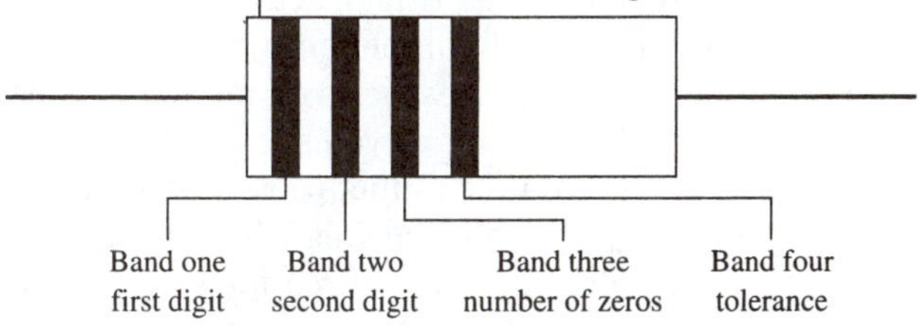

FIGURE 3–11
Resistor color code

transformer are shown in Figure 3–10d. Transformers are used in power supplies, audio and video equipment, and, in general, to isolate one ac circuit from another.

Component Packaging Styles

Most passive components, such as resistors, capacitors, and inductors, are identified as having either axial or radial leads (see Figure 3–8). If such components have polarity (positive and negative terminals), the positive terminal is usually specified with a longer lead, or the body of the component has a polarity marking clearly shown.

Leads for active components, integrated circuits, and components in the transistor family (diodes, diacs, SCRs, triacs, and so on) are identified differently. They are determined according to a packaging style that is usually associated with a specific lead configuration (see Appendix D), yet you can't always be sure that these configurations will match the particular components you are working with. To play it safe, look up the packaging style and lead pattern in Appendix D or in the **data sheet** for the appropriate component. This is the only way you can be absolutely sure of lead placement.

Electronic Component Selection and Acquisition

As an electronics technician, particularly one involved in prototype design and fabrication, you will be concerned with the selection and acquisition of electronic components, not just for the prototype, but for the mass-produced product should the prototype prove successful. With a prototype, it's simply not enough to get the circuit up and running. You must do so with electronic components and hardware that will be readily available in large quantities and at reasonable prices. In other words, the prototype technician must look ahead to the final, mass-produced product in determining component selection and acquisition.

The first step in learning to make such decisions is to gain as much knowledge as possible about electronic components: what's available, from what vendors, delivery schedules, and, of course, pricing. When you are out in industry, three sources will be of primary help to you: (1) your company's purchasing agent, (2) parts catalogs such as the EEM (Electronic Engineers Master catalog), and (3) the Internet.

When you are on the job, make it a point to get to know your company's purchasing agent. If you can, get on a first-name basis with that person. A serendipitous relationship may well develop: you will be helping each other do a better job.

Start to acquire now, while you are still in school, data manuals, line cards, and parts catalogs that will provide a valuable resource in selecting components and vendors. Such items are usually available free to those in the field. Call or write to suppliers today.

When searching the Internet for electronic components, you can take one of three approaches.

First, using your Internet provider's browser, simply name the component you want, say a 7402 IC. The trouble is, if you don't narrow the search by clearly delineating the name, you can wind up with thousands of results. A search on just the numbers 7402 turned up over 10,000 choices, including "Minnesota Rules Chapter 7402."

Second, you can simply use your preferred vendors' Web sites.

Third, you can use one of the many component search engines, such as PartMiner. Such services will list the components you are looking for by providing the part number, description, manufacturer, price, in-stock notice, quantity, and supplier. You then simply order on-line. With this approach, you have a choice of vendors and prices, both at one Internet location.

When selecting electronic components, quality and quantity must be uppermost in your mind. Although you do not want to "overdesign" (choose a Cadillac when a Chevy will do), selecting high-reliability components wherever possible can pay off and actually save money down the line. You are ahead if quality components reduce the demand for incoming inspection, if rejects are minimized, and if product failure out in the field is lessened. You may pay a little more on the front end for quality components, but in the long run, you'll often save money.

The ability to purchase in quantity doesn't just refer to the willingness of a given vendor to continue to supply parts at good prices in quantities you want when you want them—though that's important. It has more to do with the critical issue of *second sourcing*. Virtually all electronic components are "second-sourced," meaning they are available from more than one OEM (original equipment manufacturer). OEMs actually encourage this practice and often license the production of components they have designed (such as microprocessors and memory chips) to rival OEMs. They know, as you should, that manufacturers of electronic products are not going to "put all their eggs in one basket." For production houses to rely solely on one source for any item in their product lines puts them in a very vulnerable position should the source decide to discontinue the item or, worse, go out of business. The rule of thumb is simple: Never purchase any electronic component that is not second-sourced—period!

When you have selected components that might be used in your prototype, you or your company's purchasing agent can call the distributor and ask for samples. As a student, you can do the same. Don't be greedy. Ask only for what you need and be direct about who you are and why you require the item. If you are polite and positive, you'll usually get what you ask for.

What if vendors say they don't have the exact component you are looking for, but an "equivalent" substitute? Now, of course, you need a sample more than ever. When you get that sample, be sure it is not only electrically equivalent but physically the same as well.

Electronic Circuits

Active and passive components combine to make up **electronic circuits**. A schematic drawing for a three-stage audio amplifier circuit is shown in Figure 3–12. Notice the five active components—transistors Q_1–Q_5—and the passive components—resistors and capacitors—required to support them.

Though it may seem that there are hundreds, even thousands, of different types of circuits, such is not the case. All electronic circuits (just like the active components) can be grouped into two broad classifications: digital and analog circuits. **Digital** circuits switch currents on or off very rapidly; **analog** circuits use a small current to control a much larger current. All circuits, whether they are buried in a sophisticated radar system or are part of a household light dimmer, are analog or digital or a combination of both.

When we think of analog circuits, we imagine amplifiers and oscillators. Such circuits form the heart of practically all audio and video communications equipment. Chances are that your stereo, telephone, radio, and television systems are predominantly analog in design. Although the trend is clearly toward digital circuits, analog circuitry, and the designers who are familiar with it, will be needed for a long time to come.

When we turn to digital circuitry, it is computers that come quickly to mind. Virtually all the computers that you are ever likely to work with are digital, not analog. Remember, also, that if an electronic product uses a microprocessor, the device is essentially computer-based. Furthermore, with billions of microprocessors in the world, that means a large number of digital circuits to design and repair.

Computers, however, are not the only equipment to use digital circuitry. Many timers, counters, and industrial control circuits can be built with a handful of inexpensive integrated circuit gates (switching circuits combined to make logic decisions). Figure 3–13 shows a simple burglar alarm circuit. Notice that although all the active components are digital, the circuit contains no microprocessor.

Electronic Systems

As discussed, adding input and output transducers to an electronic circuit creates an **electronic sys-**

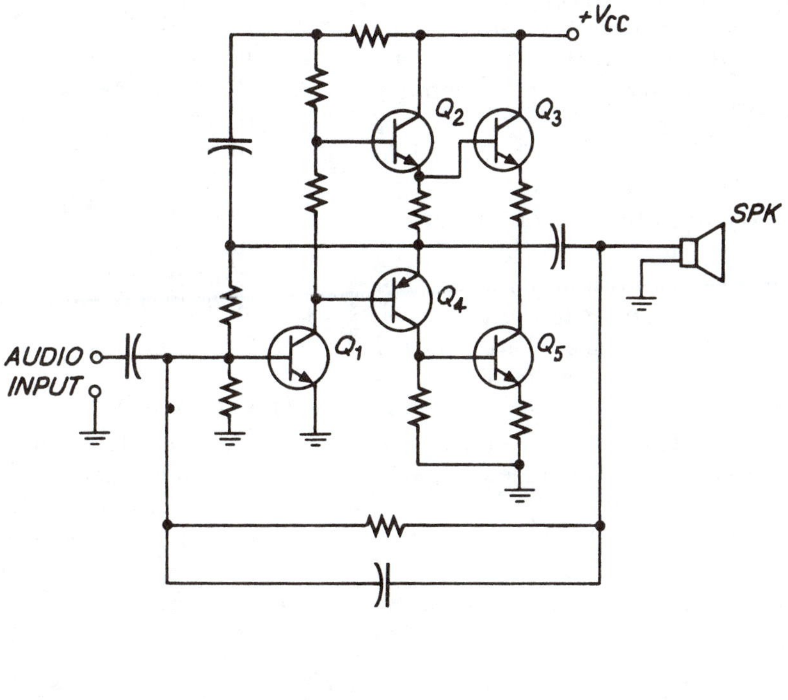

FIGURE 3–12
Three-stage audio amplifier circuit

FIGURE 3–13
Digital burglar alarm

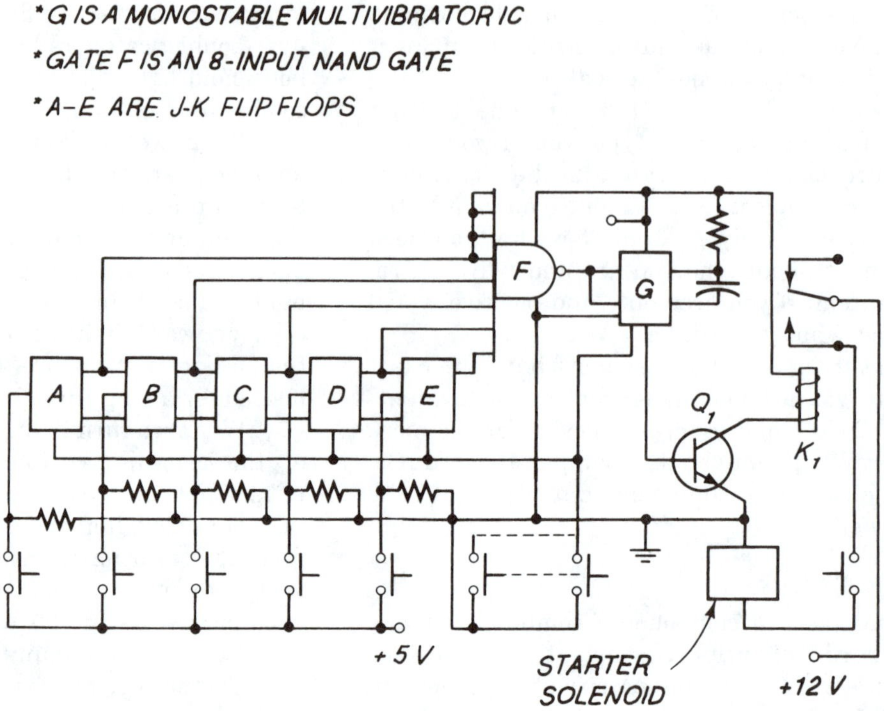

tem. Some people have found out about the need to fashion such a system the hard way. Many unsophisticated computer purchasers, lured by the "too good to be true" advertisements, bought computers at unbelievably low prices. When they got the computer home, however, and plugged it in, just like the amplifier mentioned earlier, it didn't do a thing. They forgot about the input and output transducers, known in computerese as input and output peripherals. Without a keyboard, light pen, joystick or mouse at the input and a video display unit, printer, or plotter at the output, the computer circuitry has no way of blossoming into a computer system (Figure 3–14).

Electronics designers spend a great deal of time thinking about transducers. Many of the basic circuit building blocks already exist, but determining how to sense a particular light or heat source, knowing how to actuate various valves and plungers—in other words, interfacing electronic circuitry to the outside world—that's where the real challenge often lies. For you as an electronics designer, knowing the makeup of a complete system is critical—and that means knowing about input and output transducers as well as digital and analog circuitry.

In this section we have emphasized the importance the designer must place on understanding the electronic system. Whenever you design an electronic product or service, think of how whatever it is you are doing fits into the complete system. Even though your design may seem like a small part of a much bigger picture, you will want to know where you are in that larger canvas.

Total Quality Management (TQM) and the Design Process

TQM is one of the hottest buzzwords in corporate America today. It's an umbrella term for the quality programs that have spread throughout U.S. industry in the past dozen years. It developed in response to the Japanese emphasis on superior-quality products.

Total Quality Management started with large companies but has spread to smaller ones, as the former have insisted that the latter, who often act as suppliers to their larger kin, adopt quality programs of their own. Let's see just what TQM is and how it fits into electronic design and the systems approach.

The What and Why of TQM

Total Quality Management represents, as its name indicates, a company's total commitment to quality. TQM is essentially customer- and employee-driven. What does this mean? First, there is an intense focus on customer satisfaction. Customers, however, are internal as well as external. An assembler may be the "customer" of a technician who builds a

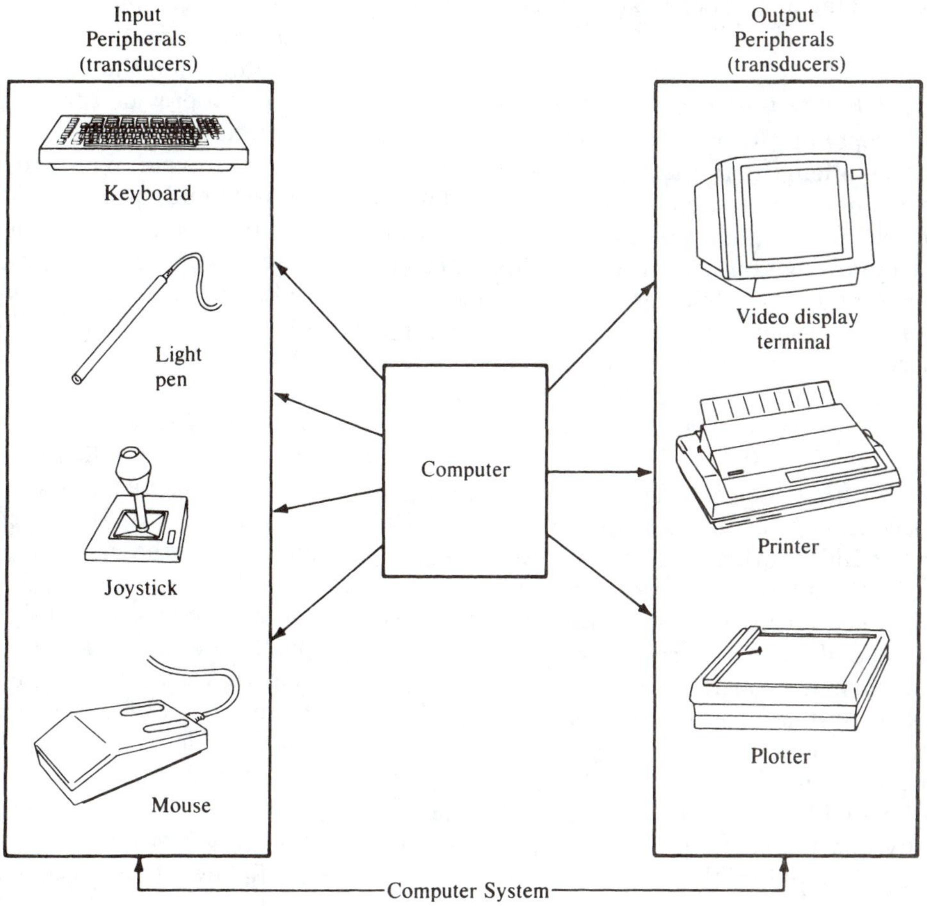

FIGURE 3–14
Computer system

prototype, for instance, just as the person who buys the final, mass-produced product is the customer of everyone in the company.

Second, TQM involves a new work relationship based on trust and teamwork. The idea centers around the term *empowerment*, which means that management gives employees wide latitude in how they go about achieving the company's goals. By getting employees involved at all levels from design to shipping, companies hope that a shift will occur from catching and correcting defects at the end of the process, to monitoring the process itself so that defects do not occur. Such an approach, the essence of TQM, represents a real change in philosophy for many U.S. companies.

The Electronics Technician's Role in TQM

Improving quality involves much more than beefing up the quality assurance (QA) department, increasing inspection and rejection at the back end—it's really about designing quality in at the front end. You'll come across this concept again and again out in industry. Obviously you, as an electronics technician dealing with prototype design and fabrication, are going to be a key player in TQM implementation, and the emphasis on "player" is significant. TQM makes considerable use of concepts such as the team method and quality circles. You might say it is the systems approach applied to people and organizations, not just an electronic circuit sandwiched between input and output transducers. In sum, you're going to be living and working with TQM for many years to come. Embrace it and find out all you can about it now, while you're still in school. It will be waiting for you out in the electronics workplace.

The Two-Step Design Process

The project design process involves two steps. We need to produce a **Concepts and Requirements Document** and a set of **design drawings** (Figure 1–3). The Concepts and Requirements Document, in addition to stating the project concept, spells out just what is to be done, by whom, and when. The design drawings consist of a system diagram, circuit design sketch (circuit schematic), and packaging plan. Let's examine both items in turn.

Concepts and Requirements Document

The Concepts and Requirements Document doesn't have to be a lengthy thesis; one or two typewritten pages will do. Its purpose is to state clearly why the project should be undertaken, what are the basic design requirements, how those requirements are to be met, and who is to do exactly what and when. First, a goals declaration is made, followed by a list of objectives, a clarification of responsibility statement, and a short discussion of the theory of operation. Here's what we mean:

Project Goals. The goals declaration simply states what the project is, why it is needed, and why it is better to build it rather than obtain it commercially. For example, suppose you want to solve the problem of break-ins in the electronics laboratory—an illustration of a need-in-search-of-a-product problem category. You conclude that by installing a burglar alarm system the incidences of theft will be reduced. The project, then, is a burglar alarm, and its purpose is to reduce break-ins. Also, because nothing is available commercially that will meet the company's particular needs, you are proposing that the company build the burglar alarm.

Project Objectives. First, you state the design requirements (objectives). For example, the system should be reliable, low in cost, safe to operate, have an entry delay, produce a loud siren sound when triggered, and protect all doors and windows. Next, you specify how those particular requirements, or objectives, will be met. Here you could say that reliability will be achieved by using solid-state components; low cost, by building the circuit on a PC board; safe operation, with the use of batteries; and so on. It's basically a question of stating specific design criteria and how they are to be met.

Project Responsibilities. It is very important, early on, to find out who is going to do what and set deadlines for the completion of the various tasks: Who will provide the design sketches? Who is going to make the complete drawing set? Who will build the prototype? Who will test and troubleshoot the project? and, of course, Who will be responsible for the documentation? Adjustments can and will be made as the project progresses, but general commitments in terms of personnel and facilities need to be made now, in the Concepts and Requirements Document.

Theory of Operation. A brief explanation of how the circuit works should be included. Although marketing personnel, and even some production people, may wish to skip this section, it is useful for all those involved in the design and prototyping phases.

After the Concepts and Requirements Document is accepted, it is signed off by the appropriate personnel and appears later as part of the Project Report. We'll look more closely at the Concepts and Requirements Document in the next section, where the Sample Project, the Variable Power Supply, is also examined.

Design Drawings

There are three design drawings: a system diagram, a circuit design sketch, and a packaging plan. The **system diagram** is a block diagram illustrating the functional units that make up the system. Each transducer is represented by its own block, as are individual circuits within the complete system. A system diagram for a standard AM transistor radio receiver is shown in Figure 3–15. The diagram is often accompanied by a brief functional statement, the purpose of which is to explain in simple terms what each block does.

The **circuit design sketch** is the rough schematic drawing of all circuits, along with input and output transducers. All components need to be

FIGURE 3–15
System diagram of an AM radio

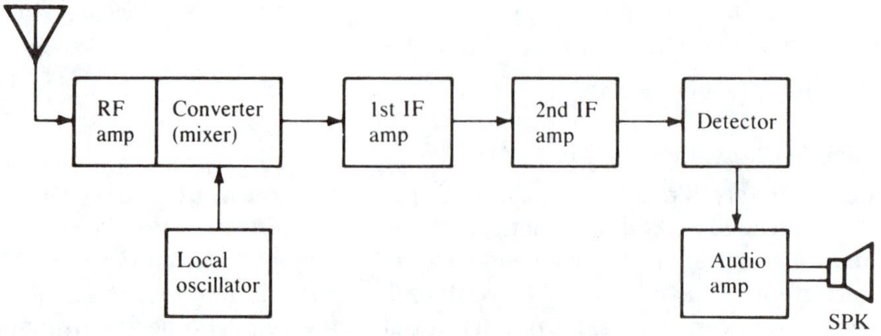

identified and their values stated, either on the drawing or in a separate parts list. A circuit design sketch for the AM transistor radio is shown in Figure 3–16.

A **packaging plan** is a sketch showing what the final project might look like. Enclosures should be chosen with aesthetics, functionality, and safety in mind. The tentative locations of panel lights, knobs, dials, jacks, and meters are identified. The type of finish to be applied must also be stated. A packaging plan for the AM transistor radio is shown in Figure 3–17.

The two-step design process, consisting of a Concepts and Requirements Document as well as a three-part design drawing set, provides the necessary information to determine if the project is worth doing. If it is a "go," the proper personnel sign off, and we move on to producing a working schematic drawing. Before we examine that procedure (in Chapter 4), let's explore some basic sketching techniques and take a look at the actual two-step design process as it applies to the Sample and Exercise Projects.

Sketching Techniques

Sketching is an important skill that every technical person should develop. The ability to get your thoughts down on paper quickly, in graphic form, for someone to evaluate is an important asset. Let's examine a few techniques that will help you do just that.

Sketching System Diagrams

Sketching a system diagram (Figure 3–15) is really quite simple. Just be sure to draw a solid block for functional units that are part of the complete system and a broken block (dotted lines) for functional units that are part of the system but not the project you will be building. (See the system diagram for the Variable Power Supply Project in Part III.) Also, don't forget to include the lines, with arrows, that indicate signal flow between functional units.

Sketching Schematic Drawings

A schematic drawing consists of electronic component symbols with interconnecting conductors. These components are identified and their lead and pin numbers indicated.

A schematic sketch differs from a working schematic drawing (see Chapter 4) primarily in two ways. One, the sketch is often incomplete in detail. Integrated circuit pin numbers are usually omitted, supply voltages are "understood," and even the identity of major components may be missing (Figure 3–16). The assumption, made by the sketcher (most often the designer), is that someone else (most often the technician) will look up this missing information when the working schematic is produced.

The second way in which the sketch differs from the working schematic is that in the sketch, little if any attention is paid to such things as component layout, line work, and scaled lettering. The idea is to put down the basic circuit as quickly as possible.

Nonetheless, the schematic sketch is no excuse for sloppiness and unorganized work. The sketch must be understandable and correct. It is one thing to leave IC pin numbers off the sketch, to be looked up at a later time, but quite another to put the wrong pin numbers on the drawing.

Keep this in mind when you are called on to produce a quick schematic sketch. Because most likely you will be sketching your schematic from one that is already drawn in books or magazines, your job will be fairly easy. Work in a logical progression, usually from left to right, and try not to forget any important details.

Sketching Pictorial Drawings

In order to sketch chassis, enclosures, electronic components, and the like, you need a basic knowledge of pictorial drawing (Figure 3–17). This often means drawing in **isometric**. In such an approach, objects are usually sketched by first developing an **isometric cube** and then "cutting the cube away" to get the final shape you want.

Isometric means equal measure. In an isometric drawing, the three common planes showing height, width, and depth are drawn true length. On an isometric drawing, vertical lines remain vertical, but horizontal lines recede at 30° angles (Figure 3–18). Any nonisometric lines (those that are not vertical or in the horizontal plane) are drawn between isometric points.

To sketch a drawing like the one in Figure 4–1 using the cutaway method, you might proceed as shown in Figure 3–19. Start with the basic cube, drawn in isometric, and then in successive steps hack away at it until the final shape emerges. As the drawing progresses, you will probably need to erase unwanted guidelines. When the final shape has emerged, you can darken the remaining object lines.

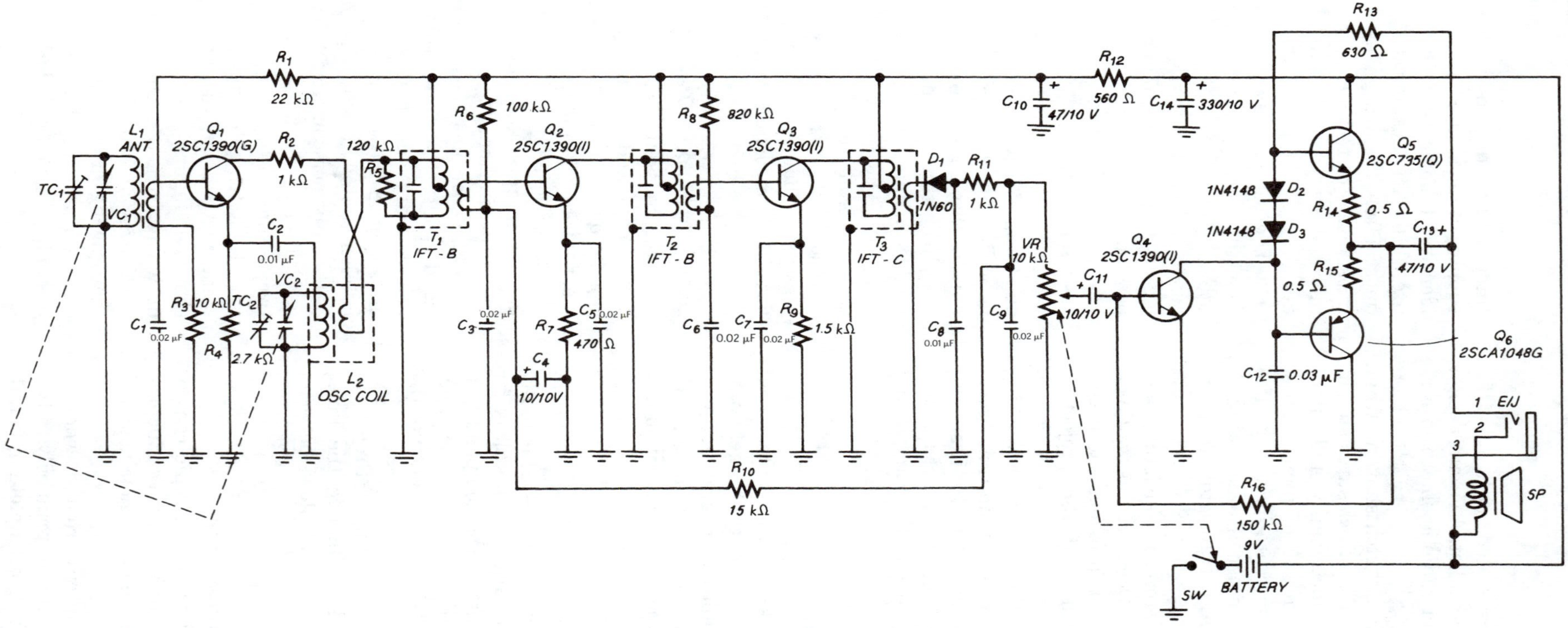

FIGURE 3–16
Circuit design sketch of an AM radio

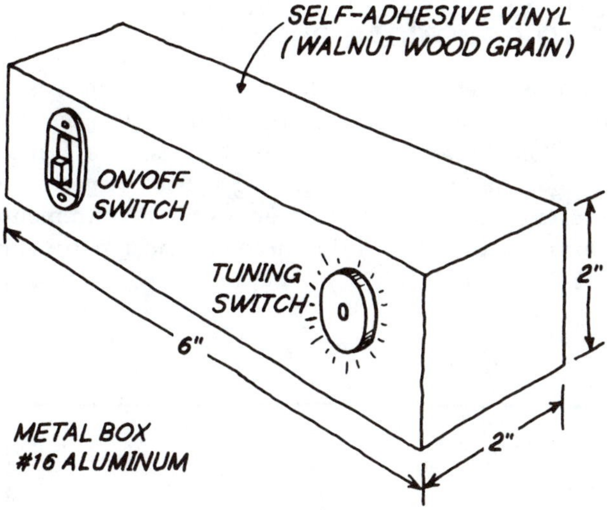

FIGURE 3–17
Packaging plan for an AM radio

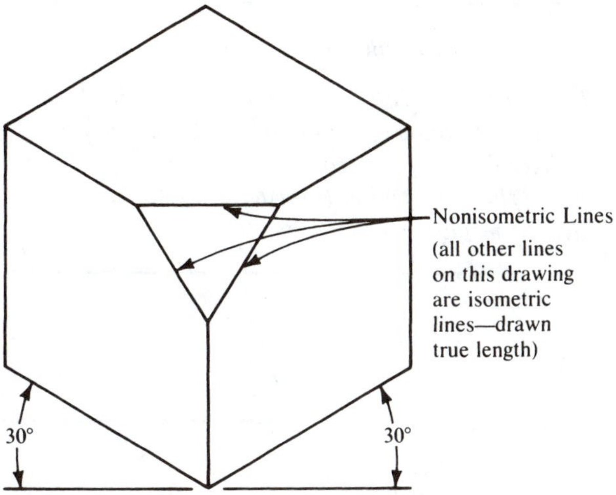

FIGURE 3–18
Isometric drawing

FIGURE 3–19
"Cutting away" an isometric cube

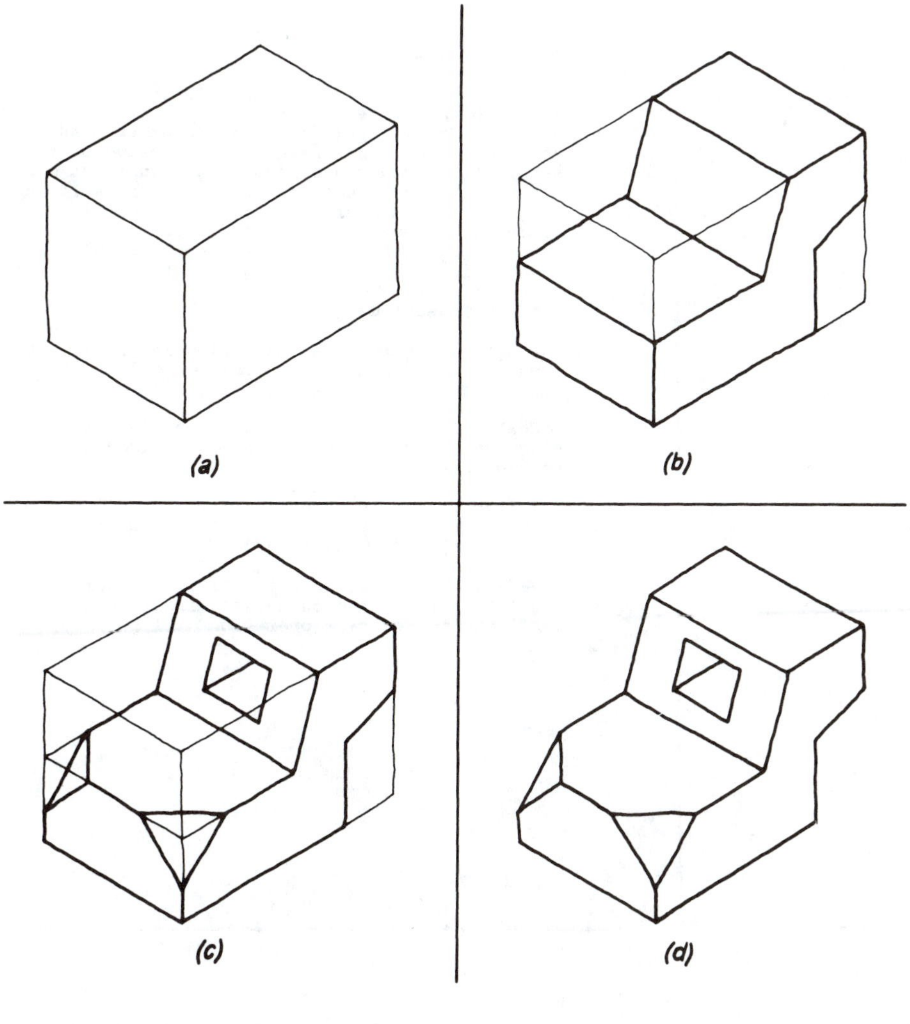

> ***Something to Think About***
>
> *Searching the Internet is a great way to determine electronic component pricing and availability for your project. Why not pick a project now, then surf the Internet to find the best deals on what you will need?*

3.3 ELECTRONICS DESIGN: TWO PRACTICAL PROJECTS

In this section we look at the two-step design process as it pertains to the Sample Project (the Variable Power Supply) and the Exercise Project (the 3-Channel Color Organ). For both projects, we present the complete Concepts and Requirements Document, as well as the three-part design drawing set.

FIGURE 3–20
Concepts and Requirements Document: Variable Power Supply

Concepts and Requirements Document

Variable Power Supply

by

Joe Smith

Project Goals

This Concepts and Requirements Document proposes that students in Electronics 150 design and build a working prototype for a Variable Power Supply that may later be mass-produced. Electronics students need an inexpensive 0- to 15-V dc power supply to power such projects as transistor radios, burglar alarms, digital counters, and a host of solid-state-based experiments. A search has failed to uncover a low-cost commercial power supply of the type required. Furthermore, undertaking such a project will provide electronics students with a valuable electronics design and fabrication experience.

Project Objectives

The project is to have the following objectives: inexpensive to produce (less than $25), reliable, safe, attractive, and easy to use. These objectives will be met in the following ways:

* **Cost.** By using noncritical, readily available hardware and electronic components, bought in bulk quantities, the cost will be kept low.

* **Reliability.** By using solid-state active components and printed circuit board construction techniques, a high degree of reliability will be obtained.

* **Safety.** By using an internal fuse, thermal shutdown voltage regulator, insulated output terminals, and a completely sealed metal enclosure, safe operation will be assured.

3

FIGURE 3–20 (cont'd)
Concepts and Requirements Document: Variable Power Supply

* **Appearance.** A metal enclosure, either painted or covered with contact paper, will ensure an attractive project.

* **Ease of Use.** With the use of an on-off switch, a front panel-mounted LED indicator, and a panel-numbered voltage indicator, the project will have a high degree of functionality and be easy to use.

Project Responsibility

Because this is to be a learning experience for the electronics student, he or she will be responsible for the design (which, in this case, is being supplied), drawings, experimenting, prototyping, and testing, troubleshooting, and final documentation phases of the Variable Power Supply. Due dates for each phase will be assigned by the electronics instructor.

Project Theory of Operation

The Variable Power Supply changes the 120 V ac from the wall outlet to a varying dc of 1.2 to 15 V. The ac line cord couples, via switch S_1 and internal fuse F_1, the 120 V ac to the primary of transformer T_1. The transformer steps down the 120 V ac to approximately 15.5 V ac. Diodes D_1–D_4 form a full-wave bridge to change (rectify) the ac to pulsating direct current (pdc). Light-emitting diode D_5 is used as a power "on" indicator; resistor R_1 limits current to the LED. Capacitor C_1 filters the pdc to smooth dc. Capacitor C_2 provides high-frequency bypassing. The variable voltage regulator U_1 sets its output voltage by a control loop consisting of resistor R_2 and potentiometer R_3. The output voltage can be varied over the 1.2- to 15-V range by adjusting the potentiometer. Finally, capacitor C_3 acts to swamp any ringing effect developed by the control loop and thereby ensures stability of the voltage regulator's output.

Electronics instructor's approval Bob Jones **Date** 4-11-01

4

Designing the Variable Power Supply

Here the Concepts and Requirements Document and design drawings—the two-step design process—for the Variable Power Supply are discussed.

Concepts and Requirements Document for the Variable Power Supply

The complete Concepts and Requirements Document for the Variable Power Supply is presented in Figure 3–20. The *project goals* state what is to be built, why it is a desirable project, and, in this case, what is to be gained by having electronics students build the device. In industry, of course, having engineers and technicians work on a project just to gain experience may not be a reasonable justification for proceeding. Nonetheless, it is important to realize that the experience factor, even in the industrial setting, is not to be discounted.

Project objectives require achieving optimum benefits with regard to cost, reliability, safety, appearance, and ease of use. How these objectives are to be realized is also stated, in general terms.

Project responsibility rests solely with you, the student. You must do it all. Again, in industry, this would rarely be the case. Designers, technicians, and technical writers would be involved, and tentative due dates would be assigned. However, because this is also to be a complete learning experience, you'll carry forward every phase of project design and construction, under your instructor's supervision.

Project theory of operation, also shown in Figure 3–20, is discussed below, after the design drawings are examined.

Design Drawings for the Variable Power Supply

The system diagram for the Variable Power Supply is shown in Figure 3–21. Notice something very interesting: the power supply project itself is not a complete electronic system, only the circuit portion of it. A power supply converts alternating current (ac) into direct current (dc). It is an all-electronic device, taking one form of electricity at its input (ac) and supplying another form at its output (dc). In that sense it is similar to an amplifier, or any other electronic circuit, that "only" manipulates electrical current.

But the power supply is part of an electrical system, nonetheless. The input transducer is the generator at the power plant supplying ac to the wall outlet. The generator changes mechanical energy into electricity. The output transducer is the load connected to the dc output terminals of the power supply. Eventually, that load, be it a radio, television, computer, or alarm, will change electricity into another form of energy. Thus, there is indeed a complete electronic system.

Figure 3–22 shows the **circuit design sketch**, or rough schematic, for the Variable Power Supply. This is a sketch that designers, technicians, and other technical personnel use to evaluate how the power supply works. In this instance, note that the drawing is quite complete. After all, the project is a simple one and the circuit design is not hard to arrive at.

The **packaging plan** for the Sample Project is illustrated in Figure 3–23. It shows the proposed size and shape of the sheet metal enclosure, suggested finishing treatment, and the locations of the on-off switch, panel light, voltage terminal posts, variable voltage control potentiometer, and dial face. Remember, this is not a final drawing, merely a first proposal showing how the complete prototype might look.

Variable Power Supply: Theory of Operation

As noted, a power supply converts ac to dc. All four active components (vacuum tubes, transistors, inte-

FIGURE 3–21
System diagram: Variable Power Supply

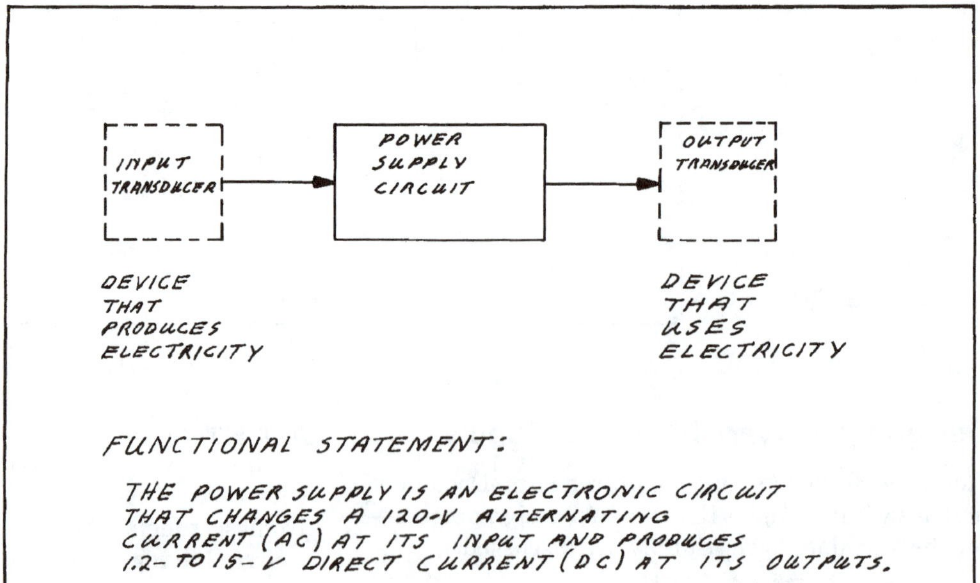